Shakespeare Bibliography

Golden Age of English Literature: Shakespeare and some of His Contemporaries

Frontispiece

Shakespeare Bibliography

A DICTIONARY OF EVERY KNOWN ISSUE
OF THE WRITINGS OF THE POET
AND OF RECORDED OPINION THEREON
IN THE ENGLISH LANGUAGE

WILLIAM JAGGARD

*With Historical Introduction, Facsimiles, Portraits
and Other Illustrations*

*"Take from this my hand . . . your crown,
And He that wears the crown immortally
Long guard it yours . . ."*

FREDERICK   UNGAR   PUBLISHING   CO.
NEW YORK

Republished 1959 by arrangement with the Shakespeare Press,
Stratford-on-Avon

To WILLIAM JAGGARD

obiit 1623

Elizabethan author, printer, publisher

to whom the world owes more than it deems for the
safe preservation of an unparalleled literary
heritage, this labour of a lifetime is
gratefully dedicated

PRINTED IN THE UNITED STATES OF AMERICA

Library of Congress Catalog Card No. 58-59877

HISTORICAL INTRODUCTION

_____

'The debt immense of endless gratitude
. . . still paying, still to owe.'—MILTON.

ALONG book needs but a short preface. Perchance, then, one may claim privilege for a tired pen, and stand excused if some necessary observations are compressed into the briefest space.

From a remote period the indispensable tribute to distinguished merit has found expression in the form of biography. Like most good things, it is often abused. What probably originated and ended in some simple tombstone inscription now sometimes extends to a set of several ponderous tomes—documentary proof, as Dr. Johnson would say, of misplaced vanity. In modern days literary genius asserts its right to a fresh prerogative in the shape of bibliography, a claim no one will grudge. That form of hero-worship honourably serves a double purpose. It fulfils the desire to pay homage where due, and, as a key to recorded knowledge, becomes a handmaid to fresh literary labour. With these few words I might fitly 'say amen betimes' did not other remarks, perhaps apropos to the place and time, press for notice.

'Man's most of might'—in Browning's expressive phrase—the transcendent genius now surveyed, is by acclaim the chosen spokesman of a race entrusted with profound and world-wide responsibilities. In addition to the labour, that fact did not lessen the serious nature of this gigantic task. But of that more anon. Among millions of Anglo-Saxons influenced by books, either at home or overseas, there can be but few who feel no quickening of the pulse at the mention of that 'great heir of fame' who left so free, so matchless a heritage. Beyond the vast numbers who have read and enjoyed, how many more millions do his happy precepts guide and cheer! How much of his wisdom and wit is woven into the common life and language of the nations! How

(v.)

his judicial sense of simple equity interlaces our laws! His æsthetics, his reverence for all that is good and beautiful, his manly courage, his patriotism—are they not reflected to-day on every side and in many an unexpected place!

Without appearing to court exaggeration, it is difficult to do justice in a few phrases to a power unique in our annals. Not only was he founder and father of our national drama—a mighty means of education, but largely of our national tongue—a still mightier means, to say nothing of our general standard of life and intercourse. To the humble 'son of toil' whose nativity in 1564 at Stratford-upon-Avon shed one of the highest honours any town or kingdom could desire, countless legions stand indebted for an impulse which defies alike calculation and valuation. Over and over again his familiar yet ever-fresh writings prove him to belong to no one age or nation, but to be infinitely royal, infinitely human in all. Not merely was he a man of extraordinary energy, both of thought and action, but the cause of boundless activity in others. Few among the legions of his debtors would dare estimate or hope to redeem their debt. Of the unnumberable myriads, over twenty thousand workers held by his magic spell stand enumerated in this census. Right through the centuries which intervene between his coming and the present year of grace, leading writers of all countries have vied in stripping the dictionary of flowers of praise to heap upon our 'ever-living poet.'

But 'hath not thy rose a thorn'? We live in days of occasional disbelief and doubt, when 'fortune in her shift and change of mood spurns down her late beloved.' A few, learned in the law (I cannot add, in literature), like to whet their wits in discoursing that black is white, despite the avalanche of evidence refuting their absurd contentions. In the United States the Baconian discussion, that pitiful waste of time, breath, and ink, has reached the advanced stage of producing its own bibliography, and in England it has brought forth the inevitable society and journal. Scattered through the following seven hundred or more pages, interested readers may find an overwhelming mass of testimony, from the sixteenth century onwards, proving that William Shakespeare was 'gentle, schooled, and learned,' that in very truth he was the surpassing genius which all sound scholars insist upon. It is not surprising that a land of extremes like America should furnish Baconian cranks and Shakespearean zealots at the same moment. Great Britain sincerely thanks the daughter-country for both. Even our friends the cranks have their uses. They encourage zealots, in the process of holding their own, to study the glorious age of Queen Elizabeth to their infinite pleasure and advantage. The annual stream of pilgrims to a shrine that kings envy sets a good example, and makes for the unity, not only of states, but of continents. At this point it may not be unacceptable to quote a few opinions from better known writers of different countries as a microcosm of this bibliography :—

> ' Thy empire changeth not, thy sceptre sways
>   A realm that widens as the years go by ;
>   A little while we love and live, but thou,
>   Thou, the all-loving, know'st not how to die.'—'Achespè,' 1897.

> ' Others abide our question. Thou art free.
>   We ask and ask—thou smilest and art still
>   Out-topping knowledge . . .
>   And thou, who didst the stars and sunbeams know,
>   Self-school'd, self-scann'd, self-honour'd, self-secure,
>   Didst tread on earth unguessed at. Better so ! . . .'
>   —*Matthew Arnold, 1853-55.*
> ' For Shakespeare was, and at his touch with light
>   Impartial as the sun's, revealed the all.'—*Mathilde Blind, 1900.*

> ' Shakespeare ! To such name's sounding what succeeds
>   Fitly as a silence ? Falter forth the spell . . .
>   Two names there are ; that which the Hebrew reads
>   With his soul only . . .
>   We voice the other name, man's most of might,
>   Awesomely, lovingly . . .
>   Shakespeare's creation rises, one remove
>   Though dread—this finite from the infinite.'
>   —*Robert Browning, 1884.*

' Shakespeare, no mere child of nature . . . first studied patiently, meditated deeply, understood minutely, till knowledge, become habitual and intuitive, wedded itself to his habitual feelings, and at length gave birth to that stupendous power by which he stands alone . . . which seated him on one of the two glory-smitten summits of the poetic mountain . . . Shakespeare becomes all things, yet for ever remaining himself . . .'—*Samuel T. Coleridge, 1817.*

Shakespeare Bibliography

'Shakespeare was one of the greatest geniuses that the world ever saw . . . One may say of him, as of Homer, that he had none to imitate and is himself inimitable.'—*John Dennis, 1712.*

'I sing the progresse of a deathlesse soule

. . . .

A worke t' outweare Seth's pillars, brick and stone,
And, holy writs excepted, made to yeeld to none.'
—*John Donne, 1633.*

'It is remarkable that on the same day (23rd April, 1616) expired in Spain his great and amiable contemporary, Cervantes, and the world was thus deprived nearly at the same moment of the two most original writers which modern Europe has produced.'—*Nathan Drake, 1828.*

'Shakespeare who, taught by none, did first impart
To Fletcher wit, to labouring Jonson art.'—*John Dryden.*

'Shakespeare's mind is the horizon beyond which at present we do not see.'—*R. W. Emerson, 1844.*

'Altogether a "manly man" (as Chaucer says) this Shakespeare: strong, tender, humorful, sensitive, impressionable, the truest friend, the foe of none but narrow minds and base . . . What can we do but bless his name, and be thankful that he came . . . a bond that shall last for ever between all English-speaking, English-reading men.'—*Dr. F. J. Furnivall, 1877.*

'In the seventeenth century Shakespeare was regarded as one of a multitude, a little more careless, and sometimes a little more felicitous, than his fellows. To the eighteenth century he became a Gothic savage, in whose "woodnotes wild" the sovereignty of nature was re-asserted as if by accident. It was left to the nineteenth century to discover in him the most magnificent of the conscious poetic artists of the world.'—*Edmund Gosse, 1903.*

'Shakespeare . . . in tragedy and comedy . . . may be said to have equalled if not excelled . . . the best writers of any age or country who have thought it glory enough to distinguish themselves in either.'—*Sir Thomas Hanmer, 1743.*

'Shakespeare glances from heaven to earth and from earth to heaven. All nature ministers to him. No poet comes near Shakespeare in the number of lines that, according to Bacon, "come home to our business and bosoms." '—*J. C. & A. J. Hare, 1827.*

'Shakespeare has surface beneath surface, to an immeasurable depth, adapted to the plummet-line of every reader. His works present many phases of truth . . . and a thousand years hence a world of new readers will possess a whole library of new books, as we ourselves do, in these volumes old already.'—*Nathaniel Hawthorne, 1863.*

Historical Introduction

'The striking peculiarity of Shakespeare's mind was its generic quality, its power of communication with all other minds . . . He was just like *any* other man but that he was like *all* other men. He turned the globe round for his amusement, and surveyed the generations of men and the individuals as they passed, with their different concerns, passions, follies, vices, virtues, actions and motives, as well those that they knew as those which they did not know or acknowledge . . . If we wish to know the force of human genius, we should read Shakespeare; if . . . the insignificance of human learning, we may study his commentators.'—*Wm. Hazlitt, 1818.*

'Mellifluous Shakespeare, whose inchanting quill
Commanded mirth or passion, was but Will.'
—*Thomas Heywood, 1635.*

'This player was a prophet from on high,
Thine own elected. Statesman, prophet, sage . . .'
—*Oliver Wendell Holmes, 1875.*

'. . . . . an immortal man,
Nature's chief darling and illustrious mate,
Destined to foil old death's oblivious plan
And shine untarnished by the fogs of fate,
Time's famous rival till the final date.'—*Thomas Hood, 1827.*

'Our love of Shakespeare, therefore, is not a monomania or unaccountable infatuation, but is merely the natural love which all men bear to those forms of excellence that are accommodated to their peculiar character, temperament, and situation . . .'—*Francis Lord Jeffrey, 1811.*

'Each change of many-coloured life he drew,
Exhausted worlds, and then imagined new.'
—*Dr. Samuel Johnson, 1747.*

'While I confess thy writings to be such
As neither man nor muse can praise too much.'
—*Ben Jonson, 1623.*

'The genius of Shakespeare was an innate universality—wherefore he had the utmost achievement of human intellect prostrate beneath his kingly gaze. He could do easily man's utmost . . .'—*John Keats.*

'. . . . . . . most great
And powerful genius! whose sublime control
Still from thy grave governs each human soul.
.   .   .   .
Shall I not bless the need to which was given
Of all the angels in the host of heaven
Thee for my guardian, spirit strong and bland,
Lord of the speech of my dear native land.'—*F. A. Kemble, 1866.*

(ix.)

Shakespeare Bibliography

' I have derived more practical Christianity from reading Shakespeare's plays and seeing them enacted than from any sermon I ever heard preached.'—*Charles Kingsley.*

' Shakespeare strengthens virtue, kills selfish and mercenary thoughts, induces sweet honourable actions and ideas, teaches benignity, courtesy, generosity, and humanity.'—*Charles Lamb.*

> ' In poetry there is but one supreme,
> Though there are many angels round his throne,
>
> .   .   .   .   .   .
>
> One crying out—" All nations spoke through me." '
> —*Walter Savage Landor, 1846.*

' Highest among those who have exhibited human nature stands Shakespeare. . . . Admirable as he is in all parts of his art, we most admire him for this—that while he has left a greater number of striking portraits than all other dramatists put together, he has scarcely left us a single caricature.'—*Lord Macaulay, 1843.*

> ' And for all time he wears the crown
>   Of lasting limitless renown ;
> He reigns, whatever monarchs fall,
>   His throne is in the hearts of all.'—*Gerald Massey.*

' Shakespeare is as astonishing for the exuberance of his genius in abstract notions and for the depth of his analytical and philosophical insight as for the scope and minuteness of his poetic imagination.'—*Prof. David Masson, 1874.*

> ' O lived the master now to paint us men
> That little twist of brain would ring a chime
> Of whence it came, and what it caused, to start
> Thunders of laughter, clearing air and heart.'
> —*George Meredith, 1883.*

' The muses would speak with Shakespeare's fine filed phrase if they would speak English.'—*Francis Meres, 1598.*

> ' What needs my Shakespeare for his honoured bones
> The labour of an age in pilèd stones ?
>
> .   .   .   .
>
> Dear son of memory, great heir of fame,
> What need'st thou such dull witness of thy name.
> Thou in our wonder and astonishment
> Hast built thyself a lasting monument.
>
> .   .   .   .
>
> And so sepulchred in such pomp dost lie,
> That kings for such a tomb would wish to die.'
> —*John Milton, 1632.*

(x.)

Historical Introduction

' The man whose prudence made him rich, whose affectionate nature made him loved almost to idolatry, and whose genius has been the wonder of the world.'—*Wm. Minto, 1874.*

' A great author . . . is one who has something to say and knows how to say it. Such pre-eminently is Shakespeare.'—*Cardinal J. H. Newman, 1873.*

> ' Our Shakespeare wrote too in an age as blest,
> The happiest poet of his time and best.
>
> .⠀⠀⠀.⠀⠀⠀.⠀⠀⠀.⠀⠀⠀.⠀⠀⠀.
>
> Most beautiful, amazing, and divine.'—*Thomas Otway, 1680.*

> ' Enthroned above the fettered souls of men,
> Sublimely great, immeasurably wise.'—*H. T. P——, 1902.*

' We turn to the " Sonnets " . . . There is, after all, nothing more remarkable or fascinating in English poetry than these personal revelations of the mind of our greatest poet. We read them again and again, and find each time some new proof of his almost superhuman insight into human nature; of his unrivalled mastery over all the tones of love.'—*F. T. Palgrave, 1865.*

' If ever any author deserved the name of an original it was Shakespeare . . . The poetry of Shakespeare was inspiration indeed . . . nature speaks through him . . . This is perfectly amazing from a man of no education or experience in those great and public scenes of life which are usually the subject of his thoughts. So that he seems to have known the world by intuition, to have looked through human nature at one glance, and to be the only author that gives ground for a very new opinion—that the philosopher and even the man of the world may be born, as well as the poet.'—*Alex. Pope, 1723.*

' The genius of Shakespeare is unlimited.'—*Prof. Wm. Richardson, 1774.*

' I believe this to be one of Shakespeare's most wondrous qualities—the humanity of his nature and heart. There is a spirit of sunny endeavour about him and an acquiescence in things as they are . . . with a cheerful resolve to make them better.' —*Frederick W. Robertson.*

' It does not matter how little, or how much, any of us have read either of Homer or Shakespeare; everything round us, in substance or in thought, has been moulded by them . . . Of the scope of Shakespeare I will say only that the intellectual measure of every man since born in the domain of creative thought may be assigned to him according to the degree in which he has been taught by Shakespeare.'— *John Ruskin.*

' The effect of the genius of an individual upon the taste of a nation is mighty, but that genius in its turn is formed according to the opinions prevalent at the period when it comes into existence. Such was the case with Shakespeare.'—*Sir Walter Scott, 1814.*

' . . . . . but, happier Stratford, thou
With uncontested laurels deck thy brow.
Thy bard was thine, unschooled, and from thee brought
More than all Egypt, Greece, or Asia taught.
Not Homer's self such matchless honours won.
The Greek has rivals, but thy Shakespeare none.'
                                        —*Anne Seward, 1782.*

     ' Divinest Shakespeare's might
       Fills Avon and the world with light,
       Like omniscient power which he
       Imaged 'mid mortality.'—*P. B. Shelley, 1818.*

' Sweet volume, stored with learning fit for saints,
    Where blissful quires imparadize their minds,
Wherein eternall studie never faints,
    Still finding all, yet seeking all it finds,
How endless is your labyrinth of blisse,
Where to be lost the sweetest finding is.'—*Robert Southwell, 1594.*

  ' Of books that have influenced me, Shakespeare has served me best.'—*Robert Louis Stevenson.*

     ' Not if men's tongues and angels' all in one
     Spake, might the word be said that might speak thee.
     Streams, winds, woods, flowers, fields, mountains, yea, the sea—
     What power is in them all to praise the sun ?
     His praise is this—he can be praised of none.'
                                        —*A. C. Swinburne, 1882.*

  ' Shakespeare stands alone, and I do not wonder he so witches the world.'—*Walt Whitman, 1898.*

  ' He speaks a language which thrills in our blood in spite of two hundred years . . . and his genius may be contemporary with the mind of every generation for a thousand years to come . . . It was Shakespeare, the most unlearned of all our writers, who first exhibited on the stage perfect images of all human characters and events . . . Except in him we look in vain for . . . perfect art.'—*Prof. John Wilson, 1857.*

  ' We may compare the mind of Shakespeare to a diamond, cut into countless polished facets, which in constant movement, at every smallest change of direction or of angle, caught a new reflection, so that not one of its brilliant mirrors could for a moment be idle, but by a power beyond its control was ever busy with the reflection of innumerable images . . .'—*Cardinal Wiseman, 1865.*

And so one might continue, almost without finality, to gyrate, as a moth, round the flashing, dazzling arc of light known as William Shakespeare. With C. E. Lawrence, ' proud may we be that this superlative genius was an Englishman, gentle-hearted, perhaps sad sometimes, but ever patriotic.' He knew the soul of man better than it is vouchsafed to mortals to know, in all its sunshine, shadow, storm, and stress. His wit was all-embracing, like a summer zephyr. It haunted the taverns with *Falstaff*, radiated the woodpaths of Arden with *Rosalind*, explored the lot of the outcast with Lear's fool, flitted hither and thither with *Ariel* and *Puck* in their madcap pranks. His wisdom touched the eternities. It peered through the tomb with *Hamlet ;* weighed, with some irony, the responsibilities of princes ; uncovered the deeds of the cunning, and deprecated the artificiality of the courtier. His sympathy was world-wide, though he had little for the quack, the insincere, the demagogue, or the unwashed mob. His humanity united all humans into one family with ' one touch of nature.' All ranks, professions, grades, and callings served him as puppets to earn our admiration, sympathy, or condemnation according to his pulling of the strings. His far-sighted vision embraced supermen in the fairies, elves, witches, and monsters employed. ' All the world's a stage ' as he saw it, and its vastness and unending variety served to deck his plots. As *Prosper* he could regard earthly existence as a dream or bubble. But they are no shadows that strut, march, dance, or sneak across his boards ; they are living beings, more actual than many we have known in the flesh ; folk of majesty or meanness, mirth or passion, and always of wonder. They exult or suffer, earning our smiles or sighs ; they ever point a moral or adorn a tale ; they illustrate, inform, or deck comedy and tragedy—irony binding the two in the human drama—and so compose and comprise human life, the unknown mighty purpose. In truth, this supreme citizen of no mean empire may stand as the eternal embodiment of all that is best and greatest in human character and achievement.

It may be well to set down something of the provenance of this book, a dictionary so long the desire and despair of scholars and collectors.

Since Francis Meres published his preliminary list in 1598 much water has run past the mill, and most of the many attempts to complete such an undertaking found a sadly common end in failure. As time progressed, the endless flow of fresh editions and new commentaries added to the task, until the mountain of work seemed one for a syndicate to attack, rather than an individual. Apart from scores of writers who have prepared lists of Shakespeareana more or less lengthy, perhaps the earliest effort towards an exhaustive key was Francis Kirkman's 'True . . . catalogue of all comedies, tragedies, and pastorals that were ever yet printed, 1671,' a work far from being so 'perfect and exact' as its title claimed. This was reprinted in 1698, with additions, by Gerard Langbaine, who was followed by W. Mears with his 'Compleat catalogue of plays, 1726.' Six years later came a work palpably founded on Kirkman, entitled the 'True and exact catalogue of all the plays and other dramatic pieces ever yet printed in English . . . 1732.' In 1740 Francis Peck added to his 'Memoirs of John Milton' a 'New catalogue of Shakespeare's writings.' Seven years after came John Mottley's 'List of all the . . . dramatic pieces ever published in English . . . 1747.' W. R. Chetwood in 1752 issued his 'British theatre, containing . . . an account of all plays . . .'; re-issued in 1756 under a fresh title. In 1767 Edward Capell added to his charming edition of the poet a 'Table of the quartos, folios, ascribed plays, and poems.' Succeeding this, in 1773, occurred Theobald's edition of Shakespeare, containing a bibliography, amusingly divided into 'editions of authority, of middle authority, of no authority,' the latter including poor Rowe's 1709 edition, from which all biographers borrow, with or without acknowledgment. Following Theobald occurred a more elaborate effort in the shape of Edward Capell's 'Catalogue of a collection intitl'd Shakesperiana, comprehending all the several editions . . . divers old prose-men and verse-men, with a variety of other articles, chiefly such as tend to illustrate him . . . 1779.' This interesting manuscript is still happily preserved at Cambridge, and was printed in 1779 under the editorship of George Steevens. In the same year appeared the 'Playhouse pocket companion, containing a catalogue of all the dramatic authors who have written for the English stage, 1779.'

A similar work, called the 'New theatrical dictionary,' was put forth in 1792, which hardly fulfilled its pretentious title. In 1803 J. Barker published a 'Complete list of plays, exhibiting at one view the title, size, date, and author from the commencement of theatrical performances . . .' About 1805, or earlier, arose a fresh Mahomet, who failed to move a mountain, in the person of the first Marquis of Bute. His manuscript is preserved at Boston, U.S., and covers fifty-two pages only. It is entitled 'Catalogue containing, or intended to contain, every edition of Shakespeare and all commentaries, etc. regarding that author.' The noble marquis was a man of caution, judged by the reservation 'intended to contain.' In 1818 John Britton added a 'bibliography of detached essays and dissertations on Shakespeare' to his edition of the bard, and remarked 'the number and variety of commentaries on the writings of Shakespeare almost exceed credibility.' If that observation fairly represented the student's library a century ago, what would Britton say now! To continue. In 1824 Robert Watt contributed his well-known but limited list in his invaluable 'Bibliotheca Britannica,' and was followed in 1827 by John Wilson's 'Catalogue of all the books, pamphlets, etc. relating to Shakespeare . . .'—a remarkably modest-looking tome for so brave a title. Two amateur collectors now set to work—one in England, one in America. Thomas Jolley, the well-known bibliophile, compiled a 'List of Shakespeareana, 1834,' a small manuscript I found at Warwick Castle; while Thomas Pennant Barton, of New York, founder of the wonderful collection at Boston, commenced at the same time (ending in 1869) his 'Shakespeariana or a complete list of all the works relating to Shakespeare.' This manuscript, now at Boston, fills over a thousand quarto pages, a treasured memento of that life-long enthusiast. In the same year, 1834, first came out Thomas William Lowndes' indispensable 'Bibliographer's manual,' with its lengthy list of Shakespeareana. He fell a martyr to the cause, and Lowndes' name will always be revered by scholars and bookmen. The year 1841 saw the two friends and co-workers, John Payne Collier and James Orchard Halliwell, both absorbed in this field of research. Collier published his studies 'On the earliest quarto editions' under the ægis of the Shakespeare Society, while Halliwell brought forth his 'Shakespeariana: a catalogue of the early editions of Shakespeare's plays and of the commentaries and other publications illustrative of his works, 1841.' Like Halliwell's many later contributions on the subject, this was exceedingly interesting, but too haphazard ever to be serviceable to any but leisured men. Next must be mentioned E. Cranwell's 'Plays of Shakespeare printed before 1623,' which came out in 1847. Following this appeared Henry George Bohn's new edition of 'Lowndes' Manual' in 1857, the Shakespearean portion of which, much enlarged, he published separately as the 'Biography and bibliography of Shakespeare . . . 1863,' and again in 1864. This Bohn proudly claimed to contain 'every known edition, translation, and commentary.' This statement was far from accurate. His dates are often wrong, while his omissions may be numbered by thousands. The year 1865 witnessed Franz Thimm's 'Shakespeariana form 1564 to 1864,' useful as a supplement to Bohn's compilation. In 1866 William Harrison, a collector, printed privately a 'Descriptive catalogue of Shakspeariana.' Clarence Hopper in 1868 prepared, under the guidance of Halliwell, the first catalogue of the contents of the birthplace library at Stratford. This was followed in 1870 by Allibone's 'Dictionary of English literature,' bearing 'Shakespeare's life and bibliography.' Then Albert Cohn commenced in 1871 his 'Shakespeare bibliographie,' English and foreign, which appeared annually until 1886. The years 1872-76 found Robert K. Dent at work upon his 'Catalogue of the Shakespeare Memorial Library, Birmingham,' and to everyone's sorrow his inventory is practically all that remains of the splendid collection destroyed by fire in 1879. To the city's eternal credit, Birmingham manfully set to work to replace its loss, and, phœnix-like, the largest Shakespeare library in the world now exists there. In 1876 Justin Winsor issued his 'Bibliography of the original quartos and folios of Shakespeare,' followed in 1879 by his similar work on the 'Poems.' At the same time Karl Knortz printed his 'American Shakespeare bibliography, 1876.' By far the most thorough and painstaking contribution next appeared in the 'Catalogue of the works of Wm. Shakespeare, original and translated. Barton Collection, Boston. By

James M. Hubbard and Arthur M. Knapp, 1878-80,' a small folio of over
two hundred closely-printed pages. In 1879 Horace H. Morgan issued
in Saint Louis a volume entitled ' Topical Shakespeariana.' This was
succeeded in 1880 by the New York ' Catalogue of the James Lenox
Library,' a compilation not to be overlooked. W. H. Wyman in 1882
produced a ' Bibliography of Bacon-Shakespeare literature,' which ran
into a second edition in 1884. Then came James A. Morgan's ' Digesta
Shakespeareana, 1886-87.' In 1889 Frederick Hawley commenced his
ambitious 'Catalogue of all the known editions of Shakespeare's plays in
every language,' and died long ere he could possibly complete it. His
folio manuscript is preserved at the Stratford Memorial Library, which
splendid institution he served as librarian. In the next year, 1890, the
writer prepared his ' Index catalogue of Shakespeareana preserved at
Warwick Castle,' which now appears (embodied herein) in print for
the first time. In 1898 the present librarian, Mr. Wm. Salt Brassington
(whose courtesy all students and visitors thankfully acknowledge)
commenced his manuscript ' Classified and indexed catalogue of the
Shakespeare Memorial Library, Stratford-on-Avon.' The next year
Mr. Marsden Jasael Perry privately printed a ' Catalogue of Shakespeareana ' [in the Perry collection]. In 1900 Mr. A. Capel Shaw
published the extensive ' Index to the Shakespeare Memorial Library,
Birmingham,' a collection now embracing about fourteen thousand
volumes. In the pages of ' The Library ' for 1903 Dr. Walter W. Greg
gave a ' Bibliographical history of the first folio ' (the Jaggard canon of
1623), and, with Mr. A. W. Pollard and others, in the same quarterly,
and in ' The Athenæum,' 1908-09, gave a series of valuable articles on
the falsely dated quartos. In 1909 appeared further welcome help from
Mr. Alfred W. Pollard in his ' Shakespeare folios and quartos,' a study
affording new light on obscure corners and phases of the subject.

One might so continue almost indefinitely, but the titles already
exhibited show that a score or more of writers in succession strove to
subdue this great toil, but in the main it subdued them, as it nearly did
the writer. The tyranny of an exacting profession leaves one little
leisure for adventure in bibliography. I was tempted in early youth

to undertake it by the fourth Earl of Warwick, and after twenty-two years' effort, chiefly in time ill-spared from rest and recreation, I have at last reconciled aim with achievement, faith with fulfilment. My sole ambition was to render the book in some measure worthy of that exquisite thinker who gave English character its greatest impetus. So vast a field can hardly prove to be perfectly gleaned at the first full attempt. Something fresh comes to light nearly every week of the year, so I hope to issue occasional supplements, like the present addenda, to keep the work up to date. Meanwhile, if readers will kindly notify omissions I shall be grateful.

Now for the aim of this conspectus. It seeks to be something more than a bibliography; in fact, to be an encyclopædia of Shakespearean information and stage history, or, as Bacon says, the ' image of men's wit and knowledge,' instantly pointing out all recorded data. In effect it is also a convergent or cumulative catalogue, annotated and indexed, of the world's twelve largest Shakespeare libraries, so simply arranged that a child can use it. It contains over thirty-six thousand distinct entries and references, including many hitherto unrecorded editions, with thousands of illustrative notes and extracts. It gives minute details and available locations of every known issue of Shakespeare's writings (whether written, printed, separate, collective, authentic, attributed, private, public, in or out of print); likewise of every tract, pamphlet, volume, or collection of Shakespearean comment; of each analogue or source, with notes of the passages affected; of every important contemporary or subsequent allusion to, or article on, the dramatist or his productions; of each autograph, genuine or forged; of all engraved Shakespeare portraits; with market values of the rarer entries. Key-references are embodied to all incidental Shakespearean actors, actresses, artists, attributes, bibliographers, bibliophiles, biographers, blind-type printings, celebrations, centenaries, clubs, collaborators, commemorations, commentators, composers, controversies, critics, editors, engravers, exhibitions, festivals, forgeries, illustrations (pictorial or literary), jubilees, managers, manuscripts, memorials, monuments, printers, prompters, pseudonyms, publishers, societies, theatres, translators, vellum-printings. [There is one exception : firms of printers and publishers still trading have not been indexed.] It will thus be seen that men of thought, of art, and of business, rightly take their place side by side in the great Shakespearean army, each having his due share of credit.

Shakespeare's best monument, like his real portrait, lies in print, at once the most fragile, imperishable, and world-wide tablet.

Finally, to whom do I owe thanks ? To some, alas ! called hence during progress ; among others, to George Guy Greville, fourth Earl of Warwick, for initial encouragement and unfailing courtesy ; to Charles Edward Flower and his good wife Sarah Flower, of Stratford-on-Avon, devoted benefactors of the town, whose forethought and generosity have made the student's path easy and pleasant ; to Alderman Timmins, of Birmingham, and to Thomas Simmons, of Leamington, whose store of knowledge was ever at my disposal.

Much do I owe Sir Edward Russell, who personifies the words of Sir Wm. Temple, another worthy knight—' the greatest medicine is a true friend.'

Specially am I indebted to that tireless enthusiast, Mrs. C. C. Stopes, beside the courteous librarians and assistants at the British Museum, the Bodleian, at Birmingham, Harvard University, Manchester, Melbourne, Stratford Memorial; also to Mr. Edmund L. Armstrong of Melbourne, Mr. George Boyden of Stratford, Mr. E. Gordon Duff of Liverpool, Mr. A. W. Pollard of the British Museum, and last, though not least, to my careful, painstaking printers, all of whom united in removing obstacles from my path.

> ' Here let us breathe and haply institute
> A course of learning and ingenious studies.'

WILLIAM JAGGARD.

Stratford-on-Avon.

Arms of William Shakespeare

NON SANZ DROICT

CONTRACTIONS ADOPTED FOR LOCATIONS

BM	British Museum, London.
BLO	Bodleian Library, Oxford.
BPL	Birmingham Public Library.
BRITWELL	*Christie Miller Library, Britwell Court.
BUS	Boston [U.S.A.] Public Library.
BUSA	,, ,, Athenæum Library.
CORPUS CH.⎫ COLL. ⎭	Corpus Christi College Library, Oxford.
CPL	Cambridge Public Library.
CTC	Cambridge, Trinity College Library.
DEVON	*Duke of Devonshire's Library.
EPL	Edinburgh Public Library.
ELLESMERE	*Earl of Ellesmere's Library, Bridgwater House.
EUL	Edinburgh University Library.
HAMBURG	Hamburg Public Library, Germany.
HCL	Harvard College Library, U.S.A.
HUTH	*Huth Library.
ISHAM	*Isham Library, Lamport Hall.
LPL	Leamington Public Library.
MPL	Melbourne Public Library, Australia.
MRL	Manchester, Rylands Library.
NY	New York, Lenox Public Library.
SION	Sion College Library, London.
SBL	Shakespeare's Birthplace Library, Stratford-on-Avon.
SKL	South Kensington Library, London, S.W.
SML	Shakespeare Memorial Library, Stratford-on-Avon.
SPL	Stratford-on-Avon Public Library.
W	*Earl of Warwick's Library, Warwick Castle.[1]
ZURICH	State Library of Zurich, Switzerland.

---

* Collections marked with an asterisk are private, and, therefore, not available for public reference.

[1] This assemblage has passed into the private library of an American collector.

ILLUSTRATIONS

VIGNETTES

ENVOI

Crown of knowledge during life,
  Crowned with honour during sleep,
Gem of England's golden era,
  Thee the world in memory keep!

—— Passionate Morrice : A sequel to Tell-Trothe's New Yeare's Gift, 1593. Ln : New Shakspere Society, 1877. 4°
BM | BPL | BUS

See also Lane (J.)
  „   „   Tell-Trothe
A—— (A.) See Adee
A—— (B.) Printer. See Habington
A—— (E.) Sh— problem : A paper for Students. Ln : Simpkin, 1909. 8°, pp. 24
BPL

A—— (S. W.) See Horn Book
A—— (T. J.) See Arnold (T. J.)
A—— (W. W.) Disputed authorship of Sh—'s Plays [In 'Pall Mall Mag.']. 1894. Roy. 8°
BPL

Abbey (E. A.) Artist—
See Rhys
  „ Sh— Works : Ext. 1896, 1900
Abbey Press Printers. See Sh— Merry Wives, 1902
Abbott (   ) Editor. See Sh— Pericles, 1864
Abbott (Dr. Edwin Abbott) Introduction. See Sh— Works : Ext. 1894, 1903
] Shakespearian Grammar : An attempt to illustrate some of the differences between Elizabethan and Modern English. Ln : Macmillan, 1869. Cr. 8°, pp. viii.-136
BM | BPL | BUS | CPL | SML
... Second edition. Ln : Macmillan, 1869. Cr. 8°
BPL
... Revised and enlarged. Ln : 1870. Cr. 8°
BM | BPL | MPL
... Ln : Macmillan, 1871. Cr. 8°
SML
... New edition. Ln : Macmillan, 1872. Cr. 8°
BPL
... Ln : Macmillan, 1873. Cr. 8°, pp. xxiv.-512
BUS
... Ln : Macmillan, 1874. Cr. 8°
SML
... Ln : Macmillan, 1875. Cr. 8°
... Ln : Macmillan, 1878. 12°
SML
... Ln : Macmillan, 1881. Cr. 8°
SML
... Ln : Macmillan, 1884. Cr. 8°, pp. xxiv.-512
... Ln : Macmillan, 1891. Cr. 8°
BPL
... White's Sh— [Review in 'North American Review']. Boston, 1859. 8°
BUS

Abbott (Dr. E. A.) Editor. See Bacon (Sir F.)

à Beckett (E. A.) Quizziology of the British drama. Ln : 'Punch' Office, 1846. 12°
à Beckett (Gilbert Abbot) King John. See Sh— King John, 1837
Abel (W. J.) Editor. See Sh— King Richard II., 1899
Abercrombie (Lascelles) Sh— as financier [In 'Liverpool Courier,' 4 Oct., p. 6]. 1909
] Sh— day [Notes on the annual festival. In 'Liverpool Courier,' 24 April, p. 6]. 1909
] The Sh— league [In 'Liverpool Courier,' 29 Sept., p. 7]. 1909
Abington (Frances) Actress—
See Molloy
  „ Sh— As you like it, 1785
  „ Sh— Much Ado, 1776
  „ Sh— Twelfth Night, 1766, 1797
Abington.] Brereton (Austin) Frances Abington [In 'The Theatre']. 1886. 8° BPL
] Life of Mrs. Abington. Ln : 1888. 8° BPL
With particulars of the 1769 Jubilee.
Abrahall (H. C. H.) Artist. See Sh— Poems, 1865, 1869
Academy of Compliments. See Sh— Cupid's cabinet unlock't. 1655
Accepted Addresses. See Smith (H. & J.)
Account of an early Italian poem on the story of Romeo and Juliet. See Sh—] Sh— Soc.
Account of the 'Boar's Head' Tavern. [Edited by J. O. Halliwell.] Privately printed [1845 ?] Roy. 8° w
Illustrates King Henry IV. and King Henry V.
Account of the Charity of 'God's Gift,' Dulwich. 1853. 8° BPL
Account of the incidents . . . . of Sh—'s Tempest. See Malone
Account of the new English Opera, taken from Sh— Tempest, Dryden, etc. [In 'Universal Visitor']. Ln : 1756. 8° BUS
Account of the New Pantomime entertainment, now performed at Sadler's Wells [Ln.] called Sh—'s choice spirits or Sir John Falstaff in Pantomime. [Ln : 1802 ?] 8° w
Excerpt [pp. 249-256] from a contemporary magazine.
Account of the origin of the [Boydell] Sh— undertaking. 1791. 8°
Accounts of performances and revels at court in the reign of Henry VIII. See Sh—] Sh— Soc.

Acheson (Arthur) Sh— and the rival poet, displaying Sh— as a satirist and proving the identity of the patron and the rival of the Sonnets . . . With a reprint of sundry poetical pieces by George Chapman bearing on the subject. Ln: Lane, 1903. Cr. 8°, pp. viii.-360 and two portraits   BPL | BUS | MPL
Chapman is here alleged to be the rival poet.
First issued by the New York Sh— Soc.

'Actæon' *pseud. See* Spenser (E.)

'Actor.' Sh— and honest King George *versus* Parson Irving and the Puritans . . . By an Actor. Ln: 1824. 8°. With coloured plate by Cruikshank   BM | BPL

Actor (The), or a treatise on the art of playing. Ln: Griffiths, 1755. Cr. 8°   SML | W
Containing ' Impartial observations on the performance, manner, perfections and defects ' of Garrick and other Shakespearean Actors.

Actor (The), or guide to the stage ; exemplifying the whole art of acting . . . 1821. 8°
References to Sh— and his works.

Actor's remonstrance or complaint, 1643. [Ed. by J. O. Halliwell. Reprinted by E. W. Ashbee.] 1869. Fcp. 4° BPL | SML

Actors by daylight, or pencillings in the pit, containing correct memoirs of forty . . . celebrated London performers . . . Ln: J. Pattie, 1838. 8°, pp. viii.-348. With woodcut portraits. Issued in weekly numbers

Actors by gaslight [Weekly Journal]. Ln: 1838. 8°   BPL

Actors.] Collection of picture postcards of Sh— Actors. 1905. 12°   BPL

Actors, Actresses and Acting—

See Abington
 ,, Accounts
 ,, Affray at Norwich
 ,, Alleyn
 ,, Anderson
 ,, Archer
 ,, Armin
 ,, Authentic Memoirs
 ,, Baddeley
 ,, Baker (H. B.)
 ,, Baker (Sir R.)
 ,, Bancroft
 ,, Bandmann
 ,, Bannister
 ,, Bellamy
 ,, Belton
 ,, Benson
 ,, Betterton
 ,, Biography

See Bond
 ,, Booth
 ,, Brewer
 ,, Brooke (G. V.)
 ,, Bruce
 ,, Brunton
 ,, Bulkeley
 ,, Calmour
 ,, Celebrities
 ,, Charke
 ,, Churchill
 ,, Cibber
 ,, Collier (J. P.)
 ,, Cooke (W.)
 ,, Cooper
 ,, Court
 ,, Crosby
 ,, Cunningham
 ,, D— (T. C.)
 ,, Darbyshire
 ,, Day

Actors, Actresses and Acting—

See Decastro
 ,, Dechmann
 ,, Derrick
 ,, Dexter
 ,, Dibdin
 ,, Dickens
 ,, Donaldson
 ,, Donne
 ,, Doran
 ,, Drama . . .
 ,, Dramatic . . .
 ,, Dramaticus
 ,, Drury Lane
 ,, Ebers
 ,, Edwards
 ,, Egan
 ,, Elizabeth
 ,, Erle
 ,, Essay . . .
 ,, Evans
 ,, Farren
 ,, Fechter
 ,, Field
 ,, Fitzgerald
 ,, Fitzpatrick
 ,, Fleay
 ,, Fletcher
 ,, Foreign
 ,, Galt
 ,, Garcia
 ,, Garrick
 ,, Geneste
 ,, Gilliland
 ,, Glasgow
 ,, Goddard
 ,, Gosson
 ,, Grant
 ,, Graves
 ,, Green (J.)
 ,, Green Room
 ,, Greenstreet
 ,, Grimaldi
 ,, Hackett
 ,, Halliwell
 ,, Harding
 ,, Harvey
 ,, Haslewood
 ,, Hawkins
 ,, Hawley
 ,, Hayns
 ,, Hedelin
 ,, Heminge
 ,, Henderson
 ,, Henslowe
 ,, Heywood
 ;, Historia . . .
 ,, History . . .
 ,, Histrionic . . .
 ,, Histrionicus

See Hitchcock
 ,, Holbrook
 ,, Holcroft
 ,, Hollingshead
 ,, Hunt
 ,, Inchbald
 ,, Irving (H. B.)
 ,, Irving (Sir J. H. B.)
 ,, Jefferson
 ,, Jemmat
 ,, Jenkin
 ,, Jones (G.)
 ,, Jordan
 ,, Kean
 ,, Kemble
 ,, Knight
 ,, Lane
 ,, Lawrence
 ,, Leighton
 ,, Lennox
 ,, Leslie
 ,, Letter . . .
 ,, Lewes
 ,, Lewis
 ,, Literary . . .
 ,, Lytton
 ,, Macklin
 ,, Mansel
 ,, Marston (W.)
 ,, Martin
 ,, Mathews
 ,, Medex
 ,, Mellon
 ,, Memoirs
 ,, Molloy
 ,, Monthly . . .
 ,, Mowatt
 ,, Munden
 ,, Munro
 ,, Murdoch
 ,, Neville
 ,, New English Theatre
 ,, New Theatrical .
 ,, Nic-Nac . . .
 ,, Notices . . .
 ,, Oldfield
 ,, Ordinance
 ,, Oxberry
 ,, Palmer
 ,, Parsons
 ,, Pascoe
 ,, Phelps
 ,, Pilgrimage
 ,, Pit
 ,, Playhouse . . .
 ,, Poel
 ,, Prynne

Actors, Actresses and Acting—

See Quin	See Sparrow
„ Rainoldes	„ Stage-Player's . .
„ Ramé	„ Stirling
„ Ratsey	„ Stratford Review
„ Rehan	„ Stuart
„ Returne . . .	„ Sullivan
„ Reynolds	„ Tallis
„ Riccoboni	„ Tarlton
„ Robertson	„ Templeton
„ Robinson	„ Terry
„ Robson	„ Theatre
„ Romney	„ Theatrical . . .
„ Rowe	„ Thespian
„ Russell	„ Tobin
„ Ryan	„ Tomlins
„ Salvianus	„ Topsell
„ Salvini	„ Tyson
„ Sayer	„ Vandenhoff
„ Scarron	„ Victor
„ Schelling	„ Waldron
„ Scott (C. W.)	„ Wallace
„ Scott (E. J. L.)	„ Ward
„ Scott (Sir W.)	„ Warren
„ Settle	„ Wells
„ *Sh*—] Sh—ana	„ Wewitzer
„ *Sh*—] Tegg	„ Whyte
„ Shaw (G. B.)	„ Wilkinson
„ Sheridan	„ Williams
„ Siddons	„ Wilson (W.)
„ Simpson (W. S.)	„ Woffington
„ Singer	„ Woodward
„ Smith (C. W.)	„ Wrighton
„ Soldene	„ Wyndham
„ Sothern	„ Young (C. M.)

Adamo (Max) *Artist.* *See* Sh— Works: Ext. 1876

Adams (E.) Handbook for Visitors to Stratford-upon-Avon. 1872. Cr. 8°   BPL

Adams (E.) Handbook for . . . Stratford. 1878. Cr. 8°   BPL

Adams (E. D.) The poets' praise from Homer to Swinburne. Ln: 1894. Cr. 8°   BPL
Sh—— occupies pp. 126-150.

Adams (George Washington) Oration pronounced before the Shakespearean Club . . . 17 April, 1826. Boston, U.S.: Dutton & Wentworth, 1826. 8°, pp. 32   BUS

Adams (John Quincy) Character of Hamlet: A letter to J. H. Hackett dated Washington, 19 Feb., 1839. Ln: Lithographed in facsimile [for private distribution] by G. E. Madeley, 1839. 4°, pp. iv.   BUS

Adams (J. Q.) & Hackett (J. H.) Character of Hamlet. Ed. by a Lady. New York: J. Mowatt, 1844 8°, pp. viii.   BUS

Adams (J. W. B.) *Editor.* *See* Sh— King Henry IV., ii. 1906

Adams (Maude) *Actress.* *See* Sh— Romeo . . . 1899

Adams.] Davies (Acton) Maude Adams. New York: Stokes, 1901. 8°   SML

Adams (T.) *Publisher*—
See Barnes
„ Ravenscroft

Adams (Wm. Hy. Davenport) Book of burlesque sketches of English stage travestie and parody. Ln: Henry, 1891. 8° SML
Concordance to the plays of Sh—. *See* Sh— Works: Ext. 1886, 1891, 1908

Adams (W. H. D.) *Editor*—
See Calmour
„ Sh— Works, 1876, 1879, 1889

Addison (Rt. Hon. Joseph) Beauties. *See* Sh— Works : Ext. 1806
Epilogue. *See* Philips
See also Dunton

Addison (John) *Composer*—
See Garrick
„ Sh— Macbeth, 1810
„ Sh— Poems, 1815
„ Sh— Works, 1855

Address of the Working Men's Sh— Committee. 1864. 8°   BPL

Addresses delivered at the Theatre Royal, Drury Lane, in aid of the People's Sh— Memorial fund. [1864.] 8°   BPL

Adee (A. A.)] Bacon's Promus [In ' The Republic ']. Washington, 1883. F°   BPL
] Hamlet's ' Dram of eale ' [In ' The Republic ']. Washington, 1883. F°   BPL
] Plea for a reference canon of the plays of Sh—. New York Sh— Soc., c. 1885. 8°

Adelaide University Sh— Society :—
Glynn (P. McM.) Some thoughts on Sh—. 1891. 8°
Proceedings from 13th Session, 1896-97. 8°
Resumé of Work, 9th and 10th Session, 1892-93. 4°
University Sh— Journal, Vol. I., Nos. 3, 4, 5, 8. 1886. 8°   BPL

Adlard ( ) *Engraver.* *See* Sh— Works, 1826

Adlard ( ) *Printer*—
See Sh— King Richard III., 1846
„ Sh— Othello, 1846

Adlard (C. & J.) *Printers.* *See* Sh— Works, 1853-65

Admiral's (Lord High) Company. *See* Battell of Alcazar

Adolphus (J.) *See* Bannister

Adolphus (J. L.) Library. *See* Catalogue, 1863

Adventures on the Black Mountains. A tale. Ln: . . . 1729. Cr. 8°   BPL
Sh—'s ' Double Falsehood ' is said to be founded upon the above.

Aery-Jacob (J.) The 'Air-drawn dagger' [In the 'Reciter and Speaker']. Ln: 1886. Cr. 8°   BPL
See ' Macbeth,' III., 4:

Æschylus—
See Cumberland   *See* Sh—] Downes

Æschylus, Sh—, and Schiller [In ' Blackwood's Edinburgh Magazine,' June]. 1851. 8°   BUS | W

Agincourt. *See* Sh—] Sh—'s library
Foundation of ' King Henry V.'

Agreeable variety. *See* Sh— Works : Ext. 1724

Ahn (F. H.) *Editor—*
 See Sh— King Richard II., 1870
 ,, Sh— Works– Ext. 1869

Aikin (Lucy) Library. *See* Catalogue, 1864

Aikin (L.) Memoirs of the Court of Queen Elizabeth. Ln : Longman, 1826. 2 vols. 8°   SML

Aikman (James). *See* Buchanan and Aikman

Ailwood (   ) *Composer. See* Dibdin (C.)

Ainger *Canon* (Alfred) A poet's responsibility. *See Sh*—] Sh— Sermons
 Lectures and Essays. Ln : 1905. 2 vols. Cr. 8°   BPL
 'Only begetter' of Sh—'s Sonnets [In 'Athenæum,' No. 3716, p. 59, and No. 3718, p. 121, Jan., 1899 ; No. 3777, p. 346, Mar., 1900]. 1899-1900

Ainger *Canon* (Alfred) *Editor. See* Sh— Works : Ext. 1881, 1883, 1886, 1904

Ainsworth (W. Harrison) Correspondence. *See* Clark (R.)
 See also Stratford] Sh—'s Birthplace

Aitken (   ) *Editor. See* Sh— Othello, 1869

Ajax *pseud. See* Caswell (J. B.)

Akenside (Mark) Remonstrance of Sh— [In his 'Works,' pp. 205-208]. Ln : 1894. Cr. 8°   BPL

Alabaster (William) Roxana : Tragedia. W. Jones, 1632. 8°
 The engraved title exhibits the first known illustration of an English stage.
 Sonnets. *See* Dobell

Alba. *See* Tofte (R.)

'Albert' *pseud. See* Armstrong (John)

Albion Knight : Fragment of a moral play. Ed. by J. P. Collier. *See Sh*—] Sh— Soc.

Albrecht (H. C.) *Editor—*
 See Sh— Poems, 1783
 ,, Sh— Venus . . . 1783

Albright (V. E.) A typical Sh— Stage ; The outer-inner stage. Ln : 1908

Aldridge *African Roscius* (F. W. K.) *See* Cole

Aldus Manutius *Venice Printer. See* Sannazaro

Alexander *Earl of Stirling* (Wm.) Julius Cæsar. *See* Sh— Julius Cæsar, 1604, 1607
 Monarchicke Tragedies . . . Newly enlarged . . . Ln : Printed by Valentine Simmes for Ed. Blovnt, 1607. Fcp. 4°   CTC
 Tragedy of Darivs. Ln : Printed by G. Elde for Edward Blount, 1604. Fcp. 4°   W
 The Shakespearean interest in this volume arises in the analogue of the celebrated passage in ' The Tempest ' at sig. H.

Alexandra Theatre, Liverpool. *See* Sh— Winter's Tale, 1876

Aleyn (Charles) Battailes of Crescey and Poictiers, under the fortunes and valour of King Edward the Third of that name and his sonne Edward Prince of Wales, named the Black. Ln : 1633. 8°
 Illustrative of ' King Richard II.'

Historie of the wise and fortunate Prince Henrie of that name the Seventh. With the famed battaile fought betweene the sayd King and Richard the Third named Crook-backe upon Redmoore neere Bosworth. Ln : T. Cotes, 1638. 8°. With portrait by W. Marshall
 Valuable for the description of Richard the Third and Bosworth field.

Alger (Wm. Rounseville) Sh— and friendship ; Sh—'s Sonnets and friendship [In 'Christian Examiner,' Sept. and Nov., 1862]. Boston, U.S.: 1862   BUS

Alias (C.) *pseud.* Scenes from Sh— for the young. *See* Sh— Works : Ext. 1885

Alicia's Diary. *See* Mulvany

Alken (Henry) *Artist. See* Sh— As you like it, 1823

All about Sh—. *See* Banks

All for Money : A Comedy. *See* Literature

All's one . . . *See* Sh— Yorkshire Tragedy, 1608

All's well that ends well. *See* Sh— All's well

Allason (W.) *Publisher. See* Sh— Works, 1819

Allde (E.) *Printer—*
 See Decker
 ,, Ravenscroft

Allde (Edward) *Printer—*
 See Batteil of Alcazar   *See* Preston
 ,, Copley   ,, Stukeley
 ,, Edwards (R.)

Allde (Elizabeth) *Printer—*
 See Prynne
 ,, Sh— Arden, 1633

Alger (W. R.) Life of Forrest. *See* Forrest

Allen (   ) *Publisher. See* Sh— Works, 1794

Allen (   ) *New York Publisher. See* Sh— Works, 1852 1860

Allen *U.S. Attorney-General* (Charles) Notes on the Bacon-Sh— question. Boston, U.S.: 1900. Cr. 8°   BPL | BUS

Allen (J. A.) The Lambda-nu : Tercentenary poem on Sh—. Stratford-upon-Avon, 1864. Cr. 8°   BPL | CPL

Allen (John W.) *See* Seccombe & Allen

Allen (John W.) *Editor—*
 See Sh— Coriolanus, 1885
 ,, Sh— King Richard II., 1885, 1895
 ,, Sh— Works, 1883-86

Allen jun. (Josiah) *Birmingham Printer. See* Sh— Hamlet, 1860

Allen (W. H.) *Publisher. See* Sh— King Henry V., 1880

Alleyn (Edward)] Extract of the Will of the benevolent . . . founder of Dulwich College . . . Ln : J. McHugh, 1829. 8°, pp. 48   BPL | BUS

Alleyn (Edward) *Actor—*
See Blanch   *See* Wilson (W.)
  ,, Garrick   ,, Young (W.)

Alleyn (Giles). *See* Stopes

Alleyn.] Alleyn Papers : A collection of original documents illustrative of the life and times of Edward Alleyn and of the early stage and drama [with the 'Additions']. Introd. by J. P. Collier. Ln : Sh— Soc., 1843-44. 2 vols. 8°
BM | BPL | BUS

] Collier (J. P.) Memoirs of Edward Alleyn, including new particulars respecting Sh—, Jonson, Massinger, Marston, Dekker, &c. Ln : Sh— Soc., 1841. 8°
BM | BPL | BUS | SML
The Stratford copy bears Collier's autograph and MS. corrections.

] Dulwich College [In ' Ladies' Cabinet of Fashion, Music and Romance.' New Series, Vol. 5, pp. 304-309]. Ln : G. Henderson, 1846. 8°. With copperplate view
Refers to Alleyn's friendship with Sh—.

] Young. Life, and Diary (1617-1622) of Edward Alleyn [In ' History of Dulwich College ']. 2 vols. 1889. 4°   BPL

Allibone (S. A.) Sh—'s life and bibliography. *See* Sh—

Allies (J.) British, Roman and Saxon antiquities and folk-lore of Worcestershire. Second edition. Ln : Smith, 1856. 8°
SML
On the ignis fatuus, or will o' the wisp, and the fairies. 1846. 8°   BPL
On the word 'scamels' in 'The Tempest.' *See* Sh— Soc.

Allingham (Wm.) Old Master Grunsey and Goodman Dodd, Stratford-on-Avon, A.D. 1597 [In ' Macmillan's Mag.,' Mar.]. Ln : 1864. 8°   BUS

Alliterative Poem on the deposition of Richard II. Edited by T. Wright. Ln : 1838. 8°
BPL

Allman (   ) *Publisher—*
See Sh— Hamlet, 1816
  ,, Sh— King Lear, 1813, 1816
  ,, Sh— Merchant . . . 1816
  ,, Sh— Othello, 1816

Allot (Robert) England's Parnassus. *See* Sh— Works : Ext. 1600

Allot (Robert) *Publisher. See* Sh— Works, 1632

Almon (J.) *Publisher. See* Sheridan

Alnwick (P.) *Publisher. See* Sh— Works, 1753

Alpenny (J. S.) 'Twelfth Night' characters from Sh—, designed and drawn on stone . . . intended as a first series of characters from the plays . . . Ln : E. C. Edlin. Und.
BUS
Consists of twelve coloured pictures on six cards, with broadside sheet of text.

Alphabet. *See* Horn-Book

Alsop (Bernard *or* Barnard) *Printer—*
See Greene (R.)
  ,, Henderson
  ,, Sh— King Henry V., 1617

Alsop (R.) *Printer. See* Goffe

Alves (R.) Sketches of a history of literature. Edinburgh, 1794. 8°   BPL
Sh— : pp. 115, 149, 187, 250.

Alvord (C. A.) *New York Publisher. See* Sh— Merchant . . . 1867

Amadis.] Treasurie of Amadis of Fraunce. Trans. from the French. Ln : A. Bynneman [Sæc. XVI.]. Fcp. 4°. Black Letter
Used by Sh— in preparing the ' Winter's Tale.'

America—
See Good Speed . . .   *See* Rhys
  ,, Ireland (J. N.)   ,, Rich
  ,, Irving (Sir J. H. B.)   ,, *Sh—*] Monument
  ,, Knortz   ,, Wall
  ,, Lodge   ,, Winsor
  ,, Lunt   ,, Wyman
  ,, Newes   ,, Wynne

American Actors. Ed. by L. Hutton —(1) E. Forrest, by L. Barrett. (2) The Jeffersons, by W. Winter. (3) The Booths, by Mrs. A. B. Clarke. (4) Mrs. Duff, by J. N. Ireland. (5) Charlotte Cushman, by Mrs. C. E. Clements. Boston, U.S : Osgood, 1881-82. 5 vols. Cr. 8°   SML

American Bibliopolist. 9 vols. 1869-1877. 8°   BPL
Contains Shakespeareana.

American Library Association. Portrait Index . . . to portraits contained in printed books and periodicals. Ed. by Wm. Coolidge Lane and Nina E. Browne. Washington : Gov. Pr. Office, 1906. Fcp. 4°, pp. lxxvi.-1602
Sh— p. 1329.

American Sh— Magazine. Ed. by Anna Randall-Diehl, Litt.D. New York : Sh— Magazine Co., 1895-98. 4 vols. Roy. 8°

Amthor (E.) Vocabulary. *See* Sh— Works : Ext. 1873

Amusements—
See Ashbee   *See Sh—*] Rolfe
  ,, Donne (W. B.)   ,, *Sh—*]Sh—'s pastimes
  ,, Douce   times
  ,, Sh—] Drake

Amyot *Bp.* (James) *Editor. See* Plutarchus

Amyot (Thomas) *Editor—*
See Dodsley   *See* Taming . . . 1844

Anagrams. *See Sh—*] Sh— Anagrams

Analysis of the ' Illustrated Sh—.' *See* White

Ancient ballad of the fair Widow of Watling Street and her three daughters . . . 1600. Edited by J. O. Halliwell. Chiswick Press : Privately printed, 1860. 8° BPL

Ancient British Drama. *See Sh—* George-a-Greene, 1810

Ancient critical essays. *See* Haslewood

Ancient documents respecting the office of Master of the Revels, and other papers relating to the early English Theatre. Edited by J. O. Halliwell. Ln : 1870. 8° BPL

Anders (H. R. D.) Sh—'s books : Dissertations on Sh—'s reading and the immediate sources of his works. Ln : Nutt, 1904. 8° BPL | BUS

Anderson (Dr. Alexander) *New York Engraver.* *See* Sh— Works, 1802-04, 1810-12

Anderson (C.) *Publisher. See* Sh— Poems, 1760

Anderson (H.) *Editor. See* Sh— Venus . . . 1847

Anderson (J.) *Artist. See* Sh— Winter's Tale, 1888

Anderson (J.) *Publisher. See* Sh— Works, 1797

Anderson (John) On the site of Macbeth's Castle at Inverness [In 'Archæologia Scotica']. Edinburgh, 1831. With plate. BUS

Anderson *Mdme.* Navarro (Mary) *Actress—*
See Humphreys
  ,, Lytton
  ,, Sh— Romeo . . . 1884
  ,, Sh— Winter's Tale, 1887, 1888
  ,, Sh— Works, 1877-87

Anderson.] Archer (W.) Miss Mary Anderson [In 'The Theatre']. Ln : 1885. Roy. 8° BPL

Anderson (R.) Life of Sh—. *See* Sh—

Anderson (Dr. R.) *Editor. See* Sh— Poems, 1793

Anderson (W.) *Stirling Publisher—*
See Sh— Taming . . . 1792
  ,, Sh— Works, 1792

Anderson (H. C. L.) & Hawkins (W. E.) Shakespearean bibliography. Sydney : New South Wales Sh— Society, 1906. 12° BPL

Anderton (Thomas) *Composer. See* Birmingham

Andrew (J.) *Editor. See* Sh— Hamlet, 1881

Andrew (Lawrence) *Printer. See* Debate and Stryfe

Andrewes (Amelia) Little Notes on Sh—'s England. Ln : Sonnenschein, 1903. Cr. 8°, pp. 124 BPL

Andrews (Francis B.) Castles of Warwickshire. *See* Memorials . . .

Andrews (R.) *Editor. See* Sh— Troilus . . . 1840

Andrews *of Coventry* (William) Ancient British place names . . . [and] Ancient British language in Warwickshire [with Glossary]. Warwick : Printed for private circulation, 1905. 8°, pp. 36. With map SML

Alderman Andrews says Warwickshire natives to-day speak a language consisting of a thick stratum of ancient British with a layer of Anglo-Saxon on top.

Andrews *of Hull* (William) Bygone Warwickshire. Hull : Andrews & Co., 1893. 8°, pp. viii.-284. Illustrated SML

Contains : Timmins (S.) Sh— at home.
    Grindon (Leo) The Sh— garden.
    Wall (A. H.) The Hathaway cottage.
    Langford (J. A.) ' Drunken Bidford.'
    Wall (A. H.) Warwickshire folk-lore.

  Report of the festival held at Hull in honour of the birthday of Sh— . . . 24th April, 1882. Hull, 1882. 8° BM | BPL

  The Doctor, in history, literature, folk-lore, etc. Hull Press, 1896. 8°, pp. viii.-288. Illust.

Contains chapter ' The Doctors Sh— knew,' by A. H. Wall, pp. 76-89.

Andriolli ( ) *Artist. See* Sh— Romeo . . . 1887

Andrus (Silas) *Hartford [U.S.] Publisher. See* Sh— Works, 1829, 1830, 1832, 1846, 1849

Andrus (S.) & Son *Hartford Publishers. See* Sh— Poems, 1852

Andrus & Judd *Hartford Publishers. See* Sh— Works, 1832, 1836

Andrus (W.) *Hartford Publisher. See* Sh— Works, 1843

Angelica. *See* Thurlow (E. A. *Lord*)

Angellier (M.) *Editor. See* Sh— Macbeth, 1876, 1881

Anglo-Saxon story of Apollonius. *See* Apollonius

Anglorum Speculum. *See* S— (G.)

Angus ( ) *Engraver. See* Sh— Works, 1787-91

Angus (J. K.) A Scotch Play-house. Second edition. Aberdeen : Wyllie, 1878. 8° SML

Anna Bullen. *See* Sh— King Henry VIII., 1680

Annalia Dubrensia : Upon . . . Robert Dover's Olimpick games upon Cotswold Hills. Written by M. Drayton, W. Denny, Ben Jonson, S. Marmyon, T. Heywood. Ln : R. Raworth for M. Wallbancke, 1636. Fcp. 4° BM

See also Ashbee

Annalia Dubrensia . . . Manchester, 1877. Fcp. 4° BUS

Annals of the life-work of Sh—. *See Sh—*] Cundall

Anners (H. F.) *Philadelphia Publisher. See* Sh— Works, 1838

Annotations. *See* Sh— Works: Criticism
Annotations illustrative of the plays of Sh —
by Johnson, Steevens, Malone, Theobald,
Warburton, Farmer, Heath, Pope, Haw-
kins, Hanmer, Sir J. Reynolds, and
Percy. Ln: J. Offor, 1819. 2 vols. 12°
                      BM | BUS | CPL
Offprinted from Scholey's edition of Sh—.
Annotations on Plays of Sh—. *See* Croft (J.)
Another essence of Malone. *See* Hardinge
Anson (J. W.) Dramatic and Musical Al-
manack. 1865. 12°   BPL
Anson (W. S. W.) Shakespearean quotations.
See Sh— Works: Ext. 1906
Answer to certain passages. *See* Warburton
Answer to Mr. Pope's preface. *See* Roberts
'Antenor.' Letter to George Chalmers, Esq.,
author of 'An apology . . .' 1800. 8°
                      BPL | W
Refers to the Ireland forgeries.
Anti-Midas. *See* Garrick
Antiquarian Magazine and Bibliographer. Ed.
by Edward Walford and George W.
Redway. Ln: Reeves, Unwin and Red-
way, 1882-87. 8 vols. 8°. Illustrated
Contains much Shakespearean lore and a portrait of
the poet alleged to have been taken just before his
death.
'Antiquary' *pseud.* Sonnets of Sh—: When,
to whom, and by whom written ? [1883.]
12°   BM | BPL
Antiquity, a farce in two acts. Ln: C.
Chapple, 1808. 8°, pp. viii.-46   BUS
A skit on Shakespearean Antiquaries. Two of the
scenes represent Falstaff and his companions at an
Eastcheap tavern.
Antony and Cleopatra. *See* Sh— Antony . . .
Aphorisms from Sh—. *See* Lofft
Apollonius.] Anglo-Saxon version of the story
of Apollonius of Tyre, upon which is
founded the play of 'Pericles' . . . from a
MS. in the library of Ch. Ch. Coll., Cam-
bridge. With a literal translation, etc.
by Benjamin Thorpe. Ln: J. and A.
Arch, 1834. 12°, pp. vi.-92
             BPL | BUS | MPL | W
] Fragment of the English translation of the
romance of Apollonius of Tyre, containing
one hundred and forty lines. [c. 1850.]
Manuscript upon 17 leaves of paper.
Fcp. 4°   W
Apollonius of Tyre—
See also Gesta Romanorum
  ,,   ,,   Gower
  ,,   ,,   *Sh*—] Sh—'s library
Apology for the believers . . . *See* Chalmers
Apology for the life of Colley Cibber. *See*
Cibber
Apolonius and Silla. *See* Rich
Resembles the foundation of ' Twelfth Night.'

Appian. Chronicle of the Romane's Warres.
Ln: 1578. 4°   BUS
Illustrates ' Julius Cæsar.'
Chronicle . . . 1578: Speeches of Brutus
and Antony. Ln: New Sh— Soc., 1875-
76. 8°
Apsley (Wm.) *Publisher. See* Decker
Aramanthus borne a leper. *See* Rich
Arber (Edward) Sh— anthology, 1592-1616.
See Sh— Works: Ext. 1899
Arber (Edward) *Editor—*
See Sh— Poems, 1899
  ,,   Stationers
  ,,   Udall
Arbor of amorous devices. *See* Breton
Arbuthnot *Archdeacon* (George) A poet's in-
spiration. *See Sh*—] Sh— Sermons
] Guide to the Collegiate Church of Stratford-
on-Avon. Stratford: W. Stanton [c.
1895]. Roy. 8°, pp. 24. Illust.   BPL
] Guide to the Collegiate Church . . . Strat-
ford: E. Fox [c. 1895]. Cr. 8°, pp. 12,
incl. pr. wrappers
Poet and historian. *See Sh*—] Sh— Sermons
] Preservation and repair of the Holy Trinity
Church . . . Stratford-on-Avon. [1884.]
4°, pp. 16 (includ. wrappers). With three
views   BPL
Two hours in Stratford-on-Avon ; An
itinerarium. Stratford: J. Morgan, 1889.
Cr. 8°. Illust.   BPL
Arbuthnot *Archdeacon* (George) *Editor—*
See Sh—] Sh— Sermons
  ,, *Stratford*] Vestry . . .
Archæology in the theatre [In ' Macmillan's
Magazine ']. 1886. 8°   BPL
Archdeacon (J.) *Cambridge Printer. See*
Farmer
Archer (Wm.) English dramatists of to-day.
1882. 12°   BPL
Henry Irving. *See* Irving (Sir J. H. B.)
Introducton. *See* Mantzius
Masks or faces: A study in the psychology
of acting. Ln: Longmans, 1888. 8° SML
Myths of ' Romeo and Juliet ' [In the
' National Review ']. 1884. 8° BPL
Ophelia and Portia [In ' The Theatre '].
1885. 8°   BPL
Sh— and the public [In 'About the Theatre,'
pp. 239-256]. 1886. 12°   BPL
Stage of Greater Britain [In ' The National
Review ']. 1885. 8°   BPL
Study and Stage: A year book of criticism.
1886. 12°   BPL
Sh— occupies pp. 77-132.
Study and Stage . . . Ln: 1899. Cr. 8°
W. C. Macready. *See* Macready
' Winter's Tale ' [In ' Nineteenth Century '].
Ln: 1887. Roy. 8°   BPL

Archer (W.)—
See Anderson
  „ Brandes
  „ Irving
  „ Lowe and Archer
  „ Macready
Archer (W.) *Editor.* *See* Macklin
Archer (W.) & Lowe (R. W.) 'Henry VIII.'
  on the stage [In ' Longman's Magazine '].
  8°. 1892   BPL
' Macbeth ' on the stage [In ' English Illust.
  Mag.']. Ln: 1888. Roy. 8°   BPL
Architecture of Sh—. *See* Green
Arden family—
See Bellew   *See* Stopes
  „ French (G. R.)   „ Tucker
Aria (Mrs. E.) Costume; fanciful, historical
  and theatrical. 1906. 8°   BPL
Ariosto. Ariodantes and Geneura. *See* Sh—
  Much Ado, 1890
  Ariodanto and Genevra. *See* *Sh*—] Sh—
  Library
  A foundation of ' Much Ado . . .'
Ariosto. *See also* Gascoigne
Aristippus. *See* Randolph
Aristophanes. *See* Hope
Aristotle. Illustrations. *See* Sh— Works:
  Ext. 1832
See Riddle
Aristotle and Sh—. *See* *Sh*—] Collection
Arlaud (B.) *Artist.* *See* Sh— Works, 1745
Arlequin Cruello. *See* Sh— Othello, 1792
Arliss (   ) *Publisher.* *See* Sh— Works, 1815
Armada. *See* Halliwell
Armin (Robert) Nest of ninnies. Simply of
  themselves without compound. Ln: John
  Deane, 1608. With Introd. and Notes by
  J. P. Collier. Ln: Sh— Soc., 1842. 8°,
  pp. xx.-68   BPL | BUS
  Armin figures in the list of Actors in the Jaggard folio
  1623. See Knight for reply to Collier's Introd.
] The fool and the ice. A brief account of
  a singular adventure . . . supposed to be
  alluded to by Sh— in his . . . ' Troilus
  and Cressida.' Edited by J. O. Halliwell.
  1883. 8°   BM | BPL
Armor of proofe . . . *See* Cotton (R.)
Arms—
See Milles   *See* Silver
  „ Saviolo   „ Tucker
  „ Segar   „ Visitation
Armstrong (   ) *Engraver.* *See* Sh— Works,
  1829
Armstrong *M.D.* (John) Imitations of Sh— . . .
  [In ' Miscellanies ']. Ln: T. Cadell, 1770.
  2 vols. 8°   BPL
  Imitations of Sh— [In ' Works,' Vol. I.,
  pp. 147-163]. 1792. Cr. 8°   BPL
] Sketches or Essays by ' Launcelot Temple.'
  1758. 12°   BPL

Armstrong *pseud.* 'Albert' (John) *Editor.* *See*
  Sh— Sonnets, 1791
Armytage-Morley (F.) *Editor.*   *See* Sh—
  Julius Cæsar, 1902
Arne (Dr. Thomas Augustine) Music in the
  ' Tempest.' *See* Sh— Poems, 1862
  Ode upon dedicating a building to Sh—
  [Stratford Town Hall]; with Music.
  [1769 ?] 8°   BPL
  Arne, with Garrick and Boswell, directed the 1769
  Jubilee.
  Songs. *See* Sh— 'As You Like It' and
  'Twelfth Night.' [1740 ?]
  Songs and duetts . . . *See* Sh— Merchant . . .
  1740
  Songs sung by Mr. Lowe. *See* Sh— ' Mer-
  chant of Venice.' [1740 ?]
Arne (*Dr.* T. A.) *Composer*—
See Dibdin (C.)
  „ Garrick
  „ Sh— As You Like It, 1740
  „ Sh— Comedy of Errors, 1819
  „ Sh— Macbeth, 1785
  „ Sh— Poems, 1850, 1875
  „ Sh— Romeo . . . 1740
  „ Sh— The Tempest, 1776, 1785
  „ Sh— Twelfth Night, 1740
  „ Sh— Winter's Tale, 1762, 1771
Arnold (   ) Verses. *See* Reprints
Arnold (C.) Index to Sh— thought. *See* Sh—
  Works: Ext. 1880
Arnold (C. S.) *Publisher.* *See* Sh— Works,
  1823
Arnold (Matthew) Sh— [A sonnet, in
  ' Poems ']. 1881. 12°   BPL
Arnold (Richard) [Chronicle] Customs of
  London . . . Ln: Richard Pynson [c.
  1496]
  Here Sh— found the source of his ' Seven Ages ' the oft-
  quoted part of ' As You Like It.' The original runs :
  ' Seven ages of man lyving in the worlde : The fyrst
  age is infancie and lastyth from the byrth unto VII.
  yere of age. The second is chyldhood and enduryth
  unto XV. yere of age. The third is adolescencye
  and enduryth unto XXV. yere of age. The fourth
  . . . The fifth age is manhood and enduryth unto
  L. yere of age. The sixth age is second infancie
  and lasteth unto LXX. yere of age. The seventh
  age of a man is crepyll and enduryth unto dethe.'
Arnold (Samuel) *Composer.* *See* Sh— Mac-
  beth, 1770
Arnold (S. J.) *Editor.* *See* Sh— Macbeth, 1814
Arnold (Thomas James I.) Ireland forgeries
  [In ' Fraser's Magazine,' Aug.]. Ln: 1860.
  8°   BUS
Sh— Bibliography in the Netherlands.
  Hague: M. Nijhoff, 1879. 16°, pp. 36
                                 BM | BUS
Shakespearian discovery : The 'old correc-
  tor': Mr. Collier's reply [In Fraser's
  Magazine,' Jan., Feb. and May]. Ln:
  1860. 8°   BPL | BUS

Arraignement of the whole creature. *See* Henderson

Arrowsmith *M.A. Camb.* ( )] The Reformation, a comedy. Acted at the Duke's Theater. Ln : Printed for Will. Cademan, 1673. Fcp. 4°, pp. 82
Mentions Sh— p. 47.

Arrowsmith (William Robson) Letter to the editor of ' Notes & Queries ' and his friend Mr. Singer, or the questionable credit of that periodical and the Sh— adulterators. Ln : Piper, Stephenson & Spence [1858]. 8°, pp. 20   BPL | BUS
On the Collier forgeries.

Sh—'s editors and commentators. Ln : J. R. Smith, 1865. 8°, pp. 52   BPL | BUS | CPL

Art of cavilling [In ' Blackwood's Magazine,' Nov.] Edin., 1856. 8°   BUS
An answer to W. H. Smith (*q. v.*) on the Bacon-Sh— question.

Art of Sh— as revealed by himself. *See* Sh—

Arte of English poesie. *See* Puttenham

Arts Club, Manchester ; Eleventh Sh— commemoration. Manchester : April 23, 1896. 4°, pp. 4. Illust.

As you like it. *See* Sh— As you like it

'As you like it' : Gossip on our Rosalinds [In 'Cornhill Magazine']. Ln : Smith, 1867. 8°   BPL

Asch (M.) Sh—'s and Voltaire's ' Julius Cæsar ' compared. [1881.] 4°   BM

Ash (T. T.) *Philadelphia Publisher. See* Sh— Works, 1838

Ashbee (C. R.) Last records of a Cotswold community, being the Weston Subedge Field Account Book for the final twenty-six years of the famous Cotswold games, hitherto unpublished and now edited with a study on the old-time sports of Campden and . . . Weston Campden. Essex House Press, 1904. Fcp. 4°

Ashbee (Edmund Wm.) *Editor—*
See Historia Histrionica
 ,, Ordinance
 ,, Stage Player
 ,, Tarlton

Ashbee (Edmund Wm.) *Printer—*
See Sh— Hamlet, 1867
 ,, Sh— King Richard II., 1862, 1869, 1870, 1871
 ,, Sh— King Richard III., 1862, 1863, 1865, 1867, 1871
 ,, Sh— Merchant . . . 1865, 1870
 ,, Sh— Merry Wives, 1866
 ,, Sh— Midsummer N. D., 1864, 1865, 1871
 ,, Sh— Much Ado, 1865
 ,, Sh— Othello, 1864
 ,, Sh— Pericles, 1862, 1871
 ,, Sh— Rape, 1866

Ashbee (Edmund Wm.) *Printer—*
See Sh— Romeo, 1865, 1866, 1868, 1869
 ,, Sh— Taming . . . 1870
 ,, Sh— Titus . . . 1866, 1867
 ,, Sh— Troilus . . . 1863, 1871
 ,, Sh— Venus . . . 1866, 1867
 ,, Sh— Works, 1862-71, 1863, 1871

Ashe (T.) *Editor. See* Coleridge (S. T.)

Ashhurst (Richard Lewis) Contemporary evidence of Sh—'s identity. Philadelphia, 1903. 8°, pp. 68   BPL | BUS

Sh— Society of Philadelphia, 1860-79. Philadelphia, 1898. 8°, pp. 36   BUS

Some remarks on W. H. Edwards' ' Shaksper not Sh—.' Philadelphia, 1901. 8°, pp. 54   BPL | BUS

Aspley (Wm.) *Publisher—*
See Marston
 ,, Sh— King Henry IV., ii., 1600
 ,, Sh— Much Ado, 1600
 ,, Sh— Sonnets, 1609
 ,, Sh— Works, 1623, 1632
 ,, Sprot

Astell (T.) *Publisher. See* Macklin

Aston Cantlow Registers. Ed. by Richard Savage. Stratford-on-Avon, 1886. F° broadside (1 sheet)   BPL

Astor (W. W.) Brabantio's love [In ' Pall Mall Magazine ']. 1896. 8°   BPL
Illustrates ' Othello.'

Astronomy. *See* Deverell

Athenæum (The) : Journal of English and foreign literature . . . and the drama. [Ed. by V. H. Rendall.] Ln : Francis, 1828-1909. 4°   BM | BPL
Contains numberless Shakespearean papers and reviews by leading writers. [*Consult its indexes.*]

See also Wright (C.)

Athenian Mercury. No. 14 of Vol. 2 for July 11th, 1691 [Contains query ' Which is the best poem ever made, and who deserves the title of the best poet that ever was ?' The editor replies ' Sh—, Milton, Spenser, Jonson, and D'Avenant ']. F° broadside

Athenian Oracle. *See* Dunton

Athenian Sport. *See* Dunton

Atkins (F.) *See* Poems

Atkins (Ion) Immortal memory of Sh—. Birmingham, 1907. 8°   BPL

Atkinson (Ernest G.) Documents relating to Sh— [Birth-house history. In ' Athenæum,' No. 3638, p. 108, July]. 1897. 4°

Atkinson (H. G.) & Cattell (C.) Authorship of Sh—. [1881.] 12°   BPL

Attempt to rescue . . . Sh—. *See* Holt

Aubrey (John) Brief lives . . . 1898. 2 vols. 8°   BPL
Sh— Vol. I., pp. 97 and 204 ; Vol. II., pp. 225-227.

Aubrey (John) Letters by eminent persons and lives of eminent men. Ln : Longman, 1813. 2 vols. 12° BPL | BUS | SML
Contains anecdotes of Sh—.

Lives. Ed. by Clark. *See* Sh— Epitaph on Combe

Manuscript papers—
See Caulfield
" Malone

Aurelio.] Historie of Avrelio and of Isabell, doughter of the Kinge of Schotlande, nyeuley translatede. In foure langagies : Frenche, Italien, Spanishe, and Inglishe. [By Jean de Flores.] Anvers : Juan Steelsio, 1556. 12° W
Frequently referred to by the commentators ; Collins stated erroneously that the plot of 'The Tempest' is found in it. The four languages are printed in parallel columns.

Authentic memoirs of the green room . . . Drury Lane, Covent Garden and the Haymarket. Ln : Und. 8°

Autographic Mirror. *See* Sh— Will . . . 1864

Autographs. *See* Birmingham

Aveling (E.) 'Hamlet' at 'The Princess's' [In 'To-day']. Ln : 1884. 8° BPL

Aveling (E. B.) On the works of Sh— : 'Hall of Science Thursday Lectures.' 1882. 8° BM | BPL

Avon (River)—
See Garrett   *See* Jaggard (W.)
" Garrick   " Jones (G.)
" Huckell   " Showell
" Ireland (S.)

Avril (P.) *Artist. See* Sh— Antony, 1891

Awdeley (John) Fraternitye of Vacabondes. *See* Viles and Furnivall

Axon (Wm. E. A.) Did Sh— visit Lancashire ? [In 'Manchester Quarterly']. Manchester, 1882. 8° BPL

Axtell (T.) *Publisher. See* Sh— Works : Ext. 1774

Ayers (E. T.) Bowls, bowling greens, bowl playing. 1894. 12° BPL
Shakespearean references pp. 106-109.

Aylesford (Jane Wightwick *Dowager Countess of*). *See* Jaggard (W.)

Ayling (S.) *Editor. See* Sh— Works, 1864

Ayling (S.) *Publisher. See* Sh— As you like it, 1864

Aylward (Theodore) Elegies and glees. Ln : [XIX. Cent.]. F° BUS
Contains from 'Much Ado' the song 'Done to death by slanderous tongues.'

Six Songs. *See* Sh— Midsummer N. D., 1765

Ayscough (Samuel) *B.M. Librarian.* Index. *See* Sh— Works : Ext. 1790, 1791, 1807, 1827, 1842

Ayscough (Samuel) *Editor. See* Sh— Works, 1784, 1790, 1791, 1792, 1807

——(A.) *Printer. See* Marvell

B—— (C.)—
See Bathurst (Charles)
" Brooke
" Ghost . . .
B—— (C.) *Publisher—*
See Allot

B—— (C.) *Publisher. See* Sh— Works : Ext. 1600

B—— (C. A. H.) Sh—'s debt to the Bible [In 'Our Own Fireside']. Ln : May, 1864. Roy. 8° BUS

B—— (G. *or* W.) Beware the Cat. *See* Baldwin (W.)

B—— (G. H. P.) Who wrote the . . . works of Sh— ? An undelivered lecture . . . Ln : Simpkin, 1903. 8°

B—— (G. S.) Prologue and epilogue in English literature : Sh— to Dryden. Ln : Kegan Paul, 1884. 8°, pp. xii.-188 BPL

B—— (H.) Loves of Venus and Adonis. *See* Clarke (R.)

B—— (I.) *Printer—*
See Marlowe
" Sh— Rape, 1624

B—— (J.) Crows of Sh—. *See* Sh— Works : Ext. 1899

B—— (J.) *Editor. See* Sh— Poems, 1872

B—— (J.) *Printer. See* Sh— Titus . . . 1687

B—— *of Selkirk* (J.) *See* Brown (James)

B—— (J. B.) *Editor. See* Shelley

B—— (J. C.) *See* Bucknill

B—— (J. D.) Hollingbury Copse. *See* Halliwell

B—— (N.) *See* Breton (Nicholas)

B—— (O.) Questions of profitable and pleasant concernings talked of by two olde seniors ; the one an ancient retired gentleman, the other a midling or new upstart frankeling, under an oak in Kenelworth Parke . . . called by the report the 'Display of vain life.' Ln : Richard Field, 1594. Fcp. 4°
Dedicated to Robert Devereux, Earl of Essex.

B—— (R.) *Printer—*
See Sh— Yorkshire Tragedy, 1608
" Willis

B—— (R.) *Publisher. See* Sh— Pericles, 1630

B—— (T.) *See* Brewer (Tony *or* Antony)

B—— (W.) Sketch of . . . Sh—. *See* Sh—

B—— (W.) *Printer. See* Barrett (Wm.)

B—— (W.) *Publisher. See* Wright (T.)

B—— and O——. *See* Baltimore

Baar (H.) Moral ideals of Sh— [In 'Historic Soc. of Lancs. and Chas. Trans.'] 1864. 8° BPL

J.Chapman sculpsit

FRANCIS LORD BACON VISCOUNT St. ALBANS.

London, Publish'd as the Act directs, Feb.10.1798, by J.Wilkes

Bacon (Delia S.) Philosophy of the plays of Sh— unfolded. With preface by N. Hawthorne. Ln: Groombridge, 1857. 8°, pp. 680

BM | BPL. | BUS | CPL | MPL | SML

Reviewed in the 'Athenæum,' 11 April, 1857. The authoress is graphically described by N. Hawthorne in 'Our old home' (q.v.). She died insane at Stratford-on-Avon. One of the first to question Sh—'s claims to greatness, Delia Bacon may be regarded as the founder of the Bacon-Sh— controversy. She spent years in preparing her voluminous MS. before kindly Hawthorne found her a publisher; meanwhile W. H. Smith (q.v.) published a small work on the subject.

Philosophy of the plays . . . Boston, U.S: Ticknor & Fields, 1857. 8°, pp. cxii.-582

BUS

Reviewed in 'North American Review,' Oct., 1857.

Wm. Sh— and his plays: An inquiry concerning them [In 'Putnam's Monthly,' Jan.]. New York, 1856 BUS

Reviewed in the 'Athenæum,' 26 July, 1856.

Bacon.] Bacon (Theodore) Delia Bacon: a biographical sketch. Boston, U.S. 1888. 8°. With portrait BUS

Chapter 10 contains 'Wm. Sh— and his plays,' first pub. in 'Putnam's Monthly,' Jan., 1856.

] Biographical sketch of Delia Bacon, with letters from Carlyle, Emerson, etc. 1888. 8° BPL

] Hawthorne (Nathaniel) Recollections of [Delia S. Bacon] a gifted woman [In 'Atlantic Monthly,' Jan.]. Boston, 1862. 8° BUS

Reprinted in Hawthorne's 'Our old home' (q.v.)

Bacon (Delia). *See also* Hawthorne

Bacon *Baron Verulam* (Francis) Conference of pleasure. Ed. from a manuscript belonging to the Duke of Northumberland by J. Spedding. Ln: Longman, 1870. 8° SML

] Declaration of the practises and treasons attempted and committed by Robert late Earle of Essex and his complices, against her Maiestie and her kingdoms, and of the proceedings as well at the arraignments and conuictions of the said late Earle, and his adherents, as after: Together with the very confessions and other parts of the evidences themselves . . . taken out of the originals. Imprinted at Ln by Robert Barker, 1601. Fcp. 4°. Sig. A to Q4 unpaged CTC | W

Upon the last page but one occurs this note of 'King Richard II.': 'That the afternoone before the rebellion Merricke with a great company of others, that afterwards were all in the action, had procured to be played before them the play of deposing 'King Richard the Second.' Neither was it casual but a play bespoken by Merricke. And not so onely, but when it was told him by one of the players that the play was olde and they should have losse in playing it because fewe would come, there was Fourty Shillings extraordinary given to play it, and so

thereupon playd it was. So earnest hee was to satisfie his eyes with the sight of that tragedie which he thought soone after his lord should bring from the stage to the state, but that God turned it upon their owne heads.'

Bacon *Baron Verulam* (Francis) Instauratio Magna [Novum Organum . . .]. Ln: John Bill, 1620. F°. With engraved title by S. Pass showing a ship under full canvas

The Baconians have discovered a passage in 'Love's labours lost' (probably written thirty years before the above was issued) which they claim supports their theories. It is in Act V., Sc. 2:—

> *Bir.* Abate a throw at Novum, and the whole world again
> Cannot pricke out five such ; take each one in his vaine.
> *King.* The ship is under sail, and here she comes amain.

Promus of formularies and elegancies, circa 1594, hitherto unpublished . . . illustrated and elucidated by passages from Sh—, by Mrs. H. Pott. With preface by E. A. Abbott . . . Ln: Longmans, 1883. 8°, pp. xx.-628. With folding facsimiles

BM | BPL | BUS | MPL | SML

'In this note-book Bacon has jotted down a great variety of memoranda, stray thoughts of his own, proverbs, quotations, phrases, and even single words. Mrs. Pott believes that many of them were intended for use, and were actually used in writing the plays of Sh—.'—*Literary World.*

See reviews in 'Athenæum,' 3 Feb., 1883, and in 'Saturday Review' on same date.

Promus of formularies and elegancies. Copied [from the Harleian MS.] and collated by Bickley. 1898. 8° BPL

Bacon.] Abbott (E. A.) Francis Bacon: An account of his life and works. Ln: Macmillan, 1885. 8° SML

] Bacon and Sh— on vivisection. *See* Thomson

] Bacon out-Shakespeared! The story of a horrifying discovery!! Sh— a loose fish!!! By A. Pimpleton Spoffkins. 1887. 12° BPL

] Bacon or Sh— ? Synopsis of some of the arguments advanced by the Baconians. [1887 ?] 4° BPL.

] Baconiana. Vol. I., numbers 1 and 2. Chicago, 1892. 8° BPL

] Baconiana. New Series, 1893. 8° BPL

] Journal of the Bacon Society, Vols. 1 and 2 [all published]. 1886-91. Ln: Redway. 2 vols. 8° BPL | BUS

Largely devoted to the Bacon-Sh— controversy.

] Life and correspondence of Francis Bacon, Viscount St. Albans, Lord Chancellor of England. By a Barrister. Ln: Saunders, Otley & Co., 1861. 8°, pp. xxiv.-568

With several references to Sh—.

] Woodward (P.) Early life of 'Lord' Bacon newly studied. 1902. 8° BPL

Bacon (Francis)—
See Adee *See* Booth
   ,, Bayley   ,, Stopes
   ,, Begley
Bacon-Sh— controversy—
See A—— (W. W.) *See* Laird
   ,, Allen   ,, Lang
   ,, Art of Cavilling   ,, 'Lector'
   ,, Beerbohm   ,, Loosen
   ,, Bormann   ,, Mallock
   ,, Browne (H. J.)   ,, Marriott
   ,, Bucke   ,, Martin
   ,, Burr   ,, Matthew
   ,, C—— (R. C   ,, Maude
   ,, Caldecott   ,, Moore
   ,, Caldwell   ,, Morgan
   ,, Calvert   ,, 'Multum'
   ,, Castle   ,, Newspaper . . .
   ,, Caswell   ,, Nicholson
   ,, Cattle   ,, Northumberland
   ,, Churcher   ,, O'Connor
   ,, Clark (E. G.)   ,, O'Neill
   ,, Clarke (J. F.)   ,, Owen
   ,, Clemens   ,, P—— (J. V.)
   ,, Corbett   ,, Penzance
   ,, Cotgrave   ,, Platt
   ,, Cox   ,, Pott
   ,, Davidson   ,, Pyle
   ,, Dawbarn   ,, Reed
   ,, Dawson   ,, Roe
   ,, De Peyster   ,, Ross
   ,, Dethroning . . .   ,, Rowlands
   ,, Dixon   ,, S—— (E. W.)
   ,, Donnelly   ,, S—— (L. H.)
   ,, Douse   ,, Sanders
   ,, Dowling   ,, Shackford
   ,, Doyle   ,, *Sh*—] Sh— allu-
   ,, Dryerre   sion book
   ,, Duggan   ,, *Sh*—] Sh— ana-
   ,, Edwards   grams
   ,, Elze   ,, *Sh*—] Sh— - Ba-
   ,, Farnaby   con
   ,, Fearon   ,, *Sh*—] Sh— or
   ,, Fiske   Bacon
   ,, Foard   ,, *Sh*—] Sh—'s se-
   ,, Follett   cret
   ,, Gallup   ,, *Sh*—] Sharpe
   ,, Gervais   ,, *Sh*—] Townsend
   ,, Greenwood   ,, Smith (W. H.)
   ,, Hackett   ,, So-called . . .
   ,, Harding   ,, Steel
   ,, Hart   ,, Stopes
   ,, Hayward   ,, Stotzenburg
   ,, Henderson   ,, Stronach
   ,, Holmes   ,, Taverner
   ,, Holzer   ,, Thayer
   ,, Hosmer   ,, Theobald (R. M.)
   ,, Irving   ,, Theobald (W.)
   ,, James   ,, Thomson
   ,, King   ,, Thorne

Bacon-Sh— controversy—
See Thorpe *See* White
   ,, Titmarsh   ,, Who wrote Sh—?
   ,, Towne   ,, Wigston
   ,, Vaile   ,, Wilkes
   ,, Varagnac   ,, Willis (W.)
   ,, Was Bacon . . .   ,, Windle
   ,, Webb   ,, Wyman
Bacon.] Famous history of Fryer Bacon.
  1637. Fcp. 4°   BPL
Baddeley (Robert) *Actor*—
See Sh— King Henry V., 1780
  ,, Sh— King Henry VI., i., 1786
  ,, Sh— The Tempest, 1778
Badger (E. W.) Monumental brasses of War-
  wickshire. Birmingham : Cornish, 1895.
  8°   SML
Badger (Richard) *Publisher.* *See* Sh— Peri-
  cles, 1630
Badham *D.D.* (Charles) Criticism applied to
  Sh— : . . . Essays, published in ' The
  Surplice.' Ln : [Privately printed by]
  J. Bohn, 1846. 8°, pp. 16
      BM | BPL | BUS | CPL | MPL | SML
Badham (Charles) Text of Sh— [In ' Cam-
  bridge Essays,' pp. 261-291]. Ln : 1856.
  8°   BPL | BUS
Bagehot (Walter) Sh— the individual. *See*
  Sh—
  Sh— the man. *See* Sh—
Bagnall (J. E.) Flora of Warwickshire . . .
  Birm : Cornish ; Ln : Gurney & Jackson,
  1891. 12°   SML
Baildon (H. Bellyse) *Editor.* *See* Sh— Titus
  . . . 1904
Bailey (Samuel) On the received text of Sh—'s
  dramatic writings and its improvement.
  Ln : Longman, 1862-66. 2 vols. 8°
        BM | BPL | BUS | CPL | W
Bailey (Sir Wm. H.) ' Bradshaw ' of Sh—
  [On ' Birm. Sh— Cat.'] Manchester [c.
  1904]. 8°   BPL
  Henry VIII. and the last work of Sh—.
  Manchester Sh— Soc., 1902. 8°   BPL
  Sh— and Montaigne. Manchester, 1895.
  8°   BPL
  Sh— and temperance. Inaugural address
  . . . Manchester Sh— Society. For pri-
  vate circulation, 1900. 8°, pp. 16. With
  Madox Brown portrait
  Sh— and temperance. Manchester [c. 1903].
  8°   BPL
  Sh— as a patriot. Manchester Sh— Soc.,
  1899. 8°   BPL
  Souvenir : ' King Henry VIII.,' Queen's
  Theatre, Manchester. Revived by R.
  Flanagan. [1903.] Fcp. 4°   BPL
  Swinburne and Sh— : Inaugural address to
  the Manchester Sh— Soc. Manchester,
  1909. 8°

Baillot (A.) *Editor.* *See* Hugo

Bain (Dr. B.) Sh—'s death. *See* Sh—

Bain (David) *Editor.* *See* Sh— The Tempest, 1892

Baker ( ) *Boston, U.S. Publisher.* *See* Sh— Merchant . . . 1866, 1871

Baker (David Erskine)] Biographia dramatica, or a companion to the playhouse . . . New edition, enlarged. Ln : Rivington, 1782. 2 vols. 8°

] Companion to the play-house, or an historical account of all the dramatic writers and their works that have appeared in Great Britain and Ireland. Composed in the form of a dictionary. Ln : T. Becket & P. A. De Hondt, 1764. 2 vols. 12°
BPL | CPL | MPL | SML
Sh— occupies five pages. The authorship of this work has been assigned to Oliver Goldsmith.

Baker (D. E.) Reed (I.) & Jones (S.) Biographia dramatica : A companion to the playhouse. Ln : Longman, 1812. 3 vols. 8° BPL | BUS | MPL | SML
Sometimes found bound in four vols.

Baker (Ernest E.) Calendar. *See* Halliwell
Halliwell-Phillipps Library. *See* Halliwell

Baker (F. T.) *Editor.* *See* Sh— Macbeth, 1901

Baker (George M.) Peddler of Very-Nice. *See* Sh— Merchant . . . 1866, 1871

Baker (George P.) Development of Sh— as a dramatist. *See* Sh—

Baker (G. P.) *Editor*—
See Sh— As You Like It, 1907
,, Sh— Midsummer N. D., 1896

Baker (Harold) Collegiate Church of Stratford-on-Avon and other buildings of interest in the town and neighbourhood. Fifty-eight illustrations, chiefly from photographs by the author. Ln : Bell, 1903. Cr. 8°, pp. 108 BPL | SML

Baker (H. Barton) Colley Cibber. *See* Cibber
London stage : its history and traditions from 1576 to 1888. Ln : Allen & Co., 1889. 2 vols. Cr. 8°. Plates BPL | SML
Contains a 'Chronological list of London theatres from the earliest period.'

Our old actors. Ln : Bentley, 1878. 2 vols. 8° SML

Baker (James) Literary and biographical studies, or 10,000 miles with Sh—. Ln : Chapman, 1908. 8°, pp. 268 BPL

Baker (Oliver) Moated houses of Warwickshire. *See* Memorials . . .

Baker (*Sir* Richard) Chronicle of the kings of England. Ln : 1660. F°. Frontispiece contains portraits SML
Refers to Sh— at p. 503.

Baker (*Sir* Richard) Theatrum triumphans, or a discourse of plays, shewing the lawfulness and excellent use of dramatique poesy wherein the vain objections of 'Histriomastix' [by Prynne] are answered and confuted. Ln : 1670. 12° SML

Baker (W. H.) *Editor.* *See* Sh— Coriolanus, 1880

Baldwin (A.) *Printer.* *See* Sh— Merry Wives, 1702

Baldwin (H.) *Printer.* *See* Sh— Works, 1790, 1798

Baldwin (H.) *Publisher.* *See* Malone

Baldwin (Richard) *Publisher*—
See Rymer
,, Sh— King Henry VIII., 1762
,, Sh— King Lear, 1768
,, Sh— Macbeth, 1770
,, Sh— Merchant . . . 1783
,, Sh— The Tempest, 1761
,, Sh— Timon . . . 1770
,, Sh— Works, 1762, 1798

Baldwin *jun.* (R.) *Publisher.* *See* Chetwood

Baldwin (William)] 'Beware the Cat, 1570': An exceedingly rare rhapsody . . . containing matters illustrative of the stage and the writings of Sh—. Edited by J. O. Halliwell. Ln : 1864. Fcp. 4°
BM | BPL | HCL | MPL
Issue restricted to ten copies.
According to Halliwell, no copy exists of the first edition, 1551, and no complete copy of the 1570 and 1584 issues.

Baldwin (Wm.) *See* Mirrour . . .

Baldwin and Cradock *Publishers.* *See* Sh— Fifth of November, 1830

Bale *Bp. of Ossory* (John) Briefe chronycle concerning the examination and death of that blessed martir of Christ Sir Iohn Oldecastell the Lord Cobham. Ln : Imprinted by Anthony Scoloker and Wyllyam Seres. [1548.] 12°. Black letter ; with portrait of Cobham on title
A supposed source of 'Sir John Oldcastle.'

Kynge Johann : a play. Ln : 1838. Fcp. 4° BUS

Bale *Bp.* (John). *See also* S—— (L.)

Balfe (M. W.) *Composer.* *See* Sh— Merry Wives, 1838

Balfour ( ) *Edinburgh Publisher.* *See* Sh— Works, 1753

Ball (John) *Publisher.* *See* Sh— All's Well, 1773

Ball (W.) Etchings round about Stratford-on-Avon. [1890 ?] 12° BPL

Ball, Arnold & Co. *Publishers.* *See* Sh— Sonnets, 1840

Ballad.] 'I'm to be married o' Sunday': Illustrative of a passage in 'Taming of the Shrew.' *See Sh*—] Sh— Soc.

Ballad intituled the 'Constancy of Susanna.'
[c. 1760.] Roy. 4°. Broadsides: two
different editions, each of two pages,
with woodcuts   w
Quoted in 'Twelfth Night.'

Ballad of the northern lord: founded on the
story of the 'Merchant of Venice.'
Coventry [c. 1800]. 4°. With woodcuts
BPL

'Ballad of two lovers,' illustrative of 'Romeo
and Juliet.' Ed. by A. Barton. *See
Sh*—] Sh— Soc.

'Ballad-Monger,' *pseud. of* Halliwell (J. O.)

Ballads.] Bundle of old ballads laid open to
view [1550-70] in modern type and
orthography. Ln: 1870. 8°. With cuts

Ballads.] Collection of seventy-nine black
letter ballads and broadsides . . . between
1559 and 1597. Accompanied with introd. and illustrative notes by J. Lilly
[J. P. Collier and J. O. Halliwell]. Ln:
Joseph Lilly, 1867. 8°, pp. xxxvi.-320
Contains the 'Faire Widow of Watling Street,' pp.
157-166, and several Sh— references in the notes.

Ballads and ballad music. *See* Barr (A. E.)

Ballads of books. Ed. by Andrew Lang.
Ln: Longmans, 1888. 12°, pp. xx.-158
Contains ballad, pp. 80-82, entitled 'My Sh—,' by
H. C. Bunner.

Ballads that illustrate Sh— [In Percy's 'Reliques of Anc. Eng. Poetry,' Vol. I., pp.
151-246]. 1891. 8°   BPL

Ballads—
See Barr   *See* Oliphant
„ Broadside   „ Rimbault
„ Chappell   „ Ritson
„ Deloney   „ *Sh*—] Sh—ana
„ Falconer   „ Somers
„ Old Ballads

Ballantyne ( ) *Edinburgh Publisher. See*
Sh— Works, 1807, 1819

Ballantyne (J. R.) *Editor. See* Sh— Macbeth,
1848

Ballard ( ) *Publisher. See* Sh— Othello,
1869

Ballard (Henry) *Printer. See* Sh— Merry
Devil . . . 1608

Ballinger (J.) Sh— and the municipal libraries
[In 'The Library,' April, pp. 181-191].
Ln: 1906. Roy. 8°   BPL

Balmanno (Mary) Lines addressed to T. C.
Croker . . . on his acquisition of Sh—'s
gimmel ring. New York: Priv. printed
. . . for the Soc. of Noviomagus by J. D.
Torrey, 1857. 4°, pp. 8 and portrait of
Croker   BUS

Balmanno (Robert) Testimonial to Mary
Cowden Clarke. New York: For sub-
scribers only, 16 Feb., 1852. 8°, pp.
xii. and portrait   BUS | w
First appeared in the 'New York Whig Review.'

Balne ( ) *Publisher. See* Sh— Works, 1825

B[altimore] and O[hio] Shakspearian Salma-
gundi. [1887 ?] 12°   BPL

Balzac (H. de). *See* Lilly (W. S.)

Bancroft (Mrs.) Gleanings from 'On and
off the stage.' Ln: Routledge, 1892. 8°,
pp. 320

Bancroft.] Mr. and Mrs. Bancroft on and off
the stage. Ln: Bentley, 1891. 12° SML

Bancroft (Thomas) Two bookes of epigrammes
and epitaphs, dedicated to two top-
branches of gentry, Sir Charles Shirley,
baronet, and William Davenport, esquire.
Ln: Printed by I. Okes for M. Wallbancke,
and are to be sold at his shop in Grayes
Lane Gate, 1639. Fcp. 4°   w
Contains two epigrams addressed to Sh—, numbered
118 and 119.
The Warwick copy came from the library of Thomas
Park, and is enriched by his manuscript notes. [*See*
Halliwell's 'Sh— reliques,' 4to., 1852, p. 125].
One of the early writers who perceived and acknow-
ledged the pre-eminence of Sh—.

Bandello (Matteo) Timbreo di Cardona. *See*
Sh—] Sh—'s Library
A foundation of 'Much Ado . . .'

Bandello (Matteo) & Brookes (Arthur)]
Tragicall history of Romeus and Iuliet,
written first in Italian by Bandell, and
now in English by Ar. Br——. Impr.
at Ln. in Flete Strete within Temble
Barre at the Signe of the Hand and
Starre by Richard Tottill, the XIX. day
of Nouember, 1562. 8°. Black letter.
Sig. A to L4, folios numbered
BLO | BUS | CTC
The foundation of 'Romeo and Juliet.'

Tragicall historie of Romeus and Iuliet.
Contayning in it a rare example of true
constancie. With the subtill counsels
and practises of an old Fryer and their ill
euent . . . At Ln: Imprinted by R.
Robinson, 1587. 8°. Black letter. Sig.
A to N8, on numbered folios   CTC

Tragical history of Romeus and Juliet.
[Edited by Edmund Malone.] Ln: C.
Bathurst . . . 1780. 8°
Twelve copies off-printed with separate pagination
from Malone's Supplement, 2 vols.

Tragical history of Romeus and Juliet, 1843.
See Sh—] Sh—'s Library

Tragical history of Romeus and Juliet.
Ed. by P. A. Daniel. Ln: New Sh—
Soc., 1875. 8°

Tragical history of Romeus and Juliet,
[and] History of Hamlet. Ln: Cassell,
1890. 12°, pp. 192

Tragical history of Romeus and Juliet, and
History of Hamlet. 1895. 12°   BPL

Tragical history of Romeus and Juliet. Ed.
by J. J. Munro. 'Sh— Classics.' Ln:
De la More Press, 1908. Fcp. 4°   BPL

Bandmann (D. E.) An actor's tour. New York, 1886. 12°   BPL

Bandow (Dr. K.) *Editor. See* Sh— Works: Ext. 1873

Bangs (J. K.) *Editor. See* Sh— Taming . . . 1888

Banks (George Linnæus)] All about Sh—. Profusely illustrated with wood engravings by T. Gilks, drawn by H. Fitzcook. In commemoration of the tercentenary [1864]. Ln: H. Lea [1864]. 8°, pp. 62. With portraits   BM | BPL | BUS | CPL

] England's minstrel king; Song and chorus written and composed expressly for performance at the tercentenary festivals at London and Stratford . . . Music by G. A. Macfarren. Sung by Sims Reeves. Ln: Music Pub. Co. [1864]. F°, 8 pp.   BUS

Banks (John) Vertue betray'd: or, Anna Bullen. A tragedy. Ln: 1682. Fcp. 4° w
A play on the subject of 'King Henry VIII.'

Banks ('Showman') Performing horse. *See* Pegasus

Bankworth (Richard) *Publisher—*
See Battell of Alcazar
  ,, Stukeley

Bannister.] Adolphus (J.) Memoirs of John Bannister, comedian. [1839.] 2 vols. 8°   BPL | SML

Barba (   ) *Paris Publisher. See* Sh— Hamlet, 1836

Barber (H.) British family names. Ln: Stock, 1894. 8°   SML

Barbier (J.) *Editor. See* Sh— Hamlet, 1869
Barbier (P. J.) *Editor. See* Sh— Romeo . . . 1867

Barclay (Alex.) *Editor. See* Brandt
Barclay (James)] Examination of Mr. Kenrick's review of Johnson's edition of Sh—. Ln: W. Johnston, 1766. 8°, pp. xii.-92   BPL | BUS
The writer was an Oxford student.

Barclay *or* Barckley (Sir Richard) Discovrse of the felicitie of man, or his summum bonum . . . Ln: Printed [by Wm. Jaggard] for Wm. Ponsonby, 1598. Fcp. 4°   w
A garner full of amusing histories and small narratives, including the foundation of 'Taming of the Shrew,' pp. 23-26, 'Antony and Cleopatra,' p. 46, 'Pyramus and Thisbe,' p. 52.

Discovrse of the felicitie of man . . . At Ln: Printed for Wm. Ponsonby [by Wm. Jaggard], 1603. Fcp. 4°, pp. xvi.-736

Felicitie of man . . . Ln: 1631. Fcp. 4° w

Bard of Avon birthday book. *See* Sh— Works: Ext. 1880, 1881, 1882

Bardi (Girolamo) *Editor. See* Mexia

Baret (John) Alvearie or quadruple dictionarie, containing . . . English, Latine, Greeke & French. Ln: Henry Denham, 1580. F°
The materials were collected in eighteen years by Baret's pupils, and entitled on that account an Alvearie or Beehive. Of considerable service for its great store of obsolete words used by Sh—.

Barham (G.) *Editor. See* Sh— Othello, 1821
Barham (Wm.) *Editor. See* Sh— Julius Cæsar, 1822

Barker (J.) Complete list of plays, exhibiting at one view the title, size, date, and author, from the commencement of theatrical performances to 1803. To which is added a continuation to the 'Theatrical Remembrancer' designed to shew collectively each author's work. Ln: J. Barker [1803]. 8°, pp. iv.-350   SML

] Drama recorded, or Barker's list of plays to 1814, [with] Notitia dramatica. 1814. 12°   BPL

Barker (J.) *Publisher—*
See Ireland (S. W. H.)
  ,, Sh— Cymbeline, 1795
  ,, Sh— Hamlet, 1800, 1820
  ,, Sh— King Henry VIII., 1790
  ,, Sh— King Richard III., 1794
  ,, Sh— Merchant . . . 1794, 1802
  ,, Sh— Othello, 1800
  ,, Sh— Romeo . . . 1794, 1803
  ,, Sh— The Tempest, 1794
  ,, Sh— Twelfth Night, 1794
  ,, Sh— Winter's Tale, 1794
  ,, Sh— Works, 1798

Barker (R.) *Publisher. See* Sh— King Richard II., 1720

Barker (Robert) *Printer—*
See Bacon
  ,, Euordanus
  ,, James I.

Barkstead (William) Mirrha the mother of Adonis, or luste's prodigies. Ln: 1607
Referring to Sh—, says: 'His song was worthie merit.'

Barley (Wm.) *Publisher. See* Sh— King Richard III., 1594

Barlow (Tymothie) *Publisher. See* Sh— King Henry V., 1617

Barnard (Alfred) Round about Warwick. Ln: Nelson, Dale & Co., 1899. Fcp. 4°, pp. 64. Illustrated
With a chapter on Sh— and Stratford. Every page headed with a running quotation from Sh—

Barnard (Francis Pierrepont) *Editor—*
See Sh— King John, 1897
  ,, Sh— King Richard III., 1897

Barnard (*Sir* John and *Lady*) Facsimile of an indenture . . . in October, 1652, in which they covenant to levy a fine settling a portion of the estates of Sh— to themselves for their lives, then to the children of Lady Barnard, and in default of such issue, to be subject to her direction. [Ed. by J. O. Halliwell.] Brighton : John George Bishop, 1883. F°. Issue limited to twenty-six copies   SML

Barnard.] Inventory A.D. 1674 of the goods of Sir J. Barnard : Record of letters of administration to Sir John Barnard's goods, 1674 ; Pedigree of Sh—'s grand-daughter and her husband's children. Ln : New Sh— Soc., 1880-86. 8°

Barnard.] Last of the Shakespeares [Barnard family and Abington Abbey]. 1889. Cr. 8°   BPL

Barnards of Abington—
See Scott (E. J. L.)
  ,, Sh—] Sh— MSS.
  ,, Taylor (John)

Barnefield (Richard) Encomion of Lady Pecunia, or the praise of money . . . Ln : G. S—— for John Jaggard, 1598. Fcp. 4°, pp. 52

At p. 44 occurs a 'Remembrance of some English poets,' with the stanza :—
  'And Sh—! thou, whose hony-flowing vaine,
  Pleasing the world thy praises doth containe,
  Whose 'Venus' and whose 'Lucrece' sweete and chaste
  Thy name in fame's immortal booke have plac't,
  Live ever you, at least in fame live ever ;
  Well may the bodye dye, but fame dye never.'
Contains also three poems reprinted in Sh—'s 'Passionate Pilgrim,' 1599.

Encomion of Lady Pecunia. Ln : 1816. Fcp. 4°   BUS

Encomion of Lady Pecunia, 1598. *See* Reprints . . . 1866

Lady Pecunia, or the praise of money . . . Newly corrected and inlarged. Ln : Printed by W. I—— [Wm. Jaggard] and are to bee sold by John Hodgets . . . 1605. Fcp. 4°, pp. 40
Reprinted by J. P. Collier in 1866.

Lady Pecunia, 1605. *See* Reprints
See Nicholson (S.)
  ,, Sh— Passionate . . . 1599, 1870, 1883

Barnes (Barnaby) Divil's charter : A tragædie. Ln : 1607. Fcp. 4°   BUS
According to Baker's 'Biog. Dram.,' this play is formed after the model of 'Pericles.' In Act V., sc. 1, Hamlet's soliloquy is imitated.

Foure bookes of offices, enabling private persons for the special service of all good princes and policies. Ln : G. Bishop, T. Adams, & C. Burbie, 1606. F°
Refers to 'King Kichard III.' at p. 113.

Barnes.] Knight (Joseph) Barnabe Barnes, poet and playwright [In 'Athenæum,' No. 4008, p. 240]. Aug., 1904

Barnes (Joseph) *Oxford Printer. See* Rider

Barnett (Miss) *Editor. See* Sh— Mid. N. D., 1866

Barnett (Morris) ' The Tempest ' as a lyrical drama. 1850. 8°   BPL | CPL | MPL

Barnett (Thomas Duff) Notes on ' As you like it.' Ln : Bell, 1895. 8°, pp. 72
   BM | BPL | BUS

Notes on ' Coriolanus.' Ln : Bell, 1891. 8°

Notes on ' Coriolanus.' Second edition. Ln : Bell, 1892. 8°, pp. 76   BPL | BUS

Notes on ' Hamlet.' Ln : Bell, 1889. 8°
   BM | BUS

Notes on ' Hamlet.' Second edition. Ln : Bell, 1893. 8°, pp. 100   BPL

Notes on ' Julius Cæsar.' Third edition. Ln : Bell, 1891. 8°, pp. 48   BPL

Notes on ' King Henry V.' Fourth edition. Ln : Bell, 1895. 8°   BPL

Notes on ' King John.' Ln : Bell, 1890. 8°
   BPL

Notes on ' King Lear.' Ln : Bell, 1891. 8°
   BM | BPL | BUS

Notes on ' King Richard II.' Ln : Bell, 1890. 8°   BM | BUS

Notes on ' King Richard II.' Second edition. Ln : Bell, 1893. 8°   BPL

Notes on ' King Richard II.' Third edition. Ln : Bell, 1896. 8°, pp. 68

Notes on ' King Richard III.' Ln : Bell, 1895. 8°, pp. 82   BM | BPL | BUS

Notes on ' Macbeth.' Ln : Bell, 1889. 8°
   BPL

Notes on the ' Merchant of Venice.' Ln : Bell, 1889. 8°   BM | BUS

Notes on the ' Merchant of Venice.' Second edition. Ln : Bell, 1892. 8°   BPL

Notes on a ' Midsummer Night's Dream.' Ln : Bell, 1887. 8°, pp. 44   BPL | BUS

Notes on a ' Midsummer Night's Dream,' Ln : Bell, 1894. 8°, pp. 44

Notes on . . . ' Much ado about nothing.' Ln : Bell, 1895. 8°, pp. 72 BM | BPL | BUS

Notes on ' The Tempest.' Second edition, revised. Ln : Bell, 1890. 8°   BPL | BUS

Notes on . . . ' Twelfth Night.' Ln : Bell, 1895. 8°, pp. 72   BM | BPL | BUS

Questions on ' The Tempest.' [1897.] 8°
   BM

Barnett (T. D.) *Editor*—
See Sh— Julius Cæsar, 1893
  ,, Sh— King Richard II., 1890
  ,, Sh— Merchant . . . 1893
  ,, Sh— The Tempest, 1893

Barnstorff (D.) Key to Sh—'s Sonnets. Trans. from the German by T. J. Graham. Bremen, Ln : Trübner, 1862. 8°, pp. 220
   BPL | SML

Barnstorff (D.) *Editor. See* Sh— Sonnets, 1860, 1862

Barr (Amelia E.)] Ballads and ballad music illustrating Sh— [In 'Harper's Mag.']. 1881. 8°   BPL

Barr (Amelia E.)] Young people of Sh—'s dramas. New York, 1882. 12°. Illust.
BUS

Barré (P. G.) Editor. See Sh— Othello, 1792

Barret (J. V.) Sh—, fresh chiselled on stone. Ln : Dean [1859]. 12°. With 14 comic plates BM | BPL | BUS
Also issued with coloured plates.

Barret (Robert) Theorike and practike of moderne warres. 1598. F°
Supposed by Chalmers to be alluded to in ' All's Well.'

Barrett (E. E.) Publisher. See Sh— Works, 1874

Barrett (L.) E. Forrest. See Forrest

Barrett (L.) Editor. See American . . .

Barrett (S. B.) Publisher. See Sh— Works, 1879

Barrett (T. S.) Who wrote ' Sh—'? 8°. 1896
BM

Barrett (William) Printer. See Sh— Venus . . 1617

Barrett (Wilson) Actor. See Scott (C. W.)

Barrett (Wilson) Editor. See Sh— Hamlet, 1884, 1886

Barrey (Lodowick) Ram Alley, or merrie trickes. A comedy . . . acted by the children of the King's revels. Ln : 1611. Fcp. 4°
Said to be 'one continuous parody of Sh—.' [See Fleay's Sh— Manual].

Barrie (J. M.) My lady nicotine. Ln : Hodder, 1892. 8°
Chapter xiii. (pp. 105-116), 'The grandest scene in history,' contains the ' Influence of tobacco on Sh—.'

Barrington (Lord) Treasurer. See Cunningham

Barrow Diggers—
See Sh— Hamlet, 1839
„ Woolls

Barry ( ) Composer. See Sh— Merry Wives, 1824

Barry (Spranger) Actor—
See Foote
„ Jemmat
„ Sh— Timon . . . 1773, 1780
„ Sh— Othello, 1777, 1780

Barry (Thomas) Editor. See Sh— The Tempest, 1856

Barry (W.) Editor—
See Sh— King Henry V., 1892
„ Sh— King Richard II., 1894
„ Sh— Works, 1893

Barrymore.] Life of the Earl of Barrymore, including a history of the Wargrave theatricals and original anecdotes of eminent persons. By 'Anthony Pasquin' [J. Williams]. Ln : 1793. 8°

Barsanti (Miss) Actress. See Sh— Midsummer N. D., 1778

Barter (A.) Editor. See Sh— Much Ado, 1903

Barth ( ) Publisher. See Sh— King Richard III., 1844

Barthel (G. E.) Halle Publisher. See Sh— Works, 1869

Barthelimon ( ) Composer. See Dibdin (C.)

Bartlet (W. S.) Lowell Sh— memorial : Exercises on the tercentenary celebration. 1864. 8° BM

Bartlett (G. B.) Mrs. Jarley's waxworks. [1840 ?] 2 vols. 12° BPL
The Shakesperian Chamber, part 2, pp. 28-32.

Bartlett (John) Book of familiar quotations. See Sh— Works : Ext. 1860, 1862, 1887
New and complete concordance . . . to the works of Sh— See Sh— Works : Ext. 1894, 1899
Sh— phrase book. See Sh— Works : Ext. 1881, 1882

Bartol (Cyrus A.) Personality of Sh—. See Sh—] Bartol

Bartolozzi (Francesco) Engraver—
See Sh— Poems, 1795, 1798
„ Sh— Works : Ext. 1792-96

Barton (A.) Editor. See Ballad

Barton (Richard) Of Sh— [In 'The Farrago']. Tewkesbury, 1792. 2 vols. 8° BUS | W

Barton (Thomas Pennant)] Description of a copy of the first folio of Sh—. New York : Privately printed by C. A. Alvord, 1862. Roy. 8°, pp. 22 BM | BUS
Issue limited to twenty copies.
Holograph letters, with replies, referring to his library, chiefly to and from booksellers. New York, 1834-64. Collection in 6 vols. 4° BUS
List of Shakespeariana and books wanted. New York [1834-69]. Holograph MS. 3 vols. 4° BUS
Lists of magazines, portraits, autographs, etc. wanted. New York [Und., 1834-69]. Holograph MS. F° BUS
Shakespeariana, or a complete list of all the works relating to Sh—. New York [1834-69]. Holograph MS. 2 vols. 4°, over 1,000 pages BUS
Classified into : Ancient quarto plays, Ancient collected editions, Modern editions, Poems, Spurious plays, Plays altered, Detached criticisms, Biographical and literary notices, Ireland forgery, Anniversaries and festivals, Engravings and autographs, Translations, Shakesperian books. Full titles and collations are given, with notes and references.

] Wanted, to purchase, the books enumerated in this catalogue [Shakespeariana]. Ln : J. R. Smith, 1857. 8°, pp. 16 BPL | BUS

Barwick (G. F.) Impresas [In ' The Library,' April, pp. 140-148]. 1906. Roy. 8° BPL

Bas (W.) Sword and buckler, 1602. See Reprints

Baskerville (John) Birmingham Printer—
See Huckell
„ Sh— Works, 1768

Basse (Wm.) Epitaph on Sh—
See Donne See Sh—] Tyrrell

Basset (Richard) *Publisher.* *See* Pix
Bateman (Stephen) *Editor.* *See* Glanvilla
Bates (K. L.) English religious drama. New
 York: Macmillan, 1893. 12° SML
Bates (W.) Collection of manuscript notes,
 newspaper cuttings, relating to Sh—.
 1854. 8° BPL
Bath. *See* Penley
Bathurst (C.) *Publisher—*
 See Edwards (T.)
 ,, Sh— As You Like It, 1786
 ,, Sh— Cymbeline, 1784
 ,, Sh— King Henry IV., i., 1785
 ,, Sh— King Lear, 1786
 ,, Sh— Macbeth, 1770, 1785
 ,, Sh— Merchant . . . 1783
 ,, Sh— Othello, 1784
 ,, Sh— Poems, 1780
 ,, Sh— Taming . . . 1786
 ,, Sh— The Tempest, 1785
 ,, Sh— Timon . . . 1770
 ,, Sh— Winter's Tale, 1785
 ,, Sh— Works, 1768, 1773, 1778, 1780, 1785
Bathurst (Charles)] On Sh—. 1854. 12°
 BPL
] Remarks on the difference in Sh—'s ver-
 sification in different periods of his life
 and on the like points of difference in
 poetry generally. Ln: J. W. Parker,
 1857. 8°, pp. 218 BM | BPL | BUS | CPL
] Remarks on . . . Sh—'s versification. Ln:
 J. W. Parker, 1859. 8°
Batley (J.) *Publisher—*
 See Sh— Poems, 1725, 1728
 ,, Sh— Works, 1725
Batman uppon Bartholome. *See* Glanville
Battell of Alcazar . . . as it was sundrie times
 plaid by the Lord high Admirall his
 seruants. Imprinted at Ln. by Edward
 Allde for Richard Bankworth and are to
 be solde at his shoppe in Pouls Church-
 yard at the signe of the Sunne, 1594.
 Ln: Malone Society, 1907. Fcp. 4°
Battle of Alcazar. *See* Halliwell
Baudissin *Count* (Wolf)] *Translator of Sh—*
 [In 'Macmillan's Magazine']. 1885. 8°
 BPL
Baudius. Moralis et civilis sapientiæ monita.
 Leydæ: L. Elzevir, 1611. *See Sh—*]
 Collection
 With Ben Jonson's autograph.
Baudry (M.) *Paris Publisher—*
 See Sh— Julius Cæsar, 1865
 ,, Sh— Works, 1827, 1830, 1835-36, 1838,
 1842, 1843, 1843-44, 1844, 1847
Baughan (Rosa) *Editor—*
 See Sh— Works, 1863-71
 ,, Sh— Works: Ext. 1871
 ,, Sh— Works, 1879

Baugust (W. F.) *Editor—*
 See Sh— Cymbeline, 1896
 ,, Sh— Midsummer N. D., 1894
Baumgartner ( ) *Leipzig Publisher—*
 See Sh— Romeo, 1833
 ,, Sh— Works, 1837-39, 1854, 1864
Baverstock (J. H.) Few words on the line in
 'Hamlet' as regards 'too too.' *See Sh—*]
 Sh— Soc.
 On a mistake in Chambers' 'Cycl. of Lit.'
 relating to 'Damon and Pythias.' *See
 Sh—*] Sh— Soc.
 Damon is mentioned in 'Hamlet.'
Bayard (E.) *Artist—*
 See Sh— As You Like It, 1887
 ,, Sh— Works, 1884-92
Bayes (Joshua ?) Reasons of Mr. Bays
 changing his religion. Ln: 1688
 Refers to Sh— at pp. 7 and 15.
Bayley (Harold) Sh— symphony; Introduc-
 tion to the ethics of the Elizabethan
 drama. Ln: Chapman, 1906. 8°, pp.
 404 BPL | SML
 Sh—symphony. Ln: Chapman, 1908. 8°,
 pp. 404
 Tragedy of Sir Francis Bacon: An appeal
 for further investigation and research.
 Ln: Richards, 1901. Cr. 8°, pp. 292.
 With illustrations, portraits, and fac-
 similes BPL | BUS
Bayne (Peter) Mr. Spedding's proposed
 arrangement of acts in 'King Lear.'
 Ln: New Sh— Soc., 1880-86. 8°
Bayne (Ronald) Sh—. *See Sh—*] Bayne
 Was Hamlet mad ? Ln: 1882. Cr. 8° BPL
Bayne (Ronald) *Editor. See* Sh— Arden, 1897
Baynes (Dr. Thomas Spencer) Life of Sh—.
 See Sh—] Baynes
 Sh— studies and essay on English dic-
 tionaries. With biog. preface by L.
 Campbell. Ln: Longmans, 1894. 8°,
 pp. xvi.-410 BM | BPL | MPL | SML
 Sh— studies . . . Ln: Longman, 1896. Cr. 8°
 What Sh— learnt at school. *See* Sh—
Baynes & Son (W.) *Publishers. See* Sh—
 Works, 1824, 1825
Baynham (George Walter) Swedenborg and
 Sh—. *See* Sh—
Beale (John) *Printer. See* Sh— Rape . . . 1624
Beale (Miles) Lecture on the times and play of
 King Richard the Third: delivered in
 Crosby Hall, 8 Nov. Ln: 1844. 8°, pp.
 40. Illust. BPL | BUS | MPL
Beamont (W.) On three dramas . . . 'Richard
 II.,' 'Henry IV., Pt. I.,' 'Henry IV.,
 Pt. II.' Warrington, 1879. 8° BM | BPL
Bear Garden—
 See Halliwell, Two old theatres
 ,, Howell
Beard (Thomas) *Editor. See* La Primaudaye

Bearsdell (A. F.) Sh— speaker. *See* Sh—
    Works : Ext. 1884
Beatty ( ) *Dublin Publisher*. *See* Griffith
Beaumont (Francis) British Muse. *See* Sh—
    Works : Ext. 1738
    Poem. *See* Sh— Poems, 1640

See Boyle	*See* Mason
,, Cartwright	,, Mercurius . . .
,, Coleridge	,, Mitford
,, Douse	,, Morehead
,, Fleay	,, Salmacis . . .
,, Heywood	,, Thorndike

Beaumont (Francis) & Fletcher (John) A
    king and no king . . . Ln : 1661. Fcp. 4°
                                        W
    For comparison with 'Coriolanus,' *see* Furnivall's
    'Allusions,' p. 612.
    Knight of the burning pestle. As it is now
    acted by her Majesties Servants at the
    Private House in Drury Lane. Ln : 1635.
    Fcp. 4°   W
    Contains allusions to Sh—.
    Poems. Ln : 1660. 8°
    With several references to Sh—, including the famous
    elegy beginning :
      'Renowned Spencer lye a thought more nye.'
    Valentinian : A tragedy. As 'tis altered
    by the late [John Wilmot] Earl of Ro-
    chester. Ln : Timothy Goodwin, 1685.
    Fcp. 4°, pp. xvi.-82
    Preface refers to 'Troilus and Cressida,' and the pro-
    logue by Mrs. Behn refers to Falstaff.
    Wild goose chase. A comedie. Retriv'd
    for the publick delight of all the ingenious,
    and private benefit of John Lowin and
    Joseph Taylor. Ln : 1652. F°   W
    Lowin and Taylor were Sh—'s friends and companions.
    In the 'Bookseller's address' it is proposed to re-issue
    'Ben Jonson' and also to reprint 'old Shakespear.'
    Woman's prize. *See* Norton
Beauties of England . . . pointing out what-
    ever is curious both in art and nature.
    Ln : Davis & Reymers, 1767. 8°, pp.
    xx.-326
    At p. 161, in describing Sh—, the author says : 'On
    his monument are inscribed some wretched verses
    and a bust of him in marble.'
Beauties of Sh—. Ed. by C. P. Berly. *See*
    Sh— Works : Ext. 1835
Beauties of Sh—. Ed. by W. Dodd. *See*
    Sh— Works : Ext. 1752 *et seq.*
Beauties of Sh— [*Rival to Dodd*] *See* Sh—
    Works : Ext. 1783, 1784, 1790, 1800,
    1805, 1810, 1812, 1819, 1830, 1838, 1853,
    1905
Beauties of Sh—, selected by Alex. Campbell.
    See Sh— Works : Ext. 1804
Beauties of the English drama. *See* Sh—
    Works : Ext. 1777
Beauties of the English stage. *See* Sh—
    Works : Ext. 1737
Beautiful Sidea. *See* Cohn

Beck (J. M.) Student of Wittenberg and his
    ' Dram of Eale.' Philadelphia, 1901.
    8°   BPL
Beck (S. W.) Gloves ; their annals and asso-
    ciations. Ln : Hamilton, 1883. 8° SML
    Refers to the poet's gloves, p. 122.
    Sh—'s gloves [In 'Antiquarian Magazine,'
    Vol. VI., pp. 101-108]. Ln : 1884. 8°
                                        BPL
Becke (G.) Against the Anabaptists, 1550.
    See Reprints
Becket (Andrew)] Concordance to Sh—. *See*
    Sh— Works : Ext. 1787
    ] Proposal for printing in two large volumes,
    octavo, ' Sh— set free, or the language of
    the poet asserted.' Ln : 1812. 8°
    Sh—'s himself again, or the language of
    the poet asserted : being a full but dis-
    passionate examen of the readings and
    interpretations of the several editors . . .
    Ln : A. J. Valpy, 1815. 2 vols. 8°
        BM | BPL | BUS | CPL | MPL | SML | W
Becket (James) *Publisher*. *See* Sharpe (L.)
Becket (T.) *Publisher*—

    See Colman
    ,, Dibdin (C.)
    ,, Garrick
    ,, Sh— King Lear, 1768
    ,, Sh— Macbeth, 1770
    ,, Sh— Timon . . . 1770, 1771
    ,, Sh— Works, 1773
    ,, Victor

Beckington (C.) Hamlet the Dane. *See* Sh—
    Hamlet, 1847
Bedell & Collins *Publishers*. *See* Sh— Merry
    Wives, 1656
Bedford (Arthur) Evil and danger of stage
    plays, shewing their natural tendency to
    destroy religion and introduce a general
    corruption of manners, in almost two
    thousand instances, taken from plays of
    the two last years, against all the methods
    lately used for their reformation. Bristol :
    W. Bonny, 1706. 8°, pp. xvi.-212 SML | W
    Contains notices of Sh—.
    Serious reflections on the scandalous abuse
    and effects of the stage. In a sermon
    preached at the Parish Church of St.
    Nicolas, Bristol . . . Bristol, 1705. 8°
                                  BPL | MPL
    Serious remonstrance . . . against the horrid
    blasphemies and impieties which are still
    used in the English playhouses. [Ln : ?]
    1719. 8°
Bee (The). *See* Repton (H.)
Beeching *Canon* (Hy. Charles) On the religion
    and the sonnets of Sh—. *See* Sh—
    Works. Stratford, 1904-07
    Sonnets of Sh— [In ' Cornhill Mag.', Vol.
    XII., pp. 244-263]. 1902. 8°   BPL

Beeching *Canon* (Hy. Charles) Wm. Sh—: player, playmaker, and poet. *See* Sh—

Beeching (H. C.) *Editor*—
See Sh— Coriolanus, 1890
„ Sh— Julius Cæsar, 1886, 1887
„ Sh— Macbeth, 1908
„ Sh— Merchant . . . 1887, 1889
„ Sh— Sonnets, 1904
„ Sh— Works, 1886-91

Beeching *Canon* (H. C.) *See also* Greenwood

Beecroft (J.) *Publisher. See* Sh— Works,1773

Beer (T. H. de) Short account of the plots . . . of Sh—'s plays. 1871. 8° BM

Beerbohm (Max) Poets' corner. Ln : Heinemann, 1904. F°. 20 coloured caricatures
No..12 represents Sh— covertly receiving from Bacon the MS. of ' Hamlet.' The title was the copyright of J. C. M. Bellew thirty-six years earlier.

Beeton (S. O.) Sh— Memorial. *See* Gibbs, Halliwell, and Rogers

Beeton (S. O.) *Editor. See* Sh— Works : Ext. 1869

Beever (Susanna) Book of reference to . . . Sh—. *See* Sh— Works : Ext. 1870

Begley (Walter) Bacon's ' Nova resuscitatio,' or unveiling of his concealed works and travels. Ln : Gay & Bird, 1906. 8°, pp. 232

Begley (Walter E.)] Is it Sh— ? The great question of Elizabethan literature answered in the light of new revelations and important contemporary evidence hitherto unnoticed. By a Cambridge Graduate. Ln : Murray, 1903. 8°, pp. 400. Portrait and facsimiles BPL | BUS | MPL | SML

Behn (*Mrs.* Aphra) Emperor of the Moon : a farce. Ln : R. Holt for Joseph Knight, 1687. Fcp. 4°
Dedication says : ' So many admirable plays heretofore as Shakespeare's, Fletcher's, and Johnson's, 'twas this alone that made the town able to keep so many playhouses alive.'

Beiro (Marquis di) *Editor. See* Sh— Othello, 1867

Beisiegel (M. K. A.) *Editor. See* Sh— Much Ado, 1904

Beisly (Sidney) Sh—'s garden, or the plants and flowers named in his works described and defined. With notes and illustrations from the works of other writers. Ln : Longman, 1864. Cr. 8°, pp. xx.-172
BM | BPL | BUS | CPL | MPL | SML

Belfast Sh— Festival : Announcement ; Concert book of words ; Catalogue of Exhibition. Belfast, 1905. Cr. 8° BPL

Bell ( ) *Edinburgh Publisher. See* Sh— Works, 1761

Bell (Allan) *Publisher. See* Sh— Works, 1837

Bell (David Charles) *Editor. See* Sh— Works, 1895-97, 1898

Bell (David Charles & Alexander Melville) Standard elocutionist. *See* Sh— Works : Ext. 1882, 1888, 1892

Bell (George Joseph). *See* Jenkin & Bell

Bell (Hy.) *Publisher. See* Greene (R.)

Bell (Henry Glassford) *Editor. See* Sh— Works, 1864, 1865, 1871, 1872, 1875, 1878, 1900

Bell (Henry & Moses) *Publishers. See* Greene (R.)

Bell (James) Biblical and Shakespearian characters compared . . . Hull : W. Andrews, 1849. 8°. Stratford portrait
BM | BPL | MPL | SML

Bell (Jane) *Printer. See* Sh— King Lear, 1655

Bell (John) *Publisher*—
See Franklin
„ Garrick
„ Gentleman
„ Sh— All's Well, 1786
„ Sh— Antony, 1776 *et seq.*
„ Sh— As you like it, 1773, 1785
„ Sh— Comedy of Errors, 1785, 1793
„ Sh— Coriolanus, 1773
„ Sh— Cymbeline, 1773
„ Sh— Hamlet, 1785
„ Sh— Julius Cæsar, 1773
„ Sh— King Henry IV., i., 1785
„ Sh— King Henry IV., ii., 1785
„ Sh— King Henry V., 1773, 1785
„ Sh— King Henry VI., i., 1786
„ Sh— King Henry VI., ii., 1774, 1786
„ Sh— King Henry VI., iii., 1774, 1786
„ Sh— King John, 1773
„ Sh— King Lear, 1785
„ Sh— King Richard II., 1774, 1777, 1786
„ Sh— Love's labours lost, 1777, 1785
„ Sh— Macbeth, 1788
„ Sh— Measure, 1773, 1778, 1785
„ Sh— Merchant, 1785
„ Sh— Merry Wives, 1773
„ Sh— Midsummer N. D., 1777, 1785
„ Sh— Much Ado, 1774, 1778
„ Sh— Othello, 1773, 1785, 1788
„ Sh— Pericles, 1796
„ Sh— Poems, 1774
„ Sh— Taming . . . 1774, 1776
„ Sh— Timon . . . 1773, 1785, 1788
„ Sh— Titus . . . 1774, 1777, 1785
„ Sh— Troilus . . . 1774, 1776
„ Sh— Twelfth Night, 1773, 1774, 1786
„ Sh— Two Gentlemen, 1774, 1786
„ Sh— Will . . . 1787
„ Sh— Winter's Tale, 1773, 1784
„ Sh—'s Works, 1773-74, 1785-87, 1786-88, 1801, 1804, 1820

Bell (J. G.) *Manchester Publisher. See* Sh— Works, 1861

Bell (R.) Macbeth modernised. *See* Sh— Macbeth, 1838

Bell (Robert) Lecture on Sh— and his times.
See Sh—
Sh—'s Sonnets. G. Massey's edition. [In
' Fortnightly Review,' Aug.]. Ln : 1866.
Roy. 8°   BUS
] Wm. Sh—.   See Sh—
Bell (Robert) Editor. See Sh— Poems, 1854,
1855, 1856, 1860, 1861, 1864, 1870
Bell (Robert Anning) Artist—
See Sh— Midsummer N. D., 1895
„   Sh— The Tempest, 1901, 1902
„   Sh— Works : Ext. 1899, 1901, 1902
Bell (T.) Publisher. See Hawkins
Bell (W.   ) Sh—'s birth. A lyric ode. Ln :
[1864].   8°, pp. 8   MPL
Bell (William) Sh—'s Puck, and his Folks
Lore, illustrated from the superstitions
of all nations, but more especially from
the earliest religion and rites of Northern
Europe and the Wends. Ln : Printed
for the author, 1852-64. 3 vols. 12°.
Illust.   BM | BPL | BUS | CPL | MPL | SML
With a chapter of proofs that Sh— visited Germany.
Bell & Bradfute Edinburgh Publishers. See
Sh— Works, 1795
Bell & Dunham. Lives of British dramatists.
2 vols.   12°   BM | MPL
Formed part of Lardner's Cabinet Cyclopædia.
Bellamy (Daniel). See Carrington & Bellamy
Bellamy Actress (George Anne) Apology for
her life. Ln : 1785. 6 vols. 8°. With
5 frontispieces
Bellamy (G. A.) Actress. See Sh— Romeo . . .
1904
Bellamy (George Somers) Essays from Sh—.
Edinburgh Publishing Co., 1879. 8°, pp.
238   BM | BPL | SML
New Sh— dictionary of quotations. See
Sh— Works : Ext. 1875
Shaksperian sermons [Magazine excerpts].
1877. 8°   BPL
Bellamy (T.) Life of Parsons. See Parsons
Bellamy & Robarts Publishers. See Sh—
Works, 1787-91, 1791, 1796
Bellchambers (E.) Editor. See Cibber
Belleforest (Francois de) Hystorie of Hamblet.
See Sh— Hamlet, 1608
Bellers (Fettiplace) Injur'd innocence : A
tragedy . . . Ln : Printed for J. Brindley
at the King's Arms in New Bond Street,
1732. 8°
' From these our stage, transplanted, took its rise,
The school of virtue and the scourge of vice ;
Rude in its youth, till Sh—'s master hand
Taught the strong scene each passion to command.'
                                —Prologue.
Bellet (M. H.) Editor. See Sh— King Richard
III., 1882
Bellew (John Chippendale Montesquieu) Poets'
corner. See Sh— Works : Ext. 1868

Bellew (John Chippendale Montesquieu)
Sh—'s home at New Place, Stratford-
upon-Avon. Being a history of the 'Great
House' built in the reign of K. Henry
VII. by Sir Hugh Clopton, and subse-
quently the property of Wm. Sh—, where-
in he lived and died. Ln : Virtue, 1863.
8°, pp. xvi.-380. With six folded pedi-
grees of the families of Sh—, Arden,
Clopton, Combe, Underhill, Hales, Nash,
Forster, and Hathaway
                   BM | BPL | BUS | CPL | MPL | SML
Sh—'s home (and grant of arms to John
Sh—) [In ' Herald and Genealogist '].
Ln : 1863. 8°   BUS
Bellini (V.) Composer. See Sh— Romeo, 1848,
1850, 1860
Belloc (Hilaire) The aftermath . . . Caliban's
guide to letters. Ln : Duckworth, 1903.
Cr. 8°, pp. viii.-194
' Wm. Sh— : An appreciation,' occupies pp. 164-169.
Belsham (William) On Sh—. See Sh—] Bel-
sham
Bolton (F.) Random Recollections of an old
actor. Ln : Hurst & Blackett, 1880. 8°
                                        BPL | SML
Belvoir household accounts—
See Round   See Stopes
Benas (B. L.) Study of Sh—. See Sh—] Benas
Bence-Jones and others (A. B.) Second folio
Sh—, 1632 [In 'Athenæum, No. 3847, p.
104 ; 3849, p. 168 ; 3850, p. 200 ; 3852,
p. 264]. July-Aug., 1901
Benecke (Ida) Editor. See Heine
Benger (Miss   ) Memoirs . . . See Tobin
Bennet (T.) Publisher—
See Sh— Antony, 1692
„   Sh— The Tempest, 1701
„   Sh— Timon, 1703
Bennett (Hannaford) Editor. See Much Ado,
1905
Bennett (J.) Master Skylark : A story of
Sh—'s time. Illust. by R. B. Birch.
New York Century Co., 1898. 8°   SML
Bennett (Dr. J. B.) Evil of theatrical amuse-
ments stated and illustrated. Dublin,
c. 1839. 8°
For reply, see Calcraft.
Bensley (Robert) Actor.   See Sh— Julius
Cæsar, 1780
Bensley (T.) Printer—
See Jones (S.)
„   Sh— Works, 1798-1800, 1800, 1803-05,
1805
Benson (Frank R.)] Mr. and Mrs. F. R.
Benson and their Sh— Company. See
Sh— Works : Ext. 1908
Speech at the Belfast Sh— festival, 2nd
Feb. Belfast, 1905. Fcp. 4°   BPL
See also Flint Castle

Benson.] Hallett (W. Hughes) Mr. Benson's
Hamlet [Rep. from ' The Pilot ']. 1900.
8°   BPL
Benson (J.) *Publisher.* *See* Malvezzi
Benson (John) *Publisher.* *See* Sh— Poems,
1640
Bent (W.) *Publisher.* *See* Sh— Works, 1798
Bentley (Richard) *Publisher*—
See Crowne (J.)
„ Dryden
„ Durfey
„ Hedelin
„ Lee (N.)
„ Mountfort
„ Otway
„ Sh— Antony, 1692 *et seq.*
„ Sh— Cymbeline, 1682
„ Sh— Hamlet, 1683, 1695
„ Sh— Julius Cæsar, 1680, 1684, 1691, 1695
„ Sh— King Henry VI., ii., 1680
„ Sh— King Lear, 1681, 1689
„ Sh— Macbeth, 1687, 1695
„ Sh— Othello, 1681, 1687, 1695
„ Sh— Romeo . . . 1696
„ Sh— The Tempest, 1690
„ Sh— Works, 1685
Bentley (Walter) *Editor.* *See* Sh— Hamlet,
1888
Bentley's Milton. *See* Verbal Criticism
Benton (Myron B.) Sh— and the musical
glasses [In ' Appleton's Journal,' April].
New York, 1879. 8°   BUS
' Benvenuto ' (*Prof.*) The Passenger [Dia-
logues in English and Italian, parallel].
Ln : J. Stepneth, 1612. Fcp. 4°
Of Shakespearean interest.
Berger (J. A.) *Publisher.* *See* Sh— Works,
1858
Bergmann (J. & F.) *Wiesbaden Publishers.* *See*
Sh— Macbeth, 1878
Berio (Marquis) *Editor.* *See* Sh— Othello,
1822, 1826
Berkenhead (*Sir* John) Assembly man. Ln :
1662. Fcp. 4°. With portrait of Hugh
Peters, by Faithorne
Peters is said to have been a player in Sh—'s company.
Berly (Carl Peter) Beauties of Sh—. *See*
Sh— Works : Ext. 1835, 1857
Bernard (John) Retrospections of the Stage.
Ln : Colburn & Bentley, 1830. 2 vols. 8°
BPL | SML
Bernard (*Saint*). *See* Edwards (R.)
Bernhardt (Sarah) *Actress*—
See Fouquier
„ Scott (C. W.)
Bernhardt.] Home of Sarah Bernhardt in
Paris. Paris, 1898. 12°   SML
Bernhardt.] Huret. Sarah Bernhardt. Ln :
Chapman, 1899. 8°   SML

Berrow (   ) *Worcester Publisher.* *See* Sh—
Works, 1768
Berry (T. W.) *Editor*—
See Sh— As you like it, 1903
„ *See* Sh— Julius Cæsar, 1899
Berthel (G. E.) *Halle Publisher.* *See* Sh—
Hamlet, 1869
Berthelet (Thomas) *Printer.* *See* Terence
Besant (*Sir* Walter) South London. Ln :
Chatto, 1901. 8°. Illust.   SML
Best (Charles). *See* Ghost . . .
Best (K. T.) Shakesperiana : Five hundred
passages. *See* Sh— Works : Ext. 1889
Best (R.) *Publisher.* *See* Husbands
Betson (A.) Origin of masquerades, plays,
poetry, etc. [c. 1799.] 8°   BPL
Betterton (*Mrs.*) *Actress.* *See* Sh— Antony,
1677
Betterton (Thomas) History of the English
stage from the restauration to the present
time. Including the lives, characters and
amours of the most eminent actors and
actresses . . . adorned with cuts. Ln :
Printed for E. Curll at Pope's Head in
Rose Street, Covent Garden, 1741. 8°
SML
Wm. Oldys is said to be the real writer.
Betterton (Thomas) *Actor-Editor*—
See Sh— Antony, 1677
„ Sh— King Henry IV., i., 1700
„ Sh— King Henry IV., ii., 1700, 1710,
1719, 1721
„ Sh— Works, 1709
Betterton.] Life and Times of Thomas Better-
ton. Ln : Reader, 1888. 12°. With por-
trait   SML
] Life of Thomas Betterton . . . wherein the
action and utterances of the stage, bar,
and pulpit are distinctly considered, to
which is added the 'Amorous widow or
wanton wife,' a comedy by Mr. Betterton.
Ln : 1710. 8°. With· portrait
Betterton (Thomas)—
See Brereton
„ Davies (T.)
„ Doran
Bettesworth (A.) *Publisher*—
See Dancing devils
„ Sh— Hamlet, 1723
„ Sh— Julius Cæsar, 1729
„ Sh— King Lear, 1723
„ Sh— Macbeth, 1729
„ Sh— Poems, 1725, 1728
„ Sh— Works, 1714, 1725, 1728, 1733
Bettesworth (W. A.) Way about Warwickshire.
Ln : Iliffe [1892]. 12°   SML
Betty.] Authentic biographical sketch of W.
H. W. Betty, the ' Young Roscius.' Ln :
1804. 8°   W

Betty.] Bisset (James) Dramatic excellencies of the 'Young Roscius' [W. H. W. Betty]. Birmingham [1804 ?]. 8°   BPL

] Harley (G. D.) Biographical sketch of W. H. W. Betty. 1804. 8°   BPL

] [Merritt (J.)] Memoirs of W. H. W. Betty, the 'Young Roscius.' Liverpool, 1804. 12°   BPL

] Young Albert the Roscius. Exhibited in a series of characters from Sh— and other authors . . . King Richard III., Hamlet, Othello, As you like it, King Henry IV. Ln : S. & J. Fuller at the Temple of Fancy, Rathbone Place, 1811. 16°, pp. 24. 7 coloured plates, with moveable heads to form the characters   BUS

] Young Albert the Roscius . . . Third edition, 1811. 12°   BPL

Bew (J.) *Publisher.* See Sh—Merchant...1783

Beware the Cat. *See* Baldwin (W.)

Bewick (Thomas) *Artist-Engraver—*
  See Jarvis (J. W.)
  ,, Sh— Hamlet, 1799
  ,, Sh— Macbeth, 1800
  ,, Sh— Measure . . . 1800

Beyle (M. H.) *See* Stendhal

Beza (Theodore) *pseud. Publisher. See* Marvell

Bibb (Grace C.) Lady Macbeth : A study in character [In ' The Western ']. St. Louis, 1875. 8°   BUS

The Theatre in Blackfriars [In ' The Western ']. 1875. 8°   BPL

Bible—
  See B— (C. A. H.)   *See* Potwin
  ,, Bell (James)   ,, Price
  ,, Brown (J.)   ,, Psalms
  ,, Bullock   ,, Schmucker
  ,, Burgess   ,, Sh—] Sh—'s Bibli-
  ,, Colton   cal knowledge
  ,, Dore   ,, Swinburne
  ,, Malcolm   ,, Wordsworth

Bible : Our Lord's Prayer. *See* Horn-Book

Bible truths . . . *See* Brown (J.)

Bibliography—
  See Cole   *See Sh*—] Sh— bibliography
  ,, Pollard   ,, Wheatley

Bickerstaff (Isaac) Extracts. *See* Sh— Works : Ext. 1822

Judith : A sacred drama as performed in the Church of Stratford-upon-Avon on occasion of the Jubilee, 6 Sept., 1769, in honour of the memory of Sh— . . . The music by Dr. Arne. Ln : W. Griffin, 1769. 4°, pp. iv.-20   BPL | BUS

Bickerstaff (Isaac) & Dibdin (Charles)] Queen Mab or the Fairies' Jubilee : A cantata, compos'd for the Jubilee at Stratford-upon-Avon, Sept. 6th and 7th . . . Ln : J. Johnston, 1769. F°, pp. viii.   BPL
Words by Bickerstaff, music by Dibdin.

Bickerton (W.) *Publisher. See* Garrick

Bickley (   ) *Editor. See* Bacon (F.)

Bickley (W. B.) *Editor. See* Knowle

Bicknell (John Laurens) Analysis of . . . ' Hamlet ' [In ' Original Miscellanies,' pp. 143-189]. 1820. 8°   BPL

] The Trial : A serious drama by ' Wm. Sh— and John Milton ' (*pseuds.*) Lithographed by J. L. Bicknell, of the Philodanberg Academy. [c. 1840.] 4°, pp. 8. illustrated   W

Bidgood (J.) *Editor. See* Sh— Merchant...1900

Bigelow (Horatio R.) Hamlet's insanity. Chicago, 1873. 8°, pp. 8   BUS
Offprinted from the 'Chicago Medical Journal,' Sept., 1873.

Bigsby (R.) On the signature of John Sh— [and] Wm. Sh—'s papers. *See Sh*—] Sh— Soc.

Bijou (The) Annual. Ln : Pickering, 1828. 12°   SML
Contains a Shakespearean story.

Bill (John) *Engraver. See* James I.

Bill (John) *Printer—*
  See Bacon (F.)
  ,, Estienne
  ,, James I.

Bill of Complaint in Chancery respecting Mr. Sh—'s legacy to the birthplace in Henley Street . . . Edited by J. O. Halliwell. 1859. Fcp. 4°

Billington (W.) *Rugby Publisher—*
  See Sh— As you like it, 1868
  ,, Sh— Hamlet, 1870
  ,, Sh— King Henry V., 1880
  ,, Sh— King Lear, 1871
  ,, Sh— Macbeth, 1869, 1872, 1881
  ,, Sh— Midsummer N. D., 1881
  ,, Sh— Romeo, 1880
  ,, Sh— The Tempest, 1870

Bindley (Frank) *Artist. See* Sh— Romeo, 1892, 1895

Binger (Gebrooeders) *Amsterdam Publishers—*
  See Sh— Othello, 1860
  ,, Sh— Works, 1860-72

Binney (T.) *See* Wilks (T. C.)

Biographic sketch of C. C. Clarke. *See* Clarke

Biographica Britannica. *See* Baker (D. E.)

Biographical Portrait Gallery. 1837. 12°. Sh—, p. 67   BPL

Biographical sketches of eminent British poets. *See* Sh—

Biography of Sh—. *See Sh*—] Biography

Biography of the British Stage, being correct . . . lives of all the principal actors and actresses at Drury Lane, Covent Garden, Haymarket, Lyceum, Surrey, Coburg, and Adelphi Theatres. Ln : 1824. 8°, with front. and woodcuts   BPL

Bioren and Madan, *Philadelphia Printers and Publishers. See* Sh— Works, 1795-96

Birch (R.) *Artist.* See Clark (I.)

Birch (Dr. T.) Houbraken (Ja.) and Vertue (George) Heads of illustrious persons, with their lives and characters. Ln : 1743-51. F°, 108 portraits (includ. Sh—)
Reprinted in 1747, 1749, 1756, and 1811.
Heads of illustrious persons . . . Ln : 1813. F°, with 108 portraits   BPL
Sh— occurs at pp. 181-182.

Birch (Wm. John) Inquiry into the philosophy and religion of Sh—. *See* Sh—

Bird (G. M.) Sh— Clubs at Stratford-upon-Avon. 'Sh— Club Paper.' Stratford, 1905. 8°, pp. 8

Birmingham.] Autographs of Contributors to the Sh— Memorial Library. Birmingham, 1864. Manuscript. 4°   BPL

] Birmingham Central Literary Association : Central Literary Magazine. Birmingham : Cornish, 1887-1908. 19 vols. 8°   BPL
Contains addresses and much other matter on the poet.

] Birmingham Dramatic Club : Address by the President [C. Green]. 1885. 8°   BPL

] Birmingham Dramatic Club : Sh— Commemoration [Programmes, Notices, etc.] 1878-93. 4°   BPL

] Birmingham Dramatic Club : Sh— Commemoration [Circulars]. 1900. 12°   BPL

] Birmingham Dramatic Club : Sh— Meeting. Toast List. 1880-82. 4°   BPL

] Birmingham Grand Theatre : Souvenir of First Shaksperian Revival, ' Romeo and Juliet.' Birm., 1906. 8°   BPL

] Birmingham Literary and Dramatic Club : Sh— dinner, with the speech by J. T. Bunce. Birmingham, 1896. 8°   BPL

] Birmingham Old Boy's Association : St. George's, Edgbaston, Annual Dinner, 23rd April [Programme, etc.] 1901. 12°   BPL

] Birmingham University Sh— Society : Cards. 1906-08. Cr. 8°   BPL

] Materials for a history of the Sh— memorial library : Collection of circulars, newspaper cuttings, etc. 1861. 4°   BPL

] Moseley Shakespearean Society : (Juvenile) Programme of ' Julius Cæsar.' Birmingham, 1907. Cr. 8°   BPL

] ' Our Sh— Club,' Birmingham. Annual Dinner [In ' Birmingham Liberal Review '] 1880. F°   BPL

] ' Our Sh— Club ' : Chronicle, 1862-93. Birmingham, 1893. 4°   BPL

] ' Our Sh— Club ' : Soiree. Nock's Royal Hotel, 22nd April. Birmingham, 1864. 8°, pp. 12   BPL | BUS
Contains a cantata based on the ' Seven Ages of Man.' Words by Sebastian Evans, music by Thomas Anderton.

] ' Our Sh— Club ' Tercentenary Dinner. Birmingham, 1864. 4°   BPL

Birmingham.] Sh— Memorial Library Committee : Letter copying book of book correspondence. Manuscript. 1868-69. 8°   BPL

] Sh— Memorial Library Opening : Collection of Newspaper Cuttings. 1868-71. 4°   BPL

Birmingham—
  See also Dent   *See also* Programme
   ,,   ,, Hill   ,,   ,, Shaw (A. C.)
   ,,   ,, Langford   ,,   ,, Timmins (S.)
   ,,   ,, Pemberton

Birt (S.) *Publisher.* See Sh— Works, 1745, 1747

Birth of Merlin. See Sh— Birth . . .

Birthday chimes from Sh—. *See* Sh— Works : Ext. 1886

Bishop (George) *Printer—*
  See Barnes   *See* La Primaudaye
   ,, Holinshed   ,, Stowe

Bishop (*Sir* Henry Rowley) *Composer—*
  See Sh— As you like it, 1825
   ,, Sh— Comedy of Errors, 1819
   ,, Sh— Midsummer N. D., 1816
   ,, Sh— Poems, 1850
   ,, Sh— Twelfth Night, 1820
   ,, Sh— Two Gentlemen, 1821
   ,, Sh— Venus, 1830

Bisset (J.) Jubilean dramatic pageant, containing the invitation or the call of the counties, Sh—'s dream, the sweet blossomed crab, the gossiping ghosts, and the joys of the jubilee. With a great variety of original comic sketches. Respectfully inscribed to . . . the Stratford Shakesperian Society. Leamington : J. Fairfax [1827]. 8°, pp. viii.-34   BPL | BUS

Bisset.] Memoir of James Bisset (written by himself) . . . Author, Royal Medallist, Poet and Inventor. With Portrait, Illustrations and Song. Edited by T. B. Dudley. Leamington : F. Glover, 1904. 8°, pp. 96   SML
Fifty copies in 4to. were done on large paper. Refers to the Sh— commemoration of 1830.

Bisset (James). *See* Betty

Black & Son (A.) *Publishers.* See Sh— Works, 1820-21, 1821

Black (John) *Editor.* See Schlegel

Black (William) Judith Shakespeare : A romance. Ln : Macmillan, 1884. 3 vols. Cr. 8°
First appeared in Harper's Magazine.
Judith Shakespeare. Ln : Macmillan, 1885. 12°   BPL
Judith Shakesepare. Ln : Low, 1893. 8°   SML

Black, Young & Young, *Publishers.* See Sh— Works, 1824, 1831

Black *Editor.* See Sh— King Henry V., 1909

Blacke Booke. *See* Middleton
Blackfriars Theatre—
   See Bibb   *See* Greenstreet
  ,, Sh— Love's Labours Lost, 1631
  ,, Sh— Othello, 1655, 1681, 1695, 1705,
    1724
  ,, Sh— Two Noble Kinsmen, 1634
  ,, *Sh*—] Halliwell
  ,, Stage Player's Complaint
  ,, Wallace
  ,, Wilson (H. S.)
Blackmore (Ed.) *Publisher*—
  See Sh— George-a-Greene, 1632
  ,, Greene (R.)
Blades (William) Account of the German mor-
  ality play, entitled ' Depositio Cornuti
  Typographici.' Ln : Trubner, 1885. Fcp.
  4°, pp. xii.-116. With 9 plates
Common typographical errors with especial
  reference to the text of Sh— [In ' Athe-
  næum,' 27 Jan., 1872, p. 114]. 1872. 4°
                              BM
Enemies of books. With preface by Richard
  Garnett. 1896. 4°, pp. xviii.-152. Illus-
  trated
  Refers to the Shakespearean discovery at Lamport
  Hall, p. 53.
Sh— and typography. *See* Sh—
Bladon (S.) *Publisher*—
  See Garrick
  ,, Interview . . .
  ,, Kenrick
  ,, New Theatrical Dictionary
  ,, Sh— King Richard III., 1784
  ,, Sh— Macbeth, 1770
  ,, Sh— Romeo, 1769, 1793
  ,, Sh— Taming . . . 1767
  ,, Sh— Timon . . . 1770
Blagrave (Obadiah) *Publisher*—
  See Cotgrave   *See* Winstanley
Blair (Hugh) *Editor. See* Sh— Works, 1753,
  1761, 1769, 1771, 1795
Blair (J. Talfourd) *Editor. See* Sh— Works,
  1886, 1900
Blake (Wm.) *Artist-Engraver*—
  See Ritson
  ,, Sh— Works : Ext. 1807, 1810, 1822
Blanch (W. H.) History of Dulwich College
  and its founder, Edward Alleyn. Ln :
  Allen, 1877. 8°   SML
Blanchard.] Scott (C.) & Howard (C.) Life
  and Reminiscences of E. L. Blanchard.
  1891. 2 vols. 8°   BPL
Blanchard (W.) *York Printer. See* Kemble
Blare (J.) *Publisher. See* Bunyan
Blatchford (A. N.) Studies in religion from
  Sh—. Ln : Stock, 1899. 12°
              BPL | MPL | SML
Blind (Mathilde) *Editor. See* Sh— Sonnets,
  1902

Blind type text—
  See Sh— Hamlet, 1871
  ,, Sh— Julius Cæsar, 1871
  ,, Sh— King Lear, 1871
  ,, Sh— Macbeth, 1871
  ,, Sh— Merchant . . . 1887
  ,, Sh— Midsummer N. D., 1870
  ,, Sh— Works : Ext. 1870
Bloom (James Harvey) Errors of the 'Avon
  Star' [Reply to Marie Corelli, *q.v.*]. Strat-
  ford : J. Morgan, 1903. 4°, pp. 54   BPL
Free School of the Gild of the Holy Cross
  . . . Stratford-on-Avon [1904]. Cr. 8°
                               BPL
Sh—'s Church, otherwise the Collegiate
  Church of the Holy Trinity of Stratford-
  on-Avon : An architectural and eccle-
  siastical history of the fabric and its
  ornaments. Illustrated by L. C. Keighly-
  Peach. Ln : Unwin, 1902. 8°, pp. xvi.-
  292   BPL | SML
Sh—'s garden. Ln : Methuen, 1903. 8°,
  pp. xii.-244, and 4 plates
           BPL | BUS | MPL | SML
  The title was already the copyright of S. Beisley about
  forty years earlier.
Sh—'s garden. Philadelphia, 1903. 8°, pp.
  256. Illust.   BUS
Topographical Notes . . . Stratford-on-Avon.
  1903-05. 3 vols. 8°   BPL
Bloom (J. H.) *Editor*—
  See Stratford] Muster *See Stratford*] Register
Bloudy Murders. *See* Fites
Blount (Edward) *Publisher*—
  See Alexander   *See* Montaigne
  ,, Florio   ,, Sh— Works, 1623
  ,, Historie . . .   ,, Silver
Blount (*Sir* Thomas Pope) De re poetica : or,
  remarks upon poetry. With characters
  and censures of the most considerable
  poets . . . Ln : 1694. Fcp. 4° BPL | BUS | W
  Includes Sh— at pp. 201-206.
Bloxam (Matthew Holbeche) & others] No-
  tices of the churches of Warwickshire . . .
  Warwick : H. T. Cooke, 1847. 2 vols.
  Imp. 8°, rubricated. With many large
  lithographed plates and textual en-
  gravings
Boaden (James) Comparative review of
  opinions . . . relative to the Sh— manuscripts [forged by W. H. Ireland]. [1796.]
  8°   BM | CPL
Inquiry . . . *See* Sh—
Letter to George Steevens containing a
  critical examination of the papers of
  Sh— published by Samuel Ireland. To
  which are added, extracts from ' Vortigern.' Ln : Martin & Bain, 1796, 8°,
  pp. iv.-72   BM | BPL | BUS | MPL | W
  First published in ' The Oracle,' a newspaper edited by
  the author.

Boaden (James) Letter to George Steevens
. . . Second edition. Ln : Martin &
Bain, 1796. 8°, pp. iv.-72   BUS | W
Life of Mrs. Jordan. *See* Jordan
Memoirs of Kemble. *See* Kemble
Memoirs of Mrs. Inchbald. *See* Inchbald
Memoirs of Mrs. Siddons. *See* Siddons
On the sonnets of Sh—, identifying the
person to whom they were addressed and
elucidating several points in the poet's
history. Ln : T. Rodd, 1837. 8°, pp.
iv.-62 BM | BPL | BUS | CPL | MPL | SML | W
See also Oulton
   „   „ Wyatt
Boaden (J.) *Editor.* *See* Oracle
' Boar's Head ' Tavern, Eastcheap, Ln :—
See Account
   „ Goldsmith
   „ Irving (W.)
Boas (Frederick Samuel) Sh— and his pre-
decessors. Ln : Murray, 1896. Cr. 8°, pp.
viii.-556   BM | BPL | BUS | MPL
Sh— and his predecessors. New impres-
sion. Ln : Murray, 1902. Cr. 8°, pp.
viii.-556
Boas (F. S.) *Editor*—
See Kyd
   „ Sh— Taming . . . 1908
   „ Sh— The Tempest, 1897
   „ Sh— Works, 1893-98
Boas (*Mrs.* F.) In Sh—'s England. Ln :
Nisbet, 1903. 8°, pp. viii.-296. With
portraits   BPL | MPL | SML
Boaster (The)—
See Sh— King Henry IV., i., 1859
   „ Shakespearean Drolls
Bobson (G.) Sh— and the drama. A letter
to T. Smith, scene painter and tragedian
at the Amphitheatre [In ' Blackwood's
Mag.,' May]. Edin., 1846. 8°   BUS
Boccaccio (Giovanni) Bernabo da Genova.
See Sh—] Sh—'s Library
A foundation of ' Cymbeline.'
Giletta of Narbona, 1843. *See Sh*—] Sh—'s
Library
A foundation of ' All's Well.'
] The Decameron. Containing an hundred
pleasant novels. Wittily discoursed be-
tween seven honourable ladies and three
noble gentlemen. Ln : Printed by Isaac
Iaggard, 1620-25. 2 vols. F°. With
woodcuts   CTC | W
The story of Juliet of Narbona, and the Count of
Roussilion gives the foundation of ' All's Well,'
ff. 107-112.
An anonymous issue of the 'great refiner of Italian
prose,' and the first English edition. It is a matter
for profound regret that the translator's name so far
has remained a buried secret.
The Decameron. *See also* Giovanni
Thirteen most pleasaunt and delectable
questions entituled a disport of diuerse

noble personages . . . written in his
booke named ' Philocopo.' Englished by
H. G— [Humphrey Gifford or H. Gran-
tham]. Ln : Imprinted by A. I. [Abel
Jeffes] and are to be solde in Paules
Churchyard by Thomas Woodcocke,
dwelling at the Signe of the Beare, 1587.
8°. Black letter. Sig. A to L8 unpaged
                                                CTC
Boccaccio (Giovanni)—
See also Novel . . .   *See also* Painter
Bocchius (Achilles). *See* Green (H.)
Bochsa (N. C.) *Composer.* See Sh— Macbeth,
1800
Boden (*Miss*) *Bridgnorth Publisher.* See
Sh— Works, 1768
Boden (N.) *Birmingham Printer.* See
Sh— Works, 1768
Bodenham (John) *Compiler*] England's helicon
. . . Ln : John Flasket in Paule's Church-
yard, 1600. Fcp. 4°
Contains three Sh— pieces : ' Passionate Sheepheard's
Song' (signed W. Sh—) ; ' On a day, alack the day ' ;
' My flocks feed not.'
] England's helicon . . . Ln : 1614. Fcp. 4°
] England's helicon : A collection of pastoral
and lyric poems first published at the
close of the reign of Elizabeth. [Ed. by
Sir S. E. Brydges.] Third edition, 1812.
Fcp. 4°   MPL
] England's helicon ; Those songs and poems
from the excessively rare first edition . . .
1600, which are connected with the works
of Sh—. Edited by J. O. Halliwell.
1865. Fcp. 4°, pp. 58
                    BM | BPL | BUS | HCL | MPL
Of twenty-five copies printed, ten only preserved.
Witt's academy. A treasurie of divine,
morall and philosophicall similes and
sentences generally usefull. But more
particularly published for the use of
schooles. Ln : W. Stansby, 1634. 12°.
Engraved title by Jo. Droeshout SBL | W
Contains references to Sh— at p. 623.
See Halliwell's ' Sh— reliques,' 1852, p. 111.
Originally appeared as part i. of Francis Meres' ' Wit's
treasury,' 1598 (*q.v.*)
Witt's Academy . . . Ln : 1636. 12°. BUS
On p. 623 the list of Sh—'s works.
Bodleian Library : Catalogue of early Eng-
lish poetry and works illustrating the
drama, collected by Edmond Malone.
Oxford, 1836. F°   BPL
] Catalogus Librorum Impressorum Biblio-
thecæ Bodleianæ in Academia Oxoniensi.
Oxonii, 1843-51. 4 vols. F°
                          BM | BLO | BUS | W
Contains detailed list of Shakespeareana at the Bodleian
See Halliwell, Hand list
   „ Macray
Bogue (D.) *Publisher.* See Sh— Works,
1839, 1841

Bohn (E. F.) *Haarlem Publisher.* *See* Sh— King Richard III., 1871

Bohn (Henry George) Bibliographical account of the works of Sh—, including every known edition, translation and commentary. Printed off separately from his enlarged edition of the 'Bibliographer's Manual,' with some additions. Ln: Privately printed, 1864. Fcp. 4°, pp. 104, on handmade paper   BM | BUS | SML
Issue restricted to twenty-five copies. Some copies are dated 1863.
So far from 'including every known edition,' its omissions may be numbered by thousands. Yet, despite this drawback and its chaotic arrangement, it remained the best available list for nearly half a century.

Biography and bibliography of Sh— ['Miscellanies of the Philobiblion Society']. Ln: 1863. Fcp. 4°. With ten engravings   BM
Impression limited to forty copies 'for presentation to persons of wealth and rank.' Apparently intellect did not count.

Bohn (H. G.) *Editor.* *See* Lowndes

Bohn (H. G.) *Publisher—*
See Sh— Sonnets, 1838
  ,, Sh— Works, 1840, 1842, 1843, 1844, 1847, 1848, 1849, 1850, 1851, 1852, 1853, 1854, 1855, 1857, 1858, 1859, 1862, 1863

Bohn (J.) Chronicles of the White Rose of York: Historical fragments, proclamations and other documents relating to the reign of K. Edward IV. Ln: Bohn, 1845. 8°   SML
Illustrates 'K. Henry VI.' and 'K. Richard III.'

Bohn (James) *Publisher.* *See* Sh— Poems, 1838

Bohte (J. H.) *Publisher.* *See* Sh— Works, 1823

Boke. *See* Booke

Bold (Henry) Latine songs, with their English, and poems. Ln: 1685. 8°
Allusions at p. 159 to the 'Merry Wives' and 'King Henry IV.'

Boler (James) *Publisher.* *See* Taylor (John)

Bolland (Baron). *See* Mirror of Literature

Bollifant (Edmund) *Printer.* *See* Montemayor

Bolton (W. G. F.) *Auctioneer.* *See* Stratford: New Place

Bompas (George Cox) Problem of the Sh— plays. Ln: Low, 1902. 8°, pp. viii.-120   BPL | BUS | SML
On the Bacon-Sh— question. This writer, who shows uncommon acquaintance with the history of the Jaggard family, was one of the first to combat the errors of 'Sidney Lee' and other Sh— 'authorities.'

Bond ( ) *Editor.* *See* Lyly

Bond (Acton) Plea for a national dramatic college. Sh— Club paper. Stratford-on-Avon, 1909. Cr. 8°, pp. 8

Bond (R.) *Gloucester Publisher.* *See* Sh— Works, 1768

Bond (R. Warwick) *Editor—*
See Sh— King Lear, 1907-08
  ,, Sh— Taming . . . 1904
  ,, Sh— Two Gentlemen, 1906

Bonian (R.) *Publisher.* *See* Sh— Troilus, 1609

Bonsal, Conrad & Co. Norfolk [U. S.] *Publishers.* *See* Sh— Works, 1805-09

Bööcke (R. L.) Shakespearian Costumes. *See* Sh— Works, 1889

Boodle (R. W.) Miscellaneous essays. Montreal Sh— Club, 1878-87. 8°   BPL
Contains 'Notes upon Romeo and Juliet.'

Book of Sh— gems. *See* Sargent (G. F.)

Booke of Common Prayer, 1596. *See* Sh— Autograph

Booke of good maners . . . [*colophon*] Here endeth and fynysshed the boke named and intytled good maners. Ln: Wynken de Worde, 1507. Fcp. 4°; without pagination; signatures A to N in eights and fours alternately; 32 lines to the full page   BM | CPL | W
Alluded to in 'As you like it' (Act V., Sc. 4): 'O sir, we quarrel in print, by the book, as you have books for good manners.' [*See* Halliwell's 'Sh— reliques,' 1852, p. 23].

Booke of merrie riddles, together with proper questions and witty proverbs to make pleasant pastimé. Ln: Roger Jackson, 1617. 8°. Black letter
An earlier edition of this work is mentioned by Slender in the 'Merry Wives,' I., 1 :—
'You have not the "Book of riddles" about you, have you?'

Booke of merrie riddles . . . Ln: T. C—— [Thomas Cotes] for Michael Sparkes. 1629. 8°
See also Literature . . .

Booke of merry riddles. Ln: [c. 1750]. 12°. Old chapbook edition, with nineteen rude woodcuts   W
See Halliwell, Sh— reliques, 1852, p. 92

Booke of merrie riddles . . . Now first reprinted from the unique edition printed in 1660. [Ed. by J. O. Halliwell]. Ln: 1866. 12°. Twenty-five copies printed; ten only preserved   BPL | HCL

Booke of Perymus and Thesbye. Ln: T. Hacket [Sæc. XVI.]. Fcp. 4°. Black letter
Illustrates 'Mid. N. Dream.' *See also* Gale.

Booke or counseill against . . . the Sweate. *See* Caius

Booker (Luke) Springs of Plynlimmon: A poem, with copious notes. Wolverhampton, 1834. 8°   BUS
Refers to 'King Henry V.' and the battle of Tewkesbury.

Bookman (The) [Monthly periodical. Edited by Dr. Robertson Nicoll]. Sh— double number. Ln: Hodder, 1903. F°., pp. 74 and xxii.-xxvi. Illustrated with portraits and scenes   BPL

Bookmart (The). A periodical. Pittsburgh, U. S., Dec., 1885. Roy. 8°., pp. 32
Contains article on Sh—'s autograph, 'Kinton' portrait, etc.

Boole ( ) Quality of mercy [In ' University Mag.,' Jan.]. Ln : 1880. 8°   BUS
On ' Merchant of Venice.'

Boone, *Bookseller*. *See* Sh— Hamlet, 1603

Booth (Barton) *Actor*—
See Cibber (T.)
 ,, Drury Lane

Booth (Edwin) Sh— League. *See Sh*—] Sh—

Booth (Edwin) *Actor-Manager*—
See American . . .
 ,, Sh— Hamlet, 1878
 ,, Sh— King Henry VIII., 1878
 ,, Sh— King Lear, 1878
 ,, Sh— King Richard II., 1878
 ,, Sh— King Richard III., 1868, 1870, 1876, 1878
 ,, Sh— Much ado, 1871
 ,, Sh— Othello, 1869, 1870, 1878
 ,, Sh— Romeo . . . 1870
 ,, Sh— Taming . . . 1876, 1878

Booth (Edwin) *Editor*—
See Sh— Hamlet, 1866
 ,, Sh— Julius Cæsar, 1871
 ,, Sh— Macbeth, 1874, 1878
 ,, Sh— Merchant . . . 1867, 1868, 1870

Booth.] Clarke (Mrs. A. B.) The elder and younger Booth. Boston : Osgood, 1881-82. 8°   SML

] Illustrations of Edwin Booth [In ' American Enterprise ']. 1875. F°   BPL

] Winter (W.) Life and art of Edwin Booth. 1893. 12°   BPL

Booth (Lionel) *Publisher*—
See Sh— As you like it, 1864
 ,, Sh— Hamlet, 1864
 ,, Sh— King Henry IV., i., 1863
 ,, Sh— King Henry IV., ii., 1863
 ,, Sh— King Henry V., 1863
 ,, Sh— King Henry VI., i.-ii.-iii., 1863
 ,, Sh— King Lear, 1864
 ,, Sh— King Richard II., 1863
 ,, Sh— King Richard III., 1864
 ,, Sh— Love's labours lost, 1862
 ,, Sh— Merchant . . . 1862
 ,, Sh— Merry Wives, 1862
 ,, Sh— Midsummer N. D., 1862
 ,, Sh— Much ado, 1862
 ,, Sh— Othello, 1864
 ,, Sh— Pericles, 1865
 ,, Sh— Romeo . . . 1864
 ,, Sh— Titus . . . 1864
 ,, Sh— Troilus . . . 1864
 ,, Sh— Works, 1862-64, 1864

Booth (W. S.) Some acrostic signatures of Francis Bacon. 1909. 4°   BPL

Bormann (August. Edwin) Sh—'s debut. *See* Sh—

Bormann (E.) Francis Bacon's cryptic rhymes and the truths they reveal. Ln : Siegle, 1906. 8°, pp. 250   BPL

Quintessence of the Sh— secret. Ln : Siegle, 1905. 8°, pp. 30

Sh— secret. Trans. from the German by Henry Brett. 1895. Roy. 8°, pp. 366
   BM | BPL | MPL | SML

Borrenstein (D. A.) *Glasgow Publisher*. *See* Sh— Works, 1841, 1844

Borsa (M.) English stage of to-day. 1908. 8°   BPL
Sh— occupies pp. 167-188.

Bosanquet (B.) Comparison of Dante and Sh— [In his ' History of Æsthetics ']. 1892. 8°   BPL
Sh—occupies pp. 152-165.

Bossiegel (Victorinus) *Gottingen Publisher*. *See* Sh— Othello, 1766

Bostocke (Robert) *Publisher*. *See* Brathwaite

Boston prize poems and other specimens of dramatic poetry, by Charles Sprague and others. Boston [U. S.]: J. T. Buckingham, 1824. 12°, pp. 130   BUS
A collection of the leading poems sent to the ' Boston Theatre' for a prize ode to be recited at a Sh—pageant.

Boston Public Library : Barton Collection. *See* Hubbard & Knapp

Boston Theatre impartial critique. Boston [U. S.]: Wilkinson, 1813-14. 2 vols. 8°   SML

Boston [U. S.] Theatre—
See Sh— Hamlet, 1794
 ,, Sh— Othello, 1823
 ,, Sh— Twelfth Night, 1794

Boswell ( ) Account of Stratford Jubilee. *See* Gentleman's . . .

Boswell *jun.* (James) Essay on the phraseology and metre of the poet and his contemporaries [In Malone's Life of Sh—]. 1821. 8°   BM | BPL | BUS
Manuscript Notes. *See* Steevens
Memoir of Malone. *See* Malone

Boswell *jun.* (James) *Editor*—
See Malone
 ,, Sh— Works, 1821

Boswell-Stone (W. G.) ' As you like it ' and Lodge's ' Rosalynde ' compared. Ln : New Sh— Soc., 1880-86. 8°

Boswell-Stone (W. G.) *Editor*—
See Holinshed
 ,, Sh— All's well . . . 1909
 ,, Sh— Comedy of Errors, 1908
 ,, Sh— Much ado . . . 1908

Bosworth (T.) *Publisher*. *See* Sh— Macbeth, 1868

Botany and Flora—
See Bagnall   *See* Burgess
 ,, Beisly   ,, Crane
 ,, Bloom   ,, Elder

Botany and Flora—
See Ellacombe   See Hancock
  ,, Gallio   ,, Oswald
  ,, Giraud   ,, Serres
  ,, Grindon
Botticelli (Sandro) *Artist.* See Sh— Sonnets,
1902
Bottom the weaver.   *See* Sh— Midsummer
N. D.
Bouncing knight.   *See* Kirkman
Bowden (Henry Sebastian).   *See Sh*—] Simp-
son & Bowden
Bowdler *Censor* (Thomas) Letter to the . . .
' British Critic ' occasioned by the cen-
sure . . . on the editions of Sh— by
Johnson, Pope, Bowdler, Warburton,
Theobald, Steevens, Reed, and Malone,
et hoc genus omne, all the herd of these
and Meibomiuses of the British School.
Ln : Longman, 1823. 8°, pp. 40   BM | BUS
] Postscript to the Fourth Edition of the
' Family Sh—.'   1824.   12°   W
Bowdler (Thomas) *Editor*—
See Sh— Hamlet, 1860
  ,, Sh— Works, 1807, 1818, 1820, 1822,
       1823, 1825, 1827, 1828, 1831, 1839,
       1843, 1847, 1849, 1850, 1852-53,
       1853-55, 1855, 1859, 1860, 1860-61,
       1860-65, 1861, 1863, 1865, 1867,
       1872, 1874, 1876, 1878, 1883, 1887
Bowdler.] " The Family Shakespeare, 1818 "
[Review in ' Edinburgh Review '].   1821.
8°   BPL | CPL
Bowen (Francis) Battle of the commentators :
Restoration of the text of Sh— [In ' North
American Review,' April].   Boston, 1854.
8°   BUS
Bowen (H. C.) Sh— reading book.   *See* Sh—
Works : Ext. 1881
Bowen (H. C.) *Editor.*   *See* Sh— Works, 1881,
1883, 1886-87
Bowen (John) Selection of favourite catches,
glees, etc. as sung at the Bath Harmonic
Society . . . Bath : R. Cruttwell, 1799.
8°, pp. xxviii.-152
Includes glees and lyrics from ' Macbeth,' ' Romeo,'
' Tempest,' ' Winter's Tale,' etc.
Bowen (W.) *Publisher.*   *See* Sh— Macbeth,
1776
Bowles (   ) *Editor.*   *See* Sh— King John,
1764
Bowles (T.) *Publisher.*   *See* Sh—Merchant . . .
1783
Bowles (Thomas) Plan of London in Queen
Elizabeth's days. Ln : J. Bowles, 1724.
Imp. f°
Bowyer (W.) *Printer.*   *See* Sh— Works, 1770-
74
Boyce (*Dr.* Wm.) *Composer*—
See Sh— Macbeth, 1750, 1760
  ,, Sh— Tempest, 1750

Boyd (H. M.)   *See* Chalmers
Boyd (L. B.) *Editor.*   *See* Sh— As you like it,
1906
Boydell (John)] Description of several pictures
presented to the Corporation of the City
of London by John Boydell, 1794.   J. &
J. Boydell, 1794-95.   8°   W
Sh— : Mr. Alderman Boydell, Josiah Boydell and George Nicol propose to publish
by subscription a most magnificent and
accurate edition of the plays . . . in eight
volumes. Ln : 1 Dec., 1786. Orig. MS.
F°, pp. 4   BUS
This was printed 1st May, 1789.
Sh— : Signatures of the subscribers. Ln :
[1789-91]. Orig. MS. 80 ff. on vellum
                             BUS
Bears the autographs of King George III., Queen
Charlotte, George Prince of Wales, Dukes of Rox-
burghe, Devonshire, Marlborough, Bedford, Rutland, Buckingham, Earl Spencer, Marquis of Bute,
C. J. Fox, Warren Hastings, Thomas Erskine, and
other notabilities.
See Jerningham
Boydell (John) *Editor.*   *See* Sh— Works,
1802, 1874
Boydell (John & Josiah)] Catalogue of small
pictures painted for the Sh— Gallery,
Pall Mall. Ln : 1795. 8°   BPL | W
] Catalogue of the collection of pictures in
the Sh— Gallery, Pall Mall. Ln : J. & J.
Boydell, 1787.   8°
] Catalogue of the Sh— Gallery. Ln : Sold
at the place of Exhibition, 1789. 8°, pp.
xvi.-96   BPL | BUS
] Catalogue of the Sh— Gallery. Ln : H.
Baldwin, 1790. 8°, pp. xx.-144
                 BM | BPL | BUS
] Catalogue of the . . . Sh— Gallery. Ln :
1791.   8°   BM | BPL
] Catalogue of the . . . Sh— Gallery. Ln :
Printed for the Proprietors, 1792. 8°,
pp. xvi.-194   BM | BPL | BUS | W
] Catalogue of the . . . Sh— Gallery. Ln :
1794.   8°   BPL | W
] Catalogue of the . . . Sh— Gallery. Ln :
J. & J. Boydell, 1796. 8°   BPL | W
] Catalogue of the . . . Sh— Gallery. Ln :
1802.   12°   BPL | CPL
Contains the passages alluded to by each picture.
] Catalogue of the . . . Sh— Gallery, to be
sold by auction May, 1805. 1805. 4°
] Exhibition of the Sh— Gallery, Pall Mall,
being the last time the pictures can ever
be seen as an entire collection, 1805. Ln :
J. & J. Boydell, 1794-1805.   8°   W
Boydell (J. & J.) *Publishers.*   *See* Sh—Works,
1786-1802, 1791-1802, 1802, 1802-03
Boydell.] Boydell Gallery. *See* Sh— Works,
1874, 1875, 1876, 1878

(29)

Boydell.] Boydell *v.* Drummond. 11th Easter 142. Court of King's Bench. 49 Geo. III. 25 May, 1809. MS. Fcp. 4°, pp. 46   BUS
Report of an action against a subscriber to the Boydell Sh—.

] Boydell's Lottery, to be drawn pursuant to Act of Parliament. Contains 22,000 tickets at three guineas each. Ln : 1804. 8°, pp. 2   BUS

] New Sh— Gallery, Pall Mall : Prospectus. [c. 1795.] 8°   BPL

] Notice to the subscribers of Boydell's edition of Sh— concerning the re-engraving of a plate. 1791. F°   W

] Plan of the Sh— Lottery. Ln : W. Bulmer, 1804. 4°, pp. 8   BUS

] Plan of the Sh— Lottery. Ln : W. Bulmer, 1804. 8°, pp. 4   BUS

] Prospectus of Boydell's edition of Sh—. Ln : 1786. F°, pp. 4   W

See also Nichol (G.)
   ,,   ,,   Public Characters
   ,,   ,,   Repton
   ,,   ,,   Spooner

Boyden (George)—
See Stopes & Boyden
   ,,   Stratford-on-Avon Herald

Boyle. *See* Dunton

Boyle (R.) ' King Henry VIII.' : An investigation into the origin and authorship of the play. Ln : New Sh— Soc., 1880-86. 8°

On Beaumont, Fletcher, and Massinger. Ln : New Sh— Soc., 1880-86. 8°

On Massinger and the ' Two Noble Kinsmen.' Ln : New Sh— Soc., 1882. 8°   BPL

On Wilkins' share in . . . Sh—'s ' Pericles.' Ln : New Sh— Soc. [1882]. 8°   BM

Boys *Publisher.* *See* Moon, Boys & Graves

Bracebridge (Charles Holte) Sh— no deer-stealer, or a short account of Fulbroke Park, near Stratford-on-Avon. Ln : Harrison, 1862. 8°, pp. iv.-32. With view of the old Deer Barn   BM | BPL | CPL

Brackett (Anna C.) A thought on Sh— [From the ' Journal of speculative Philosophy ']. 1867. 8°   BPL

Braddon *aft.* Maxwell (Mary E.) Asphodel : A novel. Ln : Maxwell [c. 1882].   BPL
Concerns Ann Hathaway's cottage and its tenant, Mrs. Baker.

Bradley (A.) *Dublin Publisher—*
See Sh— As you like it, 1741
   ,,   Sh— Merry Wives, 1730, 1739

Bradley (Andrew Cecil) Oxford lectures on poetry. Ln : 1909. 8°   BPL
Shakespearean tragedy : Lectures on 'Hamlet, Othello, King Lear, Macbeth.' Ln : Macmillan, 1904. 8°, pp. 510   BPL
Shakespearean tragedy. 2nd edition. Ln : Macmillan, 1905. 8°, pp. 510
    BUS | MPL | SML

Bradley (A. C.) *Editor. See* Sh— Works, 1886-91

Bradocke (Richard) *Publisher—*
See Essex
   ,,   Euordanus
   ,,   Sh— Hamlet, 1608

Bradshaw (Christopher B.) Sh— and Company : A comedy. 1845. 8° BPL | BUS

Bradwood (   ) *Publisher. See* Montaigne

Bradwood (M.) *Printer. See* Sprot

Brae (Andrew Edward)] Collier, Coleridge and Sh— : A review. Ln : Longman, 1860. 8°, pp. 150   BM | BPL | BUS | CPL | SML
' The Athenæum '—pp. 150, 11th Aug., 1860—describes this as ' a mere waste of passionate words.'

] Literary cookery, with reference to matter attributed to Coleridge and Sh— : A letter addressed to the ' Athenæum,' with a postscript containing some remarks upon the refusal of that journal to print it. Ln : J. R. Smith, 1855. 8°, pp. iv.-12   BPL | BUS
Collier brought an unsuccessful action for libel against the publisher. The pamphlet was suppressed.

Prospero's clothes-line, with other readings in Sh—. 1873. 8°   BPL

Prospero's clothes-line . . . with some other readings . . . [In Roy. Soc. of Literature : Trans.] Ln : 1874. 8°   BUS

' Scarre ' between Bertram and Diana [' All's Well ']. [c. 1871.] 8°   BPL

Bragge (B.) *Publisher—*
See Dunton
   ,,   Sh— Taming . . . 1708

Braithwaite (B.) Sh— ; man, dramatist and poet. *See* Sh—

Braithwaite (W. S.) Book of Elizabethan verse. *See* Sh— Works : Ext. 1908

Branch (H. E.) Welshmen in Sh—'s plays. Cheltenham [1909]. Cr. 8°   BPL

Branch (Helen *Lady*). *See* Harbert (*Sir* W.)

Brandes (*Dr.* George Morris Cohen) Life and work of Sh— *See* Sh—.
Wm. Sh— ; A critical study. Trans. by W. Archer, Diana White and Mary Morison. *See* Sh—

Brandes (*Dr.* G. M. C.) *Editor—*
See Sh— All's well, 1904
   ,,   Sh— Antony, 1904
   ,,   Sh— As you like it, 1904
   ,,   Sh— Comedy of Errors, 1904
   ,,   Sh— Cymbeline, 1904
   ,,   Sh— Hamlet, 1904
   ,,   Sh— Julius Cæsar, 1904
   ,,   Sh— King Henry IV., i., 1904
   ,,   Sh— King Henry IV., ii., 1904
   ,,   Sh— King Henry V., 1904
   ,,   Sh— King Henry VI., i., 1904
   ,,   Sh— King Henry VI., ii., 1904
   ,,   Sh— King Henry VI., iii., 1904
   ,,   Sh— King Henry VIII., 1904

Brandes (*Dr.* G. M. C.) *Editor—*
  See Sh— King John, 1904
  ,, Sh— King Lear, 1904
  ,, Sh— King Richard II., 1904
  ,, Sh— King Richard III., 1904
  ,, Sh— Love's labours . . . 1904
  ,, Sh— Macbeth, 1904
  ,, Sh— Measure for M., 1904
  ,, Sh— Merchant . . . 1904
  ,, Sh— Merry Wives, 1904
  ,, Sh— Midsummer N. D., 1904
  ,, Sh— Much ado, 1904
  ,, Sh— Othello, 1904
  ,, Sh— Pericles, 1904
  ,, Sh— Rape, 1904
  ,, Sh— Romeo, 1904
  ,, Sh— Sonnets, 1904
  ,, Sh— Taming . . . 1904
  ,, Sh— The Tempest, 1904
  ,, Sh— Timon . . . 1904
  ,, Sh— Titus . . . 1904
  ,, Sh— Troilus . . . 1904
  ,, Sh— Twelfth Night, 1904
  ,, Sh— Two Gentlemen, 1904
  ,, Sh— Venus, 1904
  ,, Sh— Winter's Tale, 1904
  ,, Sh— Works, 1904, 1905
Brandram (Samuel) Selected pieces in prose
  and verse. *See* Sh— Works : Ext. 1893
Brandram (S.) *Editor. See* Sh— Works, 1881,
  1882, 1892
Brandt (Sebastian) Ship of fooles, wherein is
  shewed the folly of all states. Trans. by
  Alex. Barclay. Ln : John Cawood, 1570.
  F°, with 118 woodcuts
  Illustrates 'Macbeth' and 'Two Gentlemen.'
Branston ( ) *Engraver. See* Sh— Works,
  1809, 1810
Brassey (*Lady*). *See Sh—*] Sh— Show Book
Brassington (William Salt) Catalogue of the
  Library at the Sh— Memorial, Stratford-
  on-Avon [Classified and indexed]. 1909.
  Typewritten MS. 15 vols. Oblong 12°
  [In progress] SML
  Charters and muniments of Stratford-upon-
  Avon. *See* Memorials . . .
  ] Hand-List of collective editions of Sh—'s
  Works published before 1800 . . . Strat-
  ford-upon-Avon : J. Morgan, 1898. Roy.
  8°, pp. 8 BM | BPL | BUS | SML
  ] Illustrated catalogue of the pictures, &c. in
  the Sh— Memorial, Stratford-upon-Avon.
  1896. Fcp. 4° BPL | SML
  Notes on ecclesiastical Seals of Warwick-
  shire. Birmingham : Privately printed,
  1893. 4°, pp. 16, illustrated SML
  Notes on portraits of Sh—. Sh— Club
  paper. Stratford, 1908. Cr. 8°, pp. 8
  See also Sh— Works, 1899

Brassington (William Salt) Picturesque War-
  wickshire. Dundee : Valentine, 1906. Cr.
  8°, pp. 168, illustrated SML
  Sh—'s home-land : Sketches of Stratford-
  on-Avon, the Forest of Arden, and the
  Avon Valley. With bust portrait in
  colours and seventy illustrations by Hy.
  J. Howard and Sidney Heath. Ln : Dent,
  1903. 8°, pp. 376 BPL | BUS | SML
Brassington (W. S.) *Editor. See* Irving (W.)
Brassington (W. S.) & Lunn (Robert) Stratford-upon-Avon illustrated. Bourne-
  mouth : Mate, 1908. Cr. 8° BPL | SML
Brathwaite (Richard) English gentleman . . .
  Ln : Printed for Felix Kyngston and to be
  sold by Rob. Bostocke. 1633. Fcp. 4°,
  pp. xxiv.-456
  P. 28 refers to 'Venus and Adonis'; pp. 178-196 relate
  to 'Stage-plays, stage-stingers, and poet-scourgers,
  objections against stage-plays, who the first come-
  dian and first tragedian?' . . .'
  Honest ghost, or a voice from the vault.
  Ln : R. Hodgkinsonne, 1658. Fcp. 4°
  Illustrates 'Measure for Measure.'
  Remains. *See* Sh— Epitaph on Combe
  Strappado for the Divell : Epigrams and
  Satyres alluding to the time, with divers
  measures of no lesse delight. Ln : 1615. 8°
  For its Shakespearean interest *see* Collier's 'Rarest
  books in the English language.' Says :
    'If I had lived but in King Richard's days,
    Crying "A horse ; a kingdom for a horse."'
?] The Whimzies or a new cast of characters ;
  from the original edition, 1631. Ed. by J.
  O. Halliwell. Ln : 1859. Fcp. 4°. BUS
  Limited to twenty-six copies.
Brayley (A. A.) *Editor—*
  See Sh— As you like it, 1902
  ,, Sh— Macbeth, 1903
  ,, Sh— Merchant . . . 1906
Brayley (E. W.) Historical and descriptive
  account of the theatres of London. Ln :
  1826. 4°, with 14 coloured plates and 2
  plans
Brereton (Austin) Life of Henry Irving. *See*
  Irving
  Sh— Scenes and characters, with descrip-
  tive notes on the plays and principal
  Sh— players from Betterton to Irving.
  See Sh— Works : Ext. 1886
  Sir Hy. Irving. *See* Irving (*Sir* J. H. B.)
  Some famous Hamlets, from Burbage to
  Fechter . . . Ln : D. Bogue, 1884. 8°,
  pp. xii.-74 BPL | BUS | SML
  Theatrical Richmond [In 'The Theatre'].
  1885. 8° BPL
Brereton (Austin) *Editor—*
  See Abington
  ,, Sh— Works, 1903, 1904
Brereton (J. Le Gay). *See* Slater, Ingram &
  Brereton

(31)

Breton (Nicholas)] Arbor of amorous devices, wherein young gentlemen may reade many pleasant fancies and fine deuices, and thereon meditate diuers sweete conceites to court the loue of faire ladies and gentlewomen. By N. B. Imprinted at Ln. by Richard Iones at the Rose and Crowne neere S. Andrewe's Church. Fcp. 4°. Sig. A to F4 unpaged   CTC

Will of wit, otherwise called wit's will or will's wit. Now first reprinted from the rare edition of 1599. Ed. by J. O. Halliwell. Ln : 1860. Fcp. 4°.   BUS
Limited to twenty-six copies.
Entered at Stationers' Hall probably in or before 1580, in which year presumably it was first printed. An edition of 1597 is recorded, but apparently the 1599 one was the earliest available to Halliwell.
It is interesting to compare it with the 'Will' sonnet, first printed in 1609.

Brett (E. J.) Editor. See Sh— Hamlet, 1881

Brett (Hy.) Editor. See Bormann

Brett (John) Publisher. See Loveling

Breuning (C. G. F.) Erlangen Publisher. See Sh— Macbeth, 1812

Brewer (Antony) Merry Devil of Edmonton. See Sh— Merry Devil . . . (heading)

Brewer (James Norris) House in which Sh— was born [In ' Histrionic Topography ']. 1818. 8°   BPL
Topographical and historical description of the county of Warwick. Ln : J. Harris, 1814. 8°, pp. 324, with copperplates SML
Stratford and Sh—, pp. 223-263.

Brewer (J. N.) & Storer (J. S.) Histrionic topography, or the birthplaces, residences, and funeral monuments of the most distinguished actors. Ln : Cole, 1818. 8°   BPL | BUS | SML

Brewer (John Sherren) English studies, or essays in English history and literature. Ed. with a prefatory memoir by Henry Wace. Ln : 1881 8°   BUS
Contains article on the ' Study of Sh—.'
Inaugural lecture before the Sh— Soc. of King's College . . . Ln : 1856. 12°   BPL

Brewster (E.) Publisher. See Sh— Works, 1685

Bridges (Robert) On the influence of the audience. See Sh— Works, 1904-07

Bridges (Wm.) Editor. See Sh— As you like it, 1850

Bridgett (T. E.) Sh—'s nuns [In ' Merry England ']. 1886. 8°   BPL

Bridgewater House Library. See Collier (J. P.)

Bridgman (T.) Editor. See Sh— King Richard III., 1820

Brief description of the Collegiate Church and choir of Saint Mary, Warwick . . . with the antiquities and curiosities . . . and of the Chapel [By W. Field ?]. Warwick, 1820. Cr. 8°
Gives English renderings of the Latin epitaphs upon Sh—'s contemporaries.

Brief enquiry into the learning of Sh—. See Sh—

Briefe conceipte. See Sh— Compendious examination

Brien (G.) The ' Œdipus in exile ' of Sophocles compared with ' King Lear ' [In ' Prolusiones Literariæ,' pp. 19-30]. 1841. 8°   BPL

Briggs (   ) Artist. See Sh— Works, 1829

Briggs (B. C.) ' King Lear ': Questions and notes. Dinglewood Manuals. [c. 1907.] 2 vols. 12°   BPL

Bright (B. H.) Library. See Catalogue, 1845

Brighton. See Porter

Brigstocke (W. Osborne) Editor. See Sh— All's well, 1904

Brindley (J.) Publisher. See Sh— Works, 1740, 1745, 1747, 1757

Brindley (J. M.) England's bard : A poem [c. 1864]. 8°   BPL

Brink (Bernhard Ten) Five lectures on Sh—. See Sh—

Brinsmead (E.) History of the Pianoforte. Ln : Simpkin, 1889. 12°   SML
Includes details of Elizabethan instruments.

Briscoe (James Potter) Elizabethan garland. See Sh— Works : Ext. 1900

Briscoe (J. P.) Editor. See Sh— Sonnets, 1900

Bristol. See Tyrer

Bristol (Frank M.) Sh—and America. Chicago, 1898. 8°, with port. and maps   BM | BPL | BUS

British curiosities in art and nature. Giving an account of rarities both ancient and modern. Ln : 1721. 8°   W
Sh— and Stratford-on-Avon, p. 71.

British drama : A collection of the most esteemed tragedies, comedies, operas, and farces. 1828. 2 vols. 8°   MPL

British drama. See Sh— Antony, 1853

British Empire Sh— Society : Liverpool centre syllabus, No. I., Oct.-Dec., 1909. 12°, pp. 4   BPL

British Empire Sh— Society : Official Report, edited by Greta Morritt (foundress) and Acton Bond. Ln : 1909. 8°, pp. 60 BPL
With particulars of the provincial branches.

British Empire Sh— Society : Reports, 1905-06. Cr. 8°   BPL

British Empire Sh— Soc : Stratford branch. Programmes. 1907. 4°   BPL

British Museum. Catalogue of Printed Books : Wm. Sh— [By G. K. Fortescue]. Ln : Clowes, 1897. 4°, pp. 116 BM | BPL | SML

] Catalogue of the Books in the Library of the British Museum printed in England, Scotland and Ireland, and of Books in English printed abroad, to the year 1640, by George Bullen and Gregory W. Eccles. 1884. 3 vols. 8°   BM | BLO | BUS | CTC

British Museum.] **Librorum** Impressorum, qui in Museo Britannico adservantur, Catalogus [Excerpt from Vol. vi., containing article 'Sh—']. Ln: 1817. 8°

BM | W

Guide to Autograph Letters [Shakespeare, pp. 15-16]. 1860. 12° BM | BPL

British Museum. *See* Thimm

British Plutarch [Vol. v., pp. 1-28, containing 'Life of Wm. Sh—']. 1762. 12° BPL

British stage, or literary cabinet. Ed. by Thomas Kenrick. Illust. by G. & R. Cruikshank. Ln: J. Marshall, 1817-22. 6 vols. 8°. With 24 character portraits, in colours

British Theatre. *See* Chetwood (W. R.)

British Theatre. *See* Sh— Works, 1808, 1816-18, 1829-31

British Theatrical Gallery [Whole-length coloured portraits of actors and actresses]. With biographical notices by D. Terry. 1825. F°

Britons, strike home. *See* Sh— Works: Ext. 1745

Brittain (J. H.) *Editor. See* Sh— Twelfth Night, 1906

Britter (C. A.) *Editor. See* Sh— Merchant . . . 1897

Britton (John) Autobiography . . . Copiously illustrated. Ln: [Privately printed] 1850. 2 vols. Roy. 8°

In vol. ii. is the 'Essay on . . . Sh—,' with bust portrait and eight woodcuts of Stratford.

Collection of papers and autograph letters on Shakespearean subjects. 1814-39. Original manuscripts. 2 vols. F° BUS

Essays on the merits and characteristics of Sh—'s writings. Ln: 1849. Roy. 8°, pp. viii.-64-viii. BPL | BUS

Issued as a separate appendix to Britton's Autobiography.

Index to Sh—. c. 1800. Manuscript BUS Library. *See* Catalogue, 1832

Life and writings of Sh—. *See* Sh— Works: Ext. 1818

Remarks on . . . Sh—. *See* Sh—

Rules for judging of Sh—, chiefly extracted from Upton. [c. 1800.] Manuscript BUS Wm. Sh—. *See* Sh—

See Eginton
  ,, Southey
  ,, Wheler
  ,, Wilkins
  ,, Wordsworth

Britton (John) *Editor. See* Sh— Works, 1808, 1813-14, 1818

Broad hints at retirement. An ode to a tragedy king, addressed to J. P. Kemble. By a theatrical rebel. [1809 ?] 8° W

Contains parodies of and references to Sh—.

Broadbent (R. J.) Annals of the Liverpool stage. L'pool: E. Howell, 1908. 8°, pp. viii.-394 and 24 plates BPL | SML

Broadside black letter ballads. Ed by J. P. Collier. Ln: Privately printed, 1868. Fcp. 4°

Issue limited to twenty-five copies.

Broadsides. *See* Ballads

Brock (H. M.) *Artist. See* Sh— King Richard II., 1899

Broderip & Wilkinson *Publishers. See* Sh— Macbeth, 1760

Brody (G. M.) Hamlet: An essay. Edinburgh, 1870. 8° BPL

Broenner (H. L.) *Frankfort Publisher. See* Sh— Works, 1846

Brome (H.) *Publisher. See* Sh— Works: Ext. 1677

Brome (Richard) Joviall crew, or the merry beggars, presented in a comedy at the Cock-pit in Drury Lane . . . Ln: Printed by J. Y— for E. D— and N. E—, and are to be sold at the Gun in Ivy Lane, 1652. Fcp. 4°

In the preliminary verses occur these lines:—
  'Beaumont and Fletcher they say perhaps might
  Passe well for currant coin in a dark night,
  But Sh—, the plebian driller, was
  Founder'd in 's *Pericles* and must not pass.'

Brome (Wm.) *Publisher. See* Scot

Bromley (W.) *Hammersmith Engraver & Publisher. See* Sh— As you like it, 1799

Bromton (*Abbot*). *See* O'Keeffe

Brönner ( ) *Frankfort Publisher. See* Sh— Works, 1829-31, 1829-43

Brook (Nathaniel) *Publisher—*
See Cotgrave
  ,, Webster & Rowley

Brooke ( ) *Artist. See* Sh— Works, 1902

Brooke (A.) *Editor. See* Sh— Works, 1790

Brooke (Arthur)—
See Bandello & Brooke *See* Turberville

Brooke (Christopher)] Ghost of Richard the third expressing himself in three parts: I. His character, II. His legend, III. His tragedie; containing more of him than hath been heretofore shewed either in Chronicles, Plays, or Poems. By C. B——. Ln: Printed for L. Lisle and are to be sold at the Tiger's Head, 1614. Fcp. 4° BLO

Collation: Title, preceded by blank leaf; Dedication, marked 3; blank leaf; Epistle to reader, A; Verses, marked O 3, 2 (the last three also paged 1 to 6); text, B to L 2 in fours.

Sheet i. is headed 'The Tragedie of Richard the third.' The whole work is in verse. Contains lines 'caught from Sh—'s King Richard III.' The dedicatory verses are signed by W. Brown, Geo. Chapman, Fr. Dyne, Geo. Wythers, Robert Daborne, and Ben Ionson.

Reprinted for the Sh— Society, with Notes by J. P. Collier, in 1844.

See also Ghost . . .

Brooke (C. F. Tucker) *Editor.* See Sh—
Works, 1908

Brooke.] Lawrence (W. J.) Life of Gustavus
Vaughan Brooke, tragedian. Belfast:
W. & G. Baird, 1892. Roy. 8°, pp. xii.-
284 and portrait   BPL

Brooke (Henry) Prologue to 'Othello' spoken
by Mr. Garrick [In his 'Collection of
Pieces']. 8°   BUS

Brooke (Henry) *Editor.* See Sh— Cymbeline,
1778

Brooke (Richard) Visits to fields of battle in
England of the fifteenth century. Ln:
1857. 8°   BUS

Brooke (Stopford A.) English literature. *See*
Sh—
Introduction. *See* Sh— Works: Ext. 1908
Introduction. *See* Treasury
On ' King Richard III.' Ln: New Sh—
Soc., 1880-86. 8°
On ten plays of Sh—. Ln: Constable, 1905.
8°, pp. 318   BPL | BUS

Brooks (Charles Shirley) Shake-scene's new
tragedy [In ' Gentleman's Magazine,'
Feb.] Ln: 1869. 8°   BUS
Upon ' Hamlet.'

Broster ( ) *Chester Publisher.* See Sh—
Works, 1768

Brough (R. B.) How the last Act of 'Hamlet'
was written [In 'A Cracker Bon-bon,' pp.
66-80]. 1861. 12°   BPL

Brough (R. B.) & Cruikshank (G.) Life of Sir
John Falstaff. With a biography of the
knight from authentic sources. Ln:
Longman, 1858. Roy. 8°, pp. xx.-196.
With 20 etchings.   BPL | BUS | CPL | SML

Brough Brothers *Editors.* See Sh— The Tempest, 1849

Brough (Wm.) *Editor.* See Sh— Winter's Tale,
1856

Brougham (John) ' Merchant of Venice '
travesty. *See* Sh— Merchant . . . 1860
Sh—'s dream : An historic pageant, with
an allegorical introduction. To which
are added a description of the costume,
cast . . . positions . . . and stage business.
As performed at the Academy of Music,
2 Aug. New York, 1858. 12°, pp. viii.
          BPL | BUS

Broughton (Hugh) Obseruations vpon the
first ten fathers. Ln: W. White, 1612.
Fcp. 4°   W
Contains signatures and notes alleged to be in Sh—'s
autograph, and to have formed part of his library.
In reality one of W. H. Ireland's fabrications.

Broughton (R.) *Editor.* See Sh— King Henry
IV., i., 1858

Brown (A.) *Editor*—
See Sh— As you like it, 1869
,, Sh— Hamlet, 1865
,, Sh— Romeo . . . 1837

Brown (Charles Armitage) *Editor*—
See Sh— Poems, 1838
,, Sh— Sonnets, 1838

Brown (D.) *Publisher*—
See Sh— Measure . . . 1700
,, Sh— Twelfth Night, 1703

Brown (Daniel) *Publisher. See* Feigned friendship

Brown (David Paul) Sketches of the life and
genius of Sh—. *See* Sh—

Brown *of Newington Butts* (Henry) Sonnets of
Sh— solved and the mystery of his friend-
ship, love and rivalry revealed . . . Ln :
J. R. Smith, 1870. 8°, pp. vi.-242
          BM | BPL | BUS | CPL | MPL | SML

Brown (Irving)] Character of the Nurse's de-
ceased husband in ' Romeo and Juliet,'
by ' Cream Curdle.' Ed. by W. Ord
Hunter. New York: Printed for the
Editor [c. 1880]. 8°, pp. 20   BUS
Iconoclasm and whitewash, and other
papers. New York, 1885. 8°   BUS
Contains Shakespearean criticism.

Brown (J.) Bible truths. *See* Sh— Works :
Ext. 1862, 1864, 1872, 1877, 1878, 1879

Brown (J.) *Publisher. See* Shore

Brown (J.) *Boston U.S. Publisher. See* Sh—
Works, 1844

Brown (J.) *Edinburgh Publisher. See* Sh—
Works, 1753

Brown (O. Phelps) Shakespearian Annual
Almanac. *See* Sh— Works : Ext. 1871-82

Brown (O. Phelps) *Editor. See* Sh— Works :
Ext. 1870

Brown (P.) *Edinburgh Publisher. See* Sh—
Works, 1837

Brown (W.) Verses. *See* Brooke (C.)

Browne (C. Elliot) Master Robert Shallow :
A study of the Sh— country [In 'Fraser's
Magazine,' April]. Ln : 1877. 8°
          BPL | BUS
Sh—'s son-in-law : A study of old Stratford
[In ' Fraser's Magazine,' April]. Ln :
1874. 8°   BPL | BUS

Browne (D.) *Publisher*—
See Pearce
,, Sh— King Henry VIII., 1758
,, Sh— Works : Ext. 1778

Browne (E. V.) ' Juliet ' and ' Othello.'
Melbourne, 1885. 8°   MPL

Browne (G.) Wm. Sh—. *See* Sh—

Browne *D.D.* (G. F.) Use of works of fiction.
See Sh—] Sh— Sermons

Browne (George H.) Notes on Sh—'s versification. With appendix on the verse tests
and a short descriptive bibliography.
Boston [U.S.], 1884. 8° BM | BPL | BUS
Notes on Sh—'s versification. Second edition. 1886. 12°   BPL

Browne (Gordon) *Artist*—
See Sh— King Lear, 1906
,, Sh— Macbeth, 1899
,, Sh— Works, 1888-90, 1895
,, Sh— Works : Ext. 1902
Browne (H. J.) Baconian authorship of Sh—'s
plays refuted. Melbourne, 1898. 8°,
pp. 18   MPL
Is it Sh—'s confession ? The cryptogram
in his epitaph. Washington, 1887. 8°
                          BM | BPL | BUS
Browne (Hablot Knight) *Artist. See* Sh—
Works, 1858, 1872, 1882, 1882-84
Browne (I.) Sh— in criticism. Read before
the Albany Institute. Albany, U.S. :
[1880]. 8°   BPL
Browne (J.) *Publisher. See* Sh— Works, 1714
Browne (Jonas) *Publisher. See* Theobald
Brownes '*Cib. Jusc.*' (*Major*) *Editor. See*
Sh— Love's Labour Won, 1841
Browning (Robert) Caliban upon Setebos
(suggested by 'The Tempest') [In
'Poetical Works,' Vol. 6, pp. 136-147].
1878. 12°   BPL
[Works] Poetical Works. Leipzig: Tauch-
nitz, 1872. 2 vols. Cr. 8°
In the poem 'Men and Women' (pp. 255-257) Browning
tries to imagine himself Sh—.
See Halliwell
,, Poet lore
,, *Sh*—] Sh— Show Book
,, Thomson
Brownsmith (T.) Dramatic time-piece. 1767.
12°   BPL
Bruce (J.) Who was ' Will, my lord of Ley-
cester's jesting player '? *See Sh*—] Sh—
Soc.
Bruce (J.) *Editor. See* Hayward
Brundage (Frances) *Artist. See* Sh— Works :
Ext. 1895, 1899, 1901
Bruney (R.) *Antwerp Publisher. See* Verste-
gan
Brunsdon *Actor. See* Sh— Comedy of Errors,
1779
Brunton *Actress* ( ) Portrait. *See* Sh—
King Lear, 1785
Bryant (Wm. Cullen) Sh—. *See Sh*—
Bryant (W. C.) *Editor. See* Sh— Works,
1888, 1896
Brydges (*Sir* Samuel Egerton) *Editor. See*
Bodenham
Brydges (*Sir* Egerton) *Editor. See* Greene (R.)
Bubble ghost and his son. *See* Sh— Hamlet,
1869
Buc (*Sir* George). *See* Cunningham
Buchan (A. W.) Poems of feeling. Glasgow :
Murray & Son, 1884. 12°   SML
Contains verses ' On reading Sh—,' p. 194.
Buchan (Peter) Secret history of Macbeth,
King of Scotland. With interesting me-
moirs of the ancient Thanes. 1828. Cr. 8°

Buchanan (George) & Aikman (James) History
of Scotland. Trans. from the Latin . . .
Edinburgh : Thomas Ireland, jun., 1829-
30. 6 vols. 8°, with portraits
Gives a very full account of the life of King Macbeth.
Buchanan was probably one of Sh—'s happiest
sources.
Buchanan (Robert) Fleshly school of poetry
and other phenomena of the day. Ln :
Strahan, 1872. 8°, pp. x.-90, pink
wrappers
On p. 1 is Dickens' reference in ' Martin Chuzzlewit,'
beginning ' Sh— 's an infernal humbug, Pip ! I
never read him. What the devil is it all about, Pip?'
Chapter two is devoted to a historical sketch of Euro-
pean poetry, tracing the 'fleshly scrofula' from the
time of Dante, Chaucer, and Sh— down to the date
of writing.
On p. vi. reference is made to an imaginary ' cast' of
' Hamlet,' with Tennyson in the title rôle.
Buchel (C. A.) *Artist. See* Sh— King Richard
II., 1903
See Sh— The Tempest, 1904
Bucher (*Dr.* J.) *Editor. See* Sh— Julius Cæsar,
1856
Büchner (A.) *Editor. See* Sh— King Richard
III., 1882
Buck (*Sir* George) History of the life and
reigne of Richard the third . . . Ln :
Printed by W. Wilson, 1647. F°. With
portrait by Cross
Probably first prepared or written in Sh—'s life-time,
as Buck died in 1623. Malone doubted the above
authorship.
Buck pourtrays King Richard as an admirable char-
acter, contrary to the view presented by Sh— and
others.
See Sh— Locrine, 1595
Buck (Peter) *Publisher. See* Rowe
Buck (Will.) Testament. *See* Literature
Bucke (R. M.) Sh— dethroned : The proof,
partly from a just-discovered anagram,
that the real author of the so-called
' Sh—' drama was Francis Bacon [In
'Pearson's Magazine,' Vol. 4, pp. 642-654].
Ln : 1897. Roy 8°, pp. 14. Illustrated
Buckham (P. W.)] Theatre of the Greeks.
Second edition. Cambridge : Grant, 1827.
8°   SML
Buckingham (John Sheffield *Duke of*) Four
Chorusses—
See Sh— Julius Cæsar, 1723, 1759
,, James I.
Buckingham (John Sheffield *Duke of*) *Editor.*
See Sh— Julius Cæsar, 1722, 1729, 1740
Buckingham (J. T.) *Printer. See* Sh— Works,
1813
Buckley (Samuel) *Publisher. See* Sh— Works :
Ext. 1708, 1710
B[ucknill] *M.D.* (John Charles) Hamlet : A
psychological study [In ' Journal of
mental science,' Oct.]. Ln : 1858. 8°
                              BPL | BUS

B[ucknill] *M.D.* (John Charles) King Lear : A psychological study [In ' Journal of mental science,' April]. Ln : 1859. 8° BUS

Macbeth : A psychological study [In ' Journal of mental science,' July]. Ln : 1858. 8° BUS

Mad folk of Sh— : Psychological essays. Ln : Macmillan, 1867. 8° BM | BPL | SML

Mad folk of Sh—. Second edition, revised. Ln : Macmillan, 1867. 8°, pp. xvi.-334 MPL

Medical knowledge of Sh—. Ln : Longmans, 1860. 8°, pp., viii.-292 BM | BPL | BUS | CPI | MPL | SML

Psychology of Sh—. Ln : Longman, 1859. 8°, pp. viii.-264 BM | BPL | BUS | CPL | MPL

Buckstone (John Baldwin) Sh—'s drinking bout : A tale of the toping at Bidford [In ' Colburn's New Monthly Magazine,' March]. Ln : 1839. 8° BUS

Budd (Thomas D.) *Editor. See* Sh— Sonnets, 1868

Budgell. *See* Philips

Bulfinch (T.) *Editor. See* Sh— Macbeth, 1877

Bulfinch (Thomas and S. G.) Sh— adapted for reading classes. *See* Sh— Works : Ext. 1865

Bulkeley *Actress* (*Mrs.*) Portrait. *See* Sh— Love's labours, 1785

Bullen (A. H.) Lyrics from the dramatists of the Elizabethan age. *See* Sh— Works : Ext. 1891

On ' A midsummer night's dream.' Sh— Club Paper. Stratford-on-Avon, 1908. 8°, pp. 8

] Sh— Head Press. Stratford, 1904. 8° BPL

Sh— Head Press : A paper read before the Birm. Univ. Sh— Soc. Stratford, 23 Jan., 1908. 8°, pp. 16 BPL

See also Powell & Bullen

Bullen (A. H.) *Editor*—

See Sh— Arden, 1887

„ Sh— Poems, 1907

„ Sh— Sonnets, 1905

„ Sh— Venus . . . 1905

„ Sh— Works, 1904-07

Bullen (Frank T.) Sack of shakings. Ln : Pearson, 1901. Cr. 8°, pp. viii.-390

Contains ' Sh— and the sea,' pp. 52 59, illustrating the poet's nautical knowledge.

Bullen (George) London theatres in 1673 [In 'Athenæum,' No. 2791, p. 569]. 1881

See British Museum

Bullen (Mark W.) Note of an action to recover £50 by John Shaxbere of Stratford-on-Avon against John Luther of Banbury, John Phippis of Stoke, and Richard Quyney of Shuckborough, 1571 [In 'Athenæum,' No. 3675, p. 447]. Ap., 1898

Bulloch (John) Studies on the text of Sh—. With emendations and appendices. Ln : Hamilton, 1878. 8°, pp. xii.-336 BM | BPL | BUS | MPL | SML

Bullock (C.) Cobler of Preston. *See* Sh— Taming of the Shrew, 1732

Bullock (Charles) Sh—'s debt to the Bible. With memorial illustrations. [1879.] 8°, pp. 66. Portraits and illustrations BM | BPL | BUS

Bullock (Christopher) *Editor. See* Sh— Taming . . . 1716, 1723, 1732, 1755, 1767

Bullokar *of Chichester* (John)] English expositor, teaching the interpretation of the hardest words used in our language. Ln : J. Legatt, 1616. Cr. 8°, sig. A1 to A6 and B1 to V8 in eights, unpaged

Quaint definitions abound ; for example :—

THEATRE : A place made half round where people sate to behold solemne playes and games.

COMEDY : A play or interlude, the beginning whereof is ever full of troubles, and the end joyfull.

ACTOR : A doer, sometime a player.

Bulmer & Co., *Printers. See* Sh— Works, 1802

Bulwer (John) View of the people of the whole world, or a short survey of their politics, dispositions, naturall deportments, complexions, customs, manners, habits, fashions . . . adorned with observations on their mutations and changes throughout all ages. Ln : 1654. Fcap. 4°

Illustrates ' Hamlet,' ' Measure for Measure,' and 'Two Gentlemen of Verona.'

Bumpus (J.) *Publisher. See* Sh— Works, 1818, 1821, 1823, 1825, 1828

Bunbury (Hy. Wm.) *Prints. See* Sh— Works : Ext. 1792-96, 1802

Bunce (J. T.) Speech. *See* Birmingham

Bunn (Alfred) Address recited at the theatre in Stratford-on-Avon . . . 3rd June, 1823, for the benefit of a fund now raising towards the erection of a monument to . . . Sh—. Birmingham : T. Knott, jun., 1823. 8°, pp. 8 BUS

The Stage ; both before and behind the curtain. 1840. 3 vols. 12° BPL

Bunn (*Mrs.*) *Actress. See* Sh— Winter's Tale, 1823

Bunner (H. C.) My Sh—. *See* Ballads of books

Bunnett (F. E.) *Editor. See* Gervinus

Bunyan (John) Meditations on the several ages of man's life . . . from his cradle to his grave . . . Ln : J. Blare at the Looking Glass on London Bridge, 1700-01. 8°

Illustrates 'As you like it.'

Burbage (Cuthbert). *See* Stopes

Burbage (James). *See* Stopes

Burbage (Richard) *Actor*—

See Brereton   *See* Davies

„ Cope   „ Flecknoe

„ Corbet   „ Malone

Burbage (Richard) *Actor*—
See Marston   *See* Returne . . .
  ,, Poems   ,, Stopes
Burbage Family. *See* Collier
Burbie *or* Burby (Cuthbert) *Publisher*—
See Barnes
  ,, Johnson (R.)
  ,, Meres
  ,, Orlando
  ,, Sh— King Edward III., 1596, 1599
  ,, Sh— Love's labours lost, 1598
  ,, Sh— Romeo . . . 1599
  ,, Sh— Taming . . . 1594, 1596
Burchard (A.) *Printer. See* Sh— Coriolanus, 1864
Burckhardt (*Prof.* G. F.) *Editor. See* Sh— Julius Cæsar, 1838
Burges (J.) *Cambridge Publisher. See* Plumptre
Burgess (James) Notes on 'King Lear' [In Milton's 'Samson Agonistes']. Calcutta, 1859.   12°   BUS
Burgess (J. Tom) Historic Warwickshire : its legendary lore, traditionary stories and romantic episodes. With numerous illustrations. Ln., Warwick, Leamington, Stratford . . . Collingwood [1876]. 8°, pp. xvi.-408   BPL | BUS | W
Contains 'The Swan of Avon' [Life of Sh—], pp. 303-317.
Historic Warwickshire.   Second edition. Edited by Joseph Hill. Birmingham : Midland Educational Co. [1893]. 4°
                           BPL | SML
Last battle of the Roses : Bosworth Field. Leamington : G. Cunnew, 1872. 4° BPL
Illustrates 'King Richard III.'
Our English wild flowers [chiefly those in the Sh— country]. Ln : Warne [1875 ?]. Cr. 8°. Eight coloured plates and other engravings
Sh—'s monument and gravestone [In 'Athenæum,' No. 2923, p. 568]. 1883
Sh—'s Warwickshire [In 'Athenæum,' No. 2963, p. 179]. 1884. 4°   BPL
Burgess *Bp.* (Thomas) Ode on the present state of English poetry, occasioned by reading a translation of select parts of Sh— . . . and others. By 'Cornelius Scriblerus Nothus.' With remarks. Oxford : J. & J. Fletcher, 1779. 4°, pp. 32
                                BUS
Burgess (W.) The Bible in Sh—. Chicago, 1903. 8°   BPL | MPL
Burghley (Feltham) *pseud. See* Ward (C. A.)
Burgoyne (F. J.) *Editor*—
See Elizabethan
  ,, Northumberland
Burke (Edmund) Oration. *See* Garrick
Burke (John & *Sir* J. B.) Heraldic illustrations. Ln : 1843. 8°   BPL
Contains Sh—'s coat-of-arms.

Burleigh (Wm. Cecil *Baron*). *See* Hulme
Burn (John) Desolate Island. *See* Sh— The Tempest, 1791
Burn (J. H.) *Editor. See* Laneham
Burnaby (Charles)] Love betray'd. *See* Sh— Twelfth Night, 1703
Burnand (*Sir* F. C.) Rise and fall of Richard III. *See* Sh— King Richard III., 1868
The A— D— C— ; Personal reminiscences of the University Amateur Dramatic Club, Cambridge. Ln : Chapman, 1880. 8°, pp. xx.-268   SML
The A— D— C—. Second edition. Ln : Chapman, 1880. 8° pp. xx.-268
Burnand (*Sir* F. C.) *Editor*—
See Sh— Antony, 1866
  ., Sh— Venus . . . 1864
Burney (   ) *Artist. See* Sh— Works, 1787-91
Burns (J. J.) Story of the English kings according to Sh—. New York, 1809. 8°
                                BUS
Burns (Robert). *See* Sh— Works, 1771
Burr (C. H.) 'Hamlet' once more [In 'Poet Lore']. Philadelphia, 1891. 8°   BPL
Burr (W. H.) Bacon and Sh— : Proof that . . . Sh— . . . could not write. The sonnets written by Bacon to the Earl of Essex and his bride A.D. 1590. Bacon identified as the concealed poet 'Ignoto,' 1589-1600. Washington, 1885. 8°   BM | BPL
Bacon and Sh—. New York : W. H. Burr, 1886. 24°   BPL | SML
Burre (Walter) *Publisher. See* Jonson
Burrell (Arthur) Selections from Sh—. *See* Sh— Works : Ext. 1905
Burrow (E. J.) Borough guide to Stratford. 1906. Cr. 8°   BPL
Handbook to Leamington, Warwick and Stratford. 1901. 8°   BPL
Burrows (Edward) Revival and practice of folk music in England. Sh— Club paper. Stratford-on-Avon, 1908. Cr. 8°, pp. 8
Burton (Francis) *Publisher. See* Nero
Burton (John Hill) Life of Spalding. *See* Spalding (W.)
Burton (Robert). *See* Henderson
Burton *of New York* (W. E.) Library. *See* Catalogue, 1860
Shakespeariana. *See* Sh—
Burton's Theatre, New York. *See* Collection . . .
Busby *or* Busbie (John) *Publisher*—
See Decker
  ,, Lodge
  ,, Sh— King Henry V., 1600
Busby (*Dr.* Thomas) *Composer. See* Sh— The Tempest, 1780, 1800

(37)

Busche *called* le Sylvain (Alexandre Vanden)
The Orator ; handling a hundred seuerall
discourses, in forme of declamations,
some of the arguments being drawne
from Titus Liuius and other ancient
writers, the rest of the author's owne
inuention . . . Written in French by
Alexander Siluayn, and Englished by
L. P— [Lazarus Piot or Pyott, *pseud. of*
Anthony Munday]. Ln : Adam Islip,
1596. Fcp. 4°   BPL | BUS | W
The 'ninety-fifth declamation,' at p. 400, is the story [of
the 'Merchant of Venice'] 'of a Jew, who would for
his debt have a pound of the flesh of a Christian.'

Jew who would . . . have a pound of flesh.
1843. *See Sh*—] Sh—'s Library
Illustrates the 'Merchant of Venice.'

Butcher (Edmund) Excursion from Sidmouth
to Chester. Ln : H. D. Symonds, 1805.
2 vols. 12°
In vol. ii. (pp. 362-363) is a brief account of New Place

Bute (John, *third Earl of*) as 'Macboote.' *See
Sh*— Macbeth, 1763

Bute (Stuart *first Marquis of*) Catalogue written by desire of the Marquis of Bute, containing or intended to contain every
edition of Sh— and all commentaries,
etc. regarding that author. Manuscript.
F°, pp. 52. [c. 1805]   BUS

Butler. *See* Deverell

Butler (Charles) Rhetoricæ libri duo . . . Cantabrigiæ : R. Danielis, 1642. 8°
In a list of poets (p. 41) figures 'Gulielmus Sh—.'

Butler (E. M.) *Editor. See Sh*— Julius Cæsar,
1896, 1897

Butler *née* Kemble (Frances Anne) Journal
[of stage life, etc. in America]. Philadelphia : Carey, Lea, & Blanchard, 1835. 2
vols. 8°
A diary which for vivid colouring and interest is perhaps
only exceeded by D'Arblay, Pepys, and Evelyn.
For her unfavourable opinion of acting, *see* 'The
Shakespearean,' vol. i., p. 10.

Journal. Ln : Murray, 1835. 2 vols. 8°
    SML

Butler (H.) Theatrical directory and dramatic
almanack. 1860. 12°   BPL

Butler (James Davie) Once-used words in
Sh—. New York Sh— Soc., 1886. 8°
    BM | BPL

Vocabulary of Sh—. Madison, 1903. 8°,
pp. 20   BUS

Butler (S.) Hudibras. *See* Grey (Z.)

Butler (S.) *Editor. See Sh*— Sonnets, 1899

Butler (Samuel) 'Only begetter' [In
'Athenæum,' No. 3717, p. 92, Jan., 1899 ;
3776, p. 315 ; 3778, p. 379, Mar., 1900].
1899-1900. 4°

Sh—'s Sonnets [When written ?], [In
'Athenæum,' No. 3692, p. 161, July,
1898]. 4°

Butler (Samuel) Sh—'s Sonnets and the Ireland
forgeries [On the 'Only begetter '], [In
'Athenæum,' No. 3713, p. 907, Dec.,
1898]. 4°

Butler (W. J.) Inspiration of Sh— : A sermon.
Stratford-on-Avon : J. Morgan, 1892. 8°
    BPL | BUS

Butter (Nathaniel) *Publisher*—
See Decker
   „   Sh— King Lear, 1608
   „   Sh— London Prodigall, 1605
   „   Sh— Pericles, 1608
   „   Speech . . .
   „   Topsell

Butters (R.) *Publisher*—
See Sh— As you like it, 1785
   „   Sh— King Lear, 1780
   „   Sh— King Richard II., 1789-90
   „   Sh— Macbeth, 1785
   „   Sh— Much Ado, 1784
   „   Sh— Othello, 1780
   „   Sh— The Tempest, 1780

By (Wm.) King Richard III. travestie. *See
Sh*— King Richard III., 1816

Byington (E. H.) Sh— and the puritans [In
the 'Puritan as a colonist and reformer,'
pp. 307-354]. 1899. 8°   BPL

Bynneman (Hy.) *Printer*—
See Amadis   *See* Painter
   „   Drout   „   Sandford
   „   Mantuan

Byrd (William) Songs of sundrie nature, some
of gravitie and others of mirth, fit for all
companies and voyces, with music. Ln :
Imprinted by Lucretia East, 1610. Fcp.
4°
The above title seems paraphrased from the secondary
one in the 'Passionate Pilgrim' of 1599. The prin-
teress, too, is reminiscent of the poems.

Byrne (P.) *Dublin Publisher. See* Mason

Bysshe (Edw.) Art of English poetry. *See
Sh*— Works : Ext. 1708, 1710

—— (   ) *Editor. See* Sh—
    Poems, 1856
C mery talys. *See* Hun-
    dred . . .
C—— (E.) *See* Capell
C—— (F.) *Printer. See*
    Winstanley

C—— (H.) *See* Chettle

C—— (I.) Saint Mary Magdalen's Conversion.
Ln : 1603
Contains the lines :—
   'Of Helen's rape and Troye's besieged towne,
   Of Troylus' faith and Cressid's falsitie,
   Of Rychard's stratagems for the English crowne,
   Of Tarquin's lust and Lucrece' chastitie.'

C—— (J.) Annals of . . . Wm. Sh—. *See* Sh—

C—— (J.) Modern receipt, or a cure for love.
See Sh— As you like it, 1739

C—— (J.) *Printer*—
See Scarron
  ,, Winstanley
C—— (J. W.) More improvements . . . *See* Collier (J. P.)
C—— (L.) Epigrames, served out in fifty-two severall dishes for every man to fast without suffering. Ln : [c. 1604]

Has the passage :—
  ' As he that calde to Sh—, Johnson, Greene,
   To write of their dead noble Queene.'

C—— (P.) *Printer. See* Chetwynd (Philip)
C—— (R.) *See* Carew (Richard)
C—— (R.) *See* Chamberlaine
C—— (R. C.) Was Bacon Sh— ? [In ' Victorian Review,' Nov.]. Melbourne, 1880. 8°   BUS

An answer to ' Thomson. Renascence . . .'

C—— (T.) Letters on Sh—: No. I., On Hamlet [In ' Blackwood's Magazine,' Feb.]. Edin : 1818. 8°   BUS
C—— (T.) *Printer*—
See Middleton
  ,, Sh— London Prodigall, 1605
  ,, Sh— Merry Wives, 1602
C—— (W.) *Polimanteia. See* Clarke (William)
C—— (W.) *Printer. See* Cartwright (W.)
C—— (W.) *Publisher. See* Marston
C—— (W. F.) Brief memorial of Sh—. *See* Sh—
C—— (W. G.) Sh— in his works. *See* Sh—
Cabe (E.) *Publisher. See* Sh— Macbeth, 1763
Cabinet (The). *See* Sh— Works : Ext. 1806
Cadell *Bristol Publisher. See* Sh— Works : Ext. 1778
Cadell ( ) *Publisher. See* Whiter
Cadell (T.) *Edinburgh Publisher. See* Sh— Comedy of Errors, 1780
Cadell (Thomas) *Publisher*—
See Giraldi
  ,, Griffith
  ,, Noorthouck
  ,, Repton
  ,, Sh— Macbeth, 1770
  ,, Sh— Merchant . . . 1783
  ,, Sh— Timon . . . 1770
  ,, Sh— Works, 1773
Cadell, jun. (T.) *Publisher. See* Malone
Cadell & Davies *Publishers. See* Sh— Works, 1798
Cademan (Wm.) *Publisher*—
See Arrowsmith
  ,, Hedelin
  ,, Settle
  ,, Sh— Macbeth, 1673
  ,, Sh— The Tempest, 1675
  ,, Sh— Two Noble Kinsmen, 1668
Caine (R. H.) Love songs of the English poets. *See* Sh— Works : Ext. 1892
Caine (R. H.) *Editor. See* Sh— Poems, 1892

Caine (T. H. Hall) ' Richard III.' and ' Macbeth ' : The spirit of romantic play in relationship to the principles of Greek and of Gothic art and to the picturesque interpretations of Henry Irving. A dramatic study. Ln : Simpkin, 1877. 8°, pp. 46   BM | BPL | BUS
Supernatural element in poetry. Liverpool, 1880. 8°   BPL
Supernatural in Sh— [In ' New Monthly Magazine ']. Ln : Colburn, 1879. 8°   BPL | BUS
The novelist in Sh— [In ' New Review ']. 1894. 8°   BPL
Two aspects of Sh—'s art [In ' Contemporary Review,' Vol. 43, pp. 883-900]. 1883. 8°   BPL
See also Hyatt
Caird (E.) Some characteristics of Sh— [In ' Contemporary Review ']. 1896. 8° BPL
Caius *of Norwich* (John)] Boke, or counseill against the disease commonly called the sweate, or sweatyng sicknesse . . . Ln : Richard Grafton, 1552. 8°. Black letter   W

It is supposed that only two other copies are known of this extremely rare book.
It is of interest as being the only English medical work by Dr. Caius, who is introduced as a character in the ' Merry Wives.'
[*See* Halliwell's ' Sh— Reliques,' 1852, p. 9].

See Halliwell
  ,, Sh— Merry Wives . . . 1602
Caius Marius. *See* Otway (T.)
Calcott (Wm. H.) *Composer. See* Sh— Macbeth, 1850
Calcraft (John Wm.) Defence of the stage, or an inquiry into the real qualities of theatrical entertainments, their scope and tendency. Being a reply to a sermon entitled the ' Evils of theatrical amusements,' by Dr. J. B. Bennett. Dublin : Milliken & Son, 1839. 8°, pp. viii.-176   BPL

With list of 157 authorities defending the stage.

Library. *See* Catalogue, 1837
Caldecott (H. S.) Spoils : Studies in Sh— . . . 1891. 8°   BM | BPL

On ' Julius Cæsar,' ' Winter's tale,' and the Bacon-Sh— controversy.

The Bacons and Sh—; their lives in parallel lines. 1908. 8°   BPL
Caldecott (Randolph) *Artist. See* Sh—] Sh— Show Book
Caldecott (Thomas)] Mr. Ireland's vindication of his conduct, respecting the publication of the supposed Sh— manuscripts. Being a preface . . . to a reply to the critical labors of Mr. Malone in his ' Enquiry into the authenticity of certain papers,' etc. Ln : R. Faulder & Mr. Robson . . . 1796. 8°, pp. iv.-48 BM | BPL | BUS | CPL | MPL | W

Caldecott (T.) *Editor. See* Hamlet, 1819, 1820, 1832

Calderon (Pedro) The mighty magician: '*Such stuff as dreams are made on.*' Trans. by Edward Fitzgerald. Ln: Pickering, 1853. 8°
See Desch
,, Ellits

Caldwell (G. S.) To Sir Walter Ralegh, the author of Sh—'s plays and sonnets? Melbourne, 1877. 8°, pp. 32 MPL

Calendar of Sh— sonnets. *See* Sh— Works: Ext. 1906

Caliban. *See* Wilson (*Sir* D.)

Calisto.] Interlude of Calisto and Melebea. Ln: Malone Society, 1908. Fcp. 4°

Calkin & Budd *Publishers. See* Sh— King Henry IV., ii., 1829

Callcott (*Lady*) *Editor. See* Sh— As you like it, 1840

Callcott (*Sir* Augustus Wall) *Artist*—
See Sh— As you like it, 1840
,, *Sh*—] Sh—'s heroes

Callcott (*Sir* A. W.) Leslie (C. R.) and others. Sh—'s heroes and heroines. [c. 1891.] Fcp. 4° BPL

Callender (Charles) Catalogue of the Sh— Circulating Library, Boston, Mass. 1820. 16° BUS

Calmour (Alfred C.) Fact and fiction about Sh—. *See* Sh—
Practical playwriting and cost of production. [With introd. by W. D. Adams.] Bristol: Arrowsmith [1891]. 12° SML

Calthrop (Annette). *See* Matthew

Calverley and the Yorkshire Tragedy, 1605. *See* Reprints

Calverley (Walter). *See* Wilkins

Calvert (Albert F.) Bacon and Sh—. Ln: Dean, 1902. Roy. 8°, pp. 146 BPL

Calvert (Charles) *Actor-Manager and Editor*—
See Sh— Antony, 1867
,, Sh— King Henry IV., ii., 1874
,, Sh— King Henry V., 1872, 1875
,, Sh— King Henry VIII., 1877, 1878
,, Sh— King Richard III., 1870
,, Sh— Merchant . . . 1871
,, Sh— Midsummer N. D., 1865
,, Sh— Twelfth Night, 1873
,, Sh— Winter's Tale, 1869, 1874

Calvert (F. B.) Ode to Sh—, suggested by his tercentenary. Edinburgh: W. Elgin & Son, 1864. 8°, pp. 32 BUS

Calvert (George Henry) Sh—. *See* Sh—

Calvert (L.) *Editor. See* Sh— Antony . . . 1878, 1897

'Calvin (John)' *pseud., Publisher. See* Marvell

Cambridge—
See Capell *See* Halliwell
,, Greg ,, Hartshorne

Cambridge—
See Pilgrimage . . . *See Sh*—] Memorial
,, Returne . . . ,, Sinker
,, Sh—Hamlet, 1603 ,, Stage condemned

Cambridge University translations which have obtained the Porson Prize . . . from 1817. 3rd ed. Cambridge, 1871. 8° MPL

Camden (William) Remaines concerning Britaine . . . . 1605. Fcp. 4° BM | W
In the chapter on ' Poems ' mentions ' Wm. Sh—' and some of his contemporaries. *See also* Sh— Epitaph on Combe.

Cameron ( ) *Glasgow Publisher*—
See Sh— King Richard III., 1859
,, Sh— Macbeth, 1859
,, Sh— Merchant . . . 1860
,, Sh— Merry Wives, 1860
,, Sh— Midsummer N. D., 1861
,, Sh— Othello, 1859
,, Sh— Romeo . . . 1859
,, Sh— Taming . . . 1861

Campbell (Alexander) *Editor. See* Beauties of Sh—

Campbell (J.) *Philadelphia Publisher. See* Sh— Sonnets, 1868

Campbell (John *Baron*) Sh—'s legal acquirements considered. In a letter to J. P. Collier. Ln: J. Murray, 1859. 8°, pp. 118 BM | BPL | CPL | MPL
An amazing plagiarism of W. L. Rushton's ' Sh— a lawyer ' (*q.v.*)
So long as Lord Campbell stuck to Mr. Rushton's text his law at least was unimpeachable.

Sh—'s legal acquirements . . . New York: D. Appleton & Co., 1859. 12°, pp. 146 BUS | SML

Campbell (L.) Biog. preface. *See* Baynes
Tragic drama in Æschylus, Sophocles, and Sh—. Ln: 1904. 8° BPL | MPL

Campbell *Poet* (Thomas) Life of Mrs. Siddons. *See* Siddons
Remarks on . . . Sh—. *See* Sh—

Campbell (Thomas) *Editor. See* Sh— Works, 1838, 1842, 1843, 1848, 1850, 1852, 1858, 1859, 1860, 1862, 1866, 1870, 1873

Campe (F.) *Nuremberg Publisher. See* Sh— Poems, 1837

Camus *Bishop* (J. P.) Nature's paradox, or innocent impostor. A pleasant Polonian history originally intituled Iphigenes . . . Englished by Major Wright. 1652. Fcp. 4°. With front. by Vaughan
Contains verses by R. Loveday, in which the reference occurs:—
' Who as thy pen has made her woo'd and wooe, Might passe for " Venus and Adonis " too.'

Can members of Christian Churches consistently take part in the Sh— tercentenary movement? [In the ' British Controversialist,' Vol. I.] Ln: 1864. 12° BPL
The writer prudently withheld his name.

Canada. *See* Rhys (H.)

Cann (Alfred L.) *Editor*—
See Sh— As you like it, 1902
" Sh— Much Ado, 1903, 1904
Cann (Alfred L.) & Lees (J.) Questions on
'King Richard II.' Ln: 1904. Cr. 8°
BPL

Canning (*Hon.* Albert S. G.) Sh— studied in
eight plays. Ln: Unwin, 1903. 8°, pp.
504 BPL
Sh— studied in six plays. Ln: Unwin,
1907. 8°, pp. 554 BPL
Sh— studied in three plays. Ln: Unwin,
1908. 8°, pp. 320 BPL
Thoughts on Sh—'s historical plays. Ln:
Allen, 1884. 8° BM | BPL | SML

Canons of criticism. *See* Edwards

Canterbury Church House Library. *See*
Catalogue, 1870

Capell (Edward) Catalogue of a collection intitl'd Shakesperiana; comprehending all
the several editions of the works of Sh—,
old and new; divers rare old editions of
writers, prose-men and verse-men; with
a variety of other articles, chiefly such as
tend to illustrate him. Made by his last
editor, E. C——, and by him deposited
in the Library of Trinity College in Cambridge this eleventh day of Iune in the
year 1779. 4°. Capell's holograph MS. CTC

History of the origin of Sh—'s fables. *See*
Sh— Poems, 1798

'King Edward III.' manuscript. *See* Sh—
King Edward III., 1753

Library. *See* Greg

Notes and various readings to Sh—. Ln:
1767-71. 3 vols. 4°. Author's holograph
MS. CTC

] Notes and various readings to Sh—: Part
the first . . . With a general glossary.
Ln: E. & C. Dilly [1774]. 4° BUS
Misdated 1759 in Lowndes.

] Notes and various readings to Sh—, by
E.C. [1779.] 4° BM | BPL
Notes and various readings to Sh—. 1779-
80. Fcp. 4° BM | BPL | W
With manuscript corrections and emendations in the
autograph of Edmund Malone.

Notes and various readings to Sh—. With
additions [by John Collins]. Ln: Printed
by H. Hughs, 1779-83. 3 vols. 4°. With
portrait BUS | MPL
The third vol. is entitled the 'School of Sh—, or
authentic extracts from divers English books that
were in print in that author's time, evidently shewing
from whence his fables were taken.'

] Notitia dramatica, or tables of ancient
plays, by E. C. [In 'Notes and Readings'].
[c. 1780.] 4° BPL
Portrait. *See* Sh— Poems, 1795, 1798
Preface. *See* Sh— Works, 1803

Capell (Edward)] Prolusions, or select pieces
of antient poetry . . . containing I. The
notbrowne mayde; Master Sackvile's
induction. II. Edward the Third: a
play thought to be writ by Sh—. III.
Those excellent didactic poems intitl'd
Nosce Teipsum, by Sir John Davis
[Davies]. With a preface . . . Ln: J. &
R. Tonson, from the Press of Dryden
Leach, 1759-60. 8°
BM | BPL | BUS | CTC | MPL
The author's holograph MS., in 2 vols., 4to., should be
in the Capell Collection at Trinity College, Cambridge (according to his Catalogue), but cannot now
be found.

Shakespeareana [Collection of notes, 1,130
entries in all, entirely in the autograph of
Edward Capell]. Manuscript on paper,
dated Sept. 16th, 1752. 6 vols. 4° W
A few of the numbered entries left blank.
Transcripts of a large number of early Sh— quartos and
those of the poet's contemporaries are given; for
instance, entry number 27 in vol. i. is that of the old
novel of 'Rhomeo aud Julietta,' taken from Painter's
'Palace of Pleasure.'
Capell's storehouse of Shakespearean lore, taken in
conjunction with the following entry.

Shakespeareana [Notes and various readings: A manuscript collection. c. 1760].
6 vols. Fcp. 4° W
Wholly in the autograph of Capell, and chiefly devoted
to the variations of the text in the Jaggard folio of
1623, that of 1632, and the early quarto versions of
the accepted plays.

Capell (Edward) *Editor*—
See Sh— Antony . . . 1758
" Sh— Julius Cæsar, 1758
" Sh— Poems, MS., 1770
" Sh— Poems, 1775, 1805
" Sh— Works, 1767-68, 1770-71, 1771

Capell.] Capell's Ghost—
See Hardinge
" School . . .

] Steevens (George) Catalogue of Mr. Capell's
Shaksperiana; presented by him to
Trinity College, Cambridge, now printed
from an exact copy of his own manuscript.
Privately printed, 1779. 8° BM | BPL | W
Thirty copies only of this Catalogue were executed.
George Steevens says: 'Thirty copies printed at the
expense of G. Steevens, who requests those to whom
he presents copies to keep it from the sight of any
bookseller, for otherwise it may be the means of rising
Shakespeariana above 100 per cent.'
Reprinted in Hartshorne's 'Book rarities.'

See Few words

Capell Collection—
See Collins (John)   *See* Halliwell
" Cranwell   " Hartshorne
" Greg   " Sinker

Capgrave (John) Book of the illustrious
Henries. Trans. by Francis Charles
Hingeston. Ln: Longman, 1858. Roy.
8°, pp. xxiv.-286 SML

Capulet and Montague. *See* Sh— Romeo . . .
1785, 1823, 1850, 1860, 1874

Capulet and Montague; or, the tragical loves
of Romeo and Juliet. [c. 1820 ?] 8°   w
A novel, founded on Sh—'s play.

Carcano (Giulio) *Editor*. *See* Sh— Macbeth,
1866, 1876

Cardenio, Cardenna, or Cardenno. *See* Sh—
Cardenio

Carew (Richard)] Excellencie of the English
tongue [In Camden's ' Remaines . . .'].
Ln : 1605. Fcp. 4°   BM | W
Bears the passage, ' Will you reade Virgil? Take the
Earle of Surrey! Catullus? Sh—, and Barlow's
fragment.'

Carew (Richard) *Editor* (?). *See* Stephen

Carey (Emily J.) *Editor*. *See* Stapfer

Carey (George Saville) Sh—'s Jubilee : A
masque. Ln : T. Becket, 1769. 8°, pp.
24   BPL | BUS | CPL | W

Carey *Earl of Monmouth* (Henry) *Editor*. *See*
Malvezzi

Carey (H. C.) *Philadelphia Publisher*. *See*
Sh— Works, 1823

Cargill (Alexander) Likenesses of Sh— [In
' Strand Magazine,' Vol. 8]. 1894. Roy.
8°, pp. 317-324 and 16 portraits BPL | SML
Mystery of the Sh— manuscripts [In
' Chambers' Journal,' 6th Ser., part 25,
pp. 5-7, Jan.]. 1900. Roy. 8°
Sh— as an actor [In ' Scribner's Magazine'].
1891. 8°   BPL

Carion (John) Thre bokes of Cronicles, 1550.
See Sh— autograph

Carleton (*Sir* Dudley). *See* Herbert

Carlhaut (C.) *Editor*—
See Sh— Julius Cæsar, 1856
,, Sh— King Lear, 1847
,, Sh— King Richard III., 1856

Carlile (R.) *Publisher*. *See* Sh— King Richard
III., 1818

Carlisle (George Howard *Earl of*)] Present condition of the stage. 1800. 8°   BPL

Carlo (Viani) *Editor*. *See* Sh— King Henry
IV., i., 1872

Carlyle (Thomas) Lectures on heroes. Ln :
1856. 12°   BPL
Contains ' Sh— the hero as poet,' pp. 243-270.
On heroes, hero worship and the heroic in
history. Ln : Chapman & Hall, 1897.
8°. With portrait of Sh—
Sh—, pp. 101-114.
On heroes . . . Ln : Chapman, 1898. 12° SML
On Sh— : From the ' Hero as poet.' Ln :
De la More Press, 1904. 18°   BPL
See Bacon (D. S.)

Carnan ( ) *Publisher*. *See* Miscellaneous

Carnegie (Andrew) An American four-in-hand
in Britain. New York : Scribner, 1886-
87. 8°, pp. 192
Sh— country, pp. 77-82.

Carpenter ( ) *Publisher*—
See Ritson
,, Sh— Works, 1827

Carpenter (E.) Souvenir of ' Romeo and
Juliet ' produced at the Lyceum Theatre,
Ln. 1908. 4°   BPL

Carpenter (F. J.) English lyric poetry, 1500-
1700. *See* Sh— Works : Ext. 1897

Carpenter (J. E.) Sh— : An ode written for
the tercentenary and recited at the
Urban Club. Ln : 1864. 8°   BPL | CPL

Carpenter *Bp*. (W. Boyd) Address on the study
of Sh—. [c. 1906.] 8°   BPL

Carpio (L. F. de Vega) *Editor*. *See* Sh—
Romeo . . . 1869

Carr (J.) *Publisher*. *See* Sh— The Tempest,
1675

Carr (J. C.) Macbeth and Lady Macbeth : An
essay. 1889. 8°   BM | BPL

Carr (R. H.) *Editor*. *See* Plutarchus

Carr (Samuel) *Publisher*. *See* Shadwell

Carré (M.) *Editor*—
See Sh— Hamlet, 1869
,, Sh— Romeo . . . 1867

Carrington (James) & Bellamy (Daniel)
Modern receipt. *See* Sh— As you like it,
1739

Carruthers (Robert) *Editor*. *See* Sh— Works,
1861-63, 1875

Carson (L.) *Editor*. *See* Stage Year Book

Carstens (*Dr*. B.) *Editor*. *See* Sh— Works,
1889

Carter (Thomas) Sh— and Holy Scripture ;
with the version he used. Ln : Hodder,
1905. Roy. 8°, pp. 498   BPL | BUS
Sh— and the Genevan Bible [In ' Leisure
Hour ']. Ln : 1903. Roy. 8°   BPL
Sh— ; puritan and recusant. *See* Sh—

Cartwright (N.) The prince and the offered
crown [Essays on Hamlet's philosophy,
etc. 1879.] 8°   BM

Cartwright *M.D.* (Robert)] Footsteps of Sh—,
or a ramble with the early dramatists,
containing much new and interesting in-
formation respecting Sh—, Lyly, Mar-
lowe, Greene, and others. Ln : J. R.
Smith, 1862. 8°, pp. vi.-186
          BM | BPL | BUS | CPL | SML | W
New readings in Sh—, or proposed emenda-
tions of the text. 1866. 8° BM | BPL | CPL
Papers on Sh—. Ln : J. R. Smith, 1877.
8°, pp. 48   BM | BPL | BUS
] Sh— & Jonson. Dramatic *versus* Wit-
Combats. Auxiliary forces :—Beaumont,
Fletcher, Marston, Decker, Chapman,
and Webster. Ln : J. R. Smith, pub.
Twelfth Night, 1864. 8°, pp. 122
          BM | BPL | BUS | CPL | SML

Cartwright *M.D.* (Robert) *Editor*. *See* Sh—
Sonnets, 1859

Cartwright (T.) *Editor—*
See Sh— King Richard II., 1903
,, Sh— King Richard III., 1902
Cartwright (W.) *Printer.* *See* Heywood
Cartwright (Wm.)—
See Sh—] Sh— Notices
,, Sh— Works, 1623
Caryl (   ). *See* Mirrour . . .
Caryl (J.) English Princess. *See* Sh— King
Richard III., 1667
Caryll (John *Lord*) Sir Salomon, or the
cautious coxcomb. A comedy, as it is
acted at . . . the Duke of York's Theatre.
Ln : Printed for H. Herringman at the
Blew Anchor . . . 1671. Fcp. 4°
'Molière, the famous Sh— of this age,'
Both when he writes and when he treads the stage.'
—*Epilogue.*

Case (R. H.) *Editor. See* Sh— Antony . . 1906
Caslon (T.) *Publisher—*
See Sh— Hamlet, 1767
,, Sh— King Henry VIII., 1762
,, Sh— King Lear, 1767, 1771
,, Sh— Macbeth, 1770
,, Sh— Merchant . . . 1783
,, Sh— Othello, 1765
,, Sh— Romeo . . . 1769
,, Sh— The Tempest, 1761
,, Sh— Timon . . . 1770
,, Sh— Works, 1757, 1762, 1773
Cassel (Hesse) *Frankfort Publisher.* *See* Sh—
Works, 1827-40
Cassell's Sh— tercentenary pocket keepsake.
1864. 16° BM
Castle (Edward James) Sh—, Bacon, Jonson,
and Greene : A study. Ln : Low, 1897.
8°, pp. 360 BM | BPL | BUS
Castle (Egerton) Schools and masters of fence,
from the middle ages to the eighteenth
century. With a sketch of the develop-
ment of the art of fencing with the rapier
and the small sword and a bibliography
of the fencing art during that period . . .
Ln : Bell, 1885. 4°, pp. lii.-256. 7 plates
and numerous cuts
At pp. 22-27 are some amusing fencing anecdotes and
manners of Sh—'s time, including an account of
Signior Rocko, an Italian who opened a fencing
college in Warwick Lane about 1586, and his son
Jeronimo, who taught fencing at Blackfriars.

Castrated letter of Sir T. Hanmer. *See* Nichols
Caswell (J. B.)] Sh— or Bacon ? Evidence of
Sh—'s authorship, by 'Ajax.' Boston
[U.S.], 1888. 8° BPL | BUS
Catalogue of a well-chosen library of books
containing near five thousand volumes,
in most languages, arts, and sciences . . .
sold 8th Dec. by Samuel Paterson, bookseller, at Sh—'s Head, opposite Durham
Yard in the Strand. Ln : 1748. 8°, pp.
60 BUS
A copy of the 1623 Jaggard folio was included.

Catalogue of Capell's Shakespeareana, 1779.
See Capell
Catalogue of the curious and distinguished
library of Thomas Crofts, A.M., which
will be sold by auction by Mr. Paterson,
April 7th, 1783. 8°
Includes eight early Sh— quartos.

Catalogue of the Sh— Gallery, Pall Mall,
1787-1805. *See* Boydell (J. & J.)
Catalogue of the neat and elegant household
furniture, portraits, pictures, drawings,
and farming stock which will be sold by
auction by Churchill & Taylor, 13-15th
June, 1797, at the College, Stratford-on-
Avon. Stratford : Morris, 1797. 8°, pp.
16 BUS | SBL
The residence of John à Combe, the usurer, who lies
buried near Sh—.

Catalogue of the curious and valuable library
of George Steevens [Sh— editor] which
will be sold by auction, May 13, 1800,
and ten following days. Ln : King, 1800.
Roy. 8° W
Large paper copy, with prices realised.
The sale was rich in Shakespeareana.

Catalogue of the books, paintings, miniatures,
drawings, prints, and curiosities, the
property of the late Samuel Ireland, of
Norfolk Street, Strand, to be sold by
auction by Leigh, Sotheby & Son, 7
May. Ln : 1801. 8°, pp. 36 BUS
The collection realised £1,322 6s. 6d.

Catalogue of the . . . library of Isaac Reed
[Sh— editor] to be sold by auction by
King & Lochee [with prices]. 2nd Nov.,
1807. 8° BPL
Catalogue of the library of John Duke of
Roxburghe to be sold by auction by R.
H. Evans [with prices]. 1812. 8° BPL
Catalogue of the valuable stock of printed
books, etc. of the late john Mason, book-
seller, of Gerrard Street, Soho, deceased.
Comprising the original Sh— manuscripts
by W. H. Ireland and various tracts re-
lating to the same. To be sold by auc-
tion by Christie . . . Ln : 1812. 8° W
Catalogue of the library of the Duke of
Grafton . . . sold by auction by R. H.
Evans, June 6/11, 1815. 8°
Includes several early Sh— quartos.

Catalogue of a portion of the library of E.
Malone [Sh— editor] to be sold by
auction by Mr. Sotheby [with prices].
1818. 8° BPL
Catalogue of Capt. Sabine's collection of
books relating to Sh— to be sold by
auction by Sotheby & Co. Ln : 1820. 8°
Catalogue of the library of J. P. Kemble to
be sold by auction by Mr. Evans [with
prices]. 1821. 8° BPL

(43)

Catalogue of books [from the library of —. Kinnard] sold by Sotheby, 17 Ap. Ln: 1822. 8°, pp. 30   BUS

Catalogue of David Garrick's library, 1823. *See* Garrick

Catalogue of the library of E. Jones to be sold by auction by Mr. Sotheby. 1824-25. 2 vols. 8°   BPL

Catalogue of the dramatic library of W. B. Rhodes to be sold by auction by Mr. Sotheby [with prices]. 1825. 8°   BPL

Catalogue of the theatrical portraits to be sold by auction by Messrs. Robins. 1825. 8°   BPL

Catalogue of old plays, among them the unique 'Taming of the Shrew,' 1594, to be sold by auction by Mr. Sotheby. Ln: 1826. 8°   BPL

Catalogue of the rarest old plays to be sold by auction by Mr. Sotheby [with prices]. 1826. 8°   BPL

Catalogue of the theatrical and miscellaneous library of John Field to be sold by auction by Sotheby & Co. Ln: 1827. Roy. 8°
                                                            W
Large and fine paper copy, marked with prices and names of purchasers. The Shakespearean portion embraced lots 388 to 622.

Catalogue of the library of a collector . . . sold by Mr. Evans, 3 Mar. [with prices]. Ln: W. Nicol, 1828. 8°, pp. ii.-28   BUS

Catalogue of the library of John Britton to be sold by auction by Southgate, Grimston & Wells [with prices]. 1832. 8° BPL

Catalogue of the miscellaneous and dramatic library of Charles Mathews to be sold by auction by Sotheby & Son. 1835. 8°
                                                 BPL | MPL

Catalogue of the library of J. W. Calcraft, comprising editions of Sh— . . . sold by Wheatley, 25 May. Ln: 1837. 8°, pp. 42   BUS

Catalogue of the pictures, the vase, and snuff boxes formed of the . . . Sh— mulberry tree, which were in the possession of Garrick . . . Sold by Christie . . . 30 March. Ln: 1838. 4°, pp. 16   BUS

Catalogue of the library of W. M. Pitt, to which is added another collection. Including Sh—'s copy, with his undoubted autograph, of 'Montaigne's Essays' . . . Sold by Mr. Evans, 9 May. Ln: 1838. 8°, pp. 78   BUS
The 'Montaigne' is now in the British Museum.

Catalogue of a series of cabinet pictures, 1839. *See* Singleton

Catalogue of the printed books and manuscripts bequeathed by Francis Douce to the Bodleian Library. Oxford: University Press, 1840. F°

Catalogue of . . . cabinet pictures, 1843. *See* Singleton

Catalogue of the library of Thomas Jolley: Theology, early English poets, dramatists, etc. To be sold by auction, 20th Feb., 1843, and 17th June, 1844. 1843-44. 8°
                                                            MPL

Catalogue of the library of B. H. Bright to be sold by auction by Sotheby & Co. [Sh— pp. 319-326]. 1845. 8°   BPL
This sale contained no fewer than 140 lots relating to Sh—.

Catalogue of the library of J. W. K. Eyton to be sold by auction by Sotheby & Co. [with prices]. Ln: 1848. 8°   BPL

Catalogue of the library of Dr. Wright, of Birmingham, to be sold by auction by Sotheby & Wilkinson. 1853. 8° BPL

Catalogue.] Bibliotheca Curiosa et Selecta: Catalogue of collections of books—Sh— and Shakespeariana—sold 12 May, 1853, by Bangs & Co. New York: 1853. 8°, pp. 96   BUS

Catalogue of a collection of antiquities, especially a ring considered to be Sh—'s betrothal ring, which will be sold by auction by Puttick . . . 21 Dec. Ln: 1854. 8°, pp. 38   BUS

Catalogue of the library of J. D. Gardner to be sold by auction by Sotheby & Wilkinson. 1854. 8°   BPL

Catalogue of the stock of publications of the Sh— Society to be sold by auction by Puttick & Simpson. [1854?] 8° BPL

Catalogue of books [Shakespeareana pp. 29-33] to be sold by auction by Sotheby & Wilkinson. 1855. 8°   BPL

Catalogue of the dramatic and miscellaneous library of R. J. Smith to be sold by auction by Puttick & Simpson [with prices]. 1855. 8°   BPL

Catalogue of the residue of the library of Thomas Jolley to be sold by auction by Sotheby & Wilkinson. 1855. 8° BPL

Catalogue of a collection of Shakespearian and dramatic literature chiefly consisting of books used for . . . Mr. Halliwell's folio ed. of Sh— . . . sold by Sotheby . . . 23 May. Ln: 1856. 8°, pp. 36
                                          BPL | BUS (priced)

Catalogue of the library of M. Gancia . . . Sold by Sotheby . . . 27 June. Ln: 1856. 8°, pp. 44   BUS

Catalogue of a singularly curious and important collection of dramatic and philological literature to be sold by auction by Sotheby, Leigh & Wilkinson, 21-23 May, 1857. 8°, pp. 74 BPL | BUS (priced) | HCL
The result of fifteen years' collection used for literary purposes, by J. O. Halliwell.

(44)

Catalogue of rare and curious books illustrative of the English drama and early English literature, the property of . . . [J. O. Halliwell], to be sold by auction by Sotheby, Leigh & Wilkinson, 14 June, 1858. 8°, pp. 32 BPL | BUS (priced) | HCL
This sale included Sh—'s mortgage deed of his Blackfriars house, with autograph, secured for £315 by the British Museum.

Catalogue of the library of J. P. Harley to be sold by auction by Mr. Robins. 1858. 8°
BPL

Catalogue of rare and curious books illustrative of the English drama . . . [the property of J. O. Halliwell] to be sold by auction by Sotheby, 13 June, 1859. 8°, pp. 38 BPL | BUS (priced) | HCL

Catalogue of the library of T. Turner, comprising a collection of standard English works . . . also the magnificent extra-illustrated Sh— in 44 vols. . . . sold by Puttick, 20 June. Ln: 1860. 8°, pp. ii.-90 BPL | BUS (priced)
The Shakespeareana occupies pp. 52-80.

Catalogue of the theatrical and miscellaneous library of W. E. Burton. New York: Sabin & Co., 1860. 8° BPL

Catalogue of early English and Shakespearean literature [including works issued by J. O. Halliwell] to be sold by auction by Sotheby & Wilkinson. 1861. 8° BPL

Catalogue of a collection of books . . . with Shakespeariana and editions of Sh—, sold 30 Jan., 1861, by Bangs, Merwin & Co. New York, 1861. 8°, pp. 40 BUS
From the collection of Richard Grant White.

Catalogue of reprints and facsimiles illustrative of early English and Shaksperian literature, the impressions of which are mostly confined to 26 or 30 copies, to be sold by auction by Sotheby . . . 2 Feb. Ln: 1861. 8°, pp. 32 BPL | BUS

Catalogue of autograph letters, including two Shakespearian documents being a counterpart of the deed in the Guildhall Library, and a conveyance to the uses of Sh—'s will. Sold 10 March by Puttick . . . Ln: 1862. 8°, pp. 102 BUS

Catalogue of books disposed of among the proprietors of the Sh— Library, Stratford-on-Avon. 1862. 8° BPL

Catalogue of the library of J. L. Adolphus, comprising Works of Sh— and Shakespeariana, to be sold by auction by Sotheby & Wilkinson, 11 June, 1863. 8°, pp. 124 BPL | BUS

Catalogue of a selection from the libraries of two eminent collectors, comprising copies of the [Sh—] folios; ' Venus and Adonis,' Edin., 1627 ; Relics from the only scion of Sh—'s mulberry tree . . . sold by Sotheby, 21 Mar. Ln: 1864. 8°, pp. ii.-28 BPL | BUS

Catalogue of fittings and effects supplied for the recent dramatic and musical performances, to be sold by auction by Puttick at Stratford-on-Avon, 31 May, 1864. 8°, pp. 12 BPL | BUS

Catalogue of pictures and drawings exhibited at the Town Hall, Stratford-on-Avon, 1864. See Flower

Catalogue of the library of A. Turner; also of Lucy Aikin ; and some Shakespeariana, sold by Sotheby . . . 12 April. Ln: 1864. 8°, pp. 50 BPL | BUS

Catalogue of the library of George Daniel to be sold by Sotheby . . . 20 July . . . 1864. 8°, pp. vi.-222 BPL (priced) | BUS
The Jaggard folio brought the then record price of £716 2s., and ' King Richard III.,' 1597, £351 15s.

Catalogue of Elizabethan and dramatic literature [from the library of J. E. Cooley] . . . sold 1st March . . . New York, 1865. 8°, pp. 44 BUS

Catalogue of a valuable library [Sh— pp. 77-92] to be sold by auction by Puttick & Simpson. 1866. 8° BPL

Catalogue of W. Harrison's Shakespeareana, 1866. See Harrison

Catalogue of Books . . . in the Sh— . . . Museum, Henley Street, 1868. See Hopper (C.)

Catalogue of the library of J. Dillon to be sold by auction by Sotheby, Wilkinson & Hodge [with prices]. 1869. 8° BPL

Catalogue of books . . . at the Church House, Canterbury . . . G. Slater, 1870. 8° BPL

Catalogue of the library of a well-known collector, comprising the Shaksperian portion, to be sold by auction by Sotheby, Wilkinson & Hodge. 1870. 8° BPL

Catalogue of a portion of the library of Gen. G. W. Whistler to be sold by auction by Sotheby, Wilkinson & Hodge. 1871. 8° BPL

Catalogue of a collection of portraits formed by T. H. Lacy to be sold by auction by Sotheby, Wilkinson & Hodge [with prices]. 1873. 8° BPL

Catalogue of the library of T. H. Lacy to be sold by auction by Sotheby, Wilkinson & Hodge [with prices]. 1873. 8° BPL

Catalogue of the private library of books relating to Sh—, the drama, etc. to be sold by auction by Bangs & Co. 1873. 8° BPL

Catalogue of a collection of play bills, the drama, etc. to be sold by auction by Sotheby, Wilkinson & Hodge [with prices]. 1874. 8° BPL

Catalogue of books, manuscripts, autograph letters, and engravings . . . sold by Sotheby, 18 May. Ln: 1874. 8°, pp. ii.-288   BUS (priced)

Catalogue of the Alexander Dyce Collection, South Kensington Museum. 1874-75. 3 vols. 8°   BPL

Catalogue of the Barton Sh— Collection. Boston, 1878-83. *See* Hubbard

Catalogue of a portion of the library of C. M. Ingleby to be sold by auction by Sotheby, Wilkinson & Hodge [with prices]. 1879. 8°   BPL

Catalogue of water-colour drawings made for the 'Illustrated Sh—,' published by Cassell, to be sold by auction by Christie, Manson & Woods. 1880. 8°   BPL

Catalogue of fine books, including . . . a series of Halliwell's reprints, to be sold by auction by Puttick & Simpson. 1881. 8°   BPL

Catalogue of the library of W. Harrison to be sold by auction 25th June . . . Ln: 1881. 8°   BUS (priced)
Mainly a Shakespearean collection.

Catalogue of the library of the Earl of Gosford to be sold by auction by Puttick & Simpson [with prices]. 1884. 8°   BPL

Catalogue of the library of R. G. White to be sold by auction by Bangs & Co. New York, 1885. 8°   BPL

Catalogue of the library of J. Crosby, Sh— student of Zanesville, Ohio, to be sold by auction by Bangs & Co. New York, 1886. 8°   BPL

Catalogue of the library of J. O. Halliwell-Phillipps to be sold by auction by Sotheby, Wilkinson & Hodge [with prices]. 1889. 8°   BPL

Catalogue of the library [further portion] of J. O. Halliwell-Phillipps to be sold by auction by Sotheby, Wilkinson & Hodge. 1891. 8°   BPL

Catalogue of Shakespeareana sold by order of the executors of J. O. Halliwell-Phillipps, to be sold by auction by Sotheby, Wilkinson & Hodge. 1895. 8°   BPL

Catalogue of Sh— relics formerly at his birthplace, to be sold by auction by Christie, Manson & Woods. 1896. 8°   BPL

Catalogue of the Dundee Sh— Exhibition [from the collection of A. C. Lamb]. 1896. 12°   BPL

Catalogue of the rare and valuable collection of drawings by old masters of the Right Hon. [George Guy Greville] Earl of Warwick to be sold by auction, May 20th, 1896. Ln: 1896. Roy. 8°, pp. 56

Catalogue.] A goodly array of books, pictures, prints, and stamps . . . on sale at Messrs. Jaggard's bookshop, Liverpool. 1899. 8°, pp. 24. Illust.   BPL
Includes a set, with duplicates, of the first four folio editions of Sh—, also a collection of books printed at the Tudor-Stuart press of Sh—'s original publishers.

Catalogue of a portion of the library of S. Timmins to be sold by auction by Sotheby, Wilkinson & Hodge. 1899. 8° BPL

Catalogue of Shakespeareana, 1899. *See* Perry

Catalogue of the library of the late Thomas Jefferson McKee, of New York: [Section] English prose and verse of the 16th and 17th centuries . . . To be sold by auction by J. Anderson. New York, 1900. 4°, pp. 254. Illust.   BPL (priced)
Sh—, pp. 653-659.

Catalogue of a very valuable and important collection of Shakespeareana . . . to be sold by auction . . . Ln: Sotheby, 1903. 8°, pp. 12. With portrait, plate, and facsimiles   BPL | BUS

Catalogue of illuminated and other manuscripts, printed books, etc. to be sold by Sotheby & Co. Ln: 1903. Roy. 8° BPL
Sh— occupies pp. 147-152.

Catalogue of books by or relating to Sh— to be sold by Sotheby & Co. Ln: 1905. Roy. 8°   BPL

Catalogue of rare and valuable books, including first and early quarto editions of Sh—'s Plays, to be sold by Sotheby & Co. Ln: 1906. Roy. 8°   BPL

Catalogue—
   See Bodleian Library
   ,, British Museum
   ,, Sh—] Sh— bibliography

Cater (W.) *Publisher. See* Sh— Merchant . . . 1783

Catharine and Petruchio. *See* Sh — Taming, 1756, 1780, 1783, 1784, 1786, 1792, 1806, 1809, 1811, 1815, 1820, 1838, 1839, 1848, 1853, 1855, 1865, 1866, 1879

Catley.] Life of Miss A. Catley. Ln: 1888. 8°   SML

Catnach (J.) *Alnwick Printer. See* Sh— The Tempest, 1791

Cattell (Charles Cockbill) Did Bacon write Sh— ? A reply to Donnelly. Birmingham, 1888. 8°   BM | BPL | BUS

— Great men's views on Sh—. With essay by Dr. Ingleby. Birmingham: G. & J. Shipway, 1879. 8°, pp. 68   BPL | SML

— Lord Bacon: Did he write Sh—'s Plays ? A reply to Judge Holmes, Miss D. Bacon, and W. H. Smith. Birmingham [1879]. 8°, pp. 16   BUS

— Sh—! Did he write the Works attributed to him ? Birmingham [c. 1879]. 8°, pp. 16

Cattell (Charles Cockbill) Sh—! Did he write the Works attributed to him ? 3rd edition. With notes on what Sh— learnt at school. Ln : [c. 1880]. 8° BUS

Sh—! Was he a myth ? or What did he write ? Ln : C. Watts [1878]. 8°, pp. 16 BPL | BUS

Cattell (C. C.) *Editor.* See Dawson

Cattell (C. C.) & Atkinson (H. G.) Authorship of Sh—. [1881 ?] 12° BPL

Caulfield (I.) *Publisher.* See Malone

Caulfield (J.)] Enquiry into the conduct of Edmond Malone, concerning the manuscript papers of John Aubrey in the Ashmolean Museum, Oxford. Ln : 1797. 8° W
An episode in the Ireland forgeries controversy.

Sam. Cowell's comic songs : Macbeth. Words by J. Caulfield. Music by J. Harroway. Ln : Davidson, und. F°, pp. 8 BUS

Vocal music in Sh—'s Plays. [c. 1862 ?] 2 vols. 8° BPL

Caulfield (John) *Composer.* See Sh— Poems, 1815

Caulfield (T.) *Publisher.* See Sh— Works, 1855

Causton (Hy. Kent Staple) Essay on Mr. Singer's ' Wormwood ' . . . and a reading of Sh—'s Sonnet CXI. supplementary to all the commentators. Ln : 1851. 12°, pp. 52. Suppressed BM | BPL | BUS

Cavendish *or* Candish. *See* Lodge's Euphues' shadow

Cavendish. Wolsey—
See Robinson
,, Wolsey

Cawood (Gabriel) *Publisher. See* Lyly

Cawood (John) *Printer. See* Brandt

Cawthorn (G.) *Publisher. See* Sh— Pericles, 1796

Cawthorn (J.) *Publisher. See* Sh— Taming . . . 1806

Caxton (W.) *Printer—*
See Evans (T.)
,, Jaggard (W.)

Cazenove (C. F.) A Shakesperian student's library [In ' New Liberal Review ']. 1896. Roy. 8° BPL

Cecil *first Earl of Salisbury* (Robert) Letter to Thomas Edmondes (on Hy. Wriothesley, third Earl of Southampton), 3rd Sept., 1598 [In 'Athenæum,' No. 3,348, p. 864]. Dec., 1891. 4°
See also Pembroke

Celebrities of the stage. Ed. by Boyle Lawrence. Ln : G. Newnes [c. 1906]. 12 parts. F°. With 49 portraits in colours

Century of acrostics [Sh— pp. 10-11]. 1855. 12° BPL

'Cerberus' *pseud. See* Theatrical Inquisitor

Certayne conceyts and jeasts, 1864. *See Sh—*] Sh— Jest books

Certificates respecting Herne's oak, Windsor, proving Mr. Jesse's Herne's oak not the real one. c. 1850. Manuscript on four leaves of paper, with two plates. F° W
Illustrates the ' Merry Wives.'

Cervantes. Don Quixote—
See Gayton
,, Sh— Double falsehood
,, Tourgenieff

Chalmers. *See* Gilchrist

Chalmers (Alex.) Life of Sh—. *See* Sh— Preface. *See* Sh— Works, 1805

Chalmers (Alex.) *Editor—*
See Sh— Poems, 1810
,, Sh— Timon . . . 1805
,, Sh— Works, 1811, 1823, 1826, 1833, 1837, 1838, 1839, 1840, 1844, 1845, 1847, 1849, 1853, 1854, 1855, 1856, 1864

Chalmers (George) Another account of the incidents from which the title and a part of the story of Sh—'s ' Tempest ' were derived and the true era of it ascertained, evincing the original connexion of the Royal family with the poet's drama. Ln : Only forty copies printed by R. & A. Taylor, but not published nor intended to be, 1815. 8°, pp. viii.-82 BM | BPL | BUS | MPL
A reply to Malone on same subject (*q. v.*).

] Apology for the believers in the Sh— papers [forged by W. H. Ireland] which were exhibited in Norfolk Street . . . Ln : T. Egerton, 1797. 8°, pp. iv.-628. With coat of arms and seal of the Office of the Revels BM | BPL | BUS | CPL | SML

Appendix to the ' Supplemental apology for the believers in the supposititious Sh— papers,' being the documents for the opinion that Hugh McAuley Boyd wrote Junius's Letters. Ln : 1800. 8° BM | BUS | MPL

Further account of the rise and progress of the English stage [In Sh— Works, 21 vols., 1803, *q.v.*]. Ln : 1803. 8°

] Supplemental apology for the believers in the Sh— papers, being a reply to Mr. Malone's 'Answer' which was early announced but never published. With a dedication to Geo. Steevens and a postscript to T. J. Mathias. Ln : T. Egerton, 1799. 8°, pp. viii.-656 W
BM | BPL | BUS | W
A complete set consists of the 'Apology, 1797,' the 'Supplemental Apology, 1799,' and the 'Appendix, 1800.'
See Owen, Jun., for reply.

See also 'Antenor'

Chalmers (George) *Editor.* *See* Sh— Pericles, 1800

Chalmers.] Chalmeriana. *See* Hardinge

Chalon (Alfred E.) *See* Sh— As you like it, 1840

Chaloner (*Sir* Thomas). *See* Mirrour . . .

Chamberlain (Mellen) A Shaksperian autograph [An article on the alleged autograph of Sh— in the Boston Public Library. With photographs and facsimiles]. c. 1890. F°. Typewriter manuscript   BUS

Notes on some Writing which may be by Sh— in the Boston Public Library. Boston [U.S.], 1890. 8°. With plates BUS

Chamberlain's (Lord) Servants—
See Sh— King Henry IV., ii., 1600
  ,, Sh— King Henry V., 1600, 1602, 1608
  ,, Sh— King Richard II., 1597, 1598, 1608
  ,, Sh— King Richard III., 1597, 1598, 1602, 1605
  ,, Sh— Merchant . . . 1600, 1637
  ,, Sh— Midsummer N. D., 1600
  ,, Sh— Romeo . . . 1599
  ,, Sh— Thomas . . . 1602

Chamberlaine (D.) *Dublin Publisher.* *See* Sh—] Dennis

Chamberlaine (Robert)] Swaggering damsell. A comedy. Written by R. C——. Ln : Printed by Thomas Cotes for Andrew Crooke [c. 1640]. Fcp. 4°   w
From the library of Wm. Mitford, historian of Greece. Contains passages illustrative of Sh—.

Chambers (David Laurance) Metre of ' Macbeth ' : Its relation to Sh—'s earlier and later work. Princeton [U.S.], 1903. 8°, pp. 70   BUS

Chambers (E. F.) *Editor.* *See* Sh— Merchant . . . 1908

Chambers (Edmund K.) English Pastorals. *See* Sh— Works : Ext. 1895
Stage of ' The Globe ' [Theatre]. *See* Sh— Works, Stratford, 1904-07. Roy. 8°

Chambers (E. K.) *Editor—*
See Sh— Coriolanus, 1898, 1904
  ,, Sh— Hamlet, 1856
  ,, Sh— King Richard II., 1891
  ,, Sh— Macbeth, 1893, 1895-96
  ,, Sh— Midsummer N. D., 1897
  ,, Sh— Works, 1886-91, 1893-98

Chambers (Robert) *Editor.* *See* Sh— Works, 1856-57

Chambers (Wm.) *Editor.* *See* Sh— Works, 1861-63, 1875

Chambers (W. & R.) History of the English language and literature. Edinburgh : W. & R. Chambers, 1877. Cr. 8°
Contains notices of Sh— and his contemporaries.

Chambers' Journal [Excerpt containing article ' Sh— : A celebration ode ']. 1864. Roy. 8°   BPL

Chambers' Journal [Excerpt containing article on the ' Sh— festival.] 1864. Roy. 8°   BPL

Sh— tercentenary number, April 23rd. 1864. Roy. 8°, pp. 32   BPL | BUS | CPL

Chandler (F. W.) Literature of roguery. 1907. 2 vols. Cr. 8°   BPL
Contains Shakespeareana.

Channing (W. E.) Sh—'s ' Hamlet ' [In ' National literature,' p. 30]. 1830. 8°   BPL

Chapman ( ) *Editor.* *See* Theatrical . . .

Chapman (Geo.) The Turtle and Phœnix. *See* Sh— The Turtle
Verses. *See* Brooke (C.)
See Acheson   *See* Levi
  " Cartwright   ,, Malone
  ,, Chettle   ,, Parrott
  ,, Dobell

Chapman (John K.) Court Theatre and Royal dramatic record, being the history of theatrical entertainments at the English Court from the time of Henry VIII. . . . Ln : 1850. Imp. 8°. With steel plates by Finden

Theatrical entertainments, etc. at the English Court. [c. 1860.] 4°   BPL

Chapman (John K.) *Publisher—*
See Sh— King Henry V., 1859
  ,, Sh— King Henry VIII., 1855
  ,, Sh— King Lear, 1858
  ,, Sh— King Richard II., 1857
  ,, Sh— Macbeth, 1853
  ,, Sh— Merchant . . . 1858
  ,, Sh— Midsummer N. D., 1856
  ,, Sh— Much Ado, 1858
  ,, Sh— The Tempest, 1857
  ,, Sh— Winter's Tale, 1856
  ,, Sh— Works, 1856-58

Chapman (Laurence) *Publisher.* *See* Randolph

Chappel (A.) *Artist.* *See* Sh— Works, 1888, 1896

Chappell (W.) Ballad literature and popular music of the olden time : A history of ancient songs, ballads, and dance tunes of England. Ln : Und. 2 vols. 8°

Chapple (C.) *Publisher—*
See Sh— Poems, 1804
  ,, Sh— Timon . . . 1816

Character of Cleopatra [In ' Cornhill Magazine ']. Ln : Smith, 1871. 8°   BPL
Illustrates ' Antony and Cleopatra.'

Character of Sir John Falstaff [In ' Fraser's Magazine ']. Ln : 1852. 8°   BPL

Character of the Nurse's deceased husband . . . *See* Brown (I.)

Character studies in Sh—'s Plays : Sh—'s servants [In ' Co-operative News ']. 1893. F°   BPL

Charades and acrostics, with key: Sh— and
Stratford. 1864. 4° BPL
Charades. *See Sh*—] Sh— charades
Chard (Thomas) *Printer—*
See Rowlands
,, Sh— Merry wives, 1630
Charke *née* Cibber (Charlotte) Narrative of
her life, by herself. Ln: W. Reeve,
1755. 8°
Charlecote, Warwickshire. [1830 ?] 4° BPL
Charlecote. *See* Lucy family
Charlemont (*Countess of*) Gruach [Lady Mac-
beth]. Ln: New Sh— Soc., 1875-76. 8°
Charles I. *of England* (*King*) Declaration. *See*
Collier (Jeremy)
See Cook (John)   *See* Husband
,, Famous tragedie   ,, James I.
,, Halford   ,, Milton
,, Havard   ,, Stage condemned
Charles II. *of England* (*King*)—
See Cunningham
,, Sh— Fair Em, 1631
,, Stage acquitted
,, Tomlins (T. E.)
Charlotte (*Queen*) Portrait. *See* Sh— Works,
1802
Charm of Sh—'s country [In 'Chambers'
Journal,' Part III., pp. 173-176, Mar.]
1907. Roy. 8°
Charms of melody, being a select collection of
. . . love and sentimental songs . . . hunt-
ing and sporting songs . . . humorous,
drinking, and loyal songs . . . [With three
frontispieces on copper]. Dublin : Printed
for John Colles at the corner of Temple
Lane, Dame Street, 1776. 3 vols. 12°
Collation: viii.-136; viii.-132; viii.-132.
At the end of the 'Hunting songs' occur 'Twelve
country dances and six cotillons composed for Sh—'s
Jubilee.'
Charters. *See* Fisher
Chase (S. C.) Sh— ; a tercentenary tribute.
See Sh—
Chaucer (Geoffrey) Knighte's tale—
A foundation of 'Two noble Kinsmen.'
See Sh—] Sh—'s library
,, Sh— Two Noble Kinsmen (*heading*)
Pyramus and Thisbe. *See* Sh— Midsummer
N. D., 1886
See Thom
Chaucer (Geoffrey) *Editor.* *See* Sh— Troilus
. . . 1679
Chaucer and Sh— [In 'Quarterly Review,'
Jan.]. Ln: 1873. 8° BPL | BUS
Chedworth (John *Baron*)—
See Howe
,, Seymour
Cheesman (Thomas) *Engraver.* *See* Sh—
Works : Ext. 1792-96
Chelard (A. H.) *Composer.* *See* Sh— Macbeth,
1832

Chesney (J. Portman) Sh— as a physician.
Saint Louis : J. H. Chambers, 1884. 8°.
Illust. BM | BPL | BUS | SML
Chester Whitsun Plays : Mysteries upon
Scriptural subjects. Ed. by T. Wright.
Ln : Sh— Soc., 1843-47. 2 vols. 8°
BPL | BUS
Chester (Robert) Annals of Great Britaine.
See Sh— Threnos, 1611
Love's martyr, or Rosalin's complaint.
Allegorically shadowing the truth of love
in the constant fate of the Phœnix and
Turtle. To these are added some new
compositions of severall modern writers,
whose names are subscribed to their
several workes. Ln : 1601. Fcp. 4°
These 'New Compositions' are by Sh—, Marston, Ben
Jonson, and others.
Halliwell wrote an account of the work in 1865 [*q. v.*].
Love's martyr . . . 1601. Including some
account . . . by J. O. Halliwell. Ed. by
A. B. Grosart. Ln : New Sh— Soc.,
1878. Fcp. 4° BPL | BUS | MPL
Issue restricted to ten copies.
Love's martyr—
See Furnivall
,, Sh— Threnos, 1601, 1611
Chettle (Henry) Englande's mourning gar-
ment, worne here by plaine shepheardes
in memorie of their sacred Mistresse
Elizabeth, Queene of Vertue while shee
liued and theame of sorrow being dead.
To which is added the true manner of her
Emperiall funerall . . . Ln : Printed by
V. S—— [Valentine Sims] for Thomas
Millington, and are to be sold at his shop
vnder Saint Peter's Church in Cornhill
[1603]. Fcp. 4°
Under assumed names, Sh—, Chapman, Drayton,
Jonson, and others are mentioned, together with
some of their works. Sh— is baptised by Chettle as
'smooth-tongued Melicent,' and again as 'silver-
tongued Melicent.'
Halliwell discovered in this work that Sh— wrote one
or more ballads on the Spanish Armada.
England's mourning garment . . . [In Sh—
Allusion books]. Ln : New Sh— Soc.,
1874. 8° BM | BPL | BUS
Hoffman, or a revenge for a father. A
tragedy, acted 1602, printed 1631.
Edited by H. B. L——. 1852. 12° BPL
Illustrates 'Hamlet.'
] Kind hart's dreame. Containing five ap-
paritions with their inuectiues against
abuses raigning. Deliuered by seuerall
ghosts vnto him to be publisht after Piers
Penilesse post had refused the carriage.
By H. C——. Ln : Printed for William
Wright . . . [1593]. Fcp. 4°. Black letter
Contains anecdotes of the literary squabbles between
Chettle, Greene, Nashe, Tarleton, and the players.
Chiefly curious for the apology to Sh— for the part
Chettle took in printing Robert Greene's posthumous
attack on the poet. *See* Greene (R.)

Chettle (Henry)—
  See Collier (J. P.)
  ,, Decker & Chettle
  ,, Halliwell
Chetwin. See Chetwynde
Chetwood Dublin Publisher. See Sh— Fair
  Em, 1750
Chetwood (W.) Prompter—
  See Sh— Comedy of Errors, 1734
  ,, Sh— Measure . . . 1734
  ,, Sh— Pericles, 1734
Chetwood (W.) Publisher—
  See Sh— As you like it, 1723
  ,, Sh— King Henry IV., ii., 1719, 1721
  ,, Sh— King Henry V., 1723
  ,, Sh— King Henry VI., i., 1724
  ,, Sh— King Henry VI., ii.-iii., 1724
  ,, Sh— King Henry VI., iii., 1724
Chetwood (William Rufus)] British theatre,
  containing the lives of the English
  dramatic poets, with an account of all
  their plays, together with lives of most
  of the principal actors as well as poets.
  To which is prefixed a short view of the
  rise and progress of the English stage.
  Ln : R. Baldwin, jun., 1752. 8°, pp.
  xvi.-iv.-200   W
  'A compilation full of the grossest blunders.'—Lowndes.
  Sh—, see p. 8
  General history of the stage, from its
  origin in Greece. With the memoirs of
  most of the principal performers that
  have appeared on the English and Irish
  stage for these last fifty years. 1749. 8°
                                   BPL | W
  With notices of Shakespearean performances.
  Theatrical records, or an account of English dramatic authors and their works.
  1756. 8°   W
Chetwynde or Chetwin (Philip) Publisher—
  See Sh— Macbeth, 1674
  ,, Sh— Merry Wives, 1664
  ,, Sh— Works, 1663, 1664
Chevalier (W. A.) Sh— and Dickens as men
  of affairs [In ' Dickensian,' Vol. 3, pp.
  44-47 and 66-69]. Ln : Chapman, 1907.
  8°   BPL
  Tribute to the Sh— Memorial at Stratford-
  on-Avon : Outlines of a scheme for re-
  forming the stage and elevating the
  actor's calling to the status of a liberal
  and legitimate profession. 8°
Cheyne (N. R.) Edinburgh Publisher. See
  Sh— Works, 1792
Cheyne (W.) Edinburgh Printer. See Sh—
  Macbeth, 1753
Chicago Public Library special bulletin :
  Sh—. 1904. 8°   BPL
Chidley (J. J.) Publisher. See Sh— Works,
  1835, 1841, 1843, 1845, 1847

Chilcot (T.) Composer. See Sh— Poems, 1800
Chilcott (Wm.) Composer. See Sh— Poems,
  1750
Child (F. J.) Editor. See Sh— Poems, 1866
Child (H.) Stratford-on-Avon new guide.
  1902. Cr. 8°   BPL
Child (Mary) Mr. Spectator and Sh— [In
  ' The Library,' Vol. 6, pp. 360-379]. Ln :
  1905. Roy. 8°   BM
Child-life as seen by the poets [In ' Saint Paul's
  Magazine']. 1872. 8°   BPL
Children of Paule's. See Sh— Puritan Widow,
  1607
Children of the King's Revels. See Barrey (L.)
Childs (George W.) Benefactor. See Davis
  (L. C.)
Childs (J. R. & C.) Bungay Printers. See
  Sh— Works, 1827, 1836
Chipping Campden, Gloucs. See Rushen
Chiswell (Richard). See Worsley
Choice ayres and dialogues. See Sh— The
  Tempest, 1675
Choice, chance, and change, or conceits in
  their colours . . . Imprinted at Ln. for
  Nathaniell Fosbrooke, and are to be sold
  at his shop in Paul's Churchyard at the
  Signe of the Helmet, 1606. Fcp. 4°
  Of Shakespearean interest. One of the dialogues
  begins : ' Why, how now ? doe you take me for a
  woman that you come upon me with a ballad of
  " Come live with me and be my love ? " '
Choice thoughts from Sh—. See Bartlett
Cholmeley (R. F.) Editor—
  See Sh— Coriolanus, 1897
  ,, Sh— King Henry V., 1903
  ,, Sh— Macbeth, 1895
  ,, Sh— Twelfth Night, 1895, 1897
Chorleton (Jeffrey) Publisher—
  See Middleton
  ,, Rich
Christie (J.) Publisher. See Sh— Coriolanus,
  1789
Christmas at Old Court. See Robinson
Christy (H. C.) Artist. See Sh— Hamlet, 1898
Chronicle history of Thomas Lord Cromwell.
  See Sh— Thomas . . .
Church performances. See Collier
Churcher (William H.) Mystery of ' Sh—'
  revealed ; Sir Francis Bacon the real
  author. Detroit : Fry, 1886. 12°
                            BPL | BUS | SML
Churches of Warwickshire. See Bloxam (M. H.)
Churchill (Charles) The rosciad and the
  apology. Edited by Robert W. Lowe.
  With eight illustrations. Ln : Lawrence
  & Bullen, 1891. 4°, pp. xxviii.-80
  Contains several references to Sh— and his plays. The
  plates are portraits of Shakespearean actors and
  actresses of the eighteenth century.
Churchill (G. B.) Richard III. up to Sh— [In
  ' Palæstra ']. Berlin, 1900. 8°   BPL

Churchill (John) *Publisher.* *See* Temple
Churchyard (Thomas) Extracts. *See* Sh—
  Works: Ext. 1845
  Reformation of rebellion and Shore's wife.
  See Reprints
  See Mirrour . . .
Chute (C. W.) *Editor.* *See* Sh— King Richard
  III., 1860
'Cib. Jusc' *pseud.* *See* Brownes (*Major*)
Cibber (Colley) Apology for the life of Colley
  Cibber. Ln: Printed by J. Watts for
  the author [1740]. 4°. With portrait by
  Van der Gucht after Vanloo   BPL | W
  'One of the most amusing specimens of biography and
  the best history of the English stage of the time.'—
  Lowndes.
  Apology . . . Ln: R. Dodsley, 1750. 12° SML
  Apology . . . with account of the English
  stage, old plays and players . . . Ln:
  R. & J. Dodsley, 1756. 2 vols. 8°. With
  portrait
  Apology . . . Edited by E. Bellchambers.
  Ln: Simpkin, 1822. 12°   SML
  Apology . . . New edition, edited by R. W.
  Lowe. 1889. 2 vols. 8°   BPL
  Autograph. *See* Cibber (Theo.)
  Cæsar in Egypt. *See* Sh— Antony, 1725
  Epilogue. *See* Sh— Taming . . . 1716
  Lives of the poets . . . to the time of Dean
  Swift. Compiled from . . . books . . . and
  manuscript notes of . . . Coxeter and
  others, by Colley Cibber. Ln: R.
  Griffiths, 1753. 4 vols. 8°
  Sh—'s life and a list of his plays occupies pp. 123-143 of
  vol. i.
  Papal tyranny. *See* Sh— King John, 1744,
  1745
  Ximena, or the heroick daughter. Ln:
  1719. 8°
  Refers to Sh—.
  The egotist, or Colley upon Cibber. Ln:
  W. Lewis, 1743. 12°   SML
  See Theatrical bouquet
Cibber (Colley) *Editor.* *See* Sh— King
  Richard III., 1700, 1718, 1734, 1736,
  1737, 1745, 1751, 1754, 1756, 1757, 1760,
  1766, 1770, 1775, 1784, 1793, 1811, 1814,
  1818, 1819, 1839, 1846, 1854, 1857, 1868,
  1870
Cibber.] Baker (H. Barton) Colley Cibber
  versus Sh— [In ' Gentleman's Magazine,'
  Mar.]. Ln: 1877   BUS
] Colley Cibber as Richard the Third: An
  essay [In the ' Dramatic Censor ']. Ln:
  [1770 ?]. 8°   W
] Colley Cibber in ' King John.' *See* Letter
  See Drury Lane   *See* History . . .
Cibber.] Account of the life of Mrs. Susannah
  Maria Cibber, also the trials of T. Cibber
  and W. Sloper. Ln: Privately printed,
  1887. 8°, pp. 56, and portrait   SML

Cibber (Theophilus) Familiar epistle to Mr.
  William Warburton. [1752 ?] 8°   W
  References to Sh—.
  Serio-comic apology for the life of Theo-
  philus Cibber. Written by himself. Ln:
  [1748 ?] 8°   W
  Theophilus Cibber to David Garrick, Esq.,
  with dissertations on theatrical subjects
  [and an appendix]. Ln: W. Reeves at
  Sh—'s Head, 1756-1759. 3 parts in 1 vol.
  8°   SML | W
  Portrait of Cibber as *Antient Pistol* ('King Henry
  VI.'), and other plates.
  The Warwick copy bears autographs of Robert Wilks,
  Barton Booth, and Colley Cibber upon a paper pasted
  on the fly-leaf.
  Two dissertations on the theatres. With
  an appendix. [1756 ?] 8°   BPL
Cibber (Theophilus) *Editor*—
  See Sh— King Henry VI., i., 1724
  ,, Sh— King Henry VI., ii.-iii., 1720, 1723,
    1724
  ,, Sh— Romeo . . . 1744, 1748
Citation of . . . Sh— touching deer stealing.
  See Landor
Clapp (H. A.) Time in Sh—'s comedies [In
  'Atlantic Monthly']. 1885. 8°   BPL
Clare ( ) *Bewdley Publisher.* *See* Sh—
  Works, 1768
Clare ('*Professor*') Bard of Avon quadrilles in
  commemoration of the tercentenary,
  composed expressly for the ' Young
  Ladies' Journal.' [1864.] 4°, pp. 8
                                  BPL | BUS
Clare ('*Prof.*') *Composer.* *See* Elliott
Claretie (*M.*) On Sh— and Moliere [In
  'Athenæum,' No. 3743, p. 139, July].
  1899
Clark (Andrew) *Printer*—
  See Sh— Hamlet, 1676
  ,, Sh— Macbeth, 1674
Clark (Edward G.) Tale of the Sh— epitaph,
  by Francis Bacon. Trans. from the
  Anglo-Phonetic. Chicago: Belford Clark,
  1888. 12°   BPL | BUS | SML
Clark (H.) *Printer.* *See* Winstanley
Clark (Imogen) Will. Sh—'s little lad. Illust.
  by R. Birch. New York: Scribner, 1897.
  8°   SML
Clark (J.) *Publisher.* *See* Sh— Venus . . . 1675
Clark (M.) *Printer.* *See* Henry VIII.
Clark (Samuel) *Editor.* *See* Sh— Julius
  Cæsar, 1860
Clark (William George) *Editor*—
  See Sh— Hamlet, 1872, 1873, 1874, 1880,
    1881, 1883, 1884, 1890, 1896
  ,, Sh— King Richard II., 1860, 1868,
    1869, 1873, 1874, 1876, 1879,
    1880, 1881, 1882, 1884, 1886,
    1889, 1892, 1893, 1895
  ,, Sh— King Richard III., 1885

Clark (William George) *Editor*—
See Sh— Macbeth, 1869, 1873, 1874, 1876,
1882, 1883, 1885, 1889, 1895,
1901
„ Sh— Merchant . . . 1868, 1869, 1874,
1876, 1880, 1881, 1883, 1884,
1886, 1887, 1889, 1891
„ Sh— Works, 1863-66, 1864, 1865, 1867,
1868-83, 1873, 1874, 1878, 1879,
1880, 1881, 1884, 1887, 1887-88,
1891, 1895, 1897
Clark (W. M.) *Publisher.* See Sh— Works,
1834-36
Clarke ( ) *Publisher*—
See Sh— Macbeth, 1770
„ Sh— Othello, 1765
„ Sh— Timon . . . 1770
Clarke (*Mrs.* A. B.) *Editor.* See American . . .
Clarke (Charles Cowden) Carmina Minima.
Ln : Simpkin, 1859. 8°, pp. iv.-34 SML
Author's presentation copy at Stratford.
Sh— characters ; chiefly those subordinate.
Ln : Smith, 1863. 8°, pp. viii.-522
BM | BPL | BUS | MPL | SML
Sh—'s philosophers and jesters [In ' Gen-
tleman's Magazine,' March-June]. Ln :
1873. 8° BM | BUS
Clarke (Charles Cowden) *Editor*—
See Sh— Poems, 1868, 1878
„ Sh— Works, 1864, 1864-68, 1865, 1865-
69, 1869, 1874, 1874-78, 1875,
1876, 1878, 1879, 1880, 1881,
1883, 1886-90
Clarke (C. C. & M. C.) Sh— key. See Sh—
Works : Ext. 1879, 1881
Clarke (Ernest) ' The Tempest ' as an opera
[In 'Athenæum,' No. 4113, p. 222, Aug.].
1906
Clarke (F. W.) *Editor.* See Sh— Works,
1904-08
Clarke (Helen A.) *Editor*—
See Poet lore
„ Sh— Midsummer N. D., 1903
„ Sh— Works, 1903, 1906
Clarke (James Freeman) Address. See New
England . . .
Did Sh— write Bacon's Works ? [In ' North
American Review,' Vol. 132, Feb.]. 1881.
8° BUS
Memorial and biographical sketches.
Boston [U.S.], 1878. 8° BUS
Tercentenary celebration of the birth of
Sh— by the New England Historic-
Genealogical Soc. at Boston, Mass., 23
April, 1864 : An address. Boston : G. C.
Rand & Avery, 1864. 8°, pp. 44 BUS
Offprinted from the Society's papers.
Clarke (Mary Cowden) Biographic sketch of
Charles Cowden Clarke. Ln : Novello,
1887. 12° BPL | SML

Clarke (Mary Cowden) Complete concordance
to Sh—. See Sh— Works : Ext. 1845,
1846, 1847, 1848, 1856, 1870, 1874, 1875,
1881
Girlhood of Sh—'s heroines [1st and 2nd
Series]. New York : G. P. Putnam.
1851-52. 8°. Illust. BUS
Girlhood of Sh—'s heroines [1st and 2nd
Series]. New York : C. S. Francis &
Co., 1857. 8°. Illust. BUS
Girlhood of Sh—'s heroines. Ln : Smith
& Son, 1864. 3 vols. 8°
BUS | CPL | MPL | SML
Girlhood of Sh—'s heroines. 1879. 8° BM
Girlhood of Sh—'s heroines . . . Condensed
by her sister, Sabilla Novello. Ln :
Bickers, 1880. 8°, pp. x.-456 and 9
plates BPL
Girlhood of Sh—'s heroines . . . Ln :
Bickers, 1887. 8°, pp. x.-456 and 9 plates
Girlhood of Sh—'s heroines. Ln : Hutchin-
son [1892]. 5 vols. Cr. 8° BM
Girlhood of Sh—'s heroines. Ln : Dent,
1906. 3 vols. 12°
Honey from the weed : Verse-waifs. 1881-
83. 2 vols. 12° BPL
Letters to an enthusiast, Robert Balmanno,
1850-61. Ln : 1904. 8° BPL
Memorial sonnets . . . Ln : Novello, 1888.
Cr. 8°, pp. 112 SML
My long life : Autobiography. Ln : Unwin,
1896. 12°, pp. 270 BPL | SML
Portia and other stories of the early days of
Sh—'s heroines. New York : Putnam,
1868. 8°, pp. iv.-486. Illust. BUS
Score of sonnets to one object. Ln : Paul,
Trench & Co., 1884. Cr. 8°, pp. 28 SML
Sh— proverbs. See Sh— Works : Ext.
1847, 1848, 1849
Sh—'s self. See Sh— Works : Ext. 1886
Verse waifs . . . Ln : Paul, Trench & Co.,
1883. Cr. 8°, pp. viii.-80 SML
With note on the orthography of Sh—'s name, and list
of works written by Charles and Mary Cowden
Clarke.
See Balmanno
Clarke (Mary Cowden) *Editor.* See Sh—
Works, 1860, 1864, 1864-68, 1865, 1865-
69, 1866, 1868, 1869, 1874, 1874-78, 1875,
1876, 1878, 1879, 1880, 1881, 1883, 1885,
1886-90, 1897
Clarke (M. C.) & Rolfe (W. J.) Sh— proverbs.
See Sh— Works : Ext. 1908
Clarke (Richard) Recollections of Herne's Oak
and Windsor. [c. 1850.] Manuscript on
20 leaves of paper, illustrated with
plates. Roy. 4° W
This manuscript forms the substance of correspondence
with W. Harrison Ainsworth upon the 'Merry
Wives.'

Clarke (Richard) Some account of the Car-
man's Whistle. 1842. Manuscript on
six unnumbered leaves of paper. 4° w
Alluded to in ' King Henry IV.'

Clarke (Richard) & others. Poems. [Manu-
script volume containing poems by
Richard Clarke and other younger Jaco-
bean contemporaries of Sh—. 1630 ?
Manuscript on 34 leaves of paper, lettered
' MS. Poems ']. F° w
Two of the poems are from Sh—'s ' Passionate Pilgrim,'
and another, signed H. B—, is entitled ' The loves of
Venus and Adonis.' [*See* Halliwell's ' Sh— reliques,'
1852, p. 6].

Clarke (Sampson) *Publisher.* See Sh— King
John, 1591

Clarke (Sidney W.) Miracle play in England :
An account of the early religious drama.
[1890 ?] 8°
With four plates, including one ' Lost souls,' taken from
a fresco in the Guild Chapel, Stratford-on-Avon. A
chapter is devoted to Coventry, the home of the
Mystery Plays.

Clarke (Wm.)] Polimanteia, or the meanes
lawfull and unlawfull to ivdge of the fall
of a common-wealth against the friuolous
and foolish coniectures of this age.
Wherevnto is added, A letter from England to her three davghters, Cambridge,
Oxford, Innes of Court, and to all the
rest of her inhabitants, perswading them
to . . . unitie of . . . religion, etc. Cambridge : Iohn Legate, Printer to the
Vniversitie. To be sold in Pauls Church-
yard in London, 1595. Fcp. 4°, without
pagination BUS | W
Remarkable as containing the second extraneous printed
notice of Sh— by name. It occurs in a marginal
note on the verso of signature R2 :—
' All praise, worthy Lucrecia [of] sweet Sh—.'
The epithet ' sweet,' peculiar as applied to the sterner
sex, appeared again in print shortly after, in the
Cambridge play entitled ' Return from Parnassus'
[*q. v.*]. thus : ' Sweet Maister Sh—,' and the adjective has clung tenaciously throughout three centuries.

Clarke & Son (W.) *Publisher.* See Sh— Works,
1798

Classical Comedy. *See* Hamilton

Classification of readers. *See* Pemberton

Clavell (John) Recantation of an ill-led life
. . . or a discoverie of the highway law.
With vehement disswasions to all in that
kind offenders. As also many cautelous
admonitions and full instructions how to
know, shun, and apprehend a theefe, etc.
[In verse.] The third edition, with additions. Ln : Printed by A. M—— [Augus-
tine Mathewes ?] for R. Meighen, 1634.
Fcp. 4° w
The author professes to discover all the villanies of his
abandoned profession, that of a highwayman. His
first depredations were on Gad's Hill. *See* ' King
Henry IV.'

Clavell (Robert) General catalogue of books
printed since the dreadful fire . . . plays
acted at both the theatres . . . Ln : 1680.
F°
Several pieces of Sh— are mentioned.

Claxton (Marshall) *Artist. See* Sh— As you
like it, 1850

Clay (C. J.) Female characters of the Greek
tragedians and Sh—. 1844. 8° BPL

Clay (F.) *Publisher*—
  See Sh— Hamlet, 1723
   „ Sh— Julius Cæsar, 1729
   „ Sh— King Lear, 1723
   „ Sh— Macbeth, 1729
   „ Sh— Poems, 1725, 1728
   „ Sh— Works, 1725, 1728, 1733

Clayden (P. W.) Macbeth and Lady Macbeth
[In ' Fortnightly Review,' Aug.]. Ln :
1867. 8° BM | BUS

Cleaver (W.) Sermon preached at the Assizes
held at Warwick. Oxford : At the
Theatre, 1739. 8° SML
The Grand Jury on this occasion included one William
Shakespeare, gent.

'Clelia' *pseud. See* Downing (Charles)

Clemens (S. L.)] Is Sh— dead ? From my
autobiography, by Mark Twain. Ln :
Harper, 1909. Cr. 8°, pp. iv.-50, and
imaginary portraits of Sh— and Bacon
BPL
A contribution to the Bacon controversy, twenty-two
pages of which were ' conveyed' from Greenwood's
' Sh— problem restated' without permission, a form
of joke which did not appeal to the author or publisher of the latter work. For reply *see Sh—*] Sh—
and the School of Assumption.

Clements (*Mrs.* C. E.) Charlotte Cushman.
See Cushman

Clements (*Mrs.* C. E.) *Editor. See* American . .

Clements (H.) *Oxford Publisher. See* Langbaine

Cleopatra [In ' Tinsley's Magazine ']. 1874.
8° BPL

Cleveland (John) Character of a London
diurnall. With several select poems . . .
Ln : Printed in the yeere 1647. Fcp. 4°
At p. 43 [misprinted 51] is a reference to Sh—'s ' Fal-
staffe's buckram-men.' On p. 7 is a ' Song to Marke
Anthony.' [*See* ' Antony and Cleopatra,' also ' Julius
Cæsar.']

Cliffe (Leigh) *pseud. See* Jones (George)

Cliffe (N.) *Publisher*—
  See Sh— Works, 1714
   „ Shore

Clifton Sh— Society : Catalogue of the
library. Bristol : H. Hill [Privately
printed]. 1881. 4°, pp. 42 [printed and
paged one side only] SML
Catalogue of the library, with supplement.
1881-87. 4° BPL

Clint ( ) *Artist. See* Sh— Works, 1829,
1875-76

Clinton. Verses. *See* Reprints

Clopton (*Sir* Hugh) New Place. *See* Bellew

Will of Sir Hugh Clopton, of New Place,
Stratford-upon-Avon, and Citizen, Mer-
cer, and Alderman of London, 1496.
Now first printed from the original manu-
script [Ed. by J. O. Halliwell]. Ln : 1865.
8° BPL | HCL | MPL
Issue restricted to twenty-five copies, of which five
were destroyed by the editor, and ten burnt at the
British Museum fire, leaving ten only in existence.

Clopton family—
See Hodgson
 ,, Howitt

Close (F.) The stage, ancient and modern : its
tendencies on morals and religion. Ln :
Hatchard, 1850. 8° BPL | SML

Clowes (A. A.) Charles Knight. *See* Knight

Clowes (W.) *Printer. See* Sh— Works, 1821

Coates *Philadelphia Publisher. See* Sh—
Works, 1860

Cobbett (Wm.) Advice to young men. Ln :
1837. Cr. 8°
Adverse criticism of Sh –, pp. 292-296.

Fragment of an essay on taste [In ' Blackwood's Magazine ']. 1818. 8° BPL

Sh—, Milton, and potatoes [In ' Political
Register,' Vol. 29]. Ln : 1816 ? 8°

Year's residence in the United States of
America. 1819
Adverse criticism of Sh—occupies six pp. of the chapter
on potatoes.

Cobham.] Life and times of the good Lord
Cobham, by Thomas Gaspey. Ln :
Cunningham & Mortimer, 1843. 2 vols.
12°
A few copies done on large paper in octavo.
Illustrates ' King Henry VI.' and ' Sir John Oldcastle.'

Cobler of Canterburie. *See* Tinker of Turvey

Cobler of Preston. *See* Sh— Taming . . .
1716, 1723, 1732, 1755, 1767, 1786

Cochran *Edinburgh Printer. See* Sh— Works,
1753

Cochrane (A. B.) Théâtre Français in the
reign of Louis XV. Ln : Hurst &
Blackett, 1879. 8° SML

Cochrane (Robert) Treasury of English literature. *See* Sh— Works : Ext. 1881

Cocking (T.) *Bristol Publisher. See* Jones (H.)

Cockpit, Drury Lane—
See Greenstreet
 ,, Sh— King John, 1655

Cogan *or* Coggan (F.) *Publisher*—
See Feigned friendship
 ,, Sh— Works : Ext. 1738

Cohn *Bookseller* (Albert). Sh— bibliographie
[English and foreign], April, 1871 bis
ende 1886. Berlin : A. Cohn, 1886. 8°
BUS | SML

Sh— in Germany in the sixteenth and
seventeenth centuries. An account of
English actors in Germany and the

Netherlands and of the plays performed
by them during the same period. Ln :
Asher, 1865. 4°, pp. viii.-cxxxviii.-422
and 2 plates BM | BPL | CPL | MPL | SML | W
An investigation of visits paid by companies of English
actors. It includes also the full text of contemporary
German plays which can be brought into relation
with Sh—, such as the ' Beautiful Sidea,' ' Julius and
Hyppolita,' and ' Titus Andronicus,' with English
translations.

Cohn (Albert) *Editor*—
See Sh— Romeo . . . 1865
 ,, Sh— Titus . . . 1865

Coinage. *See* Davis (W. J.)

Cokaine *or* Cockaine (*Sir* Aston) Small poems
of divers sorts. Ln : W. Godbid, 1658.
8°, pp. 508. With portrait W
At p. 124 occurs the ' Epigram to Clement Fisher of
Wincot' [Wilnecote] illustrating ' Taming of the
Shrew ':
 ' Sh—, your Wincot ale hath much renown'd
 That fox'd a beggar so, by chance was found
 Sleeping, that there needed not many a word
 To make him to believe he was a lord.
 But you affirm, and in it seem most eager,
 'T will make a lord as drunk as any beggar.
 Bid Norton brew such ale as Sh— fancies
 Did put Kit Sly into such lordly trances ;
 And let us meet there for a fit of gladness
 And drink ourselves merry in sober sadness.'

Small poems, 1658—
See Sh—] Sh—Miscellanies
 ,, Sh—] Sh— Notices

Coke (*Sir* Edward *or* Lord)—
See Mercurius . . .
 ,, Stopes

Coke (W.) *Leith Publisher. See* Sh— Works,
1792

Colbert (S. M. & E.) Washington, Sh—, and
Saint George. Chicago : St. George Soc.,
1893. 8° BM | SML

Coldocke (Frances) *Publisher. See* Heliodorus

Cole (George Watson) Catalogue of books,
consisting of English literature and miscellanea, including many original editions
of Sh—, forming part of the library of the
late E. Dwight Church. New York :
Dodd, Mead, 1909. Roy. 8°, pp. 755-961
BM

Sh— quartos [In the ' Boston Transcript,'
page 17, 25th Aug.]. 1909 BUS

Cole (John)] Critique on the performance of
'Othello' by F. W. Keene Aldridge, the
'African Roscius.' Scarborough : Printed
for J. Cole, 1831. 8°, pp. 4. BPL | BUS
Issue limited to thirty copies.

Cole (J. W.) Life of Kean. *See* Kean

Coleman (*Dr.* Charles) *Composer. See* Sh—
Works : Ext. 1653

Coleman (J.) Fifty years of an actor's life.
1904. 2 vols. 8° BPL

Players and playwrights I have known.
1888. 2 vols. 8° BPL

Coleman (J.) *Editor.* *See* Sh— King Henry V., 1876
Coleridge (Hartley) Essays and marginalia. Edited by his brother. Ln: Moxon, 1851. 2 vols. 8° BPL | BUS
Vol. i. Sh— a tory and a gentleman, pp. 113-150. On the character of ' Hamlet,' pp. 151-171. Critique on Retzsch's illustrations of ' Hamlet,' pp. 172-177. Sh— and his commentators, pp. 353-366.
Vol. ii. Notes on Sh—, pp. 129-198.
Coleridge (Samuel Taylor) Essays and lectures on Sh—. ' Everyman's Lib.' Ln: Dent, 1907. 12°
Lectures and notes on Sh— and other English poets. Now first collected by T. Ashe. Ln: Bell & Sons, 1883. 8°, pp. xii.-552 BM
Lectures and notes . . . Ln: Bell, 1884. 8° SML
Lectures and notes on Sh—. Collected by Ashe. Ln: Bohn, 1890. 12° BPL
Lectures and notes on Sh—. ' York Lib.' Ln: Bell, 1907. Cr. 8°, pp. 564 BPL
Lectures and notes on Sh— . . . ' New Univ. Lib.' Routledge, 1908. 12°, pp. 304
Lectures upon Sh— and other dramatists. New York, 1884. 12° BPL
Manuscript notes. *See* Sh— Works, 1807
Notes and lectures upon Sh— and some of the old poets and dramatists, with other literary remains. Edited by Sara Coleridge. Ln: W. Pickering, 1849. 2 vols. 8° BM | BPL | BUS | MPL
Seven lectures on Sh—. List of all the MS. emendations in J. P. Collier's Folio Sh— of 1632 and introductory preface by J. P. Collier. Ln: Chapman, 1856. 8°, pp. viii.-cxx.-276 BM | BPL | BUS | CPL | MPL | SML
Seven lectures on Sh— . . . Ln: Bohn, 1862. 8°
Sh—, Ben Jonson, Beaumont and Fletcher: Notes and lectures. Liverpool: E. Howell, 1874. 8°, pp. viii.-318 BPL
Sh—, Ben Jonson, Beaumont and Fletcher: Notes and lectures. Liverpool, 1875. 8°, pp. viii.-318 BPL | CPL
Sh— and Milton: List of manuscript emendations in Collier's folio 1632. With preface by J. P. Collier. 1856. 8° BPL
Sh— and the Elizabethan dramatists. Edinburgh: John Grant, 1905. 12°, pp. viii.-318, and Chandos portrait
Zapolya: A Christmas tale. In two parts: The prelude entitled ' The Usurper's Fortune ' and the sequel entitled ' The Usurper's fate.' Ln: Printed [by S. Curtis] for Rest Fenner, Paternoster Row, 1817. 8°, pp. viii.-128 W
An imitation of the ' Winter's Tale.'

Coleridge (Samuel Taylor) Zapolya. *See* Sh— Winter's Tale, 1817, 1857
See Brae
,, Detective
Coles (F.) *See* Coules (Francis)
Colet (*Mme*. L.) *Editor.* *See* Sh— Works, 1836-39
Collection and selection of English prologues and epilogues. *See* Sh— Works: Ext. 1779
Collection of all the airs, catches, glees, cantatas, and roundelays which were performed at Stratford-upon-Avon on occasion of the Jubilee held there in honour of Sh—, 1769. With the dedication ode as spoken by Mr. Garrick. 1770. 12° BM
Collection of ancient documents respecting the office of Master of the Revels and other papers relating to the early English theatre, from the original manuscripts formerly in the Haslewood Collection [Ed. by J. O. Halliwell]. Ln: 1870. 8° HCL
Issue restricted to eleven copies. The running headline title is ' Dramatic records.'
Collection of critical opinions on the popular revival of the ' Winter's Tale ' at Burton's Theatre. New York [1856]. 8° BUS
Collection of diuers and remarkable stories, tragical and comical [including Macbeth, Romeo . . . and several other plots of Sh—]. Manuscript on seventy-one leaves of paper, including index, three leaves. c. 1670. 12° W
A curious assemblage of short tales, some abridged perhaps from printed books and others from sources not now known or from oral tradition. *See* Halliwell's ' Sh—reliques,' 1852, p. 36.
Collection of farces and other afterpieces which are acted at the Theatres Royal . . . printed under the authority of the managers from the prompt book. Selected by Mrs. Inchbald . . . Ln: Longman, 1809. 7 vols. 12°
Contains ' Catharine and Petruchio,' altered from Sh— by Garrick (vol. iv., pp. 143-172).
Collection of much-esteemed dramatic pieces. *See* Sh— Works: Ext. 1795
Collection of the most celebrated prologues . . . *See* Sh— Works: Ext. 1728
Collection of the most esteemed farces and entertainments performed on the British stage. Edinburgh: C. Elliot, 1783-88. 6 vols. 8°
Contains ' Florizel and Perdita ' (' Winter's Tale ') and several other adaptations of Sh—.
Collection of the most esteemed farces. [Second edition.] Edinburgh, Silvester Doig; Stirling, Wm. Anderson, 1792. 6 vols. 8°. Vignette titles

Collection of the most esteemed farces [Garrick's 'Catharine and Petruchio' altered from ' Taming of the Shrew,' excerpt of title and pp. 290-317 from Vol. I.]. Edinburgh : S. Doig, 1792. 8°
            W

Colles (John) *Dublin Publisher.* *See* Charms
Colles (W.) *Dublin Publisher. See Sh*—] Dennis
Collet (C. D.) *Editor.* *See* Sh— Macbeth, 1862
Collet (S.) Relics of literature. 1823. 8° BPL
Collier *Bp.* (Jeremy) Defence of the ' Short View' : Being a reply to Congreve. The stage condemned and the encouragement given to the theatre by the English schools censured. King Charles the first's Sunday Mask and declaration for sports and pastimes animadverted upon ; and remarks upon divers late plays, as also on those presented by the two universities to Charles I. Ln : 1699. 8°   MPL | W

Dissuasive from the play-house, in a letter to a person of quality, occasion'd by the late calamity of ' The Tempest.' Ln : R. Sare, 1703. 8°, pp. 16   BPL | MPL

Short view of the immorality and profaneness of the English stage, together with the sense of antiquity upon this argument. Ln : Printed for S. Keble at the Turk's Head in Fleet Street, R. Sare at Gray's Inn Gate, and H. Hindmarsh against the Exchange in Cornhil, 1698. 8°. First edition   W
This work succeeded in cleansing the ' Augean stable,' a sorely-needed reform. It was answered by Congreve, Dennis, Drake, Filmer, Vanbrugh, and others.

Short view . . . . Second edition. Ln : S. Keble, 1698   SML

Short view . . . Third edition. Ln : 1698. 8°   BPL | MPL | W
Pp. 154 to 156 are devoted to Sh—.

Short view . . . 1698. *See Sh*—] Sh— Notices
Short view . . . With several defences of the same in answer to Mr. Congreve, Dr. Drake, &c. Ln : 1730. 8°

Short view . . . Ln : 1738. 12°   BPL
See Critical essays   *See* Immorality
   ,, Dennis   ,, Rymer
   ,, Drake   ,, Stage acquitted
   ,, Dunton   ,, Stage condemn'd

Collier (John Payne) Bibliographical and critical account of the rarest books in the English language. New York, 1866. 4 vols. 8°   BUS

Catalogue bibliographical and critical of early English literature in the library at Bridgewater House. Ln : 1837. 4°   BPL | MPL

Dissertation on the imputed portraits of Sh—. Ln : 1851. 8°

Collier (John Payne) Dogberry and his associates : Arrest of the conspirators with Mary Queen of Scots. *See Sh*—] Sh— Soc.
Illustrates ' Much Ado . . .'

Dryden, Killigrew, and the first company which acted at Drury Lane Theatre. *See Sh*—] Sh— Soc.

Farther particulars regarding Sh— and his works, in a letter to . . . Joseph Hunter. Ln : T. Rodd, 1839. 8°, pp. 68. With facsimile   BM | BPL | BUS | CPL | MPL
Impression restricted to fifty copies on small and a few on large paper.

History of English dramatic poetry to the time of Sh— ; and annals of the stage to the restoration. Ln : J. Murray, 1831. 3 vols. 8°. With woodcuts
          BPL | BUS | MPL | SML
Six sets were printed on large paper, in octavo.
F. G. Fleay, in ' On certain modern Sh—,' says, after counting 2,000 errors in this work, he got tired of counting.

History of English dramatic poetry . . . New edition. Ln : Bell, 1879. 3 vols. 8°
          BPL | BUS | MPL
Reprinted from 1831 edition, with ' Memoirs of actors' added from the Sh— Soc. Pub.

John Wilson the singer in ' Much Ado ': A musical composer in Sh—'s plays. *See Sh*—] Sh— Soc.

King Edward the third. *See* Sh— King Edward III.

Letter to F. W. Cosens, Esq. upon a national Sh— memorial. Manuscript. 31st Jan., 1864. 8°   BPL

Life of Sh—. With a history of the early English stage. *See* Sh—

Memoirs of Alleyn. *See* Alleyn

Memoirs of the principal actors in the plays of Sh—. *See Sh*—] Sh— Soc.

New fact regarding Sh— and his wife contained in the Will of Thomas Whittington. *See Sh*—] Sh— Soc.

New facts regarding . . . Sh—. *See* Sh—

New particulars regarding the works of Sh—. In a letter to Alex. Dyce . . . Ln : T. Rodd, privately printed, 1836. 8°, pp. 68   BPL | BUS | CPL | MPL | W
The example at Warwick is an autograph presentation copy to John Black. A few were done on large paper.

Notes and emendations to the text of Sh—'s plays from early manuscript corrections in a copy of the Folio 1632 in the possession of John Payne Collier . . . [First edition.] Ln : Sh— Soc., 1852. 8°, pp. xxviii.-512 and facsimile   BUS
Afterwards withdrawn from the Society's Proceedings and issued as a separate publication.
J. P. Collier gave an account of how he acquired what is known as the Perkins folio (containing the alleged

John Payne Collier

See p. 56

early MS. notes) in the 'Athenæum,' 31st Jan. and 7th Feb., 1852, and (with reference to the autograph of Thomas Perkins in the volume) 4th June, 1853. A stormy controversy followed, and the 'early' MS. notes proved to be Collier's own handiwork.

Collier (John Payne) Notes and emendations . . . Second edition, revised and enlarged. Ln : Whittaker, 1853. 8°, pp. xxvi.-528 and facsimile page of forged corrections
BM | BPL | BUS | CPL | MPL | SML | W
Issued as a supplement to Collier's edition of Sh—, 1853, and also by the Sh— Society.

Notes and emendations . . . Third edition. Ln : Sh— Soc., 1852. 8°   W

Notes and emendations . . . New York : Redfield, 1853. 12°, pp. ii.-542 and facsimile   BUS

Old man's diary forty years ago.   Ln : 1871-72. 4 parts. Fcp. 4°
Twenty-five copies only, printed strictly for private circulation.

On Norton and Sackville, authors of 'Gorboduc,' the earliest blank verse tragedy in our language. See Sh—] Sh— Soc.

On Sh— [In 'Fraser's Magazine,' May]. Ln : 1836. 8°   BUS
A notice of 'New facts' and 'New particulars.'

On the earliest quarto editions of Sh—. See Sh—] Sh— Soc.

On the supposed origin of 'Romeo and Juliet.' See Sh—] Sh— Soc.

Original history of the theatre in Shoreditch and connexion of the Burbadge family with it. See Sh—] Sh— Soc.

'Passing measure Pavin'; illustrative of a passage in 'Twelfth Night.' See Sh—] Sh— Soc.

Performances of early dramas by parish clerks and players in churches. See Sh—] Sh— Soc.

Players and dramatic performances in the reign of Edward IV. See Sh—] Sh— Soc.

Poetical decameron, or conversations on English poets and poetry, more particularly of the reigns of Elizabeth and James I. Ln : 1820. 2 vols. 8°
BPL | MPL

Preface—
See Coleridge (S. T.)
„ Wilkins

Reasons for a new edition of Sh—'s works, containing notices of defects of former impressions and pointing out the lately-acquired means of illustrating the plays, poems, and biography of the poet. Ln : Whittaker, 1841. 8°, pp. 52
BM | BPL | BUS | W

Reasons for a new edition of Sh— . . . Second edition. With additions. Ln : Whittaker, 1842. 8°, pp. 56
BM | BPL | BUS | MPL

Collier (John Payne) Reply to Mr. Dyce on Mr. Hunter's 'Tempest.' Ln : 1853. 8°
CPL

. . . Reply to Mr. N. E. S. A. Hamilton's 'Inquiry' into the imputed Sh— forgeries. Ln : Bell & Daldy, 1860. 8°, pp. iv.-72   BM | BPL | BUS | MPL | W

Richard Field (printer of Sh—'s 'Venus . . .' and 'Lucrece') Nathaniel Field, Anthony Munday, and Henry Chettle. See Sh—] Sh— Soc.

Sh— and the 'Passionate Pilgrim' [In 'Athenæum,' 17th May, pp. 616-617]. 1856. 4°   BM

Sh— and the 'Passionate Pilgrim' [In 'Notes and Queries,' 5th July, 2nd Ser., Vol. 2, p. 8]. 1856. Fcp. 4°   BM

Sh— emendations: Additional facsimiles from Mr. Collier's Folio of 1632 [Perkins manuscript]. Manuscript on four leaves of paper. 8°   W

Sh—'s library. See Sh— . . .

Some information regarding the Lucies of Charlcot, the Shakespeares in and near Stratford-upon-Avon, and the property of Wm. Sh— in Henley Street [In 'Archæologia']. Ln : 1853. 4°   BPL | BUS

Trilogy : Conversations between three friends on the emendations of Sh—'s text contained in Mr. Collier's corrected Folio 1632, and employed by recent editors of the poet's work. Printed for private circulation [1874]. 3 parts in 1 vol. 4°
BM | BPL | BUS

Collier (J. P.) Editor—
See Albion Knight
„ Alleyn
„ Armin
„ Ballads
„ Broadside ballads . . .
„ Decker & Chettle
„ Dodsley
„ Dowdall
„ Drout
„ Forde
„ Ghost . . .
„ Gosson
„ Greg
„ Henslowe
„ Heywood
„ Jones (I.)
„ Lodge
„ Munday
„ Nash
„ Northbrooke
„ Old ballads
„ Reprints
„ Sh— Hamlet, 1858, 1859
„ Sh— King Edward III., 1874
„ Sh— King John, 1838

Collier (J. P.) *Editor—*
   See Sh— Passionate . . . 1599, 1870
   ,, Pericles, 1857
   ,, Sh— Works, 1841-53, 1843-44, 1844-53,
       1853, 1856, 1857, 1858, 1860, 1865,
       1866, 1878
   ,, *Sh—*] Sh— Soc.
   ,, *Sh—*] Sh—'s library
   ,, Stationers
   ,, Stubbes
   ,, Thynn
Collier.] Collier controversy [Collection of
   newspaper cuttings and magazine arti-
   cles]. 1859-62. 8°   BPL
] Corrector of Sh—: Collier and Singer [In
   'Edinburgh Review,' April]. 1856. 8°
              BM | BPL | BUS
] More improvements in the text of Sh—, by
   J. W. C—— [In 'Dublin Univ. Mag.,'
   March]. Dublin, 1853. 8°   BUS
] New readings in Sh— [In 'Blackwood's
   Edin. Mag.,' Aug.-Oct.]. 1853. 8° BUS
] Recent editions of Sh—; Review of J. P.
   Collier's edition of 1842-44 [In the
   'Edinburgh Review']. 1845. 8° BPL
] Review of 'An inquiry . . . by N. E. S. A.
   Hamilton.' Also the reply of J. P.
   Collier. Reprinted from the 'Athenæum.'
   New York: Printed for private circula-
   tion by C. W. Frederickson, 1860. 8°,
   pp. 32   BUS
Attributed to J. W. Dilke.
] Review of 'Notes and emendations' [In
   'North British Review']. 1854. 8° BPL
] Sh— controversy [In the 'Universal Re-
   view,' Sept.]. Ln: 1859. 8°   BUS
] Text of Sh— [In 'North British Review,'
   Feb.]. Edin., 1854. 8°   BUS
] Text of Sh—: Mr. Collier's corrected Folio
   [In 'Putnam's Monthly']. 1853. 8° BPL
] Wheatley (Henry B.) Notes on the life of
   John Payne Collier, with a list of his
   works and an account of such Sh— docu-
   ments as are believed to be spurious.
   Ln: Stock, 1884. 8°
          BM | BPL | BUS | SML
Reprinted from the 'Bibliographer.'
] Works of Sh— [In 'Christian Examiner,'
   Nov.]. Boston [U.S.], 1853. 8°   BUS
Collier forgeries—

See Arnold (T. J.)	*See* Hamilton
,, Arrowsmith	,, Hardy
,, Brae	,, Hunter (J.)
,, Broadside	,, Ingleby
,, Coleridge (S. T.)	,, Knight (C.)
,, Detective	,, Mac Chaff
,, Dixon	,, Parrott
,, Dyce	,, Quincy
,, Fairholt	,, Rivington
,, Frederickson	,, *Sh—*] Neil

Collier forgeries—

See Singer	*See* T—— (T.)
,, Sotheby	,, White (R. G.)

For a detailed list of articles and letters on this subject
   see Lowndes' 'Manual,' p. 2337.
Collier (*Dr.* Wm. Francis) History of English
   literature . . . With supplement on
   America. Ln: Nelson, 1898. Cr. 8°,
   pp. 582
Sh—, pp. 140-149.
Collins *Editor. See* Sh— George-a-Greene,
   1905
Collins *New York Publisher. See* Sh— Works,
   1821, 1824
Collins *Publisher—*
   See Sh— Macbeth, 1770
   ,, Sh— Othello, 1765
   ,, Sh— Timon . . . 1770
Collins (Francis) *Warwick Solicitor. See* Sh—
   Will . . . 1616
Collins (John)] Letter to George Hardinge on
   the subject of a passage in Mr. Stevens's
   [*sic*] preface to his impression of Sh—.
   Ln: B. Sibthorp for G. Kearsley in
   Fleet St., 1777. 4°, pp. viii.-48
          BM | BPL | BUS
Attributed by Malone to the Rev. John Collins and by
   Nichols to William Collins.
Described by Dr. Johnson as 'a great gun without
   powder and ball.'
It defends Capell's edition.
Collins (John) *Editor. See* Capell
Collins (*Prof.* John Churton) Ephemera critica.
   Ln: 1901. 8°   BPL
Sh —'s Sonnets, pp. 219-335.
   Essays and Studies. Ln: 1895. 8° BPL
   Lectures on Sh— at the Athenæum [News-
   paper cuttings]. 1881. 8°   BPL
   Problem of Sh—'s 'Hamlet': Sh— Club
   Paper. Stratford, 1905. 8°, pp. 8
Sh—. *See* Sh—
Sh— as a ladies' man [In 'The Boudoir '].
   1905. 8°   BPL
Studies in Sh—. Westminster: Constable,
   1904. 8°, pp. 396   BPL | BUS | MPL
Collins (J. Churton) *Editor—*
   See Sh— King Henry V., 1896
   ,, Sh— Macbeth, 1895
   ,, Sh— Works, 1894, 1906
Collins (Richard) *Publisher. See* Decker
Collins (Wm.)] Verses to Sir Thomas Hanmer
   on his edition of Sh—'s Works. By a
   Gentleman of Oxford. Ln: 1743. F°
[Verses] Epistle addrest to Sir Thomas
   Hanmer on his edition of Sh—'s Works.
   To which is added a song from 'Cymbe-
   line.' Ln: R. Dodsley, 1744. F°, pp. 16
[Verses] Epistle . . . Second edition. Ln:
   Dodsley, 1744. F°, pp. 16   BUS
Works [containing 'An epistle . . .']. Ln:
   1781. 12°   W

Collins (Wm.)] Works . . . to which is prefixed a life of the author by Dr. Johnson. Ln: Printed by T. Bensley for E. Harding, 1798. 8°, pp. xvi.-166. Twenty stipple copperplates in the text
Contains the 'Epistle to Hanmer,' Dirge from 'Cymbeline,' and a song borrowed from Sh—.

Collins (Wm) *Artist. See* Sh— As you like it, 1840

Collins (Wm. Wilkie) Mr. Wray's cash box. A novel. Ln: 1852. 12°   BPL | CPL
Chapter ix. deals with a mask of Sh— taken from the Stratford bust. Pirated in Philadelphia and issued by T. B. Peterson under the title of 'The stolen mask.'

Collis.] Cunningham (F. M.) In memoriam: Rev. John Day Collis, D.D. [Principal of Stratford-on-Avon College]. Privately printed, 1879. Cr. 8°. With plate

Collyer (R.) Introduction. *See* Colton

Colman (Edward) *Composer. See* Sh— Works: Ext. 1653

Colman *1732-94* (George) Fairy Prince: A masque . . . Ln: T. Becket, 1771. 8°, pp. viii.-26
Contains passages from Sh—.

Jealous wife: A comedy. Ln: J. Newbery, 1761. 8°
Sh— is referred to in the dedication, in the prologue, and on last leaf.

] Man and wife, or the Sh— jubilee: A comedy . . . as it is performed at the Theatre Royal in Covent Garden. Ln: T. Becket, 1770. 8°, pp. xii.-64 BPL | BUS

] Man and wife . . . Second edition. Ln: T. Becket, 1770. 8°, pp. xii.-64 BPL | BUS

Man and wife . . . Dublin: Printed for A. Leathley [and others], 1770. 12°

Man and wife . . . [In his 'Works,' Vol. 2]. Ln: 1777. 8°   BPL

Man of business: A comedy. Ln: T. Becket, 1774. 8°
Refers to Sh— in the epilogue.

The spleen, or Islington spa: A comick piece. Ln: T. Becket, 1776. 8°
The prologue, written by Garrick, refers to Sh—.

Colman (George) *Editor*—
See Sh— King Lear, 1768, 1770, 1771
 ,, Sh— Midsummer N. D., 1763, 1771,1777
 ,, Sh— Winter's Tale, 1777

Colman (G.) & Garrick (D.) Clandestine marriage: A comedy. Ln: T. Becket, 1766. 8°
Several allusions to Sh— and his characters in both prologue and epilogue.

See also Garrick & Colman

Colman *1762-1836* (George) Iron chest. Ln: 1796. 8°
The preface contains passages, afterwards suppressed, of unmerited censure upon J. P. Kemble.

Colman.] Peake (R. B.) Memoirs of the Colman family, with their correspondence. Ln: 1841. 2 vols. 8°   BPL

Colnaghi & Son *Publishers. See* Sh— King Richard III., 1829

Colomb (G. H.) Prince of Army chaplains. Ln: 1899. 8°   BPL

Colomb (G. H.) *Editor. See* Sh— Hamlet, 1880

Colton (Charles Caleb) Lacon, or many things in few words. 1822. 8°
Of considerable Shakespearean interest.

Lacon . . . New edition . . . with the subjects alphabetically arranged. Ln: Wm. Tegg, 1867. Cr. 8°, pp. xvi.-352 and frontispiece

Colton (Gardner Q.) Sh— and the Bible. With introd. by R. Collyer. *See* Sh— Works: Ext. 1888

Colvile (Frederick Leigh) Worthies of Warwickshire. *See* Sh—

Colville (James) *Editor*—
See Sh— Coriolanus, 1878
 ,, Sh— Works, 1873-75

Combe. Facsimile of the original indenture of the conveyance of over a hundred acres of land which was made by William and John Combe, of Stratford-on-Avon, to Sh— on the first of May . . . 1602. [Ed. by J. O. Halliwell.] Brighton: John George Bishop, 1884. F°   BPL | SML
Issue limited to twenty-five copies.

Combe (John à) *of Stratford*—
See Catalogue, 1797   *See* Dugdale
 ,, Dobell   ,, Sh— Epitaph

Combe Abbey, Warwickshire. *See* Howitt

Combe family. *See* Bellew

Come live with me . . . *See* Sh— Passionate Pilgrim, 1570-1600

Comedians' tales, or jests, songs, and pleasant adventures of several famous players. Ln: Printed for T. Warner at the Black Boy in Paternoster Row, and W. Pepper at the Crown in Maiden Lane, Covent Garden, 1729. 12°. With frontispiece
'Contains odd anecdotes of the old actors nowhere else to be found.'—GEO. DANIEL.

Comedy of errors. *See* Sh— Comedy . . .

Comenius (John Amos) Orbis sensualium pictus: The visible world . . . and men's employments therein. Trans. by Charles Hoole. Ln: Charles Mearne, 1685. 8°. With portrait by Cross and woodcuts
Two of the woodcuts are worth notice. That at p. 76, 'Septem Ætates Hominis' [Seven Ages of Man], and that at p. 264, 'Ludus Scenicus' [A stage play], shewing the interior of a play-house of the period.

Comfort (W. W.) 'Hamlet,' III., ii.: A striking parallel [In 'Athenæum,' No. 3810, p. 588, Nov.]. 1900

Comic guide to the Royal Academy. By the Gemini. Ln: 1864. 8°   BPL
Sh— references, pp. 6-7, 18, 19.

Comic Sh—. *See* Ross

Commemorations. *See* Sh— festivals

Commentaries and Commentators. *See* Sh— Works : Criticism . . .

Companion to the bottle, or Don Jumpedo in the character of Harlequin jumping down his own throat in the pantomime entertainment of the ' Royal chace, or Merlin's cave,' acting at the Theatre Royal, Covent Garden. Ln : B. Dickinson, Mar. 20, 1748-49. F° broadside, coloured
Refers to Sh— thus :—
   ' To rescue from disgrace the noblest art
   And in invention's race still keep the start
   The French must to our drama still submit.
   Sh— drew nature, and Ben Johnson writ.
   If they can boast Racine and gay Molière
   Still they but imitate ; the standard's here.'

Companion to the playhouse. *See* Baker

Companion to the theatre, or a key to the play. Containing the stories of the most celebrated dramatick pieces. Ln : 1740. 12°   w
Originally published as the ' Dramatic historiographer.' Includes the plots of several Sh— plays.

Companion to the theatre. Second edition. Ln : 1740. 12°   BPL

Companion to the theatre, or a view of our most celebrated dramatic pieces, in which the plan, characters, and incidents are explained. Ln : 1747. 2 vols. 12°

Company of Booksellers. *See* Sh— The Tempest, 1710

Company of Stationers. *See* Stationers

Comparative review of opinions. *See* Wyatt

Comparison between the two stages. In dialogue. Ln : 1702. 8°   w
Contains several Sh— notices.

Compendious . . . examination. *See* Sh— Compendious . . .

Complaint of the Churche, 1562. *See* Reprints

Complaynte of them that ben to late maryed. *See* Reprints

Complete Sh— reciter. *See* Sh— Works : Ext. 1845

Compton (C. & E.) Memoirs of Henry Compton, comedian. Ln : Tinsley, 1879. 8°, pp. viii.-348   SML

Compton *Actor* (Edward) Rhyming address. *See Stratford*] Sh— Memorial

Compton Wynyates, Warwickshire. *See* Howitt

Conceits, clinches, flashes, and whimzies : A jest book . . . 1639. Edited by J. O. Halliwell. Ln : Privately printed, 1860. Fcp. 4°. With facsimile of the original title   BPL | BUS | HCL
On p. 30 is a jest relating to Sh—. Reprinted in Sh— jest books.

Concerning the honour of bookes. *See* Sh— Concerning . . .

Concise account of Garrick's jubilee. *See* Jarvis

Concordance to Sh—. *See* Sh— glossaries

Cond (T.) Wm. Sh—, his life and genius. *See* Sh—

Condé (J.) *Artist*. *See* Thespian Magazine

Condell *or* Kendall (Henry) *Actor*—
   See Heminge & Condell
   ,, Hosken
   ,, Scott (E. J. L.)
   ,, Sh— Works, 1623, 1632, 1663, 1664, 1685

Conduct of the stage consider'd. 1721. 12°   BPL

Cone (Helen Gray) *Editor*. *See* Sh— Macbeth, 1897

Confessions of Wm. Sh—. *See* Sh—

Confused characters of conceited coxcombs, 1661. Ed. by J. O. Halliwell. Ln : 1860. 8°   BPL

Confusion's masterpiece—
   See Ford (Thomas)
   ,, Sh— Macbeth, 1794

Congal and Fenella. *See* Sh— Macbeth, 1791

Congdon (Charles T.) Statesmanship of Sh— [In ' Harper's Mag.,' Sept.]. New York, 1863. 8°   BUS

Congreve (F. A.) Memoirs of Macklin. *See* Macklin

Congreve (William) Amendments of . . . [Bishop Jeremy] Collier's false and imperfect citations, etc. [in his ' Immorality and profaneness of the English stage ']. From ' The old bachelour,' ' The double dealer,' ' Love for love,' ' Mourning bride ' . . . Ln : J. Tonson at the Judge's Head in Fleet Street, near the Inner Temple Gate, 1698. 8°   w
Several allusions to Sh—.

Sports of the muses. *See* Sh— Works : Ext. 1752

Congreve.] Memoirs of the life, writings, and amours of William Congreve, interspersed with miscellaneous essays, letters, and characters, also some very curious memoirs of Mr. Dryden and his family. Compiled from their respective originals by Charles Wilson. Ln : Printed in the year 1730. 8°. With portrait
   See Collier (*Bp.*)
   ,, Dennis
   ,, Gildon

Conington (J.) Lectures on ' King Lear ' and ' Hamlet ' [In ' Miscellaneous Writings,' Vol. I., pp. 74-136]. Ln : 1872. 8°   BPL | BUS | MPL

Conjectural emendations on the text of Sh—. With observations on the notes of the commentators [In ' Gentleman's Mag.,' Aug. and Nov., 1844, Feb. and June, 1845]. Ln : 1844-45. 8°   BM | BUS

Conner (J.) *New York Publisher.* *See* Sh—
Works, 1834, 1835, 1839
Conolly (John) Study of 'Hamlet.' Ln:
Moxon, 1863. 8°, pp. iv.-210
BM | BPL | BUS | CPL | SML
Conrad (C. & A.) *Philadelphia Publishers.* *See*
Sh— Works, 1805-09, 1809
Conrad (*Dr.* H.) *Editor.* *See* Sh— Twelfth
Night, 1887
Conrad, Lucas & Co. *Baltimore Publishers.*
See Sh— Works, 1805-09
Considerations on the stage and on the ad-
vantages which arise to a nation from the
encouragements of arts. Ln: 1731. 8° w
Contains (chap. ii.) 'On tragedy: A criticism of 'King
Lear.'
Considerations on the state of the stage . . .
Contests at Covent Garden . . . Ln:
Chapple, 1809. 8° SML
Constable (John) *Artist.* *See* Sh— As you
like it, 1840
Contemporary depositions respecting an affray
at Norwich in 1583, in which Q. Eliza-
beth's company of players, then acting
at the Red Lion Inn, were involved. Ed.
by J. O. Halliwell. Ln: 1864. Fcp. 4° BPL
Twenty-five copies printed, fifteen of which were des-
troyed.
Contemporary notices of Sh—. *See* Sh—
'Contrast Jumble' *pseud.* *See* Sh— King
Richard III., 1823
Conway (Moncure Daniel) Mr. Wm. Sh— at
home. *See* Sh—
The 'Pound of flesh' [In ' Nineteenth
Century']. 1880. Roy. 8° BPL
Illustrates the ' Merchant of Venice.'
Cook (Dutton) Book of the play. Ln: Low,
1876. 2 vols. Cr. 8° BPL | SML
Hours with the players. Ln: Chatto, 1881.
2 vols. 12° BPL | SML
Cook (Eliza) Tercentenary ode. Written for
the Working Men's Sh— celebration,
April 23rd, 1864. Spoken by Hy. Marston.
1864. Broadside BUS
Cook *Barrister* (John) King Charls; his case,
or an appeal to all rational men concern-
ing his tryal . . . Ln: 1649. Fcp. 4°
Cook charged King Charles with paying far less atten-
tion to Scripture than to Sh— and Ben Jonson.
Cook (Richard) *Artist.* *See* Sh— Works, 1807
Cooke (B.) *Publisher.* *See* Temple
Cooke (C.) *Publisher*—
See Sh— Antony, 1817
,, Sh— Poems, 1797, 1800
Cooke.] Dunlop (W.) Life of George Frederick
Cook, with original anecdotes of his con-
temporaries. Ln: H. Colburn, 1815. 8°
] Life of G. F. Cooke, with critical remarks,
anecdotes, and an account of the morality
of the stage. Ln: Pierce Egan [1813]. 8°.
Coloured frontispiece by G. Cruikshank

Cooke (G. F.) *Actor*—
See Kean
,, Kemble
,, Remarks
,, Sh— King Richard III., 1818
Cooke (J.) Astrology of Sh— [In ' Macmillan's
Magazine']. Ln: 1885. 8° BPL
Cooke *of Warwick* (James) Mellificium chirur-
giæ, or marrow of chirurgery. Ln: T.
Hodgkin for W. Marshall, 1685. Fcp. 4°.
With portrait of Cooke
Cooke *of Warwick* (James) *Editor.* *See* Hall
Cooke (James O'Neale) Shaksperean shadow-
ings [In 'The Leader']. New York, 1863.
8° BUS
On 'Merchant of Venice,' 'Macbeth,' 'King Lear,'
'Much Ado,' 'King Henry IV.,' 'Othello.'
Cooke (Martin W.) The human mystery in
' Hamlet ': An attempt to say an unsaid
word. With suggestive parallelisms from
the elder poets. New York, 1888. 16°
BM | BPL | BUS
Cooke (T.) *Composer*—
See Garrick
,, Sh— Poems, 1862
Cooke (Thomas) Epistle to the Countess of
Shaftesbury, with a prologue and epilogue
on Sh— and his writings. Ln: T. Cooper,
1742. F°, pp. 8 BUS
Cooke (Wm.) Memoirs of Foote. *See* Foote
Cooke *Barrister* (Wm.) Elements of dramatic
criticism, containing an analysis of the
stage under the following heads : tragedy,
tragi-comedy, comedy, pantomime, and
farce. With a sketch of the education of
the Greek and Roman actors. Concluding
with some general instructions for suc-
ceeding in the art of acting. Ln: G.
Kearsly & G. Robinson, 1775. 8°, pp.
xviii.-216. Engraved title BPL
Numerous references to Sh—.
Cooke (Wm.) *Publisher.* *See* Habington
Cooledge (G. F.) *New York Publisher.* *See*
Sh— Works, 1848
Cooley (J. E.) Library. *See* Catalogue, 1865
Cooper *Actor.* *See* Sh— Pericles, 1796
Cooper *Artist.* *See* Sh— Works, 1826-29,1829
Cooper *Publisher.* *See* Ireland (S. W. H.)
Cooper (Abraham) *Artist.* *See* Sh— As you
like it, 1840
Cooper (E.) *pseud.* *See* Oldys (W.)
Cooper (John Gilbert)] Letters concerning
taste. Second edition, 1755. 12° BPL
Tomb of Sh—: A poetical vision. Ln:
R. & J. Dodsley, 1755. Fcp. 4°, pp. 12
BPL | BUS | W
Reprinted in Dodsley's Collection of Poems, vol. v.
Tomb of Sh— . . . Second edition, corrected ;
with considerable alterations. Ln: R. & J.
Dodsley, 1755. Fcp. 4°, pp. 12 BUS | W

Cooper (M.) *Publisher*—
See Edwards (T.)
,, Letter . . .
,, Novel . . .
,, Sh— King Henry VIII., 1758
,, Sh— Works : Ext. 1752
Cooper (Oliver) Explanatory notes on Sh—'s
  ' Tempest.' 1889. 8°   BM
Cooper (Stanley) Ecclesiastical dramas of the
  middle ages. Sh— Club paper. Strat-
  ford-on-Avon, 1907. 8°, pp. 8   SML
Great playwrights of the classical era. Sh—
  Club paper. Stratford-on-Avon, 1904.
  F° broadside, single sheet
Nine fancy pictures of events in Sh—'s
  country, town, and court life. Ln : Nor-
  gate, 1893. 16°, pp. 80, and view of
  Globe Theatre   BM | BPL | SML
Sh—'s dramatic predecessors [Greene, Lyly,
  and Peele]. Sh— Club paper. Stratford-
  on-Avon, 1909. 8°, pp. 8
Cooper (T.) *Publisher*—
See Cooke
  ,, Wedderburn
Cooper (W. D.) *Editor*—
See Dodsley
  ,, Norton & Sackville
  ,, Udall
Cooper & Graham *Publishers. See* Sh— King
  Lear, 1796
Coote (H. C.) On Sh—'s new map in ' Twelfth
  Night.' Ln : New Sh— Soc., 1878. 8°
       BM | BPL
Sh— and Italian law [In 'Athenæum,' No.
  2939, p. 251]. 1884
Coote (J.) *Publisher. See* Derrick
Cope *Publisher. See* Sh— King Richard III.,
  1820
Cope (C. W.) *Artist. See* Sh— Works, 1873-76,
  1875-76
Cope (*Sir* Walter) Holograph letter : ' I have
  sent and bene all thys morning huntyng
  for players, juglers, and such kind of
  creatures, but fynde them hard to finde
  . . . Burbage is come . . . Sayes there is
  no newe playe that the Quene hath not
  seene, but they have revyved an olde
  one cawlèd " Love's labors lost," which
  for wytt and mirthe he sayes will please
  her exceedingly.' [*Dated*] ' From your
  library, 1604 '
  Printed in the Historical Manuscripts Commission :
  Third Report, 1872, p. 148.
Copley (Anthony)] Wits, fits, and fancies, or
  a general and serious collection of the
  sententious speeches, answers, jests, and
  behaviours of all sortes of estates from
  the throane to the cottage . . . Newly
  corrected and augmented with many late
  true and wittie accidents . . . Ln : Pr.

by Edw. Allde, dwelling in Little Saint
  Bartholomewes neer Christ Church, 1614.
  Fcp. 4°. Black letter. Sig. A—C²   CTC
  Originally appeared in 1595.
Copping (Harold) *Artist*—
See Sh— Hamlet, 1897, 1898
  ,, Sh— Works : Ext. 1901, 1902
Copy of a letter of news. *See* Herbert (*Sir* G.)
Copyright and Stageright. *See* Coryton
Coquelin (C.) Molière and Sh— [In ' The
  Century ']. New York [c. 1889]. Roy. 8°
       BPL
Corbet. Poem on Bosworth Field. *See* Poems
Corbet *or* Corbett (C.) *Publisher*—
See Foote
  ,, Sh— Hamlet, 1767
  ,, Sh— King Henry VIII., 1762
  ,, Sh— King Lear, 1767, 1771
  ,, Sh— Macbeth, 1770
  ,, Sh— Othello, 1765
  ,, Sh— Romeo . . . 1748
  ,, Sh— The Tempest, 1761
  ,, Sh— Timon . . . 1770
  ,, Sh— Works, 1740, 1757, 1762, 1773
Corbet *Bp.* (Richard) Certain elegant poems.
  Ln : R. Cotes for Andrew Crooke, 1647.
  Fcp. 4°
  On p. 12 is a reference to Sh— and his fellow-actor
  Burbage, from which we learn that Burbage originally
  represented King Richard III. :—
  ' Mine host was full of ale and history

  And policyes not incident to hosts,
  But chiefly by that one perspicuous thing
  Where he mistook a player for a king,
  For when he would have sayd " King Richard dyed,"
  And call'd, " A horse, a horse "—he " Burbidge "
  cry'de.'
  Certain elegant poems . . . Third edition.
  Ln : 1672. 8°
Corbett (F. Saint-John) Epitome of the Sh— -
  Bacon controversy [In ' The King '].
  1905. F°   BPL
Corbin *of Harvard* (John) Elizabethan Ham-
  let : A study of the sources, and of
  Sh—'s environment, to show that the
  mad scenes had a comic aspect now
  ignored. Ln : 1895. 8°   BM | BPL | BUS
New portrait of Sh— : The case of the Ely
  Palace painting as against that of the
  so-called Droeshout original. Ln : Lane,
  1903. Fcp 4°, pp. xii.-96. With Droes-
  hout, Ely, and Flower portraits
       BPL | MPL | SML
Corbould (E. M.) *See* Rossi & Corbould
Corbould (F. H.) *Artist. See* Gold, silver, lead
Corbould (Richard) *Artist. See* Sh— Works,
  1787-91, 1803, 1821-29, 1826, 1829, 1875-
  80
Cordley (C.) Sh—'s piscine lore [In ' Gentle-
  man's Magazine']. 1895. 8°   BPL
'Corelli (Marie).' *See* Gonzalez

'Corin' *pseud.* Truth about the stage. Ln : Wyman, 1885. Cr. 8°, pp. viii.-180 SML
'A warning to moth-like persons dazzled by the artificial halo of romance surrounding theatrical life.'—*Pref.*
Coriolanus. *See* Sh— Coriolanus
Cornelianum Dolium. *See* Randolph
Corner (M.) On ' Hamlet ' [In ' New Monthly Mag.,' Mar.]. Ln : 1820. 8° BUS
Corner (Sidney) Rural churches : their histories, architecture, and antiquities. Ln : Groombridge, 1869. F°, pp. 72 and 18 large coloured plates
Sh— and the Stratford radius occupy pp. 69-72, with a coloured view of Holy Trinity Church.
Cornewallis *d. 1631* ? (*Sir* William) Essayes of certain paradoxes [in prose and verse ; two parts]. Ln : Ed. Mattes, 1600-1601. 18°
Contains the ' Prayse of King Richard the third,' in which occur references to Sh—'s plays.
Reprinted in Somers' tracts.
] Essayes of certaine paradoxes . . . Ln : Printed for Th. Thorp, 1616. Fcp. 4° W
With a manuscript transcript of the dedication to Sir Henry Neville prefixed to the original manuscript of the first essay (formerly preserved in Yarnold's collection).
] Essayes of certaine paradoxes. Second impression, inlarged. Ln : 1617. Fcp. 4° W
The list of contents finishes up by enumerating two essays—' On sadness ' and ' On the virtues of Julian the Apostate '—as following that ' On debt,' but as the word ' Finis ' follows this last composition in the text, the volume was evidently published minus the first-mentioned, and is apparently complete without them. Nevertheless, preceding the ' Paradoxes ' in this copy is a quite separate edition of the two essays in question, entitled ' Essays, or rather, Prayses on sadnesse : and of the Emperour Julian the Apostate. By Sir W. Cornewallis. 1616.'
Corney (Bolton) Argument on the assumed birthday of Sh—, reduced to shape . . . Ln : Privately printed by P. Shoberl [1864]. 8°, pp. 16 BM | BPL | BUS | MPL
Sonnets of Sh— : A critical disquisition suggested by a recent discovery. Ln : Private impression by F. Shoberl [1862]. 8°, pp. 16 BM | BPL | BUS | CPL | MPL
Refers to M. Chasle's interpretation. *See* 'Athenæum,' 25 Jan., 1862.
Cornhill Magazine. Edited by W. M. Thackeray and others. [*Consult its general indexes*]
Cornucopia ; or literary and dramatic mirror, containing critical notices of the drama. Ln : J. Jameson, Dec. 1820—Jan. 1821. Fcp. 4° (issued in 13 nos.) W
Containing notices of Shakespearean representations and a coloured plate of Vandenhoff as Caius Marcius in ' Coriolanus.'
Cornwaleys (Anne) Autograph. *See* Poems
Cornwall. *See* Sandys
'Cornwall (Barry)' *pseud.* Life of Kean. *See* Kean

'Cornwall (Barry)' *pseud. See* Procter (B. W.)
Corrall *Printer. See* Sh— Works, 1822-23, 1831
Corréard (M.) *Editor*—
See Sh— Coriolanus, 1845
,, Sh— Julius Cæsar, 1865
Corrector of Sh—. *See* Collier (J. P.)
Corson (Hiram) Introduction to the study of Sh—. Boston [U.S.], 1889. 8°
BM | BPL | BUS
Introduction . . . Boston [U.S.], 1893. 8°
BUS
Introduction . . . Ln : Harrop, 1907. 8°, pp. 404
Jottings on the text of ' Hamlet ' : First folio *v.* Camb. edition. Ithaca [U.S.], 1874. 8°, pp. 34 BM | BPL | BUS
Issue limited to 200 copies.
Note on a passage in Sh— [Reprinted from ' The Nation,' 28 Aug.]. Ithaca, 1873. 8° broadside BUS
On a disputed passage in ' Hamlet.' Ithaca, 1873. 8°, pp. 4 BUS
Cort (C. F.) Tribute to learning . . . a poem [Sh— p. 22]. 1834. 4° BPL
Cortazzo (O.) *Artist. See* Sh— Romeo . . . 1891
Coryton (J.) Stageright : Law relating to dramatic authors. Ln : Nutt, 1873. 8°
Sh—'s plots not original, etc., p. 85. BPL | SML
Cosens (F. W.) *Editor*—
See Manuel
,, Rojas y Zorrilla
,, Sh— Romeo . . . 1869, 1874
Cosens (F. W.) *See* also Collier (J. P.)
'Cosmopolite' *pseud. See* Sh— ! Was he a Christian ?
Cossins (Jethro A.) Early works of architecture in Warwickshire. *See* Memorials . . .
Costume and dress—
See Aria
,, British Theatrical Gallery
,, Brougham
,, Lacy
,, Sh— Merchant . . . 1863
,, Sh— Winter's tale, 1855, 1861
,, Sh— Works : Boocke, 1889
,, Siddons
,, Wingfield
,, Wright (T.)
Cotes (Richard) *Printer. See* Corbet
Cotes (Thomas) *Printer-Publisher*—
See Aleyn
,, Booke . . .
,, Chamberlaine
,, Sh— Pericles, 1635
,, Sh— Poems, 1640
,, Sh— Two noble kinsmen, 1634
,, Sh— Works, 1632
,, Shirley

(63)

Cotgrave (John) English treasury of wit and language, collected out of the most and best of our English dramatick poems. Methodically digested into commonplaces for generall use . . . Ln : Printed for Humphrey Moseley and are to be sold at his shop at the sign of the Princes Armes in S. Pauls Church-yard, 1655. 8°. sig. A to X4, paged   BPL | CTC

Wit's interpreter ; The English parnassus, or a sure guide to those admirable accomplishments that compleat our English gentry . . . Ln : 1662. 8°
The frontispiece contains portraits of Sh—, Bacon, Spenser, and Jonson.

Wit's interpreter. Third edition, with many new additions. Ln : Printed for N. Brook at the Angel in Cornhill and Obadiah Blagrave at the Printing Press in Little Britain, 1671. 8°

Cotswold games—
See Annalia
,, Ashbee
Cotta (J. G.) *Stuttgart Publisher. See* Sh— Macbeth, 1842
Cottage at Shottery, where Sh— wooed and won Anne Hathaway [a poem]. [1864 ?] 4°   BPL
Cotter *Dublin Publisher. See* Sh— Measure . . . 1761
Cotter (James H.) Sh—'s art. Cincinnati, 1903. Cr. 8°, pp. 184   BPL
Cotton (J.) Song and sentiment. Ln : Simpkin, 1891. 12°   SML
Contains ' Sonnets on Sh—,' p. 129
Cotton (Roger)] Armor of proofe, brought from the tower of Dauid, to fight against Spannyardes, and all enimies of the trueth. By R. C——. [In verse.] Ln : G. Simson and W. White, 1596. Fcp. 4°, without pagination   W
According to W. H. Ireland, this copy formed part of Sh—'s library. Contains the autograph and manuscript notes of Sh— forged by Ireland.
Couch & Laking *Publishers. See Sh*—] Skene
Coules *or* Coles (Francis) *Publisher*—
See Sh— Mucedorus, 1626, 1663, 1668
,, Sh— Venus . . . 1630, 1636, 1675
Counsellor Manners. *See* Dare (J.)
Court of Oberon. *See* Sh— Midsummer N. D., 1831
Court of Thespis. *See* Garrick
Court of Venus. *See* Stopes
Court revels in the reigns of Q. Elizabeth and James I. Ed. by P. Cunningham. *See Sh*—] Sh— Soc.
Courtenay (*Rt. Hon.* Thomas Peregrine) Commentaries on the historical plays of Sh—. Ln : H. Colburn, 1840. 2 vols. 12°
BM | BPL | BUS | CPL | MPL | SML | W

Courtenay (*Rt. Hon.* Thomas Peregrine) Commentaries . . . Ln : Houlston, 1861. 2 vols. 8°
Sh—'s historical plays considered historically [In ' New Monthly Mag.,' June, 1838 and Mar., 1839]. Ln : 1838-39. 8°
BUS | SML
Courthope (Wm. John) History of English poetry. 1903. 8°   BPL
Sh— occupies pp. 19-200, 455-476, vol. iv.
Three hundredth anniversary of Sh—'s birth : Prize poem recited in the Theatre, Oxford, 8 June, 1864. Oxford : T. & G. Shrimpton, 1864. 8°, pp. 16   BPL | BUS
Courtneidge (R.) Souvenir : ' As you like it' at the Prince's Theatre, Manchester. 1902. 8°   BPL
Courtney (W. L.) Idea of tragedy in ancient and modern drama. With note by A. W. Pinero. Ln : Constable, 1900. Cr. 8°, pp. xii.-132   SML
Courtney & Slie.] Life and execution of Charles Courtney, alias Hollice, and Clement Slie, fencer. With their escapes and breaking of prison. Ln : Edward Marchant, 1612. Fcp. 4°. With woodcut title
' The Slys are no rogues : look in the chronicles.'
—*Taming of Shrew*, Ind. I., iii.
Cousins (Samuel) *Engraver. See* Sh—] Portrait
Covent Garden. *See* Theatre Royal
Covent Garden Journal . . . ' The hurly-burly's done' (*Macbeth*). Ln : J. J. Stockdale, 1810. 2 vols. 8°. With plates
Contains the history of the O. P. riots, in which John Kemble took a prominent part.
Coventry—
See Dugdale   *See* Memorials . . .
,, Edwards   ,, Merridew
,, Harris   ,, O'Keeffe
,, Logismos   ,, Poole
,, Ludus Coventriæ   ,, Sharpe
Coventry (Two) Corpus Christi plays. Re-edited by W. J. Craig. [Early English Text Soc., Vol. 87.] Ln : 1902. 8° BPL
See also Ludus Coventriæ
Cowie. British drama. *See* Sh— Antony, 1833
Cowie & Co. *Publishers. See* Sh— Works, 1811, 1814
Cowley (Abraham) Tragical history of Piramus and Thisbe. *See* Sh— Midsummer N. D., 1681
] Will . . . from the registry of . . . Canterbury. Ed. by P. Cunningham. *See Sh*—] Sh— Soc.
Cowley (Abraham)—
See Dunton
,, Mercurius Britannicus
Cowley (*Mrs.*) Extracts. *See* Sh— Works : Ext. 1822
Cox *Publisher. See* Holt
Cox (*Capt.*) Book of fortune. *See* Stopes

Cox *player* (*Capt.*) Library. *See* Halliwell

Cox (Charles) *Publisher*. *See* Sh— Works, 1843-44, 1849

Cox (David) *Artist*. *See* Jaffray

Cox (E. W.) Psychology of Hamlet. [Psych. Soc. of Gr. Brit.] 1879. 8°   BM

Cox (F. A.) English madrigals in the time of Sh—. Ln : Dent, 1899. 12°, pp. 292

Cox (Frederick) Lecture on the genius, life, and character of Wm. Sh—. *See* Sh—

Cox (G.) *Publisher*. *See* Sh— Works, 1852, 1853

Cox *Mayor of Stratford* (James) The tercentenary : A retrospect. Ln : Cassell, 1865. 8°, pp. 12   BM | BPL | BUS | CPL

Cox (Robert) Merry conceited humours . . . *See* Sh— Midsummer N. D., 1646

Cox (S. A.) Sh— converted into Bacon : An extravaganza. In two acts. Dublin [1899]. Cr. 8°, pp. 32   BPL

Cox (Thomas)] Magna Britannia. Ln : Nutt, 1721-31. Fcp. 4°   SML | W
Includes a history of Warwickshire (vol. iv., pp. 457-488), containing a notice of Sh—.

Coxe (A. C.) Impressions of England. New York, 1856. 8°   BPL
Chapter xxii. includes Stratford and Sh—.

Impressions of England. 1857. 8°

Coxeter (Thomas) *forger*. *See* Cibber

Coyne (J. S.) This house to be sold—the property of the late W. Sh— : An extravaganza. [1847.] 12°   BPL

Coyne (J. S.) *Editor*. *See* Sh— King Richard III., 1844

Coyne (Wm. P.) *Editor*. *See* Sh— Works : Ext. 1895

Cradock ? (Joseph)] Letters from Snowdon, etc. Dublin, 1770. 12°   W
A notice of ' King Lear ' at p. 77.

Cradock (Joseph). *See also* Farmer (R.)

'Craft (Zachary)' *pseud*. *See* Kelsall

Craig (E. T.) Portraits . . . of Sh—. *See* Sh—] Craig

Sh— and art. *See* Sh—] Craig

Sh—'s portraits. *See* Sh—] Craig

Craig (W. J.) *Editor*—
See Coventry
,, Sh— All's well, 1904
,, Sh— Antony, 1905
,, Sh— As you like it, 1904
,, Sh— Comedy of errors, 1903
,, Sh— Coriolanus, 1904
,, Sh— Cymbeline, 1883, 1905
,, Sh— Hamlet, 1905
,, Sh— Julius Cæsar, 1905
,, Sh— King Henry IV., i., 1904
,, Sh— King Henry IV., ii., 1904
,, Sh— King Henry V., 1904
,, Sh— King Henry VI., i., 1904
,, Sh— King Henry VI., ii., 1904

Craig (W. J.) *Editor*—
See Sh— King Henry VI., iii., 1904
,, Sh— King Henry VIII., 1904
,, Sh— King John, 1904
,, Sh— King Lear, 1901, 1905
,, Sh— King Richard II., 1904
,, Sh— King Richard III., 1905
,, Sh— Love's labours lost, 1904
,, Sh— Macbeth, 1905
,, Sh— Measure . . . 1903
,, Sh— Merchant . . . 1904
,, Sh— Merry wives, 1903
,, Sh— Midsummer . . . 1903
,, Sh— Much ado, 1903
,, Sh— Othello, 1905
,, Sh— Pericles, 1905
,, Sh— Poems, 1905
,, Sh— Romeo . . . 1904
,, Sh— Sonnets, 1905
,, Sh— Taming . . . 1904
,, Sh— The Tempest, 1903
,, Sh— Timon . . . 1905
,, Sh— Titus . . . 1904
,, Sh— Troilus . . . 1905
,, Sh— Twelfth night, 1904
,, Sh— Two gentlemen, 1903
,, Sh— Winter's tale, 1904
,, Sh— Works, 1891, 1892, 1899 - 1906, 1902, 1903, 1904, 1905, 1907

Craik (George L.) English of Sh— illustrated in a philological commentary on his ' Julius Cæsar ' [with the text and an index]. Ln : Chapman & Hall, 1857. Cr. 8°, pp. xxxviii.-352   BM | BPL | BUS

English of Sh— . . . Second edition, revised and improved. Ln: 1859. Cr. 8°, pp. xvi.-350   BPL | BUS | CPL | MPL | SML

English of Sh— . . . Third edition, revised and corrected. Ln : 1864. Cr. 8°, pp. xvi.-350   SML

English of Sh—. Ed. by W. J. Rolfe. Boston [U.S.]: Crosby, 1867. Cr. 8°, pp. xvi.-386   BUS

English of Sh—. Ed. by W. J. Rolfe. Boston [U.S.]: E. Ginn, 1868. Cr. 8°, pp. xvi.-386   BUS

English of Sh— . . . Fourth edition. Ln : Chapman, 1869. Cr. 8°   BPL

English of Sh—. Ed. by W. J. Rolfe. Sixth edition. Boston [U.S.]: Ginn, 1872. Cr. 8°, pp. xvi.-386   BUS

English of Sh—. Edited by W. J. Rolfe. Boston [U.S.], 1876. 12°   BPL

English of Sh— . . . Ed. by W. J. Rolfe. Boston : Ginn, 1883. Cr. 8°, pp. xvi.-386   SML

English of Sh—. Ed. by W. J. Rolfe. Boston : Ginn, 1886. Cr. 8°, pp. xvi.-386   SML

(65)   5

Craik (George L.) Sketches of the history of literature and learning in England from the Norman conquest . . . with specimens. Ln : Knight & Co., 1844-45. 6 vols. in 3. Cr. 8°
Vols. iii. and iv. contain critical sketches of Sh— and his contemporaries.

Craik (George L.) *Editor*. *See* Sh— Julius Cæsar, 1857, 1859, 1867, 1868, 1869, 1872, 1876

Cranch (C. P.) Ariel and Caliban, with other poems. Boston & New York, 1887. 12°
Illustrates 'The Tempest.' BPL

Crane (Walter) Flowers from Sh—'s garden. *See* Sh— Works : Ext. 1906

Crane (Walter) *Artist*—
See Sh— King Richard II., 1904
,, Sh— Merry wives, 1894
,, Sh— Midsummer . . . 1904
,, Sh— The Tempest, 1893, 1898, 1904
,, Sh— Two gentlemen, 1894
,, *Sh*—] Sh— Show book

Crane (W. W.) Allegory in 'Hamlet' [In 'Poet Lore ']. 1891. 8° BPL

Cranwell (E.) Plays of Sh— printed before 1623, in the Capell collection. Cambridge, 1847. 8° BPL

Craven (Hawes) *Artist*—
See Sh— Hamlet, 1897
,, Sh— Romeo . . . 1895

Crawford *Publisher*. *See Sh*—] Fraser & Crawford

Crawford (C.) Collectanea. Stratford-on-Avon, 1906. Cr. 8° BPL

Crawfurd (O.) ' King Henry IV., Part I.' [In ' English comic dramatists ']. New York, 1884. 12° BPL

Crawley (H. Howard) *Editor*—
See Sh— Taming . . . 1891
,, Sh— Twelfth night, 1889, 1891
,, Sh— Works, 1886-91

Creahan (J.) Life of Laura Keene. *See* Keene
'Cream Curdle' *pseud*. *See* Brown (I.)

Creech (W.) *Edinburgh Publisher*—
See Richardson
,, Sh— Works, 1795

Creede (Thomas) *Printer*—
See Greene
,, Selimus
,, Sh— King Henry V., 1598, 1600, 1602
,, Sh— King Henry VI., ii., 1594
,, Sh— King Richard III., 1594, 1598, 1602, 1605, 1612
,, Sh— Locrine, 1595
,, Sh— Merry wives, 1630
,, Sh— Romeo . . . 1599
,, Spenser

Creighton M.D. (Charles) Falstaff's deathbed [In ' Blackwood's Magazine']. 1889. 8°
BPL

Creighton *M.D*. (Charles) Sh—'s story of his life. *See* Sh—

Creighton (C.) Stopes (*Mrs.*) Reynolds (E. Lionel) Hughes (Charles) ' Willobie his avisa ' [written by Lord Southampton ?], [In 'Athenæum,' No. 4053, p. 19, No. 4054, p. 49]. 1906 BM | BPL

Creighton *Bp*. (Mandell) Age of Elizabeth. Ln : Longmans, 1882. 12°, pp. xx.-236, and maps
Sh—, pp. 214-218.

Cresswell (P. T.) *Editor*. *See* Sh— Midsummer N. D., 1906

Creswick (W.) *Editor*. *See* Sh— Macbeth, 1874

Crime and criminology. *See* Goll

Crimes and remarkable trials in Scotland . . . Incidents of the earlier reigns . . . Inquiry into the character of Macbeth [In ' Blackwood's Magazine,' Mar.]. Edin., 1848. 8° BUS

Criswell (R. W.) The new Sh—, and other travesties. New York : American News Co., 1882. 8°, pp. 162 BM | BPL | SML

Critical and historical programme of the madrigals, glees, and songs to be given at the second annual musical entertainment at University College, London, 9th May. 1884. 8°, pp. 24 MPL

Critical essays of the seventeenth century. 1909. 3 vols. Cr. 8° BPL
Includes Collier's ' Short view of the stage,' 1698, and Dennis' ' Impartial critic,' 1693.

Critical examination of the performances of . . . Kean and Macready in Cibber's alteration of ' King Richard III.' Ln : Simpkin, 1819. 8°, pp. iv.-40 BUS

Critical reflections on old English dramatic writers. Ln : 1761. 8°

Croft (John)] Annotations on plays of Sh— [as edited by Johnson and Steevens]. York, 1810. 8° BM | BPL | W
] Select collection of the beauties of Sh—. *See* Sh— Works : Ext. 1792

Crofts (Thomas) Library. *See* Catalogue, 1783

Croker (Thomas Crofton) New readings of Sh—'s ' Tempest.' [c. 1850.] 12°
Original notes and a theory respecting . . . 'The Tempest.' Original holograph manuscript on seven leaves of paper. [1850.] 8° W
] Remarks on an article inserted in the papers of the Sh— Soc. on Massinger's ' Beleeve as you list.' Privately printed [1849 ?]. 8° BPI | W

Walk from London to Fulham. Illustrated by F. W. Fairholt. 1860. 8° BUS | CPL
Contains 'Sh—'s visit to the "Golden Lion Inn," Fulham, in 1595-96,' p. 182.

Croker (Thomas Crofton) *Editor*. *See* Sh— The Tempest, 1845

Croker (W.) Familiar epistles written in 1804 to F. Jones of the Dublin Theatre. Ln: Livermore, 1804. 12°   SML

Cromwell (Henry) Speech in the House. Ln: Printed anno dom. 1659. Fcp. 4°
On p. 5 (referring to 'As you like it') says: 'The players have a play where they bring in a tinker and make him believe himself a lord, and when they have satisfied their humour they make him a plain tinker again. Gentlemen, but that this was a great while agoe, I should have thought this play had been made of me, for if ever two cases were alike 'tis the tinker's and mine.' The writer was Oliver Cromwell's son.

Crook (C. W.) *Editor*—
   See Sh— Hamlet, 1908
    ,, Sh— King Henry V., 1903
    ,, Sh— King Lear, 1907
    ,, Sh— King Richard II., 1903
    ,, Sh— Macbeth, 1906
    ,, Sh— Merchant . . . 1907
    ,, Sh— Midsummer N. D., 1906
    ,, Sh— The Tempest, 1906

Crooke (Andrew) *Publisher*—
   See Chamberlaine   *See* Hermeticall . . .
    ,, Corbet   ,, Shirley

Crooke (John) *Publisher*. *See* Shirley

Crooke (Wm.) *Publisher*—
   See Scarron
    ,, Webster

Crosby (B.) Pocket companion to the play-houses, being the lives of all the principal London performers . . . to which are subjoined particulars of the life of Mr. Dibdin. Ln: B. Crosby, 4 Stationer's Hall Court, 1796. 12°, pp. xii.-106, and portrait of R. B. Sheridan   W
Remarkable for the unrestrained descriptions of its subjects' vices and failings.

Crosby (Ernest Howard) Sh—'s attitude to-wards the working classes. Syracuse, New York [c. 1900]. 8°, pp. 32   BPL | BUS
Reprinted in 'Tolstoy on Sh—,' 1907.

Crosby (J.) Introduction. *See* Leighton Library. *See* Catalogue, 1886

Crosby & Ainsworth *Boston* [*U.S.*] *Publishers.*
   See Sh—] Julius Cæsar, 1867

Cross *Engraver*—
   See Buck (G.)
    ,, Comenius

Cross *pseud.* (L.) Lorenzo of the 'Merchant of Venice'; his character. A phantasie. 1885. 8°   BM | BLP

Cross lights . . . [containing . . . 'Sh— on the stage']. Ln: 1888. 8°   BUS

Crotch (W. Duppa) Double acrostics from Sh—. *See* Sh— Works: Ext. 1875

Crouch *or* Crowch (H.) Love's court of con-science. 1637. *See* Reprints
Welch traveller [a poem], 1671. Ed. by J. O. Halliwell. 1860. 8°   BPL

Crowder (J.) *Printer*. *See* Sh— Works: Ext. 1800

Crowder (R.) *Printer*. *See* Sh— Works, 1772

Crowder (S.) *Publisher*—
   See Sh— Hamlet, 1767
    ,, Sh— King Henry VIII., 1762
    ,, Sh— Macbeth, 1770
    ,, Sh— Merchant . . . 1783
    ,, Sh— The Tempest, 1761
    ,, Sh— Timon . . . 1770
    ,, Sh— Works, 1773

Crowder & Co. (S.) *Publishers. See* Sh— Works, 1762

Crowe (Wm.) *Editor. See* Sh— Hamlet, 1819

Crown garland of golden roses gathered out of England's royal garden. Set forth in many pleasant new songs and sonnets, with new additions never before im-printed. Ln: J. M—— for W. & T. Thackeray at the sign of 'The Angel' in Duck Lane, near West Smithfield, 1662. 8°
Includes 'King Cophetua and the beggar maid,' the famous ballad quoted in 'Romeo and Juliet,' 'King Henry IV.,' Part ii., and 'Love's labours lost.'
It was reprinted by J. O. Halliwell in 1842.

Crowne (John) Misery of civil war. *See* Sh— King Henry VI., ii., 1680, 1681
Thyestes. A tragedy. Ln: R. Bently & M. Magnes, 1681. Fcp. 4°
'The world will ask, in scorn of your dispraise,
Where was your wit, sirs, before Sh—'s days?
No matter where, we'll say y'have excellent sence
If you will please to let us get your pence.'
          —*Prologue.*

Crowne (John) *Editor. See* Sh— Works, 1908

Cruikshank (George) Discovery concerning ghoets. Ln: 1863. 8°   BPL
Criticises the ghost in 'Hamlet.'

Cruikshank (George) *Artist*—
   See 'Actor'
    ,, British stage
    ,, Brough
    ,, Cooke
    ,, Elliston
    ,, Grimaldi
    ,, Scott (*Sir* W.)
    ,, Sh— As you like it, 1807
    ,, Sh— Romeo . . . 1823
    ,, Sh— Works, 1873-75, 1879
    ,, *Sh*—] Sh— Show book
    ,, Wallace

Cruikshank (Isaac) *Artist. See* Kean

Cruikshank (Isaac Robert) *Artist*—
   See British stage
    ,, Mirror . . .
    ,, O'Keeffe
    ,, Sh— Hamlet, 1823, 1829
    ,, Sh— King Henry IV., i., 1850
    ,, Sh— King Richard III., 1829
    ,, Sh— Love's labours lost, 1839
    ,, Sh— Measure . . . 1830
    ,, Sh— Taming . . . 1830, 1838, 1865
    ,, Sh— The Tempest, 1827

Cruikshank (Isaac Robert) *Artist—*
  See Sh— Two gentlemen, 1831
  „ Sh— Troilus . . . 1852
  „ Sh— Works : Ext. 1844
  „ Somerset
Crump (C. D.) *Editor. See* Landor
Crutwell *or* Cruttwell (Richard) *Bath Printer—*
  See Sh— Works, 1807
  „ Sh— Works : Ext. 1778
Crystal Palace : Sh— tercentenary féte, Sat.,
  23 April, 1864. Vocalists : Mdme. Parepa
  and Mr. Cummings. Mr. Hy. Leslie's
  Choir. Conductors : Mr. A. Manns and
  Mr. H. Leslie. Ln : R. K. Burt, Crystal
  Palace Printing Office, 1864. 8°, pp. 12
  BUS
Cuffe (Henry)] Differences of the ages of
  man's life, together with originall causes,
  progresse, and end thereof. By a Fellow
  of Merton College, Oxford. Ln : 1607.
  8°
  The author was implicated in the Essex conspiracy of
  1601.
  Illustrates ' As you like it.'
Culler (The) . . . Glasgow, 1795. 8° BPL
  Parody of Hamlet's soliloquy, p. 144, and other parodies
  of Sh— at p. 208.
Culverwell (R. J.) Pleasant ramble to Coven-
  try, Kenilworth, Warwick, and Stratford
  [In ' Leisure Moments,' pp. 7-21, April].
  1850. Roy. 8°
Cumberland (John) *Publisher—*
  See Sh— All's well, 1811 *et seq.*
  „ Sh— As you like it, 1823
  „ Sh— Comedy of errors, 1829
  „ Sh— Coriolanus, 1824
  „ Sh— Cymbeline, 1823
  „ Sh— Hamlet, 1823, 1829
  „ Sh— Julius Cæsar, 1824, 1830, 1831
  „ Sh— King Henry IV., i., 1825, 1831
  „ Sh— King Henry IV., ii., 1831
  „ Sh— King Henry V., 1825, 1830
  „ Sh— King John, 1829, 1831
  „ Sh— King Lear, 1824, 1828
  „ Sh— King Richard II., 1831
  „ Sh— King Richard III., 1822, 1823,
       1827, 1829
  „ Sh— Love's labours lost, 1839
  „ Sh— Macbeth, 1823, 1829
  „ Sh— Measure . . . 1830
  „ Sh— Merchant . . . 1824, 1831
  „ Sh— Merry wives, 1830
  „ Sh— Midsummer . . . 1816, 1830
  „ Sh— Much ado, 1829, 1831
  „ Sh— Othello, 1829, 1830
  „ Sh— Romeo . . . 1831, 1832
  „ Sh— Taming . . . 1828, 1830
  „ Sh— The Tempest, 1827, 1831
  „ Sh— Timon . . . 1831
  „ Sh— Twelfth night, 1830, 1840
  „ Sh— Two gentlemen, 1831

Cumberland (John) *Publisher—*
  See Sh— Winter's tale, 1823, 1827, 1830
  „ Sh— Works, 1829-31
Cumberland (Richard) British Theatre. *See*
  Sh— Antony, 1848
Delineation of Sh—'s characters of ' Mac-
  beth ' and ' Richard III.' : A parallel
  between him and Æschylus [In ' Ob-
  server ']. Boston, U.S., 1866. 8° BUS
  Extracts. *See* Sh— Works : Ext. 1822
Sh— in the shades. *See* Sh—
The Observer. Ln : Jones, 1822. 12°
  BPL | SML
  Contains several essays on Sh— and the drama.
Cumberland (Richard) *Editor—*
  See Sh— Antony, 1817
  „ Sh— Timon . . . 1771, 1772
Cumberlege (S. A.) *Publisher. See* Sh— Mer-
  chant . . . 1783
Cumming (J.) *Dublin Publisher. See* Sh—
  Works, 1825, 1827
Cundall *Publisher. See* Sh— Poems, 1847
Cundall (Joseph) Annals of the life and work
  of Wm. Sh—. *See* Sh—
Cundell *Editor. See* Sh— Poems, 1808
Cundell (Henry) *Editor—*
  See Sh— Twelfth Night, 1877
  „ Works, 1876-77
Cuningham (Henry) *Editor—*
  See Sh— Comedy of Errors, 1907
  „ Sh— Midsummer N. D., 1905
Cuningham (Hy.) *See also* Littledale
Cunningham. Verses. *See* Vigo
Cunningham (A.) Gallery of pictures. Ln :
  1834. 2 vols. 4° BPL
  Contains Shakespearean plates.
Cunningham (Allan) *Editor. See* Sh— Works,
  1836, 1850, 1852
Cunningham (F. M.) *See* Collis
Cunningham (Peter) Device to entertain Q.
  Elizabeth at Harefield, the house of Sir
  Thomas Egerton, 1602. *See Sh*—] Sh—
  Soc.
  ' The name of Peter Cunningham as forger might be
  appended to the ballad on the " Wreckage of the
  Cockpit Theatre." '—F. G. FLEAY, in ' On certain
  modern Sh—.'
Did General Harrison kill Dick Robinson
  the player ? *See Sh*—] Sh— Soc.
Inigo Jones. *See* Jones
Nell Gwyn and the sayings of Charles II.
  Ln : Bradbury & Evan, 1852. 12° SML
New facts in the life of Thomas Nash, prose
  satirist and poet, contemporary with
  Sh—. *See Sh*—] Sh— Soc.
Plays at Court, 1613. From the accounts
  of Lord Barrington, treasurer of the
  Chamber to James I. *See Sh*—] Sh—
  Soc.
Sir George Buc and the Office of the Revels.
  See Sh—] Sh— Soc.

Cunningham (Peter) Whitefriars Theatre, Salisbury Court Theatre, and the Duke's Theatre in Dorset Gardens. *See Sh*—] Sh— Soc.

Cunningham (Peter) *Editor*—
  See Court revels   *See* Extracts
    ,, Cowley   ,, Jonson (Ben)
    ,, Daniel   ,, Phaer

Cunningham forgeries—
  See Extracts
    ,, Ireland (S. W. H.)

'Cunny-catcher *pseud.* (Cuthbert)' Defence of coney-catching, 1592 ; being a reply . . . to R. Greene on the same subject. Ed. by J. O. Halliwell. Ln : 1859. 16°
Twenty-six copies printed.   BPL | BUS | HCL

Cupid's cabinet unlockt. *See* Sh— Cupid's cabinet

Cupid's revenge [A ballad of the king and the beggar]. Ln : 1565 ? 12°   BPL
'Is there not a ballad, boy, of the "King and the beggar"?'—*Love's labours lost*, I., ii.

Cupid's revenge [A ballad . . .]. Ln : c. 1598. 12°   BPL

Cure for a scold. *See* Sh— Taming . . . 1735, 1738

Curiosities, natural and artificial, of Great Britain. Ln : R. Snagg [c. 1750]. 4 vols. 8°. With numerous copperplates
Warwickshire, Stratford and Sh— occupy pp. 17-38 of vol. iv.

Curious paper of the time of Elizabeth, respecting the Office of the Revels. Edited by J. O. Halliwell. 1872. 8°   BPL

Curling (*Capt.* Henry) Forest youth, or Sh— as he lived. An historical tale. Ln : E. C. Eginton & Co., 1853. 12°, pp. 294 and woodcut   BPL | BUS | CPL | SML
A reprint of the second following under an altered title.

Merry wags of Warwickshire, or the early days of Sh—. A drama. Ln : G. Wright, 1854. 8°, pp. vi.-82   BUS | CPL

Sh— ; the poet, the lover, the actor, the man. A romance. Ln : R. Bentley, 1848. 3 vols. Cr. 8°   BPL | BUS

Wm. Sh— as he lived. An historical tale. Warwick [c. 1893]. Cr. 8°   BPL

Curll (Edmund) Life of Wilks. *See* Wilks

Curll (Edmund) *Publisher*—
  See Sh— Merry wives, 1725
    ,, Sh— Poems, 1710, 1714
    ,, Sh— Taming . . . 1714
    ,, Sh— Venus . . . 1710
    ,, Sh— Works, 1710, 1714

Curschmann (Frederick) *Composer*. *See* Sh— Poems, 1875

Cursory criticisms on . . . Malone's Sh—. *See* Ritson

Cursory remarks on . . . ancient English poets. . . *See* Le Neve

Cursory remarks on tragedy. *See* Richardson

Curtain Theatre—
  See Rainoldes
   ,, Tomlins

Curtis (A. C.) *Guildford Printer*—
  See Sh— Sonnets, 1902

Curtis (Dora) *Artist*—
  See Sh— As you like it, 1903
    ,, Sh— King Henry V., 1904
    ,, Sh— King John, 1905
    ,, Sh— King Richard II., 1903
    ,, Sh— Merchant . . . 1904

Curtis (Jessie Kingsley) 'Hamlet' and the 'Merchant of Venice' [a syllabus]. Albany, U.S., 1893. 8°, pp. 36   BUS
'Macbeth' and 'King Lear' [a syllabus]. Albany, U.S., 1893. 8°, pp. 24   BUS
'Romeo and Juliet' and 'The Tempest' [a syllabus]. Albany, U.S., 1894. 8°, pp. 28   BUS

Cushman (Charlotte) *Actress*. *See* American . .

Cushman.] Clements (*Mrs.* C. E.) Charlotte Cushman. Boston : Osgood, 1882. 8°   SML

Cust (Lionel) Portraits of Sh—. *See* Sh—

Customs. *See* Manners and customs

Cuthbertson (Evan J.) Wm. Sh—. *See* Sh—

Cuthell (J.) *Publisher*. *See* Sh— Works, 1798

Cutter (C. A.) Arrangement and notation of Shaksperiana [In 'Library Journal']. New York, 1884. 8°   BPL

Cyclopædias. *See* Sh—] Sh— glossaries

Cymbeline. *See* Sh— Cymbeline

—— (A. F.) *Editor*. *See* Houssaye

D—— (J. W.) Memoir of Lamb. *See* Sh—Works : Ext. 1844

D—— (Q.) *Editor*. *See* Sh— Works, 1866-67

D—— (R.) *Editor*. *See* Des Periers

D—— (R. O.) *See* Shirley

D—— (T.) *See* Deloney (Thomas)

D—— (T. C.) Familiar epistles to Frederick J——s on the state of the Irish stage. Dublin : Barlow, 1804. 8°   SML

D—— (W. G.) *See* Dix (W. G.)

Daborne (Robert) Verses. *See* Brooke (C.)

Dale (Robert William) Genius the gift of God : A sermon on the tercentenary . . . Ln : Hamilton, 1864. 8°, pp. 20
    BM | BPL | BUS | CPL

Dalgleish (*Dr.* Walter Scott) Great authors, from Chaucer to Pope . . . Ln : Nelson, 1896. Cr. 8°, pp. 272. Illust.
Sh—, pp. 46-96.

Dalgleish (*Dr.* Walter Scott) Great speeches from Sh—'s plays. With life of Sh—. *See* Sh— Works: Ext. 1891

Sh— for schools. *See* Sh— Works: Ext. 1871

Sh— reader. *See* Sh— Works: Ext. 1871, 1873

Dalgleish (W. S.) *Editor*—
 See Sh— Hamlet, 1871
 „ Sh— Macbeth, 1862, 1864

Dall (*Mrs.* Caroline W. H.) Romance of the Association [Shakespeariana pp. 3-9]. Cambridge [U.S.], 1875. 12° BPL
What we really know about Sh—. *See* Sh—

Dallas (D. C.) *Editor, Engraver, & Printer*—
 See Sh— Merry wives, 1894
 „ Sh— The Tempest, 1893, 1895
 „ Sh— Two gentlemen, 1894
 „ Sh— Works, 1895

Daly (Augustin) Woffington. *See* Woffington

Daly (Augustin) *Editor & Manager*—
 See Sh— Love's labours lost, 1891
 „ Sh— Merchant ... 1898
 „ Sh— Merry wives, 1886
 „ Sh— Midsummer ... 1888
 „ Sh— Much ado, 1897
 „ Sh— Taming ... 1887, 1888, 1900
 „ Sh— The Tempest, 1897
 „ Sh— Twelfth night, 1893
 „ Sh— Two gentlemen, 1895

Daly (Charles) *Publisher*—
 See Sh— Poems, 1841, 1850
 „ Sh— Works, 1836, 1838, 1850, 1852

Daly *Judge* (Charles P.) Letter to J. H. Hackett [on Hackett's ' Notes and Comments . . .']. 24 Feb., 1863. MS. transcript. 4°, pp. 24 BUS
 See also Sh—] Monument

Daly (F.) Henry Irving. *See* Irving (*Sir* J. H. B.)

Dambeck (Johann Heinrich) *Editor*—
 See Sh— Poems, 1856
 „ Sh— Venus ... 1856

Damm (H. C.) *Editor. See* Taming ... 1886

Dampier (Alfred) *Editor. See* Sh— King Richard III., 1879

Dana (R. H.) Kean's acting. *See* Kean

Dance (James) *Editor. See* Sh— Timon ... 1768, 1780

Dance *Artist. See* Sh— Works, 1773-74

Dancing—
 See Davies (*Sir* John) *See* Music ...
 „ Grove „ Scott
 „ Morris ...

Dancing devils, or the roaring dragon : A dumb farce. As it was lately acted at both houses, but particularly at one, with unaccountable success. [By Thomas D'Urfey ?]

' *Pray tell me whether, in a vicious age,*
 The stage corrupts the town, or town the stage,
 For both concur when folly makes its way,
 And where the fault begins 'tis hard to say.'
Ln : A. Bettesworth, 1724. 8°, pp. 70
At p. 8 occur these lines:—
 ' Here Sh— to Elizion fled,
 And o "rare Ben" should live tho' dead,
 That their inimitable plays
 In others might a genius raise
 And teach 'em to deserve the bays.'

Dandridge (B.) *Artist. See* Sh— King Lear, 1723

Daniel (George) Collection of engravings, letters, and newspaper cuttings relating to the Sh— Jubilee of 1769. Ln : 1768-69. 4° BM
 Library. *See* Catalogue, 1864

] On the second centenary of the death of Sh— [Broadside poem]. 1816. 8° BPL

Particulars of the sale of Sh—'s house and a variety of interesting and recondite lore relative to Sh—, his family, and his fellows, very curiously and copiously illustrated [Collection of newspaper cuttings, engravings, etc., with MS. title]. 1820, etc. F° BM

Poems. Vindication of poesie. Ed. by Dr. A. B. Grosart. Privately printed, 1878. 4 vols.
At pp. 28-29, vol. i., are these lines :—
 ' The sweetest swan of Avon to ye fair
 And cruel Delia passionately sings,
 Other men's weaknesses and follies are
 Honor and wit to him ; each accent brings
 A sprig to crown him poet, and contrive
 A monument, in his own work, to live.'

Daniel (George) *Editor*—
 See O'Keeffe
 „ Sh— All's well, 1828
 „ Sh— As you like it, 1823
 „ Sh— Comedy of errors, 1829
 „ Sh— Coriolanus, 1824
 „ Sh— Cymbeline, 1823
 „ Sh— Hamlet, 1823, 1829
 „ Sh— Julius Cæsar, 1824, 1830
 „ Sh— King Henry IV., i., 1823, 1831, 1850
 „ Sh— King Henry IV., ii., 1831
 „ Sh— King Henry V., 1825, 1830
 „ Sh— King Henry VIII., 1824, 1830
 „ Sh— King John, 1819, 1829, 1831
 „ Sh— King Lear, 1824, 1830
 „ Sh— King Richard II., 1831
 „ Sh— King Richard III., 1823, 1829
 „ Sh— Love's labours lost, 1839
 „ Sh— Macbeth, 1829, 1864
 „ Sh— Measure ... 1830
 „ Sh— Merchant ... 1824
 „ Sh— Merry wives, 1824, 1830
 „ Sh— Midsummer ... 1828, 1830
 „ Sh— Much ado, 1829, 1831
 „ Sh— Othello, 1819, 1823, 1829, 1838
 „ Sh— Romeo ... 1823, 1831

Daniel (George) *Editor*—
See Sh— Taming ... 1828, 1830
  ,,   Sh— The Tempest, 1827, 1831
  ,,   Sh— Timon ... 1831
  ,,   Sh— Troilus ... 1852
  ,,   Sh— Twelfth night, 1824, 1830
  ,,   Sh— Two Gentlemen, 1831
  ,,   Sh— Winter's tale, 1823, 1830, 1850, 1879
  ,,   Sh— Works, 1829-31
  ,,   Somerset
See also Moncrieff
Daniel (Peter Augustine) 'Locrine' and 'Selimus' [by Robert Greene]. [In 'Athenæum,' No. 3677, p. 512, April]. 1898. 4°
Notes and conjectural emendations. *See* Sh— Works: Ext. 1870
On Halpin's Time analysis of the 'Merchant of Venice.' Ln: New Sh— Soc., 1877-79. 8°
See Sh— Romeo [1597] 1874, [1599] 1874, [1599] 1875
Time analysis of the plots of Sh—'s plays. Ln: New Sh— Soc., 1879. 8°   BUS
Daniel (P. A.) *Editor*—
See Bandello
  ,,   Painter
  ,,   Sh— King Henry V., 1877, 1887
  ,,   Sh— King Lear, 1885
  ,,   Sh— King Richard II., 1887, 1890
  ,,   Sh— King Richard III., 1886, 1888,1889
  ,,   Sh— Merry wives, 1881
  ,,   Sh— Much ado, 1886
Daniel (R.) *Cambridge Publisher. See* Butler
Daniel (Samuel) Civile wars between the two houses of Lancaster and Yorke. Ln: 1595. Fcp. 4°   BUS
Illustrates 'King Henry VI.'
Vision of the twelve goddesses, 1604. A royall masque. Ed. by Law. 1880. 8°   BPL
Will of Samuel Daniel the poet, Sh—'s rival and contemporary. Ed. by P. Cunningham. *See* Sh—] Sh— Soc.
See also Levi
Daniel (Samuel) *Editor. See* Jovius
Danish tragedy. *See* Chettle
Dante Alighieri—
See Bosanquet
  ,,   *Sh*—] Downes
Danter (John) *Printer*—
See Orlando
  ,,   Peele
  ,,   Sh— Romeo ... 1597
  ,,   Sh— Titus ... 1594
Darby (John) *Printer & Publisher*—
See Sh— Hamlet, 1723
  ,,   Sh— Julius Cæsar, 1729
  ,,   Sh— King Lear, 1723

Darby (John) *Printer & Publisher*—
See Sh— Macbeth, 1729
  ,,   Sh— Othello, 1724
  ,,   Sh— Poems, 1714, 1725, 1728
  ,,   Sh— Venus ... 1725
  ,,   Sh— Works, 1714, 1725, 1728
Darbyshire (Alfred) Address on stage representation of Sh— at the Arts Club. Manchester: Privately printed, 1896. 8°   BPL
An architect's experiences. Manchester, 1897. 8°   BPL
References to Sh—.
Art of the Victorian stage: Notes and recollections. 1907. 8°   BPL
Notes on heraldry. *See* Sh— King Henry V., 1880
Darbyshire (A.) *Editor. See* Sh— King Henry V., 1872, 1875
Dare (Josiah)] Counsellor Manners; his last legacy to his son ... enriched and embellished with grave adviso's, pat histories, ingenious proverbs, apologues, and apophthegms. Ln: 1673. 8°
At p. 89 is a curious note upon Nathaniel Field, the colleague of Sh—: 'And be not of Nat. Feeld the player's humour, who vowed that if the old woman that crawled upon her tail at Holborn Bridge had a thousand pounds for her portion he would marry her and adorn her breech with a French velvet hood.'
] Counsellor Manners ... Ln: 1699. 8°   w
Darley (F. O. C.) *Artist. See* Sh— Works, 1888, 1896
Darlington (John) Shakespearean vademecum. *See* Sh— Works: Ext. 1890
Darmesteter (James) Sh—. *See* Sh—
Darmesteter (J.) *Editor. See* Sh— Macbeth, 1881, 1887
Darnton (S.) *Publisher. See* Sh— Works, 1753
Dar's de money [Desdemona]. *See* Sh— Othello, 1870
Daryus. *See* King Darius
'Daven (W.)' *pseud. See* Davenport (Robert)
Davenant (John) Last will and testament of John Davenant, vintner, of the Crown Tavern, Oxford, the house at which Sh— lodged in some of his journeys between Stratford-on-Avon and London. Ed. by J. O. Halliwell. Ln: 1866. 12°, pp. 20
Issue restricted to ten copies.   BPL | BUS | MPL
Davenant (*Mrs.* John). *See* Select beauties
Davenant (*Sir* William) Law against lovers—
See Sh— Measure ... 1673, 1874
  ,,   Sh— Much ado, 1673
Lisander.] Tragi-comical history of our times under the borrowed names of Lisander and Calista. Ln: Printed by R. Y—— for G. Lathum at the Bishop's Head in Paule's Churchyard, 1635. F°, pp. iv.-248
In prose and verse. The dedication signed W. D. Partly founded on a 'Midsummer Night's Dream.'

Davenant (*Sir* William) Love and honour. *See* Sh— Twelfth night, 1720

Madagascar; with other poems . . . Ln: Printed by J. Haviland for T. Walkly, 1638. 12°   BUS | W
On p. 37 is the poem, 'In remembrance of Master Wm. Sh—.'
Reprinted several times.

The rivals. *See* Sh— Two noble kinsmen, 1668

Works. Now published out of the author's originall copies. 1673. F°   BPL

Davenant (*Sir* W.) *Editor*—
See Sh— Julius Cæsar, 1719
  ,, Sh— Macbeth, 1673, 1674, 1687, 1689, 1695, 1710
  ,, Sh— Much ado, 1874
  ,, Sh— The Tempest, 1669, 1670, 1674, 1676, 1690, 1695, 1701, 1710, 1720, 1806, 1808, 1811, 1815, 1874
  ,, Sh— Works, 1908

Davenant (*Sir* Wm.)—
See also James I.
  ,, ,, Mercurius . . .

Davenant family. *See* Fletcher

Davenport *Vicar of Stratford* (James) Correspondence. *See* Malone

Davenport (Robert) King John and Matilda. *See* Sh— King John, 1655

Davenport (S.) *Engraver. See* Sh— Works, 1827

Davey (Henry) Life of Sh—. *See* Sh— Works, 1904-06
Memoir of Sh—. *See* Sh—

Davey (S.) Fools, jesters, and comic characters in Sh— [In 'Trans. of Roy. Soc. of Literature,' 2nd Ser., Vol. 23, pp. 129-190]. Ln: 1902. 8°   BPL

] Great Shaksperian forgeries [In 'The Archivist']. 1888. 8°   BPL

On Sh—'s English historical plays [In 'Trans. of Roy. Soc. of Literature,' 2nd Ser., Vol. 24, pp. 163-199]. Ln: 1903. 8°   BPL

Davidson (G. H.) *Publisher*—
See Sh— Julius Cæsar, 1825
  ,, Sh— King Henry VI., iii., 1830
  ,, Sh— King Lear, 1831
  ,, Sh— Macbeth, 1827
  ,, Sh— Merchant . . . 1823, 1830
  ,, Sh— Merry wives, 1824
  ,, Sh— Troilus . . . 1852
  ,, Sh— Twelfth night, 1825

Davidson (J.) A rosary. Ln: Richards, 1903. Fcp. 4°, pp. 220   BPL
Sh—, pp. 2-5, and Sh—'s flower, p. 192.

Davidson (J.) *Editor. See* Sh— Sonnets, 1908

Davidson (T.) Was it Bacon or Sh— ? [In 'New York World ']. 1887. F°   BPL

Davidson (T.) *Publisher. See* Sh— Poems, 1760

Davies (Acton) Maude Adams. *See* Adams

Davies *of Hereford* (John) Civile warres of death and fortune. Ln: 1603
In the margin against the line referring to players, 'Some followed her by acting all men's parts,' are the initials W. S. and R. B., doubtless intended for Sh— and Burbage.

Microcosmos: Discovery of the little world, with the government thereof. Oxford, 1603. Fcp. 4°   BUS
In the margin against the line, 'Players, I love yee,' are the initials W. S. and R. B., probably intended for Sh— and Burbage.
The full reference is so interesting as to bear repeating here :—
'Players, I love yee and your quality
As ye are men—that pastime not abused ;
And some I love for painting, poesy ;
And say fell fortune cannot be excused
That hath for better uses you refused.
Wit, courage, good shape, good parts, and all good
(As long as all these goods are no worse used) ;
And though the stage doth stain pure gentle blood,
Yet generous ye are in mind and mood.'

] Scovrge for paper-persecvtors, or paper's complaint, compil'd in rvthfull rimes against the paper-spoylers of these times. By J. D——. With a continved inqvisition against paper persecutors. By A. H——. Ln: Printed for H. H—— [Hy. Holland ?] and G. G—— [George Gibbs], 1624. Fcp. 4°   BLO | W
Alludes on p. 3 to 'Venus and Adonis':—
'Making lewd Venus, with eternal lines
To tye Adonis to her love's designs.'

] Scourge for paper persecutors . . . Ln: 1625. Fcp. 4°   BLO

Scourge of folly, consisting of satyricall epigramms. Ln: 1611. Fcp. 4°
Has the lines: 'To our English Terence, Mr. Will. Sh—':
'Some say, good Will, which I in sport do sing,
Hadst thou not play'd some kingly parts in sport
Thou hadst been a companion for a king
And been a king among the meaner sort.
Some others rail, but rail as they think fit,
Thou hast no railing but a reigning wit,
And honesty thou sow'st which they do reap
So to increase their stock which they do keep.'

Davies *Attorney General* (*Sir* John) Discoverie of the trve cavses why Ireland was neuer entirely subdued, nor brought vnder obedience of the crowne of England, vntill the beginning of his majesties happie raigne. [Ln:] Printed [by Wm. Iaggard] for Iohn Iaggard dwelling within Temple Bar at the signe of the Hand and Star, 1612. Fcp. 4°, pp. iv.-288
A second edition appeared in 1613.
Illustrates 'King Henry V.'; 'King Henry VI.,' ii. ; 'King Henry VIII.'; 'King Richard II.'

Davies *Attorney General* (*Sir* John) Nosce teipsum : This oracle expounded in two elegies ;—Of human knowledge. Of the soule of man . . . Hymnes of Astræa . . . Orchestra or a poeme of dauncing . . . Ln : 1622. 8°

A portion of ' Orchestra' is reprinted in Dr. Furness' variorum ' Romeo and Juliet.'

Nosce teipsum. *See also* Capell

Davies (Maurice) Sh—'s heroines [In ' New Monthly Magazine']. Ln : 1874. 8° BUS

Davies (R. S.) *Editor. See* Sh— Merchant, 1879

Davies *Actor & Publisher* (Thomas) Dramatic miscellanies : Consisting of critical observations on several plays of Sh. With a review of his principal characters and those of various eminent writers as represented by Mr. Garrick and other celebrated comedians. With anecdotes of dramatic poets, actors, etc. . . . Ln : Printed for the author and sold at his shop in Great Russell Street, Covent Garden, 1783-84. 3 vols. 8°. With portrait of Betterton
BM | BPL | BUS | MPL | W

Dramatic miscellanies . . . Dublin : S. Price, H. Whitestone, and others, 1784. 3 vols. 8°

Dramatic miscellanies . . . Ln : Printed for the author, 1784. 3 vols. 8°

Dramatic miscellanies. Ln : Printed for the author, 1785. 2 vols. 8°. With portrait BUS

Essay on ' Hamlet.' *See* Pilon
Memoirs of Garrick. *See* Garrick

Davies (Thomas) *Actor, Editor, & Publisher—*
See Downes
,, Lloyd
,, Miscellaneous . . .
,, Morgann
,, Sh— Macbeth, 1770
,, Sh— Timon . . . 1770
,, Sh— Works, 1773
,, Sh— Works : Ext. 1738
. Victor
,, Warner

Davies (W.) *Publisher—*
See Giraldi
,, Malone

Davis *Philadelphia Publisher. See* Sh— Works, 1824, 1828

Davis (Cushman K.) Law in Sh— . . . Saint Paul [U.S.], 1884. 12° BM

Law in Sh—. Second edition. St. Paul [U.S.], 1884. 12° BPL | BUS

Davis (H.) Sh—'s Sonnets. San Francisco, 1888. 12° BPL

Davis (Latham) Sh—: England's Ulysses. The masque of ' Love's labours won,' or the enacted will . . . dramatized from the Sonnets of 1609 . . . Seaford, Delaware [U.S.], 1905. 8°, pp. 402-xxxiv. BPL

Davis (L.) *Publisher—*
See Sh— King Henry IV., ii., 1766, 1773
,, Sh— Macbeth, 1770
,, Sh— Timon . . . 1770
,, Sh— Works, 1773

Davis (Lucius Clarke) Story of the memorial fountain to Sh— at Stratford-upon-Avon and other gifts of Geo. W. Childs. Cambridge [U.S.]: Privately printed, Riverside Press, 1890. 8° BM | BPL | SML

Davis (S.) *Coventry Printer. See* Logismos

Davis (W.) *Publisher. See* Gildon

Davis (W. J.) Philosophical explanation of Sh—'s ' Hamlet,' with observations on F. V. Hugo's French translation. First delivered at the University of Kiew. Trans. by John Millard. Amsterdam : J. D. Brouwer, 1867. 8° BM | BPL

Token coinage of Warwickshire, with descriptive and historical notes. Birmingham : Hudson, 1895. 4°. 24 plates SML
Includes Sh – tokens.

Davison (T.) *Printer—*
See Sh— Hamlet, 1816
,, Sh— King Henry VIII., 1816
,, Sh— King Richard III., 1816
,, Sh— Merry wives, 1808
,, Sh— Works, 1807

Davison (W.) *Printer. See* Sh— Works, 1807

Davy (John) *Composer. See* Sh— Six madrigals

Dawbarn (C. Y. C.) Bacon-Sh— discussion : Paper read before the Liverpool Philomathic Society. Liverpool : Young, 1903. 8°, pp. 44 BPL

Dawks (J.) *Printer. See* Sh— Troilus . . . 1695

Dawlman (Robert) *Publisher. See* Wright (T.)

Dawson (Benjamin) Sh—'s accentuation of proper nouns. Ln : New Sh— Soc., 1887-92. 8°

Dawson (B.) *Editor—*
See Sh— Coriolanus, 1891, 1907
,, Sh— Julius Cæsar, 1890, 1907
,, Sh— King Henry V., 1888, 1907
,, Sh— King John, 1887, 1907
,, Sh— Works, 1887-89

Dawson (E. A.) Bacon-Sh— controversy. Columbus [U.S.], 1885. 8° BPL | BUS

Dawson (George) Sh—, and other lectures. *See* Sh—
Speeches on Sh—, selected by C. C. Cattell. Birmingham [1878]. Cr. 8° BPL

Dawson (T.) *Publisher—*
See Florio
,, Gosson
,, Wolsey

Day (John) Humour out of breath. A comedy
now first reprinted from the edition of
1608. Ed. by J. O. Halliwell. Ln : 1860.
Cr. 8°
Limited to fifty copies.

Day (W. C.) Behind the footlights, or the
stage as I knew it . . . Ln : Warne, 1885.
8°, pp. viii.-192. Illustrated   BPL | SML
Contains an amusing sketch of Sh—'s last play.

Day & Son *Publishers*. See Much ado, 1864,
1865

Day with Herne the hunter [In ' Dublin
University Magazine ']. 1874. 8°   BPL
Illustrates the ' Merry Wives.'

Dead man's fortune. See Halliwell

Deakin (A.) Sketches in Sh— villages. Birmingham : Midland Educ. Co. [1885 ?].
F°   BPL | SML

Dean (Christopher) *Artist*.   See Sh— Sonnets,
1899

Dean (R. & W.) *Manchester Publishers—*
See Sh— As you like it, 1802
  ,,   Sh— Cymbeline, 1802
  ,,   Sh— Hamlet, 1800, 1801
  ,,   Sh— King Henry VIII., 1801
  ,,   Sh— King Lear, 1800, 1808
  ,,   Sh— King Richard III., 1800
  ,,   Sh— Macbeth, 1800
  ,,   Sh— Measure . . . 1800
  ,,   Sh— Merchant . . . 1800, 1806
  ,,   Sh— Othello, 1802
  ,,   Sh— Romeo . . . 1800, 1806
  ,,   Sh— The Tempest, 1801
  ,,   Sh— Twelfth night, 1803

Deane (John) *Publisher*.   See Armin

Dearborn (G.) *New York Publisher*.   See Sh—
Works, 1834, 1835

Death of King Leir.   See Sh—] Sh—'s Library
A foundation of ' King Lear.'

Debate and stryfe betwene somer and wynter.
Ln : Lawrence Andrew [XVI. Cent.].
Fcp. 4°, pp. 8, black letter   BM
' I cannot help thinking that some dialogue such as
the present one suggested the conclusion of "Love's
labours lost."'—HALLIWELL.

Debate and stryfe betwene somer and wynter ;
a poetical dialogue ; [reprinted] from the
unique copy printed . . . early in the sixteenth century. Ed. by J. O. Halliwell.
[Ln : Privately printed] For the editor,
1860. Fcp. 4°   BPL | BUS | HCL | W
Impression restricted to thirty copies.

Debrett (J.) *Publisher—*
See Ireland (S. W. H.)
  ,,   Sh— All's well, 1793
  ,,   Sh— King Henry V., 1789
  ,,   Sh— Sonnets, 1791
  ,,   Sh— The Tempest, 1789
  ,,   Sh— Works : Ext. 1795
Decameron.   See Boccaccio

Decastro.] Memoirs of J. Decastro, comedian,
edited by Humphreys. 1824. 12°   BPL

De Chatelain (*Le Chevalier*) Le monument
d'un Français a Sh—.   See Sh—
Notre monument.   See Sh—
Shakespearean gems.   See Sh— Works :
Ext. 1868

Dechmann (George) Histrions and the histrionic art. London Publishing Co. [c.
1870]. 8°, pp. 88

Decker *or* Dekker (Thomas) Belman of London, bringing to light the most notorious
villanies that are now practised in the
kingdome . . . Printed at London for
Nathaniell Butter, 1608. Fcp. 4°, black
letter. With woodcut of the Bellman
' Affords a useful note on "King Lear."'—J. P. COL-
LIER.

Decker's dream, in which, being rapt with
a poetical enthusiasm, the great volumes
of heaven and hell were opened to him,
in which he read many wonderful things.
Reprinted from the rare edition of 1620.
Ed. by J. O. Halliwell. Ln : 1860. Fcp.
4°   BPL | BUS
Limited to twenty-six copies.

Honest whore . . . Ln : E. Allde for N.
Butter and N. Okes for Richard Collins,
at his shop under St. Martin's Church,
neere Ludgate, 1630-35. 2 parts. Fcp. 4°
Contains a parody on ' King Richard III.' and allusions
to ' As you like it,' ' Comedy of errors,' and ' Othello.'

Lanthorne and candle-light, or the Bellman's second night's walke, in which he
brings to light a brood of more strange
villanies than euer were till this yeare
discouered. Ln : Printed for John Busby
and are to be solde at his shop in Fleete
Streete, Saint Dunstane's Churchyard,
1609. Fcp. 4°, black letter
References to ' Mad Hamlet,' the stage, actors, etc. on
sig. H 2.

Newes from hell, brought by the divel's
carriers. Ln : 1605. Fcp 4°
Refers to the ' Comedy of errors.'

Pleasant comedie of Old Fortunatus. As it
was plaied before the Queene's Maiestie
this Christmas by the . . . Earl of Not-
tingham . . . his seruants. Ln : Printed by
S. S—— for William Apsley dwelling in
Paule's Churchyard at the sign of the
Tyger's Head, 1600. Fcp. 4°, black letter
Contains five passages illustrative of Sh—.

Satiro-mastix, or untrussing of the humorous poet . . . Ln : E. White, 1602. Fcp.
4°
Refers to Sh— on A 4 verso and on E 3.
Ben Jonson is ridiculed under the name of ' Horace.'

Seven deadly sins of London.   See Reprints
See Cartwright   See Heywood
  ,, Foard   ,, Jonson & Dekker

Decker (T.) Chettle (Hy.) & Haughton (Wm.) [Patient Grissell] Pleasant comodie of Patient Grissell. As it hath beene sundrie times lately plaid by the Right Honorable the Earle of Notingham Lord High Admiral his servants. Ln: 1603. Fcp. 4°, black letter

Patient Grissil. With introd. and notes [by J. P. Collier]. Ln: Sh— Soc., 1841. 8°, pp. xvi.-96　　　　　　BPL | BUS

Decker (T.) & Webster (John) Westward hoe. As it hath beene divers times acted by the children of Paules . . . Printed at London, and are to be sold by Iohn Hodgets dwelling in Paule's Churchyard, 1607. Fcp. 4°
Contains the reference : 'Let these husbands play mad Hamlet and crie revenge.'

Decker (T.) & Wilson (Robert) Shoemaker's holiday, 1600. See 'Dramaticus'

Declaration of practices . . . See Bacon

Dedekind (Frederic)] Schoole of slovenrie, or Cato turn'd wrong side outward. Trans. into English verse. By R. F——, gent. Ln : Printed for Valentine Simmes, 1605. Fcp. 4°
'Containing many passages illustrative of Sh—. Only three copies known to exist.'—J. O. HALLIWELL.

Deeve (John) Publisher. See Sh— King Henry IV., i., 1700

Defence of coney-catching, 1592. See 'Cunny-Catcher'

Defence of dramatick poetry. See Rymer

Defence of Mr. Kenrick's review. See Kenrick

De Flores (Jean). See Aurelio and Isabell

Defoe (Daniel). See Roe

De Hondt (P. A.) Publisher. See Dibdin

Deighton (J.) Publisher. See Sh— Works, 1798, 1811

Deighton (K.) Editor—
See Sh— Antony . . . 1891
„ Sh— As you like it, 1891
„ Sh— Coriolanus, 1894
„ Sh— Cymbeline, 1890
„ Sh— Hamlet, 1891, 1896
„ Sh— Julius Cæsar, 1890
„ Sh— King Henry IV., i., 1893
„ Sh— King Henry IV., ii., 1893
„ Sh— King Henry V., 1880, 1888, 1889, 1895, 1896
„ Sh— King Henry VIII., 1895
„ Sh— King John, 1890, 1896
„ Sh— King Lear, 1891
„ Sh— King Richard II., 1896, 1901, 1903
„ Sh— Macbeth, 1890, 1896, 1901
„ Sh— Merchant . . . 1890, 1895
„ Sh— Midsummer . . . 1891, 1895
„ Sh— Much ado, 1888
„ Sh— Othello, 1890, 1893
„ Sh— Pericles, 1907

Deighton (K.) Editor—
See Sh— Romeo . . . 1893
„ Sh— The Tempest, 1889, 1895
„ Sh— Timon . . . 1905
„ Sh— Troilus . . . 1906
„ Sh— Twelfth night, 1889, 1895
„ Sh— Two gentlemen, 1905
„ Sh— Winter's tale, 1889
„ Sh— Works, 1888

Dekker (Thomas). See Decker

Delagrave (C.) Paris Publisher. See Sh— Macbeth, 1881, 1887

De la Harpe. See Franklin

'De la Mare (W. J.)' pseud. See Ramal

De Lange (J.) Deventer Publisher—
See Hamlet, 1849
„ Sh— Macbeth, 1843

Delaplaine (J.) Philadelphia Publisher. See Sh— Works, 1813

Delights of the muses, being a collection of poems. Ln: 1738. 12°　　　　BUS
Contains poem, 'To the ladies of Sh—'s club.'

Delius (Dr. Nicolaus) Sh—'s use of narration in his dramas. Englisht by E. Gordon & E. Marx. Ln: New Sh— Soc., 1875-76. 8° BUS

The quarto and folio of 'King Lear' [Trans. by Eva G. Gordon]. Ln : New Sh— Soc., 1875-76. 8°　　　　BUS

Delius (Dr. N.) Editor—
See Sh— Arden . . . 1855
„ Sh— Birth . . . 1856
„ Sh— Fair Em, 1874
„ Sh— King Edward III., 1854
„ Sh— Macbeth, 1841
„ Sh— Mucedorus, 1874
„ Sh— Two Gentlemen, 1858
„ Sh— Works, 1854, 1854-61, 1854-74, 1876, 1877, 1880, 1880-84, 1882, 1882-83, 1883, 1883-84, 1886, 1891, 1894-96, 1896, 1897, 1898, 1901, 1903

Deloney or Delone (Thomas)] Historie of the gentle craft. By T. D—— [Excerpt of signatures H and I containing the 'History of Tom Drum']. Ln : 1598. Fcp. 4°, black letter　　　　　　　W
A curious history, believed to be alluded to in 'All's well.'
'This extract is taken from one of the two copies known of the first edition of 1598.'—J. O. HALLIWELL.

History of John Winchcomb, usually called Jack of Newbury, the famous clothier . . . 1597. Ed. by J. O. Halliwell. Ln : 1859. Fcp. 4°　　　　　　BPL | BUS | HCL
Limited to twenty-six copies.
Illustrative of old manners and customs.

Three old ballads on the overthrow of the Spanish Armada, written 1588. Now first reprinted from black letter copies supposed to be unique. Ed. by J. O. Halliwell. Ln : 1860. 12° BPL | BUS | HCL
Limited to thirty copies.
Believed to be among the earliest productions of this prolific writer.

De Loyer (Peter) Treatise of specters or straunge sights . . . Ln : 1605. 8°
Dr. Farmer declared this to be the identical work which supplied Sh— with the information put into Shylock's mouth, commencing :—
'Some love not a gaping pig . . .'

Demmon (Isaac N.) Catalogue of the Shakespearian books and pamphlets in the Crosby Library, Zanesville, Ohio. Ann Arbor, Michigan, 1885. Roy. 8°, pp. 92
Limited to 100 copies.

Sh— course : References for students. 1882. 12°   BPL

'Democritus' *pseud.* *See* Ellis (*Dr.* H.)

'Democritus junior' *pseud.* *See* Versatile . . .

Demonology. *See* Superstition

Denham-(Hy.) *Printer & Publisher—*
See Baret   *See* Scot
,,   Painter   ,,   Turberville
,,   Salvianus

Denison (Henry) *Editor.* *See* Sh— Julius Cæsar, 1856, 1869

Denman (J.) The drama vindicated. Cambridge : Smith, 1835. 12°   BPL | SML

Denney (*Prof.* E. E.) *Editor—*
See Sh— Julius Cæsar, 1900
,,   Sh— King Richard III., 1902

Dennie (Joseph) *Editor.* *See* Sh— Works, 1805-09, 1809

Dennis (J.) The English sonnet [In ' Studies in English Literature,' pp. 392-444]. 1883. 12°   BPL

Dennis (J.) *Editor—*
See Sh— All's well, 1902
,,   Sh— As you like it, 1899
,,   Sh— Comedy of errors, 1902
,,   Sh— Coriolanus, 1900
,,   Sh— Cymbeline, 1901
,,   Sh— Hamlet, 1899
,,   Sh— Julius Cæsar, 1900
,,   Sh— King Henry IV., i., 1901
,,   Sh— King Henry IV., ii., 1901
,,   Sh— King Henry V., 1901
,,   Sh— King Henry VI., i., 1901
,,   Sh— King Henry VI., ii., 1902
,,   Sh— King Henry VI., iii., 1902
,,   Sh— King Henry VIII., 1902
,,   Sh— King John, 1900
,,   Sh— King Lear, 1900
,,   Sh— King Richard II., 1900
,,   Sh— King Richard III., 1902
,,   Sh— Love's labours lost, 1901
,,   Sh— Macbeth, 1899
,,   Sh— Measure . . . 1901
,,   Sh— Merchant . . . 1899, 1904
,,   Sh— Midsummer . . . 1900
,,   Sh— Othello, 1899
,,   Sh— Pericles, 1902
,,   Sh— Poems, 1902
,,   Sh— Romeo . . . 1899

Dennis (J.) *Editor—*
See Sh— Sonnets, 1902
,,   Sh— Taming . . . 1902
,,   Sh— The Tempest, 1899
,,   Sh— Timon . . . 1902
,,   Sh— Titus . . . 1902
,,   Sh— Troilus . . . 1902
,,   Sh— Twelfth night, 1900
,,   Sh— Two gentlemen, 1900
,,   Sh— Winter's tale, 1899
,,   Sh— Works, 1899-1902

Dennis (John) Causes of the decay and defects of dramatic poetry, and of the degeneracy of the publick taste. [Author's holograph unpublished MS. on thirty-seven leaves of paper, c. 1700.] F°   w
Contains many references to Sh— and other playwrights.

Comical gallant. *See* Sh— Merry wives, 1702

Essay on the genius and writings of Sh—. *See* Sh—

Heroes of literature. *See* Sh—

Impartial critick ; or, some observations upon a late book, entituled, a short view of tragedy, written by Mr. Rymer. Ln : 1692. Fcp. 4°   w
In the ' Letter to a friend,' which serves for a preface, the writer declares that the parts of his work concerning Waller ' are not written of malice or vanity or to attack Waller, so much as to vindicate Sh—.'

Impartial critick . . . Second edition. Ln : 1693. 8°   BPL

Impartial critick . . . Third edition. Ln : 1697. Fcp. 4°

Invader of his country. 1720

Letters upon several occasions : Written by and between Dryden, Wycherly, [Moyle], Congreve, and Dennis . . . Ln : 1696. 8°   w
Contains references to Rymer's Sh— criticisms.

On the genius of Sh—. *See* Eighteenth . . .

Usefulness of the stage, to the happiness of mankind, to government, and to religion. Occasioned by a late book written by [Bishop] Jeremy Collier. Ln : Parker, 1698. 8°   SML | W
Mentioning the first establishment of the drama in England [p. 40], Dennis speaks of ' so many suns at once appearing. The reader will immediately comprehend that I speak of Spencer, Bacon, and Raleigh, whose like had never been and never would be seen.'
Why Sh— should be ignored is not apparent, in view of the earlier and later writings of Dennis, unless the author's views underwent a temporary change. The omission was probably accidental ; otherwise Dennis might rank as founder of the heretics who promulgate the Bacon-Sh— theory.

Dennis.] Dennis on Sh— [In ' Blackwood's Magazine,' Sept.]. Edin., 1842. 8°
                                        BPL | BUS
A notice of ' Macbeth ' in the style of John Dennis.

Dennis.] Life of Dennis, the renowned critick, in which are some observations on most of the poets. Not written by Mr. Curll. Ln : 1734. 8°
Includes Sh—.
See Critical essays
  ,, Gildon
Denny (W.) *See* Annalia Dubrensia
Dent (Robert K.)] Catalogue of the Sh— Memorial Library. I., English editions of Sh—'s works ; II., English editions of the separate plays and poems. [Supervised] by J. D. Mullins. Birmingham : Printed by Josiah Allen, 1872-76. 2 vols. 8°, pp. iv., 1-40 and pp. iv., 41-130B
  BPL | BUS | CPL | MPL | SML | W
Though nominally prepared by J. D. Mullins, the real compiler was R. K. Dent.
A few were issued on large paper, royal octavo, of which impression one is at Stratford.
This fine collection of seven thousand volumes was practically annihilated by fire on 11th January, 1879, a fate which almost overtook the Warwick Castle library eight years earlier. With undaunted courage and public spirit the Birmingham Library committee and its officials have gradually replaced their disastrous loss.

] Catalogue of the Sh— Memorial Library, Birmingham. By J. D. Mullins. Birmingham : Printed for the Free Libraries Committee [by J. Allen], 1875. 8°, pp. iv.-344 BPL | BUS | SML
Dent (W.) *Editor*—
See Sh— Coriolanus, 1893
  ,, Sh— Julius Cæsar, 1893
  ,, Sh— Works, 1893
De Perott (Joseph) Probable source of the plot of Sh—'s 'Tempest.' Worcester, U.S. : Clark Univ. Press, 1905. Roy. 8°, pp. xii. (incl. pr. wrappers) BPL | BUS
De Peyster (J. W.) Was THE Sh—, after all, a myth ? New York, 1888. 8°
  BM | BPL | BUS
Depositio Cornuti Typographici. *See* Blades
De Quincey (Thomas) Biographies of Sh—, Pope, etc. *See* Sh—
  Last new life of Sh—. *See* Sh—
  On the knocking at the gate in ' Macbeth ' [In 'London Magazine,' Oct.]. Ln : 1823. 8° BUS
  On the knocking . . . [In ' Miscellaneous Essays']. Boston, U.S., 1851. 8° BUS
  On the knocking . . . [In 'Art of Conversation']. Edin., 1863. 8° BUS
  Sh— ; a biography. *See* Sh—
  Sh— and Wordsworth [In ' Posthumous Works,' Vol. 2, pp. 197-200]. 1893. 12°
  BPL
Derby. *See* Hoskins
Derby (Wm. Stanley *sixth Earl of*)—
  See Greenstreet
  ,, Sh— Titus, 1594

Dering (Edward) Briefe and necessarie catechisme . . . very needfull to be knowne of all housholders . . . Ln : Printed by W. Iaggard, 1614. Fcp. 4°, pp. 32
Contains the remarkable Puritanical invective against literary fiction, and 'the multitude of bookes ful of all sin and abhominations. Our forefathers had their spiritual inchantments in which they were bewitched, as Bevis of Hampton, Guy of Warwick, Arthur of the round table, Huon of Burdaux, Oliver of the Castel, Foure sons of Aymon, and other such childish folly. And yet more vanity than these, the witlesse devices of Gargantua, Howleglasse, Esope, Robin Hood, Adam Bell, Frier Rush, Fooles of Gotham, and a thousand other.'
Dering *or* Deryng *of Surrenden* (*Sir* Edward) *Editor*—
See Marriage
  ,, Sh— King Henry IV., i., 1610
Dermody (Thomas) Sh— and Milton contrasted. [Author's holograph MS. on twenty-nine leaves of paper, c. 1850.] Fcp. 4° W
Derrick. Poems. *See* Poems
Derrick (Samuel)] General view of the stage. By Mr. Wilkes. J. Coote, 1759. 8° W
Derrick officiated as 'master of the ceremonies' at Bath, and adopted the pen name of 'Thomas Wilkes' when publishing the above. It contains references to Sh—.
Desch (Cecil H.) Calderon : the national dramatist of Spain. Stratford-on-Avon, 1899. 8° BPL
  Sh— and the science of his time [Reprinted from 'Stratford Herald']. 1896. Cr. 8°
  BPL
  Sh—'s fairies. 'Sh— Club Paper.' Stratford, 1907. 8°, pp. 8
  Some phases of Shakespearean criticism in France : Sh— Club Paper. Stratford-on-Avon : G. Boyden, 1898. 4°, pp. 20 BPL
Description of Sh—'s cliff . . . Dover : T. Rigden [Sæc. XIX.]. 8°, pp. ii.-8. Illust.
  BUS
Description of . . . Warwickshire. *See* Dowdall
Descriptive account of the . . . gala festival. *See* Jarvis
Desenfans. Letter . . . to Mrs. Montagu. Ln : 1777. 8°
De Serres. *See* Serres
Desfontaines de la Vallée (G. F.) *Editor*. *See* Sh— Othello, 1792
Des Periers (Bonaventure) Mirrour of mirth and pleasant conceits, containing many proper and pleasaunt inventions, for the recreation and delight of many and to the hurt and hinderance of none . . . Englished by R. D——. At Ln : Printed by Roger Ward dwelling a litle aboue Holburne Conduite at the Signe of the Talbot, 1583. Fcp. 4°, black letter, Sig-A—O2 on numbered folios CTC
Supposed to be unique.

(77)

De Stael. *See* Stael-Holstein

Desultory notes on the national drama, by an old playgoer. 1850. 8° BPL

'Detective' *pseud.* Literary cookery, with reference to matter attributed [by J. P. Collier] to Coleridge and Sh—. Ln: 1855. 8° BM

Dethick *herald.* *See* Halliwell

Dethroning Sh—. *See* Theobald

Dethroning Sh—. Who wrote his plays? Cipher by Francis Bacon, etc. [Cuttings from the 'Daily Telegraph,' &c.]. 1887-88. 12° BPL

Devecmon (William C.) In re 'Sh—'s legal acquirements': Notes of an unbeliever therein. Sh— Soc. of New York, 1890. 12°, pp. 54 BPL | BUS

In re Sh—'s legal acquirements. New York, Sh— Press; Ln., Kegan Paul, 1899. Cr. 8°, pp. viii.-52

Non sanz droict [Reviews of Bacon-Sh— literature], [In 'New Shakespeareana,' Vol. I., No. 2, pp. 1-47, Jan.]. New York, 1902. Roy. 8°

Deverell (Robert) Discoveries in hieroglyphics and other antiquities. In treating of which many favourite pieces of Butler, Sh—, and other great writers . . . are put in a light now entirely new, by notes, dissertations, and upwards of two hundred woodcuts. Ln: T. & J. Allman, 1813-16. 6 vols. 8° BM | BPL | BUS

In vol. ii. is the text of 'Hamlet' and 'King Lear,' and in vol. iii. 'Othello' and 'Merchant of Venice,' with curious notes explaining passages by references to the moon.

Deverell (R.) *Editor*—
See Sh— King Lear, 1813, 1816
  „ Sh— Merchant . . . 1813
  „ Sh— Othello, 1813, 1816

Devereux. *See* Essex

Devonshire (Georgiana *Duchess of*). *See* Sheridan

Dewe (Thomas) *Publisher.* *See* Sh— King John, 1622

De Wickedé (C. F.) *Editor.* *See* Sh— Midsummer . . . 1875

De Wint (P.) *Artist.* *See* Jaffray

Dexter (Arthur) Plays and play-acting [In 'Atlantic Monthly,' Sept.]. Boston, U.S., 1862. 8° BUS

d'Hugnes *Editor*—
See Sh— Macbeth, 1883
  „ Sh— Othello, 1884

Dialects—
See Halliwell, Hist. Sketch
  „ Sh— Glossaries
  „ Sherwen

Diary of a lover of Sh—. Written at Sheffield. [Manuscript upon sixteen leaves of paper, with a view of Stratford-upon-Avon inserted.] 1799. Fcp. 4° w

Dibdin (Charles) Complete history of the English stage. Ln. [1795]. 5 vols. 8° BPL

] Jubilee concert, or the Warwickshire lad. Being a collection of songs performed at the jubilee in honour of Sh— at Stratford-upon-Avon. Ln. [1769]. 12°, pp. 8 BM | W

Letter . . . See Bellamy (T.)

Overture, songs, airs, and chorusses in the jubilee or Sh—'s garland, as performed at Stratford-upon-Avon and the theatre, Drury Lane. To which is added a cantata called 'Queen Mab, or the fairies jubilee.' Ln: J. Johnston [1769]. Oblong f°, pp. 40 BPL | BUS

Professional life . . . by himself. Ln: 1803. 4 vols. 8°

With portrait and sixty circular etchings by Miss Dibdin.

Queen Mab. *See* Bickerstaff & Dibdin

] Sh—'s garland, being a collection of new songs, ballads, roundelays, catches, glees, comic-serenatas, etc. performed at the jubilee at Stratford-upon-Avon. The musick by Dr. Arne, Mr. Barthelimon, Mr. Ailwood, and Mr. Dibdin. [First part.] Ln: T. Becket & P. A. De Hondt, 1769. 8°, pp. 28

BM | BPL | BUS | CPL | MPL | SML | W

Sh—'s garland, or the Warwickshire jubilee, being a collection of ballads, catches, and glees as performed in the great booth at Stratford-upon-Avon . . . [Second part.] Ln: John Johnston, 1769. F°, pp. 8. With engr. music BM | BUS | SML | W

] Sh—'s garland. Dedicated to the Shakespearian Club established at the Falcon Inn, the ancient resort of the bard himself in Stratford. Stratford-upon-Avon: J. Ward, 1826. 8°, pp. 16 BUS

] Songs, chorusses, &c. which are introduced in the new entertainment of the jubilee at the Theatre Royal, in Drury Lane. Ln: 1769. 8°

] Songs, chorusses, &c. . . . 1770. 8° BPL
] Songs, chorusses, &c. . . . 1778. 8° BPL
] Songs, chorusses, &c. . . . 1787. 8° BPL

] Songs, chorusses, &c. in the musical afterpiece called 'Garrick's Jubilee, 1769' . . . Revised. 1816. 8° BPL

] Songster's pocket book, or jubilee concert; being a choice collection of the newest and most favourite songs that has [*sic*] been sung at the Stratford jubilee, etc. Ln: 1770. 12° BUS | W

] Warwickshire lad, as perform'd at the Theatre Royal in Drury Lane in the entertainment of the jubilee. With music. [Ln: 1769.] F° broadside BPL | BUS

Dibdin (Charles) 'Would you be taught, ye feathered throng?' Leamington : J. Merridew, c. 1825. Broadside song, with view of Hathaway cottage   BUS
On Anne Hathaway.

Dibdin (C.) *Composer*. *See* Sh— Poems, 1862

Dibdin.] Life of C. Dibdin. *See* Crosby

Dibdin (J. C.) Annals of the Edinburgh stage, with an account of . . . dramatic writing in Scotland. 1888. Fcp. 4°. With portraits and facsimiles   BPL

Dibdin (Thomas) Melodrame mad ! or the siege of Troy. A new comic melange. The situations and sentiments from Mr. Homer, a blind old ballad-singer, and Sh—, a Warwickshire deer-stealer, etc. Ln : 1819. 8°   W

Reminiscences . . . of the Theatres Royal Covent Garden, Drury Lane, Haymarket, and author of ' The Cabinet.' Ln : H. Colburn, 1827. 2 vols. 8°. With portrait   SML
Sh— references, p. 12, etc.
The Index (published afterwards) is rarely found with the work.

Dibdin (Thomas) *Editor*. *See* Sh— Antony, 1818

Dicey (C.) *Publisher*. *See* Sh— Titus . . . 1780

Dick (J.)] Here and there in England, including a pilgrimage to Stratford-upon-Avon. Ln : J. R. Smith, 1871. 12°   BPL | CPL | SML

Dickens (Charles) Memoirs . . . *See* Grimaldi
On Fechter's acting : Followed by critical notices (extracted from London journals) on his 'Hamlet,' 'Othello' . . . Leeds : J. H. Clark [c. 1861]. 12°, pp. 24   BUS

Dickens (Charles)—
See Buchanan
  ,, *Stratford.*] Particulars
  ,, *Stratford.*] Sh—'s birthplace

Dickinson (B.) *Publisher*. *See* Companion . . .

Dicks. British drama. *See* Sh— Antony, 1871

Dicksee (F. B.) *Artist*—
See Sh— Othello, 1890
  ,, Sh— Romeo . . . 1884
  ,, Sh— Works, 1884-92

Dickson (J.) *Edinburgh Publisher*. *See* Sh— Works, 1795

Dictionary of quotations—
See Sh— Works : Ext. 1824, 1835
  ,, *Sh*—] Sh— glossaries
  ,, Walbran

Did Francis Bacon write 'Sh—'? *See* Pott

Did Sh— write Sh—'s plays ? *See* Sh— Works : Ext. 1869

Diderot (Denis) Paradox of acting. Trans. with notes by W. H. Pollard and preface by Hy. Irving. Ln : Chatto, 1883. Cr. 8°

Differences of the ages of man's life . . . *See* Cuffe

Digby mysteries. Ed. by F. J. Furnivall. Ln : New Sh— Soc., 1882. 4°   BPL

Digesta Shakespeareana. *See* Morgan (J. A.)

Digges (L.) Poems. *See* Sh— Poems, 1640
Verses. *See* Sh— Works, 1623, 1632, 1663, 1664, 1685

Dighton (*Mrs.* Phoebe) Sh— relics, from drawings . . . comprising the curiosities of Stratford-upon-Avon, relating to Sh— . . . Stratford-on-Avon, 1835. Oblong 4°. 10 plates   CPL
Also issued with coloured plates on tinted paper.

Dilke (*Sir* Charles Wentworth) *Editor*. *See* Dodsley

Dilke (J. W.) *See* Collier (J. P.)

Dillon (Arthur) Stage of the sixteenth century. [No place ; c. 1900.] 8°, pp. 20
See Littledale

Dillon (J.) Library. *See* Catalogue, 1869

Dilly (C.) *Publisher*—
See Johnson
  ,, Mason
  ,, Sh— King Lear, 1793
  ,, Sh— Macbeth, 1791
  ,, Sh— Merchant . . . 1783
  ,, Sh— Works, 1798

Dilly (E.) *Publisher*—
See Sh— Macbeth, 1770
  ,, Sh— Timon . . . 1770

Dilly (E. & C.) *Publishers*—
See Capell   *See* Sh— Works, 1773
  ,, Montagu   ,, Sheridan
  ,, Reflections

Dilton (R.) *Publisher*. *See* Sh— Works, 1753

Dinglewood. Sh— manuals. *See* Wood

Dircks (Hy.) On Sh—'s dramas as affording evidence of the poet's nature study [In ' Trans. of Royal Soc. of Literature ']. Ln : 1874. 8°   BPL | BUS

Direy (L.) Wm. Sh— : His poems, sonnets, and dedication. 1890. 8°   BM

'Dirrill (Charles)' *pseud*. *See* Sill

D'Israeli (Isaac) Amenities of literature, consisting of sketches and characters of English literature. Ln : E. Moxon, 1841. 3 vols. 8°
Vol. iii. contains chapters headed ' Predecessors and contemporaries of Sh—' and ' Sh—.'

Disselhoff (J.) Sh—'s tragedies a guide to faith. 1860. 8°   BPL

Distortions of the English stage : ' Macbeth ' [In ' National Review,' Oct.]. Ln : 1863. 8°   BUS

Diverting history . . . of Sir John Falstaff—
See Sh— King Henry IV., i., 1789
  ,, Sh— Merry wives, 1750, 1789

Dix (E. R. McC.) Earliest Dublin edition of Sh—'s plays [In 'Athenæum,' No. 3928, p. 177, Feb.]. 1903

Literary drama in Ireland [In 'Athenæum,' No. 4126, p. 665, Nov.]. 1906

Dix (Wm. Giles)] Imaginary conversation between Wm. Sh— and his friend Hy. Wriothesley, Earl of Southampton. Also . . . between . . . Sh— and Richard Quiney, an old associate of his, at Stratford. Boston [U.S.]: Jordan & Co., 1844. 12°, pp. 40   BM | BUS

Dixon (F. A.) *Editor. See* Sh— Midsummer . . . 1898

Dixon (T. S. E.) Francis Bacon and his Sh—. Chicago, 1895. 8°   BM | BPL | BUS

Dixon (Wm. Hepworth) Review of an 'Inquiry . . . by N. E. S. A. Hamilton.' New York, 1860. 8°, pp. 38   MPL
On the Collier controversy.

Sh—'s Windsor. The two Shakespeares: The 'Merry wives' [In 'Royal Windsor']. Ln : 1880. 3 vols. 8°   BPL | BUS

Dobell (Bertram) Newly discovered documents of the Elizabethan and Jacobean periods [In 'Athenæum,' No. 3830, p. 369; No. 3831, p. 403; No. 3832, p. 433; No. 3833, p. 465, Mar.-Ap.]. 1901
Papers by G. Chapman and B. Jonson.

Sonnets of Wm. Alabaster [In 'Athenæum,' No. 3974, p. 856, Dec.]. 1903

Unknown early allusion to Sh— [in old commonplace book, 1679-1710, by Robert Dobyns], [In 'Athenæum, No. 3821, p. 91, Jan.]. 1901
Gives a transcript of the verses on Sh—'s grave and of that originally placed on Combe's grave, attributed to the poet's pen.

Unknown (?) poem of Ben Jonson [In 'Athenæum,' No. 4014, p. 447 and p. 517, Oct.]. 1904

Dobson (H. Austin) Peg Woffington [In 'Magazine of Art']. Ln : Cassell, 1885. 4°   BPL

Dobyns (Robert) Commonplace book. *See* Dobell

Doctors of Dull-head College : A droll, 1672. Ed. by J. O. Halliwell. 1860. 8°   BPL

Dod (B.) *Publisher*—
See Sh— King Henry VIII., 1762
  ,, Sh— Othello, 1765
  ,, Sh— The Tempest, 1761
  ,, Sh— Works, 1745, 1747, 1757, 1762

Dod (Edw.) *Publisher. See* Kynder

Dodd (A.) *Publisher*—
See Pope
  ,, Shore

Dodd (James Wm.) *Actor. See* Sh— Romeo . . . 1803

Dodd *DD.* (Wm.) Beauties of Sh—. *See* Sh— Works : Ext. 1752, 1757, 1773, 1780, 1782, 1811, 1818, 1820, 1821, 1823, 1824, 1825, 1827, 1831, 1835, 1837, 1839, 1842, 1845, 1846, 1849, 1850, 1851, 1853, 1857, 1860, 1861, 1865, 1869, 1870, 1873, 1878, 1879, 1880, 1882, 1883, 1887, 1888, 1893
Dodd, the editor, was hung for forgery.

Life and beauties of Sh—. *See* Sh—

Dodd *DD.* (Wm.) *Editor. See* Sh— Works, 1769, 1771, 1795

Dodsley (J.) *Publisher*—
See Cibber   *See* Lovibond
  ,, Jago   ,, Montagu

Dodsley *Editor* (Robert) Collection of poems by several hands. Ln : R. Dodsley, 1755. 6 vols. 8°   W
Contains 'Slender's ghost, Hamlet's soliloquy imitated'; Ibbot (Dr.) 'Fit of the spleen, in imitation of Sh—'; 'Epilogue to Sh—'s King Henry IV., acted by young gentlemen at Mr. Newcombe's school at Hackney, 1748.'

Select collection of old plays. Ln : 1744. 12 vols. 8°
Vol. i. contains a preface with many references to Sh—, also Dr. Johnson's notices of playhouses from 1570 to 1629.
Vol. x. contains 'The marriage night,' by Viscount Falkland, afterwards suppressed.

Select collection of old plays. *See also* Sh— George-a-Greene, 1744

Select collection of old plays. With notes by C. W. Dilke. Ln : Rodwell & Martin, 1816. 6 vols. 8°

Select collection of old plays. Ed. by I. Reed, O. Gilchrist, and J. P. Collier. Ln : S. Prowett, 1825-27. 12 vols. 8°

[Select] Collection of old plays : Supplement. Ed. by T. Amyot, J. P. Collier, W. D. Cooper, A. Dyce, and J. O. Halliwell. Ln : Sh— Soc., 1853. 4 vols. 8°

Select collection of old English plays. Now first chronologically arranged, revised, and enlarged by W. Carew Hazlitt. Ln : Reeves & Turner, 1874-76. 15 vols. 8°

Dodsley (R.) *Editor*—
See Sh— Merry Devil . . . 1744, 1825, 1875
  ,, Mucedorus, 1744, 1874

Dodsley (R.) *Publisher*—
See Cibber
  ,, Richard III.

Dodsley (R. & J.) *Publishers*—
See Cooper
  ,, Huckell
  ,, Sh— Works : Ext. 1762

Dodsworth (Roger). *See* Dugdale & Dodsworth

Doig (Silvester) *Edinburgh Publisher*—
See Sh— Taming . . . 1792
  ,, Sh— Works, 1792

Dolan (D. G.) Pre-Reformation monastic establishments. *See* Memorials . . .

Dolby. British Theatre—
See Sh— As you like it, 1823
,, Sh— Hamlet, 1823
Dolby *Publisher*—
See Sh— King Henry VIII., 1824
,, Sh— Merry wives, 1824
,, Sh— Much ado, 1823
,, Sh— Othello, 1823
,, Sh— Romeo . . . 1823
,, Sh— Winter's tale, 1823
Dolby (Thomas) Dictionary of Sh— quotations. *See* Sh— Works: Ext. 1851, 1853, 1859, 1868
Sh—dictionary. *See* Sh— Works: Ext.1832
Thousand Sh— mottoes. *See* Sh— Works: Ext. 1856
Dolby (T. F.) Apotheosis of Sh—. Ln: Whittaker, 1848. 8°. In verse
Doll (Anton) *Vienna Publisher*. *See* Sh— Works, 1814
Dolle *Engraver*. *See* Settle
Dolman (John). *See* Mirrour . . .
Domesday book: Facsimile of the part relating to Warwickshire. Southampton: Ordnance Survey Office, 1862. F° SML
Donaldson (A.) *Edinburgh Publisher*. *See* Sh— Works, 1753, 1768, 1769, 1771
Donaldson (J. W.) Theatre of the Greeks: A treatise on the history and exhibition of the Greek drama. Seventh edition. Ln: Longman, 1860. 8°. Coloured plates and cuts
Donaldson *Comedian* (Walter) Recollections of an actor, never before published. Ln: Maxwell, 1865. 8°, pp. viii.-360 and portrait SML
Theatrical portraits. Ln: Varnham, 1870. 12° SML
Donne (Charles Edward) Essay on the tragedy of 'Arden of Feversham' . . . read at the . . . Kent Archæological Soc., July, 1872. Faversham: R. Smith, 1873. 8°, pp. 24 and facsimile BUS | SML
Donne *Dean* (John) Eighty sermons [with life of Donne by I. Walton]. Ln: R. Royston and R. Marriott, 1640. F°. With engraved title by Merian bearing a portrait of Donne BM
'Donne is an author pre-eminently illustrative of Sh—, the greatest preacher of the seventeenth century, the admired of all hearers.'—S. T. COLERIDGE.
Fifty sermons. Ln: J. Flesher & R. Marriott, 1649. F° BM
] Poems by J. D——. With elegies on the author's death. Ln: M. F—— [Miles Flesher] for John Marriot, 1633. Fcp. 4°
W

On sig. Y₃ (p. 165, mispaged 149) is the famous eulogy by William Basse :—
AN EPITAPH UPON SH—.
Renowned Chaucer, lie a thought more nigh
To rare Beaumont ; and learned Beaumond lie
A little nearer Spencer, to make roome
For Sh— in your threefold fourefold tombe.
To lie all foure in one bed make a shift
For, untill doomesday hardly will a fift
Betwixt this day and that be slaine
For whom your curtaines need be drawne againe.
But, if precedency of death doth barre
A fourth place in your sacred sepulchre
Under this curled marble of thine owne
Sleepe, rare tragedian Sh—, sleepe alone,
That unto us and others it may bee
Honor hereafter to be laid by thee.
For other references *see* 'Notes and Queries,' first series, vol. vi., p. 158, by which it will be seen this epitaph (wrongly credited to Donne) was omitted in later editions. *See* also Sh— Works (Reed), 1803, vol. ii., p. 181.
The earliest known MS. version of Basse's lines will be found entered under 'Poems.'

Polydoron. Ln: 1631. 12° BUS
Says on pp. 31-32: 'Names were first questionless given for distinction, [or] facultie . . . Armestrong, Sh—, of high quality.'

Twenty-six sermons. Ln: T. N—— for J. Maynes, 1669. F° BM
Two elegies. *See* Waldron

Donne (Wm. Bodham) Dramatic art representation [In 'Dark Blue']. 1871. 8° BPL
Essays on the drama and popular amusements. Ln: Parker, 1858. 8° SML
Essays on the drama. Second edition. 1863. 8° MPL

Donnelly (Ignatius) Cipher in the plays and on the tombstone. Minneapolis, U.S., 1900. Cr. 8°, pp. 372. With facsimiles
BM | BPL | BUS | MPL | SML
Great cryptogram: Francis Bacon's cipher in the so-called Sh— plays. Chicago, 1888. 2 vols. 8°. With portraits and facsimiles BM | BPL | BUS | MPL | SML
See Nicholson (Dr.) for decisive reply, in which Donnelly is 'hoist with his own petard.'
] His secret is revealed : Mr. Donnelly gives up the origin of his cipher numbers . . . [In ' The World ']. 1888. F° BPL
On the Bacon-Sh— controversy.
Sonnets of Sh—: An essay. Saint Paul: Printed [by G. W. Moore] for private distribution, 1859. 8°, pp. 16 BUS

Donnelly (I.)—
See Doyle
,, Pyle
,, Theobald
Donovan (T.) *Editor*—
See Sh— King Henry IV., i., 1896
,, Sh— Works, 1896
Doorne (Stephen) *Feversham Publisher*. *See* Sh— Arden, 1770
Doran (Alban) Sh— and the Medical Society [In ' British Medical Journal,' 15th May]. 1899. 4° BPL

Doran (Alban) Sh— and the Medical Society. 1899. 8°, pp. 20   BPL | BUS

Doran (*Dr.* John) History of Court fools. Ln: Bentley, 1858. Cr. 8°

In and about Drury Lane, and other papers. Ln: Bentley, 1881. 2 vols. Cr. 8°   BPL

Knights and their days . . . New York: Redfield, 1856. Cr. 8°, pp. 480
An amusing account of 'Sir Guy of Warwick,' pp. 133-147; 'Sir John Falstaff,' pp. 276-294; 'Stage knights,' pp. 295-311; 'Stage ladies,' pp. 312-328.

Love for, and the lovers of, Sh— [In 'Gentleman's Magazine,' Feb.]. Ln: 1856. 8°   BUS

Sh— in France [In 'Nineteenth Century,' Vol. 3, pp. 115-135, Jan.]. Ln: King, 1878. Roy. 8°   BPL | BUS

'Their Majesties servants': Annals of the English stage, from Thomas Betterton to Edmund Kean. Ln: Allen, 1864. 2 vols. 8°   SML

'Their Majesties' servants.' Second edition. Ln: W. H. Allen, 1865. 8°, pp. viii.-460   BPL | MPL

'Their Majesties' servants' . . . Edited and revised by R. W. Lowe. Ln: Nimmo, 1888. 3 vols. 8°. With 50 copperplate portraits and 80 wood engravings, all on India paper   BPL | SML
Some sets were done on large paper, royal octavo.

Doran (*Dr.* John) *Editor.* See Notes & Queries

Dorchester. *See* Gray (W.)

Dorchester (*Prof.*) Character of Hamlet. Ln: New Sh— Soc., 1891. 8°   BUS

Doré (Gustave) *Artist. See* Sh— The Tempest, 1860, 1861

Doré (J. R.) Old Bibles: An account of early versions of the English Bible. Ln: Eyre & Spottiswoode, 1888. Cr. 8°   SML
Gives a description of those editions which influenced Sh—.

Old Bibles . . . Second edition. Ln: Eyre & Spottiswoode, 1888. Cr. 8°, pp. xvi.-396, and 17 facsimiles

Dorrell (Hadrian) *Editor. See* Willobie

Double falsehood. *See* Sh— Double falsehood

Doubleday (H. Arthur) *Editor. See* Sh— Works, 1893-98, 1900

Douce (Francis) Illustrations of Sh— and of ancient manners, with dissertations on the clowns and fools of Sh—; on the collection of popular tales entitled 'Gesta Romanorum'; and on the English morris dance. Ln: Longman, 1807. 2 vols. 8°. With wood engravings by J. Berryman   BPL | BUS | MPL | SML | W

Illustrations of Sh— . . . Ln: Tegg, 1839. 8°, pp. xvi.-632. With wood engravings by Jackson   BPL | BUS | CPL | SML

Douce (Francis) Library—
See Catalogue, 1840
,, Halliwell, Hand list

Douce (Francis) *Editor. See* Sh— Works, 1807, 1860

Douce.] 'Douce's illustrations' [Article in 'Edinburgh Review,' July]. 1808. 8°   BUS

Doughty (J.) *Publisher. See* Theatrical Examiner

Douglas (*Sir* George Brisbane Scott) A Sh— misunderstanding: The Lucy story [Magazine excerpt, c. 1890.] 8°   BPL

Deer-stealing escapade of Sh— [In 'Belgravia,' Vol. 93, p. 198]. Ln: c. 1897. 8°

Douse (Thomas Le Marchant) Examination of an old manuscript preserved in the library of the Duke of Northumberland at Alnwick, and sometimes called the Northumberland manuscript. Ln: Taylor & Francis, 1904. 8°, pp. 16 and facsimiles   BUS
The manuscript contains matter by Francis Bacon, and has been used in support of arguments by Baconians in their controversy. *See also* Elizabethan MS.

Dove (J. F.) *Publisher*—
See Sh— Poems, 1820, 1830
,, Works, 1827, 1830

Dover (Robert). *See* Annalia Dubrensia

Dow (J. G. A.) Notes on 'All's well . . .' Ln: New Sh— Soc., 1880-86. 8°

Sh—'s fugues [In 'Fortnightly Review']. Ln: 1885. 8°   BPL

Dowdall (John)] Description of severall places in Warwickshire. [Author's holograph manuscript on ten leaves of paper.] 1693. Fcp. 4°   W
The earliest known manuscript upon Sh—'s life and native ground. [*See* Halliwell's 'Sh— reliques,' 1852, p. 57].

Traditionary anecdotes of Sh— collected in Warwickshire in the year 1693. Now first published from the original manuscript [Ed. by J. P. Collier]. Ln: T. Rodd, 1838. 8°, pp. 24, includ. pr. wrappers   BM | BPL | BUS | CPL | MPL

Dowden (*Prof.* Edward) 'Beget' and 'Begetter' in Elizabethan English [In 'Athenæum,' No. 3776, p. 315; No. 3778, p. 379, Mar.]. 1900
Illustrates the 'Sonnets.'

Chronology of the plays. *See* Sh— Works, 1881, 1882, 1882-83, 1884-92, 1890

Introduction to Sh—. Ln: Blackie, 1893. 8°, pp. viii.-136. With Droeshout portrait   BM | BPL | MPL

Sh—; a critical study. *See* Sh—

Sh—; literature primer. *See* Sh—

Sh— as a comic dramatist [In C. M. Gayley's 'Representative English Comedies,' Vol. I.]. New York, 1903. 8°   BPL | MPL

Dowden (*Prof.* Edward) Sh— scenes and characters. *See* Sh— Works : Ext. 1876
Sh—'s portraiture of women [In ‘ Contemporary Review’]. 1885. 8° BPL
Dowden (*Prof.* E.) *Editor*—
See Phin
 ,, Sh— As you like it, 1887
 ,, Sh— Cymbeline, 1903
 ,, Sh— Hamlet, 1899
 ,, Sh— King Henry IV., i., 1887
 ,, Sh— King Henry VIII., 1892
 ,, Sh— Othello, 1890
 ,, Sh— Poems, 1903
 ,, Sh— Romeo . . . 1884, 1900, 1903
 ,, Sh— Sonnets, 1881, 1882, 1889, 1896, 1897
 ,, Sh— Works, 1886, 1899, &c.
Dowland (John) Songs or ayres. *See* Nash
Dowling (Maurice G.) *Editor*—
 ,, Sh— Othello, 1834, 1856, 1884
 ,, Sh— Romeo . . . 1837
Dowling (Richard) Indolent essays. Ln : Ward & Downey, 1889. 8°, pp. viii.-226
At p. 28 occurs ‘ Zero in space,’ which deals with the Bacon-Sh— controversy.
Downes (John)] Roscius Anglicanus, or an historical review of the stage after it had been suppressed by means of the late unhappy Civil War begun in 1641, giving an account of its rise again, of the time and places the governors of both companies first erected their theatres, names of actors, actresses, and plays for forty-six years . . . Ln : H. Playford at his house in Arundel Street, near the Waterside, 1708. 8° BPL
According to Downes, Sh— took pains to train Joseph Taylor as Hamlet and John Lowine as King Henry VIII.
] Roscius Anglicanus . . . With additions by T. Davies. Ln : Egerton, 1789. 8° BPL | SML
Roscius Anglicanus . . . 1660 to 1706. 1886. 12° BPL
See also Hazlitt (W. C.)
Downes (Robert P.) Seven supreme poets. *See* Sh—] Downes
Downing (Charles) Future of Sh— and Stratford-on-Avon [with comment by Wm. Jaggard]. Sh— Club paper. Stratford, 1906. 8°, pp. 8
] God in Sh—. By ‘Clelia.’ Ln : Unwin, 1890. 8°, pp. 424 BM | BPL | BUS | SML
God in Sh—: The course of the poet's spiritual life, with his reflections thereon, and his resultant conception of his world-personality inductively established from his text. Second edition. With special preface to meet preconceptions and misconceptions. Ln : Greening, 1901. Cr. 8°, pp. 434 BPL

Downing (Charles)] Great Pan lives [Sh—'s sonnets, with paraphrases and references, pp. 20-126], by ‘Clelia.’ Ln : Luzac, 1892. 8°, pp. x.-208 BPL | BUS | SML
] Long desiderated knowledge of the life and personality of Sh—. *See* Sh—
] Messiahship of Sh—. Sung and expounded. By ‘Clelia.’ Ln : Greening, 1901. 8°, pp. xx.-104 BPL | BUS | MPL | SML
Sh— reconciliation : A lecture. Ln : Luzac, 1892. 8°, pp. xl. BPL
Downing (Charles) *Editor. See* Sh— Sonnets, 1892
Downs (*Major*) Paddy M'Shane's seven ages. *See* Sh— As you like it, 1807
See also Brownes
Doyle (*Sir* Francis Hastings) Lectures on poetry. Second series. Ln : 1877. 12° BPL | BUS | MPL
Includes lectures on ‘ King Lear,’ ‘ Macbeth,’ ‘ Othello,’ and ‘ The Tempest,’ pp. 150-229.
Doyle (J. T.) Donnelly and the Sh— cipher. 1888. 8° BPL
Drake (*Dr.* James) Antient and modern stages survey'd, or Mr. [Jeremy] Collier's ‘ View of the English stage’ set in a true light. Ln : 1699. 8°
See Collier (Jeremy)
 ,, Stage condemn'd
Drake (Nathan) Memorials of Sh—. *See* Sh—
] Noontide leisure ; or sketches in summer . . . including a tale of the days of Sh—. Ln : T. Cadell, 1824. 2 vols. 8° BPL | BUS | SML | W
Sh— and his times. *See* Sh—
Shaksperiana. *See* Sh—
Drama—
See Actors
 ,, Stage
Drama recorded. *See* Barker
Drama (The), or theatrical pocket magazine, wholly dedicated to the stage, and containing original dramatic biography, essays, criticisms, poetry, reviews, anecdotes, bon mots, chit chat. With occasional notices of the country theatres . . . Ln : T. & J. Elvey, 1821-23. 7 vols. 12°. With steel engraved character portraits, Stratford bust, &c. SML
Dramatic beauties selected from the early and modern British dramatists, forming a companion to Dodd's ‘ Beauties of Sh—.’ Ln : Orr & Smith, 1834. 16°, pp. vi.-244-vi. and portrait
Dramatic biography. *See* Baker
Dramatic censor, or critical companion [Ed. by Francis Gentleman]. Ln., J. Bell ; York, C. Etherington, 1770. 2 vols. 8° BUS | CPL
Contains lengthy accounts of various alterations of Sh—'s plays.

Dramatic characters of the English and French stages in the time of Garrick. Ln: R. Sayer, 1769-72. 2 vols. 8°. With 'character' portraits

Dramatic entertainments by Royal command at Windsor Castle, 1848-49, comprising the 'Merchant of Venice,' 'Hamlet,' &c. Edited by B. Webster. Ln: Mitchell [1850]. 8°   BPL | SML

Dramatic historiographer, or the British theatre delineated ; exhibiting the argument, conduct, and chief incidents of the most celebrated plays ; with an account of such previous circumstances as serve to illustrate each representation. Ln: 1735. 12°   BUS | W
Contains an account of 'Hamlet,' 'Julius Cæsar,' 'King Henry IV.,' 'King Henry VIII.,' 'King Lear,' 'Macbeth,' 'Merry Wives.' and 'Othello.'
This publication was re-issued in 1740, under the title of 'Companion to the theatre' (q.v.).

Dramatic history. *See* Stage

Dramatic impressions. *See* Hiatt

Dramatic muse, or jubilee songster, consisting of the songs sung at the Stratford jubilee. Canterbury, 1769. 12°   BUS
Contains also Garrick's Ode, with a frontispiece of Garrick reciting it.

Dramatic peerage : Personal notes of actors and actresses. Ln: 1892. 8°, pp. 244

Dramatic performances—
See Actors
,, Stage
,, Theatres

Dramatic songs. Selected and composed by W. Linley. *See* Sh— Works : Ext. 1800

Dramatic souvenir : being literary and graphical illustrations of Sh— and other celebrated English dramatists, etc. With engravings. Ln: C. Tilt, 1833. 8°, pp. xvi.-204. 200 woodcuts by Harvey printed within borders
    BM | BUS | CPL | SML | W
A re-issue of 'Literary and graphical illustrations,' 1831, under an altered title.

Dramatic table talk. *See* Ryan

'Dramaticus.' On the profits of old actors. *See Sh*—] Sh— Soc.
Players who acted in the 'Shoemaker's holiday, by T. Dekker & R. Wilson, 1600.' *See Sh*—] Sh— Soc.
Recusancy of John Sh— and the inclosure of Welcombe fields. *See Sh*—] Sh— Soc.

'Dramaticus' *Editor*—
See Every man
,, Jonson & Dekker
,, Salmacis . . .

Dramatists—
See Bell & Dunham
,, Dodsley

Dramatists of the present day. *See* Purnell

Draper (S.) *Publisher*—
See Sh— King Richard III., 1745
,, Sh— Midsummer . . . 1755
,, Romeo . . . 1750, 1756
,, Sh— Taming . . . 1756
,, Sh— Works, 1745, 1747

Drawing of a hand. *See Sh*—] Sh—ano

Drayton (Michael) Battaile of Agincourt fought by Henry the fift of that name . . . Ln: W. Lee, 1627. F°. With portrait by W. Hole   BM | W
At p. 206 says :—
'Sh—, thou hadst as smooth a comic vein
Fitting the sock, and in thy natural brain
As strong conception and as clear a rage
As any one that trafick'd with the stage.'

Matilda : the fair and chaste daughter of Lord Robert Fitzwater. Ln: 1594. Fcp. 4°   W
Alludes on sig. B 2 to Sh—'s newly issued work thus :—
'Lucrece, of whom proud Rome hath boasted long.'
One of the earliest printed references to Sh—.

Merry devil of Edmonton. *See* Sh— Merry devil . . . (*heading*)

Nymphidia. *See* Sh— Midsummer . . . 1886, 1894
See Annalia Dubrensia
,, Chettle
,, Hall (John)
,, Sh— Sir John Oldcastle (*heading*)

Drayton.] Elton (O.) Michael Drayton. A critical study. With bibliography. Ln: Constable, 1905. Cr. 8°, pp. 232   BPL
Refers to Sh—.

Dress. *See* Costume

Drewry (Ina L.) Hy. Irving's 'Hamlet.' *See* Irving

Dring (Thomas) *Publisher*—
See Payne
,, Sh— King Richard III., 1667

Droeshout (John) *Engraver*. *See* Bodenham

Droeshout (Martin) *Engraver*—
See Dugdale
,, Henderson
,, Heywood
,, Sh— Works, 1623, 1632, 1663, 1664,1685
,, *Sh*—] Sh— portrait

Droll of the bouncing knight. *See* Sh— King Henry IV., i., 1860

Droll of the gravemakers. *See* Sh— Hamlet, 1860

Drolls—
See Doctors
,, Sh— King Henry IV., i., 1860
,, Simpleton

Drout (John) Pityfull historie of two loving Italians, Gaulfrido and Barnardo le Vayne. Trans. out of Italian into English meter. Ln: H. Binneman, 1570. 12°, thirty leaves (unpaged), black letter
One of the supposed foundations of 'Romeo and Juliet.'

Drout (John) Pittyfull historie . . . 1570.
Privately reprinted, with introduction,
by J. P. Collier. Ln : F. Shoberl [1844].
Fcp. 4°   BPL
Issue restricted to twenty-five copies.

Druce (G.) Editor—
See Sh— King Henry V., 1842
  ,, Sh— The Tempest, 1841

Drummond of Hawthornden (Wm.) Ben Jon-
son's conversations, January MDCXIX.
Ln : Sh— Soc., 1842. 8°   BPL
See also Jonson

Drury Lane Gazette : No. I., Sept. 7th, 1816
to No. 148, April 9, 1817. Ln : 1816-17.
2 vols. 8°

Drury Lane Playhouse broke open. See
Garrick

Drury Lane Theatre [Collection of three hundred and fifty-seven wardrobe and property bills for the Theatre Royal, Drury
Lane, from 1713 to 1716, certified for
payment by Colley Cibber, Robert Wilks,
and Barton Booth, managers respectively
for that period]. Ln : 1713-1716. MS.
on paper, mounted into a volume, roy. f°
                                                   W
Illustrative of the performances of Sh—'s plays, their
costumes and cost, in the reign of Queen Anne, etc.

Early original documents relating to Shake-
spearean performances at old Drury Lane
Theatre in or about the year 1713.
Sixty-nine pieces in all. MS. on paper.
Ln : 1713. F°   W
Many of the accounts included are franked for payment
with the signatures of the managers, Robert Wilks,
Barton Booth, and Colley Cibber.

See Collier (J. P.)
  ,, Sh— Works, 1850
  ,, Theatre Royal
'Drusus' pseud. for Sh—. See Marston
Dryden (Alice) Compton Wynyates. See
Memorials . . .

Dryden (Alice) Editor. See Memorials
Dryden (John) Albion and Albanius : An
opera, performed at the Queen's Theatre
in Dorset Garden. Ln : Jacob Tonson,
1691. Fcp. 4°, pp. viii.-34
The preface contains references to Dryden's alteration
of 'The Tempest.'

All for love. See Sh— Antony, 1678 et seq.
An evening's love, or the mock astrologer.
Ln : T. N—— for H. Herringman, 1671.
Fcp. 4°
Dryden was indebted to Sh— at several points in this
play. Prefixed is an essay on the merits of the older
dramatists, in which remarks on their respective
qualities are made with fine discrimination.
The Shakespearean notices and references mention the
origin of some of his plays.

An evening's love. Ln : H. Herringman &
R. Bentley, 1691. Fcp. 4°

Dryden (John) Aureng-Zebe : A tragedy . . .
Ln : Printed by T. N—— for Henry
Herringman at the Anchor in the Lower
Walk of the New Exchange, 1676. Fcp. 4°
' But spite of all his pride, a secret shame
  Invades his breast at Sh—'s sacred name.'
                                      —Prologue.

Conquest of Granada by the Spaniards . . .
Ln : T. N—— for H. Herringman, 1672.
Fcp. 4°
The prose essays attached contain most interesting
matter relative to the drama and Sh—'s plays :
' Love's labours lost,' ' Measure for Measure,' ' Per-
icles,' and ' Winter's Tale ' being referred to.

Conquest of Granada. Third edition. Ln :
H. Hills for H. Herringman, 1678. Fcp. 4°
Conquest of Granada . . . Fourth edition.
Ln : 1687. Fcp. 4°
Conquest of Granada . . . Fifth edition.
Ln : 1695. Fcp. 4°
Conquest of Granada. Sixth edition. Ln :
1704. Fcp. 4°
Defence of the epilogue. See Sh—] Sh—ana
Love triumphant, or nature will prevail.
A tragi-comedy. Ln : Jacob Tonson, at
the Judge's Head, near the Inner Temple
Gate in Fleet St., 1694. Fcp. 4°
The prologue says :—
  ' To Sh—'s critique he bequeaths the curse,
  To find his faults, and yet himself make worse.'

Miscellany poems . . . Ln : Jacob Tonson,
1684. 8°
Contains a lengthy reference to Sh—, in which Dryden
hints that he considered ' Pericles ' the bard's first
production :—
  ' Sh —'s own muse her " Pericles " first bore.'

Mistaken husband : A comedie. Ln :
Printed for J. Magnes & R. Bentley in
Russell Street in Covent Garden, near the
Piazzas, 1675. Fcp. 4°
Introduces Sh – in the address.

Of dramatick poesie. An essay. Ln : H.
Herringman, at the Sign of the Anchor,
1668. Fcp. 4°   BPL
Dryden's greatest prose production, in which, says Dr.
Johnson, ' the account of Sh — may stand as a perpetual model of encomiastic criticism, exact without
minuteness and lofty without exaggeration. In a few
lines is exhibited a character so extensive in its com-
prehension and so curious in its limitations that
nothing can be added, diminished, or referred, nor
can the editors and admirers of Sh—, in all their
emulation of reverence, boast of much more than of
having diffused and paraphrased the epitome of excellence, or having changed Dryden's gold for baser
metal of lower value though of greater bulk.'

Of dramatick poesie. Ln : H. Herringman,
1684. Fcp. 4°
Of dramatick poesie. Ln : H. Herringman,
1693. Fcp. 4°
Of dramatick poesie. Ln : [c. 1709]. 12° w
Of dramatic poesy. Oxford : Clarendon
Press, 1889. 8°   SML

Prologue. See Harris (Joseph)

(85)

Dryden (John) Rival ladies. A tragi-comedy. Ln : T. N——— for H. Herringman, 1675. Fcp. 4°

> Dryden falls into a curious error in crediting Sh— with the invention of blank verse. In the 'Address to the Earl of Orrery,' Dryden says : 'Sh—, who with some errors not to be avoided in that age, had undoubtedly a larger soul of poesie than ever any of our nation, was the first who, to shun the pains of continual rhyming, invented that kind of writing which we call blank verse, but the French more properly "prose mesurée," into which the English tongue so naturally slides that in writing prose 'tis hardly to be avoided.'

Secret love, or the maiden queen. Ln : Henry Herringman, 1691. Fcp. 4°

> At the end is 'A catalogue of some plays printed for R. Bently,' in which several by Sh— are named.

Songs. *See* Sh— Midsummer . . . 1755
Sports of the muses. *See* Sh— Works : Ext. 1752

State of innocence and fall of man. An opera. Written in heroick verse. Ln : Printed by T. N——— for Henry Herringman at the Anchor . . . 1684. Fcp. 4°, pp. xvi.-xl.

> Refers to Sh—'s 'Midsummer Night's Dream' and 'The Tempest' in the 'Author's apology.'

The Tempest. *See* Sh— The Tempest
Troilus and Cressida. *See* Sh— Troilus and Cressida

See Collier (J. P.)   *See* Gildon
   „ Congreve   „ Juvenalis
   „ Dennis   „ Poems
   „ Dunton   „ Terence

Dryden (J.) *Editor*—
See Sh— Julius Cæsar, 1719
   „ Sh— Othello, 1670, 1674, 1681, 1695, 1697, 1701, 1705
   „ Sh— Romeo . . . 1883
   „ Sh— The Tempest, 1669, 1670, 1674, 1676, 1690, 1695, 1701, 1710, 1720, 1735, 1756, 1780, 1789, 1806, 1808, 1815, 1821
   „ Sh— Troilus . . . 1679, 1695, 1701, 1735, 1808, 1821
   „ Sh— Works, 1908

Dryerre (H.) Who wrote the Sh— plays ? Sh— or Bacon ? [In the ' People's Friend ']. 1898. 4°   BPL

Dublin—
See Sh—] Sh— Soc. of Dublin
   „ Theatre Royal
   „ Victor

Du Bois *Judge* (Edward) The wreath . . . To which are added Remarks on Sh—. Ln : 1799. 8°   BM | BPL | BUS | MPL

Du Bois (E.) *Editor*. *See* Monthly Mirror
Duchange (G.) *Engraver*. *See* Sh— Works, 1745
Ducis (Jean François). *See* K——— (A. J.)

Dudevant (Amantine Lucile Aurore Dupin)] Letter to M. Regnier, of the Théâtre Français, by ' George Sand ' upon her adaptation to the French stage of ' As you like it.' Trans. by Theodosia Lady Monson. Ln : J. Chapman, 1856. 8°, pp. 24   BM | BPL | BUS | MPL

Dudley Sh— festivals. *See* Timmins (J. F.)
Dudley (*Sir* Henry Bate & *Lady*)] Passages selected by distinguished personages on the great literary trial of ' Vortigern and Rowena ; a comi-tragedy.' ' Whether it be or be not from the immortal pen of Sh—.' Ln : J. Ridgway [1795-98]. 4 vols in 2. 8°   W

> A popular satire on the leading public characters of the day in a series of passages purporting to be extractions from Ireland's play, but in reality written by Sir Henry and Lady Dudley. The work relates to the Ireland forgeries, and is considered a felicitous imitation of Sh—'s style. Originally published in the ' Morning Herald.'
> 'Some of these characters are admirably adapted.'— LOWNDES.

] Passages . . . Fifth edition. Ln : J. Ridgway [1795-1807]. 4 vols. 8°   BM | BPL | BUS | SML

] Passages . . . Sixth edition. Ln : H. Brown [1795]. 3 vols. 12°
Sh—'s history of the times. *See* Sh— Works : Ext. 1778
See also Ireland (S. W. H.)

Dudley (R.) *Artist*. *See* Sh— Works, 1873-75, 1879
Dudley (R. & A.) Sh— pictures. Ln : Nister, 1896. 8°   BM
Dudley (T. B.) *Editor*. *See* Bisset
Duff (Edward Gordon) Catalogue. *See* Rylands library
Duff (*Mrs.*) *Actress*. *See* American . . .
Duff.] Ireland (J. N.) Mrs. Duff. Boston : Osgood, 1881-82. 8°   SML
Duff (W.) Of Sh—. *See* Sh—
Dufferin (*Marquis of*) Introduction. *See* Sheridan
Duffet (T.)] Empress of Morocco. A farce. With an epilogue after the manner of ' Macbeth.' 1674. 12°   BPL

> In 1673 Elkanah Settle wrote a play under the same title.

The mock-tempest. *See* Sh— The Tempest, 1675

Du-gard (Th.) Death and the grave, or a sermon preached at the funeral of that honorable and virtuous ladie, the Ladie Alice Lucie, August 17, 1648. By Th. Du-gard, M.A. and Rector of Barford in the Countie of Warwick. Ln : Pr. by Wm. Du-gard, anno domini 1649. Fcp. 4°, pp. ii.-54

> Of much interest for the light it throws on the general esteem in which the Lucy family was held in the early seventeenth century. It also refers to the library of books at Charlecote.

Dugard (Wm.) *Printer.* *See* Dugard (Th.)

Dugdale (*Sir* William) Antiquities of Coventrie illustrated. Coventry, 1765. F°, pp. 60

Antiquities of Warwick and Warwick Castle ... Earl of Leicester's arrival at Warwick, 1571 ... Account of Q. Elizabeth's reception in Warwick, 1572 ... Warwick, 1786. 8°, pp. iv.-164 and view of St. Mary's Church

Antiquities of Warwickshire illustrated from records, leiger books, manuscripts, charters, evidences, tombes, and armes. Beautified with maps, prospects, and portraictures. Ln: T. Warren, 1656. F°
      BM | BUS | SBL | SML
Contains the earliest view of the Stratford Church bust, probably drawn or finished from memory, as it differs in detail from the monument itself.
Has a notice of Sir Thomas Lucy of Charlecote.

Antiquities of Warwickshire ... Second edition. Augmented and continued by William Thomas, *D.D.* Ln: Osborn & Longman, 1730. 2 vols. F°   BPL

Antiquities of Warwickshire ... Coventry: J. Jones, 1765. F°   SML
An unreliable reprint of the 1656 edition.

Dugdale (*Sir* W.) & Dodsworth (Roger) Monasticon Anglicanum ... An epitome by James Wright. Ln: 1693. F°
In the preface Wright announces that Dugdale and Sh— are the two most famous English authors, placing the poet second in order of merit.

Dugdale & *others* (*Sir* Wm.) Warwickshire. Coventry: John Aston, 1817. 8°, pp. iv.-598. Map, portrait, and seven plates
Account of Sh— and Stratford, pp. 415 and 431-450.

Dugdale.] Dugdale (W. F. S.) Sir Wm. Dugdale. *See* Memorials ...

] Hamper (W.) Life, diary, and correspondence. Ln: Harding, 1827. 4°. With portrait   SML
Refers at p. 52 to visit of Queen Henrietta on 3rd July, 1643, to Stratford-on-Avon, where she slept at New Place, Prince Rupert at the same time staying at the Red Horse Hotel.
On p. 99 relates that Sh—'s and John Combe's monuments at Stratford super Avon were made by one Gerard Johnson, and gives some account of Johnson at p. 512.
On p. 511 is a curious description of 'Mychaell Drowshot ... a graver in copper.'

Duggan (John)] Fair, kind, and true, by 'Junius junior.' Scranton [U.S.], 1896. 12°. With portraits   BPL | BUS
On the Bacon-Sh— question.

Du Guernier (Lud.) *Artist-Engraver—*
See Sh— Cymbeline, 1734
 ,,   Sh— Julius Cæsar, 1734
 ,,   Sh— King Richard II., 1734
 ,,   Sh— Love's labours lost, 1735
 ,,   Sh— Macbeth, 1734
 ,,   Sh— Measure ... 1734
 ,,   Sh— Much ado ... 1734

Du Guernier (Lud.) *Artist-Engraver—*
See Sh— Othello, 1734
 ,,   Sh— The Puritan, 1714, 1734
 ,,   Sh— Thomas Lord Cromwell, 1734

Duignan (W. H.) Worcestershire place names. Ln: Frowde, 1905. 12°   SML

Duke's Theatre, Dorset Gardens—
See Cunningham
 ,,   Sh— Antony ... 1677
 ,,   Sh— King Henry V., 1672
 ,,   Sh— King Henry VI., i., 1681
 ,,   Sh— King Henry VI., ii., 1680
 ,,   Sh— King Lear, 1681
 ,,   Sh— Macbeth, 1673, 1674
 ,,   Sh— Timon ... 1678, 1688, 1732
 ,,   Sh— Troilus ... 1679, 1695

Duke of York's Theatre—
See Sh— Hamlet, 1676, 1683
 ,,   Sh— King Richard III., 1667
 ,,   Sh— The Tempest, 1670, 1676

Dulac (Edmund) *Artist.* *See* Sh— The Tempest, 1908

Dulce (Lodovico) *Editor.* *See* Mexia

Dulwich—
See Account ...   *See* Henslowe
 ,,   Alleyn   ,,   Young (W.)
 ,,   Blanch

Dumaresq de Carteret-Bisson (*Capt.* F. S.) *Editor.* *See Sh*—] Julius Cæsar, 1883

Dumas (A.) Edmund Kean. *See* Kean

Du Mont-Schauberg (M.) *Köln Publisher.* *See* Sh— Julius Cæsar, 1861

Dunbar (M. F. P.) Sh— birthday book. *See* Sh— Works: Ext. 1875, 1876, 1879, 1882, 1884, 1886

Dunbar Family. *See* Jaggard

Duncan (J. & A.) *Glasgow Publishers.* *See* Sh— Works, 1795

Duncan (T.) *Edinburgh Publisher.* *See* Sh— Works, 1795

Duncan (W.) *Glasgow Publisher.* *See* Sh— Macbeth, 1755

Dunciad (The). *See* Pope

Duncombe *Editor.* *See Sh*—] Sherlock

Duncombe (E.) *Publisher.* *See* Sh— King Richard III., 1823

Duncombe (John) The Feminiad: A poem. Ln: M. Cooper, 1754. Fcp. 4°, pp. 32
Refers to Sh—, p. 20.

Duncombe (J.) *Editor—*
See Sh— King Richard III., 1831
 ,,   Sh— Love's labours lost, 1839
 ,,   Sh— Macbeth, 1840
 ,,   Sh— Works: Ext. 1830

Duncombe (J.) *Publisher.* *See* Sh— Romeo ... 1837

Dundee.] Victoria Galleries: Sh— exhibition from the collection of A. C. Lamb. [1896?] 12°   BPL

Dunmore (John). *See* Worsley

Dunning (Edwin James) Genesis of Sh—'s art: A study of his sonnets and poems. Boston [U.S.]: Lee & Shepard, 1897. 8°, pp. xxxiv.-336   BPL | BUS | SML

Dunning (E. J.) *Editor*. *See* Sh— Sonnets, 1897

Dunton (John) Athenian gazette, or casuistical mercury . . . Ln: J. Dunton, 1691. F°
Contains this passage: ' But since we can't go through all the world, let's look home a little. Grandsire Chaucer, in spite of the age, was a man of as much wit, sense and honesty as any that have writ after him. Father Ben was excellent at humour. Sh— deserves the name of "sweetest" which Milton gave him.'

] Athenian oracle . . . Ln: Andrew Bell, 1703-04. 3 vols. 8°
Numerous references to Sh—.
• Hope, Cat. of newspapers (p. 60), attributes the authorship to Edward Smith.

] Athenian oracle . . . With supplement. Third edition. Ln: A. Bell, 1706-16. 4 vols. 8°   BM

] Athenian sport, or two thousand paradoxes merrily argued, to amuse and divert the age . . . with improvements from . . . Boyle, Lock, Norris, Collier, Cowley, Dryden, Garth, Addison, and other illustrious wits. Ln: B. Bragg in Paternoster Row, 1707. 8°, pp. xxxii.-544
Contains passages and incidents paraphrased from Sh—.

Duport (F.) *Editor*. *See* Sh— Taming . . . 1888

Durand (John) Contribution to Sh— study [on ' Hamlet,' in ' Galaxy,' April]. New York, 1873. 8°   BUS

Durell (Hy.) *New York Publisher*. *See* Sh— Works, 1817-18

D'Urfey (Thomas) Injured princess. *See* Sh— Cymbeline, 1682

Progress of honesty, or a view of the court and city: A Pindarique poem. Ln: Joseph Hindmarsh, 1681. Fcp. 4°, pp. 32
Refers on p. 25 to the ' Merchant of Venice.'

Virtuous wife, or good luck at last. A comedy. Ln: T. N. for R. Bentley, 1680. Fcp. 4°
Quotations from ' Venus and Adonis' on pp. 33-34.

See Dancing devils

Duthie (D. W.) Case of Sir John Fastolf. 1907. Cr. 8°   BPL

Duvar (Hunter) Where did Sh— get his *Ariel* ? [In ' Canadian Monthly,' Mar.]. Toronto, 1876. 8°   BUS

Du Verdier (A.) *See* Mexia, Sansovino, & Du Verdier

Duyckinck (E. A.) *Editor*. *See* Sh— Works, 1896

Duyckinck (George Long) *Editor*. *See* Sh— Works, 1866, 1867, 1872, 1876, 1888

Dyce (Alexander) Few notes on Sh—, with occasional remarks on the emendations of the manuscript-corrector in Mr. Collier's copy of the folio of 1632. Ln: J. R. Smith, 1853. 8°, pp. 156
BM | BPL | BUS | MPL | SML | W

Glossary to the works of Sh—. *See* Sh— Works: Ext. 1866, 1880, 1892, 1894, 1902, 1904

Library. *See* Catalogue, 1874-75

Memoirs of Sh—. *See* Sh—

Remarks on J. P. Collier's and C. Knight's editions of Sh—. Ln: Moxon, 1844. 8°
BPL | BUS | CPL | MPL

Strictures on Mr. Collier's new edition of Sh— . . . 1858. Ln: J. R. Smith, 1859. 8°, pp. x.-228
BM | BPL | BUS | CPL | MPL | SML | W

Dyce (Alexander) *Editor*—

See Dodsley
 ,, Jervis
 ,, Sh— Antony . . . 1907
 ,, Sh— As you like it, 1907
 ,, Sh— Hamlet, 1907
 ,, Sh— Merchant . . . 1907
 ,, Sh— Merry wives, 1908
 ,, Sh— Midsummer . . . 1907
 ,, Sh— Poems, 1832, 1856, 1857, 1870
 ,, Sh— Romeo . . . 1907
 ,, Sh— Sir Thomas More, 1844
 ,, Sh— The Tempest, 1907
 ,, Sh— Timon . . . 1842
 ,, Sh— Twelfth night, 1907
 ,, Sh— Winter's tale, 1907
 ,, Sh— Works, 1857, 1860, 1864-67, 1866, 1866-67, 1868, 1874, 1875-76, 1877, 1880-81, 1883, 1885, 1886, 1895-1901

Dyce.] Review of Alex. Dyce's edition of Sh—, 6 vols., 8°, 1857 [In ' Quarterly Review']. 1859. 8°   BPL | BUS

Dyce (Alex.)—
See Collier (J. P.)   *See* Hunter
 ,, Genée   ,, Mitford

Dyche (W.) *Editor*. *See* Sh— As you like it, 1900

Dyer (*Sir* Edward) Verses. *See* Poems

Dyer (George) Relation of poetry to the arts and sciences [In ' The Reflector ']. Ln: 1811
Reprinted in ' Poetics,' 1812.
' Sh— had the inward clothing of a fine mind ; the outward covering of solid reading, of critical observation, and the richest eloquence ; and, compared with these, what are the trappings of the schools?'

Dyer (John). *See* Nichols

Dyer (Thomas F. T.) British popular customs. Ln: Bell, 1876. Cr. 8°   SML

Folk lore of Sh—. Ln: [1883]. 8°
BM | BPL | BUS | SML

Dykes (J. Oswald) Prefatory note. *See* Carter

Dyne (Fr.) Verses. *See* Brooke (C.)

—— (A.) *See* Grey (Z.)
E—— (C.) *See* Ellis (C.)
E—— (G.) *Printer. See* Heywood
E—— (R.) *Printer. See* Lee (N.)
Eardley - Wilmot (*Sir* J. E.) Lecture on 'Othello.' Leamington, 1879. 12° BPL
Earle (John) *Editor. See* Sh— Merchant . . . 1862, 1864
Earle (W.) *Publisher. See* Sh— Works, 1811
Early authorship of Sh—. *See* Sh—
Early English literature. *See* Halliwell
Early English metrical romances. *See* Ellis
Early English poets. *See* Ellis
Early love letters. *See* Reprints
Easingwood *Printer. See* Savage & Easingwood
East (Lucretia) *Printer. See* Byrd
East (Thomas) *Printer—*
   See Glanvilla   *See* Lyly
   ,, Guazzo   ,, Vigo
East and West Junction Railway guide, including notices of Stratford. 1886. Cr. 8° BPL
Eaton (S.) Shakespearean prints. *See* Sh—
Eaton (Thomas Ray) Sh— and the Bible : showing how much the great dramatist was indebted to holy writ for his profound knowledge of human nature. Ln : J. Blackwood, 1858. 8°, pp. iv.-188 BPL | BUS | MPL | SML
   Sh— and the Bible . . . Third edition. Ln : Blackwood [1860]. 8°. With portrait BM | BPL | CPL | SML | W
Ebers (J.) Seven years of the King's Theatre. Ln : W. H. Ainsworth, 1828. 8°
Ebsworth (Joseph Woodfall). *See* Knight (J.)
Ebsworth (J. W.) *Editor. See* Sh— Midsummer . . . 1880
Eccles (Ambrose) Illustrations and variorum commentaries on three plays of Sh—, viz., ' King Lear,' 'Cymbeline,' and ' The Merchant of Venice.' Ln : 1792-1805. 3 vols. 12°
Eccles (Ambrose) *Editor—*
   See Sh— Cymbeline, 1793
   ,, Sh— King Lear, 1793, 1794, 1801, 1805
   ,, Sh— Merchant . . . 1805
   ,, Sh— Works, 1794
Eccles (Gregory W.) *See* British Museum
Eccles (John) *Composer. See* Sh— Macbeth, 1842
Ecclesiastical drama. *See* Religious drama
Echard (Laurence) *Editor. See* Terence
Eclogs of Mantuan. *See* Mantuan

Edge Hills, Warwickshire—
   See Howitt
   ,, Jago
   ,, Miller
Edinburgh. *See* New Theatre
Edinburgh essays, by members of the University. 1857. 8° BPL
   Contains Shakespeareana.
Edinburgh Review [*Consult its general indexes*]
Edinburgh Sh— Society : Annual dinners. Menu cards, 1900-05. Cr. 8° BPL
Editor, booksellers, and critic. *See* Hardinge
Editors of Sh—
   See Harding
   ,, Sh— [Works] Criticism and comment
   ,, *also under respective names*
Edmond (Brice) *Dublin Publisher. See* Sh— King Richard III., 1756
Edmondes (Thomas)—
   See Cecil
   ,, Elizabeth
Edmonds (Charles) Shakespearean discoveries [On ' Venus and Adonis, 1599,' in ' Gentleman's Magazine,' Nov.]. Ln : 1867. 8° BM | BUS
Edmonds (Charles) *Editor—*
   See Lamport
   ,, Sh— Passionate . . . 1870
   ,, Sh— Poems, 1870, 1874
   ,, Sh— Venus . . . 1870
Edmunds *Jesuit. See* Harsnet
Edward III. (*King*). *See* Sh— King Edward III.
Edward IV. (*King*)—
   See Collier (J. P.)
   ,, Heywood
Edward VI. Grammar School. *See* Stratford
Edward the black prince, attempted after the manner of Sh—. Ln : 1750. 8°
Edwardes (Marian) Pocket lexicon and concordance to the ' Temple Sh—.' Ln : Dent, 1909. 16°, pp. 282 BPL
   Contains a glossarial index, and quotations from the chief authorities interpreting obscure passages.
Edwards (E.) *Engraver. See* Sh— Works, 1773-74
Edwards (Ernest) Memorials of Sh—. *See* Sh—
Edwards (H. C.) Poems in connection with the Sh— festival at Coventry. 1864. 12° BPL
Edwards (H. S.) Famous first representations. Ln : Chapman, 1886. 8° SML
Edwards (J.) Biography of Sh—. *See* Sh—
Edwards (J.) *Publisher. See* Sh— Works, 1797, 1798
Edwards (Richard) Paradice of dainty deuises. Containing sundry pithie precepts, learned counsailes, and excellent inuentions : right pleasant and profitable for all estates, deuised by . . . M. Edwardes

[Saint Bernard, Edward Vere Earl of Oxford, Lord Vaux the Elder, W. Hunnis, Iasper Haywood, F. Kindlemarshe, D. Sande, M. Ylope]. Whereunto is added sundry new inuentions very pleasant and delightfull. At Ln : Printed by Edward Allde for Edward White, dwelling at the little north doore of Saint Paules Church at the signe of the Gunne, 1596. Fcp. 4°, black letter, sig. A—L4, unpaged CTC
Apparently the seventh edition. The first appeared in 1576. *See also* 'Waking man's dreame.'

Edwards (Thomas) *Author of 'Narcissus.' See* Stopes

Edwards (Thomas)] A supplement to Mr. Warburton's edition of Sh—. Being the canons of criticism, and glossary collected from the notes in that celebrated work and proper to be bound up with it. By another gentleman of Lincoln's Inn. Ln : M. Cooper, 1748. 8°, pp. 62 BUS | SML | W

] A supplement . . . Second edition. Ln : M. Cooper, 1748. 8°, pp. 62
BM | BPL | BUS | W

] Canons of criticism and glossary . . . Third edition. Ln : C. Bathurst, 1750. 8°, pp. xxvi.-176 BPL | BUS | MPL | W
Richard Roderick assisted Edwards with this edition.

] Canons of criticism . . . Fourth edition. Ln : C. Bathurst, 1750. 8°, pp. xxxviii.-182 BUS | W

] Canons of criticism . . . Fifth edition. Ln : C. Bathurst, 1753. 8°, pp. xl.-180-xviii. BUS | SML | W
With three sonnets prefixed and indexes added.

] Canons of criticism . . . Sixth edition, with additions. Ln : C. Bathurst, opposite St. Dunstan's Church in Fleet St., 1758. 8°, pp. lii.-238-251-325-xiv.
BPL | BUS | CTC | SML

] Canons of criticism and a glossary ; the trial of the letter ϒ, alias Y, and sonnets. Seventh edition, with additions. Ln : C. Bathurst, 1765. 8°, pp. 325-xiv.
BPL | BUS | CPL | MPL | SML | W
Contains at the end Roderick's ' Remarks on Sh—.'

Edwards.] Cambrian Sh—. [Portrait of Thomas Edwards, of Nant, known as the 'Cambrian Sh—'. E. Pugh, *pinx.*, J. Chapman, *sculp*]. Ln : E. Pugh, 1800. 8°
He was born in 1738, died in 1810. Wrote several dramas and poems in Welsh.

Edwards (William Henry) Shaksper not Sh— : A denial of the claims set up for William Shaksper of Stratford as the writer of the Sh— plays. Cincinnati, 1900. 8°. With portrait and facsimiles BPL | BUS
See also Ashhurst

Edyth.] Twelve mery jests of the wyddow Edyth. Ln : R. Ihones, 1573. 8°
Reprinted in Sh—'s Jest books, ed. by Hazlitt (*q.v.*)

Edyth.] Twelve mery jests . . . *See also* Old English jest books

Egan (M. F.) Some phases of Sh— in interpretation. Reprinted from the 'Catholic University Bulletin.' Washington, 1899. 8° BPL

The ghost in ' Hamlet ' and other essays in comparative literature. Chicago, 1906. Cr. 8° BPL

Egan (Pierce) Life of an actor. Illust. by T. Lane. Ln : 1825. 8°. With 27 coloured plates

Life of an actor. Ln : 1892. Roy. 8vo. With 27 coloured plates

Life of Lane. *See* Lane

Egerton. Theatrical remembrancer : List of dramatic performances. 1788. 12° BPL

Egerton (Daniel) *Actor. See* Hawkins

Egerton (*Sir* Thomas) *of Harefield. See* Cunningham

Egerton (T.) *Publisher—*
See Chalmers
  „ Sh— Works, 1798, 1811

Egerton (T. & J.) *Publishers. See* Kemble

Egerton (W.) Faithful memoirs. *See* Oldfield

Eginton (Harvey) Letters to James Britton on the restoration of Trinity Church chancel at Stratford. 1836-39. Holograph MSS. BUS

Eglesfield (Francis) *Publisher. See* Theatrum

Eighteenth century essays on Sh—. Ed. by D. Nichol Smith. Glasgow : Maclehose, 1903. Roy. 8°, pp. 422 BPL | BUS | MPL
Includes Dennis, On genius of Sh— ; Farmer, Essay on learning of Sh— ; Hanmer, Preface . . . 1744 ; Johnson, Preface . . . 1765 ; Morgann, Essay on . . . Falstaff, 1767 ; Pope, Preface . . . 1725 ; Rowe, Life of Sh—, 1709 ; Theobald, Preface . . . 1733 ; Warburton, Preface . . .

Eiloart (Arnold) Sh— and Tolstoy. *See* Sh—

Eld *or* Elde (George) *Printer—*
See Alexander
  „ Goulart
  „ Marston
  „ Returne . . .
  „ Sh— Merry devil . . . 1617
  „ Sh— Puritan widow, 1607
  „ Sh— Sonnets, 1609
  „ Sh— Troilus . . . 1609

Elder (W.) Shaksperean bouquet : Flowers and plants of Sh—. Paisley : Watson, 1872. 8° BPL | SML

Elegie on the death of the famous writer and actor Mr. William Sh—. [In Sh— Poems.] Ln : 1640. 8°
On sig. L an anonymous writer says :—
    'I dare not do thy memory that wrong
    Unto our larger griefs to give a tongue.
. . . .
    How can we then forget thee, when the age
    Her chiefest tutor, and the widowed stage
    Her only favourite, in thee hath lost,
    And nature's self what she did brag of most?

Figures in front row (reading from left to right)

1 Thomas, *first* Howard de Walden
2 Charles Earl of Nottingham *Lord High Admiral.*
3 George Carey *second* Lord Hunsdon *Lord Chamberlain*
4 George Clifford Earl of Cumberland
5 Henry Brooke *sixth* Lord Cobham *Warden of Cinque Ports*

6 Roger Manners Earl of Rutland
7 Lord Herbert of Cardiff
8 Edward *fourth* Earl of Worcester, *father of bridegroom*
9 Queen Elizabeth
10 Edward Russell *third* Earl of Bedford : *or the bridegroom's brother Thomas*

11 Lord Herbert, *the bridegroom*
12 Lucy Harrington Countess of Bedford
13 The Hon. Anne Russell, *the bride*
14 Lady Russell, *the bride's mother*

See p. 91

Sleep then, rich soul of numbers, whilst poor we
Enjoy the profits of thy legacy;
And thinke it happiness enough we have
So much of thee redeemed from the grave
As may suffice to enlighten future times
With the bright lustre of thy matchless rhymes.'

Elimandus ?] Gesta Romanorum . . . 1588.
F° BUS
Chapter cix. contains the foundation-story of the three caskets in the 'Merchant of Venice.' Chapter cliii. is the story of Apollonius of Tyre, one of the sources of 'Pericles.'

] Record of ancient histories, entituled in Latin ' Gesta Romanorum.' Discoursing of sundry examples for the aduancement of vertue and the abandoning of vice, no lesse pleasant in reading than profitable in practise. Now newly perused and corrected, with something added, by R. R— [Richard Robinson]. Ln: Printed by Thomas Snodham [c. 1600]. 12° BUS
For Sh—'s indebtedness to this work *see* Douce's 'Illustrations' and Warton's 'History of English poetry.' Reprinted in 'Sh—'s library,' edited by Collier.

Eliot (J.) *Editor*. *See* Loque

Elizabeth *of Eng*. (*Queen*) Letter to Thomas Edmondes, English agent at the French Court [on Hy. Wriothesley, third Earl of Southampton], 3rd Sept., 1598 [In 'Athenæum,' No. 3348, p. 864, Dec.]. 1891. 4°
Proclamation as to licences for interludes. Ln: New Sh— Soc., 1880-86. 8°

Elizabeth.] Elizabeth Regina to Victoria Regina, Greeting: Anno Domini 1847. 1847. 12° BPL
A poem, with Shakespearean references.

Elizabeth (*Queen*)—

See Aikin	*See* Livius
,, Bacon (F.)	,, Malone
,, Chettle	,, Mirrour . . .
,, Contemporary	,, Ordish
,, Cope	,, Puttenham
,, Court	,, Revels
,, Creighton	,, Rye
,, Cunningham	,, Schelling
,, Dugdale	,, Scott (E. J. L.)
,, Extracts	,, Sh—Love's labours
,, Fleay	lost, 1598
,, Greene (T.)	,, Sh— Merry wives,
,, Gregg	1602, 1702
,, Gybbys	,, Sh— Works: Ext.
,, Hall (H.)	1900
,, Halliwell	,, Smith (W. H.)
,, Hayward	,, Spalding
,, Hazlitt	,, Stopes
,, Heywood	,, Swarraton
,, Ingleby	,, Thornbury
,, Johnson	,, Waldron
,, Laneham	,, Whipple

Elizabeth's (*Queen*) players—
See Affray . . .
,, Peele

Elizabeth's (*Queen*) players—
See Sh— King Henry V., 1598
,, Sh— King John, 1591, 1611
,, Sh— King Richard III., 1594

Elizabethan manuscript preserved at Alnwick Castle, Northumberland: Collotype facsimile and type transcript. Ed. with introduction and notes by Frank J. Burgoyne. Ln: Longman, 1904. 4°
Bears on the Bacon-Sh— controversy. BPL | BUS
See also Douse

Elizabethan poets. *See* Van Dam

Ellacombe (Henry Nicholson) Plant-lore and garden-craft of Sh—. *See* Sh— Works: Ext. 1878, 1884, 1896
Seasons of Sh—'s plays. Ln: New Sh— Soc., 1880-86. 8°
Sh— as an angler. Ln: Stock, 1883. 8°
BM | BPL | SML

Ellesmere (Francis Egerton *Earl of*) *Bibliophile*. *See* Sh— Sonnets, 1862

Elliot (C.) *Edinburgh Publisher*. *See* Sh— Taming . . . 1783-88

Elliott (J.) Tercentenary national song to Sh—. With music by Prof. Clare. 1864. 8° CPL

Elliott (*Mrs*. M. Leigh). *See* Leigh-Noel

Ellis (Alexander John) On early English pronunciation, with especial reference to Sh— and Chaucer, containing an investigation of the correspondence of writing with speech in England from the Anglo-Saxon period to the present day, preceded by a systematic notation of all spoken sounds by means of the ordinary printing types. Ln: Asher & Co. for the Philological Soc., 1869-75. 4 vols. 8°
BM | BPL | BUS | MPL

Ellis (A. J.) *Editor*—
See Sh— Macbeth, 1849
,, Sh— The Tempest, 1849

Ellis (Charles) Christ in Sh—. *See* Sh— Sonnets, 1902

Ellis (Charles) *Editor*—
See Sh— Sonnets, 1896, 1897
,, Sh— Works: Ext. 1897

Ellis (Edwin J.) *Artist*—
See Sh— Sonnets, 1883
,, Sh— Winter's tale, 1888

Ellis (Frederick Startridge) New catalogue of ancient and modern books, including a collection of Shakespeareana . . . Ln: 1864. 8° BPL | BUS | MPL

Ellis (F. S.) *Editor*. *See* Sh— Poems, 1893, 1899

Ellis (George) Specimens of early English metrical romances . . . Revised by J. O. Halliwell. Ln: H. G. Bohn, 1848. 8°, pp. viii.-600 and illuminated frontispiece

Ellis (George) Specimens of early English poets
[with] . . . the rise and progress of English
poetry and language. Third edition. Ln :
Bulmer & Co., 1803. 3 vols. 8°

Ellis *M.D.* (Havelock) *Editor—*
See *Sh—*] Robertson
,, *Sh—*] Wheeler

Ellis (J.) The tercentenary : A festal song
[In 'Meletæ : Poems']. 1869. 12° BPL

Ellis (Tristram J.) *Engraver. See* Sh— Sonnets, 1883

Elliston (R. W.) Portrait. *See* Moncrieff

Elliston (R. W.) *Actor & Editor—*
See Sh— Coriolanus, 1820
,, Sh— King Henry IV., ii., 1904
,, Sh— King Lear, 1820, 1845

Elliston.] Raymond (G.) Memoirs of Robert
William Elliston, comedian. Illustrated
by G. Cruikshank and 'Phiz.' Ln : 1846.
2 vols. 8°
Reprinted in 1857.

Ellits (*Dr.*) Othello and Desdemona : their
characters, and the manner of Desdemona's death. With a notice of Calderon's
debt to Sh—. Philadelphia, 1887. 12°
BM | BPL | BUS

Elsheimer.] Hirst (S.) Life of Adam Elsheimer,
painter of Sh—'s portrait. Huddersfield,
1884. 8°

Elson (Louis Charles) Sh— in music : A collation of the chief musical allusions in
the plays . . . with an attempt at their
explanation and derivation, together with
much of the original music. Ln : Nutt,
1901. Cr. 8°, pp. 364. With portraits
and plates BPL | BUS | SML

Elson (Robert) *Editor. See* Sh— Works,
1893-98

Elstracke (Renold) *Artist & Engraver—*
See James I.
,, Mexia

Elton (Charles Isaac) Wm. Sh— ; his family
and friends. *See* Sh—

Elton (E. W.) *Editor. See* Sh— Works, 1839-
43

Elton (*Prof.* Oliver) Michael Drayton. *See*
Drayton
Recent Sh— criticism [In ' Modern Studies,'
pp. 78-121]. Ln : Arnold, 1907. 8°, pp.
350 BPL

Elton (*Prof.* Oliver) *Editor—*
See Saxo-Grammaticus
,, Sh— King Henry IV., i., 1889
,, Sh— King John, 1890
,, Sh— Works, 1886-91

Elwall (A.) *Editor—*
See Sh— Julius Cæsar, 1881
,, Sh— King Richard III., 1881
,, Sh— Macbeth, 1881

Elwert *Marburg Publisher. See* Sh— King
Lear, 1886

Elwin (Hastings) Shakespeare restored. *See*
Sh— Macbeth, 1853

Ely (G. H.) *Editor—*
See Sh— King Henry VIII., 1893
,, Sh— Merchant . . . 1893
,, Sh— Works, 1893

Elze (*Prof.* Friedrich Karl) Alexandrines in the
' Winter's tale ' and ' King Richard II.'
[1881.] 8° BM
Essays on Sh— . . . Trans. . . . by L. Dora
Schmitz. Ln : Macmillan, 1874. 8°,
pp. viii.-380 BM | BPL | BUS | MPL | SML
Letter to C. M. Ingleby . . . containing notes
. . . on Sh—'s ' Cymbeline.' 1885. 8° BM
Who was the English originator of the so-
called ' Baconian theory '? [In 'Athe-
næum,' No. 3008, p. 801]. 1885
Wm. Sh—. *See* Sh—
See also Friesen
,, ,, Halliwell

Elze (*Prof.* F. K.) *Editor. See* Sh— Hamlet,
1857, 1882

Emanuel (John) Moorish marriage. Bearing
some similarity to Sh—'s ' Taming of the
Shrew.' Ln : Privately printed, 1867.
16°, pp. 30 MPL
Impression limited to ten copies.
Poem in celebration of Sh—'s tercentenary
at the Hartley Institution, Southampton.
[1864 ?] 4° BPL

Emerson (Ralph Waldo) On Sh—. *See* Sh—
Representative men. *See* Sh—
See Bacon (D. S.)

Emery (Mary Ella Bryant) Was not Sh— a
gentleman ? Lynn [U.S.], 1903. 8°, pp.
40 BPL | BUS

Emmanuel (F. L.) *Artist. See* Sh— Merry
wives, 1895, 1897

Empress of Morocco. *See* Duffet

Enfield (W.) The speaker. *See* Sh— Works :
Ext. 1785, 1792

Engel (E.) History of English literature.
1902. 8° BPL
Sh – occupies pp. 110-203.

Engel (M.) *See* Siddons (H.)

Engelmann (W.) *Leipzig Publisher. See* Sh—
Hamlet, 1849

England (N.) *Publisher. See* Painter

England's bards, 1864, or the three poems
which were awarded the one hundred
guineas prize in the advt. ' Ho ! for a
Sh—' . . . Ln : Day & Son, 1864. 8°,
pp. 16. Illust. BPL | BUS
An advertisement of Thomson's crinoline.

England's helicon. *See* Bodenham

England's parnassus. *See* Sh— Works : Ext.
1600

England's selected characters, describing the good and bad worthies of the age, where the best may see their graces and the worst discerne their basenesse. Ln : T. S——, 1643. F°
Twenty-eight characters are depicted. No. 20, 'An unworthy lawyer,' mentions 'King Richard the Third.'

Engleheart (T. S.) *Engraver—*
See Sh— Works, 1829
,,   Sh— Works : Ext. 1841

English and American Review. Ed. by C. H. Gunn. Amsterdam, 1864
Contains at pp. 148-153 'Shakespearean studies'; at p. 385 an article entitled 'Sh—, 1564-1616.'

English and Scottish sketches, by an American 1857. 12°   BPL
Sh—'s birthplace and tomb, pp. 163-190.

English drama and the English stage, 1543-1664, under the Tudor and Stuart princes. Illustrated by documents, treatises, and poems, with preface and index. [Ed. by W. C. Hazlitt.] Ln : Roxburgh Library, 1869. 4°   MPL

English re-traced, or remarks, critical and philological, founded on a comparison of the 'Breeches' Bible with the English of the present day. Cambridge : H. Wallis, 1862. Cr. 8°, pp. xii.-228
A valuable commentary on Sh—'s English.

English plays [from the earliest times] : selected, edited, and arranged by Henry Morley. Ln : Cassell [1880 ?]. 4°, pp. viii.-440, textually illustrated with portraits and engravings

English stage from 1660 to 1830. *See* Geneste

Enquiry into the conduct of Edmond Malone. *See* Caulfield

Enslin (T. C. F.) *Berlin Publisher—*
See Sh— Julius Cæsar, 1855
,,   Sh— Macbeth, 1853
,,   Sh— Merchant . . . 1854
,,   Sh— Othello, 1853
,,   Sh— Romeo . . . 1853

Ensor (John Strong). *See* Nichols

Epistle from little Captain Brazen to the worthy Captain Plume. To which is added, an answer to the said epistle. In which the character of Iago is set forth so as to be understood by the meanest capacity. Ln : Printed for A. Moore [c. 1740]. F°.   w
In verse.

Epistle from Sh— to his countrymen [a poem]. To which are added, some stanzas upon the immortality of the soul. Ln : Richardson & Urquhart, 1777. 4°, pp. 24
                                    BM | BPL | BUS

Epistle to Mr. Pope, occasioned by Theobald's Sh— . . . Second edition. Ln : Printed by Lawton Gilliver at Homer's Head over against St. Dunstan's Church, Fleet Street, 1733. F°

Erasmus (D.) *See* Heywood

Erle (T. W.)] Letters from a theatrical scene-painter : Sketches of minor London theatres. Ln : Ward, 1880. 8°   SML

Esdaile (A.) Sh— literature, 1901-05 [In 'The Library,' Vol. 7, April]. Ln : 1906. Roy. 8°   BM | BPL

Esquiros (A.) English at home. [Second series.] Ln : 1862. Cr. 8°   BPL
Contains Shakespeareana.

Essay on acting. *See* Garrick

Essay on . . . Falstaff. *See* Morgann

Essay on 'Julius Cæsar' [In 'Dramatic Censor,' Vol. 2]. Ln : 1770. 8°   w

Essay on one particular view of tragedy, not sufficiently attended to by modern poets, namely, a more general improvement of the understanding; shewing by some examples taken from Sh— how this may be done. Together with some observations, as well on certain beauties in that poet, as on the reigning pathos of the age. The whole proposed as a means of greatly improving and extending the usefulness of the stage. Manuscript on thirty-five leaves of paper [c. 1750]. F°   w

Essay on original genius; and its various modes of exertion in philosophy and the fine arts, particularly in poetry. Ln : 1767. 8°   w
On p. 141 is an article, 'Sh—: his great genius,' and on p. 287 another on the 'Genius of Sh— and Milton.'

Essay on . . . Sh—. *See* Montagu (E.)

Essay on the authorship of the three parts of 'King Henry VI.' Cambridge, 1859. 8°

Essay on the character of Hamlet. *See* Pilon

Essay on the character of Macbeth. Ln : C. Mitchell, 1846. 8°, pp. iv.-100
                         BM | BPL | BUS | SML | W
A reply to G. Fletcher on 'Macbeth.'

Essay on the jubilee at Stratford-upon-Avon. Ln : Woodfall [1769]. 4°, pp. 16   BUS

Essay on the science of acting. *See* Grant (G.)

Essay on the theatres, or art of acting [Harleian Misc., Vol. 5]. Ln : 1810. 4°.
In verse.   BPL

Essay on the theatres . . . [Harleian Misc., Vol. 12]. Ln : 1811. 8°   BPL

Essay on tragedy, with a critical examen of 'Mahomet' and 'Irene.' 1749. 8° BPL

Essay towards fixing the true standards of wit. *See* Morris

Essay upon poetry, 1682. *See* Sh—] Sh—ana

Essayes of certaine paradoxes. *See* Cornewallis

Essays, by a society of gentlemen at Exeter. Exeter [1796]. 8° BPL
Contains Shakespeareana.

Essays ; philosophical, historical, and literary. 1789. 8° BPL
Sh—, pp. 16-32.

Essence of Malone. *See* Hardinge

Essex (Robert Devereux *Second Earl of*)] Apologie . . . against those which jealously and maliciously tax the Earl of Essex to be the hinderer of the peace and quiet of his country. Penned . . . in 1598 . . . Ln : R. Bradocke, 1603. Fcp. 4° SML

Essex.] True mannor and forme of the proceeding to the funerall of the Earl of Essex. Ln : H. Seale, 1646. Fcp. 4° SML

See B—— (O.) *See* Munro
 „ Bacon (*Sir* F.) „ Owen
 „ Cuffe   „ Stopes
 „ Hayward „ Swarraton
 „ Landor

Essex House Press. *See* Sh— Poems, 1899

Estienne (C.) & Liebault (Jean) Maison rustique, or the countrie farme. Trans. into English by Ric. Surflet . . . Also a short collection of the hunting of the harte, wild bore, hare, foxe, gray, conie, etc. Ln : Printed by A. Hatfield for J. Norton and J. Bill, 1606. Fcp. 4°. With plans of 'knots for gardens' W
' Her hedges ruined ; her knots disorder'd.'
—*King Richard II.*
' From the west corner of thy curious knotted garden.'
—*Love's labours lost*, Act I., Sc. ii.

Estienne (Henry). *See* Stephen (H.)

Etching Club *Artists. See* Sh— Poems, 1842-52, 1843, 1847, 1852

Etherington (C.) *York Publisher—*
See Garrick
 „ Gentleman
 „ Hull
 „ Sh— All's well, 1773
 „ Sh— Antony, 1776
 „ Sh— Coriolanus, 1773
 „ Sh— Cymbeline, 1773
 „ Sh— Julius Cæsar, 1773
 „ Sh— King Henry V., 1773
 „ Sh— King Henry VI., i., 1774
 „ Sh— King Henry VI., ii., 1774
 „ Sh— King Henry VI., iii., 1774
 „ Sh— King John, 1773
 „ Sh— King Lear, 1774
 „ Sh— King Richard II., 1774
 „ Sh— Measure . . . 1773
 „ Sh— Othello, 1773
 „ Sh— Poems, 1774
 „ Sh— Taming . . . 1774
 „ Sh— Timon . . . 1773
 „ Sh— Titus . . . 1774

Etherington (C.) *York Publisher—*
See Sh— Troilus . . . 1774
 „ Sh— Twelfth night, 1773, 1774
 „ Sh— Winter's tale, 1773

Ethics of ' Macbeth ' [In ' Dublin University Magazine,' Mar.] Dublin, 1865. 8° BPL | BUS

Ethics of the Sh— celebrations. *See* Gordon

Eton Shakespeareana. *See* Greg

Etymologist (The) : A comedy of three acts. Most humbly dedicated to the late Doctor Samuel Johnson's negro servant ; to all commentators that ever wrote, are writing, or will write, on Sh— ; and particularly to that commentator of commentators, the conjectural, inventive, and collatitious G. S—— [George Steevens]. Ln : J. Jarvis, 1785. 8°, pp. iv.-46 and woodcut BPL | BUS | W

Euordanus.] First and second part of the history of the famous Euordanus Prince of Denmark. With the strange aduentures of Iago Prince of Saxonie, and of both theyr seuerall fortunes in loue. Ln : Printed by J. R—— [James Roberts ?] for R. B—— [Robert Barker or Richard Bradock?], 1605. Fcp. 4°, black letter W
It is supposed that Sh— took the name of Iago from this work.'—J. O. HALLIWELL.

Euphues' golden legacie. *See* Lodge

Euripides. Iphigenia et Aulis. Trans. by [Jane] Lady Lumley [c. 1550]. Ed. by Harold H. Child and W. W. Greg. Malone Society Reprints, 1909. Fcp. 4° SML

Euripides. *See* Sh— King Richard III., 1824

Eusebius. Auncient ecclesiasticall histories . . . Trans. by Meredith Hanmer. Ln : 1585. F°
In his ' New illustrations,' vol. i., p. 247, Hunter shows how the ' Epistle dedicatory' of above illustrates a passage in ' Much ado.'

Evans (E. P.) Youth, marriage, and manhood of Sh—. *See* Sh—

Evans (Francis Wm. Ernest) Gallery influences on Sh—'s plays. Sh— Club Paper. Stratford-on-Avon, 1909. Cr. 8°, pp. 8

Evans (H. A.) *See* Stopes & Evans

Evans (Herbert Arthur) *Editor—*
See Sh— King Henry IV., i., 1881
 „ Sh— King Henry IV., ii., 1882
 „ Sh— King Henry V., 1903
 „ Sh— King Lear, 1898
 „ Sh— Midsummer . . . 1887, 1907
 „ Sh— Othello, 1885
 „ Sh— Romeo . . . [1597] 1886, [1599] 1886, [Und.] 1887
 „ Sh— The Tempest, 1889, 1907
 „ Sh— Works, 1887-89

Evans (*Dr.* John) Sh—'s ' Seven ages of man ' :
The progress of human life illustrated by
extracts. Introduced by a brief memoir
of Sh— and his writings. Chiswick : C.
Whittingham, 1818. 12°, pp. xlviii.-252
                              BPL | BUS | W
Sh—'s ' Seven ages . . .' Second edition.
Chiswick : C. Whittingham, 1820. 12°,
pp. xlviii.-252   BPL | BUS
Sh—'s ' Seven ages . . .' Ln : C. Tilt, 1834.
12°, pp. xlviii.-252. Illust.   BPL | BUS
Evans (M. B.) ' Der bestrafte brudermord '
and Sh—'s 'Hamlet' [Rep. from 'Modern
Philology']. Chicago, 1905. 8°   BPL
Evans (R. H.) *Publisher*—
  See Evans (T.)
  ,, Sh— Works, 1811
Evans (Sebastian) Sh— : A cantata. Bir-
mingham : Our Shakespeare Club, 1864.
8°, pp. xii.   BPL | BUS
  See also Birmingham
Evans *Editor* (Thomas) Old ballads, historical
and narrative, with some of modern date,
collected from rare copies and MSS.
New ed., revised and considerably en-
larged from public and private collections
by his son. Ln : Printed for R. H. Evans
by W. Bulmer . . . 1810. 4 vols. 8°.
With frontispiece from Caxton's ' Mirror
of the world, 1481 '
  See also Sh— King Henry V., 1838
Evans (Thomas) *Publisher*—
  ,, Sh— Merchant . . . 1783
  ,, Sh— Poems, 1775
  ,, Sheridan
Events in the history of New York city, with
illustrations from Sh— [Calendars]. 1880-
81. 2 vols. 12°   BPL
Evered (Elwin Everard John) Festival of
Sh— : A sermon preached in the church
of Saint James, Stratford-on-Avon. Ln :
J. Masters, 1864. 8°, pp. 16   BUS
Everybody's year book [Sh— p. 71]. 1870.
12°   BPL
Every man : An interlude. An unknown
edition printed by Pynson. Ed. by
'Dramaticus.' *See Sh*—] Sh— Soc.
Ewen (Alfred) Sh—. *See* Sh—
Ewing (George) *Dublin Publisher*—
  See Fielding
  ,, Sh— Macbeth, 1723
Ewing (George & Alexander) *Dublin Pub-
lishers*. *See* Upton
Ewing (Thomas) *Dublin Publisher*—
  See Sh— Coriolanus, 1754
  ,, Sh— Poems, 1771
  ,, Sh— Works, 1771

Examination into the structure, language, and
metre of ' Richard II.' and ' Henry IV.'
[In ' London University Magazine,' Aug.
1858. 8°   BUS
Examination of Kenrick's review. *See* Bar-
clay
Examination of . . . [Warburton's] Sh—. *See*
Grey
Excellencie of the English tongue. *See* Carew
Excerpta from the commonplace book of a
septuagenarian : Reflections on Sh—'s
' Seven ages of man ' [In ' Knickerbocker,'
May]. New York, 1835. 8°   BUS
Exhibitions—
  See Flower   *See Sh*—] Sh— museum
  ,, *Sh*—] Sh—   ,, Stratford
Explanations and emendations. *See* Morehead
Exshaw (John) *Dublin Publisher*—
  See Sh— King Lear, 1768
  ,, Sh— Timon . . . 1772
  ,, Sh— Titus . . . 1794
  ,, Sh— Works, 1766, 1794
Extemporal verses written at the birthplace
. . . [by various writers]. With a history
of the bard and family by Mary Hornby.
Stratford-on-Avon : Barnacle, 1820. 8°,
pp. 24. Illust.   BPL | CPL
Extemporal verses . . . With observations on
the comet by Mary Hornby. Fourth
edition. Stratford-on-Avon : Barnacle
[c. 1820]. 8°, pp. 24. Illust.   BUS
Extemporary verses, written at the birthplace
of Sh— at Stratford-upon-Avon by people
of genius ; to which is added, A brief
history of the immortal bard and family,
with a discourse on natural and moral
philosophy by Mary Hornby . . . Stratford : Barnacle, printer, June, 1818. 8°,
pp. 26   BM | BPL
The first known publication issued from the Birthplace, a house that continued in the possession of
the poet's family descendants until Mrs. Hornby's
husband became the tenant.
Extracts. *See* Stratford-upon-Avon
Extracts and collections from various authors.
See Sh— Works : Ext. 1834
Extracts from the accounts of the revels at
Court in the reigns of Q. Elizabeth and
K. James I., from the original office books
of the masters and yeomen. With introd.
and notes by Peter Cunningham. Ln :
Sh— Soc., 1842. 8°, pp. lii.-228 BUS
The Sh— entries proved to be forgeries, done by Cun-
ningham.
Extracts from the registers of the Stationers'
Company. *See* Stationers
Ey (A.) *Editor*. *See* Sh— Macbeth, 1879
Eyton (J. W. K.) *Bibliophile*. *See* Catalogue,
1848

—— (C.) *See* Fleming (C.)
F—— (F. J.) *See* Furnivall (F. J.)
F—— (M.) *Printer*—
See Flesher (Miles)
,, Weaver
F—— (O.) *See* Follett (O.)
F—— (T.) *Printer*. *See* Habington
F—— (T. J.) *See* Foard (T. J.)
Facetiæ—

See Adams	*See* Notes & emendations
,, Antiquity	
,, Barret	,, Old English . . .
,, Bartlett	,, P—— (J. & T. C.)
,, Beerbohm	,, Parker
,, Bobson	,, Peele
,, Brooks (C. S.)	,, Pleasant . . .
,, Brough	,, Poems . . .
,, Clemens	,, Posthumous . . .
,, Comic guide	,, Powell
,, Cox	,, R—— (S.)
,, Coyne	,, Ralegh
,, Criswell	,, Ritson
,, Culler	,, Ross
,, Davey	,, Rout (The)
,, Decker	,, Routledge
,, Des Periers	,, Rowlandson
,, Dibdin	,, S—— (T.)
,, Doctors	,, Sack . . .
,, Dodsley	,, Scarron
,, Douce	,, Seymour
,, Dowden	,, *Sh*—] Sh— Jest books
,, Drama (The)	
,, Dudley	,, *Sh*—] Sh—'s comic tricentenary
,, Dunton	
,, Edwards	,, Shaw (G. B.)
,, Edyth	,, Simpleton
,, Etymologist	,, Singer
,, Fairholt	,, Smith (H. & J.)
,, Fechter	,, Soule
,, Ford	,, Spermacetti
,, Furnivall	,, Spoffkins
,, Gilbert	,, Stephens
,, Gray	,, *Stratford*] Hoax
,, Griffin	,, *Stratford*] Notes
,, Hamilton (W.)	,, Symonds
,, Hardinge	,, T—— (T.)
,, Heath	,, Tarlton
,, Hyatt	,, Taylor (John)
,, Ignotus	,, Teetgen
,, Jacox	,, Thompson
,, Kelsall	,, Three conjurors
,, Kenrick	,, Titmarsh
,, Lawreen	,, Tom King . . .
,, Lovibond	,, Typographical
,, Meadows	,, Weiss
,, Melodrama mad	,, West Indian
,, Memoirs . . .	,, White
,, Morehead	,, Zangwill

Facts and reasons in answer to Farren. Ln:
1833. 8°
A reply to George Farren (*q. v.*)
Fair Em. *See* Sh— Fair Em
Fair, kind, and true. *See* Duggan
Fair Widow.] Ancient ballad of the fair widow of Watling Street and her three daughters: From the earliest known edition printed by Thomas Pavier about 1600. Ed. by J. O. Halliwell. Ln: 1860. 12°, thirty copies printed BPL | BUS | HCL
Entered at Stationers' Hall, 15 Aug., 1597, but no earlier edition than Pavier's is known.
Malone conjectured that the 'Puritan Widow,' attributed to Sh—, was founded on this ballad, but the story is essentially different.
Fairbairn (J. & J.) *Edinburgh Publishers*. *See* Sh— Works, 1792, 1795
Fairbanks (Charles B.)] Letter from 'Aguecheek': Sh— and his commentators, with suggestions concerning . . . 'Hamlet' [In 'Boston Saturday Evening Gazette,' 24 April]. 1858 BUS
Fairbrother *Publisher*. *See* Sh— Othello, 1844
Fairholt (Frederick William)] 'Grimaldi Sh—': Notes and emendations on the plays of Sh—, from a recently-discovered annotated copy by the late J. Grimaldi. Ln: J. Russell Smith, 1853. 8°, pp. 16
BM | BPL | BUS | CPL | MPL
A humorous satire on Collier's alleged discovery. *See* Collier controversy, also ' Notes and emendations.'
Home of Sh— illustrated and described. Ln: 1845. Cr. 8°. 33 woodcuts
Home of Sh—. Ln: Chapman & Hall, 1847. Cr. 8°, pp. ii.-32 and 33 engravings
BM | BPL | BUS | CPL
Home of Sh—. New York: W. Taylor [1847]. Cr. 8°, pp. 64 BPL | BUS
Home of Sh— . . . Ln: H. G. Bohn, 1862. Cr. 8°
Home of Sh— . . . With a few introductory observations . . . by J. O. Halliwell-Phillipps. Warwick: Cooke, 1889. Cr. 8°, pp. iv.-68 (incl. pr. wrappers) BPL
Tobacco: Its history and associations. Ln: Chapman, 1859. Cr. 8° SML
Refers to Sh—'s mulberry tree, p. 293.
See also Irving & Fairholt
Fairholt (F. W.) *Artist*—
See Croker
,, Neil
,, Sh— Works, 1853-65
Fairholt (F. W.) *Editor*. *See* Lyly
Fairies. *See* Folk-Lore
Fairies (The): An opera. *See* Sh— Midsummer . . . 1754, 1755, 1756, 1798
Fairy prince—
See Colman
,, Sh— Midsummer . . . 1771
Fairy queen: An opera. *See* Sh— Midsummer . . . 1692, 1693

Fairy queen dialogue. *See* Sh— Winter's tale, 1690

Faithorne *Artist.* *See* Sh— Works, 1816

Faithorne (W.) *Engraver.* *See* Scarron

Falbe (*Count de*) Hamlet saga, from Saxo-Grammaticus. 1882. 8°   BPL

Falconer (E.) Anne Hathaway : A tradition-ary ballad. 1864. 4°   BPL | CPL
   Fairies' festival on Sh—'s birthday. Ln : Theatre Royal, Drury Lane [1864 ?] 12°   BPL

Falkland (Lucius Cary *Viscount*) Marriage night. *See* Dodsley

Falkner (Francis) *Publisher.* *See* Sh— Merry devil . . . 1626, 1631

Fall of Mortimer. An historical play. [By —. Hatchett ?] 1763. 8°   W
  Nearly forty references to Mortimer occur in ' King Henry IV.' and ' King Henry VI.'

Falstaff.] Diverting history . . . *See* Sh— Merry wives, 1750, 1789

] Falstaff : A comedy. *See* Sh— Works : Ext. 1829

] Falstaff : Comic opera. *See* Sh— Merry wives, 1838

] Falstaff Club : [Programme of the] first soirée musicale. 1882. 8°   BPL

] Falstaff's jests. *See* Sh— Works : Ext. 1761, 1762

] Falstaff's wedding. *See* Kenrick (W.)

] Life and exploits . . . *See* Sh— Merry wives,. 1800

Falstaff, Fastolff, *or* Cobham—

See Account . . .	*See* Maynard
„ Antiquity . . .	„ Morgann
„ Bale	„ Morris
„ Beaumont	„ New comic . . .
„ Brough	„ New pantomime
„ Character	„ Oldys
„ Cleveland	„ Otway
„ Creighton	„ Phelps
„ Doran	„ Picton
„ Duthie	„ Playford
„ Flatman	„ Purveiour
„ Forbes-Robertson	„ Radford
„ Gairdner	„ Randolph
„ Giles	„ Richardson
„ Goldsmith	„ Rochester
„ Hackett	„ Rusden
„ Halliwell	„ S—— (C.)
„ Hatton	„ Shadwell
„ Heylyn	„ Sh— King Henry
„ Interview	IV., 1789
„ Irwin	„ Sh— Merry wives
„ Jackson	1789
„ Johnson	„ *Sh—*] Sh—
„ Kelly	„ Stack
„ Konewka	„ Turner
„ Mackenzie	„ Welsted
„ Marvell	„ White & Lamb

' Falstaff the Second ' *pseud.* Shakespearean characters in Liverpool. L'pool : Will-mer, 1887. 8°, pp. 24
  Extracts attached to the names of local public men.

Familiar address to the curious in English poetry, more particularly to the readers of Sh—. By ' Thersites Literarius.' Ln : Henry Payne, opposite to Marlborough House, Pall Mall, 1784. 8°
  Contains criticism of Ritson's ' Remarks.'

Familiar verses. *See* Woodward

Famous tragedie of King Charles I. basely butchered . . . Ln : 1649. Fcp. 4°
  Refers to Sh— in the prologue.

Famous victories of Henry the Fifth—
  See Sh— King Henry V., 1598
  „ Six old plays

Fane *jun.* (*Sir* Francis) Love in the dark, or the man of business : A comedy. Acted at the Theatre Royal by His Majesties servants. Ln : In the Savoy, Printed by T. N—— for Henry Herringman, 1675. Fcp. 4°, pp. viii.-184
  The epilogue has this passage :—
   ' The great wonder of our English stage,
   Whom nature seemed to charm for your delight,
   And bid him speak, as she bid Sh— write.'

The sacrifice : A tragedy. Ln : Printed by J. R—— for John Wedd at the Crown between the Temple Gates in Fleet Street, 1686. Fcp. 4°
  In the prefixed poem, by Nahum Tate, Sh— is twice mentioned, also ' Othello ':—
   ' Your monarch rages in Othello's strain,
   Iago in Ragolzan lives again.'

Farley (Charles) *Theatre Manager*—
See Garrick
  „ Sh— King Henry IV., ii., 1821

Farmer (*Dr.* Richard) Essay on the learning of Sh—, addressed to Joseph Cradock. Cambridge : Printed by J. Archdeacon . . . 1767. 8°, pp. vi.-50   BM | BUS | W
  The writer was principal of Emmanuel College, Cambridge.

Essay . . . Second edition, with additions. Cambridge : J. Archdeacon, 1767. 8°, pp. viii.-98   BPL | BUS | MPL
  Twelve copies were also printed on thick paper.

Essay . . . Third edition. Ln : T. Longman, 1789. 8°, pp. x.-96
         BPL | BUS | CPL | MPL | W

Essay . . . Ln : Merrill, 1798. 8°   SML

Essay . . . Ln : 1800. 12°   BPL

Essay . . . Basil [Switzerland] : J. J. Tour-neisen, 1800. 8°, pp. 96   BM | BUS | W

Essay . . . Ln : T. & H. Rodd, 1821. 8°, pp. 114. With portraits (of Sh— and the author)   BM | BPL | BUS | CPL | W

Essay . . .
See Eighteenth
  „ Sh— Works, 1773, 1793, 1798-1800, 1800, 1803-05

Farmer (*Dr.* Richard) Shakespearean manuscripts [A large collection of papers relating to Sh—, 1760]. Holograph manuscript on paper. 4 vols. F° w
Probably the garner used by Dr. Farmer in preparing his works.

Farmer (*Dr.* R.)—
See Annotations
,, Maginn
,, Malone

Farnaby (Thomas) Florilegium epigrammatum Græcorum, eorumque Latino versu a variis redditorum. Ln: 1629. 8°
In the Baconian controversy some dwell on the statement of John Aubrey that ' Bacon was a good poet but concealed.' The verses of Bacon (of which Aubrey quotes the opening lines) formed a parody on a Latin version of the ' Seven ages of man.' Bacon's English rendering, which seems to have fallen into the hands of Farnaby, is printed with the latter writer's Greek on parallel pages herein.

Farnie (H. B.) *Editor. See* Sh— Romeo . . . 1867

Farquhar (A. B.) Did Sh— write ' Sh—' ? [In 'American Journal of Politics']. 1893. **8°**   BPL

Farquhar (George) Extracts. *See* Sh— Works: Ext. 1822

Farrar *Dean* (F. W.) Great books : Sh—. Ln: 1898. 8°   BM | BPL
Sh—; the man and the poet. *See* Sh—]
Sh— Sermons

Farren *Actress* (Elizabeth) Portrait—
See Sh— King Richard II., 1786
,, Sh— Midsummer . . . 1785

Farren (George) Essay on Sh—'s character of Shylock . . . laws and customs of Moses, and primitive Christians, with reference to enumerations of population and the rate of interest of money. Ln: P. Richardson, 1833. 8°, pp. iv.-52
BM | BPL | BUS | W
Essays on the varieties in mania exhibited by the characters of Hamlet, Ophelia, Lear, and Edgar. Ln: 1833. 8°
Illustrations of the progress of mania, melancholia, craziness, and demonomania as displayed in Sh—'s characters of King Lear, Hamlet, Ophelia, and Edgar [In 'Observations']. Ln: Hessey & Richardson, 1826. 8°   BUS | SML
Illustrations . . . Ln: 1829. 8° BUS | CPL
Observations on the laws of mortality . . . With an appendix containing illustrations of the progress of mania, melancholia, craziness, and demonomania as displayed in Sh—'s characters of Lear, Hamlet, Ophelia, and Edgar. Printed for the author, 1829. 8°   BM | BPL
Observations . . . 1833. 8°   BM | BPL
On Hamlet's soliloquy . . . [In ' London Magazine,' June]. Ln: 1824. 8° BUS

Farren (George) On the madness of Hamlet and Ophelia [In ' London Magazine,' April]. Ln : 1824. 8°   BPL | BUS
On the madness of Lear [In ' London Magazine,' July]. Ln : 1824. 8°   BUS
On the madness of Ophelia [In ' London Magazine,' May]. Ln : 1824. 8° BUS
See also Facts and reasons

Farren (Wm.) *Actor. See* Sh— Twelfth night, 1780

Farther defence of dramatick poetry. *See* Rymer

Fastolff *or* Falstaff. *See* Falstaff

Faulder (J.) *Publisher. See* Sh— Works, 1811

Faulder (R.) *Publisher*—
See Caldecott
,, Ireland
,, Sh— Works, 1797, 1798

Faulkner (F.) *Publisher. See* Greene (R.)

Fawcett (John) Prospectus. *See* Sh— The Tempest, 1804

Fawcit (T.) *Printer. See* Goffe

Fay (Theodore Sedgwick) Sh— in France [In 'Graham's Magazine,' Oct.]. Philadelphia, 1843. 8°   BUS

Fayram (F.) *Publisher*—
See Sh— Poems, 1725, 1728
,, Sh— Works, 1725

Feales (W.) Plays and other dramatick pieces, printed in English . . . 1732. 12°   BPL

Feales (W.) *Publisher*—
See Sh— King Henry VIII., 1732
,, Sh— Works, 1733
,, True . . . catalogue

Fearon (Francis) Did Francis Bacon write Sh— ? Ln : 1885. 8°   BUS

Featherstone (J.) *Editor. See* Warwickshire . . .

Fechter.] Critical notices of Charles Fechter as Hamlet, from the London journals. [1861 ?] 12°   BPL
] Fechter in ' Hamlet ' and ' Othello ' [In ' Blackwood's Magazine']. 1861. 8° BPL
] Sh— and his latest stage interpreters [In ' Fraser's Magazine,' Dec.]. 1861. 8° BUS
] Sh— travestied [In ' Dublin Univ. Mag.,' Feb.]. 1862. 8°   BUS
] Tercentenary celebration at Stratford [Correspondence on Charles Fechter's withdrawal from 'Hamlet']. 1864. F° BPL

Fechter (Charles) *Actor & Editor*—
See Brereton   *See* Ottley
,, Dickens   ,, Sh— Hamlet, 1864
,, Field   ,, Sh— Othello, 1861

Feign'd friendship, or the mad reformer. As it was acted at the theatre in Little Lincoln's-Inn-Fields. Ln : Printed for Daniel Brown at the Bible, without

Temple Bar, F. Coggan in Inner Temple
Lane, E. Rumballd in Russel St., Covent
Garden [c. 1700]. Fcp. 4°
'Of old in England's golden age of wit,
   When godlike Ben and lofty Sh— writ.'
                          — *Prologue.*

Feis (Jacob) Sh— and Montaigne: An en-
deavour to explain the tendency of
' Hamlet ' from allusions in contemporary
works. Ln: Kegan Paul, 1884. 8°, pp.
viii.-210   BM | BPL | BUS | SML
Feldborg (Andreas Anderson) Hamlet's gar-
den [In ' Denmark delineated,' pp. 13-30].
Edinburgh, 1824. 8°   BPL | BUS
Contains also a sketch and portrait of P. Foersom,
translator of Sh—.
Felix (M.) Essence of Malone. *See* Hardinge
Feller (F. E.) *Editor*—
See Sh— King Henry IV., ii., 1830
   ,,   Sh— Romeo ... 1830, 1833
Felt (O. S.) *New York Publisher.* *See* Sh—
Works, 1864
Felton. On Sh—. *See Sh*—] Notices
Felton (H.) Dissertation on reading the
classics. Third edition. 1718. 12° BPL
Sh--, pp. 215-225.
Felton (Samuel)] Imperfect hints towards a
new edition of Sh— . . . Ln: Printed
for the author at the Logographic Press,
1787-88. 2 parts, forming 1 vol. 4°
              BM | BPL | BUS | W
Proposing a grand illustrated edition. Probably this
led to Boydell's issue. Quotes passages which sug-
gest subjects for pictures, and refers to various Sh—
portraits and illustrations.
Fencing—
See Arms
   ,, Castle
   ,, Giacomo
Fennell (James Hamilton) Sh— cyclopædia.
See Sh— Works: Ext. 1862
Fennell (J. H.) *Editor.* *See Sh*—] Sh— re-
pository
Fenner. *See* Hermeticall . . .
Fenner (Dudley) Certain godly and learned
treatises . . . for the behoofe and edifica-
tion of al those that desire to grow in true
godlines . . . Edinburgh: Robert Walde-
grave, 1592. 8°
If the poet was acquainted with this volume at the
outset of his career, it is fortunate he was unmoved
by its vigorous denunciation of stage plays.
Fenton (Elijah) Epistle to Mr. [Thomas]
Southerne, from Kent, 28th Jan., 1710-11
Contains thirty-five lines of verse on Sh—, commencing:
' Sh—, the genius of our isle, whose mind,
The universal mirror of mankind,
Express'd all images, enrich'd the stage,
But sometimes stoop'd to please a barbarous age.
          .   .   .   .   .   .
May spring with purple flowers perfume thy urn,
And Avon with his greens thy grave adorn;
Be all thy faults, whatever faults there be,
Imputed to the times, and not to thee.
          .   .   .   .   .   .

Jonson the tribute of my verse might claim
Had he not strove to blemish Sh—'s name;
But like the radiant twins that gild the sphere,
Fletcher and Beaumont next in pomp appear.
          .   .   .   .   .   .
Few moderns in the lists with these may stand,
For in those days were giants in the land;
Suffice it now by lineal right to claim,
And bow with filial awe to Sh—'s fame;
The second honours are a glorious name.
Achilles dead, they found no equal lord
To wear his armour and to wield his sword.'

Fenton (Elijah) Poems on several occasions.
Ln: B. Lintot, 1717.   8°, pp. iv.-224
and engraved front. by E. Kerhall
Several references to Sh—.
Fenton (*Sir* Geoffrey) Certaine tragicall discourses. Ln: 1567. Fcp. 4°   BUS
In his manuscript notes on Langbaine, Oldys refers to
this book as one of the sources of ' Timon of Athens.'
Fenton (Richard)] Tour in quest of genealogy
through several parts of Wales . . . and
curious fragments from a manuscript
collection ascribed to Sh—. By a Barrister. Ln: Sherwood, 1811. 8°. With
plates   BPL | BUS | W
Contains copies of letters and verses alleged to have
passed between Sh— and Anne Hathaway, in reality
part of Ireland's handiwork.
Ferbrand (W.) *Publisher.* *See* Jack of Dover
Ferguson (A.) An essay: Influence on the
writings of Sh— by his knowledge of the
Bible. Liverpool, 1867. 12°   BPL
Ferguson (*Dr.* Adam) Morality of stage-plays
seriously considered . . . Edinburgh,
1757. 8°, pp. 30
For reply, *see* Harper.
Ferguson (D.) *Editor.* *See* Sh— King Henry
V., 1900
Ferguson (J. C.) Railway readings, or prose
by a poet. 1859. 12°   BPL
Contains Shakespeareana.
Ferguson (Samuel) Shakespearean breviates.
See Sh— Works: Ext. 1882
Ferne (John) Blazon of gentrie, in two parts:
Glorie of generositie and Lacye's Nobilitie.
Wherein is treated the beginning, parts,
and degrees of gentleness, blazon of cote
armors, lawes of armes . . . Ln: J.
Windet, 1586. Fcp. 4°   W
Cited by Hunter as well known to Sh—. Its influence
may be traced in ' Merry Wives,' ' Merchant of
Venice,' ' Hamlet,' ' Othello,' ' As you like it,' and
the ' Winter's tale.'
Ferrara (A.) Sh— sacrificed, or the offering to
avarice [an engraving]. 1789. F°   BPL
Ferrers (George). *See* Mirrour . . .
Ferrers family. *See* Norris
Ferris (R.) Voyage to Bristol. *See* Reprints
Ferris-Gettemy (M. E.) Outline studies in the
Sh—drama. Chicago, 1907. Cr. 8° BPL
Few words in defence of Edward Capell,
occasioned by a criticism in ' The Times.'
Ln: Privately printed, 1861. Fcp. 4°

(99)   7—2

Few words in reply to . . . Mr. Dyce. *See* Hunter

Few words upon Sh—. *See* Lordan

Fick (*Dr.* J. C.) *Editor. See* Sh— Macbeth, 1812

Fiebig (*Dr.* Otto) *Editor*—
See Sh— Hamlet, 1857
„ Sh— Julius Cæsar, 1859
„ Sh— Romeo . . . 1859
„ Sh— Works, 1857

Fiedler (*Prof.* H. G.) Date and occasion of 'The Tempest.' Sh— Club Paper. Stratford, 1906. 8°, pp. xii.

Field. Verses. *See* Vigo

Field *pseud.* 'Oxoniensis' (Barron) Conjectures on some of the corrupt or obscure passages of Sh—. *See Sh*—] Sh— Soc.

Field (Barron) *Editor*
See Heywood
„ Legge
„ Sh— King Henry VI., iii., 1844
„ Sh— King Richard III., 1844

Field (Benjamin Rush) Medical thoughts of Sh—. *See* Sh— Works : Ext. 1885

Field (E. M.) *Editor. See* Sh— King Henry IV., i., 1874

Field (John) *Bibliophile. See* Catalogue, 1827

Field (Kate) Fechter's Hamlet [In 'Charles Albert Fechter,' pp. 87-117]. Boston [U.S.], 1882. 12°   BPL

Field *Actor* (Nathaniel) Amends for ladies, with the merry pranks of Moll Cutpurse or the humour of roaring. A comedy full of honest mirth and wit. As it was acted at the Blacke-Fryers, both by the Princes servants and the Lady Elizabeth's . . . Ln : Printed by Io. Okes for Math. Walbancke and are to be sold at his shop at Grayes Inne Gate, 1639. Fcp. 4°
Refers to ' King Henry IV.':—
    '. . . Did you never see
    The play, where the fat knight hight Oldcastle
    Did tell you truly what this honor was?'

Remonstrance of Nathan. Field, one of Sh—'s company of actors, addressed to a preacher in Southwark [Mr. Sutton] who had been arraigning against the players at the Globe Theatre in 1616. Now first edited from the original manuscript [by J. O. Halliwell]. Ln : 1865. 12°
     BPL | HCL | MPL
Twenty-five copies printed, ten only preserved.
Collier gives an account of Field in his ' Memoirs of principal actors . . . 1846,' pp. 206-223.

Field (Nathaniel) *Actor*—
See Collier (J. P.)
„ Dare (J.)

Field (Richard) *Printer*—
See B——— (O.)
„ Collier
„ Plutarchus

Field (Richard) *Printer*—
See Puttenham
„ Sh— Rape . . . 1594
„ Sh— Venus . . . 1593, 1594, 1596
„ Spenser

Field (W.)] Historical and descriptive account of . . . Warwick and Leamington. Warwick, 1817. 8°. With copperplates   BPL
] New guide to . . . Warwick and Leamington . . . towns and villages within ten miles. Warwick : H. Sharpe, 1823. 8°, pp. iv.-156. Folded map and folded plate
Stratford and Sh— occupy pp. 133-139.
See Brief description

Fielder (R. R.) Sh—! Lines written for the tercentenary anniversary festival, 1864. Ln : 1871. 8°   BM | BPL | CPL

Fielding *Composer*—
See Sh— Poems, 1800
„ Sh— Works : Ext, 1800

Fielding *Publisher. See* Kemble

Fielding (Henry) Journey from this world to the next [In his ' Miscellanies ']. Ln : A. Millar, 1743. 3 vols. 8°
In chapter viii. says : ' I then observed Sh— standing between Betterton and Booth, deciding a difference between these two great actors concerning an accent in one of his lines . . . in ' Othello ' :—
   ' Put out the light and then put out the light.'

Pasquin. A dramatic satire on the times . . . Second edition. Dublin : Printed by S. Powell for George Risk at Shakespear's Head, George Ewing at the Angel and Bible, and William Smith at the Hercules in Dame Street, 1736. 8°, pp. iv.-64. First Irish edition
Sh— referred to on pp. 38, 40, 49, 58, and also in the epilogue, thus :—
   ' Or dare the greatest genius of their stage
     With Sh— or immortal Ben engage ?'

Fielding (J.) *Publisher. See* Sh— Merchant . . . 1783

Fielding & Walker *Publishers. See* Sh— Works : Ext. 1779

Fifth of November. *See* Sh— Fifth of November

Fifty Oxford and Cambridge Local Examination papers on Sh—. Ln : Relfe [1898]. 8°, pp. 90   BUS

Filmer (E.) Defence of plays, or the stage vindicated. Ln : 1707. 8°

Filon (Augustin) English stage, being an account of Victorian drama. Trans. from the French by Fredk. Whyte. With introduction by H. A. Jones. Ln : 1897. 8°

Finck (Dennig) *Pforzheim Publisher. See* Sh— Merchant . . . 1843

Finden *Artist-Engraver*—   *302195*
See Chapman
„ Sh— Works, 1825-26, 1829

Findlay (A. G.) Bermuda or Somers Islands.
1856. 8° BPL
The supposed scene of 'The Tempest.'

Fine art gossip : Chandos portrait of Sh—.
[1849 ?] 8° BPL

Finegan (J. T.) Attempt to illustrate a few
passages in Sh—'s Works. Bath : R.
Cruttwell, 1802. 8°, pp. 58 BM | BUS | W

Fineo and Fiamma. See Rich

Finkenbrink (Dr.) Essay on the date, plot,
and sources of Sh—'s ' Midsummer night's
dream.' Muhleim a. d. Ruhr, 1884. 4°
BM | BUS

Finnemore (J.) Artist. See Sh— Merry wives,
1895, 1897

First part of the contention . . . See Sh—
King Henry VI., ii., 1594

First sitting of the committee on the proposed
monument to Sh—. See Kelsall

Fischer (Alexander) Editor. See Sh— Merchant . . . 1843

Fish (Asa Israel) Some recent helps in the
study of Sh— [In ' Penn. Monthly,' Dec.].
Philadelphia, 1874. 8° BUS

Fisher (Alexina A.) Actress. See Sh— Othello,
1838

Fisher (Clara) Remembrances of Sh— : Wood
engravings of the models . . . Ln : Trus-
cott [1820 ?] 8°. Twenty engravings

Fisher (Clement) of Wilnecote, near Stratford.
See Cokaine

Fisher (Fred. Geo.) Catalogue of . . . articles
in Clara Fisher's Shaksperean cabinet.
Ln : Printed by V. Slater for the author,
1830. 8°, pp. xii.-18. With 20 woodcuts
BPL | BUS

Fisher (F. H.) Wm. Sh—. See Sh—] Fisher

Fisher (H.) Printer. See Sh— Works, 1824,
1827, 1828

Fisher (Thomas) Series of antient, allegorical,
historical, and legendary paintings in
fresco which were discovered in the
summer of 1804 on the walls of the
chapel belonging to the Guild of the Holy
Cross at Stratford-on-Avon, with engraved facsimiles of charters, registers,
etc. Edited by J. Gough Nichols. 1836.
Roy. f°. With twenty-four large plates,
some in colours BPL | BUS | W

Series of antient . . . paintings . . . Edited
by J. G. Nichols. Ln : H. G. Bohn, 1838.
F°. Fifty-six engravings, mostly coloured

Fisher (Thomas) Publisher—
See Sh— King Richard II., 1605
,, Sh— Midsummer . . . 1600

Fisher, Son, & Co. Printers. See Sh— Works,
1829, 1830, 1832, 1833, 1834, 1839

Fishley (Edward E.) A Shakespearean tract :
' The Tempest.' Boston [U.S.], 1898.
12°, pp. 12 BUS

Fishley (Edward E.) Sh—'s rule of life. See
Sh— Works : Ext. 1891, 1892

Fishwick Col. (H.) Sh—'s London. Roch-
dale, 1905. 8° BPL

Fiske (J.) Forty years of Bacon-Sh— folly
[In the 'Atlantic Monthly']. 1897. 8°
BPL

Forty years . . . [In 'Century of Science,'
pp. 350-404]. 1899. 12° BPL

Fites.] Narrative of the bloudy murders committed by Sir John Fites, alias Fitz, 1605.
With an account of his suicide at Twicken-
ham. Ed. by J. O. Halliwell. Ln : Pri-
vately printed, 1860. 8° BAUS | BPL
Issue restricted to twenty-six copies on thick paper.

Fitton. See Herbert-Fitton

Fitton (Anne & Mary). See Newdigate

Fitton (Mary)—
See Furnivall
,, Sh—] Harris

Fitz (L.) Artist. See Sh— Romeo . . . 1892

Fitzball (Edward) Thirty-five years of a
dramatic author's life. 1859. 2 vols.
Cr. 8°

Fitzcook (H.) Artist. See Banks (G. L.)

Fitzgerald (Edward)] Polonius : A collection
of wise saws and modern instances. Ln :
W. Pickering, 1852. 8°

Fitzgerald (Edward) Editor. See Calderon

Fitzgerald (Percy Hetherington) Art of acting,
with study of character, comedy, and
stage illusion. Ln : 1892. Cr. 8°. With
portrait

Art of the stage as set out in Lamb's
'Dramatic essays.' Ln : Remington,
1885. 8° SML

Catholic jewels from Sh—. See Sh—
Works : Ext. 1890

First appearances : David Garrick [In 'The
Theatre']. 1886. 8° BPL

Garrick Club. 1904. 8° BPL

Henry Irving. See Irving (Sir J. H. B.)

Kings and queens of an hour. Ln : 1883.
2 vols. 8° MPL
Contains ' Ireland and the Sh— forgeries.'

Life of Garrick. See Garrick

Lives of the Sheridans. See Sheridan

New history of the English stage, from the
restoration to the liberty of the theatres.
Ln : Tinsley, 1882. 2 vols. 8° BPL | SML

Play bills, old and new [In ' The Theatre'].
1885. 8° BPL

Principles of comedy and dramatic effect.
1870. 8° BPL

Romance of the English stage. Ln :
Bentley, 1874. 2 vols. 8°, pp. xii.-334,
iv.-328 BPL | BUS
Contains a vivid account of the Ireland forgeries, pp.
76-95, vol. ii.

Fitzgerald (Percy Hetherington) Sh— folios and quartos [In 'Book Fancier,' pp. 253-306]. 1886. 12° BPL

Shakespearean representation: Its laws and limits. Ln: Stock, 1908. 8°, pp. 154 BM | BPL

The Kembles. *See* Kemble
See also Kemble

Fitzgerald (P. H.) *Editor. See* Lamb

Fitzgerald (Wm. G.) Finance of literary shrines . . .; How Stratford lives on the name of Sh— . . . [In ' Munsey's Mag.,' Sept.]. New York, 1907. Roy. 8°. Illust.
Occupies pp. 732-743.

Fitzgibbon (H. M.) *Editor. See* Sh— Two noble kinsmen, 1890

Fitzpatrick (*Col.* Richard) Incantation for raising a phantom. *See* Sh— Macbeth, 1789

Fitzpatrick (R. H.) *Editor. See* Shrine

Fitzpatrick (W. Routh) The drama; its influence for good or evil. Keswick: 'Guardian' Office, 1903. Cr. 8°, pp. 32, incl. pr. wrappers

Flasket (John) *Publisher—*
See Bodenham
,, Henri IV.

Flather (J. H.) *Editor. See* Sh— Works: Ext. 1898, 1903, 1904, 1906

Flatman (Thomas) Heraclitus ridens, or a dialogue between jest and earnest . . . Ln: 1681-82. F°. Issued in 82 weekly numbers
Refers to 'honest Sir John Falstaff.'

Fleay (Frederick Gard) Biographical chronicle of the English drama, 1559-1642. Ln: 1891. 2 vols. 8° BPL
Adjudged the best extant account of the English drama during Sh—'s time.

Chronicle history of the London stage, 1559-1642. Ln: 1890. 8° BPL

Chronicle history of . . . Wm. Sh—, player, poet, and playmaker. *See* Sh—

Confirmation. *See* Hickson.

Introduction to Shakespearian study. Glasgow: Collins, 1877. 8°, pp. 128 BM | BPL | BUS | SML

Metrical tests as applied to dramatic poetry. Part I., Sh—; Part II., Beaumont, Fletcher, and Massinger. Ln: New Sh— Soc., 1874. 8° BM | BPL | BUS

On certain modern Sh—ana [In ' The Library,' Vol. 2, pp. 277-381. Ed. by J. Y. W. MacAlister]. Ln: 1890. Roy. 8°
Deals with the errors of Halliwell, A. W. Ward, H. P. Stokes, and the 'D. N. B.,' also with the forgeries of Collier and his friend Cunningham.

Fleay (Frederick Gard) On certain plays of Sh— of which portions were written at different periods of his life. Ln: New Sh— Soc., 1874. 8° BM | BPL | BUS
'All's Well,' 'Two Gentlemen,' 'Twelfth Night,' 'Troilus and Cressida.'

On the authorship of the ' Taming of the Shrew,' with remarks on ' Titus Andronicus.' Ln: New Sh— Soc., 1874. 8° BM | BPL | BUS

On the authorship of ' Timon of Athens,' with a print of the genuine parts of the play. Ln: New Sh— Soc., 1874. 8° BM | BPL | BUS

On the extract from an old play in ' Hamlet' [In ' Macmillan's Magazine,' Dec.]. Ln: 1874. 8° BPL | BUS

On the motive of Sh—'s Sonnets: A defence of his morality [In ' Macmillan's Magazine,' March]. Ln: 1875. 8° BUS

On the play of ' Pericles,' with a print of the genuine parts of the play. Ln: New Sh— Soc., 1874. 8° BM | BPL | BUS

On two plays of Sh—, the verses of which, as we have them, are the results of alterations by other hands. Ln: New Sh— Soc., 1874. 8° BM | BPL | BUS

Queen Elizabeth, Croydon, and the drama. Ln: Balham Antiq. Soc., 1898. 8°, pp. 16 BPL

Sh— manual. Ln: Macmillan, 1876. 8°, pp. xxiv.-312 BM | BPL | BUS

Sh— manual. 1878. 12° BPL | MPL | SML

The text of ' Romeo and Juliet ' [In ' Macmillan's Magazine,' July]. Ln: 1877. 8° BUS

Who wrote ' [King] Henry VI.' ? [In ' Macmillan's Magazine,' Nov.] Ln: 1875. 8° BPL | BUS

Who wrote our old plays ? [In ' Macmillan's Magazine']. 1874. 8° BPL
See also Sh— London prodigall, 1605

Fleay (F. G.) *Editor—*
See Sh— King John, 1878
,, Sh— Pericles, 1874
,, Sh— Timon . . . 1874
,, Sh— Works, 1873-75

Fleay.] Ward (*Dr.* Adolphus Wm.) F. G. Fleay [obituary notice], [In 'Athenæum, No. 4248, pp. 375-376, 27th Mar.]. 1909

Fleay (F. G.) & Macpherson (J.) Land of Sh—. 31 etchings and 61 head and tail pieces. With introd. and descriptive text. Ln: 1889. F° BPL
One hundred copies were issued as 'proofs on Japanese vellum paper' in addition to the ordinary copies.

Flecknoe (Richard) Epigrams, 1670. *See* Sh—] Sh— notices

Flecknoe (Richard) Epigrams made at several
    times . . . Ln : 1673. 8°
    Refers to Sh—'s friend and fellow-actor Burbage, also
    to Sh—'s grand-nephew Charles Hart.

Love's kingdom. A pastoral trage-comedy.
    With a short treatise of the English stage.
    Ln : 1664. 12°   W
    Mentions Sh—.
Fleischer (Ernst) *Leipzig Publisher*—
    See Sh— Hamlet, 1825
    ,, Sh— Poems, 1826
    ,, Sh— Works, 1824-26, 1826, 1833, 1840
Fleischer (G.) *Leipzig Publisher*. *See* Sh—
    Macbeth, 1806
Fleischer *jun.* (G.) *Leipzig Publisher*. *See*
    Sh— Works, 1804-13
Fleming (C.) *Editor*—
    See Sh— Coriolanus, 1850
    ,, Sh— Julius Cæsar, 1866, 1873, 1881,
        1884
Fleming (William Hansell) How to study Sh—.
    With an introd. by W. J. Rolfe. New
    York, 1890. 2 vols. 8°   BUS
How to study Sh—. New York, 1898. 8°
                                         BUS
How to study Sh—. New York, 1899-1904.
    4 vols. 8°   BUS
How to study Sh—. New York, 1899-1901.
    2 vols. 8°   BUS
How to study Sh—. New York, 1903. Cr.
    8°   BPL
Sh—'s plots : A study in dramatic con-
    struction. New York : Putnam, 1902.
    Cr. 8°   BPL | BUS
Flesher (E.) *Publisher*. *See* Sh— King Lear,
    1681
Flesher (J.) *Printer*. *See* Donne
Flesher (Miles) *Printer*—
    See Donne
    ,, Wright
Fletcher (A. E.) Philosophy of art [In 'Time'].
    [1885.] 8°   BPL
Fletcher (C. J. H.) History of the church and
    parish of Saint Martin, Oxford. Oxford :
    Blackwell, 1896. 8°   SML
    Sh— and the Davenant family, p. 62.

Fletcher (G.) Character studies in ' Macbeth,'
    Ln : 1889. 8°   BM | BUS
Fletcher (George) Studies of Sh— in . . .
    ' King John,' ' Cymbeline,' ' Macbeth,'
    ' As you like it,' ' Much ado about
    nothing,' ' Romeo and Juliet.' With ob-
    servations on the criticism and acting of
    those plays. Ln : Longman, 1847. 8°,
    pp. xxiv.-384
            BM | BPL | BUS | CPL | MPL | SML
    For reply, *see* 'Essay on . . . "Macbeth."'
Study of Sh— in the ' Merchant of Venice '
    [In ' Fraser's Mag.,' May]. Ln : 1850.
    8°   BUS

Fletcher (James) *Publisher*. *See* Sh— Cym-
    beline, 1759
Fletcher (John) British Musc. *See* Sh—
    Works : Ext. 1738

Cardenio. *See* Sh— Cardenio
Faithfvll shepherdesse. Third edition, with
    addition. Ln : 1634. Fcp. 4°   W
    ' Imitates in some parts Sh—'s "Midsummer Night's
    Dream."'—J. O. HALLIWELL.

] Sea voyage. Ln : 1679. F°   W
    Written in imitation of Sh—'s ' Tempest.'

Tragœdy of Rollo Duke of Normandy.
    Oxford : Leonard Lichfield, 1640. Fcp.
    4°.   W
    In five acts, in verse. Contains at p. 65 the song intro-
    duced into ' Measure for Measure.'
    An earlier edition appeared in 1639 under the title of
    the ' Bloody Brother.'

Woman's prize, or the tamer tamed. Ln :
    1679. F°   W
    A continuation, or parody, of the ' Taming of the
    Shrew.'

Fletcher (John)—
    See Beaumont   *See* Mercurius . . .
    ,, Boyle   ,, Mitford
    ,, Cartwright   ,, Morehead
    ,, Coleridge   ,, Sh— Two noble kins-
    ,, Fleay   men, 1634
    ,, Gould   ,, Sheffield
    ,, Hickson   ,, Spalding
    ,, Lee (N.)   ,, Thorndike
    ,, Mason
Fletcher (Joseph) Christe's bloodie sweat . . .
    Ln : 1613. Fcp. 4°
    Contains a parody of a line in the ' Merchant of Venice'
    in the passage :—
        ' The crosse his stage was, and he plaid his part
        Of one that for his friend did pawne his heart.'

Fletcher (William I.) Index to general lite-
    rature : Biographical, historical, and
    literary . . . Boston [U.S.] : Houghton,
    Mifflin & Co., 1901. 4°, pp. iv.-680 BM
    With a key to minor Shakespearean contributions.

See Poole & Fletcher
Fletcher (Wm. I.) & Bowker (R. R.) Annual
    literary index, including periodicals,
    American and English. New York :
    ' Publisher's Weekly ' Office, 1904-06. 4
    vols. Roy. 8°   BM
    With a key to Shakespearean articles.

Fleury (M.) Memoirs. *See* Hook (T.)
Flexney (W.) *Publisher*—
    See Pilon
    ,, Woty
Flint Castle, 1399-1899 : Quincentenary of
    the surrender of Richard the Second.
    Programme of the performance by F. R.
    Benson's Company of scenes from Sh—'s
    ' King Richard II.,' Aug. 21, 1899. 1899.
    12°   BPL

(103)

Florio (John) First fruites, which yeelde familiar speech, merie prouerbes, wittie sentences, and golden sayings. Also a perfect introduction to the Italian and English tongues. Ln : T. Dawson, 1578. Fcp. 4°
'Florio,' says Lowndes, 'is *Holofernes* in 'Love's labours lost.'

Second frutes, to be gathered of twelve trees of divers but delightsome tastes to the tongues of Italians and Englishmen. To which is annexed his gardine of recreation, yeelding six thousand Italian prouerbs. Ln : Printed for Thomas Woodcock, 1591. Fcp. 4°
Contains the sonnet, 'Phaeton to his friend Florio,' generally attributed to Sh—.

Worlde of wordes, or most copious and exact dictionarie in Italian and English. Printed at London by Arnold Hatfield for Edw. Blount, 1598. F°   SBL
In the dedication Florio says he was taken into the pay and patronage of the Earl of Southampton (Sh—'s patron), on which he lived some years.

Florio (John) *Editor. See* Montaigne

Florizel and Perdita. *See* Sh— Winter's tale, 1754, 1757, 1758, 1762, 1784, 1785, 1786, 1792

Flower (Charles Edward)] Catalogue of pictures and drawings exhibited at the Town Hall, Stratford-upon-Avon, at the celebration of the tercentenary birthday of Wm. Sh—. Stratford-on-Avon : Pub. by the Committee, 1864. 8°, pp. 64
BM | BPL | BUS

] History of the Sh— Memorial, Stratford-on-Avon. Published for the Council of the Sh— Memorial Association. Ln : Cassell [1879]. 8°, pp. 80. With 3 plates
BM | BPL | BUS | MPL | SML

] History of the Sh— Memorial. Second edition. Ln : Cassell & Co. [1882]. 8°, pp. 40 and frontispiece   BPL

] Official programme of the tercentenary festival of the birth of Sh—, to be held at Stratford-upon-Avon, commencing 23 April, 1864. Also an account of the poet's life . . . guide to Stratford, and sundrie other matters just now of publicke interest relating thereto. Ln : Cassell, 1864. 8°, pp. 76. Portrait and illustrations
BM | BPL | BUS

] Opening of the Sh— Memorial Theatre . . . Preliminary programme. Stratford : 'Herald' Office, 1879. 8°, pp. 8   BUS

] Preliminary programme of the tercentenary festival . . . at Stratford . . . commencing April 23rd. Stratford : E. Adams, 1864. 8°, pp. 12   BPL | BUS

Flower (Charles Edward)] Sh— Memorial Buildings : Festival connected with the inauguration of the theatre portion. Stratford-on-Avon, 1879. 4°   BPL

] Sh— Memorial Library extension : Prospectus. 1887. 4°   BPL

] Sh— Memorial Theatre : Preliminary programme of the opening. Stratford-on-Avon, 1879. 8°   BPL | BUS | MPL | SML

Sh— on horseback : A paper read at the Union Club, 3rd March . . . Stratford-on-Avon : Privately printed, 1887. 8°, pp. 24   BPL | BUS
' Sh— on horseback ' and ' Sh— no dog-fancier.' Sh—Club [papers]. Stratford-on-Avon [1892]. 8°, pp. iv.-40 BPL | SML
One of the few copies done on large paper, quarto, is at S. M. L.

Flower (C. E.) *Editor—*
See Sh— All's well, 1889
  ,, Sh— Antony . . . 1891
  ,, Sh— As you like it, 1882
  ,, Sh— Comedy of errors, 1882
  ,, Sh— Coriolanus, 1890
  ,, Sh— Cymbeline, 1889
  ,, Sh— Hamlet, 1882
  ,, Sh— Julius Cæsar, 1889
  ,, Sh— King Henry IV., i., 1882
  ,, Sh— King Henry IV., ii., 1889
  ,, Sh— King Henry V., 1889
  ,, Sh— King Henry VI., i., 1889
  ,, Sh— King Henry VI., ii., 1889
  ,, Sh— King Henry VI., iii., 1889
  ,, Sh— King Henry VIII., 1889
  ,, Sh— King John, 1889
  ,, Sh— King Lear, 1883
  ,, Sh— King Richard II., 1886
  ,, Sh— King Richard III., 1884
  ,, Sh— Love's labours lost, 1885
  ,, Sh— Macbeth, 1883
  ,, Sh— Measure . . . 1882
  ,, Sh— Merchant . . . 1883
  ,, Sh— Merry wives, 1887
  ,, Sh— Midsummer . . . 1887
  ,, Sh— Much ado, 1882
  ,, Sh— Othello, 1880
  ,, Sh— Pericles, 1890
  ,, Sh— Romeo . . . 1882
  ,, Sh— Taming . . . 1888
  ,, Sh— The tempest, 1885
  ,, Sh— Timon . . . 1889
  ,, Sh— Titus . . . 1890
  ,, Sh— Troilus . . . 1889
  ,, Sh— Twelfth night, 1882
  ,, Sh— Two gentlemen, 1886
  ,, Sh— Winter's tale, 1885
  ,, Sh— Works, 1879-91

Flower.] Laffan (B. J.) C. E. Flower [In ' Leisure Hour ']. Ln : 1893. 4°. Illustrated   BM | BPL

Flower.] Laffan (R. S. de Courcy) In memoriam: C. E. Flower, d. 3 May, 1892: A sermon preached in the Guild Chapel, Stratford-on-Avon, 8th May. 1892. 8°
BPL

See also Hawley (F.)
Flowers of Sh—. *See* Giraud
Foard *Barrister* (James T.) Apocrypha of Sh—. Manchester, 1904. 8° BPL
Bacon-Sh— craze. Manchester [1895]. 8° BPL

Dramatic dissensions of Jonson, Marston, and Dekker. Manchester [1897]. 8° BPL
Genesis of 'Hamlet.' Manchester, 1889. 3 parts. 8° BPL
Joint authorship of Marlowe and Sh— [In 'Gentleman's Magazine,' Vol. 288, pp. 134-154]. 1900. 8° BPL
'Macbeth.' Manchester [1893?] 8° BPL
More silly stories about Sh—. Manchester [1898?] 8° BPL
On the law case: Shylock *v.* Antonio. Manchester [1899?] 8° BPL
On the moral dignity of the Shakesperian drama [In 'Trans. of the Literary and Philos. Soc. of Liverpool']. 1858. 8° BPL
] Plagiarism of Sh— ['Lucrece'] in a dedication. By T. J. F——. 1847. Holograph manuscript. 4° BPL
Real life of Sh—. *See* Sh—
Sh—'s alleged forgery of a coat-of-arms [In 'Manchester Quarterly Review']. 1890. 8° BPL
Sh—'s classical plays [In 'Manchester Quarterly Review']. 1893. 8° BPL
Sh—'s mission and office as the dramatic and histrionic poet of the English people. With some comments on Mr. Clement Scott's severe strictures on the stage. Being an address read at the . . . Manchester Sh— Club. Manchester: Cornish, 1898. 8°, pp. 36, including printed wrappers BPL
Sh—'s probable connection with Lancashire [In 'Manchester Quarterly Review']. 1896. 8° BPL
Some caprices of criticism. Manchester [1898]. 8° BPL
Some contemporaries of Sh— [In 'Southport Lit. & Phil. Soc. Proc., pp. 32-58]. 1901-02. 8° BPL
Some recent biographies of Sh—. Manchester, 1900. 8° BPL
Foersom (P.) *Editor. See* Feldborg
Fogerty (Elsie) *Editor. See* Sh— As you like it, 1900
Foggs (A.) On the character of Banquo. Ln: New Sh— Soc., 1875-76. 8°

Folds (W.) *Dublin Publisher. See* Hitchcock
Folk-lore—
See Bell   *See* Hazlitt (W. C.)
  ,, Halliwell &   ,, Lucy
    Ritson   ,, Morley
  ,, Harland   ,, *Sh*—] Rolfe
Folk-lore of Sh— [In 'Leisure Hour']. Ln: Rel. Tr. Soc., 1884. Roy. 8° BPL
Follett (O.)] Sh—'s plays; The theatre; Who wrote 'Sh—'? By O. F.——. Sandusky [U.S.], 1879. 16° BPL | BUS
Following extracts from the writings of pious men of different denominations and at different periods . . . exposing the evil and pernitious effects of stage plays and other vain amusements are recommended to the serious perusal of all who profess Christianity. Dublin: Robert Jackson, 1785. 12°
Folsing (*Dr.* J.) *Editor. See* Sh— Works, 1840
Fool and the ice. *See* Armin
Foote (Samuel) Satire on the jubilee. *See* Jubilee
] Treatise on the passions, so far as they regard the stage; with a critical enquiry into the theatrical merit of Mr. G . . . . k, Mr. Q . . n, and Mr. B . . . y. The first considered in the part of Lear, the two last opposed in Othello. Ln: C. Corbett [1767]. 8°, pp. 44 BUS | W
The three actors alluded to are Garrick, James Quin, and Spranger Barry.
See Garrick, Colman, & Foote
Foote.] Cooke (Wm.) Memoirs of Samuel Foote, with his bon mots, anecdotes, and three of his dramatic pieces not yet published. Ln: 1805. 3 vols. 12°. With portrait BPL
Footsteps of Sh—. *See* Cartwright
Forbes-Robertson *Actor* (J.) Falstaff's own, by Marks [a picture, from 'Art']. 1871. F° BPL

See also Scott (C. W.)
Ford (Harold) Sh—'s 'Hamlet': A new theory, or what was the poet's intention in the play? Ln: Stock, 1900. Cr. 8°, pp. iv.-108 BPL | BUS
Ford *or* Forde (John) 'Honour triumphant' and 'Line of life': Two tracts by Forde the dramatist unknown to the editors of his works. [Ed. by J. P. Collier.] Ln: Sh— Soc., 1843. 8°, pp. viii.-76
BM | BPL | BUS
Ford (John). *See* Heywood
Ford (Thomas) Confusion's masterpiece. *See* Sh— Macbeth, 1794
Foreign actors and the English drama [In 'Cornhill Magazine']. 1863. 8° BPL
Forest of Arden. *See* Warwickshire

Forgeries—
  See Collier (J. P.)   *See* Jordan
    „ Coxeter   „ Sh— autograph
    „ Cunningham   „ Steevens
    „ Ireland
Forman (H. B.) *Editor*. *See* Keats
Forman (Simon) Book of plays, or notes in
    1611 on ' King Richard II.,' ' Winter's
    tale,' 'Cymbeline,' and 'Macbeth.' With
    the Lord Treasurer's payments for the
    acting six of Sh—'s plays. Ln: New
    Sh— Soc., 1875-76. 8°   BM | BPL | BUS
Forrest.] Alger (W. R.) Life of Edwin Forrest,
    American tragedian. Philadelphia, 1877.
    2 vols. 8°. With portraits in character
    Issue limited to one hundred copies.   BUS
  ] Barrett (L.) Edwin Forrest. 'American
    actors.' Boston : Osgood, 1881. 12° SML
  See also American . . .
Forrest (H. R.) *Bibliophile*. *See Sh*—]
    Sh—ana
Forshaw (C. F.) & Garnett (*Dr.* Richard) At
    Sh—'s shrine. *See Sh*—] Forshaw
Forster (Henry Rumsey). *See* Rodd &
    Forster
Forster (John) *Editor*. *See* Sh— Works, 1875-
    76
Forster family. *See* Bellew
Forsyth (David) *Editor*. *See* Sh— Julius
    Cæsar, 1899, 1901
Forsyth (E.)] Sh— ; some notes on his charac-
    ter and writings. *See* Sh—] Forsyth
Forsyth (J.) *Publisher*. *See* Sh— Works, 1811
Fortescue (G. K.) Catalogue. *See* British
    Museum
Fortnightly Review [*Consult its general in-
    dexes*]
Fortnightly Sh—. Ed. by Mrs. Anna Randall-
    Diehl. New York, 1895. F°
    Forerunner of the 'American Sh— Magazine.'
Fortunate and unfortunate lovers. *See* Greene
    (R.)
Fortune playhouse—
  See Halliwell
    „ Stage player's complaint
Fortune telling. *See* Stopes
Fortune's tennis ball. *See* Greene (R.)
Fosbrooke (Nathaniel) *Publisher*. *See* Choice
Foster (Birket) *Artist*—
  See Sh— Merchant . . . 1860
    „ Sh— Poems, 1862
    „ Sh— The tempest, 1860, 1861, 1864
    „ Sh— Works : Ext. 1879
Foster (John) Sh— word-book. *See* Sh—
    Works : Ext. 1908
Foster (J. Gregory) *Editor*. *See* Sh— Works,
    1893-98, 1900
Foster child, or Prince of Corinth. *See* Sh—
    Pericles, 1820

Foulis (Robert & Andrew) *Glasgow Printers*—
  See Sh— King Richard III., 1766
    „ Sh— Othello, 1757
    „ Sh— The tempest, 1752
    „ Sh— Works, 1752-57, 1766
Fouquier (H.) Sarah Bernhardt as ' Hamlet' ;
    Illustrated comments. [1899 ?] 4° BPL
Fourant (C.) *Paris Publisher*. *See* Sh—
    Julius Cæsar, 1865
Fourdrinier (P.) *Engraver*—
  See Sh— Antony . . . 1734
    „ Sh— King Henry VI., i., 1735
    „ Sh— King Henry VI., ii., 1734
    „ Sh— King John, 1734
    „ Sh— King Richard III., 1734
    „ Sh— London prodigal, 1734
    „ Sh— Merchant . . . 1734
    „ Sh— Pericles, 1734
    „ Sh— Romeo . . . 1734
    „ Sh— Sir John Oldcastle, 1734
    „ Sh— Taming . . . 1734
    „ Sh— Timon . . . 1734
    „ Sh— Twelfth night, 1734
    „ Sh— Winter's tale, 1734
Fowler *Salisbury Printer*. *See* Sh— As you
    like it, 1790
Fowler (Rufus Bennett) Stratford-on-Avon :
    An address before the Lincoln Guild . . .
    Worcester, Mass. [U.S.], 1895. 8°, pp. 36
    An unpublished typewriter manuscript.
Fox *Engraver*. *See* Sh— Works, 1826
Fox (*Hon.* Charles James) Speech on the
    happy restoration of peace with France
    . . . at the Sh— Tavern, 10th Oct., 1801
    . . . Ln: J. S. Jordan, 1801. 8°, pp. 22
Fox (Edward)] Penny guide to Stratford-on-
    Avon. New edition. Stratford, c. 1885.
    12°   BPL
Fox (Henry J.) *Editor*. *See* Sh— Works, 1880
Fox (T.) *Publisher*. *See* Hedelin
Fragmenta Scoto-dramatica : Collection of
    curious memoranda relating to the Scot-
    tish stage from 1715 to 1750. Ed. by
    W. H. Logan. Edinburgh, 1835. 12°
    Privately issued ; limited to thirty copies.
France—
  See Goldsmid   *See* Hook
    „ Halliwell   „ Houssaye
    „ Hawkins   „ Jusserand
    „ Henri IV.   „ Mathews
Francis *Boston Publisher*. *See* Munroe &
    Francis
Francis (David) *Editor*. *See* Sh— Works,
    1802-04
Francis (John Collins) Notes by the Way.
    See Knight (Joseph)
Francke (*Dr.* C. L. W.) *Editor*—
  See Sh— Hamlet, 1849
    „ Sh— Macbeth, 1833
Francklin (R.) *Publisher*. *See* Theobald

Franklin *Publisher*. *See* Sh— Works, 1839

Franklin (*Dr*.) Earl of Warwick: A tragedy . . . Ln: John Bell, 1792. 12°, pp. 76. Frontispiece of Mrs. Whitelock as 'Margaret' w
Founded on a French tragedy by De la Harpe.

Franklin (Hy. A.) Einladungsschrift . . . A few observations on Sh— and his 'Merchant of Venice.' Leipzig, 1867. 8°
BM | SML

Observations . . . [In 'Sh— Museum']. Leipzig, 1870-74. 8° BUS

Franklin (Julia) *Editor*. *See* Brink

Fraser (F. J.) Merry Merchant of Venice. *See* Sh— Merchant . . . 1895

Fraser (J.) Supernatural in Sh— [In 'Mind in Nature']. 1885. 8° BPL

Fraser & Crawford *Edinburgh Publishers*. *See* Sh— Works, 1838, 1839

Fratricide punished, or Prince Hamlet of Denmark [In Cohn's 'Sh— in Germany']. Reprinted in Sh— 'Hamlet, variorum edition, edited by Furness.'

Fraunce (Abraham) Lawier's logike. Ln: 1588. Fcp. 4° BUS
Chalmers regarded this as the source of the poet's legal knowledge.

Freckelton (T. W.) The church and the drama: A sermon. 1865. 12° BPL

Frederic and Basilia. *See* Halliwell

Frederick (Cæsar) Voyage and trauaile of M. Cæsar Frederick, merchant of Venice, into the East India, the Indies, and beyond the Indies. Out of Italian by T. H—— [Thomas Hickock]. Ln: R. Iones and E. White, 1588. Fcp. 4°
The probable source of the title of Sh—'s 'Merchant of Venice.'

Fredericks (Alfred) *Artist*. *See* Sh— Midsummer . . . 1874

Frederickson (C. W.) Review of 'An inquiry . . .' by N. E. S. A. Hamilton. New York, 1860. 8° BPL
On the Collier forgeries.

Free and familiar letter to . . . Mr. Warburton. *See* Grey

Free reflections on miscellaneous papers and instruments. *See* Waldron

Freeman (Thomas) Rubbe, and a great caste, and Runne, and a great caste: The second bowle. In two hundred epigrams. Ln: 1614. Fcp. 4° BLO
Epigram xcii. on recto of sig. K 2 reads:—
'To Master W. Sh—.
Sh—, that nimble mercury, thy brain,
Lulls many hundred argus eyes asleep,
So fit for all thou fashionest thy rein.
At th' horse-foot fountain thou hast drank full deep;
Vertue's or vice's theme to thee all one is.
Who loves chaste life, there's 'Lucrece' for a teacher;
Who but read lust, there's 'Venus and Adonis,'
True model of a most lascivious leacher;
Besides, in plays thy wit winds like meander,

Whence needy new composers borrow more
Than Terence doth from Plautus or Menander.
But to praise thee aright I want thy store;
Then let thine own works thine own worth upraise,
And help to adorn thee with deserved bays.'

Freemasonry—
See Halliwell
  ,, Parkinson

French (George Russell) On the maces of the corporation of Stratford-on-Avon. [c. 1868.] 12° BPL

Shakspeareana genealogica: Part I., Identification of the 'dramatis personæ' in Sh—'s historical plays . . . notes on characters in 'Macbeth' and 'Hamlet,' persons and places belonging to Warwickshire alluded to in several plays. Part II., The Sh— and Arden families and their connections; with tables of descent. Ln: Macmillan, 1869. 8°, pp. xiv.-590 BM | BPL | BUS | CPL | MPL | SML
Issued as a supplement to the 'Cambridge Sh—.'

French (S.) Guide to selecting plays. Ln: French [1882]. 12° SML

French (S.) *London Publisher*—
See Sh— King Lear, 1838
  ,, Sh— Midsummer . . . 1853
  ,, Sh— Taming . . . 1853
  ,, Sh— Works, 1830

French (Samuel) *New York Publisher*—
See Sh— As you like it, 1846
  ,, Sh— Hamlet, 1845, 1859
  ,, Sh— Julius Cæsar, 1849
  ,, Sh— King Henry IV., i., 1848
  ,, Sh— King Henry VIII., 1848
  ,, Sh— King John, 1846
  ,, Sh— King Lear, 1848
  ,, Sh— King Richard III., 1846
  ,, Sh— Love's labours lost, 1858
  ,, Sh— Macbeth, 1843, 1847
  ,, Sh— Merchant . . . 1848, 1857, 1860
  ,, Sh— Merry wives, 1855
  ,, Sh— Much ado, 1845, 1848, 1860, 1869
  ,, Sh— Othello, 1845, 1846
  ,, Sh— Romeo . . . 1847
  ,, Sh— The tempest, 1850, 1856
  ,, Sh— Twelfth night, 1847
  ,, Sh— Two gentlemen, 1846, 1847
  ,, Sh— Winter's tale, 1857, 1860

French 'Hamlet' [In the 'Imperial Review']. 1887. 8° BPL

Frew (David) *Editor*. *See* Sh— Works: Ext. 1898

Frey (A. R.) Sh—'s autograph [In 'Daily Graphic']. New York, 1887. 4° BPL
Wm. Sh— and alleged Spanish prototypes. New York Sh— Soc., 1886. 8° BM | BPL

Friderichs (R. L.) *Elberfeld Publisher*—
See Sh— Birth . . . 1856
  ,, Sh— Fair Em, 1874

Friderichs (R. L.) *Elberfeld Publisher—*
See Sh— King Edward III., 1854
" Sh— Mucedorus, 1874
" Sh— Works, 1854-61, 1854-74, 1882
Friesen (*Baron* H. Von) Dr. K. Elze's Wm.
Sh—. 1876. 8°   BM
Friswell (James Hain) Life portraits of Wm.
Sh—. *See* Sh—
Friswell (J. H.) *Editor. See* Sh— Will . . 1864
Frith (J. C.) Sh—. *See* Sh—
Frith (W. P.) *Artist. See* Sh— Works, 1873-
76, 1875-76, 1875-80, 1879
Fritzsche (*Dr.* E.) *Editor—*
See Sh— Coriolanus, 1885
" Sh— Hamlet, 1890
Frobisher (N.) *York Publisher. See* Kemble
Frost (F. J.) *Editor. See* Sh— King Lear, 1909
Frothingham (O. B.) Worship of Sh— [In
'The Century.' 1885 ?]. 8°   BPL
Froude (James Anthony) Short studies on
great subjects. Ln : Longmans, 1867-83.
4 vols. 8°   BM
Frequently reprinted.
In vol. i., pp. 445-446, says : 'We wonder at the
grandeur, the moral majesty of some of Sh—'s
characters, so far beyond what the noblest among
ourselves can imitate, and at first thought we attri-
bute it to the genius of the poet who has outstripped
nature in his creations. But we are misunderstanding
. . . Sh— created, but only as the spirit of nature
created around him. The men whom he draws were
such men as he saw and knew ; the words they utter
were such as he heard . . . At the Mermaid with
Ralegh and with Sidney, and at a thousand unnamed
English firesides he found the living originals for his
Prince Hals, Orlandos, Antonios, Portias, Isabellas.
The closer the personal acquaintance which we can
form with the English of the age of Elizabeth, the
more we are satisfied that Sh—'s great poetry is no
more than the rhythmic echo of the life which it
depicts.'
Fuller (J.) *Publisher. See* Grey (Z.)
Fuller (Richard Frederick) Sh— as a lawyer
[In 'Monthly Law Reporter,' Nov.].
Boston [U.S.], 1862. 8°   BUS
Fuller *DD.* (Thomas) History of the worthies
of England. Ln : Printed by J G——,
W. L——, and W. G——, 1662. F°.
With portrait by Logan   W
At p. 126 says of Sh— (under *Warwickshire*):—
'He was an eminent instance of the truth of that rule,
"poeta non fit sed nascitur . . ." Indeed, his learn-
ing was very little, so that, as Cornish diamonds are
not polished, but are pointed and smoothed even as
they are taken out of the earth, so nature itself was
all the art which was used upon him.
Many were the wit-combats betwixt him and Ben
Jonson, which two I beheld like a Spanish great
galleon and an English man-of-war : Master Jonson
(like the former) was built far higher in learning,
solid but slow in all his performances. Sh—, the
English man-of-war, lesser in bulk but lighter in
sailing, could turn with all tides, tack about and
take advantage of all winds, by the quickness of his
wit and invention.'
Fullom (Stephen Watson) History of Wm.
Sh—, player and poet. *See* Sh—

Furness (Helen Kate) Concordance to Sh—'s
poems. *See* Sh— Works: Ext. 1872,
1874, 1875, 1878
Index of the pages in the volumes of Wm.
Sidney Walker on which occur citations
from the plays of Sh—. Philadelphia :
Gillin & Murphy, 1870. 12°, pp. iv.-30
BPL | BUS
Limited to fifty copies for private purposes.
Furness.] Review of H. K. Furness's Con-
cordance . . . [Rep. from ' N. American
Review']. Boston, 1874. 8°, pp. 8 BUS
Furness (*Dr.* Horace Howard) Report on the
Shakespearian collection [In ' Boston
Public Library Report,' pp. 7-10]. Bos-
ton [U.S.], 1882. 8°   BPL
Text of Sh—[In 'Poet Lore']. 1891. 8° BPL
See also Hudson
" " Williams & Furness
Furness (*Dr.* H. H.) *Editor—*
See Sh— Antony . . . 1907
" Sh— As you like it, 1890
" Sh— King Lear, 1880
" Sh— Love's labours lost, 1904
" Sh— Macbeth, 1898, 1903
" Sh— Merchant . . . 1888
" Sh— Midsummer . . . 1895
" Sh— Othello, 1886
" Sh— Romeo . . . 1898
" Sh— The tempest, 1892
" Sh— Twelfth night, 1901
" Sh— Winter's tale, 1898
" Sh— Works, 1871-1908, 1898
Furness *jun.* (Horace Howard) *Editor—*
See Sh— King Richard III., 1908
" Sh— Works, 1871-1908
Furness (W. R.) Composite photography
applied to the portraits of Sh—. Phila-
delphia, 1885. 8°   BPL
Composite photography . . . New York :
Putnam, 1903. 8°   SML
Furniture, 16th and 17th cent. *See* Halliwell
Furnivall (*Dr.* Frederick James) Allusions to
Sh— A.D. 1592-1693 : Supplement to
Sh—'s ' Centurie of prayse.' Ln : 1880.
4°   SML
[Allusions] Some three hundred fresh allu-
sions to Sh— from 1594 to 1694, gathered
by members of the New Sh— Society.
Ln : 1886. 4°   BM
Forewords. *See* Sh— Works : Ext. 1881
Introduction. *See* Gervinus
Modern Shakespearean criticism, as ex-
hibited in a letter . . . 1888. 8°   BM
Mr. Swinburne and Mr. Spedding : Sh—'s
' Henry VIII.' 1876. 8°   BPL
Mr. Swinburne's ' flat burglary ' on Sh—.
Ln : 1879. 8°   BM | BPL | BUS | MPL
On Chester's ' Love's martyr.' Ln : New
Sh— Soc., 1877-79. 8°

F. J. Furnivall   Aetat February 1825

See p. 108

Furnivall (*Dr.* Frederick James) On Puck's
'Swifter than the moon's sphere,' and
Sh—'s astronomy. Ln: New Sh— Soc.,
1877-79.   8°
Illustrates ' Midsummer Night's Dream.'
On Sh—'s signatures. [1895.] 8° BM | BPL
Preface. *See* Simpson (R.)
Proposed edition of Sh— with the original
spelling. [Ln: (*No place, printer, or date*)
1880 ?] 8°, pp. 4   MPL
Sh— and Mary Fitton [In ' The Theatre'].
1897. 8°   BM | BPL
] Sh—'s sweetheart [Reprinted from the
' Pall Mall Gazette']. 1890. 8°   BPL
Succession of Sh—'s works and the use of
the metrical tests in settling it. 1874.
8°   BM | BPL | MPL
Succession of Sh—'s works . . . Ln: Smith,
1877. 8°, pp. iv.-xx.-50   BPL | BUS
The ' Co.' of Pigsbrook and Co. 1881. 8°
                                         BPL

See also Greenhill, Harrison, & Furnivall
  ,,   ,,   Halliwell
Furnivall (*Dr.* F. J.) *Editor*—
See Digby mysteries
  ,, Harrison
  ,, Laneham
  ,, Sh— As you like it, 1908
  ,, Sh— Compendious . . . 1876
  ,, Sh— Hamlet, 1880
  ,, Sh— King Henry IV., 1909
  ,, Sh— King Henry VI., ii., 1889
  ,, Sh— King Henry VI., ii.-iii., 1886
  ,, Sh— King John, 1888
  ,, Sh— Love's labours lost, 1880, 1904,
        1907
  ,, Sh— Merchant . . . 1881, 1887, 1909
  ,, Sh— Midsummer . . . 1907
  ,, Sh— Rape . . . 1886
  ,, Sh— Taming . . . 1886, 1907
  ,, Sh— The tempest, 1895, 1909
  ,, Sh— Twelfth night, 1907
  ,, Sh— Two gentlemen, 1907
  ,, Sh— Works, 1877, 1878, 1880, 1880-84,
        1880-91, 1882, 1882-83, 1883,
        1883-84, 1887, 1891, 1894-96,
        1895, 1896, 1898, 1903, 1904-08,
        1908
  ,, Sh— Works: Ext. 1900, 1901, 1902
Furnivall.]   Furnivallos furioso! and the
' Newest Society.' A dram-attic squib.
1876. 12°   BPL
Furnivall (F. J.) & Munro (J.) Sh—'s life and
work. *See* Sh— Works, 'Century ed.,'
1908
' Fuscus (Eduardus)' *pseud.* *See* Ovid's Ghost
Fuseli (H.) On Sh— and Rembrandt
Fuseli (Henry) *Artist.* *See* Sh— Works, 1803,
1805, 1807, 1811, 1826
Fytton. *See* Fitton

 —— (C. M.) The stage
censor, 1544-1907:
An historical
sketch. Ln: Low,
1907. 8°, pp. 128
G—— (D.) *See* Daniel
(George)
G—— (E.) *Printer.* *See* Hall
G—— (G.) *Publisher.* *See* Gibbs (George)
G—— (*Dr.* I.) Elegy. *See* Oldmayne
G—— (J.) *Editor.* *See* Giacomo
G—— (J.) *Printer*—
See Fuller
  ,, Sh— Rape . . . 1655
G—— (M. F.) The poems of Sh— [In ' Metro-
politan Quarterly Mag.,' Feb.]. Ln: 1826.
8°   BUS
G—— (T. H.) *See* Gem
G—— (W.) *Printer.* *See* Fuller
Gadd & Keningale *Publishers.* *See* Sh—
Poems, 1842-52, 1843
Gager (D.) *See* Rainoldes
Gairdner (James) On the historical element in
Sh—'s Falstaff [In ' Fortnightly Review,'
March]. Ln: 1873. Roy. 8°   BUS
Sh—'s Falstaff [In ' Studies in English
History,' pp. 55-77]. 1881. 8°   BPL
Gairdner (James) & Spedding (James) Studies
in English history: On the historical
element in Sh—'s Falstaff. Edinburgh,
1881. 8°   BUS
Gale (Dunstan) Pyramus and Thisbe: A
lovely poem. Ln: 1597. Fcp. 4°
Bears on ' Midsummer Night's Dream.'
Pyramus and Thisbe. Ln: 1617. Fcp. 4°
See also Greene & Gale
Gale (Thomas). *See* Vigo & Gale
Gale & Curtis *Publishers.* *See* Sh— Works,
1811
Galindo (Catherine) Letter. *See* Siddons
Galliard (J. F.) *Composer.* *See* Sh— Julius
Cæsar, 1723
' Gallio.' Melancholy Jaques. Birmingham:
White & Pike, 1899. 12°   SML
Illustrates ' As you like it.'
Sh—'s garden. Birmingham, 1900. 8° BPL
The title had previously been copyrighted by S. Beisly
(*q.v.*) in 1864.
Gallup (*Mrs.* Elizabeth Wells) Bi-literal cipher
of Sir Francis Bacon discovered in his
works and deciphered. Detroit: Howard,
1899. Roy. 8°   BUS
Bi-literal cipher . . . Second edition. De-
troit: Howard Co., 1900. Roy. 8°
                                BPL | BUS | SML
Bi-literal cipher . . . Third edition. Detroit, Howard Co.; Ln., Gay & Bird,
1901. Roy. 8°. pp, xvi.-384. Portraits
and facsimiles   MPL

Gallup (*Mrs.* Elizabeth Wells) Bi-literal cipher . . . Ln: Gay & Bird, 1902. Roy. 8°, pp. xvi.-384

Bi-literal cipher of Sir Francis Bacon : New light on a few old books [In ' Pall Mall Mag.,' Mar., pp. 393-401]. Ln: 1902. Roy. 8°. Illust.

Bi-literal cipher . . . Replies to criticisms. [Detroit ?] 1903. 8°, pp. 40. With facsimiles   BUS

Gallup.] Bi-literal cipher . . . [Press comments on the book]. Detroit, 1899. 8°, pp. 36   BUS

Galpin Sh— Club [Members and programme]. Los Angeles, U.S.: 1904. 8°, pp. 24 and 2 plates

Galsworthy (John) Some platitudes concerning the drama [In ' Fortnightly Review,' Dec.] 1909. Roy. 8°   BM

Galt (J.) Lives of the players. 1886. 12° BPL

Sh—'s dramas [In ' The Bachelor's Wife,' pp. 321-344]. Edinburgh, 1824. 12° BPL

Games. *See* Amusements

Games of quartettes . . . Shaksperian characters. Ln : H. Greenwood [c. 1870] BUS

Games of quartettes . . . Ln : Houlston & Wright [c. 1870]   BUS

Gammon (Richard) *Publisher*—
See Hemminge
,, Sh— King John, 1662

Gancia (M.) *Bibliophile. See* Catalogue, 1856

Garcia (G.) Actor's art : A practical treatise on stage declamation, public speaking, and deportment . . . Ln : Pettitt, 1882. 8°. Illust.   SML

Actor's art . . . Ln : Simpkin, 1888. 8° SML

Gardenstone (Francis *Lord*) Travelling memorandums. Edinburgh : Bell & Bradfute, 1791. 8°, pp. xii.-268
Refers to Sh— at p. 150, etc.

Gardiner (Alfonzo) *Editor. See* Sh— Works : Ext. 1888

Gardiner (Samuel Rawson) Political element in Massinger's plays. Ln : New Sh— Soc., 1875-77. 8°   BUS

Gardiner (Wm. Nelson) *Artist. See* Sh— Works, 1803

Gardner (E. G.) Dante and Sh— [In ' Dublin Review,' Vol. 130, pp. 316-332]. 1902. 8°   BPL

Gardner (H. L.) *Publisher*—
See Sh— Merchant . . . 1783
,, Sh— Works, 1798

Gardner (J. D.) *Bibliophile. See* Catalogue, 1854

Garland (Halhed) *Publisher*—
See Sh— Othello, 1765, 1800
,, Sh— Romeo . . . 1750, 1795

Garland for the New Royal Exchange. *See* Sh— Works : Ext. 1845

Garnett (*Dr.* Richard) Date and occasion of ' The Tempest ' [In ' Essays,' pp. 29-54]. Ln : 1901. Cr. 8°   BPL

Essays of an ex-librarian. Ln : Heinemann, 1901. 8°   SML

Plays partly written by Sh—. *See Sh*—] Forshaw

Wm. Sh— ; pedagogue and poacher. *See* Sh—] Garnett

See also Blades

Garnett (*Dr.* R.) & Gosse (E.) Sh—. *See* Sh—

Garrett (G.) Gems from Sh—. *See* Sh— Works : Ext. 1894

Garrett (John Henry) Idyllic Avon : A description of the Midland river . . . from its mouth at Tewkesbury to above Stratford-on-Avon. 1906. 8°   BPL

Garrett (W. H.) Character of ' Macbeth ' [In ' Trans. of Royal Soc.,' 2nd Ser., Vol. 13, pp. 312-332]. 1886. 8°   BPL

Essay on the character of ' Macbeth.' 1886. 8°   BM | BPL

Garrick *Actor* (David) Address to the ladies at Stratford-on-Avon. *See* Jubilee

Catherine and Petruchio. *See* Sh— Taming

Dedication ode. *See* Collection

Diary of a memorable trip to Paris [with criticisms of theatres, actors, plays, notes of expenditure, &c.]. MS. on 38 leaves. 1752. Fcp. 4°
Sold (with Wm. Wright's library) in 1899 for £51.

Dialogue between an actor and a critic, by way of prologue to the English opera called ' The Tempest.' The characters Heartly the Actor (Mr. Havarde) and Wormwood the Critic (Mr. Yates). 1796. Holograph MS. 4°, 9ff.   BUS
Printed in ' St. James' Magazine,' vol. i., p. 144.

Dramatic works, now first collected and carefully corrected. Ln : 1774. 2 vols. Cr. 8°   W

Dramatic works. Ln : 1798. 3 vols. 8°

Harlequin's invasion, with transparencys, etc. 1759. Holograph MS. 8°, pp. 54 BUS
A Christmas pantomime produced 31 Dec., 1759, representing Harlequin's invasion of Parnassus and Sh—'s territory.

[Harlequin's invasion] Sh— *versus* Harlequin, or Harlequin's invasion. A broad farcical pantomimical drama . . . The overture and music composed by Mr. Reeve and T. Cooke. Now performing at the Theatre Royal, Drury Lane. Ln : Printed by J. Tabby, 1820. 8°, pp. iv.-36   BUS

] Jubilee in honour of Sh—. A musical entertainment as performed at the theatre in Waterford . . . With additions. Waterford : Esther Crowley & Son, 1773. 8°, pp. 32   BPL | BUS | MPL
Garrick's text much altered.

DAVID
GARRICK
ESQ?

See p. 110

Garrick *Actor* (David) Letters concerning Mrs. Siddons [In 'Athenæum,' No. 3399, p. 865, Dec.] 1892. 4°

] Ode upon dedicating a building and erecting a statue to Sh— at Stratford-upon-Avon. Ln: T. Becket & P. A. Le Hondt, 1769. Fcp. 4°, pp. iv.-34 BM | BPL | BUS | CPL | W
A few copies were struck off on large paper.

] Ode upon dedicating a building to Sh— which was erected by the subscription of the noblemen and gentlemen in the neighbourhood of Stratford-upon-Avon. The music composed by Dr. Arne. [1769.] Oblong f° W

Ode . . . originally spoken and sung at Stratford-upon-Avon in 1769, with a description of the grand pageant. [c. 1816.] 8° BPL

Ode . . . Stratford-upon-Avon, 1827. 8° BPL

Ode . . . *See also* Gentleman's . . .

Oration in honour of Sh— [In Wheler's ' History of Stratford ']. 1806. 8° BUS | SML
In quoting this Oration Charles Knight suggested that Edmund Burke was the real author.

] Peep behind the curtain, or the new rehearsal. As it is now performed at the Theatre Royal in Drury Lane. Ln: 1767. 8° W
With the reference to Sh— at p. 21:—
' Pray don't you adore Sh—, Sir Mac . . .?
Sir Toby and I are absolute worshippers of him ! '

Poetical works. Ln: 1785. 2 vols. 8° BUS
Contains much Sh— matter.

Portrait—
See Gentleman
    ,, Sh— Works, 1773-74
    ,, Sh— Works: Ext. 1783, 1798
Private correspondence. Ln: 1831-32. 2 vols. 4° BPL

Some unpublished correspondence. Ed. by G. P. Baker. Ln: Constable, 1907. 8°. Illust.

Songs, chorusses, etc. which are introduced in the new entertainment of the Jubilee at the Theatre Royal in Drury Lane. Ln: T. Becket, 1770. 8°, pp. ii.-18 BUS

Songs, chorusses, etc. . . . Ln: T. Becket, 1778. 8°, pp. ii.-18 BUS

Songs, chorusses, etc. in the musical afterpiece called Garrick's Jubilee as first performed at the Theatre Royal . . . 1769, and now revived (under the direction of Mr. Farley) at the Theatre Royal, Covent Garden, 23rd April, 1816, being the second centenary . . . from the death of Sh— and in commemoration of the immortal genius of England's great dramatick bard. With a plan of the grand

pageant of the characters of Sh— by the whole of the company. Ln: J. Miller, 1816. 8°, pp. 16 BUS

Garrick *Actor* (David) The Jubilee. [1769.] Holograph MS. 4°, pp. 26 BUS

] The theatres. A poetical dissection. By Sir Nicholas Niplose. Second edition. Ln., J. Bell ; York, C. Etherington, 1772. Fcp. 4°, pp. 80 and 2 engravings BPL
The first vignette pictures Garrick treading on the works of Sh—, with lines :—
' Behold the muses' Roscius sue in vain,
Tailors and carpenters usurpe their reign.'

Thou soft-flowing Avon, written in honour of Sh—. Composed by Dr. Arne. Arranged by J. Addison. Ln: c. 1800. F°, pp. 4 BUS

Warwickshire : A song [In Dibdin's ' Sh—'s garland ' (*q.v.*)]. 1769. 8°
This song is sometimes attributed to Garrick, although the more likely writer is Charles Dibdin. It has long served as the regimental ballad of the Warwickshire regiments. The lively melody brings to mind the ' native wood notes wild ' of Sh—'s country. Two of the verses are here quoted :—
' Each shire has its different pleasures,
Each shire has its different treasures,
But to rare Warwickshire all must submit,
    Warwickshire wit !
    How he writ !
For the wit of all wits was a Warwickshire wit.

    .   .   .   .

Old Ben, Thomas Otway, John Dryden,
And half a score more we take pride in ;
Of famous Will. Congreve we boast too the skill ;
But the Will of all Wills was a Warwickshire Will,
    Warwickshire Will,
    Matchless still,
For the Will of all Wills was a Warwickshire Will.

Garrick (David) *Actor-Editor*—
See Sh— Antony . . . 1758
    ,, Sh— Cymbeline, 1761
    ,, Sh— King Lear, 1779, 1786
    ,, Sh— King Richard III., 1778
    ,, Sh— Macbeth, 1780
    ,, Sh— Midsummer . . . 1754, 1755, 1756, 1763, 1771, 1777, 1798
    ,, Sh— Much ado, 1778
    ,, Sh— Romeo . . . 1748, 1750, 1756, 1758, 1763, 1766, 1769, 1770, 1778, 1780, 1784, 1787, 1800, 1803, 1811, 1812, 1819, 1823, 1827, 1832, 1847, 1904
    ,, Sh— Taming . . . 1756, 1780, 1783-88, 1784, 1806, 1809, 1810, 1811, 1815, 1820, 1831, 1838, 1866, 1879
    ,, Sh— Winter's tale, 1757, 1758, 1762, 1777, 1785

Garrick.] Airs, catches, etc. performed at Stratford on the occasion of the jubilee. With the dedication ode, as spoken by Mr. Garrick. Birmingham, 1769. Cr. 8° BPL

Garrick.] An ode to Mr. G . . r . . k. Ln:
1749. F°   W
Refers to Garrick's part of *King Richard III.*

] Anti-Midas : A jubilee preservative from
unclassical, ignorant, false, and invidious
criticism. 1769. 4°
A defence of Garrick's ode and jubilee.

] Catalogue of engravings and relics collected
by David Garrick, to be sold by auction
by Mr. Christie. Ln : 1825. 8°
The relics included the famous cup made from Sh—'s
mulberry tree presented to Garrick at the 1769
Jubilee.

] Catalogue of the library of David Garrick,
to be sold by auction on the 23rd of
April, 1823, by Mr. Saunders. Ln : 1823.
8°   BPL | SML
A large paper copy in quarto (with purchasers' names
and prices realised) is at Stratford.
According to T. F. Dibdin (*see* his 'Bibliog. Decam.,'
vol. iii., p. 313), the great Roscius formed his library
in anything but an orthodox manner : 'Garrick had
free access to the library at Dulwich College founded
by Alleyn, and pillaged it without scruple or remorse.
He did pretty nearly the same with Sir Thomas
Hanmer's library. No wonder therefore that the
Garrick collection in the British Museum presents at
once an object of vexation, envy, and despair to the
bibliomaniac.'

] Davies (T.) Memoirs of David Garrick. Ln :
1784. 2 vols. 8°   BPL | SML

] Davies (T.) Memoirs . . . Ln : 1808. 2 vols.
8°

] D . . ry L . ne p . . yh . . se broke open.
In a letter to Mr. G . . . . . . Ln : 1748.
8°   W
Contains references to Garrick's Sh— parts.

] Essay on acting, in which will be considered
the mimical behaviour of a certain
fashionable faulty actor and the laudable-
ness of such unmannerly as well as in-
humane proceedings. To which will be
added a short criticism on his acting
Macbeth. 'Oh ! Macbeth has murdered
G . . . . . k.' Ln : W. Bickerton, 1744.
8°, pp. iv.-28   BPL | BUS

] Fitzgerald (P. H.) Life of David Garrick.
Ln : 1868. 2 vols. 8°   BPL

] Garrick's jubilee in 1769 [Advertisement
from ' Stratford-on-Avon Chronicle ' containing details]. 1864. 12°   BPL

] Garrick's vagary, or England run mad.
With particulars of the Stratford jubilee.
Ln : S. Bladon, 1769. 8°, pp. viii.-56
                                    BPL | BUS | W

] H—— (J. F.) David Garrick [In ' Temple
Bar ']. 1864. 8°   BPL

] Knight (Joseph) David Garrick. Ln : 1894.
8°   BPL

] Letter to David Garrick concerning a
glossary to . . . Sh—, on a more extensive
plan than has hitherto appeared. To

which is annexed a specimen . . . Ln :
Printed for the author and sold by T.
Davies in Covent Garden . . . 1768. 8°
                                BM | BPL | MPL | W

Garrick.] Murphy (A.) Life of David Garrick.
1801. 2 vols. 8°. With portrait after Sir
Joshua Reynolds   BPL

] Parsons (*Mrs.* Clement) Garrick and his
circle. Ln : Methuen, 1906. 8°, pp. 442.
Illust.   BPL

] Sheridan (R. B.) Verses to the memory of
Garrick, spoken as a monody at the
Theatre Royal, Drury Lane. Ln : T.
Evans . . . 1779. 8°. With frontispiece W
Large paper copy at Warwick.

] The visitation, or an interview between
the ghost of Sh— and D . v . d G . rr . . k.
Ln : C. Corbett, 1755. 4°, pp. 14
                                BM | BPL | BUS

Garrick (David)—
  See Actor (The)   *See* Lovibond
   ,, Brooke (H.)   ,, Macklin
   ,, Catalogue, 1838   ,, Martin
   ,, Colman and   ,, Melmoth
      Garrick   ,, Memoirs
   ,, Davies (T.)   ,, Morehead
   ,, Dibdin (C.)   ,, Pearce
   ,, Dramatic char-   ,, Poetical . . .
      acters   ,, Reynolds
   ,, Dramatic muse   ,, Robinson
   ,, Fitzgerald   ,, Rolt
   ,, Foote   ,, Sayer
   ,, Hawkins   ,, Sh—] Sh— : An
   ,, Interview   epistle
   ,, Jarvis   ,, Sheridan
   ,, Kenrick   ,, Steevens
   ,, Lamb   ,, Warner
   ,, Lloyd   ,, Wolcot

Garrick (D.) Colman (G.) Foote (S.) Murphy
(A.) & Lloyd (R.) Court of Thespis, being
a collection of the most admired prologues
and epilogues that have appeared for
many years. Written by some of the
most approved witts of the age . . . Ln :
Richardson & Urquhart [c. 1770]. 8°,
pp. iv.-148-iv.
See also Collection . . .
  ,,   ,, Original . . .

Garth. *See* Dunton

Gascoigne (George) Alarum for London, or
the siege of Antwerp. Together with the
spoyle of Antwerpe [In Simpson's 'School
of Sh—' (*q.v.*)]. Ln : Longmans, 1872.
8°, pp. viii.-76 BM | BPL | BUS | CPL | MPL
The editor thinks this play (attributed to Marlowe) was
written by Marston, under the direction and with the
help of Sh—.

Princely pleasures, with the masque intended to have been presented before
Queen Elizabeth at Kenilworth in 1571 :

Laneham's letter describing the magnificent pageants at Kenilworth, 1575. Ln: 1821. 8°   SML | W

Gascoigne (George) Whole woorkes . . . newlye compyled into one volume, that is to say, his Flowers, Hearbes, Weedes, Fruites of Warre, Comedie called 'Supposes,' Tragedie of Iocasta, Steele glasse, Complaint of Phylomene, Storie of Fernando Ieronimi, and The pleasure at Kenelworth Castle. Ln: Imprinted by Abel Ieffes dwelling in the Fore Streete without Creeplegate, neere vnto Grubstreete, 1587. Fcp. 4°, partly black letter   CTC | W

Sh— based his 'Taming of the Shrew' on Gascoigne's 'Supposes,' of which there is no separate edition. It was a translation from Ariosto.

Gaspey (Thomas). *See* Cobham

Gastrell *Iconoclast* (Francis)—
See Halliwell, Historical account . . .
,, Levi
,, Rossetti

Gay (Walter) *Editor. See* Sh— Hamlet, 1859

Gayton. Festivous notes on ' Don Quixote,' 1654. *See Sh*—] Sh—ana

Gazette and Morning Chronicle. *See* Sh— Sonnets, 1791

Geary *Publisher. See* Scott, Webster, & Geary

Gebauer (J. J.) *Halle Publisher*—
See Sh— Poems, 1783
,, Sh— Venus, 1783

Gebhard (J. H.) *Amsterdam Publisher*—
See Sh— Macbeth, 1862
,, Sh— Othello, 1862

Geddes (W. D.) Sh— and Hector Boece. [1896 ?] 4°   BPL

Geffe (Nicholas). *See* Serres & Geffe

Gehrich (E.) *Krefeld Publisher. See* Sh— Hamlet, 1869

Geldart (W. M.) *Editor. See* Sh— King Henry V., 1890

Gem (T. H.)] Sh— as a sportsman. 1872. 8°   BPL

Gems from Sh—. *See* Sh— Works : Ext. 1856, 1907

Genée (Rudolph) Collation of the first edition of ' King Edward II., 1594 ' with Dyce's text of 1850. Ln : New Sh— Soc., 1875-76. 8°   BUS

General view of the stage. *See* Derrick

Geneste (John)] Some account of the English stage from 1660 to 1830. Bath : H. E. Carrington, 1832. 10 vols. 8°   BPL | SML

Genius of Sh—. *See* Sh—

Gent (L. C.)] Choice thoughts from Sh—. *See* Sh— Works : Ext. 1860, 1861, 1862, 1866

Gentleman (Francis)] Introduction to Sh—'s plays, containing an essay on oratory [and dramatick performances]. Ln., John Bell ; York, C. Etherington, 1773. 12°,

pp. 60. Portrait of ' Wm. Sh— at the age of forty ' and portrait of ' David Garrick,' both engraved by J. Hall   BM

Written for Bell's edition of Sh—, and also published separately.

Gentleman (Francis) Introduction . . . Ln : J. Bell, 1774. 8°, pp. 58   BM | BUS | W

] Prolegomena to Sh—'s dramatick writings. Bell's edition. Ln : Bell, 1786. 2 vols. 12°   BUS

The text resembles the introduction to Malone's edition of the works, 1790.

] Prolegomena . . . Ln : J. Bell, 1788. 2 vols. 12°. Portraits and illusts.   CPL

] Prolegomena . . . Ln : Sherwood, 1825. 8°. Portrait   W

] Stratford jubilee : A new comedy, as it has been lately exhibited at Stratford, with great applause. To which is prefixed ' Scrub's trip to the jubilee.' Ln : T. Lowndes, 1769. 8°   BPL | BUS | W

Gentleman (Francis) *Editor*—
See Dramatic censor
,, Sh— All's well, 1773
,, Sh— As you like it, 1773
,, Sh— Coriolanus, 1773
,, Sh— Cymbeline, 1773
,, Sh— Julius Cæsar, 1773
,, Sh— King Henry V., 1773
,, Sh— King Henry VI., i., 1774
,, Sh— King Henry VI., ii., 1774
,, Sh— King Henry VI., iii., 1774
,, Sh— King John, 1773
,, Sh— King Richard II., 1774, 1777
,, Sh— Love's labours lost, 1777
,, Sh— Measure . . . 1773
,, Sh— Merchant . . . 1773
,, Sh— Merry wives, 1773
,, Sh— Midsummer . . . 1777
,, Sh— Othello, 1773
,, Sh— Poems, 1774
,, Sh— Taming . . . 1774, 1776
,, Sh— Timon . . . 1773
,, Sh— Titus . . . 1774, 1777
,, Sh— Troilus . . . 1774, 1776
,, Sh— Twelfth night, 1773
,, Sh— Two gentlemen, 1774
,, Sh— Winter's tale, 1773
,, Sh— Works, 1773-74

Gentleman, according to Sh— [In ' Temple Bar,' April]. Ln : 1868. 8°   BPL | BUS

Gentleman's and London Magazine. Dublin, Oct., 1769. 8°. With rough steel engraving of Stratford pageant

Contains Boswell's 'Account of the Sh— Jubilee at Stratford' and 'Another Account . . .,' in which are given Garrick's Ode and other pieces, together with some written by Boswell intended for recitation at the masquerade.

Gentleman's companion. *See* Ramesay

Gentleman's Magazine or Monthly Intelligencer [Ed. by John Nichols and others]. With general indexes. Ln : 1731-1868. 228 vols. 8°. Illust.   BM
The first thirty-six volumes contain no fewer than ninety-nine essays on the poet and his works.

'Gentleman's Magazine' library: English topography, Warwickshire . . . Ed. by F. A. Milne. Ln : E. Stock, 1901. 8°, pp. xii.-388
Stratford-on-Avon and Sh— occupy pp. 75-103.

Geoffrey of Monmouth. British history. Ln : 1842. 8°   BUS
Book ii. (chapters 11-15) contains an account of King Leir and his daughters.
See Perrett

George III. *of England* (*King*) Portrait. *See* Sh— Works, 1802
See Sh— and honest King George

George *of England* (*Saint*)—
See Colbert
  ,, Heylyn

George of Montemayor. *See* Montemayor

George *Editor. See* Sh— King Henry V., 1909

George-a-Greene. *See* Sh— George-a-Greene

Gerard (G.) To Sh— [In ' Grace and remembrance : Poems,' pp. 3-45]. 1856. 12°   BPL

German *Composer* (Edward) Music to ' As you like it,' 1896
  Music to ' King Henry VIII.,' 1892
  Music to ' King Richard III.,' 1889
  Music to ' Much ado,' 1898
  Music to ' Romeo and Juliet,' 1895
  Symphonic poem : ' Hamlet,' 1897

Germany—
  See Cohn   *See* Herford
  ,, Goethe   ,, Thoms
  ,, Greg

Gernutus the Jew. *See Sh*—] Sh—'s library
A foundation of the ' Merchant of Venice.'

Gervais (Francis Peter) Sh— not Bacon : Some arguments from Sh—'s copy of ' Florio's Montaigne ' in the British Museum. Ln : Unicorn Press, 1901. 4°, pp. 40. With facsimiles
                   BPL | BUS | MPL | SML

Gervinus (George Gottfried) Sh—. *See* Sh— Sh— commentaries. Trans. from the second German edition by F. E. Bunnett. Ln : Smith & Elder, 1862. 2 vols. 8°
                   BM | SML
Sh— commentaries . . . Ln : Smith . . . 1863. 2 vols. 8°   BM | BPL | BUS | CPL
Sh— commentaries . . . Introd. by F. J. Furnivall. Ln : 1874. 8°   BPL
Sh— commentaries . . . Ln : Smith . . . 1875. 8°, pp. l.-942   BM | BUS
Sh— commentaries . . . New edition, revised. With introd. by J. F. Furnivall. Ln : Smith, 1877. 8°   BM | BPL | SML

Gervinus (George Gottfried) Sh— commentaries . . . Ln : Smith . . . 1883. 2 vols. 8°   MPL
Sh— commentaries . . . Ln : 1892. 8°   BUS

Gesta Grayorum. Ln : 1688. 4°   BUS
An account of the revels at Gray's Inn in 1594, with this passage : ' After such sports a " Comedy of errors," like to Plautus his " Menechmus," was played by the players.' This is the first known presentment of Sh—'s comedy.

Gesta Romanorum.] Choice of the three caskets, 1843. *See Sh*—] Sh—'s library

Gesta Romanorum—
See Apollonius of Tyre
  ,, Douce
  ,, Elimandus

Ghost of Richard the third. A poem, printed in 1614 and founded upon Sh—'s historical play. Reprinted from the only known copy in the Bodleian Library. With introduction and notes by J. P. Collier. Ln : Sh— Soc., 1844. 8°, pp. xvi.-80
                   BPL | BUS
The dedication is signed C. B., possibly Charles Best or Christopher Brooke.
See also Brooke

Ghost of Sh—: Memoirs of the ' Sh— head ' in Covent Garden. Ln : 1755. 2 vols. Cr. 8°   BPL
Shakespearean in title only.

Ghost-player's guide, or a hint to two great houses ; More ghost-playing : Banquo's spirit brought to book. By ' Umbra ' [In ' London Magazine,' April-July]. Ln : 1824. 8°   BUS

Ghost-player.] Observations on the ' Ghost-player's guide ' and on the invariable tendency to corpulence in Sh—'s ghosts ; together with cursory remarks on swearing. By ' Horrida Bella ' [In ' London Mag.,' May]. 1824. 8°   BUS

Giacomo di Grassi. His true arte of defence, plainlie teaching by infallable demonstrations, apt figures, and perfect rules, the manner and forme how a man without other teacher or master may safelie handle all sortes of weapons, as well offensive as defensive. With a treatise of disceit or falsinge, and with a waie or meane by private industrie to obtaine strength, iudgment, and activitie. First written in Italian by the foresaid author, and Englished by J. G. Printed at Ln. for I. I. [John Jaggard, by Wm. Jaggard] and are to be sold within Temple Barre at the signe of the hand and starre, 1594. Fcp. 4°   BLO
Copies of the original issue in Italian, Venice, 1570, with a portrait of the author, are at the British Museum and the Bodleian Library.
The first English work on fencing.
  ' Nay, not sure, in a thing falsing.'—
                   Comedy of errors, ii., 2.

'What's his weapon? Rapier and dagger. That's
two of his weapons.'—*Hamlet*, v., 2.
'I would I had bestowed that time in the tongues
that I have in fencing, dancing.'
—*Twelfth night*, i., 3.

Gibbs *Editor*. *See* Goldsmith
Gibbs (George) *Publisher*. *See* Davies (John)
Gibbs (Hunt) Sh— memorial. *See* Sh—
Gibbs (J.) *See* Gybbys
Gibbs (J. W. M.) *Editor*. *See* Simpson (R.)
Gibbs (Philip) Knowledge is power : A guide
to personal culture. 1903. Cr. 8°
Sh— occupies pp. 76-90.
The title was already the copyright of Charles Knight.

Gibson (C. H.) *Editor*—
See Sh— King Richard II., 1897
,, Sh— Merchant . . . 1895, 1897
Gibson (J. Paul S. R.) Sh—'s use of the
supernatural. Harness prize essay.
Author's original type - written manu-
script, on 124 leaves. 1907. F°
Sh—'s use of the supernatural. Cam-
bridge : Deighton Bell, 1908. Cr. 8°
BM | BPL

Gibson (R. L.) Shaksperean gems. *See* Sh—
Works : Ext. 1865
Gibson (Robert Lamplugh) Shakesperean
gems. *See* Sh— Works : Ext. 1865
Gibson (Strickland). *See* Madan, Turbutt, &
Gibson
Gibson (W. S.) *Editor*. *See* Sh— King Henry
IV., ii., 1870
Gifford (Humphrey) *Editor*. *See* Boccaccio
Gilbert (Allan) *Artist*. *See* Sh— Romeo . . .
1899
Gilbert (Bennet) Sh—'s dream : An opera
[Full score]. Ln : 1861. F"
Gilbert (Henry & Elizabeth). *See* Sh—]
Malone
Gilbert (*Sir* John) *Artist*—
See Sh— As you like it, 1850
,, Sh— King Henry VIII., 1892
,, Sh— Poems, 1861, 1863, 1877, 1888
,, Sh— Sonnets, 1862, 1863, 1875, 1877,
1878, 1888, 1890
,, Sh— Works, 1858-60, 1858-61, 1860,
1862-64, 1865, 1865-67, 1866,
1868, 1873-75, 1875, 1879, 1881-
82, 1882, 1883, 1888, 1891, 1897,
1899
,, Sh— Works : Ext. 1876, 1877, 1879,
1882, 1890
Gilbert (*Sir* Wm. Schwenck) An unfortunate
likeness [to Sh—], [In ' Fun,' 14 Nov.]
Ln : 1868. 4°
Rosencrantz and Guildenstern. *See* Sh—
Hamlet, 1893, 1895
Gilbertson (Wm.) *Publisher*—
See Peele
,, Sh— Merry devil . . . 1655
,, Sh— Rape . . . 1655

Gilchrist (Frederika B.) True story of Hamlet
and Ophelia. Boston [U.S.], 1889. 12°
BM | BUS
Gilchrist (Octavius) Examination of the
charges maintained by Messrs. Malone,
Chalmers, and others, of Ben Jonson's
enmity, etc. towards Sh—. Ln : Taylor
& Hessey, 1808. 8°, pp. iv.-62
BM | BPL | BUS
Gilchrist (O.) *Editor*. *See* Dodsley
Gild of the Holy Cross. *See Stratford*] Register
Gilder (Richard Watson) Five books of song.
Ln : 1894. Cr. 8°
In the poem, 'Two worlds,' p. 154, is a sonnet called
the 'Twenty-third of April':—
'A little English earth and breathèd air
Made Sh— the divine ; so is his verse
The broidered soil of every blossom fair,
So doth his song all sweet bird-songs rehearse.
But tell me then what wondrous stuff did fashion
That part of him which took those wilding flights
Among imagined worlds ; whence the white passion
That burned three centuries through the days and
nights.
Not heaven's four winds could make, nor round the
earth
The soul wherefrom the soul of Hamlet flamed,
Not anything of merely mortal birth
Could enlighten when Sh—'s name is named.
How was his body bred we know full well,
But that high soul's engendering who may tell.'

Gildon (Charles) Complete art of poetry. *See*
Sh— Works : Ext. 1718
Essay on the art, rise and progress of the
stage in Greece, Rome, and England.
See Sh— Poems, 1710, 1725
] Miscellaneous letters and essays . . . in
prose and verse, directed to Dryden,
Congreve, Dennis, and others. Ln : 1694.
8° BPL | BUS | W
At p. 64, 'Some reflections on Rymer's "Short view."'
Remarks on the plays of Sh—. Ln : [1709.]
8° W
Original edition. Issued as a supplement to Rowe's
1709 edition of Sh—'s works.
Remarks . . . Ln : 1710. 8°
Shakespeariana. *See* Sh— Works : Ext.
1718
The patriot, or the Italian conspiracy. A
tragedy. Ln : W. Davis, 1703. Fcp. 4°
In the preface Sh—'s merits and faults are discussed.
Gildon (C.) *Editor*—
See Langbaine
,, Sh— Measu э . . . 1700
,, Sh— Poems, 1709, 1710, 1714, 1725,
1728
,, Sh— Works, 1710, 1714, 1725
Giles (Henry) Falstaff : A type of epicurean
life [In ' Lectures and Essays,' Vol. I.,
pp. 1-44]. Boston [U.S.], 1851. 12°
BPL | BUS
Growing and perpetual influence of Sh—
[In ' Christian Examiner,' Sep.] Boston
[U.S.], 1859 BUS

Giles (Henry) Human life in Sh—. With
introd. by J. B. O'Reilly. Boston [U.S.],
1868 : Lee & Shepard. 16°, pp. 286
BM | BPL | BUS | MPL | SML
Gilfillan (George) Galleries of literary portraits.
See Sh—] Gilfillan
Great poem mysteries : ' Hamlet ' [In
' Eclectic Magazine,' Sep.]. New York,
1851. 8°   BUS
Life and poetry of Sh—. *See* Sh—
Third gallery of portraits. *See* Sh—
Gilfillan (G.) *Editor. See* Sh— Poems, 1856,
1862, 1878
Gilfillan.] Macrae. George Gilfillan. Glas-
gow : Morison, 1891. 8°, pp. 158
Gilkes (Arthur H.) School lectures on the
' Electra ' of Sophocles and ' Macbeth.'
Ln : Longmans, 1880. 8°, pp. xii.-148
BM | BPL | BUS
Gilks (T.) *Engraver. See* Sh— As you like it,
1850
Gillespie (J. D.) Medical notes about Sh— and
his times. Harveian address. Edinburgh,
1875. 8°   BPL
Gilliland (T.) Dramatic mirror : History of
the stage from the time of Sh—. 1808.
2 vols. 12°   BPL | BUS | CPL
Gilliver (Lawton) *Printer*--
See Epistle
  „ Mallet
  „ Sh— Taming . . . 1735
Gillmor (Clotworthy)] Reflections from Sh—'s
Cliff : with a glance at Calais Cliff. Ln :
E. Palmer & Son, 1851. 8°, pp. 36
BPL | BUS | W
Reflections . . . Second edition. Ln :
Palmer, 1853. 8°, pp. 48   BUS
Gilman (A.) History of the drama in Sh—'s
time. *See* Sh— Works, 1880, 1881, 1882
Sh—'s morals. *See* Sh— Works : Ext. 1880
Gilmore (J. H.) How shall we spell Sh—'s
name ? [In ' Scribner's Monthly,' May].
New York, 1876. 8°   BUS
Ginn (E.) *Boston [U.S.] Publisher. See* Sh—
Julius Cæsar, 1868
Ginsburg (Christian D.) Sh—'s use of the
Bible : Bishop's version, 1568 [In
'Athenæum,' No. 2896, p. 541]. 1883
Giovanni Fiorentino. Adventures of Gian-
netto, 1843. *See Sh*—] Sh—'s library
A foundation of the ' Merchant of Venice.'
Bucciuolo and Pietro Paolo. *See Sh*—]
Sh—'s library
A foundation of the ' Merry Wives.'
Novel [in the ' Pecorone '] from which the
play of the ' Merchant . . .' is taken . . .
To which is added a translation of a
novel from the ' Decamerone ' of Boc-
caccio. Ln : 1755. 8°   BPL | W

Giraldi-Cinthio (Giovanni Battista) Moor of
Venice : Cinthio's tale and Sh—'s tragedy.
By John Edward Taylor. Ln : Chapman
& Hall, 1855. 8°, pp. 36   BUS
Novella. *See* Sh—] Sh—'s library
A foundation of ' Measure for Measure.'
Story of the Moor of Venice. Translated
from the Italian. With two essays on
Sh— and preliminary observations by
Wolstenholme Parr. Ln : T. Cadell &
W. Davies, 1795. 8°, pp. 92   BM | BUS
Story of the Moorish captain, 1843. *See
Sh*—] Sh—'s library
Giraud (*Miss* J. E.) Flowers from Sh—. *See*
Sh— Works : Ext. 1846
] Flowers of Sh— [thirty fanciful groups of
flowers mentioned in the plays]. Acker-
mann, Ln : Day & Son [1845]. 4°.
Thirty large plates in colours   BPL | SML
A delightful gallery of Warwickshire flora.
Given (Walker) Further study of ' Othello' :
Have we misunderstood Sh—'s Moor ?
New York Sh— Soc., 1899. Cr. 8°
BM | BPL | BUS | SML
Gladstone (*Rt. Hon.* Wm. Ewart). *See* Kean
Glanville (Bartholomew de)] Batman vppon
Bartholome : His booke ' De proprietati-
bus rerum.' Newly corrected, enlarged,
and amended. Ln : Thomas East, 1582.
F°, black letter   BUS | W
The Batman referred to is Stephen Bateman. Douce
considered this Sh—'s text book of science and
natural history.
Glasgow Dramatic Review, 1826. 8°
Glasgow Theatrical Review, 1827. 8°
Glasgow University Album, edited by students
of the university. [1838 ?] 12°   BPL
Notes on ' Hamlet,' pp. 166-185.
Glasse of godly love. Wherein all married
couples may learne their duties, each
towards others, according to the Holy
Scriptures. [By John Rogers ?] Ln :
New Sh— Soc., 1876. 4°   BUS
Gleanings from the comedies of Sh—. *See*
Sh— Works : Ext. 1868, 1869, 1881
Gleanings from the English poets. *See* Sh—
Works : Ext. 1862
Glenny. Illustrated garden forget - me - not.
1860. 12°   BPL
Mentions Herne's Oak, p. 55 [' Merry Wives '].
Globe Theatre, London, 1594-1613.] Sh—'s
theatre : Description of the model [of
the first Globe Theatre]. Ln : c. 1901.
Broadside, with 2 photographs   BUS
] Sh—'s Globe [theatre]. In 'The Athenæum,'
No. 4286, 18 Dec., 1909. 4°   BM
Globe Theatre, London—
See Halliwell, Two old theatres
  „ Howell
  „ J—— (J. R.)
  „ Jackson

The Bear Garden.   *From the Venetian Map, 1629*   The Globe Theatre

Globe Theatre, in which William Shakespeare acted.

See p. 18

Globe Theatre, London—
  See Martin
  ,, Rendle
  ,, Sh— King Lear, 1608, 1655
  ,, Sh— King Richard II., 1608, 1615, 1634
  ,, Sh— London prodigall, 1605
  ,, Sh— Love's labours lost, 1631
  ,, Sh— Merry devill, 1608, 1617, 1626,
        1631, 1655
  ,, Sh— Othello, 1655, 1681, 1695, 1705,
        1724
  ,, Sh— Pericles, 1609, 1611
  ,, Sh— Poems, 1795
  ,, Sh— Romeo . . . 1609, 1609-37, 1637
  ,, Sh— Troilus . . . 1609
  ,, Sh— Yorkshire tragedy, 1608
  ,, Sh— Works, 1850
  ,, *Sh*—] Halliwell
  ,, *Sh*—] Knight
  ,, Stopes
  ,, Vyse
  ,, Wallace
Glossaries. *See Sh*—] Sh— glossaries
Glossary explaining the obsolete and difficult
  words in the plays of Sh—. [Und.] Manu-
  script, 63 columns. F°   BUS
Gloucester (Humphrey *Duke of*). *See* Sh—
  King Henry VI., iii., 1723
Gloucestershire—
  See Annalia . . .   *See* Huntley
  ,, Ashbee   ,, Rushen
Glover (John) *Editor. See* Sh— Works, 1863-66
Glover (Stephen) Homage to Sh— : Three
  melodies for the pianoforte. Ln : R.
  Cocks & Co., c. 1864. F°, pp. 12   BUS
Glynn (P. McM.) Some thoughts on Sh—. *See*
  Sh—
  Works of Sh— as a key to the man. *See*
  Sh—
Goadby (Edwin) Sh—'s time : A lecture at
  York Institute. With 'A pilgrimage to
  Stratford-on-Avon.' York, J. Sampson ;
  Ln : A. H. Moxon [1879]. 8°, pp. 48
                    BM | BPL
  The England of Sh—. Ln : Cassell [1881].
  Cr. 8°, pp. 192   SML
  The England of Sh—. Ln : Cassell [1889].
  Cr. 8°, pp. 224. Illustrated BM | BPL
Goadby (R.) *Sherborne Publisher. See* Sh—
  Works, 1768
God in Sh—. *See* Downing
Godbid (W.) *Printer*—
  See Cokaine
  ,, Lucy
  ,, Playford
Goddard (Arthur) Players of the period :
  Anecdotal, biographical, and critical
  monographs of the leading English actors
  of the day. Ln : 1891. 2 vols. Cr. 8°.
  Illust.

Goddard (H. P.) Lesson of ' Cymbeline ' [In
  ' Poet Lore ']. Philadelphia, 1891. 8°
                    BPL
Godfrey (Elizabeth) Children in Sh—'s plays
  [In 'Children of Olden Time,' pp. 99-114].
  1907. 8°   BPL
Godley (J. A.) *Editor. See* Sh— Cymbeline,
  1869
Godly Queene Hester : Enterlude, 1561. *See*
  Reprints
Godwin (Parke) New study of the ' Sonnets '
  of Sh—. New York : Putnam, 1900. 12°,
  pp. 314   BPL | BUS
Godwin (P.) *Editor. See* Sh— Sonnets, 1900
Godwin (W.) The enquirer. *See* Sh—
Goethe (J. W. von) Conversations with Ecker-
  mann and Soret. *See* Sh—
  On Sh— : Selections from Carlyle's trans.
  of ' Wilhelm Meister.' Ln : De la More
  Press, 1904. 18°   BPL
  Wilhelm Meister's apprenticeship, trans. by
  T. Carlyle. Ln : Chapman, 1860. 2 vols.
  Cr. 8°   BPL
  On ' Hamlet,' book v. Frequently reprinted.
Goethe.] Female characters of Goethe and Sh—
  [In ' North British Review,' Feb.] Edin-
  burgh, 1848. 8°   BUS
Goethe (J. W. von)—
  See Masson   *See* Tomlinson
  ,, Rudloff   ,, Wilson (H. S.)
Goetz *Composer. See* Sh— Taming . . . 1880
Goffe (Thomas) Covrageovs Tvrke, or Amvrath
  the first. A tragedie. Ln : Printed by
  R. Alsop and T. Fawcit for R. Meighen,
  1632. Fcp. 4°, without pagination   W
  In five acts, and all in verse.
    ' Not Amurath an Amurath succeeds.'
              —*King Henry IV.*, ii.
Goggin (S. E.) *Editor*—
  See Sh— Hamlet, 1909
  ,, Sh— Merchant . . . 1908
Gold, silver, lead : A collection of original
  stories. Ed. by Mrs. [Laura] Valentine.
  With numerous illustrations . . . Ln :
  Warne, 1867. Roy. 8°, pp. 96, with
  coloured frontis. of ' Portia and Bas-
  sanio,' by F. H. Corbould
  The title is named after the three caskets in Sh—'s
  ' Merchant of Venice.'
Golding (Arthur) *Editor. See* Ovidius
Goldsmid (E.) Dramatic works performed in
  France 1200-1800 : Part I., 1200-1529.
  Aungervyle Soc. reprints. Edinburgh,
  1883. 8°   BPL
Goldsmid (E.) *Editor. See* Kempe
Goldsmith (*Dr.* Oliver) Diverting history of
  Sir John Falstaff . . .
  See Sh— King Henry IV., 1789
  ,, Sh— Merry wives, 1789
  Extracts. *See* Sh— Works : Ext. 1822

Goldsmith (*Dr.* Oliver) History of the 'Boar's head' tavern in East Cheap [In his 'Miscellaneous Works,' Vol. 4]. Ln: 1806. 8°   BUS
Much altered from the version in the 'Diverting history.'
Short dissertation on the character of Sir John Falstaff, and a reverie at the 'Boar's head' tavern in East Cheap [In his 'Collected Essays']. Ln: 1765. 8°, pp. 16   W
'The character of old Falstaff, even with all his faults, gives me more consolation than the most studied efforts of wisdom ...'
Works. With notes by Gibbs. Ln: Bell, 1884-86. 5 vols. Cr. 8°   BPL
Contains Shakespeareana.
See Baker (D. E.)

Goll (August) Criminal types in Sh—. Trans. from the Danish by Mrs. Charles Weekes. Ln: Methuen, 1909. Cr. 8°, pp. 280 BFL
Gollancz (*Prof.* Israel) 'Hamlet' in Iceland. Ln: 1898. 8°   BPL
Shakespeariana, 1598-1602: Summary [Extracted from 'Proceedings of the British Academy,' 27 April]. Ln: Privately off-printed, 1904. Roy. 8°, pp. 8, including printed wrappers   BPL
Gollancz (*Prof.* I.) *Editor—*
See Sh— All's well, 1894
  ,, Sh— Antony ... 1896
  ,, Sh— As you like it, 1894, 1904
  ,, Sh— Comedy of errors, 1894
  ,, Sh— Coriolanus, 1896
  ,, Sh— Cymbeline, 1896
  ,, Sh— Hamlet, 1895, 1902
  ,, Sh— Julius Cæsar, 1896
  ,, Sh— King Henry IV., i.-ii., 1895
  ,, Sh— King Henry V., 1895, 1898
  ,, Sh— King Henry VI., i.-ii.-iii., 1895
  ,, Sh— King Henry VIII., 1895
  ,, Sh— King John, 1895
  ,, Sh— King Lear, 1895, 1904
  ,, Sh— King Richard II., 1895
  ,, Sh— King Richard III., 1895
  ,, Sh— Love's labours lost, 1894
  ,, Sh— Macbeth, 1896, 1904, 1906
  ,, Sh— Measure ... 1894, 1899
  ,, Sh— Merchant ... 1895
  ,, Sh— Merry wives, 1894
  ,, Sh— Midsummer ... 1894, 1895
  ,, Sh— Much ado, 1894
  ,, Sh— Othello, 1895
  ,, Sh— Pericles, 1896
  ,, Sh— Rape ... 1896
  ,, Sh— Romeo ... 1896
  ,, Sh— Sonnets, 1896
  ,, Sh— Taming ... 1894, 1895
  ,, Sh— The tempest, 1894
  ,, Sh— Timon ... 1896
  ,, Sh— Titus ... 1896

Gollancz (*Prof.* I.) *Editor—*
See Sh— Troilus ... 1896, 1904
  ,, Sh— Twelfth night, 1895
  ,, Sh— Two gentlemen, 1894
  ,, Sh— Venus ... 1896, 1897
  ,, Sh— Winter's tale, 1895
  ,, Sh— Works, 1894-96, 1899-1900, 1900-01, 1904
Goltz (B.) Sh—'s genius. [1870.] 16°   BM
Gonsales and his vertuous wife Agatha. *See* Rich
Gonzalez (Maria Coralie de la)] Avon star [Sh— miscellany], by 'Marie Corelli.' Stratford-on-Avon: A. J. Stanley, 1903. 4°, pp. iv.-146   BPL
For reply, *see* Bloom.
] Plain truth of the Stratford controversy. Concerning the fully-intended demolition of old houses in Henley Street and the changes proposed to be effected on the national ground of Sh—'s birthplace. By 'Marie Corelli.' Ln: Methuen, 1903. Roy. 8°   BPL
Refers to the proposed spoliation of Henley Street by the erection of a Carnegie free library.
For reply, *see* Levi (S. L.)
See also Hyatt
  ,,   ,,   Waters
Good speed to Virginia, 1609. *See* Reprints
Goodall (E.) *Engraver.* *See* Sh— As you like it, 1850
Goodban (Henry W.) *See* Lacy & Goodban
Goodhall (James) *Editor.* *See* Sh— King Richard II., 1772
Goodlet (I.) New word on Sh—'s 'Sonnets' [In 'Poet Lore']. Philadelphia, 1891. 4°   BPL
Goodson (H. F.) Sh—; his religious and moral sentiments. *See* Sh—
Goodson (H. F.) *Editor.* *See* Sh— Works: Ext. 1874
Goodwin (A. T.) Court revels in the reign of Henry VII. *See Sh—*] Sh— Soc.
Goodwin (T.) History of the reign of Henry V. Ln: S. & J. Sprint, 1704. F°   SML
Goodwin (Timothy) *Publisher—*
See Beaumont & Fletcher
  ,, Rochester
  ,, Saint Evremond
Goonewardena (D. G.) Companion to Sh—'s 'Julius Cæsar.' 1890. 8°   BM
Gordon (D.)] Ethics of the Sh— celebrations ... Ln: J. H. Tressider, 1864. 8°, pp. 42
                                     BPL | BUS
Gordon (Eva G.) *Editor.* *See* Delius
Gordon (G. S.) *Editor—*
See Sh— Julius Cæsar, 1909
  ,, Sh— King Richard II., 1909
  ,, Sh— Macbeth, 1909
  ,, Sh— Works, 1908

Gordon (J.) *Edinburgh Publisher.* *See* Sh—Macbeth, 1862

Gordon (J. T.) Sh— and ourselves. Edinburgh, 1863. 8°   BPL

Gordon (W.) *Edinburgh Publisher. See* Sh—Works, 1753, 1792

Gosford (Archibald *Earl of*) *Bibliophile. See* Catalogue, 1884

Gosnell (S.) *Printer. See* Sh— Coriolanus, 1806

Gosse (Edmund) From Sh— to Pope: Classical poetry in England. Cambridge: Univ. Press, 1885. 12°   BPL | SML
See Garnett & Gosse

Gosson (Henry) *Publisher—*
See Sh— Pericles, 1609
  ,,   Taylor (John)

Gosson (Stephen) Ephemerides of Phialo, divided into three books: A method to rebuke a friend; A canuagado to courtiers; Defence of a courtezan; and a short apologie of the 'Schoole of abuse' against poets, pipers, players, etc. Ln: T. Dawson, 1579. Fcp. 4°
School of abuse, containing a pleasant invective against poets, pipers, players, jesters, etc. With an introd. regarding the author and his works by J. P. Collier. *See* Sh—] Sh— Soc.   BM | BPL | BUS
See Salvianus for sequel, and Lodge, Defence . . . for reply.

Gostwick (J.) Sh—. *See* Sh—

Gough (H. T.) Ode, inscribed with reverent regard, to the memory of . . . the immortal bard. Ln: W. S. Johnson, 1848. 4°, pp. 12   BM

Goulart (Simon) Admirable and memorable histories containing the wonders of our time. Collected into French out of the best authors by J. Govlart. And out of French into English by Ed. Grimeston. Ln: George Eld, 1607. Fcp. 4°, sig. A—T4, unpaged   BUS | CTC | W
The original was the handiwork of Simon, not Jean Goulart.
A story similar to the Induction of 'Taming of the Shrew' occurs on pp. 587-589. Incidents found in 'Measure for Measure' occur on pp. 341 and 346.
Waking man's dream. *See* Sh—] Sh—'s library
A foundation of 'Taming of the Shrew.'

Goulart (S.) *Editor. See* Plutarchus

Gould (George) Corrigenda and explanations of the text of Sh—. Ln: 1881. 8°, pp. 16   BM | BPL | MPL
Corrigenda . . . New issue, showing hundreds of mistakes existing in the standard editions. Ln: Virtue, 1884. 8°, pp. 64   BPL | BUS | MPL | SML
Greek plays in their relations to the dramatic unities. 1883. 8°   BPL

Gould (George) Letters to Samuel Timmins on Sh—. [Manuscript.] 1884-89. 12° BPL
Printing of the first folio Sh— [In the 'Leisure Hour']. Ln: 1888. Roy. 8° BPL

Gould (Robert) Poems, chiefly consisting of satyres and satyrical epistles. Ln: Printed and . . . sold by most booksellers in Ln. and Westminster, 1689. 12°
In a 'Satyr against the playhouse,' p. 177, is a lengthy passage on Sh—, beginning:—
  'But if in what's sublime you take delight,
  Lay Sh—, Ben, and Fletcher in your sight,
  Where human actions are with life exprest,
  Vertue extoll'd and vice as much deprest . . .'

Goulding *Publisher. See* Sh— Twelfth night, 1820

Goulding (G.) *Publisher. See* Sh— Romeo . . . 1750

Gounod (Charles) *Composer. See* Sh— Romeo . . . 1867

Gourley (Oscar) Anniversary poem for the Sh— Club. Recited by John B. Hart at their third anniversary celebration, 17 April, 1826 [In G. W. Adams' 'Oration']. Boston: Dutton & Wentworth, 1826. 8°, pp. 25-30   BUS

Gowan (J.) Sh— and Milton compared [In 'Preaching and Preachers,' pp. 153-160]. 1902. 8°   BPL

Gower (John) De confessione amantis. Ln: 1554. F°   BUS
On ff. 175-185 of book viii. is the story of Apollonius, Prince of Tyre, one of the sources of 'Pericles.'
De confessio amantis: Apollonius of Tyre. *See* Sh—] Sh—'s library
See also Sh— Pericles, 1608, 1889

Gower (Ronald Sutherland *Baron*) Old diaries, 1881-1901. Ln: 1902. 8°   BPL
The writer designed and presented the beautiful bronze statue and group in the Memorial gardens at Stratford.

Gowrie.] Earle of Gowrie's conspiracie against the King's Maiestie of Scotland. Ln: V. Simmes, 1600. Fcp. 4°
This tract is supposed to have supplied Sh— with information for 'Macbeth.'

Gowrie conspiracy. *See* Sprot

Grabstein (*Prof.*) On the character of the Ghost in 'Hamlet' [In 'Fraser's Mag.,' Sept.]. Ln: 1845. 8°   BUS

Gracian (Lorenzo) Heroe of Lorenzo, or way to eminence and perfection . . . Ln: 1652. 8°
Contains the story of the Jew and pound of flesh.

Grädener (K.) *Hamburg Publisher. See* Sh—Works, 1879-91, 1880-91

Graebner (G.) *Leipzig Publisher—*
See Sh— Julius Cæsar, 1859
  ,,   Sh— King Lear, 1861
  ,,   Sh— Merchant . . . 1861
  ,,   Sh— Romeo . . . 1859

Græser (C.) *Editor. See* Sh— Julius Cæsar, 1870

Grafton (George Fitzroy *fourth Duke of*) *Biblio-phile.* *See* Catalogue, 1815
Grafton (Richard) *Printer*—
  See Caius   *See* Wilson
  ,, Halle
Graham *Publisher.* *See* Ireland (S. W. H.)
Graham (T. J.) *Editor*—
  See Barnstorff
  ,, Sh— Sonnets, 1862
Graham *DD.* (W.) Sh—; Tercentenary ser-mon. 1864. 8°   BM
Grahame (J.) Notice respecting Macbeth's Castle at Inverness [In 'Archæologica Scotica']. Edin., 1831. 8°   BUS
Grant (G.)] Essay on the science of acting, by a veteran stager. Ln : Cowie & Strange, 1828. 12°, pp. xii.-202. Portrait of Sh— engraved by J. Thomson from the original picture in the possession of Mr. Richard-son   SML
Grantham (H.) *Editor.* *See* Boccaccio
Granville *Baron Lansdowne* (George) Jew of Venice. *See* Sh— Merchant . . . 1701, 1711, 1713, 1721, 1732, 1736
  Songs. *See* Sh— Midsummer . . . 1755
Granville *Baron Lansdowne* (G.) *Editor. See* Sh— King Henry IV., i., 1710, 1721
Graphic gallery . . . *See* Sh— Works, 1896
Graphic illustrations of Warwickshire. *See* Jaffray
Grau (J.) *Editor.* *See* Sh— Macbeth, 1866
Gravelot (H.) *Artist-Engraver*—
  See Sh— Timon . . . 1770
  ,, Sh— Works, 1740, 1744-46, 1757, 1762, 1770-71
Graves *Publisher. See* Moon, Boys, and Graves
Graves (Henry Mercer) Essay on the genius of Sh—. 1825. 8°   BPL
  Essay on the genius of Sh—, with critical remarks on the characters of Romeo, Hamlet, Juliet, and Ophelia ; together with some observations on the writings of Sir Walter Scott. To which is annexed a critique on taste, judgment, and rheto-rical expression, and remarks on the leading actors of the day. Ln : J. Bigg, 1826. 8°, pp. viii.-206
      BM | BPL | BUS | CPL | MPL | W
Graves (Joseph) Dramatic tales. *See* Sh— Works : Ext. 1850
  Life of Wm. Sh—. *See* Sh—
Graves (Richard) On erecting a monument to Sh—, under the direction of Mr. Pope and Lord Burlington [In ' Euphrosyne ']. Ln : 1776.
  Refers to the statue in Poet's corner, Westminster Abbey, defrayed by public subscription, designed by Wm. Kent, and executed by Peter Scheemachers.
  ' To mark her Sh—'s worth and Britain's love
  Let Pope design, and Burlington approve.
  Superfluous care ! When distant time shall view
  This tomb grown old—his works shall still be new.'

Gray *Publisher. See* Hilliard & Gray
Gray (H.) *Publisher. See* Sh— Works, 1753
Gray (J.) *Publisher*—
  See Lillo
  ,, Sh— Pericles, 1738
Gray & Son (J.) *Publishers. See* Sh— Works, 1811
Gray (J. A.) *New York Printer. See* Sh— Midsummer . . . 1866
Gray (James Wm.) Sh—'s marriage, departure from Stratford, and other incidents in his life. *See* Sh—] Gray
Gray (R.) True ' Hamlet ' of Wm. Sh—. Peterhead : Brown, 1901. 12°   SML
Gray (T.)] My notes on Sh— . . . written at Stratford-on-Avon. Leamington, 1867. 12°, pp. 32   BPL | MPL
  ] Remarks on the desecration of the church-yard in which sleeps the immortal Sh—. Stratford-on-Avon, 1868. 8°   BPL
Gray *Poet* (Thomas) Beauties . . . *See* Sh— Works : Ext. 1806
  Manuscript notes. *See* Sh— Works, 1740
  Progress of poesy. A Pindaric ode. 1759
    ' Far from the sun and summer gale
    In thy [Albion's] green lap was nature's darling laid,
    What time, where lucid Avon strayed,
    To him the mighty mother did unveil
    Her awful face : The dauntless child
    Stretched forth his little arms and smiled ;
    This pencil take, she said, whose colours clear
    Richly paint the vernal year.
    Thine too these golden keys ; immortal boy,
    This can unlock the gates of joy,
    Of horror that, and thrilling fears,
    Or ope the sacred source of sympathetic tears.'
Gray (W.) Ye comic Sh—, with designs . . . Part I. [c. 1864.] 8°   BPL
Gray (Walter) Gray, 1591 : Almanacke and prognostication made for the yeere of our Lorde God 1591. Rectified for the eleua-tion and meridian of Dorchester, seruing most aptly for the West partes, and generally for all Englande . . . Ln : Richarde Watkins and James Robertes [1591]. 12°, black letter   w
  In the ' Midsummer night's dream,' Act iii., Scene 1. Bottom refers to the 'Almanacke' for the night of moon-shine, and other references occur in the ' Comedy of errors,' ' King Hy. IV.,' and in ' Antony and Cleopatra.'
Gray (Wm.) *Artist. See* Ross
Gray-Wilson (W.) To be or not to be. *See* Sh— Works : Ext. 1883
Gray's Inn—
  See Gesta Grayorum
  ,, Sh— Comedy of errors (*heading*)
  ,, Stopes
Grazia (E. N.) *Composer. See* Sh— Measure . . . 1870
Great assises holden in Parnassus, by Apollo. Ln : Spenser Soc., Issue No. 40. 1885. 4°   BPL
  Sh— is mentioned as a juror.

Great book of poetry. Ed. by S. O. Beeton.
　See Sh— Works: Ext. 1870

Great book robbery. A Warwickshire man
　implicated. By a literary thief. 1881.
　12° 　　　　　　　　　　　　　　　　　BPL
　Suggesting that Sh— was a plagiarist.

Great Sh— forgeries. *See* Davey

Greatbach *Engraver*—
　See Sh— Works, 1829
　　,,　Sh— Works: Ext. 1841

Greece and Greek drama—
　See Chetwood　　　*See* Gould
　　,, Donaldson　　　　,, Lambros

Greek ' Hamlet ' [In ' Fraser's Magazine '].
　1880. 8° 　　　　　　　　　　　　　　BPL

Green (B. E.) Sh— and Goethe on Gresham's
　law and the single gold standard. Chat-
　tanooga [U.S.], 1901. Cr. 8° 　　　　BPL

Green (C.) *See* Birmingham Dramatic Club

Green (C. F.) *Artist*. *See* Wheler

Green (Charles Frederick) Legend of Sh—'s
　crab tree, with a descriptive account,
　showing its relation to the poet's tradi-
　tional history. Ln: Privately printed
　by Metchim & Burt, 1857. 4°, pp. 50.
　With Droeshout portrait, nine tinted
　plates and map
　　　　BPL | BUS | CPL | MPL | SML | W

Sh—'s crab tree. Ln: T. H. Lacy, 1862.
　4°, pp. 50. Portrait, 9 plates, and map
　The only change is in the title. 　BM | BPL | BUS

Green (Henry) Frontispiece, vignette, and
　photo-lithographic plates in ' Sh— and
　the emblem writers.' 1870. 8° 　　BM

Sh— and the emblem writers: An exposi-
　tion of their similarities of thought and
　expression. Preceded by a view of em-
　blem literature to A.D. 1616 . . . With
　numerous illustrative devices from the
　original authors. Portrait of Sh— from
　the oil painting in the possession of Dr.
　Clay, of Manchester. Ln: Trubner, 1870.
　Roy. 8°, pp. xvi.-572
　　　　BM | BPL | BUS | CPL | MPL | SML
　This portrait was here engraved for the first time, and
　is accompanied by portraits of Sebastian Brandt,
　Paolo Giovio or Jovius, Achilles Bocchius, and John
　Sambucus.

Green (J.)] Architecture of Sh— [In ' Building
　News,' Vol. 63, p. 314]. 1892. F° 　BPL

Odds and ends about Covent Garden.
　[1820 ?] 8° 　　　　　　　　　　　　　BPL

Green (J. L.) Dramatic criticism. Ln: Green-
　ing & E. Nash, 1900-03. 5 vols. 12° BPL

Green (John Richard) History of the English
　people. Ln: Macmillan, 1878-80. 4 vols.
　8° 　　　　　　　　　　　　　　　　　BM
　Sh— occupies pp. 454-500 in vol. ii. (1461-1603), while
　vol. iii. covers the period 1603-1688. Frequently
　reprinted.

Green (Kate Richmond) Interpretations of 'A
　winter's tale' and 'King Lear.' Chicago:
　Knight & Leonard, 1890. Cr. 8°
　　　　　　　　　　　　　　　　BPL | SML

Green (Valentine) Account of the discovery of
　the body of King John, in the Cathedral
　Church of Worcester, 1797. Worcester,
　1797. Roy. 4°. With plates 　　　　　W

Green room year book. Ln: 1906-10. 4
　vols. Cr. 8°. Illust. [In progress] BPL

Greene (Joseph) Lines . . . 1746: Commemora-
　tion at Stratford-on-Avon, April, 1880.
　F° broadside 　　　　　　　　　　　BPL

Greene (Robert) Arcadia. *See* Sh— Arraign-
　ment . . . (*heading*)

Dorastus and Fawnia. *See* Sh— Winter's
　tale (*heading*), 1859

Dramatic works. *See* Sh— George-a-
　Greene, 1831

Fair Em. *See* Sh— Faire Em

] Fortune's tennis ball. By S. S—— . . .
　an early English metrical version of the
　foundation story of Sh—'s ' Winter's
　tale.' Ed. by J. O. Halliwell. Ln: 1859.
　8°, pp. 26 　　　BPL | BUS | HCL | MPL
　Private impression : limited to twenty-six copies. Re-
　printed from the sole known copy of the original
　issue of 1672. It was entered at Stat. Hall in 1656.

Groats-worth of witte, bought with a million
　of repentance, describing the follie of
　youth, the falshood of make-shift flat-
　terers, the miserie of the negligent and
　mischiefes of deceiuing courtezans. Writ-
　ten before his death and published at his
　dyeing request. *Foelicem fuisse infaus-
　tum*. Ln: Imprinted for William Wright,
　1592. Fcp. 4°, 24 unpaged leaves ; sig.
　A¹ to F⁴ in fours (the first blank) 　BM
　Contains on p. 55 the first extrinsic personal notice of
　Sh— in print. Greene, who died 3 Sept., 1592, left
　behind him for publication the above deathbed repent-
　ance, in which he exhibits envy of the rising dramatist.
　Addressing his friends Marlowe, Nash, and others,
　he says :—' There is an upstart crow, beautified with
　our feathers, that, with his *tyger's heart wrapt in a
　player's hide*, supposes he is as well able to bumbaste
　out a blanke verse as the best of you ; and being an
　absolute Johannes Factotum is, in his owne conceit,
　the only Shake-scene in a countrie ' etc. The line is
　in italics is a true travesty of that in ' King Henry VI.' :
　　' Oh, tiger's heart wrapt in a woman's hide.'
　In Dec., 1592, Henry Chettle, Greene's publisher,
　apologised for this unmerited attack. *See* Chettle—
　' Kind harte's dreame.'
　It is noteworthy that Sh— uses ' bombast' in ' Love's
　labours lost,' Act v. 2 : ' As bombast and living to the
　time.' The word is found only three times in his
　writings.

Groatsworth of witte bought with a million
　of repentance. Ln: 1596. Fcp. 4°
　　　HUTH | PETERBOROUGH CATHEDRAL

Groatsworth of witte . . . Ln: B. Alsop
　for H. Bell, 1617. Fcp. 4°

Greene (Robert) Groatsworth of witte : bovght with a million of repentance : Describing the folly of youth, the falsehood of make-shift flatterers, the miserie of the negligent and mischiefes of deceyuing cvrtezans. Pvblished at his dying reqvest : and newly corrected and of many errors pvrged . . . Ln : Printed by N. O—— [Nicholas Okes] for Henry Bell, and are to be sold at his shop in Bethlem at the signe of the Sun, 1621. Fcp. 4°, black letter, sig. A1 to F4 unpaged. Sixth edition   CTC | W
With an address 'To wittie poets or poeticall wittes,' signed 'I. H.' [possibly Joseph Hall], here first appearing.

Groatsworth of wit. Ln : 1629. Fcp. 4° BUS

Groatsworth of wit . . . Eighth edition. Ln : Printed for Henry & Moses Bell, 1637. Fcp. 4°, black letter, sig. A-F4 unpaged   CTC

Groats-worth of wit. With a preface, critical and biographical, by Sir Egerton Brydges. Printed at the Private Press of Lee Priory, 1813. Roy. 4°   W

Groats-worth of wit . . . Reprinted from the . . . edition of 1596 in the library of Henry Huth. Edited by J. O. Halliwell. Ln : 1870. 8°. Issue limited to eleven copies   BPL | HCL

Maiden's dream. An unknown poetical tract. With introd. by J. P. Reardon. See Sh—] Sh— Soc.

Mirror of modesty, 1584. See Reprints

Notable discovery of coney-catcher's cozen-age, 1591. Edited by J. O. Halliwell. Ln : 1859. 8°. Twenty-six copies printed   BPL | BUS | HCL
A picture of low life in Sh -'s day.

[Pandosto] Pleasant historie of Dorastus and Fawnia. Wherein is discovered that although by the meanes of sinister for-tune, truth may be concealed ; yet by time, in spight of fortune, it is manifestly revealed, etc. Ln : Printed for F. Faulkner, 1636. Fcp. 4°, black letter CTC
The foundation of the 'Winter's tale.' Illustrates 'As you like it,' 'Much ado,' and 'Two gentlemen.' First appeared in 1588, and subsequently under the title of ' Pandosto,' the title being altered for the first time in this issue, which is probably the eleventh ed. For fuller account see Halliwell's 'Sh— reliques, 1852,' p. 119.

[Pandosto] Pleasant history of Dorastus and Fawnia. Peasant [sic] for age to avoid drowsy thoughts, profitable for youth to avoyd other wanton pastimes, and bring to both a desired content. Ln : Printed for Ed. Blackmore and are to be sold at his shop at the sign of the Angell in Paul's Churchyard, 1655. Fcp. 4°, black letter, sig. A-G4 unpaged
Probably the twelfth edition.

Greene (Robert) [Pandosto] Pleasant history of Dorastus . . . Ln : Printed by Robert Ibbitson for John Wright and are to be sold by W. Thackery at the Black-spread Eagle and Sun in the Old Bailey. 1664. Fcp. 4°, black letter, sig. A-G4 unpaged
Probably the thirteenth edition.   CTC

[Pandosto] Pleasant history of Dorastus and Fawnia. Ln : 1684. Fcp. 4°, black letter   W

[Pandosto] Pleasant and delightful history of Dorastus and Fawnia. Ln : 1703. Fcp. 4°   BUS

[Pandosto] Fortunate and unfortunate lovers, or the history of Dorastus and Fawnia, Hero and Leander. Made Eng-lish from the originals. By a gentleman [Hugh Stanhope]. Ln : 1735. 2 parts in 1 vol. 12°. With woodcuts   W

Pandosto, 1843.' See Sh—] Sh—'s library

Pandosto : The triumph of time. 1858. 8°   MPL

Pandosto. See Sh— Winter's tale (head-ing), also 1887 ed.

Pandosto. Ed. by P. G. Thomas. 'Sh— Classics.' Ln : Chatto, 1907. Fcp. 4° BPL

[Selimus] The first part of the tragicall raigne of Selimus, sometime Emperour of the Turkes and grandfather to him that now raigneth . . . As it was play'd by the Queenes Maiesties players. Ln : Printed by Thomas Creede in Thames Streete at the signe of the Kathren Wheele, neare the olde Swanne, 1594. Fcp. 4°
For its connection with ' Locrine ' see Daniel. A copy sold for £19 5s. 0d. in Feb., 1906.

[Selimus] The first part of the tragicall raigne of Selimus . . . Ln : 1594. Malone Society, 1909. Fcp. 4°

See Cartwright   See La Primaudaye
  „ Castle   „ Peele
  „ Chettle   „ R—— (S.)
  „ Cooper   „ Scott (T. J.)
  „ Cunny-catcher   „ Sh— Mucedorus,
  „ Daniel   1598
  „ Grosart   „ Sh— Taming ..
  „ Harvey   (heading)
  „ Herford   „ Simpson
  „ Heywood   „ Tinker
  „ Hosken

Greene (Robert) Editor. See Lodge

Greene (Robert) & Gale (D.) Historie of Arbasto . . . To which is added a lovely poem of ' Pyramus and Thisbe.' Ln : 1626. Fcp. 4°

Greene Actor (Thomas) A poet's vision and a prince's glorie. Ln : 1603. Fcp. 4°
A mediocre poem, dedicated to King James. Thomas Greene was both actor and author, and it is supposed that being a distant relative of William Sh— he introduced the latter to the stage.

Greene *Actor* (Thomas)] Mourneful dittie entituled Elizabeth's losse. Together with a Welcome to King James. Ln : [c. 1603-04].
Contains the line ' You poets all, brave Sh—, Johnson, Green . . .'
See Hawkins

Greene *Stratford Town Clerk* (Thomas) Sh— and the enclosure of common fields at Welcombe. Being a fragment of the private diary . . . 1614-17. Reproduced in autotype with letterpress transcript by C. M. Ingleby. Birmingham : R. Birbeck, 1885. 4°   BM | BPL | BUS | SML

Greenhill (J.) Harrison (W. A.) & Furnivall (F. J.) List of all the songs and passages in Sh— which have been set to music . . . Ed. by F. J. Furnivall and W. C. Stone. Ln : New Sh— Soc., 1884. 4°, pp. xxxvi.-114   MPL

Greening (L. Arthur) *Editor*. *See* Scott

Greenstreet (James) Blackfriars playhouse; its antecedents [In 'Athenæum,' July, 1886, p. 81 ; Jan., 1888, pp. 25-26 ; April, 1888, pp. 445-446 and 509 ; Aug., 1889, pp. 203-204]

Documents relating to the players at the Red Bull, Clerkenwell, and the Cockpit in Drury Lane, in the time of James I. Ln : New Sh— Soc., 1880-85.   8°

Drury Lane Theatre in the reign of James I. [In 'Athenæum,' No. 2991, p. 258]. 1885

Hitherto unknown writer of Elizabethan comedies : the Earl of Derby [In the 'Genealogist']. 1891. 8°   BPL

Red Bull playhouse in the reign of James I. [In 'Athenæum,' No. 3031, p. 709]. 1885

Whitefriars theatre in the time of Sh—. Ln : New Sh— Soc., 1887-92.   8°

Greenwood (George G.) In re Sh—, Beeching *v.* Greenwood : A rejoinder on behalf of the defendant. Ln : Lane, 1909. Cr. 8°, pp. 164   BPL
See also Beeching.

Sh— problem re-stated. Ln : Lane, 1908. 8°, pp. 590   BPL
Reviewed at some length in 'Athenæum,' 4 July, '08, pp. 7-8, to which the author responded 11 July, '08, p. 43. *See also* Clemens.

Vindicators of Sh— [In ' Nineteenth Century,' No. 388, pp. 1038-1055, June]. 1909. Roy. 8°
A reply to Sir Edward Sullivan (*q.v.*)

Greenwood (William) Description of the passion of love, demonstrating its original causes, effects, signs, and remedies. Ln : Printed for Wm. Place at Grayes Inn Gate in Holborn, 1657. 12°
Refers to ' Venus and Adonis,' p. 85.

Greg (Walter Wilson) Another Baconian cipher [In ' The Library,' Vol. 10, pp. 418-442, Oct.] Ln : 1909

Bacon's bi-literal cipher and its applications [In ' The Library,' Vol. 3, pp. 41-53]. Ln : 1902. Roy. 8°

Bibliographical history of the first folio [Sh— 1623], [In ' The Library,' Vol. 4, pp. 258-285]. Ln : 1903. Roy. 8°

Catalogue of the books presented by Edward Capell to the library of Trinity College in Cambridge. Camb. Univ. Press, 1903. 8°, pp. viii.-172   BPL | MPL

] Eton Shakespeareana : A descriptive catalogue of early editions of Sh— preserved in Eton College Library. Oxford : Univ. Press, 1909. Roy. 8°   BPL

Facsimiles of Sh—'s ' Poems ' and ' Pericles ' : Two reviews [In ' The Library,' Vol. 7, pp. 192-224]. Ln : 1906. Roy. 8°

Henslowe, Collier, and the latest German criticism [In ' The Library,' Vol. 5, pp. 293-304]. Ln : 1904. Roy. 8°

List of English plays written before 1643 and printed before 1700. Ln : Bibliographical Society, 1900. Fcp. 4°, pp. xii.-158   BPL

List of masques, pageants, etc. Ln : Bibliographical Society, 1902. Fcp. 4°, pp. xii.-38-cxxxii.

On certain false dates in Sh— quartos [In ' The Library,' April and Oct.] Ln : Moring, 1908. Roy. 8°, pp. 113-131 and 2 facsimiles, and pp. 381-409, with facsimiles of watermarks
See also Jaggard

Greg (W. W.) *Editor*—
See Henslowe
  ,, Lodge
  ,, Malone Society
  ,, Phillip
  ,, Sh— King Lear, 1907-08
  ,, Sh— Locrine, 1908
  ,, Sh— Sir John Oldcastle, 1908

Greg (W. W.) Levi (S.) Pollard (A. W.) & Huth (A. H.) Sh— quartos [In 'Athenæum,' No. 4201, p. 544 ; No. 4236, p. 14 ; No. 4237, p. 43 ; No. 4238, p. 73 ; No. 4239, p. 100 ; No. 4240, p. 132]. May, 1908-Jan., 1909

Gregg (*Dr.* Tresham Dames) Queen Elizabeth, or the origin of Sh—. A drama. Ln : W. Macintosh & Co., 1872. 8°, pp. viii.-128   BPL | BUS

Gregory *Warwick Castle butler*. *See* Jaggard

Gregory (J. H. S.) Desdemona : An essay written for the Edinburgh Sh— Soc., c. 1886. Manuscript. 8°   BPL

Grein (J. I.) Dramatic criticism. Ln : 1899. Cr. 8°

Dramatic criticism. 1902. Cr. 8°   BPL

Gresley (W.) Forest of Arden. A tale . . .
Ln: J. Burns, 1841. 12°, pp. x.-304.
With frontispiece

Grey (H.) Plots of old English plays, with
index of characters. 1888. 12°   BPL

Grey *of Wilton (Lord).* *See* Stopes

Grey (Zachary) Critical, historical, and explanatory notes on Sh—, with emendations of the text and metre. Ln: R.
Manby, 1754. 2 vols. 8°
    BM | BPL | BUS | CPL | MPL | SML | W

] Examination of a late edition [Warburton's]
of Sh—, wherein several plagiarisms are
taken notice of, and the late Sir Tho.
Hanmer vindicated. Addressed to Mr.
Warburton. By a country gentleman.
Ln: 1752. 8°   W

] Free and familiar letter to that great refiner of Pope and Sh—, William Warburton. With remarks upon the epistle of
friend A. E—— in which his unhandsome
treatment of this celebrated writer is
expos'd in the manner it deserves. By
a country curate. Ln: G. Jones, 1750.
8°, pp. 32   BPL | BUS | W

] Remarks upon a late edition [by Bp. War-
burton] of Sh—, with a long string of
emendations borrowed . . . without
acknowledgment from the Oxford edition.
To which is prefixed, A defence of the late
Sir Thomas Hanmer, Bart. Addressed
to the Rev. Mr. Warburton. Ln: C.
Norris, sen. [1751]. 8°, pp. 36
    BM | BPL | BUS | MPL
Reprinted in 1752 under the fresh title of 'Examination
of a late edition.'

] Word or two of advice to Wm. Warburton;
a dealer in many words. By a friend.
With appendix containing a taste of
William's spirit of railing. Ln: J. Fuller,
1746. 8°, pp. 28   BPL | BUS | W
Upon Warburton's 'Pope, Sh— and Hudibras.'

Grierson (George) *Dublin Printer & Publisher*
See Sh— Hamlet, 1721
 ,, Sh— Julius Cæsar, 1721
 ,, Sh— Othello, 1721
 ,, Sh— Works, 1725-26

Griffin (Bartholomew) Fidessa: A collection
of sonnets. Reprinted from the edition of
1596. Chiswick, 1815. 12°   BUS
The third sonnet in above is almost identical with the
fourth in 'Passionate pilgrim,' commencing—
'Fair Venus with Adonis sitting by her.'

See Sh— Passionate . . . *(heading)*

Griffin (G. W.) Studies in literature. Baltimore, 1870. 12°   BPL

Griffin (G. W. H.) Hamlet the dainty. *See*
Sh— Hamlet, 1849, 1877

Shylock: A burlesque. *See* Sh— Merchant
. . . 1860

Griffin (R.) *Glasgow Publisher.* *See* Sh— The
Tempest, 1864

Griffin & Co. (R.) *Glasgow Publishers.* *See*
Sh— Works, 1823, 1827, 1836, 1841, 1845,
1856, 1858, 1860, 1860-61, 1861, 1866,
1867, 1874

Griffin (W.) *Publisher—*
See Sh— Works, 1773
 ,, Vega Carpio

Griffin (W. H.) *Editor.* *See* Sh— Hamlet, 1896

Griffith *Publisher.* *See* Mason

Griffith (*Mrs.* Elizabeth) Morality of Sh—'s
drama illustrated. Ln: T. Cadell, 1775.
8°, pp. xvi.-528 and portrait
    BM | BPL | BUS | CPL | MPL | SML | W

Morality . . . Dublin: Beatty, 1777.   12°
    SML

Morality . . . Ln: 1777.   8°   BM

Griffiths (L. M.) Evenings with Sh—: A
handbook to . . . his works. Bristol,
1889. Fcp. 4°   BM | BPL | BUS | SML

Sh— and the medical sciences. *See* Sh—

Shakespearean qualities of 'A king and no
king' [by Beaumont & Fletcher]. Philadelphia, 1891. 8°   BPL

Griffiths (R.) *Publisher—*
See Cibber
 ,, Stevens
 ,, Victor

Griggs (Edward Howard) Syllabus of . . .
lectures on Sh—. *See* Sh—

Griggs (E. W. M.) *Editor.* *See* Sh— King
Richard III., 1902

Griggs (W.) Old London bridge as Sh— saw
it, about 1600: A chromo-lithograph.
Ln: New Sh— Soc., c. 1890.   4°

Sh—'s monument in Stratford Church: A
chromo-lithograph. Ln: New Sh— Soc.,
c. 1890.   4°

Grignion (C.) *Engraver.* *See* Sh— Works,
1771, 1773-74

Grimaldi *Editor.* *See* Sh— Hamlet, 1712

Grimaldi.] Dickens (Charles) Memoirs of
Joseph Grimaldi. With illustrations by
G. Cruikshank. Ln: Bentley, 1838. 2
vols. Cr. 8°   SML

] Dickens. Memoirs . . . Ln: Routledge [c.
1855]. Cr. 8°, pp. xvi.-256. With portrait and plates

] Dickens. Memoirs . . . Ln: Dicks, 1883.
8°   SML

Grimaldi Sh—. *See* Fairholt

Grimestone (Ed.) *Editor.* *See* Goulart

Grimm (H.) 'Hamlet' [an essay].   1875.
8°   BM

Grimston (Madge). *See* Kendal

Grindon (Leo H.) Life: its nature, varieties,
and phenomena.   1857.   8°
Refers to Sh— and his christianity.

Grindon (Leo H.) Sh— flora. A guide to all
the principal passages in which mention
is made of trees, plants, flowers, and vege-
table productions. With comments and
botanical particulars. Manchester : Palmer & Howe, 1883. Cr. 8°, pp. xii.-318.
With plates   BM | BPL | BUS | SML
Shakespeare garden. *See* Andrews
Grindon (*Mrs.* Leo) In praise of Sh—'s 'Merry
wives . . .' Manchester [c. 1902]. 12°
       BPL

Grinfield (Charles Vaughan) Century of
acrostics [Sh—, pp. 10-11]. 1855. 8° BPL
] Pilgrimage to Stratford-upon-Avon, the
birthplace of Sh—. Coventry : Merridew,
1850. 8°, pp. 52 and portrait
     BPL | BUS | CPL | MPL | SML | W
Grinfield (Thomas) Remarks on the moral
influence of Sh—'s plays ; with illustra-
tions from ' Hamlet.' Coventry : Merri-
dew, 1850. 8°, pp. 48 and plates
     BPL | BUS | CPL | SML | W
Groppe (E.) *Treves Publisher. See* Sh— King
Richard II., 1870
Grosart (*Dr.* A. B.) Was Robert Greene sub-
stantially the author of ' Titus Andro-
nicus'? [Repr. from 'Englische studien'].
Leipzig, 1896. 8°   BM | BPL
Grosart (*Dr.* A. B.) *Editor*—
See Chester
   ,,   Sh— The turtle
   ,,   Tofte
   ,,   Willobie
Groto (L.) Hadriana. *See* Walker
Grouillard (M.) *Editor. See* Sh— Julius
Cæsar, 1875
Groundworke of conny-catching. *See* Viles
& Furnivall
Grove (Francis) *Publisher. See* Kyd
Grove (John) *Publisher. See* Chettle
Grove (Joseph) Life of Henry VIII. *See* Sh—
King Henry VIII.
Grove (*Mrs.* L.) Dancing. Badminton Library.
Ln : Longmans, 1895. Cr. 8°
Some copies done on large paper.
Grutzner (Ed.) *Artist*—
See Sh— King Henry IV., i., 1887
   ,,   Sh— Works, 1884-92
Guazzo (Stephen) Civile conversation. Trans.
into French by George Pettie. Contain-
ing the general fruits that may be reaped
by conversation, and how to know good
companie from ill. Trans. into English
by Bartholomew Young. Ln : Imprinted
by T. East, 1586. Fcp. 4°   W
For Sh—'s use of Guazzo see Douce's Illustrations.
Gubbins (T.) *Publisher. See* Lodge
Guenther (M. F.) Defence of Sh—'s ' Romeo
and Juliet ' . . . [1876.] 8°   BM

Guernsey (R. S.) Ecclesiastical law in ' Ham
let ' : Burial of Ophelia. New York Sh—
Society, 1885. 8°   BM | BPL
Guernsey (Wellington) Sh— polka. Ln : L.
Lee & Coxhead [c. 1864]. F°, pp. 8 BUS
Guiana. *See* Ralegh
Guide to places of interest round Birmingham.
Birmingham [1880 ?] 12°   BPL
Stratford-on-Avon, pp. 26-29.
Guide to selecting plays, or manager's com-
panion, giving a description of fifteen
hundred pieces. [1882 ?] 12°   BPL
Guild—
See Gild   *See* Knowle
Guilmette (Gregory C.) A Sh— epic : ' King
Richard II.' 1886. 8°   *   BPL
Guilmette (G. C.) *Editor. See* Sh— King
Richard II., 1886
Guiraud (M. J.) *Editor. See* Sh— King
Richard III., 1888
Guizot (F. P. G.) On Corneille and Sh— [In
' North British Review,' Nov.] Edin.,
1852. 8°   BUS
Sh— and his times, with notices of his
principal dramas. *See* Sh—
Gullett (H.) Making of Sh—. *See* Sh—
Study of Sh—. *See* Sh—
Gummere (F. B.) *Editor. See* Sh— Merchant
. . . 1896
Gunn (C. H.) *Editor*—
See English . . .
   ,,   Sh—] Ingram
Günther (C. F.) Sh—'s autograph [In ' Book-
mart,' p. 172]. Pittsburgh [U.S.], 1885.
Roy. 8°
Gurney (R.) *Editor. See* Sh— Romeo . . 1812
Gutenberg *Printer. See* Jaggard
Guthrie (William) Essay upon English tragedy.
With remarks upon the Abbé le Blanc's
'Observations on the English stage.'
Ln : T. Waller [1747]. 8°, pp. 34
With several references to Sh—.   BPL | BUS | W
Essay . . . Ln : 1749. 8°
Guy *of Warwick* (*Sir*)—
See Dering   *See* Doran
Gwinne (Matthew) Vertumnus sive annus
recurrens Oxonii XXIX. Augusti 1605,
coram Jacobo rege, Henrico principe pro-
ceribus. 1607. Fcp. 4°
The above is the dramatic piece which effectually lulled
King James into slumber upon his visit to Oxford in
1605. It concerns Sh— indirectly. Upon the same
occasion a Latin interlude on ' Macbeth' was per-
formed, and although no text is known the short
epilogue at the end of ' Vertumnus' refers to it.
Gwinnett (S.) *See Stratford*] Second . . .
Gwyn (Nell). *See* Cunningham
Gybbys *of Exeter* (J.) Alchemical testament,
temp. Elizabeth. Edited by J. O.
Halliwell. 1854. Fcp. 4°   BPL
Gyldendalsk *Copenhagen Publisher. See* Sh—
Taming . . . 1886

—— Sh—'s ghost. *See* Sh— Works: Ext. 1803

H—— (A.) *See* Davies (John)

H—— (A.) Proposal for erecting a monument to Sh— . . . Cundall & Addey, 1851. 8°, pp. 16

H—— (C. T. J.) *See* Hiatt

H—— (E. B.) Study of 'Hamlet.' 1875. 8° BPL

H—— (E. B.) *Editor.* *See* Sh— Hamlet, 1875

H—— (E. K.) Sh— forget-me-nots. *See* Sh— Works: Ext. 1885

H—— (H.) *Publisher.* *See* Davies (John)

H—— (I.) Address. *See* Greene (R.)

H—— (I.) *Printer*— *See* Sh— Rape . . . 1600 „ Sh— Venus . . . 1600, 1630, 1636

H—— (J.) *Printer.* *See* Malvezzi

H—— (J.) Stanzas occasioned by a late visit to Poets' Corner in Westminster Abbey . . . Sh— [In 'Westminster Magazine']. Ln: 1770. 8° BUS

H—— (J. F.) David Garrick. *See* Garrick

H—— (L.) *See* Hutchings (L.)

H—— (M.) Sh—: his humour and pathos. *See* Sh—

H—— (M. B.) *Editor.* *See* Sh— Taming . . . 1881

H—— (R.) *Publisher.* *See* Heywood

H—— (R. E.) *See* Hunter

H—— (T.) *See* Hickock (Thomas)

H—— (T.) *Printer*— *See* Sh— Merry wives, 1630 „ Sh— Works: Ext. 1653

H—— (V.) *Editor.* *See* Sh— Julius Cæsar, 1872

H—— (*Mr.* W.)— *See* Nicholson „ Sh— Sonnets (*heading*) „ Stopes „ Wilde

Habington (William) Castara . . . Ln: B. A—— & T. F—— for Will. Cooke. 1635. 8°

Refers to Sh— at p. 22: 'Of this wine should Prynne drink but a plenteous glasse, he would beginne a health to Sh—'s ghost. . . .'

Hackett (James Henry) Bacon and Sh— [In 'New York Evening Post,' 26 Jan.]. 1867 BUS

Falstaff: A Sh— tract. Ln: Privately printed by T. C. Savill, 1840. 8°, pp. 12 BM | BPL | BUS

Hamlet's soliloquy [In 'Home Journal,' Nov.-Dec.] New York, 1860. 8° BUS

Hackett (James Henry) Harvey and Sh—: Had Sh— a knowledge of the circulation of the blood [In 'New York Evening Post,' Oct.-Dec.] 1861 BUS

Notes and comments upon certain plays and actors of Sh—. With criticisms and correspondence. New York: Carleton, 1863. 12°, pp. 354 and portrait BPL | BUS

Notes and comments . . . 3rd ed. New York: Carleton, 1863. 12°, pp. 354 BUS

Notes and comments . . . 1864. 12° BM

Notes, criticism, and correspondence upon Sh—'s plays and actors. New York, 1863. 12°

Contains at pp. 217-228 President J. Q. Adams' 'Misconceptions of Sh—.'

See Daly

Hackett (John) Select and remarkable epitaphs on illustrious and other persons in several parts of Europe. Ln: 1757. 2 vols. 8°. With copper frontispiece W

Sh— occupies pp. 79-81 in vol. i. and Bacon p. 90.

Hadow (G. E. & W. H.) Growth of the drama [In 'Oxford Treas. of Eng. Lit.,' Vol. 2]. 1907. 8° BPL

Hadow (W. H.) *Editor.* *See* Sh— Sonnets, 1908

Haeusser (F. E.) Sh—'s 'Julius Cæsar': Objective dramatic table. 1879. 8° BM

Hagena (*Prof.*) Introductory scene of the second part of 'King Henry IV.' Ln: New Sh— Soc., 1877-79. 8°

Haigh (A. E.) *Editor.* *See* Sh— Julius Cæsar, 1876

Hailes (N.) *Publisher.* *See* Sh— Works, 1823

Hale (E. E.) Both their houses: 'Romeo and Juliet' retold [In 'Harper's Monthly']. 1891. Roy. 8° BPL

Hales *of Eton* (John). *See Sh*—] Hales

Hales (John Wesley) At Stratford-upon-Avon: An historical association [In 'Fraser's Magazine,' April]. Ln: 1878. 8° BPL | BUS

Essays and Notes on Sh—. Ln: Bell, 1892. 8° BM

From Stratford to London [In 'Cornhill Mag.,' Jan.]. Ln: 1877. 8° BPL | BUS

'King Lear' [In 'Fortnightly Review,' Jan.] Ln: 1875. 8° BPL | BUS

'Macbeth' note [In 'Athenæum,' No. 3907, p. 359, Sept.] 1902 BM | BPL

Notes and Essays on Sh—. Ln: 1884. 8° BM | BPL | BUS

On the porter in 'Macbeth.' Ln: New Sh— Soc., 1874. 8° BUS

Runawayes eyes: 'Romeo and Juliet' [In 'Longman's Mag.']. 1892. 8° BPL

Sh— and Puritanism [In 'Contemporary Review']. 1895. 8° BPL

Hales (John Wesley) Sh— and the Jews [In
'English Historical Review,' Vol. 9, pp.
652-661]. 1894. 8°   BPL
Sh—'s language [In 'The Antiquary,' Vol.
9, p. 63]. 1884. 4°   BPL
The name Sh— [its history, &c.], [In
'Athenæum,' No. 3955, Aug., p. 230].
1903   BM | BPL
Hales family. *See* Bellew
Halévy (F.) *Composer. See* Sh— The tem-
pest, 1850
Half-pay officers—
See Sh— King Henry V., 1720
,, Sh— Twelfth night, 1720
Halford (*Sir* Henry) Essays and orations . . .
With account of the opening of the tomb
of King Charles I. Ln : J. Murray, 1831.
8°, pp. viii.-192. With portrait of Charles
I.
Contains Sh—'s test for madness, pp. 55-64.
Hall. Verses. *See* Vigo
Hall *Publisher. See* Sh— Much ado, 1740
Hall (A.) Sh—'s handwriting, 1899. *See* Sh—
autograph
Hall (E.) Coloured drawings of Ann Hatha-
way's cottage and New Place gardens,
Stratford-on-Avon. 1882. F°   BPL
Hall (Elizabeth) *Sh—'s grand-daughter—*
See Barnard (*Lady*)
,, Hall (John)
,, Scott (E. J. L.)
Hall (Henry Thomas) Memorial of the Sh—
tercentenary in Cambridge. Manuscript
on twenty-three sheets of vellum. 8°.
[Cambridge, c. 1864]   CPL
Contents: Introduction, list of names, copy of play
bill, address [text written in gold and colours].
WATER COLOURS: i., Portrait of Sh— by Warman;
ii., *Merchant of Venice*, by R. Farren; iii., *Mer-
chant of Venice*, by W. B. Redfarn; iv., *As you like
it*, Wounded stag, by W. B. Redfarn; v., *As you
like it*, Banished duke and foresters, by H. R.
Robertson.
Shakesperean fly-leaves. Cambridge : J.
Webb, 1864. 2 vols. 12°   BPL | BUS
Shakesperean fly-leaves. Cambridge, 1869.
12°   BPL | CPL
Shakesperean fly-leaves and jottings. En-
larged edition. Ln : J. R. Smith, 1871.
8°, pp. viii.-272 BM | BPL | BUS | CPL | SML
Shakesperean fly-leaves . . . New Series.
Cambridge, 1879. 12°   BPL
Shakesperean fly-leaves . . . Cambridge,
1881. 8°, pp. 272
Shakesperean statistics. Cambridge : H.
Wallis, 1865. 8°, pp. 38   BM | BPL | CPL
Shakesperean statistics. Cambridge : H.
Wallis, 1874. 8°, pp. 100   BPL | CPL
Sh—'s plays . . . The separate editions,
with the alterations done by various
hands [a bibliography]. Cambridge : H.
W. Wallis, 1873. 8°   BPL | CPL

Hall (Henry Thomas) Sh—'s plays . . .
Second edition. Cambridge : H. W.
Wallis, 1880. 8°, pp. 76   BM | BPL
See also Pink
Hall (Hubert) Society in the Elizabethan
age. Second edition. Ln : Sonnenschein,
1887. 8°   SML
Hall (J.) Illustrations of Sh—. 1773. 8°
Hall (John) *Engraver—*
See Gentleman
,, Sh— Works, 1773, 1773-74, 1778
Hall *of Durham* (John) Horæ vacivæ, or essays.
Some occasional considerations . . . Ln :
Printed by E. G—— for J. Rothwell at
the Sun and Fountaine in Paul's Church-
yard, 1646. 12°, pp. xxiv.-204, including
portrait of the author, aged 19, by W.
Marshall
Refers to 'Venus and Adonis' on p. 142.
Hall (*Dr.* John) Select observations on English
bodies : or, cures both empericall and
historicall, performed upon very eminent
persons in desperate diseases. First
written in Latine by Mr. John Hall,
physician, living at Stratford-upon-Avon.
Now put into English by James Cooke
[of Warwick]. Ln : John Sherley, at the
Golden Pelican in Little Britain, 1657.
8°   BPL | BUS | W
By Sh—'s son-in-law and executor. It includes the
case of Elizabeth Hall, Sh—'s granddaughter (who
married, firstly, Thomas Nash, and secondly, Sir
John Barnard), and other members of the poet's
family, also Michael Drayton the poet.
Select observations . . . Second edition.
Ln : 1679. 8°   W
Select observations . . . Third edition.
Ln : 1683. 8°. With portrait by White
Hall (*Dr.* John) *Executor. See* Sh— Will . . .
1616
Hall.] Epitaph on John Hall, inscribed on
his gravestone in Holy Trinity Church,
Stratford-on-Avon, 1635
'Heere lyeth ye body of Iohn Hall, gent. Hee
marr[ied] Svsanna ye davghter and co-heire[ss] of
Will. Sh—, gent. Hee deceased Nove[mbe]r. 25 A°
1635, aged 60.
'Hallius hic situs est medica celeberrimus arte
Expectans regni gaudia læta Dei
Dignus erat meretis, qui nestor.. vinceret annis
In terris omnes, sed rapit æqua dies
Ne tumulo, quid desit adest sidissima coniux,
Et vitæ comitem nunc quoq. mortis habit.'
Hall (John G.) Sh— *versus* Ingersoll. 1888.
8°   BM | BPL
Hall.] Lewis (George) Life of Joseph Hall,
DD., Bishop of Exeter and Norwich.
Ln : Hodder, 1886. 8°, pp. xii.-452
Several references to Sh— and his contemporaries.
At p. 70 is the history of a copy of the 'Passionate
pilgrim, 1612.'
Hall (Robert) Who wrote Sh— ? [1892.]
8°   BM

Hall (Spencer) Letter to John Murray, Esq. upon an æsthetic edition of the Works of Sh—. Ln: Chapman, 1841. Roy. 8°, pp. 38   BM | BPL | BUS | CPL

Hall *née* Sh— (Susanna) *Executor. See* Sh— Will . . . 1616

Hall.] Epitaph on Susanna Hall, *née* Sh—, inscribed on her gravestone in Holy Trinity Church, Stratford, 1649.
' Heere lyeth ye body of Svsanna, wife to Iohn Hall, gent : ye davghter of William Sh— gent. Shee deceased ye 11th of Ivly, A° 1649, aged 66.
  ' Witty above her sexe, but that's not all
  Wise to salvation was good Mistris Hall.
  Something of Sh— was in that, but this
  Wholy of him with whom she's now in blisse.
  Then, passenger, hast ne're a teare
  To weepe with her that wept with all
  That wept, yet set her selfe to chere
  Them up with comforts cordiall.
  Her love shall live, her mercy spread
  When thou hast ne're a teare to shed.'

Hall (Thomas)] Henry the fifth : Manuscript notes. [1779 ?] 8°   BPL
' These notes are, I believe, in the handwriting of Thomas Hall' [MS. note by J. O. Halliwell within the volume].

Hall (William) Sh—'s grave : Notes of traditions that were current at Stratford-on-Avon in the latter part of the seventeenth century. [Ed. by J. O. Halliwell.] Brighton : For private circulation, 1884. 8°, pp. 12   BM | BLO | SML
Issue limited to fifty copies.
The substance is a letter to Edward Thwaites, the original of which is at the Bodleian.

Hallam (Henry) Introduction to the literature of Europe in the fifteenth, sixteenth, and seventeenth centuries. Ln : 1839. 2 vols. 8°
In vol. ii., pp. 382-3, says : ' Of Wm. Sh— . . . it may be truly said that we scarcely know anything. . . . The two greatest names in poetry are to us little more than names. All that insatiable curiosity and unwearied diligence have hitherto detected about Sh— serves rather to disappoint and perplex us than to furnish the slightest illustration of his character.'

Literary essays and characters. *See* Sh—

Halle (Edward) Chronicle : The union of the two noble and illustrious families of Lancastre and Yorke . . . Ln : Grafton, 1548. F°. Black letter   w
Sh—'s indebtedness to this work is too well known to need recital.

Halleck (R. P.) Education of the central nervous system. *See* Sh—

Hallen (A. W. C.) Pedigree of the family of Sh—. *See* Sh—

Hallett (W. Hughes). *See* Benson

Hallewell (E. G.) Views of the Bermudas or Somer Islands. Ln : J. Hogarth, 1848. F°. 9 large coloured plates
The reputed locality of Sh—'s ' Tempest.'

Halliday (Andrew) Everyday papers. Ln : Tinsley, 1864. 2 vols. Cr. 8°   BPL
Contains ' Sh— not a man of parts,' pp. 93-98 ; ' Sh— mad,' pp. 99-115.

Halliday (A.) *Editor*—
See Sh— Antony . . . 1873
  ,, Sh— Romeo . . . 1855, 1859

Halliwell (James Orchard) Abstract of title to the house in Henley Street. *See* Stratford
Thirty years after his elopement and marriage with Henrietta, daughter of Sir Thomas Phillipps, Halliwell added that surname to his own, and thenceforward became known as Halliwell-Phillipps. At the time of this runaway match he was librarian to Sir Thomas Phillipps.

Abstracts and copies of indentures respecting estates in Henley Street, Stratford, 1866. *See* Stratford

Account of the 'Boar's Head' tavern. *See* Account . . .

Account of the only known manuscript of Sh—'s plays, comprising some important variations and corrections in the ' Merry wives ' obtained from a playhouse copy of that play recently discovered. Ln : J. R. Smith, 1843. 8°, pp. 24
     BM | BPL | BUS | CPL | SML
The manuscript itself was secured by the fourth Earl of Warwick [*see* Sh— ' Merry wives,' 1660]. In the following year a contemporary Sh— MS. was found [*see* Sh— ' King Henry IV.,' c. 1610]. At Boston is the only copy printed on vellum.

Accounts of . . . Stratford-on-Avon, 1590-1866. *See* Stratford

Acolastus, 1600-1866. *See* Nicholson

Adventure of the fool and the ice at Evesham . . . 1883. *See* Armin

Ancient ballad of the fair widow. *See* Fair widow

Ancient documents respecting the office of the Master of the Revels. *See* Collection

Ancient inventories of furniture, pictures, tapestry, plate, etc. illustrative of the domestic manners of the English in the sixteenth and seventeenth centuries, selected from inedited manuscripts. Ln : 1854. Fcp. 4°
Restricted to twenty-five copies.
Includes an inventory of the household property at Kenilworth Castle at the death of Robert Earl of Leycester, 1588.

Attempt to discover which version of the Bible was that ordinarily used by Sh—. Ln : 1867. 8°   BPL | HCL | MPL
Issue confined to ten copies.
Halliwell concluded it was the Genevan version.

Beeton's Sh— memorial. *See Sh*—] Gibbs

Beware the cat, 1570. *See* Baldwin (W.)

Bill of complaint . . . 1859. *See* Bill . . .

Booke of merrie riddles, 1660-1866. *See* Booke . . .

Books of characters, illustrating the habits and manners of Englishmen from the reign of James I. to the Restoration. Ln : 1857. Fcp. 4°
Issue limited to twenty-five copies on thick vellum paper.

Hollingbury Copse.
Brighton
1 Jany 1881

With Mr Halliwell-Phillipps's
Kind regards.

See p. 128

Halliwell (James Orchard)] Brief guide for strangers who are visiting Stratford-on-Avon. Ln: J. E. Adlard [c. 1864]. 8°
BPL | CPL
Brief guide to the gardens of Sh— and prospectus of the Sh— fund. Chiswick: Whittingham, 1863. 8°, pp. 16
BM | BPL | BUS
Brief guide to the Sh— library and museum at Stratford. [1865.] 8° BM
Brief hand-list of books, manuscripts, etc. illustrative of the life and writings of Sh—, collected between 1842 and 1859. Ln: Printed for private circulation by J. E. Adlard, 1859. 8°, pp. viii.-112
BM | BPL | BUS | W
Impression restricted to thirty copies.
Contains 355 titles.
Brief hand-list of the collections respecting the life and works of Sh— and the history and antiquities of Stratford-upon-Avon formed by the late R. B. Wheler . . . and presented by his sister, Miss Wheler, to be preserved forever in the Sh— . . . Museum. Ln: Privately printed at the Chiswick Press, 1863. Fcp. 4°, pp. viii.-64 BM | BUS | MPL | SML
Issue confined to one hundred copies.
Brief hand list of the early quarto editions of . . . Sh—, with notices of the old impressions of the poems. [First issue.] Ln: [Privately printed] 1860. 8°, pp. vi.-24 BM | BPL | BUS | CPL | W
Impression limited to twenty-five copies.
For second edition see Halliwell, Skeleton Hand List, 1860.
Brief hand list of the records belonging to the borough of Stratford - on - Avon. Showing their general character; with notes of a few of the documents in the same collection. Ln: Privately printed by Whittingham, 1862. 8°, pp. 32
BM | BPL | BUS | HCL | MPL | W
Impression restricted to fifty copies.
Brief hand list of the selected parcels in the Sh— and dramatic collections of J. O. H. Ln: Privately printed by J. E. Adlard, 1876. 8°, pp. 32 BM | BUS | HCL | MPL
Brief history of the ancient records of Stratford-on-Avon. Brighton, 1884. 8°
BPL
Brief list of a portion of the Sh— rarities at Hollingbury Copse. Brighton, 1886. 8°
BPL
Brief list of some of the rarer and most curious old-book rarities in the library of J. O. H. . . . illustrative chiefly of early English popular literature. West Brompton, 1862. Fcp. 4°. For private circulation only HCL

Halliwell (James Orchard) Brief notices of a small number of the Sh— rarities that are preserved in the rustic wigwam at Hollingbury Copse. 1885. 12° BM | BPL
Brief notices of bibliographical rarities in . . . [his] library. Ln: Priv. printed, 1855. Fcp. 4° BPL | HCL
Issue confined to twenty-five copies.
Brief report on the interchange of books, relics, etc. between the New Place and the Birthplace Museum, and on the re-arrangement of the library . . . Stratford-on-Avon: Private and confidential, 1881. 8° BPL
Budget of notes and memoranda on the life and works of Sh—. See Sh—
Calendar of the Sh— rarities, drawings, and engravings preserved at Hollingbury Copse. Brighton: For special circulation and presents only, 1887. 8°
BM | BPL | BUS
Calendar of the Sh— rarities . . . 2nd ed. Enlarged by E. E. Baker. Ln: Longman, 1891. 8° BM | BPL | BUS | MPL
Catalogue of books . . . preserved in Henley Street . . . See Hopper (C.)
Catalogue of . . . engravings and drawings illustrative of . . . Sh—. See Sh—
] Catalogue of reprints and facsimiles illustrative of early English and Sh— literature, the impressions of which are mostly limited to twenty-six or thirty copies. Sold by auction . . . 2nd Feb., 1861. 8°
BUS (priced)
The reprints were issued in 1859-60. The notice says the entire impression will be sold, with the exception of one copy supplied to the British Museum, or reserved by the editor. It was an experiment to see if such bibliographical curiosities can thus be made to meet their expenses without the trouble attendant on subscription lists. The seven hundred lots realised £415 6s. 6d.
Catalogue of Sh— reliques: Some account of the antiquities, coins, manuscripts, rare books, ancient documents and other reliques, illustrative of the life and works of Sh— in . . . [his] possession. Brixton Hill: Printed for private circulation only, 1852. 4° BM | BPL | BUS | MPL | W
Impression restricted to eighty copies.
Catalogue of Sh— study books in . . . [his] immediate library. Ln: Privately printed by J. E. Adlard, 1876. 8°, pp. 72
BM | BPL | BUS | HCL | MPL
Catalogue of Shakespearian literature. See Catalogue, 1856, 1857, 1858, 1859, 1861, 1881, 1889, 1891, 1895
Catalogue of the Warehouse library of No. 11, Tregunter Road, West Brompton. Ln: [Privately printed by J. E. Adlard] 1876. 8°, pp. viii.-108
BPL | BUS | HCL | MPL | SML

9

Halliwell (James Orchard) Collectanea respecting the birthplace . . . *See* Wheler

Collection of ancient documents respecting the . . . Revels, 1870. *See* Collection . . .

Collection of letters illustrative of the progress of science in England from the reign of Queen Elizabeth to that of Charles the Second. Ln: 'Historical Soc. of Science,' 1841. 8°, pp. xxx.-124

Conceits, clinches, . . . 1860. *See* Conceits . . . 1860

Concordance to the 'Poems.' *See* Sh—Poems, 1867

Contemporary depositions . . . 1583-1864. *See* Contemporary . . .

Copy of a letter . . . to Sir D. Carleton. *See* Herbert

Correspondence of Malone with Davenport. *See* Malone

[Correspondence with Robert Browning, president of the New Sh— Society, relative to language used by Mr. Furnivall in speaking of Mr. Halliwell - Phillipps.] Jan.-Feb., 1881. F°, pp. 8, with no title
BPL | BUS | HCL

Curiosities of modern Sh— criticism [In reply to the 'Athenæum' review of his folio Sh—]. Ln: J. R. Smith, 1853. 8°, pp. 32, with facsimile of the Dulwich letter
BM | BPL | BUS | CPL | HCL | MPL | SML | W

Cursory memoranda on . . . 'Macbeth.' 1880. 8°
BM | BPL

Decker's dream, 1620-1860. *See* Decker

Defence of coney-catching, 1592-1859. *See* Cunny-catcher

Descriptive account of a series of churchwardens' presentments appertaining to the parish of Stratford-on-Avon. 1867. Fcp. 4°
MPL
Issue restricted to ten copies.

Descriptive calendar of the ancient manuscripts and records in the possession of the Corporation of Stratford-upon-Avon : including notices of Sh— and his family and of several persons connected with the poet. Ln: Printed for private circulation by J. E. Adlard, 1863. Roy. f°, pp. viii.-468
BM | BPL | BUS | MPL | W
Impression limited to seventy-five copies.
Includes records from the thirteenth century to 1750, now preserved at the Birthhouse library. A supplement to his folio edition of Sh—.

Descriptive notices of popular English histories. Ln: Percy Society, 1848. 8° SML

Dictionary of archaic and provincial words, obsolete phrases, proverbs and ancient customs from the fourteenth century. Ln: 1846. 2 vols. 8°
BUS | HCL
About fifty thousand words are noted, with examples from inedited manuscripts and rare books. Full of Sh— philological illustrations.

Halliwell (James Orchard) Dictionary of archaic and provincial words . . . Ln: 1847. 8°
BUS | HCL

Dictionary of archaic and provincial words . . . Ln: 1850. 8°
BUS

Dictionary of archaic and provincial words . . . Brixton Hill: Printed for private circulation only, 1852. 2 vols. 4°
W
One of the few copies done on large paper.

Dictionary of archaic and provincial words . . . Fourth edition. Ln: J. R. Smith, 1860. 2 vols. 8°
BPL | SML

Dictionary of archaic and provincial words . . . Ninth edition. Ln: 1878. 2 vols. 8°
BPL

Dictionary of misprints in printed books of the sixteenth and seventeenth centuries. Compiled . . . for those who are editing the works of Sh—, etc. Brighton, 1887. Fcp. 4°
BPL

Dictionary of old English plays existing either in print or in manuscript . . . to the close of the seventeenth century ; including also notices of Latin plays by English authors during the same period. Ln: J. R. Smith, 1860. 8°, pp. viii.-296
BPL | BUS | HCL | MPL | SML | W

Dictionary of old English plays. 1862. 8° BPL

Discovery that Sh— wrote one or more ballads or poems on the Spanish armada. Ln: 1866. Fcp. 4°
BM | BPL | HCL | MPL
Issue confined to twenty-five copies, of which fifteen were destroyed.
The evidence is drawn from Chettle's 'Englande's mourning garment.'

Discursive notes on . . . 'Romeo and Juliet.' 1880. 8°
BM | BPL

Dispute between the Earl of Worcester's players and the Corporation of Leicester in 1586, from the records of that city. *See Sh—*] Sh— Soc.

'Dorastus and Fawnia.' *See* Sh— Winter's tale, 1859

Droll of the bouncing knight . . . *See* Sh—King Henry IV., Part i., 1860

Droll of the gravemakers. *See* Sh— Hamlet, 1860

Early editions of Sh— [a bibliographical account of fourteen early quartos]. Printed for private circulation, 1857. 8°, pp. 16
BM | BPL | BUS | MPL | W
Impression limited to twenty-five copies.

Early history of freemasonry in England . . . Ln: T. Rodd, 1840. 12°, pp. 46. With facsimile
BUS | HCL
'The singing masons, building roofs of gold.'
—*King Henry V.*
'He is not his craft's master.'—*King Henry IV.*
'You and your crafts, you have crafted fair.'
Coriolanus.

Early notice of 'King Henry VIII.' *See Sh—*] Sh— Soc.

Halliwell (James Orchard) England's helicon,
1865. *See* Bodenham

Executive committee of Sh—'s birthplaec
and Mr. Halliwell-Phillipps ; Correspondence. Brighton, 1887. 8° BPL

Executive committee of Sh—'s birthplace
... Second edition. 1887. 8° BPL

Extract from a manuscript at Oxford, containing a memorandum of complaints
against Dethick the herald, who made
the grant of arms to John Sh—. *See
Sh*—] Sh— Soc.

Extract from the diary of Joseph Hunter,
1867. *See* Hunter

Extracts from ancient Subsidy Rolls,
showing the values of goods and lands
upon which assessments were made in
respect to the inhabitants of Stratford-
upon-Avon. Ln : 1864. Fcp. 4°
Limited to ten copies.

Extracts from the accounts of ... Stratford-
on-Avon, 1585 to 1608, 1866. *See* Stratford

Extracts from the accounts of ... Stratford-
on-Avon ... 1609 to 1616, 1867. *See*
Stratford

Extracts ... from the parish registers ...
of Holy Trinity, 1864. *See* Stratford

Extracts taken from the vestry book of
... Holy Trinity, 1865. *See* Stratford

Facsimile of the deed ... of Sh—'s Blackfriars estate, 1884. *See* Sh— Autograph

Facsimile of the original indenture ... *See*
Combe

Facsimiles of the plats of three old English
plays, viz. : the ' Battle of Alcazar,'
'Frederic and Basilia,' and the 'Dead
man's fortune.' Being the original directions for the actors suspended near the
prompter's station on the walls of the
Fortune playhouse, temp. Elizabeth. Ln :
1860. F° BUS
Restricted to twenty-six copies.

Fair widow of Watling Street, 1600-1860.
See Fair widow

Fairy mythology of Sh—. *See Sh*—] Sh—
Soc.

Few observations on the composition of the
' Midsummer night's dream.' *See Sh*—]
Sh— Soc.

Few remarks on the emendation ' Who
smothers her with painting ' in 'Cym-
beline' discovered by Mr. Collier in a
corrected copy of the second edition ...
Ln : J. R. Smith, 1852. 8°, pp. 16
BPL | BUS | CPL | MPL | SML
' Whose mother was her painting.'—*Cymbeline*, iii., 4.
Replied to by Collier in the ' Appendix to Notes and
Emendations.'

Halliwell (James Orchard) Few words in
defence of the memory of Edward
Capell, occasioned by a criticism in 'The
Times' newspaper, Dec. 26th, 1860.
[Ln :] Printed only for presentation, 1861.
Fcp. 4° BPL | HCL | W
Halliwell thought Charles Knight the only critic who
spoke of Capell with due respect.

First appeal to the public for the preservation of the gardens of Sh—. Ln : Oct.
15th, 1861. 8°, pp. 4 BPL | BUS
Reprinted from *The Times*.

First Sh— Society. New York Sh— Soc.,
c. 1885. 8° BPL

First sketch of the ' Merry wives,' 1842.
See Sh— Merry wives, 1842

First sketches of . . . ' King Henry the
sixth.' *See* Sh— King Henry VI., Parts
ii.-iii., 1843

Fisherman's tale, 1595-1867. *See* Sabie (F.)

Fortune's tennis ball, 1859. *See* Greene

Fragment of ' Illustrations of the life of
Sh—.' *See* Sh—

Garland of Sh—, recently added to [his]
library and museum at Avenue Lodge,
Brixton Hill : Printed by J. E. Adlard,
for private circulation, 1854. Fcp. 4°
BM | BPL | BUS | MPL
Impression confined to twenty-five copies.

General introduction to the historical plays
of Sh—. [1850.] F° W
Originally intended by Halliwell to accompany his
edition of Sh—, but eventually he issued it as a
separate publication.

Greene's ghost - haunting cony-catchers,
1626-1860. *See* R—— (S.)

' Groats-worth of wit, 1596-1870.' *See*
Greene (R.)

'Hamlet, 1603-1866.' *See* Sh— Hamlet, 1866

'Hamlet, 1604-1867.' *See* Sh— Hamlet, 1867

'Hamlet, 1605-1860.' *See* Sh— Hamlet, 1860

'Hamlet, 1605-1867.' *See* Sh— Hamlet, 1867

'Hamlet, 1611-1870.' *See* Sh— Hamlet, 1870

Hand-book index to the works of Sh—, including references to the phrases, manners, customs, proverbs, songs, and
particles which are used or alluded to by
the great dramatist. 1866. 8°
BM | BPL | HCL | MPL
Issue limited to fifty copies.

Hand-list of a curious and interesting collection of early editions of . . . Sh—,
mostly printed before the appearance of
the folio ... 1623. West Brompton, 1867.
For private circulation only. 8°

Hand-list of drawings and engravings illustrative of the life of Sh—. *See* Sh—

Halliwell (James Orchard) Hand-list of the early English literature preserved in the Douce collection in the Bodleian Library. [Ln:] Printed for private circulation only, 1860. 8° BPL | BUS | W
A list of the books collected by Douce, the Sh— critic. Impression confined to fifty-one copies.

Hand-list of the early English literature preserved in the Malone collection in the Bodleian Library, selected from the printed catalogue . . . Ln: 1860. 8° BPL | BUS | MPL | W
Issue limited to fifty-one copies for private circulation. Contains many Sh— items.

Hand-list of upwards of a thousand volumes of Sh— added to the three previous collections of a similar kind formed by J. O. H . . . and of which lists have been previously printed. Ln: Privately printed by Whittingham & Wilkins, 1862. Fcp. 4°, pp. viii.-264 BM | BPL | BUS | W
Impression restricted to twenty-five copies.

Hand-table of regnal years for the use of enquirers into the history of the Shakespeares. Privately printed, 1864. 8° MPL
Issue confined to fifteen copies, of which Halliwell destroyed five. *See also* Halliwell, 'Regnal Years,' *post.*

Harrowing of hell, 1840. *See* Harrowing . . .

Hint on the date of 'Coriolanus.' *See* New Sh— Soc.

Historical account of the birthplace . . . 1863. *See* Wheler (R. B.)

Historical account of the New Place, Stratford-upon-Avon, the last residence of Sh—. Ln: Printed by J. E. Adlard, Bartholomew Close, 1864. F°, pp. viii.-246
BM | BPL | BUS | CPL | HCL | MPL | SML | W
With plan, autograph facsimiles, woodcut illustrations, and a brief list of Halliwell's writings. Printed throughout on thick plate paper.
The only work giving an account of Gastrell the iconoclast.
'Printed at the author's expense, and presented to all who subscribed £5 and upwards to the Sh— fund, in the hope that it will prove decisively the authenticity of the estates purchased by their subscriptions.'

Historical sketch of the provincial dialects of England, illustrated by numerous examples. Ln: 1847. 8° BUS
Extracted from his 'Dictionary of archaic words.'

Historical sketch of the provincial dialects . . . Albany [U.S.] 1863. 8° BUS

History of John Winchcomb, 1597-1859. *See* Deloney (T.)

'Hystorie of Henry the fourth.' *See* Sh— King Henry IV., i., 1598

Illustrations of the fairy mythology of a 'Midsummer night's dream' [with notes]. Ln: Sh— Soc., 1845. 8°, pp. xxii.-320
BM | BPL | BUS | HCL | MPL | SML
Afterwards incorporated with Ritson's work. *See* Halliwell and Ritson.

Halliwell (James Orchard) Illustrations of the life of Sh—. *See Sh*—] Halliwell

Introduction to . . . 'Midsummer night's dream.' Ln: Wm. Pickering, 1841. 8°, pp. iv.-104
BM | BPL | BUS | CPL | HCL | MPL | W

] Inventory of certain books and manuscripts, including notes for Sh— researches, preserved at Hollingbury Copse . . . Brighton: J. G. Bishop, 1887. Fcp. 4°, pp. 8 BM

Inventory of . . . manuscripts and printed books, chiefly relating to Sh— . . . in the library of J. O. H. 1883. Fcp. 4° BM | BPL

'King Henry IV., 1598-1866.' *See* Sh— King Henry IV., 1866

'King Henry IV., 1599-1861.' *See* Sh— King Henry IV., 1861

'King Henry IV., 1600-1866,' 1st and 2nd issues. *See* Sh— King Henry IV., 1866

'King Henry IV., 1604-1871.' *See* Sh— King Henry IV., Part i., 1871

'King Henry IV., 1608-1867.' *See* Sh— King Henry IV., Part i., 1867

'King Henry IV.,' MS. c. 1610. *See* Sh— King Henry IV., Part i., 1845

'King Henry IV., 1613-1867.' *See* Sh— King Henry IV., 1867

'King Henry V., 1600-1867.' *See* Sh— King Henry V., 1867

'King Henry V., 1602-1867.' *See* Sh— King Henry V., 1867

'King Henry V., 1608-1870.' *See* Sh— King Henry V., 1870

'King Henry V., 1617-1857.' *See* Sh— King Henry V., 1857

'King Henry VI.': First sketches. *See* Sh— King Henry VI., Parts ii.-iii.

'King Lear, 1608-1868,' 1st and 2nd issues. *See* Sh— King Lear, 1868

'King Richard II.': Anterior to Sh—'s tragedy, 1870. *See* Sh— King Richard II., 1870

'King Richard II., 1597-1862.' *See* Sh— King Richard II., 1862

'King Richard II., 1598-1869.' *See* Sh— King Richard II., 1869

'King Richard II. . . . 1608-1858.' *See* Sh— King Richard II., 1858

'King Richard II., 1608-1870.' *See* Sh— King Richard II., 1870

'King Richard II., 1615-1870.' *See* Sh— King Richard II., 1870

'King Richard III., 1597-1863.' *See* Sh— King Richard III., 1863

'King Richard III., 1598-1867.' *See* Sh— King Richard III., 1867

'King Richard III., 1602-1865.' *See* Sh— King Richard III., 1865

'King Richard III., 1605-1863.' *See* Sh— King Richard III., 1863

Halliwell (James Orchard) 'King Richard III., 1612-1871.' *See* Sh— King Richard III., 1871

Last days of Sh—, 1861, and 1863. *See* Sh—] Halliwell

Last will of John Davenant, 1866. *See* Davenant

Letter to Prof. K. Elze respecting . . . his literary biography of Sh—. 1888. 16° BM

Letter to the executive committee of the birthplace of Sh—, Stratford-on-Avon. Brighton, 1880. 8° BPL

Letters of the Kings of England. Ed. with historical introd. Ln: H. Colburn, 1848. 2 vols. 8° SML
Refers to Sh—'s historical characters.

Levy made for relief of poor, 1697-1865. *See* Levy

Library. *See* Catalogue, 1856, 1857, 1858, 1859, 1861, 1889, 1891, 1895

Life of Saint Katharine . . . and an account of the magical manuscript of Dr. Caius [founder of Caius College, Cambridge: together with some observations on the character of that name in the 'Merry wives']. 1848. Fcp. 4° BM | BPL

Life of Wm. Sh—. *See Sh*—] Halliwell

Lineal concordance to the 'Poems of Sh—.' *See* Sh— Works: Ext. 1867

List of the contents of the drawers in my study . . . : Index to objects of research: List of regnal years, 1558-1649. Brighton, 1870. 3 works in 1 vol. 8° BPL | HCL
Speaks of his 'having abandoned the critical study of the text of Sh—.'

List of Sh— rarities. Ln: Privately printed, 1885. 8°. With plate BUS
Reprinted from 'Book Lore' [*see* Halliwell, 'Sh— Rarities'].

List of works illustrative of the life and writings of Sh—, History of Stratford-upon-Avon, and . . . early English drama. Printed for very limited and private circulation at the expense of J. O. H., 1850-1866. Ln: Whittingham & Wilkins, 1867. 8°, pp. 70
BM | BPL | BUS | HCL | MPL | SML
The preface explains why Halliwell issued such very limited editions of his writings, and says, 'It is the only practical plan, in the hands of one who is not a millionaire, to preserve a vast quantity of material, too diffuse or too technical for the general public.'

Literature of the sixteenth and seventeenth centuries, 1851. *See* Literature . . . 1851

'Love's labours lost, 1598-1869.' *See* Sh— Love's labours lost, 1869

'Lucrece, 1594-1866.' *See* Sh— Rape . . . 1866

Ludus Coventriæ, 1841. *See* Ludus

Halliwell (James Orchard) Lyttle boke gevinge a true and brief accounte of some reliques and curiosities added of late to Mr. Halliwell's Sh— collection. Ln: Printed for private circulation by J. E. Adlard, 1856. Fcp. 4°, pp. vi.-18 and facsimile
BM | BPL | BUS | W
Impression restricted to twenty-five copies.

Mad wooing, 1859. *See* Sh— Taming . . . 1859

Management of Covent Garden theatre vindicated from the attack of an anonymous critic in a letter to the . . . 'Cambridge Advertiser.' Ln: 1841. 8°
BPL | BUS
The 'attack' was occasioned by Halliwell's criticisms of dramatic matters.

Manifest detection of . . . dice play, 1850. *See* Walker (G.)

Manuscript rarities of the University of Cambridge. Ln: 1841. 8° BUS | HCL

Margarite of America, 1596-1850. *See* Lodge (T.)

Marriage of wit and wisdom, 1846. *See* Marriage

Memoranda intended for the use of amateurs . . . sufficiently interested . . . to make searches in the Public Record Office on the chance of discovering new facts respecting Sh—. 1884. 8° BM | BPL

Memoranda on Sh—'s 'All's well,' 'Two gentlemen,' 'Much ado,' and 'Titus Andronicus.' Brighton: Fleet & Bishop, 1879. 8°, pp. 80, with facsimile
BM | BPL | BUS | SML

Memoranda on Sh—'s 'Hamlet.' Ln: 1879. 8°, pp. 80 BM | BPL | BUS | SML | W

Memoranda on Sh—'s 'Love's labours lost,' 'King John,' 'Othello,' 'Romeo and Juliet.' Ln: Adlard, 1879. 8°, pp. 96 BM | BPL | BUS | MPL | SML

Memoranda on . . . Sh—'s . . . 'Measure for measure.' 1880. 12° BM | BPL

Memoranda on Sh—'s 'Midsummer night's dream,' 1879 and 1855. Brighton: Fleet & Bishop, 1879. 8°, pp. 48
BM | BPL | BUS | MPL | SML

Memoranda on Sh—'s 'The Tempest,' chiefly the . . . probable date of composition. Brighton, 1880. Fcp. 4°
BM | BPL

Memoranda on Sh—'s . . . 'Troilus and Cressida.' 1880. 12° BM | BPL

Memoranda on the present state of the birth-place trust [of Stratford-on-Avon]. Brighton, 1883. 8° BM | BPL | SML

'Merchant of Venice, 1600-1865.' *See* Sh— Merchant of Venice, 1865

'Merchant of Venice, 1600-1870.' *See* Sh— Merchant . . . 1870

Halliwell (James Orchard) Merry conceited humours of Bottom the weaver. *See* Sh— Midsummer . . . 1860

'Merry tales of the wise men of Gotham, 1840.' *See* Merry tales

'Merry wives': First sketch. *See* Sh— Merry wives, 1842

'Merry wives . . . 1602-1866.' *See* Sh— Merry wives, 1866

'Merry wives . . . 1619-1866.' *See* Sh— Merry wives, 1866

'Midsummer night's dream, 1600-1864.' *See* Sh— Midsummer . . . 1864

'Midsummer night's dream, 1600-1865.' *See* Sh— Midsummer . . . 1865

Moorish marriage, 1332-1867. *See* Manuel of Castile

'Much ado . . . 1600-1865.' *See* Sh— Much ado . . . 1865

Muster roll of able men, 1867. *See* Stratford-upon-Avon

Narrative of the bloudy murders . . . 1860. *See* Fites

National Shakesperian fund, 4 Nov., 1861. Fcp. 4°, pp. 4   BUS

National Shakesperian fund [With the laws of the fund and list of the subscriptions . . . promised. West Brompton, 20 Nov., 1861]. 4°   BUS | HCL

New and merry prognostication, 1623-1860. *See* New . . .

New boke about Sh— and Stratford-on-Avon. Ln: Printed for private circulation, 1850. Fcp. 4°, pp. 96-iv. With facsimile of Sh—'s marriage bond and engravings BM | BPL | BUS | HCL | MPL | W
Impression restricted to seventy-five copies; fifty on ordinary and twenty-five on very thick paper.

New evidences in confirmation of the traditional recognition of Sh—'s birth-room, A.D. 1769-1777. Brighton, 1888. 16°   BM | BPL

New lamps or old ? A few additional words on the momentous question respecting the E and A in the name of our national dramatist . . . Brighton : Fleet & Bishop, 1880. 8°, pp. 28, grey wrappers. For private circulation
    BM | BPL | BUS | HCL | MPL | W
Contains a facsimile signed page from the 'Passionate Pilgrim,' 1599. The title, 'Old Lamps or New,' was copyrighted by Charles Knight in 1853.

New lamps or old ? . . . Second edition. Brighton : Fleet & Bishop [privately printed] 1880. 8°, pp. 40 BPL | BUS | SML
See also Halliwell, Which shall it be ?

Newes from Virginia, 1610-1865. *See* Rich (R.)

Halliwell (James Orchard) Nominal index to 'Descriptive calendar of ancient manuscripts and records in the possession of the Corporation of Stratford-upon-Avon . . .' [folio 1863]. Ln : [Privately printed] 1865. 8°, pp. 72
    BPL | BUS | MPL | SML
Impression limited to twenty-five copies, of which fifteen were destroyed.

Notable discovery . . . 1591-1859. *See* Greene (R.)

Note on the recently-discovered manuscript of 'King Henry the Sixth.' *See Sh—*] Sh— Soc.

Notes from the Record Office. *See* Sh—] Halliwell

Notices of players acting at Ludlow [1554-1627] selected from the original manuscripts belonging to the Corporation of that town. Ln: 1867. 12°   HCL
Issue confined to ten copies.

Notices of the Sh— rarities preserved at Hollingbury Copse. British Archæological Association [1886]. 8°   BM | BPL

Observations on some of the manuscript emendations of the text of Sh—, and are they copyright ? Ln : Privately printed, by J. R. Smith, 1853. Fcp. 4°, pp. 16. With facsimile
    BM | BPL | BUS | CPL | HCL | SML | W
Impression restricted to twenty-five copies.
This also refers to manuscript notes and corrections in a copy of the Jaggard folio and to six original documents in the Bridgewater collection.

Observations on some of the manuscript emendations . . . [Second edition]. Ln : Privately printed by J. R. Smith, 1853. 8°, pp. 16   BPL | MPL | SML

Observations on the Charlecote traditions and on the personation of Sir T. Lucy in the character of Justice Shallow [in the 'Merry wives' and King Henry IV., Part ii.] Brighton : Bishop, 1887. 8°
    BM | BPL | SML

Observations on the Sh— forgeries at Bridgewater House. Illustrative of a facsimile of the spurious letter of H. S——. Ln : For private circulation, 1853. Fcp. 4°, pp. 8 and facsimile   BM | BPL | BUS
Issue limited to twenty-five copies.
Halliwell expresses his 'firm conviction that all the Sh— manuscripts at Bridgewater House are modern forgeries.'

Observations on 'too too' in 'Hamlet.' *See Sh—*] Sh— Soc.

On the character of Sir John Falstaff, as originally exhibited by Sh— in the two parts of 'King Henry IV.' Ln: W. Pickering, 1841. 8°, pp. 56
    BM | BPL | BUS | CPL | HCL | MPL | SML

On the life of Sh—. *See* Sh—

Halliwell (James Orchard) On the means
adopted to insure the rarity of the
privately-printed works of J. O. H. Ln :
For private circulation only, 1854. 8°
On the word ' Ducdame ' in 'As you like it.'
See Sh—] Sh— Soc.
Original collections of John Jordan, 1780-
1864. See Jordan (J.)
Original letters of Malone . . . 1864. See
Malone (E.)
'Othello, 1622-1864.' See Sh— Othello,
1864
Outlines of the life of Sh—. See Sh—]
Halliwell
Papers respecting disputes . . . 1588-1866.
See Tarleton (R.)
'Pericles, 1609-1862.' See Sh— Pericles,
1862
'Pericles, 1609-1871.' See Sh— Pericles,
1871
'Pericles, 1611.' See Sh— Pericles, 1868,
1871
Poem containing notices of Ben Jonson,
Sh—, Massinger, etc. See Sh—] Sh—
Soc.
Pretie new enterlude . . . of Kyng Daryus,
1565-1860. See King
Probate copy of the will of Sh—. See Sh—
Will, 1872
Proposed so-called restoration of the Church
of the Holy Trinity at Stratford-on-Avon.
Brighton : [Privately printed] 1888. 8°
BPL
Prospectuses of Sh—'s works : I. The folio
edition in sixteen volumes ; II. Facsimiles
of all the quarto editions issued in the life-
time of the poet. [1862-71, 48 vols.]
8° BPL
Random note on the good old times [temp.
Elizabeth : In ' The Rose, Shamrock and
Thistle']. [c. 1862.] 8° BPL
Regnal years, list of law terms, etc. during
the Sh— period. Privately printed :
Brighton, 1883. 8° BPL | SML
Remarks on the plots of Sh—'s plays, 1850.
See Simrock (K. J.)
Remarks on the similarity of a passage in
Marlowe's ' Edward II.' and one in the
first part of the 'Contention' ['King Hy.
VI.']. See Sh—] Sh— Soc.
Remonstrance of Nathan Field, 1865. See
Field (N.)
'Romeo and Juliet, 1597-1866.' See Sh—
Romeo . . . 1866
'Romeo and Juliet, 1599-1865.' See Sh—
Romeo . . . 1865
'Romeo and Juliet, 1607.' See Sh— Romeo
. . . 1868, 1871
'Romeo and Juliet, 1609-1869.' See Sh—
Romeo . . . 1869

Halliwell (James Orchard) Rough list of Sh—
rarities and manuscript collections at
Hollingbury Copse, Brighton. [Privately
printed] Brighton, April 1880. 8°
Issue confined to fifty copies. BM | BPL
Roundabout letters on Stratford-on-Avon :
Nos. 1 to 10 [In ' The Rose, Shamrock
and Thistle']. Edin., 1862-64. 8°
BPL | BUS
Second letter to the executive committee
of the birthplace . . . Brighton, 1880. 8°
BPL
Selected extracts from the ancient registry
. . . See Stratford-upon-Avon
Selected notes upon Sh—'s 'Antony and
Cleopatra.' Ln : [Privately printed] 1868.
Fcp. 4°, pp. 42
BM | BPL | BUS | HCL | MPL | SML
Issue restricted to fifty copies [on hand-made paper].
One of a contemplated series of gathered critical and
philosophical material on the plays collected before
the issue of his 1853 folio edition.
Selected notes upon Sh—'s ' The Tempest.'
Ln : 1868. Fcp. 4° BM | BPL | BUS | HCL
Issue limited to fifty copies.
Selection from an unpublished glossary of
provincial words in use in Warwickshire
in the early part of the present century.
Ln : 1865. 12° BPL
Twenty-five copies printed, ten only preserved.
Sh— autotype committee at Stratford :
Transformation scenes and a retrospect.
Brighton : Privately printed, 1883. 8°
BPL
Sh— autotype committee . . . Second
edition. Brighton : Privately printed,
1883. 8°, pp. 60 BPL
Sh— index, c. 1850. Holograph MS., with
eight proofs, corrected by the author.
F°, pp. 894 SML
A projected publication never fulfilled.
Sh— manuscript in France ? [In 'Athe-
næum,' No. 2974, p. 529]. 1884 BM | BPL
Sh— memorial, 1864. See Sh—] Gibbs
Sh— rarities [In ' Book Lore']. 1885. 4°
BPL
Sh—'s grave. See Hall (W.)
Sh—'s will. See Sh— Will . . . 1838, 1851,
1872
Shakespearian drolls. See Shakespearean . .
Shakespearian facsimiles. See Sh—
Shakespearian literature [In ' The Archæo-
logist,' pp. 193-202, Jan.] Ln : 1842.
8° BUS
Shakespearian literature [Off-printed from
' The Archæologist,' Jan.] 1842. 8°,
pp. 12 BUS
Shakespearian parallelisms, 1865. See Sh—
Works : Ext. 1865

Halliwell (James Orchard) Shakespeariana:
A catalogue of the early editions of
Sh—'s plays and of the commentaries
and other publications illustrative of his
works. Ln: J. R. Smith, 1841. 8°,
pp. 46 BM | BPL | BUS | CPL | HCL | MPL | SML
A few were done also on India paper, and one on pure
vellum, now at Boston.

Skeleton hand list of the early quarto
editions of . . . Sh— . . . Printed for
private circulation, 1860. 8°, pp. 198,
interleaved BUS | HCL | MPL | W
Printed on one side of the page only, upon blue writing
paper, leaving space for MS. notes.
Impression limited to thirty copies.
Second edition. For first issue *see* Halliwell, 'Brief
hand list . . .' 1860.
Contains the list of contents of the collection of Sh—
facsimiles, 1862-71, 48 vols.

Some account of Robert Chester's 'Love's
martyr . . . 1601,' including a remarkable
poem by Sh—. The facsimiles by E. W.
Ashbee. Ln: 1865. Fcp. 4° HCL
Twenty-five copies printed, ten only preserved.
See also Chester (R.) *ante.*

Some account of the antiquities, coins,
manuscripts, rare books, ancient documents, and other reliques illustrative of
the life and works of Sh—. Brixton Hill:
Printed [by Thomas Richards] for private
circulation only, 1852. 4°, pp. viii.-136,
with facsimile BUS | SBL | SML
Issue confined to eighty copies.

Some account of the popular belief in
animated horsehairs alluded to by Sh—,
in the play of 'Antony and Cleopatra.'
[Ln: Privately printed] 1866. 16°
BM | BPL | HCL | MPL
Issue restricted to twenty-five copies, of which Halliwell destroyed fifteen.

Some account of the popular tracts which
composed the library of Capt. Cox, a
humourist who took a part in the Hock
Tuesday play, performed before Queen
Elizabeth at Kenilworth in 1575. *See*
Sh—] Sh— Soc.

Some account of Tofte's 'Alba . . . 1598,'
an extremely rare poem, containing the
earliest extrinsic notice of . . . 'Love's
labours lost.' Ln: Privately printed,
1865. Fcp. 4° BPL | BUS | HCL | MPL
Twenty-five copies printed, ten only preserved.

Some notes on passages in Sh—. *See Sh*—]
Sh— Soc.

Stratford records and the Sh— autotypes:
A brief review of singular delusions that
are current at Stratford-on-Avon. By
the supposed delinquent. Brighton, 1884.
8° BPL
First edition, afterwards suppressed.

Stratford records and the Sh— autotypes
. . . Second edition. Brighton, 1884-85.
8° BPL

Halliwell (James Orchard) Stratford records
and the Sh— autotypes . . . Third
edition. Brighton, 1884-85. 8°
BPL | BUS | SML

Stratford records and the Sh— autotypes
. . . Fourth edition. Ln: Harrison, 1886.
8°, pp. 116, including printed wrappers
BPL

Stratford records and the Sh— autotypes
. . . Fifth edition. Ln: Harrison, 1887.
8° BPL | SML

Stratford-upon-Avon in the times of the
Shakespeares. Illustrated by extracts
from the valuable manuscript Council
Books of the Corporation, especially
selected with reference to the history of
the poet's father. Illustrated with facsimiles of the entries respecting John
Sh—, executed by E. W Ashbee, engraved
. . . by J. H. Rimbault. Ln: Printed
by J. E. Adlard, 1864. F°, pp. viii.-128
Issue limited to thirty copies. BPL | BUS | MPL

Tale of Tereus and Progne, 1866. *See*
Pettie (George)

'Taming of a shrew, 1594.' *See* Sh—
Taming . . . 1870

Tarlton's Jests, 1844. *See* Tarlton (R.)

The lost 'Hamlet' [In 'New Monthly
Magazine,' April]. Ln: 1873. 8° BUS
Refers to the play alluded to by Nash in 1589.

The Whimzies, 1631-1859. *See* Brathwaite
(R.)

Three old ballads, 1588-1860. *See* Deloney

'Titus Andronicus, 1600-1866.' *See* Sh—
Titus . . . 1866

'Titus Andronicus, 1611-1867.' *See* Sh—
Titus . . . 1867

To the trustees of Sh—'s birthplace [Letter
on the subject of the library]. Privately
printed, 1879. 8°
Issue limited to fifty copies.

'Troilus and Cressida, 1609.' *See* Sh—
Troilus . . . 1863, 1871

Two indentures, 1865. *See* Stratford

Two old theatres: Views of the Globe and
the Bear Garden, the former being the
theatre belonging to Sh—'s company . . .
which was erected on the site of the
original building . . . destroyed by fire in
. . . 1613. Brighton: For private circula-
tion, 1884. F°, pp. 4 and plate BPL | SML

'Venus and Adonis, 1593.' *See* Sh— Venus
. . . 1866

'Venus and Adonis, 1594-1867.' *See* Sh—
Venus . . . 1867

Visits of Sh—'s company of actors to the
provincial cities and towns of England.
Illustrated by extracts gathered from
Corporate records. Brighton, 1887. Fcp.
4° BM | BPL | BUS | SML

Halliwell (James Orchard) Was Nicholas ap Roberts that butcher's son of Stratford-upon-Avon who is recorded by Aubrey as having been an acquaintance of Sh— in the early days of that great poet ? And was Sh— an apprentice to Griffin ap Roberts ? 1864. 16° BM | BPL | MPL
Issue confined to ten copies.

Which shall it be ? New lamps or old ? Shaxpere or Shakespeare ? Brighton, 4 Nov., 1879. 8°, pp. 16 BM | BPL | BUS | HCL
See also Halliwell, New lamps . . .

Will of Sir Hugh Clopton, 1496-1865. See Clopton

'Will of wit, 1599-1860.' See Breton (N.)

Halliwell (J. O.) Editor—

See Account . . .	See Malone
„ Actor's . . .	„ Manuel
„ Ancient ballad	„ Marriage . . .
„ Ancient docu-	„ Marston
„ Armin [ments	„ Merry . . .
„ Ballads	„ Metrical . . .
„ Barnard	„ Moral . . .
„ Bill . . .	„ Morgan
„ Booke . . .	„ Nares
„ Chester	„ New . . .
„ Clopton	„ Newes . . .
„ Collection . . .	„ Nicholson
„ Combe	„ Notices . . .
„ Conceits	„ Parker
„ Confused . . .	„ Pettie
„ Contemporary	„ R—— (S.)
„ Crouch	„ Redford
„ Cunny-Catcher	„ Rich
„ Curious . . .	„ Sabie
„ Davenant	„ Sack . . .
„ Day	„ Sh— K. Henry IV.,
„ Debate . . .	i., 1845, 1859,
„ Decker	1860, 1866, 1867,
„ Deloney	1871
„ Doctors . . .	„ Sh— K. Lear, 1867,
„ Dodsley	1868
„ Ellis	„ Sh— K. Richard
„ Fair . . .	II., 1858, 1862,
„ Fairholt	1869, 1870
„ Field	„ Sh— K. Richard
„ Fites	III., 1862, 1863,
„ Greene	1865, 1867, 1871
„ Gybbys	„ Sh— Love's la-
„ Hall	bours lost, 1869
„ Harrowing . . .	„ Sh— Merry wives,
„ Henslowe	1875
„ Herbert	„ Sh— Rape . . . 1866
„ Hopper	„ Sh— Works, 1850,
„ Hornby	1850 - 53, 1851,
„ Jenkin . . .	1853, 1853 - 65,
„ Jordan	1854, 1856, 1858,
„ Lodge	1860, 1862 - 71,
„ Literature . . .	1863, 1866, 1875,
„ Ludus . . .	1876, 1887

Halliwell (J. O.) Editor—

See Sh—] Malone	See Stratford] Muster
„ Sh—] Sh— Drolls	„ „ Two...
„ Sh—] Sh—'s grave	„ Tarlton
„ Sharpe	„ Theatre plats
„ Shaw	„ Tinker . . .
„ Simpleton	„ Treatyse . . .
„ Simrock	„ Walker (G.)
„ Stratford] Abstract	„ West
„ „ Accounts	„ Westward . . .
„ „ Extracts	„ Wheler
„ „ Levy	„ Wyse . . .

Halliwell.] B—— (J. D.) Hollingbury Copse and its Shakesperiana [In ' Book-Lore ']. 1885. 8° BPL

] Baker (Ernest E.) Halliwell-Phillipps library : Notes on a portion which will be sold by auction. Weston-super-Mare, 1889. 8°

] Baker (E. E.) Halliwell-Phillipps library : Notes . . . Second edition. 1889. 8° BPL

] [Collection of newspaper cuttings relating to the offer to Birmingham of the Halliwell-Phillipps collection.] 1889. F°
BPL

] Collection of newspaper cuttings upon J. O. Halliwell-Phillipps. 1839-89. F°
BPL

] Hollingbury Copse, Sussex, residence of the late Mr. Halliwell-Phillipps : Particulars, views, and conditions of sale by Farebrother, Ellis, Clark & Co. 1889-93. 4°
BPL

] On Halliwell's introd. to a ' Midsummer night's dream ' [Reprinted from ' The Times,' 12 June]. 1841. 8°, pp. 8 BUS

] On Halliwell's 'Life of Sh—.' See Sh—] Halliwell

] Opinions of the press on the design of the ' Monograph edition ' of Sh—, ed. by J. O. Halliwell. Brighton [1853 ?] 8° BPL

] Smyth (A. H.) Halliwell-Phillipps collection [In ' Pennsylvania Literary Club : Occasional Papers, No. 2]. 1895. 4° BPL

] Winsor (Justin) Halliwelliana : A bibliography of the publications of J. O. Halliwell-Phillipps. 'Harvard University Bibliographical Contributions.' Cambridge : University Press [U.S.]: John Wilson & Son, 1881. F°, pp. 32 BPL | BUS

] Wright (G. R.) Brief memoir of J. O. Halliwell-Phillipps. 1889. 8° BPL

Halliwell (J. O.)—
See Drury Lane
„ Gibbs
„ Hawley (F.)
„ Hazlitt
„ Prizes . . .
„ Sh— Hamlet, 1603
„ Sh— Merry wives, 1660

Halliwell (J. O.)—
　See *Sh*—] Sh— MSS.
　,, Timmins
Halliwell (J. O.) & Ritson (Joseph) Fairy tales,
　legends, and romances illustrating Sh—
　and other early English writers. To
　which are prefixed two . . . dissertations:
　I. On pigmies, II. On fairies. With pre-
　face by W. C. Hazlitt. Ln: F. & W.
　Kerslake, 1875. 8°, pp. iv.-426 BUS | HCL
Halpin (Nicholas John) Bridal runaway:
　Essay on Juliet's soliloquy. Ln: Sh—
　Soc., 1845. 8° BPL | BUS
Dramatic unities of Sh—. Dublin: Hodges
　& Smith, 1849. 8°, pp. 58
　　　　　　　BM | BPL | BUS | W
Dramatic unities, with the time-analysis of
　the 'Merchant of Venice.' Ed. by C. M.
　Ingleby. Ln: New Sh— Soc., 1875-76.
　8° BUS
Oberon's vision in the 'Midsummer night's
　dream' illustrated by a comparison with
　Lyly's 'Endymion.' *See* Sh—]Sh— Soc.
Halstead (Caroline A.) Richard III. *See*
　Richard
Halswelle (Keeley) *Artist. See* Sh— Works,
　1861-63, 1875
Ham (J. Panton) Pulpit and stage: Four
　lectures. With illustrative notes by
　Fred. Whymper. Ln: C. H. Clarke,
　1878. 8°, pp. 184 and portrait SML
Hamer (John) Sh—'s ideal of womanhood
　[In 'Belgravia,' Vol. 77, p. 304]. Ln:
　1892. 8° BM | BPL
Sweet Swan of Avon. *See* Sh—
Hamilton *Edinburgh Publisher. See* Sh—
　Works, 1753
Hamilton (N. E. S. A.) Inquiry into the
　genuineness of the manuscript corrections
　in J. P. Collier's annotated Sh—, folio,
　1632, and of certain Sh— documents
　likewise published by Mr. Collier. Ln:
　Bentley, 1860. Fcp. 4°, pp. iv.-156, with
　facsimiles
　　　BM | BPL | BUS | CPL | MPL | SML | W
　See Rivington for reply.
See Collier (J. P.)
　,, Dixon
Hamilton (R. W.) Nugæ literariæ. 1841. 8°
　　　　　　　　　　　　BPL
　Contains 'On the tragic genius of Sh—,' p. 185, and
　'Classical comedy compared with Sh—'s,' p. 237.
Hamilton (W.) Parodies. Ln: 1885. 4° BPL
　Parts 19-21 and 23 contain imitations of Sh—.
Hamilton (Wm.) *Artist. See* Sh— Works,
　1802-03
Hamlet. *See* Sh— Hamlet
Hamlet.] Hamlet [In 'Blackwood's Magazine,'
　April]. Edinburgh, 1879. 8° BUS
]'Hamlet' [In the 'Dublin University
　Magazine']. 1876. 8° BPL

Hamlet.] 'Hamlet' . . . [In 'King Edward's
　School Chronicle']. 1898. 8° BPL
]'Hamlet, 1736' [Reprints of scarce pieces
　of Sh— criticism]. Ln: J. R. Smith,
　1863. 8°
] Hamlet: An attempt, etc. *See* Soames
]'Hamlet' at home and abroad [In 'Temple
　Bar']. 1875. 8° BPL
] Hamlet controversy: Was Hamlet mad?
　or the lucubrations of Messrs. Smith,
　Brown, Jones, and Robinson. With pre-
　face by the Editor of the 'Argus.' Mel-
　bourne, 1867. 12° BPL | MPL
]'Hamlet' from W. Sh— to J. Nowell [In
　the 'Imperial Review']. 1882. 8° BPL
] Hamlet improved. *See* Sh— Hamlet, 1880
] Hamlet, or not such a fool as he looks. *See*
　Sh— Hamlet, 1882
] Hamlet revamped. *See* Sh— Hamlet, 1879
]'Hamlet': Studies of great subjects [Rep.
　from 'Family Herald']. 1875. 8° BPL
] Hamlet the dainty. *See* Sh— Hamlet, 1849,
　1877
] Hamlet the Dane. *See* Sh— Hamlet, 1847
] Hamlet the ravin' prince . . . *See* Sh—
　Hamlet, 1866
] Hamlet travestie. *See* Sh— Hamlet, 1810,
　1849, 1880
] Hamlet: Whether the Queen were an ac-
　cessory before the fact in the murder of
　her first husband. Ln: J. R. Smith, 1856.
　8° CPL
] Hamlet's soliloquy imitated. *See* Dodsley
] Historie of Hamblet, 1843. *See* *Sh*—]
　Sh—'s library
　One of the foundations of 'Hamlet.'
] Newspaper cuttings on 'Hamlet.' 1884?
　8° BPL
] On the character of Hamlet, by an old
　bachelor [Rep. from 'Blackwood's Mag.']
　1828. 8° BPL
] On the feigned madness of Hamlet [Rep.
　from 'Blackwood's Mag.'] 1839. 8° BPL
Hamley (*Sir* Edward Bruce) Sh—'s funeral
　[In 'Blackwood's Mag.,' April]. Edin.,
　1873. 8° BUS
Sh—'s funeral [In 'Tales from Blackwood'].
　Edin., 1878. 12° BPL | BUS | SML
Sh—'s funeral and other papers. Edin.:
　Blackwood, 1889. Cr. 8°, pp. iv.-312
　　　　　　　　　　　BPL | SML
Hammond. Songs. *See* Sh— Midsummer . . .
　1755
Hancock (*Miss* L.)] Sh—'s garden: With re-
　ference to over a hundred plants. By
　'Leonard Holmesworth.' Leamington:
　F. Glover, 1903. Cr. 8°, pp. 74 BUS | SML
　This title was copyrighted by S. Beisley (*q.v.*) in 1864.
] Sh—'s garden. Leamington, 1906. Cr. 8°
　　　　　　　　　　　　BPL

Hancock (*Miss* L.)] Sh—'s songsters and other birds. With over one hundred references. By 'Leonard Holmesworthe.' Leamington Spa : F. Glover, 1905. 8°, pp. 46, including printed wrappers SML

Hancocke (Ralph) *Publisher. See* Peele

Hand and heart [Magazine]. Ln : 18th April, 1879. F° BPL
Contains Sh— matter.

Hand list of collective editions of Sh—. *See* Brassington

Handel (George Frederic) *Composer. See* Sh— Julius Cæsar, 1787

Handley (G. M.) *Editor. See* Sh— The Tempest, 1904

Haney (J.) Name of Wm. Sh— *See* Sh—

Hanmer *Speaker* (*Sir* Thomas) Castrated letter. *See* Nichols

Glossary explaining the obsolete and difficult words in the plays of Sh—. Oxford : Printed at the Theatre, 1744-46. 4° W

Preface to his edition of Sh— [Holograph manuscript]. 1743. F°, pp. 6
Sold at auction 9th December, 1905, for £50.
'Sh—, who does great honour to his country as a rare and perhaps singular genius ; one who hath attained a high degree of perfection in those two great branches of poetry, tragedy and comedy, different as they are in their natures from each other ; and who may be said without partiality to have equalled, if not excelled, in both kinds, the best writers of any age or century who have thought it glory enough to distinguish. themselves in either.'

Preface. *See* Eighteenth . . .

Preface. *See* Sh— Works, 1803-05

See Annotations

,, Collins

,, Grey

,, Johnson (*Dr.* S.)

,, Sh— Hamlet, 1603

,, Some remarks

,, Stevens

Hanmer (*Sir* T.) *Editor. See* Sh— Works, 1744-46, 1745, 1747, 1748, 1750-51, 1760, 1770-71, 1771

Hanmer (Meredith) *Editor. See* Eusebius

Hannett *Bookseller* (J.) Forest of Arden. Henley-in-Arden : J. Hannett, 1863. 12°. Numerous woodcuts BPL | SML
The title was copyrighted by W. Gresley in 1841.

Forest of Arden. Birmingham, 1894. 4° BPL

Hano (E.) Some hints about Sh—'s 'Othello.' Schellstadt, 1880. Fcp. 4° BM | BUS

Hansard (L.) Shaksperian commemoration, Stratford, 1827 [In 'Memoir of Hansard,' pp. 72-77]. 1829. 4° BPL

Hanscomb (E. W.) Sh— birthday book. *See* Sh— Works : Ext. 1892

Hansen (G. P.) Legend of Hamlet, Prince of Denmark, as found in the works of Saxo Grammaticus and other writers of the twelfth century. [Ed. by C. E. Simons.] Chicago : Kerr, 1887. 8° BM | BPL | SML

Hanway *New York Publisher. See* Sh— Works, 1821, 1824

Harbert (*Sir* William)] Epicedium : Funerall song upon the vertuous life and godly death of the Right Worshipfull the Lady Helen Branch. Ln : 1594.
With the allusion :—
'You that have writ of chaste Lucretia.'

Harcourt (*Capt.* A. F. P.) Sh— argosy. *See* Sh— Works : Ext. 1874

Harder (A.) Philosophy of Wm. Sh—. *See* Sh— Works : Ext. 1869

Hardie (Iohn) *Publisher. See* Peele

Hardie (W. R.) *Editor. See* Sh— Twelfth night, 1882

Harding (E.) *Publisher*—
See Sh— All's well, 1799
,, Sh— Antony . . . 1799
,, Sh— Works, 1800

Harding (Edward) Baconian summary. Ln : 1902. 8°, pp. 50 BPL | BUS

Harding (J.) *Publisher. See* Sh—Works, 1811

Harding (J.) *Philadelphia Publisher. See* Sh— Works, 1849

Harding (J. D.) *Artist. See* Jaffray

Harding (S.) *Artist. See* Sh— Poems, 1795

Harding (Sylvester & E.)] Sh— illustrated by an assemblage of portraits and views appropriated to the whole series of that author's historical dramas. To which are added portraits of actors, editors, etc. Ln : S. & E. Harding, 1793. 4° BM | BUS | SML | W
Largest paper copy, folio, with 137 plates on toned paper, is at the British Museum.
Some copies contain an additional plate of Jane Shore in low cut dress.
Large paper copies were done in royal quarto.

Sh— illustrated . . . With biographical anecdotes . . . and descriptions of the places mentioned, adapted to the whole series of that author's dramas. To which are added portraits of actors, editors, etc. Arranged with directions for their insertion in any edition. Ln : G. Sidney [c. 1793]. 2 vols. 8°. With 158 plates BUS

Whole historical dramas . . . illustrated by an assemblage of portraits of the royal, noble, and other persons mentioned, together with those of editors, commentators, and actors, and views of castles, towns, etc. . . . referred to, with short biographical and topographical accounts. Ln : E. Jeffery, 1811. 2 vols. 4° BPL | BUS
The copperplates in this printing shew signs of wear.
A large paper edition was also issued of this date, 2 vols., royal quarto.

Hardinge (George)] Another 'Essence of Malone,' or the 'Beauties' of Sh—'s editor [First and Second part]. Ln : T. Becket, 1801. 2 parts in 1 vol. 8° BM | BPL | MPL | W

Hardinge (George)] Capell's ghost, to Edmund Malone . . . a parody. First printed in 1799 [In 'School for Satire']. Ln: 1802. 8°   BUS

] Chalmeriana, or a collection of papers . . . occasioned by reading a late heavy 'Supplemental apology . . . by G. Chalmers.' Arranged by 'Mr. Owen, jun.,' assisted by 'Jasper Hargrave.' Ln: T. Becket, 1800. 8°, pp. viii.-94
BM | BPL | BUS
Described by Lowndes as 'an infamous attack on one of the most worthy of men.'
Contains the poem entitled, 'Capell's ghost.'

] Editor, booksellers, and critic: An eclogue 'from . . . 'Chalmeriana.' 1800. 8° BPL
Sometimes placed to the credit of T. J. Mathias, author of 'Pursuits of literature,' but Hardinge is the more probable writer.

] Essence of Malone, or the 'Beauties' of that fascinating writer extracted from his immortal work (with his accustomed felicity), entitled 'Some account of the life and writings of John Dryden.' By 'M. Felix.' Ln: 1800 BM | W
Several allusions to Sh—.
'A virulent attack.'—Lowndes.

] Essence of Malone . . . Second edition, enlarged. 1800. 12° BPL
Essay on Sh—'s character of the fool in 'King Lear': On the 'Winter's tale': On Sh—'s accentuation [In his 'Miscellaneous Works,' Vol. 3]. Ln: 1818. 3 vols. 8° BPL | BUS
In the latter of these essays he expresses regret for attacking Malone.

Hardinge (George). See Collins (John)
Hardwicke (Harriet Countess of) Court of Oberon. See Sh— Midsummer . . . 1831
Hardy (R. B.) Lectures on the drama: Sh—. See Sh—
Hardy (Sir Thomas Duffus) Review of the present state of the Sh— controversy. 1860. Ln: Longman, 8°, pp. ii.-76
On Collier controversy. BM | BPL | BUS | CPL
Hardy (T. M.) An evening with Sh—. Ln: 1908. Cr. 8° BPL
Hare (Augustus J. C.) Walks in London. 1883. 2 vols. 8°
Contains the history in outline of the theatres of Sh—'s time, and refers to the bard many times.

Hare (Julius Charles & A. J.) Guesses at truth. Ln: 1827. Cr. 8°
'Sh— glances from heaven to earth and from earth to heaven. All nature ministers to him as gladly as a mother to her child. . . . No poet comes near Sh— in the number of lines that, according to Bacon's expression, "come home to our business and bosoms," and open the door for us to look in and see what is nestling and brooding there.'

Guesses at truth, by two brothers. Ln: Macmillan & Co., 1874. Cr. 8°, pp. lvi.-576

'Hargrave (Jasper)' pseud. See Hardinge (G.)
Harington (Sir John)] New discourse of a stale subject called the metamorphosis of Ajax, written by 'Misacmos' to his friend 'Philostilpnos.' Ln: 1596. 8°. With woodcuts
'Its grossness does not atone for its wit, however poignant.'
It was reprinted in 1614.
For its connection with 'Love's labours lost' see Drake, 'Sh— and his times.'

Harkom (J. M.) Address on 'Hamlet.' Delivered before the Edin. Sh— Soc. 1902. 8° BPL
Harland (J.) & Wilkinson (T. T.) Lancashire legends, traditions, pageants, sports. With appendix on the Lancashire witches. 1882. 8°. With portrait
Illustrates 'Macbeth.'

Harleian manuscripts [No. 6395, 'Merry passages and Jests,' in B.M., contains Sh— - Jonson anecdote. Repeated in 'The Drama,' Vol. I. p. 346, II. p. 324, III. p. 281]
'W. Sh—, being at a certain time on terms of familiarity and friendship with Ben Jonson, before the latter had become jealous and envious of his rising merits, stood godfather to a child of Ben's, who demanded of him in a pleasant way what gift he would bestow, as the custom was. "I have just been thinking," replied the Warwickshire bard, "and am determined to give the boy a dozen latten spoons, and thou shalt translate them."'
The term latten, otherwise tin, still survives in the stannaries or tin mines of Cornwall.

Harley (G. D.) See Betty
Harley (J. P.) Bibliophile. See Catalogue, 1858
Harlow (Louis K.) Home of Sh—: After water-colour sketches . . . Boston [U.S.]: 1888. Oblong 8° BPL | BUS
Harman (Thomas) Caveat for common cursetors. See Viles & Furnivall
Harness (William) Sh—'s bust at Stratford. See Sh—
Widow of Sh—. See Sh— (Anne)
Harness (W.) Editor. See Sh— Works, 1825, 1833, 1838, 1839, 1842
Harness.] L'Estrange (A. G.) Literary life of Wm. Harness, editor of Sh—. 1871. 8° BPL

Harness annual prize Sh— essay for Cambridge students—
See Gibson   See Rothschild
  „ Herford   „ Stokes
  „ Rives
Harper (J. & J.) New York Publishers. See Sh— Works, 1829
Harper (Rev.   )] Some serious remarks on a late pamphlet [by Dr. Adam Ferguson] entituled the 'Morality of stage-plays seriously considered . . .' Edinburgh [sans pr.] 1757. 8°, pp. ii.-32

Harper (S. B. A.) Was Sh— a Catholic ?
See Sh—] Harper

Harper (T.) *Printer—*
See Heylyn
„ Randolph
„ Sh— Merry wives, 1630

Harper (W. H.) Sh— and the Thames. Ln :
[c. 1892]   BUS

Harris *Roy. Inst. Librarian, Editor. See* Sh—
Works, 1813

Harris (A.) National theatre [In the ' Fortnightly Review']. 1885. 8°   BPL

Harris (Frank) Sh—'s sweetheart : A play.
1909

The man Sh— and his tragic life story.
See Sh—] Harris

Harris *Actor* (George). *See* Wilson (Thomas)

Harris (J.) Most correct copies of all the
authentic autographs of Sh—. 1843. *See*
Sh— Autograph

Harris *Cornish Poet* (John) Poems in connection with the Sh— festival at Coventry.
1864. 12°   BPL
Harris won first prize for the great Sh— tercentenary
poem. He was then working as a miner at Delcoath.

Sh—'s shrine : An Indian story, with essays
and poems. Ln : Hamilton Adams, 1866.
12°   BPL | SML

Harris *Actor* (Joseph) The mistakes, or the
false reports. A tragi-comedy. Acted
by their Majesties servants. Prologue by
Dryden. Epilogue by Tate. Ln : Printed
by J. O. Hindmarsh at the Golden Ball
over against the Royal Exchange, 1691.
Fcp. 4°
' How's this ! you cry ? An actor write ! We know it ;
But Sh— was an actor and a poet.
Has not great Jonson's learning often fail'd,
But Sh—'s greater genius still prevail'd !'

Harris (M. Dormer) Historic Warwickshire,
1908. *See* Memorials . . .
The title was copyrighted by J. T. Burgess in 1876.

Manuscript treasures of Coventry. *See*
Memorials . . .

Harris (W.) History of ' Our Sh— Club.'
Birmingham, 1903. 8°   BPL

Harrison (Anthony) Infant vision of Sh—,
with an apostrophe to the immortal bard,
and other poems. Ln : Harrison & Co.,
1794. 4°, pp. 24   BM | BPL | BUS | W

Harrison (F.) New calendar of great men. *See*
Sh—

Harrison (Gabriel) Stratford bust of Wm.
Sh—. *See* Sh—

Harrison (*General*). *See* Cunningham

Harrison (J.) *Publisher—*
See Sh— All's well, 1778
„ Sh— Measure . . . 1779
„ Sh— Twelfth night, 1779

Harrison *or* Harison (John) *Printer. See*
Holinshed

Harrison *or* Harison *jun.* (John) *Printer. See*
Sh— Rape . . . 1600

Harrison *or* Harison (John) *Publisher—*
See Sh— Rape . . . 1594, 1598, 1600, 1607
„ Venus . . . 1596, 1600

Harrison (Wm.) Description of England in
Sh—'s youth. Ed. by F. J. Furnivall.
Ln : New Sh— Soc., 1877-81. 3 parts
forming 2 vols. 4°. Maps, views, and
folded coloured plate of old London
Bridge   BPL | BUS
Description of England . . . Ed. by F. J.
Furnivall. Ln : Chatto, 1908. 4°   BPL
Elizabethan England. Ed. by L. Withing-
ton. With introd. by F. J. Furnivall.
Ln : W. Scott [c. 1890]

Harrison (Wm.) *Bibliophile. See* Catalogue,
1881

Harrison.] Descriptive catalogue of a collection of Shakspeariana, consisting of
manuscripts, books, and relics illustrative of the life and writings of Sh— in
the library of Wm. Harrison, of Galli-
greaves Hall, near Blackburn . . . Ln :
Thomas Richards, 1866. Fcp. 4°, pp.
viii.-116   BPL | MPL | SML
Privately printed ; fifty copies only.

Harrison (William A.) Hamlet's ' juice of
cursed hebona.' Ln : New Sh— Soc.,
1882. 8°   BUS
See Greenhill & Harrison

Harrison (W. A.) *Editor. See* Sh— King
Richard II., 1888

Harrison (W. J.) Sh— land [In ' Irving Sh—,'
Vol. 14, pp. 135-269]. c. 1907. 8° BPL

Harrison & Co. *Publishers—*
See Sh— Comedy of errors, 1779
„ Sh— Coriolanus, 1780
„ Sh— Hamlet, 1779
„ Sh— Julius Cæsar, 1780
„ Sh— King Henry V., 1780
„ Sh— King Lear, 1779
„ Sh— Macbeth, 1780
„ Sh— Othello, 1780
„ Sh— Timon . . . 1780
„ Sh— Winter's tale, 1779
„ Sh— Works, 1791

Harrop (J.) *Manchester Publisher. See* Sh—
King Richard II., 1772

Harroway (J.) *Composer—*
See Sh— King Richard III., 1830
„ Sh— Merchant, 1830
„ Sh— Othello, 1830

Harrowing of hell : A miracle play. With
introduction, translation, and notes by
J. O. Halliwell. 1840. 8°

Harry White : his humour. *See* Parker

Harsnet *Archbp.* (Samuel) Declaration of egregious Popish impostures . . . under the pretence of casting out devils, practised by Edmunds, a Jesuit . . . with confessions of those supposed to be possessed. Ln: James Roberts, 1603. Fcp. 4°　　　　　　　　　BUS
From this work Sh— probably borrowed the fantastical names of the spirits in ' King Lear.' This conjecture is used as an argument that he was a Protestant.

Hart (Andrew) *Edinburgh Printer.* *See* Stephen

Hart *Sh—'s grand-nephew* (Charles). *See* Flecknoe

Hart (Ernest Abraham) On the tragedy of ' King Lear.' *See* Seeley, Young & Hart

Hart (H. C.) *Editor—*
See Sh— Love's labours lost, 1906
　,, Sh— Measure . . . 1905
　,, Sh— Merry wives, 1904
　,, Sh— Othello, 1903

Hart (John B.) *Reciter.* *See* Gourlay

Hart *LL.D.* (John Seely) Description of Sh—'s portraits. *See* Sh— Works, 1879

　Sh— death mask [In ' Scribner's Monthly,' July]. New York, 1874. 8°. Illust.
　　　　　　　　　BPL | BUS

Hart (Joseph C.) Romance of yachting. New York: Harper, 1848. 12°　BUS | SML
On pp. 208-242 is a discussion of the authenticity of Sh—'s plays.

Hart (W. Shakspeare) Statement as to Sh—'s birthplace. 1822. Manuscript. 4°　BPL

Hart family. *See* Sh—] Jordan

Harting (James Edward) Birds of Sh— critically examined, explained, and illustrated. Ln: Van Voorst [c. 1900]. 8°. Plates by J. G. Keulemans　　　　SML

　Ornithology of Sh— critically examined, explained, and illustrated. Ln: Van Voorst, 1871. 8°, pp. xxiv.-322 and portrait　BM | BPL | BUS | CPL | SML

Hartley (Edward). *See* Littledale

Hartmann (Sadakichi) Sh— in art. Boston [U.S.]: 1901. 8°. With portraits and plates　　　　　　　BPL | BUS

Hartshorne (Albert) Monuments and effigies in St. Mary's Church, Warwick. *See* Memorials . . .

Hartshorne (C. H.) Book rarities in the University of Cambridge, illustrated by original letters, biographical, literary, and antiquarian. 1829. 8°. With engravings
　　　　　　　BM | BUS | CTC
Contains (pp. 283-319) a reprint of Capell's ' Catalogue of Shakesperiana,' presented to Trinity Coll., Camb.

Harvard.] Shelley (H. C.) John Harvard and his times. 1907. Cr. 8°　　　BPL
Contains Shakespeariana.

Harvard memorial window. *See* Withington

Harvey *M.D.* *See* Hackett

Harvey (Gabriel) Four letters and certaine sonnets . . . especially touching Robert Green, and other parties by him abused. Ln: 1592. Fcp. 4°
The third ' Letter ' (pp. 48-49) refers to Sh—:
' Good sweete oratour, be a divine poet indeede.'

　Four letters . . . Ln: 1814. Fcp. 4°　BUS
　Third letter. *See* Sh—] New Sh— Soc.

Harvey *Actor* (J. Martin) Character and the actor: A lecture . . . Ln: Ethological Society, 1908. 8°, pp. 20, includ. printed wrappers

　Character and the actor. A lecture delivered before the British Empire Sh— Soc., Liverpool branch [In ' Liverpool Courier', p. 9, 29 Sept.]. 1909

　Character and the actor [In ' Liverpool Post and Mercury,' p. 10, 29 Sept.] 1909

Harvey (K.) *Editor—*
See Sh— As you like it, 1909
　,, Sh— Hamlet, 1909
　,, Sh— Merchant . . . 1909
　,, Sh— Midsummer . . . 1909
　,, Sh— Works, 1909

Harvey (W.) Prolegomena to the works of Sh—. 1825. 8°　　　BPL | CPL
Contains a life of the poet.

Harvey (W.) *Editor.* *See* Sh— Works, 1825

Harvey (Wm.) *Artist—*
See Dramatic souvenir
　,, Sh— Works, 1826, 1844, 1849, 1852, 1854, 1857, 1862
　,, Sh— Works: Ext. 1831, 1838

Harvey (*Sir* Wm.) identified as ' Mr. W. H—.' *See* Stopes

Harwood (*Mrs.* S.) Sh— cult in Germany. New South Wales Sh— Soc., Sydney, 1907. Cr. 8°　　　　　BPL

Haskell (Ernest) *Artist.* *See* Sh— Romeo . . . 1899

Halewood (Joseph) Ancient critical essays upon English poets and poesy. Ln: 1811-15. 2 vols. Fcp. 4°
Limited to 220 copies.

　Life of Ritson. *See* Ritson

] Secret history of the green rooms. Ln: J. Ridgway, 1790. 2 vols. 12°　BPL

] Secret history of the green rooms. Containing authentic memoirs of actors and actresses in the three Theatres Royal . . . Ln: J. Owen, 1795. 2 vols. 8°

Haslewood (J.) *Editor—*
See Meres
　,, Painter

Hatchard (J.) *Publisher.* *See* Sh— Works, 1807

Hatchett. *See* Fall of Mortimer

Hatfield (Arnold) *Printer—*
See Estienne
　,, Florio
　,, Historie . . .

Hathaway (Agnes *or* Anne)—

See Braddon	*See* Lacy
„ Cottage	„ Laffan
„ Dibdin	„ Reiss
„ Falconer	„ Severn
„ Fenton	„ Sh— (Anne)
„ Hall	„ Steer
„ Harness	„ Stopes
„ Howitt	„ Wilson

Hathaway (P.) Sermons and theological collections, together with a few verses, medical recipes, etc. Manuscript on two hundred and forty-eight leaves of paper. Tewkesbury, 1690. 8°   w

Probably written by a collateral descendant of Sh—'s wife, some of whose near relatives settled near Tewkesbury at an early date.

Hathaway family. *See* Bellew

Hathway (Thomas). *See* Sh— Sir John Oldcastle, 1600

Hatton *Editor*. *See* Sh— Much ado, 1774

Hatton. Nursery tales from Sh—. *See* Sh— Works : Ext. 1879

Hatton (Joseph) With a show in the north : Reminiscences of Mark Lemon. Together with [his] revised text of Falstaff. Ln : W. H. Allen & Co., 1871. 8°, pp. iv.-284   BUS

Hatton (Joseph) *Editor*—

  See Irving (*Sir* J. H. B.)

  „ Sh— King Henry IV., i., 1871

  „ Sh— King Henry IV., ii., 1871

Hatton (Joshua)] William Jaggard. *See* Jaggard

Hatton (J. Liptrot) *Composer*. *See* Sh— King Henry VIII., 1855

Haughton (Wm.) *See* Decker, Chettle & Haughton

Haussaire (E.) *Editor*—

  See Sh— Julius Cæsar, 1881

  „ Sh— King Richard III., 1885

Havard (W.)] King Charles the first : An historical tragedy. Written in imitation of Sh—. As it is acted at the Theatre Royal in Lincoln's Inn Fields. Ln : 1737. 8°. With frontispiece   MPL | W

Havarde *Actor*. *See* Garrick

Havell (D.) *Artist*. *See* Winston (J.)

Haviland (J.) *Printer*. *See* Davenant

Haviland (Thomas) *Printer*. *See* Sh— Merry wives, 1630

Haweis (Hugh Reginald) Introduction. *See* Sh— Works : Ext. 1899

Sh— and the stage : . . . A sermon [In 'Arrows in the air']. Ln : 1878. 8°   BM | BPL | BUS

Hawes (L.) *Publisher*—

  See Sh— All's well, 1756

  „ Sh— Hamlet, 1759, 1763

Hawes (L.) *Publisher*—

  See Sh— King Henry IV., i., 1763

  „ Sh— King Henry VIII., 1762

  „ Sh— King Lear, 1756, 1759, 1760

  „ Sh— Macbeth, 1770

  „ Sh— Othello, 1765, 1771

  „ Sh— The tempest, 1761

  „ Sh— Timon . . . 1770

  „ Sh— Works, 1757, 1762

Hawes & Co. *Publishers*. *See* Sh— Hamlet, 1767

Hawes, Clarke & Collins *Publishers*. *See* Sh— Works, 1773

Hawkey (C.) Sh— tapestry, woven in verse. Edinburgh : Blackwood, 1881. Cr. 8°   BM | BPL | BUS | SML

Hawkins. *See* Annotations

Hawkins *Publisher*. *See* Sh— Taming . . 1778

Hawkins (C. H.) *Editor*—

  See Noctes Shakesperianæ

  „ Winchester . . .

Hawkins (F.) Annals of the French stage. 1884. 2 vols. 8°   BPL

French stage in the eighteenth century. 1888. 2 vols. 8°. With portraits BPL

' Henry VIII.' on the stage [In ' English Illustrated Magazine']. 1892. Roy. 8°   BPL

' King Lear ' on the stage [In ' English Illustrated Magazine']. 1893. Roy. 8°   BPL

Hawkins (F. W.) Life of Kean. *See* Kean

Hawkins (G.) *Publisher*. *See* Upton

Hawkins (Richard) *Publisher*—

  See Sh— Othello, 1630

  „ Sh— Works, 1632

Hawkins (Thomas) Manuscript notes. *See* Sh— Works, 1752

Origin of the English drama, illustrated in its various species, viz., mystery, morality, tragedy and comedy, by specimens from our earliest writers : with explanatory notes. Oxford, 1773. 3 vols. 8°   BUS | MPL

Contains several plays regarded as Sh— sources.

Hawkins *M.A.* (William) *Editor*. *See* Sh— Cymbeline, 1759

Hawkins (W. E.) *See* Anderson & Hawkins

Hawkins (W. M.) Miscellanies in prose and verse, containing candid and impartial observations on the principal performers [Garrick, King. Egerton, Green] belonging to the two Theatres Royal from Jan., 1773 to May, 1775 . . . with . . . pastoral songs, epitaphs, &c. Ln : T. Bell, 1775. 8°, pp. xxiv.-142

Many pages relate to Sh—.

Hawley (Frederick) Catalogue of all the known editions of Sh—'s plays in every language. Stratford-on-Avon, 1889, Manuscript. F°   SML

The compiler was librarian of the Stratford Memorial Library for about three years [1886-89], and did much to develop that institution in its earlier stages. He was trained for the legal profession, admitted solicitor in 1852, but afterwards preferred the stage for a career, playing in various Sh— parts under the name of 'Haywell,' a transposition of his proper name. One of the plays he wrote, 'Agnes of Bavaria,' secured an appearance at the Gaiety Theatre.

List of Sh— rhymes, with Sh— orthography and assumed Sh— pronunciation. Stratford-on-Avon, 1884. Original holograph MS. 8°, pp. iv.-240   SML

] Mr. Halliwell-Phillipps and the 'Stratford Oligarchy' . . . By an Onlooker. Stratford-on-Avon, 1887. Orig. holograph MS. on 114 folios. 4°   SML

'What needs this iteration?
A good old man, sir, he will be talking.'

A reply to J. O. Halliwell's pamphlets on his dispute with the Stratford trustees and his remarks upon Charles E. Flower.

Hawley (F.) *Editor. See* Sh— King John, 1887

Hawthorne *U.S. Consul* (Nathaniel) Mosses from an old manse. Ln : Routledge, 1851. Cr. 8°   BM

In the essay headed 'Earth's holocaust,' pp. 146-147, says : 'The human race had now reached a stage of progress so far beyond what the wisest and wittiest men of former ages had ever dreamed of, that it would have been a manifest absurdity to allow the earth to be any longer encumbered with their poor achievements in the literary line. Accordingly, a thorough and searching investigation had swept the booksellers' shops, hawkers' stands, public and private libraries, and even the little bookshelf by the country fireside, and had brought the world's entire mass of printed paper, bound or in sheets, to swell the already mountain-bulk of our illustrious bonfire. Thick heavy folios, containing the labours of lexicographers, commentators, and encyclopædists were flung, and falling among the embers with a leaden thump, smouldered away to ashes like rotten wood. . . . From Sh— there gushed a flame of such marvellous splendour, that men shaded their eyes as against the sun's meridian glory, nor even when the works of his own elucidators were flung upon him did he cease to flash forth a dazzling radiance beneath the ponderous heaps. It is my belief that he is still blazing as fervidly as ever. . . . The chief benefit to be expected from this conflagration of past literature undoubtedly is that writers will henceforth be compelled to light their lamps at the sun or stars.'

Our old home. Ln : Smith, 1863. 2 vols. Cr. 8°   CPL

Sh—, Stratford, and recollections of Delia Bacon, pp. 143-193, vol. i.

'Sh— has surface beneath surface, to an immeasurable depth, adapted to the plummet-line of every reader ; his works present many phases of truth, each with scope large enough to fill a contemplative mind. Whatever you seek in him you will surely discover, provided you seek truth. There is no exhausting the various interpretations of his symbols ; and a thousand years hence a world of new readers will possess a whole library of new books, as we ourselves do, in these volumes old already.'

Hawthorne *U.S. Consul* (Nathaniel) Our old home. Boston [U.S.], 1866. 8°   BUS

Hawthorne (N.) *Editor—*
See Bacon (D. S.)
  ,, Smith (W. H.)

Haydn (Joseph) *Composer. See* Sh— Poems, 1862

Hayes (Laurence) *Publisher. See* Sh— Merchant . . . 1637

Hayes (S.) *Publisher. See* Sh— Merchant . . 1783

Hayes *or* Heyes (Thomas) *Publisher—*
See Sh— Merchant . . . 1600
  ,, Sh— Works : Ext. 1600

Hayley (Wm.) Poetic epistle to an eminent painter [George Romney]. Ln : 1779

In part ii., pp. 472-484, is a sonnet to Sh— beginning :
'When, mighty Sh—, to thy judging eye
Presents that magic glass whose ample round
Reflects each figure in creation's bound
And pours in floods of supernatural light
Fancy's bright beings on the charmèd sight,
This chief enchanter of the willing breast
Will teach thee all the magic he possessed.'

Hayman (Francis) *Artist—*
See Sh— Hamlet, 1773
  ,, Sh— Works, 1744-46, 1770-71

Haymarket Theatre—
See Sh— Hamlet, 1712
  ,, Sh— Julius Cæsar, 1787
  ,, Sh— Midsummer . . . 1777
  ,, Sh— Works, 1850

Hayns.] Life of the late famous comedian Jo. Hayns, containing his comical exploits and adventures. Ln : 1701. 8°

Hayter *Artist. See* Sh— Works, 1875-80

Hayward (*Sir* John) Annals of first four years of the reign of Q. Elizabeth. Ed. by J. Bruce. Ln : Camden Soc., 1840. 8°   SML

First part of the life and raigne of King Henrie IIII. . . . Imprinted at Ln : by John Wolfe and are to be solde at his shop in Pope's Head Alley neere the Exchange, 1599. Fcp. 4°   BM

Queen Elizabeth ordered Sir Francis Bacon to search this book for treason. Bacon reported he found no treason, but many felonies, 'for Hayward had stolen many of his conceits out of Tacitus.' Nevertheless Hayward was summoned before the Star Chamber and imprisoned until Essex was executed. It is supposed the Queen took offence at his passages upon hereditary right of succession.

History of . . . Henry the Fourth . . . Ln : 1642. 12°   W

Hayward (Thomas) British muse. *See* Sh— Works : Ext. 1738

Quintessence of English poetry. *See* Sh— Works : Ext. 1740

Haywell (F.) *Editor. See* Macbeth, 1827

Haywood (Jasper). *See* Edwards (R.)

Hazlitt (William) Characters of Sh—'s plays. Ln : R. Hunter, 1817. 8°, pp. xxiv.-352
  BM | BPL | BUS | SML | W

Hazlitt (William) Characters . . . Second edition. Ln: Taylor & Hessey, 1818. 8°, pp. xxiv.-352   BM | BUS | SML
Characters . . . Boston [U.S.], Wells & Lilly, 1818. 12°, pp. 324   BUS
Characters . . . Third edition. Edited by his son. Ln: J. Templeman, 1838. 8°, pp. xxviii.-326   BUS
Characters . . . New York: Wiley & Putnam, 1845. 8°, pp. xxii.-230   BUS
Characters . . . Fourth edition. Edited by his son. Ln: Templeman, 1848. 8°
   BM | BPL | CPL
Characters . . . Philadelphia: Carey & Hart, 1848. 8°, pp. xxii.-230   BUS
Characters . . . 5th ed. Ln: C. Templeman, 1854. Cr. 8°, pp. xxviii.-346   BM | MPL
Characters . . . New edition. Ed. by Wm. **Carew Hazlitt.** Ln: Bell & Daldy, 1873. 8°, pp. xx.-248
'All extracts have been collated with Dyce's text of 1868. In all former editions these quotations were corrupt beyond measure. A few notes have also been added.'—W. C. H.
Characters . . . Ln: Macmillan, 1903. 8°, **pp. 450**   BPL
Characters . . . 'Temple Classics.' Ln: Dent, 1905. 12°, pp. 238
Characters . . . Ln: Dent, 1906. 12°, pp. 292
Characters . . . Ed. with introd. and notes by J. H. Lobban. Camb. Univ. Press, 1908. Cr. 8°, pp. 304
Characters . . . See also Jeffrey
Criticisms and dramatic essays of the English stage. Ln: 1851. Cr. 8°
Criticisms . . . Second edition. Edited by his son. Ln: Routledge, 1854. Cr. 8°
   BPL | BUS | SML
Lectures on the dramatic literature of the age of Elizabeth. Ln: 1821. 8°   BPL
Lectures on the dramatic literature . . . Third edition. Ln: Templeman, 1840. 12°   MPL
Lectures on the English comic writers. Ln: 1819. 8°   BUS
The second lecture is on Sh— and Jonson.
Lectures on the English poets delivered at the Surrey Institution. Ln: Taylor & Hessey, 1818. 8°, pp. iv.-332   BPL | SML
Contains the essay on 'Sh— and Milton' at pp. 86-134.
'The striking peculiarity of Sh—'s mind was its generic quality, its power of communication with all other minds; so that it contained a universe of thought and feeling within itself, and had no one peculiar bias or exclusive excellence more than another. He was just like any other man but that he was like all other men. . . . He not only had in himself the germs of every faculty and feeling, but he could follow them by anticipation intuitively into all their conceivable ramifications through every change of fortune or conflict of passion or turn of thought. . . . He turned the globe round for his amusement, and

surveyed the generations of men and the individuals as they passed, with their different concerns, passions, follies, vices, virtues, actions and motives, as well those that they knew, as those which they did not know, or acknowledge to themselves. . . .'
Hazlitt (William) Lectures on the English poets . . . Second edition. Ln: Taylor, 1819. 8°, pp. iv.-332   BUS
Lectures on the English poets and English comic writers. Edited by W. C. Hazlitt. Ln: 1884. 8°   BPL
Lectures on the literature of the age of Elizabeth and characters of Sh—'s Plays. Ln: Bell & Daldy, 1870. Cr. 8°, pp. viii.-248
Lectures on the literature . . . Ln: 1878. 8°
   BPL
Table talk. 1821
At p. 177, vol. i., remarks: 'If we wish to know the force of human genius, we should read Sh—. If we wish to see the insignificance of human learning, we may study his commentators.'
View of the English stage. Ln: 1818. 8°
   BPL
View . . . Ln: 1819. 8°   BUS
View . . . Ln: Bell, 1906. Cr. 8°, pp. 382
   BPL
Hazlitt (Wm.) *Editor*—
  See Sh— Poems, 1852
  ,, Sh— Works, 1851-52, 1852, 1852-59, 1853, 1855, 1856, 1857, 1859, 1860, 1861, 1862, 1864, 1865, 1865-67, 1871, 1887, 1891
Hazlitt.] 'Hazlitt on Sh—' [In 'Edinburgh Review']. Aug., 1817. 8°   BUS
] 'Hazlitt on Sh— and the poets,' etc. [In 'Monthly Review']. Ln: May, 1820. 8°
   BUS
] On Hazlitt's 'Characters of Sh—'s plays' [In 'Quarterly Review']. Ln: Jan., 1818. 8°   BUS
Hazlitt (Wm. Carew) Bibliographical collections and notes on early English literature [Three Series]. Ln: 1867-87. 3 vols. 8°   BM
Bibliographical collections and notes . . . made during 1893-1903. Ln: Quaritch, 1903. 8°
Fairy tales, legends, and romances illustrating Sh—. 1875. 8°   BPL
Handbook to popular, poetical, and dramatic literature of Great Britain. Ln: 1867. 8°   BUS
With short bibliography of early editions of Sh—.
Manual for the collector and amateur of old English plays. Edited from the material formed by Kirkman, Langbaine, Downes, Oldys, and Halliwell-Phillipps. With extensive additions and corrections. Fcp. 4°   BPL
Issue limited to 250 copies.
Preface. *See* Halliwell & Ritson

Hazlitt (Wm. Carew) Sh—: [his private and
literary history]. *See* Sh—] Hazlitt
Sh— himself and his work. *See* Sh—]
Hazlitt
Hazlitt (Wm. Carew) *Editor*—
See Dodsley
  ,, English drama
  ,, Hazlitt (W.)
  ,, Hundred . . .
  ,, Sh— Merry devil . . . 1875
  ,, Sh— Mucedorus, 1874
  ,, Sh— Taming . . . 1875
  ,, *Sh—*] Sh—'s Jest books
  ,, *Sh—*] Sh—'s Library
Head (Franklin H.) Sh—'s insomnia. *See*
Sh—] Head
Head (Richard) Proteus redivivus, or the art
of wheedling or insinuation. Ln: 1679.
8°   W
Refers to 'Love's labours lost' at p. 55.
Headlam (Stewart D.) Theatres and Music
Halls. A lecture. Ln: Women's Print-
ing Society, 1877. 12°, pp. 12   BPL
Headlam (W.) 'Arden of Feversham' [In
'Athenæum,' No. 3974, p. 868, Dec.]
1903
Headley (Hy.) *Editor. See* Select beauties
Heard (Franklin Fiske) Legal acquirements of
Wm. Sh—. Boston [U.S.], J. K. Wiggin,
1865. Fcp. 4°, pp. 66   BUS
Sh— as a lawyer. Boston [U.S.], 1883.
8°   BPL
This is virtually W. L. Rushton's title, copyrighted in
1858.
Sh—'s legal acquirements [In 'Monthly
Law Reporter,' Jan.] Boston, 1864. 8°
pp. 12   BUS
Heath *Engraver. See* Johnson
Heath (Benjamin)] Revisal of Sh—'s text,
wherein the alterations introduced into
it by the more modern editors and critics
are particularly considered. Ln: W.
Johnston in Ludgate Street, 1765. 8°,
pp. xiv.-574
BM | BPL | BUS | CPL | CTC | MPL | SML | W
The Warwick exemplar is an autograph presentation
copy from the author.
Heath (B.) *See* Annotations
Heath (Charles) Heroines of Sh—: comprising
the principal female characters in the
plays of the great poet. Engraved . . .
from drawings by eminent artists. Ln:
W. D. Kent & Co., late D. Bogue, 1848.
F°   BM | BUS
Issued also with coloured plates, and as India proofs,
royal quarto.
Text, pp. 96 (unpaged), and plates, forty-five large
separate portraits.
Heroines of Sh— . . . Ln: W. Kent &
Co., 1858. F°, pp. 96 [unpaged] and 45
separate plates

Heath (Charles) Heroines of Sh—. *See* Sh—
Works : Ext. 1883
Sh— gallery. *See* Sh— Works : Ext. 1836-
37, 1860, 1862-64
Heath (C.) *Engraver. See* Sh— Works, 1836
Heath (J.) *Engraver. See* Sh— Hamlet, 1806
See Sh— Works, 1802, 1802-04, 1807, 1825-
26, 1829, 1836, 1842
Heath (W.) Studies from the stage in the
vicissitudes of life. Ln: W. Sams, 1823.
Oblong 4°. Coloured title and 20 plates
With 120 humorous illustrations of popular plays.
Heath & Robinson *Publishers. See* Sh—
Works, 1802-04
Hedelin *Abbot* (F.) Whole art of the stage,
containing not only the rules of the
dramatick art but many curious observa-
tions about it which may be of great use
to the authors, actors and spectators of
plays, together with much critical learn-
ing about the stage and plays of the
antients . . . Now made English. Ln:
Printed for the Author and sold by Wm.
Cadman at the Pope's Head in the New
Exchange, Richard Bentley, Russel
Street, Sam. Smith at the Prince's Arms
in St. Paul's Churchyard and T. Fox in
Westminster Hall, 1684. Fcp. 4°   BPL
A few were done on large paper in quarto.
Heidmann *Berlin Publisher. See* Sh— Tam-
ing . . . 1864
Heigel (C. M.) *Editor. See* Sh— Macbeth,
1832
Heine (Heinrich) On Sh—: A translation of
his Notes on Sh— heroines by Ida
Benecke. Westminster : Constable, 1895.
Cr. 8°, pp. 190   BM | BPL | BUS | SML
Sh—'s maidens and women. Trans. by C.
G. Leland [In Heine's Works, vol. i., pp.
241-442]. Ln: Heinemann, 1891. Cr. 8°
BPL
Heinse (G. H.) *Zeiz Publisher. See* Sh— King
Lear, 1794
Heire (The). *See* May (Thomas)
Heliconia ; comprising a selection of English
poetry of the Elizabethan age, 1515-1604.
Ed. by Thomas Park. Ln: 1815. 3
vols. 4°   MPL
Contains a reprint of Allot's 'England's parnassus,' 1600.
Heliodorus. Æthiopian historie, written in
Greek . . . very wittie and pleasaunt.
Englished by Thomas Vnderdoune. Im-
printed at Ln. by Henrie Wykes for
Fraunces Coldocke dwelling in Powle's
Churche-yarde at the signe of the Greene
Dragon. [c. 1569.] Fcp. 4°
In 'Twelfth Night,' Act v., Sc. i., is a direct reference
to the lines found herein :—
  'Why should I not, had I the heart to do it,
  Like to the Egyptian thief at point of death,
  Kill what I love. . . .'

Hellstrom (S.) *Hudiksvall Publisher. See* Sh— Julius Cæsar, 1872

Helme (John) *Publisher. See* Sh— King John, 1611

Helms (G.) English adjective in . . . Sh—. *See* Sh— Works: Ext. 1868

Hemans (Felicia Dorothea) England and Spain, 1807

Bears the lines :—
' Is there no bard of heavenly power possess'd
To thrill, to rouse, to animate the breast,
Like Sh— o'er the sacred mind to sway,
And call each wayward passion to obey?'

Poems. 1808

At p. 48 is the poem 'Sh—,' written at the age of eleven. Her sister relates that when only six years old Mrs. Hemans had a passion for reading Sh—. The foregoing begins :—
' I love to rove o'er history's page,
Recall the hero and the sage.
. . . .
How sweet the native wood notes wild
Of him, the muses' favourite child ;
Of him, whose magic lays impart
Each various feeling to the heart.'

Heming's Players. *See* Tyson

Heminge *Actor* (John) To the great variety of readers [preface to Sh— [Works], 1623, 1632, 1663, 1664 1685]. F°

Heminge & Condell.] Walker (Charles Clement) John Heminge and Henry Condell . . . [*First Edition.* Privately printed : Lilleshall Hall, Salop.] 1896. Fcp. 4°, pp. 26, and plate of monument

This author built a monument at St. Mary's Church, Aldermanbury, London, in recognition of the two actors' labours as editors of the Jaggard folio. As they probably never edited a single line, this generous act appears to be a deed of well-meant but mistaken zeal.

] Walker (Charles Clement) John Heminge and Henry Condell : friends and fellow-actors of Sh— and what the world owes to them. [Second edition.] Privately printed, 1896. Fcp. 4°, pp. 26. With eight plates   BM | BPL | MPL | SML

Hemminge (William) Jewes' tragedy, or their fatal and final overthrow by Vespatian and Titus his son. Agreeable to . . . Josephus. Never before published. Ln : Printed for Matthew Inman and are to be sold by Richard Gammon over against Excester House in the Strand, 1662. Fcp. 4°

Contains a parody of Hamlet's soliloquy, p. 29.

Henderson (H. L.) *Editor. See* Sh— King Henry IV., ii., 1903

Henderson *Actor* (John) Letters and Poems. With anecdotes of his life by John Ireland. Ln : 1786. 8°. With frontispiece bearing portrait   BPL | w

Some of the letters are upon Shakespearean subjects.

Shakesperiana, selected from . . . 'Letters and Poems' . . . by John Ireland. Ln : 1786. 8°

Henderson.] Essay on the character of Hamlet, as performed by Mr. Henderson. [1777 ?] 8°   BM

] Harley (G. D.) Monody on the death of John Henderson. Norwich, 1787. 4°   BPL

Henderson (John) *Actor*—
See Pilon
,, Sh— Hamlet, 1779
,, Sh— Merry wives, 1778
,, Sh— Othello, 1788

Henderson (R.)] Arraignement of the whole creature at the barre of religion, reason, and experience. Ln : B. Alsop, 1631. With engraved title by M. Droeshout. 4°

Refers at p. 44 to Sh—'s ' wanton Venus with Adonis in the fable,' and other famous authors, as Bacon, Burton, Marlowe, Montaigne, Holinshed, Purchas, Sandys, Ralegh, Spenser.

Henderson *Printer* (William) Who wrote Sh— ? 'Aye, there's the rub' [Verses], with pen and ink sketches by C. Lyall. Ln : Stott, 1887. Fcp. 4°
       BM | BPL | BUS | SML

Henderson (W. A.) Hamlet and Elsinore [In 'Athenæum,' No. 4015, p. 491, Oct.] 1904

Henley (William Ernest) 'Graphic' gallery of Sh—'s heroines. *See* Sh— Works : Ext. 1888

Henley (W. E.) *Editor*—
See Sh— Othello, 1908
,, Sh— Works, 1901-04
,, Tudor translations

Henri IV. of France.] Order of ceremonies observed in the anointing and coronation of the most Christian French King and of Navarre, Henry IIII., celebrated in the City of Chartres, 27 Feb., 1594. Trans. by E. A—. Ln : J. Windet for J. Flasket [1594]. Fcp. 4°

Rheims, which should have witnessed the coronation, was possessed by the rebels. Henri IV. was therefore crowned at Chartres 'in the midst of his true subjects.' *See* 'Merchant of Venice,' Act iii., Sc. 2, where Sh— makes use of the incident :—
' . . . He may win,
And what is musick then ? Then musick is
Even as the flourish when true subjects bow
To a new crownèd monarch.'

Henrietta (*Queen*). *See* Dugdale

Henry II. *of England* (*King*). *See* Ireland

Henry IV. (*King*). *See* Sh— King Henry IV.

Henry V. Anonymous version of 1598, 1779, 1857, 1887, 1896, etc. *See* Sh— King Henry V.

Henry V. (*King*). *See* Sh— King Henry V.

'Henry V.' (*King*) as produced under the direction of C. Calvert at the Prince's Theatre, Manchester : Opinions of the Press. Manchester, 1872. 8°   BPL

Henry VI. (*King*). *See* Sh— King Henry VI.

Henry VII. (*King*) Almshouses, Westminster.
   See Stopes
Henry VIII.] Herbert of Cherbury (Edward
   Lord) Life of King Henry the Eighth.
   Ln : M. Clark for H. Herringman and are
   to be sold by T. Passenger at the Three
   Bibles on London Bridge, 1683. F°, pp.
   vi.-636-xvi.   SML
Henry VIII. (*King*)—
   See Accounts . . .
   ,, Sh— King Henry VIII.
   ,, *Stratford*] Muster
   ,, Tyson
'Henry VIII (*King*)' at the Lyceum Theatre
   [In 'Atalanta']. 1892. 8°   BPL
Henry (Eva M.) *Lady Macbeth* : An analysis
   [In the 'Scribbler's Herald,' 1889 ?]. 4°
                                                   BPL
Henslowe (Philip) Diary, from 1591 to 1609.
   Printed from the original MS. preserved
   at Dulwich College. Ed. by J. P. Collier.
   Ln : Sh— Soc., 1845. 8°, pp. xxxiv.-
   290   BPL | BUS | SML
   Diary. Facsimile by J. O. Halliwell. F°,
   pp. 109
   Diary and papers . . . Edited by W. W.
   Greg. Stratford-on-Avon : A. H. Bullen,
   1904-07. 3 vols. 8°   BPL
Henslowe (P.)—
   See Chettle
   ,, Greg
   ,, Sh— Sir John Oldcastle (*heading*)
Henty (W.) Sh— : Some notes on his early
   biography. *See* Sh—
Her Majesty's Theatre. *See* Ebers
Heraldry—
   See Arms   *See* Milles
   ,, Burke   ,, Rodwaye
   ,, Darbyshire   ,, Sawyer
   ,, Holme   ,, Segar
   ,, Lucy   ,, Visitation
Heraud (John Abraham) New view of Sh—'s
   Sonnets [In 'Temple Bar,' April]. Ln :
   1862. 8°   BUS
Sh— ; his inner life as intimated in his
   works. *See* Sh—
Herbert *of Cherbury* (Edward *Lord*). *See*
   Henry VIII.
Herbert (*Sir* Gerrard)] Copy of a letter of
   news written to Sir Dudley Carleton at
   the Hague in May, 1619, containing . . .
   account of the performance of 'Pericles'
   at the English Court [Ed. by J. O. Halli-
   well]. Ln : 1865. 16°
                        BM | BPL | HCL | MPL
   Issue restricted to ten copies of the twenty-five printed.
Herbert-Fitton theory. *See* Tyler
Here and there in England. *See* Dick

Herford (C. H.) Notes on Sh—'s predecessors,
   with special reference to 'Hamlet.'
   [Und.] 4°   BPL
   Studies in the literary relations of England
   and Germany. Cambridge : Univ. Press,
   1886. 8°   BPL | SML
   Study of Sh— : Some hints. [Und.,
   1890 ?] 8°   BPL
   Suggestions on Greene's romances and Sh—.
   Ln : New Sh— Soc., 1887-92. 8°
Herford (C. H.) *Editor*—
   See Sh— All's well, 1900
   ,, Sh— Antony, 1900
   ,, Sh— As you like it, 1900
   ,, Sh— Comedy of errors, 1900
   ,, Sh— Coriolanus, 1900
   ,, Sh— Cymbeline, 1900
   ,, Sh— Hamlet, 1900
   ,, Sh— Julius Cæsar, 1900
   ,, Sh— King Henry IV., i., 1900
   ,, Sh— King Henry IV., ii., 1900
   ,, Sh— King Henry V., 1900
   ,, Sh— King Henry VI., i., 1900
   ,, Sh— King Henry VI., ii., 1900
   ,, Sh— King Henry VI., iii., 1900
   ,, Sh— King Henry VIII., 1900
   ,, Sh— King John, 1900
   ,, Sh— King Lear, 1900
   ,, Sh— King Richard II., 1893, 1895-96,
        1900
   ,, Sh— King Richard III., 1900
   ,, Sh— Love's labours lost, 1900
   ,, Sh— Macbeth, 1900
   ,, Sh— Measure . . . 1900
   ,, Sh— Merchant . . . 1900
   ,, Sh— Merry wives, 1900
   ,, Sh— Midsummer . . . 1900
   ,, Sh— Much ado, 1900
   ,, Sh— Othello, 1900
   ,, Sh— Pericles, 1900
   ,, Sh— Rape, 1900
   ,, Sh— Romeo . . . 1900
   ,, Sh— Sonnets, 1900
   ,, Sh— Taming . . . 1900
   ,, Sh— The tempest, 1900
   ,, Sh— Timon . . . 1900
   ,, Sh— Titus, 1900
   ,, Sh— Troilus, 1900
   ,, Sh— Twelfth night, 1900
   ,, Sh— Two gentlemen, 1900
   ,, Sh— Two noble kinsmen, 1897
   ,, Sh— Venus . . . 1900
   ,, Sh— Winter's tale, 1900
   ,, Sh— Works, 1893-98, 1899, 1900
Herford (C. H.) & Widgery (W. H.) First
   quarto edition of 'Hamlet, 1603': Two
   essays to which the Harness prize was
   awarded. Ln : 1880. 8°
                        BM | BPL | BUS | MPL

Hermeticall banquet drest by a spagiricall cook for the better preservation of the microcosme. Ln: Printed for Andrew Crooke, 1652. Cr. 8°   w

On p. 35 says: 'Poeta . . . prefers all her poor kindred to severall places in the Court. Ovid she makes a major-domo; Homer (because a merry Greek), master of the wine-cellars; Sh—, butler; Ben Johnson, clark of the kitchin; Fenner, his turn-spit; and Taylor, his scullion.'
An odd mixture of alchemy and cookery.

Hernon (J.) The query 'Was Hamlet mad?' fully answered in original and critical observations on Sh—'s 'Hamlet.' Exeter, 1864. 8°   BM | BPL

Heroines of Sh—
See Heath (C.)
,, Sh—] Sh—'s heroes

'Heron (Robert)' pseud. See Pinkerton

Herondo (F.) World's argument, or justice and the stage. Ln: Sedwyn Pub. Co., 1887. Fcp. 4°, pp. 150
Refers to 'Twelfth night,' pp. 100-101, and the 'Merry devil of Edmonton,' p. 99.

Herr (J. G.) Scattered notes on the text of Sh—. Philadelphia: W. C. Wilson, 1879. 12°, pp. 146   BPL | BUS

Herrick (Robert) Fairy poems. See Sh— Midsummer . . . 1886

Select musicall ayres. See Sh— Works: Ext. 1653

Herrick (R.) See Hesperides . . .

Herrig (Ludwig) Editor—
See Sh— Macbeth, 1853
,, Sh— Merchant . . . 1854, 1870, 1878

Herringman (Hy.) Publisher—
See Caryll
,, Dryden
,, Fane
,, Henry VIII.
,, Newcastle
,, Sh— Antony, 1678 et seq.
,, Sh— Hamlet, 1676, 1683, 1695
,, Sh— Macbeth, 1687, 1689, 1695
,, Sh— The tempest, 1670, 1674, 1676, 1690, 1695
,, Sh— Timon . . . 1678, 1688, 1696, 1703
,, Sh— Works, 1685

Herringman jun. (H.) Printer. See Sh— Julius Cæsar, 1680, 1684, 1691, 1695

Hersee (Henry) Editor. See Sh— Merry wives, 1875

Hertford (Marquis of). See Plumptre

Hesperides or the muses' garden [by Robert Herrick?], 2pp. Catalogue of the bookes from whence these collections were made, 6pp. [Original manuscript on four leaves of paper, c. 1645]. Oblong 4°   w
Extracted from some early seventeenth century commonplace book. The catalogue embraces Sh—'s plays among others.

Hessey Publisher. See Taylor & Hessey

Hetherington (J. Newby) Sh—'s fools [In 'Cornhill Mag.,' Dec.] Ln: 1879. 8°   BUS

Heussi (J.) Editor—
See Sh— Hamlet, 1868
,, Sh— Romeo . . . 1853

Hewis (J.) Survey of the English tongue taken according to the use and analogie of the Latine. Ln: Young, 1632. 12°   SML

Hewlett (Henry G.) Sheaf of verse. Ln: H. S. King & Co., 1877. 8°, pp. viii.-142
At p. 79 occurs the poem 'Sh—'s curse.'

Heyes (Thomas) Publisher. See Hayes

Heylyn (Peter) Historie of the most famous souldier Saint George, asserted from the fictions . . . Ln: T. Harper, 1633. Fcp. 4°
At p. 344 occurs 'Sir John Fastolfe . . . was a wise and valiant captaine. However, on the stage they have been pleased to make merry with him.'

Heywood (A.) Guide . . . See Wall

Heywood (John) Ballad of the green willow; the same burden as the song of 'The willow' in 'Othello' [Ed. by J. O. Halliwell]. See Sh—] Sh— Soc.

Miscellanies. See Redford

Skeltonical song. See Sh—] Sh— Soc.

Heywood (T.) Artist. See Sh— Venus . . . 1847

Heywood (Thomas) Actors' vindication. Ln: Printed by G. E—— for W. C—— [1655]. Fcp. 4°, sig. A—G4.   CTC
The publisher was William Cartwright, actor and bookseller.

Apology for actors, containing three briefe treatises: I., their antiquity; II., their ancient dignity; III., true use of their quality. Ln: Printed by Nicholas Okes, 1612. Fcp. 4°, sig. A—G4, unpaged   CTC
In this tome is to be found the supposed brief conversation with Sh—, the only fragment known, if genuine, of his personal opinion on any subject, if one excepts his dedications, his will, and his tombstone. Yet upon such insecure foundation a few reputed Shakespearean authorities, headed by the forger John Payne Collier (who afterwards withdrew his imputations), have built up an extraordinary tissue of slander and falsehood. Their allegations are remarkable for presumption rather than for judgment, justice, or knowledge, and recoil upon such writers with boomerang effect.

Apology for actors . . . from the edition of 1612, compared with that of W. Cartwright. With introd. and notes [by J. P. Collier]. See Sh—] Sh— Soc.

Fair maid of the Exchange. Ln: 1607. Fcp. 4°
Quotes stanzas iii. and xxxix. of 'Venus and Adonis.'

Fair maid of the exchange. Ed. by Barron Field. Ln: Sh— Soc., 1845-46. 8°, pp. x.-xii.-100   BUS | SML

Fair maid of the west, or a girl worth gold: First and second parts. With introd. and notes by J. P. Collier. Ln: Sh— Soc., 1850. 8°, pp. xii.-182   BUS

(149)

Heywood (Thomas) Golden . . . [and] Silver
age. With introd. and notes by J. P.
Collier. Ln: Sh— Soc., 1851. 8°, pp.
vi.-180-14   BUS
Hierarchie of the blessed angells: their
names, orders, and offices . . . Ln:
Printed by Adam Islip, 1635. F°. Illus-
trated by Marshall, Droeshout, and others
Contains the passage descriptive of the early dramatists:
' Our modern poets to that passe are driven
Those names are curtailed which they first had given
And as we wish to have their memories drowned
We scarcely can afford them halfe their sound.
Greene who had in both academies tane [taken]
Degree of Master, yet could never gaine
· To be called more than Robin : who had he
Profest ought, saved the muse, served and been free
With credit too, gone Robert to his grave.
Marlo, renowned for his rare art and wit
Could ne're attain beyond the name of Kit
Altho' his " Hero and Leander " did
Merit addition rather. Famous Kidd
Was called but Tom. Tom Watson (tho' he wrote
Able to make Apollo's selfe to dote
Upon his muse) for all that he could strive
Yet never could to his full name arrive.
Tom Nash, in his time of no small esteeme,
Could not a second syllable redeeme
Excellent Bewmont, in the foremost ranke
Of the rarest wits, was never more than Frank.
Mellifluous Sh— whose inchanting quill
Commanded mirth or passion, was but Will.
And famous Jonson though his learned pen
Be dipt in Castaly, is still but Ben.
Fletcher and Webster of that learned packe
None of the meanest, yet neither was but Jacke.
Decker is but Tom, nor May, nor Middleton
And he's but now Jacke Foord that once were John.
Nor speake I this that any here exprest
Should think themselves lesse worthy than the rest
Whose names have their full syllable and sound.
Or that Franke, Kit, or Jacke are the least wound
Unto their fame and merit. I for my part
(Thinke others what they please) accept that heart
Which courts my love in most familiar phraze.
And think it takes not from my pains or praise
If any one to me so bluntly come
I hold he loves me best that calls me Tom.'
Hierarchie . . . See Sh—] Sh—ana
[If you know not me, you know nobodie :
Two parts] Two historical plays on the
life of Q. Elizabeth. With introd. and
notes by J. P. Collier. Ln: Sh— Soc.,
1851. 8°, pp. xxviii.-178   BUS
King Edward IV.: First and second parts
. . . With introd. and notes by B. Field.
Ln: Sh—Soc., 1842. 8°, pp. x.-202 BUS
Merry devil of Edmonton. See Sh— Merry
devil . . . (heading)
Pleasant dialogves and drammas, selected
ovt of Lucian, Erasmus, Textor, Ovid,
&c. . . . Ln: Printed by R. O—— for R.
H—— and sold by T. Slater, 1637. 8° w
Contains verses on an actor in the part of ' King
Richard III.'
Poems. See Sh— Poems, 1640
Royal king and loyal subject [&] A woman
killed with kindness : Two plays. With
introd. and notes by J. P. Collier. Ln:
Sh— Soc., 1850. 8°, pp. x.-168   BUS

Heywood (Thomas)—
See Anderson
„ Annalia Dubrensia
„ Sh— Passionate . . . 1612
Heywood (Thomas) Editor—
See Lidgate
„ Marlowe
Heywood (T.) & Rowley (Wm.) Fortune by
land and sea. Ed. by B. Field. See Sh—]
Sh— Soc.
Hiatt (Charles T. J.) Dramatic impressions :
The new ' Hamlet ' [In ' World-Litera-
ture']. 1892. 8°   BPL
Ellen Terry. See Terry
Hibbert (J.) Monumenta . . . [c. 1902]. 8° BPL
Refers to ' Romeo and Juliet,' pp. 88-90.
Allusions throughout the plays to fate and metaphysical
aid, pp. 307-343.
Hickock (Thomas) Editor. See Frederick
Hickson (Samuel) Shares of Sh— and Fletcher
in the ' Two noble kinsmen.' With con-
firmation by F. G. Fleay. Ln: New Sh—
Soc., 1874. 8°   BUS
The 'Two noble kinsmen' [In 'Westminster
and Foreign Quarterly Review,' April].
Ln: 1847. 8°   BUS
Hiestand (Sarah Willard) Editor—
See Sh— Comedy of errors, 1901
„ Sh— Midsummer . . . 1900
„ Sh— The tempest, 1900
„ Sh— Winter's tale, 1901
Hiffernan MD. (Paul) Dramatic genius : An
essay. Ln: [Privately] Printed for the
author, 1772. 4°   BUS
Delineates the ' Plan of a permanent temple to be
erected to the memory of Sh—, in classical taste,
with inscriptions and decorations suitable to the
objects chosen.'
Dramatic genius. Second ed. Ln: 1772.
8°   BUS
Higgins. Queen Cordila, 1843. See Sh—]
Sh—'s library
Illustrates ' King Lear.'
Higgins (Charles H.) Who wrote the plays
ascribed to Sh— ? Leicester: Clarke &
Hodgson, 1886. 8°, pp. 54   BPL
Higgins (John). See Mirrour . . .
Higgs of Colesbourne (Thomas & Mary). See
Sh—] Malone
Hill Edinburgh Publisher. See Jackson
Hill (Aaron) Editor. See Sh— King Henry
V., 1723, 1746, 1759, 1760, 1765
Hill (Joseph) Bookmakers of old Birmingham ;
authors, printers, and book sellers.
Birmingham : Cornish Brothers, 1907.
4°, pp. 128. Illustrated   BPL | SML
Issue limited to 275 copies, numbered and signed.
Sh—'s birthplace and adjoining properties.
Stratford-upon-Avon, 1885. 12°. With
plate   BPL | BUS
Hill (Joseph) Editor. See Burgess

Hillard (Kate) On the study of Sh—'s sonnets [In 'Lippincott's Mag.,' April]. Philadelphia, 1873. 8° BUS
Hilliard & Gray *Boston [U.S.] Publishers. See* Sh— Works, 1836, 1841
Hills (H.) *Printer & Publisher*—
See Dryden
  „ Long vacation
  „ Sh— King Lear, 1699
  „ Sh— Timon . . . 1700
  „ Ward (E.)
Hilton (Wm.) *Artist*—
See Sh— As you like it, 1840
  „ Sh— Works, 1829
Hinchcliffe (W.) *Publisher. See* Sh— Taming . . . 1716, 1786
Hind *Editor. See* Sh— Macbeth, 1839
Hindmarsh (H.) *Publisher. See* Collier (Jeremy)
Hindmarsh (J.) *Publisher*—
See Mountfort
  „ Sh— Titus . . . 1687
  „ Sheffield
Hindmarsh (John) *Publisher. See* Buckingham
Hindmarsh (Joseph) *Publisher*—
See Durfey
  „ Otway
  „ Sh— Coriolanus, 1682
Hindmarsh (J. O.) *Printer. See* Harris (Joseph)
Hingeston (Francis Charles) *Editor. See* Capgrave
Hingeston (Wm.) *Publisher*
See Sh— Timon . . . 1768
  „ Sh— Works, 1773
Hingray (C.) *Paris Publisher. See* Sh— Coriolanus, 1845
Hinton (Henry L.) *Editor*—
See Sh— King Richard III., 1868, 1878
  „ Sh— Macbeth, 1868
  „ Sh— Merchant . . . 1867, 1868
  „ Sh— Much ado, 1871
  „ Sh— Othello, 1869, 1870
  „ Sh— Romeo . . . 1868, 1870
  „ Sh— Taming . . . 1876
Hinton (John) *Publisher*—
See Sh— Macbeth, 1770
  „ Sh— Timon . . . 1770
  „ Sh— Works, 1773
  „ Sh— Universal . . .
Hints respecting the character of Hamlet [In 'Literary and Statistical Mag.,' Feb.] Edin., 1819. 8° BUS
Hirst (S.) Celebration of Sh—'s natal day: An address. Huddersfield, 1884. 8° BPL
Old and new lines in the life of Wm. Sh—. *See* Sh—
See Elsheimer
His secret is revealed. *See* Donnelly
Historia histrionica: Historical account of the English stage, in a dialogue of plays and players. Ln: 1699. 8° W

Historia histrionica, 1699. Reprinted by E. W. Ashbee, 1872. Fcp. 4° BPL | MPL | W
Historian's pocket dictionary . . . Ln: J. Murray, 32 Fleet St. and G. & T. Wilkie, 71 St. Paul's Churchyard [c. 1770]. 12°, pp. viii.-352
Sh—, p. 342.
Historic doubt respecting Sh—. *See* Schmucker
Historical dramas of Sh— illustrated. *See* Harding
Historical memoir on Italian tragedy [containing an account of an old Italian play bearing a resemblance to 'Romeo and Juliet']. Ln: 1799. Fcp. 4° W
Historie of the gentle craft. *See* Deloney
Historie of the uniting of the kingdom of Portugall to the Crowne of Castill . . . Ln: Imprinted by Arn. Hatfield for Edward Blount, 1600. Fcp. 4°
Dedicated to Sh—'s patron 'Henry Earle of Southampton.'
History and fall of Caius Marius. *See* Otway (T.)
History of Jacob and his twelve sonnes. *See* Reprints
History of *Portia.* Written by a lady. Ln: R. Withy, 1759. 2 vols. 8°
Illustrates the 'Merchant of Venice.'
History of *Prospero*, Duke of Milan. Trans. from the French original. Gloucester [1750?] 12° BPL
Illustrates 'The Tempest.'
History of the Sh— Memorial. *See* Flower (C. E.)
History of the stage, with the theatrical characters of celebrated actors, and life of Colley Cibber. Ln: Miller, 1742. 8° SML
History of the theatres. *See* Victor (B.)
Histrionic topography, or the birthplaces, residences, and funeral monuments of the most distinguished actors. Ln: 1818. 8°. Plates by H. S. Storer
'Histrionicus (A. S.)' *pseud.* Answer to Mr. Pope's preface to Sh— . . . Some memoirs of Sh— and stage-history of his time are inserted. Ln: 1729. 8° BM
Hitch (C.) *Publisher*—
See Sh— All's well, 1756
  „ Sh— Hamlet, 1759
  „ Sh— King Henry IV., i., 1763
  „ Sh— King Henry VIII., 1762
  „ Sh— King Lear, 1756, 1759, 1760, 1763
  „ Sh— Macbeth, 1750
  „ Sh— Merry wives, 1756
  „ Sh— Othello, 1750
  „ Sh— The tempest, 1761
  „ Sh— Works, 1733, 1740, 1745, 1747, 1757, 1760, 1762

Hitchcock (Ethan Allan)] Remarks on the 'Sonnets' of Sh—. New York, 1865. 8° BPL

Hitchcock (E. A.) *Editor.* See Sh— Sonnets, 1865, 1867

Hitchcock (Robert) Historical view of the Irish stage from the earliest period . . . interspersed with anecdotes of Irish dramatic authors and actors. Dublin: R. Marchbank & W. Folds, 1788-94. 2 vols. 12° SML
Many references to Sh—.

Hoadly (John). *See Sh*— Arden, 1763

Hoare (Prince) On the moral fame of authors, and moral character of Sh—'s dramas [In ' Roy. Soc. of Literature; Trans. Vol. 2, pp. 290-303]. Ln: 1834. 8° BPL | BUS

Hobbes (Thomas) Leviathan. *See* Lucy

Hobbes *Solicitor* (W. J.) *See* Stratford: New Place

Hoby (C.) *Publisher.* See Sh— Works, 1845, 1851

Hoby (G.) *Publisher.* See Sh— Works, 1862

Hoby (James) *Dublin Publisher.* See Sh— King Lear, 1768

Hodges (J.) *Publisher*—
See Sh— Macbeth, 1750
„ Sh— Works, 1757

Hodgets (John) *Publisher*—
See Barnefield
„ Decker & Webster

Hodgkin (T.) *Printer.* See Cooke

Hodgkinsonne (Elizabeth) *Printer.* See Sh— Venus . . . 1675

Hodgkinsonne (R.) *Publisher. See* Brathwaite

Hodgson *Editor. See* Malam

Hodgson *Publisher. See* Sh— Romeo . . . 1823

Hodgson (*Sir* Arthur) Clopton and the Cloptons. Leamington, 1892. 8° BPL
Sh— jottings collated in a lecture delivered . . . in the Stoneleigh Institute, Warwickshire . . . Ln: Printed for private circulation at the Chiswick Press, 1902. 8°, pp. 32. With 6 process plates SML

Hodgson (J.) *Editor.* See Sh— King John, 1825

Hodgson (T.) *Publisher. See* Sh— Works, 1853, 1854-56, 1855-56

Hodson *Burton-on-Trent Publisher. See* Sh— Works, 1768

Hoe (W.) Sh— treasury of subject quotations. *See* Sh— Works: Ext. 1862, 1863

Hoehnen (A.) Sh—'s ' Passionate pilgrim '; Inaugural dissertation. 1867. 8° BM

Hoffa (*Dr.* J.) *Editor*—
See Sh— Hamlet, 1845
„ Sh— Julius Cæsar, 1848
„ Sh— Romeo . . . 1845

Hoffman. *See* Chettle (N.)

Hoffman (Alice Spencer) *Editor*—
See Sh— As you like it, 1904
„ Sh— Hamlet, 1905
„ Sh— Julius Cæsar, 1905
„ Sh— King Henry V., 1904
„ Sh— King John, 1905
„ Sh— King Lear, 1905
„ Sh— King Richard II., 1904
„ Sh— Macbeth, 1905
„ Sh— Merchant . . . 1904
„ Sh— Midsummer . . . 1904
„ Sh— Romeo . . . 1906
„ Sh— The tempest, 1904

Hofmann *Artist. See* Sh— Works: Ext. 1876

Hogarth (William) Sh— chair [Print, engraved by J. I——]. Ln: S. Ireland, 1 May, 1799 BUS
An engraving of a chair carved by Hogarth.

Hogben (John) Master passages. *See* Sh— Works: Ext. 1905

Hogg (James) Songs by the Ettrick Shepherd, now first collected. 1831
At p. 304 is a poem ' To the genius of Sh—,' commencing—
'Spirit all limitless
Where is thy dwelling place
Spirit of him whose high name we revere
Come on thy seraph wings
Come from thy wanderings
And smile on thy votaries, who sigh for thee here.'

Holbrook (Ann C.) The dramatist, or memoirs of the stage. 1809. 12° BPL

Holcroft (Thomas) Theatrical recorder. 1805-06. 2 vols. 8°. With coloured portraits and plates BPL
Contains Shakespeareana. The B. P. L. copy is imperfect.

Holder (H. W.) Marriage of Wm. Sh—. *See* Sh—

Hole (Richard)] On literary fame and the historical characters of Sh—: An apology for the character . . . of Iago . . . for Shylock [In ' Essays by a society of gentlemen at Exeter']. Ln: 1796. 8° BUS

Hole (W.) *Artist-Engraver. See* Drayton

Holford (Samuel) *Publisher. See* Marguetel

Holinshed (Raphael) Chronicles . . . Ln: John Harrison, 1577. 2 vols. F° BPL | BUS
One of the sources from which Sh— derived the incidents of ' King Lear,' ' Macbeth,' and ' K. Henry VIII.'

Chronicles . . . Ed. by J. Hooker & A. Fleming. Ln: Harrison & Bishop, 1586-87. 3 vols. F° BM
Known as the ' Sh— edition.'

Chronicles—
See Sh— King Edward III., 1596
„ Sh— King Richard II., 1870

History of Lear. *See Sh*—] Sh—'s library
A foundation of ' King Lear.'

History of Macbeth, 1843. *See Sh*—] Sh—'s library

Holinshed (Raphael) Passages. *See Sh*—]
Sh—'s library
A foundation of 'King Henry VIII.'
Sh—'s Holinshed : The 'Chronicle' and the
'Historical plays' compared, by W. G.
Boswell-Stone. Ln : 1896. 4°, pp. xxiv.-
532   BM | BPL
Sh—'s Holinshed . . . by W. G. Boswell-
Stone. New York, 1896. 4°   BUS
Sh—'s Holinshed . . . by W. G. Boswell-
Stone. New ed. Ln : Chatto, 1907.
Roy. 8°, pp. 554
Holinshed (Ralph)—
See Henderson
   „ Pell
Holl (H.)] 'Our Club' : Sh— night, April 26,
1881. Birmingham, 1881. 12°   BPL
Holland—
See Cohn
   „ Herbert
Holland (Elihu G.) Sh—'s caricature of King
Richard III. [In 'Continental Monthly,'
Sept.] New York, 1862. 8°   BUS
Holland (F. M.) Sh—'s unbelief [Rep. from
'The Index']. Boston, U.S., 1884. 4°
                                       BPL
Holland (Frederick West) Essay . . . *See* New
England . . .
Study of Sh— [In ' New England Historic
Soc. Tercentenary Celebration']. 1864.
8°, pp. 72   BUS
Holland (Henricus)] Herwologia Anglica . . .
Arnheim : Pass et Jansonii, 1620. F°
Valuable and curious as being the earliest series of
engraved English portraits, chiefly of Sh—'s con-
temporaries.
Holland (Henry) *Publisher. See* Davies (John)
Holland (Hugh) Pancharis, 1603. *See* Reprints
Upon the lines and life of the famous scenick
poet, Master Wm. Sh— [In Sh— [Works]
1623]. F°
Commendatory sonnet, thus :—
'Those hands which you so clapt go now and wring
You Britain's brave, for done are Sh—'s days
His days are done that made the dainty plays.

       .   .   .   .   .

For though his line of life went soon about
The life yet of his lines shall never out.'
Reprinted in Sh—'s Works, 1632, 1663, 1664, 1685
Holland *Canon* (H. Scott) Preface. *See* Hol-
land (L. G.)
Holland (Laurence Gifford) Some essays and
lectures [chiefly upon Sh—], with preface
by Canon H. S. Holland. Ln : Privately
printed, 1893. 8°, pp. 218 and map SML
Holland (Philemon) *Editor*—
See Livius
   „ Suetonius

Holland (Samuel) Wit and fancy in a maze,
or the incomparable champion of love
and beauty. Ln : T. W—— for Thomas
Vere, 1656. 8°
On p. 102 Sh— and other dramatists are cited, whilst
'Venus and Adonis' is introduced as a masque at
pp. 153-164.
This volume appeared in the same year under the title
of 'Don Zaro del Fogo: A mock romance,' and in
1660 as 'Romancio-mastix.'
Hollingshead (John) My lifetime. 1895. 2
vols. Cr. 8°. With portrait
Contains reminiscences of Shakespearean performances.
Plain English. Ln : Chatto, 1880. Cr. 8°,
pp. viii.-192
Much information on stage life.
Holme (Randle) Academy of armory, or a
storehouse of armory and blazon.
Chester, 1688. F°
Illustrates 'As you like it,' 'Measure for measure,'
'Much ado,' 'Taming of the shrew,' and the
'Winter's tale.'
'A heterogeneous and extraordinary composition, con-
taining a vast fund of curious information.'—*Lowndes*.
An 'Index of names' was published in 1821 (thin f°,
pp. 46), of which only fifty copies were struck off,
and in consequence is rarer than the work itself.
Academy of armory . . . Ln : Printed and
sold by the Booksellers, 1701. F°   BM
Holmes. *See* Rolfe (W. J.)
Holmes (Nathaniel) Authorship of Sh—. New
York : Hurd & Houghton, 1866. 8°, pp.
xvi.-602 and portrait of Bacon
                               BM | BUS | MPL
Authorship of Sh—. Second edition. New
York : Hurd & Houghton, 1867. 8°, pp.
xvi.-602   BM | BPL | BUS
Authorship of Sh— . . . Third edition.
With an appendix of additional matters,
including a notice of the recently-
discovered Northumberland MSS. New
York, Hurd & Houghton ; Boston, H. O.
Houghton & Co. ; Cambridge, Riverside
Press, 1875. Cr. 8°, pp. xvi.-696 and
portrait of Bacon   BM | BPL | BUS
Authorship of Sh—. Third edition . . .
New York : Hurd & Houghton . . . 1876.
Cr. 8°, pp. xvi.-696 and portrait of Bacon
Authorship of Sh—. Fourth edition. Bos-
ton : Houghton, 1882. 8°   SML
Authorship of Sh—. New and enlarged
edition. With appendix. Boston and
New York, 1886. 2 vols. 8°
                           BM | BPL | BUS | SML
Authorship of Sh—. With appendix. Bos-
ton [U.S.], 1887. 2 vols. 12°. With por-
trait   BUS
Holmes (*Dr.* Oliver Wendell) One hundred
days in Europe. Ln : Low, 1887. Cr. 8°,
pp. iv.-316
'Stratford-on-Avon' occupies pp. 134-149.

Holmes (*Dr.* Oliver Wendell) Songs of many seasons. 1875
Contains poem called the 'Sh— tercentennial celebration, 23 April, 1864,' from which these two verses are culled :—
'O land of Sh—! ours with all thy past
Till these last years that make the sea so wide
Think not the jar of battle's trumpet-blast
Has dulled our aching sense to joyous pride
In every noble word thy sons bequeathed
The air our fathers breathed.
. . . .
This player was a prophet from on high
Thine own elected. Statesman, poet, sage,
For him thy sovereign pleasure passed them by
Sidney's fair youth, and Ralegh's ripened age
Spenser's chaste soul, and his imperial mind
Who taught and shamed mankind.'

'Holmesworthe (Leonard)' *pseud. See* Hancock (L.)

Holt (John)] Attempte to rescue that aunciente English poet and play-wrighte, Maister Wme. Sh— from the maney errours faulsely charged on him by certaine new-fangled wittes and to let him speak for himself, as right well he wotteth, when freede from the many careless mistakeings of the heedless first imprinters of his workes. By a gentleman formerly of Greys-Inn. Ln : Privately printed by Manby & Cox, 1749. 8°, pp. 94   BM | BPL | BUS | W
Republished in 1750 under the title of ' Remarks on " The tempest." '

] Remarks on ' The tempest,' or an attempt to rescue Sh— from the many errors falsely charged on him by his several editors. To which is prefixed a short account of the story, plot, disposition, and chronology of the play, as a plan for a new edition of that author. Ln : Manby & Cox, 1750. 8°, pp. ii.-94
BM | BPL | BUS | MPL | W

Holy Trinity Church. *See* Stratford-on-Avon

Holzer (Gustavus) Sh—'s ' Tempest ' in Baconian light ; a new theory. Heidelberg, 1904   BUS
With facsimile frontispiece of Bacon's ' Instauratio magna, 1620.'

Home *Lord Kames* (Henry) Elements of criticism. Edin., 1788. 8°   BUS
The literary illustrations drawn chiefly from Sh—.

Homer—
See Dibdin (T.)   See Hunt (J. H. L.)
  „ Hallam   „ Melodrama
  „ Hermeticall . . . „ Sh—] Downes

Homes and haunts of Sh—. *See Sh*—] Homes
Homes of Sh—. *See* Sh—] Homes . . .
Hone (William) Ancient mysteries described, especially the English miracle plays. Ln : M'Creery, 1823. 8°   BPL | SML
Hone (W.) *See* Theatrical house . . .
Hood *Publisher. See* Vernor & Hood

Hood (E. P.) Sermons from Sh— [Rep. from the 'Christian Globe']. 1877. F° BPL
Hood *1799-1845* (Thomas) Plea of the midsummer fairies 1827.
At p. 53 says of Sh— :
'. . . . . An immortal man
Nature's chief darling and illustrious mate
Destined to foil old death's oblivious plan
And shine untarnished by the fogs of fate
Time's famous rival till the final date ! '

Hook (Theodore) French stage and French people, as illustrated in the memoirs of M. Fleury. Ln : Colburn, 1841. 2 vols. 8°   SML
Hooke (J.) *Publisher*—
See Sh— Poems, 1725, 1728
  „ Sh— Works, 1725
Hookham *Publisher. See* Ritson
Hookham (E. T.) *Publisher. See* Sh— Romeo . . . 1812
Hookham (T.) *Publisher. See* Kemble
Hookham *jun.* (T.) *Publisher. See* Sh— Romeo . . . 1812
Hoole (Charles) *Editor. See* Comenius
Hooper (S.) *Publisher. See* Jordan
Hope (Alexander J. B.) Sh— and Aristophanes [In 'Essays,' pp. 143-160]. Ln : 1844. 8°   BPL | BUS
Hope (T.) *Publisher. See* Sh— Love's labours lost, 1762
Hopkins (   ) *Editor & Prompter*—
See Sh— All's well, 1773
  „ Sh— As you like it, 1773
  „ Sh— Coriolanus, 1773
  „ Sh— Cymbeline, 1773
  „ Sh— King John, 1773
  „ Sh— King Lear, 1774
  „ Sh— Macbeth, 1773
  „ Sh— Merchant . . . 1773
  „ Sh— Merry wives, 1773
  „ Sh— Othello, 1773
  „ Sh— Timon . . . 1773
  „ Sh— Twelfth night, 1773, 1774

Hopkinson (A. F.) Essays on Sh—'s doubtful plays. Ln : Sims, 1900. 8° BPL | SML
Hopkinson (A. F.) *Editor*—
See Sh— Arden, 1898
  „ Sh— Birth . . . 1901
  „ Sh— King Henry V., 1896
  „ Sh— King Henry VI., ii.-iii., 1897
  „ Sh— King John, 1896
  „ Sh— King Richard III., 1901
  „ Sh— Sir Thomas More, 1902
  „ Sh— Works, 1890-95

Hopper (Clarence) Account of churchwardens' presentments, etc., appertaining to Stratford-upon-Avon. Edited by J. O. Halliwell. 1867. 8°   BPL

Hopper (Clarence)] Catalogue of the books, manuscripts, . . . works of art, antiquities, and relics, illustrative of the life and works of Sh— and Stratford-upon-Avon . . . which are preserved in the Sh— Library and Museum in Henley Street. Edited by J. O. Halliwell. Ln: J. E. Adlard, 1868. 8°, pp. 184
BM | BPL | BUS | CPL | MPL | SBL | SML
Published on behalf of the Sh— fund.

Hoppin (James Mason) Reading of Sh—, Part I. New Haven [U.S.] 1904. 8°   BUS

Reading of Sh—, Part I. Boston, U.S., 1906. 8°   BPL

Hopton (Arthur) Concordancy of yeares, containing a new, easie, and most exact computation of time according to the English account. Also the vse of the English and Roman Kalendar, with briefe notes, rules and tables as well mathematicall and legal as vulgar for each man's private occasion . . . Ln : Printed for the Company of Stationers, 1612. 8°. Reprinted in 1615

Horatian canons of friendship, with two dedications ; the first to that admirable critic, the Rev. Mr. W. Warburton, occasioned by his ' Dunciad ' and his ' Sh—,' and the second to my good friend the trunk maker at the corner of St. Paul's Church Yard. By Ebenezer Pentweazle. Ln : J. Newbery, 1750. 4°, pp. xii.-20
BUS

Horestes : An interlude, 1567. *See* Reprints

Horn (C. E.) *Composer—*
See Sh— As you like it, 1860
,, Sh— Merry wives, 1824
,, Sh— Midsummer . . . 1860
,, Sh— Poems, 1862

Horn-book [containing the alphabet and our Lord's prayer. Ln : *sans* printer or place, c. 1590]   W
8º : black letter broadside, framed in old oak of the period, faced with a thin translucent sheet of horn : the bottom portion of the frame carved into a handle, after the manner of hand mirrors.
The horn-book thus referred to in Act v., Sc. 1 of ' Love's labours lost ' : ' Yes, yes ; he teaches boys the horn-book,' was the first and most elementary primer for infants in Sh—'s day.
An account of this example will be found in Halliwell's ' Sh— reliques,' 1852, p. 131.
An interesting illustrated history of horn-books has been written by A. W. Tuer.
Some account of them is also to be found in W. Andrews' ' Byegone England,' 1892, pp. 157-162, with an engraving of one.

] Most easie instruction for reading, specially penned for the good of those who are come to yeares, by S. W. A——. [Ln : *sans* title, place, printer, and date, but c. 1590.] 8°, 2 ll.

Hornby (Mary) Battle of Waterloo : A tragedy. Stratford-upon-Avon, 1819. 8°
BPL
' Written in the room which gave birth to my great predecessor, the immortal Sh—.'—*Preface.*
Miss Hawkins in her ' Anecdotes' thus describes her :—
' This Mrs. Hornby, a very decent nurse-like woman in her exterior, appears very singular in mind. She writes and prints plays and verses of her own composition. From the newspapers she made a tragedy of the "Battle of Waterloo," the queerest thing imaginable. . . . Her innocent conceit is the most curious circumstance of her character. Says she has written some beautiful verses on the comet, but not satisfied with them has turned them into a play and made Sh— the comet. She writes a fair hand, and in her style of speaking there is no predominant vulgarity ; nothing to distinguish her from her own class. In speaking she always called me "lady," and began the sentence "Lady, I can show you . . ." She spoke of seeing Sh—'s plays, but with no discrimination. Speaking of her children she called them "the little Shakespeares." '

Broken vow : A comedy. Mostly founded on fact. Stratford-upon-Avon : W. Barnacle, 1820. 8°, pp. 100   W
' Written in the house of Sh—'s birth, July, 1820.'
The writer was tenant and show-woman of the birthhouse for many years. Her literary ambition soared above her power of fulfilment.

History of the bard and family—
See Extemporal verses
,, Extemporary verses

Hornby (M.) *Editor—*
See Extemporal verses
,, Extemporary verses

Hornby (T.) *Editor. See* Middleton

Hornby (W.) Scourge of drunkenness : A poem, 1614. Edited by J. O. Halliwell. Ln : 1859. 8°   BPL

Horne (Herbert P.) Brief note upon the 'Winter's tale' [In 'Century Guild Hobby Horse,' pp. 109-113, June]. Ln : Paul, Trench & Co., 1888. 4°

Horne (Richard Henry) Madness as treated by Sh—. [*Sans* place, printer, or date. Ln : 1849 ?] 8°   MPL

Was Hamlet mad ? Critiques on the acting of Walter Montgomery. [1871.] 8°
BM | BPL | CPL
See Michie, Nield, & Horne

Horne (R. H.) *Editor. See* Sh— Works, 1839-43, 1857-59, 1858

'Horrida Bella' *pseud. See* Ghost player's guide

Horsburgh (Edward Lee Stuart) Syllabus of a course of six lectures on six historical plays of Sh—. Philadelphia, 1903. 8°, pp. 16   BUS

Horsefield *or* Horsfield (Robert) *Publisher—*
See Sh— King John, 1764
,, Sh— Macbeth, 1770
,, Sh— Merchant . . . 1783
,, Sh— Poems, 1764
,, Sh— Timon . . . 1770
,, Sh— Works, 1773

Horton (Priscilla) *Actress*. *See* Sh—. The tempest, 1904

Horton-Smith (Lionel) Ars tragica Sophoclea cum Shakesperiana comparata : An essay on the tragic art of Sophocles and Sh—. Cambridge, 1896. 8°   BPL

Hosken (J. D.) 'Christopher Marlowe' and 'Belphegor.' 1896. Cr. 8°
Two tragedies in the Elizabethan vein in which Condell, Greene, and others of the period take part.

Hoskins (E. H.) Oration on Wm. Sh— delivered at the tercentenary banquet, Duffield House, Derby, April 23rd, 1864. Derby : Privately printed, 1864. 8°, pp. 16

Hosmer (H. L.) Bacon and Sh— in the 'Sonnets.' San Francisco, 1887. 8°
                BM | BPL | BUS

Houbraken (Ja.) *See* Birch & Houbraken

Houghton (A. V.) *Editor—*
See Sh— King Lear, 1906
 ,, Sh— Works, 1908

Houldgate *Sheffield Publisher*. *See* Sh— Works, 1768

House (H. H.) *Editor. See* Sh— King Henry IV., ii., 1884

Houssaye (Arsene) Behind the scenes of the Comedie Française, and other recollections. [Trans. and edited, with notes, by A. D. Vandam.] Ln : Chapman, 1889. 8°   SML

Houssaye (W.) Cleopatra : A study. Trans. from the French by A. F. D——. New York : Duprat, 1890. 8°   SML

How (W.) Commonplace book [including extracts from 'Pericles,' the 'Merchant of Venice,' and other plays]. Manuscript upon thirty-five leaves of paper. [c. 1640.] 8°   W

How Sh—'s skull was stolen. *See* Langston

Howard (C.) *See* Blanchard

Howard (Frank) Spirit of the plays of Sh— exhibited in a series of outline plates illustrative of the story of each play . . . With quotations and descriptions. Ln : Cadell, 1827-33. 5 vols. 8°. With 483 outline plates BPL | BUS | CPL | SML | W
Spirit of the plays . . . Ln : Cadell, 1827-1833. 4°, large paper   BM

Howard (Frank) *Artist—*
See Sh— King John, 1806
 ,, Sh— King Richard III., 1806
 ,, Sh— Romeo . . . 1806
 ,, Sh— Works, 1876, 1879, 1895-97

Howard (Henry) Visionary interview at the shrine of Sh—. Ln : R. Withy & J. Ryall, 1756. Fcp. 4°, pp. 12 BPL | BUS

Howard *Earl of Surrey* (Henry) Poems . . . printed from a correct copy. With the poems of Sir Thomas Wiat and others his famous contemporaries. To which are added some memoirs of his [Howard's] life and writings. Ln : Printed for W. Meares at the Lamb, and J. Brown at the Black Swan without Temple Bar, 1717. 8°, pp. xvi.-270 (pp. 225-240 are mispaged 125-140)

Songes and Sonnettes. Ln : R. Tottell, 1574. 8°, black letter
Howard's 'Songes and sonnettes' are thought to have had much influence on Sh— when preparing his own 'Sonnets,' printed in 1609.
A copy sold for £17 in March, 1906.

Songes and Sonnettes. Ln : 1587. 8°, black letter   BLO | HUTH
Only two perfect copies are recorded of this issue.

Howard (James) *Editor. See* Sh— Romeo . . . 1790

Howe *fourth Baron Chedworth* (John) Notes upon some of the obscure passages in Sh—'s plays. With remarks upon the explanations and amendments . . . in the editions of 1785, 1790, 1793 . . . Ln : W. Bulmer & Co., 1805. 8°, pp. iv.-376
    BM | BPL | BUS | CPL | MPL | SML
Privately printed by the editor, T. Penrice, because (he said) 'I have strong reason to suppose that . . . these "Notes" will be offered . . . in a less perfect form.'
His real motive, it is thought, was to prove the sanity of the author, who left him considerable property. The will, after being legally contested, was upheld.
See also Seymour (E. H.)

Howe (Joseph) Sh— : An oration. *See Sh—*] Howe

Howell *Editor. See* Sh— Works, 1848

Howell. Selections. *See* Sh— Works : Ext. 1845

Howell (James) Londinopolis or perlustration of the city of London. Ln : 1657. F°. With portrait and folding view by W. Hollar
The view exhibits Sh—'s Globe Theatre and the Bear Garden.

Howell (Thomas) Few stray thoughts upon Sh—. Ln : Batten, 1867. 8°, pp. 56
    BM | BPL | CPL | MPL | SML
Few stray thoughts . . . Ln : T. Bosworth, 1867. 8°, pp. 62   BUS | SML

Howells (William Dean) Certain delightful English towns, with glimpses of the pleasant country between. Ln : Harper, 1907. 8°, pp. 300. Illust.

Howes (E.) *Editor. See* Sh— King Richard II., 1834

Howison (Jack) 'Hamlet' : A descriptive account of its performance witnessed by J. Howison, aged twelve. 1894. 8° BM

Howitt (Wm.) Visits to remarkable places . . .
Ln: Longman, 1840. First series. 8°.
Illust.   BM | BPL
Stratford-on-Avon and the haunts of Sh—, Ann
Hathaway's Cottage, Charlecote Park, Lucy family,
Clopton Hall, Combe Abbey, pp. 81-168; Compton
Wynyates, pp. 305-328; Edgehill, pp. 367-381.
Visits . . . Second ed. Ln: 1840. 8°.
Illust.   BM | BPL
Visits . . . Third ed. Ln: 1856. 8°. Illust.
                                           BM | BPL
Visits . . . Ln: 1890. Cr. 8°   SML
Hows (J. W. S.) *Editor*—
See Sh— As you like it, 1846
„ Sh— King Lear, 1848
„ Sh— Works, 1850, 1857, 1859, 1870
Hoyer (M. A.) Sh—'s country. [1894.] Ob-
long 8°   BM
Hubaud (*Sir John*) *of Ipsley, Warwickshire.*
See *Sh*—] Malone
Hubaud (Ralph). See *Sh*—] Malone
Hubbard (E.) Sh—: Little journeys to the
homes of good men and great. New York,
1895. 8°   BPL
Hubbard (James Mascarene) [& Knapp
(Arthur Mason)] Catalogue of the works
of Wm. Sh—, original and translated.
Barton collection : Boston Public Library.
Boston [U.S.] Printed by order of the
Trustees [by Rockwell & Churchill] 1878-
80. F°, pp. iv.-228   BM | BPL | MPL
Issue restricted to 200 copies.
Hubbard (W.) Ceyx and Alcione, 1569. *See*
Reprints
Huchon (R.) Mrs. Montagu. *See* Montagu
Huckell (John)] The Avon : A poem. Bir-
mingham, J. Baskerville ; Ln., R. & J.
Dodsley, 1758. 4°, pp. 78 BPL | BUS | SML
The Avon . . . Stratford-upon-Avon : J.
Ward [1811]. 8°, pp. 60   BPL | BUS
Hudson (Henry Norman) Classical English
reader. *See* Sh— Works : Ext. 1883
English in schools. Boston [U.S.] 1881. 8°
                                           BPL
Essays on education ; English studies, and
Sh—. Boston [U.S.]: Ginn, Heath, 1884.
16°   BUS | SML
Lectures on Sh—. New York : Baker &
Scribner, 1848. 2 vols. 12°
                                 BM | BPL | BUS
On ' Furness's Sh—' [In ' North American
Review,' Jan.-Oct.] New York, 1873.
8°   BUS
On ' Hamlet ' [In 'American Review,' Jan.-
Feb.] New York, 1848. 8°   BUS
Sh—; his life, art, and characters. *See*
Sh—] Hudson
Hudson (H. N.) *Editor*—
See Sh— All's well, 1903
„ Sh— Antony . . . 1881, 1903
„ Sh— As you like it, 1880

Hudson (H. N.) *Editor*—
See Sh— Comedy of errors, 1881, 1903
„ Sh— Coriolanus, 1878
„ Sh— Cymbeline, 1881, 1903
„ Sh— Hamlet, 1878, 1879
„ Sh— Julius Cæsar, 1877, 1879, 1889,
      1908
„ Sh— King John, 1880, 1889, 1903
„ Sh— King Henry IV., i., 1889, 1903
„ Sh— King Henry IV., ii., 1889, 1903
„ Sh— King Henry V., 1876, 1889, 1903,
      1905
„ Sh— King Henry VI., i., 1903
„ Sh— King Henry VI., ii., 1903
„ Sh— King Henry VI., iii., 1903
„ Sh— King Henry VIII., 1876,1889,1903
„ Sh— King Lear, 1877, 1889, 1902
„ Sh— King Richard II., 1879, 1889, 1903
„ Sh— King Richard III., 1880, 1889,1903
„ Sh— Love's labours lost, 1903, 1908
„ Sh— Macbeth, 1877, 1889, 1901
„ Sh— Measure . . . 1903
„ Sh— Merchant . . . 1878, 1879, 1883,
      1885, 1888, 1908
„ Sh— Merry wives, 1902
„ Sh— Midsummer . . . 1876, 1880, 1889
„ Sh— Much ado, 1873, 1880, 1881, 1888,
      1902
„ Sh— Othello, 1878, 1881, 1902
„ Sh— Pericles, 1903
„ Sh— Rape . . . 1903
„ Sh— Romeo . . . 1873, 1881
„ Sh— Sonnets, 1903
„ Sh— Taming . . . 1903
„ Sh— The tempest, 1874, 1888, 1889,
      1902
„ Sh— Timon . . . 1903
„ Sh— Titus . . . 1903
„ Sh— Troilus . . . 1903
„ Sh— Twelfth night, 1880, 1881, 1889,
      1903
„ Sh— Two gentlemen, 1902
„ Sh— Two noble kinsmen, 1903
„ Sh— Venus . . . 1903
„ Sh— Winter's tale, 1880, 1888, 1902
„ Sh— Works, 1851-56, 1852-57, 1863-64,
      1871, 1873, 1874, 1878, 1880-
      81, 1886, 1900-01, 1903
„ Sh— Works : Ext. 1871-75
Hudson (Robert) Memorials of a Warwickshire
parish . . . Ln : Methuen, 1904. 8°, pp.
xvi.-312. Plates   SML
Hudson (Thomas) Four odes intended for
choruses to a tragedy altered from Sh—,
on the death of Julius Cæsar. 1759.
Fcp. 4°   BPL
Hudson (W. H.) Early mutilators of Sh— [In
'Poet Lore']. Philadelphia, 1892. 4° BPL
The church and stage. 1886. 8°   BPL

Hue and cry after those rambling protonotaries of the times. Ln: 1651. Fcp. 4°
Refers on p. 3 to ['Merry Wives,' iii. 5] 'Stewed in grease':—
'Sweating like butter'd Moors stew'd in their grease, Blenching each bush like a justice of peace . . .'

Hufford (Lois Grosvenor) Sh— in tale and verse. See Sh— Works: Ext. 1902

Huggard (Miles) Miscellanies. See Redford

Hughes Publisher. See Sh— Merchant . . . 1822

Hughes (C.) Editor. See Willobie

Hughes (Charles). See Creighton, Stopes, Reynolds, & Hughes

Hughes (Charles) Editor. See Moryson

Hughes (C. E.) Editor. See Sh—] Praise

Hughes (J.) Publisher. See Pope

Hughes (T.) Publisher—
See Sh— Measure . . . 1820
,, Sh— Winter's tale, 1820

Hughs (H.) Printer. See Capell

Hugo (François Victor Viscount) Commentary on the 'Merchant of Venice.' Trans. by Edward L. Samuel. Ln: Chapman, 1863. 8°, pp. 32   BM | BUS | CPL | MPL
Wm. Sh—. Trans. by A. Baillot. See Sh—
Hugo.] R—— (W. F.) 'Victor Hugo on Sh—' [In 'Temple Bar,' July]. Ln: 1864. 8°   BUS

Hugo (F. V. Viscount). See Davis (J. B.)

Hull Literary Club: Sh— festival programme. Hull, 1884. 8°   BPL

Hull Sh— festival. See also Andrews

Hull (Edward) Artist. See Levi (S. L.)

Hull (Thomas) Henry the Second, or the fall of Rosamond. A tragedy; as it is performed at the Theatre Royal, Covent Garden . . . Ln: Printed for John Bell, near Exeter Exchange, Strand, and C. Etherington, at York, 1774. 8°, pp. xii.-76   1774
Illustrates 'King Henry VI.'
This play passed through four editions in 1774.
See Ireland; also Mountfort, for same subject and title.

Hull (Thomas) Editor—
See Sh— Comedy of errors, 1779
,, Sh— Timon . . . 1786

Hulme (E. W.) Integrity of Lord Burghley [In 'Athenæum,' No. 4004, p. 112, July]. 1904

Hume Canon (Abraham) Who was Macbeth? [1853.] 12°   BM
Sh—; An oration. See Sh—] Hume

Hume (David) History of England from the invasion of Julius Cæsar to the revolution in 1688. Ln. & Edin., 1754-62. 6 vols. 4°
'If Sh— be considered as a man born in a rude age and educated in the lowest manner without any instruction either from the world or from books he may be regarded as a prodigy. If represented as a poet we must abate much of this eulogy. Jonson possessed all the learning wanting in Sh— and wanted all the genius

the other possessed. Both of them were equally deficient in taste and elegance, in harmony and correctness. A servile copyist of the ancients, Jonson translated into bad English the beautiful passages of the Greek and Roman authors without accommodating to the manners of his age and country. His merit has been totally eclipsed by that of Sh—, whose rude genius prevailed over the rude art of his contemporary.'

Hume (M. or A. S.) Spanish influence on English literature. 1905
Sh— pp. 118-119, 166-167, 263-274.

Humour. See Facetiæ

Humphrey Duke of Gloucester. See Sh— King Henry VI., iii., 1723

Humphreys Editor. See Decastro

Humphreys (Arthur L.) Editor. See Sh— Passionate . . . 1894

Humphreys (E. R.) Lyra Latina. See Sh— Works: Ext. 1850

Humphreys (G. E.) Voice and emotion, with reference to the 'Juliet' of Mary Anderson [In the 'National Review']. 1885. 8°   BPL

Humphreys (Hy. Noel) Sentiments and similes of Wm. Sh—. See Sh— Works: Ext. 1851, 1856, 1857, 1863

Humphreys (John) Wild flowers of Sh—: Sh— Club paper. Stratford-on-Avon, 1910. Cr. 8°, pp. 8

Humphry (O.) See Malone (E.)

Hundred merry tales, or Sh—'s Jest book. Ln: J. Chidley, 1831. 12°, pp. xvi.-106
BM | BPL | BUS | CPL
Referred to in 'Much ado,' Act ii., Sc. 1.

Hundred merry tales.] Sh—'s merry tales [Part I. A ℭ. merry tales; Part II. Tales and quick answers]. Ln: G. Routledge, 1845. 16°, pp. xv.-240   BM | BUS | SML

Hundred merry tales.] Sh—'s 'Merry tales' and 'Tales and quick answers.' New York, 1845. Cr. 8°, pp. 120   BUS

Hundred mery talys [Sh—'s Jest book] from the only perfect copy known. Edited, with introd. and notes, by Dr. Herman Oesterley. Ln: J. R. Smith, 1866. 8°, pp. xx.-162   MPL

Hundred merry tales: Sh—'s Jest book. Reproduced from the unique original. Printed by J. Rasbell, Gottingen, 1526. With introduction, notes, etc. by W. C. Hazlitt, 1887. F°   BPL | SML

Hundred mery talys, 1864, 1866, 1881—
See Sh—] Sh— Jest book
,, Sh—] Sh— notices

Hunnis (William)—
See Edwards (R.)
,, Stopes

Hunsdon's (Lord) Servants. See Sh— Romeo . . . 1597

Hunt (James Hy. Leigh) Blue-stocking revels, or the feast of the violets [In ' Monthly Repository']. Ln: 1837. 8°
In canto iii. says:—
'Than Sh— and Petrarch pray who are more living
Whose words more delight us, whose touches more touch?'

Critical essays on the performers of the London Theatre. Ln: Hunt, 1807. 8°
SML

Imagination and fancy. *See* Sh— Works: Ext. 1844, 1846, 1893

Table talk. 1851
At p. 154 is the essay ' Associations with Sh—.'
'How naturally the idea of Sh— can be made to associate itself with anything which is worth mention.'

Thoughts of the Avon on 28th Sept., 1817
Bears the lines:—
'. . . Humanity's divinest son
That sprightliest, gravest, wisest, kindest one
Sh—.'

Hunt (Richard) Bow of Jonathan. *See* Lucy

Hunt (Wm. Oakes) *Stratford Town Clerk*. *See* Stratford-cn-Avon

Hunter (*Dr.* Andrew) *Editor*. *See* Sh— Macbeth, 1797

Hunter (James) *Editor*. *See* Sh— Hamlet, 1866

Hunter (John) Examination questions on . . . the ' Merchant of Venice.' 1862. 12° BM

Studies for candidates in select plays of Sh—. 1880-87. 3 vols. 12° BM | BPL

Hunter (John) *Editor*—
See Sh— All's well, 1873
,, Sh— Antony . . . 1870
,, Sh— As you like it, 1869, 1899
,, Sh— Comedy of errors, 1873
,, Sh— Coriolanus, 1869
,, Sh— Cymbeline, 1872
,, Sh— Hamlet, 1865, 1869, 1870, 1878
,, Sh— Julius Cæsar, 1861, 1867, 1869, 1878
,, Sh— King Henry IV., i., 1871, 1878
,, Sh— King Henry IV., ii., 1871, 1878
,, Sh— King Henry V., 1871, 1878, 1881, 1892
,, Sh— King Henry VI., i., 1873
,, Sh— King Henry VI., ii., 1873
,, Sh— King Henry VI., iii., 1873
,, Sh— King Henry VIII., 1860, 1869, 1872, 1878
,, Sh— King John, 1871, 1879
,, Sh— King Lear, 1865, 1869, 1878
,, Sh— King Richard II., 1869, 1876, 1877
,, Sh— King Richard III., 1869, 1877
,, Sh— Love's labours lost, 1873
,, Sh— Macbeth, 1869, 1871
,, Sh— Measure . . . 1873
,, Sh— Merchant . . . 1861, 1869, 1878
,, Sh— Merry wives, 1872, 1878

Hunter (John) *Editor*—
See Sh— Midsummer . . . 1870, 1878, 1902
,, Sh— Much ado, 1872, 1882
,, Sh— Othello, 1869, 1877
,, Sh— Romeo . . . 1872, 1877
,, Sh— Taming . . . 1872
,, Sh— The tempest, 1869, 1873, 1877
,, Sh— Timon . . . 1873
,, Sh— Troilus . . . 1872
,, Sh— Twelfth night, 1870, 1878
,, Sh— Two gentlemen, 1873
,, Sh— Winter's tale, 1872
,, Sh— Works, 1860, 1860-73, 1866, 1872-81

Hunter (Joseph) Disquisition on the scene, origin, date, etc. of Sh—'s ' Tempest.' Ln: Privately printed by Whittingham, 1839. 8°, pp. iv.-152 BM | BPL | BUS | W
Impression confined to one hundred copies. A few were also done on large paper.

Extract from [his] unpublished diary, containing an account of a visit to Stratford-on-Avon in 1824. Ed. by J. O. Halliwell. 1867. 8° BPL | HCL | MPL
Issue restricted to ten copies.
Halliwell notes that Sh— was buried in the chancel of Holy Trinity Church by virtue of his ownership of part of the tithes of the edifice.

] Few words in reply to the animadversions of the Rev. Mr. Dyce on Mr. Hunter's ' Disquisition . . . (1839) ' and his ' New illustrations of the life . . . of Sh—, 1845.' Ln: J. R. Smith, 1853. 8°, pp. 24
BM | BPL | BUS | MPL | SML | W
On the Collier controversy.

New illustrations of the life, studies and writings of Sh—. *See Sh*—] Hunter

Hunter.] Hunter (Joseph) On ' The Tempest ' [In 'Quarterly Review,' March]. Ln: 1840. 8° BUS

Hunter (Joseph). *See* Collier (J. P.)

Hunter (L.) *Edinburgh Publisher*. *See* Sh— Works, 1753

Hunter (Robert E.) Sh— and Stratford. *See* Sh—] Hunter

] Stratford-upon-Avon and the approaching Sh— tercentenary. 1864. 4° BPL

Hunter (W. Ord) *Editor*. *See* Brown (I.)

Huntington *DD.* (Frederick D.) Religious and moral sentences. *See* Sh— Works: Ext. 1859

Huntley (R. W.) Glossary of the Cotswold dialect. Gloucester: E. Nest, 1868. 8°
BPL | SML
Contains 'Sh—'s visit to Dursley,' pp. 22-23.

Hurd *Bp.* (Richard). *See* Warburton

Hurd & Houghton *New York Publishers*. *See* Sh— Macbeth, 1868

Hurdis (James) Cursory remarks upon the arrangement of the plays of Sh—, occasioned by reading Malone's 'Essay on the chronological order of those celebrated pieces.' Ln: J. Johnson, 1792. 8°, pp. 56   BM | BPL | BUS | W
'The feeble effort of a critic unprepared.'—*T. Park.*

Huret. *See* Bernard

Hurst (J. F.) Why Americans love Sh—. 1856. 8°   BM

Hurst (T.) *Publisher. See* Sh— Works, 1816-18, 1819, 1825-26, 1826, 1827

Hurst & Robinson *Publishers—*
See Sh— Julius Cæsar, 1816
  ,, Sh— King Henry IV., ii., 1816
  ,, Sh— Much ado, 1816
  ,, Sh— The tempest, 1816

Hurton *Liverpool Publisher. See* Sh— Coriolanus, 1846

Husbands (Edward)] Exact collection of all remonstrances, declarations, votes, orders, ordinances, proclamations, petitions, messages, answers, and other remarkable passages between the King and the Parliament. Ln: E. Husbands, T. Warren, & R. Best ... 1643. Fcp. 4°, pp. x.-976 and engraved frontispiece of the Houses of Parliament assembled
At p. 593 is the singular 'Ordinance of the Lords and Commons concerning stage playes, 2 Sept., 1642.'

Hutchings (W.) Past dramatic performances in Stratford: A paper read before the Sh— Club, 6th Dec., 1894. Stratford-upon-Avon, 1895. 8°, pp. 24   BPL | BUS

Hutchings *nee* Lucy (*Mrs.* Lucy) & Lucy (Margaret)] An old sanctuary, by L. H— and M. L—. Stratford-on-Avon: [G. Boyden] 1896. 8°, pp. 28. Illust.   BPL | SML

Hutchinson.] British Empire Sh— Society; its origin, development and scope [In 'Windsor Magazine,' March, pp. 547-558]. 1910. Roy. 8°. Illust.   BM | BPL

Hutchinson (Thomas) Collection of vocal music in two, three, four, five, and six parts, principally attempted after the manner of the earlier masters ... With accompaniments for the piano. Ln: Preston [1807]. F°, pp. viii.-84   BUS
Contains four Sh— songs :—
  'You sunburnt sicklemen.'—*Tempest.*
  'How sweet the moonlight.'—*Merchant of V.*
  'If I profane.'—*Romeo & J.*
  'Lawn as white as driven snow.'—*Winter's tale.*

Hutchinson (Wm.) *Greenock Printer. See* Sh— Works, 1877-96

Huth (Alfred H.) *See* Greg, Levi, Pollard & Huth

Huth (A. H.) & Pollard (A. W.) On the supposed false dates in certain Sh— quartos [In 'The Library,' Jan., pp. 36-53]. 1910. Roy. 8°   BM | BPL

Hutton (Catharine) Welsh mountaineer: A novel. Ln: 1817. 3 vols. Cr. 8°   BPL
Deals with 'Hamlet,' Vol. i., pp. 252-264.

Hutton (L.) A century of 'Hamlet' [In 'Harper's New Monthly Mag.'] 1889. Roy. 8°   BPL

Hutton (L.) *Editor. See* American ...

Hutton *Bookseller* (William) Battle of Bosworth Field. Birmingham, 1788. 8° BUS
Illustrates 'King Richard III.'

Hyatt (Stanley P.) Is Sh— really dead? Another Druce case [In 'John Bull': Weekly magazine, 18 Jan., p. 65]. Ln: 1908. F°
An amusing jeu d'esprit, satirising Hall Caine and 'Marie Corelli.'

Hyde (J.) *Dublin Publisher. See* Sh— Double falsehood, 1728

Hyndman (F. A.) *Editor—*
See Sh— The tempest, 1895
  ,, Sh— Works, 1895

———— (B.) *See* Jonson
I—— (I.) *Publisher. See* Jaggard (John)
I—— (J. H.) *See* Ingram
I—— (W.) *Printer & Publisher. See* Jaggard (William)

Iago display'd ;—How Cassio accused Iago of corruption ; The various ways by which Iago endeavour'd to destroy Cassio ; How Iago published a libel against Cassio without a name. Second edition. [c. 1740.] 8°   W
The only apparent Sh— connection lies in the names borrowed from 'Othello.'
Its theme is alleged War Office corruption.
See 'Notes & Queries,' 1st S., Vol. 8, p. 56.

Iago display'd ... [c. 1808.] 8° BPL | BUS

Ibbitson (Robert) *Printer—*
See Greene
  ,, Shepheard ...

Ibbot (Benjamin) Fit of the spleen, in imitation of Sh— [In Dodsley's 'Collection of Old Plays,' Vol. 5]. 1775. 12° BPL
Reprinted in 1826.

'Ibef' *pseud., Editor, See* Sh— Othello, 1813

Ibsen.] 'Zanoni.' Ibsen and the drama. Ln: Digby, Long. Cr. 8°, pp. iv.-192
Chapter iii. (pp. 53-75) is headed 'Sh— vindicated.'

Iceland. *See* Gollancz

Ieffes. *See* Jeffes

'Ignotus' *pseud.* Nugæ Paddingtonienses. Paddington, 1864. 12°   BPL
Contains a parody on 'Hamlet.'

Ihne (W.) Notes and emendations to ... 'Merchant of Venice.' Braunschweig, 1862   BPL | BUS

Ihones (R.) *See* Jones (R.)
Iliffe (J. W.) *Editor. See* Sh— Midsummer ...
  1906, 1907
Illustrated birthday text book. *See* Sh—
  Works: Ext. 1881, 1883
Illustrated London News: Tercentenary number [May 14, 1864]. F° BPL
Illustrated Sporting News: Sh— tercentenary, 23rd Ap., 1864. F° BPL
Illustrations (Literary)—

See Bacon (F.)	*See* Conjectural ...
„ Baldwin	„ Cumberland
„ Ballads	„ Dall
„ Baltimore	„ Davey
„ Banks	„ Davies (M.)
„ Barton	„ Davies (T.)
„ Bates	„ Decker
„ Beale	„ Dedekind
„ Bellamy	„ Dramatic ...
„ Blades	„ Finegan
„ Borsa	„ Galt
„ Bosanquet	„ Gervinus
„ Brooke	„ Gildon
„ Brougham	„ Giles
„ Browne	„ Griffiths
„ Buchan	„ Hall (H. T.)
„ Caine	„ Halliwell
„ Cambridge ...	„ Home
„ Cartwright	„ Lennox
„ Chamberlaine	„ Literary
„ Chambers	„ Marriage ...
„ Coleridge	„ Rodenberg
„ Collet	„ Rushton
„ Collier (J. P.)	„ Sh— Works:
„ Collier (W. F.)	Comment ...
„ Collins	

Illustrations (Pictorial)—

See Barret	*See* Halliwell
„ Beerbohm	„ Harding
„ Bookman	„ Heath
„ Boydell	„ Heroes
„ Brassington	„ Holcroft
„ Brewer & Storer	„ Holland
„ Catalogue, 1839, 1880	„ Howard
„ Comenius	„ Jameson
„ Cunningham	„ Jerningham
„ Donaldson	„ Jerrard
„ Drama (The)	„ Literary ...
„ Dramatic ...	„ Liverseege
„ Dudley	„ Localities
„ Eaton	„ Meek
„ Ferrara	„ Monthly
„ Fisher	„ Mortimer
„ Fleay	„ Niven
„ Graphic	„ Old English ...
„ Green (H.)	„ Oxberry
„ Griggs	„ P— (J. & T. C.)
„ Hall (H. T.)	„ Paget
„ Hall (J.)	„ Pascoe
	„ Paton

Illustrations (Pictorial)—

See Photographic	*See* Sh—] Gibbs
„ Pictorial	„ *Sh*—] Halliwell
„ Picturesque	„ *Sh*—] Knight
„ Poole	„ Singleton
„ Repton	„ Stephens
„ Retzsch	„ Stewart
„ Rider	„ Stratford gallery
„ Rimmer	„ Stratford-on-
„ Rodd	„ Tallis [Avon
„ Rowlandson	„ Theatre
„ Ruhl	„ Thespian ...
„ Sabatini	„ Tyrrel
„ Sayer	„ Vertue
„ Seager	„ Wingate
„ Settle	„ Wingfield
„ Sh— Works: Ext.	„ Wivell
1792-96, 1836-37,	„ Wretch
1841, 1842, 1846,	
1878, 1883, 1888	

Imaginary conversation ... *See* Dix (W. G.)
Imitations of Sh— and Spenser. Ln: [1770?] 12° W
Immorality of the English pulpit [Reply to Jeremy Collier's strictures on the stage]. 1698. 8° BPL
Immortality of Sh—. *See* Sh—
Impartial remarks ... *See* Warburton
Imperfect hints ... *See* Felton
Impresas. *See* Barwick
Impressions of some Sh— characters [In 'The Century']. 1891. 8° BPL
In Sh—'s country. Illustrated. Ln: Hills, 1905. 16°
Inchbald *Actress* (Elizabeth) Portrait. *See* Sh— Comedy ... 1785
Inchbald (Elizabeth) *Editor*—
  See Collection ...
  „ Sh— Antony ... 1808 *et seq.*
  „ Sh— As you like it, 1808
  „ Sh— Comedy of errors, 1808
  „ Sh— Coriolanus, 1808
  „ Sh— Cymbeline, 1808
  „ Sh— Hamlet, 1806, 1816, 1822, 1827
  „ Sh— Julius Cæsar, 1811, 1816
  „ Sh— King Henry IV., i., 1808, 1817
  „ Sh— King Henry IV., ii., 1808, 1816
  „ Sh— King Henry V., 1808
  „ Sh— King Henry VIII., 1808, 1811, 1816
  „ Sh— King John, 1808, 1817
  „ Sh— King Lear, 1808, 1811, 1817
  „ Sh— King Richard III., 1808, 1811
  „ Sh— Macbeth, 1808, 1811, 1828
  „ Sh— Measure ... 1808, 1811, 1806
  „ Sh— Merchant ... 1808
  „ Sh— Merry wives, 1806, 1808, 1816
  „ Sh— Much ado, 1808, 1816
  „ Sh— Othello, 1808, 1821, 1822
  „ Sh— Romeo ... 1806, 1816
  „ Sh— Taming ... 1809, 1815

Inchbald (Elizabeth) *Editor*—
See Sh— The tempest, 1808, 1811, 1816
„ Sh— Twelfth night, 1808
„ Sh— Winter's tale, 1808, 1811, 1817
„ Sh— Works, 1808, 1816-18
Inchbald.] Boaden (J.) Memoirs of Mrs. Inchbald. To which are added ' The Massacre ' and ' A case of conscience.' Ln : Bentley, 1833. 2 vols. 8° SML
Inchbald (Peter) *Editor. See* Sh— Poems, 1875
Incorporated Law Society's provincial meeting at Birmingham ; Excursion to Stratford-on-Avon. Birmingham, 1896. 12° BPL
Indenture [Deed of conveyance covering the purchase of a residence at Blackfriars] 1612-13. *See* Sh— Autograph
Inderwick (F. A.) Biographical note. *See* Penzance
Index catalogue of . . . books . . . relating to the county of Warwick. *See* Jaggard
Index catalogue of . . . Sh—'s works and Shakespeareana. *See* Jaggard
Indexes. *See Sh*—] Sh— glossaries . . .
Indexes to characters. *See* Sh— Works, 1887
Ingannati (Gl'), or the deceived. A comedy, performed at Siena, 1531. Edited by Thomas Love Peacock. Ln : Chapman, 1862. 8°, pp. 78 BPL | BUS
The foundation story of ' Twelfth night.'
Ingersoll (R. G.) Sh— ; A lecture—
See Hall (J. G.)
„ Sh—] Ingersoll
Ingleby *Editor* (*Dr.* Clement Mansfield) Allusions to Sh—, 1592-1693 : Sh—'s centurie of prayse. Ln : New Sh— Soc., 1879. 4°
For other allusions see Furnivall.
„ „ Jusserand.
„ „ *Sh*—] Sh— allusion book.
[Allusions] Sh— allusion books . . . 1592-98. Ed. by C. M. Ingleby. Ln : New Sh— Society, 1874. 8° BM
Authorship of the works attributed to Sh— [In 'Trans. of the Roy. Soc.'] Ln : 1870. 8° BPL | BUS
Authorship of the works . . . [In ' Essays,' pp. 1-34]. 1888. 12° BPL
Complete view of the Sh— controversy concerning the authenticity and genuineness of manuscript matter affecting the works and biography of Sh— published by J. P. Collier as the fruits of his researches. Ln : Nattali & Bond, 1861. 8°, pp. xvi.-350 and 18 plates of facsimiles BM | BPL | BUS | MPL | SML | W
' After a few copies got out the frontispiece was suppressed at my instigation.'—*J. R. Smith.*
One of the withdrawn copies is at Warwick.
Essay. *See* Cattell
Letters to S. Timmins on Sh—. 1883.

Ingleby *Editor* (*Dr.* Clement Mansfield)—
Library. *See* Catalogue, 1879
Manuscript. 4° BPL
Notes on the history of the Sh— canon. [1889 ?] 8° BPL
Obsolete phraseology of Sh— [In ' Englishman's Mag. ' April]. Ln : 1865. 8° BUS
Occasional papers on Sh—. *See* Sh—] Ingleby
On Hamlet's ' Some dozen or sixteen lines.' Ln : New Sh— Soc., 1877-79. 8°
On Sh—'s traditional birthday [In ' Roy. Soc. of Literature : Trans.'] Ln : 1874. 8° BPL | BUS
On some peculiarities of Sh—'s language [In ' Englishman's Mag.,' Nov.] Ln : 1865. 8° BUS
On the fabrications, or the manuscript notes, of the Perkins folio shown to be of recent origin. With an appendix on the authorship of the Ireland forgeries. Ln : J. R. Smith, 1859. 8°, pp. xxviii.-116. With facsimile
BM | BPL | BUS | CPL | SML | W
Collier controversy.
Portraiture of Sh— [In ' Sh—, the man and the book']. 1876 ? 8° BPL
Sh— ; the man and the book. *See* Sh—
Sh— hermeneutics, or the still lion. Being an essay towards the restoration of Sh—'s text. Birmingham, Printed by Josiah Allen ; Ln., Trübner & Co., 1875. Fcp. 4°, pp. viii.-168 and leaf of ' Errata '
BM | BPL | BUS | SML
' The still lion ' enlarged under an altered title.
Sh—'s bones : The proposal to disinter them considered in relation to their possible bearing on his portraiture. 1883. 8° BPL
Sh—'s century of praise. *See* Sh—
The ' Scule arayed.' A letter to H. Staunton, Esq. concerning Sh—'s Sonnet 146. Ln : 1872. 8°, pp. 16 BM | BPL | MPL
The still lion : An essay towards the restoration of Sh—'s text. Ln : Trübner, 1874. 8° BM | BPL | BUS | MPL | SML
First appeared in ' Sh— Jahrbuch, 1867.'
Text of Sh— [In ' Englishman's Mag.,' Jan.] Ln : 1865. 8° BPL | BUS | CPL
Was Thomas Lodge an actor ? The social status of the playwright in the time of Queen Elizabeth. 1868. Fcp. 4° BPL
Ingleby (*Dr.* C. M.) *Editor*—
See Greene
„ Halpin
„ Prouerbes . . .
„ Sh— Cymbeline, 1886
See also Elze
Ingleby (Holcombe) *Editor. See* Sh— Cymbeline, 1889

Samuel William Henry Ireland

See p. 163

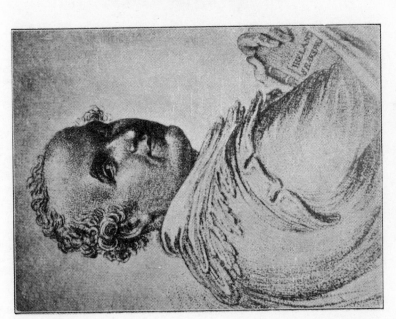

Samuel Ireland, the elder

Inglis (Robert) Dramatic writers of Scotland.
Glasgow: Mackellar, 1868. 12° SML
Inglis (Robert) Editor. See Sh— Works, 1864,
1871, 1878, 1882, 1890, 1906
Ingram (John H.) Haunted homes and family
traditions of Great Britain. Ln: Reeves
& Turner, 1905. Cr. 8°, pp. xii.-642.
Illust. SML
Contains the foundation of Sh—'s 'Yorkshire tragedy.'
Sh—; A lecture. See Sh—] Ingram
Some Marlowe riddles [In 'Athenæum,'
No. 4069, p. 552]. Ln: 1905
] Suckling and Sh— [In 'Athenæum,' No.
3586, p. 108, and No. 3590, p. 236].
1896. 4°
See also Slater & Ingram
Ingram (John Kells) On Sh—. See Sh—]
Ingram
On the weak endings of Sh—. With some
account of the history of the verse-tests
in general. Ln: New Sh— Soc., 1874.
8°
Ingratitude of a commonwealth. See Sh—
Coriolanus, 1682
Injured princess. See Sh— Cymbeline, 1682
Inman (Matthew) Publisher. See Hemminge
Innes (Arthur D.) Editor—
See Sh— Julius Cæsar, 1893, 1895
„ Sh— King Henry IV., ii., 1889
„ Sh— King Henry V., 1890, 1893
„ Sh— Twelfth night, 1895, 1895-96
„ Sh— Works, 1886-91, 1893-98
Innys (W. & J.) Publishers. See Law (W.)
Interludes—
See Elizabeth   See Religious . . .
„ Greg   „ Stage
„ Malone . . .
Interview (The), or Sir John Falstaff's ghost.
A poem, inscribed to David Garrick.
Ln: S. Bladon, 1766. 4°, pp. 24   BUS
Introduction to Sh—'s plays, 1773. See Gen-
tleman
Introduction to the new tragedy, call'd Hum-
frey Duke of Gloucester. 1723. 12° BPL
Illustrates Sh—'s 'King Henry VI.'
Introduction to the school of Sh—. See
Kenrick
Invader of his country. See Sh— Coriolanus,
1720
Inventory of certain books and manuscripts.
See Halliwell
Inverness. See Anderson (J.)
Ireland—
See Dix   See Sheridan
„ Hitchcock   „ Walker
„ Patterson
Ireland (Alexander) Manchester Printer &
Publisher—
See Sh— Hamlet, 1864
„ Sh— Sonnets, 1880

Ireland (Alexander) Manchester Printer &
Publisher—
See Sh— Twelfth night, 1873
„ Sh— Works, 1864
Ireland (Alma Maria). See Ireland (S. W. H.)
Ireland (John) Anecdotes. See Henderson
Ireland (Jane). See Ireland (S. W. H.)
Ireland (John) Editor. See Henderson
Ireland (J. N.) Mrs. Duff. See Duff
Records of the New York stage from 1750
to 1860. New York, 1860. 2 vols. 4°
Sixty copies were printed on large paper.
Ireland (J. N.) Editor. See American . . .
Ireland (Samuel) Investigation of Mr. Malone's
claim to the character of scholar or critic;
being an examination of his 'Inquiry
into the authenticity of the Sh— manuscripts, etc.' Ln: R. Faulder [1797].
8°, pp. viii.-154   BM | BPL | BUS | W
Samuel Ireland was originally a Spitalfields silk weaver,
but having a natural taste for the fine arts, forsook
that trade and embarked in business as a book-
dealer and publisher, himself writing several of the
illustrated itineraries he issued. He took a prominent
part in the gross forgeries of his son, Samuel Wm.
Henry Ireland, and though acquitted of wilful par-
ticipation by the chief criminal it is difficult to believe
him entirely free of blame.

Library. See Catalogue, 1801
Picturesque views on the upper or Warwickshire Avon from its source at Naseby
to . . . the Severn at Tewkesbury. With
observations on the public buildings and
other works of art in its vicinity. Ln:
R. Faulder, 1795. Roy. 8°, pp. xxviii.-
284, and 33 aquatint plates
BM | BPL | BUS | W
Sixty copies done on large paper, 4°, and some with
coloured plates. Lowndes quotes the date 1792 in
error (p. 2321).
A considerable portion concerns Sh— and Stratford.
Some of the plates rank among the earliest views of
Shakespearean spots unaltered since the poet's day.
One scene depicts the ancient farmhouse at Fulbroke,
the alleged temporary lock-up in the legendary
poaching expedition.
The writer 'navigated down this poetic and enchanting
stream attended by a very modest and well-informed
man, John Jordan, who is by trade a wheelwright,
and possesses considerable knowledge in history and
antiquity, and is also no mean poet. . . . It was
Jordan who gave S. W. H. Ireland the first information on which he created his visionary falsehood.'—
Gentleman's Magazine, Oct., 1800.

Play-bill and hand-bill respecting the per-
formance of 'Vortigern.' Ln: 1796
Sold at the Sabine sale for one guinea.
Vindication of his conduct. See Caldecott
Ireland (S.) Publisher. See Hogarth
Ireland (Samuel William Henry) Authentic
account of the Sh— manuscripts. [First
edition.] Ln: J. Debrett, opposite Bur-
lington House in Piccadilly, 1796. 8°,
pp. ii.-44   BM | BPL | BUS | MPL | W
The original edition became so scarce that Barker of
Ln. reprinted in imitation of it fifty copies, which
are now as valuable as the original.

Ireland (Samuel William Henry) Confessions . . . containing particulars of the fabrication of the Sh— manuscripts, together with anecdotes and opinions of many distinguished persons in the literary, political, and theatrical world. Ln: Ellerton & Byworth, 1805. 8°, pp. viii.-318-16 and 2 plates

BM | BPL | BUS | CPL | MPL | SML | W

In one of the Boston copies is a note by John Jones, of Gray's Inn, a former owner:—
'A friend, from whom I had the following verses, informed me that in 1796 Ireland was in the neighbourhood of Welchpool, and being . . . at Venor Hall -Mrs. Winder requested Ireland to write a few lines on avarice in the Sh— style—which he did impromptu.'
The forty-two lines in blank verse which follow begin:
'Men's minds I liken to an ague fit
That parches up the flesh with fev'rous heat.'

Confessions . . . Ln: Ellerton & Byworth, 1805 [Rep. c. 1870]. 8°, pp. 336. Folding and other plates   BPL
Large paper reprint.

Confessions . . . With introd. by Rd. Grant White and additional facsimiles. New York: J. W. Bouton, 1874. 12°, pp. xxxii.-vi.-318-16 and 5 plates   BUS
The Introd. gives account of the Sh— forgeries by Peter Cunningham (q.v.).

Full and explanatory account of the Shakesperian forgery, by myself, the writer, Wm. Hy. Ireland
MS., with some original forged Sh— documents, contracts, indentures, love verses, lock of hair, &c. Illustrated by Westall and others with portraits and engravings of persons or places mentioned by the poet.
Sold in White Knights' auction for £30 9s.

] Henry the Second. An historical drama, supposed to be written by [Sh—] the author of 'Vortigern.' Ln: J. Barker, 1799. 8°, pp. ii.-iv.-78   BUS | W
The forger's own annotated copy is at Boston. The title had been used previously by Wm. Mountford in 1793, and Thomas Hull in 1774.

Manuscripts. *See* Sh—] Manuscript

] Miscellaneous papers and legal instruments under the hand and seal of Wm. Sh—. [Original forged manuscripts: Collection of thirty-seven documents, on paper, mounted into a volume.] Ln: [1795]. Roy. 4°   W
With inscription on fly-leaf in W. H. Ireland's autograph. 'These specimens of my Sh— reproductions were presented to Mrs. Ireland [his mother] at her particular request in 1805, the period when I published my "Confessions," in which will be found a full account of every document herein contained.'
Further particulars of this collection may be seen in Halliwell's 'Sh— reliques,' 1852, p. 12.

] Miscellaneous papers and legal instruments . . . [Original forged manuscripts, with portrait of Sh—, lock of hair, &c.] Ln: 1795. 3 vols. F°
Purchased by Dent for £300. At the sale of his library, 1827, the collection produced £46 4s. only.

Ireland (Samuel William Henry) Miscellaneous papers . . . [Manuscript duplicate set of forgeries]. 1796. 4°, ff. 24   BUS
With a holograph letter by the forger, ending with the phrase:—'Pray excuse this scrawl but I have had another night without a moment's sleep, and am more like a man drunk than in his senses.'

Miscellaneous papers and legal instruments under the hand and seal of Wm. Sh—, including the 'Tragedy of King Lear' and a small fragment of 'Hamlet,' from the original manuscripts in the possession of Samuel Ireland, of Norfolk Street . . . Ln: Cooper & Graham . . . 1796. F°, pp. lxviii.-108-viii. and 26 plates of facsimiles, etc., some in colours

BM | BPL | BUS | CFL | MPL | SML | W

These forgeries by W. H. Ireland, postdated 1796, were issued on Christmas eve, 1795.
Of the 368 copies printed only 138 survived, including 122 to subscribers, some half-dozen as gifts, and the remainder to the State libraries. The forger's youngest sister Jane supervised the destruction of the copperplates and the rending into waste paper of the other 230 copies.
In the original forged manuscripts bought by Mr. Dent, M.P. was a note concerning the suppression of this volume:—'Upon my confessing, the sale of the folio was stopped by my father, nor had the octavo edition made its appearance. . . . In order still further to obliterate I committed to the flames the complete impression of the present reprint reserving no more than the annexed copy which, as a literary curiosity, ranks unique. . . .'

] Miscellaneous papers and legal instruments . . . [Second edition.] Ln: Cooper & Graham . . . 1796. 8°, pp. lii.-156. With folding portrait   BUS | CPL | W
The unexpected exposure of these forgeries put an early stop to the sale until Sept., 1814, when a few copies were further disposed of.

Proposals for the publication of 'Miscellaneous papers and legal instruments . . .' Ln: 1795. 8°

] Scribbleomania, or the printer's devil's polichronicon. A sublime poem. Ed. by Anser Pen-Drag-On . . . Ln: Sherwood, Neely & Jones, 1815. 8°, pp. viii.-344
Refers to Sh—, p. 10.

Sh— hunt [Delineations of leading political and fashionable personages inserted in 'The Oracle,' a newspaper edited by J. Boaden]. [1796 ?]
Ireland was employed by the editor to write these articles in rivalry to those appearing in the 'Morning Herald' by Sir Hy. and Lady Dudley (q.v.).

Sh— manuscripts. *See* Catalogue, 1812

Shakespearian forgeries and manuscript notes [A collection mounted into a volume, with one page of printed matter]. Manuscript, on 11 leaves of paper. [1796.] 4°   W

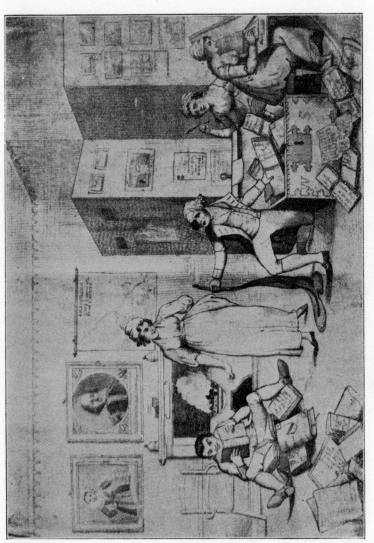

Ireland Forgeries Caricature by James Gillray

S. W. H. Ireland handing a lock of hair and original manuscripts of Shakespeare from an old chest

See p. 165

Ireland (Samuel William Henry)] Vortigern: An historical tragedy. [Original forged holograph manuscript, announced as the work of Sh—. On 21 leaves of paper. 1795.]   F°   W
The first four leaves missing ; begins p. 9, ends p. 50.

Vortigern. [Two manuscript transcripts of the play of 'Vortigern' taken from the supposed Sh— manuscript, the first, upon 108 leaves, written by Mrs. Ireland [his mother], and the second, upon 99 leaves, by Alma Maria Ireland [his sister]. Manuscript, on paper. [1795 ?] 2 vols in 1. F°   W
With S. W. H. Ireland's autograph inscription and signature.

] Vortigern: An historical tragedy in five acts. Represented at the Theatre Royal, Drury Lane, on Saturday, 2nd April, 1796. Ln: J. Barker, 1799. 8°, pp. xii.-78 . First edition   BPL | BUS | W
'Vortigern,' the alleged newly-discovered Sh— drama, was announced to appear at Drury Lane Theatre on 2nd April, 1796, with Mrs. Jordan as 'Flavia.' Before the performance began Edmund Malone distributed a handbill at the doors cautioning the public against the fraud. Samuel Ireland responded with another handbill requesting playgoers to lay aside all prejudice, &c.

Vortigern . . . With an original preface . . . Represented at the Theatre Royal, Drury Lane, on Saturday, April 2, 1796, as a supposed newly-discovered drama of Sh—. Ln: Joseph Thomas, Birchin Lane, 1832. 8°, pp. ii.-xvi.-62 (including printed wrappers) and folded facsimile of the forged MS.   BM | BPL | BUS | CPL | W

Ireland (S. W. H.) Editor. See Sh— King Lear, 1796

Ireland.] Review of W. H. Ireland's Miscellaneous papers and legal instruments [In the 'British Critic']. 1796. 8°   BPL

] Sh— Ireland forgeries [In 'London Review,' Oct.] 1860   BUS

Ireland forgeries—
See 'Antenor'   See New Monthly . .
  ,, Arnold   ,, Oulton
  ,, Boaden   ,, Payn
  ,, Broughton   ,, Porson
  ,, Butler (S.)   ,, Precious . . .
  ,, Caldecott   ,, Robinson
  ,, Caulfield   ,, Sh—] Neil
  ,, Chalmers   ,, Sh—] Sh— col-
  ,, Chandler   lection
  ,, Cotton   ,, Vorbrodt
  ,, Dudley   ,, Waldron
  ,, Fitzgerald   ,, Webb
  ,, Ingleby   ,, White (T.)
  ,, Lawrence   ,, White & Lamb
  ,, Lea   ,, Woodward
  ,, Montgomery   ,, Wyatt
'Irene.' See Essay on tragedy

Ireson (F.) Sketch of the pre-Sh— drama. Odd Volume Miscellanies, 1885. 12° BPL

Irvine (W.) En Easter ramble. Hawick, 1860. 12°   BPL
Stratford, pp. 38-51.

Irving (Henry B.) Occasional papers : dramatic and historical. Ln: Bickers, 1906. 8°, pp. viii.-252   BPL
Contains the 'English stage in the 18th century,' &c.

Irving (Sir John Henry Brodribb) Acting : An art [In the 'Fortnightly Review']. 1895. Roy. 8°   BPL

An actor's notes on Sh—: I. The third murderer in 'Macbeth' [In 'Nineteenth Century,' Vol. I., pp. 327-330]. Ln: King & Co., 1877. Roy. 8°   BPL | BUS

An actor's notes on Sh—: II. Hamlet and Ophelia [In 'Nineteenth Century,' Vol. I., pp. 524-530]. Ln: King & Co., 1877. Roy. 8°   BPL | BUS

Art of acting [In the 'English Illustrated Mag.'] Ln: 1885. Roy. 8°   BPL

English actors ; their characteristics and methods.   Oxford : Clarendon Press, 1886. 8°, pp. iv.-60

Essay on Sh— and Bacon [In 'Stage Sh—,' Vol. I.] c. 1903. 8°   BPL

Impressions of America narrated in a series of sketches, chronicles, and conversations by J. Hatton. Ln: 1884. 2 vols. Cr. 8°

Impressions of America. Ed. by J. Hatton. Boston: Osgood, 1884. Cr. 8°   SML

'Macbeth' at the Lyceum : Mr. Irving and his critics. 1875. 8°   BM

Preface. See Diderot

] Souvenir of 'King Henry the Eighth' at the Lyceum Theatre.   Illustrated by Partridge. [1892.] 8°   BPL

] Souvenir of 'King Lear' at the Lyceum Theatre. Illustrated by Partridge. [1892.] 8°   BPL

] Souvenir of 'Macbeth,' produced at the Lyceum Theatre by H. Irving, 29th Dec., 1888. Ln: [1889]. Oblong 4° BM | BPL

Study of Sh— in small communities [In 'Windsor Mag.,' pp. 100-110, Dec.] Ln: Ward & Lock, 1902. Roy. 8°

The drama : Addresses. Ln: Heinemann, 1893. Cr. 8°

The stage : An address delivered at the Perry Bar Institute, near Birmingham. 1878. 8°   BPL

The stage as it is : A lecture delivered at Edinburgh, 8th Nov., 1881. 8°

Irving.] Archer (W.) Henry Irving : A critical study. Ln: Field & Tuer [1888 ?] 12°
                                          SML

] Brereton (Austin) Life of Hy. Irving. Ln : Longmans, 1908. 2 vols. 8°, pp. 402 and 374. Illust.   BPL

Irving.] Brereton. Sir Henry Irving: A biographical sketch. Ln: Bogue, 1883. Roy. 8°. With 17 portraits by Whistler, Long, and others   SML

] Daly (Fredk.) Henry Irving in England and America, 1838-84. Ln: Unwin, 1884. Cr. 8°. With portrait   SML

] Drewry (Ina L.) Henry Irving's 'Hamlet' [In 'Victoria Mag.,' Dec.] Ln: 1874. 8°   BUS

] Fitzgerald (Percy) Henry Irving: A record of twenty years at the Lyceum. Ln: Chatto, 1893. 8°, pp. viii.-150. With portrait   BPL

] 'Hamlet' [In 'Blackwood's Mag.,' April]. Edin., 1879. 8°   BUS

] 'Hamlet' at the Lyceum [In 'Notes on the drama' in the 'Dublin University Mag']. 1875. 8°   BPL

] 'Hamlet' at the Lyceum [In the 'Kensington Mag']. 1879. 8°   BPL

] Hamlet: Criticism of Henry Irving [In 'Blackwood's Mag.'] 1879. 8°   BPL

] Henry Irving, actor and manager: A criticism of a critic's criticism, by an Irvingite. 1883. Cr. 8°

] Henry Irving: Record of twenty years at the Lyceum. Ln: 1893. 8°

] Henry Irving and Ellen Terry in America: Opinions of the press. Chicago, 1884. 8°

] Kenney (C. L.) Mr. Irving in 'Hamlet' [In 'Belgravia']. Ln: 1874. 8° BPL | BUS

] Knight (Joseph) Henry Irving, 1838-1905 [In 'Athenæum,' No. 4069, p. 551]. Ln: 1905

] 'Macbeth' at the Lyceum Theatre [In 'Belgravia,' Nov.] Ln: 1875. 8° BUS

] 'Macbeth' at the Lyceum: Mr. Irving and his critics. By two amateurs. 1875. 12°   BPL

] 'Merchant of Venice' at the Lyceum [In 'Blackwood's Mag.'] 1879. 8°   BPL

] New Hamlet and his critics [Excerpt relating to Sir Henry Irving from 'Macmillan's Mag.'] 1875. 8°

] Ophelia and Hamlet: A rejoinder to 'An Actor's Notes' [In 'Temple Bar,' Mar.] Ln: 1878. 8°   BUS

] Stoker (Bram) Personal reminiscences of Henry Irving. 1906. 2 vols. 8° BPL

] The new Hamlet [In 'Tinsley's Mag.,' Dec.] Ln: 1874. 8°   BUS

] Theatrical reform: The 'Merchant of Venice' at the Lyceum [In 'Blackwood's Mag.,' Dec.] Edin., 1879. 8°   BUS

] Willan (J. N.) First night impressions of Mr. Irving's 'Macbeth.' Bath, 1889. Cr. 8°   BPL

] Yockney (A.) Art of Sir Hy. Irving [In Sh— Works, Vol. 6]. 1907. F°   BPL

Irving]—
  See Brereton   *See* Russell
  ,, Kenney   ,, Scott (C. W.)
  ,, Knowles   ,, Yorick
  ,, Ramé

Irving (*Sir* J. H. B.) *Editor—*
  See Sh— Coriolanus, 1880
  ,, Sh— Cymbeline, 1896
  ,, Sh— Hamlet, 1878, 1880
  ,, Sh— King Henry VIII., 1892
  ,, Sh— King Lear, 1892
  ,, Sh— King Richard II., 1877
  ,, Sh— King Richard III., 1877, 1880, 1896
  ,, Sh— Macbeth, 1880, 1888, 1889, 1890
  ,, Sh— Merchant . . . 1880, 1881
  ,, Sh— Much ado, 1882, 1883
  ,, Sh— Othello, 1882
  ,, Sh— Romeo . . . 1882, 1883
  ,, Sh— Twelfth night, 1884
  ,, Sh— Works, 1877-87, 1888-90, 1895, 1905

Irving (Washington) Book of Sh— gems. *See* Sh— Works: Ext. 1854

Sketch book. Ln: Routledge, 1850
Pp. 191-206 occupied by Sh— and Stratford. Describes too the old 'Boar's head' tavern in Eastcheap, London.

Sketch book. New York, 1860. 12° BUS

Sketch book. Ln: Routledge, 1886. Cr. 8°   SML

Stratford-on-Avon [In the 'Sketch Book']. [1820 ?] 8°   BPL

Stratford-on-Avon [In the 'Sketch Book']. [1821 ?] 12°   BPL

Stratford-on-Avon, from the 'Sketch Book.' Edited by R. Savage and W. S. Brassington. Stratford-on-Avon: E. Fox, 1900. 8°   BPL | SML
Some copies done on Japanese vellum.

The Bermudas: A Sh— research [In 'The Knickerbocker,' Jan.] New York, 1840. 8°   BUS
Reprinted in his 'Wolfert's roost,' 1863. Illustrates 'The Tempest.'

See Stratford] Sh—'s birthplace

Irving (W.) & Fairholt (F. W.) Sh—'s home visited and described. With a letter from Stratford by J. F. Sabin and the complete prose works of Sh—. With etchings by J. F. & W. W. Sabin. New York: J. Sabin, 1877. 16°, pp. vi.-84 and portrait of Southampton   BM | BPL | BUS
The complete 'prose works' are the dedications of 'Venus' and 'Lucrece,' the poet's will being unaccountably omitted.

Irving.] Pemberton (T. E.) Washington Irving in England: The eleven years that author spent in the English midlands, where he found the original of Bracebridge Hall [Aston Hall] and where much of his best literary work was done [In the 'Munsey Mag.,' pp. 552-558, Jan.] 1904. Roy. 8° With portrait and Stratford views

Irwin (J. O.) Sh—'s religious belief. *See* Sh—

Irwin (T.) Falstaff's wake [In 'Dublin Univ. Mag.,' Feb.] Dublin, 1864. 8° BPL | BUS

Is it Sh— ? *See* Begley

Is there any resemblance . . . ? *See* Steel

Isaac (*Dr.* H.) *Editor. See* Sh— Merchant . . . 1884

Isaac, Tuckey & Co. *Publishers. See* Sh— Works, 1836

Isaacson (J.) *Composer. See* Sh— King Henry V., 1858

Isham (*Sir* Charles E.) *Library. See* Lamport

Isle of Man. *See* Talbot

Islip (Adam) *Printer*—
 See Busche   *See* Livius
  „ Heywood   „ Key . . .

Italian books of fortune. *See* Stopes

Italian dictionary. *See* Florio

Italy—
 See Coote
  „ Scott (M. A.)
  „ Walker

Itinerant (The). *See* Romney

—— (E. M.) Questions and exercises on Sh—'s **leading plays** [1894]. 8° BM | BPL

J—— (J. R.) Globe theatre [In ' The Olio,' 12 Nov.] Ln: 1831. 8° BUS

Contains also a poem on Sh— by R. W. S—.

J—— (S.) 'Merchant of Venice' at the Prince of Wales theatre [In 'Fraser's Magazine,' July]. Ln: 1875. 8° BUS

J—— (T.) Stratford-on-Avon Church [Rep. from the 'Literary World']. 1839. 8° BPL

J—— (T. E.) Handbook of reference and quotation. *See* Sh— Works: Ext. 1869, 1877

J—— (W.) Whipping of the satyre. Ln: 1601
Mentions 'Sir John Falstaffe' and ' John of Gaunt.' Illustrates 'King Hy. IV.,' 'King Hy. VI.,' 'King Richard II.'

J—— (Y.) On Sh—'s 'Poems' [In 'New Monthly Mag.'] c. 1823. 8° BPL

Jacke Drum's entertainment, or the comedie of Pasquill and Katherine. Ln: 1601. Fcp. 4° BUS
Referred to in 'All's well' . . . Act iii., Sc. vi.
See also Simpson.

Jacke of Dover; his quest of inquirie or his privy search for the veriest fool in England. Ln: W. Ferbrand, 1604 [In Sh— Jest books. Ed. Hazlitt, Vol. 2, *q.v.*]
'Were he the veriest antic in the world.'—*Taming of the shrew.*
See also Sh—] Sh— jest books.

Jack of Newbury. *See* Deloney

Jackman (I.) All the world's a stage [In 'Collection of farces, selected by Mrs. Inchbald,' Vol. 4, pp. 1-34]. Ln: Longman, 1809. 12° BPL

Jackson *Artist. See* Douce

Jackson *Composer. See* Sh— Poems, 1862

Jackson *Oxford Publisher. See* Sh— Works: Ext. 1778

Jackson (A.) *Printer. See* Sh— Compendious . . . 1751

Jackson (D.) *Publisher. See* Sh— Works, 1714

Jackson (J.) History of the Scottish stage from its first establishment . . . interspersed with memoirs of his own life. Edinburgh: Hill, 1793. 8° SML

Jackson (J. W.) Ethnology and phrenology as an aid to the biographer; Sh—. *See* Sh—] Jackson

Jackson (*Mrs.*) *Actress. See* Sh— Romeo . . . 1778

Jackson (Richard C.) London's national memorial to Sh— [In the 'Saturday Review,' 13 Nov., p. 598]. 1909. F° BM | BPL

Memorials to Sh—: A disclaimer [In 'Athenæum,' No. 4281, p. 602, 13 Nov.] 1909. 4°

National theatres [In the 'Saturday Review,' 20th Nov., p. 632]. 1909. F° BM | BPL

Site of Sh—'s Globe playhouse [In 'Athenæum,' 30 Oct., No. 4279, pp. 525-526]. 1909 BM | BPL
Mr. Jackson says he has the portrait of Sh— which adorned the Falcon Inn, Southwark (razed in 1828), a famous literary resort in Sh—'s days. Also that Sh—'s Sonnets, 1609, was originally sold at fivepence. The article is full of interest.
Mr. Jackson claims to be the original of Walter Pater's ' Marius the epicurean.'

Jackson (Richard C.) *See* Sh— Works, 1623

Jackson (Robert) *Dublin Publisher. See* Following . . .

Jackson (Roger) *Publisher*—
 See Booke . . .
  „ Sh— Rape, 1616

Jackson (William) Thirty letters on various subjects. Ln: 1783. 2 vols. 12° W
Sh— pp. 158-165.

Thirty letters. Third edition, with considerable additions. Ln: 1795. 8° BPL | BUS | W

Jackson (Z.) Death of Falstaff. *See* Sh— King Henry IV., ii., 1820
Few concise examples of seven hundred errors in Sh—'s plays, now corrected and elucidated, and which have afforded abundant scope for critical animadver-

sion and hitherto held at defiance the penetration of all . . . commentators. Ln : J. Harper, 1818. 8°, pp. 20

BM | BPL | BUS | MPL

Republished as 'Sh—'s genius.'

Jackson (Z.) Sh—'s genius justified : A few concise examples . . . Second edition, enlarged. Ln : J. Major, 1818. Royal 8°, pp. 34

BPL | BUS | SML | W

Sh—'s genius justified ; being restorations and illustrations of seven hundred passages in Sh—'s plays, which have afforded abundant scope for critical animadversion and hitherto held at defiance the penetration of all Sh—'s commentators. Ln : Printed by J. Johnson, Apollo Press, Brook Street, Holborn, for John Major, 18 Skinner Street, 1819. 8°, pp. xvi.-470. Third edition

BPL | CPL | MPL | SML | W

Jackson (Zachariah) *Dublin Publisher.* See Sh— Works, 1816

Jacob (Giles)] Poetical register. *See Sh—]* Jacob

Jacob and Esau. *See Stopes*

Jacox (Francis) About giving sorrow words [In 'New Monthly Mag.,' Dec.] Ln : 1867. 8°

BUS

'Give sorrow words . . .'—*Macbeth, iv. 3.*

About great griefs as a medicine to less. A cue from Sh— [In 'Bentley's Miscellany']. Ln : 1866. Roy. 8°

BPL

'Great griefs, I see, medicine the less.'—*Cymbeline iv. 2.*

About Iago and motiveless malignity [In 'New Monthly Mag.,' Feb.] Ln : 1866. 8°

BUS

About sophisms that plain sense can neither answer nor accept [In 'New Monthly Mag.,' Nov.] Ln : 1867. 8°

BUS

About the physic prescribed to pomp by ex-King Lear [In 'New Monthly Mag.,' July]. Ln : 1867. 8°

BUS

Sh— diversions : A medley of motley wear [First series]. Ln : Daldy, Isbister & Co., 1875. 8°, pp. xxii.-506

BM | BPL | BUS | MPL | SML

For index of the very varied contents see Hubbard & Knapp's Catalogue.

Sh— diversions . . . [First series]. New York : Scribner, 1875. 8°

BUS

Sh— diversions . . . [First series]. Second edition. Ln : Daldy . . . 1876. 8°, pp. xxii.-506

Sh— diversions. Second series. Ln : Daldy . . . 1877. 8°

BM | BPL | BUS | MPL | SML

For contents see Hubbard & Knapp's Catalogue.

'Jacques' *pseud.* Peeps into Sh—. Nos. i. to x. [In 'Hood's Mag.'] 1847-48. 8°

BPL

See also Jaques.

Jadis Catalogue. *See Rodd (T.)*

Jaffray (James) Graphic illustrations of Warwickshire. Ln : Beilby, 1829. F°

SML

These charming views were the work of a little band of artists which included David Cox, P. de Wint, J. D. Harding, and others. At that time Sh—'s country had undergone no very drastic change since Elizabeth held the throne.

Graphic illustrations . . . Birmingham : Thomas Underwood, 1862. 4°, pp. 120. With 45 large plates and vignettes of the Sh— country

BUS

Jaggard (Dorothy) *Printer and Publisher.* See Sh— Poems (*heading*)

Jaggard (Isaac) *Printer and Publisher—* See Boccaccio

  ,, Morgan (J. A.)
  ,, Sh— King Henry V., 1619
  ,, Sh— King Henry VI., ii.-iii., 1619
  ,, Sh— King Lear, 1619
  ,, Sh— Merchant . . . 1619
  ,, Sh— Merry wives, 1619
  ,, Sh— Midsummer . . . 1619
  ,, Sh— Pericles, 1619
  ,, Sh— Sir John Oldcastle, 1619
  ,, Sh— Yorkshire tragedy, 1619
  ,, Sh— Works, 1623

Jaggard (John) *Publisher—* See Barnefield

  ,, Davies
  ,, Giacomo
  ,, Johnson (R.)

Jaggard *1567 ?-1623* (William)] A catalogve of such English bookes, as lately haue bene, and now are, in printing for publication. From the ninth day of October, 1618, vntill Easter terme [May, 1619] next ensuing. And from this forme of beginning (though not in such perfect manner as heereafter may be performed) to be continued for euery halfe yeare. [device.] Ln : Printed by W. Iaggard, 1618. Fcp. 4°, sig. A¹ to A⁴ and B¹, B²

BLO

Somatographia anthropinii, or a description of the body of man, by artificiall figures representing the members and fit termes expressing the same. By W. I— *printer.* [Ln] : Printed by W. Iaggard, dwelling in Barbican . . . 1616. 8°, pp. vi.-310 (including 153 full-page copperplates)

To the above writer (son of a surgeon) or to the MS. of this work Sh— was perhaps indebted for much of his surgical knowledge.

Jaggard (William) *Editor.* See Sh— Works, 1623

Jaggard *1567 ?-1623* (Wm.) *Printer and Publisher—*

See Barclay   See Dering
  ,, Barnefield   ,, Giacomo
  ,, Davies   ,, Johnson (R.)

Offchurch Bury, Warwickshire

See p. 169

Jaggard *1567?-1623* (Wm.) *Printer and Pub-
lisher—*
See Levi
  ,, Mexia
  ,, Milles
  ,, Rhead
  ,, Ryland
  ,, Sh— Passionate ... 1599,1599-1612,1612
  ,, Sh— Threnos (*heading*)
  ,, Sh— Works, 1623
  ,, Swinburne

Jaggard *Bibliographer* (William) Another
Shakespearean discovery [In 'Stratford
Herald,' p. 8, 15 Oct.] 1909
Refers to the signature of William Sh— as witness to a
marriage, said to exist in the parish registers of St.
Martin Carfax, Oxford.

Avon rights and wrongs [In 'Stratford-on-
Avon Herald,' 9th April]. 1909

'Dictionary of National Biography: Epitome.' Four hundred and twenty-four
corrections, errors, and omissions [In
'Notes and Queries,' 10th Series, Vol. 9,
pp. 21, 83; Vol. 10, pp. 183, 282; Vol. 12,
pp. 24, 124, 262, 393]. Ln: 1908-09.
Fcp. 4°   BM | BPL | BUS
Gives particulars of Sh—'s parents, children, and other
relatives, omitted in the 'D. N. B.' and its 'Index-
Epitome.'

Doctor Johnson and Charles Jennens [In
the 'Athenæum,' 27 Nov., No. 4283,
p. 659]. 1909. 4°   BM | BPL

Dunbar pedigree; A biographical chart
tracing descent of the Dunbar family,
through fourteen successive centuries,
from the early English and Scottish
kings. Stratford-on-Avon: Shakespeare
Press, 1910. 4°   BM | BLO | CTC | SML
On large folded linen sheet, with the early Dunbar
arms in red and views of Dunbar Castle.
Gives particulars of Macbeth and his descent.

False dates in Sh— quartos [In 'The
Library,' pp. 208-211]. Ln: De
la More Press, 1909. Roy. 8°   BM

Folk-lore, superstition, and witchcraft in
Sh—: A bibliography. *See* Lucy (Margaret)

Folios and quartos; A review of A. W.
Pollard's 'Sh— folios and quartos' [In
'Liverpool Courier,' 24 Dec., p. 8]. 1909

Future of Sh— and Stratford-upon-Avon.
See Downing (C.)

Index catalogue of the general library at
Warwick Castle. *See* Simmons & Jaggard

Index catalogue of the library, preserved
at Offchurch Bury, of Jane Wightwick
Dowager Countess of Aylesford, Warwickshire. Leamington: T. Simmons,
1891. F°. Manuscript, on handmade
parchment
The single copy (prepared for the owner's private use)
is at Offchurch.

Jaggard *Bibliographer* (William) Index cata-
logue of the Lucy library preserved at
Charlecote, near Stratford-upon-Avon.
Leamington: Thomas Simmons, 1891.
F°. Manuscript, on handmade parchment
The one copy (executed for the owner's private use) is
at Charlecote.

Index to 'Book-Prices Current,' first ten
volumes, 1887-96, constituting a reference list of subjects and, incidentally, a
key to anonymous and pseudonymous
literature. Ln: Stock, 1901. 8°, pp. viii.-
472   BM | BLO | BPL | CTC | SML
Sh— occupies pp. 394-399.
Reviewed in 'Liverpool Daily Post,' 4 Nov., 1901, p. 4.

Index to 'Book-Prices Current' for the
second decade, 1897 to 1906, forming a
key to the ten volumes and, incidentally,
to anonymous, pseudonymous, and suppressed literature. With a supplement
of bibliophiles and bibliopoles. Ln:
Stock, 1909. 8°, pp. xvi.-1058
     BM | BLO | BPL | CTC | SML
Sh— contributes 1174 entries, occupying pp. 875-887.
Reviewed in 'Liverpool Courier,' 23 April, 1909, p. 10.

Jaggard press: A tentative bibliography of
Sh—'s publishers, 1594 - 1627. With
notes by other contributors [In 'Athenæum,' 1902, pp. 83, 145, 210; 1903,
pp. 114-115]. Ln: 1902-3. 4°   BM | BPL

Jaggard press: Some account of Sh—'s
authorised printers and publishers. Compiled from family documents and printed
sources. [In preparation]

On the 'Stratford town Sh—' [In 'Athenæum,' No. 4115, p. 274]. Ln: 1906

On the title 'Sh— press' [In 'Athenæum,'
No. 4127, p. 693; No. 4128, p. 738; No.
4129, p. 774]. Ln: 1906

Portraits of Sh— [In 'Stratford-on-Avon
Herald,' 11th Dec.] 1908

Printing: Its birth and growth. With
illuminated facsimile of the Gutenberg
Bible and a portrait of Caxton. L'pool:
Sh— Press, 1908. Roy. 8°, pp. 16 and
2 plates   BPL
Includes a detailed list of a loan exhibition at Stratford, with Sh— references.

Salvation of Sh— [Notes upon the 1623
Jaggard folio. In 'Liverpool Daily Post,'
9th Feb., p. 7]. 1903. F°   SML

Sh— collection; Index catalogue of the
manuscript and printed Shakespeareana
preserved at Warwick Castle gathered by
George Guy Greville fourth Earl of
Warwick. Leamington: Thomas Simmons, 1890. F°. Manuscript, on handmade parchment   w
Until 1910 two manuscript copies of the above alone
existed; the one described above, prepared for the
fourth Earl's personal use, and the original rough
transcript in the writer's Sh— collection.

With the advent of the volume before the reader there springs into existence a complete printed record of this fascinating assemblage. It included many duplicates which are not indicated herein for lack of space.

See also Simmons.

In 1871 the extensive library at Warwick Castle narrowly escaped destruction by fire. By the prompt thought of Gregory the butler the books were saved by being pitched through the windows upon the lawn of the inner keep. Many were scorched and battered, but none absolutely destroyed.

Jaggard *Bibliographer* (William) Sh— first folio facsimile [Discovery of the supposed unique block elsewhere. In 'Athenæum,' Oct., No. 4017, p. 559]. 1904

Sh— pilgrims and their quest [In 'Liverpool Courier,' 19 April, p. 7]. 1909
On the annual festival at Stratford.

Sh—'s country, from Roman to Tudor times, pictured and described [In 'Liverpool Post and Mercury,' 2nd March, p. 10]. 1910
A lantern lecture, illustrated by two hundred slides, presided over by Sir Edward Russell, given 1st March, 1910, before St. Paul's Literary Society, Birkenhead. Accounts also appeared the same week in the 'Liverpool Courier,' 2nd Mar. (p. 3), 'Birkenhead News,' 5th Mar. (p. 2), 'Birkenhead Advertiser,' 5th Mar. (p. 2), 'Stratford Herald,' 4th Mar. (p. 8).

Sh—'s first play : Some gleanings and conjectures upon 'Love's labours lost' : A paper delivered before the Sh— Club, Stratford - on - Avon. Liverpool : Sh— Press, 1907. 8°, pp. 12   BPL
This paper was re-delivered at their request before the Liverpool members of the British Empire Sh— Society on Feb. 9th, 1910.

Sh—'s grave [In 'Liverpool Courier,' 9 Jan.] 1908

Sh—'s publishers : A defence of the 1623 Jaggard folio [In 'Liverpool Post and Mercury,' 19 Sept.] 1907

Sh—'s publishers : Notes on the Tudor-Stuart period of the Jaggard press. Liverpool : Sh— Press, 1907. 8°, pp. 12   BPL

Sh—'s religion, and other attributes [In 'Stratford-on-Avon Herald,' 16 April]. 1909

Warwickshire Collection : Index catalogue of the books and manuscripts, historical, topographical, and biographical, relating to Warwickshire. Also of works by writers born or resident in the county, and of Warwickshire printed books. Gathered and preserved at Warwick Castle by George Guy Greville fourth Earl of Warwick. Leamington : Thomas Simmons, 1890. F°. Manuscript, written upon handmade parchment   W
Besides the compiler's rough transcript, since partly destroyed by accident, the above copy, for the owner's private use, was the only one prepared.

See also Temple

Jaggard.] A Shakespearean achievement [In 'Liverpool Post and Mercury,' ed. by Sir Edward Russell, 29 March, page 8]. 1910
BPL | SML
Describes at considerable length the work before the reader.

] Roslyn (Guy) William Jaggard [A brief memoir in 'The Biographer,' April, No. 5, Vol. 1, pp. 67-70]. 1909. 8°. With portrait

] Russell (*Sir E. R.*) William Jaggard and his Sh— bibliography [In 'L'pool Post and Mercury,' 17 Feb., 1906, p. 6]
Reprinted in the 'Stratford Herald' the following week.

Jaggard family. *See* Bompas

Jaggard press. *See* Greg

Jago (Richard) Edge Hill, or the rural prospect delineated and moralized. A poem. Ln : J. Dodsley, 1767. 4°, pp. xxiv.-164. With vignettes of the Castles of Kenilworth and Warwick and the artificial ruins at Edgehill   SML
Refers to Sh— pp. 19-21.
Contains list of subscribers, 9 pages.
R. B. Wheler's copy at Stratford bears manuscript annotations, a life of Jago, and some biographical details of the subscribers to the work.

] Hamlet's soliloquy imitated [In Dodsley's 'Collection of Poems,' Vol. 5]. 1775. 8°
BPL

Jahrbuch der Deutschen Shakespeare. *See* Stopes

James I. *of England* (*King*) Company of Actors. *See* Marston

Letter to Wm. Sh— [*See* 'The Drama,' 1822, Vol. 3, p. 28]
At the end of the advt. prefixed to Lintot's edition of the 'Poems,' 1709 [*q.v.*] it is said 'that most learned prince and great patron of learning, King James I., was pleased with his own hand to write an amicable letter to Mr. Sh—, which letter, though now lost, remained long in the hands of Sir W. D'Avenant, as a credible person now can testify.'
According to a manuscript note by Wm. Oldys in his copy of Fuller's Worthies the 'credible person' was John Sheffield Duke of Buckingham.
Dr. Farmer believed the letter to have been written in return for the compliment paid James I. in 'Macbeth.'

Portrait. *See* Sh— Works, 1728

[Proclamation] To all and singular . . . whereas . . . upon Sat. the nynth of July, 1614, there happened a sodaine and terrible fire . . . within Stratford-upon-Avon . . . which within the space of lesse than two howres consumed . . . fifty and fower dwelling houses . . . amounting to eight thowsand pounds . . . Ln : Printed by Thomas Purfoot, 1616. F°. Black letter

Workes . . . Ln : Robert Barker & John Bill, 1616. F°. Collation :—Portrait of K. James on his throne by John Bill after Simon Pass ; engraved title by Elstrack ; printed title, arms of K. James ; dedication to Charles I., with portrait by S. Pass, 2 leaves, preface 14 leaves; text pp. i.-622

Beneath the portrait of K. James are the lines ascribed to Sh—:

> 'Crownes haue their compasse
> Length of dayes their date . . .'
> Triumphes their tombes
> Felicity her fate
> Of more than earth can earth
> Make none partaker
> But knowledge makes the king
> Most like his maker.

James I. *of England* (*King*)—
See Court . . .   See Halliwell
„ Cunningham   „ Revels
„ Extracts   „ Scot
„ Greene (T.)   „ Sh— King Lear, 1608
„ Greenstreet   „ Sh— Mucedorus, 1610
„ Gwinne   „ Stopes

James (Elias). *See* Sh— Epitaph

James (George)] Bacon-Sh— controversy: I.-II., A plea for the plaintiff; III., Notes on the origin and construction of the plays; IV., Short studies on the origin of the plays; V., Francis Bacon in the sonnets; VI., New light on 'Love's labours lost' and 'Macbeth'; VII., Francis Bacon and St. Albans and new light on Dr. Caius and the 'Merry wives,' pp. 44; VIII., F. Bacon the statesman and primary causes of the alienation of the plays. Birmingham, 1894-95. 3 vols. Cr. 8°   BM | BPL

Francis Bacon in the sonnets. Birmingham, 1900. 8°, pp. 40   BPL | BUS | MPL

Francis Bacon the author of Sh—. Birmingham, 1893. 8°   BM | BPL

James (*Col. Sir* Hy.) *Printer. See* Sh— Sonnets, 1862

Jameson (Anna Brownell) Characteristics of women; moral, poetical, and historical. With fifty vignette etchings [from the author's designs]. Ln: Saunders & Otley, 1832. 2 vols. 12°. With plates   BUS | CPL
Contains many of Sh—'s female characters.

Characteristics . . . Second edition. Ln: Saunders & Otley, 1833. 2 vols. 12°. 50 vignette etchings   BPL | MPL

Characteristics . . . Third edition. Ln: Saunders & O., 1836. 2 vols. 12°   BPL | BUS

Characteristics . . . New York: Saunders & Otley, 1837. 12°, pp. ii.-viii.-382 BUS

Characteristics . . . Fourth edition. Ln: 1846. 2 vols. 8°

Characteristics . . . Fifth edition. Ln: Saunders & Otley, 1858. 2 vols. 8°. With plates re-engraved   MPL | SML

Jameson (Anna Brownell) Characteristics . . . Boston [U.S.] Ticknor & Field. 1866. 16°, pp. 468 and front. by Hayter BUS
Characteristics . . . [Review in ' Blackwood's Mag.,' Jan.-Ap.] 1833. 8°   BPL | BUS
Sh—'s female characters. 2nd ed. Bielefeld. 1843. 12°   BUS
Sh—'s heroines: Characteristics of women. ' Standard Library.' Ln: Bell, 1879. 8°   BM | BPL | MPL
Sh—'s heroines. Goupil-gravure studies. Ln: Low, 1888. 4°
Sh—'s heroines. Ln: Newnes, 1896. Cr. · 8°, pp. 332
Sh—'s heroines. With portraits of famous players in character. 1897. 8°   BM | BPL | SML
Sh—'s heroines. With decorative designs by R. A. Bell. Ln: Dent, 1901. 16°, pp. 392   BPL | BUS
Sh—'s heroines. ' Temple Classics.' Ln: Dent, 1904. 12°, pp. 350
Sh—'s heroines . . . With decorative designs by R. A. Bell. ' Miranda's library.' Ln: Dent, 1905. 8°, pp. 396
Sh—'s heroines . . . ' York library.' Ln: Bell, 1905. 12°, pp. 352

Jamieson (John) Congal and Fenella: A tale, in verse. Ln: 1791. 8°   w
Founded upon ' Macbeth.'

Jancke (Theodor) *Editor. See* Sh— Julius Cæsar, 1861

Jane, the Queen's fool. *See* Stopes

Janet (Gustave) *Artist. See* Sh— The tempest, 1860

'Jaques,' *pseud.* Modern corruptions of Sh—'s text. 1869. 8°   BM
See also Jacques.

Jarrow (J.) Sh—: A tercentenary poem. 1864. 8°

Jarvie (M.) *Edinburgh Publisher. See* Sh— Taming, 1756

Jarvis (J.)] Concise account of Garrick's Jubilee, held at Stratford-upon-Avon in 1769, and of the commemorative festivals in 1827 and 1830. With a brief notice of the . . . Sh— Club, established at the Falcon Inn in 1824. Stratford-upon-Avon: J. Ward, 1830. 8°, pp. 24   BPL | BUS | W
With a folded broadside of the 1830 festival proceedings inserted at end of Warwick copy.

Correct details of the ceremonies attending the Sh— gala, celebrated at Stratford-upon-Avon on . . . April 23rd, 24th, 25th, 1827. Together with some account of Garrick's Jubilee in 1769. Stratford-upon-Avon: J. Bacon [1827]. 8°, pp. 30 and front.   BM | BPL | BUS | CPL | W
The author describes himself as ' Reporter to the London Journals.'

(171)

Jarvis (J.)] Descriptive account of the late gala festival at Stratford-upon-Avon, in commemoration of the natal day of Sh—, the King's adopted birthday, and the festival of Saint George . . . 23rd, 24th, and 25th days of April, 1827. Stratford-upon-Avon : R. Lapworth, 1827. 8°, pp. 60
BM

Descriptive account of the second royal gala festival at Stratford-upon-Avon in commemoration of the natal day of Sh—, 23rd, 24th, 26th, and 27th April, 1830 . . . By a member of the Royal Sh— Club. Stratford-upon-Avon : R. Lapworth, 1830. 12°, pp. 88. With frontispiece
BM | BPL | BUS

] Descriptive account of the second royal gala festival . . . at Stratford. Leamington, 1830. 12°
Dedicated to the Stratford Sh— Club.

Jarvis *Bookseller* (John Wm.) Catalogue of books and pamphlets, wholly relating to Sh—. 1892. 8°
BPL
Literary collection [Sh— newspaper cuttings]. Stratford, 1879, etc. 4°
BPL
The glyptic or musee phusee glyptic . . . Jottings from Stratford-on-Avon . . . With . . . description of Henry Jones's museum. Ln : J. R. Smith, 1875. 8°, pp. 112. Illustrated by T. Bewick and others
BPL | BUS | SML

Jauncy (T.) *Publisher.* See Sh— King Henry IV., ii., 1719
Jay (M.) *Editor.* See Sh— Works, 1836-39
Jeaffreson (John Cordy) New view of Sh—'s will [In 'Athenæum,' No. 2844, p. 539 ; 2847, p. 634 ; 2848, p. 666 ; 2906, p. 18]. 1882

Sh—'s will a holograph document. See Sh— Will . . . (*heading*)
Jealousy exemplified. See Sh— Othello, 1820
Jebb (H. G.) Letters to Samuel Timmins on Sh—. Manuscript. 1890. 4°
BPL
Jebb (*Sir* R. C.) Translations into Greek and Latin verse. See Sh— Works : Ext. 1907
Jefferson *Actor* (Joseph) Autobiography. Ln : Unwin, 1890. 8°. With portraits and plates
SML
Jefferson (J.) *See also* American . . .
Jefferson.] Winter (W.) The Jeffersons. Boston : Osgood, 1881-82. 12°
SML
Jeffrey (Edward) *Publisher—*
See Sh— Poems, 1795, 1798
 ,, Sh— Works, 1811

Jeffes (Abel) *Printer—*
See Boccaccio
 ,, Gascoigne
 ,, Lodge

Jeffrey (Francis *Lord*) Critique of Hazlitt's 'Characters of Sh—'s plays ' [In ' Edinburgh Review,' Aug.] 1817. 8° BM | BLO
'More full of wisdom, ridicule and sagacity than all the moralists and satirists that ever existed, he [Sh—] is more wild, airy, and inventive, more pathetic and fantastic, than all the poets of all regions and ages of the world, and has all those elements so happily mixed up in him and bears his high faculties so temperately, that the most severe reader cannot complain of him for want of strength or of reason, nor the most sensitive for defect of ornament or ingenuity. Everything in him is in unmeasured abundance and unequalled perfection, but everything so balanced and kept in subordination as not to jostle or disturb or take the place of another. The most exquisite poetical conceptions, images, and descriptions are given with such brevity and introduced with such skill, as merely to adorn with loading the sense they accompany. Although his sails are purple and perfumed, and his prow of beaten gold, they waft him on his voyage not less but more rapidly and directly than if they had been composed of baser materials. All his excellences, like those of nature herself, are thrown out together, and instead of interfering with, support and recommend each other. His flowers are not tied up in garlands, nor his fruits crushed into baskets, but spring living from the soil in all the dew and freshness of youth ; while graceful foliage in which they lurk and the ample branches, the rough and vigorous stem, and the wide spreading roots on which they depend, are present along with them, and share in their places, the equal care of their creator.'

On Sh— [In ' Edinburgh Review.,' Aug., Vol. 18, p. 285]. 1811. 8° BM | BLO
'Our love of Sh— therefore is not a monomania or solitary and unaccountable infatuation, but is merely the natural love which all men bear to those forms of excellence that are accommodated to their peculiar character, temperament and situation, and which will always return and assert its power over their affections, long after authority has lost its reverence, fashions been antiquated, and artificial tastes passed away.'

Jemmat (Catherine) On seeing Mr. Barry perform the parts of Othello, Romeo, Jaffier, and Castalio [In ' Miscellanies ']. Ln : 1766. 4° BUS | W
Jenkin of Wales ; his love-course and perambulation, 1647. Ed. by J. O. Halliwell. Ln : Privately printed, 1861. 8° BPL
Jenkin (Fleeming) & Bell (George Joseph) Mrs. Siddons as Lady Macbeth, from contemporary notes [In the ' Nineteenth Century,' Feb.] Ln : 1878. Roy. 8°
BPL | BUS
Jenks (Tudor Storrs) In the days of Sh—. See Sh—] Jenks
Jennens (Charles)] The tragedy of ' King Lear,' as lately published, vindicated from the abuse of the critical reviewers, by the editor . . . Ln : 1772. 8°
Jennens was a millionaire grandee of Gopsall Hall, Leicestershire, described by Dr. Johnson as ' a vain fool, crazed by his wealth, who, were he in heaven, would criticize the Lord Almighty ; who lives surrounded by all the luxuries of an Eastern potentate— verily an English " Solyman the magnificent " ; who never walks abroad without a train of footmen at his heels, and, like Wolsey, with a scented sponge 'neath his nose, lest the breath of the vulgar herd should contaminate his sacred person.'

Jennens (Charles) *Editor*—
See Sh— Hamlet, 1773
,, Sh— Julius Cæsar, 1773, 1774
,, Sh— King Lear, 1770
,, Sh— Macbeth, 1773
,, Sh— Othello, 1773
,, Sh— Works, 1770-74
Jennings (H. J.) Famous Lears [In the
'Gentleman's Mag.'] 1892. 8°   BPL
'King Lear' at the 'Lyceum' [In 'Gentle-
man's Mag.'] 1892. 8°   BPL
Jennings (J. A.) Modern elocutionist. *See*
Sh— Works : Ext. 1882
Jennings (R.) *Publisher*. *See* Sh— Works,
1823, 1826-29
Jephson (J. M.) Glossary. *See* Sh— Works,
1874, 1879
Sh—; his birthplace, home and grave. *See*
Sh—] Jephson
Jephson (J. M.) *Editor*. *See* Sh— The tem-
pest, 1864, 1866, 1867, 1871, 1872, 1874
Jeremiah (John) Aid to Sh— study. Ln :
Sotheran, 1880. 8°, pp. lxiv.-8. With
Chandos portrait   BM | BPL | BUS
History of the Urban Club. Ln : Clayton,
1876. 8°   SML
Notes on Sh—. *See* Sh—] Jeremiah
Shakespearean memorabilia : Being a col-
lation of all contemporary allusions to
the bard and his works. Ln : Skipper &
East, 1877. Roy. 8°, pp. 12   BPL | BUS
Shakespearean souvenir : Report of the
festival of the Urban Club. 1877. 8° BPL
Jerningham (Edward) Sh— gallery. A poem
[dedicated to John Boydell]. Ln : J. Rob-
son, 1791. 4°, pp. viii.-24   BPL | BUS | W
Jerome (Jerome Klapka) On the stage and
off. Ln : Field & Tuer. Cr. 8°
Stage-land : Curious habits and customs of
its inhabitants. Ln : 1889. 8°. Illust.
Jerrard (Paul) Flowers from Stratford-on-
Avon [A selection from the flowers mentioned in the poems and plays of Sh—].
Richly coloured from the original drawings . . . Ln : P. Jerrard [1852]. F°. 14
plates. Text printed in gold
       BM | BPL | SML
This work was suggested to the artist, during a summer
ramble along the Avon, by the profusion of wild
flowers growing on spots where Sh— obtained his
first impressions of nature.
The plates are coloured by hand.
Jerrard invented, and bound his publications in, a
species of papier-mache which he termed 'patent
enamel binding.' It proved too brittle and heavy for
successful adoption.
] Sh— tableaux [Pictures illustrative of passages in the plays . . . Twelve compositions . . . richly coloured . . . with the
text printed in gold]. Ln : P. Jerrard
[1854]. F°. 13 plates   BPL | CPL
The plates are coloured by hand.

Jerrard (Paul) *Publisher*. *See* Sh— Works,
1854
Jerrold (Walter) Descriptive Index to Sh—'s
characters. *See* Sh— Works : Ext. 1905
Jervis (Swynfen) Dictionary of the language
of Sh— [Ed. by Alex. Dyce]. Ln : J. R.
Smith, 1868. 4°, pp. iv.-374
       BM | BPL | BUS | CPL | MPL | SML
Proposed emendations of the text of Sh—'s
plays, with confirmatory and illustrative
passages from the poet's works and those
of his contemporaries. Ln : Longman,
1860. 8°, pp. 28   BM | BPL | BUS | CPL
Proposed emendations . . . Second edition.
Ln : Longman, 1861. 8°, pp. 20
       BM | BUS
Jesse (Edward) Book of Sh— gems. *See*
Sh— Works : Ext. 1854
Jest books—
See Facetiæ
,, Pleasant taunts
,, Sh—] Sh—'s Jest book
,, Specimen
Jesters—
See Actors   *See* Jane
,, Collier (J. P.)   ,, Stage
,, Doran   ,, Tarleton
Jewitt *Editor*. *See* Sh— Works, 1853
Jews—
See Hemminge
,, Levi
,, Salaman
,, Sh— Merchant . . .
John.] Interlude of Johan the evangelist.
Imprynted at Ln : in Foster laene by
John Waley. Ln : Malone Society, 1907.
Fcp. 4°   BM | SML
John (Ivor B.) *Editor*. *See* Sh— King John,
1907
Johnson *New York Publisher*. *See* Sh—
Works, 1854-56, 1855-59
Johnson (Andrea C.) *See* Poole & Johnson
Johnson (Arthur) *Publisher*—
See Sh— Merry devil . . . 1608, 1612, 1617
,, Sh— Merry wives, 1602, 1619
Johnson *junior* (Ben) Poems . . . being a
miscelanie of seriousness, wit, mirth and
mysterie . . . composed by W. S.——,
gent. Ln : Tho. Passenger, 1672. 8°
Contains the Sh— poem 'To all the ancient family of
the Luceys and to all their honourable extractions.'
Malone describes the volume in his edition of Sh—.
Johnson (Charles) History of the lives and
actions of the most famous highwaymen.
Birmingham, 1742. F°   BUS
With lengthy account of Sir John Falstaff.
Love in a forest. *See* Sh— As you like it,
1723
Johnson (Charles) *Editor*. *See* Sh— Taming
. . . 1716, 1767, 1786

Johnson (C. F.) Sh— and his critics. Boston [U.S.], 1909. 8°   BPL

Johnson (E.) *Publisher*—
See Longinus
,, Sh— Hamlet, 1767
,, Sh— Timon . . . 1770
,, Sh— Works, 1773
,, Sh— Works : Ext. 1778

Johnson (Fanny) *Editor*—
See Sh— King Henry V., 1901
,, Sh— Twelfth night, 1904

Johnson (Gerard) *Sculptor. See* Dugdale

Johnson (Jesse) Testimony of the sonnets as to the authorship of the Sh— plays and poems. New York : Putnam, 1899. 16°
    BM | BPL | BUS

Johnson (J.) *Printer. See* Jackson

Johnson (John) *Publisher*—
See Hurdis
,, Miller
,, Ritson
,, Sh— Twelfth night, 1766
,, Sh— Works, 1790, 1798, 1803, 1811
,, Sh— Works : Ext. 1792
,, Webb

Johnson (Richard) Look on me, London ! 1613. *See* Reprints

Most famous historie of the seuen champions of Christendome. Ln : Cuthbert Burbie, 1596. Fcp. 4°
A work familiar to Sh—. On p. 4 is the prototype of a passage in 'King Lear,' and elsewhere are other parallels.
'The most complete champion that ever I heard.'—*King Henry VI., ii. 4, 10.*
It was reprinted in 1608 by Elizabeth Burbie.

Walks of Moorfields, 1607. *See* Reprints

Johnson (R. Brimley) *Editor*—
See Sh— As you like it, 1900
,, Sh— Julius Cæsar, 1899
,, Sh— King Richard II., 1898
,, Sh— Macbeth, 1903
,, Sh— Merchant . . . 1898
,, Sh— Midsummer . . . 1894, 1900
,, Sh— The tempest, 1899
,, Sh— Works, 1898, 1903

Johnson (Robert) & Botero (G.)] Historicall description of the most famous king-domes and common-weales in the worlde. Relating their scituations, manners, cus-tomes, ciuill gouernment, and other memorable matters. Translated into English and enlarged . . . in no language ever before imprinted. Printed at Ln : [by Wm. Iaggard] for Iohn Iaggard, 1603. Fcp. 4°, pp. iv.-268
Second edition. The first appeared in 1601, the third in 1608, and the fourth in 1616.
'King and commander of our commonweal,
  The wide world's emperor . . .'
     —*Titus Andronicus, I. i. 114.*

Johnson *Playwright* (Samuel) Blazing comet. Ln : 1732. 8°. With frontispiece
'In the days of Q. Elizabeth the taste of the fair sex made a Sh—; their palates like steel struck upon Sh—'s flint and forced all his fire' (p. viii.)

Johnson (*Dr.* Samuel) Dedication. *See* Lennox Irene. *See* Essay on tragedy
Life of Collins. *See* Collins (W.)
Miscellaneous observations on the tragedy of ' Hamlet, Prince of Denmark.' With a preface containing some general re-marks on the writings of Sh—. Ln : W. Clarke, 1752. 8°, pp. xii.-10-52
    BM | BUS | W

Miscellaneous observations on the tragedy of ' Macbeth,' with remarks on Sir T. H[anmer]'s edition of Sh—. To which are affix'd ' Proposals for a new edition of Shakeshear [*sic*] with a specimen.' Ln : E. Cave, 1745. 12°, pp. ii.-64
    BPL | BUS | W
The Boston copy bears manuscript comments in which the writer is unconsciously amusing in his patronage of our literary leviathan. For instance, he says :—
' Most of this man's notes are pretty tolerable and many of them very necessary.'

Notices of playhouses. *See* Dodsley

On Sh—: Essays and notes selected and set forth. With an Introd. by Walter Raleigh. Oxford : University Press, 1908. Cr. 8°

Philological tracts and prefaces. Ln : W. Baynes & Son, 1824. 12°, pp. 396 BPL
Sh— occupies pp. 71-217.

Portrait. *See* Sh—] Knight

Preface to . . . Sh—'s plays. Ln : J. & R. Tonson . . . 1765. 8°, pp. 72
    BM | BPL | BUS | W
' Addison speaks the language of poets, and Sh— of men ' (page 3).
Reprinted in 1858.

Preface . . . *See* Eighteenth . . .

Preface . . . *See* Sh— Works, 1805, 1806, 1811, 1815, 1818, 1823, 1824, 1830, 1832, 1832-34, 1835-36, 1838, 1840, 1858, 1860, 1862, 1875

Prologue spoken by D. Garrick at the open-ing of Drury Lane theatre, 1747
' When learning's triumph o'er her barbarous foes
First reared the stage, immortal Sh— rose ;
Each change of many-coloured life he drew
Exhausted worlds, and then imagined new.
Existence saw him spurn her bounded reign,
And panting time toiled after him in vain.
His powerful strokes presiding truth impressed,
And unresisted passion stormed the breast.'
  .   .   .   .   .
Drinking tea one day at Garrick's with Mr. Langton, he (Johnson) was questioned if he was not somewhat of a heretic as to Sh—? Said Garrick, ' I doubt he is a little of an infidel.' ' Sir,' said Johnson, ' I will stand by the lines I have written on Sh— in my prologue at the opening of your theatre.'
Mr. Langton suggested that in the line ' And panting time . . .' Johnson might have had in his eye the

SAM: JOHNSON LL.D.

See p. 174

passage in 'The tempest' where Prospero says of Miranda : 'She will outstrip all praise and make it halt behind her.'

Johnson said nothing. Garrick then ventured to observe, 'I do not think that the happiest line in praise of Sh—.' Johnson exclaimed, smiling, 'Prosaical rogues ! Next time I write I'll make both time and space pant.'--*Boswell's Life of Johnson (Langton's notes)*.

Johnson (*Dr.* Samuel) Proposals for printing, by subscription, the 'Dramatick works of W. Sh—, corrected and illustrated ' . . . Ln : 1756. 8°

Short strictures of the ' Plays of Sh—.' Ln : 1900. 32°, pp. 52

] The Rambler. Ln : J. Payne, 1749-52. 2 vols. F°

In the issue No. 156, 14th Sept., 1751, Johnson wrote, 'Instead of vindicating tragi-comedy by the success of Sh—, we ought perhaps to pay new honours to that transcendent and unbounded genius that could preside over the passions in sport : who, to actuate the affections, needed not the slow gradation of common means, but could fill the heart with instantaneous jollity or sorrow and vary our disposition as he changed his scenes. Perhaps the effects even of Sh—'s poetry might have been greater, had he not counteracted himself ; and we might have been more interested in the distresses of his heroes, had we not been so frequently diverted by the jokes of his buffoons.'

Johnson (*Dr.* Samuel) *Editor*—

See Sh— All's well . . . 1786

,, Sh— Antony . . . 1792

,, Sh— As you like it, 1785, 1802

,, Sh— Comedy . . . 1785

,, Sh— Coriolanus, 1818

,, Sh— Cymbeline, 1802

,, Sh— Hamlet, 1785, 1806, 1810

,, Sh— Julius Cæsar, 1777, 1800, 1803, 1807

,, Sh— King Henry IV., i., 1785, 1818

,, Sh— King Henry IV., ii., 1785, 1807

,, Sh— King Henry V., 1785, 1822

,, Sh— King Henry VI., i., 1786, 1813

,, Sh— King Henry VI., ii., 1786, 1813

,, Sh— King Henry VI., iii., 1786, 1818

,, Sh— King Henry VIII., 1809

,, Sh— King John, 1811

,, Sh— King Lear, 1785, 1822

,, Sh— King Richard II., 1786, 1812, 1822

,, Sh— King Richard III., 1812

,, Sh— Love's labours lost, 1785, 1788, 1822

,, Sh— Macbeth, 1778, 1788, 1807

,, Sh— Measure . . . 1785, 1806, 1820

,, Sh— Merchant . . . 1785, 1811, 1822, 1830

,, Sh— Merry wives, 1806

,, Sh— Midsummer . . . 1785, 1806, 1822

,, Sh— Much ado, 1818

,, Sh— Othello, 1785, 1788, 1802

,, Sh— Romeo . . . 1806

,, Sh— Taming . . . 1785, 1812

,, Sh— The tempest, 1806

Johnson (*Dr.* Samuel) *Editor*—

See Sh— Timon, 1785, 1788, 1820

,, Sh— Titus, 1785, 1809

,, Sh— Troilus . . . 1811

,, Sh— Twelfth night, 1803

,, Sh— Two gentlemen, 1786, 1812

,, Sh— Winter's tale, 1820

,, Sh— Works, 1765, 1766, 1768, 1771, 1773, 1778, 1780, 1785, 1785-87, 1786-88, 1792, 1793, 1795-96, 1798-1800, 1799-1802, 1802-04, 1803, 1805-09, 1807, 1809, 1810-12, 1813, 1817, 1817-18, 1819, 1820-21, 1821, 1822, 1823, 1824, 1824-26, 1825, 1826, 1827, 1828, 1830, 1831, 1832, 1833, 1835, 1835-36, 1836, 1837, 1840, 1841, 1842, 1843, 1844, 1845, 1846, 1847, 1848, 1849, 1850, 1851, 1851-52, 1852, 1852-59, 1854, 1855, 1857, 1858, 1859, 1860, 1861, 1863, 1864, 1866, 1868, 1897

Johnson.] Boswell (James) Life of Samuel Johnson, LL.D., comprehending an account of his studies and numerous works, in chronological order. Ln : C. Dilly, 1791. 2 vols. 4°. With portrait by Heath after Sir Joshua Reynolds, and facsimiles   BM

Constantly reprinted.

] Johnson and Garrick. *See* Reynolds

Johnson (*Dr.* S.)—

See Annotations . . .   *See* Miscellaneous . . .

,, Etymologist   ,, Reynolds

,, Jennens   ,, Ribbans

,, Kenrick   ,, Smith (H. & J.)

,, Lovibond   ,, Zetes

Johnson *and others* (*Dr.* S.) Prefaces to Sh—'s plays by Dr. Johnson, Mr. Pope, Mr. Theobald, Sir J. Hanmer, and Dr. Warburton. With some account of the life of Sh— by Mr. Rowe. Ln : 1765. 8°

Johnson (*Dr.* S.) Steevens (G.) & Malone (E.) Annotations illustrative of the plays of Sh—. 1819. 2 vols. 8°   BPL

Johnson (*Dr.* S.) Steevens (G.) and others. Annotations . . . upon ' All's well . . .' Ln : John Bell . . . 1787. 12°, pp. 92 w

Annotations upon ' Antony and Cleopatra.' Ln : J. Bell, 1787. 12°, pp. 130   w

Annotations upon ' As you like it.' Ln : J. Bell, 1787. 12°, pp. 64

Annotations upon the ' Comedy of errors.' Ln : J. Bell, 1787. 12°, pp. 42

Annotations upon ' Coriolanus.' Ln : J. Bell, 1787. 12°, pp. 72

Annotations upon ' Coriolanus.' Ln : J. Bell, 1787. 8°, pp. 72, large paper   w

Johnson (*Dr.* S.) Steevens (G.) and others. Annotations upon 'Cymbeline.' Ln : J. Bell, 1787. 12°, pp. 82

Annotations upon ' Hamlet.' Ln : J. Bell, 1787. 12°, pp. 200   SML

Annotations upon ' Julius Cæsar.' Ln : J. Bell, 1787. 12°, pp. 50   SML

Annotations upon ' Julius Cæsar.' Ln : J. Bell, 1787. 8°, pp. 50, large paper   W

Annotations upon ' King Henry IV., Part i.' Ln : J. Bell, 1787. 12°   W

Annotations upon ' King Henry IV., Part ii.' Ln : J. Bell, 1787. 12°   W

Annotations upon ' King Henry IV., Part ii.' Ln : J. Bell, 1787. 8°. Large paper   W

Annotations upon ' King Henry V.' Ln : J. Bell, 1787. 12°   W

Annotations upon ' King Henry VI., Part i.' Ln : J. Bell, 1787. 12°, pp. 46   W

Annotations upon ' King Henry VI., Part ii.' Ln : J. Bell, 1787. 12°, pp. 58   W

Annotations upon ' King Henry VI., Part iii.' Ln : J. Bell, 1787. 12°, pp. 60   W

Annotations upon ' King Henry VI.' [Parts i.-iii.] Ln : J. Bell, 1787. 3 parts. 8°. Large paper   W

Annotations upon ' King Henry VIII.' Ln : J. Bell, 1787. 12°, pp. 82   W

Annotations upon ' King John.' Ln : J. Bell, 1787. 12°, pp. 82   W

Annotations upon ' King John.' Ln : J. Bell, 1787. 8°, pp. 82. Large paper   W

Annotations upon ' King Lear.' Ln : J. Bell, 1787. 12°, pp. 164   W

Annotations upon ' King Richard III.' Ln : J. Bell, 1787. 12°, pp. 92

Annotations upon ' King Richard III.' Ln : 1787. 8°, pp. 92. Large paper   W

Annotations upon ' Love's labours lost.' Ln : J. Bell, 1787. 12°, pp. 122

Annotations upon ' Macbeth.' Ln : J. Bell, 1787. 12°, pp. 146   W

Annotations upon ' Macbeth ' . . . Ln : J. Bell, 1787. 8°. Large paper   W

Annotations upon ' Measure for measure.' Ln : J. Bell, 1787. 12°, pp. 122

Annotations upon the ' Merchant of Venice.' Ln : J. Bell, 1787. 12°, pp. 76

Annotations upon the ' Merry wives . . .' Ln : J. Bell, 1787. 12°, pp. 126

Annotations upon ' Midsummer night's dream.' Ln : J. Bell, 1787. 12°, pp. 100

Annotations upon ' Much ado . . .' Ln : J. Bell, 1787. 12°, pp. 76

Annotations upon ' Othello.' Ln : J. Bell, 1787. 12°, pp. 156   W

Annotations upon ' Romeo and Juliet.' Ln : J. Bell, 1787. 12°, pp. 124   W

Johnson (*Dr.* S.) Steevens (G.) and others. Annotations upon 'Romeo and Juliet' . . . Ln : J. Bell, 1787. 8°, pp. 124. Large paper   W

Annotations upon ' Taming of the shrew.' Ln : J. Bell, 1787. 12°, pp. 98

Annotations upon ' The tempest.' Ln : J. Bell, 1787. 12°, pp. 100

Annotations upon ' Timon of Athens.' Ln : J. Bell, 1787. 12°, pp. 84   W

Annotations upon ' Timon of Athens ' . . . Ln : 1787. 8°, pp. 84. Large paper   W

Annotations upon ' Titus Andronicus.' Ln : J. Bell, 1787. 12°, pp. 24

Annotations . . . upon ' Troilus and Cressida.' Ln : J. Bell, 1787. 12°, pp. 92   BUS

Annotations upon ' Twelfth night.' Ln : J. Bell, 1787. 12°, pp. 94

Annotations . . . upon ' Twelfth night.' Ln : J. Bell, 1787. 8°, pp. 94. Large paper   BUS

Annotations upon ' Two gentlemen of Verona.' Ln : J. Bell, 1787. 12°, pp. 48

Annotations upon the ' Winter's tale.' Ln : J. Bell, 1787. 12°, pp. 84   W

Johnson & Steevens. *See also* Mason

Johnson (Thomas) New book of new conceits, 1630. *See* Literature

Johnson (Thomas) *Printer—*
See Sh— Birth . . . 1662
   ,, Webster & Rowley

Johnson (Thomas) *Ln. and Hague Publisher—*
See Sh— Antony . . . 1720
   ,, Sh— Hamlet, 1720
   ,, Sh— King Henry IV., i., 1710, 1721
   ,, Sh— Merchant . . . 1711, 1721
   ,, Sh— Timon . . . 1712

Johnson (Thomas) *Manchester Publisher. See* Sh— Works, 1850

Johnson (W. S.) *Publisher. See* Sh— The tempest, 1850

Johnston (G.) Cupid's birthday book. *See* Sh— Works : Ext. 1875

Johnston (John) *Publisher. See* Dibdin

Johnston (W.) *Publisher—*
See Heath
   ,, Sh— Hamlet, 1767
   ,, Sh— King Henry VIII., 1762
   ,, Sh— Othello, 1765
   ,, Sh— The tempest, 1761
   ,, Sh— Works, 1762, 1773

Johnston (W. P.) Prototype of ' Hamlet,' and other Sh— problems. New York : Bedford [1890]. Cr. 8°   BPL | BUS | SML

Johnstone. Table talker, or brief essays on society and literature. Ln: 1840
Says in Vol. i., p. 183 :—'Some men can only acquire knowledge by a careful process of painstaking investigation, while the minds of others descend at once, and with a 'swoop, as it were, upon the truth of which they are in search. Others again can not only do this, but having grasped the truth they soar upward with it to the highest pinnacles of imaginative loftiness, or beyond these even to the empyrean of thought, where the minds of ordinarily gifted men may not follow them. Of this last class was Sh— the most wonderful of mere men that we know to have ever lived.'

Johnstone (A. S.) Spirit of Sh— . . . [Sonnets in the 'Water nymph']. 1905. 12°, pp. 145-146   BPL

Jolley Bibliophile (Thomas) Catalogue: Shakespearean portion. [1843-44.] 8°, excerpt of pp. 43 to 66   BUS
Library. See Catalogue, 1843-44, 1855
List of Shakespeareana [giving editions, dates and prices]. 1834. Holograph manuscript on paper. 8°, pp. 58   W

Jones. Coventry, Warwick, and Birmingham Magazine. See Sh—] Jones
Jones Publisher. See Sh— Works, 1818, 1823, 1825, 1826, 1827, 1828, 1832
Jones Dublin Publisher. See Sh— Merchant . . . 1805
Jones (B. C.) Editor—
  See Sh— Hamlet, 1846
  ,, Sh— King Richard III., 1846
  ,, Sh— Othello, 1846
Jones (Chloe B.) Lover's Sh—: Quotations. See Sh— Works: Ext. 1897, 1899, 1900
Jones (E.) Bibliophile. See Catalogue, 1824-25
Jones (F.) Croker (W.)
J——s [? Jones] (Frederick). See D—— (T. C.)
Jones (G.) Publisher. See Grey (Z.)
Jones Actor (George) First annual jubilee oration upon . . . Sh—. See Sh—] Jones
] Pilgrim of Avon, by 'Leigh Clifte.' Ln: Simpkin, 1836. 8°, pp. viii.-24 BPL | BUS
Tecumseh and the prophet of the west. See Sh—] Jones
Jones.] Mr. George Jones the American tragedian [In 'The Literary,' Nov.] New York, 1836. 8°   BUS
Jones of Stratford (Henry) The glyptic. See Jarvis
Jones of Drogheda (Henry) Clifton: A poem. With an ode to Sh— . . . Bristol, 1773. 4°   BPL
Ode to Sh—, in honour of the jubilee [with 'Arcana; A poem']. Wolverhampton: T. Smith, 1769. 8°, pp. 6   BUS | W
Ode to Sh— . . . Bristol: T. Cocking, 1779. 8°, pp. 6   BUS
Jones Dramatist (Henry Arthur) Introduction. See Filon
Renascence of the English drama. 1895. 12°   BPL

Jones (H. K.) Notes of a conversation on Sh—'s 'Tempest' [In 'Journal of speculative philosophy,' July]. St. Louis, 1875. 8°   BUS
Jones.] Cunningham (Peter) Inigo Jones: A life of the architect.; Remarks on some of his sketches for masques and dramas by J. R. Planché. Ed. from the original MSS. of Ben Jonson, John Marston, etc. by J. P. Collier. With facsimiles and portraits. See Sh—] Sh— Soc.
] Cunningham (P.) Inigo Jones and his office under the Crown. With extracts from the accounts of the Paymaster of the Crown Works preserved by the Audit Office. See Sh—] Sh— Soc.
Jones (J.) Coventry Printer. See Dugdale
Jones of Gray's Inn (John). See Ireland (S. W. H.)
Jones (John Winter) Observations on the division of man's life into stages prior to the 'Seven ages' of Sh—. Ln: 1853. 4°   BPL | BUS | MPL
Offprinted from 'Archæologia,' Vol. 35, pp. 167-189.
Observations . . . Ln : Ellis, 1861. 4°, pp. 26. Illust.   BUS
Jones (Owen) Artist—
  See Sh— Winter's tale, 1866
  ,, Warren
Jones or Ihones (Richard) Printer—
  See Breton   See Robinson
  ,, Edyth   ,, Segar
  ,, Frederick   ,, Whetstone
Jones (Robert) Composer. See Sh— Poems, 1862
Jones (R. D.) Ethical element in literature: Method of teaching illustrated by an interpretation of . . . 'Julius Cæsar.' Bloomington: Public School Co., 1891. 12°   SML
Jones (Stephen) New biographical dictionary. Ln: T. Bensley . . . 1799. 12°, pp. viii. and A¹ to OO² in sixes, unpaged
Sh— sig. II6.
Jones (T.) Publisher. See May (T.)
Jones (William) Printer—
  See Alabaster
  ,, Prynne
Jones (William) Publisher—
  See Sh— Mucedorus, 1598, 1606, 1610, 1613, 1615
  ,, Sh— Thomas . . . 1602
Jones (Wm.) Dublin Publisher—
  See Sh— Works, 1791
  ,, Sh— Works: Ext. 1791
Jones (W. H. S.) Editor. See Sh— King Richard III., 1902
Jonson (Benjamin) Additions to the 'Spanish tragedy.' See Kyd
Autograph. See Baudius

(177)   12

Jonson (Benjamin) Bartholomew fair. Ln :
1614. Fcp. 4°
Speaks of 'a servant-monster,' doubtless referring to
Caliban in 'The tempest.'

British muse. *See* Sh— Works : Ext. 1738

Epitaph on Sh—'s tomb. *See Sh*—] Epitaph

Euery man in his hvmovr. As it hath beene
sundry times publickly acted by the
right honorable the Lord Chamberlaine
his seruants . . . Imprinted at Ln : for
Walter Burre and are to be sould at his
shoppe in Paule's church-yarde, 1601.
Fcp. 4°
In the cast of this play Sh— appeareu.

] Euery man in his hvmovr. By B. I.
Ln : 1616. Fcp. 4°   BPL
Refers in the prologue to 'K. Henry V.' and 'K.
Henry VI.' in the lines :
  'Fight over York and Lancaster's long jars,
  And in the tyring-house bring wounds to scars.'
In Act v., Sc. 10, refers to K. Henry IV. 'as fat as Sir
John Falstaff.'

Extracts. *See* Sh— Works : Ext. 1845

Letter to the Earl of Newcastle, and other
matters relating to the poet [Sh—]. Ed.
by P. Cunningham. *See Sh*—] Sh— Soc.

Notes of . . . conversations with Wm. Drummond of Hawthornden, Jan., 1619 [Ed.
by David Laing]. Ln : Sh— Soc., 1842.
8°, pp. xxiv.-54 BM | BPL | BUS | SML | W

Poems. *See* Sh— Poems, 1640

Select musicall ayres. *See* Sh— Works :
Ext. 1653

Silent woman. *See Sh*—] Sh—ana

The turtle and phoenix. *See* Sh— The
turtle . . .

To the memory of my beloved the author
Mr. Wm. Sh— and what he hath left us
[Verses within Sh—'s works, 1623]. F°
The lines commence :—
  'To draw no envy, Sh—, on thy name
  Am I thus ample to thy book and fame,
  While I confess thy writings to be such
  As neither man nor muse can praise too much
  'Tis true, and all men's suffrage . . .'
Reprinted in the folio editions of 1632, 1663, 1664, and
1685.

Verses. *See* Brooke (C.)

Jonson.] Ben Jonson's quarrel with Sh— [In
'North British Review,' July]. Edin., 1870.
8°   BUS | SML

] Jonsonus Virbius, or the memorie of Ben
Jonson. Revised by the friends of the
muses. Ln : E. P— for Henry Seile,
1638. Fcp. 4°
Refers to Sh— pp. 42-43.

] Something upon an old subject, or Ben
Jonson and Mr. Drummond [In 'Fraser's
Mag.,' April]. Ln : 1842. 8°   BUS

Jonson (Benjamin)—
See Annalia . . .   *See* Chester
 ,, Cartwright   ,, Chettle
 ,, Castle   ,, Coleridge

Jonson (Benjamin)—
See Cotgrave   *See* Jusserand
 ,, Decker   ,, Menton
 ,, Dobell   ,, Mercurius . . .
 ,, Drummond   ,, Mountfort
 ,, Feigned . . .   ,, Nabbes
 ,, Fielding   ,, Pemberton
 ,, Foard   ,, Poems
 ,, Gilchrist   ,, Returne . . .
 ,, Gould   ,, Rich
 ,, Greene (T.)   ,, Sandys
 ,, Halliwell   ,, Settle
 ,, Harleian   *Sh*— Sh— Notices
 ,, Hazlitt   ,, Terence
 ,, Hermeticall   ,, Theobald (W.)
 ,, Heywood   ,, Versatile . . .
 ,, Hume   ,, Wright (C.)
 ,, Jones (I.)

Jonson (Ben) & Dekker (T.) Story of Page of
Plymouth. Ed. by 'Dramaticus.' *See
Sh*—] Sh— Soc.

Jonson *Saec. XIX.* (Ben) *Editor*—
See Sh— King Henry V., 1889, 1890
 ,, Sh— King John, 1887
 ,, Sh— Macbeth, 1889
 ,, Sh— Merchant . . . 1886
 ,, Sh— Midsummer . . . 1887
 ,, Sh— The tempest, 1889

Jonson (Henry) *Editor.* *See* Sh— Midsummer
. . . 1888

Jordan (John) Correspondence. *See Sh*—]
Malone
The author was a Stratford-on-Avon wheelwright,
poet, and forger. He was friendly with S. W. H.
Ireland the forger, and acted as guide to the latter's
father when preparing the 'Picturesque tour of the
Avon' (*q.v.*)

Original collections on Sh— and Stratford-
on-Avon. Selected from the original
MSS. written about 1780. Ed. by J. O.
Halliwell. Ln : 1864. Fcp. 4°   BM
Issue limited to ten copies.

Original memoirs and historical accounts of
families of Sh— and Hart. *See Sh*—]
Jordan

Pedigree of the Sh-- family. *See* Ryan

Welcombe hills, near Stratford-upon-Avon :
A poem, historic and descriptive . . . Ln :
S. Hooper, 1777. Fcp. 4°, pp. 48. With
vignette view   BPL | BUS | SML

Welcombe hills . . . Stratford-upon-Avon,
1827. 8°   BPL

See also Sh--] Sh— Collection

Jordan (*Mrs.* Dorothea) *Actress*—
See Molloy
 ,, Sh— Twelfth night, 1787

Jordan.] Boaden (J.) Life of Mrs. Jordan.
Ln : Bull, 1831. 2 vols. 8°   SML

Jordan (T.) Royal arbor of loyal poesie, 1664.
See Reprints

Joseph (G. F.) *Artist. See* Sh— Works, 1824

The birth place of Shakspere

WITH GARRICK'S JUBILEE PROCESSION

See p. 179

Josephus. *See* Hemminge
Jourdain (M.) Literary associations of War-
wickshire. *See* Memorials . . .
Tapestry manufacture at Barcheston. *See*
Memorials . . .
Journal of the Sh— Club, University of North
Carolina. 1886-87. 8°   BPL
Jovius *or* Giovio *Bp.* (Paulus) Worthy tracte
. . . containing a discourse of rare inven-
tions both militarie and amorous called
imprese. Whereunto is added a preface
by Samuel Daniel. At Ln : Printed for
Simon Waterson, 1585. Fcp. 4°
Illustrates 'Hamlet.'
Daniel's first appearance in print.
See also Green (H.)
Joy *Publisher. See* Sh— Works, 1811
Joyce (J. A.) Sh—; Personal recollections.
See Sh—] Joyce
Jubilee, 1769.] Anecdote of the Jubilee.
Foote's Satire on the Jubilee. Garrick's
Address to the ladies at the Stratford
Jubilee, 1769. Inscription for a cup
made of the mulberry tree. Receipt for
mulberry wood, 1770. On busts of Sh—
[and other papers relating to Sh—].
Manuscript upon 28 leaves of paper
[c. 1840.] Fcp. 4°   W
Jubilee, 1769—
  See Bickerstaff   *See* Jarvis
  ,, Charms . . .   ,, *Sh*—] Sh—festivals
  ,, Colman (G.)   ,, Stratford
  ,, Garrick   ,, Wheler
Jubilee, 1827. *See* Bisset
Jubilee . . . at Waterford. *See* Garrick
Jubilee concert. *See* Dibdin (C.)
Judd *Publisher. See* Andrus & Judd
Judith : A sacred drama. *See* Bickerstaff
Julien (*L'Abbe*) *Editor*—
  See Sh— Julius Cæsar, 1881, 1895
  ,, Sh— King Richard III., 1883
  ,, Sh— Macbeth, 1881
Julius and Hyppolita. *See* Cohn
June (J.) *Engraver*—
  See Sh— Cymbeline, 1770
  ,, Sh— King Lear, 1771
  ,, Sh— Timon . . . 1770
'Junius.' *See* Chalmers
'Junius junior,' *pseud. See* Duggan
'Junius redivivus,' *pseud.* Coriolanus no
aristocrat [In 'Monthly Repository'].
Ln : 1834. 8°   BUS
Jusserand (Jean Adrien Antoine Jules) Allu-
sions to Sh— in translations of old French
novels [In 'Athenæum,' May, '88, p. 642]
Ben Jonson's views on Sh—'s art. [*See* Sh—
Works.] Stratford, 1904-07. Roy. 8°
English novel in the time of Sh—. Trans.
by Elizabeth Lee. Enlarged by the
author. Ln : Unwin, 1890. Cr. 8°, pp.
434. With portrait and illustrations   BPL

Jusserand (Jean Adrien Antoine Jules)
Literary history of the English people,
from the Renaissance to the Civil War.
Ln : Unwin, 1909. 8°. With frontis-
piece   BM
Forms Vol. 3 of the entire work and gives a scholarly
and impartial review of the Elizabethan period.
One more first folio [In 'Athenæum,' No.
4215, p. 154]. Ln : 1908   BM | BPL
Sh— in France under the ancien régime.
Ln : Unwin, 1899. 8°, pp. xxviii.-496.
Portraits, plates, and illusts.
      BM | BPL | BUS | MPL | SML
Juvenalis (Decimus Junius) Satires. Trans.
into English verse by Dryden . . . Ln :
Jacob Tonson, 1693. F°. First edition
Allusions to Sh— in dedication, pp. ii. and vii.
See also Ingleby's ' Centurie of prayse,' p. 413.

 —— (A. J.) On the
'Hamlet' of Jean
François Ducis
compared with
that of Sh— [In
' Correspondent,'
No. 3]. Ln :
1817. 8°   BUS
K—— (J. A.) Birthday register. *See* Sh—
Works : Ext. 1876
Kastner (L. E.) Thomas Lodge as an imitator
of the French poets [In 'Athenæum,' No.
4017, p. 552, Oct.] 1904   BM | BPL
Katharine (*Saint*) Life. *See* Halliwell
Kay (J. Taylor) Emendators of Sh— [Maga-
zine excerpt. c. 1898]. 8°, pp. xii.
A plea for republication of the Jaggard folio, 1623.
Kay (T.) *Publisher. See* Sh— Works, 1798
Kay & Biddle *Philadelphia Publishers. See*
Sh— Hamlet, 1834
Kean (Charles John) Selections from the plays
of Sh—. *See* Sh— Works : Ext. 1859,
1860
Kean (C.) *Actor, Editor & Manager*—
  See Sh— Hamlet, 1851, 1859, 1869
  ,, Sh— King Henry V., 1859
  ,, Sh— King Henry VIII., 1855
  ,, Sh— King John, 1858
  ,, Sh— King Lear, 1858
  ,, Sh— King Richard II., 1857
  ,, Sh— Macbeth, 1853
  ,, Sh— Merchant . . . 1858
  ,, Sh— Midsummer . . . 1856
  ,, Sh— Much ado, 1858
  ,, Sh— The tempest, 1857
  ,, Sh— Two gentlemen, 1846
  ,, Sh— Winter's tale, 1855, 1856
  ,, Sh— Works, 1856-58, 1858, 1860

Kean.] C. J. Kean banquet, St. James' Hall, 20 July, 1859 . . . and Kean testimonial presentation, 22 Mar., 1862 . . . W. E. Gladstone in the chair. Ln: 1862. 8°, pp. 48   BUS

] Cole (J. W.) Life and theatrical times of Charles Kean, including a summary of the English stage for the last fifty years. 1859. 2 vols. 8°   BPL

] 'Much ado about nothing' [A review of C. J. Kean's 'Life.' In 'Fraser's Magazine,' Sept.] Ln: 1859. 8°   BUS

] Smythies (W. G.) Charles John Kean [In 'Golden leisures,' pp. 12-13, 1868 ?]. 12°   BPL

Kean (C. J. & *Mrs.*) Readings and recitations for the Sh— fund. 1863. 8°   BPL

Kean (Edmund) Letters [In 'Athenæum,' No. 3684, p. 735, June]. 1898. 4°

Kean (Edmund) *Actor & Editor*—
  See Sh— Hamlet, 1823
  ,,   Sh— King Henry VI., i.-ii.-iii.,1817,1830
  ,,   Sh— King Henry VI., iii., 1817, 1830
  ,,   Sh— King Richard II., 1815
  ,,   Sh— King Richard III., 1904
  ,,   Sh— Works, 1807

Kean.] Cooke sleeps!—Kean lives! Life and interesting anecdotes of [Edmund] Kean . . . Embellished with an animated likeness . . . in character of Richard . . . by I. Cruikshank. Ln: Smeeton [c. 1814]. 8°, pp. 24   BUS

] Critical remarks on the astonishing performance of Mr. Kean at Drury Lane. Ln: Fairburn [1814]. 8°   SML

] Dana (Richard Henry) Kean's acting [In 'Poems and prose writings']. Philadelphia, 1833. 8°   BUS

] Dumas (A.) Edmund Kean, or the genius and the libertine. 1847. 8°

] Hawkins (F. W.) Life of Edmund Kean. Ln: 1869. 2 vols. 8°   BPL

] Molloy (J. F.) Life and adventures of Edmund Kean. Ln: 1888. 2 vols. Cr. 8°

] Procter (B. W.)] Life of Edmund Kean, with critical remarks on his theatrical performances, by 'Barry Cornwall.' Ln: 1835. 2 vols. 8°

Kean (Edmund)—
  See Critical . . .   *See* Sh— Works, 1813
  ,, De Soligny   ,, *Stratford*] Sh—'s
  ,, Doran   [birthplace

Kearsley (C.) *Publisher*. *See* Sh— Works: Ext. 1790

Kearsley (George) *Publisher*—
  See Collins
  ,,   Sh— Macbeth, 1770
  ,,   Sh— Midsummer . . . 1777
  ,,   Sh— Timon . . . 1770
  ,,   Sh— Winter's tale, 1777

Kearsley (George) *Publisher*—
  See Sh— Works, 1806
  ,,   Sh— Works: Ext. 1783, 1784, 1790, 1798

Keate (George) Ferney: An epistle to Mons. de Voltaire. Ln: 1768
The verses begin and end thus:—
  'Yes, jealous wits may still for empire thrive,
  Still keep the flames of critick rage alive ;
  Our Sh— yet shall all his rights maintain
  And crown the triumphs of Eliza's reign.

    .   .   .   .   .

  O'er the dear vault, ambition's utmost bound
  Unheard shall fame her airy trumpet sound,
  Unheard alike nor grief nor transport raise
  Thy blast of censure, or thy note of praise ;
  As Raphael's own creation graced his hearse*
  And shamed the pomp of ostentatious verse
  Shall Sh—'s honours by himself be paid
  And nature perish ere his pictures fade.'
* Refers to the fact that Raphael's great picture of the transfiguration did impressive honour to his memory by being carried before his body to the grave.

Poetical Works. Ln: 1781. 2 vols. 12°   BPL
Includes 'Ferney'; also prologues and epilogues to several of Sh—'s plays.

Keating *Stratford-on-Avon Publisher*. *See* Sh— Works, 1768

Keats (John) Endymion. *See* Halpin
Letter to George and Georgiana Keats, 18 Feb., 1819
'Sh— led a life of allegory : his works are the comments on it.'

Note on 'Troilus and Cressida,' I., iii. ; Marginalia from the Sh— folio of 1807 [In his 'Works,' ed. by H. B. Forman (4 vols.), Vol. iii., p. 254]. 1901. 8°   BM | BPL
The genius of Sh— was an innate universality—wherefore he had the utmost achievement of human intellect prostrate beneath his indolent and kingly gaze. He could do easily man's utmost. His plan of tasks to come were not of this world. If what he purposed to do hereafter would not in his own idea 'answer the aim,' how tremendous must have been his conception of ultimates !

Sonnet on sitting down to read 'King Lear' once again [In his 'Life, letters, and literary remains,' ed. by R. M. Milnes, Vol. i., p. 96]. Ln: Moxon, 1848. 2 vols. 8°. With portrait and facsimile
'O golden-tongued romance, with serene lute
Fair plumed syren, queen of far-away !
Leave melodising on this wintry day,
Shut up thine olden pages and be mute.
Adieu ! for once again the fierce dispute
Betwixt damnation and impassioned clay
Must I burn through ; once more humbly assay
The bitter-sweet of this Shakespearian fruit.

Chief poet ! and ye clouds of Albion
Begetters of our deep eternal theme !
When through the old oak forest I am gone
Let me not wander in a barren dream,
But when I am consumed in the fire
Give me new phoenix wings to fly at my desire.'

Keble (S.) *Publisher*. *See* Collier (Jeremy)
Keene (Laura) *Editor*. *See* Sh— Midsummer . . . 1863

Keene.] Creahan (J.) Life of Laura Keene. Philadelphia : Rodgers, 1897. 8°   SML

Keightley (Thomas) Sh— expositor: An aid
to the perfect understanding of Sh—'s
plays. Ln: J. R. Smith, 1867. Cr. 8°,
pp. viii.-432   BM | BPL | BUS | MPL | SML
With life and brief bibliography.

Keightley (Thomas) *Editor.* *See* Sh— Works,
1864, 1865, 1866, 1867, 1868, 1868-79,
1884, 1892-94, 1893-95

Keith (G.) *Publisher*—
See Sh— Merchant . . . 1783
,, Sh— Works, 1773

Keller (Helen) The world I live in. Ln:
Hodder & Stoughton, 1908. Cr. 8°, pp.
xvi.-242, and portrait
The authoress, who is quite blind, writes (pp. 36-39)
upon Sh—'s references to hands.

Kellogg (Abner Otis) Cordelia. Utica, 1865.
8°, pp. 12   BUS
Appeared in 'American Journal of Insanity,' Jan.,
1865.

Sh— as a physiologist and psychologist [In
'American Journal of Insanity']. Utica,
Oct. 1859, April 1860. 8°   BUS

Sh—'s delineations of insanity, imbecility,
and suicide. New York: Hurd, 1866.
Cr. 8°, pp. viii.-204   BM | BPL | MPL | SML

Sh—'s delineations of mental imbecility as
exhibited in his fools and clowns [In
'American Journal of Insanity']. Utica,
1861-63. 8°   BUS

Sh—'s psychological delineations: His
suicides. Othello. Utica: Curtiss &
White, 1864. 8°   BUS
First appeared in 'American Journal of Insanity,' July,
1864.

Sh—'s psychological delineations: 'Jaques.'
Utica, 1863. 8°, pp. 10   BPL | BUS
Appeared in 'American Journal of Insanity,' July,
1863.

Sh—'s psychological delineations: 'Ophelia.'
Utica, 1864. 8°, pp. 16   BPL | BUS
First appeared in 'American Journal of Insanity,' Jan.,
1864.

Kellogg (Brainerd) *Editor*—
See Sh— As you like it, 1883
,, Sh— Hamlet, 1882
,, Sh— Julius Cæsar, 1882
,, Sh— King Henry V., 1883
,, Sh— King Lear, 1882
,, Sh— King Richard III., 1886
,, Sh— Macbeth, 1882
,, Sh— Merchant . . . 1882, 1899
,, Sh— The tempest, 1882
,, Sh— Works, 1882

Kelly (J. G.) The Falstaff of Sh— [In 'Overland Monthly,' Oct.] San Francisco,
1874. 8°   BUS

Kelly (Michael) Hamlet's letter to Ophelia
versified, composed for, and dedicated to
Miss Abrams. 1800. 8°

Kelly (Michael) Reminiscences . . . of the
King's Theatre and Theatre Royal, Drury
Lane, including . . . nearly half a century.
With original anecdotes of many distinguished persons, political, literary, and
musical. Ln: H. Colburn, 1826. 2 vols.
8°. Portrait and music

Kelly (Wm.) *Editor.* *See* Notices . . .

Kelmscott Press. *See* Sh— Poems, 1893

Kelsall (Charles)] First sitting of the com-
mittee on the proposed monument to
Sh—. Carefully taken in short-hand by
'Zachary Craft' . . . Cheltenham, G. A.
Williams; Stratford-upon-Avon, Ward,
1823. 16°, pp. 92
BM | BPL | BUS | CPL | MPL | SML | W
A sarcastic and amusing squib.

First sitting . . . Ln : . . . 1823. 8°, pp. 30
BUS

] First sitting . . . By 'Z. Craft' [In 'Pamph-
leteer,' Vol. 22, pp. 169-197]. 1823.
8°   BPL

Kemble (Charles) Sh— readings. *See* Sh—
Works: Ext. 1870

Kemble (Charles) *Actor & Editor*—
See De Soligny
,, Sh— King John, 1886
,, Sh— Merchant . . . 1884
,, Sh— Romeo . . . 1823
,, Sh— Works, 1870, 1878, 1879, 1883-87

Kemble (Frances Anne) 'Lady Macbeth' [In
'Macmillan's Magazine']. Ln: 1868. 8°
BPL | BUS | CPL

Notes on the characters of Q. Katharine and
Cardinal Wolsey . . . [In 'Lippincott's
Magazine']. Philad., 1875. 8°   BUS
Illustrates 'King Henry VIII.'

Notes upon some of Sh—'s plays. Ln:
Bentley, 1882. 8°
BM | BPL | BUS | MPL | SML
Includes 'King Henry VIII.' 'Macbeth,' 'Romeo,'
'Tempest.'

Poems. Ln: E. Moxon, 1866. Cr. 8°, pp.
286
Contains the sonnet 'To Sh—,' pp. 59-61, commencing
and ending thus :—
'Shelter and succour such as common men
Afford the weaker partners of their fate
Have I derived from thee—from thee, most great
And powerful genius ! whose sublime contro'
Still from thy grave governs each human sou
That reads the wondrous record of thy pen.

.   .   .   .

Shall I not bless the need to which was given
Of all the angels in the host of heaven
Thee, for my guardian, spirit strong and bland,
Lord of the speech of my dear native land.'

Some notes on Sh— [In 'Atlantic Monthly'].
Boston, 1860. 8°   BUS

Some notes upon the characters in 'Macbeth' [In 'Macmillan's Magazine']. Ln:
1867. 8°   BPL | BUS

Kemble (F. A.) *Editor. See* Sh— Midsummer
... 1855

Kemble (John Philip) Fugitive pieces . . .
'coacta prodire.' York: W. Blanchard
& Co. for the Author, and sold by Fielding
& Walker, London; and T. Wilson &
Son, & N. Frobisher, York, 1780. 8°,
pp. viii.-44
Of considerable rarity, as the author, regretting publication, suppressed the work, and destroyed every
example he could secure. On one occasion he gave
fifteen guineas for a copy.

Library. *See* Catalogue, 1821

'Macbeth' and 'King Richard the Third':
An essay, in answer to 'Remarks on some
of the characters of Sh—' [by Thomas
Whately]. Ln: J. Murray, 1817. 8°,
pp. xii.-172
       BM | BPL | BUS | MPL | SML | W
First appeared as 'Macbeth reconsidered, 1786.'
The preface incorrectly quotes William [for Thomas]
Whately.
A reply to the above appeared in the same year. *See*
'Macbeth . . .'

] 'Macbeth' reconsidered; An essay intended
as an answer to part of [Whately's]
'Remarks on some of the characters of
Sh—, 1785.' Ln: T. & J. Egerton, 1786.
8°, pp. ii.-36   BM | BPL | BUS | W

Portrait—
See Sh— Hamlet, 1785
  ,, Sh— Timon, 1785

Kemble.] Authentic narrative of Mr. [J. P.]
Kemble's retirement from the stage.
1817. 8°   BPL

] Boaden (J.) Memoirs of J. P. Kemble, Esq.,
including a history of the stage from the
time of Garrick. Ln: Longman, 1825.
2 vols. 8°. With portrait   BPL | SML

] Fitzgerald (P.) The Kembles: An account of
the Kemble family. [1875 ?] 2 vols. 8°

] Kemble and Cooke, or a critical review of a
pamphlet . . . 'Remarks on the character
of Richard the Third as played by Cooke
and Kemble.' Ln: Westley [1801]. 8°,
pp. 52. With two portraits   BUS | W

] Kemble and Cooke . . . Second edition. Ln:
Westley [c. 1801]. 8°, pp. ii.-52   BUS

] Life of John Philip Kemble . . . proprietor
and stage manager of Covent Garden
Theatre, interspersed with family and
theatrical anecdotes. Ln: [1809]. 8°.
With folding plate   W

] Mr. Kemble in the character of Hamlet [In
the 'Theatrical Review.' 1783 ?] 12°
                          BPL

] Observations on Mr. Kemble in the characters of Cato, Wolsey, and Coriolanus.
To which are added his farewell address
at Covent Garden Theatre and an account

of the dinner given at Freemason's
Tavern . . . Ln: J. Asperne, 1817. 8°,
pp. 34   BUS | W
First appeared in the 'European Magazine.'
Illustrates 'Julius Cæsar,' 'King Henry VIII.,' and
'Coriolanus.'

Kemble.] Remarks on the character of Richard
the Third, as played by Cooke and Kemble
[By H. Martin ?] Ln: Parsons, 1801. 8°,
pp. 56   BUS

] Remarks on the character of Richard the
Third . . . Second edition. Ln: Parsons
[1801]. 8°, pp. 56   BM | BPL | BUS

] Short criticism on the performance of
'Hamlet' by Mr. Kemble. Ln: T. Hookham, 1789. 8°, pp. x.-22   BUS

Kemble (John Philip) *Actor & Editor*—
See Sh— All's well, 1793, 1795
  ,, Sh— As you like it, 1794
  ,, Sh— Comedy of errors, 1811
  ,, Sh— Coriolanus, 1789, 1800
  ,, Sh— Cymbeline, 1800
  ,, Sh— Hamlet, 1796, 1800, 1804, 1808,
       1818
  ,, Sh— Julius Cæsar, 1811, 1812, 1814,
       1883
  ,, Sh— King Henry IV., i., 1803, 1804,
       1811, 1815
  ,, Sh— King Henry IV., ii., 1803, 1804,
       1815, 1821
  ,, Sh— King Henry V., 1789, 1795, 1801,
       1806, 1815
  ,, Sh— King Henry VIII., 1804, 1815
  ,, Sh— King John, 1800, 1804, 1814
  ,, Sh— King Lear, 1800, 1808, 1810, 1815
  ,, Sh— King Richard III., 1810, 1811,
       1814, 1818
  ,, Sh— Macbeth, 1794, 1803, 1814
  ,, Sh— Measure . . . 1789, 1796, 1803, 1815
  ,, Sh— Merchant . . . 1795, 1797, 1810,
       1814
  ,, Sh— Merry wives, 1797, 1804, 1815
  ,, Sh— Much ado, 1799, 1810, 1815
  ,, Sh— Othello, 1804, 1808, 1814, 1818,
       1823
  ,, Sh— Romeo . . . 1800, 1811, 1814
  ,, Sh— Taming . . . 1810, 1815, 1831
  ,, Sh— The tempest, 1789, 1795, 1806,
       1807, 1808, 1811, 1815, 1816
  ,, Sh— Timon . . . 1788
  ,, Sh— Twelfth night, 1810, 1811, 1815
  ,, Sh— Two gentlemen, 1808, 1815
  ,, Sh— Winter's tale, 1802, 1811, 1815
  ,, Sh— Works, 1815

Kemble (J. P.)—
See Broad . . .   *See* Martin
  ,, Colman   ,, Pemberton
  ,, Covent . . .   ,, Remarks
  ,, Macbeth

Kemble (*Mrs.*) *Actress. See* Sh— Taming . . .
1806

Kemp (Thomas) History of Warwick and its people. Warwick: Cooke [1905]. Fcp. 4°   SML
At p. 288 refers to one Wm. Sh— drowned in the Avon at Warwick, 6th July, 1579.

Kempe *Actor* (William) Nine daies wonder, performed in a journey from London to Norwich. Ed. by E. Goldsmid. Edinburgh: Privately printed, 1884.   12°, pp. 42   BUS
At pp. 24-25 are the verses attributed to Sh—.

See also Returne . . .

Kempston (J.) *Dublin Printer.* *See* Sh— Othello, 1813

Kemshead (*Dr.* W. B.) *Editor.* *See* Sh— King Lear, 1875

Kendal *Madge Grimston* (*Mrs.*) The drama: A paper read at Birmingham, Sept., 1881. [1885 ?]   12°   BPL

Kendall (Hy.) *See* Condell

Kendall (J.) Remarks on attending stage entertainments. 1796. 12°   BPL

Kenilworth Castle and Park, Warwickshire—
See B—— (O.)   *See* Jago
,, Gascoigne   ,, Laneham
,, Halliwell   ,, Warwickshire

Kennard (*Mrs.* A.) Mrs. Siddons. *See* Siddons

Kennedy (B. H.) *Editor*—
See Sh— King Henry VIII., 1823
,, Sh— King John, 1826
,, Sh— Merchant . . . 1824

Kennedy (C. R.) *Editor*—
See Sh— King Henry VIII., 1829
,, Sh— Romeo . . . 1830

Kennedy (G. J.) *Editor*—
See Sh— As you like it, 1831
,, Sh— King Henry VI., iii., 1831

Kennedy (Wm. Sloane) Browsings in 'Hamlet.' Philadelphia, 1897. 8°, pp. 12 BUS

Kenney (Charles Lamb) Mr. Irving in 'Hamlet.' *See* Irving
Mr. Phelps and the critics of his correspondence with the Stratford Committee. Ln: T. H. Lacy, 1864. 8°, pp. 8   BUS

Kenney (Thomas) Life and genius of Sh—. *See* Sh—] Kenney

Kenrick (Thomas) *Editor.* *See* British stage

Kenrick (William)] Defence of Mr. Kenrick's Review: containing a number of curious and ludicrous anecdotes of literary biography. By a friend. Ln: S. Bladon, 1766. 8°, pp. vi.-68   BPL | BUS | W
Falstaff's wedding. *See* Sh— King Henry IV., ii., 1760, 1766, 1773, 1781, 1795
] Introduction to the school of Sh—; held on Wednesday evenings, in the Apollo, at the Devil's Tavern, Temple Bar. To which is added a retort courteous on the critics. Ln: Privately printed for the Author [1773]. 8°, pp. vi.-40
    BM | BPL | BUS | W

Kenrick (William) Letter to David Garrick [on] the lamentations of Roscius. 1772. 4°   BPL
Proposals for a new edition of the Plays of Sh—. Illustrated by a critical review of each play [c. 1766]. Manuscript   BUS
Review of Dr. Johnson's new edition of Sh—, in which the ignorance or inattention of that editor is exposed, and the poet defended from the persecutions of his commentators. Ln: J. Payne, 1765. 8°, pp. xvi.-134   BM | BPL | BUS | W
'A very illiberal and virulent attack.'—*Lowndes.*

Kent—
See Description . . .
,, Gillmor

Kent (Charles Wm.) Sh— note book. Boston [U.S.], 1897. Fcp. 4°   BUS
Sh— note book . . . for advanced courses in colleges and universities, Sh— clubs, etc. Boston [U.S.], 1898. Fcp. 4°   BPL

Kent (William) *Sculptor.* *See* Graves

Kent (Wm. C. M.) Sh— at Shottery [In 'Dreamland: Poems,' pp. 3-9]. Ln: Longman, 1862. 12°   BUS

Keroschner (Frederick Doyle) Syllabus of . . . six lectures on the drama of Sh— [with bibliography]. Philadelphia, 1903. 8°, pp. 28   BUS

Kerr (J. G.) Scattered notes on the text of Sh—. Philadelphia, 1879. 8°   BUS

Kersten (C. R.) *Halle Publisher.* *See* Sh— Works, 1829-43

Kertland (William) *Editor.* *See* Sh— Pericles, 1820

Keulemans (J. G.) *Artist.* *See* Harting

Key to the drama, or memoirs of personages . . . chosen by celebrated poets as the fittest characters for theatrical representation . . . Containing the life, character, and secret history of Macbeth. By a gentleman. Ln: 1768. 8°
    BUS | MPL | W
Identical with 'Life of Macbeth' and 'Secret history' (*q.v.*)

Key to unknowne knowledge, or a shop of five windows :—
    Whiche if you doe open
    To cheapen and copen
    You will be unwilling
    For many a shilling
    To part with the profit
    That you shall have of it.
Treating of the judgement of urines, judiciall rules of physike, questions of oyles, opinions for curing of harquebushshot, discourse of human nature [from Hippocrates]. Ln: Adam Islip for Edward White . . . at the signe of the Gun, 1599. Fcp. 4°
Of Sh— interest.

Kidd (Thomas). *See* Heywood

Kilbourne (F. W.) Alterations and adaptations of Sh—. Boston, U.S., 1906. 8° BPL

Kilkenny.] Private Theatre of Kilkenny . . . Privately printed, 1825. 8°

Killigrew. *See* Collier (J. P.)

Kincaid (A.) *Edinburgh Publisher. See* Sh— Works, 1753, 1761

Kindlemarshe (F.) *See* Edwards (R.)

King Charles the First. *See* Havard

King Cophetua and the beggar maid— *See* Crown garland
,, Cupid's revenge

King Darius.] A pretie new enterlude, both pithie and pleasaunt, of the story of Kyng Daryus : Now first reprinted from the original edition issued in 1565. Ln : 1860. Fcp. 4° BPL | BUS
Limited to twenty-six copies.
One of the earliest English morality plays to introduce the character of ' Vice.'

King Edward II., 1594. *See* Genée

King Edward III. *See* Sh— King Edward III.

King Henry IV.— *See* Sh— King Henry IV.
,, Sh— Works : Ext. 1827

King Henry V. *See* Sh— King Henry V.

King Henry VI. *See* Sh— King Henry VI.

King Henry VIII. *See* Sh— King Henry VIII.

King John. *See* Sh— King John

King Lear. *See* Sh— King Lear

King Queer : A burlesque. *See* Sh— King Lear, 1855

King Richard II. *See* Sh— King Richard II.

King Richard III. *See* Sh— King Richard III.

King Richard IV. [*misprint*]. *See* Sh— Works, 1753

King (Alice) Sh—. *See Sh—*] King

King (E.) Poems of liberty. Coventry, 1864. 8° BPL
Charlecote, p. 60. The Sh— tercentenary, p. 61.

King (J.) Our English Sh—. *See* Sh—

King *or* Kinge (John) Lectures upon ' Jonas,' delivered at Yorke in . . . 1594. Oxford, 1597. Fcp. 4°
Contains a passage illustrative of ' Midsummer night's dream,' Act. ii., Sc. 1 (*see* Furness, variorum ed., 1895, p. 249).

King (S.) *New York Publisher. See* Sh— Works, 1825, 1831

King (Thomas) *Actor*— *See* Hawkins
,, Public characters
,, Sh— King Lear, 1767
,, Sh— Measure . . . 1779

King (Thomas D.) Bacon *versus* Sh— : A plea for the defendant. Montreal : Lovell & Co., 1875. 12°, pp. ii.-188 BPL | BUS
Bacon *versus* Sh— . . . Montreal, 1875. 8°.
Large paper copy BPL

King (Thomas D.) Shall we open Sh—'s grave ? No ! A reply. Montreal, 1884. 8°
BM | BPL

King (W.) Tragi-comedy of Joan of Hedington ['Imitations of Sh—' in Works, Vol. iii., pp. 1-23]. 1776. 8° BPL

King's Theatre, London— *See* Ebers
,, Kelly
,, Sh— King Lear, 1729, 1756, 1760

Kingdon (J. G.) *Editor. See* Sh— Pericles, 1849

Kingsley (Charles) Plays and puritans. 1873. 12° BPL

Kingsley (Rose G.) Sh— in Warwickshire [In 'Nineteenth Century and after,' May]. 1910. Roy. 8° BM | BPL
Sketches of old-time life and local colour of Avon Valley villages.

Sh—'s country [In 'English Illust. Mag.'] 1885. Roy. 8° BPL
When Sh— was a boy [In 'St. Nicholas']. 1886. 4° BPL

Kinnaird (*Hon.* Douglas) *Bibliophile*— *See* Catalogue, 1822
,, Sh— Works, 1813

Kinnear (B. G.) Cruces Shakespearianæ. *See* Sh— Works : Ext. 1883

Kinnear (M. H.) *Editor. See* Penzance

Kinney (*Mrs.* S.) *Editor. See* Sh— Macbeth, 1885

Kinney (S. S.) *Editor. See* Sh—Taming . . . 1886

Kipling (Rudyard) Letter . . . on a possible source of 'The tempest.' With an epistle to the reader by Edwin Collins Frost. Providence [U.S.], Privately printed, 1906. 16°, pp. 32
Limited to 52 copies.

Kiralfy (I.) Venice : Bride of the sea. [1891 ?] 8° BPL

Kirk (W. B.) *Artist. See* Sh— Midsummer . . . 1853

Kirkman (Francis) The wits, or sport upon sport. Ln : For H. Marsh at the sign of the Prince's Arms in Chancery Lane, 1662. 8°
The engraved frontispiece gives a representation of a stage of the period.
Droll 1 : ' The bouncing knight' illustrates the ' Merry wives.'
Droll 9 : ' Story of the gravemakers' illustrates ' Hamlet.'
Droll of ' Bottom the Weaver' illustrates ' Midsummer night's dream.'

The wits . . . Ln : 1670-72. 8° BM | W
The wits. Ln : 1672. 8° BM | W
The wits . . . Ln : 1673. Fcp. 4° BUS
See also Sh— Hamlet, 1860
True, perfect, and exact catalogue of all comedies, tragedies and pastorals that were ever yet printed and published. Ln : 1671. Fcp. 4° BPL

Kirkman (Francis) *Publisher—*
See Hazlitt (W. C.)
,, Sh— Birth . . . 1662
,, Webster & Rowley

Kirkman (J.) Animal nature *versus* human
nature in 'King Lear.' Ln: New Sh—
Soc., 1877-79. 8°   BM | BPL
True use of Sh— for a Christian man . . .
[1879]. 16°   BM

Kirkman (J. T.) Life of Macklin. *See* Macklin

Kirkup (Thomas) *Editor. See* Sh— Julius
Cæsar, 1903

Kirwan (G. R.) English grammar, to which
are added rules for scanning Sh— blank
verse. 1895. 12°   BPL

Kitchiner *M D.* (W.) *Bibliophile. See* Sh—
Poems, 1815

Klingenstein *Salzwedel Publisher. See* Sh—
Merchant . . . 1870, 1878

Klose (*Dr.* H.) *Editor. See* Sh— Julius Cæsar,
1872

Knapp (Arthur Mason). *See* Hubbard &
Knapp

Knapton (James) *Publisher—*
See Shadwell
,, Sh— Hamlet, 1754, 1756
,, Sh— King Richard II., 1691
,, Sh— Merchant . . . 1755
,, Sh— Othello, 1750, 1753
,, Sh— Works, 1714

Knapton (J. & J.) *Publishers—*
See Sh— Poems, 1728
,, Sh— Works, 1728

Knapton (J. & P.) *Publishers—*
See Sh— Macbeth, 1750, 1755
,, Sh— Works, 1731, 1745, 1747, 1748,
1750-51, 1752, 1760

Knapton (P.) *Publisher. See* Sh— Othello,
1750

Knell (T.) Piththy note to Papists, 1570. *See*
Reprints

Knibb (T.)] Guide to Leamington, its vicinity
. . . Stratford and surrounding country
[c. 1865]. Cr. 8°. Map and plates

Knight [*Sæc. XVII.*] Miscellanies. *See* Redford

Knight (Charles)] Land we live in. Ln: [c.
1847]. 4 vols. Roy. 8°   BPL
With chapters on Stratford and Sh—, Windsor and the
'Merry wives,' etc.

Life of Sh—. *See* Sh—] Knight

Old lamps, or new ? A plea for the original
editions of the text of Sh— . . . Ln:
Knight, 1853. 8°   BM | BPL | BUS
Offprinted from the Introduction to the 'Stratford
Sh—.'

Sh— and his writings. *See* Sh—

Knight (Charles) Store of knowledge for all
readers. Being a collection of treatises in
various departments of knowledge by
several authors. Ln: C. Knight & Co.,
c. 1840. Roy. 8°, pp. iv.-424. Illust.
     BUS
'Sh— and his writings, by C. Knight,' occupies pp.
3-32.

] Stratford - upon - Avon and Warwick.
'Knight's Excursion companion' [c.
1851 ?]. 8°   BPL

Studies of Sh—. *See* Sh—] Knight

To the Council of the Sh— Society . . .
Highgate, 20 Sept., 1842. 8°, pp. 4   BUS
Reply to J. P. Collier's Introduction to Armin's 'Nest
of ninnies.'

Wm. Sh— : A biography. *See* Sh—] Knight

Knight (Charles) *Editor—*
See Sh— Hamlet, 1882, 1890
,, Sh— Love's labours lost, 1851
,, Sh— Poems, 1838, 1842, 1843, 1847, 1851
,, Sh— Romeo . . . 1882
,, Sh— The tempest, 1843, 1895
,, Sh— Works, 1838-43, 1842-44, 1843,
1843-44, 1844, 1845, 1846, 1847,
1847-48, 1849, 1850-52, 1851,
1852, 1852-54, 1853, 1854, 1854-
56, 1855-56, 1855-59, 1856-57,
1857, 1857-60, 1858, 1859, 1860,
1861, 1862, 1863, 1864-67, 1866,
1867, 1868, 1869, 1870, 1871,
1873-76, 1874, 1875, 1875-76,
1876, 1878, 1879, 1880, 1882,
1883, 1884, 1885, 1888, 1889,
1890, 1890-91, 1891, 1892, 1894,
1895, 1898, 1900, 1904, 1906,
1906-07

Sh— Works : Ext. 1870

Knight.] Clowes. Charles Knight : A sketch.
Ln: Bentley, 1892. 8°, pp. 266. With
two portraits   BPL

] Recent editions of Sh— [Review of Charles
Knight's editions from the 'Edinburgh
Review']. 1845. 8°   BPL | CPL

Knight (Charles). *See* Dyce

Knight (Joseph) *Publisher—*
See Sh— Julius Cæsar, 1680, 1695
,, Sh— Works, 1685

Knight *F.S.A.* (Joseph) Barnabe Barnes. *See*
Barnes

David Garrick. *See* Garrick

Henry Irving. *See* Irving (*Sir* J. H. B.)

Theatrical notes. Ln: Laurence & Bullen,
1893. 8°   BPL
A few were done on large paper, roy. 8°.

'Twelfth night' at the Lyceum [In 'The
Theatre']. 1884. 8°   BPL

Knight *F.S.A.* (Joseph) *Editor. See* Notes &
Queries

Knight.] Francis (John Collins) Notes by the way. With memoirs of Joseph Knight, F.S.A., dramatic critic and editor of 'Notes & Queries,' 1883-1907, and of Joseph Woodfall Ebsworth, F.S.A. Ln: Unwin, 1909. Fcp. 4°. With eight illustrations

Mr. Francis relates that Joseph Knight contributed five hundred biographies of actors and actresses to the 'Dictionary of national biography.'

] Rendall (Vernon Horace) Joseph Knight [In 'Notes & Queries,' 10th series, Vol. vii., pp. 501-502]. 1907. Fcp. 4°. With two portraits   BM | BPL

Knight (W.) & Oliphant (T. T.) Sh— on golf [In 'Stories of golf,' pp. 125-146]. Ln: Heinemann, 1894. 12°   BPL | SML

Knights (Mark) Sh—'s 'Hamlet' interpreted. Ln: Jarrold & Sons, 1893. 8°, pp. xii.-136   BM | BPL | SML

Knortz (Karl) American Sh— bibliography. Boston, U.S.: Schoenhof & Moeller [1876]. 12°, pp. ii.-16
                     BM | BPL | BUS | SML

Knowle.] Register of the Guild of Knowle, 1451-1535, from the original manuscript in the Public Library, Birmingham. Transcribed and edited by W. B. Bickley. Walsall: W. H. Robinson, 1894. 4°, pp. xlviii.-272-xl.   BPL | SML

The original narrowly escaped destruction in the catastrophe which overtook the Birmingham Library. Gives particulars of the Warwickshire branch of the Jaggard family, settled near Leamington about 1500, descendants of which live near the same spot to-day.

Knowles (J. Sheridan) Lectures on dramatic literature: 'Macbeth.' Never before published. Ln: F. Harvey, 1875. Fcp. 4°, pp. iv.-82   BPL | BUS | MPL

Sheridan Knowles' conception and Mr. Irving's performance of 'Macbeth.' 1876. 8°.   BM

Koch (M.) Sh—. *See* Sh—] Koch

Köhler (*Dr.* F.) *Editor. See* Sh— Hamlet, 1856

Köhler (R.) *Editor. See* Sh— Taming . . . 1864

Kohlschein (C.) Commentary on Sh—'s 'Othello,' iii., 90-279 . . . 1879. Fcp. 4°
                                             BM

Kok (A. S.) *Editor. See* Sh— King Richard III., 1871

Konewka (Paul) Falstaff and his companions: Twenty-one illustrations in silhouette. With an introd. by Hermann Kurz. Trans. by C. C. Shackford. Boston: Roberts Brothers, 1872. 8°, pp. xviii., ff. 19, and 20 plates   BUS

Konewka (P.) *Artist. See* Sh— Midsummer . . . 1868, 1870, 1887

Kreutzberg (P.) Brutus in Sh—'s 'Julius Cæsar.' 1894. 4°   BM

Krueger (E.) Sh— entertainment; Programme and text-book. [1863 ?] 8°   BPL

Küchler *Editor. See* Sh— King Lear, 1794

Kühtmann (J.) *Bremen Publisher. See* Sh— Sonnets, 1860

Kuitert (G. B.) *Editor. See* Sh— Works, 1882

Kummel *Halle Publisher. See* Sh— Othello, 1794

Kurz (Hermann) Introduction. *See* Konewka

Kyd *or* Kydde (Thomas) Murder of John Brewen, 1592. *See* Reprints

Spanish tragedie, or Hieronimo is mad again. Containing the lamentable end of Don Horatio and Belimperia. With the pittiful death of Hieronimo. Newly corrected, amended and enlarged. Ln: W. White for I. White & T. Langley, 1615. Fcp. 4°. With woodcut title

This play closely resembles 'Hamlet,' and is reformed, it is supposed, from an older version (now lost) by the same writer, of 1589 or earlier. The vanished version is thought to have supplied Sh— with material for his greatest tragedy.

The play was the object of much contemporary contumely.

The expressions 'Go by, Jeronimy' and 'In time the savage bull doth bear the yoke' in this play are used by Sh— in 'Taming of the shrew' and 'Much ado' respectively.

'The "Spanish tragedy" bears some similarity to "Titus Andronicus," and points of resemblance to "Hamlet."'—*Saintsbury.*

Spanish tragedy . . . With new additions as it hath of late been divers times acted. Ln: Augustine Mathewes for Francis Grove, 1633. Fcp. 4°. With woodcut title

Malone attributes the 'Additions' to Ben Jonson, for Henslowe's accounts shew that he received payment for adding to the play about this time.

See also Worrall

Works. Ed. with introd., etc. by F. S. Boas. Oxford, 1901. 8°   BPL

Kynder (Philip)] The surfeit. To A. B. C. Ln: Printed for Edw. Dod at the Gun in Ivy Lane, 1656. 8°   BLO

Says 'Or that the condition of all our English women may be drawn out of Shackespeer's "Merry wifes of Windsor" . . .'

Kyngston (Felix) *Printer—*
See Brathwaite
,, Mirrour . . .

L—— Sh—'s plays in folio. [1861.] 4° BM

L—— Editor. See Sh— Macbeth, 1807

L—— (C.) Essay on 'Hamlet' [In 'The Wanderer']. 1869. 8° BPL

L—— (G.) Editor. See Nash

L—— (G. H.) See Lewes

L—— (H.) See Latham (Henry)

L—— (H. B.) Editor—
See Chettle
,, Leonard (H. B.)

L—— (L.) Oxford Printer. See Langbaine

L—— (M.) See Lucy (Margaret)

L—— (N.) See Ling (N.)

L—— (W.) Printer. See Fuller

Lacey (John) Editor. See Sh— Taming . . . 1698, 1708, 1714, 1731

Lackington (John) Publisher—
See Sh— Cymbeline, 1801
,, Sh— King Lear, 1801
,, Sh— Works, 1790, 1792, 1794, 1798

Lackington, Allen & Co. Publishers—
See Sh— Works, 1811
,, Sh— Works : Ext. 1798

Lacy (Fanny E.) & Goodban (Henry W.) Beauties of Sh—: Anne Hathaway. Ln : L. Lee & Coxhead. [Und.] Fo, pp. 8 BUS

Lacy (Thomas Hailes) Library. See Catalogue. 1873
Male and female costumes : historical, national, and dramatic, in four hundred [coloured] plates. Ln : T. H. Lacey, 1865-68. 4°

Lacy (T. H.) Publisher—
See Sh— All's well, 1850
,, Sh— Antony, 1866 et seq.
,, Sh— Comedy of errors, 1866
,, Sh— Coriolanus, 1850
,, Sh— Cymbeline, 1865
,, Sh— Julius Cæsar, 1859
,, Sh— King Henry IV., i., 1859
,, Sh— King Henry IV., ii., 1864, 1865
,, Sh— King Henry V., 1859
,, Sh— King Henry VIII., 1855, 1865
,, Sh— King John, 1859
,, Sh— King Lear, 1857
,, Sh— King Richard II., 1868
,, Sh— King Richard III., 1844, 1854, 1857, 1858, 1873
,, Sh— Macbeth, 1840, 1847, 1853, 1864, 1869
,, Sh— Merchant . . . 1840, 1855, 1856, 1860, 1870
,, Sh— Merry wives, 1840, 1865

Lacy (T. H.) Publisher—
See Sh— Midsummer . . . 1856
,, Sh— Much ado, 1858, 1866, 1870, 1877
,, Sh— Othello, 1856, 1861, 1869
,, Sh— Romeo . . . 1855, 1859, 1869, 1870
,, Sh— Taming . . . 1855, 1865, 1866
,, Sh— The tempest, 1858, 1859
,, Sh— Twelfth night, 1855, 1869
,, Sh— Venus, 1864
,, Sh— Winter's tale, 1856, 1870

Lady Macbeth. See Leigh-Noel

Lady's preceptor. See Sh— Works : Ext. 1804

Laffan (Bertha J.) C. E. Flower. See Flower

Laffan (R. S. de Courcy) Anne Hathaway's cottage [In 'All the Year Round']. 1892. 8° BPL
Sermon at Holy Trinity, Stratford-on-Avon, April 22, 1894. [1894 ?] 12° BPL
Sh— the prophet. See Sh—] Sh— Sermons

Lafond (E.) Editor. See Sh— Poems, 1836, 1856

Lahure (Ch.) Paris Publisher. See Sh— Poems, 1836

Lainé (J.) Editor. See Sh— Hamlet, 1836

Laing (David) Editor. See Jonson

Laing (Dr.) Introduction. See Lodge

Laird (J.) Sh— controversy [Bacon & Sh—]. Dundee, 1884. 8° BPL

Lake (J. W.) Editor—
See Sh— King Richard III., 1827, 1834
,, Sh— Works, 1828

Lamb (A. C.) Bibliophile. See Dundee

Lamb (Charles) Dramatic essays. Edited with introd. and notes by Brander Matthews. Ln : Chatto, 1891. Cr. 8°, pp. 266, and steel portrait
Full of Sh— matter.

Epilogue to an amateur performance of 'Richard II.' [In his Works, Vol. v., p. 128]. 1903-04
'In "sad civility" once Garrick sate
To see a play, mangled in form and state ;
Plebeian Sh— must the words supply.
The actors all were fools—of quality ;
The scenes, the dresses, were above rebuke,
Scarce a performer there below a Duke ;
He sate and mused how in his Sh—'s mind
The idea of old nobility enshrined,
Should thence a grace and a refinement have
Which passed these living nobles to conceive
Who with such apish base gesticulation,
Remnants of starts, and dregs of playhouse passion
So foul belied their great forefathers' fashion,
He saw—and true nobility confessed
Less in the high-born blood, than lowly poet's breast.'

Letter to Samuel Rogers, 21st Dec., 1833 [In his Works, Vol. vii.] 1903-04
'I am jealous of the combination of the sister arts. Let them sparkle apart. What injury, short of the theatres, did Boydell's "Sh — gallery" do me with Sh—? To have Opie's Sh—, Northcote's Sh—, light-headed Fuseli's Sh—, heavy-headed Romney's Sh—, wooden-headed West's Sh— (though he did the best in "Lear"), deaf-headed Reynolds' Sh—, instead of my and everybody's Sh—! To be tied down to an authentic face of Juliet! To have Imogen's portrait ! To confine the illimitable !

(187)

Lamb (Charles) On a passage in 'The tempest'
[In his Works, pp. 507-509]. 1876. 8°
BPL
On the tragedies of Sh— considered with
reference to their fitness for stage repre-
sentation [In his Works, Vol. ii.] Ln:
1818. 8° BUS
Frequently reprinted.
Original letters of Falstaff. *See* White &
Lamb
Specimens of English dramatic poets who
lived about the time of Sh—. With notes.
Ln: Longman, 1808. 8° SML
Specimens . . . Second edition. Ln: 1813.
12° BPL
Specimens . . . Ln: Baldwin, Cradock & Co.
[c. 1815]. 12°
Specimens . . . Ln: Moxon, 1835. 2 vols.
12° BUS
Specimens . . . Ln: Moxon, 1837. 2 vols,
12°
Specimens . . . Ln: Moxon, 1844. 2 vols.
12° BPL
Specimens . . . Including extracts from the
Garrick Plays. New edition. Ln: H.
G. Bohn, 1854. 8°, pp. viii.-552
Specimens . . . With notes. 'London Lib.'
Ln: Routledge, 1907. 8°, pp. 540
Specimens . . . With notes. Ln: Routledge,
1908. 8°
Works. Collected and edited by T. N.
Talfourd. Ln: 1876. 8° BPL
Includes the 'Essay on the tragedies of Sh—.'
Writings. With Life and Letters. Ed. by
P. H. Fitzgerald. Ln: 1876. 6 vols.
Cr. 8° BPL
Works and Life. *Ed. de luxe.* Ln: 1899-
1900. 12 vols. 8° BPL
Works. Ed. by E. V. Lucas. 1903. 8°
BPL
Works. Ed. by Macdonald. 1903. Cr.
8° BPL
Lamb (C.) *Editor*—
See Sh— Midsummer . . . 1840
,, Sh— Much ado, 1840
,, Sh— The tempest, 1840
,, Sh— Winter's tale, 1840
Lamb.] Memoir of C. Lamb, by J. W. D.
See Sh— Works : Ext. 1844
Lamb (Charles & Mary Ann) Tales from Sh—.
See Sh— Works : Ext. 1807, 1816, 1822,
1831, 1838, 1839, 1840, 1843, 1844, 1846,
1848, 1849, 1851, 1853, 1857, 1858, 1860,
1861-62, 1863, 1866, 1870, 1873, 1877,
1879, 1881, 1882, 1883, 1885, 1886, 1888,
1889, 1890, 1892, 1893, 1894, 1895, 1896,
1897, 1898, 1899, 1900, 1901, 1902, 1903,
1904, 1905, 1906, 1907, 1908, 1909
Lamb (*Hon.* George) *Editor. See* Sh— Timon
. . . 1816

Lambert (B.) Wit, humour, and pathos : A
lecture. 1861. 12° BPL
Sh—, pp. 25-38.
Lambert (Daniel Henry) Cartæ Shakes-
peareanæ. *See* Sh—] Lambert
Lambert (D. H.) *Editor. See* Sh— Julius
Cæsar, 1906
Lambert (G.) Cocked hats at Evesham and
Stratford-on-Avon. 1889. 8° BPL
'By his cockle hat and staff and sandal shoon.'—
Hamlet, iv., 5.
Lambros (S. P.) Sh— ['s Works] in Greece [In
'Athenæum,' No. 2861, p. 272]. 1882
Lamentation against London, 1548. *See*
Reprints
Lampe (I. F.) *Composer*—
See Sh— Midsummer . . . 1740, 1745, 1750
,, Sh— Romeo . . . 1750
Lampedusa, Prospero's Island. *See* Rodd
Lamport garland, from the library of Sir
Charles E. Isham. Four unique works,
edited by C. Edmonds. Ln: 'Roxburghe
Club,' 1881. Fcp. 4° BPL
Lancashire—
See Axon
,, Sh— Faire Em [*heading*]
Land we live in. *See* Knight
Landmann (F.) Sh— and euphuism. Ln:
New Sh— Soc., 1880-86. 8°
Landor *of Warwick* (Walter Savage) Antony
and Octavius. *See* Sh— Antony . . . 1856
] Citation and examination of Wm. Sh—,
Euseby Treen, Joseph Carnaby, and
Silas Gough, Clerk, before the Worshipful
Sir Thomas Lucy, Knight, touching deer-
stealing . . . Now first published from
original papers. To which is added, a
Conference of Master Edmund Spenser
. . . with the Earl of Essex touching the
state of Ireland [in] 1595. Ln: Saunders
& Otley, 1834. 8°, pp. xii.-284
BM | BPL | BUS | CPL | MPL | W
Citation . . . [In Landor's Works, Vol. ii.]
Ln: 1846. 8° MPL
Citation . . . Ln: 1853. 8°
Citation . . . [In his Works, Vol. ii.] 1876.
8° BPL | BUS
Citation . . . Boston [U.S.], 1888. 12° BUS
Citation . . . Ln: Chatto, 1891. Cr. 8°, pp.
xiv.-230
Citation . . . With Introd. by H. W. Mabie.
New York, 1891. 8° BUS
Longer prose works. Ed. by C. G. Crump.
Ln: Dent, 1892. 2 vols. 8° SML
On Sh— [Poems and epigrams. In his
Works]. 1846
'In poetry there is but one supreme,
Tho' there are many angels round his throne,
Mighty and beauteous, while his face is hid.'

Landor *of Warwick* (Walter Savage) Sh— and Milton [In 'Last fruit off an old tree']. 1853. 8°
'The tongue of England, that which myriads
Have spoken and will speak, were paralysed
Hereafter, but two mighty men stand forth
Above the flight of ages, two alone,
One crying out, "all nations spoke thro' me."'
. . . . . .
Landor.] 'Examination of Wm. Sh— touching deer stealing' [A review]. 8°   BUS

Landseer (*Sir* Edwin) *Artist. See* Sh— As you like it, 1840

Landure (Nicholas) *Publisher. See* Sh— Hamlet, 1603

Lane (John) Tom Tell-troth's message and his pen's complaint, 1600. Ln: New Sh— Soc., 1876. 8°   BUS

Lane (R. J.) *Editor—*
See Sh— Works, 1870, 1878, 1879, 1883-87
  ,, Sh— Works: Ext. 1870

Lane (T.) *Artist. See* Egan

Lane.] Egan (Pierce) Life of Theodore Lane. 8°

Laneham (Robert) Letter describing the magnificent pageants presented before Queen Elizabeth at Kenilworth Castle in 1575. Repeatedly referred to in the romance of 'Kenilworth' [by Sir W. Scott]. With introd., preface, glossarial and explanatory notes [by J. H. Burn]. Ln: Printed for J. H. Burn by S. & R. Bentley, 1821. 8°, pp. xviii.-114, and portrait of Queen Elizabeth   SML
  Letter . . . Re-edited by F. J. Furnivall. Ln: New Sh— Soc., 1890. 8°
  Letter . . . Edited with introd. by F. J. Furnivall. Ln: Chatto, 1908. 8°

Lang (Andrew) Introductory preface—
See Sh— Works: Ext. 1899, 1901
  Memoir of C. I. Elton. *See Sh*—] Elton
  Sh—-Bacon imbroglio [In the 'Valet's tragedy and other studies,' pp. 312-357]. Ln: 1903. 8°   BPL | MPL

Lang (Andrew) *Editor—*
See Ballads of books
  ,, Poet . . .

Lang (Jeanie) Stories from Sh—. *See* Sh— Works: Ext. 1905

Lang (*Mrs*. Andrew) Life of Sh—. *See Sh*—] Lang

Lang (*Mrs*. Andrew) *Editor. See* Sh— Works: Ext. 1908

Langbaine (Gerard) Account of the English dramatick poets. With observations on their comedies, tragedies, etc. . . . Oxford: Printed by L. L. for G. West & H. Clements, 1691. 8°
            BPL | BUS | MPL | SML | W
Pp. 453-470 devoted to Sh—.

Langbaine (Gerard) Lives and characters of the English dramatick poets. Also an exact account of all the plays that were ever yet printed in the English tongue, their double titles, places where acted, dates when printed, and the persons to whom dedicated . . . Improved and continued down to this time by a careful hand [C. Gildon]. Ln: 1698. 8°

Momus triumphans, or the plagiaries of the English stage exposed in a catalogue of all the comedies, etc., both ancient and modern, that were ever yet printed in English. With an account of the originals from whence most of them stole their plots. Ln: 1688. Fcp. 4°   BPL | BUS
Gives the sources of some of Sh—'s plots.

Langbaine (Gerard)—
See Hazlitt (W. C.)
  ,, Oldys
  ,, Sh— Mucedorus (*heading*)

Langford (John Alfred) Birmingham Free Libraries, Sh— Memorial Library, and the Art Gallery. Birmingham, 1871. 8°   BPL
Contains account of the Sh— Library contents.
'Drunken Bidford.' *See* Andrews
Ode to the memory of Sh—. Birmingham [1859 ?] 12°   BPL
Pleasant spots and famous places. Ln: W. Tegg, 1862. 8°, pp. viii.-288   BPL
Contains 'Pilgrimage to England's Mecca,' pp. 262-279.
Praise of books. *See* Sh— Works: Ext. 1884
Sh— tercentenary year: Poems. Stratford-on-Avon, 1864. 12°   BPL

Langford (J. A.) Mackintosh (C. S.) & Tildesley (J. C.) Staffordshire and Warwickshire, past and present. With illustrations by H. Warren. Ln: W. Mackenzie [c. 1875]. 4 vols. 4°
Several large steel plates of Stratford, etc., with descriptions.

Langley (T.) *Publisher. See* Kyd

Langston (C. J.)] How Sh—'s skull was stolen and found. By a Warwickshire man [In 'The Argosy']. Ln: 1879. 8°   BPL
  How Sh—'s skull was stolen. Ln: Stock, 1884. 8°, pp. 46   BM | BPL | BUS | SML

Langton *Editor. See* Johnson (*Dr*. S.) Prologue

'Langton (Clare)' *pseud. See* Tucker (F. J.)

Lanier (Sidney) Sh— and Chaucer [In 'Music and poetry']. 1905. Cr. 8°   BPL
  Sh— and his forerunners: Studies in Elizabethan poetry and its development from early English. Ln: Heinemann, 1903. 2 vols. Roy. 8°, pp. 698. Illust.   BPL | MPL

Lanneare (Nicholas) *Composer. See* Sh— Works: Ext. 1653

(189)

Lansdowne (*Lord*). *See* Granville

La Primaudaye (Pierre de) French academie
. . . Ln: 1586. 8°   BUS
The fifty-second chapter, headed 'Of the division of
the ages of man,' is perhaps founded on Richard
Arnold (*q.v.*), and may have suggested to Sh— the
famous passage in 'As you like it.'

French academie, wherin is discovrsed the
institution of maners and whatsoever els
concerneth the good and happie life of
all estates. Newly trans. [from the
French] by T. B. C. [Thomas Beard,
Clerk (?)] Third edition. Ln: Impensis
Georg. Bishop, 1594. Fcp. 4°, in two
parts, with separate paginations   w
In the 'Epistle to the reader' notices are found of old
English poets, and a philippic against the stage and
players. For an account of the work see Collier,
'Poetical Decameron,' and Halliwell, 'Handlist of
Sh—, 1862.'
Robert Greene, the soured critic of Sh—, filched whole
pages and passages from this work, in addition to his
plagiarisms of other writers. [*See* 'Notes and
Queries,' 1st July, 1905.]

La Rochefoucauld (*Duke de*) Maxims and
moral reflections, also Sh— aphorisms.
[c. 1850]. 12°   BPL

Latham (E.) Shakespearean quotations. *See*
Sh— Works: Ext. 1905

Latham (*Miss* G.) Julia, Silvia, Hero and
Viola. Ln: New Sh— Soc., 1887-92.
8°
Illustrates 'Romeo . . . Two gentlemen . . . Much ado
. . .' and 'Twelfth night.'

O 'poor Ophelia!' Ln: New Sh— Soc.,
1880-86. 8°

On Volumnia. Ln: New York Sh— Soc.,
1887-92. 8°
Illustrates 'Coriolanus.'

Rosalind, Celia and Helen. Ln: New Sh—
Soc., 1887-92. 8°
Illustrates 'As you like it.'

Sh—'s metaphors in the comedies. Ln:
New Sh— Soc., 1887-92. 8°

Some of Sh—'s waiting women. Ln: New
Sh— Soc., 1887-92

Latham (Henry)] Sertum Shakesperianum,
subnexis aliquot inferioris notæ floribus.
Autore H. L——. *Oblatum Amicus*, 1863.
Cr. 8°

Sertum Shakesperianum . . . Ln: Macmillan,
1864. 12°, pp. xii.-204   BUS | SML

Latham (R. G.) On the double personality of
the 'Hamlet' of Saxo Grammaticus: The
'Hamlet' of Sh—, its relation to the
German 'Hamlet.' Ln: 1874. 8°
                    BM | BPL | BUS | CPL

Plot and dramatis personæ of 'Titus Andronicus' [In 'Fraser's Magazine,' Sept.]
Ln: 1870. 8°   BPL | BUS

Two dissertations on the 'Hamlet' of Saxo
Grammaticus and of Sh— . . . Ln: Williams & Norgate, 1872. 8°, pp. 150 BUS

Lathrop (Elise) Where Sh— set his stage.
Ln: Laurie, 1906. 8°, pp. 258   BPL

Lathum (G.) *Publisher. See* Davenant

Latimer (Elizabeth W.) Familiar talks on
some of Sh—'s comedies. Boston [U.S.]:
Roberts, 1886. 8°   BM | BUS | SML

Familiar talks. New edition. Boston [U.S.],
1897. 12°   BPL

Laurie & Whittle *Publishers. See* Sh— As
you like it, 1807

Law—
    See Campbell
    ,, Devecmon
    ,, Ordinance
    ,, Rushton
    ,, *Sh*—] Sh—'s legal knowledge

Law against lovers. *See* Sh— Measure . . . 1673

Law (B.) *Publisher*—
    See Sh— Hamlet, 1767
    ,, Sh— Macbeth, 1770
    ,, Sh— Merchant . . . 1783
    ,, Sh— Othello, 1765
    ,, Sh— The tempest, 1761
    ,, Sh— Timon . . . 1770
    ,, Sh— Works, 1773, 1790, 1793

Law (C.) *Publisher. See* Sh— Works, 1798,
1811

Law (J.) Sea shore of Bohemia. With an
appendix on Sh—'s gloves. Lancaster:
Penn [U.S.], 1900. Fcp. 4°   BPL
Illustrates the 'Winter's tale.'

Law *or* Lawe (Mathew) *Publisher*—
    See Rowlands
    ,, Sh— King Henry IV., i., 1604, 1608,
        1613, 1622
    ,, Sh— King Henry IV., ii., 1605
    ,, Sh— King Richard II., 1608, 1615
    ,, Sh— King Richard III., 1605, 1612,
        1621, 1622, 1629

Law (Robert) Memorials, or the memorable
things that fell out within this Island of
Britain from 1638 to 1684. Ed. from
the orig. MS. by Charles Kirkpatrick
Sharpe. Edinburgh, 1818. 4°
A collection of witchcraft and wizardy tales. Illustrates
'Macbeth.'

Law (Wm.) Absolute unlawfulness of the stage
entertainment fully demonstrated. Ln:
Printed for W. & J. Innys at the West
End of St. Pauls, 1798. 8°   BPL

Lawes (Henry) *Composer. See* Sh— Works:
Ext. 1653

Lawes (Wm.) *Composer. See* Sh— Works:
Ext. 1653

Lawreen (J. B.) Hamlet ye Dane: A ghost
story. With music. [1877?] F°   BPL

Lawrence (Boyle) *Editor. See* Celebrities

Lawrence (F.) Remarkable literary impos-
tures [In 'Sharpe's London Magazine,'
Jan.] 1849   BUS
Includes the Ireland forgeries.

Lawrence (Wm. J.) Actresses in male Sh—
roles [In 'Universal & Ludgate Mag.,'
April]. 1901. 8°   BPL
Did Thomas Shadwell write an opera on
'The tempest' ? [In 'Anglia,' pp. 205-
217]. Halle, 1904. Roy. 8°
Life of G. V. Brooke. *See* Brooke
Players' petition to Charles II. [In 'Athe-
næum,' No. 3938, p. 508, April]. 1903
Lawson (Richard) *Edinburgh Publisher. See*
Stephen
Lawson (Wm.) *Editor*—
See Sh— King Henry VIII., 1875
  ,, Sh— King Richard III., 1874
  ,, Sh— Works, 1873-75
Lawton (G.) *Publisher. See* Pope
Lea (Henry Charles) Ireland and the Sh—
forgeries [In 'Democratic Review,' July].
New York, 1845. 8°   BUS
Lea (I.) *Philadelphia Publisher. See* Sh—
Works, 1823
Lea (R.) *Publisher. See* Sh— Works, 1798,
1811
Lea & Hurst *Publishers. See* Sh— Works, 1798
Leach (Dryden) *Printer*—
See Capell
  ,, Sh— Antony . . . 1758
  ,, Sh— Works, 1767-68
Leake (William) *Publisher*—
See Sh— Merchant . . . 1652
  ,, Sh— Othello, 1655
  ,, Sh— Passionate . . . 1599
  ,, Sh— Venus . . . 1599, 1602
Learcroft (S.) *Publisher. See* Six old plays
Leask (W. Keith) *Editor. See* Sh— King
Richard II., 1903
Leathley (A.) *Dublin Publisher*—
See Colman
  ,, Sh— Works, 1766
Leaves from the diary of a dreamer, found
among his papers. Ln : W. Pickering,
1853. 12°
Refers to 'Hamlet' on p. 59.
Leavitt *New York Publisher. See* Sh— Works,
1852, 1860
Le Blanc (*L'Abbé*) Observations on the Eng-
lish stage. *See* Guthrie
'Lector *pseud.* (Oliver)' Letters from the
dead to the dead. Boston [U.S.], 1905.
8°, pp. 88. Illust.   BPL | BUS
On the Sh—-Bacon controversy.
Lee (Alexander) Recollections of Sh—:
Dramatic overture for the piano . . . Ln :
Lee & Coxhead [c. 1864]. F°, pp. 8 BUS
Lee (Elizabeth) *Editor*—
See Jusserand
  ,, Sh— The tempest, 1894
  ,, Sh— Twelfth night, 1895
Lee (Henry T.) Sh—'s Brutus [In 'Knicker-
bocker,' May]. New York, 1861. 8° BUS
Illustrates 'Julius Cæsar.'

Lee (Jane) On the authorship of the second
and third parts of 'King Henry VI.' and
their originals. Ln : New Sh— Soc.,
1875-76. 8°   BUS
Table of Sh—'s and Marlowe's shares in
'King Henry VI.' : parts ii. and iii. Ln :
New Sh— Soc., 1875-76. 8°   BUS
Lee (John) *Editor. See* Sh— Macbeth, 1753
Lee (Nathaniel) Lucius Junius Brutus, father
of his country : A tragedy. Ln : Richard
& Jacob Tonson at Gray's Inn Gate and
at the Judge's Head in Chancery Lane,
1681. Fcp. 4°   W
Contains an imitation of the scene between Hamlet
and Polonius and several references to Tarquin and
Lucrece.
Mithridates, King of Pontus : A tragedy.
Ln : Printed by R. E. for James Magnes
and Rich. Bentley, Russell St., Covent
Garden, 1678. Fcp. 4°
'I have endeavoured to mix Sh— with Fletcher, the
thoughts of the former for majesty and true Roman
greatness, and the softness and passionate expression
of the latter, which make up half the beauties, are
never to be matched.'—*Dedication.*
Mithridates . . . Ln : R. E. for R. Bentley
and T. Magnes, 1685. Fcp. 4°
Mithridates . . . Ln : Richard Wellington
and E. Rumbold, 1702. Fcp. 4°, pp.
vi.-66   BM
'Lee (Sidney Lancelot).' *See* Levi (S. L.)
Lee (W.) *Publisher. See* Drayton
Lees (E.)] Stratford as connected with Sh—.
Stratford-upon-Avon, 1851. 8°   BPL
Stratford . . . Second edition. Stratford-
upon-Avon, 1854. 8°   BPL | CPL
Lees (John) Questions on 'As you like it.'
Ln : Allman, 1900. Cr. 8°   BPL
Questions on 'Julius Cæsar.' Ln : Allman
[1896]. Cr. 8°   BM | BPL
Questions on 'King Henry V.' Ln : All-
man, 1900. Cr. 8°   BPL
Questions on 'Midsummer night's dream.'
Ln : Allman [1894]. 8°, pp. 56
                               BM | BPL | BUS
Questions on 'The tempest.' Ln : Allman
[1897]. 8°, pp. 64   BM | BPL | BUS
Questions on 'Twelfth night.' Ln : Allman
[1896]. 8°   BM | BPL
See also Cann & Lees
Lees (John) *Editor*—
See Sh— Julius Cæsar, 1896
  ,, Sh— King Henry V., 1901
  ,, Sh— Midsummer . . . 1902
  ,, Sh— Twelfth night, 1895, 1896
Lees (J.) & Cann (A. L.) Questions on King
Richard III. [c. 1904]. Cr. 8°   BPL
Lefanse (Alicia) Memoirs of Mrs. Sheridan.
See Sheridan
Legate *or* Legatt (John) *Cambridge Printer*—
See Bullokar
  ,, Clarke (W.)

Legg (J. W.) Note upon the 'elf-locks' in 'Romeo & Juliet.' Ln : New Sh— Soc., 1875-76. 8°
'And bakes the elf-locks in foul sluttish hairs.'—*Romeo . . . i., 4.*

Legge (Thomas) The true tragedy of Richard the Third. To which is appended the Latin play of Richardus Tertius . . . Both anterior to Sh—'s drama. With introd. and notes by Barron Field. Ln : Sh— Soc., 1844. 8°, pp. x.-166 BPL | BUS | SML
Reprinted in Collier's Sh 's Library.

Le Goux *Engraver. See* Sh— Poems, 1795

Legrand (M. A.) *Editor. See* Sh— Othello, 1882

Le Hondt (P. A.) *Publisher. See* Garrick

Lêibrock (E.) *Braunschweig Publisher. See* Sh— Romeo, 1840

Leicester—
See Halliwell
 ,, Notices . . .

Leicester (Robert Dudley *Earl of*)—
See Bruce   *See* Kenilworth
 ,, Dugdale   ,, Malone
 ,, Halliwell

Leifchild (F.) Hamlet : A new reading [In 'Contemporary Review']. 1883. Roy. 8°
BPL

Leigh (*Lady*) Stoneleigh Abbey. *See* Memorials . . .

Leigh-Noel *aft.* Elliott (M.)] Lady Macbeth : A study. Ln : Wyman, 1884. 8°
BM | BPL | BUS | SML

] Sh—'s garden of girls . . . A study by the author of 'Lady Macbeth.' Ln : Remington, 1885. 8°, pp. iv.-352, and portrait of Mary Anderson as 'Juliet'
BM | BPL | BUS

Leighton (Alexander)] Shorte treatise against stage playes. Ln : Printed in the yeere of our Lord 1625. Fcp. 4°, pp. 28 ; sig. A to D² in fours   BM | EAL
According to Field this was secretly printed.

Leighton (William) Sh—'s dream and other poems. Philadelphia, 1881. 8°   BPL
The title was the copyright of Bennet Gilbert (*q.v.*) for twenty years ere this.

Sketch of Sh—. *See* Sh—
Subjection of Hamlet : An essay . . . with introd. by J. Crosby. Philadelphia : Lippincott, 1882. Fcp. 4° BPL | BUS | SML

Leisure Hour [An illustrated magazine]. Ln : Religious Tract Soc., 1886. 4°
Contains article on 'Sh—'s handwriting,' p. 431.

Leisure Hour. Ln : Religious Tract Soc., 1888. 4°
Contains the following articles :—
 'A modern Sh—,' p. 286.
 'Printing of the first folio Sh—,' p. 428.
 'Sh—'s personal fame,' p. 432.
 'Sh—'s tombstone,' p. 493.
 'Sh—'s learning,' p. 640.
 'Stratford-on-Avon mace,' p. 711.

Leisure Hour. Ln : Religious Tract Soc., 1892. 4°
Contains article :—
 'Was Sh— a roman catholic?' p. 286.

Leisure Hour. Ln : Religious Tract Soc., 1893. 4°
Contains the following :—
 'Trusteeship of Sh—'s house,' p. 52.
 'Sh—'s books and manuscripts,' p. 211.
 'Charles Edward Flower, by B. J. Laffan,' with portraits and plates, p. 473.
 'Only likeness of Sh—' [History of the Stratford bust], p. 623.

Leisure Hour : Tercentenary number. *See* Sh—

Leland (Charles Godfrey) *Editor. See* Heine

Le Loyer *Sieur de la Brosse* (Pierre) Treatise of specters. Ln : 1605. Fcp. 4°   BUS
On folio 32 is a story which may have suggested the bagpipe allusion in the 'Merchant of Venice.'

Lemoine (H.) *Publisher. See* Sh— Merry wives, 1789

Lemon (Mark) Sir John Falstaff—
See Sh— King Henry IV., i.-ii., 1868, 1871
 ,, *also* Hatton

Le Monnier *Firenze Publisher*—
See Sh— Hamlet, 1867
 ,, Sh— Macbeth, 1867
 ,, Sh— Othello, 1867
 ,, Sh— Romeo . . . 1868

Le Neve (Philip)] Cursory remarks on some of the ancient English poets, particularly Milton . . . Ln : [Privately printed], 1789. 8°, pp. vi.-146
Anonymously printed for presents. Issue restricted to two hundred copies.
Contains a chapter on Sh—.

Lennig (Thompson) 'Macbeth' [In 'Penn Monthly,' May]. Philadelphia, 1870. 8°
BUS

Lennox (*Mrs.* Charlotte)] Sh— illustrated, or the novels and histories on which the plays of Sh— are founded. Collected and translated from the original authors, with critical remarks . . . Ln : A. Millar, 1753-54. 3 vols. 12°
BM | BPL | BUS | CPL | MPL | SML | W
The dedication to John Earl of Orrery was written by Dr. Johnson. Malone thought many of the notes throughout the work also proceeded from his pen. For contents see Hubbard & Knapp, Catalogue, p. 147.

Sh— illustrated . . . with critical remarks and biographical sketches of the writers by M. M. Noah, Vol. i. Philadelphia : Bradford & Inskeep, 1809. 8°   BUS
Projected in two vols. Only one appeared.

Lennox (W. Pitt *Lord*) Plays, players, and playhouses at home and abroad. With anecdotes of the drama and the stage. Ln : Hurst & Blackett, 1881. 2 vols. 8°
SML

Lenny (C.)] Sh— for schools. *See* Sh— Works : Ext. 1847, 1851, 1865

Lenny (C.) *Editor*—
  See Sh— King Lear, 1865
  ,, Sh— Works, 1865
Lenox (James) Lenox Collection of Sh—
  folios [In 'American Bibliopolist,' June-
  July]. New York, 1870. 8° BUS
Sh—'s plays in folio [In 'Historical Maga-
  zine,' July]. New York, 1861. 8° BUS
  A few also done on large paper.
] Sh—'s plays in folio : An account of the
  folios in the Lenox Library. 1866. 4°
  BPL
Lenox.] Contributions to a catalogue of the
  Lenox Library, No. v. : Works of Sh—,
  etc. New York : Printed for the Trustees,
  1880. 4°, pp. 132 (*includ. printed wrappers*)
  BM | BPL | BUS | NY | SML
  The entertaining introduction gives a curious account
  of the variants of the name Sh—.
Leo (F. A.) Autograph of Rosenkranz and
  Güldenstern. Weimar [1890]. 4°
  BM | BUS
  Illustrative of 'Hamlet.'
Sh— notes. Ln : 1885. 8° BM | BPL | BUS
Sh—'s Coriolanus. Berlin : Trowitzsch,
  1861. 8° SML
Leo (F. A.) *Editor*—
  See Plutarchus
  ,, Sh— Coriolanus, 1864
Leonard (H. B.) *Editor.* See Sh— Hamlet :
  Hoffman, 1852
Léonard Gallery : Account of the great pic-
  ture Sh— . . . See Sh—
Leopold (*Prince*) Bibliophile. See Sh— Romeo,
  1874
Leslie (Charles Robert) *Artist*—
  See Callcott & Leslie
  ,, Sh— Works, 1829, 1873-76, 1875-76
Leslie.] Vincent (W. T.) Recollections of
  Frederick Leslie. With introd. by
  Clement Scott. Ln : K. Paul, 1894. 2
  vols. 8°. Illust.
L'Estrange (A. G.) Literary life of Wm.
  Harness. See Harness
L'Estrange (*Sir* Roger) *Editor.* See Terence
Lethbridge (J. W.) *Editor.* See Sh— Works :
  Ext. 1849-50
Leti (Gregory) Life of Pope Sixtus V. See
  Sixtus
Letter from 'Aguecheek.' See Fairbanks (C.
  B.)
Letter on Sh—'s authorship of 'Two noble
  kinsmen' . . . See Spalding
Letter to Colley Cibber on his transformation
  of 'King John.' Ln : M. Cooper, 1745.
  8°, pp. iv.-48 BPL | BUS
Letter to David Garrick. See Warner
Letter to George Hardinge on Steevens'
  preface. See Collins

Letter to Miss Mossiter, occasioned by her
  first appearance on the stage . . . [with]
  Remarks on the manner of her playing
  'Juliet' . . . [and] some other theatrical
  observations. Ln : W. Owen & G. Wood-
  fall, 1753. 8°, pp. iv.-56 BUS
Letter to Sir D. Carleton. See Herbert
Letters concerning taste. See Cooper
Letters from a late eminent prelate. See
  Warburton
Letters from a theatrical scene painter. See
  Erle
Letters from Snowdon. See Cradock
Letters on the drama. See Penn
Lettsom (W. N.) *Editor.* See Walker (W. S.)
Leuven *Comte* Ribbing (Adolphe) *Editor.* See
  Sh— Midsummer . . . 1866
Leveridge (Richard) Pyramus and Thisbe.
  See Sh— Midsummer . . . 1716
Levi *Sidney L. Lee* (Solomon Lazarus)] Alleged
  vandalism at Stratford. Ln : Constable,
  1903. 8°, pp. 82, including printed wrap-
  pers. Illustrated BPL | SBL | SML
  For reply, see Gonzalez, 'Plain truth . . .'
] 'As you like it' and Stratford-on-Avon [In
  'Gentleman's Magazine,' Vol. lix., p.
  351-363]. 1885. 8° BPL
] 'Beget' and 'Begetter' in Elizabethan
  English [In 'Athenæum,' No. 3774, p.
  250, Feb. ; No. 3777, p. 345, Mar.] 1900
  On the 'Sonnets.'
] Bibliographical curiosity [Stratford-Boston
  Sh— circular] [In 'Athenæum,' No.
  3981, p. 211, Feb.] 1904
] Census of extant copies [of the Jaggard
  folio of Sh—, 1623]. See Sh— Works,
  1902
] Elizabethan England and the Jews. Ln :
  New Sh— Soc., 1887-92. 8°
] Elizabethan plagiarism [by Geo. Chapman
  and S. Daniel] [In 'Athenæum,' No. 4076,
  p. 800, Dec.] 1905
] Four quarto editions of plays by Sh—, the
  property of the trustees and guardians of
  Sh—'s birthplace . . . Stratford-on-Avon :
  Edward Fox, 1908. Fcp. 4°, pp. 68,
  including printed wrappers and five fac-
  similes BPL | SBL | SML
  Among other errors the writer says (p. 19), 'In 1608 . . .
  William Jaggard . . . had hitherto been destitute of
  a press of his own,' although some thirty examples
  of that publisher's press, beginning at 1599, were
  exhibited at the Public Library, adjoining the birth-
  house property, for twelve months before this
  pamphlet appeared, and a lengthy list of others from
  1594 to 1627 was given in the 'Athenæum' in 1902-03.
  See Jaggard (W.)
] Great Englishmen of the sixteenth century.
  Westminster : Constable, 1904. 8°, pp.
  358. With portraits BPL | MPL
  Deals with More, Sidney, Ralegh, Spenser, Bacon,
  and Sh—.

Levi *Sidney L. Lee* (Solomon Lazarus)] Impersonal aspect of Sh—'s art. English Assoc. leaflets. Ln: 1909. 8°

Introduction. *See* Sh— Works: Ext. 1902

] 'King Henry V.': An account and an estimate. 1900. 12°　　　　BPL

] Life of Wm. Sh—. *See Sh—*] Levi

] Most popular English author [In 'London Mag.'] Ln: 1906. Roy. 8°　　　BPL

] Notes and additions to the census of copies of the Sh— first folio. Oxford Univ. Press, 1906. Roy. 8°, pp. 32　　BPL

] Notes and additions . . . [In 'The Library,' April]. Ln: 1906. Roy. 8°　　BPL

] Original Shylock [In 'Gentleman's Mag.,' Feb.] Ln: 1880. 8°　　　　BUS
Advocates the claims of Roderigo Lopez.

Preface. *See Sh—*] Praise

] Prefatory essay . . . *See* Perry

] Sh— and patriotism [In 'Cornhill Mag.,' N.S., Vol. x.] 1901. 8°　　　BPL

] Sh— and the Elizabethan playgoer [In an 'English Miscellany,' pp. 235-254]. Oxford, 1901. 8°　　　　　　BPL

] Sh— and the modern stage. With other essays. Ln: Murray, 1906. 8°, pp. 266　　　　　　　　　　　　BPL

] Sh— first folio: Some notes and a discovery [In 'Cornhill Magazine,' pp. 449-458, April]. Ln: 1899. 8°
Refers to the Sibthorp copy, originally presented by the printer, Wm. Jaggard, to his friend Augustine Vincent, and bearing Vincent's autograph inscription, of which a facsimile is given.

] Sh— quartos [In 'Athenæum,' No. 4202, p. 574]. Ln: 1908

] Sh—'s birthplace [Annual Report] [In 'Athenæum,' No. 4125, p. 619, and No. 4185, p. 43, Nov.-Jan.] 1906-1908

] Sh—'s handwriting. Ln: Smith, 1899. 8°. pp. viii., and 3 plates　　BPL | BUS
Reprinted from his 'Life of Sh—.'

Sh—'s life and work. *See Sh—*] Levi

] Stratford-on-Avon from the earliest times to the death of Wm. Sh—. With forty-five illustrations by Edward Hull. Ln: Seeley, 1885. F°, pp. vi.-78, fourteen full-page etchings and 33 etched vignettes, 47 pictures in all, not 46, as stated on title　　　　　　BM | BPL | SML
A bad blunder occurs on p. 76, where the iconoclast, Francis Gastrell, is described as 'Vicar of Stratford.'

] Stratford-on-Avon . . . Ln: Seeley, 1885. Roy. f°　　　　　　　　　　SML
Large paper. Limited to 100 copies.

] Stratford-on-Avon . . . Ln: Seeley, 1890. Illust. by E. Hull. Cr. 8°, pp. viii.-304　　　　　　　　　　　　SML

] Stratford-on-Avon. Ln: Seeley, 1904. Cr. 8°, pp. 312. Illust.

Levi *Sidney L. Lee* (Solomon Lazarus)] Stratford-on-Avon . . . Revised ed. Ln: Seeley, 1906. Cr. 8°, pp. 328

] Stratford-on-Avon . . . Illust. Ln: Seeley, 1907. Cr. 8°　　　　　BPL

] Topical side of the Elizabethan drama. Ln: New Sh— Soc., 1887-92. 8°

] Undescribed copy of the Sh— first folio [In 'Athenæum,' No. 3747, p. 267, Aug.] 1899

See Greg　　　　　　*See* Stronach
　,, Stopes　　　　　　　,, Tyler

Levi (S. L.) *Editor—*
See Sh— Coriolanus, 1909
　,, Sh— Julius Cæsar, 1908
　,, Sh— King Lear, 1909
　,, Sh— Passionate . . . 1905
　,, Sh— Pericles, 1905
　,, Sh— Poems, 1905
　,, Sh— Rape, 1905
　,, Sh— Sonnets, 1905
　,, Sh— Venus . . . 1905
　,, Sh— Works, 1902
　,, *Sh—*] Dictionary

Levins (Peter) Manipulus vocabulorum: A rhyming dictionary of the English language, 1570. With an alphabetical index by H. B. Wheatley. Ln: Camden Soc., 1867. Fcp. 4°　　　　SML
The original edition was no doubt familiar to Sh—.

Levy (Matthias) Sh— and shorthand. Ln: 1884. 8°, pp. 16　　BM | BPL | BUS
Discusses an early system of shorthand, which may have been used for procuring pirated copies of Sh—'s plays.

Levy made in 1697 . . . *See* Stratford

Lewes *Comedian* (Charles Lee) Comic sketches, or the comedian his own manager. Ln: 1804. Cr. 8°

Lewes (George Henry) On actors and the art of acting. Ln: 1875. 12°　BPL | BUS
Includes 'Sh— as actor and critic,' pp. 88-108.

On actors. Second edition. Ln: 1875. 12°　　　　　　　　　　　BPL

On actors . . . Leipzig, 1875. 16°　　BUS

On actors . . . New York, 1878. 12°　BUS

] Sh— in France, by G. H. L. [In 'Cornhill Mag.,' Jan.] Ln: 1865. 8°
　　　　　　　　　BPL | BUS | CPL

Lewes (Louis) Women of Sh—. Trans. from the German by Helen Zimmern. Ln: Hodder, 1894. 8°, pp. xx.-384
　　　　　　　　　BM | BPL | SML

Lewis *Actor*. Portrait. *See* Sh— King Henry IV., i., 1785

Lewis (C. M.) Genesis of 'Hamlet.' New York, 1907. Cr. 8°　　　　BPL

Lewis (E. Goodwin) Sh— creations. Illuminated by Samuel Stanesby. Ln: Griffin, 1864. Fcp. 4°. With 13 photographs
　　　　　　　BM | BPL | BUS | CPL

Lewis (George) Life of Bp. Hall. *See* Hall

Lewis (J. G.) Christopher Marlowe. *See* Marlowe

Lewis (L. A.) *Publisher—*
  See Sh— Poems, 1840
  ,, Sh— Works, 1841, 1851

Lewis (W.) *Publisher. See* Cibber

Lewkenor (Edward). *See* Oldmayne

Lewkenor (Lewis) *Editor. See* Nash

Lewkenor (Samuel) Discourse not altogether unprofitable . . . for such as are desirous to know the situation and customs of foraine cities without travelling to see them. Ln : 1600. 8°
  The question is sometimes asked, How did the poet acquire his knowledge of foreign parts? The above apparently supplies the answer.

Lex scripta. *See* Rushton

Lexicons. *See Sh—*] Sh— glossaries

Leyland (John) Sh— country illustrated . . . Ln : 'Country Life' Office [Newnes, 1903]. 4°, pp. 132, and coloured folding map   BPL

Library (The): A quarterly review of bibliography and library lore. Ed. by J. Y. W. Macalister & A. W. Pollard. New Series. Ln : Kegan Paul & Alex. Moring, 1900-1910. 10 vols. Roy. 8°. Illust. [In progress]   BM | BPL
  Contains many Sh— articles and reviews.

  See Ballinger   *See* Levi
  ,, Child   ,, Plomer
  ,, Esdaile   ,, Rivers
  ,, Greg   ,, Scholderer
  ,, Jaggard

Lichfield (Leonard) *Oxford Publisher. See* Fletcher

Liddell (A. C.) *Editor—*
  See Sh— The tempest, 1891
  ,, Sh— Works, 1886-91

Liddell (Mark Harvey) *Editor—*
  See Sh— Macbeth, 1903
  ,, Sh— Works, 1903

Liebault (Jean). *See* Estienne & Liebault

Life and death of Hector. *See* Lydgate

Life and death of Richard the third: Ballad. *See Sh—*] Collection

Life and death of Titus Andronicus: Ballad. *See Sh—*] Collection

Life of Sh—, 1743. *See Sh—*] Life

Life of Sh—, 1822. *See Sh—*] Life

Life of Sh—, interspersed with . . . anecdotes, 1822. *See Sh—*] Life

Life . . . of Sh—, 1850. *See Sh—*] Life

Life . . . of Sh—, 1864. *See Sh—*] Life

Life . . . of Sh—, actor and dramatist, 1864. *See Sh—*] Life

Life of Sh—, 1883. *See Sh—*] Life

Lift for the lazy. *See* Sh—] Lift . . .

Lillo (George) Arden of Feversham. *See* Sh— Arden . . . 1763, 1775, 1866

  Extracts. *See* Sh— Works : Ext. 1822

  London merchant, or history of George Barnwell. Ln : Printed for J. Gray at the Cross Keys in the Poultry and sold by J. Roberts in Warwick Lane, 1731. 8°
  Quotes 'Hamlet' thrice in the dedication.

Lillo (G.) *Editor. See* Sh— Pericles, 1738, 1775, 1810

Lilly (J.) *Editor. See* Ballads

Lilly (William) Angli rudimenta . . . Ln : Richard Pynson [1512 *or* 1513]. Fcp. 4°, pp. 16
  Cited in 'As you like it,' v., 4, and 'Taming of the shrew,' iii., 1.
  This, the original issue, was sold in Dec., 1905, for £36. Only two copies appear to be known.

  Short introduction of [Latin] grammar. Oxford, 1714. 12°   BPL

Lilly (W. S.) Studies in religion and literature. Ln : 1904. 8°   BPL | MPL
  Contains article, 'What was Sh –'s religion?' and 'A French Sh—' [H. de Balzac].

Limberd (J.) *Publisher. See* Sh— Works, 1818

Lincoln's Inn Fields Theatre. *See* Sh— Twelfth night . . . 1703

Lindo (M. P.) *Editor. See* Sh— Macbeth, 1853, 1867

Lindsey (H. W.) *Editor. See* Sh— Hamlet, 1908

Lines read before the Sh— Society at their seventh annual celebration of the birthday of the illustrious bard, Dublin, 23rd April, 1819. Written by an absent member and honoured with the prize. Dublin, 1819. 4°   W

Ling *or* Lyng (Nicholas) *Publisher—*
  See Allot
  ,, Lodge
  ,, Sh— Hamlet, 1603, 1604, 1605

Linley (Thomas) *Composer. See* Lyric ode

Linley *junior* (Thomas) Ode on the spirits of Sh— [Original manuscript score, for *Violino primo*, 15 leaves ; *Alto*, 2 copies, each of 5 leaves ; *Tenor*, 2 copies, 5 leaves and 7 leaves respectively ; *Bass*, 3 copies, each of 6 leaves ; *Canto*, 7 leaves]. [c. 1770.] 9 vols [in two sizes]. Royal 4° and oblong f°   W
  One of the tenor, both of the alto, and the violino primo parts are in Linley's holograph entirely.

  Ode on the spirits . . . Alto part [c. 1770]. Manuscript. Oblong f°, pp. 12   BUS

Linley *jun.* (T.) *Composer. See* Sh— The tempest, 1776, 1785

Linley *jun.* (T.) & Lawrence (*Dr.*) Witches and fairies : An ode in commemoration of Sh—. The words by Dr. Lawrence, set to musick by Thomas Linley junior, and performed at the Theatre in Drury Lane, March 20th, 1776. [Original holograph manuscript.] Ln : 1776. 4°, 224 pages   w
Described in Halliwell's Handlist . . . 1862, 8°, p. 211.

Linley (W.) *Composer—*
See Dramatic songs
 ,, Sh— Poems, 1790, 1800

Linley (Wm.) & Bowles (W. L.) Ariel's adieu to Prospero [In 'Eight songs for tenor or soprano']. Ln : c. 1790. F°   BUS

Linton (*Sir* J. D.) *Artist. See* Sh— King Henry VIII., 1892

Linton (W. J.) *Artist—*
See Sh— Works, 1884-92
 ,, *Sh*—] Wise

Linton (W. J.) & Stoddard (R. H.) English verse. *See* Sh— Works : Ext. 1884

Lintot *or* Lintott (Bernard) *Publisher—*
See Dennis
 ,, Rowe
 ,, Sh— King Lear, 1699
 ,, Sh— King Richard III., 1700
 ,, Sh— Merchant . . . 1701, 1713, 1732
 ,, Sh— Poems, 1709, 1709-10
 ,, Smith (E.)
 ,, Wilkinson

Lintot (H.) *Publisher—*
See Sh— Macbeth, 1750
 ,, Sh— Works, 1740, 1745, 1747, 1757

Lippmann (E. O. von) Sh—'s ignorance : Winter's tale [In the 'New Review']. 1891. 8°   BPL

Lisle (L.) *Publisher—*
See Brooke (C.)
 ,, Sh— King Richard III., 1614

Lisle (*Sieur de*) *Editor. See* Sh— Timon . . . 1733

List of all the songs and passages in Sh— which have been set to music. Ln : New Sh— Soc., 1884. 8°   BM

Lister (M.) *Publisher. See* Sh— Merchant . . . 1788

Litchfield (J.). *See* Bellamy (T.)

Literary and graphical illustrations of Sh— and the British drama : comprising an historical view of the origin and improvement of the English stage . . . Embellished with more than two hundred engravings on wood by eminent artists. Ln : E. Wilson, 1831. 8°, pp. xvi.-204
    BM | BPL | BUS | SML | W
Reprinted in 1833 as the ' Dramatic souvenir.'

Literary cookery. *See* Brae

Literary World. [*Consult its general indexes*]

Literature of the sixteenth and seventeenth centuries illustrated by reprints of very rare tracts. Edited by J. O. Halliwell. Ln : Privately printed, 1851. Fcp. 4°. With facsimiles of titles   BUS
Issue limited to seventy-five copies.
Contents :—
  I. Harry White : his humour, set forth by M. P—.
  II. Comedy of the two Italian gentlemen [by Anthony Munday ?].
  III. Taylor the Water Poet. Travels from London to the Isle of Wight, 1648.
  IV. Will Buck, his testament.
  V. Book of merrie riddles, 1629.
  VI. Comedy of 'All for money,' 1578.
  VII. Wine, beer, ale, and tobacco.
  VIII. Johnson (Thomas) New book of new conceits, 1630.
  IX. Love's garland, 1626.
  Of No. v. 'there can be scarcely a doubt that it is a later impression of the book lent by Master Slender to Alice Shortcake.'

Little (C. C.) *Boston U.S. Publisher. See* Sh— Works, 1844

Littledale (Harold) *Editor—*
See Dyce
 ,, Sh— Two noble kinsmen, 1876, 1885
 ,, Sh— Works : Ext. 1902

Littledale (Harold) Cuningham (Hy.) Payne (Francis John) Dillon (Arthur) & Hartley (Edward) On Vllorxa in 'Timon of Athens,' iii.-iv.-112 [In 'Athenæum,' No. 3839, p. 672 ; 3846, p. 71 ; 3848, p. 136 ; 3851, p. 231 ; 3852, p. 264 ; 3854, p. 327 ; 3857, p. 424, May-Sept.] 1901

Liverpool—
See Broadbent
 ,, Falstaff
 ,, Sh— Faire Em [*heading*]
 ,, Sh— Winter's tale, 1876

Liverpool Sh— Society. *See* British Empire

Liverpool Theatrical Investigator. Vol. i. Liverpool : Johnson, 1821. 12°   SML

Liverseege (Henry) Engravings from the works . . . [With memoir by Charles Swain]. Manchester : Grundy & Goadsby [1835]. F°, pp. xvi. and 37 full-page mezzotint plates   BUS
Includes seven scenes from ' As you like it,' ' Hamlet,' ' King Henry IV.,' ' Merry wives,' ' Othello.'

Lives and traits of the Bon Ton theatricals. *See* Sh— Works : Ext. 1790

Livius (Titus) Romane historie. Also the Breviaries of L. Florus. Trans. by Philemon Holland. Ln : Adam Islip, 1600. F°, with port. of Q. Elizabeth on verso of title   BUS
Known as Sh—'s edition.
Holland was a Coventry schoolmaster.

Ljunggren (Evald) Unique copy of the first edition of Sh—'s earliest tragedy ['Titus Andronicus, 1594'] [In 'Athenæum,' No. 4030, p. 91 and p. 156, Jan.-Feb.] 1905

Lloyd (Charles) Address to the genius of Sh—
[In Coleridge's Poems, 2nd ed.] Bristol,
1797. 8°   BUS
Lloyd (H. A.) *Editor.* *See* Sh— Romeo . . .
1841
Lloyd (Robert) Sh—: A poem, 1774. *See*
Miscellaneous . . .

] Sh—: An epistle to Mr. Garrick. With an
ode to genius. Ln: T. Davies, 1760. 4°,
pp. 8   BM | BUS
Commences thus:—
  'When Sh— leads the mind a dance
  From France to England, hence to France ;
  Talk not to me of time and place,
  I own I'm happy in the chase,
  Whether the drama's here or there,
  'Tis nature, Sh—, everywhere.
  The poet's fancy can create,
  Contract, enlarge, annihilate,
  Bring past and present close together
  In spite of distance, seas, or weather,
  And shut up in a single action
  What cost whole years in its transaction.

       .   .   .   .   .

See also Garrick, Colman & Lloyd
Lloyd (Robert) Saint James' Magazine. 1763.
2 vols.   8°
Contains a series of articles 'Concerning the advan-
tage of measure in comedy' ; of much Sh— interest.
Lloyd (Wm. Watkiss) Critical essays on the
plays of Sh—. 1875. 8°   BM | BPL
Essays on the life and plays of Sh—. *See*
Sh—] Lloyd
Lloyd (W. W.) *Editor—*
See Sh— Much ado, 1884
  ,, Sh— Works, 1855-56, 1869, 1875, 1879-
81, 1880
Lo ! here the gentle lark. *See* Sh— Venus . . .
1830
Lobb (S.) Notes on the 'Merchant of Venice.'
1881.   12°   BM
Lobban (J. H.) *Editor. See* Hazlitt
Localities of Sh—'s dramas [Collection of ten
views on six sheets, coloured by hand,
with Latin text on the verso ; apparently
excerpts from the 'Theatrum' of Orte-
lius.' c. 1650]. Royal f°   W
Locke. *See* Dunton
Locke (Matthew) English opera, or vocal
musick in 'Psyche,' with the instru-
mental therein intermix'd. To which is
adjoyned the instrumental musick in
'The tempest.' Ln: T. Ratcliff & N.
Thompson, 1675. 4°, pp. viii.-72   BUS
In his early days Locke was a chorister in Exeter
Cathedral, and carved on a stone screen in the organ
loft his name and the year 1638. The antique
characters were still legible in 1824.
Music in 'Macbeth.' *See* Sh— Poems, 1862
Locke (M.) *Composer—*
See Sh— Macbeth, 1675, 1750, 1760, 1785,
1810, 1840, 1853, 1860
  ,, Sh— The tempest, 1675

Locker (Frederick) Lyra elegantiarum. *See*
Sh— Works : Ext. 1867
Lockhart (John Gibson) *Editor. See* Sh—
Works, 1825
Lockwood (T. M.) *Editor. See* Sh— King
Henry V., 1877
Locrine. *See* Sh— Locrine
Loder (E. J.) *Composer. See* Sh— Macbeth,
1840
Lodge. List of desiderata [mentioning Sh—].
Manuscript on seventeen leaves of paper.
1793.   12°   W
A transcript in the autograph of George Steevens, the
critic.
Lodge (H. C.) Sh—'s Americanisms [In
'Harper's Monthly']. 1895. 8°   BPL
Lodge (Thomas) An unknown work, with
extracts from his 'Defence of stage plays,'
by J. P. Collier. *See Sh*—] Sh— Soc.
Defence of poetry, music and stage-plays.
To which are added . . . an alarm against
usurers, and the delectable history of
Forbonius and Prisceria. With introd.
and notes [by Dr. Laing]. *See Sh*—] Sh—
Soc.
A reply to Gosson's 'School of Abuse' (*q.v.*)
Euphues shadow : The battaile of the
sences. Wherein youthful folly is set
downe in his right figure and vaine
fancies are prooved to produce many
offences. Hereunto is annexed the deaf
man's dialogue contayning Philamis
Athanatos ; fit for all sortes to peruse
and the better sorte to practise. Ln :
Printed by Abell Ieffes for Iohn Busbie
and are to be sould at his shop in Paules
Churchyard, neere to the West doore of
Paules, 1592. Fcp. 4°, black letter, sig.
A—N4 unpaged   CTC
The 'Epistle dedicatory' is signed by Robert Greene,
who claims to see through the press the work of 'one
Thomas Lodge, who nowe is gone to sea with
Mayster Candish.'
Fair Em. *See* Sh— Fair Em
Margarite of America, 1596. Ed. by J. O.
Halliwell. Ln : [Privately printed], 1850.
Fcp. 4°   BPL | BUS
Limited to twenty-six copies.
] Rosalynde : Euphues golden legacie . . .
Fetcht from the Canaries by T. L. Ln :
T. Orwin, 1590. Fcp. 4°
The novel which doubtless suggested 'As you like it.'
Reprinted in Waldron's Sh— Miscellany ; in Collier's
Sh—'s Library ; and in Halliwell's folio Sh—, Vol. vi.
Rosalynde : Euphue's golden legacie, found
after his death in his cell at Silexedra.
Bequeathed to Philatus sonnes, noursed
up with their father in England. Fetcht
from the Canaries by T. L., Gent. Ln :
N. Lyng and T. Gubbins, 1596. Fcp. 4°
In June, 1904, a copy realised £295.

Lodge (Thomas) [Rosalynde] Euphues golden legacie. Imprinted at Ln : for John Smethwick and are to be sold at his shop in Saint Dustanes Churchyard in Fleetstreet vnder the Dyall, 1612. Fcp. 4°, black letter, sig. A—O⁴ unpaged
CTC | W

[Rosalynde] Euphues golden legacie . . . Imprinted at Ln : for John Smethwicke . . . in Fleetstreet vnder the Dyall, 1623. Fcp. 4°, black letter, sig. A—O⁴ unpaged
CTC

[Rosalynde] Euphues golden legacie . . . Ln : Imprinted . . . for T. Smethwicke, 1634. Fcp. 4°, black letter BUS | W

Rosalynd : Euphues' golden legacie. 1592 reprint. Ln : 1841. 8° MPL

Rosalynd, 1843. *See Sh*—] Sh—'s library

Rosalind. Ln : 1893. 12° BPL

Rosalynde. Ed. by W. W. Greg. 'Sh— Classics.' Ln : Chatto, 1907. Fcp. 4° BPL

Scilla's metamorphosis. *See* Reardon

William Longbeard, 1593. *See* Reprints

See Boswell-Stone
„ Ingleby
„ Kastner
„ Sh— Mucedorus, 1598

Loffelt (A. C.) Sh— in Holland [*See* 'De Navorscher,' 1866, Vol. xvi., p. 340]

Loffelt (A. C.) *Editor.* *See* Sh— Hamlet, 1867

Lofft (Capel)] Aphorisms from Sh—. *See* Sh— Works : Ext. 1812

On Sh—'s learning. *See Sh*—] Notices

Lofft (R. E.) Remarks on the play of 'Hamlet.' Bury St. Edmunds [1869 ?] 8°
BPL

Loft *Publisher.* *See* Sh— Othello, 1861

Loftie (W. J.) London city : its history, streets, traffic, buildings, people . . . Ln : 1891. 4°. Illustrated BM

Loftie (W. J.) *Editor.* *See* Sh— Works, 1896, 1905

Logan *Engraver.* *See* Fuller

Logan (W. H.)] Nugæ histrionicæ ; Curious tracts relating to the affairs of the Edinburgh Theatre. Privately printed, 1834. 12°

Logan (W. H.) *Editor.* *See* Fragmenta . . .

Logeman (H.) 'This too too solid flesh' [In 'An English Miscellany,' pp. 278-281]. Oxford, 1901. 8° BPL
Illustrates ' Hamlet,' i., 2.

Logismos : A ratiocination upon voting, or Sh—'s defence against Hopkins. Coventry : Printed by S. Davis for the authour, 1721. 8°

Logographic Press. *See* Felton

Lollius the Lombard. *See* Sh— Troilus . . . 1679

London—
See Arnold (R.)
„ Besant
„ Boar's head
„ Bowles
„ Croker
„ Dulwich
„ Garland
„ Globe Theatre
„ Greenstreet
„ Griggs
„ H—— (J.)
„ Hales
„ Hare
„ Harper
„ Harrison
„ Heminge
„ Hunt
„ Jackson
„ Loftie
„ Martin
„ New pantomime
„ Old and new
„ Ordish
See Pennant
„ Poet's corner
„ Rendle
„ Sadler's Wells
„ Savage
„ Scott (E. J. L.)
„ *Sh*—] Knight
„ Simpson
„ Stage
„ Stephenson
„ Stopes
„ Stowe
„ Thompson
„ Victor
„ Wheatley
„ White
„ Wilkinson
„ Williams
„ Wilson (H. S.)
„ Woolf
„ Wyndham
„ Young (W.)

London Herald : Sh— number, 1864. *See* Sh--

London prodigal. *See* Sh— London prodigal

London stage : Collection of the most reputed tragedies, comedies, melodramas, farces, and interludes, accurately printed from acting copies. Carefully collated and reviewed. Ln : [1825]. 4 vols. 8°. With portraits

London theatres in the olden time [In 'Belgravia.' 1866 ?] 8° BPL

Long desiderated knowledge. *See* Downing

Long vacation : A satyr. Addres'd to all disconsolate traders. Ln : H. Hills, 1709. 8°, pp. 16 BM
Refers to ' Hamlet ' and ' Othello.'

Longinus (Dionysius) On the sublime. Trans. with notes, observations and . . . Life, writings and character of the author by William Smith, Dean of Chester. Ln : E. Johnson, 1770. 8°, pp. xii.-xxxiv.-186
With engraved front.
Compares Sh— with Longinus.

Longman (M.) *Publisher.* *See* Sh— Works, 1757

Longman (Thomas) *Publisher*—
See Sh— Hamlet, 1767
„ Sh— King Henry VIII., 1762
„ Sh— King Lear, 1767, 1771
„ Sh— Macbeth, 1750, 1770
„ Sh— Merchant . . . 1783
„ Sh— Othello, 1750, 1765
„ Sh— Poems, 1728
„ Sh— The tempest, 1761
„ Sh— Timon . . . 1770
„ Sh— Works, 1745, 1747, 1757, 1762, 1773, 1790, 1793, 1797

Longman (T. N.) *Publisher—*
See Sh— King Henry VIII., 1804
,, Sh— King John, 1804
,, Sh— Othello, 1804
,, Sh— Works, 1798
Longman & Co. *Publishers.* *See* Sh— Works,
1811
Longworth (T.) *New York Publisher.* *See*
Sh— Taming . . . 1820
Lonsdale *Publisher—*
See Sh— Macbeth, 1850
,, Sh— The tempest, 1776, 1862
Loosen (O.) Sh—-Bacon. 1893. 8°   BM
Lopez (Roderigo). *See* Levi (S. L.)
Lopez de Vega. *See* Vega
Loque (B. de) Discourses of warre and single
combat. Trans. out of the French by J.
Eliot. Ln : John Wolfe, 1591. Fcp. 4°
Isaac Reed deemed Sh— indebted to this work for
military terms used by Parolles in ' All's well.'
Lord Chamberlain—
See Malone Society
,, *Sh*—] Halliwell
Lord's (Our) Prayer. *See* Horn-Book
Lordan (C. L.) Colloquies, desultory and
diverse. Romsey, 1843. 8°   BPL | BUS
The third ' Colloquy ' is headed ' A few words on Sh—.'
Lorenzo (G. de) Buddhist ideas in Sh— [From
'Buddhism']. Rangoon, 1903. 8° BPL
Lounsbury (*Prof.* Thomas Raynesford) First
editors of Sh— (Pope and Theobald):
The story of the first Sh— controversy
and of the earliest attempt at establishing
a critical text . . . Ln : Nutt, 1906. 8°,
pp. xxii.-580
In addition to ignoring Nicholas Rowe, the writer
seems to have overlooked the editors of the first four
folios.
Sh— and Voltaire. Ln : Nutt, 1902. Cr.
8°, pp. 476   BUS
Sh— wars : Sh— as a dramatic artist.
With an account of his reputation at
various periods. New York, 1901. 8°
        BUS | MPL
Loutherbourg *Artist.* *See* Sh— Works, 1803-
05
'Love (James)' *pseud.* *See* Dance (James)
Love-à-la-mode : A comedy . . . [By T. Shad-
well ?] Ln : 1663. Fcp. 4°
Says : ' Were Sh—, Fletcher, or renowned Ben
Alive, they'd yield to this more happie pen.'
See also Sh—] Manuscript
Love betray'd—
See Burnaby
,, Sh— All's well, 1703
,, Sh— Twelfth night, 1703
Love feigned . . . *See* Malone Society
Love songs of the English poets. *See* Sh—
Poems, 1892
Love's garland, 1626. *See* Literature

Love's labour lost regained. *See* Sh— Love's
labour won, 1841
Love's labour won. *See* Sh—'s Love's labour
won
Love's labours lost. *See* Sh— Love's labours
lost
Loveday (R.) Verses. *See* Camus
Loveling. First satire of Persius imitated.
Ln : John Brett, 1740. F°, pp. 20
Latin and English text on alternate pages.
Numerous references to Sh—.
Lovell (J.) Sh—'s birthday [In 'Social Notes'].
1879. 8°   BPL
Lovibond (Edward) Poems on several occa-
sions. Ln : J. Dodsley, 1785. 8°
Contains a facetious Sh— poem (pp. 130-135), entitled
the ' Mulberry tree,' in which Garrick and Dr.
Johnson figure.
Low *Editor.* *See* Sh— King Henry VIII., 1909
Low (W. H.) *See* Wyatt & Low
Low (Wm. H.) *Artist.* *See* Sh— As you like
it, 1900
Lowe *Vocalist.* *See* Stratford Jubilee
Lowe (Robert W.) Bibliographical account of
English theatrical literature from the
earliest times to the present day. Ln :
J. C. Nimmo, 1888. 8°, pp. xii.-384
        BPL | SML
Issue limited to 500 copies and a few on large paper.
A valuable annotated list of thousands of theatrical
books and pamphlets, from which one notes ' Sh—
literature is excluded because it has already been
fully catalogued.' Unfortunately the author failed to
add where this ' full catalogue ' is to be found.
Sh— occupies pp. 293-298.
Lowe (Robert W.) *Editor—*
See Churchill
,, Doran
Lowe (R. W.) & Archer (W.) 'Macbeth' on the
stage [From 'English Illust. Mag.'] 1888.
8°   BPL
Lowe (Thomas) Sh— under the stars, or his
genius and works in the light of astro-
nomy. Stratford-on-Avon : J. Morgan,
1887. 8°   BM | BPL | SML
Lowell (James Russell) Old English drama-
tists. 1892. 12°   BPL
'Richard the third' and the primrose
criticism. 1887. 8°   BM
Sh— once more [In 'North American Re-
view,' April]. Boston, 1868. 8° BUS
Sh— once more [In 'Among my books,'
pp. 145-217]. 1870. 8° BPL | BUS | SML
Sh— once more [In Rice's Essays from
'North American Review']. New York,
1879. 8°   BPL | BUS
White's Sh— [In 'Atlantic Monthly,' Jan.-
Feb.] Boston, 1859. 8°   BUS
Lowell Sh— memorial : Exercises on the ter-
centenary celebration . . . by the citizens
of Lowell, Mass. Lowell : Stone & Huse,
1864. 8°, pp. 52   BM | BUS | SML
Contains an oration by W. S. Bartlet.

Lowin *or* Lowine (John) *Actor—*
See Beaumont & F.
   „ Downes

Lowndes (C.) *Publisher—*
See Sh— Coriolanus, 1800
   „ Sh— Hamlet, 1800, 1811
   „ Sh— Macbeth, 1794
   „ Sh— Merry wives, 1797
   „ Sh— Twelfth night, 1792
   „ Sh— Winter's tale, 1802

Lowndes (H.) *Publisher. See* Oulton

Lowndes (T.) *Publisher—*
See Gentleman
   „ Sh— Double falsehood, 1767
   „ Sh— Hamlet, 1767
   „ Sh— King Henry VIII., 1762
   „ Sh— King Lear, 1767, 1771
   „ Sh— Macbeth, 1770
   „ Sh— Merchant . . . 1783
   „ Sh— Othello, 1765
   „ Sh— Romeo . . . 1769
   „ Sh— The tempest, 1783
   „ Sh— Timon . . . 1770
   „ Sh— Works, 1762, 1773

Lowndes (T. & W.) *Publishers. See* Sh—
King Richard III., 1784, 1793

Lowndes (W.) *Publisher—*
   „ Sh— Merchant . . . 1783
   „ Sh— Romeo . . . 1793
   „ Sh— Works, 1790, 1798, 1811

Lowndes (Wm. Thomas) Bibliographer's
manual of English literature. Ln : 1834.
3 vols. 8°   BUS
Sh— fills pp. 1644-67.

Bibliographer's manual . . . New edition,
revised . . . by H. G. Bohn. Ln : 1857-64.
11 vols. 8°   BM | BPL | BUS | CPL | W
Sh— occupies pp. 2252-2366.

Sh— and his commentators from . . .
'Bibliographer's manual.' Ln : 1831. 8°,
pp. 26, and Droeshout portrait
Fifty-two copies printed.   BM | BPL | BUS | W

Lownes (Mathew) *Publisher—*
See Mexia
   „ Suetonius

Luard (H. R.) *Editor. See* Sh— King Richard
II., 1860

Lucas (E. V.) *Editor. See* Lamb

Luce (Morton) Handbook to the works of Wm.
Sh—. Ln : Bell, 1906. Cr. 8°, pp. 474
           BPL | BUS

Luce (Morton) *Editor—*
See Sh— The tempest, 1902
   „ Sh— Twelfth night, 1906

Lucian. *See* Heywood

Lucius Camillus. *See* Sh—] Sh—'s library
A foundation of the 'Merry wives.'

Luckman *Coventry Publisher. See* Sh— Works,
1768

Lucrece. *See* Sh— Rape of Lucrece

Lucy *of Stratford* (Jane) Materials for a history
of the Lucy family. Stratford-on-Avon,
1900   SML

Lucy *of Charlecote* (John) *Bibliophile. See* Sh—
Works, 1632

Lucy.] Rubbing of the inscription on the
tomb of Joyce Lady Lucy at Charlecote
Church. Oblong f°
'Here intombed lyeth the Lady Ioyce Lvcy, wife of Sir
Thomas Lvcy Charlecot, in ye covnty of Warwick,
knight, davghter and heire of Thomas Acton, of
Svtton, in ye covnty of Worster, esquire, who
departed ovt of this wretched world to her heavenly
kingdom ye xth day of Febrvary, in ye yere of ovr
Lord God 1595, and of her age LX. and three ; all ye
tyme of her lyfe a trve and faythfvll servant of her
good God ; never detected of any cryme or·vice ; in
religion moste sovnde ; in love to her hvsband moste
faythfvll and true ; in freindship moste constant ; to
what in trust was committed vnto her moste secret ;
in wisedome excelling ; in governing of her howse
and bringing vp of yovth in ye feare of God that did
convers with her moste rare and singular ; a great
maintayner of hospitallity ; greatly esteemed of her
betters ; misliked of none vnles of the envyovs.
When all is spoken that can be saide, a woman so
fvrnished and garnished with vertve as not to be
bettered and hardly to be equaled by any ; as shee
lived moste vertvovsly, so shee died moste godly.
Set downe by him yt best did knowe what hath byn
written to be trve.—THOMAS LVCY.'
Written by the baronet supposed to have been lam-
pooned by Sh—.

Lucy *Mrs. Scriven* (Margaret) On the Sh—
authorship of the three parts of 'King
Henry VI.' Stratford-on-Avon : J. Morgan, 1900. 8°, pp. 8   BPL

Sh— and the supernatural : A brief study
of folklore, superstition and witchcraft in
'Macbeth,' 'Midsummer night's dream,'
and 'The tempest.' With a bibliography
of the subject by William Jaggard.
Liverpool : Jaggard & Co., Shakespeare
Press, 1908. 8°, pp. 40
       BM | BLO | BPL | CTC | SML
Twenty-five large paper copies were printed upon
Japanese vellum, in royal 8°.
Reviewed at length in a leader by Sir E. R. Russell in
'Liverpool Post and Mercury,' 10th Feb., 1906, p. 6.

Sh—'s allegory in folk lore : Sh— Club
Paper. Stratford-on-Avon, 1904. 4°
broadside, single sheet

The three parts of 'King Henry VI.' 'Sh—
Club paper.' Stratford, 1906. 8°, pp.
iv.

See also Hutchings & Lucy

Lucy (Mary E.) Biography of the Lucy family
of Charlecote. 1862. 4°   BPL

] Charlecote Church ; its monuments, etc.
1883. 8°   BPL

Lucy.] Heraldic document of the early part
of the seventeenth century, containing a
tricking of the coat of arms of 'Sir Thomas
Lucie of Charlcott in the County of Warr,
Knight.' Orig. manuscript upon four-

Charlecote, near Stratford-on-Avon, from the river

Charlecote Library

See p. 201

teen leaves of paper [*Sæc. XVII.*]
12°   W

Sir Thomas Lucy is popularly supposed to be ' Justice
Shallow' in 'King Henry IV., Part ii.,' and again in
the ' Merry wives,' Act i., Sc. 1, bearing, in mocking
allusion to the surname, 'three louses rampant for
his arms.'
The Lucy coat-of-arms exhibits 'three luces hauriant
argent' as a distinguishing feature. Sh— writes
('Merry wives'), 'They may give the dozen white
luces in their coat,' etc.

Lucy.] Hunt (Richard) The bow of Jonathan,
with the flower de luce: In a funeral
lamentation committed to the men of
Judah paralleled and applyed to that
worthy his compeere Robert Lucy of
Charlcote . . . In a sermon preached at
Charlcote. Ln: Printed by W. Godbid,
1657. Fcp. 4°, pp. viii.-34   BUS

Lucy (*Sir* Thomas). *See also* Sh— Merry
wives, 1602

Lucy *Bp. of St. David's* (William) Observations, censures and confutations of notorious errours in Mr. Hobbes his 'Leviathan' and other his bookes. To which
are annexed occasional animadversions
on some writings of the Socinians and
such hæreticks of the same opinions with
him. Ln: 1663. Fcp. 4°
By the son of the supposed prototype of ' Justice
Shallow.'
Treatise of the nature of a minister in all its
offices . . . Ln: 1670. Fcp. 4°

Lucy family *of Charlecote*—
See Collier (J. P.)   *See* Johnson *jun.*
,, Douglas   ,, King
,, Dugard   ;, Landor
,, Dugdale   ,, Reiss
,, Halliwell   ,, Scott (E. J. L.)
,, Howitt   ,, Stopes
,, Jaggard (W.)   ,, Tomlinson

Luders (Arthur) Essay on the character of
Henry the Fifth when Prince of Wales.
Ln: Cadell, 1813. 8°. Frontispiece
                    BPL | BUS | MPL | SML | W
Ludlow, Shropshire. *See* Notices . . .
Ludlow (Wm.) *Editor*—
See Sh— Hamlet, 1884
,, Sh— Works, 1884-86

Ludus coventriæ: Collection of mysteries
formerly represented at Coventry on the
Feast of the Corpus Christi. Ed. by J.
O. Halliwell. Ln: Sh— Society, 1841.
8°   BM | BPL | BUS | HCL
The original MS., dated 1468, is in the Cottonian Col-
lection at the British Museum.

Lumley (Henry) Sh—: A revelation. 2nd
ed. Ln: 1899   BUS
Attributes the works of Sh— to some unknown writer.

Lumley (Jane *Lady*) *Editor. See* Euripides
Lunn *Stratford Town Clerk* (Robert). *See* Brassington & Lunn

Lunt (George) 'Abraham, Abron, Auburn':
A Sh— excursus. New York [1873]. 8°
                                       MPL
Three eras of New England. Boston, U.S.,
1857. 12°   BUS
Contains ' A Sh— research,' pp. 258-264.
Lushington (H.) *Editor*—
See Sh— Julius Cæsar, 1832
,, Sh— King Richard II., 1833
Lushington (Vernon) Sh—: An address to
the Positivist Society at Stratford. *See*
Sh—
Luther *of Banbury* (John). *See* Bullen (M. W.)
Lyall (C.) *Artist. See* Henderson
Lyceum Theatre, London. *See* Irving (Sir
J. H. B.)
Lyddon-Roberts (P.) *Editor. See* Sh— Julius
Cæsar, 1900
Lyde (L. W.) *Editor*—
See Sh— As you like it, 1894
,, Sh— Hamlet, 1895
,, Sh— Julius Cæsar, 1901
,, Sh— Macbeth, 1902
,, Sh— Midsummer . . . 1897
,, Sh— Works, 1897
Lydgate (John) Falls of Princes. *See* Mirrour
Lydgate (John) [& Heywood (Thomas)] Life
and death of Hector. Ln: Thomas Pur-
foot [1614]   W
A modernised rendering of Lydgate's poem, first issued
in 1513. Contains the foundation of 'Troilus and
Cressida.'

Lyly, Lilly, *or* Lylie (John) Endymion. *See*
Halpin
Euphues: The anatomy of wit. Very
pleasant for all gentlemen to reade and
most necessary to remember; wherin
are contained the delights that wyt fol-
loweth in his youth by the pleasauntnesse
of love and the happynesse he reapeth in
age by the perfectnesse of wisedome . . .
Imprinted at Ln: [by T. East] for
Gabriell Cawood dwelling in Paules
Churchyarde [c. 1578]. Fcp. 4°, black
letter, sig. A—T4 on numbered folios
                                       CTC
The second and third editions appeared in 1579, the
latter being undated. The only known copy of this
undated issue is at Trinity College, Cambridge.
For Lyly's influence on Sh— see Rushton.

Evphves . . . 1607. Fcp. 4°   BPL
[Works] Dramatic works, with notes and
some account of his writings by F. W.
Fairholt. Ln: J. R. Smith, 1858.   2
vols. Cr. 8°
Works. Ed. with life . . . by Bond. Oxford,
1902. 3 vols. 8°   BPL
Lyly (John)—
See Cartwright
,, Cooper
,, Morris

(201)

Lyndon (Charles) Apophthegms from the plays of Sh—. *See* Sh— Works : Ext. 1851

Concordance to select quotations from Sh—. *See* Sh— Works : Ext. 1850

Lyndon (*Miss*) *Editor*. *See* Sh— Works, 1852-53

Lyng (N.) *See* Ling

Lynn (N.) Thespian papers. Ln : Scott, 1887. 12°   SML

Lyon (L.) *Editor*. *See* Sh— Merchant . . . 1830

Lyric ode on the fairies, aerial beings, and witches of Sh—. Ln : J. Wilkie, 1776. 4°, pp. 20   BM | BUS | W
Thomas Linley (*q.v.*) set the poem to music.

Lyrics for old lutenists. *See* Reprints

Lyttelton (George Wm. *fourth Baron*) Few thoughts about Sh—. *See* Sh—] Lyttelton

Lytton (Robert *Earl of*) Miss Anderson's Juliet [In the 'Nineteenth Century']. 1884. 8°   BPL

Lytton (Hon. Robert) Old criticisms on old plays and old players [In 'Fortnightly Review,' O.S., Vol. xv., pp. 221-239 and 352-362]. Ed. by John Morley. Ln : Chapman, 1871. Roy. 8°   BPL | MPL
On Garrick as Hamlet.

—— (A.) *Printer*—
See Clavell
   ,, Mathewes (Augustine)
   ,, Sh— Othello, 1630
M—— (F. A.) *See* Marshall (F. A.)

M—— (J.) Newe metamorphosis, or a feaste of fancie or poeticall legendes. [By John Marston ?] Ln : 1600
Bears the line :—
   'It seems 'tis true that W— S— said '
   'This W— S— must stand for a name which gives two trochees like William Shakespeare.'—*Ingleby*.

M—— (J.) A recantation : Supplement to Sh— self-revealed. 1909. 8°   BPL

M—— (J.) Evening-hour with Sh— [In Sh— Museum. Ed. by M. L. Moltke]. Leipzig, 1870-74. 8°   BUS

M—— (J.) *Editor*. *See* Sh— Sonnets, 1904

M—— (J.) *Printer*—
See Crown garland
   ,, Macock (James)

M—— (J. A.) Introduction to the study of Sh— and Milton. Ln : [1889]. 8°. Illust.   BUS

M—— (J. A.) *Editor*. *See* Sh— Works : Ext. 1884

M—— (J. B.) Events in the history of New York City . . . With illustrations from Sh—. New York, 1880. 12°   SML
Events in the history . . . [2nd ed.] New York, 1881. 12°   SML

M—— (T.) *Printer*. *See* Sh— Coriolanus, 1682

M—— (W.) *Engraver*. *See* Marshall (Wm.)

Mabie (Hamilton Wright) In the forest of Arden. New York : Dodd & Mead, 1899. 8°   SML
Wm. Sh— ; poet, dramatist and man. *See* Sh—] Mabie

Mabie (H. W.) *Editor*—
See Landor
   ,, Sh— Much ado, 1907

Mabille (Leroy) *Boulogne Publisher*. *See* Sh— Macbeth, 1844

MacAlister (J. Y. W.) *Editor*. *See* Library (The)

McAllen (J. E. B.) *Editor*—
See Sh— King Henry V., 1903
   ,, Sh— King Richard III., 1902

Macaulay (Thomas Babington *Lord*) Essay on the 'Diary of Madame D'Arblay' [In the 'Edinburgh Review,' Vol. lxxvi., pp. 560-561, Jan.] 1843. 8°
'Highest among those who have exhibited human nature stands Sh—. His variety is like the variety of nature, endless diversity, scarcely any monstrosity. The characters of which he has given us an impression, as vivid as that which we receive from the characters of our own associates, are to be reckoned by scores. Yet in all these scores hardly one character is to be found which deviates widely from the common standard and which we should call very eccentric if we met it in real life. The silly notion that every man has one ruling passion, and that this clue once known unravels all the mysteries of his conduct, finds no countenance in the plays of Sh—. There man appears as he is, made up of a crowd of passions, which contend for the mastery over him and govern him in turn. . . . Admirable as he is in all parts of his art we most admire him for this, that while he has left us a greater number of striking portraits than all other dramatists put together, he has scarcely left us a single caricature.'

Marginal notes. Selected and arranged by Sir G. O. Trevelyan. Ln : Longmans, 1907. 8°, pp. 64   BPL
Contains Sh— matter.

Macaulay (T. B. *Lord*). *See* Wright (C.)

Macauley (Elizabeth Wright) Tales of the drama. *See* Sh— Works : Ext. 1822, 1848

Macbeth. *See* Sh— Macbeth

Macbeth.] Life, character, and secret history of 'Macbeth' [In 'Key to the drama']. 1768. 12°   BPL
Identical with the 'Life of Macbeth' of same year, which is not concerned with Sh—'s play.

] Life of Macbeth, with account of the amours of Lady Macbeth. [c. 1768.] 8° BPL | BUS
Identical with 'Key to Drama' [*q.v.*] and 'Secret History . . .'

] Macbeth : A poem. *See* Sh— Macbeth, 1817

Macbeth.] 'Macbeth' and 'King Richard III.':
An essay in answer to J. P. Kemble. Ln :
1817. 8°
See Kemble for the inspiration of this foundling.

] Macbeth modernised. *See* Sh— Macbeth,
1838

] 'Macbeth' reconsidered. *See* Kemble

] Macbeth travestie. *See* Sh— Macbeth, 1840,
1847, 1850, 1853, 1854

MacCallum (*Prof.* M. W.) Authorship of the
early 'Hamlet' [In 'An English miscellany,' pp. 282-295]. Oxford, 1901. 8°
BPL

Sh—'s Roman plays and their background.
Ln : Macmillan, 1910. 8°

MacCarthy (E. F. M.) How a play of Sh—
should be studied. Univ. Local Exam.,
1877. 8° BPL

M'Carty *Philadelphia Publisher.* *See* Sh—
Works, 1824, 1828

MacChaff (A.) Letter to the editor of the
'Glasgow Argus' on J. Payne Collier's
new edition of Sh—. Ln : 1842. 8° BPL
The author's name is probably a pseudonym.

M'Creery (J.) *Printer.* *See* Sh— Works, 1807

M'Dermot (M.) Philosophical inquiry into the
source of pleasures derived from tragic
representations. Ln : Sherwood, 1824.
8° SML

Macdonald *Editor.* *See* Lamb

MacDonald *LL.D.* (George) Dish of orts.
Chiefly papers . . . on Sh— . . . 1893. 8°
BM

'Hamlet' : A study. With the text of the
folio of 1623. Ln : 1885. 8°
BM | BPL | MPL

Orts [contains the 'Art of Sh— as revealed
by himself,' pp. 141-169; The elder
'Hamlet,' pp. 179-181]. Ln : 1882. 8°
BPL | BUS

The elder Hamlet [In 'Macmillan's Mag.,'
Aug.] Ln : 1876. 8° BUS

Macdonald (George) *Editor—*
See Sh— Hamlet, 1885
,, Sh— King Richard III., 1896
,, Sh— Works, 1893-98

Macdonald (R.) *Publisher.* *See* Sh— As you
like it, 1850

Macdonald (Wm.) *Editor.* *See* Sh— Works :
Ext. 1903

Macdonell (P.) Essay on . . . 'Hamlet' . . .
Interspersed with reflections on the
writings and genius of Sh—. With
copious original notes as an appendix.
Ln : Cunningham & Mortimer, 1843. 8°,
pp. 80 BM | BPL | BUS | CPL | MPL | SML
Essay on . . . 'The tempest.' With remarks
on the superstitions of the Middle Ages,
some original observations on . . . 'Caliban,' with various reflections on the

writings and genius of Sh—. Read
before the Sh— Club, 6th Sept., 1839.
Ln : J. Fellowes, 1840. 8°, pp. iv.-58
BM | BPL | BUS | CPL | MPL

McDowall (W.) The mind in the face [Sh—,
pp. 35-37, 45, and 79]. Ln : L. N. Fowler
[1882]. 12° BPL | SML

Macfarland (A. S.) & Sage (A.) Stories from
Sh—. *See* Sh— Works : Ext. 1882

Macfarlane (A. R.) *Editor.* *See* Sh— Works,
1883, 1885

Macfarren (G. A.) *Composer.* *See* Banks (G. L.)

Macgillivray (Duncan) *Editor.* *See* Sh— King
Henry V., 1905

McGlashan (J.) *Dublin Publisher.* *See* Sh—
Midsummer . . . 1853

Macgowan (J.) *Publisher.* *See* Sh— Works :
Ext. 1780

MacGregor (A. Stewart) *Editor—*
See Sh— Macbeth, 1885
,, Sh— Taming . . . 1886

McGregor (Robert Guthrie) Indian leisure.
Ln : Smith, 1854. 8° BUS | SML
Includes article ' On the character of Othello.'
Othello's character. Ln : Smith & Elder,
1852. 8°

Machin (Lewis) Dumb knight. Ln : 1608
Mentions ' Venus and Adonis.'

Machray (W. D.) *Editor.* *See* Pilgrimage

MacIlwaine (H. C.) *See* Sharp & MacIlwaine

M'Ilwraith (Jean Newton) Book about Sh—
See Sh—

Mack (Robert E.) Shakespearean quotations.
See Sh— Works : Ext. 1885

Mackay (*Dr.* Charles) Glossary of obscure
words and phrases in the writings of Sh—
and his contemporaries, traced etymo-
logically to the ancient language of the
British people. Ln : 1887. 8°
BM | BPL | BUS | SML
New light on some obscure words and
phrases in the works of Sh— and his contemporaries. Ln : Reeves, 1884. 8°, pp.
68 BM | BUS | SML

Mackay (G. Eric) True story of 'Romeo and
Juliet' [In 'Gentleman's Mag.,' Jan.]
Ln : 1887. 8° BUS

McKee (Thomas Jefferson) Library—
See Catalogue, 1900
,, Roberts

Mackenzie (Henry) Criticism on the character
and tragedy of 'Hamlet' [In 'The Mirror,'
April]. Edin., 1780. 8° BUS
Critical remarks on the character of 'Falstaff' [In 'Lounger,' May]. Edin., 1786.
8° BUS

Mackenzie (Henry) *Editor.* *See* Mirror

Mackenzie (Shelton) *Editor.* *See* Maginn

McKerrow (Ronald B.) *Editor—*
See Phillip
,, Sh— Locrine, 1908

M'Kewan (D. H.) *Artist.* *See* Sh— As you like it, 1850

Mackinlay (J.) *Publisher.* *See* Sh— Works, 1811

Mackintosh (C. S.) *See* Langford & Mackintosh

Macklin (Charles)] Apology for the conduct of Charles Macklin which, it is hoped, will have some effect in favour of an aged player . . . Ln : T. Astell, 1773. 8°, pp. ii.-38   BUS

Reply to Mr. Garrick's 'Answer.' 1743. 12°
                                                            BPL

Macklin.] Congreve (F. A.) Memoirs of Charles Macklin. Ln : Barker, 1798. 8° SML

] Kirkman (J. T.) Life of Charles Macklin. 1799. 2 vols. 12°   BPL

] Memoirs of Charles Macklin, comedian. 1804. 8°   BPL

] Parry (E. A.) Charles Macklin. Ed. by Wm. Archer. Ln : 1891. Cr. 8°

Macklin (Charles) *Actor.* *See* Sh— Merchant, 1777, 1785, 1802

Macklin (T.) *Publisher.* *See* Sh— Works : Ext. 1792-96

Macknight (Thomas) Prize essay on the historical plays of Sh— . . . Ln : Wickham & Yelland, 1850. 12°, pp. iv.-90
                              BM | BPL | BUS

Maclachlan (D.) *Editor.* *See* Sh— Hamlet, 1888

Macleish (E.) *Publisher.* *See* Sh— Two gentlemen, 1790

Macleod (Mary) Sh— Story book. *See* Sh— Works : Ext. 1902

Maclise (Daniel) *Artist*—
See Sh— As you like it, 1850
,, Sh— Works, 1875-76
,, *Stratford*] Sh—'s birthplace

McLoughlin (C.) Zanga's triumph, or Harlequin and Othello at war. Dublin, 1762. 8°   BPL

Macmillan (Michael) *Editor.* *See* Sh— Julius Cæsar, 1902

M'Nicoll (D.) Operation of the stage on the morals of society. Newcastle-on-Tyne, 1823. 8°   BPL

Macock (J.) *Printer*—
See Newcastle
,, Sh— The tempest, 1670, 1676, 1690
,, Sh— Timon . . . 1678, 1688

Macpherson (J.) *See* Fleay & Macpherson

McPhun & Son (W. R.) *Glasgow Publishers.* *See* Sh— Works, 1858

Macrae. George Gilfillan. *See* Gilfillan

Macray (W. D.) Annals of the Bodleian Library. 1868. 8°   BPL
Sh—'s autograph, p. 301.

Macready (William Charles) Reminiscences and selections from diaries & letters. Edited by Sir Frederick Pollock. 1876. Cr. 8°, pp. xviii.-750 ; four portraits BPL

Macready.] Archer (Wm.) William Charles Macready. Ln : Kegan Paul, 1890. 8°, pp. x.-224   SML

] Pollock (*Lady*) Macready as I knew him. Ln : 1885. Cr. 8°

Macready (Wm. C.)—
See Critical . . .
,, De Soligny
,, Martin
,, Pemberton
,, Sh— King Henry V., 1839
,, Sh— King Richard III., 1821
,, Sh— Macbeth, 1851
,, Sh— Works, 1851
,, *Stratford*] Sh—'s birthplace

McSpadden (J. Walker) Shakespearean synopses. *See* Sh— Works : Ext. 1905

McWilliam (R.) *Editor.* *See* Sh— Macbeth, 1899

Mad wooing. *See* Sh— Taming . . . 1859

Madan (Falconer) Turbutt (G. M. R.) & Gibson (S.) Original Bodleian copy of the first folio Sh— ('The Turbutt' Sh—). Oxford : Printed at the Clarendon Press by Horace Hart, 1905. F°, pp. 14 + 4. With seven plates   BPL
Issue restricted to 200 copies.

Madden (*Rt. Hon.* Dodgson Hamilton) Diary of Master William Silence : A study of Sh— and of Elizabethan sport. Ln : Longmans, 1897. 8°, pp. 396
                    BM | BPL | BUS | MPL | SML

Diary of Master William Silence . . . [With observations on the personality of Sh— as revealed by his writings]. Ln : Longmans, 1907. 8°, pp. xxxii.-398

Madden *B.M. Keeper* (*Sir* Frederick) Observations on an autograph of Sh— and the orthography of his name. Ln : J. B. Nichols & Son, 1837. 4°, pp. 12   BPL
Offprinted from 'Archæologia,' vol. 27, with corrections.

Observations on an autograph . . . Ln : T. Rodd, 1838. 8°, pp. ii.-16
          BM | BPL | BUS | CPL | MPL | SML

Maddox. *See* Rodd & Maddox

Madrigals. *See* Music

Maggioni (M.) *Editor.* *See* Sh— Romeo, 1848

Maggioni (S. M.) Falstaff : Comic opera. *See* Sh— Merry wives, 1838

Maginn (William) Books on my table, by 'Morgan Rattler' : Of 'Hamlet' [In 'Fraser's Mag.,' July]. Ln : 1836. 8°
                                                            BUS

Dr. Farmer's 'Essay on the learning of Sh—' considered [In 'Fraser's Mag.,' Sept.-Dec.] Ln : 1839. 8°   BUS

Edmond Malone

See p. 205

Maginn (William) Miscellanies: Prose and
verse [Farmer's Essay, Vol. ii., pp. i.-116;
Lady Macbeth, pp. 117-144]. 1885.
2 vols. 12°   BPL
Sh— papers [In 'Bentley's Miscellany'].
Ln: 1837-39. Roy. 8°   BUS
Sh— papers. Annotated by Shelton Mac-
kenzie. New York: J. S. Redfield, 1856.
12°, pp. 354   BUS | SML
Sh— papers: Pictures grave and gay. Ln:
R. Bentley, 1859. Cr. 8°, pp. iv.-368
                  BM | BPL | BUS | CPL | MPL | W
Sh— papers. Ln: R. Bentley, 1860. Cr.
8°, pp. 334   BM | BPL | BUS | CPL | SML
Maginnis (D.) Of great men: Garibaldi and
Sh—: A sermon. 1864. 8°   BPL
Magnes (James) Publisher—
See Dryden   See Lee (N.)
Magnes (M.) Publisher—
See Crowne
    ,, Sh— Cymbeline, 1682
    ,, Sh— King Henry VI., ii., 1680
    ,, Sh— King Lear, 1681, 1689
    ,, Sh— Othello, 1681
Magnes (S.) Publisher—
See Otway
    ,, Sh— Othello, 1687
Magnusson (E.) Editor. See Sh— The tem-
pest, 1885
'Mahomet.' See Essay on tragedy
Mahony (J. W.) Hamlet's mission: A critical
enquiry into . . . his mode of carrying out
the command of the ghost. Birmingham,
1875. 8°   BM | BPL
Main (D. M.) Editor. See Sh— Sonnets, 1880,
1884
Mair (G. H.) Editor. See Wilson (Sir T.)
Major (John) Publisher. See Jackson
Makart Artist. See Sh— Works: Ext. 1876
Makower (Stanley V.) Perdita. See Robinson
Malam (J.) Sh— marriage picture. Edited
by Hodgson. 1873. 12°   BPL
Sh—'s wedding [In 'The Criterion']. 1876.
F°   BPL
Malam.] Scrap-books collected by J. Malam
relating to the 'Sh— marriage picture.'
v.D. 2 vols. F°   BPL
Malcolm (W. H.) Sh— and Holy Writ. See
Sh— Works: Ext. 1881
Malden (H. E.) Sh— as an historian [In
'Trans. of the Roy. Hist. Soc.'] 1896.
8°   BPL
Malins. Collection of Warwickshire portraits,
including various likenesses of Sh—. v.D.
F°   BPL
Malins (J.) Shakespearean temperance kalen-
dar. See Sh— Works: Ext. 1880, 1897
Malleson (Wm. Taylor) Which are Hamlet's
'dozen or sixteen lives'? Ln: New Sh—
Soc., 1874. 8°   BM | BPL. | BUS

Mallet (David) Of verbal criticism: An
epistle to Mr. Pope, occasioned by Theo-
bald's Sh— . . . Ln: L. Gilliver, 1733.
F°, pp. 14   BUS
Of verbal criticism [In his Works, Vol. i.,
p. 21]. 1759. 2 vols.
    'Pride of his own and wonder of this age
    Who first created and yet rules the stage;
    Bold to design, all powerful to express,
    Sh— each passion drew in every dress.
    Great above rule and imitating none,
    Rich without borrowing, nature was his own.'
Mallock (W. H.) New facts relating to the
Bacon-Sh— question [In 'Pall Mall Mag.,'
pp. 77-89 and 215-228, Jan.-Feb.] Ln:
1903. Roy. 8°. Illust.
Malone (Edmond) Account of the incidents
from which the title and part of the story
of Sh—'s 'Tempest' were derived, and
its true date ascertained. [With appendix.] Ln: Privately printed [by C. & R.
Baldwin], 1808-09. 2 vols. 8°, pp. iv.-
52 and pp. xxxviii.-52
                       BM | BPL | BUS | NPL | W
Issued restricted to 80 copies, and of the Appendix
20 copies.
An unpublished work of great rarity. On the flyleaf
is a request by Malone 'that this pamphlet may not
be inadvertently put into the hands of any person
who may be likely to publish any part of it.'
See Chalmers for reply.
The Warwick copy, a presentation exemplar, contains
a holograph letter from Malone to Samuel Lyons.
] Account of the incidents . . . [Excerpt from
the 'Variorum Sh—']. [1821.] 8°   W
Attempt to ascertain the order in which the
plays attributed to Sh— were written.
See Sh— Works, 1778
Catalogue of early English poetry. Oxford,
1836. F°   BUS
Caveat against booksellers, respecting an
edition of Sh— attributed to him. [Ln:
1795?] 8°, single sheet   BLO
Correspondence . . . with the Rev. James
Davenport, Vicar of Stratford [on the
Life of·Sh—, edited by J. O. Halliwell].
Ln: 1864. Fcp. 4°   BM | BPL | MPL
Issue limited to ten copies.
Dissertation on the three parts of 'King
Henry VI.,' tending to shew that those
plays were not written originally by Sh—.
Ln: H. Baldwin, 1787. 8°, pp. vi.-iv.-
52   BM | BUS
Only four copies printed.
Dissertation . . . Ln: 1792. 8°
Dramatic Collection. See Bodleian . . .
Historical account of the rise and progress
of the English stage and of the economy
and usages of the ancient theatres in
England. 1790. 8°   BPL
Limited issue. Offprinted from the 'Prolegomena' to
Malone's 1790 edition of Sh—.

Malone (Edmond) Historical account ... of
the English stage. Basil [Switzerland]:
J. J. Tourneisen, 1800. 8°, pp. ii.-420
BPL | BUS

Historical account ... of the English stage
... Edited by James Boswell. Ln: 1821.
8°
Limited issue. Offprinted from Malone's ' Variorum
Sh—, 1821.'

Historical account. *See also* Sh— Works,
1803-05, 1805, 1821

Inquiry into the authenticity of certain
'Miscellaneous papers and legal instruments' published Dec. 24th, 1795, and
attributed to Sh—, Queen Elizabeth, and
Henry Earl of Southampton. Illustrated
by facsimiles of the genuine handwriting
of that nobleman and of Her Majesty, a
new facsimile of the handwriting of Sh—,
never before exhibited, and other authentick documents. In a letter addressed to
the Rt. Hon. James Earl of Charlemont
... Ln: Printed by H. Baldwin for T.
Cadell, jun. and W. Davies ... 1796. 8°,
pp. viii.-424-iv., and three folding plates
BM | BPL | BUS | CPL | SML | W
At Warwick are two copies ; one on large paper in
original boards, uncut, with a number of manuscript
notes and cuttings on the subject ; the other with a
portrait inserted.
Of the large paper only 25 copies were done, of which
one is at Boston, U.S.
This work is of considerable interest because of its
facsimiles of the autographs of Sh— and some of his
contemporaries—Queen Elizabeth, Robert Dudley
Earl of Leicester, Earl of Southampton, Geo. Chapman, Philip Massinger, Richard Burbage, etc.

Letter to ... Richard Farmer relative to the
edition of Sh— published in 1790, and
some late criticisms on that work. Ln:
G. G. & J. Robinson, 1792. 8°, pp. ii.-
xl. BM | BPL | BUS | CPL | W
A reply to Ritson's ' Cursory criticisms.'

Letter to ... Richard Farmer ... Second
edition. Ln: G. G. & J. Robinson, 1792.
8°, pp. iv.-40 BPL | BUS | MPL

Library. *See* Catalogue, 1818
Life of Wm. Sh—. *See* Sh—] Malone
List of early English poets. [1800.] Holograph manuscript on twenty leaves of
paper. 12° W

Notes on Sh—. *See Sh*—] Sh—ana
Original letters [on the life of Sh—] to John
Jordan. *See* Sh—] Jordan

] Original proposals and prospectus for the
second edition of Edmond Malone's Sh—,
in 20 vols, royal 8° ... 1795. F° W
In one of the two copies at Warwick Castle is a holograph letter from Malone, dated 1783, to O. Humphrey
upon a portrait of Henry Wriothesley, Earl of
Southampton.

Prospectus of an intended edition of Sh—
in 15 vols, royal 8° ... Ln: 1792. 4°

Malone (Edmond) Preface. *See* Sh— Works,
1803

] Second appendix to Mr. Malone's 'Supplement to the last edition of Sh—': containing additional observations by the
editor of the 'Supplement.' Ln: 1783. 8°,
pp. iv.-68 BM | BPL | BUS | W
Limited to fifty copies.

Malone (Edmond) *Editor—*
See Bandello & Brooke
,, Sh— Hamlet, 1805
,, Sh— Poems, 1780
,, Sh— Works, 1780, 1786-90, 1790, 1792,
1794, 1816, 1823, 1826, 1827, 1830, 1832,
1832-34, 1833, 1834, 1835, 1836, 1837,
1838, 1839, 1840, 1842, 1843, 1845, 1846,
1847, 1849, 1850, 1851, 1852, 1853, 1855,
1856, 1857, 1858, 1861, 1862, 1864, 1880,
1881, 1882, 1886, 1887, 1888, 1888-89,
1890

Malone.] Boswell *jun.* (James) Biographical
memoir of the late Edmond Malone. Ln:
Nichols & Bentley, not published, 1814.
8°, pp. iv.-28 BPL | BUS | W
Expanded from an article in the ' Gentleman's Mag.'
At Warwick is a presentation copy with holograph
letter from Richard Lord Sunderlin (brother of Edm.
Malone).

] Enquiry into the conduct of Edmond
Malone concerning the manuscript papers
of John Aubrey, F.R.S., in the Ashmolean
Museum, Oxford. Ln: Printed for I.
Caulfield, 11, Old Compton Street, Soho,
1797. 8°

] Original crayon portrait of E. Malone. *See*
Sh—] Sh—ana

] Prior (*Sir* J.) Life of Edmond Malone,
editor of Sh—. With selections from his
manuscript anecdotes. Ln: Smith, 1860.
8°, pp. viii.-476. With portrait
BPL | CPL

] Review of Malone's 'Inquiry into the
authenticity of certain papers ... attributed to Sh—' [In the 'British Critic'].
1796. 12° BPL

Malone (E.)—
See Annotations
,, Caldecott
,, Capell
,, Caulfield
,, Chalmers
,, Felix
,, Gilchrist
,, Halliwell, Hand List
,, Harding
,, Hurdis
,, Ireland (S.)
,, Ireland (S. W. H.)
,, Johnson, Steevens & Malone
,, Lennox

Malone (E.)—
   See Malone Society   *See* Ritson
   ,, Mason   ,, Sill

Malone Society : Collections, Part i. [Ed. by
   W. W. Greg]. Ln : Malone Soc., 1907.
   Fcp. 4°
   Contains ' Love feigned and unfeigned,' a fragmentary
   morality ; ' The Prodigal Son,' a fragment, c. 1530 ;
   Elizabethan Lords Chamberlain ; and Dramatic
   Records of London.

Collections. Parts ii. [Ed. by W. W. Greg].
   Ln : Malone Society, 1908. Fcp. 4°
   Contains ' Robin Hood,' a dramatic fragment, c. 1475 ;
   ' Lucrece,' a fragmentary interlude, c. 1530 ; Dramatic
   Records from the Lansdowne Manuscripts.

Publications. Ed. by W. W. Greg. Ln :
   Privately printed for members, 1907-10.
   14 vols. Fcp. 4°. [*In progress*]
                                BM | SML
   Comprises the following (*q.v.*) :—
   Battell of Alcazar.   Phillip.
   Calisto.   Selimus.
   Euripides.   Sh— King Lear, 1907.
   John.   ,, Locrine, 1908.
   Orlando Furioso.   ,, Sir John Oldcastle, 1908.
   Peele.   Wealth.

Malvezzi *Marquess* (Virgilio) Romulus and
   Tarquin . . . Now taught English by
   Henry Cary Earl of Monmouth. Ln :
   J. H—— for J. Benson, 1637. 8°
   Sh—'s ' Rape of Lucrece ' is graphically described and
   moralised on.

Man and wife. *See* Colman

Man in the moon. Illustrated   BUS
   A periodical containing Sh— articles.

Manby *Publisher*. *See* Holt

Manby (R.) *Publisher*. *See* Grey (Z.)

Manchester—
   See Arts Club
   ,, Duff
   ,, Rowley

Manchester Public Library Bulletin : Special
   reading list. Sh—, 1901. 8°   BPL

Manchester Sh— Club. *See* Foard

Manchester Sh— Society : First annual
   report, with statement of accounts, rules
   of the society, list of members, etc. Manchester : Barber & Farnworth, 1897. 8°,
   pp. 20, including printed wrappers BPL

Manchester Sh— Society—
   See Bailey
   ,, Foard

Mangasarian (M. M.) 'Hamlet' : The drama
   of human destiny : A sermon. Philadelphia, 1887. 8°   BPL

Lord and Lady Macbeth : A sermon. 1887.
   8°   BPL

Manifest detection . . . *See* Walker

Manly (J. M.) Specimens of the pre-Sh—
   drama. Boston [U.S.], 1897. Cr. 8°
                                  BPL

Manly (J. M.) *Editor*. *See* Sh— Macbeth, 1896

Manners and customs—
   See Deloney   *See* Morley
   ,, Douce   ,, Nares
   ,, Dyer   ,, Rolfe
   ,, Halliwell   ,, *Sh*—] Drake

Manning (T. S.) *Philadelphia Publisher*. *See*
   Sh— Works, 1805-09

Manningham (John) Diary. Ln : 1602-03
   The writer was a barrister, of Middle Temple and of
   Bradbourne, Kent. Mentions Sh— by name and
   says : ' At our feast wee had a play called " Twelue
   Night or What you will," much like the " Commedy
   of Errores." '

Mansel (R.) Free thoughts upon Methodists,
   actors, and the influence of the stage.
   Hull, 1814. 12°   BPL

Mansell *Publisher*—
   See Sh— King Lear, 1870
   ,, Sh— Macbeth, 1869
   ,, Sh— Measure . . . 1870
   ,, Sh— Merchant . . . 1850
   ,, Sh— Pericles, 1830
   ,, Sh— Romeo . . . 1850
   ,, Sh— Titus, 1830
   ,, Sh— Works, 1830, 1850

Mansfield (Richard) *Editor*—
   See Sh— King Henry V., 1901
   ,, Sh— King Richard III., 1889

Manson (A.) *Publisher*. *See* Sh— Works, 1753,
   1771, 1825

Manton (Granville) *Artist*. *See* Sh— Julius
   Cæsar, 1901

Manton (H.) Letters on theatres and music-
   halls. Birmingham, 1888. Cr. 8° BPL

Mantuan (John Baptist)] Eclogs . . . turned
   into English verse, by George Turbervile.
   Ln : Henrie Bynneman, 1567. 12°   W
   The first English translation of Mantuan. Of great
   rarity.
     '. . . Ah ! good old Mantuan,
     I may speak of thee as the traveller does of Venice.
     Old Mantuan—old Mantuan !
     Who understandeth thee not, loves thee not ?
          —' *Love's labours lost*,' act iv., sc. 2.

Mantzius (Karl) History of theatrical art in
   ancient and modern times. Trans. by
   Louise von Cossel. With introd. by Wm.
   Archer. Ln : Duckworth, 1903-09. 6
   vols. 8°. Illustrated. [*In progress*]
                                  BPL
   Contents : Vol. i. Earliest times.
      ,,   ii. Middle Ages and Renaissance.
      ,,   iii. Sh— and the English drama of
               his time.
      ,,   iv. Moliere and his time.
      ,,   v.
      ,,   vi.

Manuel *of Castile* (Juan) Moorish marriage,
   1332 : Bearing some similarity to the
   'Taming of the shrew.' Translated by F.
   W. Cosens. [Edited by J. O. Halliwell.]
   Ln : 1867. 12°   BPL | HCL
   Issue limited to ten copies. Text in English and
   Spanish.

Manuscript corrections from a fourth folio.
  See Quincy

Manuscripts—
  See Birmingham
  ,, Capell
  ,, Certificates
  ,, Chamberlain
  ,, Clarke (R.)
  ,, Collection . . .
  ,, Collier (J. P.)
  ,, Cope
  ,, Cornewallis
  ,, Croker
  ,, Daly
  ,, Dennis
  ,, Dermody
  ,, Diary
  ,, Dobell
  ,, Douse
  ,, Dowdall
  ,, Drury Lane
  ,, Eginton
  ,, Essay
  ,, F—— (T. J.)
  ,, Farmer
  ,, Farren
  ,, Fowler
  ,, Garrick
  ,, Gibson
  ,, Glossary
  ,, Gould
  ,, Gregory
  ,, Hall (H. T.)
  ,, Hall (T.)
  ,, Halliwell
  ,, Hanmer
  ,, Harleian
  ,, Hart (W. S.)
  ,, Hathaway
  ,, Hawley
  ,, Hesperides
  ,, Sh— All's well, 1785
  ,, Sh— As you like it, 1770
  ,, Sh— Hamlet, 1810
  ,, Sh— Julius Cæsar, 1660
  ,, Sh— King Edward III., 1753
  ,, Sh— King Henry IV., i., 1610, 1762
  ,, Sh— King Henry VIII., 1680
  ,, Sh— King John, 1800
  ,, Sh— Merry . . . 1660
  ,, Sh— Pericles, 1820
  ,, Sh— Poems, 1660, 1770
  ,, Sh— The tempest, 1845
  ,, Sh— Timon . . . 1842
  ,, Sh— Twelfth night, 1632, 1780
  ,, Sh— Winter's tale, 1690
  ,, Sh— Works : Ext. c. 1660, 1670
  ,, *Sh*—] Collection
  ,, *Sh*—] Halliwell
  ,, *Sh*—] Jordan

  See How
  ,, Ingleby
  ,, Ireland (S. W. H.)
  ,, Jaggard
  ,, Jebb
  ,, Jolley
  ,, Jordan
  ,, Jubilee
  ,, Kenrick
  ,, Knowle
  ,, Linley
  ,, Linley & Lawrence
  ,, Lodge
  ,, Lucy
  ,, Malone
  ,, Manningham
  ,, Marriage . . .
  ,, Mathews
  ,, Middleton
  ,, Mottley
  ,, Neele
  ,, New Pantomime
  ,, Northumberland
  ,, Norris
  ,, Notes . . .
  ,, Oldys
  ,, On . . .
  ,, Pembroke
  ,, Pennyworth
  ,, Plumptre
  ,, Poems . . .
  ,, Poetical . . .
  ,, Ritson
  ,, Rodd
  ,, Rutland
  ,, Saint John
  ,, Secret . . .
  ,, Seymour

Manuscripts—
  See Sh—] Malone
  ,, *Sh*—] Manuscript
  ,, *Sh*—] Notices
  ,, *Sh*—] Portraits
  ,, *Sh*—] Sh— Collection
  ,, *Sh*—] Sh— manuscripts
  ,, *Sh*—] Sh— miscellanies
  ,, *Sh*—] Sh— notices
  ,, *Sh*—] Sh— Society
  ,, *Sh*—] Sh—'s dramatic characters
  ,, *Sh*—] Shakespeareana
  ,, *Sh*—] Steevens
  ,, *Sh*—] Tyrrell
  ,, Sherwen   *See* Theobald
  ,, Scme . . .   ,, Tournaments
  ,, Southey   ,, Wallace
  ,, Stebbing   ,, Ward (John)
  ,, Steer   ,, Warner
  ,, Steevens   ,, Warwickshire
  ,, Story   ,, Wheler
  ,, Stowe   ,, White (R. G.)
  ,, *Stratford*]Charter ,, White (T.)
  ,,   ,, Manuscripts ,, Wright (G. R.)
  ,,   ,, Transcripts ,, Wright (W. A.)
  ,, Table Book   ,, Wyman
  ,, Taylor (John)

Mapleson (J. H.) *Actor-Manager. See* Sh—
  Othello, 1876
Mapleson (T. W. Gwilt) *Artist*—
  See Sh— Poems, 1849
  ,, Sh— Works : Ext. 1849
March (F. A.) Immaturity of Sh— as shown
  in 'Hamlet.' 1875. 8°   BPL
March (J. & J.) *Printers. See* Sh— Arden,
  ·1770
Marchant (Edward) *Publisher. See* Courtney
  & Slie
Marchbank (R.) *Dublin Publisher. See* Hitch-
  cock
Marchetti (Ludovic) *Artist*—
  See Sh— Othello, 1892, 1893
  ,, Sh— Romeo . . . 1890, 1891
'Marcian.'   Relics of the late Wm. Sh—,
  broker. Birmingham, 1901. 8°, pp. 104
                                    BPL
  A narrative of a supposed Birmingham descendant of
  the poet, said to be a broken-down author, and
  eventually a broker, with verses alleged to be written
  by him.
Margerison (T. E.) *Editor. See* Sh— Much ado,
  1904
Marguetel de Saint-Denis *Seigneur de Saint-
  Evremont* (C.) & Spence (Ferrand) Mis-
  cellanea, or various discourses upon
  tragedy, comedy, the Italian (and) the
  English comedy and operas . . . Ln :
  Printed for Sam. Holford, 1686.   12°,
  pp. xl.-180
Marina. *See* Sh— Pericles, 1738, 1775, 1810,
  1820, 1902

Marindin (G. E.) Sh— and Plutarch [Parallel
passages in 'Pelopidas' and 'Hamlet,'
What's Hecuba to him...?] [In 'Athe-
næum,' No. 3572, p. 487, April]. 1896. 4°
Marks *Artist.* See Sh— Works, 1875-76
Marlowe (Christopher) Dedication. *See* Watson
Famous tragedy of the Rich Jew of Malta.
Written by Christopher Marlo [In five
acts and in verse, edited by Thomas Hey-
wood]. Ln: Printed by I. B—— for N.
Vavasour, 1633. Fcp. 4°, without pagi-
nation   w
Bears resemblance to the 'Merchant of Venice.'
] Troublesome raigne of Iohn King of Eng-
land—
See Sh— King John
„ Sh— Works: Ext. 1764
Marlowe.] Lewis (J. G.) Christopher Mar-
lowe: his life and works. Canterbury:
W. E. Goulden, 1890. 8°, pp. 28
Contains particulars of the 'Passionate pilgrim.'
Marlowe (C.)—
See Cartwright
„ Foard
„ Gascoigne
„ Henderson
„ Heywood
„ Hosken
„ Ingram
„ Lee
„ Poel
„ Sh— Passionate (*heading*)
„ Sb— Passionate ... 1883
„ Slater
„ Theobald (W.)
„ Verity
Marmion (Shackerley). *See* Annalia Dubrensia
Marnésia (*Marquis de*) *Editor. See* Sh—] Sher-
lock
Marriage of wit and wisdom: An ancient
interlude. To which are added illustra-
tions of Sh— and the early English drama.
Edited [with notes] by J. O. Halliwell.
Ln: Sh— Society, 1846. 8°, pp. xii.-148
BM | BPL | BUS | HCL | MPL
Printed from the original MS. found in the collection
of Sir Edward Dering.
Marriot (John) *Publisher*—
See Donne
„ Randolph
Marriott (Elizabeth) Bacon or Sh— ? An his-
torical enquiry. Ln: Stock, 1898. 8°,
pp. 48   BM | BPL | SML
Bacon or Sh— ? 3rd ed. With appendix.
Ln: Stock, 1899. 8°   BUS
Bi-literal cypher. Exeter: H. S. Eland,
1901. 8°   BPL | SML
Marriott (J.) New Sh— puzzle. *See* Sh—
Works: Ext. 1878
Marriott (R.) *Publisher. See* Donne

Marsh (Charles) *Editor*—
See Sh— Cymbeline, 1755
„ Sh— Winter's tale, 1756
Marsh (Charles) *Printer. See* Sh— Compen-
dious ... 1751
Marsh (Digby) Observations on the first act
of Sh—'s 'Tempest' [In 'Royal Irish
Academy: Transactions']. Dublin, 1788.
4°   BPL | BUS
Marsh (Henry) *Publisher*—
See Kirkman
„ Mirrour ...
„ Sh— Birth ... 1662
„ Webster & Rowley
Marsh (John B.) Familiar, proverbial, and
select sayings from Sh—. *See* Sh—
Works: Ext. 1863
Shakespearian playing cards. *See* Sh—
Works: Ext. 1862-63
Shakespearian riddles. *See* Sh— Works:
Ext. 1864
Marsh (John B.) *Editor. See* Sh— Works, 1864,
1874, 1879
Marsh (Luther R.) *See* New Shakespeareana
Marshall (Emma) Sh— and his birthplace.
See Sh—] Marshall
Marshall (F.) *Editor*—
See Sh— As you like it, 1904
„ Sh— Hamlet, 1905
„ Sh— King Henry V., 1900, 1902
„ Sh— King Lear, 1905
„ Sh— King Richard II., 1905
Marshall (Frank Albert) Study of 'Hamlet.'
Ln: Longman, 1875. 8°, pp. xvi.-x.-206
BM | BPL | BUS | MPL | SML
Marshall (F. A.) *Editor*—
See Sh— Hamlet, 1880
„ Sh— Works, 1888-90, 1895
Marshall *of Bishopton, Stratford* (John). *See*
Stopes & Lee
Marshall (T. P.) *Editor*—
See Sh— As you like it, 1903
„ Sh— Julius Cæsar, 1899
Marshall (Wm.) *Engraver*—
See Aleyn   *See* Sh— Poems, 1640
„ Hall   „ Swan
„ Heywood   „ Weaver
„ Randolph
Marshall (W.) *Publisher. See* Cooke
Marshe (Thomas) *Printer*—
See Mirrour ...
„ Painter
„ Sh— Compendious ... 1581
Marston (Edward) *Editor. See* Sh— Sonnets,
1888
Marston (John) Metamorphosis of Pigmalion's
image. *See* Sh— King John, 1764
Miscellaneous pieces ...
See Sh— Poems, 1764
„ Sh— Works: Ext. 1764

(209)   14

Marston (John) Parasitaster, or the fawne . . .
Ln : Printed by T. P— for W. C—, 1606.
Fcp. 4°   w
An imitation of ‘ Measure for measure,' which play it
was meant to rival.   Contains a parody of a famous
line in ‘ King Richard III.'—
    ‘ O yes, the confusion of tongues at the large table
is broke vppe, for see, the presence filles ; A foole, a
foole, my coxcombe for a foole !'

Scourge of villanie. Ln : 1599
Alludes in Satire ii. to ‘ Romeo and Juliet,' also to
‘ Drusus ' and ‘ Roscio.' ‘ Drusus' is a pseudonym
for Sh— and ‘ Roscio ' for Richard Burbage.
In Satire vii. the line from ‘ King Richard III.' again
does duty as
    ‘ A man ; a man ; a kingdom for a man.'

Scourge of villanie. See Sh— King John,
1764

Turtle and phœnix. See Sh— The turtle . .

What you will. Ln : G. Eld for Thomas
Thorppe, 1607. Fcp. 4°, A1 to H4 in
fours, unpaged (the last blank)
An example of barefaced brigandage from Sh—. In
addition to borrowing the title from ‘ Twelfth night,'
Marston imitates ‘ Love's labours lost ' by introducing
a character named Holifernes, with a boy, on sig.
D1, etc. On C1 he transfers the line ‘ A horse, a
horse ' without scruple from King Richard III.'

[Works] Dramatic works. With notes and
account of his life by J. O. Halliwell.
Ln : J. R. Smith, 1856. 3 vols. Cr. 8°
                                           SML

See Cartwright   See Jones (I.)
 ,, Chester . . .   ,, M—— (J.)
 ,, Foard   ,, S—— (L.)
 ,, Gascoigne

Marston (John) & Webster (John) The mal-
content. [A tragi-comedy in prose and
verse in five acts.] Augmented by Iohn
Marston. With the additions played by
the Kings Maiesties seruants, written by
Iohn Webster. Ln : Printed by V. S——
[Valentine Sims] for William Aspley . . .
1604. Fcp. 4°   w
‘ This rare play contains several allusions to and illustrations of Sh—'s plays. The Induction of the players
is very curious, and Sly the actor is introduced
quoting a line from the part of Osric in “ Hamlet.” '
                                  —J. O. Halliwell.
‘ Contains bits of Sh—'s “ Hamlet.” '—F. G. Fleay.

Marston (Westland) Our recent actors ; being
recollections critical and personal of distinguished performers of both sexes.
Ln : 1890. Cr. 8°

Martin Publisher—
See Sh— King Lear, 1768
 ,, Sh— Works, 1821-29, 1823

Martin Edinburgh Publisher—
See Sh— Merchant . . . 1768
 ,, Sh— Merry wives . . . 1768
 ,, Sh— Othello, 1768
 ,, Sh— Romeo, 1768

Martin New York Publisher. See Sh— Works,
1854-56, 1855-59

Martin (H.)] Remarks on John Kemble's
performance of ‘ Hamlet' and ‘ Richard
III.,' by the author of ‘ Helen of Glen-
ross.' Ln : G. & J. Robinson, 1802. 8°,
pp. ii.-40   BUS
See also Kemble.

Martin (Helena Faucit Lady) ‘ Beatrice' : Sh—'s
female characters [In ‘ Blackwood's Mag.']
1885. 8°   BPL
Illustrates ‘ Much ado.'

On Imogen [Cymbeline]. 1882. 8° BM

On Ophelia and Portia. 1880. 8° BM | BPL
Issued for strictly private circulation.
Illustrates ‘ Hamlet ' and the ‘ Merchant of Venice.'

On some of Sh—'s female characters. 1885.
Fcp. 4°   BM | BPL

On . . . Sh—'s female characters. Edin :
Blackwood, 1888. 8°   BPL | SML

On . . . Sh—'s female characters. Edin :
Blackwood, 1891. 8°   BM | BUS

On . . . Sh—'s female characters. 5th ed.
Edin : Blackwood, 1893. 8°   MPL

On . . . Sh—'s female characters. 6th ed.
Edin : Blackwood, 1899. 8°, pp. 422

On . . . Sh—'s female characters. 7th ed.
Edin : Blackwood, 1904. 8°, pp. 432

Martin.] Waller (W. F.) Helen Faucit [Lady
Martin] [In ‘ The Theatre']. 1885. Roy.
8°   BPL

] Martin (Sir Theod.) Helena Faucit. 1900.
8°   BPL

Martin (John) Editor. See Sh— As you like
it, 1848

Martin (P. J.)] Parallel between Sh— and
Scott : being the substance of three lectures on the kindred nature of their
genius, delivered before the Chichester
Literary Society. Ln : Whittaker & Co.,
1835. 12°, pp. iv.-82
                       BM | BPL | BUS | SML | W

Martin Baskerville's partner (Robert) Birmingham Printer. See Sh— Works, 1768

Martin (Sir Theodore) An eye-witness of John
Kemble [In the ‘ Nineteenth Century'].
1888. 8°   BPL

Essays on the drama. Ln : Privately
printed, 1874. 8°   SML

Monographs : Garrick, Macready, Rachel,
and Baron Stockmar. Ln : Murray, 1906.
8°, pp. 352 and 4 portraits   BPL

Sh— or Bacon ? Reprinted from ‘ Blackwood's Magazine.' 1888. Fcp. 4°
                       BM | BPL | BUS | SML

Martin (Dr. Wm.) Site of Sh—'s Globe playhouse [In ‘ Athenæum,' No. 4276, p. 425].
9 Oct., 1909

Martin & Wotherspoon Edinburgh Printers &
Publishers—
See Sh— King Richard III., 1768
 ,, Sh— Macbeth, 1768

Martin & Wotherspoon *Edinburgh Printers & Publishers*—
See Sh— Romeo . . . 1768
,, Sh— Works, 1767, 1797
'Martinus Scriblerus' *pseud. See* Morehead
Martyn (Benjamin) Timoleon. A tragedy. As it is acted at the Theatre Royal . . . Ln: J. Watts, Wild Court, 1730. 8°, pp. xvi.-72
Refers to Sh— in the Prologue and Epilogue.
Martyn (J.) *Publisher. See* Sh— Hamlet, 1676
Marvell (Andrew) The rehearsal transpos'd. Ln: Printed by A. B—— for the assigns of John Calvin & Theodore Beza at the sign of the King's Indulgence on the south side of the Lake Leman, 1672. The rehearsal transpos'd: Second part . . . Ln: Nathaniel Ponder at the Peacock in Chancery Lane near Fleet Street, 1673. 2 vols. 8°   BM | W
Refers to 'fat Sir John Falstaff.'
See vol. i., p. 191, and vol. ii., p. 47, and the 'Merchant of Venice,' p. 73.
Mary I. *of Eng.* (*Queen*). *See* Stopes
Mary Queen of Scots—
See Owen
,, Plumptre
Marx (E.) *Editor. See* Delius
Mascall (Leonard) Booke of fishing, 1600. *See* Sh— autograph
Masklin. On Sh—'s style and science. *See* Sh—] Notices
Mason (C.) *Publisher. See* Sh— Works, 1837
Mason (H. C. F.) Compositions and translations. *See* Sh— Works: Ext. 1903
Mason (John) *Bookseller. See* Catalogue, 1812
Mason (*Rt. Hon.* John Monck) Comments on the last edition of Sh—'s plays. Ln: C. Dilly, 1785. 8°, pp. xvi.-440
       BM | BPL | CPL
The edition mentioned is that of Johnson and Steevens, 1778.
Comments . . . Dublin: P. Byrne, 1785. 8°, pp. xvi.-440   BUS
Comments on the plays of Beaumont and Fletcher. With an appendix containing some further observations on Sh—, extended to the late editions of Malone and Steevens. Ln: Griffith, 1797-98. 2 parts in 1 vol. 8°. Portrait
       BM | BPL | BUS | MPL | SML | W
Comments on the plays of Beaumont and Fletcher . . . Ln: Griffith, 1798. 8°. Portrait   BUS | W
Comments on the several editions of Sh—'s plays, extended to those of Malone and Steevens. Dublin: Graisberry & Campbell, 1807. 8°, pp. xvi.-608
       BM | BPL | BUS | MPL | W
Issue restricted to 250 copies.
Preface. *See* Sh— Works, 1803-05

Mason (William) Caractacus. 1759
'How oft I cried, "Oh come, thou tragic queen ! March from thy Greece with firm, majestic tread, Such as when Athens saw thee fill her scene When Sophocles thy choral graces led.
 .   .   .   .   .
Bring then to Britain's plain that choral throng, Display thy buskined pomp, thy golden lyre ; Give her historic forms the soul of song And mingle Attic art with Sh—'s fire !"
"Ah, what, fond boy, dost thou presume to claim ?" The muse replied, " Mistaken suppliant, know, To light in Sh—'s breast the dazzling flame Exhausted all Parnassus could bestow. True, art remains ; and if from his bright page Thy mimic power one vivid beam can seize, Proceed ; and in that best of tasks engage Which tends at once to profit and to please." '

Mason & Co. *Publishers. See* Sh— Works, 1822

Masques—
See Daniel
,, Greg

Massey (Gerald) Secret drama of Sh—'s sonnets unfolded, with the characters identified. Second edition. 1872. 8° BPL
A reprint of 'Sh—'s Sonnets' (by the same author) under a fresh title.
Contains the verses :—
Our prince of peace in glory hath gone, With no spear shaken, no sword drawn, No cannon fired, no flag unfurled, To make his conquest of the world.
 .   .   .   .   .
For him no martyr-fires have blazed, No limbs been racked, no scaffolds raised ; For him no life was ever shed To make the victor's pathway red.
 .   .   .   .   .
And for all time he wears the crown Of lasting, limitless renown ; He reigns, whatever monarchs fall, His throne is in the hearts of all !

Secret drama of Sh—'s sonnets . . . 1888. Fcp. 4°   BPL | BUS | MPL | SML
Impression restricted to 100 copies.
Sh— in domestic life. Theory of the sonnets [In 'British Quarterly Review,' Jan.] Ln: 1867. 8°   BUS
Sh—'s sonnets, never before interpreted : his private friends identified, together with a recovered likeness of himself. Ln: Longmans, 1866. 8°, pp. xii.-604
       BPL | BUS | CPL | MPL
Massey (Gerald) *Editor. See* Sh— Sonnets, 1866, 1872, 1886, 1888
Massinger (Philip) Believe as you list. *See* Sh—] Sh— Soc.
Roman actor : a tragedie. Ln: 1629. Fcp. 4°
Contains passages which parallel some in 'Hamlet.'
Massinger (Philip)—
See Boyle   *See* Malone
,, Croker   ,, Sh— Double falsehood
,, Fleay   ,, Sh— Works: Ext. 1822
,, Gardiner   ,, Warner
,, Halliwell

Masson (*Prof.* David) Sh— and Goethe [In 'British Quarterly Review,' Nov.] Ln: 1852. 8°   BUS
Sh— and Goethe [In 'Essays Biographical']. Cambridge, 1856. 8°   BUS
Sh— and Goethe [In ' Three Devils,' pp. 59-121]. Ln: 1874. 8°   BPL | BUS
Wordsworth, Shelley, Keats, and other essays. 1874
> At page 242 occurs this passage:—
> 'Sh— is as astonishing for the exuberance of his genius in abstract notions and for the depth of his analytical and philosophical insight as for the scope and minuteness of his poetic imagination.
> 'It is as if into a mind poetical in form there had been poured all the matter that existed in the mind of his contemporary Bacon. In Sh—'s plays we have thought, history, exposition, philosophy, all within the round of the poet. The only difference between him and Bacon sometimes is that Bacon writes an essay and calls it his own, while Sh— writes a similar essay and puts it into the mouth of a Ulysses or a Polonius.'

Masson (Flora) *Editor. See* Sh— As you like it, 1903
Master of the Revels—
  See Ancient . . .
  ,, Revels
Mathew (A. H.) *See* Matthew
Mathewes (Augustine) *Printer*—
  See Clavell   *See* Sh— King John, 1622
  ,, Kyd   ,, Sh— Merry devil, 1626
  ,, May   ,, Sh— Othello, 1630
Mathews *Actor* (Charles) Letter to St. Aubyn [explaining that he played 'Othello' for a wager], [In 'Athenæum,' No. 3463, p. 322, Mar.] 1894. 4°
Letter to the dramatic authors of France. Translated from himself by himself. 1852. 8°   BPL
Letter upon Somerset's 'Sh—'s early days.' 1829. Manuscript. 12°   BPL
Library. *See* Catalogue, 1835
Mathews.] Mathews (Mrs.) Memoirs of Charles Mathews. Ln: 1838. 4 vols. 8°. With portrait and folded plates
] Mathews.   Life and correspondence of Charles Mathews. Abridged by Edmund Yates. Ln: Routledge, 1860. 8°, pp. xvi.-480, with portraits
Mathews (*Mrs.*) Anecdotes of actors. 1844. 8°   BPL
Mathews & Leigh *Publishers. See* Sh— Macbeth, 1807
Mathias (D.) *Editor. See* Sh— Works, 1867
Mathias (T. J.)] *Editor, Bookseller & Critic. See* Hardinge
Mathias (T. J.)—
  See Chalmers
  ,, Hardinge
Matson (Wm. Tidd) Sh—, the poet-catholic [In ' Sh— Repository']. Ln: 1853. 8°   BUS
Mattes (Ed.) *Publisher. See* Cornewallis

Matthew (Frederic D.) Account of the German Sh— Society's Jahrbuch. Ln: New Sh— Soc., 1876   8°
Matthew (F. D.) *Editor. See* Sh— Compendious . . . 1876
Matthew.] Calthrop (Annette) & Mathew (A. H.) Life of Sir Tobie Matthew, Bacon's 'Alter ego.' 1907. 8°   BPL
See also Smith (W. H.)
Matthews (G. F. Cale) Some of the songs of Sh—. 'Sh— Club Papers.' Stratford, 1905. 8°, pp. 8
Matthews (J. Brander) Books and play-books ; Essays on literature and the drama. 1895. Cr. 8°
Theatres of Paris. 1880. Cr. 8°. Illust.
Matthews (J. Brander) *Editor. See* Lamb
Mattocks (*Mrs.*) *Actress. See* Sh— Winter's tale, 1779
Maude (Francis Cornwallis) Bacon or Sh— ? Enquiries as to the authorship of the plays of Sh—. Ln: 1895. 8°, pp. 72
                                   BM | BPL | BUS
Maudsley (H.) 'Hamlet' [In 'Psychological Essays,' pp. 145-195]. 1873. 12°   BPL
Sh— testimonied. *See* Sh—] Maudsley
Mauke (F.) *Jena Publisher. See* Sh— Julius Cæsar, 1848
Maunder (Samuel) *Editor. See* Sh— Works, 1839, 1840, 1842, 1850, 1851
Maurice (D. S.) *Printer*—
  See Sh— All's well, 1820
  ,, Sh— King Richard II., 1822
  ,, Sh— Measure . . . 1822
  ,, Sh— Timon . . . 1822
  ,, Sh— Works, 1817, 1818, 1825
Mawman *York Publisher. See* Sh— Macbeth, 1797
Mawman (J.) *Publisher. See* Sh— Works, 1811
Maxcy (Carroll Lewis) *Editor. See* Sh— Hamlet, 1892
Maxwell (Caroline) *Editor. See* Sh— Works : Ext. 1828
Maxwell (H.) *Philadelphia Publisher. See* Sh— Works, 1805-09
May (George) Birth-town of Sh— . . . Evesham : Printed by the author, c. 1850. 8°, p. 100. Illust.   BUS
Guide to the birth-town of Sh— and the poet's rural haunts. Evesham : G. May, 1847. 12°, pp. 100. Illust.   BPL | BUS
Illustrated guide to Stratford-on-Avon. Evesham [c. 1847]. 12°   BPL
May (Thomas)] The heire. A comedie. A. it was acted by the Company of the Revels, 1620. Written by T. M——s Second impression. Ln : A. Mathewes for T. Jones, 1633. Fcp. 4°, without pagina-
Several portions are borrowed from Sh—.   [tion
See Heywood

Mayer (G.) *Leipzig Publisher.* *See* Sh— Hamlet, 1857

Mayhew (E.) Stage effect, or the principles which command dramatic success in the theatre. Ln: 1840. 12°   BPL

Maynard *Editor.* *See* Sh— Much ado, 1893

Maynard (Walter) Falstaff [In 'Gentleman's Mag,.' Nov.] Ln: 1868. 8°   BPL | BUS

Maynes (J.) *Publisher.* *See* Donne

Mayou (Bessie) Natural History of Sh—. *See* Sh— Works: Ext. 1877

Meadows *Engraver.* *See* Sh— Works: Ext. 1792-96

Meadows (Arthur) Hamlet: An essay. Edinburgh: Maclachlan & Stewart, 1871. 8°, pp. 32   BM | BPL | BUS

Meadows (Joseph Kenny) Shakespearian points of humour. Ln: W. S. Orr & Co., 1841-45. 8°

Meadows (Joseph Kenny) *Artist—*
See Planché & Meadows
  ,, Sh— King John, 1823
  ,, Sh— Works, 1839-43, 1843, 1844, 1845, 1846, 1849, 1852, 1853, 1854, 1857-59, 1858, 1859, 1864, 1875-80, 1879, 1886-88
  ,, Sh— Works: Ext. 1873

Meadows (J. K.) & Measom (W.) Votive tablet to Sh—. 1864. F°   BPL

Meadows (T.) Thespian gleanings. Ulverston: G. Ashburne, 1819. 12°   SML

Meares (W.) *Publisher.* *See* Howard

Mearne (Charles) *Publisher.* *See* Comenius

Mears (W.) Compleat catalogue of plays. Second edition.. 1726. 12°   BPL

Mears (W.) *Publisher—*
See Sh— King Richard II., 1720
  ,, Sh— Midsummer ... 1716
  ,, Sh— Poems, 1725, 1728
  ,, Sh— Works, 1725

Meason (W.) *See* Meadows & Measom

Measure for measure. *See* Sh— Measure ...

Medals. *See* Shakespearean medals

Medex (Fred.) Comparative morality of the clerical and theatrical professions. N. P.: Privately printed, 1877. 8°, pp. 8

Medicine and surgery—
See Caius
  ,, Jaggard
  ,, Moyes

Medwin (T. R.) History of the school. *See* *Stratford*] Grammar

Meehan (J. F.) Sh—'s visits to Bath [In 'Famous houses of Bath']. Bath, 1901. 8°   BPL
Sh—'s Visits to Bath [In 'The Beacon']. Bath, 1901. 4°   BPL

Meek (J. McK.) [A lithographed memorial of Sh—, from a pen and ink drawing, 1862.] F°. Single sheet   BM

Meeting of gallants ... *See* Rowlands

Meighen (Richard) *Publisher—*
See Clavell
  ,, Goffe
  ,, Sh— Merry wives, 1630
  ,, Sh— Works, 1632

Meighan (T.) *Publisher.* *See* Sh— King Richard II., 1720

Meijboom (L. S. P.) Hamlet [an essay]. [1870 ?] 8°   BM

Meiklejohn (J. M. D.) *Editor—*
See Sh— Coriolanus, 1896
  ,, Sh— Hamlet, 1880, 1885, 1889
  ,, Sh— Julius Cæsar, 1878, 1889, 1893, 1895
  ,, Sh— King John, 1885
  ,, Sh— King Lear, 1879, 1888
  ,, Sh— King Richard II., 1880, 1881, 1882, 1883, 1886, 1888, 1890
  ,, Sh— Macbeth, 1880, 1888, 1902, 1903
  ,, Sh— Merchant ... 1879, 1888, 1893
  ,, Sh— The tempest, 1880, 1889
  ,, Sh— Works, 1879, 1883, 1884

Meiklejohn (M. J. C.) *Editor.* *See* Sh— Julius Cæsar, 1902

Meister (H.) Of Sh—. *See* Sh—] Meister

Melbourne Sh— Society :—
Programme of the sixth anniversary meeting. 1890. 8°   BPL
Phillips (P. D.) Sh— notes of travel. 1890. 8°   BPL

'Melicent' *pseud. of Sh—.* *See* Chettle

Mellon.] Wilson (*Mrs.* Baron) Memoirs of Harriot, Duchess of Saint Albans. Ln: Colburn, 1839. 2 vols. 8°

Melmoth (Courtney) Shadows of Sh—: A monody occasioned by the death of Mr. Garrick. 1779. 4°

Melodrama mad, or the siege of Troy: The situations and sentiment from Mr. Homer, a blind old ballad singer, and one Sh—, a Warwickshire deer stealer ... Ln: 1819. 8°

Memoirs of Betty, the 'Young Roscius.' *See* Merritt

Memoirs of Humphrey Duke of Gloucester [as they relate to Mr. Phillips's Tragedy]. 1723. 12°   BPL
Illustrates 'King Henry VI.'

Memoirs of the green room. Ln: J. Roach, Theatrical Library, Russell Court, Drury Lane [c. 1810]. 8°

Memoirs of the Sh—'s Head, Covent Garden, with many entertaining adventures and remarkable characters. By the Ghost of Sh—. Ln: J. Noble, 1755. 2 vols. 8°. With frontispiece   BUS
Garrick is satirised under the name of Buskin.

(213)

Memorable conceits of diuers noble and famovs personages of Christendome, of this our moderne time. Ln: James Shaw, 1612. 12°
It enters into the Sh— series as containing two stories bearing resemblance to the 'Merchant of Venice.'— See Halliwell's 'Sh— reliques,' 1852, page 50.

Memorial of the tercentenary in Cambridge. See Sh—] Memorial

Memorials of old Warwickshire [by various writers]. Ed. by Alice Dryden. Ln: Bemrose, 1908. 8°, pp. 272. Illust. SML
Contents :—
Harris (M. Dormer) Historic Warwickshire
Leigh (Lady) Stoneleigh Abbey
Jourdain (M.) Tapestry manufacture at Barcheston
Cossins (Jethro A.) Early works of architecture
D — (R. O.) Shirleys of Ettington
Hartshorne (Albert) Monuments and effigies in St. Mary's Church and the Beauchamp Chapel, Warwick
Stanley (S. S.) Church bells of antiquity
Newdegate (F. A.) The Newdegates
Jourdain (M.) Literary associations of Warwickshire
Stanley (S. S.) Notes on Warwickshire mints
Pearson (H. S.) Origin and growth of Birmingham
Harris (M. D.) Manuscript treasures of Coventry
Treen (A. Edward) Rugby School
Dryden (Alice) Compton Wynyates
Dolan (Dom Gilbert) Pre-Reformation monastic establishments
Dugdale (W. F. S.) Sir Wm. Dugdale
Andrews (Francis B.) Castles of Warwickshire
Baker (Oliver) Moated houses of Warwickshire
Brassington (W. S.) Note upon the charters and muniments of Stratford-upon-Avon

Memorials of Sh— and his birthplace. See Sh—] Memorials

Mendelssohn (Felix) Composer—
See Sh— Midsummer... 1826,1855,1861,1898
 ,, Sh— Poems, 1862
 ,, Stratford] Sh—'s birthplace

Menken (E.) Catalogue of a collection of Shakespeariana. Ln: 1890. 8° BPL

Mennis (Sir John) & Smith (James)] Witt's recreations. See Sh—] Sh— notices.

Menship (Samuel) Publisher. See Winstanley

Menton (L.)] Money masters all things, or satyrical poems . . . Ln: 1698. 8°
At p. 119 is a notice of Sh— :—
'And banish sense with Johnson from the stage, His sacrilege should plunder Sh—'s urn.'

Menzies (Louisa L. J.) Legendary tales of the ancient Britons. Ln: 1864. 8° BUS
'Legend of Lear,' pp. 17-51.

'Mercade.' 'Hamlet,' or Sh—'s philosophy of history: A study of the spiritual soul and unity of 'Hamlet.' Ln: Williams & Norgate, 1875. 8°, pp. xxxii.-208
BPL | BUS | SML
An attempt to read into 'this stupendous tragedy' a profound symbolism—in other words, the great dynamical principle of modern history in Europe.

Merchant of Venice. See Sh— Merchant . . .
Merchant of Venice travestie—
See Baker (G. M.) See Griffin (G. W. H.)
 ,, Brougham (J.) ,, Old clothes
 ,, Fraser (F. J.) ,, Talfourd (F.)

Mercier (A.) Hamlet: his mental state [In 'Ancient essays on English poets']. New Orleans, 1887. 8° BPL

Mercurious Britannicus [Ed. by Marchamont Needham]. Ln: R. White, 1641-60. Fcp. 4°
The editor, referring to his rival 'Aulicus,' says:—
'His braines have been wonderfully blasted of late and plannet strucke, and he is not now able to provoke the meanest christian to laughter, but lies in a paire of foule sheetes, a wofull spectacle and object of dullnesse and tribulation, not to be recovered by the Protestant or Catholique liquor, either ale or strong beer, sack, claret, hippocras, muscadine, or rosa solis, which has been reputed formerly by his grandfather Ben Jonson, his uncle Sh—, his couzen germains Fletcher and Beaumont, noselesse D'Avenant, and Frier Sherley, the poets, the onely blossoms for the braine, restoratives for the wit, bathing for the nine muses ; but none of these are now able either to warme him into a quibble, or inflame him into a sparkle of invention, and all this because he hath profaned the sabbath by his pen.'
Continuing in a further passage—'He [Aulicus] says he barbarously cut his bookes into pieces ; those were only some Lady Psalters, Cosins' Devotions, Pockington's Altar, Shelford's Sermons, Sh—'s Workes, and such prelatical trash as your clergymen spend their canonicall houres on.'
This passage shows in what abhorrence Sh— was held by the Puritans and their panegyrists. About the same period Cowley, in satirizing a semi-gentleman of Westminster Hall, wishes he may—
'Be by his father in his study took At Sh—'s plays instead of my Lord Coke.'

Meredith (C.) Publisher. See Willis

Meredith (E. A.) Note on some emendations not hitherto suggested, with a new explanation of an old passage [In 'Quebec Literary and Historical Soc. Trans.'] Quebec, 1863. 8° BUS

Meredith (George) Essay on comedy and the uses of the comic spirit [In 'New Quarterly Mag.,' April]. 1877
'Sh— is a well-spring of characters which are saturated with the comic spirit ; with more of what we will call blood-life than is to be found anywhere out of Sh— ; and they are of this world, but they are of the world enlarged to our embrace by imagination, and by great poetic imagination. They are, as it were—I put it to suit my present comparison—creatures of the woods and wilds, not in walled towns, not grouped and toned to pursue a comic exhibition of the narrower world of society. . . .'

Essay on comedy . . . Westminster: Constable, 1898. Cr. 8°, pp. 106

Spirit of Sh— [In 'Poems and lyrics of the joy of earth,' pp. 161-162]. 1883. Cr. 8°
'Thy greatest knew thee, mother earth ; unsoured He knew thy sons. He probed from hell to hell Of human passions, but of love deflowered His wisdom was not, for he knew thee well.

O lived the master now to paint us man, That little twist of brain would ring a chime Of whence it came and what it caused, to start Thunders of laughter, clearing air and heart.'

Spirit of Sh— [In 'Poems,' p. 189]. 1898. 12° BPL

Merefield (Mrs.) See Sh—] Malone

Meres (Francis) Palladis tamia : Wits treasvry, being the second part of 'Wit's commonwealth' . . . At Ln : Printed by P. Short for Cuthbert Burbie and are to be solde at his shop at the Royall Exchange, 1598. 8°, sig. A1 to A4, B1, and B2 to V8 in eights on numbered folios   CTC | W

'A noted school-book,' says Ant. a Wood, 'celebrated for its list, the first printed, of Sh—'s plays, and definitely fixing the fact that six comedies and six tragedies existed in that year, if no earlier.' The volume is a collection of moral and literary reflections and admonitions. In the essay entitled a 'Comparative discourse of our English poets with the Greek, Latin and Italian poets,' he pays high tribute to Sh—, indeed Meres placed Sh— foremost among contemporary men-of-letters. At p. 298 Meres says : 'As the soul of Euphorbus was thought to live in Pythagoras, so the sweet witty soul of Ovid lives in mellifluous and honey-tongued Sh—. Witness his "Venus and Adonis," his "Lucrece," his sugred sonnets among his private friends, etc. As Plautus and Seneca are accounted the best for comedy and tragedy among the Latins, so Sh— among the English is the most excellent in both kinds for the stage. For comedy, witness his "Gentlemen of Verona," his "Errors," his "Love's labours lost," his "Love's labours wonne," his "Midsummer night's dream," and his "Merchant of Venice." For tragedy, his "Richard II.," "Richard III.," "Henry IV.," "King John," "Titus Andronicus," and his "Romeo and Juliet."

'As Epius Stolo said that the muses would speak with Plautus' tongue, if they would speak latin, so I say that the muses would speak with Sh—'s fine filed phrase, if they would speak English.'

'Wits' commonwealth' (or 'Wits' academy '), of which the above work purports to be the continuation, was written by John Bodenham (q.v.).

Palladis tamia, 1598. Ed. by J. Haslewood. Ln : 1815. 2 vols. 8°   BPL

Meres (F.)   See Peele

Merian Engraver.   See Donne

Merie tales of the mad men of Gotham. See Old English jest books

Merivale (Herman) Alleged Sh— forgeries [In 'Edinburgh Review,' April]. 1860. 8°   BUS

Merivale (Herman). See Sh—] Sh— Show book

Merivale (J. H.) Editor. See Sh— King Henry VI., i., ii., iii., 1817

Mermaid Tavern—
See Sandys
  ,, Thompson
  ,, Watts-Dunton

Merridew (John) Catalogue of a collection of Sh— literature. [1828 ?] 8°   BPL
Catalogue of engraved portraits of nobility, gentry, clergymen, and others born, resident in, or connected with the county of Warwick, including a very accurate list of all the genuine engravings of Sh—, with biographical notices. Coventry : J. Merridew, 1849. 4°

] Coventry guide . . . ancient history of the city. Coventry, 1824. Cr. 8°. Illustrated
Valuable for its description of the Coventry of Sh—'s youth.

Merriman Bp. (N. J.) On the study of Sh—. 1857. 8°   BM
Sh— as bearing on English history. 1858. 8°   BM

Merriman (Roger Bigelow) Date of 'King Lear' [In 'Athenæum,' No. 4204, p. 648, May]. 1908

Merritt (J.)   See Betty

Merry conceited humours of Bottom the weaver. See Sh— Midsummer . . . 1646, 1661, 1672, 1673, 1860, 1868, 1871

Merry devil of Edmonton. See Sh— Merry devil

Merry tales. See Sh—] Sh— Jest book

Merry tales from Sh—. See Sh— Works : Ext. 1845

Merry tales of Skelton. See Sh—] Sh— Jest book

Merry tales of the mad men of Gotham, 1864. See Sh—] Sh—'s Jest books

Merry tales of the wise men of Gotham. Ed. by J. O. Halliwell. Ln : J. R. Smith, 1840. 8°

Merry wives of Windsor. See Sh— Merry wives

Mery tales and quicke answeres, 1567. See Old English jest books

Mery talys and qvicke answers, 1881. See Sh—] Sh— Jest books

Messmer (G.) Editor. See Sh— Macbeth, 1879

Metamorphosis of tabacca, 1602. See Reprints

Metrical history of Tom Thumb the little. Ed. by J. O. Halliwell. 1860. 8°   BPL

Meurer (Dr. K.) Editor—
See Sh— Works, 1880-81
  ,, Sh— Works : Ext. 1879

Mexia and others (Pedro) Historie of all the Roman Emperors . . . collected in Spanish . . . since inlarged in Italian by Lodovico Dulce and Girolamo Bardi and now Englished by W. T—— [W. Traheron]. Ln : Mathew Lownes, 1604. F°. With woodcut portraits   BM | SML
Contains a ' Life of Julius Cæsar ' doubtless familiar to Sh—.

Mexia (P.) Sansovino (F.) Du Verdier (A.) and others. Treasvrie of avncient and moderne times . . . Time's storehouse . . . [Edited by Thomas Milles.] Ln : William Iaggard, 1613-19. 2 vols. F°. Engraved title by Elstracke, plates, and engravings   BM | SML
Vol. i., pp. 336-339 contain the ' Seaven ages of man.'
Vol. ii., pp. 364-365 contain the ' Memorable historie of faire Iulietta of Verona the Montacute and Romeo the Capulet.'

Meyer (C.) Hanover Publisher. See Sh— Macbeth, 1879

Meyer (E.) Editor. See Sh— Julius Cæsar, 1857

Meyer (G. C. E.) *Braunschweig Publisher. See* Sh— Merchant . . . 1836

Meynell *Editor. See* Sh— Works : Ext. 1904

Meyron *Engraver. See* Sh— Romeo, 1806

Michell (N.) Sh— festival, or the birth of the world's poet : An ode. 1864. 8° BM | BPL

Michie (Archibald) Nield (J. E.) & Horne (R. H.) Was Hamlet mad ? Being a series of critiques on the acting of the late Walter Montgomery : written in Melbourne in 1887. Ln : [1871]. 8° BUS

Mickle (Wm. Julius) Introduction to 'The Lusiad, or new discovery of India : An epic poem.' 1775
'When heaven decreed to soothe the feuds that tore
The wolf-eyed barons, whose unlettered rage
Spurned the fair muse, heaven bade on Avon's shore
A Sh— rise, and soothe the barbarous age.
A Sh— rose ; the barbarous heats assuage.
At distance due how many bards attend !
Enlarged and liberal from the narrow cage
Of blinded zeal, new manners wide extend,
And o'er the generous breast the dews of heaven descend.'

Middleton (Edward). *See* Middleton (Thomas)

Middleton (Thomas) An unknown pageant. Reprinted with introd. by J. L. Pearson. *See Sh*—] Sh— Scc.

] Blacke booke. Ln : Printed by T. C—— for Jeffrey Chorlton, 1604. Fcp. 4°. Partly in black letter
Illustrates 'Love's labours lost' in a reference to Bankes' horse.

Game of chess : [and] his son Edward Middleton. Ed. by T. Hornby. *See Sh*—] Sh— Soc.

Tragi-coomodie, called the Witch [an early transcript in the autograph of George Steevens. Manuscript upon forty-eight leaves of paper. c. 1770.] Fcp. 4°
Transcribed by Steevens from the original manuscript, formerly his, and now in the Malone collection. To this play Sh— was greatly indebted for the witchery scenes in 'Macbeth.'
See also Sh— Macbeth, 1674.

Tragi-coomodie, called the Witch [Edited from the original manuscript by Isaac Reed]. Ln : J. Nichols [1778]. 8°
BPL | BUS | SML | W
Impression restricted to 104 copies.
But for the preservation of the author's original manuscript in the Bodleian, this play would have been irrevocably lost.
This is the first known edition.

See Heywood
„ Pearson

Midsummer night's dream. *See* Sh— Midsummer . . .

'Midsummer night's dream' [Article in 'Edin. Review,' April]. 1848. 8°

'Midsummer night's dream' at the Prince's Theatre, Manchester : Notes by an old playgoer. 1901. 8° BPL

Midwinter (D.) *Publisher. See* Sh— Works, 1714

Mifflin (L.) After reading Sh— sonnets [Sonnet in 'At the gates of song,' p. 28]. 1901. 8° BPL

Milan, Italy. *See* Roosevelt

Miles (Alfred H.) Sh— reciter. *See* Sh— Works : Ext. 1886

Miles (George Hy.) Review of 'Hamlet.' Baltimore, 1870. 8° BM | BUS
Review of 'Hamlet.' Ln : Longmans, 1907. 8° BPL

Millar *Publisher. See* Sh— Othello, 1830

Millar (Andrew) *Publisher*—
See Fielding
„ Lennox
„ Sh— Coriolanus, 1749, 1762

Millar (J.) *New York Publisher. See* Sh— Sonnets, 1865, 1867

Millard (E.) *Editor. See* Sh— Works : Ext. 1894

Millard (J.) Sh— for schools. *See* Sh— Works : Ext. 1894

Millard (John) *Editor. See* Davis (J. B.)

Miller *New York Publisher. See* Sh— Works, 1856

Miller (George) Parishes of the diocese of Worcester ; Warwickshire. Ln : Griffith & Farran, 1889. 8°, pp. lxxxviii.-472 and map

Rambles round the Edge Hills and in the Vale of the Red Horse. Ln : E. Stock, 1900. 8°, pp. viii.-232. Illustrated SML
Contains a short Warwickshire glossary.

Miller (James)] Universal passion. *See* Sh— Much ado, 1737

Miller (John) *Publisher*—
See Sh— All's well, 1815
„ Sh— As you like it, 1815, 1825
„ Sh— Coriolanus, 1814
„ Sh— Cymbeline, 1815
„ Sh— Hamlet, 1814, 1825
„ Sh— Julius Cæsar, 1814
„ Sh— King Henry IV., i., 1815, 1824
„ Sh— King Henry IV., ii., 1815, 1821
„ Sh— King Henry V., 1815
„ Sh— King Henry VIII., 1815
„ Sh— King John, 1814, 1823
„ Sh— King Lear, 1815
„ Sh— King Richard II., 1815
„ Sh— King Richard III., 1814
„ Sh— Macbeth, 1814
„ Sh— Measure . . . 1815
„ Sh— Merchant . . . 1814, 1825
„ Sh— Merry devil . . . 1810
„ Sh— Merry wives, 1815
„ Sh— Midsummer . . . 1816
„ Sh— Much ado, 1815
„ Sh— Othello, 1794, 1814, 1825
„ Sh— Poems, 1821
„ Sh— Romeo . . . 1814

Miller (John) *Publisher*—
See Sh— Taming . . . 1815
,, Sh— The tempest, 1815
,, Sh— Twelfth night, 1815
,, Sh— Two gentlemen, 1815
,, Sh— Winter's tale, 1815
,, Sh— Works, 1815

Miller (Samuel) Brief retrospect of the eighteenth century . . . containing a sketch of the revolutions and improvements in science, arts, and literature during that period. Printed at New York. Ln: Reprinted for J. Johnson, St. Paul's Churchyard, by S. Hamilton, Shoe Lane, Fleet Street, 1805. 3 vols. 8°
Many references to Sh— in vol. 3. At pp. 48-49 gives an historical account of the editorship of Sh— in the eighteenth century.

Miller (T.) Sh—. *See* Sh—] Miller
Miller *C.I.E., LL.D.* (Wm.) ' Hamlet ' and the waste of life. Madras, 1902. 8°   BPL
'Macbeth' and the ruin of souls. Madras, 1901. 8°   BPL
'Othello' and the crash of character. Madras, 1903. 8°   BPL
Sh—'s 'King Lear' and Indian politics. Madras : Natesan, 1900. 8°
BPL | BUS | SML

Miller (Wm.) *Publisher. See* Sh— Works, 1798, 1806, 1811

Milles (Thomas) Catalogve of honor or tresvry of nobility pecvliar and proper to the Isle of Great Britaine . . . Ln : William Iaggard, 1610. F°, pp. xii.-1132. Woodcuts, coats of arms, and engravings by Renold Elstracke, etc.   BM | SML
' Awake, English nobility !
Let not sloth dim your honours new begot.'
                    —*King Henry VI.*

Milles (Thomas) *Editor. See* Mexia
Millington (E. J.) *Editor. See* Schlegel
Millingtcn (Thomas) *Publisher*—
See Chettle
,, Sh— King Henry V., 1600
,, Sh— King Henry VI., i., ii., iii., 1595, 1600
,, Sh— King Henry VI., ii., 1594, 1600
,, Sh— Titus, 1594

Milne (F. A.) *Editor. See* Gentleman's Magazine
Milne (J. T.) *See* Williams & Milne
Milnes (R. M.) Life of Keats. *See* Keats
Milton (John) Eikonoklastes : In answer to a book intitl'd 'Eikon Basilike.' Ln : M. Simmons, 1649. 8°
Many references to Sh— which illustrate not alone Charles the first's fondness for the dramatist, but also Milton's personal acquaintance with him, and, what is of equal importance, the familiarity with Sh— of the puritans, whom Milton particularly addressed (*See* pp. 10, 11).

Milton (John) Epitaph on the admirable dramatic poet, W. Sh— [In Sh—'s Comedies . . .] 1632. F°
' What needs my Sh— for his honoured bones
The labour of an age in piled stones ?
Or that his hallowed reliques should be hid
Under a starry-pointing pyramid ?
Dear son of memory, great heir of fame,
What need'st thou such dull witness of thy name ?
Thou in our wonder and astonishment
Has built thyself a lasting monument ;
For whilst to the shame of slow-endeavouring art
Thy easie numbers flow, and that each heart
Hath from the leaves of thy unvalued book
Those Delphic lines with deep impression took,
Then thou our fancy of itself bereaving
Dost make us marble with too much conceiving,
And so sepulchred in such pomp dost lie
That kings for such a tomb would wish to die.'
These lines were repeated, slightly varied, in the 1663-64 and 1685 folio editions of Sh—.

Paradise regain'd. A poem. To which is added 'Samson Agonistes' and Poems upon several occasions. Fifth edition. Ln : 1713. 12°. With plates   W
Facing the 'Epitaph . . . on Sh—,' at page 238, is a portrait of the national poet.

Songs. *See* Sh— Midsummer . . . 1755
Sports of the muses. *See* Sh— Works : Ext. 1752
Upon the effigies. *See* Sh— Works, 1632, 1663, 1664, 1685

Milton.] Milton or Sh—. Which was the greatest poet ? [In 'British Controversialist,' Vol. 4]. 1853. 12°   BPL
] Peck (Francis) New memoirs of the life . . . of John Milton. Ln : 1740. 4°
BM | BPL | BUS
Contains ' Explanatory . . . notes on Sh—'s plays' and a 'New catalogue of . . . Sh—'s writings,' pp. 22-264.

Milton (John)—
See Bicknell   *See* Salmasius
,, Coleridge   ,, Scott (E. J. L.)
,, Le Neve   ,, Sh—] Downes
,, Phillips (E.)   ,, Sh—] Three . . .

Mingle mangle, by ' Monkshood ': Caliban [In 'Bentley's Miscellany']. Ln : 1860. Roy. 8°   BUS

Mingle mangle, by 'Monkshood' : Romeo and Rosaline [In 'Bentley's Miscellany,' Feb.] Ln : 1860. Roy. 8°   BUS
On ' Romeo and Juliet.'

Minshul (Geffray) Essays and characters of a prison and prisoners. Ln : M. Walbancke . . . 1618. Fcp. 4°
Refers to Sh—.

Minto (William) Characteristics of English poets from Chaucer to Shirley. Edinburgh : Blackwood & Sons, 1874. 8°, pp. xii.-484
Sh— occupies pp. 333-421. At p. 350 the writer remarks :—' It is a favourite way with some eulogists of Sh— to deny him all individuality whatever. He was not one man, they say, but an epitome of all

(217)

men. . . . Against such a degradation of S—'s character, or of any man's character, it is our duty to protest.
On trying to make Sh— more than human, the reck-
less panegyrist makes him considerably less than
human. Instead of the man whose prudence made
him rich, whose affectionate nature made him loved
almost to idolatry, and whose genius has been the
wonder of the world, we are presented with plasticity
in the abstract, an object not more interesting than
a quarry of potter's clay.'

Miracle plays. *See* Religious drama

Mirror (The): A periodical paper. [Edited
by Henry Mackenzie.] Ln : 1782. 8° w
Vol. i., containing article 'On indecorum at the theatre
during the performance of " King Lear." '

Mirror (The): A periodical paper. Ln : 1782.
8°   BPL | W
Vol. ii., containing a critical article upon a scene in
' King Richard III.'

Mirror (The): A periodical paper. Ln : 1782.
8°   BPL | W
Vol. iii., embracing a criticism upon ' Hamlet.'

Mirror of literature, amusement, and instruction . . . Vol. 36. Ln : J. Limbird, 1840.
8°
Contains at p. 364 an article on Sh—'s ' Venus and
Adonis,' 1593, and the sale of Baron Bolland's unbound
copy in Nov., 1840, for £91 to Thorpe, the Ln. bookseller.

Mirror of princeley deedes and knighthood,
wherein is showed the worthinesse of the
Knight of the sunne and his brother
Rosicleer, etc. Translated out of the
Spanish. Ln : 1585-1601. Fcp. 4°, black
letter   w
Alluded to in ' King Henry IV.'

Mirror of the stage. Ln : 1823. 8°. With
full-length coloured portraits by I. R.
Cruikshank
Issued in 23 numbers.

Mirrour for magistrates. Wherein maye be
seen by example of other, with howe
greuous plages vices are punished, and
howe frayle and vnstable worldly pros-
perity is founde even of those whom
fortune seemeth most highly to fauor.
[By Wm. Baldwin, George Ferrers, Sir
Thomas Chaloner, — Caryl, John Skel-
ton, Thomas Sackville Earl of Dorset,
Thomas Churchyard, Francis Segar, John
Dolman, Richard Niccolls, and others.]
Imprinted at Ln. in Fletestrete nere to
Saynct Dunstan's Churche by Thomas
Marshe, 1558-63. 2 vols. Fcp. 4°. Black
letter   BM | CTC
A storehouse of tragical legends in verse, upon which
Sh— largely drew. The following headings will
suggest the connections—' How Queen Cordelia slew
herself,' ' Life and death of Julius Cæsar,' ' How
Shore's wife King Edward the Fourth's concubine
was punished,' ' Death of Edward the Fourth,'
' Murder of the Duke of Clarence,' ' Unfortunate
life of King John,' ' Life and death of Lord Cromwell,' ' Cardinal Wolsey how he rose and fell,' ' Lives
and deaths of the young Princes,' ' Death of Henry
VI.,' ' Tragical life and death of Richard III.'

The original edition (suppressed) was printed by J.
Wayland, probably in 1554 or 1555, at the end of his
ed. of Lydgate's ' Falls of Princes.'
For the authorship of the respective pieces, *see* W. F.
Trench's Dissertation on the ' Mirror.'

Mirrour for magistrates . . . Imprinted at
London for Thomas Marshe dwellynge in
Fleetstreete neare vnto S. Dustanes
Churche, 1571. Fcp. 4°, black letter, sig.
A to X4 on numbered folios   CTC

Mirrour for magistrates. [Ed. by John
Higgins & Wm. Baldwin.] At Ln. in
Fleetestreete by Henry Marsh, being
the assigne of Thomas Marsh, 1587. Fcp.
4°, black letter, sig. A to 2M8, omitting
Z, on numbered folios   CTC

Mirrour for magistrates . . . Newly inlarged
with a last part called 'A winter night's
vision,' being an addition of such tragedies especially famous as are exempted in
the former historie. With a poem annexed
called 'England's Eliza.' [Ed. by Richard
Niccols.]   Ln : Imprinted by Felix
Kyngston, 1610. Fcp. 4°, sig. A—3L6,
paged   BUS | CTC
Reprinted, with a new title-page, in 1619 and again in
1620.

'Misacmos' *pseud.* *See* Harington (*Sir John*)

Miscellaneous and fugitive pieces [including
several acknowledged and anonymous
writings of Dr. Samuel Johnson. Ed. by
T. Davies.] Ln : Printed for T. Davies,
and Cornan & Newbery, 1774. 3 vols. 8°
Contains, inter alia, ' Proposals for printing Sh—' and
' Sh – : A poem by Rob. Lloyd.'

Miscellaneous letters and essays. *See* Gildon

Miscellaneous observations on . . . 'Hamlet.'
See Johnson

Miscellaneous observations on 'Macbeth.' *See*
Johnson

Miscellaneous pieces of antient English poesie
See Sh— King John, 1764
,, Sh— Poems, 1764
,, Sh— Works : Ext. 1764

Miscellany of early notices of Sh—. *See Sh—*]
Manuscript

Misconceptions of Sh— upon the stage [In
'New England Mag.,' Dec.]   Boston,
1835. 8°   BUS

Misprints. *See* Halliwell

Mitchell *Publisher*—
See Sh— Merchant . . . 1850
,, Sh— Midsummer . . . 1855

Mitchell (Donald G.) English lands, letters,
and kings from Celt to Tudor. Ln : Low,
1890. 2 vols. 8°
Sh— referred to at p. 214, vol. i., and occupies pp.
32-85 of vol. ii.

Mitchell (J.) *Dublin Publisher.* *See* Sh—
Works, 1766

Mitchell (J.) *Newcastle-on-Tyne Printer & Publisher*—
See Sh— Coriolanus, 1825
,, Sh— King John, 1825
,, Sh— King Lear, 1825
,, Sh— Works, 1809
Mitcheson (W.) Essay on reading. Newcastle-on-Tyne, 1858. 8°   BPL
Mitford (John) Cursory notes on various passages in the text of Beaumont and Fletcher, as edited by . . . A. Dyce, and on his 'Few notes on Sh—.' Ln: J. R. Smith, 1856. 8°, pp. 56
    BM | BPL | BUS | CPL | MPL
Mitford (Wm.) *Bibliophile.* See Chamberlaine
Moberly (Charles E.) *Editor*—
See Sh— Antony . . . 1884
,, Sh— As you like it, 1872
,, Sh— Hamlet, 1870, 1873, 1880
,, Sh— King Henry V., 1880, 1884
,, Sh— King John, 1883
,, Sh— King Lear, 1871, 1876, 1883
,, Sh— Macbeth, 1869, 1872, 1881, 1883
,, Sh— Midsummer . . . 1881
,, Sh— Romeo . . . 1880
,, Sh— Works, 1872-83
Moberly (Mary Grafton) Hints for Sh— study exemplified in an analytical study of 'Julius Cæsar' . . . Cambridge: Deighton, 1881. 8°, pp. iv.-62, in printed wrappers
    BM | BPL
Modern British drama. *See* Sh— Antony . . . 1811
Modern characters from Sh—. *See* Sh— Works: Ext. 1778
Modern corruptions of Sh—'s text. Ln: Printed for private circulation, 1860. 8°, pp. 8   MPL
Moeser (L.) Few observations on . . . 'King Richard III.' 1868. Fcp. 4°   BM
Moffatt *Editor*—
See Sh— Macbeth, 1888
,, Sh— Merchant . . . 1875
Moffat (Andrew) *Publisher.* See Sh— Works, 1844
Moira (Gerald E.) *Artist. See Sh*—] Walter
Molière (J. B. P.)—
See Claretie
,, Coquelin
,, Mantzius
Molière and Sh—: An international review of the stage. No. 1, Oct. 29, 1858. 8°
    BPL
Molloy (C.) *Editor. See* Sh— Twelfth night, 1720
Molloy (J. Fitzgerald) Famous plays: their histories and authors. With a discourse by way of prologue on the playhouse of the Restoration. Ln: Ward, 1886. Cr. 8°   SML

Molloy (J. Fitzgerald) Life of Edmund Kean. *See* Kean
Life of Woffington. *See* Woffington
Romance of the Irish stage. With pictures of the Irish capital in the eighteenth century. Ln: 1897. 2 vols. 8°. With portraits of Mrs. Abington and Mrs. Jordan
Moltke (Max) *Editor*—
See Sh— Hamlet, 1869-71, 1880
,, Sh— Works, 1869
Mommsen (*Prof.* Tycho) *Editor*—
See Sh— Pericles, 1857
,, Sh— Romeo . . . 1859
,, Wilkins
'Momus Medlar' *pseud. See* Smith (James)
Monck.] Broadsides of speeches, songs, &c. delivered in the presence of General Monck, 1660. *See* Reprints
Moncrieff (W. T.) *pseud. of* W. Thomas. Excursion to Stratford-upon-Avon . . . With a compendious life of Sh— . . . account of the Jubilee. Leamington, 1824. 12°
    BM | BPL | CPL
Guide to Leamington [with 'Excursion to Stratford-upon-Avon,' pp. 202-250]. 1818. 12°   BPL
Sh—'s festival, or a new 'Comedy of errors.' A drama in two acts . . . With remarks [by Geo. Daniel]. Ln: T. Richardson [1830]. 12°. Frontispiece by Seymour (and portrait of R. W. Elliston as 'Rochester')   BPL | BUS | W
At one period the author was established as a bookseller in Leamington, the newly-discovered and fashionable Warwickshire watering-place.
Sh—'s festival, or a new 'Comedy of errors.' A drama. J. Cumberland [1831?] 12°
    BPL | MPL | SML
The 'Lear' of private life. A domestic melo-drama. [c. 1840.] 12°   BPL
Visitors' new guide to the Spa of Leamington Priors . . . Stratford-upon-Avon . . . with poetical illustrations . . . life of Sh— . . . Leamington: R. W. Elliston, 1824. 8°, pp. xii.-316-xii. With 13 plates and 2 maps
Money masters all things. *See* Menton (L.)
Mongan (R.) *Editor*—
See Sh— Othello, 1883
,, Sh— Works, 1883
'Monkshood' *pseud. See* Mingle-mangle
Monody to . . . Garrick. *See* Garrick
Monro (T.) Essays, Number XVII.: Materials for the critics still untouched in Sh—. 1790. 8°   BPL
Monson (Theodosia *Lady*) *Editor. See* Dudevant
Monson (*Sir* Thomas). *See* Sh— Works: Ext. 1600

Montagu (*Mrs.* Elizabeth) Apologie de Sh—.
Ln: 1777. 8°   BPL
] Essay on the writings and genius of Sh—
compared with the Greek and French
dramatic poets. With some remarks upon
the misrepresentations of Mons. de Voltaire. Ln: J. Dodsley, 1769. 8°, pp. iv.-
288 BM | BPL | BUS | CPL | MPL | SML | W
'The most elegant and judicious piece of criticism this
age has produced.'—*Warton.*
] Essay . . . Dublin: H. Saunders, 1769.
12°, pp. iv.-242   BM | BPL | W
'A rare edition, unnoticed in the various Sh— biblio-
graphies.'—*J. O. Halliwell.*
This is a slip. Lowndes mentions it on p. 2317.—*W. J.*
] Essay . . . Second edition. Ln: J. Dodsley,
1770. 8°, pp. iv.-288
                   BM | BPL | BUS | SML | W
] Essay . . . Third edition. Ln: E. & C.
Dilly, 1772. 8°, pp. iv.-288
              BM | BPL | BUS | CPL | SML | W
Essay . . . Fourth edition. To which are
now first added Three dialogues of the
dead. Ln: E. & C. Dilly, 1777. 8°,
pp. iv.-316   BM | BPL | BUS | SML | W
The first edition to reveal the authorship.
Large paper at BUS.
Essay . . . Dublin: J. Potts, 1778. 12°,
pp. vi.-242 and portrait   BUS
Essay . . . Fifth edition. Ln: C. Dilly,
1785. 8°, pp. iv.-316
              BM | BPL | BUS | SML | W
Essay . . . Sixth edition, corrected. Ln: R.
Priestley, 1810. 8°, pp. xxiv.-296
              BM | BPL | BUS | CPL | SML | W
Large paper copy, roy. 8°, at BUS and W.
Montagu.] Huchon (R.) Mrs. Montagu, 1720-
1800. Ln: 1907. Cr. 8°   BPL
On her 'Essay on Sh—,' p. 27-203.
Montagu (*Mrs.* Elizabeth). *See* Desenfans
Montague (Fannie S.) *Artist. See* Poole
Montaigne (Michael *Seigneur de*) Essayes or
morall, politike, and militarie discourses,
first written . . . in French and now done
into English by Iohn Florio. Ln:
Printed by Val. Sims for Ed. Blount,
1603. F°   BM
At page 102 occurs the phrase, 'music of the spheres,'
which Sh— is presumed to have used in 'The tem-
pest.'
A copy bearing Sh—'s autograph, the genuineness of
which has been questioned, is in the British Museum.
See Sh— Autograph.
Essayes . . . done into English by John
Florio. Ln: Bradwood, 1613. F°
The verses 'Concerning the honour of bookes,' ascribed
to Sh—'s pen at sig. A4, appeared here for the first
time.
See Bailey   *See* Gervais
  ,, Feis   ,, Robertson
Monte. Shakespearian swordsmanship [In
'Illustrated Sporting and Dramatic
News']. 1886. F°   BPL

Montégut (E.) *Editor*—
See Sh— Julius Cæsar, 1881
  ,, Sh— King Henry VIII., 1883
  ,, Sh— Macbeth, 1876, 1881
  ,, Sh— Othello, 1882
Montemart (Claude) *Editor. See* Sh— Poems,
1908
Montemayor (Jorge of) Diana . . . Translated
out of Spanish into English by Bartholo-
mew Yong . . . At Ln: Printed by Ed-
mund Bollifant, 1598. F°, sig. A—2S8,
paged   CTC
This old pastoral romance is credited with being the
foundation of 'Two gentlemen of Verona' and of
'Pyramus and Thisbe' in a 'Midsummer night's
dream.' The poetry with which it is bestrewn is
repeated in great part in 'England's helicon, 1600,'
and in Sir Philip Sidney's 'Arcadia.'
It is said to have been partly translated by Sir Philip
Sidney.
Diana. 1738. 12°   BPL
Shepherdess of Felismena, 1843. *See Sh—*]
Sh—'s library
A foundation of 'Two gentlemen of Verona.'
Story of the Shepherdess Felismena [Trans.
from 'Diana' by B. Yonge]. *See* Sh—
Two gentlemen, 1889
Montgomery (H. R.) Sh— forgery [In 'Literary
Impostures,' pp. 74-88]. 1884. 12° BPL
Montgomery (Philip *Earl of*) *Patron. See*
Sh— Works, 1623
Montgomery (Walter) *Actor. See* Michie
Montgomery (W. H.) Desdemona Waltz [In
'Italian Airs': Music]. [1860?] 4° BPL
Monthly mirror, reflecting men and manners,
with strictures on their epitome, the
stage. Ed. by E. Du Bois. Ln: 1795-
1810. 31 vols. 8°
With fine portraits in stipple of actors and actresses,
and biographies.
Monthly repository. *See* Hunt
Montreal Sh— Club. *See* Boodle
Montreal Sh— Club calendar: Feb. 1882 to
Dec. 1884. 1885. 12°   BPL
Monument to Sh—. *See Sh—*] Monument
Monumental bust of Sh—. *See* Britton
Moon (G. W.) *Editor. See* Sh— Merchant . . .
1887
Moon, Boys & Graves *Publishers. See* Sh—
Works, 1832
Moor (A) and an Amour. *See* Sh— Othello,
1856
Moor (J.) On the end of tragedy, according to
Aristotle. Glasgow, 1763. 12°   BPL
Moorat (Joseph) *Editor. See* Sh— The tem-
pest, 1908
Moore (A.) *Publisher. See* Epistle
Moore (A. M.) Sh— readings and their apolo-
gists. Geelong, 1868. 8°   MPL

Moore.] Smith (*Mrs.*) Life of Henry Moore

   This work contains a fresh Shakespearean anecdote :—
It is related that after John Wesley's death one of
his preachers had access to his library and found a
Sh— quarto annotated on the margins by Wesley
and designed for one of his friends. The zealous
vandal at once burnt the volume, and thus the world
lost some profoundly interesting comments.

Moore (H. L.) Baconian hypothesis [In 'The
   Gazette']. Lawrence, Kansas [U.S.] 1886-
   87. 4°   BPL

Moore (J. C.) *Publisher. See* Sh— Works, 1846

Moore (J. S.) *Editor—*
   See Sh— Poems, 1846
    ,,   Sh— Works, 1846

Moore (J. W.) *Philadelphia Publisher. See*
   Sh— Works, 1850

Moore (T.) *Dublin Publisher. See* Sh— King
   Henry IV., i., 1731

Moore (Thomas) Extracts. *See* Sh— Works :
   Ext. 1822
   Memoirs of Sheridan. *See* Sheridan

Moore (*Sir* T.) *See* More

Moore (T. Sturge) *Editor—*
   See Sh— Passionate . . . 1896
    ,,   Sh— Sonnets, 1899
    ,,   Sh— Works, 1900-03

Moorhead (Henry C.) Analysis of 'Macbeth'
   [In 'Graham's Magazine,' Sept.] Philad.,
   1850. 8°   BUS

Moorman (F. W.) Introduction to Sh—.
   'Teubner's School texts.' Ln : Nutt,
   1906. Cr. 8°

Moral character of Sh—. *See Sh*—] Moral

Moral play of wit and science. Edited by J. O.
   Halliwell. Ln : Sh— Soc., 1848. 8° BPL

Moral sentences. *See* Sh— Works : Ext. 1870

More *Editor. See* Sh— King Richard III., 1641

More (*Sir* Thomas) Life of Jane Shore. *See*
   Shore
   Tragicall historie of the life and reigne of
   Richard the Third. Ln : Printed by T.
   Payne for the Stationer's Company, 1641.
   12°   W
   Tragicall historie . . . [Ed. by S. W. Singer].
   Chiswick Press, 1821. 12°
   25 copies also printed on large paper, 8vo.
   See Levi
    ,, Sir Thomas More : a play

Moreau (John B.) Calendar of American
   chronology. *See* Sh— Works : Ext. 1872
   Events in the history of New York City.
   See Sh— Works : Ext. 1880, 1881

Morehead (R.)] Explanations and emendations of . . . the text of Sh— and of
   Beaumont & Fletcher. By 'Martinus
   Scriblerus.' Edinburgh : A. Constable,
   1814. 12°   BM | BPL | BUS
   'The present work hath cost me in printing no less
   a sum than £6 7s. 6¼d., which I have been tempted
   to throw away in the cause of literature and thus . . .
   supply the world with one hundred copies of this
   unrivalled morsel of criticism,' p. 155.

Morehead (R.)] Ode on dedicating a building
   and erecting a statue to Le Stue, cook to
   the Duke of Newcastle, at Claremont, with
   notes by ' Martinus Scriblerus.' To which
   are prefixed testimonies to the genius and
   merits of Le Stue. Ln : 1769. 4°
   A skit on Garrick's Jubilee Ode (*q.v.*)

Morel *Editor. See* Sh— Othello, 1884

Morell (J. D.) *Editor. See* Sh— Merchant . . .
   1878, 1880

Morell (T. H.) Catalogue of books relating to
   Sh— and the drama. New York, 1872.
   8°   BPL

Morgan. Humble remonstrances of Rice-ap-
   Meredith-ap-Morgan, 1652. Edited by
   J. O. Halliwell. Ln : 1861. 8°   BPL

Morgan (Aaron Augustus) Mind of Sh—. *See*
   Sh— Works : Ext. 1860, 1861, 1876, 1878,
   1894

Morgan (Horace H.) Shakespeariana [In 'The
   Western,' Sept.] St. Louis, 1876. 8° BUS
   Shakespeariana in the Mercantile Library
   [In 'The Western,' Aug.]. St. Louis, 1876
                             BUS
   Topical Shakespeariana [In 'The Western,'
   Nov. and Dec. 1876, Feb.-May, 1877].
   St. Louis, 1876-77.   BUS
   Topical Shakespeariana [In 'The Western'].
   St. Louis, 1876-79. 8°   BUS
   Topical Shakespeariana, or a collection of
   English Shakespeariana (exclusive of
   editions) arranged under headings to
   facilitate reference to special subjects of
   investigation. S. Louis : G. I. Jones &
   Co., 1879. 8°, pp. iv.-84 BM | BPL | BUS
   Reprinted from 'The Western' magazine.

Morgan (J.) *Philadelphia Publisher. See* Sh—
   Works, 1805-09

Morgan (James) Coriolanus travestie. *See*
   Sh— Coriolanus, 1846

Morgan (James Appleton)] Digesta Sh—ana ;
   being a topical index of books, reviews
   and magazine articles on Shakespearean
   subjects (exclusive of editions) from 1623
   to Jan. 1, 1898, with dates, authors, and
   publishers. New York Sh— Soc., 1886-
   87. 2 vols. 12°   BM | BPL
   First publisher of Sh—'s plays : Isaac
   Jaggard [In 'Catholic World,' Vol. 51,
   p. 428]. New York, 1890
   History of the Sh— text [In 'American
   Monthly']. Chicago, 1884. 8°   BPL
   Sh— in fact and in criticism. New York,
   1888. 12°   BPL | BUS
   Shakespearean chronology [In the 'Catholic
   World']. New York, 1896. 8°   BPL
   Shakespearean myth [In 'Appleton's Jour-
   nal,' Feb. and June]. New York, 1879
   On the Bacon-Sh— controversy.   BUS

Morgan (James Appleton) Shakespearean myth: Wm. Sh— and circumstantial evidence. Cincinnati: Clarke, 1881. 8°
BM | BPL | BUS | SML
Some Sh—· commentators. Cincinnati, 1882. 8°
BPL | BUS
Study in Warwickshire dialect. Fourth edition. New York Sh— Soc. New York, 1900. 12°
BPL
The same writer's 'Venus and Adonis' under a fresh title.
The society and the fad: An address to the NewYork Sh— Soc. 1890. Cr. 8° BPL
'Venus and Adonis.' A study in Warwickshire dialect. New York Sh— Society. New York, 1885. 8° BM | BPL
Morgan (J. A.) *Editor*—
See New Shakespeareana
,, Sh— Works, 1888-89
,, Sh— Works, 1908
Morgan (J. A.) *See* Rolfe (W. J.)
Morgan (M.) *Lichfield Publisher*. *See* Sh— Works, 1768
Morgan (Macnamara) *Editor. See* Sh— Winter's tale, 1754, 1762, 1767, 1784, 1792
Morgann (Maurice) Essay on the dramatic character of Sir John Falstaff. Ln: T. Davies, 1777. 8°, pp. iv.-viii.-186
BM | BPL | BUS | SML | W
A large paper copy also is at Boston.
An effort to whitewash Falstaff's character and courage. 'Forms a more honourable monument to the memory of Sh— than any which has been reared to him by the united labours of his commentators.'
—*Dr. Symmons.*
Essay . . . Ln: T. Boys, 1820. 8°, pp. xvi.-190
BUS | SML
Essay . . . Ln: 1822. 12° BPL
Essay . . . New edition. Ln: Wheatley & Adlard, 1825. 8°, pp. xvi.-190
BPL | BUS | MPL | SML | W
Essay . . . Ln: 1835. 8° CPL
Essay . . . Ln: Wm. Pickering, 1852. 8°
Essay. *See* Eighteenth . . .
] Sheep-shearing. *See* Sh— Winter s tale, 1762 *et seq.*
Morison (Mary) *Editor. See* Brandes
Morley *Journalist* (George) Destruction of Sh—'s greenwood [In Gonzalez's 'Avon Star,' *q.v.*] 1903. 4° BPL
] Guide to Leamington and its environs, including Warwick, Stratford-on-Avon and Kenilworth. Seventh edition. Ln: A. & C. Black, 1891. Cr. 8°. Maps and engravings
] Illustrated gossiping guide to 'leafy' Leamington, Warwick, Stratford-on-Avon, Kenilworth, Coventry. Leamington: A. E. Maisey, 1891. Cr. 8°. Illust.
In russet mantle clad: Scenes of rural [Warwickshire] life. Ln: Skeffington, 1897. 8°, pp. 196. Illust.

Morley *Journalist* (George) In rustic livery: Scenes of rural [Warwickshire] life. Ln: Dent, 1896. Cr. 8°, pp. 206
Rambles in Sh—'s land. Ln: Record Press [1893]. 12°, pp. 64 BPL | SML
Round Sh—'s table: A century of birth day festivals at Stratford-on-Avon. Birmingham, 1908. Cr. 8°, with portrait
BPL
First appeared in Gonzalez's 'Avon Star,' 1903 (*q.v.*)
Rustic's yuletide: Christmas scenes in Sh—'s greenwood [In 'Leamington Courier,' Dec. 22]. 1905. F°
Sh— commemorations again [In 'Poet Lore']. Philadelphia [c. 1890.] 8° BPL
Sh— commemorations during the Victorian dynasty [In 'Belgravia,' Vol. 82, p. 72]. Ln: 1893. 8° BM
Sh—'s greenwood: Customs of the country, language, superstitions, folk lore, birds, trees, parson, poets, novelist. Ln: D. Nutt, 1900. 12°, pp. xx.-280. Portrait and illustrations BPL | MPL
Sketches of leafy Warwickshire: rural and urban. Derby: Harpur, 1895. 4°, pp. 172 and 12 illustrations BPL
'Sh— worship' occupies pp. 61-67.
Sweet Arden: Book of the Sh— country. Edinburgh: Foulis, 1906 12°, pp. 190. Illustrated BPL
Sweet Audrey: Comedies of [Warwickshire] country life and town glamour. Norwich: Jarrold, 1897. Cr. 8°
Morley (*Prof.* Henry) Early papers, and some memories. Ln: 1891. 8°
Includes a chapter on Sh—.
English plays. Ln: 1878. 8° BUS
Contains a sketch of Sh—, with extracts from his plays.
Journal of a London playgoer, 1851 to 1866. Ln: Routledge, 1866. 8°, pp. 384 BPL
Reprinted in 1891.
Sh— and his time. *See* Sh—] Morley
Morley (*Prof.* Henry) *Editor*—
See English plays
,, Scott (*Sir* W.)
,, Sh— All's well, 1889, 1905
,, Sh— Antony, 1889, 1891
,, Sh— As you like it, 1886
,, Sh—· Comedy . . . 1889
,, Sh— Coriolanus, 1888
,, Sh— Cymbeline, 1888
,, Sh— Hamlet, 1886, 1891, 1893, 1898, 1904
,, Sh— Julius Cæsar, 1887, 1899, 1904
,, Sh— King Henry IV., i., 1888, 1905
,, Sh— King Henry IV., ii., 1888, 1905
,, Sh— King Henry V., 1888, 1895, 1904
,, Sh— King Henry VI., i., 1889, 1905
,, Sh— King Henry VI., ii., 1889, 1905
,, Sh— King Henry VI., iii., 1889, 1905

Morley (*Prof.* Henry) *Editor*—
See Sh— King Henry VIII., 1887, 1899,1905
,, Sh— King John, 1887, 1904
,, Sh— King Lear, 1888, 1904
,, Sh— King Richard II., 1888, 1899, 1903
,, Sh— King Richard III., 1889, 1898,1905
,, Sh— Love's ... 1889, 1890, 1905
,, Sh— Macbeth, 1886, 1889, 1904
,, Sh— Measure ... 1889, 1891, 1905
,, Sh— Merchant . . . 1886, 1897, 1898, 1899, 1904
,, Sh— Merry wives, 1888, 1897, 1904
., Sh— Midsummer ... 1886, 1894, 1904
,, Sh— Much ado, 1888, 1904
,, Sh— Othello, 1889, 1895, 1898, 1904
,, Sh— Pericles, 1889, 1905
,, Sh— Romeo ... 1888, 1889, 1898, 1904
,, Sh— Taming ... 1888, 1905
,, Sh— The tempest, 1887, 1904
,, Sh— Timon ... 1888, 1905
,, Sh— Titus ... 1889, 1905
,, Sh— Troilus ... 1889, 1905
,, Sh— Twelfth night, 1889, 1904
,, Sh— Two gentlemen, 1889, 1899, 1905
,, Sh— Winter's tale, 1887, 1892, 1905
,, Sh— Works, 1886-98, 1890, 1901
Morley (John & Thomas) *Composers. See* Sh—
Poems, 1709
Morning ramble, 1673. *See Sh*—] Sh—ana
Morphew (J.) *Publisher*—
See Shore
,, Warwick
Morris (Corbyn)] Essay towards fixing the true standards of wit, humour, raillery, satire, and ridicule. To which is added an analysis of the characters of an humourist, Sir John Falstaff, Sir Roger de Coverly, and Don Quixote. Ln : 1744. 8°   BPL | BUS | MPL | W
See Sh— King Richard II., 1873, 1875
,, Sh— Merchant ... 1874, 1877, 1878
,, Sh— The tempest, 1875
,, Sh— Works, 1873-75
Morris (Harrison S.) *Editor. See* Sh— Works : Ext. 1894
Morris (J. W.) John Lyly and English Euphuism. Bath : 'Chronicle' Office, 1879. 12°, pp. 28
Key notes of Sh—'s plays : 'The tempest,' 'King Henry V.,' 'Merchant of Venice.' Bath : C. Hallett, 1885. 12°   BPL | SML
Morris (M.) Hamlet and the mode.. stage [In 'Macmillan's Mag.'] 1892. 8°   BPL
Morris (Mowbray) Poets' walk. *See* Sh— Works : Ext. 1882
Morris (R.) Sermon preached at the tercentenary meeting of the Grammar School, Stratford upon-Avon : E. Adams [1864]. 12°   SML
See also Stratford : Grammar School.

Morris (Wm.) *Printer & Publisher. See* Sh— Poems, 1893
Morris dance—
See Dancing   *See* Sh— Works, 1838
,, Douce   ,, Sharp
,, Music
Morrison (A. J. W.) *Editor*—
See Schlegel
,, Ulrici
Morrison (G. E.) Othello's visage : A plea for a black Othello. Sh— Club paper. Stratford-on-Avon, 1908. 8°, pp. 8
Morrison (John) *Editor. See* Sh— Julius Cæsar, 1904
Morrison *jun.* (R.) *Perth Publisher. See* Sh— Works, 1798
Morrison (S.) British genius, with other poems. Manchester, 1845. 12°   BPL
Contains Sh— references.
Morse (W. H.) *Engraver. See* Sh— Midsummer ... 1870, 1887
Mortgage deed concerning the Blackfriars residence. 1612-13. *See* Sh— autograph
Mortimer (John Hamilton)] Sh—'s characters : A series of heads to illustrate Sh—. 1775-76. F°. Twelve plates. BPL | BUS
Sh—'s characters. Twelve plates, reduced by B. Reading. Ln : T. & H. Rodd, 1820. 2 parts. 8°. With 12 etchings   BUS
A few proof sets were issued in quarto.
Moryson (Fynes) Sh—'s Europe : Unpublished chapters of [an] itinerary, being a survey of . . . Europe at the end of the sixteenth century. With introd. and account of Moryson's career by Charles Hughes. 1903. Fcp. 4°. With facsimile
BPL
Moseley *Publisher* (Humphrey) [Catalogue with Sh— entries] Courteous reader . . . are . . . to be sold at his shop at the Prince's Armes in St. Paule's Churchyard, Ln : 1654. 8°, pp. 16
Moseley (Humphrey) *Publisher*—
See Cotgrave
,, Sh— Cardenio
,, Sh— Cupid's cabinet, 1645
,, Sh— Rape ... 1648
,, Shirley
,, Whitlock
Moser (Joseph) *Editor. See* Sh— As you like it, 1809
Moses and Son (E.) Tercentenary or . . . birthday of Sh—. Ln : 1864. 8°, pp. 30
BM | BPL | BUS | MPL
A Jewish tailor's advertisement.
Most easie instruction . . . *See* Horn book
Motives and struggles of Sh— in settling in London. *See* Sh—] Motives
Mott (J.) Old landmarks of Stratford-on-Avon : A scrip for pilgrims. 1893. 8°   BPL

Motte (B.) *Publisher.* *See* Sh— Poems, 1728

Mottley (John) List of all the dramatic authors, with some account of their lives and of all the dramatic pieces ever published in the English language to the year 1747. Also 'Scanderbeg, or love and liberty,' a tragedy, by Thomas Whincop. 1747. 8°. With portraits of dramatists, including Sh—, by N. Parr   BUS
Richard Farmer's copy, greatly annotated, with MS. notes and corrections (evidently prepared for a revised edition which never appeared), was sold at auction in Dec., 1905, for £13.
Whincop's 'Scanderbeg' formed an appendix to Mottley's work.

Moulin (Jurriaan) Analecta Shakespeariana. 1850-56. 2 vols. 4°   BUS
A collection of cuttings on the poet.

Catalogue of Sh—'s works translated into German. Kampen: M. P. Lughten, 1855. 8°

Moulton (C. W.) Wm. Sh—. *See Sh*—] Moulton

Moulton (Richard Green) Moral system of Sh—: A popular illustration of fiction as the experimental side of philosophy. Ln: Macmillan, 1903. Cr. 8°, pp. 392   BPL | BUS | MPL

On character development in Sh—, as illustrated by 'Macbeth' and 'King Henry V.' Ln: New Sh— Soc., 1880-86. 8°

On the humour of 'Love's labours lost' and 'As you like it.' Ln: New Sh— Soc., 1887-92. 8°

'Othello' as a type of plot. Ln: New Sh— Soc., 1887-92. 8°

Sh— as a dramatic artist: A popular illustration of the principles of scientific criticism. Oxford: Clarendon Press, 1885. 8°, pp. xii.-320   BM | BPL | BUS | SML

Sh— as a dramatic artist. Second edition. Oxford, 1888. 8°   BM | BPL | BUS

Sh— as a dramatic artist. Oxford: Clarendon Press, 1893. 8°   BM

Sh—'s 'Tempest' as an illustration of the theory of central ideas. Ln: New Sh— Soc., 1887-92. 8°

Some canons of character interpretation. Ln: New Sh— Soc., 1887-92. 8°

Syllabus . . . of six lectures on Sh—'s tragedies. Philadelphia, 1901. 8°, pp. 16   BUS

Mount Tabor. *See* Willis

Mountfort (William) Greenwich Park: A comedy. Ln: J. Hindmarsh at the Golden Ball in Cornhill, R. Bentley, A. Roper at the Mitre in Fleet Street, and Randal Taylor near Stationer's Hall, 1691. Fcp. 4°
Mentions Sh— and 'Hamlet' in dedication.

Mountfort (William) Henry the Second, King of England, with the death of Rosamond. A tragedy. Acted at the Theatre Royal by their majesties servants. Ln: Printed for Jacob Tonson at the Judges Head in Chancery Lane, near Fleet Street, 1693. Fcp. 4°
Illustrates 'King Henry VI.'
See Hull; also Ireland, for same subject and title.

King Edward the Third, with the fall of Mortimer, Earl of March. An historical play. Ln: J. Hindmarsh, 1691. Fcp. 4°
The prologue refers to Sh— and Ben Jonson.

Moutray (Charles) Personal courage of Macbeth [In 'Ainsworth's Mag.,' Nov.] Ln: 1851. 8°   BUS

Mowatt (Anna Cora) Autobiography of an actress, or eight years on the stage. Boston [U.S.]: Ticknor, Reed & Fields, 1854. Cr. 8°, pp. 448 and steel portrait
Sh— and Stratford occur at pp. 304-305.
Describes theatrical life in various parts of the globe, including America and Britain.

Moxon (E.) *Publisher*—
See Sh— Poems, 1840
  ,,   Sh— Sonnets, 1830
  ,,   Sh— Winter's tale, 1847
  ,,   Sh— Works, 1838, 1842, 1844, 1848, 1852, 1857, 1880

Moyes (John) Medicine and kindred arts in the plays of Sh—. *See* Sh— Works: Ext. 1896

Moyle. *See* Dennis

Moyse (C. E.) Dramatic art of Sh—. Montreal, 1879. 8°   BPL

Mozart *Composer.* *See* Sh— Comedy . . . 1819

Mucedorus. *See* Sh— Mucedorus

Much ado about nothing. *See* Much ado . . .

Mulberry tree: A tale. *See Sh*—] Collection

Mulcaster (Richard) Positions, wherin those primitive circumstances be examined which are necessarie for the training up of children, either for skill in their booke or health in their bodie . . . Ln: Thomas Vautrollier, 1581. Fcp. 4°   BUS | W
Mulcaster is supposed by Bright to be the Holofernes of 'Love's labours lost.'

Mulgrave (*Earl of*). *See* Sheffield

Mull (Mathias) 'Hamlet' . . . : Supplementary notes . . . to my edition of the play. Ln: K. Paul, 1888. 8°   BM | SML

Sh—: [Emendations on certain passages]. [1883.] 8°   BM

Mull (M. *Editor*—
See Sh— Hamlet, 1885-88
  ,,   Sh— Julius Cæsar, 1890
  ,,   Sh— Macbeth, 1889
  ,,   Sh— Works, 1885-89

Müller (*Dr.* R.) *Editor.* *See* Sh— Merchant . . 1868

Mullick (S. C.) *Editor*—
 See Sh— King Henry VIII., 1878
 ,, Sh— Works, 1878
Mulligan *New York Publisher. See* Sh—
 Works, 1856
Mullins (John D.) Catalogue . . . *See* Dent
 (R. K.)
Mulready (Wm.) *Artist*—
 See Sh— As you like it, 1840
 ,, Sh— Works : Ext. 1807, 1810
'Multum in parvo' *pseud.* Who wrote Sh— ?
 [c. 1891.] 4° ᴮᴹ
Mulvany (Alicia M.)] Alicia's diary, with Sh—
 criticisms. 1907. 8° ᴮᴾᴸ
Munday ? (Anthony) Comedy of the two
 Italian gentlemen. *See* Literature
 John - a - Kent and John - a - Cumber : A
 comedy . . . With other tracts . . . Introd.
 and notes by J. P. Collier. *See Sh*—]
 Sh— Soc.
Munday (A.) *Editor. See* Stowe
Munday *pseud.* 'Lazarus Piot' (Anthony)
 Editor. See Busche
Munday (Anthony)—
 See Collier (J. P.)
 ,, Sh— Sir John Oldcastle (*heading*)
Mundell *Edinburgh Publisher. See* Sh—
 Poems, 1793
Munden.] Memoirs of Joseph Shepherd Mun-
 den, comedian, by his son. Ln : 1844.
 Cr. 8°. With portrait
] Saker (Horatio) Memoirs of John Shepherd
 Munden, comedian. Ln : 1858
Munro (H.) The poor player : A story . . .
 Ln : W. Richards, 1858. 12° ꜱᴍʟ
Munro (J.) *Editor. See* Sh— Works, 1908
Munro (John)—
 See Furnivall & Munro
 ,, Sh—] Sh— allusion book
Munro (J. J.) Essex's entry into London [In
 'Athenæum,' No. 4235, p. 819, Dec.]
 1908
 Illustrates ' King Richard II.'
Munro (J. J.) *Editor. See* Bandello & Brooke
Munroe & Francis *Boston, U.S., Publishers*—
 See Sh— Poems, 1812
 ,, Sh— Works, 1802-04, 1807, 1810-12
Murden (A.) *Publisher. See* Sh— Poems, 1760
Murden (E. M.) *New York Publisher. See*
 Sh— Othello, 1826
Murder of Lord Bourgh, and Arnold Cosby's
 verses, 1591. *See* Reprints
 Illustrates ' Arden of Feversham.'
Murdoch (J. E.) Short study of 'Hamlet' [In
 'Poet lore']. Philadelphia, 1891. 8° ᴮᴾᴸ
 The stage : Recollections of actors and
 acting. Philadelphia, 1880. 8° ᴮᴾᴸ
Murdoch (J. G.) *Publisher. See* Sh— Works,
 1876
Murphy (A.) Life of Garrick. *See* Garrick

Murphy (A.) *See* Garrick, Colman & Murphy
Murphy (James) Extracts. *See* Sh— Works :
 Ext. 1822
Murquardt (C.) *Publisher. See* Sh— Works,
 1842
Murray *Edinburgh Printer. See* Sh— Works,
 1753
Murray (G. G. A.) *Editor. See* Sh— King
 Henry IV., ii., 1886
Murray (John) *Publisher*—
 See Hall (S.)
 ,, Historian . . .
 ,, Richardson
 ,, Sh— Works, 1790
 ,, Sh— Works : Ext. 1778
Murray & Highley *Publishers. See* Sh—
 Works, 1798
Music and dancing—

See Arne	*See* Lyric
,, Aylward	,, Matthews
,, Banks (G. L.)	,, Naylor
,, Barr	,, New Sh— Soc.
,, Bickerstaff	,, Nicolai
,, Birmingham	,, Noble
,, Byrd	,, Novello
,, Caulfield	,, Oliphant
,, Chappell	,, Playford
,, Charms	,, Purcell
,, Clare	,, Ravenscroft
,, Collection	,, Rimbault
,, Cox	,, Ritson
,, Critical	,, Roffe
,, Dibdin	,, Sh— Hamlet, c.
,, Evans	1800
,, Falstaff Club	,, Sh—Poems, 1660,
,, Garrick	1660 - 67, 1709,
,, German	1750, 1790, 1800,
,, Gilbert	1808, 1813, 1815,
,, Glover	1850, 1886, 1900
,, Greenhill	,, Sh— T w e l f t h
,, Guernsey	n i g h t, 1740,
,, Hutchinson	1766, 1800, 1820
,, Lawreen	,, Sh— Two gen-
,, Lee	tlemen, 1800
,, Linley	,, *Sh*—] Sh—Album
,, Linley & Bowles	,, Sidgwick
,, Linley & Law-	,, Songs
rence	,, Vocal
,, List . . .	,, White
,, Locke	

Music halls—
 See Headlam
 ,, Stage
Music Publishing Co. *See* Sh— Merchant . . .
 1830
Musical miscellany ; being a collection of
 choice songs, set to the violin and flute.
 1729. 6 vols. 8°. With engravings by
 Vanderbank
 Contains several songs from Sh—.

Muskett (C.) *Norwich Publisher.* *See* Sh—
Macbeth, 1853
Muster roll of able men. *See* Stratford-on-
Avon
My flocks feed not. *See* Bodenham (J.)
My notes on Sh—. *See* Gray
Mynne (Richard) *Publisher.* *See* Randolph
Mystery plays. *See* Religious drama
Mythology. *See* Superstition

——— (G. S.) Sh— diary
a n d almanack.
1869. 8° BPL
N——— (I.) *Printer*—
See Chettle
„ Sh— Pericles,
1630
„ Wilkins
N——— (S.) *See* Neil
(S.)

N——— (S.) *Editor*—
See Sh— Poems, 1710
„ Sh— Venus . . . 1710
„ Sh— Works, 1710
N——— (T.) *Printer*—
See Donne   *See* Durfey
„ Dryden   „ Fane
N——— (T.) *Publisher.* *See* Sh— Faire Em,
1605, 1635
N——— (W.) Critical remarks on the 'Othello'
of Sh— [In 'The Bee']. Edin., 1791.
8°   BUS
Nabbes (Thomas) Tottenham Court: A
pleasant comedy. Acted at the private
house in Salisberie Court. Ln: R. Oulton,
1639. Fcp. 4°
Refers to Sh— and Ben Jonson in Act III., Scene I.
Nares *Archdeacon* (Robert) Glossary; or
collection of words, phrases, names, and
allusions to customs, proverbs, etc. which
have been thought to require illustration
in the works of English authors, particularly Sh— and his contemporaries. Ln:
R. Triphook, 1822. 4°, pp. viii.-584
BM | BUS | CPL | MPL
A few were done on fine paper.
Glossary . . . Stralsund, 1825. 8°   BM
Glossary . . . New edition, with consider-
able additions by J. O. Halliwell and T.
Wright. Ln: J. R. Smith, 1859. 2 vols.
8°   BUS | HCL | MPL
Halliwell added between five and six thousand fresh
entries.
Glossary . . . Ed. by J. O. Halliwell. Ln:
J. R. Smith, 1867. 2 vols. 8°   BUS
Glossary . . . Edited by J. O. Halliwell.
1872. 2 vols. 8°   BPL
Glossary . . . Ed. by Halliwell and Wright.
Ln: 1876. 2 vols. 8°   BPL

Nares *Archdeacon* (Robert) Glossary . . . 1888.
8°   BM | SML
Nash *or* Nashe (Thomas) Anatomy of absur-
dity, 1589. *See* Reprints
Attributed poem. Ed by G. L———. *See*
Sh—] Sh— Soc.
Attributed poems contained in Dowland's
'Songs or Ayres, 1600.' Ed. by T. J.
Scott. Ln: Sh— Soc., 1845. 8°   BPL
Pierce Penniless's supplication to the Devil.
From the first edition of 1592, compared
with later impressions. With introd.
and notes by J. P. Collier. Ln: Sh—
Soc., 1842. 8°, pp. xxii.-108
BM | BPL | BUS
Sh—'s Puck: Lines illustrative of a passage
in 'A midsummer night's dream.' *See*
Sh—] Sh— Soc.
] Spanish Mandevile of miracles, or garden of
curious flowers. Whereupon are handled
sundry points of humanity, philosophy,
divinitie and geography, beautified with
many strange and pleasant histories.
Trans. by Lewis Lewkenor. Ln: 1600.
Fcp. 4°
'One of the collateral helps which served our dramatist.'
—*W. C. Hazlitt.*

Nash (Thomas)—
See Chettle
„ Cunningham
„ Heywood
„ Sh— Arraignment (*heading*)
Nash *Sh—'s grandson* (Thomas)—
See Hall (*Dr.* John)
„ Scott (E. J. L.)
Nash family. *See* Bellew
Nasmith (D.) Sh—. *See* Sh—] Nasmith
National library of entertainment and in-
struction. [c. 1840.] 12°   BPL
Sh—, pp. 159-160, 456-462.
National Sh— Committee and the late Mr.
Thackeray [Reprinted from the 'Illus-
trated Times,' 'Morning Star,' 'London
Review,' etc.] Ln: J. Clayton [1864].
8°, pp. 24   BM | BPL | BUS
Nationalities of Sh— [In the 'Old College,'
pp. 118-130]. Glasgow, 1869. 8°   BPL
Nattali *Publisher.* *See* Sh—Works, 1825
Nayler (B. S.) Review of the English per-
formances of Sh—'s plays in Amsterdam.
Amsterdam, 1826. 8°   BPL
Time and truth reconciling the . . . world
to Sh—. *See* Sh—] Nayler
Naylor (E. W.) Sh— and music. With illus-
trations from music of the 16th and 17th
centuries. Ln: Dent, 1896. 16°, pp.
238   BM | BPL | SML
Neagle *Engraver*—
See Sh— Comedy . . . 1808
„ Sh— King John, 1806
„ Sh— Works, 1803, 1805, 1807

Neale (J. P.) Views in Stratford-upon-Avon Church in Warwickshire, containing the monument of the immortal Sh—, etc. 1825. 8°

Needham (Marchamont) *Editor. See* Mercurius Britannicus

Needler (Henry) Works . . . poems, translations, essays and letters. Ln : 1728. 12°
BPL
At p. 20 occurs a ' Prologue to " Julius Cæsar." '

Neele (Hy.) Lectures on English poetry. Second edition. Ln : 1830. 8°　BUS
The third lecture treats of Sh—.

Lectures on the literary merits of Sh—, with critical remarks on his contemporary dramatic poets. Manuscript. c. 1825. F°　BUS

Lectures on the literary merits . . . Second edition. Manuscript. 1830. F°　BUS

Sh—'s supernatural characters. 1839. 12°
BPL

Neele (Henry) *Editor—*
See Sh— The tempest, 1824
　,, Sh— Twelfth night, 1824
　,, Sh— Two gentlemen, 1824
　,, Sh— Works, 1824

Neely *Publisher. See* Sh— Works, 1818

Neil (Samuel) Biography . . . *See* Sh—] Neil
Home of Sh—. Illustrated by F. W. Fairholt. Warwick : H. T. Cooke [1871]. 8°, pp. 80. With wood engravings　BM

Home of Sh—. Fifth edition. Warwick, 1891. Cr. 8°　BPL

Home of Sh—. Seventh edition. Warwick, 1893. Cr. 8°　BPL

Home of Sh—. Eighth edition. Warwick : H. T. Cooke, 1890. 12°　SML

Sh— : A critical biography. *See* Sh—] Neil

] Sh— controversies [In the 'British Controversialist,' pp. 241-255]. 1864. 12° BPL

Teaching of Sh— in schools [In 'The Schoolmaster']. 1879. F°　BPL

Neil (Samuel) *Editor—*
See Sh— As you like it, 1876
　,, Sh— Hamlet, 1877
　,, Sh— Julius Cæsar, 1877
　,, Sh— King Henry V., 1878
　,, Sh— Macbeth, 1876
　,, Sh— Midsummer . . . 1878
　,, Sh— Romeo . . . 1879
　,, Sh— Works, 1873-75, 1879

Neilson (W. A.) *Editor. See* Sh— Works, 1906

Neist (G. V.) *Engraver. See* Sh— Coriolanus, 1762

Nelson (T.) Handbook : Sh— and his birthplace. Ln : Nelson, 1859. 12°, pp. viii.-128 and 12 coloured plates　BPL

Nelson (W.) *Publisher—*
See Sh— Poems, 1760
　,, Sh— Works, 1753

Nepos (Cornelius). *See* Plutarchus

Nero.] Tragedie of Claudius Tiberius Nero, Rome's greatest tyrant. Truly represented out of the purest records of those times. Ln : Francis Burton, 1607. 8° w
' This play is quoted in the Variorum Sh—.'
　　　　　　　—*J. O. Halliwell.*
Nero is referred to in ' Hamlet,' ' King Henry VI.,' ' King John,' and ' King Lear.'

Nesbit *Engraver. See* Sh— Works, 1807

Nesbit *aft.* Bland (Edith) Children's Sh—. *See* Sh— Works : Ext. 1895, 1899, 1900, 1901

Nesbit (E.) *Editor. See* Sh— Works, 1897

Neve. *See* Le Neve

Neville (H.) The stage : its past and present in relation to fine art. Ln : Bentley, 1875. 8°　BPL | SML

New (E.) *Publisher. See* Sh— Works, 1740, 1745, 1747

New (Edmund H.) *Artist—*
See Tompkins
　,, Windle

New (J.) *Publisher. See* Sh— Macbeth, 1750

New academy of compliments. *See* Sh— Poems, 1669

New and merry prognostication ; being a metrical satire supposititiously assigned to Will Summers the Jester, and three others. Now first reprinted from the very rare edition of 1623. Ed. by J. O. Halliwell. Ln : 1860. 8°　BUS
Limited to thirty copies.

New comic annual, by 'Falstaff.' Ln : Hurst, Chance & Co., 1831. 8°, pp. xvi.-192. Illust.　BUS
Contains ' Falstaff's Festival ' and plate.

New England Historic-Genealogical Society : Tercentenary celebration of the birth of Sh— at Boston, Mass., April 23 . . . Boston, U.S : Privately printed . . . by G. C. Rand & Avery, 1864. 8°, pp. 72
BPL | BUS
Twenty-five copies were printed on large paper and 275 on small.
Includes an Address by J. F. Clarke, Remarks and Ode by John H. Sheppard, and Essay by F. W. Holland.

New English Theatre . . . [Collection of plays]. Ln : 1776-77. 12 vols. 8°. With character portraits

New exegesis of Sh— : Interpretation of his principal characters and plays on the principle of races. Edinburgh : A. & C. Black, 1859. 8°, pp. viii.-388
BM | BPL | BUS | CPL | MPL | SML | W
Includes matter on the supernatural machinery of the poet.

New exegesis of Sh— [Review in 'North British Review,' Nov.] Edin., 1859. 8°
BUS

New Monthly Magazine and Literary Journal,
Vol. 6. Ln: Colburn, 1822. 8°
At p. 162 gives transcript of a letter (forged by
Ireland) of Sh— to Anne Hathaway, and at p. 448
particulars of a portrait in oils of Sh—, found upon a
pair of bellows, in the possession of Talma the French
tragedian.

New Orleans Daily Picayune. Comus edition.
New Orleans, 1898. F°

New Orleans.] Proceedings of the Sh— entertainment at the Grand Opera House.
New Orleans, 1894. 4°　　　　BPL

] Proceedings of the Sh— entertainment
given by the . . . Association on April 23,
1894, 330th anniversary of Sh—'s birthday. Sh— Anniversary Association.
New Orleans [U.S.] 1894. 4°　　BM

New pantomime entertainment called Sh—'s
choice spirits, or Falstaff in pantomime.
1763. Manuscript. 8°　　　　BUS
Performed at Sadler's Wells in 1763 and 1768.
Unpublished, so far as is known.

New Place, Stratford—
See Bellew　　　　*See* Oswald
　,, Hall (E.)　　　　,, Stratford-on-Avon
　,, Halliwell
New readings of old authors. *See* Seymour
New Sh— gallery. *See* Boydell
New Sh— Society: Publications. Ln:
[Privately printed for the members],
1874-84. 8° and 4°:—

Series I.: Transactions, Nos. I.-II., 1874, 8°.
i.-ii. Fleay (F. G.) Metrical tests as applied
to dramatic poetry
iii. Fleay (F. G.) Authorship of ' Taming
of the Shrew,' with appendix on
'Titus Andronicus.'
iv. Fleay (F. G.) Authorship of 'Timon
of Athens'
iv.B. Fleay (F. G.) On 'Pericles'
v. Hales (J. W.) On the Porter in 'Macbeth'
vi. Fleay (F. G.) On plays of Sh— of
which portions were written at different periods of his life
vii. Fleay (F. G.) On two plays of Sh—'s,
the versions of which as we have
them are the results of alterations
by other hands: 'Macbeth' and
'Julius Cæsar'
viii. Halliwell (J. O.) Hint on the date of
'Coriolanus'
ix. Simpson (R.) Political use of the
stage in Sh—'s time
x. Simpson (R.) Politics of Sh—'s historical plays
xi. Ingram (J. K.) On the weak endings
of Sh—
xii. Malleson (W. T.) & Seeley (J. R.)
Which are Hamlet's 'dozen or sixteen lines'?

New Sh— Society: Publications—
Transactions, Nos. I.-II.: Appendix.
i. Spedding (J.) Shares of Sh— and
Fletcher in 'Henry VIII.'
ii. Hickson (S.) Shares of Sh— and
Fletcher in the 'Two noble kinsmen'
iii. Roderick. On the metre of 'Henry
VIII.'
First report of the Society's com-
mittee, July, 1875

Transactions, Nos. III.-IV., 1875-76.
i. Spedding (J.) On the corrected edition of 'Richard III.'
Pickersgill (E. H.) On the quarto and
folio of 'Richard III.'
ii. Delius (N.) On the quarto and folio
of 'King Lear'
iii. Simpson (R.) On evening mass in
'Romeo and Juliet'
iv. Simpson (R.) On some plays attributed to Sh—
v. Smith (Lucy Toulmin) On the bond
story in 'Merchant of Venice' and
a version of it in 'Cursor Mundi'
vi. Legg (J. W.) Note upon the 'elf-
locks' in 'Romeo and Juliet'
vii. Charlemont (*Countess of*) Gruach
('Lady Macbeth')
viii. Foggo (A.) On the character of
'Banquo'
ix. & xii. Delius (N.) On Sh—'s use of narration in his dramas
x. Lee (*Miss* Jane) On authorship of
second and third parts of 'King
Henry VI.'
xi. Gardiner (S. R.) Political element in
Massinger

Transactions, Nos. III.-IV.: Appendixes.
i. Sh—'s dramatic art
ii. Forman (*Dr.* S.) Book of plays, or
notes in 1611
iii. White (R. G.) On the confusion of
time in the 'Merry wives'
iv. Appian's Chronicle, 1578: Speeches
of Brutus and Antony
v. Matthew (F. D.) Account of the
German Sh— Society's Jahrbuch,
1876
vi. Genée (R.) Collation of Marlowe's
'Edward II.,' 1594, with Dyce's
text of 1850
vii. Thimm (F.) List of Shakespeareana
since Jan. 1, 1874

Transactions, Nos. 5, 6, 7, 1877-79.
i. Rose (E.) Division into acts of 'Hamlet'
ii. Spedding (J.) Division of the acts in
'King Lear,' 'Much ado,' and
'Twelfth night'

New Sh— Society : Publications—

Transactions, Nos. 5, 6, 7, 1877-79.

   iii. Spalding (T. A.) On the witch scenes in 'Macbeth'

   iv. Daniel (P. A.) Halpin's time analysis of 'Merchant of Venice'

   v. Spalding (T. A.) On the first quarto of 'Romeo and Juliet'

   vi. Coote (C. H.) Sh—'s new map [in 'Twelfth night']

   vii. Scraps

viii., ix., x. Daniel (P. A.) Time analysis of plots of Sh—'s plays

   xi. Hagena (*Prof.*) Introductory scene of second part of 'Henry IV.'

   xii. Phipson (*Miss* E.) Natural history similes in 'Henry VI.'

   xiii. Kirkman (J.) Animal *versus* human nature in 'King Lear'

   xiv. Ruskin (J.) On 'Yon grey lines that fret the clouds' in 'Julius Cæsar'

   xv. Ingleby (C. M.) On Hamlet's 'Some dozen or sixteen lines'

   xvi. Overend (G. H.) On the dispute between George Maller and Thomas Arthur

   xv. Harrison (W. A.) Hamlet's 'Juice of cursed hebona'

   xvi. Boyle (R.) On Wilkins' share in Sh—'s 'Pericles'

   xvii. Nicholson (B.) Was Hamlet mad ?

   xviii. Boyle (R.) On Massinger and the 'Two noble kinsmen'

   xix. Latham (*Miss* G.) O 'poor Ophelia !'

   xx. Ziolecki (*Dr.*) Shakspere in Poland, Russia and other Slavonic countries

   xvii. Furnivall (F. J.) On Puck's 'Swifter than the moon's sphere' and Sh—'s astronomy

   xviii. Furnivall (F. J.) On Chester's 'Love's martyr'

   xix. Pulling (F. S.) Speech-ending test applied to twenty of Sh—'s plays

   xx. Scraps

   xxi. Thimm (F.) Sh— literature, 1876 to 1879

Transactions, Nos. 5, 6, 7 : Appendix.

   i. Wager. Cruell debtter, 1566; The only three leaves left

   ii. Sh—'s Four and a half yards of cloth on March 15, 1603-4

   iii. Wilson (*Prof.*) Solution of the mystery of double-time in Sh—

   iv. Matthew (F. D.) German Sh— Society's Year Book, Vol. XI.-XIV. Second report, Aug., 1879

Transactions, Nos. 8, 9, 10, 1880-86.

   i. Rose (E.) Sudden emotion

New Sh— Society : Publications—

Transactions, Nos. 8, 9, 10, 1880-86.

   ii. Nicholson (B.) Hamlet's 'cursed hebenon'

   iii. Rose (E.) Inconsistency of time in Sh—'s plays

   iv. Nicholson (B.) Sh— and sea-glasses

   v. Nicholson (B.) Kemp and the play of 'Hamlet' : Yorick & Tarlton

   vi. Ellacombe (H. N.) Seasons of Sh—'s plays

   vii. Nicholson (B.) Relation of the quarto to the folio version of 'Henry V.'

   viii. Nicholson (B.) Number of witches in 'Macbeth,' and a note on 'King John'

   ix. Tanger (G.) First and second quartos and first folio of 'Hamlet'

   x. Nicholson (B.) On four passages in 'King Henry V.'

   xi. Bayne (P.) Mr. Spedding's proposed arrangement of acts in 'King Lear'

   xii. Dow (J. G. A.) Notes on 'All's well'

   xiii. Landmann (F.) Sh— and Euphuism

   xiv. Boswell-Stone (W. G.) 'As you like it' and Lodge's 'Rosalynde' compared

   xxi. Boyle (R.) 'King Henry VIII.' : An investigation into the origin and authorship of the play

   xxii. Greenstreet (J.) Documents relating to the players at the Red Bull, Clerkenwell, and the Cockpit in Drury Lane, in the time of James I.

   xxiii. Brooke (Stopford A.) 'King Richard III.'

   xxiv. Sharpe (H.) Prose in Sh—'s plays : Tables showing whether each person speaks in prose or metre in each scene in 'Much ado' and 'Hamlet'

   xxv. Moulton (R. G.) On character development in Sh— as illustrated by 'Macbeth' and 'King Henry V.'

   xxvi. Boyle (R.) Beaumont, Fletcher, and Massinger

   xxvii. Sullivan (*Sir* E.) Hamlet's age

Transactions, Nos. 8, 9, 10 : Appendices.

   i. Number of lines in Sh—'s works

   ii. Inventory A.D. 1674 of the goods of Sir J. Barnard

   Record of letters of administration to Sir John Barnard's goods, 1674

   Pedigree of Sh—'s grand-daughter and her husband's children

   iii. Elizabeth (Queen) Proclamation as to licenses for interludes

New Sh— Society : Publications—

Transactions, Nos. 8, 9, 10 : Appendices.

iv.-vii. Programme of the Society's musical entertainments, 1883-86
Words of the songs, catches, ballads sung May 14, 1886
Treasurer's cash accounts, 1883-85
Abstract of proceedings, Oct. 14, 1881 to June 11, 1886

Transactions, Nos. 11, 12, 13, 1887-92.

i. Levi (S. L.)] Topical side of the Elizabethan drama, by 'S. Lee'
ii. Moulton (R. G.) Sh—'s 'Tempest' as an illustration of the theory of central ideas
iii. Latham (*Miss* G.) On Volumnia
iv. Latham (*Miss* G.) Some of Sh—'s waiting women
v. Moulton (R. G.) Some canons of character interpretation
vi. Levi (S. L.)] Elizabethan England and the Jews, by 'S. Lee'
vii. Dawson (B.) Sh—'s accentuation of proper nouns
viii. Herford (C. H.) Suggestions on Greene's romances and Sh—
ix. Tyler (T.) Sh— idolatry
Wheatley (H. B.) On a contemporary drawing of the Swan Theatre, 1596
xi. Poel (W.) Stage version of 'Romeo and Juliet'
xii. Moulton (R. G.) On the humour of 'Love's labours lost' and 'As you like it'
xiii. Greenstreet (J.) Whitefriars Theatre in the time of Sh—
xiv. Latham (*Miss* G.) Rosalind, Celia, and Helen
xv. Latham (*Miss* G.) Julia, Silvia, Hero, and Viola
xvi. Phipson (*Miss* E.) Sh—'s references to natural phenomena
xvii. Dorchester (*Prof.*) Character of Hamlet
xviii. Latham (*Miss* G.) Sh—'s metaphors in the comedies
xix. Moulton (R. G.) 'Othello' as a type of plot

Transactions, Nos. 11, 12, 13 : Appendix.

i. Programme of the Society's fifth musical entertainment
Abstract of proceedings, Oct. 22, 1886 to Jan. 10, 1890

Series II. : Plays.

1. 'Romeo and Juliet'; parallel texts 1579 and 1599. Edited by P. A. Daniel, 1874

New Sh— Society : Publications—

Series II. : Plays.

2. 'Romeo and Juliet.' Reprint of 1597. Ed. by P. A. Daniel, 1874
3. 'Romeo and Juliet.' Reprint of 1599. Ed. by P. A. Daniel. 1874
4. 'Romeo and Juliet.' Revised edition of the 1599 quarto. Ed. by P. A. Daniel, 1875
5. 'Chronicle History of Henry the fifth.' Reprint of first quarto, 1600. Ed. by B. Nicholson, 1875
6. 'Life of Henry the fifth.' Reprinted from the first folio, 1623. Ed. by B. Nicholson. 1875
7. 'Two noble kinsmen.' Reprint of the first quarto, 1634. Ed. by H. Littledale. 1876
8 & 15. 'Two noble kinsmen, by Sh— and Fletcher.' Ed. from the quarto of 1634 by H. Littledale. Parts I. and II. 1876-85
9. 'King Henry V.': Parallel texts of the quarto (1600) and folio (1623) editions. Ed. by B. Nicholson. With introduction by P. A. Daniel. 1877
10. 'Life of Henry the fift,' 1623. Revised and corrected with notes by W. G. Stone. 1880
11. 'Tragedy of Cymbeline.' Reprinted from the first folio, 1623, with collations of the second, third and fourth folios, by W. J. Craig. 1883

Series III. : Originals and Analogues.

1. Romeus and Iuliet, by Arthur Brooke
Rhomeo and Iulietta, by Wm. Painter. Ed. by P. A. Daniel. 1875
[Romeus and Iuliet, written first in Italian by Bandell, and nowe in Englyshe by Arthur Brooke; Rhomeo and Iulietta, translated by William Painter from the French paraphrase by Pierre Boaistuau, on Bandello's version of 'Romeo e Giulietta']

Series IV. : Sh— Allusion Books.

1. Sh— allusion books. Part I., 1592-98. Edited by C. M. Ingleby. 1874
2, 3. Allusions to Sh—, A.D. 1592-1693. Sh—'s centurie of prayse, by C. M. Ingleby. 1879
Some three hundred fresh allusions to Sh—, 1594-1694. Ed. by F. J. Furnivall. 1879-1886

Series V. : Contemporary Drama.

[None published.]

New Sh— Society : Publications—

Series VI. : Sh—'s England.

1, 5, 8. Harrison. Description of England in Sh—'s youth. Edited by F. J. Furnivall. 1877-81

2. Tell-trothe's new yeare's gift and the passionate morrice. 1593
John Lane's Tom Tell-troth's message and his pen's complaint. 1600
Thomas Powell's Tom of all trades. 1631
Glass of godly loue [by Iohn Rogers ?], 1569. Ed. by F. J. Furnivall. 1876

3. William Stafford's Compendious or briefe examination of certayne ordinary complaints of divers of our countrymen, 1581 ('A briefe conceipt of English pollicy'). With introduction by F. D. Matthew. Ed. by F. J. Furnivall

4, 6, 12. Philip Stubbes' Anatomy of the abuses in England in Sh—'s youth, A.D. 1583. Ed. by F. J. Furnivall. 1877-82

7. Rogues and vagabonds of Sh—'s youth, described by John Awdeley in his 'Fraternitye of vacabondes, 1561-73,' Thomas Harman in his 'Caueat for common cursetors, 1567-73,' and in the 'Groundworke of conny catching, 1592.' Ed. by E. Viles and F. J. Furnivall. 1880

9. Old London Bridge as Sh— saw it about 1600 : A chromo-lithograph by W. Griggs

10. Stratford bust of Sh— : A platinotype

11. Sh—'s monument in Stratford Church : A chromo-lithograph by W. Griggs

13. Droeshout portrait of Sh— : Photogravure by Dawson

14. Robert Laneham's letter : whearin the entertainment at Killingworth Castl in Warwik Sheer 1575 is signified. Re-edited by F. J. Furnivall. 1890

Series VII. : English mysteries, miracle plays, &c.

1. Digby mysteries. Edited by F. J. Furnivall. 1882

Series VIII. : Miscellanies.

1. Spalding (W.) Letter on Sh—'s authorship of the 'Two noble kinsmen' and on the characteristics of Sh—'s style and the secret of his supremacy. Ed. by J. H. Burton. 1876

2. Chester (Robert) Love's martyr, or Rosalin's complaint, 1601, with its supplement

New Sh— Society : Publications—

Series VIII. : Miscellanies.

Sh—, Jonson, Chapman, & Marston. Diverse poeticall essaies on the turtle and phoenix. Ed. by A. B. Grosart. 1878

3. Greenhill (J.) Harrison (W. A.) & Furnivall (F. J.) List of all the songs and passages in Sh— which have been set to music. The words in old spelling from the quartos and first folio

3A. Greenhill, Harrison & Furnivall. List of all the songs . . . Edited by W. G. Stone

4. Critical and historical programme of the madrigals, glees and songs to be given at the second annual musical entertainment at University College, London, 9th May, 1884

4A. Ditto. Revised edition. 1884
BM | BPL | BUS | MPL | SML

To the uninitiated this is a puzzling series. The following is the record of a complete set :—1st Ser., Nos. 1 to 14; 2nd Ser., Nos. 1 to 11 and 15 (Nos. 12, 13, 14 never issued); 3rd Ser., No. 1 (all ever issued); 4th Ser., Nos. 1, 2, 3 (all ever issued); 5th Ser. (none issued); 6th Ser., Nos. 1 to 8 and 12 (Nos. 9, 10, 11 all burnt at Griggs' fire); 7th Ser., No. 1 (all ever issued); 8th Ser., Nos. 1 to 4 (all ever issued)—Total, 44 issues.

See also Halliwell (J. O.) Letter
    ,,   ,,   Windle (*Mrs.* C. F. A.) Discovery

New Sh— Society of London : Prospectus, List of Papers and Publications and members. 1878-80. 8° BUS

New Shakspearean interpretations [In 'Edinburgh Review,' Oct.] 1872. 8°
BPL | BUS | CPL

New Shakespeareana : A twentieth century review of Shakespearean and dramatic study. Conducted by the Sh— Society of New York. [Ed. by J. A. Morgan.] Vol. I. Westfield [U.S.] 1902. Imp. 8°
BPL | BUS

New Shakespeareana . . . [Ed. by J. A. Morgan and Willis Vickery.] Westfield, U.S., 1902-09. 8 vols. Imp. 8°. Illust. [In progress] BUS | NY

A quarterly international review, the organ of the Sh— Society of New York. Vol. viii. contains a remarkable precipitate or 'spirit' portrait of Sh— [Chandos altered] by Luther R. Marsh.

New South Wales Sh— Society : Annual Reports, 1904-09. Cr. 8° BPL

New South Wales Sh— Society—
See Gullett
    ,, Harwood

New story teller, or historical medley: Containing sundry polite stories, remarkable histories, instructive allegories, edifying tales, and entertaining poems. [Edited by Joseph Ritson?] Newcastle, 1782. 12° W

Includes the narrative of 'King Lear and his three daughters.'

New study of Sh—. *See* Wigston (W. F. C.)

New Theatre, Dublin. *See* Shirley

New Theatre, Edinburgh. *See* Sh— Macbeth, 1731

New theatrical dictionary, containing an account of all the dramatic pieces that have appeared from the commencement of theatrical exhibitions to the present time. Together with their dates when written or printed, where acted, and occasional remarks on their merits and success. To which is added an alphabetical catalogue of dramatic writers, titles . . . of pieces written . . . and a short sketch of the rise and progress of the English stage. Ln: S. Bladon, 1792. 8°, pp. viii.-400 BPL | SML

New York—
See Events . . .
,, Lenox
,, *Sh*—] Sh— Soc. of New York

New York Mirror: Dramatic festival number. Cincinnati edition. [1883 ?] F° BPL

New York, Park Theatre. *See* Sh— Othello, 1845

New York Sh— Society: Papers and Publications. 1885, &c. :—
i. Guernsey (R. S.) Ecclesiastical law in 'Hamlet': Burial of Ophelia
ii. Morgan (J. A.) 'Venus and Adonis': A study in Warwickshire dialect
iii. Frey (A. R.) Sh— and alleged Spanish prototypes
4 & 7. Morgan (J. A.) Digesta Shakespeareana
5. Vining (E. P.) Time of the play of 'Hamlet'
6. Butler (J. D.) Once-used words in Sh— Halliwell (J. O.) First Sh— Society
8. Price (T. R.) Construction and types of Sh—'s verse as seen in 'Othello' Adee (A. A.) Plea for a reference canon of the plays
9. Renan (E.) Caliban. A philosophical drama continuing 'The tempest' of Sh—. Trans. from the French by Eleanor G. Vickery. 1896
10. Morgan (A.) Study in Warwickshire dialect ['Venus and Adonis']. Fourth edition
11. Given (W.) Further study of 'Othello': Have we misunderstood Sh—'s Moor?

New York Sh— Society: Papers and Publications. 1885, &c. :—
12. Devecmon (W. C.) Sh—'s legal acquirements: Notes by an unbeliever therein. 1890
13. Acheson (A.) Sh— and the rival poet . . . With a reprint of sundry poetical pieces by George Chapman BPL | BUS

Articles of association. New York: Sh— Press, 1895. 8°, pp. 20

Articles of association, Constitution, By-laws, Lists of trustees, officers and members. New York: Sh— Press, 1896. Roy. 8°, pp. 28 and plate

New York Theatre. *See* Sh—Othello,1823,1826

Newbery *Publisher*. *See* Miscellaneous

Newbery (E.) *Publisher*—
See Sh— Merchant . . . 1783
,, Sh— Works, 1790, 1798

Newbery (F.) *Publisher*—
See Sh— Macbeth, 1770
,, Sh— Timon . . . 1770
,, Sh— Works, 1773

Newbery (J.) *Publisher*—
See Colman
,, Horatian canons
,, Poetical epistle

Newbigging (Thomas) Literary by-paths and vagaries, and other papers. Ln: Stock, 1909. Cr. 8°

One chapter is headed 'Sh— the man and his work.'

Sh—. *See* Sh—] Newbigging

Newcastle (Margaret Cavendish *Duchess of*) Two hundred and eleven sociable letters. Ln: 1664. F°

In letter 123 says—'I wonder how that person you mention could either have the conscience or confidence to disparaise Sh—'s plays as to say they were made up only with clowns, fools, watchmen, and the like; but to answer that person—though Sh—'s wit will answer for himself—I say that it seems by his judging or censuring he understands not plays or wit, for to express rightly a fool's humour is as witty as to express the life of kings and princes. . . . Sh— did not want wit to express the life of all sorts of persons of what quality or birth soever, and so well he hath expressed as one would think he had been transformed into everyone of those persons he hath described . . . indeed Sh— had a clear judgment, quick wit, spreading fancy, subtle observation, deep apprehension, and a most eloquent elocution; truly he was a natural orator as well as a natural poet....' Letter 162 also refers to Sh—.

Newcastle (William Cavendish *Duke of*) Triumphant widow, or the medley of humours. A comedy. Ln: J. M—— for H. Herringman, 1677. Fcp. 4°

At page 60 this reference—*Codshead*: 'Good Sir, try some English Poets, as Sh— . . .'

See Jonson (Ben)

Newcastle-upon-Tyne Public Libraries: Hand list of editions, commentaries, etc. [of Sh—] in the Central Reference and Lending Departments. Newcastle-on-Tyne, 1906. 4°, pp. 12 BPL

Newcomb (*Mrs.*) *Publisher.* *See* Wolcot
Newcombe's School at Hackney. *See* Sh—
Hamlet, 1748
Newdegate (F. A.) The Newdegates. *See*
Memorials . . .
Newdigate-Newdegate (*Lady*) Gossip from a
muniment room: Lives of Anne and
Mary Fytton, 1574-1618. 1897. 8° BPL
Newe court of Venus. *See* Stopes
Newell (R. H.) Zoology of the English poets.
1845. 12° BPL
Newes from Virginia. *See* Rich
Newman *Cardinal* (John Hy.) Idea of a
university defined and illustrated. 1873
At pp. 291-293 remarks—' A great author is not one
who merely has a copia verborum, whether in prose
or verse, and can, as it were, turn on at his will any
number of splendid phrases and swelling sentences,
but he is one who has something to say and knows
how to say it. . . . Such pre-eminently is Sh— among
ourselves ; such pre-eminently is Virgil among the
Latins ; such in their degree are all those writers
who in every nation go by the name of classics.'
Newman & Co. *Publishers.* *See* Sh— Works,
1811
Newnham (John) Newnam's nightcrowe: A
bird that breedeth braules in many
families and houshouldes. Ln: Iohn
Wolfe, 1590. 8°, pp. x.-54
Said to have formed part of Sh—'s library.
Newnham-Davis (N.) *Editor.* *See* Sh— Mid-
summer . . . 1891
News from the Levant Seas. 1594. *See* Re-
prints
Newspaper cuttings and Sh— play bills.
1901. F° BPL
Newspaper cuttings, play bills, &c. relating
to Sh—, mounted in a scrap book. [Und.]
F° BPL
Newspaper cuttings: Playhouse notes, his-
torical and critical. [c. 1871.] F° BPL
Newspaper cuttings, relating to Sh—. Bir-
mingham, etc., 1871-1881. 6 vols. F°
BPL
Newspaper cuttings relating to the Bacon-
Sh— controversy, including 'Was Bacon
Mr. Gladstone?' etc. 1884-85. 12° BPL
Newspaper cuttings. Sh— miscellany. 1904,
&c. F° BPL
Newspaper cuttings: Shakespeareana and
Warwickshire notes. [c. 1886-87.] F°
BPL
Newton (J.) Arrangement of Sh—'s plays
made . . . May, 1795. 8°
Newton (R.) *Publisher.* *See* Sh— Poems, 1760
Newton (T. W.) Catalogue of old ballads in
the possession of Frederic Ouvry. Ln:
Privately printed, 1877. Fcp. 4°, pp.
xvi.-58 ; in printed grey boards
Nicander and Lucilla. *See* Riche
Niccolls (Richard) England's Eliza. *See*
Mirrour . . .

Nichol (George) Letter on Boydell's edition of
Sh—. 1791. 4°
Nichols (J.) *Editor.* *See* Whetstone
Nichols *M.R.C.P.* (James) Notes on Sh—.
Ln: W. Skeffington, 1861-62. 2 parts
in 1 vol. 8° BM | BPL | BUS | CPL | SML
Nichols (John) History and antiquities of the
county of Leicester. Ln: 1795-1815. 8
vols. F° BM
Referring to John Strong Ensor, living at Cosby or
Narborough in 1767, says—' Ensor's sister was the
wife of the Rev. John Dyer, the poet, and his grand-
mother was a Sh— descended from a brother of
everybody's Sh—.'
Ensor entered Rugby School 31 March, 1729, as John
Strong, *alias* Ensor.
Illustrations of the literary history of the
eighteenth century. 1817-58. 8 vols.
8° BPL | BUS
Contains the Shakespearean correspondence of Lewis
Theobald, Dr. Thirlby, and Wm. Warburton, pp.
189-647.
Nichols (John) *Editor—*
See Gentleman's Mag.
,, Sh— King Henry V., 1779
,, Sh— King John, 1779, 1788
,, Sh— Taming . . . 1779
,, Sh— Works, 1786-90, 1797, 1798
,, Six old plays
Nichols (J.) *Printer.* *See* Sh— Works, 1770-74
Nichols (J.) *Publisher—*
See Middleton
,, Sh— King Lear, 1779
,, Sh— Macbeth, 1794
,, Sh— Merry devil . . 1819
,, Sh— Merchant . . . 1783
,, Sh— Works, 1790, 1798
Nichols & Son (J.) *Publishers.* *See* Sh—
Works, 1811, 1813
Nichols (J. Gough) *Editor.* *See* Fisher
Nichols (Philip)] Castrated letter of Sir
Thomas Hanmer in the sixth volume of
'Biographia Britannica,' wherein is dis-
covered the rise of the Bishop of Glouces-
ter's quarrel with that baronet about his
edition of Sh—'s plays, to which is added
an impartial account of the extraordinary
means used to suppress the remarkable
letter. By a proprietor of that work.
Ln: J. Pridden, 1763. Fcp. 4° BPL
Castrated letter . . . Second edition, corrected and augmented. Ln: J. Pridden,
1763. Fcp. 4°, pp. 32 BUS
Nicholson *M.D.* (Brinsley) Hamlet's 'cursed
hebenon.' Ln: New Sh— Soc., 1880-86.
8°
Kemp and the play of 'Hamlet': Yorick
and Tarlton. Ln: New Sh— Soc., 1880-
86. 8°
Number of witches in 'Macbeth' and a
note on 'King John.' Ln: New Sh—
Soc., 1880-86. 8°

Nicholson *M.D.* (Brinsley) On four passages in 'King Henry V.' Ln : New Sh— Soc., 1880-86. 8°

Relation of the quarto to the folio version of 'King Henry V.' Ln : New Sh— Soc., 1880-86. 8°

Sh— and sea-glasses. Ln : New Sh— Soc., 1880-86. 8°
' Our ship which but three glasses since.'—*The tempest.*
' Or four and twenty times the pilot's glass.'—*All's well.*

Was Hamlet mad ? Ln : New Sh— Soc., 1882. 8°   BPL
This title was the copyright of A. Michie (*q.v.*) eleven years before.

Was 'Mr. W. H——' the Earl of Pembroke ? [In 'Athenæum,' No. 3324, p. 74, July]. 1891. 4°

Nicholson *M.D.* (B.) *Editor*—
See Scot
  ,, Sh— King Henry V., 1875, 1877

Nicholson (E. W. B.) Jaggard (Wm.) & Arthur (John S.) Sh— Society of New York and the New York Sh— Society [In 'Athenæum,' No. 4121, p. 479 ; No. 4126, p. 657 ; No. 4127, p. 693 ; No. 4128, p. 738 ; No. 4129, p. 774 ; and No. 4141, p. 290, Oct., 1906 to Mar., 1907]

Nicholson *LL.D.* (John Aldwell) No cipher in Sh—, being a refutation of the Hon. Ignatius Donnelly's 'Great cryptogram']. Leamington : Burgis, 1888. 8°, pp. 68
      BM | BPL | BUS | MPL
A raking reply, in which Donnelly is ' hoist with his own petard.'

Sh— Sermon in the Church of Holy Trinity, Stratford-upon-Avon. Rugby, 1897. 12°
      BPL

The man and the poet. *See Sh*—] Sh— sermons

Nicholson (Samuel) Acolastus, his afterwitte. A poem. Ln : Baylie, 1600. Fcp. 4°
Contains passages plagiarising thoughts found in Sh—.

Acolastus, his after-witte. A poem, 1600, containing singular plagiarisms from Sh—. Ed. by J. O. Halliwell. Ln : 1866. Fcp. 4°   BPL | MPL
Issue restricted to ten copies.

Acolastus, his afterwitte (1600). A poem ... containing quotations and adaptations from Sh— and Barnfield. 1876. 4°   BM

Nicholson (T. H.) *Artist. See Sh*— Works, 1851-54, 1852-54, 1875-80, 1886-88

Nicks (G.) Ophelia's airs. *See Sh*— Hamlet, 1800

Nic-nac or literary cabinet. With a history of the English stage. 1823-28. 5 vols. 8°   BPL

Nicol (William) *Editor. See Sh*— Hamlet, 1603
Nicol (Wm.) *Printer. See Sh*— Hamlet, 1825, 1832

Nicolai (Otto) *Editor. See Sh*— Merry wives, 1875

Nicolai (Otto) Opera : Merry wives of Windsor [Music]. [1860 ?] 4°   BPL

Nicolas (*Sir* Nicholas Harris) *Editor. See* Retrospective Review

Nicoll (Henry J.) Landmarks of English literature. Third edition, with twelve portraits. Ln : John Hogg [c. 1885]. 8°, pp. xiv.-460
Sh— occupies pp. 74-86.

Nicoll *of Southgate* (John). *See Sh*—] Houbraken

Nicoll (*Sir* Wm. Robertson) *Editor. See* Bookman

Nicoll (W.) *Publisher*—
See Sh— King Lear, 1767, 1771
  ,, Sh— King Richard III., 1784
  ,, Sh— Romeo ... 1769

Nicolls (Thomas) *Editor. See* Thucydides
Nield (J. E.) *See* Michie & Nield
Nimmo (T.) & Pettigrew (T. J.) On a passage in 'Julius Cæsar.' *See Sh*—] Sh— Soc.

'Nipclose (*Sir* Nicholas)' *pseud. See* Garrick (D.)

Nisbet (J. F.) Insanity of genius and the general inequality of human faculty physiologically considered. Ln : 1893. Cr. 8°, pp. xxviii.-342   BPL
Sh— pp. 145-162. Discusses mortality in his family, unfitness of his offspring, and cause of his death.

Insanity of genius. Fourth edition. Ln : Richards, 1900. Cr. 8°, pp. xxviii.-342

Niven (William) Illustrations of old Warwickshire houses. Thirty-one copper etchings. With descriptive notes. Ln : Printed for the author at the Chiswick Press, 1878. 4°, pp. 38
Exhibits quaint buildings which must have been familiar to the poet.
Issue limited to 75 small paper and 25 large paper copies.

Notes on English houses in Sh—'s time. Privately printed, 1881. Roy. 8°, pp. 16. With 4 etched plates

Noah (M. M.) *Editor. See* Lennox
Noble (F. & J.) *Publishers. See Sh*— King Lear, 1767, 1771
Noble (J.) *Publisher. See* Memoirs ...
Noble (S.) *Engraver*—
See Sh— King Richard III., 1806
  ,, Sh— Works, 1811

Noble (S. J.) Supplementary airs. *See Sh*— Poems, 1862

Noble souldier. *See* Rowley
Noble stranger. *See* Sharpe
Nobody and somebody. [? 1600.] 1877. 8°
The preface contains Sh— references.   BPL
Nobody and somebody. *See* Simpson (R.)

Noctes Shaksperianæ: A series of papers by members of the Winchester College Sh— Society. Ed. by C. H. Hawkins. Winchester: Castle & Lamb, 1887. 8°
BM | BPL | SML
Nodes (G.) *Publisher. See* Sh— Works, 1846
Noel (M. Leigh). *See* Leigh-Noel
Noiré (*Dr.*) *Editor. See* Sh— King Richard II., 1868
Nolte & Koehler *Hamburg Publishers. See* Sh—] Julius Cæsar, 1857
Nomenclature—
See Barber
,, Taylor
Noontide leisure. *See* Drake
Noorthouck (John) Historical and classical dictionary: containing the lives and characters of the most eminent and learned persons in every age and nation. Ln: W. Strahan & T. Cadell, 1776. 2 vols. 8°, unpaged
On sigs. R4, R5 is a three-column biography of the poet.
Norden (John) Speculum Britanniæ: An historicall and chorographicall description of Middlesex . . . Ln: 1593. Fcp. 4°
Contains three folding plans—Middlesex, London, and Westminster—of Sh—'s day. The second plan exhibits the Rose Theatre, here named 'The Play Howse,' the only theatre then on the southerly side of the Thames.
Norris. *See* Dunton
Norris *senior* (C.) *Publisher. See* Grey (Z.)
Norris (H.) Baddesley Clinton; its manor, church and hall. Leamington: Art & Book Co., 1897. 8° SML
Sh—'s ancestry, p. 122.
Includes a history of the Ferrers family.
Tamworth Castle; its foundations . . . history and lords, from the Norman conquest. Tamworth: D. Smith, 1899. 8°, pp. vi.-50, illust.
'From Tamworth thither is but one day's march.'— *King Richard III., 5.*
Norris (J. Parker) Bibliography of works on the portraits of Sh—. Philadelphia, 1879. 8°, pp. 10 BM | BPL | BUS
Fifty copies privately printed.
Death mask of Sh—. Philadelphia, 1884. 8° BM | BPL | BUS | SML
Portraits of Sh.—*See* Sh—] Norris
Sh—: Various portraits of the great poet [In 'Evening Telegraph,' 17 Nov.] Philadelphia, 1873. F° BUS
Shall we open Sh—'s grave? [In 'The Manhattan']. 1884. 8° BPL
Norris.] Handlist of works relating to Sh— in the library of J. P. Norris. Philadelphia, 1874. Manuscript. 8° BPL
Norris (J. Parker) *Editor—*
See Sh— Works, 1874
,, *Sh—*] Craig

Norstedt *Stockholm Publisher. See* Sh— The tempest, 1836
'North (Christopher)' *pseud. See* Wilson (*Prof.* John)
North (L.) *See* Phelps & North
North (Thomas) *Editor. See* Plutarchus
Northall (W. K.) *Editor. See* Sh— Macbeth, 1843
Northbrooke (John) Treatise wherein dicing, daucing, vaine plaies, etc. commonly used on the Sabbath are reproued . . . Ln: 1579. Fcp. 4°
Treatise against dicing, dancing, plays, and interludes. With other idle pastimes. From the earliest edition . . . With introduction and notes [by J. P. Collier]. *See Sh—*] Sh— Soc.
Northcote (James) *Artist. See* Sh— Works, 1802
Northern lord: A ballad—
See Ballad
,, Sh— Merchant . . . 1800
,, *Sh—*] Sh—'s library
A foundation of the ' Merchant of Venice.'
Northumberland (*Duke of*). *See* Douse
Northumberland manuscripts—
See Elizabethan . . .
,, Holmes
Norton (H. G.) On Beaumont & Fletcher's 'Woman's prize'—the day when it was acted and the prologue and epilogue spoken. *See Sh—*] Sh— Soc.
Origin of the induction to Sh—'s 'Taming of the shrew.' Ln: Sh— Soc., 1845. 8° BPL
Norton (John) *Printer—*
See Sh— King Henry IV., i., 1632, 1639
,, Sh— King Richard II., 1634
,, Sh— King Richard III., 1629, 1634
,, Sh— Pericles, 1630
Norton (J.) *Publisher—*
See Estienne
,, Stephen
Norton (Thomas) Instructions for the Lord Mayor of London, 1573. *See* Reprints
Norton (Thomas) & Sackville (Thomas) Tragedie of Gorboduc . . . [Ed. by W. D. Cooper.] Ln: Sh— Soc., 1847. 8°, pp. 91-160 and facsimile (the first 90 pp. occupied by Udall's 'Ralph Roister Doister') BPL | BUS
See Collier (J. P.), *also* Udall.
Norwich—
See Contemporary . . .
,, *Sh—*] Sh— in Norwich
,, Speech . . .
Nossiter *Actress. See* Letter . . .
Notcutt (Henry C.) *Editor. See* Sh— Macbeth, 1895

Notes and emendations on the 'Grimaldi Sh—.' Ln: 1853. 12°

Notes and emendations on the 'Grimaldi Sh—.' New York, 1853. 12°

Notes and emendations to Sh—'s plays. *See* Collier

Notes and Queries. [Ed. by Wm. John Thoms, Hy. Frederic Turle, Dr. John Doran, Joseph Knight, and Vernon H. Rendall.] Ln: J. C. Francis, 1849-1910. 130 vols. Fcp. 4°. [In progress]
         BM | BPL | BUS
Contains innumerable and invaluable Sh— contributions by scholars and antiquaries in all parts of the world. Consult its general indexes.

Notes and Queries: Sh— tercentenary number [April 23]. Ln: Francis, 1864. Fcp. 4°   BPL

Notes on Sh—'s plays. [1830 ?] 4°. Anonymous manuscript   BPL

Notes on theatres [In 'London Society']. Ln: [1871 ?] 8°   BPL

Notes on 'The tempest' for the use of Rugby School. Rugby, 1870. 12°   BPL

'Nothus (Cornelius Scriblerus)' *pseud. See* Burgess (Thomas)

Notices illustrative of the drama and other popular amusements, chiefly in the sixteenth and seventeenth centuries, incidentally illustrating Sh— and his contemporaries. Extracted from the Chamberlain's accounts and other manuscripts of . . . Leicester. With introduction and notes by Wm. Kelly. Ln: J. R. Smith, 1865. 8°, pp. viii.-310 and 2 plates
    BM | BPL | BUS | CPL | MPL | SML
Large paper at B U S.

Notices of players acting at Ludlow [Shropshire], 1554-1627. Edited by J. O. Halliwell. 1867. 8°   BPL

Notices of the churches of Warwickshire. *See* Bloxam (M. H.)

Nottingham's (*Earl of*) Company of Players—
See Decker
  ,, Decker & Chettle
  ,, Sh— Sir John Oldcastle, 1600

Nottingham Sh— Society programmes. 1907. 8°   BPL

Nourry (Claude) *Lyons Publisher. See* Villanova

Nourse (J.) *Publisher*—
See Sh— King Henry VIII., 1758
  ,, Sh— Works: Ext. 1738

Novel from which the play of the 'Merchant of Venice' is taken. Trans. from the Italian. To which is added a translation of a novel from the 'Decamerone' of Boccaccio. Ln: M. Cooper at the Globe in Paternoster Row, 1755. 8°

Novello. Catalogue of Sh— music. 1893. 4°   BPL

Novello (Sabilla) *Editor. See* Clarke

Novello (Vincent) *Composer. See* Sh— Macbeth, 1862

Nowell (J.) *See* Hamlet

Noyes (John Buttrick) & Peirce (Charles Sandars) Shakespearian pronunciation [In 'North American Review,' April]. Boston, 1864. 8°   BUS

Numeration by counters [Excerpt from an early treatise on arithmetic, c. 1600]. 12°, pp. 217 to 253 inclusive; black letter   W
'What for a counter would I do but good?'
      —*As you like it.*
'I cannot do it without counters.'—*Winter's tale.*
'Will you with counters sum?'—*Troilus and Cressida.*
'Your neck, sir, is pen, book, and counters.'—*Cymbeline.*

Nunn (J.) *Publisher. See* Sh— Works, 1798, 1811

'Nuovus Homo' *pseud. See* Tercentenary

Nutbrowne mayde. *See* Capell

Nutt (Alfred) Fairy mythology of Sh— 1900. 12°   BPL

Nutt (J.) *Publisher. See* Some thoughts

—— (E.) *Printer. See* Sh— Mucedorus, 1668

O—— (I.) *Printer. See* Sharpe (L.)

O—— (N.) *Printer—*
See Okes (Nicholas)
  ,, Sh— Rape, 1607

O—— (R.) *Printer. See* Heywood

O—— (W.) *Printer & Publisher. See* Sh— Titus . . . 1700

Oakley (Benjamin) *Editor*—
See Sh— Works, 1828, 1854
  ,, Sh— Works: Ext. 1828

O'Brien (Cecilia) Sh—'s young men [In 'Westminster Review,' Oct.] Ln: 1876. 8°   BUS

O'Brien (Constance) Sh— talks with uncritical people [In 'Monthly Packet']. Ln: 1878-79. 2 vols. 8°   BUS
Deals with 'Comedy of errors,' 'King Henry VI.,' 'King Richard II.,' 'Love's labours lost,' 'Midsummer night's dream,' 'Romeo,' and 'Two gentlemen.'

Observations and conjectures. *See* Tyrwhitt

O'Carroll (J. J.) Address: Clongowes Wood College Historical Debating Soc. Dublin, 1874. 8°   BPL
Refers to Sh—.

Oclandus (C.) Anglorvm prælia. Ln: 1580. 8°   BPL
A Latin poem much used in schools in Sh—'s time.

  Elizabetha. Ln: 1582. 8°   BPL
A Latin poem of Sh—'s day.

O'Connor (E. M.) Index to the works of Sh—. *See* Sh— Works: Ext. 1887

O'Connor (T. P.) *Editor*. *See* Sh— Macbeth, 1906

O'Connor (W. D.) Hamlet's note-book [A defence of . . . Mrs. Henry Pott and Bacon's 'Promus of formularies']. New York, 1886. 8°   BM | BPL | BUS
In reply to R. G. White's criticism of Mrs. Potts' work in 'Atlantic Monthly,' April, 1883.

    Mr. Donnelly's reviewers. Chicago, 1889. 12°   BPL | BUS
Bacon-Sh— controversy.

O'Conor (W. A.) 'Hamlet': A paper read before the Manchester Literary Club. Manchester, 1878. 8°   BPL

    'Hamlet' [In 'Essays in literature and ethics,' pp. 108-136]. Manchester, 1889. 12°   BPL

Octagonal Sh— Club: Rules, list of meetings, members, &c. 1877. 8°   BPL

Ode on dedicating a building . . . to Le Stue. *See* Morehead

Ode to G . . r . . k. *See* Garrick

Ode . . . to Sh—. *See* Garrick

Odell (George C. D.) *Editor*. *See* Sh— Julius Cæsar, 1900

O'Donavan (Wm. R.) Statue of Sh— [In 'Lippincott's Magazine,' Jan.] Philad., 1874. 8°   BUS

Oechelhaeuser (W.) Shakespeareana [Essays]. 1894. 8°   BM

Oesterley (*Dr.* Herman) *Editor*—
    See Hundred . . .
    ,, *Sh*—] Sh— Jest book

Of education, especially of young gentlemen. Oxford, 1673. 8°
Refers to Sh— at p. 43—'As the fool personates the same humour, though in divers comedies and though sometimes Launce, Jodelet, or Scaramuccio, yet 'tis all but the same buffoon.'
Illustrates 'Two gentlemen.'

Of 'Macbeth.' By an apprentice of the law [In 'Fraser's Magazine']. Ln: 1840-42. 8°   BUS

Offer (G.) *Publisher*. *See* Sh— Works, 1825

Official programme . . . *See* Flower (C. E.)

O'Flanagan (Jean I.) Sh—'s self-revelation in his Sonnets. *See* Sh—] O'Flanagan

Ogden (J.) *Editor*. *See* Sh— Works, 1839-43

Ogilvy & Son (D.) *Publishers*. *See* Sh— Works, 1798

Ogilvie & Speare *Publishers*. *See* Sh— Works, 1790

Ogle & Co. (M.) *Glasgow Publishers*. *See* Sh— Works, 1871

O'Gorman (R.) Oration on Sh—. *See* Sh—] O'Gorman

O'Keeffe (John) Peeping Tom of Coventry: A musical farce . . . With remarks . . . costume . . . stage business . . . by D. G.

[*i.e.* Geo. Daniel]. Ln: J. Cumberland [1830 ?] 12°, pp. 36. Frontispiece by R. Cruikshank
Founded upon an ancient Warwickshire legend recorded by the Abbot Bromton, with which Sh— must have been familiar.

    Recollections . . . Ln: 1826. 2 vols. 8°   BPL

Okes (John) *Printer*—
    See Bancroft (T.)
    ,, Field

Okes (Nicholas) *Printer*—
    See Decker
    ,, Greene
    ,, Heywood
    ,, Sh— King Lear, 1608
    ,, Sh— Mucedorus, 1615
    ,, Sh— Othello, 1622
    ,, Sh— Rape . . . 1607
    ,, Stephens

Okes (Nicholas & Iohn) *Printers*. *See* Old-mayne

Old and new: The King's Head, Fenchurch Street. 1877. 12°   BPL
Sh—, pp. 36-40.

Old ballads and songs. Ed. by J. P. Collier. Ln: Privately printed, 1869. Fcp. 4°
Issue limited to 25 copies.

Old clothes merchant of Venice. *See* Sh— Merchant . . . 1884

Old English drama: A selection of plays from the old English dramatists. 1825. 2 vols. Cr. 8°. With frontispiece of an old theatre
Contains the 'Rape of Lucrece.'

Old English jest books. *See* Sh—] Sh—'s jest book

Old songs of the Elizabethans. With new songs in reply. Ln: Constable, 1908. 16°, pp. 66

Old wives tale. *See* Peele

Oldfield.] Egerton (W.) Faithful memoirs of the life, amours, and performances of that celebrated actress . . . Mrs. Anne Oldfield. Ln: 1751. 8°

] Robins (Edward) Palmy days of Nance Oldfield. Ln: Heinemann, 1898. 8°. With portraits

Oldham (T.) Lines on Sh—. *See* Sh—

Oldmayne (Tymothy) Life's brevitie and death's debility. Evidently declared in a sermon preached at the funerall of that hopeful and uertuous young gentleman Edward Lewkenor Esquire &c. in whose death is ended the name of that renowned family of the Lewkenors in Suffolke . . . Also an elegy and an epitaph on the death of that worthy gentleman by I. G——, Dr. of D. Ln: N. and I. Okes, dwelling in little S. Bartholmewes

neere the Hospitall gate, 1636. Fcp. 4°.
Coat of arms on verso of title. A¹ to M¹
in fours

Curious for the early metaphorical reference to the
stage almost contemporary with the poet. The
description occurs in the ' Epistle dedicatory '—
' Foure generations of your honourable family have I
seene here upon the stage, successively acting their
several parts. Angels and men were the lookers-on
and, with great applause, highly commended their
true action and generous demeanour. But now, alas !
the theater is wholy empted and all the actors quite
gone, the stage hourely expected to be pulled down,
and if it stand, yet little hope there is that ever our
eyes shall see such actors any more upon it to play
their parts so commendable as those antients did.'

* * * *

The Bishop of London's licence to print the work is
dated 10th Sept., 1625.

Oldmixon. Prologue and epilogue. *See* Sh—
Measure . . . 1700

Oldys (W.)] Historical and poetical medley.
Ed. by 'E. Cooper.' *See* Sh— Works :
Ext. 1738

] Life of Sir John Falstaff [Reprinted from
'Biographia Britannica,' c. 1793]. F° BPL
Selection from manuscript notes to Lang-
baine's 'Dramatic poets.' Ln : 1851. 8°
Sh—. *See* Sh—] Oldys
See also Hazlitt (W. C.)
  ,,   ,,   James I.
O'Leary (J.) *Editor. See* Catalogue, 1843
O'Leary (Joseph) Memoir and introduction.
See Singleton
Oliphant (Thomas) La musa madrigalesca, or
. . . madrigals, ballets, roundelays, etc.,
chiefly of the Elizabethan age, with re-
marks and annotations. Ln : Calkin &
Budd, 1837. 8°, pp. xxviii.-338
Sh— p. viii., etc.

Oliphant (T. L. Kington) New English. Ln :
Macmillan, 1886. 2 vols. 8° SML
Chapter iv., vol. 2, is on 'Sh—'s English.'

Old and middle English. Ln : Macmillan,
1878. 8°, pp. xxvi.-668 SML
Oliphant (T. T.) *See* Knight & Oliphant
Oliver & Boyd *Edinburgh Publishers—*
See Sh— As you like it, 1813
  ,, Sh— Hamlet, 1808, 1813
  ,, Sh— Macbeth, 1813
  ,, Sh— Merchant . . . 1813
  ,, Sh— Much ado . . . 1813
  ,, Sh— Othello, 1813
  ,, Sh— Romeo . . . 1813
  ,, Sh— Works, 1817
Oliver & Munroe *Boston* [*U.S.*] *Publishers—*
See Sh— Poems, 1807
Olivieri (A.) *Editor. See* Sh— Sonnets, 1890
On a day, alack the day. *See* Bodenham (J.)
On Sh—. *See* Bathurst
On the birthday of Sh—. A canto . . .
published at the first triennial meeting in
honour of Sh— [Stratford-upon-Avon],
April 23, 1827. 8°, single sheet BM

On the character of Cleopatra. 1872. 8° CPL
On the character of Coriolanus as delineated
by Plutarch and Sh—. Und. Manuscript.
F°, pp. 24 BUS
On the character of Hamlet [In 'Blackwood's
Magazine,' Nov.] Edin., 1828. 8° BUS
On the character of Imogen ('Cymbeline')
[In 'Female Mentor,' Vol. 1, pp. 212-225].
1793. 12° BPL
On the feigned madness of Hamlet [In
'Blackwood's Magazine,' Oct.] Edin.,
1839. 8° BUS
On the origin of Sh—'s 'Tempest' [In 'Corn-
hill Mag.'] Ln : 1872. 8° BPL | BUS
O'Neill *aft. Lady Becher* (Eliza) *Actress. See*
De Soligny
O'Neill (George) Could Bacon have written
the Sh— plays ? A brief study of char-
acteristics. Ln : E. Ponsonby, 1909. 8°,
pp. 32
Only likeness of Sh—. *See* Sh—] Only . . .
Opie (John) *Artist. See* Sh— Works, 1802
Optick glasse of humours. *See* Walkington
Opzoomer (C. W.) *Editor—*
See Sh— Macbeth, 1862
  ,, Sh— Othello, 1860, 1862
  ,, Sh— Works, 1860-72
Oracle (The) [Newspaper ; Ed. by J. Boaden].
See Ireland (S. W. H.)
Orchardson (Wm. Quiller) *Artist. See* Sh—
Works, 1875-76
Ord (H. W.) *Editor. See* Sh— King Henry
IV., i., 1902
Ordinance of the Lords and Commons
assembled in Parliament for the utter
suppression and abolishing of all stage
playes and interludes. With the penal-
ties to be inflicted upon the actors and
spectators herein exprest. Ln : Imprinted
for John Wright at the King's Head in
the Old Bayley, 1647. Fcp. 4°, pp. 14
Ordinance for the suppression of stage-
playes, 1647. Ln : Reprinted by E. W.
Ashbee, 1869. Fcp. 4° BPL | SML
Ordish (Thomas Fairman) Early London
theatres in the Fields. 'Camden Library.'
Ln : Stock, 1894. 12°. With maps and
illustrations BPL | SML
First folio Sh— [In 'Bookworm,' Vol. 1,
pp. 161-255]. Ln : Stock, 1888. 8° BM
Sh—'s London : A study of London in the
reign of Queen Elizabeth. Ln : Dent,
1897. 12°, pp. 270 BM | BPL | MPL | SML
Sh—'s London. A commentary on Sh—'s
life and work in London. New edition.
With chapter on Westminster and itine-
rary of sites and reliques. Ln : Dent,
1904. 8°, pp. 346 BPL | MPL
O'Reilly (J. B.) Introduction. *See* Giles

Orger (J. G.) Critical notes on Sh—'s comedies ['histories' and 'tragedies,' 1889-90].
2 vols. 8°   BM | BPL | BUS
Original letters of Falstaff. *See* White
Original prologues, epilogues and other pieces
never before printed. To which is added
a collection of such as are celebrated for
wit . . . Ln: 1756. 12°   W
Important for its reference to an unknown portrait of
the poet. A piece entitled 'On Sh—'s monument'
opens thus :—
  'Old Homer's fancy'd face, a form unknown,
  Survives in breathing brass or Parian stone,
  While of the mind such images remain
  We wish to raise the honour'd shade again.
  Immortal wit conpels us to admire
  The relique rescu'd from devouring fire.
  Such Sh— was ; from hence invention took
  The studious posture and the piercing look.'
    *   *   *   *
Following is this note in prose :—
  'There is no genuine picture of Sh—. That called
his was taken long after his death from a person
supposed extremely like him, at the direction of Sir
Thomas Clarges.'
The reference in verse clearly relates to the Stratford
Church monument ; that in prose probably to some
painting long since lost sight of.
See ' Notes and Queries,' 10th Ser., iv., 368, etc.
Original proposals . . . for Malone's Sh—. *See*
Malone
Original story of 'Rhomeo and Juliet' [In
'The Magazine']. 1750. 8°   BPL
Original story of 'Romeo and Juliet' and
'Juliet's tomb at Verona' [In 'The
Mirror']. Ln: 1823. 8°   BPL
Orlando Furioso.] Historie of Orlando Furioso
. . . as it was plaid before the Queenes
Maiestie. Ln: Printed by Iohn Danter
for Cuthbert Burbie and are to be sold
at his shop nere the Royall Exchange,
1594. Ln: Malone Society, 1907. Fcp.
4°
Orr (Wm. S.) *Publisher*—
  See Sh— King Lear, 1854
  ,, Sh— Love's labours lost, 1851
  ,, Sh— Poems, 1851
  ,, Sh— Works, 1851
Orr & Co. *Publishers*—
  See Sh— Midsummer . . . 1854
  ,, Sh— Works, 1838, 1844, 1845, 1846,
    1849, 1851, 1852, 1853, 1854
Orrery (Roger Boyle *Earl of*) *Editor*. *See*
Sh— King Henry V., 1672, 1739
Orson (S. W.) Sh— emendations. [1891.]
Fcp. 4°   BM | BPL
Ortelius. Theatrum. *See* Localities
Orton. Familiar verses. *See* Woodward
Orton *New York Publisher*. *See* Sh— Works,
1856
Orwin (Thomas) *Printer*—
  See Lodge
  ,, Warner
Osborne (C.) A haunted Hamlet [In 'Temple
Bar,' June]. Ln: 1867. 8°   BPL | BUS

Osborn (J.) *Publisher*—
  See Sh— Poems, 1728
  ,, Sh— Works, 1714
Osborn (Thomas) *Publisher*—
  See Pope
  ,, Rowe
Ospovat (H.) *Artist*—
  See Sh— Poems, 1901
  ,, Sh— Sonnets, 1899
Osteler (Thomasina). *See* Wallace
O'Sullivan (D.) *Editor*—
  See Sh— Hamlet, 1843
  ,, Sh— King Richard III., 1843
  ,, Sh— Macbeth, 1843, 1877, 1881, 1882,
    1886
  ,, Sh— Merchant . . . 1843
  ,, Sh— Othello, 1844
  ,, Sh— Romeo . . . 1844
  ,, Sh— Timon . . . 1843
  ,, Sh— Works, 1836-39
Oswald (Lina) Sh—'s garden at New Place
[In ' One and all gardening.' Ed. by
E. O. Greening]. Ln: 1907. 8°, pp. 160.
Illust.
Othello. *See* Sh— Othello
Othello in hell, and the infant with a branch
of olives. Ln: Orr, 1848. 12°
Othello travestie. *See* Sh— Othello, 1792,
1813, 1834, 1856, 1870, 1884
Otley *Publisher*. *See* Saunders & Otley
Otridge *Publisher*. *See* Sh— Works, 1824
Ottley (Hy.) Fechter's version of 'Othello'
critically analysed. With observations
on the stage, audience, and critics. Ln:
T. H. Lacy, 1861. 8°, pp. 32
    BM | BPL | BUS | CPL | MPL | SML
Ottley (Henry) *Editor*. *See* Sh— Othello, 1861
Otway. Shakespearean lectures on six of the
tragedies [In 'Marlborough Mag.,' pp.
33-40]. 1848. 8°   BPL
Otway (Thomas) History . . . of Caius Marius.
  See Sh— Romeo . . . 1680, 1692, 1696,
  1703, 1748, 1768, 1812, 1813
  Souldier's fortune. A comedy. Ln: R.
  Bentley & S. Magnes, 1683. Fcp. 4°
Refers to Falstaff in the dedication.
  Venice preserved, or a plot discovered. A
  tragedy. Ln: Joseph Hindmarsh at the
  sign of the Black Bull over against the
  Royal Exchange in Cornhill, 1682. Fcp.
  4°
Speaking of this, Otway's supreme effort, Thomson
says :—
  'See o'er the stage the ghost of Hamlet stalks,
  Othello raves, poor Monimia mourns,
  And Belvidera pours her soul in love.'
    .   .   .   .
' Otway's talents rival at least and sometimes excel
those of Sh—.'—*Sir W. Scott.*
See Poems . . .
'Ouida' *pseud*. *See* Ramée
Oulton (R.) *Publisher*. *See* Nabbes

Oulton (Walley Chamberlain)] 'Vortigern' under consideration; with general remarks on J. Boaden's letter to Geo. Steevens relative to the manuscripts, etc. ascribed to Sh— and in the possession of Samuel Ireland. Ln: H. Lowndes, 1796. 8°, pp. 68   BM | BPL | BUS | W

Oulton (W. C.) *Editor*—
See Sh— Poems, 1804
  ,, Victor

Our club. *See* Holl

Outline illustrations. *See* Retzsch (M.)

Ouvry (Frederic) *Bibliophile*. *See* Newton

Ouvry (F.) *Editor*. *See* Singer

Overend (G. H.) On the dispute between George Maller and Thomas Arthur. Ln: New Sh— Soc., 1877-79. 8°

Overthrow of stage-playes. *See* Rainoldes

Ovidius. Metamorphoseon, 1502. *See* Sh— Autograph

Pyramus and Thisbe. *See* Sh— Midsummer . . . 1886

Ovidius.] Ovid's ghost, or Venus overthrown by the Nasonian Politian, with a remedy for love sick gallants, in a poem on the dispraise of all sorts of wives by 'Eduardus Fuscus.' [Ln: Privately] Printed for the author, 1657. 12°
Refers to Sh— and his ' Lucrece.'

] Sh—'s Ovid, being Golding's trans. of the 'Metamorphoses.' Ln: Moring, 1904. 4°   BPL

Ovidius—
See Hermeticall . . . .
  ,, Heywood
  ,, Meres

Owen (F. M.) Sh— and 'George Eliot' [In 'Essays and poems,' pp. 1-43]. 1887. 12°   BPL

Owen (J.) *Publisher*. *See* Haslewood

Owen (John) Five great skeptical dramas of history. Ln: Sonnenschein, 1896. 8°
' Hamlet,' pp. 277-348.   BM | BPL | MPL

Owen (O. W.) Bacon *versus* Sh— in the court of the arena. 1893. 8°   BPL

Celebrated case : Bacon or Sh— ? Request to re-open brief for plaintiff. 1893. 8°   BPL
The same writer's ' Bacon or Sh—' under an altered title.

Historical tragedy of Mary Queen of Scots. By the author of 'Hamlet.' . . . Deciphered from the works of Sir F. Bacon. [1894.] 8°   BM

Sir F. Bacon's cipher story [Extracted from . . . Sh— and others]. 1894. 2 vols. 8°   BM | BPL

Tragical historie of our late brother Robert Earl of Essex, deciphered from the works of Sir F. Bacon. Detroit : Howard, 1895. 8°   SML

Owen (R.) *Dublin Publisher*. *See* Sh— Works, 1747

Owen (W.) *Publisher*—
See Letter . . .
  ,, Poetical epistle
  ,, Prologue
  ,, Richardson
  ,, Sh— Hamlet, 1773
  ,, Sh— Julius Cæsar, 1774
  ,, Sh— King Lear, 1772
  ,, Sh— Macbeth, 1770, 1773
  ,, Sh— Othello, 1773
  ,, Sh— Timon . . . 1770
  ,, Sh— Works, 1770-74, 1773

Owen & Son (W.) *Publishers*   *See* Sh— Merchant . . . 1783

'Owen jun.' *pseud*. *See* Hardinge

Oxberry (Wm.) *Publisher*—
See Sh— King Lear, 1820, 1823
  ,, Sh— Merchant . . . 1820, 1823
  ,, Sh— Works, 1818-22

Oxberry (Wm. Henry) Actor's budget, consisting of monologues, prologues, epilogues, and tales . . . theatrical anecdotes and comic songs. Ln: Simpkin, 1820. 8°   SML

Anecdotes of the stage. Ln: Virtue, 1827. 12°   SML

Dramatic biography and histrionic anecdotes. Ln: G. Vertue, 1825. 7 vols. 12°. With character portraits   BPL *(impft.)*

Oxberry (Wm. Henry) *Actor-Editor*—
See Sh— As you like it, 1819
  ,, Sh— Coriolanus, 1820
  ,, Sh— Cymbeline, 1821
  ,, Sh— Hamlet, 1818, 1820, 1823
  ,, Sh— Julius Cæsar, 1822, 1823
  ,, Sh— King Henry IV., i., 1822, 1823
  ,, Sh— King Henry V., 1823
  ,, Sh— King Henry VIII., 1823
  ,, Sh— King John, 1819, 1823
  ,, Sh— King Richard III., 1819, 1827
  ,, Sh— Macbeth, 1821, 1823
  ,, Sh— Measure . . . 1822, 1823
  ,, Sh— Merry wives, 1820, 1822, 1823
  ,, Sh— Much ado . . . 1823
  ,, Sh— Othello, 1819, 1823
  ,, Sh— Romeo . . . 1819, 1823
  ,, Sh— The tempest, 1823
  ,, Sh— Twelfth night, 1821, 1823
  ,, Sh— Two gentlemen, 1823
  ,, Sh— Winter's tale, 1821, 1823

Oxford—
See Fletcher
  ,, Stage condemn'd

Oxford book of English verse. *See* Quiller-Couch

Oxford University. *See* Sh— Hamlet, 1603

Oxlade (W.) *Printer & Publisher—*
See Sh— As you like it, 1777
,, Sh— Hamlet, 1776
,, Sh— King Richard III., 1775, 1778
,, Sh— Macbeth, 1776
,, Sh— Merchant . . . 1777
,, Sh— Othello, 1777
,, Sh— Romeo . . . 1775
,, Sh— The tempest, 1778
'Oxon.' *pseud.* Analysis and study of the leading characters of 'Hamlet.' Ln: Sonnenschein, 1885. 8° BM | BUS | SML
Analysis and study of the leading characters of 'Macbeth' and 'As you like it.' Ln: Sonnenschein, 1886. 8° BM | BUS | SML
'Oxoniensis' *pseud. See* Field (B.)

P—— (E.) *Printer. See* Jonson
P—— (G.) *Printer. See* Sh— George-a-Greene, 1632
P—— (I.) *Printer. See* Sh— Venus . . . 1620
P—— (J.) Sh—; his life and writings. *See* Sh—] P——
P—— (J. & T. C.) Shys at Sh— [Etched caricatures]. Philadelphia : By the author, 1869. 8° BPL | SML
P—— (J. V.) Who wrote 'Sh—' ? [In 'Fraser's Magazine,' Aug.] 1874. 8° BUS
P—— (K.) Sh—. *See* Sh—] P——
P—— (L.) *See* Piot *or* Pyott
P—— (M.) *See* Parker
P—— (M.) *Printer. See* Sh— Merchant . . . 1637
P—— (M.) *Publisher. See* Sh— King Lear, 1723
P—— (P.) *Editor—*
See Sh— Coriolanus, 1820
,, Sh— Cymbeline, 1821
,, Sh— Julius Cæsar, 1822
,, Sh— King Henry IV., i., 1822
,, Sh— King Henry V., 1823
,, Sh— King Henry VIII., 1823
,, Sh— King Lear, 1820
,, Sh— Macbeth, 1821
,, Sh— Measure . . . 1822
,, Sh— Merry wives, 1820
,, Sh— Much ado, 1823
,, Sh— Two gentlemen, 1823
,, Sh— Twelfth night, 1821
,, Sh— Winter's tale, 1823
P—— (T.) *Printer—*
See Marston
,, Purfoot (T.)
,, Purfoot jun. (Thomas)

P—— (T.) *Publisher. See* Pavier (Thomas)
Pace-Sanfelice (G.) *Editor. See* Porto
Pack (Richardson) New collection of miscellanies. *See* Sh— Merry wives, 1725
Page (Mary D.) *Artist. See* Sh— Works : Ext. 1897
Page (T.) *Editor—*
See Sh— As you like it, 1893
,, Sh— Coriolanus, 1894
,, Sh— Hamlet, 1891
,, Sh— Julius Cæsar, 1896, 1904
,, Sh— King Henry V., 1896
,, Sh— King Henry VIII., 1903
,, Sh— King John, 1889, 1892
,, Sh— King Lear, 1889, 1892
,, Sh— King Richard III., 1902
,, Sh— Merchant . . . 1898
,, Sh— Midsummer . . . 1897
,, Sh— The tempest, 1892
,, Sh— Winter's tale, 1904
Page (Thomas) Spenser and Sh—. *See* Sh—] Page
Page (Wm.) Study of Sh—'s portraits. *See* Sh—] Page
Pageants—
See Gascoigne   *See* Laneham
,, Greg   ,, Revels
,, Harland
Paget (A. H.) Elizabethan play-houses. 1891. 8° BPL
Sh—'s plays : A chapter of stage history. An essay on the Sh— drama. Ln : J. Wilson, 1875. 8°, pp. 48
BM | BPL | BUS | MPL
Paget (H. M. & W.) Sh— pictures [illustrating scenes from the plays]. Ln : E. Nister [Nuremberg printed, 1890]. Oblong 4° BM | BPL
Paget (W.) *Artist. See* Sh— Works : Ext. 1901
Paige *Editor. See* Sh— Merchant . . . 1875
Paige (J.) *Editor—*
See Sh— Hamlet, 1891
,, Sh— King John, 1889
,, Sh— King Lear, 1892
,, Sh— Works, 1890
Painter (William) Palace of pleasure, beautified, adorned, and well furnished with pleasant histories and excellent novelles, selected out of divers good and commendable authors . . . Ln : H. Denham for R. Tottell . . . H. Bynneman for N. England, 1566-67. 2 vols. Fcp. 4° MRL
Sh— and other Elizabethan dramatists were indebted to this work for their plots.
It includes Boccaccio's story, 'Giletta of Narbona' (a source of 'All's well'); also Porto's 'History of Rhomeo and Iulietta' and tales from Bandello.
Palace of pleasure . . . Imprinted at Ln. in Fletestreate neare to S. Dunstone's Church by Thomas Marshe, 1569-80. 2 vols. Fcp 4°; black letter CTC

(241)   16

Painter (William) Palace of pleasure . . . Ln : T. Marsh, 1575. Fcp. 4°

Palace of pleasure . . . From the edition . . . 1575. Ed. by Joseph Haslewood. Ln : 1813. 2 vols in 3. 4°   BUS

Palace of pleasure—
  See Sh— All's well, 1889
  ,, Sh— King Edward III., 1596
  ,, Sh— Romeo . . . 1888

Rhomeo and Iulietta. Ed. by P. A. Daniel— See New Sh— Soc.
  ,, Sh—] Sh—'s library

Palgrave (Francis Turner) Editor—
  See Sh— Poems, 1865, 1879
  ,, Sh— Sonnets, 1864, 1865, 1879

Palmer (Henrietta Lee) Stratford gallery or the Sh— sisterhood, comprising forty-five ideal portraits . . . Illust. with engravings . . . New York: D. Appleton & Co., 1859. Roy. 8°, pp. 302   BM | BPL | BUS
Copied from Heath's ' Sh— gallery.'

Palmer Actor (John) Portrait. See Sh— King Henry VI., i., 1786

Palmer (J. F.) Ethics from Homer to Christ. Homer's characters in 'Troilus & Cressida' [In ' Trans. of Roy. Soc. of Lit.,' 2nd ser., vol. 15, pp. 48-53]. 1893. 8°   BPL

Paman (Clement). See Poetical revenge

Pandin (Beauregard) Editor. See Sh— Troilus . . . 1824

Paradyse of daynty deuises. See Stopes

Parallel between Sh— and Scott. See Martin

Parish clerks. See Collier

Park (Thomas) Editor. See Heliconia

Park Theatre, New York. See Sh— Two gentlemen, 1846

Parker Boston [U.S.] Publisher. See Sh— Works, 1810-12

Parker (Henry Meredith) Bole ponjis. Ln : 1851. 2 vols. 8°   BUS
Contains ' Sketches from Sh— texts,' vol. i., pp. 254-269, and ' Scenes of the seven ages,' vol. ii., pp. 1-80. The latter is a drama founded upon the poet's lines.

Parker (John) Printer. See Sh— Venus . . . 1620

Parker (M.)] Harry White : his humour so neare as may be set forth by M. P——. Ed. by J. O. Halliwell. [c. 1846.] 12°
See also Literature . . .   BPL

Parker (P.) Publisher. See Sh— Cupid's cabinet, 1684

Parker (R.) Publisher. See Sh— Measure . . . 1700

Parker (S. W. L.) Effects of certain mental and bodily states upon the imagination, especially as illustrated by Sh—. Birmingham, 1876. 8°   BPL

Parkinson (J. C.) Sh— a freemason : Bard of Avon lodge of united, ancient, free, and accepted masons of England, province of Middlesex. [Ln.] 1872. Fcp 4°
    BPL | BUS

Parodies—
  See Barrey (L.)   See Hamilton (W.)
  ,, Facetiæ   ,, Hardinge

Parr (N.) Artist. See Sh— King Henry VIII., 1758

Parr (Wolstenholme) Observations. See Giraldi

Story of the Moor of Venice, translated from the Italian, with two essays on Sh—. Ln : 1795. 8°   BPL | W
The essays are upon ' Coriolanus' and ' Othello.'

Parrot (Henry) Epigrams. See Sh— Epitaph on Combe

Parrott (T. M.) Chapman's 'All fooles' and J. P. Collier['s forgery of the dedication] [In 'Athenæum,' No. 4209, p. 788, June]. 1908

Parry (A. W.) Editor—
  See Sh— Macbeth, 1884
  ,, Sh— King Henry V., 1904
  ,, Sh— As you like it, 1903.

Parry (E. A.) Charles Macklin. See Macklin
Story of Sh—'s life. See Sh— Works : Ext. 1903

Parry (Thomas) Editor—
  See Sh— Julius Cæsar, 1882, 1883, 1885, 1887, 1890, 1900
  ,, Sh— King John, 1884, 1886
  ,, Sh— Merchant . . . 1883, 1884, 1887, 1894
  ,, Sh— Works, 1883-86

Parsons (Mrs. Clement) Incomparable Siddons. See Siddons

Garrick. See Garrick

Parsons (Marmaduke) Printer. See Sh— Merchant . . . 1637

Parsons (Robert) Treatise on three conversions of England from paganisme to christian religion. Ln : . . . 1603-1604. 3 vols. 12°
A notice on p. 31, vol. iii., apparently refers to Sh—'s play :—'. . . Syr John Oldcastle, a ruffian knight, as all England knoweth, and commonly brought in by comedients on their stages.'

Parsons (Wm.) Actor. See Sh— King Henry IV., ii., 1785

Parsons.] Bellamy (T.) Life of Wm. Parsons. With his dramatic characters by J. Litchfield, and a letter of intelligence. Ln : Printed for the author, 1795. 8°
    SML

Parterre of poetry. Ln : 1836. 8°   BPL
Refers to Sh—.

Partridge Artist. See Irving

Partridge (J.) History of Plasidas, 1566. See Reprints

Partridge (John) Catalogue of books . . . including Sh—'s own 'Prayer Book' . . .
On sale . . . Wellington, Salop. [1865.]
8°, pp. 16   BUS
Pascal.] Blaise Pascal the moralist, the
philosopher, the theologian [Magazine
excerpt, c. 1855]. 8°   W
Several references to Sh—.
Pascoe (C. E.) Dramatic list: Principal per-
formances of living actors and actresses.
Ln: 1879. 12°   BPL
Dramatic notes: Chronicle of the London
stage, 1879-82. With 180 sketches. Ln:
Bogue, 1883. 8°   SML
Pasquil's palinodia, 1619. *See* Reprints
Pasquil's jests. *See Sh*—] Sh—'s Jest books
Pasquil's jests, with Mother Bunche's merri-
ments. *See* Old English Jest Books
'Pasquin (Anthony)' *pseud. See* Williams (J.)
Pass (Simon) *Artist-Engraver*—
See Bacon (Sir F.)
,, James I.
Passages selected by distinguished personages.
See Dudley
Passenger (Thomas) *Publisher*—
See Henry VIII.
,, Johnson jun.
,, Sandys
Passion of a discontented mind. *See* Reprints
Passionate morrice. *See* A——
Passionate pilgrim. *See* Sh— Passionate pil-
grim
Passionate shepherd's song.. *See* Bodenham
Passions of the minde. *See* Wright
Patagonian Theatre, Exeter Change. *See*
Sh— The tempest, 1780
Pater (Walter Horatio) Appreciations. With
an essay on style. Ln: Macmillan, 1889.
8°
On 'Love's labours lost,' 'Measure for measure,' and
Sh—'s English kings.
Speaking of 'Love's labours lost,' pp. 174-175, Pater
says:—'As happens with every true dramatist, Sh—
is for the most part hidden behind the persons of his
creation. Yet there are certain of his characters in
which we feel that there is something of self-por-
traiture. And it is not so much in his grander, more
subtle, and ingenious creations that we feel this, in
'Hamlet' and 'King Lear,' as in those slighter and
more spontaneously-developed figures who, while far
from playing principal parts, are yet distinguished
by a peculiar happiness and delicate ease in the
drawing of them; figures which possess above all
that winning attractiveness which there is no man
but would willingly exercise, and which resemble
those works of art which, though not meant to be
very great or imposing, are yet wrought of the
choicest material. Mercutio belongs to this group
. . . Biron is perhaps the most striking . . . In this
character, which is never quite in touch, never quite
on a perfect level of understanding with the other
persons of the play, we see perhaps a reflex of Sh—
himself, when he has just become able to stand aside
from and estimate the first period of his poetry.'
Appreciations . . . Ln: 1890. 8°   BPL
Appreciations . . . Ln: 1898. 8°

Pater (Walter Horatio) Fragment on 'Measure
for measure' [In 'Fortnightly Review,'
vol. 76, p. 652]. Ln: 1874. Roy. 8°   BPL
Paterson *Comedian* (Peter) Glimpses of real
life, as seen in the theatrical world and in
Bohemia. 1864. Cr. 8°
Paterson (S.) *Publisher. See* Sh— Poems, 1760
Paterson (Samuel) *Bookseller. See* Catalogue,
1748
Paton *Artist. See* Sh— Works, 1792
Paton (Allan Park) North's Plutarch: Notes
as to a copy in the Greenock Library sup-
posed to have been Sh—'s. Greenock,
1871. 8°   BM | BPL | BUS
Paton (A. P.) *Editor*—
See Sh— Antony, 1890
,, Sh— Coriolanus, 1880
,, Sh— Cymbeline, 1879
,, Sh— Hamlet, 1878
,, Sh— Julius Cæsar, 1881
,, Sh— Macbeth, 1877
,, Sh— Merry wives, 1896
,, Sh— Othello, 1891
,, Sh— Timon . . . 1879
,, Sh— Winter's tale, 1879
,, Sh— Works, 1877-96
Paton (*Sir* Joseph Noel) Compositions . . .
1845—
See Sh— The tempest, 1845, 1877
,, Sh— Works, 1888-89
Patrick (David) *Editor. See* Sh— Julius
Cæsar, 1903
Patterson (Robert) Letters on the natural
history of the insects mentioned in Sh—'s
plays. With incidental notices of the
entomology of Ireland. Ln: W. S.
Orr & Co., 1838. 12°, pp. xvi.-270, por-
trait and over 80 illustrations
                              BPL | BUS | MPL
Natural history of insects. Ln: A. K.
Newman, 1841. 12°, illustrated
                                    BPL | SML
Natural history of insects . . . 1842. Cr.
8°, illustrated   BM | CPL
Pattie *Publisher*—
See Sh— As you like it, 1841
,, Sh— King Henry V., 1839
,, Sh— Midsummer . . . 1840
Paul (H.) *Editor. See* Sh— Timon . . . 1908
Pavier (Thomas) *Publisher*—
See Fair widow
,, Sh— Hamlet, 1608
,, Sh— King Henry V., 1602
,, Sh— King Henry VI., ii.-iii., 1619
,, Sh— King Henry VI., iii., 1619
,, Sh— Merry devil, 1631
,, Sh— Pericles, 1619
,, Sh— Sir John Oldcastle, 1600
,, Sh— The puritan widow, 1860
,, Sh— Yorkshire tragedy, 1608, 1619

Payn (James) Talk of the town. Ln: 1885.
12° BPL
A novel dealing with the Ireland forgeries.

Payne (F. J.) Scene divisions in Sh—'s plays.
Sh— Club paper. Stratford, 1907. Cr.
8°, pp. 8

Payne (Francis John). *See* Littledale

Payne (J.) Studies in English prose. *See* Sh—]
Payne

Payne (J.) *Publisher*—
See Johnson (*Dr.* S.) The rambler
 „ Kenrick

Payne (Nevil) Morning ramble, or the town
humours : A comedy. Acted at the
Duke's Theatre. Ln : Printed for Thomas
Dring at the White Lyon next Chancery
Lane and in Fleet Street, 1673. Fcp. 4°
'The world is busie now, and some dare say
 We have not seen of late one good new play,
 And such believe Sh—, long since in his grave,
 In choicest lybraries a place will have.'—*Epilogue.*

Payne (T.) *Printer. See* More

Payne (T.) *Publisher*—
See Sh— Works, 1766, 1773, 1798
 „ Whately

Payne *jun.* (T.) *Publisher. See* Sh— Works,
1790, 1797

Payne & Foss, *Publishers & Booksellers. See*
Sh— Hamlet, 1603, 1825

Payne & Son (T.) *Publishers*—
See Remarks
 „ Sh— Merchant . . . 1783

Payne-Smith (W. H.) *Editor. See* Sh— King
Richard III., 1889, 1900

Peabody (O. W. B.) *Editor*—
See Sh— Poems, 1855
 „ Sh— Works, 1836, 1844, 1849-51, 1877

Peacock (Thomas Love) *Editor. See* Ingannati

Peak (Clara Cleone) *Artist. See* Sterling

Peake (R. B.) *See* Colman

Pearce (William) Haunts of Sh— : A poem.
Ln : D. Browne, 1778. 4°, pp. 26, and
vignette BPL | BUS
Contains also a sonnet on Garrick's retirement.

Pearls of Sh—. *See* Sh— Works : Ext. 1860,
1864, 1873

Pearson (Howard Shakespeare)] On the 'Mer-
chant of Venice' [In 'Birmingham
Examiner,' pp. 27-32]. 1876. 4° BPL
Origin and growth of Birmingham. *See*
Memorials . . .
Secret of Sh— [In 'Central Literary Maga-
zine']. Birmingham, 1900. 8° BPL
Sh— and the world unseen. Sh— Club
paper. Stratford-on-Avon, 1903. F°,
broadside ; single sheet

Pearson (J. L.) *Editor. See* Middleton

Peck (Francis) New memoirs. *See* Milton

Peck (George Washington) Hudson's lectures
on Sh— [In 'American Review,' July].
New York, 1848. 8° BUS

Peck (George Washington) Sh—'s art [In
'Atlantic Monthly,' June]. Boston, 1859.
8° BUS

Pecke (Thomas) Parnassi puerperium, or
some wellwishes to ingenuity. Ln: 1659.
8°, with portrait
At p. 66 is the 'Epitaph of Pyramus and Thisbe.'

Pedder (H. C.) Study of 'Hamlet' [In 'The
Manhattan']. New York, 1883. 8° BPL

Peele (George) Arraignment of Paris. *See* Sh—
Arraignment
Letter to Marle. *See* Steevens (G.)
Merrie conceited iests . . . wherein is showed
the course of his life, how he liued : a
man very well knowne in the city of
London and elsewhere
Buy, reade, and iudge
The price doe not grudge
It will doe thee more pleasure
Than twice so much treasure.
Ln : Printed for Henry Bell, dwelling in
the Little Old Baily in Eliot's Court
[1607]. Fcp. 4°, sig. A¹ to D⁴ unpaged
Refers to 'Venus and Adonis' on D2 (verso), and on
D3 says 'For the price of a barrel of beere I have
bought a groatsworth of wit,' ridiculing the title of
Robert Greene's work.
So far as Peele is concerned, these jests are probably
more or less apocryphal. Peele was the City poet,
and had the ordering of pageants. He died in or
before 1598, as Meres gives the cause in his 'Palladis
tamia.' Nash termed Peele the 'chief supporter of
pleasance, atlas of poetrie, and primum verborum
artifex.'
Merry conceited jests . . . Ln : 1627. Fcp.
4° ; black letter
Merry conceited jests . . . Ln : Printed for
Wm. Gilbertson at the Bible in Giltspur
Street without Newgate, 1657. Fcp. 4° ;
black letter, sig. A—C⁴ paged CTC
Merrie conceited jests . . . [1607]. Ln : Re-
printed for S. W. Singer, 13 St. James's
St. & R. Triphook, 37 St. James's St.,
1809. Fcp. 4°, pp. 34
Includes some biographical particulars of Peele.
Merrie conceited jests, 1864. *See* Sh—]
Sh— Jest books
Merrie conceited jests. *See* Old English
Jest Books
] Old wives' tale. A pleasant conceited
comedie, played by the Queene's Maies-
tie's players. Written by G. P——.
Printed at Ln. by Iohn Danter and are to
be sold by Ralph Hancocke and Iohn
Hardie, 1595. Ln : Malone Society, 1909.
Fcp. 4° BM | SML

Peele (George). *See* Cooper
See Sh— Taming . . . (*heading*)

Peep behind the curtain. *See* Garrick

Pegasus.] Third and fourth part of Pegasus. Taught by Bankes his ghost to dance in the Dorick moode. To the tune of Lachrymæ. Ln: 1648. Fcp. 4°   w
Pegasus is referred to in ' Taming of the shrew,' ' King Henry IV., Part i.,' and ' King Henry V.' Banks' horse is mentioned in ' Love's labours lost.'

Peirce (Charles Sanders). *See* Noyes & Peirce
Peleus and Thetis: A masque. *See* Sh— Merchant ... 1701

Pell (W. C.) Sh— and Hollinshed [In 'Harper's Mag.,' Sept.] New York, 1861. 8°   BUS

Pemberton (Charles Reece)] Classification of readers of Sh—. With remarks on Macready's 'King John,' by 'Pel Verjuice' [In ' Monthly Repository,' Jan.] Ln: 1834. 8°   BUS

Pemberton.] Life and literary remains of C. R. Pemberton. Ln: 1843. 8°
          BPL | BUS | CPL
Contains Macready's 'King John' and 'Coriolanus,' Macready and Kemble as ' Brutus.'

Pemberton (J.) *Publisher—*
See Sh— Coriolanus, 1720
 ,, Sh— Poems, 1725, 1728
 ,, Sh— Works, 1714, 1725

Pemberton (John) *Publisher. See* Sewell

Pemberton (T. Edgar) Ben Jonson's 'Every man in his humour.' Memorial Theatre, Stratford, 1903. 8°   BPL
Birmingham theatres; A local retrospect. Birmingham: Cornish, 1889. 12°, pp. vi.-216   SML
'King Henry VIII.' on the stage, Memorial Theatre, Stratford. 1902. 8°   BPL
Memoir of E. A. Sothern. *See* Sothern
Original portrait of Sh—. *See* Sh—] Pemberton
Sh— Memorial Theatre: Concerning the Sh— annual festival. Stratford: J. Morgan, 1901.   8°, pp. 52 (includes printed wrappers); illust.   BPL
Washington Irving. *See* Irving

Pembroke *Sh—'s patron* (Wm. Herbert *third Earl of*) Letter to Sir Robert Cecil. 2 Sept., 1601
See 'Athenæum,' Sept., 1886, p. 337.
The original manuscript is in the Salisbury library at Hatfield.

Pembroke (Wm. Herbert *third Earl of*)—
See Nicholson
 ,, Sh— Titus, 1594
 ,, Sh— Works, 1623, 1632, 1663, 1664, 1685

Pembroke's (*Earl of*) Servants—
See Sh— King Henry VI., i.-iii., 1595, 1600
 ,, Sh— Taming ... 1594, 1596, 1607

'Pendragon (Anser)' *pseud. See* Ireland (S. W. H.)

Penley (Belville S.) Bath stage: History of dramatic representations ... Bath: Lewis, 1892. Cr. 8°, pp. xvi.-180; illustrated   BPL | SML

Penn (J.) Letters on the drama. 1796. 8°   BPL

Penn (William). *See* Wright (C.)

Pennant (Thomas) Some Account of London. Second edition [enlarged]. 1791. 4°, with portraits, plates, and map   BM
Valuable for its notes on Blackfriars (where Sh— owned property) and on the early theatres.

Pennie (J. F.) Harp of Parnassus. *See* Sh— Works: Ext. 1822

Pennington (G. I.) *Editor. See* Sh— King Henry IV., ii., 1817

Penny illustrated weekly: Sh— tercentenary. 30th Ap., 1864. F°   BPL

Pennyworth of wit [A verbatim transcript from the Parkington copy, c. 1840]. Fcp. 4°; manuscript, upon five leaves of paper   w
' Sir, your pennyworth is good.'—*Love's labours lost.*
' I have a poor pennyworth in English.'—*Merchant of Venice.*
' You take your pennyworths now.'—*Romeo and Juliet.*

Penrice (T.) *Editor. See* Howe

'Pentweazle (Ebenezer)' *pseud. See* Horatian

Penzance (J. P. W. *Baron*) Judicial summing-up: On the Bacon-Sh— controversy. Edited by M. H. Kinnear. With biographical note by F. A. Inderwick. Ln: Low, 1902. 8°, pp. 214, with portrait
          BPL | BUS | MPL

Pepper (W.) *Publisher. See* Comedian ...

Pepys (Samuel) Diary and correspondence. With life and notes by Richard Lord Braybrooke. Ln: Bumpus, 1888. 6 vols. Roy. 8°; with portraits   BM
On March 1st, 1661-62, Pepys says : ' My wife and I by coach ... to the Opera, and there saw " Romeo and Juliet" the first time it was ever acted, but it is a play of itself the worst that ever I heard, and the worst acts that ever I saw these people do, and I am resolved to go no more to see the first time of acting, for they were all of them out more or less.'
29th Sept., 1662. ' To the King's Theatre, where we saw "Midsummer night's dream," which I had never seen before, nor ever shall again, for it is the most insipid, ridiculous play that ever I saw in my life.'
28th Dec., 1665. ' To the Duke's House, and there saw "Macbeth" most excellently acted, and a most excellent play for variety. I had sent my wife to meet me there, who did come : so I did go to Whitehall, and got my Lord Bellassis [Belasyse] to get me into the playhouse, and there, after all staying an hour for the players, the King and all waiting, which was absurd, saw " Henry V." well done by the Duke's people, and in most excellent habit, all new vests being put on but this night ... The play continued till twelve at night ; and then up, and a most horrid cold night it was, frosty and moonshine.'
7th Jan., 1666. ' To the Duke's House, and saw "Macbeth," which, though I saw it lately, yet appears a most excellent play in all respects, but especially in divertisement, though it be a deep tragedy, which is a strange perfection in a tragedy, it being most proper here and suitable.'

16th Oct., 1667. 'To the Duke of York's House, and I was vexed to see Young, who is but a bad actor at best, act *Macbeth* in the room of Betterton, who, poor man, is sick; but Lord! what a prejudice it wrought in me against the whole play, and everybody else agreed in disliking this fellow. . . .'

Percy. *See* Annotations

Percy (John) *Composer. See* Sh— Midsummer . . . 1760

Percy (John) *Editor. See* Sh— Romeo . . . 1750

Percy *Bp.* (Thomas) Essay on the origin of the English stage, particularly the historical plays of Sh—. Ln: 1793. 8°

Percy Society : Publications [Edited by Wm. Hy. Black, P. Bliss, W. Chappell, J. P. Collier, T. C. Croker, P. Cunningham, J. H. Dixon, A. Dyce, F. W. Fairholt, J. Goodwin, J. O. Halliwell, C. Hardwicke, C. Mackay, T. J. Pettigrew, E. F. Rimbault, W. Sandys, W. J. Thoms, and T. Wright]. Ln: Privately printed, 1840-52. 95 numbers, forming 30 vols. Cr. 8°   BM
Of extreme interest to the Shakespearean, consisting of reprints of rare old English books and tracts in prose and verse, such as fiction, poetry, folk-lore, legends, traditions, and materials generally that Sh— would be glad to avail himself of.
Two of the numbers were suppressed.

Perdita, or the royal milkmaid. *See* Sh— Winter's tale, 1856

Perdita : Artists' notes from choice pictures [In 'London Society']. 1867. 8°   BPL
Illustrates the 'Winter's tale.'

Pereira *Calcutta Publisher. See* Sh— As you like it, 1815

Performance of 'Othello' by F. W. K. Aldridge. *See* Cole

Performances at court in the reign of Henry VIII. Ln: Sh— Soc., 1847. 8°   BPL

Pericles. *See* Sh— Pericles

Perkins (L. F.) *Artist. See* Sh— Midsummer . . . 1907

Perott (J. de). *See* De Perott

Perrett (Wilfrid) Story of 'King Lear,' from Geoffrey of Monmouth to Sh— [In 'Palæstra']. Berlin, 1904. 8°, pp. 308
BPL | BUS

Perrin (J. B.) Contes moraux. *See* Sh— Works : Ext. 1783

Perring (*Sir* Philip) Hard knots in Sh—. Ln: Longmans, 1885. 8°, pp. x.-374
BM | BUS
Hard knots . . . Second edition. Ln: 1886. 8°   BM | BPL | BUS | SML

Perry (Hugh) *Publisher—*
See Chettle
,, Sh— King Henry IV., i., 1639

Perry (Marsden Jasael)] Catalogue of Shakespeareana [Perry collection]. With a prefatory essay by 'Sidney Lee.' Chiswick Press : Privately printed, 1899. 2 vols. Imp. 8°   BPL | BUS | SML
Issue limited to one hundred copies.

Perry (Wm.) Treatise on the identity of Herne's oak, shewing the maiden tree to have been the real one. Ln: 1867. 12°, pp. 68; illust.   BPL | BUS | MPL
Illustrates the 'Merry wives.'

Perry (W. G.) Botanist's guide to the county of Warwick. Warwick, 1820. 12°   SML

Persian tales. With notes by W. A. Clouston. Glasgow, 1892. 12°   BPL
Contains at pp. 36-48 'The Kazi of Emessa,' supposed to have been used by Sh— in preparing the 'Merchant of Venice.'

Persius. *See* Loveling

Pertwee (Ernest) Sh— for recitation. *See* Sh— Works : Ext. 1904

Peters *Actor* (Hugh). *See* Berkenhead

Petrarca (Francesco) Portrait. *See* Sh— Romeo, 1879

Petre (J.) Trifles. 1823. 8°   BPL
Verses on Sh— at pp. 71-80, etc.

Pettie (George)] Tale of Tereus and Progne referred to by Sh—. Edited by J. O. Halliwell. Ln: 1866. 8°, pp. 36
Ten copies printed.   BPL | HCL | MPL
This tale is the second of twelve in the collection called a 'Petite pallace of Pettie his pleasure 1576.' The title is a plagiarism of Painter's work, 'She hath been reading late the "Tale of Tereus."'—*Cymbeline, II. 2.*

Pettie (George) *Editor. See* Guazzo

Pettigrew (T. J.) *See* Nimmo & Pettigrew

Pettigrew (T. J.) *Editor. See* Percy Society

Pfeffer (C. E. M.) *Halle Publisher—*
See Sh— Romeo . . . 1853
,, Sh— Works, 1853

Pfundheller (E.) On the character of Lady Macbeth. 1873. 4°   BM

Phaer (Thomas) Will. Ed. by P. Cunningham. *See* Sh—] Sh— Soc.

Phaeton. *See* Sh— Phaeton . . .

Phelps (Charles Edward) Falstaff and equity : An interpretation. Boston, U.S., 1901. 8°   BPL | BUS | SML
Stage history of famous plays : 'Hamlet' from the actor's standpoint. New York, 1890. 8°, with portraits   BUS

Phelps (C. E. D.) & North (L.) Bailiff of Tewkesbury. Ln: A. C. McClurg, 1893. 12°   SML
A Sh— story.

Phelps (Samuel) *Actor, Editor, & Manager—*
See Kenney
,, Sh— Works, 1851-54, 1852-54, 1853, 1858, 1859, 1872, 1882, 1882-4, 1896
Phelps.] Mr. Phelps and the Stratford-upon-Avon committee. 1864. 8°   BPL
On the tercentenary.

] Phelps (W. M.) & Robertson (J. Forbes) Life and life-works of Samuel Phelps. Ln: Low, 1886. 8°, with portraits and documents   BPL

Phelps (W. L.) *Editor. See* Sh— As you like it, 1896

Pheney (R.) *Publisher. See* Sh— Works, 1811

Philadelphia. *See* Ashhurst

Philadelphia 'Edwin Forrest' home : Commemoration of Sh—'s birthday. 1895. 8°

Philadelphia Sh— League. *See Sh—*] Sh—

Philadelphia Sh— Society : Its origin and early years. Philadelphia, 1870. 8° MPL
Memorial, 1872-97. 4° BPL
Twelfth Annual Dinner [Menu ; with quotations]. 23 April, 1864. 4°, pp. 6 BUS
Twenty-first annual dinner, Wed., 23 April, 1873. 4°, pp. 8 BUS
One hundred copies privately printed.

Twenty-fifth anniversary and twenty-fourth annual dinner. 1897. 4° BPL

Thirty-first annual dinner : Menu. Philadelphia, U.S., 1903. 4° BPL

'Philalethes' *pseud. See* Webb (*Col.* F.)

'Philarchaiotētos' *pseud.* Heraldic documents respecting Sh—'s arms [In 'European Mag.'] 1816. 8° BPL

Philipp. On Sh—'s 'Julius Cæsar,' especially with respect to historical truth. Berlin, 1849. 8° BUS

Philippi (*Dr.* A.) *Editor. See* Sh— King John, 1848

Philips (Ambrose) Distrest mother : A tragedy. Ln : J. Tonson, 1712. Fcp. 4°
Has references to Sh—. The epilogue (ascribed to Budgell) was written by J. Addison.

Humphrey Duke of Gloucester : A tragedy. As it is acted at the Theatre Royal in Drury Lane, by his Majesty's servants. Ln : Printed and sold by J. Roberts near the Oxford Arms in Warwick Lane, 1723. 8°, pp. xii.-86 BPL
Illustrates 'King Henry VI.'
For sequel see Sh— King Henry VI., ii., 1723.

Philips (John) *Publisher. See* Sh— Macbeth, 1710

Phillip (John) Commodye of pacient and meeke Grissill . . . Imprinted at Ln. in Fleetstreat beneath the conduit at the signe of Saint John Euangelist by Thomas Colwell [1565-66]. Ed. by R. B. McKerrow & W. W. Greg. Malone Society Reprints, 1909. Fcp. 4° BM | SML

Phillipps, Sampson & Co. *Boston* [U.S.] *Publishers. See* Sh— Poems, 1855

Phillips *Publisher. See* Sh— King Richard III., 1868

Phillips *Boston U.S. Publisher. See* Sh— Works, 1848, 1849-51, 1850, 1854

Phillips (Augustine) *Editor. See* Sh— Works, 1908

Phillips (Bruce) Royal aquarium and Shaksperian diary. Ln : Dickens & Evans [1876]. 24°, pp. 72 BPL | BUS

Phillips (Edward) Theatrum poetarum, or a compleat collection of the poets, especially the most eminent of all ages . . . Ln : Charles Smith at the Angel near the Inner Temple Gate, 1675. 2 parts in 1 vol. 12° W
A life of Sh— occurs in part ii., at p. 194.
The Warwick copy came from the library of Thomas Park, editor of 'Heliconia,' and is enriched with many manuscript notes by him.
The master hand of John Milton may frequently be detected in this production of his elder nephew, more particularly in the descriptions of Sh— and Marlowe.
On p. 194 says, 'Wm. Sh— the glory of the English stage, whose nativity at Stratford upon Avon is the highest honour that town can boast of, from an actor of tragedies and comedies he became a maker ; and such a maker, that though some others may perhaps pretend to a more exact decorum and economy, especially in tragedy, never any expressed a more lofty and tragic height, never any represented nature more purely to the life ; and where the polishments of art are most wanting, as probably his learning was not extraordinary, he pleaseth with a certain wild and native elegance, and in all his writings hath an unvulgar style as well in his "Venus and Adonis," his "Rape of Lucrece," and other various poems, as in his dramaticks.'

Theatrum poetarum Anglicanorum . . . Canterbury, 1800. 8° MPL

Phillips (John) *Editor. See* Scarron

Phillips (P. D.) Shakesperian notes of travel. Melbourne : Sh— Soc., 1890. 8° BPL

Phillips (R.) *Publisher. See* Public Characters

Phillpots *Editor. See* Sh— Romeo . . . 1885

Phillpotts (J. Surtees) *Editor—*
See Sh— The tempest, 1870, 1876, 1885
„ Sh— Works, 1872-83

Philological Society. *See* Ellis

Phin (John) Sh— cyclopædia and new glossary. With the most important variorum readings. Intended as a supplement to all ordinary editions of Sh—'s works. Introd. by Edward Dowden. Ln : K. Paul, 1902. 8°, pp. 456 BPL | MPL | SML
Sh— notes and new readings. New York, 1901. 8° BPL

Phin (John) *Editor. See* Sh— monthly companion

Phippis *of Stoke* (John). *See* Bullen (M. W.)

Phipson (*Miss* E.) Animal lore of Sh—'s time . . . 1883. 8° BM | BPL | MPL | SML
Natural history similes in 'King Henry VI.' Ln : New Sh— Soc., 1877-79. 8°
Sh—'s references to natural phenomena. Ln : New Sh— Soc., 1887-92. 8°

Phoenix playhouse, Drury Lane, Ln. *See* Chettle

Phonographic type—
See Sh— Hamlet, 1892
„ Sh— The tempest, 1849, 1864

Photographic view album of Birmingham and the Sh— country. 1902. 8° BPL

Phylotus and Emilia. *See* Rich

Piave (F. M.) *Editor. See* Sh— Macbeth, 1850

Pichot (P. A.) Sh—. *See Sh*—] Pichot

Pickering (R.)] Reflections on theatrical expression in tragedy. With a proper introduction and appendix. Ln: 1755. 8°   BPL

Pickering (W.) *Publisher*—

See Sh— Poems, 1825, 1826, 1832, 1837, 1842, 1853

„ Sh— Works, 1822-23, 1825, 1826, 1828, 1831, 1836

Pickersgill (Edward H.) On the quarto and folio of 'King Richard III.' Ln: New Sh— Soc., 1875-76. 8°   BM | BPL | BUS
Reply. *See* Spedding (J.)

Picton (*Sir* James A.) Falstaff and his followers. Liverpool, 1880. 8°   BPL

Pictorial illustrations of Sh—. [In 'Quarterly Review']. 1876. 8°   BPL
A critique upon four publications.

Pictorial treasury. *See Sh*—] Pictorial . . .

Picture (The). *See* Sh— As you like it, 1901

Picturesque beauties of Sh—. *See* Sh— Works, 1783-86

Picturesque Europe: British Isles. With illustrations by eminent artists. Ln: Cassell [c. 1885]. F°, pp. xii.-288, and 13 steel plates
Pages 58-76 devoted to Sh— and the Stratford locality.

Picturesque Sh— land. Stratford: W. Pearce, 1890. 8°   BPL

Pierer (H. A.) *Altenburg Publisher*. *See* Sh— Midsummer . . . 1875

Pierre (H. S.) *Editor*. *See* Sh— Works, 1840

Pierre (J. M.) *Editor*—

See Sh— Julius Cæsar, 1836

„ Sh— King Henry IV., Parts i.-ii., 1833

„ Sh— King Lear, 1831

„ Sh— Merchant . . . 1831

„ Sh— Romeo . . . 1840

„ Sh— The tempest, 1833

„ Sh— Works, 1830-40

'Pilgrimage to Parnassus.' With the two parts of the 'Return from Parnassus': Three comedies performed in St. John's College, Cambridge, A.D. 1597-1601. Ed. from MSS. by W. D. Machray. Ln: 1886. Roy. 8°   BPL

Pilgrimage to Stratford. *See* Grinfield

Pillé (H.) *Artist*. *See* Sh— Works: Ext. 1901, 1902

Pilon (Frederick)] Essay on the character of Hamlet as played by Mr. Henderson at the Theatre Royal, Haymarket. Ln: W. Flexney, corner of Southampton Buildings, Holborn [1777]. 8°, pp. iv.-24   BLO | BPL | BUS
Ascribed to Thomas Davies in the Bodleian Catalogue in error.

] Essay on . . . 'Hamlet' . . . Second edition. Ln: [c. 1777]. 8°   BPL

Pilon (F.) *Editor*. *See* Sh— All's well, 1785

Pimlyco, or run red cap: Tis a mad world at Hogsdon . . . Ln: 1609
Says:—
   'So that I truly thought all these
   Came to see "Shore" or "Pericles."'

Pincherle (James) Ricordo a Sh—: Under the auspices of Sh—'s tercentenary birth. Trieste: Printed by the Aust. Lloyd's, 1864. 8°, pp. ii.-54   BUS

'Pindar (Peter)' *pseud*. *See* Wolcot

Pinder of Wakefield. *See* Sh— George-a-Greene

Pinero (*Sir* Arthur Wing) Note . . . *See* Courtney

Pink (J.) Catalogue of books in the Cambridge Free Library: Reference department. Cambridge: Foister & Jagg, 1874. Roy. 8°, pp. iv.-106   BPL | BUS | CPL
The index to the Sh— memorial collection occupies pp. 87-106. The generous founder of this collection was Hy. Thomas Hall [*q.v.*].

Pinkerton (John)] Letters on literature by 'Robert Heron.' Ln: 1785. 8°
          BPL | BUS | W
Letters 18, 26, and 38 embody 'Remarks on the last edition of Sh—'s Plays, 1778.'

Pinks (W. J.) Memorials of Sh—. *See* Sh—] Pinks

'Piot *or* Pyott (Lazarus)' *pseud*. *See* Munday

Piramus. *See* Pyramus

Pit (P.) Thespian critique or theatrical censor. Edin., 1816. 8°

Pitman (J. R.) *Editor*. *See* Sh— Works, 1822, 1834, 1845, 1851, 1862

Pitt (W. M.) Library. *See* Catalogue, 1838

Pitt-Lewis (George) Sh— story. *See* Sh—] Pitt-Lewis

Pix (Mary) Double distress: A tragedy. Ln: 1701. Fcp. 4°
Refers to Sh—.

Queen Catharine, or the ruines of love. A tragedy. Ln: William Turner at the White Horse without, and Richard Basset at the Mitre within, Temple Bar, 1698. Fcp. 4°
A tribute to Sh— is in the epilogue, beginning:—
   'Sh— did oft his countries "worthies chuse,"
   Nor did they by his pen their lustre lose . . .'

Place (Wm.) *Publisher*. *See* Greenwood

Plagiary warned: A vindication of the drama. 1824. 8°   BPL

Planché (James Robinson) Extravaganza and spectacle [In 'Temple Bar']. 1861. 8°
          BPL

Recollections and reflections: A professional autobiography. 1872. 2 vols. 8°
          BPL

Remarks on Inigo Jones' Sketches . . . *See* Jones

Planché (J. R.) & Meadows (J. K.) Costume. *See* Sh— King John, 1823

Planché (J. R.) & Scharf (*Sir* G.) Costume.
  See Sh— As you like it, 1825
Costume. *See* Sh— Hamlet, 1825
Costume. *See* Sh— King Henry IV., 1824
Costume of . . . 'Othello' and . . . 'The
  Merchant of Venice.' Ln : 1825. 12°
                                          BPL | W
Costume of Sh—'s characters, with bio-
  graphical . . . notices . . . 'King John,'
  'King Henry IV.,' 'As you like it,' 'Ham-
  let,' 'Othello,' 'Merchant of Venice' : 97
  coloured plates by G. Scharf, with bio-
  graphical and critical notices by J. R.
  Planché. Ln : J. Miller, 1823-25. 8°.
  Issued in five parts   BM (*impft.*)
Planché (J. R.) & Tomkins (C. F.) Costume.
  See Sh— King Richard III., 1829, 1830
Planché (J. R.) *Artist-Editor*—
  See Sh— King Richard III., 1829
  ,, Sh— Midsummer . . . 1840
Plantagenet's tragicall story. *See* Weaver
Plate, 16th and 17th cent. *See* Halliwell
Platt (Isaac Hull) Are the Sh— plays signed
  by Francis Bacon ? Philadelphia, 1897.
  8°, pp. 16   BUS
Bacon cryptograms in Sh—, and other
  studies. Boston, U.S., 1905. Cr. 8°
                                    BPL | BUS
Plautus. Menæcmi [A foundation of the
  'Comedy of errors'—
  See Gesta Grayorum
  ,, Sh— Comedy of errors, 1779
  ,, *Sh*—] Sh—'s library
  ,, Six old plays
  See also Meres
  ,, ,, Sonnenschein
Play-bills of performances of Sh—'s plays
  [*Collection*]. 1779-1858. 35 vols. F° BPL
Playbills of . . . Sh—'s plays [*Collection*].
  1820-51. F°   BPL | SML
Play-bills of tableaux vivans, forming a
  grand apotheosis of Sh—. 1842. F° BPL
Play-bills—
  See Fitzgerald
  ,, Ireland
  ,, Newspaper cuttings
Players—
  See Actors
  ,, Stage
Playford (H.) *Publisher*. *See* Downes
Playford (John) Musical companion, 1667.
  See Sh— Poems, 1660-67
Musical companion : . . . catches, rounds, . . .
  dialogues, glees, ayres, and songs. Ln :
  Printed by W. Godbid for John Playford
  at his shop in the Temple near the
  Church, 1673. Oblong 8°
  'Where the bee sucks,' from 'The tempest,' set to
  music by Dr. Wilson, occurs on pp. 174-175, and on
  p. 47 a song introduces Falstaff.

Playford (John) *Publisher*. *See* Sh— Works :
  Ext. 1653
Playgoer (The). 1901-04. 5 vols. 8°   BPL
Playhouses—
  See Sh— Romeo . . . 1750
  ,, Stage
Playhouse pocket companion or theatrical
  vade mecum, containing a catalogue of
  all the dramatic authors who have written
  for the English stage. Ln : 1779. 8°
Playing cards. *See Sh*—] Sh— playing cards
Plays—
  See Selection . . .
  ,, *Sh*—] Sh— bibliography
Pleasant conceits of old Hobson—
  See Old English jest books
  ,, *Sh*—] Sh— jest books
Pleasant taunts, merry tales, modern jests
  and witty jeeres . . . Ln : [c. 1620]. 12°
                                            W
  An early jest book, containing a curious reference to
  Sh— and Stratford-upon-Avon at p. 157. *See* Halli-
  well's ' Sh— reliques, 1852,' p. 2.
Plomer (Hy. R.) Printers of Sh—'s plays and
  poems [In ' The Library,' April]. Ln :
  1906. Roy. 8°   BPL
Plumptre (C. J.) Religion and morality of
  Sh—'s works. 1873. 12°   BPL
Plumptre (James) Inquiry into the lawfulness
  of the stage. Cambridge : F. Hodson,
  1812. 12°   SML
Letter to the Marquis of Hertford on a
  dramatic institution. Cambridge : J.
  Hodson, 1820. 12°   SML
Letters to the author of a tract entitled
  ' The stage.' Cambridge : J. Hodson,
  1819. 12°   SML
Observations on 'Hamlet' and on the
  motives which most probably induced
  Sh— to fix upon the story of Amleth ;
  being an attempt to prove that he de-
  signed it as an indirect censure on Mary
  Queen of Scots. Cambridge : J. Burges,
  1796. 8°, pp. iv.-44
                    BM | BPL | BUS | MPL | W
Observations on 'Hamlet' . . . Appendix.
  Cambridge : J. Burges, 1797. 8°, pp.
  ii.-86   BUS | W
Shakspeariana, or notes upon Sh—. [c.
  1800.] Holograph manuscript. 4°   BUS
Plumptre (James) *Editor*—
  See Sh— Merchant . . . 1791
  ,, Sh— Othello, 1724
  ,, Sh— The tempest, 1785
Plutarchus. Lives of the noble Grecians and
  Romanes, compared together . . . Trans-
  lated out of Greeke into French by James
  Amyot, Abbot of Bellozane, Bishop of
  Auxerre . . . and out of French into
  Englishe by Thomas North. Imprinted

at Ln. by Thomas Vautroullier, dwelling in the Blacke Friers by Ludgate, 1579. F°, sig. *8A—5F⁶ paged   BPL | CTC

'Sh—'s storehouse of learned history.'—*Warton.*

Sir Thomas North is reputed one of the first great masters of English prose.

To Englishmen these 'Lives,' beside their intrinsic value, possess the special interest of having been Sh—'s chief authority in his great classical dramas. The correspondence between the 'Lives' and the plays is traceable in incident upon incident, personage after personage, and in some places almost line for line, or word for word.

The five plays specially identified with Plutarch are :— 'Anthony and Cleopatra,' 'Coriolanus,' 'Julius Cæsar,' 'Midsummer night's dream,' and 'Pericles.' Two others less directly associated are 'Hamlet' and 'Timon.'

Plutarchus. Lives . . . Trans. by T. North. Ln : Printed by Richard Field for Thomas Wight, 1595. F°. Second edition   BPL | W

Lives . . . Translated . . . by Sir T. North. Ln : R. Field for T. Wight, 1603.   F°
                   BPL | W

For the copy said to bear Sh—'s signature see Sh— Autograph.

Lives . . . Trans. by Sir T. North. Ln : Richard Field, 1612. F°, sig. A⁸, B—5 O⁶, 5 P⁸ paged   BM | BUS | CTC | SML

With additional lives 'from Probus' [really from C. Nepos], by Simon Goulart.

[Lives] Sh—'s Plutarch, being . . . lives in North's Plutarch which illustrate Sh—'s plays. Ed. with preface, notes, index of names and glossarial index by W. W. Skeat. Ln : Macmillan, 1875. 8°, pp. xxiv.-332   BM | BPL | BUS | SML

[Lives] Four chapters . . . as sources to Sh—'s 'Coriolanus,' 'Julius Cæsar,' 'Antony and Cleopatra,' and partly to 'Hamlet' and 'Timon of Athens.' Photolithographed [from the] edition of 1595. With preface, notes comparing the . . . editions of 1579, 1595, and 1603, and reference notes to the text . . . of Sh— . . . by F. A. Leo. Ln : Trübner, 1878. 4°
       BM | BPL | BUS | MPL | SML

Lives. Ed. by North. *See* Sh—] Julius Cæsar, 1887, 1899

[Lives] Sh—'s Plutarch. Ed. by F. C. Tucker-Brooke. 'Sh— Classics.' Ln : Chatto, 1909. 2 vols. Cr. 8°, pp. 226 and 252

Life of Antonius. *See* Sh—] Sh—'s library
A foundation of 'Antony and Cleopatra.'

Life of Coriolanus. *See* Sh—] Sh—'s library
A foundation of 'Coriolanus.'

Life of Coriolanus. North's trans. Ed. with introd. and notes by R. H. Carr. Oxford : Clarendon Press, 1906. Cr. 8°, pp. xxvi.-54

Life of Julius Cæsar. *See* Sh—] Sh—'s library
A foundation of 'Julius Cæsar.'

Plutarchus. Life of Pericles.   *See* Sh—]
Sh—'s library
A foundation of 'Pericles.'

See also Marindin
     ,,   ,,   Paton
     ,,   ,,   Sh— Coriolanus, 1864

Poel (William) First quarto 'Hamlet' [In 'Athenæum,' No. 3776, p. 316, Mar.] 1900

] Playhouse of the sixteenth century. Ln : Elizabethan Stage Soc. [1904]. 8°, pp. 36, includ. pr. wrappers. Illust.

Sh—'s Jew and Marlowe's Christians. Bedford, 1909. 8°   BPL

Stage version of 'Romeo and Juliet.' Ln : New Sh— Soc., 1887-92. 8°

Poems [Collection of old English poetry written in the reign of Q. Elizabeth, containing the earliest transcript of any portion of Sh—'s works known to exist, and verses by Edward Vere Earl of Oxford, Sir Edward Dyer, Sir Philip Sidney, — Vavasor, and others]. Manuscript upon nineteen leaves of paper.   1585-90. Oblong 4°   W

A description in detail of this collection (which bears the contemporary autograph of ANNE CORNWALEYS) will be found in Halliwell's 'Sh— reliques, 1852,' page 126.

Poems [Collection of poetry of the time of Charles I., containing upwards of two hundred poems, epigrams, epitaphs, pieces of wit and humour, by F. Atkins, Ben Ionson, Derrick, and others ; many unpublished]. Manuscript upon one hundred and five leaves of paper. [Sæc. XVII.] 12°   W

Rendered curious and interesting to the Sh— collector by its copy of Corbet's poem on Bosworth Field, differing from the printed editions, and, what is perhaps of greater literary interest, a long epitaph on Burbage, Sh—'s life-long friend, mentioning the characters he impersonated in Sh—'s plays, a list which materially varies from that in the Heber manuscript, printed by J. P. Collier.

A fuller description may be seen in Halliwell's 'Sh— reliques,' 1852,' page 29.

Poems [Collection of English poetry of the Stuart period, systematically arranged]. 1625-60. Manuscript upon paper, with two independent paginations of fifty-seven and eighty-seven leaves respectively. Fcp. 4°   W

Immediately after an 'Epitaph on Sir W. Ralegh' occurs Basse's famous eulogy 'On Mr. Wm. Sh—' —first printed in Donne's Poems, 1633—but the collection possesses extraordinary interest and curiosity by containing two poetical epitaphs : one— 'Epitaph on Sir Edward Standly, ingraven on his tomb in Tong Church,' with the name of Sh— affixed, followed by another — 'On Sir Thomas Standly,' also assigned to Sh—.

We have here testimony a quarter of a century earlier than Dugdale to these epitaphs being the productions of Sh –. *See* Halliwell's 'Sh— reliques, 1852,' p. 32 ; and Sh— Epitaphs.

Poems, by J. D——. *See* Donne

Poems, ballads, lampoons and satires, upon
Dryden, Otway, and others. Manuscript
on 222 pages. c. 1690. F°
One poem, headed 'Satyr upon the poets,' contains
the line :—'The tragick fights of towering Sh—'s
witt.'
The MS. was sold 30th April, 1909.
Poems for the prize competition [Sh— ter-
centenary] offered by the Belfast weekly
'Northern Whig.' Belfast, 1864. 8° BPL
Poems, odes ... at Reading School. *See* Valpy
Poems on various subjects. Ed. by T. Tom-
kins. *See* Sh— Works : Ext. 1800
Poet lore : Monthly magazine devoted to
Sh—, Browning and the comparative
study of literature. [Conducted by Char-
lotte Porter and Helen A. Clarke.]
Philadelphia, 1889-97. 8°
BM | BPL | BUS | SML
Poet of the age : A satirical poem. 1862. 12°
The introduction refers to Sh—. BPL
Poetic review [Number relating to Sh—, Jan.]
1852. 8° W
Poetical epistle from Sh— in elysium to Mr.
Garrick, at Drury Lane theatre. To
which is added, A view from Heymon Hill,
near Shrewsbury ; a solitudinarian ode.
Ln : J. Newbery & W. Owen, 1752. 4°,
pp 30 BM
Poetical miscellanies [An early transcript of
a Jacobean anthology, c. 1630. Manu-
script upon ninety-four numbered leaves
of paper, in which the following numbers
are lacking : 7-9, 54-55, and 95]. 12° W
Contains an imitation of the sonnet quoted in the
'Merry wives,' headed 'Come live with mee and bee
my love,' from the 'Passionate pilgrim.'
Poetical preceptor. *See* Sh— Works : Ext.
1796
Poetical register. *See* Sh—] Jacob (Giles)
Poetical revenge, from the manuscript collec-
tion of Clement Paman. Ln : [c. 1600]
Contains lines from Cowley added at a later date :
' Be by his father in his studdy tooke
At Sh—'s playes instead of the Lord Cooke.'
See also Mercurius Britannicus for same quotation.
Poets' corner, Westminster Abbey. *See* Sh—]
Knight
Poets' country, by various authors. Ed. by
Andrew Lang. Edinburgh : Jack, 1907.
8°, pp. 378, with 50 coloured plates BPL
Poets of the Elizabethan age. *See* Sh—
Poems, 1862, 1875
Polimanteia. *See* Clarke (W.)
Pollard (Alfred W.) Sh— folios and quartos :
A study in the bibliography of Sh—'s
plays, 1594-1685. Ln : Methuen, 1909.
F°, pp. viii.-176. With 37 facsimile
illustrations BM | BPL | BUS | SML
Five hundred copies printed on handmade paper (at
Letchworth).
Reviewed at length in the 'Liverpool Courier,' 24 Dec.,
1909, by W. Jaggard.

Pollard (Alfred W.) Sh— quartos [In 'Athe-
næum,' No. 4237]. 1909. 4°
See also Greg, Levi, & Pollard
,, ,, Huth & Pollard
Pollard (A. W.) *Editor*. *See* Library (The)
Pollard (W. H.) *Editor*. *See* Diderot
Pollock (*Sir* Frederick). *Editor*. *See* Macready
Pollock (Juliet) The 'Hamlet' of the Seine
[In 'Nineteenth Century']. 1886. 8° BPL
Pollock (*Lady*) Macready. *See* Macready
Polonius. *See* Fitzgerald (E.)
Ponder (Nathaniel) *Publisher*. *See* Marvell
Ponsonby (Wm.) *Publisher*—
See Barclay
,, Spenser
,, Watson
Poole (Benjamin) & Taunton (Wm. Frederic)
Coventry : its history and antiquities ...
Coventry : W. F. Taunton, 1870. 4°,
pp. xviii.-424 and 58 illustrations
With illustrated chapters on the ancient sacred plays.
Poole (John) *Editor*. *See* Sh— Hamlet, 1810,
1811, 1812, 1814, 1817, 1820, 1853, 1860
Poole (Joshua) English Parnassus. *See* Sh—
Works : Ext. 1657, 1677
Poole (Louella C.) Twelve scenes from Sh—
[Pictures] by Fannie S. Montague. With
notes. Boston [U.S.] 1899. 8°, pp. 28
and plates BUS
Poole (Louella C.) & Johnson (Andrea C.)
Very seasonable kalendar. *See* Sh—
Works : Ext. 1896
Poole (*Dr.* William Frederick) Fletcher (Wm.
I.) & Poole (Mary) Index to periodical
literature. Boston [U.S.] 1882-1903. 5
vols. 4° BM | BPL
Contains a key to Sh— contributions in English and
American periodicals.
Pooler (Charles Knox) *Editor*. *See* Sh— Mer-
chant ... 1905
Pope (Alexander) Preface—
See Eighteenth ...
,, Sh— Works, 1803-05, 1805, 1823, 1830
Sports of the muses. *See* Sh— Works :
Ext. 1752
] The dunciad : An heroic poem. Dublin
printed. Ln : Reprinted for A. Dodd,
1728. 8°, pp. viii.-52 and plate of ass
loaded with books BUS
With a slighting reference to Theobald's 'Sh— re-
stored.'
Pope (A.) *Editor*—
See Sh— Hamlet, 1731, 1776
,, Sh— Othello, 1757
,, Sh— The tempest, 1725
,, Sh— Works, 1723-25, 1725-26, 1728,
1731, 1734-36, 1744-46, 1745, 1747,
1752-57, 1760, 1761, 1766, 1767,
1768, 1769, 1771, 1795, 1833
Pope.] Epistle to Mr. Pope cocasioned by
Theobald's Sh— ... Ln : 1733. F° BPL

Pope (Alex.)—
See Annotations See Lounsbury
 ,, Epistle ,, Mallet
 ,, Graves ,, Roberts
 ,, Grey ,, Theobald
 ,, Histrionicus ,, Verbal . . .
 ,, Johnson & Pope

Pope *and others* (Alex.) Miscellany of taste. Ln : G. Lawton, T. Osborn & J. Hughes, 1732. 8°, pp. 46 BPL
Contains ' Of Mr. Pope's taste of Sh—.'

Pope (Gustavus W.) Sh—, the great dramatic demonstrator of Catholic faith, doctrine and ceremonial. Washington, 1902. 8°, pp. 36 BUS

Porson.] Watson (J. S.) Life of Richard Porson. 1861. 8° BPL
Contains the story of the Ireland forgeries.

Portal (A.) *Publisher. See* Sheridan

Portbury (F. J.) *Engraver. See* Sh— Works : Ext. 1841

Porteous Brothers *Glasgow Publishers. See* Sh— Works, 1865

Porter *Artist. See* Sh— Works, 1802, 1803

Porter *Philadelphia Publisher. See* Sh— Works, 1860

Porter (Charlotte) *Editor—*
See Poet Lore
 ,, Sh— Midsummer . . . 1903
 ,, Sh— Works, 1903

Porter (H. C.) History of the theatre, Brighton, from 1774 to 1885. Brighton : King & Thorne, 1887. 8° SML

Porter (Rose) Sh—'s men and women. *See* Sh— Works : Ext. 1897, 1898

Porto (Luigi da) Original story of 'Romeo and Juliet' . . . being the Italian text of 1530 and translation, together with preface, historical and bibliographical notes and illustrations. By G. Pace-Sanfelice. Cambridge : Deighton, Bell, 1868. 8°, pp. lxiv.-80 BPL | BUS | MPL

Portugal. *See* Historie . . .

Posthumous parodies and other poems, composed by several of our most celebrated poets, but not published in any former edition of their works. Ln : 1814. 8° w
Includes Shakespeareana.

Postscript to the . . . 'Family Sh—.' *See* Bowdler

Pote (T.) *Publisher. See* Sh— King Henry VIII., 1758

Pott (*Mrs.* Hy.)] Did Francis Bacon write 'Sh—' ? Thirty-two reasons for believing he did. Ln : 1884-85. 2 vols. 12° BPL | BUS

] Did Francis Bacon write 'Sh—' ? Second edition. 1893. 8° BM | BPL

Francis Bacon and his secret society. 1891. 12° BPL

Pott (*Mrs.* Hy.) Obiter dicta of Bacon and Sh— on manners, mind, and morals. 1900. Cr. 8° BPL

Pott (*Mrs.* Hy.) *See also* O'Connor

Pott (*Mrs.* H.) *Editor. See* Bacon. Promus . .

Potts (H. J.) Notes on Sh—'s plays. Birmingham, 1879. Cr. 8° BPL

Potts (James) *Dublin Publisher—*
See Montagu
 ,, Sh— Works, 1766
 ,, *Sh—*] Dennis

Potwin (Lemuel Stoughton) Sh— glossary for our English Bible [In 'Bibliotheca Sacra,' July]. Andover, Mass., 1862. 8° BUS

Poulson (M.) *Publisher—*
See Sh— Hamlet, 1723
 ,, Sh— Othello, 1724

Powell (S.) *Dublin Printer. See* Fielding

Powell (Thomas) Tom of all trades, or the plaine pathway to preferment . . . 1631 . . . Ln : New Sh— Soc., 1876-77. 4° BM | BPL | BUS

Powell (W.) *Editor. See* Sh— Twelfth night, 1792

Powell (Walter) Recent editions of Sh—'s works [In 'Central Lit. Mag.'] Birm., 1908. 8° BPL

Powell (Walter) Jaggard (Wm.) & Bullen (A. H.) 'Stratford town Sh—' [In 'Athenæum,' No. 4114, p. 243 ; No. 4115, p. 274 ; No. 4116, p. 305, Sept.] 1906

Pownall (Alfred) Sh— weighed in an even balance. Ln : Saunders & Otley, 1864. 8°, pp. viii.-86
 BM | BPL | BUS | CPL | MPL | SML

Powys (John Cowper) Syllabus of a course of six lectures on Sh—'s historical plays. Philadelphia, 1904. 8°, pp. 8 BUS

Syllabus of a course of six lectures on the tragedies of Sh—. Philadelphia, 1904. 8°, pp. 12

Praise of Sh—. *See Sh—*] Praise

Pratt (Mary L.) Stories from Sh—. *See* Sh— Works : Ext. 1890-95

Precious relics, or the 'Tragedy of Vortigern' rehearsed. A dramatic piece in two acts written in imitation of 'The critic.' As performed at the Theatre Royal, Drury Lane. Ln : Debret, Hookham & Clarke, 1796. 8°, pp. 62 BPL | BUS | w
This piece was published but not acted on the 15th March, 1796, in order to wet-blanket Ireland's 'Vortigern,' performed on 2nd April following. It foretells the latter to be a forgery, and predicts its failure.

Prefaces and annotations of the various commentators on Sh—. Ln : 1805. 2 vols. 8° 1805
Offprinted from Vols. ix.-x. of Wallis & Scholey's edition of Sh— (10 vols., 1803-5).

Prescott (*Dr.* Kenrick) Essay on the learning of Sh—. Cambridge : Privately printed, 1774. Fcp. 4°　　　　　　W
Letters concerning Homer. Cambridge, 1773. 4°　　　　　　BUS
No. 4, 'Classic amusement,' is on Sh—.
Remarks on Sh—. Ln : 1792. 8°
Sh—. *See* Sh—] Prescott
Present condition of the stage. *See* Carlisle
Preservation of Henry VII. 1599. *See* Reprints
Preston *Publisher. See* Sh— Poems, 1790
Preston (Mary) Studies in Sh— : A book of essays. Philadelphia : Claxton, Remsen, & Haffelfinger, 1869. 12°, pp. 182　　BM | BPL | BUS
Preston (R. W.) *Printer. See* Sh— Works, 1866
Preston (South G.) Secret of Hamlet, Prince of Denmark. New York, 1897. 8° BM
Secret of Hamlet. 3rd edition. New York [c. 1902]. 8°　　　　　　BUS
Preston (Thomas) Lamentable tragedie mixed full of plesant mirth, containing the life of Cambises King of Pereia. Ln : Imprinted by Edward Allde [c. 1570]. Fcp. 4°
A play which gave rise to the expression, 'King Cambyse's vein,' employed in 'King Henry IV.'
'Price (Morton)' *pseud. See* Rhys (H.)
Price (Norman M.) *Artist. See* Sh— Works : Ext. 1905
Price (S.) *Dublin Publisher. See* Davies (T.)
Price (S. F.) Sh—'s twilights. Boston [U.S.], 1892. 12°　　　　　　BPL
Price (Thomas) Wisdom and genius of Sh—. *See* Sh— Works : Ext. 1838, 1839, 1853, 1858
Price (Thomas R.) Construction and types of Sh—'s verse as seen in 'Othello' . . . New York Sh— Society, 1888. 8°
　　　　　　BM | BPL | BUS | SML
Pridden (J.) *Publisher—*
See Ford
　,, Nichols (P.)
Prideaux (Thomas) Miscellanies. *See* Redford
Primaudaye. *See* La Primaudaye
Prince (Dan.) *Oxford Publisher. See* Tyrwhitt
Prince (J. C.) Poetical works. 1880. 2 vols. 12°　　　　　　BPL
Pages 204-206, vol. i., contain 'Stanzas suggested at the grave of Sh—.'
Princess's theatre, Ln. *See* Sh— Works, 1850
Princess's theatre, Manchester. *See* Sh— Winter's tale, 1869
Princess's theatre, Vienna. *See* Sh— Winter's tale, 1861
Prior (*Sir* J.) Life of Malone. *See* Malone
Pritchard (H. S.) Sh— manuscripts at Abington Abbey. 1889. 8°　　　　　　BPL
See also Sh—] Sh— manuscripts.

Prize essay on the historical plays of Sh—. Ln : 1830. 8°
Prizes in book collecting [In 'Book lore']. Ln : 1885. 4°　　　　　　BPL
Refers to J. O. Halliwell's lucky finds.
Probate Registry, Somerset House. *See* Sh— Will . . . (*heading*)
Probus. *See* Plutarchus
Procter (Bryan Waller) *Editor. See* Sh— Works, 1839-43, 1843, 1844, 1846, 1849, 1852, 1853, 1854, 1857-59, 1858, 1859, 1864, 1869, 1870, 1875-80, 1879, 1886-88, 1891
Procter (Richard Wright) Our turf, our stage, our ring. Manchester : Dinham, 1862. 8°, pp. 104　　　　　　SML
Procter (T.) Triumph of truth. *See* Reprints
Prodigal Son—
See Malone Society
　,, Simpson (R.)
Proescholdt (*Dr.* Ludwig) *Editor—*
See Sh— Arden, 1888
　,, Sh— Birth, 1887
　,, Sh— Faire Em, 1883
　,, Sh— Julius Cæsar, 1889
　,, Sh— Mucedorus, 1878
　,, Sh— Works, 1879-91, 1880-91, 1883-88, 1887
Proescholdt (L. E. A.) On the sources of Sh—'s 'Midsummer night's dream.' 1878. 8°
　　　　　　BM
Programme of bazaar and Sh— show, in aid of Westminster Road Church, Birchfields. Birmingham, 1884. 12°　　BPL
Progress of human life. *See* Sh— As you like it
Progress of Pertinax Puzzlewit. *See* Sh— As you like it, 1870
Prolegomena to Sh—'s plays. *See* Gentleman
Prologue and epilogue to . . . 'Romeo and Juliet' ; spoken . . . by the gentlemen of the Royal Academy at Woolwich . . . October 10, 1751. Ln : W. Owen, 1751. F°, pp. viii.　　　　　　BM
Prologues and epilogues—
See Collection
　,, Original
Prolusions. *See* Capell
Proposal for building a cenotaph to Sh— [In 'Monthly Mag.']. 1820. 8°　　BPL
Proposal for erecting a monument to Sh—. Ln : 1837. 8°
Proposal for printing . . . Sh— set free . . . *See* Becket
Proposed site for the national monument to Sh— . . . suggested to the ter-centenary celebration committee, by one of its members. [Ln :] 1863. 4°, single sheet, lithographed　　　　　　BM

Prouerbes of Syr Oracle Mar-text. Edited by C.M.Ingleby, 1882. 12° BPL

Prynne (William) Defence of stage plays, 1649 [reprint]. 1822. 12° BPL

Histrio-mastix: The player's scovrge or actor's tragædie . . . wherein it is evidenced by divers arguments, by concurring authorities . . . of Scripture, of the whole primitive church . . . of fifty-five synodes and councels, of seventy-one fathers and Christian writers . . . and of our oune English statutes, magistrates, vniversities . . . that popular stage-playes, the very pompes of the divell . . . are sinfull, heathenish, lewde, ungodly spectacles, and most pernicious corruptions. Ln: Printed by E. A—— [Elizabeth Allde] and W. I—— [William Jones] for M.Sparke, 1633. Fcp.4° BM | BPL | BUS
Prynne's unreserved attack herein on 'Women actors' was construed into lèse-majesté, the Queen being about to take part in a pastoral at Somerset House. By writ of rebellion he was summoned before the Court of Star-Chamber on 7 Feb., 1633, and condemned to lose his ears, to be degraded from the legal profession, and to pay £5,000. Sparke the publisher got off more lightly. He paid a fine of £500 and sat in Cheapside pillory.
Curious for its many allusions to the stage and to Sh—. A leaf at p. 708 respecting ladies of quality acting on the stage was ordered by the Privy Council to be cancelled before publication. Prynne says:—'Shackspeere's plaies are printed in [on] the best crowne paper, far better than most Bibles.'—['Address to Christian reader'].
For reply see 'Theatrum redivivum.'
See also Simpson (R.)

Prynne (W.) *See also* Theatrum . . .

Psalms—
See Stopes   *See* Swinburne

Public characters of 1798-99. New edition. Ln: R. Phillips, 71 St. Paul's Churchyard, 1799. 8°, pp. xvi.-598, with 30 portraits
Contains memoirs of Tom King the comedian (pp. 234-239), Mrs. Siddons (pp. 426-431), Alderman Boydell and the Sh— gallery (pp. 485-494), Isaac Disraeli (pp. 502-506).

Publishers' Circular: Sh— tercentenary number [April 15, 1864]. 1864. 8° BPL

Pudsey (Edward) Booke, temp. Q. Elizabeth and K. James I. . . . Shakespearean extracts, which include some from an unknown play by W. Sh—. Also a few unpublished records of the Shakespeares of Snitterfield and Wroxall . . . collected by Richard Savage . . . Stratford-on-Avon: John Smith, 1888. 8°, pp. viii.-84 BPL | BUS | SML
The 'unknown play by W. Sh—,' called 'Irus,' was afterwards identified as Geo. Chapman's 'Blind beggar of Alexandria,' the chief character in which is *Irus.*

Pulling (F. S.) Speech-ending test applied to twenty of Sh—'s plays. Ln: New Sh— Soc., 1877-79. 8°

Pumphrey (A.) Twelve permanent photographs of Stratford-on-Avon. Birmingham [c. 1880]. 12° BPL

Punch: Sh— tercentenary number. 23 April, 1864. 4° BPL | CPL

Punchard (C. D.) *Editor. See* Sh— Works: Ext. 1903, 1908-09

Purcell (Henry) Dialogue in the 'Fairy Queen.' *See* Sh— Winter's tale
Music. *See* Sh— The tempest, 1750
Orpheus Britannicus: Collection of all the choicest songs . . . Two parts. Ln: 1706. F°. Portrait by White
Contains settings to Sh—'s songs.
Some select songs. *See* Sh— Midsummer . . . 1692
Songs. *See* Sh— Poems, 1862

Purcell (Hy.) *Composer*—
See Sh— Poems, 1800
   ,, Sh— The tempest, 1750, 1764, 1776, 1780, 1785
   ,, Sh— Winter's tale, 1690
   ,, Sh— Works: Ext. 1800

Purchas (Samuel). *See* Henderson

Purfoot (Thomas) *Printer*—
See James I.
   ,, Lidgate
   ,, Sh— King Henry IV., 1622
   ,, Sh— King Richard III., 1621, 1622,1624
   ,, Turbervile

Purfoot *jun.* (Thomas) *Printer. See* Sh— Pericles, 1608

Puritan widow. *See* Sh— The puritan widow

Purnell (E. K.) *Editor. See* Sh— Othello, 1882, 1883

Purnell (T.)] Dramatists of the present day. By 'Q.' Reprinted from 'The Athenæum.' Ln: 1871. 12° BPL

Purveyor of tobacco: New and choice characters of several authors . . . Ln: 1615
Says:—'Sir John Falstaffe robb'd with a bottle of sacke . . .'

Puttenham (George)] Arte of English poesie . . . At Ln: Printed by Richard Field, dwelling in the Black-Friers neere Ludgate, 1589. Fcp. 4°, sig. A—M², paged. With woodcut portrait of Q. Elizabeth
See also Rushton. BM | CTC
Extracts. *See* Sh— Works: Ext. 1845

Pye (Henry James) Comments on the commentators on Sh—. With preliminary observations on his genius and writings, and labours of those who have endeavoured to elucidate them. Ln: Tipper & Richards, 1807. 8°, pp. xvi.-342 BM | BPL | BUS | CPL | MPL | SML | W
'One meets now and then with persons who are extremely learned and knotty in expounding clear cases.'—*Spectator.*

Pye (Henry James) Sketches on various subjects. Ln: 1797. 8°　　　　　　BUS
Chapter xii. is on 'Sh— and some of his commentators.'
Pye (John) *Engraver.　See* Sh— Works, 1829
Pyle (J. G.) Little cryptogram : A literal application to 'Hamlet' of the cipher . . . of Ignatius Donnelly.　St. Paul, 1888. 12°　　　　　　　　　　　　BPL
Pyne (Wm. Hy.) *Artist.　See* Sh— Works, 1803-05
Pynson (Richard) *Printer—*
　See Arnold　　　　　*See* Every man
'Pyott (Lazarus)' *pseud.　See* Munday
Pyramus and Thisbe. *See* Sh— Midsummer . . . 1681, 1716, 1740, 1745, 1750, 1798, 1886
Pythagoras.　*See* Meres

See Quiller-Couch (A. T.)
'Q' *pseud.—*
　　See Adams (J. Q.)
　　　,, Purnell
Q—— (J. P.)　　　*See*
　　Quincy (J. P.)
'Quality of mercy.'　Ln : E. Nister, 1907. Cr. 8°　　　　　　　　　　BPL
Illustrates the 'Merchant of Venice.'
Quarles (J.) Banishment of Tarquin. *See* Sh— Rape . . . 1655
Quarterly Review [Consult its general indexes for Sh— articles]
Queen Mab. A cantata. *See* Dibdin
Queen's Arms Yard, Marshalsea Gate, Southwark. *See* Sh— Troilus . . . 1715
Queen's Theatre, Haymarket, Ln.—
　See Sh— Hamlet, 1712
　　,, Sh— King Lear, 1689, 1699, 1712
　　,, Sh— Macbeth, 1710
　　,, Sh— Midsummer . . . 1692
　　,, Smith (E.)
Quiller-Couch (*Sir* A. T.) Adventures in criticism.　Ln : Cassell, 1896.　Cr. 8°, pp. viii.-428　　　　BM | BLO | CTC
Contains article on the 'Passionate pilgrim, 1599,' pp. 30-40, and another on 'Sh—'s lyrics,' pp. 41-49.
] Historical tales from Sh—.　*See* Sh— Works : Ext. 1899, 1900, 1905, 1910
Oxford book of English verse, 1250-1900. *See* Sh— Works : Ext. 1900, 1901
] Sh—'s Christmas and other stories.　Illustrated. Ln : Smith, 1905. 8°, pp. 844　BPL
Warwickshire Avon [In 'Harper's Monthly']. 1891. Roy. 8°　　　　　　　　BPL
Warwickshire Avon.　New York : Harper, 1892.　12°　　　　　　BPL | SML
Quiller-Couch (A. T.) *Editor. See* Sh— Sonnets, 1908
Quin (James) *Actor—*
　See Foote
　　,, Sh— Coriolanus, 1749

Quin.] Life of James Quin, comedian, with a history of the stage, anecdotes, and trial. Ln : Reader, 1887. Cr. 8°. With portrait　　　　　　　　　BPL
Contains Sh— references.
Quincy (Josiah Phillips)] Manuscript corrections [by J. P. Collier] from a copy of the fourth [*sic*] folio Sh—, 1632.　By J. P. Q——.　Boston [U.S.] : Ticknor, 1854. 8°, pp. 52　　　　　BM | BPL | BUS
Quiney (Richard) Letter to Mr. Wm. Sh— [requesting a loan of £30].　25th Oct., 1598.　Manuscript　　　　　　SBL
The following is a literal transcript : — 'Loveinge contreyman.　I am bolde of yow as of a ffrende, craveinge yowr helpe with xxx. pounds vppon Mr. Bushell's and my securytee or Mr. Mytton's with me. Mr. Rosswell is nott come to London as yeate and I have especiall cawse.　Yow shall ffrende me muche in helpeinge me out of all the debettes I owe in London, I thancke God, and muche quiet my mynde, which wolde nott be indebeted.　I am nowe towardes the Cowrte in hope of answer for the dispatche of buysenes.　Yow shall nether loase creddytt nor monney by me the Lorde wyllinge and nowe butt perswade yowrselfe soe as I hope and yow shall nott need to feare butt with all hartie thanckefullenes I wyll holde my tyme and content yowr ffrende, and yf we bargaine farther yow shalbe the paie mr. [paymaster] yowrself.　My tyme biddes me hasten to an ende and soe I committ thys [to] yowr care and hope of yowr helpe.　I feare I shall nott be backe thys night ffrom the Cowrte.　Haste : The Lord be with yow and with vs all, amen.　From the Bell in Carter Lane the 25 Octobr 1598.　Yowrs in all kyndenes, Ryc. Quyney.　To my loveinge good ffrend and contreymann Mr. Wm. Sh— dlr. thees [deliver this].' With armorial seal, on a bend three trefoils slipped.
Letter to Sh—, 1598.　[Reprint.]　1896. 4° broadside　　　　　　　　　BPL
See Bullen (M. W.)
　　,, Dix
Quiney family—
　See Stratford] Description . . . .
　　,, *Stratford*] Two . . .
'Quip modest.'　*See* Ritson

—— (I.) *Printer.　See* Roberts (James)
R—— (J.)　*See* Ritson
R—— (J.) *Printer. See* Fane
R—— (J. H.) On the character of Hamlet [In 'Inquirer']. 1814. 8°　　　　　　　　　　　BUS
R—— (R.)　*See* Robinson (Richard)
R—— (S.) Greene's ghost-haunting conycatchers, wherein is set down the art of humouring, &c.　With the merry conceits of Doctor Pinchback . . . 1626. Ed. by J. O. Halliwell.　Ln : 1860.　16°
Limited to twenty-six copies.　BPL | BUS | HCL
Lowndes thinks the author was Samuel Rowlands or Samuel Rid.

R—— (T.) *Printer.* *See* Theatrum . . .
R—— (W.) *Printer.* *See* Sh— Merry devil, 1819
R—— (W. M.) *See* Rooney (W. M.)
Rabone (John) Lecture on some portraits of Sh— and Sh—'s brooch . . . Birmingham, 1884. 8°, pp. 22-iv. With four plates
BPL | BUS
] Shakespearean relics : History of Sh—'s brooch . . . Stratford-on-Avon : E. Fox [1883]. 8°, pp. 20   BM | BPL | BUS | SML
Rachel (*Madame*). *See* Martin
Rackham *Publisher.* *See* Sh— Works, 1824
Rackham (Arthur) *Artist*—
See Sh— Midsummer . . . 1908
,, `Sh— Works : Ext. 1899, 1901, 1909
Radet (J. B.) *Editor.* *See* Sh— Othello, 1792
Radford (G. H.)] Falstaff [In Birrell's 'Obiter dicta,' pp. 200-233]. Ln : Stock, 1896. 12°
BPL
Falstaff [In Birrell's 'Collected Essays']. Ln : Stock, 1899. 12°   BPL
Shylock and others : Eight studies. Ln : 1894. Cr. 8°   BPL
Rae (W. F.) Sheridan. *See* Sheridan
Raffles (Robert B.) Introductory questions on Sh—'s 'As you like it.' Ln : 1884. 8°
BM | BUS
Introductory questions on the second part of 'King Henry IV.' Ln : 1883. 8°
BM | BUS
Railton (*Mrs.* Herbert) *Editor.* *See* Sh— Midsummer . . . 1901, 1902
Rainoldes *DD.* (John)] Overthrow of stage playes by way of controversie betwixt D. Gager and D. Rainoldes, wherein is manifestly proved that it is not onely unlawful to bee an actor but a beholder of those vanities . . . Whereunto are added . . . certeine Latine letters betwixt Master Rainoldes and D. Gentiles . . . Middelburge [R. Schilders ?] 1599. Fcp. 4°
W
Throws much light on the active antipathy to the drama when the poet was producing some of his best work. 'The Theatre' and 'The Curtain' [playhouses] are both referred to. Wm. Prynne (*q.v.*) copied Rainoldes in 1633.
Overthrow of stage playes. 1600. Fcp. 4°
BPL
Overthrow of stage playes . . . Second edition. Oxford, 1629. Fcp. 4° BPL | MPL
Ralegh (*Sir* Walter) Discovery of the large, rich, and bewtiful empire of Guiana, with a relation of the great and golden city of Manoa, which the Spaniards call el dorado. Ln : Robert Robinson, 1596. Fcp. 4°   MRL
From this work Sh— is supposed to have taken his 'Still vexed Bermoothes' [Bermudas?] used in 'The tempest.'

Ralegh (*Sir* Walter) Instructions to his son and to posterity. Ln : 1632. 12°. With portrait
Contains a passage apparently founded on Sh—.
Ralegh says :—'Thou shall be in as much danger in contending with a brawler in a private quarrel as in a battle . . . but if thou be once engaged, carry thyself bravely that they may fear thee.'
                    *   *   *
Sh— says :—
'Beware of entrance to a quarrel, but being in Bear't, that the opposed may beware of thee.'
                                —*Hamlet i. 6.*
Ralegh.] Raleigh wrote Sh— or the grate Crab tree-cram. Glasgow : D. Robertson, 1888.   12°, pp. 20   BPL
] Sir Walter Raleigh the author of Sh—'s plays and sonnets.   Melbourne, 1877. 8°   MPL
] Whitehead. Life and times of Sir Walter Raleigh . . . Ln : N. Cooke, 1854. Cr. 8°, pp. xii.-312.   Illustrated
The frontispiece depicts Sh— and his companions at the Mermaid Club.
Ralegh (*Sir* Walter)—
See Caldwell   *See* Poems
,, Henderson   ,, Sewell
,, Levi
Raleigh (*Prof.* Walter) Sh—.   *See* Sh—] Raleigh
Raleigh (*Prof.* W.) *Editor*—
See Johnson
,, Sh— Troilus . . . 1908
Ramal (Walter)] Ten characters from Sh—, by 'W. J. de la Mare' [*i.e.* Walter Ramal. In 'Monthly Review,' May, 1902, pp. 153-162, in verse].   1902.   Roy. 8°
Ramée (Louise de la)] Mr. Irving on the art of acting, by 'Ouida' [In the 'Nineteenth Century'].   1895.   Roy. 8°   BPL
Ramesay (*Dr.* W.)] Gentleman's companion, or a character of true nobility and gentility. By a person of quality . . . Ln : 1672. 8°
Cites Sh—.
Ramsay (A.) Sh— in Germany.   Ln : [1866]. 8°   BM | BPL
First printed in Knight's Pictorial edition of Sh—'s works, 1838-43.
Ramsay (Allan) *Publisher.* *See* Sh— Macbeth, 1731
Ramsay (Arthur) On the character of Hamlet. Liverpool : Historic Soc.   1856.   8°
BPL | BUS | SML
Forms pp. 115-126 of vol. vii. of the 'Trans. of the Historic Society.'
Randall (Rachel) *Publisher*—
See Sh— King Richard III., 1787
,, Sh— Macbeth, 1785
,, Sh— Merchant . . . 1787
,, Sh— Merry wives, 1787
,, Sh— Romeo . . . 1785
,, Sh— Twelfth night, 1787

Randall-Diehl (*Mrs.* Anna) *Editor—*
See American Sh— Magazine
,, Fortnightly Sh—
Randolph (A. M. F.) Trial of Sir John Falstaff.
New York, 1893. 12°   BPL
Randolph (Thomas)] Aristippus, or the
joviall philosopher . . . Ln: T. Harper
for John Marriot, and sold by Richard
Mynne in Little Britayne at the Signe of
Saint Paul, 1630. Fcp. 4°
Ridicules the prologue in 'Troilus and Cressida.'
] Aristippvs . . . Ln: 1639. Fcp. 4°   BPL
] Cornelianum dolium: Comoedia lepidis-
sima . . . auctore T. R——. Ln: Thomas
Harper, Tho. Slater, & Laurence Chap-
man, 1638. 8°. With frontispiece by W.
Marshall
Attributed also to Richard Brathwaite.
On p. 22 refers to Sh—'s 'wanton' book: 'Venus and
Adonis.'
Ranew (Nathaniel) *Publisher.* See Walker
Rankin (J. E.) Theology of 'Hamlet' [In the
'Boston Review']. Boston [U.S.] 1866.
8°   BPL
Rankin (Michael Henry) Philosophy of Sh—.
See Sh— Works: Ext. 1841, 1857, 1862,
1863, 1867
Rann *of Coventry* (Joseph) *Editor. See* Sh—
Works, 1786-94
Ransome (C.) Sh—'s plots . . . Ln: Mac-
millan, 1892. Cr. 8°
Short studies of Sh—'s plots: 'Tempest,'
'Macbeth,' 'Hamlet.' Ln: Macmillan,
1890. Cr. 8°   BM | BPL | BUS | MPL
Short studies . . . 'King Richard II.' Ln:
Macmillan, 1899. Cr. 8°
Short studies . . . 'King Lear.' Ln: Mac-
millan, 1899. Cr. 8°
Raper (R. W.) *Editor. See* Sh— King Henry
IV., ii., 1862
Rastell (Wm.) Collection . . . of the statutes,
1598. *See* Sh— autograph
Ratsey.] Life and death of Gamaliel Ratsey,
1605. *See* Reprints
] Ratsei's ghost, or the second parte of his
madde prankes and robberies. Ln: [1605]
A sketch of the life of Gamaliel Ratsey, a highwayman,
hanged at Bedford 26 March, 1605. He is said to
have thus addressed the head of a troop of actors
[possibly Sh—] after a compulsory performance on
the highway :—' When thou feelest thy purse well
lined buy thee some place or lordship in the country,
that, growing weary of playing, thy money may there
bring thee to dignity and reputation.' This sage
advice Sh— closely followed in due course. Elsewhere the volume says :—' My conceit is such of thee
that I durst all the money in my purse on thy head
to play "Hamlet." '
'Rattler (Morgan)' *pseud. See* Maginn (W.)
Ravenscroft *Editor. See* Sh— Works, 1908
Ravenscroft (Edward) *Editor. See* Sh— Titus
. . . 1687
Ravenscroft (Thomas) Briefe discourse of the
true use of charactering the degrees . . .

in measurable musick against the common practise . . . of these times. Ex-
amples whereof are exprest in the har-
mony of four voyces concerning the
pleasure of five usual recreations :—
hunting, hawking, dauncing, drinking
& enamouring. Ln: E. Alde for T.
Adams, 1614. Fcp. 4°
At p. 14 is an imitation of 'Take, O take those lips
away' from 'Measure for measure.'
In May, 1905, a copy realised £60.
Raworth (R.) *Printer. See* Annalia Dubrensia
Ray (Isaac) Sh—'s delineations of insanity
[In 'American Journal of Insanity,'
April]. Utica, 1847. 8°   BUS
Raymond (G.) *See* Elliston
Raymond (R. R.) Sh— for the young folk.
See Sh— Works : Ext. 1881
Typical tales of fancy and history. *See*
Sh— Works : Ext. 1892
Rayne (Lin.) *Editor. See* Sh— Macbeth, 1868
Reader (William) Warwickshire ode: Wm.
Sh— [for the tercentenary]. Coventry,
1864. Cr. 8°, pp. 4   BPL
Reader or reciter. *See* Sh— Works : Ext. 1799
Reading, Berkshire. *See* Valpy
Reading (B.) *Artist. See* Mortimer
Readings and recitations from Sh—. *See*
Sh— Works : Ext. 1870
Readings from the plays of Sh—. *See* Sh—
Works : Ext. 1848
Real 'Macbeth,' by the real Macduff. *See*
Sh— Macbeth, 1870, 1889
Reardon (J. P.) Sh—'s 'Venus and Adonis'
and Lodge's 'Scilla's metamorphosis.'
See Sh—] Sh— Soc.
Two specimens of the poetry of Philip
Stubbes (. . . enemy of theatrical per-
formances) unknown to bibliographers.
See Sh—] Sh— Soc.
Reardon (J. P.) *Editor. See* Greene
Recent editions of Sh— [In 'Quarterly Re-
view,' Mar.] Ln: 1847. 8°   BUS
Recent Sh— literature [In 'Gentleman's Maga-
zine,' Dec.] Ln: 1867. 8°   BUS
Recitations from Sh—. *See* Sh— Works :
Ext. 1886
Reclam *jun.* (P.) *Leipzig Publisher. See* Sh—
Hamlet, 1856
Record of auncient histories. *See* Elimandus
Recorde (Robert) Castle of knowledge, con-
taining the explication of the sphere,
both celestiall and materiall . . . Ln:
Reginalde Wolfe, 1556. 8°. With wood-
cut. title exhibiting the castle of know-
ledge, wheele of fortune, sphere of des-
tinye, &c.
'And certain stars shot madly from their spheres.'
—*Midsummer night's dream.*
'The music of the spheres.'—*Pericles.*
'And giddy fortune's furious fickle wheel.'
—*King Henry V., iii. 6.*

Red Bull playhouse, Clerkenwell. *See* Green-street

Redding (Cyrus) The facsimile Sh— [In 'New Monthly Magazine,' Mar.] Ln : 1865. 8°
On Booth's 1862-64 reprint of the Jaggard folio. BUS

Reddish (Samuel) *Actor. See* Sh— Cymbeline, 1777

Rede (Leman T.) Guide to the stage. New York [c. 1863]. 12° BPL
Road to the stage, or performer's preceptor, containing . . . instructions for obtaining theatrical engagements ; a description of things necessary to the profession, etc. Ln : 1827. 12°. With portrait of Kean

Redfield *New York Publisher. See* Sh— Works, 1853, 1856, 1857

Redford (John) Moral play of wit and science and early poetical miscellanies. From an unpublished manuscript. Ed. by J. O. Halliwell. Ln : Sh— Soc., 1848. 8°, pp. xii.-128 and facsimile BM | BPL | BUS
The 'miscellanies' are by John Heywood, John Thorne, Thomas Prideaux, Miles Huggard, Master Knight, and others.

Redway (Geo. W.) *Editor. See* Antiquarian Magazine

Reed *Publisher. See* Sh— Merry devil . . . 1780

Reed (*Hon.* Edwin) Bacon and Sh—: Coincidences. Ln : Gay & Bird, 1906. Roy. 8°, pp. 160 BPL
Bacon and Sh— parallelisms. Boston, U.S., 1902. 8° BPL | BUS
Bacon *versus* Sh—: Brief for the plaintiff. Seventh edition, revised. Boston [U.S.] 1897. 8°. With portraits and plates BPL | BUS
Bacon *v.* Sh— . . . Ln : Service & Paton, 1899. Cr. 8°, pp. xxiv.-296. Plates and autographs BM | SML
Francis Bacon our Sh—. Boston, U.S., 1902. 8° BPL | BUS
Noteworthy opinions pro and con Bacon *v.* Sh—. Compiled and edited . . . Ln : Gay & Bird, 1905. 8°, pp. 86 BUS
Truth concerning Stratford and Sh—. With other essays. Boston, U.S., 1907. 8° BPL

Reed (Hy.) Lectures on English history and tragic poetry, as illustrated by Sh—. Ln : J. F. Shaw, 1856. 8°, pp. 280
BPL | BUS | CPL | MPL | SML
Lectures on English history . . . Ln : 1858. Cr. 8°
Lectures on English history. Philadelphia : Claxton, 1881. 8° SML
Lectures on English literature . . . Philadelphia : Parry & McMillan, 1856. 16°, pp. 466 BUS
Lectures on the British poets. 1863. 12°
Sh— occupies pp. 97-121. BPL

Reed (Hy.) Lectures on the British poets. Philadelphia : Claxton, 1870. 2 vols. 8° SML
Lectures on the English poets. Philadelphia : Claxton, 1873. 8° SML

Reed (Isaac) Library. *See* Catalogue, 1807

Reed (Isaac) *Editor—*
See Dodsley
  „ Sh— Macbeth, 1807
  „ Sh— Works, 1778, 1785, 1793, 1799-1802, 1800, 1803, 1805-09, 1807, 1809, 1810-12, 1811, 1812-15, 1813, 1814, 1817, 1817-18, 1819, 1820, 1821, 1822, 1823, 1824, 1824-26, 1825, 1826, 1827, 1828, 1830, 1831, 1832, 1833, 1835-36, 1836, 1837, 1839, 1840, 1842, 1843, 1847, 1848, 1849, 1851, 1851-52, 1852, 1852-59, 1854, 1855, 1857, 1858, 1859, 1860, 1862, 1863, 1864, 1866, 1868, 1885, 1897

Reed (Isaac). *See* Middleton

Rees (James) Sh— and the Bible. To which is added prayer on the stage, proper and improper ; Sh—'s use of the sacred name of the Deity ; The stage viewed from a scriptural and moral point ; The old mysteries and moralities the precursors of the English stage. Philadelphia : Claxton . . . 1876. 16°, pp. 188 BUS

Rees (O.) *Publisher—*
See Sh— King Henry VIII., 1804
  „ Sh— King John, 1804
  „ Sh— Othello, 1804

Reeve *Composer. See* Garrick

Reeve (Lovell) *Publisher. See* Sh— Sonnets, 1862

Reeves (Sims). *See* Banks (G. L.)

Reeves (W.) *Publisher—*
See Charke
  „ Cibber

Reference key to the Sh— memorial. [c. 1864.] F° BPL
See also Sh—] Gibbs.

Reflections from Sh—'s cliff. *See* Gillmor

Reflections on the too prevailing spirit of dissipation and gallantry, shewing its dreadful consequences to publick freedom. Ln : E. & C. Dilly, 1771. 8°, pp. viii.-86
'The comedies of Ben Jonson betray nothing of looseness and immorality' (p. 19).
'But that particular which ought to be weighed above all the rest is that the gayest, most polite, and delightful of all genteel pastimes may be said to have absolutely commenced in this [Elizabethan] era of manliness and gravity. This was the stage, which rose under Sh—'s hands to a height of dignity it has never since surpassed. Of all diversions none was received with more approbation and applause ; none followed with more appetite and ardour. But the real reason was not because they were dramatic entertainments, but because they were calculated to

Engraved by Ridley Holl & Blood, from an original Painting by Romney.

Isaac Reed, Esq.

See p. 258

please the taste of a judicious thinking people, and
were generally fraught with an active kind of instruction. Thus the age of Queen Elizabeth was not
only virtuous and manly, but no less polite, splendid,
and even gay ' (pp. 42-43).

Reflections upon theatrical expression. *See*
Pickering

Reformation (The). *See* Arrowsmith

Regimen sanitatis . . . *See* Villanova

Registers—
See Aston Cantlow   *See* Stationers
„ Fisher   „ Stopes
„ Savage   „ Stratford

Regnal years. *See* Halliwell

Regnier (M.) *See* Dudevant

Rehan (Ada) *Editor*. *See* Sh— Taming . . .
1900

Rehan.] Winter (Wm.) Study of Ada Rehan.
Privately printed, 1891-96. Cr. 8°. Illust.

Reid (T. B.) Sh— birthday record. *See* Sh—
Works : Ext. 1894

Reilly (A.) *Dublin Printer*. *See* Sh— As you
like it, 1741

Reinach (T.) *Editor*. *See* Sh— Hamlet, 1880

Reiss (F. A.) History of the parish of Rock in
the county of Worcester [with brief
glossary]. Ln : H. Grant [c. 1900]. 8°,
pp. 48. With five plates
Refers to Sh—, Hathaway and Lucy at pp. 33-34.

Rejected articles. Ln : 1826. 8°   BUS
Contains letters on . . . 'Romeo and Juliet,' signed
T. C., pp. 111-141.

Religion—
See Bell (Wm.)   *See* Blatchford
„ Bible   „ Sh—] Sh—'s religion

Religious and moral drama—
See Albion knight   *See* Hone
„ Clarke   „ King Darius
„ Collier   „ Ludus Coventriæ
„ Cooper   „ Malone Soc.
„ Coventry   „ Moral play
„ Digby . . .   „ Poole
„ Halliwell   „ Rees
„ Harrowing . . .   „ Sharpe
„ Hawkins

Religious and moral sentences. *See* Watson

Remarkable satires. *See* Wolcot (John)

Remarks on an article . . . *See* Croker

Remarks on Kemble's performance. *See*
Martin

Remarks on . . . Sh—'s versification. *See*
Bathurst

Remarks on some of the characters of Sh—.
By the author of 'Observations on modern
gardening.' Ln : T. Payne & Son,
Mews Gate, Castle St., St. Martin's, 1785.
8°

Remarks on the bust of Sh—. *See* Britton

Remarks on the character of Richard the
Third as played by Cooke and Kemble.
[By H. Martin ?] Ln : Parsons [1801].
8°, pp. 56   BUS

Remarks on the character of Richard the
Third . . . [By H. Martin ?] Second ed.
Ln : Parsons & Son [1801]. 8°, pp. 56
See also Kemble.   BM | BPL | BUS

Remarks on the desecration of the church-
yard. *See* Gray

Remarks on . . . the last edition of Sh—. *See*
Ritson

Remarks on the 'Sonnets.' *See* Hitchcock

Remarks on 'The tempest.' *See* Holt

Remarks upon a late edition of Sh—. *See*
Grey

Rembrandt. *See* Fuseli

Rémy (G.) Sh— ; a poem [In 'Pepper and
mustard for London stomachs,' p. 34].
Ln : 1868. 12°

Renan (Joseph Ernest) Caliban : A philosophical drama continuing 'The tempest'
of Sh—. Trans. by E. G. Vickery. New
York Sh— Soc., 1896. Cr. 8°, pp. 68
BM | BUS

Rendall (Vernon Horace) Joseph Knight. *See*
Knight

Rendall (Vernon Horace) *Editor*—
See Athenæum (The)
„ Notes & Queries

Rendle (W.) Playhouses at Bankside in the
time of Sh—. [c. 1886.] 8°   BPL
The Bankside, Southwark, and the Globe
playhouse. Ln : New Sh— Soc., 1876.
4°   BM | BPL | BUS

Renger *Berlin Publisher*. *See* Sh— Julius
Cæsar, 1856

Report of the sub-committee on the available
sites for a memorial of Sh—. 1864. F°
BPL

Report on printers and stationers, 1584. *See*
Reprints

Reprints . . . *Blue Series :*—English poetical
miscellanies. Ed. by J. P. Collier. Ln :
Privately printed [c. 1867]. 25 parts,
forming 2 vols. Fcp. 4°

Reprints . . . *Green Series :*—Illustrations of
old English literature. Ed. by J. P.
Collier. Ln : Privately printed, 1866.
24 parts, forming 3 vols. Fcp. 4°
Issue limited to twenty-five sets.
Contents :—
Lamentation against London, 1548.
Pasquil's palinodia, 1619.
Respublica : An interlude, 1553.
Barnfield (R.) Lady Pecunia, 1605.
Salter (T.) Mirror of modestie.
Passion of a discontented mind, 1602.
Barnfield (R.) Encomion of Lady Pecunia, 1598.
News from the Levant seas, 1594.
Holland (Hugh) Pancharis, 1603.
Horestes : An interlude, 1567.
Preservation of Henry VII., 1599.
Churchyard (T.) Reformation of rebellion and Shore's
Dekker (T.) Seven deadly sins of London.   [wife.
Crowch (H.) Love's court of conscience, 1637.
Lodge (T.) William Longbeard, 1593.
Procter (T.) Triumph of truth.

Greene (Robert) Mirror of modesty, 1584.
Ratsey.] Life and death of Gamaliel Ratsey, a famous
Hubbard (W.) Ceyx and Alcione. 1569. [thief, 1605.
Vennar (R.) Apology for England's joy, 1614.
Partridge (J.) History of Plasidas, 1566.
Nash (Thomas) Anatomy of absurdity, 1589.
Jordan (T.) Royal arbor of loyal poesie, 1664. [1573.
Norton (T.) Instructions for the Lord Mayor of London,

Reprints . . . *Red Series :*—Early English
popular literature. Ed. by J. P. Collier.
Ln : Privately printed, 1863. 24 parts,
forming 2 vols. Fcp. 4°
Issue restricted to twenty-five sets.

Contents :—

Knell (T.) Piththy note to Papists, 1570.
Kydde (Thomas) Murder of John Brewen, 1592.
History of Jacob and his twelve sonnes.
Wyll of the deuyll and last testament.
Metamorphosis of tabacca, 1602.
Murder of Lord Bourgh and Arnold Cosby's verses,
Godly Queene Hester : Enterlude, 1561. [1591.
Complaynte of them that ben to late maryed.
Whetstone (G.) Censure of a loyal subject, 1587.
Lyrics for old lutenists.
Calverley and the Yorkshire tragedy, 1605.
Complaint of the Churche, 1562.
Report on printers and stationers, 1584.
Sherley (Sir Anthony) Travels. Ed. by W. Parry, 1601.
Becke. Against the anabaptists, 1550.
Tyde taryeth no man : Comedy, 1576.
Ferris (R.) Voyage to Bristol.
Broadsides of speeches, songs, &c. delivered in the
     presence of General Monck, 1660.
Johnson (R.) Look on me London, 1613.
Bas (W.) Sword and buckler, 1602.
Good speed to Virginia, 1609.
Copies of early love letters.
Johnson (R.) Walks of Moorfields, 1607.
Walton, Arnold, & Clinton. Verses.

Reprints . . . *Yellow Series :*—Miscellaneous
tracts. Ed. by J. P. Collier. Ln : Privately printed [c. 1868]. 17 parts,
forming 2 vols. Fcp. 4°

Reprints of scarce pieces of Sh— criticism :
I., Remarks on 'Hamlet,' 1736. Ln :
1864. 8°, pp. 52   MPL

Repton (H.)] The bee, or a companion to the
Sh— gallery in Pall Mall, containing a
Catalogue-raisonné of all the pictures,
with comments . . . Ln : T. Cadell, 1789.
8°, pp. 54   BM | BPL | BUS
See also Boydell.

Respublica : An interlude, 1553. *See* Reprints

Retrospective review : Historical and antiquarian magazine. Edited by Henry
Southern and Nicholas Harris Nicolas.
Ln : Baldwyn & Cradock, 1820-28. 16
vols. 8°
Contains a review of Sh—'s Poems, pp. 378-406, vol. 7,
1823, and much other Shakespeareana.

Retvrne from Pernassvs, or the scovrge of
simony. Publiquely acted by the stvdents
in Saint Iohn's Colledge in Cambridge.
At Ln : Printed by G. Eld for Iohn
Wright and are to bee sold at his shop at
Christchurch Gate, 1606. Fcp. 4°, sig.
A—I² on 32 unpaged leaves
                          BM | BUS | CTC | W

A dramatic satire which reflects upon the chief poets of
the time. Sh— is thus criticised :—
     'Who loves Adonis' love or Lucre's rape?
     His sweeter verse contains hart-robbing life,
     Could but a graver subject him content
     Without love's lazy foolish languishment.'
Burbage occurs, instructing a would-be actor in the
part of 'King Richard the Third,' and the familiar
lines—'Now is the winter of our discontent . . .'—
are recited by the pupil as part of his lesson. Subsequently, in a prose dialogue between Sh—'s fellow-
actors Kempe and Burbage, Kempe remarks of
university dramatists, 'Why, here's our fellow Sh—
puts them all down ; aye, and Ben Ionson too. O !
that Ben Ionson is a pestilent fellow. He brought
up Horace, giving the poets a pill, but our fellow
Sh— hath given him a purge that made him bewray
his credit !' Burbage adds, 'He is a shrewd fellow
indeed.'
Elsewhere in the play a poor student enviously com-
plains of the wealth and position which a successful
actor derived from his calling—
     'England affords those glorious vagabonds
     That carried erst their fardles on their backs
     Coursers to ride on through the gazing streets,
     Sweeping it in their glaring satin suits,
     And pages to attend their masterships
     With mouthing-words that better wits had framed
     They purchase lands and now esquires are made.'

          *   *   *

Says the character *Ingenioso* : 'What's thy judgment
of Wm. Sh—?'
In the first part Gullio exclaims, 'O sweet Mr. Sh— !
I'le have his picture in my study at the Courte.'
This expression is remarkable evidence of the exist-
ence of the poet's portrait, some years before his
death, either in the form of a print or in oils.
This play formed the foundation of Dr. Wild's comedy,
'The Benefice,' issued in 1689.
See also 'Pilgrimage to Parnassus.'
See also Ratsey for a reference to Sh—'s investments.

Retzsch (F. A. Moritz)] Outline illustrations
to Sh—, Goethe, and Schiller. Ln : Tilt
[c. 1840]. Oblong 8°. With 67 outline
plates

Retzsch (F. A. Moritz) *Artist*—
See Sh— Hamlet, 1828
   ,,   Sh— King Henry IV., i., 1845
   ,,   Sh— King Lear, 1838
   ,,   Sh— Macbeth, 1833
   ,,   Sh— Merry wives, 1844
   ,,   Sh— Othello, 1842
   ,,   Sh— Romeo . . . 1836
   ,,   Sh— The tempest, 1839
   ,,   Sh— Works, 1847

Retzsch.] Retzsch's outlines [In 'Foreign
Quarterly Review,' Oct.] Ln : 1836. 8°
                                         BUS

Retzsch's outlines : 'Hamlet' [In 'Foreign
Quarterly Review,' June]. Ln : 1828. 8°
                                         BUS

] Retzsch's outlines : 'Macbeth' [In 'Foreign
Quarterly Review,' Oct.] Ln : 1833. 8°
                                         BUS

Revels—
See Ancient . . .   *See* Gesta Grayorum
   ,, Collection . . .   ,, Goodwin
   ,, Curious paper   ,, Stage
   ,, Forman   ,, Tomlins

Revels at court: Accounts extracted from the office books of Elizabeth and James I. Ln: Sh— Soc., 1842

Revisal of Sh—'s text. *See* Heath

Reynolds (E. L.) *See* Creighton, Stopes & Reynolds

Reynolds (F.)] Songs, duettos, glees . . . *See* Sh— Two gentlemen, 1821

Reynolds.] Life and times of F. Reynolds, written by himself. 1826. 2 vols. 8° BPL

Reynolds (Frederick) *Editor*—
See Sh— Comedy of errors, 1819
„ Sh— Merry wives, 1824
„ Sh— Midsummer . . . 1816
„ Sh— Two gentlemen, 1821

Reynolds (*Sir* Joshua)] Johnson and Garrick. 1816. 8° BPL

Reynolds (*Sir* Joshua) *Artist*—
See Garrick
„ Johnson
„ Robinson
„ Sh— Works, 1802

Reynolds (*Sir* J.) *Editor*. *See* Annotations

Reynolds' Miscellany: Tercentenary number [April 30th, 1864]. 4° BPL

Rhames *Dublin Publisher*. *See* Sh— Macbeth, 1739

Rhead (G. W. & F. A.) Staffordshire pots and potters. Ln: Hutchinson, 1906. 4°, pp. xvi-384. With 210 coloured and other plates BM | BPL
Gives some account of Sh—'s 'Passionate pilgrim,' of William Jaggard, and of Richard Barnefield at pp. 83-86, paraphrased apparently from S. L. Levi's 'Life of Sh—.'

Rhetoric made familiar. *See* Sh— Works: Ext. 1748

Rhodes *Engraver*. *See* Sh— Works, 1813

Rhodes (W. B.) Library. *See* Catalogue, 1825

Rhys (Ernest) Sh—'s 'King Henry VI.': Critical comment [In Harper's 'New Monthly Magazine,' 1905]. With tinted illustrations by E. A. Abbey. New York: Harper, 1905. Roy. 8° BM

Rhys (Ernest) *Editor*. *See* Sh— Poems, 1898

Rhys (*Capt.* H.)] Theatrical trip for a wager through Canada and the United States, by 'Morton Price.' 1861. 8°

Ribbans (F. B.) Instructive copies selected from Dr. Johnson's criticisms on Sh—'s plays. [c. 1873.] 4° BPL

Ribton-Turner (C. J.) Sh—'s land: Description of central and southern Warwickshire. With maps and plans. Leamington: Glover, 1893. 12° BPL | SML
Sh—'s land. Leamington: Glover, 1897. 12°

Ribton-Turner (C. J.) *Editor*. *See* Sh— Hamlet, 1886

Riccoboni (Lewis) Historical and critical account of the theatres in Europe. Together with two celebrated essays . . . on action, or the art of speaking in public; and a companion of the antient and modern drama. Ln: Waller, 1741. 8° SML | W
Contains article, with references to Sh—, headed 'The English theatre.'

Rice (C.) *Publisher*. *See* Sh— Works, 1822, 1834

Rice (George Edward) *Editor*. *See* Sh— Hamlet, 1852, 1853

Rich *or* Riche (Barnaby) Apolonius and Silla— *See* Sh— Twelfth night, 1889
„ Sh—] Sh—'s library
Eight novels employed by English dramatic poets of the reign of Queen Elizabeth. Originally published . . . in 1581 and reprinted from a copy of that date in the Bodleian Library. Ln: Sh— Soc., 1846. 8°, pp. xvi.-224 BM | BPL | BUS | SML
Contents:—Preface and dedication; Sappho Duke of Mantona; Apolonius and Silla; Nicander and Lucilla; Fineo and Fiamma; Two brethren and their wives; Gonsales and his vertuous wife Agatha; Aramanthus, borne a leper; Phylotus and Emilia.
The second story resembles the foundation of 'Twelfth night.'
First issued under the title of ' Farewell to the militarie profession.'

Faultes, faults, and nothing else but faultes . . . Ln: Jeffrey Chorleton, 1606. Fcp. 4°
Satirical reflections upon the peculiarities and vices of the Shakespearean age. There is a notice of Jonson's ' Every man ' (in which Sh— performed, 1598), p. 4, and a reference to Tarleton.

Rich (Richard)] Newes from Virginia, 1610. A poetical tract, describing the adventures supposed to be referred to in Sh—'s 'The tempest.' Ed. by J. O. Halliwell. Ln: 1865. 8° BM | BPL | HCL
Twenty-five copies printed; ten only preserved.

Rich (Samuel). *See* R—— (S.)

Richard II. *See* Sh— King Richard II.

Richard II.] Deposition of Richard the Second. Translation of a French metrical history. By Webb. 1899. 8° BPL

] Life and death of King Richard the Second, who was deposed of his crown, by reason of his not regarding the councell of the sage and wise of his kingdom. Published by a well-wisher to the Commonwealth. Ln: 1642. Fcp. 4° W

] Life and reign of King Richard the Second. By a person of quality. Ln: 1681. 12° BPL

] 'Richard II.' at the Princess's Theatre: Newspaper cuttings. [c. 1857]. 12° BPL

Richard III. *See* Sh— King Richard III.

Richard III.] Halsted (C. A.) Richard III. as Duke of Gloucester and King of England. Ln : Longman, 1844. 2 vols. 8°, pp. xx.-458 and xii.-570, with portraits   SML

] Richard the Third and the primrose criticism. Chicago, 1887. 12°   BPL

] Walpole. Historic doubts on the life and reign of King Richard III. Ln : Dodsley, 1768. 4°   SML

Richard the Third. *See* Legge

Richard Duke of York—

See Sh— King Henry VI., iii., 1817

,, True tragedie of Richarde . . .

Richards (T.) *Publisher. See* Sh— King Richard II., 1870

Richards (T. P.) Guide to King Edward VI. School, &c. Stratford-on-Avon, 1895. Cr. 8°   BPL

Richards (Wm. C.) Sh— calendar. *See* Sh— Works : Ext. 1850

Richardson *Editor. See* Sh— Works, 1860, 1866

Richardson *Publisher. See* Garrick

Richardson (Abby Sage) Sh— as a plagiarist [In 'Galaxy,' Dec.] New York, 1870. 8°   BUS

Richardson (David Lester) Literary leaves, or prose and verse. Calcutta, 1836. 8° BUS
Contains articles on Sh—'s 'Sonnets,' 'Shylock,' 'Othello,' and 'Iago.'

Richardson (Edith) Green thoughts from Sh—. *See* Sh— Works : Ext. 1904

Richardson (J.) *Publisher. See* Sh— Works, 1811

Richardson (J. M.) *Publisher. See* Sh— Hamlet, 1810, 1812

Richardson (L.) Sh— studies : Aguecheck the 'gifted' ['Twelfth night']. New York [1897]. 12°, pp. 12   MPL

Sh— studies : New interpretation of Falstaff's dying words. New York [1897]. 12°, pp. 24   BPL | MPL

'Richardson (W.)' *pseud. See* Steevens

Richardson (W.) *Publisher—*

See Sh— Hamlet, 1770

,, Sh— Works, 1766

Richardson (*Prof.* Wm.)] Cursory remarks on tragedy, on Sh—, and on certain French and Italian poets, principally tragedians . . . Ln : Printed for W. Owen in Fleet Street, 1772. 8°, pp. x.-242
By some the authorship is ascribed to Edward Taylor, and by others to J. Ritson.

] Cursory remarks on tragedy . . . Ln : W. Owen, 1774. 8°, pp. x.-242
BPL | BUS | CPL | MPL | SML | W

Essays on Sh—'s dramatic characters of Richard the Third, King Lear, and Timon of Athens . . . [with] an essay on the faults of Sh—, and . . . observations on 'Hamlet.' Ln : J. Murray, 1784. 8°, pp. viii.-170   BM | BPL | BUS | SML

Richardson (*Prof.* Wm.) Essays on Sh—'s dramatic characters . . . Second edition. Ln : Murray, 1785. 12°   BPL | SML

Essays on Sh—'s dramatic characters . . . Ln : J. Murray, 1786. 8°, pp. viii.-iv.-170   BM | BUS | CPL | SML

Essays on Sh—'s dramatic character of Sir John Falstaff and on his imitation of female characters. To which are added, some general observations on the study of Sh—. Ln : J. Murray, 1788. 8°, pp. ii.-96   BPL | BUS

Essays . . . Ln : J. Murray, 1789. 8°, pp. ii.-96   BM | BPL | MPL | SML | W

Essays . . . Fifth edition. Ln : J. Murray & S. Highley, 1797. 8°, pp. viii.-402
BM | BPL | BUS | MPL | SML | W
This publication combines the author's three previous works : 'Philosophical analysis,' 'Essays on . . . dramatic characters,' and 'Essays on Falstaff.'

Essays . . . Fifth edition. Ln : Murray, 1798. 8°, pp. viii.-402   BPL | BUS | CPL | SML

Essays . . . With an illustration of Sh—'s representation . . . in Fluellen [King Henry V.] Sixth edition. Ln : S. Bagster, 1812. 8°, pp. viii.-iv.-448
BM | BPL | BUS | W

Essays . . . 1818. 8°   BM

Philosophical analysis and illustration of some of Sh—'s dramatic characters. Edinburgh, W. Creech ; Glasgow, 1774. 8°, pp. iv.-224   CPL
'Macbeth,' 'Hamlet,' 'Jaques,' and 'Imogen.'
'No writer has hitherto appeared who possesses in a more eminent degree than Sh— the power of imitating the passions. All of them seem familiar to him ; the boisterous no less than the gentle ; the benign no less than the malignant. There are several writers as there are many players who are successful in imitating some particular passions, but who appear stiff, awkward, and unnatural in the expression of others . . . The genius of Sh— is unlimited. Possessing extreme sensibility and uncommonly susceptible, he is the Proteus of the drama ; he changes himself into every character and enters easily into every condition of human nature. Many dramatic writers of different ages are capable occasionally of breaking out with great fervour of genius, in the natural language of strong emotion. No writer of antiquity is more distinguished for abilities of this kind than Euripides. His whole art and soul seem torn and agitated by the force of the passion he imitates. He ceases to be Euripides ; he is Medea ; he is Orestes. Sh—, however, is most eminently distinguished not only by these occasional sallies, but by imitating the passion in all its aspects, by pursuing it through all its windings and labyrinths, by moderating or accelerating its impetuosity according to the influence of other principles and of external events, and finally by combining it in a judicious manner with other passions and propensities, or by setting it aptly in opposition. He thus unites the two essential powers of dramatic invention—that of forming characters ; and that of imitating in their natural expressions the passions and affections of which they are composed.'

Philosophical analysis . . . Second edition, corrected. Ln., J. Murray ; Edinburgh, W. Creech, 1774. 8°, pp. iv.-224
BM | BPL | BUS | SML

Richardson (*Prof*. Wm.) Philosophical analysis
. . . Ln : J. Murray ; Edin. : W. Creech,
1775. 8°, pp. iv.-204   BPL | BUS
Philosophical analysis . . . Ln : J. Murray,
1780. 8°, pp. 208   BUS
Philosophical analysis . . . Third edition.
Ln : J. Murray, 1784. 8°, pp. 208 .
          BM | BUS | CPL
Philosophical analysis . . . Ln : J. Murray,
1785. 8°, pp. iv.-204   BM | BPL
Philosophical analysis . . . Philadelphia,
1788. 8°
The first known American publication on Sh—.
Philosophical analysis . . . To which is
added an essay on the faults of Sh—.
Boston [U.S.]: Munroe, Francis & Parker,
Sh— bookstore, 1808. 8°, pp. 188
          BPL | BUS
Philosophical analysis. *See* Sh— Works,
1807
Proposals. *See* Sh— Works, 1803
Richardson (W. J. & J.) *Publishers.   See*
Sh— Works, 1798
Richardson & Lord *Boston [U.S.] Publishers.*
See Sh— Othello, 1823
Richardson & Sons *Derby Publishers.   See*
Sh— Works, 1831, 1845
Richardus tertius. *See* Legge
Richter *Artist.   See* Sh— Works, 1787-91
Ricketts (Charles S.) *Artist—*
See Sh— Passionate . . . 1896
  ,, Sh— Sonnets, 1899
  ,, Sh— Works, 1900-03
Rickey & Co. *Cincinnati Publishers. See* Sh—
Works, 1864
Riddle (Joseph Esmond) Illustrations of
Aristotle on men and manners from the
dramatic works of Sh—. Oxford : S.
Collingwood, 1832. 12°, pp. 134
          BM | BPL | BUS | CPL | SML | W
Rider *Bp. of Killaloe* (John) Bibliotheca
scholastica : A double dictionarie . . .
Oxford : Printed by Joseph Barnes, 1589.
Fcp. 4°
Curious for definitions illustrative of manners and
customs in Sh—'s day. A theatre is described as 'a
place made halfe round where people assemble to
beholde plaies.'
See also Bullokar.
Rider (Wm.)] Views in Stratford-on-Avon
and its vicinity illustrative of the bio-
graphy of Sh—, with descriptions. War-
wick : H. T. Merridew, 1822. 8°
Some copies on large paper issued in roy. 4°.
Views in Stratford . . . to illustrate the life
of Sh—. With remarks. Warwick : H.
T. Merridew, 1828. F°, ff. 8. With five
etchings   BM | BPL | BUS
A few done on large paper with India proofs.
Ridgway (J.) *Publisher—*
See Dudley

Ridgway (J.) *Publisher—*
See Haslewood
  ,, Sh— Hamlet, 1804, 1805
  ,, Sh— King Henry IV., i., 1803
  ,, Sh— King Henry IV., ii., 1804
  ,, Sh— Macbeth, 1803
  ,, Sh— Measure . . . 1803
  ,, Sh— Merry wives, 1804
Ridley (J.) *Publisher. See* Sh— Works, 1773
Riechelmann (*Dr.* L.) *Editor—*
See Sh— King Richard II., 1869
  ,, Sh— Julius Cæsar, 1879
  ,, Sh— Merchant . . . 1876
Riedel (T.) *Munchen Publisher.   See* Sh—
Macbeth, 1879
Rignold (G.) *Editor. See* Sh— King Henry V.,
1880
Riley (A.) Analysis of poetry. *See* Sh— Works :
Ext. 1827
Riley & Co. (I.) *New York Publishers.   See*
Sh— Works, 1805-09
Rimbault (Edward Francis) Bibliotheca mad-
rigaliana : A bibliographical account of
musical and poetical works published in
England in the 16th and 17th centuries
under the titles of madrigals, ballets,
ayres, canzonets, etc. Ln : A. Reader
[c. 1875]. 8°, pp. xvi.-88   SML
Who was 'Jack Wilson,' the singer of Sh—'s
stage ? An attempt to prove identity
. . . with John Wilson, doctor of musick,
in the Univ. of Oxford, 1644. Ln : J. R.
Smith, 1846. 8°, pp. 20
          BPL | BUS | CPL | MPL
At Boston is the only copy printed on vellum.
Rimbault (E. F.) *Editor—*
See Percy Society
  ,, Sh— Macbeth, 1840
  ,, Sh— Poems, 1850
Rimmer (Alfred) & Smith (W. H. Payne)
Rambles round Rugby. Ln : Percival,
1892. Roy. 8°, pp. xxiv.-270. With 73
textual illustrations
Limited to 750 copies.
Describes and illustrates Warwickshire.
Risk (Geo.) *Dublin Publisher.   See* Fielding
Ritson (Joseph) Ancient songs from the time
of Henry III. to the Revolution. Ln :
1790. Cr. 8°. With six vignettes by
Stothard   BM | MPL
With observations on the early English minstrels, songs,
music, and instruments.
' The most curious and certainly the most interesting to
antiquarian readers of all Ritson's works.'—*Lowndes*.
Ancient songs . . . Ln : 1829. 2 vols. Cr.
8°   BM | MPL
Bibliographia poetica : A catalogue of
English poets of the twelfth-sixteenth
centuries. With a short account of their
works. 1802. 8°   BM
With a notice of Sh—.

Ritson (Joseph)] Cursory criticisms on the edition of Sh— published by Edmund Malone. Ln: Hookham & Carpenter, 1792. 8°, pp. x.-104 BM | BPL | BUS | W
For answer see Malone: Letter to Farmer.
See also Richardson.

Fairy tales . . . To which are prefixed dissertations on pigmies and fairies. 1831. 8° MPL
See also Halliwell & Ritson, Fairy tales, 1875.

Pieces of ancient popular poetry from authentic manuscripts and old printed copies. Ln: 1791. 8°. With cuts by Bewick
Contains the best account of Adam Bel the archer, mentioned in 'Much ado . . .'

] 'Quip modest': A few words by way of supplement to 'Remarks . . . on . . . the last edition of Sh— . . .' By J. R——. Ln: J. Johnson, 1788. 8°, pp. viii.-32
BM | BPL | BUS | W
This copy contains the rare cancelled leaf (page vii. of the preface) on which Ritson describes George Steevens as an infamous scoundrel, and predicts the gallows as his end. After a small number had been issued, the tract was reprinted with the offending phrase modified, but still caustic.

] 'Quip modest . . .' Ln: J. Johnson, 1788. 8°, pp. viii.-32 BUS | W
Second issue, with the revised preface.

] Remarks, critical and illustrative, . . . on the last edition of Sh— [Ed. by G. Steevens, 1778]. Ln: J. Johnson, 1783. 8°, pp. viii.-240
BM | BPL | BUS | CPL | SML | W
Some copies issued on large paper, of which one is in the British Museum.
At the end appear 'Proposals for publishing the plays of Sh—, in 8 vols, 12°, from the two first folios.' The orthography was to be reduced to a modern and uniform system, with glossary, vocabulary, and index.

Select collection of English songs. 1783. 3 vols. Cr. 8° MPL

Select collection of English songs. 1813. 3 vols. Cr. 8°. Vignettes by Stothard and Blake
Contains seven of Sh—'s Songs.

Stockton jubilee.] By permission of the Mayor. Vivat Rex. The St.ckt.n jubilee, or Sh— in all his glory. A choice pageant for the Christmas holidays. Veluti in speculum. Newcastle: Printed for the managers, 1781. 12°
See also Sh— Works: Ext. 1781.

Ritson (Joseph) Editor—
See New story teller
  ,, Sh— Comedy of errors, 1787

Ritson.] Haslewood (J.) Life and publications of J. Ritson. 1824. 8° BPL
Contains Sh— matter.

Ritson (J.)—
See Familiar address
  ,, Halliwell & Ritson
  ,, Malone

Rivals (The). See Sh— Two noble kinsmen, 1668

Rivers Artist. See Sh— Works, 1803

Rives (George Lockhart) Essay on the authorship of the first, second, and third parts of 'Henry the Sixth,' commonly attributed to Sh—. Cambridge: Deighton, 1874. 8°, pp. viii.-48 BM | BUS
Secured the Harness prize (q.v.)

Rivington (C.) Publisher—
See Sh— Merchant . . . 1783
  ,, Sh— Poems, 1725, 1728
  ,, Sh— Works, 1725

Rivington (Charles)] Strictures on N. E. S. A. Hamilton's 'Inquiry into . . . J. P. Collier's annotated Sh—,' by 'Scrutator.' Ln: J. R. Smith, 1860. 8°, pp. 28
BM | BPL | BUS | CPL | MPL

Rivington (C. & J.) Publishers. See Sh— Works, 1823, 1826

Rivington (F. & C.) Publishers—
See Sh— Pericles, 1800
  ,, Sh— Twelfth night, 1800
  ,, Sh— Works, 1798, 1805
  ,, Sh— Works: Ext. 1798

Rivington (F. C. & J.) Publishers. See Sh— Works, 1811, 1823

Rivington (J.) Publisher—
See Sh— Comedy of errors, 1770
  ,, Sh— Cymbeline, 1759
  ,, Sh— Hamlet, 1767
  ,, Sh— King Henry VIII., 1762
  ,, Sh— Macbeth, 1768, 1770
  ,, Sh— Measure . . . 1770
  ,, Sh— Much ado, 1776
  ,, Sh— Othello, 1765
  ,, Sh— The tempest, 1761
  ,, Sh— Timon . . . 1770
  ,, Sh— Works, 1757, 1762, 1786-90, 1790, 1805

Rivington (J. & F.) Publishers—
See Sh— Merchant . . . 1783
  ,, Sh— Works, 1773

Roach (J.) Publisher—
See Sh— Cymbeline, 1806
  ,, Sh— King Richard III., 1814
  ,, Sh— Othello, 1808
  ,, Sh— Taming . . . 1806
  ,, Sh— The tempest, 1806
  ,, Sh— Timon . . . 1806
  ,, Sh— Winter's tale, 1802

Robartes (Foulke) Revenve of the gospel, 1613. See Sh— Autograph

Roberts Publisher. See Sh— Timon . . . 1770

Roberts (A. E.) Editor. See Sh— Julius Cæsar, 1902

Roberts (Edwin F.) Sh— studies and fancies [In 'Family Friend']. Ln: 1862. 8° BUS
Contents :—'Midsummer night's dream,' 'Cymbeline,' 'Macbeth,' 'The tempest.'

Roberts (J.) Publisher. See Theobald

Roberts (James) *Printer & Publisher—*
See Euordanus
,, Gray (W.)
,, Harsnet
,, Lillo
,, Philips
,, Sh— Hamlet, 1603, 1604, 1605
,, Sh— Merchant . . . 1600
,, Sh— Midsummer . . . 1600
,, Sh— Sir John Oldcastle, 1600
,, Sh— Titus . . . 1600
,, Sh— Troilus . . . (*heading*)

Roberts (John)] Answer to Mr. Pope's preface
to Sh—. In a letter to a friend. Being
a vindication of the old actors who were
the publishers and performers of that
author's plays. Whereby the errors of
their edition are further accounted for
and some memoirs of Sh— and stage-
history of his time are inserted which
were never before collected and publish'd.
By a stroling player. Ln: . . . 1729.
8°, pp. 48   BUS | CTC | W
Lowndes (p. 2329) misquotes the date as 1829.
'One of the rarest pieces of Shakespeareana.'—*Halliwell.*

Roberts (John) *Prompter. See* Sh— King
Richard II., 1632

Roberts (P. Lyddon) *Editor. See* Sh— King
Richard III., 1902

Roberts (Wm.) Earlier history of English
bookselling. Ln: Low . . . 1889. Cr. 8°,
pp. xii.-344
'Bookselling in the time of Sh—' fills pp. 46-77. It is
disconcerting to find so experienced a writer as Mr.
Roberts in the company of less careful scribes. On
p. 73 Mr. Roberts says he is 'quite certain that Isaac
Jaggard published pirated editions [of Bacon's
Essays] in 1606, 1612, 1624.' This is 'confusion
worse confounded.' It is fairly well known, and
easily ascertainable, that Isaac Jaggard never issued
any works, pirated or permissible, of Sir Francis
Bacon. His shop, too, was not at the 'Hand and
Starre,' and his publications do not include Carew's
'Survey of Cornwall' or Fairfax's 'Godfrey of Bul-
loigne.' Some of these were the publications of his
uncle John, who succeeded Richard Tottell, and one
was issued by Elizabeth Jaggard.

Earlier history of English bookselling. Ln:
Low, 1892. Cr. 8°, pp. xii.-344
With the errors of the first impression repeated.

McKee library [In 'Athenæum,' No. 3798,
p. 195; No. 3833, p. 475; No. 3865, p.
701]. Aug. 1900, Ap. 1901, Nov. 1901

Shakespeareana [In 'Athenæum,' No. 4038,
p. 347, Mar.] 1905

Simon Trippe [Elizabethan poet], [In
'Athenæum,' No. 3797, p. 153, Aug.] 1900

Robertson (Cornwell) King Edward VI.
School [Prospectus of Sh—'s school],
Stratford-on-Avon. [c. 1908]. Oblong
8°, pp. 28 (including wrappers and twelve
plates)

Robertson (Francis) *Edinburgh Publisher. See*
Sh— King Richard III., 1766

Robertson.] Brooke (Stopford A.) Life and
Letters of Frederick W. Robertson. Ln:
1886. 2 vols. Cr. 8°   BM | BPL
At p. 289, vol. i., says:—'What I admire in Sh—, however, is that his loves are all human, no earthliness
hiding itself from itself in sentimental transcendental-
ism, no loves of the angels, which are the least angelic
things, I believe, that float in the clouds, though they
do look down upon mortal feelings with contempt
. . . Sh— is healthy, true to humanity in this, and
for that reason I pardon him even his earthly coarseness. You always know that you are on an earth
which has to be refined instead of floating in an
empyrean with wings of wax. Therein he is im-
measurably greater than Shelley. Shelleyism is very
sublime, sublimer a good deal than God, for God's
world is all wrong and Shelley is all right ; much
purer than Christ, for Shelley can criticise Christ's
heart and life ; nevertheless, Shelleyism is only
atmospheric profligacy, to coin a Montgomeryism.
I believe this to be one of Sh—'s most wondrous
qualities—the humanity of his nature and heart.
There is a spirit of sunny endeavour about him and
an acquiescence in things as they are, not incom-
patible with a cheerful resolve to make them better.'

Robertson (G. S.) *Editor. See* Sh— King
Henry IV., ii., 1894

Robertson (J.) *Edinburgh Publisher. See* Sh—
Works, 1819

Robertson (J. & M.) *Glasgow Publishers. See*
Sh— Works, 1795

Robertson (John Mackinnon) Did Sh— write
'Titus Andronicus'? A study in Eliza-
bethan literature. Ln: Watts, 1905.
8°, pp. xii.-256   BPL | BUS
Is 'Hamlet' a consistent creation ? [In
'Free Review']. 1895. Cr. 8°   BPL
Montaigne and Sh—. Ln: University
Press, 1897. 8°, pp. iv.-170
          BM | BPL | BUS
Originality of Sh—. *See* Sh—] Robertson
Religion of Sh—: Two discourses. Ln:
[1887]. 8°   BM | BUS

Robertson (Johnston Forbes) *Actor & Editor—*
See Phelps
,, Sh— Hamlet, 1897
,, Sh— Macbeth, 1898
,, Romeo . . . 1895

Robertson (Thomas) Essay on the character
of Hamlet [In 'Royal Soc. of Edin.
Trans.'] 1770. 8°   BUS
Essay on . . . Hamlet [In 'Edin. Philoso-
phical Soc. Trans.'] 1788. 4° BPL | W
Also published separately.

Robertson.] Pemberton (T. E.) Life and
writings of T. W. Robertson. 1893. 8°
          BPL

Robin Goodfellow : Fairy ballad opera. *See*
Sh— Midsummer . . . 1848

Robin Hood. *See* Malone Society

Robins (George) *Auctioneer—*
See Stratford] Auction
,, Stratford] Particulars

Robinson *Publisher*—
See Sh— Timon . . . 1770
,, Sh— Works, 1816-18, 1825-26, 1826,
1829, 1839
Robinson *& others* (Clement) Handefull of
pleasant delites. Ln: Richard Jhones,
1584. 16°
From this work Sh— quotes several songs.
Reprinted in 'Heliconia,' vol. 2, and by the Spenser
Society.
Robinson (F. S.) The connoisseur. Ln:
Redway, 1891. 8°   SML
At p. 53 is an erroneous account of the Flower portrait,
now lodged in the Sh— Memorial Gallery at Stratford.
Robinson (G.) *Publisher*—
See Sh— Merchant . . . 1783
,, Sh— Works, 1773, 1811
Robinson (George) *Printer. See* Wilson (T.)
Robinson (G. & J.) *Publishers*—
See *Sh*—] Sherlock
,, White & Lamb
Robinson (G. G. & J.) *Publishers*—
See Malone
,, Sh— Cymbeline, 1794
,, Sh— King Lear, 1794
,, Sh— Poems, 1797
,, Sh— Works, 1790, 1797, 1798
,, Sh— Works: Ext. 1787
Robinson (H. G.) *Editor. See* Sh— King
Richard II., 1867, 1874
Robinson (H. P.) Church of the Holy Trinity,
Stratford-on-Avon [In 'Warwickshire Il-
lustrated,' pp. 43-50. 1865 ?]. 4°   BPL
Robinson (J.)] Christmas at Old Court. 1864.
8°   BPL
Sh— forgery, pp. 151-286.
Robinson (J.) *Publisher. See* Sh— Works,1811
Robinson (John) *Witness. See* Sh— Will . . .
1616
Robinson (J. H.) Had Sh— read Cavendish's
'Life of Wolsey'? *See Sh*—] Sh— Soc.
Robinson *'Perdita'* (*Mrs.* Mary) Memoirs,
written by herself. Ln: 1801. 4 vols.
12°. With oval portrait in stipple
Poems . . . Ln: John Bell, 1791. 8°, pp.
xxiv.-224 and stipple portrait by T.
Smirke after Sir J. Reynolds
At p. 72 is an 'Elegy to Garrick.'
Robinson.] Makower (Stanley V.) 'Perdita' :
A romance in biography. Ln: Hutchin-
son, 1908. 8°. With portraits   BPL
Robinson (M. Bryant) *Editor. See* Sh— Mer-
chant . . . 1907
Robinson (P.) Sh—'s flower language [In the
'Monthly Packet']. [1895 ?]. 8°   BPL
Sh—'s natural history : New light on
'Titus Andronicus' [In the 'Contempo-
rary Review']. 1894. Roy. 8°   BPL
Robinson (R.) *Printer. See* Bandello & Brooke
Robinson (Richard) *Actor. See* Cunningham
Robinson (Richard) *Editor. See* Elimandus

Robinson (Robert) *Publisher*—
See Ralegh
,, Sh— Romeo . . . 1587
Robinson (T. H.) *Artist*—
See Sh— Julius Cæsar, 1902
,, Sh— Macbeth, 1902
Robinson (Wm. Clarke) Sh— ; the man and
his mind. 1890. 8°   BM
Robinson (W. Heath) *Artist*—
See Sh— Twelfth night, 1908
,, Sh— Works : Ext. 1901
Robinson & Roberts *Publishers. See* Sh—
Macbeth, 1770
Robson (J.) *Publisher*—
See Caldecott
,, Sh— Macbeth, 1770
,, Sh— Merchant . . . 1783
,, Sh— Timon . . . 1770
,, Sh— Works, 1773, 1790
Robson (William) The old play-goer. Ln:
J. Masters, 1846. 8°   BPL
Contains notices of Sh—'s plays.
Rochester (John Wilmot *Earl of*) Poems on
several occasions. 1731. 8°
Reference to Sh— at p. 31.
Sports of the muses. *See* Sh— Works :
Ext. 1752
Valentinian : A tragedy. Ln: Timothy
Goodwin at the Maidenhead against St.
Dunstan's Church, Fleet St., 1685. Fcp.
4°
The prologue says :—
'Like Falstaffe, let 'em conquer heroes dead.'
Rochester (John Wilmot *Earl of*) *Editor. See*
Beaumont & Fletcher
Rodd *Bookseller* (Horatio) Catalogue of an-
cient and modern books . . . containing
many early English plays, old poetry and
rare books. Ln: 1851. 8°, pp. 42   BUS
Catalogue of English portraits and topo-
graphy, including . . . plates to illustrate
Sh—. With a relic of the mulberry tree.
Ln: Compton & Ritchie [c. 1850]. 8°,
pp. ii.-44   BUS
Rodd (H.) & Forster (Hy. Rumsey) Few remarks on the Chandos portrait of Sh—
recently purchased at Stowe for the Earl
of Ellesmere . . . Ln: Priv. printed, 1849.
8°, pp. ii.-20 and woodcuts of the Droeshout, Stratford bust, and Chandos por-
traits   BM | BPL | BUS | MPL
Limited to 50 copies.
Rodd (H.) & Maddox. Catalogue of an extensive collection of fine and rare prints
illustrative of the works of Sh—, including all the rare portraits of the bard
and scenic prints in choice proof state.
Also a capital collection of Shakespeariana. Collected by John Tyrrel. Ln:
1850. 8°, pp. iv.-34   BUS
One of four copies done on thick paper.

Rodd *Bookseller* (Thomas)] Catalogue of some
books in the possession of H. Jadis [con-
taining a Shakespearean assemblage].
Ln : J. Moyes, 1826. 8°, pp. 48

Issue limited to 25 copies.   BPL | BUS | MPL

English dramatic literature : Catalogue of
an extensive collection of plays, early
masques and pageants . . . Shakespeariana.
Ln : 1835. 8°, pp. ii.-64   BUS

Essay on 'The tempest.' c. 1835 ? Manuscript. F°, on ff. 9. With orig. pencil
portrait of the author   BUS
The writer held the theory that Lampedusa was Prospero's island. Hunter in his 'Disquisition' acknowledges his indebtedness to Rodd for this theory.

Shakspeariana : A list of editions of . . .
Sh— and books illustrative of his life
and writings. Ln : [c. 1841]. 8°   BUS

Shakspeariana : A list of an extensive collection of the works of Sh—, including
some of great curiosity and interest, also
of . . . works illustrative of his life and
writings. On sale at the prices affixed.
Ln : [c. 1845]. 8°, pp. 24   BPL | BUS
Some of the prices quoted are modest enough to mention. Sh—'s Poems, 1640, large copy, £12/12/- ;
King Henry the Fourth, 1622, 28/- ; King Henry
the Fifth, 1608, 63/- ; King Henry the Sixth, 1619,
£5/5/- ; King Lear, 1608, £10/10/- ; Hamlet, 1637,
5/- ; Merchant of Venice, 1600, £10 ; ditto, 1637,
25/- ; Merry wives, 1619, £7/7/- ; Midsummer
night's dream, 1600, £10/10/- ; Othello, 1630, 28/- ;
Pericles, 1619, £5/15/6 ; King John, 1622, 45/-.

See Sh— Merry wives, 1660
  „   Sh— Will . . . 1830
  „   *Sh*—] Sh— Soc.

Rodenberg (Julius) England ; literary and
social. Ln : 1875. 8°   BUS

Roderick. On the metre of 'King Henry
VIII.' Ln : New Sh— Soc., 1875. 8°

Roderick (Richard) Remarks on Sh—. *See*
Edwards (T.)

Rodwaye (A. J.) Notes on the heraldry of
'King Henry V.' [In 'Mansfield acting
version,' pp. 119-124]. New York, 1901.
8°   BPL

Rodwell (T.) *Publisher*—
See Sh— Hamlet, 1818
  „   Sh— King Richard III., 1818
  „   Sh— Taming . . . 1821
  „   Sh— Twelfth night, 1822
  „   Sh— Works, 1821-29, 1823

Rodwell & Martin *Publishers. See* Sh— The
tempest, 1821

Roe (J.) *Artist. See* Warwick Castle

Roe (J. E.) 'Mortal moon,' or Bacon and his
masks : The Defoe period unmasked.
New York : Frankfort & Jacob, 1891.
8°   BPL | SML
Illustrates Sonnet 107.

Roffe *Engraver. See* Sh— Works, 1845

Roffe (Alfred T.) Essay on the ghost-belief of
Sh—. Ln : Privately printed by Hope &
Co., 1851. 8°, pp. 32   BM | BPL | BUS

Handbook of Sh— music, being an account
of three hundred and fifty pieces of
music set to words taken from the plays
and poems of Sh— ; the compositions
ranging from the Elizabethan age to the
present time. [Ed. by A. J. Waterlow].
Ln : Chatto, 1878. 4°, pp. vi.-122-vi.
        BM | BPL | BUS |MPL

Musical triad from Sh— : Clown in 'Twelfth
night,' Autolycus, Lord of Amiens ; also
Sh— upon art and nature. Somerstown,
Ln : 1872. Fcp. 4°   BM | BPL | BUS
Illustrates 'As you like it' and the 'Winter's tale.'

Real religion of Sh—, together with an
essay on 'Prospero' and his philosophy.
Somerstown, Ln : 1872. Fcp. 4°
        BM | BPL | BUS

Roffe (E. & A.) *Editors. See* Sh— Venus . . .
1876

Rogers (John). *See* Glasse of Godly love

Rogers (Mary Eliza)] Sh— memorial. *See*
Sh—] Gibbs

Rogers (Samuel) Dedication. *See* Sh— Works,
1838

Rohrbach (C.) Sh—'s 'Hamlet.' Berlin :
Schneider, 1859. 8°   SML

Rojas y Zorrilla (F. de) Los Bandos de
Verona : Montescos y Capeletas. Eng-
lished by F. W. Cosens. Ln : For private
distribution, 1874. 4°, pp. viii.-44 and
frontispiece   BPL | SML
Limited issue.
Illustrative of 'Romeo and Juliet.'

Rolfe (Richard W.) *Editor. See* Sh— Julius
Cæsar, 1907

Rolfe (William James) A witness for Wm.
Sh— [In 'North American Review'].
1891. 8°   BPL
[Articles in the 'Literary World,' Jan. 4,
Dec. 3, 1881, Feb. 5, 1882, answering
Holmes and Morgan.] Ln : 1881-82. 4°
        BM | BUS

Introduction. *See* Fleming
Life of Sh—. *See* Sh—] Rolfe
Sh— the boy. *See* Sh—] Rolfe
Rolfe (W. J.) *Editor*—
See Craik
  „   Sh— All's well, 1881
  „   Sh— Antony . . . 1881, 1891
  „   Sh— As you like it, 1878, 1883
  „   Sh— Comedy of errors, 1881
  „   Sh— Coriolanus, 1882
  „   Sh— Cymbeline, 1881
  „   Sh— Hamlet, 1878, 1879, 1883, 1902
  „   Sh— Julius Cæsar, 1867, 1868, 1872,
        1876, 1883, 1900, 1906
  „   Sh— King Henry IV., i., 1880, 1883

Rolfe (W. J.) *Editor—*
  See Sh— King Henry IV., ii., 1880
  „ Sh— King Henry V., 1878, 1883, 1902
  „ Sh— King Henry VI., i., 1882
  „ Sh— King Henry VI., ii., 1882, 1895
  „ Sh— King Henry VI., iii., 1882
  „ Sh— King Henry VIII., 1872, 1883
  „ Sh— King John, 1880, 1882, 1895, 1897, 1902
  „ Sh— King Lear, 1880, 1883, 1902
  „ Sh— King Richard II., 1876, 1882, 1895
  „ Sh— King Richard III., 1880, 1883, 1891, 1902
  „ Sh— Love's labours lost, 1882
  „ Sh— Macbeth, 1877, 1883, 1902
  „ Sh— Measure . . . 1882
  „ Sh— Merchant . . . 1871, 1883, 1902, 1903
  „ Sh— Merry wives, 1882
  „ Sh— Midsummer . . . 1877, 1883, 1902
  „ Sh— Much ado, 1878, 1879, 1883
  „ Sh— Othello, 1879, 1883, 1902
  „ Sh— Pericles, 1883
  „ Sh— Poems, 1883, 1890, 1893
  „ Sh— Romeo . . . 1879, 1883, 1899, 1902
  „ Sh— Sonnets, 1883, 1899
  „ Sh— Taming . . . 1881, 1883, 1902
  „ Sh— The tempest, 1871, 1883
  „ Sh— Timon . . . 1882
  „ Sh— Titus . . . 1884, 1892
  „ Sh— Troilus . . . 1882
  „ Sh— Twelfth night, 1879, 1881, 1883, 1895, 1902
  „ Sh— Two gentlemen, 1882
  „ Sh— Two noble kinsmen, 1883
  „ Sh— Venus . . . 1883
  „ Sh— Winter's tale, 1880, 1883, 1896
  „ Sh— Works, 1871-96, 1879-82, 1881, 1884, 1896
  See also Clarke & Rolfe
Rolls (C.) *Engraver—*
  See Sh— Works, 1829, 1836
  „ Sh— Works : Ext. 1841
Rolt (Richard) Poetical epistle from Sh— in elysium to Mr. Garrick at Drury Lane theatre. To which is added a view from Heymon Hill, near Shrewsbury . . . Ln : J. Newbery, 1752. 4°, pp. 30   BUS
Roman (E.) *Editor. See* Sh— King Henry V., 1908
Romani (F.) *Editor. See* Sh— Romeo . . . 1850, 1860
Romdahl (A.) Obsolete words in Sh—'s 'Hamlet.' 1869. 8°   BM
Romeo and Juliet. *See* Sh— Romeo and Juliet
Romeo and Juliet travesty. *See* Sh— Romeo . . . 1837, 1841, 1855, 1859, 1868, 1877
Romney (George) *Artist—*
  See Hayley
  „ Sh— Works, 1802

Romney *or* Ryley (Samuel William)] The itinerant, or memoirs of an actor. 1808-27. 9 vols. 8°. With portrait of the author in Vol. 4
Ronalds (J. & T.) *New York Publishers. See* Sh— Works, 1805-09
Rooney (Michael) *Dublin Bookseller. See* Sh— Hamlet, 1603, 1856
Roorbach *jun.* (O. A.) *New York Publisher. See* Sh— Midsummer . . . 1859
Roosevelt (Blanche) Verdi : Milan and 'Othello.' 1887. 12°   BPL
Root (Robert Kilburn) Classical mythology in Sh. New York, 1903. 8° BPL | BUS
Roper (A.) *Publisher. See* Mountford
Rosalynde. *See* Lodge
Rosbourg (C. de) Memories of Sh—. *See* Sh—] Rosbourg
'Roscio' [*pseud. for* R. Burbage]. *See* Marston
Roscius Anglicanus. *See* Downes
Roscius. *See* Kenrick
' Roscius (Young).' *See* Betty
Roscoe (Edward) Hamlet : His character and critics [In 'Victoria Mag.,' April]. Ln : 1873. 8°   BPL | BUS
  Ophelia [In 'Victoria Magazine']. 1871. 8°   BPL
Rose (Edward) A northern 'Hamlet' [In 'Fraser's Mag.,' May]. Ln : 1877. 8°   BUS
  Division into acts of 'Hamlet.' Ln : New Sh— Soc., 1877. 8°   BM | BPL | BUS
  Inconsistency of time in Sh—'s plays. Ln : New Sh— Soc., 1880-86. 8°
  Sh— and history [In 'Fraser's Magazine,' May]. Ln : 1876. 8°   BUS
  Sh— as an adapter [In 'Macmillan's Magazine']. 1878. 8°   BPL | BUS
  Sudden emotion. Ln : New Sh— Soc., 1880-86. 8°
Rose (Mary) Women of Sh—'s family. Ln : Lane, 1905. 16°, pp. 64   BPL | BUS
  Sh— in fact and tradition : A paper delivered before the Incorporated Phonographic Society, at Stratford [In 'Stratford Herald,' 11th Sept.] 1908   BPL
Rose (The), Shamrock, and Thistle, Nos. 1-10 [Containing in Feb. number a series of 'Roundabout letters from Stratford-on-Avon,' by J. O. Halliwell]. Feb.-Nov., 1863   BUS
Rose theatre—
  See Norden
  „ Sh— King Lear, 1605
Rosencrantz and Guildenstein [In 'The Library,' Vol. 2, pp. 464-465]. Ln : 1890
  See also Sh— Hamlet, 1895
Roses (The), or King Henry VI. *See* Sh— King Henry VI., iii., 1795
Roses and holly. *See* Sh— Works : Ext. 1885

Rosetti (*Signor*) *Editor*. *See* Sh— Othello, 1830

Rosicrucianism. *See* Wigston

Rosier (Joseph Bernard) *Editor*. *See* Sh— Midsummer . . . 1866

'Roslyn (Guy)' *pseud*. *See* Hatton (Joshua)

Ross (Charles H.)] Ye comic Sh—. With 12 designs by Wm. Gray. Part I. Ln : W. Oliver [1864]. 8°   BPL | BUS
No second part ever appeared apparently.

Sh— ; Mad characters in his works ; The sonnets ; His character [In 'Studies,' pp. 7-62]. Ln : [1867]. 8° BPL | BUS | CPL

Absurdity of the theory that Lord Bacon wrote the plays of Sh— [In 'Modern Thought']. 1882. 4°   BPL

Deterioration of the stage [In 'Poet-Lore']. Philadelphia, 1891. 8°   BPL

Rossetti (Wm. Michael) Lives of famous poets. *See* Sh—] Rossetti

Rossetti (W. M.) *Editor*. *See* Sh— Works, 1880, 1881, 1882

Rossi (E.) *Actor & Editor*—
See Sh— Macbeth, 1876
  „ Sh— Romeo . . . 1876, 1883

Rossi (L.) *Artist*. *See* Sh— Romeo . . . 1891

Rossi (L.) & Corbould (E. M.) Side-lights on Sh—. *See* Sh—] Rossi

Rossini *Composer*—
See Sh— Othello, 1828, 1830, 1836, 1838, 1839, 1844, 1850, 1855, 1864, 1867, 1870
  „ Sh— Poems, 1862
  „ Sh— Taming . . . 1828

Rothschild (J. A. de) Sh— and his day : Study of the topical element in Sh— and in the Elizabethan drama. 'Harness prize essay.' Ln : Arnold, 1906. Cr. 8°, pp. 264   BPL

Rothwell (J.) *Publisher*. *See* Hall

Round (J. H.) & Yeatman (J. Pym) Belvoir household accounts [In 'Athenæum,' No. 4115, p. 274 ; No. 4117, p. 325 ; No. 4118, p. 369, Sept.] 1906
Concerns the Sh— impresa. See Stopes (Mrs.) for full detail.

Round (P. Z.) *Editor*. *See* Sh— Pericles, 1886

Roundelays. *See* Music

Rous (Francis) Archæologia Atticæ . . . Oxford, 1637. Fcp. 4°
The first book to give the origin of the poet's name. 'The custom [of the Greeks] to vibrate the speare before they used it, to try the strength, was so constantly kept that enchespalos, a shake-speare, came at length to be an ordinary word in Homer and other poets to signifie a soldier.'

Archæologia Atticæ. Seventh edition. Oxford, 1670. Fcp. 4°   BPL

Rousseau.] Craddock (Thomas) Rousseau, as described by himself and others. Liverpool : James Woolard, 1877. 8°, pp. viii.-252
Sh—, p. 157.

Rousseau.] Texte (J.) Jean-Jacques Rousseau, etc. 1899. 8°   BPL
Contains Shakespeareana.

Rout (The). *See* Sh— King Richard III., 1770, 1780

Routledge (E.) Questions from Sh—. *See* Sh— Works : Ext. 1867, 1873, 1892

Readings from Sh—. *See* Sh— Works : Ext. 1876

Routledge (W.)] What's it on ? or Sh— lence teaches [a burlesque]. [c. 1870.] 12° BPL

Rowden (F. A.) Sh—. *See* Sh—] Rowden

Rowe (Hy.) *Nominal Editor*. *See* Sh— Macbeth, 1797

Rowe (John) Tragi-comoedia, being a brief relation of the strange and wonderful hand of God discovered at Witney [Oxfordshire] in the comedy acted there February the third [1652] where there were some slaine, many hurt, etc. Oxford, 1653. Fcp. 4°   BPL | W
The accident described occurred during the performance of 'Mucedorus.'
The volume affords some information upon the habits of strolling companies of the period.

Rowe (Nicholas) Ambitious step-mother : A tragedy. Ln : Peter Buck at the sign of The Temple near Inner Temple Gate in Fleet St., 1701. Fcp. 4°
Several references to Sh—.
The prologue says :—
  'Sh— whose genius to itself a law
  Could men in every height of nature draw
  And copy'd all but women that he saw.'

Ambitious stepmother . . . Second ed. With a new scene. Ln : Printed for R. Wellington at the Dolphin and Crown, west end of St. Paul's Churchyard, and Thomas Osborne, near Gray's Inn Walk, 1702. Fcp. 4°, pp. viii.-70

Extracts. *See* Sh— Works : Ext. 1822

Life of Jane Shore. *See* Shore

Life of Sh—. *See* Eighteenth . . .

Life of Sh—. *See* Sh— Works : Ext. 1792

Some account of the life of Mr. Wm. Sh—. *See* Sh—] Rowe
'The delicacy of his taste and the natural bent of his own genius, equal if not superior to some of the best of theirs [the ancients], would certainly have led him to read and study them with so much pleasure that some of their fine images would naturally have insinuated themselves into and been mixed with his own writings ; so that his not copying at least something from them may be an argument of his never having read them. Whether his ignorance of the ancients were a disadvantage to him or no may admit of a dispute, for though the knowledge of them might have made him more correct, yet it is not improbable but that the regularity and deference for them . . . might have restrained some of that fire, impetuosity, and even beautiful extravagance which we admire in Sh—, and I believe we were better pleased with those thoughts altogether new and uncommon which his own imagination supplied him so abundantly with than if he had given us the most

beautiful passages out of the Greek and Latin poets,
and that in the most agreeable manner that it was
possible for a master of the English language to
deliver them.'

Rowe (Nicholas) Tragedy of Jane Shore.
Written in imitation of Sh—'s style.
Ln: Bernard Lintott at the Cross Keys
between the two Temple Gates in Fleet
St. [c. 1710]. Fcp. 4°   w
'In such an age immortal Sh— wrote,
By no quaint rules nor hampering criticks taught,
With rough majestick force he moved the heart,
And strength and nature made amends for art.'
                                —*Prologue.*
Large paper copy at Warwick.
Tragedy of Jane Shore . . . Ln: Printed
for the company [1714]. 8°   BPL | w
Tragedy of Jane Shore . . . Third edition.
Ln: 1723. 12°. With frontispiece   w
Tragedy of Jane Shore . . . Ln: 1728. 12°
                                          w
Tragedy of Jane Shore . . . Fifth edition.
Ln: 1733. 12°. Frontispiece   w
Tragedy of Jane Shore . . . Ln: Bernard
Lintot, 1735. 12°. With frontispiece w
Tragedy of Jane Shore . . . Ln: Bernard
Lintot, 1736. 12°. Frontispiece   w
Tragedy of Jane Shore . . . Taken from the
manager's book at the Theatre Royal,
Covent Garden. Ln: 1736. 8°   w
Tragedy of Jane Shore. Ln: [c. 1750].
8°   w
Tragedy of Jane Shore . . . Ln: 1751. 12°
                                          w
Tragedy of Jane Shore. Tenth edition.
Ln: 1768. 12°   BPL
Tragedy of Jane Shore. Ln: 1774. 12°.
With frontispiece   w
Tragedy of Jane Shore. Ln: 1787. 8°
Tragedy of Jane Shore [In 'Works . . .,'
Vol. 2, pp. 131-186]. Ln: 1792. 12° BPL
Tragedy of Jane Shore [In 'Modern British
drama,' Vol. 1, pp. 583-602]. Ln: 1811.
Roy. 8°   BPL
Tragedy of . . . Jane Shore [In 'Works,'
Vol. 2, pp. 93-177]. Ln: 1811. 8° BPL
Rowe (N.) *Editor*—
See Sh— The puritan widow, 1709
 ,, Sh— The tempest, 1709
 ,, Sh— Works, 1709, 1714, 1723-25, 1771,
    1822, 1823, 1825, 1826, 1827, 1830,
    1831, 1832, 1833, 1845, 1848, 1849,
    1851, 1852, 1856, 1859
Rowlands (John) Sh— still enthroned. Ln:
A. H. Stockwell, 1903. Cr. 8°, pp. 94
On the Bacon-Sh— controversy.   BPL | SML
Rowlands (Samuel)] Meeting of gallants at an
ordinarie, or the walkes in Powles. Ln:
Printed by T. C—— [Thomas Chard] and
are to be solde by Mathew Lawe dwelling
in Paules Church-yard, 1604. Fcp. 4°,
fifteen unpaged leaves. Black letter BLO

Five copies of the original are known to survive. Reed's
copy in 1807 sold for £6/2/6 ; Chalmers' copy in 1842
sold for £15/15/-. A third occurred in the Daniel
sale. The fourth is at Oxford. The fifth, bought
for 2/6 in Jan., 1910, was privately resold for one
hundred guineas.
In it a character named *Ginglespur* says :—' This was a
prettie " Comedy of errors " my round host.'

Rowlands (Samuel)] Meeting of gallants . . .
Ed. by J. O. Halliwell. [Ln: Privately
printed for the Percy Society, c. 1842].
Cr. 8°   BM
See also R—— (S.)
Rowlandson (Thomas) Twelfth night charac-
ters. Ln: [c. 1820]. 8°. Twenty-four
illustrations
Rowlandson (Thomas) *Artist. See* Wigstead
Rowington, Warwickshire. *See* Ryland
Rowley (Charles) Workshop paradise, and
other papers. Illustrated. Manchester:
Sherratt . . . 1905. Cr. 8°, pp. viii.-280
Contains 'Portraits of Sh—,' pp. 146-148. With repro-
duction of the Madox-Brown composite portrait at
the Manchester Art Gallery.
Rowley (Samuel)] Noble souldier, or a con-
tract broken justly revenged. A tragedy.
By S. R——. Ln: Nicholas Vavasour,
at his shop in the Temple neere the
Church, 1634. Fcp. 4°
Allusions to ' Hamlet,' ' Julius Cæsar,' etc.
Originally written in Jan., 1602. It establishes the
fact that ' All's well ' was then in existence.
King: 'What think'st thou of this great day, Baltazar?'
Bal.: 'Of this day? Why—as of a new play—
        If it ends well, all's well.'
Rowley (Wm.) Birth of Merlin. *See* Sh—
Birth . . .
See also Heywood & Rowley
 ,, ,, Webster & Rowley
Roxburghe (John *Duke of*) Library. *See*
Catalogue, 1812
Royal courtly garland, in six parts. [c. 1750.]
12°   w
A chap-book in verse, containing the story of the
' Winter's tale.'
Roycroft (Thomas) *Printer. See* Whitlock
Royston (R.) *Printer. See* Donne
Ruddiman (T. & W.) *Edinburgh Printers. See*
Sh— Macbeth, 1731
Ruddiman (Wal.) *Edinburgh Publisher. See*
Sh— Works, 1769
Rudloff (F. W.) Sh—, Schiller, and Goethe
relatively considered. Brighton: H. S.
King, 1848. 12°, pp. 30
                         BM | BPL | BUS | SML
Rudolphi *Zurich Publisher. See* Sh— Son-
nets, 1881
Rugby. *See* Rimmer
Ruggles (H. J.) Method of Sh— as an artist,
deduced from an analysis of his leading
tragedies and comedies. New York:
Hurd & Houghton, 1871. 16°, pp. xx.-
298   BM | BPL | BUS | CPL

Edward Russell

William Lowes Rushton

See p. 271

Ruggles (H. J.) Plays of Sh— founded on literary forms. Boston & New York, 1895. 8° BPL

Ruggles (Julia) Metaphysical Sh—: The 'Merchant of Venice.' Pasadena [U.S.] 1908. Cr. 8° BPL

Ruhl (Ludwig S.) Gallery of Sh—. Ln: Ackermann, 1828-32. 8° SML

Ruhl (L. S.) *Artist*—
See Sh— Midsummer . . . 1829
,, Sh— Othello, 1832
,, Sh— Works, 1827-40

Rumbold (E.) *Publisher*—
See Feigned friendship
,, Lee (N.)
,, Sh— King Lear, 1690

Rumbull (E.) *Publisher.* See Sh— Hamlet, 1703

Rummio and Judy. *See* Sh— Romeo . . . 1841

Rumsey (Mary C.) *Editor. See* Tieck

Rumsey (M. E.) *Editor. See* Sh— Midsummer . . . 1854

Rupert (*Prince*). *See* Dugdale

Rusconi (Carlo) *Editor*—
See Sh— Hamlet, 1867
,, Sh— Julius Cæsar, 1868
,, Sh— King Henry VIII., 1880
,, Sh— King Lear, 1868, 1876
,, Sh— King Richard III., 1878
,, Sh— Othello, 1867
,, Sh— Romeo . . . 1868
,, Sh— The tempest, 1878

Rusden (G. W.) Lecture on the character of Falstaff . . . Melbourne, 1870. 8° BM | MPL
Wm. Sh—. *See Sh*—] Rusden

Rush (James) *Editor. See* Sh— Hamlet, 1834

Rushen (P. C.) History of Chipping Campden. Woodbridge: Booth, 1899. 8° SML

Rushfield (B.) Medical thoughts of Sh—. 2nd ed. Easton, Pa. [U.S.], 1885. 8° MPL

Rushton *Barrister* (William Lowes) Sh— a lawyer. Liverpool: Webb & Hunt, 1858. 8°, pp. 50, issued in pink printed wrappers BM | BPL | BUS | CPL | MPL | SML
W. L. Rushton showed exceptional knowledge of early English law, and Lord Campbell coolly plundered and plagiarised it a year later, in his imitation work, entitled 'Sh—'s legal acquirements,' without the least acknowledgment.

Sh— an archer. Liverpool: Lee & Nightingale, 1897. 8°, pp. 118 BPL | BUS | SML

Sh— and the 'Arte of English poesie' [by Puttenham]. Liverpool: Young, 1909. Cr. 8°, pp. 168 BPL

Sh— hymn tune book. Liverpool, 1891. 12° BPL

Sh— illustrated by old authors. Ln: Longmans, 1867-68. 2 parts. 8°, pp. iv.-84 and vi.-56 BM | BPL | BUS | CPL | SML

Rushton *Barrister* (William Lowes) Sh— illustrated by the Lex Scripta. First part. Ln: Longmans, 1870. 8°, pp. iv.-104 BM | BPL | BUS | SML

Sh—'s euphuism. Liverpool: Adam Holden, 1871. Cr. 8°, pp. viii.-108 BM | BPL | BUS | SML

Sh—'s legal maxims. Ln: Longmans, 1859 8°, pp. 34 BM | BPL | BUS | CPL | MPL | SML

Sh—'s legal maxims. Liverpool, 1907. Cr. 8°, pp. 62 BPL

Sh—'s testamentary language. Ln: Longmans, 1869. Cr. 8°, pp. viii.-56 BM | BPL | BUS | CPL | SML

Ruskin (John) Arrows of the chace. Orpington: Allen, 1880. 2 vols. 8° BPL
Contains Shakespeareana.

Fors clavigera. Orpington: Allen, 1871-87. 9 vols. 8° BPL
Contains Shakespeareana.

On 'Yon grey lines that fret the clouds,' in 'Julius Cæsar.' Ln: New Sh— Soc., 1877-79. 8°

Russell (*Sir* Edward R.) Irving as Hamlet . . . 'Now I am alone . . .' Ln: H. S. King & Co., 1875. 8°, pp. iv.-60, incl. printed wrappers BM | BPL | SML

Irving as Hamlet . . . Second edition. Ln: H. S. King & Co., 1875. 8°, pp. iv.-54 BUS | SML

Irving's King Lear [In 'Nineteenth Century']. Ln: 1893. Roy. 8° BPL

'Merchant of Venice': Minor characters [In 'Liverpool Lit. and Phil. Soc. Proc.,' Vol. 42, pp. 129-160]. 1887-88. 8°

'Merchant of Venice': Shylock [In 'Liverpool Lit. and Phil. Soc. Proc.,' Vol. 42, pp. 109-128]. 1887-88. 8°

Religion of Sh— [In 'Theological Review,' Oct.] Ln: 1876. 8° BUS

That reminds me—. Ln: Unwin, 1899. 8°, pp. xii.-334 and portrait
A curious anecdote of Lord Randolph Churchill and 'Hamlet' at p. 234; another at p. 292 on a passage in the 'Winter's tale' about nature, art, or evolution, etc.

The true Macbeth: A paper read before the Lit. and Phil. Soc., 29th Nov., 1875. Liverpool: D. Marples, 1875. 8°, pp. ii.-52 BM | BPL | BUS

William Jaggard and his 'Sh— bibliography.' *See* Jaggard

Russell (Thomas) *Overseer. See* Sh— Will . . . 1616

Russell (W. Clark) Extraordinary men. *See* Sh—] Russell

Representative actors. Ln: Warne [c. 1875]. 8°, pp. xvi.-496
Reprinted in 1888.

Rutherford (R.) Helps to the study of . . .
'Julius Cæsar' . . . Ln: Ralph, 1900.
Cr. 8°, pp. 120   BPL
Rutherford (R.) *Editor.* See Sh— Julius
Cæsar, 1899
Rutland (*Duke of*) Manuscripts [In 'Historical
MSS. Commn. Reports, Vol. 4]. 1905.
Roy. 8°   BPL
Contains Shakespearean references.
Ryall (J.) *Publisher.* See Howard (H.)
Ryan (Richard)] Dramatic table talk, or
scenes, situations and adventures . . . in
theatrical history and biography. Ln:
J. Knight & H. Lacey, 1825-30. 3 vols.
8°. With autographs of famous actors
                                          BUS
Contains matter on Sh— and (in vol. 3) a 'Pedigree of
the family of the Shakespeares by John Jordan.'
Ryder (Corbet) *Theatre Manager.* See Siddons
Ryder (Maxwell) Elocution and stage training.
Ln: 1900. 8°
Rye (Wm. B.) England as seen by foreigners
in the days of Elizabeth . . . Journals of
the two Dukes of Wirtemberg, 1592 and
1610, both illustrative of Sh— . . . Ln:
J. R. Smith, 1865. Fcp. 4°, pp. 132-300
and portraits   BPL | BUS | CPL | MPL | SML
Twenty-five copies also printed on large paper.
Ryland (John William) Records of Rowington
[Warwickshire], being extracts from the
deeds in the possession of the feoffees of
the Rowington charities, with notes from
the parish chest, churchwardens' accounts,
church registers, monuments, etc., and
appendix of manuscripts from the British
Museum, Public Record Office, Bodleian
Library, etc. Birmingham: Cooper &
Co., 1896. Roy. 8°, pp. xxviii.-240.
With map and plates, some in colours SML
Impression restricted to 100 copies, fifty only of which
were sold.
Interesting as containing the following entry:—'John,
son of Thomas Sh—, of Warwick, apprenticed to
William Jaggard the stationer of Ln., 1609.'
Many early records herein of the Sh— family, all
probably related to the bard.
Records of Wroxall Abbey and Manor
[Warwickshire]. Ln: Spottiswoode, 1903.
F°   SML
Ryland (W.) Life of Wm. Sh—. *See Sh—*]
Ryland
Rylands Library.] Duff (E. Gordon) Catalogue
of the printed books and manuscripts in
the John Rylands Library. Manchester:
J. E. Cornish, 1899. 3 vols. 4°
Sh— occupies pp. 1658-1662.   BM | BPL | SML

Rylands Library, Manchester: Catalogue of
an exhibition of original editions of the
principal English classics shown in the
main library from March to October,
1910. Manchester: Univ. Press, 1910.
8°, pp. xvi.-92, including printed wrap-
pers   BM | MRL
Gives details of the Rylands Library copies of the first
four folio editions of Sh—; of his Sonnets, 1609; of
his Poems, 1640; and of the Ireland forged autograph, 1613.
Ryley *Artist.* See Sh— Works, 1787-91
'Ryley (S. W.)' *pseud.* See Romney (S. W.)
Rymer (Thomas)] Defence of dramatick
poetry: being a review of [Jeremy]
Collier's 'View of the immorality and
profaneness of the stage.' Ln: 1698.
8°   MPL | W
Cites Sh—'s plays.
] Farther defence of dramatick poetry.
Done by the same hand. Ln: 1698. 8°
                                          W
Short view of tragedy; its original, ex-
cellency, and corruption. With some
reflections on Sh— and other practitioners
for the stage . . . Ln: Richard Baldwin,
at the Black Lyon in Fleet St. between
the two Temple Gates, 1693. 8°, pp.
xiv.-182   BPL | CPL | MPL | W
The earliest work of express Sh— criticism, 'by the
"Don Quixote" of literature.'
'As one invested with authority, to sit in judgment, he
criticizes Sh— and passes on him as decisive a sentence of condemnation as ever was awarded against a
friendless poet by a reviewer. We look now on his
work amazedly, and were it put forth by a writer of
our times should regard it as "the very ecstasy of
madness."'—*Retrospective review.*
Short view, 1693. *See Sh—*] Shakespeareana
Short view of tragedy . . . Ln: Baldwin,
1698. 8°   SML | W
Tragedies of the last age consider'd and
examined by the practice of the ancients
and by the common sense of all ages . . .
Ln: Richard Tonson under Gray's Inn
Gate, 1678. 8°   MPL | SML | W
Refers to the character of 'Cassio' in 'Othello.'
Tragedies of the last age considered [with
some reflections on Sh—] . . . Second
edition. Ln: R. Baldwin . . . 1692. 8°
                                     BM | W
Tragedies of the last age . . . Ln: 1693. 8°
                                         BM
Rymer (Thomas)—
See Dennis
,, Gildon

—— (A.) *Editor. See* Sh— Works, 1851

S—— (C.) *See* Short (C.)

S—— (E. W.) Sh—- Bacon: An essay. Ln: 1899   BM | BUS

S—— (G.) *See* Sandys (George)

S—— (G.) *Printer. See* Barnefield

S—— (I. M.) On worthy master Sh—. *See* Sh— Works, 1632, 1663, 1664, 1685
The initials are believed to represent John Milton, student (*q.v.*)

S—— (J.) On the portrait of Sh— [In 'Gentleman's Magazine,' vol. 29, p., 380]. Ln: 1759. 8°
A vigorous reply to Joseph Greene (*q.v.*)
The author, writing from Crane Court, says 'there is no genuine picture of Sh— existing, nor ever was; that called his having been taken long after his death from a person supposed extremely like him, at the direction of Sir Thomas Clarges, and this I take upon me to affirm as an absolute fact.'

S—— (J.) The 'Merchant of Venice' at the Prince of Wales Theatre [In 'Fraser's Magazine']. 1875. 8°   BPL

S—— (J. R.) A stage *Iago* [In 'Cornhill Magazine']. Ln: 1876. 8°   BPL

S—— (L.) Notes on old plays by Bale, Marston, and Sh—. *See* Sh—] Sh— Soc.

S—— (L. H.) True cryptogram of Francis Bacon. Philadelphia [c. 1887]. 12°   BPL

S—— (P.) *Printer. See* Short (Peter)

S—— (S.) Fortune's tennis ball. *See* Greene

S—— (S.) *Printer—*
See Decker
  ,, Sh— Pericles, 1611
  ,, Stafford (Simon)

S—— (S. W.) *See* Singer

S—— (T.) Fragmenta aulica, or court and state jests in noble drollery ... Ln: 1662. 8°. With frontispiece   W
Contains an amusing anecdote on p. 1 of Sh—'s 'King Henry VIII.'

S—— (T.) *Printer. See* Sh— Rape, 1616

S—— (T.) *Publisher. See* England's selected characters

S—— (V.) *Printer—*
See Sh— Sir John Oldcastle, 1600
  ,, Simmes (Valentine)
  ,, Wright

S—— (W.)—
See Johnson *jun.* (Ben.)
  ,, Smith (Wentworth)

S—— (W.) *Printer—*
See Sh— Love's labours, 1631
  ,, Sh— Taming ... 1631
  ,, Stansby (William)

Sabatini (F. L.) Pictures in colour of Warwickshire. Norwich: Jarrold, 1905. 4°   BPL

Sabie (Francis) The fisherman's tale ... 1595, founded on the story used by Sh— in the 'Winter's tale.' Printed from an early MS. in the Bodleian ... Edited by J. O. Halliwell. Ln: 1867. Fcp. 4°
Issue limited to ten copies.   BPL | HCL

Sabin (J. F.) Letter from Stratford. *See* Irving & Fairholt

Sabin (J. F. & W. W.) Artists. *See* Irving & Fairholt

Sabine (*Capt.*) Library. *See* Catalogue, 1820

Sabine *jun.* (T.) *Publisher. See* Sh— King Richard III., 1770

Sabine & Son *Publishers. See* Sh— Othello, 1780

Sachs (C.) *Editor. See* Sh— Works, 1884-87

Sack full of newes: An old jest book, 1673. Edited by J. O. Halliwell. 1861. 8°   BPL
See Old English jest book
  ,, Sh—] Sh—'s jest books

Sackville *first Earl of Dorset* (Thomas) Induction. *See* Capell
See Mirrour ...
  ,, Norton & Sackville

Sadler (Hamnet) *Witness. See* Sh— Will ... 1616

Sadler's Wells Theatre, Ln.—
See Account ...
  ,, Sh— Works, 1850

Sael (G.) *Publisher—*
See Sh— Antony, 1799
  ,, Wyatt

Sage (A.) *See* Macfarland & Sage

Saint Aubyn. *See* Mathews (C.)

Saint Clair (G.) *Editor. See* Dawson

Saint Clements Danes, Ln. *See* Stopes

Saint-Evremond (*Le Sieur de*) Mixt essays upon tragedies, comedies, Italian comedies, English comedies and operas. Ln: Timothy Goodwin, 1687. Fcp. 4°

Saint George's Athenæum Club, Ln: Dinner and entertainment programme [Sh— tercentenary]. Ln: 1864. 8°   BPL

Saint-John (James Augustus) Character of Lady Macbeth [In 'Eclectic,' Feb.] New York, 1849. 8°   BUS

Saint-John *Editor* (*Sir* Spenser) Essays on Sh— and his works. From the manuscripts and notes of a deceased relative. Ln: Smith, 1908. 8°, pp. 320   BPL

Saint Margaret's, Westminster. *See* Stopes

Saints of the stage [In 'Cornhill Magazine']. Ln: Smith, 1867. 8°   BPL

Saintsbury (George) History of English prosody. Ln: 1908. 2 vols. 8°   BPL
Vol. 2 contains 'Sh— to Crabbe.'

Short history of English literature. Ln: Macmillan, 1898. Cr. 8°, pp. xx.-818
Sh— fills pp. 313-350.

18

Saker (Edward) *Actor-Editor*—
  See Sh— Comedy of errors, 1881
  ,, Sh— Midsummer ... 1880
  ,, Sh— Much ado, 1878
  ,, Sh— Winter's tale, 1876
Saker (Horatio) Memoirs of Munden. *See*
  Munden
Sala (G. A.) On stage costume [In 'Belgravia'].
  Ln : 1869. 8°   BPL
Salaman (C. K.) Shylock from a Jewish point
  of view [In 'Jews as they are,' pp. 211-
  255]. 1882. 12°   BPL
Salisbury *Bookseller* (Jesse) Glossary of words
  and phrases used in S.E. Worcestershire.
  Ln : J. Salisbury, 1893. 8°, pp. xii.-92
  Contains 'Sh— and our dialect,' pp. 83-86. BPL | SML
Salisbury Court theatre. *See* Cunningham
'Salmacis and Hermaphroditus' not by
  Francis Beaumont. The edition of 1602.
  Ed. by 'Dramaticus.' *See Sh*—] Sh—
  Soc.
Salmasius (Claudius) Dessection and confuta-
  tion of the diabolical rebel Milton in his
  impious doctrines of falsehood against
  King Charles I. . . . Ln : 1660. Fcp. 4°
  At pp. 81-82 are mentions of Sh—'s ' King Richard III.'
  The work was suppressed.
Salter (T.) Mirror of modestie. *See* Reprints
Salusbury (John) *Publisher*. *See* Stage con-
  demned
Salvation of Sh—. *See* Jaggard
Salvianus (Massiliensis) Second and third
  blast of retrait from plaies and theaters :
  The one whereof was sounded by a
  reuerend byshop dead long since ; the
  other by a worshipful and zealous gentleman now aliue : one showing the filthi-
  nes of plaies in times past ; the other the
  abhomination of theaters in the time
  present, both expresly prouing that that
  common-weale is nigh vnto the curse of
  God, wherein either plaiers be made or
  or theaters maintained. Set forth by
  Anglo-phile Eutheo . . . Imprinted at Ln.
  by Henrie Denham dwelling in Paternoster Row at the signe of the starre
  being the assigne of William Seres . . .
  1580. 8°, sig. A-I⁸ paged   BM | CTC
  The 'Second blast' is translated from the sixth book of
  the ' De gubernatione Dei' of Salvianus, written in
  the fifth century.
  This attack was intended as a continuation of Gosson's
  'School of abuse' (*q.v.*)
Salvini (T.) On Sh—. *See* Sh—] Salvini
Salvini (T.) *Actor*—
  See Sh— Hamlet, 1873, 1875, 1876
  ,, Sh— King Lear, 1881, 1884
  ,, Sh— Othello, 1873, 1875, 1876, 1880
Salvini.] Signor Salvini's 'Hamlet,' by a
  Parisian critic [In 'Gentleman's Maga-
  zine']. Ln : 1875. 8°   BPL

Salvini.] Tommaso Salvini [In 'The Century'].
  1881. 8°   BPL
Sambucus (John). *See* Green (H.)
Sampson *Boston U.S. Publisher*. *See* Sh—
  Works, 1848, 1849-51, 1850, 1850-51,
  1854
Sams (W. R.) *Publisher*. *See* Sh— Othello,
  1861
Samuel (Edward L.) *Editor*. *See* Hugo
'Sand (George)' *pseud*. *See* Dudevant
Sande (D.) *See* Edwards (R.)
Sanders (G. A.) Sh— or Bacon ? Springfield,
  Ill., U.S. [c. 1877]. 8°   BUS
Sandford (James) Garden of pleasure, con-
  tayninge most pleasaunt tales, worthy
  deedes, and witty sayings of noble princes
  and learned philosophers, moralized. No
  lesse delectable than profitable. Done out
  of Italian . . . Imprinted at Ln. by Henry
  Bynneman . . . dwelling in Knight Riders
  Streate at the signe of the mermayde and
  are to be sold at the Northwest dore of
  Poules Church, 1573. 8°, black letter,
  sig. A⁴, B—P⁸ on numbered folios   CTC
  Probably one of Sh—'s sources.
Sands (W.) *Edin. Pub.* *See* Sh— Works, 1753
Sandys (George)] Anglorum speculum, or the
  worthies of England [Abridged from
  Fuller] alphabetically digested into shires
  . . . Ln : John Wright at the Crown on
  Ludgate Hill ; Thomas Passenger at the
  Three Bibles on London Bridge ; and
  William Thackary at the Angel in Duck
  Lane, 1684. 8°, pp. vi.-974-20
  At p. 831 under Warwickshire is a description of Sh—:
  ' His learning being very little, nature seems to have
  practised her best rules in his production . . .' The
  passage refers also to his 'many witty combats with
  Ben Jonson,' comparing them as ' an English man-of-
  war and a Spanish galleon.'
  See Henderson
Sandys (Wm.) Sh— illustrated by the dialect
  of Cornwall. *See Sh*—] Sh— Soc.
Sandys (Wm.) *Editor*. *See* Percy Society
Sandfelice (G. Pace) *Editor*. *See* Sh— Romeo
  ... 1868
Sandford (E.) *Editor*. *See* Sh— Poems, 1819
Sandford, Harroun & Co. *New York Pub-
  lishers*. *See* Sh— Macbeth, 1866
Sanger (E.) *Publisher*—
  See Sh— Poems, 1710
  ,, Sh— Venus ... 1710
  ,, Sh— Works, 1710
Sanger (K.) *Publisher*. *See* Sh— Works, 1714
Sannazaro (Jacomo) Arcadia. Vinegia : Aldus
  Manutius. 1514. 8°
  In this volume Sh— found the name ' Hamlet.' *See*
  ' Hamlet' in Furness's ' Variorum edition.'
Sansovino (F.) *See* Mexia & Sansovino
Santayana *Editor*. *See* Sh— Hamlet, 1908
Sappho Duke of Mantona. *See* Rich

Saravi (Giovanni) I quattro libri della filosofia, 1565. *See* Sh— Autograph

Sare (R.) *Publisher. See* Collier (Jeremy)

Sargent (Epes) *Editor. See* Sh— King John, 1846

Sargent (G. F.) Book of Sh— gems. *See* Sh— Works : Ext. 1846, 1854, 1869, 1871, 1872, 1880

Sh— illustrated. *See* Sh— Works : Ext. 1842

Satires of Lerna, No. ii. : 'Comedy of King John.' 1891. Cr. 8°   BPL

Sauerlænder (J. D.) *Frankfort Publisher. See* Sh— Works, 1830-40

Saunders (Francis) *Publisher—*
See Sh— Antony, 1692
  ,, Sh— Julius Cæsar, 1680, 1695
  ,, Sh— Timon, 1696
  ,, Sh— Works, 1685

Saunders (H.) *Dublin Printer & Publisher—*
See Montagu
  ,, Sh— Works, 1766
  ,, *Sh*—] Dennis

Saunders (Robert) *Publisher. See* Sh— Works, 1833

Saunders & Otley *Publishers. See* Sh— Works, 1825

Sauny the Scot. *See* Sh— Taming . . . 1698, 1708, 1714, 1731

Savage (R.) Prologue spoken at revival of 'King Henry VI.' at Drury Lane [In Works, vol. 2, p. 151]. 1777. Cr. 8° BPL

Savage *Librarian* (Richard)] Catalogue of the books, manuscripts, works of art, antiquities, and relics at present exhibited in Sh—'s birthplace. With 61 illustrations. Stratford-upon-Avon : Printed for the Trustees and Guardians . . . 1910. Cr. 8°, pp. 134
    BM | BPL | BUS | CTC | SBL | SML
It may be pointed out that this is not a complete catalogue of the birthplace collection, but merely a list of the contents of the glass cases, etc.

Stratford to London and back on horseback in Sh—'s time [In 'Athenæum,' No. 4219, p. 270]. Ln : 1908   BM | BPL

Savage *Librarian* (R.) *Editor—*
See Aston Cantlow
  ,, Irving (W.)
  ,, Pudsey
  ,, Sh— Works : Ext. 1888
  ,, *Stratford*] Registers

Savage & Easingwood *Printers—*
See Sh— Merry wives, 1806
  ,, Sh— Works, 1806

Savell (J.) *Publisher. See* Sh— Works, 1798

Savile (Jeremiah *or* Jeremy) *Composer. See* Sh— Works : Ext. 1653

Saviolo (Vincentio) His practise . . . of the rapier and dagger . . . of honor and honorable quarrels. Ln : John Wolfe, 1594-95. Fcp. 4°, sig. A—2 M4. With woodcuts   BLO | BUS | CTC
Perhaps referred to by Touchstone in 'As you like it,' act v., scene 4.
Throws light on the manners of Elizabethan gallants, and elucidates many passages of Sh—.
'Ah, the immortal passado, the punto riverso, the hay !'
  —*Romeo*, act ii , scene 4.
'Fencing by the book of arithmetic.'—*Romeo*, act iii., scene 1.

Saward (William T.) Wm. Sh— ; a play in four acts. Ln : Mathews, 1907. 12°, pp. 120   BM | BLO | BPL | CTC

Sawyer (*Sir* J.) Arms granted to John Sh—, 1596. Emblazoned. 1899. 8°   BPL

Sawyer (R.) *Engraver. See* Sh— Works, 1816

Saxelby (F.) Sh—'s sonnets [In the 'Institute Magazine']. Birmingham, 1890. 8°   BPL

Saxo Grammaticus. Danish history. Translated by Oliver Elton. Ln : Folk Lore Soc., 1894. 8°   BPL
'Amleth or Hamlet,' pp. xlvii., xcv., 106-120, 398-413.

Historiæ Danicæ. 1644-45. 2 vols. F° BPL
One of the sources of Sh—'s 'Hamlet.'
See also Hansen (G. P.)

Saxo-Grammaticus—
See Falbe
  ,, Latham

Sayer (R.) Dramatic characters, or different portraits of the English stage in the days of Garrick. Ln : [Und.] 4°

Scadding *Dr.* (Hy.) Sh— the seer, the interpreter : An address before St. George's Soc. of Toronto in the Cathedral Church of St. James, 23 April, 1864. Toronto : Rolls & Adam, 1864. 16°, pp. iv.-88
        BPL | BUS

Scarron (Paul) Comical romance, or facetious history of a company of strolling stage players. Turn'd into English [by John Phillips]. Ln : J. C—— for Wm. Crooke at the Grene Dragon, without Temple Bar, 1676. F°. With engraved frontispiece by W. Faithorne
The plate is said to represent the strolling players performing at Old Smithfield.
At p. 17 is a Shakespearean reference not found in Scarron's original and not repeated in Tom Brown's or Goldsmith's translations.

Scatcherd (J.) *Publisher—*
See Sh— Works, 1798
  ,, Sh— Works : Ext. 1798

Scatcherd & Whitaker *Publishers. See* Sh— Works, 1790

Scenes from Sh—. *See* Sh— Works : Ext. 1898

Schaeffer (Charles C.) Hamlet, Prince of Denmark : An essay (with a diagram). An earthquake of critical criticisms. Philadelphia, 1884. F°   BPL | BUS

              18—2

Scharf *the elder* (George) *Artist—*
　See Sh— As you like it, 1825
　　,, Sh— Hamlet, 1825
　　,, Sh— King Henry IV., i.-ii., 1824
　　,, Sh— Merchant of Venice, 1825
　　,, Sh— Othello, 1825
Scharf (*Sir* George) National portrait gallery
　. . . A few observations connected with
　the Chandos portrait of Sh—. [1864.]
　12°, single sheet　　　　　　　　　BM
　On the principal portraits of Sh—. Ln:
　1864. 12°　　　　　　　　BM | BPL | W
　See also Planché & Scharf
Scheemachers (Peter) *Sculptor. See* Graves
Scheinert (A.) *Dantzig Publisher. See* Sh—
　Works, 1874-81
Schelling (*Prof.* Felix Emanuel) Elizabethan
　drama, 1558-1642 [with bibliography,
　commentary, list of plays and index].
　Ln: Constable, 1908. 2 vols. 8°　BPL
　English chronicle play : A study in the
　popular historical literture environing
　Sh—. New York : Macmillan, 1902. 8°,
　pp. xii.-310　　　　　　　BPL | BUS
Schenck *Edinburgh Publisher. See* Sh—
　Antony, 1867
Scherer (E.) Essays on English literature.
　1891. 12°　　　　　　　　　　　BPL
　Sh— fills pp. 32-97.
Schilders (R.) *Middelburg Printer. See* Rain-
　oldes
Schiller (F.) 'Macbeth' [In 'Dublin Univ.
　Magazine,' Oct.] 1874. 8°　BPL | BUS
Schiller (Friedrich von) *See* Rudloff
Schlegel (August. Wilhelm von) Lectures on
　dramatic art and literature. Trans. by
　John Black. Ln: 1815. 2 vols. 8°
　　　　　　　　　　BPL | BUS | MPL
　'In this work Sh— has found one of his ablest com-
　mentators.'—*Lowndes.*
　Lectures . . . Trans. by J. Black. 2nd ed.
　Ln : J. Templeman, 1840. 2 vols. 12°
　　　　　　　　　　　　　　　　SML
　Lectures . . . Trans. by J. Black. Revised
　by A. J. W. Morrison. [3rd ed.] Ln :
　Bohn, 1846. 8°, pp. viii.-536
　　Reprinted in 1861.　　　BPL | CPL | MPL
　Lectures . . . Ln : 1879. 12°　　　BPL
Schlegel (A. W. von) *Editor—*
　See Sh— Hamlet, 1880
　　,, Sh— Works, 1881, 1884-87
Schlegel (Frederick von) Æsthetic and miscel-
　laneous works . . . Remarks on romance,
　poetry, and on Sh— . . . Trans. by E. J.
　Millington. Ln : H. G. Bohn, 1849. 8°,
　pp. xxiv.-534
Schloss (A.) *Publisher. See* Sh— The tem-
　pest, 1836
Schmeding (G. A.) Essay on Sh—'s 'King
　Henry V.' 1784. 8°　　　　　　　BM

Schmerber (S.) *Frankfort Publisher. See* Sh—
　Works, 1828-34, 1829-43
Schmid (E.) *Editor. See* Sh— Works, 1874-
　81, 1891
Schmidt (Alexander) Sh— Lexicon. *See* Sh—
　Works : Ext. 1874-75, 1886, 1902
Schmidt (I.) *Editor. See* Sh— Macbeth, 1893
Schmitz (L. Dora) *Editor—*
　See Elze　　　　　　　*See* Ulrici
　,, *Sh—*] Elze
Schmucker (S. M.)] Historic doubt respecting
　Sh— ; illustrating infidel objections
　against the Bible. Philadelphia, 1853.
　12°, pp. 480
　First published in 1848 under the title of ' Errors of
　modern infidelity.'
Scholey (Robert) *Publisher. See* Sh— Works,
　1803-05, 1807, 1811
Schonpflug (O.) *Goslar Publisher. See* Sh—
　Merchant . . . 1868
School for satire [with Capell's ghost to
　Edmond Malone, editor of Sh— : A
　parody]. Ln : 1802. 8°
School of slovenrie. *See* Dedekind
Schubert *Composer. See* Sh— Poems, 1850,
　1862
Schuler (M.) Sh—'s confession. Berlin, 1900.
　8°, pp. 42　　　　　　　　　　　BUS
　An anxious attempt to prove Sh— a Roman Catholic.
Schultz (W.) *Upsala Publisher. See* Sh—
　Macbeth, 1867
Schümann (*Brothers*) *Leipsic Publishers. See*
　Sh— Works, 1820, 1843-44
Schünemann (C.) *Bremen Publisher. See* Sh—
　Macbeth, 1841
Schwoerer *Artist. See* Sh— Works : Ext. 1876
Scogin. Jests, 1626—
　See Old English jest books
　,, *Sh—*] Sh—'s Jest books
Scoloker (Anthony) Daiphantus, or the pas-
　sions of love. Ln : 1604
　Says :—' Friendly Sh—'s tragedies . . .'
　　　　' Faith, it should please all, like Prince Hamlet.'
Scoloker (Anthony) *Printer. See* Bale
Scot *or* Scott (Reginald *or* Reynold) Discouerie
　of witchcraft, wherein the lewd dealing of
　witches and witchmongers is notably
　detected . . . and all the conueiances of
　legierdemaine and juggling are deciphered.
　Ln : Wm. Brome, 1584. Fcp. 4°, black
　letter, sig. A8—2 S8, paged　BM | CTC
　Refers to Puck (Robin Goodfellow).
　Sh— used this work in ' Macbeth' and elsewhere.
　Many copies were burnt by order of King James I.,
　who, in the preface to his ' Dæmonologie,' speaks of
　' one called Scot, an Englishman, who is not ashamed
　in publike print to denie that there can be such a
　thing as witchcraft.'
　A large paper copy was in Lord Ashburnham's library
　measuring 8⅜ by 6in.
　Probably printed by Henry Denham.

　Discouerie of witchcraft, 1584. Reprinted
　and edited by B. Nicholson, 1886. 8° BPL

Scotland—
: See Buchanan
: „ Dibdin (J. C.)
: „ Fragmenta
: „ Jackson
: „ Jaggard
: „ Logan
: „ Sh—] Sh— Society
Scott (Clement Wm.) Drama of yesterday and to-day. Ln: Macmillan, 1899. 2 vols. 8°. With numerous portraits BPL
: From 'The bells' to 'King Arthur': A critical record of first night productions at the Lyceum from 1871 to 1895. Ln: 1896. 8°. Illust.
: Introduction. *See* Leslie
: Life of E. L. Blanchard. *See* Blanchard
: Some notable Hamlets [Bernhardt, Irving, Barrett, Tree, and Forbes-Robertson]. Ed. by L. Arthur Greening. Ln: 1900. 8°. With portraits BPL | BUS | MPL
Scott (Clement Wm.) *Editor. See* Theatre
Scott (Edward). Dancing in all ages. Ln: Sonnenschein, 1899. 8°, pp. 216. With coloured plates
Scott (Edward J. L.) Elizabethan players [at Westminster School]. In 'Athenæum,' No. 3560, p. 95, and No. 3562, p. 158. 1896. 4° BM
: Original records of expenses of apparel borrowed through Henry Condell or Kendall from Sh—'s Company at Southwark.
: Elizabethan stage: Whereabouts of Sh—, 1587-91 [In 'Athenæum,' No. 2830, p. 103]. 1882 BM
: Family of Sh— in London [In 'Athenæum,' No. 3773, p. 219, Feb.] 1900 BM
: Private diary of Sh—'s cousin, Thomas Greene, town clerk of Stratford-upon-Avon. 1885
: Sh—: A seventeenth century allusion [In 'Athenæum,' No. 3902, p. 191, Aug.] 1902 BM
: Shakspeareana [In 'Athenæum,' No. 3580, p. 756, June]. 1896 BM
: Refers to Sir John Barnard and to Sh—'s deer hunting.
: Shakspeareana [In 'Athenæum,' No. 3671, p. 320, Mar.] 1898. 4° BM
: Seventeenth century allusions to Sh— in the Sloane MS. collection at the B.M.
: Shakspeareana [In 'Athenæum,' No. 3675, p. 447, Ap.] 1898. 4° BM
: Concerns Sir Thomas Lucy of Chorelcote.
: Two passing notices of Sh— and Milton in the seventeenth century [In 'Athenæum,' No. 3884, p. 434, Ap.] 1902 BM
: Westminster School and Sh—'s family [In 'Athenæum,' 3994, p. 636, May.] 1904 BM
: Alludes to Thomas Nash, who married Elizabeth Hall, the poet's grand-daughter.

Scott (G.) *Printer. See* Woty
Scott (J. W.) Sh— tercentenary draught board. 1864. 8° BPL
Scott *Ph.D.* (*Prof.* Mary Augusta) 'Book of the courtyer': A possible source of Benedick and Beatrice. Baltimore: Modern Language Association, 1901. Roy. 8°, pp. 30
: Illustrates 'Much ado . . .'
: Elizabethan translations from the Italian . . . Baltimore: Modern Language Association, 1896-99. 4 vols. Roy. 8°
Scott (T. J.) Early rarity of the works of Robert Greene. Ln: Sh— Soc., 1844. 8° BPL
Scott (T. J.) *Editor. See* Nash (T.)
Scott (*Sir* Walter) Essay on the drama [Article in 'Ency. Brit.']. 1814. 4°
: 'The English stage might be considered as equally without rule and without model when Sh— arose. The effect of the genius of an individual upon the taste of a nation is mighty; but that genius in its turn is formed according to the opinions prevalent at the period when it comes into existence. Such was the case with Sh—. With an education more extensive and a taste refined by the classical models it is probable that he also, in admiration of the ancient drama, might have mistaken the form for the essence, and subscribed to those rules which had produced such masterpieces of art. Fortunately for the full exertion of a genius as comprehensive and versatile as intense and powerful, Sh— had no access to any models of which the commanding merit might have controlled and limited his own exertions. He followed the path which a nameless crowd of obscure writers had trodden before him, but he moved in it with the grace and majestic step of a being of a superior order, and vindicated for ever the British theatre from a pedantic restriction to classical rule. Nothing went before Sh— which in any respect was fit to fix and stamp the character of a national drama, and certainly no one will succeed him capable of establishing by mere authority a form more restricted than that which Sh— used.'
: Essay on the drama [In 'Miscellaneous works,' vol. 6, pp. 217-395]. Edinburgh, 1870. 12° BPL
: Letters on demonology and witchcraft. Ln: 1830. Cr. 8°. With plates by G. Cruikshank
: Letters on demonology . . . With introduction by Hy. Morley. 2nd ed. Ln: 1885. 8°
: Refers to 'Macbeth,' p. 232.
Scott (*Sir* W.) *Editor—*
: *See* Sh— Antony, 1811
: „ Sh— Arden, 1811
: „ Sh— London prodigal, 1810
: „ Sh— Merry devil . . . 1810
: „ Sh— Sir John Oldcastle, 1810
: „ Sh— The puritan widow, 1810
: „ Sh— Thomas . . . 1810
: „ Sh— Two noble kinsmen, 1811
: „ Sh— Yorkshire tragedy, 1810
: „ Sh— Works, 1825

Scott (*Sir* Walter)—
  See Graves
    ,, Laneham
    ,, Martin
    ,, *Sh*—] Sh— and Scott
    ,, *Stratford*] Sh—'s birthplace

Scott (William Bell) *Editor. See* Sh— Works, 1875

Scott & Webster *Publishers. See* Sh— Works, 1833

Scott, Webster & Geary *Publishers. See* Sh— Works, 1836, 1838, 1839, 1840, 1842, 1849

Scourge for paper-persecutors. *See* Davies

Scribbleomania. *See* Ireland (S. W. H.)

Scribe (E.) *Editor. See* Sh— The tempest, 1850

'Scriblerus (Martinus)' *pseud. See* Morehead

'Scrutator' *pseud. See* Rivington

Scrymgeour (Daniel) Class book of English poetry. *See* Sh— Works : Ext. 1865

Scudder (Horace E.) Childhood in English literature [In 'Atlantic Monthly']. 1885. 8°   BPL
  Future of Sh— [In 'Men and letters,' pp. 215-226]. Boston, 1887. 12°
          BPL | BUS

Scvdery (G. de) Amaryllis to Tityrus. 1681. 12°   BPL
Sh— referred to upon pp. 66-67.

Sea voyage. *See* Fletcher

Seager (H. W.) Natural history in Sh—'s time : Extracts illustrative of the subjects as he knew it. Ln : Stock, 1896. 8°, pp. 366. With quaint woodcuts BM | BPL | SML

Seale (H.) *Publisher. See* Essex

Seamer (Mary). *See* Seymour (Mary)

Seccombe *Major* (Thomas S.) Military mis-readings of Sh—. *See* Sh— Works : Ext. 1880

Seccombe (Thomas S.) & Allen (John W.) Age of Sh—, 1579-1631. Ln : Bell, 1903. 2 vols. Cr. 8°, pp. 568   BPL | BUS

Second appendix to Malone's supplement. *See* Malone

Second Maiden's tragedy. *See* Sh— Second ...

Secret history of Mack-beth, King of Scotland. Taken from a very ancient original manuscript. Ln : 1708. 8°   BUS | W
Identical with 'Key to the drama' and 'Life of Macbeth.'
A romance adapted from the French.
The Shakespearean connection begins and ends with the title.

Secret history of the green room. *See* Haslewood

Secret passion. *See* Williams

Sedley (Charles) *Editor. See* Sh— King Richard III., 1844, 1854, 1858

Sedley (*Sir* Charles) Prologue [In Higden's 'The wary widdow ...']. Ln : 1693
'But against old as well as new to rage
Is the peculiar frenzy of this age,
Sh— must down and you must praise no more
Soft Desdemona, nor the jealous Moor,
Sh— whose fruitful genius, happy wit
Was framed and finished at a lucky hit,
The pride of nature and the shame of schools,
Born to create and not to learn from rules.'

Sedley (*Sir* C.) *Editor. See* Sh— Antony, 1677

Sedley (E.) *Editor. See* Sh— Macbeth, 1875

Seel (T. S.) *Engraver. See* Sh— Poems, 1795

Seeley (*Sir* John Robert) Sh—'s 'Macbeth' and another [In 'Cornhill Mag.,' Nov.] Ln : 1875. 8°   BUS
  Which are Hamlet's 'dozen or sixteen lines' ? Ln : New Sh— Soc., 1874. 8°
     BM | BPL | BUS | MPL | SML

Seeley (*Sir* J. R.) Young (Wm.) & Hart (Ernest Abraham)] Three essays on Sh—'s tragedy of 'King Lear.' By pupils of the City of London School. Ln : Bruce & Ford, 1851. 8°, pp. viii.-150
      BM | BPL | BUS | CPL

Segar (Francis). *See* Mirrour ...

Segar (*Sir* Wm.) Booke of honor and armes, wherein is discoursed the causes of quarrell and the nature of injuries, with their repulses. Also the meanes of satisfaction and pacification. At Ln : Printed by Richard Ihones, dwelling at the signe of the Rose and Crowne neere Holbourne Conduit, 1590. Fcp. 4°. With woodcuts   BM | W
Touchstone in 'As you like it' may have referred to this book when he said :—
  'O, sir, we quarrel in print by the book.'

Seguin *freres*, Avignon *Publishers. See* Sh— Works, 1809

Seile (Henry) *Publisher. See* Jonson

Selby (M. H.) Sh— classical dictionary. *See* Sh— Works : Ext. 1888, 1889

Select beauties of ancient English poetry. With remarks by Henry Headley, and a biographical sketch by Henry Kett. Ln : John Sharpe ... 1810. 2 vols. 8°. With engraved titles
With lives of many of Sh—'s contemporaries and followers. At p. xliii. occurs an account (probably the true version) of the legend connecting Sh— with the beautiful Mrs. John Davenant. At pp. xliv.-xlv. other references to Sh— include a note of the fact that in the poet's time a blanket supplied the place of a stage curtain, suggesting the line in 'Macbeth'—
'Nor heaven peep through the blanket of the dark.'

Select biography. Ln : 1821. 12° BM | BPL
Vol. x. includes a life of Sh—.

Select British theatre. *See* Sh— Works, 1815

Select collection of the beauties of Sh—. *See* Croft

Select scenes from Sh—. *See* Sh— Works : Ext. 1853

Select specimens of English poetry. With introd. by George Walker. *See* Sh— Works : Ext. 1827

Selections from Sh—. *See* Sh— Works : Ext. 1872, 1876-84

Selections from the comedies of Sh—. *See* Sh— Works : Ext. 1880

Selections from the English poets. *See* Sh— Works : Ext. 1848

Selection of plays from the old English dramatists. Ln : 1825. 2 vols. 8°. With frontispieces
A few sets were done on large and stout paper in roy. 8°.

Selimus *See* Greene (Robert)

Sellick *Bristol Publisher. See* Sh— Works, 1768

Selous (Hy. Courtney) *Artist*—
See Sh— The tempest, 1825, 1836
,, Sh— Works, 1864-68, 1874-78, 1880

Seneca. *See* Meres

Sentimental spouter, or young actor's companion. *See* Sh— Works : Ext. 1774

Seres (Wm.) *Printer. See* Bale

Serger (Richard) *Publisher. See* Shirley

Serious remonstrance on behalf of the Christian religion against the horrid blasphemies and impieties still used in the English playhouses. Ln : 1719. 8°

Serres (Oliver de) & Geffe (Nicholas) Perfect use of silk-worms and their benefit, with the exact planting and artificiall handling of mulberrie trees . . . done out of the French originall. Ln : 1607. 8°
A work which probably led to the planting by Sh—, in or about 1609, of the famous mulberry tree at New Place, Stratford, cut down by Gastrell. The site is now occupied by a similar tree, said to be a scion of the original.

Sertum Shakesperianum. *See* Latham

Seton (Matthew) Recent Shakesperian revivals : 'Hamlet' and 'Macbeth' at the Lyceum ; 'Richard III.' and 'Macbeth' at Drury Lane ; 'Henry V.' at the Queen's [In 'New Monthly Mag.'] Ln : 1877. 8°   BUS

Settle (Elkanah) Cambyses King of Persia : A tragedy. Ln : Wm. Cademan at the Pope's head in the lower walk of the new Exchange, 1672. Fcp. 4°
Says the prologue :—
  'Indifferent writers are contemned, for now
  There grow no lawrels for a common brow,
  None but great Ben, Sh—, or whom this age
  Has made their heirs, succeed now on the stage.'

Empress of Morocco : A tragedy, with sculptures. As it is acted at the Duke's theatre. Ln : W. Cademan, 1673. Fcp. 4°. With six plates by Dolle
Valuable as being the earliest book to depict an English theatre, together with play-scenes and scenery, scarcely altered since Sh—'s time.

See also Duffet

Settle (Elkanah) *Editor. See* Sh— Troilus . . . 1707, 1708, 1715, 1718

Seven ages of man. *See* Sh— As you like it

Seven champions of christendom. *See* Johnson

Severn (Charles) *Editor. See* Ward (John)

Severn (Emma) Anne Hathaway, or Sh— in love. Ln : R. Bentley, 1845. 3 vols. 12°   BUS
A novel.

Sévrette (J.) *Editor. See* Sh— Coriolanus, 1895

Seward (Anne) On Sh—'s monument at Stratford-upon-Avon [In Dodsley's 'Collection of poems by several hands,' vol. 2, p. 315]. 1782. 6 vols. Cr. 8°   BM
  'Great Homer's birth seven rival cities claim,
  Too mighty such monopoly of fame,
  Yet not to birth alone did Homer owe
  His wondrous worth ; what Egypt could bestow
  With all the schools of Greece and Asia joined,
  Enlarged the immense expansion of his mind,
  Nor yet unrivalled the Mæonian strain,
  The British eagle [*Milton*] and the Mantuan swan
  Tower equal heights ; but, happier Stratford, thou
  With uncontested laurels deck thy brow,
  Thy bard was thine unschooled, and from thee brought
  More than all Egypt, Greece, or Asia taught ;
  Not Homer's self such matchless honours won—
  The Greek has rivals, but thy Sh— none.'

Sewell (*Dr.* George) *Editor*—
See Sh— Poems, 1709, 1725, 1728
,, Sh— Venus . . . 1725
,, Sh— Works, 1725, 1725-26

Sewell (George)] Tragedy of Sir Walter Raleigh as it is acted at the theatre in Lincoln's-Inn-Fields . . . Third edition, corrected. Ln : John Pemberton at the Buck, Fleet St., 1719. 8°, pp. xvi.-64
The epilogue gives imaginary objections of Sh— to the mutilation of his plays :
  'Scenes cut and alter'd and miscall'd—his play,
  How would the reverend bard regret the shame,
  Why thus—To rob my urn, then stab my fame
  Should be a sin this learned generous age
  Ought to revenge upon the guilty stage.
  But if in vain an honest cause I plead
  Thus shall my wish and punishment succeed ;
  Fleckno, the sire of dullness, shall inspire
  His sons to scribble, without sense or fire ;
  Players turn wits, by nonsense rise or fall,
  Yet cry out boldly, " —'s blood." We'll stand 'em all.
  Thus far for Sh— and our common right,
  Now for the author's part, and then—good night !
  For I have a request before I go.
  Speak plainly :—Is our poet damn'd, or no ?
  If he is dull, the play perhaps may live,
  For wit's a crime we know you can't forgive.'

Sewell (J.) *Publisher. See* Sh— Works, 1790

Sewell (J. W.) *Cincinnati Publisher. See* Sh— Works, 1857

Sex of Ariel *The tempest* [In 'Athenæum,' No. 4014, p. 456, Oct.] 1904   BM

Sexton (G.) Psychology of 'Macbeth.' Glasgow, 1869. 12°   BM | BPL | CPL

Seymour (E. H.) Remarks, critical, conjectural, and explanatory upon the plays of Sh— resulting from a collection of the

early copies . . . with valuable extracts from the manuscripts of John Lord Chedworth. Ln: Lackington, 1805. 2 vols. 8°   BM | BPL | BUS | CPL | MPL | SML
Large paper, roy. 8°, at Warwick.

Seymour (Mary) Sh—'s stories simply told. *See* Sh— Works: Ext. 1880, 1883, 1890, 1899

Seymour (Robert) New readings of old authors. *See* Sh— Works: Ext. 1841

Seymour (Robert) *Artist. See* Moncrieff

Sh—. *See* Shakespeare (William)

Shackford (Charles Chauncey) Sh— in modern thought [In 'North American Review,' Oct.] Boston, 1857. 8°   BUS
Reviews Delia Bacon's work (*q.v.*)

Shackford (C. C.) *Editor. See* Konewka

Shadwell (Thomas) A true widow: A comedy. Ln: Benjamin Tooke at the Ship in St. Paul's Churchyard, 1679. Fcp. 4°
The dedication embodies references to Sh—.

Bury fair: A comedy. As it is acted by His Majesty's servants. Ln: James Knapton at the Crown in St. Paul's Churchyard, 1689. Fcp. 4°
On p. 26 says the character *Oldwit*, 'Come my Lord Count' . . . 'may good digestion wait on appetite and health on both.' As Macbeth says, 'Ah, I love those old wits.'

Lancashire witches and Tegue O'Divelly the Irish priest . . . The amorous bigot . . . Ln: 1691. Fcp. 4°   W
Says:—'For the magical part I had no hopes of equalling Sh— in fancy, who created his witchcraft for the most part out of his imagination, in which faculty no man ever excelled him, and therefore I resolved to take mine from authority.'

Sullen lovers, or the impertinents: A comedy. Ln: 1770. Fcp. 4°
Has a curious allusion to 'Falstaff.'

See also Sh—] Manuscript

The tempest: an opera. *See* Lawrence

Woman captain: A comedy. Ln: Samuel Carr, at the King's Head in St. Paul's Churchyard, 1680. Fcp. 4°
On p. 2 says the character:—
Fool.—' But for all that Sh—'s fools had more wit than any of the wits and criticks now-a-days.'

See also Love-a-la-mode

Shadwell (T.) *Editor*—

See Sh— The tempest, 1673
  ,, Sh— Timon . . . 1678, 1680, 1688, 1696, 1700, 1703, 1712, 1720, 1732, 1768, 1780, 1786
  ,, Sh— Works, 1908

Shaftesbury (*Countess of*). *See* Cooke

Shakespeare *née* Hathaway (Anne)] Epitaph on Sh—'s wife, inscribed on her mural bronze tablet in the chancel of Holy Trinity Church, Stratford-on-Avon, 1623 [c. 1895]. Broadside rubbing. Oblong f°   BPL

' Heere lyeth the body of Anne, wife of William Sh—, who departed this life the 6th day of August, 1623, being of the age of 67 yeares.
Vbera, tu, mater, tu lac vitamq. dedisti,
Væ mihi ; pro tanto munere saxa dabo !
Quam mallem amoueat lapidem bonus ang[e]l[us] orê
Exeat ut Christi corpus, imago tua
Sed nil vota valent ; venias cito, Christe ; resurget
Clausa licet tumulo, mater, et astra petet.'
These elegiacs were probably written by John Hall her son-in-law.

Shakespeare *née* Hathaway (Anne) Harness (W.) Widow of Sh—. Ln: Sh— Soc., 1845. 8°   BPL

] True story of Mrs. Sh—'s life [In 'Gentleman's Mag.'] 1869. 8°   BUS
A squib caricaturing Mrs. Stowe's newly published ' True story of Lady Byron's life.'

] True story . . . Boston U.S.: Loring [1869]. 12°, pp. 24   BUS

Sh— *Poet's brother* (Edmond). *See* Thompson

Sh— *of Surrey* (Geoffrey). *See* Stopes

Sh— *Poet's brother, of Saint Bride's* (Gilbert). *See* Stopes

Sh— *of Snitterfield* (Henry) *Poet's uncle. See* Stopes

Sh— *Poet's father* (John) Signature. *See* Bigsby

See also Bullen (M. W.)
  ,, Dramaticus
  ,, Halliwell
  ,, Sawyer
  ,, Stopes

Sh— *of Ingon* (John). *See* Stopes

Sh— *of Warwick* (John) *Apprentice. See* Ryland

Sh— (John) *Alderman* of Aldgate Ward, Ln., d. 1775
Mentioned in the obituary of the 'Gentleman's Magazine,' 1775, vol. 45, p. 255.

Sh— (John) *Bitmaker?* of the Strand, Ln: 1618. *See* Snell

Sh— (John) *Royal bitmaker. See* Stopes

Sh— (Jonathan) *Coal merchant*, Ln: d. 1768
Mentioned in the obituary of the 'Gentleman's Magazine,' 1768, vol. 38, p. 94.

Sh— *Poet's daughter, aft. Quiney* (Judith)— *See* Black
  ,, Quiney family

Sh— (Roger) *Yeoman of the chamber. See* Stopes

Sh— (Susanna). *See* Hall (Susanna)

Sh— (Thomas) *Royal messenger* 1572-77. *See* Stopes

Sh— *of Coventry* (Thomas). *See* Stopes

Sh— *of Warwick* (Thomas). *See* Ryland

NOTE.—Shakespeare's separate pieces now follow, arranged in alphabet, and each piece in chronological order. The pieces include adaptations, alterations, burlesques, continuations, extracts, foundations, illustrations, imitations, music, parodies, references, travesties, and variations. Many additional references to each play will be found by turning to Sh— Works: Comment and criticism.—W. J.

Shakespeare (William) A midsummer night's dream. *See* Sh— Midsummer . . .

All's one . . . *See* Sh— Yorkshire tragedy, 1608

ALL'S WELL THAT ENDS WELL.

The honour as editio princeps of this comedy belongs to the version in the Jaggard folio of 1623. It forms one of twenty dramas, more than half of Sh—'s entire work, occurring in that volume, of which no previous printing is known.

[All's well . . .] Love betray'd, or the agreable disapointment: A comedy. By Charles Burnaby. Ln: Printed for D. Brown at the Black Swan without Temple Bar . . . 1703. Fcp. 4°
First separate edition. Partly founded on 'All's well . . .' and partly on 'Twelfth night.'
'Part of the tale of this play I took from Sh—, and about fifty of the lines . . . A military critic did me the honour to say I had plundered all from Sh—.' —*Preface.*

All's well . . . Ln: 1714. 12°

All's well . . . Ln: J. Tonson, 1734. Cr. 8°
Jacob Tonson and R. Walker at this period (1734-35) were rival publishers, each claiming the sole privilege of issuing Sh—'s plays and command of the trade-sign 'Sh—'s head.' The serial issues of the competitors' respective editions contained printed notices warning the buying public against the rival's wares. These spirited and defamatory advertisements must have furnished some diversion for onlookers at the time. For instance, an extract from Walker's edition of 'Two gentlemen . . .' runs : 'Concerning J. Tonson and his accomplices . . . each volume of Tonson's may be called a gallimaufrey of scraps and nonsense.'
Some account of this copyright conflict will be found on p. 109 of Halliwell's Hand-list . . . of Shakespeareana, 1862.'

All's well . . . Ln: R. Walker, 1735. Cr. 8°
BPL

All's well . . . A comedy. Ln: Printed for C. Hitch, L. Hawes . . . 1756. 8°, pp. 84, includ. engraved frontispiece by G. Van der Gucht, after Gravelot

All's well . . . A comedy, by Sh—, as performed at the Theatre Royal, Drury Lane. Regulated from the prompt book, with permission of the Managers, by Mr. Hopkins, Manager. An introduction and notes, critical and illustrative, are added by the authors of the 'Dramatic censor' [F. Gentleman]. Ln: Printed for John Bell; York: C. Etherington, 1773. 8° [Excerpt, pp. 233-300]
Off printed from Bell's edition of Sh—'s Works for the use of playgoers.
With a list (pp. 4) of Bell's publications at end.

All's well . . . A comedy. As it is acted at the Theatres Royal in Drury Lane and Covent Garden . . . Ln: Printed for J. Harrison, 18 Paternoster Row, and sold

Sh— All's well . . .
likewise by J. Wenman, 144 Fleet St., and all other booksellers, 1778. 8°, pp. 18, and copperplate portrait of Thomas King as 'Parolles' BM | BPL

All's well . . . A comedy. Altered by Mr. [F.] Pilon and reduced to three acts. 1785. Manuscript
See Lowndes' Manual, p. 2274.

All's well . . . printed complete from the text of Sam Johnson and Geo. Steevens, and revised from the last editions . . . Ln: Printed for . . . John Bell . . . 1786. 12°, pp. 118, with engraved title and frontispiece of Mrs. Warren as 'Helena'

All's well . . . with alterations by J. P. Kemble. As it is performed by His Majesty's servants of the Theatre Royal, Drury Lane. Ln: J. Debrett, 1793. 8°, pp. 62 BM | BPL | BUS

All's well . . . [In 'Collection of much-esteemed dramatic pieces.' Ed. by J. P. Kemble]. Ln: J. Debrett, 1795. 2 vols. 8°

All's well . . . Ln: E. Harding, 1799. Cr. 8° BPL

All's well . . . Ln: J. Cumberland, 1811. 8°

All's well . . . A comedy. Adapted to the stage by J. P. Kemble, and now first published as it is acted at the Theatre Royal in Covent Garden. Ln: Printed for the theatre, 1811. 8°, pp. 74
BPL | BUS | W

All's well . . . by Will. Sh—. Printed complete from the text of Sam. Johnson and Geo. Steevens. Ln: 1812. 18° W

All's well . . . Adapted to the stage by J. P. Kemble and now published as it is performed at the Theatre Royal. Ln: J. Miller, 1815. 8°, pp. 75 BM | BPL | W

All's well . . . Correctly given, from the text of Johnson and Steevens. With remarks. Ln: Printed for the proprietors by D. S. Maurice [c. 1820]. 16°, pp. 94 BM

All's well . . . Printed from the acting copy, with remarks, biographical and critical, by D. G—— [Geo Daniel]. To which are added a . . . cast of the characters . . . and the whole of the stage business, as now performed at the Theatres Royal, etc. Ln: J. Cumberland [1828]. 12°, pp. 62 BM | BPL | BUS

All's well . . . Ln: J. Cumberland, 1831. 8° BPL

All's well . . . Lacy's acting edition. Ln: Lacy [1850]. 12° BM | BPL

All's well . . . With notes by John Hunter. Ln: Longman, 1873. Cr. 8° BPL

Sh— All's well . . .

All's well . . . Edited with notes by W. J. Rolfe. New York : Harper, 1881
BPL | BUS

All's well . . . Dicks' standard plays. Ln : John Dicks [1883]. Cr. 8°
BM

All's well . . . With the Story of Giletta [from W. Painter's ' Palace of pleasure' and an introduction by H. Morley]. ' National Library.' Ln : Cassell & Co., 1889. 16°, pp. xxxii.-160
BM

All's well . . . Edited by C. E. Flower. ' Memorial Theatre edition.' Stratford-on-Avon : Printed by G. Boyden [1889 ?]. Cr. 8°, pp. viii.-90, incl. printed wrappers
BPL | SML

All's well . . . Ed. by I. Gollancz. ' Temple edition.' Ln : Dent, 1894. 16°

All's well . . . 'Ariel edition.' Ln : Routledge, 1897. 16°

All's well . . . ' Pocket Falstaff edition.' Ln : Bliss, Sands, 1898. 16°, pp. 116
BPL | SML

All's well . . . Edited with introductions and notes by C. H. Herford. ' Eversley edition.' Ln : Macmillan, 1900. 12° BPL

All's well . . . Introd. and notes by J. Dennis. Illust. by B. Shaw. 'Chiswick edition.' Ln : Bell, 1902. 12°

All's well . . . Edited with notes by H. N. Hudson. ' Windsor edition.' Edinburgh : Jack, 1903. Cr. 8°, pp. 130

All's well . . . Introd. by George Brandes. ' Favourite classics.' Ln : Heinemann, 1904. 12°

All's well . . . Ed. by W. Osborne Brigstocke. 'Arden edition.' Ln : Methuen, 1904. 8°, pp. 204

All's well . . . Introd. and notes by W. J. Craig. ' Little quartos.' Ln : Methuen, 1904. 16°

All's well . . . ' Ellen Terry edition.' Glasgow : Bryce, 1904. 32°

All's well . . . ' National library.' Ed. by H. Morley. Ln : Cassell, 1905. 16° BPL

All's well . . . ' Waistcoat pocket edition.' Ln : Treherne, 1905. 32°

All's well . . . ' Renaissance edition.' New York : Harrap, 1907. Fcp. 4° BPL

All's well . . . Ed. by W. G. Boswell-Stone. ' Old spelling Sh—.' Ln : Chatto, 1908. 8°
BPL

'All's well . . .' references—
See Barret (R.)
  ,, Boccaccio
  ,, Brae
  ,, Davies. Dramatic . . .
  ,, Deloney

Sh— All's well . . .

'All's well . . .' references—
See Dow
  ,, Fleay
  ,, Halliwell
  ,, Jacke Drum . . .
  ,, Johnson & Steevens
  ,, Lennox
  ,, Nicholson
  ,, Rowley
  ,, *Sh*—] T—— (H.)
  ,, Thiselton

ANTONY AND CLEOPATRA.

This tragedy is found in the Jaggard folio of 1623 for the first time, and the first separate edition is Sedley's adaptation of 1677.

It was entered at Stationers' Hall on the 20 May, 1608, thus :—

' Edward Blount. Entred also for his copie by the like aucthoritie a booke called "Anthony and Cleopatra, VId." '

Antony and Cleopatra : A tragedy [founded on Sh—]. As it is acted at the Duke's theatre. Written by the Honourable Sir Charles Sedley, baronet . . . Ln : Richard Tonson . . . under Graye's Inne Gate, next Graye's Inne Lane, 1677. Fcp. 4°
BPL | W

The list of actors gives Betterton as *Antony* and his wife as *Octavia*.
' The only tragedy, except two of Jonson's and one of Sh—'s, wherein Romans speak and do like Romans.' —*Shadwell.*

[Antony and Cleopatra] All for love ; or the world well lost : A tragedy. As it is acted at the Theatre-Royal ; and written in imitation of Sh—'s stile. By John Dryden, servant to His Majesty. Ln : In the Savoy, H. Herringman, 1678. Fcp. 4°, pp. xx.-78 BPL | BUS | W

First produced in 1678 at Drury Lane by what was known as the King's Company. It was professedly written in imitation of Sh—'s style, and the author calls it ' the only play he wrote for himself,' all his other dramatic productions having been written to please the prevailing taste of the public. It is generally esteemed by critics as the best of Dryden's theatrical ventures.

[Antony . . .] All for love . . . by John Dryden. Ln : H. Herringman, R. Bentley, J. Tonson, F. Saunders, & T. Bennet . . . 1692. Fcp. 4°

Antony . . . Written by Sir Charles Sedley. Ln : Bentley, 1696. Fcp. 4° BPL

[Antony . . .] All for love . . . As it is acted by His Majesties servants and written in imitation of Sh—'s stile by Mr. Dryden. Ln : H. Herringman, 1696. Fcp. 4°, pp. xvi.-64 BPL | BUS

[Antony . . .] All for love . . . [In Dryden (J.) Comedies, tragedies and operas, now first collected together and corrected from the originals . . . Ln: Printed for Jacob Tonson at Gray's Inn Gate in Gray's Inn Lane; Thomas Bennet at the Half Moon; and Richard Wellington at the Lute in St. Paul's Churchyard], 1701. 2 vols. F°. With folded portrait of Dryden   BM | BUS

[Antony . . .] All for love . . . acted by Her Majesties Servants. Written in imitation of Sh—'s stile by Mr. Dryden. Ln: J. Tonson, 1703. Fcp. 4°, pp. xvi.-64 BUS

[Antony . . .] All for love . . . by John Dryden. Ln: Tonson, 1709. Fcp. 4° BPL

[Antony . . .] All for love. Written in imitation of Sakespear's [sic] stile by Mr. Dryden. *'Facile est verbum aliquod ardens (ut ita dicam) notare; idque restinctis animorum incendiis irridere.'* — *Cicero.* Ln: Printed [for T. Johnson] in the year 1710. Cr. 8°, pp. 108   W

[Antony . . .] All for love . . . Written in imitation of Sakespear's [sic] stile. By Mr. Dryden . . . [Ln]: Printed for T. Johnson, 1720. 8°, pp. 102   CPL | W

[Antony . . .] Cæsar in Ægypt, by Colley Cibber. Ln: 1725. 8°   BPL

Antony . . . A tragedy. By Mr. Wm. Sh—. Ln: Printed for J. Tonson and the rest of the proprietors and sold by the booksellers of Ln. and Westminster, 1734. Cr. 8°, pp. 96, and frontispiece by P. Fourdrinier   BPL | W
With the piracy notice by W. Chetwood at the end against R. Walker.

Anthony . . A tragedy. As it is acted at the Theatres . . . Ln: R. Walker, 1734. 12°   W

[Antony . . .] All for love . . . by Mr. Dryden. Ln: J. Tonson, 1740. 12°   SML | W

Antony . . . An historical play . . . fitted for the stage by abridging only and now acted at the Theatre Royal in Drury Lane by his Majesty's servants . . . Ln: Printed for J. & R. Tonson in the Strand: [Cphn.] From the Press of Dryden Leach in Crane Court, Fleet Street, 23 Oct., 1758. 8°, pp. 102 (incl. title)   BM | BPL | CTC
Edited by Edward Capell and David Garrick.

[Antony . . .] All for love . . . by Mr. Dryden. Ln: 1768. 12°. With engraved frontispiece   BPL | W

Antony . . . An introduction and notes, critical and illustrative, are added by the authors of the 'Dramatic censor' [Francis Gentleman]. Ln: John Bell; York: C. Etherington, 1776. 8°, pp. 108

[Antony . . .] All for love . . . Written by Mr. Dryden. Marked with the variations in the manager's book at the Theatre Royal in Drury Lane [In 'New English Theatre,' vol. 8]. Ln: W. Strahan, 1776. 12°, pp. 76, and portrait of Mrs. Yates as 'Cleopatra'   BUS

[Antony . . .] All for love . . . By Mr. Dryden. Ln: 1778. 8°   BPL | W

[Antony . . .] All for love . . . Ln: [c. 1784]. 12°   BPL

[Antony . . .] All for love . . . By Mr. Dryden. Adapted for theatrical representation as performed at the Theatres Royal, Drury Lane and Covent Garden. Regulated from the prompt books by permission of the managers. Ln: John Bell, 1792. 12°, pp. 114   BUS
With frontispiece, 'Mrs. Ward as Octavia.'
An edition of 100 pages, with the same title-page and date, was also issued by J. Bell.

Antony . . . Printed complete from the text of Sam. Johnson and Geo. Steevens, and revised from the last editions . . . Ln: John Bell, 1792. 12°, pp. 144; frontispiece of Mrs. Pope as 'Cleopatra,' and vignette title

Antony . . . Accurately printed from the text of Mr. Steevens' last edition. Ornamented with plates. Ln: E. Harding, J. Wright, G. Sael, Vernor & Hood . . . 1799. 8°, pp. iv.-126, and three plates

[Antony . . .] All for love [In Dryden's Works]. Ln: 1808. 8°   BUS

Antony . . . With remarks by Mrs. Inchbald. Ln: Longman . . . & Orme, 1808. 12°, pp. 88. With frontispiece   BPL | BUS

Anthony and Cloopatra [sic], by Will. Sh—. Printed complete from the text of Sam. Johnson and Geo. Steevens. Ln: 1809. 16°   W

[Antony . . .] All for love [In 'Modern British drama, edited by Sir W. Scott,' vol. i., pp. 337-365]. Ln: 1811. 8°   BPL | BUS

Antony . . . With alterations and additions from Dryden. As now performed at the Theatre Royal, Covent Garden. Ln: Longman . . . & Brown [c. 1811]. 12°, pp. 84, and plate   BUS

Antony . . . With alterations and additions by Dryden. Ln: 1813. 8°   BPL
This is Dryden's 'All for love,' printed under Sh—'s title.

Antony . . . With alterations and additions by Dryden. Second edition. Ln: 1813. 8°

Sh— Antony . . .

[Antony . . .] All for love . . . By John Dryden. Adapted for theatrical representation. As performed at the Theatres Royal, Covent Garden and Drury Lane. Regulated from the prompt books . . . With life of the author by Dr. Johnson and a critique by R. Cumberland. The lines distinguished by inverted commas are omitted in the representation. Cooke's edition. Superbly embellished [In 'Cumberland's British drama']. Ln : C. Cooke, 1817. 12°, pp. lxii.-80, and plate   BUS

[Antony . . .] All for love . . . By John Dryden. Correctly given from copies used in the theatres by Thomas Dibdin, author of several dramatic pieces [In Dibdin's 'London Theatre']. Ln : Printed at the Chiswick Press by C. Whittingham for Sherwood, Neely, & Jones, 1818. 8°, pp. 68. With vignette   BPL | BUS | W

[Antony . . .] All for love . . . [In Dryden's Works, second edition]. Edinburgh, 1821. 8°   BUS

Antony . . . Cowie's British Drama. Ln : 1833. 12°. With frontispiece

Antony . . . A burletta, by Sir C. Selby. Ln : [1842 ?]. 12°   BPL

Antony . . . 'Cumberland's British Theatre.' Ln : [1848 ?]. 12°   BPL

[Antony . . .] All for love . . . [In 'British Drama']. Philadelphia, 1853. 8°   BUS

[Antony . . .] Antony and Octavius, by W. S. Landor. Ln : Bradbury & Evans, 1856. 8°   BM | BLO | CTC

Antony . . . A burlesque, by [Sir] F. C. Burnand. Ln : 1866. Cr. 8°   BPL

Antony . . . Ln : T. H. Lacy, 1866. 12°, pp. 80, and plate

Antony . . . Arranged for representation by C. Calvert, Prince's Theatre, Manchester. Edinburgh : Schenck [1867 ?] Cr. 8° BPL

Antony . . . 'Acting edition.' Ln : T. H. Lacy [1867]. 12°, pp. 80, and plate   BM | BPL | BUS

Antony . . . Edited by John Hunter. Ln : Longman, 1870. Cr. 8°   CPL

[Antony . . .] All for love . . . by J. Dryden [' Dicks' British Drama,' vol. 7]. Ln : Dicks, 1871. 12°   BPL

Antony . . . Arranged and adapted for representation by Andrew Halliday. Ln : Tinsley, 1873. 8°, pp. viii.-64   BM | BPL

Antony . . . 'Standard plays.' Ln : John Dicks [1875 ?]. Cr. 8°

[Antony . . .] Antony and Octavius, by W. S. Landor [In Landor's Works, 8 vols.] Ln : Chapman, 1876. 8°   BPL
Forms part of vol. 7.

Sh— Antony . . .

Antony . . . as purchased by L. Calvert at the Queen's Theatre. Manchester [c. 1878]. Cr. 8°

Antony . . . With notes and extracts from the history on which the play is founded, by John Hunter. Ln : Longmans, 1878. 8°, pp. xxviii.-156   BPL

Antony . . . Edited with notes by W. J. Rolfe. New York, 1881. 12°. Illustrated   BPL | BUS

Antony . . . With introduction, and notes explanatory and critical, by H. N. Hudson. Boston [U.S.]: Ginn & Heath, 1881. 8°, pp. 224   BM
Part of the ' Annotated English classics.'

Antony . . . 'Standard plays.' Ln : John Dicks, 1883. Cr. 8°   BM | BPL

Antony . . . 'Rugby edition.' Edited by C. E. Moberly. Ln : Rivington, 1884. Cr. 8°

Antony . . . Edited for schools by H. N. Hudson. Boston [U.S.]: Ginn & Heath, 1888. Cr. 8°   BPL

Antony . . . [With an introduction by Henry Morley]. 'National library.' Ln : Cassell, 1889. 16°, pp. 192   BM

[Antony . . .] Hamnet Sh—: Part viii., The tragedy of 'Antony and Cleopatra' according to the first folio (spelling modernised), with lists of . . . the emphasis-capitals of Sh— . . . also . . . remarks on various passages . . . unnecessarily altered in many modern editions, and on the arrangement of its lines in the four folios by A. P. Paton. Greenock : W. Hutchison, 1890. 8°, pp. xliv.-102 SML

Antony . . . With notes . . . by J. Hunter. Ln : Longmans, 1890. Cr. 8°, pp. xxviii.-156

Antony . . . With introduction and notes by R. Deighton. Ln : Macmillan, 1891. 12°   BPL

Antony . . . Edited by C. E. Flower. ' Memorial theatre edition.' Stratford-on-Avon : Printed by G. Boyden ; Ln : S. French [1891 ?]. Cr. 8°, pp. viii.-108, incl. printed wrappers   BPL | SML

Antony . . . With an introduction by W. J. Rolfe and . . . illustrations by P. Avril [Also glossary and notes by J. Thomson]. Edition de luxe. New York : Duprat & Co., 1891. 8°, pp. xxii.-196   BM

Antony . . . [Ed. by Hy. Morley]. ' National library.' Ln : Cassell, 1891. 16°, pp. 192

Antony . . . Edited by I. Gollancz. ' Temple edition.' Ln : Dent, 1896. 16°, pp. viii.-186   BUS

Sh— Antony . . .

Antony . . . as produced by L. Calvert at [the Queen's theatre], Manchester. 16 Feb., 1897. Cr. 8°   BPL

Antony . . . With preface, glossary, &c. by I. Gollancz. Ln: Dent, 1897. 16°, pp. viii.-186. With frontispiece

Antony . . . ' Pocket Falstaff edition.' Ln: Bliss, Sands, 1898. 16°, pp. 140   BPL | SML

Antony . . . ' National library.' Ed. by H. Morley. Ln: Cassell, 1899. 16°   BUS

Antony . . . Edited with introduction and notes by C. H. Herford. ' Eversley edition.' Ln: Macmillan, 1900. Cr. 8°   BPL

Antony . . . Ed. with notes by H. N. Hudson. ' Windsor edition.' Edinburgh: Jack, 1903. Cr. 8°

Antony . . . With introduction by G. Brandes. ' Favourite classics.' Ln: Heinemann, 1904. 12°

Antony . . . Ed. by W. J. Craig. ' Little quartos.' Ln: Methuen, 1905. 16°

Antony . . . Ed. by H. Morley. ' National library.' Ln: Cassell, 1905. 16°   BPL

Antony . . . ' Waistcoat pocket edition.' Ln: Treherne, 1905. 32°

Antony . . . Edited by R. H. Case. 'Arden edition.' Ln: Methuen, 1906. 8°, pp. lx.-212

Antony . . . ' New variorum edition.' Ed. by H. H. Furness. Philadelphia: Lippincott, 1907. Roy. 8°, pp. 636   BM | BPL | BUS | SML

Includes a reprint of Dryden's ' All for love.'
Reviewed at length in the ' Athenæum,' 7th Mar., 1908.

Antony . . . Text revised by A. Dyce. Ln: Sonnenschein, 1907. 8°   BPL

Antony . . . ' Red letter edition.' Ln: Blackie, 1907. 12°

Antony . . . ' Renaissance ed.' Ln: G. G. Harrap, 1908. 4°   BPL

Antony . . . The text of the 1623 folio, with that of 'All for love,' by J. Dryden. 'Bankside restoration ed.' New York: Sh— Soc., 1908. 8°   BPL

'Antony and Cleopatra' references—
See Barclay
  ,, Character
  ,, Cleopatra
  ,, Cleveland
  ,, Gray
  ,, Halliwell. Selected . . .
  ,, Halliwell. Some account . . .
  ,, Johnson & Steevens
  ,, On the character . . .
  ,, Plutarchus
  ,, Sh—] Sh— notes
  ,, Sh—] Sh—'s character

Sh— Antony . . .

'Antony and Cleopatra' references—
See Snider
  ,, Thiselton
  ,, Topsell

ARDEN OF FEVERSHAM.

This play, entered at Stationers Hall 3rd April, 1592, was first issued by Edward White in that year.

[Arden of Feversham] The lamentable and trve tragedie of M. Arden of Feversham in Kent. Who was most wickedlye murdered by the meanes of his disloyall and wanton wyfe ; who, for the loue she bare to one Mosbie, hyred two desperat ruffins, Blackwill and Shakbag, to kill him. Wherin is shewed the great mallice and discimulation of a wicked woman, the vnsatiable desire of filthie lust, and the shamefull end of all murderers. Imprinted at London for Edward White, dwelling at the lyttle North dore of Paules Church at the signe of the Gun, 1592. Fcp. 4°, 37 leaves, sig. A to I[1] in fours ; black letter

' The only reason for assigning it to Sh— is its merit.'— *R. Bayne.*
' The possible work of no man's youthful hand but Sh—'s.'—*A. C. Swinburne.*
In support of the contention that the play is Sh—'s production it should be observed that two syllables from his own name (WILL and SHAK) occur in the cognomens of the characters, and that the title instantly recalls his mother's maiden name.
A copy sold in June, 1907, realised £1,210.

[Arden . . .] The lamentable and true tragedie of Arden of Feversham . . . Ln: Ed. White, 1599. Fcp. 4°
With slight textual variations from the first edition.

[Arden . . .] The lamentable and true tragedie of Arden of Feversham . . . Ln: Printed by Eliz. Allde, dwelling neere Christ's Church, 1633. Fcp. 4°. Woodcut on title verso   BM
With slight textual variations from the first and second editions. In June, 1904, a copy realised £53.

[Arden . . .] The lamentable and trve tragedie of M. Arden of Feversham in Kent . . . With a preface in which some reasons are offered in favour of its being the earliest dramatic work of Sh— now remaining, and a genuine account given of the murder from authentic papers of the time [by Edward Jacob]. Ln: Printed for Edward White, 1592 ; and reprinted verbatim by J. & J. March for Stephen Doorne, bookseller at Feversham, 1770. 8°, pp. viii.-90   BUS
A few copies were issued on large paper, of which one is at Boston.

Sh— Arden . . .

Arden . . .; An historical tragedy, taken from Holingshead's 'Chronicle,' in the reign of King Edward VI. As it is acted at the Theatre Royal in Drury Lane. By the late Mr. Lillo . . . Dublin: Printed for T. & J. Whitehouse, Booksellers, at the State Lottery Office in Nicholas Street, 1763. Cr. 8°, pp. 56
An alteration by G. Lillo, who uses most of the plot and text of the original version. At Lillo's death it is said the unfinished MS. was completed by John Hoadly.

Arden . . . [In Lillo's Dramatic Works]. Ln: 1775. 8°   BUS

Arden . . . An historical tragedy acted at the Theatre Royal in Drury Lane [In Lillo's Dramatic Works]. Ln: 1810. 12°   BUS

Arden . . . By G. Lillo. Finished by J. Hoadly [In 'Modern British Drama, edited by Sir W. Scott,' Vol. 2, pp. 105-123]. Ln: 1811. 8°   BPL | BUS

Arden . . . By G. Lillo [In 'British Drama']. Philadelphia, 1853. 8°   BUS

Arden . . . [Text and notes in English and German. Edited by N. Delius]. Elberfeld: R. L. Friderichs, 1855. 12° BUS

Arden . . . by G. Lillo. Price one penny. Ln: J. Dicks [c. 1866]. Cr. 8°, pp. 20, including printed wrappers

Arden . . . Reprinted from the edition of 1592. With an introduction by A. H. Bullen. Ln: J. W. Jarvis & Son, 1887. Fcp. 4°, pp. xx.-108 and frontispiece
Issue restricted to 250 numbered copies.   BPL | BUS

Arden . . . Revised and edited with introduction and notes by K. Warnke and L. Proescholdt. Halle, 1888. 8°   BUS

Arden . . . Edited with a preface, notes and glossary by Ronald Bayne. Ln: Dent, 1897. 12°. With etched frontispiece BPL

Arden . . . Edited with an introduction by A. F. Hopkinson. Ln: 1898. 12° BPL

'Arden of Feversham' references—
See Crawford   *See* Headlam
 ,, Donne   ,, Murder

ARRAIGNMENT OF PARIS.

This drama was included by Capell among those ascribed to Sh—, to whom F. Kirkman also attributed it: but reference to R. Greene's 'Arcadia' will shew it was written by George Peele, according to the epistle therein by Thomas Nash. It first appeared in 1584, anonymously.

[Arraignment . . .] The araygnment of Paris. A pastorall, presented before the Queenes Maiestie by the Children of her

Sh— Arraignment . . .

Chappell. London: Printed by Henrie Marsh, 1584. Fcp. 4°, sig. A¹ to E⁴ in fours   BM
An interesting account of it appears in the 'Retrospective Review,' vol. iii., pp. 97-126.

Arraignment of Paris [In G. Peele's Works]. Ln: 1829. 8°   BUS

Arraignment . . . [In Works of G. Peele, pp. 347-370]. Ln: 1860. 8°   BPL

AS YOU LIKE IT.

This comedy first made its appearance in print in the Jaggard folio of 1623, and no separate edition is known before Charles Johnson's adaptation of a century later.

The externals and local colour of the play were largely drawn from the forest of Arden and surroundings of Stratford-upon-Avon.

'As you like it' altered and entitled 'Love in a forest.' A comedy, by Mr. [Charles] Johnson. Ln: W. Chetwood, 1723. 8°   BM | BPL | BUS | W
A rare adaptation combining the plot and characters of 'As you like it'; a dialogue from 'Much ado . . .' and the interlude from a 'Midsummer night's dream.'

[As you like it] The modern receipt, or a cure for love. A comedy. Altered from Sh— . . . With original poems, letters, etc. [By James Carrington, aged 19, & Daniel Bellamy, students at Trin. Coll., Camb.] Ln: Printed for the author, 1739. 12°, pp. xvi.-178   BM | BPL | BUS | W
Carrington's autograph presentation copy to his coadjutor is at Warwick Castle. An account of the volume is given in Halliwell's 'Handlist of Sh—, 1862,' p. 225.

[As you like it] Songs in 'As you like it' [*Full score*]. Composed by Dr. T. A. Arne. Ln: W. Smith [c. 1740]. F° BPL

As you like it. A comedy; as it is acted at the Theatre-Royal in Aungier-Street, Dublin . . . Collated with the oldest copies and corrected, by Mr. Theobald. Dublin: A. Reilly for A. Bradley, 1741. 12°, pp. 72   BM

As you like it . . . As it is acted at the Theatre Royal in Smock Alley. Dublin [1750 ?]. Cr. 8°   BPL

[As you like it] Charles Macklin's part as 'Touchstone.' Manuscript, on nine leaves of paper. [c. 1770.] Fcp. 4°   W
The original stage or playhouse copy.

[As you like it] Seven ages of man. Describ'd by Sh— and adorn'd with curious cutts. Ln: 1771. Cr. 8°   BPL

As you like it. A comedy . . . As performed at the Theatre Royal, Drury Lane. Regulated from the prompt book, with permission of the managers by Mr. Hopkins,

prompter. An introduction, and notes critical and illustrative are added by the authors of the 'Dramatic censor' [F. Gentleman]. Ln: John Bell, 1773. 8°
Excerpt, pp. 73-148.
An offprint from Bell's edition for the use of play-goers.
At the end is Bell's list (8pp.) of publications.

As you like it . . . As performed at the Theatre Royal, Drury Lane. With the notes of Mr. Theobald. 1775. Cr. 8° BPL

As you like it . . . As it acted at the Theatres Royal in Drury Lane and Covent Garden. Ln: W. Oxlade, 1777. Cr. 8° BPL

As you like it. A comedy. As it is acted at the Theatres Royal in Drury Lane and Covent Garden . . . Ln: Printed for J. Wenman, 144, Fleet St., and sold by all other booksellers in town and country, 1777. 8°, pp. 24, and copperplate portrait of King as 'Touchstone' BM | BPL

As you like it . . . printed complete from the text of Sam. Johnson and Geo. Steevens, and revised from the last editions . . . Ln: Printed for . . . John Bell . . . 1785. 12°, pp. 110, with engraved title and frontispiece of Mrs. Abington in 'Rosalind'

As you like it. A comedy. Taken from the manager's book at the Theatre Royal in Drury Lane. Ln: R. Butters [c. 1785]. 12°, pp. 52 BM | BPL

As you like it . . . Marked with the variations in the manager's book at the Theatre Royal in Covent Garden. Ln: C. Bathurst, 1786. 12°, pp. 76, with engraved frontispiece BM | BPL

[As you like it] A parody on Sh—'s celebrated description of the seven stages of human life. Salisbury: Fowler [c. 1790]. 8°, single sheet BM | BUS

As you like it. Printed conformable to the representation under the inspection of J. Wrighten. Ln: 1791. 8°

As you like it. A comedy, by Sh—, as performed at the Theatres Royal. Ln: 1794. 12° W

As you like it. Altered by J. P. Kemble. As performed at the Theatre Royal, Drury Lane. Ln: 1794. 8°

[As you like it] Seven ages of man illustrated [Seven plates and title-page engraved by W. Bromley from drawings by T. Stothard, with text to each]. Hammersmith: W. Bromley, 1799. F°, pp. iv.-14. Engraved throughout BM | BUS
Some copies were issued printed in colours.

As you like it . . . from the text of Johnson and Steevens. Manchester: R. & W. Dean, 1802. 12°, pp. 72, and engraved frontispiece

[As you like it] Paddy M'Shane's 'Seven ages,' written by Major Downs and sung with unbounded applause by Mr. Johnstone at the Theatre Royal, Drury Lane. Ln: Laurie & Whittle, 1807. Broadside, with plate by G. Cruikshank BUS

As you like it. A comedy. In five acts . . . As performed at the Theatres Royal, Drury Lane and Covent Garden. Printed under the authority of the managers from the prompt book. With remarks by Mrs. Inchbald. Ln: Longman . . . & Orme, 1808. 12°, pp. 80, and frontispiece BPL | BUS

'As you like it.' An additional scene by Joseph Moser [In 'European Magazine,' vol. 55, May.] Ln: 1809. 8° BUS
Represents the scene referred to between Duke Frederic and the friar in act v., sc. 8.

[As you like it] Seven ages of man. Ln: C. Whittingham [c. 1810]. Roy. f°, pp. 20 ?

As you like it . . . Revised by J. P. Kemble for Covent Garden. Ln: 1810. 8°

As you like it . . . With remarks by Mrs. Inchbald. Ln: Longman . . . & Brown [c. 1811]. 12°, pp. 80 BUS

As you like it: A comedy . . . Edinburgh: Oliver & Boyd [c. 1813]. 12°
Issued in blue wrappers at 6d.

As you like it. With remarks by Mrs. Inchbald. Calcutta: Pereira [c. 1815]. 12° BPL

As you like it. A comedy. Revised by J. P. Kemble, and now published as it is performed at the Theatres Royal. Ln: J. Miller, 1815. 8°, pp. 76 BM | BPL | BUS | W

[As you like it] Progress of human life; Sh—'s 'Seven ages of man,' illustrated by a series of extracts in prose and poetry . . . Introduced by a brief memoir of Sh— and his writings, by John Evans. 1818. 8° BM

As you like it . . . A specimen of a new edition of Sh— [Edited by T. Caldecott]. Ln: J. Murray, 1819. Roy. 8°. Four paginations: pp. xiv.-174-136-116-42 BM | BPL | BUS
Only one hundred copies printed.
See footnote to this edition under heading of Sh— Hamlet, 1819.

As you like it. A comedy. . . With prefatory remarks [signed W. H.] marked with the stage business, and stage directions, as it is performed at the Theatres Royal, by W. Oxberry. Ln: 1819. 8°, pp. ii.-68 BM | BPL | W

Sh— As you like it . . .

[As you like it] Progress of human life :
Sh—'s 'Seven ages . . .' by John Evans.
Ln : 1820. Cr. 8°

[As you like it] 'Hamlet' and 'As you like
it' : A specimen of a new edition by T.
Caldecott. Ln : John Murray, 1820. 8°
BPL | BUS | SML

As you like it . . . 'Dolby's British Theatre.'
1823. Cr. 8° BPL

As you like it . . . With remarks by D. G——
[Geo. Daniel]. Ln : John Cumberland,
1823. 12°

[As you like it] Sh—'s ' Seven ages,' by H.
Alken. Seven coloured plates. Ln : [c.
1823]. Oblong 4°

As you like it. Marked with the stage business by W. Oxberry. Ln : 1823. 12°

[As you like it] Seven ages of man. By
Henry Alken. Ln : 1824. F°; seven
coloured plates and one sheet of text

[As you like it] Planché (J. R.) & Scharf
(G.) Costume of . . . 'As you like it,'
selected and arranged from the best
authorities, with biographical, critical,
and explanatory notices. Ln : J. Miller,
1825. 8°, pp. 28 BPL | BUS

[As you like it] Music in 'As you like it'
[*Full score*]. Composed by Sir H. R.
Bishop. Ln : [c. 1825]. F°

[As you like it] Senarii Græci [A translation
by J. Wordsworth from 'As you like it.'
In English and Greek]. Cambridge : [c.
1827]. 8° BM

As you like it . . . Printed from the acting
copy, with remarks, biographical and
critical, by D. G—— [George Daniel].
To which are added a . . . cast of the
characters . . . and the whole of the stage
business, as now performed at the
Theatres Royal. Ln : J. Cumberland,
1829. 12°, pp. 68 BM | BPL

[As you like it] Senarii Græci [A translation
by G. J. Kennedy from 'As you like it.'
In English and Greek]. Cambridge : 1831.
8° BM

[As you like it] Seven ages . . . Illustrated
by a series of extracts in prose and poetry.
Introduced by a brief memoir of Sh—.
Ln : 1831. 8° BUS

[As you like it] Hamlet, and As you like it.
A specimen of a new edition of Sh—.
By T. Caldecott. Second edition. Ln :
[Privately] Printed for the Editor, 1832.
Royal 8°, pp. xvi. +178+ 150+ 115 +43
+4 BM | BPL | BUS | CPL | MPL | W
Two hundred and fifty printed.
Large paper copy at Warwick Castle.

Sh— As you like it . . .

[As you like it] Seven ages of man, or the
Progress of human life . . . With a brief
memoir of Sh— and his writings by John
Evans, LL.D. Chiswick Press : C. Whittingham, 1834. 8°, pp. xlviii.-252 ; lllust.
BM | CPL

[As you like it] Seven ages of man [Illus-
trated]. Ln : J. T. Wood [1840]. An en-
graved card BM | SML

[As you like it] Seven ages . . . [With wood
engravings by Wm. Mulready, John Constable, Sir D. Wilkie, Wm. Collins, Alfred
E. Chalon, Abraham Cooper, Sir Augustus
Callcott, Edwin Landseer, and Wm. Hilton. Introd. by Lady Callcott. Ed. by
John Martin]. Ln : J. van Voorst, 1840.
8°, pp. 20, and 10 plates BPL | CPL | SML
Copies done on large paper, 4°, at BM | BUS.

As you like it . . . As performed by Mr. Macready. Ln : Pattie, 1841. 12°

As you like it. Leipzig : Tauchnitz, 1843.
Cr. 8°

As you like it. Cabinet edition. Ln :
1845. 24° BUS

As you like it . . . French's standard drama.
With the stage business, cast . . . relative
positions. [Ed. by J. W. S. Hows.]
New York : S. French, 1846. 12°, pp.
iv.-8-66 BUS

As you like it . . . 'Modern standard drama.'
New York : Taylor & Co., 1848. 12° BPL

[As you like it] Seven ages . . . Introduction by Lady Callcott. Ed. by John
Martin.] Ln : J. Van Voorst, 1848. 8°,
pp. 18-16 and 10 plates BM | BPL
Printed from the same plates as the 1840 edition, but
with quotations and names of artists added on separate leaves.

As you like it . . . ' Lacy's acting edition.
Ln : [c. 1849]. 12° BPL

[As you like it] Seven ages of man. Etched
by E. Goodall, after original designs by
Daniel Maclise. Ln : Art Union, 1850.
Oblong 4°, ff. 2. With 8 plates
BM | BPL | BUS | SML
Proof copies were also issued in imperial folio.

[As you like it] Seven ages . . . comically
illustrated in jest and earnest. By a
funny fellow. With engravings. Ln :
R. Macdonald [1850]. 8°, pp. 10
BM | BUS | W

[As you like it] Man : from the cradle to
the grave. Being Sh—'s Seven ages of
life. Illustrated in a series of seven
original designs on wood by John Gilbert,
Marshall Claxton and D. H. M'Kewan.
Engraved by T. Gilks. With introd. by
Wm. Bridges. Ln : W. H. Smith & Son
[c. 1850]. 4°, ff. 8 BUS

[As you like it] Seven ages of Sh— illus-
trated. 1850. 4° BPL
As you like it. Lacy's acting edition. Ln :
T. H. Lacy, 1856. 12°, pp. vi.-64 BM
[As you like it] Seven ages : Illustrated by
music and poetry [Seven songs] with· a
finale. Composed by Charles E. Horn.
Words by George Soane. Ln : Cramer
& Co. [c. 1860]. F°, pp. ii.-44 BUS
As you like it. Glasgow : Cameron [1860 ?].
12° BPL
[As you like it] Seven ages of man . . .
Depicted by R. Smirke [in photography].
Ln : L. Booth & S. Ayling, 1864. Fcp. 4°,
pp. 24 and photographs, including the
Droeshout and Stratford bust portraits
BM | BPL | CPL | SML
As you like it . . . for the use of Rugby
School. Rugby : W. Billington, 1868.
Cr. 8°, pp. viii.-82 BM | BPL
As you like it. Ln : Lacy [1868 ?] 12°
BPL
As you like it . . . With explanatory French
notes by A. Brown . . . improved with à
copious selection of notes from Johnson,
Steevens, Malone, Theobald, Warburton,
etc. Truchy's edition. Paris : J. H.
Truchy, 1869. 12°, pp. 248 BM
As you like it. With explanatory and
illustrative notes, selected criticisms on
the play, etc. Adapted for scholastic or
private study and for those qualifying
for university and government examina-
tions. By John Hunter. Ln : Longmans,
1869. 12°, pp. viii.-104 BUS | CPL
As you like it . . . ' Cumberland's British
theatre.' [1870 ?] 12° BPL
[As you like it] Progress of Pertinax Puzzle-
wit [a burlesque of the ' Seven ages of
man,' with Sh—'s text, in S. O. Beeton's
'Christmas Annual']. Ln : [c. 1870.]
Fcp. 4°. Illust.
Sh— occupies pp. 62-69.
As you like it . . . With notes by J. Hunter.
Ln : 1872. 12° BPL
As you like it. ' Rugby School edition.'
Edited by Charles E. Moberly. Ln :
Rivington, 1872. 12°, pp. 108 BPL | BUS
As you like it. From Hudson's School
Sh—. Boston [U.S.]: Ginn Brothers,
1874. 8°, pp. xxii.-96 BUS
[As you like it] Seven ages of life. Illus-
trated by Sir John Gilbert. Second edi-
tion. Ln : Dean [c. 1874]. 4°, pp. 8
BUS | CPL
As you like it . . . As arranged for Crystal
Palace. Ln : Crystal Palace Company,
1874. 8° BPL

As you like it . . . Edited by W. A. Wright.
Oxford : Clarendon Press, 1876. Cr. 8°,
pp. xxxvi.-168 BPL
As you like it . . . With explanatory re-
marks, explanatory, grammatical and
philological notes, etc. by Samuel Neil.
Ln : W. Collins, 1876. Cr. 8°, pp. 156
BM | BPL | BUS
As you like it. Ed. with notes by W. J.
Rolfe. With engravings. New York :
Harper . . . 1878. 16°, pp. 206 BUS
As you like it . . . Edited by W. A. Wright.
Oxford : Clarendon Press, 1879. Cr. 8°,
pp. xxxvi.-168 BPL | BUS
Cover dated 1877.
As you like it . . . Edited by W. A. Wright.
'Clarendon Press Series.' Oxford, 1879.
Cr. 8° BPL
Cover dated 1880.
As you like it . . . as performed under Miss
Litton's management. With remarks by
Tom Taylor. Ln : [c. 1880]. 8° BPL
As you like it . . . as played at the Imperial
Theatre, Westminster. [c. 1880.] 8°
BPL
As you like it . . . with introduction and
notes . . . by H. N. Hudson. Boston
[U.S.]: Ginn & Heath, 1880. 8°, pp.
xxvi.-160 BM | BPL
Part of the ' Annotated English classics.'
As you like it . . . Edited by C. E. Flower.
' Memorial Theatre edition.' Stratford-
on-Avon, Printed by G. Boyden ; Ln :
S. French [1882]. Cr. 8°, pp. viii.-80
BPL | SML
As you like it . . . ' Dick's standard plays.'
Ln : John Dicks, 1883. 12° BM | BPL
As you like it . . . Edited by W. J. Rolfe.
New York : Harper, 1883. 12° BPL
As you like it. With notes, examination
papers, and plan of preparation, by
Brainerd Kellogg. New York, 1883.
Illust. BUS
As you like it . . . With notes, examination
papers. . . Ln. & Edin.: W. & R.
Chambers, 1883. 8°, pp. 96 BM
As you like it . . . With notes. ' Oxford and
Cambridge Sh—.' Ln : Allman [1884].
Cr. 8° BPL
As you like it . . . Edited by C. E. Moberly.
' Rugby edition.' Ln : Rivington [1884 ?]
Cr. 8° BPL | MPL
As you like it . . . Edited by W. A. Wright.
Oxford : Clarendon Press, 1884. Cr. 8°,
pp. xxxvi.-170 MPL | SML
As you like it . . . 1623. Reprinted from
the first folio. Ln : William Ludlow,
1885. 12° BPL

Sh— As you like it . . .

[As you like it] Seven ages of man . . . Artists' edition. Illustrated with photogravures from original paintings. Philadelphia, 1885. 4°   BM | BPL | BUS

[As you like it] Seven ages of man . . . Illustrated. Ln: Unwin, 1885. Fcp. 4°, twenty unpaged leaves, including seven plates   BM

[As you like it] Seven ages of life. Illustrated by Sir J. Gilbert. Engraved by T. Gilks. Second edition. [1885 ?] 4° BPL

As you like it . . . With notes. 'Blackie's school classics.' Ln: Blackie & Son [1886]. 16°, pp. 96   BM

As you like it. . . With the 'Tale of Gamelyn' [and an introduction by H. Morley]. 'National library.' Ln: Cassell & Co., 1886. 16°, pp. 192   BM

As you like it . . . With illustrations by E. Bayard. Introduction by E. Dowden. 'International Sh—.' Ln: Cassell, 1887. F°   BPL

As you like it. Ed. by W. A. Wright. Oxford: Clarendon Press, 1887. Cr. 8°, pp. xxxvi.-170

As you like it . . . With notes. Ln: W. & R. Chambers, 1888. 12°   BPL

As you like it. 'New variorum edition.' Ed. by H. H. Furness. Philadelphia: Lippincott, 1890. Roy. 8°
   BM | BPL | BUS | SML

As you like it. Ed. by K. Deighton. Ln: Macmillan, 1891. Cr. 8°

As you like it . . With notes . . . Edinburgh: Chambers, 1892. 8°, pp. 96

As you like it . . . Ed. by C. E. Flower [With 'in memoriam' notice by Mrs. C. E. Flower]. Stratford-on-Avon: Sh— Memorial, 1893. Cr. 8°, pp. xii.-88, incl. printed wrappers   SML

As you like it . . . Edited with introduction and notes by T. Page. Ln: Moffatt [1893]. 12°   BPL

As you like it . . . With introduction and notes by K. Deighton. Ln: 1893. Cr. 8°
   BPL

As you like it . . . edited by J. C. Smith. 'Warwick Sh—.' Ln: Blackie, 1894. Cr. 8°, pp. 182   BPL

As you like it . . . With introduction, notes, etc., by Lionel W. Lyde. 'Junior School Sh—.' Ln: Blackie [c. 1894]. 12°, pp. 120   BPL

[As you like it] Seven ages of man. A series of seven reproductions from original photographs. Ln: Cassell & Co., 1894. 8°   BM

As you like it. Ed. by I. Gollancz. 'Temple edition.' Ln: Dent, 1894. 16°

Sh— As you like it . . .

As you like it . . . edited by S. E. Winbolt. 'Arnold's school Sh—' [1895]. 12° BPL

As you like it . . . Ed. by J. C. Smith. 'Arden edition.' Ln: Methuen, 1896. 8°   BM | BLO | BUS | CTC

As you like it . . . 'Ariel edition.' Ln: Routledge, 1896. 16°

[As you like it] Selections from 'As you like it.' Blackie's English classics. Ln: Blackie, 1896. 16°   BM

As you like it. With introd. and notes by W. L. Phelps. New York: 1896. 8° BUS

As you like it. Ed. by S. E. Winbolt. Ln: Arnold, 1897. 12°

As you like it. 'Pocket Falstaff edition.' Ln: Sands & Co., 1898. 12°, pp. 104
   BPL | SML

As you like it. Ed. by W. A. Wright. Oxford: Clarendon Press, 1899. Cr. 8°, pp. xxvi.-170

As you like it. With the 'Tale of Gamelyn' [Ed. by Henry Morley]. Ln: Cassell, 1899. 16°, pp. 192   BUS

As you like it. With introd. and notes by John Dennis. Illust. by Byam Shaw. Chiswick ed. Ln: Bell, 1899. 16°, pp. 130

As you like it . . . Edited with . . . notes, glossary . . . by A. W. Verity. Cambridge: University Press, 1899. 8°, pp. lii.-256
   BPL | BUS

As you like it . . . With explanatory and illustrative notes . . . by John Hunter. New impression. Ln: Longmans, 1899. Cr. 8°, pp. viii.-110

As you like it . . . 'Masterpiece library' Penny poets. Ln: [W. T. Stead, c. 1900]. Cr. 8°, pp. 62 (includ. pr. wrappers) BPL

As you like it. Ed. . . . by A. W. Verity. Cambridge: Univ. Press, 1900. Cr. 8°, pp. lii.-256

As you like it. Notes by W. Dyche. Ten illustrations by W. Shepperton. 'Swan edition.' Ln: Longmans, 1900. Cr. 8°, pp. 134   BPL

As you like it. With photogravure illustrations and decorations by Wm. H. Low. New York: 1900. 8°   BPL | BUS

As you like it. Adapted for amateur performances in girls' schools by Elsie Fogerty. 'Costume edition.' Ln: Sonnenschein, 1900. Cr. 8°, pp. 88   BPL

As you like it. Introd. notes and glossary by R. B. Johnson. Edinburgh: Blackwood, 1900. Cr. 8°, pp. 200   BPL

As you like it . . . Edited with introd. and notes by C. H. Herford. 'Eversley edition.' Ln: Macmillan, 1900. Cr. 8° BPL

As you like it. The 'picture Sh—.' Ln: Blackie, 1901. Cr. 8°, pp. 144 ; illust. BPL

Sh— As you like it . . .

'As you like it' references—
See Mexia
 „ Moulton
 „ Music
 „ Numeration
 „ 'Oxon'
 „ Parker
 „ Planché
 „ Raffles
 „ Richardson
 „ Roffe
 „ Saviolo
 „ Segar
 „ Sh— Poems, 1660
 „ Sh— Works : Ext. 1870, 1881
 „ *Sh*—] Sh— miscellanies
 „ *Sh*—] Sh—'s library
 „ Sheldon
 „ Sigerson
 „ Snider
 „ Springthorpe
 „ Stewart
 „ Whiter
 „ Wilding
 „ Wood (S.)
 „ Woodforde
 „ Wurtzburg

AUTOGRAPH.

Six indubitably genuine autographs of Sh— exist. They are attached respectively to the Montjoy deposition, 1612-13 ; Black-friars deed of conveyance, 1612-13 ; Black-friars mortgage document, 1612-13 ; and his will, 1615-16:

In every other asserted instance of genuineness more evidence is needed before the attributed signatures can be finally accepted or rejected.

[Autograph] Ovidii metamorphoseon . . . Venetiis in ædibus Aldi, 1502. 8° BLO
Bears a contracted signature, 'Wm. Sh—.' The volume was purchased at auction for the Bodleian in or about 1872 by the librarian, Dr. Coxe. At the foot of the page bearing the autograph is this note : 'This little booke of Ovid was given to me by W. Hall, who sayd it was once Will. Sh—'s. [*Signed*] T. N—, 1682.'
A full account, with facsimiles, is given by W. Carew Hazlitt in his 'Sh—, 1902,' pp. 72-74.

[Autograph] Carion (John) Thre bokes of cronicles . . . Ln : Gwalter Lynne, 1550. Fcp. 4°
The title bears two signatures, 'Wm. Shakespeare' and 'Southampton.' On the verso is a note to the effect that the Earl of Southampton presented the volume to the poet. A second note, signed 'W. S.,' is on the verso of folio LXXXIII., and a third note, signed 'Wm. Shakespeare,' appears on a blank leaf before the 'Table.' An article upon the autographs from the pen of Andrew Lang appeared in the 'Morning Post' of March 27th, 1905, p. 10.

Sh— Autograph . . .
The doubt attached to these signatures was fairly expressed in the sum the volume sold for (£32) in March, 1905.
It appears to belong to the Ireland manufactory.

[Autograph] Saravi (Giovanni) I quattro libri della filosofia. Vinegia : 1565. 8°
The name 'W. Shakespeare' is written twice upon the external vellum cover, and the signatures were first noticed in 1811 by the wife of a Mr. Taylor, who had purchased the volume for sixpence. The autograph corresponds with that in 'Montaigne' at the British Museum.
The volume occurred for sale in 1898, when it realised £102.

[Autograph] Booke of common prayer . . . Ln : 1596. Fcp. 4°
Contains three alleged signatures of the poet.
In 1864 a working man took the volume into the shop of John Partridge, bookseller, of Wellington (*q.v.*), and sold it for eighteenpence. It was re-sold by Partridge in 1865 for £300 to a collector named Rothwell, of Sharples Hall. [*See* 'N. & Q.,' 10 S. ii., pp. 248 and 332.]

[Autograph] Booke . . . 1596. Photographic copies of several pages of a 'Book of psalms and prayer' which belonged to Sh— and contains his autographs. 1864. Fcp. 4°, pp. 6 BUS

[Autograph] Rastell (Wm.) Collection in English of the statutes now in force from magna charta to XXXV. Queen Elizabeth . . . Ln : T. Wright & B. Norton, 1598. F°
With signature 'Wm. Shakespere' written longitudinally.
The volume, which realised £80 in April, 1904, had been closely compared with genuine signatures of the poet by various experts, and while none would give a definite decision in favour of its authenticity, the concensus of opinion was that it should not be regarded as one of the Ireland forgeries.
On the fly-leaf were two signatures of Thomas Bragge, a Stratford contemporary of Sh—.

[Autograph] Mascall (Leonard) Booke of fishing with hooke and line . . . Ln : Printed by Iohn Wolfe for Edw. White in Paule's . . . 1600. Fcp. 4°
Probably one of Ireland's frauds.
It realised £30 in April, 1907.

[Autograph] Plutarch. Lives of the noble Grecians and Romanes . . . Trans. by Sir Thomas North . . . Ln : R. Field for T. Wight. 1603. F° BUS
Contains a supposed Sh— autograph. For further details see 'Bulletin of Boston Public Library,' 1889, vol. 8, pp. 515-527.

[Autograph] Montaigne. Essayes . . . Done into English by John Florio. Ln : Printed by Val. Sims for E. Blount, 1603. F° BM
The authenticity of this signature is disputed.
The volume was purchased for the British Museum in 1838. *See* Catalogue . . . 1838.
A facsimile is given on p. 74 of W. Carew Hazlitt's 'Sh—, 1902.'
'An undoubted autograph of Sh—,' says Lowndes, 'the interest of which is increased by its having been shown that Sh— used Florio's translation of Montaigne in "The tempest, Act ii., Sc. 2."'

Sh— Autograph . . .

[Autograph] True and perfect relation of
proceedings at the several arraignments
of the late most barbarous traitors [Gun-
powder plot] Garnet and his confederates
. . . Ln : R. Barker, 1606. Fcp. 4°
With a doubtful signature of the poet.
The volume realised £13 10s. in May, 1905.

[Autograph] Deposition in the suit Bellot v.
Mountjoy, entered in the Court of Requests, 1612-13
A contracted signature, quite genuine, attached to a
document preserved in the Public Record Office, of
which a facsimile is given in 'Harper's Magazine'
for March, 1910 [see Wallace], and in 'The Sphere,'
26 Feb., 1910.

[Autograph] Indenture [Vendor's deed of
conveyance covering the purchase of a
residence on the West side of Saint
Andrew's Hill formerly named Puddle
Hill, near Ireland Yard, Blackfriars, for
£140, dated]. Ln : . . . 10th March,
1612-13
This document, with a veritable signature of Sh—'s,
was bought for £145 on the 13th May, 1843, for the
Guildhall Library, Ln., where it may now be seen.
It is curious that the deed thus sold for £5 more than
the property it represented.

[Autograph] Mortgage deed [contracting
that sixty pounds of the purchase money
of the Blackfriars residence shall remain
on mortgage, dated], 11th March, 1612-13
BM
Bears Sh—'s undoubted autograph.
Purchased for the National Museum at J. O. Halliwell's sale, 14 June, 1858, at £315. See Catalogue,
1858.

[Autograph] Robartes (Foulke) Revenve of
the gospel in tythes, due to the ministrie
of the word, by that word. Cambridge :
Printed by Cantrel Legge . . . 1613. Fcp.
4°   MRL
Sh—'s signature herein is one of Ireland's forgeries.

[Autograph] Last will and testament of
William Sh— of Stratford-vpon-Avon,
[dated] Jan.-March, 1616
SOMERSET HOUSE
Written on three sheets of paper, each signed by the
poet.
These three signatures admit of no doubt as to their
genuineness. Critics and Baconians of slight reading
or discernment sometimes point to these autographs
as the sign manual of an illiterate man, forgetful or
ignorant of the fact that they were written hurriedly
on his deathbed by the poet ; careless, too, of the
fact that few writers of Sh—'s output write a clear or
legible hand—particularly when using a quill pen.
See also Sh— Will . . .

Autograph [In Sh— Works]. Sæc. XVII.
F°
Referred to in 'The Bookmart,' Dec., 1885, as a Sh—
folio, formerly the property of John Ward, vicar of
Stratford, and now in the possession of C. F. Günther,
in the United States.

[Autograph] Letter to Anne Hathaway.
See New Monthly Mag., 1822

Sh— Autograph . . .

[Autograph] The most correct copies of all
the authentic autographs. Copied . . .
and enlarged to four times the original
size upon the same sheets by J. Harris.
Ln : T. Rodd, 1 Sept., 1843. 4°
BPL | BUS

[Autograph] Memorials of Sh—. Comprising the poet's will . . . Indentures of conveyance and mortgage . . . With annotations by H. Staunton. Ln : Day & Son
[1864]. F°, ff. 19   BPL | BUS | CPL | SML

[Autograph] Facsimile of the deed of bar-
gain and sale of Sh—'s Blackfriars estate
. . . [Edited, with a preface, by J. O.
Halliwell-Phillipps]. Brighton : Printed
for private circulation, 1884. F°, pp. 6
Issue restricted to fifty copies.   BM | BPL

Autograph signature to a deed of purchase
of a house in Blackfriars, 10 March,
1612-13 [Facsimile prepared for the
library committee of the Ln. Corpora-
tion]. Ln : 1896. F°, single sheet
BM | BPL

[Autograph] Facsimiles of five authentic
autograph signatures of the poet . . .
Ln : Smith . . . 1899. Cr. 8°, pp. 12

[Autograph] Hall (A.) Sh—'s handwriting
further illustrated. With facsimiles. Ln :
Asher, 1899. 8°, pp. 16

[Autograph] Signature as a marriage witness in parish register of Saint Martin
Carfax, Oxford. See Jaggard

Autograph references—
See Bigsby   See Madden
  „ Bookmart   „ Malone
  „ Broughton   „ Sh— Works, 1778
  „ Catalogue, 1862   „ Sh—] Drake
  „ Chamberlain   „ Sh—] Hall
  „ Frey   „ Sh—] Halliwell
  „ Furnivall   „ Sh—] Lambert
  „ Günther   „ Sh—] Memorials
  „ Indenture   „ Sh—] Sharpe
  „ Leisure Hour   „ Smith (J. T.)
  „ Levi   „ Theobald
  „ Macray   „ Wise

Ballad upon the Spanish armada—
See Deloney
  „ Chettle
  „ Halliwell, Discovery . . .

BIRTH OF MERLIN.

*No edition of this play is known anterior
to that printed by Thomas Johnson in 1662.
The authorship has been assigned to the
joint hands of Sh— and Rowley.*

Sh— Birth of Merlin . . .

Birth of Merlin, or the childe hath found his father. As it hath been several times acted with great applause. Written by William Sh— and William Rowley. *Placere cupio*. Ln: Printed by Tho. Johnson for Francis Kirkman and Henry Marsh and are to be sold at the Princes Arms in Chancery Lane, 1662. Fcp. 4°, on twenty-eight leaves, including title; sig. A to G4 in fours, unpaged

> BM | BLO | BUS | CTC | NY | W

Doubtless written by William Rowley alone.
'Sh— is said on the title-page to have assisted in this play, which is not probable from the poorness of the composition.'—*Halliwell*.

Birth of Merlin . . . [Text and notes in English and German, edited by N. Delius.] Elberfeld: R. L. Friderichs, 1856. 12° BUS | SML

Birth of Merlin . . . Ed. by K. Warnke and L. Proescholdt. Halle: Germany, 1887. 8° BUS

Birth of Merlin . . . Edited with introduction by A. F. Hopkinson. Ln: Sims & Co., 1901. 12° BPL | SML

Bottom the weaver. *See* Sh— Midsummer night's dream

CARDENIO [*otherwise* CARDENNA *or* CARDENNO].

A lost Sh— play. Twice performed by Sh—'s company at court in 1613, in the May marriage celebrations of the Princess Elizabeth, and again on the 8th of June before the Duke of Savoy's ambassador. It is believed to be a dramatised version of an episode in Cervantes' 'Don Quixote,' which appeared in English for the first time in 1612. The piece is found entered in the Stationers' Registers in 1653 by Humphrey Moseley and described as the joint production of Sh— and Fletcher, but beyond this no evidence is forthcoming as to the existence of any printed version.

See also Sh— Double falsehood

Chronicle history of Thomas Lord Cromwell. *See* Sh— Thomas . . .

Come live with me . . .

  See Choice

  ,, Sh— Passionate . . .

COMEDY OF ERRORS.

Unprinted until it appeared in the Jaggard canon of 1623. It is referred to in Gesta Grayorum (q.v.) as having been performed in Gray's Inn in 1594: is men-

Sh— Comedy of errors . . .

tioned by F. Meres (q.v.) in 1598: and named again by Decker (q.v.) in 1605. The earliest separate edition recorded was issued by J. Tonson in 1734.

Comedy of errors, by Mr. Wm. Sh—. London: Printed for J. Tonson and the rest of the proprietors and sold by the booksellers of Ln. and Westminster, 1734. 12°, pp. 60. With frontispiece BPL | W

Following the title is this definite disclaimer:—'Whereas R. Walker and his accomplices have printed and published several of Sh—'s plays, and, to screen their innumerable errors, advertize that they are printed as they are acted, and industriously report that the said plays are printed from copies made use of at the theatre,—I therefore declare, in justice to the proprietors, whose right is basely invaded, as well as in defence of myself, that no person ever had, directly or indirectly, from me any such copy or copies, neither would I be accessory on any account to the imposing on the publick such useless, pirated, and maimed editions as are published by the said R. Walker. W. Chetwood, prompter to H.M. company of commedians, Theatre Royal, Drury Lane.'

Comedy of errors . . . Now acted at the Theatre Royal in Covent-Garden. Ln: J. Rivington . . . 1770. 12°, pp. 60

> BM | BPL

Comedy of errors . . . Adapted for the stage by Thomas Hull. Ln: 1779. 8°

[Comedy of errors] Plautus. Menæcmi 1595 [In 'Six old plays on which Sh— founded his . . . "Comedy of errors," edited by J. Nichols, Vol. I.'] Ln: 1779. Cr. 8° BPL

Comedy of errors. As it is acted at the Theatres Royal in Drury Lane and Covent Garden . . . Ln: Printed for Harrison & Co., 18, Paternoster Row, and sold likewise by J. Wenman, Fleet St., and all other booksellers, 1779. 8°, pp. 16 and copperplate portrait of Brunsdon as 'Dromio of Syracuse' BM | BPL

[Comedy of errors] The twins, or which is which? A farce. In three acts. Altered [and abridged] from Sh—'s 'Comedy of errors' by W. Woods. As it is performed at the Theatre Royal, Edinburgh. Edinburgh: T. Cadell, 1780. 8°, pp. 68

> BM | BUS | W

[Comedy of errors] The twins, or which is which? . . . [by W. Woods]. Ln: 1784. 12° BM | BPL

Comedy of errors . . . printed complete from the text of Sam. Johnson and Geo. Steevens, and revised from the last editions . . . Ln: Printed for . . . John Bell . . . 1785. 12°, pp. 76, with engraved title and frontispiece of Mrs. Inchbald as the 'Lady Abbess'

[Comedy of errors] The twins, or which is which? . . . [by W. Woods]. 1786. 12°

> BM

Comedy of errors. Two sheets of this play, with notes by Joseph Ritson. Ln: 1787. 8°

[Comedy of errors] The twins . . . by W. Woods [In 'Collection of farces']. Edinburgh, 1792. 12°   BPL | BUS

Comedy of errors. With alterations from Sh—. Adapted for theatrical representation by Thomas Hull. As performed at the Theatre Royal, Covent Garden. A new edition. Ln: J. Bell, 1793. 8°, pp. 52   BPL | BUS | W
Originally issued in 1780 as ' The twins.'

Comedy of errors [An excerpt from the 'English Magazine']. 1797. 8°, pp. 52 BM

Comedy of errors. As performed at Covent Garden . . . With remarks by Mrs. Inchbald. Ln: Longman [1808]. 12°, pp. 64. With frontispiece by Neagle after Singleton   BPL | BUS

Comedy of errors, adapted to the stage by T. Hull; revised by J. P. Kemble, and now first published as it is acted at the Theatre Royal in Covent Garden. Ln: Printed for the Theatre, 1811. 8°, pp. 56   BM

Comedy of errors. Adapted . . . by Thomas Hull. Revised by J. P. Kemble, and now published as it is performed at the Theatres Royal. Ln: J. Miller, 1815. 12°, pp. 58   BM | BPL | BUS

[Comedy of errors] Music in the 'Comedy of errors' [Full score] by Sir H. R. Bishop. Ln: [1819]. F°

Comedy of errors. In five acts. With alterations, additions, and with songs, duet, glees, and chorusses, selected entirely from the plays, poems, and sonnets of Sh—. Performed at the Theatre Royal, Covent Garden. The overture and new music composed and the glees arranged by Mr. Bishop. The selections from Dr. Arne, Sir J. Stevenson, — Stevens, and Mozart [Ed. by Frederick Reynolds]. Ln: S. Low, 1819. 8°, pp. iv.-86   BPL | BUS

[Comedy of errors] Airs, duets, glees, and chorusses introduced in the 'Comedy of errors' . . . entirely selected from the plays, poems and sonnets of Sh—, etc. Ln: S. Low [c. 1820]. 8°, pp. 16 BM

Comedy of errors . . . Printed from the acting copy, with remarks . . . by D. G—— [George Daniel]. To which are added, a . . . cast of the characters . . . and the whole of the stage business, as now performed at the Theatres Royal, etc. Ln: J. Cumberland, 1829. 12°, pp. 52   BM | BPL | BUS

Comedy of errors . . . A comedy, in three acts . . . With editorial remarks, original casts, costumes, scene and property plots, and the whole stage business. Boston [U.S.]: W. V. Spencer, 1856. 12°, pp. 56   BUS | CPL

Comedy of errors . . . as arranged for the Royal Princess's Theatre, under the management of Mr. Vining. 1864. 8°   BPL

Comedy of errors. 'Lacy's acting edition.' Ln: T. H. Lacy [1866]. 12°, pp. 38   BM | BPL

Comedy of errors. A comedy, in five acts . . . Ln: S. French [late Lacy] 1866. 12°, pp. 38   BUS

Comedy of errors . . . With notes by John Hunter. Ln: Longmans, 1873. Cr. 8°   BPL

Comedy of errors . . . produced at the Alexandra Theatre [Lime St.], Liverpool, June 13th, 1881, arranged by E. Saker. Liverpool, 1881. Cr. 8°   BPL

Comedy of errors . . . Edited by W. J. Rolfe. New York: Harper, 1881. 12°   BPL

Comedy of errors . . . edited by H. N. Hudson. Boston: Ginn & Heath, 1881. 12°

Comedy of errors . . . Edited by C. E. Flower. 'Memorial theatre edition.' Stratford-on-Avon: Printed by G. Boyden [1882]. Cr. 8°, pp. viii.-60, including printed wrappers   BPL | SML

Comedy of errors. 'Standard plays.' Ln: Dicks [1883]. 12°, pp. 16   BM

'Comedy of errors,' produced by Robson & Crane. Prospectus. Detroit, U.S. [c. 1885]. 8°   BPL

Comedy of errors. Ed. by W. J. Rolfe. New York, 1886. 16°   BUS

Comedy of errors . . . With a pleasant and fine conceited comoedie, called Menechmus, taken out of the most excellent poet Plautus. [With introduction by Henry Morley.] 'National library.' Ln: Cassell, 1889. 16°, pp. 192   BM

Comedy of errors. [Ed. by Henry Morley.] Ln: Cassell, 1892. 16°, pp. 192

Comedy of errors. With preface and glossary by I. Gollancz. Ln: J. M. Dent, 1894. 12°

Comedy of errors. 'Pocket Falstaff edition.' Ln: Bliss, Sands, 1898. 16°, pp. 76   BPL | SML

Comedy of errors . . . Edited with introduction and notes by C. H. Herford. 'Eversley edition.' Ln: Macmillan, 1900. Cr. 8°   BPL

Sh— Comedy of errors . . .

Comedy of errors . . . Abridged and edited by Sarah Willard Hiestand. 'Beginner's Sh—.' Boston [U.S.]: Heath, 1901. 8°. Illustrated   BPL | BUS

Comedy of errors. Ed. by W. J. Rolfe. New York [1902]. 8°. Illustrated BUS

Comedy of errors. Introduction and notes by John Dennis. Illustrated by B. Shaw. 'Chiswick edition.' Ln : Bell, 1902. 12°

Comedy of errors. Introductory notes by W. J. Craig. Ln : Methuen, 1903. 32°

Comedy of errors. Ed. with notes by H. N. Hudson. 'Windsor edition.' Edinburgh : Jack, 1903. 8°, pp. 74

Comedy of errors. 'Ellen Terry edition.' Glasgow : Bryce, 1904. 32°

Comedy of errors. Introduction by G. Brandes. 'Favourite classics.' Ln : Heinemann, 1904. 12°

Comedy of errors. 'Waistcoat pocket edition.' Ln : Treherne, 1905. 32°

Comedy of errors. Ed. by H. Morley. 'National library.' Ln : Cassell, 1905. 16°, pp. 192   BPL

Comedy of errors . . . 'Renaissance edition.' New York, 1907. Fcp. 4°   BPL

Comedy of errors. 'Red letter edition.' Ln : Blackie, 1907. 12°

Comedy of errors. Ed. by Hy. Cuningham. 'Arden edition.' Ln : Methuen, 1907. 8°, pp. 228

Comedy of errors. Ed. by W. G. Boswell-Stone. 'Old spelling edition.' Ln : Chatto, 1908. Fcp. 4°   BPL

'Comedy of errors' references—

See Decker   See Meres
,, Gesta Grayorum   ,, O'Brien
,, Giacomo   ,, Plautus
,, Gray   ,, Rowlands
,, Johnson & Steevens   ,, Shirley
,, Lennox   ,, Six . . .
,, Manningham

COMPENDIOUS . . . EXAMINATION.

Attributed to Sh— on account of the identity of initials. The writer was William Stafford, and the subject political economy.

Compendious or briefe examination of certayne ordinary complaints, of diuers of our country men in these our dayes : which although they are in some part vniust and friuolous, yet are they all by way of dialogues throughly debated and discussed. By W. S., *gentleman*. [*Coat of arms*.] Imprinted at Ln. in Fleetstreate, neere vnto Saincte Dunstones Church by Thomas Marshe, 1581. Fcp. 4°, on fiftynine unpaged leaves   BUS | W

Sh— Compendious . . .

The running head-title reads :—'A briefe conceipte of English pollicy.'
A copy so lettered on the morocco binding is at Warwick.

Compendious or briefe examination of certayne ordinary complaints of diuers of our countrymen in these our dayes : which although they are in some parte vnjust and friuolous, yet are they all, by way of dialogue, throughly debated and discussed by William Sh—, *gentleman*. Imprinted at Ln. . . . by T. Marshe, 1581. Reprinted by Charles Marsh and Λ. Jackson, 1751. 8°, pp. x.-10-120   BM | BUS | SML

The reference by Stafford in the dedication to Queen Elizabeth to ' her clemency in pardoninge certayne my vndutifull misdemeanour' (he having been engaged in a conspiracy against her), has led the editors to ascribe the work to Sh—, on the assumption that his supposed deer-stalking was the offence referred to.

Compendious . . . examination . . . 1581 [In 'Harleian Miscellany,' Vol. 9]. Ln : 1812. 4°   BPL

Compendious or briefe examination of certayne ordinary complaints . . . With introduction by Frederic D. Matthew. Ed. by F. J. Furnivall. Ln : New Sh— Soc., 1876. 4°, pp. xx.-114   BM | BPL | BUS

Concerning the honour of bookes. *See* Montaigne, Essayes, 1613

CORIOLANUS.

This tragedy appeared in print for the first time in the Jaggard folio of 1623. Nahum Tate's adaptation of 1682 is the first known separate edition, while Tonson's printing of 1734 is the first separate issue with unadulterated text.

[Coriolanus] The ingratitude of a commonwealth, or the fall of Caius Martius Coriolanus. As it is acted at the Theatre-Royal. [Adapted from Sh—] By Nahum Tate. Ln : Printed by T. M—— for Joseph Hindmarsh, 1682. Fcp. 4°, pp. viii.-64   BM | BPL | BUS | W

In the 'Epistle dedicatory' to Charles Marquess of Worcester, Tate says he has 'launch't out in Sh—'s Bottom,' and intends the play as a lesson and rebuke to the political parties of the day.
The fifth act is wholly by Tate.

[Coriolanus] The invader of his country, or the fatal resentment. A tragedy. As it is acted at the Theatre Royal in Drury Lane. By His Majesty's servants. By Mr. [John] Dennis. Ln : J. Pemberton & J. Watts, 1720. 8°, pp. xvi.-80   BPL | BUS | W

Somewhat less than half of the play is from 'Coriolanus.'

[Coriolanus] The invader of his country:
or the fatal resentment. A tragedy. By
Mr. [John] Dennis. Second edition. 1721.
8°   w

Coriolanus . . . Ln : J. Tonson, 1734. 12° BPL
Coriolanus . . . Ln : R. Walker, 1735. 12°
                                                    BPL

Coriolanus . . . With alterations by James
Thomson. Acted at Covent Garden.
Ln : 1748. 8°

Coriolanus. A tragedy. As it is acted at
the Theatre Royal in Covent Garden.
By the late James Thomson. Ln :
Printed for A. Millar, at Buchanan's
Head in the Strand, 1749. 8°, pp. iv.-62
                                          BPL | BUS

This posthumous play was presented 13 Jan., 1749,
the leading part being taken by Quin, friend of
Thomson. Quin is said to have broken down on
reaching these lines in Lyttelton's prologue :—
  ' Not one unmoral, one corrupted thought,
   One line which, dying, he could wish to blot.'

        .   .   .   .   .

The proceeds were sent to Thomson's sisters.

Coriolanus . . . An opera. [*Sans place or
printer*] 1749. 8°

Coriolanus . . . Adapted by James Thomson. Dublin : Ewing, 1754. 8°   BPL

Coriolanus, or the Roman matron. A
tragedy [by Thomas Sheridan]. Taken
from Sh— and Thomson. As it is acted
at the Theatre-Royal in Covent-Garden.
To which is added, the order of the
ovation. Ln : A. Millar, 1755. 8°, pp.
vi.-78   BM | BPL | BUS |w

Coriolanus . . . Adapted by James Thomson.
Ln : 1757. 12°

Coriolanus . . . Taken from Sh— and
Thomson [by T. Sheridan]. Dublin,
1757. 12°   BPL

Coriolanus : A tragedy [In ' Works of
James Thomson,' 4 vols.] Ln : A. Millar,
1762. Cr. 8° ; occupies pp. 203 to 288
of Vol. 4, with copperplate eng. by G. V.
Neist

Coriolanus. A tragedy. . . As it is now
performed at the theatres in London and
Dublin. Dublin : Printed for R. Watts
& W. Whitestone in Skinner Row, 1762.
12°

Coriolanus . . . As performed at the Theatre
Royal, Drury Lane. Regulated from the
prompt book, with permission of the
managers, by Mr. Hopkins, prompter.
An introd. and notes, critical and illustrative, added . . . [by F. Gentleman].
Ln. : John Bell ; York : C. Etherington,
1773. 8°. With frontispiece

Excerpt, pp. 227-312.
Part of Bell's ed. of the works issued separately for
theatre-goers.

Coriolanus. A tragedy. As it is acted at
the Theatres-Royal in Drury-Lane and
Covent-Garden. Ln : Harrison & Co.,
1780. 8°, pp. 22   BM | BPL
With frontispiece portrait of ' Mr. Sheridan in the
character of Coriolanus.'

Coriolanus . . . Altered from Sh— by Mr. T.
Sheridan. [1780 ?] Cr. 8°   BPL

Coriolanus ; or, the Roman matron. A
tragedy. Altered from Sh—. Printed
exactly conformable to the representation
at the Theatre Royal, Drury Lane.
With the order of the ovation. By permission of the managers, under the inse-
spection [*sic*] of James Wrighten, prompter. Ln : J. Christie, 1789. 8°, pp. 80
                                  BPL | BUS | W

In the dramatis personæ Kemble takes the part of
' Coriolanus ' and Mrs. Siddons that of ' Volumnia.'
A stage adaptation rather than an alteration, mainly
agreeing with Kemble's version (published later),
which was probably altered from Sheridan's edition,
in turn founded partly on Thomson's.

Coriolanus . . . [In ' Works of James
Thomson,' Vol. 3, pp. 237-310]. Ln :
1798. 12°   BPL

Coriolanus . . . Edited by J. P. Kemble.
Ln : C. Lowndes [c. 1800]. 8°

Coriolanus . . . Adapted to the stage. With
additions from Thomson, by J. P. Kemble,
as acted at Drury Lane Theatre. Ln :
1801. 8°

Coriolanus, or the Roman matron. A historical play. Adapted to the stage, with
additions from Thomson by J. P. Kemble,
and now first published as it is acted at
the Theatre Royal in Covent Garden.
Ln : Printed [by S. Gosnell] for Longman,
Hurst, Rees & Orme, Paternoster Row,
and sold in the Theatre, 1806. 8°, pp.
66   BPL | W

Coriolanus . . . In five acts. As performed
at the Theatre Royal, Covent Garden.
Printed . . . from the prompt book.
With remarks by Mrs. Inchbald. Ln :
[Printed by Savage & Easingwood for
Longman [1808]. 12°, pp. 70 and frontis-
piece   BPL | BUS

Coriolanus . . . Adapted to the stage, with
additions from Thomson by J. P. Kemble,
and published as it is acted at the Theatre
Royal, Covent Garden. Ln : For the
Theatre, 1812. 8°, pp. 62   BPL | BUS

Coriolanus ; a historical play . . . As performed at the Theatres-Royal, Drury
Lane and Covent Garden. Printed under
the authority of the managers from the
prompt books . . . Edinburgh : Oliver &
Boyd [1813 ?] 12°, pp. 54
Published at 6d. in printed blue wrappers.

Sh— Coriolanus . . .

Coriolanus, or the Roman matron ; Adapted to the stage, with additions from Thomson, by J. P. Kemble, and now published as it is performed at the Theatres Royal. Ln : J. Millar, 1814.   12°, pp. 64

BM | BPL | BUS | W

Coriolanus . . . Printed complete from the text of Samuel Johnson and George Steevens. Ln : 1818. 16°   W

[Coriolanus] Senarii Græci [A translation by H. Waddington from 'Coriolanus,' in English and Greek]. Cambridge, 1819. 8°   BM

Coriolanus. An historical play. From the prompt copy of the Theatre Royal, Drury Lane. [Edited by R. W. Elliston.] Ln : J. Tabby, Theatre Royal, 1820. 12°, pp. viii.-62   BM

The play is preceded on p. viii. by an 'Ode of triumph.' The preface deals with the difficulty of staging and costuming this tragedy.

Elliston says :—To represent ' Coriolanus' in its original form would, from the length of the play, be impossible. But though we cannot bring upon the stage all that the great poet has written, there yet appears no just cause for interpolating his text with the works of others. Any alteration but that of omission seems a sin against the majesty of our poet. . . . The ' Coriolanus' of the modern edition is very freely interpolated with extracts from Thomson.

Coriolanus . . . With prefatory remarks [signed P. P.] . . . Marked with the stage business and stage directions, as it is performed at the Theatres Royal, by W. Oxberry. Ln : 1820. 8°, pp. iv.-62 BM | BPL

Coriolanus. ' Oxberry's edition.' Boston [U.S.] 1822. 24°   BUS

Coriolanus . . . Printed from the acting copy, with remarks, biographical and critical, by D. G. [i.e. Geo. Daniel]. To which are added a . . . cast of the characters . . . and the whole of the stage business, as now performed at the Theatres Royal. Ln : J. Cumberland [1824]. 12°, pp. 58

Published at 6d.   BM

Coriolanus . . . Ln : Published and sold by Vernor & Hood ; Newcastle-on-Tyne ; printed by and for J. Mitchell [c. 1825]. 12°   BPL

Coriolanus . . . 'Cumberland's British theatre.' Ln : [1831 ?] 12°   BPL

Coliolan : Tragédie . . . accompagnée de notes grammaticales et explicatives, par M. Corréard. Coriolanus : A tragedy . . . [In English and French]. Paris : C. Hingray, 1845. 12°, pp. viii.-152   BM

Coriolanus travestie.   A burlesque by James Morgan.   Liverpool : Hurton, 1846. 8°

Published at 1s.

Apparently the first Liverpool Shakespearean publication, and rather unworthy of the occasion.

Sh— Coriolanus . . .

Coriolanus . . . Printed from the acting copy, with remarks . . . by D. G—— [George Daniel] . . . ' Lacy's acting edition.' Ln : T. H. Lacy, 1850. 12°   BM

Coriolanus [The text juxtalinear in French and English. Translated and annotated by C. F—— (C. Fleming)]. Paris : L. Hachette & Cie, 1850. 8°, pp. xviii.-662

BM | BUS

Coriolanus, or the Roman matron . . . In five acts. With original casts, costumes and all the stage business. As performed at the principal theatres in the United States. Marked and arranged by J. B. Wright, assistant manager, Boston Theatre. Boston [U.S.] : W. V. Spencer [1855]. 12°, pp. 50   BUS

Coriolanus . . . In five acts . . . With original casts . . . arranged by J. B. Wright. New York : S. French [1855]. 12°, pp. 50 BUS

A reprint of the Boston 1855 edition, with changed title and introductory pages.

Coriolanus.   'Spencer's theatre.'   Boston [U.S.] : Spencer, 1860. 12°

Coriolanus . . . Edited by F. A. Leo . . . With a quarto-facsimile of the tragedy of 'Coriolanus' from the folio of 1623, photolithographed by A. Burchard, and with extracts from North's ' Plutarch.' Ln : J. R. Smith, 1864. Fcp. 4°, pp. x.- 128-30-10, and Droeshout portrait

BM | BPL | BUS

' The proceeds of the sale will be appropriated towards the Sh— monument.'

Coriolanus.   Leipzig : Tauchnitz, 1868. Cr. 8°

Coriolanus . . . With notes by J. Hunter. Ln : Longman, 1869. 12°

Coriolanus.   With illustrative notes and extracts from the history on which the play is founded, by John Hunter. Ln : Longmans, 1870. 8°, pp. xxviii.-154

Coriolanus . . . ' Lacy's acting edition.' Ln : Lacy [c. 1870]. 12°   BPL

Coriolanus . . . Edited by R. Whitelaw [with glossary]. ' Rugby edition.' Ln : Rivingtons, 1872. Cr. 8°, pp. xvi.-156

BUS | MPL

Coriolanus.   With notes prepared for the Oxford and Cambridge local examinations. Ln : Allman & Son [c. 1875]. 8°, pp. 130

Coriolanus . . . With notes, etc. by J. Hunter. Ln : Longman [c. 1878]. 12°   BPL

Coriolanus . . . With introduction and notes by H. N. Hudson. Boston [U.S.] : Ginn & Heath, 1878. 12°, pp. 440-550 [excerpt]

BUS

Coriolanus . . . With introd. remarks; explanatory, grammatical, and philological notes, by James Colville. Ln. & Glasgow: W. Collins, 1878. Cr. 8°, pp. 164
BM | BPL

Coriolanus. Ed. by W. A. Wright. Oxford: Clarendon Press, 1879. Cr. 8°, pp. xliv.-256

Coriolanus . . . Edited by R. Whitelaw. 'Rugby edition.' Ln: Rivington [c. 1880]. 12°
BPL

Coriolanus . . . Arranged especially for school use by H. Irving. Edited by W. H. Baker. Ln: Wightman & Co., 1880. 8°, pp. 38
BM

[Coriolanus] 'Hamnet Sh: Part VI.' The tragedy of 'Coriolanus,' according to the first folio (spelling modernised), with introduction (including two phototypes) and relative lists by A. P. Paton. Ln: Longmans, 1880. 8°, pp. lxx.-106
SML

Coriolanus . . . Ed. by Dr. W. A. Wright. Oxford: Clarendon Press, 1880. Cr. 8°, pp. xliv.-256

Coriolanus . . . Edited by W. A. Wright. Oxford: Clarendon Press, 1881. 8°, pp. xliv.-256
BPL

Coriolanus . . . With notes for Oxford and Cambridge examinations. Ln: Allman, 1881. 12°
BUS

Coriolanus . . . With introduction and notes . . . by H. N. Hudson. 'Annotated English classics.' Boston [U.S.]: Ginn & Heath, 1881. 8°, pp. 222
BM | BPL

Coriolanus . . . Edited with notes by W. J. Rolfe. New York, 1882. 12° BPL | BUS
Author's proof-sheets at Boston, U.S.

Coriolanus . . . Edited by W. A. Wright. Oxford: Clarendon Press, 1883. Cr. 8°
SML

Coriolanus . . . 'Dicks' standard plays.' Ln: John Dicks, 1883. 12°
BM

Coriolanus . . . 'School edition.' Ln. & Edin.: W. & R. Chambers, 1884. Cr. 8°, pp. ii.-128

Coriolanus. Ed. by W. A. Wright. Oxford: Clarendon Press, 1884. Cr. 8°, pp. xliv.-258

Coriolanus . . . With introduction . . . glossary . . . and appendix . . . by John W. Allen. Ln: Longmans, 1885. 8°, pp. xvi.-208. Illustrated
BM | BUS

Coriolanus. With illustrative and explanatory notes and numerous extracts from the history on which that play is founded, by John Hunter . . . Ln: Longmans, Green & Co. [c. 1885]. Cr. 8°, pp. xxviii.-154

[Coriolanus] Sh—'s Coriolan. Für den Schulgebrauch bearbeitet von Dr. E. Fritsche [In English and German]. Leipzig: O. Wigand, 1885. 8°, pp. 128
BM

Coriolanus. Ed. by W. A. Wright. Oxford: Clarendon Press, 1886. Cr. 8°, pp. xliv.-258

Coriolanus . . . Ed. with notes by W. J. Rolfe. New York, 1886. 16° BUS

Coriolanus . . . With introduction and notes. 'Oxford & Cambridge Shakespeare.' Ln: G. Gill, 1886. 12°, pp. 148. Illust.
BM | BPL

Coriolanus . . . With notes, examination papers, and plan of preparation. Ln. & Edinburgh: W. & R. Chambers, 1887. 8°, pp. 132
BM | BPL

Coriolanus [With an introduction by H. Morley]. 'National library.' Ln: Cassell, 1888. 16°, pp. 192
BM

Coriolanus. Ed. by Henry Irving. Oxford: Clarendon Press [c. 1890?] Cr. 8°

Coriolanus . . . Edited by H. C. Beeching. 'Falcon edition.' Ln: Rivington, 1890. 12°
BPL

Coriolanus . . . Edited by C. E. Flower. 'Memorial theatre edition.' Stratford-on-Avon: printed by G. Boyden; Ln: S. French [1890]. Cr. 8°, pp. viii.-108
BPL

Coriolanus . . . With introduction and notes. Ln: Macmillan, 1891. 12°

Coriolanus. Ed. by W. A. Wright. Oxford: Clarendon Press, 1891. Cr. 8°, pp. xliv.-258

Coriolanus. 'Oxford & Cambridge series.' Ln: Gill, 1891. Cr. 8°

Coriolanus . . . Edited with notes by B. Dawson. 'University Shakespeare.' Ln: R. Sutton, 1891. 12°
BPL

Coriolanus. Ed. by H. C. Beeching. Ln: Longman, 1891. Cr. 8°

Coriolanus . . . With notes . . . Edinburgh: Chambers, 1892. 8°, pp. 132

Coriolanus . . . With introduction and notes by W. Dent. 'Junior school Shakespeare.' Ln: Blackie, 1893. 12°
BPL

Coriolanus . . . Edited by W. A. Wright. Oxford: Clarendon Press, 1893. Cr. 8°, pp. xliv.-258
BPL

Coriolanus . . . With introduction and notes by K. Deighton. Ln: Macmillan, 1894. 12°
BPL

Coriolanus . . . Edited with introduction and notes by T. Page. Ln: Moffatt, 1894. Cr. 8°
BPL

Sh— Coriolanus . . .

Coriolanus. Ed. by H. C. Beeching. 'Falcon edition.' Ln: Longmans & Co., 1894. Cr. 8°, pp. xvi.-172

Coriolanus. Ed. by H. C. Beeching. 'Falcon edition.' Ln: Longmans, 1894. Cr. 8°, pp. 172

Coriolanus. With notes, examination papers and plan of preparation, by Alex. M. Trotter. Ln. & Edinburgh: W. & R. Chambers, 1894. Cr. 8°, pp. 132

[Coriolanus] Coriolan. Avec une notice littéraire et des notes par J. Sévrette [In English and French]. Paris: Bélin frères, 1895. 12°, pp. 184   BM

Coriolanus. Ed. by I. Gollancz. 'Temple edition.' Ln: Dent, 1896. 16°, pp. 204   BUS

Coriolanus . . . Edited by R. F. Cholmeley. 'School Sh—' [Gen. Ed., J. Churton Collins]. Ln: Arnold [1897]. 12°, pp. xxviii.-172   BPL

Coriolanus . . . Edited by Edmund K. Chambers. 'Warwick Sh—.' Ln: Blackie, 1898. 12°, pp. 250   BPL

Coriolanus. With intro. notes by W. Dent. Ln: Blackie, 1898. 12°

Coriolanus. 'Pocket Falstaff edition.' Ln: Bliss, Sands, 1898. 16°, pp. 144   BPL | SML

Coriolanus. Introd. and notes by John Dennis. Illust. by B. Shaw. 'Chiswick edition.' Ln: Bell, 1900. 12°, pp. 178

Coriolanus . . . Edited with introduction and notes by C. H. Herford. 'Eversley edition.' Ln: Macmillan, 1900. 12°   BPL

Coriolanus. With introd. and footnotes by W. J. Craig. 'Little quartos.' Ln: Methuen, 1904. 16°

Coriolanus. Ed. by E. K. Chambers. 'Warwick edition.' Ln: Blackie [1904]. Cr. 8°, pp. xviii.-232

Coriolanus. Ed. by H. Morley. 'National library.' Ln: Cassell, 1905. 16°, pp. 192   BPL

Coriolanus. 'Waistcoat pocket edition.' Ln: Treherne, 1905. 32°

Coriolanus. Ed. for . . . students by A. W. Verity. Cambridge: Univ. Press, 1905. 8°, pp. xxxvi.-308   BPL

Coriolanus. Ed. by W. A. Wright. Oxford: Clarendon Press, 1905. Cr. 8°, pp. xliv.-256

Coriolanus. Ed. by Stanley Wood. Ln: Gill & Sons [1906]. Cr. 8°, pp. lxiv.-240. Illustrated   BPL

Coriolanus . . . Ed. by Benjamin Dawson. Ln: R. Sutton, 1907. Cr. 8°

Coriolanus . . . 'Plain text edition.' Ln: Chambers, 1907. Cr. 8°   BPL

Sh— Coriolanus . . .

Coriolanus . . . 'Texts without notes.' Ln:' Chambers, 1908. Cr. 8°, pp. 96

Coriolanus. With introduction by 'S. Lee.' 'Renaissance edition.' Ln: Harrap, 1909. Fcp. 4°   BPI

'Coriolanus' references—

See Barnett (T. D.)

,, Beaumont & Fletcher

,, Cornucopia

,, Halliwell

,, Johnson & Steevens

,, Junius . . .

,, Kemble

,, Latham

,, Leo

,, On . . .

,, Parr

,, Pemberton

,, Plutarchus

,, *Sh*—] Urwick

,, Sidgwick (H.)

,, Spiers

,, Universal

,, Wood (S.)

———

Crownes haue their compasse . . . *See* James I. of Eng.

CUPID'S CABINET UNLOCK'T.

Except for extracts from the poet, this cannot be numbered among Sh—'s productions. It appears to have been reprinted under the title of the 'Academy of compliments.'

Cupid's cabinet unlock't, or the new accademy of compliments. Odes, epigrams, songs and sonnets, poesies, presentations, congratulations, ejaculations, rhapsodies, etc. With other various fancies. Created partly for the delight but chiefly for the use of all ladies, gentlemen, and strangers who affect to speak elegantly or write queintly. By W. Sh—. [Ln: Humphry Moseley, c. 1645.] 12°, pp. ii.-148   BUS (impft.)

The Boston copy lacks printer's name, place, and date. It wants pp. 33-56 and all after p. 148.

Bound up with it is a fragment of another work, printed in the same style, the headline of which is the 'Art of courtship.'

[Cupid's cabinet . . .] Academy of compliments, enriched with many witty poems and pleasant songs, excellent similitudes, comparisons, fancies, devices, and delightful fictions. Ln: 1655. 8°

[Cupid's cabinet . . .] Academy of compliments . . . Ln: 1670. 8°

[Cupid's cabinet . . .] Academy of compliments . . . Ln: 1680. 8°

Sh— Cupid's cabinet unlock't . . .

[Cupid's cabinet . . .] Academy of compliments . . . songs, catches . . .witty dialogues . . . discourses amorous and jovial,
by refined wits. Ln: P. Parker, 1684.
8°

At p. 261 occurs Sh—'s ' Under the greenwood tree.'

[Cupid's cabinet . . .] Academy of compliments . . . Ln: 1713. 8°

CYMBELINE.

*The first known printing of this tragedy
is to be found in the Jaggard folio of 1623,
and the first separate edition was issued by
Jacob Tonson in 1734. An adaptation
appeared as early as 1682.*

[Cymbeline] The injured princess, or the
fatal wager. As it was acted at the
Theatre Royal by His Majesties servants.
By Thomas Durfey . . . Ln: Printed
for R. Bentley and M. Magnes in Russel
Street in Covent Garden near the Piazza,
1682. Fcp. 4°   BM | W
An adaptation of ' Cymbeline.'

Cymbeline: A tragedy. By Mr. Wm. Sh—.
Ln: Printed for J. Tonson and the rest
of the proprietors, and sold by the book-
sellers of Ln. and Westminster, 1734.
Cr. 8°, pp. 96. With engraved frontis-
piece by Lud. Du Guernier   W
Contains a piracy warning against R. Walker by W.
Chetwood at the end.

Cymbeline . . . Ln: R. Walker, 1735. Cr.
8°

Cymbeline: King of Great Britain . . .
With some alterations by Charles Marsh.
Ln: . . . 1755. 8°

Cymbeline: King of Britain. A tragedy
. . . With some alterations by C. Marsh.
As it was agreed to be acted at the
Theatre Royal in Covent Garden. Ln:
. . . [c. 1758]. 8°, pp. 82   BM

Cymbeline. A tragedy, altered from Sh—
by William Hawkins, M.A. As it is
perform'd at the Theatre-Royal in Covent
Garden. Ln: James Rivington & James
Fletcher, at the Oxford Theatre in Paternoster Row, 1759. 8°, pp. xii.-92. With
engraved frontispiece   BM | BPL | BUS | W
In the preface the adapter is engagingly frank. He
remarks:—' I have retained in many places the very
language of the author, and in all others endeavoured
to supply it with a diction similar thereunto.'

Cymbeline . . . With alterations by C. Marsh.
Ln: . . . 1759. 8°   BPL

Cymbeline . . . With alterations by David
Garrick. Ln: . . . 1761. 12°   BPL

Sh— Cymbeline . . .

Cymbeline. A tragedy. By Sh—. With
alterations [by David Garrick]. Ln:
J. & R. Tonson, 1762. 12°, pp. 78. With
rude vignette portrait on title, the latter
printed in red and black   BPL | BUS | W
' The admirers of Sh— must not take it ill that there
are some scenes and consequently many fine passages
omitted in this edition. It was impossible to retain
more and bring it within the compass of a night's
entertainment.'—*Preface.*

Cymbeline . . . With some alterations by C.
Marsh. Ln: . . . 1762. 8°

Cymbeline. A tragedy by Sh—. With
alterations by David Garrick. Ln: . . .
1767. 8°   W

Cymbeline . . . With alterations by David
Garrick. Ln: Printed for J. Rivington,
W. Strahan . . . 1770. 8°, pp. 72, includ.
engr. front. by J. June   BPL

Cymbeline. A tragedy . . . As performed
at the Theatre Royal, Drury Lane.
Regulated from the prompt book with
permission of the managers by Mr.
Hopkins, prompter.   An introduction
and notes, critical and illustrative, are
added by the authors of the ' Dramatic
censor' [F. Gentleman]. Ln., John Bell ;
York, C. Etherington, 1773. 8°
Excerpt, pp. 231-312.
An off-print from Bell's edition of Sh— for the use of
playgoers. At the end is a list (2 pp.) of Bell's publications.

Cymbeline. A tragedy. As it is acted at
the Theatres Royal in Drury Lane and
Covent Garden . . . Ln: J. Wenman,
1777. 8°, pp. 22   BM | BPL | BUS | W
With an engraved portrait, as frontispiece, of 'Mr.
Reddish in the character of " Posthumous." '

Cymbeline . . . Altered by Henry Brooke.
Ln: . . . 1778. 8°
This version was never acted.

Cymbeline. A tragedy. Written by Sh—.
With alterations. Ln: 1780. 8°   W

Cymbeline. A tragedy. Altered from Sh—
by David Garrick, Esq. Marked with the
variations in the manager's book at the
Theatre Royal in Drury Lane. Ln: C.
Bathurst, 1784. 12°, pp. 70   BM | BPL

Cymbeline. A tragedy. By Sh—. Taken
from the manager's book at the Theatre
Royal, Drury Lane [by David Garrick].
Ln: . . . 1788. 8°   BPL | W

Cymbeline. A play. [*Sans place or printer
or date, but* c. 1790.] 8°, pp. 102
Probably issued for the use of theatre-goers.

[Cymbeline] The plays of ' Lear ' and
' Cymbeline.' With notes and illustrations selected from the various commentators and remarks by the editor [Am-
brose Eccles]. Dublin, 1793. 2 vols. 8°

Sh— Cymbeline . . .

Cymbeline . . . With notes and illustrations . . . and remarks by the editor [Ambrose Eccles]. Ln: G. G. & J. Robinson, 1794. 2 vols. 8°   BM | BUS | W

Cymbeline . . . Ln: Printed for the proprietors [c. 1795]. 8°

Cymbeline. A tragedy . . . With an introduction and notes . . . Ln: Printed [by assignment] for J. Barker, 1795. 8°, pp. 72   BM

Cymbeline . . . Revised by J. P. Kemble. Acted at Drury Lane. Ln: . . . 1800. 8°

Cymbeline . . . Written by Sh—. With alterations . . . Ln: . . . 1800. 12°   BPL

Cymbeline . . . Revised by J. P. Kemble, as it is acted [at] the Theatre Royal, Drury-Lane. Ln: . . . [c. 1801]. 8° BPL

[Cymbeline] 'King Lear' and 'Cymbeline' . . . With notes, etc. selected by A. Eccles. Ln: Lackington, 1801. 2 vols. 8° BPL

Cymbeline . . . from the text of Johnson & Steevens. Manchester: R. & W. Dean, 1802. 12°, pp. 98. With engraved frontispiece

[Cymbeline] The plays of 'Lear' and 'Cymbeline' [Edited by A. Eccles]. Dublin, 1805. 2 vols. 8°

Cymbeline. A tragedy . . . adapted for theatrical representation [by J. P. Kemble]. As performed at the Theatres Royal . . . Regulated from the prompt books by permission of the managers. The lines distinguished by inverted commas are omitted . . . Ln: J. Roach, 1806. 12°, pp. 72 and portrait of Miss Smith as 'Imogen'   BUS

Cymbeline . . . With remarks by Mrs. Inchbald. Ln: Longman . . . [1808]. 12°, pp. 90. With frontispiece   BPL | BUS

Cymbeline: King of Britain; A historical play. Revised by J. P. Kemble; and now first published as it is acted at the Theatre Royal in Covent Garden. Ln: Printed for the Theatre, 1810. 8° CPL | W

Cymbeline: King of Britain. An historical play. Revised by J. P. Kemble and now published as it is performed at the Theatres Royal. Ln: J. Miller, 1815. 8°, pp. 86   BM | BPL | BUS | W

Cymbeline, by Will. Sh—. Printed complete from the text of Samuel Johnson and George Steevens. Ln: . . . 1818. 16°   W

Cymbeline . . . With prefatory remarks [signed P. P.] . . . Marked with the stage business, and stage directions, as it is performed at the Theatres Royal, by W. Oxberry. Ln: . . . 1821. 8°, pp. iv.-80   BM | BPL

Sh— Cymbeline . . .

Cymbeline . . . With remarks by D—G— [i.e. Geo. Daniel]. Ln: John Cumberland, 1823. 16°
Published at 6d.

Cymbeline . . . With remarks and stage directions by W. Oxberry. Ln: . . . 1823. 12°. With portrait

Cymbeline . . . Printed from the acting copy, with remarks . . . by D. G— [George Daniel]. To which are added a . . . cast of the characters, and the whole of the stage business, as now performed at the Theatres Royal. Ln: J. Cumberland, 1829. 12°, pp. 74   BM | BPL

Cymbeline. A tragedy . . . Nuremberg . . . ; New York . . . 1839. 12°

Cymbeline: King of Britain. A play, in five acts. 'Acting edition.' Ln: T. H. Lacy [1865]. 12°, pp. 86. With plate   BM | BPL | BUS
With a bibliography, and record of its production on the London stage from 1682 to 1864, by G. Daniel.

Cymbeline . . . Act IV., Sc. 2, trans. into Greek Theocritean verse by J. A. Godley. Gaisford prize. Oxford . . . 1869. 12° BPL

Cymbeline . . . arranged for representation at the Queen's Theatre . . . 1872. 12° BPL

Cymbeline . . . Edited by John Hunter. Ln: Longman, 1872. Cr. 8°   CPL

Cymbeline . . . With notes . . . by J. Hunter. Ln: Longmans, 1878. Cr. 8°   BPL

[Cymbeline] 'Hamnet Sh— part III.':— The tragedy of Cymbeline. According to the first folio (spelling modernised). With lists of such of the emphasis-capitals . . . as were omitted by each of the second, third, and fourth folios, and of new emphasis-capitals shewn by it in each of these. Also a few remarks on the consideration due to such emphasis-capitals as may be found in obscure passages, by A. P. Paton. Edin.: Edmonston & Co., 1879. 8°, pp. xxxvi.-108, includ. printed wrappers   SML

Cymbeline . . . Edited with notes by W. J. Rolfe. New York . . . 1881. 12°   BPL | BUS

Cymbeline . . . With introduction and notes . . . by . . . H. N. Hudson. Boston [U.S.]: Ginn & Heath, 1881. 8°, pp. 224   BM | BPL

Cymbeline . . . 'Standard plays. Ln: John Dicks [1883]. 12°, pp. 32   BM

[Cymbeline] The tragedie of Cymbeline. Reprinted from the first folio, 1623, with collations of the second, third, and fourth folios, by W. J. Craig. Ln: New Sh—Society, 1883. 8°, pp. viii.-146
BM | BPL | BUS | MPL | SML

Cymbeline. The text revised and annotated by C. M. Ingleby. Ln: Printed by Robert Birbeck, Birmingham, for Trübner & Co., 1886. Fcp. 4°, pp. xxiv.-214; printed on Pirie's handmade paper
BM | BPL | BUS

Cymbeline. With notes critical and explanatory . . . by John Hunter. Ln: Longmans, 1887. Cr. 8°, pp. xii.-148

Cymbeline [with introduction by Henry Morley]. 'National library.' Ln: Cassell, 1888. 16°, pp. 192
BM

Cymbeline . . . Edited with notes by C. M. Ingleby . . . Revised and adapted for the use of schools by H. Ingleby. Ln: Trübner & Co., 1889. 8°, pp. xvi.-200
BM | BPL

Cymbeline . . . Edited by C. E. Flower. 'Memorial Theatre edition.' Stratford-on-Avon: Printed by G. Boyden [1889]. Cr. 8°, pp. viii.-108, includ. printed wrappers
BPL | SML

Cymbeline . . . With introduction by K. Deighton. Ln: Macmillan, 1890. Cr. 8°

Cymbeline . . . Edited by E. Winckler. 'Indian university series.' Madras: V. Kalyanaram Iyer, 1893. 8°, pp. xx.-282
BM

Cymbeline . . . With introduction and notes by K. Deighton. Ln: Macmillan, 1894. Cr. 8°
BPL

Cymbeline. With preface, glossary, &c. by I. Gollancz. Ln: J. M. Dent & Co., 1896. 16°, pp. xvi.-186. With frontispiece
BUS

Cymbeline . . . With introduction and notes by W. F. Baugust. 'Junior school Sh—.' Ln: Blackie, 1896. Cr. 8°, pp. 152 BPL

Cymbeline . . . As arranged for the stage by Henry Irving and presented at the Lyceum Theatre on Tuesday, 22nd Sept., 1896. Ln: Chiswick Press, 1896. 8°, pp. viii.-70, includ. printed wrappers
Large paper copy at the British Museum. BM | BPL

Cymbeline. Ed. by I. Gollancz. 'Temple edition.' Ln: Dent, 1896. 16°, pp. 200

Cymbeline . . . Edited by A. J. Wyatt. 'Warwick Sh—.' Ln: Blackie, 1897. 12°, pp. 110
BPL

Cymbeline. 'Pocket Falstaff edition.' Ln: Bliss, 1898. 16°, pp. 144
BPL | SML

Cymbeline . . . Edited with introduction and notes by C. H. Herford. 'Eversley edition.' Ln: Macmillan, 1900. 12° BPL

Cymbeline. Introd. notes by John Dennis. Illust. by B. Shaw. 'Chiswick edition.' Ln: Bell, 1901. 12°, pp. 170

Cymbeline. Edited with notes by H. N. Hudson. 'Windsor edition.' Edinburgh: Jack, 1903. 8°

Cymbeline. Edited by Edward Dowden. 'Arden edition.' Ln: Methuen, 1903. 8°, pp. 256

Cymbeline. With introduction by George Brandes. 'Favourite classics.' Ln: W. Heinemann, 1904. Cr. 8°, pp. xviii.-144. With plate of Smith as 'Iachimo'

Cymbeline . . . Introd. and notes by W. J. Craig. 'Little quartos.' Ln: Methuen, 1905. 16°

Cymbeline . . . Edited by H. Morley. 'National library.' Ln: Cassell, 1905. 16°
BPL

Cymbeline. 'Waistcoat pocket edition.' Ln: Treherne, 1905. 32°

Cymbeline. 'Renaissance edition.' New York: Harrap, 1907. Fcp. 4° BPL

'Cymbeline' references—
See Boccaccio
,, Collins (W.)
,, Eccles
,, Elze
,, Fletcher
,, Forman
,, Goddard
,, Halliwell
,, Jacox
,, Johnson & Steevens
,, Lennox
,, Martin
,, Numeration
,, On . . .
,, Pettie
,, Poetical preceptor
,, Richardson
,, Roberts
,, *Sh—*] Sh—'s library
,, Snider
,, Thiselton
,, Vaughan
,, Westward . . .
,, Windle
,, Young . . .

DOUBLE FALSEHOOD.

A double meaning lies in this title. No known record of any kind exists of the play by way of entry, manuscript, printed version, or performance, before Lewis Theobald produced it in 1728 as a precious salvage.

Sh— Double falsehood . . .

The plot is founded upon the story of Cardenio in Cervantes' 'Don Quixote.'
See also Sh— Cardenio

Double falsehood, or the distrest lovers. A play. As it is acted at the Theatre Royal in Drury Lane. Written originally by William Sh—, and now revised and adapted to the stage by Mr. [Lewis] Theobald, the author of ' Sh— restored.' Ln: Printed by W. J. Watts at the Printing Office in Wild Court near Lincoln's Inn Fields, 1728. 8°, pp. 64

BPL | BUS | SML | W

Malone attributed this play to Massinger, Farmer to Shirley, and Reed thought that Theobald himself was the writer. Reed's surmise was probably the shrewdest.

Double falsehood . . . Second edition. Ln: Printed by W. J. Watts . . . 1728. 8°, pp. 64

W

Double falsehood . . . Revised . . . by L. Theobald. Dublin: J. Hyde, 1728. 12°, pp. 58

BM

Double falsehood . . . Revised by L. Theobald. As it is acted at Drury Lane. Ln: 1740. 8°

Double falsehood . . . Revised . . . by L. Theobald. Ln: T. Lowndes, 1767. 8°, pp. xvi.-64

BM | NY | SML

Double falsehood . . . *See* Adventures . . .

Edward III. *See* Sh— King Edward the third

Epitaph on a monument erected to Sir Thomas Stanley, knight, in Tong Church, Salop, c. 1600

Preserved in a collection of epitaphs at the end of Sir Wm. Dugdale's 'Visitation of Salop, 1664,' a manuscript now at the Heralds' College.

'Not monumental stone preserves our fame,
Nor skye-aspiring pyramids our name ;
The memory of him for whom this stands
Shall outlive marble and defacer's hands
When all to time's consumption shall be geaven,
Standley for whom this stands shall stand in heaven.

*   *   *

The west side says :—
' Ask who lyes here but do not weep,
He is not dead, he doth but sleepe ;
This stony register is for his bones,
His fame is more perpetuall than stones,
And his own goodness with himself being gone
Shall lyve when earthlie monument is none.'

*   *   *

In the latter lines is a thought which recurs in 'King Henry VIII.' :—
' And when old time shall lead him to his grave
Goodness and he fill up one monument.'
The opening of the second stanza is reminiscent of the verse on John Combe (who lies in Stratford Parish Church chancel), attributed to Sh— :
' If any man ask who lies in this tomb . . .'
Another manuscript version exists (*see* Poems, 1625-60), written a generation or more before Dugdale, which also attributes these lines to Sh—.

Sh— [Epitaph] Upon one John Coombe of Stratford-upon-Aven, a notable usurer, fastened upon a tombe, that he had caused to be built, in his life-time [1614]:
' Ten in the hundred the devil allows,
But Combe will have twelve he sweares and he vowes ;
If any man asks, who lies in this tomb ?
"Oh, ho !" quoth the devil, "'tis my John-a-Combe."'
[*See* Parrot (Hy.) Epigrams, 1608 ; Camden's Remaines, 1614 ; R. Brathwaite's Remains, 1618 ; and Aubrey's Lives, ed. by Clark II., 226].
Rowe's version differs in the opening lines, thus :—
' Ten in the hundred lies here engraved,
'Tis a hundred to ten his soul is not saved. . . .'
The inscription engraved on the tomb is given in Wheler's History of Stratford, 1806, pp. 70-71.

Epitaph on Sh—'s tomb, 1616, supposed to be written by himself [Set to music]. Composed at Coughton Court, Warwickshire. 1801. F°   BPL

The well-known curse-verse which has effectually protected the poet's grave for three centuries :—
' Good frend for Iesvs' sake forbeare
To digg the dvst enclosed heare,
Blese be ye man yt. spares thes stones,
And curst be he yt. moves my bones.'
No true Shakespearean believes the poet capable of having written this doggerel, but he may have expressed a dying wish that his resting place should be undisturbed by sacrilegious sextons. Until about 1800 it was a too-common custom to remove human remains to the charnel house adjoining Trinity Church, and there burn them.

Epitaph on Elias James [In a manuscript volume of poems by W. Herrick and others, *temp.* Charles I. *Rawlinson Collection,* c. 1625]   BLO
' When God was pleas'd, the world unwilling yet,
Elias James to nature payd his debt,
And here reposeth : As he liv'd he dyde,
The saying in him strongly verified,
Such life, such death : Then the known truth to tell,
He liv'd a godly life and dyde as well.'—*Wm. Sh—*.

[Epitaph] On Sir Edward Standly. *See* Poems, 1625-60.

FAIRE EM.

Attributed to Sh—, to Robert Greene, Thomas Lodge, and Robert Wilson respectively.

'In "Faire Em," says Charles Knight, 'we look in vain for all that sets Sh— so high above his contemporaries : his wit, humour, poetry, philosophy, intimate knowledge of man, and his exquisite method.'

It can hardly be Greene's work, seeing that the author is ridiculed and attacked in Greene's 'Farewell to folly,' 1591.

It is clearly the product of some prentice hand, and in places bears a rough resemblance to 'Love's labours lost,' particularly in Act I., Sc. iv., where lovers, talking aloud to themselves, are overheard.

The play is remarkable as being the first to mention Liverpool and Manchester.

In Act III., Sc. iv. it says :—'Since

*fortune hath thus spitefully crost our hope
let vs leaue this quest and harken after our
King who is at this daie landed at Lirpoole.'*

The earliest issue known is the undated
quarto printed for T. N—— and I. W——
[John Wright] circa 1605.

It was first staged in or about 1590 by a
company to which Sh— was attached, whose
patron was Lord Strange [Ferdinando fifth
Earl of Derby].

'In this same year [1590] was produced
a play ["Faire Em"] in which although I
cannot detect Sh—'s hand as coadjutor with
its probable author, R. Wilson, he most
likely appeared as an actor. "Faire Em"
is the earliest play we certainly know of
which was acted by Lord Strange's Company. It is alluded to by Robert Greene
[the profligate parson], to whom it gave
offence, in the address to his "Farewell to
folly." '—F. G. Fleay.

The library of K. Charles II. contained a
copy bound up with 'Mucedorus' and
lettered 'Shakespeare, Vol. I.'

Phillips, Dyce, and Winstanley attri-
bute the authorship to Greene. Richard
Simpson argues that Sh— wrote it as an
allegorical attack on Greene and his school.
He tries to prove that William I. represents
Wm. Kempe, who took a company to Den-
mark, that Mountney stands for Marlowe,
Manvile for Greene, and the successful
Valingford for Sh—, while Faire Em sym-
bolises the Manchester public.

F. G. Fleay agrees in the main with
Simpson, but regards R. Wilson as the
author, Valingford as Peele, and Faire
Em as typifying the company of Queen's
players.

[Faire Em] A pleasant commodie of faire
Em, the millers daughter of Manchester:
With the loue of William the conqueror:
As it was sundrie times publiquely acted
in the honourable citie of London, by the
right honourable the Lord Strange his
seruaunts. [Printer's device.] Imprinted
at Ln. for T. N—— and I. W—— [John
Wright], and are to be solde in S. Dun-
stones Church-yarde in Fleete-streete [c.
1605]. Fcp. 4°, sig. A¹ to F⁴ in fours
(the last blank)   BLO

The only copy known measures 6¾ by 4½ in. Its title
is slightly damaged, and blank last leaf missing.

[Fair Em] A pleasant comedie of faire Em
the millers daughter of Manchester.
With the loue of William the conqueror.
As it was sundty [sic] times publiquely
acted in the honourable citie of London

by the right honourable the Lord Strange
his seruants.   Ln: Printed for Iohn
Wright and are to be sold at his shop at
the signe of the Bible in Guilt-spur Street
without New-gate, 1631.   Fcp. 4°, on
twenty-three unpaged leaves, including
title ; sig. A to F in fours (F4 being blank)
In June, 1907, a copy sold for £14.   BUS | CTC | W

Fair Em . . . the miller's daughter . . . [In
W. R. Chetwood's 'Old plays']. Dublin:
Chetwood, 1750.   Cr. 8°

Faire Em [In Sh— Works: Doubtful plays.
Ed. by Hy. Tyrrell.   See Sh— Works].
c. 1850.   8°

Fair Em . . . [Text and notes in English
and German, edited by N. Delius].
Elberfeld: R. L. Friderichs, 1874.   12°
                                           BUS

Fair Em . . . [In Simpson, 'School of Sh—,'
q.v.] Ln: Chatto, 1878. 2 vols. 8° SML

[Faire Em] Comedie of Faire Em. Revised
and edited with notes by K. Warnke and
L. Proescholdt. Halle, 1883. 8° BUS

Fair Em . . . [In Brooke, 'Sh—apocrypha.'
See Sh— Works].   1908

FIFTH OF NOVEMBER.

The first printed edition known is that
issued by Baldwin & Cradock in 1830.

Fifth of November ; or the gunpowder plot.
An historical play, supposed to be written
by William Sh—.   Ln: Baldwin &
Cradock, etc., 1830. 8°, pp. iv.-114
                            BM | BPL | BUS | W
'This play is supposed to have been written by Sh—
during the short period between his retirement into
the country and his death in 1616, and about ten
years after the discovery of the plot. The reasons of
it not being published in his life-time are sufficiently
obvious.'—Advertisement.

GEORGE-A-GREENE.

The earliest known recorded version of
this was printed in 1599.   It is attributed
to Sh—'s pen by Tieck and others on the
strength of an old tradition, although the
more probable writer was Robert Greene.

[George-a-Greene] The pinder of Wakefield
. . . Ln: . . . 1599.   Fcp. 4°

[George-a-Greene] The pinder of Wakefield,
being the merry history of George-a-
Greene, the lusty pinder of the north,
briefly shewing his manhood and his brave
merriments amongst his boone companions. A pill fit to purge melancholy in
this drooping age. With the great battel
fought betwixt him and Robin Hood,
Scarlet and Little John, and after of his

Sh— George-a-Greene . . .

living with them in the woods. Full of pretty histories, songs, catches, jests, and ridles. Ln : Printed by G. P—— [George Purslow ?] for E. Blackamore in Paul's Church-yard at the Angell, 1632. Fcp. 4°
BM | BLO
Only three copies said to be known, one of which sold for £45 in June, 1900.

[George-a-Greene] History of George-à-Green, pindar of the town of Wakefield. With divers pleasant as well as serious passages in his life. Ln : . . . 1706. 8°. With curious woodcuts
A copy in May, 1897 sold for £1 17s. od.

[George-a-Greene] History of George-a-Green, pindar of the town of Wakefield, his birth, calling, valour and reputation in the country. Ln : . . . [c. 1716]. 8°
A copy in March, 1906 realised 21s.

[George-a-Greene] A pleasant conceyted comedie of George-a-Greene the pinner of Wakefield [In Dodsley's Collection of plays]. Ln : . . . 1744. 12° BUS

George-a-Greene, the pinner of Wakefield [In 'Ancient British drama, edited by Sir W. Scott']. Ln : . . . 1810. Roy. 8°
BUS

George-a-Greene the pinner of Wakefield [In Dodsley's Collection of plays]. Ln : 1825. 8° BUS

George-a-Greene the pinner of Wakefield [In Greene's Dramatic works, with notes by A. Dyce]. Ln : . . . 1831. 8° BUS

George-a-Greene the pinner of Wakefield [In ' Works of R. Greene,' pp. 249-271]. Ln : . . . 1861. 8° BPL

George-a-Greene . . . [In R. Greene's Plays and poems, edited by J. C. Collins, Vol. 2, pp. 159-218]. Oxford : Clarendon Press, 1905. 8° BM | BPL

HAMLET.

Popularly accepted as the greatest play ever written. The earliest known printed version (which has barely survived the passage of time) is that of 1603, printed by N. L—— [Nicholas Ling] and published by John Trundell. It contains far fewer lines than subsequent issues. Four allusions given by Elizabethan writers prove, however, that an earlier tragedy under the same title was known to them in or before 1598.

[Hamlet] The Tragicall Historie of Hamlet, Prince of Denmarke. By William Shakespeare. As it hath beene diuerse times acted by his Highnesse seruants in the Cittie of London : as also in the two Vniuersities of Cambridge and Oxford,

Sh— Hamlet . . .

and else-where. [*Honeysuckle device.*] At London : Printed for N. L—— [Nicholas Ling] and Iohn Trundell, 1603. Fcp. 4°, thirty-three unpaged leaves ; sig. B to I⁴ in fours BM | DEVON
This immortal tragedy was first entered at Stationers Hall, 26th July, 1602, by James Roberts. Thus runs the entry :—' A booke called the Revenge of Hamlett, Prince [of] Denmark, as yt was latelie Acted by the Lord Chamberleyne his seruantes, VId.'
The British Museum copy lacks the title-page, but is interleaved, and contains MS. notes by J. O. Halliwell, along with printed extracts from subsequent editions.
The sole other copy known lacks the final leaf, and is in the Devonshire Library.
An atmosphere of romance surrounds these surviving copies. Until within so recent a period as 1856 the only known copy of the original 1603 ' Hamlet ' was that named the ' Devonshire ' copy, bound up with twelve other old plays, bought by the Duke in 1825. It formerly belonged to Sir Thomas Hanmer (*q.v.*) From his library it passed eventually to the old book firm of Payne and Foss for £180, and thence to the Duke of Devonshire for £250, although it lacked the last leaf. From the ' Devonshire ' copy William Nicol prepared a careful and accurate reprint, minus the final leaf. Over thirty years passed, until one day a Nottinghamshire youth, studying at Trinity College, Dublin, entered the shop of M. W. Rooney, a Dublin bookseller, with some old books for sale. Among these reposed another copy (unbound) of the ' unique ' 1603 Hamlet, this time lacking the title-page, but possessing the priceless last leaf. Rooney secured the copy for one shilling, reprinted the last leaf, and then sold the volume for £70 to Boone, a London bookseller, from whom J. O. Halliwell bought it for £120, and transferred it to the British Museum at a further advance, where it now rests for aye. Rooney asserted the initials of the publisher, N. L., stood for Nicholas Landure (not Ling, as is generally supposed). Landure's name does not occur in Arber's Index.
Reproduced by Payne and Foss, 1825 ; by Collier, 1858 ; by Timmins, 1860 ; by Ashbee, 1866 ; and several times subsequently.

[Hamlet] The Tragicall Historie of Hamlet Prince of Denmarke. By William Shakespeare. Newly imprinted and enlarged to almost as much againe as it was, according to the true and perfect Coppie. [*Device.*] At London : Printed by I. R— [James Roberts] for N. L— (Nicholas Ling) and are to be solde at his shoppe vnder Saint Dunstons Church in Fleetstreet, 1604. Fcp. 4°, fifty-one unpaged leaves, including title ; sig. B to O² (the latter erroneously marked G²)
DEVON | HUTH
Some passages in this version are omitted from the Jaggard folio of 1623. Together the two foregoing editions form the standard text of ' Hamlet.'
Three copies only are known. Apart from the two quoted, the third copy, from Earl Howe's collection at Gopsall, passed to an American collector in Dec., 1907, along with thirteen other early quartos, at a ransom said to be in the neighbourhood of £10,000. The size of the Howe example is 7 by 5in., bound in modern half blue morocco, and on the title occurs this manuscript addition, in an old hand, following the name WILLIAM SHAKESPEARE : ' Who (with

some errors not to be avoided in that age, had
undoubtedly a larger soule of poesie then for any of
our nation) was the first who, to shun ye pain of con-
tinuall rhyming, invented that kinde of writing which
we call blanch verse, but ye French more properly
prose mesurée, into which the English tongue so
naturally falls.'
These are the well-known words of Dryden (*q.v.*), and
it would be easy for the present owner to ascertain
whether the handwriting is his.

[Hamlet] The Tragicall Historie of Hamlet
Prince of Denmarke. By William Shakespeare. Newly imprinted and enlarged to
almost as much againe as it was, according to the true and perfect Coppie.
[*Honeysuckle device.*] London: Printed
by I. R—— [Iames Roberts] for N. L——
[Nicholas Ling] and are to be sold at his
shoppe vnder Saint Dunston's Church in
Fleetstreet, 1605. Fcp. 4°, on fifty-one
unpaged leaves; sig. B to N⁴, O¹ and O²
BM | CTC
Halliwell issued facsimiles in 1860 to prove this issue
identical with the 1604 edition, except in date, but
H. H. Furness gives a number of instances where the
two texts vary.
The British Museum copy lacks the last leaf.

[Hamlet] The Tragedy of Hamlet Prince
of Denmark. Newly Imprinted and in-
larged, according to the true and perfect
Copy lastly Printed. By William Shake-
speare. Ln: Printed by W. S. [William
Stansby ?] for Iohn Smethwicke and are
to be sold at his Shop in Saint Dunstans
Church-yard in Fleetstreet: Vnder the
Diall [1607 ?] Fcp. 4°, fifty-one unpaged
leaves; the last page is sig. N³ verso
BM | BLO | NY | W
This edition is supposed to be that entered on the
Stationers' Registers, 19th Nov., 1607.
On the contrary, Heber, Thomas Rodd, and George
Daniel assigned it to the years 1636-1637, but the
distinctive spelling, ' I ' for J and ' V ' for U, had practically passed out of common use years before that
period. No other edition is known which at all
coincides with the official entry, presuming publication really took place.

[Hamlet] Hystorie of Hamblet. London:
Imprinted by Richard Bradocke for
Thomas Pauier and are to be sold at his
shop in Corne-hill, neere to the Royall
Exchange, 1608. Fcp. 4°; black letter;
sig. A to I² in fours   CTC
Translated from the third ' Histoire ' of François de
Belleforest's collection. For an account of this issue
see Farmer, Learning . . . 1767, p. 59. Supposed to
be unique.

[Hamlet] The Tragedy of Hamlet Prince
of Denmark. London: Iohn Smethwicke, 1609. Fcp. 4°
The existence at any time of this edition is doubtful.
On the strength of Lowndes' entry of an issue bearing
this date, Halliwell inserted it in his ' Shakespeareana, 1841,' but apparently no one has ever seen a
copy.

Sh— Hamlet . . .

[Hamlet] The Tragedy of Hamlet Prince
of Denmark. By William Shakespeare.
Newly imprinted and enlarged to almost
as much againe as it was, according to
the true and perfect Coppy. [*Device.*]
At London: Printed for Iohn Smethwicke and are to be sold at his shoppe in
Saint Dunston's Church yeard in Fleet-
street: Vnder the Diall, 1611. Fcp. 4°,
fifty-one unpaged leaves; sig. B to O² in
fours, exclusive of title
BM | BLO | BUS | CTC | DEVON | HUTH
Earl Howe's copy, 7 by 5¼ in., half blue morocco, sold
for £400 in Dec., 1907.

[Hamlet] The Tragedy of Hamlet Prince
of Denmarke. Newly Imprinted and inlarged, according to the true and perfect
Copy lastly Printed. By William Shakespeare. London: Printed by W. S——
[William Stansby ?] for Iohn Smethwicke
and are to be sold at his Shop in Saint
Dunstans Church-yard in Fleetstreet:
Vnder the Diall [c. 1636]. Fcp. 4°, fifty-
one leaves, unpaged; sig. A to N⁴ in fours
(the last leaf blank)   BM | BUS | CTC
A copy in April, 1907, realised £172.

[Hamlet] The Tragedy of Hamlet Prince
of Denmark. Newly imprinted and inlarged according to the true and perfect
Copy last Printed. By William Shakespeare. London: Printed by R. Young
for John Smethwicke & are to be sold at
his Shop in Saint Dunstans Church-yard
in Fleet-street, under the Diall, 1637.
Fcp. 4°, on fifty-two unpaged leaves, including title; sig. A to N⁴ in fours
BM | BUS | CTC | NY | W
A copy measuring 7 and five-sixteenths by 5⅜ in.
realised £107 in Nov., 1906.

[Hamlet] The Tragedy of Hamlet Prince of
Denmark, as it is now Acted at His
Highness the Duke of York's Theatre.
By William Shakespeare. London:
Printed by Andrew Clark for J. Martyn
and H. Herringman at the Bell in St.
Paul's Churchyard and at the Blue
Anchor in the Lower Walk of the New
Exchange, 1676. Fcp. 4°, pp. 88
BM | BPL | BUS | W

[Hamlet] The tragedy of Hamlet prince of
Denmark. As it is now acted at his
highness the Duke of York's Theatre . . .
Ln: Printed for H. Heringham [*sic*] and
R. Bentley at the Blew Anchor in the
New Exchange . . . 1683. Fcp. 4°, pp. 88
BM | BUS | BPL | W
In the cast Betterton takes ' Hamlet.' The play is
abbreviated for stage purposes, Hamlet's instructions
to the players being marked for omission.

Sh— Hamlet . . .

[Hamlet] The tragedy of Hamlet prince of Denmark. As it is now acted at the Theatre Royal by their Majesties servants. By Wm. Sh—. Ln : H. Herringman and R. Bentley, 1695. Fcp. 4°, pp. iv.-88   BM | BPL | BUS | W
A reprint, with slight changes, of the 1676 edition.

[Hamlet] The tragedy of Hamlet prince of Denmark. As it is now acted by Her Majestie's servants . . . Ln : Richard Wellington at the Dolphin and Crown in Paul's Churchyard, and E. Rumbull in Covent Garden, 1703. Fcp. 4°, pp. iv.-82   BM | BPL | BUS | W
There are two issues of this edition which may be identified by the spelling of the name 'Barnardo' at the foot of page 1. The first spells it as above written, and has numerous errors in the text.
In June, 1904, a copy realised £11.

Hamlet, prince of Denmark. A tragedy. Written by Mr. Wm. Sh—. Ln : Printed in the year 1710. Cr. 8°   W

Hamlet . . . [Excerpt from a 'Collection of the best English plays']. 1711. 8°   BM

Hamlet . . . Ln : J. Tonson, 1712. 8°

Hamlet . . . An opera, as it is performed at the Queen's Theatre in the Haymarket. Ln : J. Tonson, 1712. 8°, pp. viii.-12   BPL

Hamlet . . . As it is now acted by his Majesty's servants. Ln : 1718. Cr. 8°   BPL

Hamlet, prince of Denmark A tragedy by Mr. Wm. Sh—. Ln : T. Johnson, 1720. Cr. 8°   W

Hamlet, prince of Denmark : A tragedy . . . Dublin : Reprinted by George Grierson at the 'Two Bibles' in Essex Street, 1721. 8°, pp. 108
Believed to be the first piece of Sh— printed in Ireland. *See* also Sh— 'Julius Cæsar' and 'Othello' of same year.

Hamlet prince of Denmark ; A tragedy as it is now acted by his Majesty's servants . . . Ln : Printed by J. Darby for A. Bettesworth in Paternoster Row and F. Clay without Temple-Bar. Price One Shilling. 1723. 12°, pp. 108, including title and half-title ; the last page bears a list of books printed for M. Poulson   BPL | CPL
In the variorum 'Hamlet,' Dr. Furness doubted the existence of this edition. Nevertheless, three different copies occurred for sale between July, 1902 and June, 1906, in addition to two in above public libraries and one in the writer's collection—six in all.

Hamlet, prince of Denmark. A tragedy . . . Revised by Mr. Pope. Dublin . . . 1731. 8°

Hamlet . . . [Excerpt from 'Life of the stage' (8 vols.), Vol. I.] 1733. Cr. 8° BPL

Sh— Hamlet . . .

Hamlet, prince of Denmark. A tragedy. As it is now acted by his Majesty's servants. Written by Wm. Sh—. Ln : Printed for J. Tonson and the rest of the proprietors and sold by the booksellers of Ln. and Westminster, 1734. Cr. 8°, pp. 108 and frontispiece by Lud. Du Guernier   BUS | W
Piracy notice at end against R. Walker.

Hamlet prince of Denmark : A tragedy. As it is now acted by His Majesty's servants . . . Ln : Printed and sold by the booksellers of Ln. and Westminster, 1736. Cr. 8°, pp. 110   BUS
A reprint of the 1734 edition, with small changes.

Hamlet . . . Ln : Printed for the trade, 1739. 12°

Hamlet . . . As it is now acted by His Majesty's servants. Ln : . . . 1743. 12° BPL

[Hamlet] Slender's ghost ; Hamlet's soliloquy imitated : A fit of the spleen in imitation of Sh—. Acted by young gentlemen at Mr. Newcombe's school at Hackney. Ln : . . . 1748. 8°

Hamlet, prince of Denmark. A tragedy. By Wm. Sh—. Collated with the best editions. Dublin : Peter Wilson, 1750. 8°   BPL | W
The original prompter's copy is at Warwick, from the Theatre Royal, Crow Street, Dublin, bearing additional interest in its interleaved manuscript notes, alterations, and additions.

Hamlet, prince of Denmark. A tragedy. As it is now acted by His Majesty's servants. Written by Wm. Sh—. Ln : Knapton [and others] 1754. 8°   W

Hamlet, prince of Denmark : A tragedy. As it is now acted at the Theatres Royal in Drury Lane and Covent Garden. Ln : Printed for T. Witford, 1755. 8°, pp. 72

Hamlet . . . As it is now acted by his Majesty's servants. Ln : Knapton . . . 1756. Cr. 8°   BPL

Hamlet, prince of Denmark. A tragedy. As it is now acted by his Majesties' servants. Written by Wm. Sh—. Ln : C. Hitch ; L. Hawes ; Rivington, 1759. 8° W

Hamlet . . . [Excerpt from a volume entitled 'Plays']. 1762. 12°   BPL

Hamlet . . . As it is now acted at the Theatres Royal in Drury Lane and Covent Garden. Ln : L. Hawes . . . [c. 1763]. 12°   BPL

[Hamlet] The tragicall historie of Hamlet prince of Denmarke. By Wm. Sh—. Newly imprinted, and enlarged to almost as much againe as it was, according to the true and perfect coppie. At Ln : Printed for Iohn Smethwicke, 1611. Steevens' reprint, 1766. 8°   BPL

Hamlet prince of Denmark. A tragedy. As it is now acted at the Theatres Royal in Drury Lane and Covent Garden. Ln: Printed for H. Woodfall, Mess. Hawes & Co., E. Johnson, W. Johnston, J. Rivington, S. Crowder, T. Longman, B. Law, T. Caslon, T. Lowndes, and C. Corbett, 1767. 8°, pp. 72 and frontispiece on copper
Hitherto unchronicled elsewhere.

Hamlet . . . Ln: Richardson . . . 1770. 8°
BPL

Hamlet . . . Altered by David Garrick. Acted at Drury Lane. Ln: Not printed . . . 1771

Hamlet, prince of Denmark. Collated with the old and modern editions [by Charles Jennens]. Ln: Printed by W. Bowyer and J. Nichols, 1773. 8°, pp. 208. Frontispiece by Hayman   BM | BPL | W

Hamlet, prince of Denmark. A tragedy . . . Collated with the old and modern editions [by Charles Jennens]. Ln: W. Owen, 1773. 8°, pp. xviii.-208. With plate   BUS

Hamlet . . . As performed at Covent Garden. Regulated from the prompt book by Mr. Younger. Second edition. Ln: . . . 1774. Cr. 8°   BPL

Hamlet . . . as now acted at the Theatres Royal in Drury Lane and Covent Garden. Ln: Printed for and sold by W. Oxlade at Sh—'s Head in George St., Old Baily, 1776. 8°, pp. vi.-62   BPL
Unrecorded elsewhere.

Hamlet . . . as performed at Covent Garden. Regulated from the prompt-book by Mr. Younger. Belfast, 1776. 12°   BPL

Hamlet . . . According to Mr. Pope's second edition. Glasgow, 1776. 12°   BPL

Hamlet . . . A tragedy . . . As it is acted at the Theatres-Royal in Drury Lane and Covent-Garden. Ln: Harrison & Co., 1779. 8°, pp. 22. With frontispiece portrait of 'Mr. Henderson in the character of Hamlet'   BM | BPL

Hamlet . . . marked with the variations in the manager's book, Drury Lane. Ln: . . . 1782. Cr. 8°   BPL

Hamlet . . . printed complete from the text of Sam. Johnson and Geo. Steevens, and revised from the last editions. Ln: John Bell . . . 1785. 12°, pp. 160. With engraved title and portrait of J. P. Kemble as Hamlet

Hamlet . . . taken from the manager's book at the Theatre Royal, Drury Lane. Ln: . . . 1787. Cr. 8°   BPL

Hamlet . . . As it is acted at the Theatres Royal. Ln: . . . [1788 ?] 12°   BPL

Hamlet, prince of Denmark. A tragedy. Written by Wm. Sh—. With the variations in the manager's book at the Theatre-Royal in Drury-Lane. Ln: . . . 1789. 8°   W

Hamlet, prince of Denmark. A tragedy. In five acts. By Wm. Sh—. As performed at the Theatre in Boston. Boston [U.S.]: Printed for David West, 36, Marlborough Street, & John West, 75, Cornhill [1794]. 12°, pp. 72   BUS
One of the first separate plays of Sh— produced in America. [See also Sh— 'Twelfth night,' 1794].

Hamlet . . . Regulated from the prompt-book at the Theatres Royal. Ln: . . . [1794]. Cr. 8°   BPL

Hamlet . . . Revised by J. P. Kemble. Acted at Drury Lane. Ln: . . . 1796. 8°

Hamlet . . . a tragedy. Manchester: R. & W. Dean, 1799. 12°. With frontispiece and woodcut by Bewick

[Hamlet] 'Doubt thou that the stars are fire?' [Song, with music. Ln: 1800 ?]. F°   BPL

Hamlet . . . Revised by J. P. Kemble, as performed at the Theatres Royal. Regulated from the prompt books. Ln: . . . [c. 1800]. Cr. 8°   BPL

Hamlet . . . Ln: Barker [c. 1800]. 12°

Hamlet . . . Revised by J. P. Kemble; and now first published as it is acted by their majesties' servants of the Theatre Royal, Drury Lane. Ln: C. Lowndes [1800]. 8°, pp. 92   BM | BPL

[Hamlet] Ophelia's airs in 'Hamlet' arranged by G. Nicks. Ln: Lonsdale [c. 1800]. F°

Hamlet . . . Manchester: R. & W. Dean, 1800. 12°   BPL

Hamlet . . . 'British theatre.' Manchester: R. & W. Dean, 1801. 12°   BPL

Hamlet . . . As performed at the Theatres-Royal. Regulated from the prompt book. Ln: . . . [1802 ?] 12°   BPL

Hamlet prince of Denmark. A tragedy. Revised by J. P. Kemble, and now first published as it is acted at the Theatre Royal in Covent Garden. Ln: J. Ridgway, 1804. 8°, pp. 84   BUS

Hamlet . . . As it is acted at the Theatre Royal in Drury Lane. Ln: J. Ridgway, 1805. 8°   BPL

Hamlet, prince of Denmark. A tragedy. . . . Printed from the text of Mr. Malone's edition. Boston [U.S.]: Printed by Hosea Sprague, 1805. 8°, pp. 112   BUS

Sh— Hamlet ...

Hamlet ... Printed complete from the text of Samuel Johnson and George Steevens and revised. Ln: ... 1806. 16°   w

Hamlet. A tragedy. In five acts ... As performed at the Theatres Royal, Drury Lane and Covent Garden. Printed under the authority of the managers from the prompt books [Ed. by J. P. Kemble]. Edinburgh: Oliver & Boyd [c. 1808]. 12°, pp. 64   BUS

Hamlet ... As performed at the Theatres Royal ∴. With remarks by Mrs. Inchbald. Ln: Longman ... [1806]. 12°, pp. 94. With frontispiece by J. Heath after R. Smirke   BPL | BUS

Hamlet travestie: In three acts. With [burlesque] annotations by Dr. Johnson and Geo. Steevens and other commentators [By John Poole]. Ln: J. M. Richardson, 1810. 8°, pp. xiv.-94   BM | BPL | BUS | W

The original holograph manuscript of this work is in the Barton Collection, Boston, U.S.

[Hamlet] Hamlet travestie: With burlesque annotations, by J. Poole. Second edition. Ln: ... 1811. 12°   BM | BPL

[Hamlet] Hamlet travestie: With burlesque annotations by J. Poole. Third edition. Ln: ... 1811. 12°   BM | BPL

Hamlet ... With the variations in the manager's book at the Theatre Royal in Covent Garden. Ln: Lowndes, 1811. 8°   BPL

[Hamlet] Hamlet travestie ... With burlesque annotations ... by J. Poole. Fourth edition. Ln: J. M. Richardson, 1812. 8°, pp. xii.-110   BPL | BUS | MPL

Hamlet: A tragedy ... Edinburgh: Oliver & Boyd [1813 ?] 12°, blue wrappers
Published at 6d.

[Hamlet] Hamlet travestie: With burlesque annotations by J. Poole. Fifth edition. Ln: ... 1814. 12°   BPL

Hamlet, prince of Denmark ... Revised by J. P. Kemble, and now published as it is performed at the Theatres Royal. Ln: J. Miller, 1814. 8°, pp. 86 BM | BUS | W

Hamlet ... put in a light entirely new ... [In 'Deverell, Hieroglyphics,' q.v.] Ln: Allman, 1816. 8°   BM | BPL

Hamlet ... With remarks by Mrs. Inchbald ... Ln: [Printed by T. Davison for] Longman ... [c. 1816]. 12°, pp. 94. With frontispiece   BPL | BUS
The plate differs from that in the 1811 edition.

Sh— Hamlet ...

Hamlet travestie: In three acts. With burlesque annotations ... By John Poole ... Sixth edition. Ln: Sherwood, Neely & Jones, 1817. Cr. 8°, pp. xii.-110   BM | BPL | BUS | W

Hamlet: A tragedy. Revised by J. P. Kemble. As it is acted at the Theatre Royal, Drury Lane. Ln: T. Rodwell, 1818. 12°, pp. 88   BUS

Hamlet ... Oxberry's edition. The only edition existing which is faithfully marked with the stage business and stage directions, as it is performed at the Theatres Royal. Ln: Published for the proprietors by W. Simpkin & R. Marshall, Stationer's Court, Ludgate St.; C. Chapple, 66, Pall Mall; and sold by W. & J. Lowndes, 9, Brydges St., Covent Garden, 1818. Cr. 8°, pp. xxviii.-84 and portrait of Kean   BM | BPL

'Hamlet' and 'As you like it.' A specimen of a new edition of Sh— [by T. Caldecott]. Ln: J. Murray, 1819. Roy. 8°, four paginations: pp. xiv.-174, 136, 116, 42   BM | BPL | BUS

Issue restricted to one hundred copies.
The British Museum possesses three copies, two of which contain copious manuscript corrections and additions by the author. Caldecott is said to have been assisted by Wm. Crowe, author of 'Lewesdon Hill.' [See 'Notes and Queries,' II. S., vi., 43].
The first edition of 'Hamlet' with the text of the 1623 Jaggard folio as a basis, and in Charles Knight's opinion a distinct advance on all previous issues.

'Hamlet' and 'As you like it.' A specimen of a new edition by T. Caldecott. Ln: John Murray, 1820. 8° BPL | BUS | SML

Hamlet travestie ... With [burlesque] annotations [by J. Poole]. New York ... 1820. 12°   BPL

Hamlet. As performed at the Theatres Royal. By W. Oxberry. Ln: 1820. 8°

Hamlet ... Ln: Barker ... [1820 ?] 12°

Hamlet ... With remarks by Mrs. Inchbald. Ln. & Paris: 1822. 12°

Hamlet ... 'Dolby's British theatre.' 1823. 12°

Hamlet ... Edited by D. G—— [Geo. Daniel] ... Ln: J. Cumberland, 1823. 12°, pp. xii.-x.-78 and plate by R. Cruikshank   BM | BUS

Hamlet ... With prefatory remarks by W. Oxberry. Ln: 1823. 12°. With portrait of Kean

[Hamlet] The first edition of the tragedy of Hamlet prince of Denmark ... Ln: Printed for N. L. [Nicholas Ling] and Iohn Trundell, 1603. Reprinted at the

Sh— Press by William Nicol for Payne and Foss . . . 1825. 8°, pp. 72 (unpaged)

BM | BPL | BUS | MPL | W

At the time this reprint appeared the only known original lacked the last leaf. By an almost miraculous recovery in a Dublin bookshop of another copy, imperfect, but possessing the precious final leaf, the hiatus in the reprint was made good at a later date. *See* Sh— ' Hamlet,' 1856.

[Hamlet] The first edition of the tragedy of Hamlet. Ln : Printed for N. L—— and Iohn Trundell, 1603. Reprinted for Ernst Fleischer, Leipsic, 1825. 8° BM | W

[Hamlet] Costume of . . . ' Hamlet.' With . . . notices by J. R. Planché. The figures by G. Scharf. Ln : J. Miller, 1825. 8°

BPL

Hamlet . . . With remarks by Mrs. Inchbald. Ln : . . . 1827. 12°

[Hamlet] Outlines to illustrate . . . ' Hamlet.' With explanations in English, German, French, and Italian. By Moritz Retzsch. Leipzig . . . ; Ln . . . 1828. 4°. 13 plates

Hamlet . . . Printed from the acting copy, with remarks by D. G—— [Geo. Daniel]. To which are added, a . . . cast of the characters and the whole of the stage business as performed at the Theatres Royal. Ln : J. Cumberland, 1829. 12°, pp. 78. Frontispiece by R. Cruikshank

BM | BPL

Hamlet . . . ' Mansell's Pocket Sh.' [1830 ?] 12°

BPL

' Hamlet ' and ' As you like it.' A specimen of a new edition of Sh—. By T. Caldecott, Esq. Second edition. Ln : [Privately] printed for the editor by W. Nicol, 1832. Roy. 8° ; five paginations : pp. xvi.+178+150+115+43+4. With facsimiles

BM | BPL | BUS | CPL | MPL | SML | W

Large paper copy at Warwick.

Hamlet . . . in English and French [with costume and stage directions]. Paris . . . 1833. 18°

Hamlet : A dramatic prelude. In five acts. By James Rush. Philadelphia : Key & Biddle, 1834. 12°, pp. 122 BPL | BUS

Intended as a preliminary to the tragedy, beginning with Hamlet's schooldays.

In the Boston copy is inserted a printed broadside bearing a severe criticism of this imitation, written apparently to satisfy some personal or professional end.

[Hamlet] Une scène d' ' Hamlet ' [The play scene from Act III., Sc. ii.] . . . traduite en vers par J. Lainé [In English and French]. Paris : Barba, 1836. 8°, pp. 26 BM

Hamlet. . . Adapted for the use of schools [by E. Slater]. Ln : . . . [1836]. 12° BPL

Hamlet . . . A new burlesque. Ln : . . . 1838. 12°

Hamlet . . . Hind's acting edition, with accurate stage directions . . . Ln : Simpkin & Co., 1839. 12°, pp. 76 BUS

[Hamlet] The barrow diggers : A dialogue in imitation of the grave diggers in ' Hamlet.' With numerous explanatory notes. Ln : Whittaker & Co., 1839. 4°, pp. 112 and 12 plates (views of Dorsetshire tumuli) BUS

Written by the Rev. C. Woods, on the occasion of opening a barrow near Shapwick, Dorset.

Hamlet . . . [1840 ?] 12°

Hamlet . . . Nouvelle édition, précédée d'une notice critique et historique et accompagnée de notes par O'Sullivan [In English and French]. Paris : L. Hachette, 1843. 12°, pp. xxiv.-188 BM

Hamlet . . . Leipzig : B. Tauchnitz, 1843. 12°

Hamlet, prince of Denmark. Grammatisch und sachlich zum schul-und privatgebrauch erläutert von J. Hoffa. Braunschweig : G. Westermann, 1845. 8°, pp. 168 BM | BUS

Text in English and notes in German.

Hamlet . . . ' Modern standard drama ' . . . With the stage business, characters, costumes . . . New York : S. French [c. 1845]. 12°, pp. viii.-8-78 BPL | BUS

Published at 12 cents.

Hamlet . . . As compressed and arranged for public reading. With notes by B. C. Jones. 1846. 12° BPL

[Hamlet] Hamlet the Dane : A burlesque burletta by C. Beckington. Newcastle-on-Tyne . . . 1847. 8° BPL

Hamlet . . . Mit sprache und sachen erläuternden anmerkungen . . . von Dr. C. L. W. Francke. Leipzig : W. Engelmann, 1849. 8°, pp. vi.-150 BM | BUS

Text in English, with notes in German.

Hamlet . . . Ten gebruike der gymnasia. Met ophelderingen voorzien door S. Susan. Deventer : J. De Lange, 1849. 8°, pp. viii.-124 BM | BUS

Text in English and notes in Dutch.

[Hamlet] Hamlet travestie : A burlesque. In two acts. Oxford : J. Vincent, 1849. 12°, pp. 60 BPL | BUS

Hamlet . . . As performed at the Theatre Royal, Haymarket, 1849. 'Acting national drama.' Ln : . . . 1849. 12° BPL

Published at 6d.

[Hamlet] Hamlet the dainty : An Ethiopian burlesque, by G. W. H. Griffin. New York . . . [1849 ?] 12° BPL

Sh— Hamlet . . .

Hamlet . . . a travesty. In two acts. Ln : Whittaker, 1849. 12°
Published at 1s.

Hamlet. A tragedy . . . Leipzig, 1849. 8°
Text in English, with notes in German.

[Hamlet] Thin slice of Ham let ! By the cooker-up of ' The duck's motto.' [1850 ?] 12°   BPL

Hamlet . . . ' Dramatic entertainments at Windsor Castle, 1848-49 ' [1850 ?] Fcp. 4°   BPL

Hamlet . . . Willoughby's edition. [1850 ?] 8°

Hamlet . . . With notes. Ln : Routledge, 1850. 8°   BPL

Hamlet ; with portrait of Mr. C. Kean as ' Hamlet,' and memoir [Part one of 'Acting edition of Sh—']. Ln : Tallis & Co. [1851]. 8°   BM
Only two parts published.

Hamlet . . . Edited by E. W. Sievers. Leipzig . . . 1851. 8°

[Hamlet] An old play in a new garb. Hamlet . . . In three acts. [By George Edward Rice.] Boston [U.S.]: Ticknor, Reed & Fields, 1852. 12°, pp. 60. Illustrated [by L. M. Sargent, jun.]   BPL | BUS

[Hamlet] Hoffman ; or a revenge for a father, by Henry Chettle, acted 1602, printed 1631. Now first edited by H. B. L[eonard]. Ln : Lacy, 1852. 12°   BPL

[Hamlet] An old play in a new garb : Hamlet . . . By G. E. Rice. Second edition. Boston [U.S.]: Ticknor, Reed & Fields, 1853. 12°, pp. 60. Illustrated   BUS

Hamlet . . . With preliminary notes. Ln : Lacy [1853]. 12°

Hamlet travestie . . . 'Acting edition.' By J. Poole. Ln : T. H. Lacy [1853]. 12°, pp. 48   BM | BUS

[Hamlet] An old play in a new garb : Hamlet . . . By G. E. Rice. Third edition. Boston [U.S.]: Ticknor, Reed & Fields, 1853. 12°, pp. 60. Illustrated   BUS

Hamlet . . . ' Lacy's acting edition.' Ln : T. H. Lacy [1855]. 12°, pp. vi.-80 BM

Hamlet . . . Edited by W. R. Chambers. Ln : . . . 1856. 12°

Hamlet ; first edition, 1603. The last leaf of the lately discovered copy, carefully reprinted. With a narrative of its discovery, remarks on its probable date, on the date of the first edition of ' Lear,' and on the pirated quartos. By W. M. R[ooney]. Dublin : W. M. Rooney, Sign of Sh—'s head, 1856. 8°, pp. 16 (the last leaf blank)   BM | BPL | BUS | MPL

Sh— Hamlet . . .

Hamlet . . . Deutsch durch Dr. F. Köhler. Leipzig : P. Reclam, jun., 1856. 16°, pp. vi.-226   BM | BUS
The first of a projected series of the plays. No more issued. English and German texts on parallel pages.

Hamlet . . . With copious English explanatory notes by Dr. O. Fiebig [Vol. I. of 'College Sh—']. Leipsic : T. Thomas, 1857. 8°, pp. vi.-232   BM
No more published.

Hamlet . . . Willoughby's cheap and popular edition. ´Ln : . . . [c. 1857]. 8°   BPL

[Hamlet] Hamlet . . . herausgegeben von K. Elze. Leipzig : G. Mayer, 1857. 8°, pp. lxiv.-272   BM | BUS
English text, with German notes.

[Hamlet] The tragicall historie of Hamlet . . . 1603. [Ed. by J. P. Collier.] Reprinted 1858. Fcp. 4°, on 33 leaves
                                      BM | BPL | BUS
A private issue, limited to forty copies, on behalf of the Duke of Devonshire, for presentation purposes.

[Hamlet] The tragicall historie of Hamlet, 1604. [Ed. by J. P. Collier.] Reprint, 1859. Fcp. 4°, on 51 leaves BM | BUS
One of the forty copies privately executed by direction of the Duke of Devonshire for presentation.

Hamlet . . . With notes, glossarial, grammatical and explanatory [for scholastic study]. Ln : Routledge & Co., 1859. 8°, pp. 126   BM | BPL | BUS

Hamlet . . . Adapted and condensed by Walter Gay [in three acts]. New York : Samuel French [c. 1859]. 12°, pp. 48
                                      BPL | BUS

Hamlet . . . Arranged for representation at the Royal Princess's Theatre. With explanatory notes by C. Kean. Ln : Bradbury & Evans, 1859. 12° BPL | SML
The editor's autograph copy is at Stratford.

Hamlet travestie, with [burlesque] annotations by J. Poole. ' Lacy's plays.' [1860 ?] 12°   BPL

Hamlet . . . [Expurgated] by T. Bowdler. 1860. 12°   BPL

Hamlet, 1603 . . . Hamlet, 1604 . . . Being exact reprints of the first and second editions of Sh—'s great drama, from the very rare originals in the possession of his grace the Duke of Devonshire ; with the two texts printed on opposite pages, and so arranged that the parallel passages face each other. And a bibliographical preface by Samuel Timmins. ' Looke heere vpon this picture, and on this.' Ln : [Printed by Josiah Allen, jun., Birmingham, for] S. Low, Son & Co., 1860. 8°, pp. xvi.-200 BM | BPL | BUS | MPL
Known as the ' Devonshire Hamlets.'
One of the two copies in the British Museum contains copious manuscript notes by J. O. Halliwell.

[Hamlet] Facsimile copies from the edition of 'Hamlet,' dated 1605, made for the purpose of showing that it is the same impression as that of 1604, the date only being altered. Edited by J. O. Halliwell. The facsimiles by Ashbee & Dangerfield. Ln : Printed for private circulation, 1860. Fcp. 4°, pp. xvi.   BM | BPL | BUS | HCL
Issue limited to 26 copies.

[Hamlet] Droll of the gravemakers. Reprinted from F. Kirkman's 'The wits, or sport upon sport,' about A.D. 1647. Edited by J. O. Halliwell. Ln : Privately printed, 1860. Fcp. 4°   BM | BPL | BUS

Hamlet . . . Leipzig : B. Tauchnitz, 1862. 16°, pp. ii.-142 and woodcut   BUS

Hamlet . . . 'Lacy's acting edition.' [1864 ?] 12°   BPL

Hamlet . . . 1623. The text from the folio of 1623. Ln : Printed for L. Booth, 1864. Fcp. 4°   BPL

Hamlet . . . 'People's penny library.' Manchester : Ireland [1864 ?] 8°   BPL

Hamlet . . . par le Chevalier de Chatelain. As performed by Salvini and his Italian Company. Ln : Rolandi, 1864. 12°   BPL

Hamlet . . . performed at the Royal Lyceum Theatre, under the management of Mr. Fechter, 21 May, 1864. [1864.] 8°   BM

Hamlet . . . With notes, extracts from the old 'Historie of Hamblet,' selected criticisms on the play, etc. Adapted for use in schools and for private study by John Hunter. Ln : Longman . . . & Green, 1865. 12°, pp. xxxviii.-164   BPL | BUS

Hamlet . . . With explanatory French notes, etc. by A. Brown. New edition, improved with new notes. Paris : J. H. Truchy, 1865. 12°, pp. 178   BM

Hamlet . . . As produced by E. Booth. 'Acting plays, No. I.' New York . . . [1866 ?] 8°   BPL

Hamlet . . . 1603. Facsimiled by E. W. Ashbee. [Ed. by J. O. Halliwell.] Ln : For private circulation, 1866. Fcp. 4°   BPL | MPL | W
Fifty copies produced, of which the editor destroyed nineteen to increase their scarcity.

[Hamlet] Hamlet the ravin' prince of Denmark, or the Baltic swell and the diving belle [a travesty]. 1866. 12°   BPL

Hamlet . . . 'Standard plays.' New and complete edition. Price one penny. Ln : J. Dicks [c. 1866]. Cr. 8°, pp. 36, includ. printed wrappers

[Hamlet] Story of 'Hamlet.' Condensed and interwoven with the text, by James Hunter. Leicester [1866 ?] 8°   BPL

Hamlet . . . 1604. Facsimiled by E. W. Ashbee. [Ed. by J. O. Halliwell.] Ln : For private circulation, 1867. Fcp. 4°   BPL | MPL | W
Fifty copies produced, nineteen of which the editor destroyed.

Hamlet . . . 1605. Facsimiled by E. W. Ashbee. Ed. by J. O. Halliwell. Ln : For private circulation only, 1867. Fcp. 4°, on ninety-nine leaves   BM | BPL | W
One of the thirty-one copies to which the impression was finally limited. The editor destroyed nineteen of the fifty copies produced.

[Hamlet] Amleto, principe di Danimarca : . . . tragedia . . . voltata in prosa Italiana da C. Rusconi. Settima edizione col testo Inglese di riscontro. Firenze : Successori Le Monnier, 1867. 8°, pp. 272   BM
English and Italian text.

Hamlet . . . Uitgegeven en verklaard door A. C. Loffelt. Utrecht [Holland] : J. L. Beijers en J. van Boekhoven, 1867. 8°, pp. viii.-202   BM
English text, with Dutch notes.

Hamlet . . . Erklärt von J. Heussi. Parchim : J. Heussi, 1868. 8°, pp. vi. - 308   BM | BUS
English text, with German notes.

Hamlet . . . Leipzig : B. Tauchnitz, 1868. Cr. 8°

[Hamlet] The bubble ghost and his son, by A. Teetgen . . . 1869. 12°   BPL

Hamlet . . . 'Acting edition.' Ln : Lacy [1869]. 12°   BPL | SML.

Hamlet . . . Edited by C. Kean. Ln : . . . 1869. 8°

Hamlet . . . By M. Carré and J. Barbier. The Italian version by A. de Lauzières . . . Translated into English by T. J. Williams. Music by A. Thomas. Ln : J. Miles & Co. [1869]. 8°   BM | BPL

Hamlet . . . Edited by J. Hunter for scholastic or private study . . . and examinations. Ln : Longmans, 1869. 12°, xxxviii.-164
Save in the title, identical with the 1865 edition.   BUS

[Hamlet] The tragicall historie of Hamlet . . . Edited according to the first printed copies, with the various readings and critical notes, by F. H. Stratmann. Ln : N. Trübner & Co. ; Krefeld : E. Gehrich & Co., 1869. 8°, pp. vi.-118   BM | BPL | BUS

Hamlet . . . 'Acting edition.' Ln : Lacy [1869 ?] 12°   BPL

[Hamlet] Sammtliche Werke. Englischer text, berichtigt und erklart von Benno Tschischwitz. Nebst historisch-kritischen einleitungen [I. Hamlet]. Halle : G. E. Berthel, 1869. 8°   BUS
English text, with German notes.

Sh— Hamlet . . .

Hamlet . . . Englisch und Deutsch. Neu übersetzt und erlautert von M. Moltke. Leipzig: A. Fritsch, 1869-71. Hefte I.-IV. 8° BM
No more published.

[Hamlet] A throw for a throne, or the prince unmasked. By . . . 'Sergeant Zinn,' with introduction and references by 'Chancery Lane.' Ln: Wilson [c. 1870]. 8°, pp. ii.-144 BUS

Hamlet . . . Edited by J. Hunter. Ln: Longman, 1870. 12°

Hamlet . . . for the use of Rugby School. [Edited by C. E. Moberly.] Rugby: W. Billington, 1870. Cr. 8°, pp. iv.-xii.-140

Hamlet, 1611. Facsimiled by E. W. Ashbee. Ed. by J. O. Halliwell. Ln: For private circulation only, 1870. Fcp. 4° BPL | W
Fifty copies printed, nineteen of which Halliwell destroyed.

[Hamlet] Plays of 'Hamlet' and 'Julius Cæsar.' Two parts. Boston [U.S.]: Perkins Institution for the blind, 1871. F°, printed on 122 folios in embossed Roman type BM | BUS

Hamlet . . . With notes and glossary by W. S. Dalgleish. 'Sh— for schools.' 1871. 12° BPL

Hamlet . . . Edited by W. G. Clark and W. A. Wright. Oxford: Clarendon Press, 1872. Cr. 8°, pp. xvi.-232 BPL
First 'Clarendon Press' edition, and forming part of a series called 'English classics.'

Hamlet . . . Edited by Charles E. Moberly. 'Rugby School edition.' Ln., Oxford, & Cambridge: Rivingtons, 1873. Cr. 8°, pp. xvi.-140 BUS | MPL | SML

Hamlet . . . Edited by W. G. Clark and W. A. Wright. Second edition. Oxford: Clarendon Press, 1873. Cr. 8°, pp. xvi.-232 BUS | CPL

Hamlet . . . As abridged and arranged for acting at the Crystal Palace by Tom Taylor. 1873. 12° BPL

Hamlet . . . As played by Salvini . . . In Italian and English. New York: George F. Nesbitt & Co., 1873. 8° BPL

Hamlet. Ed. by W. G. Clark and W. A. Wright. Oxford: Clarendon Press, 1874. Cr. 8°, pp. xvi.-232

Hamlet . . . Libretto by M. Carré and J. Barbier. Music by A. Thomas. Ln: J. Miles & Co., 1874. Cr. 8° BPL

Hamlet . . . As performed by Salvini and his Italian company. Ln: Clayton & Co., 1875. 8° BPL
Text in Italian and English.

Sh— Hamlet . . .

[Hamlet] . . . A study of 'Hamlet' [for stage representation] by E. B. H——. 1875. 8° BPL

Hamlet . . . As performed by Salvini and his Italian company. Ln: Clayton & Co., 1876. 8° BPL

[Hamlet] Amleto . . . Trad. e ridotta . . . da C. Rusconi [In Italian and English]. Ln: Theatre Royal, Covent Garden, 1876. Fcp. 4° BPL

[Hamlet] Hamlet the dainty: An Ethiopian burlesque, by G. W. H. Griffin. [1877.] Cr. 8° BM | BPL

Hamlet . . . With introductory remarks . . . notes, etc. by S. Neil. 'School and college classics.' Glasgow: W. Collins, 1877. 8°, pp. 224 BM | BPL

Hamlet . . . Edinburgh: Chambers, 1877. Cr. 8°, pp. iv.-140

[Hamlet] Plays of Sh— selected and prepared for use in schools. With introductions and notes by Henry N. Hudson. Number 3, 'Hamlet.' Boston [U.S.]: Ginn & Heath, 1878. 12°, (excerpt) pp. 511-636 BUS

Hamlet . . . With notes, etc. by J. Hunter. Ln: Longman [c. 1878]. 12° BPL

Hamlet . . . 'French's acting edition, late Lacy's.' Ln: . . . [1878 ?]. 12° BPL

Hamlet . . . As arranged for the stage by Henry Irving and presented at the Lyceum Theatre. Ln: . . . 1878. 8° BPL

Hamlet . . . As presented by Edwin Booth: The prompt book, edited by Wm. Winter. New York: F. Hart & Co., 1878. 16°, pp. 136 BPL | BUS
Printed on one side of paper only. Contains preface and appendix, but no notes.

[Hamlet] 'Hamnet edition.' The tragedy of Hamlet . . . according to the first folio (spelling modernised), with further remarks on the emphasis-capitals of Sh— by A. P. Paton. Edinburgh: Edmonston & Co., 1878. 8°, pp. xxxvi.-106 BUS | SML

Hamlet . . . Ed. with notes by W. J. Rolfe. With engravings. New York: Harper, 1878. 16°, pp. 286 BUS

Hamlet . . . Ed. by W. J. Rolfe. New edition. New York: Harper, 1878. 8°, pp. 286

Hamlet . . . Edited with notes by W. J. Rolfe. New York, 1879. 12° BPL

[Hamlet] Hamlet revamped: A travesty without a pun [by C. C. Soule]. St. Louis . . . 1879. 8° BPL

Hamlet . . . With introd. and notes explanatory and critical by H. N. Hudson. Boston [U.S.]: Ginn & Heath, 1879. 8°, pp. xviii.-258 BM | BPL

Hamlet . . . Edited by W. G. Clark and W. A. Wright . . . Second edition. Oxford : Clarendon Press, 1880. Cr. 8°, pp. xvi.-232   BPL

[Hamlet] Hamlet travestie : with [burlesque] annotations. 'Acting edition.' Ln : French [c. 1880]. 12°   BPL

Hamlet . . . Edited by C. E. Moberly. ' Rugby School edition.' Rugby : Billington [c. 1880]. 12°   BPL

Hamlet . . . as arranged for the stage by Henry Irving . . . Revised edition, with a preface by F. A. M—— [F. A. Marshall]. Eighth thousand. Ln : Chiswick Press, 1880. 8°, pp. xiv.-32   BM

Hamlet . . . traduite en prose et en vers, avec une préface et un commentaire . . . par T. Reinach. Text révise en regard. Paris : Hachette & Co., 1880. 8°, pp. xxxii.-428   BM

[Hamlet] Hamlet improved : A travesty, by G. H. Colomb. Ln : French [1880]. 12°   BPL

Hamlet . . . English and German according to the translation of A. W. von Schlegel, edited by Max Moltke. Leipzig : O. Lenz [c. 1880]. 32°, pp. 320   BM
Part of the 'Salon-Bibliothek.'

Hamlet . . . With notes, examination papers, and plan of preparation. Edited by J. M. D. Meiklejohn. Ln. & Edinburgh : W. & R. Chambers, 1880. 8°, pp. 192   BM | BPL

Hamlet . . . The first quarto, 1603. A facsimile in photo-lithography by Wm. Griggs . . . With fore-words by F. J. Furnivall. ' Sh— quarto facsimiles, No. I.' Ln : W. Griggs [1880]. Fcp. 4°, pp. xii.-64   BM | BPL | BUS | MPL

Hamlet . . . The second quarto, 1604. A facsimile in photo-lithography by W. Griggs . . . With forewords by F. J. Furnivall. ' Sh— quarto facsimiles, No. II.' Ln : W. Griggs [1880]. Fcp. 4°, pp. xx.-100   BM | BPL | BUS

Hamlet . . . Arranged for reading in schools, with notes by J. Andrew. Montreal, 1881. 12°   BPL

Hamlet . . . Ed. by W. G. Clark and W. A. Wright. Oxford : Clarendon Press, 1881. 8°, pp. xvi.-232

[Hamlet] Stories from Sh—'s plays. No. 2, 'Hamlet.' By E. J. Brett. [1881.] 4°   BPL

Hamlet . . . Edited by C. E. Flower. ' Memorial Theatre edition.' Stratford-on-Avon : Printed by G. Boyden [1882]. Cr. 8°, pp. viii.-116, includ. printed wrappers   BPL | SML
A duplicate at Birmingham is marked for playing at the Haymarket by Sir H. B. Tree.

Hamlet . . . Edited by C. Knight. Illustrated. Ln : Virtue, 1882. 8°

Hamlet, or not such a fool as he looks. Cambridge . . . 1882. 8°   BPL

Hamlet . . . Ed. by K. Elze. Halle : M. Niemeyer, 1882. Roy. 8°, pp. xvi.-258   BM | BPL | BUS

Hamlet, with notes, examination papers, and plan of preparation by Brainerd Kellogg. New York . . . 1882. 24°. With portrait   BUS

Hamlet. ' Standard plays.' Ln : John Dicks [1883 ?] 12°, pp. 32   BM | BPL

Hamlet . . . Edited with notes by W. J. Rolfe. New York : 1883. 12°   BPL

Hamlet . . . Edited by W. G. Clark and W. A. Wright. Oxford : Clarendon Press, 1883. Cr. 8°   SML

Hamlet . . . 1623. Reprinted [from the Jaggard folio] for William Ludlow. Ln : . . . 1884. 12°   BPL

Hamlet . . . Edited by W. G. Clark and W. A. Wright. Oxford : Clarendon Press, 1884. Cr. 8°   MPL

Hamlet . . . as arranged for the stage by Wilson Barrett. Represented at the Princess's Theatre, Oct. 16th, 1884. Ln : D. Bogue [1884]. 8°, pp. 96   BM | BPL | BUS

[Hamlet] The tragedie of Hamlet . . . A study, with the text of the folio of 1623, by George Macdonald. Ln : Longman, 1885. 8°, pp. xiv.-278   BM | BPL | BUS | MPL

Hamlet . . . Edited with plans for study by H. B. Sprague. Chicago . . . [1885]. 12°   BPL | BUS

Hamlet . . . ' People's penny Sh—.' Manchester . . . [1885 ?] 8°   BPL

Hamlet. With notes, exam. papers, and plan of preparation, by J. M. D. Meiklejohn. Ln. & Edin. : W. & R. Chambers, 1865. Cr. 8°, pp. 192

Hamlet . . . Lines pronounced corrupt restored and mutilations before unsuspected amended ; also, some new renderings. With preface and notes, Hamlet's 'Antic-disposition,' and an account of some Sh— classes. By Matthias Mull. Two parts. Ln : Kegan Paul & Co., 1885-88. 2 vols. 8°   BM | BPL | BUS

Hamlet . . . [With an introduction by Henry Morley] Ln : Cassell, 1886. 16°, pp. 192   BM | BPL | BUS

Hamlet . . . as arranged for the stage by Wilson Barrett . . . With notes and an introduction by C. J. Ribton-Turner. Ln : J. S. Virtue & Co. [1886]. 8°, pp. 96   BM

Sh— Hamlet . . .

Hamlet. With notes. 'Modern school series.' Ln: Cassell [1886]. 8°, pp. 62
BM

Hamlet . . . Edited by H. B. Sprague. Chicago: Winchell, 1886. 8°

Hamlet . . . Edited by Wilson Barrett. Chicago: Dramatic Publishing Co. [1886]. 8°
BUS

Hamlet . . . Edited by W. Barrett. Ln: Virtue, 1886. 12°

Hamlet . . . Arranged for stage representation from the 'famous folio of 1623' by Walter Bentley. Belfast: D. Allen & Sons [1888]. 8°, pp. 60
BM

Hamlet . . . With notes. 'School classics.' Ln:.Blackie & Sons [1888]. 16°, pp. 128
BM

Hamlet . . . With introduction, emendations, notes and appendix by D. Maclachlan. Ln: Reeves & Turner, 1888. 8°, pp. xxiv.-176
BM | BFL

Hamlet . . . With notes, etc. Edited by J. M. D. Meiklejohn. Ln: W. & R. Chambers, 1889. 12°
BPL

Hamlet . . . With notes. Ln: Allman, 1890. Cr. 8°

Hamlet . . . With notes. 'Oxford & Cambridge Sh—.' Ln: Gill [1890]. 12° BPL

Hamlet. Ed. by W. G. Clark and W. A. Wright. Oxford: Clarendon Press, 1890. Cr. 8°, pp. xvi.-256

Hamlet . . . Mit einleitung und anmerkungen von Dr. Fritsche [In English and German]. Leipzig [c. 1890]. 8°, pp. 164
BPL

Hamlet . . . C. Knight's pictorial Shakspere. 'People's edition.' Ln: . . . [c. 1890]. 8°
BPL

Hamlet. Ed. by H. Morley. 'National library.' Ln: Cassell, 1891. 16°, pp. 192

Hamlet . . . With introduction and notes by T. Page and J. Paige. Ln: Moffatt [1891]. 12°
BPL

Hamlet . . . With introd. and notes by K. Deighton. Ln: Macmillan, 1891. Cr. 8°, pp. xxxii.-292

Hamlet . . . 'Phonographic edition; National phonographic library.' Ln: Pitman, 1892. 16°, pp. 96
BM | BPL

Hamlet . . . A study for classes in English literature [with the text]. By Carroll Lewis Maxcy. Boston [U.S.]: Ginn & Co., 1892. 16°, pp. viii.-196
BM | BPL

[Hamlet] Rosencrantz and Guildenstern, by W. S. Gilbert. 'Acting edition.' Ln: T. H. Lacy, 1893. 12°
BM
A travesty of the tragedy.

Hamlet . . . Ed. by H. Morley. 'National library.' Ln: Cassell, 1893. 16°, pp. 192

Sh— Hamlet . . .

Hamlet . . . Edited by E. K. Chambers. 'Warwick Sh.—' Ln: Blackie & Son, 1894. 12°, pp. 224
BPL

[Hamlet] Rosencrantz and Guildenstern, by W. S. Gilbert [In 'Original plays; third series']. Ln: 1895. 12°
BPL
A travesty, issued previously in 1893.

Hamlet . . . Edited by L. W. Lyde. 'Junior school Sh—.' Ln: Blackie, 1895. 12°
BPL

Hamlet. 'Ariel edition.' Ln: Routledge, 1895. 16°

Hamlet. Ed. by I. Gollancz. 'Temple edition.' Ln: Dent, 1895. 16°

Hamlet . . . With introduction and notes by K. Deighton. Ln: Macmillan, 1896. 12°
BPL

Hamlet . . . Edited by W. H. Griffin. 'School Sh—.' Ln: Arnold [c. 1896]. 12°
BPL

Hamlet . . . Edited by W. G. Clark and W. A. Wright. Oxford: Clarendon Press, 1896. Cr. 8°
BPL

Hamlet. With notes, exam. papers, and plan of preparation, by J. M. D. Meiklejohn. Ln. & Edin.: W. & R. Chambers, 1896. Cr. 8°, pp. 192

Hamlet . . . As arranged for the stage by Forbes Robertson and presented at the Lyceum Theatre, 11th Sept., 1897. Illust. by Hawes Craven. Ln: Nassau Press, 1897. Fcp. 4°, pp. 96
BM | BPL | BUS

Hamlet . . . Illustrated by H. Copping. Ln: Tuck [1897]. 4°
BM | BPL

Hamlet. 'Pocket Falstaff edition.' Ln: Bliss, Sands, 1898. 16°, pp. 152
BPL | SML

Hamlet . . . Illust. by Harold Copping. Ln: Tuck [1898]. 4°

Hamlet. 'National library.' Ed. by H. Morley. Ln: Cassell, 1898. 16°, pp. 192

Hamlet. Illust. by H. C. Christy. New York, 1898. 12°

Hamlet. With introd. and notes by John Dennis. Illust. by Byam Shaw. Ln: Bell, 1899. 12°, pp. 174

Hamlet. Ed. by E. Dowden. Ln: Methuen, 1899. 8°, pp. 266

Hamlet . . . Edited with introduction and notes by C. H. Herford. 'Eversley edition.' Ln: Macmillan, 1900. 12° BPL

Hamlet . . . E. H. Sothern's acting version. New York: McClure, Phillips & Co., 1901. 8°. With portraits and plates BPL | BUS

Hamlet . . . Ed. by W. J. Rolfe. New York . . . 1902. 8°
BUS

Hamlet . . . 'Picture Sh—.' Ln: Blackie, 1902. Cr. 8°, pp. 210
BPL

[Hamlet] The new 'Hamlet,' intermixed and interwoven with a revised version of ' Romeo and Juliet ' as first produced by the Smiths. Chicago, 1902. Cr. 8° BPL

Hamlet . . . 'Sh— for schools.' Ln: Dent, 1903. Cr. 8° BPL

Hamlet . . . With preface, glossary, etc. by Israel Gollancz. ' Temple edition.' Ln: Dent & Co., 1902. 16°, pp. xvi.-216

Hamlet . . . notes, introd. and glossary by Oliver Smeaton. With six illustrations and coloured frontis. by Patten Wilson. Ln: Dent, 1903. Cr. 8°

Hamlet. ' Waistcoat pocket edition.' Ln: Treherne, 1904. 32°

Hamlet. Introduction by G. Brandes. ' Favourite classics.' Ln: Heinemann, 1904. 12°

Hamlet. ' Pocket book classics.' Ln: Bell, 1904. 16° BPL

Hamlet. ' Ellen Terry edition.' Glasgow: Bryce, 1904. 32°

Hamlet . . . Edited for students by A. W. Verity. Cambridge: Univ. Press, 1904. 8°, pp. 412 BPL | BUS

Hamlet. Ed. by H. Morley. ' National library.' Ln: Cassell, 1904. 16°, pp. 192 BPL

Hamlet . . . Introd. and notes by W. J. Craig. ' Little quartos.' Ln: Methuen, 1905. 16°

Hamlet. Retold for children by A. S. Hoffman. Illustrated. Ln: Dent, 1905. 16°

Hamlet . . . With notes by Wood and F. Marshall. ' Oxford and Cambridge edition.' Ln: G. Gill & Sons, 1905. Cr. 8° BPL

Hamlet . . . Text revised by A. Dyce. Ln: Sonnenschein, 1907. 8° BPL

Hamlet. ' Red letter edition.' Ln: Blackie, 1907. 12°

Hamlet. ' Texts without notes.' Ln: Chambers, 1907. Cr. 8°, pp. 128 BPL

Hamlet . . . Complete paraphrase by H. W. Lindsey. Ln: Normal Press, 1908. Cr. 8°, pp. 98

Hamlet . . . With introd. by Santayana. ' Renaissance edition.' Ln: Harrap, 1908. Fcp. 4° BPL

Hamlet . . . With introduction, text and notes, etc. by C. W. Crook. Ln: Ralph & Holland, 1908. Cr. 8°, pp. 240, inter-leaved

Hamlet . . . Ed. by K. Harvey. 'Sh— for home reading.' Ln: Routledge, 1909. 12° BPL

[Hamlet] The tragedy of Hamlet prince of Denmark. Ed. by S. E. Goggin. ' Univ. tutorial series.' Ln: Clive, 1909. Cr. 8°, pp. 256 BPL

[Hamlet] The tragicall historie of Hamlet prince of Denmarke, 1604-23. Doves Press [S. J. Cobden-Sanderson], 1909. 8° BPL

Reviewed in ' The Athenæum,' 24 July, 1909.

' Hamlet ' references—

See Adams	*See* Dorchester
„ Adee	„ Dramatic En-tertainments
„ Archer	
„ Aveling	„ Dramatic His-toriographer
„ Bandello & Brooke	
	„ Durand
„ Barnes	„ Egan
„ Barnett (T. D.)	„ Evans
„ Baverstock	„ Fairbanks
„ Bayne	„ Falbe
„ Benedict	„ Farren
„ Betty	„ Fechter
„ Bicknell	„ Feldborg
„ Bigelow	„ Ferne
„ Bradley	„ Field
„ Brereton	„ Fleay
„ Brody	„ Foard
„ Brooks (C. S.)	„ Ford
„ Brough	„ Fouquier
„ Buchanan	„ Fatricide
„ Bucknill	„ French (G. R.)
„ Bulwer	„ French 'Hamlet'
„ Burr	„ German
„ C—— (T.)	„ Ghost Player's Guide
„ Carstens	
„ Cartwright	„ Giacomo
„ Channing	„ Gilbert
„ Chettle	„ Gilchrist
„ Coleridge	„ Gilfillan
„ Collins (J. C.)	„ Glasgow
„ Comfort	„ Goethe
„ Conington	„ Gollancz
„ Conolly	„ Grabstein
„ Cooke	„ Graves
„ Corbin	„ Gray
„ Corner	„ Greek
„ Corson	„ Griffin
„ Cox	„ Grimm
„ Crane	„ Grinfield
„ Cruikshank	„ Guernsey
„ Culler	„ H—— (E. B.)
„ Curtis	„ Hackett
„ Davies	„ Halliwell
„ Davis (J. B.)	„ Hamlet
„ Davis (W. J.)	„ Hansen
„ Decker	„ Harkom
„ Decker&Webster	„ Harrison
„ Deverell	„ Hemminge
„ Dickens	„ Henderson (J.)

Sh— 'Hamlet' references—

See Henderson (W.
    A.)
 ,, Herford
 ,, Hernon
 ,, Hiatt
 ,, Hints . . .
 ,, Horne
 ,, Howison
 ,, Hudson
 ,, Hutton
 ,, Ignotus
 ,, Ingleby
 ,, Ireland (S. W.H.)
 ,, Irving (*Sir* J. H.
    B.)
 ,, Jago
 ,, Johnson (*Dr.* S.)
 ,, Johnson & Stee-
    vens
 ,, Johnston
 ,, Jovius
 ,, K—— (A. J.)
 ,, Kelly
 ,, Kemble
 ,, Kennedy
 ,, Kenney
 ,, Kirkman
 ,, Knights (M.)
 ,, L—— (C.)
 ,, Lambert
 ,, Latham
 ,, Lawreen
 ,, Leaves
 ,, Lee (N.)
 ,, Leifchild
 ,, Leighton
 ,, Lennox
 ,, Leo
 ,, Lewis
 ,, Lillo
 ,, Liverseege
 ,, Lofft
 ,, Logeman
 ,, Long . . .
 ,, Mac Callum
 ,, Macdonald
 ,, Macdonell
 ,, Mackenzie
 ,, Maginn
 ,, Mahony
 ,, Malleson
 ,, Mangasarian
 ,, March
 ,, Marindin
 ,, Marshall
 ,, Marston
 ,, Martin
 ,, Massinger
 ,, Maudsley

See Meadows
 ,, Meijboom
 ,, 'Mercade'
 ,, Mercier
 ,, Michie
 ,, Miles
 ,, Miller
 ,, Mirror
 ,, Miscellaneous . .
 ,, Morris
 ,, Mountfort
 ,, Mull
 ,, Murdoch
 ,, Nero
 ,, Nicholson
 ,, O'Connor
 ,, On . . .
 ,, Osborne
 ,, Otway
 ,, Owen
 ,, 'Oxon'
 ,, Pedder
 ,, Phelps
 ,, Pilon
 ,, Planché
 ,, Plumptre
 ,, Plutarchus
 ,, Poel
 ,, Pollock
 ,, Preston
 ,, Pyle
 ,, R—— (J. H.)
 ,, Ralegh
 ,, Ramsay
 ,, Rankin
 ,, Ransome
 ,, Ratsey
 ,, Reprints
 ,, Retzsch
 ,, Richardson
 ,, Robertson
 ,, Rohrbach
 ,, Romdahl
 ,, Roscoe
 ,, Rose
 ,, Rosencrantz
 ,, Rowley
 ,, Russell
 ,, Sannazaro
 ,, Saxo Gramma-
    ticus
 ,, Schæffer
 ,, Scoloker
 ,, Scott (C. W.)
 ,, Seeley
 ,, Seton
 ,, Sh— Works:
    E x t. 1798,
    1799

Sh— 'Hamlet' references—

See Sh—] Sh—'s li-
    brary
 ,, Sharpe (H.)
 ,, Shaw (J. H.)
 ,, Simpson
 ,, Snider
 ,, Soames
 ,, Some remarks . .
 ,, Something . . .
 ,, Songs
 ,, Soule
 ,, Spermacetti
 ,, Stefansson
 ,, Stopes
 ,, Strachey
 ,, Studies
 ,, Sullivan
 ,, Table Book
 ,, Tanger
 ,, Teetgen
 ,, Teichmann
 ,, Templar
 ,, Templeton
 ,, Theobald
 ,, Thom
 ,, Thomas
 ,, Thring
 ,, Tolman
 ,, Tomlinson

See Tourgenieff
 ,, Tragedy . . .
 ,, Tree
 ,, Turnbull
 ,, Tyler
 ,, Van Wart
 ,, Very
 ,, Vining
 ,, Vocal . . .
 ,, Voltaire
 ,, W—— (P.)
 ,, Wade
 ,, Walters
 ,, Walton
 ,, Watts
 ,, Webster
 ,, Welch
 ,, Werder
 ,, Whately
 ,, White (E. H.)
 ,, White (R. G.)
 ,, Widgery
 ,, Wilson (H. S.)
 ,, Wilson (J. E.)
 ,, Wood (S.)
 ,, Wood (W. D.)
 ,, Woods
 ,, Woolls
 ,, Zornlin

Henry IV. *See* Sh— King Henry IV.

Henry V. *See* Sh— King Henry V.

Henry VI. *See* Sh— King Henry VI.

Henry VIII. *See* Sh— King Henry VIII.

History of the times. *See* Sh— Works:
Extracts, 1778

Indenture . . . betweene William Combe of
Warrwicke . . . John Combe of olde Stret-
ford on the one partie . . . and William
Sh— of Stretford-uppon-Avon . . . on
thother partie [*dated*] 1st May, 1602.

An unexecuted deed, with seal appended, printed at
length in Wheler's History of Stratford (*q.v.*), pp.
139-144. Relates to the purchase of 107 acres of land
at Stratford by the poet for £320.

Indenture. *See also* Sh— autograph

[Jests] Sh—'s jests, or the jubilee jester;
being a curious collection of funny jokes,
merry stories, droll adventures, frolick-
some tales, witty quibbles, youthful
pranks, ridiculous bulls, &c. With jovial
songs, facetious dialogues, toasts, and
hob nobs. Ln: R. Sharpe [c. 1769].
8°, pp. 152; sig. B to O. With frontispiece   BUS

'It is difficult to account for the extreme rarity of this
quaint but very gross collection, in which a number
of anecdotes are fathered on Sh—.'—*J. O. Halliwell*.
Probably the volume met with natural suppression on
account of its coarseness.
In March, 1906, a copy realised £45.

Sh— [Jests] Sh—'s jests, or the jubilee jester
  . . . Ln: 1770. Cr. 8°, pp. 152

[Jests] Sh—'s jests, or the jubilee jester.
Ln: 1795. 8°

JULIUS CÆSAR.

*This tragedy is believed to have made its
first appearance in type in the Jaggard
canon of 1623. No separate edition is
known before that issued by Hy. Herringman of 1680, though an earlier play under
the same title, written by Wm. Alexander,
came out in 1604.*

Julius Cæsar . . . by William Alexander of
Menstrie (afterwards Earl of Stirling).
Ln: [Printed by Valentine Simmes ?]
1604. Fcp. 4°

[Julius Cæsar] The tragedy of Ivlivs Cæsar.
By W. Alexander [Earl of Stirling]. Ln:
. . . 1607. Fcp. 4°   BPL

Julius Cæsar [Manuscript, c. 1660]. 8°   W
The earliest known manuscript of this play, and trans-
scribed, probably from an old playhouse copy, in the
reign of K. Charles II. It occupies sixty-seven
pages of a volume of manuscript poetical miscellanies,
numbering in all eighty-six leaves. The last scene of
the fifth act is missing. This manuscript exhibits so
many departures from all the known printed editions
that it is safe to assume it was transcribed from some
independent version. To judge by a technical direction, 'Pindarus descends,' in the fifth act, it is almost
certainly copied from a prompter's copy long since
lost. The first and larger part of the volume, including the 'Julius Cæsar,' clearly belongs to the restoration period; but the last portion is in a later hand.
A prefixed note in the autograph of J. O. Halliwell,
dated 1870, reads :—'Presented to the library at
Warwick Castle, where are preserved, now this
volume is added, all known manuscript copies of
Sh—'s plays written before the close of the seventeenth century.'

Julius Cæsar: A tragedy. As it is now
acted at the Theatre Royal . . . Ln:
Printed by H. H——, jun. for Hen.
Herringman and R. Bentley in Russel
Street in Covent Garden and sold by
Joseph Knight and Francis Saunders at
the Blew Anchor in the Lower Walk of
the New Exchange in the Strand [1680].
Fcp. 4°, pp. 64   BM | BPL | BUS | NY | W
The cast, on verso of title, includes Betterton as
'Brutus.'
This is the first separate edition of Sh—'s 'Julius
Cæsar.'

Julius Cæsar. A tragedy. As it is now
acted at the Theatre Royal. Written
by Wm. Sh—. Ln: Printed by H. H——,
jun. for Hen. Herringman and R. Bentley,
1684. Fcp. 4°, pp. 62 BM | BPL | BUS | W

Julius Cæsar. A tragedy. As it is now
acted at the Theatre Royal. Written by
Wm. Sh—. Ln: Printed by H. H——,
jun. for Hy. Herringman & Rd. Bently,

Sh— Julius Cæsar . . .
at the Post House in Russel Street,
Covent Garden, 1691. Fcp. 4°, pp. 60
              BM | BPL | BUS | W
Reprinted and slightly altered from the 1680 edition.
The date has been tampered with in the Warwick copy
and altered to 1661, but 1691 is the correct year of
issue.

Julius Cæsar . . . Ln: Printed by H. H——,
jun. for Hen. Herringman and R. Bentley
in Russel Street in Covent Garden and
sold by Joseph Knight and Francis
Saunders at the Blew Anchor in the
Lower Walk of the New Exchange in the
Strand. [c. 1695.] Fcp. 4°

Julius Cæsar . . . [An excerpt from a
'Collection of the best English plays'].
Ln: . . . 1711. 8°, pp. 90   BM

[Julius Cæsar] The tragedy of Julius Cæsar,
with the deaths of Brutus and Cassius.
Written originally by Sh—, and since
altered by Sir Wm. Davenant and John
Dryden. As it is now acted by his
majesty's company of comedians at the
Theatre Royal. To which is prefixed the
life of Julius Cæsar abstracted from
Plutarch and Suetonius. Ln: . . . 1719.
12°, pp. xii.-78   BM | BPL

Julius Cæsar: A tragedy . . . Dublin:
Printed by and for George Grierson at
the 'Two Bibles' in Essex Street, 1721.
8°, pp. 72
No Irish issue of Sh— is known before this year.

[Julius Cæsar] The tragedy of Julius Cæsar
. . . Altered, with a prologue and chorus,
by his grace John Duke of Buckingham.
Ln: Printed for the Company [c. 1722].
8°   W

Julius Cæsar . . . Ln: . . . 1723. 8°

[Julius Cæsar] Four choruses in . . . 'Julius
Cæsar,' written by John Sheffield Duke
of Buckinghamshire. Set to music by
J. F. Galliard. [Original manuscript.]
1723. Fcp. 4°
Sold in July, 1903, for £2 2s.

Julius Cæsar. A tragedy. As it is now
acted by his majesty's servants. Written
by Wm. Sh—. Ln: Printed for J.
Tonson, and also for J. Darby, A. Bettesworth, and F. Clay, in trust for Richard,
James, and Bethel Wellington, 1729.
Price 1s. Cr. 8°, pp. 84 (the last leaf
containing a list of plays and other publications)
An unrecorded edition hitherto.

[Julius Cæsar] The tragedy of Julius Cæsar.
Altered, with a prologue and chorus, by
his grace John Duke of Buckingham.
Ln: Tonson [c. 1729]. 8°   BPL | W
An excerpt from the 'Works of the Duke of Buckingham.'

Sh— Julius Cæsar . . .

Julius Cæsar. A tragedy. As it is acted at the Theatre Royal in Drury Lane by his majesty's servants . . . Ln: Printed for J. Tonson and the rest of the proprietors, and sold by the booksellers of Ln. and Westminster, 1734. 12°, pp. 72, and frontispiece by Lud. Du Guernier w

Julius Cæsar . . . Altered, with prologue and chorus. By John Sheffield Duke of Buckingham [In Buckingham's Works, 3rd ed., 2 vols.] Ln: T. Wotton, 1740. 8°

Julius Cæsar. A tragedy. As it is acted at the Theatre Royal in Drury-Lane, by Wm. Sh—. Ln: J. & R. Tonson, 1741. 12°, pp. 70 BM | BPL | W

Julius Cæsar . . . Ln: J. Tonson [c. 1745]. 8°

Julius Cæsar. Altered by John Sheffield Duke of Buckingham [In his ' Plays']. Glasgow: 1751. 12° BUS

Julius Cæsar . . . Edited by E. Capell. Ln: . . . 1758. 8°

[Julius Cæsar] Four odes, intended for choruses to a tragedy altered from Sh— on the death of Julius Cæsar [By John Sheffield Duke of Buckingham]. Ln: 1759. Fcp. 4° BPL

Julius Cæsar . . . Dublin . . . 1762. 12° MPL

Julius Cæsar. A tragedy . . . Ln: D. Williams, 1766. 12°, pp. 74 BM | W

Julius Cæsar. A tragedy . . . As performed at the Theatre Royal, Covent Garden. Regulated from the prompt book, with permission of the managers, by Mr. Younger, prompter. An introduction and notes critical and illustrative are added by the authors of the ' Dramatic censor' [F. Gentleman]. Ln: John Bell; York: C. Etherington, 1773. 12°, pp. 76. Frontispiece of Sheridan as ' Brutus'
Part of Bell's edition of the Works, issued separately for theatre-goers.

Julius Cæsar . . . Collated with the old and modern editions [by Charles Jennens]. Ln: . . . 1773. 8°

Julius Cæsar. A tragedy. Collated [by Charles Jennens] with the old and modern editions. Ln: W. Owen, 1774. 8°, pp. 144. With plate BM | BPL | BUS

Julius Cæsar . . . With explanatory notes selected from Dr. Johnson's and Mr. Steevens's commentaries. Gottingen: A. Vandenhoek's widow, 1777. 8°, pp. 94 BM

Julius Cæsar. A tragedy . . . As it is acted at the Theatres Royal in Drury-Lane and Covent-Garden. Ln: Harrison & Co., 1780. 8°, pp. 20 BM | BPL
With frontispiece portrait of Mr. Bensley in the character of ' Mark Antony.'

Sh— Julius Cæsar . . .

Julius Cæsar. A tragedy, written by Wm. Sh—, taken from the manager's prompt book at the Theatre Royal, Drury Lane. Ln: . . . [c. 1780]. 8° w

[Julius Cæsar] Giulio Cesare in Egitto. A serious opera, as performed at the King's Theatre in the Hay-market. The music by Handel. 1787. 8° w
Italian and English text on parallel pages.

Julius Cæsar. A tragedy by Wm. Sh—, accurately printed from the text of Johnson & Steevens. Manchester: R. & W. Dean, 1800. 12° BPL | W

Julius Cæsar . . . from the text of Johnson and Steevens. Manchester: R. & W. Dean, 1803. 12°

Julius Cæsar . . . Printed complete from the text of Sam. Johnson and Geo. Steevens. [Ln.] 1807. 16° w

Julius Cæsar. A tragedy. In five acts. As performed at the Theatre Royal, Covent Garden. Printed under the authority of the managers from the prompt book. With remarks by Mrs. Inchbald. Ln: Longman . . . & Orme [1808]. 12°, pp. 72 and plate BPL | BUS

Julius Cæsar . . . With remarks by Mrs. Inchbald. Ln: Longman . . . & Brown [c. 1811]. 12°, pp. 72 and plate BUS

Julius Cæsar . . . As performed at Covent Garden . . . Adapted to the stage by J. P. Kemble, as acted at Covent Garden Theatre. Ln: . . . 1811. 8°

Julius Cæsar . . . Adapted to the stage by J. P. Kemble, and published as it is acted at the Theatre Royal. Ln: Printed for the theatre, 1812. 8°

Julius Cæsar. A tragedy . . . Adapted to the stage by J. P. Kemble, and now published as it is performed at the Theatres Royal. Ln: J. Miller, 1814. 12°, pp. 74 BPL | BUS | W

Julius Cæsar . . . With remarks by Mrs. Inchbald. Ln: Hurst, Robinson & Co. [c. 1816]. 12°, pp. 78 and plate BUS

Julius Cæsar . . . With prefatory remarks [signed P. P.] . . . Marked with the stage business, and stage directions, as it is performed at the Theatres Royal, by W. Oxberry. Ln: . . . 1822. 8°, pp. 80 BM | BPL

[Julius Cæsar] Versus præmio Porsoniano . . . dignati, auctore Gulielmo Barham [An excerpt, in English and Greek, from Act IV., Sc. iii.] Cambridge . . . 1822. 8° BM

Julius Cæsar . . . Edited by W. Oxberry. Ln: Simpkin, 1823. 12°. With portrait

Julius Cæsar . . . With remarks by D. G——
[Geo. Daniel]. Ln : John Cumberland,
1824. 18°
Julius Cæsar . . . ' Cumberland's British
theatre.' Ln : Davidson [c. 1825]. 12°
BPL
Julius Cæsar . . . Printed from the acting
copy, with remarks . . . by D. G——
[Geo. Daniel]. To which are added a
. . . cast of the characters . . . the whole
of the stage business as now performed
at the Theatres Royal. Ln : J. Cumber-
land [c. 1830]. 12°, pp. 64 BM | BUS
Julius Cæsar . . . Ln : J. Cumberland,
1831. 12° BPL
[Julius Cæsar. A translation in Greek
iambics, by H. Lushington, from Act II.,
Sc. 2. English and Greek.] Cambridge
. . . 1832. 8° BM
Julius Cæsar . . . Printed from the text of
Geo. Steevens. With historical and
critical notes in German by J. M. Pierre.
Frankfort . . . 1836. 12°
Julius Cæsar . . . Nuremberg & New York
. . . 1836. 12°
Julius Cæsar. A tragedy . . . Revised and
corrected by Prof. G. F. Burckhardt.
Boston [U.S.] . . . 1838. 8°
Julius Cæsar . . . ' Penny acting Sh— ' . . .
[c. 1845.] 12° BPL
Julius Cæsar . . . grammatisch und sachlich
. . . erläutert von Dr. J. Hoffa [In English
and German]. Jena : F. Mauke, 1848.
8°, pp. iv.-130 BM
Julius Cæsar . . . With the stage business,
cast of characters, costumes, relative
positions, etc. Modern standard drama.
New York : S. French, 1849. 12°, pp. 66
BUS
Julius Cæsar . . . erklärt von Dr. E. W.
Sievers [In English and German]. Berlin :
T. C. F. Enslin, 1855. 8°, pp. iv.-140
BM | BUS
Julius Cæsar . . . Latine reddidit Henricus
Denison. Oxford : J. H. & J. Parker,
1856. 8°, pp. 170 BPL | BUS
English and Latin text on parallel pages.
[Julius Cæsar] Jules César, tragédie traduite
en vers français, avec le texte Anglais au
bas des pages, précédée d'une étude et
suivie de notes, par C. Carlhaut [In English and French]. Paris : Firmin Didot
frères, 1856. 8°, pp. lxxx.-168 BM
Julius Cæsar . . . grammatisch und sachlich
zum schulund privatgebrauch erläutert
und mit einem ausführlichen worterbuche
versehen von Dr. J. Bucher [In English
and German]. Berlin : Renger'sche buchhandlung, 1856. 8°, pp. iv.-132 BM

[Julius Cæsar] The English of Sh— illustrated in a philological commentary on
his ' Julius Cæsar ' [with the text and an
index]. By George L. Craik. Ln : Chapman & Hall, 1857. Cr. 8°, pp. xxxviii.-
352 BM | BPL | BUS
Julius Cæsar . . . mit sprach-und sachanmer-
kungen begleitet von E. Meyer [In English and German]. Hamburg : Nolte &
Koehler, 1857. 8°, pp. xiv.-154 BM
[Julius Cæsar] The English of Sh—. . . .
' Julius Cæsar ' . . . By G. L. Craik.
Second edition, revised and improved.
1859. Cr. 8°, pp. xvi.-350
BPL | BUS | CPL | MPL | SML
In the first edition the text appeared at the end. In
this issue it is dispersed through the work.
Julius Cæsar. A tragedy . . . With notes
by Dr. Otto Fiebig. Leipzig : G. Græb-
ner, 1859. 8°, pp. iv.-96 BM | BUS
Julius Cæsar . . . ' Lacy's acting edition.'
Ln : T. H. Lacy [1859]. 12°, pp. 70
BM | BPL
Julius Cæsar . . . For the use of Sydney
grammar school. Sydney, N.S.W., 1860.
12° MPL
The earliest Australasian printing of Sh—.
Julius Cæsar . . . With notes by Samuel
Clark, principal of Battersea Training
College. Ln : 1860. 8°, pp. 341-432.
Illust.
An excerpt, with MS. notes.
Julius Cæsar . . . erklärt von Theodor
Jancke. Köln : M. Du Mont-Schauberg,
1861. 8°, pp. iv.-96 BM | BUS
English text, with German notes.
Julius Cæsar . . . With introd. remarks,
copious interpretation of the text,
critical and grammatical notes, and
numerous extracts from the history on
which the play is founded. Adapted for
scholastic or private study and . . .
middle class examinations by John
Hunter. Ln : Longman . . . & Roberts,
1861. Cr. 8°, pp. xxxvi.-136 BUS
[Julius Cæsar] English of Sh—. . . . Edited
by G. L. Craik. Third edition. Ln :
Chapman, 1864. Cr. 8°, pp. xvi.-350
SML
Julius Cæsar . . . With grammatical and
explanatory notes by Corréard. Paris :
C. Fourant . . . [1865]. 12°, pp. 72 BM
Julius Cæsar. A tragedy . . . New edition,
with notes. Revu et adapté a l'enseigne-
ment dans les Lycées . . . par C. Witcomb.
Paris : Baudry's European Library, 1865.
8°, pp. 80 BM
Julius Cæsar . . . Ln : Lacy [c. 1866]. 12°

Sh— Julius Cæsar . . .

[Julius Cæsar] Jules César. Nouvelle édition, publiée avec une notice, un argument analytique et des notes en français par C. Fleming. Paris : Hachette & Cie, 1866. 16°, pp. 174   BM
In English and French.

[Julius Cæsar] Jules César . . . trad. en vers Français par le Chevalier de Chatelain. 1866. 12°   BPL

Julius Cæsar . . . With remarks, notes and extracts . . . by John Hunter. Ln : Longmans, 1867. 8°, pp. xxxvi.-136

[Julius Cæsar] The English of Sh—. Illustrated in a philological commentary on his 'Julius Cæsar.' By G. L. Craik. Edited by W. J. Rolfe. Boston [U.S.]: Crosby & Ainsworth, 1867. Cr. 8°, pp. xvi.-386   BUS

[Julius Cæsar] The English of Sh— . . . by G. L. Craik. Ed. by W. J. Rolfe. Boston [U.S.]: E. Ginn, 1868. Cr. 8°, pp. xvi.-386   BUS

[Julius Cæsar] Giulio Cesare, tragedia . . . voltata in prosa Italiana da C. Rusconi. Quinta edizione col testo inglese di riscontro [In English and Italian]. Firenze : Successori Le Monnier, 1868. 8°, pp. 182   BM

Julius Cæsar . . . Leipzig: Tauchnitz, 1868. Cr. 8°

Julius Cæsar . . . [Edited] for scholastic study by J. Hunter. Ln : Longman & Co., 1869. 12°, pp. xxxvi.-136 BUS | CPL

Julius Cæsar . . . Latine reddidit Henricus Denison. 2nd edition. Oxford : J. H. & J. Parker, 1869. 8°, pp. 170   BPL
English and Latin text parallel.

[Julius Cæsar] The English of Sh— . . . 'Julius Cæsar' . . . By G. L. Craik. Fourth ed. Ln : Chapman, 1869. Cr. 8°   BPL

Julius Cæsar, annoté par C. Græser [In English and French]. Leipzig: F. A. Brockhaus, 1870. 8°, pp. 84   BM

Julius Cæsar . . . Ln : Lacy . . . [1870 ?] 12°

Julius Cæsar [Printed for the use of the blind at the Perkins Institution]. Boston [U.S.] 1871. F°, on 82 unpaged folios   BUS
Printed together with 'Hamlet,' without a separate title-page.

Julius Cæsar . . . As performed by E. Booth. 'Booth's acting plays.' Ln : . . . [c. 1871]. 8°   BPL

Julius Cæsar . . . 'School edition.' Ln : W. & R. Chambers, 1871. Cr. 8°   BPL

Sh— Julius Cæsar . . .

Julius Cæsar . . . Edited with notes by W. J. Rolfe. With engravings. New York : Harper Brothers, 1872. 16°, pp. 190   BUS

[Julius Cæsar] The English of Sh— . . . by G. L. Craik. Ed. by W. J. Rolfe. Sixth edition, revised and corrected. Boston [U.S.]: Ginn Brothers, 1872. 8°, pp. xvi.-386   BUS

Julius Cæsar. Tragedi . . . Med inledning och anmärkningar [by V. H], [In English and Norse ? Icelandic ?]. Hudiksvall : S. Hellströms Förlag, 1872. 8°, pp. xviii.-116   BM

Julius Cæsar . . . zur uebersetzung in's Deutsche bearbeitet . . . von Dr. H. Klose. Heidelberg . . . 1872. 8°, pp. 36   BM

[Julius Cæsar] Jules César. Nouvelle édition publiée avec une notice, un argument analytique et des notes en Français par C. Fleming. Paris : Hachette & Cie, 1873. 16°, pp. ii.-174   BUS
English text, with French notes.

Julius Cæsar . . . Nouvelle édition, avec une notice sur la pièce et des notes philologiques et littéraires par M. Grouillard. Paris : C. Delagrave, 1875. 12°, pp. 154   BM | BUS
English text, with French notes.

Julius Cæsar [Act I., Sc. ii.] In Greek verse, by A. E. Haigh. Gaisford prize. Oxford : Shrimpton & Son, 1876. 12°   BPL
In Greek and English.

Julius Cæsar . . . Ed. by W. A. Wright. Oxford : Clarendon Press, 1876. Cr. 8°, pp. xlvi.-204

[Julius Cæsar] The English of Sh— . . . By G. L. Craik. Edited by W. J. Rolfe. Boston [U.S.] 1876. Cr. 8°   BPL

Julius Cæsar . . . with introductory remarks ; explanatory, grammatical, and philological notes, etc. by Samuel Neil. 'School and college classics.' Glasgow : W. Collins & Co., 1877. 8°, pp. 160   BM | BPL | BUS

Julius Cæsar. With introductions and notes by H. N. Hudson. Boston [U.S.]: Ginn & Heath, 1877. 12°   BUS
Excerpt pp. 427-509 inclusive.

Julius Cæsar . . . With notes, examination papers and plan of preparation. Edited by J. M. D. Meiklejohn. Ln. & Edinburgh : W. & R. Chambers, 1878. Cr. 8°, pp. 130   BM

Julius Cæsar . . . With notes . . . by J. Hunter. Ln : Longman [1878]. Cr. 8°   BPL

Julius Cæsar . . . Edited by W. A. Wright. Oxford : Clarendon Press, 1878. 8°, pp. xlviii.-204　　　　BUS

Julius Cæsar . . . Für den schulgebrauch erklärt von Dr. L. Riechelmann . . . Zweite Auflage [In English and German]. Leipzig : B. G. Teubner, 1879. 8°, pp. xl.-124　　　　BM

Julius Cæsar . . . With introduction and notes . . . for use in schools . . . by H. N. Hudson. Boston [U.S.] : Ginn & Heath, 1879. 12°, pp. 206　　　　BM

[Julius Cæsar] A Selection from Sh—'s ' Julius Cæsar ' . . . 1880. 16°, pp. 46　　　　BM

[Julius Cæsar] Jules César : Tragedie . . . édition classique précédée d'une notice litteraire par A. Elwall [In English and French]. Paris : Delalain frères [1881]. 12°, pp. xxiv.-116　　　　BM

Julius Cæsar . . . Edited by W. A. Wright. Oxford : Clarendon Press, 1881. Cr. 8°　　　　BPL

[Julius Cæsar] Jules César : tragédie. Nouvelle édition avec notice biographique, sommaires, notes . . . par E. Haussaire [In English and French]. Paris : P. Dupont, 1881. 12°, pp. 214　　　　BM

[Julius Cæsar] Jules César, traduction Française [in prose] par E. Montégut. Avec le texte Anglais. Paris : Hachette et Cie, 1881. 8°, pp. viii.-129　　　　BM

[Julius Cæsar] Jules César . . . par C. Fleming. Nouvelle edition [In English and French]. Paris : Hachette & Cie, 1881. 8°, pp. 174　　　　BM

[Julius Cæsar] Hamnet Sh—, part vii. The tragedy of Julius Cæsar : according to the first folio (spelling modernised), with relative lists of emphasis capitals and introduction, including remarks on the deviation of modern editors from Sh—'s punctuation, as it is shewn in the original edition (1623), by A. P. Paton. Ln : Longmans, 1881. 8°, pp. xxxvi.-76　　　　SML

[Julius Cæsar] Jules César : tragedie en cinq actes. Texte Anglais revu et annoté par M. l'Abbe Julien [In English and French]. Paris : Poussilegue frères, 1881. 12°, pp. xii.-142　　　　BM

Julius Cæsar . . . for schools and colleges. Ln : Simpkin, 1882. Cr. 8°

Julius Cæsar . . . With notes, examination papers, and plan of preparation, by Brainerd Kellogg. New York . . . 1882. 24°. With portrait　　　　BUS

Julius Cæsar . . . with introduction, notes, examination papers, and an appendix of prefixes and terminations, by Thomas Parry. Ln : Longmans, 1882. 8°, pp. viii.-150　　　　BM

Julius Cæsar . . . edited by W. J. Rolfe. New York : Harper Brothers, 1883. 12°　　　　BPL

Julius Cæsar . . . Edited by W. A. Wright. Oxford : Clarendon Press, 1883. Cr. 8°, pp. xlvi.-204　　　　BPL | MPL | SML

Julius Cæsar . . . Edited by J. P. Kemble . . . Abridged. Ln : Bell, 1883. 12°

Julius Cæsar. ' Standard plays.' Ln : John Dicks [1883]. 12°　　　　BM

[Julius Cæsar] Sh—. Dumaresq series. By Captain F. S. Dumaresq de Carteret-Bisson . . . and R. Mongan. Part I., ' Julius Cæsar.' Ln : Simpkin, Marshall & Co. [1883]. 8°, pp. 176　　　　BM
No more published.

Julius Cæsar . . . With introduction, notes . . . and appendix by Thomas Parry. Ln : Longmans, 1883. 8°, pp. viii.-150. Illustrated　　　　BUS

[Julius Cæsar] Selections from ' Julius Cæsar.' With introduction, notes, and an appendix . . . by T. Parry. Ln : Longmans, 1883. 8°, pp. 52　BM | BPL

Julius Cæsar . . . With notes. Ln : Blackie & Son [1884]. 8°, pp. 96　　　　BM

[Julius Cæsar] Jules César . . . par C. Fleming [In English and French]. Paris : Hachette & Cie, 1884. 8°, pp. 174　BM

Julius Cæsar . . . With notes, glossary and questions. 'Oxford & Cambridge Sh—.' Ln : Allman & Son [1885]. Cr. 8°, pp. 128　　　　BPL

[Julius Cæsar] Selections from ' Henry the Eighth ' and ' Julius Cæsar.' Ln : Blackie & Son [1885]. 16°　　　　BM

Julius Cæsar. With introductory notes and appendix by T. Parry. Ln : Longmans, 1885. 8°, pp. 154. Illustrated

Julius Cæsar. With introduction, notes, and tables of prefixes and suffixes. Ln : Gill & Sons [c. 1885]. Cr. 8°, pp. 144. Illustrated

Julius Cæsar . . . edited by H. C. Beeching. ' Falcon edition.' Ln : Longmans & Co., 1886. Cr. 8°　　　　BPL

[Julius Cæsar] English of Sh— . . . by G. L. Craik. Edited by W. J. Rolfe. Boston [U.S.] : Ginn, 1886. Cr. 8°, pp. xvi.-386　　　　SML

Julius Cæsar . . . With illustrations from Worth's Plutarch [and introduction by Henry Morley]. ' National library.' Ln : Cassell, 1887. 16°, pp. 192　　　　BM

Sh— Julius Cæsar . . .

Julius Cæsar . . . With introd., notes . . . by
T. Parry. Ln : Longmans, 1887. Cr. 8°,
pp. 154. Illustrated

Julius Cæsar . . . edited by H. C. Beeching.
[Second] ' Falcon edition.' Ln : Rivington, 1887. Cr. 8°

Julius Cæsar . . . for school use. With
notes and tables of prefixes. Ln : Gill,
1887. Cr. 8°

Julius Cæsar . . . Moffatt's edition. With
introduction and notes. Third edition,
revised. [1888 ?] Cr. 8°   BPL

Julius Cæsar . . . With introduction and
notes by H. N. Hudson. Boston [U.S.]
. . . 1889. Cr. 8°   BPL

Julius Cæsar . . . herausgegeben von Dr. L.
Proescholdt [In English and German].
Gera : Dr. H. Schlutters Verlag, 1889.
8°, pp. 82   BM

Julius Cæsar . . . With notes, etc. Edited
by J. M. D. Meiklejohn. Ln : W. & R.
Chambers, 1889. Cr. 8°   BPL

Julius Cæsar . . . Ed. by W. A. Wright.
Oxford : Clarendon Press, 1889. Cr. 8°,
pp. xlvi.-204

Julius Cæsar . . . Edited by C. E. Flower.
' Memorial theatre edition.' Stratford-
on-Avon : Printed by G. Boyden [1889].
Cr. 8°, pp. viii.-82, including printed
wrappers   BPL | SML

Julius Cæsar. With notes arranged and
classified. Third edition. Ln : Moffatt,
1890. Cr. 8°

Julius Cæsar . . . With notes, also fresh
renderings, punctuation amended, etc.,
by M. Mull. 1890. 8°   BPL

Julius Cæsar . . . edited with notes, etc. by
B. Dawson. ' University Sh—.' Ln :
Sutton, 1890. Cr. 8°   BPL

Julius Cæsar . . . with an introduction and
notes by K. Deighton. Ln : Macmillan,
1890. Cr. 8°, pp. xxxii.-184   BM | BPL

Julius Cæsar . . . With notes . . . by Thomas
Parry. Ln : Longmans, 1890. Cr. 8°,
pp. 154

Julius Cæsar . . . Ed. by W. A. Wright.
Oxford : Clarendon Press, 1892. Cr. 8°,
pp. xlvi.-204

Julius Cæsar . . . With introduction and
notes, etc. by W. Dent. ' Junior school
Sh—.' Ln : . . . 1893. Cr. 8°   BPL

Julius Cæsar . . . edited by Arthur D.
Innes. ' Warwick Sh—.' Ln : Blackie
& Son, 1893. Cr. 8°, pp. 144   BPL

Julius Cæsar . . . ' Pitt Press Sh—' for
schools ; with introduction, notes, glossary and index. Edited by A. W. Verity.
Cambridge : University Press, 1893.
Cr. 8°   SML

Sh— Julius Cæsar . . .

Julius Cæsar. With notes . . . by J. M. D.
Meiklejohn. Ln : Chambers, 1893. Cr.
8°, pp. 130

Julius Cæsar . . . Edited by T. D. Barnett.
' English classics.' Ln : Bell, 1893.
Cr. 8°, pp. 134   BM | BPL

Julius Cæsar. With notes by Homer B.
Sprague. Boston [U.S.] 1894. Cr. 8°

Julius Cæsar . . . edited by Arthur D.
Innes. Ln : Blackie, 1895. Cr. 8°, pp.
144

Julius Cæsar . . . With notes . . . by A. W.
Verity. ' Pitt Press Sh—.' Cambridge :
University Press, 1895. Cr. 8°, pp. xxx.-
208   BPL

Julius Cæsar . . . edited by J. M. D. Meiklejohn. Ln : W. & R. Chambers, 1895.
Cr. 8°, pp. 130

[Julius Cæsar] Jules César . . . par M.
l'Abbe Julien. Troisieme édition [In
English and French]. Paris : Poussielgue
frères, 1895. 12°, pp. xii.-142   BM

Julius Cæsar . . . edited by A. D. Innes.
' Arden Sh—.' Ln : Methuen, 1895-96.
8°   BM | BLO | BUS | CTC

Julius Cæsar. Ed. by I. Gollancz. ' Temple
edition.' Ln : Dent, 1896. 16°, pp. 146
          BM | BLO | BUS | CTC

Julius Cæsar . . . edited with introduction
and notes by Thomas Page. Ln : Moffatt
[1896]. 12°, pp. 174   BPL

Julius Cæsar . . . edited by E. M. Butler.
Ln : E. Arnold [c. 1896]. Cr. 8°, pp.
xxxiv.-124   BPL

[Julius Cæsar] Selections from ' Julius
Cæsar.' Ln : Blackie & Son [1896].
16°, pp. 32   BM

Julius Cæsar . . . ' Ariel edition.' Ln :
Routledge, 1896. 16°

Julius Cæsar . . . edited by J. Lees. Ln :
Allman, 1896. Cr. 8°

Julius Cæsar . . . edited by C. E. Flower.
' Memorial theatre edition.' Ln : Jarrold ;
Stratford-on-Avon : Sh— Memorial, 1896.
Cr. 8°, pp. viii.-82, including printed
wrappers   SML

Julius Cæsar . . . Prepared specially for the
Oxford and Cambridge local examinations. Ln : . . . [1897]. Cr. 8°   BUS

Julius Cæsar . . . ' Masterpiece library of
penny poets.' Ln : W. T. Stead, 1897.
Cr. 8°   BPL

Julius Cæsar . . . edited by E. M. Butler.
Ln : Arnold, 1897. Cr. 8°, pp. xxiv.-124

Julius Cæsar . . . edited by A. W. Verity.
Fourth edition. Cambridge : University
Press, 1898. 8°   BUS

Julius Cæsar . . . As arranged for the stage by H. B. Tree. Ln : Nassau Press, 1898. 8°, pp. 108 BM

Julius Cæsar . . . 'Pocket Falstaff edition.' Ln : Sands & Co., 1898. 12°, pp. 100 BPL | SML

Julius Cæsar . . . 'School Sh—.' Edinburgh : Blackwood, 1898. Cr. 8° BPL

Julius Cæsar . . . With illustrations from North's Plutarch . . . Ln : . . . 1899. 8° BUS

Julius Cæsar . . . with notes by David Forsyth. 'Swan edition.' Ln : Longman, 1899. Cr. 8°, pp. 140 BPL

Julius Cæsar . . . With introd., notes and glossary by R. B. Johnson. Ln : Blackwood, 1899. 12°, pp. 182

Julius Cæsar . . . edited by T. W. Berry and T. P. Marshall. Ln : Simpkin, 1899. Cr. 8°, pp. 216 BM

Julius Cæsar . . . With helps to its study ; introduction and notes by R. Rutherford. Ln : Ralph, 1899. Cr. 8°, pp. 120 BM

Julius Cæsar [Edited by Hy. Morley]. 'National library.' Ln : Cassell, 1899. 16°, pp. 192

Julius Cæsar . . . edited with introduction, notes, glossary, and indexes by A. W. Verity. Fifth edition. Cambridge : University Press, 1900. Cr. 8°, pp. xxiv.-222

Julius Cæsar . . . introduction and notes by John Dennis. Illust. by B. Shaw. 'Chiswick edition.' Ln : Bell, 1900. 12°

Julius Cæsar . . . Complete paraphrase by Prof. E. E. Denney and P. Lyddon-Roberts. Ln : Simpkin, 1900. Cr. 8° BPL

Julius Cæsar . . . edited with introduction and notes by C. H. Herford. 'Eversley edition.' Ln : Macmillan, 1900. 12° BPL

Julius Cæsar . . . 'Masterpiece library . . . penny poets.' Ln : [W. T. Stead, c. 1900.] Cr. 8°, pp. 58

Julius Cæsar . . . With introduction, notes, examination papers, appendix of prefixes and terminations, by Thomas Parry. Ln : Longmans, 1900. Cr. 8°, pp. 154. Illust.

Julius Cæsar . . . edited with notes by W. J. Rolfe. Ln : W. B. Clive [c. 1900]. Cr. 8°, pp. 200. Illustrated

Julius Cæsar . . . Ed. by George C. D. Odell. New York . . . 1900. 8°. With portrait BUS

Julius Cæsar . . . Parsed and analysed by E. E. Denney and P. Lyddon - Roberts. Ln : . . . [c. 1901]. Cr. 8° BPL

Julius Cæsar . . . With notes, etc. by David Forsyth, and ten full-page illustrations by Granville Manton. 'Swan edition.' Ln : Longmans, 1901. Cr. 8°, pp. xxiv.-116

Julius Cæsar . . . Ed. by W. A. Wright. Oxford : Clarendon Press, 1901. Cr. 8°, pp. xlvi.-204

Julius Cæsar. Ed. by L. W. Lyde. Ln : Blackie, 1901. Cr. 8°

Julius Cæsar . . . Ed. by S. Wood and A. Syms-Wood. 'Oxford & Camb. edition.' Ln : Gill, 1901. Cr. 8°, pp. lxiv.-180. Illustrated BPL

Julius Cæsar . . . Newport, Salop : Bennion, Horne, Smallman & Co. [1902]. Cr. 8° BPL

Julius Cæsar . . . with notes, introduction and glossary. Edited by F. Armytage-Morley. Illustrated by T. H. Robinson. Ln : Dent, 1902. Cr. 8°

Julius Cæsar . . . Introductory notes and appendices by A. E. Roberts. 'Normal tutorial series.' Ln : Simpkin, 1902. Cr. 8° BPL

Julius Cæsar . . . introduction and notes by M. J. C. Meiklejohn. Ln : Holden, 1902. 'Blackfriars edition.' Cr. 8°, pp. 156 BPL

Julius Cæsar . . . edited by Michael Macmillan. Ln : Methuen, 1902. Cr. 8°, pp. 274

Julius Cæsar . . . edited by A. W. Verity. Cambridge : Univ. Press, 1902. Cr. 8°, pp. xxxiv.-222

Julius Cæsar . . . 'Temple edition for schools.' Ln : Dent, 1903. Cr. 8° BPL

Julius Cæsar . . . Introduction and notes by David Patrick and Thomas Kirkup. 'Academy edition.' Ln : Chambers, 1903. Cr. 8°, pp. 180 BPL

Julius Cæsar . . . 'Ellen Terry edition.' Glasgow : Bryce, 1904. 32°

Julius Cæsar. Academy edition, specially adapted for use in Indian schools and colleges, by John Morrison. Ln : Chambers, 1904. Cr. 8°, pp. 204

Julius Cæsar . . . edited by A. W. Verity. Cambridge : University Press, 1904. Cr. 8°, pp. xxxiv.-222

Julius Cæsar . . . introduction by G. Brandes. 'Favourite classics.' Ln : Heinemann, 1904. 12°

Julius Cæsar . . . With introduction and notes, arranged and classified by T. Page. Ln : Simpkin, 1904. Cr. 8°

Julius Cæsar . . . edited by H. Morley. 'National library.' Ln : Cassell, 1904. 16° BPL

Sh— Julius Cæsar . . .

Julius Cæsar . . . Retold for children by A. S. Hoffman. Illustrated. Ln : Dent, 1905. 16°   BPL

Julius Cæsar . . . 'Waistcoat pocket edition.' Ln : Treherne, 1905. 32°

Julius Cæsar . . . Introduction and notes by W. J. Craig. 'Little quartos.' Ln : Methuen, 1905. 16°

Julius Cæsar . . . 'Red letter edition.' Ln : Blackie, 1906. 12°

[Julius Cæsar] Julio Cezaro . . . Tradukita de D. H. Lambert. Ln : British Esperantist Association, 1906. Cr. 8°, pp. x.-86   BPL
Printed in the hybrid language called 'Esperanto.'

Julius Cæsar . . . introduction and notes by W. J. Rolfe. Ln : Clive, 1906. Cr. 8°

Julius Cæsar . . . Edited by Benjamin Dawson. Ln : R. Sutton, 1907. Cr. 8°

Julius Cæsar . . . introduction and notes by Richard W. Rolfe. Ln : Clive, 1907. Cr. 8°

Julius Cæsar . . . Ed. by A. W. Verity. Camb. Univ. Press, 1907. Cr. 8°, pp. xxxiv.-222

Julius Cæsar . . . 'Texts without notes.' Ln : Chambers, 1907. Cr. 8°   BPL

Julius Cæsar . . . With introduction by W. H. Hudson. 'Elizabethan Sh—.' Ln : Harrap, 1908. Cr. 8°

Julius Cæsar . . . with introd. by 'S. Lee.' 'Renaissance edition.' Ln : Harrap, 1908. Fcp. 4°   BPL

Julius Cæsar . . . Ed. with introd. and notes by G. S. Gordon. Oxford : Clarendon Press, 1909. Cr. 8°, pp. 288

'Julius Cæsar' references—
See Appian
  ,, Asch
  ,, Barnett
  ,, Birmingham
  ,, Caldecott
  ,, Carstens
  ,, Cleveland
  ,, Craik
  ,, Dramatic historiographer
  ,, Essay . . .
  ,, Goonewardena
  ,, Haeusser
  ,, Hudson
  ,, Johnson & Steevens
  ,, Jones (R. D.)
  ,, Kemble
  ,, Kreutzberg
  ,, Lee
  ,, Lees (J.)
  ,, Mexia
  ,, Mirrour . . .
  ,, Moberly

Sh— 'Julius Cæsar' references—
See Needler
  ,, Nimmo
  ,, Philipp
  ,, Plutarchus
  ,, Rowley
  ,, Ruskin
  ,, Rutherford
  ,, Sh— Works : Ext. 1799, 1880, 1881
  ,, Sheffield
  ,, Sidgwick (H.)
  ,, Snider
  ,, Suetonius
  ,, Tree
  ,, Wilken
  ,, Wood
  ,, Woodforde
  ,, Zollmann

KING EDWARD THE THIRD.

This anonymous play, licensed at Stationers' Hall the first of Dec., 1595, was first issued by Cuthbert Burby in 1596. It is thought to be the work of Christopher Marlowe, assisted by Sh—.

[King Edward III.] The Raigne of King Edward the third : as it hath bin sundrie times plaied about the Citie of London. Ln : Printed for Cuthbert Burby, 1596. Fcp. 4° ; sig. A to K² unpaged   BM | CTC | W

Published anonymously, and attributed to Sh—.
'That it was indeed written by Sh— it cannot be said with candour that there is any external evidence at all. Something of proof arises from resemblance between the stile of his earlier performances and of the work in question, and a more conclusive one yet from consideration of the time it appear'd in, in which there was no known writer equal to such a play.'— *Capell.*

'If the play is not Sh—'s, as the English critics maintain, then truly it is a disgrace to them not to have done anything to rescue from forgetfulness this second Sh—, this twin brother of their great poet.'— *Ulrici.*

The parts which perhaps most resemble the work of such a pen as Sh—'s are the various speeches introduced, and the scene in which the king is spurned by the Countess of Salisbury.

The plot is taken from Holinshed's Chronicles and Painter's 'Palace of pleasure.'

[King Edward III.] The Raigne of King Edward the third. As it hath bene sundry times played about the Citie of London. Imprinted at Ln. by Simon Stafford for Cuthbert Burby. And are to be sold at his shop neere the Royall Exchange, 1599. Fcp. 4° ; sig. A to I4, unpaged   BM | CTC | W

This, the second issue, contains some important additions to, and variations from, the text of the first edition.

Sh— King Edward the third . . .

[King Edward III.] The Raigne of King Edward the third [as it hath bin sundrie times plaied about the Citie of London. Ln: Printed for Cuthbert Burby, 1596]. Manuscript transcript by Edward Capell, 1753. Fcp. 4°, pp. 86, upon paper   W
The original holograph transcript by Edward Capell, dated Oct. 8th / Nov. 6th, 1753, on eighty-six pages, with preliminary blank, prepared for the purpose of inclusion in his 'Prolusions,' which appeared in 1760. Together with the issues of 1596 and 1599, these are the only early editions known.

King Edward the third; A play thought to be writ by Sh— [In Capell's 'Prolusions']. Ln: . . . 1760. 8°, pp. 94
           BM | BPL | BUS | CTC

King Edward the third. A play attributed to Sh—. Edited by N. Delius. Elberfeld: R. L. Friderichs, 1854. 12° BUS

King Edward the third . . . Attributed by E. Capell to Sh—, and now proved to be his work, by J. P. Collier. Ln: Richards [privately printed] 1874. Fcp. 4°   BM | BPL

King Edward the third . . . [In Donovan, 'English historical plays arranged for acting,' Vol. I.] Ln: Macmillan . . . 1896. 2 vols. Cr. 8°   BM | MPL

King Edward III. . . . Edited with preface, notes, and glossary by G. C. M. Smith. Ln: Dent, 1897. 8°, pp. xxii.-128   BM

'King Edward III.' references—
See Capell
  ,, Mountfort
  ,, Teetgen
  ,, Sh— Works: Ext. 1836
  ,, Worrall

KING HENRY THE FOURTH;
FIRST PART.

The first known edition is that of 1598, printed by P. S. [Peter Short] for Andrew Wise, and no fewer than six separate editions were issued before the play appeared in the Jaggard canon of 1623. A coeval version in writing also exists, the only contemporary manuscript known to survive.

[King Henry IV., i.] The History of Henrie the Fovrth; With the battell at Shrewsburie, betweene the King and Lord Henry Percy, surnamed Henrie Hotspur of the North. With the humorous conceits of Sir Iohn Falstalffe. [Device.] London: Printed by P. S—— [Peter Short] for Andrew Wise dwelling in Paules Churchyard at the signe of the

Sh— King Henry the fourth . . .

Angell, 1598. Fcp. 4°, forty unpaged leaves; sig. A to K4 in fours
          BM | CTC | DEVON
For long this was accepted as the editio princeps, but Halliwell announced in 'The Athenæum,' Jan., 1875, that he had found a fragment of an earlier edition, fcp. 4°, the headline reading, 'The hystorie of Henry the fourth.' [See Halliwell's 'Catalogue of Sh— study books, 1876,' p. 18.]
This fragment, however, may be only a cancelled proof of the 1598 issue.
The edition was reproduced by Halliwell in 1861.
The British Museum copy is imperfect, lacking signs. E4 and K4.

[King Henry IV., i.] The History of Henrie the Fovrth; With the battell at Shrewsburie, betweene the King and Lord Henry Percy, surnamed Henry Hotspur of the North. With the humorous conceits of Sir Iohn Falstalffe. Newly corrected by W. Shake-speare. [Device.] At London: Printed by S. S—— [Simon Stafford] for Andrew Wise dwelling in Paules Churchyard, at the signe of the Angell, 1599. Fcp. 4°, forty unpaged leaves; sig. A¹ to K4 in fours   BM | BLO | CTC | DEVON

[King Henry IV., i.] The History of Henrie the Fourth. With the battell at Shrewsburie, betweene the King and Lord Henry Percy, surnamed Henry Hotspur of the North. With the humorous conceits of Sir Iohn Falstalffe. Newly corrected by W. Shake-speare. [Ornament.] London: Printed by Valentine Simmes for Mathew Law and are to be solde at his shop in Paules Churchyard at the signe of the Fox, 1604. Fcp. 4°, forty unpaged leaves; sig. A¹—K4   BLO | CTC
The Bodleian copy lacks leaf C1.

[King Henry IV., i.] The History of Henry the fourth. With the battell at Shrewseburie, betweene the King, and Lord Henry Percy, Surnamed Henry Hotspur of the North. With the humorous conceites of Sir Iohn Falstalffe. Newly corrected by W. Shake-speare. London: Printed for Mathew Law and are to be sold at his shop in Paules Church-yard, neere unto S. Augustines gate, at the signe of the Foxe, 1608. Fcp. 4°, forty unpaged leaves; sig. A¹—K4, in fours
          BM | BLO | DEVON | W
The Warwick copy has the last leaf in facsimile, and bears the autograph of 'John Cooper, 1688,' and another, 'Mr. Thomas Middleton, Esq., of Silkswoorth,' of the same period.
The British Museum possesses one of the two perfect copies known.
A copy in July, 1905, realised £1,000.

[King Henry IV., i.] History of King Henry the fourth [Two parts condensed into one; original manuscript written upon

(327)

Sh— King Henry the fourth . . .

paper, fifty-five leaves, with blank preliminary leaf, c. 1610]. F°   w

The sole contemporary manuscript of any of Sh—'s literary productions known to survive. Presumably it is in the holograph of Sir Edward Deryng or Dering, of Surrenden, Kent, who died in 1644, and, conjecturally, transcribed from Sh—'s own MS., or some coeval playhouse copy, as no known printed copy contains its various corrections and alterations. This almost priceless relic was discovered among the charters and papers of the present baronet at Surrenden in 1844, just two centuries after the original owner's death.

It is particularly interesting as showing that private performances existed at this period. This is proved by two lists of dramatis personæ in the 'Spanish curate' in the manuscript, the characters being sustained by Kentish gentlemen of the day.

Possibly Surrenden then possessed its own stage, for which this transcript may have been intended.

It was first printed in 1845 by the Sh— Soc. [*q.v.*]

In 1843, a year before this discovery, a unique playhouse manuscript (c. 1660) of the 'Merry wives' was secured by Halliwell from bookseller Rodd. This was accepted as the earliest Sh— play in manuscript until the foregoing occurred.

Sir Ed. Dering was the author of 'Godly private prayers,' published by Isaac Iaggard in 1624.

[King Henry IV., i.] The History of Henrie the fourth. With the Battell at Shrewseburie, betweene the King and Lord Henrie Percy, surnamed Henrie Hotspur of the North. With the humorous conceites of Sir Iohn Falstaffe. Newly corrected by W. Shake-speare. [*Device.*] London: Printed by W. W—— for Mathew Law and are to be sold at his shop in Paule's Church-yard, neere vnto S. Augustine's Gate, at the signe of the Foxe, 1613. Fcp. 4°, forty unpaged leaves (including title); sig. A¹ to K⁴ in fours   BM | BLO | CTC | NY

At the date of printing there were three printers in business whose initials tally with W. W——, *i.e.*, William Welby, William White, and William Wright, jun.

This edition supplied the text for the Jaggard canon of 1623.

One of the two copies in the British Museum bears the autograph of George Steevens on the title-page. The other exhibits variations at sig. H1, line five from foot, and at sig. H4 verso, line four, apparently corrections made after issuing the preliminary copies.

The last mentioned lacks the original last leaf, which is supplied in manuscript.

[King Henry IV., i.] The Historie of Henry the Fourth. With the Battell at Shrewseburie betweene the King and Lord Henry Percy, surnamed Henry Hotspur of the North. With the humorous conceits of Sir Iohn Falstaffe. Newly corrected. By William Shake-speare. [*Ornament.*] London: Printed by T. P—— [Thomas Purfoot] and are to be sold by Mathew Law, dwelling in Pauls Churchyard at the Signe of the Foxe, neere S. Austine's Gate, 1622. Fcp. 4°, forty unpaged leaves; sig. A¹ to K⁴ in fours

BM | BLO | BUS | CTC | W

Sh— King Henry the fourth . . .

[King Henry IV., i.] The Historie of Henry the Fourth. With the battell at Shrewesbury be-tweene the King, and Lord Henry Percy, surnamed Henry Hotspur of the North. With the humorous conceits of Sir Iohn Falstaffe. Newly corrected. By William Shake-speare. London: Printed by Iohn Norton and are to bee sold by William Sheares at his shop at the great South doore of Saint Pauls-Church, and in Chancery Lane neere Sericants-Inne, 1632. Fcp. 4°, forty unpaged leaves, including title; sig. A¹ to K⁴ in fours   BM | BUS | CTC | W

A copy sold in December, 1907, for £66.

[King Henry IV., i.] The Historie of Henry the Fourth: With the Battel at Shrewsbury, betweene the King and Lord Henry Percy, surnamed Henry Hotspur of the North. With the humorous conceits of Sir Iohn Falstaffe. Newly corrected. By William Shake-speare. London: Printed by John Norton and are to be sold by Hvgh Perry at his shop next to Ivie-bridge in the Strand, 1639. Fcp. 4°, forty unpaged leaves; sig. A¹ to K⁴ in fours   BM | BLO | BUS | CTC | NY | W

Upon the fly-leaf of the Warwick Castle copy J. O. Halliwell has written, 'By far the largest copy I ever saw.'

King Henry IV. With the humours of Sir John Falstaff. A tragi-comedy. As it is acted at the Theatre in Little Lincoln's Inn Fields by his Majesty's servants. Revised with alterations [by T. Betterton]. Written originally by Mr. Sh—. Ln: Printed by R. W—— and sold by John Deeve, 1700. Fcp. 4°, pp. ii.-54

BM | BPL | BUS | W

The 'alterations' are mainly abridgments.

King Henry the fourth. With the humours of Sir John Falstaff . . . Ln: . . . 1710. 16°, pp. 100   BM | BPL

King Henry the fourth . . . With the humours of Sir John Falstaff. Edited by the Hon. Mr. Granville [Lord Lansdowne]. The Hague: T. Johnson, 1710.   8°

The first piece of Sh— in English printed outside Britannia.

King Henry IV. With the humours of Sir John Falstaff. A tragi-comedy. By Mr. W. Sh—. Ln: Printed for T. Johnson, 1721. 8°, pp. 92   BM | BUS | W

An adaptation, probably from the pen of George Granville, afterwards Lord Lansdowne.

King Henry the fourth. With the humours of Sir John Falstaff . . . Dublin: T. Moore, 1731. 12°, pp. 82   BM

[King Henry IV., i.] The first part of Henry IV. With the life and death of Henry sirnamed Hot-spur. By Mr. Wm. Sh—. Ln: Printed for J. Tonson and the rest of the proprietors, and sold by the booksellers of Ln. and Westminster, 1734. Cr. 8°, pp. 96. Frontispiece by P. Fourdrinier and rude vignette port of Sh— BM | W
With piracy notice against R. Walker by W. Chetwood.

King Henry the fourth, part i. . . . Ln: R. Walker, 1734. Cr. 8°

[King Henry IV.] The first part of Henry IV., with the life and death of Henry, sirnamed Hot-Spur, by Sh—. Ln: J. & P. Knapton . . . 1751. 8°, pp. vi.-96 and frontispiece BPL | W

King Henry IV. [Portion of a playhouse copy containing Falstaff's part. Manuscript, written upon sixteen leaves of paper]. Kidderminster: May, 1762. Fcp. 4° W

[King Henry IV.] The first part of Henry IV. With the life and death of Henry, sirnamed Hot-Spur, by Sh—. With alterations as perform'd at the Theatres. Ln: Printed for C. Hitch, L. Hawes, etc., 1763. 12°, pp. 70 BPL | W

[King Henry IV., i.] History of Henry the fourth, with the battell at Shreweseburie . . . Ln: Printed by W. W—— for Mathew Law, 1613. [Reprinted by Geo. Steevens, 1766.] 8°, pp. 98, unpaged; sig. CC to HH in eights BM | BPL | BUS | W

King Henry IV., part i. . . . printed complete from the text of Sam. Johnson and Geo. Steevens, and revised from the last editions . . . Ln: Printed for . . . John Bell . . . 1785. 12°, pp. 122. With engraved title and frontispiece of Mr. Lewis as the 'Prince of Wales'

[King Henry IV., i.] The first part of Henry IV. . . . marked with the variations in the manager's book at the Theatre-Royal in Drury-Lane. Ln: C. Bathurst, 1785. 12°, pp 84. BM | BPL

[King Henry IV., i.] Diverting history of the life, memorable exploits, pranks and droll adventures of the most heroic, valiant and renowned Sir John Falstaff of facetious memory; his jests, drolleries, comical humours, queer conceits and most miraculous escapes from the wanton contrivances of the 'Merry wives of Windsor,' as written by Sh—. To which is added, a short dissertation on his character and the history of the 'Boar's Head'

tavern in East Cheap, by Dr. Goldsmith. Ln: H. Lemoine, 1789. 8°, pp. xii.-48 and plate BM | BUS | MPL
The first edition to contain Goldsmith's supplement.

King Henry the fourth [Part i.]: A historical play. Revised by J. P. Kemble and now first published as it is acted at the Theatre Royal in Covent Garden. Ln: J. Ridgway, 1803. 8°, pp. ii.-68 BUS

King Henry the fourth . . . as performed at Drury Lane and Covent Garden . . . Revised by J. P. Kemble. Ln: . . . 1804. 8°

King Henry the fourth . . . first part. With remarks by Mrs. Inchbald. Ln: Longman [1808]. 16°, pp. 82. With frontispiece BPL

King Henry the fourth . . . Revised by J. P. Kemble, as acted at . . . Covent Garden. Ln: Printed for the theatre, 1811. 8° CPL

King Henry IV., first part . . . As performed at the Theatres Royal. Edinburgh . . . [c. 1812]. 12° BPL

King Henry the fourth; The first part. An historical play. Revised by J. P. Kemble, and now published as it is performed at the Theatres Royal. Ln: J. Miller, 1815. 8°, pp. 76 BM | BPL | BUS | W

King Henry IV. The first part . . . As performed at the Theatre Royal, Covent Garden. Printed under the authority of the managers from the prompt book. With remarks by Mrs. Inchbald. Ln: Longman . . . & Brown [c. 1817]. 12°, pp. 82. With plate BUS

King Henry IV., part i. . . . Printed complete from the text of Samuel Johnson and George Steevens. Ln: . . . 1818. 16° W

King Henry the fourth . . . Ln: . . . [c. 1820]. 2 vols. 8° W
The play transformed into a prose novel.

King Henry the fourth, part i. . . . With prefatory remarks [signed P. P.] . . . marked with the stage business and stage directions, as it is performed at the Theatres Royal, by W. Oxberry. Ln: . . . 1822. 8°, pp. ii.-82 BM | BPL

King Henry the fourth: part i. . . . Edited by W. Oxberry. Ln: . . . 1823. 12°

King Henry IV,, part i. . . . 'Dolby's British theatre.' With remarks by D. G—— [Geo. Daniel]. [c. 1823.] 12° BPL
Published at 6d.

Sh— King Henry the fourth . . .

King Henry IV., part i. . . . 'Cumberland's
British theatre.' Ln: J. Cumberland [c.
1825]. 12°   BPL

[King Henry IV.] Sh—'s romances, collected and arranged by Sh— II. Ln:
Sherwood, Gilbert & Piper, 1825. 2 vols.
8°   BUS
Contents: Proem, King Henry IV.

[King Henry IV.] Life and humours of
Falstaff: A comedy, formed out of Sh—'s
'King Henry IV.' . . . [by C. Short].
1829. Cr. 8°   BPL

King Henry the fourth, part i. . . . printed
from the acting copy, with remarks . . .
by D. G—— [Geo. Daniel], to which are
added a . . . cast of the characters . . .
and the whole of the stage business as
performed at the Theatres Royal. Ln:
J. Cumberland [c. 1831]. 12°, pp. 68
                                        BM | BPL

King Henry the fourth. A Sh— novel.
Ln: Sherwood, Gilbert & Piper [c. 1834].
2 vols. 8°   BUS | W
Reprinted from the 1825 issue, the 'Proem' being left
out.

[King Henry IV., i.] Reprint of a unique
contemporary manuscript, circa 1610, of
the first part . . . Edited by J. O. Halliwell.
Ln: Sh— Soc., 1845. 8°, pp. xx.-122.
With facsimiles
                    BM | BPL | BUS | HCL | MPL | W

[King Henry IV.] Outlines to illustrate
. . . 'King Henry the fourth,' by Moritz
Retzsch. With text in English and Ger-
man. Leipzig . . . 1845. 4°. 13 plates

King Henry the fourth, part i. In five
acts. Also the stage business, casts, costumes, positions, etc. New York: S.
French [c. 1848]. 12°, pp. ii.-66
                                        BPL | BUS
Also issued in the series 'Modern standard drama' in
the same year, with slight change in title.

King Henry IV., part i. . . . printed from
the acting copy, with remarks, biographical and critical, by D. G—— [G. Daniel],
to which are added . . . the costume
. . . cast . . . entrances, exits, relative
positions . . . and the whole of the stage
business as performed at the Theatres
Royal, London. Embellished with a fine
engaving [sic] by . . . R. Cruikshank.
Ln: G. H. Davidson, Peter's Hill,
Doctors Commons, between St. Paul's and
Upper Thames Street [1850]. 12°, pp.
68 and plate

King Henry IV., part i. [Act II., Sc. 4],
trans. into Greek iambics by R. Broughton. Gaisford prize. Oxford: T. & G.
Shrimpson, 1858. 12°   BPL
In Greek and English.

Sh— King Henry the fourth . . .

King Henry the fourth, part i. 'Lacy's
acting edition.' With preliminary notes.
Ln: T. H. Lacy [1859]. 12°, pp. 70.
With frontispiece   BM | BPL

[King Henry IV.] The boaster, or Bully-
Huff catch'd in a trap [In 'Shaksperian
drolls,' ed. J. O. Halliwell]. Ln: Pri-
vately printed, 1859. 8°   BM | BUS
An extract, with adaptations from K. Henry IV., part
i., act ii., sc. 4, reprinted from the 'Theatre of ingenuity,' issued circa 1698.

[King Henry IV.] Droll of the bouncing
knight, or the robbers robbed . . . Ed. by
J. O. Halliwell. Privately printed
for the editor, 1860. 8°, pp. 44
                        BM | BPL | BUS | HCL | MPL
Reprinted from Kirkman's 'The wits, or sport upon
sport, 1672' [q.v.] An extract from 'K. Henry IV.,
part i., act ii., sc 4.'

[King Henry IV.] First part of Sh—'s
Henry the fourth . . . 1599. Facsimiled
. . . by E. W. Ashbee. [Ed. by J. O.
Halliwell.] 1861. Fcp. 4°, seventy-eight
unpaged leaves   BPL | BUS | W
Limited to fifty copies, of which Halliwell destroyed
nineteen.

[King Henry IV.] First part of Henry the
fourth . . . The text from the folio of
1623; with notices of the known editions
previously issued. Ln: L. Booth, 1863.
Fcp. 4°, pp. iv.-26, interleaved   BM

King Henry IV., part i. . . . 'Acting edition.'
Ln: Lacy [c. 1864]. 12°   BPL

King Henry the fourth: first part, 1598 . . .
Facsimiled by E. W. Ashbee. Ed. by
J. O. Halliwell. Ln: For private circu-
lation, 1866. Fcp. 4°   BPL | MPL | W
Fifty copies produced, nineteen of which the editor
destroyed.

King Henry the fourth: first part, 1608 . . .
Facsimiled by E. W. Ashbee. [Ed. by
J. O. Halliwell.] Ln: For private cir-
culation, 1867. Fcp. 4°   BPL | MPL | W

King Henry IV., first part, 1613. Facsimiled by E. W. Ashbee. Ed. by J. O.
Halliwell. Ln: For private circulation,
1867. Fcp. 4°   BPL | W
Fifty copies printed, nineteen of which Halliwell
destroyed.

King Henry IV.: part i. . . . Leipzig:
Tauchnitz, 1868. Cr. 8°

[King Henry IV.] First part of Henry the
fourth, 1604. Facsimiled . . . by E. W.
Ashbee. Ed. by J. O. Halliwell. Ln:
For private circulation only, 1871. Fcp.
4°   BM | BPL
Limited to fifty copies, of which nineteen were destroyed
by Halliwell.

King Henry IV., part i. [with introd. and
notes]. Ln: W. & R. Chambers, 1871.
Cr. 8°, pp. 106. Illustrated

[King Henry IV., part i.] Story of Falstaff [In Hatton's 'Reminiscences of Mark Lemon,' pp. 197-284]. Ln: . . . 1871. 12° BPL

King Henry IV., part i. With explanatory and illustrative notes and numerous extracts from the history on which the play is founded . . . by John Hunter. Ln: Longmans . . . 1871. 8°, pp. xii.-128 CPL

King Henry IV., part i. . . . con tante note spiegative ed osservazioni sulla grammatica di Sh— da rendere il dramma intelligibile a chiunque conosce anche solo mezzanamente l'inglese. Saggio del padre Viani Carlo. Torino: E. Loescher, 1872. 8°, pp. viii.-108 BM | BUS
English text, with Italian introduction and notes.

King Henry IV. [Act v., Sc. 4], trans. into Greek comic iambics, by E. M. Field. Gaisford prize. Oxford: Thomas Shrimpton & Son, 1874. Cr. 8° BPL
In Greek and English.

King Henry IV., part i. [from 'Hudson's school Sh—']. Boston [U.S.]: Ginn Brothers, 1874. 12°, [excerpt] pp. 247-337 BUS

King Henry IV., part i. With notes. Edinburgh: W. & R. Chambers [c. 1875]. 12°, pp. 108

King Henry IV., part i. . . . With notes and extracts by John Hunter. Ln: Longman [c. 1878]. 12°, pp. xiv.-128 BPL

King Henry the fourth: part i. . . . edited by W. J. Rolfe. New York: Harper, 1880. 12°. Illustrated BPL | BUS

King Henry the fourth, part i.: The first quarto, 1598, a facsimile in photolithography by W. Griggs . . . with forewords by H. A. Evans. 'Sh— quarto facsimiles.' Ln: W. Griggs [1881]. Fcp. 4°, xiv.-80 BM | BPL | BUS

King Henry the fourth: first part . . . edited by C. E. Flower. 'Memorial Theatre edition.' Stratford-on-Avon: Printed by G. Boyden [1882]. Cr. 8°, pp. viii.-92, including printed wrappers BPL | SML

King Henry the fourth: part i. . . . edited by W. J. Rolfe. New York . . . 1883. 12° BPL

King Henry the fourth, part i. 'Standard plays.' Ln: John Dicks [1883]. Cr. 8° BM

King Henry the fourth, part i. . . . arranged for performances at the A. D. C. [Amateur Dramatic Club], Michaelmas term, 1886. Cambridge: University Press, 1886. 8°, pp. 70 BM

[King Henry IV.] First part of King Henry IV. . . . and the old play of the 'Famous victories of Henry V.' [with introduction by Hy. Morley]. 'National library.' Ln: Cassell, 1888. 16°, pp. 192 BM

King Henry the fourth: First part . . . Edited by O. Elton. 'Falcon edition.' Ln: Rivingtons . . . 1889. Cr. 8°, pp. xxiv.-142 BPL

King Henry IV.: part first . . . With introduction and notes by H. N. Hudson. Boston [U.S.] . . . 1889. Cr. 8° BPL

King Henry the fourth: first part . . . With introduction and notes by K. Deighton. Ln: Macmillan, 1893. Cr. 8°, pp. xl.-200 BPL

King Henry IV. . . . [In Donovan's 'English historical plays arranged for acting,' Vol. I.] Ln: Macmillan, 1896. 2 vols. Cr. 8°, pp. 480 and 474
BM | BLO | CTC | MPL

King Henry IV.: first part . . . edited by W. A. Wright . . . Oxford: Clarendon Press, 1897. Cr. 8°, pp. 202 BPL

King Henry IV.: part i. 'Pocket Falstaff edition.' Ln: Bliss, Sands, 1898. 16°, pp. 116 BPL | SML

King Henry the fourth: first part . . . edited with introduction and notes by C. H. Herford. 'Eversley edition.' Ln: Macmillan, 1900. Cr. 8°
BM | BLO | BPL | CTC

King Henry IV.: part i. . . . Introductory notes by John Dennis. Illustrated by B. Shaw. 'Chiswick edition.' Ln: Bell, 1901. 12°

King Henry IV.: part i., edited by H. W. Ord. Ln: Black, 1902. Cr. 8°, pp. 156 BPL

King Henry IV.: part i., edited with notes by H. N. Hudson. 'Windsor edition.' Edinburgh: Jack, 1903. Cr. 8°

King Henry IV., part i. . . . 'Warwick Sh—.' Ln: Blackie, 1904. Cr. 8° BPL

King Henry IV.: part i. With introduction by G. Brandes. 'Favourite classics.' Ln: Heinemann, 1904. 12°, pp. xviii.-118 and port. of Macready

King Henry IV.: part i. Introduction and notes by W. J. Craig. 'Little quartos.' Ln: Methuen, 1904. 16°

King Henry IV.: part i. 'Ellen Terry edition.' Glasgow: Bryce, 1904. 32°

King Henry IV.: part i. Edited by H. Morley. 1905. 16° BPL

King Henry IV.: part i. . . . 'Waistcoat pocket edition.' Ln: Treherne, 1905. 32°

Sh— King Henry the fourth . . .

King Henry IV., part i. ' Stage edition.'
Glasgow : Collins, 1905. 16°

King Henry IV. : part i. ' Red letter
edition.' Ln : Blackie, 1906. 12°

King Henry IV. : part i. ' Renaissance
edition.' Ln : Harrap, 1908. Fcp. 4° BPL

KING HENRY THE FOURTH : SECOND PART.

*The first edition known is that printed
by V. S—— [Valentine Sims] for Andrew
Wise and William Aspley in 1600, of
which two varying issues exist. Apparently
no subsequent impression appeared until
that of 1623 in the Jaggard canon.*

[King Henry IV. : part ii.] The Second
part of Henrie the fourth, continuing to
his death, and coronation of Henrie the
fift. With the humours of sir Iohn Falstaffe, and swaggering Pistoll. As it
hath been sundrie times publikely acted
by the right honourable, the Lord Chamberlaine his seruants. Written by William Shakespeare. [*Ornament.*] London :
Printed by V. S—— [Valentine Sims] for
Andrew Wise, and William Aspley, 1600.
Fcp. 4°, forty-three leaves unpaged ; sig.
A to L² in fours, except sheet E, which
consists of six leaves
BM | BLO | CTC | DEVON | HUTH
In the earliest copies struck off the compositor omitted
the entire first scene of the third act. To rectify this
blunder sheet E (four leaves) was reprinted upon six
leaves, and the deficiency made good. One of the
two copies in the British Museum contains the auto-
graph of George Steevens.
When the play appeared in the Jaggard folio of 1623 it
received considerable and important additions.
Reproduced by Halliwell in 1866.
A copy of the first issue realised £1,035 in April, 1904.

[King Henry IV., ii.] The Second Part of
the History of King Henry the Fourth.
London : Printed for Mathew Law, 1605.
Fcp. 4°
In July, 1905, a copy realised £500. The title was
missing and supplied in manuscript, the top corner of
one leaf defective, and some headlines shaved. The
collation tallied with the 1600 issue, and the written
date may therefore have been an error. No other
record of this edition is extant.

[King Henry IV., ii.] The sequel to Henry
IV. With the humours of Sir John
Falstaff and Justice Shallow. As it is
acted at the Theatre Royal, Drury Lane.
Altered by Mr. Betterton. Ln : R.
Walker, 1700. Fcp. 4°

[King Henry IV., ii.] The sequel to Henry
the fourth. With the humours of Sir
John Falstaff and Justice Shallow. As
it is acted at the Theatre Royal, Drury
Lane. Altered by the late Mr. Betterton.
Ln : . . . [c. 1710]. 8°

Sh— King Henry the fourth . . .

[King Henry IV., ii.] The sequel of Henry
the fourth ; with the humours of Sir
John Falstaffe, and Justice Shallow. As
it is acted by His Majesty's company of
comedians at the Theatre-Royal in Drury
Lane. Altered from Sh— by the late
Mr. Betterton. Ln : W. Chetwood and
T. Jauncy, 1719. 8°, pp. 82 BM | CPL

[King Henry IV., ii.] The sequel of Henry
the fourth. With the humours of Sir
John Falstaffe and Justice Shallow. As
it is acted by his majesty's company of
comedians at the Theatre Royal in Drury
Lane. Alter'd from Sh— by the late
Mr. Betterton. Ln : W. Chetwood [c.
1721]. 8°, pp. viii.-82 BPL | BUS
Baker's ' Biographia dramatica' assigns 1719 as the
date, but Geneste says it could not have been printed
until after the 17th Dec., 1720.

[King Henry IV., ii.] Prologue and epilogue
to ' Henry IV., part 2,' spoken Dec. 27,
1728 in the presence of the Free-Masons
at the Theatre Royal, Drury Lane.
Ln : . . . 1728. F°, pp. 4 BUS

[King Henry IV., ii.] The second part of
Henry IV. Containing his death and the
coronation of King Henry V. Ln : J.
Tonson . . . 1733. 8°, pp. vi.-94 and
frontispiece BPL | W

[King Henry IV., ii.] The second part of
Henry IV. Containing his death, and
the coronation of King Henry V. By Mr.
Wm. Sh—. Ln : Printed for J. Tonson
and the rest of the proprietors ; and sold
by the booksellers of Ln. and Westminster, 1734. Cr. 8°, pp. 94 and frontis-
piece BM | BPL | W
Piracy notice against R. Walker on verso of title.

[King Henry IV., ii.] Henry IV. : The
second part. Containing his death and
the coronation of King Henry V. . . .
Ln : R. Walker . . . 1734. 12°. Frontispiece

[King Henry IV., ii.] Falstaff's wedding.
a comedy, being a sequel to the second
part of the play of ' King Henry the
fourth.' Written in imitation of Sh—
by William Kenrick. Ln : J. Wilkie,
1760. 8°, pp. viii.-84 BM | BPL | BUS | W
According to the preface, dated 1 Jan., 1766, this work
was written in 1751, printed in 1760, and published in
1766.

[King Henry IV., ii.] Falstaff's wedding ;
a comedy, as it is acted at the Theatre
Royal in Drury Lane. Being a sequel to
the second part of the play of ' King
Henry the fourth.' Written in imitation
of Sh— by W. Kenrick. Second edition.

Ln : L. Davis & C. Reymers, 1766. 8°,
pp. viii.-70   BM | BPL | BUS | W
In this edition the parts of the King and Courtiers
have been omitted, while prologue and epilogue are
added.

[King Henry IV., ii.] Falstaff's wedding . . .
By W. Kenrick.   Dublin . . . 1766.
Cr. 8°   BPL

[King Henry IV., ii.] The second part of
Henrie the fourth . . . [Reprinted by G.
Steevens]. Ln : 1600[-1766]. 8°, pp. 92,
unpaged ; sig. II¹ to OO⁶ in eights
    BPL | W

[King Henry IV., ii.] Falstaff's wedding . . .
By W. Kenrick. A new edition. Ln :
L. Davis, etc., 1773. 8°, pp. viii.-64
    BPL | BUS | W

[King Henry IV., ii.] Falstaff's wedding . . .
As it is acted at the Theatre Royal.
By W. Kenrick. Ln : 1781. 8°   BPL

King Henry IV., part ii. . . . printed complete from the text of Sam. Johnson and
Geo. Steevens, and revised from the last
editions . . . Ln : Printed for . . . John
Bell . . . 1785. 12°, pp. 132. With engraved title and frontispiece of ' Mr.
Parsons as Justice Shallow '

[King Henry IV., ii.] Falstaff's wedding.
A comedy . . . By W. Kenrick. Adapted
for theatrical representation, as performed
at the Theatre Royal, Covent Garden.
Regulated from the prompt book by permission of the manager. Ln : G. Cawthorn, 1795. 12°, pp. 92. Illustrated
    BUS

[King Henry IV., ii.] Falstaff's wedding . . .
As performed at Drury Lane. By W.
Kenrick . . . Ln : G. Cawthorn . . . 1795.
8°, pp. 80. Illustrated   BPL | BUS

[King Henry IV., ii.] The second part of
King Henry the fourth, altered from
Sh— [by Dr. Richard Valpy], as it was
acted at Reading School, 1801. Published, as it was performed, for the
benefit of the Humane Society. Reading :
Smart and Cowslade, 1801. 8°, pp. x.-96
    BM | BPL | BUS | W

King Henry the fourth : Part ii. . . . As
performed at Covent Garden. Revised
by J. P. Kemble . . . Ln : . . . 1803. 8°

King Henry IV. [second part], a historical
play. Revised by J. P. Kemble ; and
now first published as it is acted at the
Theatre Royal in Covent Garden. Ln :
J. Ridgway, 1804. 8°, pp. 64   BUS | W

King Henry IV. : second part . . . Printed
complete from the text of Samuel
Johnson and George Steevens. Ln : . . .
1807. 16°   W

King Henry the fourth : part ii. . . . As
performed at Covent Garden . . . Edited
by Mrs. Inchbald. Ln : Longman [c.
1808]. 12°   BPL

[King Henry IV., ii.] Falstaff's wedding . . .
By W. Kenrick [In ' Modern British
drama,' Vol. 4]. Ln : . . . 1811. 8°
    BPL | BUS

King Henry IV. [second part] : an historical play . . . Revised by J. P. Kemble
and now published as it is performed at
the Theatres Royal. ' Select British
theatre.' Ln : J. Miller, 1815. 12°, pp.
70   BPL | BUS | W

King Henry IV., second part . . . As performed at the Theatre Royal, Covent
Garden. Printed under the authority of
the managers from the prompt book.
With remarks by Mrs. Inchbald. Ln :
Hurst, Robinson & Co. [c. 1816]. 12°,
pp. 74 and plate   BUS

[King Henry IV., ii.] Senarii Græci [a
translation from ' Henry IV.,' part ii.,
act iii., sc. i. . . In English and Greek]
. . . auctore G. I. Pennington. Cambridge . . . 1817. 8°, pp. 8   BM

[King Henry IV., ii.] Death of Falstaff : A
melodrame. Ln : Printed for the author,
1820. 8°, pp. ii.-58   BUS
Issue confined to twenty copies.

King Henry IV., second part. An historical
play. Revised by J. P. Kemble and
printed as it was revived at the Theatre
Royal, Covent Garden, on Monday, June
25th, 1821 ; With the representation of
the coronation, as arranged by Mr.
Farley. Published with the stage directions. Ln : Printed [by W. Smith] for
John Miller, Fleet Street, 1821. 8°, pp.
68   BM | BPL

King Henry IV., part ii. [a prose romance
founded upon Sh—'s play], collected and
arranged by ' Sh— II.' [pseud.] Ln :
Sherwood, 1825. 8°   BM
No more published.

King Henry IV. [part ii.] A drama in two
parts . . . With introduction and notes
[in German] by F. E. Feller. Leipsic . . .
1830. 8°

King Henry the fourth : The second part.
Printed from the acting copy, with remarks . . . by D. G—— [Geo. Daniel].
To which are added a . . . cast of the
characters . . . and the whole of the stage
business as now performed at the Theatres
Royal. Ln : J. Cumberland [c. 1831].
12°, pp. 60   BM | BPL | BUS

King Henry IV. : part ii. . . . Ln : J. Cumberland & Son [c. 1831]. 12°   BPL

Sh— King Henry the fourth . . .

[King Henry IV., ii.] Programme of the airs, duets, &c. in the grand musical festival! introduced in ' King Henry IV., part the second,' at the Theatre Royal, Drury Lane, 1834. With a drawing of the plan of the orchestra. Ln : . . . 1834. 8°   w

King Henry IV., part ii. [Act iv., Sc. 3]. In Greek iambics, by R. W. Raper. Gaisford prize.   Oxford : T. & G. Shrimpton, 1862.   12°   BPL
In Greek and English.

[King Henry IV.] The second part of Henry the fourth . . . The text from the folio of 1623 ; with notices of the known editions previously issued. Ln : L. Booth, 1863. Fcp. 4°, pp. 28, interleaved   BM | BPL

King Henry IV., part ii. . . . With . . . remarks. 'Acting edition of plays.' Ln : T. H. Lacy [c. 1864].   12°, pp. 72
                          BPL | BUS

King Henry the fourth : part ii. . . . 'Acting edition.' Ln : T. H. Lacy [1865]. 12°, pp. 72   BM | BPL

King Henry the fourth : second part, 1600. Facsimiled from the first edition by E. W. Ashbee. [Ed. by J. O. Halliwell.] Ln : For private circulation, 1866.   Fcp. 4°
                 BPL | MPL | W
Of the fifty copies produced, the editor destroyed nineteen.

King Henry the fourth : second part, 1600. Facsimiled from the second edition by E. W. Ashbee. Ed. by J. O. Halliwell. Ln : For private circulation, 1866. Fcp. 4°   BPL | W
Fifty copies produced, nineteen of which the editor destroyed.

King Henry IV., part ii. [Act v., Sc. i.]. In comic iambic verse, by W. S. Gibson. Gaisford prize.   Oxford : T. & G. Shrimpton, 1870.   12°   BPL

King Henry IV., part ii. . . . [With introd. and notes]. ' Household edition.' Ln : W. & R. Chambers, 1871. 8°, pp. 110
Illustrated

King Henry IV., part ii. . . . edited by J. Hunter. Ln : Longman . . . 1871.   12°

[King Henry IV., ii.] Story of Falstaff [In Hatton's ' Reminiscences of Mark Lemon,' pp. 197-284]. Ln : 1871.   12°
                           BPL

King Henry the fourth : second part . . . Arranged by Charles Calvert and produced at the Prince's Theatre, Manchester, Sept., 1874.   Manchester : J. F. Wilkinson, 1874. 8°, pp. 64
               BM | BPL | BUS

Sh— King Henry the fourth . . .

King Henry IV. : part ii. . . . With notes, etc. by J. Hunter. Ln : Longmans . . . [c. 1878].   Cr. 8°   BPL

King Henry the fourth : part ii. . . . edited by W. J. Rolfe. New York : Harper . . . 1880.   12°   BPL | BUS

King Henry IV. : part ii. . . . Ln : W. & R. Chambers [c. 1882].   8°, pp. 110

King Henry the fourth, part ii. . . . The quarto of 1600. A facsimile in photolithography by W. Griggs . . . with forewords by H. A. Evans. ' Sh— quarto facsimiles.' Ln : W. Griggs [1882]. 8°, pp. xii.-86   BM | BPL | BUS

King Henry the fourth : part ii. . . . 'Standard plays.' Ln : John Dicks [1883]. 12°   BM

[King Henry the fourth, part ii., act i., sc. i.] The Gaisford verse, 1884 [translated into Greek iambics]. By H. H. House.   Oxford : B. H. Blackwell, 1884. 8°, pp. 12   BM | BPL
English and Greek text.

King Henry IV., part ii. [act iii., sc. 2]. In Greek comic verse. By G. A. Murray. Gaisford prize. Oxford : B. H. Blackwell, 1886. 8°, pp. 10   BM | BPL

[King Henry IV.] Second part of King Henry IV. [With introduction by H. Morley.] ' National library.' Ln : Cassell, 1888.   16°, pp. 192   BM

King Henry the fourth : Second part . . . Edited by A. D. Innes. ' Falcon edition.' Ln : Longmans, 1889.   12°   BPL

King Henry the fourth : Second part . . . Edited by C. E. Flower. ' Memorial theatre edition.'   Stratford-on-Avon : Printed by G. Boyden ; Ln : S. French [1889]. Cr. 8°, pp. viii.-84, incl. printed wrappers   BPL | SML

King Henry IV. : part second . . . With introduction and notes by H. N. Hudson. Boston [U.S.], 1889.   12°   BPL

King Henry the fourth : second part . . . With introduction and notes by K. Deighton. Ln : Macmillan, 1893.   Cr. 8°
                          BPL

King Henry IV., part ii. [act ii., sc. 2, lines 1-100]. Trans. into comic iambic verse by G. S. Robertson. Oxford : B. H. Blackwell, 1894. 8°, pp. 16   BM | BPL

King Henry IV. : part ii. . . . . ' Pocket Falstaff edition.' Ln : Bliss, Sands, 1898. 16°, pp. 128   BPL | SML

King Henry the fourth : second part . . . Edited with introduction and notes by C. H. Herford. ' Eversley edition.' Ln : Macmillan, 1900.   12°   BPL

King Henry IV.: part ii. Introductory notes by John Dennis. Illustrated by B. Shaw. 'Chiswick edition.' Ln: Bell, 1901. 12°, pp. 148

King Henry IV., part ii. [act iii., sc. ii.] In comic iambics, by H. L. Henderson. Gaisford prize. Oxford: B. H. Blackwell, 1903. 12°   BPL

King Henry IV.: part ii. Edited with notes by H. N. Hudson. 'Windsor edition.' Edinburgh: Jack, 1903. Cr. 8°

King Henry IV.: part ii. With introduction by G. Brandes. 'Favourite classics.' Ln: Heinemann, 1904. 12°, pp. 126 and portrait of Elliston as Falstaff

King Henry IV.: part ii. 'Ellen Terry edition.' Glasgow: Bryce, 1904. 32°

King Henry IV.: part ii. . . . With introduction and notes by W. J. Craig. 'Little quartos.' Ln: Methuen, 1904. 16°

King Henry IV.: part ii. 'Waistcoat pocket edition.' Ln: Treherne, 1905. 32°

King Henry IV.: part ii. Edited by H. Morley. 'National library.' Ln: Cassell, 1905. 12°   BPL

King Henry IV.: part ii. 'Stage edition.' Glasgow: Collins, 1905. 16°

King Henry IV.: part ii. Edited by J. W. B. Adams. 'Carmelite classics.' Ln: H. Marshall, 1906. 12°

King Henry IV.: part ii. . . . 'Red letter edition.' Ln: Blackie, 1906. 12°

King Henry IV.: part ii. 'Renaissance edition.' Ln: Harrap, 1908. Fcp. 4° BPL

KING HENRY THE FOURTH: PARTS I. & II.

[King Henry IV.] Costume of 'King Henry IV., Parts i. and ii.,' selected . . . from the best authorities, with . . . notices by J. R. Planché. The figures . . . by G. Scharf. Ln: J. Miller, 1824. 8°, pp. 36   BPL | BUS

[King Henry IV.] Life and humours of Falstaff; A comedy formed out of the two parts of Sh—'s 'Henry the fourth' and a few scenes of 'Henry the fifth.' Compiled, etc. by C. S—— [C. Short]. Ln: Calkin & Budd, 1829. 12°, pp. ii.-94   BM | BPL | BUS | W
Issue restricted to a few copies, for presentation purposes.

King Henry the fourth . . . Two parts. With . . . notes [in German] by J. M. Pierre. Frankfort . . . 1833. 12°

King Henry the fourth: parts i.-ii. . . . Nuremberg and New York . . . 1841. 12°

King Henry the fourth . . . Printed from a contemporary manuscript, circa 1610 [Consisting of part i. and a portion of part ii.] Edited by J. O. Halliwell. Ln: Sh—Soc., 1845. 8° BM | BPL | MPL | W
The original is at Warwick Castle. See Sh— King Henry IV., i., 1610.

[King Henry the fourth] Sir John Falstaff, in selected scenes from 'Henry the fourth,' parts i. and ii.: Readings, in costume, by Mark Lemon. Ln: . . . 1868. 12°   BPL

[King Henry IV.] Story of Falstaff, selected from 'King Henry IV.' for drawing-room representation, by Mark Lemon. Ln:... 1871. 8°   BM

[King Henry IV.] Selections from 'King Richard II.' and 'Henry IV.' Ln: Blackie & Son [1885]. 16°   BM

King Henry IV. . . . parts i. and ii. Introduction by E. Dowden. With 12 illustrations by Ed. Grützner. Ln: Cassell, 1887. F°   BPL

King Henry the fourth . . . two parts. Edited by I. Gollancz. 'Temple edition.' Ln: Dent, 1895. 16°

King Henry IV. . . . two parts [In Donovan, 'English historical plays,' Vol. I.] Ln: Macmillan, 1896. 2 vols. Cr. 8° BM | MPL

[King Henry IV.] Historie of Henrie the fourth, parts i. and ii., edited by F. J. Furnivall. 'Old spelling library edition.' Ln: Chatto, 1909. 2 vols. 8°   BPL

'King Henry IV.' references—

See Account of the	See Hayward
'Boar's Head'	„ J—— (W.)
„ Beamont	„ Johnson & Stee-
„ Betty	vens
„ Bold	„ Jonson
„ Brown	„ Liverseege
„ Capgrave	„ Lucy
„ Cibber	„ Meres
„ Clarke (R.)	„ Mirror
„ Clavell	„ Pegasus
„ Cooke	„ Planché
„ Crawfurd	„ Preston
„ Crown garland	„ Raffles
„ Dodsley	„ S—— (C.)
„ Dramatic histo-	„ Sh— Works:
riographer	Ext. 1799
„ Examination	„ Sh—] Sh— drolls
„ Fall . . .	„ Shirley
„ Field	„ Six old plays
„ Goffe	„ Skeat
„ Goldsmith	„ Stopes
„ Gray	„ Stukeley
„ Hagena	„ Table book
„ Halliwell	„ Towndrow

Sh—] KING HENRY THE FIFTH.

The first known edition is that printed by 'Thomas Creede for Thomas Millington and John Busby, 1600,' which was unregistered at Stationer's Hall. This reappeared in 1602, and in 1619; the latter with the fictitious date of 1608. This last quarto gives a total of eighteen hundred lines only, as compared with three thousand five hundred in the next printing of this play in the Jaggard folio of 1623.

[King Henry V.] The Famous Victories of Henry the Fifth, containing the honourable Battel of Agin Court. As it was plaide by the Queene's Maiesties Players. Ln: Printed by Thomas Creede, 1598. Fcp. 4°   BLO
This play furnished Sh— with an outline for 'King Henry IV.' and 'King Henry V.'

[King Henry V.] The Cronicle History of Henry the fift. With his battell fought at Agin Court in France. Togither with Auntient Pistoll. As it hath bene sundry times playd by the Right honorable the Lord Chamberlaine his seruants. [*Device with motto 'Viressit vulnere veritas.'*] Ln: Printed by Thomas Creede for Tho. Millington and Iohn Busby. And are to be sold at his house in Carter Lane, next the Powle head, 1600. Fcp. 4°, twenty-eight unpaged leaves; sig. A¹ to G⁴ in fours; sig. G² is erroneously marked G³, while sig. G³ is unmarked and its verso is blank; G⁴ is blank
                    BM | BLO | CTC | DEVON
Sh—'s name does not appear in this edition.

[King Henry V.] The Chronicle History of Henry the fift. With his battell fought at Agin Court in France. Together with Auntient Pistoll. As it hath bene sundry times playd by the Right honorable the Lord Chamberlaine his seruants. [*Device and motto.*]   Ln: Printed by Thomas Creede for Thomas Pauier and are to be sold in Cornhill at the signe of the Cat and Parrets neare the Exchange, 1602. Fcp. 4°, twenty-six unpaged leaves; sig. A¹ to G² in fours
                    CTC | DEVON

[King Henry V.] The Chronicle History of Henry the fift, with his battell fought at Agin Court in France. Together with ancient Pistoll. As it hath bene sundry times playd by the Right Honourable the Lord Chamberlaine her Seruants. ['*Heb Ddieu*' block. Ln:] Printed for T. P—— [Thomas Pavier by Isaac Jaggard, 1619], 1608. Fcp. 4°, twenty-eight unpaged

Sh— King Henry the fifth . . . leaves; sig. A¹ to G⁴ in fours (the last leaf blank)
BM | BLO | BPL | BUS | CTC | DEVON | NY | W
Sh—'s name is unmentioned in this issue. Although dated 1608, the real year of publication was 1619. *See* A. W. Pollard's 'Sh— folios and quartos' for further particulars.
For the Jaggard folio of 1623 the play was either set from an unknown version, or entirely recast, so great is the difference between that and the earlier printings.
A copy, measuring 7 by 5¼ in., sold in May, 1906 for £150; another, Dec., 1907, for £104.

[King Henry V.] The Famous Victories of Henry the Fifth. Containing the Honourable Battell of Agincourt. As it was Acted by the Kinges Maiesties Servantes. London: Imprinted by Barnard Alsop dwelling in Garter Place in Barbican, 1617. Fcp. 4°, on twenty-six unpaged leaves, including title; sig. A to G² in fours   CTC
The second edition of this foundation of Sh—'s play. The first appeared in 1598.

[King Henry V.] The Famous Victories of Henry the Fifth. Containing the Honourable Battell of Agin-Court. As it was Acted by the Kinges Maiesties Seruants. London: Imprinted by Barnard Alsop and are to be sold by Tymothie Barlow at his shop in Paules Church-yard, at the Signe of the Bull-Head, 1617. Fcp. 4°, on twenty-six unpaged leaves   BM
Similar to the foregoing, save in imprint.
Not more than two or three copies are known of this issue. Reproduced by Halliwell in 1857.
One sold in June, 1902 for £107.

King Henry the Fifth . . . A tragedy as performed at the Duke's Theatre . . . by the Earle of Orrery. Ln: . . . 1672. F°

[King Henry V.] Two-part song in the play call'd 'Harry the fifth.' Set by H. Purcell. Within compass of the flute. Ln: . . . [c. 1700]. F° broadside   BUS

[King Henry V.] Half-pay officers [A play, altered from Davenant's ' Love and honour,' with some scenes taken from Sh—'s 'King Henry V.'] Ln: . . . 1720. 12°   BM

King Henry V., or the conquest of France by the English. A tragedy. As it is acted at the Theatre-Royal in Drury Lane by his majesty's servants. By Aaron Hill. Ln: Printed for W. Chetwood & J. Watts, 1723. 8°, pp. xvi.-64 BM | BPL | BUS | W
Hill created a famous phrase. After handsomely acknowledging his indebtedness to the poet in the above adaptation, he remarked that 'Shakespeare spelt ruin to theatrical managers.' This dictum passed into a truism, to be repeated by successive generations of managers for nearly two centuries. The end of the 19th century witnessed a change. New men and methods restored Sh— to his rightful position on the throne of the English drama.

Sh— King Henry the fifth . . .

Hill attacked the fashionables of his day for their devotion to the ballet, for ' wit in the heels rather than in the head.' Much the same criticism applies to-day to the masses which frequent music halls and football fields.

[King Henry V.] The life of Henry V. By Mr. Wm. Sh—. Ln : Printed for J. Tonson, and the rest of the proprietors, and sold by the booksellers of Ln. and Westminster, 1734. Cr. 8°, pp. 96 and frontispiece   BM

King Henry the fifth . . . Edited by the Earl of Orrery. Ln : . . . 1739. 8°

King Henry the fifth, by A. Hill. Second edition. Ln : . . . 1746. 12°   BPL

King Henry V. . . . As it is acted at the Theatre Royal in Drury Lane by his majesty's servants. [Altered] by Aaron Hill. Edinburgh : Printed for A. Donaldson at Pope's Head, opposite to the Exchange, 1759. 8°, pp. 60
Unchronicled elsewhere.

King Henry the fifth . . . [In Aaron Hill's ' Dramatic works,' Vol. I., pp. 219-282]. Ln : . . . 1760. 8°   BPL

King Henry the fifth, by A. Hill. Third edition. Ln : . . . 1765. 12°   BPL

[King Henry V.] Chronicle History of Henry the fift . . . [Ln :] Printed for T. P., 1608 ; Reprinted by George Steevens, 1766. 8°   BPL | W

King Henry V. . . . As it is acted at the Theatre Royal in Drury Lane and Covent Garden. Ln : . . . 1769. 12°   BPL

King Henry V. . . . As performed at the Theatre Royal, Covent Garden. Regulated by Mr. Younger, prompter of that theatre. An introduction and notes critical and illustrative are added by the authors of the ' Dramatic censor ' [F. Gentleman]. Ln : John Bell ; York : C. Etherington, 1773. 8°, pp. 80
An off-print from Bell's edition for the use of playgoers.

[King Henry V.] Famous victories of Henry the fifth . . . 1617 [In ' Six old plays . . . edited by J. Nichols,' Vol. 2]. Ln : . . . 1779. 8°   BPL | BUS | W
From this play, which first appeared in 1598, Sh— obtained his foundation for both parts of ' King Henry IV.' and for ' King Henry V.'

King Henry the fifth. A tragedy . . . As it is acted at the Theatres Royal in Drury-Lane and Covent-Garden. Ln : Harrison & Co., 1780. 8°, pp. 20. With engraved portrait of ' Mr. Baddeley in the character of Pistol '   BM | BPL

King Henry V. . . . printed complete from the text of Sam. Johnson and Geo. Steevens, and revised from the last

editions . . . Ln : Printed for . . . John Bell . . . 1785. 12°, pp. 132. With engraved title and frontispiece of Mrs. Siddons as Princess Katherine '

King Henry V., or the conquest of France. A tragedy, written by Sh—. Printed exactly conformable to the representation, on its revival at the Theatre Royal, Drury Lane, Oct. 1, 1789. [Adapted to the stage by J. P. Kemble. Edited by J. Wrighten, prompter.] Ln : J. Debrett, 1789. 8°, pp. 62   BM | BPL | W

King Henry V. A tragedy. Written by Sh—. Taken from the manager's book at the Theatre Royal, Drury Lane. Ln : . . . [c. 1790]. 12°   W

King Henry V. [In ' Collection of . . . dramatic pieces. Ed. by J. P. Kemble']. Ln : J. Debrett, 1795. 2 vols. 8°

King Henry V. [In ' Collection of much-esteemed dramatic pieces ']. Ln : J. Debrett, 1795. 2 vols. 8°

King Henry the fifth . . . Revised by J. P. Kemble. Ln : . . . 1801. 8°

King Henry the fifth . . . Revised by J. P. Kemble and now first published as it is acted at the Theatre Royal in Covent Garden. Ln : Longman . . . 1806. 8°, pp. 66   BM | BPL

King Henry the fifth . . . With remarks by Mrs. Inchbald. Ln : Longman [1808]. 12°. With frontispiece   BPL

King Henry the fifth . . . An historical play. Revised by J. P. Kemble ; and now first published as it is acted at the Theatre Royal in Covent Garden. Ln : J. Miller, 1815. 8°, pp. 68   BM | BUS | W

King Henry the fifth . . . from the text of Johnson and Steevens. With remarks. Ln : . . . [1822]. 12°   BPL

King Henry the fifth . . . With prefatory remarks [signed P. P——] . . . Marked with the stage business, and stage directions, as it is performed at the Theatres Royal, by W. Oxberry. Ln : . . . 1823. 8°, pp. x.-68   BM | BPL

King Henry V. . . . With remarks by D. G—— [G. Daniel]. ' British theatre.' Ln : J. Cumberland [c. 1825]. 12°
          BPL | BUS

[King Henry V.] Life and humours of Falstaff : A comedy [by C. Short] formed out of Sh—'s 'King Henry IV.' and 'King Henry V.' Ln : . . . 1829. Cr. 8°   BPL

King Henry the fifth . . . Printed from the acting copy, with remarks, biographical and critical, by D. G——[Geo. Daniel]. To which are added a . . . cast of the characters . . . and the whole of the stage

Sh— King Henry the fifth . . . .
business, as now performed at the
Theatres Royal. Ln: J. Cumberland
[c. 1830]. 12°, pp. 56   BM | BPL
King Henry the fifth [A translation, in
Greek iambics, by Thomas Evans, from
'King Henry V., act iv., sc. i.'] Cam-
bridge . . . 1838. 8°   BM
King Henry the fifth . . . as performed by
Mr. Macready. Ln: Pattie . . . 1839. 12°
King Henry the fifth [A translation, into
Greek iambics, by G. Druce, from 'King
Henry V., act iv., sc. i.'] Ln: . . . 1842.
8°   BM
King Henry the fifth . . . Acting edition.
Ln: Sherwood . . . 1849. 12°
King Henry the fifth . . . 1617 [Facsimile,
edited by J. O. Halliwell]. Ln: For
private circulation, 1857. 12° BPL | W
Issue limited to ten copies.
One of the 'first attempts to photograph old books,
before photolithography and photozincography were
used.' Some of the pages are now illegible.

[King Henry V.] Music in 'King Henry
the fifth,' as performed at the Princess's
Theatre [Full score]. Composed by J.
Isaacson. Ln: Cramer & Co., 1858. F°
King Henry the fifth . . . arranged for re-
presentation at the Princess's Theatre,
with historical and explanatory notes, by
Charles Kean, as first performed on March
28th, 1859. Second edition. Ln: T. K.
Chapman & Co. [1859]. 8°, pp. 96
                    BM | CPL | W
King Henry the fifth . . . Arranged . . . by
Charles Kean . . . Third edition. Ln:
J. K. Chapman & Co., 1859. 8°, pp. 96
                    BUS
King Henry the fifth . . . 'Acting edition.'
Ln: T. H. Lacy [1859]. 12°, pp. 76
                    BM | BPL | BUS
King Henry the fifth . . . With . . . notes by
C. Kean. Third edition. Ln: Chapman
& Co. [1859]. 8°, pp. 96   BM | BPL
[King Henry V.] Life of Henry the fift . . .
text from the folio of 1623; with notices
of the known editions previously issued.
Ln: L. Booth, 1863. Fcp. 4°, pp. iv.-28
                    BM | BPL
King Henry the fifth . . . 1600. Facsimiled
by E. W. Ashbee. Edited by J. O.
Halliwell. Ln: Printed for private cir-
culation, 1867. Fcp. 4°   BPL | W
Limited to fifty copies, nineteen of which the editor
destroyed. Some copies were dated 1858.

King Henry the fifth . . . 1602. Facsimiled
by E. W. Ashbee. Ed. by J. O. Halliwell.
Ln: Printed for private circulation, 1867.
Fcp. 4°   BPL | W
Edition limited to fifty copies, of which only thirty-one
survive, the editor having destroyed nineteen.

Sh— King Henry the fifth . . .
King Henry the fifth, 1608. Facsimiled
by E. W. Ashbee. Ed. by J. O. Halliwell.
Ln: Printed for private circulation, 1870.
Fcp. 4°   BPL | W
Edition limited to fifty copies, of which nineteen were
destroyed by the editor.

King Henry the fifth, 1608. Facsimiled
by E. W. Ashbee. 1870. Fcp. 4°   W
The sole large paper copy is at Warwick Castle.

King Henry V. . . . With explanatory and
illustrative notes and numerous extracts
from the history on which the play is
founded.   Adapted for scholastic or
private study. By . . . John Hunter. Ln:
Longmans, 1871. Cr. 8°, pp. xxiv.-124 CPL
King Henry the fifth . . . Arranged . . . by
Charles Calvert, and produced at the
Prince's Theatre, Manchester, Sept., 1872.
[With notes on the heraldry displayed
. . . by A. Darbyshire.]   Manchester:
Henry Blacklock [1872].   8°, pp. 80, in
pictorial pink wrappers   BPL | CPL
[King Henry V.] Chronicle history of Henry
the fifth. Reprint of first quarto, 1600.
Edited by Dr. B. Nicholson.   'New Sh—
Soc.'   Ln: N. Trubner & Co., 1875.
Fcp. 4°, on forty-eight unpaged folios
                    BM | BPL | BUS
[King Henry V.] Life of Henry the fifth.
Reprinted from the first folio, 1623.
[Edited by B. Nicholson.]   Ln: New
Sh— Soc., 1875. Fcp. 4°, pp. iv. and
folios 69-95   BPL | BUS
[King Henry V.] Famovs victories of
Henry the fifth. Containing the honour-
able battell of Agincourt. As it was
plaide by the Queenes Maiesties players.
Ln: Printed by Thomas Creede, 1598
[Reprinted in Hazlitt's 'Sh—'s library'].
1875. 8°   BUS
King Henry the fifth . . . Arranged for
representation in five acts by Charles Cal-
vert and produced under his direction at
Booth's Theatre, February, 1875. [With
notes on heraldry by Alfred Darbyshire.]
New York: S. French [1875].   12°, pp.
68   BUS
King Henry V. . . . With notes. Edinburgh: W. & R. Chambers [c. 1875].
12°, pp. 217 to 234
An excerpt from the 'Cabinet edition.'

King Henry V. . . . With introductions and
notes. By Henry N. Hudson. Boston
[U.S.]: Ginn & Heath, 1876. 12° [ex-
cerpt], pp. 171-262   BUS
King Henry V. . . . Preceded by a prologue
taken from 'Henry IV.' Arranged for
representation at the Queen's Theatre by
J. Coleman. Ln . . . . [c. 1876]. 12° BPL

[King Henry V.] Story of the battle of Agincourt . . . arranged by T. M. Lockwood. Chester: E. Thomas, 1877. 8°, pp. 42   BPL
The first and only known Cestrian printing of the poet.

King Henry the fifth . . . Parallel texts of the first quarto (1600) and first folio (1623) editions. Edited by Dr. B. Nicholson. With an introduction by P. A. Daniel. Ln: New Sh— Soc., 1877. 4°, pp. xvi.-214   BM | BPL | BUS

King Henry the fifth . . . With introductory remarks, explanatory . . . notes, etc. by S. Neil. 'School and college classics.' Glasgow: W. Collins, 1878. 8°, pp. 160   BM | BPL

King Henry the fifth . . . Edited with notes by William J. Rolfe. With engravings. New York: Harper brothers, 1878. 16°, pp. 192   BUS
The illustrations partly borrowed from Knight's pictorial edition.

King Henry V. With . . . notes by John Hunter. Ln: Longmans [c. 1878]. Cr. 8°, pp. xxiv.-124   BPL

King Henry V. . . . As produced by Mr. George Rignold at Drury Lane Theatre, Nov. 1st, 1879. Ln: Aubert, 1880. 8°, pp. viii.-viii.-64   BPL | MPL
Includes A. Darbyshire's 'Notes on heraldry' and press opinions.

King Henry the fifth . . . 'Rugby school edition.' Edited by C. E. Moberly. Rugby: Billington; Ln: Rivingtons, 1880. 12°   BPL | BUS | MPL

King Henry the fifth . . . With notes and an introduction by K. Deighton. Ln: W. H. Allen & Co., 1880. 8°, pp. xxxii.-288   BM | BPL | BUS

[King Henry V.] Life of Henry the fift . . . The edition of 1623 newly revised and corrected, with notes and an introduction by W. G. Stone. Ln: New Sh— Soc., 1880. 8°, pp. cvi.-180   BM | BPL | MPL

King Henry V. With notes by John Hunter. Ln: Longmans . . . 1881. 8°, pp. xxiv.-124

King Henry the fifth . . . Edited by W. A. Wright. Oxford: Clarendon Press, 1882. Cr. 8°, pp. xl.-196   BPL

King Henry the fifth . . . With notes prepared for the Oxford and Cambridge local examinations. Ln: Allman & Son, 1882. Cr. 8°, pp. 128   BPL | BUS

King Henry the fifth . . . with notes, examination papers, and plan of preparation. Ln. & Edinburgh: W. & R. Chambers, 1882. Cr. 8°, pp. 128   BM

King Henry V. With notes, examination papers and plan of preparation, by Brainerd Kellogg. New York, 1883. 24°. With portrait and illustrations   BUS

King Henry the fifth . . . Edited by W. A. Wright. Oxford: Clarendon Press, 1883. Cr. 8°, pp. xl.-196   MPL | SML

King Henry the fifth . . . Edited by W. J. Rolfe. New York: Harper, 1883. 12°   BPL

King Henry the fifth . . . 'Standard plays.' Ln: John Dicks [1883]. 12°   BM

King Henry V. . . . Edited by C. E. Moberly. Ln: Rivington, 1884. Cr. 8°

King Henry the fifth . . . abridged to 673 lines. With notes and introduction. Ln: W. & R. Chambers, 1885. Cr. 8°, pp. 32   BM

King Henry the fifth . . . The first quarto, 1600. A facsimile from the British Museum copy . . . by C. Prætorius . . . With an introduction by A. Symons. 'Sh— quarto facsimiles.' Ln: C. Prætorius, 1886. Fcp. 4°, pp. xviii.-54   BM | BPL | BUS

King Henry the fifth . . . The third quarto, 1608. A facsimile from the British Museum copy . . . by C. Prætorius. With an introduction by Arthur Symons. 'Sh— quarto facsimiles.' Ln: C. Prætorius, 1886. Fcp. 4°, pp. viii.-54   BM | BPL | BUS

King Henry the fifth . . . With notes. 'Modern school series.' Ln: Cassell [1886]. Cr. 8°, pp. 60   BM

[King Henry V.] Famous victories of Henry the fifth. The earliest known quarto, 1598. A facsimile in photo-lithography (from the unique copy in the Bodleian), With introduction by P. A. Daniel. Ln: C. Prætorius, 1887. Fcp. 4°   BPL | BUS

King Henry the fifth . . . With notes and glossary by B. Dawson. 'University Sh—.' Ln: Simpkin, 1888. 12°   BPL

King Henry V. . . . With notes, etc. Ln. & Edinburgh: W. & R. Chambers, 1888. 12°   BPL

King Henry V. . . . With introduction and notes by K. Deighton. Ln: Macmillan, 1888. 12°   BPL

King Henry the fifth . . . [With introduction by Henry Morley]. 'National library.' Ln: Cassell, 1888. 16°, pp. 192   BM

King Henry the fifth . . . Ed. by W. A. Wright. Oxford: Clarendon Press, 1889. Cr. 8°, pp. xl.-196

Sh— King Henry the fifth . . .

King Henry V. With introduction and notes by K. Deighton. Second edition. Ln: Macmillan, 1889. 12°

King Henry V. . . . Edited by C. E. Flower. 'Memorial theatre edition.' Stratford-on-Avon: Printed by G. Boyden [1889]. Cr. 8°, pp. viii.-94   BPL | SML

King Henry the fifth . . . With introduction and notes by H. N. Hudson. Boston [U.S.], 1889. 12°   BPL

King Henry the fifth . . . With introduction and notes by B. Jonson. Ln: G. Gill & Sons, 1889. 12°, pp. 128   BM

King Henry V. . . . With notes by Ben Jonson. Ln: Gill, 1890. Cr. 8°

King Henry the fifth . . . Edited by A. D. Innes. 'Falcon edition.' Ln: Longmans, 1890. 8°   BPL

King Henry V. . . . With notes, examination papers, and plan of preparation. Ln: Chambers, 1890. Cr. 8°, pp. iv.-128

King Henry V. . . . Abridged to 673 lines. With notes and introduction. Ln: W. & R. Chambers, 1890. Cr. 8°, pp. 32, in pictorial violet wrappers

King Henry V. [act ii., sc. iii.] translated into comic iambics, by W. M. Geldart. Gaisford prize. Oxford: B. H. Blackwell, 1890. 8°, pp. 8   BM | BPL

King Henry the fifth . . . edited by W. A. Wright. Oxford: Clarendon Press, 1892. Cr. 8°, pp. xl.-196

King Henry the fifth . . . With introduction and notes by W. Barry. Ln: Blackie, 1892. Cr. 8°, pp. 128   BM | BPL

King Henry V. With . . . notes by John Hunter. Ln: Longmans, 1892. Cr. 8°, pp. xxiv.-132

King Henry the fifth. Ed. by A. D. Innes. 'Falcon edition.' Ln: Longmans, 1893. 8°, pp. xvi.-150

King Henry V. . . . With notes . . . for the Oxford and Cambridge local examinations. Ln: Allman [c. 1895]. Cr. 8°, pp. 128

King Henry the fifth . . . With introduction and notes by K. Deighton. Ln: Macmillan & Co., 1895. Cr. 8°, pp. xxxvi.-234

King Henry V. . . . edited by I. Gollancz. 'Temple edition.' Ln: Dent, 1895. 16°

King Henry V. [Edited by H. Morley.] 'National library.' Ln: Cassell, 1895. 16°, pp. 192   BUS

King Henry V. . . . Ed. by G. C. Moore Smith. 'Arden Sh—.' Ln: Methuen, 1895-96. 8°   BUS

Sh— King Henry the fifth . . .

[King Henry V.] Famous victories of Henry the fifth . . . Edited with an introduction by A. F. Hopkinson. 'Old English plays.' Ln: . . . 1896. 12°   BPL

King Henry V. . . . Edited with introduction and notes by T. Page. 'Moffatt's plays.' Ln: . . . [1896]. 12°   BPL

King Henry V. . . . Edited by S. E. Winbolt and J. Churton Collins. 'School Sh—.' Ln: Arnold [c. 1896]. Cr. 8°, pp. lii.-168   BPL

King Henry the fifth . . . Edited by G. C. Moore Smith. 'Warwick Sh—.' Ln: Blackie, 1896. Cr. 8°, pp. 264   BPL

King Henry the fifth . . . [In Donovan, 'English historical plays,' Vol. I.] Ln: Macmillan, 1896. 2 vols. Cr. 8°   BM | MPL

King Henry V. With introd. and notes by K. Deighton. Ln: Macmillan, 1896. Cr. 8°, pp. xxxvi.-308   BM

King Henry V. 'Ariel edition.' Ln: Routledge, 1898. 16°

King Henry V. 'Pocket Falstaff edition.' Ln: Bliss, Sands, 1898. 16°, pp. 124   BPL | SML

King Henry the fifth . . . With preface, glossary, &c. by I. Gollancz. Ln: J. M. Dent & Co., 1898. 16°, pp. xii.-174. With frontispiece

King Henry V. . . . Edited by G. C. Moore Smith. Ln: Blackie, 1899. Cr. 8°, pp. 264

King Henry V. . . . With notes by D. Ferguson. Ten illustrations by R. Wheelwright. 'Swan edition.' Ln: Longmans, 1900. Cr. 8°, pp. 190   BPL

King Henry the fifth . . . With introduction and notes for the examinations by F. Marshall and Stanley Wood. 'Oxford & Cambridge series.' Ln: Gill & Sons [c. 1900]. 8°, pp. lii.-204. Illustrated with coloured maps, etc.

King Henry the fifth . . . edited with introduction and notes by C. H. Herford. 'Eversley edition.' Ln: Macmillan, 1900. Cr. 8°   BPL

King Henry V. Edited . . . by A. W. Verity. Cambridge: University Press, 1900. Cr. 8°, pp. xxxvi.-256   BPL | BUS

King Henry the fifth. Edited by W. A. Wright. Oxford: Clarendon Press, 1900. Cr. 8°, pp. xl.-196

King Henry V. . . . edited by G. C. M. Smith. Ln: Blackie, 1900. Cr. 8°, pp. 264

King Henry V. . . . With an introduction and notes by K. Deighton. Ln: Macmillan, 1900. Cr. 8°, pp. xxxvi.-308

King Henry V. . . . 'Picture Sh—.' Ln:
Blackie, 1901. Cr. 8°   BPL
King Henry V. . . . with introduction and
notes by Fanny Johnson. Edinburgh:
Blackwood, 1901. Cr. 8°   BPL
King Henry V. 'Richard Mansfield acting
version.' A history in five acts. New
York . . . 1901. 8°. With portrait and
illustrations   BPL | BUS
King Henry V. . . . with introductory notes
by John Dennis. Illustrated by B. Shaw.
'Chiswick edition.' Ln: Bell, 1901. 12°,
pp. 158
King Henry the fifth. Edited with intro-
duction and notes by J. Lees. Ln: All-
man, 1901. Cr. 8°, pp. xviii.-136
King Henry V. Edited by G. C. M. Smith.
'Picture Sh—.' Ln: Blackie, 1901. 8°,
pp. 264   BPL
King Henry V. . . . Introduction, etc. by
F. Marshall and Wood. Ln: Gill . . .
1902. Cr. 8°   BPL
King Henry V. . . . edited by W. J. Rolfe.
New York . . . 1902. 8°. Illustrated
                                         BUS
King Henry V. . . . edited by A. W. Verity.
Cambridge: University Press, 1902. Cr.
8°, pp. xxxvi.-256
King Henry V. . . . edited by J. E. B.
McAllen. 'Normal tutorial series.' Ln:
Simpkin, 1903. Cr. 8°   BPL
King Henry V. . . . Full text, with intro-
duction and notes by C. W. Crook. Ln:
Ralph & Holland, 1903. Cr. 8°   BPL
King Henry V. . . . with introduction and
notes by R. F. Cholmeley. 'Blackfriars
edition.' Ln: A. M. Holden, 1903. Cr.
8°   BPL
King Henry V. . . . edited with notes by
H. N. Hudson. 'Windsor edition.' Edin-
burgh: Jack, 1903. Cr. 8°
King Henry V. . . . edited by G. C. M.
Smith. Ln: Blackie, 1903. Cr. 8°, pp.
264
King Henry V. . . . edited by Herbert
Arthur Evans. 'Arden edition.' Ln:
Methuen, 1903. 8°, pp. 222   BM
King Henry V. . . . edited by H. Morley.
'National library.' Ln: Cassell, 1904.
16°, pp. 192   BPL
King Henry V. . . . Retold by Alice Spencer
Hoffman. Illustrated by Dora Curtis.
Ln: Dent, 1904. 16°   BPL
King Henry V. . . . A complete paraphrase
by I. F. Young. 'Normal tutorial series.'
Ln: Simpkin, 1904. Cr. 8°   BPL
King Henry V. . . . Parsed and analysed
by A. W. Parry. 'Normal tutorial
series.' Ln: Simpkin, 1904. Cr. 8° BPL

King Henry V. . . . With introduction and
notes by W. J. Craig. 'Little quartos.'
Ln: Methuen, 1904. 16°   BM
King Henry the fifth . . . With introduction by G. Brandes. 'Favourite classics.'
Ln: W. Heinemann, 1904. 12°, pp. x.-
126 and frontispiece of Lewis Waller in
the title role   BM
King Henry V. . . . with introduction and
notes by Duncan Macgillivray. 'Academy
edition.' Ln: Chambers, 1905. Cr. 8°,
pp. 208   BPL
King Henry V. . . . edited by H. N. Hudson.
Additional grammatical and metrical
notes by W. H. Weston. Edinburgh:
Jack, 1905. Cr. 8°, pp. 142   BPL
King Henry V. . . . 'Waistcoat pocket edi-
tion.' Ln: Treherne, 1905. 32°
King Henry V. 'Red letter edition.' Ln:
Blackie, 1905. 12°
King Henry the fifth . . . edited by A. W.
Verity. Cambridge: University Press,
1905. Cr. 8°, pp. xxxvi.-256
King Henry V. . . . 'Texts without notes.'
Ln: Chambers, 1907. Cr. 8°   BPL
King Henry V. . . . edited by Benjamin
Dawson. Ln: R. Sutton, 1907. Cr. 8°
King Henry V. . . . Parallel texts of the
first and third quartos and first folio,
edited by E. Roman. Ln: Nutt, 1908. 8°
King Henry V. . . . 'Renaissance edition.'
Ln: Harrap, 1908. Fcp. 4°   BPL
King Henry V. 'Elementary school books.'
Oxford: Clarendon Press, 1908. Cr. 8°
King Henry V. . . . 'Sh— for schools.'
Ln: Dent, 1908. Cr. 8°   BPL
King Henry V. . . . edited and revised by
Black and George. 'New Hudson Sh—.'
1909. Cr. 8°   BPL
'King Henry V.' references—

Sh—] KING HENRY THE SIXTH;

FIRST PART.

This play doubtless made its first printed appearance in the Jaggard folio of 1623. No untampered separate edition is chronicled before the 1735 issue of Tonson's. An adaptation was issued in 1681.

King Henry the sixth: The first part. With the murder of Humphrey Duke of Gloucester. As it was acted at the Duke's Theatre. Written by Mr. [John] Crowne. Ln: Printed for R. Bently and M. Magnes in Russel Street in Covent Garden, 1681. Fcp. 4°   BM | BPL
Plot and text partly borrowed from Sh—'s play.

[King Henry VI., i.] The first part of Henry VI. By Mr. Wm. Sh—. Ln: Printed for J. Tonson and the rest of the proprietors, and sold by the booksellers of Ln. and Westminster, 1735. Cr. 8°, pp. 82 and frontispiece, engraved by P. Fourdrinier   BM

King Henry VI.: first part. A tragedy . . . An introduction, and notes critical and illustrative, are added by the authors of the 'Dramatic censor' [F. Gentleman]. Ln: John Bell; York: C. Etherington, 1774. 8°, (excerpt) pp. 87-174
An off-print, from Bell's edition, for playgoers.

King Henry VI., part i. . . . printed complete from the text of Sam. Johnson and Geo. Steevens and revised from the last editions . . . Ln: Printed for . . . John Bell . . . 1786. 12°, pp. 116. With engraved title and frontispiece of Miss Stuart as Joan la pucelle

King Henry VI.: part i. . . . Printed complete from the text of Samuel Johnson and George Steevens. Ln: . . . 1813. 16°   w

King Henry VI.: part i. . . . With notes by J. Hunter. Ln: Longmans . . . 1873. Cr. 8°   BPL

King Henry VI.: part i. . . . edited with notes by W. J. Rolfe. New York . . . 1882. Cr. 8°   BPL

King Henry VI.: part the first . . . 'Standard plays.' Ln: John Dicks [1883]. 12°   BM

King Henry VI.: first part . . . edited by C. E. Flower. 'Memorial theatre edition.' Stratford-on-Avon: G. Boyden; Ln: S. French [1889]. Cr. 8°, pp. viii.-84, including printed wrappers   BPL

[King Henry VI.] First part of King Henry VI. [With an introduction by Henry Morley]. 'National library.' Ln: Cassell, 1889. 16°, pp. 192   BM

Sh— King Henry the sixth . . .

King Henry the sixth: first part . . . [In Donovan, ' English historical plays,' Vol. 2]. Ln: Macmillan . . . 1896. 2 vols. Cr. 8°   BM | BLO | CTC | MPL

King Henry VI.: part i. . . . 'Ariel edition.' Ln: Routledge, 1898. 16°

King Henry the sixth: first part . . . ' Pocket Falstaff edition.' Ln: Bliss, Sands & Co., 1898. 16°, pp. 112
   BPL | SML

King Henry the sixth: first part . . . edited with introduction and notes by C. H. Herford. 'Eversley edition.' Ln: Macmillan, 1900. Cr. 8°   BPL

King Henry VI.: part i. . . . with introductory notes by John Dennis. Illustrated by B. Shaw. ' Chiswick edition.' Ln: Bell, 1901. Cr. 8°

King Henry VI.: part i. Edited with notes by H. N. Hudson. ' Windsor edition.' Edinburgh: Jack, 1903. Cr. 8°, pp. 110

King Henry VI.: part i. . . . with introduction and notes by W. J. Craig. ' Little quartos.' Ln: Methuen, 1904. 16°

King Henry VI.: part i. . . . with introduction by G. Brandes. ' Favourite classics.' Ln: Heinemann, 1904. 12°, pp. xii.-110 and frontispiece of ' Mrs. Baddeley as Jeanne D'Arc'

King Henry VI.: part i. ' Waistcoat pocket edition.' Ln: Treherne, 1905. 32°

King Henry VI.: part i. Edited by H. Morley. ' National library.' Ln: Cassell, 1905. 16°   BM | BLO | BPL | CTC

King Henry VI.: part i. ' Renaissance edition.' Ln: Harrap, 1907. Fcp. 4°   BPL

KING HENRY THE SIXTH;

SECOND PART.

Believed to have first appeared in its entirety in the Jaggard folio of 1623. It is mainly a revision of the ' First part of the contention' issued in 1594. The second and third parts of ' King Henry VI.' were published together in 1619 under the title of ' The whole contention . . .' [printed by Isaac Jaggard for Thomas Pavier]. In this play Sh— makes a curious slip, which turned out an accurate forecast, in referring to ' all the wealthy kingdoms of the west.'

[King Henry VI.: part ii.] The First part of the Contention betwixt the two famous Houses of Yorke and Lancaster, with the death of the good Duke Humphrey: and the banishment and death of the Duke of Suffolke and the Tragicall end of the proud Cardinall of Winchester, with the notable Rebellion of Jacke Cade: and the Duke of Yorkes first claime vnto the Crowne. [*Device*.] Ln: Printed by Thomas Creede, for Thomas Millington, and are to be sold at his shop vnder Saint Peter's Church in Cornwall [Cornhill], 1594. Fcp. 4°; sig. A¹ to H⁴ in fours, on thirty-two unpaged leaves   BLO | BUS

There are two varying impressions of this issue, one showing differences in spelling and punctuation from the other in the title.

The date and device are repeated at the end of the play. It was reprinted by the Sh— Soc. in 1843 under the editorship of J. O. Halliwell (*q.v.*); in Halliwell's folio ed. of the Works, 1853; and in the Cambridge ed., 1863-66.

The copy, which changed hands in June, 1907, for £1,910, represents the topmost financial tide-mark for an early quarto sold publicly so far, but that sum has been exceeded privately. [*See* Sh— Passionate pilgrim, 1599; *also* Sh— Titus Andronicus, 1594.]

[King Henry VI., ii.] The First Part of the Contention betwixt the two famous Houses of Yorke and Lancaster. With the death of the good Duke Humphrey and the banishment and death of the Duke of Suffolke and the Tragical end of the prowd Cardinall of Winchester, with the notable Rebellion of Jacke Cade. And the Duke of Yorkes first clayme to the Crowne. Ln: Printed by Valentine Simmes for Thomas Millington and are to be sold at his shop vnder S. Peters Church in Cornewall, 1600. Fcp. 4°; sig. A¹ to H⁴ unpaged
BLO | CTC

Another edition of the same year is mentioned, in which the imprint runs:—'London: Printed by W. W—— [William White?] for Thomas Millington . . .'

[King Henry VI., ii.] Misery of civil war. A tragedy. As it was acted at the Duke's Theatre by his royal highnesses servants. Written by Mr. [John] Crown. Ln: Printed for R. Bentley and M. Magnes in Russel Street in Covent Garden, 1680. Fcp. 4°   BM | BPL | W

'A portion of the second part of "King Henry VI." is introduced . . . In the prologue, however, the author unblushingly asserts he has borrowed nothing from Sh—.'—*J. O. Halliwell.*

Crowne says:—
'For by his feeble skill 'tis built alone,
The divine Sh— did not lay one stone.'

[King Henry VI., ii.] Humfrey, Duke of Gloucester. A tragedy. By Mr. [A.] Philips. Ln: . . . 1723. 12°   BPL

[King Henry VI., ii.] The second part of Henry the sixth. With the death of the good Duke Humphrey. A tragedy. By Mr. Wm. Sh—.   Ln: Printed for J. Tonson and the rest of the proprietors and sold by the booksellers of Ln. and Westminster, 1734. Cr. 8°, pp. 84 and frontispiece eng. by P. Fourdrinier   BM

King Henry VI.: second part. A tragedy . . . an introduction and notes critical and illustrative are added by the authors of the ' Dramatic censor ' [F. Gentleman]. Ln: John Bell; York: C. Etherington, 1774. 8°, (excerpt) pp. 175-272

An off-print for playgoers, from Bell's edition.

King Henry VI.: part ii. . . . printed complete from the text of Sam. Johnson and Geo. Steevens and revised from the last editions . . . Ln: Printed for . . . John Bell . . . 1786. 12°, pp. 132. With engraved title and frontispiece of ' Mr. Baddeley as Peter '

King Henry VI.: part ii. . . . Printed complete from the text of Samuel Johnson and George Steevens. Ln: . . . 1813. 16°   W

King Henry VI.: part ii. . . . With notes by John Hunter. Ln: . . . Longmans . . . 1873. Cr. 8°   BPL

King Henry the sixth: part ii. . . . Edited with notes by W. J. Rolfe. New York . . . 1882. Cr. 8°   BPL

King Henry the sixth: part the second . . . ' Standard plays.' Ln: John Dicks [1883]. 12°   BM

[King Henry VI., ii.] The first part of the contention . . . The first quarto, 1594, from the unique copy in the Bodleian Library, Oxford. A facsimile, by photolithography. With forewords embodying the late L. Grant White's argument on Sh—'s right to the whole of 2 & 3 Henry VI., by F. J. Furnivall. Ln: C. Prætorius, 1889. Fcp. 4°   BM | BPL | BUS

King Henry VI.: second part . . . Ed. by H. Morley. ' National library.' Ln: Cassell . . . 1889. 16°, pp. 192

King Henry VI.: second part . . . edited by C. E. Flower. ' Memorial theatre edition.' Stratford-on-Avon: Printed by G. Boyden; Ln: S. French [1889]. Cr. 8°, pp. viii.-92, incl. printed wrappers
BPL | SML

King Henry the sixth: part ii. . . . edited with notes by W. J. Rolfe. New York: Harper Brothers, 1895. Cr. 8°, pp. 184. Illustrated

Sh— King Henry the sixth . . .

King Henry the sixth: second part [In Donovan, ' English historical plays,' Vol. 2]. Ln: Macmillan, 1896. 2 vols. Cr. 8°
BM | BLO | CTC | MPL

King Henry VI.: part ii. ' Pocket Falstaff edition.' Ln: Bliss, Sands, 1898. 16°, pp. 128
BPL | SML

King Henry the sixth: second part . . . edited with introduction and notes by C. H. Herford. ' Eversley edition.' Ln: Macmillan, 1900. Cr. 8°
BPL

King Henry VI.: part ii. . . . with introduction and notes by John Dennis. Illust. by B. Shaw. ' Chiswick edition.' Ln: Bell, 1902. Cr. 8°

King Henry VI.: part ii. . . . edited with notes by H. N. Hudson. ' Windsor edition.' Edinburgh: Jack . . . 1903. Cr. 8°

King Henry VI.: part ii. . . . with introduction and notes by W. J. Craig. ' Little quartos.' Ln: Methuen, 1904. 16°

King Henry VI.: part ii. . . . with introduction by G. Brandes. ' Favourite classics.' Ln: Heinemann, 1904. 12°, pp. iv.-124 and portrait of Henry VI.

King Henry VI.: part ii. Edited by H. Morley. ' National library.' Ln: Cassell, 1905. 16°
BPL

King Henry VI.: part ii. ' Waistcoat pocket edition.' Ln: Treherne, 1905. 32°

King Henry VI.: part ii. ' Renaissance edition.' Ln: Harrap, 1907. Fcp. 4° BPL

KING HENRY THE SIXTH; THIRD PART.

The version in the Jaggard folio of 1623 is accepted as the earliest in print. It largely consists of the 'True tragedy . . .' of 1595 in revised form.

An adaptation in separate shape came out in 1723, but the first unspoilt separate text was issued by Tonson in 1734.

[King Henry VI., part iii.] Humphrey, Duke of Gloucester. A tragedy. As it is acted at the Theatre Royal in Drury-Lane, by Mr. [Ambrose] Philips. Ln: . . . 1723. 8° w
Some of the lines and speeches borrowed from Sh—.

King Henry VI. [iii.] A tragedy. As it is acted at the Theatre Royal in Drury Lane, by his majesty's servants. Altered from Sh— in the year 1720 by Theophilus Cibber. Second edition. Ln: W. Chetwood, 1724. 8°, pp. iv.-60 BUS
Altered from the third part of ' King Henry VI.,' with the addition of the final act of part two.

Sh— King Henry the sixth . . .

[King Henry VI., iii.] The third part of Henry the sixth. With the death of the Duke of York. By Mr. Wm. Sh—. Ln: Printed for J. Tonson and the rest of the proprietors, and sold by the booksellers of Ln. and Westminster, 1734. Cr. 8°, pp. 96 and frontispiece BM

[King Henry VI., iii.] Third part of King Henry VI. With the death of the Duke of York, by W. Sh—. Ln: R. Walker . . . 1735. 12° w

King Henry VI.: third part. A tragedy . . . An introduction and notes critical and illustrative are added by the authors of the ' Dramatic censor' [F. Gentleman]. Ln: John Bell; York: C. Etherington, 1774. 8°, (excerpt) pp. 273-364
An off-print for playgoers, from Bell's edition.

King Henry VI., part iii. . . . printed complete from the text of Sam. Johnson and Geo. Steevens, and revised from the last editions. Ln: Printed for . . . John Bell . . . 1786. 12°, pp. 136. With engraved title and frontispiece of ' Mr. Palmer in the Earl of Warwick '

[King Henry VI., iii.] The roses, or King Henry the sixth: An historical tragedy. Represented at Reading School, October 15, 16, 17, 1795. Compiled principally from Sh—[by Richard Valpy]. Published as it was performed, for the benefit of the cheap repository for moral and instructive tracts. Reading: Smart & Cowslade [1795]. 8°, pp. viii.-48
BM | BPL | BUS
Taken chiefly from the last four acts of ' King Henry VI., part iii.,' with passages from ' King Richard II., parts i. and ii.'

King Henry VI.: part iii. . . . Ln: . . . [c. 1800]. 8°

[King Henry VI., iii.] The roses, or King Henry the sixth. An historical tragedy. Represented at Reading School, Oct., 1795. Compiled principally from Sh— [by R. Valpy]. Second edition. Ln: Longman, 1810. 8°, pp. viii.-60

King Henry the sixth; part iii., by Will. Sh—. Printed complete from the text of Sam. Johnson and Geo. Steevens. Ln: . . . 1818. 16° w

[King Henry VI., iii.] Richard Duke of York. Altered [by Edmund Kean] from Sh—'s ' Henry VI.' As performed at the Theatre Royal, Drury Lane. Ln: . . . 1817. 8°

King Henry VI., part iii. . . . Ln: . . . 1818. 12°

King Henry VI., part iii. . . . Edited by E. Kean. Ln: Davidson [c. 1830]. 12°

[King Henry VI., iii.] A translation, into Greek iambics, by G. J. Kennedy, from 'King Henry VI., part iii., act ii., sc. 2' [In English and Greek]. Cambridge . . . 1831. 8°   BM

[King Henry VI., iii.] A translation, into Greek iambics, by E. M. Cope, from 'King Henry VI., part iii., act ii., sc. 5' [In English and Greek]. Cambridge . . . 1839. 8°   BM

King Henry VI., part iii. [Reprinted from the first edition. Edited by Barron Field]. Ln: Sh— Soc., 1844. 8°   BM | BPL | BUS | W

King Henry VI.: part iii. . . . With notes by J. Hunter. Ln: Longman . . . 1873. Cr. 8°   BPL

King Henry VI., part iii. . . . Edited with notes by W. J. Rolfe. New York: Harper . . . 1882. Cr. 8°   BPL

King Henry the sixth, part the third. 'Standard plays.' Ln: John Dicks [1883]. 12°   BM

King Henry VI.: third part . . . edited by C. E. Flower. 'Memorial theatre edition.' Stratford-on-Avon: G. Boyden [1889]. Cr. 8°, pp. viii.-92, including printed wrappers   BPL | SML

[King Henry VI.] Third part of King Henry VI. [With an introduction by Henry Morley.] 'National library.' Ln: Cassell, 1889. 16°, pp. 192   BM

[King Henry VI., iii.] True tragedy . . . The first quarto, 1595; facsimile by C. Prætorius. With introduction by T. Tyler. 'Sh— quarto facsimiles.' Ln: C. Prætorius, 1891. Fcp. 4° BPL | BUS

King Henry the sixth: third part [In Donovan, 'English historical plays,' Vol. 2]. Ln: Macmillan, 1896. 2 vols. Cr. 8°   BM | BLO | CTC | MPL

King Henry VI.: part iii. 'Pocket Falstaff edition.' Ln: Bliss, Sands, 1898. 16°, pp. 124   BPL | SML

King Henry the sixth: third part . . . edited with introduction and notes by C. H. Herford. 'Eversley edition.' Ln: Macmillan, 1900. Cr. 8°   BPL

King Henry VI.: part iii. With introduction and notes by John Dennis. Illustrated by B. Shaw. 'Chiswick edition.' Ln: Bell, 1902. Cr. 8°

King Henry VI.: part iii. . . . edited with notes by H. N. Hudson. 'Windsor edition.' Edinburgh: Jack . . . 1903. Cr. 8°

King Henry VI.: part iii. With introductory notes by W. J. Craig. 'Little quartos.' Ln: Methuen, 1904. 16°

King Henry VI.: part iii. . . . with introduction by G. Brandes. 'Favourite classics.' Ln: Heinemann, 1904. 12°, pp. iv.-124 and portrait of 'G. F. Cooke as Gloster'

King Henry VI.: part iii. Edited by H. Morley. 'National library.' Ln: Cassell, 1905. 16°   BM | BLO | BPL | CTC

King Henry VI., part iii. 'Renaissance edition.' Ln: Harrap, 1907. Fcp. 4°   BPL

King Henry VI.: part iii. 'Waistcoat pocket edition.' Ln: Treherne, 1905. 32°

King Henry VI., part iii. 'Arden edition.' Ln: Methuen, 1910. 8°, pp. 220   BM | BLO | BPL | CTC

KING HENRY THE SIXTH;
PARTS I.-II.-III.

[King Henry VI.: i.-ii.-iii.] The true Tragedie of Richard Duke of Yorke and the Death of good King Henry the Sixt, with the whole Contention betweene the two Houses Lancaster and Yorke, as it was sundrie times acted by the Right Honorable the Earle of Pembrooke his Seruants. Printed at London by P. S—— [Peter Short] for Thomas Millington and are to be sold at his shoppe vnder Saint Peters Church in Cornwal, 1595. Fcp. 4°, on forty unpaged leaves   BUS
Reprinted in 1844 (edited by Barron Field) for the Sh— Soc.; in Halliwell's folio ed. of Sh—'s Works, 1853; and in the Cambridge edition, 1863-66.

[King Henry VI., i.-ii.-iii.] The True Tragedie of Richarde Duke of Yorke and the Death of good King Henrie the Sixt: With the Whole Contention between the two Houses, Lancaster and Yorke; As it was sundry times acted by the Right Honourable the Earl of Pembrooke his Seruantes. The second edition. Printed at Londou by W. W—— for Thomas Millington, and are to be sold at his shoppe vnder Saint Peter's Church in Cornewall [Cornhill], 1600. Fcp. 4°, on 32 unpaged folios, including title; sig. A¹ to H⁴ in fours   BM | BLO | BUS
Sh—'s name does not occur herein.
'Of the greatest rarity in an absolutely perfect state.'— *Halliwell.*
The British Museum copy bears the autograph of George Steevens.

[King Henry VI., part i.-ii.-iii.] The true Tragedie of Richard Duke of Yorke and the death of good King Henry the Sixt . . . London: Printed [by Isaac Iaggard] for T. P—— [Thomas Pavier, 1619]. Fcp. 4°   BM | BLO
Issued with Part ii. [1619], *q.v.*

Sh— King Henry the sixth . . .

[King Henry VI., parts i.-ii.-iii.] Richard, Duke of York; or, the contention of York and Lancaster. As altered from Sh—'s three parts of ' Henry VI.' In five acts. As it is performed at the Theatre Royal, Drury-Lane. Ln: R. White, 1817. 8°, pp. xxviii.-82   BM | BPL | BUS
<small>Lowndes ascribes this adaptation to Edmund Kean, while Burton's catalogue attributes it to Soane, and the copy now at Boston bought at his sale is so lettered on the back. Hawkins in his ' Life of Kean' says J. H. Merivale was the editor.</small>

King Henry VI. [part i.-iii.] . . . As adapted by E. Kean. Ln : . . . [c. 1830]. 12°   BPL

King Henry VI. . . . In three parts. From the folio of 1623. Ln: L. Booth, 1863. Fcp. 4°   CPL

King Henry VI. . . . Three parts. Edited by I. Gollancz. ' Temple edition.' Ln : Dent, 1895. 16°

KING HENRY THE SIXTH; PARTS II.-III.

[King Henry VI., parts ii.-iii.] The Whole Contention betweene the two Famous Houses, Lancaster and Yorke. With the Tragicall ends of the good Duke Humfrey, Richard Duke of Yorke, and King Henrie the Sixt. Diuided into two Parts : And newly corrected and enlarged. Written by William Shake-speare, Gent. [*Device.*] Printed at London [by Isaac Jaggard] for T. P—— [Thomas Pavier, 1619]. Fcp. 4°; sig. A¹ to Q⁴ in fours, without pagination
     BM | BLO | BPL | BUS | CTC | NY | W
<small>First edition of these parts combined.
The supplementary portion of the Warwick copy entitled the ' History of Pericles', occupying sig. R1 to BB1, was removed and bound up separately. *See* Sh— Pericles, 1619.
It was reprinted by Steevens in 1766, and by Charles Knight in his ' Pictorial edition of Sh—'s Works.'
Isaac Jaggard's name does not appear on the title, but he is said to be the printer by W. A. Wright in the ' Cambridge Sh—' (1892, Vol. v., p. ix.), and again by Sir H. Irving and F. A. Marshall in the ' Henry Irving Sh—' (1888, Vol. ii., p. 4).
A copy measuring 7 by 5¼ in., in May, 1906, realised £110, and another, in Dec., 1907, £120.
In the Bodleian copy, which measures 7⅛ by 4⅞ in., is a plate depicting Henry VI.</small>

[King Henry VI., ii.-iii.] An historical tragedy of the civil wars in the reign of King Henry VI. [in five acts] . . . Alter'd from Sh— by Theo. Cibber. Ln: J. Walthoe, jun. [1720]. 8°, pp. 60
           BM | BPL | W

[King Henry VI., ii.-iii.] An historical tragedy of the civil wars in the reign of King Henry VI. . . . Alter'd from Sh— by T. Cibber. Second edition. Ln: J. Walthoe, jun. [c. 1720]. 8°   BM

Sh— King Henry the sixth . . .

[King Henry VI., ii.-iii.] An historical tragedy of the civil wars in the reign of King Henry VI. Being a sequell to the tragedy of ' Humphrey Duke of Gloucester.' Altered in the year 1720 by Theophilus Cibber. Ln : . . . [1723]. 8°

[King Henry VI., ii.-iii.] An historical tragedy of the civil wars . . . by T. Cibber. Second edition. Ln : W. Chetwood, 1724. 8°   BPL

[King Henry VI., ii.-iii.] The whole contention . . . Written by Wm. Sh—. Printed at Ln. for T. P—— [Thomas Pavier, 1619]; Reprinted by George Steevens, 1766. 8°   BPL | W

[King Henry VI., ii.-iii.] First sketches of the second and third parts of King Henry the sixth [as printed in 1594-95]. Edited by J. O. Halliwell [with introduction and notes]. Ln : Sh— Soc., 1843. 8°, pp. xl.-224
   BM | BPL | BUS | HCL | MPL | W

[King Henry VI., ii.-iii.] The whole contention . . . 1619, Parts I. and II.. The third quarto, 1619 . . . A facsimile by photo-lithography from the British Museum copy . . . by C. Prætorius. With forewords by F. J. Furnivall. ' Sh— quarto facsimiles.' Ln : C. Prætorius, 1886. 2 vols. Fcp. 4°   BM | BPL | BUS

[King Henry VI., ii.-iii.] ' The contention' and ' The true tragedy' [1619] . . . edited with an introduction by A. F. Hopkinson. 'Old English plays.' Ln : . . . 1897. 12°
           BPL

' King Henry VI.' references—

See Bohn	See Lucy
,, Capgrave	,, Malone
,, Cobham	,, Memoirs
,, Daniel (S.)	,, Mirrour . . .
,, Davies	,, Mountford
,, Essay	,, Nero
,, Fall . . .	,, O'Brien
,, Fleay	,, Philips
,, Greene (R.)	,, Phipson
,, Halliwell	,, Rhys
,, Hull	,, Rives
,, Introduction	,, Savage
,, J—— (W.)	,, Sh— Poems,
,, Johnson (R.)	1660-67
,, Johnson & Steevens	,, Solly-Flood
	,, White
,, Jonson	,, Zornlin
,, Lee (J.)	

KING HENRY THE EIGHTH.

Unprinted until it appeared in the Jaggard canon of 1623. The first separate

Will Sommers *Kinge Henryes Jester*

What though thou think'st mee clad in strange attire
And yet I am suted to my owne desire
And yet the Characters describ'd upon mee
May shewe thee that a King bestow'd them on mee

This Horne I have betoken't Sommers game
Which sportive tyme will bid thee reade my name
All withiny Nature well agreeing too
As both the Name and Tyme and Habit doe

William Sommers, jester to King Henry viii.

*edition was issued by Jacob Tonson in
1732, but an adaptation, in manuscript,
exists, which was prepared as early as 1680.*

[King Henry the Eighth] Anna Bullen. A
tragedy in five acts [founded on ' King
Henry VIII.' Original manuscript, c.
1680]. Fcp. 4°, fifty leaves
This manuscript was sold for £18 10s. in Dec., 1906.

[King Henry VIII.] Life of Henry VIII., by
Mr. Wm. Sh—. Ln : Printed for J. Tonson, and sold by W. Feales at Rowe's
Head over against Clement's Inn Gate,
1732. Cr. 8°   BPL

[King Henry VIII.] Life and death of King
Henry the eighth . . . Ln : J. Tonson, 1734.
12°, pp. 96, with frontispiece   BM

[King Henry VIII.] Life of Henry VIII.
By Mr. Wm. Sh—. In which are inter-
spersed historical notes, moral reflections
and observations, in respect to the unhappy fate Cardinal Wolsey met with.
Never before publish'd. Adorned with
several copperplates. By the author of
the ' History of the life and times of
Cardinal Wolsey ' [Joseph Grove]. Ln :
Printed for D. Browne, J. Whiston, B.
White, J. Nourse, W. Withers, T. Pote,
M. Cooper, and B. Tovey, 1758. 8°, pp.
viii.-116 ; six plates by N. Parr
                    BM | BPL | BUS | SML | W
The portraits represent Henry VIII., Wolsey, Catharine of Arragon, Thomas Cromwell, Earl of Essex,
and Anne Boleyn.

King Henry the eighth. With the corona-
tion of Anne Bullen. Written by Sh—.
With alterations. As it is performed at
the Theatre Royal in Drury Lane. Ln :
C. Hitch & L. Hawes, J. & R. Tonson,
B. Dod, G. Woodfall, J. Rivington, R.
Baldwin, T. Longman, S. Crowder & Co.,
W. Johnston, C. Corbet, T. Lownds, T.
Caslon, 1762. 12°, pp. 72, engraved
frontispiece   BUS
A stage adaptation, with many omissions.

King Henry the eighth. With the coronation of Anne Bullen. Written by Sh—
With alterations. As it is performed at
Drury Lane. Dublin . . . 1762. 12° BPL | W

King Henry the eighth. As it is acted at
the Theatres-Royal in Drury-Lane and
Covent-Garden . . . Ln : Printed for J.
Wenman, 144, Fleet St., and sold by all
other booksellers in town and country,
1778. 8°, pp. 18. Copperplate portrait
of Clarke as ' Henry VIII.'   BM | BPL

King Henry VIII., by Sh—, as performed
at the Theatres Royal. Regulated from
the prompt book. By permission of the
managers. Ln : Barker [c. 1790]. 12° W

King Henry VIII. . . . Manchester : R. & W.
Dean, 1801. 12°   BPL

King Henry the eighth . . . Revised by J. P.
Kemble ; and now first published as it is
acted at the Theatre Royal in Covent
Garden. Ln : T. N. Longman & O. Rees,
1804. 8°, pp. 64   BM | BPL

King Henry VIII. A historical play in five
acts . . . As performed at the Theatre
Royal, Covent Garden. Printed under
the authority of the managers from the
prompt book. With remarks by Mrs.
Inchbald. Ln : Longman, Hurst, Rees,
and Orme [1808]. 12°, pp. 76. With
steel frontispiece   BPL | BUS

King Henry VIII., by Will. Sh—. Printed
complete from the text of Sam. Johnson
and Geo. Steevens. Ln : . . 1809. 16° W

King Henry VIII. Edinburgh : Oliver &
Boyd [c. 1810]. 12°

King Henry VIII. . . . With remarks by Mrs.
Inchbald. Ln : [J. Ballantyne & Co. for]
Longman . . . & Brown [c. 1811]. 12°,
pp. 76. With frontispiece   BUS

King Henry VIII. With remarks by Mrs.
Inchbald. New York . . . 1811. 12° BUS

King Henry the eighth . . . revised by J. P.
Kemble, and now published as it is performed at the Theatres Royal. Ln : J.
Miller, 1815. 8°, pp. 68 BM | BPL | BUS

King Henry VIII. . . . With remarks by Mrs.
Inchbald. Ln : [Printed by T. Davison
for] Longman . . . and Brown [c. 1816].
12°, pp. 76, and steel plate   BUS

[King Henry VIII.] Senarii Græci [A trans-
lation, by G. S. Walker from ' Henry
VIII., Act ii., Sc. 2 ' . . . In English and
Greek]. Cambridge . . . 1818. 8°, pp. 8
                                          BM

[King Henry VIII.] Senarii Græci [A trans-
lation by B. H. Kennedy from ' Henry
VIII.,' Act v., Sc. 4. In English and
Greek]. Cambridge . . . 1823. 8°   BM

King Henry the eighth . . . With prefatory
remarks [signed P. P——] . . . Marked
with the stage business, and stage directions, as it is performed at the Theatres
Royal, by W. Oxberry. Ln : . . . 1823.
8°, pp. xvi.-70

King Henry VIII. . . . ' Cumberland's
theatre ' . . . Edited by D. G—— [Geo.
Daniel] . . . Ln : . . . 1824. 12°

King Henry the eighth . . . ' British theatre.'
Ln : Dolby . . . 1824. 12°   BPL

King Henry the eighth . . . As performed at
the Theatres Royal, Drury Lane and
Covent Garden. Printed . . . from the
prompt books. Edinburgh : Oliver &
Boyd [c. 1825]. 12°, pp. 52   BM

Sh— King Henry the eighth . . .

[King Henry VIII.] Senarii Græci [A translation, by C. R. Kennedy, from ' Henry VIII., Act. iv., Sc. 2.' In English and Greek]. Cambridge . . . 1829. 8° BM

King Henry the eighth . . . Printed from the acting copy, with remarks . . . by D. G—— [George Daniel]. To which are added a . . . cast of the characters . . . and the whole of the stage business, as now performed at the Theatres Royal. Ln : J. Cumberland [c. 1830]. 12°, pp. 64 BM | BPL

King Henry VIII. . . . 'Pocket Sh—.' The whole play for one penny. Ln : G. Mansell, 115, Fleet Street [c. 1830]. 32°, pp. 129-192 (excerpt), in printed wrappers

King Henry VIII. . . . Nuremberg and New York . . . 1837. 12°

King Henry VIII. . . . With the stage business, casts of characters, costumes, relative positions, etc. ' Modern Standard drama.' New York : S. French, 1848. 12°, pp. 60 BUS

King Henry the eighth . . . arranged for representation at the Princess's Theatre, by Charles Kean. First performed on Wednesday, 16th May, 1855 . . . Ln . J. K. Chapman & Co. [1855]. 8°, pp. 94 (including printed wrappers)
With historical preface. BM | BPL | BUS

[King Henry VIII.] Sh—'s historical play of ' King Henry the eighth . . .' Third edition. Ln : J. K. Chapman & Co. [1855]. 8°, pp. 90 BM | BUS
Sc. i., act v., is omitted in this issue.

King Henry the eighth . . . [With notes]. ' Lacy's acting edition.' Ln : T. H. Lacy [1855]. 12°, pp. xxvi.-64 BM | BPL

[King Henry VIII.] Overture and music to ' King Henry the eighth' as performed at the Royal Princess's Theatre. [Full score.] Composed by J. L. Hatton. Ln : Campbell, Ransford & Co., 1855. F°, pp. 54 BUS

King Henry VIII. . . . The costumes as represented at the Princess's Theatre, Vienna. Ln : . . . 1858. Oblong f°. With 18 plates

King Henry the eighth. With introductory remarks, copious interpretation of the text, critical, historical and grammatical notes, specimens of parsing, analysis, examination questions, and life of Cardinal Wolsey. Adapted for scholastic or private study and . . . middle class examinations. By John Hunter. Ln : Longman . . . & Roberts, 1860. Cr. 8°, pp. xl.-188 BUS | CPL

Sh— King Henry the eighth . . .

King Henry the eighth . . . 'Acting edition.' Ln : T. H. Lacy [c. 1865]. 12° BPL

King Henry VIII. . . . Leipzig : B. Tauchnitz, 1868. 16°

King Henry VIII. . . . edited for scholastic or private study by J. Hunter. Ln : Longmans, 1869. 12°, pp. xl.-188 BUS

King Henry VIII. . . . edited by J. Hunter for scholastic study. Ln : Longmans, 1872. Cr. 8° CPL

King Henry the eighth . . . edited with notes by W. J. Rolfe. With engravings. New York : Harper brothers, 1872. 16°, pp. 210 BUS

King Henry the eighth . . . With explanatory, grammatical and philological notes, critical remarks and historical extracts by William Lawson. Ln : W. Collins & Co., 1875. Cr. 8°, pp. 122 BM | BPL | BUS

King Henry VIII. . . . With introductions and notes. By H. N. Hudson. Boston [U.S.] : Ginn brothers, 1876. 12°, pp. 139-235 BUS

King Henry the eighth . . . arranged for representation . . . by Charles Calvert, and first produced at the Theatre Royal, Manchester . . . Ln : W. S. Johnson, 1877. 8°, pp. 78, in pictorial wrapper BPL

King Henry VIII. . . . Arranged for representation by C. Calvert, and produced at the Prince of Wales Theatre, Birmingham. Ln : Johnson, 1878. 12° BPL

King Henry the eighth . . . part two [edited by S. C. Mullick]. Calcutta : Sonatun Press, 1878. 8° BM

King Henry the eighth . . . With introductory remarks and critical and explanatory notes by John Hunter. Ln : Longman [c. 1878]. Cr. 8°, pp. xii.-136 BPL

King Henry VIII., as presented by Edwin Booth [In the ' Prompt book, edited by Wm. Winter']. New York : F. Hart, 1878. 16°, pp. 6, ff. 8-60 and pp. 62-72 BUS

[King Henry VIII.] Il Re Enrico VIII. dramma . . . voltato in prosa Italiana da C. Rusconi. Ottava edizione, col testo Inglese di riscontro. Firenze : Successori Le Monnier, 1880. 8°, pp. 226 BM
In English and Italian.

[King Henry the eighth] Henri VIII. . . . traduction Française [in prose] par E. Montégut, avec le text Anglaise. Paris : Hachette et cie, 1883. 8°, pp. iv.-184 BM

[King Henry the eighth] Henri VIII. [Expliqué litteralement par M. Morel . . . traduction Française [in prose] . . . de M. E. Montégut. Paris : Hachette et cie, 1883. 8°, pp. x.-322 BM
In English and French.

King Henry the eighth . . . 'Standard plays.' Ln : John Dicks [1883]. 12° BM
King Henry VIII. . . . 'School series.' Ln : Blackie . . . 1883. Cr. 8°
King Henry VIII. . . . edited with notes by W. J. Rolfe. New York : Harper . . . 1883. 12° BPL
[King Henry VIII.] The play of Henry VIII. . . . with notes. Ln : Blackie [1884]. Cr. 8°, pp. 100 BM
King Henry the eighth. With notes, examination papers . . . Ln. & Edin. : W. & R. Chambers, 1884. Cr. 8°, pp. 116 BM
King Henry VIII. . . . abridged. With notes. 'Educational series.' Ln. and Edin. : Blackwood & Sons [c. 1885]. Cr. 8°, pp. 68, clay wrappers
[King Henry VIII.] Selections from ' Henry the eighth' and 'Julius Cæsar' . . . With . . . notes. Ln : Blackie [1885]. 16°, pp. 32 BM
King Henry the eighth. [With introduction by H. Morley.] Ln : Cassell, 1887. 16°, pp. 192 BM
[King Henry VIII.] 150 lines from Sh—'s play of Henry VIII. With . . . notes. ' World school series.' Ln : . . . [1888]. 16°, 8°, and f°, pp. 8 BM
King Henry the eighth . . . With introduction and notes by H. N. Hudson. Boston [U.S.] . . . 1889. 12° BPL
King Henry VIII. . . . With notes, etc. Ln. and Edin. : W. & R. Chambers, 1889. Cr. 8° BPL
King Henry the eighth . . . edited by C. E. Flower. ' Memorial theatre edition.' Stratford-on-Avon : Printed by G. Boyden [1889]. Cr. 8°, pp. viii.·100, including printed wrappers BPL | SML
King Henry the eighth . . . Edited by W. H. Low. ' Tutorial series.' Ln : W. B. Clive [1890]. Cr. 8°, pp. 124 BM
King Henry the eighth . . . Edited by W. A. Wright. Oxford : Clarendon Press, 1891. Cr. 8° BPL
King Henry VIII. . . . with introduction by E. Dowden. Illustrations by Sir J. D. Linton. ' International Sh—.' Ln : . . . 1892. F° BPL
King Henry VIII. . . . As arranged for the stage by Henry Irving and presented at the Lyceum Theatre, 5th Jan. Ln : Nassau Press, 1892. 8°, pp. 72 BM | BPL
King Henry VIII. Illust. by Sir J. Gilbert. Ln : Routledge, 1892. Roy. 8°
King Henry the eighth . . . With introduction and notes by G. H. Ely. ' Junior school Sh—.' Ln : Blackie, 1893. Cr. 8°, pp. 128 BPL

King Henry VIII. Edited by I. Gollancz. ' Temple edition.' Ln : Dent, 1895. 16°
King Henry the eighth, with introduction and notes by K. Deighton. Ln : Macmillan, 1895. Cr. 8°, pp. xlvi.-184 BM | BPL
[King Henry VIII.] Selections from ' King Henry VIII.' Ln : Blackie [1896]. 16°, pp. 32 BM
King Henry the eighth . . . [In Donovan, ' English historical plays,' Vol. 2]. Ln : Macmillan, 1896. 2 vols. Cr. 8° BM | MPL
King Henry VIII. . . . ' Pocket Falstaff edition.' Ln : Bliss, Sands, 1898. 16°, pp. 128 BPL | SML
King Henry VIII. . . . [Edited by H. Morley.] ' National library.' Ln : Cassell, 1899. 16°, pp. 192
King Henry the eighth . . . Edited by D. Nichol Smith. ' Warwick Sh—.' Ln : Blackie, 1899. 12°, pp. 200 BPL
King Henry the eighth . . . Edited with introduction and notes by C. H. Herford. ' Eversley edition.' Ln : Macmillan, 1900. Cr. 8° BPL
King Henry VIII. With introduction and notes by John Dennis. Illust. by B. Shaw. ' Chiswick edition.' Ln : Bell, 1902. 12°
King Henry VIII. . . . ' Moffat's plays ' . . . Leeds : E. J. Arnold, 1903. 12°, pp. 236 BPL
First Leeds printing of Sh—.
King Henry VIII. Edited with introduction, and notes arranged and classified, by Thomas Page. Ln : Simpkin, 1903. Cr. 8°
King Henry VIII. Edited with notes by H. N. Hudson. ' Windsor edition.' Edinburgh : Jack, 1903. Cr. 8°
King Henry VIII. With introduction and notes by W. J. Craig. ' Little quartos.' Ln : Methuen, 1904. 16°
King Henry VIII. With introduction by G. Brandes. ' Favourite classics.' Ln : Heinemann, 1904. 12°
King Henry VIII. . . . ' Picture Sh—.' Ln : Blackie, 1905. 16° BPL
King Henry VIII. . . . edited by H. Morley. ' National library.' Ln : Cassell, 1905. 16°, pp. 192 BPL
King Henry VIII. ' Waistcoat pocket edition.' Ln : Treherne, 1905. 32°
King Henry VIII. . . . ' Renaissance edition.' Ln : ·Harrap, 1908. Fcp. 4° BPL
King Henry VIII. . . . ' Red letter edition.' Ln : Blackie . . . 1908. 16°

Sh— King Henry the eighth . . .

King Henry VIII. . . . 'Plain text Sh—.'
Ln : Blackie, 1909. Cr. 8°   BPL

King Henry VIII. . . . edited by Low.
'Universal tutorial series.' Ln : Clive,
1909. Cr. 8°   BPL

'King Henry VIII.' references—

See Archer & Lowe	See Johnson & Stee-
„ Bailey	vens
„ Banks (J.)	„ Kemble
„ Boyle	„ Mirrour
„ Capgrave	„ Pemberton
„ Davies	„ Roderick
„ Dramatic . . .	„ S—— (T.)
„ Furnivall	„ Sh— Epitaph
„ German	„ Sh— Works :
„ Halliwell	Ext. 1800
„ Hawkins	„ Spedding
„ Henry VIII.	„ Vaughan
„ Holinshed	„ Wolsey
„ Irving	

KING JOHN.

A manuscript or playhouse copy of this tragedy existed in or before 1598, yet no printed version is known before it appeared in the Jaggard canon of 1623. An inferior but somewhat similar play, called " The troublesome raigne of King Iohn" (attributed to Christopher Marlowe), appeared in 1591, 1611, and 1622. The earlier play was undoubtedly made use of by Sh— in shaping his own drama on the same subject.

[King John] The Troublesome Raigne of Iohn King of England, with the discouerie of King Richard Cordelion's Base Sonne (vulgarly named The Bastard Fawconbridge) : Also the Death of King Iohn at Swinstead Abbey. As it was (sundry times) publikely acted by the Queene's Maiesties Players in the honourable Citie of London. [*Device.*] Imprinted at London for Sampson Clarke, and are to be solde at his shop on the backe-side of the Royall Exchange, 1591. Fcp. 4° ; sig. Aꟾ to G4 on twenty-eight unnumbered leaves ; black letter   CTC

The title of this first part, an anonymous issue, was closely followed in succeeding editions bearing Sh—'s name. It was reprinted in Hazlitt's 'Sh—'s library.' Only one perfect copy known.

[King John] The Second part of the troublesome Raigne of King Iohn, conteining the death of Arthur Plantaginet, the landing of Lewes and the poysning of King Iohn at Swinstead Abbey. As it was (sundry times) publikely acted by the Queenes Maiesties Players, in the

Sh— King John . . .

honourable Citie of London. [*Device.*] Imprinted at London for Samson Clarke and are to be solde at his shop, on the backe-side of the Royall Exchange, 1591. Fcp. 4° ; sig. Aꟾ to E4 on twenty unpaged leaves   CTC

Only one perfect copy known.

[King John] The First and Second Part of the Troublesome Raigne of Iohn King of England. With the Discouerie of King Richard Cordelion's Base Sonne (vulgarly named The Bastard Fawconbridge). Also the Death of King Iohn at Swinstead Abbey. As they were (sundry times) lately acted by the Queenes Maiesties Players. Written by W. Sh—. Imprinted at London by Valentine Simmes for Iohn Helme and are to be sold at his shop in Saint Dunstan's Churchyard in Fleete-street, 1611. Fcp. 4° ; sig. Aꟾ to L4 in fours and M² on 45 unpaged folios
BM | BLO | BUS | CTC | DEVON

Attributed to Christopher Marlowe. Reprinted in 1764 in ' Miscellaneous pieces,' in 1766 by Geo. Steevens, in 1788 by John Nichols, and in 1853-65 by Halliwell in his folio Sh—.

[King John] The First and Second Part of the troublesome Raigne of Iohn, King of England. With the discouerie of King Richard Cordelion's Base sonne (vulgarly named the Bastard Fauconbridge). Also the death of King John at Swinstead Abbey. As they were (sundry times) lately acted. Written by W. Shakespeare. Ln : Printed by Aug. Mathewes, for Thomas Dewe, and are to be sold at his shop in St. Dunstan's Churchyard in Fleet Street, 1622. Fcp. 4° ; sig. Aꟾ to M² in fours ; 46 leaves without pagination BM | BUS | CTC | DEVON

A reprint of the 1611 edition, according to George Steevens, with slight changes. The second part has an independent title-page :—
'The Second Part of the Troublesome Raigne of King Iohn. Containing the entrance of Lewis the French King's Sonne : with the Poysoning of King Iohn by a Monke. Written by W. Shakespeare. London . . . 1622.'
Although stated to be ' Written by W. Shakespeare,' this is not his work, but the third edition of the older ' King John,' probably by Marlowe, which forms the basis of Sh—'s finer conception.
In April, 1907, a copy realised £80. In Dec., 1907, the Howe copy, 7⅛ by 5in., sold for £60.

[King John] The Second Part of the troublesome Reigne of King John. Written by W. Shakespeare. Ln : Printed by Aug. Mathewes for Thomas Dewe, 1622. Fcp. 4° ; sig. Hꟾ to M² in fours   W

The absent ' First part' occupies signatures A to G.

[King John] King John and Matilda. A tragedy. As it was acted at the Cock-pit in Drury Lane by her majesties servants. Written by Robert Davenport. Ln : . . . 1655. Fcp. 4°

[King John] King John and Matilda: A tragedy. Written by W. Daven, Gent. [*i.e.*, Robert Davenport]. Ln : Rich. Gammon [?] 1662. Fcp. 4°   w
The publisher's name may be fictitious.

[King John] The life and death of King John. A tragedy. By Mr. Wm. Sh—. Ln : Printed for J. Tonson and the rest of the proprietors, and sold by the book-sellers of Ln. and Westminster, 1734. Cr. 8°, pp. 72 and frontispiece by P. Fourdrinier   BM | W

[King John] The life and death of King John. A tragedy by Sh—. Ln : R. Walker, 1735. Cr. 8°   w

[King John] Papal tyranny in the reign of King John. A tragedy, as it was acted by Colley Cibber. Ln : . . . 1744. 8°

[King John] Papal tyranny in the reign of King John. A tragedy. As it is acted at the Theatre-Royal in Covent-Garden by his majesty's servants. By Colley Cibber. Ln : Printed for J. Watts, 1745. 8°, pp. xii.-72   BPL | BUS | CPL | W
The first act of Sh—'s play is omitted, and the interest of the plot turns upon the conflict between John and the Legate. Scarcely a line of the original is retained intact.
Reprinted in 'Cibber's dramatic works,' in 1760 and 1777.

[King John] Life and death of King John, with a new set of choruses in the manner of the ancients as they are to be sung at the end of each act. Dublin . . . 1750. 12°

[King John] Miscellaneous pieces of antient English poesie, viz., The troublesome raigne of King John, written by Sh—, extant in no edition of his writings [1611]; The metamorphosis of Pigmalion's image and certain satyres by John Marston; The scourge of villanie, by the same. All printed before the year 1600. [Ed. by J. Bowles.] Ln : Printed for Robert Horsefield at the Crown in Ludgate Street, 1764. 8°, pp. iv.-234
                    BM | BPL | BUS | W
Gifford in his edition of Ben Jonson styles Marston 'the most scurrilous, filthy, and obscene writer of his time.'

[King John] The first and second part of the troublesome raigne of John King of England . . . Imprinted at Ln. by Valentine Simmes . . . 1611; [Reprinted by Geo. Steevens, 1766]. 8°, pp. 100, unpaged; sig. N7 to T8 in eights   BPL | W

[King John] Life and death of King John. A tragedy. Written by Sh—. Ln : H. Woodfall, 1769. 8°   BPL | W
The 'Dramatis personæ' is dated 1754.

King John. A tragedy. . . As performed at the Theatre Royal, Drury Lane. Regulated from the prompt book, with permission of the managers, by Mr. Hopkins, prompter. An introduction and notes, critical and illustrative, are added by the authors of the 'Dramatic censor' [F. Gentleman]. Ln : John Bell; York : C. Etherington, 1773. 8°, pp. 64   BPL
An off-print from Bell's edition for the use of playgoers. With list of Bell's publications (8 pp.) at end.

[King John] Troublesome raigne of John king of England. First and second part, 1611 [In 'Six old plays, edited by J. Nichols,' Vol. 2]. Ln : . . . 1779. 8°
                    BPL

[King John] Life and death of King John. A tragedy. Written by Wm. Sh—. Marked with the variations of the manager's book at the Theatre Royal in Drury Lane. Ln : . . . 1784. 8°   BPL | W

[King John] First and second part of the troublesome raigne of John king of England. Imprinted at Ln. by Valentine Simmes for Iohn Helme, 1611; Reprinted by J. Nichols, 1788. 8°   w

[King John] First and second part of the troublesome raigne of John King of England . . . Written by W. Sh—. Imprinted at Ln. by Valentine Simmes for Iohn Helme and are to be sold at his shop in Saint Dunston's Churchyard in Fleetestreet, 1611. [Manuscript transcript on 45 leaves of paper, c. 1800, from the original quarto in the Zurich library.] F°
                    w
'First printed in 1591, and reprinted in 1611 and 1622 with the letters 'W. Sh.' affixed, that it might be mistaken for the work of Sh—, who has made very slight use of it in his play on the same subject.'— *J. O. Halliwell.*

King John . . . Revised by J. P. Kemble. As acted at Drury Lane Theatre. Ln : . . . 1800. 8°

King John . . . altered from Sh— [by Richard Valpy] as it was acted at Reading School for the subscription to the naval pillar to be erected in honor of the naval victories of the present war. Reading: Smart & Cowslade, 1800. 8°, pp. xii.-82-vi.   BM | BPL | BUS | W
Sh—'s first act omitted, as in Cibber's version, and with other changes, mostly in the language and versification. On account of the passages referring to the renewal of war with France it had afterwards a great success.

Sh— King John . . .

King John . . . Altered [by R. Valpy] from Sh—. As it was acted at Reading School and is now performing at Covent Garden with distinguished applause. Second edition. Reading: Smart & Cowslade, 1803. 8°, pp. xvi.-82-vi. BM | BPL | BUS
With a new prologue and epilogue; otherwise the same as the 1800 edition.

King John . . . Revised by J. P. Kemble, and now first published as it is acted at the Theatre Royal in Covent Garden. Ln: T. N. Longman & O. Rees, 1804. 8°, pp. 62 BPL | BUS

King John . . . As performed at the Theatre Royal, Covent Garden. Printed under the authority of the managers from the prompt book. With remarks by Mrs. Inchbald. Ln: Longman . . . & Orme [1806]. 12°, pp. 70 and frontispiece by Neagle after Howard BPL | BUS

King John, by Will. Sh—. Printed complete from the text of Sam. Johnson and Geo. Steevens. Ln: . . . 1811. 16° W

King John. An historical play. Revised by J. P. Kemble, and now published as it is performed at the Theatres Royal. Ln: John Miller, 1814. 8°, pp. 64 BPL | BUS | W

King John . . . With remarks by Mrs. Inchbald. Ln: Longman . . . & Brown [c. 1817]. 12°, pp. 70 and plate BUS

King John . . . With prefatory remarks . . . by D. G—— [Geo. Daniel]. Marked with the stage business, and stage directions, as it is performed at the Theatres Royal, by W. Oxberry. Ln: . . . 1819. 8°, pp. ii.-62 BM | BPL

King John . . . Edited by W. Oxberry . . . Ln: . . . 1823. 12°. With portrait

[King John] Costume of . . . ' King John ' selected . . . from the best authorities. With . . . notices by J. R. Planché. The figures . . . by J. K. Meadows. Ln: J. Miller, 1823. 8°, pp. ii.-36 BUS

King John . . . Ln: Published and sold by Vernor & Hood; Newcastle-upon-Tyne: Printed by and for J. Mitchell [1825]. 12° BPL

[King John] Senarii Græci [A translation by J. Hodgson from ' King John, act iv., sc. 2.' In English and Greek]. Cambridge . . . [1825]. 8° BM

[King John] Senarii Græci [A translation, by B. H. Kennedy, from ' King John, act iii., sc. 3 ']. Cambridge . . . 1826. 8°
In English and Greek. BM

King John . . . Printed from the acting copy with remarks . . . by D. G. [Geo. Daniel]. To which are added a . . . cast of the

Sh— King John . . .

characters . . . and the whole of the stage business as performed at the Theatres Royal. Ln: J. Cumberland, 1829. 12°, pp. 60 BM

King John . . . Edited by D. G—— [Geo. Daniel]. Ln: J. Cumberland [c. 1831]. 12° BPL

King John . . . Adapted for the use of schools [by E. Slater]. Ln: . . . [1836]. 12° BPL

King John (with the benefit of the act). A burlesque in one act, by Gilbert Abbot à Beckett. Printed from the acting copy, with description of the costume, cast of the characters, exits and entrances, and the whole of the business. As performed at the St. James Theatre. With a portrait of H. Hall. Ln: W. Strange, 1837. 12°, pp. xxii. BPL | BUS

[King John] Kynge Iohan, by J. Bale. Edited by J. Payne Collier. Ln: Camden Society, 1838. Fcp. 4° BPL

King John . . . Nurnberg & New York . . . 1841. 12°

King John. A historical play in five acts . . . Ln: Sherwood & Bowyer, 1844. 16°, pp. ii.-64 BUS

King John . . . With the stage business, cast of characters, costumes, relative positions, etc. Also a list of authorities for costumes by Charles Kean. As produced with great splendour at the Park Theatre. ' Modern standard drama.' Edited by Epes Sargent. New York: W. Taylor & Co., 1846. 12°, pp. 68 BUS

King John . . . ' French's standard drama.' New York: S. French [c. 1846]. 12°, pp. 68 BUS

King John . . . Edited by Dr. A. Philippi for the use of families and schools. Dusseldorf . . . 1848. 12°

King John . . . arranged for representation at the Princess's Theatre, with notes by Charles Kean, as performed on Oct. 18th, 1858. Ln: Bradbury . . . 1858. 8° BPL | W

King John . . . ' Lacy's acting edition.' Ln: T. H. Lacy [1859]. 12°, pp. 72 BM | BPL

King John . . . As performed at the Theatre Royal, Drury Lane. Ln: . . . 1865. 8° BPL

King John . . . Edited by John Hunter. With notes . . . for scholastic or private study. Ln: Longmans, 1871. Cr. 8°, pp. xvi.-114 CPL

[King John] Life and death of King John . . . together with the troublesome reign of King John, as acted by the Queen's players, c. 1589 . . . edited, with notes . . . by F. G. Fleay. 'School and college classics.' Glasgow: W. Collins, 1878. Cr. 8°, pp. 224　　　　BM | BPL | BUS

[King John] A selection from Sh—'s ' King John.' ' Lines from the poets.' Ln : . . . 1879. 16°, pp. 30　　　　BM

King John . . . With notes by J. Hunter. Ln : Longmans . . . 1879. Cr. 8°　　BPL

[King John] History of the life and death of King John . . . edited, with notes, by W. J. Rolfe. New York : Harper, 1880. 16°, pp. 190　　　　BM | BPL

[King John] History of King John. With introduction and notes . . . by . . . H. N. Hudson. Boston [U.S.]: Ginn & Heath, 1880. 16°, pp. xxvi.-166　　BM

King John . . . School edition. Ln : W. & R. Chambers, 1882. Cr. 8°, pp. 98. Illustrated

King John . . . edited with notes by W. J. Rolfe. New York . . . 1882. 12°　BPL

King John . . . Ln : Simpkin . . . 1882. Cr. 8°

King John . . . ' Standard plays.' Ln : John Dicks [1883 ?]. 12°　　　　BPL

King John . . . Edited by C. E. Moberly. ' Rugby school edition.' Rugby: Billington . . . 1883. Cr. 8°
　　　　　　　BPL | BUS | MPL

King John . . . ' School edition.' Ln. and Edin. : W. & R. Chambers, 1883. Cr. 8°, pp. 98. Illust.

King John. With . . . notes. ' World school series.' Ln : . . . [1883]. 16°, pp. vi.-48　　　　BM

[King John] Selections from Sh—'s ' King John ' . . . An English text-book . . . by T. Parry. Ln : Longmans, 1884. Cr. 8°, pp. 48　　　　BM

King John . . . with introduction, notes, examination papers, and an appendix . . . Edited . . . by T. Parry. Ln : Longmans, 1884. Cr. 8°, pp. 152　　BM

[King John] The play of King John . . . With notes. Ln : Blackie [1885]. 16°, pp. 96　　　　BM

King John . . . abridged, with notes by J. M. D. Meiklejohn. Ln : W. Blackwood & Sons, 1885. Cr. 8°, pp. 64　BM

King John . . . With notes, examination papers, and plan of preparation. Edinburgh : W. & R. Chambers, 1885. Cr. 8°, pp. 88　　　　BM

King John . . . With introduction, notes, examination papers . . . by Thomas Parry. Ln : Longmans, 1886. Cr. 8°, pp.152. Illustrated

[King John] Sh—'s play of ' King John ': with the meaning of the words, paraphrase of difficult passages, and . . . notes . . . for standards v., vi. and vii. Manchester: J. B. Ledsham [1886]. Cr. 8°, pp. vi.-48　　　　BM

[King John] ' Sh— for schools ': ' King John,' as abridged by C. Kemble, with notes for school use. Ln : Bell, 1886. Cr. 8°, pp. 52　　　　BM

King John . . . edited by W. A. Wright. Oxford : Clarendon Press, 1886. Cr. 8°, pp. viii.-160　　BPL | BUS | SML

[King John] Selections from ' King John.' With introductory notes and appendix by T. Parry. Ln : Longman, 1886. Cr. 8°, pp. 48, including printed wrappers

King John . . . With notes. Ln : Blackie, 1887. Cr. 8°　　　　BUS

King John . . . With notes for the Oxford and Cambridge examinations. Ln : Allman [1887]. Cr. 8°　　BPL | BUS

King John . . . edited by B. Dawson. ' University Sh—.' Ln : Simpkin, 1887. 12°　　　　BPL

[King John] Life and death of King John. [With an introduction by Henry Morley.] ' National library.' Ln : Cassell, 1887. 16°, pp. 192　　　　BM

King John . . . with restorations of text by F. Haywell [F. Hawley]. Ln : Cumberland [1887 ?]. 12°

King John . . . With introduction and notes [by Ben Jonson]. Ln : Gill, 1887. 12°, pp. 112　　　　BM

King John . . . ed. by W. A. Wright. Oxford : Clarendon Press, 1887. Cr. 8°, pp. viii.-160

[King John] Troublesome raigne of John, King of England. The first quarto, 1591, parts i. and ii., which Sh— rewrote about 1595 as his ' Life and death of King John.' A facsimile by C. Prætorius. Forewords by F. J. Furnivall. ' Sh— quarto facsimiles.' Ln : 1888. 2 vols. Fcp. 4°
　　　　　　　BM | BPL | BUS

King John . . . With notes, etc. Ln. and Edin. : W. & R. Chambers, 1889. 12°
　　　　　　　BPL

King John . . . With introduction and notes by H. N. Hudson. Boston [U.S.] . . . 1889. 12°　　　　BPL

King John . . . edited by C. E. Flower. ' Memorial theatre edition.' Stratford-on-Avon : G. Boyden [1889]. Cr. 8°, pp. viii.-84, including printed wrappers
　　　　　　　BPL | SMI.

Sh— King John . . .

King John . . . with notes arranged and classified by T. Page. Edited by J. Paige. Ln: Moffatt & Paige, 1889. 8° SML

King John . . . With notes by K. Deighton. Ln: Macmillan, 1890. 12°

King John . . . edited by O. Elton. 'Falcon edition.' Ln: Longmans, 1890. 8° BPL

King John . . . With introduction and notes by T. Page. 'Moffatt's plays.' Ln: . . . [1892]. 12° BPL

King John . . . With introduction and notes by F. E. Webb. 'Junior school Sh—.' Ln: Blackie, 1894. Cr. 8°, pp. 112 BPL

King John . . . edited with notes by W. J. Rolfe. New York . . . 1895. 12° BPL

King John . . . Edited by I. Gollancz. 'Temple edition.' Ln: Dent, 1895. 16°

[King John] Troublesome reign of King John. Edited with an introduction by A. F. Hopkinson. 'Old English plays.' Ln: . . . 1896. 12° BPL

King John . . . With introduction and notes by K. Deighton. Ln: Macmillan, 1896. 12° BPL

King John . . . [In Donovan, 'English historical plays,' Vol. I.] Ln: Macmillan, 1896. 2 vols. Cr. 8° BM | MPL

King John . . . edited by Francis Pierrepont Barnard. 'School Shakespeare.' Ln: Arnold [1897]. 12°, pp. 204 BPL

King John . . . edited with notes by W. J. Rolfe. Ln: Clive, 1897. Cr. 8°

[King John] Life and death of King John. 'Pocket Falstaff edition.' Ln: Sands & Co., 1898. 16°, pp. 104 BPL | SML

King John . . . 'Swan edition.' Ln: Longmans, 1899. Cr. 8° BPL

King John . . . with notes by W. Young. 'Swan edition.' Ln: Longmans, 1900. Cr. 8°

King John . . . edited by G. C. Moore Smith. 'Warwick edition.' Ln: Blackie, 1900. Cr. 8°, pp. 222 BPL

King John . . . with introduction and notes by John Dennis. Illust. by B. Shaw. 'Chiswick edition.' Ln: Bell, 1900. Cr. 8°, pp. 128

King John . . . edited with introduction and notes by C. H. Herford. 'Eversley edition.' Ln: Macmillan, 1900. Cr. 8° BPL

King John . . . edited by W. J. Rolfe. New York . . . [1902]. Cr. 8°. Illust. BUS

King John . . . 'Picture edition.' Ln: Blackie . . . 1903. Cr. 8° BPL

Sh— King John . . .

King John, edited with notes by H. N. Hudson. 'Windsor edition.' Edinburgh: Jack, 1903. Cr. 8°, pp. 110

King John . . . edited by H. Morley. 'National library.' Ln: Cassell, 1904. 16°, pp. 192 BPL

King John . . . with introduction and notes by W. J. Craig. 'Little quartos.' Ln: Methuen, 1904. 16°

King John . . . with introduction by G. Brandes. 'Favourite classics.' Ln: Heinemann, 1904. 12°

King John. 'Ellen Terry edition.' Glasgow: Bryce . . . 1904. 32°

King John. 'Waistcoat pocket edition.' Ln: Treherne . . . 1904. 32°

King John . . . 'Stage edition.' Glasgow: Collins . . . 1905. 16°

King John . . . Retold for children by A. S. Hoffman. Illust. by D. Curtis. Ln: Dent, 1905. 16° BPL

King John . . . 'Red letter edition.' Ln: Blackie, 1906. 12°

King John . . . edited by Benjamin Dawson. Ln: R. Sutton, 1907. Cr. 8°

King John . . . edited by Ivor B. John. 'Arden edition.' Ln: Methuen . . . 1907. 8°, pp. 106

King John . . . 'Renaissance edition.' Ln: Harrap . . . 1907. Fcp. 4° BPL

King John . . . Text without notes. Ln: Chambers . . . 1908. Cr. 8°, pp. 68

King John . . . 'Plain text Sh—.' Ln: Blackie, 1909. Cr. 8° BPL

'King John' references—

See Bale	See Mirrour . . .
,, Barnett (T. D.)	,, Nero
,, Davies	,, Nicholson
,, Fletcher	,, Pemberton
,, Green (V.)	,, Planché
,, Halliwell	,, Satires
,, Johnson & Steevens	,, Six old . . .
	,, Smith (G. C. M.)
,, Letter . . .	,, Tree
,, Meres	

KING LEAR.

The 1608 impression of this tragedy issued by Nathaniel Butter, bearing his business address, is accepted as the first edition. An anonymous play entitled 'The true chronicle history of King Leir,' published three years earlier, together with William Warner's 'Albion's England,' printed in 1592, furnished Sh— with essentials.

It was entered thus at Stationer's Hall: 26 Nov., 1607. Nathanael Butter, John

Busby.   Entred for their copie under thandes of Sir George Buck knight ann Thwardens A booke called Master William Sh— his historye of Kinge Lear, as yt was played before the Kinges maiestie at Whitehall vppon Sainct Stephens night at Christmas Last, by his maiesties servantes playinge vsually at the Globe on the Banksyde.

[King Lear] The True Chronicle History of King Leir and his Three Daughters, Gonerill, Ragan, and Cordella. As it hath bene diuers and sundry times lately acted. [*Printer's ornament.*] London: Printed for Simon Stafford for Iohn Wright and are to bee sold at his shop at Christes Church dore, next Newgate Market, 1605. Fcp. 4°; sig. A¹ to I⁴ in fours; thirty-six unpaged leaves   BM

In verse.
Of extreme rarity. This is the oldest known impression, although acted as early as the Rose Theatre as early as 1593.
As the precursor of Sh—'s tragedy on the same subject, and a play which he must have known and used, its great interest is palpable.
A copy [with these defects: title-page in facsimile, margins of next four leaves slightly repaired, and sig. H and I barely cut into, but otherwise sound, bound by W. Pratt in light blue morocco] sold in July, 1905, for £480.
Reprinted by Steevens in 1766, by Nichols in 1779, by Victor in 1886, and by the Malone Society in 1907-8.

[King Lear] M. William Shak-speare: his True Chronicle Historie of the life and death of King Lear and his three Daughters. With the vnfortunate life of Edgar, sonne and heire to the Earle of Gloster, and his sullen and assumed humor of Tom of Bedlam. As it was played before the Kings Maiestie at Whitehall vpon S. Stephans night in Christmas Hollidayes. By his Maiesties seruants playing vsually at the Gloabe on the Bancke-side. [*Pegasus emblem.*] London: Printed [by Nicholas Okes ?] for Nathaniel Butter, and are to be sold at his shop in Pauls Church-yard at the signe of the Pide Bull, neere St. Austins Gate, 1608. Fcp. 4°, forty-one unpaged leaves; sig. B¹ to L⁴ in fours (title unsigned) BM | BLO | CTC | DEVON | NY

This edition formed the basis of the text in the 1623 folio.
An inlaid copy sold for £900 in July, 1905.

[King Lear] M. William Shake-speare, His True Chronicle Historie of the life and death of King Lear, and his three Daughters. With the vnfortunate life of Edgar, sonne and heire to the Earle of Glocester, and his sullen and assumed humour of Tom of Bedlam. As it was plaid before the Kings Maiesty at White-

Hall, vppon S. Stephens night, in Christmas Hollidaies. By his Maiesties Seruants, playing vsually at the Globe on the Banckside, 1608. . . . London: Printed for Nathaniel Butter and are to be sold at his shop in Pauls Church-yard at the signe of the Pide Bull neere St. Austins Gate, 1608. Fcp. 4°, forty-one leaves; sig. B¹ to L⁴ in fours   BM

The British Museum copy lacks the original title-page; replaced by one in facsimile. The impression presents several textual variations from the foregoing, particularly on G2 verso, H3 verso, and H4 recto.
It also bears a manuscript note by J. O. Halliwell.
Known as the second issue of the first edition.

[King Lear] M. VVilliam Shake-speare; His True Chronicle History of the life and death of King Lear and his three Daughters. With the vnfortunate life of Edgar, sonne and heire to the Earle of Glocester and his sullen and assumed humour of Tom of Bedlam. As it was plaid before the Kings Maiesty at White-Hall, vppon S. Stephens night, in Christmas Hollidaies. By his Maiesties Seruants, playing vsually at the Globe on the Banck-side. [' *Heb Ddieu* ' block. Ln.] Printed for Nathaniel Butter [by Isaac Jaggard] 1608 [otherwise 1619]. Fcp. 4°, forty-four unpaged leaves, including title; sig. A to L in fours
BM | BLO | BUS | CTC | DEVON | NY | SBL | W

The date 1608 is fictitious [for fuller particulars see A. W. Pollard's 'Sh— folios and quartos']. The real year of issue was 1619.
It was reprinted by Steevens in 1766, who observed, 'There is besides this edition a third of the same year (1608), which with that published by Jane Bell in 1655 is but a copy from the first, and retains even the printer's errors.' It was also reprinted by Halliwell in 1867, and by Daniel in 1885.
At the Bodleian is a copy, lacking the title, which exhibits variations from other examples. In May, 1906, one measuring 7 by 5¼ in. sold for £395, while Earl Howe's copy, in Dec., 1907, realised £200.

[King Lear] M. William Shake-speare. His True Chronicle History of the life and death of King Lear and his three Daughters. With the Vnfortunat life of Edgar, sonne and heire to the Earle of Glocester and his sullen assumed humour of Tom of Bedlam. As it was plaid before the Kings Maiesty at Whit-hall, vpon S. Stephens night in Christmas Hollidaies. By his Maiesties servants playing vsually at the Globe on the Bank-side. London: Printed by Jane Bell and are to be sold at the East-end of Christ-Church, 1655. Fcp. 4°; sig. A to L⁴ in fours; forty-four unpaged leaves, with publisher's list of books on verso of title
BM | BLO | BPL | BUS | CTC | NY

Reprinted from the second edition of 1608.

23—I

Sh— King Lear . . .

[King Lear] The history of King Lear. Acted at the Duke's Theatre. Reviv'd with alterations. By Nahum Tate. Ln: Printed for E. Flesher and are to be sold by R. Bentley and M. Magnes in Russel Street near Covent Garden, 1681. Fcp. 4°, pp. 68   BPL | BUS | W

The changes mainly consist of threading 'through the whole a love between Edgar and Cordelia,' and ending the play with their marriage and Lear's triumph. The part of the Fool is entirely omitted. Addison protested against this outrage on Sh—, and Johnson defended it on the ground of poetical justice, as his feelings were too much agitated by the death of Cordelia.

[King Lear] The history of King Lear, acted at the Queen's Theatre. Reviv'd with alterations by N. Tate. Ln: Printed for R. Bentley and M. Magnes in Russel Street near Covent Garden, 1689. Fcp. 4°, pp. vi.-58   BPL | W

[King Lear] The history of King Lear. Revived with alterations. By N. Tate. Ln: Printed for Rich. Wellington at the Dolphin and Crown in St. Paul's Church-Yard & E. Rumbold at the Post House, Covent Garden: and Tho. Osborne at Gray's Inn, near the Walks [c. 1690]. Fcp. 4°, pp. 60   BPL | BUS | SML

The epilogue says :—
' But still so many master-touches shine,
Of that vast hand that first laid this design,
That in great Sh—'s right, he's bold to say,
If you like nothing you have seen to-day,
The play your judgment damns, not you the Play.
Beneath the imprint runs a list of publications, as follow :—' There is newly published, Mr. Glanvil's Discourse of plurality, of the third edition . . . Memoirs of the court of France and city of Paris, giving an account of the intrigues of the court . . . all Mrs. Behin's plays in two volumes . . . A satyr against dancing . . . Architecture illustrated, with fifty-two copper plates, being much enlarged . . . Where gentlemen and ladies may have all sorts of novels and plays.'

[King Lear] The history of King Lear. Acted at the Queens Theatre. Reviv'd with alterations. By N. Tate. Ln: Printed by H. Hills for Rich. Wellington at the Lute in St. Paul's Church-Yard, and E. Rumbold at the Post House, Covent Garden, and sold by Bern. Lintott at the Cross Keyes in St. Martin's Lane, 1699. Fcp. 4°   BM | SML | W

[King Lear] The history of King Lear . . . Reviv'd with alterations. By N. Tate. Ln: Printed for R. Wellington [c. 1710]. Fcp. 4°, pp. 60   BM

[King Lear] The history of King Lear. Acted at the Queen's Theatre. Revived with alterations. By N. Tate. Ln: Printed for Richard Wellington, 1712. Fcp. 4°, pp. 60   BM | BPL | W

Sh— King Lear . . .

King Lear . . . By N. Tate . . . Ln : . . . 1717. 8°

King Lear . . . A tragedy. Ln: Printed by J. Darby for M. P—— and sold by A. Bettesworth in Paternoster Row and F. Clay without Temple Bar. Price 1/-. 1723. 8°, pp. 84 and frontispiece, B. Dandridge inv., J. Van der Gucht sc.
                                     BPL | W

[King Lear] The history of King Lear. A tragedy. As it is now acted at the King's Theatre. Reviv'd with alterations by N. Tate. Ln: Printed in the year 1729. 8°, pp. 72   BPL

[King Lear] The history of King Lear . . . Reviv'd with alterations. By N. Tate. Dublin: William Smith, 1733. 12°, pp. 78   BM

[King Lear] The life and death of King Lear. By Mr. Wm. Sh—. Ln: Printed for J. Tonson and the rest of the proprietors and sold by the booksellers of Ln. and Westminster, 1734. Cr. 8°, pp. 92 and frontispiece by Lud. Du Guernier
Piracy notice at end against R. Walker.   W

[King Lear] The life and death of King Lear . . . Ln: R. Walker . . . 1735. 12°

King Lear . . . By N. Tate. Ln : . . . 1745. 12°

[King Lear] The history of King Lear . . . Reviv'd with alterations by N. Tate. Ln : . . . 1749. 12°   BPL

[King Lear] The history of King Lear . . . Revived with alterations by N. Tate. Ln : . . . 1750. 12°   BPL
Differs from the preceding edition of same year.

[King Lear] The history of King Lear. A tragedy. As it is now acted at the King's Theatres. Revived, with alterations, by N. Tate. Ln: Printed for C. Hitch and L. Hawes, 1756. 12°, pp. 70   BUS | W
The cast differs from those in preceding editions.

[King Lear] The history of King Lear . . . Reviv'd with alterations by N. Tate. Ln : . . . 1757. 12°   BPL

[King Lear] The history of King Lear . . . Reviv'd with alterations. By N. Tate. Ln: C. Hitch & L. Hawes, 1759. 12°, pp. 70   BM | BPL

[King Lear] The history of King Lear. A tragedy. As it is now acted at the King's Theatre. Revived, with alterations, by N. Tate. Ln: Printed for C. Hitch and L. Hawes, 1760. 12°   W

[King Lear] The history of King Lear . . . Revived with alterations by N. Tate. Cork . . . 1761. 12°   BPL
The first piece of Sh— printed at Cork.

[King Lear] The history of King Lear . . . Revived with alterations by N. Tate. Ln: C. Hitch, 1763. 12°, pp. 70   BUS
The cast is identical with that in the first edition.

[King Lear] M. Wm. Sh— his true chronicle history of . . . King Lear . . . Printed for Nathaniel Butter, 1608 [Reprinted by George Steevens. Ln: J. & R. Tonson, 1766]. 8°, pp. 102, unpaged; sig. G6 to N6 in eights   BPL | W

[King Lear] The true chronicle history of King Leir . . . Printed by Simon Stafford for Iohn Wright, 1605 [Reprinted by George Steevens. Ln: J. & R. Tonson, 1766]. 8°   BPL | W

[King Lear] The true chronicle history of King Leir . . . Simon Stafford for Iohn Wright, 1605 [Reprinted by George Steevens. Ln: J. & R. Tonson, 1766]. Fcp. 4°, large paper   W

[King Lear] The history of King Lear. A tragedy. As it is now acted at the Theatres Royal in Drury Lane and Covent Garden. Revived with alterations by N. Tate. Ln: F. & J. Noble, T. Lowndes, T. Longman, T. Caslon, C. Corbett, T. King, W. Nicoll, 1767. 8°, pp. 72   SML | W
With preface, prologue, and epilogue. In the first-named Tate says:—' Nothing but . . . my zeal for . . . Sh— could have wrought me to so bold an undertaking . . . Lear's real and Edgar's pretended madness have so much of extravagant nature as could never have started but from our Sh—'s creating fancy . . . None but Sh— could have formed such conceptions . . . I found the whole a heap of jewels unstrung and unpolish'd, yet so dazzling in their dis-order that I soon perceived I had seized a treasure.'

[King Lear] The life and death of King Lear, by Mr. Wm. Sh— . . . [Edited by N. Tate]. Ln: . . . 1767. 12°. With frontispiece   BPL | W

[King Lear] The history of King Lear. As it is performed at the Theatre Royal in Covent Garden [with a preface by George Colman]. Ln: R. Baldwin and T. Becket, 1768. 8°, pp. vi.-72
BM | BPL | BUS | SML | W
Except in the love of Edgar and Cordelia this altera-tion follows Tate's version.

[King Lear] Life and death of King Lear. A tragedy . . . Edinburgh: Printed by and for Martin & Wotherspoon . . . 1768. 12°, pp. 108   BPL | SML
The Stratford copy bears J. O. Halliwell's autograph inscription.

[King Lear] The history of King Lear . . . Dublin: James Hoby & John Exshaw, 1768. 8°

King Lear. A tragedy. By Wm. Sh—. Collated with the old and modern editions [by Charles Jennens]. Ln: W. White,

1770. 8°, pp. xiv.-192. With portrait after Jansen, engraved by R. Earlom
BM | BPL | BUS | NY | SML | W
A version meeting with some hostility, to which the editor responded. See Jennens, also Sh— King Lear, 1772. The dedication is by the editor to himself. Jennens died in 1773, after issuing five of the plays, before he could carry out his idea of editing all. This is the first known appearance of the Jansen portrait in print.

King Lear . . . By N. Tate and G. Colman. Ln: . . . 1770. 12°

King Lear. Written by Sh—. With al-terations by Geo. Colman. Ln: . . . [1771]. 8°   BPL

[King Lear] The history of King Lear. A tragedy. As it is now acted at the Theatres Royal in Drury Lane and Co-vent Garden. Revived with alterations by N. Tate. Ln: Printed for F. & J. Noble, T. Lowndes, T. Longman, T Caslon, C. Corbett, & W. Nicoll, 1771. 8°, pp. 72, including engraved frontis-piece by J. June   W

[King Lear] The tragedy of King Lear, as lately published, vindicated from the abuse of the critical reviewers . . . By the editor of ' King Lear ' [C. Jennens]. Ln: W. Owen, 1772. 8°, pp. 42   BM

King Lear . . . As performed at the Theatre Royal, Drury Lane. Regulated from the prompt book by Mr. Hopkins, prompter. Ln: John Bell; York: Bell & Ethering-ton, 1774. 8°   BPL

[King Lear] The history of King Lear . . . Revived with alterations by N. Tate. Ln: . . . 1775. 12°   BPL

King Lear . . . [In Colman's ' Dramatic works,' Vol. 3]. Ln: . . . 1777. 8°
BPL | BUS

King Lear . . . As it is acted at the Theatres-Royal in Drury-Lane and Covent-Garden. Ln: Harrison & Co., 1779. 8°, pp. 20
BM | BPL
With frontispiece portrait of ' Mr. Garrick as King Lear.'

[King Lear] The true chronicle history of King Leir . . . [In ' Six old plays ']. Ln: 1605; Rep. by J. Nichols, 1779. 8°
BPL | W

King Lear . . . Ln: Butters . . . [c. 1780]. 12°

King Lear . . . printed complete from the text of Sam. Johnson & Geo. Steevens and revised from the last editions . . . Ln: John Bell . . . 1785. 12°, pp. 152. With engraved title, one other plate, and frontispiece of 'Miss Brunton in Cordelia.'
BPL

Sh— King Lear . . .

King Lear: altered from Sh— by David
Garrick. Marked with the variations in
the manager's book at the Theatre-Royal
in Drury Lane. Ln: C. Bathurst, 1786.
12°, pp. 68   BM | BPL | W

[King Lear] The plays of 'Lear' and
'Cymbeline.' With notes and illustrations selected from the various commentators. To which are added remarks by
the editor [Ambrose Eccles]. Ln: C. Dilly,
1793. 2 vol. 8°   BUS

[King Lear] The plays of 'Lear' and
'Cymbeline.' With notes . . . illustra-
tions . . . remarks by . . . [Ambrose
Eccles]. Dublin . . . 1793. 2 vols. 8°

[King Lear] The plays of 'Lear' and
'Cymbeline.' With notes and illustra-
tions . . . remarks by . . . [Ambrose
Eccles]. Ln: G. G. & J. Robinson, 1794.
2 vols. 8°   BM | BUS | W

King Lear. A tragedy by Sh— as performed at the Theatres Royal. Regulated from the prompt-book. With an
introduction and notes [by Ambrose
Eccles]. Ln: . . . 1794. 12°   W

King Lear . . . [English and German texts].
Leipzig . . . 1794. 12°

King Lear . . . With explanatory annotations by Küchler. Zeiz: G. H. Heinse,
1794. 8°, pp. 188   BM

King Lear . . . [In W. H. Ireland's ' Miscellaneous papers ']. Ln: Cooper & Gra-
ham . . . 1796. 8° BM | BPL | CPL | MPL

King Lear . . . Manchester: R. & W. Dean,
1800. 12°, pp. 100. With woodcut
frontispiece   BPL

King Lear . . . as altered by N. Tate. Newly
revised by J. P. Kemble. As acted at
Drury Lane. Ln: . . . [c. 1800]. 8° BPL

[King Lear] The plays of 'Lear' and
'Cymbeline.' . . . With notes, etc. selected
by Ambrose Eccles. Ln: . . . Lackington . . . 1801. 2 vols. 8°   BPL

[King Lear] The plays of 'Lear' and
'Cymbeline.' . . . [Edited by Ambrose
Eccles]. Dublin . . . 1805. 2 vols. 8°

King Lear . . . With remarks by Mrs. Inchbald. Ln: Longman [c. 1808]. 12°, pp.
78. With frontispiece   BPL | BUS
An adaptation of Tate's version.

King Lear . . . Manchester: R. & W. Dean,
1808. 12°

King Lear [with Nahum Tate's alterations].
A tragedy, revised by J. P. Kemble ; and
now published as it is acted at the Theatre
Royal in Covent Garden. Ln: Printed
for the theatre, 1808. 8°   W

King Lear . . . By N. Tate and J. P. Kemble.
Ln: . . . 1810. 8°

Sh— King Lear . . .

King Lear . . . With remarks by Mrs. Inchbald. Ln: Longman . . . & Brown [c.
1811]. 12°, pp. 78, and plate   BUS
During George the third's illness, about this period,
the public performance of ' King Lear' was banned
by the lord chamberlain.

King Lear . . . As performed at the Theatres
Royal, Drury Lane and Covent Garden.
Edinburgh . . . [c. 1812]. 12°   BPL

King Lear [In Deverell's ' Discoveries in
hieroglyphics and other antiquities']. Ln:
Allman . . . 1813. 8°   BUS
With notes and illustrations intended to explain the
play by reference to the moon.

King Lear . . . Ln: Chiswick Press, 1813.
12°

King Lear: A tragedy . . . Edinburgh:
Oliver & Boyd [1813 ?]. 12°, blue wrappers. Pub. at 6d.

King Lear, from Nahum Tate's alterations.
A tragedy. Revised by J. P. Kemble and
now published as it is performed at the
Theatres Royal. Ln: J. Miller, 1815.
8°, pp. 76   BM | BPL | SML | W

King Lear. Put in a light now entirely
new [In Deverell's ' Hieroglyphics '].
Ln: Allman, 1816. 8°   BM | BPL

King Lear . . . With remarks by Mrs. Inchbald. Ln: Longman . . . & Brown [c.
1817]. 12°, pp. 78, and plate   BUS

King Lear. Printed chiefly from N. Tate's
edition, with some restorations from the
original text, [edited] by R. W. Elliston.
Ln: J. Tabby, 1820. 12°, pp. xii.-68
                                BPL | BUS

King Lear, altered from Sh— by N. Tate.
With prefatory remarks [signed P. P.]
. . . Marked with the stage business, and
stage directions, as it is performed at the
Theatres Royal by W. Oxberry. Ln:
Simpkin, 1820. Cr. 8°, pp. x.-72
                        BM | BPL | MPL | SML

King Lear . . . from the text of Johnson &
Steevens. With remarks. Ln: . . . [c.
1822]. 12°   BPL

King Lear . . . Altered by N. Tate. ' Oxberry's edition.' Boston [U.S.], 1822.
12°   BUS

King Lear . . . With remarks and stage
directions by W. Oxberry . . . Ln: . . .
1823. 12°

King Lear . . . With remarks by D. G——
[Geo. Daniel]. Ln: John Cumberland,
1824. 16°. Pub. at 6d.

King Lear . . . Ln: Published and sold by
Vernor & Hood ; Newcastle-on-Tyne:
Printed by J. Mitchell [c. 1825]. 12° BPL

King Lear . . . ' Acting edition.' Ln: J.
Cumberland, 1828. 12°   SML

King Lear . . . A tragedy in five acts, as
performed in Paris. Paris . . . 1828. 18°
The first English text of Sh— produced in Paris.

King Lear . . . printed from the acting copy,
with remarks . . . by D. G—— [Geo.
Daniel]. To which are added a . . . cast
of the characters . . . and the whole of the
stage, as now performed at the Theatres
Royal. Ln : J. Cumberland [c. 1830].
12°, pp. 68. Frontispiece by R. Cruik-
shank   BM | BPL

[King Lear] King Lear and his daughters
queer . . . versified, vocalized, and sung
. . . by Hugo Vamp. Ln : Davidson [c.
1830]. F°, pp. 8   BUS

King Lear . . . With historical notes [in
German] by J. M. Pierre. Frankfort . . .
1831. 8°   BPL

King Lear . . . 'Cumberland's theatre.' Ln :
Davidson . . . [c. 1831]. 12°   SML

King Lear . . . With notes by S. W. Singer.
Frankfort . . . 1834. 12°   BPL

King Lear . . . Nuremberg & New York :
. . . 1835. 12°

King Lear [A translation into Greek iambics by C. J. Vaughan from 'King Lear,
act iii., sc. 2']. Cambridge . . . 1837.
8°   BM
In English and Greek.

King Lear . . . Ln : French, 1838. 12°   SML
W. Creswick's copy is at Stratford.

King Lear . . . Ln : Lacy . . . 1838. 12° SML
W. Creswick's copy is at Stratford.

[King Lear] Outlines to Sh—: 'King
Lear': Thirteen plates by Moritz
Retzsch. Leipsic : E. Fleischer ; Ln :
Black & Armstrong, 1838. 4°, pp. xxii.,
and 13 plates   BPL
With text in English, French, German, and Italian,
parallel.

King Lear . . . With notes and glossary.
Ln : . . . 1839. 12°. With eleven sketches
by Creswick   BUS | SML
W. Creswick's copy is at Stratford.

King Lear . . . Leipzig : Bernard Tauchnitz,
1843. 16°   SML

King Lear . . . Edited by N. Tate and R. W.
Elliston. Ln : Hayward & Adam, 1845.
12°, pp. 80   BUS
Partly Tate's and partly Elliston's version.

King Lear . . . [Text in English and French.]
Edited by M. Carlhaut. Paris . . . 1847.
12°

King Lear. 'Standard drama.' With the
stage business, casts of characters, costumes, relative positions, etc. [with introduction by John W. S. Hows]. New
York : S. French [c. 1848]. 12°, pp. 70
                    BPL | BUS
Founded upon Tate's version, but ending differently.

Sh— King Lear . . .

King Lear . . . Ln : Orr & Co., 1854. 12°
                    SML
The prompter's marked copy from the library of W.
Creswick is at Stratford.

King Lear . . . burlesqued as 'King Queer
and his daughters three.' As performed
at the Strand Theatre. Ln : 1855. 12°

King Lear . . . A tragedy. 'Acting edition.'
Ln : T. H. Lacy [1857]. 12°, pp. 80
                    BM | BPL

[King Lear] Tragedy of King Lear, arranged
for representation at the Princess's
Theatre, with historical and explanatory
notes by Charles Kean, F.S.A., as first
performed on April 17, 1858. Ln : J. K.
Chapman & Co. [1858]. 8°, pp. 90
        BM | BPL | BUS | SML | W

King Lear . . . with explanatory notes
founded on the best commentators.
Edited by R. H. Westley. Leipzig : G.
Græbner, 1861. 8°, pp. 114
                    BM | BPL | SML

King Lear . . . The text from the folio of
1623. Ln : Printed for L. Booth, 1864.
4°   BPL

King Lear . . . Edited by C. Lenny for
schools. Second edition. Ln : . . . 1865.
12°

King Lear . . . With explanatory and illustrative notes . . . by John Hunter. Ln :
Longman, 1865. Cr. 8°, pp. xvi.-142
                    BUS | CPL

King Lear. A tragedy . . . New edition,
with notes. Revu et adapté à l'enseigne-
ment dans les lycées . . . par C. Witcomb.
Paris : Baudry's European library, 1865.
8°, pp. 120   BM

King Lear . . . 1608. Facsimiled from the
edition printed for N. Butter (sans
address) by E. W. Ashbee. Ed. by J. O.
Halliwell. Ln : For private circulation,
1867. Fcp. 4°   BPL
Edition limited to fifty copies, of which nineteen were
destroyed by the editor.

King Lear. Leipzig : Tauchnitz, 1868. 16°

King Lear, 1608. Facsimiled from the
edition 'printed for Nathaniel Butter at
the Pide Bull' by E. W. Ashbee. Ed. by
J. O. Halliwell. Ln : For private circu-
lation, 1868. Fcp. 4°   BPL | W
Limited to fifty copies, nineteen of which were destroyed by the editor.

[King Lear] Re Lear, tragedia . . . voltata
in prosa Italiana da C. Rusconi. Sesta
edizione col testo Inglese de'riscontro.
Firenze : Successori Le Monnier, 1868.
8°, pp. 248   BM
In Italian and English.

Sh— King Lear . . .

King Lear . . . Adapted for scholastic study . . . by John Hunter. Ln : Longmans . . . 1869. Cr. 8°, pp. xvi.-142
BUS | SML

King Lear, or the undutiful children. A tale in twelve chapters. Ln : Bull, Simmons & Co., 1870. 12°, pp. 62 BPL | BUS

King Lear . . . ' Pocket Sh—.' Ln : Mansell [c. 1870]. 12° SML

King Lear . . . Edited by C. E. Moberly for the use of Rugby School. Rugby : Billington . . . 1871. Cr. 8° SML

King Lear . . . Louisville [U.S.]: American Printing House for the blind, 1871. 4°; printed in embossed Roman type BM

King Lear . . . 'Standard plays.' Ln : Dicks . . . [c. 1875]. 12° SML

King Lear . . . Edited by W. A. Wright. Oxford : Clarendon Press, 1875. Cr. 8°, pp. xx.-200

King Lear. With . . . notes . . . by Dr. W. B. Kemshead. Glasgow : W. Collins, 1875. Cr. 8°, pp. 136 BM | BPL | BUS

King Lear . . . [As played by Rossi; text in Italian and English; Italian version by Carlo Rusconi]. Ln : Drury Lane Theatre, 1876. 4°, pp. viii.-38, in yellow wrappers SML

King Lear . . . Ed. by W. A. Wright. Oxford : Clarendon Press, 1876. Cr. 8°, pp. xx.-200 BUS

King Lear . . . edited by Charles E. Moberly. Rugby : Billington ; Ln., Oxford, & Cambridge ; Rivingtons, 1876. Cr. 8°, pp. 150 BPL | BUS | MPL | SML

King Lear . . . edited for schools by H. N. Hudson. Boston : Ginn & Heath, 1877. 12°, pp. 375-486 [excerpt] BUS | SML

King Lear . . . As presented by Edwin Booth. Edited by W. Winter. New York : F. Hart & Co., 1878. 16°, pp. 120 BUS | SML
Printed on one side of the leaf only.

King Lear . . . with notes, etc. by J. Hunter. Ln : Longman [1878]. Cr. 8°, pp. xvi.-142 BPL

King Lear . . . 'Acting drama.' Ln : French . . . [1879 ?] 12° SML
The prompt copy from W. Creswick's library is at Stratford.

King Lear . . . with notes, examination papers, and plan of preparation. Edited by J. M. D. Meiklejohn. Ln. & Edin. : W. & R. Chambers, 1879. Cr. 8°, pp. viii.-148 BM | BPL

King Lear . . . With introduction and notes by H. N. Hudson. Boston [U.S.] 1879. 12° BPL

Sh— King Lear . . .

King Lear . . . edited by W. A. Wright. Oxford : Clarendon Press, 1879. Cr. 8°, pp. xx.-200 MPL

King Lear . . . edited by W. A. Wright. Oxford : Clarendon Press, 1880. Cr. 8°, pp. xx.-200 BPL | SML

King Lear . . . Edited by W. J. Rolfe. New York : Harper . . . 1880. 16°. Illust. BUS

King Lear . . . ' New variorum edition.' Edited by H. H. Furness. Philadelphia : Lippincott, 1880. Roy. 8°, pp. viii.-504 BM | BPL | BUS | SML

King Lear . . . As played by Signor Salvini. Ln : . . . 1881. 8° SML
Text in Italian and English.

King Lear . . . edited by W. A. Wright. Oxford : Clarendon Press, 1881. Cr. 8°, pp. xx.-200 BPL

King Lear . . . with notes for the Oxford and Cambridge examinations. Ln : Allman [1881]. Cr. 8° BPL | BUS

King Lear . . . with notes, examination papers, and plan of preparation, by Brainerd Kellogg. New York . . . 1882. 24° BUS

King Lear . . . edited by C. E. Flower. ' Memorial theatre edition.' Stratford-on-Avon : Printed by G. Boyden [1883]. Cr. 8°, pp. viii.-102, including printed wrappers BPL | SML

King Lear . . . edited by C. E. Moberly. Ln : Rivington . . . [c. 1883]. 12°

King Lear . . . edited with notes by W. J. Rolfe. New York . . . 1883. Cr. 8° BPL

King Lear. ' Standard plays.' Ln : John Dicks [1883]. 12°, pp. 32 BM | BPL

King Lear . . . edited by W. A. Wright. Oxford : Clarendon Press, 1884. Cr. 8°

King Lear . . . As performed by Signor Salvini at Covent Garden Theatre, season 1884. Manchester & Ln : Emmott's Printing Works, 1884. 8°, pp. 56
With an Italian verse translation. BM | BPL

[King Lear] M. Wm. Sh—'s ' King Lear.' The first quarto, 1608. A facsimile, with an appendix . . . introduction, by P. A. Daniel. ' Sh— quarto facsimiles.' Ln : C. Prætorius, 1885. Fcp. 4°, pp. xxii.-80 BM | BPL | BUS

[King Lear] M. Wm. Sh—'s ' King Lear.' The second quarto, 1608. A facsimile . . . with introductory notice by P. A. Daniel. ' Sh— quarto facsimiles.' Ln : C. Prætorius, 1885. Fcp. 4°, pp. 88 BM | BPL | BUS

King Lear . . . Parallel texts of the first
quarto and first folio. With collations of
the later quartos and folios. Ed. by
Wilhelm Victor. Marburg: Elwert, 1886.
8°   BUS
King Lear: Parallel texts. Ln: Whit-
taker, 1887. 16°
King Lear . . . with notes, etc. Edited by
J. M. D. Meiklejohn. Edinburgh: W. &
R. Chambers, 1888. 12°   BPL
King Lear [with introduction by Henry
Morley]. 'National library.' Ln: Cas-
sell, 1888. 16°, pp. 192   BM
King Lear . . . With notes. Ln: Blackie
[1888]. 16°, pp. 128   BM
King Lear . . . With notes arranged and
classified by T. Page. Ln: Moffatt &
Paige, 1889. Cr. 8°   SML
King Lear . . . With introduction and notes
by K. Deighton. Ln: Macmillan, 1891.
Cr. 8°   BPL
King Lear . . . edited with introduction and
notes by T. Page and J. Paige. Ln:
Moffatt [1892]. Cr. 8°   BPL
King Lear . . . souvenir . . . presented at
the Lyceum Theatre, 10th Novr., by
Henry Irving. Ln: 1892. Oblong 8° BM
King Lear . . . edited by I. Gollancz.
'Temple edition.' Ln: Dent, 1895. 16°
King Lear . . . 'Ariel edition.' Ln: Rout-
ledge, 1896. 16°
King Lear . . . edited by D. C. Tovey.
'School Sh—.' Ln: Arnold [c. 1896].
Cr. 8°   BPL
King Lear . . . edited with introd. notes,
glossary and index by A. W. Verity.
Cambridge: Pitt Press, 1897. Cr. 8°,
pp. 300   BPL | BUS
King Lear. 'Pocket Falstaff edition.' Ln:
Bliss, Sands, 1898. 16°, pp. 138
                                         BPL| SML
King Lear . . . With introduction and notes
by H. A. Evans. 'Junior school Sh—.'
Ln: Blackie, 1898. Cr. 8°   BPL
King Lear . . . edited by P. Sheavyn. Ln:
Black, 1898. 12°, pp. 164   BPL
King Lear. Edited by F. Spencer. 'Plays
for young actors.' Ln: Dean, 1898. 8°
King Lear . . . Ln: . . . 1899. 8°   BUS
King Lear . . . edited with introduction
and notes by C. H. Herford. 'Eversley
edition.' Ln: Macmillan, 1900. Cr. 8°
                                                BPL
King Lear. With introduction and notes
by John Dennis. Illust. by B. Shaw.
'Chiswick edition.' Ln: Bell, 1900. Cr
8°, pp. 170
King Lear . . . edited by W. J. Craig. Ln:
Methuen, 1901. 8°, pp. 314

King Lear . . . edited by D. Nicol Smith.
'Warwick edition.' Ln: Blackie, 1902.
Cr. 8°   BPL
King Lear . . . edited with notes by H. N.
Hudson. 'Windsor edition.' Edinburgh:
Jack, 1902. Cr. 8°, pp. 148
King Lear . . . edited by W. J. Rolfe.
New York . . . [1902]. Cr. 8°   BUS
King Lear. With preface and glossary by
I. Gollancz. Ln: Dent, 1904. 16°, pp.
xvi.-190
King Lear . . . edited by H. Morley.
'National library.' Ln: Cassell, 1904.
16°, pp. 192   BPL
King Lear. 'Waistcoat pocket edition.'
Ln: Treherne, 1904. 32°
King Lear . . . with introduction by George
Brandes. 'Favourite classics.' Ln:
Heinemann, 1904. 12°, pp. xviii.-142
and plate of ' Mrs. Cibber as Cordelia'
King Lear . . . with introduction and notes
by W. J. Craig. 'Little quartos.' Ln:
Methuen, 1905. 16°
King Lear . . . with introduction and notes
. . . by A. J. Spilsbury and F. Marshall.
'Oxford and Cambridge edition.' Ln:
Gill, 1905. 8°   BPL
King Lear . . . Retold for children by A. S.
Hoffman. Ln: Dent, 1905. 16°, pp. 90
                                                BPL
King Lear . . . edited by A. W. Verity.
Cambridge: University Press, 1906.
Cr. 8°, pp. xl.-260
King Lear . . . with notes by A. V. Hough-
ton. Illust. by Gordon Browne. 'Swan
edition.' Ln: Longman, 1907. Cr. 8°
                                                BPL
King Lear. With introductory notes, glos-
sary, examination questions, and index,
by C. W. Crook. Interleaved. Ln:
Ralph, 1907. Cr. 8°, pp. 224   BPL
King Lear. 'Red letter edition.' Ln:
Blackie, 1907. 12°
[King Lear] The history of King Leir, 1605
[Prepared by W. W. Greg and checked
by R. Warwick Bond]. Ln: Malone
Society, 1907-08. Fcp. 4°, pp. xii.-A¹ to
I⁴ in fours. With facsimile of original
title   BM | SML
King Lear . . . A complete paraphrase by
Jean F. Terry. 'Normal tutorial series.'
Ln: Normal Press, 1908. Cr. 8°   BPL
King Lear. With introd. by W. Archer.
'Renaissance edition.' Ln: G. G.
Harrap, 1908. Fcp. 4°   BPL
King Lear. With introduction and notes
by F. J. Frost. 'Normal tutorial series.'
Ln: 1909. Cr. 8°   BPL

Sh— King Lear . . .

[King Lear] Chronicle history of King Leir
. . . Ed. by 'S. Lee.' 'Sh— classics.'
Ln : Chatto, 1909. Roy. 8°, pp. 180 BPL
King Lear . . . 'Plain text Sh—.' Ln :
Blackie, 1909. Cr. 8°   BPL
King Lear . . . edited by S. E. Goggin.
'University tutorial series.' Ln : Clive,
1910. Cr. 8°, pp. 244

            BM | BLO | BPL | CTC

' King Lear ' references—

See Barnett	See Jennens
,, Bayne	,, Jennings
,, Bradley	,, Johnson (R.)
,, Brien	,, Johnson & Stee-
,, Briggs	vens
,, Bucknill	,, Keats
,, Burgess	,, Kirkman
,, Conington	,, Lennox
,, Considerations	,, Letters
,, Cooke	,, Menzies
,, Cradock	,, Merriman
,, Curtis	,, Miller
,, Death . . .	,, Mirror
,, Decker	,, Mirrour . . .
,, Delius	,, Moncrieff
,, Deverell	,, Nero
,, Doyle	,, New story teller
,, Dramatic . . .	,, Perrett
,, Eccles	,, Ransome
,, Farren	,, Richardson
,, Foote	,, Russell
,, Geoffrey	,, Seeley
,, Green	,, Sh—] Sh—'s li-
,, Hales	brary
,, Hardinge	,, Sidney
,, Harsnet	,, Six . . .
,, Hart	,, Spedding
,, Hawkins	,, Three . . .
,, Higgins	,, Thring
,, Holinshed	,, Turnbull
,, Ireland	,, Warner
,, Irving	,, Warton
,, Jacox	,, Young (W.)

KING RICHARD THE SECOND.

*No earlier impression of this tragedy is
known than the anonymous one printed by
Valentine Wise in 1597.
It was registered at Stationers' Hall thus :
—1597, 29th Aug. Andrew Wise. Entred
for his copie by appoyntment from master-
warden Man the tragedye of Richard the
second.*

[King Richard II.] The Tragedie of King
Richard the Second. As it hath beene
publikely acted by the right Honourable
the Lorde Chamberlaine his Seruants.
[*Pictorial device.*] London : Printed by

Sh— King Richard the second . . .
Valentine Simmes for Androw Wise, and
are to be sold at his shop in Paules
church yard at the signe of the Angel,
1597. Fcp. 4°, on thirty-seven unpaged
leaves, the last being sig. K²   CTC
Sh—'s name is omitted.
Only two copies known to exist ; one in the Capell
collection, and another formerly in the Daniel collection.

[King Richard II.] The Tragedie of King
Richard the second. As it hath beene
publikely acted by the Right Honourable
the Lord Chamberlaine his seruants. By
William Shake-speare. [*Pictorial device.*]
London : Printed by Valentine Simmes for
Andrew Wise, and are to be sold at his
shop in Paules churchyard at the signe of
the Angel, 1598. Fcp. 4°, sig. A to I⁴
(in fours), on thirty-six unpaged leaves,
including title   BM | BLO | BUS | CTC
The first issue to announce the authorship. A few of
the errors of the first issue corrected, but many fresh
misprints occur.

[King Richard II.] The Tragedie of King
Richard the Second . . . London : Printed
for Thomas Fisher, 1605. Fcp. 4°
A copy sold in July, 1905 for £250. It wanted sig. A4,
and the title was in MS.

[King Richard II.] The Tragedie of King
Richard the Second. As it hath been
publikely acted by the Right Honourable
the Lord Chamberlaine his seruantes. By
William Shake-speare. [*Device.*] London :
Printed by W. W— [William White ?]
for Mathew Law, and are to be sold at his
shop in Paules Churchyard, at the signe
of the Foxe, 1608. Fcp. 4°, forty unpaged leaves, sig. A to K⁴ (the last blank)
                            BM
There are two issues of 1608, the second being distinguished by additions to the title, and the parliament scene in act iv., sc. i., now published for the first
time.

[King Richard II.] The Tragedie of King
Richard the second. With new additions of the Parliament Sceane and the
deposing of King Richard. As it hath
been lately acted by the Kinges Maiesties
seruantes, at the Globe. By William
Shake-speare. [*Device.*] At London :
Printed by W. W— [William White ?]
for Mathew Law, and are to be sold at
his shop in Paules church-yard at the
signe of the Foxe, 1608. Fcp. 4°, forty
unpaged leaves, sig. A to K⁴ in fours (the
last blank)   BM | BLO | DEVON

[King Richard II.] The Tragedie of King
Richard the Second : With new additions of the Parliament Sceane, and the
deposing of King Richard. As it hath
been lately acted by the Kinges Maiesties

seruants, at the Globe. By William
Shake-speare. [*Ornament.*] At London:
Printed for Matthew Law, and are to be
sold at his shop in Paules church-yard at
the signe of the Foxe, 1615. Fcp. 4°,
forty leaves, sig. A to K⁴ in fours (last leaf
blank), unpaged   BM | BLO | BUS | CTC | NY
Reprinted by Geo. Steevens in 1766 after collation with
the editions of 1598 and 1634.
This edition supplied the text, corrected by a superior
one, for the 1623 folio.

[King Richard II.] The Life and Death of
King Richard the Second [An excerpt
from the second folio of 1632, with the
stage directions as cut from the prompt
book of Drury lane theatre by John
Roberts, prompter, 1727, and sketched
positions of the respective players at the
termination of each act. Ln : Printed by
Tho. Cotes for Robert Allot, 1632]. F°,
12 leaves, pp. 23-46   W
Bound up with a Drury Lane playbill of 1815, announcing a performance of 'King Richard the third,' and
other interesting Shakespearean fragments.

[King Richard II.] The Life and Death of
King Richard the Second. With new
Additions of the Parliament Scene, and
the Deposing of King Richard. As it
hath beene acted by the Kings Majesties
Servants, at the Globe. By William
Shakespeare. London : Printed by Iohn
Norton, 1634. Fcp. 4°, forty unpaged
leaves, sig. A to K⁴ in fours
BM | BLO | BUS | CTC | NY
The earliest quarto to present the play divided in acts
and scenes, as first given by the Jaggard canon of
1623.
In May, 1907, a copy realised £29.

[King Richard II.] The history of King
Richard the second. Acted at the Theatre
Royal under the name of the 'Sicilian
usurper.' With a prefatory epistle in
vindication of the author. Occasion'd by
the prohibition of this play on the stage.
By N. Tate. Ln : Printed for Richard
Tonson and Jacob Tonson at Gray's Inn
Gate, and at the Judge's Head in Chancery Lane near Fleet Street, 1681. Fcp.
4°, pp. xii.-52   BM | BPL | BUS | SML
The character of Richard is changed, and additions are
made to the text in order to render the play more
acceptable to the English court. The dedication
gives the origin of the drama, and how Tate altered
the text.

[King Richard II.] The history of King
Richard the second. Acted at the Theatre
Royal under the name of the 'Sicilian
usurper'; A tragedy . . . With a prefatory
epistle . . . by N. Tate. Ln : R. & J. Ton-
son, 1691. Fcp. 4°   BM | BPL
After two representations at Drury Lane this play was
stopped by the lord chamberlain.

[King Richard II.] The Sicilian usurper. A
tragedy. As it was acted at the Theatre
Royal. With a prefatory epistle . . .
Written by N. Tate. Ln : J. Knapton,
1691. Fcp. 4°, pp. xii.-52   BUS
A reprint of the 1681 edition, with a variant title.

[King Richard II.] The tragedy of King
Richard the second, as it is acted at the
Theatre in Lincoln's Inn Fields. Alter'd
from Sh— by Mr. [Lewis] Theobald. Ln :
Printed for G. Strahan, W. Mears, T.
Meighan, & R. Barker, 1720. 8°, pp. 60
BM | CPL | W
Owing probably to the rarity of the work, the preface
(on Sh—'s learning) seems to have escaped the notice
of all writers on the subject.

[King Richard II.] The life and death of
Richard the second. By Mr. Wm. Sh—.
Ln : Printed for J. Tonson, and the rest
of the proprietors, and sold by the book-
sellers of Ln. and Westminster, 1734.
Cr. 8°, pp. 84, and frontispiece by Lud.
Du Guernier   BM | W

[King Richard II.] The life and death of
Richard II. by Sh—. Ln : R. Walker,
1735. 12°   W

[King Richard II.] Life and death of
Richard II. As it is acted at the Theatres.
Ln : . . . 1736. 8°, pp. 84

King Richard the second . . . 1615 [In
'Twenty of the plays of Sh—, reprinted
by G. Steevens,' Vol. 2]. At Ln : Printed
for Mathew Law . . . 1615 [1766]. 8°, pp.
94 (unpaged excerpt)   BPL

King Richard the second. A tragedy.
Alter'd from Sh— and the stile imitated
by James Goodhall. Manchester: J.
Harrop, 1772. 8°, pp. iv.-52
BM | BPL | W
The interpolated lines are asterisked.
The first piece of Sh— printed in Manchester.

King Richard II. A tragedy . . . An introduction and notes, critical and illustrative, are added by the authors of the
'Dramatic censor' [F. Gentleman]. Ln :
John Bell; York: C. Etherington, 1774.
8°, pp. 86
An off-print from Bell's edition for playgoers.

King Richard the second . . . Edited by
. . . [F. Gentleman]. Ln : John Bell,
1777. 12°

King Richard II. . . . printed complete
from the text of Sam. Johnson and Geo.
Steevens and revised from the last
editions . . . Ln : Printed for . . . John
Bell . . . 1786. 12°, pp. 116. With engraved title and frontispiece of 'Mrs.
Farren as the Queen'

King Richard the second . . . Ln : Butters
. . . 1789-90. 8°

Sh— King Richard the second . . .

King Richard II.   A tragedy, by Wm.
Sh—. Adapted for theatrical represen-
tation. As performed at the Theatres
Royal. [c. 1810.] 12°   W

[King] Richard II., by Will. Sh—. Printed
complete from the text of Sam. Johnson
and Geo. Steevens. Ln: . . . 1812.   16°
                                                W

King Richard the second; an historical
play. Adapted to the stage, with alterations and additions, by Richard Wroughton. And published as it is performed at
the Theatre-Royal, Drury Lane. Ln:
John Miller, 1815.   8°, pp. 72
                    BM | BPL | BUS | SML | W

The following passage, from the preliminary advertisement, is noteworthy:—'The play of "Richard the
second" has been hitherto neglected by the managers
of the London theatres, being considered too heavy
for representation. As it stood it certainly was so,
and might also be felt as bordering too much on the
mono-drama. That so exquisite a production of our
immortal bard should not grace, among his other
works, the boards of our national theatres was
almost theatrical treason. The present attempt has
been made by a few alterations and additions (and
those taken from the writings of Sh—) to rescue
it from neglect. Whoever is curious may find the
introduced passages in the plays of "Henry the
sixth," "Titus Andronicus," and "King Lear";
other lines are here and there necessarily interpolated. The event has justified the deed, and, like
Colley Cibber's alteration of "Richard the third,"
now acted at both theatres, the tragedy of "Richard
the second" will also most probably long keep possession of the English stage. It has likewise given
an opportunity of fully evincing the complete powers
and distinguished judgment of a young actor, Mr.
Kean, whose merit is deservedly rewarded by the
loudest plaudits of a discriminating publick.'
The cast includes Kean as 'Richard II.'

King Richard the second . . . from the
text of Johnson and Steevens. With
remarks. Ln: D. S. Maurice [c. 1822].
12°   BPL

King Richard the second . . . Printed from
the acting copy with remarks . . . by
D. G—— [Geo. Daniel]. To which are
added a . . . cast of the characters . . .
and the whole of the stage business as
performed at the Theatres Royal. Ln:
J. Cumberland [1831].   12°, pp. 54
                                      BM | BPL

King Richard the second [A translation,
into Greek iambics, by H. Lushington
from ' King Richard II., act iii., sc. 2.'
In English and Greek]. Cambridge . . .
1833.   8°   BM

King Richard the second [A translation,
into Greek iambics, by E. Howes, from
' King Richard II., act iii., sc. 2.' In
English and Greek]. Cambridge . . .
1834.   8°   BM

Sh— King Richard the second . . .

King Richard the second [A translation,
into Greek iambics, by C. J. Vaughan
from ' King Richard II., act ii., sc. 1.'
In English and Greek]. Cambridge . . .
1836.   8°   BM

King Richard the second . . . Brunswick
. . . 1850.   16°, pp. 140   BM

[King Richard the second] Sh—'s play of
King Richard II., arranged for repre-
sentation at the Princess's Theatre, with
historical and explanatory notes by
Charles Kean. As first performed on
Thursday, March 12, 1857. Ln: J. K.
Chapman, 1857.   8°, pp. 92, including
printed wrappers   BM | BPL | SML

King Richard the second . . . arranged . . .
with notes . . . by C. Kean. Second
edition. Ln: J. K. Chapman, 1857.
8°, pp. 92   CPL

King Richard the second . . . arranged . . .
with notes . . . by C. Kean . . . Third
edition. Ln: J. K. Chapman, 1857.
8°, pp. 92   BUS

King Richard the second . . . arranged . . .
by C. Kean . . . Fourth edition. Ln:
J. K. Chapman, 1857.   8°, pp. 92

King Richard the second . . . arranged . . .
by C. Kean. Fifth edition. Ln: J. K.
Chapman, 1587.   8°, pp. 92   SML

[King Richard II.] The tragedie of King
Richard the second . . . 1608. Photographic copy [by J. O. Halliwell]. Privately printed, 1858.   8°, on seventy-
seven unpaged folios   BPL | BUS | W

Halliwell stated this to be 'the first complete photograph of an old book ever executed,' but see 'Sh—
King Henry V., 1857,' which Halliwell must have
forgotten.
A further note says 'the negatives are destroyed, and
only ten perfect copies of this facsimile have been
preserved.' In the Boston copy all the pages have
faded, and portions are entirely illegible.

King Richard the second . . . first act.
Intended as a specimen of a new edition
of Sh—. [Edited by W. G. Clark & H. R.
Luard.] Cambridge: University Press,
private and confidential, 1860.   8°, pp.
32   BUS

King Richard the second. Facsimiled from
the edition printed . . . in 1597 by Edmund William Ashbee. [Ed. by J. O.
Halliwell.] Ln: For private circulation
only, 1862.   8°   BM | BPL | BUS | W

Impression restricted to fifty copies, of which nineteen
were destroyed by the editor.
As the name of E. W. Ashbee occurs repeatedly in
connection with facsimiles, it may be of interest to
state here that two others were concerned with him
in these reproductions of the early quartos, viz., John
Tuckett and J. O. Halliwell, and that the signatures
of all three were appended to some of their facsimiles.

[King Richard II.] Life and death of King Richard the second . . . The text from the folio of 1623; with notices of the known editions previously issued. Ln: L. Booth, 1863. Fcp. 4°, pp. 24, interleaved BM | CPL

King Richard the second. With historical and critical introductions; grammatical, philological, and miscellaneous notes. Adapted for . . . examinations and students . . . By H. G. Robinson. Edinburgh: Oliver & Boyd; Ln: Simpkin, . . . 1867. 8°, pp. xxviii.-104 BM | BUS | CPL

King Richard the second . . . Edited by W. G. Clark & W. A. Wright. Oxford: Clarendon Press, 1868. Cr. 8° SML
The first Clarendon Press edition.

King Richard II. . . . Leipzig: B. Tauchnitz, 1868. 16°

King Richard the second . . . A tragedy. 'Acting edition.' Ln: T. H. Lacy [1868]. 12°, pp. 68 BM | BPL | SML

King Richard the second . . . Mit einleitung und erklärungen herausgegeben von Dr. Noiré. Mainz: V. V. Zabern, 1868. 16°, pp. 128 BM
In English and German.

King Richard the second . . . edited by W. G. Clark & W. A. Wright. Second edition. Oxford: Clarendon Press, 1869. Cr. 8° CPL

[King Richard II.] The tragedie of King Richard the second . . . 1598. Facsimiled . . . by E. W. Ashbee. Ed. by J. O. Halliwell. 1869. Fcp. 4° BPL | W
One of the fifty copies printed 'for private circulation only,' nineteen of which were destroyed by the editor.

King Richard the second . . . With notes. Adapted for scholastic study by John Hunter. Ln: Longman, 1869. Cr. 8°, pp. xxiv.-120 CPL

[King Richard II.] The tragedy of King Richard II. . . . fur den schulgebrauch erklärt von Dr. L. Riechelmann. Leipzig: B. G. Teubner, 1869. 8°, pp. viii.-150 BM
In English and German.

King Richard the second, 1608. Facsimiled by E. W. Ashbee. Ed. by J. O. Halliwell. Ln: For private circulation, 1870. Fcp. 4° BPL | W
One of the fifty copies produced, nineteen of which the editor destroyed.

King Richard the second . . . 1615. Facsimiled by E. W. Ashbee. Ed. by J. O. Halliwell. Ln: For private circulation, 1870. Fcp. 4° BPL | W
One of the fifty copies produced, nineteen of which the editor destroyed.

King Richard the second . . . 1615. [Ed. by J. O. Halliwell.] Facsimiled by E. W. Ashbee. For private circulation, 1870. Fcp. 4° W
Large paper copy. The sole example so done is at Warwick Castle.

King Richard the second, concluding with the murder of the Duke of Gloucester at Calais. A composition anterior to Sh—'s tragedy on the same reign. Now first printed from a contemporary manuscript. [Edited by J. O. Halliwell.] Ln: T. Richards [privately printed], 1870. 8°, pp. iv.-100 HCL | SML
Issue restricted to eleven copies.

[King Richard II.] The tragedy of King Richard II. . . . With a memoir of the author, an introduction, explanatory notes, and appendixes comprising a prosody of Sh— and extracts from Holinshed's Chronicle, by F. H. Ahn. 'British and American standard authors.' Treves: E. Groppe, 1870. 8°, pp. vi.-168 BM

King Richard the Second . . . 1608. [Edited by J. O. Halliwell.] Facsimiled by E. W. Ashbee. For private circulation, 1871. Fcp. 4° BPL
Differs from Ashbee's facsimile of 1870.

King Richard the second . . . Edited by W. G. Clark & W. A. Wright. Oxford: Clarendon Press, 1873. 8°, pp. xviii.-158 BPL | BUS

King Richard the second. With . . . notes, remarks and extracts . . . by D. Morris. Glasgow & Ln: W. Collins, 1873. 8°, pp. 128 BM | BUS

King Richard II. . . . edited by W. G. Clark & W. A. Wright. Oxford: Clarendon Press, 1874. Cr. 8°, pp. xviii.-158

King Richard II. With introduction by H. G. Robinson. Ln: Simpkin, 1874. 12°

King Richard the second . . . With notes, etc. by D. Morris. 'School and college classics.' Glasgow: Collins . . . 1875. 12° BPL

King Richard II. . . . edited by W. G. Clark & W. A. Wright. Oxford: Clarendon Press, 1876. Cr. 8°, pp. xviii.-158

King Richard II. . . . With notes and extracts . . . adapted for scholastic study . . . by John Hunter. New edition. Ln: Longmans . . . [1876]. Cr. 8°, pp. xxiv.-120 BUS

King Richard the second . . . edited with notes by W. J. Rolfe. With engravings. New York: Harper Brothers, 1876. 16°, pp. 226 BUS

Sh— King Richard the second . . .

King Richard the second . . . Edited by Sir Henry Irving. Ln: . . . 1877. 12°

King Richard the second . . . With notes, etc. by J. Hunter. Ln: Longmans . . . [c. 1877]. Cr. 8° BPL

King Richard the second . . . As presented by Edwin Booth. 'The prompt book,' edited by William Winter. New York: F. Hart & Co., 1878. 16°, pp. 4-iv., 9-61, 63-72 BPL | BUS
Printed on one side of the leaf only.

King Richard the second . . . edited by H. N. Hudson for use in schools. Boston [U.S.]: Ginn & Co., 1879. 12°

King Richard II. . . . edited by W. G. Clark & W. A. Wright. Oxford: Clarendon Press, 1879. Cr. 8°, pp. xviii.-158

King Richard II. Ed. by W. G. Clark & W. A. Wright. Oxford: Clarendon Press, 1880. Cr. 8°, pp. xviii.-158

King Richard the second . . . 'Acting edition.' Ln: French [c. 1880]. 12° SML

King Richard the second. With notes . . . Edited by J. M. D. Meiklejohn. Ln. & Edinburgh: W. & R. Chambers, 1880. Cr. 8°, pp. 136 BM

King Richard II. . . . with notes by J. M. D. Meiklejohn. Edinburgh: Chambers, 1881. Cr. 8°, pp. 136

King Richard the second . . . edited by W. G. Clark & W. A. Wright. Oxford: Clarendon Press, 1881. Cr. 8°, pp. xviii.-158

King Richard the second . . . Edited with notes by W. J. Rolfe. New York: Harper . . . 1882. 12° BPL

King Richard the second . . . edited by W. G. Clark & W. A. Wright. Oxford: Clarendon Press, 1882. Cr. 8°, pp. xviii.-158 BPL | MPL

King Richard the second . . . with notes for the Oxford and Cambridge examinations. Ln: Allman [1882]. Cr. 8° BPL | BUS

[King Richard II.] The tragedy of King Richard II. . . . With notes. Ln: Blackie & Son [1882]. 16°, pp. 96 BM

King Richard II. . . . With notes, examination papers and plan of preparation, by J. M. D. Meiklejohn. Ln. & Edin.: W. & R. Chambers, 1882. Cr. 8°, pp. 136

King Richard the second . . . 'Standard plays.' Ln: John Dicks [1883]. 12° BM

King Richard the second . . . With illustrations, notes, etc. 'Granville series.' [1883.] Cr. 8°, pp. 136 BM | BPL

Sh— King Richard the second . . .

King Richard the second. With notes, examination papers . . . by J. M. D. Meiklejohn. Ln. & Edin.: W. & R. Chambers, 1883. Cr. 8°, pp. 136

King Richard the second . . . edited by W. G. Clark & W. A. Wright. Oxford: Clarendon Press, 1884. Cr. 8° SML

King Richard II. . . . for school use, edited by Charlotte M. Yonge. Ln: National Society, 1884. 12°

[King Richard II.] Selections from 'King Richard II.' and 'King Henry IV., part ii.' . . . with . . . notes. Ln: Blackie [1885]. 16°, pp. 32 BM

King Richard the second. With introduction, story of the play, notes . . . and appendix . . . to meet the requirements of the new code in 'English,' by J. W. Allen. Ln: Longmans . . . 1885. Cr. 8°, pp. xx.-164 BM | BUS | SML

King Richard II. . . . edited by W. G. Clark & W. A. Wright. Oxford: Clarendon Press, 1886. Cr. 8°, pp. xx.-158

[King Richard II.] A Shakespearean epic: 'King Richard II.,' being a condensed narrative of the play. With a prose key and a calendar of Sh—, by Gregory C. Guilmette. New edition. Ln: . . . 1886. 8° BUS

King Richard the second . . . edited by Charles E. Flower. 'Memorial theatre edition.' Stratford-on-Avon: G. Boyden; Ln: French, 1886. Cr. 8°, pp. viii. 84, including printed wrappers BPL | SML

King Richard the second . . . With notes, examination papers . . . by J. M. D. Meiklejohn. Ln. & Edin.: W. & R. Chambers, 1886. Cr. 8°, pp. 136

[King Richard II.] Life and death of King Richard the second. By W. Sh—. Quarto 5, 1634. A facsimile in photolithography by C. Prætorius. With an introductory notice by P. A. Daniel. 'Sh— quarto facsimiles.' Ln: C. Prætorius, 1887. Fcp. 4°, pp. iv.-80 BM | BPL | BUS | SML

King Richard the second . . . Ln: Burns . . . 1887. 12°

King Richard the second. [With introduction by Henry Morley.] 'National library.' Ln: Cassell, 1888. 16°, pp. 192 BM

King Richard the second . . . With notes, etc. Edited by J. M. D. Meiklejohn. Ln: W. & R. Chambers, 1888. Cr. 8° BPL

King Richard II. . . . The first quarto, 1597; a facsimile in photo-lithography by C. Prætorius, from the copy in the possession of H. Huth . . . With an introductory notice by . . . W. A. Harrison. ' Sh— quarto facsimiles.' Ln: C. Prætorius, 1888. Fcp. 4°, pp. 76

BM | BPL | BUS | SML

King Richard II. . . . The third quarto, 1608; a facsimile in photo-lithography by C. Prætorius, from the copy in the British Museum . . . With an introductory notice by . . . W. A. Harrison. Ln: C. Prætorius, 1888. Fcp. 4°, pp. iv.-78 BM | BPL | BUS

King Richard the second . . . edited by W. G. Clark & W. A. Wright. Oxford: Clarendon Press, 1889. Cr. 8°, pp. xviii.-158

King Richard the second . . . With introduction and notes by H. N. Hudson. Boston [U.S.] . . . 1889. Cr. 8° BPL

King Richard the second . . . ' Moffatt's edition.' With introduction and notes. Second edition. Ln: . . . [c. 1889]. 12° BPL

King Richard the second . . . The first quarto, 1597. A facsimile from the Devonshire copy by W. Griggs . . . With an introduction by P. A. Daniel. Ln: W. Griggs, 1890. Fcp. 4°, pp. xxiv.-74

BM | BPL | BUS

King Richard II. . . . With notes by T. D. Barnett. Ln: Bell . . . 1890. 12°

King Richard the second . . . With illustrations, notes, questions, etc. Sixth edition. ' Granville series.' Ln: . . . [c. 1890]. 12° BPL

King Richard II. . . . With notes . . . by J. M. D. Meiklejohn. Ln: Chambers, 1890. Cr. 8°, pp. 136

King Richard II. . . . With introduction and notes. Fourth edition. Ln: Moffatt, 1890. 12°

King Richard the second . . . Edited by E. K. Chambers. ' Falcon series.' Ln: Longmans, 1891. Cr. 8°, pp. xxviii.-188

BPL

King Richard the second . . . edited by W. G. Clark & W. A. Wright. Oxford: Clarendon Press, 1892. Cr. 8°, pp. xviii.-158

King Richard the second . . . edited by C. H. Herford. ' Warwick Sh—.' Ln: Blackie, 1893. Cr. 8°, pp. viii.-212 BPL

King Richard II. . . . for school and home use. Abridged. Ln: Cassell, 1893. Cr. 8°

King Richard the second . . . abridged. ' Modern school series.' Ln: . . . [c. 1893]. 12° BPL

King Richard II. . . . edited by W. G. Clark & W. A. Wright. Oxford: Clarendon Press, 1893. Cr. 8°, pp. xviii.-158

King Richard the second . . . With introduction and notes by W. Barry. ' Junior school Sh—.' Ln: Blackie, 1894. Cr. 8°, pp. 128 BPL

King Richard II. . . . edited by W. G. Clark & W. A. Wright. Oxford: Clarendon Press, 1895. Cr. 8°, pp. xviii.-158

King Richard II. . . . with notes . . . by John W. Allen. Ln: Longmans, 1895. Cr. 8°, pp. 164. Illustrated

King Richard the second . . . edited with notes by W. J. Rolfe. New York . . . 1895. 12° BPL

King Richard the second . . . edited by I. Gollancz. ' Temple edition.' Ln: Dent, 1895. 16°

King Richard II. . . . edited by C. H. Herford. ' Arden Sh—.' Ln: Methuen, 1895-96. 8° BM | BLO | BUS | CTC

King Richard the second . . . With introduction and notes by K. Deighton. Ln: Macmillan, 1896. Cr. 8° BPL

King Richard the second . . . [In Donovan, ' English historical plays,' Vol. I.] Ln: Macmillan, 1896. 2 vols. Cr. 8° BM | MPL

[King Richard II.] Selections from ' King Richard II.' Ln: Blackie [1896]. 16°, pp. 32 BM

King Richard the second . . . edited by C. H. Gibson. ' School Sh—.' Ln: Arnold [1897]. 12°, pp. 198 BPL

King Richard II. . . . ' Pocket Falstaff edition.' Ln: Bliss, Sands, 1898. 16°, pp. 112 BPL | SML

King Richard II. . . . With introduction, notes and glossary by R. B. Johnson. Edinburgh: Blackwood, 1898. 12°, pp. 150 BPL

King Richard II. . . . edited by H. Morley. ' National library.' Ln: Cassell, 1899. 16°, pp. 192 BM | BLO | CTC

King Richard the second . . . Edited with introduction, notes, glossary, and appendix by A. W. Verity. Cambridge: University Press, 1899. Cr. 8°, pp. xxx.-232

BPL | BUS

King Richard II. With notes by W. J. Abel. Illustrated by H. M. Brock. ' Swan edition.' Ln: Longman, 1899. Cr. 8°, pp. 202 BPL

King Richard II. . . . edited . . . by A. W. Verity. Cambridge: University Press, 1900. Cr. 8°, pp. xxx.-244

Sh— King Richard the second . . .

King Richard the second . . . Edited with introduction and notes by C. H. Herford. 'Eversley edition.' Ln : Macmillan, 1900. Cr. 8°   BPL

King Richard II. . . . edited by C. H. Herford. 'Warwick Sh—.' Ln : Blackie [c. 1900]. 12°, pp. 212

King Richard II. . . . with introduction and notes by John Dennis. Illust. by B. Shaw. 'Chiswick edition.' Ln : Bell, 1900. Cr. 8°, pp. 134

King Richard II. . . . with introduction and notes by K. Deighton. Ln : Macmillan, 1901. Cr. 8°, pp. xxiv.-192

King Richard II. . . . 'Picture Sh—.' Ln : Blackie, 1902. Cr. 8°, pp. 186   BPL

King Richard II. . . . with introduction, notes, and glossary by C. W. Crook. Ln : Ralph & Holland, 1903. Cr. 8° BPL

King Richard II. . . . with notes, introduction, and glossary by W. Keith Leask. With coloured frontispiece and other illustrations from contemporary prints by Dora Curtis. Ln : Dent, 1903. Cr. 8° BPL

King Richard II. Edited by H. Morley. 'National library.' Ln : Cassell, 1903. 16°, pp. 192   BPL

King Richard II. . . . edited with notes by H. N. Hudson. 'Windsor edition.' Edinburgh : Jack, 1903. Cr. 8°

King Richard II. : Water-colour drawing of H. B. Tree's reproduction, by C. A. Buchel. Ln : . . . 1903. F°   BPL

King Richard II. . . . edited by A. W. Verity. Cambridge : University Press, 1903. Cr. 8°, pp. xxx.-244

King Richard the second. With introduction and notes by K. Deighton, appendix by T. Cartwright. Ln : Macmillan & Co., 1903. Cr. 8°, pp. xxiv.-234

King Richard II. . . . retold for children by A. S. Hoffman. Illustrated by W. Crane. Ln : Dent, 1904. 16°   BPL

King Richard II. . . . edited by A. W. Verity. Cambridge : University Press, 1904. Cr. 8°, pp. xxx.-244

King Richard II. . . . 'Ellen Terry edition.' Glasgow : Bryce, 1904. 32°

King Richard II. . . . with introduction and notes by W. J. Craig. 'Little quartos.' Ln : Methuen, 1904. 16°

King Richard II. . . . Complete paraphrase by N. Stockwell. 'Normal tutorial series.' Ln : Simpkin, 1904. Cr. 8°   BPL

King Richard II. . . . 'Swan edition.' Edited with notes, etc. by W. J. Abel and eleven illustrations by H. M. Brock. Ln : Longmans, 1904. Cr. 8°, pp. xxviii.-174

Sh— King Richard the second . . .

King Richard II. . . . with introduction by G. Brandes. 'Favourite classics.' Ln : Heinemann, 1904. 12°

King Richard II. . . . 'Oxford and Cambridge edition.' With introduction and notes by S. Wood and F. Marshall. Ln : Gill . . . [c. 1905]. 8°, pp. xlii.-188. Illustrated   BPL

King Richard II. . . . 'Waistcoat pocket edition.' Ln : Treherne, 1905. 32°

King Richard II. . . . edited by A. F. Watt. 'University tutorial series.' Ln : Clive, 1907. Cr. 8°, pp. xxx.-158   BPL

King Richard II. Revised by A. Dyce. Ln : Sonnenschein, 1907. 8°   BPL

King Richard II. 'Penny poets' [edited by W. T. Stead]. Ln : Stead [c. 1907]. Cr. 8°   BPL

King Richard II. . . . 'Texts without notes.' Ln : Chambers, 1907. Cr. 8°, pp. 96

King Richard II. . . . 'Renaissance edition.' Ln : Harrap, 1907. Fcp. 4°   BPL

King Richard II. . . . 'Plain text Sh—.' Ln : Blackie, 1909. Cr. 8°   BPL

King Richard II. . . . edited with introduction and notes by G. S. Gordon. Oxford : Clarendon Press, 1909. Cr. 8°, pp. 288

'King Richard II.' references—

See Aleyn	See Guilmette
„ Alliterative . . .	„ J—— (W.)
„ Barnett (T. D.)	„ Lennox
„ Beamont	„ Meres
„ Cann	„ Munro
„ Davies	„ O'Brien
„ Declaration	„ Ransome
„ Elze	„ Richard II.
„ Estienne	„ Swinburne
„ Examination	„ Tree
„ Flint Castle	„ Weever
„ Forman	„ Wood (S.)

KING RICHARD THE THIRD.

Of Sh—'s tragedy no issue is known earlier than the anonymous one 'printed by Valentine Sims for Andrew Wise,' which was registered at Stationer's Hall, 29th Aug., 1597, and published immediately after, but an inferior 'True tragedie of Richard the third,' also anonymous, had appeared some three years earlier, from the press of Thomas Creede.

[King Richard III.] The true Tragedie of Richard the Third, wherein is showne the Death of Edward the Fourth, with the Smothering of the two yoong Princes in the Tower. With a Lamentable Ende of Shore's Wife, an example for all wicked

Sh— King Richard the third . . .

women; and lastly the Coniunction and
ioyning of the two noble Houses of Lancaster and Yorke. As it was playd by the
Queene's Maiesties Players. London:
Printed by Thomas Creede and are to be
sold by William Barley at his shop in
Newgate Market neare Christ Church
doore, 1594. Fcp. 4°

This anonymous play was unquestionably used by Sh—
in preparing his own production on the subject. It
was reprinted in 1844 by the Sh— Soc., and edited by
Barron Field; some years later facsimiled by E. W.
Ashbee for J. O. Halliwell; and again by Hazlitt in
his Sh—'s library, 1876.
No known copy is available in any public collection.

[King Richard III.] The Tragedy of King
Richard the third. Containing His
treacherous Plots against his brother
Clarence; the pittiefull murther of his
iuuocent [sic] nephewes; his tyrannical
vsurpation; with the whole course of his
detested life and most deserued death.
As it hath been lately Acted by the Right
Honourable the Lord Chamberlaine his
seruants. [Ornament.] At London:
¶ Printed by Valentine Sims for Andrew
Wise, dwelling in Paules Church-yard at
the Signe of the Angell, 1597. Fcp. 4°,
forty-eight leaves, including title (the last
blank); sig. A¹ to M⁴ in fours
 BM | BLO | DEVON

The editio princeps of Sh—'s tragedy, of which only
three complete copies are within ken. The British
Museum possesses a fragment only, consisting of two
sheets: sigs. C and D. Sh—'s name does not occur
in this edition.
Earl Howe's copy, measuring 7¼ by 5in., half blue
morocco, was secured in Dec., 1907, by an American
collector.

[King Richard III.] The Tragedie of King
Richard the third. Conteining his
treacherous Plots against his brother
Clarence: the pitiful murther of his innocent Nephewes: his tyranicall vsurpation: with the whole course of his
detested life, and most deserued death.
As it hath beene lately Acted by the
Right honourable the Lord Chamberlaine his seruants. By William Shakespeare. [Device.] London: Printed by
Thomas Creede for Andrew Wise, dwelling in Paules Church-yard at the signe
of the Angell, 1598. Fcp. 4°; sig. A¹ to
M⁴ in fours (last leaf blank?) on forty-
eight unpaged leaves   BM | BLO | CTC

The first issue to announce the authorship.

[King Richard III.] The Tragedie of King
Richard the third. Conteining his
treacherous Plots against his brother
Clarence: the pittifull murther of his
innocent Nephewes: his tyrannicall vsurpation: with the whole course of his
detested life, and most deserued death.

Sh— King Richard the third . . .

As it hath bene lately Acted by the Right
Honourable the Lord Chambérlaine his
seruants. Newly augmented. By William Shakespeare. [Device.] London:
Printed by Thomas Creede for Andrew
Wise dwelling in Paules Church-yard at
the signe of the Angell, 1602. Fcp. 4°,
forty-six unpaged leaves; sig. A¹ to M²
in fours   BM | CTC

Although 'newly augmented,' according to the title,
no fresh text appears.

[King Richard III.] The Tragedie of
King Richard the third. Conteining his
treacherous Plots against his brother
Clarence: the pittifull murther of his
innocent Nephewes: his tyrannicall vsurpation: with the whole course of his
detested life and most deserued death.
As it hath bin lately Acted by the Right
Honourable the Lord Chamberlaine his
seruants. Newly augmented, by William
Shakespeare. [Device.] London: Printed
by Thomas Creede and are to be sold by
Mathew Lawe dwelling in Paules Church-
yard at the Signe of the Foxe, neare S.
Austin's gate, 1605. Fcp. 4°, forty-six
unpaged leaves; sig. A¹ to M² in fours
 BM | BLO

In making up the forme for the inner side of sheet G,
the compositor apparently got confused, as the
second and seventh pages were made to change
places with the sixth and third. The sheet was then
folded to bring the catchwords in order. Consequently the signatures should run in this curious
order to be correct: G, G3 verso, G2, G4 verso, G3,
G verso, G4, and G2 verso.
This volume temporarily supplanted the Jaggard folio
on the 12th July, 1905, by achieving the record price
up to that date ever paid for a piece of English
literature. It was secured for the United States at
£1,750, being an advance of £30 on the figure given
for the 1623 folio in 1901. It may be described as
almost priceless, being the sole known copy still possessing freedom outside two English public libraries.
It bears five autographs of Wm. Penn, believed to be
Admiral Penn, father of the founder of Pennsylvania.

[King Richard III.] The Tragedie of King
Richard the Third. Containing his
treacherous Plots against his brother
Clarence: the pittifull murther of his
innocent Nephewes: his tyrannicall vsurpation: with the whole course of his
detested life, and most deserued death.
As it hath beene lately Acted by the
Kings Maiesties seruants. Newly augmented, by William Shake-speare. [De-
vice.] London: Printed by Thomas
Creede, and are to be sold by Mathew
Lawe dwelling in Pauls Church-yard, at
the Signe of the Foxe, neare S. Austin's
gate, 1612. Fcp. 4°, forty-six unpaged
leaves; sig. A¹ to M² in fours
 BM | BLO | CTC | NY

24

Sh— King Richard the third . . .

The Bodleian copy is apparently dated 1613, the figure 2 being blurred. Most of the existing copies have had the imprint cut off.

Reprinted in 1766 by Geo. Steevens after collation with the editions of 1598, 1602, 1624, 1629, 1634, and another (lacking title) differing from the rest.

[King Richard III.] Ghost of King Richard the third . . . Ln: L. Lisle, 1614. *See* Brooke

[King Richard III.] The Tragedie of King Richard the Third . . . By William Shakespeare. Ln: Printed by Thomas Purfoot and are to be sold by Matthew Law, 1621. Fcp. 4°

Mentioned in Halliwell's 'Shakespeareana, 1841,' but untraceable elsewhere. Its existence at any time is doubtful.

[King Richard III.] The Tragedie of King Richard the Third. Contayning his treacherous Plots against his brother Clarence: The pittifull murder of his innocent Nephewes: his tyrannicall vsurpation: with the whole course of his detested life, and most deserued death. As it hath been lately Acted by the Kings Maiesties Seruants. Newly augmented. By William Shake-speare. London: Printed by Thomas Purfoot and are to be sold by Mathew Law dwelling in Paul's Church-yard, at the Signe of the Foxe, neere S. Austines gate, 1622. Fcp. 4°, forty-six unpaged leaves ; sig. A¹ to M² in fours

BM | BLO | CTC

Formed the foundation of the text in the 1623 Jaggard canon.

[King Richard III.] The Tragedie of King Richard the Third . . . London: Printed by Thomas Purfoot, 1624. Fcp. 4°

Referred to by Geo. Steevens in his list prefixed to 'Twenty of the plays,' 1766, and again by Alex. Dyce.

[King Richard III.] The Tragedie of King Richard the Third. Contayning his treacherous Plots, against his brother Clarence: The pittifull murther of his inocent Nephewes: his tiranous vsurpation: with the whole course of his detested Life and most deserued death. As it hathe beene lately Acted by the Kings Maiesties Sernaūts [*sic*]. Newly agmented [*sic*]. By William Shake-speare. London: Printed by Iohn Norton and are to be sold by Mathew Law, dwelling in Pauls Church-Yeard at the Signe of the Foxe neere St. Anstines gate, 1629. Fcp. 4°, forty-six unpaged leaves, including title ; sig. A¹ to M² in fours

BM | BLO | CTC | NY | W

In July, 1903, a copy realised £111. Earl Howe's copy, 7⅛ by 5in., bound in half blue morocco, sold for £115 in Dec., 1907.

Sh— King Richard the third . . .

[King Richard III.] The Tragedie of King Richard the Third. Contayning his treacherous Plots, against his brother Clarence: The pitifull murder of his innocent Nephewes: his tyranous vsurpation: with the whole course of his detested life and most deserued death. As it hath beene Acted by the Kings Maiesties Seruants. Written by William Shakespeare. Ln: Printed by Iohn Norton, 1634. Fcp. 4°, forty-six unpaged leaves, including title ; sig. A¹ to M² in fours

BM | BPL | BUS | CTC | NY

Earl Howe's copy, in half blue morocco, 7 by 5in., sold in Dec., 1907, for £68.

[King Richard III.] The Tragical Historie of King Richard the Third . . . by . . . More. Ln: . . . 1641. Fcp. 4°

[King Richard III.] The English Princess, or the Death of Richard the III. A Tragedy written in 1666 and acted at the Duke of York's Theatre. [Altered] By J. Caryl. Ln: T. Dring . . . 1667. Fcp. 4°

[King Richard III.] The Tragical History of King Richard III., as it is acted at the Theatre Royal. Altered from Sh— by Colley Cibber. Ln: B. Lintott [1700]. Fcp. 4°, pp. 56   BM

'When this piece was first introduced the censor expunged the whole first act, assigning as his reason that the distresse of King Henry VI. killed by Richard in that part would put weak people too much in mind of King James, then living in France. In this mutilated state it was acted for several years, before the proscribed part was admitted.'

[King Richard III.] Life and death of King Richard the third, with the landing of the Earl of Richmond and the battel at Bosworth Field . . . Ln: . . . 1709. 8°

CPL

[King Richard III.] Tragical history of King Richard III., as it is acted at the Theatre Royal. Reviv'd with alterations by Mr. Colley Cibber. Ln: . . . 1718. 12°, pp. 72   BM | BPL

[King Richard III.] Life and death of Richard III. With the landing of the Earl of Richmond and the battle at Bosworth Field. Ln: Printed for J. Tonson and the rest of the proprietors and sold by the booksellers of London and Westminster, 1734. 12°, pp. 96 and frontispiece by P. Fourdrinier   BM | W

King Richard the third . . . Reviv'd with alterations by Mr. Cibber. Ln: . . . 1734. 12°   BPL

Colley Cibber borrowed part of the first act from the last of 'King Henry the sixth: third part,' and numerous passages from other parts of Sh—. A considerable portion, however, is original.

[King Richard the third] The tragical history of King Richard III. As it is acted at the Theatre-Royal in Drury Lane. Containing the distresses and death of King Henry the sixth; the artful acquisition of the crown by King Richard; the cruel murder of young King Edward the fifth and his brother in the tower; the landing of the Earl of Richmond, and the death of King Richard in the memorable battle of Bosworth Field; being the last that was fought between the houses of York and Lancaster. With many other historical passages. Alter'd by Mr. Cibber... Ln : Printed for J. Tonson, and J. Watts, and sold by W. Feales, the corner of Essex Street in the Strand, 1736. Cr. 8°, pp. 72, and frontispiece   BPL | SML

King Richard the third . . . alter'd by Mr. Cibber. Ln : ... 1737.   12°   BPL

[King Richard III.] Tragical history of King Richard III. as it is acted at the Theatre Royal in Drury Lane. Alter'd from Sh— by Colley Cibber. Ln : Printed for J. & R. Tonson, S. Draper, and J. Watts, 1745. 8°, pp. 72, including engraved frontispiece   W

King Richard the third . . . As it is acted at the Theatre Royal in Drury Lane. Alter'd from Sh— by C. Cibber. Ln : J. & R. Tonson and J. Watts, 1751. 12°, pp. 72 and plate   BPL | BUS | SML

[King Richard III.] Tragical history of King Richard III. As it is acted at the Theatre-Royal in Drury-Lane. Altered from Sh—, by C. Cibber. [Ln.] ... 1754. 12°, pp. 62   BM

[King Richard III.] Tragical history of King Richard III. As it is now acted at the Theatres Royal in Drury Lane, Covent Garden, and Smock Alley. Altered from Sh— and cut for the Theatre Royal, Drury Lane, by C. Cibber. Dublin : Printed for Brice Edmond, at Addison's Head in Dame Street, 1756. 12°. With character frontispiece

King Richard the third . . . as it is acted at the Theatre-Royal in Drury-Lane. Ln : ... 1756.   12°   BPL

King Richard the third . . . alter'd from Sh— by Colley Cibber . . . 1757.   12°   BPL

[King Richard III.] Tragical history of King Richard III., by Sh—. As it is acted at the Theatre Royal in Drury Lane. Ln : ... 1759.   8°   W

King Richard III. . . . [In Cibber's Dramatic works]. Ln : ... 1760. 2 vols.   12°   BUS

[King Richard III.] Tragical history of King Richard III. Alter'd from Sh— by Colley Cibber. 'Domestica facta.' Edinburgh : Printed at Glasgow by Robert & Andrew Foulis for Francis Robertson in the year 1766. 12°, pp. 56
An edition which has eluded other bibliographers.

[King Richard III.] Tragical history of King Richard III. Altered from Sh—. By Colley Cibber. Ln : J. & R. Tonson, 1766. 12°, pp. 72. With frontispiece; title in red and black   SML

[King Richard III.] Tragedie of King Richard the third . . . 1612. Ln : Reprinted by G. Steevens, 1766. 8°, pp. 38   BPL | BUS | W

[King Richard III.] Life and death of Richard III. A tragedy, by Wm. Sh—. Edinburgh : Martin & Wotherspoon, 1768. 12°, pp. 118   BM | SML | W

King Richard the third . . . as it is acted at the Theatre-Royal in Drury-Lane. Ln : ... 1769. 12°. With frontispiece BPL

[King Richard III.] The rout, or desparing candidate. A parody on Sh—'s 'King Richard III., act v.' Ln : ... [c. 1770]. F°, single leaf   W
A rare broadside travesty.

[King Richard III.] Tragical history of King Richard III. Altered from Sh— by Colley Cibber. Now acted at the Theatres Royal in Drury Lane and Covent Garden. Ln : T. Sabine, jun. [c. 1770]. 8°, pp. 60

King Richard the third . . . Altered from Sh— by Colley Cibber. Ln : W. Oxlade . . . 1775.   12°   BPL

King Richard the third . . . [In Cibber's 'Dramatic Works']. Ln : ... 1777. 8°   BUS

King Richard the third . . . as it is acted at the Theatres-Royal in Drury-Lane and Covent-Garden. Ln : W. Oxlade . . . 1778.   12°   BPL

King Richard the third. A tragedy. As it is acted at the Theatres-Royal in Drury-Lane and Covent-Garden. Ln : J. Wenman, 1778. 8°, pp. 20 BM | BPL
With frontispiece portrait of 'Mr. Garrick in the character of King Richard.'

[King Richard III.] Tragical history of King Richard III. Altered from Sh— by Colley Cibber . . . Marked with the variations in the manager's book at the Theatre Royal in Drury Lane. Ln : Printed for T. & W. Lowndes, W. Nicoll, & S. Bladon, 1784. 8°, pp. 70

24—1

Sh— King Richard the third . . .

King Richard the third . . . taken from the
manager's book at the Theatre Royal,
Covent Garden. Ln : Printed for the
proprietors and sold by Rachael Randall
. . . and all booksellers in England, Scotland and Ireland, 1787. Cr. 8°, pp. 58,
and frontispiece of ' Mr. Holman as
Richard '   BPL | SML

King Richard the third. A tragedy by
Sh— as performed at the Theatres Royal.
Regulated from the prompt books by
permission of the managers, etc., with
introduction and notes. Ln : . . . [c.
1790]. 12°   BPL | W

King Richard the third . . . altered from
Sh— by Colley Cibber. Marked with the
variations in the manager's book at the
Theatre - Royal, Drury Lane. Ln :
Lowndes . . . 1793. 12°   BPL

King Richard the third. A tragedy, by
Sh—, as performed at the Theatres Royal.
Regulated from the prompt book. By
permission of the managers. With an
introduction and notes, critical and illustrative. Ln : Printed by assignment for
J. Barker at the dramatic repository,
Russell Court, Drury Lane, 1794. 12°,
pp. 60

King Richard the third . . . Manchester :
R. & W. Dean, 1800. 12°, pp. 106. With
woodcut frontispiece   BPL

King Richard the third . . . Ln : . . . [1806].
8°, pp. iv.-142   SML
Prompt copy, interleaved and annotated, at Stratford
from the library of W. Creswick the actor.

King Richard the third . . . As performed
at the Theatres Royal . . . With remarks
by Mrs. Inchbald. Ln : Longman [1806].
12°, pp. 80. With frontispiece by S.
Noble after Howard

King Richard the third. A historical play,
adapted to the stage by Colley Cibber ;
revised by J. P. Kemble ; and now first
published as it is acted at the Theatre
Royal in Covent Garden. Ln : Printed
for the Theatre, 1810. 8°, pp. 80   W
Interleaved copy, with manuscript stage directions and
notes, at Warwick Castle.

King Richard III. . . . As performed at
the Theatres Royal, Drury Lane and
Covent Garden . . . With remarks by Mrs.
Inchbald. Ln : Printed [by J. Ballantyne & Co.] for Longman . . . [c. 1811].
12°, pp. 80 and plate   BUS
Cibber's adaptation.

King Richard the third. Adapted to the
stage by Colley Cibber. Revised by
J. P. Kemble. Ln : . . . 1811. 8°

Sh— King Richard the third . . .

King Richard III., by Will. Sh—. Printed
complete from the text of Sam. Johnson
and Geo. Steevens. Ln : . . . 1812. 16°
                      W

King Richard the third ; a historical play.
Adapted to the stage by Colley Cibber ;
Revised by J. P. Kemble ; and now pub-
lished as it is performed at the Theatres
Royal. Ln : J. Miller, 1814. 8°, pp. 72
    BM | BPL | BUS | SML | W

King Richard III. A tragedy . . . adapted
for theatrical representation, as performed
at the Theatres Royal, Drury Lane and
Covent Garden. Regulated from the
prompt books. By permission of the
managers. Ln : J. Roach, 1814. 12°,
pp. 72

King Richard III. . . . With remarks by
Mrs. Inchbald. Ln : Printed [by T.
Davison] for Longman . . . [c. 1816].
12°, pp. 80 and plate   BUS

King Richard the third travestie. In three
acts. With annotations. By William By.
Ln : Sherwood, Neely & Jones, 1816.
12°, pp.viii.-92   BUS

King Richard the third : A historical play.
Adapted to the stage by Colley Cibber ;
revised by J. P. Kemble ; and now published as it is performed at the Theatres
Royal. ' Oxberry's edition.' Ln : . . .
1818. 8°, pp. iv.-68 and portrait of
Cooke   BM | BPL

King Richard the third . . . revised by J. P.
Kemble, as acted at Drury Lane. Ln : T.
Rodwell . . . 1818. Cr. 8°, pp. iv.-68   SML

[King Richard III.] A parody on the tent-
scene in ' Richard the third.' Principal
characters—Lord Castlebrag [i.e. Castle-
reagh], Cashman, Brandreth, Turner, and
Ludlam. From the ' Independent Whig.'
Ln : R. Carlile, 1818. 8°, pp. 8   BUS | W
' Time : The night before Hone's third trial.'

Richard the third . . . A tragedy in five
acts, as it is performed at Paris. Paris
. . . 1818. 16°

King Richard the third . . . Adapted to the
stage by Colley Cibber. With prefatory
remarks. The only edition existing which
is faithfully marked with the stage business and stage directions. As it is performed at the Theatres Royal. By W.
Oxberry, comedian. Ln : W. Simpkin &
R. Marshall, 1819. Cr. 8°, pp. viii.-70,
issued in printed wrappers   SML

King Richard the third . . . Adapted by
Colley Cibber. Ln : J. Tabby . . . 1819.
12°

[King Richard III.] Historical play of King Richard the third : Newly altered, and adapted for representation, from the original of Sh—. By T. Bridgman. Ln : Cope . . . 1820. 8°, pp. 80   w

King Richard the third, or the battle of Bosworth Field. 'Hodgson's juvenile drama.' Ln : . . . [c. 1820]. 12°   BPL

King Richard the third . . . Altered from Sh— by W. C. Macready. Ln : . . . 1821. 8°

King Richard the third . . . restored and re-arranged from the text of Sh—, as performed at the Theatre Royal, Covent Garden. Ln : . . . 1821. 12°   BPL

King Richard the third . . . Ln : J. Cumberland, 1822, 12°   SML
Describes the costumes.

King Richard the third travestie : A burlesque, operatic, mock-terrific tragedy. In two acts. Marked with the stage business and directions by the author. Ln : E. Duncombe, 1823. 12°, pp. 58   BM | BPL | BUS

King Richard the third travestie. With [burlesque] annotations by 'Contrast Jumble.' Ln : . . . 1823. 12°   BPL

King Richard the third . . . With remarks by D. G—— [Geo. Daniel]. 'British theatre.' Ln : J. Cumberland [1823]. 12°   BPL

[King Richard III.] Richard the third, after the manner of the ancients [In 'London Magazine,' June]. Ln : 1824. 8°   BUS
An attempt to reconstruct the play on the model of Euripides.

King Richard the third . . . Ln : J. Cumberland, 1827. 12°   SML
A prompt copy with MS. interpolations is at Stratford.

King Richard the third . . . edited by W. Oxberry. Ln : Simpkin . . . 1827. 12°   SML

King Richard the third . . . With explanatory notes [in French] by J. W. Lake. Paris . . . 1827. 18°   BPL

King Richard the third . . . conforme aux representations données à Paris. Anglais-Français. Paris : Madame Vergne, 1828. 12°, pp. 150   BM
The French text is in prose.

King Richard the third . . . Printed from the acting copy, with remarks . . . by D. G—— [Geo. Daniel]. To which are added a . . . cast of the characters . . . and the whole of the stage business, as performed at the Theatres Royal. Ln : J. Cumberland [1829]. 12°, pp. 66. With frontispiece by R. Cruikshank   BM | BPL

[King Richard III.] Twelve designs for the costume of 'King Richard III.,' by C. F. Tomkins. After the drawings and with the descriptions of J. R. Planché. Ln : Colnaghi & Son, 1829. 4°, pp. x.-20 and 12 coloured plates   CPL

[King Richard III.] Twelve designs for the costume . . . by C. F. Tomkins . . . With descriptions of J. R. Planché. Ln : Colnaghi, 1830. 4°, pp. x.-20 and 12 plates   BM | BPL | BUS

King Richard III. . . . Music arranged by J. Harroway. Hugo Vamp's comic dramatic Shakesperean scenas. Ln : Davidson, 1830. F°, pp. 8   BUS

King Richard the third . . . Ln : Cumberland, 1831. 12°   SML
Prompt copy from W. Creswick the actor is at Stratford.

King Richard the third . . . The only edition correctly marked . . . from the prompter's book . . . as performed at the London theatres. Edited by J. Duncombe. Ln : . . . [1831]. 12°, pp. 54   BM

King Richard the third . . . 'Lloyd's juvenile drama.' Ln : . . . 1831. 12°   BPL

King Richard the third . . . With explanatory notes [in French] by J. W. Lake. Paris . . . 1834. 16°

King Richard the third . . . Nuremberg . . . ; New York . . . 1835. 12°

King Richard the third . . . Acting edition, with accurate stage directions. 'Hinds' English stage' [Cibber's version]. Ln : Simpkin . . . 1839. 12°, pp. 64 and plate   BPL | BUS

King Richard the third . . . Nouvelle édition précédée d'une notice critique et historique, et accompagnée de notes par O'Sullivan. [In English and French.] Paris : L. Hachette, 1843. 12°, pp. xxxii.-170   BM

[King Richard III.] True sketch of King Richard the third . . . 1594. Edited by B. Field. Ln : Sh— Society, 1844. 8°   BM | BPL | CPL | MPL | SML

King Richard the third . . . burlesqued by Charles Sedley. As performed at the Strand. 'Duncombe's theatre.' Ln : T. H. Lacy . . . 1844. 12°   CPL

King Richard the third burlesqued. By J. S. Coyne. As performed at the Adelphi. Ln : Barth . . . 1844. 12°

King Richard the third . . . as compressed and arranged for public reading by B. C. Jones, from Colley Cibber's acting edition. Ln : Adlard . . . 1846. Cr. 8°, pp. 44   BPL | SML

Sh— King Richard the third . . .

King Richard III. . . . Adapted to representation by Colley Cibber. As played by Kemble, Cooke, and Kean and reproduced at the Park Theatre, New York, Jan. 7th, 1846. With the stage business, cast . . . costumes, positions, etc. New York : S. French [1846]. 12°, pp. viii.-3-65   BUS
Also issued with a change of title in the ' Modern standard drama.'

King Richard the third . . . adapted to representation by Colley Cibber. ' French's standard drama.' New York : S. French . . . [1846]. 12°, pp. viii.-3-65   BPL

King Richard the third . . . Adapted by Colley Cibber. ' Lacy's acting edition.' Ln : T. H. Lacy [1854]. Cr. 8°, pp. 68   BM | BPL | SML

Kinge Richard ye third or ye battel of Bosworth Field. Being a familiar alteration of the celebrated history by a gentleman from Stratford in Warwickshire, called Ye true tragedie of King Richard ye third . . . together with ye landing of ye Earl of Richmond and ye battel of Bosworth Field. A merrie mysterie in one act by Charles Sedley, comedian. Ln : T. H. Lacy [c. 1854]. · 12°, pp. 36 and plate   BUS

King Richard the third . . . Edited by Carlhaut. Paris . . . 1856. 8°
Text and notes in English and French.

King Richard the third . . . adapted by Colley Cibber. Ln : T. H. Lacy [c. 1857]. 12°   BPL

Kinge Richard ye third, or ye battel of Bosworth Field, by C. Sedley [a travesty]. 'Acting edition.' Ln : Lacy [c. 1858]. 12°   BPL

King Richard the third . . . Glasgow : Cameron [c. 1859]. 8°

King Richard III. (act iv., sc. 4). In Greek iambics, by C. W. Chute. Gaisford prize. Oxford : T. & G. Shrimpton, 1860. 12°   BM | BPL

King Richard the third . . . With historical and other explanatory notes founded on the best commentators. Edited by R. H. Westley. Leipzig : G. Græbner, 1861. 8°, pp. ii.-114   BM | BUS | SML

[King Richard III.] True tragedie of Richard the third, 1594 : Facsimiled by E. W. Ashbee. [Edited by J. O. Halliwell.] Ln : For private circulation, 1862. Fcp. 4°   BUS | W
Issue limited to thirty-one subscribers. Fifty copies printed, of which number Halliwell destroyed nineteen.

Sh— King Richard the third . . .

King Richard the third. Facsimiled from the edition printed . . . in 1597 by E. W. Ashbee. [Edited by J. O. Halliwell.] Ln : For private circulation, 1863. Fcp. 4°, on 92 unpaged leaves   BM | BPL | BUS
Issue restricted to thirty-one subscribers.

King Richard the third . . . 1605. Facsimiled by E. W. Ashbee. Edited by J. O. Halliwell. Ln : For private circulation only, 1863. Fcp. 4°   BPL | BUS | MPL | W
Issue restricted to thirty-one subscribers.

King Richard the third . . . from the folio of 1623. Ln : L. Booth, 1864. Fcp. 4°   BPL | CPL

King Richard the third . . . 1602. Facsimiled by E. W. Ashbee. Ed. by J. O. Halliwell. Ln : For private circulation, 1865. Fcp. 4°   BPL | MPL | W
Of the fifty copies done the editor destroyed nineteen.

King Richard the third . . . 1598. Facsimiled by E. W. Ashbee. Edited by J. O. Halliwell. Ln : For private circulation, 1867. Fcp. 4°   BPL | MPL | W
Of the fifty copies done the editor destroyed nineteen.

King Richard III. . . . Leipzig : B. Tauchnitz . . . 1868. 16°

King Richard the third . . . adapted by Colley Cibber. 'Acting edition.' Ln : French . . . [c. 1868]. 12°   BPL

[King Richard III.] Rise and fall of Richard III. : A Richardsonian burlesque, by F. C. Burnand. Ln : Phillips . . . [c. 1868]. 12°   BPL | SML

King Richard the third, as produced by Edwin Booth. Adapted from the text of the Cambridge editors, with introductory remarks, etc. by Henry L. Hinton. ' Booth's acting plays.' New York : Hurd & Houghton [1868]. 12°, pp. 98   BM | BUS

King Richard the third . . . With notes . . . adapted for scholastic study by John Hunter. Ln : Longmans . . . 1869. Cr. 8°, pp. xxviii.-144   BUS | CPL

King Richard the third . . . adapted by C. Cibber ; as produced by E. Booth. New York : French . . . [c. 1870]. Cr. 8°

King Richard the third. A tragedy in five acts . . . With . . . remarks by D. G—— Ln : T. H. Lacy . . . [c. 1870]. 12°, pp. 64 and frontispiece ; issued in printed green wrappers

King Richard the third . . . Arranged for representation, from the text, by Charles Calvert, and first produced at the Prince's Theatre, Manchester. Manchester : Alex. Ireland & Co., 1870. Cr. 8°, pp. xii. 82, in pictorial blue wrappers   BPL | SML

[King Richard III.] Tragedie of King Richard the third . . . 1612. Facsimiled . . . by E. W. Ashbee. Edited by J. O. Halliwell. Ln : . . . 1871. Fcp. 4°
BPL | W
Fifty copies printed 'for private circulation only,' of which nineteen were destroyed by the editor.

[King Richard III.] Tragedy of King Richard III. . . . uitgegeven met verklarende aanteekeningen en eene beschouwing van het treurspel door A. S. Kok. Haarlem : E. F. Bohn, 1871. 8°, pp. 226
BM
In English and Dutch.

King Richard the third . . . ' School edition of Sh—.' Ln : W. & R. Chambers [1871]. 12°
BPL

Kinge Richard ye third or ye battel of Bosworth Field . . . by C. Sedley. Ln : T. H. Lacy [c. 1873]. 12°
BPL

King Richard the third. With . . . notes, critical remarks, and historical extracts, by Wm. Lawson. Glasgow : W. Collins, 1874. 8°, pp. 142
BM | BPL | BUS

King Richard the third . . . 1594 [In Hazlitt, ' Sh—'s library,' 6 vols.] Ln : . . . 1875. 8°
BPL

King Richard the third . . . as produced by E. Booth. Edited by W. Winter. New York : Hart & Co., 1876. 12°

King Richard the third. Arranged for the stage exclusively from the author's text by Henry Irving, and originally produced January 29, 1877 at the Lyceum Theatre. Ln : E. S. Boot [1877]. 16°, pp. 94
BM | BPL

King Richard the third . . . With notes by J. Hunter. Ln : Longman . . . [c. 1877]. 12°
BPL

King Richard the third . . . As presented by Edwin Booth. ' The prompt book.' Edited by William Winter. New York : F. Hart & Co., 1878. 16°, ff. vi.-viii.-102, pp. 103-110, printed on one side of leaf only
BPL | BUS

King Richard the third . . . as presented by E. Booth. Edited by H. L. Hinton. New York : S. French [c. 1878]. 12°
SML

King Richard III. [In the ' Prompt book,' edited by W. Winter]. New York . . . 1878. 12°
BUS

King Richard the third . . . [Text and notes in Italian and English, edited by C. Rusconi]. Firenze : Le Monnier . . . 1878. 12°
SML

King Richard the third . . . arranged from the text by Alfred Dampier. Melbourne . . . 1879. 12°
MPL

King Richard the third . . . as produced at the Lyceum Theatre by Henry Irving. Ln : Chiswick Press [c. 1880]. 8°

King Richard the third . . . ' Acting edition.' Ln : French . . . [1880]. 12°
SML

King Richard the third . . . edited for schools by H. N. Hudson. Boston [U.S.]. Ginn & Co., 1880. 12°

King Richard the third. Edited by W. A. Wright. Oxford : Clarendon Press, 1880. Cr. 8°
BPL | MPL | SML

King Richard III. . . . edited by W. J. Rolfe. New York . . . 1880. 16°. Illustrated
BUS

King Richard the third . . . Edition classique précédée d'une notice littéraire par A. Elwall. Paris : Delalain frères [1881]. 12°, pp. xxiv.-168
BM
In English and French.

King Richard the third . . . Tragédie. Texte Anglais, publié, avec un avant-propos et des notes en Français, par A. Büchner. Paris : P. Dupont, 1882. 12°, pp. 364
BM

[King Richard III.] Le Roi Richard III. Piece traduite en Français et annotée par M. H. Bellet. Paris : L. Hachette et cie, 1882. 8°, pp. 444
BM
In English and French.

King Richard the third . . . Text and notes in English and French, edited by the Abbé Julien. Paris : Poussielgne . . . 1883. 12°

King Richard the third . . . With notes, examination papers, and plan of preparation. Ln. & Edin. : W. & R. Chambers, 1883. Cr. 8°, pp. 128
BM

King Richard the third . . . edited with notes by W. J. Rolfe. New York . . . 1883. 12°
BPL

King Richard the third . . . ' Standard plays.' Ln : John Dicks [1883]. 12°, pp. 32
BM

King Richard the third . . . Edited by Charles E. Flower. ' Memorial theatre edition.' Stratford-on-Avon : Printed by G. Boyden ; Ln : French, 1884. Cr. 8°, pp. viii.-112, including printed wrappers
BPL | SML

King Richard the third . . . Nouvelle édition collationnée sur les textes originaux avec des notes en Français . . . par Haussaire. Paris : Garnier frères [1885]. 12°, pp. x.-170
BM
In English and French.

King Richard III. . . . condensed and arranged in three acts for public reading. Ln : Stewart & Co. [c. 1885]. 8°, pp. 56

Sh— King Richard the third . . .

King Richard III. . . . edited by W. G. Clark & W. A. Wright. Oxford: Clarendon Press, 1885. Cr. 8° BUS

King Richard the third . . . With introduction, notes, examination papers, etc. by B. Kellogg. New York . . . 1886. 12° BPL

King Richard the third. With notes and illustrations. Ln: Cassell . . . [1886]. 8°, pp. 62 BM

King Richard the third . . . The first quarto, 1597. A facsimile in photo-lithography . . . With an introduction by P. A. Daniel. 'Sh— quarto facsimiles.' Ln: W. Griggs [1886]. Fcp. 4°, pp. xxii.-94
BM | BPL | BUS

King Richard the third . . . With notes. Ln: W. & R. Chambers . . . 1887. 12° BPL

King Richard the third . . . with introduction and notes by C. H. Tawney. Ln: Macmillan, 1888. 12° BPL

King Richard the third . . . The third quarto, 1602. A facsimile in photo-lithography by C. Prætorius. With an introductory notice by P. A. Daniel. 'Sh— quarto facsimiles.' Ln: C. Prætorius . . . 1888. Fcp. 4°, pp. iv.-92 BM | BPL | BUS | SML

King Richard the third . . . Avec une introduction et des notes par M. J. Guiraud. Paris: Vve. E. Belin et fils, 1888. 8°, pp. 158 BM
In English and French.

King Richard the third [With an introduction by Henry Morley]. 'National library.' Ln: Cassell, 1889. 16°, pp. 192 BM

King Richard the third. As arranged for production at the Globe Theatre . . . 1889, Mr. R. Mansfield appearing as the Duke of Gloucester. [Edited by R. Mansfield, with a preface signed ' F. S. A.'] Ln: . . . [1889]. Fcp. 4°, pp. 32 BM

King Richard the third . . . The sixth quarto, 1622. A facsimile . . . by C. Prætorius. With an introductory notice by P. A. Daniel. 'Sh— quarto facsimiles.' Ln: C. Prætorius, 1889. Fcp. 4°, pp. iv.-92
BM | BPL | BUS | SML

King Richard the third . . . With introduction and notes by H. N. Hudson. Boston [U.S.] . . . 1889. 12° BPL

King Richard III. With introduction and notes by C. H. Tawney. Ln: Macmillan . . . 1890. 12°

King Richard the third . . . edited by W. H. Payne-Smith. 'Falcon edition.' Ln: Rivington . . . 1889. 12° BPL

Sh— King Richard the third . . .

King Richard the third. With notes, examination papers, and plan of preparation. Ln. & Edin.: W. & R. Chambers, 1890. Cr. 8°, pp. 128

King Richard the third . . . edited with notes by W. J. Rolfe. New York . . . 1891. 12° BPL

King Richard the third . . . edited by I. Gollancz. ' Temple edition.' Ln: Dent, 1895. 16°

King Richard the third. Arranged by Henry Irving for the Lyceum Theatre, 19th Dec., 1896. Ln: . . . 1896. 8°

King Richard the third . . . [In Donovan, ' English historical plays,' Vol. 2]. Ln: Macmillan, 1896. 2 vols. Cr. 8°

King Richard the third . . . Edited by G. Macdonald. ' Warwick Sh—.' Ln: Blackie, 1896. 12°, pp. 204 BPL

King Richard the third . . . edited by F. P. Barnard. ' School Sh—.' Ln: Arnold [1897]. 12° BPL

King Richard the third . . . 'Ariel edition.' Ln: Routledge, 1897. 16°

King Richard III. . . . ' Pocket Falstaff edition.' Ln: Bliss, Sands, 1898. 16°, pp. 152 BPL | SML

King Richard the third. ' National library.' [Edited by Hy. Morley.] Ln: Cassell . . . 1898. 16°, pp. 192

King Richard the third . . . edited by W. H. Payne-Smith. ' Falcon edition.' Ln: Longmans . . . 1900. Cr. 8°, pp. xvi.-170

King Richard the third . . . edited with introductions and notes by C. H. Herford. ' Eversley edition.' Ln: Macmillan, 1900. 12° BPL

King Richard III. . . . with introduction and notes by C. H. Tawney. Ln: Macmillan, 1901. Cr. 8°, pp. 278

King Richard III. . . . 'Junior school Sh—.' Ln: Blackie . . . 1901. Cr. 8° BPL

[King Richard III.] True tragedy of King Richard III. . . . 1594. Edited by A. F. Hopkinson. Ln: Sims & Co., 1901. 12°
BPL | SML

King Richard III. . . . edited by W. J. Rolfe. New York . . . [1902]. 8° BUS

King Richard III. . . . with introduction and notes by J. Dennis. Illust. by B. Shaw. ' Chiswick edition.' Ln: Bell, 1902. 12°

King Richard III. . . . With introduction and notes arranged and classified by T. Page. Ln: Moffatt, 1902. Cr. 8° BPL

King Richard III. . . . with introduction and notes by F. E. Webb. Ln: Blackie, 1902. 12° BPL

Sh— King Richard the third . . .

King Richard the third. With introduction and notes by C. H. Tawney . . . With appendix by T. Cartwright. Ln: Macmillan, 1902. Cr. 8°, pp. xxii.-316

King Richard III. . . . with introductory notes and appendices by J. E. B. McAllen. 'Normal tutorial series.' Ln: Simpkin, 1902. Cr. 8°

King Richard III. [act i., sc. 2] In Greek iambic verse by E. W. M. Griggs. Gaisford prize. Oxford: B. H. Blackwell, 1902. Cr. 8°   BPL

King Richard III. Complete paraphrase by I. F. Young. 'Normal tutorial series.' Ln: Simpkin . . . 1902. Cr. 8°
                                            BPL

King Richard III. . . . parsed and analysed by Prof. E. E. Denney and P. Lyddon-Roberts. 'Normal tutorial series.' Ln: Simpkin, 1902. Cr. 8°   BPL

King Richard III. . . . With introduction by W. H. S. Jones. Ln: Ralph & Holland, 1902. Cr. 8°   BPL

King Richard III. Edited with notes by H. N. Hudson. 'Windsor edition.' Edinburgh: Jack, 1903. Cr. 8°

King Richard III. Introduction by G. Brandes. 'Favourite classics.' Ln: W. Heinemann, 1904. 12°, pp. xvi.-150 and frontispiece of Kean in the title role

King Richard III. . . . Introduction and notes by W. J. Craig. 'Little quartos.' Ln: Methuen, 1905. 32°

King Richard III. . . . 'Stage edition.' Glasgow: Collins, 1905. 16°

King Richard III. . . . edited by H. Morley. 'National library.' Ln: Cassell . . . 1905. 16°, pp. 192   BPL

King Richard III. 'Waistcoat pocket edition.' Ln: Treherne, 1905. 32°

King Richard III. . . . 'Red letter edition.' Ln: Blackie, 1905. 12°

King Richard III. . . . 'Plain text Sh—.' Ln: Blackie [c. 1907]. Cr. 8°   BPL

King Richard III. . . . edited by A. Hamilton Thompson. 'Arden edition.' Ln: Methuen, 1907. 8°, pp. 240

King Richard III. . . . . 'Renaissance edition.' New York: Harrap, 1907. Fcp. 4°   BPL

King Richard III. . . . 'Variorum edition.' Edited by Horace Howard Furness, jun. Philadelphia: Lippincott . . . 1908. Roy. 8°, pp. 656   BM | BPL

'King Richard III.' references—

See Aleyn	*See* Betty
,, Barnes	,, Bohn
,, Barnett	,, Brathwaite
,, Beale	,, Brooke

Sh— King Richard the third . . .

'King Richard III.' references—

See Buck	*See* Martin
,, Burgess	,, Meres
,, C—— (I.)	,, Mirror
,, Caine	,, Mirrour . . .
,, Carstens	,, Moeser
,, Churchill	,, More
,, Cibber	,, Pickersgill
,, Corbet	,, Pimlyco
,, Cornewallis	,, Remarks
,, Critical	,, Returne . . .
,, Cumberland	,, Richard
,, England's . . .	,, Richardson
,, Garrick	,, Rout
,, German	,, Salmasius
,, Ghost . . .	,, Seton
,, Halsted	,, Shore
,, Heywood	,, Spedding
,, Holland	,, Stonehouse
,, Hutton	,, Stuart
,, Johnson & Steevens	,, Taylor
	,, Throsby
,, Kemble	,, True discoverie
,, Lees & Cann	,, Turner
,, Legge	,, Vaughan
,, Life . . .	,, Weaver
,, Lowell	,, Weever
,, Macbeth	,, Wessel
,, Marston	,, Wilson (John)

Life and death of Thomas Lord Cromwell. *See* Sh— Thomas . . .

LOCRINE.

This tragedy is first found entered on the Stationers' Registers 22nd July, 1594, and was printed in the following year by Thomas Creede, under the initials of 'W. S.' The play was not definitely claimed as Sh—'s until introduced in the Chetwynde folio, 1663-64.

The authorship has been attributed to Charles Tilney.

It bears some likeness to the characteristic style of Greene and Peele. Passages found in 'Selimus' are also found repeated in 'Locrine' with slight alteration.

Sh—'s connection with the composition probably amounted only to general oversight or editorship.

[Locrine] The Lamentable Tragedie of Locrine, the eldest sonne of King Brutus, discoursing the warres of the Britaines, and Hunnes, with their discomfiture: The Britaines victorie with their Accidents, and the death of Albanact. No lesse pleasant than profitable. Newly set foorth, ouerseene and corrected. By

Sh— Locrine . . .

W. S——. [*Printer's device.*] London :
Printed by Thomas Creede, 1595. Fcp.
4°; sig. A¹ to K in fours, without pagination (A¹ being blank)

BLO | BM | BPL | CTC | DEVON

In five acts, in verse.
Sir Geo. Buck, master of the revels, assigned the
authorship to Charles Tylney. This is the sole
edition known before inclusion in the Chetwynde
folio of 1663-64. One of the three copies in the
British Museum bears manuscript notes by George
Steevens.
Earl Howe's copy, in half blue morocco, 6⅞ by 5in.,
realised £120 in Dec., 1907.

[Locrine] The tragedy of Locrine, the eldest
Son of King Brutus. By Mr. Wm. Sh—.
Ln : Printed for J. Tonson and the rest
of the proprietors, and sold by the booksellers of Ln. and Westminster, 1734. 12°,
pp. 60. With engraved frontispiece, also
piracy warning against R. Walker at end

BM | BPL | SML

[Locrine] The tragedy of Locrine, the eldest
son of King Brutus. By Sh—. Ln : R.
Walker . . . 1734. 12°, pp. 58   BM | CPL

Locrine . . . Ln : Tonson . . . 1735.   12°

[Locrine] Tragedy of Locrine, 1595. [Ed.
by Ronald B. McKerrow & W. W. Greg.]
Malone Society reprints : Oxford University Press, 1908. Fcp. 4°, pp. xii.-84
(unpaged), with facsimile of the original
title   BM | BLO | CTC | SML

' Locrine ' references—
See Crawford   *See* Greene
  ,, Daniel   ,, Lennox

LONDON PRODIGAL.

*The earliest known edition of this comedy
is that printed by T. C—— [Thomas
Creede ?] for Nathaniel Butter in 1605,
and it first found a place in Sh—'s collected
works in the Chetwynd folio of 1663-64.*

London Prodigall. As it was plaide by the
Kings Maiesties seruants. [*Device.*] By
VVilliam Shakespeare. London : Printed
by T. C—— [Thomas Creede ?] for
Nathaniel Butter and are to be sold
neere S. Austins gate at the signe of the
pyde Bull, 1605. Fcp. 4°; sig. A¹ to G⁴
in fours   BLO | BM | CTC | DEVON | NY | W
Twenty-eight unpaged leaves.
' The London Prodigal . . . written and perhaps acted
at the Globe this year [1604] . . . Its publication was
unlicensed and surreptitious . . . in 1605, with the
name of Wm. Sh— on the title-page. This surely
shows some connection of Sh— with the authorship.
It is true that in 1600 his name had been attached to
" Sir John Oldcastle " . . . and he could not have
written that play . . . but the peculiar relation in
which it stands to his historical plays places it in a
very different category from a play which was acted
by his own company, and over the publication of
which he may be supposed to have had some control,

Sh— London Prodigal . . .

direct or indirect. Perhaps he " plotted " it. It
should be noticed that the publisher, Butter, was the
same man who issued the quarto " King Lear " in
1608, which was certainly derived from an authentic
copy, however carelessly printed.'—*F. G. Fleay.*
The printer's emblem is the motto ' Viressit vulnere
veritas,' in an oval enclosing the figure of truth
receiving a birching. This emblem was used on the
title of the first edition of Spenser's ' Colin Clouts
come home againe, 1595.'
A copy of the ' London Prodigal ' in May, 1907 realised
£51. The Warwick Castle copy's title and last leaf
are both in facsimile.

London prodigal. A comedy . . . Ln : . . .
1709. 8°   BM
Published anonymously.

London prodigal. A comedy. By Mr. Wm.
Sh—. Ln : Printed for J. Tonson and
the rest of the proprietors and sold by
the booksellers of Ln. and Westminster,
1734. Cr. 8°, pp. 58 (some leaves wrongly
paginated). Frontispiece engraved by P.
Fourdrinier   BM | BPL | SML
Piracy notice by W. Chetwood at end against ' R.
Walker and his accomplices.'

London prodigal . . . Ln : Tonson . . . 1735.
12°

London prodigal . . . [In ' Ancient British
drama, edited by Sir W. Scott']. Ln :
. . . 1810. Roy. 8°

London prodigal references. *See* Sh—
Works : Ext. 1836

LOVE'S LABOURS LOST.

*Presumedly the first play to proceed from
Sh—'s pen, and one of the fifteen issued
before he died. The earliest known edition
appeared in 1598 from the press of W.
W—— [William White] for publication by
Cuthbert Burby.*
It was unregistered at Stationers' Hall.

[Love's labours lost] A pleasant Conceited
Comedie called, Loues labors lost. As it
vvas presented before her Highnes this
last Christmas. Newly corrected and
augmented. By W. Shakespere. [*Ornament.*] Imprinted at London by W. W——
[William White] for Cutbert Burby, 1598.
Fcp. 4°, thirty-eight unpaged leaves ; sig.
A¹ to K² in fours   BM | BLO | CTC | DEVON
This issue supplied the text for the 1623 folio, where
the play was divided into acts and scenes. When
preparing his twenty reprints in 1766, Geo. Steevens
was unable to get a copy of this, the original issue,
although one subsequently appeared for sale.
Reprinted by Halliwell in 1869.

Loues Labours Lost. A wittie and pleasant
Comedie. As it was Acted by his Maiesties Seruants at the Blacke-Friers and
the Globe. Written by William Shakespeare. London : Printed by W. S——
[Wm. Sheares ?] for Iohn Smethwicke

Sh— Love's labours lost . . .

and are to be sold at his shop in Saint Dunstoones Church-yard vnder the Diall, 1631. Fcp. 4°, thirty-eight leaves, including title; sig. A to K² in fours, unpaged   BM | BUS | CTC | DEVON | NY | SML
Reprinted by Geo. Steevens in 1766. A copy sold for £82 in July, 1903.
Earl Howe's copy, in half blue morocco, 7⅛ by 5in., realised £201 in Dec., 1907.

Love's labours lost . . . Ln: Printed for J. Tonson and the rest of the proprietors and sold by the booksellers of London and Westminster, 1735.   12°, pp. 84. With frontispiece by L. du Guernier   SML
Issued in paper wrappers, uncut.
The third separate edition of this play. The earliest pictorial representation of it is found in Rowe's edition of Sh—'s Works, 1709.

Love's labours lost. A comedy by Mr. Wm. Sh—.   Ln: R. Walker . . . 1735. 12°   W

[Love's labours lost] A Pleasant Conceited Comedie called Loues labors lost . . . Imprinted at London by W. W—— for Cutbert Burby, 1598 [First three leaves only: Reprinted c. 1760]. Fcp. 4°   W

[Love's labours lost] The students . . . altered from Sh—'s 'Love's labours lost' and adapted to the stage. Ln: T. Hope, 1762.   8°, pp. iv.-78
BM | BPL | BUS | W
The alteration mainly lies in the introduction of a love scene in act 3 between Biron and Jaquenetta.

Loues labours lost, 1631 [In 'Twenty of the plays . . . reprinted by G. Steevens']. Ln: . . . 1766.   8°   BPL | SML

Love's labours lost . . . An introduction and notes, critical and illustrative, are added, by the authors of the 'Dramatic censor' [F. Gentleman]. Ln: J. Bell, 1777.   12°, pp. 88   BM | BPL
An excerpt from Bell's edition of Sh—'s works for playgoers.

Love's labours lost . . . printed complete from the text of Sam. Johnson and Geo. Steevens and revised from the last editions . . . Ln: Printed for . . . John Bell . . . 1785.   12°, pp. 114. With engraved title and frontispiece of 'Mrs. Bulkeley as the Princess of France'

Love's labours lost . . . printed complete from the text of Sam. Johnson and Geo. Steevens and revised from the last editions. Ln: J. Bell, 1788.   12°, pp. 114. With plates   BUS

Love's labours lost . . . from the text of Johnson and Steevens. With remarks. Ln: . . . [c. 1822].   12°   BPL

Love's labours lost . . . printed from the acting copy, with remarks . . . by D. G—— [Geo. Daniel]. To which are added

Sh— Love's labours lost . . .

the costume . . . cast of the characters . . . and the whole of the stage business, as performed at the Theatres Royal. Ln: J. Cumberland [1839].   12°, pp. 58. Frontispiece by R. Cruikshank
BM | BPL | SML

Love's labours lost. A comedy . . . As performed at the Theatre Royal, Covent Garden. Ln: Chapman & Hall, 1839. 8°, pp. vi.-66   BM

Love's labours lost . . . marked . . . from the prompter's book . . . as performed at the London theatres. Ed. by J. Duncombe. Ln: . . . [1839]. 12°   BM | BUS

Love's labours lost . . . edited by C. Knight. Ln: Orr . . . [c. 1851].   12°, pp. 149-244 (excerpt)   SML
Phelps' prompt copy, interleaved and annotated, is at Stratford.

Love's labours lost . . . With original casts, costumes, and . . . stage business, correctly marked and arranged by J. B. Wright, assistant manager of the Boston Theatre. New York: S. French [c. 1858]. 12°, pp. 48   BUS

Love's labours lost . . . 'Spencer's Boston theatre.' Boston [U.S. . . . . c. 1860].   12° BUS

Loues labours lost . . . [in five acts, prose and verse]. The text from the folio of 1623; with notices of the known editions previously issued.   [Device.]   Ln: L. Booth, 1862. Fcp. 4°, pp. iv.-24, interleaved with blank writing paper
BM | BUS | W

Love's labours lost . . . 1598, facsimiled . . . by E. W. Ashbee . . . edited by J. O. Halliwell. Ln: . . . 1869. Fcp. 4°
BPL | W
Fifty copies privately printed, of which the editor destroyed nineteen, as was his wont.

Love's labours lost . . . edited by J. Hunter for scholastic study. Ln: Longman, 1873. Cr. 8°   BPL

[Love's labours lost] Sh—'s Loues labors lost: The first quarto, 1598: A facsimile in photo-lithography . . . With forewords by F. J. Furnivall. 'Sh— quarto facsimiles.' Ln: W. Griggs [1880]. Fcp. 4°, pp. xvi.-76   BM | BPL | BUS | SML

Love's labours lost . . . edited with notes by W. J. Rolfe. New York . . . 1882. 12°. Illustrated   BPL | BUS

Love's labours lost . . . 'Standard plays.' Ln: John Dicks [1883].   12°   BM

Love's labours lost . . . edited by Charles E. Flower. 'Memorial theatre edition.' Stratford-on-Avon: Printed by G. Boyden; Ln: S. French, 1885. Cr. 8°, pp. viii.-80, including printed wrappers   SML

Sh— Love's labours lost . . .

Love's labours lost. [With an introduction by H. Morley.] 'National library.' Ln: Cassell, 1889. 16°, pp. 192   BM

[Love's labours lost] Sh—'s Song of spring and winter. [With illustrations.] Ln: [Printed in Germany for] R. Tuck & Sons [1890]. 8°   BM

Love's labours lost . . . 'Acting edition.' Ln: French [c. 1890]. 12°   BPL

Love's labours lost. [Ed. by Hy. Morley.] 'National library.' Ln: Cassell, 1890.] 16°, pp. 192

Love's labours lost. A comedy . . . arranged in four acts for the present stage by Augustin Daly. Produced at Daly's Theatre, Mar. 28, 1891, and here printed from the prompter's copy. With a few prefatory thoughts . . . by William Winter. New York: Privately printed, 1891. F°, pp. 64   SML
Of very limited issue. An extra-illustrated inlaid copy, the gift of the editor, is at Stratford, and contains many plates, photographs of characters in costume, copy of the original programme printed on satin, etc. The cost of the few copies produced worked out at £20 each.

Love's labours lost . . . edited by I. Gollancz. 'Temple edition.' Ln: Dent, 1894. 16°

Love's labours lost . . . 'Pocket Falstaff edition.' Ln: Bliss, Sands, 1898. 16°, pp. 108   BPL | SML

Love's labours lost . . . edited with introduction and notes by C. H. Herford. 'Eversley edition.' Ln: Macmillan, 1900. Cr. 8°   BPL

Love's labours lost . . . with introduction and notes by John Dennis. Illust. by B. Shaw. 'Chiswick edition.' Ln: Bell, 1901. 12°

Love's labours lost . . . edited with notes by H. N. Hudson. 'Windsor edition.' Edinburgh: Jack . . . 1903. Cr. 8°

Love's labours lost . . . 'First folio edition.' Ln: Harrap, 1903. 12°

Loves labours lost . . . with introduction and notes by W. J. Craig. 'Little quartos.' Ln: Methuen, 1904. 16°

Love's labours lost. With introduction by George Brandes. 'Favourite classics.' Ln: W. Heinemann, 1904. 16°, pp. xii.-110. Frontispiece of Mrs. Bulkeley as 'Princess of France'

Love's labours lost . . . 'Ellen Terry edition.' Glasgow: Bryce . . . 1904. 32°

Love's labours lost . . . edited by F. J. Furnivall. 'Old spelling edition.' Ln: De la More Press, 1904. Fcp. 4°
Also issued on handmade paper.

Sh— Love's labours lost . . .

Love's labours lost. 'New variorum edition,' edited by H. H. Furness. Philadelphia: Lippincott . . . 1904. Roy. 8°, pp. xx.-402. With frontispiece   BM | BPL | BUS | SML
Reproduced from Rowe's 1709 edition of Sh—'s works.

Love's labours lost. 'Waistcoat pocket edition.' Ln: Treherne, 1905. 32°

Love's labours lost . . . edited by H. Morley. 'National library.' Ln: Cassell, 1905. 16°, pp. 192   BPL

Love's labours lost . . . edited by H. C. Hart. 'Arden edition.' Ln: Methuen, 1906. 8°, pp. 240

Love's labours lost. 'Old spelling edition.' Edited by F. J. Furnivall. Ln: Chatto, 1907. Fcp. 4°   BPL

Love's labours lost . . . 'Renaissance edition.' New York: Harrap . . . 1907. Fcp. 4°   BPL

Love's labours lost . . . edited by H. N. Hudson. 'Elizabethan Sh—.' Ln: Harrap . . . 1908. Cr. 8°

'Love's labours lost' references—

See Bacon	*See* Johnson & Steevens
,, Cope	
,, Crown garland	,, M—— (I.)
,, Cupid's revenge	,, Mantuan
,, Debate . . .	,, Meres
,, Dryden	,, Middleton
,, Estienne	,, Moulton
,, Florio	,, Mulcaster
,, Greene (R.)	,, O'Brien
,, Halliwell, Memoranda	,, Pater
,, Halliwell, Some account	,, Pegasus
	,, Pennyworth . . .
,, Harington	,, Stopes
,, Head	,, Table talk
,, Horn-book	,, Tofte
,, Jaggard	,, Tyrer
,, James	,, Versatile . . .
	,, Wellesley

LOVE'S LABOURS WON.

Francis Meres in his 'Palladis tamia' of 1598 mentions a play by Sh— bearing the above title, but the allusion is thought to refer to 'All's well . . .' inasmuch as no other record exists within knowledge.

[Love's labours won] Love's labours lost regained. A comedy. A continuation of Sh—'s play of 'Love's labours lost,' by 'Cib. Jusc.' [Major Brownes]. Ln: . . . 1841. 8°   BPL | W

'Love's labours won' references—
See Davis (L.)
,, Meres
,, Tolman

Sh— Lucrece. *See* Sh— Rape of Lucrece

MACBETH.

*This tragedy was first presented in type
in the Jaggard canon of 1623. The earliest
separate text appeared in 1711, but an
adaptation by Sir Wm. Davenant was first
issued in 1673.*

[Macbeth] The tragedie of Macbeth. [An
excerpt from the second folio edition,
with manuscript alterations of the text
in a coeval hand.] Ln: Printed by
Thomas Cotes for Robert Allot, 1632.
F°, ten leaves (lacking the eleventh, containing on verso the first page of ' Hamlet')   W
Macbeth. A tragedy . . . With all the
alterations, amendments, additions, and
new songs [by Sir W. Davenant] acted
at the Duke's Theatre. Ln : Printed for
William Cademan at the Pope's Head in
the New Exchange in the Strand, 1673.
Fcp. 4°, pp. 68   BM | BPL
An anonymous adaptation and the first issue in quarto.
An uncut copy, bound with other plays, realised £113
in July, 1900.
Macbeth . . . With all the alterations,
amendments, additions, and new songs
[by Sir W. Davenant] as it is now acted
at the Duke's Theatre. Ln : Printed for
A. Clark, 1674. Fcp. 4°, pp. iv.-60 BUS
Some of the additions came from Middleton's 'The
witch.'
[Macbeth] Epilogue ; being a new fancy
after the old and most surprising way of
Macbeth, perform'd with new and costly
machines which were invented and
managed by the most ingenious operator,
Mr. Henry Wright, P.G.Q. Ln : A. Clark,
1674. Fcp. 4°   W
A rare and curious burlesque on ' Macbeth.'
See also Duffet.
Macbeth. A tragedy. With all the alterations, amendments, additions, and new
songs [by Sir Wm. Davenant] as it is
now acted at the Duke's Theatre. Ln :
Printed for P. Chetwin and are to be sold
by most booksellers, 1674. Fcp. 4°, pp.
66   BM | BUS | NY | SML | W
An anonymous edition.
[Macbeth] Musick in the tragedy of ' Macbeth ' . . . [With text, c. 1675]. Manuscript. Oblong f°, pp. 72   BUS
Macbeth : A tragedy. With all the alterations, amendments, additions and new
songs [by Sir Wm. Davenant]. As it is
now acted at the Theatre Royal. Ln :
H. Herringman and R. Bentley, 1687.
Fcp. 4°   BPL | SML | W
Betterton [misprinted Batterton] appeared as ' Macbeth'
in the cast.
An anonymous issue.

Sh— Macbeth . . .

Macbeth : A tragedy. With all the altera-
tions, amendments, additions and new
songs [by Sir Wm. Davenant]. As it is
now acted at the Theatre Royal. Ln :
Printed for Hen. Herringman, 1689.
Fcp. 4°, pp. 60   BM
An anonymous issue.
] Macbeth : A tragedy. With all the alterations, amendments, additions and new
songs [by Sir Wm. Davenant]. As it is
now acted at the Theatre Royal. Ln :
Printed for H. Herringman and R.
Bentley, 1695. Fcp. 4°, pp. iv.-60
An anonymous issue.   BM | BUS | W
Macbeth : A tragedy. With all the altera-
tions, amendments, additions and new
songs [by Sir Wm. Davenant]. As it is
now acted at the Queen's Theatre. Ln :
Printed for J. Tonson and sold by John
Philips at the Black Bull, Royal Ex-
change, Cornhill, 1710. Fcp. 4°, pp. iv.-
52   BM | BPL | BUS | SML | W
An anonymous issue and a verbatim reprint of the 1687
edition.
The *dramatis personæ* herein differs from the previous
editions.
[Macbeth] The tragedy of Macbeth. Ln :
. . . 1711. 8°, pp. 84   BM
Macbeth . . . Ln : J. Tonson . . . 1714. 12°
                                        SML
The text varies from that in Tonson's edition of Sh—'s
Works issued in the same year.
[Macbeth] The tragedy of Macbeth. Writ-
ten by Mr. W. Sh—. Ln : Printed for the
Company [c. 1720]. 12°   W
[Macbeth] The tragedy of Macbeth . . .
Dublin : Printed for George Ewing at the
sign of the ' Angel and Bible ' in Dame's
Street, 1723. 8°, pp. 66, and leaf of pub-
lications
Macbeth. A tragedy. As it is now acted
by his majesty's servants. Written by
Wm. Sh—. Ln : Printed for J. Tonson
and also for J. Darby, A. Bettesworth,
and F. Clay in trust for Richard, James,
and Bethel Wellington, 1729. Cr. 8°, pp.
84 (last leaf containing list of publica-
tions)   BM | BPL
Macbeth. As it is now acted at the New
Theatre of Edinburgh. Written by Mr.
Sh—, with alterations by Mr. Tate.
Edinburgh : Printed by T. & W. Ruddi-
mans for Allan Ramsay, and sold at his
shop, 1731. Price one shilling. 8°, pp.
72   BPL
The first of Sh—'s plays printed in Scotland.
In June, 1904, a copy realised £25.
[Macbeth] The tragedy of Macbeth . . . To
which are added, all the original songs.
Never printed in any of the former edi-

Sh— Macbeth . . .

tions. [*Crude portrait of the poet.*] Ln:
Printed for J. Tonson and the rest of the
proprietors and sold by the booksellers
of London and Westminster, 1734. 12°,
pp. iv.-68, and frontispiece by Lud. Du
Guernier   BUS

Macbeth . . . Edited by L. Theobald.
Dublin : Rhames . . . 1739. 12°

[Macbeth] The tragedy of Macbeth . . . To
which are added all the original songs.
Ln : Printed for J. & P. Knapton, S.
Birt, T. Longman, H. Lintot, C. Hitch,
J. Hodges, J. Brindley, J. & R. Tonson &
S. Draper, B. Dod, C. Corbet, and J.
New, 1750.   Cr. 8°, pp. 72, including
copper frontispiece of the witches by Du
Guernier & G. Vander Gucht
                              BPL | CPL | W

Macbeth . . . Dublin . . . 1750. 12°   MPL

[Macbeth] Introductory symphony, airs,
recitatives, dance, and choruses in . . .
'Macbeth,' in complete score. Composed
by Matthew Locke.   First performed
about . . . 1674.   The whole revised and
corrected by Dr. Boyce [c. 1750].   F°
                                           BPL

[Macbeth] The historical tragedy of Macbeth . . . Newly adapted to the stage,
with alterations [by John Lee], as performed at the Theatre in Edinburgh.
Edinburgh : Printed by W. Cheyne, 1753.
8°, pp. iv.-68   BM | BPL | BUS | SML

[Macbeth] The tragedy of Macbeth . . . As
acted at the Theatre Royal, Drury Lane.
With all the original songs. Glasgow :
W. Duncan . . . 1755.   8°
First edition printed in Glasgow.

[Macbeth] The tragedy of Macbeth, by Wm.
Sh—.   To which are added all the
original songs. Ln : J. & P. Knapton,
1755.   12°   W

[Macbeth] Original songs, airs, and
chorusses which were introduced in the
tragedy of ' Macbeth ' in score.   Composed by Matthew Locke, chapel organist
to Queen Catharine, consort to King
Charles II.   Revised and corrected by
Dr. Boyce.   Dedicated to David Garrick.
Ln : Broderip & Wilkinson [c. 1760].   F°,
pp. 32, engraved throughout   BUS

Macbeth . . . To which is added all the
original songs. Ln : . . . 1761.   12°, with
frontispiece   BUS

[Macbeth] Three conjurers : A political
interlude. Stolen from Sh—.   As it was
performed at sundry places in Westminster on Sat., 30th of April, and Sund.,
1st May.   Most humbly dedicated to

Sh— Macbeth . . .

that distressed and unfortunate gentle-
man John Wilkes . . . Ln : E. Cabe, 1763.
Fcp. 4°, pp. ii.-26   BUS
A satire against Lord Bute, who figures as ' Macboote.'

Macbeth . . . To which are added all the
original songs. Ln : J. & R. Tonson . . .
1765.   12°   BPL

Macbeth : A tragedy . . . To which is added
all the original songs, with the life of the
author [written by Mr. Rowe]. Edinburgh : Martin & Wotherspoon . . . 1768.
12°, pp. xii.-72   BM

Macbeth . . . To which are added all the
original songs. Ln : Printed for H.
Woodfall, J. Rivington, etc., 1768.   12°,
pp. iv.-68   BUS | W

Macbeth. A tragedy . . . To which are
added all the original songs.   As per-
formed at the Theatres Royal in Drury
Lane and Covent-Garden. Ln : Printed
for J. Rivington, W. Strahan, J. Hinton,
C. Bathurst, L. Hawes, Clarke & Collins,
W. Owen, T. Longman, R. Baldwin, T.
Davies, L. Davis, B. White, B. Law, S.
Crowder, Robinson & Roberts, T.
Lowndes, T. Caslon, J. Wilkie, C. Cor-
bett, T. Becket, J. Robson, R. Horsfield,
F. Newbery, E. Dilly, G. Kearsly, S.
Bladon, and T. Cadell, 1770.   12°, pp. 72
A few copies were done on large paper, demy 8°.   BPL

[Macbeth] Scotch airs used in ' Macbeth '
in score . . . by Samuel Arnold [c. 1770].
F°

Macbeth . . . as performed at the Theatre
Royal, Drury Lane.   Regulated from the
prompt book by Mr. Hopkins, prompter.
Ln : John Bell . . . 1773.   8°, pp. 72.   With
frontispiece

Macbeth . . . Collated [by Charles Jennens]
with the old and modern editions.   Ln :
W. Owen . . . 1773.   8°, pp. 134, and
plate   BM | BPL | BUS | NY

Macbeth . . . as performed at the theatres
Royal in London and Edinburgh.   Glasgow : Printed in the year 1776.   12°, pp.
iv.-60   BPL

Macbeth . . . To which are added all the
original songs.   As performed at the
Theatres Royal in Drury Lane and Covent
Garden. Ln : Printed by W. Oxlade for
W. Bowen, 1776.   8°, pp. 68   BPL

Macbeth . . . as performed at the Theatre
Royal, Drury Lane, regulated from the
prompt book, with permission of the
managers, by Mr. Hopkins, prompter.
An introduction and notes, critical and
illustrative, are added by the authors of
the ' Dramatic censor ' [F. Gentleman].
Third edition. Ln : Printed for John Bell

near Exeter Exchange, in the Strand,
1778. 8° (excerpt), pp. 57-130, including
copperplate frontispiece of ' Garrick as
Mackbeth '
Off-printed from Bell's edition of Sh—'s Works, for
playgoers. An issue previously unnoticed.

Macbeth . . . With explanatory notes
selected from Dr. Johnson's and Mr.
Steevens' commentaries. Goettingen:
A. Vanderhoek's widow, 1778. 8°, pp.
112   BM

Macbeth . . . as it acted at the Theatres-
Royal in Drury-Lane and Covent-Garden.
Ln: Harrison & Co. . . . 1780. 8°, pp. 20.
With frontispiece portrait of ' Mr. Gar-
rick in the character of Macbeth '
                                        BM | BPL

Macbeth . . . with the additions set to
music by Mr. Locke and Dr. Arne.
Marked with the variations in the manager's book at the Theatre Royal in Drury
Lane. Ln: C. Bathurst . . . 1785. 12°,
pp. 66   BPL | SML

Macbeth . . . Taken from the manager's
book at the Theatre Royal, Drury Lane.
Ln: Printed by R. Butters, 1785. 12°,
pp. viii.-44   BUS
Probably issued on the benefit night of Mrs. Siddons,
2nd Feb., 1785, when she appeared as ' Lady Macbeth.'

Macbeth. A tragedy . . . Taken from the
manager's books at the Theatres, Drury-
Lane and Covent-Garden. Ln: R. Ran-
dall . . . 1785. 8°, pp. 60   BM

Macbeth . . . As it is acted at Drury Lane
and Covent Garden. Ln: Simmons . . .
1785. 12°   SML

Macbeth . . . as it is performed at the
Theatres Royal . . . 1788. 12°   BPL

Macbeth . . . printed complete from the
text of Sam. Johnson and Geo. Steevens,
and revised from the last editions . . .
Ln: John Bell, 1788. 12°, pp. 104:
frontispiece of Mrs. Siddons as ' Lady
Macbeth,' and vignette title

[Macbeth] Incantation for raising a phantom, imitated from ' Macbeth ' and lately
performed by H.M. servants in Westminster. By Colonel Richard Fitzpatrick [Original manuscript, in the autograph of Horace Walpole]. 1789. F°,
pp. 2
Sold in April, 1902.

[Macbeth] Congal and Fenella. A tale; in
two parts. Ln: C. Dilly, 1791. 8°, pp.
iv.-68   BUS
Founded on ' Macbeth.'

Macbeth . . . as performed at the Theatres
Royal. Regulated from the prompt
book . . . 1794. 12°   BPL

Macbeth . . . As represented by their
majesties servants, on opening the Theatre
Royal, Drury Lane. [Arranged for the
stage by J. P. Kemble.] Ln: C. Lowndes
[1794]. 8°, pp. 64   BM | BPL

Macbeth . . . As represented . . . on opening
the Theatre Royal, Drury Lane [arranged
. . . by J. P. Kemble]. Second edition.
Ln: C. Lowndes [1794]. 8°, pp. 58   BM

[Macbeth] Confusion's masterpiece: or
paine's labours lost. Being a specimen
of some well-known scenes in Sh—'s
' Macbeth.' Revived and improved; as
enacted by some of his majesty's servants
before the pit of Acheron. By the writer
of the parodies in the ' Gentleman's
Magazine ' [Thomas Ford]. Ln: J.
Nichols, 1794. Fcp. 4°, pp. 16   BM | BUS
Some copies have J. Pridden's name instead of J.
Nichols in the imprint.

Macbeth . . . with [satirical] notes by H.
Rowe. York: Printed for the annotator,
1797. 12°, pp. 88. With portrait of
Rowe   BM
The real editor was Dr. Andrew Hunter, of York, who
published it with the object of assisting Rowe during
his long illness and impoverished position.

Macbeth . . . with [satirical] notes and
emendations by Harry Rowe, trumpet
major to the high sheriffs of Yorkshire
and master of a puppet show. Second
edition. York: Wilson, Spence and Mawman, 1799. 8°, pp. 112, and portrait of
Rowe   BM | BPL | NY | W

Macbeth . . . Manchester: R. & W. Dean,
1800. 12°, pp. 70. With woodcut frontispiece and title engraved by T. Bewick
                                             BPL

Macbeth . . . Ln: Whitworth . . . [c. 1800].
12°

[Macbeth] Music to ' Macbeth ' for the harp,
by N. C. Bochsa. Ln: . . . [c. 1800]. F°,
pp. 4

[Macbeth] New songs in the pantomime of
' The witches ' . . . By Mr. Vernon. [Full
score.] Ln: . . . [c. 1800]. F°

Macbeth . . . As it is performed at the
Theatres Royal, Drury Lane and Covent
Garden. Revised by J. P. Kemble. Ln:
J. Ridgway [1803]. 8°   BPL | SML

Macbeth . . . revised by J. P. Kemble and
now first published as it is acted at the
Theatre Royal in Covent Garden. Ln:
J. Ridgway, 1803. 8°, pp. 64   BUS

[Macbeth] The tragedy of Macbeth . . .
Accurately printed from the text of Mr.
Steevens' last edition; with a selection
of the most important notes. Leipsick:
G. Fleischer the younger, 1806. 16°, pp.
254   BM | SML

Sh— Macbeth . . .

Macbeth . . . printed from the text of S. Johnson and G. Steevens, as last revised by I. Reed. With selected and original anecdotes and annotations, biographical, explanatory, critical and dramatic [signed 'L']. Ln: Mathews & Leigh, 1807. 8°, pp. 228. Illustrated with engraved portraits BM | BPL | BUS | SML

Macbeth . . . from the text of Johnson and Steevens [In 'The Cabinet']. Ln: . . . 1807-8. 2 vols. 8°

Macbeth . . . As performed at the Theatres Royal, Covent Garden & Drury Lane. Printed under the authority of the managers from the prompt books. With remarks by Mrs. Inchbald. Ln: Longman [c. 1808]. 12°, pp. 72, and frontispiece BPL | BUS

Macbeth . . . [English text and notes in French]. Avignon . . . 1809. 12°

[Macbeth] Introductory symphony, airs, recitatives, dance, and choruses, in the tragedy of 'Macbeth,' in complete score by Matthew Locke. First performed about the year 1674. Revised and corrected, and an accompaniment for the piano-forte or organ added by John Addison. [Ln: c. 1810.] F° BPL | W

Macbeth . . . With remarks by Mrs. Inchbald. Ln: Longman . . . [c. 1811]. 12°, pp. 72, and plate BUS

Macbeth . . . With notes in German by Dr. J. C. Fick. Erlangen: C. G. F. Breuning, 1812. 12°, pp. 102 BM | BPL

[Macbeth] Macbeth travestie, in three acts, with burlesque annotations [In 'Accepted addresses' . . . pp. 65-164]. Ln: . . . 1813. 12° BM | BPL | W

Macbeth travestie [In 'Accepted addresses, by different hands,' 2nd ed.] With burlesque annotations. Ln: . . . 1813. 12° BUS

Macbeth travestie . . . [In 'Accepted addresses,' 3rd ed.] Ln: . . . 1813. 12° BUS

Macbeth: A tragedy . . . Edinburgh: Oliver and Boyd [c. 1813]. 12°; issued in blue wrappers at 6d.

Macbeth: A tragedy; revised by J. P. Kemble and now published as it is performed at the Theatres Royal. Ln: J. Miller, 1814. 8°, pp. 68 BM | BPL | BUS

Macbeth . . . Revived at the Theatre Royal, Drury Lane, November, 1814, under the superintendence of S. J. Arnold. Ln: John Miller . . . 1814. 8°, pp. 68 BUS | W

Macbeth . . . [text in English: notes in German]. Berlin . . . 1815. 12°

Sh— Macbeth . . .

[Macbeth] Tragical history of Macbeth: A new song. [Sans place or printer], 1815. 8° BPL

Macbeth . . . A poem, in six cantos. Ln: Sherwood . . . 1817. 12° CPL

[Macbeth] Trochaici Græci, præmio Porsoniano . . . dignati . . . auctore G. H. F. Talbot. Cambridge . . . 1820. 8° BM
A translation from 'Macbeth, act i., sc. 7,' in English and Greek.

Macbeth . . . With prefatory remarks [signed P. P.] . . . Marked with the stage business, and stage directions, as it is performed at the Theatres Royal by W. Oxberry. Ln: . . . 1821. 8°, pp. iv.-74 BM | BPL | SML

Macbeth . . . [edited] by W. Oxberry. Ln: John Cumberland . . . 1823. 18°

Macbeth . . . With remarks . . . by W. Oxberry. 'British theatre.' Ln: Dolby . . . 1823. 12°. With portrait BPL

Macbeth . . . 'Acting edition.' Ln: Davidson . . . 1827. 12° SML
The prompt copy, with F. Haywell's restorations, is at Stratford.

Macbeth . . . With remarks by Mrs. Inchbald. Paris . . . 1828. 18°

Macbeth . . . printed from the acting copy, with remarks . . . by D. G—— [Geo. Daniel]. To which are added a . . . cast of the characters . . . and the whole of the stage business as performed at the Theatres Royal. Ln: J. Cumberland, 1829. 12°, pp. 60 BM | BPL

[Macbeth] Macbeth be-witched: Celebrated comic scena, being a mellow-dram of Scotch spirits as distilled from the shades of Acheron by Hugo Vamp. Ln: Musical Bouquet Office [c. 1830]. F°, pp. 8 BUS

Macbeth . . . Mansell's Pocket Sh—. Ln: Mansell . . . [c. 1830]. 12°

Macbeth . . . an heroic opera, by C. M. Heigel. Music by A. H. Chelard. 1832. 12° BPL
In English and German.

Macbeth. A tragedy . . . sprachlich und sachlich erläutert für schuler von Dr. C. L. W. Francke. Braunschweig: G. C. E. Meyer sen., 1833. 8°, pp. 168 BM
In English and German.

[Macbeth] Outlines to illustrate . . . 'Macbeth,' with explanations in English, German, French, and Italian by Moritz Retzsch. Leipzig & Ln: . . . 1833. 4°. 13 plates

Macbeth . . . Select plays . . . adapted for the use of schools [by E. Slater]. Ln: . . . [1836]. 12° BPL

Sh— Macbeth . . .

[Macbeth] Macbeth modernised : A most illegitimate drama [by R. Bell], diversified with songs. Ln : [Privately] printed for the author, 1838. 12°   BPL | CPL

Macbeth . . . 'Hind's acting edition' . . . With accurate stage directions . . . Ln : Simpkin . . . 1839. 8°, pp. 60, and plate   BUS

Macbeth : A tragedy . . . marked . . . from the prompter's book . . . as performed at the London Theatres. Ed. by J. Duncombe. Ln : . . . [1840]. 12°, pp. 54 BM

Macbeth travestie . . . By Francis Talfourd. Ln : Lacy . . . [c. 1840]. 12°

Macbeth travestie . . . By F. Talfourd. Second edition. Ln : Lacy . . . [c. 1840]. 12°

[Macbeth] Music of ' Macbeth,' attributed to Matthew Locke, in full score, with accompaniment for piano by E. J. Loder : to which is prefixed an historical account of the music by E. F. Rimbault . . . [c. 1840]. F°

Macbeth . . . [text in English : notes in German by N. Delius]. Bremen : C. Schünemann, 1841. 8°, pp. viii.-86   BM | BUS

[Macbeth] Sh— al vermittler zweier nationen. Von K. Simrock. Probeband ; Macbeth. Stuttgart und Tubingen : J. G. Cotta, 1842. 8°, pp. xx.-192   BM | BUS | SML
Translated in verse ; English and German on parallel pages.

[Macbeth] Selections from the music in ' Macbeth ' [John Eccles, 1696] from an ancient manuscript score. Ln : Novello . . . 1842. F°

Macbeth . . . Ten gebruike der gymnasia met ophelderingen voorzien door S. Susan. Deventer : J. De Lange, 1843. 8°, pp. vi.-84   BM | BUS
English text, with notes in Dutch.

Macbeth . . . Nouvelle édition, précédée d'une notice critique et historique et accompagnee de notes par O'Sullivan. Paris : L. Hachette, 1843. 12°, pp. xx.-106   BM | BPL
In English and French.

Macbeth travestie . . . Edited by W. K. Northall. New York : S. French [c. 1843]. 12°, pp. vi.-36   BUS

Macbeth travestie . . . Edited by W. K. Northall. New York : W. Taylor & Co., 1843. 12°, pp. 36   BUS

Macbeth . . . [text in English and notes in French]. 1844. 12°

[Macbeth] Sh—'s tragedy of Macbeth, with emendations and notes . . . a biographical notice of the author, an account of his

Sh— Macbeth . . .

contemporaries and critics, and a dissertation on the popular belief in witchcraft and magic, by Charles Travers [pseud. of Charles Tweedie]. Boulogne : Leroy Mabille . . . 1844. 8°, pp. 184 BM

Macbeth . . . With the stage business, cast of characters, relative positions. 'Modern standard drama.' New York : S. French . . . 1847. 12°, pp. 60   BPL | BUS

Macbeth travestie . . . by F. Talfourd. Fourth edition. Ln : Lacy . . . 1847 SML

Macbeth . . . With introduction and notes in Dutch by Dr. S. Susan. Deventer . . . 1848. 8°   BPL

[Macbeth] Sh—'s play of 'Macbeth.' With an explanatory paraphrase. Printed by direction of the Benares schoolbook society. [Edited by J. R. Ballantyne.] Mirzapore [India] : 1848. 8° SML | W
The first piece of Sh— printed in India.

Macbeth : a trajedi. Fonetic famili edijun, with bref ecsplanaturi nots bi Alecs. J. Elis. Ln : F. Pitman . . . 1849. 12°, pp. 78   BM | BPL | BUS

Macbeth : A melodrama [founded on Sh—'s tragedy, by F. M. Piave] in four acts. The music by Giuseppe Verdi. Ln : G. Stuart . . . [c. 1850]. 8°, pp. 54   BM

Macbeth travestie : A burlesque. In two acts. As performed at Henley Regatta, 17 June, 1847. By the author of 'Mammon and gammon ' [Francis Talfourd]. Third edition. Oxford : E. T. Spiers . . . 1850. 12°, pp. 28 BM | BPL | BUS | CPL

[Macbeth] Music in 'Macbeth,' by Matthew Locke, arranged for the piano by Wm. H. Calcott. Ln : Lonsdale . . . [c. 1850]. F°

[Macbeth] Witches' glee ; from the first scene in ' Macbeth.' New edition, revised. Ln : Goulding & D'Almaine [c. 1850]. F°, pp. 8   BUS

Macbeth ; with portrait of Mr. Macready as ' Macbeth,' and memoir. Ln : Tallis & Co. . . . 1851. 8°   BM
Forms part 2 of Tallis's ' acting edition,' of which two parts only were published.

Macbeth. With an introduction, critical and historical, and notes by M. P. Linde. Arnheim : D. A. Thieme, 1853. 8°, pp. vi.-xxvi.-112   BUS | W

[Macbeth] Sh— restored : The play of ' Macbeth,' with introduction and notes ; A ' Lamp for the reader,' etc. [By Hastings Elwin]. Norwich : Privately printed, C. Muskett, 1853. Fcp. 4°, pp. xxvi.-108   BM | BPL | BUS | CPL | W
Impression restricted to 100 copies.

Sh— Macbeth . . .

[Macbeth] Sh—'s tragedy of 'Macbeth,'
with Locke's music; arranged for representation at the Princess's Theatre, with
historical and explanatory notes, by C.
Kean...Ln: J. K. Chapman [1853]. 8°,
pp. 96, incl. pr. wrappers BM | BPL | SML

Macbeth: A tragedy. 'Acting edition.'
Ln: T. H. Lacy [1853]. 12°, pp. 64
BM | BPL

Macbeth . . . erklärt von Ludwig Herrig.
Berlin: T. C. F. Enslin . . . 1853. 8° BM
In English and German.

Macbeth travestie: A burlesque . . . By
. . . [F. Talfourd]. Fourth edition, completely revised. 'Acting edition.' Ln:
T. H. Lacy . . . [1853]. 12° BM | CPL

Macbeth . . . somewhat removed from the
text of Sh—, by F. Talfourd ['Acting
plays']. Ln: T. H. Lacy . . . [c. 1854].
12° BPL

Macbeth; somewhat removed from the
text of Sh—, by F. Talfourd. Fourth
edition. Ln: . . . [c. 1854]. 12° BPL

Macbeth . . . Glasgow: Cameron [c. 1859].
8°

[Macbeth] Complete edition of Matthew
Locke's music for 'Macbeth.' Ln:
Boosey . . . 1860. F°, pp. 24, with vig-
nette title BUS

Macbeth . . . An opera. Music by Verdi.
Melbourne . . . 1860. 8°, pp. 24 MPL

Macbeth. With the chapters of Holinshed's
'Historie of Scotland,' on which the play
is based. Adapted for educational purposes with an introduction and notes
philological and analytic by Walter Scott
Dalgleish. Edinburgh: J. Gordon . . .
1862. 8°, pp. 112 BM | BPL

Macbeth . . . uitgegeven en verklaard door
C. W. Opzoomer. Amsterdam: J. H.
Gebhard & Co., 1862. 12°, pp. iv.-146
English text, with notes in Dutch. BUS

[Macbeth] Celebrated music introduced in
. . . 'Macbeth,' commonly attributed to
Matthew Locke. Edited by C. D. Collet.
The piano accompaniment by Vincent
Novello. Ln: Novello & Co. . . . 1862.
Imp. 8°

[Macbeth] Sh— album, or Warwickshire
garland for the piano . . . including the
music in 'Macbeth' . . . Ln: Lonsdale
. . . 1862. F°

Macbeth . . . par le Chevalier de Chatelain,
. . . 1862. 12° BPL

Macbeth, King of Scotland. A tragedy in
five acts [prose and verse]. With remarks
by D. G—— (Geo. Daniel]. Ln: T. H.
Lacy, 1864. Cr. 8°, pp. xii.-64 BM | SML

Sh— Macbeth . . .

Macbeth: with the chapters of Holinshed's
'Historie of Scotland,' on which the play
is based. Adapted for educational purposes, with an introduction, notes, and
a vocabulary, by W. S. Dalgleish . . .
Second edition, re-arranged. Ln: T.
Nelson & Sons . . . 1864. 8°, pp. 118 BM

Macbeth . . . as performed at the Theatre
Royal, Drury Lane, under the manage-
ment of Messrs. Falconer & Chatterton.
Ln: T. H. Lacy [c. 1864]. Cr. 8°, pp.
xii.-64, and frontispiece BPL
Issued in printed clay wrappers.

Macbeth, a tragedy . . . New edition, with
notes. Revu . . . par C. Witcomb. Paris:
Baudry's European Library, 1865. 8°,
pp. 92 BM

Macbeth . . . Adapted expressly for Madame
Ristori and her Italian dramatic com-
pany, under the management of J. Grau.
The Italian translation by Giulio Carcano.
New York: Sanford, Harroun & Co., 1866.
8°, pp. 32 BUS
With many scenes omitted.

Macbeth . . . With an introduction, critical
and historical notes, etc. by M. P. Lindo.
Second revised edition. Arnheim: D. A.
Thieme, 1867. 8°, pp. 140
BM | BPL | SML

Macbeth . . . [Text in English and notes in
Italian]. Firenze: Successori Le Mon-
nier, 1867. 8°, pp. 176 BM | BPL | SML

Macbeth . . . [Text in English: Notes in
Swedish]. Upsala: W. Schultz, 1867.
12°, pp. lxxvi.-162 BM

Macbeth . . . as produced by Edwin Booth.
Adapted from the text of the Cambridge
editors. With introductory remarks, etc.
by Henry L. Hinton. New York: Hurd
and Houghton, 1868. 12°, pp. 80 BUS

Macbeth . . . arranged for dramatic reading,
with short sketches of some of the omitted
scenes, by Lin. Rayne. Ln: T. Bosworth
. . . 1868. 12°, pp. 40 BM | BUS

Macbeth . . . Leipzig: Tauchnitz, 1868. 16°

Macbeth . . . With explanatory and illustrative notes . . . for scholastic study by John
Hunter. Ln: Longmans, 1869. Cr. 8°,
pp. xxiv.-108 BUS | CPL

Macbeth . . . 'Cumberland's theatre.' Ln:
Lacy [c. 1869]. 12° SML

Macbeth . . . Edited by C. E. Moberly for
the use of Rugby School. Rugby: Billington, 1869. 12°

Macbeth . . . edited by W. G. Clark. Ln:
Macmillan & Co. . . . 1869. Cr. 8°

Macbeth travestie, by Momus Medlar [i.e.,
James Smith. In 'Rejected addresses,'
pp. 171-174]. Ln: . . . 1869. 12° BPL

Macbeth . . . edited by W. G. Clark and W. A. Wright. Oxford: Clarendon Press, 1869. Cr. 8°   CPL

[Macbeth] Real Macbeth, by the real Macduff. [c. 1870.] 12°   BPL

Macbeth . . . edited by J. Hunter. Ln: Longman & Co., 1871. 12°

Macbeth . . . Louisville [U.S.] American Printing House for the Blind, 1871. 4°
Printed in embossed Roman type.   BM

Macbeth . . . edited by Charles E. Moberly. 'Rugby edition.' Ln: Rivingtons; Rugby: Billington, 1872. Cr. 8°, pp. 102
                              BPL | BUS | MPL

Macbeth . . . erklärt von W. Wagner. Leipzig: B. G. Teubner, 1872. 8°, pp. l.-116   BM
In English and German.

Macbeth . . . edited by W. G. Clark & W. A. Wright. Oxford: Clarendon Press, 1873. Cr. 8°, pp. xliv.-180

Macbeth . . . edited by W. G. Clark and W. A. Wright. Oxford: Clarendon Press, 1874. Cr. 8°, pp. xliv.-180
                              BPL | BUS | MPL

Macbeth [In D'Avenant's Dramatic Works, vol. 5]. Edinburgh . . . 1874. 8°
                              BPL | BUS

Macbeth . . . edited by H. B. Sprague. 'Masterpieces in English literature.' New York . . . 1874. 8°   BUS

Macbeth . . . As performed at the Crystal Palace, under the direction of W. Creswick. Sydenham: Crystal Palace Co., 1874. 12°   SML

Macbeth . . . As produced by E. Booth. New York: French [c. 1874]. Cr. 8° SML

Macbeth . . . précédée d'une notice littéraire par E. Sedley. Paris: J. Delalain et fils [1875]. 12°, pp. 104   BUS
English text, with introduction and notes in French.

Macbeth . . . 'Standard plays.' Ln: Dicks . . . [c. 1875]. 12°

Macbeth . . . expliqué littéralement par M. Angellier . . . La traduction Française est celle de M. E. Montégut [In English and French]. Paris: Hachette & Cie, 1876. Cr. 8°, pp. viii.-266   BM | BPL | BUS

Macbeth . . . Translated and adapted for the Italian stage by G. Carcano. As played by Rossi. Ln: . . . 1876. 4°   BPL | SML
In Italian and English.

Macbeth . . . With introductory remarks . . . and . . . notes, etc. by Samuel Neil. Glasgow: W. Collins, 1876. Cr. 8°, pp. 152   BM | BPL | BUS

Macbeth . . . edited by W. G. Clark & W. A. Wright. Oxford: Clarendon Press, 1876. Cr. 8°, pp. xliv.-180

Macbeth . . . précédée d'une notice critique . . . et de notes par O'Sullivan. Paris: Hachette & Cie, 1877. 12°, pp. iv.-xx.-106   BUS
English text, with French notes.

Macbeth . . . edited for the use of schools by Henry N. Hudson. Boston: Ginn & Heath, 1877. 12°, pp. 487-569 [excerpt]
                              BUS

Macbeth. 'Hamnet edition' . . . according to the first folio (spelling modernised). With remarks on Sh—'s use of capital letters in his manuscript, and a few notes by Allan Park Paton. Edinburgh: Edmonston & Co., 1877. 8°, pp. xx.-72-xviii.   BUS | SML

Macbeth . . . edited with notes by William J. Rolfe. New York: Harper Brothers, 1877. 16°, pp. 260   BUS

Macbeth . . . adapted for schools and classes by T. Bulfinch. Boston [U.S.], 1877. 12°. With frontispiece   BUS

Macbeth . . . as presented by E. Booth [In the 'Prompt book, edited by W. Winter']. New York: Hart & Co., 1878. 12°, pp. 104   BUS

Macbeth, rendered into metrical German, with English text adjoined, by G. Solling. Wiesbaden: J. F. Bergmann, 1878. 8°, pp. x.-160   BM | BUS | SML

Macbeth . . . Acting edition. Ln: French . . . [c. 1879]. 12°   SML

Macbeth . . . für den schul-und privatgebrauch herausgegeben und mit anmerkungen, sowie mit einem auszug aus Holinshed's History of Scotland versehen von A. Ey. Hanover: C. Meyer . . . 1879. 8°, pp. 92   BM | BPL | SML
English text and German notes.

Macbeth . . . metrisch übersetzt von G. Messmer. Zweite vielfach verbesserte auflage mit gegenüberstehendem. Orig. text. Munchen: T. Riedel, 1879. 8°, pp. 194   BM | BPL
In English and German.

Macbeth . . . As played at the Lyceum Theatre. Edited by Henry Irving. Ln: Chiswick Press [c. 1880]. 8°

Macbeth, with notes, examination papers, and plan of preparation, edited by J. M. D. Meiklejohn. Ln. & Edin: W. & R. Chambers, 1880. Cr. 8°, pp. 144   BM

Macbeth . . . edited for the use of Rugby School by C. E. Moberly. Rugby: Billington . . . 1881. 12°

Macbeth . . . edited by O'Sullivan. Paris: Hachette & Cie . . . 1881. 12°
Text in English and notes in French.

Sh— Macbeth . . .

Macbeth . . . texte Anglais revu et annoté par l'Abbé Julien [In English and French]. Paris : Poussielgue frères . . . 1881. 12°, pp. xiv.-124   BM | BPL

Macbeth. Expliqué littéralement par M. Angellier . . . La traduction Française est celle de M. E. Montégut. 1881. Cr. 8°, pp. viii.-266   BM
In English and French.

Macbeth . . . edition classique précédée d'une notice litteraire par A. Elwall. Paris : Delalain frères [1881]. 12°, pp. xxiv.-104   BM
In English and French.

Macbeth . . . édition classique avec une préface et des notes par . . . A. Talandier. Paris : C. Delegrave . . . 1881. 12°, pp. xvi.-112   BM
In English and French.

Macbeth . . . édition classique par J. Darmesteter. Paris : C. Delagrave, 1881. 12°, pp. xciv.-172   BM
In English and French.

Macbeth . . . edited by O'Sullivan. Paris : Hachette & Cie . . . [1882]. 12°
Text in English and notes in French.

Macbeth . . . With notes. ' Oxford and Cambridge Sh—.' Ln : Allman & Son [1882]. 8°, pp. 128   BPL

Macbeth . . . edited by W. G. Clark and W. A. Wright. Oxford : Clarendon Press, 1882. Cr. 8°, pp. xliv.-180   BPL

Macbeth . . . With notes, examination papers, and plan of preparation, by Brainerd Kellogg. New York . . . 1882. 12°. With portrait   BUS

Macbeth . . . edited by Charles E. Flower. ' Memorial theatre edition.' Stratford-on-Avon : Printed by G. Boyden ; Ln : S. French, 1883. Cr. 8°, pp. viii.-82 SML

Macbeth . . . edited for the use of Rugby school by C. E. Moberly. Rugby : Rivington . . . [1883]. 12°

Macbeth . . . edited by d'Hugnes. Paris : Garnier . . . 1883. 12°
Text in English and notes in French.

Macbeth . . . edited with notes by W. J. Rolfe. New York . . . 1883. 12°   BPL | SML

Macbeth . . . edited by W. G. Clark & W. A. Wright. Oxford : Clarendon Press . . . 1883. Cr. 8°, pp. xliv.-180   SML

Macbeth . . . ' Standard plays.' Ln : John Dicks [1883]. 12°   BM | BPL

Macbeth . . . with notes, for the Oxford and Cambridge examinations. Ln : Allman [1883]. Cr. 8°   BUS

Macbeth . . . edited by T. Parry. Ln : Longman [c. 1884]. Cr. 8°

Sh— Macbeth . . .

Macbeth . . . edited by W. G. Clark & W. A. Wright. Oxford : Clarendon Press, 1885. Cr. 8°, pp. xliv.-180

Macbeth . . . med gloser og anmærkninger af A. Stewart MacGregor og Mrs. S. Kinney. Kjobenhavn : Gyldendalske boghandels forlag, 1885. Cr. 8°, pp. 136   BM
In English and Danish.

Macbeth . . . edited by O'Sullivan. Paris : Hachette & Cie . . . 1886. 12°
Text in English and notes in French.

Macbeth . . . with the ' Historie of Macbeth' from Ralph Holinshed's ' Chronicle of Scotland, 1577 ' [with an introduction by H. Morley]. ' National library.' Ln : Cassell, 1886. 16°, pp. 192   BM | SML

Macbeth . . . edited by Darmesteter. 'Edition classique.' Paris : Delagrave . . . 1887. 12°   SML

Macbeth . . . arranged for the stage by Henry Irving and presented at the Lyceum Theatre 29th Dec., 1888, with music by Arthur Sullivan. Ln : W. S. Johnson, 1888. 8°, pp. 72   BPL

Macbeth . . . with notes, etc., edited by J. M. D. Meiklejohn. Ln : W. & R. Chambers, 1888. 12°   BPL

Macbeth . . . with introduction and notes by Moffatt. Ln : Blackie [1888]. 16°, pp. 96   BM | BPL

Macbeth . . . Lines pronounced corrupt restored, and mutilations before unsuspected amended ; also some new renderings. With preface and notes. Also papers on Sh—'s supposed negations, the apparitions, and the temptation of Macbeth. By Matthias Mull. Ln : Kegan Paul, 1889. 8°, pp. cxvi.-90 BM | BPL | BUS

Macbeth . . . [with introd. by H. Morley]. ' National library.' Ln : Cassell . . . 1889. 16°, pp. 192

Macbeth . . . with introduction and notes by H. N. Hudson. Boston [U.S.] . . . 1889. 12°   BPL

Macbeth . . . with introd. and notes, arranged and classified. Ln : Moffatt & Paige, 1889. 8°

Macbeth, edited by H. B. Sprague. Chicago : S. R. Winchell & Co. [1889]. Cr. 8°, pp. 238   BM

Macbeth . . . with introduction and notes [by B. Jonson] for the use of students. Ln : G. Gill . . . 1889. 12°, pp. 128   BM | BPL

[Macbeth] The real Macbeth, by the real Macduff, from the text of the late Wm. Sh—. Ln : Sonnenschein [1889]. Oblong 8° ; lithographed throughout   BM
An illustrated satire on Henry Irving's performance of ' Macbeth.'

[Macbeth] The tragedie of Macbeth. With illustrations and notes by J. Moyr Smith. Ln : Low, 1889. F°, pp. xxx.-88. With 27 copper etchings   BM | BPL

Macbeth . . . edited by W. G. Clark & W. A. Wright. Oxford : Clarendon Press, 1889. Cr. 8°, pp. xliv.-180

Macbeth . . . with illustrations and notes by J. Moyr Smith. New York . . . 1889. F°. With 27 plates   BUS

Macbeth . . . arranged for the stage by H. Irving and presented at the Lyceum Theatre. Ln : . . . 1889. 8°   BPL

Macbeth . . . with introduction and notes. Third edition. Ln : Moffatt & Paige [c. 1890]. 8°, pp. 160

Macbeth . . . with notes by K. Deighton. Ln : Macmillan, 1890. Cr. 8°

Macbeth, as arranged for the public readings of Henry Irving and Ellen Terry. Ln : . . . 1890. F° ; printed in very large type

Macbeth nach der folio von 1623, mit den varianten der anderen folios, herausgegeben von A. Wagner. Halle : M. Niemeyer, 1890. 8°, pp. iv.-96   BM
In English and German.

Macbeth . . . edited by E. K. Chambers. 'Warwick Sh—.' Ln : Blackie . . . 1893. 12°, pp. 188   BPL

Macbeth . . . 'Student's Tauchnitz edition.' Mit deutschen erklärungen von I. Schmidt. Leipzig : B. Tauchnitz . . . 1893. 8°, pp. xx.-168   BM
In English and German.

Macbeth . . . 'Ariel edition.' New York : Putnam . . . 1894. 16°

Macbeth . . . edited by R. F. Cholmeley & J. Churton Collins. 'School Sh—.' Ln : E. Arnold [c. 1895]. 8°, pp. xxvi.-110   BPL

Macbeth . . . edited by Henry C. Notcutt. 'Junior school Sh—.' Ln : Blackie & Sons . . . 1895. Cr. 8°, pp. 110   BPL

Macbeth . . . with introduction and notes, arranged and classified. Fifth edition. Ln : Moffatt & Paige [c. 1895]. Cr. 8°, pp. 160

Macbeth . . . edited by W. G. Clark & W. A. Wright. Oxford : Clarendon Press, 1895. Cr. 8°, pp. xliv.-180

Macbeth . . . edited by E. K. Chambers. 'Arden Sh—.' Ln : Methuen . . . 1895-96. 8°   BUS

Macbeth . . . with introduction and notes by K. Deighton. Ln : Macmillan . . . 1896. Cr. 8°   BPL

Macbeth . . . edited by I. Gollancz. 'Temple edition.' Ln : Dent . . . 1896. 16°, pp. 138   BUS

Macbeth . . . edited by J. M. Manly. New York . . . 1896. 8°   BUS

Macbeth . . . edited by R. Grant White. With additional notes by Helen Gray Cone. Boston [U.S.] . . . 1897. 16°

Macbeth . . . 'Variorum edition.' Edited by H. H. Furness. Ln : Dent . . . 1898. 8°, pp. xx.-492   BM

Macbeth . . . 'Pocket Falstaff edition.' Ln : Bliss, Sands . . . 1898. 16°, pp. 100   BPL | SML

Macbeth . . . As arranged for the stage by Forbes Robertson, and presented at the Lyceum Theatre on Sat., 17 Sept. Ln : Nassau Press, 1898. 4°, pp. 72. With portraits   BM

Macbeth . . . edited by Homer B. Sprague. Boston [U.S.] . . . 1898. 8°. With portraits   BUS

Macbeth . . . with introduction and notes by J. Dennis. Illust. by B. Shaw. 'Chiswick edition.' Ln : Bell . . . 1899. 12°, pp. 124

Macbeth . . . 'Ariel edition.' Ln : Routledge . . . 1899. 16°

Macbeth . . . with notes, etc. by R. McWilliam. Illust. by Gordon Browne. 'Swan edition.' Ln : Longman, 1899. Cr. 8°, pp. 126   BPL

Macbeth . . . edited with introduction and notes by C. H. Herford. 'Eversley edition.' Ln : Macmillan, 1900. Cr. 8°   BPL

Macbeth . . . edited by E. K. Chambers. 'Warwick Sh—.' Ln : Blackie . . . [c. 1900]. 12°, pp. 188

Macbeth . . . edited with introductory notes, glossary, appendix, and indexes, by A. W. Verity. Cambridge : Univ. Press, 1901. Cr. 8°, pp. 336   BPL | BUS

Macbeth . . . edited by W. G. Clark & W. A. Wright. Oxford : Clarendon Press, 1901. Cr. 8°, pp. xliv.-180

[Macbeth] The tragedy of Macbeth. With an appendix containing suggestions for its study by F. T. Baker. New York : . . . 1901. 8°   BUS

Macbeth . . . with introduction and notes, for use in schools and classes, by H. N. Hudson. Boston [U.S.] . . . 1901. 8°   BUS

Macbeth . . . 'Picture Sh—.' Ln : Blackie . . . 1901. 12°   BPL

Macbeth . . . with introduction and notes by K. Deighton. Ln : Macmillan . . . 1901. Cr. 8°, pp. xxx.-224

Macbeth . . . 'Temple edition for schools.' Ln : Dent . . . 1902. Cr. 8°   BPL

Macbeth . . . 'School Sh—.' Ln : Blackie . . . 1902. Cr. 8°   BPL

Sh— Macbeth . . .

Macbeth . . . edited by W. J. Rolfe. New York . . . [1902]. 8°   BUS
Macbeth . . . edited by L. W. Lyde. Ln: Black, 1902. Cr. 8°
Macbeth . . . edited with introduction and notes by S. Wood. Ln: G. Gill [1902]. 8°, pp. xxxvi.-166. Illustrated   BPL
Macbeth . . . with notes, introduction, and glossary, by George Smith. Illust. by T. H. Robinson. Ln: Dent, 1902. Cr. 8°
Macbeth. With notes, examination papers . . . by J. M. D. Meiklejohn. Ln. and Edin.: W. & R. Chambers, 1902. Cr. 8°, pp. 144
Macbeth . . . edited for the use of students by A. W. Verity. Cambridge: Univ. Press, 1902. Cr. 8°, pp. xlviii.-288
Macbeth . . . edited . . . by A. W. Verity. Cambridge: Univ. Press, 1902. Cr. 8°, pp. xxxvi.-208   BPL | BUS
Macbeth . . . with introduction and notes by M. J. D. Meiklejohn. 'Blackfriars edition.' Ln: A. M. Holden, 1903. Cr. 8°, pp. 196   BPL
Macbeth . . . edited by A. A. Brayley. 'Normal tutorial series.' Ln: Simpkin, 1903. Cr. 8°   BPL
Macbeth. 'New variorum edition,' edited by H. H. Furness. Revised edition, by Horace Howard Furness, jun. Philadelphia: Lippincott, 1903. Roy. 8°. With plate   BM | BPL | BUS | SML
Macbeth . . . new edition. With critical text in Elizabethan English and brief notes illustrative of Elizabethan life, thought, and idiom, by Mark Harvey Liddell. New York . . . 1903. 8°   BUS
Macbeth . . . edited by R. B. Johnson. Edinburgh: Blackwood, 1903. Cr. 8° BPL
Macbeth . . . edited by A. W. Verity. 'Students' edition.' Cambridge: Univ. Press, 1903. 8°, pp. 338
Macbeth . . . 'Waistcoat pocket edition.' Ln: Treherne, 1904. 32°
Macbeth . . . edited by H. Morley. 'National library.' Ln: Cassell, 1904. 16°, pp. 192   BPL
Macbeth . . . 'Ellen Terry edition.' Glasgow: Bryce, 1904. 32°
Macbeth . . . with introduction by G. Brandes. 'Favourite classics.' Ln: Heinemann, 1904. 12°
Macbeth . . . edited by A. W. Verity. Cambridge: University Press, 1904. 8°, pp. xxxvi.-208
Macbeth. With preface, glossary, etc. by I. Gollancz. Ln: Dent, 1904. 16°, pp. xii.-128

Sh— Macbeth . . .

Macbeth . . . Retold for children by A. S. Hoffman. Ln: Dent, 1905. 16°. Illustrated   BPL
Macbeth . . . 'Stage edition.' Glasgow: Collins . . . 1905. 16°
Macbeth . . . with introduction and notes by W. J. Craig. 'Little quartos.' Ln: Methuen, 1905. 16°
Macbeth . . . edited with introduction and notes by Stanley Wood. Ln: Gill & Sons [c. 1905]. 8°, pp. xxxvi.-166. Illustrated
Macbeth . . . edited by A. W. Verity. Camb.: Univ. Press, 1906. Cr. 8°, pp. xxxvi.-208
Macbeth . . . with introduction, notes, appendix, examination questions, glossary, and index by W. C. Crook. Ln: Ralph, 1906. Cr. 8°, pp. 186; interleaved   BPL
Macbeth . . . Complete paraphrase. Normal tutorial series. Ln: . . . 1906. Cr. 8°   BPL
[Macbeth] Fireside reading in 'Macbeth' [From 'T. P. [O'Connor's] Weekly,' Oct.] Ln: 1906. 4°
Macbeth . . . with preface, glossary, etc. by I. Gollancz. 'Temple edition.' Ln: Dent & Co., 1906. 12°, pp. xii.-128
Macbeth . . . 'Text without notes.' Ln: Chambers . . . 1907. Cr. 8°, pp. 88 BPL
Macbeth . . . Text revised by A. Dyce. Ln: Sonnenschein, 1907. 8°
Macbeth. 'Renaissance edition.' With introduction by H. C. Beeching. Ln: G. G. Harrap, 1908. Fcp. 4°   BPL
Macbeth . . . edited with introd. and notes by G. S. Gordon. Oxford: Clarendon Press, 1909. Cr. 8°, pp. 288
'Macbeth' references—

See Aery-Jacob   See Collection . . .
  „ Anderson   „ Cooke
  „ Archer & Lowe   „ Crimes
  „ Barnett (T. D.)   „ Cumberland
  „ Bibb   „ Curtis
  „ Bowen   „ Dennis
  „ Bradley   „ De Quincey
  „ Brandt   „ Distortions . . .
  „ Brown   „ Doyle
  „ Buchan   „ Dramatic . . .
  „ Buchanan   „ Duffett
  „ Bucknill   „ Essay . . .
  „ Caine   „ Ethics
  „ Carr   „ Fletcher
  „ Carstens   „ Foard
  „ Caulfield   „ Foggo
  „ Chambers   „ Ford
  „ Charlemont   „ Forman
  „ Clayden   „ French

Sh— Macbeth . . .

'Macbeth' references—

MEASURE FOR MEASURE.

Of this comedy no edition is known earlier than the version in the Jaggard canon of 1623. Two adaptations followed, in 1673 and 1700 respectively. The first separate unaltered issue of the play was published by Jacob Tonson in 1734.

[Measure for measure] The law against lovers [excerpt from the Works of Sir William Davenant]. Ln : . . . 1673. F°
BPL | BUS | W

A blending of Sh—'s two plots of 'Measure for measure' and 'Much ado . . .'

Sh— Measure for measure . . .

Measure for measure, or beauty the best advocate. As it is acted at the Theatre in Lincoln's Inn Fields. Written originally by Mr. Sh— . . . and now very much alter'd. With additions of several entertainments of musick [By Charles Gildon]. Ln : D. Brown at the Black Swan without Temple Bar, and R. Parker, 1700. Fcp. 4°, pp. viii.-48
BM | BPL | BUS | SML | W

Pages 47-48 are erroneously paged 39-84.
From Davenant 'Gildon has borrowed whatever suited him without acknowledgment.'—*Geneste. English stage, vol. II, p. 221.* He has left out the parts of 'Much ado . . .' and introduced the 'Loves of Dido and Æneas : A mask.'
The prologue and epilogue were written by Oldmixon. An account of this issue may be seen in 'The Athenæum,' No. 3994.
George Steevens stated this to be 'the only alteration of the play,' quite ignoring Davenant's adaptation. Kemble's revision of 1815 must also not be lost sight of.

Measure for measure. By Mr. Wm. Sh—. Ln : Printed for J. Tonson and the rest of the proprietors, and sold by the booksellers of London and Westminster, 1734. Cr. 8°, pp. 84 ; frontispiece engraved by L. du Guernier
SML | W

With the caveat following title :—' Whereas R. Walker and his accomplices have printed and published several of Sh—'s plays, and to screen their innumerable errors advertise that they are printed as they are acted, and industriously report that the said plays are printed from copies made use of at the theatres. I therefore declare in justice to the proprietors, whose right is basely invaded, as well as in defence of myself, that no person ever had directly or indirectly from me any such copy or copies, neither would I be accessary on any account to the imposing on the publick such useless, pirated, and maimed editions as are published by the said R. Walker. W. Chetwood, prompter to his Majestys company of comedians at the Theatre Royal in Drury Lane.'

Measure for measure . . . as it is acted at the theatres of London and Dublin. Dublin : Cotter . . . 1761. 12° BPL

Measure for measure . . . now acted at the Theatre Royal in Covent Garden. Ln : Printed for J. Rivington & W. Strahan, etc., 1770. 8°, pp. 84

Measure for measure. As performed at the Theatre Royal, Covent Garden. Revised by Mr. Younger, prompter of that theatre. An introduction and notes, critical and illustrative, are added by the authors of the 'Dramatic censor' [F. Gentleman]. Ln : John Bell ; York : C. Etherington, 1773. 8°, pp. 72, & front. of 'Mrs. Yates as Isabella,' E. Edwards, *del.* ; J. Basire, *sc.*
An off-print from Bell's edition of Sh—'s Works for playgoers

Measure for measure . . . edited by L. Theobald. Edin. & Ln : John Bell . . . 1778. 12° BPL

Sh— Measure for measure . . .

Measure for measure. A comedy. As it is acted at the Theatres Royal in Drury Lane and Covent Garden . . . Ln : Printed for J. Harrison, 18 Paternoster Row, and sold likewise by J. Wenman, Fleet St., and all other booksellers, 1779. 8°, pp. 20, and copperplate portrait of ' King as Lucio '   BM | BPL

Measure for measure . . . printed complete from the text of Sam. Johnson and Geo. Steevens and revised from the last editions. Passages omitted in representation are distinguished by inverted commas thus " . . . Ln : Printed for . . . John Bell . . . 1785. 12°, pp. 116, with engraved title, and frontispiece of Mrs. Siddons as Isabella

Measure for measure . . . As acted at Drury Lane . . . Revised by J. P. Kemble. Ln : . . . 1789. 8°

Measure for measure . . . as acted at Drury Lane . . . Revised by J. P. Kemble. Ln : . . . 1796. 8°

Measure for measure . . . Manchester : R. & W. Dean . . . 1800. 12°, pp. 78, and engraved frontispiece ; engraved title by T. Bewick   BPL

Measure for measure . . . revised by J. P. Kemble, and now first published as it is acted at the Theatre Royal in Covent Garden. Ln : J. Ridgway, 1803. 8°, pp. 68   BUS

Measure for measure . . . as altered by J. P. Kemble, and acted by their majesties servants at the Theatre Royal, Drury Lane. Ln : C. Lowndes [1803]. 8°, pp. 62   BM | BPL

Measure for measure, by Will. Sh—. Printed complete from the text of Sam Johnson and Geo. Steevens. Ln : . . . 1806. 16°   W

Measure for measure . . . with remarks by Mrs. Inchbald . . . Ln : Longman . . . [c. 1808]. 12°, pp. 76. With frontispiece   BPL | BUS

Measure for measure . . . with remarks by Mrs. Inchbald. Ln : Longman [c. 1811]. 12°, pp. 76. With plate   BUS

Measure for measure . . . Revised by J. P. Kemble and now published as it is performed at the Theatres Royal. Ln : J. Miller, 1815. 8°, pp. 72   BM | BPL | SML | W

Measure for measure . . . with remarks by Mrs. Inchbald. Ln : Longman . . . [c. 1816]. 12°, pp. 76, and plate   BUS

Measure for measure . . . correctly given, from the text of Johnson and Steevens. With remarks. Ln : T. Hughes [c. 1820]. 16°, pp. 92   BM | BPL

Sh— Measure for measure . . .

Measure for measure . . . with prefatory remarks [signed P. P——], marked with the stage business and stage directions, as it is performed at the Theatres Royal, by W. Oxberry. Ln : Simpkin, 1822. 8°, pp. xii.-70   BM

Measure for measure . . . Ln : D. S. Maurice . . . [c. 1822]. 12°

Measure for measure . . . ' Dolby's British theatre,' [edited] by W. Oxberry. Ln : . . . [1823]. 12°   BPL

Measure for measure . . . printed from the acting copy. With remarks, biographical and critical, by D. G—— [George Daniel]. To which are added . . . the costume, cast . . . exits and entrances, relative positions . . . and stage business, as now performed at the Theatres Royal. With engraving by R. Cruikshank. Ln : J. Cumberland [c. 1830]. 12°, pp. 62   BM | BPL | BUS

Measure for measure . . . ' Pocket Sh—.' Ln : Mansell . . . [c. 1830]. 32°

Measure for measure . . . Nurenberg ; New York . . . 1841. 12°

Measure for measure . . . ' Cumberland's theatre.' Ln : Lacy . . . [c. 1870]. 12°

[Measure for measure] ' Take, oh ! take those lips away.' Song, with music by E. N. Grazia. Ln : . . . [c. 1870]. F°   BPL

Measure for measure . . . Edited by John Hunter for scholastic study. Ln : Longmans . . . 1873. Cr. 8°   BPL

Measure for measure . . . Acting edition. Ln : . . . [c. 1874]. 12°   SML
W. Creswick's prompt copy is at Stratford.

[Measure for measure] The law against lovers [In D'Avenant's Dramatic Works, vol. 5]. Edinburgh . . . 1874. 8°   BPL | BUS

Measure for measure . . . edited by Charles E. Flower. ' Memorial theatre edition.' Stratford-on-Avon : G. Boyden ; Ln : French [1882]. Cr. 8°, pp. viii.-88, including printed wrappers   BPL | SML

Measure for measure . . . edited with notes by W. J. Rolfe. New York : Harper . . . 1882. Cr. 8°   BPL | BUS

Measure for measure . . . ' Standard plays.' Ln : John Dicks . . . [1883]. Cr. 8°   BM

Measure for measure . . . with the ' Historie of Promos and Cassandra ' [by G. Whetstone, and an introduction by H. Morley]. ' National library.' Ln : Cassell . . . 1889. 16°, pp. 192   BM

Measure for measure . . . French's acting edition. Ln : . . . [c. 1890]. 12°   BPL

Measure for measure . . . edited by H.
Morley. 'National library.' Ln: Cassell, 1891. 16°, pp. 192

Measure for measure . . . edited by I. Gollancz. 'Temple edition.' Ln: Dent . . .
1894. 16°

Measure for measure. 'Pocket Falstaff
edition.' Ln: Bliss, Sands, 1898. 16°,
pp. 110

Measure for measure . . . with preface,
glossary, and notes by I. Gollancz.
'Temple edition.' Ln: Dent & Co., 1899.
12°, pp. x.-144

Measure for measure . . . edited with introducton and notes by C. H. Herford.
'Eversley edition.' Ln: Macmillan,
1900. 12°   BPL

Measure for measure . . . with introduction
and notes by John Dennis. Illust. by B.
Shaw. 'Chiswick edition.' Ln: Bell,
1901. 12°

Measure for measure . . . with introductory
notes by W. J. Craig. Ln: Methuen . . .
1903. 32°

Measure for measure, edited with notes by
H. N. Hudson. 'Windsor edition.'
Edinburgh: Jack . . . 1903. Cr. 8°
                                    BM | BLO | CTC

Measure for measure . . . 'Ellen Terry edition.' Glasgow: Bryce . . . 1904. 32°

Measure for measure . . . with introduction
by G. Brandes. 'Favourite classics.'
Ln: Heinemann, 1904. 12° BM | BLO | CTC

Measure for measure. 'Waistcoat pocket
edition.' Ln: Treherne . . . 1905. 32°

Measure for measure . . . edited by H.
Morley. 'National library.' Ln: Cassell
. . . 1905. 16°, pp. 192   BPL

Measure for measure . . . edited by H. C.
Hart. 'Arden edition.' Ln: Methuen
. . . 1905. 8°, pp. 184   BM | BLO | CTC

Measure for measure . . . 'Red letter edition.' Ln: Blackie . . . 1906. 12°

Measure for measure . . . 'Renaissance edition.' New York: Harrap . . . 1907.
Fcp. 4°   BPL

'Measure for measure' references—

*Of this comedy two differing editions
exist, each dated 1600. The first was
printed by I. R—— [James Roberts] on
behalf of Thomas Heyes, and the second,
said to be 'printed by James Roberts, 1600,'
was really prepared and issued in 1619.*

*The play was originally registered at
Stationers' Hall, 22nd July, 1598, but
apparently not proceeded with. It was
freshly entered 28th Oct., 1600, when Heyes
published it.*

The two entries read as follow :—

*'22nd Jul. 1598 . . . James Roberts.
Entred for his copie vnder the handes of
bothe the wardens, a booke of the "Mar-
chaunt of Venyce, or otherwise called the
Jewe of Venyce." Prouided that yt bee not
prynted by the said James Robertes or anye
other whatsoeuer without lycence first had
from the Right honorable the lord Chamberlen . . . VId.'*

*'28 Oct. 1600. Thomas Haies. Entred
for his copie under the handes of the wardens and by consent of master Roberts, a
booke called the booke of the "Merchant of
Venyce" . . . VId.'*

[Merchant of Venice] The most excellent
Historie of the Merchant of Venice. With
the extreame crueltie of Shylocke the
Iewe towards the sayd Merchant, in cutting a iust pound of his flesh : and the
obtayning of Portia by the choyse of
three chests. As it hath beene diuers
times acted by the Lord Chamberlaine
his Seruants. Written by William Shakespeare. [*Small ornament.*] At London :
Printed by I. R—— [James Roberts] for
Thomas Heyes, and are to be sold in
Paules Church-yard, at the signe of the
Greene Dragon, 1600. Fcp. 4°, thirty-
eight unpaged leaves, sig. A¹ to K² in
fours
BM | BLO | BUS | CTC | DEVON | HUTH | NY | W
Thomas Heyes was the father-in-law of the printer.
In May, 1907, a copy realised £510. Reprinted by
Halliwell in 1870, and by Furnivall in 1887.

[Merchant of Venice] The excellent History
. . . ['*Heb Ddiev*' block. Ln :] Printed by
J. Roberts, 1600
This date has been shown to be fictitious. It should be
1619 (*q.v.*) For a full account see A. W. Pollard's
'Sh— folios and quartos.'

[Merchant of Venice] The excellent History
of the Merchant of Venice. With the
extreme cruelty of Shylocke the Iew
towards the saide Merchant, in cutting a
iust pound of his flesh. And the obtaining of Portia, by the choyse of three
Caskets. Written by W. Shakespeare.

Sh— Merchant of Venice . . .

['*Heb Ddiev*' block. Ln :] Printed by J. Roberts [otherwise Isaac Jaggard], 1600 [or rather 1619]. Fcp. 4°, forty unpaged leaves, sig. A¹ to K⁴ in fours

BM | BLO | BUS | CTC | DEVON | HUTH | NY | SBL | W

The running headlines read :—'The comical history of the Merchant of Venice.'
Reprinted by Steevens in 1766, by Halliwell in 1870, and by Furnivall in 1881.
A copy, measuring 7 by 5¼ in., sold in May, 1906, for £460. Earl Howe's copy, 7⅛ by 5¼ in., half blue morocco, was secured in Dec., 1907, by an American collector.

[Merchant of Venice] The most excellent Historie of the Merchant of Venice. With the extreame crueltie of Shylocke the Iewe towards the said Merchant in cutting a just pound of his flesh : and the obtaining of Portia by the choice of three Chests. As it hath beene divers times acted by the Lord Chamberlaine his Servants. Written by William Shakespeare. London : Printed by M. P——— [Marmduke Parsons ?] for Laurence Hayes and are to be sold at his Shop on Fleetbridge, 1637. Fcp. 4°, on thirty-six unpaged leaves, sig. A¹ to I⁴ in fours

BM | BLO | BUS | CTC | NY | SBL | W

In May, 1907, a copy sold for £40.

[Merchant of Venice] The most excellent Historie of the Merchant of Venice : With the extreame cruelty of Shylocke the Jew towards the said Merchant, in cutting a just pound of his flesh : and the obtaining of Portia by the choyce of three Chests. As it hath been diverse times acted by the Lord Chamberlaine his Servants. Written by William Shakespeare. [*Emblem of a crown.*] Ln : Printed for William Leake and are to be solde at his shop at the signe of the Crown in Fleetstreet, between the two Temple Gates, 1652. Fcp. 4°, sig. A¹ to I⁴, on thirty-six unpaged leaves, including title   BM | CTC | NY | SML

A reprint or remainder of the 1637 edition, save a new first leaf (bearing a fresh title-page, with personæ and stationer's advt. on the verso).
In Dec., 1906, a cropped copy realised £72. It measured 7¼ by 4⅝ in.

[Merchant . . .] The Jew of Venice. A comedy. As it is acted at the theatre in Little-Lincoln's-Inn-Fields by His Majesty's Servants [Adapted and altered from Sh—'s ' Merchant of Venice ' by George Granville, Baron Lansdowne]. Ln : Printed for Bernard Lintott at the Post-House in the Middle Temple Gate, Fleet St., 1701. Fcp. 4°, pp. 46

BM | BPL | BUS | NY | SML | W

Sh— Merchant of Venice . . .

Nearly the whole of act 2 and parts of others omitted. The character of Shylock is essentially unchanged. Assertions to the effect that he is here made a comic character seem to have arisen from a misunderstanding of Rowe's remark by D. E. Baker in ' Biographia Britannica.'
' Peleus and Thetis ; A masque ' is inserted between acts 2 and 3.
The profits of the play were given to Dryden's family.

[Merchant . . .] The Jew of Venice. A comedy. Written originally by Sh—. Now altered and very much improved. By the Hon. [G.] Granville [Lord Lansdowne]. Printed for T. Johnson, bookseller at the Hague, 1711. 8°, pp. 68

BPL | W

[Merchant . . .] The Jew of Venice : A comedy. As it is acted at the theatre in Little Lincoln's Inn Fields by his majesty's servants [Adapted by G. Granville Baron Lansdowne]. Ln : Printed for Benj. Tooke and Bern. Lintott, 1713. 8°   SML | W

Forms the final part, pp. 171-240, of ' Three plays . . . by Lord Lansdowne,' the other two being the 'She gallants' (afterwards re-issued under the title of ' Once a lover always a lover ') and ' Heroick love.'

Merchant of Venice . . . Ln : Printed for and sold by the booksellers . . . [c. 1720]. 12°

BPL

[Merchant . . .] The Jew of Venice. A comedy. Written originally by Mr. W. Sh—. Now altered and very much improved by the Hon. M. Granville. The Hague : T. Johnson . . . 1721. 12°

SML

[Merchant . . .] The Jew of Venice. A comedy . . . [adapted and altered . . . by Geo. Granville, Lord Lansdowne]. Ln : B. Lintot . . . 1732. 12°, pp. 165-226 [excerpt]   BM | BPL | BUS | SML

[Merchant . . .] The Jew of Venice, by G. Granville, Lord Lansdowne [In ' Works . . . vol. 2, pp. 129-221']. 1732. Fcp. 4°   BPL

Merchant of Venice . . . Ln : Printed for J. Tonson and the rest of the proprietors, and sold by the booksellers of London and Westminster, 1734. 12°, pp. 72, and frontispiece by P. Fourdrinier

Merchant of Venice, by Sh—. Ln : R. Walker, 1735. 12°. With frontispiece

W

[Merchant . . .] ' The Jew of Venice : A comedy,' and ' Epilogue to the Jew of Venice ' [In ' Genuine works in verse and prose of George Granville, Lord Lansdowne, vol. i., p. 137,' etc.] Ln : . . . 1736. 3 vols. 12°   W

[Merchant . . .] Songs and duetts in the ' Blind beggar of Bethnal Green ' . . . at Drury Lane. With the favourite songs

Sh— Merchant of Venice . . .

sung by Mr. Lowe in the "Merchant of Venice' at the same Theatre. Composed by Tho. Aug. Arne. Ln : . . . [c. 1740]. F° BPL

Merchant of Venice . . . Ln : J. & P. Knapton, 1750. 8° BPL

Merchant of Venice . . . Ln : J. & P. Knapton . . . 1755. 12° SML

Merchant of Venice . . . Ln : Printed for J. & R. Tonson, 1764. 12° BPL

Merchant of Venice, 1600 [In ' Twenty of the plays of Sh— reprinted by G. Steevens, vol. 1']. Ln : . . . 1766. 8° BPL

Merchant of Venice . . . Edinburgh : Printed by and for Martin & Wotherspoon, 1768. Cr. 8° BPL

Merchant of Venice . . . as performed at the Theatre-Royal, Drury Lane. Regulated from the prompt book by Mr. Hopkins, prompter. An introduction and notes are added by the authors of the ' Dramatic censor ' [F. Gentleman]. Ln : J. Bell . . . 1773. 8°, pp. 78, & front. W
The Warwick copy is annotated with manuscript stage directions in an old hand.

Merchant of Venice. A comedy . . . As it is acted at the Theatres Royal in Drury Lane and Covent Garden . . . Printed for J. Wenman, 144 Fleet St., and sold by all other booksellers in town and country, 1777. 8°, pp. 20, and copperplate portrait of ' Macklin as Shylock '
BM | BPL | BUS | SML | W

Merchant of Venice . . . As it is acted at the Theatres-Royal in Drury-Lane and Covent Garden. Ln : W. Oxlade . . . 1777. 12° BPL

Merchant of Venice : A comedy. Written by Wm. Sh—. Marked with the variations in the manager's book, at the Theatre-Royal in Drury-Lane. Ln : C. Bathurst, W. Strahan, J. F. and C. Rivington, L. Davis, T. & W. Lowndes, R. Horsfield, W. Owen & Son, T. Caslon, S. Crowder, B. White, T. Longman, B. Law, C. Dilly, T. Cadell, G. Keith, T. Bowles, J. Robson, G. Robinson, T. Payne & Son, R. Baldwin, H. L. Gardner, J. Nichols, J. Bew, W. Cater, W. Stuart, S. A. Cumberlege, J. Fielding, T. Evans, S. Hayes, E. Newbery, 1783. 12°, pp. 72
With list of plays at end, 4 pp. BPL | W

Merchant of Venice . . . printed complete from the text of Sam. Johnson and Geo. Steevens and revised from the last editions . . . Ln : Printed for . . . John Bell . . 1785. 12°, pp. 120. With engraved title and frontispiece of ' Macklin as Shylock '

Sh— Merchant of Venice . . .

Merchant of Venice. A comedy . . . Taken from the manager's book at the Theatre-Royal, Covent Garden. Ln : Rachel Randall . . . 1787. 12° BPL | CPL | W

Merchant of Venice . . . As it is performed at the Theatres Royal . . . Ln : M. Lister . . . 1788. 12°, pp. 32, and plate
BPL | BUS

Merchant of Venice . . . A play in three acts. Altered from Sh— [by James Plumptre of Clare Hall, Cambridge], 1791. Fcp. 4°. Manuscript on 79 folios
The alterations chiefly consist of omissions. BUS

Merchant of Venice . . . as it is performed at Drury Lane and Covent Garden. Ln : Barker . . . 1794. 12°

Merchant of Venice . . . Revised by J. P. Kemble, as performed at Drury Lane Theatre. Ln : . . . 1795. 8°

Merchant of Venice . . . Revised by J. P. Kemble . . . Ln : . . . 1797. 8°

[Merchant of Venice] The Northern lord : A ballad [founded on the ' Merchant of Venice ']. Coventry . . . [c. 1800]. Fcp. 4°. With woodcuts

Merchant of Venice . . . Manchester : R. & W. Dean . . . 1800. 12° BPL

[Merchant . . .] ' How sweet the moonlight sleeps.' Arranged [with music] by S. Webbe . . . 1801. F° BPL

Merchant of Venice . . . As performed at the Theatre Royal. Regulated from the prompt book. With introduction and notes, critical and illustrative. Ln : Barker & Son . . . 1802. 12°. With portrait of Macklin SML

Merchant of Venice. A comedy, altered from Sh— [by Richard Valpy], as it was acted at Reading School, 1802, for the benefit of the literary fund. Reading : Smart & Cowslade, 1802. 8°, pp. viii.-82-iv. BM | BPL | BUS | SML | W
Several scenes omitted, and changes are made in act 5.

Merchant of Venice . . . with the notes and illustrations of various commentators and remarks by the editor [Ambrose Eccles]. Dublin : Jones . . . 1805. 8°, pp. iv.-328 BM | BPL | SML | W

Merchant of Venice . . . Manchester : R. & W. Dean . . . 1806. 12°

Merchant of Venice . . . with remarks by Mrs. Inchbald. Ln : Longman . . . [c. 1808]. 12°, pp. 72. With frontispiece
BPL | BUS

Merchant of Venice . . . as performed at Covent Garden. Revised by J. P. Kemble. Ln : For the theatre . . . 1810. 8° SML
W. Creswick's prompt copy is at Stratford.

Sh— Merchant of Venice . . .

Merchant of Venice, by Will. Sh—. Printed complete from the text of Sam. Johnson and Geo. Steevens. Ln : . . . 1811. 16° w

Merchant of Venice [In R. Deverell's Discoveries in hieroglyphics and other antiquities]. Ln : . . . 1813. 8° BUS
With notes explaining the play 'by reference to appearances in the moon.'

Merchant of Venice : A comedy . . . Edinburgh : Oliver & Boyd [c. 1813]. 12° ; issued in blue wrappers at 6d.

Merchant of Venice. Revised by J. P. Kemble, and now published as it is performed at the Theatres Royal. Ln : J. Miller, 1814. 8°, pp. 70 BM | BPL | W

Merchant of Venice. Put in a light now entirely new . . . [In ' Deverell, Hieroglyphics ']. Ln : Allman, 1816. 8°
BM | BPL

Merchant of Venice . . . with prefatory remarks [signed P. P——] . . . Marked with the stage business, and stage directions, as it is performed at the Theatres Royal, by W. Oxberry. Ln : Simpkin . . . 1820. Cr. 8°, pp. ii.-66 BM | SML

Merchant of Venice . . . from the text of Johnson and Steevens. With remarks. Ln : Hughes . . . [c. 1822]. 12° BPL

Merchant of Venice . . . ' Penny acting edition.' Ln : G. H. Davidson, Peter's Hill, 1823. 12°, pp. 62 SML
A prompt copy, with MS. variations by F. Haywell the actor, is at Stratford.

Merchant of Venice . . . with remarks by W. Oxberry. Ln : . . . 1823. 12°. With portrait

Merchant of Venice . . . with remarks by D. G—— [Geo. Daniel]. Ln : John Cumberland . . . 1824. 18°. Pub. at 6d.

[Merchant . . .] Senarii Græci, præmio Porsoniano . . . dignati . . . auctore B. H. Kennedy. Cambridge . . . 1824. 8° BM
A translation from the ' Merchant of Venice.' In English and Greek.

[Merchant . . .] Costume of . . . ' The Merchant of Venice ' . . . With notices by J. R. Planché . . . The figures by G. Scharf. Ln : J. Miller . . . 1825. 8° BPL | W

Merchant of Venice . . . as performed at the Theatres Royal, Drury Lane and Covent Garden. With explanatory French notes. Paris . . . 1827. 18° BPL

Merchant of Venice . . . correctly given from the text of Johnson et [sic] Steevens. With remarks . . . selected from the most eminent commentators, and a German vocabulary . . . [Edited by L. Lyon]. Gottingen : Vandenhoeck und Ruprecht : 1830. 8°, pp. vi.-138 BM | BPL

Sh— Merchant of Venice . . .

Merchant of Venice . . . printed from the acting copy, with remarks . . . by D. G—— [Geo. Daniel]. To which are added a . . . cast of the characters . . . and the whole of the stage business, as performed at the Theatres Royal. Ln : G. H. Davidson [c. 1830]. 12°, pp. 62. Portrait of Mrs. West as ' Portia ' BM | BPL
Issued in engraved wrappers at 6d.

Merchant of Venice, as performed at the Theatres Royal. Ln : Music Publishing Co. [c. 1830]. 12° BPL

Merchant of Venice . . . Music arranged by J. Harroway. Hugo Vamp's comic dramatic Shakesperean scenas. Ln : Davidson [c. 1830]. F°, pp. 8 BUS

Merchant of Venice . . . ' Pocket Sh—.' Ln : Mansell [c. 1830]. 12°

Merchant of Venice . . . Ln : J. Cumberland, 1831. 12°

Merchant of Venice . . . with historical and grammatical notes in German by J. M. Pierre. Frankfort . . . 1831. 8° BPL

Merchant of Venice . . . Nuremberg . . . New York . . . 1835. 12°

Merchant of Venice . . . Der Kaufmann von Venedig, schauspiel in fünf akten. Mit untergelegtem kritischem commentare, einer einleitung und einem anhange, enthaltend : historische erläuterungen des stücks und eine biographie des Dichters in Englischer sprache. Braunschweig : G. C. E. Meyer, sen., 1836. 12°, pp. xl.-246 BM | SML
In English and German.

Merchant of Venice . . . ' Acting edition.' Ln : T. H. Lacy . . . [c. 1840]. 12° SML
W. Creswick's prompt copy is at Stratford.

[Merchant . . .] Le Marchand de Venise . . . nouvelle édition, précédée d'une notice critique et historique, et accompagnée de notes par O'Sullivan. Paris : L. Hachette, 1843. 12°, pp. xx.-116 BM | BPL
In English and French.

[Merchant . . .] Kaufman von Venedig. Englisch-Deutsche ausgabe, mit 27 scenen und vignetten in feinstem Holzstich. Die Deutsche uebertragung von Alexander Fischer. Pforzheim : Dennig Finck & Co., 1843. Fcp. 4°, pp. 86
BM | BUS
With English and German texts in parallel columns.

Merchant of Venice . . . with the stage business, cast, costumes, positions, etc. New York : S. French . . . [c. 1848]. 12°, pp. 64 BUS

Merchant of Venice . . . ' Modern standard drama.' New York : S. French [c. 1848]. 12°, pp. 64 BUS

Merchant of Venice . . . Ln : Webster . . . 1849. 12°

Merchant of Venice travestie. A burlesque, in one act, by the author of ' Macbeth travestie' [F. Talfourd]. Oxford : E. T. Spiers, 1849. 12°, pp. 34
BM | BPL | BUS | CPL

Merchant of Venice [In ' Dramatic entertainments at Windsor Castle, 1848-49,' pp. 1-58. Edited by Webster]. Ln : Mitchell . . . [c. 1850]. Fcp. 4° BPL | SML

[Merchant . . .] Shylock or the Merchant of Venice preserved . . . An entirely new reading of Sh— from an edition hitherto undiscovered by modern authorities. [Travesty.] By Francis Talfourd. Lacy's acting plays. Ln : T. H. Lacy . . . 1853. 12° BM | CPL

Merchant of Venice . . . erklärt von Ludwig Herrig. Berlin : T. C. F. Enslin, 1854. 8°, pp. iv.-112 BM | SML
English text, with German notes.

Merchant of Venice . . . Ln : T. H. Lacy, 1855. 12°

Merchant of Venice . . . 'Acting edition.' Ln : T. H. Lacy . . . 1856. 12°, pp. 64
BM | BPL

[Merchant . . .] Shylock or the Merchant of Venice preserved. An entirely new reading of Sh— from an edition hitherto undiscovered by modern authorities and which it is hoped may be received as the stray leaves of a Jerusalem hearty-joke. By Francis Talfourd. As performed in the London and American Theatres. To which are added . . . the costume, cast, entrances, exits, positions, and stage business. New York : S. French [c. 1857]. 12°, pp. 30 BUS

Merchant of Venice . . . arranged for representation at the Princess's Theatre, 12th June, 1858, with historical and explanatory notes by C. Kean. Second edition. Ln : J. Chapman [c. 1858]. 8°, pp. viii.-88 BPL | MPL | SML

Merchant of Venice . . . arranged . . . with notes by C. Kean. Fourth edition. Ln : . . . 1858. 8° CPL

Merchant of Venice . . . illustrated by Thomas . . . Ln : Low & Co., 1859. 8°
The first separate edition with the text illustrated.

[Merchant . . .] The most excellent Historie of the Merchant of Venice . . . Ln : Low, 1860. Fcp. 4°, pp. viii.-96. Illustrated by Birket Foster and others
BM | BPL | BUS | CPL | MPL | SML
The editor has omitted 'a few lines which might be thought objectionable.'

[Merchant . . .] Shylock or the Merchant of Venice preserved, by F. Talfourd. 'Acting edition.' Ln : T. H. Lacy [c. 1860]. 12° BPL | CPL

[Merchant . . .] Shylock or the Merchant of Venice preserved, by F. Talfourd. Third edition. 'Acting edition.' Ln : . . . Lacy . . . [c. 1860]. 12° BPL

[Merchant . . .] Shylock. A burlesque, as performed by Griffin and Christy's minstrels. Arranged by G. W. H. Griffin. New York . . . [c. 1860]. 12° BPL

Merchant of Venice . . . New York : D. Appleton & Co., 1860. Fcp. 4°, pp. viii.-96 BPL
Identical with Low's London edition of this year, except in imprint. The text is 'expurgated.'

Merchant of Venice . . . from the original text—a long way, by John Brougham. New York : French [c. 1860]. Cr. 8° BPL

Merchant of Venice . . . Glasgow : Cameron . . . 1860. 8°

Merchant of Venice . . . with . . . remarks and notes . . . adapted for scholastic study by J. Hunter. Ln : Longman . . . 1861. 12°, pp. xxii.-144 BUS

Merchant of Venice . . . with explanatory notes founded on the best commentators. Edited by R. H. Westley. Leipzig : G. Græbner, 1861. 8°, pp. 82
BM | BPL | BUS | SML

Merchant of Venice . . . The text from the folio of 1623 ; with notices of the known editions previously issued. Ln : L. Booth, 1862. Fcp. 4°, pp. vi.-22 ; interleaved with blank writing paper BUS | W

Merchant of Venice . . . abbreviated and adapted for social reading in parts by the Swanswick Sh— circle and edited by John Earle. Bath : Peach ; Ln : Longman, 1862. Cr. 8°, pp. xvi.-48 BPL | BUS | SML

[Merchant . . .] The costumes as represented at the Princess's Theatre. Ln : . . . [c. 1863]. 4°. Four plates

Merchant of Venice . . . adapted for social reading in parts by the Swanswick Sh— circle, and edited by J. Earle. Ln : Longman, 1864. Fcp. 4°, pp. xiv.-48 BM

Merchant of Venice, 1600. Facsimiled from the edition printed by J. Roberts by E. W. Ashbee. Edited by J. O. Halliwell. Ln : For private circulation, 1865. Fcp. 4° BPL
Fifty copies produced, nineteen of which the editor destroyed.

[Merchant . . . travesty] The peddler of very-nice : A burlesque . . . . [By George M. Baker]. Boston [U.S.] : Baker & Co. . . . [1866]. 12°, pp. ii.-202-214 [excerpt]
BUS

Sh— Merchant of Venice . . .

Merchant of Venice, as produced at the Winter Garden Theatre of New York, Jan., 1867, by Edwin Booth. A new adaptation to the stage. With notes, original and selected, and introductory articles by Hy. L. Hinton. New York: C. A. Alvord, 1867. 8°, pp. 46. Illustrated   BM | BPL | BUS

Merchant of Venice . . . edited by W. G. Clark. Ln: Macmillan & Co. . . . 1868. 12°

Merchant of Venice . . . edited by W. G. Clark & W. A. Wright. Oxford: Clarendon Press, 1868. Cr. 8°, pp. xxiv.-130
    BPL | BUS | CPL | SML

Merchant of Venice . . . As produced by E. Booth, adapted from the text of the Cambridge editors. With remarks by H. L. Hinton. 'Booth's acting plays.' New York: Hurd & Houghton [1868]. 12°, pp. 88   BPL | BUS

Merchant of Venice . . . Leipzig: B. Tauchnitz, 1868. 16°

Merchant of Venice . . . für den schulgebrauch bearbeitet von Dr. R. Müller. Goslar: O. Schonpflug . . . 1868. 16°, pp. viii.-84   BM
In English and German.

Merchant of Venice . . . With remarks . . . and notes . . . by John Hunter. Ln: Longman . . . 1869. Cr. 8°, pp. xxiv.-144
    BUS | CPL

Merchant of Venice . . . edited by W. G. Clark & W. A. Wright. Oxford: Clarendon Press, 1869. Cr. 8°

Merchant of Venice . . . As produced by E. Booth. New York: French . . . [c. 1870]. 8°   SML

Merchant of Venice . . . 'Cumberland's theatre.' Ln: Lacy . . . [c. 1870]. 12°
    SML
The prompt copy from W. Creswick's library is at Stratford.

Merchant of Venice . . . [text in English and notes in German by L. Herrig]. Salzwedel [Saxony]: Klingenstein, 1870. 8°

[Merchant . . .] The most excellent Historie of the Merchant of Venice . . . Printed by I. R. for Thomas Heyes, 1600; facsimiled . . . by E. W. Ashbee; edited by J. O. Halliwell, 1870. Fcp. 4°   BPL | W
Fifty copies printed for private circulation, nineteen of which the editor destroyed.

[Merchant . . . travesty] The peddler of very-nice: A burlesque . . . By G M. Baker. Boston [U.S.]: Baker & Co., 1871. 12° [excerpt]   BUS

Sh— Merchant of Venice . . .

Merchant of Venice . . . arranged for representation at the Princess's Theatre, Manchester, by Charles Calvert. With essay by Dr. Ulrici. Manchester: Ireland & Co. . . . 1871. 12°   BPL | CPL | SML

Merchant of Venice . . . edited with notes by W. J. Rolfe. New York: Harper brothers, 1871. 12°, pp. 168, and portraits
Some lines are omitted.   BPL | BUS

Merchant of Venice . . . purified and arranged for the use of schools by A. Zimmermann. Berlin: O. Struwe . . . 1873. 8°, pp. 70   BM

Merchant of Venice . . . With introductory remarks and . . . notes, by D. Morris. Glasgow: W. Collins . . . 1874. 8°, pp. 106   BM | BPL | BUS | SML
With some passages omitted.

Merchant of Venice . . . re-arranged by and produced at the Crystal Palace under the direction of C. Wyndham. Ln: . . . 1874. 8°   BPL

Merchant of Venice . . . edited by W. G. Clark & W. A. Wright. Oxford: Clarendon Press, 1874. Cr. 8°, pp. xxiv.-130
    BPL

Merchant of Venice . . . 'Standard plays.' Ln: J. Dicks [c. 1875]. 12°

[Merchant . . .] The trial, from Sh—'s 'Merchant of Venice.' With life of the author, explanatory notes, and examination questions by Moffatt & Paige. Ln: . . . 1875. 12°, pp. 22   BM

Merchant of Venice . . . edited by W. G. Clark & W. A. Wright. Oxford: Clarendon Press, 1876. Cr. 8°, pp. xxiv.-130

Merchant of Venice . . . für den schulgebrauch erklärt von Dr. L. Riechelmann. Leipzig: B. G. Teubner, 1876. 8°, pp. xx.-118   BM | BPL | BUS
English text, with German notes.

Merchant of Venice . . . with notes, etc. by D. Morris. Glasgow: W. Collins . . . 1877. 12°   BPL

Merchant of Venice . . . with notes, critical, etc., by J. D. Morell. Ln: Stewart & Co. . . . 1878. 12°

Merchant of Venice . . . [Text in English and notes in German. Edited by L. Herrig]. Salzwedel [Saxony]: Klingenstein, 1878. 8°   SML

Merchant of Venice . . . Acting edition. Ln: French . . . [1878]. 12°   SML

Merchant of Venice . . . edited by D. Morris. Glasgow: W. Collins . . . 1878. 12°

Merchant of Venice . . . with notes . . . by J. Hunter. Ln: Longman . . . [c. 1878]. Cr. 8°   BPL

Sh— Merchant of Venice . . .

Merchant of Venice . . . with introduction and notes by H. N. Hudson. Boston [U.S.]: Ginn & Heath . . . 1878. 12°, pp. 97-172 [excerpt]   BUS

Merchant of Venice . . . selections by R. S. Davies. Hull: Brown . . . 1879. 12°

Merchant of Venice . . . for use in schools. Edited by H. N. Hudson. Boston [U.S.]: Ginn & Co. . . . 1879. 12°

Merchant of Venice, with notes, examinatio papers, an ' plan of preparation. Edited by J. M. D. Meiklejohn. Ln. & Edin.: W. & R. Chambers, 1879. 8°, pp. 122   BM | BPL | SML

[Merchant . . .] A selection from Sh—'s ' Merchant of Venice.' ' Lines from the poets.' Ln: National society . . . 1879. 16°, pp. 44   BM | BPL

Merchant of Venice [Selections from acts I., III., IV. . . .] With prefatory and explanatory notes. Ln: Blackie . . . 1879. 16°, pp. 32   BM | BPL

Merchant of Venice . . . as presented at the Lyceum Theatre under the management of Henry Irving. Ln: Chiswick Press . . . 1880. 8°, pp. 74   BM | BPL

Merchant of Venice . . . Med anmærkninger og indledning, udgivet af G. Wiesener [In English and Danish]. Christiania: J. W. Cappelens forlag, 1880. 8°, pp. 192
                          BM | BPL | SML
The first English piece of Sh— printed in Norway.

Merchant of Venice . . . with explanatory notes, paraphase, criticism, etc. by J. D. Morell. Ln: . . . [c. 1880]. 12°   BPL

Merchant of Venice . . . edited by W. G. Clark & W. A. Wright. Oxford: Clarendon Press, 1880. Cr. 8°, pp. xxiv.-130

Merchant of Venice . . . as presented at the Lyceum Theatre . . . by Henry Irving. Ln: Chiswick Press . . . 1881. 8°

Merchant of Venice . . . Selections . . . New York: Clark . . . 1881. 12°

Merchant of Venice . . . edited by W. G. Clark and W. A. Wright. Oxford: Clarendon Press, 1881. Cr. 8°, pp. xxiv.-130   BPL | MPL

Merchant of Venice: the first (and worst) quarto, 1600: A facsimile in photo-lithography by W. Griggs . . . With forewords by F. J. Furnivall. ' Sh— quarto facsimiles.' Ln: W. Griggs [1881]. Fcp. 4°, pp. xii.-78   BM | BPL | BUS
By the ' first' Dr. Furnivall meant the second issue of 1619, falsely dated 1600.

Merchant of Venice . . . with notes, examination papers, and plan of preparation by Brainerd Kellogg. New York . . . 1882. 12°   BUS

Sh— Merchant of Venice . . .

Merchant of Venice . . . edited by Charles E. Flower. ' Memorial theatre edition.' Stratford-on-Avon: Printed by G. Boyden; Ln: S. French [1883]. Cr. 8°, pp. viii.-82, incl. printed wrappers   BPL | SML

Merchant of Venice . . . for use in schools. Edited by H. N. Hudson. Boston [U.S.]: Ginn & Co. . . . 1883. 8°

Merchant of Venice . . . with . . . notes by T. Parry. Ln: Longmans, 1883. Cr. 8°, pp. xviii.-146   BM

[Merchant . . .] Selections from Sh—'s ' Merchant of Venice.' With . . . notes . . . by T. Parry. Ln: Longmans, 1883. Cr. 8°, pp. 48   BPL

Merchant of Venice . . . edited with notes by W. J. Rolfe. New York: Harper . . . 1883. 12°   BPL

Merchant of Venice . . . edited by W. G. Clark & W. A. Wright. Oxford: Clarendon Press, 1883. Cr. 8°, pp. xxiv.-130

Merchant of Venice. ' Standard plays.' Ln: John Dicks . . . [1883]. 12° BM | BPL

Merchant of Venice. As abridged by Charles Kemble. With notes for school use. Ln: Bell & Sons, 1884. Cr. 8°, pp. 50

Merchant of Venice . . . Selections . . . by T. Parry. Ln: Longman . . . 1884. 12°
                          SML

Merchant of Venice . . . Together with the prose narrative . . . from Lamb's Tales . . . Ln: Blackie . . . [1884]. Cr. 8°, pp. 104   BM | BPL

Merchant of Venice . . . edited by W. G. Clark & W. A. Wright. Oxford: Clarendon Press, 1884. Cr. 8°, pp. xxiv.-130 SML

[Merchant of Venice] The (old clothes) Merchant of Venice; or the young judge and old Jewry. A burlesque sketch [in verse, founded on Sh—'s ' Merchant of Venice '] for the drawing-room. 'Acting plays.' New York: De Witt . . . 1884. Cr. 8°, pp. 16   BM

Merchant of Venice . . . mit einleitung, anmerkungen und wörterbuch herausgegeben von Dr. H. Isaac [Two parts: In English and German]. Berlin: Friedberg & Mode, 1884. 8°   BM

Merchant of Venice . . . Abridged . . . with notes. Ln. & Edinburgh; W. & R. Chambers, 1884. 8°, pp. 32   BM

Merchant of Venice . . . with introduction, notes, examination papers, and appendix of prefixes and terminations, by T. Parry. Ln: Longmans & Co., 1884. 8°, pp. xiv.-146   SML

Merchant of Venice . . . for use in schools. Boston [U.S.]: Ginn & Co. . . . 1885. 12°
                          SML

Sh— Merchant of Venice . . .

Merchant of Venice . . . with introduction and notes by H. N. Hudson. Boston [U.S.]: Ginn & Co. . . . 1885. 12° SML

Merchant of Venice . . . edited by W. G. Clark & W. A. Wright. Oxford: Clarendon Press, 1886. Cr. 8°, pp. xxiv.-130

Merchant of Venice . . . with the 'Adventures of Giannetto,' from the 'Pecorone' of Ser Giovanni Fiorentino, and other illustrative pieces. Ed. by H. Morley. 'National library.' Ln: Cassell . . . 1886. 16°, pp. 192 BM | BUS | SML

Merchant of Venice . . . abbreviated for school use, with introduction, notes, and illustrations [by B. Jonson]. 'Whitehall series.' Ln: G. Gill . . . [1886]. Cr. 8°, pp. 112 BM | BPL

Merchant of Venice . . . The second (and better) quarto (printed for I. R. for Thomas Heyes), 1600. A facsimile in photo-lithography from the Duke of Devonshire's copy. With forewords by F. J. Furnivall. 'Sh— quarto facsimiles.' Ln: C. Prætorius, 1887. Fcp. 4°, pp. xiv.-76 BM | BPL | BUS
By the 'second' Dr. Furnivall meant the first quarto, which, until recently, was thought to have appeared after the falsely-dated one.

Merchant of Venice . . . printed in embossed type for the blind. Edited by G. W. Moon. Brighton . . . [1887]. 4° BPL
The editor himself was blind.

Merchant of Venice . . . edited by H. C. Beeching for schools. 'Falcon edition.' Ln: Rivington . . . 1887. 12° BPL

Merchant of Venice. With introduction, notes and appendix . . . by T. Parry. Ln: Longmans . . . 1887. Cr. 8°, pp. xviii.-146. Illustrated

Merchant of Venice . . . abbreviated for school use. Ln: Gill . . . 1887. Cr. 8°

Merchant of Venice . . . edited by W. G. Clark & W. A. Wright. Oxford: Clarendon Press, 1887. Cr. 8°, pp. xxiv.-130

Merchant of Venice . . . with notes, etc. Edited by J. M. D. Meiklejohn. Ln: Chambers . . . 1888. Cr. 8° BPL

Merchant of Venice . . . with introduction and notes by H. N. Hudson. Boston [U.S.] . . . 1888. 12° BPL

Merchant of Venice . . . Moffatt's handbooks for students . . . [c. 1888]. 12° BPL

Merchant of Venice . . . New variorum edition. Edited by H. H. Furness. Philadelphia: Lippincott . . . 1888. Roy. 8°, pp. 480 BM | BPL | BUS | SML

Merchant . . . edited by H. C. Beeching. 'Falcon edition.' Ln: Rivingtons . . . 1889. Cr. 8°, pp. xvi.-134

Sh— Merchant of Venice . . .

Merchant of Venice . . . edited by W. G. Clark & W. A. Wright. Oxford: Clarendon Press, 1889. Cr. 8°, pp. xxiv.-130

Merchant of Venice. With notes . . . Ln: Moffatt . . . 1890. Cr. 8°

Merchant of Venice . . . with notes by K. Deighton. Ln: Macmillan . . . 1890. Cr. 8°

Merchant of Venice . . . edited by W. G. Clark & W. A. Wright. Oxford: Clarendon Press, 1891. Cr. 8°, pp. xxiv.-130

Merchant of Venice . . . with notes . . . Ln: Moffatt . . . 1891. Cr. 8°

Merchant of Venice . . . with notes. 'Oxford and Cambridge Sh—.' Ln: Allman & son [1891]. Cr. 8°, pp. 128 BPL

Merchant of Venice . . . In the easy reporting style of phonography. 'National phonographic library.' Ln: Pitman & sons . . . 1892. 16°, pp. 64 BM | BPL

Merchant of Venice . . . annotated for school use by S. Thurber. 'Riverside literature series.' Boston [U.S. . . . . c. 1892]. 12° BPL

Merchant of Venice. With introduction and notes by G. H. Ely. 'Junior school Sh—.' Ln: Blackie . . . 1893. Cr. 8°, pp. 112 BM | BPL

Merchant of Venice . . . edited by T. D. Barnett. 'English classics.' Ln: Bell . . . 1893. Cr. 8°, pp. 142 BM | BPL

Merchant of Venice . . . 'Eclectic English classics.' New York . . . 1893 ? 12° BPL

Merchant of Venice. With notes . . . by J. M. D. Meiklejohn. Ln: Chambers . . . 1893. 8°, pp. ii.-122

Merchant of Venice . . . with introduction, notes, examination papers, and an appendix of prefixes and terminations by Thomas Parry. New edition. Ln: Longmans . . . 1894. Cr. 8°, pp. xviii.-146. Illustrated

[Merchant . . .] A burlesque extravaganza . . . entitled the merry 'Merchant of Venice,' by F. J. Fraser. Allahabad: Railway theatre [1895]. 8° BM

Merchant of Venice . . . 'Ariel edition.' Ln: Routledge . . . 1895. 16°

Merchant of Venice . . . with introduction and notes by K. Deighton. Ln: Macmillan . . . 1895. Cr. 8° BPL

Merchant of Venice . . . edited by I. Gollancz. 'Temple edition.' Ln: Dent . . . 1895. 16°

Merchant of Venice . . . edited by C. H. Gibson. Ln: Arnold . . . 1895. Cr. 8°

Merchant of Venice . . . edited by F. B. Gummere. New York: Longmans, 1896. 8° BUS

Sh— Merchant of Venice . . .

[Merchant . . .] Selections from the 'Merchant of Venice.' Ln : Blackie . . . [1896]. 16°, pp. 32   BM

Merchant of Venice, acts III. and IV. With introduction and notes . . . edited by C. A. Britter. Port Louis, Mauritius, 1897. 8°, pp. 52

Remarkable for place of publication.

Merchant of Venice . . . edited by H. L. Withers. 'Warwick Sh—.' Ln : Blackie . . . 1897. 12°, pp. xxxvi.-142   BPL

Merchant of Venice. With the 'Adventures of Giannetto' and other illustrative pieces. [Ed. by Hy. Morley.] 'National library.' Ln : Cassell . . . 1897. 16°, pp. 192

Merchant of Venice . . . edited by C. H. Gibson. Ln : E. Arnold . . . 1897. 12°   BPL

Merchant of Venice . . . edited with introduction, notes, glossary, and index by A. W. Verity. Cambridge : University Press, 1898. Cr. 8°, pp. xlviii.-212   BPL | BUS

Merchant of Venice. With introduction, notes, and glossary by R. B. Johnson. Edinburgh : Blackwood, 1898. Cr. 8°, pp. 144   BPL

Merchant of Venice . . . A comedy in five acts. As arranged for representation at Daly's theatre by Augustin Daly, and there produced for the first time on Sat., Nov. 19th, 1898. With a few prefatory words by William Winter. New York : Privately printed [by Douglas Taylor & Co.], 1898. Fo°, pp. 68, inlaid and extra-illustrated with portrait of Ada Rehan and portraits of other characters, and character scenes   SML

One of the twenty-five copies to which the impression was limited.

The Stratford copy was 'presented by Augustus Toedteberg in memory of Augustin Daly, who died in Paris, 7 June, 1899.'

Merchant of Venice. With the 'Adventures of Giannetto' . . . [Ed. by Henry Morley]. 'National library.' Ln : Cassell, 1898. 16°, pp. 192

Merchant of Venice . . . edited with introduction and notes . . . by T. Page. New edition. Ln : Moffatt . . . 1898. 12°, pp. 182   BPL

Merchant of Venice . . . 'Pocket Falstaff edition.' Ln : Bliss . . . 1898. 16°, pp. 100   BPL | SML

[Merchant . . .] Scenes from Sh— for use in schools. Selected and arranged by Mary A. Woods : Story of the caskets and rings from the 'Merchant of Venice.' Ln : Macmillan, 1898. 8°, pp. 78   BM | BPL

Sh— Merchant of Venice . . .

Merchant of Venice . . . with introduction, notes, and exam. papers by Brainerd Kellogg. New York . . . [1899]. 8°. With portrait and plates   BUS

Merchant of Venice . . . with introduction and notes by John Dennis. Illust. by B. Shaw. 'Chiswick edition.' Ln : Bell . . . 1899. 12°, pp. 126

Merchant of Venice . . . edited by J. Strong. 'School Sh—.' Ln : Black . . . 1899. 12°, pp. 128   BPL

Merchant of Venice . . . [edited by Hy. Morley]. 'National library.' Ln : Cassell . . . 1899. 16°, pp. 192

Merchant of Venice . . . with notes by J. Bidgood. 'Swan edition.' Ln : Longmans . . . 1900. Cr. 8°   BPL

Merchant of Venice . . . edited with introduction and notes by C. H. Herford. 'Eversley edition.' Ln : Macmillan . . . 1900. 12°   BPL

Merchant of Venice . . . 'Picture Sh—.' Ln : Blackie . . . 1901. Cr. 8°   BPL

Merchant of Venice . . . edited by A. W. Verity. Cambridge : Univ. Press, 1901. Cr. 8°, pp. xlviii.-212

Merchant of Venice . . . edited by W. J. Rolfe. New York . . . [1902]. Cr. 8°. Illustrated   BUS

Merchant of Venice . . . edited by W. J. Rolfe. New York . . . [1903]. 8°. With portrait and illustrations   BUS

Merchant of Venice . . . with introduction by G. Brandes. 'Favourite classics.' Ln : Heinemann, 1904. 16°

Merchant of Venice . . . edited by Hy. Morley. 'National library.' Ln : Cassell . . . 1904. 16°, pp. 192   BPL

Merchant of Venice . . . Retold by Alice S. Hoffman. Illust. by D. Curtis. Ln : Dent . . . 1904. 16°   BPL

Merchant of Venice . . . 'Ellen Terry edition.' Glasgow : Bryce . . . 1904. 32°

Merchant of Venice . . . 'Waistcoat pocket edition.' Ln : Treherne . . . 1904. 32°

Merchant of Venice . . . with introduction and notes by W. J. Craig. 'Little quartos.' Ln : Methuen . . . 1904. 16°

Merchant of Venice . . . with introduction and notes by J. Dennis. Illust. by B. Shaw. 'Chiswick edition.' Ln : Bell, 1904. 12°

Merchant of Veni e . . . edited by A. W. Verity. Cambridge : University Press, 1904. Cr. 8°, pp. xlviii.-212

Merchant of Venice . . . with introduction, notes, and illustrations. 'Whitehall series.' Ln : Gill . . . 1905. Cr. 8°, pp. 112

Sh— Merchant of Venice . . .

Merchant of Venice . . . edited by Charles Knox Pooler. 'Arden edition.' Ln: Methuen, 1905. 8°, pp. 232

Merchant of Venice . . . 'Masterpiece library of penny poets.' Ln: W. T. Stead [1906]. Cr. 8°   BPL

Merchant of Venice . . . 'Oxford and Cambridge edition.' Ln: Gill . . . 1906. Cr. 8°   BPL

Merchant of Venice . . . 'Blackfriars edition.' Ln: A. M. Holden . . . 1906. Cr. 8°   BPL

Merchant of Venice . . . edited by A. A. Brayley. 'Normal tutorial series.' Ln: Simpkin, 1906. Cr. 8°, pp. 166   BPL

Merchant of Venice . . . parsed and analysed by M. Bryant Robinson. 'Normal tutorial series.' Ln: Simpkin, 1907. Cr. 8°   BPL

Merchant of Venice . . . 'Texts without notes.' Ln: Chambers . . . 1907. Cr. 8°   BPL

Merchant of Venice . . . Complete paraphrase by Jean F. Terry. 'Normal tutorial series.' Ln: Simpkin . . . 1907. Cr. 8°

Merchant of Venice . . . with introductory notes and glossary by C. W. Crook. Ln: Ralph . . . 1907. Cr. 8°, pp. 202   BPL

Merchant of Venice . . . Text revised by A. Dyce. Ln: Sonnenschein . . . 1907. 8°   BPL

Merchant of Venice . . . edited by A. W. Verity. Cambridge: Univ. Press, 1907. Cr. 8°, pp. xlviii.-218

Merchant . . . 'Renaissance edition.' New York & Ln: G. G. Harrap . . . 1907. Fcp. 4°   BPL

Merchant of Venice . . . edited by W. H. Hudson. Ln: Harrap . . . 1908. Cr. 8°

Merchant of Venice . . . Carefully adapted for school use. Ln: Pitman . . . 1908. Cr. 8°, pp. 64. Illustrated

Merchant of Venice . . . In large type, slightly abridged, for reading aloud. With a musical appendix. Ln: Rees . . . 1908. Cr. 8°, pp. 72

Merchant of Venice . . . edited by E. K. Chambers. Ln: Blackie . . . 1908. Cr. 8°   BPL

Merchant of Venice . . . edited with notes by S. E. Goggin. Ln: Clive [1908]. Cr. 8°, pp. xlviii.-130   BPL

Merchant of Venice . . . 'Sh— for home-reading,' edited by K. Harvey. Ln: Routledge, 1909. Cr. 8°   BPL

Merchant of Venice . . . edited by F. J. Furnivall. 'Old spelling edition.' Ln: Chatto . . . 1909. 8°   BM | BLO | CTC

Sh— Merchant of Venice . . .

Merchant of Venice . . . illustrated by Sir James D. Linton. Ln: Hodder, 1909. Roy. 8°, pp. 178   BM | BLO | CTC
A few were issued on large paper.

Merchant of Venice . . . 'Langham booklets.' Ln: Siegle & Hill, 1910. 32°   BM | BLO | CTC

'Merchant of Venice' references—

See Archer	See Kiralfy
,, Ballad . . .	,, Le Loyer
,, Barnett (T.D.)	,, Leti
,, Boole	,, Levi
,, Busche	,, Lobb
,, Carstens	,, Marlow
,, Clarke	,, Martin
,, Conway	,, Marvell
,, Cooke	,, Memorable . . .
,, Cross	,, Meres
,, Curtis	,, Morris
,, Daniel	,, Northern . . .
,, Deverell	,, Novel
,, Dramatic Entertainments	,, Pearson
	,, Pennyworth
,, Durfey	,, Persian . . .
,, Eccles	,, Planché
,, Elimandus	,, Poel
,, Farren	,, Quality . . .
,, Ferne	,, Radford
,, Fletcher (Geo.)	,, Richardson
,, Fletcher (Jos.)	,, Ruggles
,, Foard	,, Russell
,, Franklin	,, S—— (J.)
,, Frederick	,, Salaman
,, Gernutus	,, Sh— Works: Ext.
,, Giovanni	1799, 1880
,, Gold . . .	,, Sh—] Sh—
,, Gracian	,, Sh—] Sh—'slibrary
,, Hall (H. T.)	,, Sh—] Shakespeare-
,, Halpin	ana
,, Henri IV.	,, Shylock
,, History of	,, Sixties
Portia	,, Skeffington
,, Hole	,, Smith (L. T.)
,, How	,, Snider
,, Hugo	,, Spedding
,, Hunter	,, Triumph . . .
,, Hutchinson	,, Underdown
,, Ihne	,, Valesco
,, Irving	,, Versatile . . .
,, J—— (S.)	,, Walkington
,, Johnson and	,, Wood (S.)
Steevens	

MERRY DEVIL OF EDMONTON.

This comedy in prose and verse was performed by Shakespeare's company in 1597. It was first entered on the Stationers' Registers, thus :—'22nd Oct., 1607. Arthur

Sh— Merry devil of Edmonton . . .

Iohnson. Entred for his copie vnder thandes of Sir George Buck knight and the Wardens a plaie called the Merry devill of Edmonton . . . VId.' A prose history by Thomas Brewer under the same title was entered 5th April, 1608, and has been confused by J. O. Halliwell and others with the play itself, which was first printed in that year.

First ascribed to Shakespeare by F. Kirkman the bookseller; the authorship has since been credited to Antony Brewer, Michael Drayton, Thomas Heywood, and George Wilkins, among others. Tieck believed Sh— wrote it, while Hazlitt thought the more likely writer to be Thomas Heywood.

Merry Devill of Edmonton.   As it hath beene sundry times acted by his Maiesties Seruants at the Globe on the Banckeside.   London : Printed by Henry Ballard for Arthur Iohnson dwelling at the signe of the White-horse in Paules Church Yard over against the great North doore of Paules, 1608. Fcp. 4°, sig. A¹ to F⁴ unpaged   CTC

The prose narrative under the same title was entered at Stationers' Hall in 1608 by Thomas Hunt and Thomas Archer, who assigned the authorship to T. B—— [probably Tony (or Antony) Brewer].
On the 9th Sept., 1653, the publisher, Humphrey Moseley, recorded this play, with another, entitled the 'History of Cardenio,' both of which he stated were the productions of Sh—.
Modern critics credit Michael Drayton with the comedy, and Sh— may have assisted him with it. Drayton was a native of Sh—'s county.
The earliest known reference to the play occurs in the 'Black book, by T. M——' [Thomas Middleton], 1604, which runs: 'Give him leave to see the "Merry devil of Edmonton" or a "Woman kill'd with kindness."'
Ben Jonson in his prologue to 'The devil is an ass' says :—

'. . . If you'll come
To see new plays, pray you afford us room
And show this but the same face you have done
Your dear delight the " Devil of Edmonton." '
In June, 1902, a copy realised £300.

Merry Divel of Edmonton . . . London : A. Iohnson . . . 1612. Fcp. 4°   HUTH
[Merry devil . . .] The Merry Divel of Edmonton. As it hath beene sundry times Acted, by his Maiesties' Seruants at the Globe on the Banke-side. At London : Printed for G. Eld for Arthur Johnson dwelling at the signe of the White Horse in Paules Churchyard ouer against the Great North Doore of Paules, 1617. Fcp. 4°, sig. A¹ to F⁴ unpaged BM | BLO | CTC
Merry Deuill of Edmonton.   As it hath been sundry times Acted by his Maiesties Seruants, at the Globe on the Banke-side. London : Printed by A. M—— [Augus-

Sh— Merry devil of Edmonton . . .

tine Mathewes] for Francis Falkner and are to be sold at his Shoppe neere vnto S. Margarites-hill in Southwarke, 1626. Fcp. 4°, sig. A¹ to F⁴ in fours (A¹ being blank)   BM | BUS | CTC
Merry Deuill of Edmonton.   As it hath beene sundry times Acted by his Maiesties Seruants at the Globe on the Bancke-Side.   London : Printed by T. P—— [Thomas Pavier] for Francis Falkner and are to be sold at his Shoppe neere vnto S. Margaret's hill in Southwarke, 1631. Fcp. 4°, sig. A¹ to F⁴ unpaged (A¹ being blank)   BM | BLO | BUS | CTC
A reprint, with slight changes of the 1626 edition.
In May, 1904, a copy realised £25.

Merry Devil of Edmonton.   As it hath been sundry times Acted, by His Majesties Servants at the Globe on the Bank side.   London : Printed for William Gilbertson and are to be sold at his Shop at the sign of the Bible in Giltspur Street without Newgate, 1655. Fcp. 4°, sig. A¹ to F⁴ unpaged.   With woodcut title

This edition is full of literal errors.   BM | CTC
Merry devil of Edmonton . . . [In R. Dodsley's Collection of plays].   Ln : . . . 1744. 12°   BUS
Merry devil of Edmonton [In Dodsley's ' Select collection of old plays, edited by Coxeter, vol. ii.']   Ln : 1744.   12 vols. 12°   BM
Merry devil of Edmonton . . . [In Dodsley's ' Select collection of old plays, edited by Isaac Reed, vol. v.']   Ln : 1780.   8°
Merry devil of Edmonton . . . [In 'Ancient British drama, edited by Sir W. Scott']. Ln : Miller . . . 1810.   8°   BUS
[Merry devil . . .] Life and death of the merry deuill of Edmonton, with the pleasant pranks of Smug the smith, Sir John, and mine host of the George about the stealing of venison. By T. B. [Thomas Brewer].   [*Woodcut of Smug and the Keepers.*]   Ln : Printed in the Black Letter by T. P—— for Francis Faulkner . . . Reprinted by W. R—— for J. Nichols & Son, 1819.   8°, pp. iv.-52   SML
Merry devil of Edmonton [In Dodsley's ' Select collection of old plays, vol. v., pp. 217-274 '].   Ln : Septimus Prowett . . . 1825   BM | BLO | CTC | SML
Merry devil of Edmonton [In Sh—'s doubtful plays . . . edited by Hy. Tyrrell]. Ln : Tallis [c. 1851].   8°, pp. 300-323
Merry devil of Edmonton [In Dodsley's ' Select collection of Old English plays, revised by W. C. Hazlitt,' Vol. 10].   Ln : Reeves . . . 1874-76.   15 vols.   8° BPL | BUS

Sh— Merry devil of Edmonton . . .

Merry devil of Edmonton . . . revised and edited with introduction and notes by K. Warnke and L. Proescholdt. Halle, 1884. 8°

Merry devil of Edmonton, edited with an introduction by A. F. Hopkinson. Ln : M. E. Sims & Co., 1891. Cr. 8°, pp. xiv.-56   SML

Merry devil of Edmonton . . . edited with a preface, notes and glossary by Hugh Walker. 'Temple dramatists.' Ln : Dent, 1897. 16°, pp. xii.-80

       BM | BLO | CTC | SML

'Merry devil' references—

See. Herondo   See Hopkinson
  ,,   Sh— [Works] Sh— apocrypha, 1908

MERRY WIVES OF WINDSOR.

The earliest known edition of this comedy came from the press of T. C—— [Thomas Creede] and was published by Arthur Johnson in 1602.

It was entered at Stationers' Hall :— '18th Jan., 1601-2. John Busby. Entred for his copie vnder the hand of Master Seton a booke called "An excellent and pleasant conceited commedie of Sir Iohn Faulstof and the merry wyves of Windesor, VId."' 'Arthur Johnson. Entred for his copye by assignement from John Busbye, a booke called "An excellent and pleasant conceyted Comedie of Sir John Faulstafe and the merye wyves of Windsor, VId."'

Prof. Arber thinks it is quite clear that the 'Merry wives' was printed by J. Busby before this date, but not entered in the registers until he came to assign it to A. Johnson. If so, every copy of Busby's printing appears to have vanished. Mr. Pollard, on the contrary, says 'it seems probable that Johnson preferred that Busby should take the responsibility of entering the book.'

The circumstance recalls the sharp order about the entry of all plays issued by the Archbp. of Canterbury and Bishop of London to the Master and Wardens of Stationers' Hall, found on the registers under date 1st June, 1599.

In this comedy Shakespeare is supposed to have caricatured Sir Thomas Lucy of Charlecote as Justice Shallow, and 'Dr. Caius' is thought to represent John Caius of Norwich (author of 'De canibus Britannicis'), who flourished in 1558.

The singular spelling of fleur-de-lis on the title may be an overt allusion to the Lucy family.

The play, as moderns know it, first

Sh— Merry wives of Windsor . . .

fully appeared in the Jaggard canon of 1623, where it contained twice as many lines as in the early quartos. While the scenes remained practically the same, the speeches were almost invariably elaborated.

[Merry wives . . .] A most pleasaunt and excellent conceited Comedie of Syr Iohn Falstaffe and the merrie Wiues of Windsor. Entermixed with sundrie variable and pleasing humors, of Syr Hugh the Welch Knight, Iustice Shallow, and his wise Cousin M. Slender. With the swaggering vaine of Auncient Pistoll and Corporall Nym. By William Shakespeare. As it hath bene diuers times Acted by the Right Honorable my lord Chamberlaines seruants. Both before her Maiestie, and else-where. [Ornament.] London : Printed by T. C—— [Thomas Creede] for Arthur Iohnson and are to be sold at his shop in Powles Church-yard, at the signe of the Flower de Leuse and the Crowne, 1602. Fcp. 4°, on twenty-seven unpaged leaves, sig. A¹ to G⁴ in fours (A¹ blank, except signature)

       BLO | CTC

Four copies only were known to Halliwell. Reprints of this issue were produced by J. O. Halliwell in 1842 and in his folio Sh—, 1854 ; in the Cambridge Sh—, 1863 ; by E. W. Ashbee, 1866 ; in Hazlitt's 'Sh—'s library' ; and elsewhere.

[Merry wives . . .] A Most pleasant and excellent conceited Comedy of Sir Iohn Falstaffe, and the merry Wiues of Windsor. With the swaggering vaine of Ancient Pistoll and Corporall Nym. Written by W. Shakespeare ['Heb Ddieu' block. Ln :] Printed for Arthur Johnson [by Isaac Jaggard ?], 1619. Fcp. 4°, twenty-eight unpaged leaves, including title, sig. A¹ to G⁴ in fours

   BM | BLO | BUS | CTC | NY | SBL | SML | W

Reprinted from the 1602 issue, with very slight alterations.

This issue forms one of the nine 'suspects.' For fuller information see A. W. Pollard's 'Sh— folios and quartos.'

In March, 1903, a copy realised £165. In May, 1906, another, measuring 7 by 5¾ in., sold for £295. Earl Howe's copy, 7⅛ by 5¼, sold in Dec., 1907, for £160. The Warwick copy having sustained a little damage to the title, extending to the type, bears inserted a facsimile copy of the original leaf for reference purposes.

Merry wives of Windsor. With the humours of Sir Iohn Falstaffe. As also the swaggering vaine of Antient Pistoll and Corporall Nym. Written by William Shake-Speare. Newly corrected. London : Printed by T. H—— [Thomas Haviland ? or Thomas Harper ?] for R. Meighen, and are to be sold at his Shop, next to the Middle

Temple Gate and in S. Dunstan's Church yard in Fleet-street, 1630. Fcp. 4°, sig. A¹ to K⁴ in fours (K⁴ blank), forty unpaged leaves including title

BM | BLO | BUS | CTC | NY

Reprinted by Geo. Steevens in 1766. The Boston copy has numerous MS. stage directions, apparently contemporary.

Merry wives of Windsor . . . London: Bedell & Collins, 1656

The sole record of this edition appears in a catalogue of publications at the end of Thomas Goff's 'Three excellent tragedies, 1656,' 8°. It may therefore have been projected and never printed.

Merry wives of Old Windsor. Written by Mr. William Shakespeare. [With] Lines upon the famous Scenicke-Poet, the author, by Hu. Holland [upon the title-page]. Original manuscript, upon twenty-one leaves of paper. c. 1660. Fcp. 4°, pp. 42   W

When discovered by Rodd the bookseller, in 1843, it was secured by J. O. Halliwell, and announced as the earliest Shakespearean MS. known, and the only MS. of this play. It is probably a long-lost acting version, prepared for some private performance. Its great interest lies in the fact that it is not a mere transcript, but presents many variations, and its value is enhanced by the descriptive list of 'dramatis personæ.' Halliwell has described the treasure fully in his 'Account of the only known manuscript . . . 1843' (q.v.)
In the following year the manuscript 'King Henry IV.,' of 1610, came to light, and found a worthy home by the side of the above in Warwick Castle.

Merry wives of Windsor [The text from the third folio edition. With contemporary manuscript corrections and stage directions; apparently an old playhouse copy]. Ln: Printed for P. C—— [Philip Chetwynd], 1664. F°   W

[Merry wives . . .] The comical gallant, or the amours of Sir John Falstaffe. A comedy. As it is acted at the Theatre Royal in Drury Lane. By his Majesty's servants. By Mr. [John] Dennis. To which is added, A large account of the taste in poetry and the causes of the degeneracy of it. Ln: Printed and sold by A. Baldwin, 1702. Fcp. 4°, pp. xvi.-50

BM | BPL | BUS | W

The dedication contains the earliest version of the famous tradition connecting Queen Elizabeth with this play, as follows :—'This comedy was written at her [the Queen's] command, and by her direction, and she was so eager to see it acted that she commanded it to be finished in fourteen days, and was afterwards, as tradition tells us, very well pleas'd at the representation.' The prologue also mentions this tradition.
'Dennis has re-written about half the dialogue and materially changed the conduct of the piece.'— *Halliwell.*

Merry wives . . . with the amours of Sir John Falstaff. A comedy. Written by Mr. W. Sh—. Ln: Printed for the company [1710]. 8°   W

Merry wives . . . with the amours of Sir John Falstaff. Written by Mr. W. Sh—. Ln: Printed for the company [c. 1720]. 8°, pp. 88   BM

[Merry wives . . .] New collection of miscellanies in prose and verse, by Richardson Pack. Ln: E. Curll, 1725. 8°, pp. xxx.-128

On pp. 56-61 occurs the 'Prologue to the "Merry wives . . ." acted by the young gentlemen of Bury school, 1723,' and 'Epilogue on the same occasion.'

Merry wives . . . A comedy. As it is acted at the theatres. Dublin: Printed for A. Bradley at the 'Golden Ball and Ring' opposite Sycamore Alley in Dame Street, Bookseller, 1730. 8°, pp. 72

First Irish edition of this play.

Merry wives . . . Ln: J. Tonson . . . 1733. 12°. With frontispiece

Merry wives . . . A comedy. By Mr. Wm. Sh—. Ln: Printed [for J. Tonson] and sold by the booksellers of Ln. and Westminster, 1734. Cr. 8°, pp. 72, and frontispiece

On the last page is a curious notice dated 6 Sept., 1734, in which one learns that these plays were supplied to hawkers at one penny per sheet, or fourpence each play, by R. Walker, and to stop the piracy J. Tonson offered the plays complete at one penny each.

Merry wives . . . A comedy. As it is acted at the theatres. By Sh—. Ln: Printed by R. Walker, 1734. 12°, pp. 70   W

Merry wives . . . With notes explanatory and critical by Mr. [Lewis] Theobald. Dublin: A. Bradley . . . 1739. 12°, pp. 84   BM

Merry wives . . . Ln: Printed for C. Hitch . . . 1756. 12°   BPL

Merry wives . . . A comedy, by Wm. Sh—. Ln: Tonson . . . 1766. 12°. With frontispiece   BPL | SML | W

Merry wives . . . 1602 [In 'Twenty of the plays of Sh—, reprinted by G. Steevens,' vol. 1]. Ln: . . . 1766. 8°   BPL

Merry wiues . . . 1619 [In 'Twenty of the plays of Sh—, reprinted by G. Steevens,' vol. 1]. Ln: . . . 1766. 8°   BPL

Merry wives . . . 1630 [In 'Twenty of the plays of Sh—, reprinted by G. Steevens,' vol. 1]. Ln: . . . 1766. 8°   BPL

Merry wives . . . Edinburgh: Printed by and for Martin & Wotherspoon, 1768. Cr. 8°, pp. 72   SML

Merry wives . . . As performed at the Theatre-Royal, Drury-Lane. Regulated from the prompt-book. . . . by Mr. Hopkins . . . An introduction and notes critical and illustrative are added by the authors of the 'Dramatic censor' [F.

Sh— Merry wives of Windsor . . .

Gentleman]. Ln : Printed for John Bell . . . and C. Etherington at York, 1773. 8°, pp. 72. With copperplate frontispiece, E. Edwards *del.*, J. Hall *sc.*   BM

Merry wives . . . A comedy. As it is acted at the Theatres Royal in Drury Lane and Covent Garden . . . Ln : Printed for J. Wenman, 144 Fleet St., and sold by all other booksellers in town and country, 1778. 8°, pp. 20, and copperplate of Henderson as 'Falstaff'   BM | BPL

Merry wives . . . A comedy . . . taken from the manager's book at the Theatre Royal, Covent Garden. Ln : Printed for the proprietors and sold by Rachel Randall . . . and all booksellers in England, Scotland, and Ireland, 1787. Cr. 8°, pp. 56
                         BPL | CPL | SML | W
With holograph presentation inscription by J. O. Halliwell.

[Merry wives . . .] Diverting history of the life, memorable exploits, pranks, and droll adventures of . . . Sir John Falstaff . . . as written by Sh—. To which is added a short dissertation on his character, and the history of the ' Boar's head ' tavern in East Cheap by Dr. Goldsmith. Ln : H. Lemoine . . . 1789. 8°, pp. xii.-48, and plate BM | BUS | MPL

Merry wives . . . A comedy. Written by Sh— and revised by J. P. Kemble. As acted at Drury Lane. Ln : Published by C. Lowndes . . . 1797. 8°, pp. 70 BUS | W

[Merry wives . . .] Life and exploits of that extraordinary character Sir John Falstaff, the hero of Sh— and companion of Henry prince of Wales, with an account of the numerous robberies and offences committed by them, particulars of his amorous adventures. Ln : . . . [c. 1800]. 8°. With portrait of ' Falstaff '

Merry wives . . . revised by J. P. Kemble and now first published as it is acted at the Theatre Royal in Covent Garden. Ln : J. Ridgway . . . 1804. 8°, pp. iv.-72
                                          BUS | CPL

Merry wives . . . with remarks by Mrs. Inchbald. Ln : Printed [by Savage & Easingwood] for Longman . . . [c. 1806]. 12°, pp. 84, and plate   BUS

Merry wives . . . by Will. Sh—. Printed complete from the text of Sam. Johnson and Geo. Steevens. Ln : . . . 1806. 16°
                                                W

Merry wives . . . with remarks by Mrs. Inchbald. Ln : [Printed by T. Davison for] Longman . . . [c. 1808]. 12°, pp. 84. With frontispiece   BPL | BUS

Sh— Merry wives of Windsor . . .

Merry wives . . . Edinburgh : Oliver & Boyd [c. 1813]. 12°, pp. 60, including blue printed wrappers issued at 6d.

Merry wives . . . revised by J. P. Kemble ; and now published as it is performed at the Theatres Royal. Ln : J. Miller . . . 1815. 12°, pp. 80   BM | BUS | SML | W

Merry wives . . . with remarks by Mrs. Inchbald. Ln : Longman . . . [c. 1816]. 12°, pp. 82, and plate   BUS
The frontispiece differs from the 1806 and 1808 editions.

Merry wives . . . A comedy : By W. Sh—. With prefatory remarks [signed P. P——] . . . Marked with the stage business and stage directions, as it is performed at the Theatres Royal, by W. Oxberry. Ln : Simpkin & Marshall, 1820. 8°, pp. iv.-76, and portrait of Wewitzer as Dr. Caius
                         BM | BPL | BUS | SML | W

Merry wives . . . edited by W. Oxberry. Boston [U.S.] . . . 1822. 12°   BUS

Merry wives . . . As performed . . . with remarks by W. Oxberry. Ln : . . . 1823. 12°

Merry wives . . . ' Cumberland's theatre.' With remarks by D. G—— [Geo. Daniel]. Ln : Davidson . . . 1824. 12° BPL | SML

[Merry wives] Songs, duetts, etc. introduced in . . . revised play of the ' Merry wives . . .' selected . . . (with one exception) from . . . Sh—. Acted at the Theatre Royal, Drury Lane. The music composed and adapted by Mr. Horn, with . . . four pieces composed and selected by Mr. Barry. Ln : S. Low . . . 1824. 8°, pp. 16   BPL | BUS
The play was edited by F. Reynolds.

Merry wives . . . ' British theatre.' Ln : Dolby . . . [c. 1824]. 12°   BPL

Merry wives . . . printed from the acting copy, with remarks . . . by D. G—— [Geo. Daniel]. To which are added, a . . . cast of the characters . . . and the whole of the stage business, as now performed at the Theatres Royal. Ln : J. Cumberland . . . [c. 1830]. 12°, pp. 64   BM

[Merry wives . . .] Falstaff. A comic opera. By S. M. Maggioni. [Founded on Sh—'s ' Merry wives . . .'] Music by M. W. Balfe . . . 1838. 12°   BM

Merry wives . . . [Acting edition]. Ln : T. H. Lacy . . . 1840. With frontispiece

Merry wives . . . Nuremberg & New York . . . 1841. 12°

[Merry wives . . .] First sketch of Sh—'s ' Merry wives . . .' With the novels on which it was founded, introduction and notes. Ed. by J. O. Halliwell. Ln : Sh— Society . . . 1842. 8°, pp. xxxii.-142
                         BM | BPL | BUS | HCL | MPL

Sh— Merry wives of Windsor . . .

[Merry wives] Outlines to illustrate . . .
' The merry wives . . .' by Moritz Retzsch.
With text in English and German.
Leipzig . . . 1844. 4°. 13 plates

Merry wives . . . ' Spencer's Boston theatre'
. . . With editorial remarks, original casts,
costumes, scene and property plots, and
all the stage business. New York &
Boston : S. French . . . 1855. 12°, pp. 72
BPL | BUS

Merry wives . . . Glasgow : Cameron . . .
1860. 8°

Merry wives . . . The text from the folio of
1623 ; with notices of the known editions
previously issued. [*Printer's emblem.*]
Ln : L. Booth, 1862. Fcp. 4°, pp. iv.-22.
Interleaved with blank writing paper
BM | BUS | W

Merry wives . . . A comedy, in five acts.
'Acting edition.' Ln : T. H. Lacy . . .
[1865]. 12°, pp. 72 BM | BPL

Merry wives . . . 1619, facsimiled by E. W.
Ashbee ; edited by J. O. Halliwell. Ln :
For private circulation only, 1866. Fcp.
4° BPL | W
Fifty copies produced, nineteen of which the editor
destroyed later.

Merry wives . . . 1602, facsimiled by E. W.
Ashbee ; edited by J. O. Halliwell. Ln :
Printed for private circulation, 1866. Fcp.
4° BM | BPL | W
Fifty copies printed, nineteen of which were destroyed
by the editor.

Merry wives . . . edited by J. Hunter for
scholastic study. Ln : Longman . . .
1872. Cr. 8° BPL | CPL

Merry wives . . . ' Standard plays.' Ln :
J. Dicks [c. 1875]. 12°

Merry wives . . . 1875. With introduction
by J. O. Halliwell. *See Sh*—] Sh—'s
library, vol. 6

Merry wives . . . English adaptation by
Henry Hersee of ' Die lustigen weiber von
Windsor.' Opera in three acts by Otto
Nicolai. Ln : Carl Rosa Opera Co. [c.
1875]. 8°, pp. 36, including printed
wrappers

Merry wives . . . edited for scholastic study
by John Hunter. Ln : Longman [c.
1878]. Cr. 8°

Merry wives . . . Acting edition. Ln : French
. . . [c. 1878]. 12° SML

Merry wives . . . Adapted by the Carl Rosa
Opera Company. Ln : . . . 1880. 8° SML

Merry wives . . . The first quarto, 1602 ; A
facsimile in photo-lithography . . . with
introduction by P. A. Daniel. ' Sh—
quarto facsimiles.' Ln : W. Griggs . . .
[1881]. Fcp. 4°, pp. xvi.-54
BM | BPL | BUS

Sh— Merry wives of Windsor . . .

Merry wives . . . edited with notes by W. J.
Rolfe. New York : Harper . . . 1882.
12°. Illustrated BPL | BUS

Merry wives . . . ' Standard plays.' Ln :
John Dicks . . . [1883]. 12° BM | BPL

Merry wives . . . 1602 ; Facsimile in photo-
lithography of the first quarto. Together
with a reprint of the prompt copy prepared for use at Daly's Theatre. The
alterations and emendations by Augustin
Daly. To which is added an introduction by W. Winter. The play produced
at Daly's theatre, Jan., 1886. New York :
Printed for Mr. Daly . . . 1886. Roy. 8°,
pp. xii.-54-xii.-76, including printed
wrappers BPL | SML

Merry wives . . . edited, with notes from the
collections of the late J. F. Stanford . . .
by Henry B. Wheatley. Ln : Bell . . .
1886. 8°, pp. lxviii.-240
BM | BPL | BUS | SML

Merry wives . . . edited by C. E. Flower.
' Memorial theatre edition.' Stratford-on-
Avon : Printed by G. Boyden ; Ln : S.
French [1887]. Cr. 8°, pp. viii.-84, in-
cluding printed wrappers BPL | SML

Merry wives . . . [with introduction by H.
Morley]. ' National library.' Ln : Cassell, 1888. 16°, pp. 192 BM

Merry wives . . . with preface, glossary, and
notes by I. Gollancz. ' Temple edition.'
Ln : Dent & Co., 1894. 16°, pp. x.-148 SML

Merry wives . . . presented in eight pen
designs by Walter Crane. Engraved and
printed by D. C. Dallas. Ln : G. Allen
. . . 1894. F° BM | BPL | BUS

Merry wives . . . 'Ariel edition.' New York :
Putnam . . . 1894. 16°

Merry wives . . . edited by Edric Vreden-
burg. Illustrated by J. Finnemore and
F. L. Emmanuel. Ln : Tuck . . . [1895].
Roy. 8° BPL

[Merry wives] ' Hamnet Sh—,' part x.
The ' Merry wives . . .' according to the
first folio (spelling modernised). With lists
of such of the emphasis-capitals of Sh—
. . . as were omitted by each of the second,
third, and fourth folios, and of new
emphasis-capitals shewn by it in each of
these, also introduction, including remarks on the running titles and paging
of the first folio, by A. P. Paton.
Greenock : W. Hutchinson . . . 1896. 8°,
pp. xliv.-72 BUS | SML

Merry wives . . . 'Ariel edition.' Ln : Routledge . . . 1897. 16°

Merry wives . . . [edited by Hy. Morley].
' National library.' Ln : Cassell, 1897.
16°, pp. 192

Sh— Merry wives of Windsor . . .

Merry wives . . . Illustrated by J. Finnemore and F. L. Emanuel; edited by E. Vredenburg. Ln : Tuck [1897]. 8°, pp. 110
BM

Merry wives . . . 'Pocket Falstaff edition.' Ln : Bliss, Sands, 1898. 16°, pp. 108
BPL | SML

Merry wives . . . edited with introduction and notes by C. H. Herford. 'Eversley edition.' Ln : Macmillan, 1900. Cr. 8°
BPL

Merry wives . . . edited with notes by H. N. Hudson. 'Windsor edition.' Edinburgh : Jack, 1902. 8°, pp. iv.-102 SML

Merry wives . . . 'Abbey text.' Ln : Bell & Sons; Edinburgh : Abbey Press, 1902. Fcp. 4°, pp. viii.-136 BM | BLO | CTC | MPL
Issue restricted to 500 copies on fine paper and 50 numbered copies on Japanese vellum, the latter being bound in gilt vellum with crimson silk tie thongs.

[Merry wives . . .] A most pleasant and excellent conceited comedy of Sir John Falstaff and the merry wives of Windsor. 'Vale Sh—' [edited] by T. S. Moore. Decorated by C. Ricketts. Ln : Hacon & Ricketts, 1902. Roy. 8°, pp. 94
BM | BLO | CTC | SML

Merry wives . . . with introduction and notes by W. J. Craig. Ln : Methuen, 1903. 16°

Merry wives . . . [with] introduction by Austin Brereton. Eight pages of illustrations, glossary, etc. 'Stage Sh—.' Ln : Wm. Collins [1903]. 16°, pp. xvi.-124
SML

Merry wives . . . edited by H. Morley. 'National library.' Ln : Cassell . . . 1904. 16°, pp. 192 BPL

Merry wives . . . 'Ellen Terry edition.' Glasgow : Bryce . . . 1904. 32°

Merry wives . . . edited by H. C. Hart. 'Arden edition.' Ln : Methuen, 1904. 8°, pp. 314 BM | BLO | CTC

Merry wives . . . 'Waistcoat pocket edition.' Ln : Treherne, 1904. 32°

Merry wives . . . with introduction by G. Brandes. 'Favourite classics.' Ln : Heinemann, 1904. 16° BM | BLO | CTC

Merry wives . . . 'Red letter edition.' Ln : Blackie . . . 1906. 12°

Merry wives . . . Text revised by A. Dyce. Ln : Sonnenschein, 1908. Fcp. 4° BPL

Merry wives . . . 'Old spelling edition,' edited by F. J. Furnivall. Ln : Chatto . . . 1908. 8° BM | BLO | CTC

Merry wives . . . 'Renaissance edition.' New York : Harrap . . . 1908. Fcp. 4°
BPL

Sh— Merry wives of Windsor . . .

Merry wives . . . 1620, edited by W. W. Greg. Oxford : University Press, 1910
Printed with types given to the University by Dr. Fell in 1660.

'Merry wives' references—

See Bold	See Lucy
„ Booke . . .	„ Nicolai
„ Caius	„ Perry
„ Certificates	„ Poetical . . .
„ Clark	Sh— Passionate
„ Dixon	. . . 1570-1600
„ Dramatic . . .	Sh— Sir John Old-
„ Ferne	castle (*heading*)
„ Giovanni	*Sh*—] Gibbs
„ Glenny	*Sh*—] Sh— miscel-
„ Goldsmith	lanies
„ Grindon	*Sh*—] Sh—'s li-
„ Halliwell	brary
„ Howard	„ Shenstone
„ Hue and Cry	„ Short . . .
„ James	„ Smith
„ Johnson &	„ Stopes
Steevens	„ Stowe
„ Kirkman	„ Straparola
„ Knight	„ Tarlton
„ Kynder	„ Tighe . . .
„ Liverseege	„ Tree
„ Lucius Camil-	„ White (R. G.)
lus	

MIDSUMMER NIGHT'S DREAM.

Two differing impressions of this comedy exist, each dated 1600. The first came from the press of James Roberts on behalf of Thomas Fisher, and the second, also purporting to proceed from the same press in 1600, was actually printed nineteen years later (doubtless by Isaac Jaggard), and should properly be dated 1619. It was registered at Stationers' Hall thus :—
'1600, 8 Oct. Thomas Fyssher. Entred for his copie vnder the handes of Master Rodes and the Wardens a booke called A mydsommer nighte's dreame, VId.'

[Midsummer . . .] A Midsommer nights dreame. As it hath beene sundry times publickely acted, by the Right honourable, the Lord Chamberlaine his seruants. Written by William Shakespeare. [*Herring Gull block, with motto.*] ¶ Imprinted at Ln. [by Iames Roberts] for Thomas Fisher, and are to be soulde at his shoppe, at the Signe of the White Hart in Fleetestreete, 1600. Fcp. 4°, thirty-two unpaged leaves, sig. A¹ to H⁴ in fours
BM | BLO | BUS | CTC

Reprinted by Steevens in 1766, by Halliwell in 1865, and by Ebsworth in 1880.

The long standing controversy as to which of the 1600 editions was the earliest found solution in the discovery by Mr. Pollard (*q.v.*) that the Roberts imprint was fictitious.

[Midsummer . . .] A midsommer nights dreame . . . [*Half-eagle and key block, with motto, 'Post tenebras lux.'* Ln :] Printed by Iames Roberts, 1600. *See* note to preceding entry

The correct date of this issue is 1619, under which year fuller particulars will be found.

[Midsummer . . .] A midsommer nights dreame. As it hath beene sundry times publikely acted by the Right Honourable, the Lord Chamberlaine his seruants. Written by William Shakespeare. [*Half-eagle and key block.* Ln :] Printed by Iames Roberts [or Isaac Jaggard], 1600 [otherwise 1619]. Fcp. 4°, thirty-two leaves, sig. A¹ to H⁴ in fours, unpaged

BM | BLO | BUS | CTC | NY | SBL

For a detailed account of this mysterious issue, with its false date, see A. W. Pollard's 'Sh— folios and quartos.'
A copy in brown morocco sold in Dec., 1905 for £480.

[Midsummer . . .] The merry conceited humours of Bottom the weaver, by Robert Cox. Ln : . . . [c. 1646]. Fcp. 4°

An adaptation of the humorous scenes from Sh—'s comedy.

[Midsummer . . .] The merry conceited humors of Bottom the weaver. As it hath been often publikely acted by some of his Majesties comedians. Ln : . . . 1661. Fcp. 4°   BM

[Midsummer . . .] Merry conceited humours of Bottom the weaver . . . [In 'The wits or sport upon sport, by Francis Kirkman']. Ln : . . . 1672. 8°   BM | W

[Midsummer . . .] Merry conceited humours of Bottom the weaver [In 'The wits . . . by F. Kirkman, 1673']. Ln : . . . 1673. Fcp. 4°   BUS

[Midsummer . . .] Tragical history of Piramus and Thisbe, by Abraham Cowley. Fifth edition. Enlarged by the author. Ln : . . . 1681. F°, title, dedication and four leaves   W

An excerpt [pp. 25-32] from Cowley's Works.

[Midsummer . . .] The fairy-queen. An opera. Represented at the Queen's-Theatre. By their Majesties servants. Ln : Printed for Jacob Tonson, 1692. Fcp. 4°, pp. vi.-52

BM | BPL | BUS | SML | W

An adaptation of a 'Midsummer night's dream.'
Contains a 'Dance of six monkeys,' a 'Grand dance of twenty-four Chineses,' and examples of curious slang of the period.
With preface and prologue.

[Midsummer . . .] Some select songs as they are sung in the 'Fairy queen.' Composed by Henry Purcell. Ln : . . . 1692. F°

[Midsummer night's dream] Song in the opera called the 'Fairy queen,' sung by Mrs. Dyer, 1692. *See Sh*—] Manuscript

[Midsummer . . .] The fairy-queen. An opera. With alterations, additions, and several new songs. Ln : Printed for Jacob Tonson, 1693. Fcp. 4°   BM | W

The only edition known to contain the additional songs. The Warwick copy was declared by J. O. Halliwell to be unique.

[Midsummer . . .] Comick masque of Pyramus and Thisbe [adapted . . . by Richard Leveridge]. As it is perform'd at the Theatre in Lincoln's-Inn Fields. Ln : W. Mears . . . 1716. 8°, pp. viii.-16

BM | BPL | BUS

'The interlude in the "Midsummer night's dream" dressed out in recitative, with airs after the present Italian mode.'—*Preface.*

Midsummer night's dream . . . Ln : Printed for J. Tonson and the rest of the proprietors and sold by the booksellers of London and Westminster, 1734. 12°, pp. 60. With frontispiece   BUS | SML

The plate is copied, and somewhat altered, from Rowe's 1609 edition.

[Midsummer . . .] Pyramus and Thisbe. A mock-opera, as it is performed at the Theatre Royal in Covent-Garden. The words taken from Sh—. Set to musick by I. F. Lampe. Ln : I. Walsh . . . [c. 1740]. F°   BPL | W

Consists of the interlude, introduced in act v., with slight alterations, and an introduction.

[Midsummer . . .] Pyramus and Thisbe. A mock opera. The words taken from Sh—. Set to music by I. F. Lampe. Ln : H. Woodfall, jun. . . . 1745. 8°, pp. viii.-24   BUS

[Midsummer . . .] Pyramus and Thisbe : A mock opera, set to music by I. F. Lampe. The words from Sh—. Ln : [c. 1750]. F°   BPL | W

[Midsummer . . .] The fairies. An opera. Taken from a 'Midsummer night's dream' . . . As it is performed at the Theatre Royal in Drury Lane. [Edited by David Garrick.] The music composed by J. C. Smith. Second edition. Ln : Tonson . . . 1754. 8°   CPL

[Midsummer . . .] The fairies : An opera. The words taken from Sh—, etc. Set to music by Mr. [J. C.] Smith. Ln : I. Walsh . . . [1755]. F°, pp. 92   BUS

[Midsummer . . .] The fairies. An opera . . . As it is performed at the Theatre Royal in Drury Lane. The songs from

Sh— Midsummer night's dream . . .

Sh—, Milton, Waller, Dryden, Lansdown, Hammond, etc. [Edited by David Garrick]. The music composed by [J. C.] Smith. Ln : J. & R. Tonson & S. Draper, 1755. 8°, pp. 48

BM | BPL | BUS | MPL | W

There are two issues of this edition at Boston, the first omitting the interlude, and the second omitting Garrick's prologue.

[Midsummer . . .] The fairies. An opera . . . [By D. Garrick.] Second edition. Ln : S. Draper . . . 1755. 8°, pp. 48 BM

[Midsummer night's dream] The fairies . . . [By D. Garrick.] Ln : . . . 1756. 12° BPL

[Midsummer . . .] 'I know a bank . . .' With music by John Percy . . . Ln : [c. 1760]. F°

Midsummer night's dream . . . With alterations and additions [by David Garrick] and several new songs. As it is performed at the Theatre Royal in Drury Lane. Ln : J. & R. Tonson, 1763. 8°, pp. 48

BM | BPL | BUS | CPL | W

The interlude in act v. is omitted.

[Midsummer . . .] A fairy tale, in two acts. Taken from Sh—. As it is performed at the Theatre-Royal in Drury-Lane [by David Garrick & George Colman the elder]. Ln : J. & R. Tonson, 1763. 8°, pp. 24 BPL | BUS | W

A further 'amendment' of Garrick's alteration, with slight changes and a fresh title.

[Midsummer . . .] Six songs in 'Harlequin's invasion, Cymbeline,' and 'Midsummer night's dream.' By Theodore Aylward. In score. [c. 1765.] F°

Midsummer night's dreame [The second quarto], 1600 [In 'Twenty of the plays . . . of Sh— reprinted by G. Steevens, vol. 1']. Ln : . . . 1766. 8° BPL

[Midsummer . . .] The fairy prince : A masque. As it is performed at the Theatre Royal in Covent Garden [by Geo. Colman and David Garrick] . . . 1771. 8° BPL

A reprint under a fresh title of 'A fairy tale.'

Midsummer night's dream . . . as performed at the Theatre Royal, Covent Garden. Regulated from the prompt book, with permission of the managers, by Mr. Hopkins, prompter. An introduction, and notes critical and illustrative, are added by the authors of the 'Dramatic censor' [F. Gentleman]. Ln : Printed for John Bell . . . and C. Etherington at York, 1773. 8°. With frontispiece

An edition not previously mentioned elsewhere.

[Midsummer . . .] A fairy tale. In two acts. Taken from Sh— [adapted . . . by George Colman the elder, and David Garrick].

Sh— Midsummer night's dream . . .

As it is performed at the Theatre-Royal in the Hay-Market. Ln : G. Kearsley . . . 1777. 8°, pp. 24 BM | BPL

With a few unimportant omissions it is the same as the 1763 issue.

Midsummer night's dream . . . [edited by F. Gentleman]. Ln : John Bell . . . 1777. 12°. With frontispiece

Midsummer night's dream. A comedy. As it is acted at the Theatres-Royal in Drury-Lane and Covent-Garden . . . Ln : Printed for J. Wenman, 144 Fleet St., and sold by all other booksellers in town and country, 1778. 8°, pp. 20, and copperplate portrait of 'Miss Barsanti as Helena' BM | BPL

Midsummer night's dream . . . printed complete from the text of Sam. Johnson and Geo. Steevens and revised from the last editions . . . Ln : Printed for . . . John Bell . . . 1785. 12°, pp. 90, with engraved title, and frontispiece of 'Miss Farren as Hermia'

[Midsummer . . .] The fairies. By J. C. Smith [In Garrick's Dramatic Works, vol. 1]. 1798. 8° MPL

[Midsummer . . .] Pyramus and Thisbe. A pantomime acted at Birmingham. Birmingham . . . 1798. 8°

Midsummer night's dream, by Will. Sh—. Printed complete from the text of Sam. Johnson and Geo. Steevens. Ln : . . . 1806. 16° W

Midsummer night's dream. With alterations, additions, and new songs [by Frederick Reynolds]. As it is performed at the Theatre Royal, Covent-Garden. Ln : J. Miller . . . 1816. 8°, pp. iv.-58

BM | BPL | BUS

One whole scene and part of another added to this version.

[Midsummer . . .] The music in a 'Midsummer night's dream.' Composed and selected by Sir H. R. Bishop. Ln : . . . [1816]. F°

Midsummer night's dream . . . Acting edition. Ln : J. Cumberland . . . 1816. 12°

Midsummer night's dream . . . from the text of Johnson & Steevens. With remarks. Ln : . . . [c. 1822]. 12° BPL

[Midsummer . . .] Music to a 'Midsummer night's dream.' Composed by Felix Mendelssohn-Bartholdy. [Full score.] Ln : . . . [1826-43]. F°

Midsummer night's dream . . . 'Cumberland's British theatre.' With remarks by D. G—— [Geo. Daniel]. Ln : Mus. Pub. Co. [1828]. 12° BPL | SML

[Midsummer . . .] Gallery of Sh—: 'Midsummer night's dream.' Six plates, by L. S. Ruhl, 1829. 12° BPL

Midsummer night's dream . . . Printed from the acting copy, with remarks . . . by D. G—— [Geo. Daniel]. To which are added, a . . . cast of the characters . . . and the whole of the stage business, as now performed at the Theatres Royal. Ln : J. Cumberland . . . [c. 1830]. 12°, pp. 68
BM | BPL

[Midsummer . . .] Court of Oberon, or the three wishes. A drama [by Harriet, Countess of Hardwicke]. Ln : . . . 1831. Fcp. 4°
BPL

Midsummer night's dream . . . Nurenberg . . . New York . . . 1839. 12°

Midsummer night's dream. As revived at the Theatre Royal, Covent Garden, 16th Nov., 1840 [edited by J. R. Planché]. Ln : . . . 1840. 8°
BPL | W

Midsummer night's dream . . . As performed at Covent Garden. Ln : Pattie . . . 1840. 12°

Midsummer night's dream . . . with historical and grammatical explanatory notes in German. Frankfort . . . 1840. 12°
BPL

Midsummer night's dream. A tale from Sh—, by C. Lamb [In ' The Romancist . . .' vol. 4, pp. 223-224]. 1840. 4° BPL

Midsummer night's dream . . . Reprinted from the ' Family Sh—,' with a glossary. Berlin . . . 1841. 8°
BPL

Midsummer night's dream . . . Nurenberg . . . New York . . . 1841

[Midsummer night's dream] Songs, chorusses, etc. in a fairy ballad opera, entitled ' Robin Goodfellow.' Ln : . . . [c. 1848]. 8°
BPL

Midsummer night's dream. With illustrations, as designed and modelled . . . by W. B. Kirk. Dublin : J. McGlashan, 1853. 8°, pp. iv.-36. With 12 plates
Privately printed. BM | BPL | BUS | CPL | SML

Midsummer night's dream . . . To which are added . . . the costume, cast of characters, entrances and exits, relative positions and . . . stage business, as performed for upwards of sixty consecutive nights at the Broadway Theatre. New York : S. French [c. 1853]. 12°, pp. 48 BPL | BUS

Midsummer night's dream . . . Ln : Orr & Co. . . . 1854. 12°

[Midsummer . . .] The midsummer night, or Sh— and the fairies. By L. Tieck. Translated by M. E. Rumsey. With notice by S. W. Singer. Ln : Privately printed by Whittingham, 1854. 12°
BPL | CPL

Midsummer night's dream . . . as read by Mrs. Fanny Kemble [at Exeter Hall]. Music by F. Mendelssohn. Ln : Mitchell . . . 1855. Fcp. 4° BPL | SML

Midsummer night's dream ; arranged for representation at the Princess's Theatre ; with historical and explanatory notes, by Charles Kean. As first performed, Oct. 15, 1856. Ln : J. K. Chapman & Co. [1856]. 8°, pp. 60 BM | BPL | BUS | CPL | SML

Midsummer night's dream. A comedy. 'Acting edition.' With preliminary notes. Ln : T. H. Lacy [1856]. 12°, pp. 62. Pub. at 6d. BM | BPL

Midsummer night's dream. Arranged for representation at Laura Keene's Theatre. With historical and explanatory notes . . . To which are added the costumes, cast, entrances and exits, relative positions and . . . stage business. New York : O. A. Roorbach, jun., 1859. 12°, pp. 60
BPL | BUS

[Midsummer . . .] Merry conceited humours of Bottom the weaver. A droll composed out of the comic scenes of the ' Midsummer night's dream,' about A.D. 1646. [By Robert Cox.] Edited by J. O. Halliwell. Ln : Printed for the editor, 1860. 16° BM | BPL | BUS | HCL | MPL | W
One of the thirty copies printed for private circulation. This droll was first printed separately in or about 1646, and afterwards included in Kirkman's ' The wits . . . 1670-72,' from which this edition is copied.

[Midsummer . . .] Songs of the fairies . . . [Full score] by C. E. Horn, words by George Soane. Ln : Cramer & Co. [c. 1860]. F°

Midsummer night's dream . . . Glasgow : Cameron . . . 1861. 8°

[Midsummer . . .] Music for ' Midsummer night's dream ' for the piano. By Felix Mendelssohn. Ln : Boosey & Co. . . . 1861. 4°, pp. 40 BUS

Midsummer night's dreame. The text from the folio of 1623 ; with notices of the known editions previously issued. Ln : L. Booth, 1862. Fcp. 4°, pp. vi.-18, interleaved with blank writing paper
BM | BPL | BUS | W

Midsummer night's dream. With . . . notes, collected . . . by L. Keene. New York : S. French . . . 1863. 12°, pp. 60 BM

Midsommer night's dream, 1600. Facsimiled by E. W. Ashbee from the edition ' *imprinted for Thomas Fisher* ' [edited by J. O. Halliwell]. Ln : For private circulation, 1864. Fcp. 4°, on sixty-two unpaged leaves BPL | BUS
Limited to fifty copies, of which nineteen were destroyed by the editor.

Sh— Midsummer night's dream . . .

Midsommer nights dreame . . . [*Printed by Iames Roberts, 1600*]. Facsimiled . . . by E. W. Ashbee. Edited by J. O. Halliwell. Ln : . . . 1865. Fcp. 4°   BPL | W
Fifty copies printed for private circulation, nineteen of which were destroyed.

Midsummer night's dream . . . arranged for representation at the Prince's Theatre, Manchester, by C. Calvert. Manchester : Ireland & Co., 1865. 12°   BPL | SML

Midsummer night's dream . . . A comic opera in three acts by J. B. Rosier and Adolphe Leuven. Music by Ambrose Thomas. Presented for the first time in Paris on April 20th, 1850, and in New York at the French Theatre on Oct. 30th, 1866 . . . English translation by Miss Barnett. New York : J. A. Gray & Green, 1866. 8°, pp. 46 and vi. pp. of music   BUS

Midsummer night's dream . . . illustrated with 24 silhouettes by P. Konewka on wood by A. Vogel. Ln. & Heidelberg : Longmans . . . 1868. F°, pp. ii.-88
BM | BPL | BUS | SML

Midsummer night's dream. Illustrated with 24 silhouettes by P. Konewka . . . engraved by A. Vogel. Ln : Longman, 1868. 4°, pp. ii.-88

[Midsummer night's dream] Merry conceited humors of Bottom the weaver [In Ashbee, Occasional facsimile reprints, vol. 1]. Ln : . . . 1868. Fcp. 4°   MPL

Midsummer night's dream. Designs by P. Konewka. Engraved by W. H. Morse. Vignette by H. W. Smith. Boston : Roberts Brothers, 1870. Fcp. 4°, pp. vi.-88. With 24 silhouettes engraved by A. Vogel   BUS | SML

Midsummer night's dream . . . edited for scholastic study by John Hunter. Ln : Longman . . . 1870. 12°   CPL

Midsummer night's dream. Louisville [U.S.] American Printing House for the blind, 1870. 4°, pp. 62. Printed in embossed Roman type   BM

[Midsummer . . .] Merry conceited humors of Bottom the weaver, 1661. Reprinted by E. W. Ashbee. For private circulation, 1871. Fcp. 4°   BPL

Midsummer night's dream . . . as produced at the Theatre Royal . . . Birmingham : Theatre Royal Printing Office, 1873. 12°
BPL | SML

Midsummer night's dream. With illustrations by Alfred Fredericks. New York : D. Appleton & Co., 1874. Fcp. 4°, pp. 102   BUS

Midsummer night's dream . . . With illustrations by Alfred Fredericks. Ln : Bickers, 1874. 4°, pp. 102   BM | BPL

Sh— Midsummer night's dream . . .

Midsummer night's dream. The school edition of Sh—, in which all those words are omitted that cannot with propriety be read . . . With memoirs and German notes, edited by C. F. de Wickedé. Altenburg : H. A. Pierer, 1875. 8°, pp. 82   BM

Midsummer night's dream . . . edited for use in schools by H. N. Hudson. Boston [U.S.] : Ginn Bros., 1876. 12°, pp. viii.-66   BUS

Midsummer night's dream . . . edited by W. A. Wright. Oxford : Clarendon Press, 1877. Cr. 8°, pp. xxiv.-148   BUS

Midsummer night's dream . . . edited with notes by W. J. Rolfe. With engravings. New York : Harper brothers, 1877. 16°, pp. 196   BUS

Midsummer night's dream . . . Illustrated. Ln : Low & Co. . . . 1877. Roy. 8°

Midsummer night's dream . . . edited by W. A. Wright. Oxford : Clarendon Press . . . 1878. Cr. 8°

Midsummer night's dream . . . 'Acting edition.' Ln : French . . . [1878]. 12°   SML

Midsummer night's dream. With introductory remarks . . . and notes, etc. by S. Neil. Glasgow : W. Collins . . . 1878. Cr. 8°, pp. 158   BM | BPL | BUS

Midsummer night's dream . . . With notes by J. Hunter. Ln : Longmans . . . [1878]. 12°   BPL

Midsummer night's dream . . . produced at the Alexandra Theatre [Lime Street], Liverpool, Mar. 29th, 1880. Arranged for representation by E. Saker. [With introduction by Sir Edward Russell.] Liverpool : ' Daily Post ' Office, Cable Street, 1880. Cr. 8°, pp. viii.-48
BPL | SML

Of all the dramas of Sh— there is none more entirely harmonious than a ' Midsummer night's dream.' All the incidents, all the characters, are in perfect subordination to the will of the poet. It is here that he first felt the greatness of his creative power. . . . We venture to offer an opinion that if any single composition were required to exhibit the power of the English language for purposes of poetry, that composition would be the ' Midsummer night's dream.'—*Sir Edward Russell.*

Midsummer night's dream. The first quarto, 1600 : A facsimile in photo-lithography . . . with introduction by J. W. Ebsworth. ' Sh— quarto facsimiles.' Ln : W. Griggs, 1880. Fcp. 4°, pp. xxii.-64
BM | BPL | BUS

Midsummer night's dream. The second quarto, 1600 : A facsimile in photo-lithography . . . With introduction by J. W. Ebsworth. ' Sh— quarto facsimiles.' Ln : W. Griggs, 1880. Fcp. 4°, pp. xxiv.-64   BM | BPL | BUS

Midsummer night's dream. With introduction and notes . . . by . . . H. N. Hudson. 'Annotated English classics.' Boston [U.S.]: Ginn & Heath, 1880. 8°, pp. xxxvi.-128   BM | BPL

Midsummer night's dream . . . edited by C. E. Moberly, for the use of Rugby School. Rugby: W. Billington, 1881. 12°   BPL | BUS | MPL

Midsummer night's dream . . . edited by W. A. Wright. Oxford: Clarendon Press, 1881. Cr. 8°, pp. xxiv.-148   BPL | MPL

Midsummer night's dream . . . edited with notes by W. J. Rolfe. New York: Harper Brothers, 1883. 12°   BPL

Midsummer night's dream . . . edited by W. A. Wright. Oxford: Clarendon Press, 1883. Cr. 8°, pp. xxiv.-148 SML

Midsummer night's dream. 'Standard plays.' Ln: John Dicks [1883]. Cr. 8°   BM

Midsummer night's dream . . . with notes . . . for the Oxford and Cambridge local examinations. Ln: Allman & Son [c. 1885]. 8°, pp. 122

Midsummer night's dream . . . adapted for open-air representation. Ln: Merritt . . . 1885. 12°   SML

Midsummer night's dream. With notes, examination papers, and plan of preparation. Ln. & Edin.: W. & R. Chambers, 1886. 8°, pp. 112   BM

Midsummer night's dream . . . With 'Nymphydia; or the court of fairy' [by Michael Drayton], &c. [With a selection of fairy poems by Herrick, other versions of the story of Pyramus and Thisbe by Chaucer, Ovid, etc., and an introduction by H. Morley.] 'National library.' Ln: Cassell, 1886. 16°, pp. 192   BM

Midsummer night's dream . . . edited by W. A. Wright. Oxford: Clarendon Press, 1886. Cr. 8°, pp. xxiv.-148

Midsummer night's dream. With short notes and glossary by F. C. Woodforde. Market Drayton: Bennion & Horne; Ln: Simpkin [1887]. 8°, pp. lviii.-42   BM

The first piece of Sh— produced in Shropshire.

Midsummer night's dream . . . edited by C. E. Flower. 'Memorial theatre edition.' Stratford-on-Avon: G. Boyden; Ln: S. French [1887]. Cr. 8°, pp. viii.-62   BPL | SML

Midsummer night's dream . . . edited by Herbert A. Evans. 'University Sh—.' Second edition. Ln: Simpkin . . . 1887. 12°   BPL | SML

Midsummer night's dream . . . With notes, examination papers . . . Edin.: W. & R. Chambers, 1887. Cr. 8°, pp. 112   BPL

Midsummer night's dream . . . Designs by P. Konewka. Engraved by W. H. Morse. Boston [U.S.] . . . 1887. Fcp. 4°   BPL

Midsummer night's dream . . . With notes for Oxford and Cambridge examinations. Ln: Allman . . . 1887. 12°

Midsummer night's dream . . . with introduction and notes [by B. Jonson]. Ln: G. Gill, 1887. Cr. 8°, pp. 128   BM | BPL

Midsummer night's dream . . . edited by W. A. Wright . . . Oxford: Clarendon Press, 1887. Cr. 8°, pp. xxiv.-148

[Midsummer . . .] The comedy of a 'Midsummer night's dream' . . . arranged for representation at Daly's Theatre by A. Daly, produced there for the first time Jan. 31, 1888. [New York] Privately printed for A. Daly, 1888. F°, pp. 74; interleaved, inlaid, and extra-illustrated with photographs of character-scenes SML
This edition-de-luxe, which contains a programme printed on satin, was produced for presentation purposes only, at a cost of about £20 per copy. The issue was confined to twenty-five copies.

Midsummer night's dream . . . Arranged for representation at Daly's Theatre. New York . . . 1888. 8°. Illustrated   BPL | BUS

Midsummer night's dreame . . . Facsimile reprint of the text of the first folio . . . With foot-notes giving every variant in spelling and punctuation occurring in the two quartos of 1600 . . . With introduction and notes by Henry Johnson. Boston [U.S.]: Houghton, Mifflin & Co., 1888. 8°, pp. xviii.-62   BM | BPL | BUS | SML

Midsummer night's dream [illustrated in colours]. New York: Dutton & Co; Ln: Printed at Nuremberg for E. Nister [1888]. F°, pp. 46   BM | BPL

Midsummer night's dream . . . With introduction and notes by H. N. Hudson. Boston [U.S.] . . . 1889. 12°   BPL

Midsummer night's dream . . . adapted to pastoral representation by N. Newnham-Davis. Calcutta: Thacker & Spink . . . 1891. 8°, pp. 64   BM | BPL

Midsummer night's dream. With notes by K. Deighton. Ln: Macmillan, 1891. Cr. 8°

Midsummer night's dream . . . edited by W. A. Wright. Oxford: Clarendon Press, 1892. Cr. 8°, pp. xxiv.-148

Sh— Midsummer night's dream . . .

Midsommer night's dreame . . . illustrated by J. Moyr Smith. [With historical introduction.] Ln: B. Quaritch . . . 1892. F°. pp. xviii.-36   BM | BUS
Issue limited to ten copies at £10 10s. each. The plates signed by the artist.

Midsummer night's dream. 'Pitt Press Sh—.' With introduction, notes, glossary and index, edited by A. W. Verity. Third edition. Cambridge: Univ. Press . . . 1893. Cr. 8°, pp. xl.-158   SML

Midsummer night's dream, edited . . . by A. W. Verity. 'Pitt Press Sh—.' Fourth edition. Cambridge: University Press . . . 1894. Cr. 8°, pp. xl.-158   BPL | BUS

Midsummer night's dream . . . With introduction, notes, etc. by W. F. Baugust. 'Junior school Sh—.' Ln: Blackie . . . 1894. Cr. 8°, pp. 96   BPL

Midsummer night's dream . . . edited by R. Brimley Johnson. Ln: Arnold . . . [1894]. Cr. 8°, pp. xxviii.-108   BPL

Midsummer night's dream . . . edited by W. A. Wright. Oxford: Clarendon Press, 1894. Cr. 8°, pp. xxiv.-148

Midsummer night's dream . . . with 'Nymphydia or the court of fairy,' etc. [edited by H. Morley]. Ln: Cassell . . . 1894. 16°, pp. 192

Midsummer night's dream . . . edited by I. Gollancz. 'Temple edition.' Ln: Dent . . . 1894. 16°, pp. xvi.-112   BM | BLO | CTC | SML

Midsummer night's dream . . . with introduction and notes by K. Deighton. Ln: Macmillan, 1895. 12°   BPL

Midsummer night's dream . . . illustrated by R. Anning Bell. Edited with introduction by Israel Gollancz. Ln: Dent, 1895. Fcp. 4°, pp. lii.-128 BM | BPL | BUS
An edition of fifty copies on handmade paper, with duplicate set of plates on China paper.

Midsummer night's dream . . . edited by H. H. Furness. 'New variorum edition.' Philadelphia: Lippincott, 1895. Roy. 8°   BM | BPL | BUS | CTC | SML

Midsummer night's dream . . . edited with notes by H. B. Sprague, etc. Boston [U.S.]: Silver, Burdett & Co., 1896. 8°, pp. 128   BM

Midsummer night's dream. 'Ariel edition.' Ln: Routledge . . . 1896. 16°

Midsummer night's dream . . . edited by G. P. Baker. New York . . . 1896. 8°   BUS

Midsummer night's dream . . . edited by E. K. Chambers. 'Warwick Sh—.' Ln: Blackie . . . 1897. 12°, pp. 200   BPL

Sh— Midsummer night's dream . . .

Midsummer night's dream . . . edited with introduction and notes by T. Page. 'Moffatt's Plays of Sh—.' . . . 1897. 12°   BPL

Midsummer night's dream . . . edited by L. W. Lyde. 'School Sh—.' Edin.: A. & C. Black . . . 1897. 12°, pp. 110 BPL

Midsummer night's dream . . . Ln: Arnold . . . 1897. 12°

Midsummer night's dream, edited . . . by A. W. Verity. Cambridge: University Press . . . 1898. 8°

Midsummer night's dream . . . 'Pocket Falstaff edition.' Ln: Bliss . . . 1898. 16°, pp. 84   BPL | SML

[Midsummer . . .] Episode of the quarrel between Titania and Oberon . . . specially arranged for representation with the Mendelssohn music by F. A. Dixon. Ottawa: Free Press Office [1898]. 8°, pp. 32   BM

Midsummer night's dream . . . Introduction and notes by John Dennis. Illust. by B. Shaw. 'Chiswick edition.' Ln: Bell . . . 1900. Cr. 8°, pp. 114

Midsummer night's dream . . . edited with introduction and notes by C. H. Herford. 'Eversley edition.' Ln: Macmillan, 1900. Cr. 8°   BPL

Midsummer night's dream . . . edited . . . by A. W. Verity. Cambridge: University Press . . . 1900. Cr. 8°, pp. lii.-172

Midsummer night's dream . . . edited by R. B. Johnson. Ln: E. Arnold . . . [1900]. Cr. 8°, pp. xxviii.-108

Midsummer night's dream. Abridged and edited by Sarah W. Hiestand. Boston, U.S.: D. C. Heath, 1900. 8°. With portrait and plates   BPL | BUS

Midsummer night's dream . . . 'Beginner's Sh—.' Boston [U.S.] . . . 1900. Cr. 8°   BPL

Midsummer night's dream . . . Specially decorated throughout for children. Introduction by Mrs. Herbert Railton. Ln: Freemantle, 1901. 4°, pp. 142   BPL

Midsummer night's dream . . . edited with introduction, notes, glossary, and index by A. W. Verity. Cambridge: University Press . . . 1901. 8°, pp. lii.-172

Midsummer night's dream . . . 'Oxford and Cambridge edition.' Ln: Gill . . . [1902]. 12°   BPL

Midsummer night's dream . . . Introduction by Mrs. H. Railton. Ln: Constable . . . 1902. 4°

Midsummer night's dream . . . Illustrated. With introduction by Mrs. H. Railton. Ln: Freemantle . . . 1902. 4°, pp. 142

Midsummer night's dream . . . edited with introduction and notes by J. Lees. Ln : Allman . . . 1902. Cr. 8°

Midsummer night's dream . . . edited by W. J. Rolfe. New York . . . [1902]. 8°   BUS

Midsummer night's dream . . . with notes . . . by John Hunter. New impression. Ln : Longmans . . . 1902. Cr. 8°, pp. xii.-96

Midsummer night's dream. Introductory notes by W. J. Craig. Ln : Methuen, 1903. 32°

Midsummer night's dream. 'First folio edition.' Edited by Charlotte Porter and Helen A. Clarke. New York : Harrap . . . 1903. 12°   BUS

Midsummer night's dream . . . edited by A. W. Verity. Cambridge : University Press, 1903. Cr. 8°, pp. lii.-172

Midsummer night's dream . . . 'Ellen Terry edition.' Glasgow : Bryce, 1904. 32°

Midsummer night's dream. Introduction by G. Brandes. 'Favourite classics.' Ln : Heinemann, 1904. 12°, pp. xii.-84 and plate

Midsummer night's dream. Retold for children by A. S. Hoffman. Illustrated by W. Crane. Ln : Dent, 1904. 16°   BPL

Midsummer night's dream . . . edited by H. Morley. 'National library.' Ln : Cassell . . . 1904. 16°, pp. 192   BPL

Midsummer night's dream . . . edited by Henry Cuningham. 'Arden edition.' Ln : Methuen . . . 1905. 8°, pp. 246
                          BM | BLO | CTC

Midsummer night's dream . . . 'Red letter edition.' Ln : Blackie . . . 1905. 16°

Midsummer night's dream . . . 'Picture Sh—.' Ln : Blackie . . . 1905. Cr. 8°, pp. 140. Illust.   BPL

Midsummer night's dream . . . edited by A. W. Verity. Cambridge : University Press, 1905. Cr. 8°, pp. lii.-172

Midsummer night's dream . . . Pictured. Ln : Blackie . . . 1906. 12°

Midsummer night's dream . . . complete paraphrase by A. W. Parry. 'Normal tutorial series.' Ln : Simpkin . . . 1906. Cr. 8°   BPL

Midsummer night's dream . . . Edited by P. T. Cresswell. Ln : Macmillan, 1906. 12°   BPL

Midsummer night's dream . . . Introduction and notes by A. F. Watt. 'University tutorial series.' Ln : Clive . . . 1906. Cr. 8°, pp. 138

Midsummer night's dream . . . Notes by J. W. Iliffe. Illust. by C. A. Shepperson. 'Swan edition.' Ln : Longman . . . 1906. Cr. 8°

Midsummer night's dream . . . Introduction, etc. by C. W. Crook. Ln : Ralph & Holland, 1906. Cr. 8°   BPL

Midsummer night's dream . . . With notes by J. W. Iliffe. Illust. by C. A. Shepperson. 'Swan edition.' Ln : Longman, 1907. Cr. 8°   BPL

Midsummer night's dream . . . text revised by A. Dyce. Ln : Sonnenschein . . . 1907. 8°   BPL

Midsummer night's dream . . . 'Lamb Sh—.' Ln : Chatto . . . 1907. 12°

Midsummer night's dream for children. Illustrated by L. F. Perkins. Ln : Harrap . . . 1907. 4°   BPL

Midsummer night's dream . . . 'Text without notes.' Ln : Chambers . . . 1907. Cr. 8°, pp. 72   BPL

Midsummer night's dream. Introduction by F. J. Furnivall. 'Old spelling edition.' Ln : Chatto . . . 1907. Fcp. 4°
                          BM | BLO | BPL | CTC

Midsummer night's dream . . . edited by Herbert A. Evans. Ln : R. Sutton, 1907. 8°

Midsummer night's dream. 'Renaissance edition.' New York : Harrap . . . 1907. Fcp. 4°   BPL

Midsummer night's dream ; sources and analogues, edited by Frank Sidgwick. 'Sh— classics.' Ln : De la More Press, 1908. Fcp. 4°

Midsummer night's dream. With forty plates in colour and other illustrations by Arthur Rackham. Ln : Heinemann, 1908. Roy. 8°, pp. 140
                          BM | BLO | BPL | CTC
In two states ; 1000 copies on handmade paper and an unlimited issue on machine-made paper.

Midsummer night's dream . . . edited by A. F. Watt. 'University tutorial series.' Ln : . . . 1909. Cr. 8°   BPL

Midsummer night's dream . . . 'Sh— for home reading.' Edited by K. Harvey. Ln : Routledge . . . 1909. Cr. 8°   BPL

'Midsummer night's dream' references—

See Allies	See Folly
,, Barclay	,, Furnivall
,, Barnett	,, Gale
,, Booke . . .	,, Gray
,, Bullen	,, Greene
,, Davenant	,, Halliwell, Illustrations
,, Dryden	trations
,, Finkenbrink	,, Halliwell, Introduction
,, Fletcher	duction

Sh— Midsummer night's dream . . .

'Midsummer night's dream' references—

MUCEDORUS.

This play made its first printed appear-
ance apparently in 1595, but every copy
seems to have perished. It was credited to
Sh— as early as 1661, and again in 1691
by Gerard Langbaine (q. v.) It played no
mean part as a foundation for 'The Tem-
pest,' the two plays bearing a marked
resemblance in sundry places and passages.
Fleay thought Thomas Lodge, assisted by
G. Wilkins, wrote it. Malone ascribed it
to Robert Greene. Although the 1598
edition is commonly described as the first
edition, the words 'newly set foorth' in-
dicate the existence of an earlier printing.

In early popularity it appears to have
rivalled 'Hamlet.' No fewer than fourteen
editions appeared before the civil war
commenced.

No entry of the play is found at Sta-
tioners' Hall until the following date :—
'17 Sept., 1618. John Wright. Assigned
ouer vnto him by Mistris Sara Jones, late
wife of William Jones deceased, and by
direction from Master warden Adames by
a note vnder his hand theis two bookes fol-
lowing, viz., "The schoole of good manners,"
"The comedy called Mucedorus," XIId.'

[Mucedorus] A Most pleasant Comedie of
Mucedorus, the Kings Sonne of Valentia
and Amadine the Kings daughter of
Arragon, with the merie Conceites of
Mouse. Newly set foorth, as it hath bin
sundrie times plaide in the honorable
Cittie of London. Very delectable and
full of mirth. London : Printed for William Iones, dwelling neare Holborne Con-

Sh— Mucedorus . . .

duit, at the signe of the Gunne, 1598.
Fcp. 4°, twenty-four (?) unpaged leaves

BM | CTC | W

A portion of sig. A and all of the last leaf supplied in
manuscript in the Warwick copy.
Written in verse and prose.
One of the later versions contained in the additions
some uncomplimentary allusions to Ben Jonson (in
reply to his satire in 'Volpone'), in which he is termed
'a lean, hungry cannibal' and 'the scrambling raven
with a needy beard.' As some soreness is believed
to have existed between the rival writers, Sh— and
Jonson, about this period, these personalities seem to
support the contention that Sh— was concerned in
the production.
The passage which most resembles Sh—'s hand is that
beginning :—
  'If thou wilt love me thou shalt be my queene,
   I'll crowne thee with a chaplet made of ivie.'
The lines are reminiscent of those commencing :—
  'Come, live with me and be my love . . .'
in Sh—'s 'Passionate pilgrim' (q.v.)

[Mucedorus] A Most pleasant Comedie of
Mucedorus . . . London : Printed for William Iones . . . 1606. Fcp. 4°, twenty-
four (?) unpaged leaves   SOUTH KENS

No copy available.
Mentioned in Beauclerc's Catalogue, 1781, and again
by Dyce.

[Mucedorus] A Most pleasant Comedie of
Mucedorus the Kings Sonne of Valentia,
and Amadine the Kings daughter of
Aragon. With the merry conceites of
Mouse. Amplified with new additions,
as it was acted before the King's Maiestie
at White-hall on Shroue-Sunday night.
By his Highes Seruants vsually playing
at the Globe. Very delectable and full of
conceited mirth. Amplefied with new
additions, etc. Imprinted at London for
William Iones, dwelling neare Holborne
Conduit, at the signe of the Gunne, 1610.
Fcp. 4°, twenty-four (?) unpaged leaves

BM | CTC

[Mucedorus] A Most pleasant Comedie of
Mucedorus . . . London : Printed for William Jones . . . 1611. Fcp. 4°, twenty-
four (?) unpaged leaves   BLO

[Mucedorus] A most pleasant Comedie of
Mucedorus the Kings Sonne of Valencia
and Amadine the Kings daughter of
Aragon. With the merry conceits of
Mouse. Amplefied with new additions,
as it was acted before the Kings Maiestie
at White-hall on Shroue-sunday night.
By his Highnesse Seruants, vsually
playing at the Globe. Very delectable
and full of conceited mirth. Imprinted
at London for William Iones, dwelling
neere Holborne Conduit at the signe of
the Gunne, 1613. Fcp. 4°, twenty-four
unpaged leaves   BM | BUS

Sh— Mucedorus . . .

[Mucedorus] A most pleasant Comedie of Mucedorus the King's Sonne of Valencia, and Amadine the King's Daughter of Aragon. With the Merry Conceits of Mouse. Amplified with new additions as it was acted before the King's Maiestie at White-hall on Shrove-Sunday Night by his Highnesse Servants, usually playing at the Globe. London: N. O—— [Nicholas Okes] for W. Jones dwelling near Holborn Conduit, 1615. Fcp. 4°
BM | CTC

In a copy of this issue (sold in June, 1902 for £80) was an old manuscript note ascribing the authorship to Sh—.

[Mucedorus] A Most pleasant Comedie of Mucedorus . . . London : Printed for John Wright . . . 1618. Fcp. 4°, twenty-four unpaged leaves HUTH

[Mucedorus] A Most Pleasant Comedy of Mucedorus the Kings Sonne of Valentia and Amadine the Kings Daughter of Aragon. With the merry conceits of Mouse. Amplified with new Additions as it was acted before the Kings Maiesty, at White-hall, on Shroue-sunday night. By his Highnesse Seruants, vsually playing at the Globe. Very delectable, and ful of conceited mirth. London : Printed for Iohn Wright and are to bee sold at his shop without Newgate, at the signe of the Bible, 1619. Fcp. 4°, twenty-four unpaged leaves BM | BLO | BUS

A reprint of the 1613 edition, with slight changes, princ pally in the spelling.

[Mucedorus] A most pleasant Comedy of Mucedorus . . . London . . . 1621. Fcp. 4°, twenty-four (?) unpaged leaves DANTZIC

[Mucedorus] A most pleasant Comedy of Mucedorus, the Kings sonne of Valencia, and Amadine the Kings Daughter of Arragon. With the Merry Conceits of Mouse. Amplified with new additions, as it was acted before the Kings Majesty at Whitehall, on Shrove Sunday night. By his Highnesse servants, usually playing at the Globe : very delectable and full of conceited mirth. London : Printed for Francis Coles . . . [c. 1626]. Fcp. 4°
S. KENS.

Lowndes gives 1598 as the year of this undated edition, oblivious of the fact that Francis Coles only commenced publishing in or about February, 1626.

[Mucedorus] A most pleasant Comedy of Mucedorus . . . London . . . 1629. Fcp. 4°
BM | DANTZIC

A perfect copy is preserved in the municipal library at Dantzic. The B.M. copy lacks the title.

[Mucedorus] A most pleasant Comedy of Mucedorus . . . London : Printed for I. Wright . . . 1631. Fcp. 4° BM

Sh— Mucedorus . . .

[Mucedorus] A most pleasant Comedy of Mucedorus . . . London : Printed for I. Wright . . . 1634. Fcp. 4° BM

[Mucedorus] A Most pleasant Comedy of Mucedorus the Kings sonne of Valentia, and Amadine the Kings Daughter of Arragon. With the merry conceits of Mouse. Amplified with new Additions, as it was acted before the Kings Majestie at Whitehall, on Shrove-sunday night. By his Highnesse servants usually playing at the Globe. Very delectable and full of conceited mirth. London : Printed for John Wright and are to be sold at his shop, at the signe of the Bible in Gilt-spurre-Street without Newgate. 1639. Fcp. 4°, twenty-four unpaged leaves
BUS | CTC

Reprinted from the 1613 edition, with slight changes.

[Mucedorus] A Most pleasant Comedy of Mucedorus The Kings Son of Valentia, and Amadine the Kings Daughter of Aragon. With the merry Conceits of Mouse. Amplifyed with new Additions, as it was Acted before the Kings Majestie at White-hall on Shrove-sunday night. By his Highness servants usually playing at the Globe. Very delectable and full of conceited mirth. London : Printed for Francis Coles, and are to be sold at his shop, at the Lamb in the Old Bayly, 1663. Fcp. 4°, twenty-four unpaged leaves
BLO | BUS

Reprinted from the 1613 issue, with little variation.

[Mucedorus] A Most pleasant Comedy of Mucedorus The Kings Son of Valentia, and Amadine the King's Daughter of Aragon. With the merry Conceits of Mouse. Amplifyed with new Additions, as it was Acted before the King's Majestie at White-hall on Shrove-sunday night. By His Highness's Servants usually playing at the Globe. Very delectable and full of conceited mirth. London : Printed by E. O—— for Francis Coles and are to be Sold at his Shop in Wine-street near Hatton Garden, 1668. Fcp. 4°, on twenty-four unpaged leaves
BM | BLO | BUS | CTC | NY

Reprinted from the 1613 issue, with but little change.

[Mucedorus] A most pleasant Comedy of Mucedorus . . . Amplified with new Additions as it was acted before the Kings Majesty at Whitehall, on Shrove-sunday Night. London : Printed for Francis Coles [c. 1688]. Fcp. 4°, sig. A¹ to F⁴ in fours ; the last leaf bears a list of romances published by Coles BM | CTC

Sh— Mucedorus . . .

Mucedorus . . . [In Dodsley's 'Collection of plays . . .'] Ln : Dodsley . . . 1744. 12°

Mucedorus . . . edited by John Payne Collier. Ln : . . . 1824
Stated to be transcribed from a quarto text of 1609, which is probably a fiction, as this edition cannot be traced.

Mucedorus . . . [Text and notes in German and English, edited by H. Delius]. Elberfeld : R. L. Friderichs . . . 1874. 12° BUS

Mucedorus . . . [In 'Dodsley's Collection of old English plays, revised by W. C. Hazlitt,' Vol. 7]. Ln : Reeves & Turner, 1874-76. 8° BPL | BUS

[Mucedorus] Comedy of Mucedorus. Revised and edited with introduction and notes by Karl Warnke and Ludwig Proescholdt. Halle : Max Niemeyer, 1878. Roy. 8°, pp. viii.-80 BUS | SML

Mucedorus . . . Sh—'s doubtful plays. Edited with an introduction by A. F. Hopkinson. Ln : [Privately printed by] M. E. Sims & Co., 1893. Cr. 8°, pp. xx.-62 SML

' Mucedorus ' references—
See Hopkinson   *See* Rowe
,, Sh— [Works] Sh— Apocrypha, 1908

MUCH ADO ABOUT NOTHING.

The first known edition of this comedy was printed by V. S—— [Valentine Sims] in 1600 for Andrew Wise and William Aspley. The play seems to have met with slender approval, as no other separate edition is recorded until Tonson issued his in 1734.
The play was registered at Stationers' Hall :—'1600, Aug. 14. Andrewe Wyse, William Aspley. Entred for their copies vnder the handes of the wardens two bookes, the one called Muche a doo about nothinge . . . wrytten by Master Shakespere XIId.' Probably printed from a playhouse copy with Sh—'s consent and that of his company. The entry is notable as being the first play on the registers to mention Sh—'s name.

Much adoe about Nothing. As it hath been sundrie times publikely acted by the right honourable, the Lord Chamberlaine his seruants. Written by William Shakespeare. [*Ornament.*] London : Printed by V. S—— [Valentine Sims] for Andrew Wise, and William Aspley, 1600. Fcp. 4°, thirty-six unpaged leaves ; sig. A¹ to I⁴ in fours
BM | BLO | BUS | CTC | ELLESMERE

Sh— Much ado about nothing . . .

A copy bound in crushed crimson morocco sold for £1,570, 9th Dec., 1905. It measured 7in. by 4¾in., was 'washed,' and had one top line mended. It crossed the Atlantic. It had previously sold for £130 only, at the disposal of the Gaisford library in 1890. This edition was reprinted by Geo. Steevens in 1766 ; by H. Staunton, 1864 ; by E. W. Ashbee, 1865. George Steevens' copy with his autograph on the title is at Boston, U.S.

[Much ado . . .] The law against lovers [In Sir Wm. Davenant's Works]. Ln : . . . 1673. F° (excerpt) BPL | W
An amalgamation of Sh—'s two plots of ' Measure for measure ' and ' Much ado . . .' ; the excerpt was extracted from a copy of Davenant's Works, 1672-73.

Much ado about nothing. By Mr. Wm. Sh—. Ln : Printed for J. Tonson and the rest of the proprietors, and sold by the booksellers of Ln. and Westminster, 1734. Cr. 8°, pp. 72 and frontispiece by Lud. Du Guernier BPL | SML

Much ado about nothing . . . Ln : R. Walker . . . 1735. Cr. 8°

[Much ado . . .] The universal passion. A comedy. [By James Miller.] As it is acted at the Theatre Royal in Drury Lane by his majesty's servants. Ln : J. Watts . . . 1737. 8°, pp. viii.-76 BUS | W
Much of the plot and language is from ' Much ado,' and the balance appears to be copied nearly verbatim from Miller and Johnson's translation of Molière's ' Princess d'Elide,' first issued in 1732.

Much ado about nothing. To which is added 'All's well that ends well.' By the ghost of Sh—. Ln : Hall . . . [c. 1740]. Fcp. 4° W
A pamphlet of a political nature.

Much ado about nothing . . . Edinburgh . . . 1754. 12° BUS

Much ado . . . [*crude portrait of the poet*]. Ln : Printed for C. Hitch and L. Hawes ; H. Lintot ; J. & R. Tonson ; J. Hodges ; B. Dod ; J. Rivington ; M. & T. Longman ; J. Brindley ; C. Corbet ; and T. Caslon, 1757. Cr. 8°, pp. 72. With frontispiece by Van der Gucht after H. Gravelot

Much ado about nothing . . . Ln : J. & R. Tonson . . . 1766. 12° BPL | SML

Much adoe about nothing . . . 1600 [Reprinted by George Steevens, Ln., 1766]. 8°, pp. 38 BPL | SML | W

Much ado about nothing . . . as performed at the Theatre Royal, Drury Lane. Regulated from the prompt-book with permission of the managers by Mr. Hopkins, prompter An introduction, and notes critical and illustrative, are added by the authors of the ' Dramatic censor ' [F. Gentleman]. Ln : Printed for John

Sh— Much ado about nothing . . .

Bell . . . and C. Etherington at York, 1773. 8°, pp. 72, and frontispiece engraved by C. Grignion after E. Edwards
An edition previously unnoticed.

Much ado about nothing . . . edited by . . . Hatton. Edinburgh: Williamson . . . 1774. 12°

Much ado about nothing . . . Second edition. Ln: John Bell . . . 1774. 8° SML

Much ado about nothing . . . As performed at the Theatre Royal, Drury Lane. Notes by L. Theobald. Ln: J. Rivington . . . 1776. 12°. With portrait of Frances Abington SML

Much ado about nothing . . . edited by L. Theobald. Ln: [Printed at Edinburgh for] John Bell . . . 1778. 12°

Much ado about nothing . . . As it is acted at the Theatres Royal in Drury-Lane and Covent-Garden . . . Ln: Printed for J. Wenman, 144, Fleet St., and sold by all other booksellers in town and country, 1778. 8°, pp. 20 and copperplate
Portrait of Garrick as 'Benedick.' BM | BPL

Much ado about nothing . . . Taken from the manager's book at the Theatre Royal, Drury Lane. Ln: Butters . . . [c. 1784]. 12° BPL

Much ado about nothing . . . adapted to the stage by J. P. Kemble, as it is performed at the Theatre Royal, Drury Lane. Ln: . . . [c. 1799]. 8°

Much ado . . . with remarks by Mrs. Inchbald. Ln: Longman . . . [c. 1808]. 12°. With frontispiece BPL

Much ado . . . revised by J. P. Kemble, and now first published as it is acted at the Theatre Royal in Covent Garden. Ln: Printed for the theatre . . . 1810. 8°, pp. 68 BUS

Much ado . . . as performed at the Theatres-Royal, Drury Lane and Covent Garden. Edinburgh . . . [c. 1812]. 12° BPL

Much ado . . . A comedy. . . As performed at the Theatres Royal, Drury Lane and Covent Garden. Printed under the authority of the managers from the prompt books . . . Edinburgh: Printed at the Caledonian Press by Oliver & Boyd, Baron Grant's Close, Netherbow, 1813. 12°, pp. 60 (includ. printed wrappers) and frontispiece of Dogberry

Much ado . . . revised by J. P. Kemble, and now published as it is performed at the Theatres Royal. Ln: J. Miller, 1815. 8°, pp. 70 BM | BPL | BUS

Much ado . . . as performed at the Theatres Royal, Drury Lane and Covent Garden. Printed under the authority of the managers from the prompt book. With remarks by Mrs. Inchbald. Ln: Hurst, Robinson & Co. [c. 1816]. 12°, pp. 74 and plate

Much ado . . . by Will. Sh—. Printed complete from the text of Sam. Johnson and Geo. Steevens. Ln: . . . 1818. 16° w

Much ado . . . 'British theatre.' Ln: Dolby . . . 1823. 12° BPL

Much ado . . . With prefatory remarks [signed P. P.] . . . marked with the stage business, and stage directions, as it is performed at the Theatres Royal, by W. Oxberry. Ln: . . . 1823. 8°, pp. viii.-72 BM | BPL | SML

Much ado . . . With remarks . . . Edinburgh: Stirling & Kenney . . . 1829. 12°. With frontispiece BPL | SML

Much ado . . . printed from the acting copy, with remarks . . . by D. G—— [Geo. Daniel]. To which are added, a . . . cast of the characters . . . and the whole of the stage business, as now performed at the Theatres Royal. Ln: J. Cumberland . . . 1829. 12°, pp. 62 BM | BPL | BUS

Much ado . . . With remarks by D. G—— [Geo. Daniel]. Ln: John Cumberland . . . 1831. 12°

Much ado . . . Nuremberg & New York . . . 1839. 12° BPL

Much ado . . . A tale . . . by C. Lamb [In 'The romancist,' Vol. 4, p. 410-411]. 1840. 4° BPL

Much ado . . . 'Modern standard drama.' New York: S. French [c. 1845]. 12°, pp. 64

Much ado . . . 'Modern standard drama.' New York: S. French . . . 1848. 12°, pp. 64

Much ado . . . A comedy. 'Acting edition.' With preliminary notes. Ln: T. H. Lacy [1858]. 12°, pp. 62 BM | CPL | SML

Much ado . . . arranged for representation at the Princess's Theatre, with explanatory notes, by Charles Kean. Ln: J. K. Chapman & Co. [1858]. 8°, pp. 68 BM | BPL | SML

Much ado . . . 'Standard drama.' New York: S. French . . . [c. 1860]. 12°
W. Creswick's prompt copy is at Stratford. BPL | SML

Much adoe . . . text from the folio of 1623; with notices of the known editions preuiously issued. Ln: L. Booth, 1862. Fcp. 4°, pp. vi.-22; interleaved with blank writing paper BM | BUS

Much ado . . . 1600 . . . photo-lithographed . . . under the superintendence of H. Staunton, from the matchless original of

Sh— Much ado about nothing . . .

1600, in the library of the Earl of Ellesmere, by R. Preston. Ln : Day & Son
. . . 1864. Fcp. 4°, on 36 unpaged folios
BM | BPL | BUS | CPL

Much ado . . . 1600, facsimiled by E. W.
Ashbee. [Edited by J. O. Halliwell.]
For private circulation, 1865. Fcp. 4° ;
A¹ to I⁴ in fours, unpaged   BPL | MPL
One of the fifty copies produced, nineteen of which the
editor destroyed.

Much ado . . . edited by H. Staunton.
Ln : Day & Son . . . 1865. 8°

Much ado . . . Ln : T. H. Lacy . . . 1866.
12°

Much ado . . . With the stage business,
cast, costumes, positions, etc. New
York : S. French . . . [c. 1869]. 12°, pp.
64   BUS

Much ado . . . 'Cumberland's theatre.'
Ln : T. H. Lacy . . . [c. 1870]. 12°

Much ado . . . edited by H. L. Hinton . . .
New York : H. L. Hinton, Booth's
Theatre [c. 1871]. 12°, pp. 64 and por-
trait of E. Booth   BUS

Much ado . . . edited for scholastic study
by John Hunter. Ln : Longman . . .
1872. Cr. 8°   BM | CPL

Much ado . . . edited for schools by H. N.
Hudson. Boston [U.S.] : Ginn Brothers
. . . 1873. 12°, pp. ii.-68-138 [excerpt]
BUS

Much ado . . . 'Acting edition.' Ln :
French . . . [c. 1873]. 12°   BPL

[Much ado . . .] The law against lovers [In
Davenant's Works, Vol. 5]. Ln : . . .
1874. 8°   BPL

Much ado . . . as performed at the Crystal
Palace. Ln : . . . 1874. 8°   BPL

Much ado . . . 'Standard plays.' Ln : J.
Dicks [c. 1875]. 12°

Much ado . . . as produced at the Crystal
Palace. Ln : . . . 1876. 8°

Much ado . . . 'Acting edition.' Ln : Lacy
. . . 1877. 12°   SML
The prompt copy used by W. Creswick on his Australian tour is at Stratford.

Much ado . . . produced at the Alexandra
Theatre [Lime St.], Liverpool, on Monday, April 22nd, 1878. Arranged for representation by Edward Saker. Liverpool : ' Daily Post,' Cable St., 1878. Cr.
8°, pp. iv.-52   BPL | SML

Much ado . . . from the text of the 1600
quarto. Edited by W. J. Rolfe. New
York : Harper . . . 1878. 12°. With engravings

Much ado . . . edited by W. J. Rolfe. New
York : Harper, 1879. 16°, pp. 178.
With engravings and portrait from
Ward's statue of Sh—   BUS

Sh— Much ado about nothing . . .

Much ado . . . with introduction and notes
. . . by . . . H. N. Hudson. Boston [U.S.] :
Ginn & Heath . . . 1880. 8°, pp. xii.-138
BM | BPL

Much ado . . . with notes by H. N. Hudson.
Boston [U.S.] . . . 1881. 12°

Much ado . . . edited . . . by John Hunter.
Ln : Longman . . . 1882. 12°

Much ado . . . as arranged for the stage by
Henry Irving and presented at the
Lyceum Theatre, Wed., Oct. 11th, 1882.
Ln : Chiswick Press . . . 1882. 8°, pp. 74
BPL | SML

Much ado . . . edited by C. E. Flower.
' Memorial theatre edition.' Stratford-
on-Avon : Printed by G. Boyden ; Ln :
S. French, 1882. Cr. 8°, pp. viii.-80,
incl. printed wrappers   BPL | SML

Much ado . . . edited with notes by W. J.
Rolfe. New York . . . 1883. 12°   BPL

Much ado . . . as arranged for the stage by
Henry Irving and presented at the Lyceum Theatre on Wed., 11th Oct., 1883.
Ln : Chiswick Press . . . 1883. 8°, pp.
82, includ. printed wrappers
11,000 copies were sold of this edition.

Much ado . . . ' Standard plays.' Ln :
John Dicks [1883]. 12°   BM | BPL

Much ado . . . now first published in fully
recovered metrical form, and with a
prefatory essay, by W. Watkiss Lloyd.
Ln : F. Norgate, 1884. 8°, pp. xvi.-92
BM | BPL | BUS | SML
A specimen of the projected ' Princeps edition.'

Much adoe . . . the quarto edition, 1600.
A facsimile. With introduction by P. A.
Daniel. ' Sh— quarto facsimiles.' Ln :
Charles Prætorius . . . 1886. Fcp. 4°,
pp. xii.-72   BM | BPL | BUS | SML

Much ado . . . with introduction and notes
by K. Deighton. Ln : Macmillan . . .
1888. 12°   BPL

Much ado . . . With introduction and notes
by H. N. Hudson. Boston [U.S.] . . .
1888. 12°   BPL

Much ado . . . [With introduction by H.
Morley]. ' National library.' Ln : Cassell . . . 1888. 16°, pp. 192   BM

Much ado . . . Philadelphia : Lopez &
Wemyss [c. 1890]. 12°   BUS

Much ado . . . [&] 'Ariodantes and
Geneura' [edited by H. Morley]. ' National library.' Ln : Cassell . . . 1890.
16°, pp. 192

Much ado . . . edited by A. W. Verity.
' Falcon edition.' Ln : Rivington . . .
1890. 12°   BPL

Much ado . . . edited by Maynard. New
York : A. H. Kellogg . . . 1893. 12° SML

Much ado . . . edited by I. Gollancz. 'Temple edition.' Ln : Dent . . . 1894. 16°

Much ado . . . edited by W. A. Wright. Oxford : Clarendon Press, 1894. Cr. 8° BPL

Much ado . . . 'Ariel edition.' Ln : Routledge . . . 1896. 16°

Much ado . . . a comedy in five acts . . . as arranged for production at Daly's theatre by Augustin Daly. With an introductory chapter by W. Winter. New York : Privately printed . . . 1897. F°, pp. 76, inlaid and extra-illustrated, with portraits in character of Ada Rehan and others, and programme SML

Edition-de-luxe, limited to twenty-five copies and prepared for presentation only by Mr. Daly at a cost of £20 each.

Much ado . . . 'Pocket Falstaff edition.' Ln : Bliss, Sands, 1898. 16°, pp. 100 BPL | SML

Much ado . . . edited with introduction and notes by C. H. Herford. 'Eversley edition.' Ln : Macmillan, 1900. Cr. 8° BPL

Much ado . . . 'Warwick edition.' Edited by J. C. Smith. Ln : Blackie . . . 1901. Cr. 8° BPL

Much ado . . . edited with notes by H. N. Hudson. 'Windsor edition.' Edinburgh : Jack . . . 1902. Cr. 8° BM | BLO | CTC

Much ado . . . with introduction and notes by Alfred L. Cann. Ln : Ralph & Holland, 1903. Cr. 8° BPL

Much ado . . . with introductory notes and appendices by A. Barter. 'Normal tutorial series.' Ln : Simpkin, 1903. Cr. 8° BPL

Much ado . . . with introductory notes by W. J. Craig. Ln : Methuen . . . 1903. 16°

Much ado . . . edited by H. Morley. 'National library.' Ln : Cassell . . . 1904. 16°, pp. 192 BPL

Much ado . . . Complete paraphrase by W. F. Smith. 'Normal tutorial series.' Ln : Simpkin, 1904. Cr. 8° BPL

Much ado . . . parsed and analysed by M. K. A. Beisiegel. 'Normal tutorial series.' Ln : Simpkin . . . 1904. Cr. 8° BPL

Much ado . . . parsed . . . by M. K. A. Beisiegel. Second edition. Ln : Simpkin, 1904. Cr. 8°

Much ado . . . edited by E. J. Thomas. With introduction and notes. Ln : Clive, 1904. Cr. 8°, pp. 138

Much ado . . . with introduction and notes by Alfred L. Cann. Ln : Ralph & Holland, 1904. Cr. 8°

Much ado . . . with introduction by G. Brandes. 'Favourite classics.' Ln : W. Heinemann, 1904. 12°, pp. x.-102 and frontispiece

Much ado . . . 'Academy edition.' With introduction and notes by T. E. Margerison. Ln : Chambers . . . 1904. Cr. 8°, pp. 164 BPL

Much ado . . . 'Waistcoat pocket edition.' Ln : Treherne . . . 1904. 32°

Much ado . . . 'Ellen Terry edition.' Glasgow : Bryce . . . 1904. 32°

Much ado . . . 'Red letter edition.' Ln : Blackie . . . 1905. 12°

Much ado . . . 'Carlton classics.' Ln : Long . . . 1905. 12°

Much ado . . . 'Swan edition.' Ln : Longmans . . . 1905. Cr. 8° BPL

Much ado . . . With biographical introduction by Hannaford Bennett. Ln : J. Long . . . 1905. Cr. 8° BPL

Much ado . . . 'Moffatt's plays.' . . . Leeds : E. J. Arnold . . . [1906]. Cr. 8° BPL

Much ado . . . with introduction by H. W. Mabie. 'Renaissance edition.' New York : Harrap . . . 1907. Fcp. 4° BPL

Much adoe . . . edited by W. G. Boswell-Stone. 'Old spelling edition.' Ln : Chatto . . . 1908. 8° BM | BLO | BPL | CTC

'Much ado about nothing' references—

See Ariosto	See Johnson & Stee-
„ Aylward	„ Kean [vens
„ Bandello	„ Kyd
„ Barnett (T. D.)	„ Latham
„ Collier	„ Martin
„ Cooke	„ Ritson
„ Eusebius	„ Scott (M. A.)
„ Fletcher	„ Sharpe (H.)
„ German	„ Spedding
„ Greene (R.)	„ Tournaments
„ Halliwell	„ Towndrow
„ Holme	„ Turbervile
„ Hundred . . .	„ Wigstead

My flocks feed not, 1600. *See* Bodenham
On a day, alack the day, 1600. *See* Bodenham

OTHELLO.

The earliest traceable edition of this tragedy is that printed by N. O—— [Nicholas Okes] and published by Thomas Walkley in 1622, just a year before the first collective edition of Sh—'s Works was ushered forth. The play thus originally appeared posthumously, some six

Sh— Othello . . .

years after the author's death. It was en-
tered at Stationers' Hall, as follows :—'6th
Oct., 1621. Thomas Walkley. Entred for
his copie vnder the handes of Sir George
Buck and Master Swinhowe, warden, The
tragedie of Othello the Moore of Venice,
VId.' This was not the text employed by
W. Jaggard in preparing the 1623 folio.

[Othello] The Tragœdy of Othello, The
Moore of Venice. As it hath beene diuerse
times acted at the Globe, and at the
Black-Friers, by his Maiesties Seruants.
Written by William Shakespeare.
[*Pegasus device.*] London : Printed by
N. O—— [Nicholas Okes] for Thomas
Walkley and are to be sold at his shop,
at the Eagle and Child, in Brittan's
Bursse, 1622. Fcp. 4°, pp. iv.-92 on
forty-eight leaves, irregularly paged :
pages 74 and 75 are numbered 78 and 77
in error, and pages 78 to 91 are erroneously paginated 80, 81, 80, 89, 90 to
99 ; sig. A two leaves, then B to N² in
fours   BM | BLO | BUS | CTC | NY

The publisher's address, headed 'The stationer to the
reader,' is perhaps sufficiently curious to quote at
length :—' To set forth a booke without an epistle
were like to the old English prouerbe, "A blew coat
without a badge," and the author being dead I
thought good to take that piece of worke vpon mee.
To commend it I will not, for that which is good I
hope euery man will commend without intreaty ; and
I am the bolder because the author's name is sufficient
to vent his worke. Thus leauing euery one to the
liberty of iudgement I haue ventered to print this
play and leaue it to the generall censure . . .'
An imperfect copy realised £104 in July, 1903. Reprinted by Steevens in 1766, after collation with the
1630 edition.

[Othello] The Tragœdy of Othello, The
Moore of Venice. As it hath beene diuerse
times acted at the Globe, and at the
Black-Friers by his Maiesties Seruants.
Written by William Shakespeare. London : Printed by A. M—— [? Augustine
Mathewes] for Richard Hawkins, and are
to be sold at his shoppe in Chancery-Lane,
neere Sergeants-Inne, 1630. Fcp. 4°, pp.
ii.-92, forty-eight leaves ; sig. A¹ to M⁴
in fours (the last leaf blank)
          BM | BLO | CTC | NY | W
This edition contains readings varying importantly from
the 1622 issue.
In May, 1907, a copy sold for £101.

[Othello] The Tragœdy of Othello, The
Moore of Venice. As it hath beene divers
times acted at the Globe, and at the
Black-Friers, by his Majesties Servants.
Written by William Shakespeare. The
Fourth Edition. London : Printed for
William Leak, at the Crown in Fleet-
street between the two Temple Gates,

Sh— Othello . . .

1655. Fcp. 4°, pp. ii.-94, paged from 1
to 93 ; sig. A¹ to M in fours (the last leaf
bearing a ' List of books printed or sold
by William Leake')
          BM | BLO | BUS | CTC | NY | W
A re-issue of the 1630 edition.
In Dec., 1905, Sir Henry Irving's copy realised £200.

Othello, the Moor of Venice . . . [Altered
by John Dryden]. Ln : . . . 1670. Fcp.
4°

Othello, the Moor of Venice . . . [Altered
by John Dryden]. Ln : . . . 1674. Fcp.
4°

Othello, the Moor of Venice. A Tragedy.
As it hath been divers times acted at the
Globe, and at the Black-Friers : And
now at the Theater Royal, by His
Majesties Servants. Written by William
Shakespear. [Edited by John Dryden.]
Ln : Printed for W. Weak [? W. Leake]
and are to be sold by Richard Bentley
and M. Magnes in Russel Street near
Covent Garden, 1681. Fcp. 4°, pp. iv.-
76   BPL | BUS | W

Othello, the Moor of Venice . . . As it hath
been divers times Acted at the Globe,
and at the Black-Friers ; . . . and now at
the Theatre Royal. [Altered by John
Dryden.] Ln : R. Bentley & S. Magnes,
1687. Fcp. 4°, pp. iv.-76 BM | BPL | BUS

Othello, the Moor of Venice. A Tragedy.
As it hath been divers times Acted at the
Globe, and at the Black-Friers : and now
at the Theatre Royal, by His Majesties'
Servants. Written by William Shake-
spear. [Edited by John Dryden.] Ln :
Printed for Richard Bentley in Russel
St. near Covent Garden, 1695. Fcp. 4°,
pp. iv.-76   BM | BPL | BUS

Othello, the Moor of Venice . . . [Altered
by John Dryden.] Ln : . . . 1697. Fcp.
4°

Othello, the Moor of Venice . . . [Altered
by John Dryden.] Ln : . . . 1701. Fcp.
4°

Othello, the Moor of Venice. A tragedy.
As it hath been divers times acted at the
Globe and at the Black-Friers : and now
at the Theatre Royal, by her majesties
servants. Written by W. Sh—. [Edited
by John Dryden.] Ln : Printed for R.
Wellington at the Dolphin and Crown at
the West End of St. Paul's Churchyard,
1705. Fcp. 4°, pp. iv.-76
          BM | BPL | BUS | NY | W

Othello . . . [An excerpt from a 'Collection
of the best English plays']. Ln : . . .
1710. 8°, pp. 114   BM

Othello, the Moor of Venice. A tragedy. Written by Mr. W. Sh—. Ln : Printed for the Company [c. 1720]. 12° w

Othello, the Moor of Venice : A tragedy . . . Dublin : Printed by and for George Grierson at the 'Two Bibles' in Essex Street, 1721. 8°, pp. 96
No Irish-printed piece of Sh— recorded before this year.

Othello, the Moor of Venice. A tragedy. As it hath been divers times acted at the Globe and at the Black-Friers : and now at the Theater Royal, by his majesties servants. Written by W. Sh—. Ln : Printed by John Darby in Bartholomew Close for M. Poulson, 1724. 12°, pp. 96
BM | BPL | BUS | W
At Boston is James Plumptre's interleaved copy with MS. preface, alterations, and notes. The changes chiefly consist in 'doing away with the prodigality of death in the original.'

Othello, the Moor of Venice. A tragedy. By Mr. Wm. Sh—. Ln : Printed for J. Tonson and the rest of the proprietors, and sold by the booksellers of Ln. and Westminster, 1734. Cr. 8°, pp. 96 and frontispiece by Lud. Du Guernier
BPL | BUS | SML

Othello . . . As it is acted at the Theatres. Ln : Printed in the year 1735. 12° BPL

Othello . . . As it is acted at the Theatres. Ln : Printed in the year 1736. 12° BPL

Othello, the Moor of Venice. A tragedy. Written by William Sh—. Ln : 1747. 12° w
With manuscript variorum readings in the margins taken from the first edition of 1622 and the second folio edition of Sh—'s Works, 1632.

Othello, the Moor of Venice. A tragedy. As it is now acted by his majesty's servants. Written by Wm. Sh—. Ln : Printed for J. & P. Knapton, T. Longman, C. Hitch, and the rest of the proprietors, 1750. Cr. 8°, pp. 96 (the first leaf blank and the last bearing list of Hitch's publications) SML | W

Othello . . . Ln : D. Williams in St. Paul's Churchyard [c. 1750]. 12° BPL

Othello, the Moor of Venice . . . Dublin : Printed for Peter Wilson in Dame St., 1751. 8°, pp. 94 (last leaf advertising Wilson's publications)

Othello . . . As it is now acted by his majesty's servants. Ln : Printed for J. & P. Knapton, T. Longman, C. Hitch, and the rest of the proprietors . . . 1753. 12°, pp. 56 SML

Othello . . . As it is now acted at the Theatre Royal in Covent Garden. Ln : . . . 1755. 12° BPL

Othello . . . As it is now acted by His Majesty's servants. Ln : . . . 1756. 12° BPL

Othello . . . According to Mr. Pope's second edition. Glasgow : Printed and sold by R. & A. Foulis, 1757. Cr. 8°

Othello, the Moor of Venice. A tragedy. As it is now acted at the Theatres Royal in Drury-Lane and Covent-Garden. Written by W. Sh—. Ln : H. Woodfall, L. Hawes, Clarke, & Collins ; W. Johnston ; B. Dod ; J. Rivington ; T. Longman ; T. Caslon ; B. Law ; T. Lownds ; C. Corbett, 1765. 12°, pp. 72, & frontispiece

Othello, the Moor of Venice . . . Printed exactly agreeable to the representation. Ln : Halhed Garland [c. 1765]. 8°, pp. 86 BM | BPL

[Othello] The tragœdy of Othello . . . 1622. Ln : [Reprinted by G. Steevens] 1766. 8°, pp. 38 BPL | W

Othello, the Moor of Venice. A tragedy . . . Gottingen : Printed for Victorinus Bossiegel, 1766. 8°, pp. 158 BPL

Othello, the Moor of Venice. A tragedy, by Wm. Sh—. Dublin : . . . 1767. 8° w

Othello, the Moor of Venice. A tragedy, by Wm. Sh—. Edinburgh : Printed by and for Martin & Wotherspoon, 1768. 12° w

Othello, the Moor of Venice. A tragedy. As it is now acted at the Theatres Royal in Drury Lane and Covent Garden . . . Ln : Printed for the proprietors and sold by all the booksellers of London and Westminster, 1770. 12°, pp. 70 and plate BUS

Othello . . . As it is now acted at the Theatres Royal in Drury Lane and Covent Garden. Ln : L. Hawes . . . 1771. 12° BPL

Othello, the Moor of Venice. A tragedy . . . collated with the old and modern editions [by Charles Jennens]. Ln : W. Owen . . . 1773. 8°, pp. xviii.-182 and plate BM | BPL | BUS | NY

Othello . . . as performed at the Theatre Royal, Drury Lane. Regulated from the prompt-book, with permission of the managers, by Mr. Hopkins, prompter. An introduction, and notes critical and illustrative, are added by the authors of the ' Dramatic censor ' [F. Gentleman]. Ln : Printed for John Bell . . . and C. Etherington at York, 1773. 8°, pp. 84, and frontispiece designed and engraved by Isaac Taylor
An edition previously unchronicled.
Offprinted from Bell's edition of Sh—'s Works for play-goers.

Sh— Othello . . .

Othello . . . Ln : W. Oxlade . . . 1777. 12°

Othello, the Moor of Venice. A tragedy. As it is acted at the Theatres Royal in Drury Lane and Covent Garden. Ln : Printed for J. Wenman, 144, Fleet Street, and sold by all other booksellers in town and country, 1777. 8°, pp. 22 and plate of 'Barry as Othello'   BM | BPL | SML
The Stratford copy presented by J. O. Halliwell, with inscription.

Othello. A tragedy . . . As it is acted at the Theatres-Royal in Drury Lane and Covent Garden . . . Ln : Harrison & Co. . . . 1780. 8°, pp. 22 and portrait of 'Barry as Othello'   BPL | BUS

Othello . . . taken from the manager's book at the Theatre Royal, Covent Garden. Ln : Sabine & Son . . . [c. 1780]. 8°   BPL

Othello . . . taken from the manager's book at the Theatre Royal, Covent-Garden. Ln : R. Butters . . . [c. 1780]. 12°   BPL

Othello, the Moor of Venice. A tragedy . . . marked with the variations in the manager's book at the Theatre-Royal in Drury Lane. Ln : C. Bathurst, W. & A. Strahan, J. F. & C. Rivington, L. Davis, T. & W. Lowndes, W. Owen & Son, S. Crowder, B. White, T. Longman, B. Law, C. Dilly, T. Cadell, T. Payne & Son, J. Robson, G. Robinson, T. Davies, T. Bowles, R. Baldwin, H. L. Gardner, J. Nicholls, J. Bew, W. Cater, J. Murray, W. Stuart, S. Hayes, W. Bent, S. Bladon, W. F. & E. Newbery, 1784. 12°, pp. 92. With engraved frontispiece BM | BPL | SML
The Stratford copy presented by J. O. Halliwell, with inscription.

Othello . . . By Will. Sh—. Printed complete from the text of Sam. Johnson and Geo. Steevens and revised from the last editions. Ln : John Bell . . . 1785. 12°, pp. 144   BUS

Othello . . . printed complete from the text of Sam. Johnson and Geo. Steevens and revised from the last editions . . . Ln : John Bell, 1788. 12°, pp. 144. Frontispiece of ' Mr. Henderson as Iago' and vignette title

[Othello] Arlequin cruello, parodie d'Othello [par J. B. Radet, G. F. Desfontaines de la Vallée et P. G. Barré]. 1792. 8°   BM
In English and French.

Othello, the Moor of Venice . . . with notes . . . for the use of lectures by T. Miller. Halle [Germany]: Kummel, 1794. 8°, pp. 134   BM

[Othello] The story of the Moor of Venice, translated from the Italian . . . by W. Parr. Ln : . . . 1795. 8°   BPL | W

Sh— Othello . . .

Othello . . . Ln : Garland . . . [c. 1800]. 8°

Othello . . . Ln : Barker . . . [c. 1800]. 12°

Othello . . . from the text of Johnson & Steevens. Manchester : R. & W. Dean, 1802. 12°, pp. 90, and engraved frontispiece

Othello . . . adapted to the stage by J. P. Kemble. As acted at the Theatre Royal, Covent Garden. Ln : Longman . . . 1804. Cr. 8°   CPL

Othello, the Moor of Venice. A tragedy, revised by J. P. Kemble, and now first published as it is acted at the Theatre Royal in Covent Garden. Ln : T. N. Longman & O. Rees, 1804. 8°, pp. 80   BUS

Othello . . . adapted to the stage by J. P. Kemble. Ln : . . . 1808. 8°

Othello, a tragedy. By Wm. Sh—. Ln : J. Roach, 1808. 12°   W

Othello, the Moor of Venice. A tragedy in five acts . . . As performed at the Theatres Royal in Drury Lane and Covent Garden. Printed under the authority of the managers from the prompt book. With remarks by Mrs. Inchbald. Ln : Longman . . . [1808]. 12°, pp. 90 and plate   BPL | BUS | SML
The Stratford copy presented by J. O. Halliwell, with inscription.

Othello : A tragedy . . . Edinburgh : Oliver & Boyd [c. 1813]. 12°
Issued in blue wrappers at sixpence.

Othello . . . [In R. Deverell's ' Discoveries in hieroglyphics and other antiquities]. Ln : . . . 1813. 8°   BUS
The notes explain the play ' by reference to appearances in the moon.'

Othello-travestie : In three acts. With burlesque notes, in the manner of the most celebrated commentators : and other curious appendices [by ' Ibef ']. Ln : J. J. Stockdale, 1813. 12°, pp. 88   BM | BUS | SML | W
The author's advt. is signed ' Ibef.'
The Stratford copy bears an autograph inscription by J. O. Halliwell presenting the volume.

[Othello] Othello-travestie : with burlesque notes . . . Second edition. 'Hic niger est.' Ln. printed, and Dublin reprinted, by J. Kempston, 1813. 12°, pp. 84 and folded plate   BPL | BUS

Othello, the Moor of Venice. A tragedy . . . Revised by J. P. Kemble, and now published as it is performed at the Theatres Royal. Ln : J. Miller, 1814. 12°, pp. 82   BM | BPL | BUS | SML | W
The Stratford copy presented by J. O. Halliwell, with inscription.

Othello . . . put in a light now entirely new . . . [In Deverell, ' Hieroglyphics']. Ln : Allman, 1816. 8°   BM | BPL

Othello . . . revised by J. P. Kemble. Ln : . . . 1818. 8°

Othello . . . With prefatory remarks by D. G—— [Geo. Daniel]. The only edition existing which is faithfully marked with the stage business and stage directions, as performed at the Theatres Royal. By W. Oxberry, comedian. Ln : W. Simpkin & R. Marshall, 1819. 12°, pp. viii.-76. With stipple portrait of ' Mrs. West as Desdemona '   BM | CPL | W

[Othello] Jealousy exemplified in the awful, tragical, and bloody history of the lives and untimely deaths of Othello and Desdemona. Ln : . . . [c. 1820]. 8°   W

Othello . . . with remarks by Mrs. Inchbald. Ln : Longman . . . [1821]. 12°, pp. 90 and plate   BUS

Othello . . . with remarks by Mrs. Inchbald. Paris . . . 1821. 8°   BPL

[Othello] Versus præmio Porsoniano . . . dignati . . . auctore G. Barham ['Othello, act I., sc. 3,' In English and Greek]. Cambridge . . . 1821. 8°   BM

Othello. A tragic opera [founded upon Sh—. By the Marquis di Berio. In English and Italian]. The translation by W. J. Walter. 1822. 12°   BM

Othello. A tragedy . . . Ln : Simpkin & Marshall, 1822. Cr. 8°, pp. vi.-76   BM | SML

Othello . . . with remarks by Mrs. Inchbald. Ln., Paris . . . 1822. 12°   BPL

Othello . . . revised by J. P. Kemble. As performed at the Covent Garden, New York, and Boston Theatres. Boston [U.S.] : Richardson & Lord, 1823. 12°, pp. 80   BUS

Othello . . . with remarks by W. Oxberry. Ln : . . . 1823. 12°

Othello . . . ' British theatre.' With remarks by D. G—— [Geo. Daniel]. Ln : Dolby . . . 1823. 12°   BPL

[Othello] Costume of . . . ' Othello ' . . . with notices by J. R. Planché. The figures by G. Scharf. Ln : J. Miller, 1825. 8°   BPL | W

Othello . . . A tragic opera. In two acts. As performed at the New York Theatre. New York : E. M. Murden . . . 1826. 12°, pp. 60   BUS
English and Italian texts on parallel pages.

Othello. A tragic opera [founded upon Sh—. By the Marquis di Berio. In English and Italian]. The translation by W. J. Walter. 1826. 12°   BM
First issued in 1822.

Othello. A tragic opera. The music by Rossini. Ln : . . . 1828. 8°   BUS
Text in Italian and English.

Othello . . . printed from the acting copy, with remarks . . . by D. G—— [Geo. Daniel]. To which are added, a . . . cast of the characters, and the whole of the stage business, as now performed at the Theatres Royal. Ln : J. Cumberland . . . 1829. 12°, pp. 72   BM | BPL

Othello . . . ' British theatre.' Ln : . . . [c. 1830]. 12°

[Othello] Otello : A tragic opera in three acts. Music by Rossini. The translation in easy verse, line for line with the Italian. With explanatory remarks and a guide to every particular piece of the opera. With a preface by a distinguished amateur. As performed at the King's Theatre, Haymarket. A new edition, revised and corrected by Signor Rosetti. Ln : Printed for H. N. Millar, 2, Norris St., Haymarket [c. 1830]. 8°, pp. 34, including printed blue wrappers   BPL

Othello . . . Music arranged by J. Harroway. Hugo Vamp's comic dramatic Shakesperean scenas. Ln : Davidson [c. 1830]. F°, pp. 6   BUS

[Othello] Outlines to Sh—: Othello. Thirteen plates. By L. S. Ruhl. Franc'-fort-o-Main : F. Wilman, 1832. 4°, pp. xii.   BM | BUS

Othello travestie. An operatic burlesque burletta, by Maurice G. Dowling. The only edition correctly marked, by permission from the prompter's book . . . Ln : J. Duncombe & Co. [c. 1834]. 12°, pp. 34 and engraving   BPL | BUS | SML
The Stratford copy presented by J. O. Halliwell, with inscription.

[Othello] Otello : A tragic opera. Music by Rossini . . . [In Italian and English]. Ln : . . . 1836. 12°   BPL

Othello . . . Acting edition. With accurate stage directions. ' Hind's English stage.' Ln : Simpkin . . . 1838. 12°, pp. 72 and frontispiece   BPL | BUS | SML
W. Creswick's prompt copy is at Stratford.

Othello . . . correctly printed from the most approved acting copy, with . . . the costume, cast . . . entrances, exits, positions, and . . . stage business. To which are added properties and directions, as now performed in the principal theatres . . . Philadelphia : Turner & Fisher [c. 1838]. 16°, pp. viii.-vi.-xiv.-6-74 and portrait of ' Alexina A. Fisher as Desdemona '   BUS
The introduction is by Geo. Daniel.

Sh— Othello . . .

[Othello] Otello : A tragic opera. Music by Rossini. Represented at Her Majesty's Theatre, Haymarket. 1838. 12° BPL
In Italian and English.

Othello. A tragic opera. In three acts. Music by Rossini . . . As represented at her majesty's theatre, Haymarket, May, 1839. Authorized edition. Ln : W. Clowes & Sons, 1839. 12°, pp. 60
In Italian and English. BPL | BUS

[Othello] Outlines to illustrate . . . 'Othello' by Moritz Retzsch. With introduction in English and German. Leipzig . . . 1842. Oblong 4°. 13 plates

Othello. A tragic opera [founded upon Sh—] . . . Translated and adapted from the Italian by G. Soane. Ln : Fairbrother . . . 1844. 8° BM | BPL

Othello . . . As performed at the Princess's Theatre. Ln : . . . 1844. 8°

Othello . . . [Text in English and notes in French]. Edited by O'Sullivan. Paris : Hachette . . . 1844. 12°

[Othello] Otello : A serious opera. Music by Rossini . . . [c. 1844]. 12° BPL

Othello . . . French's edition. Ln : S. French [c. 1845]. 8° BUS

Othello . . . With the stage business, cast . . . costumes, positions, etc., as played at the Park Theatre. New York : S. French [c. 1845]. 12°, pp. 74 BUS

Othello . . . as compressed and arranged for public reading. With notes by B. C. Jones. Ln : Adlard . . . 1846. 12° BPL | SML

Othello . . . 'Modern standard drama.' New York : S. French . . . 1846. 12° BPL

Othello . . . 'Pocket Sh—.' Ln : Mansell . . . [c. 1850]. 12°

[Othello] Otello : A lyric tragedy. Music by Rossini. Libretto translated by J. W. Tibbert. Ln : . . . [c. 1850]. 12° BPL
In Italian and English.

Othello . . . 'National edition.' Ln : Knight & Co. [1851]. 8° (excerpt), pp. 241-352 SML
W. Creswick's prompt copy is at Stratford.

Othello . . . erklärt von E. W. Sievers. Berlin : T. C. F. Enslin, 1853. 8°, pp. iv.-148 BUS | SML
English text with German notes.

Othello . . . erklärt von [Dr.] E. W. Sievers. Brunswick . . . 1853. 8° BM
English text with German notes.

[Othello] Otello : A lyric tragedy. Music by Rossini. Libretto translated by J. W. Tibbert. 1855. 12° BPL
In Italian and English.

Sh— Othello . . .

[Othello travestie] A Moor and an amour. Liverpool : Smith . . . 1856. 12°

Othello, the Moor of Venice. A tragedy. 'Acting edition.' Ln : T. H. Lacy [1856]. 12°, pp. 80. Portrait of Young as Iago
BM | BPL | MPL | SML
W. Creswick's prompt copy, interleaved, is at Stratford.

Othello travestie . . . by M. G. Dowling. 'Acting edition.' Ln : Lacy [c. 1856]. 12°, pp. 36 and plate BPL | BUS | CPL

Othello . . . Glasgow : Cameron . . . 1859. 8°

Othello . . . uitgegeven en verklaard door C. W. Opzoomer. Amsterdam : Gebroeders Binger, 1860. 12°, pp. xl.-212
BUS | SML
English text with Dutch introduction and notes.

Othello . . . 'Charles Fechter's acting edition.' [Ln :] W. R. Sams, 1861. Cr. 8°, pp. vi.-114 BUS | SML
The Stratford copy presented by J. O. Halliwell, with inscription.

[Othello] Fechter's version of 'Othello' critically analysed . . . by Hy. Ottley. Ln : Lacy . . . 1861. 8°
BM | BPL | MPL | SML

Othello . . . 'Charles Fechter's acting edition.' Second edition. Ln : W. R. Sams . . . 1861. Cr. 8°, pp. iv.-114 BM | BPL | CPL

Othello . . . 'Illustrated British drama.' Ln : Loft . . . [c. 1861]. 12° BPL

Othello . . . [uitgegeven en verklaard door C. W. Opzoomer. Amsterdam : J. H. Gebhard & Co., 1862. 12°, pp. xl.-212
BUS | SML
Between this and the 1860 edition the only noticeable change is in the imprint.

Othello . . . from the folio of 1623. Ln : L. Booth . . . 1864. Fcp. 4° BPL | CPL

Othello, 1622 . . . facsimiled by E. W. Ashbee, edited by J. O. Halliwell. Ln : For private circulation only, 1864. Fcp. 4°, pp. iv.-92 BPL | BUS | W
Fifty copies printed, nineteen of which the editor destroyed.

[Othello] Otello. Music by Rossini. With the music of the principal airs. [c. 1864.] Fcp. 4° BPL
Text in Italian and English.

[Othello] Rossini's opera of 'Otello,' containing the Italian text with an English translation and the music . . . Boston [U.S.] : O. Ditson & Co., 1867. 4°, pp. 24 BUS
The Italian text is by the Marquis di Berio.

[Othello] Otello . . . tragedia . . . voltata in prosa Italiana da C. Rusconi. Sesta edizione col testo Inglese di riscontro. Firenze : Successori Le Monnier, 1867. 8°, pp. 240 BM
In English and Italian.

Othello . . . Leipzig : B. Tauchnitz, 1868. 16°

Othello . . . 'Acting edition.' Ln : French [c. 1868]. 12°   SML

Othello . . . 'Cumberland's theatre.' Ln : Lacy . . . [c. 1869]. 12°   SML

Othello . . . edited by . . . Aitken. Ln : Ballard . . . 1869. 8°

Othello . . . With notes . . . adapted for scholastic study and . . . examinations by John Hunter. Ln : Longmans, 1869. Cr. 8°, pp. xxii.-144   BUS | CPL

Othello . . . as produced by Edwin Booth. Adapted from the text of the Cambridge editors, with introductory remarks by H. L. Hinton. 'E. Booth's acting plays.' New York : Hurd & Houghton [1869]. 12°, pp. 96   BM | BUS

Othello . . . As produced by E. Booth. Edited by H. L. Hinton. New York : French . . . [c. 1870]. 8°

[Othello] ' Dar's de money '—Burlesque on 'Othello' [Darkey drama, first part, edited by H. L. Williams, jun., pp. 21-27. c. 1870]. 12°   BPL

Othello : A burlesque, as performed by Griffin and Christy's Minstrels at their Opera House, New York . . . [c. 1870.] 12°   BPL

[Othello] Otello : A tragic opera. Music by Rossini . . . [c. 1870.] Cr. 8°   BPL
Text in Italian and English.

Othello . . . traduit en vers Français par le Chevalier de Chatelain . . . 1871. Cr. 8°   BPL

Othello . . . as performed by Salvini and his Italian company during the American tour. New York . . . 1873. 8°   BPL
In Italian and English.

Othello . . . The Italian version as performed by Signor Salvini and his Italian company at Drury Lane Theatre under the management of J. H. Mapleson. Ln : Clayton & Co., 1875. 8°, pp. 136 ; issued in printed violet wrappers
Italian and English texts on parallel pages.

Othello . . . ' Standard plays.' Ln : Dicks . . . [c. 1875]. 12°

Othello . . . as performed by Signor Salvini and his Italian company under the management of J. H. Mapleson. Ln : . . . 1876. 8°   BPL
In Italian and English.

Othello . . . With notes, etc. by J. Hunter. Ln : Longman . . . [c. 1877]. 12°   BPL

Othello . . . as presented by Edwin Booth. Edited by W. Winter. New York : F. Hart & Co. . . . 1878. 12°, pp. 126   BUS

Othello . . . prepared . . . for schools by H. N. Hudson. With introduction and notes. Boston : Ginn & Heath, 1878 12°, pp. ii.-551-655 [excerpt]   BUS

Othello . . . edited by W. J. Rolfe. New York : Harper . . . 1879. 12°

Othello . . . as performed by Salvini and the American company. New York, 1880. 8°   BPL
In Italian and English.

Othello . . . edited by Charles E. Flower. ' Memorial theatre edition.' Stratford-on-Avon : Printed by G. Boyden ; Ln : S. French, 1880. Cr. 8°, pp. viii.-100, including printed wrappers   BPL | SML

Othello . . . With introduction and notes . . . by . . . H. N. Hudson. 'Annotated English classics.' Boston [U.S.] : Ginn & Heath . . . 1881. Cr. 8°, pp. 210   BM | BPL

Othello . . . As produced at the Lyceum Theatre by Henry Irving. Ln : Chiswick Press [c. 1882]. 8°

Othello . . . edited by E. K. Purnell. Ln : Rivington . . . 1882. Cr. 8°

Othello . . . expliqué littéralement par M. A. Legrand . . . Traduction Française . . . de M. E. Montégut. Paris, 1882. 8°, pp. 344   BM
In English and French.

Othello . . . edited by E. K. Purnell. Ln : Rivingtons . . . 1883. Cr. 8°, pp. xii.-116   BM

Othello . . . edited with notes by W. J. Rolfe. New York . . . 1883. 12°   BPL

Othello . . . ' Standard plays.' Ln : John Dicks [1883]. 12°   BM | BPL

Othello . . . edited, with notes, by R. Mongan. ' Student's Sh—,' part I. Ln : Sonnenschein . . . 1883. Cr. 8°, pp. x.-180   BM
No more published.

Othello . . . [Text in English and notes in French by Morel]. Paris : Hachette . . . 1884. 12°

Othello . . . [Text in English and notes in French by d'Hugnes]. Paris : Garnier . . . 1884. 12°

Othello travestie. A burlesque burletta. By M. G. Dowling. ' Standard plays.' Ln : John Dicks [1884]. 12°, pp. 14   BM

Othello . . . The first quarto, 1622. A facsimile . . . with introduction by H. A. Evans. ' Sh— quarto facsimiles.' Ln : C. Prætorius . . . 1885. Fcp. 4°, pp. xvi.-92   BM | BPL | BUS | SML

Sh— Othello . . .

Othello . . . The second quarto, 1630. A facsimile . . . with introduction by H. A. Evans. ' Sh— quarto facsimiles.' Ln : C. Prætorius . . . 1885. Fcp. 4°, pp. viii.-94   BM | BPL | BUS | SML

Othello . . . ' New variorum edition.' Edited by H. H. Furness. Philadelphia : Lippincott . . . 1886. Roy. 8°   BM | BPL | BUS | SML

Othello . . . [With an introduction by H. Morley.] ' National library.' Ln : Cassell . . . 1889. 16°, pp. 192   BM

Othello . . . edited by K. Deighton. Ln : Macmillan . . . 1890. Cr. 8°

Othello . . . with introduction by E. Dowden. Twelve illustrations by F. Dicksee, A.R.A. ' International edition.' Ln : Cassell . . . 1890. F°, pp. xxii.-58, including 12 plates   BPL | SML

Othello . . . für den schulgebrauch eingerichtet und erklärt von Dr. C. Wünder. Döbeln : C. Schmidt, 1891. 8°, pp. 180

In English and German.   BM

[Othello] ' Hamnet Sh—, part IX.' The tragedy of Othello . . . according to the first folio (spelling modernised), with lists of . . . the emphasis-capitals of Sh—, also . . . notices of strange press-room matters in the Sh— folios, by A. P. Paton. Greenock : W. Hutchison . . . 1891. 8°, pp. xlviii.-102   BUS | SML

Othello . . . Illustrated [in colours] by Ludovic Marchetti. Reproduced by G. Whitehead & Co. Ln : Simpkin . . . [c. 1892]. F°   BPL | SML

Othello . . . with introduction and notes by K. Deighton. Ln : Macmillan, 1893. 12°   BPL

Othello . . . Illustrated by L. Marchetti. Ln : Simpkin [1893]. Fcp. 4°, pp. 42   BM

Othello. ' Ariel edition.' Ln : Routledge . . . 1895. 16°

Othello . . . [edited by Henry Morley]. ' National library.' Ln : Cassell, 1895. 16°, pp. 192

Othello . . . edited by I. Gollancz. ' Temple edition.' Ln : Dent . . . 1895. 16°, pp. xii.-178   BM | BLO | CTC | SML

Othello [edited by Hy. Morley]. ' National library.' Ln : Cassell, 1898. 16°, pp. 192

Othello . . . ' Pocket Falstaff edition.' Ln : Bliss, Sands, 1898. 16°, pp. 136   BPL | SML

Othello. ' Ariel edition.' Ln : Routledge, 1899. 16°

Othello . . . with introductory notes by J. Dennis. Illust. by B. Shaw. ' Chiswick edition.' Ln : Bell, 1899. 16°, pp. 156   BUS

Sh— Othello . . .

Othello . . . edited with introduction and notes by C. H. Herford. ' Eversley edition.' Ln : Macmillan, 1900. 12°   BPL

Othello . . . edited by W. J. Rolfe. New York . . . [1902]. 8°   BUS

Othello . . . edited with notes by H. N. Hudson. ' Windsor edition.' Edinburgh : Jack, 1902. Cr. 8°, pp. 138

Othello . . . edited by H. C. Hart. ' Arden edition.' Ln : Methuen, 1903. 8°, pp. 300

Othello . . . ' Ellen Terry edition.' Glasgow : Bryce . . . 1904. 32°

Othello . . . edited by H. Morley. ' National library.' Ln : Cassell . . . 1904. 16°, pp. 192   BPL

Othello. ' Waistcoat pocket edition.' Ln : Treherne . . . 1904. 32°

Othello . . . with introduction by G. Brandes. ' Favourite classics.' Ln : Heinemann, 1904. 16°

Othello . . . with introduction and notes by W. J. Craig. ' Little quartos.' Ln : Methuen, 1905. 16°

Othello . . . with introduction by W. E. Henley. ' Renaissance edition.' Ln : Harrap, 1908. Fcp. 4°   BPL

'Othello' references—

See Adams	*See* Johnson & Steevens
,, Astor	
,, Betty	,, Kohlschein
,, Bradley	,, Lennox
,, Brooke	,, Liverseege
,, Browne (E. V.)	,, Long . . .
,, Cooke	,, McGregor
,, Decker	,, McLoughlin
,, De Soligny	,, Mathews
,, Deverell	,, Miller
,, Dickens	,, Montgomery
,, Doyle	,, Morrison
,, Dramatic . . .	,, Moulton
,, Eardley-Wilmot	,, N—— (W.)
,, Ellits	,, Othello
,, Epistle . . .	,, Ottley
,, Euordanus	,, Otway
,, Fane	,, Parr
,, Fechter	,, Planché
,, Ferne	,, Price
,, Foote	,, Richardson
,, Giraldi	,, Roosevelt
,, Given	,, Rymer
,, Gregory	,, Sedley
,, Halliwell	,, Sh— Poems,
,, Hano	1660-67
,, Heywood	,, *Sh*—] Sh—'s
,, Hole	library
,, Iago . . .	,, Smart
,, Jacox	,, Some notes . . .
,, Jemmat	,, Sweet Robin

'Othello' references—

See T—— (W. L.) *See* White
" Taylor (J. E.) " Wilmot
" Turnbull " Wilson (John)

PASSIONATE PILGRIM.

Composition is conjectured to have taken place between 1594 and 1598. In addition to Sh—, the contributors included Richard Barnefield, Bartholomew Griffin, Christopher Marlowe, and others.

The first edition came from the press of William Jaggard in 1599, and this happy introduction to Sh— culminated in the same press producing his collected writings in 1623.

Of the second edition every copy seems to have disappeared.

John Payne Collier sought to establish [see 'Athenæum,' 17th May, 1856, and 'Notes & Queries,' 5th July, 1856] that the three sonnets erroneously attributed to Richard Barnefield were in reality Sh—'s. The three poems in question are :—'As it fell upon a day,' 'If music and sweet poetry agree,' and 'Whilst as fickle fortune smiled,'—and they appeared the previous year in Barnefield's 'Encomion of Lady Pecunia,' issued by John Jaggard.

For fifty years much silly abuse has been showered upon William Jaggard because for some reason he failed to distinguish the different authors represented in the volume, supposing that he knew them. It has not struck these sagacious critics that the manuscript brought to the printer may have been written entirely in Sh—'s hand. It is quite feasible that Sh— copied the others' poems and added them to his own for some ulterior purpose, as an anthology, like 'Tottel's Miscellany,' or jotted them down for use in unborn plays. Collier originated this unfair attack, and he was the only man with sufficient courage or honesty to withdraw the charge and admit he did Wm. Jaggard a grievous wrong. A score of superficial writers posing as Shakespearean authorities copied Collier's calumny and earned for themselves some ridicule. It is always unwise to condemn before hearing both sides.

Now Thomas Cotes added in 1640 some of Ovid's writings to Sh—'s poems, possibly in ignorance or innocence of the true authorship, a proceeding which evoked little or no comment.

[Passionate pilgrim] 'Come, live with me, and be my love' [A contemporary manuscript version differing from every known

printed rendering. Entered in an Elizabethan commonplace book]. 1570-1600. Fcp. 4°, pp. 232

The first printing of this delightful song is found in William Jaggard's edition of 1599. The verses were repeated with variations in ' England's helicon ' in 1600. In or about 1601 it was sung by Sir Hugh Evans in the ' Merry wives.' Presumably it appeared in the lost second edition of the ' Passionate pilgrim,' as it figured in the third edition of 1612.

The manuscript described above was disposed of in June, 1903, for £192.

[Passionate pilgrim] The Passionate Pilgrime [and Sonnets to Sundry Notes of Musicke]. By W. Shakespeare. [*Ornament.*] At London : Printed for W. Iaggard, and are to be sold by W. Leake, at the Greyhound in Paules Churchyard, 1599. 16°, on thirty unpaged leaves (printed on one side only, except the three last leaves) ; sig. A¹ to D⁸ in eights (A¹ and D⁸ being blanks)

CTC [4½ × 3¼in.] | BRITWELL [4⅝ × 3⅛]

The Cambridge copy bears an early MS. note stating that the copy cost the then owner three-halfpence. Trifling though this sum appears, it will be found, if calculated from 1600 at 5% compound interest, to work out to several thousand pounds, or, roughly, its market value to-day. A copy changed hands privately in 1907 at £2,000, and crossed the Atlantic. This transaction thus represents the highest price yet paid for a separate piece of Sh—.

Including the foregoing, only three copies are known to survive, and one of these is enshrined where collectors may covet in vain.

Passionate pilgrim . . . By W. Shakespeare. Second edition. At London : Printed by William Iaggard [c. 1604 ?] 16°

Issued presumably between 1599 and 1612.

Every copy appears to have vanished, despite diligent search for the last century or more. Collier suggested 1604 as the year of issue.

Passionate Pilgrime. Or Certaine Amorous Sonnets, betweene Venvs and Adonis, newly corrected and augmented. By W. Shakespere. The third edition. Wherevnto is newly added two Loue-Epistles, the first from Paris to Hellen, and Hellens answere backe againe to Paris. [London] : Printed by W. Iaggard, 1612. 16°, on sixty-two pages, without pagination BLO

In some copies Sh—'s name does not occur on the title, and adverse critics allege this is due to Thomas Heywood's complaint in the postscript to his ' Apology for actors, 1612,' where he raises objection against the insertion of some lines from Ovid, taken from ' Troia Britannica.' But as this work was published by W. Jaggard in 1609, it is quite likely it had been purchased outright from Heywood, and the publisher had absolute right in that case to use a scrap of his own property, if short of matter to complete a given sheet. The triviality has created more abuse than all the criticism levelled against Shakespearean forgers put together.

The Bodleian copy contains the two titles, one with and one without Sh—'s name.

Sh— Passionate pilgrim . . .

[Passionate pilgrim] Come live with mee and bee my love [An early imitation, in a volume of poetical miscellanies. c. 1630]. 12°, original manuscript on 94 leaves   W

Passionate pilgrime. A collection of fugitive poetry published under the name of Sh—. New edition, accurately reprinted from the original impression of 1599 . . . With a preface in which the claims of R. Barnfield to the authorship of two of the pieces are vindicated from the objections of Mr. J. P. Collier. By Charles Edmonds. ' Isham reprints.'   Ln : Chiswick Press, 1870.· 12°   BM | BPL | SML
Six copies (three quarto and three octavo) were printed on vellum and 131 ordinary copies, signed and numbered by the editor, also twenty-five copies in 8°, on large paper, bound in vellum boards, with deckle edges.

Passionate pilgrim. By Sh—, Marlowe, Barnfield, Griffin, and other writers unknown. The first quarto [sic] 1599. A facsimile in photo-lithography . . . With an introduction by E. Dowden. ' Sh— quarto facsimiles.'   Ln : W. Griggs . . . [1883]. Fcp. 4°   BM | BPL | BUS | SML
The sole copy of this issue printed on pure vellum is in the writer's possession, bound in polished brown morocco.

Passionate pilgrim, 1599. Reprinted, with a note about the book, by Arthur L. Humphreys. Ln : Privately printed for A. L. Humphreys, 1894. 16°, pp. xvi.-32   BM | SML

[Passionate pilgrim] (Colophon) Here ends this edition of the ' Passionate pilgrim ' and the songs in Sh—'s plays, edited by T. S. Moore and decorated . . . by C. Ricketts. Ln : Hacon & Ricketts, 1896. Cr. 8°, pp. 80   BM | BPL

Passionate pilgrim. Being a reproduction in facsimile of the first edition 1599 from the copy in the Christie-Miller library at Britwell. With introduction and bibliography by ' S. Lee.' Oxford : Clarendon Press . . . 1905. Fcp. 4°, pp. 58-64 (the latter unpaged and chiefly printed on one side of the leaf only)   BM | BPL | BUS | SML

' Passionate pilgrim ' references—

See Byrd	See Marlowe
,, Clarke	,, Quiller-Couch
,, Collier	,, Rhead
,, Griffin	,, Sh— Poems, 1808
,, Hall	,, Sh— Sonnets, 1885
,, Halliwell	,, Sh— Works
,, Hoehnen	

Passionate sheapheard's song, 1600.   See Bodenham

Sh—]   PERICLES.

The earliest Sh— version yet unearthed is that published by Henry Gosson in 1609.

Omitted from the Jaggard folio, 1623, and from the Cotes folio, 1632, it first secured its rightful place in the bard's works in the Chetwynde folio of 1663-64. Yet doubt of its authenticity continued to cling to the play until the dawn of the nineteenth century [See Cawthorn's 1796 ed.]

It was registered at Stationers' Hall 20th May, 1608 :—' Edward Blount.   Entred for his copie vnder thandes of Sir George Buck knight and Master Warden Seton a booke called the booke of "Pericles prynce of Tyre . . . VId." '

The composition is so disfigured by error as to suggest it was surreptitiously obtained by faulty shorthand writers at the theatre. Nevertheless, it is the only available text.

[Pericles] The Painfull Adventures of Pericles, Prince of Tyre. Being the true History of the Play of Pericles, as it was lately presented by the worthy and ancient Poet, John Gower [by George Wilkins]. London : Printed by T. P— [Thomas Purfoot, junior] for Nat. Butter, 1608. Fcp. 4°, sig. A¹ to K, forty leaves without pagination ; woodcut portrait of Gower on the title-page   BM
A romance by George Wilkins, apparently founded upon the dramatised form of Sh—'s play, or upon some earlier version than any now known.
Reprinted by Mommsen in 1857.

[Pericles] The late, And much admired Play, Called Pericles, Prince of Tyre. With the true Relation of the whole Historie, aduentures, and fortunes of the said Prince : As also, The no lesse strange, and worthy accidents, in the Birth and Life of his Daughter Mariana. As it hath been diuers and sundry times acted by his Maiestics Seruants, at the Globe on the Banck-side. By William Shakespeare.   [Device.]   Imprinted at London for Henry Gosson, and are to be sold at the signe of the Sunne in Paternoster row, &c., 1609. Fcp. 4°, thirty-six leaves (including title) unpaged ; sig. A to I⁴ in fours (the last blank)
      BM | BLO | BUS | CTC | HAMBURG | SML
A duplicate in the British Museum exhibits numerous small textual variations ; in many cases these are corrections of errors. The woodcut initial at sig. A2 is also different.
Geo. Steevens' copy with his autograph is at Boston. Earl Howe's copy, in half blue morocco, 6¾ in. by 4⅞ in., was secured by an American collector in Dec., 1907.

[Pericles] The late, and much admired Play, Called Pericles, Prince of Tyre. With the true Relation of the whole

History, aduentures, and fortune of the
sayd Prince : As also, The no lesse
strange, and worthy accidents, in the
Birth and Life, of his Daughter Mariana.
As it hath beene diuers and sundry times
acted by his Maiestyes Seruants at the
Globe on the Banck-side. By William
Shakespeare. [*Three ornaments.*] London : Printed . . . by S. S—— [Simon
Stafford], 1611. Fcp. 4°, thirty-six unpaged leaves ; sig. A¹ to I⁴ in fours (the
last leaf blank)   BM | ZURICH

Halliwell says the copy at the B.M. is the only one
known, but a more interesting example is said to be
preserved in the state library at Zurich, bearing a
dedication [believed to be unique] to Henry Fermor,
J.P., of Middlesex. The composition is stated to be
of a quality such as Sh— alone could have written.

[Pericles] The late, And much admired
Play called Pericles, Prince of Tyre.
With the true Relation of the whole His-
tory, aduentures, and fortunes of the
saide Prince. Written by W. Shake-
speare. [*'Heb Ddieu' device.* Ln :]
Printed for T. P—— [Thomas Pavier, by
Isaac Jaggard ?] 1619. Fcp. 4°, thirty-
three unpaged leaves ; sig. R to Z and
Aᴬ to Bᴮᴵ in fours
BM | BLO | BUS | CPL | CTC | NY | S. KENS. L |
SML | W

The signatures are continued from 'King Henry VI.,
parts II.-III.,' of the same date, which contained
sig. A¹ to Q. 'Pericles' formed a supplement to
that play, although not mentioned on the first title.
This issue forms part of the set of nine suspects. For
fuller information see A. W. Pollard's 'Sh— folios
and quartos.'
The Warwick copy bears manuscript corrections,
apparently in the hand of Lewis Theobald. The
British Museum exemplar came from David Garrick's
collection, and that at the Stratford Memorial from
Halliwell's library.
In May, 1906, a copy measuring 7in. by 5¼in. sold for
£161, and Earl Howe's example in Dec., 1907,
realised £65.

[Pericles] The Late, And much admired
Play, called Pericles, Prince of Tyre.
With the true Relation of the whole History, aduentures, and fortunes of the
sayd Prince : Written by Will. Shakespeare. London : Printed by I. N——
[? Iohn Norton] for R. B— [? Richard
Badger] and are to be sould at his shop
in Cheapside, at the signe of the Bible,
1630. Fcp. 4°, sig. A to I² in fours,
thirty-four unpaged leaves
BM | BLO | BUS | CTC | CANTERBURY |
EDIN. PL. | NY | S. KENS. L.
Halliwell's copy is at Boston.

[Pericles] The Late And much admired
Play Called Pericles, Prince of Tyre.
With the true Relation of the whole His-
tory, aduentures, and fortunes of the

sayd Prince : Written by Will Shakespeare. London : Printed by I. N——
for R. B——, 1630. Fcp. 4°, sig. A¹ to
I² in fours ; thirty-four leaves. Sig. E²
is wrongly marked D²   NY

This issue is set in a different fount to the preceding
edition of 1630.

[Pericles] The late, And much admired
Play, called Pericles, Prince of Tyre.
With the true Relation of the whole History, adventures, and fortunes of the
said Prince. Written by W. Shakespeare.
Printed at London by Thomas Cotes,
1635. Fcp. 4°, thirty-four unpaged
leaves ; sig. A¹ to I² in fours
BM | BLO | BUS | CTC | NY

The last of the early issues in quarto of this play.
A copy in May, 1907, realised £30.

Pericles . . . Ln : . . . 1639. Fcp. 4°
Referred to in Thimm's 'Shakspeariana' as the seventh
edition, but untraceable elsewhere.

Pericles, prince of Tyre. By Mr. Wm.
Sh—. Ln : Printed for J. Tonson, and
the rest of the proprietors, and sold by
the booksellers of Ln. and Westminster,
1734. Cr. 8°, pp. 68 and frontispiece
engraved by P. Fourdrinier   BM | W
Contains two piracy notices against 'R. Walker and
his accomplices,' by W. Chetwood.

Pericles, prince of Tyre, by Sh—. Ln : R.
Walker . . . 1734. 12°, pp. 60   BM | W

Pericles, prince of Tyre. By Sh—. Ln :
Printed in the year MDCCXXXV. 12°,
pp. 60   SBL
A copy of this rare edition was presented by J. O.
Halliwell to Stratford in 1864.

[Pericles] Marina : A play of three acts.
Taken from 'Pericles, prince of Tyre,' by
Mr. [G.] Lillo. Ln : J. Gray . . . 1738.
8°   BM
Consists of the last two acts of 'Pericles' considerably
altered and added to.

[Pericles] Marina [An alteration of 'Pericles'
in Lillo's Works]. Ln : . . . 1775. 8° BUS

Pericles, prince of Tyre. A tragedy. Supposed to be written by Mr. Wm. Sh—.
Adapted for theatrical representation, as
intended to be performed at the Theatre
Royal, Covent Garden. The lines distinguished by inverted commas are
omitted in the representation. Ln : G.
Cawthorn, 1796. 12°, pp. 92, and portrait of 'Cooper as Pericles'   BUS

Pericles, prince of Tyre . . . As intended to
be performed at the Theatre Royal,
Covent Garden. Regulated from the
prompt-book. Ln : J. Bell . . . 1796.
Cr. 8°, pp. 82   BM | BPL

[Pericles] Marina [An adaptation of 'Pericles'
in Lillo's Dramatic Works]. Second edition. Ln : . . . 1810. 12°   BUS

Sh— Pericles . . .

Pericles . . . [Edited by Alex. Chalmers].
Ln: Rivington [c. 1811]. 8° (excerpt)
W. Creswick's prompt copy is at Stratford. SML

Pericles . . . Ln: Chiswick Press . . . 1813.
12°

[Pericles] Marina, or the foster child. A
tragic play. Founded upon and altered
for the stage from Sh—'s 'Pericles.' By
William Kertland. 1820. Fcp. 4°. Manuscript on 101 folios BUS
With a variant title, 'The foster child, or the prince of
Corinth.' The plot is altered, and of the two thousand
lines over thirteen hundred are original.

Pericles . . . 'Pocket Sh—.' Ln: Mansell
. . . [c. 1830]. 12° BPL

Pericles . . . [In Greek and English by] . . .
J. G. Kingdon [In 'Prolusiones literariæ '. . .] Ln: . . . 1849. 8° BPL

[Pericles] The painfull adventures of
Pericles, 1608 . . . [by George Wilkins,
founded on Sh—'s play]. Edited by
Prof. Tycho Mommsen, with a preface
. . . and an introduction by J. P. Collier.
Oldenburg . . . 1857. Roy. 8°
BM | MPL | W
The preface contains an account of some original Sh—
editions extant in Germany and Switzerland, and a
few remarks on the Latin romance of 'Apollonius of
Tyre.'
Reprinted from the copy at Zurich.

Pericles, 1609, first issue, facsimiled by E.
W. Ashbee. [Edited by J. O. Halliwell.]
Ln: For private circulation only, 1862.
Fcp. 4°, on 68 unpaged leaves
BPL | BUS | MPL | SML | W
Issue restricted to fifty copies [lithographed], and nine-
teen were afterwards destroyed by the editor.

Pericles . . . [act v., sc. i.] In Greek tragic
iambics, by E. Abbott. Gaisford prize.
Oxford: T. & G. Shrimpton, 1864. 8°,
pp. 10 BM | BPL
English and Greek text.

Pericles, prince of Tyre . . . The text from
the third folio edition published in 1664;
with notices of former editions. Ln: L.
Booth, 1865. Fcp. 4°, pp. vi.-20
BM | BPL | BUS | CPL | SML

Pericles, 1609, second issue. Facsimiled . . .
by E. W. Ashbee. Edited by J. O. Halliwell. Ln: For private circulation only,
1871. Fcp. 4° BPL | W
Fifty copies printed, nineteen of which the editor
destroyed.

Pericles, 1611. Facsimiled by E. W. Ashbee. Ed. by J. O. Halliwell. Ln: For
private circulation only, 1871. Fcp. 4°
BPL | SML | W
Fifty copies printed, nineteen of which the editor
destroyed.

Sh— Pericles . . .

[Pericles] Strange and worthy accidents in
the birth and life of Marina. Extracted
by F. G. Fleay from . . . 'Pericles' . . .
1609. With emendations and notes. Ln:
New Sh—Society, 1874. 8° BM | BPL | BUS

Pericles . . . 'Standard plays.' Ln: John
Dicks . . . [1883]. 12° BM

Pericles . . . edited with notes by W. J.
Rolfe. New York: Harper . . . 1883. 12°
BPL

Pericles: by Wm. Sh— and others. The
first quarto, 1609. A facsimile from the
British Museum copy . . . with introduction by P. Z. Round. 'Sh— quarto
facsimiles.' Ln: Charles Prætorius, 1886.
Fcp. 4°, pp. xiv.-70 BM | BPL | BUS | SML

Pericles: by Wm. Sh— and others. The
second quarto . . . 1609. A facsimile from
the British Museum copy . . . with introduction by P. Z. Round. 'Sh— quarto
facsimiles.' Ln: C. Prætorius, 1886. Fcp.
4°, pp. xii.-70 BM | BPL | BUS | SML

Pericles . . . With the story of the prince of
Tyre from John Gower's 'Confessio
amantis' [and an introduction by H.
Morley]. 'National library.' Ln: Cassell,
1889. 16°, pp. 192 BM

Pericles . . . edited by C. E. Flower. 'Memorial theatre edition.' Stratford-on-
Avon: G. Boyden; Ln: Samuel French
[1890]. Cr. 8°, pp. viii.-70 BPL | SML

Pericles . . . edited by I. Gollancz. 'Temple
edition.' Ln: Dent, 1896. 16°, pp.140 BUS

Pericles. 'Pocket Falstaff edition.' Ln:
Bliss, Sands, 1898. 16°, pp. 96 BPL | SML

Pericles . . . edited with introduction and
notes by C. H. Herford. 'Eversley edition.' Ln: Macmillan, 1900. 12° BPL

Pericles . . . with introduction and notes by
J. Dennis. Illust. by B. Shaw. 'Chiswick
edition.' Ln: Bell . . . 1902. 12°

[Pericles] Marina: A dramatic romance.
Being the Shakespearian portion of . . .
'Pericles.' Edited by S. Wellwood. Ln:
Richards, 1902. 8°, pp. 48 BPL | BUS

Pericles . . . edited with notes by H. N.
Hudson. 'Windsor edition.' Edinburgh:
Jack . . . 1903. 8°, pp. 102 SML

Pericles . . . with introduction by G.
Brandes. 'Favourite classics.' Ln:
Heinemann, 1904. 12°

Pericles. Being a reproduction in facsimile
of the first edition, 1609, from the copy
in the Malone Collection in the Bodleian
library. With introduction and bibliography by 'Sidney Lee.' Oxford:
Clarendon Press, 1905. 4°, Introd. pp.
48; list of subscribers pp. 8; text pp. 70
BM | BPL | BUS | SML

Pericles . . . with introduction and notes by W. J. Craig. 'Little quartos.' Ln : Methuen, 1905. 32°

Pericles . . . edited by H. Morley. 'National library.' Ln : Cassell, 1905. 16°, pp. 192
BPL

Pericles. 'Waistcoat pocket edition.' Ln : Treherne, 1905. 32°

Pericles . . . edited by K. Deighton. 'Arden edition.' Ln : Methuen . . . 1907. 8°, pp. 188

Pericles. 'Renaissance edition.' New York : Harrap . . . 1907. Fcp. 4° BPL

'Pericles' references—

See Apollonius
,, Barnes
,, Boyle
,, Brome
,, Dryden
,, Elimandus
,, Fleay
,, Gower
,, Greg
,, Herbert

See How
,, Pimlyco
,, Plutarchus
,, *Sh*—] Sh—'s library
,, Smyth (A. H.)
,, Taylor (John)
,, Taylor (R.)
,, Twine
,, Wilkins

Phaeton to his friend Florio
A sonnet appearing in Florio's 'Second frutes, 1591' (*q.v.*) attributed to the poet's pen.

POEMS.

The pieces which together compose Sh—'s poems were first issued separately as follow: Venus and Adonis, 1593 ; Rape of Lucreece, 1594 ; Passionate pilgrim, 1599 ; Sonnets, 1609.

The first collective edition of Sh—'s poems was issued by Thomas Cotes, successor to Dorothy Jaggard, in 1640.

The poems found no place in the first five collective editions of Sh—'s works. Although issued uniform with Rowe's 1709 edition, the 'Poems' do not form an integral part of that issue of the poet's works.

Poems : VVritten by Wil. Shake-speare, Gent. ['*Heb Ddiev*' device.] Printed at London by Tho. Cotes and are to be sold by Iohn Benson, dwelling in St. Dunstans Church-yard, 1640. 8°, pp. 192. Preceded by a portrait of the poet engraved by W. M—— [William Marshall]
BM | BLO | BPL | BUS | CTC | HUTH | MRL
NY | W

Collation : Portrait, 1 leaf
Title, with imprint, 1 leaf
'To the reader,' sig. I.B., 2 pages
'Poems by L. Digges,' 3 pages
'Poem by Iohn Warren,' 1 page
'Poems' (text), A to L, in eights, and M, 4 leaves.

On L2 commences a head title, 'An addition of some excellent poems to those precedent of renowned Sh—, by other gentlemen.'

'Principally consisting of translations which never proceeded from Sh—'s pen,' says Lowndes. This seems a hasty assertion. Granted the translations could not be Sh—'s work, it is yet possible he may have copied them for some purpose ; that such copies found among his papers, or in his hand-writing, were too readily but innocently attributed to him by an over-zealous publisher.

The 'Poems . . . by other gentlemen' include excerpts from Thomas Heywood's 'General history of women,' two signed B. I. (Ben Jonson), one F. B. (Francis Beaumont), and one I. G.

Upon the last leaf of the copy belonging to Dr. H. H. Furness, of Philadelphia, is an additional verse in MS. not found in any printed version :—

'Aske me no more whither doth run
When day is done the poasting sun,
For in your bright and sparkling eyes
[His fires remain in love's disguise]'
[*or* His light remains in slight disguise]
Last lines conjectured. J. H[eber].

Dr. Bliss had a leaf of this edition with a contemporary manuscript note which stated it passed through the press in 1639, and was issued ready bound for fifteen pence.

In Nov., 1906, a copy brought £220. Another in Mar., 1907, £215. Another, 5½in. by 3¾in., Dec., 1907, £260.

[Poems] Collection of early manuscript music accompanying the songs found in the 'Winter's tale,' 'As you like it,' and 'Twelfth night.' [With the text. Written upon nine leaves of paper. c. 1660.] Oblong fcap. 4° W

[Poems] Collection of early music accompanying the songs found in Sh—'s plays. Text and music. Ln : 1660-67. Oblong fcp. 4° W

Contents : Airs [from Playford's Musical companion, 1667] in the 'Winter's tale'; 'King Henry VI.,' part II. ; 'As you like it'; 'The tempest'; 'Othello'; and [from Wilson's Cheerfull ayres, 1660] introduced into the 'Winter's tale,' 'Measure for measure,' and 'The tempest.'

[Poems] New academy of complements, erected for ladies, gentlewomen, courtiers, gentlemen, scholars, souldiers, citizens, countrymen, and all persons of what degree soever, of both sexes, stored with variety of courtly and civil complements, eloquent letters of love and friendship. With an exact collection of the newest and choices songs a la mode, both amorous and jovial. Compiled by the most refined wits of this age. Ln : Printed for Samuel Speed near the Inner Temple Gate in Fleet Street, 1669. 12°

Contains some of Sh—'s best songs.
For other editions *see* Sh— Cupid's cabinet.

[Poems] Purcell (Hy.) Orpheus Britannicus : Collection of all the choicest songs [by Sh— and others] . . . Ln : 1706. F°. With portrait

Contains musical settings to Sh—'s songs.

28

Sh— Poems . . .

[Poems] A collection of poems, viz.: I. Venus and Adonis; II. The rape of Lucrece; III. The passionate pilgrim; IV. Sonnets to sundry notes of musick. By Mr. Wm. Sh—. [Edited by Charles Gildon.] Ln: Printed for Bernard Lintott at the Cross-Keys between the two Temple Gates in Fleet street [1709]. 8°, pp. iv.-156   BM | BPL | BUS | SML

This is really the first of the two volumes forming the succeeding edition. Its four divisions have separate titles, dated respectively 1630, 1632, 1599, and 1599. Rodd said there were two editors, Gildon and Dr. George Sewell. Malone stated it was edited by Gildon, that he found it full of errors, and that the sonnets were separately set to music by John and Thomas Morley, according to a manuscript of Oldys. In the next issue the four early dates were cancelled. Lowndes was apparently unaware of the two-volume issue, and describes this as 'forming the seventh volume of the first small edition of Sh—'s works.' In this he is wrong. It was doubtless a separate venture, in which Rowe had no hand, for he remarks in the final paragraph of his life of the poet:—'There is a book of poems publish'd in 1640 under the name of Mr. William Sh—, but as I have but very lately seen it, without an opportunity of making any judgment upon it, I wont pretend to determine whether it be his or no.'

The following curious notice is on the opening page:—
'*Advertisement*. The remains of Mr. Wm. Sh—, called the "Passionate pilgrim and sonnets to sundry notes of musick," at the end of this collection, came to my hands in a little stitch'd book printed at London for W. Jaggard in 1599. It is generally agreed he [Sh—] dy'd about the year 1616, so that it appears plainly they were published by himself, being printed seventeen years before his death. I will say nothing of "Venus and Adonis" nor of the "Rape of Lucrece," they being universally allowed to be Sh—'s, only that I have printed them from very old editions which I procur'd, as the reader will find by my keeping close to the spelling. The writings of Mr. Sh— are in so great esteem that several gentlemen have subscribed to a late edition of his "Dramatic Works" in six volumes, which makes me hope that this little book will not be unacceptable to the publick. I shall not take upon me to say anything of the author, an ingenious person [Rowe] having compil'd some memoirs of his life and prefixed it [them] to the late above-mentioned edition. But I cannot omit inserting a passage of Mr. Sh—'s life very much to his honour and very remarkable, which was either unknown or forgotten by the writer of it. That most learn'd prince and great patron of learning King James the first [of England] was pleas'd with his own hand to write an amicable letter to Mr. Sh—, which letter tho' now lost remain'd long in the hands of Sir William Davenant, as a credible person now living can testify.'

See James I. for further particulars.

[Poems] A collection of poems, in two volumes; being all the miscellanies of Mr. Wm. Sh— which were publish'd by himself in the year 1609, and now correctly printed from those editions. The first volume contains: I. Venus and Adonis; II. The rape of Lucrece; III. The passionate pilgrim; IV. Some sonnets set to sundry notes of musick. The second volume contains one hundred and

fifty-four sonnets, all of them in praise of his mistress; II. A lover's complaint of his angry mistress. Ln: Bernard Lintott [1709-10]. 2 vols. 8° (vol. I.), pp. vi.-156, (vol. II.) pp. iv.-98   BM | BUS

Volume one is a reprint of the 1709 edition, and each of the four separate titles bears the erratic inscription, 'Printed in the year 1709.'

[Poems] . . . Venus and Adonis, Tarquin and Lucrece, and his miscellany poems. With critical remarks on his plays, etc. To which is prefix'd, an essay on the art, rise and progress of the stage in Greece, Rome, and England [by C. Gildon. Edited by S. N——]. Ln: E. Curll and E. Sanger, 1710. 8°, pp. xiv.-lxxii.-472 and plate   BM | BPL | BUS

'One of the piratical productions of Edmund Curll,' according to *Notes and Queries*, S. 2, XII., 349.
One of the few copies struck off on large paper is at Birmingham.
The independent titles are dated 1709.

[Poems] Works of Mr. Wm. Sh—, volume the ninth. [*Ornament.*] Ln: Printed by J. Darby in Bartholomew Close for E. Curll, K. Sanger, and J. Pemberton. Sold by J. Tonson in the Strand, J. Knapton and D. Midwinter in St. Paul's Churchyard, A. Betsworth on London Bridg, W. Taylor in Paternoster Row, N. Cliff and D. Jackson near the Poultry, T. Varnam and J. Osborn in Lombard Street, and J. Browne near Temple Bar, MDCCXIV. 12°, pp. iv.-lvi.-406, and two copperplates engraved by Van der Gucht

Formed the ninth volume to Jacob Tonson's 1714 edition of Sh—'s works.

[Poems] A collection of poems, in two volumes: being all the miscellanies of Mr. Wm. Sh—, which were publish'd by himself in the year 1609 and now correctly printed from those editions. [Edited by Charles Gildon.] Ln: Printed by J. Darby for E. Curll, 1714. 2 vols. bound in 1. 8°   BUS

This issue formed the ninth and final volume of Rowe's edition of Sh—'s Works, 1714.

[Poems] . . . Venus and Adonis, Tarquin and Lucrece, and Mr. Sh—'s miscellany poems. To which is prefix'd, an essay on the art, rise, and progress of the stage in Greece, Rome, and England [by C. Gildon] and a glossary of the old words used in these works. The whole revis'd and corrected, with a preface by Dr. Sewell. Ln: Printed by J. Darby for A. Bettesworth, F. Fayram, W. Mears, J. Pemberton, J. Hooke, C. Rivington, F. Clay, J. Batley, E. Symon, 1725. 4°
                    BM | BPL

Published as part of Pope's first issue of Sh—'s Works, 1723-25.

[Poems] Works . . . Tenth volume, containing Venus and Adonis, Tarquin and Lucrece, with his miscellany poems. To which are added critical remarks . . . by Mr. Gildon. The whole revis'd and corrected with a preface by Dr. Sewell. Ln: Printed for J. & J. Knapton, J. Darby, A. Bettesworth, F. Fayram, W. Mears, J. Pemberton, J. Osborn, T. Longman, B. Motte, J. Hooke, C. Rivington, F. Clay & J. Batley, 1728. 12°
BM | BPL | SML
The tenth or supplementary volume to the nine-volume edition of Sh—'s Works, 1728, edited by Pope.

Poems . . . Ln: Jacob Tonson . . . 1728. 12°
Often found accompanying Pope's second issue of Sh—'s Works. Identical with the preceding issue, save in imprint.

[Poems] Songs, set to music. The words chiefly taken from Sh—. [Full score.] By William Chilcott, organist at Bath . . . [c. 1750]. F°

Poems on several occasions . . . Ln: Sold by A. Murden, R. Newton, T. Davidson, C. Anderson, W. Nelson & S. Paterson [c. 1760]. 8°, pp. xii.-250. With portrait of Sh— by Hulett BM | BPL | SML

[Poems] Miscellaneous pieces of antient English poesie . . . by Sh— and John Marston. [Edited by J. Bowles.] Ln: R. Horsefield, 1764. Cr. 8°, pp. iv.-234
BM | BPL | BUS | W
For full title see Sh—'s King John, 1764.

[Poems] A collection of poems. In two volumes; being all the miscellanies of Mr. Wm. Sh—, which were publish'd by himself in the year 1609 and now correctly printed from those editions. The first volume contains: I. Venus and Adonis; II. The rape of Lucrece; III. The passionate pilgrim; IV. Some sonnets set to sundry notes of musick. The second volume contains one hundred and fifty four sonnets, all of them in praise of his mistress; II. A lover's complaint of his angry mistress. Ln: Printed for Bernard Lintott at the Cross Keys between the two Temple Gates in Fleet street [c. 1770]. 2 vols in one. 8° CTC
This is Capell's manuscript, prepared from Gildon's 1709 issue for a fresh edition of the poems, corrected and annotated throughout.

Poems, containing I. Venus and Adonis; II. The rape of Lucrece; III. The passionate pilgrim; IV. Sonnets. Dublin: T. Ewing . . . 1771. 8°, pp. 212 BPL | BUS
Uniform with Ewing's 1771 edition of Sh—'s Works. Includes the doubtful Shakespearean poems in the 1640 edition, and follows that issue in arrangement.

Poems written by Sh—. [With life and introduction. Edited by F. Gentleman.] Ln: Published Sept. I. for J. Bell and C. Etherington [of York] . . . 1774. Cr. 8°, pp. xl.-222. Vignette portrait on engraved title and two plates engraved by J. Hall BPL | CPL | SML | W
This edition is uniform with Bell's 1774 edition of Sh—.
A list of books (2 pp.) issued by John Bell is sometimes found appended.
The large paper copy at Warwick Castle bears manuscript notes in the autograph of Dr. Sherwin, of Bath.

Poems, written by Mr. Wm. Sh—. [Ln:] Reprinted for Thomas Evans, No. 50 Strand, near York Buildings [1775]. Cr. 8°, pp. viii.-250 and engraved title bearing vignette portrait of Sh— by A. Bannerman BM | BPL | BUS | SML | W
Follows the 1640 edition in arrangement, but bears an index naming every poem.
This edition was printed in the same style as Capell's 1767-68 issue of the Works, and intended to be supplementary to it. Perhaps edited by E. Capell.
A large paper copy (the only one recorded), measuring 7⅛in. by 4½in., is in the writer's collection.

Poems . . . viz., Venus and Adonis; The rape of Lucrece; Sonnets; The passionate pilgrim; The lover's complaint. [Edited by E. Malone.] Ln: C. Bathurst, W. Strahan . . . 1780. 8° BM | BPL | MPL
Formed part of Malone's supplement to the edition of Sh—'s plays, 1778-80.

[Poems] Venus und Adonis; Tarquin und Lukrezia. Zwei gedichte von Shakespeare. Aus dem Englischen übersezt [von H. C. Albrecht]. Mit beigedrucktem original. Halle: J. J. Gebauer, 1783. 8°, pp. xviii.-306 BUS

[Poems] Dramatic songs, consisting of all the songs, duets, trios and chorusses, in character . . . in his various dramas, partly new and partly selected, with new symphonies and accompaniments for the piano from the works of Purcell, Fielding, Boyce, Nares, Arne, Cooke, J. Smith, I. S. Smith, T. Linley jun., and R. I. S. Stevens. To which are prefixed a general introduction . . . and explanatory remarks . . . by Wm. Linley. Ln: Preston . . . [c. 1790]. 2 vols. F° BUS | SML

[Poems] Poetical works . . . containing his Venus and Adonis; Tarquin and Lucrece; Sonnets; Passionate pilgrim; and a lover's complaint. To which is prefixed the life of the author. Edited by R. Anderson, M.D. [In 'British poets']. Ln., Edinburgh: Mundell . . . 1793. 8°
BM | BPL | BUS | MPL | SML

Poems . . . viz., Venus and Adonis, the rape of Lucrece, Sonnets, the passionate pilgrim, and the lover's complaint. With Mr. Capell's History of the origin of

28—1

Sh— Poems . . .

Sh—'s fables. To which is added a glossary. Ornamented with three portraits by Bartolozzi, &c. Ln: Printed for Edward Jeffery, 11 Pall Mall [1795]. 8°, pp. iv.-xxiv.-234-xxx., and three stipple copperplates [Chandos portrait, surmounting a view of the old Globe Theatre (S. Harding *del.*, Le Goux *sculp.*) ; Henry Wriothesly third Earl of Southampton (T. S. Seel *sculp.*) ; Edw. Capell (F. Bartolozzi *del. et sculp.*)] BM | BPL | BUS
Printed on specially made paper, watermarked ' W. S., 1795.'
A large paper copy (9½in. by 5½in.) is in the writer's collection.

Poems . . . [from the text of Geo. Steevens] with a glossary. Ln: G. G. & J. Robinson, 1797. Roy. 8°   BPL | SML
Formed the seventh volume of Robinson's large type edition of Sh—'s Works, 1797.

[Poems] Poetical works . . . With the life of the author. ' Cooke's edition.' Ln: C. Cooke . . . [1797]. 12° BPL | SML | W
With portrait and three engravings in stipple on copper.

[Poems] . . . Dramatic songs, edited by W. Linley: Music from the works of Purcell, Fielding, etc. [c. 1800.] 2 vols. F° BPL

[Poems] Poetical works . . . With the life of the author . . . Ln: C. Cooke . . . 1800. 12°

[Poems] Six madrigals, for four voices . . . [The words from Sh—] Composed by John Davy. Ln: J. Balls [c. 1800]. F°, pp. 38   BUS

[Poems] Twelve English songs. The words by Sh—, set to musick by T. Chilcot . . . [c. 1800]. F°   BPL

Poems . . . with illustrative remarks, original and select. To which is prefixed a sketch of the author's life. [Edited by W. C. Oulton.] Ln: C. Chapple . . . 1804. 2 vols. 8°. With altered Chandos portrait and five plates
BM | BPL | CPL | SML

Poems . . . with the origin of Sh—'s fables, and glossary . . . edited by E. Capell. Ln: . . . 1805. 12°

Poems . . . To which is added an account of his life. Boston [U.S.]: Oliver & Munroe . . . 1807. 12°   BPL | SML
First American edition of the poems.

Poems . . . edited by . . . Cundell ? Ln: . . . 1808. 12°

[Poems] Sh—'s Duel and Loadstars. Set to music by Mr. [Wm.] Shield. Ln: Preston & Son . . . [c. 1808]. F°, pp. vi.
Consists of ' It was a lording's daughter' [' Passionate pilgrim '] and ' O happy fair' [' Midsummer night's dream '].

Sh— Poems . . .

Poems of Wm. Sh— [with the life of Sh— by A. Chalmers]. ' Johnson's English poets.' Ln: . . . 1810. 8° BM | BPL | BUS

Poems . . . Boston, U.S.: Munroe & Francis . . . 1812. Cr. 8°, pp. 204   BPL

[Poems] Poetry of various glees, songs, &c. as performed at the Harmonists, [by Sh— and others]. 1813. 8°   BPL

[Poems] Collection of the vocal music in Sh—'s plays, including the whole of the songs, duets, glees, choruses . . . Engraved from original manuscripts and early printed copies, chiefly from the collection of W. Kitchiner, M.D. Revised and arranged (with an accompaniment for the piano by Mr. Addison) by John Caulfield. Ln: J. Caulfield, 7 Fountain Court, Strand [1815]. 4°
The first collected form of Shakespearean music. Projected originally as seven distinct pieces, with individual titles and paginations, they were ultimately bound together and issued with the foregoing general title.

[Poems] Select poems of Wm. Sh—. With a life of the author by E. Sanford. Ln: . . . 1819. 12°   BM

Poems . . . With three engravings. Ln: Printed and published by J. F. Dove . . . [1820]. Cr. 8°, pp. 226 and three steel plates   BPL | SML | W

[Poems] Miscellaneous poems . . . to which is prefixed a life of the author. Ln: Miller . . . 1821. 12°

[Poems] Miscellaneous poems of Wm. Sh—. To which is prefixed the life of the author. Ln: Sherwin, 1821. 12°, pp. viii.-167
BPL | W

[Poems] Sonnets, songs, and minor poems . . . Whitehaven: Steel . . . 1822. 8°
The first piece of Sh— printed in Cumberland.

[Poems] Songs, duetts, &c. introduced in Sh—'s revived . . . ' Merry wives of Windsor.' Selected entirely, with one exception, from Sh—. 1824. 12° BPL

Poems . . . Ln: W. Pickering . . . 1825. 12°
BPL | SML

[Poems] Miscellaneous poems . . . With life by A. Skottowe and glossary after Nares. Leipzig: Fleischer . . . 1826. Roy. 8°. With Chandos portrait   SML

Poems . . . Ln: Wm. Pickering . . . 1826. Cr. 8°
Issued uniform with Pickering's 1826 edition of Sh—, 10 vols.

Poems of Wm. Sh—. Illustrated. Ln: J. F. Dove, 1830. 8°, pp. 152 BM | BPL

Poems and songs. Ln: W. Strange [c. 1830]. 16°, pp. viii.-96   BM | CPL

Poems of Sh— [with memoir . . . by Alex. Dyce]. 'Aldine edition.' Ln : William Pickering . . . 1832. 8°, *pp*. xc.-288
BM | BPL | SML

Poëmes et sonnets de Wm. Sh—; traduits en vers, avec le texte Anglais au bas des pages, précédés d'une notice et suivis de notes, par E. Lafond. [In English and French.] Paris : Ch. Lahure . . . 1836. 12°, pp. liv.-300
BM

Poems . . . [with memoir by A. Dyce]. 'Aldine edition.' Ln : William Pickering . . . 1837. 8°
CPL | W

[Poems] Poetical Works . . . Campe's edition. Nuremberg & New York : F. Campe & Co. [1837]. 12°, pp. 156 BM | BUS | SML

[Poems] Autobiographical poems . . . being his sonnets clearly developed, with his character drawn chiefly from his works by Charles Armitage Brown. Ln : James Bohn . . . 1838. 8°, pp. viii.-306
BPL | BUS | CPL

Poems . . . [edited by Charles Knight]. Ln : C. Knight . . . 1838. Roy. 8°

Poems . . . With life. Ln : J. Duncombe . . . 1839. Cr. 8°, pp. 222. Also frontispiece and engraved title
BPL

Poems . . . A new edition. [With historical notices.] Ln : L. A. Lewis . . . 1840. Cr. 8°, pp. vi.-282
BPL
A few were done on large paper in 8°.

[Poems] Miscellaneous poems, with a memoir. Ball, Arnold & Co., 1840. 12°
BPL

Poems . . . 'Standard library.' Ln : E. Moxon [and] W. Smith, 1840. 8° BPL

Poems . . . Ln : C. Daly, 1841. 12° BPL

Poems . . . [With memoir by A. Dyce.] 'Aldine edition.' Ln : W. Pickering . . . 1842. 8°

Poems . . . [edited by Charles Knight]. Ln : Knight & Co. . . . 1842. Roy. 8°. With engravings
BM | BPL | CPL | MPL | SML

[Poems] Songs from Sh—. Illustrated by the Etching Club. [Two parts.] Ln : Gadd & Keningale . . . 1842-52. F° BM

[Poems] Songs and ballads of Sh—. Illustrated by the Etching Club [John Ball and others. The text printed in red ink]. Ln : Gadd & Keningale . . . 1843. Roy. 4°, with 17 plates ; f°, India proofs
BPL | BUS | CPL

Poems . . . with facts connected with his life ; abridged from 'Wm. Sh—,' a biography [by Charles Knight]. Ln : C. Knight & Co. . . . 1843. 16°, pp. 404 BM

Poems . . . with introductory notices. Illustrated from designs by W. G. Standfast. Edited by J. S. Moore . . . 1846. 8°, pp. 60 BPL | CPL

[Poems] Songs . . . Illustrated by the Etching Club. Ln : Cundall . . . 1847. 4°
A few copies done in folio on large paper.

Poems . . . 'Cabinet edition' [Ed. by C. Knight]. Ln : Knight & Co. . . . 1847. 12°

[Poems] Songs and ballads . . . Illuminated by T. W. Gwilt Mapleson. New York : Lockwood & Co. [1849]. Fcp. 4°, on 24 unpaged leaves BPL | BUS | CPL

[Poems] . . . Songs. Thirteen standard songs . . . The music by Purcell, Arne, Bishop, Schubert, &c. Edited by E. F. Rimbault [c. 1850]. 4°, pp. 48 CPL

Poems . . . Ln : C. Daly [c. 1850]. 32°, pp. 238. With vignette title and engraved frontispiece BM

Poems . . . Ln : Bell . . . 1850. 12°

[Poems] Seven Sh— songs. Set to music in four and five parts by G. A. Macfarren [In Novello's Part song book, pp. 70-105]. Ln : Novello [c. 1850] BUS | CPL

Poems . . . with facts connected with his life [by C. Knight]. Ln : Wm. S. Orr & Co., 1851. 12°, pp. viii.-404 and bust portrait

Poems . . . 'Cabinet edition.' Ln : Chambers . . . 1851. 16°

Poems . . . C. Little, 1851. 12° BPL

Poems . . . Hartford [U.S.] : S. Andrus & Son, 1852. 16°, pp. 182 BUS

[Poems] Supplementary works of Wm. Sh—, comprising his poems and doubtful plays, with glossarial and other notes. A new edition by W. Hazlitt. Ln : G. Routledge & Co., 1852. 8°, pp. vi.-526 BM | SML

[Poems] Songs and ballads . . . Illustrated by the Etching Club. Ln : Longman . . . 1852. Roy. 4°

Poems . . . [with memoir by A. Dyce]. 'Aldine edition.' Ln : W. Pickering . . . 1853. 8° BPL

[Poems] Songs from the dramatists, edited by Robert Bell. Ln : Parker & Son . . . 1854. Cr. 8°, pp. 268 BUS
Sh— occupies pp. 77-109.

[Poems] Poetical works . . . With notes illustrative and explanatory, together with a supplementary notice to the Roman plays. Boston [U.S.] : Phillipps, Sampson & Co., 1855. 12°, pp. 442 BUS
Formed the eighth volume of Sh—'s Works, edited by O. W. B. Peabody.

Poems . . . Philadelphia : J. B. Smith & Co. [c. 1855]. 16°, pp. ii.-138 BUS

Sh— Poems . . .

Poems . . . edited [with annotations and sketch of his life] by Robert Bell. Ln: J. W. Parker & Son, 1855. 12°, pp. 252
    BUS

Poems . . . edited by Robt. Bell. 'Annotated edition of the English poets.' Ln: Charles Griffin & Co., 1855. 12°, pp. 252
    BM | MPL

Poems and sonnets . . . [Text in English and French, edited by E. Lafond]. Paris . . . 1856. 8°
    SML

Poems . . . edited by R. Bell. Ln: Griffin [c. 1856]. 8°

Poems . . . edited by A. Dyce. Ln: . . . 1856. 8°

[Poems] Venus und Adonis, Tarquin und Lukrezia . . . von W. Sh—. Uebersetzt von Johann Heinrich Dambeck. Mit genenübergedrucktem original. Leipzig: F. A. Brockhaus . . . 1856. 8°, pp. viii.-238
    BUS

Poems of Sh—. With memoir by A. Dyce [and] a few corrections and additions. Boston [U.S.]: Little, Brown & Co., 1856. 8°, pp. c.-288
    BM | BPL | W
The preface by the American editor is signed 'C.'

[Poems] Poetical works of Wm. Sh— and the Earl of Surrey. With memoirs, critical dissertations, and explanatory notes by George Gilfillan. 'British poets.' Edinburgh: J. Nichol . . . 1856. 8°, pp. xl.-316
    BM | BPL | BUS | SML
Contains a transcript of Sh—'s will.

Poems . . . 'Aldine edition' [edited by A. Dyce]. Ln: Bell & Daldy . . . 1857. 12°
    BPL | CPL | MPL | SML

Poems . . . Ln: C. Little, 1858. 12°. With engraved title and frontispiece
    SML

Poems . . . edited with a memoir by R. Bell. 'Bell's English poets.' Ln: [c. 1860]. 12°
    BPL

Poems . . . with annotations and sketch of his life by Robert Bell. Ln: Griffin & Co. . . . 1861. 12°
    BPL | CPL | SML

[Poems] Songs and sonnets . . . illustrated by John Gilbert. Ln: [Printed by J. Cundall for] Low, Son, & Co., 1861. F°, pp. 32. With coloured plates
    BM | BPL

[Poems] Poetical works . . . with glossarial notes by A. J. Valpy. Ln: H. G. Bohn . . . 1862. 12°. With portrait and two plates

Poems . . . edited by G. Gilfillan. Edinburgh: Nichol . . . 1862. 8°, pp. xl.-316

[Poems] Poets of the Elizabethan age: A selection of their most celebrated songs and sonnets. Illustrated with thirty engravings [by Birket Foster and others]. Ln: S. Low, 1862. 8°, pp. 84
Sh— at pp. 32-38.

Sh— Poems . . .

[Poems] Sh— album, or Warwickshire garland. Consisting of ancient, modern and traditional songs illustrative of Sh—. Arranged for the pianoforte by the most eminent masters. Ln: C. Lonsdale [1862]. F°, pp. xii.-68. With Chandos portrait and illustrations
    BUS | CPL
Contains Arne's music in 'The tempest,' Locke's music in 'Macbeth,' both arranged by W. H. Callcott, songs by Purcell, and 'Supplementary airs illustrative of Sh—'s Works and time selected by S. J. Noble' from the following composers:—Arne, Cooke, Dibdin, Haydn, Horn, Jackson, Robert Jones, Mendelssohn, Purcell, Rossini, Schubert, Shield, R. I. S. Stevens, Sir J. Stevenson, Verdi, and Wilson.

[Poems] Songs and sonnets. Illustrated by John Gilbert. Ln: S. Low, 1863. Cr. 8°, pp. 56

Poems . . . edited by R. Bell. Ln: Griffin . . . 1864. 12°

Poems . . . with a memoir by A. Dyce. Boston [U.S.] . . . 1864. 12°
    BPL

[Poems] Songs and sonnets . . . edited by F. T. Palgrave. 'Gem edition.' Ln: Macmillan . . . 1865. 16°
The introduction says:—'Only three or four generations of fairly long-lived men lie between us and Sh—. Literature in his own time had reached a high development; his grandeur and sweetness were freely recognised; within seventy years of his death his biography was attempted; yet we know little more of Sh— himself than we do of Homer. Like several of the greatest men, Lucretius, Virgil, Tacitus, Dante, a mystery never to be dispelled hangs over his life. He has entered into the cloud. With a natural and an honourable diligence other men have given their lives to the investigation of his, and many external circumstances, mostly of a minor order, have been thus collected; yet of "the man Sh—," in Hallam's words, we know nothing. Something which seems more than human in immensity of range and calmness of insight moves before us in the plays, but from the nature of dramatic writing the author's personality is inevitably veiled; no letter, no saying of his, or description by an intimate friend, has been preserved, and even when we turn to the "Sonnets," though each is an autobiographical confession, we find ourselves equally foiled. . . . Yet there is after all nothing more remarkable or fascinating in English poetry than these personal revelations of the mind of our greatest poet. We read them again and again, and find each time some new proof of his almost superhuman insight into human nature; of his unrivalled mastery over all the tones of love.'

[Poems] Songs of Sh— . . . illuminated by H. C. H. Abrahall. Ln: Day & Son [1865]. F°. With chromo-lithographic borders
    BM | SML

[Poems] Songs of Sh— illuminated. Ln: Routledge . . . 1866. 4°

[Poems] Poetical works. With a memoir [by A. Dyce; edited with notes by F. J. Child]. 'British poets.' Boston [U.S.]: Little, Brown & Co., 1866. 16°, pp. c.-288 and Marshall portrait
    BUS
A few were done on large paper.

Poems . . . [With memoir of Sh— by A. Dyce. 'Aldine edition']. Ln: Bell & Daldy . . . 1866. Cr. 8°, pp. xcvi.-288
BM | BPL

[Poems] Concordance to the poems of Sh—, by J. O. Halliwell . . . 1867. 8° BPL

[Poems] Poetical works . . . With memoir and critical dissertation by C. Cowden Clarke. Edinburgh . . . 1868. 8° MPL

[Poems] Songs . . . illuminated by H. C. Hoskyns Abrahall. [c. 1869.] Fcp. 4° BPL

[Poems] 'Venus and Adonis,' from the hitherto unknown edition of 1599; 'The passionate pilgrime,' from the first edition of 1599; of which only two copies are known; Epigrammes written by Sir John Davies, and certaine of Ovid's elegies, translated by Christopher Marlowe from a rare early edition. Edited by Charles Edmonds. Ln: Chiswick Press, 1870. 12° BM | BLO | CTC | SML
Impression limited to 131 signed and numbered copies, twenty-five being on large paper, 8°, and six on pure vellum.

Poems . . . edited with memoir by Robert Bell. Ln: Griffin . . . [1870]. 12°

Poems . . . 'Aldine edition,' edited by A. Dyce. Ln: Bell & Daldy [1870]. Cr. 8°

Poems . . . Philadelphia: Porter . . . [c. 1870]. 12°

[Poems] Songs of Sh—. Selected from his poems and plays [by J. B——]. Ln: Virtue, 1872. 16°, pp. vi.-188. With portrait BPL | CPL

[Poems] A concordance to Sh—'s poems . . . by Mrs. H. H. Furness. Philadelphia: J. B. Lippincott, 1874. 8°, pp. iv.-422
BUS

The poems are included at the end, pp. 369-422. Reviewed in *North American Review*, Oct., 1874.

[Poems] Concordance to the poems . . . designed to supplement Mrs. Cowden Clarke's Concordance to . . . works. Boston, U.S. [c. 1874]. Manuscript. 6 vols. 4° BUS
A lost labour, being forestalled by Mrs. Furness's work of the same year, and therefore not printed.

Poems . . . 'Isham reprints,' edited by C. Edmonds . . . 1874. Fcp. 4°

[Poems] Songs . . . selected from his poems and plays. Ln: Virtue . . . 1875. 12°

Poems . . . New York: Cassell . . . 1875. 12°

[Poems] Where the bee sucks . . . with music by Dr. Arne. Ln: Cocks [c. 1875]. F°, pp. 8

[Poems] Hark! hark! the lark . . . Adapted by Peter Inchbald. Music by Frederick Curschmann. Ln: Metzler [1875]. F°, pp. 8

[Poems] Poets of the Elizabethan age . . . Illustrated. Ln: S. Low & Co. [c. 1875]. 12° BPL
Sh—, pp. 31-37.

Poems . . . illustrated by Sir J. Gilbert. Boston [U.S.]: Osgood & Co., 1877. 12°

Poems. 'Aldine edition.' Ln: Bell . . . 1878. Cr. 8° BPL

[Poems] Poetical works of Mr. Wm. Sh— and the Earl of Surrey. With memoir and critical dissertation [by G. Gilfillan]. The text edited by C. C. Clarke. Ln: Cassell [1878]. 8°, pp. xl.-316 BM
Forms part of Cassell's 'library edition of British poets.' Reprinted from the Edinburgh edition of 1856 with a fresh title-page.

[Poems] Songs and sonnets . . . edited by F. T. Palgrave. Ln: Macmillan, 1879. 8°, pp. vi.-254 BUS

Poems . . . 'English poets,' edited by A. W. Ward. Ln: Macmillan . . . 1880. Cr. 8°

[Poems] Venus and Adonis, Lucrece, &c. With notes by W. J. Rolfe. New York . . . 1883. 12°

Poems, written by Wil. Shake-speare, gent. Ln: Tho. Cotes, 1640; Reprinted by A. R. Smith, 1885. Cr. 8°, pp. iv. and A¹ to M⁴ in eights [unpaged]
BM | BPL | BUS | SML
Issue: 225 copies on small paper and twenty-five on large paper.

[Poems] Songs, poems and sonnets. With critical introduction by W. Sharp. 'Canterbury poets.' Newcastle-on-Tyne: W. Scott . . . 1885. 12° BPL | BUS | SML
Also issued rubricated.

[Poems] Songs from Sh— [with music]. Illustrated. Ln: Cassell, 1886. Fcp. 4°, pp. 24-26 BM | BPL | BUS

[Poems] Songs, poems and sonnets, edited by W. Sharp. 'Canterbury poets.' Ln: W. Scott, 1888. 12° BUS

[Poems] Songs and sonnets. Illustrated by Sir John Gilbert. Philadelphia [1888]. Fcp. 4° BUS

Poems . . . Boston [U.S.]: Houghton [c. 1889]. 12° SML

Poems and sonnets . . . 'Elzevir series.' Ln: Bell & Sons . . . 1889. 12° BPL

[Poems] Song of spring and winter [from 'Love's labours lost']. Ln: Tuck . . . 1890. 4°

Poems: Venus and Adonis, Lucrece, and Sonnets. With notes by W. J. Rolfe, &c. New York . . . 1890. 12° BUS

[Poems] Love songs of the English poets, 1500-1800. With notes by R. H. Caine. Ln: Lawrence & Bullen, 1892. 12° BPL
Sh— pp. 61-69.

Sh— Poems . . .

Poems . . . printed after the original copies of 'Venus and Adonis, 1593,' 'The rape of Lucrece, 1594,' 'Sonnets, 1609,' 'The lover's complaint.' [Edited by F. S. Ellis.] Ln : [Printed by William Morris at the Kelmscott Press] Reeves & Turner, 1893. 8°, pp. 216. Woodcut borders and initials   BM | BPL
A few copies were printed on pure vellum.

[Poems] Venus and Adonis, Lucreece, and other poems . . . edited with notes by W. J. Rolfe. New York . . . 1893. 12°
                                                        BPL

Poems. With memoir by Alex. Dyce. 'Aldine edition.' Ln : Bell . . . 1894. 12°   BPL

Poems . . . edited with introduction and notes by George Wyndham. Ln : Methuen . . . 1898. 8°, pp. cxlviii.-344
                    BM | BPL | BUS | MPL | SML

[Poems] Songs from the plays [with preface by Ernest Rhys]. Illustrated by Paul Woodroffe. Ln : Dent . . . 1898. 12°, pp. 86   BM | BPL | BUS

[Poems] Songs from the plays . . . Ln : Dent . . . 1899. 12°, pp. 86

Poems . . . according to the text of the original copies [arranged by F. S. Ellis]. Ln : Essex House Press, 1899. Fcp. 4°
Issue limited to 450 copies.   BPL

[Poems] . . . Sh— anthology, 1592-1616, edited by Edward Arber . . . Ln : H. Frowde . . . 1899. Cr. 8°, pp. viii.-312
                                                        SML

Poems, according to the text of the original copies, including lyrics, songs, and snatches found in the dramas. Ln : Arnold . . . 1900. Roy. 8°, pp. 254

[Poems] Songs, etc. in Sh— which have been set to music. Edited by H. K. White. Great Fencote . . . 1900. 12°
Curious for its place of origin.   BPL

[Poems] Songs from Sh—'s plays. Guildford : A. C. Curtis, Astolat Press ; Ln : R. B. Johnson, 1901. 32°, pp. 64   BPL
A few copies also done on Japanese vellum.

[Poems] Songs. With drawings by H. Ospovat. Ln : Lane . . . 1901. 16°, pp. 148   BPL | BUS

Poems . . . Introduction and notes by J. Dennis. Illust. by B. Shaw. 'Chiswick edition.' Ln : Bell . . . 1902. 12°

[Poems] Songs . . . Ln : Treherne, 1903. 32°

Poems and sonnets. Introduction by E. Dowden. Ln : K. Paul . . . 1903. 8° BPL
A few copies also printed on pure vellum.

Poems and songs. ' Pocket classics.' Ln : Newnes . . . 1904. 12°, pp. 260   BPL

Sh— Poems . . .

[Poems] Songs . . . [with notes glossarial and explanatory]. ' Kelkel edition.' Ln : J. J. Keliher . . . 1904. 12°, pp. viii.-186. Illustrated   BPL

[Poems] Songs of Sh—. Second edition. Ln : Treherne & Co., 1905. 64°, printed on India paper

[Poems] A collotype facsimile of those portions of Sh— which found no place in the first folio, viz., ' Pericles ; Venus and Adonis ; Lucrece ; Sonnets ; The passionate pilgrim.' With introduction by ' S. Lee.' Oxford : At the Clarendon Press ; Ln., Edinburgh, Glasgow, New York, and Toronto : Henry Frowde, 1905. 4° (10in. × 8in.) With facsimiles of the original titles BM | BLO | CTC | SML
1000 copies printed, all numbered and signed. With list of subscribers.
A puzzling publication to the uninitiated. Each piece has a separate title and pagination. Some sets, either in vellum or paper boards, were sold in five volumes. Other sets, in rough calf or paper boards, were sold bound up in one volume, apparently lacking a general title-page, but, as none was printed, the volume is normally complete without that necessary leaf. It likewise possesses no index, an inexcusable defect. The above entry is copied from the prospectus.
Space will not permit of attempting to correct the errors in this reprint. The editor appears to supply the deficiencies of his knowledge with 'flights of fancy, far from fact.'

Poems . . . Introduction by W. J. Craig. ' Little quartos.' Ln : Methuen . . . 1905. 2 vols. 16°

[Poems] Songs . . . ' Broadway booklets.' Ln : Routledge, 1905. 16°

[Poems] Fifty Sh— songs. Edited by C. Vincent for low voices. Boston [U.S.] . . . 1906. Fcp. 4°   BPL

Poems . . . ' Red letter edition.' Ln : Blackie . . . 1906. 2 vols. 12°

[Poems] A lover's complaint, and The phoenix and the turtle [edited by A. H. Bullen]. Stratford-on-Avon : Sh— head press booklets, 1906. 16°, pp. 32
                    BM | BLO | CTC | SML

[Poems] Songs from . . . Sh—'s plays. Ln : Siegle, Hill . . . 1907. 16°, pp. 64

Poems, songs, and sonnets . . . [With short biography by Claude Montemart.] ' Everyday books.' Ln : Sisley . . . 1908. 12°, pp. xxii.-280   BPL

[Poems] Songs . . . [With a note by Arthur Henry Bullen.] Stratford-on-Avon : Sh— head press, 1908.
                BM | BLO | BPL | CTC | SML
One of 110 copies printed on hand-made paper.

Poems . . . with introduction by Alfred Austin. ' Renaissance edition.' Ln : Harrap, 1908. 2 vols. Fcp. 4°   BPL

[Poems] Songs . . . 'Langham booklets.'
Ln : Siegle & Hill, 1910. 32°
BM | BLO | CTC

'Poems' references—

See Boaden	*See* Quiller Couch
,, Bodenham	,, Retrospective . . .
,, Byrd	,, Ritson
,, C—— (I.)	,, Robinson
,, Clarke (R.)	,, Roffe
,, Davies	,, Sh— Passionate . .
,, Drayton	,, Sh— Rape . . .
,, G—— (M. F.)	,, Sh— Sonnets
,, Greg	,, Sh— Venus . . .
,, Halliwell	,, Sh— Works
,, J—— (Y.)	,, Sh— Works : Ext.
,, Kempe	,, White
,, Matthews	,, Winsor
,, Musical . . .	

Progress of human life. *See* Sh— As you
like it

Prose works. *See* Irving & Fairholt

RAPE OF LUCRECE.

*The first edition is that printed in 1594
by Sh—'s fellow-townsman and friend,
Richard Field. It forms one of the two
narrative poems which may be assumed to
have gone to press by the poet's express
wish and under his personal supervision.*

*The incident is recorded in Ovid's
'Fasti,' in Livy's 'History of Rome,' in
'Gesta Romanorum,' in Gower's 'Confessio
amantis,' in Boccaccio's 'De claris mulieri-
bus,' in St. Augustine's 'Civitas Dei,' in
Lydgate's 'Fall of Princes,' in Bandello,
and again in Chaucer's 'Legend of good
women.'*

*It was registered at Stationers' Hall on
May 9, 1594, as 'Master Harrison senior.
Entred for his copie vnder thand of Master
Cawood, warden, a booke intituled the
Ravyshement of Lucrece, VId.'*

[Rape of Lucrece] Lucrece. [*Ornament.*]
London : Printed by Richard Field, for
Iohn Harrison ; and are to be sold at the
signe of the white Greyhound in Paules
Churchyard, 1594. Fcp. 4°, forty-eight
unpaged leaves (the last blank) ; sig. A¹,
A², B to N² in fours
BM [7 × 4 15/16 in.] | BLO | DEVON | HUTH |
SION COLL.
Sig. A2 recto bears the prefatory dedication signed,
'William Shakespeare,' to his friend and patron the
Earl of Southampton.
Some copies of this edition exhibit slight textual
variations.

It will be observed that the publisher's sign was 'The
White Greyhound,' in St. Paul's Churchyard. That
of William Leake, publisher of 'The passionate
pilgrim,' 1599, was 'The Greyhound,' also in the
Churchyard.
The copy bequeathed by Capell to Trinity College,
Cambridge, is missing.
Reprinted in the series of Ashbee-Halliwell facsimiles,
1866 ; and by Dr. Furnivall in 1886.

[Rape of Lucrece] Lucrece . . . London . . .
1596
Mentioned (though never seen) by Malone, and untraceable elsewhere.

[Rape of Lucrece] Lucrece . . . At London :
Printed by P. S—— [Peter Short ?] for
Iohn Harrison, 1598. 8°, on 36 unpaged
leaves CTC
Collation :—Title ; Epistle dedicatory to Hy. Wriothes-
ley Earl of Southampton, signed 'William Shake-
speare'; The argument ; Text, sig. A4 to E4.
No other copy known.

[Rape of Lucrece] Lucrece . . . London :
Printed by I. H. [John Harison jun. ?]
for Iohn Harison, 1600. 24°, on thirty-
six unpaged leaves BLO

[Rape of Lucrece] Lucrece . . . London . . .
1602
Mentioned by Malone, but untraceable elsewhere.

[Rape of Lucrece] Lucrece . . . At London :
Printed be [*sic*] N. O—— [Nicholas
Okes] for Iohn Harison, 1607. 8°, on
thirty-two unpaged leaves ; sig. A to D⁸
(A⁴ is misprinted B⁴) BRIDGWATER | CTC

[Rape of Lucrece] Lucrece . . . London . . .
[c. 1610]
Halliwell mentions an edition issued about this date,
which so far has eluded search.

Rape of Lucrece. By Mr. William Shakespeare. Newly reuised. London : Printed
by T. S—— [Thomas Snodham ?] for
Roger Iackeson, and are to be solde at
his shop neere the Conduit in Fleet-street,
1616. 8°, thirty-two unpaged leaves ;
sig. A¹ to D⁸ in eights (sig. A⁴ is erroneously marked B⁴)
BM (5 8/16 × 3 8/16 in.) | BLO | NY
This edition is supposed to have appeared before the
author's death, 23rd April, 1616, and is described by
Malone as 'the most inaccurate and corrupt of the
ancient copies.'

Rape of Lucrece. By Mr. William Shakespeare. Newly Reuised. [*Device.*] London : Printed by I. B—— [John Beale ?]
for Roger Iackson, and are to be sold at
his shop neere the Conduit in Fleet-street,
1624. 8°, on thirty-two unpaged leaves ;
sig. A¹ to D⁸ in eights (sig. A⁴ is erroneously marked B⁴) BM (5 9/16 × 3 9/16 in.)
Issued at fourpence.
In June, 1903, a copy realised £130.

Rape of Lucrece . . . London . . . 1632. 12°
BUS | CORPUS CHRISTI COLL., OXF.

Sh— Rape of Lucrece . . .

Rape of Lucrece [In Sir John Suckling's 'Fragmenta aurea . . .']. Ln : Printed for Humphrey Moseley and are to be sold at his Shop at the Signe of the Princes Arms in S. Paul's Church-yard, 1648. 8°, pp. vi.-120, vi.-82-64, iv.-52, and portrait by Marshall   HCL | W
At p. 29 of ' Poems ' is found a ' Supplement of an imperfect copy of verses of Mr. Wil. Sh—, by the author.
These verses correspond with the stanza in the ' Rape of Lucrece ' beginning, '*Her lily hand her rosy cheek lies under,*' and the next following, at the end of which in the margin occur the words, '*Thus far Sh—.*'

Rape of Lucrece, committed by Tarquin the sixt, and the remarkable judgments that befel him for it. By the incomparable master of our English poetry, Will. Sh— *gent.* Whereunto is annexed the banishment of Tarquin, or, the reward of lust. By J. Quarles. [Two parts.] Ln : Printed by J. G—— for John Stafford in George-Yard neer Fleetbridge and Will. Gilbertson at the Bible in Giltspur-Street, 1655. 8°, pp. vi.-iv.-12 ; sig. B¹ to F⁸ in eights, and G¹ to G⁴ ; with frontispiece which ranks as A¹
BM (5 8/16 × 3 8/16 in.) | BLO | BUS | W
The portrait is the Droeshout reversed, in an oval, by W. Gilbirson.
With these lines beneath :—
' The fates decree that 'tis a mighty wrong
To woemen-kinde to have more greife then tongue.'
In the Warwick copy (which is bound in contemporary vellum) the last leaf is damaged.
J. O. Halliwell said that only four copies were known. A fifth occurred at auction in Dec., 1902. In June of that year also a title-page only sold for £13 10s.

Rape of Lucrece . . . [Included in ' Poems on affairs of state']. Ln : . . . 1707. 8°
    BM

Rape of Lucreece [In 'Old English drama']. Ln : . . . 1825. 2 vols. Cr. 8°. With frontispiece of an early English theatre

[Rape . . .] Lucrece . . . 1594. Facsimiled by E. W. Ashbee. Edited by J. O. Halliwell. Ln : For private circulation, 1866. Fcp. 4°   BPL | MPL | W
Fifty copies produced, of which the editor destroyed nineteen.

[Rape . . .] Lucrece. The first quarto, 1594. A facsimile . . . With forewords by F. J. Furnivall. ' Sh— quarto facsimiles.' Ln : C. Prætorius [1886]. Fcp. 4°, pp. xxvi.-94   BM | BPL | BUS | SML

Rape of Lucrece. [Lover's complaint ; Phœnix and turtle.] With preface and glossary by I. Gollancz. 'Temple edition.' Ln : Dent . . . 1896. 16°, pp. 136
    BM | BLO | BUS | CTC | SML

[Rape . . .] ' Venus and Adonis ' and ' The rape of Lucreece ' . . . Edited with in-

Sh— Rape of Lucrece . . .

troduction and notes by C. H. Herford. ' Eversley Sh—.' Ln : Macmillan, 1900. 12°   BPL

Rape of Lucrece [In ' English tales in verse,' pp. 64-123]. ' Warwick library.' 1902. Cr. 8°   BPL

Rape of Lucrece . . . edited with notes by H. N. Hudson. 'Windsor edition.' Edinburgh : Jack . . . 1903. 8°   SML

[Rape of] Lucrece, [and] A lover's complaint. With an introduction by G. Brandes. Ln : Heinemann, 1904. 12°, pp. viii.-86 and Droeshout portrait

[Rape of Lucrece] . . . Lucrece. Being a reproduction in facsimile of the first edition, 1594, from the copy in the Malone collection in the Bodleian Library. With introduction and bibliography by ' Sidney Lee.' Oxford : Clarendon Press . . . 1905. Fcp. 4°, pp. 56-92 (the latter unpaged)   BM | BLO | BPL | BUS | CTC | SML

' Rape of Lucrece ' references—
See Camden   *See* Malone Soc.
 ,, Drayton   ,, Malvezzi
 ,, Foard   ,, Meres
 ,, Freeman   ,, Ovid's ghost
 ,, Harbert   ,, Phillips
 ,, Irving & Fair-   ,, Sh— Poems
     holt   ,, Sh— Works
 ,, Lee (N.)   ,, Topsell

Richard II.   *See* Sh— King Richard II.
Richard III.   *See* Sh— King Richard III.

ROMEO AND JULIET.

This tragedy is not to be found entered at Stationers' Hall. The editio princeps is that produced by John Danter in 1597. The first four editions—1597, 1599, 1607, and 1609—are all anonymous, the earliest announcement of the authorship occurring in the Jaggard folio of 1623.

[Romeo and Juliet] The tragicall history of Romeus and Iuliet, written first in Italian by Bandell and now in English by Ar— Br— [Arthur Broke]. London : Richard Tottill . . . 1562. Fcp. 4°   BLO | CTC
In verse.
The foundation of Sh—'s ' Romeo and Juliet.'

[Romeo and Juliet] The tragicall history of Romeus and Iuliet, written first in Italian by Bandell and now in English by Ar— Br— [Arthur Broke]. London : Robert Robinson . . . 1587. Fcp. 4°
In verse.
The foundation of Sh—'s ' Romeo and Juliet.'

[Romeo and Juliet] An excellent conceited Tragedie of Romeo and Iuliet. As it hath been often (with great applause) plaid publiquely, by the right Honourable the L. of Hunsdon his Seruants. [*Pictorial device.*] London : Printed by Iohn Danter, 1597. Fcp. 4°, forty unpaged leaves, including title ; sig. A to K⁴ in fours (A¹ blank ?)   BM | BLO | CTC

Published anonymously.
From sheet E onwards a smaller fount of type was employed.
Reprinted by Geo. Steevens in 1766, by Mommsen 1859, in the 'Cambridge Sh—' 1865, by E. W. Ashbee 1866, by Furness 1871, and P. A. Daniel in the New Sh— Soc. Publications 1874.

[Romeo and Juliet] The most excellent and lamentable Tragedie, of Romeo and Iuliet. Newly corrected, augmented, and amended : As it hath bene sundry times publiquely acted, by the right Honourable the Lord Chamberlaine his Seruants. [*Pictorial device.*] London : Printed by Thomas Creede for Cuthbert Burby, and are to be sold at his shop neare the Exchange, 1599. Fcp. 4°, sig. A to M² in fours ; forty-six leaves without pagination, including title and prologue
    BM | BLO | W

Published anonymously.
Reprinted by Mommsen 1859, by E. W. Ashbee 1865, and P. A. Daniel 1874 and 1875.
The Warwick copy is unbound, lacking title and prologue, but bears the autograph of Geo. Steevens.
Earl Howe's copy, in half blue morocco, realised £165 in Dec., 1907.

[Romeo and Juliet] The most Excellent and Lamentable Tragedie of Romeo and Juliet. As it hath beene sundrie times publiquely Acted by the Kings Maiesties Seruants at the Globe. Newly corrected, augmented, and amended. [*Ornament.*] London : Printed for Iohn Smethwick and are to be sold at his Shop in Saint Dunstanes Church-yard, in Fleetestreete vnder the Dyall, 1609. Fcp. 4°, forty-six unpaged leaves ; sig. A to M² in fours
    BM | BLO | CTC | DEVON

Published anonymously.
The B. M. copy bears manuscript notes by J. O. Halliwell.
This edition was reprinted by Geo. Steevens in 1766.

[Romeo and Juliet] The most Excellent and Lamentable Tragedie of Romeo and Iuliet. As it hath beene sundrie times publikely Acted, by the Kings Maiesties Seruants at the Globe. Written by W. Shake-speare. Newly Corrected, augmented, and amended. London : Printed for Iohn Smethwicke and are to bee sold at his Shop in Saint Dunstanes Church-yard in Fleetestreete vnder the Dyall

[1609-37]. Fcp. 4°, on forty-four unpaged leaves (includ. title) ; sig. A¹ to L⁴ in fours   BM | BLO | BUS | CTC

The B. M. copy bears an anonymous title, but is otherwise identical with this. This issue belongs to the period 1609-1637, and not 1607 as stated in the B.M. catalogue.
According to Dyce, it has readings divergent from other editions.
The heading of sig. A2 reads, 'Tragedy . . .' whereas in the 1637 issue it runs, 'Historie . . .'
Reprinted in 1868 by E. W. Ashbee.

[Romeo and Juliet] The most Excellent And Lamentable Tragedie of Romeo and Juliet. As it hath been sundry times publikely Acted by the Kings Majesties Servants at the Globe. Written by W. Shake-speare. Newly corrected, augmented, and amended. London : Printed by R. Young for John Smethwicke and are to be sold at his shop in St. Dunstans Churchyard in Fleet Street under the Dyall, 1637. Fcp. 4°, sig. A¹ to L⁴ in fours ; forty-four leaves (including title) unpaged   BM | BLO | BPL | CTC | NY | W

A reprint, with slight alterations, of the undated [1609-37] edition.
A copy measuring 7 9/16in. by 4⅞in. brought £119 in Nov., 1904. Another in May, 1905, £120. Earl Howe's mended copy, in Dec., 1907, sold for £40.
The two copies at Warwick are bound in red and green morocco respectively.

[Romeo and Juliet] History and fall of Caius Marius. As it is acted at the Duke's Theatre. By Thomas Otway. Ln : . . . 1680. Fcp. 4°   BPL

The parts of Romeo, Juliet, and the Nurse, barring the names, are borrowed from Sh— almost word for word.
In the prologue, Otway says :—
'Our Sh— wrote too in an age as blest
The happiest poet of his time, and best ;
A gracious prince's favour cheered his muse,
A constant favour he ne'er feared to lose,
Therefore he wrote with fancy unconfined
And thoughts that were immortal as his mind ;
And from the crop of his luxuriant pen
E'er since succeeding poets humbly glean.'

. . . .

'Our this day's poet fears he's done him wrong,
Like greedy beggars that steal sheaves away ;
You'll find he's rifled him of half a play,
Amidst his baser dross you'll see it shine
Most beautiful, amazing, and divine.'

[Romeo and Juliet] History and fall of Caius Marius. A tragedy by Thomas Otway. Ln : . . . 1692. Fcp. 4°   BPL | W

[Romeo and Juliet] History and fall of Caius Marius. As it is acted at the Theatre Royal. By Thomas Otway. Ln : R. Bentley . . . 1696. Fcp. 4°, pp. vi.-66   BUS

[Romeo and Juliet] History and fall of Caius Marius. A tragedy, by Thomas Otway. Ln : . . . 1703. Fcp. 4°   BPL | W

Sh— Romeo and Juliet . . .

Romeo and Juliet. By Mr. Wm. Sh—. Ln : Printed for J. Tonson and the rest of the proprietors, and sold by the booksellers of Ln. and Westminster, 1734. Cr. 8°, pp. 84 and frontispiece engraved by P. Fourdrinier

Romeo and Juliet. A tragedy. By Sh—. Ln : R. Walker . . . 1735. 12°   W

[Romeo and Juliet] The solemn dirge in ' Romeo and Juliet ' as perform'd in the Theatre Royal in Covent Garden [Full score]. By T. A. Arne. Ln : . . . [c. 1740]. F°

Romeo and Juliet . . . Adapted by T. Cibber. Ln : . . . 1744. 8°

Romeo and Juliet . . . Revis'd and alter'd from Sh— by Mr. Theophilus Cibber. First reviv'd in Sept., 1744 at the Theatre in the Haymarket : now acted at the Theatre Royal in Drury Lane. To which is added a serio-comic apology for part of the life of T. Cibber, comedian . . . by himself. Interspersed with memoirs and anecdotes relating to stage management, theatrical revolutions, etc. Also cursory observations on some principal players. Concluding with a copy of verses call'd ' The contrite comedian's confession.' Ln : Printed for C. Corbett & G. Woodfall [1748]. 8°, pp. iv.-108

BM | BPL | BUS | SML | W

The alterations embrace an affection between Romeo and Juliet before the play commences. Some lines are borrowed from Otway's ' Caius Marius,' as well as the whole scene in the last act in which Juliet awakes. Geneste says the play was not acted at Drury Lane.

Romeo and Juliet . . . Revis'd and alter'd . . . by T. Cibber. London, 1748. 8°, pp. iv.-68   SML

This edition is without the Apology.

Romeo and Juliet, by Sh—. With some alterations and an additional scene [by David Garrick]. As it is performed at the Theatre Royal in Drury Lane. Ln : . . . 1748. 12°   W

The points differentiating Garrick's version from the original are these :—The allusion to Romeo's earlier love Rosaline is omitted, and an additional tomb scene between Romeo and Juliet is introduced.

Romeo and Juliet . . . With alterations and an additional scene by David Garrick. Ln : . . . [c. 1748]. 8°

Romeo and Juliet . . . The garden scene versified, set to music and humbly dedicated to the Hon. Mrs. Milbank by John Percy. Ln : G. Goulding . . . [c. 1750]. F°. With engraved title exhibiting a play scene

[Romeo and Juliet] The dirge in ' Romeo and Juliet.' Composed by I. F. Lampe. [Full score.] Ln : [c. 1750]. F°

Sh— Romeo and Juliet . . .

Romeo and Juliet. A tragedy [with alterations by David Garrick]. Printed exactly agreeable to the representation. Ln : H. Garland [c. 1750].   BM | BPL

Romeo and Juliet. With alterations and an additional scene [by David Garrick]. As it is performed at the Theatre-Royal in Drury Lane. Ln : J. & R. Tonson and S. Draper, 1750. 12°, pp. 70

BM | BPL | SML | W

Romeo and Juliet. [Five plates] Anty. Walker, inv. del. et sculp. Ln : 15 Jan., 1754   BUS

Romeo and Juliet . . . With alterations, and an additional scene, by D. Garrick. As it is performed at the Theatre Royal in Drury Lane. Ln : Printed for J. & R. Tonson and S. Draper, 1756. 12°, pp. 68 and plate   BPL | BUS

Next to the title Garrick adds this sarcastic memorandum :—' The persons who, from great good-nature and love of justice, have endeavoured to take away from the present editor the little merit of this [additional] scene by ascribing it to Otway have unwittingly, from the nature of the accusation, paid him a compliment which he believes they never intended.'

Romeo and Juliet, by Sh—. With alterations and an additional scene, by D. Garrick. Ln : . . . 1758. 12°   W

Romeo and Juliet . . . With alterations . . . by D. Garrick. Ln : J. & R. Tonson . . . 1763. 12°

[Romeo & Juliet] An excellent conceited tragedie of Romeo and Iuliet . . . 1597. Ln : Rep. by G. Steevens, 1766. 8°, pp. 78   BPL | W

[Romeo and Juliet] The most excellent and lamentable tragedie of Romeo and Juliet, 1609. Ln : Rep. by G. Steevens, 1766. 8°   BPL | W

Romeo and Juliet, by Sh—. With alterations and an additional scene by D. Garrick . . . Ln : J. & R. Tonson . . . 1766. 12°, pp. 72 and plate BPL | BUS | W

Romeo and Juliet. A tragedy . . . Edinburgh : Printed by and for Martin & Wotherspoon, 1768. 12°, pp. 96

BPL | SML

[Romeo and Juliet] History and fall of Caius Marius [In Otway's Works, Vol. 3, pp. 111-215]. Ln : 1768. 8°   BPL

Romeo and Juliet. By Sh—. With alterations and an additional scene by D. Garrick. As it is performed at the Theatre Royal in Drury Lane. Ln : Printed for T. Lowndes, T. Caslon, S. Bladon and W. Nicoll, 1769. 12°, pp. 72. With frontispiece   BPL

Romeo and Juliet. With alterations and an additional scene. By D. Garrick. Dublin . . . 1769. 12°   W

Romeo and Juliet . . . With alterations and an additional scene by D. Garrick. Illustrated with notes and copper plates. Birmingham . . . 1770. 8°   BPL

Romeo and Juliet . . . as performed at the Theatre Royal, Drury Lane. Regulated from the prompt book, with permission of the managers by Mr. Hopkins, prompter. An introduction, and notes critical and illustrative, are added by the authors of the 'Dramatic censor' [F. Gentleman]. Ln : Printed for John Bell . . . and C. Etherington at York, 1773. 8°, pp. 72, and copperplate frontispiece engraved by W. Walker after E. Edwards
Until now an unrecorded issue, off-printed from Bell's edition of Sh—'s Works for playgoers.

Romeo and Juliet . . . as it is now acted at the Theatres Royal in Drury Lane and Covent Garden. Ln : Oxlade . . . 1775. 12°   BPL

Romeo and Juliet . . . as it was performed at the Theatre Royal in Drury Lane . . . 1775. 12°   BPL

Romeo and Juliet . . . with alterations by David Garrick. Ln : . . . 1778. 12°

Romeo and Juliet. A tragedy. As it is acted at the Theatres-Royal in Drury Lane and Covent Garden. By Sh—. Ln : J. Wenman, 1778. 8°, pp. 20. With an engraved portrait as frontispiece of 'Mrs. Jackson in the character of Juliet'
     BM | BPL | W

Romeo and Juliet. A tragedy. Ln : J. Whitworth [c. 1780]. 12°, pp. 60   BM

Romeo and Juliet, altered from Sh— by D. Garrick. Marked with the variations in the manager's books at the Theatres Royal . . . [c. 1780]. 12°   BPL

Romeo and Juliet, altered from Sh— by D. Garrick. Marked with the variations in the manager's book at Drury Lane. Ln : . . . 1784. 12°   BPL | BUS

Romeo and Juliet. A tragedy. Ln : R. Randall [c. 1785]. 12°, pp. 60   BM

[Romeo and Juliet] Capulet and Montague, or the tragical loves of Romeo and Juliet. Ln : . . . [c. 1785]. 8°

Romeo and Juliet, altered from Sh— by David Garrick. As it is acted at the Theatres Royal . . . 1787. 12°   BPL

Romeo and Juliet. New edition . . . Marked with the variations in the managers' books at the Theatres Royal, Drury Lane and Covent Garden. Ln : Printed for the author, 1788. 12°, pp. 60   BM
A singular imprint, and probably the work of a wag.

Romeo and Juliet . . . Altered into a tragi-comedy by James Howard. Ln : . . . [c. 1790]. 8°

Romeo and Juliet. A tragedy . . . Ln : W. Lowndes & S. Bladon, 1793. 12°, pp. 60   BM

Romeo and Juliet. A tragedy. Dublin . . . 1793. 12°   BPL | W

Romeo and Juliet . . . As it is acted at . . . Drury Lane and Covent Garden. Ln : J. Barker . . . 1794. 12°

Romeo and Juliet . . . Ln : H. Garland . . . [c. 1795]. 8°

Romeo and Juliet . . . Manchester : R. & W. Dean . . . 1800. 12°, pp. 86 and woodcut frontispiece   BPL

Romeo and Juliet . . . adapted to the stage by D. Garrick. Revised by J. P. Kemble . . . [c. 1800]. 12°   BPL

Romeo and Juliet . . . [With alterations by D. Garrick]. Regulated from the prompt book. With introduction and notes, critical and illustrative. Ln : J. Barker . . . [c. 1803]. 12°, pp. 60 and portrait of Dod as Mercutio   BUS

Romeo and Juliet . . . Manchester : R. & W. Dean . . . 1806. 16°

Romeo and Juliet, by Will. Sh—. Printed complete from the text of Sam Johnson and Geo. Steevens. Ln : . . . 1806. 16°   W

Romeo and Juliet . . . With remarks by Mrs. Inchbald. Ln : Longman [1806]. 12°, pp. 78. With frontispiece by Meyron after Howard   BM | BPL | BUS

Romeo and Juliet . . . adapted to the stage by David Garrick. Revised by J. P. Kemble, and published as it is acted at the Theatre Royal, Covent Garden. Ln : Printed for the Theatre . . . 1811. 8°, pp. 76   BUS

Romeo and Juliet . . . Adapted to the stage by D. Garrick. Revised by J. P. Kemble . . . Ln : Longman . . . [c. 1811]. 12°, pp. 78 and plate

Romeo and Juliet . . . as performed at the Theatre Royal, Edinburgh. Printed from the prompt books [altered by D. Garrick]. Edinburgh . . . 1812. 12°   BPL

Romeo and Juliet travesty. In three acts. [By R. Gurney.] Ln : T. Hookham, jun. & E. T. Hookham, 1812. 12°, pp. xii.-72   BM | BPL | BUS | SML

[Romeo and Juliet] History and fall of Caius Marius [In Otway's Works]. Ln : . . . 1812. 8°   BUS

Romeo and Juliet . . . Ln : Chiswick Press, 1813. 12°

Sh— Romeo and Juliet . . .

[Romeo and Juliet] History and fall of Caius Marius [In Otway's Works]. Ln : . . . 1813. 8°   BUS

Romeo and Juliet : A tragedy . . . Edinburgh : Oliver & Boyd [c. 1813]. 12° Issued in blue wrappers at 6d.

Romeo and Juliet . . . adapted by D. Garrick. Revised by J. P. Kemble . . . Ln : J. Miller . . . 1814. 12°, pp. 74   BM | BPL | BUS | W

Romeo and Juliet . . . With remarks by Mrs. Inchbald. Ln : Longman . . . [c. 1816]. 12°, pp. 82 and plate   BUS

Romeo and Juliet. A tragedy . . . adapted to the stage by David Garrick. With prefatory remarks . . . marked with the stage business . . . as it is performed at the Theatres Royal, by W. Oxberry. Ln : Simpkin . . . 1819. Cr. 8°, pp. 68   BM | BPL | SML

[Romeo and Juliet] Capulet and Montague, or the tragical loves of Romeo and Juliet. Ln : Hodgson . . . 1823. 8°. Coloured frontispiece by G. Cruikshank

Romeo and Juliet . . . As performed . . . With remarks by W. Oxberry . . . Ln : Simpkin . . . 1823. 12°. With portrait of C. Kemble

[Romeo and Juliet] Funeral procession in 'Romeo and Juliet' : Set of 12 tableaux in colours on six sheets. Ln : Hodgson . . . 1823. 4°

Romeo and Juliet . . . 'British theatre' [altered by D. Garrick]. With remarks by D. G—— [Geo. Daniel]. Ln : Dolby . . . 1823. 12°   BPL

[Romeo and Juliet] Romeo e Giulietta : A serious opera [founded on Sh—'s play]. [c. 1824.] 8°   BM

Romeo and Juliet . . . as now performed at the Theatres Royal [altered by D. Garrick]. Paris : J. Smith . . . 1827. 12°   BPL

Romeo and Juliet . . . As performed at Paris. Paris . . . 1827. 16°

Romeo and Juliet. A tragedy . . . With notes [in German] by F. E. Feller. Leipsic . . . 1830. 12°

[Romeo and Juliet] Senarii Græci [A translation by C. R. Kennedy from 'Romeo and Juliet, act II., sc. 2.' In English and Greek]. Cambridge . . . 1830. 8°   BM

Romeo and Juliet . . . Ln : . . . 1831. 12°   SML

A prompter's copy with MS. alterations is at Stratford.

Romeo and Juliet . . . Printed from the acting copy, with remarks . . . by D. G—— [Geo. Daniel]. To which are added a . . . cast of the characters . . . and the whole

Sh— Romeo and Juliet . . .

of the stage business as now performed at the Theatres Royal. Ln : J. Cumberland [1831]. 12°, pp. 70 BM | BPL | SML

[Romeo and Juliet] Giulietta e Romeo. A serious opera. Music by Vaccai. 1832. 12°   BPL In Italian and English.

Romeo and Juliet [altered by D. Garrick]. Ln : J. Cumberland . . . [c. 1832 ?] 12°   BPL

Romeo and Juliet . . . A tragic opera. [Text in Italian and English.] Ln : . . . 1833. 12°

Romeo and Juliet. A tragedy . . . Mit erklärenden noten, einer erläuterung und einem wörterbuche von F. E. Feller. [In English and German.] Leipzig : Baumgartner's buchhandlung, 1833. 12°, pp. xvi.-138   BM

[Romeo and Juliet] Outlines to illustrate . . . 'Romeo and Juliet,' by M. Retzsch. With text in English and German. Leipzig, Ln : 1836. 4°. 13 plates

Romeo and Juliet . . . With explanatory notes [in French] by A. Brown. Paris . . . 1837. 12°

[Romeo and Juliet] Romeo e Giulietta . . . A tragic opera in three acts. Music by Nicolo Zingarelli. With preface by a distinguished amateur. As represented at the King's Theatre, Haymarket. Ln : . . . 1837. 8°

Romeo and Juliet : 'as the law directs.' An operatical burlesque burletta in one act. By M. M. G. Dowling. The only edition correctly marked by permission from the prompter's book. To which is added the costume, cast, stage business . . . properties and directions. As performed at the New Strand Theatre . . . Ln : J. Duncombe & Co. [1837]. 12°, pp. 24 and plate   BPL | BUS

Romeo and Juliet . . . printed from the text of Geo. Steevens, with historical and critical notes by J. M. Pierre. Frankfort . . . 1840. 12°

Romeo and Juliet. A tragedy . . . Mit . . . anmerkungen von Dr. Edward Winter. [In English and German.] Braunschweig : E. Leibrock, 1840. 12°, pp. vi.-218   BM | SML

[Romeo and Juliet] Rummio and Judy : A serio-comic-parodi-tragedi-farcical burlesque by H. A. Lloyd. Edinburgh : Menzies . . . 1841. 8°   BPL

[Romeo and Juliet] Romeus and Juliet . . . 1562 [In Sh—'s library, edited by Hazlitt]. Ln : . . . 1843. Cr. 8°   BM | BLO | BPL | CTC

Romeo and Juliet . . . text in English, and notes in French by O'Sullivan. Paris . . . 1844. 12°

Romeo and Juliet . . . grammatisch und Sachlich zum schul- und privatgebrauch erläutert von J. Hoffa [In English and German]. Braunschweig: G. Westermann, 1845. 8°, pp. 140   BM | SML

Romeo and Juliet . . . [with alterations by D. Garrick]. 'Modern standard drama.' With stage business, cast, costumes, positions, etc. New York: W. Taylor & Co. [1847]. 12°, pp. 70   BUS

Romeo and Juliet . . . 'Modern standard drama.' [Altered by D. Garrick.] With the stage business . . . New York: S. French . . . [c. 1847]. 12°, pp. 68
BPL | BUS

[Romeo and Juliet] I Capuletti ed i Montecchi. Music by Bellini. Libretto by M. Maggioni. Ln: . . . 1848. Cr. 8°   BPL
Operatic text in Italian and English.

Romeo and Juliet . . . 'Pocket Sh—.' Ln: Mansell . . . [c. 1850]. 12°

[Romeo and Juliet] I Capuletti ed i Montecchi. A tragic opera [founded upon Sh—'s play]. . . . The poetry by F. Romani. Music by V. Bellini. [c. 1850.] 8°   BM | BPL
Italian and English text.

Romeo and Juliet . . . erklärt von J. Heussi. Berlin: T. C. F. Enslin . . . 1853. 8°, pp. iv.-128   BUS
English text with German notes.

Romeo and Juliet . . . with notes in German by Dr. H. Ulrici. Halle: C. E. M. Pfeffer . . . 1853. 8°, pp. x.-200   BM

Romeo and Juliet . . . edited according to the most correct editions by Dr. J. Heussi. Halle, 1853. 8°   BM
In English and German.

Romeo and Juliet. A tragedy . . . 'Acting edition.' Ln: T. H. Lacy . . . [c. 1855]. 12°, pp. ii.-72   BM | BPL

' Romeo and Juliet ' travestie, or the cup of cold poison. A burlesque . . . by Andrew Halliday. 'Acting edition.' Ln: Lacy . . . [1855]. 12°   CPL

Romeo and Juliet . . . Glasgow: Cameron . . . [c. 1859]. 8°

Romeo and Juliet . . . A critical edition of the two first editions, 1597 and 1599, on opposite pages with various readings to the time of Rowe. With an introduction [in German] by Dr. T. Mommsen. Oldenburg: G. Stalling . . . 1859. 8°, pp. xii.-174-184-xii.   BM | BUS | SML
A reprint of the editions of 1597 and 1599.

Romeo and Juliet. A tragedy . . . With notes by Otto Fiebig. Leipzig: G. Græbner, 1859. 8°, pp. iv.-100   BM | BUS

' Romeo and Juliet ' travestie, or the cup of cold poison, by A. Halliday. Ln: Lacy . . . [c. 1859]. 12°   BPL

[Romeo and Juliet] Romeo e Giulietta. I Capuletti ed i Montecchi. A serious opera. Words by F. Romani. Music by V. Bellini. [c. 1860.] 12°   BPL
In Italian and English.

[Romeo and Juliet] Romeo e Giulietta [an opera]. Composed by N. Zingarelli. With the music of the principal airs. [c. 1860.] Fcp. 4°   BPL
In Italian and English.

Romeo and Juliet . . . The text from the folio of 1623, with notices of the known editions previously issued. Ln: L. Booth . . . 1864. Fcp. 4°, pp. iv.-26   BPL | CPL

Romeo and Juliet, acted in Germany in . . . 1626 by English players [In Cohn's ' Sh— in Germany,' q.v.] Ln: Asher . . . 1865. 4°, pp. viii.-138-422, and 2 plates
BM | BPL | BUS | CPL | MPL | SML | W
With English and German texts, parallel.

Romeo and Juliet . . . 1599. Facsimiled by E. W. Ashbee. Edited by J. O. Halliwell. For private circulation, 1865. Fcp. 4°
BPL | BUS | W
Fifty copies produced, nineteen of which the editor destroyed.

Romeo and Juliet . . . 1597. Facsimiled by E. W. Ashbee. Edited by J. O. Halliwell. For private circulation, 1866. Fcp. 4°   BPL | W
Fifty copies produced, nineteen of which the editor destroyed.

[Romeo and Juliet] Romeo e Giulietta; An opera [founded on Sh—'s play. Translated into English and Italian, from the French of P. J. Barbier and M. Carré]. . . . The English libretto by H. B. Farnie. Music by Gounod. Ln: Miles . . . [1867]. 8°   BM | BPL

Romeo and Juliet . . . [1607] facsimiled . . . by E. W. Ashbee. Edited by J. O. Halliwell. Ln: For private circulation, 1868. Fcp. 4°   BPL | W
Fifty copies printed, nineteen of which the editor destroyed.

Romeo and Juliet. As produced by Edwin Booth. Adapted from the text of the Cambridge editors, with introductory remarks, etc. by H. L. Hinton. 'Booth's acting plays.' New York: Hurd & Houghton [1868]. 12°, pp. 88   BM | BUS
Some passages are omitted.

Sh— Romeo and Juliet . . .

[Romeo and Juliet] Romeo e Giulietta, tragedia . . . voltata in prosa Italiana da C. Rusconi. Sesta edizione col testo Inglese di riscontro. Firenze : Successori Le Monnier, 1868. 8°, pp. 228   BM | SML
In English and Italian.

Romeo and Juliet. The original story . . . by Luiga da Porto, from which Sh— evidently drew the subject of his drama. By G. Pace Sanfelice. Cambridge . . . 1868. 8°   CPL

' Romeo and Juliet ' travestie . . . An atrocious outrage. Oxford : Shrimpton . . . 1868. 8°

Romeo and Juliet . . . 1609. Facsimiled by E. W. Ashbee. Edited by J. O. Halliwell. Ln : For private circulation, 1869. Fcp. 4°, pp. 82   BPL | W
Fifty copies printed, nineteen of which the editor destroyed.

Romeo and Juliet . . . Ln : Lacy . . . [c. 1869]. 12°

Romeo and Juliet. With explanatory notes and introduction by C. Stoffel. Deventer : A. J. van den Sigtenhorst, 1869. 8°

[Romeo and Juliet] Castelvines y Monteses [da J. L. F. de Vega Carpio]. Translated by F. W. Cosens. Ln : Chiswick Press . . . 1869. Fcp. 4°   BPL

Romeo and Juliet . . . As produced by E. Booth. Edited by H. L. Hinton. New York : French . . . [c. 1870]. 8°   SML

Romeo and Juliet . . . 'Cumberland's theatre.' Ln : Lacy . . . [c. 1870]. 12°

Romeo and Juliet [1607]. Facsimiled by E. W. Ashbee. [Edited by J. O. Halliwell.] Ln : For private circulation, 1871. Fcp. 4°   BPL

Romeo and Juliet . . . edited for scholastic study by John Hunter. Ln : Longman, 1872. 12°   CPL

Romeo and Juliet . . . edited for school use by H. N. Hudson. Boston [U.S.] : Ginn brothers . . . 1873. 12°, pp. 237-327 [excerpt]   BUS

Romeo and Juliet. Reprint of quarto I., 1597. Edited by P. A. Daniel. Ln : New Sh— Society . . . 1874. Fcp. 4°   BM | BPL | SML

Romeo and Juliet. Reprint of quarto 2, 1599. Edited by P. A. Daniel. Ln : New Sh— Society ; N. Trubner & Co. : 1874. Fcp. 4°, pp. viii.-142   BM | BPL | BUS | SML

Romeo and Juliet : Parallel texts of the first two quartos (Q° I.) 1597, (Q° 2) 1599. Edited by P. A. Daniel. 'New Sh— Society.' Ln : [Printed by Childs & Son] N. Trubner & Co., 1874. Fcp. 4°, pp. viii.-184 (including printed wrappers)   BM | BPL | SML

Sh— Romeo and Juliet . . .

A few copies of this edition were privately printed on large and thick paper for Prince Leopold, vice-pres. of the Soc., for presentation purposes. The autograph copy sent by the Prince to the Rev. H. O. Coxe, Bodley's librarian, is in the writer's possession.

[Romeo and Juliet] Los Bandos de Verona. Montescos y Capeletes [da] F. Rojas y Zorrilla. Englished by F. W. Cosens. 1874. Fcp. 4°   BPL

Romeo and Juliet. Revised edition of the second or 1599 quarto. Edited by P. A. Daniel. Ln : New Sh— Society . . . 1875. Fcp. 4°, pp. 142   BM | BPL

Romeo and Juliet . . . Adapted for the Italian stage by E. Rossi [In parallel Italian and English]. Ln : Drury Lane Theatre . . . 1876. 4°, pp. iv.-36   BPL | SML

Romeo and Juliet. A new travesty . . . as originally presented before the University Club of St. Louis, Jan. 16, 1877. [By Charles C. Soule.] St. Louis [U.S.] : G. I. Jones & Co., 1877. 8°, pp. 54   BM | BPL | BUS

Romeo and Juliet . . . With notes, etc. by J. Hunter. Ln : Longman . . . 1877. 12°   BPL

Romeo and Juliet . . . new variorum edition, edited by H. H. Furness. Philadelphia : J. B. Lippincott & Co., 1878. Roy. 8°, pp. xxiv.-480   BM | BLO | BUS | CTC | SML

[Romeo and Juliet] Katharine and Petruchio as presented by Edwin Booth. Edited by W. Winter. New York : F. Hart, 1878. 16°, pp. 50   BUS
An alteration of Garrick's version.

Romeo and Juliet . . . 'Acting edition.' Ln : French . . . [c. 1879]. 12°   SML

Romeo and Juliet. Edited with notes by W. J. Rolfe. With engravings. New York : Harper . . . 1879. 16°, pp. 222, and portrait of Petrarch   BUS

Romeo and Juliet. With introductory remarks . . . notes, etc. by S. Neil. Glasgow : W. Collins . . . 1879. 8° and f°, pp. 160   BM | BPL

Romeo and Juliet . . . edited by C. E. Moberly. ' Rugby edition.' Rugby : Billington ; Ln : Rivington, 1880. 12°   BPL | BUS | MPL

Romeo and Juliet . . . With introduction and notes by H. N. Hudson. Boston [U.S.] : Ginn & Co. . . . 1881. 12°   BPL

Romeo and Juliet . . . edited by C. Knight. Ln : Virtue . . . 1882. 8°. Illustrated

Romeo and Juliet . . . edited by C. E. Flower. ' Memorial theatre edition.' Stratford-on-Avon : Printed by G. Boyden ; Ln : French, 1882. Cr. 8°, pp. viii.-94 (incl. printed wrappers)   BPL | SML

Romeo and Juliet . . . As arranged for the stage by Henry Irving and presented at the Lyceum Theatre . . . 1882. Ln : Chiswick Press . . . 1882. 8°, pp. vi.-80
BM | SML

Romeo and Juliet. With introduction and notes, explanatory and critical, for use in families and schools, by H. L. Hudson. Boston [U.S.] : Ginn, Heath & Co., 1882. Cr. 8°, pp. 190, including printed wrappers

Romeo and Juliet . . . as arranged by H. Irving and presented at the Lyceum Theatre. Second edition. Ln : Bickers . . . 1882. 8°
BPL

Romeo and Juliet . . . [In Dryden's Works]. Ln : . . . 1883. 8°

Romeo and Juliet . . . as arranged by H. Irving . . . Provincial tour. Ln : . . . 1883. 8°
BPL

Romeo and Juliet . . . edited with notes by W. J. Rolfe. New York . . . 1883. 12° BPL

Romeo and Juliet . . . adapted for the Italian stage and performed by E. Rossi. [c. 1883]. 8°
BPL
In Italian and English.

Romeo and Juliet. 'Standard plays.' Ln : John Dicks . . . [1883]. 12° BM | BPL

Romeo and Juliet. With . . . illustrations by F. Dicksee . . . Introduction by E. Dowden. Ln : Cassell, 1884. F°, pp. xxvi.-54. With photogravures
An edition-de-luxe.
BM | BPL | SML

Romeo and Juliet . . . 'Oxford and Cambridge edition.' Ln : Allman . . . 1884. 12°

Romeo and Juliet . . . As performed by Miss Mary Anderson and company at the Lyceum theatre . . . 1884. Ln : W. S. Johnson . . . 1884. 8°, pp. 72
BM | BPL | SML

Romeo and Juliet . . . As performed by Miss Mary Anderson and company . . . Second edition. Ln : W. S. Johnson . . . 1884. 8°
SML

[Romeo and Juliet] Mr. Wm. Sh—'s tragedie of Romeo & Juliet. Reprinted from the first folio, 1623. Ln : William Ludlow . . . 1884. Cr. 8°, pp. vi.-122
BPL | SML

Romeo and Juliet . . . edited by Phillpots. Ln : Rivington . . . 1885. 12°

Romeo and Juliet . . . The first quarto, 1597. A facsimile from the British Museum copy . . . With introduction by H. A. Evans. 'Sh— quarto facsimiles.' Ln : C. Prætorius . . . 1886. Fcp. 4°, pp. xvi.-78
BM | BPL | BUS | SML

Romeo and Juliet . . . The second quarto, 1599. A facsimile from the British Museum copy . . . With introduction by H. A. Evans. 'Sh— quarto facsimiles.' Ln : C. Prætorius . . . 1886. Fcp. 4°, pp. viii.-92
BM | BPL | BUS | SML

Romeo and Juliet . . . with illustrations by Andriolli. Boston [U.S.] . . . 1887. Fcp. 4°
BPL | BUS

Romeo and Juliet . . . The undated quarto. A facsimile from the British Museum copy . . . With introductory notice by H. A. Evans. 'Sh— quarto facsimiles.' Ln : C. Prætorius . . . 1887. Fcp. 4°, pp. iv.-88
BM | BPL | BUS | SML

[Romeo and Juliet] The goodly history of the true and constant love between Romeus and Julietta. Abridged from Painter's 'Palace of pleasure.' [With an introduction by H. Morley.] 'National library.' Ln : Cassell, 1888. 16°, pp. 192
BM | BLO | CTC

Romeo & Juliet . . . edited by H. Morley. 'National library.' Ln : Cassell . . . 1889. 16°, pp. 192

Romeo and Juliet . . . painted by L. Marchetti. Ln : R. Tuck & Sons [1890]. Fcp. 4°, pp. 44
BM | SML

Romeo and Juliet . . . With illustrations by L. Marchetti, L. Rossi, and O. Cortazzo. Ln : Simpkin [1891]. F°. Coloured plates
BPL | SML

Romeo and Juliet . . . With nine illustrations in photogravure from designs by Frank Bindley. Ln : Marcus Ward [1892]. F°

Romeo & Juliet . . . With introduction by R. H. Stoddard. Illustrated by J. Wagrez & L. Fitz. New York . . . 1892. 8°
BPL
Issue limited to 300 ordinary copies on Holland paper and fifty on Japan vellum.

Romeo and Juliet . . . with introduction and notes by K. Deighton. Ln : Macmillan . . . 1893. 12°
BPL

Romeo & Juliet . . . 'Penny poets.' Ln : W. T. Stead [1895]. Cr. 8°, pp. 58 BPL

Romeo & Juliet . . . 'Ariel edition.' Ln : Routledge . . . 1895. 16°

Romeo and Juliet . . . with illustrations. Ln : Routledge, 1895. 12°, pp. viii.-198

Romeo and Juliet . . . as arranged for the stage by Forbes Robertson, and presented at the Lyceum Theatre . . . Sept. 21st, 1895. With illustrations by Hawes Craven. Ln : Nassau Press, 1895. 8°, pp. 78
BM

Sh— Romeo and Juliet . . .

Romeo and Juliet . . . with nine illustrations in photogravure from designs by Frank Bindley. Ln : Marcus Ward [1895]. Fcp. 4°, pp. 118   BM

Romeo and Juliet . . . edited by I. Gollancz. ' Temple edition.' Ln : Dent, 1896. 16°, pp. 174   BM | BLO | BUS | CTC | SML

Romeo and Juliet . . . 'Variorum edition.' Edited by H. H. Furness. Ln : Dent . . . 1898. 8°, pp. xxiv.-480   BM

Romeo & Juliet . . . edited by Hy. Morley. ' National library.' Ln : Cassell, 1898. 16°, pp. 192

Romeo and Juliet. ' Pocket Falstaff edition.' Ln : Bliss, Sands, 1898. 16°, pp. 122   BPL | SML

Romeo & Juliet . . . edited by W. J. Rolfe. New York . . . 1899. 8°. Illust.   BUS

Romeo & Juliet . . . Maude Adams' acting edition. With drawings by Ernest Haskell and Allan Gilbert. New York . . . 1899. 8°   BUS

Romeo & Juliet . . . with introduction and notes by J. Dennis. Illustrated by B. Shaw. ' Chiswick edition.' Ln : Bell, 1899. 12°, pp. 148   BUS

Romeo and Juliet . . . edited with introduction and notes by C. H. Herford. 'Eversley Sh—.' Ln : Macmillan, 1900. 12° BPL

Romeo and Juliet . . . edited by E. Dowden. 'Arden edition.' Ln : Methuen, 1900. 8°, pp. 240   BM | BLO | CTC

Romeo & Juliet . . . edited by W. J. Rolfe. New York . . . [1902]. 8°. Illust.   BUS

Romeo and Juliet . . . 'Abbey text.' Ln : Bell & Sons ; Edinburgh : Abbey Press, 1902. 4°, pp. viii.-166
Issue restricted to 500 copies on fine paper and fifty numbered copies on Japanese vellum ; the latter bound in gilt vellum, with crimson tie-thongs.

Romeo & Juliet . . . edited by Edward Dowden. Indianapolis . . . [1903]. 8° BUS

Romeo & Juliet . . . ' Ellen Terry edition.' Glasgow : Bryce . . . 1904. 32°

Romeo & Juliet . . . edited by H. Morley. ' National library.' Ln : Cassell, 1904. 16°, pp. 192   BPL

Romeo & Juliet, with introduction and notes by W. J. Craig. ' Little quartos.' Ln : Methuen . . . 1904. 16°

Romeo and Juliet. With introduction by G. Brandes. ' Favourite classics.' Ln : W. Heinemann . . . 1904. 12°, pp. xvi.-122, and frontispiece of D. Garrick and Mrs. Bellamy

Romeo & Juliet . . . ' Thumbnail series.' New York : Century Co. . . . 1904. Cr. 8°   BPL

Sh— Romeo and Juliet . . .

Romeo and Juliet. Retold for children by A. S. Hoffman. Ln : Dent, 1906. 16°, pp. 112   BPL

Romeo & Juliet . . . Revised by A. Dyce. Ln : Sonnenschein [1907]. 8°   BPL

Romeo and Juliet . . . ' Renaissance edition.' New York : Harrap, 1908. Fcp. 4° BPL

Romeo & Juliet . . . edited by L. E. Wright. ' Lamb Sh—.' Ln : Chatto . . . 1909. Fcp. 4°

Romeo & Juliet . . . with introduction, notes, and appendices. ' Normal tutorial series.' Ln : Normal Press . . . 1910. Cr. 8°, pp. 184   BM | BLO | CTC

' Romeo and Juliet ' references—
See Account . . .   See Letter . . .

,, Archer	,, Mackay
,, Ballad	,, Marston
,, Bandello and	,, Meres
Brooke	,, Mexia
,, Birm. Grand	,, Mingle . . .
Theatre	,, O'Brien
,, Bowen	,, Original . . .
,, Browne (E. V.)	,, Otway
,, Capell	,, Painter
,, Capulet . . .	,, Pennyworth
,, Collection . . .	,, Pepys
,, Collier	,, Poel
,, Crown Gar-	,, Porto
land	,, Prologue
,, Curtis	,, Rejected . . .
,, Davies	,, Rojas . . .
,, Drout	,, Saviolo
,, Fleay	,, Sh—] Sh—criticism
,, Fletcher	,, Silver
,, German	,, Simpson (R.)
,, Graves	,, Snider
,, Guenther	,, Spalding
,, Hale	,, Stael-Holstein
,, Hales	,, Story
,, Halliwell	,, Swan
,, Halpin	,, Vega Carpio
,, Hibbert	,, Walbran
,, Historical . . .	,, Walker
,, Humphreys	,, Weever
,, Hutchinson	,, Whately
,, Jemmat	,, Wheatley
,, Johnson and	,, White
Steevens	,, Woodward
,, Kemble	,, Young (J. T.)
,, Latham	,, 'Young Adam'
,, Legg	

SECOND MAIDEN'S TRAGEDY.

The original manuscript is preserved at the British Museum and was licensed for acting by Sir George Buck, 31st Oct., 1611, On the last leaf it is stated to be written by

Sh— Second maiden's tragedy . . .

*Thomas Goff, George Chapman, and Will.
Sh—. The first two names are erased,
leaving Sh— as the author, but the latter's
name was not added until 1700 or later.*

Second maiden's tragedy, 1611. Edited by
W. W. Greg. Oxford: Malone Society's
reprints, 1909-10. Fcp. 4°, pp. xvi.-78,
and six plates of facsimiles
BM | BLO | CTC | SML

Seven ages of man. *See* Sh— As you like it

SIR JOHN OLDCASTLE.

*Doubtless a joint literary production.
According to the first-class evidence of
Henslowe's diary, it was composed by
Michael Drayton, Anthony Munday,
Robert Wilson, and Thomas Hathway.*
Henslowe says :—'*16th Oct. 1599. Re-
ceved by me Thomas Downton of Phillip
Henslow, to pay Mr. Monday, Mr. Drayton,
Mr. Wilson and [Mr.] Hathway for the first
parte of the lyfe of Sr. Jhon Ouldcastell and
in earnest of the second parte, for the use
of the company, I say receved £10.*'
*A further entry says :—'Receved of Mr.
Hinchloe [Henslowe] for Mr. Mundaye
and the rest of the poets, at the playnge of
Sr. John Oldcastell, the ferst tyme, as a
geft, ten shillings.*'
*In the earliest versions of 'King Henry
IV.' Sh— utilised Oldcastle as a character,
and presumably gave offence to the Cobham
family, as the name was afterwards changed
to Falstaff. It is conjectured that Sh—'s
share in the authorship of 'Sir John Oldcastle' at the most consisted of editorial
revision.*
*It is entered in the Stationers' Registers
twice in 1600, and the second entry is
thought to be a fraud, enacted in 1619, by
Thomas Pavier.*
*'11th Aug. 1600. Thomas Pavier.
Entred for his copies vnder the handes of
Master Vicars and the wardens these III.
copies, viz., "The first parte of the history
of the life of Sir John Oldcastell lord Cobham." Item ; the "Second and laste parte
of the history of Sir John Oldcastell lord
Cobham with his martyrdom." Item ; "Ye
history of the life and deathe of Captaine
Thomas Stucley" . . .'*
*No edition is known of the 'Second
part.'*

[Sir John Oldcastle] The first part of the
true and honorable historie, of the life of
Sir John Old-castle, the good Lord Cob-

Sh— Sir John Oldcastle . . .
ham. As it hath been lately acted by the
right honorable the Earle of Notingham
Lord high Admirall of England his seruants. [*Device.*] London : Printed by
V. S—— [Valentine Simmes] for Thomas
Pauier, and are to be solde at his shop at
the signe of the Catte and Parrots neere
the Exchange, 1600. Fcp. 4°, sig. A¹ to
K⁴ in fours, unpaged, including title
BM | BLO | DEVON | ELLESMERE
This issue does not bear Sh—'s name, but contains more
lines than the 1619 entry, in addition to superior
readings.

[Sir John Oldcastle] The first part . . .
Written by William Shakespeare. Ln :
printed by T. P—— [Thomas Pavier, by
Isaac Jaggard ? 1619], 1600
Although dated 1600, the real year was 1619 (*q.v.*). For
a fuller account of the transaction, see A. W. Pollard's
' Sh— folios and quartos.'

[Sir John Oldcastle] The first part of the
true & honorable history, of the Life of
Sir Iohn Old-castle, the good Lord Cob-
ham. As it hath bene lately acted by the
Right honorable the Earle of Notingham
Lord High Admirall of England his Ser-
uants. Written by William Shakespeare.
['*Heb Ddieu' device.*] Ln : Printed [by
Isaac Jaggard ?] for T. P—— [Thomas
Pavier, 1619], 1600. Fcp. 4°, sig. A¹ to
K⁴ in fours, unpaged, including title
BM | BLO | BUS | CTC | NY | SBL | W
A copy measuring 7in. by 5⅛in. sold in May, 1906, for
£110. Earl Howe's copy, 7in. by 5¼in., in half blue
morocco, sold in Dec., 1907, for £57.

[Sir John Oldcastle] The history of Sir John
Oldcastle, the good Lord Cobham. By
Mr. Wm. Sh—. Ln : Printed for J. Tonson and the rest of the proprietors and
sold by the booksellers of Ln. and Westminster, 1734. Cr. 8°, pp. 72, and frontis-
piece by P. Fourdrinier BM | BPL | SML |W
Piracy notice by J. Tonson against R. Walker on verso
of title.

Sir John Oldcastle . . . Ln : J. Tonson . . .
1735. Cr. 8°

[Sir John Oldcastle] History of Sir John
Oldcastle, the good Lord Cobham. By
Sh—. Ln : R. Walker . . . 1735. Cr. 8°,
pp. 72 BM

Sir John Oldcastle . . . [In 'Ancient British
drama, edited by Sir Walter Scott ').
Ln : . . . 1810. Roy. 8° BM | BUS

[Sir John Oldcastle] Sh—'s doubtful plays.
The first part of Sir John Oldcastle.
Edited with an introduction by A. F.
Hopkinson. Ln : [Privately printed by]
M. E. Sims & Co., 1894. Cr. 8°, pp. xxiv.-
98 SML

Sh— Sir John Oldcastle . . .

[Sir John Oldcastle] Life of Sir John Oldcastle, 1600. [Edited by Percy Simpson
and W. W. Greg.] Malone Society reprints. Whittingham, Chiswick Press,
1908. Fcp. 4°, pp. xvi.[-88, unpaged],
including facsimiles of orig. titles
BM | BLO | CTC | SML
Gives list of variants in the early editions.

'Sir John Oldcastle' references—
See Bale	*See* Parsons
„ Cobham	„ Sh— [Works] Sh—
„ Hopkinson	Apocrypha, 1908

SIR THOMAS MORE.

*An anonymous tragedy, ascribed in part
to Sh—. The original manuscript, from
the Harleian collection, is in the British
Museum.*

Sir Thomas More [Original manuscript,
written in several hands, on twenty
varying sheets of paper, c. 1600] BM
First edited and published in 1844. Since then some
words and lines have crumbled away and become
illegible.
The portions ascribed by Simpson and Spedding to
Sh— are act II., sc. iii.-iv., lines 1-172, and act III.,
sc. ii.-iii.
Dyce's transcript and arrangement is exact and excellent, and for the illegible portions is now the sole
authority.

Sir Thomas More. A play, now first printed.
Edited by A. Dyce. Ln : ' Sh— Society '
. . . 1844. 8°, pp. xxvi.-102
BM | BPL | BUS | SML

Sir Thomas More . . . 'Old English plays.'
Edited with an introduction by A. F.
Hopkinson. For private circulation. Ln :
M. E. Sims & Co. . . . 1902. Cr. 8°, pp.
xxiv.-122   BPL | SML
The Stratford copy contains a holograph letter, pre-
senting the book, from the editor.

Six madrigals. *See* Sh— Poems, 1800
Songs. *See* Sh— Poems
[Sonnet] Phaeton to his friend Florio [In
Florio : 'Second frutes,' *q.v.*] Ln : T.
Woodcock . . . 1591. Fcp. 4°

SONNETS.

*The earliest known printed version of
the 'Sonnets' is the quarto printed by
George Eld in 1609, although copies,
apparently in manuscript, were referred to
by Francis Meres in 1598 as 'Sh—'s
sugred sonnets among his private friends.'*

*It was registered at Stationers' Hall thus :
'20th May, 1609. Thomas Thorpe.
Entred for his copie vnder thandes of*

Sh— Sonnets . . .

*Master Wilson and Master Lownes warden
a booke called Shakespeare's Sonnettes,
VId.'*

[Sonnets] Shake-speares Sonnets. Neuer
before Imprinted. [A Louers Complaint.
By William Shake-speare.] At London :
By G. Eld for T. T—— [Thomas Thorpe]
and are to be solde by William Aspley,
1609. Fcp. 4°, forty unpaged leaves, and
generally identical, save in imprint, with
the next entry
BM | CPL | CTC | ELLESMERE | MRL
The dedication to 'Mr. W. H.' has caused much
expenditure of breath and ink. It was almost cer-
tainly indited to William Herbert Earl of Pembroke,
as may be seen by the similar dedication in St.
Augustine's 'De Civitate Dei, 1610,' signed Th. Th.
[Thomas Thorpe].
With more ingenuity than reason, it was suggested by
D. Barnstorff that 'W. H.' stands for 'William
Himself.'
In April, 1907, a cropped copy sold for £800, a remark-
able advance on the published price of fivepence.
The original cost was found in a manuscript at Dulwich
College, where Edward Alleyn noted the purchase at
the time thus :—
 'A book of Shaksper Sonnets, 5d.'
This is confirmed elsewhere by Lord Spencer, of
Althorpe fame.
The B.M. copy measures 7 1/16in. by 5 3/16in.
It was reprinted in 1766 by G. Steevens, in 1850, 1862,
1870, 1886, 1901, twice in 1905, in 1908, and again in
1909.

[Sonnets] Shake-speares Sonnets. Neuer
before Imprinted. [A Louers Complaint.
By William Shake-speare.] At London :
By G. Eld for T. T—— [Thomas Thorpe]
and are to be solde by Iohn Wright,
dwelling at Christ Church gate, 1609.
Fcp. 4°, on forty unpaged leaves ; sig. A,
two leaves ; sig. B¹ to L² in fours
BM | BLO | CTC | HUTH
The Sonnets end on the recto of sig. K1 and 'A Louer's
Complaint' begins on verso of the same.
The recto of the second leaf bears inscription which
runs :—
 'To . the . onelie . begetter . of . these . insuing .
 sonnets . Mr. W. H. all . happinesse . and . that .
 eternitie . promised . by . our . everliving . Poet .
 wisheth . the . well-wishing . adventurer . in .
 setting . forth . T. T. [Thomas Thorpe].
Wright's name in the imprint is much rarer than that
of Aspley.

Sonnets, 1609. Reprinted by G. Steevens.
Ln : 1766. 8°, pp. 38   BPL | SML | W
Sonnets from Sh—, forty in number, by
'Albert' [Rev. John Armstrong]. Ln : J.
Debrett . . . 1791. 8°, pp. viii.-76
BM | BPL | BUS
Originally appeared in the columns of *The Gazette* and
Morning Chronicle.

Sonnets . . . to which are added, his minor
poems and the songs from his plays.
Whitehaven : James Steel . . . 1822. 8°,
pp. iv.-124   BUS | W
The only piece of Sh— known to have issued from
Cumberland.

[Sonnets] Sonnets of Sh— and Milton . . . Ln: Edward Moxon . . . 1830. Cr. 8°, pp. vi.-186   BPL | BUS

Sonnets, 1833. *See* Sh— Works: Ext. 1833

[Sonnets] Autobiographical poems. Being his sonnets clearly developed ; with his character drawn chiefly from his works. By Charles Armitage Brown. Ln: H. G. Bohn . . . 1838. 8°   MPL | W

Sonnets . . . Ln: W. Smith . . . 1839. Roy. 32°

Sonnets . . . A new edition. Ln: Ball, Arnold & Co. . . . 1840. 12°   BPL

Sonnets. With the lover's complaint . . . Facsimile reprint of the first edition. [Ln. . . ?] 1850. Fcp. 4°
Limited to fifty copies. A copy sold, with others, 12th Nov., 1909.

Sonnets . . . re-arranged and divided into four parts. With an introduction and explanatory notes. [By Robert Cartwright]. Ln: J. R. Smith . . . 1859. 8°, pp. 120   BM | BPL | BUS | CPL | SML

[Sonnets] Schlüssel zu Sh—'s sonnetten von D. Barnstorff. Bremen : J. Kühtmann & Co., 1860. 8°, pp. 180   BM | BUS
Text in English with commentary in German.

[Sonnets] Songs and sonnets . . . Illustrated by John Gilbert [with coloured plates]. Ln: S. Low, Son, & Co., 1862. F°, pp. x.-32   BM | BPL | BUS | CPL | SML

[Sonnets] A key to Sh—'s sonnets, by D. Barnstorff. Translated from the German by T. J. Graham [with the text]. Ln: [Bremen printed], Trübner & Co. . . . 1862. 8°, pp. 216   BM | BUS

Sonnets . . . [Aspley, 1609], reproduced in facsimile by the new process of photo-zincography in use at H.M.'s Ordnance Survey Office, from the unrivalled original in the library of Bridgewater House, by permission of the Earl of Ellesmere. Ln: Lovell Reeve & Co. . . . 1862. Fcp. 4°, on forty unpaged leaves   BM | BPL | BUS | CPL | MPL
Executed under the direction of Col. Sir Hy. James, and edited by Howard Staunton.

[Sonnets] Sh—'s songs and sonnets. Illustrated by John Gilbert. [With a preface signed 'H. S——' [*i.e.*, Howard Staunton]. Ln: S. Low, Son, & Co., 1863. 8°, pp. 56   BM | BPL | BUS | SML

[Sonnets] Songs and sonnets . . . edited by F. T. Palgrave. Boston [U.S.] . . . 1864. 12°

[Sonnets] Songs and sonnets . . . edited by F. T. Palgrave. 'Gem edition.' Ln. & Cambridge : Macmillan & Co. . . . 1865. 8°, pp. vi.-256   BM | BPL | BUS | CPL

Sonnets . . . Boston [U.S.]: Ticknor & Fields, 1865. 16°, pp. 160   BUS

[Sonnets] Remarks on the sonnets of Sh—; with the sonnets. Shewing that they belong to the Hermetic class of writings, and explaining their general meaning and purpose. By the author of 'Remarks on alchemy' [Ethan Allan Hitchcock]. New York: J. Miller . . . 1865. 12°, pp. 258
                BM | BPL | BUS | CPL | SML

Sonnets, never before interpreted ; his private friends identified ; together with a recovered likeness of himself. By Gerald Massey. Ln: Longmans . . . 1866. 8°, pp. xii.-604   BUS
Includes the Sonnets, printed in groups.

[Sonnets] Remarks on the sonnets of Sh— . . . by the author of ' Remarks on alchemy ' [E. A. Hitchcock]. Second edition, enlarged. New York: J. Miller . . . 1867. 12°, pp. xxvi.-366   BM

Sonnets . . . With commentaries by Thomas D. Budd. Philadelphia: J. Campbell . . . 1868. 12°, pp. 172   BPL | BUS | SML
The editor maintains ' the Sonnets were addressed to the soul materialized, and are thus applicable to mankind generally, individually, and to the poet in particular.'
A few were done on large paper, fcp. 4°, of which one is at Boston.

Sonnets . . . solved, and the mystery of his friendship, love, and rivalry revealed. Illustrated by numerous extracts from the poet's works, contemporary writers, and other authors. Ln: J. R. Smith . . . 1870. 8°, pp. vi.-242
                BM | BPL | BUS | CPL | MPL

Sonnets and 'A lover's complaint.' Reprinted in the orthography and punctuation of the original edition of 1609. Ln: J. Russell Smith . . . 1870. 8°, on forty-one unpaged leaves; sig. A¹ to L² in fours   BPL | BUS | MPL | SML

[Sonnets] Songs . . . selected from his poems and plays. Ln: Virtue & Co. . . . 1872. 8°, pp. vi.-188   BUS

Sonnets, never before interpreted . . . Second and enlarged edition. The secret drama of Sh—'s sonnets unfolded, with the characters identified, by Gerald Massey. Ln: Longmans . . . 1872. 8°, pp. xii.-604-56   BM

[Sonnets] Sh—'s songs and sonnets. Illustrated by John Gilbert. Ln: S. Low [1875]. 8°, pp. 56   BM | BPL

[Sonnets] Songs . . . illustrated by John Gilbert. [Edited by Benjamin Howard Ticknor.] Boston [U.S.]: J. R. Osgood & Co., 1877. 16°, pp. 94   BM | BUS

Sh— Sonnets . . .

Sonnets . . . With a frontispiece. [Ed. by
B. H. Ticknor.] Boston [U.S.]: J. R.
Osgood & Co., 1877. 16°, pp. 104
BM | BUS

Sonnets . . . illustrated by Sir John Gilbert
and others. 'Emerald series.' Ln :
Routledge . . . 1878. 12°, pp. 96
BM | BUS

[Sonnets] Songs and sonnets . . . edited by
F. T. Palgrave. 'Golden treasury series.'
Ln : Macmillan . . . 1879. 8°, pp. 254
BM | BPL | SML

[Sonnets] A treasury of English sonnets,
edited by D. M. Main. Manchester :
Ireland & Co. . . . 1880. Fcp. 4°
Sh— occupies pp. 26-54. BM | BLO | CTC

Sonnets . . . 'English library.' Zurich :
Rudolphi . . . 1881. 12°

Sonnets . . . edited by E. Dowden. 'Parchment library.' Ln : Kegan Paul . . . 1881.
Cr. 8°, pp. lxii.-252. With portrait copied
from the Page bust at the Sh— Memorial
BM | BPL | BUS | SML
Fifty copies of this edition were printed on large paper.

Sonnets . . . edited by E. Dowden. [Second
edition.] 'Parchment library.' Ln :
Kegan Paul . . . 1881. Cr. 8°, pp. x.-306
BM | BPL

Sonnets . . . 'English library.' Zurich . . .
1882. 12°

Sonnets . . . 'Parchment library.' Edited
by E. Dowden. Ln : Kegan Paul . . .
1882. Cr. 8°

Sonnets . . . with notes by W. J. Rolfe.
New York : Harper . . . 1883. 12°

[Sonnets] Some well-known 'sugar'd sonnets ' . . . Re-sugar'd with ornamental
borders designed by Edwin J. Ellis and
etched by Tristram J. Ellis. 'Put a
spirit of youth in everything . . .' Ln :
Sotheran . . . Produced by Field & Tuer
[1883]. Fcp. 4°, pp. 72 (unpaged). With
twelve etchings ; printed on one side of
the leaf only BM | BPL | SML

Sonnets . . . [In Three hundred English
sonnets. Edited by D. M. Main]. Edinburgh : Blackwood . . . 1884. 12° SML

[Sonnets] Songs, poems, and sonnets . . .
edited with a critical introduction by
William Sharp. 'Canterbury poets.' Ln :
Walter Scott . . . 1885. 16°, pp. xxxvi.-
278 BM | BPL | SML
Two varying editions exist, both dated 1885 and both
at Stratford. One is printed within red rules
throughout, and the other is without red ink.
The introduction gives some interesting theories on
Wm. Jaggard's edition of the ' Passionate pilgrim.'

Sh— Sonnets . . .

Sonnets . . . The first quarto, 1609. A facsimile in photo-lithography (from the
copy in the British Museum) . . . With an
introduction by T. Tyler. ' Sh— quarto
facsimiles.' Ln : C. Prætorius [1886].
Fcp. 4°, pp. xxxii.-80
BM | BPL | BUS | SML

Sonnets . . . never before interpreted : his
private friends identified : together with
a recovered likeness of himself. By G.
Massey. Ln : Longmans, 1886. 8°, pp.
xii.-604 BM

Sonnets . . . never before interpreted . . .
[Another edition.] Edited by G. Massey.
Ln : Printed for subscribers only, 1888.
8°, pp. viii.-482 BM

[Sonnets] Songs and sonnets. Illustrated
by Sir John Gilbert. [Edited by Edward
Marston.] Ln : Low [1888]. 4°, pp. 44.
Printed in colours BPL | BM
The illustrations are reduced reproductions of those in
the 1862 edition.

Sonnets . . . edited by E. Dowden. 'Parchment library.' Ln : Kegan Paul . . . 1889.
Cr. 8° BUS

Sonnets . . . edited, with notes and introduction, by T. Tyler. Ln : D. Nutt . . . 1890.
8°, pp. xx.-316 BM | BPL | BUS | SML

[Sonnets] I Sonetti di Wm. Sh—. Tradutti
per la prima volta in Italiano da A.
Olivieri . . . Col testo Inglese a fronte.
Palermo : S. Clausen . . . 1890. 8°, pp.
xxxviii.-318 BM

[Sonnets] Songs and sonnets. Illustrated by
Sir John Gilbert. Philadelphia : Gebbie &
Co. . . . [c. 1890]. Fcp. 4°, pp. 44. Containing 45 engravings, ten of which are in
colours

[Sonnets] 'Great Pan lives': Sh—'s
sonnets, 20-126. With paraphrase and
references by 'Clelia' [Charles Downing].
Ln : Luzac & Co. . . . 1892. 8°, pp. x.-208
BM

[Sonnets] Songs and sonnets. 'Golden
treasury series.' Ln : Macmillan . . .
1893. 12°

Sonnets . . . with decorations by Ernest G.
Treglown, engraved on wood by Charles
Carr, of the Birmingham guild of handi-
craft. Printed at the press of the same
guild and published by G. Napier and
Co. . . . Birmingham, and by Tylston &
Edwards and A. P. Marsden, Ln., Nov.,
1895. Fcp. 4°, pp. iv.-154
BM | BPL | SML
Of the fifty also done on large paper one is at Stratford.

Sonnets . . . edited by E. Dowden. 'Parchment library.' Ln : K. Paul . . . 1896.
12°, pp. 316 BPL

Sonnets. Edited by I. Gollancz. 'Temple edition.' Ln: Dent, 1896. 12°, pp. 200
BM | BLO | BPL | BUS | CTC

[Sonnets] Sh— and the Bible. Fifty sonnets with their scriptural harmonies. Interpreted by C. E—— [Charles Ellis]. Ln: Bagster, 1896. 16°, pp. 144
BM | BPL

[Sonnets] Genesis of Sh—'s art : A study of his sonnets and poems [with the text] by E. J. Dunning. Boston [U.S.]: Lea & Shephard, 1897. 8°, pp. xxxiv.-336 BM

Sonnets . . . Boston [U.S.] : Copeland & Day . . . 1897. 8°, pp. 166
BM

[Sonnets] Sh— and the Bible : Fifty sonnets with their scriptural harmonies, interpreted by C. E—— [C. Ellis]. Ln: Bagster, 1897. 16°, pp. 144. With portrait
BPL | BUS | SML

Sonnets . . . edited by E. Dowden. 'Parchment library.' Ln: Kegan Paul, 1897. 12°, pp. 316

Sonnets and poems. 'Pocket Falstaff edition.' Ln: Bliss Sands . . . 1898. 16°, pp. 128
BPL | SML

Sonnets . . . reconsidered and in part rearranged with introductory notes, etc., and a reprint of the original 1609 edition. Edited by S. Butler. Ln: Longman . . . 1899. 8°, pp. 340 BM | BPL | BUS | MPL
This edition is entered in the Boston annual library list, 1899-1900, in error as bearing the date 1809.

Sonnets . . . illustrated by Henry Ospovat. Ln: Lane . . . 1899. 16°
BM | BPL | BUS | MPL

Sonnets . . . edited by Thomas Tyler. With notes, appendix, introduction upon the identity of the 'dark lady' and interpretation of the ' Sonnets.' With new appendix in answer to ' Sidney Lee's ' criticism of the Herbert Fitton theory. Ln: Nutt . . . 1899. 8°, pp. 360, and plates
BPL | MPL

Sonnets . . . [With decorated borders and initials by Christopher Dean]. Ln: G. Bell & Sons . . . 1899. 8°, sig. A¹ to A⁴, sig. B to I, and sig. K to L in eights, unpaged
SML

Sonnets . . . reprinted from the edition of 1609. Edited by T. S. Moore. Decorated by C. S. Ricketts. Ln: Hacon & Ricketts, 1899. Fcp. 4°, pp. 160
BM

Sonnets . . . edited with notes by W. J. Rolfe. New York . . . 1899. Cr. 8°
BPL

Sonnets . . . [In a ' New study of the " Sonnets " by P. Godwin,' pp. 227-306]. New York . . . 1900. Cr. 8°
BPL

Sonnets . . . edited with introduction and notes by C. H. Herford. ' Eversley edition.' Ln: Macmillan . . . 1900. 12° BPL

Sonnets . . . edited by J. P. Briscoe. 'Bibelot edition.' Ln: Gay & Bird . . . 1900. Cr. 8°
BPL

Sonnets . . . new newly imprinted from the first edition of 1609 . . . New Rochelle . . . [1901]. 8°
BUS

Sonnets . . . ' Lover's library.' Ln: Lane . . . 1902. 16°, pp. 236
BPL

Sonnets . . . with introduction and notes by J. Dennis. Illustrated by B. Shaw. 'Chiswick edition.' Ln: Bell . . . 1902. 12°

Sonnets . . . edited by Mathilde Blind. Ln: De la More Press . . . 1902. 16°

Sonnets . . . Guildford : A. C. Curtis, Astolot Press, 1902. Cr. 8°, pp. viii.-154, and etched frontispiece after Sandro Botticelli
BM | BLO | BPL | CTC
Reprinted from the 1609 edition, with ' correction of a few obvious misprints.'
Sixty numbered copies in red and black were printed on Japanese vellum.

[Sonnets] Christ in Sh— : The dramas and sonnets interpreted. By Charles Ellis. Third edition. With . . . supplement. Ln: Stoneman . . . 1902. Cr. 8°, pp. 370. With portrait
BPL | SML

Sonnets . . . edited with notes by H. N. Hudson. 'Windsor edition.' Edinburgh: Jack . . . 1903. 8°, pp. iv.-116. With portrait of Michael Drayton
BM | BLO | CTC | SML

Sonnets . . . 'Ariel booklets.' New York : Putnam . . . 1903. 16°
BPL

Sonnets . . . and 'A lover's complaint.' Seen through the press by T. S. Moore. Decorated by C. Ricketts. 'Vale Press edition.' Ln: Hacon & Ricketts . . . 1903. Roy. 8°, pp. 72
BM | BLO· | CTC | SML

Sonnets . . . Ln: Astolat Press, 1904. Cr. 8°, pp. 164

Sonnets . . . with introduction and notes by H. C. Beeching. 'Athenæum press series.' Ln: Ginn . . . 1904. Cr. 8°
BPL

Sonnets, lover's complaint, etc. ' Ellen Terry edition.' Glasgow: Bryce . . . 1904. 32°

Sonnets . . . with introduction and notes by Mrs. C. C. Stopes. 'King's Sh—.' Ln: De la More Press, 1904. 16°, pp. 300
BM | BLO | CTC

Sonnets . . . with introduction by G. Brandes. ' Favourite classics.' Ln: Heinemann . . . 1904. 12°

[Sonnets] Sh— self-revealed in his 'Sonnets' and ' Phoenix & turtle.' Text with introduction and analysis by J. M——. Manchester: Sherratt & Hughes, 1904. 8°, pp. 286
BPL

Sh— Sonnets . . .

Sonnets and poems. 'Carlton classics.' Ln :
Long . . . 1905. 12°   BPL

Sonnets . . . with introduction and notes by
W. J. Craig. 'Little quartos.' Ln :
Methuen, 1905. 32°

Sonnets. Being a reproduction in facsimile
of the first edition, 1609, from the copy in
the Malone collection in the Bodleian
library. With introduction and bibliography by 'Sidney Lee.' Oxford :
Clarendon Press, 1905. Fcp. 4°, pp. 72-
80 (the latter unpaged)
BM | BLO | BPL | BUS | CTC | SBL | SML

The impertinent patronage of Sh— by 'Sidney Lee' is
(in his own words) 'not to be matched elsewhere.'
In the opening lines of the introduction he says :—
'Though Sh—'s sonnets are unequal in literary merit,
many reach levels of lyric melody and meditative
energy which are not to be matched. . . . If a few of
the poems sink into inanity beneath the burden of
quibbles and conceits, others are almost overcharged
with mellowed sweetness. . . .'
This editor's overflowing self-satisfaction is patent in
his further remark :—'The abundant criticism lavished
on my comments has not modified my faith in my
general position or in the fruitfulness of my investigation.'
The 'bibliography' (save the mark) alleged on the title
to be given in the volume appears to consist of a few
remarks on the original editions. Nevertheless,
within his very limited effort he achieves a pretty
blunder. The Sh— Memorial Library at Stratford
is credited with a 1640 copy it never (unfortunately)
possessed of Sh—'s Poems.

Sonnets. 'Waistcoat pocket edition.' Ln :
Treherne . . . 1905. 32°

Sonnets . . . [edited by Arthur Henry Bul-
len]. Stratford-on-Avon : Sh— head press,
1905. Cr. 8°, pp. vi.-160   BPL | SML
Issue limited to 510 copies on handmade paper and
twelve on pure vellum, all numbered.
' "Mr. Sidney Lee" argues that the sonnets were
written simply as literary exercises. The mere statement of such views would seem to carry their refutation. When he seeks to persuade us that the most
impassioned utterances in these sonnets are to be
taken *cum grano salis*, and that Sh—'s devotion to
his friend was merely servile adulation, we lose
patience, and have to recall the yeoman service that
Mr. Lee has rendered to literature before we can
pardon this affront offered to Sh—'s memory and to
our intelligence.'—*A. H. Bullen.*

Sonnets . . . 'Royal library.' Ln : A. L.
Humphreys, 1906. Cr. 8°, pp. 208 BPL

Sonnets . . . with kalendar. Ln : Hills . . .
1907. 12°, pp. 32 (unpaged) and Chandos portrait

Sonnets and A lover's complaint [1609].
With introduction by W. H. Hadow.
'Tudor & Stuart library.' Oxford :
Clarendon Press, 1908. Fcp. 4° BPL

[Sonnets] Complete sonnets. A new arrangement. With introduction and notes by C.
M. Walsh. Ln : Unwin, 1908. Cr. 8°, pp.
286   BPL

Sh— Sonnets . . .

Sonnets and poems. With introduction by
J. Davidson. 'Renaissance edition.' Ln :
Harrap . . . 1908. Fcp. 4° BPL

Sonnets and songs, chosen by A. T. Quiller-
Couch. Oxford : Clarendon Press, 1908.
Cr. 8°   BPL

Sonnets : A recantation. A supplement to
'Sh— self-revealed,' by J. M——. Ln :
. . . 1909   BPL

Sonnets. 'Tercentenary edition,' from the
first edition of 1609. Doves Press . . .
1909. Fcp. 4°   BM | BLO | CTC
Fifteen copies were also produced on pure vellum,
priced at £7 10s. each.

Sonnets . . . Ln : Sidgwick & Jackson, 1909.
16°

'Sonnets' references—

See Ainger	*See* Howard
,, Alger	,, Ingleby
,, 'Antiquary'	,, Johnson (J.)
,, Barnstorff	,, Levi
,, Beeching	,, Massey
,, Bell	,, Meres
,, Boaden	,, Mifflin
,, Breton	,, O'Flanagan
,, Brown (Hy.)	,, Richardson
,, Butler (S.)	,, Roe
,, Collins (J. C.)	,, Ross
,, Causton	,, Saxelby
,, Corney	,, Sh— Poems
,, Davis (H.)	,, Sh— Works
,, Davis (L.)	,, *Sh*—] Sh— and his
,, Dennis	sonnets
,, Direy	,, Shepherd
,, Donnelly	,, Shindler
,, Dowden	,, Simpson
,, Downing	,, Sonnet
,, Dunning	,, Spalding
,, Ellis	,, Stopes
,, Fleay	,, Swinburne
,, Godwin	,, Theobald (W.)
,, Goodlet	,, Towndrow
,, Heraud	,, Travers
,, Hillard	,, Tyler
,, Hitchcock	,, Walters
,, Hosmer	

Sports of the muses. *See* Sh— Works :
Extracts, 1752
Take, oh, take those lips away ! *See* Sh—
Measure . . . 1870
Tales. *See* Sh— Works : Ext. 1807 (*et seq.*)

TAMING OF THE SHREW.

*This comedy first appeared in the
Jaggard canon of 1623. [An earlier version, under an almost identical title, to
which the dramatist is alike indebted for*

plot, scenery, and name, thrice appeared, and its authorship has been variously assigned to Sh—, George Peele, and R. Greene.]

It was originally entered on the Stationers' registers by Peter Short, 2nd May, 1594; secondly by Nicholas Ling, 22 Jan., 1606; thirdly by John Smethwicke, 19 Nov., 1607.

An interval occurred of over a century before any untampered separate edition of Sh—'s text succeeded Smethwicke's of 1631.

[Taming of the shrew] A Pleasant Conceited Historie called the Taming of a Shrew. As it was sundry Times acted by the Right Honorable the Earle of Pembrook his Seruants. Printed at London by Peter Short and are to be sold by Cutbert Burbie, at his shop at the Royall Exchange, 1594. Fcp. 4°, on fourteen unpaged leaves, including title DEVON

Anonymous, and supposed to be the play used by Sh— as the foundation of his ' Taming of the shrew.' The difference of the respective texts is as marked as that between the 1603 and 1604 editions of ' Hamlet '; or that between the ' Merry wives ' of 1602 and 1623.
Malone assigns 1594 as the year of composition of Sh—'s ' Taming of the shrew,' and when the play was reprinted in 1607 it bore the name of Sh— as author.
' In whatever light it may be considered, whether as the play remodelled by Sh— or as the first draft of his comedy, it is unquestionably of the highest literary interest and curiosity in a Shakespearian library.'—*Heber.*
' Sh— has made very slight use of it in the composition of his drama on the same subject.'—*Halliwell.*
' There is scarce a line the same with the present play, yet the plot and scenery scarce differ at all.'—*Steevens.*
' The "Taming of a shrew" was revised by Sh— and another into the "Taming of the shrew." '—*Furnivall.*
The title is thought to have been borrowed from an older story, called ' The wyf lapped in morell's skin, or the taminge of a shrew.'
Reprinted by the Sh— Society 1844; by J. O. Halliwell, in his folio Sh—, 1853; by E. W. Ashbee 1870; by W. C. Hazlitt, in Sh—'s library, 1875; and by C. Prætorius 1886.
Only one original known to survive.—(See Catalogue . . . 1826.)

[Taming . . .] A Pleasant conceited Historie called The taming of a Shrew. As it was sundrie times acted by the Right honorable the Earle of Pembrook his servants. Imprinted at London by P. S—— [Peter Short] and are to be sold by Cutbert Burbie, 1596. Fcp. 4°, unpaged BM
In prose and verse.

[Taming . . .] A Pleasaunt Conceited Historie called the Taming of a Shrew. As it hath beene sundry Times acted by the right Honourable the Earle of Pembrooke

his Servants. Printed at London by V. S—— [Valentine Simmes] for Nicholas Ling and are to be sold at his shop in Saint Dunstons Church-yard in Fleet street, 1607. Fcp. 4° ARBURY | DEVON
Reprinted in ' Six old plays,' by John Nichols, 1779 (*q.v.*)

[Taming . . .] A Wittie and pleasant Comedie Called The Taming of the Shrew. As it was acted by his Maiesties Seruants at the Blacke Friers and the Globe. Written by Will. Shakespeare. [*Device.*] London: Printed by W. S—— [Wm. Sheares ?] for Iohn Smethwicke and are to be sold at his Shop in Saint Dunstones Churchyard vnder the Diall, 1631. Fcp. 4°, sig. A¹ to I⁴ in fours; 36 unpaged leaves, including title BM | BUS | CTC | NY | W
The first known separate edition of Sh—'s play.
Reprinted by Geo. Steevens in 1766.
In March, 1907, a copy realised £651.

[Taming . . .] Sauny the Scott, or the Taming of the Shrew: A Comedy [Founded upon Sh—'s play]. As it is now acted·at the Theatre Royal. Written by John Lacy, Servant to His Majesty, and never before printed.

' Then I'll cry out, swell'd with poetick rage, 'Tis I, John Lacy, have reform'd your stage.'

London: Printed and Sold by E. Whitlock, near Stationers Hall, 1698. Fcp. 4°, pp. iv.-48 BM | BPL | BUS | SML
Much of the original text is retained, but the ' Induction ' is omitted. Some of the characters are changed and new incidents are added.
On the fly-leaf of the Stratford copy J. O. Halliwell has written:—' This is the rarest of all the Shakespearean alterations of the latter part of the seventeenth century.'

[Taming . . .] Sauny the Scot; or the taming of the shrew: A comedy. As it is now acted at the Theatre Royal in Drury Lane by Her Majesty's Company of Comedians. Written by John Lacy. Ln: B. Bragge ✓ . . 1708. Fcp. 4°, pp. vi.-64 BUS | SML | W
In this issue is added a ' Dedicatory epistle to the Earl of Bradford.'

[Taming . . .] Sauny the Scot, or the taming of the shrew. Written originally by Mr. Sh—. Alter'd and improv'd by Mr. [John] Lacey. Ln: E. Curll . . . 1714. 12° BPL | W
Described by J. O. Halliwell, in a note written within the Warwick copy, as ' an amazingly rare edition.'

Taming of the shrew. A comedy. [Ln: Jacob Tonson] Printed in the year MDCCXIV. Cr. 8°, pp. 291-362 (excerpt), and copperplate frontispiece

Sh— Taming of the shrew . . .

[Taming . . .] The cobler of Preston. As it is acted at the Theatre-Royal in Drury-Lane by his majesty's servants. Written by Mr. [Charles] Johnson. Ln: Printed by W. Wilkins at the Dolphin in Little Britain and sold by W. Hinchcliffe at Dryden's Head under the Royal Exchange, 1716. 8°, pp. vi.-48, and frontispiece   BPL | BUS | W
The first edition of this farce, founded on the 'Induction' to Sh—'s 'Taming of the shrew,' and much of the language borrowed therefrom.
The Epilogue is by C. Cibber.

[Taming . . .] The cobler of Preston . . . Written by Mr. Johnson. Second edition. Ln: W. Hinchcliffe . . . 1716. 8°, pp. vi.-48   BUS

[Taming . . .] The cobler of Preston. As it is acted at the Theatre Royal in Drury Lane. Written by Mr. [Charles] Johnson. The second edition. Ln: W. Wilkins, 1716. 8°, pp. 84   W
The Warwick copy is inlaid to quarto size.

[Taming . . .] The cobler of Preston, by Mr. [Charles] Johnson. The third edition. Ln: . . . 1716. 8°   BM | W

[Taming . . .] The cobler of Preston. A farce. As it is acted at the New Theatre, Lincoln's Inn Fields. By Christopher Bullock. Ln: . . . 1716. 12°
Entirely different from Charles Johnson's compilation, except in title.
'I did hear there was a farce in rehearsal at Drury Lane Theatre call'd 'The Cobler of Preston,' . . . so I set to work on Friday, the 20th Jan., finished it on the Saturday following, and it was acted the Tuesday after.'—*Preface.*
Much of the language is taken from the 'Induction,' but there are some new incidents.

[Taming . . .] The cobler of Preston, by C. Bullock. Fourth edition. Ln: . . . 1723. 12°   BPL

[Taming . . .] Sauny the Scot . . . By J. Lacey. Ln: . . . 1731. 12°

[Taming . . .] The cobler of Preston. An opera [founded on Sh—'s 'Induction,' by C. Bullock]. Ln: . . . 1732. 12° BM

Taming of the shrew . . . Ln: Printed for J. Tonson and the rest of the proprietors and sold by the booksellers of London and Westminster, 1734. 12°, pp. 84, and frontispiece by P. Fourdrinier
With the piracy advertisement, following title, against R. Walker.

Taming of the shrew. A comedy by Sh—. Ln: R. Walker . . . 1735. 12°   W

[Taming . . .] A cure for a scold. A ballad farce of two acts. Founded upon Sh—'s Taming of the shrew. As it is acted by His Majesty's Company of Comedians at the Theatre Royal in Drury Lane. By

Sh— Taming of the shrew . . .

J. Worsdale, portrait painter. Ln: L. Gilliver [1735]. 8°, pp. x.-16-25-60   BM | BPL | BUS | SML
A great part is taken without acknowledgment from Lacey's 'Sauny the Scot.'
The pagination is faulty.

[Taming . . .] A cure for a scold . . . by J. Worsdale. Dublin: Faulkner . . . 1738. 8°

[Taming . . .] A cure for a scold . . . by J. Worsdale. Ln: . . . 1738. 8°   BM

[Taming . . .] The cobler of Preston . . . by C. Bullock. Glasgow . . . 1755. 12° SML

[Taming . . .] Catharine and Petruchio. A comedy. In three acts. As it is perform'd at the Theatre Royal in Drury-Lane. Alter'd from Sh—'s 'Taming of the shrew' [by David Garrick]. Ln: J. & R. Tonson and S. Draper, 1756. Cr. 8°, pp. viii.-56   BPL | BUS | W
First edition.
Garrick's version differs from the original in the omission of the 'Induction' and in the suppression of scenes which do not relate to Katharine and Petruchio, in addition to minor alterations.

[Taming . . .] Catharine and Petruchio . . . Altered from Sh— . . . by D. Garrick . . . Edinburgh: M. Jarvie . . . 1756. 8°, pp. iv.-28   BUS
A copy formerly belonging to N. Creswick (who acted Petruchio at Edinburgh) is at Boston.

Taming of the shrew. Ln: [Reprinted by G. Steevens], 1631-1766. 8°, pp. 84 (unpaged), sig. B¹ to G⁴ in eights   BPL

[Taming . . .] The cobler of Preston. A farce [Founded on . . . Sh—] . . . By C. Bullock. Fifth edition. Ln: S. Bladon . . . 1767. 8°, pp. 30   BM | BUS

[Taming . . .] The cobler of Preston . . . By C. Johnson. 1767. 12°   BM

Taming of the shrew. A comedy . . . An introduction, and notes critical and illustrative, are added by the authors of the 'Dramatic censor' [F. Gentleman]. Ln: John Bell; York: C. Etherington, 1774. 8° (excerpt), pp. 69-152
An off-print for the use of playgoers, from Bell's edition of Sh—'s Works.

Taming of the shrew . . . [Edited by F. Gentleman]. Ln: J. Bell . . . 1776. 12°

Taming of the shrew: Eight plates, with verses descriptive of the comedy. Ln: Hawkins . . . 1778. 8°

Taming of a shrew, 1607 [In 'Six old plays' . . . Edited by J. Nichols, vol. i.] Ln: . . . 1779. 8°   BPL | BUS

[Taming . . .] Catharine and Petruchio . . . Alter'd [by David Garrick] from Sh— . . . Taken from the manager's book at the Theatre Royal, Covent Garden. Ln: J. Wenman . . . [c. 1780]. 8°   BM | BPL

[Taming . . .] Katherine and Petruchio . . . by David Garrick [In 'Collection of farces,' *q.v. ante*]. Edinburgh: C. Elliot . . . 1783-88. 8° SML

[Taming . . .] Catharine and Petruchio. Altered [by David Garrick] from Sh— [In 'Supplement to Bell's "British theatre"']. 1784. 12° BM

Taming of the shrew . . . printed complete from the text of Sam. Johnson and Geo. Steevens. Ln: Printed for . . . John Bell . . . 1785. 12°, pp. 120, with engraved title and frontispiece of ' Mrs. Wrighten in Katharina '

[Taming . . .] Cobler of Preston . . . by C. Johnson. Ln: Hinchcliffe . . . 1786. 8°

Taming of the shrew, or Catherine and Petruchio. Ln: C. Bathurst . . . 1786. 12°, pp. 34 BM

[Taming . . .] Catherine and Petruchio [In ' British stage ']. 1786. 12° BM

[Taming . . .] Katharine and Petruchio . . . by David Garrick [In ' Collection of farces ']. Edinburgh & Stirling: S. Doig & W. Anderson, 1792. 8° BUS

[Taming . . .] Catharine and Petruchio . . . Ln: Roach . . . [c. 1806]. 12°

[Taming . . .] Catherine and Petruchio. Altered from Sh— by D. Garrick. As performed at the Theatres Royal, Drury Lane and Covent Garden . . . Ln: J. Cawthorn . . . 1806. 8°, pp. 56, and portrait of ' Mrs. Kemble as Catherine ' BM | BUS

[Taming . . .] Catherine and Petruchio. A comedy. Altered from Sh— by D. Garrick. [In E. S. Inchbald's ' Collection of farces' (7 vols.), Vol. 4]. Ln: Longman . . . 1809. 12° BUS | MPL

[Taming . . .] Katherine and Petruchio: Altered from the ' Taming of the shrew ' by D. Garrick. Revised by J. P. Kemble. Ln: Printed for the Theatre . . . 1810. 8° SML

[Taming . . .] Catherine and Petruchio, or the taming of the shrew. Altered from Sh— by David Garrick. Ln: . . . 1811. 12° BPL | W

Taming of the shrew, by Will. Sh—. Printed complete from the text of Sam. Johnson and Geo. Steevens. Ln: . . . 1812. 16° W

[Taming . . .] Katharine and Petruchio. A comedy. Taken by David Garrick from the ' Taming of a shrew.' Revised by J. P. Kemble, and now published as it is performed at the Theatres Royal. Ln: J. Miller . . . 1815. 8°, pp. 34 BM | BUS

[Taming . . .] Catherine and Petruchio, by D. Garrick. Edited by Mrs. E. S. Inchbald [In ' Collection of farces ']. Ln: Longman . . . 1815. 12° BM

[Taming . . .] Catharine and Petruchio . . . As altered by D. Garrick from Sh—. New York: T. Longworth . . . 1820. 12°, pp. 36 BUS

Taming of the shrew . . . With embellishments by R. Smirke, R.A. Ln: Rodwell . . . [1821]. 8° BPL | SML

Taming of the shrew . . . as performed at the Theatre Royal, Drury Lane. Rossini's celebrated overture to the ' Siege of Corinth ' is performed . . . Ln: J. Willis . . . [1828]. F° BUS

Taming of the shrew . . . As performed . . . With remarks by D. G—— [Geo. Daniel]. Ln: Musical Publishing Co., 1828. 18° SML

Taming . . . or Katharine and Petruchio . . . Printed from the acting copy, with remarks, biographical and critical, by D. G—— [Geo. Daniel]. . . . To which are added a . . . cast of the characters . . . and the whole of the stage business, as now performed at the Theatres Royal. Ln: J. Cumberland [c. 1830]. 12°, pp. 36; frontispiece by R. Cruikshank BM | BUS | SML

A prompt copy, with MS. alterations by F. Hawley, is at Stratford.

Taming of the shrew, or Katharine and Petruchio. Altered by D. Garrick and revised by J. P. Kemble. Ln: . . . [c. 1831]. 12° BPL

[Taming . . .] Katharine and Petruchio. Thomas's burlesque drama. Ln: . . . 1838. 12°

[Taming . . .] Katharine and Petruchio, taken by David Garrick from the 'Taming of the shrew.' Illustrated with original designs by Robert Cruikshank. . . . With introductory remarks. Ln: J. Thomas, 1838. 12°, pp. 50 BM | BPL | W

[Taming . . .] Katharine and Petruchio. ' Hind's English stage.' With accurate stage directions, etc. Ln: Simpkin . . . 1839. 8°, pp. 32 BUS

[Taming . . .] The old ' Taming of a shrew,' upon which Sh— founded his comedy, reprinted from the edition of 1594, and collated with the subsequent editions of 1596 and 1607 [and the ' Woman lapped in morel's skin]. Edited by Thomas Amyot. Ln: Sh— Society . . . 1844. 8°, pp. xii.-92 BM | BPL | MPL | SML | W

Sh— Taming of the shrew . . .

[Taming . . .] Katherine and Petruchio. As performed . . . ' Modern standard drama.' New York . . . [1848]. 12°

[Taming . . .] Katharine and Petruchio. . . . Edited by F. C. Wemyss. 'Standard drama.' With the stage business, cast of costumes, positions, etc. New York : S. French . . . [c. 1853]. 12°, pp. vi.-34
BUS

[Taming . . .] Katherine and Petruchio. 'Acting edition.' With preliminary notes. Ln : T. H. Lacy . . . [1855]. 12°

[Taming . . .] The mad wooing, or a way to win and tame a shrew ; being the course a gentleman took to gain a young lady with a great fortune, on whom by reason of her frowardness none before would venture. The lady's advice to froward women, minding them by her example of their duties towards their husbands [In Shaksperian drolls. Edited by J. O. Halliwell]. Ln : Privately printed by Whittingham, 1859. 8°   BM | BUS
Consists of acts II. and V., with some changes. The droll first appeared in the 'Theatre of ingenuity,' about 1698.

Taming of the shrew . . . Glasgow : Cameron . . . 1861. 8°

[Taming . . .]
    Kunst über alle künste
    Ein bös weib gut zu machen.
Eine Deutsche bearbeitung von Sh—'s The taming of the shrew aus dem jahr 1672. Neu herausgegeben, mit beifügung des Englischen originals und anmerkungen von R. Köhler. [In English and German.] Berlin : Weidmannsche buchhandlung, 1864. 8°, pp. xliv.-268 BM

[Taming . . .] Katharine and Petruchio. With illustrations by R. Cruikshank. 'Acting edition.'. Ln : T. H. Lacy . . . [1865]. 12°, pp. 42   BM

[Taming . . .] Katharine and Petruchio. . . . Altered by D. Garrick. 'Acting edition.' Ln : T. H. Lacy . . . 1866. 12° BPL

[Taming . . .] Taming of a shrew, 1594. Dramatic facsimiles. [Ed. by J. O. Halliwell.] Superintended by E. W. Ashbee. Ln : For private circulation [c. 1870]. Fcp. 4°   BPL | BUS | MPL | W
Edition restricted to one hundred copies.

Taming of the shrew . . . edited for scholastic study by J. Hunter. Ln : Longmans . . . 1872. 12°   BPL | CPL

Taming of a shrew, 1594 [In Sh—'s library, edited by Collier & Hazlitt]. Ln : Reeves & Turner, 1875. 6 vols. 8°
BM | BLO | BPL | BUS | SML

Sh— Taming of the shrew . . .

Taming of the shrew . . . as played by E. Booth. Edited by H. L. Hinton. New York . . . [1876]. 8°

[Taming . . .] Katharine and Petruchio . . . as presented by E. Booth. Edited by W. Winter. New York : Hart & Co. . . . 1878. 12°

Taming of the shrew. Der widerspänstigen zähmung. A comic opera in four acts, freely arranged from Sh—'s comedy . . . by J. V. Widmann . . . The English version by J. Troutbeck . . . 1878. 8°   BM

[Taming . . .] Katharine and Petruchio . . . altered by D. Garrick. With illustrations by R. Cruikshank. 'Acting edition.' Ln : S. French . . . [c. 1880]. 12°, pp. 46 (including printed wrappers) SML
Haywell's prompt copy is at Stratford.

Taming of the shrew . . . A comic opera. Music by Goetz. Edited by J. Troutbeck. Ln : Augemer & Co. . . . 1880. 8°

Taming of the shrew . . . A comic opera. With music by Goetz. Edited by J. Troutbeck. New York : Koppel . . . [c. 1880]. 8°

Taming of the shrew . . . edited with notes by W. J. Rolfe. New York : Harper . . . 1881. 12°   BUS

Taming of the shrew. A comedy in five acts . . . Arranged for drawing room acting . . . by M. B. H——. Ln : S. Low & Co. . . . 1881. 8°, pp. 78
BM | BPL | BUS

Taming of the shrew . . . edited with notes by W. J. Rolfe. New York . . . 1883. 12°
BPL

Taming of the shrew. 'Standard plays.' Ln : John Dicks . . . [1883]. 12°   BM

[Taming . . .] Taming of a shrew. The first quarto, 1594. The play revized by another writer and Sh— into the 'Taming of the shrew.' A facsimile by photo-lithography . . . With forewords by F. J. Furnivall. 'Sh— quarto facsimiles.' Ln : C. Prætorius . . . 1886. Fcp. 4°, pp. xiv.-52
BPL | BUS | SML

Taming of the shrew . . . Med gloser og anmærkninger af A. S. Mac Gregor, S. S. Kinney og H. C. Damm. Kjobenhavn : Gyldendalsk boghandels forlag, 1886. 8°, pp. 182   BM
In English and Danish.

Taming of the shrew . . . as arranged by Augustin Daly. First produced at Daly's theatre, Jan. 18, 1887 ; receiving its one hundredth representation April 13th, 1887, and here printed from the prompter's copy. With an introduction by William Winter [and] an additional word

by A. Daly. ' Memorial edition.' Privately printed for Mr. Daly. New York : 1887. F°, pp. 76 ; inlaid and extra-illustrated with photographic portraits of A. Daly, Ada Rehan as ' Katharine,' and of the other characters in the caste SML
This edition-de-luxe was restricted to twenty-five copies for presentation only, and the cost per copy worked out at about £20.
That at Stratford bears Daly's autograph inscription.

Taming of the shrew . . . arranged to be played in four acts by Augustin Daly. Produced at Daly's theatre Feb., 1887. With an introduction by Wm. Winter. New York : Privately printed [by the Trow Co.], 1887. Roy. 8°, pp. iv.-74, including printed wrappers BPL | SML
The copy at Stratford bears Daly's autograph inscription.

Taming of a shrew . . . 1594 . . . ' Bankside Sh—.' New York : New York Sh— Society, 1888

Taming of the shrew . . . edited by C. E. Flower. ' Memorial theatre edition.' Stratford-on-Avon : Printed by G. Boyden ; Ln : S. French [1888]. Cr. 8°, pp. viii.-84, incl. printed wrappers BPL | SML

Taming of the shrew [With introduction by H. Morley]. ' National library.' Ln : Cassell . . . 1888. 16°, pp. 192 BM

Taming of the shrew . . . as arranged by A. Daly. Special edition for Paris. La Mégère apprivoisée . . . traduction de F. Duport. [In English and French.] Paris . . . 1888. 12°, pp. 194 BM

[Taming . . .] Katharine. A travesty, by J. K. Bangs . . . 1888. 8° BM

[Taming . . .] Sh—'s part in the ' Taming of the shrew,' by A. H. Tolman. 1890. 8° BM

Taming of the shrew . . . edited by H. Howard Crawley. ' Falcon series.' Ln : Longmans . . . 1891. 12°, pp. xvi.-168 BPL | SML

Taming of the shrew. With preface, glossary, etc. by I. Gollancz. Ln : J. M. Dent & Co. . . . 1894. 16°, pp. xii.-134. With frontispiece BM | BLO | CTC | SML

Taming of the shrew. With preface, glossary, etc. by I. Gollancz. Ln : J. M. Dent & Co. . . . 1895. 16°, pp. xii.-134. With frontispiece

Taming of the shrew. ' Pocket Falstaff edition.' Ln : Bliss, Sands . . . 1898. 16°, pp. 104 BPL | SML

Taming of the shrew. ' Player's edition.' With introduction by Ada Rehan. Photogravure pictures and scenes from the play as produced by Augustin Daly. New York : 1900. 12°. With portraits and plates BUS

Taming of the shrew . . . edited with introduction and notes by C. H. Herford. ' Eversley edition.' Ln : Macmillan, 1900. 12° BPL

Taming of the shrew, with introduction and notes by J. Dennis. Illustrated by B. Shaw. ' Chiswick edition.' Ln : Bell . . . 1902. 12°

Taming of the shrew, edited by W. J. Rolfe. New York . . . [1902]. 8°. Illustrated BUS

Taming of the shrew . . . edited with notes by H. N. Hudson. ' Windsor edition.' Edinburgh : Jack . . . 1903. Cr. 8°

Taming of the shrew. ' Ellen Terry edition.' Glasgow : Bryce . . . 1904. 32°

Taming of the shrew . . . with introduction and notes by W. J. Craig. ' Little quartos.' Ln : Methuen . . . 1904. 16°

Taming of the shrew . . . edited by R. Warwick Bond. ' Arden edition.' Ln : Methuen . . . 1904. 8°, pp. 214

Taming of the shrew . . . ' Arden edition.' Indianopolis : Bowen-Merrill Co., 1904. 8° BPL

Taming of the shrew . . . with introduction by G. Brandes. ' Favourite classics.' Ln : Heinemann . . . 1904. 12°

Taming of the shrew . . . edited by H. Morley. ' National library.' Ln : Cassell . . . 1905. 12° BPL

Taming of the shrew . . . ' Red letter library.' Ln : Blackie . . . 1905. 12°

Taming of the shrew . . . ' Renaissance edition.' New York : Harrap . . . 1907. Fcp. 4° BPL

Taming of the shrew . . . with introduction by F. J. Furnivall. ' Old spelling edition.' Ln : Chatto . . . 1907. Fcp. 4° BPL

[Taming . . .] Taming of a shrew . . . edited by F. S. Boas. ' Sh— classics.' Ln : Chatto . . . 1908. Cr. 8° BPL
The foundation of Sh—'s play.

' Taming of the shrew ' references—

See		See	
Amyot		Kyd	
,,	Ballad . . .	,,	Lilly
,,	Barclay	,,	Manuel
,,	Cokaine	,,	Norton
,,	Collection . . .	,,	Pegasus
,,	Courtney	,,	Sh—] Sh— drolls
,,	Emanuel	,,	Short . . .
,,	Fleay	,,	Six . . .
,,	Fletcher	,,	Stopes
,,	Gascoigne	,,	Taming
,,	Goulart	,,	Terence
,,	Holme	,,	Theatre
,,	Jack . . .	,,	Tolman
,,	Johnson and Steevens	,,	Waking . . .
		,,	Wife . . .

Sh— The arraignment of Paris. *See* Sh—
Arraignment . . .
The birth of Merlin. *See* Sh— Birth . . .
The comedy of errors. *See* Sh— Comedy . . .
The merchant of Venice. *See* Sh— Merchant . . .
The merry devil of Edmonton. *See* Sh—
Merry devil . . .
The merry wives . . . *See* Sh— Merry wives . .

THE PURITAN WIDOW.

One of the seven fresh plays introduced as of Sh—'s composition in the Chetwynde folio of 1663-64. The earliest known version is that published by George Eld in 1607.
The real writer was probably Wentworth Smith.
It was registered at Stationers' Hall :—
'6th Aug. 1607. George Elde. Entred for his copie vnder thandes of Sir George Bucke, knight, and the wardens, a book called the comedie of "The puritan widowe" . . . VId.'

The Pvritaine, Or the Widdow of Watling-streete. Acted by the Children of Paules. Written by W. S——. [*Floral device.*] Imprinted at London by G. Eld, 1607. Fcp. 4°, sig. A¹ to H⁴ in fours, the text beginning on A3, A¹ being blank ; thirty-two unpaged leaves
BM | BUS | CTC | DEVON | NY | SBL | SML
The running headline title of the play is 'The Pvritaine Widdow.'
Attributed to Sh— on account of the identity of his initials with those of the actual writer.
It is in five acts, in prose and verse.
Earl Howe's copy, in half blue morocco, 6⅞ by 4⅞in., realised £72 in Dec., 1907.

The puritan, or the widow of Watling Street [edited by Nicholas Rowe]. Ln : J. Tonson . . . 1709. 8° (an excerpt from Sh—'s Works of same date) SML
The puritan, or the widow of Watling-Street. [No place or printer, but Ln : Jacob Tonson] Printed in the year 1714. Cr. 8° [excerpt pp. 250-314]. With frontispiece by Lud. Du Guernier
The puritan, or the widow of Watling Street. By Mr. Wm. Sh—. Ln : Printed for J. Tonson and the rest of the proprietors and sold by the booksellers of Ln. and Westminster, 1734. Cr. 8°, pp. 60. With engraved frontispiece signed Lud. Du Guernier BM
The puritan . . . Ln : J. Tonson . . . 1735. 12° BPL
The puritan . . . [In 'Ancient British drama, edited by Sir W. Scott ']. Ln : . . . 1810. Roy. 8° BM | BLO | BUS | CTC

Sh— The puritan widow . . .
[The puritan widow] The ancient ballad of the fair widow of Watling Street and her three daughters, from the earliest known edition printed by Thomas Pavier, about 1600. Edited by J. O. Halliwell. Chiswick Press : Privately printed . . . 1860. 8° BPL
Impression restricted to thirty copies.
The puritan . . . 'Sh—'s doubtful plays.' Edited with an introduction by A. F. Hopkinson. Ln. [Privately printed by] M. E. Sims & Co. . . . 1894. Cr. 8°, pp. xvi.-92 SML
'The puritan widow ' references—
See Ballads   *See* Hopkinson
  „ Fair widow

THE TEMPEST.

Probably Sh—'s final play. This comedy occupies the premier place in the Jaggard canon of 1623, and in most subsequent editions. So far as is known, it was not printed before that date. Over a century passed away before a separate unadulterated edition was born, and that appeared in Dublin in 1725.

The tempest, or the enchanted island. A comedy, as it is now acted in Dorset Gardens [Altered by John Dryden and Sir William D'Avenant]. Ln : . . 1669. Fcp. 4°
The tempest, or the enchanted island. A comedy. As it is now acted at his highness the Duke of York's theatre. [Altered by John Dryden & Sir W. Davenant]. Ln : Printed by J. M[acock] for Henry Herringman at the blew anchor in the lower walk of the new exchange, 1670. Fcp. 4°, pp. viii.-82 BM | BUS | W
Mainly, the alterations are the introduction of scenes between 'Hippolyto . . . one that never saw woman . . .' and 'Dorinda . . . that never saw man,' also the allotment of 'comical parts to the sailors' by Davenant.
The tempest . . . Made into an opera. By T. Shadwell. Ln : . . . 1673. Fcp. 4°
The tempest, or the enchanted island. A comedy as it is now acted . . . [Altered by John Dryden and Sir W. Davenant]. Ln : H. Herringman . . . 1674. Fcp. 4°
[The tempest] Vocal musick in Psyche, with the instrumental terms intermixed. To which is subjoined the musick of ' The tempest.' By Matthew Locke. Ln : J. Carr . . . 1675. 4°
[The tempest] Choice ayres and dialogues to sing to the theorbo or bass-viol, etc. To which in this new edition are added many score new songs and also those songs sung in the famous play called ' The tempest.' Ln : . . . 1675. F°

[The tempest] The mock-tempest, or the enchanted castle. Acted at the Theatre Royal. Written by T. Duffett. Ln: Printed for Wm. Cademan at the Pope's Head in the Lower Walk of the New Exchange in the Strand, 1675. Fcp. 4°, pp. vi.-56   BM | BUS | W
A travesty of Dryden and Davenant's version of 'The tempest.'

The tempest, or the enchanted island. A comedy [Altered by John Dryden and Sir W. Davenant]. As it is now acted at his highness the Duke of York's Theatre. Ln: J. Macock for Henry Herringman, 1676. Fcp. 4°, pp. viii.-82
BM | BPL | BUS | NY | W

The tempest, or the enchanted island. A comedy. As it is now acted at their majesties theatre in Dorset Garden [Altered by John Dryden and Sir Wm. Davenant]. Ln: Printed by J. M—— [Macock] for H. Herringman and R. Bentley at the Post House in Russel Street, Covent Garden, 1690. Fcp. 4°, pp. vi.-62   BM | BUS |NY | SML
The prologue contains an enthusiastic tribute to Sh—.
The text follows the 1676 edition, and not that of 1670.
The two versions differ considerably.

The tempest, or the enchanted island [Altered from Sh— by J. Dryden and Sir W. Davenant]. Ln: T. Warren for H. Herringman...1695. Fcp. 4°   BPL | NY

[The tempest] A song sung by the girl in 'The tempest.' Set by H. Purcell and exactly engrav'd by Tho. Cross. [c. 1700 ?]. F°, broadside   BUS

The tempest, or the enchanted island [Altered from Sh— by Dryden and Davenant]. A comedy. As it is now acted by His Majesties Servants. Ln: J. Tonson & T. Bennet, 1701. Fcp. 4°, pp. vi.-60   BM | BUS
Differs considerably from the text of the 1670 edition.

The tempest . . . [In Dryden's Comedies, tragedies and operas]. Ln: . . . 1701. F°   BUS

The tempest . . . edited by N. Rowe. Ln: J. Tonson . . . 1709. 8°   SML
A prompt copy with MS. alterations by W. Creswick, the actor, is at Stratford.

The tempest, or the enchanted island. A comedy. First written by Mr. Wm. Sh— and since altered by Sr. William Davenant and Mr. John Dryden. Ln:...1710. 8°, pp. 112   BPL | W

The tempest, or the enchanted island. A comedy. First written by Mr. Wm. Sh— and since altered by Sr. William Davenant and Mr. John Dryden. Ln: Printed for the company [c. 1710]. 8°, pp. 86   W

The tempest, or the enchanted island [Altered from Sh— by Dryden and Davenant]. In 'English plays' [c. 1720]. 8°, pp. 104   BM

The tempest. A comedy. Collated and corrected by former editions by Mr. Pope. Dublin . . . 1725. 8°

The tempest, or the enchanted island. A comedy. As it is acted at his Highness the Duke of York's theatre. [Vignette of Sh—.] Ln: Printed for J. Tonson and sold by W. Feales at Rowe's head, the corner of Essex Street, in the Strand, 1733. Cr. 8°, pp. 94, including frontispiece by Lud. Du Guernier
An unknown edition until a copy came into the writer's possession.

The tempest. By Mr. Wm. Sh—. Ln: Printed for J. Tonson and the rest of the proprietors, and sold by the booksellers of Ln. and Westminster, 1734. Cr. 8°, pp. 60, and frontispiece by Lud. Du Guernier   SML

The tempest, or the enchanted island. A comedy. By Mr. Dryden. Ln: Printed for Jacob Tonson, 1735. 12°, pp. 86. With frontispiece   W

The tempest . . . Ln: R. Walker . . . 1735. 12°

[The tempest] The masque in . . . 'The tempest.' Composed by Wm. Boyce. In full score. Ln: . . . [c. 1750]. Oblong 4°

[The tempest] Music composed for 'The tempest,' by Henry Purcell. [Ln: . . . c. 1750.] F°   W

The tempest . . . according to Mr. Pope's second edition. Glasgow: Printed and sold by R. & A. Foulis, 1752. 8°

The tempest . . . with notes by L. Theobald. Ln: . . . 1755. 12°

The tempest. An opera taken from Sh—. As it is performed at the Theatre Royal in Drury Lane. The songs from Sh—, Dryden . . . The music by Mr. [J. C.] Smith. Ln: J. & R. Tonson in the Strand and J. Walsh, 1756. 8°, pp. vi.-48
BM | BPL | BUS
This adaptation is commonly attributed to Garrick, who, however, denied responsibility in a letter to J. M. French, which ran :—'If you mean that I was the person who altered the "Midsummer night's dream" and "The tempest" into operas, you are much mistaken.'

The tempest: An opera . . . set to music by Mr. [J. C.] Smith. Ln: I. Walsh . . . 1756. F°, pp. iv.-110   BUS

The tempest. A comedy. As written by Sh—. Ln: C. Hitch & L. Hawes, J. & R. Tonson, B. Dod, G. Woodfall, J. Riving-

Sh— The tempest . . .

ton, R. Baldwin, T. Longman, S. Crowder & Co., W. Johnston, C. Corbet, T. Caslon, B. Law & Co., 1761. 12°, pp. 72. With engraved frontispiece and title in red and black
With ' Epilogue, spoken by Prospero.'

[The tempest] The masque in 'The tempest,' set to music by H. Purcell. Ln : . . . 1764. 8°   BPL

The tempest . . . as performed at the Theatre Royal, Drury Lane ; regulated from the prompt book, with permission of the managers, by Mr. Hopkins, prompter. An introduction and notes, critical and illustrative, are added by the authors of the ' Dramatic censor ' [F. Gentleman]. Ln : Printed for John Bell and C. Etherington at York, 1773. Cr. 8°, pp. 64. With copper frontispiece engraved by W. Byrne after E. Edwards
The last leaf (pp. 63-64) bears a list of Bell's publications. Reprinted from Bell's edition of Sh—'s works for playgoers.

[The tempest] Music in ' The tempest ' . . . by Purcell, Arne, and Linley. Ln : Lonsdale . . . [c. 1776]. F°

The tempest . . . altered by R. B. Sheridan. The songs only, with music by T. Linley, jun. Ln : . . . 1776. 8°

The tempest. A comedy. As it is acted at the Theatres Royal in Drury Lane and Covent Garden . . . Ln : Printed for J. Wenman, 144 Fleet St., and sold by all other booksellers in town and country, 1778. 8°, pp. 18, and copperplate portrait of Baddeley as ' Trinculo '   BPL

The tempest . . . A comedy as acted at the Theatre Royal in Drury Lane and Covent Garden. Ln : W. Oxlade . . . 1778. 12°   SML

The tempest . . . altered by R. B. Sheridan. Ln : . . . 1778. 12°

[The tempest] The shipwreck, altered from Sh— and Dryden as performed at the Patagonian Theatre, Exeter Exchange. Ln : . . . 1780. 8°   BPL

[The tempest] A new edition of the celebrated music in ' The tempest,' composed by Henry Purcell. Revised and corrected by Doctor Busby. [Ln : c. 1780.] F°   w

The tempest . . . Taken from the manager's book at the Theatre Royal, Drury Lane. Ln : Butters . . . [c. 1780]. 12°   BPL

The tempest . . . From the manager's book at the Theatre Royal, Drury Lane. Ln : [T. Lowndes, 1783]. 12°. With frontispiece on which is inscribed, ' Pubd. by T. Lowndes, 1783 '   BUS

Sh— The tempest . . .

The tempest. A comedy . . . The music by Purcell and Dr. Arne. With the additional airs and chorusses by the late Mr. Linley, jun. Marked with the variations in the manager's book at the Theatre Royal in Drury Lane. Ln : C. Bathurst . . . 1785. 12°, pp. 62   BUS
The Boston copy is interleaved, and bears MS. alterations and additions by James Plumptre for an intended new edition.

The tempest, or the enchanted island. Written by Sh—, with additions from Dryden. As compiled by J. P. Kemble and first acted at the Theatre Royal, Drury Lane . . . Oct. 13th, 1789. Ln : J. Debrett . . . 1789. 8°, pp. iv.-56
BM | BUS | W

[The tempest] The desolate island. A mask. By John Burn. In imitation of Sh—. To which are added two poems. Alnwick : Printed by J. Catnach . . . 1791. 12°, pp. 24   BUS
The poems are ' The parting of Hotspur and Lady Percy' and the ' Battle of Shrewsbury.'

The tempest . . . as it is acted at Drury Lane and Covent Garden. Ln : Barker . . . 1794. 12°

The tempest, or the enchanted island . . . with additions from Dryden. As compiled by J. P. Kemble and first acted at the Theatre Royal, Drury Lane, Oct. 13th, 1789 [In 'Collection of . . . dramatic pieces,' Vol. i., pp. 233-282]. Ln : J. Debrett . . . 1795. 2 vols. 8°

[The tempest] The virgin queen. A drama in five acts. Attempted as a sequel to Sh—'s ' The tempest ' [By Francis Godolphin Waldron]. Ln : Printed for the author, 1797. 8°, pp. iv.-104
BM | BUS

[The tempest] A new edition of the music in ' The tempest.' Revised by Dr. Busby. Ln : . . . [c. 1800]. 4°   BPL

The tempest . . . A comic opera. Manchester : R. & W. Dean . . . 1801. 12°, pp. 66, and woodcut frontispiece   BPL

[The tempest] Prospectus : With the songs, choruses, &c. of ' The enchanted island or dramatic ballet.' Founded on Sh—'s ' The tempest.' By Mr. [John] Fawcett. Ln : Printed for the author by John Woodfall [1804]. 8°, pp. 28
BPL | BUS | W
On every alternate page, extracts from ' The tempest' illustrate the action of the ballet.

The tempest . . . Ln : Roach . . . 1806. 12°

The tempest, or the enchanted island . . . Adapted to the stage from Dryden and Davenant by J. P. Kemble, and now first published as it is acted at the Theatre Royal in Covent Garden. Ln: Longman . . . 1806. 8°, pp. 62   BUS

The tempest, by Will. Sh—. Printed complete from the text of Sam. Johnson and Geo. Steevens. Ln : . . . 1806. 16°   W

The tempest . . . revised by J. P. Kemble. Ln : Longman . . . 1807. 8°

The tempest, or the enchanted island . . . Adapted to the stage, with additions from Dryden and Davenant by J. P. Kemble. As performed at the Theatre Royal, Covent Garden. Printed under the authority of the managers from the prompt book. With remarks by Mrs. Inchbald. Ln : Longman [1808]. 12°, pp. 72. With frontispiece   BPL | BUS | SML

The tempest . . . [In Dryden's Works]. Ln : . . . 1808. 8°   BUS

The tempest . . . adapted . . . with additions from Dryden and Davenant by J. P. Kemble . . . with remarks by Mrs. Inchbald. Ln : Longman . . . [c. 1811]. 12°, pp. 72   BUS

The tempest . . . adapted . . . with additions from Dryden and Davenant by J. P. Kemble and now published as it is performed at the Theatres Royal. Ln : J. Miller . . . 1815. 12°, pp. 62   BM | BUS | SML

The tempest . . . adapted . . . with additions . . . by J. P. Kemble . . . with remarks by Mrs. Inchbald. Ln : Hurst Robinson & Co. [c. 1816]. 12°, pp. 72, and plate   BUS

The tempest . . . [In Dryden's Works . . . Second edition]. Edinburgh . . . 1821. 8°   BUS

The tempest . . . with embellishments by Robert Smirke, R.A. Ln : Rodwell & Martin, 1821. 8°, pp. 84   BPL | BUS
The first of a projected edition of Sh—'s Works in thirty-seven numbers, of which only four appeared.

[The tempest] Angelica, or the rape of Proteus. A poem [By Edward Hovell Lord Thurlow]. Ln : . . . 1822. 8°   W
An attempt to continue Sh—'s ' The tempest.'

The tempest . . . with prefatory remarks [signed P. P.] . . . marked with . . . stage business . . . and directions, as it is performed at the Theatres Royal, by W. Oxberry. Ln : Simpkin . . . 1823. Cr. 8°, pp. xviii.-56; with portrait   BM

The tempest . . . edited by Hy. Neele. Ln : . . . 1824. 12°. With plates

[The tempest] Outlines to Sh—: ' The tempest ' . . . by H. C. Selous. Ln : C. Knight . . . 1825. 4°, ff. 13 and 12 plates   BPL | BUS | SML

The tempest . . . printed from the acting copy, with remarks, biographical and critical, by D. G—— [G. Daniel]. To which are added the . . . costume, cast . . . entrances and exits, and . . . stage business, as performed at the Theatre Royal, London. With . . . engraving by R. Cruikshank. Ln : J. Cumberland [c. 1827]. 12°, pp. x.-viii.-50   BUS

The tempest . . . printed from the acting copy, with remarks, biographical and critical, by D. G—— [Geo. Daniel]. To which are added a . . . cast of the characters . . . and the whole of the stage business as now performed at the Theatres Royal. Ln : J. Cumberland . . . [1831]. 12°, pp. 50   BM | BPL

The tempest . . . printed from the text of Geo. Steevens. With historical and grammatical notes in German by J. M. Pierre. Frankfort . . . 1833. 12°

The tempest. An outline sketch of the play. With introductory remarks and an analysis of the characters [by G. Stephens]. Stockholm : Norstedt & Sons . . . 1836. Fcp. 4°, pp. 34 ; large paper, printed on pink paper   BM

[The tempest] Outlines to Sh—'s ' The tempest ' [by H. C. Selous]. With text in English, German, French and Italian. Ln : A. Schloss ; Leipsic : Brockhaus [1836]. Oblong f°, ff. 12, and 12 plates   BM | BPL | BUS | SML
A few copies were done as ' proofs on India paper.'

The tempest . . . Ln : . . . 1839. 12°   BUS

[The tempest] Outlines to illustrate . . . ' The tempest,' by Moritz Retzsch. With text in English and German. Leipzig . . . 1839. 4°. 13 plates

The tempest . . . Nuremberg . . . New York . . . 1840. 12°

The tempest . . . A tale . . . by C. Lamb [In ' The romancist,' Vol. iii., pp. 140-141]. 1840. 4°   BPL

The tempest, or the enchanted isle. Ln ? [Sans place, printer, and date, but c. 1840]. 8°   BPL

The tempest [A translation into Greek iambics, by G. Druce, from 'The tempest, act iv., sc. i.']. Cambridge . . . 1841. 8°
In English and Greek.   BM

The tempest . . . edited by C. Knight. Ln : . . . [1843]. 8°   SML
A prompt copy is at Stratford, with alterations by W. Creswick.

[The tempest] Compositions from Sh—'s ' The tempest.' By J. Noel Paton. Ln : Chapman & Hall . . . 1845. Oblong f°, pp. xxii., and 15 outline plates   BPL | BUS | CPL
With illustrative extracts from the play.

Sh— The tempest . . .

The tempest. A play . . . Ln : . . . 1845. 24°
W
With manuscript 'New readings' in the autograph of Thomas Crofton Croker.

The tempest . . . 'Sherwood's dramatic library.' Ln : W. Strange . . . 1846. 16°, pp. 84, including printed wrappers

The tempest : A pla . . . 'Fonetic famili edisun,' with bref ecsplánaturi nots, bi Alecs J. Elis. Ln : F. Pitman . . . 1849. 12°, pp. 72   BM | BPL | BUS

The tempest burlesqued, as 'The enchanted isle.' By the brothers Brough. 'Acting edition.' Ln : Webster . . . 1849. 12°

The tempest . . . As performed . . . 'Modern standard drama.' New York : French . . . [1850]. 12°

[The tempest] La tempesta : Grand opera in three acts. With a prologue. [Music by F. Halévy. Words by E. Scribe.] Founded on 'The tempest' of Sh—. Ln : W. S. Johnson, 1850. 8°, pp. 80   BPL | BUS
English and Italian texts on parallel pages.

[The tempest] La tempesta. An entirely new grand opera . . . The poem by [A. E.] Scribe. Founded on 'The tempest' of Sh— . . . 1850. Fcp. 4°   BM | BPL | SML
In Italian and English.

The tempest. A comedy . . . Kampen : K. van Hulst . . . 1854. 8°, pp. iv.-80
BM | BUS
Text and notes in English and Dutch. Edited by S. Susan.

The tempest . . . Arranged and adapted for . . . the Boston theatre by Thomas Barry. To which are added the costume, cast . . . positions and . . . stage business. New York : S. French . . . [c. 1856]. 12°, pp. 44
BUS

The tempest . . . Arranged for representation at the Princess's Theatre. With historical and explanatory notes by C. Kean. As first performed July 1, 1857. Ln : J. K. Chapman & Co. [1857]. 8°, pp. 74
Somewhat abridged in the text.   BM | BUS | CPL

The tempest . . . arranged . . . for the Princess's Theatre . . . with notes by C. Kean. Second edition. Ln : J. K. Chapman & Co. [1857]. 8°, pp. 70
BPL | BUS | SML
Differs from the preceding issue both in text and notes.

The tempest . . . With . . . notes by C. Kean. Third edition. Ln : J. K. Chapman & Co. [1857]. 8°, pp. 70   BM

The tempest. With notes . . . Edinburgh : W. & R. Chambers, 1857. 12°. Issued in green wrappers, illustrated

The tempest . . . 'Acting edition.' Ln : T. H. Lacy . . . [1858]. 12°, pp. 56. Pub. at 6d.

Sh— The tempest . . .

The tempest . . . 'Acting plays.' Ln : T. H. Lacy [1859]. 12°, pp. 56   BM

The tempest . . . illustrated by Birket Foster, Gustave Doré, Frederick Skill, Alfred Slader, and Gustave Janet. Ln : Bell & Daldy [1860]. Fcp. 4°, pp. 92. 18 plates   BM | BPL | BUS | CPL | SML
The first separate illustrated issue, if editions with a single plate are ignored.

The tempest . . . illustrated by B. Foster, G. Doré . . . New York : D. Appleton & Co. [c. 1861]. Fcp. 4°, pp. 90. With 18 plates   BPL | BUS
Similar to the preceding issue save in title.

[The tempest] Music in 'The tempest.' Composed by Arthur Sullivan. In vocal score. Ln : Cramer & Co. . . . 1862. F°

[The tempest] Sh— album, or Warwickshire garland for the piano . . . including the music in . . . 'The tempest.' Ln : Lonsdale . . . 1862. F°

The tempest . . . Illustrated by Birket Foster. Glasgow : R. Griffin . . . 1864. Fcp. 4°

The tempest. Reprinted from the 'Phonetic Journal' for 23rd April, 1864, as an offering to the Sh— tercentenary festival. Bath : Isaac Pitman . . . 1864. Fcp. 4°, pp. 16   BPL | BUS | SML
In phonetic characters.

The tempest . . . Edited with glossarial and explanatory notes by J. M. Jephson. Ln : Macmillan & Co. . . . 1864. 8°, pp. xvi.-120   BM | BPL | BUS | CPL | SML

The tempest . . . with bibliographical preface, selected criticisms, explanatory and illustrative notes. Adapted for use in schools and for private study by John Hunter. Ln : Longman . . . 1865. Cr. 8°, pp. xii.-94

The tempest . . . edited with . . . notes by J. M. Jephson. Ln : Macmillan . . . 1866. 8°, pp. xvi.-120

[The tempest] La tempête . . . traduit en vers Français, par le Chevalier de Chatelain . . . 1867. Cr. 8°

The tempest . . . With . . . notes by J. M. Jephson. Ln : Macmillan . . . 1867. 8°, pp. xvi.-120

The tempest . . . With bibliographical preface, selected criticisms, and explanatory notes. Adapted for private study . . . and . . . examinations by John Hunter. Ln : Longmans . . . 1869. Cr. 8°, pp. xii.-94
BUS | CPL

The tempest . . . 'Acting edition.' Ln : French . . . [c. 1870]. 12°   SML

The tempest . . . edited by J. Surtees Phillpotts. Rugby : Privately printed [by W.
Billington], 1870. 12°

The tempest . . . edited with notes by J. M.
Jephson. Ln : Macmillan . . . 1871. 12°

The tempest . . . edited with notes by W. J.
Rolfe. New York : Harper brothers . . .
1871. 16°, pp. 148. Illustrated   BUS

The tempest . . . edited with . . . notes by
J. M. Jephson. Second edition. Ln :
Macmillan . . . 1872. 8°, pp. xvi.-110
                                              BUS

The tempest . . . With critical and explanatory notes . . . by John Hunter. Ln :
Longmans . . . 1873. 8°, pp. xii.-94

The tempest . . . With introduction and
notes by H. M. Hudson. Boston [U.S.] :
Ginn Brothers . . . 1874. 12°, pp. viii.-
74   BUS

The tempest . . . edited with . . . notes by
. . . J. M. Jephson. Third edition. Ln :
Macmillan & Co. . . . 1874. 16°, pp. xvi.-
110   BM

The tempest . . . edited by W. A. Wright.
Oxford : Clarendon Press, 1874. Cr. 8°,
pp. xx.-156

The tempest [Altered from Sh—. In 'Davenant's Dramatic Works,' Vol. v.] 1874.
8°   BPL

The tempest . . . edited by W. A. Wright.
Oxford : Clarendon Press . . . 1875. Cr.
8°, pp. xx.-156   BUS

The tempest . . . with introduction and
explanatory . . . notes. Edited by D.
Morris. Glasgow & Ln : W. Collins . . .
1875. Cr. 8°, pp. 84   BM | BPL | BUS

The tempest . . . edited by J. Surtees Phillpotts. 'Rugby edition.' Ln : Rivington
. . . 1876. 12°, pp. xxviii.-94
                        BPL | BUS | MPL

[The tempest] Compositions from ' The
tempest,' by Sir J. N. Paton. Ln : . . .
1877. 4°   SML

The tempest . . . With notes by J. Hunter.
Ln : Longmans . . . 1877. Cr. 8°   BPL

The tempest . . . [Text in English and
Italian, with notes by Rusconi]. Firenze
. . . 1878. 12°   SML

The tempest . . . edited by W. A. Wright.
Oxford : Clarendon Press . . . 1879. 8°,
pp. xx.-156   MPL

The tempest . . . ' Oxford & Cambridge
Sh—.' Ln : Allman . . . [c. 1880]. 12°
                                              SML

The tempest . . . with notes, examination
papers, and plan of preparation. Edited
by J. M. D. Meiklejohn. Ln. & Edin :
Chambers . . . 1880. Cr. 8°, pp. iv.-126
                                              BM

The tempest . . . edited by W. A. Wright.
Oxford : Clarendon Press . . . 1881. Cr.
8°   BPL

The tempest . . . with notes, examination
papers, and plan of preparation by
Brainerd Kellogg. New York . . . 1882.
12°. With portrait   BUS

The tempest . . . edited with notes by W. J.
Rolfe. New York . . . 1883. 12°   BPL

The tempest. ' Standard plays.' Ln : John
Dicks . . . [1883]. 12°   BM

The tempest . . . With notes for the Oxford
and Cambridge examinations. Ln : All-
man . . . [1884]. 12°   BPL

The tempest . . . edited by W. A. Wright.
Oxford : Clarendon Press . . . 1884. Cr.
8°, pp. xx.-156

The tempest . . . edited by Charles E.
Flower. ' Memorial theatre edition.'
Stratford : Printed by G. Boyden ; Ln :
S. French [1885] Cr. 8°, pp. viii.-72, incl.
printed wrappers   BPL | SML

The tempest . . . With notes. Ln : Blackie
. . . [1885]. 16°, pp. 96   BM

[The tempest] Stormurinn (Útgefinn med
skyringum af E. Magnússyni). Reyk-
javik : S. Gudmundsson . . . 1885. 8°
In English and Icelandic. Two parts.   BM

The tempest . . . With notes by J. S.
Phillpotts. Ln : Rivington . . . 1885.
Cr. 8°

The tempest . . . edited by W. A. Wright.
Oxford : Clarendon Press . . . 1885. Cr.
8°, pp. xvi.-156   SML

The tempest, 1623 . . . Reprinted from the
first folio for William Ludlow. Ln :
Simpkin . . . 1886. 16°   BPL | SML

The tempest . . . with Jacob Ayrer and
' The fair Sidea.' Montaigne's Essay on
the Caniballes. [With introduction by
H. Morley.] ' National library.' Ln :
Cassell . . . 1887. 16°, pp. 192   BM | SML

The tempest. With notes. ' School classics.' Ln : Blackie . . . [c. 1887]. Cr. 8°
                                              BUS

The tempest . . . edited by W. A. Wright.
Oxford : Clarendon Press . . . 1888. Cr.
8°, pp. xx.-156

The tempest . . . With introduction and
notes by H. N. Hudson. Boston [U.S.]
. . . 1888. 12°   BPL

The tempest . . . With introduction and
notes by K. Deighton. Ln : Macmillan
. . . 1889. 12°

The tempest . . . edited by H. A. Evans.
' University Sh—.' Ln : Sutton & Co. . . .
1889. 12°   SML

Sh— The tempest . . .

The tempest . . . for the use of students preparing for examinations. With introduction and notes by Ben Jonson. Ln: G. Gill . . . 1889. Cr. 8°, pp. 128 BM

The tempest . . . edited by W. A. Wright. Oxford: Clarendon Press . . . 1889. Cr. 8°, pp. xx.-156

The tempest . . . with notes, examination papers . . . by J. M. D. Meiklejohn. Ln. & Edin.: W. & R. Chambers . . . 1889. Cr. 8°, pp. 126 BPL

The tempest . . . With introduction and notes . . . by H. N. Hudson. Boston, U.S.: Ginn, 1889. Cr. 8°, pp. 172

The tempest . . . edited by W. A. Wright. Oxford: Clarendon Press . . . 1891. Cr. 8°, pp. xx.-156

The tempest . . . edited by A. C. Liddell. 'Falcon series.' Ln: Longman . . . 1891. 12° BPL

The tempest . . . With introduction, notes, and glossary by David Bain. 'Annotated Sh—.' Ln: Low . . . 1892. 12° BPL

The tempest . . . edited with introduction and notes by T. Page. Ln: Moffatt . . . [1892]. 12° BPL

The tempest . . . edited by H. H. Furness. 'Variorum edition.' Philadelphia: Lippincott . . . 1892. Roy. 8°, pp. xii.-466 BM | BPL | SML
With list of books and materials bearing on the play.

The tempest . . . edited by T. D. Barnett. 'English classics.' Ln: Bell . . . 1893. 8°, pp. 130 BM | BPL

The tempest, 1623 edition: Reduced facsimile, with modern text. 'Dallastype edition.' Ln: G. Redway . . . 1893. F°

[The tempest] Eight illustrations to Sh—'s 'The tempest' [with selections from the text]. Designed by Walter Crane. Engraved and printed by D. C. Dallas. Ln: J. M. Dent & Co. . . . 1893. F° BM

The tempest . . . With introduction and notes by Elizabeth Lee. 'Junior school Sh—.' Ln: Blackie . . . 1894. 12°, pp. 104 BPL

The tempest . . . With preface, notes, and glossary by I. Gollancz. 'Temple edition.' Ln: Dent & Co. . . . 1894. 16°, pp. xii.-118 BM | BLO | CTC | SML

The tempest . . . With introduction and notes by K. Deighton. Ln: Macmillan . . . 1895. 12° BPL

The tempest . . . Reduced Dallastype facsimile from the first folio (1623) edition, and facing each page thereof the text as determined by . . . Charles Knight. Introduction by F. J. Furnivall. Edited by F. A. Hyndman and D. C. Dallas. Ln: G. Redway . . . 1895. F° BPL | BUS

Sh— The tempest . . .

The tempest . . . edited by W. E. Urwick. 'School Sh—.' Ln: Arnold . . . [1896]. 8°, pp. xxvi.-92 BPL

The tempest . . . edited with introduction, notes, glossary, and index by A. W. Verity. 'Pitt Press Sh—.' Cambridge: University Press . . . 1896. 8°, pp. xxxvi.-176 BPL

[The tempest] Caliban: A philosophical drama, continuing Sh—'s 'The tempest,' by Joseph Ernest Renan. Trans. by Willis [Eleanor G.] Vickery. New York: Sh— Society, 1896. Cr. 8°, pp. 68 BM | BUS

The tempest . . . Arranged for four acts by A. Daly. Here printed from the prompt book as acted at Daly's theatre, New York, April 6th, 1897. With preface by W. Winter. New York: Privately printed . . . 1897. F°, pp. iv.-52; inlaid and extra-illustrated with programme and portraits of Ada Rehan and others in character SML
Edition-de-luxe, limited to twenty-five copies and prepared at a cost of £20 each, for presentation purposes.

The tempest . . . edited by F. S. Boas. 'Warwick Sh—.' Ln: Blackie . . . 1897. Cr. 8°, pp. xxxii.-128 BPL

The tempest . . . edited with introduction . . . by A. W. Verity. Cambridge: University Press . . . 1897. 8°, pp. xxxvi.-176

The tempest . . . edited by W. E. Urwick. Ln: Arnold . . . 1897. 12°

The tempest . . . With eight illustrations by Walter Crane. Ln: D. C. Dallas, 1898. F°

The tempest. 'Pocket Falstaff edition.' Ln: Bliss, Sands . . . 1898. 16°, pp. 92 BPL | SML

The tempest . . . 'Swan edition.' Notes by G. W. Stone. Ln: Longmans . . . 1899. Cr. 8° BPL

The tempest . . . With introduction and notes by J. Dennis. Illustrated by B. Shaw. 'Chiswick edition.' Ln: Bell . . . 1899. 12°, pp. 118

The tempest. With introduction, notes, and glossary by R. B. Johnson. Edinburgh: Blackwood . . . 1899. Cr. 8°, pp. 162 BPL

The tempest . . . edited by F. S. Boas. 'Warwick Sh—.' Ln: Blackie . . . 1899. Cr. 8°, pp. xxxii.-128

The tempest. With notes prepared specially for the . . . examinations. 'Oxford & Cambridge Sh—.' Ln: Allman . . . [c. 1900]. Cr. 8°, pp. 128

The tempest . . . edited with introductions and notes by C. H. Herford. 'Eversley edition.' Ln: Macmillan, 1900. 12° BPL

The tempest . . . with notes by G. W. Stone 'Swan edition.' Ln: Longmans, 1900. Cr. 8°

The tempest . . . 'Beginner's Sh—.' Arranged and edited by Sarah Willard Hiestand. Boston [U.S.] 1900. 8°. With portrait and plates   BPL | BUS

The tempest . . . Decorated by R. A. Bell. Ln: Freemantle . . . 1901. Roy. 8°, pp. 120   BPL

The tempest . . . edited with notes by H. N. Hudson. 'Windsor edition.' Edinburgh: Jack . . . 1902. 8°, pp. 110   BM | BLO | CTC | SML

The tempest . . . With notes, introduction, and glossary by Oliphant Smeaton. With eight illustrations by W. Crane and . . . illustrations from contemporary prints. Ln: Dent . . . 1902. Cr. 8°, pp. xxxvi.-80 (unpaged)-64-28   BPL

The tempest . . . Decorated by R. A. Bell. Ln: Freemantle, 1902. Roy. 8°

The tempest . . . edited by Morton Luce. 'Arden edition.' Ln: Methuen . . . 1902. 8°, pp. 254

The tempest . . . 'Arden edition.' Indianapolis: Bowen, Merrill Co., 1902. 8°   BPL

The tempest . . . edited by F. S. Boas. 'Warwick Sh—.' Ln: Blackie . . . 1902. Cr. 8°, pp. xxxii.-128

The tempest . . . with introduction and notes by W. J. Craig. Ln: Methuen, 1903. 16°

The tempest . . . 'Lamb edition.' Ln: De la More press, 1904. Fcp. 4°, pp. 44. Illustrated

The tempest . . . Complete paraphrase by J. Terry. 'Normal tutorial series.' Ln: Simpkin, 1904. Cr. 8°   BPL

The tempest . . . edited by G. M. Handley. 'Normal tutorial series.' Ln: Simpkin, 1904. Cr. 8°   BPL

The tempest . . . edited by H. Morley. 'National library.' Ln: Cassell . . . 1904. 12°   BPL

The tempest . . . Retold for children by A. S. Hoffman. Illustrated by W. Crane. Ln: Dent . . . 1904. 16°   BPL

The tempest . . . with introduction by G. Brandes. 'Favourite classics.' Ln: Heinemann, 1904. 12°, pp. xviii.-86, and frontispiece of ' Priscilla Horton as Ariel'

The tempest. 'Waistcoat pocket edition.' Ln: Treherne . . . 1904. 32°

The tempest . . . 'Ellen Terry edition.' Glasgow: Bryce . . 1904. 32°

The tempest . . . arranged for the stage by H. B. Tree. Illustrated by C. A. Buckel. Ln: . . . 1904. Cr. 8°   BPL

The tempest . . . H. M. Theatre [Descriptive programme by H. B. Tree]. Ln: . . . 1904. 8°   BPL

The tempest . . . edited by F. S. Boas. 'Warwick Sh—.' Ln: Blackie . . . 1904. Cr. 8°, pp. xxxii.-128

The tempest. ' Stage edition.' Glasgow: Collins . . . 1905. 16°

The tempest . . . ' Red letter edition.' Ln: Blackie . . . 1905. 16°

The tempest . . . With ' Jacob Ayrer and the fair Sidea.' With introduction by H. Morley. ' National library.' Ln: Cassell . . . 1905. 16°, pp. 192 and frontispiece

The tempest. ' Lamb Sh—.' Illustrated by Helen Stratton. Ln: Moring . . . 1905. Cr. 8°   BPL

The tempest . . . with introduction, notes, glossary, examination questions, and index by C. W. Crook. Ln: Ralph . . . 1906. Cr. 8°, pp. 166   BPL

The tempest . . . 'Oxford and Cambridge edition.' Ln: Gill . . . 1906. Cr. 8° BPL

The tempest . . . ' Texts without notes.' Ln: Chambers . . . 1907. Cr. 8°, pp. 78   BPL

The tempest . . . edited by Herbert A. Evans. Ln: R. Sutton . . . 1907. 8°

The tempest . . . ' Renaissance edition.' New York: Harrap . . . 1907. Fcp. 4°   BPL

The tempest. ' Penny poets.' Ln: W. T. Stead . . . [1907]. Cr. 8°   BPL

The tempest . . . revised by A. Dyce. Ln: Sonnenschein . . . 1907. 8°   BPL

The tempest. ' Picture Sh—.' Ln: Blackie . . . 1907. Cr. 8°   BPL

The tempest . . . illustrated. ' Lamb Sh—.' Ln: Chatto . . . 1908. 8°, pp. 66

The tempest . . . With illustrations in colour by Paul Woodroffe and songs by Joseph Moorat. Ln: Chapman & Hall, 1908. Imp. 8°, pp. 140   BPL

The tempest . . . with illustrations by Edmund Dulac. Ln: Hodder & Stoughton, 1908. Roy. 8°, pp. 168   BPL

The tempest . . . edited by F. J. Furnivall. 'Old spelling edition.' Ln: Chatto . . . 1909. 8°   BM | BLO | BPL | CTC | SML

The tempest . . . edited by A. R. Weekes. 'University tutorial series.' Ln: Clive . . . 1909. Cr. 8°, pp. 150   BPL

Sh— The tempest . . .

'The tempest' references—

[The turtle . . .] Diverse poeticall essaies on the turtle and phoenix, by Sh—, Jonson, Chapman, and Marston. Edited by A. B. Grosart. Ln : New Sh— Soc. . . . 1878. 4°, pp. xvi.-lxxxiv.-x.-254

BM | BLO | BPL | CTC | MPL | SML

The poem occurs on p. 176, signed by Wm. Sh—.

The two gentlemen . . . *See* Sh— Two gentlemen

The winter's tale. *See* Sh— Winter's tale

Sh—] THOMAS LORD CROMWELL.

A drama in verse published for the first time by William Jones in 1602. It was registered at Stationers' Hall :—'11th Aug. 1602. William Cotton. Entred for his copie vnder thandes of Master Jackson and Master Waterson, warden, a booke called the Lyfe and deathe of the Lord Cromwell as yt was lately acted by the Lord Chamberleyn his servantes . . . VId.'

It was not recognised as Sh—'s production until given a place in the Chetwynde folio, 1663-64. Since then it has been ascribed to Sh—'s pen frequently, by virtue perhaps of the similar initials on the original title rather than through any intrinsic merit. The real writer was probably Wentworth Smith.

Before its inclusion in the Chetwynde folio only two editions had appeared.

[Thomas Lord Cromwell] The True Chronicle Historie of the whole life and death of Thomas Lord Cromwell. As it hath beene sundrie times publikely acted by the Right Honourable the Lord Chamberlaine his Seruants. Written by W. S——. Imprinted at London [by William Cotton] for William Iones, and are to be solde at his house neere Holburne conduct at the Signe of the Gunne, 1602. Fcp. 4°, on twenty-eight unpaged leaves (including title) ; sig. A¹ to G⁴ in fours (last leaf blank) NY

The Lenox copy came originally from the Roxburghe collection, *viâ* the Heber sale.

Earl Howe's exemplar, in modern half blue morocco, sold in Dec., 1907, for £222.

[Thomas Lord Cromwell] The True Chronicle Historie of the whole life and death of Thomas Lord Cromwell. As it hath beene sundry times publikely Acted by the Kings Maiesties Seruants. Written by W. S——. London : Printed by Thomas Snodham, 1613. Fcp. 4°, 28 unpaged leaves ; sig. A¹ to G⁴ in fours (last leaf blank) BM | BLO | CTC | DEVON

Earl Howe's copy, in modern half blue morocco, sold for £40 in Dec., 1907.

[Thomas Lord Cromwell] The life and death of Thomas Lord Cromwell. By Mr. Wm. Sh—. [Together with Rowe's life of Sh—.] Ln : Printed for J. Tonson and the rest of the proprietors, and sold by the booksellers of Ln. and Westminster, 1734. Cr. 8°, pp. xxiv.-46. With frontispiece by Lud. Du Guernier, and portrait of Sh—, in addition to crude vignette likeness on title BPL|SML

Sh— Thomas Lord Cromwell . . .

[Thomas Lord Cromwell] Life and death of Thomas Lord Cromwell. A tragedy. By Sh—. Ln : R. Walker . . . 1734. 12°, pp. 48   BM

Thomas Lord Cromwell . . . Ln : J. Tonson . . . 1735. 12°

[Thomas Lord Cromwell] Life and death of Thomas Lord Cromwell [In 'Ancient British drama, edited by Sir W. Scott']. Ln : . . . 1810. Roy. 8°   BM | BUS

[Thomas Lord Cromwell] Life and death of Thomas Lord Cromwell. 'Sh—'s doubtful plays.' Edited with an introduction by A. F. Hopkinson. Ln : [Privately printed by] M. E. Sims & Co. . . . 1891. Cr. 8°, pp. xx.-66   SML

Thomas Lord Cromwell . . . [In 'Sh— apocrypha']. Ln : Frowde, 1908. Cr. 8°   BM | BLO | CTC | SML

'Thomas Lord Cromwell' references—
See Hopkinson
,, Mirrour . . .
,, Sh— [Works] Sh— apocrypha, 1908
,, Sh— Works : Ext. 1836

THRENOS.

This poem first saw the light in Sh—'s little anthology, 'The passionate pilgrim, 1599.' It is next found in Robert Chester's 'Love's martyr, 1601,' and again in 1611, where it is supposed to have been used without permission.

Threnos [In Robert Chester's 'Love's martyr, or Rosalin's complaint']. Ln : . . . [1601]. Fcp. 4°
The title is undated, but the year of issue occurs on p. 165. The poem by Sh— is given on p. 171.

Threnos . . . [In Chester's (Love's martyr, or) The annals of Great Brittaine . . . excently figured out in a worthy poem . . .] Ln : Printed for Mathew Lownes . . . 1611. Fcp. 4°

Threnos . . . [In Chester's 'Love's martyr. Edited by A. B. Grosart.]. Ln : New Sh— Soc. . . . 1878. Fcp. 4°, pp. xvi.- lxxxiv.-x.-254
    BM | BLO | BPL | CTC | MPL | SML
The poem occurs on p. 176, signed by Wm. Sh—.

TIMON OF ATHENS.

Until it figured in the Jaggard canon of 1623 this tragedy appears to have been unprinted. It there bears the title of 'The life of Tymon of Athens.'
Eleven editions of Shadwell's adaptation were published before Tonson issued the first separate edition with a text untampered.

Sh— Timon of Athens . . .

An early manuscript version, said to have been written about 1600, and to resemble Sh—'s text at various points, supplied the basis of Alex. Dyce's edition of 1842.

[Timon of Athens] History of Timon of Athens the man-hater [Altered from Sh—]. As it is acted at the Duke's Theatre. Made into a play by Tho. Shadwell. Ln : J. M[acock] for H. Herringman at the blew anchor in the lower walk of the new exchange, 1678. Fcp. 4°, pp. viii.-88   BM | BPL | BUS
Refers to Sh— in the dedication, prologue, and epilogue in this manner :—
'Old English Sh— stomachs you have still, And judge, as our forefathers writ, with skill.'

. . . .

After alluding to the 'inimitable hand of Sh—,' Shadwell condescendingly adds, 'Yet I can truly say I have made it into a play.'

Timon of Athens, the man-hater . . . [Founded upon Sh—]. By T. Shadwell. Ln : . . . [c. 1680]. 12°   BM

[Timon . . .] A two-part song between Cupid and Bacchus in 'Timon of Athens.' Set by Henry Purcell.] [c. 1680.] F°; broadside   BUS

[Timon . . .] The history of Timon of Athens the man hater. As it is acted at the Dvke's Theatre. Made into a play by Tho. Shadwell. Ln : Printed by J. M—— [acock] for Henry Herringman, 1688. Fcp. 4°, pp. viii.-72   BM | BUS | SML | W
On the Warwick copy's title is this inscription :—' Lord Arthur Somerset. Gift to A. Price.'

[Timon . . .] The history of Timon of Athens the man-hater. As it is acted by his majesties servants. Made into a play by Tho. Shadwell. Ln : Printed by Tho. Warren for Henry Herringman and sold by R. Bentley, J. Tonson, F. Saunders, and T. Bennet, 1696. 4°, pp. viii.-72   BM | BUS | W

[Timon . . .] The history of Timon of Athens the man hater . . . As it is acted by her majesty's servants. Made into a play. By Tho. Shadwell. Ln : H. Hills . . . [c. 1700]. 12°, pp. 88   BUS

Timon of Athens . . . As it is acted by her majesties servants . . . by Tho. Shadwell. Ln : Tho. Warren for H. Herringman and sold by Thomas Bennet at the Half Moon in St. Paul's Churchyard, 1703. Fcp. 4°   BM | BPL

[Timon . . .] The history of Timon of Athens the man-hater. First written by Mr. Wil. Sh— and since altered by Mr. Tho. Shadwell. [Printer's 'W.S.' device.] Printed

Sh— Timon of Athens . . .

for T. Johnson, bookseller at the Hague, 1712. 12°, pp. 108; sig. A¹ to G⁶ in sixes, including title   BPL | SML
The first separate Shakespearean play printed beyond Britannia. It was produced for the use of the English colony in Holland, and has hitherto escaped the notice of all bibliographers and biographers of the poet.

Timon of Athens, the man-hater. [Founded upon Sh—'s play.] By T. Shadwell. [In ' Collection of best English plays.']   Ln : . . . 1712. 8°, pp. 108   BM

Timon of Athens. A tragedy. [Ln : Jacob Tonson] Printed in the year MDCCXIV. Cr. 8°, pp. 91-160 (excerpt)

[Timon . . .] The history of Timon of Athens the man hater . . . [In Shadwell's Works]. Ln : . . . 1720. 12°   BUS

[Timon . . .] The history of Timon of Athens the man-hater. First written by Sh— and since altered by T. Shadwell. Ln : Printed for the company [c. 1720]. 12°, pp. 92
Reprinted in Shadwell's Works, 1720, 4 vols.

[Timon . . .] The history of Timon of Athens, the man-hater. As it is acted at the Duke's Theatre. Made into a play [by Thomas Shadwell]. Ln : . . . 1732. 12°   w

[Timon . . .] Timon in love, or the innocent theft. A comedy. Taken from ' Thimon misanthrope' of the Sieur de Lisle. Ln : . . . 1733. 8°   w

Timon of Athens. A tragedy. By Mr. Wm. Sh—. Ln : Printed for J. Tonson and the rest of the proprietors and sold by the booksellers of Ln. and Westminster, 1734. Cr. 8°, pp. 72, and frontispiece by P. Fourdrinier   SML | W
The first separate edition of this play with an unadulterated text.
The copy at Stratford was presented by Halliwell.

Timon of Athens. As it is acted at the Theatre-Royal on Richmond-Green. [A tragedy in five acts, in prose and verse.] Altered [by ' James Love '] from Sh— and Shadwell. Ln : M. Hingeston . . . 1768. 8°, pp. iv.-100   BM
First edition of this alteration.
James Love was the pseudonym of James Dance, who borrowed from Shadwell most of the scenes in which Evandra figures. With a little original matter interspersed here and there, the rest of the text is Sh—'s.

Timon of Athens . . . Altered from Sh— and Shadwell [by ' James Love '].   The second edition. Ln : M. Hingeston . . . 1768. 8°, pp. iv.-100 BM | BPL | BUS | W

Timon of Athens . . . as . . . acted at . . . Drury Lane and Covent Garden. Ln : Rivington . . . 1770. 12°   SML

Timon of Athens. As it is acted at the Theatres Royal in Drury Lane and Covent Garden. Ln : Printed for J. Rivington, W. Strahan, J. Hinton, C. Bathurst, L.

Sh— Timon of Athens . . .

Hawes, Clarke & Collins, E. Johnson, W. Owen, T. Longman, T. Davies, L. Davis, B. White, B. Law, S. Crowder, T. Lowndes, T. Caslon, Robinson & Roberts, J. Wilkie, C. Corbet, T. Becket, J. Robson, W. Horsefield, F. Newbery, E. Dilly, R. Baldwin, G. Kearsley, S. Bladon, T. Cadell, and W. Woodfall [c. 1770]. 8°, pp. 72, including engraved frontispiece after H. Gravelot by J. June, and a list of plays   SML
The Stratford copy was presented, with inscription, by J. O. Halliwell.

Timon of Athens . . . altered from Sh— [by Richard Cumberland] . . . as it is acted at the Theatre-Royal in Drury-Lane. Ln : Printed for the proprietors of Sh—'s works and sold by T. Becket, 1771. 8°, pp. viii.-62   BPL | BUS | CPL
Cumberland says in the preface : — ' I wish I could have brought this play upon the stage with less violence to its author. . . . Many original passages of the first merit are still retained, and in the contemplation of them my errors I hope will be overlooked.   In examining the brilliancy of a diamond, few people throw away any remarks upon the dullness of the soil.'
The alteration consists chiefly in the introduction of Evanthe, daughter of Timon. The fifth act is almost entirely original.

Timon of Athens, altered [by R. Cumberland] from Sh—. As it is acted at the Theatre-Royal in Drury Lane. Dublin : J. Exshaw . . . 1772. 12°, pp. 60   BM

Timon of Athens . . . as performed at the Theatre Royal, Drury Lane. Regulated from the prompt book, with permission of the managers, by Mr. Hopkins, prompter. An introduction, and notes critical and illustrative, are added by the authors of the ' Dramatic censor ' [F. Gentleman]. Ln : Printed for John Bell . . . and C. Etherington at York, 1773. 8°, pp. 72, and frontispiece of Mr. Barry as 'Timon' engraved by W. Byrne after E. Edwards

Timon of Athens . . . altered [by ' J. Love'] from Sh— and Shadwell. As it is acted at the Theatres-Royal in Drury-Lane and Covent-Garden. Ln : Harrison & Co. . . . 1780. 8°, pp. 20. With frontispiece portrait of ' Mr. Barry in the character of Timon'   BM | BPL

Timon of Athens . . . printed complete from the text of Sam. Johnson and Geo. Steevens and revised from the last editions . . . Ln : Printed for and under the direction of John Bell, British library, Strand, 1785. 12°, pp. 104. With engraved title and frontispiece of ' Kemble as Timon'

Timon of Athens, altered from Sh— and Shadwell by Mr. [Thomas] Hull. Acted at Covent Garden. Ln. [Privately printed . . .], 1786
Not published. Mentioned by Lowndes, p. 2299.

Timon of Athens . . . Printed complete from the text of Sam. Johnson and Geo. Steevens and revised from the last editions . . . Ln: John Bell . . . 1788. 12°, pp. 104. With frontispiece of 'Mr. Kemble as Timon,' and vignette title

Timon of Athens . . . edited by A. Chalmers. Ln: Rivington . . . [1805]. 8° (excerpt) SML
A prompt copy is at Stratford, with alterations by W. Creswick, the actor.

Timon of Athens . . . as it is acted at Drury Lane and Covent Garden. Ln: Roach . . . 1806. 12° SML

Timon of Athens . . . Ln: W. Tegg . . . [1815]. 8° (excerpt) SML
W. Creswick's prompt copy, interleaved and annotated, is at Stratford.

Timon of Athens . . . as revived at the Theatre Royal, Drury Lane, on Oct. 28, 1816 . . . altered and adapted for representation, by [the Hon.] George Lamb. Ln: C. Chapple . . . 1816. 8°, pp. iv.-54 BM | BUS
The editor remarks that 'the present attempt has been to restore Sh— to the stage with no other omissions than such as the refinement of manners has made necessary.'

Timon of Athens . . . from the text of Johnson and Steevens. With remarks. Ln: T. Hughes . . . [c. 1820]. 16°, pp. 78 BM | BPL

Timon of Athens . . . Ln: Maurice . . . 1822. 12°

Timon of Athens . . . printed from the acting copy, with remarks . . . by D. G—— [Geo. Daniel]. To which are added the costume . . . cast . . . positions . . . and stage business. As performed at the Theatres Royal, London. Ln: J. Cumberland . . . [c. 1831]. 12°, pp. 72 BM | BPL | BUS

[Timon . . .] The old play of Timon. Now first printed. Edited by Alex. Dyce. Ln: Sh— Society . . . 1842. 8°, pp. viii.-96 BM | BPL | BUS | SML | W
Printed from a manuscript written about 1600, which resembles Sh—'s text in many respects.
It also appeared in Sh—'s library, edited by Hazlitt, 1875.

[Timon . . .] Timon d'Athènes. Tragédie. Nouvelle edition, précédée d'une notice critique et historique, et accompagnée de notes, par D. O'Sullivan. Paris: L. Hachette . . . 1843. 12°, pp. xviii.-112 BM
In English and French.

Timon of Athens . . . edited for scholastic study by John Hunter. Ln: Longmans . . . 1873. Cr. 8° BPL | CPL

[Timon . . .] Life of Tymon of Athens. Edited by F. G. Fleay, from the folio of 1623 (the usual insertions by another hand being left out). Ln: New Sh— Soc., 1874. 8° BM | BPL | BUS | SML

[Timon . . .] Hamnet Sh—, part IV.: Life of Timon of Athens, according to the first folio (spelling modernised), with tables shewing the number of emphasis-capitals lost and gained . . . under each of the second, third, and fourth folios, and a few interim remarks upon the facts these tables present, and the questions they suggest, by A. P. Paton. Edinburgh: Edmonston & Co. . . . 1879. 8°, pp. xl.-72 SML

Timon of Athens . . . edited with notes by W. J. Rolfe. New York: Harper . . . 1882. 12°. Illustrated BPL | BUS

Timon of Athens . . . 'Standard plays.' Ln: John Dicks . . . [1883]. 12° BM

Timon of Athens . . . [Another play on Timon. From a manuscript of Sh—'s time. With introduction by Hy. Morley.] 'National library.' Ln: Cassell . . . 1888. 16°, pp. 192 BM

Timon of Athens . . . edited by Charles E. Flower. 'Memorial theatre edition.' Stratford-on-Avon: G. Boyden; Ln: French, 1889. Cr. 8°, viii.-78, including printed wrappers BPL | SML

Timon of Athens . . . edited by I. Gollancz. 'Temple edition.' Ln: Dent . . . 1896. 16°, pp. 142 BM | BLO | BPL | BUS | CTC

Timon of Athens . . . 'Pocket Falstaff edition.' Ln: Bliss, Sands . . . 1898. 16°, pp. 100 BPL | SML

Timon of Athens . . . edited with introduction and notes by C. H. Herford. 'Eversley edition.' Ln: Macmillan . . . 1900. Cr. 8° BPL | SML

Timon of Athens . . . seen through the press by T. S. Moore. Decorated by Charles Ricketts . . . 'Vale Sh—.' Ln: Hacon & Ricketts . . . 1900. Roy. 8°, pp. 88 BM | BLO | CTC | SML

Timon of Athens . . . with introduction and notes by J. Dennis. Illustrated by B. Shaw. 'Chiswick edition.' Ln: Bell . . . 1902. 12°

Timon of Athens . . . edited with notes by H. N. Hudson. 'Windsor edition.' Edinburgh: Jack . . . 1903. 8°, pp. 114. With frontispiece of the Stratford Sh— Memorial SML

Timon of Athens . . . with introduction by G. Brandes. 'Favourite classics.' Ln: Heinemann . . . 1904. 12°

Sh— Timon of Athens . . .

Timon of Athens . . . with introduction and
notes by W. J. Craig. 'Little quartos.'
Ln : Methuen . . . 1905. 16°
Timon of Athens . . . edited by H. Morley.
'National library.' Ln : Cassell . . .
1905. 16°, pp. 192   BPL
Timon of Athens . . . edited by K. Deighton.
'Arden edition.' Ln : Methuen . . . 1905.
8°, pp. 182   BM | BLO | CTC
Timon of Athens . . . 'Waistcoat pocket
edition.' Ln : Treherne . . . 1905. 32°
Timon of Athens . . . with introduction by
H. Paul. 'Renaissance edition.' Ln :
G. G. Harrap . . . 1908. Fcp. 4°   BPL
'Timon of Athens' references—

See Fenton   See Richardson
  ,, Fleay   ,, Snider
  ,, Johnson & Steevens   ,, Study
  ,, Littledale   ,, Wilkins
  ,, Plutarchus

TITUS ANDRONICUS.

*This anonymous tragedy was first en-
tered at Stationers' Hall :—'6th Feb. 1593-
94. John Danter. Entred for his copye
vnder thandes of bothe the Wardens a booke
intituled a noble Roman historye of Tytus
Andronicus . . . VId.'*

*It was freshly registered as follows :—
'19th April 1602. Tho. Pavier. Entred
for his copies by assignment from Thomas
Millington these bookes folowing, saluo
jure cuiuscunque . . . a booke called "Titus
and Andronicus" . . . VId. Entred by
warrant vnder master Seton's hand.'*

*'8th Nov. 1630. Mr. Bird assigns to
Ric. Cotes all his estate, right, title, and
interest in the copies hereafter menconed . . .
Titus and Andronicus . . .'*

*'4 Aug. 1626. Thomas Pavier assigns
his right in "Titus Andronicus" to Edw.
Brewster and Rob. Birde.'*

*Although actually printed in 1594, and
referred to by Gerard Langbaine (q.v.) in
1691, the edition was regarded by students
for about two centuries as either a myth or
a lost work.*

*In December, 1904, the Shakespearean
world was astonished and delighted to hear
from the librarian of Lund University that
a copy had been providentially found in a
Swedish country cottage. Truly one of the
strangest literary rescues on record, and a
fitting companion-romance to that connected with the recovery of the 1603
'Hamlet' in 1856.*

*Sh—'s share of the authorship is thought
to be much less than that respectively of Kyd,
Marlowe, or Greene.*

Sh— Titus Andronicus . . .

*Edward Ravenscroft (q.v.), who edited
in 1687 a fresh version of this play, remarks therein :—'I have been told by some
anciently conversant with the stage that it
was not originally his [Sh—'s], but brought
by a private author to be acted, and he only
gave some master touches to one or two of
the principal parts or characters.'*

[Titus Andronicus] The most lamentable
Romaine Tragedie of Titus Andronicus :
As it was Plaide by the Right Honourable
the Earle of Darbie, Earle of Pembrooke,
and Earle of Sussex their Seruants.
[*Printer's device, with motto 'Aut nunc aut
numquam.'*] London : Printed by Iohn
Danter and are to be sold by Edward
White and Thomas Millington at the
little North doore of Paules at the signe
of the Gunne, 1594. Fcp. 4°, forty unpaged leaves, sig. A¹ to K⁴ in fours
Sh—'s name is not given.
A copy, doubtless unique, happily discovered in Sweden,
was conveyed to London, and there sold, in Dec., 1904,
to a well-known American collector for £2,000 in
Feb., 1905. It is perfect, with the exception of about
ten words scraped or erased.

[Titus Andronicus] The most lamentable
Romaine Tragedie of Titus Andronicus.
As it hath sundry times beene playde by
the Right Honourable the Earle of Pem-
brooke, the Earle of Darbie, the Earle of
Sussex, and the Lorde Chamberlaine
theyr Seruants. [*Ornament.*] At London :
Printed by I. R—— [James Roberts ?]
for Edward White and are to bee solde at
his shoppe at the little North doore of
Paules at the signe of the Gun, 1600.
Fcp. 4°, forty unpaged leaves ; sig. A¹
to K⁴ in fours   EUL | ELLESMERE
Issued anonymously.
A copy lacking the title, bound in modern brown
morocco, edges untouched, occurred for sale on the
9th Dec., 1905, but appears to have been withdrawn.

[Titus Andronicus] The most lamentable
tragedie of Titus Andronicus. As it hath
svndry times beene plaide by the Kings
Maiesties Seruants. [*Device.*] London :
Printed for Eedward White and are to
be solde at his shoppe nere the little
North dore of Pauls, at the signe of the
Gun, 1611. Fcp. 4°, forty unpaged leaves ;
sig. A¹ to K⁴ in fours
                 BM | BLO | BUS | CTC | DEVON
Issued anonymously.
Reprinted by Geo. Steevens in 1766.
'The difference between the editions of 1600 and 1611
(says Charles Knight) is trifling, but between then
and the 1623 folio the variations are important.
Scene II. (about 80 lines) of Act III. is only found
in the folio.
In March, 1906, a copy wanting the title realised £106.
Earl Howe's copy in half blue morocco, 7½ by 5¼ in.,
was secured by an American collector in Dec., 1907.

Titus Andronicus, or the rape of Lavinia. Acted at the Theatre Royall. A tragedy. Alter'd from Mr. Sh—'s Works. By Edward Ravenscroft. Ln : Printed by J. B—— for J. Hindmarsh, 1687. Fcp. 4°, pp. viii.-56   BM | BPL | BUS | W
The plot and much of the text taken from Sh—. The alterations chiefly occur in the last act, the original horrors of which are intensified.

[Titus Andronicus] The lamentable and tragical history of Titus Andronicus, with the fall of his sons in the wars of the Goths . . . To the tune of ' Fortune my foe, etc.' Ln : Printed by and for W. O—— and sold by the booksellers of Pye Corner and London Bridge [c. 1700 ?]. F° broadside in black letter, with wood-cut   BUS

Titus Andronicus. A tragedy. [Ln : Jacob Tonson] Printed in the year MDCCXIV. Cr. 8°, pp. 397-468 (excerpt), and copper-plate frontispiece by Lud. du Guernier

Titus Andronicus . . . [Ln : Printed for J. Tonson, and the rest of the proprietors, and sold by the booksellers of Ln. and Westminster, 1734]. 12°, pp. 70, and frontispiece by Lud. Du Guernier   SML
With piracy warning by W. Chetwood at end against R. Walker.

[Titus Andronicus] The most lamentable tragedie of Titus Andronicus . . . 1611. Ln : [Reprinted by G. Steevens, 1766]. 8°, pp. 38   BPL | SML

Titus Andronicus. A tragedy . . . An introduction, and notes, critical and illus-trative, are added by the authors of the ' Dramatic censor' [F. Gentleman]. Ln : John Bell . . .; York : C. Etherington . . . 1774. 8°, pp. 78, and copperplate frontispiece
An off-print for playgoers from Bell's edition of Sh—'s works.

Titus Andronicus . . . [edited by F. Gen-tleman]. Ln : Printed for John Bell . . . 1777. 12°, pp. 80   SML

[Titus Andronicus] History of Titus An-dronicus . . . Newly translated from the Italian copy. Ln : C. Dicey, Bow Church-yard [c. 1780]. 12°. With woodcuts

Titus Andronicus . . . printed complete from the text of Sam. Johnson and Geo. Steevens and revised from the last editions. Ln : Printed for John Bell . . . 1785. 12°, pp. 108. With engraved title, one other plate, and frontispiece of 'Mrs. Wells as Lavinia'

Titus Andronicus . . . Dublin : J. Exshaw . . . 1794. 12° (excerpt)   SML

Titus Andronicus . . . by Will Sh—. Printed complete from the text of Sam. Johnson and Geo. Steevens and revised from the last editions. Ln : . . . 1809. 16°   W

Titus Andronicus . . . ' Pocket Sh—.' Ln : Mansell . . . [c. 1830]. 16°   BPL

Titus Andronicus . . . from the folio of 1623. Ln : L. Booth . . . 1864. Fcp. 4°   BPL | CPL

Titus Andronicus . . . [In Cohn's ' Sh— in Germany,' q.v.] Ln : Asher . . . 1865. Fcp. 4°   BM | BPL | BUS | CPL | MPL | SML | W
English and German texts given parallel.

Titus Andronicus, 1600. Facsimiled by E. W. Ashbee. [Edited by J. O. Halli-well.] Ln : [Privately printed] 1866. Fcp. 4°   BM | BPL | W
One of fifty copies, of which nineteen were destroyed by the editor.

Titus Andronicus . . . 1611. Facsimiled by E. W. Ashbee. Edited by J. O. Halliwell. Ln : For private circulation, 1867. Fcp. 4°   BPL | W
Impression restricted to fifty copies, nineteen of which the editor destroyed.

Titus Andronicus. ' Standard plays.' Ln : John Dicks . . . [1883]. 12°   BM

Titus Andronicus . . . edited by W. J. Rolfe. New York : Harper . . . 1884. 12°. Illus-trated   BUS | SML
F. Haywell's prompt copy is at Stratford.

Titus Andronicus, partly by Wm. Sh—. The first [sic] quarto, 1600. A facsimile . . . with an introduction by Arthur Symons. ' Sh— quarto facsimiles.' Ln : C. Prætorius . . . [1885]. Fcp. 4°, pp. xviii.-80   BM | BPL | BUS | SML

Titus Andronicus . . . With the ' True tragedie of Richard the third.' [Intro-duction by Hy. Morley.] ' National library.' Ln : Cassell, 1889. 16°, pp. 192   BM

Titus Andronicus . . . edited by C. E. Flower. 'Memorial theatre edition.' Stratford-on-Avon : G. Boyden ; Ln : French, 1890. Cr. 8°, pp. viii.-78 (including printed wrappers)   BPL | SML

[Titus Andronicus] ' Bankside Sh— VII.' The lamentable tragedie of Titus Androni-cus. (The player's text of 1600, with the Heminges and Condell text of 1623.) With an introduction touching the ques-tion as to whether this was Wm. Sh—'s first dramatic work and as to its stage adaptability and reception, by A. Morgan . . . New York : Sh— Society of New York, 1890. Roy. 8°, pp. iv.-236   BPL | BUS | NY | SML

Titus Andronicus . . . edited with notes by W. J. Rolfe. New York . . . 1892. 12°   BPL

Sh— Titus Andronicus . . .

Titus Andronicus . . . edited by I. Gollancz. 'Temple edition.' Ln: Dent . . . 1896. 16°, pp. 136
BM | BLO | BPL | BUS | CTC | SML

Titus Andronicus . . . 'Pocket Falstaff edition.' Ln: Bliss, Sands . . . 1898. 16°, pp. 104
BPL | SML

Titus Andronicus . . . edited with introduction and notes by C. H. Herford. 'Eversley edition.' Ln: Macmillan . . . 1900. 12°
BPL

Titus Andronicus . . . seen through the press by T. S. Moore. Decorated by Charles Ricketts. 'Vale Sh—.' Ln: Hacon & Ricketts, 1901. Roy. 8°, pp. 84
BM | BLO | SML

Titus Andronicus . . . with introduction and notes by J. Dennis. Illustrated by B. Shaw. 'Chiswick edition.' Ln: Bell . . . 1902. 12°

Titus Andronicus . . . edited with notes by H. N. Hudson. 'Windsor edition.' Edinburgh: Jack . . . [1903]. 8°, pp. 94. With portrait of W. C. Macready
BM | BLO | CTC | SML
'Lucrece' and 'Titus' occupy the same volume.

Titus Andronicus . . . edited by H. Bellyse Baildon. 'Arden edition.' Ln: Methuen . . . 1904. 8°, pp. 182   BM | BLO | CTC | MPL

Titus Andronicus . . . with introduction and notes by W. J. Craig. 'Little quartos.' Ln: Methuen . . . 1904. 16°

Titus Andronicus . . . with introduction by G. Brandes. 'Favourite classics.' Ln: Heinemann . . . 1904. 12°

Titus Andronicus . . . 'Waistcoat pocket edition.' Ln: Treherne . . . 1905. 32°

Titus Andronicus . . . edited by H. Morley. 'National library.' Ln: Cassell . . . 1905. 12°, pp. 192
BPL

Titus Andronicus . . . 'Red letter edition.' Ln: Blackie . . . 1907. 12°

Titus Andronicus . . . 'Renaissance edition.' Ln: Harrap . . . 1908. Fcp. 4°
BM | BLO | BPL | CTC

'Titus Andronicus' references—

See Fleay	See Life . . .
„ Grosart	„ Ljunggren
„ Halliwell	„ Meres
„ Johnson (R.)	„ Robertson
„ Johnson & Steevens	„ Robinson
„ Kyd	„ Titus
„ Latham	

TROILUS AND CRESSIDA.

No edition of this tragedy is known before that printed by George Eld in 1609 for Richard Bonian and Henry Walley. It was registered at Stationers' Hall :—'7th

Sh— Troilus and Cressida . . .

Feb. 1602-03. Mr. Roberts. The booke of "Troilus and Cressida" as yt is acted by my Lord Chamberlen's men. When he hath gotten sufficient aucthority for yt . . . VId.' Whether Roberts ever proceeded any further in publication is not traceable. It was freshly entered :—' 28 Jan. 1608-09. Richard Bonion. Henry Walleys. Entred for their copie vnder thandes of Master Segar, deputy to Sir George Bucke, and Master Warden Lownes, a booke called the history of Troylus and Cressida . . . VId.'

The early quartos were not employed by William Jaggard in preparing his 1623 canon, some independent and unknown original being used.

[Troilus and Cressida] The Historie of Troylus and Cresseida. As it was acted by the Kings Maiesties seruants at the Globe. Written by William Shakespeare. [*Ornament.*] London: Imprinted by G. Eld for R. Bonian and H. Walley, and are to be sold at the spred Eagle in Paules Church-yeard, ouer against the great North doore, 1609. Fcp. 4°, forty-six unpaged leaves; sig. A¹ to M² (the last blank ?)
BM

[Troilus and Cressida] The Famous Historie of Troylus and Cresseid. Excellently expressing the beginning of their loues, with the conceited wooing of Pandarus Prince of Licia. Written by William Shakespeare. [*Ornament.*] London: Imprinted by G. Eld for R. Bonian and H. Walley, and are to be sold at the Spred Eagle in Paules Church-yeard, ouer against the great North doore, 1609. Fcp. 4°, forty-six unpaged leaves   BM | BLO | CTC | DEVON
The collation is rather singular. The title has been cut out of the first sheet and replaced by two leaves, bearing a fresh title in which the word 'Famous' is introduced and the letter 'a' omitted from 'Cresseida.' The second of these new leaves is marked ¶2 instead of A2, and contains a preface. Otherwise the signatures are the same as in the first issue. In the preface we glean the interesting fact that the published price of these early quartos was a tester (*i.e.* sixpence). Reprinted by Steevens in 1766; by Halliwell in 1863 and 1871; and by Stokes in 1886.

Troilus and Cressida, or trvth found too late. A tragedy. As it is acted at the Duke's Theatre. To which is prefix'd a preface containing the grounds of criticism in tragedy. [Founded on Sh—.] Written by John Dryden, servant to his majesty. Ln: Printed for Jacob Tonson at the Judge's Head in Chancery Lane near Fleet St., and Abel Swall at the Unicorn at the west end of S. Paul's, 1679. Fcp. 4°, pp. xxvi.-90
BPL | BUS | NY | W

Says Dryden (in the preface):—' The original story was written by Lollius, a Lombard, in latin verse, and translated by Chaucer into English.
'Sh—, in the apprenticeship of his writing, modelled it into that play which is now called by the name of "Troilus and Cressida."
'I new model'd the plot; threw out many unnecessary persons, improv'd those characters which were begun and left unfinish'd . . .
'The whole fifth act, both plot and writing, are my own additions.'

Troilus and Cressida, or truth found too late. A tragedy. As it is acted at the Dukes Theatre. To which is prefix'd a preface containing the grounds of criticism in tragedy. Written by Mr. Dryden. Second edition. Ln: Printed by J. Dawks for Jacob Tonson, 1695. Fcp. 4°, pp. xxvi.-70   BUS | W

Troilus and Cressida . . . [In Dryden's Comedies . . . Vol. i., pp. 199-256]. Ln: J. Tonson . . . T. Bennet . . . and R. Wellington . . . 1701. 2 vols. F°   BM | BUS

[Troilus and Cressida] The siege of Troy. A dramatic performance by Elkanah Settle [based on Sh—'s Troilus and Cressida]. Ln: . . . 1707. 8°
Settle held the office of 'poet to the city of London.'

[Troilus and Cressida] The siege of Troy . . . [Subjoined to a ' History of the destruction of Troy']. By E. Settle. Ln: . . . 1708. 12°

Troilus and Cressida. A tragedy. [Ln: Jacob Tonson] Printed in the year MDCCXIV. Cr. 8°, pp. 199-294 (excerpt) and copperplate frontispiece

[Troilus and Cressida] The siege of Troy: A dramatic performance, presented in Mrs. Mynn's great booth in the Queen's Arms Yard, near the Marshalsea Gate, Southwark, during the time of the fair. By Elkanah Settle. Ln: . . . 1715. 8°

[Troilus and Cressida] The siege of Troy. A tragi-comedy, as it has been often acted. [By E. Settle.] Ln: . . . 1718. 8°   BUS

Troilus and Cressida. A tragedy. By Mr. Wm. Sh—. Ln: Printed for J. Tonson, and the rest of the proprietors and sold by the booksellers of Ln. and Westminster, 1734. 12°, pp. 96, and frontispiece by P. Fourdrinier   SML

Troilus and Cressida, or truth found too late . . . A tragedy. By Mr. Dryden. To which is prefix'd a preface containing the grounds of criticism in tragedy . . . (Crude portrait of Sh—). Ln: Printed for J. Tonson in the Strand . . . 1735. 12°, pp. 120, and frontispiece engraved by G. Van der Gucht after Gravelot
    BM | BPL | SML | W
The Stratford copy was presented, with inscription, by J. O. Halliwell.

[Troilus & Cressida] The famous historie of Troylus and Cresseid . . . 1609. Ln: [Reprinted by G. Steevens, 1766]. 8°, pp. 38,   BPL | W

Troilus and Cressida. A tragedy . . . An introduction, and notes critical and illustrative, are added by the authors of the ' Dramatic censor ' [F. Gentleman]. Ln: John Bell; York: C. Etherington, 1774. 12°, pp. 104. With copperplate frontis.

Troilus and Cressida . . . [edited by F. Gentleman]. Ln: J. Bell . . . 1776. 12°
    SML

Troilus and Cressida . . . [In Dryden's Works]. Ln: . . . 1808. 8°   BUS

Troilus and Cressida, by Will. Sh—. Printed complete from the text of Sam. Johnson and Geo. Steevens, and revised from the last editions. Ln: . . . 1811. 16°   W

Troilus and Cressida . . . [In Dryden's Works. Second edition]. Edinburgh: . . . 1821. 8°   BUS

Troilus and Cressida . . . edited with notes [in German] by Beauregard Pandin. Berlin . . . 1824. 12°   SML

[Troilus and Cressida] Senarii Græci [A translation by Christopher Wordsworth from ' Troilus and Cressida, act iii., sc. 3']. Cambridge, 1828, 8°   BM
In English and Greek.

Troilus and Cressida . . . With remarks . . . by D. G—— [G. Daniel]. Adapted for stage representation. With the proper costumes . . . positions . . . and stage business. Embellished with an engraving . . . by R. Cruikshank. Ln: Davidson . . . [c. 1830]. 12°, pp. 76, and plate   BPL | BUS

Troilus and Cressida [A translation in Greek verse, by R. Andrews, from ' Troilus and Cressida, act i., sc. 3']. Cambridge . . . 1840. 8°   BM
In English and Greek.

Troylus and Cressid . . . 1609. Facsimile by E. W. Ashbee. [Edited by J. O. Halliwell.] Ln: For private circulation, 1863. Fcp. 4°, on eighty-eight unpaged leaves
    BPL | BUS | W
Fifty copies produced; nineteen were destroyed by the editor.

Troilus and Cressida . . . from the folio of 1623. Ln: L. Booth . . . 1864. Fcp. 4°
    BPL | CPL

Troylus and Cresseida . . . 1609. [Edited by J. O. Halliwell.] Facsimiled by E. W. Ashbee. Ln: For private circulation, 1871. Fcp. 4°   BPL

Troilus and Cressida . . . With notes by J. Hunter. Ln: Longman . . . 1872. 12°
    BPL | CPL

Sh— Troilus and Cressida . . .

Troilus and Cressida . . . edited with notes by W. J. Rolfe. New York : Harper . . . 1882. 12°; illustrated   BPL | BUS

Troilus and Cressida . . . 'Standard plays.' Ln : John Dicks . . . [1883]. 12° BM

Troilus and Cressida . . . The first quarto, 1609. A facsimile in photo-lithography . . . With an introduction by . . . H. P. Stokes. 'Sh— quarto facsimiles.' Ln : W. Griggs . . . [1886]. Fcp. 4°, pp. xii.-91 and two facsimiles   BM | BPL | BUS | SML

Troilus and Cressida [With introduction by Hy. Morley]. 'National library.' Ln : Cassell . . . 1889. 16°, pp. 192 BM

Troilus and Cressida . . . edited by C. E. Flower. 'Memorial theatre edition.' Stratford-on-Avon : G. Boyden ; Ln : French . . . [1889]. Cr. 8°, pp. viii.-104 (including printed wrappers)   BPL | SML

[Troilus . . .] 'Bankside Sh— IV.' Troilus and Cressida. (The player's text of 1609, with the Heminges and Condell text of 1623.) With an introduction touching the question as to whether the play held Sh—'s stage or was printed with his concurrence, by A. Morgan. New York : Sh— Society of New York, 1889. Roy. 8°, pp. viii.-240   BPL | BUS | NY | SML

Troilus and Cressida . . . edited by I. Gollancz. 'Temple edition.' Ln : Dent . . . 1896. 16°, pp. 192 BUS

Troilus and Cressida . . . 'Ariel edition.' Ln : Routledge . . . 1897. 16°

Troilus and Cressida . . . edited with introduction and notes by C. H. Herford. 'Eversley edition.' Ln : Macmillan . . . 1900. Cr. 8° BPL | SML

Troilus and Cressida . . . seen through the press by T. S. Moore. Decorated by Charles Ricketts. 'Vale Sh—.' Ln : Hacon & Ricketts . . . 1900. Roy. 8°, pp. 120 BM | BLO | CTC | SML

Troilus and Cressida . . . with introduction and notes by J. Dennis. Illustrated by B. Shaw. 'Chiswick edition.' Ln : Bell . . . 1902. 12°

Troilus and Cressida . . . edited with notes by H. N. Hudson. 'Windsor edition.' Edinburgh : Jack . . . 1903. 8°, pp. 142, and Ely portrait SML

Troilus and Cressida . . . with preface and glossary by I. Gollancz. 'Temple edition.' Ln : Dent, 1904. 16°, pp. xii.-180

Troilus and Cressida . . . with introduction by G. Brandes. 'Favourite classics.' Ln : Heinemann . . . 1904. 12°

Troilus and Cressida . . . edited by H. Morley. 'National library.' Ln : Cassell, 1905. 16°, pp. 192 BPL

Sh— Troilus and Cressida . . .

Troilus and Cressida . . . with introduction and notes by W. J. Craig. 'Little quartos.' Ln : Methuen . . . 1905. 32°

Troilus and Cressida . . . 'Waistcoat pocket edition.' Ln : Treherne . . . 1905. 32°

Troilus and Cressida . . . edited by K. Deighton. 'Arden edition.' Ln : Methuen . . . 1906. 8°, pp. 240 BM | BLO | CTC

Troilus and Cressida . . . 'Red letter edition.' Ln : Blackie . . . 1907. 12°

Troilus and Cressida . . . With introduction by W. Raleigh. 'Renaissance edition.' Ln : Harrap . . . 1908. Fcp. 4° BPL

'Troilus and Cressida' references—

See Armin	*See* Lennox
„ Beaumont	„ Lydgate
„ C—— (I.)	„ Numeration
„ Fleay	„ Palmer
„ Halliwell	„ Randolph
„ Johnson &	*Sh*—] Sh— notes
Steevens	„ Snider
„ Keats	„ Young (K.)

TWELFTH NIGHT, OR WHAT YOU WILL.

According to Manningham's Diary (q.v.) this comedy was performed in the Middle Temple 2nd Feb., 1602. So far as can be gleaned, it remained unprinted until the Jaggard canon presented it in 1623. No separate untampered text is known earlier than Jacob Tonson's issue of 1714. Burnaby's adaptation appeared in 1703, and Molloy's in 1720.

Twelfe night, or what you will . . . Ln : Printed by Tho. Cotes for Robert Allot, 1632. F°, eleven leaves (an excerpt from second folio edition) W
A curious early playhouse copy, used some time before 1640, with manuscript stage directions and notes. Upon page 115 of Halliwell's 'Catalogue of Sh—reliques, 1852,' 4°, will be found matter relating to it.

[Twelfth night] Love betray'd, or the agreable disapointment. A comedy. As it was acted at the theatre in Lincoln's Inn Fields. By the author of 'The ladies' visiting day' [Charles Burnaby]. '*Jam te sequetur.*' Ln : Printed for D. Brown at the Black Swan without Temple Bar ; F. Coggan in the Inner Temple Lane, Fleet Street ; W. Davis at the Black Bull ; and G. Strahan at the Golden Ball against the Exchange in Cornhill, 1703. Fcp. 4°, pp. xiv.-64 BPL | BUS
The first separate form of Sh—'s 'Twelfth night' considerably ' adapted.'
The editor says :—' Part of the tale of this play I took from Sh—, and about fifty of the lines. Those that are his I have marked with inverted commas, to dis-

Sh— Twelfth night . . .

tinguish 'em from what are mine. I endeavour'd, where I had occasion to introduce any of 'em, to make 'em look as little like strangers as possible.'

Pages 13 and 63 contain lists of plays and other publications issued by Brown, Coggan, and Strahan aforesaid.

Twelfth night; or, What You will. A comedy. [Ln: Jacob Tonson.] Printed in the year MDCCXIV. Cr. 8°, pp. 74 and copper frontispiece

Until now an unrecorded issue, offprinted from Tonson's anonymous edition of Sh—'s works, for the use of playgoers.

[Twelfth night] The half-pay officers. A comedy [by C. Molloy; altered from Davenant's ' Love and honour,' with some scenes taken from ' Twelfth night' and ' King Henry V.'] Ln: . . . 1720. 12° BM

Twelfth night . . . Ln: J. Tonson . . . 1728. 12° (excerpt from Sh—'s Works, vol. 3) BPL

Twelfth night, or what you will. By Mr. Wm. Sh—. Ln: Printed for J. Tonson and the rest of the proprietors, and sold by the booksellers of Ln. and Westminster, 1734. Cr. 8°, pp. 72 and frontispiece by P. Fourdrinier SML | W
Piracy notice at end against R. Walker.

Twelfth night, or what you will, by Sh—. Ln: R. Walker . . . 1735. 12°, pp. 90 W

[Twelfth night] Songs in ' Twelfth night' [Full score]. Composed by Dr. T. A. Arne. Ln: [c. 1740]. F° BPL

[Twelfth night] New songs in the pantomime of the witches, the celebrated epilogue in ' Twelfth night,' and a song in ' Two gentlemen of Verona.' Composed by J. Vernon and sung by Mr. Vernon and Mrs. Abington at Vauxhall. Ln: John Johnson [c. 1766]. F°. With words and music engraved

Twelfth night . . . Ln : . . . [c. 1770]. 12°

Twelfth night . . . as performed at the Theatres Royal. Regulated from the prompt book, with permission of the managers, by Mr. Hopkins, prompter. An introduction, and notes critical and illustrative, are added by the authors of the ' Dramatic censor ' [F. Gentleman]. Ln : Printed for John Bell . . . and C. Etherington at York, 1773. 8°, pp. 74 and copperplate frontispiece by C. Grignion after E. Edwards

Off-printed, for the use of playgoers, from Bell's edition of Sh—'s works.

Hitherto an unchronicled edition.

Twelfth night . . . [edited by F. Gentleman]. Ln: John Bell . . . ; York : C. Etherington . . . 1774. 8°, pp. 74 and copper frontispiece BPL

Sh— Twelfth night . . .

On the last page is the announcement of the completion of Bell's edition, in which it is stated some of the plates were engraved by Sherwin under the direction of F. Bartolozzi.

Twelfth night, or what you will. A comedy. As it is acted at the Theatres Royal in Drury Lane and Covent Garden . . . Ln : Printed for J. Harrison, 18 Paternoster Row, and sold likewise by J. Wenman, Fleet St., and all other booksellers, 1779. 8°, pp. 20 and copperplate portrait of ' Mrs. Abington as Olivia ' BM | BPL

[Twelfth night] The part of Malvolio [c. 1780]. Fcp. 4°, manuscript on seventeen leaves of paper W
A copy written for the personal use of Wm. Farren, the actor.

Twelfth night . . . Ln : J. Bell . . . 1786. 8° SML

Twelfth night, or what you will. Taken from the manager's book at the Theatre-Royal, Drury Lane. Ln : Rachel Randall . . . 1787. 8°. With plate of ' Mrs. Jordan as Viola ' BPL | CPL | SML | W

Twelfth night . . . Printed conformable to the representation [at the Drury Lane Theatre] under the inspection of J. Wrighten, prompter. Ln : . . . 1791. 8°

Twelfth night . . . Printed conformable to the representation at the Theatre Royal, Drury Lane, by J. Wrighten, prompter. Ln : C. Lowndes . . . 1792. 12°, pp. 60
With manuscript notes by W. Powell. BM

Twelfth night, or what you will. A comedy. In five acts. Written by Wm. Sh—. As performed at the Theatre in Boston. With notes critical and illustrative. Boston [U.S.] : Printed for David West, 36 Marlborough Street, and John West, 75 Cornhill [1794]. 12°, pp. 60 BUS
The first play of Sh— printed and produced in America.
' Hamlet' [q.v.], also issued by D. and J. West in that year, differs from ' Twelfth night' in that it bears no footnotes.

Twelfth night . . . as it is acted at Drury Lane and Covent Garden . . . Ln : Barker . . . 1794. 12°

[Twelfth night] New songs in . . . the celebrated epilogue of 'Twelfth night' . . . By Mr. Vernon. [Full score.] Ln : . . . [c. 1800]. F°

Twelfth night . . . as it is acted at the Theatres Royal in Drury Lane and Covent Garden. Ln : Rivington . . . [c. 1800]. 12° BPL

Twelfth night . . . from the text of Johnson and Steevens. Manchester : R. & W. Dean . . . 1803. 12°, pp. 70 and engraved frontispiece

(479)

Sh— Twelfth night . . .

Twelfth night, or what you will . . . As performed at the Theatres Royal, Drury Lane and Covent Garden. Printed under the authority of the managers from the prompt book. With remarks by Mrs. Inchbald. Ln : Longman [1808]. 12°, pp. 76. With frontispiece   BPL | SML
The Stratford copy was presented, with inscription, by J. O. Halliwell.

Twelfth night, or what you will. Revised by J. P. Kemble. Ln : . . . 1810. 8°

Twelfth night, or what you will . . . revised by J. P. Kemble. As now performed at the Theatre Royal, Covent Garden. Ln : Longman . . . [c. 1811]. 12°, pp. 76 and plate   BUS

Twelfth night, or what you will. A comedy. Revised by J. P. Kemble, and now published as it is performed at the Theatres Royal. Ln : J. Miller . . . 1815. 12°, pp. 74   BM | BUS | SML

[Twelfth night] Songs, duetts and glees in . . . 'Twelfth night,' performed at the Theatre Royal, Covent Garden. The words selected entirely from Sh—'s 'Plays, poems, and sonnets.' The music by H. R. Bishop. Ln : Goulding . . . 1820. F°, pp. viii.-84   BUS

Twelfth night . . . With prefatory remarks [signed P. P——] . . . Marked with the stage business and stage directions, as it is performed at the Theatres Royal, by W. Oxberry. Ln : Simpkin . . . 1821. Cr. 8°, pp. ii.-72   BM | BPL | SML

Twelfth night . . . with plates by Smirke. Ln : Rodwell . . . 1822. 8°

Twelfth night . . . as performed . . . . With remarks by W. Oxberry. Ln : . . . 1823. 12°. With portrait

Twelfth night . . . edited by Hy. Neele. Ln : . . . 1824. 12°. With plates

Twelfth night . . . as performed . . . With remarks by D. G—— [Geo. Daniel]. Ln : Musical Publishing Co., 1824. 18°
   SML

Twelfth night . . . With remarks. Edinburgh : Stirling & Kenney, 1829. 12°, pp. 62. With frontispiece   SML

Twelfth night . . . Acting edition. Ln : Davidson . . . 1830. 12°, pp. 64 ; embellished with a fine engraving by Mr. Bonner from a drawing taken in the theatre by R. Cruikshank   SML
A copy with manuscript additions by F. Haywell is at Stratford.

Twelfth night, or what you will . . . Printed from the acting copy, with remarks, biographical and critical, by D. G—— [Geo.

Sh— Twelfth night . . .

Daniel]. To which are added a cast . . . and the stage business . . . as now performed at the Theatres Royal. Ln : J. Cumberland [c. 1830]. 12°, pp. 64
   BM | BPL

Twelfth night . . . 'British theatre.' Ln : Cumberland . . . [c. 1840]. 12°   BPL

Twelfth night . . . as performed at Covent Garden. Ln : . . . 1841. 12°

Twelfth night. A comedy . . . Nuremberg . . . ; New York . . . 1841. 12°

Twelfth night, or what you will . . . With the stage business, cast, costumes, positions . . . 'Modern standard drama.' New York : S. French . . . [c. 1847]. 12°, pp. 64   BUS

Twelfth night, or what you will . . . With the stage business . . . 'Standard drama.' New York : S. French [c. 1847]. 12°, pp. 64   BUS
Identical with foregoing entry except in title.

Twelfth night, or what you will : A comedy, in five acts. With preliminary notes. 'Acting plays.' Ln : T. H. Lacy . . . [1855]. 12°, pp. 66   BM | BPL | MPL

Twelfth night . . . Ln : Lacy . . . [c. 1869]. 12°

Twelfth night . . . with explanatory and illustrative notes, selected criticisms on the play, etc. Adapted for scholastic or private study and for those qualifying for university and government examinations, by John Hunter. Ln : Longmans, 1870. Cr. 8°, pp. viii.-104   CPL

Twelfth night . . . for amateurs. Edited by . . . Shield. Newcastle-on-Tyne . . . 1871. 8°   SML

Twelfth night . . . arranged for representation by Charles Calvert and produced . . . at the Prince's Theatre, Manchester, Sept. 1873. Manchester : Alex. Ireland . . . [1873]. Cr. 8°, pp. 68, in printed blue wrappers   BPL | SML

Twelfth night . . . 'Boudoir Sh—,' edited by Henry Cundell. Carefully bracketed for reading aloud. Freed from all objectionable matter, and altogether free from notes. Ln : S. Low . . . 1877. Cr. 8°, pp. 85-156 (excerpt), in printed boards

Twelfth night . . . With . . . notes . . . by J. Hunter. Ln : Longman . . . [c. 1878]. Cr. 8°, pp. viii.-104   BPL

Twelfth night . . . 'Acting edition.' Ln : French . . . [c. 1879]. 12°   SML

Twelfth night . . . edited with notes by W. J. Rolfe. New York : Harper . . . 1879. 12°   BPL

Twelfth night . . . with introduction and notes . . . by . . . H. N. Hudson. 'Annotated English classics.' Boston [U.S.]: Ginn & Heath . . . 1880. 8°, pp. xxvi.-152   BM

Twelfth night . . . edited by W. J. Rolfe. New York: Harper . . . 1881. 12°   SML

Twelfth night . . . With notes by H. N. Hudson. Boston [U.S.] . . . 1881. 12°

Twelfth night (act II., sc. 5). Translated into [Greek] comic iambics by W. R. Hardie. Gaisford prize. Oxford: B. H. Blackwell, 1882. 8°, pp. 16   BM | BPL

Twelfth night . . . edited by C. E. Flower. 'Memorial theatre edition.' Stratford-on-Avon: Printed by G. Boyden; Ln: S. French [1882]. Cr. 8°, pp. viii.-80, including printed wrappers   BPL | SML

Twelfth night . . . edited with notes by W. J. Rolfe. New York: Harper . . . 1883. 12°   BPL

Twelfth night . . . 'Standard plays.' Ln: John Dicks [1883]. 12°   BM

Twelfth night . . . as arranged by Hy. Irving and presented at the Lyceum Theatre, 8th July, 1884. Ln: Chiswick Press, 1884. 8°   BPL | SML

Twelfth night . . . Ed. by W. A. Wright. Oxford: Clarendon Press . . . 1885. Cr. 8°, pp. xvi.-172   BPL | BUS | SML

Twelfth night . . . 'Handbooks for students.' Ln: Moffatt & Page . . . [1887]. 12°   BPL | SML

Twelfth night . . . edited by W. A. Wright . . . Oxford: Clarendon Press, 1887. Cr. 8°, pp. xvi.-172   BPL

Twelfth night, or what you will . . . 'Students' Tauchnitz edition.' Mit Deutschen erklärungen . . . von Dr. H. Conrad. Leipzig: B. Tauchnitz . . . 1887. Cr. 8°, pp. xxiv.-172   BM
In English and German.

Twelfth night, or what you will . . . [Also 'Apolonius and Silla.' By Barnaby Rich. With an introduction by H. Morley.] 'National library.' Ln: Cassell . . . 1889. 16°, pp. 192   BM

Twelfth night . . . edited by H. H. Crawley. 'Falcon edition.' Ln: Rivington . . . 1889. 12°   BPL

Twelfth night . . . With introduction and notes by H. N. Hudson. Boston [U.S.] . . . 1889. 12°   BPL

Twelfth night . . . With notes by K. Deighton. Ln: Macmillan . . . 1889. 12°

Twelfth night . . . 'Falcon edition,' edited by H. H. Crawley. Ln: Longman . . . 1891. 12°

Twelfth night, or what you will . . . Arranged to be played in four acts by Augustin Daly. Printed from the prompt book, and as produced at Daly's theatre, Feb. 21st, 1893. With an introductory word by William Winter. New York: Privately printed . . . 1893. F°, pp. 74, inlaid and extra illustrated with programmes, Stratford bust, portrait of Wm. Winter, music, and forty-eight photographs of scenes and characters   SML
Edition-de-luxe, limited to twenty-five copies, prepared by A. Daly for presents only at a cost of £20 each.

Twelfth night. 'Pitt Press Sh—.' With introduction, notes, glossary and index, edited by A. Wilson Verity. Cambridge: University Press . . . 1893. Cr. 8°, pp. xxx.-174   SML

Twelfth night . . . edited by A. W. Verity. Cambridge: University Press . . . 1894. Cr. 8°, pp. xl.-174

Twelfth night. With preface, glossary, &c. by I. Gollancz. 'Temple edition.' Ln: J. M. Dent & Co. . . . 1895. 16°, pp. xii.-136. With frontispiece

Twelfth night . . . edited by R. F. Cholmeley. 'School Sh—.' Ln: Arnold . . . [1895]. 12°   BPL

Twelfth night . . . With introduction and notes by Elizabeth Lee. 'Junior school Sh—.' Ln: Blackie . . . 1895. 12°   BPL

Twelfth night . . . with notes, examination papers, &c. Ln: W. & R. Chambers . . . 1895. 12°, pp. 120   BM | BPL | SML

Twelfth night . . . With introduction and notes by K. Deighton. Ln: Macmillan . . . 1895. Cr. 8°, pp. xvi.-184   BPL

Twelfth night . . . With introduction, notes, glossary and index by A. W. Verity. Second edition. 'Pitt Press Sh—.' Cambridge: University Press . . . 1895. 8°, pp. xxx.-174   BPL

Twelfth night . . . edited with notes by W. J. Rolfe. New York . . . 1895. 12°   BPL

Twelfth night . . . edited by Arthur D. Innes. 'Warwick Sh—.' Ln: Blackie . . . 1895. 8°, pp. 154   BPL

Twelfth night . . . with notes by J. Lees. Ln: Allman . . . [1895]. Cr. 8°, pp. x.-118   BM

Twelfth night . . . edited by A. D. Innes. 'Arden Sh—.' Ln: Methuen. 1895-96. 8°   BUS

Twelfth night . . . 'Ariel edition.' Ln: Routledge . . . 1896. 16°

Twelfth night . . . With notes by J. Lees. 'Local examination series.' Ln: Allman . . . [1896]. 12°   BPL

Sh— Twelfth night . . .

Twelfth night . . . edited by R. F. Cholmeley . . . Ln : Arnold . . . 1897. 12°

Twelfth night . . . ' Pocket Falstaff edition.' Ln : Bliss, Sands . . . 1898. 16°, pp. 100
BPL | SML

Twelfth night . . . Ln : . . . 1899. 8° BUS

Twelfth night . . . with introduction and notes by John Dennis. Illustrated by B. Shaw. ' Chiswick edition.' Ln : Bell . . . 1900. 12°, pp. 126

Twelfth night . . . edited with introductions and notes by C. H. Herford. ' Eversley edition.' Ln : Macmillan . . . 1900. Cr. 8°
BPL | SML

Twelfth night : Souvenir . . . of the comedy . . . produced at Her Majesty's Theatre by H. B. Tree, 5 Feb., 1901. Ln : Hentschel . . . 1901. Oblong 4°

Twelfth night . . . ' New variorum edition,' edited by H. H. Furness. Philadelphia : Lippincott . . . 1901. Roy. 8°, pp. 456
BM | BPL | BUS | SML

Twelfth night . . . seen through the press by T. S. Moore. Decorated by Charles Ricketts. ' Vale Sh—.' Ln : Hacon & Ricketts . . . 1901. Roy. 8°, pp. 88
BM | BLO | CTC | SML

Twelfth night . . . edited by W. J. Rolfe. New York . . . [1902]. 8° BUS

Twelfth night . . . With introduction, notes, glossary and index, by A. W. Verity. Cambridge : University Press . . . 1902. Cr. 8°, pp. xxx.-174

Twelfth night . . . edited with notes by H. N. Hudson. 'Windsor edition.' Edinburgh : Jack . . . 1903. 8°, pp. iv.-102. With Stratford Bust portrait SML

Twelfth night . . . with introduction and notes by W. J. Craig. ' Little quartos.' Ln : Methuen . . . 1904. 16°

Twelfth night . . . with introduction by G. Brandes. ' Favourite classics.' Ln : Heinemann . . . 1904. 12°

Twelfth night . . . ' Ellen Terry edition.' Glasgow : Bryce . . . 1904. 32°

Twelfth night . . . edited by H. Morley. 'National library.' Ln : Cassell . . . 1904. 16°, pp. 192 BPL

Twelfth night . . . edited by A. W. Verity. Cambridge : University Press, 1904. Cr. 8°, pp. xxx.-174

Twelfth night . . . with introduction by Fanny Johnson. Edinburgh : Blackwood . . . 1904. Cr. 8° BPL

Twelfth night . . . ' Picture Sh—.' Ln : Blackie . . . 1905. Cr. 8°, pp. 144. Illustrated BPL

Sh— Twelfth night . . .

Twelfth night . . . ' Waistcoat pocket edition.' Ln : Treherne . . . 1905. 32°

Twelfth night . . . Complete paraphrase by Jean F. Terry. ' Normal tutorial series.' Ln : Simpkin . . . 1905. Cr. 8° BPL

Twelfth night . . . with introduction and notes by S. Wood. ' Oxford and Cambridge edition.' Ln : Gill . . . 1905. 8°
BPL

Twelfth night . . . ' Swan edition.' Ln : Longman . . . 1905. Cr. 8° BPL

Twelfth night . . . With introduction, &c. by J. H. Brittain. Ln : Ralph & Holland, 1906. Cr. 8° BPL

Twelfth night . . . with introduction, &c. by A. A. Brayley. ' Tutorial series.' Ln : Normal Press . . . 1906. Cr. 8° BPL

Twelfth night . . . edited by Morton Luce. 'Arden edition.' Ln : Methuen . . . 1906. 8°, pp. 236 BM | BLO | CTC

Twelfth night . . . with introduction, notes, appendix, examination questions, and index. Ln : Ralph . . . 1907. Cr. 8°, pp. 186

Twelfth night . . . revised by A. Dyce. Ln : Sonnenschein . . . [1907]. 8° BPL

Twelfth night . . . ' Renaissance edition.' Ln : Harrap . . . 1907. Fcp. 4° BPL | SML

Twelfth night . . . edited by W. G. Boswell-Stone. ' Old spelling edition.' Ln : Chatto . . . 1907. Fcp. 4°, pp. xiv.-78
BPL | SML

Twelfth night . . . ' Penny poets.' Ln : W. T. Stead . . . [1907]. Cr. 8° BPL

Twelfth night. With illustrations by W. H. Robinson. Ln : Hodder . . . 1908. Roy. 8°, pp. 168 and plates BPL
An edition-de-luxe of this issue was also prepared.

Twelfth night . . . ' Plain text Sh—.' Ln : Blackie . . . 1909. Cr. 8° BPL

' Twelfth night ' references—

Sh—] TWO GENTLEMEN OF VERONA.

Until its appearance in 1623 in the Jaggard canon, no printed version of this comedy is known, and no separate text is recorded earlier than those issued in 1734 by the rival publishers, Jacob Tonson and R. Walker.

Two gentlemen of Verona. By Mr. Wm. Sh—. Ln: Printed for J. Tonson and the rest of the proprietors, and sold by the booksellers of Ln. and Westminster, 1734. Cr. 8°, pp. 72 and frontispiece engraved by P. Fourdrinier   SML
Contains a piracy notice by W. Chetwood against R. Walker.

Two gentlemen of Verona. A comedy, by Sh—. Ln: R. Walker at 'Sh—'s head,' 1734. Cr. 8°   W

Two gentlemen of Verona: A comedy [in five acts, prose and verse] . . . With alterations and additions [by Benjamin Victor]. As it is performed at the Theatre-Royal in Drury - Lane. Ln: J. & R. Tonson . . . 1763. Cr. 8°, pp. vi.-56
      BM | BPL | BUS
Victor says:—'It is the general opinion that this comedy abounds with weeds, and there is no one I think will deny . . . that it is adorned with poetical flowers such as the hand of a Sh— alone could raise. The rankest of those weeds I have endeavoured to remove.'

Two gentlemen of Verona . . . [edited by F. Gentleman]. Ln: J. Bell and C. Etherington at York . . . 1774. 12°, pp. 68   SML

Two gentlemen of Verona, by Will. Sh—. Printed complete from the text of Sam. Johnson and Geo. Steevens and revised from the last editions. Ln: J. Bell . . . 1786. 8°, pp. 96   BUS

[Two gentlemen . . .] New songs in . . . 'The witches, . . . Twelfth night, . . . Two gentlemen of Verona . . .' [Full score.] By Mr. Vernon. Ln: . . . [c. 1800]. F°

Two gentlemen of Verona . . . Taken from the manager's book at the Theatre Royal, Drury Lane. Ln: . . . [c. 1800]. 12°   BPL

Two gentlemen of Verona . . . Revised by J. P. Kemble. As acted at Covent Garden. Ln: For the theatre . . . 1808. 8°
      CPL

Two gentlemen of Verona, by Will. Sh—. Printed complete from the text of Sam. Johnson and Geo. Steevens. Ln: . . . 1812. 16°   W

Two gentlemen of Verona. A comedy, revised by J. P. Kemble; and now published as it is performed at the Theatres Royal . . . Ln: J. Miller . . . and sold in the theatres, 1815. 8°, pp. 74
      BM | BUS | SML | W

Sh— Two gentlemen of Verona . . .

The Warwick copy bears manuscript notes by R. S. White.
In some passages Kemble has adopted Victor's alterations of 1763 [*q.v.*]

Two gentlemen of Verona . . . 'Acting edition.' Ln: Cumberland . . . 1821. 12°
      SML

[Two gentlemen . . .] Overture, songs, duetts, glees, and choruses in Sh—'s play of the 'Two gentlemen of Verona,' as performed at the Theatre Royal, Covent Garden. [Full score.] By Sir Henry R. Bishop [1821]. F°, pp. 92
The words are supplied entirely by Sh—.

[Two gentlemen . . .] Songs, duettos, glees, and choruses introduced in Sh—'s revived play of 'Two gentlemen of Verona,' selected entirely from the plays, poems, and sonnets of Sh— [by Frederick Reynolds], acted at the Theatre Royal, Covent Garden. The overture and whole of the music (excepting two melodies) composed by Sir H. R. Bishop. Ln: E. Macleish . . . [1821]. 8°, pp. 16 BPL | BUS

Two gentlemen . . . With prefatory remarks [signed P. P——] . . . Marked with the stage business, and stage directions, as it is performed at the Theatres Royal, by W. Oxberry. Ln: Simpkin . . . 1823. 8°, pp. viii.-70. With portrait BM | BPL | SML

Two gentlemen of Verona . . . edited by Hy. Neele. Ln: . . . 1824. 12°. With plates

Two gentlemen . . . Ln: J. Cumberland . . . 1830. 12°, pp. 64; 'embellished with a fine wood engraving by Mr. Bonner from a drawing taken in the theatre by R. Cruikshank'   SML
Haywell's corrected copy is at Stratford.

Two gentlemen . . . Printed from the acting copy, with remarks, biographical and critical, by D. G—— [Geo. Daniel]. To which are added a cast . . . and the . . . stage business, as now performed at the Theatres Royal. Ln: J. Cumberland . . . [1831]. 12°, pp. 64 and frontispiece by R. Cruikshank   BM | BPL | CPL

Two gentlemen . . . Nuremberg . . . ; New York . . . 1841. 12°

Two gentlemen . . . with the stage business, cast . . . costumes, positions, etc. As produced at the Park Theatre by Mr. and Mrs Charles Kean. 'Standard drama.' New York: S. French [c. 1846]. 12°, pp. 60   BUS

Two gentlemen . . . 'Modern standard drama.' New York: S. French [c. 1847]. 12°, pp. 60   BUS
Identical with French's 'Standard drama' issue, except in title.

Sh— Two gentlemen of Verona . . .

Two gentlemen of Verona . . . [Text and notes in English and German, edited by N. Delius]. Elberfeld . . . 1858. Cr. 8°, pp.   SML

Two gentlemen . . . 'Cumberland's theatre.' Ln: Lacy . . . [c. 1870]. 12°   SML

Two gentlemen . . . with notes, critical and explanatory. Adapted for scholastic or private study and for those qualifying for university or government examinations. Ln: Longmans . . . 1873. Cr. 8°, pp. viii.-94   BPL | CPL

Two gentlemen . . . edited with notes by W. J. Rolfe. New York: Harper . . . 1882. 12°   BPL | BUS

Two gentlemen . . . 'Standard plays.' Ln: John Dicks [1883]. 12°   BM | BPL

Two gentlemen . . . edited by Charles E. Flower. 'Memorial theatre edition.' Stratford-on-Avon: Printed by G. Boyden; Ln: S. French . . . 1886. Cr. 8°, pp. viii.-72, including printed wrappers   BPL | SML

Two gentlemen . . . With the story of the 'Shepherdess Felismena' [from the 'Diana' of George de Montemayor, translated by B. Yonge. With introduction by H. Morley. 'National library.' Ln: Cassell, 1889. 16°, pp. 192   BM

Two gentlemen . . . edited with preface and glossary by I. Gollancz. 'Temple edition.' Ln: Dent & Co. . . . 1894. 16°, pp. x.-112   SML

[Two gentlemen . . .] Eight illustrations to Sh—'s 'Two gentlemen . . .' By Walter Crane. Engraved and printed by D. C. Dallas. Ln: Dent . . . 1894. F° BM | BPL

Two gentlemen of Verona . . . [edited by Augustin Daly. With a word of preface by Wm. Winter. New York: Privately printed for A. Daly] 1895. F°, pp. 60, inlaid and extra-illustrated with the Droeshout portrait, portraits in character of Ada Rehan and others in the caste   BPL | SML

The Stratford copy bears Daly's autograph inscription.
Edition-de-luxe, limited to twenty-five copies for presentation only.

Two gentlemen . . . 'Pocket Falstaff edition.' Ln: Bliss, Sands . . . 1898. 16°, pp. 92   BPL | SML

Two gentlemen . . . [edited by Hy. Morley]. 'National Library.' Ln: Cassell . . . [1899]. 16°, pp. 192

Two gentlemen . . . with introduction and notes by John Dennis. Illustrated by B. Shaw. 'Chiswick edition.' Ln: Bell . . . 1900. Cr. 8°, pp. 112

Sh— Two gentlemen of Verona . . .

Two gentlemen . . . edited with introduction and notes by C. H. Herford. 'Eversley edition.' Ln: Macmillan . . . 1900. 12°   BPL

Two gentlemen . . . seen through the press by T. S. Moore. Decorated by Charles Ricketts. 'Vale Sh—.' Ln: Hacon & Ricketts . . . 1901. Roy. 8°, pp. 82   BM | BLO | CTC | SML

Two gentlemen . . . edited with notes by H. N. Hudson. 'Windsor edition.' Edinburgh: Jack . . . 1902. 8°, pp. iv.-80, and frontispiece of the Hathaway cottage interior   SML

Two gentlemen . . . with introduction and notes by W. J. Craig. Ln: Methuen . . . 1903. 16°

Two gentlemen . . . 'Ellen Terry edition.' Glasgow: Bryce . . . 1904. 32°

Two gentlemen . . . with introduction by G. Brandes. 'Favourite classics.' Ln: Heinemann . . . 1904. 16°

Two gentlemen . . . edited by H. Morley. 'National library.' Ln: Cassell . . . 1905. 16°, pp. 192   BPL

Two gentlemen . . . with introduction and notes by K. Deighton. Ln: Macmillan . . . 1905. Cr. 8°   BPL

Two gentlemen . . . 'Waistcoat pocket edition.' Ln: Treherne . . . 1905. 32°

Two gentlemen . . . edited by R. Warwick Bond. 'Arden edition.' Ln: Methuen . . . 1906. 8°, pp. 162   BM | BLO | CTC

Two gentlemen . . . edited by W. G. Boswell-Stone. 'Old spelling edition.' Ln: Chatto . . . 1907. Fcp. 4°, pp. xiv.-68   BM | BLO | BPL | CTC | SML

Two gentlemen . . . 'Renaissance edition.' New York: Harrap . . . 1907. Fcp. 4°   BPL

'Two gentlemen of Verona' references—

See Brandt	*See* Meres
,, Bulwer	,, Montemayor
,, Fidele	,, O'Brien
,, Fleay	,, Of education
,, Greene (R.)	,, Sh—Twelfth night,
,, Halliwell	1766
,, Johnson &	,, *Sh*—] Sh—'s library
Steevens	,, Short discourse
,, Latham	

TWO NOBLE KINSMEN.

This play is founded on Chaucer's 'Knight's tale,' and probably was first acted in 1625. It was originally printed in 1634 by Thomas Cotes, successor to Dorothy Jaggard.

Its omission from the Chetwynde folio 1663-64 is as remarkable as the exclusion of 'Pericles' from the Jaggard canon. Its claims to a place in Sh—'s works are stronger than those of most of the seven fresh plays introduced in 1663-64.

The authorship is attributed by the best critics variously to Sh—, Fletcher, Massinger, Beaumont, and Rowley, among others.

It was registered at Stationers' Hall :— '8th April 1634. Master John Waterson. Entred for his copy vnder the hands of Sir Henry Herbert and Master Aspley warden a tragi-comedy called the " Two noble kinsmen, by John Fletcher and William Shakespeare " . . . VId.'

Two Noble Kinsmen: Presented at the Blackfriers by the Kings Maiesties servants with great applause. Written by the memorable Worthies of their time
    Mr. John Fletcher, and ⎱ Gent.
    Mr. William Shakspeare ⎰

['*Heb Ddieu*' device.] Printed at London by Tho. Cotes, for Iohn Waterson: and are to be sold at the signe of the Crowne in Paule's Church-yard, 1634. Fcp. 4°, fifty-one unpaged leaves; sig. A¹ and B¹ to N² in fours (including title and leaf of ' Epilogue')

    BM | BLO | BPL | BUS | CTC | NY | SML

In five acts: in verse.
' If Beaumont, whose name is absent, did not assist Fletcher, it was beyond the reach of anyone else but Sh—.'—*F. G. Fleay.*
' It is now generally allowed to have been partly written by Sh—.'—*F. Locker.*
Lamb, Coleridge, and Spalding considered Sh— responsible for a large portion of the play, and Dyce included it in his edition of the poet.
Hazlitt, Hallam, and others, on the contrary, think Massinger or even Rowley had a hand in it.
A copy measuring 7⅛ by 5½in. brought £50 in Dec., 1906. Earl Howe's copy in half blue morocco realised £62 in Dec., 1907.

[Two noble kinsmen] The rivals. A comedy. Acted by his highnes the Duke of York's servants. Ln : Printed for William Cademan at the Pope's head in the lower walk of the new Exchange, 1668. Fcp. 4°, pp. iv.-56   BUS

An alteration of ' Two noble kinsmen' by Sir W. Davenant, who has retained little of the original. Langbaine says, ' Have heard Mr. Cademan . . . say it was writ by Sir William D'Avenant.'

Two noble kinsmen . . . [In Beaumont & Fletcher's Comedies]. Ln : . . . 1679. F°   BUS

Two noble kinsmen . . . [In Beaumont & Fletcher's Works]. Ln : . . . 1750. 8°   BUS

Two noble kinsmen . . . By Sh— and Fletcher [In ' Modern British drama, edited by Sir W. Scott']. Ln : . . . 1811. Roy. 8°   BM | BPL | BUS

Two noble kinsmen . . . [In Beaumont & Fletcher's Works]. Edinburgh : Ballantyne . . . 1812. 8°   BUS

Two noble kinsmen . . . [In Beaumont & Fletcher's Works]. Ln : . . . 1846. 8°   BUS

Two noble kinsmen . . . [In Beaumont & Fletcher's Works]. Boston [U.S.] . . . 1854. 8°   BUS

Two noble kinsmen . . . [In Beaumont & Fletcher's Works]. Ln : . . . 1866. 8°   BUS

Two noble kinsmen . . . [In Davenant's Dramatic works . . .] Edinburgh . . . 1874. 8°   BUS

Two noble kinsmen. By Sh— and Fletcher. Edited by W. W. Skeat. ' Pitt press series.' Cambridge : University Press . . . 1875. Cr. 8°, pp. xxiv.-160

    BM | BPL | BUS | SML
An expurgated edition, with introduction, notes, and index.

Two noble kinsmen. [Facsimile] Reprint of the quarto, 1634. Edited by Harold Littledale. ' New Sh— Society.' Ln : N. Trübner & Co. . . . 1876. 4°, pp. xiv.-112 (including printed wrappers)

    BM | BPL | SML
With bibliography and list of variations.

Two noble kinsmen, by Mr. John Fletcher and Mr. Wm. Sh—. Edited with notes by W. J. Rolfe. New York : Harper . . . 1883. Cr. 8°   BPL

Two noble kinsmen, by Sh— and Fletcher. With an introduction, and glossarial index of all the words, distinguishing Sh—'s from Fletcher's. By Harold Littledale. ' New Sh— Soc.' Ln : N. Trübner & Co. . . . 1885. 4°   BM | BPL

Two noble kinsmen [In ' Best Elizabethan plays,' edited by . . . Thayer]. Ln : . . . 1890. Cr. 8°   BPL

Two noble kinsmen [' Famous Elizabethan plays,' by H. M. Fitzgibbon]. Ln : . . . 1890. 8°   BM

Two noble kinsmen . . . ' Sh—'s doubtful plays.' Edited with an introduction by A. F. Hopkinson. Ln : [Privately printed by] M. E. Sims & Co. . . . 1894. Cr. 8°, pp. xxxviii.-118   SML

Two noble kinsmen . . . edited with preface, notes, and glossary by C. H. Herford. ' Temple dramatists.' Ln : Dent . . . 1897. 16°, pp. xvi.-148   BM | BPL | SML

Sh— Two noble kinsmen . . .

Two noble kinsmen . . . edited with notes
by H. N. Hudson. ' Windsor edition.'
Edinburgh : Jack . . . 1903. 8°, pp. iv.-
124   SML

' Two noble kinsmen ' references—
See Boyle   *See* Hopkinson
  ,, Chaucer   ,, Spalding
  ,, Hickson

Typographical sketches. *See* Sh— Works :
Ext. 1791

VENUS AND ADONIS.

*Sh—'s first publication. This and his
next effort, 'Lucrece,' are probably the only
compositions which can be said with any
degree of certainty to have gone to press by
his desire, unless, as some think, the
Jaggard canon of 1623 can be added.*

*It was licensed by the Archbishop of
Canterbury and registered at Stationers'
Hall :—' 18th April 1593. Richard Feild.
Entred for his copie vnder thandes of [John
Whitgift] the Archbisshop of Canterbury and
Master warden Stirrop a booke intituled
" Venus and Adonis " . . . VId. Assigned
ouer to Master Harrison senior 25 Jun.
1594.'*

*The original edition appeared immedi-
ately after in that year from the workshop
of Sh—'s friend, Richard Field, a Stratfordian settled in London. It was executed
with such mechanical purity as to leave
little doubt that the poet piloted it through
the press. The presence of the dedication
supports that view.*

Venvs and Adonis.

*Vilia miretur vulgus : mihi flauus Apollo
Pocula Castalia plena ministret aqua.*

[*Printer's ' Anchor' device.*] London Imprinted by Richard Field, and are to be
sold at the sign of the white Greyhound
in Paules Church-yard, 1593. Fcp. 4°,
twenty-eight unpaged leaves ; sig. A¹, A²,
B¹ to H² in fours   BLO

The leaf following title bears the dedication ' to the Rt.
Hon. Henrie Wriothesley Earle of Southampton,'
signed by Sh—.
The selection of the motto from Ovid's ' Amores ' is held
by some to lend colour to Ben Jonson's assertion that
Sh— had ' small latin.'
The quotation has been thus rendered :—
     ' Vulgar people love low things,
     But my cup from purest springs
     Mid the fair Castalian rills,
     Golden-haired Apollo fills.'
The Bodleian copy measures 7⅜ by 5¼ in., and is the
only exemplar known to survive.
Reprinted by Halliwell in 1866, by Griggs in 1886, and
again in 1905.
It is distinguished from the 1594 issue by having no
period after ' London ' in the imprint.

Sh— Venus and Adonis . . .

Venvs and Adonis.

*Vilia miretur vulgus : mihi flauus Apollo
Pocula Castalia plena ministret aqua.*

[*' Anchor' device.*] London : Imprinted
by Richard Field, and are to be sold at
the signe of the white Greyhound in
Paules Church-yard, 1594. Fcp. 4°,
twenty-eight unpaged leaves, viz., title-
page and dedication two leaves, then sig.
B¹ to H² in fours (the last blank)
BM (6 ¹³/₁₆ × 4⁷/8in.) | BLO (6³/₄ × 4³/8 in.) |
                HUTH (7¹/₄ × 4¹³/₁₆ in.)

Collier remarks :—' It is a distinct re-impression ; affords
some various readings and not a few important
confirmations of the correctness of the older text,
corrupted more or less in all subsequent editions.'
Edmonds says :—' Its new readings are always improvements, which seems to show this impression had the
benefit of the author's revision.'
Reprinted in the Ashbee-Halliwell series in 1867.

Venvs and Adonis.

*Vilia miretur vulgus : mihi flauus Apollo
Pocula Castalia plena ministret aqua.*

[*' Anchor' device.*] London : Imprinted
. . . by R. F—— [Richard Field] for Iohn
Harison, 1596. 16°, twenty-eight unpaged leaves (the last blank) ; sig. A¹. to
Diii. in eights
BM (4¹⁴/₁₆ × 2¹⁵/₁₆ in.) | BLO (4¹/₄ × 3 in.)

The British Museum copy bears manuscript notes by
George Daniel and Thomas Rodd, the bookseller.

Venvs and Adonis.

*Vilia miretur vulgus : mihi flauus Apollo
Pocula Castalia plena ministret aqua.*

Imprinted at London [by William Jaggard ?] for William Leake dwelling in
Paules Churchyard at the signe of the
Greyhound, 1599. 8°, on twenty-eight
unpaged leaves   LAMPORT

The sole copy known was providentially discovered in
Sept., 1867, by Charles Edmonds, and was reprinted
in 1870.

Venvs and Adonis.

*Vilia miretur vulgus : mihi flauus Apollo
Pocula Castalia plena ministret aqua.*

London : Printed by I. H—— [John
Harison, jun. ?] for Iohn Harison, 1600.
16°, on twenty-eight unpaged leaves
             BLO (4⁹/₁₆ × 2⁹/₁₀ in.)

The sole example known lacks the printed title, which
is replaced in MS. The date is thought by Halliwell
and Edmonds to be an error, as Harison sold the
copyright to Leake some four years earlier.

Venus and Adonis.

*Vilia miretur vulgus, mihi flauus Apollo
Pocula Castalia plena ministret aqua.*

[*Printer's device with motto, ' I live to dy,
I dy to live.'*] Imprinted at London [by
William Jaggard ?] for William Leake

Sh— Venus and Adonis . . .

dwelling at the Signe of the Holy Ghost in Paule's Church yard, 1602. 16°, twenty-eight unpaged leaves; sig. A¹ to D⁴ in eights (the last blank)
BM (5³/₁₆ × 3²/₁₆ in.)

Venvs and Adonis.

Vilia miretur vulgus : mihi flavus Apollo Pocula Castalia plena ministret aqua.

[*Printer's device, 'I live to dy . . .'*] Imprinted at London [by Wm. Jaggard ?] for William Leake, dwelling at the signe of the Holy Ghost, in Paules Churchyard, 1602. 16°, on twenty-eight unpaged leaves   SHIRBURN CASTLE
Beside little variations in the title, the text differs from preceding entry.

Venvs and Adonis.

Vilia miretur vulgus, mihi flauus Apollo Pocula Castalia plena ministret aqua.

[*Printer's 'Anchora spei' device.*] Imprinted at London [by Iohn Norton ?] for William Leake dwelling at the Signe of the Holy Ghost, in Paules Churchyard, 1602. 8°, on twenty-eight unpaged leaves
BLO (5⁹/₁₆ × 3³/₈ in.)

Venus and Adonis . . . London . . . 1616. 8°
Mentioned by Alex. Dyce, but not elsewhere. Its existence is doubtful.

Venus and Adonis . . . London : Printed for W. B—— [William Barrett]. 1617. 8°, twenty-eight unpaged leaves   BLO
Bohn states this is in the Bodleian, and 'Annals of the Bodleian,' p. 247, duly acknowledges its receipt from Thomas Caldecott in 1833, but no further record of it is traceable.

Venus and Adonis.

Vilia miretur vulgus, mihi flauus Apollo Pocula Castalia plena ministret aqua.

London : Printed for I. P—— [John Parker ?] 1620. 18°, on twenty-eight unpaged leaves; sig. A¹ to C⁸, D¹ to D⁴ (last leaf blank) BLO | CTC (4¹/₂ × 3¹/₄ in.)
Only two copies recorded, and of these the copy purchased by Dr. Bandinel for the Bodleian cannot now be found.

Venus and Adonis.

Uilia miretur vulgus, mihi flavus Apollo Pocula Castalia plena ministret aqua.

Edinbvrgh : Printed by Iohn Wreittoun and are to bee sold in his shop a little beneath the Salt Trone, 1627. 8°, pp. 46 (the last page misprinted 47)
BM (5⁵/₁₆ × 3²/₁₆ in.)
In Beloe's Anecdotes the date is misquoted as 1607.
After a fairly lengthy interval, and the appearance of a score of other popular pieces from the poet's pen, it is curious that the first work of Sh— printed in England should in Scotland also first receive the honour of publication.
Only two copies are known to survive.

Sh— Venus and Adonis . . .
See Catalogue . . . 1864. In his 'Handlist . . . 1859,' Halliwell mentions a unique facsimile in his possession. This was secured by the Earl of Warwick for his famous collection at the castle. *See* Sh— Venus . . . 1859.

Venus and Adonis . . . [London :] Printed by I. H—— [John Harison ?] and are to be sold by Francis Coules, 1630. 8°, on twenty-eight leaves BLO (4⁵/₈ × 3⁵/₁₆ in.)
The Bodleian copy is unfortunately imperfect.

Venus and Adonis, by William Sh—.

Vilia miretur vulgus, mihi flavus Apollo Pocula Castalia plena ministret aqua.

London : Printed [by F. Coules] in the year 1630. 8°, on twenty-eight leaves
BLO (4¹¹/₁₆ × 2⁵/₁₆ in.)

Venvs and Adonis.

Vilia miretur vulgus : mihi flauus Apollo Pocula Castalia plena ministret aqua.

[*Woodcut of a Cupid.*] London : Printed by I. H—— [John Harrison, and are to be sold by Francis Coules in the Old Bailey, without Newgate, 1636. 16°, on twenty-eight unpaged leaves; sig. A to Dⁱᵛ. in eights (the last blank)
BM (4⁵/₁₆ × 3²/₁₆ in.) | BLO

Venus and Adonis . . .

Vilia miretur vulgus, mihi fluvus Apollo Pocula Castalia plena ministret aqua.

[*Woodcut figure of Cupid.*]   London : Printed by Elizabeth Hodgkinsonne for F. Coles, T. Vere, J. Wright, and J. Clark, 1675. 8°
The Nassau copy, bound in green morocco (sold in 1824), passed into the library of T. J. McKee, and was sold in New York in December, 1901.
The copy in the Bodleian catalogue cannot be found, which makes three early editions all lost there.
In his 1905 facsimile, 'Sidney Lee' asserts, with his usual infallibility, that 'the only copy which seems traceable is now in America,' but see next entry, which discloses a copy in Liverpool.

Venus and Adonis.

Vilia miretur vulgus, mihi flavus Apollo Pocula Castalia plena ministret aqua.

[*Woodcut of Cupid.*] London : Printed by Elizabeth Hodgkinson, for F. Coles, T. Vere, J. Wright, and J. Clark, 1675. 16°
(4³/₄ × 3¹/₂ in.)
The imprint varies slightly from the foregoing entry.
The only perfect copy known to the writer is bound in blue morocco, edges gilt on the rough, and is in the library of Mr. E. Gordon Duff.

Venus and Adonis [In ' Poems on affairs of state']. Ln : . . . 1707. 8°   BM

Venus and Adonis. Tarquin and Lucrece. Miscellany poems. With critical remarks, etc. [Edited by S. N—— and issued as a seventh volume supplementary to Rowe's

Sh— Venus and Adonis . . .

edition of Sh—'s Works, 6 vols.]   Ln :
E. Curll & E. Sanger . . . 1710.   8°, pp.
lxxii.-472
                                        BM

Venus and Adonis ; Tarquin and Lucrece,
and Mr. Sh—'s Miscellany poems . . .
Revis'd . . . by Dr. Sewell [Issued as a
seventh volume supplementary to Pope's
six volume edition of Sh—'s Works].
Ln : Printed by J. Darby . . . 1725.   4°
                                        BM

Venus and Adonis ; Tarquin und Lukrezia.
Zwei gedichte von Sh—.   Aus dem Eng-
lischen ubersetzt [von H. C. Albrecht] mit
beigedruktem original.   Halle :   J. J.
Gebauer . . . 1783.   8°, pp. xviii.-306 BM
In English and German.

[Venus and Adonis] 'Lo ! here the gentle
lark' : Words from Sh— ; music by Sir
Henry Rowley Bishop. Ln : . . . [c. 1830].
F°, pp. 8
                                        BUS

Venus and Adonis illustrated by his contemporary, Thomas Heywood.   Edited
by H. Anderson [In Sh— Society's
papers, Vol. iii., pp. 54-57].   Ln : Sh—
Soc., 1847.   8°   BM | BPL | SML

Venus and Adonis. Tarquin und Lukrezia
. . . ueberstezt von J. H. Dambeck.   Mit
gegenübergedrucktem original.   Leipzig :
F. A. Brockhaus . . . 1856.   8°, pp. vi.-
238   BM | SML
In English and German.

[Poems] Venus and Adonis.

Vilia miretur vulgus, mihi flavus Apollo
Pocula Castalia plena ministret aqua.
Edinburgh : John Wreittoun, 1627 [Fac-
simile, executed upon tracing paper, 1859].
8°, pp. 46
                                         W
Unique, being specially executed for J. O. Halliwell in
this manner.

Venus and Adonis . . . Burlesque by F. C.
Burnand.   Ln : T. H. Lacy . . . [1864].
Cr. 8°

Venus and Adonis . . . 1593.   Facsimiled by
E. W. Ashbee.   Edited by J. O. Halliwell.
[Ln.] For private circulation, 1866.   Fcp.
4°   BPL | W
Limited to fifty copies, of which the editor destroyed
nineteen.

Venus and Adonis.   Facsimiled from the
copy printed at London in the year 1594.
By E. W. Ashbee.   Edited by J. O.
Halliwell.   Ln. [Privately printed] 1867.
Fcp. 4°   BM | BPL | MPL | W
One of fifty copies, of which nineteen were destroyed
by the editor.

Venus and Adonis, from the hitherto un-
known edition of 1599 . . . [Edited by
Charles Edmonds].   'Isham reprints.'
Ln : Chiswick Press, 1870.   12°

                          BM | BPL | SML

Sh— Venus and Adonis . . .

Six copies were printed on vellum (in two sizes, 4° & 8°)
and twenty-five copies were executed on large paper,
8°.

Entire issue restricted to 131 copies, numbered and
signed.

Venvs and Adonis . . . wyth ye prynter,
hys dyvers reasons for assignynge unto
hym the authorship, or the re-doynge of
ye 'Chevy Chase' ballad, 'Pancredge,'
by E. and A. Roffe. [Ln : . . . c. 1876.]
8°   BUS

Venus and Adonis, Lucrece, and other
poems . . . edited by W. J. Rolfe.   New
York : Harper . . . 1883.   12°.   Illustrated
                                       BUS

Venus and Adonis.   The first quarto, 1593
. . . A facsimile in photo-lithography . . .
with an introduction by A. Symons.
'Sh— quarto facsimiles.'   Ln : W. Griggs
. . . [1886].   Fcp. 4°, pp. xx.-52
                     BM | BPL | BUS | SML

Venus and Adonis [and the 'Passionate
pilgrim'].   With preface, glossary, etc.
by I. Gollancz.   'Temple edition.'   Ln :
Dent . . . 1896.   16°, pp. xvi.-108
              BM | BLO | BUS | CTC | SML

Venus and Adonis . . . With preface, glossary, etc. . . . by I. Gollancz.   'Temple
edition.'   Ln : Dent, 1897.   16°, pp. xvi.-
108

Venus and Adonis.   'Pocket Falstaff
edition.'   Ln : Bliss, Sands . . . 1898.
16°, pp. 126   BM | BLO | CTC

Venus and Adonis, and The rape of Lucreece
. . . edited with introduction and notes
by C. H. Herford.   'Eversley edition.'
Ln : Macmillan . . . 1900.   Cr. 8°, pp. 52
              BM | BLO | BPL | CTC | SML

Venus and Adonis [In Sh—'s Poems], seen
through the press by T. S. Moore.   Decorated by Charles Ricketts.   'Vale Sh—.'
Ln : Hacon & Ricketts, 1903.   Roy. 8°,
pp. 120   BM | BLO | CTC | SML

Venus and Adonis . . . edited with notes
by H. N. Hudson.   'Windsor edition.'
Edinburgh : Jack . . . 1903.   8°, pp. 124,
and portrait of Edmund Kean by Drum-
mond   BM | BLO | CTC | SML

Venus and Adonis . . . with introduction by
G. Brandes.   'Favourite classics.'   Ln :
Heinemann . . . 1904.   12°

Venus and Adonis . . . [Edited with note by
A. H. Bullen.]   Stratford-on-Avon : Sh—
head press, 1905.   8°, pp. vi.-58   SML
Limited to 510 copies on handmade paper, all numbered.

Venus and Adonis, being a reproduction in
facsimile of the first edition, 1593, from
the unique copy in the Malone collection
in the Bodleian Library.   With intro-

Sh— Venus and Adonis . . .

duction and bibliography by ' Sidney Lee.' Oxford : Clarendon Press . . . 1905. 4°, pp. 76-54 (the latter unpaged)

BM | BLO | BPL | BUS | CTC | SBL | SML

Of the alleged 'bibliography' herein perhaps the less said the better.

Venus and Adonis . . . ' Waistcoat pocket edition.' Ln : Treherne . . . 1905. 32°

'Venus and Adonis' references—

See Anderson	See Irving & Fairholt
,, Barkstead	,, Machin
,, Brathwaite	,, Meres
,, Camus	,, Mirror
,, Clarke	,, Morgan
,, Davies	,, Phillips
,, Durfey	,, Randolph
,, Edmonds	,, Reardon
,, Freeman	,, Sh— Poems
,, Greenwood	,, Sh— Works
,, Hall	,, Sharpe
,, Henderson	,, Watson
,, Heywood	,, Weever
,, Holland	

VORTIGERN.

An imposture which was quickly exposed. The manuscript and printed editions are entered under the name of the fabricator, W. H. Ireland (q.v.)

WILL AND TESTAMENT.

The original document is now preserved in the National Probate Registry, London, and bears the poet's autograph upon each of its three sheets.

Some years since, J. C. Jeaffreson tried to demonstrate in 'The Athenæum' that the above document is in the poet's holograph throughout.   More recently Sir Edwin Durning Lawrence attempted to show that not an atom was written by Sh—, but that the signatures were the work of a law clerk.

[Will] I William Shackspeare of Stratford vpon Avon in the countie of Warr . . . doe make and ordayne this my last will and testament . . . . . Ian | March 1616. Written on three sheets of paper fastened together at the top, and each signed by the testator   SOMERSET HOUSE

The executors were John (son-in-law) and Susanna Hall (Sh -'s eldest daughter). OVERSEERS, Thomas Russell and Francis Collins. WITNESSES, Francis Collins, Julius Shawe, John Robinson, Hamnet Sadler, and Robert Whattcott.
Francis Collins was the solicitor of Warwick who pre-pared the Will.

Sh— Will and testament . . .

[Will] Sh—'s Will. Extracted from the registry of the Archbishop of Canterbury . . . A.D. 1616 [In ' Prolegomena to the dramatick writings of Will. Sh—, part II.'] Ln : John Bell . . . 1787. 12°. With portraits

[Will] Sh—'s Will, faithfully copied from the original in the Prerogative Court of Canterbury : with facsimiles of the three autographs annexed. Ln : T. Rodd . . . 1830. 8°. Suppressed   BM | BPL

[Will] Sh—'s Will, copied from the original in the Prerogative Court of Canterbury, with facsimiles of the three autographs and preliminary observations by J. O. Halliwell. Ln : T. Rodd . . . 1838. 8°, ff. 8   BPL | BUS | CPL

[Will] Sh—'s Will, copied from the original in the Prerogative Court, preserving the interlineations and facsimiles of the three autographs of the poet. With a few pre-liminary observations by J. O. Halliwell. Ln : J. R. Smith, 1851. Fcp. 4°, pp. iv.-ff. 3   BM | BPL | BUS | MPL

Only one hundred copies done.
Originally printed by Rodd in 1830, as the Prerogative court authorities refused to allow the making of a facsimile. Discovering some errors, Rodd suppressed publication. Halliwell secured the sheets and issued copies, with a prefatory list of the mistakes, in 1838.

[Will] Sh—'s Will [photographed from the original document, with a printed tran-script, and facsimiles of the six known autographs of the poet. In the 'Auto-graphic mirror']. Ln : Cassell, Petter & Galpin, 1864. 2 vols. F°   BPL | BUS

[Will] Photographic reproduction of Sh—'s will. Taken by special permission of the Judge of the Court of Probate and Divorce. With descriptive letterpress by J. Hain Friswell. Ln : S. Low . . . 1864. Fcp. 4°, pp. 12 and 3 plates

BM | BPL | BUS | MPL

'The document here presented is not a copy [in the ordinary acceptation of that word], but an absolute reflection of the original document, which contains not only an expression of the last wishes of the poet, but also the three entirely undisputed signatures from his pen which are known to exist. The docu-ment is in itself of inestimable value, and a reproduc-tion so perfect that in it neither the acutest lawyer nor the best microscopist could discover the slightest difference must be also of comparatively great value.'

[Will] Memorials of Sh—. Comprising the poet's will . . . letterpress copy of same and record of the will in the register book . . . With annotations by H. Staunton. Ln : Day & Son . . . [1864]. F°, ff. 19

BPL | BUS | CPL | SML

[Will] Probate copy of the will of Sh—, now first printed from a manuscript copy of it made by the Rev. Joseph Greene of

Sh— Will and testament . . .

Stratford-on-Avon in the year 1747. [Edited by J. O. Halliwell.] Ln : [Privately printed] 1872. 8°, pp. 14
BM | BPL | BUS | HCL | MPL
Issue restricted to fifteen copies.

[Will] Facsimile [and transcript] of Sh—'s will, from the original in the Probate Registry . . . Ln : . . . [c. 1894]. Fcp. 4°
BM

'Will and testament' references—
See Rushton
„ Sh— Poems, 1856
„ Sh— Works, 1795-96, 1903
„ *Sh—*] Sh—'s legal knowledge

WINTER'S TALE.

This tragedy was unprinted until it appeared in the Jaggard canon of 1623. The plot is borrowed from Robert Greene's 'Pandosto' of 1588 (q.v.), afterwards renamed 'Dorastus and Fawnia.' Sh— copied Greene's strange error in placing Bohemia on the seaboard. No separate edition is recorded before Jacob Tonson's of 1714.

[Winter's tale] A dialogue in ' The fairy queen' [with music] by Henry Purcell. [Ln : c. 1690.] F°. Manuscript score, filling five pages of three leaves   w
The original score of a part song introduced into the rustic scene in act IV. of a ' Winter's tale.'

Winter's tale. A comedy. [Ln : Jacob Tonson] Printed in the year MDCCXIV. Cr. 8°, pp. 75-164 (excerpt) and copperplate frontispiece

Winter's tale. By Mr. Wm. Sh—. Ln : Printed for J. Tonson, and the rest of the proprietors, and sold by the booksellers of Ln. and Westminster, 1735. Cr. 8°, pp. 84, and frontispiece by P. Fourdrinier
SML

Winter's tale, by Mr. Wm. Sh—. Ln : Printed by R. Walker at Sh—'s head, 1735. 12°, pp. 92   w

[Winter's tale] Florizel and Perdita, or the sheep shearing. Altered from ' The winter's tale ' [by Macnamara Morgan]. Dublin . . . 1754. 8°
This alteration is founded on the fourth and fifth acts of the original, with little change in the text beyond the addition of a few fresh incidents.

Winter's tale. A play. Alter'd from Sh—. By Charles Marsh. Ln : Printed for Charles Marsh at Cicero's head, 1756. 8°, pp. 92   BM | BUS | w
The changes mainly consist of omitting the first part of the original and altering the last act.

Sh— Winter's tale . . .

Winter's tale. A play. Alter'd from Sh—, by Charles Marsh. Second edition. With a preface giving some account of this alteration.
'Think'st thou the swan of Avon spreads
her wings,
Her brooding wings, for thee alone to plume
And nestle there, O Garrick ? Thou de-
serv'st
Indeed much cherishing : Thy melody
Charms every ear. But sure, it ill beseems
One cygnet thus to stretch its little pinions
Ambitiously intent to fill that nest
Whose roomy limits well may shelter num-
bers.
Ln : Printed for Charles Marsh at Cicero's head, Round Court, Strand, 1756. 8°, pp. vi.-78   BM | BPL | BUS | SML
' The commentators call Homer a divine poet because he describes the manners of mankind in poetry, which they style the language of the gods, like one who seems inspired. Surely the father of the British drama, the great Sh—, may deserve that appellation in as high a degree as the illustrious Greek, since there is not a passion, . . . nor scarce a character, but is depicted in his works.'—*Preface.*

[Winter's tale] Florizel and Perdita . . . Altered from the 'Winter's tale' by D. Garrick. Ln : . . . 1757. 8°

[Winter's tale] Florizel and Perdita. A dramatic pastoral, in three acts. Alter'd from ' The winter's tale ' of Sh—. By David Garrick. As . . . performed . . . at Drury Lane. Ln : J. & R. Tonson . . . 1758. 8°, pp. iv.-66 BM | BUS | CPL | SML
The text is mostly from the original. The first part omitted, as in Marsh's adaptation. Some incidents have been added and others altered.

[Winter's tale] Florizel and Perdita. A dramatic pastoral. Altered from the ' Winter's tale.' By David Garrick. Ln : . . . 1762. 8°

[Winter's tale] The sheep-shearing, or Florizel and Perdita. Taken from Sh— [by M. Morgan]. Songs by Mr. Arne. 1762. 8°   BPL | w

[Winter's tale] The sheep shearing, or Florizel and Perdita. A pastoral comedy [by M. Morgan]. Taken from Sh—. As it is acted at the Theatre-Royal in Dublin. Dublin : P. Wilson . . . 1767. 12°, pp. 28   BM | BUS

Winter's tale . . . As performed at the Theatre Royal, Covent Garden. Regulated from the prompt book, with permission of the managers, by Mr. Younger, prompter. An introduction, and notes critical and illustrative . . . [by F. Gentleman]. Ln : John Bell . . . ; York :

C. Etherington, 1773. 8°, pp. 84. With frontispiece engraved by W. Byrne after E. Edwards

Forms part of Bell's edition of Sh—'s Works, issued separately for playgoers, with list at end (6 pp.) of Bell's publications.

[Winter's tale] The sheep-shearing, or Florizel and Perdita. Taken from Sh—. The songs set by Mr. Arne. Ln : . . . 1771. 12°   BPL

[Winter's tale] The sheep-shearing ; A dramatic pastoral in three acts. [By D. Garrick. Abbreviated by G. Colman, the elder.] Taken from Sh—. As it is performed at the Theatre Royal in the Hay-Market. Ln : G. Kearsley . . . 1777. 8°, pp. 40   BM | BUS

Winter's tale. A tragedy . . . As it is acted at the Theatres-Royal in Drury-Lane and Covent-Garden. Ln : Harrison & Co. & J. Wenman . . . 1779. 8°, pp. 22. With frontispiece portrait of ' Mrs. Mattocks as Hermione '   BM | BPL

[Winter's tale] Florizel and Perdita. A dramatic pastoral [Abridged from Morgan's adaptation entitled ' The sheep shearing ']. Ln : John Bell . . . 1784. 12°   BM

Winter's tale, or Florizel and Perdita. A dramatic pastoral, altered from Sh— by D. Garrick. Ln : Bathurst . . . 1785. 8°   BPL | SML

[Winter's tale] Florizel and Perdita. A dramatic pastoral [In 'Collection of the most esteemed farces']. Edinburgh . . . 1786. 12°   BM | SML

[Winter's tale] Florizel and Perdita, or the sheep-shearing. In two acts [In ' Collection of farces . . . edited by M. Morgan']. Edinburgh . . . 1792. 12°   BUS

Winter's tale . . . As it is acted at Drury Lane and Covent Garden. Ln : Barker . . . 1794. 12°

Winter's tale. A comedy, by Wm. Sh—, accurately printed from the text of Mr. Steevens' last edition. Ln : . . . 1799. 12°   W

Winter's tale . . . As performed at the Theatres Royal, Drury Lane and Covent Garden. Ln : J. Roach . . . 1802. 12°   CPL

Winter's tale . . . With alterations by J. P. Kemble ; now first published as it is acted by their majesties servants of the Theatre Royal, Drury Lane. Ln : C. Lowndes . . . 1802. 8°, pp. 86   BM | BUS | SML

Winter's tale. A play in five acts . . . As performed at the Theatre Royal, Drury Lane. Printed under the authority of the managers from the prompt book. With remarks by Mrs. Inchbald. Ln : Longman . . . [c. 1808]. 12°, pp. 90 and frontispiece   BPL | BUS

Winter's tale . . . adapted to the stage by J. P. Kemble and now first published as it is acted at the Theatre Royal in Covent Garden. Ln : Printed for the theatre, 1811. 8°, pp. 80   SML

W. Creswick's prompt copy, interleaved and annotated, is at Stratford.

Winter's tale . . . As performed at the Theatre Royal, Drury Lane. Printed under the authority of the managers from the prompt book, with remarks by Mrs. Inchbald. Ln : Longman . . . [c. 1811]. 12°, pp. 90 and frontispiece   BUS

Winter's tale. A play . . . adapted to the stage by J. P. Kemble ; and now published as it is performed at the Theatres Royal. Ln : J. Miller . . . 1815. 12°, pp. 84   BM | BPL | BUS | SML | W

Winter's tale . . . With remarks by Mrs. Inchbald. Ln : Hurst, Robinson & Co. [c. 1817]. 12°, pp. 90 and plate   BUS

[Winter's tale] Zapolya . . . by S. T. Coleridge. Ln : . . . 1817. Cr. 8°, pp. viii.-128   BM | W

An imitation of the ' Winter's tale.'

Winter's tale. A play . . . from the text of Johnson and Steevens. With remarks. Ln : T. Hughes [c. 1820]. 16°, pp. 100   BM

Winter's tale . . . With remarks by W. Oxberry. Ln : Simpkin . . . 1821. 12°

Winter's tale . . . With prefatory remarks [signed P. P——] . . . Marked with the stage business and stage directions, as it is performed at the Theatres Royal, by W. Oxberry. Ln : Simpkin . . . 1823. Cr. 8°, pp. x.-88. With portrait of Mrs. Bunn   BM | BPL | SML

Winter's tale . . . ' British theatre.' Ln : Dolby . . . 1823. 12°   BPL

Winter's tale . . . As performed . . . With remarks by D. G—— [Geo. Daniel]. Ln : John Cumberland . . . 1823. 16°

Winter's tale . . . Acting edition. Ln : J. Cumberland, 1827. 12°   SML

A copy with MS. restorations by F. Haywell is at Stratford.

Winter's tale . . . printed from the acting copy, with remarks . . . by D. G—— [Geo. Daniel]. To which are added a . . . cast of the characters and the . . . stage business as it is performed at the Theatres

Sh— Winter's tale . . .

Royal. Embellished with a portrait of ' Mrs. Bunn in Hermione,' engraved on steel by Mr. Woolnoth from an original drawing by Mr. Wageman. Ln : J. Cumberland . . . [c. 1830]. 12°, pp. 72, and plate   BM | BPL | BUS | SML
Haywell's corrected prompt copy is at Stratford.

Winter's tale . . . A tale . . . by C. Lamb [In ' The romancist,' vol. 4, pp. 383-384]. Ln : . . . 1840. 4°   BPL

Winter's tale . . . Nuremberg . . . ; New York . . . 1841. 12°

Winter's tale . . . printed from the acting copy, with remarks, biographical and critical, by D. G—— [G. Daniel]. To which are added . . . the costume, cast . . . entrances, exits, relative positions, and the whole of the stage business as performed at the Theatres Royal, London. Embellished with portrait of Mrs. Bunn in character of Hermione, by Wageman and Woolnoth. Ln : John Cumberland . . . [1850]. 12°, pp. 72 and plate

[Winter's tale] Costumes in the ' Winter's tale ' . . . designed [by Charles Kean]. Ln : Joseph, Myers & Co. [c. 1855]. Oblong f°. Twenty-four large plates in colours, depicting 133 different costumes   BPL

Winter's tale . . . arranged for representation at the Princess's Theatre, with historical and explanatory notes, by Charles Kean. As first performed 28th April, 1856. Ln : J. K. Chapman & Co. [1856]. Cr. 8°, pp. 106   BM | BPL | CPL
Ellen Terry made her début in 1856 in this presentment.

Winter's tale . . . with . . . notes by C. Kean . . . Second edition. Ln : J. K. Chapman [1856]. Cr. 8°, pp. 100   BM | BPL | BUS | SML

[Winter's tale] Perdita or the royal milkmaid, being the legend upon which Sh— is supposed to have founded his 'Winter's tale.' A new and original burlesque, by Wm. Brough. Ln : T. H. Lacy . . . [1856]. 12°, pp. 40   BPL | BUS | CPL

[Winter's tale] Zapolya . . . by S. T. Coleridge. Ln : Moxon . . . 1857. Cr. 8°
First issued in 1817.

Winter's tale . . . With original casts, costumes, and . . . stage business correctly marked and arranged by J. B. Wright. ' Standard drama.' New York : S. French [c. 1857]. 12°, pp. 68   BUS

Winter's tale . . . As performed . . . Spencer's theatre . . . [edited] by J. B. Wright. Boston [U.S.] : Spencer . . . 1859. 12°, pp. 68   BUS

Sh— Winter's tale . . .

[Winter's tale] Dorastus and Fawnia : The foundation story of Sh—'s ' Winter's tale.' Edited by J. O. Halliwell. Ln : Privately printed . . . 1859
Impression restricted to twenty-six copies.

Winter's tale . . . ' Standard drama ; Acting edition.' New York : French . . . [c. 1860]. 12°   BPL

Winter's tale . . . The costumes as represented at the Princess's Theatre. Vienna . . . 1861. Oblong 4°. Twenty-four plates

[Winter's tale] Shakespearian costumes [Four plates, without descriptive letterpress]. Ln : . . . 1861. Oblong 4°   BM

[Winter's tale] Scenes from the ' Winter's tale ' [Selections from the text, illuminated in colours by Owen Jones and A. Warren]. Ln : Day & Smith [1866]. Roy. 4°   BM | CPL | MPL

Winter's tale . . . arranged for representation at the Princess's Theatre, Manchester, by Charles Calvert. Manchester : Heywood . . . [1869]. 12°   BPL | CPL | SML

Winter's tale . . . 'Cumberland's theatre.' Ln : Lacy . . . [c. 1870]. 12°   SML

Winter's tale . . . With notes, critical and explanatory, by John Hunter. Ln : Longman . . . 1872. 12°   BPL | CPL

Winter's tale . . . arranged . . . by C. Calvert. Manchester . . . 1874. 12°

Winter's tale . . . arranged for representation at the Alexandra Theatre [Lime Street], Liverpool, by E. Saker. Liverpool : ' Daily Post,' Cable St., 1876. Cr. 8°, pp. viii.-78   BPL | SML
The first play of Sh— printed in Liverpool. It was, however, preceded by a burlesque or two, and some pieces of criticism.

[Winter's tale] Hamnet Sh—, part V. : The winter's tale, according to the first folio (spelling modernised), with introduction and relative lists by A. P. Paton. Edinburgh : Edmonston & Co. ; Ln : Hamilton, Adams & Co., 1879. 8°, pp. lx.-96   SML

Winter's tale . . . 'Acting edition.' Ln : French . . . [1879]. 12°   SML

Winter's tale . . . A play in five acts [prose and verse] . . . with an illustration, and remarks by D. G—— [Geo. Daniel]. ' Acting edition.' Ln : T. H. Lacy . . . [1879]. 12°, pp. 72   BM

Winter's tale . . . edited with notes by W. J. Rolfe. New York : Harper . . . 1880. 16°, pp. 218. Illustrated   BUS
Editor's copy, with corrections and plate proofs, at Boston.

Winter's tale . . . With introduction and notes . . . by . . . H. N. Hudson. 'Annotated English classics.' Boston [U.S.]: Ginn & Heath . . . 1880. 16°, pp. 196
BM

Winter's tale . . . 'Standard plays.' Ln: John Dicks . . . [1883]. 12° BM | BPL

Winter's tale . . . edited with notes by W. J. Rolfe. New York: Harper . . . 1883. 12° BPL

Winter's tale . . . edited by C. E. Flower. 'Memorial theatre edition.' Stratford-on Avon: Printed by G. Boyden . . . ; Ln: S. French . . . [1885]. Cr. 8°, pp. viii.-100 BPL | SML

Winter's tale . . . With 'Pandosto or the triumph of time, by R. Greene' [Introduction by H. Morley]. 'National library.' Ln: Cassell, 1887. 16°, pp. 192 BM

Winter's tale . . . as performed by Miss Mary Anderson and company at the Lyceum Theatre. Ln: W. S. Johnson . . . 1887. Cr. 8°, pp. 66 BPL | SML

Winter's tale . . . as arranged by Miss Mary Anderson, with illustrations by E. J. Ellis and J. Anderson, and selections from the incidental music. Ln: Field & Tuer [1888]. Oblong 8°, pp. 56 BM | BPL

Winter's tale . . . With introduction and notes by H. N. Hudson. Boston [U.S.] . . . 1888. 12° BPL

Winter's tale . . . With introduction and notes by K. Deighton. . Ln: Macmillan . . . 1889. 12° BM | BLO | BPL | CTC

Winter's tale . . . With 'Pandosto . . .' edited by H. Morley. 'National library.' Ln: Cassell, 1892. 16° pp. 192 BM | BLO | CTC

Winter's tale . . . edited by I. Gollancz. 'Temple edition.' Ln: Dent . . . 1895. 16°, pp. xii.-162. With view of Sh—'s kitchen BM | BLO | CTC | SML

Winter's tale . . . 'Ariel edition.' Ln: Routledge . . . 1895. 16° BM | BLO | CTC

Winter's tale . . . edited with notes by W. J. Rolfe. Ln: Clive . . . [1896]. 16° BPL

Winter's tale . . . 'Pocket Falstaff edition.' Ln: Bliss, Sands . . . 1898. 16°, pp. 124 BM | BLO | CTC | SML

Winter's tale . . . edited by H. H. Furness. 'New variorum edition.' Philadelphia: Lippincott . . . 1898. Roy. 8°, pp. xvi.-432 BM | BPL | BUS | SML
With list of books and materials bearing on the play.

Winter's tale. With introductory notes by J. Dennis. Illustrated by B. Shaw. 'Chiswick edition.' Ln: Bell . . . 1899. 12°, pp. 152 BM | BLO | CTC

Winter's tale . . . edited with introduction and notes by C. H. Herford. 'Eversley edition.' Ln: Macmillan . . . 1900. Cr. 8° BM | BLO | BPL | CTC | SML

Winter's tale . . . edited by Sarah Willard Hiestand. 'Beginner's Sh—.' Boston [U.S.] . . . 1901. 8°. With portrait and plates BPL | BUS

Winter's tale . . . edited with notes by H. N. Hudson. 'Windsor edition.' Edinburgh: Jack . . . 1902. 8°, pp. iv.-132. With portrait of J. P. Kemble BM | BLO | CTC | SML

Winter's tale . . . 'Stage Sh—.' Introduction by Austin Brereton. With illustrations, glossary, etc. Ln: Wm. Collins . . . [c. 1903]. 16°, pp. xvi.-140, and 8 plates BM | BLO | CTC | SML

Winter's tale . . . 'Moffatt's plays . . .' Leeds: E. J. Arnold . . . [c. 1904]. Cr. 8° BPL

Winter's tale . . . 'Ellen Terry edition.' Glasgow: Bryce . . . 1904. 32° BM | BLO | CTC

Winter's tale . . . with introduction by G. Brandes. 'Favourite classics.' Ln: Heinemann . . . 1904. 16° BM | BLO | CTC

Winter's tale . . . with introduction and notes by W. J. Craig. 'Little quartos.' Ln: Methuen . . . 1904. 16° BM | BLO | CTC

Winter's tale . . . with introduction and notes, arranged and classified, by T. Page. Ln: Simpkin . . . 1904. Cr. 8°

Winter's tale . . . edited by H. Morley. 'National library.' Ln: Cassell . . . 1905. 16°, pp. 192 BPL

Winter's tale . . . 'Swan edition.' Ln: Longmans . . . 1905. Cr. 8° BM | BLO | BPL | CTC

Winter's tale . . . revised by A. Dyce. Ln: Sonnenschein . . . [c. 1907]. 8° BPL

Winter's tale . . . 'Lamb Sh—.' Ln: Chatto . . . 1907. 12° BM | BLO | CTC

Winter's tale . . . 'Renaissance edition.' New York: Harrap . . . 1907. Fcp. 4° BM | BLO | BPL | CTC

Winter's tale . . . 'Red letter edition.' Ln: Blackie . . . 1908. 12° BM | BLO | CTC

Winter's tale . . . 'Old spelling edition.' Edited by F. J. Furnivall. Introduction and notes by F. W. Clarke. Ln: Chatto . . . 1908. 8°, pp. xviii.-94 BM | BLO | CTC | SML

Winter's tale . . . 'Elizabethan Sh—.' Ln: Harrap . . . 1909. Cr. 8° BM | BLO | CTC

Sh— Winter's tale . . .

'Winter's tale' references—

See Amadis	See Law
„ Archer	„ Lennox
„ Bowen	„ Lippmann
„ Coleridge	„ Numeration
„ Collection . . .	„ Perdita
„ Dryden	„ Roffe
„ Elze	„ Royal . . .
„ Ferne	„ Sabie
„ Forman	„ Sh— Poems, 1660
„ Green (K. R.)	„ *Sh—*] Sh—'s library
„ Greene (R.)	„ Snider
„ Hardinge	„ Table book
„ Holme	„ Warren
„ Horne	„ Webster
„ Hutchinson	„ Wright (W. A.)
„ Johnson & Steevens	

YORKSHIRE TRAGEDY.

One of the seven ascribed plays, freshly published as Sh—'s productions in the Chetwynde folio of 1663-64. It was registered at Stationers' Hall :—'2nd May 1608. Master Pavyer. Entred for his copie vnder the handes of Master Wilson and Master warden Seton a booke called a " Yorkshire tragedy written by Wylliam Shakespere " . . . VId.'

The first edition was printed in 1608 by R. B—— [Richard Bonian ?] for Thomas Pavier.

[Yorkshire tragedy] A Yorkshire Tragedy. Not so New as Lamentable and True. Acted by his Maiesties Players at the Globe. Written by W. Shakespeare. London : Printed by R. B—— [Richard Bonian ?] for Thomas Pauier, 1608. Fcp. 4°, sixteen unpaged leaves, including title (the last blank) ; sig. A¹ to D⁴ in fours
BM | BLO | DEVON

The subsidiary title on A2 varies from the chief, and runs :—' All's One, or, One of the foure Plaies in one called a York-shire Tragedy : as it was plaid by the King's Maiesties Plaiers.'
This rendering seems to indicate the original playhouse title for the drama.
For an account of the tragedy, see Whitaker's ' Loidis and Elmete.'

[Yorkshire tragedy] A Yorkshire tragedie. Not so New, as Lamentable and True. Written by W. Shakespeare. ['*Heb Ddieu*' device.] Printed [at Ln. by Isaac Jaggard ?] for T. P—— [Thomas Pavier] 1619. Fcp. 4°, sixteen unpaged leaves (including unsigned title) ; sig. A¹ to D⁴ in fours   BM | BLO | CTC | DEVON | NY | W

The head-title runs :—' All's One, or, One of the four Plaies in one, called a Yorkshire Tragedy. As it was plaid by the King's Maiesties Players.'

Sh— Yorkshire tragedy . . .

This issue forms one of the set of nine ' suspects.' For fuller information, see A. W. Pollard's 'Sh— folios and quartos.'
A copy measuring 7 by 5¼ in. sold for £125 in May, 1906. Earl Howe's copy, 7 by 5¼ in., half blue morocco, realised £71 in Dec., 1907.

Yorkshire tragedy, by Mr. Wm. Sh—. Ln : Printed for J. Tonson and the rest of the proprietors, and sold by the booksellers of Ln. and Westminster, 1735. 12°, pp. 22, and copperplate frontispiece
BM | BPL | SML

The Stratford copy was presented, with inscription, by J. O. Halliwell.

Yorkshire tragedy . . . Ln : R. Walker . . . 1735. Cr. 8°   CPL

Yorkshire tragedy [In 'Ancient British drama, edited by Sir W. Scott ']. Ln : . . . 1810. Roy. 8°   BM | BUS

Yorkshire tragedy [A review in the ' Retrospective Review,' vol. 9]. Ln : . . . 1824. 8°   BM | BLO | BUS | CTC

Yorkshire tragedy . . . ' Sh—'s doubtful plays.' Edited with an introduction by A. F. Hopkinson. Ln : [Privately printed by] M. E. Sims & Co. . . . 1891. Cr. 8°, pp. xx.-30   SML

' Yorkshire tragedy ' references—

See Calverley
„ Hopkinson
„ Ingram
„ Sh— [Works] Sh— apocrypha, 1908
„ Whitaker
„ Wilkins

NOTE.—Collective editions of Sh—'s writings now follow, in chronological order, with a reference key to commentaries and criticism thereon.—W. J.

WORKS.

The first edition of Sh—'s collected works appeared posthumously in Nov. 1623, nearly eight years after his death, and three months after his widow's decease. It came from the press of its probable editor, William Jaggard, whose death on the eve of publication brought his son Isaac's name upon the title-page in place of his own. The volume is of transcendent importance. Not merely is it the editio princeps of England's greatest genius. Among the thirty-six masterpieces presented, no fewer than twenty appeared in print here for the first time. From a literary standpoint it is the most priceless contribution, beyond all bounds and limits, to the whole world's secular literature, and to those giant forces which promote the welfare of humanity.

*It was registered at Stationers' Hall :—
'8th Nov. 1623. Mr. Blount : Isaak
Jaggard. Entred for their copie under the
hands of Master Doctor Worrall and Master
Cole wardens, Mr. William Shakspeer's
Comedyes, Histories, and Tragedyes, soe
manie of the said copyes as are not formerly
entred to other men, vizt. Comedyes : The
tempest, The two gentlemen of Verona,
Measure for measure, The comedy of errors,
As you like it, All's well that ends well,
Twelft night, The winter's tale. Histories :
The thirde parte of Henry the sixt, Henry
the eight. Tragedies : Coriolanus, Timon
of Athens, Julius Cæsar, Mackbeth, Anthonie and Cleopatra, Cymbeline.'*

*The premature death of Isaac Jaggard in
1627 caused this fresh entry in the registers :
—'1627 [June]. Thomas Cotes. Richard
Cotes. Assigned ouer vnto him [them] by
Dorathye Jaggard and consent of a full
court holden this day, all the estate, right,
title, and interest which Isaacke Jaggard her
late husband had in the copies following . . .
her parte in Shacksphere's plays . . . 11/6.'*

*Horne Tooke remarked :—'The first
edition is the only one in my opinion worth
regarding . . . By the presumptuous licence
of dwarfish commentators, who are for ever
cutting him down to their own size, we risk
the loss of Sh—'s genuine text which that
folio assuredly contains.'*

*Between 1623 and 1709 only five
editions of Sh—'s collective works appeared,
but between the latter year and 1910 about
twelve hundred different editions (in English) emerged from the press.*

[Works] Mr. William Shakespeares Comedies, Histories, & Tragedies [Collected by
John Heminge and Henry Condell.
Edited by William Jaggard ?] Published
according to the True Originall Copies.
[*Copperplate portrait signed*] *Martin Droeshout, sculpsit, London.* London : Printed
by [William and] Isaac Iaggard [in Barbican and published by the latter] and
Ed. Blount [in November] 1623. [*Colophon*] Printed at the Charges of W. Jaggard, Ed. Blount, I. Smithweeke, and
W. Aspley, 1623. F° [about 13 × 8in.],
pp. xviii.-304-232-xxx.-(unpaged)-400
BM | BLO | BPL | BUS | CTC | MRL | NY | SBL
SML | W
Collation : Nine unpaged leaves, consisting of :—1, leaf
bearing verses 'To the Reader' [signed] 'B. I.' [Ben
Jonson] ; 2, Title ; 3, [Dedication to] 'William Earle
of Pembroke and Philip Earle of Montgomery,'
signed by Iohn Heminge and Henry Condell ; 4,
[Preface by John Heminge and Henry Condell] 'To

the great variety of Readers' ; 5, 'To the Memorie of
. . . W. Shakespeare' [signed L. Digges] ; 6, Names
of the Principall Actors ; 7, 'To the Memory of my
beloued . . . by Ben Ionson' ; 8, 'Vpon . . . the
Famous Scenicke Poet . . . by Hvgh Holland' ; 9,
Catalogve of the seuerall Comedies, Histories and
Tragedies contained in this Volume.'
Then ensues the text, paged in three parts, with numerous irregularities in the pagination and signatures.
A full list of press errors of the first four folio editions
may be found in the B.M. Sh—Catalogue, 1897 (*q.v.*)
For highly detailed collations see Allibone, American
Bibliopolist 1870, Lowndes and Winsor's Bibliography. For an account of the original Bodleian
copy (in which the order of the prefatory matter
varies), see Madan. For a census of existing copies
(which by no means includes all the known copies),
see the folio pamphlet attached to the Oxford facsimile, under Sh— Works, 1902.
A copy varying from others is in the B.M., with a title
bearing the word 'and' in place of the usual contrac-
tion '&.'
The two copies dated 1622, mentioned by Lowndes,
have had the final figure mended or tampered with.
This edition was produced in Barbican (and not in Fleet
Street, as so often asserted by 'Sidney Lee.') William
Jaggard left Fleet Street for Barbican about twenty
years before this book appeared. But (as Mr. Pollard
remarks on p. 117 of his 'Sh— folios and quartos')
'As usual, Mr. Lee offers a . . . confident account of
everything.'
The published price was twenty shillings. This information is kindly supplied by Mr. R. C. Jackson
(originator of the idea of the Bankside national
memorial to Sh— at Southwark). He discovered it
at Dulwich, on a letter from Wm. Cartwright to
Edward Alleyn, founder of the College. Cartwright
was an intimate friend and guest of Alleyn's from
1617 onwards. The memorandum runs :—
'Paid a sover-in for Shaksper's booke of Plaies.'
The letter is dated 30th Nov., 1623, the very week of
publication.
A curious early allusion is found in Wm. Prynne's
Histrio-mastix, 1633 (*q.v.*), which runs :—'Some
play-books are grown from quartos into folios ; Ben
Jonson, Sh— and others . . . Sh—'s plays are
printed in [on] the best crowne paper, far better than
most Bibles. Above forty thousand play-books have
been printed and vented within these two years.'
Dr. Furness remarks :—'Practically the text of the
first four editions is the same.'
'This edition is greatly prized by amateurs, as it contains the only portrait which requires no evidence to
support its authenticity.'—*Anniversary Calendar*
1832, p. 737.
The folio was reprinted more or less accurately in
1767-68, 1807, 1808, 1862-64, 1866, 1876, 1887, 1888-89,
1902, and 1910, under which years full details will be
found.
For an index to the characters in the 1623 edition, see
Smith (A. R.)
For criticism, and a history of the venture, see Greg
(W. W.) ; Morgan (J. A.) ; Pollard (A. W.) : *Sh.*]
Sh— bibliography ; and Wright (C.) ; in addition to
the lengthy list of critics following the entries of
Sh—'s works.
The Warwick copy, measuring 13¼ by 8½in., and
bound by Bedford in scarlet morocco, gold tooled,
leaves gilt, and enclosed in an olive green morocco
slip case, is perfect from beginning to end, and the
condition unusually crisp and fine.
The Rylands copy was used by Theobald, from whom
it passed in 1744 to Martin Folkes the antiquary (who
assisted Theobald to edit Sh—). In 1756 George
Steevens secured it for 63s., and about 1790 it passed
into Earl Spencer's library, now happily and perma-
nently housed at Manchester.

Sh— Works . . .

The first edition probably consisted of 500 copies, of which about 250 survive, but fewer than twenty are perfect. The Van Antwerp copy, in March, 1907, realised £3,600. Earl Howe's copy, 13 by 8¼ in., bound in contemporary calf, brought £2,025 in Dec., 1907. One sold in July, 1910, for £2,000, and another which had been repaired was disposed of in the same month for £1,800.

[Works] Mr. William Shakespeares Comedies, Histories and Tragedies. Published according to the true Originall Copies. The second Impression. [*Droeshout portrait on copper*.] London : Printed by Tho. Cotes, for Robert Allot, and are to be sold at the signe of the Blacke Beare in Pauls Church-yard, 1632. [*Colophon*] Printed at London by Thomas Cotes for John Smethwick, William Aspley, Richard Hawkins, Richard Meighen and Robert Allot, 1632. F°, pp. xx. (un-numbered)-304-232-420

BM | BPL | BUS | CTC | LEAMINGTON PL | MRL | NY | SML | W

Collation : 1, 'To the Reader. This Figure . . .' (signed) B.I.; 2, [Title, bearing Droeshout portrait]; 3, [Dedication] 'To the most Noble and Incomparable Paire' (signed) John Heminge, Henry Condell; 4, 'To the great variety of Readers' [signed] Iohn Heminge, Henrie Condell; 5, 'Upon the Effigies . . .' (and) 'An Epitaph . . .' [by John Milton]; 6, 'To the memorie of the deceased' (signed) L. Digges, (and) 'To the Memory . . .' (signed) I. M.; 7, 'The Workes . . .' 'Names of the Principall Actors . . .'; 8, 'To the memory of my beloved . . .' (signed) Ben Ionson; 9, 'On Worthy Master Shakespeare . . .' (signed) I.M.S.; 10, 'Upon the Lines and Life . . .' (signed) Hugh Holland; 'Catalogue of all the Comedies, Histories & Tragedies . . .'
Text (numbered in three sections) pp. 1-304 (the last one blank), 1-232, 1-420 (the last one blank).
The text follows the first edition, with some corrections. For a list of signatures and irregularities, see 'B. M. Sh— catalogue 1897.'
Lowndes says :—' There were several proprietors of this edition [*i.e.*, sharing the cost and profits], and each one seems to have had a title printed with his own name, so that some bear the name of Robert Allot, others William Aspley, Richard Hawkins, Richard Meighen, or John Smethwick.' Six variations of this kind are in the Lenox Library at New York. Lowndes avers a copy is in existence dated 1631, but gives no particulars. It might be a trial proof of 1631 or a misprint. No other record exists of a copy so dated.
The leaf of Ben Jonson's lines opposite title differs from the first issue in that the letter ' v ' takes the place of ' u ' in ' Grauer,' and capital letters replace the lower case ones in the words ' With, Wit, Brasse, Face.'
For variations between the first and second editions, see Capell's Shakespeareana, c. 1760, 6 vols.
At Warwick Castle are three copies in all of this folio. The first and finest measures 13⅜ by 9in., bound by Bedford in scarlet morocco, gold tooled, with leaves gilt. The second example bears many manuscript emendations in an old hand on the margins, and came from the library of S. W. Singer (*q.v.*) It is bound in calf, measures 13 by 8½ in., lacks a leaf (pp. 149-150) in the first pagination, and lacks pp. 401-412 in the last part. The third copy is complete, bound in russia, and measures 12½ by 8¾ in.
A copy bearing the Wm. Aspley imprint (rarest of the variations), originally in the Lucy library at Charlecote, was sold for £210 in March, 1907. It was

disposed of many years previously in the sale at Hampton Lucy Rectory, upon the death of its former owner the Rev. John Lucy.
The second edition was reprinted in 1909.

Works . . . Ln : Printed for J. Tonson . . . 1635. 9 vols. Cr. 8°
The date is a compositor's error for 1735, under which year this edition will be found.

[Works] Mr. William Shakespear's Comedies, Histories and Tragedies. Published according to the true Original Copies. The Third Impression. [*Droeshout portrait*.] London : Printed for Philip Chetwinde, 1663. F°, pp. xx.-ii.-878 (the last blank)   BM | BPL | BUS | NY

The preliminary leaf of verses is signed ' B. J.' (instead of ' B. I.' as in the two earlier editions), and the words ' drawne, out-doo, looke, booke,' now appear as ' drawn, out-doe, look, book.' The prefatory leaves are set in a larger fount than before. This is the first edition to exhibit the final ' E ' clipped from the poet's name, an ugly fashion which lasted until the dawn of the nineteenth century.
' Copies with this date,' says Lowndes, ' do not contain the seven spurious plays, and in some a space is left in the title-page for the portrait, but in a few copies the portrait is engraved [*i.e.* printed] on the title-page, and the verses by Ben Jonson in large type appear on a leaf opposite.'
Lowndes is hardly accurate. A few copies were issued with the ascribed plays.
The excessive rarity of the 1663 and 1664 issues is due to destruction of almost the entire impressions in the great London fire of 1666, as they lay unsold in the printer's warehouse. In point of rarity they are much scarcer than the first edition.
An example dated 1663 (possessing the seven attributed plays) sold in May, 1907 for £1,550. Earl Howe's copy, in contemporary calf, some edges rough, 13½ by 8½ in., realised £525 in Dec., 1907.

[Works] Mr. William Shakespear's Comedies Histories and Tragedies. Published according to the true Original Copies. The third Impression. And unto this Impression is added seven Playes, never before Printed in Folio. Viz. Pericles Prince of Tyre, The London Prodigall, The History of Thomas Ld Cromwell, Sir John Oldcastle Lord Cobham, The Puritan Widow, A York-shire Tragedy, The Tragedy of Locrine. [*Printer's intrascutal crest :* Two serpents coiled round the circular motto '*Spera tendo ad ardua per*,' enclosing a spread eagle ; with the leaf opposite bearing the Droeshout portrait and verses by Ben Ionson.] London : Printed by P. C—— [Philip Chetwynde] 1664. F°, pp. xx. (un-numbered)-878-20-100

BM | BPL | BUS | CTC | MRL | NY | SML | W

Collation : 1, 'To the Reader' [bearing Droeshout portrait as in 1623]; 2, Title; 3, Dedication 'To the Earle of Pembroke . . .' (signed) John Heminge & Henry Condell ; 4, [Preface] 'To the great Variety of Readers' (signed) Iohn Heminge & Henry Condell ; 5, ' To the Memory of the deceased Authour ' (signed)

L. Digges, 'Upon the Effigies . . .' (and) 'To the Memory . . .' (signed) I. M. ; 6, 'To the Memory of my beloved the Authour' [signed] Ben Johnson ; 7 & 8, 'On Worthy Mr. Shakespeare and his Poems' [signed] J. M. S. ; 9, 'Epitaph' [by John Milton, unsigned, and] 'Upon the . . . Famous Scenick Poet' (signed) Hugh Holland ; 10, 'The Works . . .' 'Names of the principal Actors . . .' (and) 'Catalogue of all the Comedies, Histories, and Tragedies.'

Text, pp. 1-877, 1-20, 1-100.

For index of the irregularities in the pagination and list of signatures, see 'B.M. Sh— Catalogue, 1897.'

The Warwick Collection includes two copies. The finest, bound by Bedford in scarlet morocco, gold tooled, gilt leaves, measures 13½ by 8⅝in., and is in perfect order. The second is minus the leaf of verses facing title, but has two extraneous leaves added (the 1663 leaf of verses and the title-page to that issue). In March, 1907, a copy realised £650.

[Works] Mr. William Shakespear's Comedies, Histories, and Tragedies. Published according to the true Original Copies. Unto which is added, Seven Plays, Never before Printed in Folio : viz.

Pericles, Prince of Tyre
The London Prodigal
The History of Thomas Lord Cromwel
Sir John Oldcastle Lord Cobham
The Puritan Widow
A Yorkshire Tragedy
The Tragedy of Locrine

The Fourth Edition. [In three parts. *Printer's 'fleur de lis' crest.*] London : Printed for H. Herringman, E. Brewster, and R. Bentley at the Anchor in the New Exchange, the Crane in St. Pauls Church-Yard, and in Russel-Street, Covent Garden, 1685. F°

BM | BPL | BUS | CTC | MRL | NY | SML | W

Collation: 1, 'To the Reader . . .' (signed) B. J. [This leaf bears the Droeshout portrait, which has been retouched, cross lines appearing for the first time on the shading of the forehead and on the hair]; 2, [Title, now set for the first time within rules]; 3, [Dedication] 'To the most Noble and Incomparable pair . . .' (signed) John Heminge, Henry Condell ; 4, 'To the Great Variety of Readers' (signed) J. Heminge, H. Condell ; 'To the Memory . . .' (etc.) ; 5, 'On Worthy Mr. Shakespear' (signed) J. M. S. ; 'An Epitaph' (by John Milton, unsigned); 'Upon the Lines and Life . . .' (signed) Hugh Holland ; 6, 'The Works . . .' 'Names of the principal Actors . . .' 'A Catalogue of all [*sic*] the Comedies, Histories, and Tragedies' [The publisher omits all mention in this list of the seven attributed Plays]. [Text, in three sections] pp. 1-272 [then an unpaged leaf bearing the] 'Names of the Actors' [characters], pp. 1-328, pp. 1-304 (the last one blank).

The type throughout is in a larger fount than the three earlier editions, and more liberally spaced. It was executed on Dutch paper, some of the title-pages exhibiting a watermark with the maker's name, Van Duvantegard.

The imprint varies. One as follows sold for £215 in Dec., 1903, '. . . and are to be sold by Joseph Knight and Francis Saunders at the Anchor in the Lower Walk of the New Exchange 1685.'

The pagination errors of this variation differ from the ordinary copies, likewise the ornament above the imprint, indicating that the title-page was re-set. A copy of this variation is at Boston.

For a list of errors peculiar to the fourth edition, see the 'B. M. Sh— Catalogue 1897.'

Of the two copies at Warwick, the first, in faultless order, measures 14¼ by 9¾in., and is bound by Bedford in scarlet morocco, gold tooled, leaves gilt. The second copy exhibits minor variations, some of the errors in the first issue being corrected. It measures 14½ by 9in., and is bound in gold tooled russia. The writer's copy measures 14¼ by 9⅜in., and is partially rough-edged as issued.

Earl Howe's copy in contemporary calf, 14¼ by 9in., sold in Dec., 1907 for £82.

Works of Mr. Wm. Sh— in six volumes. Adorn'd with cuts. Revis'd and corrected, with an account of the life and writings of the author by N. Rowe, Esq. Ln : Printed for Jacob Tonson within Gray's Inn Gate near Gray's Inn Lane, 1709. 6 vols. 8°, pp. 3,324. With a frontispiece portrait, engraved on copper, by Van der Gucht, together with a separate letterpress title and a copper-plate scene to every play

BM | BPL | BUS | CTC | NY | SML | W

In importance and interest, this edition ranks second perhaps to the editio princeps. It is the first manual text, the first to present a biography of the poet, the first to bear an editor's name, the first to possess illustrations, and the first of the endless army of editions in octavo. The text is copied from the fourth folio of 1685, and a companion (or seventh) volume was issued by another firm containing the 'Poems.' See next entry.

Rowe commissioned Thomas Betterton, the actor, to glean for him in and around Stratford particulars of Sh—'s life. At that period it was rather late in the day, but still possible to get a few authentic details. The attributed plays are found also in this version, and the plates are of no small value because of their contemporary costume. In this issue will also be found the earliest effort to trace parallels between Sh— and other classics.

A few sets were printed on large paper (in roy. 8°), one of which is at Birmingham.

[Works : Poems] Volume the seventh. Containing Venus and Adonis, Tarquin and Lucreece, and his miscellany poems. With critical remarks on his plays, &c., to which is prefix'd, an essay on the art, rise and progress of the stage in Greece, Rome and England [by Charles Gildon. Edited by S. N——]. Ln : E. Curll and E. Sanger, 1710. 8°, pp. lxxii.-472

BM | BPL | BUS | CPL | NY

Issued as a supplementary volume to Rowe's 1709 edition of the Works.

A few copies were struck off on large paper, one of which is at Birmingham.

John Philip Kemble's copy, extra-illustrated, is in the Cambridge Public Library.

Stated in 'Notes & Queries, II. s., vol. xii., p. 349,' to be a 'piratical production of Edmund Curll.'

Works of Mr. Wm. Sh— . . . [*Oval woodcut portrait of the poet.*] Ln : Printed for Jacob Tonson in the Strand, 1714. 9 vols. 12°. With portrait, and a separate copperplate illustration preceding each play

32

Sh— Works . . .

The ninth volume contains the 'Poems . . . Essay on the art . . . of the stage, and Remarks on the plays of Sh—.' Each of the sonnets and poems is given a subject heading. The volume bears an imprint, differing from the preceding eight, as follows:—
'Ln : Printed for J. Darby in Bartholomew Close, for E. Curll, K. Sanger, and J. Pemberton. Sold by J. Tonson in the Strand ; J. Knapton ; and D. Midwinter in St. Paul's Churchyard ; A. Betsworth on London Bridg ; W. Taylor in Paternoster Row ; N. Cliff and D. Jackson near the Poultry ; T. Varnam and J. Osborn in Lombard Street ; and J. Browne near Temple Bar MDCCXIV.'
It is illustrated with two copperplates engraved by Van der Gucht.

This edition of Sh—'s Works was sold also as separate plays, with the anonymous legend at foot of each title, 'Printed in the year MDCCXIV.' The first stage edition, being produced for sale at the theatres, and for disposal to pedlars who distributed the plays in rural districts.

Works of Mr. Wm. Sh— in nine volumes : with his life, by N. Rowe, Esq. Adorn'd with cuts. To the last volume is prefix'd, I. An essay on the art, rise, and progress of the stage in Greece, Rome, and England [by C. Gildon] ; II. Observations upon the most sublime passages in this author [by C. Gildon] ; III. A glossary, explaining the antiquated words made use of throughout his works. Ln : Printed for J. Tonson, E. Curll, J. Pemberton, and K. Sanger, 1714. 9 vols. 12°. With frontispiece - portrait and copperplates   BM | BPL | SML
The ninth volume embraces the 'Poems, essay on the stage, and remarks on the plays,' and is fully entered under Sh— Poems, 1714 (q.v.) It is identical with the ninth tome in the preceding entry.

Works . . . In six volumes. Collated and corrected by the former editions by Mr. Pope [with 'Some account of the life, &c. of Mr. Wm. Sh—. Written by Mr. Rowe']. Ln : Printed for Jacob Tonson in the Strand, 1723-25. 6 vols. 4°. With portraits
    BM | BPL | BUS | CTC | MPL | NY | SML | W
Seven hundred and fifty sets were printed for sale at £6 6s. each.
The first edition in quarto, and the earliest edited by Alexander Pope. It embraces Pope's preface, the life by Rowe, an index of characters, sentiments, speeches, and descriptions, and a list of subscribers, in addition to the matter set forth on title. Of the two portraits engraved by G. Vertue, one is said by Boaden to represent King James in a large ruff, and the other, supposed to be the Stratford bust, is unlike it, inasmuch as it gives the poet a profusion of hair.
Volume one is dated 1725 ; the other five 1723.
'Pope (says Lowndes) is said to have been deficient in the industry of collation, and indulged too much in fanciful alterations. His edition did not satisfy the great expectations raised of it, and Theobald, who followed him, with less ability but more industry, was justly preferred, although he too has ventured upon many innovations.'
In the preface Pope says :—' If ever any author deserved the name of an original it was Sh—. Homer himself drew not his art so immediately from the fountains of

Sh— Works . . .

nature ; it proceeded through Egyptian strainers and channels and came to him not without some tincture of the learning or some cast of the models of those before him. The poetry of Sh— was inspiration indeed : he is not so much an imitator as an instrument of nature, and it is not so just to say that he speaks from her as that she speaks through him . . . Every single character in Sh— is as much an individual as those in life itself. The power over our passions was never possessed in a more eminent degree or displayed in so many instances. Yet all along there is seen no labour, no pains to raise them, no preparation to guide our guess to the effect or be perceived to lead towards it, but the heart swells and the tears burst out just at the proper places. . . . Nor does he only excel in the passions : in the coolness of reflection and reasoning he is full as admirable. . . . This is perfectly amazing from a man of no education or experience in those great and public scenes of life which are usually the subject of his thoughts. So that he seems to have known the world by intuition, to have looked through human nature at one glance and to be the only author that gives ground for a very new opinion – that the philosopher and even the man of the world may be born as well as the poet. . . .'

[Works : Poems] The seventh volume. Containing Venus and Adonis, Tarquin and Lucreece, and Mr. Sh—'s miscellany poems. To which is prefix'd, an essay on the art, rise, and progress of the stage, in Greece, Rome, and England [by C. Gildon]. And a glossary of the old words used in these works. The whole revis'd and corrected, with a preface by Dr. Sewell. Ln : Printed by J. Darby for A. Bettesworth, F. Fayram, W. Mears, J. Pemberton, J. Hooke, C. Rivington, F. Clay, J. Batley, E. Symon, 1725. 4°
    BM | BPL | BUS | W
Issued as a supplementary volume to Pope's first edition of Sh—'s Works 1723-25.

Works of Sh—. Collated and corrected by the former editions, by Mr. Pope [Vol. VIII. revised by Dr. Sewell]. Dublin : G. Grierson . . . 1725-26. 8 vols. 8° BM | BPL
The first edition of Sh—'s works published in Ireland. and, almost needless to add, a piracy.
Although dated 1725-26, no sets were issued until the latter year. It appears to have met with poor encouragement, only 162 subscribers offering the needful support.

Works of Sh—. Collated and corrected . . . by Mr. Pope. Ln : J. & J. Knapton . . . 1728. 10 vols. 12°. With plates
    BM | BPL | SML
The tenth volume includes the 'Poems.'

Works of Sh—. Collated and corrected . . . by Mr. Pope [An excerpt of pp. 1-109 from vol. 7, embodying 'Antony and Cleopatra,' and containing copious manuscript notes and additions by L. Theobald]. Ln : J. & J. Knapton . . . 1728. 12°   BM

Works of Mr. Wm. Sh—. In eight volumes. Collated and corrected by the former editions by Mr. Pope. Second edition.

Ln : Printed for J. Tonson in the Strand ; and for J. Darby, A. Bettesworth, and F. Clay in trust for Richard, James, and Bethel Wellington, 1728. 9 vols. 12°. With plates engraved on copper BM | SML

This second edition of Pope is said to contain additional notes and corrections.

The ninth volume, issued as a supplement, embraces ' Pericles ' and the attributed plays, and (at end) a catalogue of publications, pp. vi.

According to Boaden, King James is really represented in the " portrait of Sh—."

The British Museum set formed part of Horace Walpole's library and bears MS. notes in his autograph.

A tenth volume was issued afterwards containing the Poems.

Works . . . volume the ninth [Pericles, London prodigal, Thomas Lord Cromwell, Sir John Oldcastle, The puritan, Yorkshire tragedy, Locrine]. Ln : J. Tonson in the Strand, & for J. Darby, A. Bettesworth and F. Clay, in trust for Richard, James and Bethel Wellington . . . 1728. 12° With plates [copied from Rowe's 1709 ed.] BM | BUS | SML

[Works] Plays . . . With a glossary [Edited by Alex. Pope.] Ln : J. & P. Knapton . . . 1731. 9 vols. Cr. 8°. With portrait

Works . . . In seven volumes. Collated with the oldest copies and corrected. With notes explanatory and critical by Mr. Theobald [and Martin Folkes]. Ln : Printed for A. Bettesworth and C. Hitch, J. Tonson, F. Clay, W. Feales, and R. Wellington, 1733. 7 vols. 8° BM | BLO | BPL | BUS | CTC | SML

The first edition edited by Lewis Theobald.

' An edition of considerable merit, notwithstanding the abuse of it by Pope and Warburton.'—Lowndes.

The plates are accepted, together with those in Rowe's 1709 edition, as the earliest authentic pictures of the contemporary dress of the characters.

Seventy-five sets were done in royal 8° on large paper, 9½ by 5½in.

A list of subscribers is prefixed.

Theobald is stated to have aroused enmity by his outspoken criticism of Pope's edition, earning thereby for himself principal part in Pope's ' Dunciad.'

Works of Sh— [edited by Alex. Pope]. In eight volumes. [With some account of the life . . . by Rowe.] Ln : Printed for J. Tonson and the rest of the proprietors, 1734-36. 8 vols. 12°. With copperplates BM | BPL | SML

The second stage edition, being produced for sale at the theatres and for supplying pedlars.

Each play has a separate title-page and pagination.

The British Museum and Stratford Memorial possess sets dated in error 1635.

Considerable friction existed between the rival publishers of Sh—, Jacob Tonson and R. Walker. Appended to Tonson's edition of the separate plays of this period was the following notice :—

ADVERTISEMENT.— Jacob Tonson and the other proprietors of Sh—'s plays, designing to finish their edition now publishing with all speed, give notice, that

with the last play they will deliver gratis general titles to each volume of the whole work so that each play may be bound in its proper place. And also do give further notice, that any play of Sh—'s that now is or hereafter shall be out of print will be reprinted without delay. So that all gentlemen who have bought these plays shall not be disappointed, but may depend on having their sets compleated.

N.B.—Whereas one R. Walker has proposed to pirate all Sh—'s plays but through ignorance of what plays are Sh—'s did in several advertisements propose to print ŒDIPUS KING OF THEBES,' as one of Sh—'s plays, and has since printed Tate's 'King Lear' instead of Sh—'s, and in that and ' Hamlet ' has omitted almost one half of the genuine editions printed by Tonson and proprietors, the world will therefore judge how likely they [sic] are to have a compleat collection of Sh—'s plays from the said R. Walker.

A ninth volume containing the attributed plays was issued.

[Works] Dramatick works of Wm. Sh—. Ln : R. Walker . . . 1734-35. 7 vols. 12° BM | BPL

Works . . . Ln : Printed for J. Tonson and the rest of the proprietors, 1635 [sic pro 1735]. 9 vols. Cr. 8°. With portrait, and frontispiece to each play BM | SML

The ninth vol. contains the attributed plays.

Works of Sh— : Collated with the oldest copies and corrected. With notes by Mr. Theobald. The second edition. Ln : H. Lintott, C. Hitch, J. & R. Tonson, C. Corbet, R. & B. Wellington, J. Brindley, and E. New, 1740. 12 vols. 12°. With Chandos portrait by Van der Gucht and copperplates by Gravelot BM | BPL | BUS | MPL | SML | W

A duplicate set is at Warwick Castle enriched with many manuscript notes by the poet Thomas Gray. The set is enclosed in red morocco slip cases (by Bedford), and was secured for £12 10s. in 1851 by J. O. Halliwell for the fourth Earl of Warwick.

Works . . . carefully revised and corrected [by Sir Thomas Hanmer, Speaker in the House of Commons] by the former editions and adorned with sculptures designed and executed by the best hands. Oxford : Printed at the theatre, 1744-46. 6 vols. 4° BM | BPL | BUS | CTC | MPL | NY | SML

Contains the Chandos portrait, views of the Westminster Abbey monument and Stratford bust, by Gravelot after Hayman (the latter altered as in Pope's edition), prefaces by Hanmer and Pope, and Rowe's life of Sh—.

The first edition edited by Hanmer and issued apparently under the auspices of the University delegates.

A few were done on large paper.

The first edition to contain the Westminster and Stratford monuments.

' This edition,' says Lowndes, ' though founded on Pope's and wilder even in conjectural criticism, rose to the value of ten guineas before it was reprinted in 1770-71, while Pope's six quartos were at the same period sold off at Tonson's sale at sixteen shillings per set.'

The British Museum and Birmingham sets are dated 1743-44.

Sh— Works . . .

Works of Sh—. In six volumes. Carefully revised and corrected by the former editions. 'Nil ortum tale.'—*Horace.* Ln : J. & P. Knapton, S. Birt, T. Longman, H. Lintot, C. Hitch, J. Brindley, J. & R. Tonson, S. Draper, R. & B. Wellington, E. New, B. Dod, 1745. 6 vols. 8°. Portrait by G. Duchange after B. Arlaud

BM | BPL | SML

Reprinted from the Oxford (1744) edition. Edited by Sir Thomas Hanmer, with life, Pope's preface, and glossary.

Works . . . in eight volumes. The genuine text, collated with all the former editions and then corrected and emended, is here settled ; being restored from the blunders of the first editors, and the interpolations of the two last : With a comment and notes, critical and explanatory, by Mr. Pope and Mr. Warburton [Edited by William Warburton]. Ln : J. & P. Knapton, S. Birt, T. Longman & T. Shewell, H. Lintott, C. Hitch, J. Brindley, J. & R. Tonson & S. Draper, R. Wellington, E. New, and B. Dod, 1747. 8 vols. 8°. With portrait by Vertue

BM | BPL | BUS | CTC | SML

The first edition from the pen of Bishop Warburton, who first pillories Theobald on the title-page and then pillages his best readings without acknowledgment, in fact adhering to Theobald's text throughout. Warburton received a well-deserved castigation in the sarcastic 'Supplement to Warburton's Sh—' by T. Edwards [*q.v.*]

Bearing these facts in mind, one may the better appreciate the humour of the flattering epitaph on Warburton in Gloucester cathedral.

'This edition, founded on Pope's, is thought to be the worst of all (says Lowndes) and was never esteemed. The editor does little more than make his author a stalking horse for the display of his own learning, though some of his conjectures and illustrations are happy.'.

Works of Sh—, in nine volumes. With a glossary. Carefully printed from the Oxford edition in quarto, 1744. 'Nil ortum tale.'—*Horace.* [Edited by Sir Thomas Hanmer.] Ln : J. & P. Knapton, S. Birt, T. Longman & T. Shewell, H. Lintott, C. Hitch, J. Brindley, J. & R. Tonson, S. Draper, R. Wellington, E. New, and B. Dod, 1747. 9 vols. 12°

BM | BPL | BUS

With Chandos portrait by G. Van der Gucht and plates repeated from Theobald's 1740 edition.

Works . . . The genuine text (collated with all the former editions and then corrected and amended), with a comment and notes, critical and explanatory, by Mr. Pope and Mr. Warburton. Dublin : Printed for R. Owen . . . 1747. 8 vols. Cr. 8°

BPL | SML | W

Sh— Works . . .

Works of Sh—, in nine volumes. With a glossary. [Edited by Sir T. Hanmer.] Carefully printed from the Oxford edition in quarto, 1744. Ln : J. & P. Knapton . . . 1748. 9 vols. 12° BM | BPL | SML

With the Chandos portrait.

Works . . . with a glossary. Carefully printed from the Oxford edition in quarto, 1744. [Edited by Sir T. Hanmer.] 'Nil ortum tale.'—*Horace.* Ln : Printed for J. & P. Knapton, S. Birt, T. Longman, H. Lintott, C. Hitch, J. Hodges, J. Brindley, J. & R. Tonson and S. Draper, B. Dod, and C. Corbet, 1750-51. 9 vols. 12°. With portrait and view of the Westminster monument BPL | SML

Works of Sh—. With notes by Mr. Theobald. The third edition [with portrait and plates]. Ln : J. & P. Knapton . . . 1752. 8 vols. 12°. With the Droeshout (altered) portrait and the Westminster statue BPL | NY | SML | W

With a number of manuscript notes by Thomas Hawkins. Reprinted with fresh title-pages from the second Theobald edition of 1740.

Works . . . collated and corrected by the former editions, by Mr. Pope. Printed from his second edition . . . Glasgow : Printed by Robert & Andrew Foulis, 1752-57. 16 vols. Cr. 8°

This first Scottish edition of the poet has eluded all previous bibliographers and the chief public collections of the poet. The plays were issued individually at intervals with separate paginations and titles, commencing with 'The tempest' in 1752 and ending with 'Othello' in 1757. It was re-issued in 1766 (uniformly dated) in 8 vols. with general titles, but still retaining the individual pagination and titles.

Works . . . In which the beauties observed by Pope, Warburton, and Dodd are pointed out. Together with the author's life ; a glossary ; copious indexes ; and a list of the various readings. In eight volumes. [Edited by Hugh Blair.] Edinburgh : Printed by Sands, Murray and Cochran for W. Sands, Hamilton & Balfour, Kincaid and Donaldson, L. Hunter, J. Yair, W. Gordon and J. Brown, 1753. 8 vols. 12° BM | BPL | BUS

The first edition edited by Dr. Blair, whose famous sermons were once almost infallibly to be found on the shelves of every bookshop and library in the kingdom. Said to be the first Scottish issue, but see previous entry. It would be more correctly described as the first Edinburgh edition.

Works . . . In which the beauties observed by Pope, Warburton and Dodd are pointed out. Together with the author's life ; a glossary, copious indexes ; and a list of the various readings. [Edited by Hugh Blair.] Ln : Sold by A. Manson,

R. Dilton, J. Thomson, P. Alnwick, W. Nelson, S. Darnton and H. Gray [1753]. 8 vols. 12° BPL

The first Edinburgh edition with a London imprint.
A strange misprint occurs in vol. 4, p. 83, the headline there reading ' King Richard IV.'

Works . . . collated with the oldest copies and corrected : With notes, explanatory and critical, by Mr. Theobald. ' I, decus, i, nostrum : melioribus utere fatis.'— *Virgil.* Ln : Printed for C. Hitch and L. Hawes, H. Lintot, J. & R. Tonson, J. Hodges, B. Dod, J. Rivington, M. & T. Longman, J. Brindley, C. Corbet, & T. Caslon, 1757. 8 vols. Cr. 8°. Copper portrait engraved by G. Van der Gucht and frontispiece to each play by H. Gravelot, engraved by G. Van der Gucht BPL | BUS

The only apparent difference between this and Theobald's 1740 issue is the omission of the words ' Second edition' from the title-page, a revised imprint, and the addition of the poet's will to vol. 1.

Works . . . from the Oxford edition of 1744 [with a glossary]. Ln : C. Hitch and L. Hawes, J. & R. Tonson, B. Dod, J. Rivington, R. Baldwin, T. Longman, S. Crowder and Co., C. Corbet, and T. Caslon . . . 1760. 9 vols. 12° BPL | SML

Text edited by Hanmer, with Pope's preface and Rowe's life of Sh—.
The imprint of vol. 9 includes the name of ' B. Law & Co.'

Works . . . with the author's life, glossary, and copious indexes [The Scots editor's preface (by Hugh Blair), Pope's preface, and life by Rowe]. Edinburgh : A. Kincaid, J. Bell, J. Brown, W. Gordon, C. Wright, and R. Fleming. 1761. 8 vols. 12° BPL | SML

Works . . . In eight volumes. Collated with the oldest copies and corrected. With notes, explanatory and critical, by Mr. Theobald. Ln : Printed for C. Hitch & L. Hawes, J. & R. Tonson, B. Dod, G. Woodfall, J. Rivington, R. Baldwin, T. Longman, S. Crowder & Co., W. Johnston, C. Corbet, T. Lownds, and T. Caslon, 1762. 8 vols. Cr. 8°. With Chandos portrait engraved by G. Vandergucht and other copperplates by Gravelot and Vandergucht BM | BPL | SML

[Works] Plays of Wm. Sh—, in eight volumes. With the corrections and illustrations of various commentators. To which are added notes by Samuel Johnson. Ln : Printed for J. & R. Tonson, H. Woodfall, J. Rivington, R. Baldwin, L. Hawes, Clark & Collins, T. Longman, W. Johnston, T. Caslon, C. Corbet, T.

Lownds, and the executors of B. Dodd, 1765. 8 vols. 8°. With Chandos portrait by G. Vertue BM | BPL | BUS | NY | SML

The first edition edited by the famous lexicographer, the first variorum edition, and the foundation of hundreds of subsequent issues.
' Though this edition disappointed public expectation it was acknowledged superior to any of its predecessors, and the preface commanded universal admiration.' — *Lowndes.*
Issue took place in Oct., 1765.
Johnson appears to have received £1,312 10s. as remuneration for his editorial labours. [*See* Wheatley.]
The Stratford set formerly belonged to the Rev. Joshua Brookes, the eccentric chaplain of Manchester Collegiate Church (now the Cathedral), and he extra-illustrated it with old Shakespearean prints of interest and value.
At Warwick is a set interleaved and extended to twenty-four volumes, octavo. A note in vol. 1 in the hand of J. O. Halliwell remarks : ' This copy is in contemporary half calf binding . . . and contains manuscript notes which I believe to be unpublished and to contain useful criticism. A few of the notes have been purposely mutilated [by a former owner] by tearing the pages containing them.'

Works . . . collated and corrected by the former editions by Mr. Pope. Printed from his second edition. Glasgow : Printed by Robert and Andrew Foulis, 1766. 16 parts, forming 8 vols. Cr. 8° BPL

Originally issued as separate plays for the use of playgoers. See Sh— Works 1752-57.

[Works] Plays . . . [With corrections of various commentators and notes by Dr. Samuel Johnson]. Dublin : A. Leathley, C. Wynne, P. Wilson, J. Exshaw, H. Saunders, James Potts, S. Watson, J. Mitchell, J. Williams, 1766. 10 vols. 8° BPL | SML

[Works] Twenty of the plays of Sh—. Being the whole number printed in quarto during his life-time, or before the restoration ; collated where there were different copies, and publish'd from the originals, by George Steevens. Ln : Printed for J. and R. Tonson, T. Payne and W. Richardson . . . 1766. 4 vols. 8° BM | BPL | BUS | MPL | W

Contents : Vol. 1, Midsummer night's dream, 1600
Merry wives . . . 1619
Merry wives . . . 1630
Merry wives . . . 1602
Much ado . . . 1600
Merchant of Venice, 1600
Love's labours lost, 1631
Vol. 2, Taming of the shrew, 1631
King Lear, 1608
King John, 1611
King Richard the second, 1615
King Henry the fourth, 1613 [1600 second part,
" " "
Vol. 3, King Henry the fifth, 1608
King Henry the sixth [*undated*]
King Richard the third, 1612
Titus Andronicus, 1611
Troilus and Cressida, 1609

Sh— Works . . .

Vol. 4, Romeo and Juliet, 1597
Romeo and Juliet, 1609
Hamlet, 1611
Othello, 1622
Sonnets, 1609
King Lear, 1605

The first edition edited by George Steevens and the first set of reprints of the early quartos.
Twelve sets only were printed on fine or large and thick paper in roy. 8°.

Works of Sh—. With corrections and illustrations from various commentators. Edinburgh : Printed by and for Martin & Wotherspoon, 1767. 10 vols. 12°
BM | BPL | SML
With Pope's preface, and Rowe's life of Sh—.

Works . . . In eight volumes. Collated with the oldest copies and corrected. With notes explanatory and critical. By Mr. Theobald. Printed verbatim from the octavo edition. Ln : H. Woodfall . . . 1767. 8 vols. 12° BPL | NY | SML

[Works] Mr. Wm. Sh—, his comedies, histories, and tragedies, set out by himself in quarto or by the players his fellows in folio and now faithfully republish'd from those editions in ten volumes, octavo ; with an introduction [by Edward Capell]. Whereunto will be added, in some other volumes, notes critical and explanatory and a body of various readings entire . . . Ln : Printed by Dryden Leach for J. & R. Tonson in the Strand, 1767-68. 10 vols. Cr. 8°
BM | BPL | BUS | CTC | MPL | NY | SML | W

The first issue under the editorship of Edward Capell, and the first to contain an attempt towards a bibliography.
'Capell, a careful and industrious editor' (remarks Lowndes) 'is praised for the purity of his collations, but not for any ingenuity ; the notes and various readings promised on the title-page were not printed until 1779-80 and then only in quarto.'
A medallion portrait appears in vol. 1, p. 74, engraved by J. Miller. Capell's introduction occupies 74 pp., and he gives a bibliography, vol 1, pp. 84-88.
The British Museum set is dated in error 1760-68, and a duplicate set in the same institution bears manuscript notes and corrections by Edward Malone, with a portrait of Capell inserted.
Capell's holograph MS. of this work in 6 vols. 4° is preserved at Trinity College, Cambridge.
The fine presswork is suggestive of Baskerville's or of W. Pickering's best efforts.
A large paper set, measuring 7⅝ by 4½in. (the only one recorded), is in the collection of the writer.

[Works] Plays of Wm. Sh—, in eight volumes, with the corrections and illustrations of various commentators ; to which are added notes by Sam. Johnson. Second edition. Ln : H. Woodfall, C. Bathurst, etc., 1768. 8 vols. 8°
BM | BPL | BUS
No obvious difference between this and Johnson's first edition except in the title.

Sh— Works . . .

Works of Sh— [from Mr. Pope's edition] in nine volumes. With notes selected from the best authors, explanatory and critical. Birmingham : Printed by Robert Martin and sold by A. Donaldson, London ; R. Goadby, Sherborne ; R. Bond, Glocester ; M. Morgan, Lichfield ; and T. Smith, Wolverhamton, and by all country booksellers, 1768. 9 vols. 12°. With portrait
BM | BPL | BUS | MPL | NY | W

An edition of unusual interest. It was produced at the suggestion of David Garrick, for sale at the great Stratford jubilee of 1769, and is the first Warwickshire edition of its deathless native.
The portrait by an unknown artist, specially engraved for this edition (not repeated elsewhere), presents the poet at the age of forty-five or thereabouts, a bust within an oval frame at the base of a monument, supported by the figures of 'Comedy,' 'Tragedy,' and 'Cupid,' the latter bearing Sh—'s coat-of-arms. Emblems of the sister arts 'Literature' and 'Music' bestrew the base of the column.
The first volume bears a general title in addition, which differs somewhat from the nine ordinary ones. The compositor omitted the letter 'p' from Wolverhamton and the letter 'u' from Glocester, in order perhaps to preserve the symmetry of the lines.
Robert Martin was Baskerville's foreman, and took over his business at this period. The issue appeared monthly in blue paper wrappers at 2/- per volume, and was produced in the great Birmingham printer's own workshop with his fine types.

Works of Sh—. With illustrations . . . Birmingham : Printed by N. Boden, and sold by Mr. Williams in Shrewsbury ; Mr. Taylor in Stafford ; Mr. Smith in Newcastle ; Mr. Morgan in Lichfield ; Mr. Shelton in Tamworth ; Mr. Smart in Walsall & Wolverhampton ; Mr. Sharp in Warwick ; Mr. Keating in Stratford ; Mr. Luckman in Coventry ; Miss Boden in Bridgnorth ; Mr. Hodson in Burton ; Mr. Clare in Bewdley ; Mr. Berrow in Worcester ; Mr. Sellick in Bristol ; Mr. Sibbald in Liverpool ; Mr. Broster in Chester ; and Mr. Houldgate in Sheffield [c. 1768. Probably 9 vols.] 12°. With a frontispiece on copper preceding each play

Only fragments of this edition are available for public reference : at Stratford vol. 1, which contains 'The tempest, Midsummer night's dream, Two gentlemen of Verona, Measure for measure'; at Birmingham vol. 3, embracing 'Twelfth night, Merry wives, Taming of the shrew, Comedy of errors.'
Footnotes by Johnson, Warburton, Theobald, and others are appended
The first edition to bear a Stratford imprint, and the only edition so far naming most of the other towns mentioned on the title.
Nicholas Boden was a trade rival of Baskerville's, and by issuing a folio Bible caused the latter to resume busine s after announcing his first retirement.

Works of Sh—. [Edited by Hugh Blair.] With the author's life, glossary, indexes, etc. Edinburgh : A. Donaldson . . . 1769. 8 vols. Cr. 8° BPL

Works . . . in which the beauties observed by Pope, Warburton, and Dodd are pointed out. With the author's life, glossary, indexes, etc. [Edited by Hugh Blair.] Edinburgh : Wal. Ruddiman & Co. . . . 1769. 8 vols. Cr. 8°   BPL | MPL

Works . . . [Edited by Sir T. Hanmer, with the various readings of Theobald and Capell, preface by Pope, and life by Rowe]. Adorned with sculptures [by F. Hayman and H. Gravelot]. Second edition. ' Nil ortum tale.'—*Horace.* Oxford : Printed at the Clarendon Press, 1770-71. 6 vols. Roy. 4°

BM | BPL | BUS | SML | W

The copperplates include the Chandos portrait, Stratford bust (as altered for Pope's edition), and the Westminster monument. The introduction says :—
' The first impression of 1744 having been small, was suddenly bought up and the original price advanced to a very exorbitant sum. The great demand of the publick for so elegant an edition induced the delegates of the press to set about this republication. . . . The glossary has received very considerable additions . . . besides which the reader will find notes by Dr. Percy . . . Prof. Warton, and John Hawkins . . . and the [poetical] epistle by Collins. . . .'
A few sets were issued on large paper, f°, of which one is at Warwick Castle, and a second is in the writer's collection.
Lowndes was clearly mistaken when he doubted whether a large paper set ever existed.
Some sets are entirely dated 1771.

[Works] King Lear . . . Hamlet . . . Julius Cæsar . . . Othello . . . Macbeth . . . Collated with the old and modern editions [by Charles Jennens. Five plays only. With annotations]. Ln : Printed by W. Bowyer and J. Nichols, and sold by W. Owen, between the Temple Gates, Fleet Street, 1770-74. 2 vols. 8°, each play separately paged. With portrait and frontispiece   SML

[Works] Plays of Sh—, from the text of Dr. S. Johnson. With the prefaces, notes, &c. of Rowe, Pope, Theobald, Hanmer, Warburton, Johnson, and select notes from many other critics. Also the introduction of the last editor, Mr. Capell, and a table shewing his various readings. [Includes Sh—'s poems.]   Dublin : Thomas Ewing . . . 1771. 7 vols. 8°. With portraits and vignettes

BM | BPL | BUS

Each of the first six vols. is in two parts.
Sometimes found bound in twelve or (with the Poems) thirteen volumes.
Vol. 1 contains two portraits (the Garrick statue as frontispiece, engraved by P. Halpin, and a vignette on p. 3 by Picot and Reilly which presents the poet with a humorous and distinctly Irish appearance. In addition, each part possesses an engraved title and a pretty vignette on copper by C. Grignion.
Some curious misprints occur. For example, p. 180

vol. 1 quotes an edition of the ' Passionate pilgrim dated 1559,' or just forty years before it appeared. Further on, the ' Pape of Lucrece ' startles the eye. All the preliminary matter is pirated from Capell's edition, 1767-68.

Works of Sh—. In which the beauties observed by Pope, Warburton, and Dodd are pointed out. Together with the author's life ; a glossary, copious indexes, and a list of the various readings. [Edited by Hugh Blair.] Edinburgh : Printed by A. Donaldson, and sold at his shop, corner of Arundel Street, Strand, London, and at Edinburgh, 1771. 8 vols. Cr. 8°   BM | BPL | SML

David Garrick possessed a set on large paper.
A set given by the editor to Robert Burns, and bearing his (Burns') autograph, was sold at auction in New York in 1901.

Works . . . In which the beauties observed by Pope, Warburton and Dodd are pointed out. Together with the author's life, glossary, &c. Ln : A. Manson . . . [c. 1771]. 8 vols. 12°   SML

Works of Sh—. Collated with the oldest copies, and corrected : with notes, explanatory and critical : By Mr. Theobald. Ln : Printed for R. Crowder . . . 1772. 12 vols. 12°   BM | BPL | SML | W

Works of Sh—. In eight volumes. Collated with the oldest copies and corrected. With notes explanatory and critical by Mr. Theobald. Printed verbatim from the octavo edition . . . Ln : Printed for C. Bathurst, J. Beecroft, W. Strahan, J. & F. Rivington, J. Hinton, L. Davis, Hawes, Clarke & Collins, R. Horsfield, W. Johnston, W. Owen, T. Caslon, E. Johnson, S. Crowder, B. White, T. Longman, B. Law, E. & C. Dilly, C. Corbett, W. Griffin, T. Cadell, W. Woodfall, G. Keith, T. Lowndes, T. Davies, J. Robson, T. Becket, F. Newbery, G. Robinson, T. Payne, J. Williams, M. Hingeston, and J. Ridley, 1773. 8 vols. 12°. With portrait by J. Hall of ' Wm. Sh— at the age of 40 '   BM | BPL | NY | SML

The last volume contains a bibliography of early editions (commencing with the Jaggard canon). It is divided into three sections, headed :—' Editions of authority, of middle authority, of no authority.' The latter includes Rowe's edition (with presumably the biography) of 1709.
The British Museum set bears MS. notes in the autograph of S. T. Coleridge.

[Works] Plays . . . In ten volumes. With the corrections and illustrations of various commentators ; To which are added notes by Samuel Johnson and George Steevens. With an appendix [by Richard Farmer]. Ln : Printed for C. Bathurst

Sh— Works . . .

. . . 1773. 10 vols. Cr. 8°. With portrait
by G. Vertue   BM | BPL | BUS | MPL | SML
Remainder of imprint identical with preceding entry of
same year.
'This edition, in which were united the native powers
of Dr. Johnson with the activity, sagacity, and
antiquarian learning of George Steevens, superseded
all previous editions and became the standard for
future editors and publishers.'—*Lowndes*.

[Works] Bell's edition of Sh—'s plays, as
they are now performed at the Theatres
Royal in London, regulated from the
prompt books of each house . . . [and the
' Poems ']. With notes critical and illustrative [an essay on oratory and the life
of Sh—] by the authors of the ' Dramatic
censor ' [Francis Gentleman]. Ln : John
Bell . . . 1773-74. 9 vols. 12°. With portrait, also scene and character plates by
Sherwin, Grignion, E. Edwards, and
Isaac Taylor, engraved on copper by J.
Hall and others ; forty plates in all, prepared under the superintendence of F.
Bartolozzi   BM | BPL | SML
A general title-page appears in each of the volumes, in
addition to the independent title to each play. All the
plays were paginated and printed separately for the
use of playgoers. The ' Poems ' fill the whole of the
ninth volume, with a special title-page.
Like that of 1747, this edition (dedicated to Garrick)
was accused of being the worst ever published.
To be ' damned with faint praise ' sometimes proves the
best aid to sales, as in this case. It scored a greater
success than any previous issue, one week alone wit-
nessing the sale of eight hundred sets. Doubtless the
beautiful copperplates helped the output considerably.
The list of subscribers' names and addresses in vol. 1
occupies 23 pages, and includes Garrick, Tate Wilkinson, Douce, and other familiar names. One
American figure in it, Benjamin Guarred of South
Carolina, who ordered a ' Royal paper set.'
Of these ' Royal' or large paper sets, 8°, 134 were subscribed for, and thirteen hundred ordinary sets, of
which 98 were ordered from Edinburgh alone.
In the publisher's announcement (p. 24) the volumes
were offered ' sewn ' (*i.e.* unbound) at 3/- each.
In 1794 some of the plays were reprinted with that date,
added to older issues dated 1774, and published collectively with the former engraved general title.
The publishers asserted the portrait of Sh— was copied
from the 'most authenticated painting of the poet,'
while that of Garrick was after an 'original picture
just finished by Mr. Dance, which is esteemed the
best likeness that has yet been taken.'
It is the first edition with artistic illustrations, and
clearly influenced by the unrivalled French school of
the period.

[Works] Bell's edition [Excerpt of the forty
plates alone, including the ' Portrait of
Wm. Sh— at the age of 40 ']. Ln : John
Bell . . . 1773-74. 12°   w

Works . . . With notes by L. Theobald.
[Ninth edition ?] Ln : . . . [c. 1777]. 12
vols. Cr. 8°
'It appears (says Lowndes) that Theobald received
£652 10s. as his share of profits on his various
editions, of which no fewer than 12,860 copies were
printed. No other editor gained so much.'
Lowndes is wrong in this. Dr. Johnson received more
than double this amount. (*See* Sh— Works, 1765.)

Sh— Works . . .

[Works] Plays of Wm. Sh—. In ten
volumes. With the corrections and illustrations of various commentators ; to
which are added notes by S. Johnson
and G. Steevens. The second edition, re-
vised and augmented [by Isaac Reed].
Ln : C. Bathurst . . . 1778. 10 vols. 8°
BM | BPL | MPL | SML | W
The first edition edited by Isaac Reed.
Contains plates, Chandos portrait engraved by John
Hall, Droeshout portrait, Marshall's portrait from the
' Poems 1640,' and Sh—'s autographs from his Will.
The preliminary matter is repeated with additions
from Johnson and Steevens' edition of 1773.
Includes an ' Attempt to ascertain the order in which
the plays attributed to Sh— were written, by E.
Malone.'

[Works] Supplement to the edition of
' Sh—'s plays ' published in 1778 by S.
Johnson and G. Steevens . . . containing
additional observations by several of the
former commentators : to which are sub-
joined the genuine poems of the same
author, and seven plays that have been
ascribed to him ; with notes by the editor
[Edmond Malone] and others. Ln : C.
Bathurst, W. Strahan . . . 1780. 2 vols.
8°   BM | BPL | BUS | MPL | NY | W
With portrait of the Earl of Southampton.
The first edition edited by E. Malone.

[Works] A second appendix to Mr. Malone's
' Supplement to the last edition of Sh—,'
containing additional observations [by
Edmond Malone]. Ln : . . . 1783. 8°
BM | BPL | BUS | W
Issue restricted to fifty copies.

[Works] Picturesque beauties of Sh—, being
a selection of scenes [from drawings by
T. Stothard and R. Smirke], engraved
under the direction of Charles Taylor.
Ln : . . . 1783-86. 4°. 32 plates

[Works] Stockdale's edition of Sh—, including in one volume the whole of his
dramatic works ; with explanatory notes
compiled from various commentators.
[Edited by S. Ayscough.] Embellished
with a striking likeness of the author
[*James I. type*]. Ln : J. Stockdale . . .
1784. 8°, pp. 1,079. With Droeshout
portrait engraved by W. Sherwin
BM | BPL | SML
The first octavo edition entirely in one volume.
For this issue the buyer paid one-and-a-half guineas, or
about fifteen times the cost of a similar (but better
printed) edition to-day.

[Works] Plays of Wm. Sh—, in ten volumes.
With the corrections and illustrations of
various commentators ; to which are
added notes by Samuel Johnson and
George Steevens. Third edition, revised
and augmented by the editor of Dods-

ley's 'Collection of old plays' [Isaac Reed]. Ln: Printed for C. Bathurst, 1785. 10 vols. 8° BM | BPL | BUS | SML
With plates as in Reed's foregoing edition.
'This edition, owing to some arbitrary alterations and omissions, is not preferred to its predecessors.'— *Lowndes.*
With the Droeshout, Marshall, and Chandos portraits, also woodcuts.

[Works] Bell's edition: Dramatic writings of Will Sh—, from the text of Johnson & Steevens. Ln: J. Bell . . . 1785-87. 16 vols. 12°. With portraits and vignettes
BUS | SML
The dates on the separate titles to the various plays differ, some bearing 1785, others 1786, or 1787.

[Works] Bell's edition of Sh—. [Vol. 1-2] Prolegomena to the dramatick writings of Will. Sh—. [Vol. 3-18] Dramatick writings of Will. Sh—, with the notes of all the various commentators; printed complete from the best editions of Sam. Johnson and Geo. Steevens. Ln: J. Bell . . . 1786-88. 76 parts, forming 20 vols. 12°. With portraits, vignettes and character plates BM | BPL | SML
Published at £3 16s.
Some sets were done on fine paper; others on large paper with proof plates.

[Works] Plays . . . 1786. *See* Sh— Works, 1790-86

[Works] Dramatic works . . . in six volumes. With notes by Joseph Rann, Vicar of St. Trinity, Coventry. Oxford: Clarendon Press . . . 1786-94. 6 vols. 8°
BM | BPL | NY | SML
Some sets are dated 1786-91.
The first edition under the auspices of Joseph Rann.

[Works: Three papers relating to the publication of Boydell's Sh—, 1802] Prospectus, 4 pp., 1786; Notice to subscribers concerning the re-engraving of a plate, 1791; Receipt for Mr. Cabanell's subscription for a set, 1792. Ln: J. & J. Boydell . . . 1786-1802. F° W

[Works] Plays . . . Complete in eight volumes . . . Ln: Printed for Bellamy & Robarts, 138 Fleet Street and 4 Peterborough Court, Fleet Street, 1787-91. 8 vols. 8° BUS
Issued serially, with separate pagination and two stipple plates to each play (except 'King Richard III.' and 'Romeo,' which have one plate each); allegorical pictures of the poet, and the Chandos portrait engraved by W. and J. Walker. The artists of the scenes are Corbould, Burney, Richter, Ryley, the plates being engraved by Angus
In vol. vi. after 'K. Hen. IV.' is a publisher's announcement (2 pp.), which shews that a portion of this edition appeared in fortnightly parts. The promoters refer to it as the 'General magazine Sh—,' and state it will 'never be reprinted' [but see 1791 and 1796 editions].

[Works] Plays and Poems of Wm. Sh—, in ten volumes; collated verbatim with the most authentick copies . . . With the corrections and illustrations of various commentators, to which are added, an essay on the chronological order of his plays; an essay relative to Sh— and Jonson; a dissertation on the three parts of 'King Henry VI.'; an historical account of the English stage; and notes by E. Malone. [Including also the 'Tragicall hystory of Romeus and Iuliet,' translated from the Italian by A. Brooke, appendix and glossarial index.] Ln: Printed by H. Baldwin for J. Rivington & Sons [and others], 1790. 10 vols (Vol. I. is in two parts). 8°. With portraits, woodcuts, and facsimile BM | BPL | BUS | NY
'Malone is generally accredited as a very painstaking and faithful, though not brilliant, editor. But Dr. Symmons, a more recent critic, thought otherwise when he wrote:—"Neither the indulged fancy of Pope, nor the fondness for innovation in Hanmer, nor the arrogant and headlong self-confidence of Warburton has inflicted such cruel wounds on the text of Sh— as the assuming dulness of Malone. Barbarism and broken rhythm dog him at the heels wherever he treads." '—*Lowndes.*
Some sets were done on fine paper for presents.

[Works] . . . Dramatic works. With explanatory notes. A new edition. To which is now added a copious index to the remarkable passages and words. By . . . Samuel Ayscough, F.S.A. and assistant librarian of the British Museum. Embellished with a striking likeness of Sh— [engraved by W. Sherwin] from the original folio edition. Ln: Printed for John Stockdale, Piccadilly, 1790. 3 vols. Roy. 8° BM | BPL | NY | W
With Droeshout portrait, two short prefaces, list of subscribers, and life by Rowe.
Issued at £3 13s. 6d.

[Works] Plays . . . accurately printed from the text of Mr. Malone's edition, with select explanatory notes. [Edited by John Nichols.] In seven volumes . . . Ln: Printed for J. Rivington & Sons, L. Davis, B. White & Son, T. Longman, B. Law, H. S. Woodfall, C. Dilly, J. Robson, J. Johnson, T. Vernor, G. G. J. & J. Robinson, T. Cadell, J. Murray, R. Baldwin, H. L. Gardner, J. Sewell, J. Nichols, J. Bew, T. Payne jun., S. Hayes, R. Faulder, W. Lowndes, G. & T. Wilkie, Scatcherd & Whitaker, T. & J. Egerton, C. Stalker, J. Barker, J. Edwards, Ogilvie & Speare, J. Cuthell, J. Lackington, and E. Newbery, 1790-86. 7 vols. Cr. 8° BM | BPL | SML
Volume i. is dated 1790, and the remainder 1786.
The first edition under the supervision of John Nichols

Sh— Works . . .

[Works] Sh—'s dramatic works, with explanatory notes, to which is now added, a copious index to the remarkable passages and words, by Samuel Ayscough. Embellished with a striking likeness of Sh— from the original folio edition, and another from the collection of his grace the Duke of Chandos. A new edition . . . Dublin: Printed for Wm. Jones, 86 Dame St., 1791. 3 vols. 8°, pp. xii.-62-1,754 (the text pagination continuous). With Droeshout and Chandos portraits

BM | BPL | SML

[Works] Plays. . .Complete in eight volumes. Ln : Printed for Bellamy & Robarts . . . 1791. 8 vols. 8°. Illustrated with stipple plates

Identical with the 1787-91 edition, save in da e.

[Works] Plays of Wm. Sh—. Complete in eight volumes. 'Bellamy's edition.' Ln : Harrison . . . 1791. 8 vols. 8°. With plates dated 1786-89   BM | BPL | SML

[Works] Dramatic works. Revised by G. Steevens. 'Boydell's edition.' Ln : J. & J. Boydell . . . 1791-1802. 18 parts, forming 9 vols. F°. With 100 engravings

The first part appeared in 1791. It is now rarely found in the original paper-wrappered parts as issued.

See ' Account of the origin   ,.' also Boydell.

The sumptuous plates, the production of which swallowed up a fortune, were afterwards issued separately in 1802. The original paintings filled the great Sh— gallery in Pall Mall, and made the name of Boydell famous.

[Works] Sh— gallery: containing a select series of scenes and characters, accompanied by criticisms and remarks . . . on fifty plates [designed by H. Singleton]. Ln : C. Taylor . . . 1792. 8°, pp. ii.-260

BM | BPL

Works . . . with index by S. Ayscough. Ln : . . . 1792. 2 vols. 8°

[Works] Dramatick works . . . printed complete from the best editions of Samuel Johnson, George Stevens [sic] and E. Malone. To which is prefixed the life of the author [by N. Rowe]. Edinburgh: Printed for W. Gordon, N. R. Cheyne, I. & I. Fairbairn, and Silvester Doig; Ln : I. Lackington; Leith : W. Coke; Stirling : W. Anderson, 1792. 8 vols. 12°. With engraved titles bearing portrait of Sh— after Paton, altered to look like a Scotsman   BM | BPL | SML

[Works] Plays of Wm. Sh—. In fifteen volumes. With the corrections and illustrations of various commentators. To which are added notes by Samuel Johnson and George Steevens. The fourth edition. Revised and augmented with a glossarial index by the editor of Dodsley's

Sh— Works . . .

'Collection of old plays' [Isaac Reed] . . . Ln : Printed for T. Longman, B. Law & Son, C. Dilly, J. Robson, J. Johnson, T. Vernor, G. G. J. & J. Robinson, T. Cadell, J. Murray, R. Baldwin, H. L. Gardner, J. Sewell, J. Nicholls, F. & C. Rivington, W. Goldsmith, T. Payne jun., S. Hayes, R. Faulder, W. Lowndes, B. & J. White, G. & T. Wilkie, J. & J. Taylor, Scatcherd & Whitaker, T. & J. Egerton, E. Newbery, J. Barker, J. Edwards, Ogilvy & Speare, J. Cuthell, J. Lackington, J. Deighton, and W. Miller, 1793. 15 vols. 8°

BM | BLO | BPL | MPL | MRL | SML | W

Contains Felton portrait by T. Trotter, the preliminary matter of the 1778-80 issue, and, in addition, an essay upon Sh—, Ford and Jonson ; Farmer's essay on the learning of Sh—, etc.

Lowndes writes :—' This, generally called Steevens' own edition, is by many considered the most accurate and desirable of all.'

A copy of this issue, with manuscript notes by Steevens, Reed, and Malone, is in the Bodleian.

Steevens' own set on large paper, with MS. additions in his hand, and extra-illustrated with hundreds of portraits and plates, was bequeathed by him to Earl Spencer, and passed with the famous Althorpe library to the Rylands library, Manchester. It has a manuscript general index in a separate volume. The set is enlarged to 19 vols. roy. 8°, and is bound in blue straight-grained morocco, with Steevens' initials on the sides.

Twenty-five sets were printed on large paper.

[Works] Plays of ' King Lear and Cymbeline ' . . . With the notes and illustrations of various commentators. To which are added remarks by the editor [Ambrose Eccles]. Second edition. Ln : Lackington, Allen & Co., 1794. 2 vols. 8°

[Works] Plays and poems . . . collated verbatim with the most authentick copies and revised : With the corrections and illustrations of various commentators. To which are added, an essay on the chronological order of his plays ; an essay relative to Sh— and Jonson ; a dissertation on the three parts of ' King Henry VI.' ; an historical account of the English stage ; and notes, by Edmond Malone . . . Dublin : Printed by John Exshaw, 98 Grafton St., 1794. 16 vols. 8°. With portraits and plates

BM | BPL | SML

The last vol. includes the ' Poems, Romeus and Juliet, and a glossorial index.'

Works . . . in eight volumes. In which the beauties observed by Pope, Warburton and Dodd are pointed out. Together with the author's life, a glossary, copious indexes, and a list of the various readings. [Edited by Hugh Blair.] Edinburgh & Glasgow : Printed for J. & A. Duncan, J. & M. Robertson, & J. & W. Shaw, booksellers, 1795. 8 vols. 12° BPL | SML

Works . . . in eight volumes. In which the beauties observed by Pope, Warburton, and Dodd are pointed out. Together with the author's life, a glossary, copious indexes, and a list of the various readings. Edinburgh : Printed for Bell & Bradfute, J. Dickson, W. Creech, J. & J. Fairbairn, and T. Duncan, booksellers, 1795. 8 vols. Cr. 8°   BPL | BUS | SML
Includes the 'Scots editors' preface,' Pope's preface, and Rowe's life of Sh—.

[Works] Plays and poems of Wm. Sh—, corrected from the latest and best London editions, with notes by Samuel Johnson, LL.D. To which are added a glossary and life of the author. Imbellished with a striking likeness from the collection of his grace the Duke of Chandos. Philadelphia : Printed and sold by Bioren and Madan, 1795-96. 8 vols. 12° [6¾ × 4in.]   BUS | NY | SML
The oval portrait is in stipple on copper, supported by two cupids, engraved by R. Field from the original picture in the collection of the Duke of Chandos.
Vol. 1 contains a critical 'Preface to the American edition' [pp. iii-xii.], a 'life of Sh—' [pp. xiii-xvii.], and 'Sh—'s Will' [pp. xviii-xx.]
The first edition of Sh— produced outside the British Isles and (quite appropriately) the first to be published in America. The portrait of the poet is also the first produced in the United States.
There are no introductions to the plays, but brief notes are appended.
The first piece of Sh— printed outside the United Kingdom will be found under Sh— King Henry IV., 1, 1710.

[Works] Plays . . . complete, in eight volumes. Ln : Bellamy and Robarts . . . 1796. 8 vols. 8°   BM | BPL | SML | W
With Chandos portrait altered by Walker, the engraver.
Gives two scenes to each play, sixteen 'allegories,' and a life of the dramatist.
Reprinted from the 1791 edition issued by the same publishers, with fresh title-pages.
The plates are dated 1787-89.

[Works] Plays and poems [from the text of George Steevens], to which is added a glossary. Ln : Printed for T. Longman, B. Law, C. Dilly, J. Robson, J. Johnson, G. G. & J. Robinson, R. Baldwin, H. L. Gardner, J. Sewell, W. Richardson, J. Nichols, F. & C. Rivington, J. Edwards, T. Payne jun., S. Hayes, R. Faulder, W. Lowndes, B. & J. White, G. & T. Wilkie, J. & J. Taylor, J. Scatcherd, T. Egerton, E. Newbery, W. Bent, J. Walker, W. Clarke & Son, J. Cuthell, J. Nunn, J. Lackington & Co., T. Kay, J. Deighton, W. Miller, Vernor & Hood, Cadell & Davies, Murray & Highley, and Lee & Hurst . . . 1797. 7 vols. Roy. 8°, large type   BPL | NY | SML
Some copies on large paper 4° were issued at seven guineas.

[Works] Plays . . . Ln : T. Longman . . . 1797. 6 vols. 8°   BPL | SML
Reprinted from Robinson's edition of the same year, without the Poems and glossary.

[Works] Plays . . . with corrections. Edinburgh : [Printed by Martin & Wotherspoon ?] 1797. 8 vols. 12°

[Works] Plays . . . accurately printed from the text of Mr. Steevens' last edition. With a selection of the most important notes [collected by John Nichols]. Ln : Printed for T. Longman, B. Law, C. Dilly, J. Johnson, G. G. & J. Robinson, R. Baldwin, H. L. Gardner, J. Sewell, W. Richardson, J. Nichols, F. & C. Rivington, T. Payne jun., R. Faulder, W. Lowndes, B. & J. White, G. & T. Wilkie, J. & J. Taylor, J. Scatcherd, T. Egerton, E. Newbery, W. Bent, J. Walker, W. Clarke and Son, J. Barker, J. Edwards, D. Ogilvy & Son, J. Cuthell, J. Nunn, J. Anderson, J. Lackington & Co., T. Kay, J. Deighton, W. Miller, Vernor and Hood, Cadell and Davies, Murray and Highley, and Lee and Hurst . . . 1797. 8 vols. 12°   BPL | BUS | SML

Works . . . from the text of G. Steevens. Ln : . . . 1797. 12 vols. 8°

[Works] Dramatic works of Sh—, in eight volumes : the last containing select explanatory notes . . . by C. Wagner. Brunswick . . . 1797-1801. 8 vols. 8° BM
The first edition in English produced on the continent, likewise the first 'made in Germany.'

Works . . . accurately printed from the text of Mr. Steevens' last edition. In nine volumes [with glossary and notes by John Nichols . . . and life by Rowe]. Ln : Printed by H. Baldwin & Son for C. Dilly, J. Johnson, G. G. & J. Robinson, R. Baldwin, H. L. Gardner, J. Sewell, W. J. & J. Richardson, J. Nichols, F. & C. Rivington, T. Payne, R. Faulder, W. Lowndes, G. Wilkie, J. & J. Taylor, J Scatcherd, T. Egerton, E. Newbery, W. Bent, J. Walker, W. Clarke & Son, J. Barker, J. Edwards, D. Ogilvy & Son, J. Cuthell, R. Lea, J. Nunn, J. Lackington & Co., T. Kay, J. Deighton, J. White, W. Miller, Vernor & Hood, Cadell & Davies, T. N. Longman, C. Law, Murray & Highley, Lea & Hurst, 1798. 9 vols. 12°   BPL

Works . . . Edited by John Nichols. With prefaces and life by N. Rowe. Ln : D. Ogilvie & Son . . . 1798. 9 vols. 8° BPL

Works . . . Ln : D. Ogilvie & Son . . . 1798. 9 vols. 8°   BPL
Some textual differences from the preceding edition of the same year occur herein.

Sh— Works . . .

[Works] Dramatic writings . . . with preface to each play. Perth: R. Morrison jun. . . . 1798. 9 vols. 12° BPL | SML
The first edition printed at Perth.

[Works] Harding's edition: Plays of Wm. Sh—. Ln: Printed by T. Bensley, Bolt Court, Fleet Street, for Vernor and Hood, Poultry; E. Harding, Pall Mall; and J. Wright, Piccadilly, 1798-1800. 12 vols. 12° BPL | SML
Possesses portrait by Ridley, vignette of a swan on the Avon on title, plates by Stothard and others; the life by Rowe, Dr. Johnson's preface, Farmer's essay, and brief preliminary observations on each play.
Probably the plays were published separately for playgoers, having independent paginations and distinct dates 1798-99. The general title-page is dated 1800. One of the few sets on large paper, demy 8°, is at Stratford.

[Works] Plays of Wm. Sh—. With the corrections and illustrations of various commentators. To which are added notes by S. Johnson and G. Steevens. A new edition, revised and augmented, with a glossarial index, by the editor of Dodsley's 'Collection of old plays' [I. Reed]. Basil: J. J. Tourneisen, MDCCCC [*sic pro*] 1799-1802. 23 vols. 8° BM | BPL
A reprint of the 1793 London edition, with fresh title-pages.
Some sets are enriched by sixty added plates.
A copy in the British Museum contains copious manuscript notes by the German critic, Ludwig Tieck.

[Works] Dramatic works . . . with life by Mr. Rowe. Brunswick: C. Wagner . . . 1799-1801. 8 vols. 8° BPL
Reprinted from the 1797 issue.

Works . . . Berwick: Printed by John Taylor, 1800. 9 vols. 12°. With vignette portraits BPL | BUS | SML
The first edition of Sh— printed at Berwick-on-Tweed.

[Works] Plays . . . With glossarial notes. Ln: Sharpe . . . [1800]. 9 vols. 16°
The first miniature edition of the poet.

[Works] Plays . . . from the correct edition of Isaac Reed. Ln: Vernor, Hood & Co. . . . 1800. 12 vols. 12°

[Works] Plays . . . containing Rowe's life . . . preface . . . Farmer's essay . . . and glossary. Ln: Printed by T. Bensley for Vernor & Hood . . . E. Harding . . . & J. Wright . . . 1800. 12 vols. 12°. Portrait by Ridley and 123 stipple plates by Stothard and others
Known as Harding's edition. The plays have separate titles and paginations. Reprinted from the 1798 issue.

Works . . . With life by N. Rowe. Zurich . . . 1801. 8 vols. 8°

[Works] Bell's edition. Dramatick writings of Will. Sh—. Ln: John Bell. . . . 1801. 20 vols. 12° BPL
The separate titles to the plays are dated 1784, etc.

Sh— Works . . .

[Works] Dramatic works of Sh—. Revised by George Steevens. [Edited by J. Boydell.] Ln: Printed by Bulmer & Co. for John & Josiah Boydell and Nicol, 1802. 18 parts, forming 9 vols. F° BM | BPL | BUS | MPL | NY | SML
This set contains Boydell's series of one hundred large copperplates from paintings by leading English artists of the time, Reynolds, Smirke, Northcote, Porter, Stothard, Hamilton, Bunbury, Opie, and Westall.
According to the prospectus, issued in 1786, a type foundry, an ink factory, and a printing house were all specially erected for the production of this edition. As a matter of fact, issue of this work began serially in 1791 (*q.v.*)
During the last decade or two, complete surviving sets have greatly decreased in number owing to a curious utilitarian development. Print dealers have discovered that this edition can be profitably broken up, the plates when framed being specially adapted for wall decoration.

[Works] Graphic illustrations of the dramatic works of Sh—, consisting of a series of prints engraved from pictures purposely painted by the first artists, lately exhibited at the Sh— gallery. Ln: J. & J. Boydell . . . 1802. Roy. f°. One hundred plates
Published at sixty guineas.
Open letter proof sets contain ninety-eight etchings only.
The set is reprinted from Boydell's edition of Sh— works, 1802.
A smaller extra plate, entitled 'Sh— nursed by tragedy and comedy,' engraved by Smith after Romney, is sometimes found with the set, making 101 plates in all. The full collection embraces the 'Seven ages'; Sh— as painted by Smirke; portraits of King George III. and Queen Charlotte.

[Works] Series of engravings to illustrate the works of Sh—. Painted by T. Stothard. Engraved by J. Heath. Ln: . . . 1802. 4° CPL

[Works] A collection of prints from pictures painted for the purpose of illustrating the dramatic works of Sh— [published by J. & J. Boydell in 1802] by the artists of Great Britain. Ln: J. & J. Boydell, 1802-03. 2 vols. F°. One hundred plates BM | BPL | BUS | MPL
The dedication is dated 1805.
The artists and plates are identical with those described in the 1802 issue.

[Works] Dramatic works . . . Printed complete with Dr. Samuel Johnson's preface and notes. To which is prefixed the life of the author. Boston [U.S.]: Munroe & Francis . . . 1802-04. 8 vols. 12°. With portrait BUS | SML
The first Boston edition, probably edited by David Francis, one of its printer-publishers, 'all his life a lover and careful reader of Sh—.' It passed through two subsequent editions [see 1807 and 1810-12]. In the Lenox Library set of the third edition, at New York, is this interesting manuscript entry by D. Francis the publisher:— 'In 1802 Munroe and Francis issued proposals for publishing an edition of Sh— in serial numbers, two plays to a volume, at fifty cents

per number, complete in 16 numbers. Two editions were printed. A third was demanded and we added the "Poems," making 18 numbers. These editions were all printed from types, reset every edition, as stereotype was not then known. The presswork was mostly done by Munroe and Francis personally, on a hand press with inking balls of sheepskin, the ink distributed by hand. These volumes are a specimen of the paper and print. Paper demy size (19in. by 20in.), costing five dollars a ream, made by hand. Ink and type imported, none worth using being made here. The engravings were executed by Dr. Alexander Anderson of New York,' the first professional wood engraver in America.

The titles, copied from the 1792 Edinburgh edition, have vignette portraits, and each play is separately paged.

[Works] A new edition of Sh—'s plays from the corrected text of Johnson and Steevens, with prints engraved by Mr. Heath. [Ten plays.] Ln : Heath & Robinson, 1802-04. 10 parts. 4°   BM

The B.M. copy is without title-page. The above particulars are taken from the prospectus inserted in the first number.

[Works] Dramatic works of Sh—. Revised by G. Steevens. With plates from designs by Henry Fuseli. Ln : J. & J. Boydell . . . 1803. 2 vols. F°   BPL

[Works] Plays . . . accurately printed from the text of the corrected copy left by the late George Steevens, Esq. With glossarial notes [life by Rowe and Dr. Johnson's preface]. Ln : Printed for J. Johnson, A. Baldwin, H. L. Gardner, W. J. & J. Richardson, J. Nichols & Son, F. C. & J. Rivington, T. Payne, R. Faulder, G. & J. Robinson, W. Lowndes, G. Wilkie, J. Scatcherd, T. Egerton, J. Walker, W. Clarke & Son, J. Barker & Son, D. Ogilvy & Son, Cuthell & Martin, R. Lea, P. M'Queen, J. Menn, Lackington, Allen & Co., T. Kay, J. Deighton, J. White, W. Miller, Vernor & Hood, D. Walker, B. Crosby & Co., Longman & Rees, Cadell & Davies, T. Hurst, J. Harding, R. H. Evans, I. Bagster, J. Mawman, Blacks & Parry, R. Bent, J. Badcock, J. Asperne, and T. Ostell, 1803. 10 vols. 8°

BM | BPL | CPL | NY | SML

' These notes are original and not taken from any other edition.'—*Dibdin.*

In the writer's collection is a set extra-illustrated with portrait by C. Warren, *sc.*, and 119 stipple copperplates by Corbould, Gardiner, Porter, Rivers, Singleton, Stothard, Thurston, and others.

[Works] Plays . . . In twenty-one volumes. With the corrections and illustrations of various commentators. To which are added, notes by Samuel Johnson and George Steevens. Fifth edition. Revised and augmented by Isaac Reed, with a glossarial index. Ln : Printed for J. Johnson . . . 1803. 21 vols. 8°

BM | BPL | BUS | MPL | NY | SML | W

Felton portrait engraved by Neagle. Includes the ' advertisement' by Reed, Mr. Richardson's proposals, Capell's introduction, Malone's preface, and other preliminary matter as in the previous editions by Johnson and Steevens. From Lowndes we learn this issue is an amplification of the 1793 edition, and was left in an advanced state of preparation by George Steevens, who died in 1800. Reed received £300 for editing it, and Harrison £100 for correcting the press. Some of the original proof sheets, with manuscript corrections, are in the British Museum.

The gross sum produced by the output of fifteen hundred copies was £5,844.

For comment on this issue see Howe.

[Works] Plays . . . Fifth edition. Revised by Isaac Reed . . . Ln : Printed for J. Johnson, 1803. [21 vols.] Vol. I. only. 8°   W

This volume, containing the prolegomena, came from the library of R. B. Wheler, historian of Stratford-on-Avon, and is preserved on account of the numerous manuscript notes in his autograph it contains.

[Works] Plays of Wm. Sh— in miniature. Sharpe's edition. Ln : C. Whittingham . . . 1803-04. 9 vols. 12°   BPL

[Works] Plays . . . Ln : Printed by T. Bensley for Wynne & Scholey and J. Wallis, 1803-05. 8 vols. 8°. Illustrated

BM | BPL | MPL | NY | SML

Some sets were issued on large paper (with two extra volumes), royal 8° size, one of which is at Warwick Castle.

The woodcuts by J. Thurston, after W. H. Pyne, and P. J. Loutherbourg are unworthy of the fine letter-press work.

Includes Rowe's life of the poet.

Each play is separately paged, and selected observations are appended.

Of the two additional volumes found with large paper sets vol. 9 contains the prefaces by Heminge and Condell, Pope, Theobald, Hanmer, Warburton, and Johnson; two 'advertisements' by Steevens; Capell's introduction; Monck Mason's preface to his comments; Farmer's essay on Sh—; Malone's preface, Essay on the chronology of Sh—'s plays, and a history of the stage. Volume 10 includes selected annotations from various commentators and a glossary.

A set of this issue (extended to 20 vols.) printed on vellum [said to be the ' only edition on vellum,' but this is far from correct] was sold 2nd March, 1906, for £106, to an American collector.

[Works] Plays of Wm. Sh—. Ln : P. Wynne & Son . . . 1803-07. 10 vols. 8°. With plates   BM | BPL | SML

A reprint of Wynne and Scholey's 1803-5 edition, with new title-page to vol. 1 bearing the date 1807, and new frontispieces to ' Much ado' and a ' Midsummer night's dream.'

[Works] Plays . . . in nine volumes. Edinburgh : Printed by Thomas Turnbull . . . 1804. 9 vols. 12°   BPL

In vol. 4 occurs a singular slip, the title stating it contains a ' Winter night's tale.'

Works . . . Ln : John Bell . . . 1804. 20 vols. 12°. With copperplates

A set printed on vellum is mentioned by A. H. Wall (formerly librarian to the Stratford Memorial), but it is untraceable elsewhere.

Sh— Works . . .

[Works] Plays of Wm. Sh—, accurately printed from the text of Mr. Steevens' last edition, with a selection of the most important notes. Leipsick : Printed for Gerhard Fleischer the younger . . . 1804-13. 20 vols. 16°   BM | BPL | NY | SML
First Leipzig edition.
With oval stipple (Chandos) portrait (altered) engraved on copper by Heinrich Schmidt.

[Works] Plays . . . illustrated by the prefaces and annotations of the various commentators [Volume the ninth]. Ln : T. Bensley for James Wallis . . . 1805. 8°, pp. 782
A supplementary volume to Sh—'s works, 1803-5.

[Works] Plays of Wm. Sh— from the text of G. Steevens. With notes from the most eminent commentators, life, &c. by A. Chalmers. Thirty-seven engravings [after Fuseli's designs]. Ln : Printed for the trade . . . 1805. 9 vols. 8°. With portrait   BPL

[Works] Plays of Wm. Sh— accurately printed from the text of the corrected copy left by the late George Steevens, Esq. With a series of engravings from original designs of Henry Fuseli and a selection of explanatory and historical notes from the most eminent commentators ; a history of the stage [by E. Malone] ; a life of Sh—, &c. by Alexander Chalmers. Ln : F. C. & J. Rivington, 1805. Forty parts, forming 10 vols. 8°. Felton portrait by Neagle, and plates after Fuseli. Prefaces by Johnson, Pope, and Chalmers   BM | BPL | NY | SML | W
Some sets done on large paper, roy. 8°, of which one is at Warwick. A few also issued on largest paper, imp. 8°.

[Works] Plays . . . In seventeen volumes. With the corrections and illustrations of various commentators. To which are added notes by S. Johnson and G. Steevens. Revised and augmented by I. Reed. With a glossarial index [Ed. by Joseph Dennie]. Philadelphia : C. & A. Conrad & Co. ; Baltimore : Conrad, Lucas & Co. ; Petersburg : Somervell & Conrad ; Norfolk : Bonsal, Conrad & Co. ; New York : J. & T. Ronalds ; I. Riley & Co. ; Philadelphia : H. Maxwell, T. S. Manning, & J. Morgan, 1805-09. 17 vols. 12°   BPL | NY | SML
The imprints vary in the respective titles of the entire set.

[Works] Dramatic works . . . Complete in two volumes. Ln : Printed by Savage & Easingwood for William Miller, 1806. 2 vols. Roy. 8°, pp. xvi.-544, vi.-618
With prefatory account of Sh—.   BPL | SML

Sh— Works . . .

[Works] Plays of Wm. Sh—, with notes of various commentators. Edited by Manley Wood. Ln : Printed for George Kearsley . . . 1806. Issued in parts, forming 14 vols. 8°. With 72 plates   BM | BPL | MPL | NY | SML | W
Portrait and plates by J. Thurston, engraved by Warren, Life by Rowe, and preface by Dr. Johnson.
A few issued on large paper, with open letter proofs.

[Works] Illustrations to Sh— : A series of copperplate engravings published in Manley Wood's edition of Sh—. Ln : . . . 1806. 8°. Seventy-five plates by C. Warren and others after Thurston, Stothard and others, including the Felton portrait   BUS
Also issued in proof state.

[Works] Comedies, histories and tragedies. Published according to the true originall copies . . . Isaac Iaggard and Ed. Blount, 1623. Ln : Reprinted by E. & J. Wright, 1807. F°   BM | BPL | BUS | MPL | SML | W
Edited by Francis Douce.
This, the first reprint of the first edition in its original form, was executed by J. Wright, St. John's Square, Ln. Wm. Upcott discovered errors, and set to work to collate it with the original. After one hundred and forty-five days' attention, he compiled a list of 368 errors. This fact coming to the notice of John and Arthur Arch, the Cornhill booksellers, two promoters of the supposed facsimile, they importuned him to sell the list to them. Eventually he consented, expecting fair remuneration for his five months' close work. All he received was a copy of the reprint, published at five guineas. [See *Notes and Queries*, 1st s., vol. vii., p. 47, and 3rd s., vol. 7, p. 139.]
The paper used was specially made, and bears the watermark of 'Sh— 1806.'
The Warwick copy is extra-illustrated with one hundred and twenty-seven plates (from Harding's 'Sh— illustrated,' largest paper), the Felton portrait of Sh— engraved by T. Trotter, 1793, in three differing proof states ; two portraits of Edmund Kean as *Richard the third* ; and others.
One of the two copies at Stratford contains a manuscript list of errata by Wm. Upcott.
Of the three copies printed on India paper one is in the British Museum.
John Keats (*q.v.*) wrote some 'Marginalia' upon this reprint.

[Works] Illustrations of Sh— and other dramatists after Smirke, Stothard, and Richard Cook, engraved by Heath, Neagle, Warren, and others. Edinburgh : Ballantyne . . . [1807]. 4°
Forty-eight plates reprinted from Ballantyne's edition of Sh—.
Also issued in proof state.

[Works] Dramatic works of Wm. Sh— with explanatory notes. To which is added a copious index to the remarkable passages and words, by S. Ayscough. [Third edition.] Ln : J. Stockdale . . . 1807. 2 vols. 8°. With Droeshout portrait engraved by W. Sherwin   BM | BPL | MPL | SML
The British Museum copy is enriched with manuscript notes in the autograph of S. T. Coleridge.

[Works] The family Sh—. Bath: Printed by R. Cruttwell for J. Hatchard, London, 1807. 4 vols. 12° BM | BPL

First Bowdler edition. Contains twenty plays only, all carefully expurgated by Thomas Bowdler, a deed which gave rise to the modern verb "to bowdlerise." The first edition printed in the Western spa.
Two leading reviews of the day form a sharp contrast :—
'We are of opinion that it requires nothing more than a notice to bring this very meritorious publication into general circulation.'—*Edin. Review.*
'Among the most extraordinary attempts at moral improvement none perhaps is better calculated to excite a sarcastic smile than a "Family Sh—," from which all objectionable passages are expunged.'—*Quarterly Review.*

[Works] Plays . . . Ln: Printed by T. Davison for Peter Wynne & Son, 45, and Robert Scholey, 46 Paternoster Row, 1807. 4 vols. 8°
The paper labels on the backs state 'Select plays in four volumes.'

[Works] Dramatic works . . . from the corrected text of Johnson & Steevens. Embellished with plates. Ln: J. Stockdale . . . 1807. 6 vols. 4°. With copperplates engraved by J. Heath after Stothard and Fuseli BPL | BUS | MPL | NY | SML
The set at Stratford is extra-illustrated with about five hundred plates, and expanded into 12 vols. It was presented by W. O. Hunt in 1865.

[Works] Plays . . . [with woodcuts by J. Thurston and Nesbit]. Ln: Printed by W. Davison for P. Wynne & Son and R. Scholey, 1807. 8 vols. 8° BPL | SML
Vols. 1, 5, 6, 7, 8 are printed by T. Davison, and vols. 2, 3, 4 by J. M'Creery.
Two supplementary volumes of readings and notes were added to this issue.

[Works] Dramatick works [with poems]. Preface by Dr. Johnson, notes . . . and life. Boston [U.S.]: Munroe & Francis . . . 1807. 9 vols. 12° BPL | BUS | SML
Volume 9 contains the Poems and Richardson's Philosophical analysis of some of Sh—'s characters.

[Works] Plays . . . from the text of Johnson, Steevens and Reed. Edinburgh: Ballantyne's edition; Ln: Longman, 1807. 12 vols. 8°. Felton portrait (altered) and 48 plates by R. Smirke and others BPL | MPL | NY
Some sets were produced on large paper.

[Works] . . . Comedies, histories, and tragedies . . . 1623. With corrections, annotations, and illustrations by John Britton. Ln: Reprinted by E. & J. Wright for Vernor & Hood, 1808. 4 vols. F°, interleaved. With plates BUS

[Works] British theatre. Printed, under the authority of the managers from the prompt books . . . With biographical and critical remarks by Mrs. Inchbald. Ln:

Longman, Hurst, Rees, & Orme, 1808. 24 parts in 8 vols. 12° BM | BUS | MPL
Twenty-four plays only. Also issued independently with special titles.

[Works] . . . Selected plays, from the best edition of Johnson & Steevens. [Nine plays.] With brief explanatory notes extracted from various commentators. Avignon: Seguin frères . . . 1809. 12° BM
The first English version of Sh— printed in France.

[Works] Twelve plays . . . Newcastle-on-Tyne: Mitchell . . . 1809. 3 vols. 12°
The first Newcastle-on-Tyne edition.

[Works] Popular dramatic works of Wm. Sh—. Ln: Vernor, Hood & Sharpe [c. 1809]. 4 vols. 12° W

[Works] Plays of Wm. Sh— from the correct edition of Isaac Reed . . . Ln: Vernor, Hood, & Sharpe, Poultry; Taylor & Hessey, Fleet St., 1809. 12 vols. 12°. Chandos portrait (somewhat altered) and woodcuts BM | BPL | SML | W
A few sets were issued on large paper, demy 8°, of which one is at Stratford.

[Works] Plays . . . With the corrections and illustrations of various commentators . . . notes by Johnson and Steevens. Revised and augmented by Isaac Reed. With a glossarial index. Philadelphia: C. & A. Conrad & Co., 1809. 17 vols. 8°. With Felton portrait BUS
Said to have been edited by Joseph Dennie.

[Works] Sh— illustrated by thirty-seven engravings on wood by Branston from new designs by J. Thurston. Ln: Vernor, Hood & Sharpe [1809]. 8°
One set was printed on vellum, and a few on India paper.

[Works] Plays . . . With glossarial notes. Ln: Sharpe . . . 1810. 9 vols. 18°

[Works] Illustration of Sh—: Thirty-eight engravings by Branston from new designs by John Thurston. Ln: Vernor, Hood & Sharpe [1810]. 8° BUS

Works . . . with the corrections and illustrations of Dr. Johnson and G. Steevens. Revised by I. Reed. 3rd Boston edition, from the 5th London edition. Boston [U.S.]: Munroe, D. Francis, & Parker, 1810-12. 9 vols. 12° BPL | NY | SML
With portrait and wood engravings by Dr. A. Anderson.

[Works] Whole historical dramas . . . Illustrated by an assemblage of portraits of persons mentioned, with those of editors, commentators, and actors, views of castles, towns, etc. Ln: E. Jeffery . . . 1811. 2 vols. Roy. 8°
Some copies were done on large paper, 4°.

Sh— Works . . .

[Works] Dramatic works of Wm. Sh—.
With [123] copperplates. Ln: J. Stockdale . . . 1811. 4 vols. 8°   BPL

[Works] Plays . . . accurately printed from
the text of the corrected copy left by the
late George Steevens, Esq. With glos-
sarial notes [by A. Chalmers] and a sketch
of the life of Sh— [by N. Rowe]. Ln:
Printed for J. Nichols & Son, F. C. & J.
Rivington, J. Stockdale, W. Lowndes, G.
Wilkie & J. Robinson, T. Egerton, J.
Walker, J. Nunn, W. Clarke & Son, J.
Barker & Son, J. Cuthell, R. Lea, Lack-
ington & Co., J. Deighton, J. White & Co.,
C. Law, B. Crosby & Co., W. Earle, J.
Gray & Son, G. Robinson, Longman &
Co., Cadell & Davies, J. Harding, R. H.
Evans, J. Booker, S. Bagster, J. Mawman,
Black & Co., J. Richardson, J. Booth,
Newman & Co., R. Pheney, R. Scholey,
J. Asperne, J. Faulder, R. Baldwin,
Cradock & Joy, J. Mackinlay, J. Johnson
& Co., Gale & Curtis; York: Wilson &
Son, 1811. 8 vols. 12°. With steel
frontispieces and vignette titles engraved
by S. Noble after T. Uwins
    BM | BPL | SML | W
The engraved titles bear the names, as publishers, of
'F. C. & J. Rivington and partners.'
This edition was issued in cream-coloured boards, deckle
edges. A few sets were done on 'superfine woven
royal paper,' 5½ by 3in.

[Works] Plays . . . With glossarial notes.
'Walker's classics.' Ln: J. Walker . . .
1811. 8 vols. 24°

[Works] Plays . . . accurately printed from
the text . . . of Geo. Steevens. With
select notes and a sketch of . . . Sh—.
Ln: Wm. Miller . . . 1811. 8 vols. 12°.
Illustrated by Uwins   CPL

[Works] Plays . . . printed from the text of
Johnson, Steevens, and Reed. Ln: J.
Forsyth . . . 1811. 9 vols. 12°   BPL

[Works] Plays . . . accurately printed from
the text of . . . G. Steevens. With a
selection of explanatory and historical
notes from the most eminent commentators, a history of the stage, life of Sh—,
etc., by Alex. Chalmers. Ln: J. Nichols
& Son . . . 1811. 9 vols. 8°. With en-
gravings after Fuseli   BPL | NY | SML

[Works] Plays . . . from the text of Geo.
Steevens. With glossarial notes [by A.
Chalmers]. Ln: J. Nichols . . . 1811.
10 vols. 12°. With Droeshout portrait
    BPL | SML

Works . . . from the text of Isaac Reed.
Ln: Cowie & Co. . . . 1811. 12 vols. 12°

Sh— Works . . .

Works . . . from the text of Isaac Reed.
Ln: Thomas Tegg . . . 1812-15. 12 vols.
8°   BPL | NY
With engravings after J. Thurston's designs.
Some sets were done on large paper, 8°.

[Works] Plays . . . complete in one vol.
Accurately printed from the text of Isaac
Reed. Boston: C. Williams; Philadel-
phia: J. Delaplaine, 1813. 8°, pp. 914.
With engraved title and Felton portrait
    BPL | NY | SML
The first single volume edition published in the United
States.

[Works] . . . Dramas illustrated by a series
of copperplate engravings, from J. Thurston's designs, by Rhodes. Ln: T. Tegg
. . . 1813. Imp. 8°. Fifty plates
Some copies issued as India proofs.

[Works] Plays . . . printed from the text of
Isaac Reed. Boston [U.S.]: Printed by
J. T. Buckingham for C. Williams . . .;
Philadelphia: J. Delaplaine . . . 1813.
6 vols. 12°. With Felton portrait
(altered) and vignettes
    BM | BPL | BUS | SML
Published also at New York.

[Works] Plays . . . With the corrections and
illustrations of various commentators.
To which are added notes by Samuel
Johnson and George Steevens. Revised
and augmented by Isaac Reed. With a
glossarial index. Sixth edition. Ln. &
Weybridge: Printed for Nichols & Son,
1813. 21 vols. 8°
    BM | BPL | MPL | NY | SML | W
Felton portrait engraved by W. Holl. The proof sheets
of this edition, writes Lowndes, were corrected by
Mr. Harris, librarian of the Royal Institution. Volume
two has an engraving of a figure seated contemplating
Sh—'s bust.
The preliminary matter is the same as in the 21 vol.
edition of 1803.
The Warwick set is of especial interest, having belonged
to Edmund Kean. A manuscript note on the fly-
leaf, signed by J. P. Harley, states:—'This edition
of Sh— was presented to Edmund Kean of the
Theatre Royal, Drury Lane, by the Honble. Douglas
Kinnaird.'
Volumes 11 to 21 were printed at Weybridge. Sets
should possess half-titles to be perfect.
Sets on large paper, roy. 8°, were issued at £18 18s. each.

[Works] Dramatic works . . . Whittingham's
edition [With remarks on the life and
writings of Wm. Sh— . . . by J. Britton].
Chiswick: C. Whittingham, 1813-14. 7
vols. 16°. Woodcuts by Thompson
    BM | BPL | SML
Some sets contain the 230 embellishments on India
paper.

Works . . . from the text of Isaac Reed.
[Boston]: C. Williams . . . 1814. 8°

Works . . . from the text of Isaac Reed.
Ln: Cowie & Co. . . . 1814. 12 vols. 8°

Sh— Works . . .

[Works] Plays of Wm. Sh—, accurately printed from the text of Mr. Steevens' last edition, with a selection of the most important notes. Vienna: Anton Doll . . . 1814. 20 vols. 16°. With plates   BM
First Austrian edition of Sh— in English.

[Works] Dramatic works of Wm. Sh—. With preface by Dr. Johnson. Ln: Whittingham & Arliss, 1815. 7 vols. 12°   BPL

[Works] Select British theatre. Containing all the plays formerly adapted to the stage by Mr. Kemble. Revised by him, with additional alterations. Ln: J. Miller . . . 1815. 8 vols. 12°   BUS
Contains twenty-six of Sh—'s plays, which were also issued independently and may be found entered separately under their respective titles.

Works . . . collated verbatim from the most authentic copies and revised. With the corrections and illustrations of various commentators. To which are added, an essay on the chronological order of his plays; an essay relative to Sh— and Jonson; a dissertation on . . . ' King Henry VI.'; an historical account of the English stage, and notes by Edmond Malone . . . Ln: Printed for the proprietors [by Zachariah Jackson, of Dublin], 1816. 16 vols. 8°. With portrait by Faithorne engraved by R. Sawyer, and seven other plates   BPL

[Works] British theatre, or a collection of plays . . . with biographical and critical remarks by Mrs. Inchbald. Ln: T. Hurst, Robinson & Co. [1816-18]. 20 vols. 12°. Illustrated   BUS
Reprinted from the first edition of 1808. The plates alone are dated.
Also issued separately with independent titles.

[Works] Dramatic works of Sh—. Ln: Printed by D. S. Maurice [c. 1817]. 8 vols. 12°   BPL

Works . . . from the text of Johnson, Steevens, and Reed. Edinburgh: Oliver & Boyd . . . 1817. 9 vols. 12°   BPL

[Works] Illustrations to Sh—'s plays, by J. Thurston. Ln: . . . 1817. 4°. Thirty-eight plates and portrait   CPL

[Works] Dramatic works . . . With the corrections and illustrations of Dr. Johnson, G. Steevens, and others. Revised by I. Reed. New York: Hy. Durell . . . 1817-18. 10 vols. 8°. With Chandos portrait and illustrations   BPL | BUS | NY
Stereotype edition.

[Works] Complete dramatic works and miscellaneous poems . . . With glossarial notes, and life by N. Rowe. Ln: J.

Sh— Works . . .

Limbird . . . 1818. 8°, pp iv.-viii.-794. With Chandos portrait and engraved title by Roffe   BPL | CPL

[Works] Dramatic works . . . With life [by John Britton, preface by Dr. Johnson, glossarial index and bibliography of detached essays and dissertations on Sh—.] Whittingham's edition. Chiswick: C. Whittingham for Sherwood, Neely & Jones . . . 1818. 7 vols. 16°. Stratford bust portrait and 230 woodcuts by Thurston   BM | BPL
Some sets issued not illustrated, and twenty-five sets done with the engravings on India paper.

Works . . . edited by Alex. Chalmers. Ln: [Printed by D. S. Maurice for J. Bumpus, although ostensibly printed by] Whittingham, Chiswick, 1818. 9 vols. 8°   BPL

[Works] The family Sh—; in which nothing is added to the original text, but those words and expressions are omitted which cannot with propriety be read aloud in a family. By Thomas Bowdler. [Second edition.] Ln: Longman . . . 1818. 10 vols. 12°   SML

[Works] ' Oxberry's theatre ' [Thirteen plays only]. Ln: Wm. Oxberry . . . 1818-23. 12 vols. 12°   MPL
These plays were issued independently for playgoers, and will be found entered under their respective titles also.

[Works] Plays . . . from the text of Johnson, Steevens, and Isaac Reed. Ln: [Printed at Edinburgh by Ballantyne for] Hurst . . . 1819. 2 vols. Roy. 8°   BPL

Works . . . from the text of Johnson, Steevens, and Reed. Edinburgh: J. Robertson . . . 1819. 9 vols. 12°   BPL

Works . . . carefully revised from the best editions. Ln: W. Allason . . . 1819. 9 vols. 12°   BPL

[Works] Dramatic works . . . Leipsic: Brothers Schumann [c. 1820]. 8 vols. 24°   BPL

[Works] The family Sh—, in ten volumes . . . By T. Bowdler. Second edition. Ln: Longman & Co. . . . 1820. 10 vols. 12mo   BM | BPL
A fresh date only distinguishes this from Bowdler's previous edition.

[Works] Dramatic works . . . from the correct edition of Isaac Reed. With copious annotations. Ln: Printed for J. Walker, G. Offor, Sharpe & Sons. Edinburgh: J. Sutherland. Dublin: J. Cumming, 1820. 12 vols. 8°. With singular portrait engraved by Rhodes after Thurston   BPL | BUS | SML
At Stratford Memorial is a large paper set, 8°.

Works . . . Ln: John Bell . . . 1820. 20 vols. 12°

Sh— Works . . .

[Works] Dramatic works of Sh—. New pocket edition. [From the text of Johnson and Steevens.] Ln : Black & Son, 1820-21. 3 vols. 12°. With engravings BPL | SML

[Works] Dramatic works . . . to which are added his miscellaneous poems [life by N. Rowe] and a portrait. Ln : Sherwin & Co. . . . 1821. 8°, pp. xii.-794. With Droeshout portrait BM | BPL | SML

[Works] Dramatic works . . . Ln : Printed by W. Clowes for A. Black, G. & W. B. Whittaker . . . 1821. 3 vols. 12° BPL

[Works] Dramatic works of Wm. Sh—, to which are added his miscellaneous poems. Ln : Printed for J. Walker, J. Richardson & Co., J. Sharpe & Son, J. Johnston. Glasgow : R. Griffin & Co., 1821. 6 vols. 12° BM | BPL | SML

Contains the life of Sh— by N. Rowe.
Issued in printed yellow boards, deckle edges, at thirty shillings per set.

[Works] Dramatic works . . . correctly given from the text of Johnson and Steevens, with a preface by S. Johnson and a complete glossarial index. Ln : Printed for J. Bumpus, 6 Holborn Bars ; Andrews, New Bond St. ; Butler, Bruton St. ; Sharpe, King St. ; Reid, Charing Cross ; Clarke, Royal Exchange, 1821. 9 vols. 16°. With woodcuts SML

[Works] Dramatic works . . . with the corrections and illustrations of Johnson, Steevens and others. Revised by I. Reed. New York : Collins & Hanway, 1821. 10 vols. 8° BUS

[Works] Dramatic works . . . from the correct edition of Isaac Reed, Esq. With copious annotations [Stereotype edition]. Ln : J. Walker . . . 1821. 12 vols. 8°
The date 1820 appears on title of vol. xi. BM | BPL

[Works] Plays and poems of Wm. Sh—, with the corrections and illustrations of various commentators : comprehending a life of the poet and an enlarged history of the stage by the late Edmund Malone, with a new glossarial index. Seventh edition. [Edited by James Boswell. Malone's ' Variorum edition.'] Ln : F. C. & J. Rivington . . . 1821. 21 vols. 8° BM | BPL | MPL | NY | SML

The first edition edited by James Boswell, junior.
At his death in 1812 Malone bequeathed his MS. collections for a fresh edition of Sh— to his friend Boswell the younger, and this issue was the result. It forms a valuable mine of Shakespearean information which time has scarcely affected.
It includes the Chandos portrait, the Burgess miniature, the Stratford bust, and facsimiles.

Sh— Works . . .

[Works] Illustrations to Sh—, by Wright, Smirke, Stephanoff, Westall, and Corbould. Engraved by Heath, Bacon, Rolls, Chevalier, Greatbach, and Engleheart. Ln : Rodwell & Martin, 1821-29. 4°. Ninety-six plates BUS | CPL
India proof sets also done in folio.

[Works] Illustrations to Sh—, by Robert Smirke. Ln : Rodwell & Martin, 1821-29. F°. Engraved title and forty-four plates BPL (impft.) | BUS | CPL | SML | W

Contents :—The tempest, 6 plates
    Taming of the shrew, 6 plates
    Merry wives, 6 plates
    Twelfth night, 6 plates
    Measure for measure, 5 plates
    Midsummer night's dream, 5 plates
    King Henry IV., I., 5 plates
    Romeo and Juliet, 5 plates.
A ' largest paper ' copy with plates on India paper is at Warwick.

[Works] Dramatic works . . . from the text of Johnson, Stevens [sic] and Reed, with notes, a critique on Sh—'s writings and genius, by N. Rowe. Ln : Mason & Co. . . . 1822. 8° BPL | SML

[Works] School Sh—, or plays and scenes from Sh— illustrated for the use of schools, with glossarial notes selected from the best annotators by J. R. Pitman. Ln : C. Rice . . . 1822. 8°, pp. xxiv.-596 BM | BPL | BUS
Contains twenty-six plays, with selected passages from nine others and from the Sonnets.

[Works] ' Bowdler's family edition ' . . . Third edition. Ln : Longman . . . 1822. 8 vols. 8°

[Works] ' Bowdler's family edition ' . . . Third edition. Ln : Longman, 1822. 10 vols. 18°
An alternate size for buyers, issued at the same time as the preceding entry.

[Works] Dramatic works . . . from the edition of I. Reed. Ln : J. Walker . . . 1822. 12 vols. 12° BPL

[Works] Plays . . . Ln : Printed [by Corrall for] William Pickering, 1822-23. 9 vols, issued in 36 parts. 32°. With portrait BM | BPL | SML

Miniature edition, set in diamond type.
The smallest form, up to the end of the nineteenth century, in which Sh— appeared ; in contradistinction to the largest edition, issued by Halliwell, 1853-65.
Some sets were issued with thirty-eight engravings after Stothard, and a few sets were impressed entirely upon India paper and published in silk boards.
By some strange oversight the whole of a ' Midsummer night's dream ' was omitted from the earliest printings of this edition. The error was afterwards made good by the play being inserted, its pagination being marked with full-points.

[Works] Dramatic works . . . With a glossary. Chiswick : C. Whittingham . . . 1823. 12°, pp. 666 NY

[Works] Dramatic works . . . With a glossary. [*Vignette*.] Chiswick, Printed by C. Whittingham for Thomas Tegg, R. Jennings, Rodwell & Martin, N. Hailes, C. S. Arnold, London. Edinburgh: J. Sutherland. Glasgow: R. Griffin & Co., 1823. 12°, pp. ii.-666

[Works] Complete dramatic works and miscellaneous poems of Wm. Sh—. With notes and life by N. Rowe. Ln: J. H. Bohte, 1823. 8°　　　　　　　BPL

[Works] Dramatic works of Wm. Sh—, from the text of Johnson, Steevens, and Reed. With glossarial notes, his life, and a critique on his genius and writings by N. Rowe. Ln: Jones & Co., 1823. 8°, pp. 972　　　　　　　BM | BPL

[Works] Plays . . . from the text of G. Steevens and E. Malone, with life and glossary. Ln: C. & J. Rivington, 1823. 8°　　　　　　　BPL | SML

[Works] Plays . . . Ln: Sherwin . . . 1823. 8°

[Works] Plays . . . accurately printed from the text of correct copies left by Steevens and Malone, with a sketch of his life and a glossary [by Alex. Chalmers]. Ln: Printed for the trade, 1823. 8°. With portrait

[Works] Bowdler's family edition . . . Ln: Longman . . . 1823. 6 vols. 8°

[Works] Plays of Wm. Sh—, accurately printed from the text of the corrected copies left by the late George Steevens, Esq., and Edmund Malone, Esq., with Mr. Malone's various readings; a selection of explanatory and historical notes from the most eminent commentators; a history of the stage, and a life of Sh— by Alexander Chalmers. A new edition. Ln: F. C. & J. Rivington, 1823. 8 vols. 8°　　　　BPL | SML | W
With Chandos portrait engraved by Fry; also plates, prefaces by Pope and Johnson, and a glossary.
Some sets were done on fine paper.

[Works] Plays . . . accurately printed from the text of the corrected copy left by the late George Steevens. With glossarial notes and a sketch of the life of Sh—. Philadelphia: H. C. Carey & I. Lea, 1823. 8 vols. 12°　BPL | BUS | SML

[Works] Dramatic works . . . correctly given from the text of Johnson and Steevens, with preface by Dr. Johnson and glossarial index. Ln: J. Bumpus . . . 1823. 9 vols. 12°. With plates and vignettes　　　　　　　BPL | SML

[Works] Plays of Wm. Sh—, accurately printed from the text of the corrected copy left by the late G. Steevens, Esq. With glossarial notes. [Some account of the life of Sh— by N. Rowe and Dr. Johnson's preface.] Ln: F. C. & J. Rivington, 1823. 10 vols. 12° BM | BPL
A few sets were done on large paper.

[Works] Dramatic works . . . from the text of Isaac Reed, Ln: J. Walker . . . 1823. 12 vols. 8°　　　　　　　BPL

[Works] Dramatic works . . . from the text of Johnson and Stevens [*sic*]. Ln: Black, Young & Young, 1824. 12°, pp. xii.-1,062　　　　　　　BM | BPL

[Works] Dramatic works . . . edited by Charles Henry Wheeler. Ln: W. Baynes & Son . . . 1824. 8°. With Droeshout portrait　　　　　　BPL | SML

[Works] Dramatic works, from the text of Johnson, Steevens, and Reed, with glossarial notes, sketch of his life, and estimate of his writings. Edited by Ch. Hen. Wheeler. Ln: H. Fisher's Caxton Press, 1824. 8°　　　　　　　BPL
The first edition edited by C. H. Wheeler.

[Works] Plays . . . with notes original and selected by Henry Neele. [Four plays only] embellished by G. F. Joseph. Ln: J. Smith . . . 1824. Nos. 1-4. 8°, pp. ii.-322. With engraved plates
　　　　　　　BM | BPL | BUS
Contains 'The tempest, Two gentlemen, Merry wives, and Twelfth night.' No more published.

[Works] Dramatic works . . . With the corrections and illustrations of Johnson, Steevens, and others. Revised by I. Reed. New York: Collins & Hanway, 1824. 10 vols. 12°　　BPL | BUS

[Works] Plays . . . from the text of the corrected copy left by George Steevens, with glossarial notes, life by Rowe, and Dr. Johnson's preface. Ln: Otridge & Rackham, 1824. 10 vols. 8° BPL | SML | MPL

[Works] Dramatic works of Sh—, printed from the text of S. Johnson, G. Steevens and I. Reed. [With an appendix, list of contents, life of the author by A. Skottowe, his miscellaneous poems, critical glossary, etc.] Leipsic: E. Fleischer . . . 1824-26. 2 vols. 8°　BM | BPL | SML

[Works] Dramatic works . . . from the text of G. Steevens, with glossarial notes and life. Philadelphia: M'Carty & Davis . . . 1824-28. 2 vols. 12°　　BPL | SML

[Works] Dramatic works . . . with glossarial notes, a sketch of his life, and an estimate of his writings. Newly arranged and

Sh— Works . . .

edited by Charles Henry Wheeler . . . Ln : Printed for Wm. Baynes & Son . . . and H. S. Baynes, Edinburgh, 1825. 8°, pp. 908 and Droeshout portrait, engraved by Thomson   SML

[Works] Select comedies from Sh—. Boston [U.S.] . . . 1825. 12°   BPL

[Works] Dramatic works . . . from the text of Johnson, Steevens and Reed. With glossarial notes, life, and critique . . . by N. Rowe. Ln : Mason & Co. . . . 1825. 8°, pp. 972

[Works] Plays . . . from the text of Johnson, Steevens and Reed. With embellishments by Thurston. Ln : W. Sharpe & Co. . . . 1825. 8°   BPL

Works . . . from the text of Johnson, Steevens and Reed. With a biographical memoir and a variety of interesting matter, illustrative of his life and writings. By W. Harvey. Ln : Published for the proprietors of the ' London Stage ' by Sherwood, Jones & Co., 1825. 8°, pp. lxxx.-896. Jansen portrait, frontispiece, and rough woodcuts   BM | BPL | NY | SML

[Works] Plays . . . edited by C. H. Wheeler from the text of Johnson, Steevens and Reed. With copious glossary and embellishments by Thurston. Ln : J. Bumpus . . . 1825. Roy. 8°   BPL | SML

[Works] Illustrations of Sh— and the British drama, comprised in 230 vignette engravings by Thompson, chiefly from designs by Thurston. Adapted to all editions. Ln : Printed for Sherwood, Gilbert & Piper by D. S. Maurice, 1825. Roy. 8°, pp. 84, including wrappers
A few proof copies were done on India paper, imp. 8°.

[Works] Dramatic Works . . . from the text of Johnson, Steevens and Reed. New York : S. King . . . 1825. 2 vols. 8° BPL

[Works . . . edited by Sir Walter Scott and John Gibson Lockhart. Edinburgh : Printed by J. Ballantyne & Co. for A. Constable, 1825.] [Vols. 2 to 4.] 3 vols. 8°. [All ever printed]   BUS
In a letter dated 1822, A. Constable suggested to Scott a plan for issuing ' Sh— in twelve or fourteen volumes, with a set of readable and amusing notes.' After further correspondence it was decided to publish it in ten vols., the first to contain a general introduction and life of the dramatist by Scott, while the editing and notes were to be done by Lockhart. Scott was to receive £2,500. The sequel to the project is found in a letter from Constable's son, who wrote :—' Three volumes of the edition were completed before the sad crisis in 1826 and then laid aside, and ultimately, I have been told, the sheets were sold in London as waste paper. It is even doubted whether one copy be now in existence.'
Fortunately one set did survive. It was bought by the

Sh— Works . . .

bookseller Thomas Rodd at an Edinburgh sale, who wrote in vol. 2 :—' The book bears marks of Scott's usual inaccuracies.' This copy is now at Boston.
There are no title-pages. Each play has a brief introduction and foot-notes.

[Works] Dramatic works . . . with notes . . . selected from the most eminent commentators, to which is prefixed a life of the author by W. Harness. Ln : Saunders & Otley . . . 1825. 8 vols. 8°. With Droeshout portrait   BM | BPL | BUS
Some sets done on fine paper.

[Works] Plays . . . Diamond type edition. Ln : W. Pickering . . . 1825. 9 vols. 48°. Droeshout portrait engraved by A. Fox and plates by T. Stothard   BUS | NY
Printed on India paper. One of the smallest sets of the poet ever printed. See also Sh— Works, 1822-23.

[Works] Family Sh— . . . by Thomas Bowdler. Fourth edition. Ln : Longman, Hurst . . . 1825. 10 vols. 12°   BPL | NY

[Works] Plays and poems . . . [with preface by Dr. Samuel Johnson]. ' Wreath edition.' Ln : Pickering, Talboys, & Nattali, 1825. 11 vols. 8°   BM | BPL | BUS | NY | SML
This edition contains the attributed plays.
A few sets were printed on straw-coloured paper.

[Works] Dramatic works . . . from the correct edition of Isaac Reed. With copious annotations [borrowed from preceding commentators]. Ln : J. Walker, G. Offor, Sharpe & Sons. Edinburgh : J. Sutherland. Dublin : J. Cumming, 1825. 12 vols. 8°   BPL | SML
Issued at £3 3s. in drab boards, with linen backs and paper labels.

[Works] Illustrations of the plays of Sh— from pictures painted by R. Smirke, engraved by Heath, Finden and others. Ln : Hurst, Robinson & Co. . . . 1825-26. Roy. 8°. Forty plates
Issued in numbers, each having six plates and illustrating one play. The work was discontinued and the plates incorporated into the Sh— portfolio (q.v. under Sh— Works, 1829). A few sets were issued as ' proofs before letters.'
It was published in three states : ordinary (as above) ; French proofs ; and India proofs.

[Works] Dramatic works . . . [With life by A. Chalmers.] Ln : Wm. Pickering . . . 1826. 12°, pp. 783   BM | BPL | BUS | NY | SML
Printed in diamond type.
With a second title-page, engraved. Droeshout portrait by W. Marshall, and thirty-seven engravings by Fox, Adlard, etc.
Fifty copies were issued on India paper, and a few on large paper.

[Works] Dramatic works . . . from the text of Johnson, Steevens and Reed. With notes, etc. by N. Rowe. Ln : . . . 1826. 8°   BPL

[Works] Plays . . . accurately printed from the text of the corrected copies left by the late G. Steevens, Esq. and E. Malone, Esq. With a glossary. Ln: Hurst, Robinson & Co. . . . 1826. 8°, pp. xii.-792
With a second title-page, engraved.   BM | BPL

Works . . . from the text of N. Rowe. Ln: Jones & Co. . . . 1826. 8°

[Works] Plays . . . from the text of G. Steevens and E. Malone, with life and glossary. Ln: C. & J. Rivington . . . 1826. 8°. With Chandos portrait
BPL | SML

[Works] Plays . . . accurately printed from the text of . . . G. Steevens and E. Malone. With Mr. Malone's various readings; a selection of explanatory and historical notes from the most eminent commentators; history of the stage [by E. Malone; life of Sh— and glossary. By A. Chalmers. A new edition. Ln: C. & J. Rivington . . . 1826. 8 vols. 8°. With Chandos portrait   BM | BPL | SML

[Works] Dramatic works . . . With notes, original and selected, by Samuel Weller Singer, F.S.A., and a life of the poet by Charles Symmons. Chiswick: Printed by C. Whittingham for Wm. Pickering, 1826. 10 vols. 12°. With portrait and sixty woodcuts after Stothard, Corbould, Harvey, &c.   BM | BPL
The first edition to possess Singer's notes.

[Works] Appendix to Sh—'s dramatic works. Contents; life of the author, by Aug. Skottowe; his miscellaneous poems; a critical glossary. Leipsic: E. Fleischer . . . 1826. Roy. 8°. With Chandos portrait   W

[Works] Illustrations of Sh.— A series of 39 engravings on steel, principally from designs by T. Stothard. Ln: W. Pickering . . . 1826. 8°
Afterwards used to illustrate the 'Lansdowne rubricated Sh—' (q.v.)

[Works] Illustrations of Sh—, by J. Thurston. Ln: . . . 1826. 8°   BPL

[Works] Illustrations to Sh—, designed and etched by Lady Wharncliffe. Ln: Privately printed [c. 1826]. Oblong f°

[Works] Union Sh— illustrations. Ln: R. Jennings . . . 1826-29. 8°. Portrait and thirty-seven plates after Smirke, Cooper, etc.
Issued in numbers for a time; then discontinued and incorporated in the Sh— portfolio (q.v. under Sh— Works, 1829).
Published in two other states: proofs, folio; and India proofs before letters, folio.

[Works] Dramatic works . . . *Perennis et fragrans.* [With glossary.] Ln: [Printed by Corrall, Charing Cross, for] Wm. Pickering, 1826-32. 12°, pp. iv.-784 and Marshall portrait engraved by H. Robinson, dated 1832

Works . . . printed from the text of the corrected copies of Steevens and Malone, with life by C. Symmons, and glossary. Ln: T. Hurst . . . 1827. 12°   SML

[Works] Plays . . . accurately printed from the text of the corrected copies left by the late George Steevens and Edward Malone. With a glossary. Ln: Printed [at Bungay by J. R. & C. Childs] for Thomas Tegg. Glasgow: R. Griffin & Co. Dublin: J. Cumming. Paris: M. Baudry, 1827. Cr. 8°, pp. 792-xii., and frontispiece of Falstaff by T. Stothard and S. Davenport   BPL | NY

[Works] Dramatic works . . . 'London stereotype edition.' Ln: J. F. Dove . . . 1827. Cr. 8°   BPL

[Works] Dramatic works of Wm. Sh—, accurately printed from the text of Dr. S. Johnson, G. Steevens, Esq., and I. Reed, Esq. Edited by C. H. Wheeler. Ln: Printed at the Caxton Press by H. Fisher, 1827. 8°   BM

[Works] Dramatic works . . . from the text of Johnson, Steevens, and Reed. With notes by N. Rowe. Ln: Jones & Co. . . . 1827. 8°   BPL

[Works] Dramatic works . . . accurately printed from the text of Dr. S. Johnson, G. Steevens, Esq., and I. Reed, Esq., with explanatory and glossarial notes, a sketch of his life, an essay on his writings, and a literary and historical notice prefixed to each play. Newly arranged . . . and . . . edited by Charles Henry Wheeler. Illustrated by . . . engravings by Thompson from designs by J. Thurston. 'London stereotype edition.' Ln: R. Thurston, 1827. 8°, pp. xii.-908. With Jansen portrait   BM | BPL | BUS

[Works] Family Sh—, in which nothing is added to the original text, but those words and expressions are omitted which cannot with propriety be read aloud in a family. By Thomas Bowdler. Fifth edition. Ln: Longman, Rees, 1827. 8 vols. 8°   BPL | MPL | SML | W

[Works] Dramatic works . . . With life by Charles Symmons and glossary. Ln: Printed by Whittingham, Chiswick Press, for Carpenter . . . 1827. 8 vols. 16°. Chandos portrait and vignettes by Thurston   BPL

Sh— Works . . .

[Works] Outline sketches for Sh—'s plays.
By L. S. Ruhl. With descriptive text in
English, German, and French. Frankfurt: Hesse Cassel . . . 1827-40. 6 parts.
Oblong 4°
Contents :—Othello, 13 plates ; Merchant of Venice,
10 plates ; The tempest, 9 plates ; Midsummer night's
dream, 6 plates ; Romeo and Juliet, 6 plates ; As you
like it, 12 plates.

[Works] Dramatic works . . . in one volume.
With life . . . by C. Symmons, a glossary,
and fifty embellishments. Chiswick: C.
Whittingham . . . 1828. 16°   BUS
To some copies thirty-eight steel engravings after
Stothard were added.

[Works] Dramatic works . . . from the text
of Johnson and Steevens [with life . . . by
Rowe]. Complete in one volume. Philadelphia: T. Wardle . . . 1828. 12°, pp.
xii.-1,062   BUS | SML

Works . . . edited by C. H. Wheeler. Ln :
H. Fisher, Caxton Press . . . 1828. 8° BPL

[Works] Dramatic works . . . from the text
of Johnson, Stevens and Reed. With
glossarial notes, life, and critique on his
genius and writings by N. Rowe. Ln :
Jones & Co., 1828. 8°, pp. 972. With
compartment frontispiece

[Works] Selections from Sh—'s plays, by
Benjamin Oakley. Ln : Longman . . .
1828. 8°, pp. xxii.-182   BPL | W

Works . . . edited by G. Steevens. Philadelphia : M'Carty & Davis, 1828. 2 vols.
8°   BPL | SML
Vol. 2 is dated 1824.

[Works] Dramatic works of Sh—. With a
life [by C. Symmons] and a glossary.
Chiswick : C. & C. Whittingham . . . 1828.
8 vols. 16°. With Chandos portrait and
woodcuts   BM | BPL | BUS | SML

Works . . . Bowdler's family edition. Ln :
Longman . . . 1828. 8 vols. 8°

[Works] Plays . . . ' Diamond type edition.'
Ln : W. Pickering . . . 1828. 9 vols. 32°

[Works] Dramatic works . . . from the text
of Johnson and Steevens. Ln : J.
Bumpus . . . 1828. 9 vols. 12°   BPL

[Works] Gallery of Sh—, by F. A. M.
Retzsch. With explanations by Lake . . .
1828. 12°   BPL

[Works] Dramatic works . . . with notes . . .
by S. W. Singer and life by Charles
Symmons. Frankfurt : S. Schmerber . . .
1828-34. 10 vols. 12°   BPL
The first edition printed at Frankfort.

[Works] Dramatic works of Wm. Sh—,
with glossorial notes, a sketch of his
life, and an estimate of his writings.
Newly arranged and edited [by C. H.
Wheeler.] Ln., Paris, New York :

Sh— Works . . .

Fisher, Son & Co., Caxton Press [1829].
8°, pp. xii.-908. With 230 woodcuts after
Thurston   BM | BPL | SML
Reprinted from the 1827 edition.

[Works] Dramatic works . . . from the text
of G. Steevens, with glossary, notes, and
life. Hartford : Published by Silas Andrus. New York : J. & J. Harper, 1829.
2 vols. Roy. 8°. With engraved frontispiece, engraved title, and numerous plates
on wood   SML

[Works] Sh— portfolio : A series of ninety-
six graphic illustrations of the plays of
Sh— after designs by the most eminent
British artists, including Smirke, Stothard, Westall, Hilton, Leslie, Griggs,
Stephanoff, Cooper, Corbould, Clint, &c.,
engraved in the line manner by Heath,
Greatbach, Robinson, Pye, Finden, Engleheart, Armstrong, Rolls, and others. Ln :
. . . [1829]. Roy. 8°. Ninety-six plates
Issued in two other states : French proofs, folio ; and
India proofs, folio.
An amalgamation of several earlier collections of Shakespearean engravings, executed for Joshua Walmesley,
an enthusiast, who died before he could complete his
idea of issuing a sumptuously-illustrated edition of
the poet.

[Works] British theatre, with remarks,
biographical and critical, by D. G——
[George Daniel]. Printed from acting
copies, as performed at the Theatres
Royal. Ln : John Cumberland [c. 1829-
31]. 33 vols. 12°   BM | MPL

[Works] Dramatic works of Wm. Sh—.
With notes, original and selected, by S. W.
Singer. Francfort on Main : Printed for
Brönner, 1829-31. 10 vols. 8° BM | SML

[Works] Dramatic works . . . With notes . . .
by S. W. Singer. Francfort o. M.
Brönner. Halle : C. R. Kersten. Francfort o. M. : S. Schmerber, 1829-43. 10
vols. 8°
The imprints in this set run as follow :—Vols. 1, 2, 3,
Brönner, Francfort, 1829-30 ; vol. 4, C. R. Kersten,
Halle, 1843 ; vols. 5 and 6, Brönner, Francfort, 1831 ;
vols. 7, 8, 9, 10, Schmerber, Francfort, 1832-34.

Works . . . with life by C. Symmons, and
woodcuts. Chiswick : C. Whittingham . . .
1830. 12°   BPL

[Works] Dramatic works . . . from the text
of Johnson, Steevens and Reed. With a
biographical memoir and summary of
each play, copious glossary, and variorum
notes. Francfort . . . 1830. 8°. With
portrait

Works . . . Hartford [U.S.] : Silas Andrus,
1830. 8°

[Works] Dramatic works . . . edited by C.
H. Wheeler. Ln : Caxton Press . . . 1830.
8°   BPL

[Works] Dramatic works . . . edited by C. H. Wheeler. Ln : Fisher, Son & Co., 1830. 8° BPL

Works . . . from the text of Johnson and Steevens, with memoir, remarks, glossary, and notes. Paris : Baudry [printed by Smith], 1830. 8° SML

[Works] Plays and poems . . . from the text of Johnson, Steevens, Reed and Malone, with notes selected from the most eminent commentators and a supplement by Lewis Tieck. Leipzig . . . 1830. Roy. 8°

[Works] Dramatic works . . . with a life of the author and a selection of notes, critical, historical, and explanatory, by W. Harness. To which are added the author's poems. [Second edition.] Ln : J. F. Dove, 1830. 8 vols. 8°
BPL | MPL | NY | SML | W
Droeshout portrait, engraved by Swaine; the Stratford bust and the Chandos portrait, engraved by E. Scriven; prefaces by Rowe, Pope and Johnson.

[Works] . . . Cumberland's British theatre. 'Acting edition of Sh—'s plays.' Ln : S. French [c. 1830]. 25 vols. 12° SML

[Works] 'Pocket Sh—.' Ln : Mansell . . . [c. 1830]. 43 parts. 12° BPL | SML

[Works] Illustrations of Sh—, comprised in two-hundred-and-thirty vignette engravings [on wood] by Thompson from designs by J. Thurston. Adapted to all editions. Ln : Printed for Sherwood, Gilbert & Piper by Maurice & Co., 1830. Roy. 8°, ff. 40 BUS | W
The frontispiece depicts the Jubilee procession passing the birth-house in 1769.

[Works] Illustrations of Sh— . . . by Thompson [and] Thurston. Philadelphia : T. Wardle . . . 1830. 8°, ff. 40 BUS
Copied from the London edition.

[Works] Plays of Wm. Sh—, accurately printed from the text of Mr. Steevens' last edition, with historical and grammatical explanatory notes in German by J. M. Pierre. Francfort o. Main : J. D. Sauerlænder, 1830-40. Vols. 1 to 8. 12°
No more published. BM

[Works] Dramatic works . . . With life by C. Symmons. Chiswick : C. Whittingham . . . 1831. 12° BPL

Works . . . from the text of Johnson and Steevens. Ln : Black, Young & Young, 1831. 12° BPL

[Works] Comedies, histories and tragedies of Sh—. Ln : Printed by Corrall for William Pickering, 1831. 8°. With engravings after designs by T. Stothard and others, and an engraved title BM | BPL
A few were printed on India paper.

[Works] Complete dramatic works and poems . . . with notes and life by N. Rowe. Ln : Richardson & Sons [c. 1831]. 8°
SML

[Works] Dramatic works of Sh— from the text of Johnson and Steevens. Ln : T. Tegg . . . 1831. 8°. With engraved title-page BM

Works . . . from the text of Isaac Reed. Ln : . . . 1831. 8°

[Works] . . . 'Bowdler's family edition.' New York . . . [c. 1831]. 8°

[Works] The family Sh— . . . By T. Bowdler . . . Sixth edition. Ln : Longman . . . 1831. Roy. 8°, pp. viii.-910. With woodcuts BM | BPL | NY

Works and poems . . . With notes by S. W. Singer and life by C. Symmons. New York : S. King . . . 1831. 2 vols. 8° BPL

[Works] Dramatic works . . . from the text of Johnson and Steevens. Philadelphia : T. Wardle . . . 1831. 2 vols. 8° CPL

[Works] Illustrations of Sh— and the British drama comprised in 230 vignette engravings . . . by Thurston. Ln : . . . 1831. 8°

[Works] Complete works . . . consisting of his plays and poems. With a critical preface by Dr. Johnson and a glossary . . . Halifax : Milner & Sowerby . . . 1832. 8° CPL

Works . . . edited by C. H. Wheeler, with glossarial notes. Ln : Fisher, Son & Co., 1832. 8° BPL

Works . . . from the text of Johnson, Steevens and Reed. With preface and life by N. Rowe. Ln : Jones . . . 1832. 8°. With portrait BPL
Stereotyped edition.

[Works] Plays . . . from the text of Steevens and Malone. With glossary. Ln : T. T. & J. Tegg . . . 1832. 8°, pp. 792-xii. With engraved title BPL
Set in diamond type and printed on India paper.

[Works] Dramatic works . . . with glossarial notes, sketch of his life, and estimate of his writings. Newly arranged and edited [by C. H. Wheeler]. Ln : Moon, Boys & Graves, 1832. Roy. 8°, pp. xii.-908. Stratford bust portrait and plates by Westall BM | BPL | BUS

[Works] Dramatic works . . . from the text of G. Steevens. Hartford [U.S.]: Silas Andrus, 1832. 2 vols. 8° BPL

[Works] Dramatic works . . . from the text of Steevens. Hartford [U.S.]: Andrus & Judd [c. 1832]. 2 vols. 8° BPL

Sh— Works . . .

[Works] Plays and poems . . . [from Malone's text of 1821], with life, Dr. Johnson's preface, glossarial notes, historical digests of each play, and a general index. 'Cabinet pictorial edition.' Ln : A. J. Valpy . . . 1832-34. 15 vols. 12°. With 171 outline plates from Boydell's 1802 edition, Chandos portrait, and another in vol. 15 engraved by T. Starling   BM | BPL | BUS | MPL | NY | SML
The first edition under the auspices of A. J. Valpy.

Works . . . edited by S. W. Singer. Second edition. Halle . . . 1833. 8°

[Works] Plays and poems . . . from the text of Johnson, Steevens, Reed and Malone . . . With notes by L. Tieck. Leipsic : E. Fleischer . . . 1833. 8°   BPL

Works . . . edited by C. H. Wheeler. Ln : Fisher, Son & Co., 1833. 8°   BPL

[Works] Complete works . . . with Johnson's preface, glossary, life, &c. Ln : Scott & Webster . . . 1833. 8°   BPL

[Works] Plays . . . from the text of G. Steevens and E. Malone. With a glossary. Ln : T. T. & J. Tegg, 1833. 12°, pp. iv.-792-xii. and vignette title   BPL
The engraved title is dated 1832.

Works . . . With life by Alex. Chalmers. Ln : [Printed for the trade] 1833. 8°

[Works] Dramatic works . . . Ln : Vertue . . . [c. 1833]. Roy. 8°. With plates by A. Wivell

Works . . . edited by W. Harness . . . Ln : R. Saunders . . . 1833. Imp. 4°. With 100 plates [from Boydell's 1802 edition]

[Works] Dramatic works and poems . . . With life and select notes of the best commentators, the prefaces of Rowe, Pope, Johnson . . . With life by W. Harness. Ln : Robert Saunders . . . 1833. 8 vols. 8°

[Works] Poems and plays . . . With life of the author and a selection of notes . . . from Rowe, Pope, and other eminent commentators. With three portraits and forty superior illustrations by Heath and others. Edited by W. Harness. Ln : Scott & Webster . . . 1833. 8 vols. 8°   BPL

[Works] Select plays . . . edited by Edward Slater. Ln : J. Souter . . . 1834. 12°

[Works] Plays . . . from the text of Steevens and Malone. Ln : T. Tegg & Son . . . 1834. 12°   BPL

[Works] Dramatic works . . . from the text of Steevens and Malone, with life and glossary by C. Symmons. New York : J. Conner . . . 1834. 12°   SML

Sh— Works . . .

Works . . . edited by C. H. Wheeler. Ln : Fisher & Co., Caxton Press, 1834. 8°

[Works] School Sh— . . . with notes by J. R. Pitman. Second edition. Ln : C. Rice . . . 1834. 8°   BPL

[Works] Dramatic works and poems . . . with notes, original and selected, and introductory remarks to each play, by S. W. Singer, F.S.A., and a life of the poet, by C. Symmons. New York : G. Dearborn . . . 1834. 2 vols. 8°   BM | BPL

[Works] Illustrations to Sh—, from the plates in Boydell's edition, as published in the edition recently edited . . . by A. J. Valpy. Ln : Valpy . . . 1834. 12°. With 150 outline plates   BM

[Works] Plays and poems . . . with historical notices, glossarial notes, etc. 'Magnet edition.' Ln : W. M. Clark . . . 1834-36. 5 vols. 16°   BM | BPL | SML

[Works] Plays . . . from the text of Steevens and Malone. Ln : T. Tegg & Son . . . 1835. 12°   BPL

Works . . . from the text of Dr. Johnson. With notes, glossary, and preface. Ln : J. J. Chidley . . . 1835. 8°

[Works] Penny Sh—; complete with life, glossary, &c. Ln : G. H. Davidson . . . [c. 1835]. 8°   BM | BPL (imp/t.)

[Works] Complete dramatic works and miscellaneous poems . . . Ln : Simpkin, Marshall & Co. [c. 1835]. 8°   BPL

Works . . . With woodcuts. New York : J. Conner . . . 1835. 8°

Dramatic works and poems . . . with notes, original and selected, and introductory remarks by S. W. Singer, and a life . . . by C. Symmons. New York : G. Dearborn . . . 1835. 2 vols. 8°. With Chandos portrait and illustrations   BUS

Works . . . edited by A. J. Valpy. Ln : A. J. Valpy . . . 1835. 15 vols. 12°. With outline plates

[Works] . . . Dramatic works, from the text of Johnson, Steevens and Reed. With biographical memoir, summary remarks on each play, copious glossary and variorum notes. Paris : Baudry . . . 1835-36. 8°   BPL

[Works] Dramatic works . . . from the text of . . . Steevens and Malone. With life by C. Symmons, glossary and embellishments. Chiswick : Printed for C. Tilt by C. Whittingham . . . 1836. 12°   BPL

Works . . . from the text of Steevens and Malone. With life, historical, critical and explanatory notices by A. Cunningham,

glossary, and illustrations. Ln: Charles Daly . . . [1836]. 12°. Burdett-Coutts portrait   SML
The first edition edited by Allan Cunningham.

Works . . . [with plates]. Ln: W. Pickering . . . 1836. 12°

[Works] Select plays from Sh— adapted chiefly for the use of schools and young persons; with notes from the best commentators [Six plays, edited by Edward Slater]. Ln: J. Souter . . . 1836. 12°, pp. xii.-580   BM | BPL | CPL

[Works] Plays . . . accurately printed from the text of the corrected copies left by the late George Steevens and Edmond Malone. With a glossary. Ln: Thomas Tegg & Son, 73 Cheapside. Glasgow: R. Griffin & Co. Dublin: T. T. & H. Tegg. Sydney & Hobart Town: J. & S. A. Tegg, 1836. 12°, pp. iv.-792-xii. and engraved title   BPL
The first Sh— with an Australian imprint. It is printed on India paper, and was produced by J. R. and C. Childs of Bungay.

Works . . . from the text of Johnson and Steevens. Philadelphia: T. Wardle . . . 1836. 12°   BPL

Works . . . from the text of Isaac Reed, with notes and preface by Steevens, Malone, Johnson, etc., and glossary. Ln: Isaac, Tuckey & Co. . . . 1836. 8°. With Zoust portrait   BPL | SML

[Works] Complete works . . . with Dr. Johnson's preface, a glossary, . . . account of each play, and a memoir of the author by . . . Wm. Harness . . . Ln: Printed for Scott, Webster & Geary, 1836. Roy. 8°, pp. xxxvi.-926. Chandos portrait and forty steel plates engraved by C. Heath, C. Rolls, F. Bacon, etc. from designs by Smirke, Westall, Corbould, Stephanoff, and Wright   SML
A cheaper edition was issued without plates.

Works . . . from the text of G. Steevens, with glossary, notes, and life. Hartford [U.S.]: Andrus & Judd . . . 1836. 2 vols. 8°   SML

[Works] Dramatic works . . . with life and notes [New facts, by J. P. Collier; Sh—'s will, etc., edited by O. W. B. Peabody]. Boston [U.S.]: Hilliard, Gray & Co., 1836. 7 vols. 8°   BPL | BUS | SML
First edition produced by Peabody.
The text is based on the first folio, the notes and life on Singer's edition of 1826. Reprinted in 1837 and 1839, and frequently afterwards, without alteration.

[Works] Chefs-d'œuvre de Sh—. Jules César et La tempête; la traduction Française [in prose] en regard, par M. Jay et Mme. L. Colet. Avec des notices,

critiques et historiques, accompagnées de traductions et imitations en prose et en vers de trent drames du tragique Anglais, par la plupart des collaborateurs et D. O'Sullivan . . . Précédées d'un nouvel essai sur Sh— par M. Villemain. Paris, 1836-1839. 3 vols. 8°   BM
In French and English. Forms part of the 'Bibliothèque Anglo-Française ou collection des poëtes Anglais les plus estimes,' edited by D. O'Sullivan.

Works . . . accurately printed from the text of Samuel Johnson, George Steevens and Isaac Reed, with the preface of Dr. Johnson and a copious glossary . . . Edinburgh: Published by Peter Brown . . . 1837. 8°, pp. xiv.-964. With Chandos portrait engraved by Thomas Clerk   SML

Works . . . Ln: . . . 1837. 8°. With plates

[Works] Dramatic works . . . With the text of Steevens and Malone. With a life of the poet by C. Symmons, glossary, and sixty embellishments. Ln: . . . ; Berlin . . . 1837. 8°
The first edition produced in Germany's capital.

Works . . . from the editions of Steevens, Malone and Johnson. Ln: C. Mason . . . 1837. Roy. 8°. With Chandos portrait   BPL | SML

[Works] Dramatic works and poems . . . with notes by S. W. Singer and life by C. Symmons. New York: Harper & Brothers, 1837. 2 vols. 8°   BPL

Works . . . with plates and vignettes [outline engravings from Boydell's plates]. Ln: Allan Bell & Co. . . . 1837. 7 vols. 48°   BPL | SML

[Works] Plays . . . accurately printed from the text of the corrected copies left by the late G. Steevens, Esq. and E. Malone, Esq. With Mr. Malone's various readings; a selection of explanatory and historical notes from the most eminent commentators; a history of the stage [by E. Malone]; and a life of Sh— by A. Chalmers, F.S.A. New edition. Ln: Longman . . . 1837. 8 vols. 8°   BM | BPL

[Works] Plays . . . accurately printed from the text of Geo. Steevens . . . edited by Alex. Chalmers. Ln: C. Tilt . . . [1837]. 8 vols. 12° With woodcuts

[Works] Complete works . . . Printed from the text of the most renowned editors, with 270 engravings, accounts historical and explanatory of each play, a copious and elaborate glossary, and the author's life [by C. Symmons]. Leipzig: Baumgärtner . . . 1837-39. Roy. 8°
    BM | BPL | SML

Sh— Works . . .

[Works] Complete works . . . with life by Alex. Chalmers and forty illustrations in outline. Edinburgh: Printed and edited by Andrew Shortrede for Fraser & Crawford. Ln: W. S. Orr & Co., 1838. 12°
BPL | SML
Set in diamond type in double columns. Stereotyped edition.

[Works] Plays . . . from the text of Steevens and Malone. Ln: T. Tegg & Son . . . 1838. 12°
BPL

[Works] Dramatic works, collated from Steevens, Malone, Johnson, etc., with life of the author and proemial notes on each play. Ln: C. Daly . . . 1838. 8°. Chandos portrait
BPL | SML

[Works] Plays . . . from the text of Steevens and Malone. With life and glossary by A. Chalmers. Ln: Longman . . . 1838. 8°
BPL

Works . . . with Dr. Johnson's preface, glossary, and memoir by W. Harness. Ln: Scott, Webster & Geary . . . 1838. 8°
SML

[Works] Dramatic works . . . With remarks on his life and writings [and glossary] by Thomas Campbell. Ln: E. Moxon . . . 1838. Roy. 8°, pp. lxx.-960. With a second [engraved] title and Chandos portrait [somewhat altered] engraved by H. Robinson on steel
BM | BPL | SML
First edition edited by the poet Campbell.

[Works] Dramatic works . . . With remarks . . . by Thomas Campbell. New edition. Ln: Routledge . . . [1838]. Roy. 8°, pp. lxxx.-960
NY
Dedication to Samuel Rogers dated May, 1838.

[Works] Complete works . . . with explanatory and historical notes by the most eminent commentators. Accurately printed from the correct and esteemed edition of Alex. Chalmers. Paris: Baudry . . . 1838. 2 vols. Roy. 8° (vol. I. pp. cxxxiv.-466, vol. II. pp. iv.-732). Nearly 200 wood and steel engravings, including Chandos portrait [altered] engraved by Hopwood, portraits of famous commentators and actors; also a plate of the Morris dance
BPL
Memoirs of Sh—'s contemporaries, his fellow-actors, and of Sh— himself are given.
Issued in printed yellow wrappers.

[Works] Dramatic works . . . 'Illustrated British classics.' Second edition. Ln: Published for the proprietor . . . 1838. 5 vols. 48°
BPL

Works . . . 'Diamond edition.' Ln: T. Tegg & Son . . . 1838. 5 vols. 12°

Sh— Works . . .

[Works] Dramatic works . . . embellished with plates and vignettes. Philadelphia: T. T. Ash & H. F. Anners, 1838. 6 vols. 32°. With Chandos portrait
BM | BUS
The plays are independently paged.

[Works] Dramatic works . . . with life by Charles Symmons, glossary, and fifty-three illustrations. Ln: Charles Tilt; Berlin . . . 1838. 8 vols. 12°. Fifty-three plates

[Works] 'Pictorial edition' of the works of Sh—, edited by Charles Knight [Histories, 2 vols.; Comedies, 2 vols.; Tragedies and poems, 2 vols.; Doubtful plays, 1 vol.; Biography, 1 vol.] Ln: C. Knight & Co., 1838-43. 56 parts, forming 8 vols. Roy. 8°
BM | BPL | BUS | MPL | NY | SML
Contains introductory notices, notes, variorum readings, glossary, biography, music to the songs, and many hundreds of wood engravings.
The first edition edited by Charles Knight. Text founded on the Jaggard canon, with critical introductions and notes.

Works . . . With life by A. Chalmers. Edinburgh: A. Shortrede, Fraser & Crawford, 1839. 8°, pp. xii.-708. Portrait and outline plates
BPL

Works . . . with glossarial notes. Newly arranged and edited. Ln: Fisher, Son & Co. [c. 1839]. 8°. Portraits and illustrations
BPL | SML

[Works] Family Sh—, by Thomas Bowdler. Seventh edition. Ln: Longman, Orme . . . 1839. 8°
BPL

[Works] Complete works . . . With Johnson's preface, glossary, account of each play, and memoir of the author. Edited by . . . W. Harness. Ln: Scott, Webster & Geary, 1839. Roy. 8°
BPL | SML

[Works] Plays . . . edited by S. Maunder. Ln: J. W. Southgate . . . 1839. 8°. With portrait
BPL
The first edition edited by Samuel Maunder.

[Works] Dramatic works . . . From the text of the corrected copies of Steevens and Malone, with a life of the poet by C. Symmons, D.D. The 'Seven ages of man,' embellished with elegant engravings and a glossary. New York: J. Conner . . . 1839. 8°, pp. xx.-844
BM

[Works] Dramatic works and poems . . . from the text of G. Steevens. With glossary, notes, and life. New York: Robinson & Franklin . . . 1839. 2 vols. 12° SML

[Works] Dramatic works and poems . . . With notes by S. W. Singer, and life by C. Symmons. New York: Harper & Brothers . . . 1839. 2 vols. 8°
BPL

[Works] Dramatic works . . . 'Fine edition.' Revised by I. Reed. New York: Harper . . . 1839. 6 vols. 8°   BPL

Works . . . With woodcuts. Ln: D. Bogue . . . 1839. 8 vols. 16°. With fifty-three woodcuts

[Works] Sh— gallery; Engravings illustrative of Sh— from pictures by eminent British artists. Ln: . . . 1839. 8°   BPL

Works . . . revised from the best authorities [Edited by J. Ogden]. With a memoir and essay on his genius by Barry Cornwall [B. W. Procter]; also annotations and introductory remarks on the plays by distinguished writers. Illustrated with [nearly 1,000] engravings on wood from designs by Kenny Meadows. Ln: R. Tyas, 1839-43. 3 vols. Roy. 8°   BM | BUS | SML

The first edition under the auspices of 'Barry Cornwall' [Bryan Waller Procter] and Kenny Meadows.
Issued serially in paper parts.
Twelve copies were printed on India paper, on one side of the leaf only, with proof plates.
The introductions were written by R. H. Horne, T. Wade, E. W. Elton, C. Whitehead, and J. Ogden.

[Works] Plays and poems . . . With notes, glossary, and preface by Dr. Johnson. Ln: H. G. Bohn . . . 1840. Cr. 8°. With Jansen portrait

[Works] Select plays . . . 'Romeo and Juliet,' 'Midsummer night's dream,' 'Julius Cæsar,' and 'Macbeth.' Halle . . . 1840. 8°

[Works] Complete works . . . with Dr. Johnson's preface, a glossary, an account of each play, and a memoir of the author by W. Harness. Ln: Scott, Webster & Geary . . . 1840. 8°, pp. xxxvi.-926
    BM | BPL

[Works] Plays . . . revised by S. Maunder. Ln: Southgate & Son . . . 1840. 8°   BPL

Works . . . from the text of Johnson, Steevens and Reed. With preface . . . and copious glossary. Edinburgh: Thomas Nelson . . . 1840. Roy. 8°, pp. xvi.-964
    SML

[Works] Plays and poems . . . with preface, notes by E. Malone, life, and glossary by A. Chalmers. Leipsic: E. Fleischer . . . 1840. Roy. 8°. With 13 steel engravings
    BPL | SML

[Works] . . . Plays, arranged by Dr. J. Folsing. Berlin . . . 1840. 2 vols. 12°
Contains four plays. [See Lowndes, p. 2273.]

[Works] Selection of . . . plays. With historical and grammatical explanatory notes [in German] by H. S. Pierre. Frankfort . . . 1840. 8 vols. 12°
Contains eight plays. [See Lowndes, p. 2273.]

[Works] Plays and poems . . . Valpy's 'Cabinet edition.' Ln: H. G. Bohn . . . 1840. 15 vols. Cr. 8°. With 171 outline plates

[Works] . . . Dramatic works. Glasgow: D. A. Borrenstein . . . 1841. 12°   BPL

[Works] Dramatic works . . . Ln: Printed by C. Whittingham for D. Bogue . . . 1841. 12°
Set in diamond type.

[Works] Complete works . . . with notes and preface by Dr. Johnson, life by Alex. Chalmers, and forty illustrations [in outline]. Ln: I. J. Chidley . . . 1841. 12°, pp. xii.-708   BPL
The plates include the Jansen portrait engraved by R. Bell, and the alto relievo monument at the Sh— gallery in Pall Mall.

[Works] Dramatic works . . . from the text of Johnson, Steevens and Reed. Edinburgh: T. Nelson . . . 1841. 8°   BPL

[Works] Dramatic and poetical works . . . New edition. With introductory essay and notes. Ln. & Glasgow: R. Griffin & Co. [c. 1841]. 8°, pp. xiv.-908-48

Works . . . accurately printed from the text of the corrected copy left by G. Steevens. With glossary, notes, and life. Philadelphia . . . 1841. 2 vols. 8°. With plates
    BUS

[Works] . . . Dramatic works . . . with life of the poet and notes. Boston [U.S.] Hilliard, Gray & Co. . . . 1841. 7 vols. 8°
    BPL | MPL

[Works] Plays . . . Ln: L. A. Lewis . . . 1841. 14 vols. 12°   BPL

Works . . . The text formed from an entirely new collation of the old editions: with the various readings, notes, life of the poet, and a history of the early English stage by John Payne Collier. [Notes and emendations to the text of Sh—'s plays, from early manuscript corrections in a copy of the folio, 1632, in the possession of J. P. Collier . . . forming a supplemental volume.] Ln: Whittaker & Co., 1841-53. 9 vols. 8°
    BM | BPL | BUS | SML
The first edition edited by John Payne Collier.
The British Museum possesses two sets, one containing manuscript notes by the editor and bearing on the title-page of the supplemental volume the words 'Second edition, revised and enlarged.'
The 'early manuscript corrections' proved to be an elaborate forgery by Collier (q.v.).

Works . . . from the text of Steevens and Malone. Ln: T. Tegg . . . 1842. 12° BPL

Works . . . revised by S. Maunder. Ln: . . . 1842. Cr. 8°. With portrait

Works . . . from the text of Dr. Johnson. Ln: H. G. Bohn . . . 1842. Cr. 8°

Sh— Works . . .

Works . . . edited by W. Harness. [With plates.] Auburn . . . [U.S., c. 1842]. 8°

[Works] Dramatic works . . . With remarks on his life by T. Campbell. Ln : E. Moxon . . . 1842. 8°   BPL

[Works] Plays . . . revised by S. Maunder. Ln., Brussels & Leipzig : C. Murquardt . . . 1842. 8°   BPL

[Works] Plays . . . from the editions of Steevens, Malone and Johnson. Ln : Printed for the proprietors . . . 1842. 8°   BPL

[Works] Dramatic works . . . Paris : Baudry . . . 1842. 8°   BPL

[Works] Dramatic works . . . from the text of Johnson, Steevens and Reed, with glossary. Edinburgh : T. Nelson . . . 1842. Roy. 8°   SML

Works . . . with memoir by W. Harness. Ln : Scott . . . 1842. Roy. 8°. With forty illustrations by Heath   BPL
The whole of this edition was sent to America.

Works . . . with Johnson's preface, a glossary, and memoir by W. Harness. New York . . . [c. 1842]. Roy. 8°. With portrait and forty illustrations   BUS

[Works] Dramatic works . . . from the text of Johnson, Steevens, and Reed. Leipsic . . . 1842. 2 vols. 8°. With steel and wood engravings

[Works] Complete works . . . illustrated with many valuable literary notes from distinguished commentators, with large introductory notices prefixed to each play, and a new life. Paris : Baudry . . . 1842. 10 vols. 8°
Also issued with forty-two steel and thirty-eight wood engravings, which were sold separately on ordinary and on India paper.

[Works] Plays and poems . . . from the text of Malone, with revisions, life, notes, and index. Edited by A. J. Valpy. [Chandos portrait and outline illustrations.] Ln : H. G. Bohn . . . 1842. 15 vols. 12°
   BPL | SML

[Works] Comedies, histories, tragedies, and poems . . . edited by C. Knight. Second edition [with notes and glossary]. Ln : C. Knight & Co. . . . 1842-44. 12 vols. 8°. Numerous woodcuts
   BM | BPL | BUS | SML
The 'library edition,' afterwards re-christened the 'National edition.'

[Works] Dramatic works . . . from the text of . . . Steevens and Malone. With life by C. Symmons, the 'Seven ages of man,' . . . and a glossary. Hartford [U.S.] : W. Andrus . . . 1843. 12°, pp. xx.-844. With plate of medal and woodcuts   BUS

Sh— Works . . .

Works . . . With notes and preface by Dr. Johnson. Ln : J. J. Chidley . . . 1843. Cr. 8°   BPL

Works . . . from the text of Johnson, Steevens and Reed, with glossary. Edinburgh : T. Nelson . . . 1843. 8°. Chandos portrait   BPL | SML

Works . . . with life by C. Symmons. [With engravings.] Ln : Andrews . . . 1843. 8°

[Works] Dramatic works. With remarks on his life and writings by T. Campbell. Paris : Baudry's European library . . . 1843. 8°, pp. 828. With plates   BM

[Works] Doubtful plays . . . edited by Charles Knight. Ln : C. Knight & Co., 1843. Roy. 8°   BM | W
Forms a supplement to Knight's 'Pictorial edition of Sh—,' issued in 1839-42, 8 vols.

[Works] Family Sh—, by T. Bowdler. Eighth edition. Ln : Longman, Brown . . . 1843. Roy. 8°   BPL

Works . . . revised from the best authorities . . . [Thirty-five etched plates by Kenny Meadows, with descriptive extracts]. Ln : R. Tyas . . . 1843. Roy. 8°   W

[Works] Dramatic works and poems . . . with notes . . . by S. W. Singer and life by C. Symmons. New York : Harper & Brothers . . . 1843. 2 vols. 8°. Chandos portrait and sixteen outline illustrations by Retzsch, Northcote, etc.
   BPL | BUS | SML

Works . . . revised from the best authorities, with a memoir and essay . . . by 'Barry Cornwall' . . . Illustrated by Kenny Meadows. Ln : R. Tyas . . . 1843. 3 vols. Roy. 8°   BM | BPL
The set in the British Museum is printed on one side of the page only, upon India paper.

[Works] Harper's fine edition. Numerous steel engravings. Dramatic works of Sh—, with the corrections and illustrations of Dr. Johnson, G.' Steevens, and others. Revised by I. Reed. New York : Harper Brothers, 1843. 6 vols. 12°. With Chandos portrait   BUS

[Works] Dramatic works . . . with notes by S. W. Singer and life by C. Symmons. Halle . . . 1843. 37 parts, forming 10 vols. 12°

Works . . . edited by A. J. Valpy. 'Cabinet pictorial edition.' Ln : H. G. Bohn . . . 1843. 15 vols. 12°. Illustrated with outline plates

[Works] Plays and poems . . . from the text of J. P. Collier. Leipzig : B. Tauchnitz . . . 1843-44. 37 parts, forming 7 vols. 12°   BPL | BUS

[Works] Dramatic works [with life by C. Symmons, D.D.] Leipsic: Brothers Schumann [1843-44]. 37 parts, forming 8 vols. 16°   BM

[Works] Complete works . . . Paris: Baudry . . . 1843-44. 9 vols. 8° BPL

[Works] Knight's 'Cabinet edition' . . . Ln: Charles Cox . . . 1843-44. 41 parts, forming 11 vols. 16°   BM | BPL | SML
The final volume contains the poems and life.

[Works] Dramatic works . . . A new edition. With numerous illustrative engravings and a sketch of his life by Alexander Chalmers. Glasgow: D. A. Borrenstein. Ln: Andrew Moffat, 1844. Cr. 8°, pp. iv.-xvi.-652   BPL

Works . . . from the text of Dr. Johnson. Ln: . . . 1844. 8°

[Works] Dramatic works . . . with remarks on his life by T. Campbell. Ln: E. Moxon . . . 1844. 8°   BPL

Works . . . containing his plays and poems from the text of the editions by Charles Knight. With glossarial notes and facts connected with his life and writings, abridged from his larger biography. Ln: Knight & Co. . . . 1844. Roy. 8°. With forty large woodcuts by W. Harvey

[Works] Complete works . . . with explanatory and historical notes by the most eminent commentators accurately printed from the . . . edition of A. Chalmers [with life]. Paris: Baudry's European library . . . 1844. 2 vols. 8°   BM

Works . . . revised with memoir and essay on his genius by 'Barry Cornwall.' Woodcut designs by Kenny Meadows. Ln: W. S. Orr & Co. . . . 1844. 3 vols. 8°   BPL | SML

[Works] Dramatic works . . . with a life of the poet [abridged from that by Dr. Symmons] and notes, original and selected [mainly from Singer's edition. Edited by O. W. Peabody.] Boston [U.S.]: C. C. Little & J. Brown, 1844. 7 vols. 8°   BM
The first edition edited by Peabody.

Works . . . edited by A. J. Valpy. Illustrated. Ln: H. G. Bohn . . . 1844. 15 vols. 12°   BPL

[Works] Plays. With his life. Edited by Gulian C. Verplanck. With critical introductions, notes, etc., original and selected. New York: Harper & Brothers . . . [1844]-47. 3 vols. Roy. 8°. With portraits and hundreds of woodcuts
    BPL | BUS | NY | SML
The first edition edited by Verplanck. Text founded upon J. P. Collier's, and the illustrations mainly borrowed from Knight's 'Pictorial edition.' Issued serially.

Works . . . The text formed from an entirely new collation of the old editions . . . by J. P. Collier. Second edition. Ln: Whittaker . . . 1844-53. 8 vols. 8°

Works . . . With notes and preface by Dr. Johnson. Edited by A. Chalmers. With plates. Ln: J. J. Chidley . . . 1845. Cr. 8°   BPL

[Works] Complete dramatic works and miscellaneous poems . . . with glossarial notes and life by N. Rowe. Derby: . . . Richardson & Son [c. 1845]. 8°, pp. viii.-976. With engraved title, Chandos portrait (altered), engraved by Roffe, and facsimile autograph
The first Derby edition.

[Works] Dramatic works . . . Edinburgh: T. Nelson . . . 1845. 8°   BPL

[Works] Plays . . . from the text of Steevens and Malone. With a glossary. Ln: T. Tegg. Glasgow: R. Griffin, 1845. 8°, pp. 792-xii. With engraved title dated 1839   BPL

[Works] School Sh— . . . for the use of schools, with notes by J. R. Pitman. Ln: C. Hoby . . . 1845. 8°

Works . . . containing his plays and poems, the text of the editions by Charles Knight. With glossarial notes, and facts connected with his life and writings, abridged from ' Wm. Sh—, a biography.' Complete in one volume. Ln: C. Knight & Co., 22 Ludgate Street, 1845. Roy. 8°, pp. iv.-1,080. Illustrated   BPL

[Works] Etchings to the ' Illustrated Sh— ' designed by Kenny Meadows. Ln: Orr . . . 1845. Roy. 8°. With 36 plates

[Works] Dramatic works . . . edited by Dr. H. Stebbing. Ln: George Virtue [c. 1845]. Roy. 8°. With plates

Works . . . ' Pictorial edition,' edited by C. Knight. Ln: C. Knight & Co. [1845]. 8 vols. Roy. 8°   BUS
Apparently identical with the first ' Pictorial edition' of 1838-43, except in imprint.

[Works] Select plays . . . Adapted to the use of youth [Four plays]. Franckfort-on-Main: H. L. Broenner . . . 1846. 12°, pp. 358   BM

[Works] Dramatic works . . . with life by C. Symmons. Hartford [U.S.]: S. Andrus 1846. 12°   BPL

[Works] Plays . . . from the editions of Steevens, Malone and Johnson. Ln: G. Nodes . . . 1846. 8°   BPL

Works . . . Edinburgh: T. Nelson . . . 1846. 8°   BPL | SML

Sh— Works . . .

[Works] Plays . . . from the text of G. Steevens and E. Malone, with life and glossary [by A. Chalmers]. Ln : Longman . . . 1846. 8°. With Chandos portrait   BPL | SML

[Works] Dramatic works . . . with an original memoir. The text enriched by many valuable notes and a copious glossary. Also an enquiry into the authenticity of the Sh— portraits by A. Wivell. Ln : George Virtue . . . 1846. 2 vols. Roy. 8°. With the Hilliard portrait and forty-eight steel engravings from the Boydell gallery   CPL

Works . . . revised from the best authorities. With memoir . . . by ' Barry Cornwall.' Illustrated . . . by K. Meadows. Second edition. Ln : W. S. Orr & Co., 1846. 3 vols. Imp. 8°   BPL

[Works] Plays and poems . . . with introductory notices, glossary, notes, illustrations . . . edited by J. S. Moore. Ln : J. C. Moore . . . 1846. 4 parts. 8°   BM

Works . . . edited by Charles Knight. Ln : C. Knight & Co. . . . 1846. 7 vols. 8° BPL

Works . . . edited by Charles Knight. 'Pictorial edition.' Ln : C. Knight & Co. . . . 1846. 8 vols. Roy. 8°. With hundreds of wood engravings

Works . . . from the text of Dr. Johnson. Ln : H. G. Bohn . . . 1847. Cr. 8°

[Works] Complete works . . . With a selection of notes, and preface by Dr. Johnson. Ln : J. J. Chidley . . . 1847. Cr. 8° CPL

[Works] Dramatic works . . . from the text of Dr. Johnson, Steevens and Reed. With glossary. Edinburgh : T. Nelson . . . 1847. 8°. With portrait   BPL

[Works] Plays . . . collated from the editions of Steevens, Malone and Johnson, preceded by a sketch of the author's life and glossarial notes, with introductory observations on each play. Ln : Printed for the booksellers, 1847. 8°   BPL
Printed in small type on bad paper.

[Works] . . . ' Bowdler's Family Sh—.' Ninth edition. Ln : Longman, Brown & Co., 1847. Roy. 8°   BPL

Works . . . Boston [U.S.] : Harper . . . 1847. 2 vols.

[Works] . . . Select tragedies. Consisting of ' Romeo and Juliet,' ' Hamlet,' ' Othello,' ' King Lear,' ' Macbeth,' ' Julius Cæsar,' ' King Richard the third.' With many valuable notes by the most distinguished commentators. Paris : Baudry's European library . . . 1847. 7 parts. 8°
      BM | SML

Sh— Works . . .

Works . . . edited by C. Knight. ' Standard edition.' Ln : C. Knight & Co., 1847. 7 vols. Roy. 8°. With woodcuts
In this issue the ' Biography ' is abridged, and the attributed plays are omitted.

[Works] Plays . . . from the text of Steevens and Malone, with notes, history of the stage, and life . . . by A. Chalmers. Ln : Longman & Co. . . . 1847. 8 vols. 8°. With Chandos portrait   BPL | MPL | SML

[Works] Outline illustrations to Sh—'s plays, by F. A. Moritz Retzsch. A new edition from the original plates. With English and German explanations. Leipzig . . . ; Ln : . . . 1847. Oblong 4°. With 100 plates   BPL

Works . . . edited by Charles Knight. 'Cabinet edition.' Ln : . . . 1847-48. 16 vols. 12°

[Works] Select plays . . . [Five plays]. With notes, and an introduction to each play, and a life of Sh— [Edited by J. Howell]. Ln : J. Burns [1848]. 12°, pp. xxviii.-404   BM | BPL
From the Roman Catholic standpoint.

[Works] Complete works . . . with memoir by A. Chalmers. Ln : H. G. Bohn, 1848. Cr. 8°, pp. xii.-708 and portrait   BPL
Printed in diamond type.
An alternate issue was published simultaneously with forty outline plates.

Works . . . from the text of Johnson, Stevens [sic] and Reed. With glossarial notes and life by Nicholas Rowe. Ln : G. Routledge & Co., 1848. 8° BPL | SML

[Works] Supplement to the plays . . . comprising the seven dramas which have been ascribed to his pen, but which are not included with his writings in modern editions, namely, ' Two noble kinsmen,' ' London prodigal,' ' Thomas Lord Cromwell,' ' Sir John Oldcastle,' ' The puritan or widow of Watling Street,' ' Yorkshire tragedy,' ' Tragedy of Locrine.' Edited with notes and an introduction to each play by William Gilmore Simms. New York : G. F. Cooledge & Brother, 1848. 8°, pp. 178. Illustrated
      BM | BPL | BUS | NY
First American edition of the attributed plays.

[Works] Dramatic works . . . With remarks on his life and writings by T. Campbell. A new edition. Ln : E. Moxon . . . 1848. Roy. 8°, pp. lxxx.-960   BM | SML

[Works] Dramatic works . . . Boston [U.S.] : Phillips & Sampson, 1848. 7 vols. 8°   BPL

Works . . . edited by A. J. Valpy. Illustrated. Ln : . . . 1848. 15 vols. 12°

Sh— Works . . .

[Works] Dramatic works . . . from the text of the corrected copies of Stevens [*sic*] and Malone. With a life of the poet by C. Symmons, D.D.; . . . the 'Seven ages of man,' embellished with engravings; also, a glossary. Hartford [U.S.]: S. Andrus & Son . . . 1849. 12°, pp. xx.-844   BM | BPL

[Works] Plays and poems . . . with notes, glossary, and preface by Dr. Johnson. Ln: H. G. Bohn . . . 1849. Cr. 8°. With Chandos portrait   BPL | SML

Works . . . from the . . . editions by C. Knight. Illustrated by W. Harvey. Ln: Charles Cox . . . 1849. 8°   BPL

[Works] . . . Bowdler's Family Sh—. Ln: Longman . . 1849. 8°

Works . . . from the text of Dr. Johnson. Ln: Thomas Nelson . . . 1849. 8°   BPL

[Works] Dramatic works . . . from the text of Johnson, Stevens [*sic*] and Reed. With glossarial notes, his life, etc., by N. Rowe. Ln: Routledge . . . 1849. 8°, pp. ii.-972 and frontispiece in ten compartments   BPL | SML

[Works] Plays . . . accurately printed from the text of the corrected copies, left by the late G. Steevens, Esq. and E. Malone, Esq. With a glossary. Ln: W. Tegg & Co. . . . 1849. 8°, pp. xii.-792   BM

[Works] Plays . . . edited by A. Chalmers from editions of Steevens, Malone and Johnson. Ln: Printed for the booksellers, 1849. 8°   BPL

[Works] Dramatic works, from the text of G. Steevens, with memoir by A. Chalmers. Philadelphia: J. Harding . . . 1849. 8°   SML

[Works] Sh—'s complete works . . . Ln: Scott & Webster . . . 1849. Roy. 8°, pp. 926

Works . . . from the text of Geo. Steevens. Philadelphia . . . 1849. 2 vols. 8°

Works . . . With memoir by 'Barry Cornwall.' With plates by Kenny Meadows. Ln: W. S. Orr & Co. . . . 1849. 3 vols. Imp. 8°

[Works] Dramatic works . . . edited by O. W. B. Peabody. Boston [U.S.]: Phillips, Sampson & Co., 1849-51. 8 vols. 8°   BPL | BUS

Identical except in date with the first edition of 1836.

[Works] Complete works . . . with memoir by A. Chalmers. Ln: H. G. Bohn . . . 1850. 12°   BPL

[Works] Shakespearian reader; A collection of the most approved plays of Sh—; carefully revised, with introductory and explanatory notes and a memoir of the

author . . . by J. W. S. Hows. [Sixteen plays.] New York: D. Appleton & Co. . . . 1850. 12°, pp. xvi.-448   BM

Works . . . from the text of Geo. Steevens. Ln: . . . 1850. 8°

[Works] Doubtful plays . . . revised from the original editions, with notes critical and explanatory by H. Tyrrell. Ln: . . . [c. 1850]. 8°

Works . . . edited by A. Cunningham. With plates. Ln: C. Daly . . . [c. 1850]. 8°

[Works] Dramatic works . . . edited by T. Campbell. Ln: E. Moxon . . . 1850. 8°   BPL

[Works] Dramatic works . . . with numerous illustrative engravings, and sketch of his life by A. Chalmers. Manchester: Thomas Johnson, 1850. 8°, pp. xvi.-652. With portrait, engraved title, twelve full-page plates, and cuts in the text BPL
The illustrations are adapted from the Boydell series. First Manchester collective edition.

[Works] The family Sh—, edited by T. Bowdler, from the sixth London edition. Philadelphia: J. W. Moore . . . 1850. 8°. Chandos portrait   SML

[Works] Plays . . . from the texts of G. Steevens, E. Malone and Dr. Johnson, with notes and life by S. Maunder. Philadelphia: G. S. Appleton. New York: D. Appleton, 1850. 8°   SML

[Works] Dramatic works . . . from the text of George Steevens. With glossary, notes, and life . . . Boston [U.S.]: Phillips, Sampson & Co., 1850. 2 vols. 8°   BUS

[Works] Dramatic works . . . with introductions, notes, and biographical sketch by H. Stebbing; also an enquiry into the authenticity of the Sh— portraits by A. Wivell. Ln. & New York: G. Virtue . . . 1850. 2 vols. 8°. With fifty-one steel engravings   BPL | SML

[Works] Complete works . . . revised from the original editions, with historical and analytical introductions to each play, also notes explanatory and critical, and a life of the poet, by J. O. Halliwell and other eminent commentators. Elegantly . . . illustrated by portraits engraved on steel from daguerreotypes of the greatest and most intellectual actors of the age, taken in the embodiment of the varied and life-like characters of our great national poet. [Edited by Hy. Tyrrell.] Ln: Printed and published by John Tallis & Co., 1850. 3 vols. 4°, pp. xxxii.-576, iv.-488, and iv.-496. With bust,

Sh— Works . . .

Chandos and Somerset portraits of Sh—, views of the birthplace, and of Drury Lane, Globe, Haymarket, Princess's, and Sadlers Wells theatres, and numerous full-page character portraits
The first edition edited by Hy. Tyrrell.
An entirely unsanctioned use of Halliwell's name and matter. The offence was repeated in the four-volume edition. *See* Sh— Works, 1850-53.

Works . . . With a glossary. Carefully printed from the Oxford edition, 1744, in quarto. Ln : . . . 1850-51. 9 vols. 12°
CPL

[Works] Dramatic works . . . illustrated. Embracing a life of the poet and notes, original and selected. Boston [U.S.] : Phillips, Sampson & Co., 1850-52. 8 vols. 8°
BPL | NY | SML

[Works] Comedies, histories, tragedies, and poems . . . edited by Charles Knight. 'National edition.' Ln : C. Knight . . . 1850-52. 8 vols. 8°. With illustrations
BM | BPL | MPL | SML
The seventh and eighth volumes consist of the 'Biography' and 'Studies' respectively. Sometimes found dated 1851-52.

[Works] Complete works . . . revised from the original editions. With historical and analytical introductions to each play, also notes explanatory and critical, and a life of the poet and introductory essay on his phraseology and metre. By J. O. Halliwell and other eminent commentators [Edited by Henry Tyrrell]. Ln. & New York : [Tallis & Co.] Ln. Printing & Publishing Co., 1850-53. 4 vols. 4°. With 100 portraits and illustrations
BM | BPL | BUS | NY | SML
An unauthorised use of Halliwell's name. *See* 'The Times,' Oct., 1850, and preface to his edition of the 'Comedies,' 1854. The American issue was discontinued because of this piracy.
The portraits embrace many well-known actors and actresses in character.
Issued serially in 52 parts, and named 'Tallis's library edition.'

[Works] Complete works . . . [edited by A. S—— [Anna Swanwick ?]. With a memoir by A. Chalmers. Ln : H. G. Bohn . . . 1851. Cr. 8°, pp. xii.-708
BM | BPL

[Works] Plays . . . from the text of Steevens and Malone. Ln : W. Tegg & Co. . . . 1851. 12°
BPL

Works . . . from the text of Johnson, Steevens and Reed. With glossary. Edinburgh : Nelson . . . 1851. 8°. With portrait

[Works] Student's and school Sh—. Plays . . . with notes, etc. by J. R. Pitman. Third edition. Ln : C. Hoby . . . [c. 1851]. 8°, pp. xxiv.-572   BM | BPL | SML
Expurgated and curtailed.

Sh— Works . . .

[Works] Plays . . . collated from the editions of the late G. Steevens, Esq., E. Malone, Esq., and Dr. Samuel Johnson. A sketch of the author's life and glossarial notes, with introductory observations on each play written expressly for this edition. The whole revised by S. Maunder. Ln : L. A. Lewis . . . 1851. 8°, pp. x.-716
BM | BPL

Works . . . from the text of N. Rowe. Ln : G. Routledge & Co., 1851. 8°
BPL

Works . . . 'Lansdowne edition.' Ln : W. White . . . 1851. 8°

[Works] Dramatic works . . . Philadelphia : Lippincott, Grambo & Co., 1851. 8°
BPL | BUS

[Works] Plays . . . edited with introductions and notes critical and explanatory by James O. Halliwell. Ln. & New York : Tallis . . . 1851. Roy. 8°

Works . . . edited by Dr. Stebbing. Ln : Virtue . . . 1851. Roy. 8°. With plates

[Works] Tallis's 'Acting edition' of Sh—, as produced at the Theatres Royal, Covent Garden and Drury Lane, whilst under the management of W. C. Macready, etc. Parts 1 and 2 ['Hamlet' and 'Macbeth']. Ln : J. Tallis & Co. [1851]. 2 parts. 8°
BM
No more published.

[Works] Dramatic works . . . Philadelphia : Hogan & Thompson . . . 1851. 4 vols. 8°
BPL

Works . . . Knight's 'Cabinet edition' [edited with life and notes by C. Knight]. Ln : Wm. S. Orr & Co., 1851. 12 vols. 12°. With portraits and cuts on wood
BPL | SML
The 'Works' occupy ten volumes. The other two consist of 'Studies of Sh—' and the 'Poems . . . with facts connected with his life.'

[Works] Dramatic works . . . from the text of Johnson, Stevens [*sic*] and Reed ; with glossarial notes, life, etc. A new edition, by W. Hazlitt. Ln : G. Routledge & Co. . . . 1851-52. 4 vols. Cr. 8°   BM | NY
The first edition edited by William Hazlitt.
A supplement holding the 'doubtful' plays was issued in 1852 (*q.v.*)

[Works] . . . Dramatic works, revised from the original text, with introductory remarks and copious notes, critical, general and explanatory, produced under the immediate supervision of S. Phelps. With illustrations by T. H. Nicholson. Ln : Willoughby & Co. . . . 1851-54. 2 vols. Roy. 8°
Issued in parts. Some sets have coloured plates.
The first edition edited by Samuel Phelps, and the first Sh— issued with the plates in colours.

Works . . . The text carefully restored according to the first editions. With introductions, notes original and selected, and life of the poet, by H. N. Hudson. Boston [U.S.]: J. Munroe & Co. . . . 1851-56. 11 vols. 12°. With Chandos portrait and woodcuts
BM | BPL | BUS | MPL
First edition produced by H. N. Hudson. A reprint of the illustrated Chiswick edition.

[Works] Dramatic works and poems . . . from the text of Steevens and Malone, with life and notices by A. Cunningham [*pseud.*], glossary, and illustrations. Ln: Charles Daly . . . [1852]. Cr. 8°, pp. xxxvi.-924, and Ashborne portrait   BPL | SML

[Works] Complete works . . . With memoir by A. Chalmers. Ln: H. G. Bohn . . . 1852. Cr. 8°, pp. xii.-708 and forty outline steel plates   BPL

[Works] Plays and poems . . . Ln: H. G. Bohn . . . 1852. Cr. 8°   BPL

[Works] Supplementary works . . . comprising his poems and doubtful plays, with glossarial . . . notes. A new edition by William Hazlitt. Ln: Routledge & Co. . . . 1852. Cr. 8°, pp. vi.-526
BM | BPL | BUS
Forms an appendix to Sh—'s Works, 1851-52, 4 vols. (*q.v.*)

Works . . . Halifax: Milner . . . 1852. 8°

Works . . . from the text of C. Knight. Illustrated by W. Harvey. Sixth edition. Ln: G. Cox . . . 1852. 8°   BPL | MPL

[Works] Dramatic works. With a glossary. [Edited by W. White.] 'Lansdowne edition.' Ln: W. White . . . 1852. 8°, pp. viii.-1,124. Droeshout portrait
BM | BPL | BUS
With names of the characters rubricated.

[Works] Dramatic works . . . from the text of Johnson and Steevens. With glossary [and life by Rowe]. New York: Leavitt & Allen . . . 1852. 8°, pp. xii.-1,062 BUS

Works . . . from the text of Steevens and Malone. With life and notices by A. Cunningham [*pseud.*] With portrait, glossary, and illustrations. Philadelphia: J. B. Smith, 1852. 8°   BUS

Works . . . edited by Thomas Campbell. Ln: E. Moxon . . . 1852. Roy. 8°. With Chandos portrait

Works . . . edited by 'Barry Cornwall' . . . Illustrated by Kenny Meadows. Ln: Orr . . . 1852. 2 vols. Imp. 8°. With thirty-five steel etchings, and woodcuts

[Works] Dramatic works . . . from the text of Johnson, Stevens [*sic*] and Reed. With glossarial notes, life, etc. A new edition by William Hazlitt. Ln: G. Routledge & Co., 1852. 4 vols. Cr. 8°   BPL

Works . . . edited by A. Cunningham. Ln: C. Daly . . . 1852. 8 vols. 16°

[Works] 'Penny Sh—' [Thirty-three plays]. Ln: G. Vickers . . . [1852]. 33 numbers. 12°   BM | BPL (*impft.*)

[Works] Etchings to the 'Illustrated Sh—' by Kenny Meadows. Ln: W. S. Orr [c. 1852]. Roy. 8°, ff. 37 and thirty-five plates   BPL | BUS
Each plate is accompanied by an appropriate quotation.

[Works] Family Sh—. By T Bowdler. Ln: Longman & Co., 1852-53. 6 vols. 12° BM

Works . . . [edited by Miss Lyndon ?]. Isle of Wight: 'Observer' Office, 1852-53. 10 parts
Referred to under Lyndon in the Boston Catalogue (p. 151), but unknown elsewhere.

[Works] Histories . . . edited by C. Knight . . . With facts connected with Sh—'s life and writings. 'Companion edition.' Ln: C. Knight . . . 1852-54. 2 vols. 8°
BM

[Works] Complete works . . . revised from the original text. With introductory remarks and copious notes . . . by S. Phelps, Esq. . . . With portrait and engravings, designed by T. H. Nicholson. Ln: Willoughby & Co., 1852-54. 2 vols. 8°   BM | SML

Works . . . The text carefully restored according to the first edition. With introductory notes, original and selected, and a life . . . by H. N. Hudson. Boston & Cambridge [U.S.]: Munroe & Co., 1852-57. 11 vols. 12°

Works . . . from the text of Johnson, Stevens [*sic*] and Reed. With notes and life . . . by W. Hazlitt. Ln: Routledge & Co. . . . 1852-59. 12°   SML
Vol. 5 contains the 'Poems' and 'Doubtful plays,' and is dated 1852.

[Works] *Specimen.* The Stratford Sh—. Edited by C. Knight. To be published in twelve monthly volumes . . . Ln: [T. Hodgson] 1853. 12°   BM | BPL

[Works] Plays and poems . . . Ln: H. G. Bohn . . . 1853. Cr. 8°   BPL

[Works] Dramatic works . . . with a glossary. A new edition, corrected and improved. [Edited by J. P. Collier. 'Lansdowne (second) edition.] Ln: Wm. White . . . 1853. Cr. 8°, pp. xii.-1,124. With Droeshout portrait, engraved by F. C. Robinson   BPL | SML
Stereotyped and rubricated edition.

Sh— Works . . .

[Works] Werke in Englischen, nach den besten quellen berichtigten text. Mit kritischen und erläuternden anmerkungen von Dr. H. Ulrici. Erst s bändchen: 'Romeo und Julie.' Halle: C. E. M. Pfeffer, 1853. 8°, pp. x.-200   BM
No more published.

[Works] Plays . . . from the text of G. Steevens and E. Malone, with life and glossary [by A. Chalmers]. Ln: Longman & Co. . . . 1853. 8°, pp. xx.-968. With Chandos portrait   BPL | SML

Works [dramatic] . . . accurately printed from the text of corrected copies. Ln: Simpkin . . . 1853. 8°

Works . . . edited by A. Chalmers. New edition. Ln: Printed for the trade, 1853. 8°

Works . . . edited by Jewitt. New York . . . 1853. 8°

[Works] Plays . . . The text regulated by the old copies and by the recently discovered folio of 1632 containing early manuscript emendations. Edited by J. P. Collier. Ln: Whittaker . . . 1853. Roy. 8°, pp. xvi.-884. With Droeshout portrait and a facsimile [of Collier's forgeries]   BM | BPL | BUS | MPL | NY
This edition fanned the controversial breeze occasioned by the forgeries.

[Works] Plays . . . carefully revised from the best authorities. With a numerous selection of engravings on wood from designs by K. Meadows. With a memoir of, and essay on the genius of, Sh—, by 'Barry Cornwall.' Edited by J. O——. Ln: W. S. Orr & Co., 1853. 2 vols. 8°   BM | BPL

Works . . . edited by Samuel Phelps. Ln: Willoughby & Co., 1853. 2 vols. Roy. 8°

[Works] Complete works . . . revised from the original editions, with historical and analytical introductions to each play by J. O. Halliwell. The 'Doubtful plays,' with notes, etc. by Henry Tyrrell. Ln: Printing & Publishing Co. [c. 1853]. 4 vols. 4°   BPL | MPL
J. O. Halliwell's name was used without his permission.

[Works] Dramatic works . . . edited by W. Hazlitt. Ln: Routledge & Co., 1853. 5 vols. Cr. 8°   BPL | BUS
The fifth volume contains the attributed plays.

[Works] Comedies, histories, tragedies, and poems . . . with a biography, and studies of his works by C. Knight. 'Pictorial and national edition.' Boston [U.S.]: Little, Brown & Co., 1853. 8 vols. 8°
Reprinted from the London issue.   BUS

Sh— Works . . .

[Works] Comedies, histories, tragedies, and poems . . . with a biography and studies of his works by C. Knight. 'Pictorial and national edition.' Ln: G. Cox . . . 1853. 8 vols. 8°. With portraits and woodcuts   BPL | SML

Works . . . The text regulated by the recently discovered folio of 1632 . . . by J. P. Collier. To which are added glossarial and other notes and readings of former editions. New York: Redfield . . . 1853. 8 vols.   BUS

[Works] Sh— gallery of engravings, intended as a supplementary volume, or to illustrate all existing editions of the works of the immortal bard of Avon. With essays on the plays . . . forming a history of the sources . . . and a critical analysis of every drama produced by his inspired pen. Ln: [Tallis] Printing & Publishing Co. [c. 1853]. Roy. 8°   BUS
Short memoirs are added of E. Forrest and G. V. Brooke.

[Works] Family Sh—, by T. Bowdler. Tenth edition. Ln: Longman . . . 1853-55. 6 vols. 12°   BPL

Works . . . the text formed from a new collation of the early editions: to which are added all the original novels and tales on which the plays are founded; copious archæological annotations on each play; an essay on the formation of the text; and a life of the poet. By James O. Halliwell. . . . The illustrations and wood engravings by Frederick William Fairholt . . . Ln: Printed for the editor by C. & J. Adlard, 1853-65. 16 vols. Roy. 1°. With Stratford bust portrait and numerous facsimiles of early title-pages
  BM | BPL | BUS | MPL | NY
Issued by subscription, with list of buyers, and plates on plain paper, at £105, or with India paper plates (25 sets done) at £150. The whole impression was numbered and signed by the editor and printers, and the issue strictly confined to one hundred and fifty sets. All the blocks and plates employed were afterwards destroyed. There are 142 plates, in addition to the numerous textual woodcuts.
The most extensive repository of literary, historical, and archæological information regarding Sh— and his writings to be found in any single work, and, typographically, the most sumptuous edition.
'Titus Andronicus' and 'King Henry VI.' are printed in smaller type, as Halliwell doubted their Shakespearean authorship.
A critical review in the 'Athenæum' (1853, p. 796) provoked a pamphlet retort from Halliwell entitled, 'Curiosities of modern Shaksperian criticism' [q.v. under Halliwell].
The first issue actually edited by Halliwell, three previous editions bearing his name being fraudulent.
The largest form in which the bard has yet appeared, in contradistinction to Bryce's tiny edition of 1908 (q.v.)
Half a century after publication the set largely retained its original value. An exemplar sold in July, 1903, brought £70.

Sh— Works . . .

[Works] Complete works . . . with memoir by A. Chalmers. Ln: H. G. Bohn . . . 1854. 12°   BPL

[Works] Selections from Sh—'s plays. Edited by B. Oakley. [Second edition.] Ln: Longman . . . 1854. Cr. 8°

[Works] Complete works . . . The text regulated by the old copies and by the recently discovered folio of 1632, containing early manuscript emendations. With notes, selected and original, a . . . glossary, the poet's life [by C. Symmons] and portrait. Edited by Dr. D—— [i.e. Nicolaus Delius]. Leipzig: Baumgärtner . . . 1854. 8°, pp. xx.-1,060
The first edition edited by Delius. BM | BPL | SML

Works . . . from the text of C. Knight. Edited by A. Chalmers. Illustrated by W. Harvey. Sixth edition. Ln: H. G. Bohn . . . 1854. 8°   BPL

[Works] Dramatic works . . . from the text of Johnson, Steevens and Reed. With preface of Dr. Johnson and a copious glossary. Ln: T. Nelson & Sons . . . 1854. 8°, pp. 964. With Chandos portrait   BPL

[Works] Dramatic works . . . from the text of Johnson, Stevens [sic] and Reed. With glossarial notes, life by N. Rowe, etc. Ln: Routledge . . . 1854. 8° CPL

[Works] Dramatic works, accurately printed from the text of the corrected copies, with a glossary. Philadelphia . . . 1854. 8°

[Works] Comedies . . . Edited with introductions and notes . . . by James Orchard Halliwell. New York . . . 1854. 4°   BPL | MPL
This is the first and only American edition projected by the editor, which he abandoned on account of the piratical proceedings of Tallis & Co. (trading as the London Printing and Publishing Co.). See Sh— Works, 1850-53, 4 vols.

[Works] Comedies . . . edited with introductions and notes . . . by J. O. Halliwell. Reprinted from the American edition. Ln: Printed for private circulation, 1854. 4°, pp. 624   BM | BUS | MPL
One of twenty copies, to which the issue was restricted. Part of the pirated edition of Tallis & Co., of which Halliwell secured twenty copies, added notes, and issued them as a private venture to his friends.

Works . . . revised from the best authorities. With memoir and essay on his genius by 'Barry Cornwall,' also annotations and remarks . . . by distinguished writers. Illustrated . . . by Kenny Meadows. Ln: Wm. S. Orr & Co., 1854. 3 vols. Roy. 8°   NY

Sh— Works . . .

[Works] Dramatic works . . . with life of the poet and notes original and selected. Boston [U.S.]: Phillips, Sampson & Co., 1854. 8 vols. Cr. 8°. With Chandos portrait   BUS
Apparently printed from stereotypes of the 1836 edition, with the 'Poems' added in vol. 8.

[Works] Dramatic works. Ln: C. Daly . . . [1854]. 8 vols. Cr. 8°   BPL

[Works] Illustrations of Sh—. Ln: P. Jerrard . . . 1854. F°. 12 plates BUS

[Works] Illustrations of Sh—. By Kenny Meadows. With selected letterpress. Ln: . . . 1854. Imp. 8°

[Works] Shakesperian tableaux. Ln: P. Jerrard [1854]. 8°. Twelve plates, with illustrative quotations from Sh—'s works

Works . . . edited by C. Knight. With notes by R. Grant White. New York: Martin, Johnson & Co., 1854-56. 3 vols. 4° BPL
First issue edited by R. G. White.

[Works] The 'Stratford Sh—' . . . edited by C. Knight [with life, notes, glossary, and notices of original editions]. Ln: Thomas Hodgson . . . 1854-56. 20 vols. 12°. Stratford bust portrait and vignette woodcuts   BM | SML
Sometimes found bound in ten volumes.

[Works] Werke . . . herausgegeben und erklärt von Nicolaus Delius. Elberfeld: R. L. Friderichs, 1854-61. 7 vols. 8°
  BM | BPL | BUS
English text, with notes and introductions in German. An eighth vol. was added, containing the attributed plays.

[Works] . . . Pseudo-Shakspere'sche dramen [' Edward III.' . . . 'Arden of Feversham' . . . 'Birth of Merlin'] herausgegeben von Dr. N. Delius. 3 hefte. Elberfeld: R. L. Friderichs, 1854-74. 2 vols. 8°. Chandos portrait   BM | BUS | SML
English text, with German introductions and notes.

[Works] Complete works . . . with memoir by A. Chalmers. Ln: H. G. Bohn, 1855. 12°   BPL

[Works] Plays . . . from the text of Steevens and Malone. Ln: W. Tegg & Co. . . . 1855. 12°   BPL

[Works] Family Sh—, by T. Bowdler. Eleventh edition. Ln: Longman, Brown & Co., 1855. 8°

[Works] Dramatic works . . . from the text of Johnson, Steevens and Reed. With preface by Johnson, and glossary. Ln: T. Nelson & Sons, 1855. 8°   BPL

[Works] A supplement to the plays . . . comprising the seven dramas which have been ascribed to his pen, but which are not included with his writings in modern

Sh— Works . . .

editions . . . edited with notes and introduction to each play by W. G. Simms.
Philadelphia : J. B. Smith & Co., 1855.
8°, pp. 180   BUS
Similar to the New York edition of 1848, except in title.

Works . . . New York . . . 1855.   4°

Works . . . edited by W. Hazlitt.   Ln :
Routledge & Co. . . . 1855.   5 vols.   8°

[Works] Dramatic works . . . With life,
glossary, and poems.   Philadelphia : J.
B. Smith & Co., 1855.   8 vols.   16°.
With portraits and forty-two steel illustrations   BUS

[Works] Collection of vocal music in Sh—'s
plays, from the original MSS. and early
printed copies in the possession of Dr.
Kitchiner.   Revised and arranged for the
piano by Mr. Addison.   Ln : T. Caulfield
. . . [c. 1855].   7 numbers, forming 1 vol.
8°

[Works] 'Stratford Sh—,' edited by Charles
Knight.   Ln : T. Hodgson . . . 1855-56.
10 vols.   12°   BPL

[Works] Dramatic works . . . The text carefully revised with notes by S. W. Singer.
Life of the poet and critical essays by
William Watkiss Lloyd.   Ln : Bell &
Daldy . . . 1855-56.   10 vols.   8°.   With
wood vignettes after T. Stothard, engraved by J. Thompson ; Stratford bust
portrait and facsimiles
                          BM | BPL | BUS | MPL
A few sets were issued on large paper.

[Works] Complete works . . . from the
original text, carefully collated and compared with the editions of Halliwell,
Knight, and Collier.   With historical and
critical introductions, notes to each play,
and life, by C. Knight.   New York :
Martin, Johnson & Co., 1855-59.   3 vols.
4°, pp. liv.-1,725.   Chandos portrait and
many steel portraits of celebrated
American actors in character, drawn
from life   BUS
The titles are dated 1856, and the plates 1855-59.

[Works] Dramatic works and poems . . .
with notes . . . and remarks . . . by S. W.
Singer and a life . . . by C. Symmons.
New York : Harper Brothers, 1855-71.
2 vols.   8°.   With Chandos portrait   BUS

[Works] Dramatic works . . . New edition.
With introductory essay and notes.   Ln.
& Glasgow : R. Griffin & Co., 1856.   8°,
pp. xii.-908 and steel portrait   BPL

[Works] Dramatic works . . . Ln : T. Nelson
& Sons . . . 1856.   8°   BPL

Works . . . With notes by N. Rowe.   New
edition.   Ln : G. Routledge & Co., 1856.
8°   BPL

Sh— Works . . .

[Works] Complete works . . . dramatic and
poetic : The text from the corrected copy
of G. Steevens.   With glossarial notes
and memoir by A. Chalmers.   New York :
Miller, Orton & Mulligan, 1856.   8°, pp.
x.-viii.-988.   With Chandos portrait and
forty illustrations   BUS

Works . . . The text regulated by the recently discovered folio of 1632 . . . With
a history of the stage, a life of the poet,
and an introduction to each play, by J.
P. Collier.   To which are added, glossarial and other notes and the readings
of former editions.   New York : Redfield
. . . 1856.   8°, pp. cviii.-968   BM

[Works] Plays . . . with introductions and
notes . . . by J. O. Halliwell.   Ln. &
New York : Tallis . . . 1856.   Roy. 8°
A fraudulent use of Halliwell's name.

Works . . . edited by Wm. Hazlitt.   Ln :
G. Routledge . . . 1856.   4 vols.   Cr. 8°

[Works] Plays . . . accurately printed from
the text of the corrected copies left by G.
Steevens and Ed. Malone ; a selection of
explanatory and historical notes ; a history of the stage and a life of Sh—, by
Alex. Chalmers.   New edition.   Ln :
Longman & Co., 1856.   8 vols.   8°.   With
portrait   BPL | SML | W

Works . . . dramatic and poetical, with an
account of his life and writings.   Edited
by Charles Knight.   'Cabinet edition.'
With additional notes [by R. Chambers].
Edinburgh : W. & R. Chambers, 1856-57.
12 vols.   16°.   With twelve different por-
traits (and woodcuts)   BM | BPL | SML

[Works] Plays . . . arranged for representation at the Princess's Theatre by Charles
Kean ['King Lear,' 'King John,' 'Merchant of Venice,' 'Winter's tale'].   Ln :
Chapman . . . [1856-58].   12°   SML

[Works] The college Sh—.   In which . . .
those words and expressions are omitted
which cannot with propriety be read before young students.   With copious English explanatory notes by Dr. O. Fiebig.
Vol. 1, containing 'Hamlet.'   Leipsic :
T. Thomas, 1857.   Cr. 8°, pp. vi.-232 BM
No more published.

Works . . . edited by Charles Knight, with
glossarial notes.   Woodcuts by W.
Harvey.   7th edition.   Ln : H. G. Bohn,
1857.   Cr. 8°.   With portraits in a group
                                        BPL | SML

[Works] Dramatic works.   New edition.
Ln. : Ward & Lock . . . 1857.   8°   MPL

Works, complete, accurately printed from
the text of the corrected copy left by the

late G. Steevens. With a memoir by A. Chalmers. Cincinnati [U.S.]: J. W. Sewell, 1857. 8° BM

Works . . . The text regulated by the recently discovered folio of 1632 . . . by J. P. Collier. To which are added glossarial and other notes and the readings of former editions. New York: Redfield . . . 1857. 8°, pp. iv.-cviii.-966. With Droeshout portrait and illustrations BUS

[Works] Shakspearian reader . . . Approved plays . . . By J. W. S. Hows. New York . . . 1857. 8° BM
A reprint of the 1850 edition with a fresh title-page.

[Works] Plays . . . 'Cheap and popular edition.' Ln: Willoughby & Co., 1857. 2 vols. 8° BPL

[Works] Dramatic works . . . from the text of Johnson, Stevens [sic] and Reed, with glossarial notes, life, etc. by W. Hazlitt. New edition. Ln: G. Routledge . . . 1857. 4 vols. Cr. 8° SML

Works . . . edited by C. Knight. 'Students' edition.' Ln: Routledge . . . 1857. 6 vols. Cr. 8°

Works . . . The text revised by Alexander Dyce. Ln: E. Moxon . . . 1857. 6 vols. 8°. Stratford bust portrait
BM | BPL | BUS | MPL | NY | SML
Printed on very thick paper.
The first edition under the editorship of Dyce. Contains life, notices of early editions, account of the plays, etc.

Works . . . edited by C. Knight. 'Stratford edition.' Ln: . . . 1857. 10 vols. Cr. 8°

[Works] Plays and poems, according to the improved text of Edmund Malone, with life, glossarial notes, and index. Edited by A. J. Valpy. Ln: H. G. Bohn, 1857. 15 vols. 12°. With Chandos portrait and 170 illustrations BUS
Identical with the first issue of 1832-34, except the titles.

[Works] Complete works . . . With a memoir and essay on his genius by 'Barry Cornwall,' also historical and critical studies of Sh—'s text, characters, and commentators; annotations and introductory remarks on the plays, by R. G. White, R. H. Horne, and various other distinguished writers. Illustrated by K. Meadows. Ln: [Tallis] Printing & Publishing Company [1857-59]. 3 vols. Roy. 8° BM | BPL | MPL

[Works] 'Companion Sh—' . . . edited by Charles Knight. With facts connected with Sh—'s life and writings. Ln: Routledge . . . 1857-60. 3 vols. Cr. 8° BPL

Works . . . The plays edited from the folio of MDCXXIII., with various readings from all the editions and commentators; notes, introductory remarks, historical sketch of the text, account of the rise and progress of the English drama, memoir of the poet and essay upon his genius, by R. G. White. Boston [U.S.]: Little, Brown & Co., 1857-66. 12 vols. 8°
BM | BPL | BUS
The best American issue produced up to this date. It was financed by T. P. Barton, founder of the Boston Sh— library.
Contains 117 emendations from Collier's alleged annotations of 1632.
Of the fifty copies done on large paper, one is at Boston.

[Works] Dramatic works . . . 'Lansdowne edition.' Based on Collier's edition and compared with Johnson, Steevens, Malone, Boswell, and Knight. Ln: H. G. Bohn . . . 1858. Cr. 8°, pp. viii.-1,124, rubricated BPL | BUS | MPL | NY
The Lansdowne rubricated edition of 1852 unchanged except in imprint.
Also issued with Stothard's plates.

Works . . . from the text of G. Steevens. With memoir by A. Chalmers. Cincinnati . . . 1858. 8°. With portrait and illustrations BUS

Works . . . with preface by Dr. Johnson, life, verses by contemporary poets, and a glossary. Halifax [Eng.]: Milner & Sowerby; Ln: Simpkin . . . 1858
BPL | SML
An interleaved copy with MS. notes by S. Timmins is at Birmingham.

[Works] Dramatic Works . . . new edition, with introductory essay and notes. Ln. and Glasgow: Richard Griffin & Co., 1858. 8°, pp. iv.-xii.-908, and Jansen portrait (altered) SML

Works . . . from the text of Isaac Reed. With glossary, essay, and notes by Steevens, Malone and Johnson. Ln: W. Tegg. Glasgow: R. Griffin & Co., 1858. 8°. With Jansen portrait BPL

Works . . . edited by J. O. Halliwell. Ln: Tallis & Co., 1858. 8°
An unauthorised use of Halliwell's name.

Works . . . Ln: Simpkin . . . 1858. 8°

Works . . . edited by T. Campbell. Ln: Routledge . . . 1858. Roy. 8°. With Chandos portrait

[Works] Plays . . . as arranged for representation at the Princess's Theatre. With historical and explanatory notes by Charles Kean. Ln: . . . 1858. 2 vols. 8°

[Works] Complete works . . . revised from the original text. With . . . remarks and copious notes, critical, general, and ex-

Sh— Works . . .

planatory, by S. Phelps. Engravings by Hablot K. Browne ['Phiz']. Glasgow: W. R. McPhun & Son. Ln: J. A. Berger . . . 1858. 2 vols. Roy. 8°. With coloured plates   BPL

[Works] Complete dramatic and poetical works . . . With memoir and essay by ' Barry Cornwall,' historical and critical studies by Richard Grant White, R. H. Horne, and other writers. Illustrated by Kenny Meadows. Ln: Printing and Publishing Co., 1858. 3 vols. 4°   CPL

Works . . . edited by C. Knight. ' National edition.' Ln: Routledge . . . 1858. 6 vols. 8°. With woodcuts

[Works] Comedies, histories, tragedies, and poems, edited by J. P. Collier. Second edition. Ln: Whittaker & Co., 1858. 6 vols. 8°. With Droeshout portrait
BM | BPL | BUS | MPL | NY | SML
Identical save in date with the second edition of 1844-53.

[Works] Plays . . . edited by Howard Staunton; illustrations by John Gilbert, engraved by the brothers Dalziel. Ln: G. Routledge & Co., 1858-60. 3 vols. Roy. 8°. Stratford bust portrait
BM | BPL | BUS | MPL | SML
The first issue edited by Howard Staunton and the first to bear Sir John Gilbert's adornments. Issued serially in 50 numbers.

[Works] Plays . . edited by H. Staunton. Illustrations by J. Gilbert. Ln: G. Routledge & Co., 1858-61. 3 vols. 8°   BPL

[Works] Shakspearian reader. With notes by J. W. S. Hows. New York . . . 1859. 12°   BPL

Works . . . edited by C. Knight. With woodcuts by W. Harvey. Seventh edition. Ln: H. G. Bohn . . . 1859. Cr. 8° BPL

[Works] Complete works . . . Halifax [Eng.]: Milner & Sowerby, 1859. 8°   BPL

[Works] Dramatic works . . . Ln: T. Nelson & Sons . . . 1859. 8°   BPL

[Works] Dramatic works . . . from the text of Johnson, Stevens [sic] and Reed. With glossarial notes, life . . . by N. Rowe. Ln: Routledge, Warnes & Routledge, 1859. 8°, pp. xii.-972. With five portraits and autograph

Works . . . from the text of Geo. Steevens. Ln: W. Tegg . . . 1859. 8°

[Works] Family Sh— . . . by T. Bowdler. Ln: Longman . . . 1859. Roy. 8°

[Works] Dramatic works . . . with remarks on his life by T. Campbell. Ln: Routledge & Co. . . . 1859. 2 vols. 8°
BPL | SML
With forty-five steel portraits of Sh—'s heroines.

Sh— Works . . .

Works . . . edited by ' Barry Cornwall.' Illustrated by Kenny Meadows. Ln: Griffin & Co. . . . 1859. 3 vols. Roy. 8°

Works . . . edited by W. Hazlitt. Ln: Routledge . . . 1859. 5 vols. Cr. 8°
Includes the attributed plays.

[Works] Bowdler's ' Family Sh—.' Ln: Longmans . . . 1859. 7 vols. Cr. 8°

Works . . . The text regulated by the folio of 1632. Boston [U.S.]: W. Veazie, 1859. 8 vols. 8°   BPL
Contains the forged emendations by Collier.

Works . . . edited by C. Knight. ' Standard edition.' Ln: Routledge . . . 1859. 8 vols. Roy. 8°
Includes the attributed plays.

[Works] Plays . . . carefully revised from the original text. By S. Phelps. With a life and portrait. ' Cheap and popular edition.' Ln: Willoughby & Co. [c. 1859]. 38 parts (pub. 2d. each). 8°   CPL

[Works] Dramatic works . . . for use in schools, etc., by T. Bowdler. Ln: Griffin & Co. [1860]. 12°   BPL

[Works] Complete works . . . with preface by Dr. Johnson, life of the author, commendatory verses by contemporary poets, and a glossary. Halifax [Eng.]: Milner & Sowerby, 1860. 8°   BPL | SML

[Works] Dramatic and poetical works . . . New edition. With introductory essay and notes. Ln. & Glasgow: Richard Griffin & Co., 1860. 8°, pp. xii.-(c.)900

Works . . . edited by T. Campbell. Ln: Routledge . . . 1860. 8°

[Works] Supplementary works . . . comprising his ' Poems ' and ' Doubtful plays.' With glossarial and other notes. A new edition by William Hazlitt. Ln: Routledge . . . 1860. 8°, pp. viii.-526

[Works] Dramatic works . . . from the text of Johnson, Steevens and Reed. New York: Leavitt & Allen, 1860. 8°   BPL

[Works] Family Sh— . . . by T. Bowdler. Ln: Longman . . . 1860. Roy. 8°

[Works] Selections from the plays . . . as arranged . . . at the Princess's Theatre by Charles Kean. Ln: Bradbury & Evans, 1860. 2 vols. 8°   BPL

Works . . . edited, with a scrupulous revision of the text, by Mary Cowden Clarke. New York: D. Appleton & Co., 1860. 2 vols. 8°, pp. lxii.-1,002. Droeshout portrait and forty-eight portraits of female characters in the plays
BM | BPL | BUS
The first issue edited by Mary Cowden Clarke.

[Works] Dramatic works . . . with notes by
W. Hazlitt. Ln : Routledge & Co., 1860.
5 vols. Cr. 8°   BPL
Includes the attributed plays.

Works . . . edited by Howard Staunton.
Illustrated by J. Gilbert. Ln : . . . 1860.
6 vols. 8°
The pretended discovery of J. P. Collier (*q.v.*) was
adversely criticised by Staunton in the preface and
'life' contained herein.

[Works] 'Stratford Sh—' . . . edited by
C. Knight. Ln : R. Griffin & Co., 1860.
6 vols. 12°   BPL

Works . . . edited by Charles Knight.
'Companion edition.' Ln : Routledge . . .
1860. 6 vols. Cr. 8°

Works . . . The text regulated by the
[forged] folio of 1632. With readings
from former editions, history of the stage,
life of the poet, and an introduction to
each play. To which are added glossorial
and other notes by Knight, Dyce, Douce,
Collier, Halliwell, Hunter, and Richardson. Boston [U.S.]: Crosby, Nichols, Lee
& Co., 1860. 8 vols. 8°. With Stratford
bust portrait   BUS | MPL
Founded on the text of Collier's 1858 edition. Much of
the introductory matter is pirated from Collier's
1842-44 issue.

Works . . . edited by C. Knight. ' Pictorial
edition.' Ln : Routledge . . . 1860. 8
vols. Roy. 8°

Works . . . The text regulated by the
[forged] folio of 1632. Philadelphia :
Porter & Coates [c. 1860]. 8 vols. 12°
                                      BPL

[Works] Dramatic works . . . adapted for
family reading by T. Bowdler . . . New
edition, with steel engravings [and Jansen portrait]. Ln. & Glasgow : R. Griffin
& Co. [1860]-61. 8°, pp. 864
                      BM | BPL | NY | SML

[Works] Family Sh—. Plays . . . edited by
T. Bowdler [with woodcuts repeated from
the Harness edition of 1836]. Ln : Longman & Co., 1860-65. 6 vols. 12°
                               BPL | SML

[Works] Plays . . . uitgegeven en verklaard
door C. W. Opzoomer. 3 stuk [Three
plays]. Amsterdam : Gebroeders Binger,
1860-72. 12°   BM

[Works] Sh—'s select plays. With explanatory and illustrative notes by John
Hunter. Ln : Longmans, Green & Co.,
1860-73. 31 vols. Cr. 8°   BM

[Works] Complete . . . works . . . With
thirty-seven illustrations and a memoir.
Ln : J. Dicks . . . 1861. Cr. 8°, pp. xii.-
1,006   CPL

According to a letter in the *Bookseller*, 1st July, 1868,
John Dicks sold within a few years nearly a million
copies of this shilling edition, which appears to be the
highest record of the kind.

Works . . . from the text of Geo. Steevens
and E. Malone. Ln : T. Tegg, 1861. Cr. 8°

[Works] Plays . . . collated from the editions
of Steevens, Malone and Johnson, with
life, glossarial notes, and introductory
observations. Ln : Griffin & Co. . . .
1861. 8°

[Works] Family Sh— . . . edited by Thomas
Bowdler. Ln : Longman . . . 1861. 8°.
With Chandos portrait   SML

[Works] Complete works . . . New edition.
Manchester : J. G. Bell . . . 1861. 8° BPL

Works . . . edited by W. Hazlitt. Ln :
Routledge . . . 1861. 5 vols. Cr. 8°
Includes the attributed plays.

[Works] 'Stratford Sh—,' edited by C.
Knight. Ln : Griffin, Bohn & Co. . . .
1861. 6 vols. 12°   BPL

[Works] Chambers' ' Household edition ' of
the dramatic works . . . edited by Robt.
Carruthers and Wm. Chambers. Illustrated by Keeley Halswelle. Ln. &
Edinburgh : W. & R. Chambers, 1861-63.
10 vols. Cr. 8°. With portrait and wood-
cuts   BM | BPL | BUS | MPL | SML
The first edition under the auspices of R. Carruthers
and W. Chambers. Expurgated text.

[Works] Complete works . . with critical
preface by Dr. Johnson, life of the author
. . . verses, glossary [and anecdotes].
Halifax [Eng.]: Milner & Sowerby . . .
1862. 8°, pp. xxiv.-742. With the
Chandos portrait on steel and Falstaff
vignette   BPL | SML

[Works] Complete works . . . edited by
Charles Knight. With memoir by A.
Chalmers. Woodcuts by W. Harvey.
Eighth edition. Ln : H. G. Bohn . . .
1862. Cr. 8°. With grouped portraits
                               BPL | SML

Works . . . edited by J. R. Pitman. New
edition. Ln : G. Hoby . . . 1862. 8°

[Works] Plays . . . from the text of Steevens
and Malone. Ln : Longman & Co., 1862.
8°   BPL

Works . . . Ln : Macmillan & Co., 1862. 8°

Works . . . from the text of G. Steevens and
E. Malone. Ln : Rivington . . . 1862. 8°

Works . . . with remarks by T. Campbell.
Ln : Routledge & Co., 1862. Roy. 8°.
Illustrated   SML

[Works] Dramatic works . . . from the text
of Johnson, Steevens and Reed. With
glossarial notes by Wm. Hazlitt. Ln :
G. Routledge . . . 1862. 5 vols. Cr. 8°
Includes the attributed plays.   BPL | MPL

Sh— Works . . .

Works . . . The text regulated by the [forged] folio of 1632 . . . To which are added glossarial and other notes . . . New York: Sheldon & Co. . . . 1862. 8 vols. 8°. With Stratford bust portrait   BUS
Known as the 'Riverside edition.' Identical with the Boston 1860 edition (save that it is on smaller paper) and printed from the same stereotype plates.

Works . . . edited by Howard Staunton. Illustrations by J. Gilbert. Ln: G. Routledge & Co., 1862-64. 3 vols. 8° BPL

[Works] Sh— as put forth in 1623. A reprint of Mr. Wm. Sh—'s comedies, histories, and tragedies. Published according to the true originall copies. Ln: Reprinted for Lionel Booth, 1862-64. 3 vols. Fcp. 4°. With Droeshout portrait
   BM | BPL | BUS | MPL | SML
A disastrous undertaking from a pecuniary standpoint. Writing in 1884, Lionel Booth said he 'had never been able to guess what made him undertake it.'
[See 'New Shakespeareana,' 1909, vol. 8, p. 55.]

[Works] Sh— as put forth in 1623. A reprint . . . Ln: Reprinted for L. Booth . . . 1862-64. 4°. Large paper copy
   BPL | SML
Two of the large paper copies were also done on pure vellum.

[Works: Sh— as put forth in 1623] Extracts from various reviews of the above-named reproduction which have appeared in the public press. Ln: L. Booth [1862-64]. 8°, pp. 8   BM

Works . . . edited from the folio of 1623, with various readings from all the editions and commentators, notes, introductory remarks, historical sketch, account of the . . . English drama, memoir of the poet, and essay on his genius, by Richard Grant White. Boston [U.S.] . . . 1862-66. 12 vols. 8°   NY
Fifty copies were also printed on thick paper.

[Works] Collection of lithographic facsimiles of the early quarto editions of the separate works of Sh—, including every known edition of all the plays which were issued during the life-time of the great dramatist, by Edmund William Ashbee. Edited by J. O. Halliwell. Ln: Privately printed, 1862-71. 48 vols. Fcp. 4°
   BM | BPL | MPL | NY
Issue limited to fifty sets; of which Halliwell destroyed nineteen, and as a fire at the Pantechnicon, 13th Feb., 1874 (where the stock was stored) destroyed others, Halliwell concluded that no more than fifteen complete sets exist. Printed on one side of the leaf only. Subscribed at £5 5s. per volume.
'Every single letter has been traced from the originals by hand, and for practical uses this series is as valuable as a collection of the early quartos themselves.'
A full list of the series may be seen in Halliwell's 'Skeleton handlist 1860.'
The series does not include 'Titus Andronicus, 1594,' as the only known copy was not found until 1904.

Sh— Works . . .

Works . . . illustrated. Ln: H. G. Bohn . . . 1863. Cr. 8°

[Works] Complete works . . . With preface by Dr. Johnson. Halifax [Eng.]: Milner & Sowerby . . . 1863. 8° BPL | MPL

[Works] Family Sh—, by T. Bowdler. 'School edition.' Ln: Longman, 1863. 8°   BPL

[Works] Dramatic works . . . with life and a copious glossary. Ln., Edinburgh & New York: T. Nelson & Sons, 1863. 8°, pp. xxiv.-1,062. With plates
   BM | BPL | MPL

[Works] Dramatic works . . . edited by T. Campbell. Ln: Routledge . . . 1863. 8°
   BPL

[Works] Dramatic works . . . from the text of Johnson, Steevens and Reed. With glossarial notes, life, etc. by N. Rowe. Ln: Routledge, Warne & Routledge, 1863. 8°, pp. ii.-972 and frontispiece bearing five grouped portraits of the bard
   BPL | BUS

[Works] Shakespearian facsimiles, selected by J. O. Halliwell. Ln: [Printed] by E. W. Ashbee, 1863. F°   BPL

[Works] Plays . . . 'Penny library edition.' Manchester: Ireland & Co., 1863. 2 vols. 8°   BPL

Works . . . edited by H. Staunton. Ln: G. Routledge . . . 1863. 4 vols. 8°

Works . . . 'Cabinet edition,' edited by C. Knight. Edinburgh: Chambers . . . 1863. 12 vols. 12°

Works . . . The text restored, with notes and life by H. N. Hudson. Boston [U.S.]: Crosby & Nichols, 1863-64. 11 vols. 12°. With Chandos portrait
   BPL | SML
The last volume contains the biography, history of the drama, and the 'Poems.'

Works . . . edited by Wm. George Clark, John Glover [and Wm. Aldis Wright]. Cambridge & Ln: Macmillan & Co., 1863-66. 9 vols. 8°
   BM | BPL | BUS | MPL | NY | SML
First edition of the 'Cambridge Sh—.'
Volumes 2 to 6 were edited by W. G. Clark and W. A. Wright, and vol. 1 by J. Glover.
Reviewed in Dublin Univ. Mag., Feb., 1864. For many years this was considered the purest text available.
G. R. French's laborious 'Shakespeareana genealogica' was issued as a supplement to this edition, and like many other good books failed to find a market until too late, when practically the whole edition had been sacrificed as a 'job lot.'
'. . . Or my Sh—; my great Cambridge Sh—; it has an odour which carries me yet further back in life, for these volumes belonged to my father, and before I was old enough to read them with understanding it was often permitted me to take down one of them from the bookcase and reverently to turn the leaves. . . . What

a strange tenderness comes upon me when I hold one of them in hand. For that reason I do not often read Sh—in that edition. . . .—*George Gissing* [in 'Private papers of Hy. Rycroft'].

[Works] Sh—'s plays . . . abridged and revised for the use of girls, by R. Baughan. Ln : T. J. Allman . . . 1863-71. 2 vols. 8° BM
The title of vol. 2 varies from that in vol. 1. It bears the words 'Second edition' and the imprint, 'R. Washbourne, Ln.'

Works . . . edited by A. Chalmers. Ln : Bell & Daldy, 1864. 12°

Works . . . from the text of Steevens and Malone. Ln : Macmillan . . . 1864. 12°
Issued in two states ; with and without plates.

[Works] Plays . . . from the text of Steevens and Malone. Ln : W. Tegg . . . 1864. 12° BPL

[Works] Complete works . . . edited by A. Chalmers. With memoir by 'Barry Cornwall.' 'Commemoration edition.' New York : O. S. Felt . . . [c. 1864]. 12° BPL

[Works] 'Globe edition.' The works of Wm. Sh— . . . edited by W. G. Clark and W. A. Wright. Cambridge & Ln : Macmillan & Co., 1864. Cr. 8°, pp. viii.-1,080 BM | BPL | NY | SML
An edition founded on the 'Cambridge Sh—' of 1863-66, and which, through the purity of its text, achieved an enormous sale.
'My eyes being good as ever I take the Globe volume, which I bought in days when such a purchase was something more than an extravagance ; wherefore I regard the book with that peculiar affection which results from sacrifice.'—*George Gissing* [in 'Private papers of Hy. Rycroft'].

[Works] Dramatic works . . . with copious glossarial notes and biographical notice. By Robert Inglis. Eight steel engravings. Edinburgh : Gall & Inglis [1864]. Cr. 8°, pp. x.-934 BM | BPL

[Works] 'Dicks' complete edition ' . . . works. With a memoir. Ln : J. Dicks —*One shilling*—1864. Cr. 8°, pp. 1,022. Illustrated BPL

Works . . . edited by A. Chalmers. With plates. Cincinnati : Rickey & Co. . . . 1864. 8°

[Works] Complete works . . . From the text of Johnson, Steevens and Reed. With biographical sketch [character index and glossary] by M. Cowden Clarke. Edinburgh : W. P. Nimmo, 1864. 8°, pp. xx.-716. With portraits and vignettes BM | BPL | BUS | MPL

[Works] Complete works . . . Leipzig : Baumgartner . . . 1864. 8° BPL

[Works] Plays . . . complete in one volume. Manchester : Alex. Ireland & Co., Pall Mall Court, 1864. 8°, pp. iv.-920 BPL
The first complete Manchester edition in one volume.

Works . . . complete. Accurately printed from the text of the corrected copy left by the late G. Steevens, Esq. With a memoir by A. Chalmers. New York : D. Appleton & Co. [1864]. 8°, pp. x.-980. With portrait and illustrations BM

Works . . . dramatic and poetical . . . complete, from the text left by G. Stevens [*sic*]. With glossàry, notes, and memoir by A. Chalmers. New York : O. S. Felt . . . [1864]. 8°, pp. xii.-1,028. Chandos portrait and steel plates BUS

[Works] Dramatic works . . . With biographical introduction by Henry Glassford Bell. Glasgow : W. Collins . . . 1864. Roy. 8° BPL | MPL
First issue edited by H. G. Bell.

Works . . . edited by Thomas Keightley. Ln : Bell & Daldy . . . 1864. Roy. 8°

Works . . . edited . . . by C. and M. C. Clarke. Ln : Bickers . . . 1864. Roy. 8°, pp. lxii.-1,002 BM | BPL

[Works] 'Reference Sh—': A memorial edition of Sh—'s plays. Containing 11,600 references, compiled by John B. Marsh. Ln : Simpkin . . . 1864. Roy. 8°, pp. vi.-925 BM | BPL | MPL | SML

[Works] Dramatic works . . . Edinburgh : Gall & Inglis [1864]. 2 vols. 16° BM | BPL

Works . . . from the text of Johnson, Steevens and Reed. Edited by M. C. Clarke. Ln : Simpkin . . . 1864. 2 vols. 12°

[Works] Complete works . . . with memoir by 'Barry Cornwall.' Illustrated by K. Meadows and portraits of eminent actors. Ln : Printing and Publishing Co. [1864]. 3 vols. Roy. 8° BPL

Works . . . edited, with a scrupulous revision of the text, by C. and M. Cowden Clarke. Ln : Bickers . . . 1864. 4 vols. 8° BM | BPL | NY

Works . . . edited by H. Staunton. With copious notes, glossary, life, etc. 'Library edition.' Ln : Routledge, Warne & Routledge, 1864. 4 vols. 8° BM | BPL | MPL

[Works] Dramatic works . . . from the text of Johnson, Stevens [*sic*] and Reed. With notes and life by W. Hazlitt. Ln : Routledge . . . 1864. 5 vols. 12° BPL | SML
Includes the attributed plays.

[Works] Plays . . . carefully edited by T. Keightley. Ln. [Chiswick]: Bell & Daldy, 1864. 6 vols. Cr. 8°. With Droeshout portrait BM | BPL | MPL | NY | SML
First edition edited by Keightley.

Sh— Works . . .

Works . . . ' Bijou edition.' With forty-five photographs from Boydell's edition. Ln: L. Booth . . . 1864. (?) vols. 32° (in case)

[Works] Sh— album. Berlin: H. Graf . . . [c. 1864]. 8°. Forty-eight photographs of German actors in character and one of Sh—'s Stratford bust   BUS

[Works] Sh— album. Containing all the characters in costume as represented at the Sh— festival, celebrated April 23th [sic], 1864, by the Malkasten Society of Artists at Dusseldorf . . . Dusseldorf: G. & A. Overbeck, 1864   BUS

[Works] Sh— gallery: A reproduction [by S. Ayling] in commemoration of the ter-centenary anniversary of the poet's birth [Photographs, with selections from the plays]. Ln: Booth & Ayling . . . 1864. 4°, pp. xxx.-374   BM | BPL | BUS | CPL

Works . . . The text revised by A. Dyce . . . Second edition. Ln: Chapman & Hall, [1863] 1864-67. 9 vols. 8°. Droeshout and Stratford bust portraits and facsimile
      BM | BPL | BUS | MPL | NY
Part of this edition was issued with fresh titles dated 1866-67.

Works . . . ' Pictorial edition,' edited by C. Knight. Second edition [with biography. Third edition]. Ln: Routledge . . . 1864-67. 8 vols. 8°   BPL

[Works] ' Cassell's illustrated Sh—.' The plays of Sh—. Edited and annotated by Charles and M. Cowden Clarke . . . Illustrated by H. C. Selous. [With] The story of Sh—'s life. Ln: Cassell, Petter & Galpin [1864-68]. 3 vols. 4°. Jansen and Stratford bust portraits   BM | BUS
'Expurgated, and "Titus Andronicus" omitted not only on account of its grossness, but because of our strong conviction that it is not Sh—'s writing.'

Works . . . edited by W. G. Clark and W. A. Wright. Boston [U.S.] . . . 1865. Cr. 8°

Works . . . edited by W. G. Clark and W. A. Wright. ' Globe edition.' Cambridge & Ln: Macmillan . . . 1865. Cr. 8°, pp. viii.-1,080

[Works] Supplementary works . . . comprising his poems and 'doubtful' plays. With glossarial and other notes. A new edition, by Wm. Hazlitt. Ln: Routledge, Warne & Routledge, 1865. Cr. 8°, pp. viii.-526

[Works] Sh— [eight plays] adapted for reading classes and for the family circle. By T. Bulfinch and S. G. Bulfinch. Boston [U.S.]: J. E. Tilton & Co., 1865. 8°, pp. xii.-436   BM

Works . . . edited by C. and M. C. Clarke. Edinburgh . . . 1865. 8°

Sh— Works . . .

[Works] Complete works . . . revised from the original editions. With notes. Ln: . . . 1865. 8°   CPL

Works . . . edited by H. Staunton. Illustrated by J. Gilbert. Ln: . . . 1865. 8°

[Works] Sh— for schools and families. Being a selection and abridgment of the principal plays . . . edited by T. Shorter. Ln: T. J. Allman . . . 1865. 8°, pp. vi.-640   BM

[Works] Plays and poems. Edited by Thomas Keightley. Ln: Bell & Daldy . . . 1865. 8°, pp. viii.-944   BM | BPL

Works . . . edited for schools by C. Lenny. Second edition. Ln: Relfe . . . 1865. 8°

[Works] Cassell's illustrated Sh—. The plays . . . edited by C. and M. C. Clarke. Ln: Cassell & Co., 1865. 3 vols. 4°
      BPL

[Works] Dramatic works. With biographical introduction by Henry Glassford Bell. Glasgow: Porteous Brothers, 1865. 6 vols. 12°   BM | BPL

[Works] Family Sh—, edited by T. Bowdler. New edition. Ln: Longman . . . 1865. 6 vols. 12°

Works . . . edited . . . by R. G. White. Boston [U.S.]: Little, Brown & Co., 1865. 12 vols. Cr. 8°   BM | BPL

Works . . . edited by J. P. Collier. New York: Routledge . . . 1865-66. 8 vols. 8°   BPL
Includes the volume of ' doubtful ' plays.

Works . . . edited by H. Staunton. Illustrated by J. Gilbert. Ln: G. Routledge . . . 1865-67. 3 vols. 8°

Works . . . edited by W. Hazlitt. Ln: G. Routledge . . . 1865-67. 5 vols. Cr. 8°
Includes the attributed plays.

[Works] Cassell's illustrated Sh—. . Plays . . . edited and annotated by C. and M. C. Clarke. Illustrated by H. C. Selous. Ln: Cassell, Petter & Galpin [1865-69]. 3 vols. 4°   CPL | NY

Works . . . ' Dicks' complete edition ' . . . With 37 illustrations and a memoir. Ln: J. Dicks . . . 1866. Cr. 8°, pp. xii.-1,008 and portrait   BPL | BUS

[Works] ' Globe edition.' Works . . . Edited by W. G. Clark and W. A. Wright. Ln. & Cambridge: Macmillan . . . 1866. Cr. 8°, pp. viii.-1,076   BM | BPL | SML

[Works] Complete works . . . from the text of Johnson, Steevens and Reed. With biographical sketch by Mary Cowden Clarke [and index to characters]. Edinburgh: W. P. Nimmo . . . 1866. 8°, pp. xx.-716   BPL | BUS | SML

[Works] Complete works . . . Halifax [Eng.] :
Milner & Sowerby . . . 1866. 8°   BPL

[Works] Dramatic works . . . edited by C.
Knight. With remarks on his life by T.
Campbell. 'Blackfriars edition.' Ln :
G. Routledge . . . 1866. 8°

Works . . . edited by George Long
Duyckinck. Philadelphia . . . 1866. 8°.
With plates
First edition under this editor.

Works . . . edited by H. Staunton. Illustrated by J. Gilbert. Ln : G. Routledge
. . . 1866. 3 vols. 8°   BPL | NY

[Works] Dramatic works . . . With life and
notes, together with a copious glossary.
Philadelphia : J. B. Lippincott & Co.,
1866. 4 vols. 8°. With Chandos portrait
and plates   BUS

[Works] Plays . . . carefully edited by
Thomas Keightley. Boston [U.S.] :
Ticknor & Fields . . . 1866. 6 vols. 12°.
With Droeshout portrait by Marshall BUS
Reprinted from the London 1864 issue.

Works . . . 'Stratford edition,' edited by C.
Knight. Ln : Griffin . . . 1866. 6 vols.
12°

Works . . . edited by T. Keightley. Ln :
Chiswick Press . . . 1866. 7 vols. 8°

Works . . . 'Pictorial edition,' edited by C.
Knight. Ln : Routledge . . . 1866. 8
vols. Roy. 8°

Works . . . The text regulated by the folio
of 1632 ; with readings from former
editions, a history of the stage, a life of
the poet, and an introduction to each
play. To which are added glossorial and
other notes by Knight, Dyce, Collier,
Halliwell, Hunter and Richardson. New
York [U.S.] : W. J. Widdleton, 1866. 8
vols. 8°   BM | SML
The text founded on the forged annotations of J. P.
Collier.

[Works] Sh—. The first collected edition
of the dramatic works . . . A reproduction
in exact facsimile of the famous first folio,
1623, by the newly-discovered process of
photo-lithography. Executed by R. W.
Preston under the superintendence of
Howard Staunton. Ln : Day & Son . . .
1866. 16 parts, forming 1 vol. F°
    BM | BPL | BUS | MPL | SML
The first faithful reproduction of the Jaggard canon.
It was executed (from the originals at Bridgewater
House and the British Museum) at H.M. ordnance
survey office.
Issue began serially in 1864.

Works . . . edited by A. Dyce. Ln : Chapman & Hall, 1866-67. 9 vols. 8°   BPL
See note under Sh— Works, Dyce, 1864-67.

[Works] The 'Handy-volume Sh—.' Works
. . . [edited by Q. D——]. Ln : Bradbury,
Evans & Co., 1866-67. 13 vols. 16°
    BM | BPL | BUS | NY

[Works] 'Prince's Sh—' : A selection of
the plays . . . carefully expurgated and
annotated for the use of families and
schools. By D. Mathias. [Three plays.]
Ln : R. Bentley . . . 1867. 12°, pp. xii.-
112-112-116   BM | BPL | CPL | SML

[Works] 'Globe edition ' . . . edited by
W. G. Clark and W. A. Wright. Ln :
Macmillan . . . 1867. Cr. 8°   BPL

Works . . . [with glossarial index] edited by
C. Knight. 'Blackfriars edition.' Ln :
Routledge . . . 1867. Cr. 8°, pp. viii.-1,074
    BM | BPL | SML

Works . . . edited by G. L. Duyckinck.
With plates. Philadelphia . . . 1867. 8°

[Works] Sh— gallery : A reproduction
commemorative of the tercentenary anniversary. Ln : Routledge . . . 1867.
Fcp. 4°   MPL

Works . . . edited by T. Keightley. Ln :
Bell & Daldy . . . 1867. 6 vols. 32°, in
case

[Works] The 'Stratford Sh—,' edited by
C. Knight. Ln : C. Griffin & Co. . . .
1867. 6 vols. 12°   BPL | SML

[Works] 'Family Sh—.' Plays . . . edited
by T. Bowdler. [13th edition ?] Ln :
Longmans . . . [c. 1867]. 6 vols. 12°.
With woodcuts   SML

[Works] 'Pictorial edition ' . . . edited by
C. Knight. The second edition, revised.
Ln : G. Routledge & Sons, 1867. 7 vols.
8°   BM | MPL

Works . . . 'Handy volume edition.' Boston
[U.S.] . . . ; Ln : Bradbury & Evans, 1867.
13 vols. 18°, in case

[Works] Plays and poems . . . edited by
A. J. Valpy. With plates. Ln : Bell &
Daldy . . . 1867. 15 vols. 12°   BPL

Works . . . edited by C. Knight. 'Shilling
Sh—.' Ln : G. Routledge & Sons . . .
1868. 12°, pp. iv.-764   BM | BUS
Another shilling rival to Dicks' original shilling issue of
1861.

[Works] Complete works . . . with a memoir.
Ln : J. Dicks . . . 1868. Cr. 8°, pp. xii.-
1,008   BM | NY

Works . . . poems, life, glossary, etc. Reprinted from the original edition, and
compared with all recent commentators.
[Edited by Valentine.] 'Chandos classics.'
Ln : Warne . . . 1868. Cr. 8°, pp. xvi.-748
    BM | BPL | BUS | NY | SML
A shilling edition, put out as a rival to Dicks' successful
edition of 1861.

Sh— Works . . .

Works . . . with life, glossary, etc. Reprinted from the early editions and compared with recent commentators. ' Chandos poets.' Ln : F. Warne [1868]. Cr. 8°, pp. xii.-1,124 and steel portrait NY

[Works] Sh— for schools . . . Edited by T. Shorter. Ln : Allman . . . 1868. 8°

[Works] Complete works . . . from the text of Johnson, Steevens and Reed. With biographical sketch by M. C. Clarke. Ln : C. Griffin & Co. [1868]. 8°, pp. xx.-716 BM

[Works] ' Family Sh— ' . . . edited by T. Bowdler. Ln : Longmans . . . 1868. 8° BPL

Works . . . edited by C. Knight. Illustrated by John Gilbert. Ln : G. Routledge & Sons . . . 1868. 8° BM | BPL

Works . . . from the text of . . . A. Dyce's second edition [Tauchnitz edition]. Leipzig : B. Tauchnitz . . . 1868. 7 vols. 16°. With Chandos portrait BM | BPL | NY | SML
The next year the ' doubtful ' plays were added in vol. 8.

[Works] Plays . . . edited by T. Keightley. Ln : Bell & Daldy . . . 1868. 7 vols. Cr. 8° BPL
Sometimes found bound in 13 vols.

Works . . . text revised by A. Dyce. Ln : Chapman & Hall, 1868. 9 vols. 8°
Fresh impression (with altered date) of the ' Second edition.'

[Works] Dramatic works . . . The text carefully revised with notes by S. W. Singer. Ln : Bell & Daldy, 1868. 10 vols. 8° NY

Works . . . ' Handy volume Sh—.' Ln : Bradbury, Evans & Co., 1868. 13 vols. 16° BPL

[Works] Plays . . . edited by T. Keightley. Ln : G. Bell & Sons . . . 1868-79. 7 vols. 8°. With Droeshout portrait by Marshall SML
Vol. 7 is dated 1868.

[Works] Sh—'s select plays, edited by W. G. Clark and W. Aldis Wright [the fifth and subsequent plays edited only by W. A. Wright]. Oxford : Clarendon Press . . . 1868-83. 10 vols. 8° BM | BPL | BUS | SML
An expurgated edition for school use, entered individually in detail under the separate plays.

[Works] Doubtful plays . . . [edited by Max Moltke]. Leipzig : B. Tauchnitz . . . 1869. Cr. 8°, pp. viii.-352 BM | BUS | SML
Contains six plays :— ' King Edward III.; Thomas Lord Cromwell ; Locrine ; Yorkshire tragedy ; London prodigal ; Birth of Merlin.'
' In the present volume, intended as a supplement to Sh—'s works, I have selected those six pieces which, according to my firm conviction, bear the most unmistakeable traces of Sh—'s authorship.'—Preface.

Sh— Works . . .

Works . . . [Plays, poems, sonnets, ' Passionate pilgrim,' will and testament] life, glossary, etc. Reprinted from the original edition and compared with all recent commentators [edited by Valentine]. Ln : F. Warne & Co. . . . 1869. Cr. 8°, pp. xvi.-748. With Chandos portrait and five steel plates

[Works] Sämmtliche werke . . . Englischer text, berichtigt und erklärt von Benno Tschischwitz. Nebst historisch-kritischen einleitungen [I. ' Hamlet ']. Halle : G. E. Barthel, 1869. 8° BUS
No more issued.

Works . . . edited by C. and M. C. Clarke. Ln : Bickers . . . 1869. 8° BPL

Works . . . edited by C. Knight. Ln : Routledge . . . 1869. 8°

Works . . . edited by C. and M. C. Clarke. Ln : Bickers & Son . . . 1869. 4 vols. 8° BPL

Works . . . edited according to the first printed copies, with the various readings, and critical notes by F. H. Stratmann. Ln. & Krefeild . . . 1869. 8° NY
First edition under this editor.

Works . . . with introductions, notes, and life by C. Knight. New York [c. 1869]. 3 vols. Roy. 8°. With steel plates, chiefly portraits of American actors BUS

Works . . . edited by ' Barry Cornwall.' Illustrated. Ln : . . . 1869. 6 vols. 8°

Works . . . edited by H. Staunton. With copious notes, glossary, life, etc. Ln : Routledge & Sons, 1869. 8 vols. 8° BPL

[Works] Dramatic works . . . with notes by S. W. Singer, life by W. W. Lloyd. ' Aldine edition.' Ln : G. Bell & Sons . . . 1869. 10 vols. 8°

[Works] Handy volume Sh—. Ln : Bradbury & Evans, 1869. 13 vols. 12° BPL

[Works] Dramatic works . . . Ln : T. Nelson & Sons . . . 1870. 8° BPL

Works . . . edited by T. Campbell. Ln : Routledge [c. 1870]. 8°

[Works] Historical Shakspearian reader : comprising the ' histories ' or ' chronicle plays ' of Sh—, carefully expurgated and revised, with introductory and explanatory notes . . . by J. W. S. Hows. New York : D. Appleton & Co., 1870. 8°, pp. 504 BM

Works . . . Ln : Virtue . . . 1870. 2 vols. 8°

[Works] Charles Kemble's Sh— readings, being a selection of the plays of Sh—, as read by him in public. Edited by R. J. Lane. Ln : Bell & Daldy, 1870. 3 vols. Cr. 8° BM | SML

Sh— Works . . .

Works . . . edited by ' Barry Cornwall.' Illustrated. Ln : Publishing Co. [c. 1870]. 3 vols. 8°

Works . . . edited by C. Knight [Including the ' Doubtful plays.' With engravings]. Ln : Virtue [c. 1870]. 8 vols. 8°

Works . . . Ln : . . . 1870. 9 vols. 8°

Works . . . edited by A. J. Valpy. 'Cabinet edition.' Ln : . . . 1870. 15 vols. Cr. 8°

[Works] Dramatic works . . . with copious glossarial notes, and a biographical notice by Robert Inglis. Six steel engravings. Edinburgh : Gall & Inglis [1871]. Cr. 8°, pp. 944   BM | BPL | BUS
With the text censored.

[Works] Facsimiles of quarto editions of separate works of Sh— [Preface, contents, and three title-pages, showing variations, by E. W. Ashbee]. Ln : . . . 1871. Fcp. 4°   BPL | BUS

[Works] Dramatic works . . . edited by W. Hazlitt. Ln : Routledge & Sons [c. 1871]. 5 vols. Cr. 8°
Includes the attributed plays.

Works . . . With notes by H. N. Hudson. Boston [U.S.] : Estes & Lauriat . . . 1871. 6 vols. 12°   BPL

[Works] Dramatic works . . . with biographical introduction by H. G. Bell. Glasgow : M. Ogle & Co., 1871. 6 vols. 8°   SML

Works . . . edited by H. G. Bell. New edition. New York : Appleton . . . 1871. 6 vols. 8°

Works . . . edited by Charles Knight. ' Pictorial edition,' revised. Ln : . . . [c. 1871]. 8 vols. 8°   CPL

Works . . . edited by H. N. Hudson. New edition. Boston [U.S.] : Noyes . . . 1871. 11 vols. Cr. 8°
Also issued with illustrations.

[Works] Outlines to Sh—'s dramatic works . . . by M. Retzsch. Third edition, with explanations by C. A. Boettiger, V. Miltitz and H. Ulrici. Leipzig : E. Fleischer, 1871. Oblong f°   BUS

Works . . . edited by W. J. Rolfe. New York [U.S.] : Harper Brothers, 1871-96. 40 vols. 8°   BM

[Works] New variorum edition of Sh—, edited by Horace Howard Furness and H. H. Furness jun. Philadelphia : J. B. Lippincott & Co. . . . 1871-1908. 16 vols. Roy. 8°. [In progress]
  BM | BLO | BPL | BUS | MPL | NY | SML
Contents :—1 Romeo and Juliet
  2 Macbeth
  3 Hamlet (text)
  4 ,, (appendix)
  5 King Lear
  6 Othello

Sh— Works . . .

Contents :—7 Merchant of Venice
  8 As you like it
  9 The tempest
  10 Midsummer night's dream
  11 Winter's tale
  12 Much ado . . .
  13 Twelfth night . . .
  14 Love's labours lost
  15 King Richard III.
  16 Antony and Cleopatra.
A supplemental volume contains Mrs. Furness's Concordance to Sh—'s Poems.
Supersedes all previous versions in its collation of varying texts, in fulness and richness of references and in copiousness of extracts from the vast mass of books illustrating the poet. No student would willingly forego a set which has such claims upon him as this.

Works . . . ' Chandos edition.' Ln : Warne . . . 1872. Cr. 8°

[Works] . . . ' Bowdler's family Sh—.' Ln : Longmans . . . 1872. 8°

Works . . . with . . . life, history of the early drama, introduction to each play, readings of former editions, glossarial and other notes . . . edited by George Long Duyckinck. Philadelphia : Porter & Coates . . . 1872. Roy. 8°, pp. cxvi.-968   NY

[Works] Werke . . . Elberfeld : R. L. Friderichs . . . 1872. 2 vols. 8°   BPL

[Works] Complete works . . . revised from the original text. With remarks and copious notes . . . by S. Phelps. With engravings on steel by H. K. Browne ['Phiz']. Ln : J. A. Berger . . . [1872]. 2 vols. Roy. 8°   SML
With life of Sh—, 14 pp.

[Works] Dramatic works . . . with biographical introduction by Hy. Glassford Bell. New York : Appleton . . . 1872. 6 vols. Cr. 8°   NY

Works . . . New York . . . 1872. 12 vols. 16°

[Works] Select plays of Sh—. ' Rugby edition.' [Ten plays, edited by C. E. Moberly, R. Whitelaw, J. S. Phillpotts and R. W. Taylor.] Ln. & Edinburgh : Rivingtons . . . 1872-83. 10 vols. Cr. 8°
Abridged and expurgated.   BM | BUS

[Works] 'Annotated Sh—.' Plays . . . edited by John Hunter. Ln : Longman . . . 1872-81. 35 vols. Cr. 8°   SML
The plays of ' Pericles' and ' Titus Andronicus' are omitted.

[Works] 'Globe edition.' Works of Wm. Sh—, edited by W. G. Clark and W. A. Wright. Ln : Macmillan . . . 1873. Cr. 8°, pp. viii.-1,076   BM | BPL

[Works] Dramatic works . . . with life and a copious glossary. Ln : Nelson . . . 1873. Roy. 8°, pp. xxiv.-968 and Chandos portrait

Sh— Works . . .

Works . . . edited by T. Campbell. Ln:
Routledge . . . 1873. Roy. 8°

Works . . . edited by H. Staunton. With
copious notes, glossary and life. Ln:
Routledge . . . 1873. 6 vols. 8°   BPL

[Works] 'Library Sh—' [edited by S. Neil].
Illustrated by Sir J. Gilbert, G. Cruik-
shank and R. Dudley. [*Portrait.*] Ln:
W. Mackenzie [1873-75]. 3 vols. 4°.
With portrait, woodcuts and coloured
plates   BM | BPL | SML

[Works] 'English classics.' Plays . . .
edited by D. Morris, S. Neil, W. Lawson,
J..Colville and F. G. Fleay. With notes,
critical remarks and historical extracts.
Ln. & Glasgow: Collins . . . 1873-75. 15
vols. 8°   SML

Works . . . 'Imperial edition,' edited by C.
Knight. With illustrations on steel from
pictures by C. W. Cope, W. P. Frith, C.
R. Leslie . . . and others . . . [with] a bio-
graphy of Sh— by C. Knight . . . revised.
Ln: Virtue . . . [1873-76]. 2 vols. F°
                                  BM | MPL

Works . . . edited by W. G. Clark and W. A.
Wright. 'Globe edition.' [With glossary
by J. M. Jephson.] Ln: Macmillan . . .
1874. Cr. 8°, pp. viii.-1,076   BPL | BUS

[Works] Family Sh— . . . by T. Bowdler.
Ln: Longman . . .; Glasgow: Griffin . . .
1874. 8°, pp. xii.-910. With sixteen
steel plates   BUS | CPL

Works . . . edited by C. Knight. Illustrated.
Ln: Routledge . . . 1874. 8°

[Works] 'Chandos poets.' Works . . .
with life, glossary, etc. Reprinted from
the early editions and compared with recent commentators. Ln: Warne . . .
1874. 8°. Steel portrait   CPL

[Works] 'Reference Sh—': A self-inter-
preting edition of Sh—'s plays, containing
11,600 references, compiled by J. B.
Marsh. [Second edition.] Ln: E. E.
Barrett . . . 1874. Fcp. 4°   BM | BPL

Works . . . edited by C. and M. C. Clarke.
With illustrations from the 'Boydell
gallery.' Ln: Bickers . . . 1874. 2 vols.
8°   BPL | NY

[Works] Plays . . . selected and prepared
for use in schools, clubs, classes, and
families. With introduction and notes
by H. N. Hudson. Boston [U.S.] . . .
1874. 3 vols. 12°   MPL

[Works] 'School Sh—.' Plays . . . selected
and prepared for use in schools, clubs,
classes, and families. With introduction
and notes by H. N. Hudson. Boston
[U.S.]: Ginn . . . 1874. 3 vols. 8° SML

Sh— Works . . .

Works . . . edited by C. and M. C. Clarke.
Ln: Bickers & Son, 1874. 4 vols. 8° BPL

Works . . . edited by A. Dyce. Third
edition. Ln: Chapman & Hall, 1874.
10 vols. 8°

[Works] Gallery of illustrations . . . originally projected and published by John
Boydell, reduced and re-engraved by the
heliotype process, with selections from
the text. Ed. by J. Parker Norris.
Philadelphia: Gebbie & Barrie, 1874.
4°, pp. xvi. ff. 100, and one hundred plates
                                      BUS

[Works] Boydell gallery: Engravings illus-
trating Sh— by the artists of Great
Britain. Reproduced in Woodburytype.
Ln: Bickers . . . 1874. F°   BPL

[Works] Plays . . . edited and annotated
by C. and M. C. Clarke. Illustrated by
H. C. Selous. Ln: Cassell [1874-78]. 3
vols. 4°   BM | BPL | BUS | NY
A reprint of the 1864-68 edition with slight differences.
The type and paper are larger, and there is no letterpress on the verso of plates, contrary to the earlier
issue.

[Works] Sammlung Sh— 'scher stücke.
Für schulen herausgegeben von E.
Schmid . . . dritte verbesserte auflage.
Danzig: A. Scheinert . . . 1874-81. 12
parts. 8°   BM
In English and German.
Part 1 reached a third edition and part 3 a second edition.

Works . . . edited by C. Knight. 'Red
line edition.' Ln: Routledge . . . 1875.
Cr. 8°

Works . . . With life, glossary, etc. 'Red
line edition.' Ln: Warne . . . 1875. Cr. 8°

Works . . . with life, glossary, etc. Reprinted from the early editions, and compared with recent commentators. With
a steel portrait. [Edited by Valentine.]
Ln: F. Warne . . . [1875]. Cr. 8°, pp.
xii.-1,124   BM

[Works] Dramatic works. Printed in
phonography or phonetic shorthand [Con-
taining 'The tempest,' 'Two gentlemen,'
and part of 'Macbeth']. Birmingham:
J. Thomas . . . 1875. 8°, pp. 128
No more published.   BM | BPL

Works . . . 'Excelsior edition.' Edinburgh:
W. P. Nimmo . . . 1875. 8°

Works . . . edited with . . . revision of the
text by C. and M. C. Clarke. 'Leicester
Square edition.' With portrait and . . .
illustrations from the 'Boydell gallery'
in permanent photography. Ln: Bickers
& Son . . . 1875. 8°, pp. lxii.-1,002 BM

Works . . . from the text of the first folio,
edited by J. O. Halliwell. Ln: Chatto
& Windus . . . 1875. 8°

[Works] Dramatic works . . . The ' Lansdowne rubricated Sh—.' Ln : Chatto & Windus . . . 1875. 8°   BPL

[Works] Complete works . . . With preface by Dr. Johnson, life, commendatory verses by contemporary poets, and glossary. Ln. [& Halifax] : Milner . . . [c. 1875]. 8°, pp. xxiv.-742 and Chandos portrait on steel

Works . . . edited by C. Knight. With . . . illustrations by Sir John Gilbert [and preface signed W. B. S——, i.e. William Bell Scott]. Ln : G. Routledge & Sons . . . 1875. 2 vols. 8°   BM

Works . . . Edited by H. Staunton. Illustrated by Sir J. Gilbert. Ln : Routledge [c. 1875]. 3 vols. Roy. 8°. Stratford bust portrait   BPL | BUS
Apparently an unaltered reprint of the 1st ed., 1858-60, except that the introductory matter is in a different position.

[Works] Dramatic works . . . with life, notes and glossary. Philadelphia : Claxton & Co. . . . 1875. 4 vols. 12°. With portrait by Croome   SML

Works . . . edited by C. Knight. ' Stratford edition.' New edition. Ln : Ward & Lock . . . 1875. 6 vols. 12°

[Works] Dramatic works . . . With biographical introduction by H. G. Bell. Glasgow : Collins . . . 1875. 6 vols. 8°. With Stratford bust port.   BM | BPL | BUS | SML
Reprinted with fresh title-pages from the 1865 edition issued by Porteous Brothers, of Glasgow.

[Works] ' Household edition.' Dramatic works . . . Edited by R. Carruthers and W. Chambers. Illustrated by K. Halswelle. Ln. & Edinburgh : W. & R. Chambers . . . 1875. 10 vols. 8°   BPL

[Works] 'Aldine edition.' Works . . . revised by S. W. Singer, with notes, life [and essays on the plays] by W. W. Lloyd. Ln : G. Bell & Sons . . . 1875. 11 vols. 12°   BM | BPL | SML

Works . . . edited from the folio of 1623, with various readings, by Richard Grant White. Boston [U.S.] . . . 1875. 12 vols. 12°   MPL

[Works] ' Imperial edition.' Works . . . edited by C. Knight. Ln : Virtue & Co. . . . 1875-76. 2 vols. F°   BPL | SML
With numerous full-page steel plates after Cope, Frith, Leslie, Maclise, Ward, Clint, Marks, and Orchardson.

Works . . . edited by C. Knight. ' Imperial edition.' New York . . . 1875-76. 2 vols. 4°. Illustrated   BUS

Works . . . Text revised by A. Dyce. Third edition [with preface by John Forster]. Ln : Chapman & Hall . . . 1875-76. 9 vols. 8°   BPL | BUS | NY
Contents identical with the 1864-67 edition.

[Works] Complete works . . . containing the celebrated illustrations of Kenny Meadows, Frith, T. H. Nicholson, Corbould, Hayter, etc., and portraits from photographs of eminent actors, [also] a memoir of and essay on the genius of Sh— by B. W. Procter. Ln : Printing & Publishing Co. [1875-80]. 3 vols. 4° BM

Works . . . Illustrated. Brooklyn [U.S.] : Holmes . . . 1876. 8°

Works . . . edited by C. and M. C. Clarke. Ln : Bickers . . . 1876. 8°   BPL | SML

[Works] First edition of Sh— in reduced facsimile from the famous first folio edition of 1623. With an introduction by J. O. Halliwell-Phillipps. [Three parts in 1 vol.] Ln : Chatto & Windus . . . 1876. 8°, pp. xii.-304 × 262 × 400
                          BM | BPL | BUS | MPL
A reduced reproduction of the Staunton facsimile of 1866 by photography.

Works, arranged for family reading by T. Bowdler. Ln : Griffin . . . 1876. 8°

[Works] Dramatic works . . . With 370 illustrations by the late F. Howard, R.A., and explanatory notes, parallel passages, historical and critical illustrations, copious glossary, biographical sketch, and indexes. ' Howard Sh— ' [edited by W. H. Davenport Adams]. Ln : Nelson . . . 1876. 8°, pp. xvi.-1,422   BM | BPL | BUS
The half-title reads the 'Annotated household Sh—.'
The illustrations were originally issued alone under the title of 'Spirit of the plays of Sh—,' in 1827-33.

[Works] Dramatic works . . . with remarks on his life by T. Campbell. Ln : Routledge . . . 1876. 8°   BPL | SML

Works . . . complete. With life and glossary. Ln : Ward, Lock & Tyler [1876]. 8°, pp. viii.-974   BM

Works . . . with life, history of the drama, introduction, readings, notes . . . edited by G. L. Duyckinck. Philadelphia : C. H. Davis & Co. . . . 1876. 8°. With forty illustrations, including Chandos portrait
Edition restricted to 600 copies.   SML

Works . . . edited with a scrupulous revision of the text by M. C. Clarke. New York : D. Appleton & Co., 1876. Roy. 8°, pp. lxii.-1,002. With Droeshout portrait and illustrations   BPL | BUS

[Works] Complete works . . . With life . . . glossarial and other notes from the works of Collier, Knight, Dyce, Douce, Halliwell, Hunter, Richardson, Verplanck and Hudson, edited by George Long Duyckinck. Philadelphia : Porter & Coates . . . 1876. Roy. 8°, pp. vi.-968. With Droeshout portrait and illustrations   BUS
Copyrighted in 1866.

Sh— Works . . .

[Works] Werke, herausgegeben und erklärt von Delius. Vierte auflage. Elberfeld . . . 1876. 2 vols. 8°   BPL
English text with German notes.

[Works] Complete works . . . with explanatory and critical notes and a . . . biography . . . Illustrated with . . . chromo-engravings designed expressly for this edition. Ln: J. G. Murdoch . . . 1876. 2 vols. 4°   BM

Works . . . edited by C. and M. C. Clarke. With illustrations from the 'Boydell gallery.' Ln: Bickers . . . 1876. 4 vols. 8°   BPL

Works . . . from the text of the 1623 folio. 'Falstaff edition.' Philadelphia: Porter & Coates . . . 1876. 4 vols. 8°

[Works] Stratford Sh—, edited by C. Knight. With life . . . New York: D. Appleton & Co., 1876. 6 vols. 12°. With vignettes   BUS

Works . . . from the text of the folio of 1623. With engravings. 'Windsor edition.' Philadelphia: Porter & Coates . . . 1876. 8 vols. 12°

Works . . . [Including the poems and a glossary]. 'Handy volume edition.' Ln: Bradbury, Agnew & Co. . . . 1876. 13 vols. 12°

[Works] 'Boudoir Sh—': carefully prepared for reading aloud. Freed from all objectionable matter, and altogether free of notes. Edited by Henry Cundell. [Eight plays.] Ln: Low . . . 1876-77. 3 vols. 8°   BM | BPL | BUS | SML
First edition edited by Hy. Cundell.

Works . . . 'Cabinet Boydell edition.' Philadelphia: Gebbie & Barrie . . . 1876-77. 15 vols. 12°   BPL (lacks vol. 15)

[Works] New readings and new renderings of [his] tragedies by H. H. Vaughan. Ln: Kegan Paul . . . 1876-86. 3 vols. 8°   BM | BPL | BUS | MPL

[Works] 'Leopold Sh—.' The poet's works, in chronological order, from the text of Professor Delius, with the 'Two noble kinsmen' and 'Edward III.,' and an introduction by F. J. Furnivall. Illustrated. Ln., Paris & New York: Cassell, Petter & Galpin [1877]. Fcp. 4°, pp. cxxvi.-1,056. With Jansen portrait
BM | BPL | BUS | MPL | NY | SML
In a re-issue in the same year the frontispiece was changed.
The first edition under the auspices of Dr. Furnivall.
'Altogether a "manly man," as Chaucer says, this Sh—, strong, tender, humorful, sensitive, impressionable, the truest friend, the foe of none but narrow minds and base. . . . What can we do but bless his name, and be thankful that he came to be a delight, a lift, and strength to us and

Sh— Works . . .

our children's children to all time, a bond that shall last for ever between all English-speaking, English-reading men, the great Teutonic brotherhood which shall yet long lead the world in the fight for freedom and for truth.'—Introduction.

[Works] Plays . . . edited by T. Keightley. Ln: Bell & Sons . . . 1877. 7 vols. in 13. 12°   BPL

[Works] Complete dramatic and poetic works. With life . . . and notes, original and selected [edited by O. W. B. Peabody]. New York: World Publishing House, 1877. 8 vols. 8°. With Chandos portrait   BUS
Contents identical with the 1836 issue, but paper smaller.

Works . . . The text revised by A. Dyce. Third edition [with an altered date]. Ln: Chatto & Windus . . . 1877. 9 vols. 8°. With portraits   BPL | SML

[Works] 'Lyceum acting edition.' [Sh—'s plays] as presented at the Lyceum Theatre under [Sir] Henry Irving [and Miss Mary Anderson]. Ln: Lyceum Theatre . . . 1877-87. 7 vols. 8°   BPL | SML
Comprises: 'Hamlet, King Richard III., Merchant of Venice, Much ado, Romeo and Juliet, Twelfth night, Winter's tale.'

[Works] 'Hamnet edition.' Plays . . . according to the first folio [spelling modernised]. With tables shewing the number of emphasis-capitals lost and gained by each of Sh—'s plays under each of the second, third and fourth folios, and a few interim remarks upon the facts these tables present and the questions they suggest, by Allan Park Paton. Edinburgh: Edmonston & Company. Ln: Longman & Co. Greenock: William Hutchison, 1877-96. 10 vols. 8°
BM | BPL | BUS | MPL | SML
The editor's theory is that the lavish use of capitals in Sh—'s manuscripts and the Jaggard canon was for the express purpose of emphasis.
This excellent venture was never completed.

Works . . . with notes, etc. by R. Inglis. Edinburgh: Galt & Inglis . . . 1878. 12°

Works . . . from the text of Clark and Wright, with copious glossary and index to familiar passages and . . . to the characters . . . New York: T. Y. Crowell . . . [1878]. 12°, pp. viii.-1,098   BUS

Works . . . 'Red line edition.' Ln: Routledge . . . 1878. Cr. 8°

[Works] Complete works . . . from the text left by G. Steevens. With glossary, notes and memoir by A. Chalmers. Illustrated with historical steel engravings. Boston [U.S.]: Lee & Shepard . . . 1878. 8°, pp. 828 and portrait   BUS

[Works] Plays and poems . . . edited by S. C. Mullick. Calcutta [India]: Sonatun Press . . . 1878. 8°   BM

Works . . . edited by C. Knight. Ln: . . . 1878. 8°

[Works] Charles Kemble's Sh— readings, being a selection of the plays of Sh— . . . edited by R. J. Lane. Ln: G. Bell & Sons . . . 1878. 8°, pp. viii.-932   BM

Works . . . edited by C. and M. C. Clarke. 'Leicester Square edition,' with illustrations from the 'Boydell gallery.' Ln: Bickers . . . 1878. 8°   BPL

[Works] . . . 'Bowdler's family Sh—.' Ln: Longman . . . 1878. 8°

Works . . . with life and glossary. 'Chandos poets.' Ln: Warne . . . [1878]. 8°, pp. xii.-1,124 and Chandos portrait   BUS | SML

Works . . . in chronological order, from the text of Delius. With the 'Two noble kinsmen' and 'Edward III.' Introduction by F. J. Furnivall. Ln: Cassell . . . [1878]. Fcp. 4°, pp. cxxvi.-1,056. Illustrated

Works . . . carefully prepared from the earliest and more modern editions. Selected, where commentators have differed, as to . . . obscure . . . passages from those readings which the ablest critics believe to be the most Shakespearean and best suited to a popular edition. New York: T. O'Kane [1878]. Roy. 8°, pp. 358 and portrait   BUS

Works . . . edited by C. Knight. Philadelphia: Amies . . . 1878. 2 vols. 8°

Works . . . edited by H. G. Bell. Glasgow & Edinburgh: W. Collins . . . 1878. 6 vols. 8°

Works . . . edited by H. G. Bell. New York: Baker & Co. . . . 1878. 6 vols. 8°

[Works] Plays and poems . . . with the purest text and briefest notes, edited by J. P. Collier. Ln. [Maidenhead]: Privately printed for the subscribers, 1878. 8 vols. Fcp. 4°   BM | BPL
Edition limited to fifty-eight copies.

Works . . . edited by H. N. Hudson. 'Illustrated revised [cabinet] edition.' Boston [U.S.] . . . 1878. 11 vols. 8°

[Works] Plays and poems . . . edited by A. J. Valpy. Philadelphia: Gebbie & Barrie, 1878. 15 vols. 12°. With 170 outline plates   BUS
A reprint of the 1832-34 issue with insignificant changes.

[Works] Charles Kemble's Sh— readings, edited by R. J. Lane. Second edition. Ln: G. Bell & Sons, 1879. 12°   SML

[Works] 'Reference Sh—,' compiled by J. B. Marsh. Ln: S. B. Barrett . . . 1879. 8°   BPL

Works . . . edited by W. G. Clark and W. A. Wright. 'Globe edition.' Ln: Macmillan & Co. . . . 1879. 8°

[Works] Dramatic works . . . with explanatory notes, parallel passages, historical and critical illustrations, contemporary allusions, copious glossary, biographical sketch, and indexes, by W. H. D. Adams. With 370 illustrations by Frank Howard. Ln: Nelson . . . 1879. 8° BPL | BUS | SML

[Works] Comedies . . . expurgated for schools, by R. Baughan. Ln: Washbourne . . . 1879. 8°

[Works] Complete works . . . edited by Clark and Wright. 'Arundel poets.' New York: Arundel Co. . . . 1879. 8°   BPL

Works . . . from the text of W. G. Clark and W. A. Wright. With a copious glossary [by J. M. Jephson] . . . and an index to the characters in each play. 'American edition.' New York: T. Y. Crowell [1879]. 8°, pp. vi.-1,098 BM | BPL

Works . . . edited by C. Knight. Illustrated. New York: Johnson . . . 1879. 8°

Works . . . edited by C. Knight. Illustrated. Philadelphia: Amies . . . [1879]. Fcp. 4°

Works . . . edited by C. and M. C. Clarke. Ln: Bickers . . . 1879. Roy. 8°

[Works] 'Avon edition.' Complete dramatic and poetical works . . . With a summary outline of the life . . . and description of his most authentic portraits, collected . . . by John S. Hart. To which is appended a descriptive analysis of the plot of each play, together with an . . . index to the characters . . . to familiar passages, and a . . . glossary. Edited by W. G. Clark & W. A. Wright. With illustrations by Meadows, Frith and others. Philadelphia: Claxton, Remsen & Haffelfinger . . . 1879. Roy. 8°, pp. lxx.-896, and portraits BUS | NY

Works . . . edited by W. H. D. Adams. Illustrated by Frank Howard. Ln: Nelson . . . 1879. 2 vols. 8°

[Works] 'Library Sh—,' with notes, critical and explanatory, by Samuel Neil. Ln: Wm. Mackenzie . . . [1879]. Nine divisions, forming 3 vols. 4°. With Droeshout portrait, coloured and other plates by Sir John Gilbert, George Cruikshank and R. Dudley   BUS

Works . . . edited by 'Barry Cornwall.' Illustrated. Ln: . . . 1879. 6 vols. 8°

Sh— Works . . .

Works . . . edited by H. Staunton. With copious notes, glossary, life, etc. Ln: Routledge [1879]. 6 vols. 8° BM | BPL

Works . . . edited by J. M. D. Meiklejohn. Ln: W. & R. Chambers . . . [c. 1879]. 15 vols. 12° SML

[Works] Sh— gallery; being a collection of forty-five steel engravings after pictures by eminent artists [with selections from his plays]. Ln: Virtue & Co. [1879]. F° BM

Works . . . with notes by S. W. Singer and life by W. W. Lloyd. Third 'Aldine edition.' Ln: Bell & Sons . . . 1879-81. 10 vols. 8° BPL
Also issued with illustrations.

Works . . . edited by W. J. Rolfe. New York . . . 1879-82. 8°

Works . . . edited, with critical notes and introductory notices, by W. Wagner [and L. Proescholdt]. Hamburg: K. Grädener . . . 1879-91. 12 vols. 8° BM
Forms part of Asher's 'Collection of British authors.'

Works . . . 'Memorial theatre edition,' edited by Charles E. Flower [and Samuel Timmins]. Stratford-on-Avon: Printed by G. Boyden; Ln: S. French . . . 1879-91. 37 vols. Cr. 8° BPL | SML
An acting edition, set in two founts of type, the stage text being in larger print and the unspoken text in smaller type.

Works . . . edited by W. G. Clark and W. A. Wright. 'Globe edition.' Ln: Macmillan . . . 1880. Cr. 8°, pp. viii.-1,076
Includes a glossary.

[Works] Complete works . . . with a critical biography by W. M. Rosetti [*sic*], glossary and . . . illustrations. Ln: E. Moxon [1880]. Cr. 8°, pp. xvi.-984 BM

[Works] Complete works . . . with glossary and a critical biography by W. M. Rossetti. Ln: Ward, Lock & Co. [1880]. Cr. 8°. Illustrated BPL | SML

Works . . . edited by C. Knight. Ln: Routledge . . . [1880]. Cr. 8°, pp. 764 BM | BPL
Forms part of the 'Excelsior series.'

Works . . . carefully collated and compared with the editions of Halliwell, Knight, Collier and others. With life by C. Knight. 'America's standard edition.' Philadelphia & New York . . . 1880. 8°. With engravings, chiefly character portraits of American actors BUS

[Works] 'Leopold Sh—,' from the text of Prof. Delius. With introduction by Dr. F. J. Furnivall. Ln: Cassell . . . [c. 1880]. Fcp. 4° BPL

[Works] 'Student's Sh—': Thirty-seven plays analyzed and topically arranged, by Henry J. Fox. Boston [U.S.] . . . 1880. Roy. 8° BUS

Sh— Works . . .

[Works] Plays . . . edited by Steevens and Malone. With biographical sketch and glossary. Ln: Nimmo & Bain, 1880. Roy. 8°, pp. viii.-960-xvi. With Stratford bust portrait and vignette BPL

Works . . . 'Avon edition.' Philadelphia . . . 1880. 2 vols. 8°

Works . . . edited by C. Knight. Ln: Routledge . . . 1880. 2 vols. Roy. 8°

[Works] Plays . . . edited by Charles and Mary Cowden Clarke. Illustrated by H. C. Selous. Ln: Cassell & Co. [c. 1880]. 3 vols. 4° SML

Works . . . with notes by S. W. Singer and life by W. W. Lloyd. Ln: . . . 1880. 10 vols. 8°

Works . . . edited from the best texts. With a glossary. Ln: W. Kent & Co. . . . 1880. 12 vols. 16° (enclosed in case) BM | BPL | SML

Works . . . 'Handy volume edition.' New York: Cogswell . . . 1880. 13 vols. 12°

Works . . . edited by A. J. Valpy. 'Handy edition.' New York: Worthington . . . [1880]. 15 vols. 8°

[Works] 'Pocket Sh—.' Ln: W. Kent & Co. [1880]. 36 vols. 12° (enclosed in box) SML

[Works] Sh— für schulen . . . ausgewählte dramen. Mit einleitungen, erklärenden anmerkungen, und abriss der Sh— grammatik. Bearbeitet und herausgegeben von Dr. K. Meurer. Coeln: C. Roemke & Cie . . . 1880-81. 2 parts. 8° BM
Two plays, in English. No more issued.

Works . . . text revised by A. Dyce. Fourth edition. Ln: Bickers & Son . . . 1880-81. 10 vols. 8° BPL | MPL

[Works] Complete works . . . With a life of the poet, explanatory footnotes, critical notes and a glossarial index. 'Harvard edition,' edited by . . . H. N. Hudson. Boston [U.S.]: Ginn, Heath & Co . . . 1880-81. 20 vols. 8° BM | BPL
Some sets are dated 1881 only.

[Works] 'Royal Sh—.' The poet's works in chronological order, from the text of Professor Delius. With the 'Two noble kinsmen,' 'Edward III.,' and an introduction by F. J. Furnivall . . . With illustrations . . . Ln., Paris & New York: Cassell . . . [1880-84]. 3 vols. 8° BM

Works . . . edited by W. Wagner and L. Proescholdt. Hamburg: K. Gradener . . . 1880-91. 12 vols. 12° BPL

[Works] Plays and poems in quarto. Facsimiles of forty-three Sh— quartos, with introduction, line numbers . . . by Sh— scholars. Issued under the super-

intendence of Dr. F. J. Furnivall. Ln:
W. Griggs & C. Prætorius . . . 1880-91.
44 vols. Fcp. 4°   BM | BPL | MPL | SML

Works . . . edited by W. J. Rolfe. New
York : Harper . . . 1881.   12°

[Works] 'Globe edition' . . . edited by
W. G. Clark and W. A. Wright. Ln:
Macmillan . . . 1881. Cr. 8°, pp. viii.-
1,076   SML

[Works] 'Rossetti Sh—' . . . edited, with
a biography, by W. M. Rossetti . . .
chronology of the plays by E. Dowden
. . . history of the drama in Sh—'s time
by A. Gilman . . . introduction by Von
Schlegel. Boston [U.S.]: D. Lothrop &
Co. [1881]. 8°   SML

[Works] Plays . . . edited by Steevens and
Malone. Edinburgh : Nimmo & Bain . . .
1881. 8°   BPL

[Works] Sh— reading book ; being seventeen of Sh—'s plays, abridged for the use
of schools and public readings. By H. C.
Bowen. Ln : Cassell . . . [1881]. 8°, pp.
vi.-572   BM | BPL

[Works] Certain selected plays, abridged
for the use of the young by S. Brandram.
[Nine plays.] Ln : Smith . . . 1881. 8°,
pp. xiv.-382   BM | BUS | SML

Works . . . edited by W. M. Rossetti.
'Library edition.' Ln : Ward & Lock
. . . 1881. 8°

Works . . . 'Albion edition,' With life and
glossary. Ln : Warne . . . 1881. 8° BPL

Works, dramatic and poetic, with notes,
etc. by A. Dyce. New York : R. Worthington . . . 1881. 8°   BPL

Works . . . edited by Clark and Wright.
New York : American Book Exchange
[1881]. 3 vols. 8°

Works . . . edited by C. and M. C. Clarke.
Illustrated. Ln : Bickers . . . 1881. 4
vols. 8°

Works . . . edited by H. Staunton. Illustrated by Sir J. Gilbert. 'Edition de
luxe.' Ln : Routledge . . . 1881-82. 15
vols. Imp. 8°   BPL | BUS
Of limited issue.

[Works] 'Oxford and Cambridge Sh—'
. . . with notes, prepared specially for
the . . . local examinations. [Twelve
plays.] Ln : Allman & Son [1881-91].
12 parts. Cr. 8°   BM

[Works] Dramatic works . . . with copious
glossarial notes and a biographical notice
by Robert Inglis. Edinburgh : Gall &
Inglis [1882]. Cr. 8°, pp. 944 (printed

within tinted pictorial borders) and four
steel plates   BM

[Works] Selected plays . . . abridged by S.
Brandram. Second edition. Ln : Smith
& Elder . . . 1882. Cr. 8°   BPL | SML

Works . . . edited with biography by Wm.
M. Rossetti. With essay on the chronology of . . . [his] plays by E. Dowden,
history of the drama in England in the
time of Sh— by A. Gilman. Boston
[U.S.] . . . 1882. 8°. Illustrated   BUS

[Works] Meesterstukken onder Sh—'s
pseudo-dramas ['Arden of Feversham'
and a 'Yorkshire tragedy'] vertaald en
toegelicht door G. B. Kuitert. Leiden
. . . 1882. 8°, pp. 226   BM
In English and Dutch.

Works . . . from the text of Geo. Steevens.
Ln : Longman . . . 1882. 8°

[Works] Plays . . . from the text of G.
Steevens and E. Malone, with life and
glossary. Ln : Nimmo & Bain . . . 1882.
8°   BPL | SML

[Works] 'Shilling Sh—' . . . edited by C.
Knight. Ln : Routledge . . . [c. 1882].
8°. With portrait and sixty-three plates
by Sir John Gilbert   SML

Works . . . edited by S. Phelps. Illustrated.
Ln : Ward, Lock & Co. . . . 1882. 8°

Works . . . edited by J. F. Furnivall.
Illustrated. 'Leopold edition.' Ln :
Cassell . . . 1882. Fcp. 4°

Works, edited by H. Staunton, with . . .
illustrations by Sir John Gilbert. Ln :
Routledge . . . 1882. 10 parts, forming 1
vol. 4°, pp. 676   BM | SML

[Works] Sh—'s werke, herausgegeben und
erklärt von N. Delius. Fünfte . . auflage
Elberfeld : R. L. Friderichs . . . 1882. 2
vols. 8°   BM

Works . . . with notes, examination papers,
and plan of preparation, selected by B.
Kellogg. New York : Clark & Maynard
. . . 1882. 19 vols. 12°   SML

Works . . . 'Miniature edition.' Ln : Kent
& Co. . . . 1882. 36 parts. 16°

[Works] Sh— album [Outline sketches of
scenes from the works of Sh— to form
borders for photographs]. Berlin . . .
1882. 4°   BM

[Works] 'Royal Sh—': The poet's works
in chronological order from the text of
Prof. Delius. With the 'Two noble kinsmen,' 'Edward III.,' and introduction
by F. J. Furnivall. Illustrations on steel
and wood. Ln : Cassell . . . 1882-83. 3
vols. 4°   BPL

Sh— Works . . .

Works [edited from the text of Delius by Prof. Edward Dowden]. Ln: Kegan Paul . . . 1882-83. 12 vols. 8°
BM | BLO | BPL | BUS | CTC
Formed part of the series known as the 'Parchment library.' Fifty numbered and signed sets were issued on large paper, and six sets on pure vellum, the latter at one-hundred-and-forty-four guineas per set.

[Works] Complete works, revised from the original text; with introductory remarks and copious notes . . . by S. Phelps. With illustrations by H. K. Browne. Ln: Ward, Lock . . . [1882-84]. 8° BM | BPL

Works . . . 'Parchment library.' New York: D. Appleton & Co. . . . 1882-84. 12 vols. 12°
BUS | SML

[Works] Plays . . . vol. I.-II. [Ten plays]. Glasgow: J. Cameron . . . [1883]. 8° BM

Works . . . edited by C. and M. C. Clarke. Ln: Bickers & Son . . . 1883. 8° BPL

[Works] Sh—'s plays [Abridged, with notes. Three plays, edited by J. M. D. Meiklejohn]. Ln: Blackwood . . . 1883. 8° BM

[Works] . . . Bowdler's family Sh—. Ln: Longman . . . 1883. 8°

Works . . . edited by C. Knight. 'Blackfriars edition.' Ln: Routledge . . . 1883. 8°, pp. x.-1,074 BM | BPL

[Works] 'Student's Sh—,' part I. 'Othello' . . . edited, with notes, by R. Mongan. Ln: Sonnenschein . . . 1883. 8°, pp. x.-180 BM
No more published.

[Works] 'Leopold Sh—' . . . from the text of Professor Delius. With the 'Two noble kinsmen,' 'Edward III.,' and an introduction by F. J. Furnivall. Illustrated. Thirty-second thousand. Ln: Cassell . . . [1883]. Fcp. 4°, pp. cxxxvi.-1,056 BM

[Works] 'Riverside Sh—': The text newly edited with notes and glossary by R. G. White. Boston [U.S.] . . . 1883. 3 vols. Cr. 8° BUS

[Works] Comedies, histories, tragedies and poems. The text newly edited with . . . notes by R. G. White. 'Riverside Sh—.' [Cambridge, U.S. printed] Ln: Low . . . 1883. 3 vols. 8° BM | BPL

[Works] . . . Historical plays. Roman and English. With revised text, introductions and notes . . . by C. Wordsworth, etc. Edinburgh: Blackwood . . . 1883. 3 vols. 8° BM | BPL | BUS | SML

[Works] Sh— reading book; being a selection of Sh—'s plays abridged for the use of schools and public readings . . . by H. C. Bowen. [Seventeen plays] in three series. Ln: Cassell . . . [1883]. 3 vols. 8° BM

Sh— Works . . .

Works . . . edited by C. Knight . . . With illustrations by Sir John Gilbert. Ln: Routledge . . . 1883. 3 vols. 8° BM | BPL

Works . . . edited with a scrupulous revision of the text by Charles and Mary Cowden Clarke. Ln: Bickers & Son . . . 1883. 4 vols. 8°. With Droeshout portrait SML

Works . . . from the text of . . . Dyce's fourth edition, and an arrangement of his glossary in each volume. With a life of the poet and an account of each play, by A. R. Macfarlane. New York [U.S.]: H. Holt & Co. . . . 1883. 7 vols. 8° BM

[Works] Dramatic works . . . Text of the first edition. Illustrated with portrait and etchings. Edinburgh: W. Paterson . . . 1883. 9 vols. 8° BM | BPL | BUS | SML
Edition limited to 550 copies on small and 75 copies on large paper. A few issued with plates in two states.

[Works] 'Royal Sh—' . . . in chronological order, from the text of Prof. Delius, with the 'Two noble kinsmen,' 'King Edward III.,' and introduction by F. J. Furnivall. Ln: Cassell & Co. . . . 1883-84. 3 vols. 4° SML

[Works] 'Riverside Sh—' . . . edited with notes by R. G. White. Boston & New York: Houghton, Mifflin & Co., 1883-84. 6 vols. 8° BPL | SML

[Works] Sh—'s plays for schools. Abridged and annotated by C. M. Yonge. [Five plays.] Ln: National Society's depository [1883-85]. 5 parts. 8° BM

[Works] 'Longman's modern series.' Plays . . . edited by T. Parry and J. W. Allen. To meet the requirements of the new code in 'English.' Ln: Longman . . . 1883-86. 5 vols. 8° SML
No more published.

Works . . . edited from the folio of 1623, with notes, memoir, essay . . . by R. B. White. Boston [U.S.]: Little, Brown & Co. . . . 1883-86. 12 vols. 8°. With Felton and Droeshout portraits SML

[Works] Charles Kemble's Sh— readings; being a selection of the plays of Sh— . . . edited by R. J. Lane. Ln: G. Bell & Sons . . . 1883-87. 6 parts. 8° BM
No more published.

[Works] Pseudo-Shakespearian plays, edited by K. Warnke and L. Proescholdt. Halle: M. Niemeyer . . . 1883-88. 5 parts. 8° BM | SML
Contains nineteen plays.

Works . . . including life, glossary, etc. Ln: Simpkin . . . 1884. Cr. 8°

Works . . . life, glossary, etc; reprinted from the early editions and compared

Sh— Works . . .

with recent commentators. 'Albion edition.' Ln : Warne . . . [1884]. Cr. 8°, pp. xii.-1,124

Works . . . 'Red line edition.' Illustrated. Boston [U.S.] : Bradley & Co. . . . 1884. 8°

Works . . . abridged by J. M. D. Meiklejohn. Edinburgh : Blackwood . . . 1884. 8°

Works . . . with thirty-seven illustrations and a memoir. 'Dick's complete edition.' Ln : John Dick . . . [c. 1884]. Cr. 8° SML

Works . . . edited by Clark and Wright. Ln : Macmillan . . . 1884. 8°

Works . . . edited by Thomas Keightley. Ln : Virtue . . . 1884. Roy. 8°

[Works] Knight's 'Cabinet edition' . . . with life and notes. Edinburgh : W. & R. Chambers . . . 1884. 12 vols. 8° SML

Works. 'Friendly edition' . . . edited by W. J. Rolfe [with introductions and notes]. New York : Harper & Brothers . . . 1884. 20 vols. 12°. Illustrated
BPL | SML

[Works] . . . reprinted, from the first folio, for William Ludlow : 'As you like it,' 'Hamlet,' 'Romeo and Juliet,' 'The tempest.' Ln : Simpkin . . . 1884-86. 4 vols. 12° BPL | SML
No more published.

[Works] Lewis's penny Sh—. Liverpool : Lewis, Ranelagh St., 1884-86. 15 parts. Fcp. 4° SML
Issued in penny monthly parts, each in a differently tinted wrapper.
So far the first and only Liverpool edition of the poet.

[Works] 'People's penny Sh—' . . . with a life. Manchester : Lewis [1884-86]. 15 parts. Fcp. 4° BPL

Works . . . translated into German by A. W. von Schlegel and L. Tieck. With a preface and introduction by C. Sachs [and the English text]. Leipzig & Philadelphia : M. Schaefer . . . [1884-87]. 37 parts. 8° BM | BPL

Works . . . translated into German by A. W. von Schlegel and L. Tieck. With preface and introduction by C. Sachs [and the English text]. Ln : Whittaker [1884-87]. 37 parts. 8° BM

Works . . . edited by Howard Staunton. Ln : Routledge . . . 1884-89. 6 vols. 8°

Works . . . 'International Sh—,' edited by Edward Dowden. Illustrated by F. Dicksee, Emile Bayard, Eduard Grützner and Sir James D. Linton. Ln : Cassell . . . 1884-92. 5 vols. F°
BM | BLO | BPL | CTC | SML
No more issued.
The proof sets were limited to 250 numbered copies.

Sh— Works . . .

Contents :—Romeo and Juliet, 1884
As you like it, 1887
King Henry IV., 1887
Othello, 1890
King Henry VIII., 1892.

[Works] . . . Plays for school and home use . . . with notes and illustrations. 'Modern school series.' Ln : Cassell . . . 1885. 8°
BM

Works . . . edited by C. Knight [with glossarial index]. Ln : Routledge . . . [1885]. 8°, pp. 832 (printed within coloured borders). Illustrated

Works . . . from the text of Johnson, Steevens and Reed. With biographical sketch by M. C. Clarke. Edinburgh : W. P. Nimmo [1885]. Roy. 8°, pp. xx.-716 and portrait BPL

Works . . . from the text of A. Dyce, with life and account of each play by A. R. MacFarlane. New York : H. Holt & Co. . . . 1885. 7 vols. 12° BM | SML

[Works] Dramatic works . . . text of the first edition. Ln : Chatto & Windus . . . 1885. 8 vols. 8° BPL

Works . . . from the authentic folio ; edited by R. G. White. Boston [U.S.] : Little, Brown & Co. . . . 1885. 12 vols. 16°

Works . . . with lines pronounced corrupt restored, and mutilations unsuspected emended. Preface and notes by M. Mull. Vol. I. 'Hamlet,' vol. II. 'Macbeth.' With supplementary notes to 'Hamlet.' Ln : Kegan, Paul & Co. . . . 1885-89. 3 vols. 8° SML
No more published.

Works . . . Ln : Rivington . . . 1886. 8°

[Works] Sh— reprints . . . edited by W. Victor. Marburg : N. G. Elwert'sche Verlagsbuchhandlung . . . 1886. 8° BM

[Works] Complete works . . . with notes by Malone, Steevens and others. Together with a biography [by A. Chalmers], concordance of familiar passages, index to characters, and glossary . . . Illustrated. Philadelphia : D. McKay . . . 1886. 4 vols. 8° BM | BPL

[Works] 'Illustrated pocket Sh—.' With glossary . . . edited and compared with the best texts by J. Talfourd Blair. Glasgow : D. Bryce & Son [c. 1886]. 8 vols. 32° (enclosed in a case)
BM | BPL | BUS | SML
Sometimes found bound in 2 vols.

Works . . . edited by A. Dyce. Fifth edition. Ln : Sonnenschein . . . 1886. 10 vols. 8° BPL

Works . . . 'Avon edition,' mainly founded on the text of Delius [edited by E.

Sh— Works . . .

Dowden]. Ln : Kegan, Paul & Co. . . . 1886. 12 vols. 12°   BM | BPL | SML
A stereotype reprint (under a fresh name) of the 'Parchment library' edition of 1882-83.

[Works] 'Harvard edition.' Works . . . with life, notes and glossarial index by H. N. Hudson. Boston [U.S.] : Ginn & Co. . . . 1886. 20 vols. 8°   SML

[Works] Sh— for schools, edited by H. C. Bowen. [Seventeen plays.] Ln : Cassell . . . 1886-87. 8°

[Works] 'Reader's Sh—.' Ln. & Oxford : [Printed at the Clarendon Press] Walter Smith . . . 1886-87. 9 vols. 8°. With Chandos portrait   BM | BPL | BUS | SML
The text unexpurgated.

Works . . . with a memoir and essay on his genius by B. W. Procter . . . and . . . illustrative engravings from designs by K. Meadows and T. H. Nicholson. Ln. & Glasgow : Blackie . . . [1886-88]. 6 vols. 4°   BM

[Works] Plays . . . edited and annotated by C. and M. Cowden Clarke. Ln : Cassell . . . [1886-90]. 3 vols. 4°   BM

[Works] Plays of Sh—. 'Falcon edition' [edited by H. C. Beeching, O. Elton, A. D. Innes, W. H. Payne Smith, H. Howard Crawley, A. W. Verity, E. K. Chambers, A. C. Bradley and A. C. Liddell. Thirteen plays]. Ln : Rivingtons . . . 1886-91. 13 vols. Cr. 8°   BM | SML

[Works] 'National library' . . . [Plays] edited by Henry Morley. Ln : Cassell . . . 1886-98. 37 vols. 16°   BM | BPL | SML
Reprinted subsequently at intervals.

[Works] Indexes to the characters in Sh—'s plays for the use of Sh— reading clubs. York : J. Sampson, 1887. 12°   BPL | SML

[Works] Doubtful plays . . . with glossarial and other notes by Wm. Hazlitt. Ln : Routledge . . . 1887. Cr. 8°, pp. iv.-376   BM

[Works] 'Globe edition' . . . edited by W. G. Clark and W. A. Wright. Ln. & New York : Macmillan . . . 1887. 8°   SML

[Works] Doubtful plays . . . With notes by W. Hazlitt. Ln : Routledge . . . 1887. 8°   BPL

[Works] University Sh—. Ln : Simpkin . . . 1887. 8°   BM

Works . . . Ln : Suttaby & Co. . . . 1887. Cr. 8°

Works . . . from the text of the corrected copies left by . . . G. Steevens and E. Malone. With a glossary of terms. 'Moxon's library of poets.' Ln : Ward, Lock & Co. [1887]. 8°, pp. 832   BM | BPL | SML

Sh— Works . . .

[Works] Dramatic works . . . adapted for family reading by T. Bowdler. New edition. Ln : Ward, Lock & Co. [1887]. 8°, pp. 864   BM | BPL

Works . . . with life, glossary, etc. 'Albion edition.' Ln. & New York : Warne . . . [1887]. 8°   SML

Works . . . Reduced facsimile from the first folio edition. With introduction by J. O. Halliwell-Phillipps. New York : Funk & Wagnalls . . . 1887. 8°   BPL | BUS

[Works] Complete dramatic and poetical works . . . with a summary outline of the life of the poet . . . collected . . . by J. S. Hart . . . The text by W. G. Clark and W. Aldis Wright. With . . . illustrations. ['Avon edition.'] Philadelphia [U.S.] : E. Meeks . . . 1887. 8°, pp. lxx.-896   BM

Works . . . 'Leopold edition,' edited by F. J. Furnivall. Ln : Cassell . . . 1887. Fcp. 4°

[Works] Pseudo-Shakespearean plays, edited by K. Warnke and L. Proescholdt. Halle . . . 1887. Roy. 8°

Works . . . 'Victoria edition' [Text from the 'Globe Sh—,' edited by Clark and Wright. With glossary]. Ln : Macmillan, 1887. 3 vols. Cr. 8°, pp. viii.-544, vi.-644, vi.-666   BM | BPL | SML

Works . . . edited from the best texts. With illustrations and a glossary. Ln : Cassell . . . [1887]. 12 vols. 16°   BM | BPL
Formed part of the 'Miniature library of the poets.'

Works . . . New York : D. Appleton & Co. . . . 1887. 12 vols. 12°   BPL

Works . . . 'Ideal edition,' edited by W. G. Clark and W. A. Wright. New York : J. B. Alden . . . 1887-88. 13 vols. 12°   BPL

[Works] 'University Sh—' . . . Edited with notes and glossary by H. A. Evans and B. Dawson. Ln : Simpkin . . . 1887-89. 4 vols. 12°   SML
No more published.

Works . . . edited by Charles Knight. 'Shilling Sh—.' Ln : Routledge . . . [c. 1888]. Cr. 8°   BPL

Works . . . edited by C. Knight. Illustrated by Sir J. Gilbert. Ln : G. Routledge & Sons . . . 1888. Roy. 8°, pp. viii.-1,073   BM | BPL
Forms part of the 'Popular library of standard authors.'

[Works] Complete works . . . edited by W. C. Bryant, assisted by E. A. Duyckinck, containing . . . photogravure illustrations from original designs by F. O. C. Darley and A. Chappel. New York [U.S.] : Amies Publishing Co. . . . 1888. 3 vols. 4°   BM

[Works] Complete works . . . with notes by E. Malone. Philadelphia: D. McKay . . . 1888. 4 vols. 8°   BPL

Works . . . ' Parchment library edition.' Ln : Kegan Paul . . . 1888. 6 vols. Cr. 8°

Works . . . edited by C. Knight. ' Library pictorial edition.' Ln : Virtue & Co. . . . 1888. 8 vols. 8°

Works . . . ' Bedford edition.' With life and glossary. Ln : Warne . . . 1888. 12 vols. 32°   BPL

Works . . . edited by R. G. White. Boston [U.S.]: Little, Brown & Co., 1888. 12 vols. 12°   BPL

[Works] ' National Sh—': Plays of Wm. Sh— . . . illustrated by Sir J. Noel Paton. Ln : W. Mackenzie . . . 1888-89. 3 vols. F°. With Chandos and Droeshout portraits   BPL | SML
A reprint of the 1623 Jaggard canon.

[Works] Complete works . . . with notes by Malone, Steevens and others. Together with a biography, concordance of familiar passages, index to characters, and glossary of obsolete terms. Illustrated. Philadelphia : David McKay . . . 1888-89. 8 vols. 8°   BM | BPL

Works. ' Henry Irving Sh—' . . . edited by [Sir] Henry Irving and F. A. Marshall. With notes and introductions . . . by F. A. Marshall and other Shakespearian scholars and . . . illustrations by Gordon Browne. Ln : Blackie . . . 1888-90. 8 vols. Fcp. 4°   BM | BPL | BUS | MPL | SML
An 'edition-de-luxe,' limited to 150 copies, was also issued of this version, with India paper proof plates.

[Works] . . . with an introduction and notes by K. Deighton [and C. H. Tawney]. Ln. & Glasgow : Macmillan . . . 1888-96. 26 vols. Cr. 8°   BM

[Works] Comedies, histories and tragedies . . . as presented at the Globe and Blackfriars Theatres circa 1591-1623, being the text furnished the players, in parallel pages with the first revised folio text, with critical introductions. The 'Bankside Sh—,' edited by [James] Appleton Morgan. New York : Sh— Society of New York. Ln : Trübner & Co., 1888-1906. 22 vols. Roy. 8°. With facsimiles. [In progress]   BM | BPL | BUS | NY | SML
Issue stated to be restricted to 500 sets. Each volume is dedicated to a different Sh— scholar or actor.
This edition is sometimes confused with the 'Bankside restoration Sh—' (q.v.), 1898-1908.
Contents :—

I.	Merry wives,	edited by A. Morgan,	1888
II.	Taming . . .	,,	A. R. Frey, 1888
III.	Merchant . . .	,,	W. Reynolds, 1888
IV.	Troilus . . .	,,	A. Morgan, 1889
V.	Romeo . . .	,,	B. R. Field, 1889

VI. Much ado . edited by W. H. Fleming, 1889
VII.	Titus . . .	,,	A. Morgan, 1890
VIII.	Midsummer . . .	,,	W. Reynolds, 1890
IX.	Othello . . .	,,	T. R. Price, 1890
X.	King Lear . . .	,,	A. A. Adee, 1890
XI.	Hamlet . . .	,,	E. P. Vining, 1890
XII.	King Hen. IV., I.	,,	W. H. Fleming, 1890
XIII.	,, ,, II.	,,	W. H. Fleming, 1890
XIV.	Pericles . . .	,,	A. Morgan, 1891
XV.	King Richard III.	,,	E. A. Calkins, 1891
XVI.	King Henry V. . . .	,,	H. P. Stokes, 1892
XVII.	King Richard II.	,,	A. Waites, 1892
XVIII.	King John . . .	,,	A. Morgan, 1892
XIX.	King Hen. VI., II.	,,	C. W. Thomas, 1892
XX.	,, ,, III.	,,	A. Morgan, 1892
XXI.	Love's labours lost	,,	I. H. Platt, 1906
XXII.	Comedy of errors .	,,	A. Morgan, 1894

[Works] Sh— primer ; ' Julius Cæsar,' ' Merchant of Venice,' ' King Richard II.,' ' Macbeth,' ' Hamlet,' in gekürzter form mit anmerkungen herausgegeben von Dr. B. Carstens . . . Mit einer kopie und einer abbildung. Hamburg: O. Meissner . . . 1889. Cr. 8°, pp. xvi.-156   BM | SML

Works . . . ' Universal edition.' With life, glossary, etc. Ln : Warne . . . 1889. Cr. 8°

[Works] Family Sh— . . . edited by T. Bowdler. Ln : Longmans . . . 1889. 8°   BPL

[Works] Dramatic works . . . with notes, parallel passages, contemporary allusions, glossary and biographical sketch by W. H. D. Adams. Ln : T. Nelson & Sons . . . 1889. 2 vols. 8°. Illustrated   BPL | SML

Works . . . edited by C. Knight. Ln : Routledge . . . 1889. 3 vols. 8°   BM
Formed part of Routledge's ' Popular library.'

Works . . . with life and glossary. Carefully edited from the best texts. ' Bedford edition.' Ln. & New York : Warne . . . 1889. 12 vols. 8°

[Works] Shakespearian costumes : Illustrations of the whole of the characters in each play, in correct costume, by R. L. Bööcke. 1889. 8°   BM

Works . . . with glossarial notes by R. Inglis. Edinburgh : Gall & Inglis . . . 1890. Cr. 8°

Works . . . edited by C. Knight. Ln : Routledge . . . 1890. Cr. 8°, pp. viii.-1,074   BM | BLO | CTC | SML
Formed one of a series known as Sir John Lubbock's ' best hundred books.'

[Works] ' Universal edition ' . . . with life, glossary . . . Ln. & New York : Warne . . . 1890. Cr. 8°   BPL

[Works] . . . ' Sixpenny Sh—' . . . from the text of Steevens and Malone, with glossary. Ln : Ward, Lock & Co. [1890]. 8°   SML

Sh— Works . . .

Works . . . edited by H. Staunton. Ln:
Routledge . . . 1890

[Works] 'Pictorial edition' . . . edited by
C. Knight. Ln: Virtue & Co. . . . [c.
1890]. 8 vols. 8°   BPL

Works . . . edited by Prof. Hy. Morley.
Ln: Cassell . . . 1890. 13 vols. 16°

Works . . . Edited by C. Knight. ['Red line
edition.'] Ln: Routledge . . . 1890-91.
6 vols. Cr. 8°   BM

[Works] Moffatt's plays of Sh—, edited by
J. Paige. Ln: Moffatt & Paige [1890-
92]. 4 vols. Cr. 8°   BM

[Works] Sh—'s doubtful plays, edited . . .
by A. F. Hopkinson. Ln: M. E. Sims &
Co. [*pseud.*] 1890-95. 11 parts. 8°
                                   BM | BPL
Printed by the editor for private circulation.
The imprint is fictitious.

[Works] 'Pitt Press Sh—' for schools,
edited by A. W. Verity. Cambridge:
University Press . . . 1890-1905. 13 vols.
Cr. 8°. [In progress]   BM | BLO | CTC

Works . . . edited by Clark and Wright.
'Globe edition.' Ln: Macmillan . . .
1891. Cr. 8°

Works . . . edited by C. Knight. With
concordance by W. H. D. Adams. Ln:
Routledge . . . 1891. Cr. 8°

[Works] Doubtful plays . . . with notes by
Wm. Hazlitt. Ln: Routledge . . . 1891.
Cr. 8°

Works . . . edited by 'Barry Cornwall.' With
essay on his genius. Ln: Ward & Lock
. . . 1891. Cr. 8°

[Works] 'Oxford Sh—.' Complete works
. . . edited with a glossary by W. J. Craig.
Oxford: Clarendon Press [1891]. Cr. 8°,
pp. viii.-1,264   BM | BPL | BUS | SML
Also issued on India paper.

[Works] Sh— schulausgabe. Sammlung
Sh— 'scher stücke . . . herausgegeben
von E. Schmid [In English]. Danzig . . .
1891. 8°   BM

[Works] Plays . . . Revised edition. Ln:
J. Burns . . . 1891. 8°. With Chandos
portrait   SML

Works . . . [from the text of Delius. With
index]. 'Avon edition.' Ln: Kegan
Paul & Co. . . . 1891. 8°, pp. viii.-1,112
                                   BM | BPL

Works . . . Illustrated. Edited by F. J.
Furnivall. 'New Leopold edition.' Ln:
Cassell . . . 1891. Fcp. 4°

Works . . . edited by C. Knight. With . . .
illustrations by Sir John Gilbert. 'Mignon
edition.' Ln: Routledge . . . 1891. 6
vols. 12°   BM | BPL

Sh— Works . . .

Works . . . edited by H. Staunton. Ln:
Routledge . . . [1891]. 6 vols. 8°

Works . . . edited by W. A. Wright . . .
[Third edition.] Ln: Macmillan . . .
1891-93. 9 vols. Roy. 8° BM | BPL | SML
Reprinted from the 'Cambridge Sh—' of 1863-66, that
edition being out of print and considerably advanced
in price.

Works . . . by C. Knight. ['Lubbock
series.'] Ln: Routledge . . . 1892. Cr.
8°, pp. viii.-1,074   BM

[Works] Plays . . . abridged by Samuel
Brandram. Fourth edition. Ln: Smith
& Elder, 1892. Cr. 8°

[Works] Complete works . . . edited by W.
J. Craig. 'Miniature Sh—.' Oxford:
Clarendon Press [1892]. 6 vols. 32° BM
Printed on India paper.

[Works] Plays . . . edited by T. Keightley.
[New edition. With portraits of actors of
the day.] Ln: J. S. Virtue & Co. [1892-
94]. 4 vols. 8°   BM

[Works] 'Junior school Sh—' [edited by
G. H. Ely, W. Barry, W. Dent and
others]. Ln: Blackie . . . 1892-94. 6
vols. Cr. 8°   BM

[Works] Glossary and bibliographical notes
to the works of Sh—. Ln: . . . 1893.
16°

Works . . . with life and glossary, prepared
from the texts of the first folio and the
quartos, compared with recent commentators, by the editor of the 'Chandos
classics' [— Valentine]. 'Albion edition.'
Ln: Warne . . . 1893. Cr. 8°, pp. xvi.-
1,136   SML

[Works] 'Dallastype Sh—'; a reduced
facsimile of the first folio (1623) edition
in the British Museum [Parts 1 to 3, containing introductory matter, 'The tempest,' and part of 'Two gentlemen . . .'].
Ln: D. C. Dallas [1893]. F°   BM
A large paper copy is at the British Museum.

[Works] . . . historical plays . . . Roman and
English. With revised text and notes . . .
By Charles Wordsworth . . . New edition.
Ln. & Sydney: Remington & Co., 1893.
3 vols. 8°   BM | BPL
A repetition of the 1883 edition, with the date altered.

[Works] 'Reader's Sh—.' Ln: Innes & Co.
. . . 1893. 9 vols. 8°   BM
An unexpurgated edition.

[Works] Plays . . . edited by T. Keightley.
[With 28 photogravure plates and portraits of modern Shakespearean actors
and actresses.] Ln: J. S. Virtue & Co.
. . . 1893-95. 4 vols. 4°   BPL | SML

Works . . . edited by W. Aldis Wright. 'Cambridge Sh—.' Ln : Macmillan . . . 1893-95. 40 vols. Fcp. 4°   BM | BPL
500 sets were done on handmade paper, and a few on large paper.

Works . . . edited . . . by H. Arthur Doubleday, J. Gregory Foster and Robert Elson. [With index of characters and glossary.] 'Whitehall edition.' Westminster : A. Constable & Co., 1893-98. 12 vols. Cr. 8°   BM | BPL | SML

[Works] 'Warwick Sh—' . . . edited by C. H. Herford, J. C. Smith, E. K. Chambers, A. D. Innes, A. J. Wyatt, F. S. Boas, G. C. M. Smith, H. L. Withers and G. Macdonald. Ln : Blackie . . . 1893-98. 13 vols. 12°. [In progress]   BM | SML

Works . . . 'Hearth and home library,' edited by C. Knight. Ln : Routledge . . . 1894. Cr. 8°

[Works] 'School Sh—' . . . general editor : J. Churton Collins. Ln : E. Arnold . . . 1894. (?) vols. Cr. 8°   BM

Works . . . with life and glossary. 'Lansdowne pocket Sh—.' Ln : Warne, 1894. 6 vols. 32°   BM | BPL
Printed on India paper.

Works . . . edited by H. Staunton. Ln : Routledge . . . [1894]. 6 vols. 8°   BM

[Works] 'Royal Sh—.' The poet's works in chronological order, from the text of Professor Delius. With the 'Two noble kinsmen,' 'Edward III.,' and an introduction by F. J. Furnivall. With illustrations. Ln : Cassell . . . 1894-96. 3 vols. 8°   BM

[Works] 'Temple Sh—' [edited by Israel Gollancz, with preface, notes and glossary]. Ln : Dent . . . 1894-96. 40 vols. 16°. With portrait and frontispieces
  BM | BLO | BPL | CTC | SML
Some sets were issued on large paper, 8°.

Works . . . with glossary [edited by C. Knight]. Ln : R. E. King . . . 1895. Cr. 8°, pp. 770   SML

Works . . . carefully edited from the best texts, with a memoir, glossary, etc. 'Chandos classics.' Ln : Warne . . . [c. 1895]. Cr. 8°, pp. xvi.-748

Works . . . edited by C. Knight. ['People's Sh—.'] Ln : Routledge . . . 1895. 8°, pp. 770   BM

Works . . . from the text of Clark and Wright. With glossary, index of familiar passages, and index to the characters. New York : T. Y. Crowell & Co. [1895]. 8°   SML

Works . . . carefully edited from the best texts, with a glossary. Birmingham : Lewis & Co. . . . [1895]. Cr. 8°, pp. iv.-748. With frontispiece   SML

[Works] Double text Dallastype Sh— . . . A reduced Dallastype facsimile . . . from the first folio (1623) edition and, facing each page thereof, the modern text as determined by the late Charles Knight. Introduction by Dr. F. J. Furnivall . . . edited, with a glossarial index, by F. A. Hyndman and D. C. Dallas. Ln : George Redway, 1895. F°   BM

Works . . . 'Victoria edition.' Ln : Macmillan . . . 1895. 3 vols. Cr. 8°   BM | BLO | CTC

Works . . . edited by [Sir] Henry Irving and Frank A. Marshall. With notes and introductions to each play by F. A. Marshall and other Shakespearian scholars, and life of Sh— by Edward Dowden. With illustrations by Gordon Browne. Ln : Blackie . . . 1895. 8 vols. Fcp. 4°
The illustrations comprise portrait, etchings, and 600 wood plates.

[Works] Bell's reader's Sh—, condensed, connected and emphasized for school, college, parlour and platform by D. C. Bell. Ln : Hodder & Stoughton . . . 1895-97. 3 vols. Cr. 8°. Expurgated
  BM | BPL | BUS | SML

Works . . . 'Ariel edition.' Illustrated [by Frank Howard]. Ln : Routledge . . . 1895-97. 40 vols. 16°   BM | SML

Works . . . edited by A. Dyce. With glossary. Ln : Sonnenschein . . . 1895-1901. 10 vols. 8°

Works . . . with life, glossary, etc. . . . [by — Valentine]. 'Universal edition.' Ln : Warne . . . 1896. Cr. 8°, pp. xii.-1,124
  BM | BPL | SML

Works . . . with life, glossary, etc. [Prepared by . . . Valentine.] 'Victorian edition.' Ln : Warne . . . 1896. Cr. 8°, pp. xvi.-1,136   BM | BPL | SML
This should not be confused with the superior 'Victoria edition,' published by Macmillan nine years earlier.

Works . . . 'Falstaff edition.' Ln : Bliss, Sands & Co. . . . 1896. 8°, pp. 1,100
  BM | BPL | SML

[Works] . . . Comedies, histories, tragedies and sonnets. 'Savoy edition.' Newly edited [by W. J. Loftie]. Ln : Eyre & Spottiswoode . . . 1896. 8°, pp. xxviii.-1,086, printed with red rules   BM | BPL
A large quantity was prepared of this edition, the bulk being disposed of in 1905 (some 15,000 copies) at a 'remainder' price to Charles Taylor, who attached a fresh title-page, renaming it the 'Brooke house Sh—,' but on the half-title the words 'Savoy edition' still remained.

Sh— Works . . .

[Works] 'Leopold Sh—,' from the text of Delius. With introduction by F. J. Furnivall. Ln : Cassell . . . [1896]. Fcp. 4° BPL

Works . . . with introductory remarks and notes, critical, general and explanatory, by S. Phelps. Ln : Ward & Lock, 1896. Roy. 8°. Illustrated

[Works] English historical plays by Sh— [and others] arranged for acting, by T. Donovan. Ln : Macmillan . . . 1896. 2 vols. Cr. 8°, pp. 480 and 474

[Works] Comedies . . . with many drawings by E. A. Abbey. New York : Osgood & Co., Harper Brothers . . . 1896. 4 vols. Roy. 8° BUS | SML

Works . . . edited by W. C. Bryant, assisted by E. A. Duyckinck. Illustrated by F. O. C. Darley and A. Chappel. 'Stratford edition.' Philadelphia . . . [1896]. 6 vols. 8° BUS

[Works] 'Stratford-on-Avon Sh—' . . . comedies, histories, tragedies and poems. Ln : George Newnes . . . 1896. 12 vols. 12° BM | BPL | SML

Works . . . 'Avon Sh—.' Ln : Kegan Paul, Trench & Co. . . . 1896. 12 vols. 12° BPL

Works . . . edited by W. J. Rolfe. Ln : W. B. Clive . . . [1896]. 40 vols. 8° BM
Reprinted from the New York edition of 1871-96.

[Works] Graphic gallery of Sh—'s heroines : Studies by the greatest British painters. Ln : Low . . . 1896. F°. Coloured plates

Works . . . edited by W. G. Clark and W. A. Wright. 'Globe edition.' Ln : Macmillan . . . 1897. Cr. 8° BUS

Works . . . edited by C. Knight [with glossary]. Ln : Standard Library Co. . . . [1897]. Cr. 8°, pp. 770 BPL

Works . . . 'Albion edition.' Ln : Warne . . . [1897]. Cr. 8° BPL

Works . . . with life, glossary, etc. . . . 'Chandos edition.' Ln : Warne . . . 1897. Cr. 8°, pp. 1,152

Works . . . from the text of Johnson, Steevens and Reed. With biographical sketch by M. C. Clarke. 'Edinburgh library.' Edinburgh : Nimmo . . . 1897. Roy. 8°, pp. 736

Works . . 'Avon edition.' Ln : Kegan Paul . . . 1897. Roy. 8°, pp. 1,120
Mainly the text of Delius. BPL | BUS | SML

[Works] 'Children's Sh—,' edited by E. Nesbit [*afterwards* Bland]. Ln : . . . 1897. 4° BM

[Works] Complete works . . . Price one shilling and sixpence. Ln : Western Mail. Cardiff : Tudor Printing Works, 1897. F°, pp. iv.-366

Sh— Works . . .

[Works] Sh— for sixpence, complete. Cardiff : Western Mail . . . 1897. F°, pp. iv.-366 BPL | SML

Works . . . edited by H. Staunton. Illustrated by Sir J. Gilbert. Ln : Pearson . . . 1897. 3 vols. Roy. 8°, pp. 2,392

[Works] School Sh—, edited by L. W. Lyde. Ln : Blackie, 1897-1902. 5 vols. Cr. 8° BM

[Works] 'Reader's Sh—': Comedies . . . condensed, connected and emphasised for school, college, parlour and platform, by David Charles Bell. Ln : Hodder . . . 1898. Cr. 8°, pp. 522

Works . . . edited by C. Knight. 'Indispensable series.' Ln : Routledge . . . 1898. Cr. 8°, pp. 770

Works . . . edited by C. Knight. ['Lubbock series.'] Ln : Routledge . . . 1898. Cr. 8°, pp. 1,082

Works . . . 'Falstaff edition.' New edition. Ln : Bliss, Sands . . . 1898. Roy. 8°, pp. 1,100

[Works] Complete works . . . edited by G. L. Duyckinck. Philadelphia : H. T. Coates & Co. [c. 1898]. 8° BPL

Works . . . New variorum edition, edited by H. H. Furness. 'Student's edition.' Ln : Dent . . . 1898. 2 vols. 8° BM | BLO | BPL | CTC
A modified form of Dr. Furness's great variorum edition, 1871-1908 (*q.v.*) This student's issue was not further proceeded with.

[Works] 'Royal Sh—': The poet's works in chronological order from the text of Prof. Delius. With introduction by F. J. Furnivall. Ln : Cassell . . . 1898. 3 vols. Roy. 8°, pp. 1,634 and plates BM

Works . . . 'Handy volume edition.' Ln : Bradbury, Agnew & Co. [c. 1898]. 39 vols. 16° (in case) BPL

Works . . . 'Pocket Falstaff edition.' With glossary and bibliographical notes. Ln : Bliss, Sands & Co. . . . 1898. 40 vols. 16° BPL | SML

[Works] School Sh—, edited by R. Brimley Johnson. Edinburgh : Blackwood . . . 1898-1903. 8° BM

[Works] Plays . . . 'Bankside restoration Sh—.' Edited by J. A. Morgan. New York : Sh— Society of New York, 1898-1908. (?) vols. Fcp. 4°. [In progress] BUS | NY
The text is taken from the adaptations and alterations produced by Crowne, Davenant, Dryden, Augustine Phillips, Ravenscroft, Shadwell, Shirley, Tate, and others at the Duke's Theatre at the restoration period.
The issue is stated to be limited to 250 sets, numbered and signed.

Sh— Works . . .

Works . . . edited by Prof. Edw. Dowden. Ln : . . . 1899. 2 vols. 8°   BPL | MPL

Works . . . edited by H. Staunton. Illustrated by Sir J. Gilbert. Ln : Routledge . . . 1899. 3 vols. Roy. 8°, pp. 2,384

[Works] Shakespearian plays of Edwin Booth, edited by William Winter. 'Acting edition.' Philadelphia : Penn Publishing Co. . . . 1899. 3 vols. 8°. With portraits   BUS | SML

Works . . . 'Portrait edition.' Glasgow : Bryce . . . 1899. 8 vols in 4. 32°
Also issued on India paper.

[Works] 'Pocket portrait Sh—' [with eight portraits, biographical sketch, glossary, index to quotations, forty illustrations, and notes on the portraits, by W. S. Brassington]. Glasgow : D. Bryce & Son [1899]. 8 vols. 32°   BM | BPL | SML

[Works] Dramatic works . . . edited by S. W. Singer. Ln : G. Bell & Sons . . . 1899. 10 vols. 12°   BPL | SML

Works . . . 'Eversley edition,' with introduction and notes by C. H. Herford. Ln : Macmillan . . . 1899. 10 vols. 8°   BM | BLO | BPL | CTC | SML

[Works] 'Swan Sh—' [with notes, grammatical and critical, and examination papers, by various editors. Illustrated]. Ln : Longman . . . 1899-1900. 8 vols. 8°   BM | SML

Works . . . New edition. Ln : Newnes . . . 1899-1900. 12 vols. 12°

Works . . . edited by I. Gollancz. 'Larger temple edition.' Ln : Dent . . . 1899-1900. 12 vols. 8°. With portraits, antiquarian and topographical illustrations   BM | BPL | BUS | SML
Limited to 175 numbered sets on handmade paper.

Works . . . 'Chiswick edition.' With introduction and notes by John Dennis. Illustrations by Byam Shaw. Ln : Bell . . . 1899-1902. 41 vols. 8° BM | BPL | SML
Two hundred sets also were done on Japanese vellum.

Works . . . 'Arden edition,' edited by W. J. Craig. Ln : Methuen, 1899-1906. 32 vols. 8°   BM | BLO | BPL | CTC
The aim of this edition is to meet the requirements of three classes of readers :—I., A clear text undisturbed by notes ; II., A separate body of explanatory notes ; III., A collation with exhibition of variations.

Works . . . 'Clear type edition,' with biographical introduction by Henry Glassford Bell. With sixty-five photo-engravings of eminent histrionic artists. Ln. & Glasgow : W. Collins [1900]. 8°, pp. xxviii.-1,312   BPL | SML

Works . . . edited by C. Knight. Ln : Routledge . . . 1900. 3 vols. 8°, pp. 2,414

Sh— Works .

[Works] Comedies . . . With many drawings by E. A. Abbey, R.A. New York : Harper . . . 1900. 4 vols. Roy. 8° BPL

[Works] 'Illustrated pocket Sh—.' Complete with glossary. Carefully edited and compared with the best texts by J. Talfourd Blair. Glasgow : Bryce & Son [c. 1900]. 8 vols. 16° (in case)

[Works] Plays . . . Basil, MDCCCC. 23 vols. 8°
The date is a misprint for 1799-1802 [q.v.]

Works . . . edited by C. H. Herford. 'Eversley edition.' Ln : Macmillan, 1900. 37 vols. Cr. 8°   BUS
With this was issued a Supplement, edited by S. Eaton, in 12 parts, containing 146 Shakespearean prints.

Works . . . 'Whitehall edition' [edited by H. A. Doubleday and J. G. Forster]. Ln : Constable . . . 1900. 39 vols. 12°   BPL

Works . . . 'Ariel edition.' Ln : Routledge . . . 1900. 40 vols. 16°   BPL

Works . . . 'New century edition.' The text of the Cambridge edition. With notes and introductions by Israel Gollancz. Boston [U.S.] . . . 1900-01. 24 vols. 8°
Some sets done on large paper.

Works . . . edited by H. N. Hudson. [With life and history of each play.] Illustrated from paintings of great artists. 'Windsor edition.' Ln : Caxton Press [T. & C. Jack], 1900-01. 40 vols. 8°   BM | BLO | BPL | CTC | SML

Works . . . seen through the press by T. Sturge Moore, and decorated by Charles Ricketts. Vale Press [Printed at the Ballantyne Press], 1900-03. 39 vols. Roy. 8°   BPL | SML
Issue limited to 310 sets.

Works . . . Ln : R. E. King, Ld. . . . 1901. Cr. 8°   BPL

[Works] Complete works . . . Ln : Yardley & Hanscomb [1901]. Cr. 8°, pp. xvi.-748

Works . . . 'Avon edition' [edited by Dr. N. Delius]. Ln : Kegan Paul . . . 1901. 8°, pp. viii.-1,112

Works . . . 'Thin paper edition.' Ln : Newnes . . . 1901. 3 vols. 12°   BPL

Works . . . Ln : Constable . . . 1901. 20 vols. Cr. 8°

Works . . . 'National library,' edited by Hy. Morley. Ln : Cassell . . . 1901. 37 vols. Cr. 8°

Works . . . 'Edinburgh folio edition,' edited by William Ernest Henley. Ln. [Edinburgh, printed by Constable for] Grant Richards . . . 1901-04. 40 parts,

Sh— Works . . .

forming 10 vols. F°. With portraits and plates   BM | BLO | BPL | BUS | CTC
One thousand sets printed, at £10 each. More than half the sets came on the market at a reduced price, owing to the failure of the publisher, and were chiefly exported to America.

Works . . . edited with glossary by W. J. Craig. 'Oxford edition.' Oxford : Clarendon Press, 1902. Cr. 8°, pp. 1,272
BPL | BUS

[Works] . . . Comedies, histories and tragedies, being a reproduction in facsimile of the first folio edition, 1623, from the Chatsworth copy, in the possession of the Duke of Devonshire, K.G. With introduction and census of copies by ' Sidney Lee.' [*Droeshout portrait.*] Oxford : At the Clarendon Press, 1902. 2 vols. F°. [The 'Census' occupying a thin separate volume, pp. 48], pp. xxxvi.-908
BM | BPL | BUS | CTC | MPL | SML
One thousand numbered copies, signed by the editor, were issued, in two styles of binding : linen boards, and rough undyed calf with tie thongs, both with deckle edges. Only a small portion of the impression was done in boards.
The introduction is disfigured by blunders and inaccuracies.
Reviewed in 'The Athenæum,' Jan., 1903, p. 19, and in 'The Times' supplement.

Works . . . with introduction by Shervyn. Ln : Black . . . 1902. (?) vols. Cr. 8°

Works . . . 'Abbey Sh—.' Edinburgh : Abbey Press . . . 1902. 2 vols. Fcp. 4°
BPL
Vol. I., Romeo ; Vol. II., Merry wives. No more issued.

Works . . . 'Thin paper edition.' Ln : Newnes . . . 1902. 3 vols. 12°

Works . . . Coloured illustrations by Brooke, Shaw, etc. Ln : Constable . . . 1902. 20 vols. Cr. 8°   BPL

Works . . . 'Student's Sh—,' edited by A. W. Verity. Cambridge : University Press, 1902-05. 3 vols. 8°   BPL
I., Macbeth ; II., Hamlet ; III., Coriolanus.

Works . . . new edition, with critical text in Elizabethan English and brief notes illustrative of Elizabethan life, thought and idiom, by Mark Harvey Liddell. I., 'Macbeth.' New York . . . 1903. 8°
No more issued.   BPL | BUS | NY

Works . . . 'Oxford miniature edition,' edited with glossary by W. J. Craig. Oxford : Clarendon Press, 1903. 3 vols. 32°   BPL

[Works] 'Royal Sh—': The poet's works in chronological order from the text of Prof. Delius. Including the 'Two noble kinsmen' and '[King] Edward III.' With introduction by F. J. Furnivall [and facsimile of his Will]. Ln : Cassell . . .

Sh— Works . . .

1903. 34 parts, forming 3 vols. Roy. 8°. With sixty-eight Rembrandt photogravures and tinted plates

[Works] Complete works . . . ' Illustrated Sh—.' Glasgow & Ln : W. Collins . . . [c. 1903]. 6 vols. 12°   BPL

Works . . . 'Stage Sh—.' With introduction and glossary by A. Brereton. Illustrated. Ln. & Glasgow : W. Collins & Sons [1903]. 6 vols. 12°   SML

Works . . . edited by H. N. Hudson. 'Windsor edition.' Edinburgh : Jack, 1903. 40 vols. Cr. 8°. Illustrated   BPL

Works . . . 'Stage Sh—,' edited by A. Brereton. Glasgow : Collins . . . 1903-05. 40 vols. 12°   BPL | SML

[Works] Comedies, tragedies, histories . . . 'Little quarto Sh—.' Ln : Methuen . . . 1903-05. 40 vols. 12°   BPL

Works . . . 'Pembroke edition,' edited by Charlotte Porter and H. A. Clarke. With introduction by J. C. Collins. New York : T. Y. Crowell. Ln : G. G. Harrap, 1903-08. 13 vols. Cr. 8°. [In progress]
BPL

Works . . . 'Red letter edition.' Ln : Blackie . . . 1904. 12°   BPL

Works . . . edited with a glossary by W. J. Craig. 'Oxford edition.' Ln : H. Frowde . . . 1904. Cr. 8°, pp. viii.-1,264. With Droeshout portrait

Works . . . 'Leopold edition,' edited by F. J. Furnivall. Ln : Cassell [c. 1904]. Fcp. 4°   BPL

[Works] . . . Comedies, histories and tragedies, faithfully reproduced from the edition of 1685 . . . Ln : Methuen . . . 1904. F°, pp. 998
BM | BLO | BPL | MPL | SML
The first facsimile of the Herringman folio of 1685.

[Works] Comedies, histories, poems and tragedies. 'Thin paper classics.' Ln : Newnes, 1904. 3 vols. 12°, pp. 966, 980 and 1,068

Works . . . edited by Charles Knight. Ln : Routledge . . . 1904. 3 vols. Cr. 8° BPL

Works . . . with life by ' S. Lee.' 'Hampstead edition.' Ln : Finch . . . 1904. 4 vols. Cr. 8°, pp. 2,398   BPL

Works . . . 'Oxford miniature edition.' Oxford : Clarendon Press, 1904. 12 vols. 32° (in case)

Works . . . 'Stage edition.' With introduction and glossary by Austin Brereton. Glasgow : Collins . . . 1904. 24 vols. 16°. Illustrated

Works . . . ' Ellen Terry miniature edition.' Glasgow : Bryce . . . 1904. 40 vols. 32° (in case)   BPL

Works . . . ' Temple edition,' edited by I. Gollancz. Ln : Dent . . . 1904. 40 vols. 18° (in case)

Works . . . edited by George Brandes. ' Favourite classics.' Ln : Heinemann . . . 1904. 40 vols. 18° (in case) BPL

Works . . . ' Waistcoat pocket Sh—.' Ln : Treherne & Co. . . . 1904-05. 40 vols. 32° Printed on India paper. BPL

Works . . . In ten volumes. [' Stratford town edition.' The text revised by Arthur Henry Bullen.] With memoir of Sh—, by Henry Davey ; ' Ben Jonson's views on Sh—'s art,' by J. J. Jusserand ; ' On the influence of the audience,' by Robert Bridges ; ' On the religion of Sh—' and ' On the sonnets,' by Canon Beeching ; ' The stage of the Globe,' by E. K. Chambers ; ' Portraits of Sh—,' by M. H. Spielmann. Stratford-on-Avon : Sh— Head Press, 1904-07. 10 vols. Roy. 8°. With ten portraits
BM | BLO | BPL | CTC | SML
Limited to one thousand sets on Alton handmade paper and twelve sets on pure vellum. The text is set in Caslon type, ' English ' fount. The vellum issue was subscribed at one hundred guineas per set.
Reviewed in the 'Athenæum,' 1907 (No. 4159, p. 51).

Works . . . with essay on Sh— and Bacon by Sir Hy. Irving, and a biographical introduction. ' India paper edition.' Illustrated with 64 photo-engravings of eminent Shakespearean artists. Glasgow : Collins . . . 1905. Cr. 8°, pp. xlvi.-1,312

[Works] ' Lamb Sh—' for the young, based on Lamb's tales. Ln : Chatto . . . 1905. Cr. 8° BPL

Works . . . edited by W. J. Craig. 'Oxford edition.' Ln : H. Frowde . . . 1905. Cr. 8°, pp. x.-1,350 and plates

Works . . . edited with glossary by W. J. Craig. ' India paper edition.' Oxford : Clarendon Press, 1905. Cr. 8°, pp. x.-1,350 and plates BPL

Works . . . carefully edited from the best texts. With a memoir, glossary, etc. Ln : Warne . . . [c. 1905]. Cr. 8°, pp. xvi.-748

Works . . . with life, glossary, etc., prepared from the texts of the first folio and the quartos, compared with recent commentators [by . . . Valentine]. 'Albion edition.' Ln : Warne [c. 1905]. Cr. 8°, pp. xvi.-1,136 and Chandos portrait

[Works] ' Brooke house Sh—.' Comedies, histories, tragedies and sonnets [edited with an introduction by W. J. Loftie]. Ln : Charles Taylor . . . [1905]. 8°, pp. xxviii.-1,086, printed within red rules
See Sh— Works, ' Savoy edition,' 1895.

[Works] Complete works . . . [with glossary and notes]. ' Falstaff edition.' Birmingham : Eld & Blackham . . . 1905. Roy. 8°, pp. 1,128

[Works] . . . Comedies, histories and tragedies, faithfully reproduced in facsimile from the edition of 1664. Ln : Methuen . . . 1905. F° BPL | MPL
The first facsimile reprint of the Chetwynde folio.

Works . . . ' New universal library.' Ln : Routledge . . . 1905. 6 vols. Cr. 8°

Works . . . ' Garrick Sh—.' With introductions by G. Brandes. Ln : W. Heinemann . . . 1905. 12 vols. 8°. With photogravure plates BPL

Works . . . ' Standard library.' Ln : Methuen . . . 1905-08. 7 vols. Cr. 8° BPL

Works . . . With life, glossary, etc. Prepared from the texts of the first folio, the quartos, and compared with recent commentators [by . . . Valentine]. 'Victorian edition.' Ln : Warne . . . 1906. Cr. 8°, pp. xvi.-1,136

[Works] Standard operas, edited by G. P. Upton [' Falstaff,' ' Othello,' ' Romeo . . .,' ' Taming . . .'] . . . 1906. Cr. 8° BPL

[Works] Complete dramatic and poetic works . . . edited by W. A. Neilson. Boston [U.S.] : Houghton, Mifflin & Co., 1906. 8° BPL

[Works] Dramatic works . . . With notes by Robert Inglis. Ln : Gall & Inglis [c. 1906]. 8° BPL

[Works] Comedies, histories, plays, poems, sonnets and tragedies. ' Everyman's library.' Ln : Dent . . . 1906. 3 vols. 12°, pp. 856, 896, and 990 BPL

Works . . . ' New century library.' Ln : Nelson . . . 1906. 6 vols. 12° BPL

[Works] Plays and poems, edited by C. Knight. ' New universal library.' Ln : Routledge . . . 1906. 6 vols. 12° BPL

Works . . . ' Chiswick edition.' Ln : Bell . . . 1906. 12 vols. 16°

Works . . . reprinted from the first folio. Edited by Charlotte Porter and H. A. Clarke. With an introduction by John Churton Collins. Ln : G. G. Harrap . . . 1906. 13 vols. Cr. 8°. With portraits and plates BM | BLO | CTC | SML
Seventy-five numbered sets were also printed on handmade paper, of which one is at Stratford.

[Works] Plays . . . with notes and illustrations by C. Knight. Ln : Virtue . . . 1906-07. 6 vols. F° BPL

Sh— Works . . .

[Works] Complete works . . . edited with glossary by W. J. Craig. Oxford: University Press, 1907. Cr. 8°, pp. viii.-1,264 and Droeshout portrait

[Works] 'Old spelling Sh—'; being the works of Sh— in the spelling of the best quarto and folio texts. Edited by F. J. Furnivall, the late W. G. Boswell-Stone and F. W. Clarke. Ln: Chatto . . .; New York: Duffield & Co., 1907-08. 12 vols. Fcp. 4°. [In progress]
BM | BLO | BPL | CTC | SML

Projected for completion in 40 vols. Five hundred sets were also to be done on linen paper.
Contents :—
  1. Love's labours lost, 1907
  2. Taming of the shrew, 1907
  3. Midsummer night's dream, 1907
  4. Two gentlemen, 1907
  5. Twelfth night, 1907
  6. Comedy of errors, 1908
  7. As you like it, 1908
  8. Merchant of Venice, 1908
  9. Much ado . . . 1908
 10. Merry wives . . . 1908
 11. The tempest, 1908
 12. Winter's tale, 1908

[Works] Complete works . . . 'University Press Sh—. Renaissance edition.' New York: G. D. Sprout. Ln: G. G. Harrap, 1907-08. 32 vols. 4°   BPL

[Works] 'Little Sh—.' Glasgow: Bryce . . . 1908. 32° (3¾ × 2¾ in.), pp. 1,024. With eight portraits and forty illustrations   BPL
Stated to be the smallest edition of Sh— in one vol.

[Works] 'School Sh—,' consisting of twelve of the most suitable plays for school reading. Edited with glossary by A. V. Houghton. Ln: Longmans . . . 1908. Cr. 8°, pp. 820   BPL

[Works] Sh— apocrypha; being a collection of fourteen plays which have been ascribed to Sh—. Edited with introductory notes and bibliography by C. F. Tucker Brooke. Oxford: Clarendon Press . . . 1908. Cr. 8°, pp. lvi.-456
BM | BLO | BPL | CTC | SML
The title plagiarises that of J. T. Foard issued four years earlier, called the 'Apocrypha of Sh—.'
Contents:—
  1. Arden of Feversham
  2. Locrine
  3. King Edward III.
  4. Mucedorus
  5. Sir John Oldcastle
  6. Thomas Lord Cromwell
  7. London prodigal
  8. The puritan
  9. Yorkshire tragedy
 10. Merry devil of Edmonton
 11. Fair Em
 12. Two noble kinsmen
 13. Birth of Merlin
 14. Sir Thomas More

Sh— Works . . .

[Works] Nine plays: Merchant of Venice, Midsummer . . ., As you like it, The tempest, King Richard II., King Henry V., Julius Cæsar, Hamlet, and Macbeth. Edited with introduction and brief notes by G. S. Gordon. Oxford: Clarendon Press, 1908. Cr. 8°

[Works] Comedies, histories and tragedies. Facsimile reproduction of the lettering and design shown on title-page of the first issue of the fourth folio, 1685. Postal Literary Alliance, 1908. F° BPL

Works . . . 'Elizabethan edition.' Ln: G. G. Harrap . . . 1908. 2 vols. 8° BPL
I., Merchant of Venice; II., Love's labours lost.

Works . . . 'People's library.' Ln: Cassell . . . 1908. 4 vols. Cr. 8° BPL

Works . . . 'Century edition.' Edited by Dr. Furnivall and J. Munro, with introductions, notes, life and glossaries. Ln: Cassell . . . 1908. 40 vols. Cr. 8°. Illustrated BPL

[Works] Comedies, histories, and tragedies, faithfully reproduced in facsimile from the edition of 1632. Ln: Methuen, 1909. F° BM | BLO | BPL | CTC | SML
Reviewed in the 'Athenæum,' 2nd Oct., 1909, pp. 393-394.
The first facsimile reprint of the Cotes folio.

[Works] Sh— for home reading, edited by K. Harvey. Ln: Routledge, 1909. 37 parts. Cr. 8° BPL (*impft.*)

[Works] Comedies, histories and tragedies. Published according to the true originall copies . . . 1623. Reproduced in facsimile. Ln: Methuen, 1910. F°
BM | BLO | CTC

Works . . . 'Caxton edition.' Edited by 'S. Lee.' With annotations and general introduction. Illustrated in colour. Ln: Caxton Co., 1910. 20 vols. 8°
BM | BLO | BPL | CTC

Works . . . edited by H. N. Hudson. 'Era edition.' Ln: Jack . . . 1910. 42 vols. 12°. Illustrated BM | BLO | BPL | CTC

Works; references, criticism and comment
See Abbott   See Archer & Lowe
 ,, Acheson   ,, Astor
 ,, Adams   ,, Aveling
 ,, Adee   ,, B—— (J.)
 ,, Adelaide   ,, Baar
 ,, Alger   ,, Bacon (D. S.)
 ,, Allies   ,, Bacon contro-
 ,, American . . .   versy
 ,, Anders   ,, Badham
 ,, Annotations   ,, Bailey (S.)
 ,, Antiquarian   ,, Bailey (*Sir* W.
 ,, Antiquary   H.)
 ,, Archer   ,, Baker (*Sir* R.)

See Barclay (J.)
,, Barton (R.)
,, Bathurst
,, Baudissin
,, Baynes
,, Becket
,, Bowdler
,, Bowen
,, Brackett
,, Bradley
,, Brae
,, Brewer
,, Britton
,, Brooke (S. A.)
,, Brown (I.)
,, Browne (G. H.)
,, Bulloch
,, Caine
,, Caldecott
,, Canning
,, Capell
,, Carpenter
,, Cartwright
,, Cobbett
,, Collier (J. P.)
,, Conjectural . . .
,, Cooke (W.)
,, Cooper
,, Corrector
,, Corson
,, Courtenay
,, Courthope
,, Craik
,, Crawford
,, Croft
,, Cruikshank
,, Daniel
,, Davey
,, Davies
,, Delius
,, Demmon
,, De Quincey
,, Desch
,, Dircks
,, D'Israeli
,, Dowden
,, Drama
,, Dramatic . . .
,, Drayton
,, Dryden
,, Dubois
,, Durand
,, Dyer
,, Eccles
,, Edinburgh . . .
,, Egan
,, Elegie
,, Ellis
,, Elton

See Elze
,, Engel
,, English
,, Esquiros
,, Essays
,, Ewen
,, Fairbanks
,, Familiar . . .
,, Farrar
,, Felton
,, Fenton
,, Ferguson
,, Ferris
,, Field
,, Fielding
,, Fifty . . .
,, Finegan
,, Fish
,, Fleay
,, Fleming
,, Fletcher (G.)
,, Fletcher (W. I.)
,, Foard
,, Freeman
,, Froude
,, Fuller
,, Furness
,, Furnivall
,, Gervinus
,, Gilder
,, Gildon
,, Giles
,, Giraldi
,, Glynn
,, Goethe
,, Goldsmith
,, Gollancz
,, Gosse
,, Gould
,, Graves
,, Gray
,, Green (J. L.)
,, Grein
,, Grey
,, Griffin
,, Griffiths
,, Guthrie
,, Hackett
,, Hales
,, Hall (H. T.)
,, Halliwell
,, Hamlet
,, Harness
,, Harvey
,, Haslewood
,, Hazlitt
,, Heath
,, Henderson
,, Herford

See Herr
,, Hoare
,, Holinshed
,, Holland (F. W.)
,, Holland (L. G.)
,, Holt
,, Home
,, Hopkinson
,, Horsburgh
,, Howard
,, Howe
,, Hudson
,, Hume
,, Hunter
,, Hurdis
,, Ingleby
,, Irving (*Sir* J. H. B.)
,, J—— (E. M.)
,, Jackson
,, Jacox
,, Jaggard
,, 'Jaques'
,, Jeremiah
,, Jervis
,, Johnson (*Dr.* S.)
,, Jolley
,, Journal
,, Jusserand
,, Kay
,, Kemble
,, Kenrick
,, Kent
,, Kerr
,, Kerschner
,, Kilbourne
,, Kinnear
,, Knight
,, L——
,, Latham
,, Latimer
,, Leisure hour
,, Le Neve
,, Lennox
,, Lenox
,, Leo
,, Levi
,, Lloyd
,, Lordan
,, Lounsbury
,, Lowell
,, Luce
,, Lunt
,, M—— (J.)
,, M—— (J. A.)
,, MacCarthy
,, Macdonald
,, Macknight
,, McSpadden

See Madden
,, Maginn
,, Malden
,, Man . . .
,, Mason
,, Matson
,, Meredith
,, Meres
,, Merriman
,, Milton
,, Minto
,, Moberly
,, Modern
,, Montagu
,, Moor
,, Moorman
,, Morehead
,, Morgan
,, Morley (H.)
,, Moulin
,, Moulton
,, Mull
,, Mullins
,, Mulvany
,, Neele
,, New exegesis
,, New Sh— interpretations
,, New Sh— Soc.
,, New Sh—ana
,, New York Sh— Soc.
,, Newspaper cuttings
,, Newton
,, Nichols
,, Nicoll
,, Notes . . .
,, O'Carroll
,, Oechelhaeuser
,, Ordish
,, Orger
,, Orson
,, Otway
,, Paget
,, Pater
,, Payne
,, Peck
,, Percy
,, Perring
,, Phin
,, Pickering
,, Pinkerton
,, Plumptre
,, Poet lore
,, Poole & Fletcher
,, Pott
,, Potts
,, Pownall

Sh—Works; references, criticism and comment

NOTE.—Extracts from Sh—'s writings now follow, in chronological sequence, with a terminal key to references.—W. J.

[Works : Extracts] England's parnassus, or the choysest flowers of our moderne poets, with their poeticall comparisons, &c., whereunto are annexed various other discourses, both pleasant and profitable

Sh— [Works : Extracts]—

[edited by Robert Allot]. Ln : Printed for N. L——, C. B——, and Th. Hayes, 1600. Cr. 8°   BUS | CTC | W
Collation : Two blank leaves (one sig. A), title, dedication 'to Syr Thomas Mounson,' 'to the reader,' and 'errata' (should read 'contents'); 6 leaves in all. Text, B1 to Kk8 (pp. 510), the last leaf blank.
With seventy-nine extracts from Sh—; perhaps the most remarkable evidence of contemporary appreciation of his worth.
Collier's 'Bibliog. account of early English literature' says Allot used over fifty different writers for his compilation. Spenser stands first with 255 quotations, and Sh— is eighth on the list.
It was reprinted in 'Heliconia' (*q.v.*)
See 'Notes and Queries,' 1908-09, for a valuable dissection of and key to the volume by Charles Crawford.

[Works : Ext.] Jonson (B.) Herrick (Robert) Suckling (Sir J.) & others. Select musicall ayres and dialogues [with music by John Wilson, Dr. Charles Coleman, Henry Lawes, William Lawes, William Webb, Nicholas Lanneare, William Smegergil, Edward Colman, and Jeremy Savile]. Ln : Printed by T. H—— for John Playford and are to be sold at his shop in the Inner Temple near the Church doore, 1653. F°
Many of these songs were rendered by Jack Wilson, the earliest recorded singer of 'Sigh no more, Ladies.,

[Works : Ext.] Poole (Joshua) English parnassus, a helpe to English poesie. Containing a collection of all the rhythming monosyllables, the choicest epithets and phrases. With some general forms upon all occasions, subjects and themes, alphabetically digested. Ln : . . . 1657. 8°, pp. 598   BPL | W
An early collection of extracts from Sh— and his contemporaries.

[Works : Ext.] Early excerpts from Sh—'s works, seventy entries in all, extracted from a manuscript commonplace book of the Restoration period. c. 1660. 8°. Manuscript on seventeen leaves of paper
                                        W

[Works : Ext.] Early excerpts from Sh—'s writings, one hundred and fifteen in all, extracted from a manuscript commonplace book of the Restoration period. c. 1670. Fcp. 4°. Manuscript on fifteen leaves of paper   W

[Works : Ext.] Poole (Joshua) English parnassus, or a help to English poesie . . . Ln : H. Brome . . . 1677. 8°, pp. 640. With frontispiece   BPL | W

[Works : Ext.] Bysshe (Edward) Art of English poetry, containing rules for making verses, collection of . . . thoughts . . . found in the best English poets, dictionary of rhymes. Third edition, with large

improvements. Ln : Sam. Buckley, at the Dolphin in Little Britain, 1708. 8°, pp. xii.-482-viii.-36
Numerous extracts from Sh—.

[Works : Ext.] Bysshe (E.) Art of English poetry . . . Fourth edition. Ln : S. Buckley, 1710. 8°, pp. xii.-38-482-viii.-36

[Works : Ext.] Gildon (Charles) Shakespeareana : Most beautiful topics, descriptions, and similes that occur throughout Sh—'s plays [In ' Complete art of poetry,' Vol. 2]. Ln : 1718. 2 vols. 8°
BPL | BUS

[Works : Ext.] Agreeable variety : being a miscellaneous collection from the works of the most celebrated authors [Sh—, Milton . . .] Collected and published by a lady. Second edition. Ln : . . . 1724. 8°
W
Includes pieces from Sh— at pp. 118 and 178.

[Works : Ext.] Collection of the most celebrated prologues spoken at the theatres of Drury-Lane and Lincolns-Inn. By a young lady. Second edition. Ln : . . . 1728. 8°
W
Some of the prologues are Shakespearean.

[Works : Ext.] Beauties of the English stage, consisting of all the celebrated passages, soliloquies, similes, descriptions, and other poetical beauties in the English plays, ancient and modern . . . digested under proper heads . . . with names of plays and . . . authors. Ln. & Scarborough : Ward & Chandler. Ln : C. Corbett at ' Addi son's head '; E. Withers at the ' Seven stars,' 1737. 2 vols. 12°. With two views of old playhouses, and plays in progress
BPL

[Works : Ext.] Hayward (Thomas) British muse, or a collection of thoughts, moral, natural, and sublime, of our English poets who flourished in the sixteenth and seventeenth centuries. With several curious topicks and beautiful passages, never before extracted, from Sh—, Johnson [sic], Beaumont, Fletcher, and above a hundred more. The whole digested alphabetically under their respective heads, according to the order of time in which they wrote, to show the gradual improvements of our poetry and language. With an historical and critical review of this and all the collections of this kind hitherto published. Ln : F. Cogan, Middle Temple Gate, Fleet Street ; J. Nourse, The Lamb, without Temple Bar, 1738. 3 vols. 12°. With titles in red and black
BUS

[Works : Ext.] Historical and poetical medley, or muses' library . . . edited by E. Cooper [i.e., Wm. Oldys]. Ln : T. Davies, 1738. 8°, pp. xvi.-400
Sh— (a notice with extracts from his poems) occupies pp. 376-380.

[Works : Ext.] Hayward (Thomas) Quintessence of English poetry. Ln : . . . 1740. 3 vols. 12°
Hayward's ' British muse, 1738,' under a fresh title.

[Works : Ext.] Britons, strike home ! or Sh—'s ghost to the British armies. Ln : 1745. F° ; broadside, engraved BM
Extracts from Sh—'s historical plays.

[Works : Ext.] Rhetoric made familiar . . . illustrated with orations from Sh— . . . 1748. 12°
BPL

[Works : Ext.] Beauties of Sh—, regularly selected from each play, with a general index digesting them under proper heads. Illustrated with explanatory notes and similar passages from ancient and modern authors. By Wm. Dodd . . . Ln : T. Waller, opposite Fetter Lane, Fleet St., 1752. 2 vols. Cr. 8°
BPL | BUS | W
First edition of a famous compilation which passed through a regiment of editions. Dodd was hung for forgery in 1770, despite many petitions for his reprieve, including one from Dr. Johnson. He was buried in an unmarked grave in the little Saxon churchyard of Cowley, Middlesex.

[Works : Ext.] Sports of the muses, or a minute's mirth for any hour of the day. Containing select . . . English and Scotch songs, ballads, tales, epigrams, riddles, bon mots . . . By Spenser, Sh—, Milton, Rochester, Dryden, Pope, Swift, Congreve . . . Ln : M. Cooper . . . 1752. 8°

[Works : Ext.] Beauties of Sh—. By Wm. Dodd. Second edition, with additions. Ln : T. Waller . . . 1757. 2 vols. Cr. 8°
BPL | CPL | W

[Works : Ext.] Falstaff's jests, or the quintessence of wit and humour, with a collection of buckish songs. Ln : . . . 1761. 12°. With frontispiece

[Works : Ext.] Falstaff's jests . . . Ln : . . . 1762. 12°

[Works : Ext.] Webb (Daniel) Remarks on the beauties of poetry. Ln : R. & J. Dodsley, 1762. 8°, pp. iv.-124 BUS
With extracts largely from Sh—.

[Works : Ext.] Miscellaneous pieces of antient English poesie, by Sh—, Marston, &c. Ln : . . . 1764. Cr. 8°, pp. iv.-234
BM | BPL | BUS | W
Includes the ' Troublesome raigne of King Iohn' (by Chris. Marlowe?).

Sh— [Works : Extracts]—

[Works : Ext.] Beauties of Sh— . . . By W. Dodd. Third edition. With additions. Dublin . . . 1773. 2 vols. 12°   BPL

[Works : Ext.] Sentimental spouter, or young actor's companion . . . Ln : Printed for J. Wheble and T. Axtell . . . 1774. 8°, pp. xx.-124. With engraved frontispiece by J. Taylor
Includes scenes from eight of Sh—'s plays.

[Works : Ext.] Beauties of the English drama [with passages from Sh—]. 1777. 4 vols. 12°   BPL

[Works : Ext.] Modern characters from Sh—, alphabetically arranged, in two parts. [By Sir H. B. & Lady Dudley.] Ln : E. Johnson, 1778. Bath : Crutwell. Bristol : Cadell. Oxford : Jackson. 2 vols. 12°   BM | BPL | SML | W
Public characters of the period [under initials] described haphazard by passages found in Sh—. In the writer's possession is a copy with a MS. key to the real names.

[Works : Ext.] Modern characters . . . Second edition. Ln : D. Brown . . . 1778. 12°, pp. 80   BUS

[Works : Ext.] Modern characters for 1778, by Sh— . . . Third edition. Ln : D. Brown . . . 1778. 12°, pp. 84 BPL | BUS

[Works : Ext.] Modern characters . . . New edition. Ln : E. Johnson . . . 1778. 12°, pp. iv.-88 BM | BPL | BUS | CPL
Reprinted in Price's Wisdom and genius (Sh— Works : Ext. 1839).

[Works : Ext.] Sh—'s history of the times, or the original portraits of that author, adapted to modern characters, with notes and observations. [By Sir H. B. & Lady Dudley ?] Ln : D. Brown & J. Murray . . . 1778. 12°, pp. iv.-76 BM | BUS | W
Differs from 'Modern characters,' though the running title is the same.

[Works : Ext.] Collection and selection of English prologues and epilogues, commencing with Sh— and concluding with Garrick. Ln : Fielding & Walker . . . 1779. 6 vols. 8°   BUS | W

[Works : Ext.] Beauties of Sh—. By William Dodd . . . Third edition, with large additions and the author's last corrections. Ln : J. Macgowan . . . 1780. 3 vols. 12° BPL | BUS | W
Contains a satirical dedication to Lord Chesterfield, cancelled in most copies.

[Works : Ext.] The St . ckt . n jubilee, or Sh— in all his glory . . . Newcastle : Printed for the managers . . . 1781. 12°
By Joseph Ritson. Contains passages from Sh— applied to the principal inhabitants of Stockton-on-Tees.

[Works : Ext.] Beauties of Sh— . . . By Wm. Dodd. Fourth edition. Ln : . . . 1782. 3 vols. 12°

[Works : Ext.] Beauties of Sh—, selected from his plays and poems. To which are added the principal scenes. Ln : Kearsley . . . 1783. 12°   BPL
A rival to Wm. Dodd's collection (which was first issued thirty-one years earlier).

[Works : Ext.] Beauties of Sh— : Selected from his plays and poems. ' He was a man, take him for all in all . . .' New [second] edition [vignette portraits of Sh— and Garrick]. Ln : G. Kearsley . . . 1783. 12°, pp. xxiv.-276
With life of the poet.

[Works : Ext.] Beauties of Sh—, selected from his plays and poems. Dublin : Printed for the company of booksellers, 1783. 12° BPL | SML | W

[Works : Ext.] Perrin (J. B.) Contes moraux . . . tires des tragedies de Sh—. 1783. Cr. 8°   BPL

[Works : Ext.] Picturesque beauties of Sh—, being a selection of scenes from the works of that . . . author. Engraved under the direction of C. Taylor [from drawings by R. Smirke and T. Stothard. Forty plates.] Ln : C. Taylor, 1783-87. 4°. With 40 plates   BM | BPL

[Works : Ext.] Beauties of Sh— . . . Third edition. Corrected, revised, and enlarged. Ln : G. Kearsley . . . 1784. 12°, pp. ii.-viii.-342, and vignette portrait BUS | SML
Not by Dodd.

[Works : Ext.] Enfield (W.) The speaker. 1785. 8°   BPL
Contains selections from Sh—.

[Works : Ext.] Concordance to Sh— : suited to all the editions ; in which the distinguished and parallel passages in the plays . . . are methodically arranged. To which are added three hundred notes and illustrations, entirely new. [By Andrew Becket.] Ln : G. G. J. & J. Robinson . . . 1787. 8°, pp. viii.-470   BM | BPL | BUS | MPL | SML
First edition of the earliest concordance to Sh—.

[Works : Ext.] Ayscough (Samuel) Index to the remarkable passages and words made use of by Sh—, calculated to point out the different meanings to which the words are applied. Ln : J. Stockdale, 1790. Roy. 8°, pp. 672   BUS | MPL | SML | W
First edition.

[Works : Ext.] Beauties of Sh— ; selected from his works. Fifth edition, corrected, revised, and enlarged. Ln : C. & G. Kearsley . . . [c. 1790]. 12°, pp. xii.-394, and frontispiece engraved on copper BUS
Not by Dodd.

Sh— [Works : Extracts]—

[Works : Ext.] Lives and traits of the bon ton theatricals. Number one. To be continued weekly. Printed for the authors, 1790. 8°   w
With numerous quotations from Sh—.

[Works : Ext.] Ayscough (S.) Index to remarkable passages and words made use of by Sh— . . . Dublin : Wm. Jones . . . 1791. 8°   CPL | MPL

[Works : Ext.] Typographical sketches by Wm. Sh—. Number 1 to 4. Ln : [c. 1791]. 4°; broadside, done in two sizes of type   BUS
Quotations applied to master printers of the 1791 period, with a satirical handbill offering £105 reward for the discovery of the author.

[Works : Ext.] Enfield (Wm.) The speaker, or miscellaneous pieces selected from the best English writers and disposed under proper heads . . . Ln : J. Johnson, St. Paul's Churchyard, 1792. Cr. 8°, pp. lx.-436
Contains thirty-eight pieces from Sh—.

[Works : Ext.] Select collection of the beauties of Sh— [by John Croft], with some account, &c. of the life of Sh— [by N. Rowe]. York . . . 1792. 8°, pp. 38   BM | W

[Works : Ext.] Beauties of ancient poetry; intended as a companion to the 'Beauties of English poetry.' Ln : . . . 1794. 12°   W
Contains extracts from Sh—.

[Works : Ext.] Collection of much-esteemed dramatic pieces as performed at the Theatres Royal, Drury Lane and Covent Garden, containing . . . The tempest . . . King Henry V., All's well . . . Ln : J. Debrett . . . 1795. 2 vols. 8°

[Works : Ext.] Poetical preceptor, or a collection of select pieces of poetry; extracted from the works of the most eminent English poets [including Sh—]. Fifth edition. Ln : . . . 1796. 8°   w

[Works : Ext.] Beauties of Sh—. Selected from his works. To which are added the principal scenes in the same author. Sixth edition, corrected, revised, and enlarged [*vignette portraits of the poet and Garrick*]. Ln : G. Kearsley, F. & C. Rivington, J. Walker, J. Scatcherd, Lackington, Allen & Co., Hamilton & Co., Lee & Hurst [c. 1798]. 12°, pp. xii.-394   BM | BPL
With two copperplates, including one of the ghost scene in 'Hamlet' (p. 295).

[Works : Ext.] Reader or reciter, to which are added instructions for reading plays on a plan never before attempted. Ln : . . . 1799. 8°   w
Contains extracts from 'Hamlet,' 'Julius Cæsar,' 'King Henry IV.,' and the 'Merchant of Venice.'

Sh— [Works : Extracts]—

[Works : Ext.] Beauties of Sh—. Seventh edition. Ln : . . . [c. 1800]. 12° BPL | MPL

[Works : Ext.] Dramatic songs to all Sh—'s dramas. Selected and composed by W. Linley. [With music from the works of Purcell, Fielding. c. 1800.] 2 vols. F°   BPL

[Works : Ext.] Poems on various subjects . . . with a. view to comprise . . . the beauties of English poetry by Thomas Tomkins. Ln : Pr. for J. Wallis at Yorick's Head by J. Crowder, 1800. 12°, p. viii.-208
At p. 202, Wolsey's lamentation from 'King Henry VIII.'

[Works : Ext.] Sh—'s ghost, by ' H.' Ln : L. Hansard [1803]. F°; broadside BM
Extracts from Sh— applied to the threatened Napoleonic invasion.

[Works : Ext.] Tomkins (Thomas) Poems on various subjects; selected to comprise in one volume the beauties of English poetry. Eleventh edition. Ln : . . . 1803. 12°   w

[Works : Ext.] Beauties of Sh— selected . . . by Alexander Campbell. Ln : Tegg & Castleman, 1804. 12°, pp. ii.-238, and plate   BUS | SML

[Works : Ext.] Lady's preceptor, or exercises in reading. Ln : G. & J. Robinson, 1804. 12°   SML
With selections from Sh—.

[Works : Ext.] Beauties of Sh— . . . Paris . . . 1805. 2 vols. 12°

[Works : Ext.] Twiss (Francis) Complete verbal index to the plays of Sh—, adapted to all the editions. Comprehending every substantive, etc. used by Sh—; with a distinct reference to every passage. Ln : T. Bensley & T. Egerton, 1805. 2 vols. 8°   BM | BPL | BUS | MPL | SML | W
' Of 750 copies printed, 542 were destroyed by a fire at Bensley's in 1807.'—*Thimm*.

[Works : Ext.] The cabinet, containing the select beauties of Addison, Gray, Sh—, etc. Coventry . . . 1806. 18°; illustrated

[Works : Ext.] Ayscough (S.) Index to Sh— . . . Ln : . . . 1807. Roy. 8°

[Works : Ext.] Tales from Sh—, designed for the use of young persons by Charles [and Mary Ann] Lamb. Ln : Thomas Hodgkins, 1807. 2 vols. 12°. With twenty illustrations designed by W. Mulready and engraved by W. Blake
The fact of Lamb's sister having assisted in the compilation was disclosed in a copyright action brought by Baldwin & Co against Charles Tilt for infringement. First edition of a compilation which did, perhaps, more to popularise Sh—, especially with children, than any other.

Sh— [Works : Extracts]—

[Works : Ext.] Beauties of Sh—. Stereotype edition . . . 1810. 12°   BPL

[Works : Ext.] Tales from Sh—, by C. & M. A. Lamb. 2nd edition. Ln : . . . 1810. 2 vols. 12°. Plates by Mulready & Blake   MPL

[Works : Ext.] Beauties of Sh— . . . By Wm. Dodd. Chiswick . . . 1811. 16°   SML

[Works : Ext.] Beauties of Sh— [By Wm. Dodd.] With life . . . Stereotype edition. Ln : A. Wilson, 1811. Cr. 8°, pp. viii.-392   BPL
The 'life' says Sh— had 'three daughters,' but omits to mention his son Hamnet.

[Works : Ext.] Aphorisms from Sh—. Arranged according to his plays. With preface, notes, numerical references . . . and index. [By Capell Lofft.] Bury . . . Ln : Longman, 1812. 12°, pp. xxxiv.-456-xxxvi. With portrait   BM | BPL | BUS | CPL
The first piece of Sh— printed at Bury.

[Works : Ext.] Beauties of Sh— . . . Stereotype edition. Ln : A. Wilson . . . 1812. 12°
Not Dodd's.

[Works : Ext.] Tales from Sh— . . . by C. & M. A. Lamb. Third edition. Ln : M. J. Godwin & Co. . . . 1816. 2 vols. 12°. Illustrated   BPL | BUS

[Works : Ext.] Beauties of Sh—, regularly selected from each play. With a general index digesting them under proper heads. By . . . Wm. Dodd. Ln : Printed for J. Walker [and others named] by S. Hamilton, Weybridge, 1818. 12°. pp. xii.-408. With engraved title and front. of 'Falstaff in the clothes basket,' after T. Stothard

[Works : Ext.] Beauties of Sh— . . . By W. Dodd. (With remarks on the life and writings of Sh— by J. Britton.) Ln : Sherwood, Neely and Jones . . . 1818. 12°, pp. xliv.-378-xviii.   BM | BPL | BUS | SML

[Works : Ext.] Beauties of Sh— and Sterne. Ln : . . . 1819. 2 vols. 12°

[Works : Ext.] Beauties of Sh— . . . With a general index. By W. Dodd. Ln : J. F. Dove . . . [c. 1820]. 12°, pp. 378, and 2 plates   BPL

[Works : Ext.] Beauties of Sh—. By W. Dodd. Chiswick : C. Whittingham, 1821. 12°, pp. x.-354-18. Illustrated   BPL | BUS

[Works : Ext.] Sh—'s genius . . . Vienna : C. Armbruster . . . 1821. 2 vols. 16°. With portrait and vignettes   BUS | SML
Quotations from the plays, with a biography taken from Voss's Leipzig edition of the works of 1818.

Sh— [Works : Extracts]—

[Works : Ext.] Harp of parnassus : A new selection of classical English poetry [including Sh—] . . . by J. F. Pennie. Ln : G. & W. B. Whittaker . . . 1822. 12°, pp. viii.-404

[Works : Ext.] Macauley (E. W.) Tales of the drama, founded on the tragedies of Sh—, Massinger, Shirley, Rowe, Murphy, Lillo and Moore, and on the comedies of Steele, Farquhar, Cumberland, Bickerstaff, Goldsmith, and Mrs. Cowley. Chiswick : C. Whittingham, 1822. Cr. 8°, pp. xii.-424. Illustrated   BM | BPL | BUS

[Works : Ext.] Tales from Sh— . . . by C. & M. A. Lamb. Fourth edition. Ln : Godwin & Co. . . . 1822. 2 vols. 12°. Plates by W. Mulready & Wm. Blake   CPL

[Works : Ext.] Beauties of Sh—, selected from each play by Wm. Dodd. Ln : Sherwin & Co. . . . 1823. 12°   MPL | SML

[Works : Ext.] Beauties of Sh— . . . By W. Dodd. Ln : Baynes . . . 1824. 12°, pp. 336. Illustrated   BUS | SML

[Works : Ext.] Beauties of Sh—. By W. Dodd. Ln : J. Bumpus . . . 1824. 12°   BPL

[Works : Ext.] Beauties of Sh—. By W. Dodd. Ln : C. & J. Rivington . . . 1824. 24°, pp. xii.-408   BM | SML

[Works : Ext.] Dictionary of quotations from the British poets, part I., Sh—. Ln : G. & W. B Whittaker, 1824. 12°, pp. xx.-276-xxiv.   BM | BPL | BUS

[Works : Ext.] Sh—'s romances : King Henry the fourth. Collected and arranged by 'Shakspeare II.' Ln : Sherwood . . . 1825. 2 vols. 12°   BPL
No more published.

[Works : Ext.] Beauties of Sh— . . . By . . . W. Dodd. 'Whittingham's cabinet library.' Ln : T. Tegg . . . 1825. 16°, pp. x.-354-xviii. With woodcuts   BM | BPL | BUS

[Works : Ext.] Ayscough (S.) Index to Sh— . . . Second edition, revised and enlarged. Ln : T. Tegg . . . 1827. Roy. 8°, pp. 674   BPL | BUS | W

[Works : Ext.] Beauties of Sh— . . . By W. Dodd. Boston [U.S.] : T. Bedlington . . . 1827. 12°, pp. 346. Illustrated   BUS

[Works : Ext.] Beauties of Sh— . . . By W. Dodd. Ln : . . . 1827. 16°   CPL

[Works : Ext.] King Henry the fourth and his times : being the first of a series of romances from Sh— . . . 1827. 2 vols. 12°   BPL
No more published. First issued in 1825 under a rather different title.

Sh— [Works : Extracts]—

[Works : Ext.] Riley (A.) Analysis of poetry
. . . 1827. 12° BPL
Contains quotations from Sh—.

[Works : Ext.] Select specimens of English
poetry from the reign of Elizabeth . . .
With introduction by George Walker.
Ln : Longman . . . 1827. Cr. 8°, pp. xxxii.-
620
Sh—, pp. 56-230.

[Works : Ext.] Howard. Spirit of the plays
of Sh—. 1827-33. See Howard

[Works : Ext.] Juvenile edition of Sh—,
adapted to the capacities of youth.
Edited by Caroline Maxwell. Ln : C.
Chapple . . . 1828. 12°, pp. vi.-360
Extracts, with connecting prose passages. BUS | SML

[Works : Ext.] Selections from Sh—'s plays,
by Benjamin Oakley. Ln : Longman . . .
1828. 8°, pp. xxiv.-182 BUS | SML
'If learning were to suffer a general shipwreck and I
had choice of preserving one author only, who should
I preserve? I answer, Sh—.' - B. Oakley.

[Works : Ext.] Falstaff : A comedy, formed
out of Sh—'s ' King Henry the fourth '
and ' King Henry the fifth.' 1829. 12°
BPL

[Works : Ext.] Beauties of Sh—, selected
from the most correct editions of his
works. Ln : Sainsbury . . . 1830. 12°,
pp. viii.-194 BM | BPL
The original edition appeared in 1783.

[Works : Ext.] Dramatic tales from Sh—.
Edited by J. Duncombe. [c. 1830.] 12°
BPL

[Works : Ext.] Shakesperian anthology,
comprising the choicest passages and
entire scenes . . . with a biographical
sketch. Ln : Sainsbury . . . 1830. 12°,
pp. xii.-392
BM | BPL | BUS | MPL | SML | W

[Works : Ext.] Beauties of Sh—. By W.
Dodd. Ln : J. Smith & Co. . . . 1831.
Cr. 8° BPL | CPL

[Works : Ext.] Tales from Sh— . . . by C.
[& M. A.] Lamb. Fifth edition. Ornamented with engravings from designs by
W. Harvey. Ln : Baldwin & Cradock,
1831. Cr. 8°, pp. viii.-376

[Works : Ext.] Dolby (Thomas) Shakespearian dictionary ; forming a general
index to all the popular expressions and
most striking passages in the works of
Sh— from a few words to fifty or more
lines : an appropriate synonym being
affixed to each extract, with a reference
to the context. The whole designed to
introduce the beauties of Sh— into the

Sh— [Works : Extracts]—

familiar intercourse of society. Ln :
Smith, 1832. Cr. 8°, pp. viii.-368, and
Droeshout portrait
BM | BPL | BUS | MPL | SML
A few copies were done on large paper, of which one is
at Boston.

[Works : Ext.] Riddle (J. E.) Illustrations
of Aristotle on men and manners from
the dramatic works of Sh— [a compari-
son]. Oxford : Printed by S. Collingwood, 1832. Cr. 8°, pp. 134

[Works : Ext.] Dyce (Alexander) Specimens
of English sonnets, selected . . . Ln : Wm.
Pickering . . . 1833. Fcp. 4°, pp. viii.-224
Selections from Sh—'s sonnets fill pp. 53-90.

[Works : Ext.] Extracts and collections from
various authors [including Sh—]. Dorchester . . . 1834. 8° BUS

[Works : Ext.] Beauties of Sh— . . . By W.
Dodd. Baltimore : W. H. Hickman . . .
1835. 12°, pp. 378 BUS

[Works : Ext.] Beauties of Sh—. By W.
Dodd. Ln : C. Daly . . . 1835. 16°, pp.
iv.-380. With frontispiece and vignette
title BPL

[Works : Ext.] Dictionary of quotations
from Sh—. Second edition, improved.
Ln : . . . 1835. 12°

[Works : Ext.] Musterstücke aus Sh—'s
dramen. Englisch und Deutsch. The
beauties of Sh— [edited by C. P. Berly].
Frankfurt-am-Main : J. D. Sauerländer
. . . 1835. 2 vols. 12° BM

[Works : Ext.] Sh— romances, collected and
arranged by ' Sh— the second.' Ln :
1835. 2 vols. Cr. 8°

[Works : Ext.] Heath (Charles) Sh— gallery,
containing the principal female characters
in the plays of that great poet engraved
. . . from drawings by the first artists
[with passages . . . opposite each print].
Ln : C. Tilt . . . 1836-37. 4°, pp. 94, and
45 plates BM | BPL | BUS
Also issued with the plates coloured, and further as
India proofs before letters.

[Works : Ext.] Streams of knowledge from
the fountains of wisdom . . . choice extracts culled from . . . Sh— and the wisest
men since . . . King Solomon. Part 2.
Ln : W. Kidd [c. 1836]. 12°, pp. 36 BUS

[Works : Ext.] Vier schauspiele von Sh—
. . . Eduard der dritte ; Leben und tod
des Thomas Cromwell ; Sir John Oldcastle ; Der Londoner verlorne sohn . . .
uebersetzt von L. Tieck. Stuttgart und
Tubingen . . . 1836. 8°, pp. 366 BM

[Works : Ext.] Beauties of Sh—. By W.
Dodd. Ln : F. J. Mason . . . 1837. 12°
BPL

(565)

Sh— [Works : Extracts]—

[Works : Ext.] Selections . . . by . . . Slater. [Ln. ?] : C. H. Law . . . 1837. 12°

[Works : Ext.] Watson (J. T.) Dictionary of poetical quotations, consisting of elegant extracts on every subject compiled from various authors and arranged . . . Philadelphia . . . 1837. 8°

[Works : Ext.] Beauties of Sh—. Frankfurt & Ln : Schloss . . . 1838. 2 vols. 12°   BM
In English and German.

[Works : Ext.] Price (Thomas) Wisdom and genius of Sh—, comprising moral philosophy, delineations of character, paintings of nature and the passions, and miscellaneous pieces . . . With . . . notes and scriptural references . . . By Thomas Price. Ln : Scott, Webster & Geary . . . 1838. 12°, pp. x.-462   BM | CPL | W

[Works : Ext.] Tales from Sh—. By Mr. & Miss Lamb. Ornamented with engravings, from designs by Wm. Harvey. Ln : Baldwin & Cradock, 1838. 8°, pp. viii.-376, and portrait of Sh—   BUS

[Works : Ext.] Tayler (C.) Art of composing Greek iambics. 1838. 12°   BPL
With quotations from Sh—.

[Works : Ext.] Beauties of Sh— . . . By Wm. Dodd. Ln : Scott & Webster . . . 1839. 8°. With 21 engravings

[Works : Ext.] Price (Thomas) Wisdom and genius of Sh— . . . Philadelphia : E. L. Carey & A. Hart . . . 1839. 8°, pp. viii.-460   BM | BUS

[Works : Ext.] Smart (B. H.) Shaksperian readings, selected and adapted for young persons and others . . . First series, illustrative of English and Roman history. Ln : J. Richardson . . . 1839. 12°, pp. xxiv.-454, and plate   BM | BUS | SML

[Works : Ext.] Tales from Sh— . . . by C. & M. A. Lamb. Ln : Baldwin & Co. . . . 1839. 12°

[Works : Ext.] Tales from Sh— . . . by C. & M. A. Lamb. Ln : Bohn . . . 1840. 12°

[Works : Ext.] Tales from Sh— . . . By C. Lamb. Ln : E. Moxon, 1840. Cr. 8°, pp. iv.-104   BUS

[Works : Ext.] Beauties of Sh—, selected by Wm. Dodd. With twenty-one illustrations [on steel]. Ln : Scott, Webster & Geary, 1841. Cr. 8°, pp. xxii.-378 BPL
Contains an essay on the 'life and writings of Sh—,' pp. iv.-xxii.

The drawings are by Wright, Stephanoff, Corbould and Westall, and engraved by Heath, Rolls, Bacon, Greatbach, Engleheart, Chevalier and F. J. Portbury.

Sh— [Works : Extracts]—

[Works : Ext.] Rankin (Michael Henry) Philosophy of Sh—, extracted from his plays and interspersed with remarks. Ln : Whittaker & Co. . . . 1841. Cr. 8°, pp. xvi.-238   BM | BPL | BUS | CPL

[Works : Ext.] Seymour (Robert) New readings of old authors : Sh—. Ln : Tilt & Bogue . . . [1841]. 25 parts. 12°; each with ten plates   BPL | BUS
Humorous sketches illustrating passages from the poet.

[Works : Ext.] Smart (B. H.) Shakspearian readings, embodying the most interesting parts of English & Roman history. Ln : Rivington . . 1841. 12°, pp. xxiv.-454, and plate   BUS | SML

[Works : Ext.] Ayscough. Index to Sh—. Ln : Tegg . . . 1842. 8°

[Works : Ext.] Beauties of Sh—. By W. Dodd . . . 1842. 12°   BPL

[Works : Ext.] Sargent (G. F.) Sh— illustrated, in a series of landscape and architectural designs. With notices of the several localities from various authors. Ln : How & Parsons . . . 1842. Roy. 8°; 45 plates   BPL | CPL | SML
Republished in the same author's ' Book of Sh— gems.' Contains selections from the plays bearing upon the scenes portrayed.

[Works : Ext.] Sh— treasury of subject quotations arranged synonymously. Ln : Hodson & Son . . . 1842. 12°   SML

[Works : Ext.] Smart (B. H.) Shakspearian readings . . . intended also as exercises in elocution . . . Ln : J. G. & F. Rivington . . . 1842. 12°, pp. xxiv.-454, and plate   BM | BPL | BUS | CPL

[Works : Ext.] Dictionary of quotations from Sh— [by C. J. Walbran]. Ln : Simpkin . . . 1843. 12°

[Works : Ext.] Dictionary of quotations from Sh—. Second edition [by C. J. Walbran]. Ln : H. G. Bohn . . . 1843. 12°, pp. xii.-298   BM | BUS

[Works : Ext.] Religious and moral sentences culled from . . . Sh— compared with . . . holy writ, being . . . religious sentiments and moral precepts . . . [by Sir Fredk. Beilby Watson]. Ln : Calkin & Budd . . . 1843. 8°, pp. 224, and Jansen portrait BM | BPL | BUS | CPL | SML | W
Compiled to prove Sh— not a Papist, but a member of the Church of England.

[Works : Ext.] Smart (B. H.) Shakspearian readings . . . New edition. Ln : . . . 1843. 12°

[Works : Ext.] Tales from Sh— . . . by C. & M. A. Lamb. 7th edition. Ln : H. G. Bohn . . . 1843. 12°, pp. viii.-376, with portrait and plates by Harvey   BUS

Sh— [Works : Extracts]—

[Works : Ext.] Tales from Sh— ... By C. & M. A. Lamb. Stuttgart ... 1843. 16°

[Works : Ext.] Hunt (J. H. Leigh) Imagination and fancy, or selections from the English poets. Ln : Smith, 1844. 8°
In the chapter headed 'What is poetry?' Hunt says :— 'It is to be doubted whether even Sh— could have told a story like Homer, owing to that incessant activity and superfœtation of thought, a little less of which might be occasionally desired even in his plays, if it were possible, once possessing anything of his, to wish it away.'

[Works : Ext.] Tales from Sh—, by C. & M. Lamb. With ... memoir of C. Lamb ... by J. W. D——. Ln : Joseph Smith, 1844. 12°, pp. xxxii.-328. Illustrated by R. Cruikshank

[Works : Ext.] Tales from Sh— ... by C. & M. A. Lamb. Ln : Knight & Co. ... 1844. 2 vols. 12°   BPL | SML

[Works : Ext.] Beauties of Sh— ... By W. Dodd. Ln : Washbourne ... 1845. 18°

[Works : Ext.] Clarke (Mary Cowden) Complete concordance to Sh—. Ln : C. Knight ... 1845. Roy. 8°   BM | BPL
Issued for the first time in 1844-45, serially in eighteen parts.

[Works : Ext.] Complete Shakesperian reciter. Birmingham ... [c. 1845]. 12°
                                                          BPL

[Works : Ext.] Garland for the New Royal Exchange, composed of the pieces of divers excellent poets made in memory of the first opening thereof in 1571, with the choice verses and devices of sundry fine wits of later time, etc., now first collected and printed complete Ln : J. D. White, 1845. Fcp. 4°
Issue limited to 50 copies.
Includes pieces by Sh—, Churchyard, Jonson, Puttenham, Sidney, and Spenser.

[Works : Ext.] Merry tales from Sh-—. Ln : Routledge ... 1845. 12°   BPL

[Works : Ext.] Selections ... by ... Howell. Ln : Burns & Oates ... 1845. 12°

[Works : Ext.] Beauties of Sh—. By W. Dodd. New edition. Halifax ... 1846. 12°   BPL

[Works : Ext.] Book of Sh— gems. [Ed. by G. F. Sargent.] Ln : H. G. Bohn ... 1846. 8°, 45 plates   BUS
With quotations from the poet.

[Works : Ext.] Clarke (M. C.) Complete concordance to Sh—, being a verbal index to all the passages in the dramatic works ... New York : Wiley & Putnam, 1846. Roy. 8°, pp. viii.-860   BUS

[Works : Ext.] Flowers of Sh—. With appropriate quotations. [Coloured plates by I. E. Giraud.] Ln : ... [1846]. F°; ff. 30, on thick plate paper   BM | SML

Sh— [Works : Extracts]—

[Works : Ext] Hunt (J. H. L.) Imagination and fancy ... 3rd ed. Ln : ... 1846. 8°
Sh— fills pp. 149-194.   BUS

[Works : Ext.] Tales from Sh—. By C. & M. Lamb. Leipzig ... 1846. Cr. 8°

[Works : Ext.] Tales from Sh—. By Mr. and Miss Lamb ... To which are now added scenes illustrating each tale. Ln : C. Knight & Co. ... 1846. 2 vols. Cr. 8°
                                                          BUS

[Works : Ext.] Clarke (M. C.) Complete concordance to Sh—. [2nd English ed.] Ln : Knight ... 1847. Roy. 8°
                                            BM | BUS | SML

[Works : Ext.] Clarke (M. C.) Sh— proverbs, or the wise saws of our wisest poet, altered into modern instances. Ln : Chapman & Hall ... 1847. 16°

[Works : Ext.] Religious and moral sentences from ... Sh— ... compared with passages of holy writ. [By Sir F. B. Watson.] 2nd ed. Ln : Hatchard, 1847. 8°, pp. xx.-224, and portraits
                                            BPL | BUS | MPL

[Works : Ext.] Sh— for schools : Passages selected by a clergyman ... [C. Lenny]. Ln : Relfe ... 1847. 12°   BPL | SML

[Works : Ext.] Watson (J. T.) Poetical quotations ... With illustrations. Philadelphia ... 1847. Roy. 8°. With 9 steel plates

[Works : Ext.] Clarke (M. C.) Concordance ... Ln : Kent ... 1848. Roy. 8°

[Works : Ext.] Clarke (M. C.) Sh— proverbs collected ... Ln : Chapman & Hall ... 1848. 16°, pp. 144
                        BM | BPL | CPL | MPL | SML

[Works : Ext.[Clarke (M. C.) Sh— proverbs ... New York : Wiley & Putnam, 1848. Cr. 8°, pp. ii.-144   BUS

[Works : Ext.] Macauley (E. W.) Tales of the drama. Hartford [U.S.], 1848. Cr. 8°   BPL

[Works : Ext.] Readings from the plays of Sh— in illustration of his characters. Edited by the author of 'Aids to developement.' Ln : J. W. Parker ... 1848. 16°, pp. viii.-434   BM | BPL | BUS

[Works : Ext.] Selections from the English poets : Sh—, Pope, etc., rendered into Latin verse. Thirty-seventh edition. Lewes : Privately printed, 1848. 12° w
The editor evidently penned a transatlantic kind of joke when he mentioned the 'thirty-seventh edition.'

[Works : Ext.] Tales from Sh— ... by C. & M. A. Lamb. Ln : Tilt's miniature classical library, 1848. 2 vols. 12°   BPL

[Works : Ext.] Beauties of Sh— ... by W. Dodd. Ln : Moxon ... 1849. 24°

Sh— [Works : Extracts]—

[Works : Ext.] Clarke (M. C.) Sh— proverbs, or wise saws . . . Ln : Chapman & Hall . . . 1849. 16°

[Works : Ext.] Sh— and Milton for schools. Ln : Relfe . . . 1849. 12°   SML

[Works : Ext.] Sh— calendar . . . New York . . . 1849. 18°

[Works : Ext.] Tales from Sh— . . . by C. & M. A. Lamb. Ln : Bohn . . . 1849. 12°. Illustrated by W. Harvey

[Works : Ext.] Walbran (C. J.) Dictionary of Sh— quotations, being a collection of the maxims, proverbs, and most remarkable passages . . . arranged in alphabetical order. Ln : Simpkin . . . 1849. Cr. 8°, pp. iv.-218   BM | BPL | BUS

[Works : Ext.] Sh— almanack [edited by J. W. Lethbridge]. Ln : D. Bogue . . . 1849-50. 2 vols. 12°   BPL | CPL

[Works : Ext.] Concordance to select quotations from the plays of Sh—, alphabetically arranged with full references . . . Ln : Simpkin . . . [1850]. Nos. 1 and 2. 12°   BM
No more appear to have been issued.

[Works : Ext.] Graves (Joseph) Dramatic tales founded on Sh—'s plays. [c. 1850.] 116 numbers. 16°   BM

[Works : Ext.] Humphreys (E. R.) Lyra Latina. Edinburgh . . . 1850. 8°   BPL
With appendix containing passages from Sh—.

[Works : Ext.] Life and beauties of Sh— . . . by W. Dodd. Boston [U.S.] : Phillips & Co., 1850. 12°, pp. lx -x -346, and portrait   BPL | BUS

[Works : Ext.] Moral sentences and sentiments from Sh— compared with holy writ [by Sir F. B. Watson]. Ln : Hatchard . . . [1850]. 8°. With portrait, two engravings, and ornamental borders   BPL
First issued in 1843.

[Works : Ext.] Richards (Wm. C.) Sh— calendar, or wit and wisdom for every day in the year. New York : G. P. Putnam . . . 1850. 16°, pp. 118   BM | BPL | BUS

[Works : Ext.] Sh— almanack . . . Ln : Bogue . . . 1850. 18°

[Works : Ext.] Shakespearian readings : Shakespearian number of the 'Town and country reciter.' [1850 ?]. 4° BPL

[Works : Ext.] Translations from Sh—. English and Greek. Porson prize essay. Cambridge : Grant . . . 1850. 12°   SML

[Works : Ext.] Beauties of Sh— . . . by W. Dodd. Ln : . . . 1851. 12°

[Works : Ext.] Dolby (T.) Dictionary of Shakespearian quotations. Philadelphia . . . 1851. 12°   BPL

Sh— [Works : Extracts]—

[Works : Ext.] Humphreys (H. N.) Sentiments and similes of Wm. Sh— . . . A classified selection of similes, definitions, descriptions, and other remarkable passages in the plays and poems . . . Ln : Longman . . . 1851. Fcp. 4°, pp. vi.-100. With decorated borders in gold and colours   BM | BPL | BUS

[Works : Ext.] Lyndon (Charlotte) Apophthegms from the plays of Sh—. Ln : Simpkin . . . [1851]. Cr. 8°, pp. vi.-236   BM | BPL

[Works : Ext.] Sh— for schools : Passages selected . . . [by C. Lenny]. Ln : . . . 1851. 12°

[Works : Ext.] Smart (B. H.) Shakespearian readings . . . Ln : Rivington . . . 1851. 12°

[Works : Ext.] Tales from Sh—. By Lamb. Ornamented with engravings . . . by W. Harvey. Ln : H. G. Bohn . . . 1851. Cr. 8°, pp. viii.-376, and portrait   BUS

[Works : Ext.] Tales from Sh— . . . by C. & M. A. Lamb. Ln : Tegg & Co., 1851. Cr. 8°   BPL

[Works : Ext.] Beauties of Sh—. Ln : Clarke, Beeton & Co. [1853]. 16°, pp. 220   BM | BPL

[Works : Ext.] Beauties of Sh—, by W. Dodd. Ln : E. Law . . . 1853. 12°

[Works : Ext.] Beauties of Sh—, by W. Dodd. Ln : Washbourne . . . 1853. 12°

[Works : Ext.] Dolby (T.) Dictionary of Shakespearian quotations . . . Philadelphia : F. Bell, 1853. 12°, pp. xii.-418   BUS

[Works : Ext.] Price (T.) Wisdom and genius of Sh— . . . with . . . notes and scriptural references . . . Second edition, enlarged. Ln : A. Scott . . . 1853. 8°, pp. xvi.-576   BM | BUS
First published in 1838.

[Works : Ext.] Select scenes from Sh—. Ln : Clarke, Beeton & Co. [1853]. 16°, pp. iv.-204   BM

[Works : Ext.] Sh— character cards, providing an intellectual and withal a merry game for the social circle. Ln : . . . Mead & Powell [1853]. 12°   BM | BUS

[Works : Ext.] Sh— laconics : A selection of pithy sentences . . . designed as a manual of reference . . . Philadelphia : C. G. Henderson . . . 1853. 12°, pp. 288 BUS

[Works : Ext.] Tales from Sh— . . . by C. & M. A. Lamb. Ln : Bohn . . . 1853. 12°. Illustrated by W. Harvey

[Works : Ext.] Truths illustrated by great authors : A dictionary of nearly four thousand aids to reflection, maxims, metaphors, counsels, cautions, aphorisms, proverbs, in prose and verse, compiled from Sh— and other great writers. Second edition. Ln : W. White . . . 1853. 8°

[Works : Ext.] Beauties of Sh— [by W. Dodd]. Ln : E. Moxon . . . 1854. 8°, pp. xii.-372   BM | CPL

[Works : Ext.] Beauties of Sh— . . . By W. Dodd. Ln : Washbourne . . . 1854. Cr. 8°, pp. 380   BUS | SML

[Works : Ext.] Gems from Sh—. Ln : Clarke, Beeton & Co. [1854]. 16°, pp. 204   BM

[Works : Ext.] Passages from Sh— to be committed to memory. Ln : Relfe . . . 1854. 12°

[Works : Ext.] Poetical quotations . . . edited by John T. Watson. Philadelphia . . 1854. 12°   BUS

[Works : Ext.] Sargent (G. F.) Book of Sh— gems . . . landscape illustrations of the most interesting localities of Sh—'s dramas, with historical and descriptive accounts by W. Irving, E. Jesse, W. Howitt, C. Wordsworth, and others. Ln : H. G. Bohn . . . 1854. 8°. 45 steel plates   CPL

[Works : Ext.] Clarke (M. C.) Complete concordance to Sh—. New edition. Ln : Kent [1855]. Roy. 8°, pp. viii.-860   BM | BPL | BUS

[Works : Ext.] Hows (John W. S.) Shakespearean reader : A collection of the most approved plays . . . carefully revised with introductory and explanatory notes and a memoir of the author. Prepared expressly for the use of classes and the family reading circle. New York : D. Appleton & Co. . . . 1855. 12°, pp. xvi.-448   BUS

[Works : Ext.] Shakesperian tableaux. [Selections, with coloured illustrations, 1855]. 8°   BM

[Works : Ext.] Songs from the dramatists, edited by Robert Bell. Ln : J. W. Parker . . . 1855. 12°, pp. xii.-268   MPL

[Works : Ext.] Stephens (George) Sh— story teller, with extracts in the words of the poet and analysis of the characters. Copenhagen : C. G. Iversen. Ln : J. R. Smith . . . 1855-56. 6 parts, forming 1 vol. 8°   BM | BUS | SML

[Works : Ext.] Clarke (M. C.) Concordance to Sh— : being a verbal index to all the passages in the dramatic works of the poet. New and revised edition. 1856. 8°   MPL

[Works : Ext.] Dolby (Thomas) A thousand Shakesperian mottoes, selected and arranged for instant reference and application. Ln : H. Dolby . . . [1856]. 32°, pp. viii.-96   BUS

[Works : Ext.] Humphreys (H. N.) Sh—'s sentiments and similes. Ln : . . . 1856. Cr. 8° ; illuminated in gold and colours

[Works : Ext.] Gems from Sh—; Beauties of Sh—; Scenes from Sh—. Ln : Clarke, Beeton & Co. [c. 1856]. 12°   BPL

[Works : Ext.] Beauties of Sh—, compiled by Carl Peter Berly. Francfort-on-Main . . . 1857. 2 vols. 32°   BUS
Text in English and German.

[Works : Ext.] Beauties of Sh— . . . By W. Dodd. Ln : . . . 1857. 12°

[Works : Ext.] Beauties of Sh—. A lecture, by John R. Wise. Ln : Whittaker . . . [1857]. 8°   BM

[Works : Ext.] Humphreys (H. N.) Sentiments and similes. Second edition. Ln : . . . 1857. Cr. 8°   BPL | CPL

[Works : Ext.] Philosophy of Wm. Sh—, delineating, in seven hundred and fifty passages, selected from his plays, the multiform phases of the human mind [by M. H. Rankin]. Ln : W. White . . . 1857. 8°, pp. lii.-644. With engraved title   BM | BUS | CPL | SML
A few were done on large paper.

[Works : Ext.] Tales from Sh— . . . By C. & M. A. Lamb. Ln : Bohn . . . 1857. 12°. Illustrated by W. Harvey

[Works : Ext.] Price (Thomas) Wisdom and genius of Sh—. With notes. Ln : E. Law . . . 1858. 12°
First appeared in 1838.

[Works : Ext.] Tales from Sh— . . . By C. & M. A. Lamb. Ln : Bohn . . . 1858. 12°

[Works : Ext.] Dolby (T.) Dictionary of Sh— quotations, exhibiting the most forcible passages . . . Philadelphia : F. Bell . . . 1859. 12°, pp. xii.-418   BUS
Reprinted from the 1853 edition.

[Works : Ext.] Kean (Charles) Selections from the plays . . . Ln : Bradbury . . . 1859. 2 vols. 12°

[Works : Ext.] Religious and moral sentences culled from . . . Sh—, compared with . . . holy writ. From the English edition. With an introduction by Frederic D. Huntington, D.D. Boston & Camb. [U.S.] : Munroe . . . 1859. Cr. 8°, pp. 226, and Chandos portrait   BUS
Gives the text of a fraudulent will once exhibited at Stratford purporting that the poet was a Papist.

Sh— [Works : Extracts]—

[Works : Ext.] Sh—'s household words : A selection from the wise saws of the immortal bard. Illuminated by S. Stanesby [in gold and colours]. Ln : Griffith & Farran [1859]. 16°, pp. 28　　BM | CPL

[Works : Ext.] Beauties of Sh—, by W. Dodd. Halifax : Milner & Sowerby . . . 1860. Cr. 8°, pp. 384. Illust.　　BUS

[Works : Ext.] Beauties of Sh— . . . by W. Dodd. Ln : W. Tegg . . . 1860. Cr. 8°

[Works : Ext.] Book of familiar quotations . . . popular extracts and aphorisms from . . . the best authors. [Edited by John Bartlett.] 2nd ed. Ln : Whittaker . . . 1860. Cr. 8°, pp. viii.-242

[Works : Ext.] Choice thoughts from Sh— [edited by L. C. Gent]. Ln : Whittaker . . . 1860. 12°

[Works : Ext.] Heath (Charles) Heroines of Sh— . . . with letterpress extracts in English and French and critical essays . . . Ln. Printing and Publishing Co. [c. 1860]. F°, pp. 168 [unpaged] and 49 full-page plates

[Works : Ext.] Kean (Charles) Selections from the plays of Sh— . . . as arranged for representation at the Princess's Theatre . . . Ln : Bradbury & Evans . . . 1860. 2 vols. 8°　　BM | BUS | CPL
Contains twelve of the plays, more or less abridged.

[Works : Ext.] Morgan (A. A.) Mind of Sh—, as exhibited in his works. Ln : Chapman & Hall . . . 1860. Cr. 8°, pp. xxiv.-322　　BM | BPL | BUS | CPL

[Works : Ext.] Pearls of Sh— ; A collection of the most brilliant passages found in his plays. Illustrated by Kenny Meadows. Ln : Cassell . . . 1860. 12°, pp. viii.-160. With 48 woodcuts　　BM | BUS | CPL | SML

[Works : Ext.] Philosophy of Wm. Sh— . . . in 750 passages . . . Ln : Lockwood & Co. . . . 1860. Cr. 8°

[Works : Ext.] Readings and recitations from Sh—. Glasgow : J. Cameron, 1860. Cr. 8°　　BPL

[Works : Ext.] Sh— hand-book. 1860. 12°　　BPL

[Works : Ext.] Shakespearian tales in verse. Edited by Mrs. Valentine. [c. 1860.] 4°. Illustrated　　BPL

[Works : Ext.] Shaksperiana quædam Græce tentata. 1860. 4°　　BM
In English and Greek.

[Works : Ext.] Six tales from Sh—, by C. & Miss Lamb. Altenburg : Schnuphase . . . [1860]. Cr. 8°, pp. viii.-112　　BUS

[Works : Ext.] Beauties of Sh—. By W. Dodd. New edition. Ln : W. Tegg . . . 1861. 12°, pp. 380　　BM | CPL

Sh— [Works : Extracts]—

[Works : Ext.] Choice thoughts from Sh—. [Edited by L. C. Gent.] Ln : Whittaker . . . 1861. Cr. 8°, pp. viii.-334　　BM | BUS | CPL | SML

[Works : Ext.] Morgan (A. A.) Mind of Sh— . . . Second edition. Ln : Chapman . . . 1861. Cr. 8°, pp. xxiv.-268　　BM | MPL

[Works : Ext.] Tegg (W.) Sh—'s memorial, undertaken with a view to popularise Shakesperian literature amongst all classes. Melbourne : J. J. Blundell & Co. . . . 1861. 12°, pp. vi.-136　　BM

[Works : Ext.] Tales from Sh—, by C. & M. Lamb. Rotterdam : H. Altmann . . . 1861-62. Cr. 8°

[Works : Ext.] Bible truths with Shakespearean parallels ; being selections from scripture . . . with passages illustrative of the text, from . . . Sh—. [By J. Brown.] Ln : Whittaker . . . 1862. Cr. 8°, pp. xx.-142　　BM | BPL | BUS | CPL

[Works : Ext.] Book of familiar quotations, edited by John Bartlett. Ln : . . . 1862. 8°　　BUS
Often reprinted.

[Works : Ext.] Choice thoughts . . . [edited by L. C. Gent]. 1862. Cr. 8°　　BPL

[Works : Ext.] Extracts from Sh— for the use of schools. Ln : Whittaker & Co. . . . 1862. Cr. 8°　　BM | BPL | CPL

[Works : Ext.] Gleanings from the English poets : Chaucer to Tennyson, with biographical notices. Edinburgh : Gall & Inglis [1862]. Cr. 8°, pp. xvi.-544. Illustrated
Sh— pp. 53-63, with memoir.

[Works : Ext.] Hoe (W.) Shakspere treasury of subject quotations, synonymously indexed. [Ln.?] : Hodson & Son . . . 1862. 16°, pp. xxvi.-70　　BM | BPL | CPL

[Works : Ext.] Rankin (M. H.) Philosophy of Sh— . . . Ln : Lockwood . . . 1862. Cr. 8°
First issued in 1841.

[Works : Ext.] Sh— album, or Warwickshire garland for the piano, containing above one hundred favourite ancient, modern, and traditional airs illustrative of Sh— and his time, including the music in 'Macbeth' and 'The tempest.' Arranged by the most eminent artists. Ln : Lonsdale . . . [1862]. F°

[Works : Ext.] Sh— cyclopædia, or a classified and elucidated summary of Sh—'s knowledge of the works and phenomena of nature. Part I. : Zoology-Man, by J H. Fennell. Ln : Smith . . . 1862. 8°　　BM | BPL | BUS | CPL
Intended to extend to twenty parts, but it ended apparently with the first.

[Works: Ext.] Sh—'s household words, illuminated by S. Stanesby. New edition. Ln : Griffith & Farran [1862]. 12°. With coloured plates   BPL

[Works: Ext.] Marsh (J. B.) Shaksperian playing cards . . . selected and arranged. Manchester : J. Heywood [1862-63]. 2 parts. 16°   BM | BUS
No more published.

[Works: Ext.] Heath (Charles) Heroines of Sh— . . . With letterpress extracts from the text, in English and French, and critical essays on each of the characters. Ln : Ward & Lock [1862-64]. 4°
                                        BM | MPL

Works : Ext.] Hoe (Wm.) Shakspere treasury of subject quotations, synonymously indexed. Ln : Lockwood & Co. . . . 1863. Cr. 8°, pp. xvi.-70
                                BM | BPL | BUS

[Works: Ext.] Humphreys (H. N.) Sentiments and similes. Second edition. Ln : Longman . . . 1863. 16°

[Works: Ext.] Marsh (J. B.) Familiar, proverbial, and select sayings from Sh—. Ln : Simpkin [1863]. Cr. 8°, pp. viii.-162
                        BM | BPL | BUS | MPL

[Works: Ext.] Rankin (M. H.) Philosophy of Sh—, delineating in seven hundred and fifty passages the multiform phases of the human mind. Collated, elucidated and alphabetically arranged. Third edition. Ln : Lockwood & Co. . . . 1863. 8°, pp. lii.-644
                                BPL | MPL | SML

[Works: Ext.] Tales from Sh—. By C. & M. Lamb . . . Leipzig : B. Tauchnitz . . . 1863. 16°, pp. viii.-346, and portrait
                                        BUS

[Works: Ext.] Watson (J. T.) Poetical quotations . . . Philadelphia . . . 1863. 12°
                                        BUS

[Works: Ext.] Brown (J.) Bible truths, with Shakespearian parallels. Second edition . . . with index. Ln : Whittaker . . . 1864. Cr. 8°, pp. xxiv.-208   BM | BUS | SML

[Works: Ext.] Household words, edited by S. Stanesby. Ln : Griffith & Farran . . . 1864. 16°   SML

[Works: Ext.] Marsh (J. B.) Shakespearian riddles. Ln : Simpkin . . . 1864. 64°

[Works: Ext.] Pearls of Sh—. Ln : Cassell . . . 1864. 12°

[Works: Ext.] Sh— tercentenary pocket keepsake [almanac with quotations]. Ln : Cassell, 1864. 32°, pp. 32   BUS

[Works: Ext.] Beauties of Sh—, by W. Dodd. Ln : Moxon . . . 1865. 18°

[Works : Ext.] Gibson (R. L.) Shakesperean gems, newly collected and arranged, with a life of Wm. Sh— . . . Halifax : Wm. Nicholson & Sons . . . 1865. 16°, pp. 350. With Chandos portrait and vignette view of birthplace on title   BM | BPL | CPL

[Works : Ext.] Scrymgeour (Daniel) Class book of English poetry from Chaucer to Tennyson. With biographical notices and explanatory notes. Edinburgh : A. & C. Black . . . 1865. Cr. 8°, pp. xxxviii.-598. With portraits
Pages 86-135 contain a brief life of and extracts from Sh—.

[Works : Ext.] Sh— adapted for reading classes and for the family circle, by Thomas and S. G. Bulfinch. Boston : J. E. Tilton & Co., 1865. Cr. 8°, pp. xii.-436. Illustrated   BUS
Selections from eight of the plays.

[Works : Ext.] Sh— for schools and families ; being a selection and abridgment . . . edited by Thomas Shorter. Ln : Allman . . . 1865. 12°   CPL

[Works : Ext.] Sh— for schools, being passages from his works to be committed to memory. With notes, original and selected, by C. Lenny . . . Second edition. Ln : Relfe Brothers . . . 1865. 12°, pp. iv.-104   BM | SML

[Works : Ext.] Sh—'s magic bijou post office. Ln : Johns & Son [c. 1865]. Four broadsides, f°. Illust.   BUS
Twenty questions, with answers from Sh—.

[Works : Ext.] Shaksperian parallelisms. chiefly illustrative of ' The tempest ' and a ' Midsummer night's dream,' from Sir Philip Sidney's ' Arcadia.' Compiled by Eliza M. West. Edited by J. O. Halliwell. [Ln.] : 1865. 8°   BPL | BUS | MPL
Issue restricted to ten copies of the 25 originally printed.

[Works : Ext.] Warburton's Sh— copybooks for schools. No. I. 1865. 8°   BPL

[Works : Ext.] Watson (J. T.) Poetical quotations . . . Philadelphia . . . 1865. 12°   BUS

[Works : Ext.] Stephens (G.) Sh— story teller . . . 1865-66. 6 parts. 8°   CPL

[Works : Ext.] Ausgewählte stellen aus Sh—'s werken . . . passages from the works of Sh—, selected and translated into German . . . by G. Solling. Leipzig : F. A. Brockhaus . . . 1866. 8°, pp. x.-156
                                        BM

[Works : Ext.] Choice thoughts from Sh— . . . [edited by L. C. Gent]. Ln : Routledge . . . 1866. Cr. 8°, pp. viii.-334
                                BM | BPL | BUS

Sh— [Works : Extracts]—

[Works : Ext.] Dyce (Alex.) Glossary to the works of Sh—. Ln : Chapman & Hall . . . 1866. 8°

[Works : Ext.] Sh—'s mental photographs. New York : Hurd & Houghton . . . 1866. Cr. 8°, pp. 36   BM | BUS | SML
A game of ten questions, with twenty answers from Sh—.

[Works : Ext.] Tales from Sh—. By C. & M. Lamb. Illustrated by John Gilbert. Ln : . . . 1866. 8°   CPL

[Works : Ext.] Treasury of thought from Sh— : The choice sayings of his principal characters, analytically and alphabetically arranged. Ln. & Glasgow : G. Griffin & Co. . . . 1866. Cr. 8°, pp. viii.-368   BM | BPL | BUS

[Works : Ext.] Halliwell (J. O.) Lineal concordance to the poems of Sh— ; the paginal references adapted to the variorum edition of Malone of 1821. [Ln. ?] 1867. 8°   BPL | HCL
Issue confined to ten copies.

[Works : Ext.] Lyra elegantiarum ; Collection of . . . vers de société and vers d' occasion, edited by Fredk. Locker. Ln : Moxon . . . 1867. Cr. 8°, pp. xx.-346
Contains 'My flocks feed not' (p. 4) and 'O mistress mine, where are you roaming?' (p. 11).

[Works : Ext.] Rankin (M. H.) Philosophy of Sh—. Edinburgh . . . Ln : Lockwood . . . 1867. Cr. 8°

[Works : Ext.] Routledge (E.) Quotations from Sh—. A collection of passages from the works . . . selected and arranged. Ln : Routledge, 1867. 16°, pp. iv.-176   BM | BPL | CPL

[Works : Ext.] Bellew (J. C. M.) Poets' corner : A manual for students in English poetry, with biographical sketches. Ln : Routledge . . . 1868. 8°, pp. viii.-920
Sh— pp. 169-180.

[Works : Ext.] Dolby (T.) Dictionary of Shakespearian quotations. Philadelphia . . . 1868. 12°   BPL

[Works : Ext.] Gleanings from the comedies of Sh—. Edinburgh : W. P. Nimmo [1868]. 16°, pp. 128   BM

[Works : Ext.] Helms (G.) English adjective in the language of Sh—. Bremen : Printed by F. C. Dubbers, 1868. Cr. 8°, pp. 56   BM | BUS | SML

[Works : Ext.] Shakespearean gems in French and English settings, edited by the Chevalier de Chatelain. Ln : W. Tegg, 1868. Cr. 8°, pp. xx.-468   BM | BPL | MPL | SML

[Works : Ext.] Shakespearian texts illuminated. Ln : T. Nelson & Sons [1868]. Oblong 4°.   Six plates   BM

Sh— [Works : Extracts]—

[Works : Ext.] Sh— almanack . . . with a quotation from his works for every day in the year. 1868-75. Cr. 8°   BM
Published annually.

[Works : Ext.] Ahn (F. H.) Class-book of English poetry and prose, comprising select specimens of the most distinguished poets and prose writers from Chaucer to the present time, with biographical notices, explanatory notes and introductory sketches of the history of English . . . and American literature. Cologne : M. Dumont-Schauberg, 1869. 8°, pp. xvi.-1,136
Sh— occupies pp. 39-137.

[Works : Ext.] Beauties of Sh—, by W. Dodd. Ln : Tegg . . . 1869. 12°

[Works : Ext.] Beauties of Sh— . . . By W. Dodd . . . With large additions . . . Philadelphia : Porter & Coates [c. 1869]. 16°, pp. iv.-380   BUS

[Works : Ext.] Gleanings from the comedies of Sh—. Edinburgh . . . [1869]. 12°   BPL

[Works : Ext.] Handbook of reference and quotation : mottoes and aphorisms from Sh— arranged alphabetically, with a copious index of words and ideas by T. E. J——. Ln : James Hogg & Son [1869]. Cr. 8°, pp. vi.-246   BM | BPL | BUS | SML

[Works : Ext.] Harder (A.) Philosophy of Wm. Sh— in three hundred passages from his plays. Magdeburg : Heinrichshofen . . . 1869. 8°, pp. 156   BM
In English and German.

[Works : Ext.] Sh— gems [edited by G. F. Sargent. c. 1869]. 12°   BPL

[Works : Ext.] Stearns (C. W.) Sh—treasury of wisdom and knowledge. New York : Putnam . . . 1869. 12°, pp. viii.-436   BM | BPL | BUS | SML
Includes article, 'Did Sh— write Sh—'s plays?' pp. 394-413.

[Works : Ext.] Almanack and companion. Ln : W. Kent & Co., 1869-76. 18 vols. 12°   BPL

[Works : Ext.] Beauties of Sh—. By W. Dodd. With portrait and illustrations. Ln : Warne . . . [1870]. 8°   BPL

[Works : Ext.] Beeton (S. O.) Great book of poetry. Ln : . . . 1870. 8°   BUS
The Sh— quotations are Nos. 165-211.

[Works : Ext.] Beaver (Susanna) Book of reference to remarkable passages in Sh— . . . with a separate index to each play. Ln : Bull & Simmons . . . 1870. Cr. 8°, pp. viii.-184   BPL | CPL

[Works : Ext.] Brown (O. Phelps) Shakespearian annual almanac. Jersey City, 1870. 16°. Illustrated   BUS
Contains the 'Seven ages . . .' from 'As you like it.'

[Works: Ext.] Clarke (M. C.) Complete concordance to Sh— . . . Ln: Kent . . . 1870.
Roy. 8°   BUS

[Works: Ext.] Daniel (P. A.) Notes and conjectural emendations of certain doubtful passages in Sh—'s plays, by P. A. Daniel. Ln: Hardwicke . . . 1870. Cr.
8°, pp. 94   BM | BPL | CPL | MPL | SML

[Works: Ext.] Kemble (Charles) Sh— readings, being a selection . . . as read by him in public, edited by R. J. Lane. Ln: Bell & Daldy, 1870. 3 vols. 8°
                    BPL | BUS | CPL | MPL
Afterwards reprinted in one volume, 8°, pp. xii.-932.

[Works: Ext.] Life and beauties of Sh—, from the approved selections of W. Dodd. Philadelphia: National Association for publishing . . . works for the blind, 1870. Fcp. 4°; printed in embossed Roman type   BM

[Works: Ext.] Moral sentences culled from the works of Sh—. Second edition. Ln: . . . [c. 1870]. 8°; illustrated   W

[Works: Ext.] Readings and recitations from Sh— . . . Glasgow: Cameron & Ferguson [c. 1870 ?]. Cr. 8°, pp. 64   BUS

[Works: Ext.] Tales from Sh—-. By C. & M. Lamb. With scenes illustrating each tale, edited by Charles Knight. Ln: Blackwood & Co. [c. 1870]. 8°, pp. vi.-504

[Works: Ext.] West Indian illustrations of Sh—. 'Laughter for a month.' . . . Georgetown, Demerara: J. Thomson. Ln: J. Haddon & Co. [1870]. Oblong 4 , pp. iv., and forty-eight plates   BM | BPL
Comic caricatures of negro life in the West Indies, with quotations from the plays.
The first Shakespearean work produced in Jamaica.

[Works: Ext.] Sh— almanack. Ln: Kent . . . 1870-73. 3 vols. Cr. 8°   CPL

[Works: Ext.] Sh— almanack and companion, containing quotations from Sh— illustrating events. Ln: 1870-76. 6 vols. Cr. 8°. Illustrated   BUS

[Works: Ext.] Dalgleish (W. S.) Sh— for schools, with notes and glossary. Ln: T. Nelson . . . 1871. Nos. 1 to 5. 8° and 12°   BM

[Works: Ext.] Dalgleish (Walter Scott) Sh— reader, with notes, historical and grammatical. Ln: T. Nelson & Sons, 1871. 3 vols. 8°, pp. x.-418
                    BM | BPL | BUS | CPL | SML
The text is abridged and expurgated.

[Works: Ext.] Plays . . . abridged and revised for the use of girls, by Rosa Baughan. Second edition. Ln: R. Washbourne . . . 1871. 8°, pp. ii.-168   BPL | BUS
Contains extracts from seventeen plays, the 'Sonnets, and the 'Passionate pilgrim.'

[Works: Ext.] Sargent (G. F.) Book of Sh— gems. Ln: Routledge, 1871. 8°
                    BM | BPL | SML

[Works: Ext.] Plays . . . selected and prepared for use in schools, clubs, classes, and families. With introductions and notes by H. N. Hudson. Boston [U.S.]: Ginn brothers, 1871-75. 3 vols. 12°
Selections from twenty-one of the plays.   BM | BUS

[Works: Ext.] Brown (O. P.) Shakespearian annual almanac. 1871-82. 12°   BPL

[Works: Ext.] Bible truths, with Shakespearian parallels. By J. B. of Selkirk. . . . Third edition. Ln: Hodder . . . 1872. Cr. 8°, pp. xx.-244
                    BM | BPL | BUS | SML

[Works: Ext.] Blumenlese aus Sh—'s werken. Eine Mustersammlung der edelsten gedanken des grossen dichters. Mit beigefügtem. Original text. Magdeburg: A. Harder . . . 1872. 8°, pp. 156
                                    BM

[Works: Ext.] Everybody's sayings from Sh—, collected by John Alfred Sweny. Rochester: Edwin Harris . . . 1872. 8°, pp. 24, including wrappers   SML

[Works: Ext.] Furness (Helen Kate) Concordance to Sh—'s poems: An index to every word therein contained. 'Venus and Adonis.' Philadelphia: Lippincott . . . 1872. Roy. 8°, pp. 72   BPL | BUS
'Printed as an experiment in order that certain details which types alone can render clear may be mastered.'

[Works: Ext.] Moreau (J. B.) Calendar of American chronology illustrated by quotations from Sh—. New York . . . 1872. 4°   BPL

[Works: Ext.] Selections from Sh— [In 'Chambers' miscellany,' vol. 5]. Ln. & Edin., 1872. Cr. 8°   BPL

[Works: Ext.] Shakespearian gems [edited by G. F. Sargent]. Ln: Routledge [1872]. 12°, pp. viii.-334   BUS

[Works: Ext.] Bandow (Dr. K.) Readings from Sh—: Scenes, passages, analyses . . . Berlin: R. Oppenheim . . . 1873. 8°, pp. vi.-214   BM
In English and German.

[Works: Ext.] Beauties of Sh— . . . by W. Dodd. Ln: Routledge . . . [1873]. Cr. 8°, pp. vi.-384   BM
First edition appeared in 1752.

[Works: Ext.] Beauties of Sh— . . . by W. Dodd. Ln: Warne . . . 1873. 8°

[Works: Ext.] Pearls of Sh— . . . illustrated by K. Meadows. Ln: J. Blackwood & Co. [1873]. 8°, pp. xii.-160   BM | BPL
An earlier edition appeared in 1860.

Sh— [Works : Extracts]—

[Works : Ext.] Routledge (E.) Shakespearean quotations, selected and arranged. Ln : Routledge . . 1873. 12°

[Works : Ext.] Sh— in Norwich [Selections applicable to the principal persons in Norwich]. Fifth edition. Norwich : Miller & Leavin . . . 1873. 8°, pp. 12 BM

[Works : Ext.] Shakespearian reader, with notes historical and grammatical by W. S. Dalgleish. Ln : Nelson . . . 1873. 12° BPL

[Works : Ext.] Tales from Sh—, by C. Lamb. With a copious vocabulary compiled by E. Amthor. Fourth edition. Berlin : Renger . . . [1873]. 8°, pp. viii.-260
BUS

[Works : Ext.] Clarke (M. C.) Concordance to Sh— . . . Ln : Bickers . . . 1874. Roy. 8°

[Works : Ext.] Furness (Mrs. H. H.) Concordance to Sh—'s poems : An index to every word therein contained. Philadelphia : J. B. Lippincott & Co., 1874. Roy. 8°, pp. iv.-422   BM | BPL | BUS
Contains the 'Poems' at the end.

[Works : Ext.] Goodson (H. F.) Sh—; his religious and moral sentiments. Gems gathered from his writings. Ln : Simpkin . . . 1874. Cr. 8°, pp. 56   BM | BUS

[Works : Ext.] Harcourt (Capt. A. F. P.) Sh— argosy; containing much of the wealth of Sh—'s wisdom and wit. Alphabetically arranged and classified. Ln : H. S. King . . . 1874. 8°, pp. viii.-260
BM | BPL | BUS | SML

[Works : Ext.] Sh— lore : Fine art almanac. Ln : Virtue . . . 1874. 12°   BPL

[Works : Ext.] Schmidt (Alexander) Sh— lexicon ; A complete dictionary of all . . . words, phrases, and constructions in the works of the poet. Berlin : G. Reimer . . . 1874-75. 2 vols. Roy. 8°
BPL | BUS | MPL

[Works : Ext.] Bellamy (G. S.) New Shaksperian dictionary of quotations . . . Ln : Charing Cross Publishing Co. . . . 1875. 8°, pp. xxvi.-272   BM | BPL | BUS

[Works : Ext.] Clarke (M. C.) Complete concordance . . . Boston [U.S.] . . . 1875. Roy. 8°   BPL

[Works : Ext.] Crotch (W. Duppa) Double acrostics from Sh—. Ln : Hatchards . . . 1875. 16°, pp. 108   BM | BPL

[Works : Ext.] Furness. Concordance to Sh—'s poems. Philadelphia : Lippincott . . . 1875. Roy. 8°   MPL | SML

[Works : Ext.] Johnston (G.) Cupid's birthday book : One thousand love-darts from Sh—, gathered and arranged for every day in the year. Ln. & Edinburgh : W. P. Nimmo . . . 1875. 32°   BM | BPL

Sh— [Works : Extracts]—

[Works : Ext.] Sh— birthday book [compiled by M. F. P. Dunbar]. Third thousand. Ln : Hatchards . . . 1875. 16°, pp. vi.-278   BM | BUS

[Works : Ext.] Sh— daily gem book, and journal for birthdays. Ln : Ward, Lock & Tyler [1875]. 32°   BM

[Works : Ext.] Sh—'s household words : A selection from the wise saws of the immortal bard. Illuminated by Samuel Stanesby. Ln : Griffith & Farran . . . 1875. 16°, pp. ii.-28, and portrait BUS

[Works : Ext.] Stanford (W. B.) English verses for repetition [Sh— pp. 2-5]. 1875. 12°
BPL

[Works : Ext.] Birthday register, with sentiments from Sh— [edited by J. A. K——]. Ln : Marcus Ward & Co. . . . 1876. 16°, pp. 286   BM | BUS

[Works : Ext.] Dowden (Prof. E.) Sh— scenes and characters. A series of illustrations. Designed by Max Adamo, Hofmann, Makart, Schwoerer, and Spiess. Engraved on steel . . . with explanatory text selected and arranged. Ln : Macmillan . . . 1876. F°, pp. xvi.-276, and 36 plates   BM | BPL | BUS | SML

[Works : Ext.] Morgan (A. A.) Mind of Sh— as exhibited in his works. With illustrations by Sir John Gilbert. Ln : Routledge, 1876. 8°, pp. xxiv.-360   BM
First appeared in 1860.

[Works : Ext.] Routledge (E.) Readings from Sh— selected and arranged. Ln : Routledge . . . [1876]   BPL

[Works : Ext.] Sh— birthday book [compiled by M. F. P. Dunbar. Illustrated with photographs]. Ln : Hatchards . . . 1876. 16°   BM

[Works : Ext.] Selections from Sh— . . . with notes for teachers and scholars. Ln : T. J. Allman . . . 1876-84. Seven parts. 8°   BM

[Works : Ext.] Brown (J.) Bible truths with Shakespearian parallels. Fourth edition. Ln : Whittaker . . . [1877]. 12°   SML

[Works : Ext.] Brown (O. P.) Shakespearian annual almanac [with quotations from ' The tempest ']. Jersey City . . . 1877. 16°. Illustrated   BUS

[Works : Ext.] Handbook of reference and quotation, mottoes and aphorisms, arranged alphabetically, with index by T. E. J——. Second edition. Ln : Hogg . . . 1877. 8°, pp. 246   BM

[Works : Ext.] Mayou (Bessie) Natural history of Sh—; being selections of flowers, fruits, and animals. Manchester : E. Slater . . . [1877]. Cr. 8°, pp. viii.-220 BM | BPL | BUS | SML

[Works : Ext.] Sweet silvery sayings of Sh— on the softer sex. Compiled by an old soldier. Ln : H. S. King & Co. . . . 1877. Cr. 8°, pp. viii.-328 BM | BPL | BUS

[Works : Ext.] Tales from Sh—. By C. & M. Lamb. Boston [U.S.] : J. R. Osgood & Co. . . . 1877. 16°, pp. viii.-366 BUS

[Works : Ext.] Tales from Sh— . . . By C. Lamb. With 184 illustrations by Sir J. Gilbert. Ln : Routledge . . . [1877]. Cr. 8°, pp. xii.-372 BUS

[Works : Ext.] Beauties of Sh— . . . by W. Dodd. New edition, with 12 illustrations in permanent photography from the Boydell gallery. Ln : Bickers & Son . . . 1878. 8°, pp. xii.-356 BM | MPL

[Works : Ext.] Brown (J.) Bible truths with Shakesperian parallels. Fifth edition. Ln : [c. 1878]. Cr. 8° BPL | SML

[Works : Ext.] Ellacombe (H. N.) Plant-lore and garden craft of Sh— [reprinted, with additions, from ' The garden ' newspaper]. Exeter : Printed for the author by W. Pollard [1878]. 8°, pp. iv.-304 BM | BPL | BUS

[Works : Ext.] Furness (Mrs. H. H.) Concordance to the poems of Sh—. Philadelphia : Lippincott . . . 1878. Roy. 8°, pp. iv.-422

[Works : Ext.] Marriott (J.) New Shakesperian puzzle. [A packet of cards, bearing selections from Sh—]. With directions. Ln : F. Passmore . . . 1878. 24° BM

[Works : Ext.] Morgan (A. A.) Mind and genius of Sh—. Brighton . . . 1878. 8° BPL

[Works : Ext.] Shakspearian gems. Six illuminated designs, suitable for Christmas and New Year's greetings or for presentation. [With selections.] Ln : . . . [1878]. 16° BM

[Works : Ext.] Beauties of Sh— . . . by W. Dodd. With 120 illustrations by Sir J. Gilbert, Birket Foster, and others. Ln : Routledge . . . 1879. 8°, pp. x.-372, and plates BM
First appeared in 1752.

[Works : Ext.] Brown (J.) Bible truths with Shakspearian parallels. Fourth edition. [1879]. 16° BM

[Works : Ext.] Clarke (C. C. & M. C.) Sh— key, unlocking the treasures of his style, elucidating the peculiarities of his con-

struction, and displaying the beauties of his expression, forming a companion to the ' Complete concordance to Sh—.' Ln : Low . . . 1879. 8°, pp. xii.-810 BM | BPL | BUS | MPL | SML

[Works : Ext.] Nursery tales from Sh—, by ' Guy Roslyn ' [J. Hatton]. [In ' New monthly magazine.'] Ln : 1879. 8° BUS

[Works : Ext.] Sh— birthday book [compiled by M. F. Dunbar]. Fifty-ninth thousand. Ln : Hatchards . . . 1879. 16°, pp. 278 BM

[Works : Ext.] Sh— for children ; Tales from Sh— by C. & M. Lamb. Illustrated by J. M. Smith. Ln : Chatto . . . 1879. Fcp. 4°, pp. xl.-270 BUS | SML

[Works : Ext.] Sh—lesebuch . . . mit erklärenden änmerkungen und einem abriss der Sh—-grammatik versehen von Dr. K. Meurer . . . Wörterbuch zu dem Sh—lesebuch. Coeln : Roemke & Cie . . . 1879. 2 parts. 8° BM

[Works : Ext.] Tales from Sh—. By C. & M. A. Lamb. Ln : . . . 1879. 8° BPL | MPL

[Works : Ext.] Arnold (C.) Index to Shakespearian thought ; A collection of passages from the plays and poems of Sh—, classified . . . and alphabetically arranged. Ln : Bickers, 1880. 8°, pp. 422 BM | BPL | BUS | MPL | SML

[Works : Ext.] Bard of Avon birthday text-book. Compiled from Sh—'s plays and poems. Ln : Routledge . . . 1880. 16°, pp. 256 BM

[Works : Ext.] Beauties of Sh— . . . by W. Dodd. Ln : Routledge . . . [1880]. Cr. 8°, pp. 384 BM

[Works : Ext.] Dyce (A.) Glossary to the works of Sh—. Ln : Bickers . . . 1880. 8°, pp. viii.-514 SML

[Works : Ext.] Gilman (A.) Sh—'s morals : Suggestive selections, with brief collateral readings and scriptural references . . . New York : Dodd, Mead . . . 1880. 8°, pp. xiv.-viii.-266 BM | BPL | BUS

[Works : Ext.] Gilman (A.) Sh—'s morals . . . Ln : J. F. Shaw & Co. [c. 1880]. 8° BM

[Works : Ext.] Main (D. M.) Treasury of English sonnets, edited from the original sources, with notes and illustrations. Manchester . . . 1880. 8° BUS
Sonnets 50 to 106 culled from Sh—.

[Works : Ext.] Malins (J.) Shakespearean temperance kalendar and birthday autograph album. Containing a daily Shakespearean quotation, illustrating a record of temperance events . . . Ln : Kempster & Co. [1880]. 16° BM | BPL

Sh— [Works: Extracts]—

[Works: Ext.] Moreau (John B.) Events in the history of New York city. With illustrations from Sh—. New York . . . 1880. 12° BUS

[Works: Ext.] Sargent (G. F.) Sh— gems. Ln: Routledge . . . [1880]. 8°, pp. viii.-334 BM

[Works: Ext.] Seccombe (*Major*) Military misreadings of Sh—. Printed in colours by Edmund Evans. Ln: Routledge . . . [1880] Oblong 4°, pp. 102
BM | BPL | BUS | SML

[Works: Ext.] Selections from the comedies of Sh—. Ln: Diprose . . . [c. 1880]. 12°, pp. 128

[Works: Ext.] Sh— daily gem book . . . [c. 1880]. 12° BPL

[Works: Ext.] Sh—'s stories simply told, by Mary Seamer (*afterwards* Seymour). Ln: Nelson [1880]. 8° BM | BUS

[Works: Ext.] Swinton (Wm.) Masterpieces of English literature. New York : . . . 1880. 8°. With Chandos portrait
BUS
Selections from 'Julius Cæsar' and 'Merchant of Venice.'

[Works: Ext.] Wykes (C. H.) Sh— reader; being extracts from the plays . . . Ln: Blackie . . . 1880. Cr. 8°, pp. 160
BM | BPL

[Works: Ext.] Bard of Avon birthday textbook. Ln: Routledge . . . 1881. 16°, pp. 256 BM

[Works: Ext.] Bartlett (John) Sh— phrasebook. Ln: Macmillan . . . 1881. Cr. 8°, pp. 1,034 BM | BPL | BUS | SML

[Works: Ext.] Bowen (H. C.) Sh— reading book: Plays for schools and public reading. Ln: Cassell . . . 1881. Cr. 8°

[Works: Ext.] Clarke (M. C.) Complete concordance to Sh—. Ln: . . . 1881. 8° BPL

[Works: Ext.] Clarke (C. C. & M. C.) Sh— key. 1881. 4° BPL
Author's copy, with manuscript title, cancelled leaves, and corrections.

[Works: Ext.] Cochrane (Robert) Treasury of English literature from Chaucer to the present time, with brief biographies. Edin: W. P. Nimmo . . . 1881. Roy. 8°, pp. 576, and 10 portraits
Sh— fills pp. 46-61, with Chandos portrait.

[Works: Ext.] Gleanings from Sh—'s comedies. Philadelphia . . . 1881. 16°
BUS

[Works: Ext.] Illustrated birthday text book, with quotations from Sh—. Ln: Eyre & Spottiswoode [1881]. 16°, A to S⁸ in eights (unpaged). With Chandos portrait and illustrations BUS

Sh— [Works: Extracts]—

[Works: Ext.] Malcolm (W. H.) Sh— and holy writ. Parallel passages, tabularly arranged . . . With forewords by F. J. Furnivall. Ln: Marcus Ward & Co. . . . 1881. 16°, pp. 158 BM | BPL | SML

[Works: Ext.] Moreau (J. B.) Events in the history of New York city, with illustrations from Sh—. New York . . . 1881. 12° BUS

[Works: Ext.] Sh— for the young folk : ' Midsummer night's dream,' ' As you like it,' ' Julius Cæsar,' edited by R. R. Raymond. [Selections . . . with a connecting narrative.] New York: Fords, Howard & Halbert [1881]. 8°, pp. viii.-224 BM | BPL | SML

[Works: Ext.] Shaw (T. B.) Specimens of English literature . . . 1881 BPL
Sh— at pp. 83-102.

[Works: Ext.] Tales from Sh—, by C. & M. Lamb. With introduction by A. Ainger. Ln: Macmillan . . . 1881. 12° SML

[Works: Ext.] Tales from Sh—. By C. & M. Lamb. Ln: Routledge . . . 1881. Cr. 8°. With coloured frontispiece

[Works: Ext.] Tales from Sh—. By C. & M. Lamb. Illustrated. Ln: Warne . . . 1881. Cr. 8°

[Works: Ext.] Tales from Sh— in verse by Mrs. Valentine [with coloured illustrations]. Ln: Warne, 1881. 4 parts. 4°, unpaged BM | BUS | SML

[Works: Ext.] Bard of Avon birthday textbook . . . Ln: Routledge . . . 1882. 16°
BUS

[Works: Ext.] Bartlett (J.) Sh— phrase Book. Boston [U.S.]: Little, Brown & Co., 1882. 12° SML

[Works: Ext.] Beauties of Sh—, by W. Dodd. Knight's penny books. Gouband & Son [c. 1882]. 2 vols. 12° BPL

[Works: Ext.] Beauties of Sh—, by William Dodd. ' Chandos classics.' Ln: Warne [c. 1882]. Cr. 8°

[Works: Ext.] Bell (David C. & Alex. M.) Standard elocutionist. Ln: Hodder & Stoughton, 1882. Cr. 8°, pp. xvi.-536
Sh— occupies pp. 396-461.

[Works: Ext.] Ferguson (Samuel) Shakespearean breviates. An adjustment [in verse] of twenty-four of the longer plays of Sh— to convenient reading limits. Dublin: Hodges . . . 1882. 8°, pp. x.-84
BM | BPL | BUS

[Works: Ext.] Jennings (J. A.) Modern elocutionist. Dublin [c. 1882]. Cr. 8°
Sh— at pp. 409-443. BPL

[Works: Ext.] Macfarland (A. S.) & Sage (A.) Stories from Sh—. [1882.] 8° BM

Sh— [Works : Extracts]—

[Works : Ext.] Morris (Mowbray) Poet's walk : An introduction to English poetry, chosen and arranged. Ln : Remington . . . 1882. 16°, pp. xxxii.-382
From Sh— and others.

[Works : Ext.] Queen Mab : Gems from Sh— [with preface signed C. W——]. Ln : Griffith & Farran [1882]. 16°, pp. 96
BM

[Works : Ext.] Sh— [selected passages]. Coles & Tomlin [1882]. 8° & 16°, pp. 8
BM

[Works : Ext.] Sh— birthday book, edited by Mary F. P. Dunbar. 84th thousand. Ln : Hatchards . . . 1882. 16°

[Works : Ext.] Sh— birthday book. 'Stratford edition.' Ln : Warne . . . [1882]. 32°, pp. 128
BM

[Works : Ext.] Tales from Sh—, by C. & M. Lamb. Illustrated by Sir J. Gilbert. Ln : Routledge . . . 1882. 4°

[Works : Ext.] Beauties of Sh—, by W. Dodd. Illustrated by Sir J. Gilbert. Ln : Routledge . . . 1883. 4°

[Works : Ext.] Beauties of Sh— . . . by W. Dodd. Ln : Ward, Lock [1883]. Cr. 8°, pp. xii.-372
BM

[Works : Ext.] Flowers of Sh—: depicted by 'Viola.' [Coloured plates ; with extracts.] Ln : S. Low . . . [1883]. 8°

[Works : Ext.] Grey-Wilson (W.) To be, or not to be ? An amusing record of your friends' convictions. With most unreliable statistics. Ln : . . . 1883. 16°
With Sh— extracts.
BM | BUS

[Works : Ext.] Heath (Charles) Heroines of Sh—: Engravings, etc., with extracts, essays on the characters . . . [c. 1883]. 4°
BPL

[Works : Ext.] Hudson (H. N.) Classical English reader. Boston [U.S.] : Ginn . . . 1883. 12°
SML

[Works : Ext.] Illustrated Sh— birthday book. Ln : Routledge . . . 1883. 16°, pp. 352
BM

[Works : Ext.] Kinnear (Benjamin Gott) Cruces Shakespearianæ : Difficult passages in Sh—. The text of the folio and quartos collated with the lections of recent editions and the old commentators. With original emendations and notes. Ln : Bell . . . 1883. 8°, pp. viii.-508
BM | BPL | BUS | SML

[Works : Ext.] Sh— and Milton reader. Ln : Moffatt & Paige [1883]. Cr. 8°, pp. 192
BM

[Works : Ext.] Sh— birthday book. Twentieth thousand. Ln : Marcus Ward & Co. . . . 1883. 16°, pp. 252
BM

Sh— [Works : Extracts]—

[Works : Ext.] Sh—'s stories simply told [comedies] by M. Seamer [aft. Seymour]. Ln : Nelson . . . 1883. 8°, pp. 236. Illustrated
BM

[Works : Ext.] Sh—'s stories simply told [tragedies and histories] by M. Seamer. Ln : Nelson . . . 1883. 8°

[Works : Ext.] Sherlock (Fredk.) Sh— on temperance. With brief annotations. Ln : 'Home words' office [1883]. 12°
BPL | BUS

[Works : Ext.] Tales from Sh— by C. & M. Lamb. Selected for schools. Ln : Bell . . . 1883. 12°

[Works : Ext.] Tales from Sh—, by C. & M. Lamb. Ln : Bickers . . . 1883. Cr. 8°

[Works : Ext.] Tales from Sh—. By C. & M. Lamb. Edited by Alfred Ainger. Ln : Macmillan . . . 1883. Cr. 8°

[Works : Ext.] Tales from Sh—. By C. & M. Lamb. Ln : Routledge . . . 1883. 4°

[Works : Ext.] Tales from Sh—, by C. & M. Lamb. Ln : Whittaker . . . 1883. 12°

[Works : Ext.] Timmins (J. F.) The poet-priest : Shakespearian sermons compiled . . . Ln : Blackwood [1883]. Cr. 8°, pp. 56
BM
Extracts from the works of Sh— put into a connected form.

[Works : Ext.] Bearsdell (A. F.) Sh— speaker, with introduction and notes. New York . . . 1884. 24°
BUS

[Works : Ext.] Dunbar (M. F. B.) Sh— birthday book. Ln : . . . 1884. 12°
BPL

[Works : Ext.] Ellacombe (H. N.) Plant-lore and garden-craft of Sh—. Second edition. Ln : Satchell . . . 1884. 8°, pp. xii.-438
BM | BPL | BUS | SML

[Works : Ext.] English verse ; Dramatic scenes and characters, edited by W. J. Linton and R. H. Stoddard. Ln : Kegan Paul . . . 1884. Cr. 8°, pp. xxviii.-342
Sh— occupies pp. 73-111.

[Works : Ext.] Field (B. R.) Medical thoughts of Sh—. Easton [U.S.] : Andrews & Clifton, 1884. 8°
BPL | SML

[Works : Ext.] Introduction to the study of Sh— and Milton. [By J. A. M——. With selections from their works.] Ln : Philip . . . [1884]. 8°, pp. 140
BM

[Works : Ext.] Langford (J. A.) Praise of books, as said and sung by English authors. Ln : Cassell . . . [1884]. 12°
Sh— occupies pp. 67-72.

[Works : Ext.] Select readings from Sh— and Milton. With introductory remarks and explanatory . . . notes. Glasgow : W. Collins . . . [1884]. Cr. 8°, pp. 124
BM

37

Sh— [Works : Extracts]—

[Works : Ext.] Sh— diary and almanack for 1885. Ln : W. Kent & Co., 1884. 24°
                       BM | BPL

[Works : Ext.] Sherlock (F.) Sh— on temperance : with brief annotations. Ln : ' Home words ' office [1884]. Cr. 8°, pp. 210   BM | SML

[Works : Ext.] Field (B. R.) Medical thoughts of Sh—. Second edition . . . enlarged. Easton [U.S.] : Andrews & Clifton, 1885. 8°, pp. 86   BPL | BUS

[Works : Ext.] Mack (Robert E.) Shakespearean quotations . . . Ln : Griffith & Farran, 1885. 64°

[Works : Ext.] Roses and holly : Pen and pencil pictures from the poets. Edinburgh : Nimmo [c. 1885]. Fcp. 4°, pp. xii.-152. Illustrated
With extracts from Sh—.

[Works : Ext.] Scenes from Sh— for the young, by ' C. Alias.' Illustrated by Sidney. Ln : . . . 1885. Oblong f°
                       BM | BPL

[Works : Ext.] Sh— forget-me-nots. A text-book of Sh— quotations. [With preface signed E. K. H——.] Ln : Griffith, Farran & Co. [1885]. 16°   BM

[Works : Ext.] Sh— on golf. With special reference to the Saint Andrews links. Edinburgh : D. Douglas . . . 1885. 24°, pp. 24   BM

[Works : Ext.] Sherlock (Frederick) Sh— on temperance . . . Ln : . . . 1885. 8° BUS

[Works : Ext.] Tales from Sh—. By C. & M. Lamb. Boston [U.S.] : Ginn & Co., 1885. 12°   SML

[Works : Ext.] Tales from Sh—, by C. & M. Lamb. Ln : Bell & Sons, 1885. Cr. 8°, pp. 126 and portrait

[Works : Ext.] Tales from Sh—. By C. & M. Lamb. Engravings by W. Harvey. Ln : . . . Lockwood . . . 1885. 12°

[Works : Ext.] Adams (W. H. D.) Concordance to the plays of Sh—. Ln : . . . 1886. 8°. With portrait   BM | BUS | MPL

[Works : Ext.] Birthday chimes from Sh—. A text-book of choice extracts . . . for every day. Edinburgh : Nimmo . . . 1886. 16°, pp. 248   BM |BPL

[Works : Ext.] Brereton (A.) Shakespearean scenes and characters : with descriptive notes on the plays, and the principal Shakespearean players, from Betterton to Irving. Illustrated by thirty steel plates, ten wood engravings, and portrait. Ln : Cassell, 1886. 4° BM | BUS | MPL | SML

[Works : Ext.] Clarke (M. C.) Sh—'s self as revealed in his writings. [Excerpt from ' Shakespeariana.' 1886. 12°   BPL

Sh— [Works : Extracts]—

[Works : Ext.] Dunbar (M. F. P.) Birthday book. Ln : Hatchards . . . 1886. 32°

[Works : Ext.] Miles (Alfred H.) Sh— reciter. Ln : . . . [1886]. Fcp. 4°, pp. 128   BM | BPL

[Works : Ext.] Recitations from Sh— for school and home. [Ln. ?] : Boot . . . 1886. 12°

[Works : Ext.] Schmidt (A.) Sh— lexicon : Second edition. Berlin & Ln : Reimer & Co., 1886. 2 vols. 8°   BPL | SML

[Works : Ext.] Six floral Shakespearean mottoes . . . 1886. 8°   BPL

[Works : Ext.] Tales from Sh—, by C. & M. Lamb, edited by A. Ainger. Ln : Macmillan . . . 1886. Cr. 8°

[Works : Ext.] Tales from Sh—. By C. & M. Lamb. ' World library.' Ln : Routledge . . . 1886. Cr. 8°, pp. viii.-372, and coloured frontispiece

[Works : Ext.] Two indexes to the characters in Sh—. Ln : Simpkin . . . 1886. 12°

[Works : Ext.] Bartlett (J.) Familiar quotations. Boston [U.S.] : Little, Brown & Co. . . . 1887. 12°   SML
Frequently reprinted since.

[Works : Ext.] Beauties of Sh— . . . by W. Dodd. Ln : John Dicks . . . [1887]. Fcp. 4°   BM

[Works : Ext.] O'Connor (Evangeline M.) Index to the works of Sh—, giving references, by topic, to notable passages and significant expressions. With brief histories of the plays. New York . . . 1887. 8°   BM | BPL | BUS | SML

[Works : Ext.] Somers (A.) Shakespearean ballads. Manchester : Faulkner . . . 1887. 8°   BUS | SML

[Works : Ext.] Stokes (F. A.) Sh— calendar for 1888 . . . 1887. 8°   BPL

[Works : Ext.] Two indexes to the characters in Sh—'s plays, chiefly intended for the use of Sh— reading clubs. York : J. Sampson, 1887. 12°, pp. x.-116
                       BM | SML

[Works : Ext.] Ward (Clarence S.) Wit, wisdom and beautie of Sh—. Boston [U.S.] . . . 1887. 12°
              BPL | BUS | SML

[Works : Ext.] Beauties of Sh— . . . by W. Dodd. Ln : Dicks . . . 1888. Cr. 8°

[Works : Ext.] Bell's standard elocutionist. Ln : Hodder . . . 1888. Cr. 8°, pp. xvi.-536
Sh— occupies pp. 396-461.

[Works : Ext.] Colton (G. Q.) Sh— and the Bible. Parallel passages and passages suggested by the Bible. With the religious

sentiments of Sh—. With an introduction
by . . . R. Collyer. New York : Knox &
Co. [1888]. 8°, pp. 162   BM | BUS

[Works : Ext.] Henley (W. E.) 'The graphic'
gallery of Sh—'s heroines. A series of
studies in Goupilgravure. With the stories
of the plays. Ln : . . . 1888. F°, pp. 58
BM | BPL | MPL

[Works : Ext.] Savage (R.) Shakespearean
extracts from ' Edward Pudsey's booke '
. . . which include some from an unknown
play by Wm. Sh— . . . 1888. 8°
BM | SBL | SML
The 'unknown' play proved to be Geo. Chapman's
'Blind beggar of Alexandria.'

[Works : Ext.] Selby (H. M.) Sh— classical
dictionary, or mythological allusions in
the plays of Sh— . . . [1888] 8°   BM | BPL

[Works : Ext.] Sh— birthday text book.
Ln : Mack . . . 1888. 32°

[Works : Ext.] Sh— souvenir. Ln : M.
Ward . . . 1888. 16°

[Works : Ext.] Tales from Sh—, by C. & M.
Lamb. Ln : Bell . . . 1888. 12°

[Works : Ext.] Tales from Sh—. ' People's
edition.' Ln : Dicks . . . 1888. 8°

[Works : Ext.] Tales from Sh—, by C. & M.
Lamb. ' Standard library.' Ln : Ward
& Lock, 1888. Cr. 8°

[Works : Ext.] Tales from Sh—, by C. & M.
Lamb. Edited with notes . . . by Alfonzo
Gardiner. Manchester : John Heywood,
1888. Cr. 8°, pp. xii.-220

[Works : Ext.] Webb (Fredk. Geo.) New
reciter, reader and orator . . . with choice
recitations. 2nd ed. Ln : Dean [1888].
Cr. 8°, pp. xiv.-368
With several extracts from Sh—.

[Works : Ext.] Best (K. T.) Shakesperiana,
being 500 passages from Sh—, selected.
Hastings : A. H. Barker [1889]. Cr. 8°,
pp. 34   BM | BPL

[Works : Ext.] Colton (G. Q.) Sh— and the
Bible . . . New York . . . [1889]. 12° BPL

[Works : Ext.] Selby (M. H.) Sh— classical
dictionary, or mythological allusions in
the plays of Sh— explained. Ln : . . .
1889. Sm. 8°

[Works : Ext.] Sh— on golf. Edinburgh :
D. Douglas . . . 1889. Cr. 8°   BM

[Works : Ext.] Tales from Sh—, by C. & M.
Lamb. Ln : Bickers . . . 1889. Cr. 8°

[Works : Ext.] Tales from Sh—, by C. & M.
Lamb. Ln : Routledge . . . 1889. 12° BPL

[Works : Ext.] Darlington (John) Shakespearian vade-mecum, containing collo-
quial expressions and proverbial sayings
taken from the works. Ln : Beaumont
& Co. [c. 1890]. 8°, pp. iv.-150

[Works : Ext.] Fitzgerald (P.) Catholic
jewels from Sh—. Ln : Burns & Oates
[1890]. Cr. 8°, pp. 32   BM

[Works : Ext.] Sh—'s stories simply told,
by M. Seamer [aft. Seymour]. Ln : Nelson . . . 1890. 8°   BM

[Works : Ext.] Somers (Alex.) Shakspearean ballads [being the stories of
Sh—'s tragedies in ballad form]. . . . 1890.
16°   BM

[Works : Ext.] Tales from Sh—. By C. &
M. Lamb. Illustrated by Sir J. Gilbert.
Ln : Routledge . . . 1890. 12°

[Works : Ext.] Tales from Sh—, by C. & M.
Lamb. Paisley : Alex. Gardner [c. 1890].
Cr. 8°, pp. 310

[Works : Ext.] Timmins (J. F.) The poet-
priest. Shakespearian sermons compiled
. . . Fourth edition. Ln : Simpkin, Mar-
shall & Co. [1890]. 8°, pp. 80   BM | BPL

[Works : Ext.] Pratt (Mary L.) Stories from
Sh—. Boston [U.S.], 1890-95. 3 vols.
8°. Illustrated   BUS

[Works : Ext.] Adams (W. H. D.) Concordance to the plays of Sh—. ' Word for
word, without book.'—Twelfth night, I.
3. Ln : Routledge, 1891. Cr. 8°, pp. iv.-
496

[Works : Ext.] Bullen (A. H.) Lyrics from
the dramatists of the Elizabethan age.
Ln : 1891. Cr. 8°   BPL
Sh— fills pp. 31-60.

[Works : Ext.] Dalgleish (W. S.) Great
speeches from Sh—'s plays, with notes
and a life of Sh— . . . 1891. Cr. 8°, pp.
158   BM | BPL

[Works : Ext.] Fishley (E. E.) Sh—'s rule of
life. Boston [U.S.] : F. S. Collins . . .
1891. Cr. 8°, pp. 32   BM | BPL | BUS

[Works : Ext.] Shakespearean daily calendar for 1892. Ln : Bemrose . . . 1891.
12°

[Works : Ext.] Sweny (J. A.) Everyday
sayings from Sh—. Chatham : D. Collins . . . 1891. Cr. 8°, pp. 30   BM

[Works : Ext.] Caine (R. H.) Love songs of
the English poets, with notes . . . 1892.
12°   BPL
Sh— takes up pp. 61-69.

[Works : Ext.] Dyce (Alex.) Glossary to the
works of Sh—. Revised with notes by H.
Littledale. Ln : Sonnenschein . . . 1892.
Cr. 8°   BPL | BUS

[Works : Ext.] Hanscomb (E. W.) Sh—
birthday book. Ln : Griffith & Farran
[1892]. 16°, pp. 250   BM | BPL

[Works : Ext.] Raymond (R. R.) Typical
tales of fancy and history. New edition.
New York . . . 1892. 8°

Sh— [Works: Extracts]—

[Works: Ext.] Routledge (E.) Quotations from Sh—. Third edition. Ln: Routledge ... 1892. 8°   SML

[Works: Ext.] Tales from Sh—, by C. & M. Lamb. Edited by A. Ainger. Ln: Macmillan ... 1892. 12°

[Works: Ext.] Beauties of Sh— ... by W. Dodd. Ln: Routledge ... 1893. 8°, pp. 384   BM

[Works: Ext.] Brandram (S.) Selected pieces in prose and verse ... Ln: Routledge ... 1893. Cr. 8°   BPL

[Works: Ext.] Brandram (S.) Selections from Sh— suitable for recitation. With an introductory essay on elocution. Ln: Routledge ... 1893. 8°, pp. 156
BM | BPL

[Works: Ext.] Hunt (J. H. L.) Imagination and fancy. Edited by A. S. Cook. Ln: ... 1893

[Works: Ext.] Sh— birthday book. Ln: Routledge ... 1893. 16°. Illustrated

[Works: Ext.] Short stories of Sh—'s plots. Ln: Macmillan ... 1893. Cr. 8°   SML

[Works: Ext.] Sim (Adelaide C. G.) Phoebe's Sh—: Stories simply told. Ln: Bickers ... 1893. Cr. 8°

[Works: Ext.] Tales from Sh— for children, by C. & M. Lamb. Ln: Chatto, 1893. Fcp. 4°

[Works: Ext.] Tales from Sh—, by C. & M. Lamb. Illustrated. Ln: Routledge ... 1893. 8°

[Works: Ext.] Tales from Sh— (including C. & M. Lamb's Tales). Philadelphia ... 1893. 4 vols. 16°

[Works: Ext.] Bartlett (John) New and complete concordance or verbal index to words, phrases, and passages in the dramatic works of Sh—, with a supplementary concordance to the poems. Ln. & New York: Macmillan ... 1894. 4°, pp. viii.-1,910

BM | BLO | BPL | CTC | MPL | SML
By far the most extensive labour within the limits of a single volume ever devoted to Sh—. The achievement is alike remarkable for its extent, its accuracy, and as the fruit of eighteen years leisure taken from active duties. John Bartlett was greatly assisted by his wife in this labour of love.

[Works: Ext.] Dyce (Alex.) Glossary to the works of Wm. Sh—. Ln: ... [1894]. 8°   BM

[Works: Ext.] Garrett (G.) Gems from Sh—. A book for registering the birthdays of one's friends ... selected and arranged. Ln: H. J. Drane [1894]. 16°, pp. 126
BM

Sh— [Works: Extracts]—

[Works: Ext.] Millard (J. & E.) Sh— for recitation ... selections ... arranged for ... schools. Introduction ... by E. A. Abbott. Ln: Sonnenschein ... 1894. 8°, pp. xvi.-270   BM | BPL

[Works: Ext.] Morgan (A. A.) Mind of Sh— as exhibited in his works. Ln: Chapman & Hall [1894]. Cr. 8°, pp. xxiv.-360 BM

[Works: Ext.] Reid (T. B.) Sh— birthday record ... selected and arranged. Ln: H. J. Drane [1894]. 16°   BM

[Works: Ext.] Sh— on golf. Edinburgh: D. Douglas ... 1894. Cr. 8°   BM

[Works: Ext.] Sim (A. C. G.) Phoebe's Sh—. [Stories from the plays] arranged for children. Ln: Bickers ... 1894. Cr. 8°   BM | BPL | SML

[Works: Ext.] Tales from Sh—, by C. & M. Lamb. 'School and home library.' Ln: Blackie ... 1894. Cr. 8°

[Works: Ext.] Tales from Sh—, by C. & M. A. Lamb, with continuation by Harrison S. Morris. Ln: Dent ... 1894. 4 vols. 12°   BPL

[Works: Ext.] Chambers (E. K.) English pastorals. Ln: ... 1895. Cr. 8°   BPL
Sh— fills pp. 97-109.

[Works: Ext.] Nesbit (Edith) Children's Sh—. Illustrated by Frances Brundage. Ln: Tuck ... [1895]. Roy. 8°. With coloured plates   BPL | BUS

[Works: Ext.] Tales from Sh—, by C. & M. Lamb. Edited by W. P. Coyne. Third edition. Dublin: Browne & Nolan, 1895.
SML

[Works: Ext.] Tales from Sh—, by C. & M. Lamb. Edited by William P. Coyne. Second edition. Ln: Simpkin ... 1895. Cr. 8°

[Works: Ext.] Ellacombe (H. N.) Plant lore and garden-craft of Sh—. New edition. Ln. & New York: E. Arnold [1896]. 8°, pp. xvi.-384   BM | BPL | MPL

[Works: Ext.] Moyes (J.) Medicine and kindred arts in the plays of Sh—. Glasgow: MacLehose ... 1896. Cr. 8°, pp. xiv.-124   BM | BPL | BUS

[Works: Ext.] Poole (Louella C.) & Johnson (Andrea C.) A very seasonable kalendar for ... 1897. Designed to bee vsed by ye manie louers of ye great poet. Boston [U.S.]: 1896. 8°   BUS

[Works: Ext.] Tales from Sh—, by C. & M. Lamb. Boston [U.S.] ... 1896. 8° BUS

[Works: Ext.] Carpenter (F. J.) English lyric poetry, 1500-1700. Ln: ... 1897. Cr. 8°   BPL
Sh— pp. 80-94.

Sh— [Works: Extracts]—

[Works: Ext.] Ellis (Charles) Sh— and the Bible. Sh—: A reading from the 'Merchant of Venice' Shakespeariana; Sonnets, with their scriptural harmonies. . . . Ln: Houlston. Plymouth: W. Brendon & Son, 1897. 8°, pp. 288, and Chandos portrait

[Works: Ext.] Jones (Chloe B.) Lover's Sh—: Quotations. Chicago: McClurg . . . 1897. 16°   BUS | SML

[Works: Ext.] Light of Sh—: Passages illustrative of the higher teaching of Sh—'s dramas, by 'Clare Langton' [Miss F. J. Tucker]. Ln: Stock, 1897. 8°, pp. xx.-116   BM | BPL | SML

[Works: Ext.] Malins (J.) Shakespearean temperance kalendar. Birmingham . . . [c. 1897]. 12°   BPL

[Works: Ext.] Poole & Johnson. A very seasonable kalendar for 1898, designed to bee used by ye manie lovers of Master Wm. Sh—. Illustrated by Mary D. Page. Ln: Low . . . 1897. Fcp. 4°

[Works: Ext.] Porter (Rose) Sh—'s men and women . . . [Quotations]. New York . . . 1897. Cr. 8°   BPL

[Works: Ext.] Tales from Sh—, by C. & M. A. Lamb, with introduction by H. R. Haweis. [c. 1897.] 12°   BPL

[Works: Ext.] Wood (R. S.) New scenes from Sh— for reading, recitation, and for further studies in literature. With prose introductions from Lamb's tales. Third edition. Ln: . . . [1897]. 8°, pp. 60 BUS

[Works: Ext.] Porter (Rose) Sh—'s men and women: An everyday book, chosen and arranged. New York . . . 1898. 8°

[Works: Ext.] Scenes from Sh— [In 'Daily Picayune, Comus edition']. New Orleans . . . 1898. F°   BPL

[Works: Ext.] Select tales from Sh—, by C. & M. Lamb. With introduction and notes by David Frew. Ln: Blackie . . . 1898. Cr. 8°, pp. 190

[Works: Ext.] Selection of tales from Sh—, by C. & M. A. Lamb. Edited with notes by J. H. Flather. Cambridge: University Press, 1898. 12°, pp. xii.-154   BPL

[Works: Ext.] Webb (J. Stenson) Sh— reference-book: Quotations . . . Ln: Stock . . . 1898. Cr. 8°, pp. vi.-118
                                          BM | BPL | SML

[Works: Ext.] Bartlett. Concordance . . . to Sh—. Ln: Macmillan . . . 1899. 4°, pp. viii.-1,910

[Works: Ext.] Bell. Standard elocutionist. Ln: Hodder . . . 1899. Cr. 8°   BPL
Sh— fills pp. 396-425.

Sh— [Works: Extracts]—

[Works: Ext.] Crows of Sh—, by J. B——. Edinburgh: D. Douglas . . . 1899. F°, pp. 42, and plates   BM
Extracts from Sh—, with illustrations.

[Works: Ext.] Historical tales from Sh—, by 'Q' [A. T. Quiller-Couch]. Ln: Arnold . . . 1899. Cr. 8°, pp. 382
                                    BM | BPL | MPL

[Works: Ext.] Jones (C. B.) Lover's Sh—. Ln: Gay & Bird, 1899. 12°, pp. 194

[Works: Ext.] Nesbit (E.) Children's Sh—. Illustrated by F. Brundage. Ln: Tuck . . . 1899. Roy. 8°, pp. 96

[Works: Ext.] Sh— anthology, 1592-1616, edited by Edward Arber. Ln: Frowde, 1899. Cr. 8°, pp. vi.-312   BPL | BUS

[Works: Ext.] Sh— daily gem-book and journal for birthdays. Ln: Ward & Lock . . . 1899. 16°   BM

[Works: Ext.] Sh—'s stories simply told, by Mary Seymour . . . 1899. 2 vols Cr. 8°   BPL

[Works: Ext.] Stories from Sh—, edited by M. Surtees Townsend. Boston [U.S]: 1899. 8°   BUS

[Works: Ext.] Stories from Sh—, by M. S Townsend . . . Ln: 1899. 8°
                                    BM | BPL | BUS

[Works: Ext.] Tales from Sh—, by C. & M. Lamb. Illustrated by A. Rackham. Ln: Dent . . . 1899. 12°, pp. 370

[Works: Ext.] Tales from Sh—, by C. & M. Lamb. Introductory preface by A. Lang. Illustrated by Robert Anning Bell. Ln: S. T. Freemantle . . . 1899. Cr. 8°, pp. xxviii.-372   BPL

[Works: Ext.] Tales from Sh—, by C. & M. Lamb, designed for the use of young people. With introduction by H. R. Haweis. Ln: Routledge . . . 1899. 16°, pp. 160

[Works: Ext.] Elizabethan garland, edited by James Potter Briscoe. Ln: Gay & Bird . . . 1900. 16°, pp. xvi.-146, and portrait of Queen Elizabeth

[Works: Ext.] Historical tales from Sh—, by 'Q' [A. T. Quiller-Couch]. Ln: Arnold . . . 1900. Cr. 8°, pp. 382   BUS

[Works: Ext.] Jones (C. B.) Lovers' Sh— . . . 1900. Cr. 8°   BPL

[Works: Ext.] Nesbit (E.) Children's Sh—. Ln: Tuck . . . 1900. 8°

[Works: Ext.] Oxford book of English verse, 1250-1900, chosen and edited by A. T. Quiller-Couch. Oxford: Clarendon Press, 1900. Cr. 8°, pp. xii.-1,084
Sh— fills pp. 175-200.

Sh— [Works : Extracts]—

[Works : Ext.] Tales from Sh—, by C. & M. Lamb. With introduction and additions by F. J. Furnivall. Ln : Tuck . . . 1900. 2 vols. 8°   SML

[Works : Ext.] Historical tales from Sh—, by ' Q ' [A. T. Quiller-Couch]. New York . . . 1901. 8°   BUS

[Works : Ext.] Nesbit (E.) Children's Sh—. Illustrated by F. Brundage. Ln : Tuck . . . 1901. Imp. 8°

[Works : Ext.] Oxford book of English verse, edited by A. T. Quiller-Couch. Oxford : Clarendon Press, 1901. Cr. 8°
Sh— fills pp. 86-87 and 175-200.   BPL

[Works : Ext.] Sonnet kalendar for 1902 . . . Ln : Simpkin . . . 1901. 16°

[Works : Ext.] Tales from Sh—, by C. & M. Lamb. With introduction by Elizabeth S. P. Ward. Illustrated by H. Pillé. Boston [U.S.] . . . 1901. 8°   BPL | BUS

[Works : Ext.] Tales from Sh—, by C. & M. Lamb. Illustrated by A. Rackham. Ln : . . . 1901. 12°   BPL

[Works : Ext.] Tales from Sh—, by C. & M. Lamb. Illustrated by H. Pillé. Ln : Duckworth . . . 1901. 2 vols. 12°, pp. 758

[Works : Ext.] Tales from Sh—, by C. & M. Lamb. With introductory preface by Andrew Lang. Illustrated by R. Anning Bell. Ln : Freemantle . . . 1901. Cr. 8°, pp. 400

[Works : Ext.] Tales from Sh—, by C. & M. Lamb. With six coloured plates and seventy half-tone illustrations by W. Paget. Ln : Nister . . . 1901. 8°, pp. 320

[Works : Ext.] Tales from Sh—, by C. & M. Lamb. With sixteen illustrations by W. H. Robinson. Ln : Sands . . . 1901. 8°, pp. 296

[Works : Ext.] Tales from Sh—, by C. & M. Lamb. With introduction and additions by F. J. Furnivall. Illustrated by Harold Copping. Ln : Tuck . . . 1901. 2 vols. Roy. 8°, pp. 690. With portraits
                                            BPL | BUS

[Works : Ext.] Children's Sh—, edited by A. B. Sidolph. Ln : . . . 1902

[Works : Ext.] Dyce (A.) Glossary to . . . Sh— : The references made applicable to any edition of Sh—. The explanations revised and new notes added by H. Littledale. Ln : . . . 1902. 8°   MPL

[Works : Ext.] English songs and ballads. Compiled by T. W. H. Crosland. Ln : G. Richards . . . 1902. 12°, pp. xvi.-352
Sh— takes up pp. 79-91.

Sh— [Works : Extracts]—

[Works : Ext.] Macleod (Mary) Sh— story book. With introduction by ' S. Lee.' Ln : Wells Gardner, 1902. 8°, pp. 482. Illustrated by Gordon Browne BPL | BUS

[Works : Ext.] Schmidt (A.) Sh— lexicon . . . Berlin . . . 1902. 2 vols. 8°

[Works : Ext.] Sh— in tale and verse, edited by Lois Grosvenor Hufford. Ln : Macmillan . . . 1902. Cr. 8°, pp. 456
                                            BPL | BUS

[Works : Ext.] Some tales from Sh—, by C. & M. Lamb. ' Penny poets.' Ln : Stead [c. 1902]. Cr. 8°   BPL

[Works : Ext.] Sonnet kalendar for 1903. Ln : Simpkin . . . 1902. 16°   BPL

[Works : Ext.] Tales from Sh—, by C. & M. Lamb. Ln : Bell . . . 1902. Cr. 8°

[Works : Ext.] Tales from Sh—, by C. & M. Lamb. Illustrated by R. A. Bell. Ln : Constable . . . 1902. Cr. 8°

[Works : Ext.] Tales from Sh—, by C. & M. Lamb. Illustrated by H. Pillé. Ln : Duckworth . . . 1902. 2 vols. 12° BPL

[Works : Ext.] Tales from Sh—, by C. & M. Lamb. With introduction and additions by F. J. Furnivall. Illustrated by H. Copping. Ln : Tuck . . . 1902. 2 vols. Roy. 8°

[Works : Ext.] Compositions and translations, edited by H. C. F. Mason . . . 1903. Cr. 8°   BPL

[Works : Ext.] Sh— for recitation : 135 selections. With introduction by Dr. E. A. Abbott. Ln : Sonnenschein [c. 1903]. Cr. 8°

[Works : Ext.] Sh— remembrance kalendar for 1904. Ln : Simpkin . . . 1903. 16° BPL

[Works : Ext.] Tales from Sh—, by C. & M. Lamb. With extracts from the plays, edited by J. H. Flather. Cambridge : University Press, 1903. Cr. 8°, pp. xii.-154

[Works : Ext.] Tales from Sh—, by C. & M. Lamb. Illustrated by B. Shaw. Ln : Bell . . . 1903. Cr. 8°, pp. 376 BPL | BUS

[Works : Ext.] Tales from Sh—, by C. & M. Lamb. With introduction by Wm. Macdonald. With the original illustrations reproduced. Ln : Dent, 1903. Cr. 8°, pp. 372

[Works : Ext.] Tales from Sh—, by C. & M. Lamb. With introduction and notes by C. D. Punchard. Ln : Macmillan . . . 1903. Cr. 8°, pp. 192

[Works : Ext.] Tales from Sh—, by C. & M. Lamb. ' Evening hour library.' Ln : Nimmo . . . 1903. Cr. 8°, pp. 350

[Works: Ext.] Tales from Sh—, by C. & M. Lamb. With the story of Sh—'s life, by E. A. Parry. Manchester: Sherratt & Hughes, 1903. Cr. 8°, pp. 212

[Works: Ext.] Dyce (A.) Glossary . . . to Sh—. Boston [U.S.] . . . 1904. 8°. With portraits

[Works: Ext.] Meynell (Alice) Flower of the mind: A choice among the best poems. Ln: Richards . . . 1904. Cr. 8°, pp. 372
Sh— fills pp. 32-45. BPL

[Works: Ext.] Richardson (Edith) Green thoughts from Sh—, arranged and decorated. Ln: Simpkin . . . 1904. 16°

[Works: Ext.] Sh— calendar for 1905. Ln: Anacker . . . 1904. 16°

[Works: Ext.] Sh— for recitation. Selected scenes and passages. Edited by Ernest Pertwee. Ln: Routledge . . . 1904. 8°, pp. 224 BPL

[Works: Ext.] Sh— remembrance kalendar for 1905. Ln: Simpkin . . . 1904. 8° BPL

[Works: Ext.] Smith (A. R.) Handbook index to those characters who have speaking parts assigned to them in the first folio . . . Ln: Smith . . . 1904. 8° BPL
Some copies also done on large paper, 4°.

[Works: Ext.] Tales from Sh—, by C. & M. Lamb . . . selected and edited by J. H. Flather. Cambridge: Univ. Press . . . 1904. Cr. 8°, pp. xii.-154

[Works: Ext.] Tales from Sh—, by C. & M. Lamb. Edinburgh: Oliver & Boyd, 1904. 12°

[Works: Ext.] Tales from Sh—, by C. & M. Lamb. 'Standard library.' Ln: Blackie . . . 1904. Cr. 8°

[Works: Ext.] Tales from Sh—, by C. & M. Lamb, for preliminary students. 'Oxford and Cambridge edition.' Ln: Gill . . . 1904. Cr. 8°

[Works: Ext.] Tales from Sh—, by C. & M. Lamb. With introduction by A. Ainger. 'Golden treasury series.' Ln: Macmillan, 1904. 12°, pp. 388

[Works: Ext.] Tales from Sh—, by C. & M. Lamb. Ln: Routledge . . . 1904. Cr. 8°, pp. 416

[Works: Ext.] Beauties of Sh— . . . 'Beauties of literature.' Ln: Library press, 1905. 12°

[Works: Ext.] Beauties of Sh—. 'Cameo classics.' Ln: Library press, 1905. 12°

[Works: Ext.] Historical tales from Sh—, edited by A. T. Quiller-Couch. Ln: Arnold . . . 1905. Cr. 8°, pp. 384. Illustrated

[Works: Ext.] Hogben (John) Master passages: Guide in miniature. Treasury of 100 specimens. Ambrose . . . 1905. 12°, pp. 234

[Works: Ext.] Jerrold (Walter) Descriptive index to Sh—'s characters in Sh—'s words. Ln: Routledge . . . 1905. 32°, pp. xvi.-176

[Works: Ext.] Latham (E.) Shakespearean quotations, with the correct versions of all passages commonly misquoted. Ln: Routledge . . . 1905. 32°

[Works: Ext.] McSpadden (J. W.) Shakespearean synopses: Outlines or arguments of the plays . . . Ln: Chapman . . . 1905. 12°, pp. 224 BPL

[Works: Ext.] Selections . . . edited by Arthur Burrell. Ln: Dent . . . 1905. 12°, pp. 268

[Works: Ext.] Sh— remembrance kalendar for 1906. Ln: Simpkin . . . 1905. 16°

[Works: Ext.] Stories from Sh—, by Jeanie Lang. Pictures by N. M. Price and others. Edinburgh: Jack . . . 1905. 16°, pp. 156 BPL

[Works: Ext.] Tales from Sh—, by C. & M. Lamb. Illustrated by B. Shaw. Ln: Bell . . . 1905. Cr. 8°, pp. 376 BPL

[Works: Ext.] Tales from Sh—, by C. & M. Lamb. 'Oxford edition.' Ln: H. Froude, 1905. 8°, pp. 382 BPL

[Works: Ext.] Tales from Sh—, by C. & M. A. Lamb. With twenty original coloured illustrations by N. M. Price. Ln: T. C. & E. C. Jack . . . 1905. Roy. 8°, pp. 336. Portrait and plates BPL | BUS

[Works: Ext.] Anson (W. S. W.) Shakespearean quotations . . . [1906]. Cr. 8° BPL

[Works: Ext.] Calendar of Sh— sonnets for 1907. Ln: Anacker . . . 1906. 16°

[Works: Ext.] Flowers from Sh—'s garden. A posy from the plays, pictured by Walter Crane. Ln: Cassell . . . 1906. Roy. 8° BPL

[Works: Ext.] Sh— birthday and anniversary book. Ln: Hills . . . 1906. 18°, pp. 128

[Works: Ext.] Sh— reader, in the old spelling and pronunciation . . . 1906. Cr. 8° BPL

[Works: Ext.] Simpson (P.) Scenes from old play-books arranged as an introduction to Sh—. Oxford . . . 1906. Cr. 8° BPL | BUS

[Works: Ext.] Stobart (J. C.) Sh— epoch, 1600-25 . . . Ln: E. Arnold, 1906. Cr. 8°, pp. 160 BPL

Sh— [Works: Extracts]—

[Works: Ext.] Tales from Sh—, by C. & M. Lamb. Second selection. Edited by J. H. Flather. Cambridge: Univ. Press, 1906. Cr. 8°, pp. 176

[Works: Ext.] Tales from Sh—, by C. & M. Lamb. 'Everyman's library.' Ln: Dent . . . 1906. Cr. 8°, pp. 340

[Works: Ext.] Tales from Sh—, by C. & M. Lamb. Second selection. Ln: McDougall . . . 1906. Cr. 8°, pp. 64

[Works: Ext.] Tales from Sh—, by C. & M. Lamb. Illustrated. Ln: Pearson . . . 1906. Cr. 8°, pp. 348

[Works: Ext.] Tales from Sh—, by C. & M. Lamb. 'New universal library.' Ln: Routledge . . . 1906. 12°, pp. 384

[Works: Ext.] Gems from Sh—. Ln: C. Tilt [c. 1907]. 12°   BPL

[Works: Ext.] Sh— gem birthday book. Ln: Nister . . . 1907. 16°   BPL

[Works: Ext.] Sh— remembrance kalendar for 1908. Ln: Simpkin . . . 1907. 16°

[Works: Ext.] Tales from Sh—, by C. & M. Lamb, edited by Alfred Ainger. 'Golden treasury series.' Ln: Macmillan . . . 1907. 12°   BPL

[Works: Ext.] Translations into Greek and Latin verse, edited by [Sir] R. C. Jebb. Cambridge . . . 1907. 8°   BPL
Includes selections from Sh—.

[Works: Ext.] Adams (W. H. D.) Concordance to the plays . . . Ln: Routledge . . . [c. 1908]. Cr. 8°   BPL

[Works: Ext.] Braithwaite (W. S.) Book of Elizabethan verse. Edited with notes. Ln: Chatto . . . 1908. 12°   BPL

[Works: Ext.] Foster (John) Sh— wordbook, being a glossary of archaic forms and varied usages of words employed by Sh—. Ln: Routledge . . . 1908. 8°, pp. 748   BPL

[Works: Ext.] Gateway to Sh—: Selections from the plays, and Lamb's tales, with life of Sh— by Mrs. Lang . . . 1908. 8° BPL

[Works: Ext.] Mr. and Mrs. F. R. Benson and their Shakespearean company [by F. R. Benson]. Liverpool: Shakespeare Theatre . . . 1908. Cr. 8°, pp. 36, including 15 character and scene portraits   BPL

[Works: Ext.] Selections from Sh—, edited by A. Burrell . . . 1908. Cr. 8°   BPL

[Works: Ext.] Sh— proverbs, edited by M. C. Clarke and W. J. Rolfe. Ln: Putnam . . . 1908. Cr. 8°   BPL

[Works: Ext.] Short studies in English literature. 'Comedies' and 'Tragedies' from Lamb's tales from Sh— . . . 1908. 2 vols. 12°   BPL

Sh— [Works: Extracts]—

[Works: Ext.] Songs from Sh—: A calendar for 1909. Ln: Anacker . . . 1908. Cr. 8°

[Works: Ext.] Tales from Sh—, by C. & M. Lamb. 'People's library.' Ln: Cassell . . . 1908. Cr. 8°

Works: Ext.] Tales from Sh—, by C. & M. Lamb. 'Illustrated pocket classics.' Ln: Collins . . . 1908. 12°, pp. 424

[Works: Ext.] Tales from Sh—, by C. & M. Lamb. Second selection for preliminary students, edited by A. Syms-Wood. Ln: G. Gill . . . 1908. Cr. 8°, pp. 216

[Works: Ext.] Tales from Sh— by C. & M. Lamb. With introduction and notes by C. D. Punchard. Ln: Macmillan . . . 1908-09. 2 vols. 12°   BPL

[Works: Ext.] Treasury of English literature, selected and arranged by Kate M. Warren. With introduction by Stopford Brooke. Ln: Constable . . . 1908. 8°

[Works: Ext.] Children's Sh—. Ln: H. Frowde . . . 1909. Roy. 8°, pp. 56

[Works: Ext.] Disjecta [edited by Sidney Humphries]. Edinburgh: Privately printed by R. & R. Clark, 1909. F°, pp. xvi.-426, and frontispiece bearing coat-of-arms   SML

[Works: Ext.] Sh— remembrance kalendar. Ln: Simpkin . . . 1909. New York: F. A. Stokes. 16°, pp. 36, in red and black

[Works: Ext.] Tales from Sh—, by C. & M. Lamb. Illustrated by Arthur Rackham. New edition. Ln: Dent . . . 1909. 8°, pp. 316
Some done on large paper, roy. 8°.

[Works: Ext.] Tales from Sh—, by C. & M. Lamb. Ln: Siegle & Hill, 1909. Cr. 8°, pp. 402

[Works: Ext.] Tales from Sh—, by C. & M. Lamb. Oxford: Clarendon Press, 1909. Cr. 8°, pp. 264

[Works: Ext.] Historical tales from Sh—, by A. T. Quiller-Couch. Ln: Arnold, 1910. Cr. 8°

[Works: Ext.] Sh— day by day, selected by Agnes Caldwell Way. Ln: Harrap . . . 1910. 12°, pp. 110   BM | BLO | CTC

[Works: Ext.] Stories from Sh—, edited by Thomas Carter. Ln: Harrap . . . 1910. 8°, pp. 294. Illustrated

[Works: Ext.] Tales from Sh—, by C. & M. Lamb. Illustrated by J. A. Walker. Ln: Peacock . . . 1910. Cr. 8°

[Works: Ext.] Tales from Sh—, by C. & M. Lamb. 'World library.' Ln: Ward, Lock . . . 1910. Cr. 8°

Sh— Works : Ext. references—

NOTE. — *The succeeding sub-alphabet deals with the poet individually, and chiefly consists of biography.*—W. J.

Shakespeare.] Allibone (Samuel Austin) Sh—'s life and bibliography [In ' Dictionary of English literature,' pp. 2006-2054]. Philadelphia . . . 1870. Imp. 8° BM | BPL | BUS] Allusions and personal references to the poet—

Shakespeare.] Allusions and personal references to the poet—

Shakespeare.] Allusions and personal references to the poet—

See Sh—] Sh— allusion book
,, Sharpe
,, Sheffield
,, Shirley
,, Silsby
,, Smith (E.)
,, Southwell
,, Spenser (E.)
,, Steele
,, Stephens (G.)
,, Stephens (J.)
,, Sterne
,, Tate
,, Tatham
,, Temple (Sir W.)
,, Terence
,, Theatrical . . .

See Thomson
,, Trench
,, Tymms
,, Universal . . .
,, Valpy
,, Visions . . .
,, W—— (J.)
,, Ward (E.)
,, Webster
,, Wedderburn
,, Weever
,, Welsted
,, Westall
,, Whitlock
,, Wild
,, Wilkinson
,, Willobie
,, Yates

] Anderson (R.) Life of Sh— [In ' Works of the British poets,' Vol. 2]. 1795. 8°
BPL

] Art of Sh— as revealed by himself [In 'Victoria Magazine,' Oct., 1863]. 8° BUS

] B—— (W.) Sketch of the life and works of Sh—. [1860 ?] F° BPL

] Bagehot (Walter) Sh— the individual [In ' Estimates of some Englishmen and Scotchmen,' pp. 222-273]. Ln: Chapman . . . 1858. 8° BPL | BUS

] Bagehot (W.) Sh— the man [In 'Literary studies,' edited by R. H. Hutton, Vol. 1, pp. 126-172]. Ln: Longman . . . 1879. 8° BPL | BUS
The same article as the preceding, under an altered title.

] Bagehot (W.) Sh—: the man [In ' Literary studies ']. Ln: Longman . . . 1884. 2 vols. 8° SML

] Bagehot (Walter) Sh— the man. New York . . . 1901. 8°, pp. 82, and portrait
BPL | BUS

] Bain (*Dr.* Beattie) Sh—'s death [In ' The lancet ']. 1902. 4° BPL

] Baker (George P.) Development of Sh— as a dramatist. Ln: Macmillan, 1907. 8°, pp. 342 BPL

] Bartol (Cyrus A.) Personality of Sh— [In his ' Principles and portraits ']. Boston [U.S.] . . . 1880. 8° BUS

] Bayne (R.) Sh— [In ' God's Englishmen, edited by Stubbs,' pp. 127-154]. Ln: S.P.C.K. [1887]. 12° BPL

] Baynes (T. S.) Sh— [In ' Encyclopædia Britannica ']. Ln: Black, 1873. 4°
BM | BPL | SML

] Baynes (T. S.) Sh— [In ' Encyclopædia Britannica,' 9th ed., Vol. 21]. Ln: Black, 1886. 4° BM | BPL

Shakespeare]—

] Baynes (T. S.) What Sh— learnt at school [In ' Fraser's magazine ']. Ln: Nov., 1879. 8° BPL | BUS

] Baynham (George Walter) Swedenborg and Sh—: A comparison. Ln: J. Speirs, 1894. 8°, pp. 48 BM | BUS

] Beeching (H. C.) Wm. Sh—: player, playmaker and poet. A reply to G. Greenwood. Ln: Smith, 1908. Cr. 8°, pp. 114
BM | BLO | BPL | CTC
Reviewed in ' The Athenæum,' No. 4,240, Jan., 1909, p. 143.

] Bell (Robert) Lecture on Sh— and his times, delivered at Farnham [In ' Literary gazette,' 1857, pp. 206-9]. 1857. 4° BM

] [Bell (Robert)] William Sh— [In Lardner's ' Cabinet cyclopædia ']. 1837. 12°
BM | BPL | BUS

] Belsham (William) On Sh— [In ' Essays,' Vol. 2]. 1799. 2 vols. 8° BPL | BUS

] Benas (B. L.) Study of Sh—: A lecture. Liverpool . . . [1875]. 8° BPL

] Bensusan (S. L.) Wm. Sh—; his homes and haunts. Ln: Jack . . . 1910. Fcp. 4°, pp. 88 BM | BLO | CTC

] Biographical sketches of eminent British poets, with criticisms on their works . . . Dublin: A. Thom & Sons, 1854. 8°, pp. viii.-508
Sh— fills pp. 56-82.

] Biography of Sh— [In ' Saturday Review,' 8/15 Sept., 27 Oct., 22 Dec.] Ln: 1866. F° BUS

] Birch (Wm. John) Inquiry into the philosophy and religion of Sh—. Ln: C. Mitchell, 1848. 8°, pp. viii.-548-iv.
BM | BPL | BUS | CPL | SML
' Doubts have been entertained as to Sh—'s religious belief, because few or no notices of it occur in his works. This ought to be attributed to a tender and delicate reserve about holy things, rather than to inattention or neglect.'—*Charles Knight.*
This work seeks to prove Sh— an atheist.

] Blades (Wm.) Sh— and typography; being an attempt to shew Sh—'s personal connection with and technical knowledge of the art of printing. Also remarks upon some common typographical errors, with special reference to the text of Sh—. Ln: Trübner . . . 1872. 8°, pp. viii.-78
BM | BPL | BUS | CPL | SML
This subject was also treated of by an anonymous writer in the 'Scottish Typographical Circular,' Aug. 2, 1862.

] Boaden (James) Inquiry into the authenticity of various pictures and prints which, from the decease of the poet to our own times, have been offered as portraits of Sh—. Containing a careful examination of the evidence on which they claim to be received; by which the pretended portraits have been rejected, the genuine

confirmed and established. Illustrated
. . . by the ablest artists, from such
originals as were of indisputable authority
. . . Ln : R. Triphook . . . 1824. Roy. 8°,
pp. viii.-206, and five portraits
BM | BPL | BUS | CPL | MPL | SMI | W

] Boaden (J.) Inquiry into . . various pictures
and prints . . . Ln : R. Triphook . . . 1824.
4°, pp. viii.-144 BPL | BUS | W
Large paper copy, with India proofs.

] Bormann (August Edwin) Sh—'s debut,
1598. Leipzig . . . 1898. 8°, pp. 32
BM | BUS

] Braithwaite (B.) Sh—; man, dramatist,
and poet. Epsom : Birch & Whittington,
1900. 8° SML

] Brandes (Georg Morris Cohen) William
Sh—; A critical study. Ln : Heinemann,
1896. 2 vols. 8° BM | BPL | BUS | MPL
Tries to demonstrate that the poet has incorporated his
whole individuality in his works.

] Brandes. William Sh— . . . Trans. by W.
Archer, Diana White, and Mary Morison.
Ln : Heinemann, 1898. 2 vols. 8°, pp.
850 BM | BUS | SML

] Brandes. Sh—; A critical study. Ln :
Heinemann, 1899. 8°, pp. 720

] Brandes. Life and work of Wm. Sh—
[In ' Garrick edition ' of Sh—'s Works,
Vol. 12]. 1905. 8° BPL

] Brink (Bernhard Ten) Five lectures on Sh—
. . . Translated by Julia Franklin. Ln :
Bell . . . 1895. Cr. 8°, pp. vi.-248
BM | BPL | BUS | SML

] Britton (John) Remarks on the life and
writings of Sh—. With a list of essays
. . . on his dramatic writings. Ln : Chiswick Press [*Not for sale*], 1814. 8°, pp. 34
BM | BPL | BUS | MPL
Impression limited to twenty-five copies (for presents).
These notes were afterwards added to Whittingham's
edition of Sh—'s Works, 1814 and 1818.

] Britton (John) Remarks on . . . Sh—. [Re-
vised and enlarged.] Ln : Chiswick Press.
Not for sale, 1818. 8° BM | BUS | CPL | W
Large paper copy. Issue limited to twenty-five copies.
Printed for presents only.

] Britton (John)] Remarks on the monumental bust of Sh— at Stratford-upon-
Avon. Chiswick : C. Whittingham,
privately printed, 1816. 8°, pp. 8. With
two woodcuts representing the front and
profile of the bust BPL | BUS | W

] Britton (John) William Sh— [Article in
Rees' Cyclopædia]. Ln : . . . 1816. 4°
BUS

] Brooke (Stopford A.) English literature
from A.D. 670 to 1832. Ln : Macmillan,
1905. 12°, pp. 192
Sh— pp. 62-145.

] Brown (David Paul) Sketches of the life
and genius of Sh—. With illustrations.
Philadelphia : Rackliff & King, 1838. 8°,
pp. 68 BUS

] Browne (G.) William Sh— [In shorthand,
from ' The phonograph ']. 1880. 12°
BPL

] Bryant (William Cullen) Sh— [In ' Orations
and addresses,' pp. 369-378]. 1873. 12°
BPL

] C—— (J.) Annals of the life and works of
William Sh—. Ln : Low . . . 1886. 8°,
pp. xii.-146 BM | BPL

] C—— (J.) Brief annals of . . . life and works
of Sh—. Ln : Low . . . 1888. 8°, pp. xii.-
146. Illustrated

] C—— (W. F.) Brief memorial of Sh—.
Stratford-upon-Avon [1865]. 12° BPL

] C—— (W. G.) Sh— in his works [In
' Chambers' Journal ']. 1864. Roy. 8°
BPL

] Calmour (Alfred C.) Fact and fiction about
Sh—. With some account of the playhouses, players, and playwrights of his
period. Stratford-on-Avon : G. Boyden.
Ln : H. Williams [1894]. 4°, pp. viii.-
112. Portraits and illustrations
BM | BPL | BUS | MPL | SML

] Calvert (George Hy.) Sh—; A biographic
æsthetic study. Boston U.S. : Lee &
Shepard, 1879. 16°, pp. 212, and por-
trait BM | BPL | BUS

] Cambrian Sh—. *See* Edwards of Nant

] Campbell (Thomas) Remarks on the life and
writings of Wm. Sh—. Ln : Moxon . . .
1838. 8°, pp. x.-72 BUS
For a mistake herein see *Sh—*] Sh— Soc.

] Campbell. Life of Sh—. *See* Sh— Works,
1844, 1876

] Carter (T.) Sh—; puritan and recusant.
With prefatory note by J. Oswald Dykes.
Edinburgh : Oliphant, 1897. Cr. 8°, pp.
iv.-208 BM | BPL | BUS | SML

] Chalmers (Alex.) Life of Sh— [In ' English
poets,' by Chalmers, Vol. 5]. 1810. 8°
BPL

] Chalmers. Life of Sh—. *See* Sh— Works,
1805, 1811, 1837, 1838, 1841, 1844, 1846,
1848, 1849, 1850, 1851, 1852, 1857, 1858,
1862, 1886

] Chambers' Journal [containing article on
' Sh—; his birth, birthplace, life, and
writings ']. 1864. Roy. 8°, pp. 32.
Illustrated

] Chase (S. C.) Sh—; A tercentenary tribute.
[1864.] 12° BPL

] Coleridge (H.) Sh— a tory and a gentleman
[In ' Blackwood's magazine '] . . . 1828.
8° BPL

Shakespeare]—

] Collection :—Aristotle and Sh—. The mulberry tree ; A tale. Sharp (Thomas) Affidavit respecting the mulberry relics, 1769-1840. Three [unpublished ?] manuscripts on 29 leaves of paper. Fcp. 4° w

] Collection of original pieces upon Shakespearean subjects :—' Sh— *versus* Sh— ' ; ' Supposititious letter to Mistress Judith Hathaway ' ; Copies of letters from W. H. Ireland to John Jordan upon Sh— matters ; ' Upon Sh—'s chair,' etc. 1794-1840. Manuscript, upon twenty-eight leaves of paper. Fcp. 4° w

] Collection of twenty-seven manuscript and printed pieces illustrative of Sh— and his plays, mounted into an album, 1611-1772. Imp. 4° w
Contents : Steevens (George) Holograph letter dated 3rd Dec., 1772, on a new edition of Sh—. Baudius, Moralis et civilis sapientiæ monita, 1611, title-page only, with the autograph of Ben Ionson. *Ballad :* ' Wooing of the fair maid of London by King Edward.' *Ballad :* ' Life and death of Richard the third.' *Ballad :* ' Life and death of Titus Andronicus ' ; and other old ballads, together with an engraving of the Ellesmere portrait of Sh—.

] Collier (John Payne) Life of Sh—, with a history of the early English stage. Ln : T. Rodd . . . 1844. 8°

] Collier. New facts regarding the life of Sh— in a letter to Thomas Amyot. Ln : T. Rodd, privately printed, 1835. 8°, pp. 56   BPL | BUS | CPL | MPL | W
Twenty-five copies were also printed on large paper.

] Collier. Life of Sh—. *See* Sh— Works, 1836

] Collins (John Churton) Sh— [In ' Poet's country, edited by Andrew Lang ']. 1907. 8°, pp. 378. With coloured plates   BPL

] Colvile (Frederick Leigh) Worthies of Warwickshire who lived between 1500 and 1800. Warwick : Cooke . . . [1869]. Fcp. 4°, pp. 900   SML | W
Over forty pages devoted to Sh—.

] Cond (T.) Wm. Sh— : his life and genius. Appreciations. 1897. 4°   BPL

] Condition of the Sh— family [In ' Monthly magazine ']. 1820. 8°   BPL

] Confessions of Wm. Sh— [In ' New monthly magazine,' Jan., Mar., July, Sept.] Ln : 1835. 8°   BUS
A critique on the sonnets.

] Contemporary notices of Sh— [In British ' Quarterly Review,' July]. Ln : . . . 1857. 8°   BUS

] Conway (Moncure Daniel) Mr. Wm. Sh— at home : Tercentenary, 23 April, 1864 [In ' Harper's magazine,' Aug. New York, 1864]. 8°   BUS

Shakespeare]—

] Corbin (John) Facts about Sh— [In the ' Munsey ' magazine, pp. 277-285]. Dec., 1905. Roy. 8°. With plates of the New York statue, Jansen, Ely, Westminster Abbey, Droeshout bust, and Chandos portraits
Says that ' instead of being a divinity out-topping knowledge, the great Elizabethan dramatist is one of the clearest-cut figures in literary biography.'

] Cox (Frederick) Lecture on the genius, life, and character of Wm. Sh—, delivered to the Mutual Improvement Society of Welford. Leicester : T. C. Browne . . . 1853. 8°, pp. 66   BM | BPL | BUS

] Craig (E. T.) Portraits, bust, and monument of Sh—. 1860. 12°   BPL

] Craig (E. T.) Portraits, bust, and monuments of Sh—. [1886.] 8°   BM

] Craig (E. T.) Sh— and art, or the portraiture of the poet and the heritage of genius. Second edition [1884 ?]. 12° BPL
A reprint of " Sh—'s portraits " under an altered title.

] Craig (E. T.) Sh— and his portraits, bust, and monument. Second edition. Ln : F. Pitman [c. 1866]. 8°, pp. 64   BUS

] Craig (E. T.) Sh—'s portraits considered phrenologically ; part i., Sh— and art ; part ii., Sh—, or the Ardens of Warwickshire and the heritage of genius. 1864. 12°   BPL | CPL

] Craig (E. T.) Sh—'s portraits phrenologically considered . . . Reprinted by J. Parker Norris. Philadelphia : For private circulation, 1875. 8°, pp. ii.-8
Limited to fifty copies.   BM | BPL | BUS

] Creighton *M.D.* (Charles) Sh—'s story of his life. Ln : Richards . . . 1904. 8°, pp. 462   BPL | BUS | SML

] Cumberland (Richard) Sh— in the shades [In ' Memoirs,' p. 40]. 1806. 4°   BPL

] [Cundall (Joseph)] Annals of the life and work of Wm. Sh—. Illustrations and portraits. Ln : Low . . . 1886. 8° BUS | SML
The preface is signed ' J.C.'

] Cust (Lionel) Portraits of Sh— [In Bibliographical Society's Transactions, Vol. 9, pp. 117-119]. Ln : Privately printed, 1908. Fcp. 4°

] Cuthbertson (Evan J.) Wm. Sh— ; his life and times. Ln : Chambers, 1897. 8°, pp. 144. Portrait and illustrations   BM | BPL | BUS

] Dall (*Mrs.* Caroline W. H.) What we really know about Sh—. Boston [U.S.] : Roberts, 1886. 12°   BM | BPL | BUS | SML

] Darmesteter (James) Sh— . . . 1889. 8° BM

] Davey (Hy.) Memoir of Sh—. [*See* Sh—'s Works. Stratford, 1904-07.] Roy. 8°

] Dawson (George) Sh— and other lectures. Edited by G. St. Clair. Ln: K. Paul, 1888. 8°   BM | BPL | BUS | SML

] De Chatelain (*Chevalier*) Le monument d'un Français a Sh— . . . Ln: Rolandi, 1867. 8°, pp. xvi.-166   BPL
In French and English.

] De Chatelain (Le Chev.) Notre monument . . . [Tercentenary] . . . 1868. Cr. 8°   BPL

] Dennis (John) Essay on the genius and writings of Sh—: With some letters of criticism to 'The Spectator.' Ln: B. Lintott . . . 1712. 8°, pp. xii.-66
    BPL | BUS | MPL | W
'This is one of the rarest pieces in early Shakespeareana.' *J. O. Halliwell.*
' Sh— was one of the greatest geniuses that the world ever saw for the tragic stage. Though he lay under greater disadvantages than any of his successors, yet had he greater and more genuine beauties than the best and greatest of them. And what makes the brightest glory of his character, those beauties were entirely his own, and owing to the force of his own nature ; whereas his faults were owing to his education, and to the age that he lived in. One may say of him, as they did of Homer, that he had none to imitate, and is himself inimitable.'

] Dennis (J.) Essay on the genius and writings of Sh— [In ' Original letters,' pp. 361-436]. 1721. 12°   BPL | BUS

] Dennis. Essay on the writings and genius of Sh— compared with the Greek and French dramatic poets. With some remarks upon the misrepresentations of Mons. de Voltaire. Dublin: Printed for H. Saunders, J. Potts, W. Sleater, D. Chamberlaine, and J. Williams, 1769. Cr. 8°, pp. iv.-242

] Dennis. Essay . . . Dublin: Printed for J. Potts, W. Sleater, D. Chamberlaine, J. Williams, and W. Colles, 1778. Cr. 8°, pp. iv.-242

] Dennis (John) Heroes of literature: English poets. Ln: S.P.C.K. . . . 1883. 8°, pp. viii.-406
Sh— occupies pp. 62-73.

] De Quincey (Thomas) Sh— [In ' Encyclopædia Britannica,' seventh edition. Ln: Black, 1838]. 4°   BM | BUS

] De Quincey. Sh—: a biography. Edinburgh: Black . . . 1864. 8°, pp. iv.-100, and portrait   BM | BPL | BUS | SML
Contains also observations ' On the knocking at the gate in Macbeth.'

] De Quincey. Sh— [In ' Biographical essays ']. Boston [U.S.], 1857. 8°   BUS

] De Quincey. Sh— [In ' Biographical essays ']. Boston [U.S.], 1860. 8°   BUS

] De Quincey. Biographies of Sh—, Pope, etc. Edinburgh . . . 1862. 8°   BUS

] De Quincey. Biographies of Sh—, Pope, etc. Edinburgh, 1863. 12°   BPL | BUS

] De Quincey. Last new life of Sh— [In ' Fraser's magazine ']. Ln: July, 1841. 8°   BUS

] Dictionary of national biography, edited by Sir Leslie Stephen & ' Sidney Lee.' Ln: Smith, 1885-1904. 67 vols. Roy. 8°
    BM | BPL | SML
Sh— occupies pp. 348-397 in vol. 51, also a column or two in the volume of ' Errata.'

] Dictionary of national biography. *See also* Fleay. On certain modern Sh—ana

] Dictionary of national biography : Epitome. Edited by ' S. Lee.' Ln: Smith, 1903. Roy. 8°, pp. viii.-1,456
Contains (pp. 1183-1185) a life of Sh— by the editor, which is chiefly remarkable for crediting the poet with one child only, no mention being made of his twins Hamnet and Judith.
The volume likewise omits lives of the poet's father, mother, brothers and sisters.
This is going one better than Dodd (Beauties of Sh—, 1811) who says, ' Sh— had three daughters,' and ignores his son Hamnet.
See Jaggard (W.) for corrections.

] Dodd (Wm.) Life and beauties of Sh— . . . Boston [U.S.], Phillips, Sampson & Co., 1850. 12°, pp. lx.-x.-346, and portrait
    BUS

] Dowden (*Prof.* E.) Life of Sh—. *See* Sh—'s Works, 1895

] Dowden (*Prof.* E.) Sh—. Green's 'literature primer.' Ln: Macmillan, 1877. 12°, pp. 168   BM | BPL | BUS

] Dowden (*Prof.* E.) Sh—. Green's ' literature primer.' New York: Appleton, 1878. 12°, pp. 168   BUS

] Dowden (*Prof.* E.) Sh—. Green's ' literature primer.' New edition. Ln: Macmillan, 1879. 12°   BPL | SML

] Dowden (*Prof.* E.) Sh—. Green's ' literature primer.' 1886. 12°

] Dowden (*Prof.* E.) Sh—. Green's ' literature primer.' Ln: Macmillan, 1895. 12°, pp. 168

] Dowden (*Prof. E.*) Sh—. Green's 'literature primer.' Ln: Macmillan, 1905. 12°, pp. 168   BPL

] Dowden (*Prof.* E.) Sh—: A critical study of his mind and art. Ln: King & Co., 1875. 8°, pp. xii.-430   BM | BUS
' There are certain problems which Sh— at once pronounces insoluble. . . . Little solutions of your large difficulties can readily be obtained from priest or philosopher. Sh— prefers to let you remain in the solemn presence of a mystery. He does not invite you into his little church or his little library, brilliantly illuminated by philosophical or theological rushlights. You remain in the darkness. But you remain in the vital air. And the great night is overhead.'

] Dowden (*Prof.* E.) Sh—: A critical study. Second edition. Ln: Macmillan . . . 1876. 8°   BPL | MPL

Shakespeare]—

] Dowden (*Prof. E.*) Sh—: A critical study. Ln : Kegan Paul . . . 1880. 8°   SML

] Dowden (*Prof.* E.) Sh—: A critical study . . . New York . . . 1881. 8°   BUS

] Dowden (*Prof.* E.) Sh—: A critical study . . . Seventh edition. Ln : Kegan Paul, 1883. 8°   BPL

] Downes (Robert P.) Seven supreme poets. Ln : C. H. Kelly [1905]. Cr. 8°, pp. xii.-336, and seven portraits
Contents : Homer, Æschylus, Sophocles, Virgil, Dante, Sh—, and Milton.
Sh— occupies pp. 215-268, with bust portrait (altered).

] Downing (Charles)] Long desiderated knowledge of the life and personality of Sh—. Preceded by mental optics. By ' Clelia.' Ln : Luzac [1892]. 8°, pp. 34, and folding diagram   BM | BPL

] Drake. Memorials of Sh—, or sketches of his character and genius by various writers. With essay and notes. Ln : Colbourn . . . 1828. 8°, pp. viii.-494
BPL | BUS | CPL | MPL | SML | W
' It is remarkable ' (says Drake, talking of Sh—'s birthday) ' that on the same day expired in Spain his great and amiable contemporary Cervantes, and the world was thus deprived nearly at the same moment of the two most original writers which modern Europe has produced.'

] Drake. [Memorials.] Shaksperiana, or sketches of Sh—'s character and genius . . . Ln : Colburn, 1828. 8°, pp. viii.-494
BUS
Identical with preceding entry, except fresh title-page.

] Drake (Nathan) Sh— and his times : including the biography of the poet ; criticisms on his genius and writings ; new chronology of his plays ; disquisition on the object of his sonnets ; and history of the manners, customs, amusements, superstitions, poetry, and elegant literature of his age. Ln : Cadell & Davies . . . 1817. 2 vols. 4°. With Stratford bust and plate of autographs
BPL | BUS | CPL | MPL | SML | W
A few done on large paper.

] Drake (N.) Sh— and his times. 1843. 8°
BM

] Drake. Sh— and his times. Paris : Baudry, 1838. 8°, pp. xxviii.-660   BUS | SML

] Duff (W.) Of Sh— [In ' Critical observations,' pp. 126-196]. 1770. 12°   BPL

] Dyce (Alex.) Memoir of Sh—. [c. 1832.] 12°   BPL

] Dyce. Memoir of Sh—. *See* Sh— Poems, 1832, 1837, 1842, 1853, 1856, 1864, 1866, 1894

] Early authorship of Sh— [In ' North British Review ']. Ln : April, 1870. 8°
BUS

Shakespeare]—

] Eaton (S.) Shakespearean prints. ' Connoisseur edition.' Ln : . . . 1900. 12 parts. 4°. Containing 146 plates   BPL
Issued as a supplement to the ' Eversley edition ' of Sh—'s ' Works,' 1900.

] Edwards (Ernest) Memorials of Sh—, photographed for the tercentenary festival. Ln : E. Edwards . . . 1864. F° Eight views   BUS

] Edwards (J.) Biography of Sh—. New York [1900]. 12°

] Eiloart (Arnold) Sh— and Tolstoy ; by a lover of both. Letchworth : Garden City Press, 1909. Cr. 8°   BPL

] Elton (Charles Isaac) Wm. Sh— ; his family and friends. Edited by A. Hamilton Thompson. With a memoir of the author by Andrew Lang. Ln : Murray . . . 1904. 8°, pp. x.-522
BPL | BUS | MPL | SML
A weighty contribution to Shakespearean scholarship.

] Elze (*Dr.* Karl) Wm. Sh—: A literary biography. Translated by L. D. Schmitz. Ln : Bell . . . 1888. 8°, pp. viii.-588
BM | BPL | SML

] Elze. Wm. Sh—. Halle . . . 1876. 8°
BM | BPL

] Emerson (Ralph Waldo) On Sh—. From ' Essays on representative men.' Ln : De la More Press, 1904. 18°   BPL

] Emerson (Ralph Waldo) Representative men. 1844
At page 154 contains an essay on ' Sh—, or the poet.'
' Sh— is the only biographer of Sh—, and even he can tell nothing except to the Sh— in us ; that is, to our most apprehensive and sympathetic hour. . . . Now literature, philosophy, and thought are Shakspeare-ised. His mind is the horizon beyond which, at present, we do not see.'

] Emerson (R. W.) Representative men. Ln : Bohn, 1850. Cr. 8°   SML

] Emerson (R. W.) Sh—, or the poet [In ' Representative men,' pp. 93-106]. 1870. 12°   BPL | MPL | SML

] Emerson (R. W.) Representative men. Boston [U.S.] . . . 1857. 12°   BUS

] Epitaph on Sh—. Monumental inscription on the mural tablet in Holy Trinity Church, Stratford-on-Avon, 1623
The lines, which are anonymous (but probably written by Ben. Jonson), run :—
Ivdicio Pylivm, genio Socratem, arte Maronem, Terra tegit, popvlvs mæret, Olympvs habet.
Stay, passenger, why goest thov by so fast
Read if thov canst whom envious death hath plast
Within this monvment ; Sh— with whome
Qvick natvre dide ; whose name doth deck ys tombe
Far more then cost : Sieh [since] all yt he hath writt
Leaves living art bvt page to serve his witt.
OBIIT ANO. DOI. 1616. ÆTATIS 53 DIE 23 AP.

] Evans (E. P.) Youth . . . marriage, and manhood of Sh— ; Sh— as player and poet [In ' Western monthly,' July-Sept.] Chicago, 1869. 8°   BUS

] Ewen (A.) Sh— in the country and in the town [In ' Architectural Soc. Reports,' Vol. 28, pp. 538-568]. Ln : 1905-06. 8°
BPL

] Ewen (Alfred) Sh—. ' Great writers.' Ln : Bell . . . 1904. 12°, pp. 126. With portrait, plates, and facsimiles   BPL | BUS

] Family of Sh— [In ' Tewkesbury yearly register and magazine ']. 1834. 8°   BUS

] Fisher (F. H.) Wm. Sh—. A poem. [c. 1891.] 12°

] Fleay (Frederick Gard) Chronicle history of the life and work of Wm. Sh—, player, poet, and playmaker. With two etched illustrations. Ln : J. C. Nimmo . . . 1886. 8°, pp. viii.-364   BM | BPL | BUS | SML

] Foard (J. T.) Real life of Sh— [In ' Southport Literary and Philosophical Soc. Proc.'] 1904. 8°   BPL

] Forshaw (C. F.) At Sh—'s shrine : A poetical anthology. With ' Plays partly written by Sh—,' by Richard Garnett. Ln : E. Stock . . . 1904. 8°, pp. 396
BPL | MPL | SML

The title, 'Sh—'s shrine,' was copyrighted by John Harris (*q.v.*) nearly forty years before this.

] [Forsyth (E.)] Sh—: Some notes on his character and writings. By a student. Edinburgh . . . 1867. 8°   BM | BPL

] Friswell (James Hain) Life portraits of Wm. Sh—: History of the various representations of the poet, with an examination into their authenticity. Ln : S. Low, 1864. 8°, pp. xii.-128
BM | BPL | BUS | CPL | MPL | SML
Also issued with a facsimile of the poet's will.

] Frith (J. C.) Sh— [A sonnet in ' Leaves by the way.']. Birmingham, 1901. Cr. 8°
BPL

] Fullom (Stephen Watson) History of Wm. Sh—: Player and poet. With new facts and traditions. Ln : Saunders & Otley, 1862. 8°, pp. viii.-372
BM | BPL | BUS | CPL | MPL | SML

] Fullom. History . . . Second edition. Ln : Saunders . . . 1864. 8°, pp. viii.-372   BUS

] Furnivall (F. J.) & Munro (J.) Sh—'s life and work. *See* Sh—'s Works. ' Century ed.,' Vol. 1.   1908

] Garnett (Richard) Wm. Sh—, pedagogue and poacher ; A drama. Ln : Lane . . . 1905. 8°, pp. 112   BPL | BUS | SML

] Garnett (*Dr.* R.) & Gosse (E.) Sh— [In ' History of English literature,' Vol. 2]. Ln : Heinemann, 1903. 4 vols. 4°   BPL

] Genius of Sh—: A summer dream [In verse]. Ln : Couch & Laking [1793]. 4°, pp. ii.-34   BM

] Gervinus (G. G.) Sh—. 1849. 8°   BM

] Gervinus (G. G.) Sh—. 1872. 8°   BM

] Gibbs (Hunt) Halliwell (J. O.) & Rogers (M. E.)] Sh— memorial. Ln : S. O. Beeton, 1864. F°, pp. 48. With four coloured plates and other illustrations
BM | BPL | BUS | CPL | MPL | SML
According to S. Timmins, the writer was M. E. Rogers, who borrowed her documents and dates from Halliwell. It was issued in two forms, the shilling edition having but one coloured plate.
The Birmingham collection includes a copy bound in oaken boards (taken from Herne's oak), with MS. identifications of the engravings.
See also Reference key . . .

] Gibson (R. L.) Life of Sh—. *See* Sh—'s Works : Ext. 1865

] Gilfillan (George) Third gallery of portraits. Edinburgh : J. Hogg . . . 1854. 8°   BPL
Sh— fills pp. 501-536.

] Gilfillan (George) Life and poetry of Sh— [In ' Nichols' Poets,' Vol. 10]. 1856. 8°   BPL

] Gilfillan. Galleries of literary portraits. Edinburgh : James Hogg. Ln : R. Groombridge, 1856. 2 vols. Cr. 8°
Sh— vol. 1, pp. 17-36.

] Glynn (P. McM.) Disposition of Sh— [In ' Trans. of the Library Assoc. of Australasia ']. 1902. 8°   BPL

] Glynn (P. McM.) Some thoughts on Sh—. Adelaide Univ. Sh— Soc. . . . 1891. 8°
BPL

] Glynn (P. McM.) Works of Sh— as a key to the man [In ' Trans. of the Library Assoc. of Australasia ']. 1901. 8°   BPL

] Godwin (W.) The enquirer. 1823. 8°   BPL
Sh— pp. 342-346.

] Goethe (Johann Wolfgang von) Conversations with Eckermann and Soret. 1875. 12°   BPL
Sh— pp. 50-310.

] Goodson (H. F.) Sh— . . . Second edition . . . 1874. 12°   BPL

] Goodson (H. F.) Sh—: his religious and moral sentiments . . . 1874. 12°   BPL

] Gostwick (J.) Sh— [In ' English poets : Twelve essays,' pp. 17-49] . . . 1876. 8°
BPL

] Graves (Joseph) Life of Wm. Sh—. [c. 1830.] 12°   BM | BPL

] Gray (James William) Sh—'s marriage, his departure from Stratford, and other incidents in his life. Ln : Chapman & Hall, 1905. 8°, pp. 298. With facsimiles
BPL | BUS | MPL
Reviewed in ' The Athenæum,' 1906, No. 4,048 (p. 648).

] Griffiths (L. M.) Sh— and the medical sciences. Bristol, 1887. 8°   BUS

] Griggs (Edward Howard) Syllabus of a course of twelve lectures on Sh—. Philadelphia . . . 1904. 8°, pp. 42   BPL | BUS

Shakespeare]—

] Guizot (F. P. G.) Sh— and his times, with notices of his principal dramas. Trans. from the French. Ln : Bentley . . . 1852. 8°, pp. viii.-424   MPL | SML
Partly reprinted from 'North British Review.'

] Guizot (F. P. G.) Sh— and his times . . . Second edition. Ln : . . . 1852. 8°, pp. viii.-424   BUS | CPL

] Guizot. Sh— and his times. New York : Harper . . . 1852. 12°, pp. 360   BUS

] Guizot. Sh— and his times. New York : Harper . . . 1855. 8°   SML

] Guizot. Sh— and his times. Ln : Bentley . . . 1857. 8°

] Guizot. Sh— and his times. [Magazine review.] Ln : . . . [c. 1852]. 8°   BPL | W

] Gullett (H.) Study of Sh—. New South Wales Sh— Society, Sydney, 1906. 8°   BPL

] Gullett (H.) Making of Sh— and other papers. New South Wales Sh— Society, Sydney, 1905. 8°   BPL

] H—— (M.) Sh—; his humour and pathos. [c. 1879.] 8°   BPL

] Hales (John) Defence of Sh— [In Rowe's Life of Sh—]. See Sh—'s Works, 1709. 7 vols. 8°
At p. xiv., vol. 1, says :—
'In a conversation between Sir John Suckling, Sir W. D'Avenant, Endymion Porter, Mr. Hales of Eton, and Ben Jonson—Sir John Suckling, who was a professed admirer of Sh—, had undertaken his defence against Ben Jonson with some warmth. Mr. Hales, who had sat still for some time, hearing Ben frequently reproaching him [Sh -] with want of learning and ignorance of the ancients, told him at last that if Mr. Sh— had not read the ancients he had likewise not stolen anything from 'em [a fault the other made no conscience of], and that if he would produce any one topic finely treated by any of them, he would undertake to show something upon the same subject at least as well written by Sh—.'

] Hall (Arthur) Sh—'s handwriting further illustrated : Facsimiles of his own supposed autograph, with a short note of his early career as a dramatist. Ln : Asher . . . 1899. 8°, pp. 16   BPL | BUS | SML

] Hallam (H.) Literary essays and characters. Ln : J. Murray, 1852. 8°   SML
Contains an 'Essay on Sh—.'

] Halleck (R. P.) Education of the central nervous system. New York : Macmillan, 1904. Cr. 8°, pp. xii.-258
Valuable for the insight shown in chapter x., headed 'How Sh—'s senses were trained' (pp. 171-208), which sets forth the growth and formation of earth's greatest mind, in Warwickshire farm, field, and forest life, by Stratford lanes and hedgesides, in rustic festival and merrymaking, on the Avon's twenty-mile course between Kenilworth and Bidford, or about the stately castles of Warwick and Kenilworth, where for centuries English history revolved.
Gives insight also into the probable cause of Sh—'s death and the extinction of his direct race.

Shakespeare]—

] Hallen (A. W. C.) Pedigree of the family of Sh—. Stratford-on-Avon, 1885. 8°   BPL

] Halliwell (J. O.) Budget of notes and memoranda on the life and works of Sh—. 1880. 8°   BM | BPL

] Halliwell (J. O.) Catalogue of a small portion of the engravings and drawings illustrative of the life of Sh—, preserved in the collection formed by J. O. H. [Ln :] For presents only, 1868. 8°, pp. 92
          BM | BPL | BUS | HCL | MPL | SML
Only a few copies printed.

] Halliwell (J. O.) Fragment of 'Illustrations of the life of Sh—.' Ln : For presents only, printed by J. E. Adlard, 1874. F°, pp. iv.-86-92   BPL | BUS
Fifty copies printed.
Consists of documents found in the Lord Chamberlain's office illustrating the poet's connection with the Globe and Blackfriars theatres.

] Halliwell (J. O.) Hand-List of the drawings and engravings illustrative of the life of Sh—, preserved at Hollingbury Copse, Brighton. For private circulation only, 1884. 8°   BM | BPL | BUS | SML

] Halliwell (J. O.) Illustrations of the life of Sh— in discursive . . . essays on . . . the personal and literary history of the great dramatist. Part I. Ln : Longmans . . . 1874. F°, pp. viii.-128. Illustrated with woodcuts of Shakespearean London and particulars of Elizabethan theatres
          BM | BPL | BUS | MPL | SML

] Halliwell (J. O.) Last days of Sh— [In 'Saint James' magazine,' conducted by Mrs. S. C. Hall, Vol. i., pp. 285-288]. Ln : W. Kent & Co., 1861. 8°   BPL | BUS

] Halliwell (J. O.) Last days of Sh—. [Ln : Whittingham & Wilkins, 1863.] 16°, pp. 24   BM | BPL | BUS | HCL
'The first paper in which the gardens of Sh— were brought before . . . the public.'

] Halliwell (J. O.) Life of Wm. Sh—. Including many particulars respecting the poet and his family never before printed. Ln : J. R. Smith . . . 1848. 8°, pp. xvi.-336. 76 woodcuts by Fairholt and autograph facsimiles
          BM | BPL | BUS | HCL | MPL | SML | W

] Halliwell (J. O.) Notes from the Record Office illustrating the life and times of Wm. Sh—. [Author's holograph manuscript. c. 1870.] 3 vols. 8°   BPL

] Halliwell (J. O.) On the life of Sh— [Proposed publication : In 'The Athenæum,' No. 2737, p. 471]. 1880

] Halliwell (J. O.) Outlines of the life of Sh—. Ln : Longmans . . . 1874. 8°

] Halliwell (J. O.) Outlines . . . Brighton [Privately printed], 1881. 8°. Illustrated
BM | BPL | BUS | SML

] Halliwell (J. O.) Outlines . . . Second edition. Ln : . . . 1882. 8°
BM | BPL | BUS | MPL | SML

] Halliwell (J. O.) Outlines . . . Third edition . . . 1883. 8°
BM | BPL | BUS | SML

] Halliwell (J. O.) Outlines . . . Fourth edition. Ln : . . . 1884. 8°. Illustrations and facsimiles
BM | BPL | BUS | SML

] Halliwell (J. O.) Outlines . . . Fifth edition. Ln : . . . 1885. 8°. Illustrated
BM | BPL | SML

] Halliwell (J. O.) Outlines . . . Sixth edition . . . 1886. 2 vols. 8°. Illustrated
BM | BPL | BUS | SML

] Halliwell (J. O.) Outlines . . . Seventh edition. Ln : . . . 1887. 2 vols. 8°. Illustrated
BM | BPL | BUS | SML

] Halliwell (J. O.) Outlines . . . Eighth edition. Ln : Longman . . . 1889. 2 vols. Roy. 8°
SML

] Halliwell (J. O.) Outlines . . . Tenth edition. Ln : Longmans . . . 1898. 2 vols. Roy. 8°
SML

] Halliwell (J. O.) Shakespearian facsimiles. A collection of curious and interesting documents, plans, signatures, etc. illustrative of the biography of Sh— and the history of his family . . . from the originals chiefly preserved at Stratford-upon-Avon. Selected by J. O. Halliwell. Facsimiled by E. W. Ashbee. Ln. [Privately printed by J. E. Adlard], 1863. F°, pp. 8 and 16 plates
BM | BPL | BUS | MPL
Issue limited to thirty copies.

] Halliwell (J. O.) ' Life of Sh— ' [Critique in ' Gentleman's magazine,' May. Ln : 1848]. 8°
BUS

] Hamer (John) ' Sweet swan of Avon ' [In ' Belgravia,' Vol. 78, p. 398. Ln : 1892]. 8°
BM

] Haney (J. L.) Name of Wm. Sh— : A study in orthography. Philadelphia . . . 1906. Cr. 8°
BPL

] Hardy (R. B.) Lectures on the drama : First Series : Sh—. Glasgow, 1834. 8°
BPL

] Harness. Life of Sh—. *See* Sh—'s Works, 1836, 1840, 1842

] Harness (W.) Sh—'s bust at Stratford-upon-Avon. Ln : Sh— Soc. . . . 1845. 8°
BPL

] Harper (S. B. A.) Was Sh— a catholic ? [In ' American Catholic Quarterly Review,' Jan. Philadelphia . . . 1879]. 8°
BUS

] Harris (Frank) The man Sh— and his tragic life story. Ln : F. Palmer, 1909. 8°, pp. 446
BM | BPL
' Sh—'s tragic story is summed up in his insensate and prolonged love for Mary Fitton, the maid of honour, who had originally betrayed him by yielding to his noble friend Herbert. To the torments of frustrate desire, exquisite in a nature at once acutely sensitive and sensual, are due the last reaches and terrible scope of the great tragedies. . . . That Mr. Harris has realised Sh— more actually than any previous writer —a great achievement—is past doubt.'—*Saturday Review*, 20th Nov., 1909, pp. 633-634.
A contrary view is taken in the review by ' The Bookman,' Feb., 1910, pp. 232-233, which discourteously declares that ' such judgment would be incapable of measuring a puddle.'

] Harrison (F.) New calendar of great men. 1892. 8°
BPL
Sh— fills pp. 423-428.

] Harrison (Gabriel) Stratford bust of Wm. Sh— and a critical inquiry into its authenticity and artistic merits. Illust. with two photographic views, front and profile. Brooklyn, N.Y. : J. M. Bradstreet & Son, 1865. Fcp. 4°, pp. 14
BM | BUS
Issue limited to seventy-five copies.

] Hart (J. S.) Life of Sh—. *See* Sh—'s Works, 1887

] Hazlitt (Wm. Carew) Sh— [his private and literary history]. Ln : Quaritch . . . 1902. Roy. 8°, pp. xxxii.-288
BM | BLO | BPL | BUS | CTC | MPL | SML
In reply to a private query, Mr. Hazlitt tells the writer that in this revised edition the altered paging was not corrected in the index, which is all at sea.

] Hazlitt (W. C.) Sh— himself and his work A study. Second edition. Ln : Quaritch . . . 1903. 8°
BPL

] Hazlitt. Sh— himself and his work. 3rd edition. Ln : . . . 1908. 8°
BPL

] Head (F. H.) Sh—'s insomnia and the causes thereof. Chicago . . . 1886. 8°
BM | BPL | BUS
A satire on Shakespearean criticism.
Contains copies of forged Shakespearean correspondence which the author pretends to treat most seriously.

] Head (F. H.) Sh—'s insomnia . . . Boston and New York : Houghton. Chicago : Maxwell & Co., 1887. Cr. 8°, pp. 64
BPL | SML

] Head (F. H.) Sh—'s insomnia. Boston [U.S.] : Houghton, 1899. 8°
SML

] Henty (W.) Sh— : Some notes on his early biography. *For private circulation*, 1862. 8°
BPL

] Heraud (J. A.) Sh— ; his inner life as intimated in his works. Ln : J. Maxwell . . . 1865. 8°, pp. xiv.-522, and portrait
BM | BPL | BUS | CPL | MPL | SML

] Hirst (S.) Old and new lines . . . in the life of Wm. Sh—. Huddersfield [1884]. 8°
BM | BPL

Shakespeare]—

] Holder (H. W.) Marriage of Wm. Sh— [*re* Mr. Malam's picture]. 1872. F° BPL

] Homes and haunts of Sh—. 1892. 5 vols., in portfolios. Roy. f°. With coloured and other plates

] Homes of Sh—: his birthplace and New Place. Birmingham . . . 1899. Cr. 8° BPL

] Houbraken (J.) Portrait of Sh—, 1747. *See* Birch
This is the Chandos portrait, stated to be copied from a painting in the possession of John Nicoll, of Southgate.

] Howe (Joseph) Sh—: an oration at the Temperance Hall, Halifax, 23 April, 1864. Halifax, Nova Scotia, 'Citizen' Office, 1864. 8°, pp. 26 BM | BUS

] Hudson (H. N.) Sh—: his life, art, and characters. With historical sketch of the origin and growth of the drama in England. Boston [U.S.]: Ginn Brothers, 1872. 2 vols. 12° BM | BUS

] Hudson (H. N.) Sh—: his life, art, and characters. 4th edition. Boston [U.S.] . . . 1888. 2 vols. 12° BPL | MPL

] Hudson (H. N.) Sh—: his life, art, and characters. With an historical sketch of the drama in England. 4th edition. Boston [U.S.], 1895. 2 vols. 8° BUS

] Hugo *Viscount* (Victor Marie) Wm. Sh—. English translation by A. Baillot. Ln: Hurst & Blackett, 1864. 8°, pp. viii.-366 BM | BPL | BUS | CPL | MPL

] Hugo (Victor M.) Wm. Sh—. 'New universal library.' Ln: Routledge . . . 1905. 16°, pp. 352

] Hugo. Sh— [In 'North American Review,' Vol. 173, pp. 289-293]. 1901. 8° BPL

] Hume *Canon* (Abraham) An oration . . . delivered 20th April, 1864. Liverpool: T. Brakell . . . 1864. 8°, pp. 20. Cream wrappers
A few copies privately printed for presents.

] Hume *Canon* (Abraham) Sh— [In 'Trans. of the Hist. Soc. of Lancs. and Cheshire']. Liverpool . . . 1864. 8° BPL

] Hunter (Joseph) New illustrations of the life, studies, and writings of Sh—. First part . . . 1844. 8° BPL

] Hunter (Joseph) New illustrations of the life, studies, and writings of Sh—: supplementary to all editions. Ln: J. B. Nichols & Son . . . 1845. 2 vols. 8°
BM | BPL | BUS | CPL | MPL | W

] Hunter (Robert E.) Sh— and Stratford-upon-Avon: A chronicle of the time. Comprising the salient facts and traditions, biographical, topographical, and historical, connected with the poet and his birthplace. Together with a full record of the tercentenary celebration

Shakespeare]—

. . . Stratford-upon-Avon: E. Adams, 1864. Cr. 8°, pp. viii.-246. With the Church bust, and plan of pavilion
BM | BPL | BUS | CPL | MPL | SML
The life of the poet occupies pp. 1-57; Stratford: a walk through the town, pp. 58-72; Former jubilees and the tercentenary festival, pp. 73-246.

] Immortality of Sh—, in which is introduced an episode [a poem]. Ln: S. Highley . . 1784. 4°, pp. 16 BUS

] Ingersoll (R. G.) Sh—: A lecture. [c. 1897. 12° BPL

] Ingleby (C. M.) Sh—'s centurie of prayse: Being materials for a history of opinion on Sh— and his works, culled from writers of the first century after his rise. Birmingham . . . Ln: Trübner & Co., 1874. 4°, pp. xx.-362
BM | BPL | BUS | SML
Only 250 copies were printed and a few on large paper.

] Ingleby (C. M.) Sh—, the man and the book; being a collection of occasional papers on the bard and his writings. Birmingham: Printed by Josiah Allen. Ln: Trübner . . . 1877-81. 2 vols. Fcp. 4°, pp. viii.-172 & x.-194 BM | BPL | BUS | SML

] Ingleby (C. M.) Occasional papers on Sh—: The man and the book. Part 2. Ln: Trübner . . . 1881. 8° SML

] Ingleby (C. M.) Sh—'s centurie of praise. Second edition. Revised with many additions by Lucy Toulmin Smith. Ln: New Sh— Soc. . . . 1879. 8° BPL | BUS
Twenty-six copies were done on large paper, 4°.
See Furnivall, 'Some fresh allusions,' for supplement to above.

] Ingram (John Kells) On Sh— [In 'Afternoon lectures on English literature']. Dublin . . . 1863. 8°
BM | BPL | BUS | MPL

] Ingram (J. K.) Sh—: A lecture delivered at the Museum of Industry, Dublin [*See* pp. 161-171 & 241-252 of 'English and American Review,' edited by C. H. Gunn]. 1864

] Irwin (J. O.) Sh—'s religious belief [In 'Overland monthly,' Aug.-Sept.] San Francisco, 1875. 8° BUS

] Jackson (J. W.) Ethnology and phrenology as an aid to the biographer: Sh— [In 'Anthropological review,' May]. Ln: 1864. 8° BUS

] [Jacob (Giles)] Poetical register, or the lives and characters of the English dramatick poets, with an account of their writings. Ln: . . . 1719-20. 2 vols. 8°
BPL | MPL | W
Includes a 'Life of Sh—,' pp. 226-236, and portrait.

] [Jacob (Giles)] Poetical register . . . 1723. 8° BPL

] Jenks (Tudor Storrs) In the days of Sh—
[with a brief bibliography, pp. 275-279].
New York . . . 1905. Cr. 8°   BUS
Aims at presenting the poet as he was known to his
friends and neighbours, to tell the story of his life,
and so record the happenings that influenced him.

] Jenks (T.) Lives of great writers. New York
. . . 1905. Cr. 8°   BPL
Contains chapter headed 'In the days of Sh—.'

] Jephson (J. M.) Sh—: his birthplace, home,
and grave. A pilgrimage to Stratford-on-
Avon . . . Ln : L. Reeve . . . 1864. Fcp.
4°, pp. x.-204. With photographic illus-
trations   BM | BPL | BUS | CPL | MPL

] Jephson. Sh— . . . Ln : Bennett . . . 1865.
Fcp. 4°

] Jeremiah (John) Notes on Sh— . . . Comprising a succinct account of the life and
times of the great dramatist . . . History
of the Urban Club. Ln : Clayton, 1876.
8°, pp. 130. With portrait and illustra-
tions   BM | BPL | BUS | MPL | SML

] Jeremiah (J.) Notes on Sh— . . . Ln : . . .
1877. Roy. 8°   BPL
Large paper copy.

] Jones. Coventry, Warwick, and Birmingham Magazine. 1764. 12°   BPL
Contains Nicholas Rowe's 'Life of Sh—,' pp. 117-121.

] Jones *American actor* (George) Tecumseh
and the prophet of the west. An historical Israel-Indian tragedy . . . With
. . . the first oration upon the life, character, and genius of Sh—. Ln : . . . 1844.
Roy. 8°   BM | BUS

] Jones (George) First annual jubilee oration
upon the life, character, and genius of
Sh—. Delivered at Stratford-upon-Avon,
April 23rd, 1836. Ln : E. Churton . . .
1836. 8°, pp. 52   BM | BPL | BUS | W

] Jones (G.) First oration . . . 2nd ed. 1836.
8°   BPL

] Jones (George) First annual Jubilee oration
. . . Fourth edition. [c. 1844.] 8°   BPL

] Jordan (John) Original Memoirs and historical accounts of the families of Sh—
and Hart, deduced from an early period.
1790. 4°. Author's holograph manuscript   BPL
The forger of John Sh—'s will, and a writer whose
statements need to be carefully verified.
Jordan was a Stratford wheelwright and a friend of the
forgers Ireland.

] Jordan (J.) Original memoirs and historical
accounts of the families of Sh— and Hart.
Edited by J. O. Halliwell . . . 1865. Fcp.
4°   BPL
Issue limited to ten copies.

] Joyce (J. A.) Sh—: Personal recollections.
New York . . . [c. 1904]. 8°   BPL

] Kenny (Thomas) Life and genius of Sh—.
Ln : Longman, 1864. 8°, pp. viii.-414.
With portrait and facsimile
    BM | BPL | BUS | CPL | MPL | SML

] King (Alice) Sh— [In 'The Argosy'].
Ln : 1873. 8°   BUS

] King (J.) Our English Sh— [In 'Canadian
monthly ']. Toronto, 1876. 8°   BUS

] Knight (Charles) Sh— and his writings.
[c. 1840.] 8°   BPL

] Knight (C.) Sh— and his writings [In 'Store
of knowledge for all readers,' pp. 3-32].
Ln : Knight . . . 1841. Roy. 8°. With
twelve illustrations of the Globe theatre,
Sh—'s handwriting, Poet's corner, etc.

] Knight (C.) Studies and illustrations . . .
See Knight

] Knight (C.) Wm. Sh—: A biography . . .
Ln : Knight . . . 1842. Roy. 8°, pp. 544.
Illustrated throughout

] Knight (Charles) Wm. Sh—: A biography.
Ln : Knight, 1843. Royal 8°, pp. viii.-544.
Illustrated   BUS | MPL | W
First issued as a supplement to Knight's 'Pictorial
edition' of Sh—'s works, 1839-42.

] Knight (C.) Life of Sh—. 'Standard edition.' Ln : Routledge . . . 1846. 8°   CPL

] Knight (C.) Wm. Sh—. Ln : C. Knight,
1850. Roy. 8°, pp. x.-330. Illustrated

] Knight (C.) Studies of Sh— . . . containing a
history of opinion on the writings of Sh—,
with the chronology of his plays. Ln :
Wm. S. Orr & Co., 1851. 12°, pp. 300, and
woodcut portrait of Dr. S. Johnson
    BPL | SML
Prepared as an introductory volume to the 'Cabinet
edition' of Sh—'s works, 1851.

] Knight (C.) Studies . . . Ln : Routledge . . .
1868. 8°, pp. ii.-560   BUS

] Knight (Charles) Studies and biography of
Sh— . . . Ln : Routledge . . . 1857. 8°

] Knight (C.) Studies . . . Ln : . . . 1856. 12°
    CPL

] Knight (C.) Studies . . . Ln : . . . 1851. 8° BPL

] Knight (Charles) Studies . . . Ln : Knight . . .
1850. 2 vols. 8°. With portraits and
engravings   BM | BUS

] Knight (Charles) Studies of Sh—, forming a
companion to every edition of the text.
Ln : Knight, 1849. 8°, pp. viii.-560.
Frontispiece of portraits
    BM | BPL | BUS | MPL
A reprint, with increment, of the critical notes in
Knight's editions of Sh—.

] Knight (Charles) Wm. Sh—: A biography.
Ln : Knight . . . 1851. 8°, pp. xii.-330
    BPL

] Knight (C.) Wm. Sh—: A biography. Ln :
Routledge . . . 1857. Roy. 8°

Shakespeare]—

] Koch (M.) Sh— . . . [1886]. 8° BM

] Lambert (Daniel Henry) Cartæ Shakespeareanæ; Sh— documents. A chronological catalogue of extant evidence relating to the life and works of Wm. Sh—, collated and arranged. Ln : Bell . . . 1904. Cr. 8°, pp. xxii.-108. With eleven portraits and illustrations BPL | BUS | MPL

] Lang (*Mrs.* Andrew) Life of Sh—. *See* Sh— Works : Ext. 1908

] Last of the Shakespeares [In ' Northamptonshire Notes and Queries,' c. 1889]. 8°
Refers to Lady Barnard, of Abington Abbey. BPL

] Law (Ernest) Sh— as a groom of the chamber. Illustrated. Ln : Bell . . . 1910. Fcp. 4°, pp. viii.-64, and six plates
 BM | BLO | CTC | SML
The illustrations embrace (i.) a facsimile of the entry at the Public Record Office of the grant of red cloth to Sh— on the occasion of James the first's coronation ; (ii.) a facsimile of the entry of the payment made to the players for attending on the Constable of Castile in Aug., 1604 ; (iii.) conference of English and Spanish commissioners, Aug., 1604, when Sh— was in waiting ; and three old views of Somerset House.

] Leighton (W.) Sketch of Sh—. 1879. 8°
 BM

] Leisure hour : Sh— Tercentenary number [April, 1864]. Ln : . . . 1864. 4°
 BPL | CPL

] Léonard gallery : Account of the great picture, ' Sh—, or the glory of Great Britain.' [c. 1875.] 8° BPL

] Levi (Solomon Lazarus)] Life of Wm. Sh—, by ' Sidney Lee.' Ln : Smith . . . 1898. 8° BM | BPL | BUS | MPL | SML
Reviewed by J. C. Collins in his ' Ephemera critica,' pp. 211-218.
' It is a possibility that some of these adventurers [referring to the Baconians] if they were to settle down at Stratford and purchase Halliwell-Phillipps' ' Outlines,' or even (which is much the same thing—not quite so good) " Lee's Life," and digest the contents, they might grow disposed to reconsider their signally precipitate and unwise verdict.'—*W. Carew Hazlitt.*

] Levi (S. L.)] Life of William Sh—, by ' S. Lee.' ' Illustrated library edition.' Ln : Smith & Elder, 1899. Roy. 8°
 BM | BPL | MPL

] Levi (S. L.)] Sh—'s life and work. An abridgment, by ' S. Lee.' Ln : Smith . . . 1900. Cr. 8°, pp. xvi.-232 BPL

] Levi (S. L.)] Life of Wm. Sh—. ' Hampstead edition.' Ln : Finch, 1904. 8° BPL

] Levi (S. L.)] Life of Sh—. 5th edition. Ln : Smith . . . 1905. 8°, pp. 524 BPL

] Levi (S. L.)] Life of Wm. Sh—. ' Illustrated library edition, newly revised.' Ln : Smith, 1908. Roy. 8°, pp. 426
The author says in the preface ' this issue gives him an opportunity of correcting errors,' an opportunity he made careless use of, seeing that his time-worn

Shakespeare]—

blunder that the Jaggard canon was produced in Fleet St. still appears on p. 251, although the writer has pointed out the mistake over and over again.

] Levi (S. L.)] Life of Wm. Sh—. 6th edition. With a new preface. Ln : Smith, 1908. 8°, pp. 544

] Levi (S. L.)] Life of Sh—. *See* Sh—'s Works, 1904

] Levi (S. L.)] Sh—'s life and work. ' New edition.' Ln : Smith . . . 1907. Cr. 8°, pp. 246

] Life and beauties of Shakespeare. Boston [U.S.] . . . 1850. 12° BUS

] Life and times of Sh—, actor and dramatist. Ln : H. Vickers [1864]. Cr. 8°, pp. 16, and Chandos portrait BM | BUS

] Life of Sh—. *See* Sh—'s Works, 1795-96

] Life of Sh—. ' Select biography.' Ln : Wetton & Jarvis . . . 1822. 12° CPL

] Life of Wm. Sh—. Interspersed with a variety of authentic and interesting anecdotes. Dublin : A. O'Neil, 1822. 12°, pp. vi.-40 BUS

] Life of Mr. Wm. Sh— . . . 1743. 12° BPL

] Life of Sh— [In ' Illustrations of Stratford-upon-Avon '] . . . 1827. 8° BPL

] Life and times of Wm. Sh—. Ln : Sonnenschein . . . [c. 1883]. Cr. 8° BPL

] Life and times of Wm. Sh—. With an account of his plays and their plots . . . Second edition. Ln : Sonnenschein . . . 1888. Cr. 8°, pp. xii.-244 BPL | SML

] Lift for the lazy [Sh—, pp. 77-158]. New York . . . 1849. 12° BPL

] Lloyd (W. W.) Essays on the life and plays of Sh—. Chiswick Press : Privately printed, 1858. 8°, pp. 640
 BM | BPL | BUS | CPL
Issue limited to fifty copies. First separate issue. Appeared in Singer's edition of Sh—'s Works.

] London herald : Sh— number . . . April 23rd, 1864. 4° BPL | CPL

] Lushington (Vernon) Sh—: An address to the Positivist Society of London on 2nd Aug. at Stratford-on-Avon. Ln : 1885. 8° BM | BPL | BUS

] Lyttelton (George Wm. *fourth Baron*) Few thoughts about Sh—. Stourbridge . . . [1885]. 12° BPL

] Lyttelton (Geo. Wm. *fourth Baron*) Few thoughts about Sh— [In ' Ephemera,' pp. 285-321]. 1865. 12° BPL

] Mabie (Hamilton Wright) Wm. Sh—: poet, dramatist, and man. New York . . . 1900. 8°. With portraits, maps, and illustrations BPL | BUS | MPL

] Mabie (H. W.) Wm. Sh—: poet, dramatist, and man. Ln : Macmillan . . . 1901. Roy. 8°, pp. 442. With nine photogravure and ninety-one other illustrations BUS | SML

] Mabie. Wm. Sh—. New edition, with a new preface. Ln: Macmillan, 1904. Cr. 8°, pp. 364

] M'Ilwraith (Jean Newton) Book about Sh—, written for young people. Ln: Nelson, 1898. 12°, pp. 222   BM | BPL | BUS | SML

] Malone (Edmond) Life of Wm. Sh—. With an essay on the phraseology and metre of the poet and his contemporaries. Ln: [Printed by C. Baldwin for] F. C. & J. Rivington, 1821. 8°, pp. iv.-586, and portraits as in Boaden's 'Inquiry'
BM | BPL | BUS

Off-printed from Malone's 'Variorum Sh—,' 1821.

As presents, twenty-one copies were executed on fine paper, roy. 8°, for Boswell.

The four-page prospectus of this 'Life,' issued as a supplement to his 'Inquiry . . . 1796' contains some useful hints to original searchers. Malone points out that Lady Barnard appointed her kinsman, Edward Bagley, of London, as her executor and residuary legatee. He would become possessed of her coffers, cabinets, and grandfather's papers in 1670. If one could trace his death and legatees, it is just possible the history of Lady Barnard's effects might be followed.

Again, on the death of Sir John Barnard, in 1674, administration of his effects was granted to his daughters (by a former wife) and their husbands. Some of the poet's papers might have fallen into their hands. They were (1) Elizabeth, who married Henry Gilbert, of Locko, Derbyshire; (2) Mary, who married Thomas Higgs, of Colesborne; (3) Eleanor, who married Samuel Cotton.

Sh— purchased property of Ralph Hubaud, brother of Sir John Hubaud, of Ipsley, Warwickshire. Some instrument executed or attested by the poet may still lie buried among the papers of that estate.

If any descendant of John Heminges, the actor, still survives, possessing his ancestor's deeds, papers, account books, or theatrical contracts, these would throw light on the stage history of Sh—'s period.

John Heminges died in Oct., 1630, leaving a son (1) named William (the latter died about 1650) and four married daughters (2) Alice, who married John Atkins; (3) Rebecca, who married Capt. Wm. Smith; (4) Margaret, who married Thomas Sheppard; (5) name untraced, who became Mrs. Merefield.

] Malone (E.) Original letters [on the life of Sh—] to John Jordan the poet, now first printed from the autograph MSS. preserved at Stratford-on-Avon, edited by J. O. Halliwell. Ln: 1864. Fcp. 4°

Issue limited to ten copies.   BM | BPL

] Manuscript miscellany of early notices of Sh—: A large collection of manuscript and printed references relating to the poet, chiefly of the restoration period, 1663-1796. Contained in 6 vols. Fcp. 4°
W

CONTAINS EXCERPTS FROM Shadwell's Sullen lovers, 1668; Love à-la-mode, 1663; The triumphant widow, 1677; Some original manuscript Ireland forgeries, 1796; A song in the opera called 'The fairy queen,' sung by Mrs. Dyer, 1692, from an alteration of 'A Midsummer night's dream'; and other pieces.

] Marshall (Emma) Sh— and his birthplace. Nuremberg: Nister [1890]. Oblong 4°
BM | BPL | SML

] Marshall (*Mrs.* E.) Sh— and his birthplace. Ln: Nister, 1899. Oblong 4°

] Maudsley (H.) Sh— ' testimonied in his own bringings forth ' [in heredity, variation, and genius] . . . 1908. Cr. 8°   BPL

See ' Measure for measure,' act iii., sc. 2.

] Meister (H.) Of Sh— [In ' Letters written during a residence in England,' pp. 91-101]. 1799. 8°   BPL

] Memorial of the tercentenary of Sh— in Cambridge. Cambridge, 1864. 12°   BPL

] Memorials of Sh— and his birthplace at Stratford-on-Avon. Ln: . . . 1847. F°; single sheet   BM

] Memorials of Sh—: The poet's will in photolithography. Indentures of Sh—'s house, and photographs of his portraits. With annotations by H. Staunton. Ln: Day & Son [1864]. F°, ff. 19
BPL | BUS | CPL | SML

] Miller (T.) Sh— [In ' Poems,' pp. 84-87] . . . 1841. 8°   BPL

] Misconceptions of Sh—. *See* Adams

] Monument to Sh—. New York . . . June, 1864. 8° pp. 8   BUS

] Monument commemorative of the tercentenary anniversary of the birth of Sh— in the Central Park. New York . . . 1864. 8°, pp. 8   BUS

The Chairman of the Committee was Judge Charles P. Daly. The corner stone was laid 23rd April, 1864, and the erection dedicated 23rd May, 1872. It consists of a statue by Ward.

] Moral character of Sh— [In ' Meliora,' April]. Ln: 1874. 8°   BUS

] Morley (Henry) Sh— and his time [In ' English writers, Vols. 10, 11]. Ln: Cassell, 1893-95. 2 vols. 8°   BPL | MPL

] Motives and struggles of Sh— in settling in London [In ' National Quarterly Review,' March. New York, 1873]. 8°   BUS

] Moulton (C. W.) Wm. Sh— [In ' Library of literary criticism,' Vol. 1., pp. 447-557]. Buffalo . . . 1901. 8°   BPL

] Nasmith (D.) Sh— [In ' Makers of modern thought,' pp. 188-219. 1892] 12°   BPL

] Naylor (B. S.) Time and truth reconciling the moral and religious world to Sh—, the greatest poet and dramatist, moral philosopher and philanthropist that ever lived in the tide of times, whose greatness like an Alpine avalanche continues increasing . . . as the wonderful revelations of his overwhelming genius roll down the steep of time. Ln: W. Kent & Co. . . . 1854. 12°, pp. xii.-232
BM | BPL | BUS | SML

Shakespeare]—

] Neil (Samuel) Sh—; a critical biography, and an estimate of the facts, forgeries, etc. which have appeared in remote and recent literature. Ln : Houlston & Wright ... 1861. Cr. 8°, pp. iv.-124
BM | BPL | BUS | SML
On the Ireland and Collier controversies.

] Neil (S.) Sh— ... Ln : Houlston ... 1863. Cr. 8°, pp. iv.-124 BUS

] Neil (S.) Biography of Sh—. Warwick ... 1869. Cr. 8° BPL

] New Sh— Society. See New ...

] Newbigging (T.) Sh— [Rep. from ' Rossendale Free Press ']. Rawtenstall, 1907. 8° BPL

] Norris (J. Parker) Portraits of Sh—. Philadelphia : Robert M. Lindsay, 1885. 4°, pp. xxviii.-266. With 33 plates
BM | BPL | BUS | SML

] Notices of Sh— [Collection of original manuscript papers, comprising :—Felton on Sh—, Fuseli on Sh— and Rembrandt, Masklin on Sh—'s style & Sh—'s science, Capel Lofft on Sh—'s learning. Symmons' Sh— and Milton compared. [Sæc. XIX.] Fcp. 4°; holograph manuscripts, on twenty-eight leaves of paper W

] Ode on Sh—, and testimonies to the genius and merits of Sh—. [Sæc. XIX.] 4°

] O'Flanagan (Mrs. Jean I.) Sh—'s self-revelation in his ' Sonnets.' Paper prepared for the Stratford Sh— club and read 11th March, 1902. Stratford-on-Avon : E. Fox ... 1902. 8°, pp. 44

] O'Gorman (R.) Oration on Sh—. Dublin ... 1857. 8° BPL

] Oldham (T.) Lines on Sh— [In ' Poetry,' pp. 142-144]. Ln : Bailey & Co., 1840. 12° BPL

] Oldys (Wm.) Sh— [In Yeowell's Memoir of W. Oldys, pp. 43-47]. 1862. 8° BPL

] Only likeness of Sh—: The bust in the church of Stratford-on-Avon [In ' Leisure hour,' pp. 623-625]. 1893. Roy. 8° BPL

] P—— (J.) Sh—: his life and writings. A lecture given at the Tattenhall Reading Room, 5 March. Ln : Longman ... 1855. 8°, pp. 36 BM | BPL | BUS

] P—— (K.) Sh—. 1774. 4° BM

] Page Schoolmaster (Thomas) Spenser and Sh—: their lives and literary work. Ln : ... [1894]. 8°, pp. 32 BM | BUS

] Page (William) Study of Sh—'s portraits. Illustrated. [In ' Scribner's monthly,' Sept.] New York, 1875 BUS
Deals specially with the alleged Sh— death mask.

] Page (William) Study of Sh—'s portraits. Ln : Chiswick Press [1876]. 16°, pp. iv.-76, and two portraits BM | BPL | BUS | SML

Shakespeare]—

] Payne (J.) Studies in English prose. 1872, 12° BPL
Sh— pp. 121-126.

] Pemberton (T. Edgar) Original portrait of Sh— [In ' The theatre ']. 1896. 8° BPL

] Pichot (P. A.) Sh— ... [1889]. 8° BM

] Pictorial treasury of famous men and famous deeds. Ln :. J. G. Murdoch [c. 1885]. Roy. 8°
The life of Sh— occupies the first eleven pages, with Chandos portrait and four illustrations of Stratford-on-Avon.

] Pinks (W. J.) Memorials of Sh— [In ' Country trips,' pp. 59-91]. Ln : [1860]. 12° BPL

] Pitt-Lewis (George) The Sh— story: An outline. Ln : Sonnenschein ... 1904. 8°, pp. 120 BPL

] Praise of Sh—: An English anthology. Edited by C. E. Hughes. With preface by ' S. Lee.' Ln : Methuen ... 1905. 8°, pp. xvi.-342 BPL | BUS | MPL | SML

] [Prescott (Dr. Kenrick)] Sh—. ' Rara avis in terris.' Juvenal. Cambridge [Privately printed], 1774. Fcp. 4°, pp. 16
BPL | BUS | W
' The rarest of all in the list of modern Shakespereana, I believe.'—J. O. Halliwell.

] Proposal for conferring an annuity on the descendants of Sh—'s family [In 'Monthly magazine ']. 1820. 8° BPL

] Raleigh (Prof. Walter) Sh—. ' English men of letters.' Ln : Macmillan, 1907. Cr. 8°, pp. 238 BPL

] Raleigh (Prof. Walter) Sh—. ' Eversley series.' Ln : Macmillan ... 1909. Cr. 8°, pp. 310 BPL

] Robertson (John M.) Originality of Sh— [In ' University magazine,' edited by ' Democritus ' (i.e., Dr. Havelock Ellis), Vol. x., pp. 577-608]. Ln : 1898. Roy. 8°

] Rolfe (Wm. James) Life of Sh—. Boston [U.S.]: Dana ... 1904. 8°, pp. 550. Portrait of Dr. Rolfe and other illustrations BPL | BUS | SML

] Rolfe (W. J.) Life of Wm. Sh—. Ln : Duckworth ... 1905. 8°, pp. viii.-552. With bust portrait, Gower statue, portrait of Rolfe, and five other plates MPL
In questionable taste, but unquestioned ignorance, Rolfe slavishly copies from Swinburne and ' Sidney Lee ' unmerited attacks upon Wm. Jaggard, Sh—'s accredited publisher. The volume appears to be a hasty compilation. One of the plates purports to be a view from the Stratford ' Memorial chapel,' which exists only in Rolfe's imagination. He may mean the Memorial theatre.

] Rolfe (W. J.) Sh— the boy: Sketches of home and school life, games, sports, manners and folk-lore of the time ...

New York : Harper . . . 1896. Cr. 8°, pp. viii.-252. Illustrated BUS | SLM
First proof sheets with corrections and additions at Boston.

] Rolfe (W. J.) Sh— the boy . . . New York : Harper . . . 1897. Cr. 8°, pp. viii.-252. Illustrated BM | BPL | MPL

] Rolfe (W. J.) Sh— the boy . . . With new index of plays and passages referred to. Ln : Chatto, 1900. Cr. 8°, pp. 266, and 41 illustrations BPL

] Rolfe (W. J.) Sh— the boy. New York, 1902. 8°. Illustrated BUS

] Rosbourg (C. de) Memories of Sh— [In ' Charing Cross magazine ']. Ln : 1876. 8° . BPL

] Rossetti (William Michael) Lives of famous poets. Ln : Moxon . . . 1878. Cr. 8°, pp. 406, and portrait
Sh— fills pp. 35-63.

] Rossetti (W. M.) Life of Sh— [In Shakespeare's Works, pp. v.-xvi.] Ln : . . . [c. 1880]. 12° BPL

] Rossi (L.) & Corbould (E. M.) Side-lights on Sh—. Ln : Sonnenschein . . . 1897. Cr. 8°, pp. 304, and two plates
BM | BPL | BUS | SML

] Rossi & Corbould. Side-lights on Sh—, with two illustrations. Ln : Sonnenschein . . . 1900. Cr. 8°, pp. 302 BPL

] Rossi & Corbould. Side-lights on Sh—. Ln : Sonnenschein . . . 1901. Cr. 8°, pp. 302

] Rowden (F. A.) Sh— [In ' Biographical sketch of distinguished writers,' pp. 113-118]. 1820. 12° BPL

] Rowe (Nicholas) Some account of the life of Sh—. *See* Sh—'s Works, 1709 *et seq.*

] Rowe (N.) Some account . . . Ln : . . . [1714]. 12° W
Formed a supplement to Rowe's edition of Sh—'s works, 1714.

] Rowe (N.) Some account . . . [In ' Works of Sh—, collated by Pope ']. 1725. 4° BPL

] Rowe (N.) Life of Sh—. *See* Sh—'s Works, 1734-36, 1744-46, 1760, 1761, 1767, 1790, 1792, 1795, 1798, 1798-1800, 1799-1801, 1800, 1801, 1803-05, 1806, 1811, 1818, 1821, 1823, 1824, 1828, 1852, 1854, 1863

] Rowe (N.) Life. *See* Sh— Macbeth, 1768

] Rowe (N.) Life of Sh—. *See also* Johnson

] Rusden (G. W.) Wm. Sh— : his life, works, and teachings. Melbourne . . . 1903. 8°
BPL | MPL

] Russell (W.) Extraordinary men. Ln : . . . 1853. 12° BPL
Sh— fills pp. 27-40.

] Ryland (W.) Life of Wm. Sh—. [1890.] 8° BM

] S—— Brief enquiry into the learning of Sh— [In ' Universal Visiter ']. Ln : c. 1756. 8° BUS

] Salvini. On Sh—, with sketch of Salvini [In ' The century,' Nov., 1881]. Manchester . . . 1884. 8° BPL

] Sh— [In ' North British Review,' Nov.] Edinburgh, 1849. 8° BUS
Refers to the ' Merchant of Venice.'

] Sh— [article in the ' Quarterly Review,' July]. Ln : 1871. 8° BUS

] Sh— [In ' Cabinet portrait gallery of British Worthies ']. Ln : . . . 1845. 12° BUS

] Sh— [article in 'British Quarterly Review,' Ap.] Ln : 1864. 8° BUS

] Sh— [article in ' London Quarterly Review,' April]. Ln : . . . 1864 8° BUS

] Sh—; a celebration ode [In ' Chambers' Journal '] . . . 1864. Roy. 8° BPL

] Sh—; a revelation, by ——? Ln : Skeffington . . . 1897. 8°, pp. 160
BM | BPL | SML

] Sh— . . . ' Pilgrim books.' Illustrated by A. Forestier. Ln : Jack . . . 1910. 16°
BM | BLO | CTC

] Sh— a butcher. *See* Halliwell, Was Nicholas

] Sh— a freemason. *See* Parkinson

] Sh— a gentleman—
See Coleridge (H.)
,, Emery
,, *Sh—*] Sh—

] Sh— a lawyer. *See* Sh—'s legal knowledge

] Sh— a poacher—
See Bracebridge *See* Garnett
,, Collier ,, Landor

] Sh— a printer. *See* Blades

] Sh— a puritan. *See* Carter

] Sh— a recusant. *See* Carter

] Sh— a Roman Catholic. *See* Fitzgerald

] Sh— a sailor. *See* Bullen (F. T.)

] Sh— a Scotsman. *See* Thompson

] Sh— a seaman [In ' Saint James' Magazine,' July]. Ln : . . . 1862. 8° BUS

] Sh— a soldier. *See* Thoms

] Sh— a tory. *See* Coleridge (H.)

] Sh— acrostics—
See Century *See* Crotch
,, Charades ,, Grinfield

] Sh— adversaria. *See* Wall (A. H.)

] Sh— album—
See Sh— Macbeth, 1862
,, Sh— Poems, 1862
,, Sh— The tempest, 1862
,, Sh— Works, 1882
,, Sh— Works : Ext. 1862

] Sh— allusion book : Collection of allusions to Sh— from 1591 to 1700. By C. M. Ingleby and others. Now re-edited, re-

] Sh— and Stratford-upon-Avon. With portraits and illustrations. Glasgow : Bryce, 1905. Cr. 8°   BPL

] Sh— and Swedenborg. *See* Baynham

] Sh— and temperance. *See* Bailey (*Sir* W. H.)

] Sh— and the Bible—

See Bible	*See* Ferguson
,, Carter	,, Gilman
,, Colton	,, Ginsburg
,, Dore	,, Glasse
,, Eaton	,, Halliwell
,, Ellis	,, Rees
,, English . . .	,, Sh— autograph

] Sh— and the emblem writers. *See* Green

] Sh— and the Jews. *See* Hales

] Sh— and the puritans. *See* Milton

] Sh— and the school of assumption [In ' The Library,' pp. 314-327, No. 39, Vol. x., July]. 1909. Roy. 8°
A critique of Mark Twain's ' Is Sh— dead,' which combats the Baconian theory.

] Sh— and the stage. A vexed question. By Sir Nathaniel . . . [In ' New Monthly Magazine.' Ln : 1864]. 8°   BUS

] Sh— and the supernatural [In ' Chambers' Journal.' Edin. . . . 1874]. Roy. 8° BUS

] Sh— and the Thames. *See* Harper

] Sh— and the working classes. *See* Crosby

] Sh— and time. *See* Clapp

] Sh— and tobacco. *See* Barrie

] Sh— and Tolstoy. *See Sh*—] Eiloart

] Sh— and Venice [In ' Quarterly Review ']. 1889. 8°   BPL

] Sh— and Voltaire. *See* Lounsbury

] Sh— and Washington. *See* Colbert

] Sh— and Whitman. *See* Trumbull

] Sh— and Wordsworth. *See* De Quincey

] Sh— annals from the most recent authorities. Ln : Low . . . 1886. Cr. 8°

] Sh— annals from the most recent authorities. New edition. Ln : Low . . . 1888. Cr. 8°

] Sh— anniversary. Hen and Chickens Hotel. Birmingham . . . 1865. 12°   BPL

] Sh— anniversary. Plough and Harrow Hotel. Birmingham . . . 1882-83. 4° BPL

] Sh— anniversary. Royal Hotel. Birmingham . . . 1873-1880. 4°   BPL

] Sh— as a business man [In ' Chambers' Journal,' 6th series, Vol. 9, pp. 820-822]. Roy. 8°

] Sh— as a comic dramatist. *See* Dowden

] Sh— as a ladies' man. *See* Collins (J. C.)

] Sh— as a physician. *See* Chesney

] Sh— as a sportsman—

    See Flower
    ,, Gem

] Sh— as 'Actæon.' *See* Spenser (E.)

] Sh— as actor. *See Sh*—] Sh—'s acting

] Sh— as actor-trainer. *See* Downes

] Sh— as an angler. *See* Ellacombe

] Sh—, as bearing on English history. Grahamstown, South Africa : 'Anglo-African' Office [c. 1858]. 8°, pp. 16   BM

] Sh— as critic. *See* Lewes

] Sh— as dramatic artist—

See Halpin	*See* Moyse
,, Moulton	,, New Sh— Soc.

] Sh— as dramatic model. *See* Spink

] Sh— as financier. *See* Abercrombie

] Sh— as historian—

    See Malden
    ,, Merriman

] Sh— as horseman. *See* Flower

] Sh— as ' Johannes factotum.' *See* Greene

] Sh— as ' priest of cupid.' *Ses* Seymar

] Sh— as seer—

    See Scadding
    ,, Skipsey

] Sh— as ' Shake-scene.' *See* Greene (R.)

] Sh— as singer. *See* Skipsey

] Sh— Association of New Orleans. *See* New Orleans

] Sh— at the ' Mermaid.' *See* Ralegh

] Sh— - Bacon : An essay. Ln : Sonnenschein . . . 1899. 12°, pp. 152   BPL

] Sh— - Bacon : An essay. Ln : Sonnenschein . . . 1900. 12°, pp. 152

] Sh— - Bacon controversy [In ' Scribner's monthly '] . . . 1875. 8°   BPL

] Sh— - Bacon controversy. *See* Bacon

] Sh— bibliography—

See Allibone	*See* Clifton . . .
,, Arnold	,, Cohn
,, Anderson	,, Collier (J. P.)
,, Bailey	,, Cranwell
,, Ballinger	,, Cutter
,, Barker	,, Demmon
,, Barton	,, Dent
,, Bence-Jones	,, Dix
,, Blades	,, Dryden, Secret
,, Bodleian . . .	love
,, Bohn	,, Ellis
,, Boydell	,, Esdaile
,, Brassington	,, Eton
,, British . . .	,, Felton
,, Browne	,, Fitzgerald
,, Bullen	,, Fleay
,, Burton	,, Fletcher (W. I.)
,, Bute	,, Flower
,, Callender	,, Furness
,, Capell	,, Furnivall
,, Catalogue	,, Garrick
,, Cazenove	,, Greg
,, Chetwood	,, Grey
,, Chicago	,, Guide
,, Clarke (M. C.)	,, Hall (H. T.)
,, Clavell	,, Hall (S.)

Shakespeare]—

] Sh— club of London. *See* Macdonell
] Sh— club of Los Angeles [U.S.] *See* Galpin
] Sh— club of Montreal. *See* Montreal
] Sh— club of North Carolina [U.S.] *See* Journal
] Sh— club of Scotland : Laws . . . instituted 1827. Edinburgh : A. Cannon [1827]. 8°, pp. 24 BUS
] Sh— club of Sheffield. *See* Sheffield
] Sh— club of Stratford-on-Avon—

See Bird	*See* Jaggard (W.)
„ Bond	„ Jarvis
„ Brassington	„ Lucy
„ Bullen	„ Matthews
„ Burrows	„ Morrison
„ Collins	„ Payne
„ Cooper	„ *Sh*—] O'Flanagan
„ Desch	„ Sidgwick
„ Dibdin	„ Sonnenschein
„ Downing	„ *Stratford*] Royal
„ Evans	„ *Stratford*] Stratford
„ Fiedler	„ Temple
„ Flower	„ Urwick
„ Hudson	„ Ward
„ Hutchings	„ Yardley

] Sh— commemorated [In ' Temple Bar,' March. Ln : 1864]. 8° BM | BUS
] Sh— concordances, cyclopædias, dictionaries, glossaries, indexes, lexicons, tables, etc.—

See Abbott	*See* Hoe
„ Adams	„ Humphreys
„ Andrews	„ Jaggard
„ Arnold	„ Jerrold
„ Ayscough	„ Jervis
„ Baret	„ Keightley
„ Bartlett	„ Kinnear
„ Baynes	„ Levins
„ Becket	„ List
„ Bellamy	„ Lyndon
„ Best	„ Mackay
„ Britton	„ Miller
„ Bullokar	„ Morgan
„ Clarke	„ Morley
„ Cunliffe	„ Nares
„ Dictionary	„ O'Connor
„ Dolby	„ Oliphant
„ Dyce	„ Phin
„ Edwards	„ Poole
„ Edwardes	„ Potwin
„ Fennell	„ Rankin
„ Fleay	„ Rider
„ Foster	„ Romdahl
„ Furness	„ Routledge
„ Garrick	„ Schmidt
„ Glossary	„ Sh— Works, 1880,
„ Griffiths	1887, 1893
„ Halliwell	„ *Sh*—] Rolfe [book
„ Hanmer	„ *Sh*—] Sh— hand-

Shakespeare.] Sh— concordances, cyclopædias, dictionaries, glossaries, indexes, lexicons, tables, etc.—

See Sharpe	*See* Truths
„ Siddons	„ Twiss
„ Smith (G. A.)	„ Two . . .
„ Smith (A. R.)	„ Walbran
„ Stearns	„ Warner
„ Sweny	„ Watson
„ Thomasius	„ Webb

] Sh—; containing the traits of his characters. Ln : Printed for the author and sold by J. Bew [c. 1770]. 3 parts. 8°, pp. 48 BM | BUS
Deals with Miranda and Falstaff. A weekly publication. No more issued.
] Sh— controversies—

See Bacon	*See* Ireland
„ Collier	„ Lounsbury
„ Halliwell	„ Neil

] Sh— criticism [In ' Ladies' companion ']. Ln : . . . 1863. 8° BUS
] Sh— daily gem book. *See* Sh—'s Works : Ext., 1875, 1880, 1899
] Sh— diary. *See* Sh— Works : Ext.
] Sh— documents—
See Sh— Autograph
„ Wallace
] Sh— engravings. *See* Ferrara
] Sh— epilogues—
See Keate
„ Prologues . . .
] Sh— examination papers—
See Fifty
„ Hunter
„ *See* J—— (E. M.)
] Sh— exhibition in the British Museum [In ' The Athenæum,' No. 3992, p. 562, April, 1904]
] Sh— exhibitions—
See Belfast
„ Boydell
„ Catalogue, 1864, 1896
„ Dundee
„ *Sh*—] Sh— memorial
„ Stratford-on-Avon
] Sh— festival [In ' Chambers' Journal,' 1864]. Roy. 8° BPL
] Sh—festivals. *See Sh*—] Sh— celebrations
] Sh— for schools. *See* Lenny
] Sh— for recitations. *See* Sh— Works : Ext., 1903
] Sh— forgeries and frauds—

See Collier	*See* Fitzgerald
„ Coxeter	„ Halliwell
„ Cunningham	„ Hamilton
„ Davey	„ Holder
„ Detective	„ Ireland
„ Extracts	„ Jaggard
„ Fenton	„ Jordan

Shakespeare.] Sh— forgeries and frauds—
 See Merivale   *See* Steevens
 ,, Montgomery   ,, Theobald
 ,, Sh— Autograph   ,, Zincke
] Sh— gallery, Pall Mall—
 See Boydell
 ,, Sh— Works, 1792, 1839, 1841, 1864,
 1867, 1879
] Sh— gallery company's prospectus. 1862.
 F°   BPL
] Sh— garland: A roundabout paper on
 tercentenary matters relating to litera-
 ture and art [In ' The reliquary,' April,
 1864]. 8°   BUS
] Sh— gazette; A weekly record of pro-
 ceedings relating to the tercentenary cele-
 bration, No. I., 3rd Dec. Ln : H. Thomas,
 1863. 8°   BPL | BUS
] Sh— gem birthday book. *See* Sh— Works :
 Ext., 1907
] Sh— gems. *See* Sh— Works : Ext.
] Sh— glossaries. *See Sh*—] Sh— concor-
 dances ...
] Sh—hand book. *See* Sh—Works: Ext., 1860
] Sh—: his life and times, with a critical
 account of his writings and a description
 of Stratford and the neighbourhood. Ln :
 S. Grieves ... [c. 1847]. 8°, pp. 8   BUS
] Sh— idolatry. *See Sh*—] Sh— worship
] Sh— illustrated—
 See Lennox
 ,, Sh— Works, 1793
] Sh— imitations. *See* Facetiæ
] Sh— in France—
 See Doran   *See* Lewes
 ,, Fay   ,, Ware
 ,, Jusserand
] Sh— in Germany—
 See Cohn   *See* Moulin
 ,, Harwood   ,, Ramsay
 ,, Matthew   ,, Thoms
] Sh— in Griechenland. *See* Wagner
ᴊ Sh— in Holland—
 See Loffelt
 ,, Nayler
] Sh— in India. *See* Tarakanatha
] Sh— in Lancashire. *See* Axon
] Sh— in Norwich. *See* Sh— Works : Ext.,
 1873
] Sh— in Poland. *See* Ziolecki
] Sh— in Russia. *See* Ziolecki
] Sh— in schools—
 See Hudson
 ,, Neil
 ,, Wood
] Sh— in the class-room. *See* Thom
] Sh— in the shades. *See* Woty
] Sh—: Journal of the Edwin Booth Sh—
 League. Philadelphia ... 1894-95. 12
 parts. 4°   SML

Shakespeare]—
] Sh— jubilee at Stratford-on-Avon [In the
 ' Town and Country magazine,' pp. 341-4,
 473-8, and 545-50]. Ln : ... 1769. 8°
                                        BM
] Sh— jubilee, 1769. *See* Sh— Works, 1830
] Sh— jubilees, festivals, and commemora-
 tions [In ' Chambers' Journal.' c. 1864].
 Roy. 8°   BPL
] Sh— laconics. *See* Sh— Works : Ext., 1853
] Sh— lottery. *See* Boydell
] Sh— made easy. *See* Turner
] Sh— memorial—
 See Sh—] Monument
 ,, Stratford-on-Avon
] Sh— memorial and theatrical exhibition
 [catalogue], Whitechapel Art Gallery
 [Ln.] 12 Oct.-20 Nov., 1910. Cr. 8°, pp.
 52 ; including printed wrappers
] Sh— memorial : National theatre, 1616-
 1916. Appeal for £500,000. Ln : 1909.
 F°, pp. 4   BPL
] Sh— memorial : National theatre com-
 mittee. Ln : June, 1909. 8°, pp. 24 BPL
] Sh— memorial : National theatre. Illus-
 trated handbook. Ln : Executive com-
 mittee. [1909.] Oblong 8°, pp. 44 (incl.
 wrappers). With bust portrait and eight
 views of foreign national theatres   BPL
] Sh— memorial : National theatre. Petition
 to Ln. County Council. Ln : June, 1909.
 F°, pp. 4   BPL
] Sh— memorial : National theatre. Report
 of Executive Committee. Ln : Mar.,
 1909. 4°, pp. 4   BPL
] Sh— memorial number of 'Academy and
 Literature ']. 1904. 4°. Illustrated BPL
] Sh— memorial scheme [In 'The Athenæum,'
 No. 4280, pp. 567-568]. 6 Nov., 1909. 4°
 Points out that the plan to raise half-a-million for a
 Sh— memorial, inaugurated 23rd March, 1904, is an
 imitation of Mr. R. C. Jackson's Southwark scheme,
 commenced in 1903, estimated to cost just half that
 amount.
] Sh— monthly and literary companion.
 Edited by John Phin. Vol. I., Nos. 1
 and 2. New York ... 1906. 8°   BPL
] Sh— mottoes. *See* Dolby
] Sh— museum. Leipzig ... 1873. 8° SML
] Sh— national memorial—
 See Collier (J. P.)   *See* Report
 ,, Hiffernan   ,, *Sh*—] Sh—'s day
] Sh— National memorial fund, 1864—
 See Addresses   *See* Hopper
 ,, Bunn   ,, Kean
 ,, Halliwell
] Sh— newspaper. Ln : ... 1847. F°, pp. 8.
 Illustrated   BM | BUS
 Published in aid of the fund for the public purchase of
 Sh—'s birth-house.

Shakespeare]—

] Sh— night: In aid of the fund for the purchase and preservation of Sh—'s house, Tuesday, December the seventh, 1847, at the Royal Italian Opera, Covent Garden [Programme]. Ln: Bradbury & Evans, 1847. 8°, pp. 16

BM | BPL | BUS | SML

] Sh— no dog-fancier. *See* Flower
] Sh— not an impostor. *See* Townsend
] Sh— odes—

See Boston	*See* Linley
„ Bunner	„ Linley & Lawrence
„ Calvert	„ Lloyd
„ Carpenter	„ Michell
„ Chambers	„ Petre
„ Cook	„ Poems
„ Cotton	„ Prince
„ Courthope	„ Reader
„ Garrick	„ Rémy
„ Gentleman's ..	„ *Sh*—] Ode
„ Gerard	„ *Sh*—] Oldham
„ Gough	„ *Sh*—] Sh—
„ H—— (J.)	„ Sheppard
„ Harrison	„ Swinburne
„ Hudson	„ Tupper
„ J—— (J. R.)	„ Ward
„ Jarrow	„ Warlow
„ Jones (H.)	„ Whiter
„ Kemble	„ Williams & Milne
„ Langford	„ Winstanley
„ Lines ...	„ Yarrow

] Sh— on golf. *See* Sh— Works: Ext., 1885, 1889, 1894
] Sh— on hands. *See* Keller
] Sh— on horseback. *See* Flower
] Sh— on the Durbar. From an original MS. found in the ' Pratibasi ' office. Calcutta ... [c. 1903]. 8° BPL
] Sh— or Bacon [In ' New York Herald,' Sept. 9-11]. 1874 BUS
] Sh— performances. *See* Stage ...
] Sh— prize [with answers by Miss Mertins and Miss Wilson to questions upon ' Hamlet ' by H. H. Furness. Cutting from ' The album.' Edited by W. T. Thom]. Salem [U.S.A.], 1881. 4° BUS
] Sh— prologues—
See Keate
„ Valpy
] Sh— proverbs—
See Clarke & Rolfe
„ Sh— Works: Ext., 1847
] Sh— quartos. *See Sh*—] Sh—'s falsely-dated quartos
] Sh— rare print collection, edited by S. Eaton. Published for private circulation, 1900. 4° BPL
] Sh— reader. *See* Sh— Works: Ext., 1906

Shakespeare]—

] Sh— reading and elocution—
See Hoppin
„ Indexes
] Sh— relics—
See Deighton
„ Tregaskis
] Sh— repository, edited by J. H. Fennell. Nos. 1 to 4. Ln: Thomas Scott ... 1853. 4 parts. F° [No more issued]

BPL | BUS | CPL

An eight-page periodical, full of interesting matter, much of it from early sources.

] Sh— sermons, preached in the Collegiate Church of Stratford-on-Avon. Edited by George Arbuthnot. Ln: Longmans ... 1900. Cr. 8°, pp. viii.-138. With frontispiece of the chancel and bust BPL | BUS

Contents:—
  I. Browne (G. F.) Use of works of fiction.
  II. Laffan (R. S. de C.) Sh— the prophet.
  III. Ainger (A.) A poet's responsibility.
  IV. Nicholson (J. A.) The man and the poet.
  V. Stubbs (C. W.) A thanksgiving for Sh—.
  VI. Arbuthnot (G.) A poet's inspiration.
  VII. Farrar (F. W.) Sh—: the man and the poet.
  VIII. Arbuthnot (G.) Poet and historian.

] Sh— sermons—

See Bellamy	*See* Morris
„ Dale	„ Nicholson
„ Evered	„ Stubbs
„ Haweis	„ T—— (W. G.)
„ Hood	„ Timmins (J. F.)
„ Laffan	„ Trench
„ Maginnis	„ Wordsworth
„ Mangasarian	

] Sh— Shapleigh entanglement. *See* Winsor
] Sh— societies and clubs—

See Bird	*See* New ... [ana
„ Birmingham	„ *Sh*—] Shakespeare-
„ British ...	„ Stratford-on-Avon
„ Delights ...	„ Sunday

] Sh— society of Adelaide—
See Adelaide
„ *Sh*—] Glynn
] Sh— society of Birmingham university—
See Birmingham
„ Bullen
] Sh— society of Clifton. *See* Clifton
] Sh— society of Dublin. *See* Lines ...
] Sh— society of Edinburgh—
See Edinburgh
„ Gregory
„ Harkom
] Sh— society of Germany. *See* Matthew
] Sh— society of King's College, Ln. *See* Brewer
] Sh— society of Ln. [Autograph letters of members, chiefly to T. Rodd, the Society's business agent]. 1841-53. Original manuscripts. ·4 vols. 4° BUS

Shakespeare]—

] Sh— society of Ln.; Publications [edited by John Payne Collier]. Ln : Printed for the Sh— Society, 1841-53. 48 pieces, bound and issued in 19 vols. 8°

BM | BPL | BUS | CPL | MPL | SML | W

Contents: Vols. I. to IV. :—

Dodsley's Old plays : supplement
Chester Whitsun plays. Edited by T. Wright
Ludus Coventriæ. Coventry mysteries. Edited by J. O. Halliwell
Marriage of wit and wisdom
Moral play of ' Wit and science.' Ed. by Halliwell
Udall (N.) ' Ralph Roister Doyster.' Edited by W. D. Cooper
Norton and Sackville, 'Tragedie of Gorboduc.' Edited by W. D. Cooper
'Timon ': an old play. Edited by A. Dyce
'Sir Thomas More ': a play. Edited by A. Dyce
Dekker, Chettle, and Haughton, ' Patient Grissil.' Edited by J. P. Collier
Old ' Taming of a shrew.' Edited by T. Amyot
First sketch of the ' Merry wives of Windsor.' Edited by J. O. Halliwell
First sketch of ' King Henry VI.,' Parts II., III. Edited by J. O. Halliwell
True tragedie of Richard III. Edited by B. Field

Vols. V., VI. :—

Heywood (Thomas) Dramatic Works. Edited by B. Field.

Vols. VII., VIII. :—

Henslowe (Philip) Diary, from 1591 to 1609. Edited by J. P. Collier
Memoirs of Edward Alleyn. Edited by J. P. Collier
Alleyn papers. Edited by J. P. Collier.

Vols. IX., X. :—

Rich, Farewell to the military profession
Nash, Pierce Pennilesse. Edited by J. P. Collier
Armin, Nest of ninnies. Edited by J. P. Collier
Thynn, Debate between pride and lowliness
Ghost of Richard the third. By C. B[rooke].
Forde (John) Inedited tracts : ' Honor triumphant' and ' Line of life.' Edited by J. P. Collier.

Vol. XI. : Papers of the Sh— Soc. too short for publication. First Series. Contents :—

1. Collier (J. P.) Dogberry and his associates. Arrest of the conspirators with Mary Queen of Scots
2. Halliwell (J. O.) Remarks on the similarity of a passage in Marlowe's ' Edward II.' and one in the first part of ' The contention ' [' King Henry VI.']
3. Jonson (Ben) Letter to the Earl of Newcastle and other matters relating to the poet. Edited by P. Cunningham
4. Ballad illustrative of ' Romeo and Juliet,' entitled a ' Pleasant new ballad of two lovers.' Edited by A. Barton
5. Alleyn papers : additions from the originals in the possession of J. F. Herbert
6. ' Dramaticus' pseud., On the profits of old actors
7. Collier (J. P.) ' The passing measure Pavin'; illustrative of a passage in ' Twelfth night '
8. Tomlins (T. E.) Origin of the Curtain Theatre and mistakes regarding it
9. Mistake by Campbell in his ' Life of Sh—'
10. Halliwell (J. O.) Observations on ' too too' in ' Hamlet '
11. Ballad of the ' Green willow,' by John Heywood, with the same burden as the song of ' The willow ' in ' Othello.' By a ballad-monger [J. O. H.]
12. Goodwin (A. T.) Court revels in the reign of Henry VII.
13. Shelley, Imitations of Sh— in his tragedy of ' The cenci.' Edited by J. B. B.

Shakespeare]—

14. ' Albion knight ': fragment of a moral play. Edited by J. P. Collier
15. Sh—'s Puck : Lines by Thomas Nash illustrative of a passage in a ' Midsummer night s dream '
16. Heywood (John) Skeltonical song
17. Sh—'s bust at Stratford and a proposal for restoring it to its primitive state
18. L— (G.) On a poem attributed to Thomas Nash
19. ' I'm to be married o' Sunday' : ballad illustrative of a passage in the ' Taming of the shrew '
20. Scott (T. J.) Early rarity of the works of Robert Greene
21. Bruce (J.) Who was ' Will, my Lord of Leycester's jesting player?'
22. Tomlins (T. E.) Corrections of Sh—'s text suggested by Judge Blackstone
23. Cunningham (P.) Inigo Jones and his office under the crown, with extracts from the accounts of the paymaster of the crown-works, preserved by the audit office
24. Halliwell (J. O.) On the word ' Ducdame' in ' As you like it '
25. Bigsby (R.) On the signature of John Sh— [and] Wm. Sh—'s papers.

Second Series. Contents :—

1. Norton (H. G.) Origin of the Induction to ' Taming of the shrew '
2. Harness (W.) Sh—'s bust at Stratford
3. Cunningham (P.) Did General Harrison kill Dick Robinson the player ?
4. Halpin (N. J.) Bridal runaway : Essay on Juliet's soliloquy
5. Collier (J. P.) John Wilson, the singer in ' Much ado ' ; a musical composer in Sh—'s plays
6. Baverstock (J. H.) On a mistake in Chambers' ' Cyclopædia of literature,' relating to ' Damon and Pythias '
7. Field (B.) Conjectures on some of the corrupt or obscure passages of Sh—
8. Scott (T. J.) Poems attributed to Thomas Nash contained in Dowland's ' Songs or ayres,' 1600
9. Cunningham (P.) Device to entertain Queen Elizabeth at Harefield, the house of Sir Thomas Egerton, 1602
10. Redford (John) Marriage of wit and science : an interlude. By a ballad-monger [J. O. Halliwell]
11. Jonson (Ben) and Dekker (Thomas) Story of Page of Plymouth. Edited by ' Dramaticus'
12. Halliwell (J. O.) Note on the recently-discovered manuscript of ' Henry the sixth'
13. Collier (J. P.) Players and dramatic performances in the reign of Edward IV.
14. Middleton (Thomas) An unknown pageant. Reprinted with introduction by J. L. Pearson
15. Middleton (Thomas) Game of chess : [and] his son Edward Middleton. By T. Hornby
16. Harness (W.) The widow of Wm. Sh—
17. Nimmo (T.) and Pettigrew (T. J.) On a passage in ' Julius Cæsar '
18. Recusancy of John Sh—, and on the inclosure of Welcombe fields. By ' Dramaticus'
19. Collier (J. P.) On the supposed origin of ' Romeo and Juliet '
20. Cunningham (P.) Plays at court, 1613, from the accounts of Lord Barrington, treasurer of the chamber to James I.
21. Greene (R.) Maiden's dream. An unknown poetical tract, with introduction by J. P. Reardon
22. Cowley]. Will of Cowley, the poet, extracted from the registry of the Prerogative Court of Canterbury by P. Cunningham
23. Halliwell (J. O.) Early notice of ' King Henry the eighth '
24. Baverstock (J. H.) Few words on the line in ' Hamlet ' as regards ' too too'

25. Lodge (Thomas) An unknown work, with extracts from his 'Defence of stage plays' by J. P. Collier.

Third Series. Contents :—

1. Tomlins (T. E.) New document regarding the authority of the master of the revels over play makers, plays and players in 1581
2. Illustration of 'Fortune by land and sea': a play by Heywood and Rowley. Edited by 'Oxoniensis' [B. Field]
3. Tyson (W.) Heming's players at Bristol in the reign of Henry VIII.
4. Stubbes (Philip) An unknown tract. Edited by J. P. Collier
5. Sandys (W.) Sh— illustrated by the dialect of Cornwall
6. Halliwell (J. O.) Some notes on passages in Sh—
7. Collier (J. P.) Performance of early dramas by parish clerks and players in churches
8. Zornlin (Miss G. M.) Remarks on discrepancies in the character of Jack Cade in 'King Henry VI.'
9. Anderson (H.) Sh—'s 'Venus and Adonis,' illustrated by his contemporary Thomas Heywood
10. Collier (J. P.) On the earliest quarto editions of Sh—
11. S— (L.) Notes on old plays by Bale, Marston, and Sh—
12. Accounts of performances and revels at court in the reign of Henry VIII.
13. 'Salmacis and Hermaphroditus,' not by Francis Beaumont: the edition of 1602. By 'Dramaticus'
14. Collier (J. P.) New fact regarding Sh— and his wife, contained in the will of Thomas Whittington
15. Field (B.) Conjectures on passages of Sh—
16. Reardon (J. P.) Sh—'s 'Venus and Adonis' and Lodge's 'Scilla's metamorphosis'
17. 'Every man': an interlude. An unknown edition printed by Pynson. Edited by 'Dramaticus'
18. Zornlin (Miss G. M.) On the conduct of Hamlet towards Ophelia
19. Tomlins (T. E.) Original patent for the nursery of actors and actresses in the reign of Charles II.
20. Allies (J.) On the word 'scamels' in Sh—'s 'The tempest'
21. Halliwell (J. O.) Poem containing notices of Ben Jonson, Sh—, Massinger, etc.
22. Robinson (J. H.) Had Sh— read Cavendish's 'Life of Wolsey'?
23. Cunningham (P.) New facts in the life of Thomas Nash, prose satirist and poet, contemporary with Sh—.

Fourth Series. Contents :—

1. Phaer] Will of Thomas Phaer, the poet and translator from Virgil. Ed. by P. Cunningham
2. Account of an early Italian poem on the story of 'Romeo and Juliet'
3. Halliwell (J. O.) Some account of the popular tracts which composed the library of Capt. Cox, a humourist who took a part in the Hock Tuesday play performed before Queen Elizabeth at Kenilworth, in 1575
4. Collier (J. P.) Richard Field (the printer of Sh—'s 'Venus and Adonis' and 'Lucrece'), Nathaniel Field, Anthony Munday, and Henry Chettle
5. Tomlins (T. E.) Three new privy seals, for players in the time of Sh—
6. Zornlin (G. M.) Two additional notes on 'King Henry VI., Part II.'
7. Halliwell (J. O.) Extract from a manuscript at Oxford containing a memorandum of complaints against Dethick, the herald, who made the grant of arms to John Sh—
8. Collier (J. P.) Original history of the theatre in Shoreditch, and connexion of the Burbadge family with it

9. Reardon (J. P.) Two specimens of the poetry of Philip Stubbes (author of 'Anatomy of abuses, 1583,' and enemy of theatrical performances) unknown to bibliographers
10. Cunningham (P.) Whitefriars theatre, Salisbury Court theatre, and the Duke's theatre in Dorset Gardens
11. Players who acted in the 'Shoemaker's holiday, 1600': a comedy by Thomas Dekker and Robert Wilson. Edited by 'Dramaticus'
12. Collier (J. P.) On Norton and Sackville, authors of 'Gorboduc,' the earliest blank verse tragedy in our language
13. Halliwell (J. O.) Few observations on the composition of the 'Midsummer night's dream'
14. On Massinger's 'Believe me as you list': a newly-discovered manuscript tragedy printed by the Percy Society
15. Norton (H. G.) On Beaumont and Fletcher's 'Woman's prize': the day when it was acted and the prologue and epilogue spoken
16. Cunningham (P.) Sir George Buc and the office of the revels
17. Halliwell (J. O) Dispute between the Earl of Worcester's players and the Corporation of Leicester in 1586, from the records of that city
18. Collier (J. P.) Dryden, Killigrew, and the first company which acted at Drury Lane theatre
19. Daniel] Will of Samuel Daniel, the poet, Sh—'s rival and contemporary. Ed. by P. Cunningham.

Vol. XII. :—Stationers' Company Registers. Extracts by J. P. Collier.

Vol. XIII. :—
Court revels in the reigns of Q. Elizabeth and James I. Edited by P. Cunningham
Tarlton, 'Jests' and 'Newes out of purgatory.' Edited with life by J. O. Halliwell.

Vol. XIV. :—
Halliwell, Fairy mythology of Sh—
Halpin (N. J.) Oberon's vision in a 'Midsummer night's dream' illustrated by comparison with Lyly's 'Endymion.'

Vol. XV. :—
Northbrooke, Treatise against dicing, dancing, plays, and interludes. Edited by J. P. Collier
Gosson, School of abuse
Lodge, Defence of stage plays.

Vol. XVI. :—
Collier (J. P.) Memoirs of the principal actors in Sh—'s plays.

Vol. XVII. :—
Cunningham (P.) Life of Inigo Jones
Jonson (Ben) Conversations with Drummond, of Hawthornden. Edited by D. Laing.

Vol. XVIII. :—
Munday (Anth.) John-a-Kent and John-a-Cumber, with other tracts. Edited by J. P. Collier
Heywood (Thomas) Apology for actors.

Vol. XIX. :—
Simrock (Karl) On the plots of Sh—
Sh—'s 'King Henry IV.,' from a contemporary manuscript. Edited by J. O. Halliwell.

This society was founded by J. O. Halliwell and J. P. Collier in 1841, and came to an end in 1853, shortly after the exposure of Collier's manuscript frauds. In 1872 Howard Staunton tried in vain to revive it. Two more years elapsed and 1874 saw the New Sh— Soc. founded, which lasted for ten years.

] Sh— society of Ln. : Publications [edited by John Payne Collier. Parts one to thirty inclusive]. Ln : Printed for the Sh— Society, 1841-1846. 30 parts, bound in 29 vols. 8°   w

This collection is bound in chronological order as published, irrespective of the Society's later method of attempted classification.

Shakespeare]—

] Sh— society of Ln. Plays edited by the Sh— Society [In 'Gentleman's magazine']. Ln: ... 1845. 8° BUS

] Sh— society of Ln. [Report of the Council for the first year]. Ln: 26 April, 1842. 8°, pp. 16 BUS

] Sh— society of Ln. Report of the Council at the eleventh annual meeting ... Ln: 26 April, 1852. 8°, pp. 16 BUS

] Sh— society of Ln.—
See Catalogue, 1854
   ,, Croker

] Sh— society of Manchester—
See Bailey
   ,, Foard
   ,, Manchester

] Sh— society of Melbourne—
See Melbourne
   ,, Phillips
   ,, Tucker

] Sh— society of New York—
See Acheson   See Halliwell
   ,, Adee   ,, Morgan
   ,, Butler   ,, New Sh—ana
   ,, Devecmon ,, New York
   ,, Frey   ,, Nicholson
   ,, Given   ,, Price
   ,, Guernsey   ,, Vining

] Sh— society of Nottingham. See Nottingham

] Sh— society of Philadelphia—
See Ashhurst
   ,, Philadelphia

] Sh— society of Stockton. See Stockton-on-Tees

] Sh— society of Winchester College—
See Hawkins
   ,, Winchester

] Sh— souvenir. See Sh— Works: Ext., 1888

] Sh— tavern. See Fox
] Sh— temple. See Sh— national memorial
] Sh— tercentenary, 1864 [Collection of newspaper cuttings]. 1864. 8° BPL

] Sh— tercentenary. Newspaper cuttings, play bills, etc. 1864. F° BPL

] Sh— tercentenary, 1564-1864: Poems for the prize competition offered by the ... 'Belfast Weekly Northern Whig.' Belfast, 1864. 8°, pp. 64 BUS

] Sh— tercentenary celebration. Lancashire and Cheshire Historic Society ... 1864. 8° BPI

] Sh— tercentenary programme. See Flower (C. E.)

] Sh— the hero as poet. See Carlyle
] Sh— tokens. See Davis (W. J.)
] Sh— treasury. See Sh— Works: Ext. 1842, 1869

Shakespeare]—

] Sh— versus Colley Cibber. See Cibber
] Sh— versus harlequin, or harlequin's invasion. A broad, farcical, pantomimical drama. Founded on Garrick's celebrated drama called 'Harlequin's invasion.' Now performing at the Theatre Royal, Drury Lane. Ln: 1820. 8° W

] Sh— versus Ingersoll. See Hall (J. G.)
] Sh— vindicated. See Ibsen
] Sh— vocal album. With music. [c. 1864.] F° BPL

] Shakespeare! was he a christian? by a cosmopolite. Newcastle-under-Lyme: T. Bayley, 1862. 8°, pp. 16
               BM | BPL | BUS

] Sh— worship—
See Frothingham   See Sh—] Praise
   ,, Ingleby   ,, Thoughts
   ,, Morley   ,, Tyler

] Sh—'s accentuation—
See Dawson   See Noyes
   ,, Hardinge   ,, Sh— Works, 1877-
   ,, Hawley   96

] Sh—'s acting—
See Brassington   See Lewes
   ,, Cargill   ,, Sh—] Vyse
   ,, Davies   ,, Sparrow
   ,, Jonson

] Sh—'s actresses—
See Actors
   ,, Lawrence

] Sh—'s adaptations—
See Kilbourne
   ,, Rose

] Sh—'s adaptors—
See King
   ,, Stage ...

] Sh—'s adjectives. See Helms
] Sh—'s affinities. See Swinburne
] Sh—'s age. See Sh—] Sh—'s time
] Sh—'s almanack. See Sh—] Sh—'s calendar
] Sh—'s Americanisms. See Lodge
] Sh—'s ancestors—
See Norris   See Sh—] Sh—'s family
   ,, Pudsey   ,, Sh—] Sh—'s pedigree
   ,, Rose

] Sh—'s angling lore. See Cordley
] Sh—'s animals. See Sh—] Sh—'s nature study
] Sh—'s aphorisms. See Rochefoucald
] Sh—'s apocrypha—
See Foard
   ,, Sh— Works, 1908
   ,, Simpson

] Sh—'s apotheosis. See Dolby
] Sh—'s architecture—
See Green
 -,, Sh—] Was ...

] Sh—'s arithmetic. See Numeration

Shakespeare]—

] Sh—'s characters—
 See Adams   *See* Moulton
   ,, Brereton   ,, New exegesis
   ,, Clarke (C. C.)   ,, Porter
   ,, Falstaff II.   ,, Remarks . . .
   ,, Games   ,, *Sh*—] Sh—
   ,, Garrick   ,, *Sh*—] Sh— char-
   ,, Goethe   acter cards
   ,, Halliwell, Let-   ,, *Sh*—] Sh— play-
    ters   ing cards
   ,, Hazlitt   ,, *Sh*—] Sh—'s dra-
   ,, Heath   matic . . .
   ,, Hole   ,, Stebbing
   ,, Impressions   ,, Two indexes
   ,, Indexes   ,, Whately
   ,, Jerrold   ,, White (R. G.)
   ,, Mortimer   ,, Wood (S.)
] Sh—'s children—
 See Godfrey
   ,, Scudder
   ,, *Sh*—] Sh—'s family
   ,, Wright
] Sh—'s christianity. *See* Sh—'s religion
] Sh—'s Christmas. *See* Quiller-Couch
] Sh—'s chronology—
 See Hurdis   *See* Stokes
   ,, Newton   ,, Theisen
   ,, *Sh*—] Sh—'s calendar
] Sh—'s church. *See* Stratford
] Sh—'s cipher—
 See Donnelly
   ,, Gallup
   ,, Nicholson
] Sh—'s classical knowledge—
 See Selby
   ,, *Sh*—] Hales
   ,, Stapfer
] Sh—'s cliff—
 See Description
   ,, Gillmor
   ,, Walk
] Sh—'s clowns—
 See Kellogg
   ,, Waller
] Sh—'s coat-of-arms—
 See Bellew   *See* Philarchaiotêtos
   ,, Burke   ,, Sawyer
   ,, Foard   ,, Tucker
] Sh—'s coincidences. *See* Reed
] Sh—'s comic tricentenary, or quaint memo-
 ries of ye bard. [1864.] 12°   BPL
] Sh—'s commentators. *See Sh*—] Sh—'s
 critics
] Sh—'s confession
 See Schuler
   ,, *Sh*—] Confessions
   ,, *Sh*—] Harris

Shakespeare]—

] Sh—'s contemporaries—
 See Cartwright   *See Sh*—] Tweddell
   ,, Craik   ,, Stephenson
   ,, D'Israeli   ,, Stokes
   ,, Foard   ,, Stopes
   ,, Holland   ,, Traill
   ,, Lamb   ,, Underhill
   ,, Neele   ,, Wager
   ,, Notices . . .   ,, Walker
   ,, Select beauties   ,, Wall
   ,, *Sh*—] Contem-   ,, Watson
    porary
] Sh—'s correspondents—
 See Greene
   ,, Heywood
   ,, Quiney
] Sh—'s corruptors. *See* Modern . . .
] Sh—'s country
 See Bradley   *See* Knight
   ,, Burgess   ,, Leyland
   ,, Jaggard   ,, Tytler
   ,, Kingsley   ,, Warwickshire
] Sh—'s court service—
 See Sh—] Law
   ,, Stopes
] Sh—'s creations. *See* Lewis
] Sh—'s criminals. *See* Goll
] Sh—'s critics—
 See Monro   *See* Sh— Works: re-
   ,, Morgan   ferences
   ,, Shackford   ,, Whipple
] Sh—'s critics, English and foreign [In
 ' Edinburgh Review,' July]. 1849.   8°
          BPL | BUS
] Sh—'s crows. *See* B—— (J.)
] Sh—'s curse verse—
 See Hewlett   *See* Sh— Epitaph
   ,, Leisure hour   ,, Wilson (J.)
] Sh—'s day : A plea for a monument. With
 a lyric from ' Romeo and Juliet.' Ln :
 Hatton & Son . . . 1864. 12°, pp. 12
       BM | BPL | BUS
] Sh—'s day. *See Sh*—] Sh—'s time
] Sh—'s death—
 See Bain   *See* Nisbet
   ,, Clemens   ,, *Sh*—] Halleck
   ,, Hyatt   ,, Ward
] Sh—'s 'death mask'—
 See Collins (W. W.) *See Sh*—] Page
   ,, Hart   ,, *Sh*—] Sh—'s por-
   ,, Norris   trait
] Sh—'s début. *See* Bormann
] Sh—'s deer-hunting—
 See Bracebridge   *See* Landor
   ,, Douglas   ,, Melodrama
   ,, Ireland (S.)   ,, Scott (E. J. L.)
] Sh—'s defamers. *See* Sullivan
] Sh—'s delineations. *See* Kellogg

] Sh—'s descendants—
See Barnard   See Pudsey
„ Cleaver   „ Rose
„ 'Marcian'   „ *Sh*—] Sh—'s family
„ Nisbet
] Sh—'s dialect—
See Salisbury
„ Sandys
] Sh—'s disposition. *See Sh*—] Glynn
] Sh—'s doctors. *See* Andrews
] Sh—'s documents—
See Sh— Autograph
„ *Sh*—] Lambert
] Sh—'s domestic life. *See* Massey
] Sh—'s dramatic art. *See* Baker
] Sh—'s dramatic characters ; their connec-
tions . . . acts and scenes . . . together
with inductions, prologues, epilogues, and
scenery, rendered into alphabetical order ;
also a list of his XXXVII. plays, accom-
panied by remarks of different commen-
tators on each. [*Sæc. XIX.*] Manu-
script. F°   BUS
] Sh—'s dramatic predecessors. *See* Cooper
] Sh—'s dramatic situations and characters.
1872. 8°   CPL
] Sh—'s dramatic unities. *See* Halpin
] Sh—'s dramas on ancient history [magazine
review. c. 1852.] 8°   W
] Sh—'s dream—
See Gilbert
„ Leighton
] Sh—'s drinking bout—
See Buckstone
„ Green
] Sh—'s early days : A play. *See* Somerset
] Sh—'s editors—
See Lounsbury
„ Miller
„ Sh— Works : references
„ Verbal criticism
] Sh—'s education—
See Baynes   See Sh—] Halleck
„ Dyer   „ *Sh*—] Rolfe
„ Seward   „ *Stratford*] Grammar
] Sh—'s educative excellence. *See* Hudson
] Sh—'s emblems. *See* Green
] Sh—'s emphasis. *See Sh*—] Sh—'s accentua-
tion
] Sh—'s England—
See Andrewes   See Rye
„ Boas   „ Thornbury
„ Goadby   „ Waterhouse
„ Harrison   „ Winter
„ Reflections
] Sh—'s English—
See Craik   See English . . .
„ Ellis   „ Oliphant

] Sh—'s English history—
See Holinshed   *See Sh*—] Sh—'s history
„ Pater   „ Warner
„ Reed
] Sh—'s entomology. *See Sh*—] Sh—'s insects
] Sh—'s epitaph—
See Browne (H. J.) *See* Hackett
„ Clark (E. G.)   „ Sh— Epitaph
„ Dobell   „ Thorpe
„ Donnelly
] Sh—'s epoch. *See* Sh—'s time
] Sh—'s estate—
See Combe
„ Pennant
„ *Stratford*] Act
] Sh—'s euphuism—
See Landmann   *See* Morris
„ Lyly   „ Rushton
] Sh—'s Europe. *See* Moryson
] Sh—'s face. *See* Sh—'s portraits
] Sh—'s fairies—
See Desch
„ Halliwell & Ritson
] Sh—'s faith. *See Sh*—] Sh—'s religion
] Sh—'s falsely-dated quartos—
See Cole   *See* Jaggard
„ Greg   „ Levi
„ Huth   „ Pollard
] Sh—'s fame. *See* Leisure hour
] Sh—'s family—
See Bellew   *See Sh*—] Sh—'s des-
„ French   cendants
„ Godfrey   „ Stopes
„ Jaggard   „ *Stratford*] Extracts
„ Rose   „ Thompson
„ Ryland   „ Warwickshire
„ Scott (E. J. L.) „ Waters
„ Scudder   „ Wheler
„ *Sh*—] Halliwell „ Wright
„ *Sh*—] Sh—'s ancestors
] Sh—'s faults—
See Richardson
„ Rose
] Sh—'s fellow-actors—
See Actors   *See* Heminge
„ Alleyn   „ Singer
„ Collier   „ Stopes
„ Field
] Sh—'s female characters. *See Sh*—] Sh—'s
women
] Sh—'s fiction. *See* Moulton
] Sh—'s first play. *See* Jaggard (W.)
] Sh—'s fish-lore. *See Sh*—] Sh—'s angling
lore
] Sh—'s flowers—
See Davidson
„ *Sh*—] Sh—'s botany

Shakespeare]—

] Sh—'s folk-lore—
  See Bell   *See* Folk-lore
    ,, Dyer   ,, Thoms
] Sh—'s fools—
  See Hetherington
    ,, Kellogg
] Sh—'s forerunners. *See Sh*—] Sh—'s pre-
  decessors
] Sh—'s friends—
  See Alleyn   *See* Stopes
    ,, *Sh*—] Elton ,, Williams (R. F.)
    ,, *Sh*—] Sh—'s ,, Williams (S. F.)
      contemporaries
] Sh—'s fugues. *See* Dow
] Sh—'s funeral—
  See Hamley
    ,, *Sh*—] Watchman
] Sh—'s future—
  See Downing & Jaggard
    ,, Scudder
] Sh—'s games [In ' Belgravia,' Feb.] Ln :
  1874. 8°   BPL | BUS
] Sh—'s games. *See Sh*—] Sh—'s sports
] Sh—'s garden craft—
  See Bagnall   *See* Grindon
    ,, Beisley   ,, Hancock
    ,, Bloom   ,, Oswald
    ,, Burgess   ,, Serres
    ,, Crane   ,, Sh— Works : Ext.,
    ,, Elder   1906
    ,, Ellacombe ,, *Sh*—] Halliwell
    ,, Gallio   ,, *Sh*—] Sh—'s bo-
    ,, Giraud   tany
] Sh—'s garden of girls. *See* Leigh-Noel
] Sh—'s garland. *See* Dibdin (C.)
] Sh—'s genius—
  See Brown   *See* Lloyd
    ,, Cond   ,, Nisbet
    ,, Cox   ,, Price
    ,, Dennis   ,, Pye
    ,, Drake   ,, Sh— Works : Ext.,
    ,, Essay   1821
    ,, Genius   ,, *Sh*—] Ode
   , Goltz   ,, *Sh*—] Testimonial
    ,, Graves   ,, *Sh*—] White
    ,, Jackson   ,, Skene
] Sh—'s gentleman. *See* Gentleman
] Sh—'s geography—
  See Johnson (R.)
    ,, Law
    ,, Lewkenor
] Sh—'s ghost—
  See Garrick
    ,, Memoirs
    ,, Sh— Works : Ext. 1803
] Sh—'s gimmel ring. *See* Balmanno
] Sh—'s girls. *See* Sh—'s women

Shakespeare]—

] Sh—'s gloves—
  See Beck
    ,, Law
] Sh—'s golf. *See* Knight (W.)
] Sh—'s grammar. *See* Abbott
] Sh—'s grand-daughter. *See* Barnard
] Sh—'s grave : Traditions current in Strat-
  ford-on-Avon in the seventeenth century.
  Edited by J. O. Halliwell. Brighton . . .
  1884. 8°   BPL
] Sh—'s grave—
  See Cooper   *See* King
    ,, Dugdale   ,, Langston
    ,, Gray   ,, Leisure hour
    ,, Hackett   ,, Norris
    ,, Hall (Wm.) ,, Prince
    ,, Hunter (J.) ,, Sh— Epitaph
    ,, Ingleby   ,, *Sh*—] Good . . .
    ,, Jaggard   ,, *Sh*—] Jephson
] Sh—'s Greek names [In 'Cornhill Magazine,'
  Feb.] Ln : Smith . . . 1876. 8°   BUS
] Sh—'s handwriting—
  See Sh— Autograph
    ,, *Sh*—] Knight
] Sh—'s haunts—
  See Pearce
    ,, Warwickshire
] Sh—'s heraldry—
  See Arms   *See Sh*—] Sh—'s coat-
    ,, Ferne   of-arms
    ,, Heraldry
] Sh—'s heroes and heroines. Illustrated by
  Callcott, Leslie, etc. Ln : Tuck . . .
  1891. 8°. With coloured plates BUS
] Sh—'s heroes—
  See Heroes . . .
    ,, Wingate
] Sh—'s heroines. *See Sh*—] Sh—'s women
] Sh—'s higher teaching. *See* Victory
] Sh—'s history—
  See Rose   *See* Stebbing
    ,, *Sh*—] Sh—   ,, Terry
    ,, *Sh*—] Sh—'s sources
] Sh—'s home—
  See Stratford
    ,, Timmins (S.)
] Sh—'s human life. *See* Giles
] Sh—'s humour—
  See Falstaff   *See* Meadows
    ,, Lambert   ,, Sh—] H—— (M.)
] Sh—'s hypocrites. *See* Waller
] Sh—'s identity—
  See Ashhurst   *See* Bormann
    ,, Atkinson   ,, Cattell
    ,, B— (G. H. P.) ,, Farquhar
    ,, Bacon   ,, Follett
    ,, Barrett   ,, Gervais
    ,, Begley   ,, Greenwood
    ,, Bompas   ,, Hall (R.)

See Hart
  ,, Henderson
  ,, Higgins
  ,, Holmes
  ,, Ingleby
  ,, James
  ,, Lumley
  ,, 'Multum'
  ,, P—— (J. V.)
  ,, Ralegh
  ,, Rolfe

See S—— (E. W.)
  ,, Sh— Works : Ext., 1869
  ,, *Sh—*] Townsend
  ,, Stearns
  ,, Surtees
  ,, Thayer
  ,, Theobald (W.)
  ,, Who wrote Sh— ?
  ,, Winsor

] Sh—'s ignorance. *See* Lippmann

] Sh—'s illustrations. *See* Sh— Works : Ext., 1832

] Sh—'s imagination. *See* Parker

] Sh—'s imitators—
See Sheffield
  ,, Shelley
  ,, Shirley (J.)
  ,, Shirley (W.)

See Theobald
  ,, Useful . . .
  ,, W—— (T.)

] Sh—'s immaturity. *See* March

] Sh—'s imposture. *See Sh*—] Townsend

] Sh—'s imprecation. *See Sh*—] Sh—'s curse verse

] Sh—'s impresa—
See Camden
  ,, Round
  ,, Stopes

] Sh—'s inconsistencies. *See* Rose
] Sh—'s industry. *See* Webster
] Sh—'s infidelity. *See* Schmucker
] Sh—'s influence—
See Giles
  ,, Reflections
] Sh—'s inner life. *See* Heraud
] Sh—'s inns. *See* Corner
] Sh—'s insects. *See* Patterson
] Sh—'s insomnia. *See* Head
] Sh—'s inspiration. *See* Butler
] Sh—'s irreligion. *See Sh*—] Wheeler
] Sh—'s Italian inspiration. *See* Walters
] Sh—'s jest book : part I. ' Tales and quicke answeres, very mery and pleasant to rede.' With preface and glossary. Part II. 'A C. mery talys.' With preface and glossary. Part III. [supplement] 'Mery tales, wittie questions, and quicke answeres, very pleasant to be readde.' 1567. Edited by S. W. S[inger]. Chiswick : C. Whittingham, 1814-16. 3 parts, forming 1 vol. 8°   BM | BUS

Issue restricted to 250 copies.
Six copies were done on blue paper (one at B.U.S.) and a few entirely on India paper.
See 'Retrospective Review,' 1854, vol. 2, p. 313.
Contents : Glossary ; Tales and quicke answeres ; Hundred mery talys ; Supplement to ' Tales and quicke answers' ; Mery tales, wittie questions and quicke answeres.

] Sh—'s jest book [edited by S. W. Singer]. Chiswick : C. Whittingham . . . 1824. 3 vols. Cr. 8°

] Sh—'s jest book [Review in ' Retrospective Review,' Aug.] Ln : 1854. 8°   BUS

] Sh—'s jest books : Reprints of the early and very rare jest books supposed to have been used by Sh—. Edited with introduction and notes by W. Carew Hazlitt. Ln : Willis . . . 1864. 3 vols. Cr. 8°, (Vol 1) xii.-162, (vol. 2) xii.-368, (vol. 3) xii.-108-84-52-86-76-xvi.
    BM | BPL | BUS | CPL | MPL | SML
Contents :—
Hundred mery talys, from the only known copy
Mery tales and quicke answeres, 1567
Merie tales of Skelton
Jests of Scogin
Sackfull of newes
Tarlton's jests
Merrie conceited jests of George Peele
Jacke of Dover
Merie tales of the mad men of Gotham
Twelve mery jests of the wydow Edyth
Pasquil's jests, with Mother Bunches merriments
Pleasant conceits of old Hobson
Certayne conceyts and jeasts
Taylor's wit and mirth
Conceits, clinches, flashes and whimzies.

] Sh—'s jest book : Hundred mery talys. Edited with introduction and notes by Dr. A. Oesterley. Ln : J. R. Smith . . . 1866. Cr. 8°, pp. xx.-162 BM|CPL|MPL|SML

] Sh—'s jest books : Reprints of the early and very rare jest-books supposed to have been used by Sh—. I. A hundred mery talys, from the only known copy. II. Mery talys and quicke answers, from the rare edition of 1567. Edited with introduction and notes by W. Carew Hazlitt . . . Ln : Sotheran . . . 1881. 8°, pp. xii.-x.-162   BM | BLO | BPL | CTC

] Sh—'s jesters. *See* Clarke
] Sh—'s jests. *See* Sh— Jests . . .
] Sh—'s journeys—
See Savage
  ,, *Stratford*] From . . .
] Sh—'s jubilee. *See* Sh—] Sh— celebrations
] Sh—'s knots. *See* Perring
] Sh—'s language—
See Andrews
  ,, Hales
  ,, Halliwell

See Ingleby
  ,, *Sh*—] Sh—'s vocabulary
] Sh—'s last days—
See Sh—] Halleck
  ,, *Sh*—] Halliwell
] Sh—'s last play. *See* Day
] Sh—'s learning—
See Anders
  ,, Farmer
  ,, Leisure hour
  ,, Lofft
  ,, Maginn

See Prescott
  ,, *Sh*—] Rolfe
  ,, *Sh*—] Sh—'s library
  ,, Whalley

Shakespeare]—

] Sh—'s legal knowledge—

See Campbell	*See* Heard
,, Coote	,, Rushton
,, Davis (C. K.)	,, *Sh*—] T—— (H.)
,, Devecmon	,, *Sh*—] White
,, Fraunce	,, Sprague
,, Fuller	,, Stopes
,, Green (B. E.)	,, Swinburne (H.)
,, Guernsey	,, Wilkes

] Sh—'s library; A collection of the romances, novels, poems and histories, used by Sh— as the foundation of his dramas. Now first collected and printed. With introductory notes . . . by J. P. Collier. Ln : T. Rodd . . . [1843]. 2 vols. 8°

BM | BPL | CPL | MPL | SML | W

Twelve copies were done on fine paper, of which one is at Boston.

Contents :—
Greene, Pandosto
Lodge, Rosalynd
Historie of Hamblet
Apollonius prince of Tyre
Bandello, Romeus and Juliet
Painter, Rhomeo and Julietta
Boccaccio, Giletta of Narbona
Tarlton, Story of the two lovers of Pisa
Rich, Historie of Apollonius and Silla
Whetstone, Historie of Promos and Cassandra
Giovanni, Adventures of Giannetto
Busche, Jew who would . . . have a pound of flesh
'Gesta Romanorum' : Choice of the three caskets
Giraldi-Cinthio, Story of the Moorish captain
Higgins, Queen Cordila
Sidney, Paphlagonian unkind king
Holinshed, History of Makbeth
Montemayor, Shepherdess of Felismena
Westward for smelts: Story told by the fishwife of
    Stand-on-the-green.

] Sh—'s library . . . Edited by J. P. Collier. Ln : T. Rodd, 1850. 2 vols. 8° BUS

] Sh—'s library: A collection of the plays, romances, novels, poems, and histories employed by Sh— in the composition of his works. With introductions and notes. Second edition. Carefully revised and greatly enlarged. The text now first formed from a new collation of the original copies. Edited by J. P. Collier and W. Carew Hazlitt. Ln : Reeves & Turner, 1875. 6 vols. 8°

BM | BLO | BPL | BUS | SML

Contents :—
Plutarch, Life of Theseus
Bandello and Brooke, Romeus and Iuliet
Painter, Rhomeo and Iulietta
Agincourt
Montemayor, Shepherdess Felismena
Giovanni, Adventures of Giannetto
'Gesta Romanorum' : Three caskets
Busche, Jew who would have a pound of flesh
Northern lord
Gernutus the Jew
Rich, Apolonius and Silla
Lodge, Rosalynde
Holinshed, History of Makbeth
Boccaccio, Bernabo da Genova
Westward for smelts : Tale by the fishwife

Shakespeare]—

Hystorie of Hamblet
Giraldi-Cinthio, Moor of Venice
Holinshed, History of Lear
Higgins, Queen Cordila
Sidney, Paphlagonian unkind king
Death of King Leir
Straparola, Filenio Sisterna
Giovanni, Bucciuolo and Pietro Paolo
Lucius Camillus
Straparola, Story of Nerino
Tarlton, Story of two lovers of Pisa
Ariosto, Ariodanto and Genevra
Bandello, Timbreo di Cardona
Boccaccio, Giletta of Narbona
Whetstone, Promos and Cassandra
Giraldi-Cinthio, Novella
Plutarch, Life of Julius Cæsar
    ,,   Life of Coriolanus
    ,,   Life of Antonius
Greene, History of Pandosto
Holinshed, Passages
Chaucer, Knighte's tale
Gower, Apollonius of Tyre
Twine, Patterne of painefull aduentures
Plutarch, Life of Pericles
Goulart, Waking man's dream
Wife lapped in morel's skin
Plautus, Menechmi. Edited by W. W[arner]
Legge (T.) Richardus tertius
Troublesome raigne of King Iohn
Famous victories of Henry the fifth
First part of the contention between Yorke and
    Lancaster
True tragedie of Richard Duke of Yorke
Whetstone, Historie of Promos and Cassandra
True chronicle history of King Leir . . .
'Timon of Athens,' by an unknown author about 1600
'Taming of a shrew,' by an unknown author.

] Sh—'s library—

See Anders	*See* Sh— autograph
,, Bible	,, *Sh*—] Drake
,, Cotton	,, *Sh*—] Sh—'s school
,, Glanville	books
,, Jaggard	,, Smith (J. T.)
,, Jones (T.)	,, Stopes
,, Leisure hour	,, Swinburne (H.)
,, Levins	,, Thomasius
,, Newnham	,, Thucydides
,, Partridge	,, Topsell
,, Paton	,, Tudor
,, Robinson	,, Villanova
,, Rushton	,, White (T.)

] Sh—'s little lad. *See* Clark (I.)

] Sh—'s localities—
See Localities
,, Warwickshire

] Sh—'s London—

See Fishwick	*See* Ordish
,, Griggs	,, *Sh*—] Halliwell
,, Norden	,, Stephenson

] Sh—'s life—

See Acheson	*See* British Museum
,, Aubrey	,, British Plutarch
,, Bookman	,, Burgess
,, Borsa	,, Caldecott
,, Bosanquet	,, Chetwood
,, British curiosi-	,, Cibber
ties	,, Collier

See Cooper
  ,, Corner
  ,, Cottage
  ,, Coxe
  ,, Craik
  ,, Creighton
  ,, Curiosities
  ,, Curling
  ,, Dalgleish
  ,, Dixon
  ,, Dowdall
  ,, Drake
  ,, Dryden
  ,, Engel
  ,, English . . .
  ,, Evans
  ,, Extemporary . .
  ,, Fay
  ,, Field
  ,, Fisher
  ,, Fishley
  ,, Fleay
  ,, Fletcher
  ,, Foard
  ,, French
  ,, Friesen
  ,, Frothingham
  ,, Gentleman's
     magazine
  ,, Gentleman's
     magazine
     library
  ,, Gray
  ,, Green
  ,, Greene (R.)
  ,, Greene (T.)
  ,, Gregg
  ,, Grinfield
  ,, Hales
  ,, Hall (E.)
  ,, Halliwell
  ,, Harleian
  ,, Harrison
  ,, Harvey
  ,, Hazlitt
  ,, Histrionicus
  ,, Hodgson
  ,, Hopper
  ,, Hornby
  ,, Hugo
  ,, Hunter (J.)
  ,, Ireland (S.)
  ,, Irving (W.)
  ,, Jaggard (W.)
  ,, Jones (S.)
  ,, Keightley
  ,, Kemp
  ,, Kent
  ,, Knight

See Langbaine
  ,, Lees (E.)
  ,, Le Neve
  ,, Levi
  ,, Lordan
  ,, Lumley
  ,, Macdonell
  ,, Madden
  ,, Mathews
  ,, May
  ,, Meadows
  ,, Meek
  ,, Minto
  ,, Mitchell
  ,, Moncrieff
  ,, Montagu
  ,, National library
  ,, New Sh— So-
  ,, Newell [ciety
  ,, Newspaper cut-
     tings
  ,, Nichols
  ,, Nicoll
  ,, Nisbet
  ,, Noorthouck
  ,, Old and new
  ,, Ordish
  ,, Parry
  ,, Phillips
  ,, Pictorial
  ,, Picturesque . . .
  ,, Poetic . . .
  ,, Prince
  ,, Pye
  ,, Reed
  ,, Rémy
  ,, Ribton-Turner
  ,, Rider
  ,, Roberts
  ,, Saintsbury
  ,, Sandys
  ,, Scherer
  ,, Select beauties
  ,, Select biography
  ,, Sh— Poems,
     1908
  ,, Sh— Works:
     Ext. 1870
  ,, Stratford-on-
     Avon
  ,, Taine
  ,, Tieck
  ,, Timmins (J. F.)
  ,, Traill
  ,, Ward
  ,, Westover
  ,, Wheler
  ,, Winstanley
  ,, Yeatman

] Sh—'s mad folk—
  See Bucknill   *See* Kellogg
  ,, Halford   ,, Ray
  ,, Horne   ,, Ross
] Sh—'s magic bijou Post Office. *See* Sh—
  Works : Ext. 1865
] Sh—'s making. *See* Tucker
] Sh—'s manuscripts—
  See Cargill   *See Sh*—] Sh— forgeries
  ,, Leisure hour   ,, Taylor (John)
  ,, Prichard   ,, Webb
  ,, *Sh*—] Malone
] Sh—'s Manx knowledge. *See* Talbot
] Sh—'s marriage—
  See Evans   *See* Malam
  ,, Halliwell, New ,, *Sh*—] Gray
     boke . . .   ,, *Sh*—] Holder
] Sh—'s mask. *See Sh*—] Sh—'s 'death mask'
] Sh—'s medical knowledge—
  See Bucknill   *See* Jacox
  ,, Doran   ,, Key . . .
  ,, Field   ,, Moyes
  ,, Gillespie   ,, Rushfield
  ,, Griffiths   ,, Stearns
  ,, Hackett   ,, Wadd
] Sh—'s mental photographs. *See* Sh—
  Works : Ext. 1866
] Sh—'s merry tales. *See* Hundred . . .
] Sh—'s metaphors. *See* Latham
] Sh—'s methods—
  See Ruggles
  ,, Sidgwick (H.)
  ,, Snider
] Sh—'s metre—
  See Boswell   *See* Lloyd
  ,, Fleay   ,, *Sh*—] Malone
  ,, Furnivall
] Sh—'s military knowledge—
  See Loque
  ,, Seccombe
] Sh—'s mind—
  See Morgan
  ,, Robinson
] Sh—'s minor poems [Article in 'Oxford &
  Cambridge Magazine,' Feb.] 1856. 8°
                      BUS
] Sh—'s misprints. *See* Jackson
] Sh—'s mission. *See* Foard
] Sh—'s monuments—
  See Burgess   *See* Proposed . . .
  ,, H—— (A.)   ,, Ward
  ,, Kelsall   ,, Wilson (W.)
  ,, Proposal
] Sh—'s morality—
  See Baar   *See* Moulton
  ,, Gilman   ,, Plumptre
  ,, Griffith   ,, *Sh*—] Moral . . .
  ,, Grinfield   ,, Sharp
  ,, Hoare

Shakespeare]—

] Sh—'s mulberry tree—
  See Catalogue . . . 1838, 1864
  ,, Fairholt
  ,, Garrick
  ,, Jubilee
  ,, Serres
  ,, *Sh*—] Shakespeareana
  ,, Sharp
  ,, *Stratford*] Transcripts
  ,, Sweet Robin
] Sh—'s musical knowledge—
  See Naylor
  ,, Willetts
] Sh—'s mutilators—
  See Hudson
  ,, Sewell
] Sh—'s mythology—
  See Root
  ,, *Sh*—] Sh—'s fairies
] Sh—'s name—
  See Camden   See Rous
  ,, Clarke (M. C.) ,, Stopes
  ,, Gilmore ,, Van Winkle
  ,, Hales ,, Verstegan
  ,, Halliwell ,, White (R. G.)
  ,, Haney ,, Wise
  ,, Madden
] Sh—'s nationalities. *See* Nationalities
] Sh—'s nature study—
  See Dircks   See Robinson
  ,, Glanvilla ,, Roffe
  ,, Mayou ,, Seager
  ,, Phipson ,, Topsell
] Sh—'s nautical knowledge. *See* Bullen (F. T.)
] Sh—'s ' New Place '—
  See Bellew   See Halliwell
  ,, Brassington ,, Stratford
  ,, Butcher
] Sh—'s nomenclature. *See* Taylor
] Sh—'s non-dramatic work. *See* Wilson
] Sh—'s nuns. *See* Bridgett
] Sh—'s occult knowledge. *See* Supernatural
] Sh—'s originality. *See Sh*—] Robertson
] Sh—'s ornithology. *See Sh*—] Sh—'s birds
] Sh—'s orthography. *See* Hawley
] Sh—'s Ovid. *See* Ovidius
] Sh—'s papers. *See Sh*—] Malone
] Sh—'s parallels
  See Halliwell
  ,, Reed
] Sh—'s pastimes. *See* Ward (H. S.)
] Sh—'s pathos—
  See H—— (M.)
  ,, Lambert
] Sh—'s patriotism—
  See Bailey
  ,, Levi

Shakespeare]—

] Sh—'s pedigree—
  See Bellew   See Sh—] Jordan
  ,, Jordan ,, *Sh*—] Sh—'s family
  ,, *Sh*—] Hallen ,, Wheler
] Sh—'s personal history [In ' Southern Review,' July]. Baltimore .. 1868. 8° BUS
] Sh—'s personality—
  See Clarke   See Sh—] Cox
  ,, Hallam ,, *Sh*—] Downing
  ,, Madden ,, *Sh*—] Glynn
  ,, Nisbet ,, *Sh*—] Halliwell
  ,, Robinson ,, *Sh*—] Sh—
  ,, Ross ,, *Sh*—] Smith
  ,, *Sh*—] Bartol ,, Stephens
  ,, *Sh*—] C— (W. G.) ,, Thomson
] Sh—'s philosophy—
  See Bacon (D. S.) See Rankin
  ,, Birch ,, Roffe
  ,, Clarke (C. C.)
] Sh—'s phraseology—
  See Boswell
  ,, Ingleby
  ,, *Sh*—] Malone
] Sh—'s phrenology. *See Sh*—]
] Sh—'s physiology. *See* Kellogg
] Sh—'s pilgrims. *See* Jaggard
] Sh—'s plagiarism—
  See Great . . . See Richardson
  ,, Langbaine ,, *Sh*—] Robertson
] Sh—'s plagiarists—
  See Foard
  ,, Nicholson
] Sh—'s plays in folio. *See* Lenox
] Sh—'s plots—
  See Beer   See Sh— Works : Ext. 1893
  ,, Fleming ,, *Sh*—] Life
  ,, Langbaine ,, *Sh*—] Skottowe
  ,, Ransome ,, *Sh*—] Tegg
] Sh—'s politics—
  See Coleridge
  ,, Simpson
] Sh—'s popularity—
  See Thiel
  ,, Three centuries
] Sh—'s portrait, by Arlaud and Duchange. *See* Sh— Works, 1745
] Sh—'s portrait by Bannerman. *See* Sh— Poems, 1775
] Sh—'s portrait. Burdett-Coutts' picture. *See* Sh— Works, 1836
] Sh—'s portrait. Burgess miniature. *See* Sh— Works, 1821
] Sh—'s portrait. Chandos picture, engraved by F. Bartolozzi. *See* Sh— Poems, 1798
] Sh—'s portraits. Chandos picture, engraved by A. Bourgeois. Paris : Furne [c. 1840]. 4°. On steel

] Sh—'s portrait. Chandos picture, engraved by Samuel Cousins. Ln : Sh— Society . . . 1849. 4°

] Sh—'s portrait, engraved by Croome. *See* Sh— Works, 1875

] Sh—'s portrait. Chandos picture, engraved by R. Field. *See* Sh— Works, 1795-96

] Sh—'s portrait. Chandos picture, engraved by H. Gravelot. *See* Sh— Works, 1744-46, 1770-71

ᵢ Sh—'s portrait. Chandos picture, engraved by J. Hall. *See* Sh— Works, 1778

] Sh—'s portrait. Chandos picture, engraved by H. Robinson. *See* Sh— Works, 1838

] Sh—'s portrait. Chandos picture, engraved by Roffe. *See* Sh— Works, 1818

] Sh—'s portrait. Chandos picture, engraved by E. Scriven. *See* Sh— Works, 1830

] Sh—'s portrait. Chandos picture, engraved by T. Starling. *See* Sh— Works, 1832-34

] Sh—'s portrait. Chandos picture, engraved by G. Vertue. *See* Sh— Works, 1723-25, 1765

] Sh—'s portrait. Chandos portrait, engraved by W. & J. Walker. *See* Sh— Works, 1787-91, 1796

] Sh—'s portrait. Chandos picture—
   See Fine art . . .
   ,, Rodd & Forster
   ,, Scharf
   ,, Sh— Poems, 1804, 1826, 1862
   ,, Sonnets, 1907
   ,, Sh— Works, 1748, 1762, 1785, 1791, 1804-13, 1809, 1817-18, 1821, 1826, 1828, 1835, 1836, 1837, 1838, 1842, 1843, 1845, 1846, 1847, 1849, 1850, 1851-56, 1852, 1853, 1854, 1854-74, 1855-59, 1855-71, 1856, 1857, 1858, 1862, 1863-64, 1864, 1866, 1868, 1869, 1875, 1876, 1877, 1878, 1886-87, 1888-89, 1891
   ,, Sh— Works : Ext. 1865, 1881, 1897
   ,, *Sh*—] Corbin
   ,, *Sh*—] Houbraken
   ,, *Sh*—] Life . . .
   ,, *Sh*—] Portrait
   ,, *Sh*—] Tegg
   ,, Traill
   ,, Walters

] Sh—'s portrait. Droeshout picture, painted upon a prepared surface of white jesso upon an old panel of elm [probably by an Italian ceiling artist, settled in Ln. c. 1623 ?]   SML

Sir Wm. Richmond, R.A. believes this to be the un-doubted original of the clumsy Droeshout engraving. It was purchased by Mrs. Charles E Flower for the low sum of £150, and presented to the Sb— Memorial. It was reproduced in colours in 1910, and has frequently been engraved.
It is also known as the Flower portrait.

] Sh—'s portrait. Droeshout picture, engraved by A. Fox. *See* Sh— Works, 1825

] Sh—'s portrait. Droeshout picture, engraved by W. Gilbirson. *See* Sh— Rape, 1655

] Sh—'s portrait. Droeshout picture, engraved by Wm. Marshall—
   See Sh— Poems, 1640, 1866
   ,, Sh— Works, 1778, 1785, 1826, 1866, 1868-79

] Sh—'s portrait. Droeshout picture, engraved by W. Marshall and H. Robinson. *See* Sh— Works, 1826-32

] Sh—'s portrait. Droeshout picture, engraved by W. Sherwin. *See* Sh— Works, 1790

] Sh—'s portrait. Droeshout picture, engraven by Swaine. *See* Sh— Works, 1830

] Sh—'s portrait. Droeshout picture, photographed and printed in colours. Ln : Medici Society . . . 1910. 4°   SML

An exact copy of the Flower picture, the supposed original of the Droeshout engraving, by an unknown artist, at the Sh— Memorial, Stratford-on-Avon.

] Sh—'s portrait. Droeshout picture—
   See Corbin
   ,, Dowden
   ,, Green
   ,, Lowndes
   ,, New Sh— Soc.
   ,, Robinson
   ,, Rodd
   ,, Sh— As you like it, 1864
   ,, Sh— Two gentlemen . . . 1895
   ,, Sh— Works, 1623, 1632, 1663, 1664, 1750-51, 1773, 1785, 1791, 1811, 1821, 1824, 1825, 1852, 1853, 1857 1858, 1860, 1864, 1864-67, 1876, 1879, 1883, 1883-86, 1888-89, 1902, 1904, 1907
   ,, Sh— Works : Ext. 1832
   ,, *Sh*—] Corbin
   ,, Sh—] Shakespearean show book

] Sh—'s portrait. Ellesmere picture. *See* Sh—] Collection

] Sh—'s portrait. Ely Palace picture. *See* Sh—] Corbin

] Sh—'s portrait, engraved by W. Faithorne and R. Sawyer. *See* Sh— Works, 1816

] Sh—'s portrait. Felton picture, engraved by W. Holl. *See* Sh— Works, 1813

] Sh—'s portrait. Felton picture, engraved by Neagle. *See* Sh— Works, 1803, 1805

] Sh—'s portrait. Felton picture, engraved by Trotter. *See* Sh— Works, 1793, 1807

] Sh—'s portrait. Felton picture—
   See Sh— Works, 1806, 1807, 1809, 1813, 1883-86
   ,, *Sh*—] Steevens

] Sh—'s portrait. Flower picture. *See* Sh—] Sh—'s portrait, Droeshout picture

Shakespeare]—

] Sh—'s portrait. Garrick statue, engraved by P. Halpin. *See* Sh— Works, 1771
] Sh—'s portrait. Gower statue. *See Sh—*] Rolfe
] Sh—'s portrait. Grafton picture. *See Sh—*] Spielmann
] Sh—'s portrait, engraved by H. Gravelot. *See* Sh— Works, 1757
] Sh—'s portrait, engraved by J. Hall— *See* Gentleman
   ,, Sh— Poems, 1774
   ,, Sh— Works, 1773
] Sh—'s portrait, engraved by Hilliard. *See* Sh— Works, 1846
] Sh—'s portrait, engraved by Hulett. *See* Sh— Poems, 1760
] Sh—'s portrait. Janssen (or Somerset) picture—
   See Sh— Works, 1825, 1827, 1840, 1841, 1850, 1858, 1864-68, 1877
   ,, *Sh—*] Corbin
] Sh—'s portrait. Kinton picture. *See Sh—*] Walford
] Sh—'s portrait. Madox-Brown picture— *See* Bailey
   ,, Rowley
] Sh—'s portrait, engraved by J. Miller. *See* Sh— Works, 1767-68
] Sh—'s portrait. Miniature picture [In 'Catalogue of an exhibition of portraits, 1800']. 4°   BPL
] Sh—'s portrait in oils, painted on an old oak panel 23in. by 14in.
With inscription beneath, painted on another panel, commencing :—
   'How speak thatte browe soe pensive yet serene
     The lucidde teare just startynge to thine eyne...'
It was reproduced and described in 'The Antiquarian,' Oct., 1885, by E. Walford; also in 'Sale Prices,' Jan., 1904.
Sold in Dec., 1903, for £131.
Bears a strong resemblance to the numerous frauds perpetrated by W. F. Zincke.
] Sh—'s portrait. Pall Mall alto relievo monument. *See* Sh— Works, 1841
] Sh—'s portrait : Page bust. *See* Sh— Sonnets, 1881
] Sh—'s portrait, engraved by N. Parr— *See* Mottley (John)
   ,, Whincop
] Sh—'s portrait, by Paton. *See* Sh— Works, 1792
] Sh—'s portrait, by Picot & Reilly. *See* Sh— Works, 1771
] Sh—'s portrait. Precipitate or 'spirit' picture, by L. R. Marsh. *See* New Shakespeareana
] Sh—'s portrait, by Ridley. *See* Sh— Works, 1798-1800, 1800

Shakespeare]—

] Sh—'s portrait, by Sanders. *See Sh—*] Spielmann
] Sh—'s portrait, by Sherwin & Grignion. *See* Sh— Works, 1773-74
] Sh—'s portrait. Somerset picture. *See Sh—*] Sh—'s portrait, Janssen picture
] Sh—'s portrait. Stratford bust of Sh—, a platinotype. Ln : New Sh— Soc. . . . 1882. F°   BPL
] Sh—'s portrait. Stratford bust— *See* Beauties . . .
   ,, Bell
   ,, Brassington
   ,, Britton
   ,, Dugdale
   ,, Greene
   ,, Jubilee
   ,, Leisure hour
   ,, Neale
   ,, New Sh— Soc.
   ,, Rodd
   ,, S—— (J.)
   ,, Sh— As you like it, 1864
   ,, Sh— Poems, 1851
   ,, Sh— Works, 1744-46, 1770-71, 1818, 1821, 1830, 1832, 1850, 1853-65, 1854-56, 1855-56, 1857, 1860, 1862, 1864-67, 1864-68, 1875, 1880
   ,, *Sh—*] Corbin
   ,, *Sh—*] Downes
   ,, *Sh—*] Drake
   ,, *Sh—*] Harness
   ,, *Sh—*] Harrison
   ,, *Sh—*] Hunter
   ,, *Sh—*] Rolfe
   ,, *Sh—*] Sh— sermons
   ,, *Sh—*] Smith
   ,, *Sh—*] Stratford
   ,, Taylor
   ,, Tompkins
   ,, Wivell
] Sh—'s portrait, engraved by J. Thomson. *See* Grant
] Sh—'s portrait, engraved by Thurston & Warren. *See* Sh— Works, 1806
] Sh—'s portrait, engraved by Van der Gucht. *See* Sh— Works, 1709, 1740, 1747
] Sh—'s portrait, engraved by G. Vertue— *See* Sh— Works, 1747, 1773
   ,, Vertue
] Sh—'s portrait. Ward's New York statue. *See* Sh— Much ado . . . 1879
   ,, *Sh—*] Corbin
   ,, *Sh—*] Ward
] Sh—'s portrait, by Warman. *See* Hall (H. T.)
] Sh—'s portrait, engraved by C. Warren. *See* Sh— Works, 1803

Shakespeare]—

] Sh—'s portrait. Westminster Abbey monument—
  See Graves
   ,, *Sh*—] Corbin
   ,, Sh—Works, 1744-46, 1750-51, 1770-71
] Sh—'s portrait. Zoust picture. *See* Sh—
  Works, 1752, 1836
] Sh—'s portraits : Various pictures—
  See Bookman
   ,, Sh— Poems, 1797, 1862, 1872
   ,, Sh— Works, 1750-51, 1768, 1784, 1790, 1794, 1800, 1818, 1823, 1826, 1830, 1832, 1832-34, 1839, 1842, 1847, 1850, 1851, 1853, 1855, 1856-57, 1857, 1858, 1859, 1862, 1863, 1864, 1866, 1868, 1873-75, 1874, 1875, 1877, 1880, 1882, 1883, 1899, 1899-1900, 1901-04
   ,, Sh— Works : Ext. 1783, 1784, 1798, 1838, 1850

See Sh—] Bagehot	*See Sh*—] Lambert
,, *Sh*—] Calmour	,, *Sh*—] Levi
,, *Sh*—] Calvert	,, *Sh*—] Mabie
,, *Sh*—] Cundall	,, *Sh*—] Malone
,, *Sh*—] Cuthbert-son	,, *Sh*—] Memorials
	,, *Sh*—] Norris
,, *Sh*—] De Quincey	,, *Sh*—] Portrait
	,, *Sh*—] Steevens
,, *Sh*—] Ewen	,, Taylor (John)
,, *Sh*—] Jacob	,, Timmins (S.)
,, *Sh*—] Jeremiah	,, Townesend

] Sh—'s portrait literature—

See American	*See* Malins
,, Antiquarian ...	,, Massey
,, Biographical	,, Merridew
,, Birch	,, Milton
,, Bookmart	,, Norris
,, Brassington	,, Original ...
,, Cargill	,, Patterson
,, Catalogue, 1873	,, Rabone
,, Collier	,, Reed
,, Corbin	,, Returne
,, Cotgrave	,, Robinson
,, Edwards	,, Rowley
,, Ellis	,, Scharf
,, Elsheimer	,, *Sh*—] Boaden
,, Farmer	,, *Sh*—] Craig
,, Felton	,, *Sh*—] Cust
,, Furness	,, *Sh*—] Friswell
,, Green	,, *Sh*—] Norris
,, Hart	,, *Sh*—] Only ...
,, Hartmann	,, *Sh*—] Page
,, Ingleby	,, *Sh*—] Pemberton
,, Ireland	,, *Sh*—] Portraits
,, Jaggard	,, *Sh*—] Sh— notes
,, Jeremiah	,, *Sh*—] Spielmann
,, Knight	,, *Sh*—] Wheatley
,, Leisure hour	,, Smith (J. R.)
,, McDowall	,, Steevens

Shakespeare.] Sh—'s portrait literature—

See Stoddard	*See* Wilson (John)
,, Stopes	,, Wivell
,, Turbutt	,, Wordsworth
,, Wall	,, Wright (C.)
,, Wheler	

] Sh—'s portraits ; a list. [c. 1850.] F°.
  Original manuscript   BPL
] Sh—'s praise—
  See Sh—] Ingleby
   ,, *Sh*—] Praise
] Sh—'s prayer book, 1596. *See* Sh— Autograph
] Sh—'s prayer book [Collection of news cuttings relating thereto. c. 1870.] 4°
              BPL
] Sh—'s predecessors—

See Boas	*See* Manly
,, D'Israeli	,, Rushton
,, Herford	,, Sonnenschein
,, Ireson	,, Symonds
,, Lanier	

] Sh—'s printer-publishers—

See Bompas	*See* Jaggard (Wm.)
,, Gould	,, Morgan
,, Holt	,, Plomer
,, Jaggard (Dorothy)	,, Roberts
,, Jaggard (Isaac)	,, Stationers
,, Jaggard (John)	

] Sh—'s prologues and epilogues. *See* Sh—
  [Works : Ext.] Collection ... 1779
] Sh—'s pronunciation—

See Ellis	*See* Noyes
,, Hawley	Victor

] Sh—'s property—
  See Sh—] Sh—'s estate
   ,, Wallace
] Sh—'s prophecies—
  See Scadding
   ,, Skipsey
] Sh—'s prose—
  See Sharpe (H.)
   ,, Sill
] Sh—'s prototypes. *See* Frey
] Sh—'s provincialisms. *See* Surtees
] Sh—'s psychology—
  See Bucknill
   ,, Kellogg
] Sh—'s puritanism—
  See Byington
   ,, Hales
   ,, Mercurius ...
] Sh—'s qualities. *See* Griffiths
] Sh—'s quarrel. *See* Jonson
] Sh—'s readers. *See* Pemberton
] Sh—'s recreations. *See* Ward (H. S.)
] Sh—'s relatives. *See Sh*—] Sh—'s family

Shakespeare]—

] Sh—'s speeches. *See* Pulling
] Sh—'s spirit—
   See Johnstone
   ,, Meredith
] Sh—'s spiritual life. *See* Downing
] Sh—'s sports—
   See Ayers
   ,, Madden
   ,, *Sh*—] Sh—
] Sh—'s stage—
   See Alabaster   *See* Mantzius
   ,, Albright   ,, Stage
] Sh—'s stagecraft—
   See Lamb
   ,, Lathrop
] Sh—'s statesmanship. *See* Congdon
] Sh—'s statues——
   See Garrick
   ,, O'Donavan
] Sh—'s stoicism. *See* Sonnenschein
] Sh—'s struggle. *See Sh*—] Motives
] Sh—'s style—
   See Masklin
   ,, Taverner
] Sh—'s successors. *See* Sonnenschein
] Sh—'s suicides. *See* Kellogg
] Sh—'s superstition—
   See Bell   *See* Lucy
   ,, Caine   ,, Spalding
   ,, Hall
] Sh—'s supremacy. *See* Spalding
] Sh—'s surgical knowledge—
   See Jaggard
   ,, Vigo
   ,, West
] Sh—'s sweetheart—
   See Fitton   *See Sh*—] Harris
   ,, Furnivall   ,, Sterling
   ,, Sh— (Anne)
] Sh—'s swordsmanship—
   See Arms
   ,, Fencing
   ,, Monte
] Sh—'s teaching. *See Sh*—] Rusden
] Sh—'s temperance—
   See Malins
   ,, Sherlock
] Sh—'s testamentary language—
   See Rushton
   ,, *Sh*—] Sh—'s legal knowledge
] Sh—'s text—
   See Adee   *See* Jervis
   ,, Ingleby   ,, Morgan
   ,, 'Jaques'
] Sh—'s time—
   See Bell   *See* Halliwell
   ,, Drake   ,, Hare
   ,, Goadby   ,, Jusserand
   ,, Greene (R.)   ,, Niven

Shakespeare.] Sh—'s time—

   See Rich   *See Sh*—] Tweddell
   ,, Rothschild   ,, Stobart
   ,, Rye   ,, Stopes
   ,, Seccombe   ,, Stubbes
   ,, *Sh*—] Jenks   ,, Swinburne
   ,, *Sh*—] Morley   ,, Willis
] Sh—'s tithes. *See* Hunter (J.)
] Sh—'s tomb. *See Sh*—] Sh—'s grave
] Sh—'s topical elements. *See* Rothschild
] Sh—'s tragic genius. *See* Hamilton
] Sh—'s twilights. *See* Price
] Sh—'s unbelief. *See* Holland
] Sh—'s use of narration. *See* Delius
] Sh—'s uses. *See* Uses . . .
] Sh—'s vagabonds. *See* Viles & Furnivall
] Sh—'s versification—
   See B—— (C.)   *See* Ingram
   ,, Browne (G. H.)   ,, Walker
] Sh—'s vindicators. *See* Greenwood
] Sh—'s visits to Bath. *See* Meehan
] Sh—'s visits to Coventry. *See* Merridew
] Sh—'s visits to Dursley. *See* Huntley
] Sh—'s visits to Fulham. *See* Croker
] Sh—'s visits to Oxford. *See* Davenant
] Sh—'s visits to Stratford. *See* Savage
] Sh—'s vocabulary—
   See Butler   *See* Helms
   ,, Halliwell   ,, Hewis
] Sh—'s vocabulary and style [In ' Fraser's
   Magazine']. Ln. . . . 1869. 8°   BUS
] Sh—'s waiting women. *See* Latham
] Sh—'s wars. *See* Lounsbury
] Sh—'s Warwickshire. *See Sh*—] Sh—'s
   country
] Sh—'s weak endings. *See* Ingram
] Sh—'s wedding—
   See Malam
   ,, *Sh*—] Gray
] Sh—'s whereabouts. *See* Scott (E. J. L.)
] Sh—'s wild flowers [In the ' Nature lover'].
   1893. 8°   BPL
] Sh—'s wisdom. *See* Price
] Sh—'s wit—
   See Lambert
   ,, Ward
] Sh—'s women—
   See Clarke (M. C.)   *See* Kellogg
   ,, Clay   ,, Latham
   ,, Davies (M.)   ,, Leigh-Noel
   ,, Dowden   ,, Lewes
   ,, Goethe   ,, Martin
   ,, Graphic . . .   ,, Palmer
   ,, Hamer   ,, Richardson
   ,, Heine   ,, Springthorpe
   ,, Heroes . . .   ,, Wingate
   ,, Jameson   ,, Yardley

Shakespeare]—

] Sh—'s young people—
   See Barr
    ,, O'Brien
] Sh—'s youth—
   See Evans
    ,, Kingsley
    ,, Rolfe
    ,, *Sh*—] Sh—'s character
    ,, Somerset
    ,, Williams

] Shakespearean [a magazine], edited by A. H. Wall. Stratford-on-Avon [Printed by George Boyden for] Edith Wall, 1895-96. 2 vols. 4°   BPL
A periodical commenced 15th May, 1895, with the financial aid of Mr. R. H. Fitzpatrick, a Stratford resident. After eighteen numbers had appeared, it changed its publisher and shape in Oct., 1896. Fourteen more numbers brought the publication to a close in Dec., 1897.

] Shakespearean [a magazine], edited by A· H. Wall. Ln: Dawbarn & Ward, Roxburghe Press, 1896-97. Vol. 3. 8°, pp. iv.-448. Illustrated   BPL | SML

] Shakespearean anthology. *See* Sh— Works: Ext. 1830

] Shakespearean character cards. *See* Sh— Works: Ext. 1853

] Shakespearean charades, with solutions [In ' Family pastime ']. 2 vols. 12°   BPL

] Shakespearean Christmas card : ' Post Office Savings Bank.' Views of Stratford, etc. 1901. 12°   BPL

] Shakespearean criticism [In 'American Church Review,' Oct.] Hartford [U.S.] 1874. 8°   BUS

] Shakespearean criticism and acting : 'Romeo and Juliet' [In 'Westminster Review,' Sept.] Ln : 1845. 8°   BUS

] Shakespearean drolls, from a rare book printed about A.D. 1698, entitled the ' Theatre of ingenuity,' containing the mad wooing from the ' Taming of the shrew' and the ' Boaster or bully huff catch'd in a trap taken from the first part of "King Henry the fourth."' Edited by J. O. Halliwell. Chiswick Press: Privately printed, 1859. 12°, pp. 28
         BPL | BUS | HCL | MPL | W
Impression restricted to thirty copies.

] Shakespearean drolls. *See also* Theatre
] Shakespearean extracts from ' Edward Pudsey's booke.' *See* Sh— Works: Ext. 1888

] Shakespearean facsimiles [Collection of seven facsimile leaves from early quarto Sh— plays and other works concerning the poet, 1600-1640. Ln: c 1870]. Roy. 4°   W
A private impression, restricted to twelve copies.

Shakespeare]—

] Shakespearean glossaries [In ' Edinburgh Review' . . .] 1869. 8°   CPL

] Shakespearean literature [In ' Bentley's Quarterly Review,' Oct.] Ln : 1859. 8°
             BUS

] Shakespearean manuscripts at Abington Abbey : Mr. Halliwell-Phillipps' theory and Mr. Pritchard's refutation [In 'Northamptonshire Notes & Queries'] . . . 1889. 8°   BPL
See also Pritchard.

] Shakespearean mares-nests. *See* White
] Shakespearean medals. *See* Hubbard, Catalogue, 1878-80, p. 157

] Shakespearean miscellanies [Collection of over thirty pieces respecting Sh—, including the air of ' Under the greenwood tree,' with new words from the ' Village opera, 1729'; excerpts from Sir A. Cokain's Poems, 1658; print of Herne's oak, etc.; mounted into an album]. Various years. Fcp. 4°. Manuscript and printed   W

] Shakespearean museum . . . Ln : . . . 1794. 4°. Portraits and plates

] Shakespearean notes [In ' Dublin University Magazine,' March]. 1864. 8° BUS
Contents: Sh—'s portrait, ' Hamlet,' 'Antony and Cleopatra,' ' Troilus and Cressida,' ' Macbeth.'

] Shakespearean notices : Collection of eight excerpts from early editions of Wm. Cartwright, Ben Jonson, Taylor the waterman, 'Witt's recreations' [by Mennis & Smith], etc. Mounted into a volume. Ln : [*Sæc. XVII.*] 8°   W

] Shakespearean notices [Collection of fragments, a few in manuscript, many in print, with some old engravings, all relating to Sh—: including excerpts from Collier's Short view of the stage, 1698 ; Cokain (*Sir* Aston) Poems, 1658 ; Sheppard, Epigrams, 1651 ; Flecknoe, Epigrams, 1670 ; Suckling (*Sir* John) Goblins, 1646 ; Wandering Jew, 1647 ; Turberville, Noble arte of venerie or hunting, 1611 ; Hundred mery tales ; etc.] *Sæc. XVII.-XVIII.* Mounted into 4 vols. 8° ; interleaved   W

] Shakespearean oracle [A set of nine cards, with a sheet of answers. Ln : . . . 1840]. F°   BM

] Shakespearean playing cards [The coloured court cards representing Sh— characters. Midland Railway Co., c. 1904]. 53 cards (including the ' Joker') in case
] Shakespearean playing cards—
   See Sh— Works: Ext. 1878
    ,, Tilney

] Shakespearean readings. *See* Sh— Works: Ext. 1850

] Shakespearean recitals. *See* Williams

] Shakespearean relics. *See* Rabone

] Shakespearean show book, with original literary contributions, illustrations and music from the following writers, artists, and composers: Lord Tennyson, Lady Brassey, Robert Browning, Herman Merivale, Oscar Wilde, R. Caldecott, W. Crane, G. Cruikshank . . . edited by J. S. Wood. Manchester: Falkner, 1884. Oblong roy. 8°, pp. xii.-124-lxviii. With Droeshout portrait   BPL | BUS

Produced for charity on behalf of the Chelsea Hospital for Women.
The sonnet by Robert Browning, headed ' The names,' is as follows :—
' Sh— ! to such name's sounding, what succeeds
Fitly as a silence? Falter forth the spell,
Act follows word, the speaker knows full well,
Nor tampers with its magic more than needs.
Two names there are : that which the Hebrew reads
With his soul only ; if from lips it fell,
Echo, back thundered by earth, heaven and hell,
Would own ' Thou didst create us.' Nought impedes.
We voice the other name, man's most of might,
Awesomely, lovingly ; let awe and love
Mutely await their working, leave to sight
All of the issue, as below, above,
Sh—'s creation rises ; one remove
Though dread—this finite from that infinite.'

] Shakespearean sketches. *See* Wallace

] Shakespearean tableaux. *See* Jerrard

] Shakespeareana [In ' Monthly Magazine,' Feb. Ln : 1818]. 8°. Illustrated   BPL | BUS

] Shakespeareana. New York & Philadelphia : Leonard Scott Co., 1883-1893. 10 vols. 8° and 4°. Illustrated   BM | BPL | BUS | SML

A monthly magazine which began in Nov., 1883, containing Shakespearean notes and queries, notices of the drama, Sh— societies and reviews.

] Shakespeareana [from the ' Stratford Herald ']. Stratford-on-Avon : G. Boyden, 1883. 12°   BPL

] Shakespeareana. *See* Barton (T. P.)

] Shakespeareana and Warwickshire notes [from the ' Stratford-on-Avon Herald ']. Stratford-on-Avon : G. Boyden, 1886-87. F°   BPL

] Shakespeareana Burtoniensis : Being a catalogue of the extensive collection of the late W. E. Burton, forming part of his histrionic library. New York : J. Sabin & Co., 1860. 8°, pp. 72 BUS | W

] Shakespeareana [Collection of manuscript and printed pieces relating to Sh— : including letters from R. B. Wheler. Dryden's ' Defence of the epilogue : An original chiromantic drawing of a hand, XV. cent. ; and other excerpts, men-

tioning Sh— or his writings, from rare books]. *Sæc. XV.-XIX.* Mounted into 3 vols. 4°   W

In the ' Merchant of Venice,' ii., 4, is the passage :—
' I know the hand ; in faith, 'tis a fair hand
And whiter than the paper it writ on . . .'

] Shakespeareana [Collection of manuscript and printed pieces relating to Sh—, embracing excerpts from Rymer's ' Short view of tragedy, 1693 ' ; ' Morning ramble, 1673 ' ; ' Essay upon poetry, 1682 ' ; Shirley's ' Royal master, 1638,' etc., together with an original crayon portrait of Edmond Malone]. 1638-1793. Fcp. 4°   W

] Shakespeareana [Collection of manuscript and printed pieces relating to Sh—, mounted into three folio volumes. *Sæc. XVII.-XIX.*] 3 vols. F°   W

The contents include manuscript notes on Sh— in Edmund Malone's autograph ; letters of Robert Bell Wheler to John Britton on Sh—'s biography ; excerpt of title and various leaves from Sh—'s Works, 1685 ; title and leaves from Ben Ionson's ' Silent Woman, 1616 ' ; excerpt from Gayton's ' Festivous notes on Don Quixote, 1654 ' ; excerpt from Thomas Heywood's ' Hierarchie of the blessed angels, 1635 ' ; broadside ballads, etc.

] Shakespeareana [Collection formed by H. R. Forrest of Manchester. 1830-86]. 76 vols. F°. Mounted and bound uniformly   BPL

Described at some length in the ' Antiquarian Magazine, edited by E. Walford,' 1886. The subjects of the cuttings, illustrations, and pieces are as follow :— Comedies, 21 vols. ; Histories, 20 vols. ; Tragedies, 21 vols. ; Poems and Sonnets, 2 vols. ; Attributed plays, 1 vol. ; Introductions, 1 vol. ; Prospectuses, titlepages, etc., 1 vol. ; Biography, 2 vols. ; Portraits of Sh—, 1 vol. ; Portraits of editors, 1 vol. ; Portraits of Sh—'s contemporaries, 2 vols. ; Portraits of actors, 3 vols.

] Shakespeareana [Collection contained in scrap-books. *Sæc. XIX.*] 4 vols. F° BPL

] Sharp (W.) Literary geography. 1904. 8°

Sh— fills pp. 56-60, etc.   BPL

] Sharpe (R. Farquharson) Architects of English literature : Biographical sketches of great writers from Sh— to Tennyson. Illustrated with facsimiles from autograph manuscripts. Ln : Sonnenschein . . . 1900. 8°, pp. viii.-386, and plates

Sh— fills pp. 1-14, with facsimile autograph ; and Bacon occupies pp. 15-28, with facsimile letter.

] Shaw (George Bernard) Letter to V. Tchertkoff on Sh— [In ' Tolstoy on Sh—']. New York, 1906. Cr. 8°   BPL

] Shaw (G. B.) Sh— [In ' Tolstoy on Sh—']. 1907. 8°   BPL

] Shaw (T. B.) History of English literature, edited by A. H. Thompson . . . 1901. Cr. 8°   BPL

Sh—, pp. 180-213.

Shakespeare]—

] Shaw (T. B.) Student's manual of English
literature . . . 1878. Cr. 8°   BPL
Sh— fills pp. 134-159.

] Sherlock (Martin) Fragment sur Sh—. Ln :
. . . 1780. Cr. 8°   BPL

] Sherlock (M.) Fragment on Sh—, extracted
from 'Advice to a young poet,' trans.
from the French [by . . . Duncombe]. Ln :
G. & J. Robinson, 1786. 8°, pp. 38
    BM | BPL | BUS
Originally published in Italian under the title of
' Consiglio . . .'

] Sherlock (M.) Fragment on Sh— . . . Four
letters on Sh— [In ' Letters from an
English traveller, written originally in
French ']. Ln : . . . 1802. 2 vols. 8°
    BUS | W
Nichols in his ' Literary anecdotes ' says, ' This edition
of 1802 is now among the scarcest of scarce books.'
The Marquis de Marnésia is said to have assisted in the
composition.

] Silsby *Compiler* (Mary R.) Tributes to Sh—.
New York : Harper, 1892. 16°
    BM | BPL | BUS | SML

] Simpson (Richard) & Bowden (Henry Se-
bastian) Religion of Sh—. Ln : Burns &
Oates. New York : Benziger Brothers,
1899. Cr. 8°, pp. xvi-428   BPL | SML
An endeavour to show that Sh— belonged to the Roman
Church.

] Skene (G.) Genius of Sh— : A summer
dream. Ln : Couch & Laking . . . 1793.
4°, pp. ii-34   BUS

] Skottowe (Augustine) Life of Sh— : Enquiries into the originality of his dramatic
plots and characters, and essays on the
ancient theatres and theatrical usages.
Ln : Longman, 1824. 2 vols. 8°
    BM | BPL | BUS | CPL | MPL | SML

] Skottowe (A.) Life of Sh—
See Sh— Poems, 1826
  ,,   Sh— Works, 1824-26, 1826

] Smith (Charles Roach) Remarks on Sh—,
his birthplace, etc. Suggested by a visit
to Stratford . . . Privately printed, 1868-
69. 8°   BPL

] Smith (C. R.) Remarks on Sh—, his birthplace . . . Second edition. Ln : Bell . . .
1877. 8°, pp. 36   BM | BPL | MPL

] Smith (C. R.) Rural life of Sh— as illustrated by his works . . . 1870. 8°
    BM | BPL | CPL

] Smith (C. R.) Rural life of Sh—. Second
edition. Ln : Bell . . . 1874. 8°, pp.
viii.-68   BM | BPL | BUS

] Smith (George Barnett) Wm. Sh— : Eulogy
spoken at the Urban Club, April 23, 1888.
Ln : 1888. 8°   BM | BPL

] Smith (*Prof.* Goldwin) Sh— the man : An
attempt to find traces of the dramatist's
personal character in his dramas.

Shakespeare]—

Toronto : G. N. Morang, 1899. Cr. 8°,
pp. 78. With bust portrait
    BPL | MPL | SML

] Smith (Goldwin) Sh— the man . . . Ln :
Unwin . . . 1900. Cr. 8°, pp. 78

] Smith (Goldwin) Sh— the man . . . New
York . . . 1900. Cr. 8°, pp. 60   BUS

] Spielmann (M. H.) ' Grafton ' and ' Sanders ' portraits of Sh— [In ' The Connoisseur,' Feb., pp. 97-102, and 2 plates].
1909. 4°

] Spielmann (M. H.) ' Janssen ' or ' Somerset ' portrait of Sh— [In ' The Connoisseur ']. Ln : 1909. 4°   BPL

] Steevens (George) Manuscript collections in
illustration of the life and writings of
Wm. Sh—, with other dramatic notes
[including some in the autograph of
James Boswell, mounted into a volume.
c. 1790]. F°. Manuscript, on paper,
interleaved with eight early portraits of
Sh— and two other plates inserted   W

] Steevens (G.) Sh—. Ln : Plymsell & Young
[c. 1795]. 8°, pp. 8   BUS
Reprinted from the ' European Magazine, Dec., 1794.'
Relates to the Felton portrait.

] Stephen (*Sir* Leslie) Sh— as a man [In
' Studies of a biographer,' Vol. 4, pp. i.-
44]. Ln : Smith . . . 1902. 8°   BPL | MPL

] Stubbs *Bp.* (C. W.) Sh— [In ' The Christ of
English poetry,' pp. 123-165]. ' Hulsean
lectures ' . . . 1906. 8°

] Sturges (R. Y.) Sh— : A poem. Birmingham . . . 1864. Cr. 8°   BPL

] Swinburne (Algernon Charles) Sh—. Ln :
Chatto . . . 1909. Cr. 8°
    BM | BLO | BPL | CTC

] Swinburne (A. C.) Sh—. Written in 1905
and now first published. Oxford : Clarendon Press, 1909. 16°, pp. 84
    BM | BLO | CTC
Reviewed in ' The Athenæum,' 11th Sept., 1909, pp.
289-290.

] Swinburne (A. C.) Study of Sh—. Ln :
Chatto . . . 1880. Cr. 8°, pp. viii.-310
    BM | BPL | BUS | MPL | SML
' In the heaven of our tragic song, the first born star on
the forehead of its herald god was not outshone till
the full midsummer meridian of that greater godhead
before whom he [Marlowe] was sent to prepare a
pathway for the sun. Through all the forenoon of
our triumphant day, till the utter consummation and
ultimate ascension of dramatic poetry incarnate and
transfigured in the master singer of the world, the
quality of his tragedy was as that of Marlowe's, broad,
single, and intense ; large of hand, voluble of tongue,
direct of purpose. With the dawn of its latter epoch,
a new power comes upon it, to find clothing and
expression in new forms of speech and after a new
style. The language has put off its foreign decorations of lyric and elegiac ornament ; it has found
already its infinite gain in the loss of those sweet,
superfluous graces which encumbered the march and
enchained the utterance of its childhood.'

] Swinburne (A. C.) Study of Sh—. New York : R. Worthington, 1880. 12°, pp. vi.-320   BPL | BUS

] Swinburne (A. C.) Study of Sh—. Third edition. Revised. Ln : Chatto ... 1895. Cr. 8°

] Swinburne (A. C.) Three stages of Sh— [In ' Fortnightly Review,' Vol. 23, p. 613 ; Vol. 25, p. 24]. 1875-76. Roy. 8°   BM | BLO | BPL | BUS

] Swinburne (A. C.) ' Wm. Sh— ' [In ' Tristram of Lyonesse and other poems.' Ln : Chatto ... 1882]. Cr. 8°   BM | BLO | CTC

At p. 280 is the sonnet :—
' Not if men's tongues and angels' all in one
Spake, might the word be said that might speak thee.
Streams, winds, woods, flowers, fields, mountains, yea, the sea
What power is in them all to praise the sun?
His praise is this—he can be praised of none.
Man, woman, child, praise God for him ; but he
Exults not to be worshipped, but to be.
He is, and, being, beholds his work well done.
All joy, all glory, all sorrow, all strength, all mirth
Are his ; without him, day were night on earth.
Time knows not his from time's own period.
All lutes, all harps, all viols, all flutes, all lyres
Fall dumb before him ere one string suspires.
All stars are angels ; but the sun is God.'

] Swinburne (A. C.) Wm. Sh— [In ' Tristram of Lyonesse.' Ln : ... 1884]. Cr. 8° BPL

] Symmons (Charles) Life of Sh—. *See* Sh— Works, 1826, 1827, 1828, 1828-34, 1830, 1831, 1834, 1835, 1836, 1837, 1837-39, 1839, 1843, 1843-44, 1844, 1846, 1849, 1854, 1855-71

] T—— (H.) Was Sh— a lawyer ? being a selection of passages from ' Measure for measure ' and ' All's well ' . . . which point to the conclusion that their author must have been a practical lawyer, and in which many obscurities are made clear, and some apparent corruptions in the text are attempted to be restored by an application of a knowledge of English law. Ln : Longman, 1871. 8°, pp. iv.-42   BM | BPL | BUS | CPL

This author (or plagiarist) clearly found both title and inspiration in Rushton's work of 1858 (*q.v.*) following Lord Campbell's bad example.

] Tegg *F.R.H.S.* (Wm.) Sh— and his contemporaries ; together with the plots of his plays, theatres, and actors . . . Ln : Tegg & Co., 1879. Cr. 8°, pp. xii.-244. With Chandos portrait etched by Robert Graves, and 10 illustrations   BM | BPL | SML

] Terry (C. S.) Sh— the historian . . . 1899. 8°   BM

] Testimonies to the genius and merits of Sh—. [c. 1790]. 4°   BPL

] Thomson (W.) Wm. Sh— in romance and reality. Melbourne . . . 1881. 8°, pp. 96   BPL | MPL

] Three great English poets : Spenser, Sh—, and Milton [In ' Victoria Magazine,' Sept.-Oct.] Ln : 1875. 8°   BUS

] Tillotson (J.) Wm. Sh— [In ' Lives of eminent men,' pp. 91-104. c. 1855]. 12°   BPL

] Tolstoy (*Count* Leo N.) Sh—. New York . . . 1906. Cr. 8°   BPL
Contains E. H. Crosby's article on ' Sh— and the working classes.'

] Tolstoy (*Count* Leo N.) Sh—. Ln : Everett . . . 1907. Cr. 8°

] Townsend (G. H.) Wm. Sh— not an impostor. By an English critic. Ln : Routledge . . . 1857. 8°, pp. viii.-122   BM | BPL | BUS | CPL | SML
Bacon-Sh— controversy : A reply to W. H. Smith (*q.v.*) Reviewed in ' The Athenæum,' 14th Feb., 1857.

] Tupper (Martin Farquhar) Sh— : An ode for his three-hundredth birthday. Ln : Hatchard, 1864. 8°, pp. 8   BUS

] Tupper (M. F.) Sh— : An ode . . . 2nd ed. Ln : Hatchard, 1864. 8°, pp. 8   BUS

] Tupper (M. F.) Sh— : An ode . . . 4th ed. Ln : Hatchard, 1864. 8°, pp. 8   BPL

] Turner (James) Few fragmentary thoughts on Sh—. A paper read before the Erdington Literary Association. Printed for private circulation. Birmingham : J. Allen . . . 1882. 8°, pp. 28, including printed wrappers   SML

] Turner (J.) Fragmentary thoughts about Sh—. Birmingham . . . 1885. 8°   BPL

] Tweddell (G. M.) Sh— : his times and contemporaries. Ln : G. Kershaw, 1852. 12°, pp. 224   BM | BPL | BUS | CPL

] Tweddell (G. M.) Sh— : his times and contemporaries. Second edition. Bury : J. Heap, 1861. 3 parts. 8°, pp. 120. Illustrated   BUS | CPL
The first three of ten projected parts. No more issued.

] Tyrrell (*Sir* James) Commonplace book : containing a collection of poetry, culinary recipes, and other miscellanies [*Sæc.* XVII.] 4°. Manuscript on paper
Portions of the MS. only are in the autograph of Sir J. Tyrrell (the Whig historian, born 1642). The volume contains Basse's epitaph ' Upon poet Sh—,' first printed with Donne's ' Poems, 1633,' and this written version differs from the printed one. Some of the pieces are signed ' W. S.'
The MS. sold for £45 in July, 1900.

] Urwick (Hy.) Sh— and politics : A lecture [In ' Malvern News,' 13 Nov., p. 5]. 1909
Comparing ' Coriolanus,' a struggle between aristocracy and democracy, with the struggle in 1909-10 between the British peers and people.

] Van Dam (B. A. P.) & Stoffel (C.) Sh—: prosody and text. An essay in criticism, being an introduction to a better editing and a more adequate appreciation of the works of the Elizabethan poets. Ln: Williams & Norgate, 1900. Roy. 8°, pp. viii.-438

BPL | BUS | MPL | SML

] Van Winkle (Edward S.) Spelling of Sh—'s name [In ' International Review,' New York . . . 1878]. 8° BUS

] Vyse (B.) William Sh— behind the scenes of the Globe Theatre. 1864. 8° BPL

] W—— (E. N.) Sh— and the stage [In 'Progress.' c. 1885]. 8° BPL

] Wadsworth (M. A.) Sh— and prayer. Second edition. Chicago: Welch . . . 1903. 12° SML

] Walford (Edward) ' Kinton ' portrait of Sh— [In ' Bookmart,' pp. 171-172, Dec.] Pittsburg, U.S., 1885. Roy. 8°

] Wall (A. H.) Sh—'s face : a monologue on the portraits of Sh— in comparison with the death-mask at Darmstadt. Stratford-on-Avon : G. Boyden . . . 1890. 4°, pp. 16 BPL
The author was librarian of the Stratford memorial library for some years.

] Wallace (A.) Wm. Sh— [In the ' Irvine Express.' c. 1885]. 12° BPL

] Walter (James) Sh—'s home and rural life. With illustrations of localities and scenes around Stratford-upon-Avon by the heliotype process. Ln: Longmans . . . 1874. 4°, pp. 168 and 72 engravings
BM | BPL | BUS | MPL | SML | W

] Walter. Sh—'s true life. Illustrated by Gerald E. Moira. Ln: Longmans . . . 1890. F°, pp. viii.-iv.-396 and hundreds of illustrations BM | BPL | BUS | SML
'The fact is recorded that an important recent book, called ' Sh—'s true life . . . ,' incorporates into its text, without credit, several passages of original description and reflection taken from the present writer's sketches of the Sh— country, and also quotes, as his work, an elaborate narrative of a nocturnal visit to Anne Hathaway's cottage, which he never wrote and never claimed to have written.'—*W. Winter*, in preface to ' Gray days and gold.'
One of the ' Royal edition' on large paper, imperial quarto (of which only a few were done), is at Birmingham.

] Walter. Sh—'s true life. Second edition. Ln: Longman . . . 1896. 8°, pp. 412. Illustrated

] Walter. Sh—'s true life. Ln: Longman . . . 1900. 8°

] Ward. Statue [of Sh—] in the Central Park, New York. New York . . . 1873. F°. Portrait and plates BPL | BUS
Issue limited to twelve copies.

] Warlow (J.) Ode in commemoration of the Sh— tercentenary. Liverpool . . . 1864. 8° BPL

] Was Sh— a builder ? [In ' The Builder ']. Ln : . . . 1879. F° BPL

] Was Sh— a [Roman] Catholic ? [In ' American Catholic Quarterly Review']. 1896. 8° BPL

] Was Sh— a Roman Catholic ? [In ' Edinburgh Review,' Jan., 1866]. 8°
BPL | BUS | CPL

] Was Sh— a [Roman] Catholic ? [In ' The rambler,' Roman Catholic periodical, No. 7, July]. 1854. 8° BUS

] Was Sh— a scholar ? [In ' British controversialist,' pp. 442-448] . . . 1868. 12° BPL

] Was Sh— Shapleigh ? *See* Winsor

] Watchman and reflector [American newspaper, c. 1800 ?]
Contains this anecdote (according to R. L. Gibson):—
' A very old lady, a native of the Stratford neighbourhood, told me fifty years ago that she learnt from her grandmother, who heard the sermon at Sh—'s funeral [in 1616], that the congregation in attendance on that occasion was very large, and very serious in their feelings : that the preacher, after describing the intellectual character of Sh— at great length, and having avowed his opinion that no man since the days of the Apostle Paul had possessed so profound an acquaintance with all the diversified forms of human nature, he burst into tears and exclaimed, " Would to God he had been a divine."'

] Waters (Robert) Wm. Sh— portrayed by himself : a revelation of the poet in the career and character of one of his own dramatic heroes [King Henry V.] New York : Worthington . . . 1888. 12°
BM | BPL | BUS | SML

] Webb *Judge* (Thomas Ebenezer) Mystery of Wm. Sh—: Summary of evidence. Ln : Longmans . . . 1902. 8°, pp. 308
BPL | BUS | MPL | SML

] Wendell (Barrett) Wm. Sh—: a study in Elizabethan literature. New York . . . 1894. 8° BM | BPL

] Wendell (B.) Wm. Sh—: a study . . . New York, 1901. 8° BUS

] West (J. F.) Wm. Sh— from a surgeon's point of view. Birmingham Dramatic Club [1881]. 8° BPL

] Whalley (Peter) Enquiry into the learning of Sh—. With remarks on several passages of his plays . . . Ln : Printed for T. Waller at the Crown and Mitre opposite to Fetter Lane in Fleet Street, 1748. 8°, pp. 84 BM | BPL | BUS | MPL | W

] What was the religion of Sh— [In ' The rambler,' March, 1858]. 8° BPL | BUS

] Wheatley (H. B.) Historical portraits. Ln : Bell . . . 1897. 8° SML

] Wheeler (J. M.) Irreligion of Sh— [In 'University Magazine,' edited by 'Democritus,' *i.e.* Dr. Havelock Ellis, Vol. X., pp. 26-35]. Ln : . . . 1898. Roy. 8°

] Wheler (Robert Bell) Notes on Sh—'s pedigree [addressed to John Britton. With a folding genealogical chart]. Stratford-upon-Avon, 14 Feby., 1814. Fo. Manuscript, on ten leaves of paper **W**

] Whipple (E. P.) Sh— [In 'Atlantic Monthly']. Boston, U.S., 1867. 8° BUS

] White (Richard Grant) Anatomizing of Wm. Sh— [In the 'Atlantic Monthly']. 1884. 8° BPL

] White (R. G.) Memoirs of . . . Sh—. With an essay toward the expression of his genius and an account of . . . the English drama. Boston, U.S.: Little, Brown & Co., 1865. 8°, pp. xii.-426 BM | BPL | BUS | CPL | MPL

] White (R. G.) Memoirs of Sh— . . . Cambridge [U.S.]: Privately printed, 1865. 8°, pp. xxxiv.-296, with woodcuts and facsimiles BUS
Two copies printed only.

] White (R. G.) Wm. Sh—, attorney-at-law and solicitor in chancery [In 'Atlantic Monthly']. Boston . . . 1859. 8° BUS

] White (R. G.) Wm. Sh— [In 'New American Cyclopædia']. New York, 1862. 8° ' US
Three copies only off-printed.

] White (T. W.) Our English Homer, or Sh— historically considered. Ln : Low . . . 1892. 8°, pp. xvi.-298 BM | BPL | SML
On the Bacon-Sh— controversy.

] Whiter (Walter) Verses in commemoration of Sh—'s birthday, 1815-18. Norwich : Booth & Ball [1819]. 12°, pp. 20 BPL | BUS

] Wilder (D. W.) Life of Sh— copied from the best sources, without comment, for the use of schools. Boston [U.S.]: Little, Brown . . . 1893. 8° BM | BPL | SML

] Wilkes (George) Sh—, from an American point of view : including an enquiry as to his religious faith and his knowledge of law. With the Baconian theory considered. Ln : S. Low, 1877. 8°, pp. x.-472 BM | BPL | BUS | MPL | SML
First issued in the 'Spirit of the age.'
Reviewed in the 'Catholic world,' June, 1877.
Contains also the 'Styles of Sh— and Bacon, by J. W. Taverner.'

] Wilkinson (Thomas Read) Sh—: An address delivered at the Arts Club. Manchester : Privately printed, 1898. Cr. 8°, pp. 16 BM | BPL

] Wm. Sh— [In 'Pleasant hours' magazine, pp. 71-74, May. 1864]. Roy. 8°. Illustrated

] Williams (James Leon) & Furness (H. H.) Homes and haunts of Sh—. Illustrated. Ln : Low, 1892. F° BM | BPL

] Williams (Langton) & Milne (J. T.) How shall we honour him ? Song for the Sh— tercentenary. Ln : W. Williams . . . [1864]. F°, pp. 6 BUS

] Williams (S. Fletcher) Times and associates of Sh—. Birmingham . . . [1886]. 8° BM | BPL

] Wilson (R. G.) Select biography, containing . . . the lives, characters and actions of eminent persons. Ln : J. S. Pratt . . . 1843. 16°, pp. 384 and portrait
Sh— occupies pp. 239-250.

] Winstanley (William) Lives of the most famous English poets, or the honour of parnassus in a brief essay on the works and writings of above two hundred of them . . . Ln : Printed by H. Clark for Samuel Manship at the sign of the Black Reel in Cornhill, 1687. 8°. With portrait by Van Hove BPL | BUS
Sh— occupies nearly four pages.

] Wise (G.) Autograph of Wm. Sh— . . . together with four thousand ways of spelling his name. Philadelphia . . . 1869. 8° BPL

] Wise (John R.) Sh—: his birthplace and its neighbourhood. Illustrated by W. J. Linton. Ln : Smith & Elder, 1861. Cr. 8°, pp. x.-164. With 25 wood engravings BM | BPL | BUS | CPL | MPL
'Written in good taste and with good feeling.'—*Lowndes.*

] Wise (J. R.) Sh— . . . Cheap edition. Ln : Smith . . . 1861. Cr. 8°, pp. x.-164 BUS | SML

] Wise (J. R.) Sh— . . . Ln : Smith . . . 1862. Cr. 8°

] Wiseman *Cardinal* (N. P. S.) Wm. Sh— [a lecture]. Ln : Hurst & Blackett . . . 1865. 8°, pp. viii.-80 BUS | SML
' We may compare the mind of Sh— to a diamond, pellucid, bright, and untinted, cut into countless polished facets, which, in constant movement, at every smallest change of direction or of angle, caught a new reflection, so that not one of its brilliant mirrors could be for a moment idle, but by a power beyond its control was ever busy with the reflection of innumerable images, either distinct or running into one another, or repeated each so clearly as to allow him, when he chose, to fix it in his memory.'

] Wiseman. Wm. Sh—. Boston [U.S.]: P. Donahoe, 1865. 16°, pp. 64 BUS

] Wiseman. Wm. Sh— [Review in 'Catholic World']. New York, 1865. 8° BM | BPL | BUS | CPL

] Yarrow (John) Sh—; a tercentenary poem. Ln : A. M. Pigott, 1864. 8°, pp. 30 BPL | CPL

Sh— (Wm.) & Milton (John) *pseuds.* The trial. *See* Bicknell

'Shakspeare II.' *pseud.* Sh—'s romances collected and arranged . . . Vol. I. King Henry IV., part ii. Ln : Sherwood, Gilbert & Piper, 1825. 8°　　　　　BM
Re-issued under the title of ' King Henry IV. : a Sh— novel.

Sharp *Warwick Publisher. See* Sh— Works, 1768

Sharp (C. J.) & MacIlwaine (H. C.) The morris [dancing] book. 1907. Cr. 8°　　　BPL

Sharp (Frank Chapman) Sh—'s portrayal of the moral life. New York : Scribner . . . 1902. 12°　　　BPL | BUS | MPL | SML

Sharp (J.)] Account of the second commemoration of Sh— celebrated at Stratford-upon-Avon on Friday the 23rd of April, 1830, and three subsequent days, including full particulars of the various festivities given . . . in honour of the poet and the adopted birthday of the august patron of the club, H.M. George the fourth. Dedicated to members of the Royal Shakspearean Club. Leamington : J. Sharp, 'Courier' Office, 1830. 8°, pp. 62　BM | BPL | BUS

Sharp *of Stratford* (Thomas) Affidavit respecting the mulberry relics—
　See Sh—] Collection
　,, Sh—] Shakespeareana

Sharp (W.) Literary geography. *See Sh*—] Sharp

Sharp (W.) *Editor—*
　See Sh— Poems, 1885, 1888
　,, Sh— Sonnets, 1885

Sharpe *Publisher. See* Sh— Works, 1800, 1809, 1810

Sharpe. Diamond dictionary, with [Shakespearean] decorations. Ln : Tilt & Bogue, 1841. 12°　　　　　SML

Sharpe (Charles Kirkpatrick) *Editor. See* Law

Sharpe (H.) Prose in Sh—'s plays : Tables showing whether each person speaks in prose or metre in each scene in ' Much ado' and ' Hamlet.' Ln : New Sh— Society, 1880-86. 8°

Sharpe (Lewis)] The noble stranger. As it was acted at the private house in Salisbury Court by her majesties servants. By L. S——. Ln : I. O—— for James Becket . . . at the Inner Temple Gate in Fleet Streete, 1640. Fcp. 4°
Contains the reference at sig. G4 :—' Oh, for the book of " Venus and Adonis " to court my mistris by.' On G3 verso is an interesting description of a playhouse.

Sharpe (R.) *Publisher. See* Sh— Jests, 1769

Sharpe (R. Farquharson) Architects of English literature. *See Sh*—] Sharpe

Sharpe (T.) Dissertation on the pageants and dramatic mysteries anciently performed at Coventry, with the pageant of the Shearman and Taylors company. Coventry : Merridew . . . 1825. F°　　SML

Epitome of the county of Warwick. Ln : Pickering . . . 1835. 8°　　　SML

Glossary of provincial words in use in Warwickshire. Edited [from the manuscript] by J. O. Halliwell . . . 1865. 8°　BPL

Sharpe (W.) Consecrated poem to commemorate the tricentenary of Sh—. [1864.] 12°　　　　　BPL | CPL

Sharpe & Sons (W.) *Publishers. See* Sh— Works, 1825

Shaw. Tourist's picturesque guide to Leamington and Stratford . . . 1876. Cr. 8°　　　　　　　　BPL

Shaw (A. Capel)] Birmingham Free Libraries : Index to the Sh— memorial library. *First part*, English editions of Sh—'s works, separate plays and poems; *Second part*, English Shakespeareana; *Third part*, Foreign. Birmingham . . . 1900-03. 3 vols. 4°
　　　　BM | BLO | BPL | BUS | SML

Index to the [catalogue of the] Sh— memorial library. Birmingham : Jones . . . 1903. 4°, pp. 8
The preface, which gives some interesting statistics, says :—' The proposal for a Sh— library was made by Samuel Timmins in 1858, and publicly advocated by George Dawson in 1861. . . . Mr. Dawson said, " I want to see founded in Birmingham a Sh— library which should contain every edition and every translation of Sh— ; all the commentators, good, bad, and indifferent ; in short, every book connected with the life or works of our great poet. I would add portraits of Sh— and all the pictures, etc. illustrative of his works." '
How faithfully the city has lived up to this noble ideal is to be seen by its great assemblage, completely recorded in print for the first time in this bibliography.

Shaw] Inventory of the goods and chattels of Ann Shaw, friend and neighbour of Sh—, 1630. Edited by J. O. Halliwell . . . 1880. 8°　　　　　BPL

Shaw (Byam) *Artist—*
　See Sh— All's well, 1902
　,, Sh— As you like it, 1899
　,, Sh— Comedy of errors, 1902
　,, Sh— Coriolanus, 1900
　,, Sh— Cymbeline, 1901
　,, Sh— Hamlet, 1899
　,, Sh— Julius Cæsar, 1900
　,, Sh— King Henry IV., i., 1901
　,, Sh— King Henry IV., ii., 1901
　,, Sh— King Henry V., 1901
　,, Sh— King Henry VI., i., 1901
　,, Sh— King Henry VI., ii., 1902
　,, Sh— King Henry VI., iii., 1902
　,, Sh— King Henry VIII., 1902
　,, Sh— King John, 1900
　,, Sh— King Lear, 1900

Shaw (Byam) *Artist*—
  See Sh— King Richard II., 1900
    ,, Sh— King Richard III., 1902
    ,, Sh— Love's labours lost, 1901
    ,, Sh— Macbeth, 1899
    ,, Sh— Measure . . . 1901
    ,, Sh— Merchant . . . 1899, 1904
    ,, Sh— Midsummer . . . 1900
    ,, Sh— Othello, 1899
    ,, Sh— Pericles, 1902
    ,, Sh— Poems, 1902
    ,, Sh— Romeo . . . 1899
    ,, Sh— Sonnets, 1902
    ,, Sh— Taming . . . 1902
    ,, Sh— The tempest, 1899
    ,, Sh— Timon . . . 1902
    ,, Sh— Titus . . . 1902
    ,, Sh— Troilus . . . 1902
    ,, Sh— Twelfth night, 1900
    ,, Sh— Two gentlemen, 1900
    ,, Sh— Winter's tale, 1899
    ,, Sh— Works, 1899-1902, 1902
    ,, Sh— Works: Ext. 1903, 1905
Shaw (George Bernard) Dramatic opinions and
  essays. With an apology. Ln: 1907.
  2 vols. Cr. 8°   BPL
Sh—. *See Sh*—] Shaw
  Three plays for puritans . . . Ln: Richards
  . . . 1901. Cr. 8°, pp. xxxviii.-308 and 2
  plates
  Contains (pp. 27-38) 'Better than Sh—.'
  Three plays for puritans. Ln: 1906. Cr.
  8°   BPL
Shaw (J. H.) Sh—'s idea in 'Macbeth' and
  'Hamlet' [In 'New Zealand Magazine'].
  1877. 8°
Shaw (J. & W.) *Glasgow Publishers. See* Sh—
  Works, 1795
Shaw (James) *Publisher. See* Memorable con-
  ceits
Shaw (Julius) *Witness. See* Sh— Will . . . 1616
Shaw (T. B.) History of English literature.
  See Sh—] Shaw
  Specimens of English literature. *See* Sh—
  Works: Ext. 1881
  Student's manual. *See* Sh—] Shaw
Sheares (Wm.) *Printer and Publisher*—
  See Sh— King Henry IV., i., 1632
    ,, Sh— Love's labours lost, 1631
    ,, Sh— Taming . . . 1631
    ,, Wolsey
Sheavyn (Phoebe) The literary profession in
  the Elizabethan age. Manchester:
  Sherratt, 1909. 8°, pp. 234
Sheavyn (P.) *Editor. See* Sh— King Lear,
  1898
Sheep shearing. *See* Morgan (M.)
Sheffield *Duke of Buckingham* (John) Essay
  on poetry. Ln: Jo. Hindmarsh, 1691.
  F°, pp. 32
  References to Sh— pp. 21-23.

Sheffield *Duke of Buckingham* (John) Works.
  Third edition, corrected . . . 1740. 2
  vols. 8°. With folding portrait and
  vignettes
  Contains 'Julius Cæsar altered,' pp. 211-302, vol. 1,
  with vignettes.
    'Hope to mend Sh—, or to match his style?
    'Tis such a jest—would make a stoick smile.'
Sheffield *Duke of Buckingham* (John) *Editor*—
  See Sh— Julius Cæsar, 1751
  See also Buckingham
Sheffield *Earl of Mulgrave* (John) Essay upon
  poetry. Ln: Printed for Joseph Hind-
  marsh at the Black Bull in Cornhill near
  the Roy. Exch., 1682. Fcp. 4°
  Says:—
    'Sh— and Fletcher are the wonders now,
    Consider them, and read them o'er and o'er,
    Go see them play'd, then read them as before. . . .
Sheffield. *See* Diary . . .
Sheffield Sh— Club; Proceedings . . . from
  its commencement in 1819 to January,
  1829. By a member. Sheffield: H. & G.
  Crookes . . . 1829. 8°, pp. xii.-164 and
  portrait   BPL | BUS | SML | W
Sheldon (Charles) Notes to 'As you like it' . . .
  Manchester: J. Galt & Co. . . . 1877. 8°,
  pp. 48, in printed wrappers BM | BPL | BUS
Sheldon & Co. *New York Publishers. See* Sh—
  Works, 1862
Shelley (H. C.) John Harvard. *See* Harvard
Shelley (Percy Bysshe) Imitations of Sh— in
  his tragedy of 'The Cenci.' Edited by
  J. B. B——. *See Sh*—] Sh— Soc.
  Lines written among the Euganean hills
  . . . October, 1818
    'Divinest Sh –'s might
    Fills Avon and the world with light
    Like omniscient power which he
    Imaged 'mid mortality.'
Shenstone (W.)]] Slender's ghost. *See* Sh—
  Hamlet, 1748
  Slender's ghost [In Dodsley's Collection of
  poems, Vol. 5]. 1775. Cr. 8°   BPL
  Illustrates the 'Merry wives.'
Shepheard's kalendar. Newly augmented and
  corrected. Ln: Robert Ibbitson . . . 1656.
  F°
  Illustrates 'Measure for measure' and a 'Midsummer
  night's dream.'
Shepherd (R. H.) 'In memoriam' and Sh—'s
  sonnets [In 'Tennysoniana,' pp. 52-72].
  Ln: . . . 1879. 12°   BPL
Sheppard (John H.) Tercentenary celebra-
  tion . . . remarks and ode . . . 'New
  England Historic Genealogical Society.'
  Boston [U.S.] . . . 1864. 8°   BM
  See also New England.
Sheppard (Samuel) Epigrams; theological,
  philosophical and romantick. Six books,
  etc., with other select poems. Ln: . . .
  1651. 8°   BUS

Epigram 17, lib. vi., p. 150, is 'In memory of our famous Sh—,' and runs:—

'Sacred spirit, whiles thy lyre
Echoed o'er the Arcadian plains,
Even Apollo did admire,
Orpheus wondered at thy strains.

.   .   .   .   .   .

Thou wert truly priest elect,
Chosen darling to the nine,
Such a trophy to erect
By thy wit and skill divine.

.   .   .   .   .   .

Where thy honoured bones do lie,
As Statius once to Maro's urn,
Thither every year will I
Slowly tread and sadly mourn.'

Sheppard (Samuel) Epigrams. *See Sh*—] Sh— notices

Sheppard (Thomas & Margaret). *See Sh*—] Malone

Shepperson (C. A.) *Artist. See* Sh— Midsummer . . . 1906, 1907

Shepperton (W.) *Artist. See* Sh— As you like it, 1900

Sheridan.] Lefanse (Alicia) Memoirs of the life and writings of Mrs. Frances Sheridan, mother of R. B. Sheridan. With remarks upon a late 'Life of R. B. S——' and biographical anecdotes . . . 1824. 8°

Sheridan (Richard Brinsley) Portrait. *See* Crosby

Verses to the memory of Garrick. Spoken as a monody at the Theatre Royal in Drury Lane. Ln : T. Evans, J. Wilkie, E. & C. Dilly, A Portal, & J. Almon, 1779. 8°. With frontispiece
Large paper copy at Warwick.
It went through several later editions, in quarto.

Sheridan (R. B.) *Actor-Editor*—
See Sh— Coriolanus, 1780
   ,,   Sh— The tempest, 1776, 1778

Sheridan.] Fitzgerald (Percy) Lives of the Sheridans. Ln : . . . 1886. 2 vols. 8°. With steel portraits

] Moore (Thomas) Memoirs of the life of Richard Brinsley Sheridan . . . 1825. 2 vols. 8°   BPL

] Moore. Memoirs . . . 1827. 2 vols. 8°

] Rae (W. F.) Sheridan : A biography. With introduction by the Marquess of Dufferin. Ln : . . . 1896. 2 vols. 8°   BPL

] Sheridan and his times. By an octogenarian who stood by his knee in youth, and sat at his table in manhood . . . 1859. 2 vols. Cr. 8°

] Sheridaniana, or anecdotes of the life of R. B. Sheridan, his table talk and bon mots . . . 1826. Cr. 8°. With portrait

] Sichel (Walter) Sheridan ; from new and original material, including a manuscript diary by Georgiana Duchess of Devonshire, and hitherto unpublished correspondence and compositions. Ln : Constable, 1909. 2 vols. 8°. With 52 illustrations   BM | BLO | BPL | CTC

Sheridan.] Watkin (John) Memoirs of the public and private life of R. B. Sheridan . . . 1818. 2 vols. 8°

Sheridan (Thomas) Humble appeal to the public . . . on the present critical and dangerous state of the stage in Ireland, 1758. Case of the stage in Ireland, containing reasons for and against a bill for limiting the number of theatres in Dublin. 1758. 8°, pp. 124-48

Sheridan (Thomas) *Editor. See* Sh— Coriolanus, 1755

Sherley (*Sir* Anthony) Travels, edited by W. Parry, 1601. *See* Reprints

True report of . . . iourney ouerland to Venice, from thence by sea to Antioch, Aleppo, and Babilon, and soe to Casbine in Persia : his entertainment there by the great Sophie ; his oration ; his letters of credence to the great christian princes ; and the priuiledg obtained of the great Sophie for the quiet passage and trafique of all christian marchants throughout his whole dominions [Printer's emblem, clenched fist, with motto ' Ex avaritia bellum ']. Ln : Printed by R. B—— [Ralph Blore] for I. I—— [Isaac Jaggard], 1600. Fcp. 4°, pp. 12 (the first blank, marked A1), suppressed
                                                       BM
This curious and rare tract, of which only two copies are known [one at the British Museum and the other in the writer's collection], may have suggested to Sh— his immortal ' Merchant of Venice.'

Sherley (*Sir* Anthony). *See* Surtees

Sherley (John) *Publisher. See* Hall (John)

Sherlock (Frederick) Sh— on temperance. *See* Sh— Works : Ext., 1883, 1884, 1885

Sherlock (Martin) Fragment on Sh—. *See* Sh—] Sherlock

Sherman (Lucius Adelno) Analytic questions on the art of Sh—. Lincoln [U.S.], 1896. 8°, pp. x.-60   BUS

What is Sh— ? Introduction to the great plays. New York : Macmillan . . . 1902. Cr. 8°, pp. 428   BPL

Shervyn *Editor. See* Sh— Works, 1902

Sherwen (John) Vindicatio Shakespeariana, or supplementary remarks on the editions of Sh— by Reed and others, with occasional illustrations of some obscure and disputed passages. [1800.] 2 vols. 4°. Author's manuscript
This manuscript (referred to by Dibdin in his ' Library companion ' as being at the Bath Literary Institution) is stated to be written with the view that Sh— is to be greatly elucidated by means of the Northern dialects of our country.

Sherwin (W.) *Engraver. See* Sh— Works, 1773-74, 1784, 1790, 1807

Sherwin & Co. *Publishers*—
  See Sh— Poems, 1821
  ,, Sh— Works, 1821, 1823
Sherwood *Publisher*—
  See Sh— King Henry IV., ii., 1825
  ,, Sh— King Henry V., 1849
  ,, Sh— Macbeth, 1817
  ,, Sh— Works, 1818, 1825
Sherwood & Bowyer *Publishers*. *See* Sh— King John, 1844
Sherwood, Gilbert, & Piper *Publishers*. *See* Sh— Works, 1825, 1830
Sherwood, Neely, & Jones *Publishers*— See Sh— Hamlet, 1817
  ,, Sh— King Richard III., 1816
Shewell (T.) *Publisher*. *See* Sh— Works, 1747
Shield *Editor*. *See* Sh— Twelfth night, 1871
Shield (Wm.) *Composer*. *See* Sh— Poems, 1808, 1862
Shindler (R.) The stolen key [to the Sonnets. In the 'Gentleman's Magazine.' 1892]. 8°   BPL
Shipwreck (The). *See* Sh— The tempest, 1780
Shirley *Editor*. *See* Sh— Works, 1898-1908
Shirley (Evelyn Philip) Lower Ettington : Its Manor House and Church. Ln : Whittingham, 1869. Fcp. 4°   SML
Probably a familiar spot to Sh—, being an easy walking distance from Stratford.

Lower Ettington . . . Second edition. Ln : Pickering, 1880. Fcp. 4°   SML

Verse inscribed on a stone indicator at the entrance to Ettington Park, Shipston Road, near Stratford-on-Avon [c. 1864]
  'Six miles to Sh—'s town, whose name
    Is known throughout the earth ;
  To Shipston four, whose lesser flame
    Boasts no such poet's birth.'

Shirley.] D—— (R. O.) Shirleys of Ettington. *See* Memorials . . .
Shirley (James) Extracts. *See* Sh— Works : Ext. 1822
The example. Ln : . . . 1637. Fcp. 4°
At sig. C4 is a quotation from Sh—'s 'King Henry IV.'

The opportunitie. A comedy. Ln : Thomas Cotes for Andrew Crooke . . . at the signe of the Greene Dragon in Paul's Churchyard. [c. 1640.] Fcp. 4°
Partly founded on the 'Comedy of errors.'

The royall master. As it was acted in the new theater in Dublin and before the Right Honorable the Lord Deputie of Ireland in the Castle. Ln : Printed by T. Cotes and are to be sold by John Crooke and Richard Serger at the Grayhound in Paul's Churchyard, 1638. Fcp. 4°
Several references to Sh— in the commendatory verses.

The royal master, 1638. *See* Sh—] Shakespeareana

Shirley (James) The sisters . . . Ln : . . . [c. 1640]
The prologue says :—
  'You see what audience we have, what company
  To Sh— comes, whose mirth did once beguile
  Dull hours and buskin'd make even sorrow smile,
  So lovely were the wounds that men would say
  They could endure the bleeding a whole day,
  He has but few friends lately.'

Triumph of beautie, as it was personated by some young gentlemen for whom it was intended, at a private recreation. Ln : Humphrey Moseley . . . at the signe of the Princes Armes in St. Paul's Churchyard, 1646. 8°
Partly borrowed from a 'Midsummer night's dream.'
See Mercurius . . .
  ,, Sh— Double falsehood

Shirley (William) Edward the black prince, or the battle of Poictiers. An historical tragedy, attempted after the manner of Sh—. Ln : . . . 1750. 8°   BPL | W

Shore.] Life and character of Jane Shore. Collected from our best historians, chiefly from the writings of Sir Thomas More, who was her contemporary and personally knew her. Humbly offer'd to the readers and spectators of her tragedy, by Mr. Rowe. Inscrib'd to Mrs. Oldfield. Second edition. Ln : J. Brown at the Black Swan ; W. Taylor at the Ship ; N. Cliffe ; J. Morphew ; and A. Dodd at the Peacock, 1714. Fcp. 4°
Illustrative of Sh—'s 'King Richard III.'

Shore (Jane)—
See Harding (S. & E.)
  ,, Rowe

Short (C.)] Life and humours of Falstaff. *See* Sh— King Henry IV., ii., 1829
Short (Peter) *Printer*—
See Meres
  ,, Sh— King Henry IV., i., 1598
  ,, Sh— King Henry VI., i.-ii.-iii., 1595
  ,, Sh— Rape, 1598
  ,, Sh— Taming . . . 1594, 1596

Short discourse of fashions of apparel [containing a 'Poem against farthing-gales']. Ln : . . . [1750]. 12°   W
  'What compass will you wear your farthingale?'—*Two gentlemen*.
  'In a semi-circled farthingale.'—*Merry wives*.

Short stories of Sh—'s plots. *See* Sh— Works : Ext. 1893
Short studies in English literature. Ln : . . . 1908. Cr. 8°   BPL
Contains 'Introductions to Sh—'s comedies and tragedies.'

Shorte treatise against stage playes. *See* Leighton
Shorter (Thomas) Sh— for schools . . . *See* Sh— Works : Ext. 1865, 1868
Shorthand. *See* Phonographic . . .

Shortrede (Andrew) *Editor and Printer. See*
Sh— Works, 1838, 1839

Showell (Charles) Sh—'s Avon from source to
Severn. With 180 pen drawings by the
author. Birmingham : Cornish ... 1901.
Fcp. 4°, pp. iv.-208, and folded map
BPL (L.P.) | SML (L.P.)

Shrewsbury—
See Poetical epistle
,, Rolt
,, Sh— King Henry IV., 1608 (*et seq.*)

Shrine (The) : A quarterly magazine of life,
literature, and art [chiefly Shakespearean,
edited by R. H. Fitzpatrick]. Stratford :
G. Boyden. Birmingham : Hudson & Son.
Ln : E. Stock, 1902-03. 4 parts. 4° BPL

Shylock the Jew-ed [In ' Temple Bar,' Sept.]
Ln : 1875. 8° BPL | BUS
' Shylock ' versus ' Antonio ' [In ' Albany
Law Journal ' ... 1874]. 8° BPL

Sibbald *Liverpool Publisher. See* Sh— Works,
1768

Sibthorp (B.) *Printer. See* Collins (J.)

Sichel (Walter) Sheridan. *See* Sheridan

Sicilian usurper. *See* Sh— King Richard II.,
1691

Siddons (Henry) Practical illustrations of
rhetorical gesture and action, adapted to
the English drama, from a work by M.
Engel. Embellished with numerous engravings representing theatrical costumes. Ln : R. Phillips, 1807. 8°, pp. iv.-
410, and sixty-eight stipple copperplates
Rhetorical gesture and action . . . Ln :
Sherwood ... 1822. 8° BPL | SML

Siddons (J. H.) Shakespearean referee : A
cyclopædia of 4,200 words, obsolete and
modern, occurring in the plays of Sh—,
with explanations, commentaries [etc.]
Washington ... 1886. 12° BPL | BUS

Siddons *Actress* (*Mrs.* Sarah) Portrait—
See Sh— King Henry V., 1785
,, Sh— Measure ... 1785

Siddons.] Boaden (J.) Memoirs of Mrs.
Siddons, with anecdotes of authors and
actors. Ln : Colburn ... 1827. 2 vols.
8° SML

] Boaden. Memoirs of Mrs. Siddons. With
portraits. Ln : Gibbings ... 1895. Cr.
8°, pp. viii.-472. With portraits

] Boaden. Memoirs ... Ln : Gibbings, 1896.
Cr. 8°. With portraits

] Campbell (T.) Life of Mrs. Siddons. Ln :
Wilson ... 1834. 2 vols. 8°. With
portrait SML
An extra-illustrated copy with twenty-eight plates is at
Stratford.

] Campbell. Life of Mrs. Siddons. Ln : ...
1839. 8°. With portrait BPL | SML

Siddons.] Galindo (Catherine) Letter to Mrs.
Siddons, being a circumstantial detail of
Mrs. Siddons' life for the last seven years.
Ln : Privately printed ... 1809. 8°
A libellous charge of improper conduct with Mr. Galindo.

] Critique on the theatrical performance of
Mrs. Siddons. Edinburgh, July, 1788.
4°, pp. 18

] Kennard (*Mrs.* A.) Mrs. Siddons. ' Eminent
women series.' Ln : Allen ... 1887. Cr.
8°, pp. viii.-268 BPL

] Parsons (*Mrs.* Clement) The incomparable
Siddons. Ln : Methuen, 1909. 8°, pp.
318 BM | BLO | CTC

] Siddons *v.* Ryder : Case of Mrs. H. Siddons
of the Edinburgh theatre Royal against
Corbet Ryder of the Caledonian Theatre
for infringement of patent rights. 1825.
8°
Includes a history of the Edinburgh theatre, with copies
of the original patent and other documents.

Siddons (*Mrs.* S.)—
See Garrick
,, Jenkin
,, Public ...
,, Sh— Coriolanus, 1789
,, Sh— Macbeth, 1785, 1788

Sidgwick (Frank) Songs and snatches quoted
by Sh—. ' Sh— club papers.' Stratford :
Privately printed, 1906. Cr. 8°, pp. 16
Sources and analogues of a ' Midsummer
night's dream.' Ln : Chatto ... 1908.
Cr. 8°, pp. 208 BPL

Sidgwick (Frank) *Editor. See* Sh— Midsummer ... 1908

Sidgwick (H.) Miscellaneous essays and
addresses. Ln : 1904. 8° BPL | MPL
Contains articles ' Sh— and the romantic drama, with
special reference to "Macbeth,"' and 'Sh—'s
methods, with reference to "Julius Cæsar" and
"Coriolanus."'

Sidney *Artist. See* Sh— Works : Ext. 1885

Sidney (*Sir* Philip) [Arcadia] Shaksperian
parallelisms . . . illustrative of ' The
tempest ' and a ' Midsummer night's
dream,' collected from . . . 'Arcadia.'
Ln : ... 1865. 16° BM
Arcadia. *See* West
Extracts. *See* Sh— Works : Ext. 1845
Paphlagonian unkind king, 1843. *See Sh*—]
Sh—'s library
Some sonnets . . . from Charles Lamb's
' Last essays of Elia.' [Edited by Sydney
Humphries.] Edinburgh : Privately
printed by R. & R. Clark, 1910. F°, pp.
12 (printed on recto only). With portrait
of Sydney and editor's coat of arms SML
Limited to twenty copies on hand-made paper, vellum
bound, for presentation only.

Verses. *See* Poems

Sidney (*Sir* Philip) Works. Ln: 1725. 3 vols. 8° BUS
In his ' Arcadia, book 2., chap. 10,' is the ' Story of the Paphlagonian unkind king,' regarded as one of the sources of ' King Lear.'

Sidney (*Sir* Philip)—
See Crawford
,, Levi
,, Montemayor

Sidolph (A. B.) Children's Sh—. *See* Sh— Works: Ext. 1902

Siege of Troy. *See* Sh— Troilus . . . 1707, 1708, 1715, 1718

Sievers (*Dr.* E. W.) *Editor*—
See Sh— Hamlet, 1851
,, Sh— Julius Cæsar, 1855
,, Sh— Othello, 1853

Sigerson (George) ' Ducdame ' [identified with ' Tiucfai me '—*I will come*], [In ' The Athenæum,' No. 3,558, p. 27, Jan. 1896]. 4°
Illustrates ' As you like it.'

Sigtenhorst (A. J. Van den) *Deventer Publisher*.
See Sh— Romeo . . . 1869

Sill (Edward Rowland) Sh—'s prose [In ' Overland Monthly']. San Francisco . . . 1875. 8° BUS

Sill (Richard)] Remarks on Sh—'s ' The tempest '; containing an investigation of Mr. Malone's attempt to ascertain the date of that play and various notes . . . of abstruse readings and passages by Charles Dirrill [*i.e.* R. Sill]. Ln: . . . 1797. 8° BM

Silsby (Mary R.) Tributes to Sh—. *See Sh—*] Silsby

Silvayn (Alexander) *pseud. See* Busche

Silver (George) Paradoxes of defence, wherein is proved the true grounds of fight to be in the short auncient weapons and that the short sword hath advantage of the long sword or long rapier . . . Ln: Printed for Edward Blount, 1599. Fcp. 4°. With woodcuts BM | BLO
In an amusing story of Signor Rocco, an Italian fencing master of Blackfriars, says, ' Thou that takest upon thee to hit anie Englishman with a thrust upon anie button.'
This elucidates the passage in ' Romeo . . .,' ' the very butcher of a silk button.'
The Ashburnham copy sold for £72 in May, 1898.

Sim (Adelaide C. G.) Phoebe's Sh—: Stories simply told. *See* Sh— Works: Ext. 1893, 1894

Simmes, Simms, *or* Sims (Valentine) *Printer and Publisher*—
See Alexander
,, Chettle
,, Dedekind
,, Gowrie
,, Marston
,, Montaigne

Simmes, Simms, *or* Sims (Valentine) *Printer and Publisher*—
See Sh— Julius Cæsar, 1604
,, Sh— King Henry IV., i., 1604
,, Sh— King Henry IV., ii., 1600
,, Sh— King Henry VI., ii., 1600
,, Sh— King John, 1611
,, Sh— King Richard II., 1597, 1598
,, Sh— King Richard III., 1597
,, Sh— Much ado . . . 1600
,, Sh— Taming . . . 1607

Simmons *Publisher*. *See* Sh— Macbeth, 1785

Simmons (M.) *Publisher*. *See* Milton

Simmons (Thomas) & Jaggard (William)] Index catalogue of the manuscript and printed literature gathered by George Guy Greville fourth Earl of Warwick, designated the ' General library,' at Warwick Castle. Leamington Spa: T. Simmons, 1890. Manuscript, written upon handmade parchment and bound in green vellum, deckle edges. F° W
This collection of books is rich in early printed and early English literature, much of it illustrative of Sh—'s time and works. The books repose on bookcases fashioned by the Earl's workmen from cedar of Lebanon, grown on the estate by the Avon.
The arrangement, collation, and cataloguing occupied about twelve months. The above is now the only copy existing, the first rough transcript being accidentally destroyed.

Simms (William Gilmore) *Editor*. *See* Sh— Works, 1848, 1855

Simons (C. E.) *Editor*. *See* Hansen

Simpleton the smith: A droll, composed about A.D. 1647. Edited by J. O. Halliwell . . . 1860. 8° BPL

Simpson (D.) Discourse on stage entertainments . . . 1788. 8° BPL

Simpson (Percy) Rosencrantz and Guildenstern [In ' The Athenæum,' No. 3,997, p. 731, June, 1904]. 4° BM | BPL
Scenes from old play books. *See* Sh— Works: Ext. 1906

Simpson (Percy) *Editor*. *See* Sh— Sir John Oldcastle, 1908

Simpson (Richard) Evening mass in ' Romeo and Juliet.' Ln: New Sh— Soc., 1875-76. 8°
Introduction to the philosophy of Sh—'s sonnets. Ln: Trübner, 1868. 8°, pp. viii.-82 BM | BPL | BUS | CPL | MPL | SML
On some plays attributed to Sh—. Ln: New Sh— Soc., 1875-76. 8°
BM | BPL | BUS
Political use of the stage in Sh—'s time. Ln: New Sh— Soc., 1874. 8°
BM | BPL | BUS
Politics of Sh—'s historical plays. Ln: New Sh— Soc., 1874. 8° BM | BPL | BUS
Religion of Sh—, edited by H. S. Bowden. Ln: . . . 1899. Cr. 8° BM | BPL | BUS | MPL

Simpson (Richard) School of Sh—; including the 'Life and death of Captain Thomas Stukeley,' with a new life of Stucley from unpublished sources; 'Nobody and somebody'; 'Histrio-mastix'; 'The prodigal son'; Jack Drum's entertainment'; 'A warning for fair women'; with reprints of the accounts of the murder, and 'Faire Em.' Edited, with introductions and notes, and an account of Robert Greene, his prose works, and his quarrels with Sh—. Ln: Chatto . . . 1878. 2 vols. Cr. 8°

BM | BPL | BUS | CPL | MPL | SML

The author's premature death caused this work to be edited and indexed by J. W. M. Gibbs, with preface by Dr. Furnivall.
The title 'School of Sh—' was invented and used in 1779 by Edward Capell (q.v.)

Simpson (R.) *Publisher. See* Temple

Simpson *Dean* (W. Sparrow) Gleanings from old St. Paul's. Ln: Stock . . . 1889. 8°, pp. xii.-308. Illust.
Refers to Sh— pp. 102-103, and gives a list of plays performed by the 'Children of Paule's,' pp. 113-116.

Simpson-Blaikie (Edwin) Dramatic unities. Third edition. Ln: Trübner . . . 1878. Cr. 8°, pp. iv.-108   SML

Simrock (Karl Joseph) Remarks . . . on the plots of Sh—'s plays. With notes and additions by J. O. Halliwell. *See Sh—*] Sh— Soc.

Simrock (K. J.) *Editor. See* Sh— Macbeth, 1842

Simson (G.) *Printer. See* Cotton

Sinclair (Thomas) The mount: Speech from its English heights. Ln: Trübner . . . 1878. 8°, pp. viii.-302   BUS

Singer *Comedian* (J.) Quips upon questions, or a clowne's conceite on occasion offered, bewraying a morallised metamorphoses of changes upon interrogatories, shewing a little wit with a good deal of will in verse. Edited from the unique original, 1600, by F. Ouvry. Ln: Privately printed . . . 1875. Fcp. 4°
Limited issue.

Singer (Samuel Weller) Introduction. *See* Tieck

Text of Sh— vindicated from the interpolations and corruptions advocated by J. P. Collier in his 'Notes and emendations' . . . Ln: W. Pickering . . . 1853. 8°, pp. xx.-312

BM | BPL | BUS | CPL | MPL | SML | W

S. W. Singer, originally a bookseller in St. James' St., London, S.W., became librarian to the Royal Institution from 1827 to 1835. He was the first to doubt the genuineness of J. P. Collier's alleged discoveries.

Singer (S. W.) *Editor—*
See More
    „ Peele

Singer (S. W.) *Editor—*
See Sh— King Lear, 1834
    „ Sh— Midsummer . . . 1854
    „ Sh— Works, 1826, 1828-34, 1829-31, 1829-43, 1831, 1833, 1834, 1835, 1836, 1837, 1839, 1843, 1844, 1855-56, 1855-71, 1868, 1869, 1875, 1879-81, 1880, 1899
    „ Sh—] Sh— Jest books
See also Arrowsmith
    „   „ Causton
    „   „ Collier (J. P.)

Singleton (Henry)] Analytical catalogue of a series of cabinet pictures illustrating the plays of Sh—. With a memoir and introduction by Joseph O'Leary. Ln: J. Hogarth . . . 1843. 8°, pp. xii.-54

BM | BUS | CPL | W

] Catalogue of pictures . . . Ln: 1839. 8°, pp. 34   BM | BPL | BUS

] Catalogue of pictures . . . Stratford-upon-Avon, 1848. 8°   BPL

Singleton (Henry) *Artist—*
See Sh— Comedy . . . 1808
    „ Sh— Works, 1792, 1803

Sinker (*Dr.* Robert) Library of Trinity College. Cambridge: Deighton . . . 1891. Fcp. 4°, pp. xii.-136 and 10 plates   BPL
Chap. vi., pp 115-124, deals with Edward Capell and his Sh— collection.

Sir John Oldcastle. *See* Sh— Sir John Oldcastle

Sir Thomas More. *See* Sh— Sir Thomas More

Six floral Sh— mottoes. *See* Sh—'Works: Ext. 1886

Six old plays on which Sh— founded his 'Measure for measure,' 'Comedy of errors,' 'Taming of the shrew,' 'King John,' 'King Henry the fourth,' 'King Henry the fifth,' 'King Lear' [Edited by John Nichols]. Ln: S. Learcroft . . . 1779. 2 vols. 8°

BPL | BUS | MPL | SML | W

Contents:—
1. Whetstone (Geo.) Promos and Cassandra.
2. Plautus, Menæcmi. Written in English by W. W. [W. Warner].
3. Taming of a shrew.
4. Troublesome raigne of John King of England. Parts i. and ii.
5. Famous victories of Henry the fifth.
6. True chronicle history of King Leir.
Reprinted at the suggestion of George Steevens. The collection forms a valuable supplement to Hawkins' English drama (q.v.)
The Warwick copy bears the autograph of Samuel Ireland, the forger.

Six old plays . . . Ln: Nichols . . . 1788

Sixteenth century women students. *See* Stopes

Smith (Charles) *Publisher.* *See* Phillips
Smith (Charles Roach) Remarks on Sh—. *See* Sh—] Smith
Retrospections, social and archæological. 1883-89. 3 vols. 8°   BPL
Contains Shakespeareana.
Rural life of Sh—. *See Sh*—] Smith
Smith (Charles W.) The actor's art: its requisites and how to obtain them; its defects and how to remove them
Smith (D. Nichol) *Editor*—
See Eighteenth . . .
  „ Sh— King Henry VIII., 1899
  „ Sh— King Lear, 1902
Smith, 1672-1710 (Edmund) Phædra and Hippolitus: A tragedy. As it is acted at the Queen's theatre in the Hay Market by her Majesty's sworn servants. Ln: Bernard Lintott, 1707. Fcp. 4°, pp. x.-64
In the prologue by Addison reference is made to Sh—.
Smith (F.) Warwickshire delineated . . . Second edition. Southam: F. Smith [c. 1810]. 8°. Illustrated   SML
The earliest book published in Southam, a Warwickshire village twice mentioned in 'King Henry VI.'
Smith (F. A.) The critics *v.* Sh—: A brief for the defendant. New York . . . 1907. Cr. 8°   BPL
Smith (George) *Editor.* *See* Sh— Macbeth, 1902
Smith (G. A.) Compendium and concordance of the works of Sh—. Philadelphia . . . 1889. 12°   BPL
Smith (George Barnett) Wm. Sh—. *See Sh*—] Smith
Smith (G. C. Moore) English miscellany . . . Oxford . . . 1901. 8°   BPL
Contains Sh—'s 'King John' and the 'Troublesome raigne,' pp. 335-337.
Smith (G. C. Moore) *Editor*—
See Sh— King Edward III., 1897
  „ Sh— King Henry V., 1895-96, 1896, 1899, 1900, 1901, 1903
  „ Sh— King John, 1900
  „ Sh— Works, 1893-98
Smith (Goldwin) Sh— the man. *See Sh*—] Smith
Smith (Horatio & James)] Accepted addresses, or præmium poetarum. To which are added, ' Macbeth travestie, in three acts,' and ' Miscellanies, by different hands.' With burlesque annotations after the manner of Dr. Johnson, G. Steevens . . . Ln: Tegg . . . 1813. 12° BM | BPL | W
] Rejected addresses. Ln: 1812. 12° BUS
Contains ' Macbeth travesty' and ' Punch's apotheosis.'
Smith (J.) *Publisher.* *See* Sh— Works, 1824
Smith (J.) *Paris Publisher.* *See* Sh— Romeo . . . 1827

Smith ' *Momus Medlar* ' (James) *Editor.* *See* Sh— Macbeth, 1869
Smith (John) *Dramatist.* *See* Vince
Smith (J. B.) *Philadelphia Publisher*—
See Sh— Poems, 1855
  „ Sh— Works, 1852, 1855
Smith (J. C.)] The fairies: An opera. *See* Sh— Midsummer . . . 1754, 1755, 1756, 1798
Smith (J. C.) *Composer*—
See Sh— Midsummer . . . 1754, 1755
  „ Sh— The tempest, 1756
Smith (J. C.) *Editor*—
See Sh— As you like it, 1894, 1896
  „ Sh— Much ado, 1902
  „ Sh— Works, 1893-98
Smith (J. Moyr) *Editor and Artist*—
See Sh— Macbeth, 1889
  „ Sh— Midsummer . . . 1892
  „ Sh— Works: Ext. 1879
Smith (John Russell) Catalogue of engraved portraits . . . on sale. Ln: [c. 1865]. 8°, pp. 32   BUS
Sh—: Wanted, to purchase. *See* Barton (T. P.)
Shakesperiana: A catalogue of books, pamphlets . . . illustrating the life and writings of Sh— . . . Ln: . . . 1864-70. 8°, pp. 74 BM | BPL | BUS | MPL
Smith (John Russell) *Publisher*—
See Sh— Sonnets, 1859, 1870
  „ Sh— Will . . . 1838, 1851
Smith (Joseph) *Publisher.* *See* Sh— Works: Ext. 1844
Smith (Joshua Toulmin) Sh— autographs . . . [1864-65]. 4° BM | BPL
Sh— autographs. [1865.] 4° and f° BM
Sh—'s own Prayer book . . . [1864]. F°; single sheet   BM
Smith (Lucy Toulmin) On the bond story in the ' Merchant of Venice ' and a version of it in the ' Cursor mundi.' Ln: New Sh— Soc., 1875-76. 8° BM | BPL | BUS
Smith (L. T.) *Editor.* *See Sh*—] Ingleby
Smith (*Miss*) *Actress.* *See* Sh— Cymbeline, 1806
Smith (*Mrs.*) Life of Moore. *See* Moore
Smith (R. J.) *Bibliophile.* *See* Catalogue, 1855
Smith (Samuel) *Publisher.* *See* Hedelin
Smith.] Memoir of Teena Rochfort-Smith, 1861-1883. 1883. 8°   BPL
Smith (T.) *Wolverhampton Publisher*—
See Jones (H.)
  „ Sh— Works, 1768
Smith (W.) Evesham and the neighbourhood. Illustrated by E. H. New and B. C. Boulter. Ln: Homeland Association, 1902. 12°   SML
Smith (W.) *Printer.* *See* Sh— King Henry IV., ii., 1821

Smith (W.) *Publisher.* *See* Sh— As you like it, 1740

Smith (Wentworth). *See* Sh— The puritan widow (*heading*)

Smith *Dean of Chester* (Wm.) *Editor.* *See* Longinus

Smith (Wm.) *Dublin Publisher*—
See Fielding
  „ Sh— King Lear, 1733

Smith (*Capt.* Wm. and Rebecca). *See* Sh—] Malone

Smith (W. F.) *Editor.* *See* Sh— Much ado, 1904

Smith (Wm. Henry) [*pseud. of* Albert Smith ?] Bacon and Sh—: An inquiry touching players, playhouses, and playwriters in the days of Elizabeth . . . To which is appended an abstract of a MS. respecting Tobie Matthew. Ln: J. R. Smith . . . 1857. Cr. 8°, pp. viii.-162
BM | BPL | BUS | CPL | MPL | SML | W

Bacon and Sh— . . . Second edition. Ln: J. R. Smith, 1857. Cr. 8°, pp. viii.-iv.-162 BUS
Contains Smith's reply to Hawthorne's charge of plagiarism.

Bacon and Sh—: William Sh—; his position as regards the plays. 1884. 8°
BM | BUS

Was Lord Bacon the editor of Sh—'s plays ? A letter to Lord Ellesmere. Ln: W. Skeffington, 1856. 8°, pp. 16
BM | BPL | BUS | CPL
Reviewed in 'The Athenæum,' 13th Sept., 1856; 'Blackwood,' Nov., 1856; 'Illustrated Ln. News' (by C. M. Ingleby), 6th Dec., 1856.

Smith (W. H. Payne). *See* Rimmer & Smith

Smith (W. H. Payne) *Editor*—
See Sh— King Richard III., 1889, 1900
  „ Sh— Works, 1886-91

Smith (W. L.) Historical notices and recollections relating to the parish of Southam. Illustrated . . . Ln: Stock . . . 1894. 2 parts. 4°
Projected for completion in eight parts. Poor Smith's unexplained suicide left it incomplete, and his executors refused to allow the work to be finished from his MSS.

Smyth (Albert Hy.) Halliwell-Phillipps collection. *See Halliwell*] Smyth
Sh—'s Pericles and Apollonius of Tyre : A study in comparative literature. Philadelphia : MacCalla . . . 1898. 8°
BM | BPL | SML
Syllabus of a course of six lectures on Sh—. Philadelphia, 1897. 8°, pp. 8 BUS

Smythies (W. G.) Life of Kean. *See* Kean
Snagg (R.) *Publisher.* *See* Curiosities
Snell (F. S.) London Shakespeares [John Sh— 'dwellinge in the Strande,' 1618 (bit-maker ?), his 'two sonnes' and 'fower

prentices'], [In 'The Athenæum,' No. 4,313, p. 772, 25 June, 1910]. 4°
BM | BPL
Referred to as legatees in the will of Wm. Shere of Fetter Lane, 20th Mar., 1618[-19].

Snider (Denton J.) 'Antony and Cleopatra' [In 'Journal of speculative philosophy']. St. Louis, 1876. 8° BUS
'As you like it' [In 'Journal of speculative philosophy']. 1873. 8° BUS
'Cymbeline' [In 'Journal of speculative philosophy']. 1875. 8° BUS
'Hamlet' [In 'Journal of speculative philosophy']. 1873. 8° BPL | BUS
'Julius Cæsar' [In 'Journal of speculative philosophy']. 1872. 8° BUS
'Macbeth' [In 'The Western']. 1875. 8°
BPL
'Measure for measure' [In 'Journal of speculative philosophy']. St. Louis, 1875. 8° BPL | BUS
'Merchant of Venice' [In 'Journal of speculative philosophy']. 1872. 8° BUS
'Midsummer night's dream' [In 'Journal of speculative philosophy']. 1874. 8° BUS
'Romeo and Juliet' [In 'The Western']. 1875. 8° BPL
Sh—'s tragedies. Philadelphia [1876]. 8°
BM | SML
Shakesperian drama : A commentary. Boston & St. Louis, 1887-91. 3 vols. 8°
BUS | SML
System of Sh—'s dramas. St. Louis : G. I. Jones, 1877. 2 vols. 16°
BM | BPL | BUS | MPL
'The tempest' [In 'Journal of speculative philosophy']. 1874. 8° BUS
'Timon of Athens' [In 'The Western']. 1875. 8° BPL
'Troilus and Cressida' [In 'Journal of speculative philosophy']. 1876. 8° BUS
'Two gentlemen of Verona' [In 'Journal of speculative philosophy']. 1876. 8° BUS
'Winter's tale' [In 'Journal of speculative philosophy']. 1875. 8° BPL | BUS

Snodham (Thomas) *Printer*—
See Elimandus
  „ Sh— Rape . . . 1616
  „ Sh— Thomas . . . 1613

Soames (C.)] 'Hamlet' : An attempt to ascertain whether the queen were an accessory . . . in the murder. Ln : J. R. Smith . . . 1856. 8°, pp. 48 BPL | BUS | MPL

Soane (George) Songs. *See* Sh— Midsummer . . . 1860

Soane (George) *Editor*—
See Sh— As you like it, 1860
  „ Sh— King Henry VI., i.-ii.-iii., 1817
  „ Sh— Othello, 1844

So-called Shakespearian myth [In 'Canadian Monthly,' July, 1879]. 8°   BUS
Occasioned by Morgan's articles.

Soldene (Emily) My theatrical and musical recollections. Ln : . . . 1897. 8°

Solling (G.) *Editor—*
See Sh— Macbeth. 1878
,, Sh— Works : Ext. 1866

Solly-Flood (F.) Prince Henry of Monmouth and Chief Justice Gascoigne. 1886. 8°   BPL
Illustrates 'King Henry V.' and 'King Henry VI.'

Somatographia anthropinii . . . See Jaggard (W.)

Some account of the English stage. *See* Geneste

Some notes on 'Othello' [In 'Cornhill Magazine,' Oct. Ln : 1868]. 8°
BPL | BUS | CPL

Some remarks on the tragedy of 'Hamlet prince of Denmark,' written by Mr. Wm. Sh—. Ln : W. Wilkins . . . 1736. 8°, pp. viii.-64   BM | BUS
Ascribed to Sir Thomas Hanmer.
Said to be the earliest piece of express Shakespearean criticism.

Some remarks on the tragedy of ' Hamlet ' . . . Ln : W. Wilkins, 1736 [Reprinted by J. R. Smith, 1864]. 8°, pp. vi.-52
BM | BUS | CPL | MPL

Some serious remarks. . . . *See* Harper

Some Shakespearian and Spenserian manuscripts [In 'American Whig Review']. New York . . . 1851-52. 8°   BUS

Some thoughts concerning the stage, in a letter to a lady. Ln : J. Nutt . . . 1704. 8°, pp. 16   SML
'The licentious and unbounded liberty the players have taken of late years, and particularly in their daring to act ' The tempest' within a very few days after the late dreadful storm, has rais'd such an abhorrence that we may possibly see the stage brought under regulations.'—*Extract.*

Somers (Alexander) Shakespearean ballads. *See* Sh— Works : Ext. 1887, 1890

Somerset (C. A.) Sh—'s early days : An historical play. With remarks by D. G—— [Geo. Daniel]. Ln : J. Cumberland [1830]. 12°, pp. 48 and frontispiece by R. Cruikshank   BPL | BUS | MPL | SML
Sh—'s early days . . . ' Lacy's acting edition.' [1865.] 12°   BPL
See also Mathews.

Somerset House. *See Sh—*] Law

Somervall & Conrad *Petersburg* [*U.S.*] *Publishers. See* Sh— Works, 1805-09

Somerville (H. G.) Wanderings in Worcestershire. Illustrated by A. H. Wall. Ln : Simpkin . . . 1894-95. 12°   SML

Somerville *of Edreston* (*Sir* Wm.) *See* Stopes

Something that Sh— lost ; Touching the Lord Hamlet ; Retouching the Lord Hamlet [In ' Household Words,' 17 Jan., 17 Oct., 5 Dec. Ln : . . . 1857]. Roy. 8°   BUS

Sonatun Press, Calcutta *Publishers. See* Sh— Works, 1878

Songes and Sonettes. *See* Howard

Songs—
See Ballads .... See Greenhill
,, Charms .... ,, Linley
,, Crown . . . . ,, List . . .
,, Dibdin .... ,, Old . . .
., Dramatic . . . . ,, Ritson
,, Garrick .... ,, Stevens
,, Glover .... ,, White

Songs, chorusses, etc. in the entertainment of the jubilee. *See* Dibdin

Songs, duetts, etc. . . . *See* Sh— Merry wives, 1824

Songs from Sh— : Calendar . . . *See* Sh— Works : Ext. 1908

Songs in the opera . . . *See* Sh— Hamlet, 1712

Songster's pocket book. *See* Dibdin

Sonnenschein (*Prof.* E. A.) Sh— and stoicism [In 'University Review'] . . . 1905. 8°   BPL
Sh—'s debt to Plautus. ' Sh— Club paper.' Stratford-on-Avon : Privately printed, 1908. Cr. 8°

Sonnenschein (W. S.) Sh—'s debt to his predecessors and his successors' debt to him : A collection of parallel passages, with translations of the foreign examples. Ln : Routledge . . . 1905. Cr. 8°
A projected publication.

Sonnet kalendar. *See* Sh— Works : Ext. 1901, 1902

Sonnet (The). [Excerpt notice from the 'Quarterly Review' . . . 1873.] 8° BPL

Sonnets. *See* Sh— Sonnets

Sonnets of Sh— [Article in 'Westminster Review']. Ln : 1857. 8°   BUS

Sophocles. Electra. *See* Gilkes
Œdipus. *See* Brien
See Horton-Smith
,, *Sh—*] Downes

Sotheby (S. L.) Sh— : Collier controversy. A collection of Collier's autograph letters, pamphlets, facsimiles, extracts, cuttings, reviews, etc. mounted into a volume. [c. 1855.] F°

Sothern.] Pemberton (T. Edgar) Memoir of Edward Askew Sothern. Ln : Bentley . . . 1889. 8°   BPL
] Pemberton. Memoir of E. A. Sothern. New edition. Ln : Bentley & Son, 1890. Cr. 8°, pp. viii.-346. With facsimiles

Sothern (E. H.) *Editor. See* Sh— Hamlet, 1901

HENRY WRIOTHESLEY,
EARL of SOUTHAMPTON.

*Engraved by A. Ferguson, from an original Picture
in the collection of His Grace the Duke of Bedford*

See p. 639

Soule (Charles C.) Hamlet revamped. *See* Sh— Hamlet, 1879

Romeo . . . travesty. *See* Sh— Romeo . . . 1877

] Travesty without a pun ! 'Hamlet' re-vamped, modernized, and set to music. By the author of 'Romeo and Juliet.' St. Louis [U.S.]: G. I. Jones & Co., 1880. 8°   BM

Souter (J.) *Publisher. See* Sh— Works, 1834, 1836

Southam, Warwickshire—
See Smith (F.)
  ,, Smith (W. L.)

Southampton (Henry Wriothesly *third Earl of*) Portrait—
See Sh— Poems, 1795
  ,, Sh— Works, 1780

Southampton (Hy. Wriothesley, *third Earl of*)
See Cecil
  ,, Creighton
  ,, Dix
  ,, Elizabeth
  ,, Florio
  ,, Historie . . .
  ,, Irving & Fairholt
  ,, Malone
  ,, Sh— Rape . . . 1594, 1598
  ,, Sh— Venus . . . 1593
  ,, Stopes
  ,, Wright

Southampton Hartley Institution. *See* Emanuel

Southern (Henry) *Editor. See* Retrospective Review

Southerne (Thomas). *See* Fenton

Southey (Robert) Holograph letter to J. Britton [declining to write a poem com-memorative of Sh—]. 13 March, 1816. Manuscript. 8°   BUS

Southgate (J. W.) *Publisher. See* Sh— Works, 1839

Southgate & Son *Publishers. See* Sh— Works, 1840

Southwark—
See Corner
  ,, Jackson
  ,, London

Southwell (Robert) Saint Peter's complaint. With other poems. Ln : Printed by I. R—— [James Roberts] for G. C——, 1595. Fcp. 4°
Alludes to Sh— thus :—
  'Still finest wits are stiling Venus' rose.'

Spain—
See Cervantes
  ,, Historie . . .
  ,, Hume
  ,, Mexia

See Sh— Ballad
  ,, Sh— Cardenio
  ,, Spanish . . .

Spalding (Thomas Alfred) Elizabethan de-monology. An essay in illustration of the belief in the existence of devils . . . with special reference to Sh— and his works. Ln : Chatto . . . 1880. 8°, pp. xiv.-152
                  BM | BPL | BUS | MPL | SML

On Sh—'s sonnets [In 'Gentleman's maga-zine' . . . 1878]. 8°   BUS | SML

On the first quarto of 'Romeo and Juliet' : Is there any evidence of a second hand in it ? Ln : New Sh— Soc., 1877-79. 8°
                            BM | BPL | BUS

On the witch-scenes in 'Macbeth.' Ln : New Sh— Soc., 1877-79. 8°
                            BM | BPL | BUS

Spalding (*Prof.* Wm.)] Letter on Sh—'s authorship of the 'Two noble kinsmen,' a drama commonly ascribed to John Fletcher. Edinburgh: Black . . . 1833. 8°   BM | BPL | MPL | SML | W

Letter on the . . . 'Two noble kinsmen,' and the characteristics of Sh—'s style and the secret of his supremacy. With life of the author by John Hill Burton. Ln : New Sh— Soc., 1876. 8°
                            BM | BPL | BUS

Recent Shakspearian literature [In 'Edin-burgh Review']. 1840. 8°   BUS

Spanish Mandevile of miracles. *See* Nash

Sparke (Michael) *Publisher*—
See Booke . . .
  ,, Prynne

Sparrow (W. S.) Life in a Shakespearian com-pany on tour [In 'Atalanta' magazine, 1892]. Roy. 8°   BPL

Speare *Publisher. See* Sh— Works, 1790, 1793

Specimen of a commentary. *See* Whiter

Spedding (James) On the corrected edition of 'King Richard III.' With a reply by E. H. Pickersgill. Ln : New Sh— Soc., 1875. 8°   BM | BPL | BUS | SML

On the division of the acts in 'King Lear,' 'Much ado,' and 'Twelfth night.' Ln : New Sh— Soc., 1877-79. 4°
                            BM | BPL | BUS

On the several shares of Sh— and Fletcher in . . . 'Henry VIII.' Ln : New Sh— Soc., 1874. 8°   BM | BPL | BUS

Reviews and discussions. Ln : . . . 1879. 8°   BUS
On 'Merchant of Venice,' 'Twelfth night,' etc.

Who wrote Sh—'s Henry VIII. ? [In 'Gentleman's Magazine']. Ln : 1850. 8°
                                                  BUS

Spedding (James) *Editor. See* Bacon

Spedding (James)—
See Furnivall
  ,, Gairdner & Spedding

(639)

Speech and charge at Norwich assizes, with a discoverie of the abuses and corruption of officers. Ln : Nathaniell Butter, 1607. Fcp. 4°
On the verso of sig. H2 will be found an entry upon stage plays.

Speed (Samuel) *Publisher.* *See* Sh— Poems, 1669

Spence *York Publisher.* *See* Sh— Macbeth, 1797

Spence (Ferrand). *See* Marguetel . . .

Spencer (F.) *Editor.* *See* Sh— King Lear, 1898

Spencer (Herbert) Alexander Smith *v.* Sh— [In 'The Athenæum,' Mar., No. 3570, p. 415]. 1896. 4°   BM | BPL

Spencer (W. V.) *Boston* [*U.S.*] *Publisher*— *See* Sh— Comedy of errors, 1856
  , Sh— Coriolanus, 1855

Spencer's Theatre, Boston [U.S.] *See* Sh— Winter's tale, 1859

Spenser (Edmund) Extracts . . . *See* Sh— Works : Ext. 1845
Colin Clouts come home againe. Ln : Printed [by T. Creed] for William Ponsonbie, 1595. Fcp. 4°, sig. A¹ to H4, unpaged   BM | BPL
At sig. C2 is the allusion to Sh—, under the name of 'Actæon' :— 'A gentler shepherd may no where be found . . .'
In Sh—'s days it was customary to speak of poets as shepherds.

Complaints, containing sundrie small poemes of the world's vanitie. Whereof the next page maketh mention. Ln : Imprinted for William Ponsonbie, dwelling in Paule's Churchyard at the Signe of the Bishop's head, 1591. Fcp. 4°, sig. A¹ to Z4, unpaged (the last leaf blank)   BM | CTC
Refers to 'Our pleasant Willy' in 'Teares of the muses,' p. 8 ; but opinion is divided as to whether Sh— is meant or not.

Faerie queene. Disposed into twelve books, fashioning XII. moral vertues. Ln : Printed [by Iohn Wolfe and Richard Field] for William Ponsonby, 1590-96. 2 vols. Fcp. 4°   BM | CTC
Book IV., canto iii., stanza 10, bears a passage employing Sh—'s name :—
  'He all enraged his shivering *speare* did *shake,*
  And charging him afresh thus felly him bespake.'

Sports of the muses. *See* Sh— Works : Ext. 1752

Spenser (Edmund)—
See Cotgrave
  ,, Henderson
  ,, Imitations
  ,, Landor
  ,, Levi
  ,, Sh— Works : Ext. 1600
  ,, *Sh*—] Three . . .
  ,, Some Shakespearian MSS.

' Spermacetti *the elder* (Marcus) ' *pseud.* Specimen of a new jest book, containing interesting and original bon mots, etc., also annotations upon Sh— [Hamlet], etc. 1810. Cr. 8°   BPL | BUS | W

Spielmann (M. H.) ' Grafton ' and ' Sanders ' portraits of Sh—. *See Sh*—] Spielmann Janssen portrait. *See Sh*—] Sh—'s portrait

Portraits of Sh—. *See* Sh— Works, 1904-06

Portraits of Sh— : An essay. 1907. Roy. 8°   BPL
Reprinted from Sh— works, Stratford ed., vol. 10, 1907.

Spiers (E. T.) *Oxford Publisher*—
See Sh— Macbeth, 1850
  ,, Sh— Merchant . . . 1849

Spiers (R. P.) Architecture of ' Coriolanus ' at the Lyceum Theatre [In ' Architectural Review ']. 1901. F°   BPL

Spiess *Artist. See* Sh— Works : Ext. 1876

Spilsbury (A. J.) *Editor. See* Sh— King Lear, 1905

Spink (W.) Sh— as a dramatic model [In ' National Review.' Ln : . . . 1885]. 8°   BPL

Spoffkins (A. Pimpleton) *pseud.* Bacon out-Shakespeared. *See* Bacon

Spooner (Shearjashub) Prospectus for publishing an American edition of Boydell's Illustrations of Sh—. New York : J. J. Reed, 1848. 16°, pp. 18   BUS
Prospectus . . . [with appendix]. New York : J. J. Reed [c. 1850]. 16°, pp. 32   BUS

Sports—
See Annalia . . .
  ,, Harland
  ,, Ravenscroft
  ,, *Sh*—] Sh—'s sports
  ,, Ward (H. S.)

Sports of the muses. *See* Sh— Works : Ext. 1752

Sprague (Charles) Prize ode . . . recited at the representation of the Sh— jubilee. Boston [U.S.], 13 Feb., 1824. 8°, pp. 8   BM | BUS
' Who now shall grace the glowing throne
Where all unrivalled, all alone,
Bold Sh— sat, and looked creation through—
The minstrel monarch of the worlds he drew?
That throne is cold, that lyre in death unstrung
On whose proud note delighted wonder hung ;
Yet old oblivion, as in wrath he sweeps,
One spot shall spare, the grave where Sh— sleeps.
Rulers and ruled in common gloom may lie,
But nature's laureate bards shall never die ;
Art's chiselled boast and glory's trophied shore
Must live in numbers, or can live no more.
While sculptured Jove some nameless waste may claim,
Still roars the Olympic car in Pindar's fame ;
Troy's doubtful walls, in ashes passed away,
Yet frown on Greece in Homer's deathless lay ;
Rome, slowly sinking in her crumbling fanes,
Stands all immortal in her Maro's strains.

So, too, yon giant empress of the isles,
On whose broad sway the sun for ever smiles,
To time's unsparing rage one day must bend,
And all her triumphs in her Sh— end !

Still o'er our land shall Albion's sceptre wave,
And what her mighty lion lost, her mightier swan shall
save.'

Sprague (Charles). *See also* Boston prize poems

Sprague (Homer Baxter) Sh—'s alleged blunders in legal terminology.   New York, 1902.   8°, pp. 16   BUS

Sprague (Homer B.) *Editor*—
See Sh— Hamlet, 1885, 1886
,, Sh— Julius Cæsar, 1894
,, Sh— Macbeth, 1874, 1889, 1898
,, Sh— Midsummer . . . 1896

Sprague (Hosea) *Boston Printer.   See* Sh— Hamlet, 1805

Springthorpe (J. W.) A perfect woman [' Rosalind ']. Melbourne . . . 1897.   8°, pp. 22   MPL
Illustrates ' As you like it.'

Sprint (S. & J.) *Publishers.   See* Goodwin

Sprot.] Examinations, arraignment and conviction of George Sprot, notary [*in re* Gowrie conspiracy].   Ln : M. Bradwood for William Aspley, 1609.   Fcp. 4°
Both Knight and Elze consider the Gowrie plot tracts supplied Sh— with local colour for ' Macbeth.'

Stack (Richard) Examination of [Morgann's] Essay on the dramatic character of ' Sir John Falstaff.' [1788.] 4°   BPL | BUS
Issued in the ' Transactions of the Royal Irish Academy,' vol. ii.

Stael-Holstein (Anne L. G. N.) Influence of literature upon society.   Boston [U.S.] 1813.   12°   BUS

Stael-Holstein (L. G. N.) Corinna or Italy. Ln : A. K. Newmann . . . 1822.   12° SML
Describes a performance of ' Romeo and Juliet ' in Italy.

Stafford (John) *Publisher.   See* Sh— Rape . . . 1655

Stafford (Simon) *Printer*—
See Sh— King Edward III., 1599
,, Sh— King Henry IV., i., 1599
,, Sh— King Lear, 1605
,, Sh— Pericles, 1611

Stafford (Wm.)] Briefe conceipte . . . *See* Sh— Compendious examination
Compendious examination. *See* Sh— Compendious . . .

Stage acquitted : being a full answer to [Bp. Jeremy] Collier and the other enemies of the drama. With a vindication of King Charles the martyr and the clergy from the abuses of a scurrilous book called the ' Stage condemned.' Ln : . . . 1699. 8°   MPL
A reply to Collier's ' Stage condemned ' (*q.v.*).

Stage adaptations of Sh— [In 'Cornhill Magazine']. Ln : 1863. 8°   BPL | BUS

Stage condemned.   *See* Collier (Jeremy)

Stage enemies—
See Collier (*Bp.*)   *See* Reardon
,, Prynne   ,, Stubbes
,, Rainoldes

Stage-player's complaint in a pleasant dialogue between Cane of the *Fortune* [theatre] and Reed of the *Friers* [Blackfriar's theatre] deploring their sad and solitary conditions for want of imployment in this heavie and contagious time of the plague . . . Ln : . . . 1641.   Fcp. 4°. With curious woodcut on title-page
' Only two copies of this tract (relating to the stage and drama just before the closing of theatres by the puritans) are known.   The plague was prevailing, and the enemies of plays availed themselves of the visitation as if sent by heaven as a punishment for indulging in such profanations.'—J. P. COLLIER, in ' Rarest books . . .'

Stage-player's complaint, 1641.   Reprinted by E. W. Ashbee. Ln : . . . 1868. Fcp. 4°
                                      BPL | SML

Stage, theatre, and drama—
See Accounts . . .   *See* Buckham
,, Actors   ,, Bullen
,, Albright   ,, Bullokar
,, Ancient   ,, Bunn
,, Angus   ,, Burnand
,, Archæology   ,, Butler
,, Archer   ,, Calcraft
,, B—— (G.)   ,, Calmour
,, Baker (H. B.)   ,, Campbell
,, Baker (*Sir* R.)   ,, Capell
,, Bancroft   ,, Carlisle
,, Barker   ,, Catalogue, 1825
,, Barrymore   ,, Celebrities
,, Bates   ,, Chalmers
,, Bayley   ,, Chambers
,, Beauties   ,, Chapman
,, Bedford   ,, Chetwood
,, Bennett   ,, Chevalier
,, Bernard   ,, Cibber
,, Betson   ,, Clarke
,, Betterton   ,, Close
,, Betty   ,, Cochrane
,, Bibb   ,, Cohn
,, Biography   ,, Cole
,, Blades   ,, Coleman
,, Bodleian   ,, Coleridge
,, Bond   ,, Collection
,, Borsa   ,, Collier (Jer.)
,, Boston . . .   ,, Collier (J. P.)
,, Brathwaite   ,, Comedian . . .
,, Brayley   ,, Comenius
,, Brereton   ,, Companion . . .
,, Bridges   ,, Comparison . . .
,, British . . .   ,, Conduct . . .
,, Broadbent   ,, Considerations . .
,, Brownsmith   ,, Contemporary . .
,, Bruce   ,, Cook

Stage, theatre, and drama—

See Roberts
,, Robertson
,, Robson
,, Romney
,, Ross
,, Rothschild
,, Rowe
,, Russell
,, Ryan
,, Ryder
,, Rymer
,, S—— (L.)
,, Saint-Evremond
,, Saints
,, Sala
,, Salvianus
,, Scarron
,, Schelling
,, Schlegel
,, Scott (C. W.)
,, Scott (E. J. L.)
,, Scott (*Sir* W.)
,, Select . . .
,, Selection
,, Serious . . .
,, Settle
,, *Sh*—] Hudson
,, *Sh*—] Law
,, *Sh*—] Sh— me-
   morial
,, *Sh*—] Shake-
   speareana
,, *Sh*—] Skottowe
,, *Sh*—] Tegg
,, *Sh*—] White
,, Sharpe
,, Shaw
,, Sheridan
,, Simpson (R.)
,, Simpson (W. S.)
,, Smith
,, Soldene
,, Sothern
,, Sparrow
,, Speech . . .
,, Stirling
,, Stopes

See Stratford
,, Styles
,, Symonds
,, Symons
,, Tallis
,, Tarlton
,, Taylor
,, Tegg
,, Theatre
,, Theatrical . . .
,, Thespian . . .
,, Thoms
,, Thomson
,, Tom King
,, Tomlins
,, Topsell
,, Tyson
,, Vandenhoff
,, Victor
,, W—— (E. N.)
,, Waldron
,, Walker
,, Wallace
,, Waller
,, Ward
,, Watt
,, Weaver
,, Webster . . .
,, Wemyss
,, Whyte
,, Wigston
,, Wilde
,, Wilkinson
,, Wilks
,, Williams
,, Willis
,, Wilson (H. S.)
,, Wilson (W.)
,, Wingate
,, Winston
,, Winter
,, Wiss
,, Woffington
,, Woodward
,, Woolf
,, Wyndham
,, Young

Stage year book . . . Edited by L. Carson.
Ln : Carson . . . 1908-10. 3 vols. Cr. 8°.
[In progress]   BM | BLO | CTC
Stalker (C.) *Publisher*. *See* Sh— Works, 1790
Stalling (G.) *Oldenburg Publisher*. *See* Sh—
Romeo . . . 1859
Standfast (W. G.) *Artist*. *See* Sh— Poems,
1846
Stanesby (Samuel) Sh—'s household words.
See Sh— Works : Ext. 1859, 1862, 1864,
1875

Stanesby (Samuel) *Artist*. *See* Lewis
Stanford (J. F.) *Editor*. *See* Sh— Merry
wives, 1886
Stanford (W. B.) English verses. *See* Sh—
Works : Ext. 1875
Stanhope (Hugh) *Editor*. *See* Greene (R.)
Stanley (S. S.) Church bells of antiquity. *See*
Memorials . . .
Notes on Warwickshire mints. *See* Memo-
rials . . .
Stanley (*Sir* Thomas). *See* Sh— Epitaph
Stansby (Wm.) *Printer*—
See Bodenham
,, Sh— Hamlet, 1607, 1636
,, Topsell
,, Willobie
Stapfer (Paul) Sh— and classical antiquity.
Translated . . . by Emily J. Carey. Ln :
Kegan Paul, 1880. Cr. 8°, pp. x.-484
                    BM | BPL | BUS | MPL | SML
Star chamber. *See* Hayward
Starkey (John) *Publisher*. *See* Wilson (John)
Stationers.] Extracts from the registers of the
Stationers' Company . . . between 1557
and 1587. With notes . . . by J. P. Collier.
See Sh—] Sh— Soc.
] Transcript of the registers of the stationers
of London, 1554-1640. Edited by Ed-
ward Arber. Ln : Printed for subscribers,
1875-94. 5 vols. 4°   BM
Limited issue. In this may be found the original pub-
lication entries of most of Sh—'s works, and notes of
their transfer to fresh owners.
See Hopton
,, More
Staunton (Howard) Memorials of Sh—. *See*
Sh—] Staunton
Staunton (H.) *Editor*—
See Sh— Much ado . . . 1864, 1865
,, Sh— Sonnets, 1862, 1863
,, Sh— Will . . . 1864
,, Sh— Works, 1858-60, 1858-61, 1860,
1862-64, 1863, 1864, 1865, 1865-67,
1866, 1869, 1875, 1879, 1881-82,
1882, 1884-89, 1890, 1891, 1894,
1897, 1899
See also Ingleby
Stearns (Charles Woodward) Sh— treasury of
wisdom and knowledge. *See* Sh— Works :
Ext. 1869
Sh—'s medical knowledge. New York :
Appleton . . . 1865. 12°, pp. 78 BPL | BUS
Stebbing (*Dr.* Henry) Arguments of such of
the plays of Sh— as are not founded on
historic facts. With casual observations
on some of the characters. Manuscript.
[c. 1795.] 4°, pp. 100   BUS
Stebbing (*Dr.* H.) *Editor*. *See* Sh— Works,
1845-51, 1850, 1851

Steel (C. F.)] Is there any resemblance between Sh— and Bacon ? Ln : Field &
Tuer, 1888. 8°, pp. 302

BM | BUS | MPL | SML

Steel (James) *Whitehaven Publisher.* See Sh—
Sonnets, 1822

Steele (*Sir* Richard) Essay on Ravenscroft's
' The London cuckolds ' [In ' The Tatler,'
No. 8, 28 April, 1709]

'The play of the "London cuckolds" was acted this
evening before a suitable audience, who were extremely well diverted with that heap of vice and
absurdity ... The amendment of these low gratifica-
tions is only to be made by people of condition, by
encouraging the presentation of the noble characters
drawn by Sh— and others, from whence it is impossible to return without strong impressions of
honour and humanity. On these occasions distress is
laid before us with all its causes and consequences,
and our resentment placed according to the merit of
the persons afflicted. Were dramas of this nature
more acceptable to the taste of the town, men who
have genius would bend their studies to excel in them.'

Extracts. *See* Sh— Works : Ext. 1822

] The tatler. Ln : . . . 1709-11

Issued in 289 numbers. Nos. 8, 41, and 167 contain
references to Sh—.

Steer (W. C.) Ballad of Anne Hathaway.
1858. Manuscript. 12° BPL

Steevens (George). Catalogue of Capell's
Shakespeareana. *See* Capell

Holograph letter on a new edition of Sh—,
3 Dec., 1772. *See Sh*—] Collection

] Letter from George Peele to Christopher
Marlowe [In 'Annual Register,' p. 107].
Ln : 1770. 8°

Reprinted in ' The drama,' 1822, vol. ii., p. 87.
The second attempt in the lengthy series of Shake-
spearean forgeries. Steevens was imitated by the
Irelands, Jordan, Collier, Cunningham, and others.
The letter is as follows :—

'Friend Marlo,—I must desyre that my syster hyr
watche and the cookerie book you promysed may be
sent bye the man. I never longed for thy company
more than last night. We were all very merry at the
Globe, when Ned Alleyn did not scruple to affyrme
plesauntely to thy friende Will that he had stolen his
speeche about the qualityes of an actor's excellencye
in "Hamlet" hys trajedye from conversations many-
fold which had passed between them and opinyons
given by Alleyn touchinge the subjecte.

'Shakespeare did not take this talke in good sorte
but Jonson put an end to the strife, with wittylye
remarkinge :—" This affaire needeth no contentione ;
you stole it from Ned, no doubte ; do not marvel ;
have you not seen him act tymes out of number ?"
Believe me most syncerilie, yours,—G. Peel.'

Such a document would hardly deceive an amateur
to-day.

Library. *See* Catalogue, 1800

Manuscript annotations. *See* Sh— Works,
1793

Manuscript collections. *See Sh*—] Steevens

On the early quarto editions of Sh—'s plays
[being the introduction to 'Twenty of the
plays of Sh—']. Ln : J. & R. Tonson . . .
1766. 8° W

Steevens (George)] Proposals . . . for the publication of two plates . . . [Felton por-
trait] by 'W. Richardson' [*i.e.* Geo.
Steevens]. Ln : Privately printed [1794].
8°, pp. 16 BPL | BUS

Sh—. *See Sh*—[Steevens

To the public : Proposals for publishing an
edition of Sh—'s plays. Ln : Feb. 1, 1766.
F°, pp. 4 BUS | W

Garrick intended to contribute to this venture.

Steevens (G.) *Editor*—

See Sh— All's well . . . 1786

 ,, Sh— Antony . . . 1792 *et seq.*

 ,, Sh— As you like it, 1785, 1802

 ,, Sh— Comedy . . . 1785

 ,, Sh— Coriolanus, 1818

 ,, Sh— Cymbeline, 1802

 ,, Sh— Hamlet, 1766, 1785, 1806, 1810

 ,, Sh— Julius Cæsar, 1777, 1800, 1803, 1807

 ,, Sh— King Henry IV., i., 1766, 1785, 1818

 ,, Sh— King Henry IV., ii., 1766, 1785,
    1807, 1813

 ,, Sh— King Henry V., 1766, 1785, 1822

 ,, Sh— King Henry VI., i., 1786, 1813

 ,, Sh— King Henry VI., ii., 1786, 1813

 ,, Sh— King Henry VI., iii., 1786, 1818

 ,, Sh— Hing Henry VIII., 1809

 ,, Sh— King John, 1766, 1811

 ,, Sh— King Lear, 1766, 1785, 1822

 ,, Sh— King Richard II., 1766, 1786, 1812,
    1822

 ,, Sh— King Richard III., 1766, 1812

 ,, Sh— Love's labours lost, 1766, 1785,
    1788, 1822

 ,, Sh— Macbeth, 1778, 1788, 1806, 1807

 ,, Sh— Measure . . . 1785, 1806, 1820

 ,, Sh— Merchant . . . 1766, 1785, 1811,
    1822, 1830

 ,, Sh— Merry wives, 1766, 1806

 ,, Sh— Midsummer . . . 1766, 1785, 1806,
    1822

 ,, Sh— Much ado . . . 1766, 1818

 ,, Sh— Othello, 1766, 1785, 1788, 1802

 ,, Sh— Romeo . . . 1766, 1806, 1840

 ,, Sh— Sonnets, 1609

 ,, Sh— Taming . . . 1766, 1785, 1812

 ,, Sh— The tempest, 1806, 1833

 ,, Sh— Timon . . . 1785, 1788, 1820

 ,, Sh— Titus . . . 1766, 1785, 1809

 ,, Sh— Troilus . . . 1766, 1811

 ,, Sh— Twelfth night, 1803

 ,, Sh— Two gentlemen . . . 1786, 1812

 ,, Sh— Winter's tale, 1799, 1820

 ,, Sh— Works, 1766, 1773, 1778, 1780,
    1785, 1785-87, 1786-88, 1791-1802,
    1792, 1793, 1797, 1798, 1799-1802,
    1802, 1803, 1804-13, 1805, 1805-09,
    1807, 1809, 1810-12, 1811, 1813,
    1814, 1817, 1817-18, 1819, 1820-21,
    1821, 1822, 1823, 1824, 1824-26,
    1825, 1826, 1827, 1828, 1829, 1830,

G. STEEVENS.

See p. 644

1830-40, 1831, 1832, 1833, 1834,
1835, 1835-36, 1836, 1837, 1838,
1839, 1840, 1841, 1842, 1843, 1845,
1846, 1847, 1848, 1849, 1850, 1851,
1851-52, 1852, 1852-59, 1853, 1854,
1855, 1856, 1857, 1858, 1859, 1860,
1861, 1862, 1863, 1864, 1866, 1868,
1880, 1881, 1882, 1885, 1886, 1887,
1888-89, 1890, 1897

Steevens (G.)—
  See Annotations   *See* Oulton
  ,, Boaden   ,, Ritson
  ,, Etymologist   ,, Sh—Measure . . .
  ,, Johnson & Steevens   1700
  ,, Lodge   ,, Smith (H. & J.)
  ,, Mason   ,, Waldron
  ,, Middleton

Stefansson (J.) Sh— at Elsinore [In 'Con-
temporary Review']. 1896. 8°   BM | BPL
Illustrates 'Hamlet.'

'Stendhal' (M. de) *pseud. of* M. H. Beyle.
Racine and Sh—: A review [In 'Magazine of foreign literature,' pp. 197-203].
1823. 8°   BPL

Stephanoff (F. P.) *Artist*—
  See Sh— Works, 1821-29, 1829, 1836
  ,, Sh— Works : Ext. 1841

Stephen *or* Estienne (Henry) World of wonders
. . . Translated by R. C—— [Richard
Carew ?] Ln : John Norton . . . 1607.
F°
'The phraseology of Sh— is better illustrated by this
book than any other.'—*Beloe.*
Also referred to by Wm. Hazlitt and Caldecott.

  World of wonders . . . Trans. out of the
French . . . by R. C—— [Richard Carew ?]
Edinburgh : Imprinted by Andrew Hart
& Richard Lawson, 1608. F°
See also Estienne

Stephen (*Sir* Leslie) Sh— as a man. *See Sh*—]
Stephen

Stephen (*Sir* Leslie) *Editor. See Sh*—] Dictionary

Stephens (G.) Macbeth, Earl Siward and
Dundee. 1876. 4°   BPL
  Sh— story teller. *See* Sh— Works : Ext.
1865-66
  The patriot : A tragedy. 1849. 8°   BPL
Sh— pp. viii.-xii.

Stephens (G.) *Editor. See* Sh— The tempest,
1836

Stephens (Henry L.) Illustrations of the poets
. . . Philadelphia : S. Robinson, 1849.
16°, pp. 32   BUS
Comic sketches, many illustrating passages in Sh—.

Stephens (J.) Satyrical essayes and characters
. . . Ln : N. Okes . . . 1615. 12°
The character of a 'Worthy poet' is supposed to be a
sketch of Sh—.

Stephens (P.) *Publisher. See* Willis

Stephenson *of Indiana* (Henry Thew) Eliza-
bethan people. Ln : Bell . . . 1910.
Illustrated
Reviewed in 'The Athenæum,' 16th April, 1910, p. 454.
  Sh—'s London ; with maps, plans, and
illustrations of the well-known topo-
graphical landmarks of Sh—'s day. Ln :
Constable . . . 1905. 8°   BPL
With illustrations reproduced from contemporary books.
The title already belonged to T. F. Ordish in 1897 (*q.v.*)

Stephenson (H. W.) The fickle wheel : A tale
of Elizabethan London. Indianapolis . . .
1901. Cr. 8°   BPL

Sterling (John) Poems . . . Ln : Moxon . . .
1839. 12°
At p. 151 are verses headed 'Sh—' which run :—
  ' How little fades from earth when sink to rest
  The hours and cares that moved a great man's breast !
  Though nought of all we saw the grave may spare,
  His life pervades the world's impregnate air.

      .   .   .   .   .

  Above the goodly land more his than ours
  He sits supreme, enthroned in skyey towers,
  And sees the heroic brood of his creation
  Teach larger life to his ennobled nation.
  O ! shaping brain ! O ! flashing fancy's hues ;
  O ! boundless heart, kept fresh by pity's dews ;
  O ! wit humane and blythe ! O ! sense sublime
  For each dim oracle of mantled time !
  Transcendent form of man ! in whom we read
  Mankind's whole tale of impulse, thought, and deed,
  Amid the expanse of years beholding thee,
  We know how vast our world of life may be
  Wherein, perchance, with aims as pure as thine,
  Small tasks and strengths may be no less divine.'

Sterling (Sarah Hawks) Sh—'s sweetheart [a
novel]. Illust. by Clara Cleone Peak.
Philadelphia & Ln : . . . 1905. 8°, pp.
282. With 6 coloured plates   BPL
The title already belonged to Dr. Furnivall in 1890.

  Sh—'s sweetheart. Ln : Port Pub. Co.,
1907. 8°

Sterne (L.) Beauties. *See* Sh— Works : Ext.
1819

Sterne.] Sterne and his sentimentalism
[Magazine article, c. 1855]. 8°   w
Contains Sh— references.

Stevens (George Alexander)] Distress upon
distress, or tragedy in true taste. A
heroi - comi - parodi - tragedi - farcical
burlesque in two acts . . . With all the
similies, rants, groans, sighs, etc. entirely
new. With annotations, dissertations,
explanations, observations, emendations,
quotations, restorations, etc., by Sir
Henry Humm, and notes critical, classical, and historical by Paulus Purgantius
Pedasculus, who has carefully revised,
corrected, and amended it ; expunged the
several errors and interpolations ; reconciled the various readings, and restored
the author to himself. Ln : Reprinted
from the Dublin edition for R. Griffiths
in St. Paul's Churchyard, 1752. 8°, pp.
100

An amusing satire on Sir Thomas Hanmer and pretentious Warburton.
The 'genealogy of the author' is in the author's wittiest vein.

Stevens (George Alexander) Songs, comic and satirical ... 1801. 12°. With engravings
With numerous Shakespearean references. For instance, on page 17 occurs :—
'As to Sh— or Purcell, why, you may allow
They were well enough once, but they will not do now.'

Stevens (R. I. S.) *Composer.* *See* Sh— Poems, 1862

Stevenson (*Sir* J.) *Composer*—
See Sh— Comedy of errors, 1819
,, Sh— Poems, 1862

Stewart. Metrical history of Scotland. *See* Stopes

Stewart (Helen Hinton) Supernatural in Sh—. Ln : J. Ouseley, 1908. 8°, pp. 164 BPL

Stewart (James) Plocacosmos, or whole art of hair dressing. Ln : Privately printed, 1782. Roy. 8°. With plates
The frontispiece in red depicts Sh—'s 'Seven ages.'

Stirling (Edward) Old Drury lane : Fifty years' recollection of author, actor, and manager. Ln : Chatto ... 1881. 2 vols. Cr. 8° BPL | SML
Contains an amusing anecdote of Stratford, vol. i., pp. 205-208.

Stirling & Kennedy *Edinburgh Publishers*—
See Sh— Much ado ... 1829
,, Sh— Twelfth night, 1829

Stirrop (Thomas) *Stationers' warden.* *See* Sh— Venus ... (*heading*)

Stobart (J. C.) Sh— epoch, 1600-25. *See* Sh— Works : Ext. 1906

Stockdale (John) *Publisher*—
See Sh— Works, 1784, 1790, 1807, 1811
,, Sh— Works : Ext. 1790

Stockdale (J. J.) *Publisher.* *See* Sh— Othello, 1813

Stockmar (*Baron*). *See* Martin

Stockton-on-Tees jubilee. *See* Sh— Works : Ext. 1781

Stockton-on-Tees Shaksperian Society : Annual commemoration supper programmes. 1903. Cr. 8° BPL

Stockwell (N.) *Editor.* *See* Sh— King Richard II., 1904

Stoddard (Richard Henry) Sh— portraits [In 'Aldine']. New York ... 1872. 8° BUS

Stoddard (R. H.) *Editor.* *See* Sh— Romeo ... 1892

Stoddard (R. H.) *See* Linton & Stoddard

Stoffel (C.) *Editor.* *See* Sh— Romeo ... 1869

Stoffel (C.) *See* Sh—] Van Dam & Stoffel

Stoker (Bram) Personal reminiscences ... *See* Irving (*Sir* J. H. B.)

Stokes (F. A.) Sh— calendar. *See* Sh— Works : Ext. 1887

Stokes (Henry Paine) Attempt to determine the chronological order of Sh—'s plays. Harness essay. Ln : Macmillan, 1878. 8°, pp. xvi.-220 BM | BPL | BUS | MPL | SML

Sh— and his contemporaries [In 'The Athenæum,' No. 3,551, p. 690, Nov.] 1895. 4°

Stokes (H. P.) *Editor.* *See* Sh— Troilus ... 1886

Stokes (H. P.) *See* Fleay, On certain ...

Stone (G. W.) *Editor.* *See* Sh— The tempest, 1899, 1900

Stone (W. C.) *Editor.* *See* Greenhill

Stone (W. G.) *Editor.* *See* Sh— King Henry V., 1880

Stone (W. G. Boswell). *See* Boswell-Stone

Stonehouse (James) Characters of ' Macbeth ' and ' King Richard III.' . . . compared [In ' Lancs. & Ches. Hist. Soc. Trans., Vol. 9]. Ln : Parker ... 1851. 8° BUS | SML

Stopes (*Mrs.* Charlotte Carmichael) 'Adolescens' and 'Adolocentula' in Stratford-on-Avon register, in relation to Gilbert Sh— [In 'Archiv für das studium der neueren sprachen und literaturen,' band CXXIII., pp. 159-161]. Braunschweig ... 1909. 8°
Tends to show that the natural explanation of the omission of Gilbert Sh—'s name in the poet's will is that he died on or about Feb. 1st, 1611-12.

Anne Hathaway's kindred [In ' The Athenæum,' No. 4,027, p. 904, 31st Dec., 1904]. 4° BM | BPL

Ardens of Park Hall [In 'Genealogical Magazine,' 1898]. 4°

Authorship of the ' Newe court of Venus ' [In ' The Athenæum,' No. 3,740, p. 38, 1st July, 1899]. 4° BM | BPL

Bacon-Sh— question. Ln : T. G. Johnson ... 1888. 8°, pp. xii.-150 BM | BUS | SML

Bacon-Sh— question answered. Second edition. Ln : Trübner ... 1889. 8°, pp. 266 BM | BPL | BUS | SML
'With this book the whole question is closed.'—*Prof. Leo.*

Bell-ringer's notes on the history of St. Margaret's, Westminster [In ' The Athenæum,' No. 3,586, p. 106, 18 July, 1896]. 4° BM | BPL

Burbage's theatre [In ' Fortnightly Review,' edited by W. L. Courtney, p. 148, July, 1909]. Roy. 8°
On James Burbage, the first English playhouse builder, and 'The Theatre' playhouse. *See also* article on 'The Burbages,' by same writer, a page or two further.

Captain Cox's book of fortune [In ' The Athenæum,' No. 3,786, p. 625, 19 May, 1900]. 4° BM | BPL

City marching watch in 1854. *See* Harrison (Wm.) England ... Vol. 4

Yours sincerely
Charlotte C. Stopes.

See p. 646

Stopes (*Mrs.* Charlotte Carmichael) Date of Sh—'s sonnets [In ' The Athenæum,' No. 3,673, p. 374, and No. 3,674, p. 405, 19-26 March, 1898 .   4°   BM | BPL

Description of England in Sh—'s youth. *See* Harrison

Dr. Frederick James Furnivall: An obituary. *See* Furnivall

Earliest official record of Sh—'s name [In ' Sh— Jahr-buch,' Vol. 32. Weimar, 1896].   8°   BM | BPL

Early Piccadilly [In ' The Athenæum,' No. 3,848, p. 125, 27 July, 1901]. 4° BM | BPL

Edward Arden of Park Hall [In ' The Athenæum,' No. 3,563, p. 190, 8 Feb., 1896].   4°   BM | BPL

Elizabethan lawsuit :—The Rose and the Swan [theatres], 1597 [In ' The Stage,' 6 Jan., 1910].   F°   BM

Elizabethan stage scenery [In ' Fortnightly Review,' June, 1907]. Roy. 8° BM | BPL

Friends in Sh—'s ' Sonnets ' [Reprinted from the Royal Society of Literature : Transactions]. 1908. 8°, pp. 36 [including printed wrappers]

Giles and Christopher Alleyn of Holywell [In ' Notes & Queries,' 10 S. xii., pp. 341-343, Oct., 1909]. Fcp. 4°   BM | BPL

The Alleyn family were the ground landlords of and closely concerned in 'The Theatre,' re-named 'The Globe,' after its removal, in which Sh—'s company performed.

Gleanings from Saint Clements Danes [In ' The Athenæum,' No. 4,111, p. 159, 11 Aug., 1906].   4°   BM | BPL

Guildenstern [In ' The Athenæum,' No. 3,439, p. 418, 23 Sept., 1893]. 4°

Illustrates ' Hamlet.'   BM | BPL

' Hamlet ' and ' Macbeth ' : An intended contrast [In ' The Athenæum,' No. 3,995, p. 666, 21 May, 1904]. 4° BM | BPL

Henry Sh—'s death [In ' The Athenæum,' No. 4,308, pp. 608-609, 21 May, 1910]. 4°   BM | BPL

Remarks :—' We know little of any of the poet's relatives, but from what we do know none of them touches our imagination so keenly as does his uncle, Henry Sh— of Snitterfield.'

Henry the seventh's almshouse, Westminster [In ' The Athenæum,' No. 4,079, 30 Dec., 1905].   4°   BM | BPL

' Honorificabilitudinitatibus ' in Warwickshire : Pillerton registers [In ' The Athenæum,' No. 4,221, p. 334, 19 Sept., 1908].   4°   BM | BPL

Illustrates ' Love's labours lost.'

Interlude or comedie of Jacob and Esau [In ' The Athenæum,' No. 3,783, p. 538, April, 1900].   4°   BM | BPL

A drama supposed to be written by Wm. Hunnis.

Stopes (*Mrs.* Charlotte Carmichael) Italian and English books of fortune [In ' The Athenæum,' No. 3,800, p. 249, 25 Aug., 1900].   4°   BM | LBP

Jane, the queen's tool [In ' The Athenæum,' No. 4,059, p. 209, 12 Aug., 1905]. 4°
                                        BM | BPL

John Sh— of Ingon and Gilbert of Saint Brides [In ' The Athenæum,' No. 3,818, p. 867, 29 Dec., 1900]. 4° BM | BPL | BUS

Lampoon on the oppo ents of Essex, 1601. With notes [In ' Sh— Jahrbuch ']. Berlin . . . April, 1910.   8°, pp. 12, including printed wrappers

Literary expenses in St. Margaret's, Westminster [In ' The Athenæum,' No. 3,633, p. 777, 12th June, 1897]. 4° BM | BPL

Locks and weirs on the Thames in Sh—'s time [In ' The Field.' Ln : . . . 9 Feb., 1895].   F°

London Shakespeares [A reply to F. S. Snell (*q.v.*), in ' The Athenæum,' No. 4,316, 16 July, 1910]. 4°   BM | BPL

London Shakespeares about the poet's time [In ' The Athenæum,' No. 3,790, p. 763, 16th June, 1900]. 4°   BM | BPL

Mary Arden's arms [In ' The Athenæum,' No. 3,537, p. 202, 10 Aug., 1895]. 4°
                                        BM | BPL

Mary's Chapel Royal and her coronation play [In ' The Athenæum,' No. 4,063, p. 346, 9th Sept., 1905]. 4°   BM | BPL

Metrical psalms and the 'Court of Venus' [In ' The Athenæum,' No. 3,739, p. 784, 24th June, 1899]. 4°   BM | BPL

Mr. Shaksper, one book [In ' The Athenæum,' No. 4,239, p. 104, 23 Jan., 1909]. 4°   BM | BPL

Mr. Sh—, about my lorde's impresa [In ' The Athenæum,' No. 4,203, p. 604, 16th May, 1908].   4°   BM | BPL

Mr. W. H—— [thought to be Sir Wm. Harvey], [In ' The Athenæum,' No. 3,797, p. 154, 4 Aug., 1900]. 4° BM | BPL

Mrs. Shaxspere in the law courts [In ' The Athenæum,' No. 4,242, p. 199, 13th Feb., 1909]   BM | BPL

Other William Shakespeares [In ' The Athenæum,' No. 4,112, p. 188; No. 4,113, p. 214; 18th/25th Aug., 1906]. 4°
                                        BM | BPL

Overseers of the poor, St. Margaret's, Westminster [In ' The Athenæum,' p. 148, 3 Feb., 1894]. 4°   BM | BPL

' Paradise of daynty deuises ' (by Richard Edwards *q.v.* and others) [In ' The Athenæum,' No. 3,747, p. 256, 19th Aug., 1899].   4°   BM | BPL

Stopes (*Mrs.* Charlotte Carmichael) Pre-Shakespearean London Shakespeares [In ' The Athenæum,' No. 3,365, p. 543, 23rd April, 1892]. 4°   BM | BPL

Quarrel between the Earl of Southampton and Lord Grey of Wilton [In ' The Athenæum,' No. 4,020, p. 658, and No. 4,021, p. 695, 12th / 19th Nov., 1904]. 4°   BM | BPL

Representation of Sh—. *See* Dowden

Richard Watts, curate of Stratford-on-Avon [In ' Stratford Herald,' 19th Aug., 1910]   SML

Roll of Coventry. Arrest of Prince Henry [In ' The Athenæum,' No. 4,328, pp. 420-421, and No. 4,331, pp. 520-521, 8-29 Oct.] Ln: 1910. 4°   BM | BPL
Describes a small manuscript roll at the Birmingham Public Library containing a list of the bailiffs or mayors of that city, with brief historical notes, for three centuries, 1352-1650.
Illustrates ' King Henry IV.' and ' King Henry V.'
In 1512-13 the roll notes that King Henry VIII. and Queen Katherine visited Coventry, lodging at the Priory. Two pageants and a stage play were presented in their honour.
For reply *see* Stronach, *also* Ramsay (*Sir* W.)

Scottish and English Macbeth [In Royal Soc. of Literature : Proceedings, 24 Feb., 1897]. F°   BM | BPL

Sh— and Gray's Inn revels, 1594 [In ' The Athenæum,' No. 3,992, p. 570, 30th April, 1904]. 4°   BM | BPL
For further matter on this subject see ' The Times,' 13th Dec., 1895.

' Sh— of the court ': Roger, Thomas, John, William [In ' The Athenæum,' No. 4,298, pp. 319-320, 12 March, 1910]. 4°   BM | BPL
Points out that Sh— was a court official as groom of the privy chamber. Gives details of Roger Sh—, yeoman of the chamber to Edward VI. ; Thomas Sh—, royal messenger, 1572-77 ; John Sh—, royal bitmaker.

Sh—'s aunts and the Snitterfield property [In ' The Athenæum,' No. 4,265, pp. 95-97, and No. 4,268, pp. 181-183, July-Aug., 1909]. 4°   BM | BPL

Sh—'s bust at Stratford ; its restoration in 1748 [In ' Pall Mall Gazette,' 18 Nov. and 25 Nov., 1910]. F°   BM
Points out the difference between the present monument, altered in 1748, and the original one, engraved in Dugdale's Warwickshire, 1656, and explains why the ' restoration' was carried out. The information is gleaned from manuscripts (in the Wheler collection at the Birthplace) by Joseph Greene, headmaster of the Stratford grammar school.

Sh—'s family [In 'Genealogical Magazine,' Vol. I.] Ln : 1898. 4°   BPL

Sh—'s family, being a record of the ancestors and descendants of Wm. Sh—, with some account of the Ardens. Ln : Stock . . . 1901. 8°, pp. xii.-258. Droeshout portrait and 14 plates
                    BPL | MPL | SML

Expanded from the article on same subject in ' Genealogical magazine.'
The earliest Sh— recorded herein is Geoffrey Sh— of Surrey, 1268, and the earliest Warwickshire example Thomas Sh— of Coventry, 1359.
Reviewed in ' The Athenæum,' No. 3,832, p. 426, April, 1901, which drew a reply from the authoress in No. 3,833, p. 467.

Stopes (*Mrs.* Charlotte Carmichael) Sh—'s fellows and followers : A special set of facts collected from the Lord Chamberlain's papers [From ' Jahrbuch der Deutschen Sh— gesellschaft']. Berlin, 1910. 8°, pp. 20, including printed wrappers

Sh—'s ' Macbeth ' in relation to Stewart's ' Metrical history of Scotland ' [In ' Notes & Queries,' 8th Series, Vol. XI. Ln : . , . 24 May, 1897]. Fcp. 4°   BM | BPL

Sh—'s materials for ' Macbeth ' [In ' The Athenæum,' No. 3,587, p. 138, 25 July, 1896]. 4°   BM | BPL

Sh—'s signatures [Correspondence in ' The Scotsman,' 18th Aug., 1910]   BM

' Sh—'s " Sonnets," edited by T. Tyler ' [Review in ' Sh— Jahrbuch,' Vol. 25, pp. 185-204]. Weimar . . . 1890. 8°   BM

Sh—'s Warwickshire contemporaries. Stratford-upon-Avon : G. Boyden, 1897. 8°, pp. iv.-114   BM | BPL | SML

Sh—'s Warwickshire contemporaries [with additions and corrections]. Stratford : Sh— Head Press, 1907. 8°, pp. viii.-274
                    BM | BPL | CTC | SML
Reviewed in ' The Athenæum,' 1907, No. 4,185, p. 36.
For reply see next issue, No. 4,186, 18th Jan., 1907, p. 78.

Should Sh—'s plays be acted with scenery. *See* Poel

Sir Edward Coke's widow [In ' Law Times.' Ln : . . . 1909]. 4°

Sir Thomas Lucy [In ' The Athenæum,' p. 67, 13 July, 1895]. 4°   BM | BPL

Sir Thomas Lucy not the original of ' Justice Shallow' [In ' Fortnightly Review,' Feb., 1903]. Roy. 8°   BM | BPL
Illustrates ' King Henry IV.' and the ' Merry wives.'

Sir William Somerville of Edreston [In ' The Athenæum,' No. 4,165, p. 211, 24 Aug., 1907]. 4°   BM | BPL

Sixteenth century women students [In ' Royal Society of Literature : Proceedings,' Vol. 25. Ln : . . . June, 1904]. 8°
                    BM

Spring pilgrimages to Sh—'s town [In ' Poet lore ']. Philadelphia . . . 1892. 8°
                    BPL | BUS | NY

Stratford's ' bookless neighbourhood' [In ' The Athenæum,' No. 4,139, p. 226, 23rd Feb., 1907]. 4°   BM | BPL
Gives inventory of the library of John Marshall, curate of Bishopton, near Stratford, who died in 1607.

Stopes (*Mrs.* Charlotte Carmichael) ' Taming of the shrew ' [In ' The Athenæum,' No. 3,998, p. 762, 11 June, 1904]. 4° BM | BPL

The Burbages and the transportation of ' The Theatre ' [In ' The Athenæum,' No. 4,277, pp. 470-472, 16 Oct., 1909]. 4° BM | BPL

Concerns James, Richard, and Cuthbert Burbage, Peter Street, Giles Alleyn, Sir F. Bacon, and the playhouse re-named ' The Globe.' It partly explains where Sh— learnt practical law. *See also* article by same writer on ' Burbage's theatre,' *ante.*

The theatre [In ' Archiv für das studium der neueren sprachen und literaturen, Vol. 124. 1910]. 8°, pp. 8

Says :—' It is now twenty-one years since I felt that if I wanted to understand the life and environment of Sh— I must get behind the bewildering multiplicity of books which either copy or contradict one another, and devote the rest of my working life to the study of manuscripts concerning his period.'

Thomas Edwards, author of ' Narcissus ' [In ' Fortnightly Review,' edited by W. L. Courtney. Ln : Chapman . . . 1911]. Roy. 8°

Mentions one of the earliest references to Sh—.

Thomas Witham's commonplace book [In ' The Athenæum,' No. 3,521, p. 505, 20 April, 1895]. 4° BM | BPL

True story of the Stratford bust [In ' Monthly Review,' pp. 150-159, April. Ln : 1904]. Roy. 8°. With 7 portraits

True story of the Stratford bust : A contemporary likeness of Sh—. Ln : Murray, 1904. Roy. 8°, pp. 16 (including printed wrappers) and 7 portraits
BM | BPL | CTC | MPL

Weirs on the Thames in 1584. *See* Harrison (Wm.) England . . . Vol. 4

West-end of Queen Elizabeth and King James [In ' The Athenæum,' p. 286, 31 Aug., 1901]. 4° BM | BPL

William Hunnis [In ' Sh— Jahrbuch,' Vol. 27. Weimar . . . 1892]. 8°

William Hunnis and the revels of the Chapel Royal : A study of his period and the influences which affected Sh—. Louvain : A. Uystpruyst. Leipzig : O. Harrassowitz. Ln : D. Nutt, 1910. Roy. 8°, pp. xvi.-364, including printed wrappers BM | SML

The frontispiece is Hunnis's new coat of arms, from a manuscript in the Bodleian. The volume is dedicated to ' Dr. F. J. Furnivall, comrade and inspirer of all faithful workers towards the understanding of Sh—.' Reviewed in the ' Stratford Herald,' 29th July and 12th Aug., 1910; ' Glasgow Herald,' 9th Aug., 1910; ' Scotsman,' 28th July, 1910; and in the ' Morning Post,' 22nd Dec., 1910 (by Andrew Lang).

William Hunnis the dramatist [In ' The Athenæum,' 21 Feb., 1891, p. 249; 21 March, 1891, p. 676; 31 March, 1900, p. 410. 1891-1900]. 4° BM | BPL

Stopes (*Mrs.* C. C.) *Editor—*
See Harrison
" Sh— Sonnets, 1904

Stopes (*Mrs.* C. C.) & Boyden (G.) Sh— commemoration week : Stratford letters [In ' Poet lore ']. Philadelphia, 1891. 8°
BPL | BUS | NY

Stopes (*Mrs.*) & Evans (H. A.) Sh—'s Warwickshire contemporaries : Correspondence [In ' The Athenæum,' No. 4,186, p. 78, and No. 4,187, p. 102 and p. 104, Jan., 1908]. 4° BM | BPL

Stopes (*Mrs.*) ' Lee (S.)' & Stronach (Geo.) Stratford's ' bookless neighbourhood' [In ' The Athenæum,' No. 4,139, p. 226, No. 4,140, p. 254, No. 4,141, p. 290, Feb.-March, 1907] BM | BPL

Stopes (*Mrs.* C. C.)—
See also Creighton & Stopes
" " Greenwood

Storer (H. S.) *Artist. See* Histrionic . . .

Storer (James Sargant). *See* Brewer & Storer

Storer (T.) Life of Wolsey. *See* Wolsey

Story (Wm. Wetmore) Poems . . . Ln : Blackwood, 1886. 2 vols. 12°

In vol. 2, pp. 273-274, is the sonnet headed the ' Mighty makers ' :—
' And such was Sh—, whose strong soul could climb
Steeps of sheer terror, sound the ocean grand
Of passions deep, or over fancy's strand
Trip with his fairies, keeping step and time ;
His, too, the power to laugh out full and clear
With unembittered joyance, and to move
Along the silent shadowy paths of love
As tenderly as Dante, whose austere
Stern spirit through the worlds below, above,
Unsmiling strode, to tell their tidings here.'

' Runaways eyes ' [c. 1870 ?]. 8°, manuscript, pp. 10 BUS

Suggests ' Evening's eyes may wink ' as an emendation for ' Romeo and Juliet,' act iii., sc. 2.

Stothard (Thomas) *Artist—*
See Ritson
" Sh— As you like it, 1799
" Sh— Works, 1783-86, 1798-1800, 1800, 1802, 1803, 1806, 1807, 1822-23, 1825, 1826, 1827, 1828, 1829, 1831, 1855-56, 1858
" Sh— Works : Ext. 1783-87

Stotzenburg (John Hawley) Impartial study of the Sh— title. Louisville [U.S.], 1905. 8°. With facsimiles BPL | BUS

Stourbridge Sh— commemorative banquets : Souvenirs . . . 1903. 8° BPL

Stowe (*Mrs.* Harriet Beecher) Sunny memories of foreign lands. Ln : . . . 1854. Cr. 8°
BPL | SML

Chapter on ' Stratford and Sh—,' pp. 145-164.

Stowe (John) Annales of England, faithfully collected out of the most autenticall authors. Ln : George Bishop . . . 1605. Fcp. 4°

For its Shakespearean interest see Dr. Furnivall's notes to the ' Merry wives,' New Sh— Soc., 1877-79, and Malone's notes in Steevens' ed. of Sh—'s Works, 1790, vol. iii., p. 128.

Stowe (John) Svrvay of London, contayning the originall, antiquity, increase, moderne estate and description of that citie . . . Also an apologie or defence against the opinion of some men concerning that citie, the greatnesse thereof. With an appendix containing in latin ' Libellum de situ & nobilitate Londini,' written by Wm. Fitzstephen . . . Imprinted at Ln. by Iohn Wolfe, printer to the honourable citie of Ln. and are to be sold at his shop within the Pope's head alley in Lombard Street, 1598. Fcp. 4°   BM | MRL

Survey of London. With additions by Anthony Munday. Ln : . . . 1633. F°
A volume of contemporary manuscript extracts from above, and giving an account of Sh—, was sold for £51 in Dec., 1906.

Survey of London . . . edited by William J. Thoms. Ln : Chatto . . . 1876. Roy. 8°, pp. xviii.-222. Portrait, plates, and index

Strachey (Sir Edward) Analysis of Sh—'s ' Hamlet.' Ln : J. W. Parker . . . 1849. 8°

Sh—'s Hamlet : An attempt to find the key to a great moral problem, by methodical analysis of the play. Ln : J. W. Parker . . . 1848. 8°, pp. iv.-104
          BM | BPL | BUS | CPL | MPL | W

Strachey (J. Saint Loe) New way of life. Ln : Macmillan . . . 1909. 12°, pp. viii.-144
Chap. v. (pp. 84-95) deals with ' Sh— and national service.'

Strahan (Alexander) Publisher. See Sh— Othello, 1784

Strahan (G.) Publisher. See Sh— King Richard II., 1720

Strahan (W.) Publisher—
See Noorthouck
„ Sh— Antony . . . 1776
„ Sh— Cymbeline, 1770
„ Sh— Macbeth, 1768
„ Sh— Measure . . . 1770
„ Sh— Merchant . . . 1783
„ Sh— Poems . . . 1780
„ Sh— Timon . . . 1770
„ Sh— Works, 1773, 1780

Strange fifth Earl Derby (Ferdinando Lord) Company of actors. See Sh— Faire Em, 1605, 1631

Strange (W.) Publisher—
See Sh— King John, 1837
„ Sh— Poems, 1830

Straparola. Filenio sisterna. See Sh—] Sh—'s library
A foundation of the ' Merry wives.'

Story of Merino of Portugal. See Sh—] Sh—'s library
A foundation of the ' Merry wives.'

Stratford-on-Avon.] Abstract of title to the house in Henley Street, Stratford-upon-Avon, in which Sh— was born ; drawn up by the vendor's solicitors, when the premises were about to be sold in the year 1847; the first document recited being the poet's will of 1616. [Edited by J. O. Halliwell.] Ln : T. Richards . . . 1865. Fcp. 4°, pp. 66   BM | HCL | MPL
Issue restricted to ten copies.
' The object was to prove the descent of the estate from the poet.'—J. O. H.

] Abstracts and copies of indentures respecting estates in Henley Street, Stratford-on-Avon, which illustrate the topography and history of the birthplace of Sh—. Edited by J. O. Halliwell. Ln : . . . 1866. Fcp. 4° BM | BPL | BUS | HCL | MPL
Issue restricted to ten copies.

] Account of the Stratford jubilee [In ' London Magazine,' 1769]. 8°   BPL

] Accounts of the chamberlain of the borough of Stratford-on-Avon, from 1590 to 1597, now first edited from the original manuscripts [by J. O. Halliwell]. Ln : . . . 1866. Fcp. 4°
Issue limited to ten copies.

] Act for dividing and inclosing certain common fields . . . meadows, pastures, and other . . . lands within the parish of Old Stratford . . . 1774. F°, pp. 22 BUS
Covers part of Sh—'s estate.

] Auction sale of Sh—'s house at Stratford-on-Avon . . . by George Robins . . . 1847. F°. Broadside poster   BPL | SBL

] Borough receipts and payments, 1864-65. Stratford-on-Avon . . . 1866. 8°.   BPL

] Brief account of Stratford-upon-Avon. With a . . . description . . . of the collegiate church, the mausoleum of Sh—, containing all the armorial bearings and inscriptions therein. To which is added . . . some account of . . . three eminent prelates who derive their sirnames from Stratford, the place of their nativity. Stratford : E. Walford [c. 1790]. 12°, pp. 98, and frontis.   BM | BPL | BUS | W

] Catalogue of pictures, drawings, etc. exhibited in the gallery of the Sh— Memorial. Stratford-on-Avon : G. Boyden, 1881. Cr. 8°, pp. 28, including printed wrappers   SML

] Catalogue of the exhibition of armour, arms, and heraldry, illustrative of Sh—'s histories in the ancient hall of the Guild of the Holy Cross, Stratford-upon-Avon, 25 April-14 May . . . opened by Lord Howard de Walden . . . with a lecture by Charles Foulkes . . . Stratford : E. Fox, 1910. Cr. 8°, pp. 24, including printed wrappers

Stratford - on - Avon.] Charity commission scheme for management of King Edward VI. school . . . 1901. F° BPL

] Charter of the grammar school of King Edward VI., 1553. [*Sæc. XIX.*] Manuscript transcript. Cr. 8° BPL

] Church of the Holy Trinity . . . [In Neale & Le Keux's ' Views of . . . Churches ']. Ln : . . . 1824. 4°, pp. 12, and 4 plates BUS

] Church of the Holy Trinity: American Window [In ' Church bells.' Ln : . . . 1896]. F° BPL

] Collector's duplicate of assessments for the borough, 1822-24. Stratford, 1823-24. 4° BPL

] Complete record of the festival connected with the inauguration of the theatre portion of the Sh— memorial buildings from April 23rd to May 3rd. Reprinted from the ' Stratford Herald ' . . . 1879. 4°, pp. 44, including printed wrappers
' Record it with your high and worthy deeds,
'Twas bravely done . . .'

] Corporation records : Guild accounts. Stratford : G. Boyden, 1886. 4°, pp. iv.-58, and frontispiece BPL | SML

] Description of the Sh— - Quiney house, Stratford-on-Avon . . . 1896. 12° BPL

] Extenta manerii de veteri Stratford [Extenta burgi de Stratford, 1252] 1840. F° BPL

] Extracts from ancient subsidy rolls of Stratford-upon-Avon. Edited by J. O. Halliwell . . . 1864. 8° BPL

] Extracts from the accounts of the chamberlains of Stratford-upon-Avon, 1585-1608 and 1608-1619. Selected and edited from the original manuscripts [by J. O. Halliwell]. Ln : . . . 1866-67. 2 vols. Fcp. 4° BPL
Issue limited to ten copies.

] Extracts of entries respecting Sh—, his family and connexions . . . taken from the . . . parish registers preserved in the Church of the Holy Trinity at Stratford-upon-Avon, by J. O. Halliwell . . . 1864. Fcp. 4° BM | BPL | HCL | MPL
Issue restricted to ten copies.

] Extracts.] Selected extracts from the ancient registry of the causes tried in the Court of Record in the time of Sh—, including many entries respecting the poet's family [edited by J. O. Halliwell]. Ln : 1867. 8° BPL | BUS | HCL
Issue limited to ten copies.

] Extracts taken from the vestry book of the Church of the Holy Trinity at Stratford-upon-Avon, containing entries illustrative of the history of that Church, with several notices of the Sh— family, from the original inedited manuscript by J. O. Halliwell. Ln : [Privately printed] . . . 1865. Fcp. 4° BPL | BUS | MPL
Issue limited to twenty-five copies, of which fifteen were destroyed.

Stratford-on-Avon.] Fine day at Stratford [and] another day at Stratford [In ' Fraser's Magazine ']. Ln : . . . 1844. 8° BUS

] From Stratford to London [In ' Cornhill Magazine ']. Ln : . . . 1877. 8° BUS

] Grammar school of King Edward VI. Tercentenary volume :—The sermon, by Rev. R. Morris ; History of the school, by Rev. T. R. Medwin ; Report of proceedings at the tercentenary meeting, 30 June, 1853. Stratford : E. Adams, 1853. 12° BPL | SML

] Halliwell (J. O.) Brief guide . . . *See* Halliwell

] Hoax of the Sh— birth-house and relic trade at Stratford. By a Warwickshire man [In ' Bentley's Miscellany ']. Ln : . . . 1848. 8° BPL | BUS

] Illustrated guide to Stratford-on-Avon. Ln : Ward & Lock [c. 1870]. 12° BPL

] Illustrations of Stratford . . . With notices of the town, church, Sh—'s house, life of Sh—, and account of the jubilee. Stratford : J. Ward, 1827. 8°. Vignette title and 10 lithographic plates BPL

] Illustrations of Stratford-upon-Avon as connected with Sh—. Stratford : F. & E. Ward [c. 1840]. 12° BPL

] Illustrations of Stratford . . . and the life of Sh—, from original drawings [with descriptive letterpress]. Stratford : F. & E. Ward, 1851. F°, pp. 12, and 6 full-page plates in colours BM | BPL | BUS

] Illustrations of Stratford as connected with Sh—. 1864. Cr. 8° BPL

] Illustrations of Stratford-on-Avon : A collection. [c. 1884.] F° BPL

] Levy made in July, 1697, for the relief of the poor at Stratford-upon-Avon, the earliest one yet discovered. Now first printed from the original manuscript, edited by J. O. Halliwell. Ln : . . . 1865. Fcp. 4° BPL | MPL
Issue restricted to ten copies.

] List of places of interest associated with Sh— at Stratford-on-Avon. [*Sæc. XIX.*] Fcp. 4°, pp. 8

] Little modeller, or how to make Sh—'s birthplace. Ln : H. G. Clarke [*Sæc. XIX.*] 8°. Folded sheet BUS

] London committee for the purchase of Sh—'s house. Ln : Bradbury & Evans, 1847. 8°, pp. 8. Illustrated BUS

Stratford-on-Avon.] Manuscripts belonging to the Stratford Corporation [In 'Historical Manuscripts Commission reports,' Vol. 9, part i., pp. 289-293 ... 1883]. F°
BPL

] Muster roll of able men at Stratford-on-Avon and its neighbourhood in the twenty-eighth year of King Henry VIII. Now first printed [by J. O. Halliwell]. Ln : Privately printed ... 1867. Fcp. 4°
Issue limited to ten copies. BPL | BUS | MPL

] Muster roll of the hundreds of Barlichway and Kineton. Transcribed by J. H. Bloom ... 1905. Cr. 8°
BPL

] New Place : Particulars of valuable and important freehold property at Stratford to be sold by auction by W. G. F. Bolton at the Red Horse Hotel ... on Tues., 23rd April, 1861, at half-past one p.m. precisely. W. J. Hobbes, solicitor. Stratford ... 1861. F°, pp. 2
BUS

] Notes drawn on the Avon Bank for general circulation [In 'London Society,' with one plate]. Ln : ... 1864
BUS
A humorous article on Stratford.

] Particulars of properties of the Corporation of Stratford-upon-Avon ... E. Fox ... June, 1895. 4°, pp. 20, including printed wrappers

] Particulars of Sh—'s house at Stratford-on-Avon, for sale by auction by Mr. Robins at the mart, London, on Thursday, September 16th, 1847, at 12 o'clock [with plan]. Ln : ... 1847. Roy. 4°, pp. 16. Illust.
BM | BPL | BUS | MPL | SBL | SML | W
'Both houses,' writes Sidney Lee, 'were purchased in behalf of subscribers to a public fund in 1846 [*sic*], and after extensive restoration were converted into a single domicile for the purposes of a public museum.' Funds were collected by means of public lectures for the purchase. Charles Dickens helped considerably by lecturing in Liverpool and elsewhere.

] Picture postcards of Stratford and Shottery : Collection. 1905. 12°
BPL

] Preservation of Sh—'s tomb and monument : List of donations, etc. Stratford-on-Avon ... 1835. F°
BPL

] Proposed national monument to Sh— at Stratford, initiated by Dr. Wade [In 'Gentleman's Magazine,' part i., pp. 545-6, part ii., p. 263]. Ln : ... 1830. 8°

] Public library controversy : Collection of newspaper cuttings. 1903-04. F° BPL

] Public library reports, 1906-07. 8° BPL

] Register of the Gild of the Holy Cross ... Stratford-on-Avon. Edited by J. H. Bloom. Ln : Phillimore ... 1907. 8°
BPL | SML

Stratford-on-Avon.] Registers of Stratford-on-Avon : Baptisms, 1558-1652 ; Marriages, 1558-1812. Transcribed by Richard Savage. Ln : Parish Register Society, 1897. 8° BPL | SBL | SML

] Registers of Stratford, transcribed by R. Savage. Burials, 1558-1623. Ln : Parish Register Society, 1897-1905. 3 vols. 8°
BPL

] Royal Sh— Club, established at the Falcon Inn ... April 23, 1824. Certificate of membership. F°. Broadside on parchment
BUS

] Second commemorative festival under the auspices of the Stratford Sh— Club [In 'Gentleman's Magazine,' pt. i., pp. 457-8]. Ln : ... 1830. 8°

] Second commemorative festival at Stratford-upon-Avon in honour of the natal day of Sh— ... Stratford-upon-Avon ... 1830. 4°, pp. 2
BM
Broadside programme of the pageant by S. Gwinnett, secretary.

] Sh— Club papers [Privately reprinted from the 'Stratford Herald,' 1903]. Cr. 8°
BPL

] Sh— Club rules. Stratford-on-Avon ... 1904. Cr. 8°, pp. 8

] Sh— Club rules. Stratford-on-Avon ... 1905. Cr. 8°, pp. 8

] Sh— Club : Sh— festival celebrations, Stratford-upon-Avon, April 22 to May 11, 1907. Official programme. Stratford : E. Fox, 1907. Cr. 8°, pp. 24

] Sh— festival celebrations : Official programme, 22 April to 14 May, 1910. Cr. 8°, pp. 40, including printed wrappers

] Sh— Hotel, Stratford-upon-Avon : [Prospectus of] this valuable freehold family and commercial hotel ... comprising about 3,452 square yards, with a frontage of 113 feet to the main street and adjoining the town hall. To be sold by auction on the premises on Wednes. the 21st Sept., 1910, by Hutchings & Deer. F°, pp. 16, including printed wrappers. With two folded coloured ground plans and six photogravure plates
'It was originally a manor house, but for the last two hundred years has been an hotel, and in the hands of the late Mr. Justins and his family for the last forty years ... One of the finest specimens of half-timbered houses in the town.'—*Preface.*

] Sh— memorial ; catalogue of pictures, drawings, etc. exhibited in 1881. Stratford : G. Boyden, 1881. 12° BPL | SML

] Sh— memorial : Illustrated catalogue of the pictures, etc. With historical and descriptive notes [by W. S. Brassington]. Stratford : Memorial Association, 1896. Fcp. 4°, pp. 94. With engravings SML

Stratford-on-Avon.] Sh— memorial: Illustrated catalogue of pictures, etc. [by W. S. Brassington]. Stratford: Memorial Association, 1898. Fcp. 4°, pp. 90. With engravings SML

] Sh— memorial: Illustrated catalogue of the pictures . . . [by W. S. Brassington]. Stratford: Memorial Association, 1901. Fcp. 4°, pp. 94. Illustrated SML

] Sh— memorial: Laying the first stone [In 'Leamington . . . Chronicle,' 28 April . . . 1877]. F° BUS

] Sh— memorial: Librarian's annual report. Stratford-on-Avon: J. Morgan, 1888-1909. 12 parts. 8°. [In progress] BM | BPL | BUS | SML

] Sh— memorial library. Interesting and important donation from the Indian Government [List of translations of works of Sh— into the languages of India]. Stratford-on-Avon, 1890. F°, single sheet BM

] Sh— memorial: Original Shakespearian rhyming address by Edward Compton. Spoken by him on his benefit . . . 1881. 8° BPL

] Sh— memorial: Play bills, posters, and programmes . . . 1883. F° BPL

] Sh— memorial: Stratford festival club. Catalogue of paintings by E. Grubb and others. 1902. *See* Brassington

] Sh— memorial. *See also* Wall (A. H.)

] Sh— tercentenary celebration at Stratford . . . 1864 [Collection containing newspaper cuttings, official programme, sermons of Archbishop Trench and Bishop Wordsworth at Holy Trinity Church, together with other printed matter. Mounted into one volume. 1864]. Roy. f° W

] Sh—'s birthplace [its income, obligations, and assessment], [In 'The Athenæum,' No. 4,054, p. 50, July, 1905]. 4° BM | BPL

] Sh—'s birthplace and adjoining properties: A plan. [c. 1880.] F° BPL | SBL

] Sh—'s birthplace and museum: Reports of annual meetings. 1869-76. F° BPL | SBL

] Sh—'s birthplace and New Place: Oil paintings on exhibition at the louvre, Stratford. Birmingham, 1899. Cr. 8° BPL

] Sh—'s birthplace. Collection of newspaper cuttings relating thereto. [Various dates.] 4° BPL

] Sh—'s birthplace committee reports. 1866-67. F° BPL | SBL

] Sh—'s birthplace, museum, and New Place trust: Annual reports, 1890-91. F° BPL | SBL

Stratford-on-Avon.] Sh—'s birthplace, museum, and New Place: Report of annual meeting, 1877, and annual reports, 1877-90. 1877-90. F° BPL | SBL

] Sh—'s birthplace trust: Bill to vest in trustees certain lands and other property in Stratford-on-Avon . . . [draft with manuscript corrections]. 1891. F° BPL

] Sh—'s birthplace trust: Bill to vest in trustees . . . [*later draft*]. 1891. F° BPL

] Sh—'s birthplace trust: Recommendations of sub-committee upon New Place. 1876. F° BPL | SBL

] Sh—'s birthplace trust act, 1891: Act to incorporate the trustees and guardians of Sh—'s birthplace and to vest in them certain lands and other property in Stratford-upon-Avon, including the property known as Sh—'s birthplace, and to provide for the maintenance in connection therewith of a library and museum, and for other purposes. 1891. F° BPL | SBL

] Sh—'s birthplace trustees: Annual meeting, 6th May. Stratford-on-Avon: 'Herald' Office, 1910. 8°, pp. 20 SBL

] Sh—'s birthplace trustees and Hornby cottages: Report of meeting, 12 Oct., 1904. Cr. 8° BPL

] Sh—'s birthplace visitors' books [from May, 1821 to Sept., 1847, containing signatures of royal, antiquarian, literary, and theatrical celebrities, with poetical inscriptions]. Stratford-on-Avon . . . 1821-47. 5 vols. 4°
The autographs include Sir W. Scott, Dickens, Ainsworth, Mendelssohn, Edmund Kean, W. C. Macready, W. Irving, Maclise. (An alphabetical index is added.) Sold in 1898 for £56.

] Short account of Stratford-on-Avon . . . Birmingham: Pumphrey brothers [c. 1878]. 12° BPL

] Six views in Stratford . . . Coventry: J. Merridew [c. 1825]. 8° BUS

] Stratford-on-Avon and Hatton railway: Collection of news cuttings. 1858-79. 4° BPL

] Stratford-on-Avon and its neighbourhood. Ln: T. Nelson [c. 1864]. 12° BPL

] Stratford-on-Avon and the approaching tercentenary. *See* Hunter

] Stratford-on-Avon and Warwick. *See* Knight

] Stratford-on-Avon as connected with Sh—. *See* Lees

] Stratford-upon-Avon Chronicle: An independent [weekly] journal . . . Stratford: John Morgan, 4 Jan., 1861 to 25 Dec., 1885. 24 vols. Atlas f°. Illustrated
John Morgan ran this organ for twenty-four years successfully, but towards the end became embarrassed financially, for on the 18th Dec., 1885 he

announced the forthcoming suspension of publication and added, 'For a long time we have been greatly hampered by the lack of adequate office accommodation and by want of modern machinery and appliances. In consequence of these hindrances we have been unable to devote more than four of our pages to local and district news and topics...' Before his death Morgan stated he lost £1,000 on the venture ultimately.

It gives a full illustrated account of the Sh— tercentenary of 1864, and a mass of other Shakespearean and Stratfordian historical matter.

Stratford-on-Avon.] Stratford-on-Avon Chronicle: Tercentenary supplement, April 23, 1864. F°   BPL

] Stratford-on-Avon commemorative festival: Programme. Stratford-on-Avon, 1830. F° broadside poster   BUS

] Stratford-on-Avon commemorative festival, under the auspices of the Stratford Sh— Club [In 'Gentleman's Magazine,' pt. i., pp. 2 and 456]. Ln: ... 1827. 8°

] Stratford-on-Avon guide. Ln: Whittaker & Co. [c. 1838]. 8°, pp. 44. Illustrated   BUS

] Stratford-on-Avon Herald [edited by Edward Adams & George Boyden]. 1860-1910. 50 vols. Atlas f°. [In progress]   BPL

A weekly newspaper containing innumerable Sh— articles. It was founded by Edward Adams in 1860 as a small four-page paper, partly printed in London. On the death of Adams it was purchased by a small Stratford syndicate, William Hutchings, Edward Downing, and Robert Lunn, in or about 1876, and was enlarged to eight pages, entirely produced in Stratford. This syndicate erected the present suite of offices and workshops, and lost about £3,000 on the venture. In 1880 the property passed to the present editor and proprietor, George Boyden, by purchase.

] Stratford jubilee: A comedy. *See* Gentleman (F.)

] Stratford jubilee. As sung by Mr. Lowe with great applause at Finch's Gardens [Ln., 1769]. F° broadside   BUS

] Stratford-on-Avon public library, 1810-20 [*afterwards the*] Sh— library, 1820-61: Accounts, catalogue of books, and list of subscribers. Stratford-on-Avon, 1810-61. F°. Original MS. on paper, 250 leaves, some blank   SML

] Stratford-upon-Avon, the home of Wm. Sh— pictorially illustrated. Ln: Rock & Payne, 1864. 8°, pp. 16 and 12 plates   BPL | BUS

] Stratford Theatrical review and stage reporter, No. I., 10 Dec. Stratford: J. Bacon, 1827. 8°, pp. 4   BUS

] Tercentenary of Sh—. Ln: Stereoscopic Co., 1864. 8°. 12 plates   BUS

] Transcripts of original letters, written in 1788, etc., chiefly upon Sh—'s mulberry tree at Stratford-on-Avon. Manuscript, on 23 leaves of paper. [1850 ?] Fcp. 4°   W

Stratford-on-Avon.] Trusteeship of Sh—'s house. [c. 1892.] 4° broadside   BPL

] Two indentures respecting 'The cage,' ... High Street, Stratford-on-Avon, inhabited by Thomas Quiney, son-in-law to Sh—, 1616-33. Now first printed from the original manuscripts, edited by J. O. Halliwell. [Ln.] 1865. 8°, pp. 22   BPL | HCL | MPL

Impression restricted to twenty-five copies; ten only preserved.

] Vestry minute book of the parish ... from 1617 to 1699. Edited by G. Arbuthnot. Ln: Bedford Press, 1899. 8° pp. iv.-158   BPL

] Views in Stratford. Ln: T. Nelson [1859]. 8°, pp. 16 and 11 plates   BUS

] Visitor's guide to Stratford-on-Avon. [c. 1885.] 12°   BPL

Stratford-on-Avon—

Sse Abercrombie	*See* Daniel
,, Adams	,, Davenant
,, Allingham	,, Davis
,, Arbuthnot	,, Deighton
,, Arne	,, Diary
,, Atkinson	,, Dibdin
,, Baker	,, Dick
,, Ball	,, Downing
,, Barnard	,, Dramatic ...
,, Beauties ...	,, 'Dramaticus'
,, Bickerstaff	,, Dugdale
,, Bird	,, East ...
,, Bloom	,, Eginton
,, Bracebridge	,, English ...
,, Brassington	,, Essay
,, Brewer	,, Evans
,, British ...	,, Evered
,, Browne	,, Extemporal ...
,, Bullen	,, Fairholt
,, Bunn	,, Fechter
,, Burrow	,, Field
,, Burrows	,, Fisher
,, Butcher	,, Fitzgerald
,, Carnegie	,, Fleay
,, Catalogue, 1797,	,, Flower
1862, 1864, 1896	,, Fowler
,, Charades	,, Fox
,, Chevalier	,, French
,, Child	,, Garrett
,, Clarke	,, Garrick
,, Clopton	,, Gentleman
,, Collection	,, Gentleman's ...
,, Collier	,, Goadby
,, Collis	,, Gray
,, Compton	,, Greene
,, Corelli	,, Griggs
,, Corner	,, Grinfield
,, Cox	,, Guide
,, Coxe	,, Hales
,, Culverwell	,, Hall

Stratford-on-Avon—

See Halliwell
,, Harlow
,, Harrison
,, Hart
,, Hawley
,, Hawthorne
,, Hewlett
,, Hill
,, Hodgson
,, Holmes
,, Homes . . .
,, Hopper
,, Hornby
,, Howard
,, Howells
,, Howitt
,, Hoyer
,, Hubbard
,, Hunter
,, Hutchings
,, In . . .
,, Incorporated . . .
,, Ireland
,, Irvine
,, Irving
,, J—— (T.)
,, Jaffray
,, Jaggard
,, James I.
,, Jarvis
,, Jerrard
,, Jordan
,, Jubilee
,, Kenney
,, Kent
,, King
,, Knibb
,, Knight
,, Laffan
,, Lambert
,, Langford
,, Lees
,, Leisure . . .
,, Levi
,, Lucy
,, Malone
,, May
,, Medwin
,, Memorials . . .
,, Moncrieff
,, Morley
,, Morris
,, Mott
,, Mowatt
,, Neale
,, Neil
,, Nelson
,, On . . .
,, Oswald

See Pemberton
,, Photographic . . .
,, Pictorial
,, Picturesque
,, Pleasant
,, Pumphrey
,, Reed
,, Ribton-Turner
,, Richards
,, Rider
,, Robertson
,, Robinson
,, Rose . . .
,, Savage
,, Serres
,, Seward
,, Sh— Works, 1850
,, Sh— Works : Ext.
      1865
,, *Sh*—] Gray
,, *Sh*—] Hallen
,, *Sh*—] Homes
,, *Sh*—] Hunter
,, *Sh*—] Jephson
,, *Sh*—] Lushington
,, *Sh*—] Marshall
,, *Sh*—] Memorials
,, *Sh*—] Only . . .
,, *Sh*—] Sh— and his
      birthplace
,, *Sh*—] Sh— and
      Stratford
,, *Sh*—] Sh— Christ-
      mas . . .
,, *Sh*—] Sh— : his life
      and times
,, *Sh*—] Sh— sermons
,, *Sh*—] Sh—'s grave
,, *Sh*—] Smith
,, *Sh*—] Walter
,, *Sh*—] Wise
,, Sharp
,, Shaw
,, Shirley
,, Showell
,, Shrine
,, Smith
,, Stirling
,, Stopes
,, Stowe
,, Sumner
,, Thorne
,, Tompkins
,, Tourist . . .
,, Tymms
,, Vicinity
,, Views
,, Vigo
,, Waite

Stratford-on-Avon—

See Wall
,, Ward
,, Waters
,, Way
,, Wheler
,, White
,, Williams . . .

See Wilson
,, Windle
,, Winter
,, Wivell
,, Wordsworth
,, Yarranton

Stratmann (F. H.) *Editor*—
   See Sh— Hamlet, 1869
   ,, Sh— Works, 1869
Stratton (Helen) *Artist. See* Sh— The tempest,
   1905
Streamer (V.) Book titles from Sh—. New
   York : Privately printed, 1901. 16° BPL
Streams of knowledge. *See* Sh— Works : Ext.
   1836
Street (Peter). *See* Stopes
Strictures on Hamilton's ' Enquiry . . .' by
   ' Scrutator.' *See* Rivington
Stronach (George) Did Lord Bacon write
   Sh—'s plays ? The case for Bacon [In
   ' Pall Mall Magazine,' Feb., pp. 244-256.
   Ln : 1902]. Roy. 8°. Illustrated
   Roll of Coventry [In ' The Athenæum,' 22
   Oct.-5 Nov., No. 4330, pp. 488-489 ; No.
   4332, pp. 554-555. 1910]. 4° BM | BPL
   A reply to Mrs. Stopes' article on same subject (*q.v.*)
   Illustrates Sh—'s ' King Henry IV.'

   ' Sidney Lee ' and the Baconians ; a critic
      criticised. Ln : 1904. 8°, pp. 24 BUS
Stronach (George)—
   See Stopes
   ,, Stopes, 'Lee,' & Stronach
Strong (J.) *Editor. See* Sh— Merchant . . .
   1899
Struwe (O.) *Berlin Publisher. See* Sh— Mer-
   chant . . . 1873
Stuart (G.) *Publisher. See* Sh— Macbeth,
   1850
Stuart *Actress* (*Miss*) Portrait. *See* Sh—
   King Henry VI., i., 1786
Stuart (Thomas) Sh—'s ' Tragedy of Richard
   III.' considered dramatically and his-
   torically, and in comparison with Cib-
   ber's alteration at present in use on the
   stage . . . Liverpool . . . [c. 1840]. 12° BPL
   The first piece of Liverpool criticism of Sh—.
Stuart (W.) *Publisher*—
   See Sh— Merchant . . . 1783
   ,, Sh— Othello, 1784
Stubbes (Philip) An unknown tract. Edited
   by J. P. Collier. *See Sh*—] Sh— Soc.
Anatomie of abuses in England in Sh—'s
   youth, 1583. Ln : New Sh— Society,
   1877-82. 3 vols. 8°. With numerous
   woodcuts BM | BPL | BUS
   Condemns 'stage playes, enterludes, maie games,
   dauncing, feasts of musick, cards, dice, tenisse,
   bowles, cockfighting, hawking, football, reading of
   wicked books, men's dress and its absurdities . . .'

Stubbes (Philip) Poetry. *See* Reardon
Two wunderfull and rare examples. *See*
Sh—] Sh— Soc.

Stubbs *Bp.* (Charles Wm.) A thanksgiving for
Sh—: Birthday sermon in the Church of
the Holy Trinity, Stratford-on-Avon, 23
April, 1899. Birmingham: Cornish, 1899.
Cr. 8°, pp. 28   BPL | SML
A thanksgiving for Sh—. *See also Sh—]*
Sh— Sermons
Sh—. *See Sh—]* Stubbs
Sh— sermons. 1900. Cr. 8°   BPL

Stucley *or* Stukeley. *See* Simpson (R.)

Students (The). *See* Sh— Love's labours lost,
1762

Studies of Sh—: No. I., Of the ghost and
Hamlet. Lincoln: A. Stark . . . 1809.
16°, pp. 54   BUS
Apparently no more issued.

Study in Sh—: 'Timon of Athens' [In
'Oxford and Cambridge Magazine'].
1856. 8°   BUS

Study in Sh—: 'Twelfth night' [In 'Oxford and Cambridge Magazine']. 1856.
8°   BUS

Stukeley *or* Stucley (*Capt.* Thomas) Life. *See*
Simpson (R.)

Stukeley (*Sir* Thomas) Battell of Alcazar,
fovght in Barbarie, betweene Sebastian
king of Portugall, and Abdelmelec king of
Marocco. With the death of Captaine
Stukeley. As it was sundrie times plaid
by the Lord high Admirall his seruants.
Ln: Printed by Edward Allde for Richard
Bankworth . . . 1594. Fcp. 4°   W
Sh— ridiculed this play in the passage or parody com-
mencing, 'Then feed and be fat, my fair Calipolis'
(*King Henry IV.*)
See also 'Battell . . .'

Sturges (R. Y.) Sh—; a poem. *See Sh—]*
Sturges

Styles (J.) Essay on the character, immoral
and anti-Christian tendency of the stage.
Newport, Isle of Wight . . . 1806. 12° BPL
'The great dramatic favourites have generally been
men of libertine principles, Sh—, Congreve, Dryden,
Kotzebue . . . We cannot but lament the luckless hour
in which Sh— became a writer for the stage' (p. 55).

Essay on the character of the stage. Second
edition . . . 1807. 12°   BPL
The stage: its character and influence.
Ln: Ward . . . 1838. 8°   SML

Suckling (*Sir* John) Select musical ayres. *See*
Sh— Works: Ext. 1653
The goblings, 1646. *See Sh—]* Sh— notices
The goblings. A comedy. Ln: . . . 1658.
12°   W
This volume is quite perfect, although a hiatus exists
in the pagination between pages 12 and 81. Probably
some of the spare copies were made up from the
'Fragmenta aurea.'

'Part of the play is indebted to Sh—'s "The tempest,"
the character of "Reginella" being a clear imitation
of "Miranda," and his goblins are copied from
Ariel.'—*J. O. Halliwell.*

Suckling (*Sir* John). *See also* Ingram

Suetonius (G. C.) History of the twelve Cæsars.
Newly translated by Philemon Holland.
Ln: Lownes . . . 1606. F°   SML
A very likely source of Sh—'s 'Julius Cæsar.'

Sullivan (*Sir* Arthur) *Composer*—
See Sh— Macbeth, 1888
„ Sh— The tempest, 1862

Sullivan.] Sillard (R. M.) Barry Sullivan and
his contemporaries. 1901. 2 vols. 8°
BPL

Sullivan (*Sir* Edward) Defamers of Sh—.
Part I. [In 'Nineteenth Century,' March,
No. 385, pp. 419-434]. 1909. Roy. 8°
Defamers of Sh—. Part II. [In 'Nineteenth
Century,' April, No. 386, pp. 630-647].
1909. Roy. 8°
For reply *see* Greenwood.

Hamlet's age. Ln: New Sh— Soc., 1880-
86. 8°

Summers (Will.) *Jester. See* New and merry . .

Sumner (Heywood) The Avon, from Naseby
to Tewkesbury. Twenty-one etchings
[with descriptions]. Ln: Seeley . . . 1882.
F°, pp. 58, and 21 plates BM | BLO | CTC

Sunday Sh— society, in connection with the
National Sunday league. Prospectus . . .
1874. 12°   BPL

Sunderlin (Richard *Lord*) Holograph letter.
See Malone

Supernatural element in Sh— [In 'Westminster Review']. Ln: 1877. 8°   BUS

Superstition and witchcraft—
See Bell   *See* New . . .
„ Caine   „ Nutt
„ Cruikshank   „ Pearson
„ De Loyer   „ Ritson
„ Desch   „ Roe
„ Fraser   „ Root
„ Gibson   „ Scot
„ Halliwell   „ Scott
„ Harland   „ Selby
„ Hazlitt   „ Shadwell
„ Ingram   „ *Sh—]* Drake
„ Law   „ Spalding
„ Le Loyer   „ Stewart
„ Lucy   „ Supernatural
„ Lyric . . .   „ Temple
„ Morley   „ Waller
„ Neele   „ Wilson

Supplement to Warburton's Sh—. *See*
Edwards

Supplemental apology. *See* Chalmers

Surfeit (The). *See* Kynder (P.)

Surflet (Richard) *Editor. See* Estienne

Surrey (*Earl of*). *See* Howard (Henry)

Surtees (Scott F.) Sh—'s provincialisms.
[1889.] 8°   BM
   Wm. Sh—, of Stratford-on-Avon; his
   epitaph unearthed, and the author of the
   plays [Sir Anthony Sherley] run to ground.
   Ln : H. Gray . . . 1888. 8°, pp. 44
                     BM | BPL | BUS | SML

Susan (*Dr. S.*) *Editor*—
   See Sh— Hamlet, 1849
   ,, Sh— Macbeth, 1843, 1848
   ,, Sh— The tempest, 1854

Sussex (Robert Radcliffe *fifth Earl of*) Company of actors. *See* Sh— Titus, 1594

Sutherland (J.) *Edinburgh Publisher. See* Sh—
   Works, 1823, 1825

Sutton (W. A.) Sh— enigma. Dublin : Sealy,
   Bryers & Walker, 1904. 8°, pp. 208 BPL

Swaggering damsell. *See* Chamberlaine

Swall (Abel) *Publisher. See* Sh— Troilus . . .
   1679

Swan (John) Specvlvm mundi, or a glasse
   representing the face of the world . . .
   Cambridge : Printed by the printers to
   the universitie, 1635. Fcp. 4°. With
   title engraved by W. Marshall   w
   On p. 299 is a quotation from 'Romeo and Juliet'
   differing from all extant versions.
   The volume was reprinted in 1643, 1665, and 1670.

Swan theatre, 1596—
   See Stopes
   ,, Wheatley

Swanwick (Anna) *Editor. See* Sh— Works,
   1851

Swanswick Sh— circle. *See* Sh— Merchant
   . . . 1862, 1864

Swarraton (Thomas of) Noble traytour : A
   chronicle [of the Earl of Essex]. Ln :
   Smith . . . 1857. 3 vols. Cr. 8°
   Chapters 18 and 20 introduce Sh— and the glove
   episode between Elizabeth and himself at the Globe
   Theatre.
   Perhaps written by Anne Manning.

Swartz (Stephen) *Amsterdam Publisher. See*
   Versatile ingenium

Sweet robin, or the children in the wood. A
   select collection of the choicest songs,
   ancient and modern. Ln : J. Roach, 1794.
   8°, pp. 72. With engraved front.
   Contains Sh—'s 'Mulberry tree' and 'Willow, willow,
   willow' (from whence his song in 'Othello').

Sweet silvery sayings of Sh— on the softer sex.
   See Sh— Works : Ext. 1877

Sweny (John Alfred) Everyday sayings . . .
   See Sh— Works : Ext. 1872, 1891

Swift *Dean* (Jonathan) Sports of the muses.
   See Sh— Works : Ext. 1752

Swift *Dean* (Jonathan) *Editor. See* Temple

Swinburne (Algernon Charles) Age of Sh—.
   Ln : Chatto . . . 1908. Cr. 8°, pp. 296 BPL
   One hundred copies also done on large paper.
   Reviewed in 'The Athenæum,' Nov., 1908, p. 674.

Swinburne (Algernon Charles) John Webster
   [In 'Nineteenth century']. Ln : . . .
   1886. Roy. 8°   BM | BPL
   Sh—. *See Sh*—] Swinburne

Sonnets of Sh— [In 'Miscellanies,' pp. 10-
   13]. Ln : . . . 1886. Cr. 8°
                 BM | BLO | BPL | CTC

Studies in prose and poetry. Ln : Chatto
   . . . 1894. Cr. 8°, pp. vi.-298   BM | BPL
   On p. 90 is the violent invective against Sh—'s
   'Passionate pilgrim' and his publisher, William
   Jaggard. The charges are as unsustained as the
   language is unrestrained, and serve to illustrate how
   pitifully unsuited Swinburne's nature at times was for
   calm literary criticism.

Study of Sh—. *See Sh*—] Swinburne

Three plays of Sh—. Ln : Harper, 1909.
   Cr. 8°, pp. 102   BPL

Three stages of Sh—. *See Sh*—] Swinburne

Wm. Sh—. *See Sh*—] Swinburne
   See Furnivall

Swinburne (Charles Alfred) Sacred and Shakespearian affinities, being analogies between the writings of the psalmists and
   of Sh—. Ln : Bickers . . . 1890. 8°
                 BM | BPL | MPL | SML

Swinburne (H.) Briefe treatise of testaments
   and last willes, very profitable to be
   understoode of all subjects of this realme
   of England. Ln : . . . 1590. Fcp. 4°
   'It is probable,' says J. O. Halliwell, 'this was a
   valuable book of reference in Sh—'s library, from the
   similarity of expression used.'
   See also Rushton's 'Sh—'s testamentary language.'
   A portion of the title seems woven into John of Gaunt's
   magnificent peroration : 'This realm, this England,'
   in 'King Richard II.'

Swinhowe (George) *Stationers' warden. See*
   Sh— London prodigal (*heading*)

Swinton (Wm.) *Editor. See* Sh— Works :
   Ext. 1880

Sykes (Fredk. Hy.) Syllabus of a course of
   six lectures on Sh—. Philadelphia, 1898.
   8°, pp. 8   BUS

Symmons. Sh— and Milton compared

Symon (E.) *Publisher. See* Sh— Works, 1725

Symonds (A. G.) Comic characters of Sh—
   [In 'Dramatic reform association journal,'
   pp. 221-223]. 1882. 8°   BPL

Symonds (John Addington) Sh—'s predecessors in the English drama. Ln : Smith,
   1884. 8°   BM | BPL | BUS | SML

Sh—'s predecessors . . . New edition. Ln :
   Smith . . . 1900. 8°, pp. xx.-552   BUS

Symons (Arthur) Studies in two literatures.
   Ln : Simpkin, 1897. 8°, pp. 322
   Includes 'Studies in the Elizabethan drama.'

Symons (Arthur) *Editor*—
   See Sh— King Henry V., 1886
   ,, Sh— Titus . . . 1886

Syms-Wood (Arthur) *Editor*—
   See Sh— Julius Cæsar, 1901
   ,, Sh— Venus . . . 1886
   ,, Sh— Works : Ext. 1908

—— (H. Was Sh— a
lawyer. *See Sh*—]

T—— (H.)

T—— (R.) *See* Tofte
(Robert)

T—— (T.) Postscript to
the 'Child's own
book.' Ln: Richards
... 1842. 8°, pp. 8
BUS

A squib, ridiculing J. P. Collier's 'Reasons for a new edition ...'

T—— (T.) *Publisher*—
See Sh— Sonnets, 1609
  ,, Thorpe (Thomas)

T—— (W.) *See* Thomson

T—— (W.) *See* Traheron (W.)

T—— (W. G.) Sh— sermons [In the 'Birmingham Examiner,' pp. 387-391, 535-540]. Birmingham [1877 ?] 4° BPL

T—— (W. L.) Iago: A critical study [In 'Monthly Repository']. Ln. [c. 1850].
8° BUS

Tabby (J.) *Publisher*—
See Sh— Coriolanus, 1820
  ,, Sh— King Lear, 1820
  ,, Sh— King Richard III., 1819

Table book, or memorandum book. Manuscript, on sixteen leaves of paper, suitable for erasure. 1701-02. 12° W

Traces remain of the removal of older entries than those now appearing in this example. Old table books are of the greatest rarity. Douce possessed one, and only two others are traceable, both in private museums. They were clearly familiar to Sh—, who wrote :
'Brooch, table book, ballad, knife, tape, glove.'—*Winter's tale*.
'If I had play'd the desk or table book, or given my heart a winking.'—*Hamlet*.
'Lisping to his master's old tables, his note book, his counsel keeper.'—*King Henry IV*.
'Therefore will he wipe his tables clean
And keep no tell-tale to his memory.'—*King Henry IV*.
'From the table of my memory I'll wipe away all trivial fond records.'—*Hamlet*.
'My tables—meet it is I set it down,
That one may smile, and smile, and be a villain.'
—*Hamlet*.

Table talk on Sh—: 'Love's labours lost' [In 'Fraser's Magazine,' Jan.] 1858. 8°
BUS | SML

Table talker, or brief essays on society and literature. Ln: Wm. Pickering, 1840. 2 vols. Cr. 8°
In vol. 1, pp. 108-111, is an essay on the 'Midsummer night's dream.'

Tacitus. *See* Hayward

Tagg (William) Sh—'s memorial, undertaken with a view to popularize Shakesperian literature amongst all classes. Melbourne ... 1861. 8° MPL

Taine (Hippolyte Adolphe) History of English literature. Edinburgh ... 1873. 8°
Afterwards reprinted. BM | BLO | BUS | CTC

Take, oh, take those lips away. *See* Sh— Measure ... 1870

Talandier (A.) *Editor*. *See* Sh— Macbeth, 1881

Talbot (G. H. F.) *Editor*. *See* Sh— Macbeth, 1820

Talbot (T.) English history *versus* Sh— and Manx history [In the 'Manx Sun' ... 1885]. 12° BPL

Talboys *Publisher*. *See* Sh— Works, 1825

Tale of Tereus and Progne. *See* Pettie (G.)

Talfourd (Francis) Macbeth travestie—
See Sh— Macbeth, 1840, 1847, 1853, 1854
Merchant of Venice travestie. *See* Sh— Merchant ... 1849
Shylock. *See* Sh— Merchant ... 1853, 1857, 1860

Talfourd (*Sir* Thomas Noon) *Editor*. *See* Lamb

Tallis (John) Dramatic magazine and general theatrical and musical review. Ln: Tallis & Co., 1850-51. 4°. With steel portraits
Drawing room table book of theatrical portraits, memoirs, and anecdotes: Sh— gallery of engravings. Ln: Tallis & Co. [c. 1850]. Imp. 8°. With 52 large steel portraits of actors and actresses in character
Illustrated life in London. Tercentenary number, April 23, 1864. F° BPL

Tallis (John) *Printer & Publisher*. *See* Sh— Works, 1850

Tallis & Co. (John) *Publishers*. *See* Sh— Works, 1850-53, 1851, 1856, 1858

Talma *Actor*—
See De Soligny
  ,, New Monthly Magazine

Taming of a shrew—
See Sh— Taming ... 1594
  ,, Six old plays
A foundation of Sh—'s play.

Taming of the shrew. *See* Sh— Taming ...

'Taming of the shrew' [Article in 'Temple Bar']. Ln: ... 1872. 8° BPL

'Taming of the shrew' travesty. *See* Sh— Taming ... 1888

Tanger (G.) First and second quartos and first folio of 'Hamlet.' Ln: New Sh— Society, 1880-86. 8°

Tapestry, 16th and 17th century. *See* Halliwell

Tārakanātha Sānyāla. Shakespearian study in India ... [1887.] 8° BM

Tarleton *Actor* (Richard) Jests, 1638. Facsimile ... by E. W. Ashbee. [Ln: ... c. 1870.] Fcp. 4° BUS
One hundred printed for private circulation.

Jests, 1864. *See* Sh—] Sh— Jest books

Tarleton *Actor* (Richard) Jests and news out of purgatory. With notes and some account of the life of Tarlton by J. O. Halliwell. Ln: Sh— Society . . . 1844. 8°, pp. xlviii.-136 and woodcuts

Reprinted from the 1611 edition, which, though not the first, is the earliest known to still exist.

Story of the two lovers of Pisa, 1843. *See Sh—]* Sh—'s library

Illustrates the 'Merry wives.'

Tarleton.] Papers respecting disputes which arose from incidents at the death-bed of Richard Tarleton the actor in 1588. Edited by J. O. Halliwell. Ln : . . . 1866. 12°   BPL | SML

Issue limited to ten copies.

Tarleton *Actor* (Richard)—
See Chettle
  ,, Rich
  ,, Wright

Tasso. *See* Wilson (H. S.)

Tate (Nahum) Epilogue. *See* Harris (Joseph)
Ingratitude of a commonwealth. *See* Sh— Coriolanus, 1682
Loyal general. A tragedy. Ln : 1680. Fcp. 4°   W

With a Shakespearean preface.

Sicilian usurper. *See* Sh— King Richard II., 1691

Tate (Nahum) *Editor—*
See Sh— King Lear, 1681, 1689, 1690, 1699, 1710, 1712, 1717, 1729, 1733, 1745, 1749, 1750, 1756, 1759, 1760, 1761, 1763, 1767, 1768, 1770, 1771, 1775, 1808, 1810, 1815, 1820, 1822, 1845, 1848
  ,, Sh— King Richard II., 1681, 1691
  ,, Sh— Macbeth, 1731
  ,, Sh— Works, 1898-1908

Tatham (John) The rump or mirrour of the late times : A new comedy . . . Ln : . . . 1660. Fcp. 4°

Bears passages, at pp. 7, 34, 49, and 53, of Shakespearean interest.

Tatler (The). *See* Steele (*Sir* R.)

Taunton (W. F.) *See* Poole & Taunton

Taverner (J. W.) Styles of Sh— and Bacon, judged by the laws of elocutionary analysis and melody of speech [In 'Sh—, by G. Wilkes ']. 1877. 8°

                   BM | BPL | BUS | MPL

Tawney (C. H.) *Editor—*
See Sh— King Richard III., 1888, 1890, 1901, 1902
  ,, Sh— Works, 1888

Taylor. Wit and mirth. *See* Old English jest books

Taylor *Stafford publisher. See* Sh— Works, 1768

Taylor (Bayard) Poetical works . . . Boston [U.S.] 1880. 12°

At p. 224 is the poem entitled 'Sh—'s statue, Central Park, New York, 23 May, 1872.'
  'Here, in his right, he stands !
  No breadth of earth-dividing seas can bar
  The breeze of morning, or the morning star
    From visiting our lands:
  His wit the breeze, his wisdom as the star
  Shone where our earliest life was set, and blew
    To freshen hope and plan
    In brains American.
  To urge, resist, encourage, and subdue
  He came, a household ghost we could not ban.
  He sat, on winter nights, by cabin fires ;
  His summer fairies linked their hands
    Along our yellow sands ;
  He preached within the shadow of our spires ;
  And when the certain fate drew nigh, to cleave
  The birth-cord, and a separate being leave,
  He, in our ranks of patient-hearted men,
  Wrought with the boundless forces of his fame
    Victorious, and became
  The master of our thought, the land's first citizen.
    If, here, his image seem
  Of softer scenes and grayer skies to dream,
  Thatched cot and rustic tavern, ivied hall,
    The cuckoo's April call
  And cowslip-meads beside the Avon stream,
  He shall not fail that other home to find
    We could not leave behind !'

Sh— : New York Central Park, 23 May, 1872 [In ' Harper's Magazine ']. 1872. 8°   BUS

Tayler (C.) Art of composing Greek iambics. *See* Sh— Works : Ext. 1838

Taylor (C.) *Publisher—*
See Sh— Works, 1792
  ,, Sh— Works : Ext. 1783-87

Taylor (Edward) Cursory remarks on tragedy. *See* Richardson

Taylor (Isaac) Names and their histories ; Historical and topographical nomenclature. Ln : Rivington . . . 1898. 12° SML
Scenes in England for the amusement and instruction of little tarry-at-home travellers. Ln : J. Harris [c. 1825]. Cr. 8°, pp. xvi.-150. Illust.

At p. 60 is an article on Stratford and Sh—, with a copperplate of the church bust.

Taylor (Isaac) *Artist & Engraver—*
See Sh— Othello, 1773
  ,, Sh— Works, 1773-74

Taylor (J.) List of plays and tracts on Richard III. and the battle of Bosworth. 1885. 8°   BPL

Taylor (J.) *Engraver. See* Sh— Works : Ext. 1774

Taylor (John) *Berwick-on-Tweed Printer & Publisher. See* Sh— Works, 1800

Taylor *Bookseller* (John) Concise history of Abington ; the abbey, park, church, and parish ; with notes on the . . . Shakespearean associations. Northampton . . . 1897. 8°, pp. iv.-68. Illustrated   SML

With conjectures on Lady Barnard's disposal of Sh—'s manuscripts.

Taylor *Bookseller* (John) Local Shakspearean names [In ' The Athenæum,' Feb., 1889, pp. 189-190, and July, 1892, p. 172]. 1889-92   BM | BPL.

Taylor *Waterman* (John)] Heads of all fashions, being a plain desection or definition of diverse and sundry sorts of heads, butting, jetting, or pointing at vulgar opinion. Ln : John Morgan . . . 1642. Fcp. 4°
The engraved title presents seventeen different heads, two of which are doubtless meant for Sh—. Next to the Droeshout (1623) and Marshall (1640) portraits, these rank as the earliest pictorial representations of the poet.
' Yes indeed shall you, and taste gentlemen of all fashions.'—*Pericles* iv., 2.

Praise of hemp seed . . . Ln : H. Gosson . . . 1620. Fcp. 4°
In the above occurs the line :—
    ' Spencer and Sh— did in art excel.'

Travels from London to the Isle of Wight, 1648. *See* Literature
Wit and mirth, 1864. *See* Sh—] Sh— jest book
Workes . . . being sixty and three in number. Ln : James Boler . . . 1630. F°. With engraved title bearing portrait
Refers to Sh—.
See Hermeticall . . .
   ,, *Sh—*] Sh— notices
   ,, Westward for smelts

Taylor *Printer* (John Edward) The Moor of Venice : Cinthio's tale and Sh—'s tragedy. Ln : . . . 1855. 8°   BM | BPL | CPL
Taylor (John Edward) *Editor. See* Giraldi
Taylor *Actor* (Joseph)—
See Beaumont
   ,, Downes
Taylor (J & J.) *Publishers. See* Sh— Works, 1793, 1797, 1798
Taylor (Robert) The hog hath lost his pearl Ln : . . . 1614. Fcp. 4°
Says :—' And if it prove so happy as to please
    We'll say 'tis fortunate like *Pericles*.'

Taylor (R. W.) *Editor. See* Sh— Works, 1872-83
Taylor *M.A.* (Tom) The theatre in England ; some of its shortcomings and possibilities. Reprinted from the ' Dark blue.' Ln : British and Colonial Publishing Co., 1871. 8°, pp. 16, including printed wrappers
Taylor (Tom) *Editor—*
See Sh— As you like it, 1880
   ,, Sh— Hamlet, 1873
Taylor (W.) *Publisher—*
See Sh— Works, 1714
   ,, Shore
Taylor (W.) *New York Publisher—*
See Sh— King John, 1846
   ,, Sh— Macbeth, 1843
   ,, Sh— Romeo . . . 1847

Taylor & Hessey *Publishers. See* Sh— Works, 1809
Tchertkoff (V.) *Editor. See* Tolstoy
Tedder (Henry R.) Classification of Shakespeareana [In ' Library Chronicle ']. Ln : Library Association, 1886. Roy. 8°
Teetgen (Alex. T.) Bubble ghost . . . *See* Sh— Hamlet, 1869
   Sh—'s ' King Edward the third ' absurdly called and scandalously treated as a ' doubtful play ' : An indignation pamphlet . . . Ln : Williams & Norgate, 1875. 8°, pp. iv.-52   BM | BPL | BUS
Tegg (J.) *Publisher. See* Sh— Works, 1832, 1833
Tegg (J. & S. A.) *Sydney Publishers. See* Sh— Works, 1836
Tegg (Thomas) The O. P. war poetic epistle. Ln : Tegg . . . 1810. 12°   SML
Tegg (Thomas) *Publisher. See* Sh— Works, 1812-15, 1813, 1823, 1827, 1831, 1832, 1842, 1845, 1861
Tegg & Son (T.) *Publishers. See* Sh— Works, 1834, 1835, 1836, 1838
Tegg (T. T.) *Publisher. See* Sh— Works, 1833
Tegg (T. T. & H.) *Dublin Publishers. See* Sh— Works, 1836
Tegg (Wm.) Sh— and his contemporaries. *See* Sh—] Tegg
   Sh—'s memorial. *See* Sh— Works : Ext. 1861
Tegg (Wm.) *Publisher—*
See Sh— Timon . . . 1815
   ,, Sh— Works, 1849, 1851, 1855, 1858, 1859, 1864
Teichmann (E.) On Sh—'s ' Hamlet' : History of the old tale of ' Hamlet.' Borna . . . 1880. Fcp. 4°   BM | BUS
Tell-trothe's new yeare's gift . . . Ln : New Sh— Society, 1877. 4°   BM | BPL | BUS
See also A ——. Passionate morrice.
   ,, Lane (J.)
Tempest (The). *See* Sh— The tempest
' Tempest (The).' A Shakespearian tract. Boston [U.S.] . . . 1898. 12°   BPL
' Tempest (The)' travesty. *See* Sh— The tempest, 1675, 1849
Templar (A.) The new Hamlet and his critics [In ' Macmillan's Magazine,' Jan.] Ln : 1875. 8°   BUS
' Temple (Launcelot) ' *pseud. See* Armstrong
Temple (T. W.) Witchcraft in ' Macbeth ' : A paper read by William Jaggard before the Sh— Club, Stratford-on-Avon. [Privately printed.] 1907. Cr. 8°, pp. 8 SML
Temple (*Sir* Wm.) Miscellanea . . . Published by Jonathan Swift. Ln : J. Tonson, John Churchill, R. Simpson, & B. Cooke, 1693-1701. Three parts, forming 2 vols. 8°
Contains two references to Sh—.

Templeton.] Some account of William Templeton's acting in the play of ' Hamlet '
[1802]. 8°   w
Excerpt of six leaves from a magazine contemporary
with Templeton's appearance.

Ten Brink. *See* Brink
Tennyson (Alfred *Lord*)—
See Sh—] Sh— Show book
,, Shepherd
Tennyson.] Tennyson (Hallam *Lord*) Life and
works of Alfred Lord Tennyson. Ln :
Macmillan, 1898. 12 vols. Roy. 8°
                         BM | BLO | CTC
In vol. 4, p. 39, Tennyson says :—There are three
repartees in Sh— which alway bring tears to my
eyes from their simplicity. One is in ' King Lear,'
when Lear says to Cordelia, ' So young and so
untender,' and Cordelia lovingly answers, ' So young,
my lord, and true.' And in the ' Winter's tale,'
when Florizel takes Perdita's hand to lead her to the
dance, and says, ' So turtles pair that never mean to
part,' and the little Perdita answers, giving her hand
to Florizel, ' I'll swear for 'em.' And in ' Cymbeline,'
when Imogen in tender rebuke says to her husband,
' Why did you throw your wedded lady from you ?...'
and Posthumus does not ask forgiveness, but answers,
kissing her, ' Hang there like fruit, my soul, till the
tree die.'

Tercentenary, 1864. *See Sh*—] Sh— commemorations
Tercentenary celebration. *See* New England ..
Tercentenary of Corydon : A bucolic drama
of three acts. By ' Nuovus homo.' Oxford : T. & G. Shrimpton ... 1864. 8°,
pp. iv.-30   BUS
Terence. Comedies. Made English, with his
life, and remarks by several hands [L.
Echard and Sir R. L'Estrange]. Ln : ...
1705. 8°
The preface contains an ' Essay on dramatic history,'
and refers to Sh—, Jonson, Dryden, etc.

Flovres for Latine spekynge. Selected and
gathered ... by Nicolas Udall and the
same translated in to Englysshe. Ln :
Tho. Berthelet ... 1544. 8°. Black
letter
Adjudged to be one of Sh—'s school books, as he quotes
a passage from it in the ' Taming of the shrew.'
Reprinted in 1568 and 1581.

Tereus and Progne. *See* Tale ...
Terry (C. S.) Sh— the historian. *See Sh*—]
Terry
Terry (Daniel) *Editor*. *See* British theatrical
gallery
Terry.] Ellen Terry and her impersonations ;
An appreciation by Charles Hiatt. Ln :
Bell, 1898. Cr. 8°, pp. x.-274. With 31
different portraits of Ellen Terry
] Pemberton (T. E.) Ellen Terry and her
sisters. 1902. 8°   BPL
Terry (Ellen)—
See Irving (*Sir* J. H. B.)
,, Sh— Macbeth, 1890
,, Sh— Winter's tale, 1856

Terry (J.) *Editor*. *See* Sh— The tempest, 1904
Terry (Jean F.) *Editor*—
See Sh— King Lear, 1908
,, Sh— Merchant ... 1907
,, Sh— Twelfth night, 1905
Terry.] Kate Terry in *Viola* [In ' Fraser's
Magazine']. Ln : 1865. 8°   BPL
On ' Twelfth night.'
Testimonial to Mrs. Mary Cowden Clarke. *See*
Clarke
Text of Sh— [In ' North British Review,'
pp. 281-318, Feb.] 1854   SML
Criticises the Jaggard canon of 1623, and Collier's
forgeries.
Text of Sh— vindicated. *See* Singer
Textor. *See* Heywood
Thackary (Wm.) *Publisher*. *See* Sandys
Thackeray (W. & T.) *Publishers*. *See* Crown
garland
Thackeray (William Makepeace). *See* National
committee
Thackeray (Wm. Makepeace) *Editor*. *See*
Cornhill
Thames (River). *See* London
Thayer *Editor*. *See* Sh— Two noble kinsmen,
1890
Thayer (Wm. R.) The Sh— hoax ; A startling
prospectus. Cambridge [U.S.] ... 1888.
12°   BUS
Theatre (National). *See* Stage
Theatre of ingenuity [Excerpt containing the
' Mad wooing, or a way to win and tame
a shrew']. Ln : ... 1704. 12°   w
Theatre of ingenuity. *See Sh*—] Sh— drolls
Theatre plats of three old English dramas,
with facsimiles. Edited by J. O. Halliwell
... 1860. F°   BPL
Theatre Royal, Covent Garden—
See Dibdin
,, Halliwell
,, Hawkins
,, Kemble
,, Sh— All's well 1778
,, Sh— As you like it, 1777, 1794
,, Sh— Comedy ... 1770, 1779, 1793
,, Sh— Coriolanus, 1748, 1749, 1755, 1780
,, Sh— Cymbeline, 1758, 1759, 1777
,, Sh— Hamlet, 1755, 1763, 1767, 1774,
      1776, 1779, 1788, 1794, 1800
,, Sh— Julius Cæsar, 1773, 1780
,, Sh— King Henry IV., ii., 1803
,, Sh— King Henry V., 1769, 1773, 1780
,, Sh— King Henry VIII., 1778
,, Sh— King John, 1745
,, Sh— King Lear, 1767, 1768, 1771, 1779,
      1794
,, Sh— King Richard III., 1756, 1770,
      1778, 1787, 1790, 1794
,, Sh— Macbeth, 1770, 1776, 1780, 1785,
      1788, 1794
,, Sh— Measure ... 1770, 1773, 1779

Theatre Royal, Covent Garden—
See Sh— Merchant ... 1777, 1787, 1788, 1794
  ,, Sh— Merry wives, 1778, 1787
  ,, Sh— Midsummer ... 1740, 1778
  ,, Sh— Othello, 1765, 1770, 1771, 1777, 1780
  ,, Sh— Pericles, 1796
  ,, Sh— The tempest, 1778, 1794
  ,, Sh— Timon ... 1770, 1780, 1786
  ,, Sh— Twelfth night, 1773, 1774, 1779, 1794, 1800
  ,, Sh— Winter's tale, 1773, 1779, 1794, 1802

Theatre Royal, Drury Lane—
See Dibdin   *See* Hawkins
  ,, Garrick   ,, Kelly
  ,, Greenstreet   ,, Philips
  ,, Havard
  ,, Sh— All's well, 1773, 1778, 1793
  ,, Sh— Antony ... 1678, 1758, 1776, 1792
  ,, Sh— Arden ... 1810
  ,, Sh— As you like it, 1773, 1775, 1777, 1785, 1786, 1794
  ,, Sh— Comedy ... 1779
  ,, Sh— Coriolanus, 1682, 1773, 1780, 1789
  ,, Sh— Cymbeline, 1682, 1773, 1777, 1784, 1800
  ,, Sh— Double falsehood, 1728, 1740
  ,, Sh— Hamlet, 1695, 1755, 1763, 1767, 1771, 1776, 1779, 1782, 1787, 1788, 1789, 1794. 1796, 1800
  ,, Sh— Julius Cæsar, 1680, 1684, 1691, 1719, 1734, 1741, 1780
  ,, Sh— King Henry IV., i., 1785
  ,, Sh— King Henry IV., ii., 1700, 1719, 1721, 1728, 1766, 1773, 1781, 1795
  ,, Sh— King Henry V., 1723, 1769, 1780, 1789, 1790
  ,, Sh— King Henry VI., i., 1724
  ,, Sh— King Henry VI., iii., 1723
  ,, Sh— King Henry VIII., 1762, 1778, 1790
  ,, Sh— King John, 1773, 1784, 1800
  ,, Sh— King Lear, 1767, 1771, 1774, 1779, 1786, 1794, 1800
  ,, Sh— King Richard II., 1632, 1691, 1720
  ,, Sh— King Richard III., 1700, 1718, 1745, 1751, 1754, 1756, 1759, 1769, 1770, 1778, 1784, 1790, 1793, 1794
  ,, Sh— Macbeth, 1687, 1689, 1695, 1755, 1773, 1776, 1780, 1785, 1788, 1794
  ,, Sh— Measure ... 1761, 1779, 1796
  ,, Sh— Merchant ... 1773, 1777, 1783, 1788, 1794, 1795
  ,, Sh— Merry wives, 1702, 1773, 1778, 1797
  ,, Sh— Midsummer ... 1754, 1755, 1763, 1778
  ,, Sh— Othello, 1695, 1724, 1765, 1770, 1771, 1777, 1780
  ,, Sh— The tempest, 1675, 1690, 1756, 1778, 1780, 1783, 1789, 1794

Theatre Royal, Drury Lane—
See Sh— Timon ... 1770, 1771, 1772, 1773, 1780
  ,, Sh— Titus ... 1687
  ,, Sh— Twelfth night, 1773, 1774, 1779, 1787, 1791, 1794, 1800
  ,, Sh— Two gentlemen ... 1763, 1800
  ,, Sh— Winter's tale, 1758, 1779, 1794, 1802

Theatre Royal, Haymarket—
See Dibdin
  ,, Sh— Winter's tale, 1777

Theatre [Royal], Lincoln's Inn Fields—
See Sh— Measure ... 1700
  ,, Sh— Merchant ... 1701

Theatre Royal, Richmond Green. *See* Sh— Timon ... 1768

Theatre Royal, Dublin—
See Sh— As you like it, 1741, 1750
  ,, Sh— King Richard III., 1756
  ,, Sh— Measure ... 1761
  ,, Sh— Winter's tale, 1767

Theatre Royal, Edinburgh—
See Sh— Comedy ... 1780
  ,, Sh— Macbeth, 1753
  ,, Siddons

' Theatre (The) ' playhouse—
See Rainoldes
  ,, Stopes

Theatre (The) : A weekly review [edited by Clement William Scott]. Ln : ... 1877-78. 3 vols. F°   BPL
Commenced as a weekly, and was then changed into a monthly.

Theatre (The) : A monthly review [containing photographic portraits of the chief actors and actresses of the day, with biographies. Edited by C. W. Scott]. Ln : ... 1878-97. 39 vols. Roy. 8°   BPL | SML

Theatres. *See* Stage

Theatres.] Foreign national theatres. *See* Sh—] Sh— memorial

Theatres (The). *See* Garrick

Theatric tourist. *See* Winston (J.)

Theatrical biography : Memoirs of the principal performers of the three Theatres Royal ... 1772. 2 vols. 12°   BPL

Theatrical bouquet, containing an alphabetical arrangement of the prologues and epilogues ... by distinguished wits, from the time that Colley Cibber first came on the stage ... Ln : Printed for T. Lowndes, No. 77 in Fleet Street, 1778. 8°, pp. iv.-312
The dedication to Garrick compares him with the 'immortal Sh—,' and adds ' that the poet as much excelled the actor in the one as the actor excelled the poet in the other ; in his own excellence each equally inimitable.'

Theatrical examiner : An enquiry into the merits and demerits of the present Eng-

Lewis Theobald (as the 'Distrest poet'), By William Hogarth

See p. 663

lish performers in general, substance of theatric character, public taste, conduct of managers, advice to actors, slight remarks on late productions . . . Ln : J. Doughty, 1757. 8°, pp. 98
Numerous references to the poet, and a trenchant criticism of Garrick and other actors of the time.

Theatrical house that Jack built. [By W. Hone ?] Ln : . . . 1819. 8°

Theatrical inquisitor or literary mirror. By 'Cerberus.' Ln : . . . 1812-20. 17 vols. 8°. With full-length portraits

Theatrical journal and stranger's guide : A weekly record of the drama . . . Ln : Gilbert & Vickers, 1839-71. 32 vols. 8°

Theatrical looker-on . . . Birmingham . . . 1823. 12°   SML

Theatrical monthly mirror. Ln : . . . 1795-1811. 30 vols. 8°. With portraits of players

Theatrical observer . . . ' Nothing extenuate nor set down aught in malice' . . . Dublin : J. J. Nolan . . . 1821. 2 vols. 12°
Issued in penny daily sheets, each of 4 pp.
Gives copies of play-bills, casts, and songs.

Theatrical observer and daily bills of the play . . . 1821-30. 8°. With 18 coloured portraits

Theatrical records, or an account of English dramatic authors and their works. Ln : . . . 1756. 8°

Theatrical remembrancer, containing a complete list of all the dramatic performances in the English language . . . 1788. 12°
                                                             MPL

Theatrical review, or new companion to the playhouse. By a society of gentlemen independent of managerial influence . . . 1772. 2 vols. Cr. 8°

Theatrum illustratum. See Wilkinson (R.)

Theatrum redivivum, or the theatre vindicated : In answer to Pryn's ' Histriomastix,' wherein his groundless assertions against stage-plays are discovered. Ln : T. R—— for Francis Eglesfield at the Marigold in St. Paul's Churchyard, 1662. 8°

Theisen (C.) A chapter from an attempt at a critique of the chronologies of Sh—'s plays . . . [1886 ?]. 8°   BM

Theobald (Lewis) Cave of poverty : A poem written in imitation of Sh— . . . Ln : Printed for Jonas Browne at the Black Swan without Temple Bar and sold by J. Roberts at the Oxford Arms in Warwick Lane, 1715. 8°, pp. vi.-48 BUS | SML
It would be a matter of some difficulty to find the part of Sh— this is supposed to resemble.

Double falsehood, 1728. See Sh— Double falsehood

Manuscript notes. See Sh— Works, 1728

Theobald (Lewis) Miscellany of taste, by Pope ; Of Mr. Pope's taste of Sh—, etc. . . . 1732. Cr. 8°   BPL

Preface—
    See Eighteenth . . .
      „ Sh— Works, 1733
' In how many points of light must we be obliged to gaze at this great poet ! In how many branches of excellence to consider and admire him ! Whether we view him on the side of art or nature, he ought equally to engage our attention ; whether we respect the force and greatness of his genius, the extent of his knowledge and reading, the power and address with which he throws out and applies either nature or learning, there is ample scope both for our wonder and pleasure. If his diction and the clothing of his thoughts attract us, how much more must we be charmed with the richness and variety of his images and ideas ! If his images and ideas steal into our souls and strike upon our fancy, how much are they improved in price when we come to reflect with what propriety and justness they are applied to character. If we look into his characters and how they are furnished and proportioned to the employment he cuts out for them, how are we taken up with the mastery of his portraits. What draughts of nature ! What variety of originals and how differing each from the other ! Each of them the standard of fashion for themselves.'

Sh— restored, or a specimen of the many errors, as well committed as unamended, by Mr. Pope in his late edition of this poet. Designed . . . to restore the true reading of Sh— in all the editions ever yet published. Ln : R. Francklin . . . 1726. 4°, pp. vi.-viii.-194
                     BM | BPL | BUS | W
Consists of a critical examination of ' Hamlet.'
In the course of his notes Theobald calmly asserted that whoever edited Sh—, be he Pope or any other, he (Theobald) would at the end still be able to give five hundred emendations which would escape any other editor. Pope retaliated by creating Theobald hero of ' The dunciad,' while Hogarth has given us the only known portrait of him in his print, ' The distrest poet.'
Valuable for its text of ' Hamlet,' formed from that of the Jaggard canon and the second quarto. Theobald's foundation was adopted for the Cambridge edition of 1863-66, and is now the accepted text.

Sh— restored . . . Second edition . . . 1740. 4°   BPL

Shakespearean note book [evidently used for the preparation of his edition of Sh—, c. 1730]. 8°. Manuscript on thirty leaves
Sold 8th Dec., 1905, for £26.
On the question of Sh—'s knowledge of the ancients, Theobald favoured the view that Sh—'s classical knowledge was considerable. He remarks :—' The result of the controversy must certainly, either way, terminate to our author's honour : how happily he could imitate them, if that point be allowed : or how gloriously he could think like them, without owing anything to imitation.'

Theobald (Lewis) Editor—
    See Sh— As you like it, 1741
      „ Sh— King Richard II., 1720
      „ Sh— Macbeth, 1739
      „ Sh— Measure . . . 1778
      „ Sh— Merry wives, 1739
      „ Sh— Much ado . . . 1776, 1778

Theobald (Lewis) *Editor*—
See Sh— The tempest, 1755
  „ Sh— Works, 1733, 1740, 1752, 1757,
     1762, 1767, 1771, 1772, 1773, 1777
See Annotations   *See* Mallet
  „ Epistle   „ Pope
  „ Johnson   „ Sh— Works, 1623
  „ Lounsbury „ Verbal . . .
Theobald (L.) Thirlby (*Dr.*) & Warburton *Bp.*
(W.) Shakespearean correspondence [In
Nichols' ' Literary history,' Vol. 2, pp.
189-654]. 1817. 8°   MPL
Theobald (Robert M.) Bacon the poet: In-
dications of Bacon's mind in the Shake-
spearean poems [In ' Transactions of the
Royal Society,' 2nd Series, Vol. 16, pp.
135-193]. [1893 ?] 8°   BPL
Dethroning Sh—: A selection of letters
to the ' Daily Telegraph.' Edited with
notes and comments. Ln: Low, 1888.
        BM | BPL | BUS | SML
Baconian correspondence elicited by the appearance of
Donnelly's ' Great cryptogram.'
Ethics of criticism illustrated by Mr.
Churton Collins. 1904. 8°   BPL
On the Bacon-Sh— controversy.
Sh— studies in Baconian light. Ln: Low
. . . 1901. 8°, pp. 512   BPL | BUS
Sh— studies . . . New impression. Ln:
Low . . . 1904. 8°, pp. 512
Sh—'s handwriting [In ' Literary opinion'].
Ln: 1889. 4°   BPL
Theobald (William) Authorship of the plays
attributed to Marlowe. Budleigh Salter-
ton . . . 1895. 8°   BPL
Authorship of the plays attributed to Sh—.
Budleigh Salterton . . . 1894. 8°   BPL
Authorship of the ' Sonnets ' attributed to
Sh—. Budleigh Salterton . . . 1896. 8°
                   BPL
Bacon *versus* Sh—: An examination of
certain current errors and mis-statements
regarding the above controversy, especi-
ally as respects the true sentiments of
Ben Jonson towards Wm. Sh—. Bud-
leigh Salterton . . . 1899. 8°, pp. 28
        BM | BPL | BUS
Bacon *versus* Sh— . . . Budleigh Salterton:
F. N. Parsons, 1900. Cr. 8°, pp. 28
Classical element in Sh—'s plays. Ln:
Banks . . . 1909. 8°   BPL
' Thersites literarius.' *See* Familiar address
Thespian dictionary, or dramatic biography
of the eighteenth century; containing
. . . the lives, productions, etc. of all the
principal managers, dramatists, composers, commentators, actors, and actresses of the United Kingdom . . . with
anecdotes, forming a concise history of
the English stage. Ln: J. Candie for
T. Hurst, 1802. 8°, pp. 300, unpaged

Thespian dictionary, or dramatic biography
of the present age . . . Second edition.
Ln: James Candie & C. Chapple, 1805.
8°. With 22 sepia portraits BPL | SML
Thespian magazine and literary repository.
Ln: Wilkins, June 1792-Sept. 1794. 3
vols. 8°. With circular portraits by J.
Condé   SML
Thew (William) Poems on various subjects,
chiefly theatrical . . . 1825. 8°   W
Contains Sh— references.
Thiel (B.) Principal reasons for Sh—'s re-
maining unpopular longer than a century,
even in England. [1874.] 8°   BM
Thieme (D. A.) *Arnheim Publisher*. *See* Sh—
Macbeth, 1853, 1867
Thimm *Bookseller* (Franz) Sh— in the British
Museum . . . [1887.] 8°   BM | BPL
Sh— literature, 1876 to 1879. Ln: New
Sh— Society,. 1879. 8°
Shakspeariana from 1564 to 1864: An
account of the Shakspearian literature
of England, Germany, France, and other
European countries during three cen-
turies. With bibliographical introduc-
tions. Ln: F. Thimm . . . 1865. Roy. 8°,
pp. vi.-92   BM | BPL | BUS | MPL
Shakspeariana . . . Second edition. Con-
taining the literature from 1864 to 1871.
Ln: F. Thimm, 1872. Roy. 8°, pp. viii.-
120-x.   BPL | BUS
Shakspeariana published during 1874 and
1875. Ln: New Sh— Society, 1875-76.
8°   BM | BPL | BUS
Thin slice of ham let. *See* Sh— Hamlet, 1850
Thirlby (*Dr.*) Shakespearean correspondence.
See Nichols
Thiselton (Alfred Edward) Notulæ criticæ . . .
1904. 8°   BPL
Some textual notes on 'All's well . . .'
Ln: . . . 1900. 8°, pp. 32   BPL | BUS
Some textual notes on a ' Midsummer
night's dream' . . . 1903. 8°   BPL
Textual notes on 'Anthony and Cleopatra.'
With other Sh— memoranda. Ln: . . .
1899. 8°, pp. 42   BPL | BUS
Textual notes on 'Cymbeline.' 1902. Cr.
8°   BPL
Textual notes on ' Measure for measure.'
1901. 8°   BPL
Thom (William T.) Sh— and Chaucer exami-
nations, with remarks on the class-room
study of Sh—. Boston [U.S.]: Ginn &
Heath, 1888. 8° BM | BPL | BUS | SML
Two Sh— examinations, with some re-
marks on the class-room study of Sh—.
Boston [U.S.]: Ginn & Heath, 1883. 12°
            BM | BUS | SML
Thomas *Artist*. *See* Sh— Merchant . . . 1859

Thomas (Ambrose) *Composer*—
See Sh— Hamlet, 1869, 1874
,, Sh— Midsummer . . . 1866
Thomas (E. J.) *Editor.* See Sh— Much ado . . . 1904
Thomas (J.) *Publisher.* See Sh— Taming . . . 1838
Thomas (J.) *Birmingham Publisher.* See Sh— Works, 1875
Thomas (Joseph) *Printer.* See Ireland
Thomas (Moy) Hamlet's age [In 'The Athenæum,' No. 2,979, p. 703, 1884]. 4°   BM | BPL
Thomas (P. G.) *Editor.* See Greene (R.)
Thomas (T.) *Leipzig Publisher*—
See Sh— Hamlet, 1857
,, Sh— Works, 1857
Thomas (W.) See Moncrieff
Thomas DD. (Wm.) *Editor.* See Dugdale
Thomas Lord Cromwell. See Sh— Thomas . .
Thomasius (Thoma) Dictionarium . . . Cantabrigiæ . . . 1596. Fcp. 4°
Sold for £15 in July, 1903. The copy was stated to have formed part of Sh—'s library. It was bound in original calf, richly decorated with gold tooling, and bore the letters 'W. S.' impressed at the four corners of each side.
Thompson *Engraver.* See Sh— Works, 1813-14, 1825, 1827, 1830
Thompson (A. Hamilton) *Editor*—
See Sh— King Richard III., 1907
,, Sh—] Elton
Thompson '*Dangle*' (Alexander M.) Haunts of old Cockaigne. Ln: 'Clarion' Office, 1898. 12°, pp. 240 and 12 illustrations
'Mermaid tavern,' pp. 78-86; 'Was Sh— a Scotsman?' pp. 87-115.
Thompson (Edward)] Trinculo's trip to the Stratford jubilee. Ln: Printed for C. Morgan, W. Flexney, and R. Riddley, 1769. 4°, pp. 48   BPL | BUS
] Trinculo's trip . . . Second edition . . . 1770. 4°   BPL
Thompson (J.) *Engraver.* See Sh— Works, 1855-56
Thompson (W.) History and antiquities of Saint Saviour, Southwark. Ln: Ash . . . 1894. 12°   SML
Refers to the poet's brother Edmond Sh—, pp. 81 and 97.
Thompson (Wm.) Garden inscriptions . . . Poetical calendar . . . 1763
Contains the poem, ' In Sh—'s walk.'
Reprinted in Anderson's ' Poets of Great Britain, 1794,' vol. 10, p. 993.
The lines run :—
By yon hills with morning spread,
Lifting up the tufted head ;
By those golden waves of corn
Which the laughing fields adorn ;
By the fragrant breath of flowers
Stealing from the woodbine bowers ;
By this thought-inspiring shade ;
By the gleamings of the glade ;
By the babblings of the brook,
Winding slow in many a crook ;

By the rustling of the trees ;
By the humming of the bees ;
By the woodlark ; by the thrush,
Wildly warbling from the bush ;
By the fairy's shadowy tread,
O'er the cowslip's dewy head—
Father, monarch of the stage,
Glory of Eliza's age :
Sh— ! deign to lend thy face
This romantic nook to grace,
Where untaught nature sports alone,
Since thou and nature are but one !

Thoms (William John) Anecdotes and traditions. Ln: Camden Society . . . 1839. Fcp. 4°   SML
Folk-lore of Sh— [In ' The Athenæum']. Ln: 1847. 4°   BUS
On the connexion between the early English and early German drama and on the probable origin of Sh—'s ' The tempest ' [In ' New Monthly Magazine']. Ln: . . . 1841. 8°   BUS
Three notelets on Sh—. Ln: J. R. Smith, 1865. 8°, pp. viii.-136
BM | BPL | BUS | CPL | MPL | SML
Contents :—Sh— in Germany
Folk-lore of Sh—
Was Sh— ever a soldier?
Was Sh— ever a soldier ? Ln: Privately printed [1859]. 12°, pp. 24
BM | BPL | BUS | W
First appeared in ' Notes and Queries,' 23-30 April, 1859.
Thoms (Wm. John) *Editor*—
See Notes & Queries
,, Percy Society
,, Stowe
Thomson (Alexander) Random relations of Browning to Sh— [In ' Gentleman's Magazine,' Vol. 299, pp. 581-588]. Ln: . . . 1905. 8°   BM
Thomson (J.) *Editor.* See Sh— Antony . . . 1891
Thomson (J.) *Publisher.* See Sh— Works, 1753
Thomson (James) Tancred and Sigismunda. A tragedy . . . Ln: A. Millar, 1745. 8°, pp. iv.-84
The ' Prologue' refers to Sh—.
The seasons. Ln: . . . 1730. Fcp. 4°. With plates after Kent
In the verses on ' Summer' he says :—
' . . . for lofty sense,
Creative fancy, and inspection keen,
Through the deep windings of the human heart,
Is not wild Sh— thine and nature's boast ?'
Thomson (James) *Editor.* See Sh— Coriolanus, 1748, 1798
Thomson (W.) Orpheus Caledonius, or a collection of the best Scotch songs set to musick. [c. 1730.] F°
Contains the songs, with settings, from ' Macbeth.'
Thomson (William)] Bacon and Sh— on vivisection. Melbourne . . . 1881. 8°
BM | BPL

Thomson (William)] Bacon, not Sh—. In rejoinder to the 'Sh—, not Bacon, by J.
S——.' Melbourne ... 1881. 8°   BPL

Minute among the amenities. Melbourne
... 1883. 8°   BPL
On the Bacon-Sh— controversy.

On renascence drama, or history made
visible. Melbourne ... 1880. 8°
  BPL | BUS
The author claims to give ample proof of Bacon's
authorship of Sh—'s Works.

Political allegories in the renascence drama
of Francis Bacon. Melbourne ... 1882.
8°, pp. 46   BPL | MPL
On the Bacon-Sh— controversy.

Political purpose of the renascence drama
the key to the argument. Melbourne ...
1878. 8°, pp. xii.-58   MPL

Wm. Sh— in romance and reality. See
Sh—] Thomson

Thornbury (G. Walter) Sh—'s England, or
sketches of our social history in the
reign of Elizabeth. Ln: Longman ...
1856. 2 vols. 8°
  BPL | BUS | CPL | MPL | SML

Thorndike (A. H.) Influence of Beaumont
and Fletcher on Sh—. Worcester [U.S.]
... 1901. 8°   BPL

Thorne (James) Rambles by rivers: The
Avon. Ln: C. Knight ... 1845. 12°,
pp. vi.-254. Illustrated with woodcuts
  BPL | SML

The Avon of Sh— ... With illustrations
redrawn from old prints. Ln: De la
More Press, 1902. 8°, pp. 80   BPL

Thorne (John) Miscellanies. See Redford

Thorne (W. H.) Sh— versus Bacon [In 'The
Globe']. Philadelphia ... 1890. 8° BPL

Thorney Abbey. See W—— (T.)

Thorpe (Benjamin) Editor. See Apollonius

Thorpe Bookseller (Thomas) Catalogue of a
very curious collection of early plays,
pageants, etc. now selling ... Ln : ...
[c. 1825]. 8°   BPL
No fewer than fifteen early Sh— quartos figure herein.

Thorpe (Thomas) Publisher—
See Cornewallis
  ,, Marston
  ,, Sh— Sonnets, 1609

Thorpe (Thomas Bangs) Case of Lady Macbeth medically considered [In 'Harper's
Magazine']. New York ... 1854. 8° BUS

Thorpe (Wm. George) Did Bacon write Sh—'s
epitaph? [In 'Middle Temple table talk,'
pp. 41-72]. 1894. 8°   BPL

Hidden lives of Sh— and Bacon, and their
business connection, with some revelations of Sh—'s early struggles, 1587-1592.
Ln : Whittingham ... 1897. 8°, pp. 114
  BM | BPL | BUS | SML

Thoughts on Sh— worship [In 'Christian
Spectator']. Ln: ... 1864. 8°   BUS

Thrale (Richard) Publisher. See Wilkins

Three centuries of Sh— [In 'National Quarterly Review']. New York ... 1868. 8°
  BUS

Three conjurers. See Sh— Macbeth, 1763

Three great English poets: Spenser, Sh—,
and Milton. See Sh—] Three ...

Three prize essays on Sh—'s ... 'King Lear.'
By pupils of the city of London school.
Ln : Privately printed ... 1851. 8°
  BPL | W
Contents :—
Seeley (J. R.) Parallel between 'King Lear' and the
'Œdipus' of Sophocles.
Young (W.) Religious belief and feeling which pervade
'King Lear.'
Hart (E. A.) On the tragedy of 'King Lear.'

Thring (E.) Principles of grammar. Oxford,
1868. 12°   BPL
Contains 'Mood sentences of "Hamlet," "Macbeth,"
"King Lear,"' etc., pp. 99-149.

Throsby (John) Battle of Bosworth. Hinckley
... 1862. 8°   BUS
Illustrates 'King Richard III.'

Throw for a throne—
See Sh— Hamlet, 1870
  ,, Wilson (J. E.)

Thucydides. History ... of the warre
betweene the Peloponesians and the
Athenyans. Translated by Thomas
Nicolls. Ln : ... 1560. F°
See Sh— Works, Johnson and Steevens, 1773, vol. 2,
p 93, for account of this, the first, English translation
of Thucydides.

Thurber (S.) Editor. See Sh— Merchant ...
1892

Thurlow (Edward Hovell Lord)] Angelica ...
See Sh— The tempest, 1822

Thurston (John) Artist. See Sh— Works,
1803, 1803-05, 1806, 1807, 1809, 1810,
1812-15, 1813, 1817, 1818, 1825, 1826,
1827, 1829, 1830, 1831

Thurston (R.) Publisher. See Sh— Works,
1827

Thwaites (Edward). See Hall (Wm.)

Thynn (Francis) Debate between pride and
lowliness. With introduction and notes
by J. P. Collier. Ln : Sh— Society, 1841.
8°, pp. xvi.-88   BM | BPL | BUS

Tibbert (J. W.) Editor. See Sh— Othello,
1850, 1855

Ticknor (Benjamin Howard) Editor. See Sh—
Sonnets, 1877

Tieck (Lewis) Life of poets. A novel [part i.]
Leipzig: E. Fleischer, 1830. 8°, pp. ii.-
140   BUS

Tieck (Lewis) Editor. See Sh— Works, 1830,
1833, 1836, 1884-87

Tieck (Ludwig) Manuscript notes. *See* Sh—
Works, 1799-1802
Midsummer night, or Sh— and the fairies.
See Sh— Midsummer . . . 1854
Tighe (R. R.) & Davis (J. E.) Annals of
Windsor, being a history of the castle
and town, with some account of Eton,
etc. . . . 1858. 2 vols. Roy. 8°   w
Chapter 24 in vol. i. consists of 'Local illustrations of
the "Merry wives."'
Tildesley (J. C.) *See* Langford, Mackintosh &
Tildesley
Tillotson (J.) Wm. Sh—. *See* Sh—] Tillotson
Tilney (Charles). *See* Sh— Locrine (*heading*)
Tilney (F. C.) Shakespearean playing cards
. . . 1902. Cr. 8°   BPL
Tilt (C.) *Publisher. See* Sh— Works, 1836,
1837
Tilton & Co. (J. E.) *Boston* [*U.S.*] *Publishers.*
See Sh— Works, 1865
Time and truth . . . *See* Naylor
Timmins (J. F.) Dudley Sh— commemora-
tions. Reprinted from the 'Dudley
Herald ' . . . 1899-1901. 8°. With
frontispiece   BPL
Dudley Sh— commemorations . . . Brierly
Hill . . . 1901. 8°   BPL
Dudley Shakespearean souvenir . . . 1905.
8°   BPL
The poet priest: Shakespearean sermons,
compiled for the use of students and
public readers. Ln: James Blackwood
[c. 1880]. 8°, pp. 56   BPL | SML
The poet-priest . . . Ln: Blackwood . . .
[1883]. Cr. 8°, pp. 56   BM
The poet-priest . . . Ln: . . . 1884. 8°. With
portrait   BUS
The poet-priest . . . Fourth edition. Ln:
Simpkin [1890]. 8°, pp. 80   BM | BPL
Timmins (Samuel) Books on Sh—. ' Birmingham Reference Library lectures.' Birmingham: Midland Educ. Co. . . . [1885].
8°, pp. 24   BM | BPL | SML
The Birmingham library possesses a copy on large paper.
Collection of Sh—'s portraits. [*Various
dates.*] F°   BPL
Halliwell-Phillipps collection of Sh— rari-
ties: Statement prepared for the Free
Libraries committee. Birmingham . . .
1889. 8°, pp. 8   BPL
History of Warwickshire. ' Popular county
histories.' Ln: Stock . . . 1889. 8° pp.
viii.-300   BM | BLO | BPL | CTC | SML
Library. *See* Catalogue, 1899
Sh— at home [In ' Mid-England ' . . . 1879].
8°   BPL
Sh— at home [In ' Bygone Warwickshire,
edited by W. Andrews ']. Hull . . . 1893.
8°, pp. viii.-284. Illustrated   BPL | SML
] The Sh— year [Reprinted from ' Birming-
ham Daily Post ']. 1886-98. 4°   BPL

Timmins (Samuel) *Editor*—
See Sh— Hamlet, 1860
,, Sh— Works, 1879-91
Timmins (Samuel)—
See Gould   *See* Jebb
,, Ingleby   ,, Wyman
Timon in love. *See* Sh— Timon . . . 1733
Timon of Athens. *See* Sh— Timon . . .
Tinckam (C. W.) Sh— and modern fiction:
Fourth list of titles suggested by pas-
sages, scenes, and characters from Sh—
[In ' Publisher's circular,' 24th April,
p. 607. 1909]. 4°
Sh— and titles in fiction suggested by pas-
sages, scenes, or characters in the works
of Sh— [In ' Publisher's circular,' 29
June, 1907; 11 April and 24 Oct., 1908].
Ln: . . . 1907-08. 4°
' Tinker of Turvey, or Canterbury tales, 1630.'
An early collection of English novels.
Edited by J. O. Halliwell. Ln: . . . 1859.
Fcp. 4°   BPL | BUS | HCL
Twenty-six copies printed.
First issued in 1590 and again in 1608 under the title of
the 'Cobler of Caunterburie'; it appeared in 1630
with the title of the 'Tinker of Turvey: his merry
pastime in his passing from Billingsgate to Graves-End.'
It was ascribed to Robert Greene, who repudiated it in
'Greene's vision.'
' Titmarsh (Belgrave) ' *pseud.* Sh—'s skull
and Falstaff's nose. A fancy in three
acts. Ln: Stock . . . 1889. Cr. 8°, pp.
80   BPL | SML
A farce, upon the Bacon-Sh— controversy.
Titus Andronicus. *See* Sh— Titus Andronicus
Titus Andronicus.] The tragedy of Titus
Andronicus. Acted in Germany about
the year 1600 by English players. Ln:
. . . [c. 1850]. Fcp. 4°   w
A totally different play to Sh—'s ' Titus Andronicus.'
English and German text in parallel columns.
Tobin.] Benger (*Miss*) Memoirs of J. Tobin,
with selections from his unpublished
writings. Ln: Longman . . . 1820. 12°
                                         SML
Tofte (Robert)] Alba; The month's minde of a
melancholy lover . . . By R. T——*gentle-
man.* Ln: . . . 1598. 8°   HUTH
Contains the earliest allusion to Sh—'s first play :—
' "Love's labours lost." I once did see a play ycleped
so, so called to my pain . . .'
Halliwell was cognisant of two copies only. See his
'Some account of Tofte's "Alba."'

Alba . . . 1598, edited with introduction,
notes and illustrations by Alex. B.
Grosart. [Manchester: Charles E. Simms:
Privately] printed for the subscribers,
1880. Fcp. 4°, pp. lxx.-160, including
printed wrappers   BM | BLO | BUS
Issue rigidly limited to sixty-two copies.
Gives biographical details of Tofte; also his Will, 1618,
in full, where occurs one of the earliest known references to umbrellas.

Tolman (Albert Harris) Sh—'s part in the 'Taming of the shrew.' Ripon [U.S.], 1890. Cr. 8°   BM | BPL
Studies in 'Macbeth' [In the 'Atlantic Monthly'... 1892]. 8°   BPL
Views about 'Hamlet' and other essays. Boston [U.S.A.], 1904. 8°. With facsimiles   BUS
What has become of Sh—'s play, 'Love's labours won'? [In 'Chicago Univ. Decennial Pub.,' 1st series, Vol. vii., pp. 159-190]. Chicago... 1903. 4°   BPL

Tolstoy *Count* (Leo) On Sh— and the drama. First part [In 'Fortnightly Review']. Ln:... 1906. Roy. 8°   BM | BPL
On Sh— and the drama. Second part [In 'Fortnightly Review,' pp. 62-91]. Trans. by V. Tchertkoff. Ln: 1907. Roy. 8°   BM | BPL
On Sh—. Christchurch, Hants [c. 1907]. Cr. 8°   BPL
Includes E. H. Crosby on 'Sh— and the working classes,' 'The press against Sh—,' etc.

Sh—. *See Sh*—] Tolstoy

Tom King's, or the Paphian Grove. With the humours of Covent Garden, theatre, gaming house... A mock-heroick poem. Ln:... 1741. 8°. With three plates

Tom Thumb. *See* Metrical history...
Tomkins (C. F.) *Editor. See* Sh— King Richard III., 1829
Tomkins (C. F.) *See* Planché & Tomkins
Tomkins (P. W.) *Engraver. See* Sh— Works, 1792-96
Tomkins (Thomas) Poems. *See* Sh— Works: Ext. 1803
Tomkins (Thomas) *Editor. See* Poems on various subjects
Tomlins (F. G.) Brief view of the English drama from the earliest period. Ln: C. Mitchell... 1840. 12°, pp. viii.-152   BPL | SML
Nature and state of the English drama. 1841. 12°   BPL

Tomlins (Richard) *Publisher. See* Weaver
Tomlins (T. E.) Corrections of Sh—'s text, suggested by Judge Blackstone. *See Sh*—] Sh— Soc.

New document regarding the authority of the master of the revels over play-makers, plays, and players in 1581. *See Sh*—] Sh— Soc.
Origin of the Curtain Theatre, and mistakes regarding it. *See Sh*—] Sh— Soc.
Original patent for the nursery of actors and actresses in the reign of Charles II. *See Sh*—] Sh— Soc.
Three new privy seals for players in the time of Sh—. *See Sh*—] Sh— Soc.

Tomlinson (C.) On Goethe's proposed alterations in Sh—'s 'Hamlet'... 1889. 8°   BM

Tomlinson (Francis) Holy salvtation of the blessed Apostle Saint Jude, to the saints and seruants of God, preached at Pavls Crosse, 1611. Ln: 1612. Fcp. 4°   W
Dedicated 'to Sir Thomas Lucie, high sheriff of Warwickshire,' the owner of Charlecote.

Tompkins (H. W.) Stratford-on-Avon. With illustrations by Edmund H. New. Ln: Dent, 1904. Cr. 8°, pp. xii.-70. With bust and other sketches   BPL

Tonson (Jacob) *Publisher*—
  See Dryden   *See* Mountfort
  ,, Juvenalis   ,, Philips
  ,, Sh— All's well... 1714, 1734
  ,, Sh— Antony... 1692, 1701, 1714
  ,, Sh— As you like it, 1714, 1734
  ,, Sh— Comedy of errors, 1734
  ,, Sh— Coriolanus, 1714, 1734
  ,, Sh— Cymbeline, 1714, 1734
  ,, Sh— Hamlet, 1712, 1714, 1734
  ,, Sh— Julius Cæsar, 1714, 1729, 1734, 1741, 1745
  ,, Sh— King Henry IV., i., 1714, 1734
  ,, Sh— King Henry IV., ii., 1733, 1734
  ,, Sh— King Henry V., 1734
  ,, Sh— King Henry VI., i., 1735
  ,, Sh— King Henry VI., ii., 1734
  ,, Sh— King Henry VI., iii., 1734
  ,, Sh— King Henry VIII., 1714, 1732,1734
  ,, Sh— King John, 1714, 1734
  ,, Sh— King Lear, 1714, 1734
  ,, Sh— King Richard II., 1681, 1691, 1714, 1734
  ,, Sh— King Richard III., 1714, 1734, 1736, 1745, 1751, 1766
  ,, Sh— Locrine, 1734, 1735
  ,, Sh— London prodigal, 1734, 1735
  ,, Sh— Love's labours lost, 1714, 1735
  ,, Sh— Macbeth, 1710, 1714, 1729, 1734, 1750
  ,, Sh— Measure... 1734
  ,, Sh— Merchant... 1714, 1734
  ,, Sh— Merry wives... 1733, 1766
  ,, Sh— Midsummer... 1692, 1714, 1734
  ,, Sh— Much ado... 1734
  ,, Sh— Othello, 1714, 1734
  ,, Sh— Pericles, 1734
  ,, Sh— Poems, 1728
  ,, Sh— Romeo... 1714, 1734
  ,, Sh— Sir John Oldcastle, 1734, 1735
  ,, Sh— Taming... 1714, 1734
  ,, Sh— The puritan widow, 1709, 1734, 1735
  ,, Sh— The tempest, 1701, 1709, 1733, 1734, 1735
  ,, Sh— Thomas... 1734, 1735
  ,, Sh— Timon... 1696, 1714, 1734

Tonson (Jacob) *Publisher—*
See Sh— Titus . . . 1714, 1734
  ,, Sh— Troilus . . . 1679, 1695, 1714, 1734,
    1735
  ,, Sh— Twelfth night, 1714, 1728, 1734
  ,, Sh— Two gentlemen . . . 1734
  ,, Sh— Winter's tale, 1714, 1735
  ,, Sh— Yorkshire tragedy, 1735
  ,, Sh— Works, 1709, 1714, 1723-25, 1728,
    1733, 1734-36
  ,, Temple

Tonson (Jacob & Richard) *Publishers—*
See Capell
  ,, Lee (N.)
  ,, Sh— Macbeth, 1765
  ,, Sh— Merchant . . . 1764
  ,, Sh— Midsummer . . . 1754, 1755, 1763
  ,. Sh— Much ado . . . 1757, 1766
  ., Sh— Romeo . . . 1750, 1756, 1763, 1766
  ,, Sh— Taming . . . 1756
  ,, Sh— Two gentlemen . . . 1763
  ,, Sh— The tempest, 1756, 1761
  ,, Sh— Winter's tale, 1758
  ,, Sh— Works, 1740, 1745, 1747, 1750-51,
    1757, 1760, 1762. 1765, 1766, 1767-
    68

Tonson (Richard) *Publisher—*
See Rymer
  ,, Sh— Antony . . . 1677
  ,, Sh— Julius Cæsar, 1741
  ,, Sh— King Richard II., 1681, 1691
  ,, Sh— King Richard III., 1745, 1751, 1766
  ,, Sh— Macbeth, 1750

Tooke (Benjamin) *Publisher—*
See Shadwell
  ,, Sh— Merchant . . . 1713
Tooke (Horne) On the Jaggard folio. *See*
Sh— Works, 1623

Topsell (Edward) Time's lamentation, or an
exposition upon the prophet Joel. Ln :
William Stansby for Nathaniel Butter,
and are to be sold at his shop at Saint
Austen's gate, 1613. Fcp. 4°, pp. xl.-502
Refers to Lucrece and Cleopatra, p. vii. verso ; fables
of poets, p. 62 ; histrionicall players, p. 69 ; shaking
of a speare, p. 249 ; bauderie in print, p. 429 ; plays
on the sabbath, p. 426.

Topsell (Edward) & Gesner (Conradus) Historie of fovre-footed beastes. Describing
the true and liuely figure of euery beast,
with a discourse of their seuerall names,
conditions, kindes, vertues, both naturall
and medicinall, countries of their breed,
their loue and hate to mankinde, and the
wonderfull worke of God in their creation, preseruation, and destruction.
Necessary for all diuines and students,
because the story of euery beast is amplified with narrations out of scriptures,
fathers, phylosophers, physitians, and

poets ; wherein are declared diuers
hyerogliphicks, emblems, epigrams, and
other good histories . . . Ln : Printed by
William Iaggard, 1607. F°, pp. xliii.-758-
xii. Illustrated on wood throughout
BM | SML
One of Sh—'s reference books for natural history.

Topsell (Edward) & Gesner (Conradus) Historie of serpents, or the second booke of
liuing creatures ; wherein is contained
their diuine, naturall, and morall descriptions, with their liuely figures, names,
conditions, kindes, and natures of all
venemous beasts : with their seuerall
poysons and antidotes ; their deepe
hatred to mankind, and the wonderfull
worke of God in their creation and destruction. Necessary and profitable to
all sortes of men. Collected out of diuine
scriptures, fathers, phylosophers, physitians, and poets : amplified with sundry
accidentall histories, hieroglyphicks, epigrams, emblems, and ænigmaticall obseruations. Ln : Printed by William
Jaggard, 1608. F°, pp. xii.-316-viii. (the
first blank). Illustrated on wood BM | SML

Tottell (Richard) Tottel's miscellany. *See*
Howard

Tottell (Richard) *Printer & Publisher—*
See Bandello & Brooke
  ,, Painter
  ,, Sh— Romeo . . . 1562
Tour in quest of genealogy. *See* Fenton
Tourgenieff (I.) ' Hamlet ' and ' Don Quixote'
[In ' Fortnightly Review']. 1894. Roy.
8° BPL
Tourist's guide, or rambles round Leamington
. . . [c. 1865]. Cr. 8°. With plates
Includes Stratford-on-Avon, with an illustration.

Tournaments of love : A series of eight joco-
serious challenges and answers used in
the tournaments of love in the XVII.
century [The original papers, manuscript
and printed, mounted into a volume].
1614-15. F° W
' He set up his bills here in Messina and challenged
Cupid at the flight ; and my uncle's fool, reading the
challenge, subscribed for Cupid, and challenged him
at the bird-bolt.'—*Much ado,* act i., sc. 1.

Tourneisen (J. J.) *Basle Printer—*
See Farmer
  ,, Malone
Tovey (B.) *Publisher. See* Sh— King Henry
VIII., 1758
Tovey (D. C.) *Editor. See* Sh— King Lear,
1896
Towndrow (Richard F.) Canker-blooms [In
' Madresfield Agric. Club Quarterly'].
1904. Cr. 8° BPL
' You canker-blossom ! you thief of love.'—*Midsummer
night's dream,* iii., 2.

Towndrow (R. F.) & Birdwood (*Sir* Geo.) Canker-blooms and canker [In ' The Athenæum,' No. *4,004*, p. 123, No. *4,005*, p. 156, No. *4,006*, p. 188, No. *4,007*, p. 219, No. *4,009*, p. 284, July-Aug.] 1904
BM | BPL
Illustrates the ' Sonnets,' ' King Henry IV.,' and ' Much ado.'

Towne (E. C.) Bacon-Sh— [In ' Boston Evening Transcript,' Jan. 19, 23, 25, 1883] BUS

Townsend (G. H.) Wm. Sh— not an impostor. *See* Sh—

Townsend (Mabel Surtees) Sh— and sentiment [In the 'Animal's friend,' Sept. Ln : 1896]. Roy. 8° pp. 4. With portrait

Stories from Sh—. *See* Sh— Works : Ext. 1899

Toynbee (Paget) Dante and Sh— [In ' The Athenæum,' p. 759, Dec., 1899]. 4°
Illustrates ' Love's labours lost.' BM | BPL

Tragedy of fratricide punished, or Prince Hamlet of Denmark. Acted in Germany about the year 1603 by English players. Ln : [c. 1850]. Fcp. 4° W
English and German text in parallel columns.
A play quite different to Sh—'s ' Hamlet.'

Tragedy of Sir Walter Ralegh. *See* Sewell

Tragical history of Macbeth : A new song. Ln : J. Miller . . . 1815. 8°, pp. 20 BUS

Tragi-comical history of . . . Lisander and Calista. *See* Davenant

Traill (H. D.) & Mann (J. S.) Social England : A record of the progress of the people in religion, laws, learning, arts, industry, commerce, science, literature, and manners, from the earliest times . . . Ln : Cassell . . . 1902-04. 6 vols. 4°. Profusely illustrated (in colours and otherwise), including Chandos portrait
Francis Bacon, vol. i., p. 70 ; vol. iii., p. 724 *et seq.* ; vol. iii., pp. 8-224.
Sh— and his contemporaries, vol. iii., pp. 481-719 ; vol. iv., pp. 149-211.

Translations from Sh—. *See* Sh— Works : Ext. 1850

Translator of Sh—. *See* Baudissin

Travers (Charles) *pseud. See* Tweedie (C.)

Travers (S. Smith)] Sh—'s sonnets : To whom were they addressed ? Hobart, Tasmania : Davies Brothers, 1881. 8°, pp. 28 (including printed wrappers) BM

Travesties—
See Facetiæ
,, Sh— Separate pieces

Treasury of English literature. Edited by Kate M. Warren. Introduction by Stopford Brooke. Ln : Constable . . . 1908. 6 vols. 8°

Treasury of thought from Sh—. *See* Sh— Works : Ext. 1866

Treatise on the passions. *See* Foote (S.)

Treatyse of a galaunt. Edited by J. O. Halliwell . . . 1860. 8° BPL

Tree (*Sir* Herbert Beerbohm) Hamlet. From an actor's prompt-book [In ' Fortnightly Review,' Dec.] 1895 Roy. 8° BM | BPL

Hamlet. From an actor's prompt-book. New York : De Vinne Press, 1896. Cr. 8°, pp. 44 (including printed wrappers)

] Souvenir : ' Julius Cæsar.' Ln : Her Majesty's Theatre, 1898. 4° BPL

] Souvenir : 'King John.' Ln : H.M. Theatre, 1899. 4° BPL

Souvenir : ' King Richard II.' Ln : H.M. Theatre, 1903. 8° BPL

Souvenir : ' Merry wives of Windsor.' Ln : H.M. Theatre, 1902. 8° BPL

Souvenir : ' Midsummer night's dream.' Ln : H.M. Theatre, 1900. 4° BPL

Souvenir : 'The tempest.' Ln : H.M.Theatre, 1904. 8° BPL

Souvenir : ' Twelfth night.' Ln : H.M. Theatre, 1901. 8° BPL

Tree (*Sir* H. B.) *Actor*—
See Scott (C. W.)
,, Sh— Hamlet . . . Flower, 1882

Treen (A. Edward) Rugby School. *See* Memorials . . .

Treglown (Ernest G.) *Artist. See* Sh— Sonnets, 1895

Trench (H.) Deirdre wedded, Sh—, and other poems . . . Ln : Methuen, 1908. Cr. 8° BPL

Trench *Archbp.* (Richard Chenevix) Every good gift from above : A tercentenary sermon, 24 April, 1864 . . . Second edition. Ln : Macmillan . . . 1864. 8°, pp. 20 BPL | BUS

Trevelyan (*Sir* George Otto) *Editor. See* Macaulay

' Trinculo's ' trip to the jubilee. *See* Thompson

Triphook (R.) *Publisher. See* Peele

Trippe *Poet* (Simon). *See* Roberts

Triumph of envy, or the vision of Shilock the Jew. Ln : . . . 1712. 8°. With folding plate

Triumphant widow, 1677. *See* Sh—] Manuscript

Troilus and Cressida. *See* Sh— Troilus and Cressida

Trotter (Alex. M.) *Editor. See* Sh— Coriolanus, 1894

Trotter (T.) *Engraver. See* Sh— Works, 1793, 1807

Troublesome raigne of John King of England. *See* Six old plays
A foundation of Sh—'s play.

Troutbeck (J.) *Editor. See* Sh— Taming . . . 1878

Truchy (J. H.) *Paris Publisher—*
See Sh— As you like it, 1869
,, Sh— Hamlet, 1865

True and exact catalogue of all the plays and other dramatic pieces that were ever yet printed in the English tongue, in alphabetical order [including Sh—'s plays] . . . Ln : Printed for W. Feales at Rowe's Head over against Clement's Inn Gate, 1732. 8°, pp. 36   SML | W

True and perfect relation . . . of the late . . . [gunpowder plot]. 1606. *See* Sh— Autograph

True chronicle history of King Leir. *See* Sh— King Lear, 1605

True discoverie of the king's majestie's proceedings against the parliament and against this kingdome. Ln : . . . 1643. Fcp. 4°
Refers on p. 6 to the 'Tragedie of King Richard III.'

True tragedie of Richarde Duke of Yorke—
See Sh— King Henry VI., iii., 1595
,, Sh— King Henry VI.,i.-ii.-iii., 1619,1817

True tragedie of Richard the third. *See* Sh— King Richard III., 1595

Trumbull (J.) The Whitman-Sh— question [In ' Poet lore ']. Philadelphia . . . 1891. 8°   BPL

Trundell *or* Trundle (John) *Publisher—*
See Sh— Hamlet, 1603
,, Westward for smelts

Truths illustrated by great authors : A dictionary . . . *See* Sh— Works : Ext. 1853

Tschischwitz (Benno) *Editor—*
See Sh— Hamlet, 1869
,, Sh— Works, 1869

Tucker (F. J.)] Light of Sh— : Passages illustrative of the higher teaching of Sh—'s dramas. *See* Sh— Works : Ext. 1897

Tucker (S.) Assignment of arms to Sh— and Arden, MDXCVI.-MDXCIX. With introductory notes. Ln : Mitchell & Hughes . . . 1884. 4°   BPL | SML

Tucker (T. G.) Making of a Sh—. An address delivered by invitation of the Melbourne Sh— Society . . . 1908. 8°   BPL

Tucker-Brooke (C. F.) *Editor—*
See Plutarch
,, Sh— Works, 1908

Tuckerman (H. T.) Castles and Sh— [In ' Month in England,' pp. 170-199. 1854]. 12°   BPL

Tuckett (John) *Printer. See* Sh— King Richard II., 1862

Tuckey *Publisher. See* Isaac & Tuckey

Tudor translations, edited by W. E. Henley. Ln : D. Nutt . . . 1892 *et seq.* 38 vols. 8°
     BM | BLO | BPL | CTC

Tupper (Martin Farquhar) Sh— : An ode. *See Sh—*] Tupper

Turbervile (George) Book of falconrie or hawking . . . [with poem by George Gascoigne commending the sport]. Ln : T. Purfoot . . . 1611. Fcp. 4°. With woodcuts   W
Originally dedicated in 1575 to Ambrose Dudley Earl of Warwick.
Illustrates ' Much ado.'

Epitaphs, epigrams, songs, and sonets. With a discourse of the friendly affections of Trymetes to Pyndare his ladie. At Ln : Imprinted by Henry Denham . . . 1570. 8°
A rare Shakespearean volume, dedicated to Anne Countess of Warwick. At p. 143 is an ' Epitaph on Arthur Brooke, drownde in passing to New Haven.' Brooke was the first translator of the story of ' Romeo and Juliet ' from the Italian. Turberville says :—
' In proufe that he for myter [metre] did excell,
  As may be iudged by Iuliet and hir mate,
For there he shewyde his cunning passing well
  When he the tale to English did translate.'
A copy sold July, 1900, for £105.

Noble arte of venerie. 1611. *See Sh—*] Sh— notices

Turbervile (George) *Editor. See* Mantuan

Turbutt (G. M. R.) Droeshout portrait of Sh— [In ' The Athenæum,' No. 4,039, p. 380, Mar., 1905]. 4°   BM | BPL

Turbutt (G. M. R.) *See* Madan & Turbutt

Turle (Henry Frederic) *Editor. See* Notes & Queries

Turnbull (Monica P.) Short day's work. Ln : Unicorn Press, 1902. Cr. 8°, pp. 140 BPL
Treats of ' Hamlet,' ' King Lear,' ' Macbeth,' ' Othello.',

Turnbull (Thomas) *Edinburgh Printer. See* Sh— Works, 1804

Turnbull (W. R.) Othello : A critical study. Edinburgh . . . 1892. 8° BM | BPL | MPL

Turner (A.) *Bibliophile. See* Catalogue, 1864

Turner (G.) Falstaff letters [In ' The Theatre ' . . . 1885]. Roy. 8°   BPL

Turner (Godfrey Wordsworth) Sh— made easy [In ' Tinsley's Magazine.' Ln : 1877]. 8°   BUS

Turner (J.) Address delivered before the Birmingham Sh— Reading Club at the annual dinner. Birmingham . . . 1885. 8°   BPL

Fragmentary thoughts about Sh—. *See Sh—*] Turner

Thoughts about Sh—. *See Sh—*] Turner

Turner (Sharon) Richard the third ; a poem . . . 1845. 12°   BPL

Turner (T.) *Bibliophile. See* Catalogue, 1860

Turner (William) *Publisher. See* Pix

Turner & Fisher *Philadelphia Publishers. See* Sh— Othello, 1838

' Twain (Mark) ' *pseud. See* Clemens (S. L.)

Tweddell (G. M.) Sh— ; his times and contemporaries. *See Sh—*] Tweddell

Tweedie *pseud.* '*Charles Travers*' (Charles) Editor. *See* Sh— Macbeth, 1844

Twelfth night . . . *See* Sh— Twelfth night . . .

Twelve merry jests of the wydow Edyth. 1864. *See Sh*—] Sh—'s jest books

Twine (L.) Patterne of painefull adventures. *See Sh*—] Sh—'s library
A foundation of ' Pericles.'

Twins (The). *See* Sh— Comedy of errors, 1780

Twiss (Francis) Complete verbal index to the plays of Sh—. *See* Sh— Works : Ext. 1805

Two brethren and their wives. *See* Rich

Two gentlemen of Verona. *See* Sh— Two gentlemen . . .

Two indexes to characters in Sh—. *See* Sh— Works : Ext. 1886, 1887

Two Italian gentlemen. *See* Munday

Two noble kinsmen. *See* Sh— Two noble kinsmen

Tyas (R.) *Publisher. See* Sh— Works, 1839-43, 1843

Tyde taryeth no man, 1576. *See* Reprints . . .

Tyler (James Endell) Henry of Monmouth : Memoirs of Henry V. Ln : Bentley,1838. 2 vols. 8°. With portrait   BUS | SML

Tyler (Moses Coit) Direct study of English masterpieces : Sh— course . . . Ann Arbor [U.S.], Sheehan . . . 1877. 8°, pp. 12 BUS

Tyler (Thomas) Herbert-Fitton theory of Sh—'s ' Sonnets ' : A reply. Ln : Nutt . . . 1898. 8°, pp. 24   BM | BPL | BUS
Philosophy of ' Hamlet.' Ln : Williams & Norgate, 1874. 8°, pp. 32
   BM | BPL | BUS | SML
Sh— idolatry. Ln : New Sh— Society, 1887-92. 8°   BM
' Sonnets of Sh—.' Appendix on the Herbert-Fitton theory : A reply to ' Sidney Lee.' Ln : Nutt, 1899. 8°, pp. 24

Tyler (T.) *Editor*—
See Sh— King Henry VI., iii., 1891
 ,, Sh— Sonnets, 1886, 1890, 1899

Tylney (Charles). *See* Sh— Locrine, 1595

Tymme (Thomas) Silver watch bell . . . Ln : . . . 1612. 8°. Black letter
Contains an account of ' Bermuda or the isle of devils,' the supposed scene of ' The tempest.'

Tymms (Samuel) Compendium of the ancient and present state of . . . Warwickshire. Ln : J. B. Nichols . . . 1835. 8°
Several references to Sh— and Stratford.

Typographical sketches. *See* Sh— Works : Ext. 1791

Tyrer (C. E.) Dante and Sh— [In ' The Athenæum,' Nov., No. 3,761, p. 722. 1899]. 4°   BM | BPL
Illustrates the sesquipedalian word in ' Love's labours lost,' v., 1.

Tyrrel (John) *Bibliophile. See* Rodd & Maddox

Tyrrell (Henry) *Editor*—
See Sh— Faire Em, 1850
 ,, Sh— Merry devil, 1851
 ,, Sh— Works, 1850, 1850-53, 1853

Tyrrell (*Sir* James) Manuscript. *See Sh*—] Tyrrell

Tyrwhitt (Thomas)] Observations and conjectures upon some passages of Sh—. Oxford : At the Clarendon Press, sold by Dan Prince . . . 1766. 8°, pp. 54
   BM | BPL | BUS | W

Tyson (W.) Heming's players at Bristol in the reign of Henry VIII. *See Sh*—] Sh— Society

Tytler (Sarah) American cousins ; a story of Sh—'s country. [c. 1897.] 12°   BPL

UDALL (Nicholas) Ralph Roister Doister : A comedy. And the ' Tragedie of Gorboduc,' by T. Norton and T. Sackville. Edited by W. D. Cooper. Ln : Sh— Society, 1847. 8°, pp. lxviii.-160
   BM | BPL | BUS | SML
Ralph Roister Doister. Edited by E. Arber. ' English reprints.' . . . 1869. 8°   BPL

Udall (Nicholas) *Editor. See* Terence

Ulrici (*Dr.* Hermann) Sh—'s dramatic art and his relation to Calderon and Goethe. Translated by A. J. W. Morrison. Ln : Chapman . . . 1846. 8°, pp. xvi.-554
   BM | BPL | BUS | MPL | SML
Sh—'s dramatic art. History and character of Sh—'s plays . . . Translated . . . by L. Dora Schmitz. Ln : Bell . . . 1876. 2 vols. Cr. 8°   BM | BPL | BUS | CPL | SML

Ulrici (*Dr.* H.) *Editor*—
See Sh— Merchant . . . 1871
 ,, Sh— Romeo . . . 1853
 ,, Sh— Works, 1853

Ulrici.] Review of 'Sh—'s dramatic art' [extracted from ' The Inquirer,' 11 April]. Ln : Chapman . . . 1846. 8°, pp. 8 BUS

' Umbra ' *pseud. See* Ghost player's guide

Umbrellas. *See* Tofte

Underdown (Thomas) Excellent historye of Theseus. and Ariadne. Wherein is declared her feruent loue to hym and his trayterous dealynge toward her. Written in English meeter in comendacion of all good women and to the infamie of such lyght huswyues as Phedra the sister of Ariadne was, which fled away with Theseus, her sister's husbande, as is declared in this. Imprinted at Ln. by Rycharde Iohnes and are to be sold at his shop,

ioyning to the southwest doore of Paule's
Church, 28 of Ianuarie 1566 [1567]. 8°
MRL
The picturesque title of Sh—'s 'Merchant . . . 1600,'
was apparently founded on Underdown.

Underdown (Thomas) *Editor.* *See* Heliodorus

Underhill (G. F.) Literary epochs: Chapters
on periods of intellectual activity. Ln :
Stock . . . 1887.   12°   BM | BLO | CTC
Has a chapter on Sh— and his contemporaries.

Underhill family. *See* Bellew

Universal magazine of knowledge and
pleasure . . . Vol. 62. Ln : John Hinton
. . . 1778.   8°
At pp. 20-21 is an account of Coriolanus from Livy and
Plutarch, ending up, 'for what Milton somewhere
says of himself is perhaps even more unquestionably
true of Sh—, that his "mother bore him a speaker of
what God made his own, and not a translator."'

Universal passion. *See* Miller (James)

Upcott (Wm.) Press errors. *See* Sh— Works,
1807

Upon Sh—'s chair. *See* Sh—] Collection . . .

Upton (G. P.) *Editor.* *See* Sh— Works, 1906

Upton *Prebendary of Rochester* (John) Critical
observations on Sh— . . . Ln : Printed
for G. Hawkins in Fleet Street, 1746.
8°, pp. iv.-362
BM | BPL | BUS | CTC | MPL | SML | W

Critical observations . . . Dublin : Geo. &
Alex. Ewing at the Angel and Bible in
Dame Street, 1747.   12°, pp. 300, partly
in black letter   BPL | W

Critical observations . . . Second edition,
with alterations and additions. Ln : G.
Hawkins . . . 1748. 8°, pp. lxii.-416-
xviii.   BM | BPL | BUS | SML | W
The ' Reverie' is omitted from this edition.

Urban club ; Fourth Sh— festival proceedings . . . 1863. 8°   BPL

Urban club [Collection of Shakespearean pro-
grammes]. 1876. 12°   BPL

Urban club. *See also* Jeremiah

Urquhart *Publisher.* *See* Garrick

Urwick (Henry) On ' Twelfth night ': Sh—
Club paper. Stratford-on-Avon : [Pri-
vately printed] 1908. Cr. 8°, pp. 12
Sh— and politics. *See* Sh—] Urwick

Urwick (W. E.) *Editor.* *See* Sh— The tempest, 1896, 1897

Useful miscellanies, containing the tragi-
comedy of Joan of Hedington. In imitation of Sh—, etc. [part I.] Ln : . . . 1712.
8°   W

Uses of Sh— off the stage [In Harper's ' New
Monthly Magazine,' 1882]. Roy. 8° BPL

Uwins (T.) *Artist.* *See* Sh— Works, 1811

 —— (R.) *See* Verstegan (R.)
Vaccai *Composer.* *See* Sh—
Romeo . . . 1832
Vaile (E. O.) Sh— - Bacon con-
troversy [In ' Scribner's
Monthly,' 1875]. Roy. 8°
BUS

Valentine (*Mrs.* Laura) Tales from Sh—. *See*
Sh— Works : Ext. 1881

Valentine (*Mrs.* Laura) *Editor*—
See Gold, silver, lead
,, Sh— Works, 1868, 1869, 1875, 1896,
1905, 1906
,, Sh— Works : Ext. 1860

Valesco. Iewe's prophesy, or newes from
Rome. Ln : . . . 1607. Fcp. 4°   BUS
The prophesy which closes the work is headed, 'Caleb
Shilock his prophesie for the yeere 1607.'

Valpy (A. J.) *Editor*—
See Sh— Poems, 1862
,, Sh— Works, 1832-34, 1834, 1835, 1840,
1842, 1843, 1844, 1848, 1857, 1867,
1870, 1877-78, 1880

Valpy (*Dr.* Richard)] Poems, odes, prologues,
and epilogues spoken on public occasions
at Reading school . . . Ln : J. Nichols &
Son, 1804. 8°, pp. viii.-264   BPL
Contains several Shakespearean prologues and references.

The roses. *See* Sh— King Henry VI., iii.,
1795, 1810

Valpy (*Dr.* R.) *Editor*—
See Sh— King Henry IV., ii., 1801
,, Sh— King John, 1800, 1803
,, Sh— Merchant . . . 1802

Vamp (Hugo) *Editor*—
See Sh— King Lear, 1830
,, Sh— Macbeth, 1830
,, Sh— Merchant . . . 1830
,, Sh— Othello, 1830

Vandam (A. D.) *Editor.* *See* Houssaye

Van Dam (B. A. P.) & Stoffel (C.) Sh—. *See*
Sh—] Van Dam

Vandenhoek's widow (A.) *Gottingen Pub-
lisher*—
See Sh— Julius Cæsar, 1777
,, Sh— Macbeth, 1778

Vandenhoeck & Ruprecht *Gottingen Publishers.* *See* Sh— Merchant . . . 1830

Vandenhoff *Actor* (George) Dramatic reminiscences, or actors and actresses in England and America . . . 1860. Cr. 8°

Vandenhoff (John) *Actor.* *See* Cornucopia

Vanderbank *Artist.* *See* Musical . . .

Van der Gucht (G.) *Engraver*—
See Cibber
,, Sh— King Lear, 1723
,, Sh— Macbeth, 1750
,, Sh— Much ado . . . 1757
,, Sh— Works, 1709, 1747, 1762

Van Hulst (K.) *Kampen Publisher.* *See* Sh—
The tempest, 1854
Vanloo *Artist.* *See* Cibber
Van Voorst (J.) *Publisher.* *See* Sh— As you
like it, 1840
Van Wart (Albert) Studies on the character
of Hamlet. Sheffield: Leng . . . 1889.
8°, pp. 16
Van Winkle (Edward S.) Spelling of Sh—'s
name. *See Sh*—] Van Winkle
Varagnac (Bernard) Sh— and the Baconian
theory [In 'Christian register.' Boston
[U.S. 1878]. 8°   BUS
Variorum editions. *See* Sh— Works, 1765,
1766, 1767, 1767-68, 1768, 1771, 1773,
1778, 1785, 1790, 1793, 1794, 1795, 1799-
1802, 1803, 1805, 1805-09, 1809, 1813,
1816, 1821, 1826, 1835-36, 1837, 1838-43,
1871-1908
Varnam (T.) *Publisher.* *See* Sh— Works, 1714
Vaughan *Engraver.* *See* Camus
Vaughan (C. J.) *Editor*—
See Sh— King Lear, 1837
„ Sh— King Richard II., 1836
Vaughan (*Prof.* Henry Halford) New readings
and new renderings of Sh—'s tragedies.
Ln : Kegan Paul . . . 1878-86. 3 vols. 8°
BM | BPL | BUS | MPL
New readings . . . Ln : Kegan Paul, 1886.
8°   BM | BPL | BUS | SML
Contents :—' King Henry VIII.,' ' King Richard III.,'
and ' Cymbeline.'
Vaughan (*Prof.* H. H.) *Editor.* *See* Sh—
Works, 1876-86
Vautrollier (Thomas) *Printer*—
See Mulcaster
„ Plutarchus
Vaux *the elder* (*Lord*). *See* Edwards (R.)
Vavasor. Verses. *See* Poems
Vavasour (Nicholas) *Publisher*—
See Marlowe
„ Rowley
Veazie (W.) *Boston* [*U.S.*] *Publisher.* *See*
Sh— Works, 1859
Vega Carpio (Lope Felix de) Romeo and
Juliet. A comedy . . . built upon the
same story on which that greatest dra-
matic poet . . . founded his tragedy. Ln :
W. Griffin, 1770. 8°, pp. iv.-30 BPL | BUS
Vega Carpio (Lopez F. de) *Editor.* *See* Sh—
Romeo . . . 1770, 1869
Vellum printing—
See Sh— Passionate . . . 1883
„ Sh— Sonnets, 1909
„ Sh— Works, 1803-05, 1804, 1809, 1904-07
Venice—
See Sh— Merchant . . .
„ Sherley
Vennar (R.) Apology for England's joy, 1614.
See Reprints
Venus and Adonis. *See* Sh— Venus . . .

' Venus and Adonis ' travesty. *See* Sh—
Venus . . . 1864
Verbal criticism : An epistle to Mr. Pope,
occasioned by Theobald's Sh— and
Bentley's Milton. Ln : . . . 1733. F° w
A satire on Sh—'s commentators.
Verdi (Giuseppe) *Composer*—
See Sh— Macbeth, 1850, 1860
„ Sh— Poems, 1862
Vere *Earl of Oxford* (Edward) Verses. *See*
Poems
Vere *Earl of Oxford* (Edward). *See also*
Edwards (R.)
Vere (Thomas) *Publisher*—
See Holland (S.)
„ Sh— Venus . . . 1675
Vergne (*Mdme.*) *Paris Publisher.* *See* Sh—
King Richard III., 1828
Verity (Arthur Wilson) Influence of Christo-
pher Marlowe on Sh—'s earlier style . . .
Harness prize essay. Cambridge . . .
1886. 8°   BM | BPL | BUS
Verity (A. W.) *Editor*—
See Sh— As you like it, 1899, 1904
„ Sh— Coriolanus, 1905
„ Sh— Hamlet, 1904
„ Sh— Julius Cæsar, 1893, 1895, 1898,
1900, 1902, 1904
„ Sh— King Henry V., 1900, 1902, 1905
„ Sh— King Lear, 1897, 1906
„ Sh— King Richard II., 1899, 1900, 1903,
1904
„ Sh— Macbeth, 1901, 1902, 1903, 1904,
1906
„ Sh— Merchant . . . 1898, 1901, 1904, 1907
„ Sh— Midsummer . . . 1893, 1894, 1898,
1900, 1901, 1903, 1905
„ Sh— Much ado . . . 1890
„ Sh— The tempest, 1896, 1897
„ Sh— Twelfth night, 1893, 1894, 1895,
1902, 1904
„ Sh— Works, 1886-91, 1890-1905
' Verjuice (Pel) *pseud.* *See* Pemberton
Verlaine (P.) Sh— and Racine [In ' Fortnightly
Review,' 1894]. Roy. 8°   BM | BPL
Vernon (J.) New songs in ' The witches.' *See*
Sh— Macbeth, 1800
Vernon (J.) *Composer.* *See* Sh— Twelfth
night, 1766, 1800
Vernor (T.) *Publisher.* *See* Sh— Works, 1790,
1793, 1797, 1798, 1798-1800
Vernor & Hood *Publishers*—
See Sh— Antony . . . 1799
„ Sh— Coriolanus, 1825
„ Sh— Works, 1798, 1800, 1808, 1809
Vernor, Hood & Sharpe *Publishers.* *See* Sh—
Works, 1810
Verplanck (Gulian C.) *Editor.* *See* Sh—
Works, 1844-47

(674)

Versatile ingenium ; The wittie companion, or jests of all sorts from city and countrie, court and universitie. With . . . life of the laughing philosopher Democritus of Abdera, by ' Democritus junior.' Amsterdam : Stephen Swartz, 1679. 8°
At p. 86 a paraphrase of the 'Merchant of Venice' is given. At p. 95 Bankes' performing horse (mentioned in ' Love's labours lost ') is referred to, and Ben Jonson's ' Sejanus' at p. 29.

Verses to Sir Thomas Hanmer. *See* Collins

Verstegan (Richard)] Restitution of decayed intelligence in antiquities concerning the most noble and renowned English nation by the study and travel of R. V——. Antwerp : R. Bruney . . . 1605. Fcp. 4°. With curious engravings BM
In the ' Epistle to the English nation,' dated ' Antwerp, 7th Feb., 1605,' it is stated :—' Breakspear, Shakspear, and the like have been sirnames imposed upon the first bearers of them for valour and feates of armes.' Some commendatory verses herein, signed ' R. B.,' have been attributed to Richard Barnefield. Reprinted in 1628, in 1634, and since.

Vertue (George) Effigies . . . [Sh——, Chaucer, Gower, Spenser, Beaumont, Fletcher, Jonson, Milton, Cowley, Butler, Waller, and Dryden]. Ln : . . . 1727. F°. Twelve large portraits

Vertue (George) *Engraver*—
See Birch
  ,, Sh— Works, 1723-25, 1747

Verulam (*Baron*). *See* Bacon (Francis)

Very (Jones) Essays and poems. Boston [U.S.] . . . 1839. 12° BPL | BUS
Contains articles : ' Sh—,' pp. 39-82; and ' Hamlet,' pp. 83-104.

Vestry book of . . . Holy Trinity. *See* Stratford-upon-Avon

Vicars (Samuel ?) *Stationers' warden. See* Sh— Sir John Oldcastle (*heading*)

Vicinity of Leamington : A guide to Warwick, Coventry, and Stratford. Leamington . . . 1840. 12° BPL

Vickers (G.) *Publishers. See* Sh— Works, 1852

Vickery (Eleanor G. *or* Willis) *Editor*—
See Renan
  ,, Sh— The tempest, 1896

Vickery *Judge* (Willis) *Editor. See* New Shakespeareana

Victor (Benjamin)] History of the theatres of London and Dublin from 1730 to the present time. To which is added an annual register of all the plays performed at the Theatres Royal in London from 1712. With notes and anecdotes. Ln : T. Davies, R. Griffiths & T. Becket, 1761-71. 3 vols. Cr. 8° BPL | SML
Contains much about Shakespearean performances and Garrick's jubilee of 1769.

History of the theatres of London, containing an annual register of tragedies, comedies, operas, performed in London 1771-95 . . . Ln : . . . 1796. 2 vols. 8°

Victor (Benjamin) History of the theatres . . . containing an annual register of new pieces, revivals, pantomimes. With occasional notes and anecdotes by W. C. Oulton. Ln : . . . 1818. 3 vols. Cr. 8°

Victor (Benjamin) *Editor. See* Sh— Two gentlemen . . . 1763

Victor (Wilhelm) Sh—'s pronunciation. Ln : Nutt . . . 1906. Cr. 8° BPL
Part I. Sh— phonology with a rime index.
  ,, II. Sh— reader in the old spelling.

Victor (Wilhelm) *Editor*—
See Sh— King Lear, 1886
  ,, Sh— Works, 1886

Victoria (*Empress*). *See* Elizabeth (*Queen*)

Victoria history of the county of Warwick. Ln : Constable . . . 1904. Vol. I. [all yet issued]. F°, pp. xxiv.-416. Illustrated
BM | BLO | BPL | CTC | SML
This volume deals chiefly with the natural history and physical features of the county. Its chapter headings comprise :— Botany, Zoology, Insects, Crustacea, Fishes, Reptiles, Birds, Mammals, Early man, Anglo-Saxon remains, Domesday survey, Holders of lands, Ancient defensive earthworks, and an index to Domesday.

Victory (Louis H.) Higher teaching of Sh—. Ln : Stock . . . 1896. Cr. 8°, pp. 202
BM | BPL | BUS

Views in Stratford-on-Avon. *See* Rider

Views in Stratford-upon-Avon [Sh— and Stratford, with descriptive letterpress]. [1859.] 8° BM

Vigo *or* Vigon (John) & Gale (Thomas) Whole worke of chirurgerie . . . Ln : T. East . . . 1586. 8°
Known at Stratford in Sh—'s life-time. It was the subject of an action against Philip Rogers in 1604, when that individual was sued by Wm. Sh— for £1 15s. 10d., balance of a malt debt.
It also contains some unnoticed verse on pp. 33, 65, and 77, by Hall, Field, and Cunningham.

Viles (Edward) & Furnivall (F. J.) *Editors.* Rogues and vagabonds of Sh—'s youth. Described by Jn. Awdeley in his ' Fraternitye of vacabondes, 1561-73,' Thos. Harman in his 'Caveat for common cursetors, 1567-73,' and in the 'Groundworke of conny catching, 1592 ' . . . Ln : New Sh— Society, 1880. 4°, pp. xxx.-112. Illustrated BM | BPL

Rogues and vagabonds . . . Ln : Chatto . . . 1907. 8°, pp. 150

Village opera. *See Sh*—] Sh— miscellanies

Villanova (Arnaldus de)] Regimen sanitatis en Francoys. Souuerain remede contre lepydimie. Traictee pour congnoistre les vrines. Remede tresutile pour la grosse verole. Lyon : Claude Nourry . . . 1514 W
According to Ireland, this volume formed part of Sh—'s library.
On the fly-leaf is a ' signature of Sh—' from the Ireland factory.
Attached is an autograph letter from Thomas Caldecott to Dr. Sherwen, presenting him with the book.

Villemain (M.) Essay on Sh—. *See* Sh— Works, 1836-39

Vince (C. A.) John Smith, dramatist [In ' Central Literary Magazine ']. Birmingham . . . 1898. 8° BPL

Vincent (Augustine). *See* Levi (S. L.)

Vincent (C.) *Composer*. *See* Sh— Poems, 1906

Vincent (J.) *Oxford Publisher*. *See* Sh— Hamlet, 1849

Vincent (W. T.) Recollections of Leslie. *See* Leslie

Vining *Editor*. *See* Sh— Comedy . . . 1864

Vining (Edward P.) Mystery of Hamlet: An attempt to solve an old problem. Philadelphia . . . 1881. 8° BM | BPL | BUS
The author's theory is that Hamlet was a woman, educated and dressed as a man.

Time in the play of 'Hamlet.' New York Sh— Society, 1886. 8° BM | BPL

' Viola.' Flowers of Sh—. *See* Sh— Works: Ext. 1883

Virgil. *See* Sh—] Downes

Virgin queen. *See* Waldron

Virginia. *See* Good speed

Virtue (George) *Publisher*. *See* Sh— Works, 1845-51, 1846, 1850, 1851

Visions of the western railways. 1838. 4° BPL
Contains Shakespeareana.

Visitation (The). *See* Garrick

Visitation of Warwickshire. Edited by J. Fetherston. Warwick: Cooke . . . 1859. Roy. 8° BM | BLO | BPL | CTC | SML | W

Visitors' books. *See* Stratford] Sh—'s birthplace

Vocal music to Sh—'s plays: 'Hamlet.' [c. 1880.] 8° BPL

Vogel (A.) *Artist & Engraver*. *See* Sh— Midsummer . . . 1868, 1870

Voltaire *pseud*. (F. M. Arouet de) Critical essays on dramatic poetry. Glasgow . . . 1761. 12° BPL
Contains the essay 'Of Sh—,' pp. 129-131.

Letter to the French Academy, containing an appeal on the merits of Sh— . . . and preface by the editor. 1777. 8° BPL

Plan of ' Hamlet ' [In his Works, Vol. 25, pp. 128-145]. 1770. 8° BPL

Voltaire (F. M. A. de)—
See Asch (M.)   *See* Montagu
,, Keate (G.)   ,, Sh—] Dennis

Von Cossel (Louise) *Editor*. *See* Mantzius

Vorbrodt. Ireland's forgeries. [1885.] 4° BM

Vortigern. *See* Ireland (W. H.)

' Vortigern ' under consideration. *See* Oulton

Vredenburg (Edric) *Editor*. *See* Sh— Merry wives . . . 1895, 1897

—— (C.) Queen Mab. *See* Sh— Works: Ext. 1882

W—— (I.) *Publisher See* Sh— Faire Em, 1605
,, Wright (John)

W—— (J.) The valiant Scot . . . Ln : . . . 1637
Shakespearean allusions at pp. 3, 22, and 69.

W—— (P.) A query on ' Hamlet.' With reply [In ' Fraser's Magazine, 1879.'] 8° BM | BPL

W—— (R.) *Printer*. *See* Sh— King Henry IV., i., 1700

W—— (T.) *See* Walkington (Thomas)

W—— (T.) Thorney abbey, or the London maid. A tragedy. Ln : . . . 1662. 12° W
An imitation of Sh—'s ' Macbeth.'

W—— (T.) *Printer*. *See* Holland (S.)

W—— (Th.) *See* Wright (Thomas)

W—— (W.) *See* Warner (W.)

W—— (W.) *Printer*—
See Sh— King Henry IV., i., 1613
,, Sh— King Henry VI., ii., 1600
,, Sh— King Richard II., 1608
,, Sh— Love's labours lost, 1598
,, White (William)

Wadd (W.) Medico-chirurgical commentary on Sh— [In ' Quarterly Journal of Science of the Royal Inst.,' p. 234, 1824]. 8°

Waddington (H.) *Editor*. *See* Sh— Coriolanus, 1819

Wade (*Dr.*) *See* Stratford] Proposed . . .

Wade *Poet* (Thomas) What does ' Hamlet ' mean ? A lecture . . . Jersey : ' British Press ' Office [1840]. 8°, pp. 38 BM | BPL | BUS | MPL | W

Wade (Thomas) *Editor*. *See* Sh— Works, 1839-43

Wadsworth (W.) Under the greenwood tree with Sh—. New York [c. 1888]. 8° BPL

Wageman *Artist*. *See* Sh— Winter's tale, 1850

Wager (Wm.) Cruell debtter, 1566; the only three leaves left. *See* New Sh— Society

Wagner (A.) *Editor*. *See* Sh— Macbeth, 1890

Wagner (C.) *Editor*. *See* Sh— Works, 1797-1801, 1799-1801

Wagner *Ph.D.* (Wilhelm) Sh— in Griechenland [c. 1875.] 8° BM

Wagner (W.) *Editor*—
See Sh— Macbeth, 1872
,, Sh— Works, 1879-91, 1880-91

Wagrez (J.) *Artist*. *See* Sh— Romeo . . . 1892

Waite (W. Hallsworth) Sh—'s Stratford : A pictorial pilgrimage. Birmingham : J. L. Allday, 1895. 8° SML

Sh—'s Stratford. Birmingham : J. L. Allday [1897]. 8°, pp. 70 BM | BPL | SML

Wake (*Sir* Isaac) Rex Platonicus, sive musæ
regnantes. Oxon. . . . 1607. Fcp. 4°
BPL | BUS
On p. 18 mention is made of an interlude embracing the
story of Macbeth, performed before K. James VI. &
I. at Oxford, in 1605, said to have led Sh— to write
his play on the subject.

Waking man's dreame. Ln: . . . [c. 1630].
Fcp. 4°, pp. 59-68
BUS
Contains the story on which the induction to 'Taming
of the Shrew' is founded.
Supposed to be a fragment of Richard Edwards' 'Comic
stories.'

Walbancke (M.) *Publisher—*
See Annalia Dubrensia
,, Bancroft (T.)
,, Minshul

Walbancke (Nathaniel) *Publisher. See* Field

Walbran (C. J.)] Dictionary of quotations
from Sh—. *See* Sh— Works: Ext. 1843,
1849
Thoughts on 'Romeo and Juliet.' Ripon
. . . 1852. 12°
BPL

Waldegrave (Robert) *Edinburgh Printer. See*
Fenner

Walden (Ernest) Shakespearian criticism,
textual and literary, from Dryden to the
end of the 18th century. Harness prize
essay. Bradford: Brear & Co., 1895. Cr.
8°, pp. 136
BPL

Waldron (Francis Godolphin) Ancient and
modern miscellany, containing a republication of scarce and valuable tracts;
biographical anecdotes of theatrical performers; with portraits of actors; scarce
and original poetry; and other interesting . . . articles. Ln: E. & S. Harding,
1794. 4°. With 10 plates
BUS
For contents see Hubbard, Catalogue, p. 212.

] Free reflections on 'Miscellaneous papers
. . . of Wm. Sh— in the possession of
Samuel Ireland.' To which are added,
extracts from an unpublished manuscript play, called 'The virgin queen,'
written by, or in imitation of, Sh— [On
the Ireland forgeries]. Ln: F. G. Wal-
ron . . . 1796. 8°, pp. 56
BM | BPL | BUS | CPL | W
The author is said to have been greatly assisted by Geo.
Steevens.

Shakespearean miscellany, containing a collection of scarce and valuable tracts,
biographical anecdotes of theatrical performers, with portraits of ancient and
modern actors, of many of whom there
are no prints extant . . . Two elegies by
Dr. Donne . . . not in his works, a concise
history of the English stage . . . printed
chiefly from manuscripts. Ln: Lackington, Allen & Co., 1802. 4°, pp. iv.-50-4-24.
With plates
BPL | BUS | SML

Shakespearean miscellany . . . Ln: J. Manson, 1804. 4°
BUS

Waldron (Francis Godolphin)] The virgin
queen. A drama in five acts. Attempted
as a sequel to Sh—'s 'The tempest.' Ln:
Printed for the author, 1797. 8°, pp. iv.-
104
BM | BPL | BUS

Waldron (F. G.) & Dibdin (T.) Compendious
history of the English stage from the
earliest period . . . and a sketch of the
most eminent in the profession . . . 1800.
12°. With engraved title and frontispiece
BPL
Many references to Sh—.

Wales—
See Branch   *See* Flint Castle
,, Fenton   ,, Wigstead

Waley (John) *Printer. See* John

Walford (E.) *Stratford Publisher. See* Stratford

Walford (Edward) 'Kinton' portrait of Sh—.
See Sh—] Walford

Walford (Edward) *Editor. See* Antiquarian
magazine

Walk under the Sh— [cliff] and other poems.
Dover . . . 1836. 12°
BPL

Walker *Publisher. See* Kemble

Walker *DD.* (Anthony) ΕΥΡΗΚΑ-ΕΥΡΗΚΑ:
The virtuous woman found, her loss be-
wailed, and character exemplified, in a
sermon preached at Felsted in Essex,
April 30, 1678, at the funeral of that
most excellent lady the right honourable
and eminently religious and charitable
Mary, countess dowager of Warwick, the
most illustrious pattern of sincere piety
and solid goodness this age hath produced. With so large additions as may
be stiled the life of that noble lady. To
which are annexed some of her ladyships
pious and useful meditations. Ln:
Nathaniel Ranew at the King's Arms in
S. Paul's Church-Yard, 1678. Cr. 8°, pp.
224. Portrait by S. Harding, 1798, inserted
W
With 'Catalogue of books,' 12 pp., at end.
Refers to the stage at p. 41 thus:—'As the cryer used
to call spectators to the secular plays, 'Come, see
those shews.'

Walker (Antony) *Artist & Engraver. See*
Sh— Romeo . . . 1754

Walker (Charles Clement) Heminge & Condell.
See Heminge

Walker (George) *Editor. See* Select specimens

Walker (Gilbert)] Manifest detection of the
most vyle and detestable use of dice play.
Edited [with notes] by J. O. Halliwell.
Ln: Percy Society . . . 1850. 8°
BUS | HCL
Affords an explanation of obscure gaming terms used by
Sh—.

Walker (G. S.) *Editor. See* Sh— King Henry
VIII., 1818

Walker (Hugh) *Editor.* *See* Sh— Merry devil
. . . 1897
Walker (J.) *Publisher*—
See Sh— Works, 1797, 1798, 1811, 1820,
1821, 1822, 1823, 1825
,, Sh— Works : Ext. 1798
Walker (Joseph Cooper) Historical essay on
the Irish stage. Dublin . . . 1789. 4°,
pp. 20
Historical memoir on Italian tragedy. Ln :
. . . 1799. 4°   BUS
Contains a parallel between L. Groto's tragedy
'Hadriana' and 'Romeo and Juliet.'

Revival of the drama in Italy . . . 1805.
8°   BPL
Walker (R.) *Publisher*—
See Sh— All's well . . . 1734
,, Sh— Comedy . . . 1734
,, Sh— Coriolanus, 1735
,, Sh— Cymbeline, 1735
,, Sh— King Henry IV., i., 1734
,, Sh— King Henry IV., ii., 1700, 1734
,, Sh— King Henry VI., iii., 1735
,, Sh— King John, 1735
,, Sh— King Lear, 1735
,, Sh— King Richard II., 1735
,, Sh— Locrine, 1734
,, Sh— Love's labours lost, 1735
,, Sh— Merchant . . . 1735
,, Sh— Merry wives . . . 1734
,, Sh— Much ado . . . 1735
,, Sh— Pericles, 1734
,, Sh— Romeo . . . 1735
,, Sh— Sir John Oldcastle, 1735
,, Sh— Taming . . . 1735
,, Sh— The tempest, 1735
,, Sh— Thomas . . . 1734
,, Sh— Twelfth night, 1735
,, Sh— Two gentlemen . . . 1734
,, Sh— Winter's tale, 1735
,, Sh— Yorkshire tragedy, 1735
,, Sh— Works, 1734-35
Walker (W.) *Engraver. See* Sh— Romeo . . .
1773
Walker (Wm. Sidney) Critical examination of
the text of Sh—, with remarks on his
language and that of his contemporaries,
together with notes . . . Edited by W. N.
Lettsom. Ln : J. R. Smith, 1860. 3 vols.
Cr. 8°   BM | BPL | BUS | CPL | MPL | W
Sh—'s versification and its apparent irre-
gularities explained by examples from
early and late English writers. Edited
by W. N. Lettsom. Ln : J. R. Smith . . .
1854. 12°, pp. xxiv.-296
                         BM | BPL | BUS | MPL | W
Walker (Wm. S.) *See also* Furness (H. K.)
Walkington (Thomas)] Optick glasse of
humours, or touchstone of a golden tem-
perature. By T. W——. Oxford . . .

[c. 1605]. 8°. With woodcut title and
frontispiece
Includes the story from Scaliger of one who could not
endure bagpipes, mentioned in the 'Merchant of
Venice.'
Reprinted in 1664.
Walkley (A. B.) Dramatic criticism : Three
lectures delivered at the Royal Institu-
tion, Feb., 1903. Ln : J. Murray, 1903.
8°, pp. 126   BM | BLO | CTC
Playhouse impressions. Ln : Unwin . . .
1892. Cr. 8°, pp. viii.-262
Gives critiques of 'Much ado,' pp. 15-18 ; 'Hamlet,'
pp. 19-30 ; 'As you like it,' pp. 31-34 ; 'Taming of the
shrew,' pp. 35-41 ; 'Antony and Cleopatra,' pp. 43-46.
Walkley (Thomas) *Publisher*—
See Davenant
,, Sh— Othello, 1622
Wall (Alfred H.) Davenant bust of Sh— [In
'Saint Louis Public Library Magazine '].
1897. 8°   BPL
Doctors Sh— knew. *See* Andrews
] Guide to Kenilworth, Warwick, and Strat-
ford-on-Avon. Manchester . . . 1868.
Cr. 8°. With map
] Guide to Stratford-on-Avon, its church and
vicinity . . . Manchester : H. Heywood
[c. 1885]. Cr. 8°, pp. 28. Illustrated BPL
Hathaway cottage. *See* Andrews
] Sh— adversaria, part I. Stratford-upon-
Avon . . . 1890. 4°   BM
] Sh— memorial library ; List of the editions
of Sh—'s works published in America . . .
[1890.] 8°   BM
Visitor's brief guide to Stratford-on-Avon.
Stratford : W. Stanton [c. 1894]. 12°,
pp. 8. Illustrated
Warwickshire folk-lore. *See* Andrews
Wall (A. H.) *Artist. See* Somerville
Wall (A. H.) *Editor. See* Sh—] Shakespearean
Wallace (*Prof.* Charles Wm.) *Advance sheets
from* ' Sh—, The Globe, and Blackfriars.'
Stratford-on-Avon : A. H. Bullen, 1909.
Roy. 8°, pp. 20 (including printed wrap-
pers)   SML
Gives a transcript of a plea at common law by Thomasina
Osteler, in Feb., 1616, which reveals the origin and
history of the Globe and Blackfriars theatres, the
shares owned by Sh— and his associates, and an
estimate of the profits.
New Shakespearean discoveries ; Sh— as a
man among men [In ' Harper's Monthly
Magazine,' pp. 489-510, March], 1910.
Roy. 8°. Illustrated   BM | BPL
With facsimile of a fresh Sh — signature attached to a
deposition in the Montjoy case, found at the Record
Office.
Newly-discovered Sh— documents. Lincoln, Nebraska [U.S.], 1905. 8°   BPL
Sh— and the Blackfriars, based on documents lately discovered by the writer [In
' Century Magazine,' pp. 742-752, Sept.]
1910. Roy, 8°. Illustrated
                                BM | BLO | CTC

Wallace (*Prof.* Charles Wm.) Sh—'s money interest in the Globe theater: Newly discovered records of a suit-at-law which show that his profits as part owner were smaller than has been supposed [In 'Century Magazine,' pp. 500-512, Aug., 1910]. Roy. 8°. Illustrated   SML
Wm. Sh—. *See Sh—*] Wallace
Wallace (James)] Shakesperian sketches by James W . . . . . e, of Christ's College, Cambridge. Ln : Printed for the author's private use, 1795. 8°, pp. xii.-88-iv. With coloured plates by Isaac Cruikshank   BPL | BUS | W
The word 'Shakesperian' was added to the title by the author's friends, who thought the work resembled that poet's style.
Waller *Publisher.* *See* Riccoboni
Waller (Edmund) Songs. *See* Sh— Midsummer . . . 1755
Waller (H. F.) Helen Faucit. *See* Martin
Waller (J. G.) Prospero of ' The tempest ' [In 'Gentleman's Magazine,' 1853]. 8° BUS
Waller (J. J.) Prize essays: chiefly Shakespearean studies. Aberystwyth : J. Gibson, 1882. 8°   BM | BPL | SML
On Sh—'s clowns ; the supernatural in Sh— ; Sh—'s hypocrites ; The drama : its decline and reformation.
Waller (T.) *Publisher—*
See Guthrie
,, Sh— Works : Ext. 1752
,, Whalley
Walley (Henry) *Publisher—*
See Sh— Troilus . . . (*heading*)
,, Sh— Troilus . . . 1609
Wallis (James) *Publisher—*
See Sh— Works, 1803-05, 1805
,, Sh— Works : Ext. 1800
Walmesley (Joshua) *Editor. See* Sh— Works, 1829
Walpole *Earl of Orford* (Horace) Letter to George Montagu, 14 Oct., 1756 [In ' Letters, edited by Peter Cunningham,' Vol. 3, p. 36, 1857]. 8°   BM
Says :—' John and I are just going to Garrick's with a grove of cypresses in our hands, like the Kentish men at conquest. He has built a temple to his master, Sh—, and I am going to adorn the outside, since his modesty would not let me decorate it within, as I proposed with these mottoes:
   " Quod spiro et placeo, si placeo, tuum est."
    " That I spirit have and nature,
     That sense breathes in every feature ;
     That I please, if please I do ;—
     Sh—, all I owe to you !" '
Walpole (Horace) *Editor. See* Sh— Macbeth, 1789
Walsh (C. M.) *Editor. See* Sh— Sonnets, 1908
Walsh (J.) *Publisher—*
See Sh— Midsummer . . . 1740, 1755
,, Sh— The tempest, 1756
Walter (W. J.) *Editor. See* Sh— Othello, 1822, 1826

Walters (C. F.) Italian influence on Sh— [In 'Gentleman's Magazine,' 1895]. 8° BPL
Walters (Frank) ' Hamlet ' and ' The tempest' : A Shakespearian contrast [In ' Modern Review,' 1882]. 8°   BPL
Studies of some of Sh—'s plays. Ln : Sunday School Assoc., 1889. Cr. 8°, pp. 192   BM | BLO | BPL | CTC | SML
Studies . . . Second edition. Ln : Sunday School Assoc., 1902. Cr. 8°, pp. 192 and Chandos portrait   BM | BLO | CTC
Walters (James Cuming) Mystery of Sh—'s sonnets ; An attempted elucidation. Ln : New Century Press, 1899. Cr. 8°, pp. 120   BPL | BUS | MPL | SML
Walthoe *jun.* (T.) *Publisher. See* Sh— King Henry VI., ii.-iii., 1720
Walton. Verses. *See* Reprints
Walton (C.) A brief for ' Ophelia ' [In ' Poetlore.' Philadelphia, 1891]. 8°   BPL
Walton (Izaak) Life of Donne. *See* Donne
Wandering Jew, 1647. *See Sh—*] Sh— notices
Warburton. Sh— copy book. *See* Sh— Works : Ext. 1865
Warburton *Bp.* (Wm.)] Letters from a late eminent prelate to one of his friends [Richard Hurd *Bp.*]. Kidderminster [c. 1808]. 4°   BPL
Says De Quincey (in his Works, vol. vi., p. 259) of Warburton :—' The natural vegetation of his intellect tended to that kind of fungus which is called "crochet," so much so that if he had a just and powerful thought (as sometimes in germ he had), or a wide and beautiful thought, yet by the mere perversity of his tortuous brain it was soon digested into a crochet.'
Preface—
See Eighteenth . . .
,, Sh— Works, 1747 *et seq.*
' Of all literary exercitations of speculative men, whether designed for use or entertainment, there are none of so much importance than those which let us into the knowledge of our nature. Others may exercise the reason or amuse the imagination ; but these only can improve the heart and form the mind to wisdom. Now, in this science our Sh— is confessed to occupy the foremost place ; whether we consider the amazing sagacity with which he investigates every hidden spring and wheel of human action, or his happy manner of communicating this knowledge in the just and living paintings which he has given us of all our passions, appetites, pursuits. These afford a lesson which can never be too often repeated or too constantly inculcated.'
Shakespearean correspondence. *See* Nichols
Warburton *Bp.* (William) *Editor. See* Sh— Works, 1747, 1769, 1771, 1795, 1803-05
Warburton.] Answer to certain passages in Mr. W.'s preface to his . . . Sh—. Together with some remarks of the many errors and false criticisms in the work itself. Ln : . . . 1748. 8°   BM | W
An attack on Bp. Warburton for his presumption in undertaking a task for which he was unfitted.
] Impartial remarks upon the preface of Dr. Warburton. Ln : . . . 1758. 8°
] Watson (J. S.) Life of [*Bishop*] Warburton. 1863. 8°   BPL

Warburton *Bp.* (W.)—
　See Annotations　　*See* Johnson
　,, Cibber (T.)　　　,, Nichols
　,, Grey　　　　　,, Stevens
　,, Horatian . . .　　,, Theobald
Ward *Artist.* *See* Sh— Works, 1875-76
Ward *Editor.* *See* Sh— Poems, 1880
Ward *Sculptor.* Statue [of Sh—] in the Central Park, New York—
　See Sh—] Monument
　,, Sh—] Ward
Ward (*Dr.* Adolphus William) F. G. Fleay. *See* Fleay
　History of English dramatic literature to the death of Queen Anne. Ln: Macmillan . . . 1875. 2 vols. 8°
　　BM | BLO | BPL | BUS | CTC | MPL | SML
　Chapter iv. (pp. 270-513) is on Sh—.
　History of English dramatic literature . . . Ln: Macmillan, 1899. 3 vols. 8°
　　BM | BLO | CTC | SML
　Proposed monument to Sh— at Weimar [In ' The Athenæum,' No. 3,869, p. 841, Dec., 1901]. 4°　　　BM | BPL
Ward (*Dr.* A. W.) *See also* Fleay, On certain . . .
Ward (C. A.) Sonnets by ' Feltham Burghley.' Ln: 1855. 8°　　　　　　BUS
　Sonnet 140 is 'To Sh—.'
Ward (Catharine Weed)] Sh— festival; Plays and players at Stratford-on-Avon [In ' Windsor Magazine,' May, 1907]. Roy. 8°, pp. 765-781. Illustrated　　BPL
　Sh— festival [In ' Windsor Magazine.' Ln: . . . 1909. Roy. 8°. Illustrated　BPL
Ward (Clarence S.) Wit, wisdom, and beauties of Sh—. *See* Sh— Works: Ext. 1887
Ward (Edward)] The libertine's choice, or mistaken happiness of the fool in fashion. Ln: H. Hills, 1709. 8°, pp. 16
　Refers to Sh— and Ben Jonson.
Ward (Elizabeth Stuart Phelps) *Editor.* *See* Sh— Works: Ext. 1901
Ward (F. & E.) Handbook for visitors to Stratford-upon-Avon. Stratford: Ward . . . 1851. 8°, pp. 40 and two plates
Ward (H. Snowden) Sports and pastimes of Sh—'s day. ' Sh— Club paper.' Stratford: Privately printed, 1906. Cr. 8°, pp. 8
Ward (H. S. & C. W.) Sh— and Stratford-on-Avon. New York . . . 1896. 8°. Illustrated　　　　　　　　　　BUS
　Sh—'s town and times. Ln: Dawbarn & Ward, 1896. Fcp. 4°, pp. 174. Illustrated
　　BM | BPL | BUS | MPL | SML
　Sh—'s town and times. Second edition, enlarged. Ln: Dawbarn & Ward, 1901. Roy. 8°, pp. 184 and 4 plates　BUS

Ward (H. S. & C. W.) Sh—'s town and times. Third edition, enlarged. Ln: Dawbarn, 1905. 4°, pp. 184 and 4 photogravure plates　　　　　　　　　BPL
　Issued again in 1908 with fresh imprint.
　Shakespearean guide to Stratford-on-Avon . . . [1897.] Ln: Dawbarn. 12°, pp. 138. With map and plates　　BPL | SML
Ward *Vicar of Stratford* (John) Diary . . . extending from 1648 to 1679. From the original manuscripts preserved in the library of the Medical Society of London. Arranged by Charles Severn. . . Ln: H. Colburn . . . 1839. 8°, pp. xx.-316
　　BPL | BUS | CPL | MPL | SML | W
　Pages 31 to 87 are devoted to Sh—.
Ward (John). *See also* Sh— Autograph, *Sæc.* XVII.
Ward (Roger) *Printer.* *See* Des Periers
Wardle (T.) *Philadelphia Publisher.* *See* Sh— Works, 1828, 1831, 1836
Ware (John R.) Sh— done into French [In ' Atlantic Monthly,' Aug. Boston [U.S.] 1860]. 8°　　　　　　　BUS
Wargrave theatricals. *See* Barrymore
Warlow (J.) Ode . . . *See* Sh—] Warlow
Warner *Editor* (B.) Famous introductions to Sh—'s plays. New York . . . 1906. 8°
　　　　　　　　　　　　BPL
Warner (Beverley E.) English history in Sh—'s plays. New York . . . 1894. 8°
　　　　　BM | BPL | BUS | MPL
　English history in Sh—'s plays. New York: Longman, 1899. 12°　　SML
　English history in Sh—'s plays. New York: Longman, 1903. 12°　　SML
Warner (Charles Dudley) The people for whom Sh— wrote [In ' Atlantic Monthly,' June-July. Boston [U.S.] 1879]. 8°　BUS
　The people for whom Sh— wrote. New York: Harper, 1897. 12°, pp. 194. Illustrated　　BM | BPL | BUS | MPL | SML
Warner (G. F.) Autograph play of Philip Massinger, ' Believe as you list ' [In ' The Athenæum,' No. 3,821, p. 91, Jan., 1910]. 4°　　　　　　BM | BPL
Warner *Botanist* (Richard)] Letter to David Garrick concerning a glossary to the plays of Sh— . . . to which is annexed a specimen . . . including letter 'A.' Ln: Printed for the author by T. Davies, 1768. 8°, pp. 110 BM | BPL | BUS | MPL | SML | W
　Sh— glossary. Author's original manuscript, c. 1768
　Said by Lowndes to be in the British Museum, but the B. M. Sh-- catalogue does not mention it.
Warner (T.) *Publisher.* *See* Comedian . . .
Warner (William) Albion's England: The third time corrected and augmented. Continuing an history of the same

George Guy Greville fourth Earl of Warwick

See p. 681

countrey and kingdome from the originals
of the same until her nowe maiestie's
moste blessed raigne, with intermixture
of histories and invention, performed in
verse. Imprinted at Ln. by Thomas
Orwin . . . 1592. Fcp. 4°, black letter

Of exceeding Shakespearean interest, as the poet's 'King
Lear' closely follows in plot the poetical story of Lear
narrated herein.
This important source has been entirely overlooked by
the poet's biographers.

Warner (William) Albion's England : A con-
tinued historie of the same kingdome
from the originals of the first inhabitants
thereof. Ln : . . . 1597. Fcp. 4°
Albion's England : A continued historie.
Ln : . . . 1602. Fcp. 4°   BUS
Warner (W.) Editor. See Plautus
Warning for fair women. See Simpson (R.)
Warnke (Karl) Editor—
See Sh— Arden, 1888
   „ Sh— Birth, 1887
   „ Sh— Faire Em, 1883
   „ Sh— Merry devil . . . 1884
   „ Sh— Mucedorus, 1878
   „ Sh— Works, 1883-88, 1887
Warren Engraver. See Sh— Works, 1806, 1807
Warren (A.) Artist. See Sh— Winter's tale,
   1866
Warren (H.) Artist. See Langford
Warren (John) Poem. See Sh— Poems, 1640
Warren (Kate M.) Treasury of English litera-
   ture. See Sh— Works : Ext. 1908
Warren Actress (Mrs.) Portrait. See Sh—
   All's well . . . 1786
Warren (Thomas) Printer & Publisher—
See Dugdale
   „ Husbands
   „ Sh— The tempest, 1695
   „ Sh— Timon . . . 1696, 1703
Warton (Joseph) Observations on ' King
   Lear ' [In ' The Adventurer,' edited by
   Dr. S. Johnson. Ln : . . . 1753-54]. 8°
                                         BUS
Observations on ' The tempest ' [In ' The
   Adventurer.' Ln : . . 1753]. 8° BUS
Observations on ' The tempest ' and ' King
   Lear ' [In ' British Essayists,' Vol. 21,
   and ' The Adventurer ']. 1823. 12° BPL
The enthusiast, or the lover of nature . . .
   1740
' What are the lays of artful Addison,
Coldly correct, to Sh—'s warblings wild ?
Whom on the winding Avon's willow'd banks
Fair fancy found and bore the smiling babe
To a close cavern (still the shepherds show
The sacred place, whence with religious awe
They hear, returning from the field at eve,
Strange whisperings of sweet music through the air).
Here as with honey gathered from the rock
She fed the little prattler and with songs
Oft soothed his wondering ears with deep delight,
On her soft lap he sat and caught the sounds.'

Warton the younger (Thomas) Miscellaneous
   odes . . . 1777
Contains a 'Monody written near Stratford-upon-Avon':
' Avon, thy rural view, thy pastures wild,
The willows that o'erhang thy twilight edge,
Their boughs entangling with the embattled sedge,
Thy brink with watery foliage quaintly fringed,
Thy surface with reflected verdure tinged
Soothe me with many a pensive pleasure mild ;
But while I muse that here the bard divine,
Whose sacred dust yon high arched aisles enclose,
Where the tall windows rise in stately rows
Above the embowering shade,
Here first at fancy's fairy-circled shrine
Of daisies pied his infant offering made,
Here playful yet in stripling years unripe
Framed of thy reeds a shrill and artless pipe ;
Sudden thy beauties, Avon, all are fled,
As at the waving of some magic wand.'

. . . .

Warton (Prof. Thomas) Editor. See Sh—
   Works, 1770-71
Warwick (Ambrose Dudley Earl of). See Tur-
   bervile
Warwick (Anne Countess of). See Turberville
Warwick (Frances Evelyn Countess of) War-
   wick castle and its earls, from Saxon
   times to the present day. Ln : Hutchin-
   son . . . 1903. 2 vols. Roy. 8°, pp. 914.
   With 174 illustrations
                    BM | BLO | BPL | CTC
Warwick (George Guy Greville Earl of) Col-
   lection of drawings. See Catalogue, 1896
General library. See Simmons
Sh— collection. See Jaggard (W.)
Warwickshire collection. See Jaggard (W.)
Warwick (Mary Countess of). See Walker
Warwick.] History of the Earl of Warwick,
   sirnamed the king-maker, containing his
   amours and other memorable transac-
   tions, by the author of ' Memoirs of the
   English court.' To which is added the
   remaining part of the unknown lady's
   pacquet of letters. Ln : J. Woodward
   . . . & J. Morphew, 1708. 8°, pp. 198-
   174-80   SML | W
] Warwick and its castle . . . their familiar
   scenes . . . with sketches . . . of local
   characters. By a young student. 1827.
   Cr. 8°. With plate   W
] Warwick castle. A poem. Embellished
   with engravings from drawings by J. Roe.
   Stratford-on-Avon . . . 1812. Fcp. 4° W
With views of Warwick and Kenilworth not to be found
elsewhere.
Warwick castle—
See also Dugdale   See also Jago
   „ „ Jaggard   „ „ Warwickshire
Warwickshire—
See Andrews   See Barnard
   „ Aston Cantlow   „ Bettesworth
   „ Badger   „ Birmingham
   „ Bagnall   „ Bloxam

Warwickshire—

See Brassington
 „ Brewer
 „ Brief . . .
 „ Browne
 „ Burgess
 „ Burrow
 „ Carnegie
 „ Charlecote
 „ Charm
 „ Clarke
 „ Colvile
 „ Corner
 „ Coventry
 „ Cox .
 „ Culverwell
 „ Curiosities
 „ Curling
 „ Davis
 „ Deakin
 „ Dibdin
 „ Domesday
 „ Dowdall
 „ Dugdale
 „ East . . .
 „ Edwards
 „ Fairholt
 „ Field
 „ Fisher
 „ Fleay
 „ French
 „ Garrett
 „ Gascoigne
 „ Giraud
 „ Graphic
 „ Green
 „ Gresley
 „ Guide
 „ Halliwell, Selection . . .
 „ Hannett
 „ Harris
 „ Harrison
 „ Hawthorne
 „ Hill
 „ Hodgson
 „ Homes . . .
 „ Howells
 „ Howitt
 „ Hoyer
 „ Hubaud
 „ Huckell
 „ Hudson
 „ In . . .
 „ Irving (W.)
 „ Jaffray
 „ Jaggard
 „ Jago
 „ Jones
 „ Jordan

See Kemp
 „ King
 „ Kingsley
 „ Knight
 „ Laneham
 „ Langford
 „ Leyland
 „ Logismos
 „ Lucy
 „ Mabie
 „ Malins
 „ May
 „ Memorials . . .
 „ Merridew
 „ Miller
 „ Moncrieff
 „ Morgan
 „ Morley
 „ Mott
 „ Newspaper . . .
 „ Niven
 „ Norris
 „ O'Keeffe
 „ Pearce
 „ Perry
 „ Photographic . . .
 „ Pictorial . . .
 „ Picturesque . . .
 „ Poet . . .
 „ Poole
 „ Pudsey
 „ Questions
 „ Quiller-Couch
 „ Ramsay
 „ Reader
 „ Ribton-Turner
 „ Rimmer
 „ Ryland
 „ Sabatini
 „ Sandys
 „ Savage
 „ Scott (E. J. L.)
 „ Sh—] Shakespeareana
 „ Sh—] Walter
 „ Sh—] Wise
 „ Sharp
 „ Sharpe
 „ Shaw
 „ Shirley
 „ Showell
 „ Smith
 „ Stopes
 „ Stratford-on-Avon
 „ Stronach
 „ Sumner
 „ Thorne
 „ Timmins

Warwickshire—

See Tompkins
 „ Tourist . . .
 „ Tymms
 „ Tytler
 „ Vicinity . . .
 „ Victoria . . .
 „ Views
 „ Visitation . . .
 „ Wadsworth
 „ Waite

See Wall
 „ West
 „ Wheler
 „ White
 „ Williams
 „ Wilson
 „ Windle
 „ Winter
 „ Wivell
 „ Yarranton

Warwickshire antiquarian magazine. Edited by John Featherstone. Warwick : Cooke, 1859-77. 8 parts. Roy. 8°. Illustrated
BM | BPL | SML | W
The plates consist of old armorial bearings (with folded pedigrees), monuments, and views.

Warwickshire ; Collection of thirty-five original papers relating to Warwickshire and mentioning the Sh— family, 1620-1710. F°. Original manuscripts mounted into one volume W
On the fly-leaf Halliwell has noted that these papers 'prove there was another William Sh— contemporary with the great poet.'

Warwickshire lad. See Dibdin (C.)
Warwickshire language. See Andrews
Warwickshire place names. See Andrews
Was Bacon Mr. Gladstone ? See Newspaper cuttings . . .
Was Hamlet mad ?—
 See Hamlet
 „ Watts
Was Sh— a builder ? See Sh—] Was . . .
Was Sh— a Catholic ? See Sh—] Was . . .
Was Sh— a lawyer. See Sh—] T—— (H.)
Was Sh— a Roman Catholic? See Sh—] Was . . .
Was Sh— a scholar ? See Sh—] Was . . .
Watchman and reflector. See Sh—] Watchman
Waterford [Ireland] jubilee. See Garrick
Waterhouse (N.) England of Sh— [In ' Transactions of the Historic Society of Lancashire & Cheshire ' . . . c. 1865]. 8° BPL
Waterlow (A. J.) Editor. See Roffe
Waters (H. F.) Genealogical gleanings in England. Boston : New England Genealogical Society, 1888. 2 vols. 8° BUS
With particulars of Sh— and a view of Harvard House, Stratford-on-Avon, before Miss Marie Corelli purchased and restored it.

Waters (Robert) Wm. Sh— portrayed by himself. See Sh—] Waters
Waterson (John) Publisher. See Sh— Two noble kinsmen, 1634
Waterson (Simon) Publisher—
 See Jovius
 „ Sh— Thomas . . . (heading)
Watkin (John) Memoirs of Sheridan. See Sheridan

Watkins (Richard) *Printer*. *See* Gray

Watson (*Sir* Fredk. Beilby)] Religious and moral sentences culled from Sh—. *See* Sh— Works: Ext. 1843, 1847, 1850

Watson (J. S.) Life of Porson. *See* Porson
Life of Warburton. *See* Warburton

Watson (J. T.) Dictionary of poetical quotations. *See* Sh— Works: Ext. 1837, 1847, 1863, 1865

Watson (S.) *Dublin Publisher*. *See* Sh— Works, 1766

Watson (Thomas) Amintæ gaudia . . . Ln: Gul. Ponsonbei . . . 1592. Fcp. 4°
With long dedication by Christopher Marlowe to 'Sidney's sister, Pembroke's mother,' at A2, A3. Watson is pointed out in 'Polimanteia, by W. Clarke' (*q.v.*), 1595, as having inspired Sh—'s 'Venus and Adonis.' He is distinguished also as the pioneer of the Italian school of poetry in England.

See also Heywood

Watson (Wm.) Some literary idolatries; Contemporaries of Sh— [In 'Excursions in criticism.' Ln: . . . 1893]. Cr. 8°
BM | BLO | BPL | CTC

Watt (A. F.) *Editor*—
See Sh— King Richard II., 1907
,, Sh— Midsummer . . . 1906, 1909

Watt (Lauchlan M.) Attic and Elizabethan tragedy. Ln: Dent . . . 1908. 8°, pp. x.-356
BPL

Watt (Robert) Bibliotheca Britannica, or general index to British and foreign literature. Edinburgh: Coustable . . . 1824. 4 vols. 4°
BM | BLO | BPL | BUS | CTC
With interesting Sh— list.

Watts (J.) *Printer*. *See* Cibber

Watts (John) *Publisher*—
See Martyn
,, Sh— Coriolanus, 1720
,, Sh— King Henry V., 1723
,, Sh— King John, 1745
,, Sh— King Richard III., 1745
,, Sh— Much ado . . . 1737
,, Welsted

Watts (N.) Was Hamlet mad ? . . . 1888. 8°
BM | BPL

Watts (R.) *Dublin Publisher*. *See* Sh— Coriolanus, 1762

Watts (W. J.) *Printer*. *See* Sh— Double falsehood, 1728

Watts-Dunton (Theodore) Christmas at the 'Mermaid' . . . 1902. Cr. 8°   BPL
Christmas . . . [In 'Coming of love,' pp. 115-181]. 1906. Cr. 8°   BPL

Way (Agnes Caldwell) *Editor*. *See* Sh— Works: Ext. 1910

Way (A. E.) Reliques of Stratford-on-Avon: A souvenir of Sh—'s home. Ln: Lane . . . 1902. 12°   BPL | SML

Wayland (J.) *Printer*. *See* Mirrour . . .

Weak [? Leake] (W.) *Publisher*. *See* Sh— Othello, 1681

Wealth.] Interlude of wealth and health. Ln: Malone Society . . . 1907. Fcp. 4°
BM | SML

Weaver (J.) History of the mimes and pantomimes . . . 1728. 8°

Weaver (Thomas)] Plantagenet's tragicall story, or the death of King Edward the fourth. With the unnaturall voyage of Richard the third through the red sea of his nephews innocent bloud to his usurped crowne. Metaphrased by T. W——. Ln: Printed by M. F—— for Richard Tomlins at the Sun and Bible neer Pie Corner, 1649. 12°. With portrait by W. Marshall
W
The description of K. Richard III. entitles the volume to a place in any Sh— library.

Webb *Editor*. *See* Richard II.

Webb (Daniel) Remarks on the beauties of poetry. *See* Sh— Works: Ext. 1762

Webb (*Colonel* F.)] Sh—'s manuscripts, in the possession of Mr. Ireland, examined . . . respecting . . . their authenticity. By 'Philalethes.' Ln: J. Johnson . . . 1796. 8°, pp. iv.-34   BM | BPL | BUS | MPL | W

Webb (F. E.) *Editor*—
See Sh— King John, 1894
,, Sh— King Richard III., 1902

Webb (Frederick George) New reciter. *See* Sh— Works: Ext. 1888

Webb (J. Stenson) Sh— reference book: Quotations. *See* Sh— Works: Ext. 1898

Webb (S.) *Composer*. *See* Sh— Merchant . . . 1801

Webb *Judge* (Thomas Ebenezer) Mystery of Wm. Sh—. *See* Sh—] Webb

Webb (Wm.) *Composer*. *See* Sh— Works: Ext. 1653

Webster *Editor*. *See* Sh— Merchant . . . 1850

Webster *Publisher*—
See Scott & Webster
,, Sh— Merchant . . . 1849
,, Sh— The tempest, 1849

Webster (B.) *Editor*. *See* Dramatic entertainments

Webster (Evelyn) In Sh—'s world: Autolycus [In 'The Idler']. 1898. 8°   BPL
Illustrates the 'Winter's tale.'

Webster (John) Vittoria Corombona, or the white devil: A tragedy. Ln: 1612. Fcp. 4°
Pays a notable compliment in the preface to Sh—'s industry. 'For mine own part I have ever truly cherished my good opinion of other men's worthy labours, especially of that free and heightened style of Master Chapman, the laboured and understanding works of Master Jonson, the no less worthy composures of the both worthily excellent Master Beaumont and Master Fletcher, and lastly (without wrong last to be named) the righte happie and copious industrie of M. Shakespeare, M. Dekker, and M. Heywood—wishing what I may write may be read by their light.'

Webster (John) Vittoria Corombona . . . Ln :
Printed for W. Crooke at the Green
Dragon without Temple Bar, 1672. Fcp.
4°

Webster (John)—
See Cartwright   See Marston
,, Decker & Webster   ,, Swinburne
,, Heywood

Webster (John) & Rowley (Wm.) Cure for a
cuckold. A pleasant comedy. As it
hath been several times acted with great
applause. Ln : Printed by Tho. Johnson
and are to be sold by Nath. Brook at the
Angel in Cornhil and Francis Kirkman at
the John Fletcher's Head, on the Back
side of St. Clements, and Tho. Johnson
at the Golden Key in Paul's Churchyard,
and Henry Marsh at the Princes Arms in
Chancery Lane near Fleet Street, 1661.
Fcp. 4°
Quoted for the sake of the 'Address' by Francis Kirkman, wherein he says : – The pleasure I have taken in
plays hath bin so extraordinary that it hath bin much
to my cost ; for I have been, as we term it, a gatherer
of plays for some years, and have more . . . than any
man in England, bookseller or other. I can at any
time shew seven hundred in number, which is within
a small matter all that were ever printed. Many of
these I have several times over, and intend, as I sell,
to purchase more ; all or any of which I shall be ready
either to sell or lend to you upon reasonable consideration.

Wedd (John) Publisher. See Fane

Wedderburn. Incle and Yarico. A tragedy
. . . Ln : T. Cooper at the Globe in
Paternoster Row, 1742. 8°
The preface has references to Sh—.

Weekes (A. R.) Editor—
See Sh— As you like it, 1910
,, Sh— The tempest, 1909

Weekes (Mrs. Charles) Editor. See Goll

Weever (John) Epigrammes in the oldest cut
and newest fashion. Ln : . . 1599.
Epigram 22 runs :–
AD GULIELMUM SH—.
Honey-tongued Sh—, when I saw thine issue
I swore Apollo got them, and none other ;
Their rosy-tinted features clothed in tissue,
Some heaven-born goddess said to be their mother.
Rose-cheeked Adonis, with his amber tresses ;
Fair, fire-hot Venus, charming him to love her ;
Chaste Lucretia, virgin-like her dresses ;
Proud, lust-strong Tarquin, seeking still to prove her ;
Romeo, Richard ; more whose names I know not,
Their sugared tongues, and power, attractive beauty,
Say they are saints, although that saints they show not,
For thousands vow to them subjective duty.
They burn in love, thy children, Sh—, het [? let] them
Go ; woo thy muse, more nymphish brood beget them.

Weever's verse seems to be based on Meres' judgment
(q.v.) of the previous year.
An edition of 1595 is spoken of, but no copy can be traced.

Weiss (John) Wit, humor, and Sh— : Twelve
essays. Boston [U.S.] : Roberts Bros.,
1876. 8°, pp. iv.-428   BM | BPL | BUS | SML
First appeared in the 'New York tribune,' 1873.

Welby (F. A.) Editor. See Hastings

Welch (C.) 'Hamlet' and the recorder
[In 'Musical Association's Proceedings,'
pp. 105-137 . . . 1902]. 8°   BPL

Wellesley DD (Hy.) Stray notes on the text
of Sh—. Ln : J. Murray, 1865. Fcp.
4°, pp. iv.-34   BM | BPL | BUS | CPL | MPL
Gives a portrait of the dwarf Gradasso, from the hall of
Constantine at the Vatican, supposed to be referred
to in 'Love's labours lost,' act iii., sc. 1, in the line,
'This signior Iunios gyant dwarfe Don Cupid.'

Wellington (Bethel) Publisher—
See Sh— Julius Cæsar, 1729
,, Sh— Macbeth, 1729
,, Sh— Works, 1728, 1740, 1745

Wellington (James) Publisher—
See Sh— Julius Cæsar, 1729
,, Sh— Macbeth, 1729
,, Sh— Works, 1728

Wellington (Richard) Publisher—
See Lee (N.)
,, Rowe
,, Sh— Antony . . . 1701
,, Sh— Hamlet, 1703
,, Sh— Julius Cæsar, 1729
,, Sh— King Lear, 1690, 1699, 1710, 1712
,, Sh— Macbeth, 1729
,, Sh— Othello, 1705
,, Sh— Works, 1728, 1733, 1740, 1745, 1747

Wells Actress (Mrs.) Portrait. See Sh—
Titus . . . 1785

Wellwood (S.) Editor. See Sh— Pericles, 1902

Welsted (Leonard) Dissembled wanton, or
my son, get money. A comedy. As it is
acted at the Theatre Royal in Lincoln's
Inn Fields. Ln : Printed for John Watts,
1727. 8°, pp. xii.-72-iv.
The prologue mentions Sh— and Falstaff.
Of false fame : an epistle [in verse] to the
Earl of Pembroke. Ln : T. Cooper, 1732.
8°, pp. 24
Refers several times to Sh—.

Wemyss (F. C.) Theatrical biography . . .
1848. 12°   BPL

Wemyss (F. C.) Editor. See Sh— Taming . . .
1853

Wendell (Barrett) Seventeenth century in
English literature . . . 1904. Cr. 8° BPL
Wm. Sh—. See Sh—] Wendell

Wenman (J.) Publisher—
See Sh— All's well . . . 1778
,, Sh— As you like it, 1777
,, Sh— Comedy of errors, 1779
,, Sh— Cymbeline, 1777
,, Sh— King Henry VIII., 1778
,, Sh— King Richard III., 1778
,, Sh— Measure . . . 1779
,, Sh— Merchant . . . 1777
,, Sh— Merry wives, 1778
,, Sh— Midsummer . . . 1778
,, Sh— Much ado . . . 1778
,, Sh— Othello, 1777
,, Sh— Romeo . . . 1778

(684)

Wenman (J.) *Publisher*—
See Sh— Taming . . . 1780
„ Sh— The tempest, 1778
„ Sh— Twelfth night, 1779
„ Sh— Winter's tale, 1779
Werder (K.) Heart of Hamlet's mystery.
New York . . . 1906. Cr. 8°   BPL
Wesley (John). *See* Moore
Wessel (C.) Richard III. in Sh—'s plays [*i.e.*
' King Henry VI.' and ' King Richard
III.'] compared with Richard III. in
history. Eschwege . . . 1876. Fcp. 4°
                                   BM | BUS
West (David) *Boston* [*U.S.*] *Publisher. See*
Sh— Twelfth night, 1794
West (Eliza M.) Shaksperian parallelisms
chiefly illustrative of ' The tempest ' and
a ' Midsummer night's dream,' from Sir
Philip Sidney's 'Arcadia.' Edited by
J. O. Halliwell. *See* Sh— Works : Ext.
1865
West (G.) *Oxford Publisher. See* Langbaine
West (John) *Boston* [*U.S.*] *Publisher*—
See Sh— Hamlet, 1794
„ Sh— Twelfth night, 1794
West (J. F.) Wm. Sh— from a surgeon's
point of view. *See Sh*—] West
West *née* Cooke (*Mrs.*) *Actress*—
See Sh— Merchant . . . 1830
„ Sh— Othello, 1819
West (W.) History, topography and directory
of Warwickshire. Birmingham : Wright-
son, 1830. 8°   SML
West Indian illustrations of Sh—. *See* Sh—
Works : Ext. 1870
Westall (Richard) Day in spring and other
poems. Ln : . . . 1808. 8°   BUS
The poem headed 'Sh—' at pp. 207-211.
Westall (Richard) *Artist*—
See Sh— Works, 1802, 1821-29, 1826, 1829,
1832, 1836
„ Sh— Works : Ext. 1841
Westermann (G.) *Braunschweig Publisher*—
See Sh— Hamlet, 1845
„ Sh— Romeo . . 1845
Westley (R. H.) *Editor*—
See Sh— King Lear, 1861
„ Sh— King Richard III., 1861
„ Sh— Merchant . . . 1861
Westminster Abbey. *See* H—— (J.)
Westminster School. *See* Scott (E. J. L.)
Weston (Stephen) Short notes on Sh— by
way of supplement to Johnson, Steevens,
Malone, and Douce. Ln : Privately
printed by C. & R. Baldwin, 1808. 8°,
pp. iv.-18   BM | BPL | BUS | MPL | W
Weston (W. H.) *Editor. See* Sh— King Henry
V., 1905
Westover (C. C.) Romance of gentle Will.
New York . . . 1905. Cr. 8°   BPL

Westward for smelts, or the waterman's fare
of mad-merry western wenches, whose
tongues, albeit like bell-clappers, they
neuer leave ringing, yet their tales are
sweet and will much content you. Written by ' Kinde Kit of Kingstone' [John
Taylor the waterman ?].   Ln : Printed
for Iohn Trundle and are to be sold at his
shop in Barbican at the signe of the Nobody. 1620. Fcp. 4°, black letter, sig.
A—F² unpaged   CTC | HUTH
From an earlier edition Sh— is supposed to have
borrowed incidents for ' Cymbeline.'
Westward for smelts ; Story told by the fish-
wife of Strand-on-the-green, 1843. *See*
Sh—] Sh—'s library
Westward for smelts . . . [Edited by J. O.
Halliwell]. Percy Society : Privately
printed, 1848. 8°   BPL | BUS | W
Wewitzer (*Miss*) *Actress. See* Sh— Merry
wives, 1820
Wewitzer (R.) Dramatic chronology of actors
. . . 1817. 12°   BPL | MPL
Whalley (Peter) Enquiry into the learning of
Sh—. *See Sh*—] Whalley
Wharncliffe (*Lady*) *Artist & Engraver. See*
Sh— Works, 1826
What is it on ? *See* Routledge
What was the religion of Sh— ? *See Sh*—]
What . . .
Whately (E.) ' Romeo and Juliet ' [In
'Afternoon lectures on English litera-
ture']. Ln : . . . 1869. 8°   BM | MPL
Whately (E. W.) Character of *Hamlet* : A
lecture. [1863.] 8°   BM | BPL
Whately (Joseph) *Editor. See* Whately
(Thomas)
Whately *Archbp.* (R.) *Editor. See* Whately
(T.)
Whately (Thomas)] Remarks on some of the
characters of Sh— [Edited by Joseph
Whately]. Ln : T. Payne & Son . . . 1785.
8°, pp. ii.-82 BM | BPL | BUS | CPL | MPL
Remarks on some of the characters of
Sh— . . . 1790. 8°
Remarks on some of the characters of Sh—.
Second edition. Oxford : J. Parker . . .
1808. 8°, pp. viii.-92
          BM | BPL | BUS | CPL | SML | W
Remarks on some of the characters of Sh—.
Edited by [Archbp.] Richard Whately.
Third edition. Ln : J. W. Parker, 1839.
12°, pp. 128   BPL | BUS | CPL | SML
See also Kemble (J. P.)
Whattcott (Robert) *Witness. See* Sh— Will
. . . 1616
Wheatley (H. B.) Historical portraits. *See*
Sh—] Wheatley
Johnson's edition of Sh— [In ' The Athe-
næum,' No. 4,272, 11 Sept., 1909]. 4°
                                  BM | BPL

Wheatley (H. B.) Notes on the life of J. P.
Collier. *See* Collier

On a contemporary drawing of the Swan
theatre, 1596. Ln: New Sh— Society,
1887-92. 8°

Story of ' Romeo and Juliet ' [In ' The
Antiquary,' Vols. 5 and 6. Ln: Stock,
1882]. 4°   BM | BPL

Wheatley (H. B.) *Editor*—
See Levins
,, Sh— Merry wives, 1886

Wheble (J.) *Publisher. See* Sh— Works: Ext.
1774

Wheeler (Charles Henry) *Editor. See* Sh—
Works, 1824, 1825, 1827, 1828, 1829,
1830, 1831, 1832, 1833, 1834

Wheeler ˙(J. M.) Irreligion of Sh—. *See Sh*—]
Wheeler

Wheelwright (R.) *Artist. See* Sh— King
Henry V., 1900

Wheler *of Stratford-on-Avon* (*Miss*). *See* Halliwell

Wheler (Robert Bell) Collectanea respecting
the birthplace of Sh—. Copied . . . with
a few additions by J. O. Halliwell. Ln:
1865. Fcp. 4°   BM | BPL | HCL | MPL
Issue limited to ten copies.

Guide to Stratford-on-Avon. Printed and
sold by J. Ward, Stratford . . . 1814.
Cr. 8°, pp. iv.-160 and folded map
            BPL | BUS | MPL | SBL | SML
Interesting for its account of the alleged seal ring of the
poet.

Guide to Stratford-upon-Avon . . . Coventry: H. Merridew [1825]. Cr. 8°
                                  BPL | SML

Guide to Stratford-upon-Avon . . . New
edition. Coventry: H. Merridew [c.
1827]. Cr. 8°, pp. ii.-58. Illustrated
                                  BPL | BUS

Historical account of the birthplace of
Sh—. With lithographic prints by C. F.
Green. Stratford: J. Ward, 1824. 8°,
pp. 14 and plan   BUS | MPL | SBL | SML
A few copies were done in 4° on large paper, of which
one is at Birmingham.

Historical account of the birth-place of
Sh—. With prefatory remarks by J. O.
Halliwell. Stratford: Sold at the poet's
birthplace, 1863. 8°, pp. 28 (including
printed wrappers), with etched plate of
the birthplace   BM | BPL | BUS

History and antiquities of Stratford-upon-
Avon, comprising a description of the
collegiate church, the life of Sh—, and
copies of several documents relating to
him and his family, never before printed.
With a biographical sketch of other
eminent characters, natives of, or who
have resided in Stratford. To which is
added a particular account of the jubilee

. . . in honour of our immortal bard. With
eight engravings. Stratford-upon-Avon
. . . [1806]. 8°, pp. iv.-230. Eight aqua-
tint plates   BPL | BUS | CPL | SML | W
Gives an account of the monuments, with copies of in-
scriptions, in the church ; of the monastic college,
dissolved in 1546, and demolished in 1799 ; of the
chapel and guild of the Holy Cross ; and transcripts
of legal documents connected with Sh— and his
descendants.
The eight plates consist of :—
   View of Waterside and Sheep Street from the Avon
   Holy Trinity Church
   Sh—'s mural monument
   Stratford monastic college
   Clopton bridge
   Sh—'s home, before restoration
   New Place, Guild chapel, and grammar school
   Garrick's Jubilee amphitheatre.
In a few copies the frontispiece was issued prettily
coloured by hand.

Wheler (Robert Bell) History . . . of Stratford-upon-Avon [Abridged] . . . 1814.
8°. With folded plan of the town

Letters. *See Sh*—] Shakespeareana

Letters to John Britton on Sh—'s biography. *See Sh*—] Shakespeareana

Manuscript notes. *See* Sh— Works, 1803

Notes on Sh—'s pedigree. *See Sh*—] Wheler
See also Halliwell

Where the bee sucks . . . *See* Sh— Poems, 1875

Whetstone (George) Censure of a loyal subject,
1587. *See* Reprints

[Historie] The right excellent and famous
historye, of Promos and Cassandra . . .
Imprinted at Ln. by Richard Ihones and
are to be solde ouer agaynst Saint Sepul-
chres Church, without Newgate, Aug. 20,
1578. 4°, black letter, sig. A to M⁴ un-
paged (last leaf blank ?)   BM | CTC | W
The probable foundation of ' Measure for measure.'

Historie of Promos and Cassandra, 1578
[In ' Six old plays . . .' (*q.v.*), Vol. I.] . . .
1779. 12°   BPL

Historie of Promos and Cassandra, 1843—
See Sh—] Sh—'s library
,, Six old plays

Historie of Promos and Cassandra. *See*
Sh— Measure . . . 1889

Whimzies (The). *See* Brathwaite (R.)

Whincop (Thomas) Scanderbeg, or love and
liberty. A tragedy. 1747. 8°
                        BPL | BUS | MPL | W
With eighteen medallion portraits, including one of Sh—
by N. Parr.
Issued as part of Mottley's List . . . [*q.v.*]

Whipple (Edwin Percy) Literature of the age
of Elizabeth. Boston [U.S.] 1869. 8°
                                        BUS

Literature of the age of Elizabeth. Boston
[U.S.] 1881. 12°   BPL

Sh—. *See Sh*—] Whipple

Sh—'s critics [In ' Essays and reviews,' Vol.
2, pp. 209-249. 1885]. 12°   BPL

Whipple (Edwin Percy) Verplanck and Hudson: Sh—'s plays [In ' North American Review.' Boston, 1848]. 8° BUS

Whistler *General* (G. W.) *Bibliophile. See* Catalogue, 1871

Whistler (J. N. M.) *Artist. See* Irving

Whiston (J.) *Publisher. See* Sh— King Henry VIII., 1758

Whitaker *Publisher. See* Sh— Works, 1790, 1793

Whitaker (Thomas Dunham) Loidis and Elmete, or an attempt to illustrate the districts described in those words by Bede . . . Aredale, Wharfdale . . . Vale of Calder, in the county of York. Ln : . . . 1816. 2 vols. F° BM | BLO | BPL | CTC
Contains an account of the ' Yorkshire tragedy,' a play attributed to Sh—.

White *Engraver. See* Hall (John)

White (B.) *Publisher—*
See Sh— King Henry VIII., 1758
,, Sh— Macbeth, 1770
,, Sh— Merchant . . . 1783
,, Sh— Othello, 1784
,, Sh— Timon . . . 1770
,, Sh— Works, 1773

White & Son (B.) *Publishers. See* Sh— Works, 1790

White (B. & J.) *Publishers. See* Sh— Works, 1793, 1797

White (Diana) *Editor. See* Brandes

White (Edward) *Publisher—*
See Decker   *See* Frederick
,, Edwards (R.)   ,, Key . . .
,, Sh— Arden . . . 1592
,, Sh— Titus . . . 1594, 1600, 1611

White (E. H.) Sh— and his ' Hamlet ' [In 'Athelstan, and other poems,' pp. 87-95. 1847]. 12° BPL

White (F.) History, gazetteer, and directory of Warwickshire. Sheffield . . . 1850. 8°
Contains probably the earliest detailed directory of Stratford.

White (Frederick M.) The doubting D——, or a cranky cryptogram : A defence of the great bard in three fyttes. Revised and corrected up to date by himself. Also containing evidence . . . as given by Bacon, Ben Jonson, and others. Ln : . . . 1888. 8° BM | BPL | BUS

White (George) Portrait of a boy violinist after Fran. Hals. Ln : . . . 1732. 4° (15 × 10½ in.), engraved in mezzotint
Beneath the portrait are engraved some verses in which occurs this line :—
' O Sh—! for thy soul to raise my flame.'

White.] Harry White, his humour . . . set forth. *See* Parker

White (Holt) Notes on the plays of Sh— . . . 1790. Fcp. 4°, manuscript upon eighteen leaves of paper W

White (H. Kelsey) Essays and poems. Hull . . . 1907. Cr. 8° BPL
Contains Shakespeareana.

Index to songs, snatches and passages in Sh— which have been set to music. Great Fencote : J. R. Tutin . . . 1900. 8°, pp. 16
300 copies done.

White (H. K.) *Editor. See* Sh— Poems, 1900

White (I. or J.) *Publisher. See* Kyd

White (J.) *Publisher. See* Sh— Works, 1797, 1798

White & Co. (J.) *Publishers. See* Sh— Works, 1811

White (James) & Lamb (C.)] Original letters, etc. of Sir John Falstaff and his friends ; now first made public by a gentleman, a descendant of Dame Quickly, from genuine manuscripts. Ln : G. & J. Robinson . . . 1796. 12°, pp. xxiv.-124 and frontispiece
 BPL | BUS | W
'A humorous and ingenious satire [on the Ireland forgeries], with a "Dedicatione to Master Samuel Irelaunde,"' written by James White, a friend of Charles Lamb, who refers to him in ' Essays of Elia.' Lamb is supposed to have assisted in the composition.

] Original letters of Sir John Falstaff . . . Second edition. Ln : . . . 1797. 12°
The text unaltered.

Original letters . . . Philadelphia : R. Desilver, 1813. 12°, pp. xxii.-130 BUS

[Original letters . . .] Falstaff's letters. With notices of the author . . . 1877. 12° BPL

White (J. G.) Churches and chapels of old London. With a short account of those who have ministered in them. Ln : Printed for private circulation, 1901. 8°, pp. x.-170-104

White (R.) *Publisher—*
See Mercurius Britannicus
,, Sh— King Henry VI., i.-ii.-iii., 1817
,, Woodward

White (Richard Grant) Anatomizing of Wm. Sh—. *See Sh—*] White

Bacon-Shakespeare craze [In 'Atlantic Monthly,' Vol. 51, 1883]. 8° BUS
'A literary bee in the bonnet of ladies of both sexes.'

Case of Hamlet the younger [In the 'Galaxy.' New York . . . 1870]. 8° BUS

Collier's folio . . . Its most plausible manuscript corrections [In ' Putnam's Monthly.' New York, 1853]. 8° BUS

Collier folio Sh—; is it an imposture ? [In 'Atlantic Monthly.' Boston [U.S.] 1859]. 8° BUS

Essay on the authorship of the three parts of ' King Henry the sixth.' Cambridge [U.S.]: H. D. Houghton, 1859. 8°, pp. iv.-100 BUS
Twenty-five copies printed.

White (Richard Grant) Florentine arithmetician: Cassio [In the ' Galaxy.' New York, 1878]. 8°   BUS
Introduction. *See* Ireland (S. W. H.)
Lady Gruach's husband: *Macbeth* [In the ' Galaxy.' New York, 1870]. 8° BUS
Library. *See* Catalogue, 1861, 1885
Library catalogue . . . 1870. 8°   BPL
Sh— occupies pp. 154-175.
On reading Sh— [In the ' Galaxy.' New York, 1876-77]. 8°   BPL | BUS
On the confusion of time in the ' Merry wives.' Ln: New Sh— Society, 1875-76. 8°
Memoirs of Sh—. *See Sh*—] White
Sh— mystery [In 'Atlantic Monthly.' Boston . . . 1861]. 8°   BUS
Sh—'s scholar; being historical and critical studies of his text, characters, and commentators. With an examination of Mr. Collier's folio of 1632. New York, Appleton. Ln: Trübner & Co., 1854. 8°, pp. xliv.-504   BM | BPL | BUS | MPL
Sh—'s scholar [an answer to a critical notice in ' New York Albion,' 1854]. 8°, pp. 12   BUS
Shakespearean mare's nests [In the ' Galaxy.' New York, 1869]. 8°   BUS
Studies in Sh—. Boston [U.S.]: Houghton, 1885. 8°   BM | BPL | BUS | SML
Text of Sh—: Mr. Collier's corrected folio . . . [In ' Putnam's Monthly.' New York, 1853]. 8°   BUS
The two ' Hamlets ' [In the 'Atlantic Monthly.' 1881]. 8°   BPL
Visit to Stratford-on-Avon [In the ' Galaxy,' New York, 1877]. 8°   BPL | BUS
Visit to Stratford-on-Avon [In ' England without and within,' pp. 509-530. 1881]. 12°   BPL
Who was Juliet's runaway ? Quincy folio of 1685. Collier's folio, 1632. Sh—'s name [In ' Putnam's Monthly.' New York . . . 1854]. 8°   BUS
Wm. Sh—. *See Sh*—] White
White (R. G.) *Editor*—
See Sh— Macbeth, 1897
  ,, Sh— Works, 1854-56, 1857-59, 1857-66, 1858, 1862-66, 1865, 1875, 1883, 1883-84, 1883-86, 1885
White of Sion College (Thomas) Discoverie of Brownisme . . . Ln: . . . 1605. Fcp. 4°   W
Alleged to have belonged to Sh—'s library, and bears the autograph of Sh— and manuscript notes (forged by S. W. H. Ireland). The lettering on the binding says, 'Sh—'s MS. notes.'
White (Thomas) Notes on Sh—. 1793. 8°. Manuscript   BPL
White (T. W.) Our English Homer. *See Sh*—] White

White (W.) *Editor & Publisher.* *See* Sh— Works, 1852
White (Wm.) *Printer*—
See Kyd
  ,, Sh— King Henry VI., i.-ii.-iii., 1600
  ,, Sh— Love's labours lost, 1598
White (W.) *Publisher*—
See Cotton
  ,, Sh— King Lear, 1770
  ,, Sh— Works, 1851, 1853
Whitefriars theatre—
See Cunningham
  ,, Greenstreet
Whitehead. Life of Sir W. Raleigh. *See* Ralegh
Whitehead (C.) *Editor.* *See* Sh— Works, 1839-43
Whitehead *Poet laureate* (Wm.) Charge to the poets. Ln : . . . 1762
' But chief avoid the boisterous roaring sparks. The sons of fire ! you'll know them by their marks.
. . . .
Hear them on Sh—! there they foam, they rage, Yet taste not half the beauties of his page, Nor see that art, as well as nature, strove To place him foremost in the Aonian grove ; For there, there only, where the sisters join, His genius triumphs and the work's divine. Or would ye sift more near these sons of fire, 'Tis Garrick and not Sh— they admire ; Without his breath inspiring every thought, They ne'er perhaps had known what Sh— wrote. Without his eager, his becoming zeal To teach them, though they scarce know why, to feel A crude unmeaning mass had Jonson been, And a dead letter Sh—'s noblest scene.'
Whitehouse (T. & J.) *Dublin Publishers.* *See* Sh— Arden . . . 1763
Whitelaw (R.) *Editor*—
See Sh— Coriolanus, 1872
  ,, Sh— Works, 1872-83
Whitelock (*Mrs.*) *Actress.* *See* Franklin
Whiter (Walter)] Specimen of a commentary on Sh—, containing I. Notes on 'As you like it,' II. An attempt to explain and illustrate various passages on a new principle of criticism, derived from Mr. Locke's Doctrine of the association of ideas. Ln: Cadell . . . 1794. 8°, pp. viii.-258
          BM | BPL | BUS | CPL | MPL | SML | W
Verses in commemoration of Sh—'s birthday. *See Sh*—] Whiter
Whitestone (H.) *Dublin Publisher.* *See* Davies (T.)
Whitestone (W.) *Dublin Publisher.* *See* Sh— Coriolanus, 1762
Whitgift *Archbp.* (John) *Censor.* *See* Sh— Venus . . . (*heading*)
Whitlock (E.) *Printer & Publisher.* *See* Sh— Taming . . . 1698
Whitlock (Richard) Zootomia, or observations on the present manners of the English, briefly anatomising the living by the

dead, with an usefull detection of the mountebanks of both sexes. Ln : Printed by Tho. Roycroft and sold by Humphrey Moseley at the Prince's Armes, 1654. 8°

At p. 318 says :—' Nor can my poore reason but assent-
ingly pronounce, since man's inventions have brought
him to this sad loss, that his speculations are but a
"Comedy of errors" and his imployments "Much
ado about nothing" (to borrow our comedian's titles),
that the world's busy man is the grand impertinent.'
Mentions likewise Bacon and Ben Jonson.

Whitman (Walt) Complete prose works. Boston [U.S.] . . . 1898. Cr. 8°

Remarks :—' The inward and outward characteristics of
Sh— are his vast and rich variety of persons and
themes, with his wondrous delineation of each and
all, not only limitless funds of verbal and pictorial
resource, but great excess . . . But to the deepest soul,
it seems a shame to pick and choose from the riches
Sh— has left us, to criticise his infinitely royal, multiform quality ; to gauge, with optic glasses, the dazzle
of his sun-like beams . . . he stands alone, and I do
not wonder he so witches the world.'

Democratic vistas. 1888. 12°   BPL

Contains ' A thought on Sh—' (pp. 106-108) and ' Sh—'s
historical plays ' (pp. 109-112).

Whittaker & Co. *Publishers. See Sh—* Works, 1841-53, 1844-53, 1853, 1858

Whittaker (G. & W. B.) *Publishers. See Sh—* Works, 1821

Whittingham (C.) *Chiswick Printer—*
See Sh— Antony . . . 1818
  ,, Sh— As you like it, 1810
  ,, Sh— Works, 1803-04, 1813-14, 1815, 1818, 1823, 1826, 1827, 1828, 1830, 1831, 1836, 1841

Whittington (Thomas) Will. *See* Collier

Whittsitt (W. H.) Lady Macbeth ⌊In ' Louis-ville Courier.' 1885]. 12°   BPL

Whitworth (J.) *Publisher—*
See Sh— Macbeth, 1800
  ,, Sh— Romeo . . . 1780

Who wrote Sh— ? [In ' Chambers' Journal', 7th Aug. Edin., 1852]. Roy. 8°   BUS

Whymper (Fred.) Notes. *See* Ham (J. P.)

Whyte (Frederic) Actors of the century : A play-lover's gleanings from theatrical annals. Ln : Bell . . . 1898. 4°. Por-traits and illustrations   BM | BLO | CTC

Whyte (Fredk.) *Editor. See* Filon

Widgery (W. H.) First quarto edition of Hamlet,' 1603. Harness prize essay. Cambridge . . . 1880. 12°
     BM | BLO | BPL | CTC

Widmann (J. V.) *Editor. See Sh—* Taming . . . 1878

Wiesener (G.) *Editor. See Sh—* Merchant . . . 1880

Wife lapped in morel's skin. *See Sh—*] Sh—'s library

A foundation of ' Taming of the shrew.'

Wight (Thomas) *Publisher. See* Plutarchus

Wigstead (Henry) Remarks on a tour to North and South Wales in 1797 . . . 1799. 8°. With plates by Thomas Rowlandson and others   W

Contains the plate of the turnspit illustrative of the passages :—
  ' The capon burns, the pig falls from the spit.'
  —*Comedy of errors.*
  ' Like a rabbit on a spit.'—*Love's labours lost.*
  ' Weke, weke ! So cries a pig prepared to the spit.'—*Titus Andronicus.*
  ' Thou mayst cut a morsel off the spit.'—*Pericles.*

Wigston (W. F. C.) Bacon, Sh—, and the Rosicrucians. Ln : Redway . . . 1888. 8°, pp. xxiv.-284 and 2 plates
     BM | BPL | SML

Columbus of literature, or Bacon's new world of sciences. Chicago : F. J. Schulte, 1892. 8°, pp. 218 and 2 plates
     BPL | BUS | MPL | SML

Discoveries in the Bacon problem. Edin-burgh [c. 1893]. 8°   BPL

Francis Bacon ; poet, prophet, philosopher, *versus* Phantom Captain Sh—, the Rosi-crucian mask. Ln : [Privately printed] 1890. 8°, pp. xlviii.-436. With portrait of Bacon and facsimiles   SML

Francis Bacon . . . Ln : Kegan Paul, 1891. 8°   BM | BPL | MPL

Hermes stella, or notes and jottings upon the Bacon cipher. Ln : Redway, 1890. 8°   BM | BPL | BUS | SML

] New study of Sh— : An inquiry into the connection of the plays and the poems with the origins of the classical drama, and with the Platonic philosophy, through the mysteries [Rosicrucian theories, etc.] Ln : Trübner & Co. [1884]. 8°, pp. xii.-372. With Stratford bust portrait
     BM | BPL | BUS | SML

Wild *DD.* (Robert) Iter boreale . . . Ln : Printed 23rd April . . . 1660. Fcp. 4°
Refers to Sh— at p. 63.

Iter boreale, with large additions of several other poems. Ln : Printed for the book-sellers, 1668. 12°

Iter boreale . . . Ln : . . . 1670. 12°

] The benefice. A comedy . . . now made publick for promoting innocent mirth. Ln : . . . 1689. Fcp. 4°
At sig. B is a reference to Sh— and Sir John Falstaff.

Wilde (Oscar O'Flahertie Wills) Portrait of Mr. W. H—— [Willie Hughes]. Privately printed, 1889. Cr. 8°   BPL

Portrait of Mr. W. H——. Portland, U.S., 1901. 8°, pp. 76   BUS

Portrait of Mr. W. H—— [In ' Lord Arthur Savile's crime.' Ln : . . . 1908]. Cr. 8°
     BM | BLO | BPL | CTC

Reviews. Ln : . . . 1908. 8°
     BM | BLO | BPL | CTC

Contains references to Sh—.

Wilde (Oscar O'Flahertie Wills) Sh— and stage costume [In the 'Nineteenth century.' Ln : . . . 1885]. 8° BPL

 Truth of masks : On Sh— and stage costume [In 'Intentions.' Ln : . . . 1908]. 8° BM | BLO | BPL | CTC

 See Sh—] Shakespearean show book

Wilder (D. W.) Life of Sh—. *See Sh*—] Wilder

Wilding (C. J.) Forked heads [In 'The Athenæum,' No. 3,735, p. 667, May, 1899]. 4° BM | BPL
 Illustrates 'As you like it,' ii., 1.

Wilken. Historical and metrical introduction to the study of Sh—'s Works, with particular regard to his 'Julius Cæsar.' Beidenkopf . . . 1883. 4° BM | BUS

Wilkes (George) Sh— from an American point of view. *See Sh*—] Wilkes

Wilkes (John). *See* Sh— Macbeth, 1763

'Wilkes (Thomas)' *pseud. See* Derrick (S.)

Wilkie (*Sir* David) *Artist. See* Sh— As you like it, 1840

Wilkie (G.) *Publisher. See* Sh— Works, 1798, 1811

Wilkie (G. & T.) *Publishers*—
 See Historian . . .
  ,, Sh— Works, 1790, 1793, 1797

Wilkie (J.) *Publisher*—
 See Lyric ode
  ,, Sh— Macbeth, 1770
  ,, Sh— Timon . . . 1770

Wilkins *Dramatist* (George) Merry devil of Edmonton. *See* Sh— Merry devil . . . (*heading*)

 Miseries of inforst marriage, playd by his majesties servants. Ln : Printed by I. N—— for Richard Thrale and are to be sold at his shop at Paul's Gate next to Cheapside, 1637. Fcp. 4°
 Based on the story concerning Walter Calverley, which served also for the plot of Sh—'s 'Yorkshire tragedy.' It passed through four editions, and after being altered and adapted by Mrs. Behn appeared under the title of 'The town fop' in 1677.
 Wilkins was a fellow-member with Sh— of the King's company of actors, and is believed to have contributed to 'Pericles' and 'Timon of Athens.'
 Bearing in mind the poet's unconventional marriage and suspected subsequent estrangement, this play bears special interest.

 Pericles prince of Tyre. A novel . . . founded upon Sh—'s play. Edited by Prof. Tycho Mommsen. With preface and introduction by J. P. Collier. Oldenburg : G. Stalling . . . 1857. Roy. 8°, pp. xxxvi.-82 and facsimile
   BM | BPL | BUS | MPL | W
 With brief account of some original editions of Sh— extant in Germany and Switzerland.
 See also Sh—'s 'Pericles,' 1608.

 See Boyle
  ,, Sh— Mucedorus (*heading*)

Wilkins *Sæc. XIX.* (Geo.) Autograph letters to John Britton [on the 'imposture' of Sh—'s Birth-house]. Manuscripts BUS

Wilkins (W.) *Printer. See* Sh— Taming . . . 1716

Wilkins (W.) *Publisher. See* Some remarks . .

Wilkinson (R.) Theatrum illustratum : Graphic and historic memorials of ancient playhouses, modern theatres, etc. in London and Westminster. Ln : R. Wilkinson . . . 1825. 4°

Wilkinson (Richard) Vice reclaimed, or the passionate mistress. A comedy as it is acted at the Theatre Royal by her majesty's servants. Ln : Bernard Lintott at the Middle Temple Gate in Fleet Street, 1703. Fcp. 4°
 Afterwards appeared as 'The quaker's wedding.' Refers to Sh— in the prologue.

Wilkinson *Actor* (Tate) Memoirs of his own life. York . . . 1790. 4 vols. 8°

 Original anecdotes respecting the stage. [c. 1790.] 8° BPL

 Wandering patentee, or history of the Yorkshire theatres from 1770 . . . York . . . 1795. 4 vols. 8°

Wilkinson (Thomas Read) Sh—; an address. *See Sh*—] Wilkinson

Wilkinson (T. T.) *See* Harland & Wilkinson

Wilks (Robert) Autograph. *See* Cibber (T.)

Wilks.] Curll (E.)] Life of R. Wilks. Ln : E. Curll . . . 1733. 12° SML

Wilks (Robert). *See* Drury Lane

Wilks (T. C.) Letter to the Rev. T. Binney in defence of the drama . . . 1838. 8° BPL

Will and testament of Wm. Sh—. *See* Sh— Will . . .

Willan (J. N.) First night impressions of . . . 'Macbeth.' *See* Irving

 'Macbeth' [Excerpts from the 'Bath Chronicle' . . . 1885]. 12° BPL

Willetts (Ada) Sh—'s thoughts on music. Ballarat . . . 1889. 12° BPL

William I. *of Eng.* (*King*). *See* Sh— Faire Em . . . 1605

Williams *Shrewsbury Printer. See* Sh— Works, 1768

Williams (Bransby) An actor's story. Ln : Chapman & Hall, 1909. Cr. 8°, pp. xiv.-272 and plates
 Chap. ix. deals with 'Shakespearean and other performances' (pp. 114-126).

Williams (C.) *Boston* [*U.S.*] *Publisher. See* Sh— Works, 1813, 1814

Williams (D.) *Publisher*—
 See Sh— Julius Cæsar, 1766
  ,, Sh— Othello, 1750

Williams (G. & M. M.) Shakespearian recitals. Birmingham [c. 1900]. 8° BPL

Williams *jun.* (H. I.) *Editor. See* Sh— Othello, 1870

Williams *pseud.* ' Pasquin ' (J.) *Editor.* *See* Barrymore

Williams (J.) *Publisher. See* Sh— Works, 1773

Williams (J.) *Dublin Publisher—*
See Sh— Works, 1766
,, *Sh—*] Dennis

Williams (J. L.) & Furness (H. H.) Homes and haunts of Sh—. *See Sh—*] Williams

Williams (J. M.) Dramatic censor, or critical and biographical illustrations of the British stage. Ln : Brimmer . . . 1811. 8°   SML

Williams (Langton) & Milne (J. T.) How shall we honour him ? *See Sh—*] Williams

Williams (Michael) Some London theatres, past and present. Ln : Low, 1883. 12°   SML

Williams (Robert Folkstone)] Sh— and his friends, or the golden age of merry England. Ln : H. Colburn . . . 1838. 3 vols. 12°   BM | BPL | BUS | SML
A sequel to the 'Youth of Sh—.'

] Sh— and his friends . . . Paris : Baudry . . . 1838. 8°. pp. 484   BM | CPL | SML

] Sh— and his friends. New York . . . 1839. 3 vols. 12°

] Sh— and his friends. Philadelphia . . . 1839. 3 vols. 12°

] Sh— and his friends. Ln : Bohn . . . 1846. 12°

] The secret passion [a novel]. Ln : H. Colburn . . . 1844. 3 vols. 12° BPL | BUS | SML
A sequel to 'Sh— and his friends.'

] Youth of Sh— [a novel]. Ln : H. Colburn . . . 1839. 3 vols. 12°
            BM | BPL | BUS | MPL | SML
An imaginary story of the poet's boyhood.

] Youth of Sh—. Paris : Baudry . . . 1839. 8°, pp. ii.-416   CPL

] Youth of Sh—. Philadelphia . . . 1840. 3 vols. Cr. 8°   BUS

] Youth of Sh—. Ln : Newman & Co., 1846. 3 vols. 12°   SML

] Youth of Sh—. Ln : Bohn . . . 1846. Cr. 8°

] Youth of Sh—. New York . . . 1847. 8°

Williams (S. Fletcher) Times and associates of Sh—. *See Sh—*] Williams

Williams (T. J.) *Editor. See* Sh— Hamlet, 1869

Williamson *Edinburgh Publisher. See* Sh— Much ado . . . 1774

Willis. Current notes. 1852-58. 7 vols. Fcp. 4°   BPL
Contains Shakespeareana.

Willis (R.)] Mount Tabor, or private exercises of a penitent sinner. Serving for a daily practice of the life of faith, reduced to speciall heads, comprehending the chiefe comforts and refreshings of true

christians. Written in a time of a voluntary retrait from secular affaires, by R. W., Esq. Published in the yeare of his age 75. Ln : Printed by R. B—— for P. Stephens and C. Meredith, 1639. 12°   W
In prose and verse.
Gives a graphic account of boy and school life, dramatic performances in country towns, cock-fighting, etc. of exactly Sh—'s own time.
' Dost thou live by thy tabor ?'—*Twelfth night.*

Willis *Judge* (William) Baconian mint ; its claims examined . . . Ln : Privately printed [by Miller] 1903. 4°, pp. iv.-110
            BPL | BUS | SML

Baconian mint : A further examination of its claims . . . 1908

Sh— - Bacon controversy : A report of the trial of an issue in Westminster Hall, June 20, 1627. Read in the Inner Temple Hall, Thursday, May 29th, 1902, and prepared for publication . . . Ln : Low, 1902. Fcp. 4°, pp. 88-164 BPL | BUS | SML
An imaginary action at law.
Gives seventy-six facsimiles of titles and leaves from the early quartos, etc.
A few done on large paper.

Willobie (Henry) Avisa, or the true picture of a modest maid and of a chast and constant wife. In hexamiter verse [and prose. Edited by Hadrian Dorrell] . . . Imprinted at Ln. by Iohn Windet, 1594. Fcp. 4°, pp. xvi.-68   BM | BRITWELL | W
Two of the commendatory verses read thus :—
' Though Collatine haue deerely bought
    To high renowne a lasting life,
And found that most in vaine haue fought
    To haue a faire and constant wife ;
Yet Tarquyne pluckt his glistering grape,
And Sh— paints poore Lucreece rape.
    *   *   *   *   *
Then Aui-Susan ioyne in one,
    Let Lucres-Auis be thy name ;
This English eagle sores alone,
    And farre surmounts all others fame,
Where high or low, where great or small,
This Brytan bird out-flies them all.
At pp. 40-41 is the first extraneous and direct printed notice of Sh—, and the most convincing vision of his personality known throughout all literature. It is written in autobiographic form :—' H. W—, being sodenly affected with the contagion of a fantasticall fit at the first sight of A—, pyneth awhile in secret griefe. At length, not able any longer to indure the burning heate of so feruent a humour, bewrayeth the secresy of his disease vnto his familiar friend W. S—, who not long before tryed the curtesy of the like passion, and was now newly recouered of the like infection* ; yet, finding his frend let blood in the same vaine, he took pleasure for a tyme to see him bleed, and instead of stopping the issue, he inlargeth the wound with the sharp razor of a willing conceit, perswading him that he thought it a matter very easy to be compassed, and no doubt with payne, diligence, and some cost in tyme, to be obtained. Thus this miserable comforter comforting his frend with an impossibilitie, eyther for that he now would secretly

* These pleasant girds reveal personal friendship and intercourse with Sh—, and specially point to his sonnets and love-poems.

laugh at his frend's folly, that had giuen occasion not
long before vnto others to laugh at his owne, or
because he would see whether another could play his
part better then himselfe, and in vewing afar off the
course of this louing comedy, he determined to see
whether it would sort to a happier end for this new
actor then it did for the old player. But at length
this comedy was like to haue growen to a tragedy, by
the weake and feeble estate that H. W. was brought
vnto, by a desperate vewe of an impossibility of obtaining his purpose, till time and necessity, being his
best phisitions, brought him a plaster, if not to heal
yet in part to ease his maladye. In all which discourse is liuely represented the vnrewly rage of
vnbrydeled fancy, hauing the raines to roue at liberty
with the dyuers and sundry changes of affections and
temptations which Will, set loose from reason, can
deuise,' etc.
The initials ' H. W.' fit his friend and patron, Henry
Wriothesley, Earl of Southampton.
The 'eagle' metaphor is also thought to refer to Sh—.
Dr. Grosart believed 'Henry Willobie' to be the pseudonym of the real author Dorrell, and that his christian
name 'Hadrian' was likewise borrowed.
The book was reprinted in 1596, and again before 1605,
but no exemplars are now known of those issues.

Willobie (Henry) Avisa . . . The fourth time
corrected and augmented. Imprinted at
Ln. by Iohn Windet, 1605. Fcp. 4°
BRITWELL

Avisa . . . whereunto is added an apologie
shewing the true meaning of ' Willobie
his Avisa,' with the victorie of English
chastitie, never before published. The
fourth time corrected and amended.
Imprinted at Ln. by Iohn Windet, 1609.
Fcp. 4°
Halliwell's copy sold July, 1889 for £24 10s.

Avisa . . . The fifth time corrected and
augmented. Ln : Printed by Wm. Stansby, 1635. 12°   BM
The only copy known to exist.

Avisa . . . 1594 ; Apologie, 1596 ; Victorie of
English chastitie, 1596 ; [also] ' Penelope's complaint,' by Peter Colse. Edited
with introduction, notes and illustrations
by Alex. B. Grosart. [Manchester :
Charles E. Simms ; privately] Printed
for the subscribers, 1880. Fcp. 4°, pp.
xxxii.-xvi.-204, including printed wrap-
pers   BM | BLO | BUS | CTC
Issue limited to sixty-two copies.

Avisa . . . 1635. Ln : Spenser Society,
1886. 8°   BPL

Avisa . . . With an essay towards its interpretation by C. Hughes. 1904. 8° BPL
Avisa. See Creighton

Willoughby & Co. Publishers. See Sh—
Works, 1851-54, 1852-54, 1853, 1857, 1859

Wilmot. Retrospective glance at Fechter's
' Iago ' and the acting edition of 'Othello.'
Ln : Lacy . . . 1862. 8°, pp. 32
BPL | BUS | CPL | SML

Wilson York Publisher. See Sh— Macbeth,
1799

Wilson & Son York Publishers. See Sh—
Works, 1811

Wilson (A.) Short studies in Sh—. Dunedin
. . . 1898. Fcp. 4°   MPL

Wilson (Mrs. Baron) Memoirs . . . See Mellon

Wilson (Charles). See Congreve

Wilson of Toronto (Sir Daniel) Anne Hathaway : A dialogue [In ' Canadian
Monthly']. Toronto . . . 1872   BPL

Caliban ; the missing link. Ln : Macmillan
& Co., 1873. 8°, pp. xvi.-274
BPL | BUS | CPL | MPL | SML
A commentary on 'The tempest' and Sh—'s monsters,
ghosts, witches, fairies, folk-lore, etc.
The Boston copy is on large paper.

Wilson (H. Schuetz) Discontents of a dramatist [In ' The Theatre.' 1886]. Roy. 8°
BM | BLO | BPL

Goethe on ' Hamlet ' [In ' London Society'].
Ln : 1875. 8°   BPL | BUS

Studies and romances. Ln : H. S. King . . .
1873. Cr. 8°   BM | BLO | BPL
Contains ' Sh— in Blackfriars, or the first performance
of " Hamlet,"' pp. 1-28.

Tasso [In the ' Fortnightly Review.' Ln :
. . . 1885]. Roy. 8°   BM | BLO | BPL
Contains Shakespeareana.

The non-dramatic in Sh— [In ' International Review']. New York . . . 1877.
8°   BUS

Three desperate deaths in Sh— [In ' The
Theatre.' Ln : . . . 1885]. Roy. 8°
BM | BLO | BPL

Wilson (J.)] Sh—'s curse, and other poems.
Ln : Bosworth & Harrison . . . 1861.
16°, pp. viii.-68   BM | BPL | BUS | SML
Attributed to J. Wilson.

Wilson (J. E.)] Throw for a throne, or the
prince unmasked, by ' Zinn, Sergeant at
law.' Ln : Wilson . . . 1897. 8°
BM | BPL | SML
Maintains that Claudius (in ' Hamlet ') was innocent of
murder.

Wilson Vocalist (Jack)—
See Rimbault
,, Sh— Works : Ext. 1653

Wilson (James Grant) Stratford-upon-Avon
[In ' Harper's Magazine ']. New York,
1861. 8°   BM | BLO | BPL | BUS

Wilson Bookseller (John)] Catalogue of all the
books, pamphlets, etc. relating to Sh—.
To which are subjoined an account of the
early quarto editions of the great dramatist's plays and poems ; the prices at
which many copies have sold in public
sales. Together with a list of the leading
and esteemed editions of Sh—'s collected
works. Ln : Printed for John Wilson . . .
1827. Cr. 8°, pp. xlii.-70
BM | BPL | BUS | CPL | MPL | SML | W
A few copies were done on large paper 8°, of which
examples are at Warwick Castle and Birmingham.
The first distinct effort towards a complete Sh— biblio-

graphy. It was preceded by Capell's limited sketch in his edition of the poet's works, 1767-68, and by the Marquis of Bute in 1805.
The preface contains an account of spurious Sh— portraits and manuscripts.
An interleaved copy, with MS. additions, from the library of Charles E. Flower, is at Stratford.

Wilson *Bookseller* (John) Miscellaneous catalogue of useful, interesting and curious old books, including . . . Shakespeareana, etc. Ln : . . . Dec., 1863.   8°, pp. 48
BUS

Miscellaneous catalogue of useful . . . old books, including many relating to Sh—. Ln : . . . 1864.   8°, pp. 48   BUS

Wilson *Composer* (John) Cheerfull ayres, 1660 *See* Collier (J. P.)
  ,, Sh— Poems, 1660-67, 1862
  ,, Sh— Works : Ext. 1653

Wilson *Dramatist* (John) Andronicus Comnenius. A tragedy. Ln : Printed for John Starkey at the Mitre between the Middle Temple Gate and Temple Bar in Fleet Street, 1664. Fcp. 4°
A passage between Andronicus and Anna, act iv., sc. 3, seems to have been inspired by a famous scene in 'King Richard III.'

Wilson *Christopher North* (*Prof.* John) Dies boreales ; Christopher under canvas [In ' Blackwood's Magazine,' 1849-50].   8°
On ' Macbeth ' and ' Othello.'   BUS

Double time analysis of ' Macbeth ' and ' Othello.' Ln : New Sh— Society, 1875-76.   8°   BM | BPL | BUS

] Essays, critical and imaginative, by 'Christopher North.' Edinburgh : Blackwood . . . 1857.   4 vols.   Cr. 8°
BM | BLO | BPL | BUS | CTC
Contains ' A few words on Sh—, May, 1819,' in vol. iii., pp. 420-431, in which Wilson remarks :—' Sh— is of no age. He speaks a language which thrills in our blood in spite of the separation of two hundred years. His thoughts, passions, feelings, strains of fancy, all are of this day as they were of his own, and his genius may be contemporary with the mind of every generation for a thousand years to come. He, above all poets, looked upon man and lived for mankind. His genius, universal in intellect, could find in no more bounded circumference its proper sphere . . . Whatever in nature or life was given to man was given in contemplation and poetry to him also, and over the undimmed mirror of his mind passed all the shadows of our mortal world. Look through his plays and tell what form of existence, what quality of spirit he is most skilful to delineate. Which of all the manifold beings he has drawn lives before our thoughts, our eyes in most unpictured reality? . . . It was Sh—, the most unlearned of all our writers, who. first exhibited on the stage perfect models, perfect images of all human characters and all human events. We cannot conceive any skill that could from his great characters remove any defect or add to their perfect composition. Except in him, we look in vain for the entire fulness, the self-consistency, and self-completeness of perfect art.'

] Essays . . . Edinburgh : Blackwood, 1866. 4 vols.   Cr. 8°   BM | BLO | CTC

Wilson *Christopher North* (*Prof.* John)] Noctes ambrosianæ.   Edinburgh : Blackwood, 1855-56.   4 vols.   Cr. 8°   BPL
For Shakespearean references see index in vol. iv.

Wilson (Patten) *Artist. See* Sh— Hamlet, 1903

Wilson (Peter) *Dublin Printer & Publisher—*
  See Sh— Hamlet, 1750
  ,, Sh— Othello, 1751
  ,, Sh— Winter's tale, 1767
  ,, Sh— Works, 1766

Wilson (Robert) Fair Em.   *See* Sh— Fair Em, 1631
See Sh— Sir John Oldcastle (*heading*)

Wilson (R. G.) Select biography.   *See* Sh—] Wilson

Wilson & Son (T.) *York Publishers.   See* Kemble

Wilson (Thomas)] Analysis of the illustrated Sh— of Thomas Wilson, accompanied by a portrait of George Harris in the character of 'Cardinal Wolsey.' Ln : W. J. White . . . 1820.   4°, pp. viii.-68-viii.
BM | BPL | BUS | CPL
Issue restricted to twenty-five copies, on large paper.

Wilson *Sec. of State* (*Sir* Thomas) Arte of rhetorique for the use of all such as are studious of eloquence. Ln : R. Grafton . . . 1553.   Fcp. 4°, black letter
Reprinted seven times between 1553 and 1586.
Writers of similar experience will readily agree with the author when he says, ' If others neuer gette more by books than I haue doen, it wer better to be a carter than a scholer for worldlie profite.'
Wilson was imprisoned as a presumptuous and dangerous heretic by the Inquisitors of the holy see at Rome.
For evidence of Sh—'s use of this work, see Drake's ' Sh— and his times,' pp. 440 and 473.

Arte of rhetorique, now newly set forth againe, with a prologue to the reader. Imprinted at Ln. by George Robinson . . . 1585.   Fcp. 4°

Arte of rhetorique. Edited by G. H. Mair. Oxford : University Press, 1909.   Cr. 8°
BM | BLO | CTC

Wilson (W.) *Printer. See* Buck (G.)

Wilson (Wm.) A house for Sh— : A proposition for the consideration of the nation. Reprinted from ' Hood's Magazine.' Ln : H. Hurst, 1848.   8°, pp. 8   BPL | BUS | W
Advocates the ' building of a theatre where . . . Sh— . . . may be constantly performed.'

A house for Sh— . . . Second . . . paper . . . Ln : C. Mitchell [1849].   8°, pp. 16
BPL | BUS | W

Wilson (William) Sh— and astrology from a student's point of view. Boston [U.S.] . . . 1903.   8°, pp. 12   BUS

Wilson *Actor* (Wm.) Letter to Edward Alleyn [Oct., 1617 ?] at Dulwich [In ' The Athenæum,' No. 3,960, Sept., 1903].   4°
BM | BPL

Winbolt (S. E.) *Editor*—
  See Sh— As you like it, 1895
  ,, Sh— King Henry V., 1896
Winchester College Sh— Society's publications: Noctes Shaksperianæ; a series of papers by late and present members. Edited by C. H. Hawkins. Winchester . . . 1887. 8°. With folded plate
  BPL | BUS
Winckler (E.) *Editor. See* Sh— Cymbeline, 1893
Windet (J.) *Printer*—
  See Ferne
  ,, Henri IV.
  ,, Willobie
Windle (Bertram Coghill Alan) School history of Warwickshire. Ln : Methuen . . . 1906. Cr. 8°, pp. 236. Illustrated BPL
Sh—'s country. Illustrated by Edmund H. New. Ln : Methuen, 1899. 12°, pp. 230. With maps and plates
  BM | BPL | BUS | SML
Windle (*Mrs.* Catharine F. A.) Address to the New Sh— Society . . . Discovery of Lord Verulam's undoubted authorship of the 'Sh—' Works. San Francisco . . . 1881. 8° BM | BUS
  Reviewed in 'Literary World,' 5th Nov., 1881.
Discovery of Lord Verulam's undoubted authorship of the 'Sh—' Works. San Francisco . . . 1881. 8° BPL
  An 'under' reading of 'Cymbeline.'
Report to the British Museum . . . Discovery . . . of the cipher of F. Bacon, Lord Verulam, alike in his prose writings and in the 'Sh—' dramas. 1882. 8° BM
Wine, beer, ale, and tobacco. *See* Literature
Wingate (Charles Edgar Lewis) Sh—'s heroes on the stage. New York, 1896. 8°. With portraits BUS | MPL
Sh—'s heroines on the stage. New York, 1895. 8°. With portraits
  BM | BPL | BUS | MPL
Sh—'s heroines on the stage. 'Holiday edition.' New York . . . 1901. 2 vols. 12°. With portraits and illustrations
Wingfield (L.) English costumes, A.D. 1070-1820. Ln : Hope . . . [1897]. 4°. Nineteen coloured plates SML
Winslow (C. M. Reignolds) Readings from the old English dramatists. Boston [U.S.] . . . 1895. 2 vols. Cr. 8° BPL
Winsor (Justin) Bibliography of the original quartos and folios of Sh—, with particular reference to copies in America. Boston [U.S.]: J. R. Osgood, 1876. F°, pp. 110. With 68 facsimiles BPL | BUS | MPL
  Reprinted from the Boston public library reports.
Halliwelliana. *See* Halliwell

Winsor (Justin)] Sh— - Shapleigh entanglement [In the 'Atlantic Monthly.' 1887]. 8° BPL | BUS
Sh—'s poems : A bibliography of the earlier editions. 'Harvard University Bibliographical Contributions' . . . Cambridge [U.S.]: University Press, 1879. F°, pp. 12 BM | BPL | BUS
Was Sh— Shapleigh ? A correspondence in two entanglements. Boston [U.S.]: Houghton, 1887. 8° BM | BPL | BUS | SML
Winstanley (William) England's worthies : Select lives of the most eminent persons of the English nation . . . Ln : J. C—— & F. C—— for Obadiah Blagrave at the Bear in St. Paul's Churchyard, 1684. 8°. With frontispiece containing portraits of the worthies SML
  Refers to Sh— on pp. 174, 343, 345-347, and contains a poem upon him.
Lives of the most famous English poets . . . *See* Sh—] Winstanley
Winston (James)] Theatric tourist : Views of the principal theatres of the United Kingdom. With historical accounts. Ln : . . . 1805. 4°. With 25 coloured plates by D. Havell
Winter (*Dr.* Edward) *Editor. See* Sh— Romeo . . . 1840
Winter (William) English rambles and fugitive pieces . . . Boston [U.S.]: Osgood, 1884. 12° SML
  Includes 'Shrines of Warwickshire.'
Gray days and gold. Edinburgh : D. Douglas, 1891. 16° SML
  Several chapters are devoted to Stratford-on-Avon and the Sh— country.
Gray days and gold. Edinburgh : D. Douglas, 1899. 16°
  Complaint is made in the preface that Major Walter pirated portions of the author's work in his 'Sh—'s true life.'
Old shrines and ivy. New York : Macmillan . . . 1892. 16° BPL | SML
Preface. *See* Sh— Two gentlemen . . . 1895
Shadows of the stage. New York : Macmillan, 1892-95. 3 vols. 12° SML
Sh—'s England. Edinburgh : Douglas . . . 1886. 8° BM | BPL | SML
  As pointed out in the preface to the 1910 edition, the author unintentionally plagiarises the title of G. W. Thornbury's work (*q.v.*), which was copyrighted thirty years earlier.
Sh—'s England. Boston [U.S.], 1886. 12° BUS
Sh—'s England. Revised. With illustrations. 1893. 8° BM | BPL
Sh—'s England. Edinburgh : D. Douglas, 1900. 8°
Sh—'s England. Illustrated. New York : Moffat, Yard & Co., 1910. 8°, pp. 344 and 33 plates, chiefly of well-known scenes in the Sh— country BUS | NY

Winter (William) Stratford-upon-Avon [In 'Harper's Monthly.' New York, 1879]. Roy. 8°   BM | BPL | BUS
Stratford-upon-Avon [In 'Harper's Magazine,' pp. 28-53, Dec., 1881]. Roy. 8°. With 22 illustrations   BM | BPL | BUS
Study of Ada Rehan. *See* Rehan
The press and the stage. New York: Lockwood & Combes, 1889. 8°   SML
Trip to England. Boston [U.S.], 1879. 12°   BPL

Trip to England. Second edition. Boston [U.S.]: Osgood, 1881. 12°   SML
Winter (Wm.) *Editor*—
See American . . .
  ,, Booth
  ,, Sh— Hamlet, 1878
  ,, Sh— King Henry VIII., 1878
  ,, Sh— King Lear, 1878
  ,, Sh— King Richard II., 1878
  ,, Sh— King Richard III., 1876, 1878
  ,, Sh— Love's labours lost, 1891
  ,, Sh— Macbeth, 1878
  ,, Sh— Merchant . . . 1898
  ,, Sh— Merry wives, 1886
  ,, Sh— Much ado . . . 1897
  ,, Sh— Othello, 1878
  , Sh— Romeo . . . 1878
  ,, Sh— Taming . . . 1878, 1887
  ,, Sh— Twelfth night, 1893
  ,, Sh— Works, 1899
Winter night's tale [*sic*]. *See* Sh— Works, 1804
Winter's tale. *See* Sh— Winter's tale
'Winter's tale' travesty. *See* Sh— Winter's tale, 1856
Wirtemberg (*Duke of*). *See* Rye
Wise *or* Wyse (Andrew) *Publisher*—
See Sh— King Henry IV., i., 1598, 1599
  ,, Sh— King Henry IV., ii., 1600
  ,, Sh— King Richard II., 1597, 1598
  ,, Sh— King Richard III., 1597, 1598, 1602
  ,, Sh— Much ado . . . 1600
Wise (G.) Autograph of Wm. Sh—. *See Sh*—] Wise
Wise (John Richard) Beauties of Sh—: A lecture before the . . . Royal Shakespearean Club, 23 April, 1857 . . . Stratford. Stratford: E. Adams. Ln: Whitaker, 1857. 8°, pp. 20 BM | BPL | BUS | CPL
Sh—; his birthplace and neighbourhood. *See Sh*—] Wise
Wiseman *Cardinal* (N. P. S.) Wm. Sh—; a lecture. *See Sh*—] Wiseman
Wiss (James) On the rudiments of the Shakespearian drama . . . Frankfort . . . 1828. 8°   BM
Witchcraft. *See* Superstition
Witches (The). *See* Sh— Macbeth, 1800

Witches (The) : Pantomime. *See* Sh— Twelfth night, 1766
Witcomb (C.) *Editor*—
See Sh— Julius Cæsar, 1865
  ,, Sh— King Lear, 1865
  ,, Sh— Macbeth, 1865
Witford (T.) *Publisher*. *See* Sh— Hamlet, 1755
Witham's (Thomas) Commonplace book. *See* Stopes
Withers (Geo.) Verses. *See* Brooke (C.)
Withers (H. L.) *Editor*—
See Sh— Merchant . . . 1897
  ,, Sh— Works, 1893-98
Withers (W.) *Publisher*. *See* Sh— King Henry VIII., 1758
Withington (Leonard) Sh—; old and new criticism upon him [In 'Bibliotheca sacra']. Andover [U.S.], 1847. 8° BUS
Withington (L.) *Editor*. *See* Harrison
Withington (Lothrop) Harvard memorial window at St. Saviour's [In 'The Athenæum,' No. 4,049, p. 690, June, 1905]. 4°   BM | BPL
Withy (R.) *Publisher*—
See History of Portia
  ,, Howard (H.)
Witney, Oxfordshire. *See* Rowe
Wits, fits, and fancies. *See* Copley
Witt's academy. *See* Bodenham
Witt's recreations. *See* Mennis
Wivell (Abraham)] Account of A. Wivell's portrait of Sh— from the Stratford bust. Ln: . . . 1825. 8°
Historical account of the monumental bust . . . in the church at Stratford. With critical remarks on the authors who have written on it. Ln: Pub. by the author, 1827. 8°, pp. 28. Illustrated   BPL | BUS | CPL
Inquiry into the history, authenticity, and characteristics of the Sh— portraits, in which the criticisms of Malone, Steevens, Bowden, and others are examined, confirmed or refuted. [With 7 portraits.] With supplement [and 15 additional plates]. Warwick: John Merridew. Stratford-on-Avon: J. Bacon, 1827. 8°, pp. iv.-254. With portraits of Sh— and Wivell   BM | BPL | BUS | CPL | MPL | SML

Inquiry into . . . the Sh— portraits . . . Ln: C. Knight, 1840. 8°, pp. 48 and 2 portraits   BPL | BUS
Supplement to 'Inquiry . . .' Ln: Simpkin . . . 1827. 8°, pp. iv.-52 and portraits   BUS

Wivell (Abraham) *Engraver. See* Sh— Works, 1833, 1846, 1850

Woffington.] Daly (Augustus) Woffington : A tribute to the actress and the woman. Ln : . . . [1891]. 4°
BM | BLO | BPL | BUS | NY

] Molloy (J. F.) Life and adventures of Peg Woffington, with pictures of the period in which she lived. Ln : Downey, 1897. Cr. 8°, pp. 348. With portrait
BM | BLO | CTC

Woffington (Peg). *See* Dobson

Wolcot (John)] Remarkable satires : The causidicade, triumvirade, porcupinade, processionade, piscopade, scandalizade, and pasquinade. With notes variorum. By 'Peter Pindar.' Ln : Mrs. Newcomb . . . 1760. 8°, pp. 172
Refers to Garrick in Shakespearean parts, pp. 115-116.

Wolfe (John) *Printer*—
See Hayward   *See* Saviolo
„ Loque   „ Spenser (E.)
„ Newnham   „ Yates

Wolfe (Reginalde) *Publisher. See* Recorde

Wolsey.] Cavendish. Negotiations of Thomas Woolsey the great cardinall, containing his life and death. Ln : William Sheares, 1641. Fcp. 4°
Illustrates 'King Henry VIII.' Many of the phrases and incidents, especially the Advice to Master Kingston (p. 113), are remarkably similar to passages in Sh—'s play.

] Storer (T.) Life and death of Thomas Wolsey, cardinall. Ln : T. Dawson . . . 1599. 8°. In verse
Sh— was indebted to this volume (Malone thought) for his knowledge of Wolsey's character.

Wolsey *Cardinal* (Thomas). *See* Robinson

Wood (J. S.) *Editor. See Sh*—] Shakespearean show book

Wood (J. T.) *Publisher. See* Sh— As you like it, 1840

Wood (Manley) *Editor. See* Sh— Works, 1806

Wood (R. S.) New scenes from Sh— for reading, recitation and further studies. *See* Sh— Works : Ext. 1897

Wood (Stanley) 'As you like it' : Questions and notes. 'Dinglewood Sh— manuals.' [c. 1894.] 12°   BPL | SML

'Coriolanus' : Questions and notes. Manchester : Heywood . . . [1894]. 12°
BPL | SML

Dinglewood Sh— manuals [Questions and notes on Sh—'s works . . . 1891]. 12°   BM

'Hamlet' : Questions and notes. With supplement. [c. 1894.] 12°   BPL | SML

'Hamlet' : Two hundred and fifty questions on 'Hamlet.' [c. 1894.] 12°
BPL | SML

Wood (Stanley) 'Julius Cæsar' : Questions and notes . . . With supplement. Manchester : J. Heywood [c. 1894]. 12°, pp. 46   BPL | SML

'King Henry the fifth' : Questions and notes. Manchester : J. Heywood [1895], 12°   BPL | SML

'King Richard II.' : Questions and notes. With supplement. [c. 1894.] 12°
BPL | SML

'Merchant of Venice' : Questions and notes. With supplement. [c. 1894.] 12°   BPL | SML

'Midsummer night's dream' : Questions and notes. Manchester : J. Heywood [c. 1894]. Cr. 8°, pp. 56

On the teaching of Sh— in schools. Manchester : Heywood [1895]. 12°   BPL

Studies of Sh—'s characters as revealed in twelve representative plays. Ln : Gill . . . 1907. Cr. 8°, pp. 322   BPL

'The tempest' : Questions and notes. With supplement. Manchester : J. Heywood [c. 1894]. 12°, pp. 46   BPL | SML

Wood (Stanley) *Editor*—
See Sh— As you like it, 1904
„ Sh— Coriolanus, 1906
„ Sh— Hamlet, 1905
„ Sh— Julius Cæsar, 1901
„ Sh— King Henry V., 1900, 1902
„ Sh— King Richard II., 1905
„ Sh— Macbeth, 1902, 1905
„ Sh— Twelfth night, 1905

Wood (W. D.) 'Hamlet,' from a psychological point of view. 1870. 8° BM | BPL | CPL | SML

Woodcocke (Thomas) *Publisher*—
See Boccaccio
„ Florio
„ Sh— Sonnet : Phaeton, 1591

Woodfall (G.) *Publisher*—
See Letter . . .
„ Sh— King Henry VIII., 1762
„ Sh— Romeo — 1748
„ Sh— The tempest, 1761
„ Sh— Works, 1762

Woodfall (H.) *Publisher*—
See Sh— Hamlet, 1767
„ Sh— King John, 1769
„ Sh— Macbeth, 1768
„ Sh— Othello, 1765
„ Sh— Works, 1767, 1768

Woodfall *jun.* (H.) *Publisher. See* Sh— Midsummer . . . 1745

Woodfall (H. S.) *Publisher. See* Sh— Works, 1790

Woodfall (John) *Publisher. See* Sh— The tempest, 1804

Woodfall (W.) *Publisher*—
See Sh— Timon . . . 1770
„ Sh— Works, 1773

Woodforde (F. C.) Etymological index to 'As you like it.' Market Drayton : Bennion & Horne, 1884. 12°, pp. 24 BM
Etymological index to 'Julius Cæsar.' Market Drayton [1886]. 8° BM
Etymological index to ' King Henry V.' Market Drayton [1888]. 8° BM
Etymological index to ' King Henry V.' Second edition. Market Drayton [c. 1888]. 12° BPL
Etymological index to ' The tempest.' Market Drayton ... 1885. 12° BM | BPL
Notes to a ' Midsummer night's dream.' [c. 1887.] 12° BPL
Woodforde (F. C.) Editor. See Sh— Midsummer ... 1887
Woodroffe (Paul) Artist—
See Sh— Poems, 1898
   ,, Sh— The tempest, 1908
Woods (G. B.) Essays ... Boston [U.S.], 1873. 12° BPL
Contains articles entitled ' How old was Hamlet?' (pp. 90-102) and ' The time of Hamlet' (pp. 102-106).
Woods (Mary A.) Editor. See Sh— Merchant ... 1898
Woods (W.) The twins, or which is which ? See Sh— Comedy of errors, 178c
Woodward Caricaturist (George M.)] Familiar verses from the ghost of Willy Sh— to Sammy Ireland. To which is added, Prince Robert, an auncient ballad. Ln : R. White ... 1796. 8°, pp. 16 BM | BPL | BUS | W
By some the authorship is assigned to one Orton. A skit on the Ireland forgeries.
Woodward (Henry)] Mr. Woodward in the character of Mercutio in ' Romeo and Juliet.' Ln : W. Herbert, 1753. Engraving, with quotation BUS
Songs, chorusses, etc. . . . performed . . . in Harlequin's jubilee at . . . Covent Garden. Ln : W. Griffin, 1770. 8°, pp. iv.-14 BUS
Woodward (J.) Publisher—
See Secret history of Mack-beth
   ,, Warwick
Wooing of the fair maid of London by King Edward. See Sh—] Collection ..
Woolf (Arthur Harold) Sh— and the old Southwark playhouses. Ln : . . . 1903. 8°, pp. 20 BPL | BUS
Woolls (C.)] The barrow diggers. See Sh— Hamlet, 1839
Worcester's players (Earl of). See Halliwell
Worcestershire—
   See Allies   See Reiss
   ,, Duignan   ,, Salisbury
   ,, Lambert   ,, Smith (W.)
   ,, May   ,, Somerville
Word . . . of advice to William Warburton. See Grey

Worde (Wynkyn de) Printer. See Booke . . .
Wordsworth (Charles) Editor. See Sh— Works, 1883, 1893
Wordsworth Bp. (Charles) Man's excellency a cause of praise . . . A sermon at Stratford, 24 Ap., 1864. Ln : Smith . . . 1864. 8°, pp. 28 BPL | BUS
On Sh—'s knowledge and use of the Bible. Ln : Smith, 1864. Cr. 8°, pp. xii.-310. Illustrated BM | BPL | BUS | CPL | MPL
On Sh—'s knowledge . . . of the Bible. Ln : Smith, 1880. 8° BM | BPL | SML
On Sh—'s knowledge . . . of the Bible. Fourth edition. Ln : Eden . . . 1892. 8° BM
Wordsworth (Christopher) Editor. See Sh— Troilus . . . 1828
Wordsworth (J.) Editor. See Sh— As you like it, 1827
Wordsworth Poet (Wm.) Holograph letter to John Britton [criticising the Stratford bust]. 12 Oct., 1816. 4°. Manuscript BUS
Poems. Ln : Longman . . . 1807. 2 vols. Cr. 8° BM | BLO | CTC
In the 'Sonnets dedicated to liberty,' Wordsworth writes :—   '. . . In our halls is hung Armoury of the invincible knights of old. We must be free, or die, who speak the tongue That Sh— spake ; the faith and morals hold Which Milton held. In everything we are sprung Of earth's first blood, have titles manifold.'
Sh— and Goethe [In ' Memoirs of Wm. Wordsworth, by Christopher Wordsworth,' Vol. 2, pp. 437-438, 1851]. 2 vols. Cr. 8°
' He (Goethe) does not seem to me to be a great poet in either of the classes of poets. At the head of the first class I would place Homer and Sh—, whose universal minds are able to reach every variety of thought and feeling without bringing their own individuality before the reader. They infuse, they breathe light into every object they approach, but you never find themselves. At the head of the second class, those whom you can trace individually in all they write, I would place Spenser and Milton. In all that Spenser writes you can trace the gentle, affectionate spirit of the man ; in all that Milton writes you find the exalted, sustained being that he was . . .'
Worrall (Walter) Kyd's ' Spanish tragedy' : A note [In ' The Athenæum, No. 4,203, p. 616, May, 1908]. 4° BM | BPL
On a passage in ' [King] Edward III.' [In The Athenæum,' No. 4,206, p. 708, June, 1908]. 4° BM | BPL
Worsdale (J.) Editor. See Sh— Taming . . . 1735, 1738
Worsley.] Catalogus librorum . . . Doctoris Benjaminis Worsley . . . quoram auctio habebitur Londin . . . per Joan. Dunmore & Ric. Chiswell bibliopolas, 1678. Fcp. 4°
Said to be the fifth English book auction and the first containing Sh—'s works.
' Lot 303, Sh—, 1632,' realised 16/-, and lot 304, ' Sh—, 1663,' 28/6.
The first known recorded appearance at auction of the Jaggard canon of 1623 was in Sir Wm. Coventry's library, sold in the Haymarket, Ln., in May, 1687.

Wotton (J.) *Publisher. See* Sh— Julius Cæsar, 1740

Woty (William) Poetical works . . . '*Favete.*' Ln : G. Scott for W. Flexney, 1770. 2 vols. Cr. 8°

At p. 74, vol. i., occurs the curious 'Familiar epistle from the shades below, giving an account of the station of the poets' [from Chaucer to Derrick], twice referring to the national poet, thus :—

'And Sh—·and Spenser appear pretty tight, They've each a small freehold, tho' bounded in sore.
* * *
As to Sh— himself, he's so modest a man, He would not declare what he thought of the plan ; With so much applause, and benevolence crushed, He made his obeisance, retreated, and blushed.
* * *

In the list of subscribers prefixed occur the names of Addison, Boswell, Colman, Garrick, Johnson, Langhorne, and Reynolds.

Wrangler (The). Cambridge . . . 1836-37. 8° SML

A periodical with Shakespearean articles, signed 'G.'

Wreittoun (John) *Edinburgh Printer. See* Sh— Venus . . . 1627, 1860

'Wretch' *pseud.* Illustrations of Sh—. [1829.] F° BM

A skit on F. A. M. Retzsch's Illustrations (*q.v.*)

Wright *Artist. See* Sh— Works, 1821-29, 1836

Wright (Amy Payton) Children of Sh— : An account of the child-characters appearing in Sh—'s plays. Ln : Moring . . . 1905. Cr. 8° BPL

Wright (C.) *Publisher. See* Sh— Works, 1761

Wright (Charles) Sh— : Reprint of the first collected edition of the plays, and ' The Athenæum' of 25 Jan., 1862 [a letter] . . . 1862. 4°, pp. 4 BM | BUS

Sh— and Ben Jonson, Wm. Penn, Lord Macaulay and ' The Athenæum'—or its editor. Ln : *Not published*, 1861. 8°, pp. 4

Stratford portrait of Sh— and ' The Athenæum' . . . [1861.] 8°, pp. 20 BM | BPL | BUS

Stratford portrait . . . : Copies of communications to ' The Times ' . . . 1861. 8°, pp. 4 BUS

Wright *of Birmingham (Dr.) Bibliophile. See* Catalogue, 1853

Wright (E. & J.) *Printers. See* Sh— Works, 1807, 1808

Wright (E. R.) Archæological and historic fragments, including a manuscript list of plays, 1638, having reference to ' Julius Cæsar' and ' Merry wives.' Ln : 1887. Cr. 8°. With facsimiles

Wright (George R.) Archæologic and historic fragments, containing inter alia a facsimile of a rare manuscript page, dated 1638, having reference to two of Sh—'s most famous plays, with notes. Ln : . . . 1887. 8° BUS

Brief memoir. *See* Halliwell

Wright (Henry) *Editor. See* Sh— Macbeth, 1674

Wright (Henrietta C.) Children's stories in English literature from Taliesin to Sh—. Ln : Ward . . . 1890. Cr. 8° SML

Children's stories in English literature : Sh— to Tennyson. Ln : Unwin, 1892. Cr. 8° BPL

Wright (J.) *Publisher. See* Sh— Works, 1798, 1798-1800

Wright (James) *Editor. See* Dugdale

Wright (John) *Publisher*—
See Greene (R.) *See* Returne . . .
,, Ordinance ,, Sandys
,, Sh— Antony . . . 1799
,, Sh— Fair Em, 1605, 1631
,, Sh— King Lear, 1605
,, Sh— Mucedorus, 1619, 1631, 1634, 1639
,, Sh— Sonnets, 1609
,, Sh— Venus . . . 1675
,, Sh— Works, 1800

Wright (J. B.) *Editor*—
See Sh— Coriolanus, 1855
,, Sh— Love's labours lost, 1858
,, Sh— Winter's tale, 1857, 1859

Wright (J. M.) *Artist. See* Sh— Works : Ext. 1841

Wright (L. E.) *Editor. See* Sh— Romeo . . . 1909

Wright (*Major*). *Editor. See* Camus

Wright (Thomas)] Passions of the minde, by Th. W——. Ln : V. S—— for W. B——, 1601. 8°

At p. 298 is an account of the costume of Sh—'s fellow-actor, Richard Tarlton.

Passions of the minde in general . . . Corrected, enlarged, and with sundry new discourses augmented. Ln : Printed by Miles Flesher and . . . sold by Robert Dawlman at the Brazen Serpent in Paul's Churchyard, 1630. Fcp. 4°

Dedicated to the Earl of Southampton, one of Sh—'s patrons.

Wright (Thomas) *Editor*—
See Alliterative poem *See* Nares
,, Chester plays ,, Percy Society

Wright (Wm.) *Publisher*—
See Chettle
,, Greene

Wright (Wm. Aldis) A disputed reading in the ' Winter's tale.' 1890. 4°. Manuscript BPL

Wright (W. A.) *Editor*—
See Sh— As you like it, 1876, 1899
,, Sh— Coriolanus, 1879, 1905
,, Sh— Hamlet, 1872, 1873, 1874, 1880, 1881, 1883, 1884, 1890, 1896
,, Sh— Julius Cæsar, 1876, 1878, 1881, 1883, 1889, 1892, 1901
,, Sh— King Henry IV. i., 1897

Wright (W. A.) *Editor—*
  See Sh— King Henry V., 1882, 1883, 1889,
      1892, 1900
  ,, Sh— King Henry VIII., 1891
  ,, Sh— King John, 1886, 1887
  ,, Sh— King Lear, 1875, 1876, 1879, 1880,
      1881, 1884
  ,, Sh— King Richard II., 1868, 1869, 1873,
      1874, 1876, 1879, 1880, 1881,
      1882, 1884, 1886, 1889, 1892,
      1893, 1895
  ,, Sh— King Richard III., 1880, 1885
  ,, Sh— Macbeth, 1869, 1873, 1874, 1876,
      1882, 1883, 1885, 1889, 1895, 1901
  ,, Sh— Merchant . . . 1868, 1869, 1874,
      1876, 1880, 1881, 1883, 1884,
      1886, 1887, 1889, 1891
  ,, Sh— Midsummer . . . 1878, 1881, 1883,
      1886, 1887, 1892, 1894
  ,, Sh— Much ado . . . 1894
  ,, Sh— The tempest, 1874, 1875, 1879,
      1881, 1884, 1885, 1889, 1891
  ,, Sh— Twelfth night, 1885, 1887
  ,, Sh— Works, 1863-66, 1864, 1865, 1866,
      1867, 1868-83, 1873, 1874, 1878,
      1879, 1880, 1881, 1884, 1887,
      1887-88, 1888, 1891, 1891-93,
      1893-95, 1895, 1897
Wrighten (J.) *Editor & Prompter—*
  See Sh— As you like it, 1791
  ,, Sh— Coriolanus, 1789
  ,, Sh— King Henry V., 1789
  ,, Sh— Twelfth night, 1791, 1792
Wrighten *Actress (Mrs.)* Portrait. *See* Sh—
    Taming . . . 1785
Wroughton (Richard) *Editor. See* Sh— King
    Richard II., 1815
Wünder (*Dr.* C.) *Editor. See* Sh— Othello,
    1891
Würtzburg (C. A.) The plot of 'As you like it'
    [In 'Poet-lore']. Philadelphia . . . 1891.
    Roy. 8°   BPL | BUS | NY
Wyatt (A. J.) *Editor—*
  See Sh— Cymbeline, 1897
  ,, Works, 1893-98
Wyatt (A. J.) & Low (W. H.) Intermediate
    text-book of English literature. Ln: W.
    B. Clive, 1903. Cr. 8°, pp. xx.-658
    Sh— pp. 203-240.
Wyatt (Mat. *or* John ?)] Comparative review
    of the opinions of Mr. James Boaden . . .
    in 1795 and . . . 1796 relative to the Sh—
    manuscripts. By a friend to consistency.
    Ln: G. Sael . . . [1796]. 8°, pp. ii.-60
                              BPL | BUS | W

Wyatt (*Sir* Thomas) Poems, 1717. *See*
    Howard
Wycherly (Wm.) *See* Dennis
Wykes (C. H.) Sh— reader. *See* Sh— Works:
    Ext. 1880
Wykes (Henry) *Printer. See* Heliodorus
Wylie (J. H.) The Agincourt 'chaplain'
    [identified as Thomas Elmham, Cluniac
    prior of Lenton, near Nottingham]. [In
    'The Athenæum,' No. 3,904, p. 254, Aug.,
    1902]. 4°   BM | BPL
    Illustrates 'King Henry V.'
Wyman (W. H.) Bibliography of the Bacon-
    Sh— literature. Cincinnati, U.S., 1882.
    8°, pp. 8   BM | BPL | BUS | MPL
    Bibliography of the Bacon-Sh— literature.
    With notes and extracts. Cincinnati:
    Thomson, 1884. 8° BM | BPL | MPL | SML
    Letters to Samuel Timmins on Sh—. 1886.
    4°. Manuscript   BPL
Wyndham (Charles) *Editor. See* Sh— Mer-
    chant . . . 1874
Wyndham (George) *Editor. See* Sh— Poems,
    1898
Wyndham (Horace) The magnificent mum-
    mer: Some reflections on the twentieth
    century stage; its status and pretensions.
    Ln: F. V. White, 1909. Cr. 8°, pp. 158
    Several Shakespearean references.
Wyndham (H. S.) Annals of Covent Garden
    theatre, 1732-1897. Ln: 1906. 2 vols.
    8°. With 43 full-page caricatures, por-
    traits, and other plates
                      BM | BLO | BPL | CTC
Wyll of the deuyll and last testament. *See*
    Reprints
Wynne (C.) *Dublin Publisher. See* Sh—
    Works, 1766
Wynne (J.) Private libraries of New York.
    New York [c. 1890]. 8°   BUS
Wynne & Scholey *Publishers. See* Sh— Works,
    1803-05
Wynne & Son (Peter) *Publishers. See* Sh—
    Works, 1803-07, 1807
Wyntown (Andrew) Orygynale cronykil of
    Scotland. Edited by D. Macpherson.
    Ln: . . . 1795. 4°   BUS
    The story of 'Macbeth' occurs in book vi., chap. 18.
    250 copies printed on small, and 25 on large paper, 4°.
    It was reprinted in 1872-79.
    'This metrical chronicle, written in the pure language
    of the country, throws great light on many Scottish
    transactions.'—*Lowndes.*
Wyse chylde and the Emperor Adrian. A
    dialogue. Edited by J. O. Halliwell. . .
    1860. 8°   BPL

 —— (R.) *Printer.* See Davenant

Yair (J.) *Edinburgh Publisher.* See Sh— Works, 1753

Yardley (W. R.) Sh—'s heroines. Sh— Club paper. Stratford-on-Avon: [Privately printed] 1909. Cr. 8°, pp. 8

Yarranton (Andrew) England's improvement by sea and land. To outdo the Dutch without fighting; to pay debts without moneys . . . Ln: . . . 1677-81. Fcp. 4°. With folding plate   w
Contains interesting suggestions respecting Stratford-on-Avon.

Yarrow (John) Sh—; a tercentenary poem. *See Sh*—] Yarrow

Yates *Actor.* See Garrick

Yates (Edmund) *Editor.* See Mathews

Yates *Servingman* (James) Castell of courtesie, hould of humilitie, chariot of chastitie, & Diana and Venus. Ln: Iohn Wolfe . . . 1582. Fcp. 4°
At p. 16 is a poem dedicated to the memory of W. S—, with punning allusions to his christian name. Being unknown to Sh—'s biographers, and strongly reminiscent of the famous 'Will' sonnets 135, 136, and 143, the lines are here given in full :—

'*Verses written at the departure of his friend, W. S—, when hee went to dwell at London.*

The absence of a friend
    Is griefe unto the hart ;
The presence of him worketh joy,
    And putteth backe the smart.
So Will, my onely Will,
    The absence now of thee
Doth make me waile in woful wise,
    To thinke that it should bee.

But when thy friendly corpes
    Shall present be to view,
Then shall I joy, as now I mourne
    That absence makes me rue.
But, Will, I must content
    My dolefull minde with this :
We subject are to fortune's lore,
    As certain true it is.

Yet this I doe persuade,
    That absence hath no force
A faithful friende to make unkinde,
    That were without remorse.
I doe not thinke that Will
    Will soe his friende forget ;
But will remain in former will,
    And be not over set.

By any light conceite,
    Which doth procure unrest,
To bring disdaine, whereas delight
    Should build within the brest.
No, no, I am disposed
    To speake this by the way ;
But trust me, Will, beleeve me now,
    I doubt not as I say.

For I am firmly fixt,
    Thy friendship will not faile,
Although that absence might procure
    The same for to prevaile.

Well, for a vauntless vow,
    Accept this at my hand :
As I have beene so will I bee,
    Good Will to understand.'

Yates (*Mrs.*) *Actress.* See Sh— Measure . . . 1773

Yeatman (John Pym) Gentle Sh—: A vindication. Ln: Roxburghe Press, 1896. Roy. 8°, pp. 442   BM | BPL | SML
Is William Sh—'s will holographic ? With remarks upon the recent action for libel of Yeatman *v.* 'Saturday Review' . . . and photographs of the poet's will. Second edition. Darley Dale . . . 1901. Roy. 8°, pp. 72   BPL | BUS

Yeatman (J. Pym). See Round & Yeatman

Ylope (M.) *See* Edwards (R.)

Yockney (A.) Art of Sir Hy. Irving. *See* Irving (*Sir* J. H. B.)

Yong. *See* Young

Yonge (Charlotte M.) *Editor*—
    See Sh— King Richard II., 1884
    ,, Sh— Works, 1883-85

'Yorick' *pseud.* Letter concerning Henry Irving addressed to E. R. H. . . . 1877. 12°   BPL

York's (*Duke of*) servants. *See* Sh— Two noble kinsmen, 1668

York (Duke of) theatre—
    See Pepys
    ,, Sh— The tempest, 1733

Yorkshire—
    See Whitaker
    ,, Wilkinson

Yorkshire tragedy. *See* Sh— Yorkshire tragedy

Young. Life of E. Alleyn. *See* Alleyn

Young *Publisher.* *See* Black & Young

Young *or* Yonge (Bartholomew) *Editor*—
    See Guazzo
    ,, Montemayor

Young.] Memoir of Charles Mayne Young, tragedian. With extracts from his son's journal by J. C. Young. With portraits and sketches. Ln: Macmillan, 1871. 2 vols. 8°. With seven plates   BPL

Young (C. M.)—
    See De Soligny
    ,, Pepys

Young (Isabel F.) *Editor*—
    See Sh— As you like it, 1903
    ,, Sh— King Henry V., 1904
    ,, Sh— King Richard III., 1902

Young (John T.) Lecture on 'Romeo and Juliet.' Ln: 'Warehousemen's Journal' [c. 1885]. 8°, pp. 16

Young (K.) Origin of the story of 'Troilus and Criseyde.' Ln: Chaucer Society (2nd Series, Vol. 40), 1908. 8°   BPL

Young (R.) *Printer*—
    See Sh— Hamlet, 1637
    ,, Sh— Romeo . . . 1637

Young (W.) History of Dulwich College.
With life of Edward Alleyn. Edinburgh :
Morrison & Gibb, 1889. 2 vols. 4° SML
Religious belief and feeling which pervade
' King Lear.' *See* Three prize essays
Young (W.) *Editor. See* Sh— King John, 1900
Young Adam Cupid [In ' Penn Monthly'].
Philadelphia, 1873. 8° BPL
Illustrates ' Romeo and Juliet,' act ii., sc. 1.
Young Albert the Roscius. *See* Albert
Young gentleman and lady's poetical precep-
tor. Coventry . . . 1807. 16° W
Contains the dirge from ' Cymbeline.'
Young ladies' journal : Sh— tercentenary.
20th April, 1864. 4° BPL
Younger *Editor & Prompter—*
See Sh— Hamlet, 1773, 1774, 1776
„ Sh— Julius Cæsar, 1773
„ Sh— King Henry V., 1773
„ Sh— King Henry VIII., 1773
„ Sh— Winter's tale, 1773
Youth of Sh—. *See* Williams

ABERN (V. V.) *Mainz Publisher.*
See Sh— King Richard II.,
1868
Zangwill (Israel) The English Sh—
[In ' The Idler,' Vol. I., pp.
61-73. Ln : . . . 1892]. 8°.
Illustrated BM | BPL
A humorous sketch.
' Zanoni ' *pseud. See* Ibsen
' Zetes ' *pseud.* A word with Dr. Johnson
[on his edition of Sh—. In ' Hood's
Magazine.' 1846]. 8° BPL
Zimmermann (A.) *Editor. See* Sh— Merchant
. . . 1873
Zimmern (Helen) *Editor. See* Lewes
Zincke (W. F.) *Forger—*
See Jaggard
„ *Sh—*] Portrait
Zingarelli (Nicolo) *Composer. See* Sh— Romeo
. . . 1837, 1860
' Zinn (*Sergeant*) ' *pseud. See* Wilson (J. E.)
Ziolecki (*Dr.*) Sh— in Poland, Russia, and
other Slavonic countries. Ln : New Sh—
Society, 1880-86. 8°
Zollmann (W.) Marcus Brutus in Sh—'s
' Julius Cæsar' . . . 1867. 4° BM
Zornlin (*Miss* G. M.) On the conduct of
Hamlet towards Ophelia. *See Sh*—] Sh—
Society
Remarks on discrepancies in the character
of Jack Cade in ' King Henry VI.' *See
Sh*—] Sh— Society
Two additional notes on ' King Henry VI.,
part ii.' *See Sh*—] Sh— Society

AFTERMATH:

An alphabet of additions and corrections while printing.—W. J.

'Achespè.' Sh— (a sonnet). *See* Birmingham

Actors—
  See Cane
  ,, Reed

Adams *President* (John Quincy)] Character of Desdemona, by J. Q. A—— [In 'American Monthly Magazine,' Vol. 7, New Ser. Vol. I., pp. 209-217, March, 1836]. 8°
  Reprinted in Griswold's Prose writers of America, Philadelphia, 1847, 8°, pp. 103-106.

] Misconceptions of Sh— upon the stage, by 'Q' [In 'New England Magazine,' Vol. 9, pp. 435-440, Dec., 1835]. 8°

Misconceptions of Sh— upon the stage. New York, 1835. 8°, pp. 8
  Reprinted in J. H. Hackett's 'Notes, criticism, and correspondence on Sh—'s plays, 1863,' pp. 217-228.

Notes and comments upon certain plays and actors of Sh—. With criticisms and correspondence. New York, 1863. 12°

] Personations of the characters of Sh—. Extracts from the MS. letters of a celebrated personage [In 'American Monthly Magazine,' Vol. VII., New Ser. Vol. I., pp. 38-40 and one plate, Jan.] 1836. 8°

Personations of the characters of Sh—. New York, 1836. 8°, pp. 4
  Reprinted in J. H. Hackett's Notes, 1863, pp. 229-233.

Adee (Alvey Augustus) *Editor*—
  See Sh— King Lear, 1890
  ,, Sh— Works, 1888-94

Ainger *Canon* (Alfred) *Editor*. *See* Sh— Works: Ext. 1907

Akenside (Mark) An inscription [In his 'Poetical Works,' Vol. 2, pp. 136-137. 1805]. 12°
  'Say to each other, "this was Sh—'s form
  Who walk'd in every path of human life,
  Felt every passion, and to all mankind
  Doth now, will ever, that experience yield
  Which his own genius only could acquire." '

Albright (V. E.) Shakespearean stage. Columbia [U.S.] Univ. Press . . . 1909. 8°
  BUS | NY

Allde (Edward) *Printer*. *See* Denmark

Allot (Robert)] Wit's theatre of the little world . . . Ln : . . . 1599

Anders. Sh—'s books. Ln : Nutt . . . (*p. 6, read*) Berlin : G. Reimer . . . 1904. Roy. 8°, pp. viii.-316

Anderson (J.) *Publisher*. *See* Sh— Works 1797

Andrews *of Hull* (Wm.) Report of the festival . . . (*p. 6, read*) Hull : M. C. Peck & Son, 1882. Cr. 8°, pp. 44, including printed wrappers. With portrait and view of old birthplace

Anglo-Saxon remains in Warwickshire. *See* Victoria . . .

Anniversary calendar, natal book, and universal mirror, embracing anniversaries of persons, events, institutions and festivals, of all denominations, historical, sacred and domestic, in every period and state of the world, from the creation . . . Ln : Wm. Kidd . . . 1832. 2 vols. in 1. 8°, pp. vi.-1 016
  Sh— occupies p. 737, where it is noted that the collected 'Comedies, histories, tragedies of this "great heir of fame" were first published in 1623.'

Arch (John & Arthur) *Booksellers*. *See* Sh— Works, 1807

Archer (W.) *Editor*. *See* Sh— King Lear, 1908

Ariosto. Supposes. Translated by George Gascoigne, 1566. *See* Hawkins

Arms. *See* Castle

Armstrong (C.) *Engraver*. *See* Sh— Works, 1807

Armstrong (John) Of the dramatic unities [In his 'Works, 1770,' Vol. 2, p. 242]
  'Sh— indeed, without one perfect plan, has perhaps excelled all other dramatic poets as to detached scenes. But he was a wonder! His deep knowledge of human nature, his prodigious variety of fancy and invention, and of characters drawn with the strongest, truest, and most exquisite strokes, oblige you to forget his most violent irregularities.'

Of the versification of English tragedy [In his 'Works, 1770,' Vol. 2, pp. 164-165]

Arnold (Matthew) Essays in criticism. Ln : Macmillan . . . 1865. Cr. 8°
  At p. 108, comments upon Sh—'s double faculty of interpreting the physiognomy and movement of the outward world and the ideas and laws of man's moral and spiritual nature.

Essays in criticism : Second series [Wordsworth]. Ln : Macmillan, 1888. Cr. 8°
  At pp. 129-131 remarks :—' Let me have the pleasure of quoting a sentence about Sh— which I met with by accident not long ago in "The Correspondant," a French review which not a dozen English people, I suppose, look at.' The writer is praising Sh—'s prose.

'With Sh—,' he says, ' prose comes in whenever the subject being more familiar is unsuited to the majestic English iambic.' And he goes on :—' Sh— is the king of poetic rhythm and style, as well as the king of the realm of thought. Along with his dazzling prose, Sh— has succeeded in giving us the most varied, the most harmonious verse which has ever sounded upon the human ear since the verse of the Greeks.' Henri Cochin, the writer of this sentence, deserves our gratitude for it ; it would not be easy to praise Sh— in a single sentence more justly.

Poems. Ln: Longmans . . . 1853-55. 2 vols. Cr. 8°   BM | BLO | CTC
Contains the beautiful sonnet headed 'Sh—' :—
'Others abide our question. Thou art free,
We ask and ask—thou smilest and art still
Out-topping knowledge. For the loftiest hill,
Who to the stars uncrowns his majesty,
Planting his steadfast footsteps in the sea,
Making the heaven of heavens his dwelling-place,
Spares but the cloudy border of his base
To the foil'd searching of mortality.

    .   .   .   .   .

And thou, who didst the stars and sunbeams know,
Self-school'd, self-scann'd, self-honour'd, self-secure,
Didst tread on earth unguessed at. Better so !
All pains the immortal spirit must endure,
All weakness which impairs, all griefs which bow,
Find their sole speech in that victorious brow !'

Asperne (J.) *Publisher.* *See* Sh— Works, 1811
Aspley (William) *Publisher.* *See* Sh— King Henry IV., ii. (*heading*)
Aston Hall, Warwickshire. *See* Irving (W.)
Atkins (Ion) The immortal memory. *See* Birmingham
Atkins (John & Alice). *See Sh*—] Malone
Aubrey (J.) Brief lives, chiefly of contemporaries, set down between the years 1669 and 1696. Edited from the author's MS. by Andrew Clark. Oxford : Clarendon Press, 1898. 2 vols. 8°, pp. 818, with facsimiles   SBL
Includes a most interesting sketch of Sh—, the second earliest biography known, Fuller being first.
Austin (Alfred) *Editor.* *See* Sh— Poems, 1908
Avon club, for the study of literature, science, and the arts, Sh— memorial, Stratford-on-Avon [founded by Wm. Jaggard]. Syllabus, 1910-11. 16°, pp. 4   BPL | SML
See also Baker
  ,, ,, Brassington
  ,, ,, Bullen
  ,, ,, Elliott
  ,, ,, Field
  ,, ,, Savage
Avon river. *See* Hunt (J. H. L.)

B—— (A.) *Editor.* *See* Bodenham
B—— (N.) *See* Breton (Nicholas)
B—— (O.) Questions (*p.* 10, *read*) Questions of profitable and pleasant concernings talked of by two olde seniors, the one a retired gentleman, the other an upstart frankeling, under an oake in Kenelworth Parke, where they met by accident to defend the partching heate on a hoate day, in grasse or buckhunting time. Called by the reporter a display of vaine life. Together with a panacea or suppling plaister to cure if it were possible the principle diseases wherewith this present time is especially vexed. Ln : Printed by Richard Field dwelling in the Blackfriars by Ludgate, 1594. Fcp. 4°, sig. A to M² in fours
One of the few Warwickshire pieces of Sh—'s lifetime. The dramatist may have had a hand in its production. The scene is laid within walking distance of his birthplace. The printer was his friend and fellow townsman, who published his 'Venus and Adonis' in 1593 and ' Lucrece ' in 1594. The phrase 'Upstart frankeling' reminds one that two years before Robert Greene termed the bard an 'Upstart crow.' Sh— uses the terms 'Upstart' and 'Franklin' several times in the plays.

B—— (R.) *Printer.* *See* Blore (Ralph)
Bacon.] Bacon (Theodore) Delia Bacon : A biographical sketch . . . (*p.* II, *read*) Boston and New York : Houghton, Mifflin . . . 1888. Cr. 8°, pp. viii.-324 and portrait   BPL | BUS | NY | SML
Bacon (F.) *Engraver*—
  See Sh— Works, 1836
  ,, Sh— Works : Ext. 1841
Bacon *Baron Verulam* (Francis). *See* Traill
Bacon.] Steeves (*Dr.* G. Walter) Francis Bacon ; a sketch of his life, works, and literary friends, chiefly from a bibliographical point of view. With forty-three illustrations. Ln : Methuen [1910]. Cr. 8°, pp. xvi.-232   BM | BLO | CTC | SML
Contains title-facsimiles of early editions of Bacon. Refers to Sh— at pp. 36, 47, and 204.
Bacon-Sh— controversy—
  See Birmingham   *See* Marvin
  ,, Bradley   ,, Mendenhall
  ,, Crawford   ,, Ross
  ,, Greg   ,, Vince
  ,, Lawrence
Bacon (Mathew) *Defendant.* *See* Public . . .
Bagley *London* (Edward). *See Sh*—] Malone
Bagster (S.) *Publisher.* *See* Sh— Works, 1811
Bailey (*Sir* W. H.) Sh— as a patriot. Inaugural address by the President . . . Manchester Sh— Society, 10th Oct., 1899. Manchester : Herald & Walker, 1899. 8°, pp. 20, including printed wrappers ; privately printed
Baker (G. P.) *Editor.* *See* Garrick
Baker (George P.) & Cole (G. W.) Some bibliographical puzzles in Elizabethan quartos. With notes. A paper delivered before the Bibliographical Society of America. [New York : Privately printed, 1910.] Roy. 8°   BM | BUS | NY | SML
Baker (H. Barton) History of the London stage and its famous players, 1576-1903. Ln : Routledge . . . 1904. 8°, pp. 574. With ten copperplates   BM | BLO | CTC

Baker (J.) *Engraver.* *See* Cibber

Baker (Oliver) Baddesley Clinton hall. *See* Birmingham

Old midland manor-house: Baddesley Clinton. Avon Club lecture [In 'Stratford Herald,' 3rd Feb., 1911]   BPL | SML

Baldwin (R.) *Publisher—*
See Sh— Macbeth, 1785
,, Sh— Othello, 1784
,, Sh— Works, 1760, 1790, 1793, 1797, 1811

Ballads—
See Evans
,, Newton

Ballantyne (*p. 14, read*) Ballantyne & Co. (James) *Edinburgh Printers*

Barker (J.) *Publisher.* *See* Sh— Works, 1790, 1793, 1797

Barker & Son (J.) *Publishers.* *See* Sh— Works, 1811

Barker (Robert) *Printer.* *See* Hakluyt

Barnard (Eleanor). *See Sh—*] Malone

Barnard (Elizabeth *Lady*). *See Sh—*] Malone

Barnard (*Sir* John). *See Sh—*] Malone

Barnard (*Sir* John & *Lady* Elizabeth) Indenture between John and Elizabeth Barnard on thone part, and Henry Smyth of Stratford and William Fetherston of the same towne, yeoman, witnesseth that it is covenanted that the said John and Elizabeth Barnard shall levy . . . one fine or fines . . . of all that messuage with the appurtenances knowne by the name of New Place . . . 20 Oct., 1652
Printed in extenso in Wheler's 'History of Stratford' (*q.v.*)
This is followed by the transcript of a later deed, dated 18th May, 1675, showing the further history of the poet's property.

Barnard (Mary). *See Sh—*] Malone

Barnard.] Higgins (*Mrs.* Napier) The Bernards of Abington and Nether Winchendon: A family history. Ln: Longman, 1903-04. 4 vols. 8°   SBL

Barnefield (Richard)—
See Bodenham   *See* Rhead
,, Crawford   ,, Verstegan

Bartlet (W. S.) Lowell Sh— memorial (*p. 17. add*) *See also* Lowell

Bartolozzi (F.) *Artist-Engraver.* *See* Sh— Works: Ext. 1792-96 (*p. 17, read*) Sh— Works, 1792-96

Bartolozzi (F.) *Artist-Engraver. See also* Sh— Works, 1773-74

Barton (Thomas Pennant). *See* Hubbard

Basire (James) *Engraver—*
See Sh— Julius Cæsar, 1773
,, Sh— Measure . . . 1773

Battell of Alcazar. *See* Stukeley

Baylie *Publisher. See* Nicholson (S.)

Baynes (H. S.) *Edinburgh Publisher. See* Sh— Works, 1825

Baynes & Son (Wm.) *Publishers. See* Sh— Works, 1825

Beaumont (Francis). *See* Gentleman

Belasyse (John *Lord*). *See* Pepys

Bell (Henry) *Publisher. See* Peele

Bell (John) *Publisher—*
See Hull
,, Sh— Hamlet, 1773
,, Sh— King Henry IV., i., 1773
,, Sh— King Henry IV., ii., 1773
,, Sh— King Henry VIII., 1773
,, Sh— King Lear, 1773
,, Sh— King Richard III., 1773
,, Sh— Macbeth, 1778
,, Sh— Merry wives . . . 1773
,, Sh— Much ado . . . 1773
,, Sh— Othello, 1773
,, Sh— Romeo . . . 1773
,, Sh— The tempest, 1773
,, Sh— Works, 1761

Bell (R.) *Engraver. See* Sh— Works, 1841

Bellot *v.* Mountjoy. *See* Sh— Autograph, 1612-13

Benedict (Robert Russell) Mystery of Hamlet, prince of Denmark. New York (?) . . . 1910   BUS

Bennet (Thomas) *Publisher—*
See Sh— Antony . . . 1701
,, Sh— Timon . . . 1696

Benson (Francis Robert) On 'Two gentlemen of Verona' from an actor's point of view. 'Sh— Club paper.' Stratford-on-Avon: Privately printed, 1910. Cr. 8°, pp. 8

Popularity of Sh—; an address at the 'Courier' book exhibition [In 'Liverpool Courier,' p. 11, 27 Nov., 1909].

Sh— and the fuller life of the people [An address to the Arts Students' Assoc. of the Liverpool University. In 'Liverpool Courier,' 26 Nov., 1909]

Bensusan (S. L.) Wm. Sh—. *See Sh—*] Bensusan

Bent (W.) *Publisher—*
See Sh— Macbeth, 1785
,, Sh— Othello, 1784
,, Sh— Works, 1797

Bentley (R.) *Publisher—*
See Sh— King Henry VI., i., 1681
,, Sh— Timon . . . 1696

Betterton (Thomas) *Actor—*
See Fielding
,, Pepys

Bew (J.) *Publisher—*.
See Sh— Macbeth, 1785
,, Sh— Othello, 1784
,, Sh— Works, 1790

Bible.] Holy Bible . . . 1584. *See* Sh— Autograph

Bonner *Engraver*—
  See Sh— Twelfth night, 1830
  ,, Sh— Two gentlemen . . . 1830
Booker (J.) *Publisher.* *See* Sh— Works, 1811,
Booth (Edwin) *Actor.* *See* Fielding
Booth (J.) *Publisher.* *See* Sh— Works, 1811
Boswell (James) Life of Johnson. *See* Johnson
Boswell-Stone (W. G.) *Editor*—
  See Sh— Twelfth night, 1907
  ,, Two gentlemen . . . 1907
Botero (G.) *See* Johnson & Botero
Bowles *Editor* (*p. 29, read*) Bowles (J.)
Bowles (T.) *Publisher*—
  See Sh— Macbeth, 1785
  ,, Sh— Othello, 1784
Bowles (Wm. Lisle) Sonnets and other poems.
  Third edition. Ln : . . . 1794.
  At pp. 67-70 contains a poem 'On Sh—,' commencing :
  'O sovereign master, who with lovely state
  Dost rule as in some isle's enchanted land,
  On whom soft airs and shadowy spirits wait,
  Whilst scenes of faerie bloom at thy command,
  On thy wild shores forgetful could I lie
  And list, till earth dissolved, to thy sweet minstrelsy.'
Bradley (A. G.) The Avon and Sh—'s country.
  Ln : Methuen [1910]. 8°, pp. x.-366 and
  30 plates in colours BM | BLO | BPL | CTC
  The author begins at Tewkesbury, where the river
  merges into the Severn, and finishes at Rugby, some
  distance from the source.
Bradley (Isaac) Sh— and Bacon once more.
  See Birmingham
  The immortal memory. *See* Birmingham
Brandon (Samuel) Vertuous Octauia [A tragi-
  comoedi . . .] Ln : Printed for William
  Ponsonbye and are to be sould at his
  shop in S. Paule's Churchyarde, 1598. 8°
  BLO | DEVON | S. KENS.
Vertuous Octavia. Edited by R. B.
  McKerrow & W. W. Greg. Oxford :
  Malone Society reprints, 1909-10. Fcp.
  4°, pp. x.-128 (unpaged) and five plates
  of facsimiles BM | BLO | CTC | SML
Brassington (Wm. Salt) A Warwickshire
  library of Sh—'s time [In ' Stratford
  Herald,' p. 8, 15 July, 1910] BPL
] Catalogue of an exhibition of paintings by
  Edward Grubb and others. Sh— Memo-
  rial festival club. Stratford-on-Avon : J.
  Morgan, 1902. 8°, pp. 16 BPL | SML
  Edward Grubb, b. 1740, d. 1816, who lies in Trinity
  Churchyard at Stratford, was a self-taught amateur,
  who painted everyone of note in the town, from the
  'parson and squire, down to the beadle.' Among
  others, he portrayed John Lord, the mayor, and his
  wife, and their portraits are to be seen at the Sh—
  Memorial.
  When New Place was demolished by Gastrell in 1759,
  a bronze lock with iron key, and a bronze sundial
  therefrom, were secured by John Lord, who inscribed
  the information upon them. These articles, although
  they probably date back only to the re-erection of
  Sh—'s residence, about 1700, have considerable
  interest, and are to be seen (on loan) at the Sh—
  Memorial, Stratford.

Brassington (Wm. Salt) Notes on the old houses
  of Stratford. [Contributed to the Trans.
  of the Birmingham Midland Institute :
  Archæological Section, Birmingham, 16
  Nov., 1898.] 4°, pp. 16, including printed
  wrappers. With eight plates SML
Note on the Sh— family records. *See* Bible
Sh— as an actor. 'Avon Club paper' [In
  ' Stratford Herald,' 25th Nov., 1910] BPL
Brereton (Austin) *Editor.* *See* Sh— Winter's
  tale, 1903
Breton (Nicholas)] Court and country, or a
  briefe discourse betweene the courtier
  and countryman of the manner, nature,
  and condition of their liues. Ln : Printed
  by G. Eld for Iohn Wright and are to be
  sold at his shoppe at the signe of the
  Bible without Newgate, 1618. Fcp. 4°
  Reprinted in ' Inedited tracts' (*q.v.*) BLO
Breton (Nicholas). *See* Bodenham
Brewster (Edward) *Publisher.* *See* Sh—
  Titus . . . (*heading*)
Brierley (Leonard) The immortal memory.
  See Birmingham
Brindley (J.) *Publisher*—
  See Sh— Macbeth, 1750
  ,, Sh— Much ado . . . 1757
  ,, Sh— Works, 1750-51
British Empire Sh— Society. *See* Hutchinson
Bromley (W.) *Engraver.* *See* Sh— Works,
  1807
Brown (J.) *Publisher*—
  See Howard
  ,, Sh— Works, 1761
Brown (Peter) *Edinburgh Publisher.* *See* Sh—
  Works, 1837
Brown *Satirist* (Thomas) Collection of miscel-
  lany poems. Ln : . . . 1699. Cr. 8°
  BM | W
  At p. 318 refers to ' Macbeth' thus :—'Then when we
  have mixed all these noble ingredients, which gener-
  ally speaking are as bad as those the witches in
  "Mackbeth" jumble in the cauldron together to
  make a charm . . .'
  At p. 327 mentions ' King Henry IV.' :—' I can answer
  for nobody's palate but my own, and cannot help
  saying with the fat knight in " Harry the fourth," if
  sack and sugar is a sin, the Lord have mercy on the
  wicked.' At p. 338 is a further reference :—' Even
  that pink of courtesie, Sir John Falstaff in the play,
  who never was a niggard of his lungs, yet would not
  answer one word when the must was put upon him.'
  ' Were reasons,' says that affable knight, ' as cheap as
  blackberries, I would not give you one upon compul-
  sion, which is but another word for duty.'
Browne (H K.) *Artist.* *See* Sh— Works (*p.
  35, delete*) 1882
Browne *1591-1643* (Wm.) *See* Gentleman
Buc *or* Buck (*Sir* George) *Censor*—
  See Sh— Second . . . (*heading*)
  ,, Sh— The puritan . . . (*heading*)
Buckhurst (Thomas *Lord*) & Norton (Thomas)
  Ferrex and Porrex. *See* Hawkins

Bullen (Arthur Henry) A Warwickshire celebrity; Michael Drayton. 'Avon Club paper' [In 'Stratford Herald,' 23 Dec., 1910]   BPL
Bulmer (W.) *Printer.* *See* Evans
Bunbury (Hy. Wm.) *Prints* . . . *See* Sh— Works: Ext. 1792-96 (*p. 36, read*) Sh— Works, 1792-96
Burbage (Richard) *Actor.* *See* Public . . .
Burleigh (Wm. Cecil *Baron*). *See* Public . . .
Burlington (Richard Boyle *third Earl of*). *See* Graves
Burrell (A.) *Editor.* *See* Sh— Works: Ext. 1908
Byrne (W.) *Engraver*—
  See Sh— The tempest, 1773
  ,, Sh— Timon . . . 1773
  ,, Sh— Winter's tale, 1773

C—— (G.) *Publisher.* *See* Southwell
C—— (T.) *Printer.* *See* Chard
Cadell (T.) *Publisher*—
  See Sh— Macbeth, 1785
  ,, Sh— Othello, 1784
  ,, Sh— Works, 1790, 1793, 1797
Cadell & Davies *Publishers.* *See* Sh— Works, 1811
Calkins (Elias A.) *Editor*—
  See Sh— King Richard III., 1891
  ,, Sh— Works, 1888-94
Cambises King of Percia. *See* Preston
Camden (Wm.) Remaines concerning Britaine . . . Ln: Iohn Legatt for Simon Waterson, 1614. Fcp. 4°   BM | W
] Remaines concerning Britaine but especially England, and the inhabitants thereof, their languages, names, surnames, allusions, anagrammes, armories, monies, empreses, apparell, artillary, wise speeches, prouerbs, poesies, epitaphs. The third impression reviewed, corrected, and encreased. [*Device*.] Ln: Printed by Nicholas Okes for Simon Waterson and are to be sold at his shop at the signe of the Crowne in Paul's Churchyard, 1623. Fcp. 4°, pp. iv.-346   BM | W
At p. 86 refers to the 'chaste lady Lucretia.'
On p. 111 gives the origin of Sh—'s surname.
'Impreses,' their origin and meaning, with details of a great number, fill pp. 181-197.
On p. 289 (in the chapter on 'Poemes' and poets) says: 'These may suffice for some poeticall descriptions of our ancient poets; if I would come to our time what a world could I present to you, out of Sir Philip Sidney, Edward Spencer [*sic*], Iohn Owen, Samuel Daniel, Hugh Holland, Ben Iohnson, Thomas Campion, Mich. Drayton, George Chapman, Iohn Marston, William Sh—, and other most pregnant wits of these onr times, whom succeeding ages may iustly admire.'
Campion (Thomas). *See* Camden
Candlemas day. *See* Parfre
Cane *Actor.* *See* Stage-player's . . .

Capell (E.) Portrait (*p. 41, delete*) 1798
Carr (Charles) *Engraver.* *See* Sh— Sonnets, 1895
Carter (Thomas) *Editor.* *See* Sh— Works: Ext. 1910
Caslon (T.) *Publisher*—
  See Sh— Much ado . . . 1757
  ,, Sh— Works, 1760
Castile (Constable of). *See Sh*—] Law
Catalogue of . . . paintings by Edward Grubb. *See* Brassington
Catalogue of the books . . . *See* Savage
Catalogue of the curious, valuable, and extensive library in print and manuscript of the late Rev. Richard Farmer *DD*. sold by Mr. King . . . in King Street, Covent Garden, May . . . 1798. 8°
Catalogue.] Shakespeariana: A calatogue of books, pamphlets, etc. illustrating the life and writings of Sh— . . . on sale by A. R. Smith, 36 Soho Square, Ln., 1871. 8°, pp. 54, including printed wrappers. With bust portrait, old houses in Chapel Lane, Henley Street, Sh—'s autograph, Sh—'s grave slab, Stratford College interior, Stratford boundary elm, Stratford College, New Place in 1740, Harvard House, Birthplace, Hathaway Cottage, etc.   SML
Cater (W.) *Publisher*—
  See Sh— Macbeth, 1785
  ,, Sh— Othello, 1784
Chalmers (G.) [*p. 48, read*] Chalmers (Alex.) *Editor.* *See* Sh— Pericles, 1811
Chambers (Edmund K.) Introduction. *See* Lee
Chapman (George)—
  See Camden
  ,, Gentleman
Chappell (W.) *Editor.* *See* Percy Society
Character of wit's squint-ey'd maid, pasquimakers . . . Ln: . . . 1681. Broadside
Appears to criticise Davenant and Dryden in the lines:
'Our English writers are all transmigrate
In pamphlet penners and diurnal scribes,
Wanton comedians and foul gypsy tribes,
Not like those brave heroick sublime strains
That wrote the Cæsars and their noble reigns,
Nor like those learned poets so divine
That pen'd "Macduff" and famous "Cataline."'
Charlewood (John) *Printer.* *See* Phillip
Cheesman (Thomas) *Engraver.* *See* Sh— Works: Ext. 1792-96 (*p. 49, read*) Sh— Works, 1792-96
Chettle (Hy.) [Hoffman] The tragedy of Hoffman, or a reuenge for a father. As it hath bin diuers times acted with great applause at the Phenix in Druery lane. Ln: Printed by I. N—— for Hugh Perry and are to bee sold at his shop at the signe of the Harrow in Btittaine's-burse,

1631. Fcp. 4°, A¹, A², B¹ to I⁴, and K¹ to L² in fours, unpaged

On the 7th July, 1602, Henslowe paid Chettle twenty shillings for a piece called the 'Danish tragedy,' which cannot be traced. The record may refer to the foregoing play or to some lost fore-runner of 'Hamlet.' It is entered in the Stationers' Registers, 26 Feb., 1629-30, on behalf of John Grove.

Chettle (Hy.) *See also* Gentleman

Chevalier (W.) *Engraver. See* Sh— Works: Ext. 1841

Child (Harold H.) *Editor. See* Euripides

Children of Paule's—
See Denmark
  ,, Simpson

Chovil (A. S.) Sh— (a sonnet). *See* Birmingham

Cibber. Apology . . . with an historical view of the stage during his own time . . . Second edition. Ln : Printed by John Watts for the author, and sold by W. Lewis in Russel Street near Convent Garden, 1740. 8°, pp. xxiv.-488 and portrait of Cibber, aged 67, Vanloo *pinx.*, J. Baker *sculpt.*

Clarence (Reginald) 'The Stage' cyclopædia : An alphabetical list of plays, operas, oratorios, sketches, and other stage pieces of which any record can be found, since the commencement of the English stage. Ln : Carson & Comerford, 1910

A projected publication, said to contain mention of over forty thousand plays.

Clarges (*Sir* Thomas) *Patron. See* Original . . .

Clark (Andrew) *Editor. See* Aubrey

Clarke (F. W.) *Editor. See* Sh—'s Winter's tale, 1908

Clarke (M. C.) Complete concordance . . . (*p. 52, add*) 1910

Clarke & Son (W.) *Publishers. See* Sh— Works, 1797, 1811

Clavell (Roger) *Publisher. See* Seymar

Clements (H. B.) Miserere seats in the chancel of Holy Trinity Church, Stratford [In 'Sh—'s home and rural life,' by J. Walter, p. 35, *q.v.*]

Clerk (Thomas) *Engraver. See* Sh— Works, 1837

Clifford Chambers, near Stratford-on-Avon. *See* Maclean

Cockpit, Drury Lane (*p. 54, add*) *See* Massinger

Cole (George Watson) Census of the Sh— quartos of 1619 [In A. W. Pollard's 'Sh— folios and quartos,' pp. 165-166. Ln : . . . 1909, *q.v.*]

First folio of Sh—: A further word regarding the correct arrangement of its preliminary leaves . . . New York :

Printed for the author, 1909. Roy. 8°, pp. 28, including printed wrappers

BM | SML

Issue restricted to 100 copies.
Reviewed at some length in 'The Library,' 3rd Ser., Vol. i., p. 211.

Cole (George Watson) Notes on 'Some bibliographical puzzles.' *See* Baker & Cole

Coleridge (Hartley) Poems. Ln : . . . 1833

BM

At p. 28 is a sonnet 'To Sh—':
'. . . . Great poet, 'twas thy art
To know thyself and in thyself to be
Whatever love, hate, ambition, destiny,
Or the firm fatal purpose of the heart
Can make of man. Yet thou wert still the same,
Serene of thought, unhurt by thy own flame.'

Coleridge (Samuel Taylor) Biographia literaria, or biographical sketches of my literary life and opinions. Ln : . . . 1817. 2 vols. 8°

BM | BLO | CTC

In chapter xv. says :—'Sh—, no mere child of nature . . . first studied patiently, meditated deeply, understood minutely, till knowledge, become habitual and intuitive, wedded itself to his habitual feelings, and at length gave birth to that stupendous power by which he stands alone . . . which seated him on one of the two glory-smitten summits of the poetic mountain, with Milton as his compeer, not rival . . . Sh— becomes all things, yet for ever remaining himself. O, what great men hast thou not produced, England, my country !'

Collier *Bp.* (Jeremy) Short view . . . Fourth edition. Ln : Printed for S. Keble . . . and R. Sare . . . 1699. 8°, pp. xvi.-288

] Stage condemned and the encouragement given to the immoralities and profaneness of the theatre by the English schools, universities and pulpits censur'd. King Charles I. Sunday's mask and declaration for sports and pastimes on the sabbath largely related . . . The arguments . . . against Mr. Collier consider'd, and the sense of the fathers, councils, antient philosophers and poets . . . Greek and Roman states, and of the first christian emperours concerning the drama . . . together with the censure of the English state and . . . Church of England upon the stage and remarks on diverse late plays, as also on those presented by the two universities to King Charles I. Ln : Printed for John Salusbury at the Angel in St. Paul's Church-Yard, 1698. 8°, pp. viii.-216

From the historical standpoint a valuable document.

Collier (John Payne)—
See Jaggard
  ,, Percy Society

Collins (Wm.) Verses. *See* Sh— Works, 1770-71

Colse (Peter) Penelope's complaint. *See* Willobie

Colwell (Thomas) *Printer. See* Philip

Cond (Thomas) Appreciations of . . . Sh—.
See Birmingham

Constable & Co. *Edinburgh Publishers.* See
Sh— Works, 1807

Cook (A. S.) *Editor.* See Hunt (J. H. L.)

Cooper (R.) *Engraver.* See Gentleman

Cooper (Stanley) Sh—'s dramatic predecessors.
8°, pp. 8 (*p. 62, read*) Cr. 8°, pp. 12

Corbet (C.) *Publisher,*—
See Sh— Macbeth, 1750
,, Sh— Much ado . . . 1757
,, Sh— Works, 1750-51, 1760

Corbett (W.) Elizabethan village surveys [In
' Royal Historical Society's Transactions,'
New Series, Vol. XI., pp. 67-88]. 1897.
8°   BM

Corbould (H.) *Artist*—
See Sh— Works, 1836
,, Sh— Works: Ext. 1841

Corner (George R.) On some of the ancient
inns of Southwark. Read at the . . .
Surrey Archæological Society, 12th May,
1858. 8°, pp. 32 and 2 plates of the
' George ' and 'White Hart '

Corrall *Printer* (*p. 63, add*) 1826

Cotes (Richard) *Printer & Publisher.* See
Sh— Titus . . . (*heading*)

Cotton (John) Sonnet in praise of Sh—. *See*
Birmingham

Cotton (Samuel & Eleanor). *See Sh*—] Malone

Cotton (Wm.) *Publisher.* See Sh— Thomas
. . . (*heading*)

Country club ; a poem . . . 1679
At p. 2 says :—
' Such noise, such stink, such smoke there was, you'd
swear
" The tempest " surely had been acted there . . .'

Covent Garden theatre. *See* Wyndham

Coventry—
See Ramsay
,, Stopes
,, Stronach

Coventry leet book, or mayor's register, containing the records of the city court leet
or view of frankpledge A.D. 1420-1555,
with divers other matters, transcribed
and edited by Mary Dormer Harris. Ln :
Early English Society, 1907-08. 2 vols.
8°, pp. xii.-viii.-580   BM | SPL

Coventry leet book : Transcribed and edited
for the Early English Text Society, by
Mary Dormer Harris. Ln : 1910. Fcp.
4°   BM

Coventry leet book : A paper read before
the British Archæological Association by
M. H. Harris [In 'Coventry Herald,' p.
12, 1st July, 1910]
Contains many glimpses of the gallery of Shakespearean
heroes.
See also Coventry.

Cowley (Abraham) Works . . . consisting of
those which were formerly printed and
those which he design'd for the press.
Now published out of the author's original
copies. Ln : Printed by J. M—— for
Henry Herringman . . . 1668. F°. With
portrait eng. by W. Faithorne
In the preface Cowley remarks :—' I began to reflect on
the fortune of almost all writers, especially poets,
whose works, commonly printed after their deaths,
we find stuffed out, either with counterfeit pieces,
like false money put in to fill up the bag, though it
add nothing to the sum ; or with such which though
of their own coyn they would have called in themselves for the baseness of the alloy : whether this
proceed from the indiscretion of their friends, who
think a vast heap of stones or rubbish a better monument than a little tomb of marble, or by the unworthy
avarice of some stationers who are content to diminish
the value of the author so they may encrease the price
of the book ; and, like vintners with sophisticate
mixtures, spoil the whole vessel of wine, to make it
yield more profit. This hath been the case with
Sh—, Fletcher, Johnson [Jonson], and many others ;
part of whose poems I should take the boldness to
prune and lop away if the care of replanting them in
print did belong to me ; neither would I make any
scruple to cut off from some the unnecessary young
suckers and from others the old withered branches ;
for a great wit is no more tyed to live in a vast volume
than in a gigantick body ; on the contrary, it is commonly more vigorous the less space it animates.'

Works . . . Seventh edition. Ln : J. M——
for Henry Herringman . . . 1681. F°.
With portrait by Faithorne

Coxeter (Thomas) *Editor & Forger.* See Sh—
Merry devil . . . 1744

Cradock & Joy *Publishers.* See Sh— Works,
1811

Crawford (Charles) Collectanea. Stratford-
on-Avon : Sh— Head Press, 1906-07.
2 vols. Cr. 8°, pp. viii.-136 and viii.-154
BPL | SML
Contents of Vol. i. :—Barnfield, Marlowe, and Sh— ;
Ben Jonson's method of composing verse ; John
Webster and Sir Philip Sidney ; Edmund Spenser,
'Locrine' and 'Selimus' ; Authorship of 'Arden of
Feversham.' *Vol. ii.* :—Montaigne, Webster, and
Marston ; Donne and Webster ; The Bacon-Sh—
question.

Key to Allot's ' England's parnassus.' *See*
Sh— Works : Ext. 1600

Creede (Thomas) *Printer.* See Sh— Locrine
(*heading*)

Croker (T. Crofton) *Editor.* See Percy Society

Cromek *Engraver.* See Sh— Works, 1807

Crosby & Co. (B.) *Publishers.* See Sh—
Works, 1811

Crosland (T. W. H.) *Editor.* See Sh— Works :
Ext.

Crowder (S.) *Publisher.* See Sh— Othello,
1784

Crowder & Co. (S.) *Publishers.* See Sh—
Works, 1760

Crowne (John) *Editor* (*p. 67, read*) *See* Sh—
Works, 1898-1908

Cruikshank (Robert) *Artist*—
 See Sh— Taming . . . 1880
 ,, Sh— Twelfth night, 1830
 ,, Sh— Two gentlemen . . . 1830
Cumberland (J.) *Publisher. See* Sh— Two
 gentlemen . . . 1830
Cumming (J.) *Dublin Publisher. See* Sh—
 Works, 1820
Cunliffe (Richard John) New Shakespearean
 dictionary. Ln : Blackie, 1910. Fcp. 4°,
 pp. 356   BM | BLO | CTC
Cunningham (Peter)—
 See Jaggard
 ,, Percy Society
 ,, Public . . .
Curtis *Publisher. See* Sh— Works, 1811
Cuthell (J.) *Publisher. See* Sh— Works, 1790,
 1793, 1797, 1811

Daly (Augustin) *Editor. See* Sh— Two gentle-
 men . . . 1895
Dance (N.) *Artist. See* Hardinge
Daniel (Samuel)—
 See Camden
 ,, Gentleman
Danter (John) *Printer. See* Sh— Titus . . .
 (*heading*)
Davenant (*Sir* W.) *Editor* (*p. 72, read*) *See*
 Sh— Works, 1898-1908
Davenant (*Sir* Wm.) *See* Gentleman
Davenport (Robert). *See* Gentleman
David and Bethsabe. *See* Hawkins
Davies (*Sir* John) & Marlowe (C.)] Epi-
 grammes and elegies, by I. D. and C. M.
 At Middleborough [c. 1598]. 12°, on
 twenty-eight unpaged leaves; sig. A¹ to
 G⁴ in fours (last blank)   ISHAM
 Middleborough is the capital of the Isle of Walcheren,
 a spot much used at that time for international commerce, especially in English cloth. It proved a convenient centre for printing books which might meet
 with censure from the Church authorities of England,
 but there is reason to suppose the name of Middleborough was sometimes affixed to books secretly
 produced in London.

] Epigrammes and elegies by I. D. and C. M.
 At Middleborough [c. 1599]. 12°, ten
 unpaged leaves; sig. A¹, A², sig. B and
 C in fours   BM
] Ovid's elegies; three bookes . . . Epigrams
 . . . At Middleborough [c. 1599]. 12°,
 forty-eight leaves; sig. A¹ to F⁸ in eights
] Ovid's elegies . . . Epigrams . . . At Middle-
 borough [c. 1640]. 12°
Davies (T.) *Publisher*—
 See Sh— Macbeth, 1785
 ,, Sh— Othello, 1784
 ,, Sh— Works, 1797
Davis (L.) *Publisher*—
 See Sh— Macbeth, 1785
 ,, Sh— Othello, 1784
 ,, Sh— Works, 1790

Day (John). *See* Gentleman
Decker *or* Dekker (Thomas)—
 See Gentleman
 ,, Hawkins
Deighton (J.) *Publisher. See* Sh— Works,
 1793, 1797
Deighton (K.) *Editor. See* Sh— King Henry
 V., 1900
Denmark.] The King of Denmarke's welcome,
 containing his ariuall, abode, and enter-
 tainment, both in the citie and other
 places. Ln : Edward Allde . . . 1606.
 Fcp. 4°
 Describes the entertainments and shows given in honour
 of the king's visit, including the songs. At p. 16 is
 mentioned a play called ' Abuses . . .' containing both
 ' comedie and tragedie,' acted by the Children of
 Paul's.
 According to Hazlitt, this piece was produced by Sh—'s
 fellow-actor, John Heminge. It is more than likely
 that Sh— assisted, as his company gave three representations before the King of Denmark.
 In any case, Sh— and the King of Denmark must have
 possessed unusual interest for each other, for ' Hamlet '
 had passed through three editions in the trio of years
 preceding that king's visit to England.
De Soligny (Victoire *Count*) Letters on England. Trans. from the original MSS.
 Ln : Colburn & Co., 1823. 2 vols. 8°
 Chapter xiv., vol. 1, English drama ; chap. xv., Kean
 and Talma ; chap. xvi., Othello and Desdemona ;
 chap. xvii., Kean's performance of ' Othello ' ; chap.
 xviii., Miss O'Neil ; chap. xix., Charles Kemble and
 Young ; chap. xx., Macready.
Devil and Saint Dunstan inn. *See* Birming-
 ham
Dighton (*Mrs.* Phoebe) Relics . . . (*p. 79, read*)
 Stratford-on-Avon : Published by Phoebe
 Dighton, June, 1835. Oblong 4°, pp. vi.
 and 12 plates
Dilly (C.) *Publisher*—
 See Sh— Macbeth, 1785
 ,, Sh— Othello, 1784
 ,, Sh— Works, 1790, 1793, 1797
Disjecta. *See* Sh— Works : Ext. 1909
Dixon (James H.) *Editor. See* Percy Society
Dod (B.) *Publisher*—
 See Sh— Macbeth, 1750
 ,, Sh— Much ado . . . 1757
 ,, Sh— Works, 1750-51, 1760
Domesday book of Warwickshire. *See* Vic-
 toria history
Donne (John). *See* Crawford
Douglas *Countess of Lennox* (Margaret). *See*
 Phillip
Dowden (*Prof.* E.) Kirwan (Patrick) Levi (S.
 L.) Madden (*Rt. Hon.* D. H.) Stopes (*Mrs.*
 C. C.) Ward (*Dr.* A. W.) & Watts-Dunton
 (Theodore) Representation of Sh—; a
 series of papers [In the ' New Age,' 17
 Nov., 1910]   BM
Draper (S.) *Publisher*—
 See Sh— Macbeth, 1750
 ,, Sh— Works, 1750-51

Drayton (Michael) Portrait. *See* Sh— Sonnets, 1903
Drayton (M.)—

See Bodenham   *See* Gentleman
 ,, Bullen   ,, Maclean
 ,, Camden

Drinkwater (John) Stage presentation of Sh—. A defence of the draped stage. ' Sh— Club paper.' Stratford-on-Avon : Privately printed, 1910. Cr. 8°, pp. 12

Dryden (John) Portrait. *See* Sh— Antony . . . 1701
Works. *See* Sh— Antony . . . 1701

Dryden (J.) *Editor* (*p. 86, read*) *See* Sh— Works, 1898-1908

Du Guernier (Lud.) *Artist-engraver*—
See Sh— Coriolanus, 1714, 1734
 ,, Sh— Cymbeline, 1714
 ,, Sh— King Lear, 1714
 ,, Sh— King Richard II., 1714
 ,, Sh— Love's labours lost, 1714
 ,, Sh— Macbeth, 1750
 ,, Sh— Othello, 1714
 ,, Sh— The tempest, 1733
 ,, Sh— Titus . . . 1714

Duncombe (J.) *Publisher. See* Sh— Antony . . . 1837

Duvantegard (Van) *Papermaker. See* Sh— Works, 1685

Dyce (Alex.) Specimens of English sonnets. *See* Sh— Works : Ext. 1833

Dyce (Alexander) *Editor. See* Percy Society

Earlom (Richard) *Engraver. See* Gentleman
Earthworks of Warwickshire. *See* Victoria . .
Edsone *of Coventry* (Jane). *See* Harris
Edward III. (*King*) Charter. *See* Halliwell, Few hints . . .
Edwards (E.) *Artist*—
See Sh— All's well . . . 1773
 ,, Sh— As you like it, 1773
 ,, Sh— Coriolanus, 1773
 ,, Sh— Cymbeline, 1773
 ,, Sh— Hamlet. 1773
 ,, Sh— Julius Cæsar, 1773
 ,, Sh— King Henry IV., i., 1773
 ,, Sh— King Henry IV., ii., 1773
 ,, Sh— King Henry V., 1773
 ,, Sh— King Henry VIII., 1773
 ,, Sh— King John, 1773
 ,, Sh— King Lear, 1773
 ,, Sh— Measure . . . 1773
 ,, Sh— Merry wives . . . 1773
 ,, Sh— Much ado . . . 1773
 ,, Sh— Romeo . . . 1 73
 ,, Sh— The tempest, 1773
 ,, Sh— Timon . . . 1773
 ,, Sh— Twelfth night, 1773
 ,, Sh— Winter's tale, 1773

Edwards (J.) *Publisher. See* Sh— Works, 1790, 1793, 1797
Edwards (T.) A supplement . . . (*p. 90, add*)
'The best piece of facetious criticism in the language.' —*Disraeli.*
Egerton (T.) *Publisher. See* Sh—Works, 1797
Egerton (T. & J.) *Publishers. See* Sh— Works, 1790, 1793
Eld *or* Elde (George) *Printer. See* Sh— The puritan . . . (*heading*)
Elizabeth (*Queen*). *See* Public . . .
Elizabeth's (*Queen*) players (*p. 91, add*)—*See* Massinger
Elizabethan architecture. *See* Bloom
Elizabethan villages. *See* Corbett
Elliot (*Dr.* Wm.) Shells and shell-life of the Stratford district. Avon Club lecture [In ' Stratford Herald,' 14th April, 1911]
                          BPL | SML
Engleheart (T. S.) *Engraver. See* Sh— Works, 1807
English courtier and the countrey gentleman . . . wherein is discoursed what order of lyfe best beseemeth a gentleman . . . Imprinted at Ln. by Richard Iones dwelling at the signe of the Rose and Crowne neere vnto Holborne Bridge, 1586. Fcp. 4°   BLO
Reprinted in ' Inedited tracts' (*q.v.*)
Etherington (C.) *York Publisher*—
See Sh— Hamlet, 1773
 ,, Sh— King Henry IV., i., 1773
 ,, Sh— King Henry IV., ii., 1773
 ,, Sh— King Henry VIII., 1773
 ,, Sh— King Lear, 1773
 ,, Sh— King Richard III., 1773
 ,, Sh— Merry wives . . . 1773
 ,, Sh— Othello, 1773
 ,, Sh— Romeo . . . 1773
 ,, Sh— The tempest, 1773
 ,, Sh— Two gentlemen . . . 1774
Everyman ; a morality. *See* Hawkins

Fairholt (F. W.) *Editor. See* Percy Society
Falcon tavern, Bankside. *See* Gentleman
Farmer (*Dr.* Richard) Library. *See* Catalogue, 1798
Faulder (R.) *Publisher. See* Sh— Works, 1790, 1793
Feales (W.) *Publisher. See* Sh— The tempest, 1733
Featherstone (John) *Editor. See* Warwickshire . . .
Ferrex and Porrex. *See* Hawkins
Fetherston *of Stratford* (Wm.) *See* Barnard
Fidele and Fortunio : The deceiptes in love discoursed in a commedia of two Italian gentlemen and translated into Englishe.

Ln: Thomas Hackett, 1584. Fcp. 4°, black letter DEVON

The few first and few last pages are missing, so the title is gathered from the entry at Stationers' Hall, 12th Nov., 1584.
From this play possibly Sh— derived his title and idea of 'Two gentlemen of Verona.'

Fidele and Fortunio . . . Edited by Percy Simpson and W. W. Greg. Oxford: Malone Society reprints, 1909-10. Fcp. 4°, pp. xii.-48 (unpaged) and two plates of facsimiles BM | BLO | CTC | SML

Field (B. Rush) *Editor*—
See Sh— Romeo . . . 1889
,, Sh— Works, 1888-94

Field (Nathaniel). *See* Gentleman

Field (Richard) *Printer & Publisher. See* Sh— Venus . . . (*heading*)

Field (Samuel G.) Art of book illumination in the middle ages. 'Avon Club paper' [In 'Stratford Herald,' 9 Dec., 1910] BPL | SML

Filmer (*Dr.* Edward) Defence of plays, or the stage vindicated (*p. 100, add*) from several passages in Mr. Collier's 'Short view . . .' wherein is offered the most probable method of reforming our plays, with a consideration how far vicious characters may be allowed on the stage. Ln: . . . 1707. 8°
Refers on p. 129 to the 'incomparable Sh—.'

Findlay *Artist. See* Sh— Antony . . . 1837

Finnemore (Wm.) Shakespearean criticism. *See* Birmingham

Fittler *Engraver. See* Sh— Works, 1807

Fitton (Anne) Autograph signature SML
The Fittons are held by some to have inspired Sh— in his 'Sonnets.' *See* Sh— 'Sonnets' references; *also* Tyler.

Fitzpatrick (R. H.) *Patron. See Sh*—] Shakespearean magazine

Fitzstephen (Wm.) Libellum de situ et nobilitate Londini. *See* Stowe

Fleming (R.) *Publisher. See* Sh— Works, 1761

Fleming (Wm. H.) *Editor*—
See Sh— King Henry IV., i., 1890
,, Sh— King Henry IV., ii., 1890
,, Sh— Much ado . . . 1889
,, Sh— Works, 1888-94

Fletcher (John). *See* Gentleman

Fletcher (Phineas). *See* Gentleman

Florio (John). *See* Phæthon

Flower (C. E.) Sh— on horseback: A paper [read (for the second time) by A. D. Flower before the Sh— Club]. Stratford-on-Avon: Privately printed, 1909. Cr. 8°, pp. 8

Fogerty (E.) *Editor. See* Sh— Twelfth night, 1911

Folkes (Martin) *Editor. See* Sh— Works, 1623, 1733

Folly of priest-craft: A comedy. Ln: . . . 1690
At p. 18 the character *Leucasia* says: 'It seemed to me as preposterous as . . . the woman in Sh— kissing the fellow with the asses' head' ('Midsummer night's dream').

Ford *or* Forde (John). *See* Gentleman

Forgeries and frauds. *See* Jaggard

Fortune theatre. *See* Gentleman

Foster *MD.* (Philip) Sh— day; the monuments and portraits reviewed. [Leeds: Privately printed, 1910.] 8°, pp. 16. With Droeshout portrait SML

Foulkes (Charles). *See* Stratford: Catalogue

Fourdrinier (P.) *Engraver*—
See Sh— All's well . . . 1734
,, Sh— As you like it, 1734
,, Sh— Taming . . . 1734

Fox (W.) *Publisher. See* Sh— Macbeth, 1785

Frey (Albert R.) *Editor. See* Sh— Taming . . . 1888

Frith (J. Cartwright) The immortal memory. *See* Birmingham

Fuller (T.) History . . . 1662 (*p. 108, add*)—
The earliest biography of Sh—.

Furness (H. H.) *Editor. See* Sh— Romeo . . . 1898 (*p. 108, add*) 1878

Furnivall (*Dr.* F. J.) *Editor. See* Sh— Winter's tale, 1908

Furnivall.] Dr. Furnivall [An *in memoriam* notice in 'The Athenæum,' No. 4315, p. 42, 9 July, 1910] BM | BPL

] Stopes (*Mrs.* C. C.) Dr. Frederick James Furnivall: An obituary. With note by Prof. A. Brandl [In 'The Archiv.' Braunschweig: G. Westermann, Aug., 1910]. 8°, pp. 12, including printed wrappers and portrait of Furnivall

G—— (C.) Sonnet to April 23rd. *See* Birmingham

'Gabble (Gridiron)' *pseud. See* Green room

Gager (Wm.) *See* Gentleman

Gallup (*Mrs.* E. W.) Bi-literal cipher . . . Ln: Gay . . . 1910. 8°

Gammer Gurton's needle. *See* Still

Gardner (H. L.) *Publisher*—
See Sh— Macbeth, 1785
,, Sh— Othello, 1784
,, Sh— Works, 1790, 1793, 1797

Garnett (Henry). *See* Sh— Autograph, 1606

Garnett (*Dr.* Richard) Memoir of M. Blind. *See* Blind

Garrick (David) Portrait. *See* Sh— Macbeth, 1778

Gascoigne (George) Poem commending hawking. *See* Turbervile

Gascoigne (George)—
See Ariosto
,, Gentleman

Gascoigne *Lord Chief Justice* (*Sir* Wm.) *See* Solly-Flood

Gastrell (Francis) *Iconoclast*. *See* Brassington

Geddes (*Sir* W. D.) Sh— and Hector Bocce [Magazine excerpt]. 1896. 4°, pp. 12 SML Concerns 'Macbeth.'

Gentleman (F.)] Prolegomena to the Works of Sh—, 1825 (*p. 113, add*) Embellished with a mezzotinto portrait of Sh— (engraved by R. Cooper from a print by R. Earlom after an original painting by Cornelius Jansen); Sh—'s birthplace; view of New Place, the last residence of Sh—; monument in Stratford Church; monument in Westminster Abbey; eight portraits of eminent performers of Sh—'s characters; Globe theatre; interior of Red Bull playhouse, Clerkenwell; Fortune theatre; Falcon tavern, Bankside; amphitheatre erected by Garrick for the Stratford jubilee. Ln : Published for the proprietors by Sherwood & Co., Paternoster Row, and sold by all booksellers, 1825. 8°, pp. 80, two plates, and several woodcuts in the text.

A few were done on large paper, roy. 8°, with earliest impressions of the Jansen portrait.
Chiefly valuable for its biographies of Sh—'s contemporaries: Spenser, Jonson, Massinger, Beaumont, J. Fletcher, Marlowe, Chapman, Webster, Marston, Middleton, Rowley, John Heywood, Thomas Heywood, Forde, Decker, Shirley, Drayton, Phineas Fletcher, Daniel, Chettle, Browne, Day, Davenport, Field, Peele, Quarles, Nash, Sackville, Lodge, Lyly, Greene, Gascoigne, Gager, Preston, Whetstone, Warner, Taylor the Waterman, Sir Wm. Davenant, Sir Philip Sidney, and Mary Herbert Countess of Pembroke.

Gentleman (F.) *Editor*—
See Sh— Hamlet, 1773
  ,, Sh— King Henry IV., i., 1773
  ,, Sh— King Henry IV., ii., 1773
  ,, Sh— King Henry VIII., 1773
  ,, Sh— King Richard III., 1773
  ,, Sh— Macbeth, 1778
  ,, Sh— Merry wives . . . 1773
  ,, Sh— Much ado . . . 1773
  ,, Sh— Othello, 1773
  ,, Sh— Romeo . . . 1773
  ,, Sh— The tempest, 1773

Gesner (Conradus). *See* Topsell & Gesner

Globe playhouse—
See Gentleman
  ,, Public . . .

Goggin (S. E.) *Editor*. *See* Sh— King Lear, 1910

Goldsmith (W.) *Publisher*. *See* Sh— Works, 1793

Goodere (Anne). *See* Maclean

Goodere (Frances). *See* Maclean

Goodere (*Sir* Henry). *See* Maclean

Goodwin (J.) *Editor*. *See* Percy Society

Gorboduc—
See Hawkins
  ,, Udall

Gordon (W.) *Publisher*. *See* Sh— Works, 1761

Gough (Alfred) The immortal memory. *See* Birmingham

Gravelot (H.) *Artist*—
See Sh— Much ado . . . 1757
  ,, Sh— Troilus . . . 1735

Graves (A. P.) *Editor*—
See Sh— As you like it
  ,, Sh— Merchant . . .

Gray (Robert) The immortal memory. *See* Birmingham

Green (Charles) Some aspects of Shakespearean characterization. *See* Birmingham

Green room gossip, or gravity, galliment, and gallimaufrey, consisting of theatrical anecdotes, bon-mots, chit-chats, drollery, entertainment, fun, gibes, humour, jokes, kickshaws, lampoons . . . gathered and garnished by 'Gridiron Gabble' . . . 1809. Cr. 8°

Greene (Robert) Plays and poems. Edited by J. C. Collins. Oxford : Clarendon Press, 1905. 2 vols. 8°, pp. 752   BM | BPL
Includes the play 'George-a-Greene' (attributed to Sh—) in vol. ii., pp. 159-218.

Greene (Robert). *See* Gentleman

Greenwich. *See* Public . . .

Greg (W. W.) *Editor*—
See Fidele . . .
  ,, Sh— Merry wives . . . 1910
  ,, Sh— Second . . . 1909-10

Griffin & Co. (R.) *Glasgow Publishers*. *See* Sh— Works, 1821

Grignion (C.) *Engraver*—
See Sh— Much ado . . . 1773
  ,, Sh— Twelfth night, 1773

Griswold. Prose writers of America. *See* Adams

Grubb (Edward) *Stratford-on-Avon Artist*. *See* Brassington

Hackett (Thomas) *Printer*. *See* Fidele . . .

Hakluyt (Richard) Principal navigations, voiages, traffiques, and discoueries of the English nation made by sea or ouerland to the remote and farthest distant quarters of the earth at any time within the compasse of these fifteen hundred yeeres. Deuided into three seuerall volumes, according to the positions of the regions whereunto they were directed. Imprinted at Ln. by George Bishop, Ralph Newberie, and Robert Barker, 1598[-1600]. 3 vols. F°   BM | MRL
The second edition, much enlarged.

Hall (J.) *Engraver*—
  See Sh— Hamlet, 1773
  ,, Sh— King Henry IV., i., 1773
  ,, Sh— King Henry IV., ii., 1773
  ,, Sh— King Henry V., 1773
  ,, Sh— King Henry VIII., 1773
  ,, Sh— King Lear, 1773
  ,, Sh— Merry wives... 1773

Hall (John)] Poesie in forme of a vision, briefly inueying against the moste hatefull and prodigious artes of necromancie, witchcraft, sorcerie, incantations, and diuers other detestable and deuilishe practises, dayly vsed vnder colour of iudiciall astrologie. Compiled in metre by I. H——. Printed at Ln. by Rouland Hall dwellyng in Gutter Lane at the signe of the Halfe Egle and the Keye, 1563. 8°   MRL
No other existing copy is recorded.

Hall (Rouland) *Printer. See* Hall (John)
Halliwell (J. O.) Few hints to novices in manuscript literature. Ln : T. Rodd ... Cambridge : Thomas Stevenson, 1839. 8°, pp. 12 and facsimile of charter of I. Edward III.   SML
Halliwell (J. O.) *Editor. See* Percy Society
Hamilton (S.) *Printer. See* Miller
Harding (E.) *Publisher. See* Sh— Works, 1798, 1798-1800
Hardinge (George) Essay ... (*p. 140, read*) With memoirs of the author by J. Nichols. [In Hardinge's Miscellaneous works (3 vols.), Vol. I.] Ln : Printed by and for Nichols & Bentley, 1818. 8°, pp. xliv.-86 and stipple portrait by H. Meyer after N. Dance
Hardwicke (C.) *Editor. See* Percy Society
Harison. *See* Harrison
Harness annual prize (*p. 140, add*) A prize given every year for the best English essay upon some subject connected with Shakespearean literature, the competitors being restricted to the undergraduates, or graduates, of not more than three years' standing, in Cambridge University
Harris (Frank) Sh— and his love : A play in four acts and an epilogue. Ln : F. Palmer ... 1910. Cr. 8°, pp. 96   BM | BLO | CTC
Harris (Mary Dormer) Sh— and Coventry [In 'The Athenæum,' No. 4,330, p. 489, 22 Oct., 1910]. 4°   BM | BPL
Speaks of '8 Nov., 1545. Sh—'s house in the new rent vak' [vacant]. Mentions ' Richard Sh— of Hinckley and Jane Edsone of Coventry marryed 20 Aug. 1656.' The article also bears on Sh—'s ' King Henry IV.' and ' King Henry V.'
Harris (M. D.) *Editor. See* Coventry ...
Harrison (John) *Printer. See* Sh— Venus ... (*heading*)

Harrison (Wm.) Description of England in Sh—'s youth. Edited by F. J. Furnivall and Mrs. Stopes. Part 4. Ln : Chatto ... 1908. Roy. 8°   BM
This volume completed the work. Mrs. Stopes has added two interesting articles of her own—one on the ' City marching watch, 1584 '; the other, ' Weirs on the Thames, 1584.'
Harvey (K.) *Editor. See* Sh— King Lear, 1910
Haslehurst (E. W.) *See* Jerrold & Haslehurst
Hastings (C.) The theatre ; its development in France and England and a history of its Greek and Latin origins. Translated by Frances A. Welby. Ln : Duckworth ... 1901. 8°, pp. 384   BM | BLO | CTC
Hatton (Joshua)] Nursery tales from Sh—, by 'Guy Roslyn.' *See* Sh— Works : Ext. 1879
Hawes (L.) *Publisher*—
  See Sh— Much ado ... 1757
  ,, Sh— Works, 1760
Hawkins (John) *Editor. See* Sh— Works, 1770-1771
Hawkins (Thomas) Origin of the English drama (*p. 143, add*) pp. viii.-320 ; ii.-352 ; iv.-378, and three plates
Contents :—' Candlemas day, or the killing of the Children of Israel : A mystery, by Ihan Parfre, 1512.' 'Everyman ; A morality' (*temp.* Henry VIII.) ' Hycke-Scorner ; A morality.' ' Lusty Juventus ; A morality, by R. Wever.' ' Gammer Gurton's needle ; A comedy (by Bp. John Still).' ' Cambises King of Percia ; A lamentable tragedy, by Thomas Preston.' ' Spanish tragedy, by Thomas Kyd.' ' King David and fair Bethsabe, with the tragedy of Absalon, by George Peele, 1599.' ' Soliman and Perseda (by Thomas Kyd?), 1599.' ' Ferrex and Porrex, or Gorboduc, by Thomas Lord Buckhurst and Thomas Norton.' ' Supposes, by Ariosto, translated by George Gascoigne, 1566.' ' Satiro-mastix, or the untrussing of the humorous poet, by Thomas Dekker.' ' Return from Parnassus, or the scourge of simony, 1606.' ' Wily beguiled ; A pleasant comedy.'
Hayes (Alfred) Gentle Sh—. *See* Birmingham
Hayes (S.) *Publisher*—
  See Sh— Macbeth, 1785
  ,, Sh— Othello, 1784
  ,, Sh— Works, 1790, 1793, 1797
Hazlitt (W. C.) Manual ... (*p. 145, add*) Ln : Pickering ... 1892
Hazlitt (Wm. Carew) *Editor. See* Inedited ...
Heath (C.) *Engraver. See* Sh— Works : Ext. 1841
Heath (Frank R.) Sh—'s day. *See* Birmingham
Heath (J.) *Engraver. See* Sh— Works, 1807
Heminge *or* Heminges (Alice). *See* Sh—] Malone
Heminge *or* Heminges (John) *Actor-Manager*—
  See Denmark
  ,, Public ...
  ,, *Sh*—] Malone
Heminges (Margaret). *See* Sh—] Malone

Heminges (Rebecca). *See Sh*—] Malone
Heminges (Wm.) *See Sh*—] Malone
Henry *of Monmouth* (*Prince*). *See* Solly-Flood
Herbert (F. A.) *Editor*. *See* Lawrence
Herne's oak—
 See Perry
 ,, Sh— Merry wives . . .
 ,, *Sh*—] Shakespearean miscellanies
Herringman (Henry) *Publisher*. *See* Cowley,
 1668, 1681
Heywood (John). *See* Gentleman
Heywood (Thomas). *See* Gentleman
Highley *Publisher*. *See* Sh— Works, 1797
Hitch (C.) *Publisher*—
 See Sh— Much ado . . . 1757
 ,, Sh— Othello, 1753
 ,, Sh— Works, 1750-51
Hodges (J.) *Publisher*—
 See Sh— Much ado . . . 1757
 ,, Sh— Works, 1750-51
Holder *Forger*. *See* Jaggard
Holinshed (R.) Chronicles . . . 1577 (*p. 152,
 add*)—   BM | MRL
Holland (Hugh). *See* Camden
Homer. *See* Seward
Hood *Publisher*. *See* Sh— Works, 1797, 1798,
 1798-1800
Hopkins *Editor & Prompter*—
 See Sh— King Henry IV., i., 1773
 ,, Sh— King Henry IV., ii., 1773
 ,, Sh— King Richard III., 1773
 ,, Sh— Macbeth, 1778
 ,, Sh— Merry wives . . . 1773
 ,, Sh— Midsummer . . . 1773
 ,, Sh— Much ado . . . 1773
 ,, Sh— Othello, 1773
 ,, Sh— Romeo . . . 1773
 ,, Sh— The tempest, 1773
Hopkinson (A. F.) Essays (*p. 154, read*) Ln :
 [Privately printed by] M. E. Sims & Co.
 . . . 1900. Cr. 8°, pp. viii.-44, xlii.-64, 52,
 32, 20, 26, 24, 38, 42, 48
 Deals with 'Arden of Feversham, Birth of Merlin, Fair
 Em, King Edward III., Locrine, London prodigal,
 Merry devil of Edmonton, Mucedorus, Sir John Old-
 castle, The puritan, Thomas Lord Cromwell, Two
 noble kinsmen, Yorkshire tragedy.'
 The Stratford copy bears a holograph letter from the
 author presenting the volume.
Hopkinson (A. F.) *Editor*—
 See Sh— Birth . . . 1892
 ,, Sh— Fair Em, 1895
 ,, Sh— King Edward III., 1891
 ,, Sh— Locrine, 1892
 ,, Sh— London prodigal, 1893
 ,, Sh— Sir John Oldcastle, 1894
 ,, Sh— The puritan, 1894
 ,, Sh— Thomas . . . 1891
 ,, Sh— Two noble kinsmen, 1894
 ,, Sh— Yorkshire tragedy, 1891
Howard (H.) *Artist*. *See* Sh— Works, 1807

Howard *Earl of Surrey* (Henry) Poems. *See*
 Sh— Poems, 1856, 1878
Howard *Earl of Surrey, and others* (Henry)
 Songes and sonettes. [*Cn.*] Imprinted at
 Ln. in Flete-strete within Temple barre
 at the signe of the hand and starre by
 Richard Tottell, anno 1567. 8°   MRL
 This publication, better known as 'Tottel's miscellany,'
 began a new epoch in English literature. It contains
 two hundred and seventy-one poems, never previously
 printed, by a number of authors, the chief of whom
 were Sir Thomas Wyatt (who died in 1542) and
 Henry Howard (by courtesy Earl of Surrey), executed in 1547. These two were easily the first poets
 of the period, and were indeed pioneers of a more
 brilliant school of verse than any since Chaucer's day.
 Howard first imitated Italian models, especially
 Petrarca, and, with Wyatt, first brought the sonnet
 into vogue in England.
 The volume may be regarded as the silver-throated
 herald of the great dawn of Elizabethan poetry.
 How long-lived and popular the venture proved is
 shown by Slender's reference in the 'Merry wives'
 (I., i.), 'I had rather than forty shillings I had my
 book of *Songs and sonnets* here.' Before 1587 eight
 editions were printed. Only four copies in all of the
 first three issues are now known.
Howard de Walden (Thomas *Lord*) *Editor*.
 See Sh— As you like it, 1910
 See also Stratford : Catalogue . . .
Hudson (H. N.) *Editor*. *See* Sh— Works, 1910
Hudson (Reginald) Notes on Sh—'s birds.
 'Sh— Club paper.' Stratford-on-Avon :
 Privately printed, 1911. Cr. 8°, pp. 8
Hudson (W. H.) *Editor*. *See* Sh— Midsummer
 . . . 1910
Humorous poet. *See* Hawkins
Humphreys (John) Wild flowers, 1910, cr. 8°,
 pp. 8 (*p. 158, read*) pp. 24. Privately
 printed
Humphries (Sidney) Disjecta. *See* Sh—
 Works : Ext. 1909
Hunter (John) *Editor*—
 See Sh— King John, 1877
 ,, Sh— King Richard III., 1872, 1878
 ,, Sh— The tempest, 1865
Hurst *Publisher*. *See* Sh— Works, 1797
Hurst (John G.) The immortal memory. *See*
 Birmingham
Hutton (R. H.) *Editor*. *See Sh*—] Bagehot
Hutton (Wm.) Battle of Bosworth Field
 between Richard III. and Henry Earl of
 Richmond, 22 Aug., 1485 ; wherein is
 described the approach of both armies
 . . . 1813. 8°. With plan and plates   BPL
 Illustrates 'King Richard III.'
Hycke-Scorner ; a morality. *See* Hawkins

Impreses. *See* Camden
Inedited tracts : Illustrating the manners,
 opinions and occupations of Englishmen
 during the sixteenth and seventeenth
 centuries. Now first republished from the
 original copies with a preface and notes

[by W. C. Hazlitt. Ln:] Printed for the
Roxburghe Library, 1868. Fcp. 4°
Contents :—
   'English courtier and the countrey gentleman . . .
      1586.'
   'M——(I.) A health to . . . seruingmen, 1598.'
   'B——(N.) The court and country, 1618.'
Inns and taverns—
   See Boar's head   *See* Falcon
   ,, Birmingham   ,, Mermaid
   ,, Devil & St. Dunstan
Ireland (Samuel) *Forger*. *See* Jaggard
Ireland (S. W. H.) *Forger*—
   See Jaggard
   ,, Sh— Autograph
   ,, *Sh*—] Manuscript . . .
Ireland forgeries. *See* William IV.

J—— (A.) Sh—'s English. *See* Birmingham
Jackson (*Master*) *Stationers' Warden*. *See*
   Sh— Thomas . . . (*heading*)
Jaffray (J.) Graphic illustrations . . . 1829
   (*p. 168, read*) [Edited by C. W. Radclyffe].
   Birmingham : Beilby, Knott, & Beilby.
   Warwick : John Merridew. Coventry :
   Merridew & Son, 1829. 4°, pp. viii.-128.
   Thirty-two etched copperplates and
   twelve vignettes
   Stratford-on-Avon fills pp. 119-128, with views of old
   Clopton House, Trinity Chancel, and Blythe Hall.
Jaggard (Dorothy) *Printer & Publisher*. *See*
   Sh— Works (*heading*)
Jaggard (Isaac) *Publisher*. *See* Sherley
Jaggard *1567 ?-1623* (Wm.) *Printer & Pub-
   lisher*—
   See Sh— Sonnets, 1885
   ,, Sh— Venus . . . 1599, 1602
   ,, Topsell & Gesner
Jaggard *Bibliographer* (Wm.) Avon Club
   syllabus. *See* Avon Club
Sh—'s Bible [In ' Notes and Queries,' 11th
   Series, Vol. 2, pp. 430-431. Ln : . . .
   1910]. Fcp. 4°   BM | BLO | BPL | CTC
   Refers to the 1584 Bible, purporting to be Sh—'s copy,
   at the Stratford Memorial Library.
Shakespearean frauds : The story of some
   famous literary and pictorial forgeries.
   ' Sh— Club paper.' Stratford-on-Avon :
   [Privately printed] 1911. Cr. 8°, pp. 20,
   including printed wrappers
   Deals with the frauds of J. P. Collier, Peter Cunning-
   ham, Holder, Samuel Ireland, Wm. Hy. Ireland,
   John Jordan, George Steevens, Lewis Theobald, W.
   F. Zincke, and others.
See also Powell
James I. *of Eng.* (*King*)—
   See Public . . .
   ,, Sh— Romeo . . . 1680
   ,, *Sh*—] Law
Janssen (Cornelius) *Artist*. *See* Gentleman

Jerrold (Walter) & Haslehurst (E. W.) Shake-
   speareland described and pictured. Ln :
   Blackie, 1910. Roy. 8°, pp. 56
                    BM | BLO | BPL | CTC
Johnson (J.) *Publisher*. *See* Sh— Works,
   1793, 1797
Johnson (*Dr*. Samuel). *See* Raleigh
Johnston (J.) *Publisher*. *See* Sh— Works, 1821
Jones *or* Iohnes (Richard) *Printer*. *See* Under-
   down
Jones (Tom) Sh—'s Bible [In ' Notes and
   Queries,' 11th Series, Vol. 2, p. 430. Ln :
   . . . 1910]. Fcp. 4°   BM | BLO | BPL | CTC
   Written to show that the Bible used by the poet was
   the ordinary quarto Genevan version.
Jonson (Ben)—
   See Camden   *See* Crawford
   ,, Character . . .   ,, Gentleman
Jordan (John) Original collections . . . 1864
   (*p. 178, add*)—   BPL
Jordan (John) *Forger*. *See* Jaggard
Jubilee, 1769. *See* Gentleman

Kay (T.) *Publisher*. *See* Sh— Works, 1797
Kean (Edmund) *Portrait*—
   See Rede
   ,, Sh— Venus . . . 1903
Kempe (Wm.) *Actor*. *See* Public . . .
Kent *Artist*. *See* Thomson
Kidd (Wm.) *Publisher*. *See* Anniversary . . .
King Cambises—
   See Hawkins
   ,, Preston
King (Thomas) *Actor*. *See* Sh— All's well . . .
   1778
King's theatre. *See* Pepys
Kirwan (Patrick) Representation of Sh—.
   See Dowden
Kyd (Thomas) Soliman and Perseda. *See*
   Hawkins
Spanish tragedy. *See* Hawkins

Lackington (J.) *Publisher*. *See* Sh— Works,
   1793
Lackington & Co. (J.) *Publishers*. *See* Sh—
   Works, 1797
Lamb (C. & M.) Tales from Sh—. *See* Sh—
   Works : Ext. (*p. 188, add*) 1910
Lambert (John) *Defendant*. *See* Public . . .
Langford (*Dr*. J. A.) Sh— (a poem). *See*
   Birmingham
Sh— in our daily life. *See* Birmingham
The immortal memory. *See* Birmingham
Law (B.) *Publisher*—
   See Sh— Macbeth, 1785
   ,, Sh— Othello, 1784
   ,, Sh— Works, 1760, 1797
Lawrence (*Sir* Edwin Durning) Bacon is Sh—!
   Together with a reprint of Bacon's Pro-
   mus of formularies and elegancies. Col-

lated with the original manuscript by the late F. B. Bickley and revised by F. A. Herbert. Ln: Gay & Hancock, 1910. 8°, pp. 302   BM | BLO | CTC

Lee *Publisher. See* Sh— Works, 1797

Lee (Elizabeth) School history of English literature. With an introd. by E. K. Chambers . . . Chaucer to Marlowe. Ln: Blackie, 1896. Cr. 8°, pp. 206
                         BM | BLO | CTC
'Early Elizabethan poets' fill pp. 118-129, and 'Beginnings of the English drama,' pp. 171-197.

Lees (E. Antony) The immortal memory. *See* Birmingham

Legate *or* Legatt (John) *Printer. See* Camden

Legge (Cantrel) *Cambridge Printer. See* Sh— Autograph, 1613

Levi (S. L.) *Editor*—
  See Sh— Works, 1910
  ,, *also* Dowden
  ,,   ,,   Sh— Sonnets, Bullen, 1905

Lewes (G. H.) Sh— in France (*p. 194, add*) SML

Lewis (W.) *Publisher. See* Cibber

Liart (M.) *Engraver*—
  See Sh— As you like it, 1773
  ,,   Sh— Coriolanus, 1773
  ,,   Sh— Cymbeline, 1773

Liddell (Andrew) Sh— anniversary, 1896. *See* Birmingham

Lindsey (H. W.) *Editor. See* Sh— Cymbeline, 1910

Linge (Nicholas). *See* Sh— London prodigal (*heading*)

Linton (*Sir* James D.) *Artist. See* Sh— Merchant . . . 1909

Lintot (H.) *Publisher*—
  See Sh— Much ado . . . 1757
  ,,   Sh— Works, 1750-51

Lobban (J. H.) *Editor*—
  See Sh— King Henry IV., i., 1910
  ,,   Sh— Macbeth, 1910
  ,,   Sh— Twelfth night, 1910
  ,,   Sh— Winter's tale, 1910
  ,,   Sh— Works, 1910

Lodge (Thomas)—
  See Bodenham
  ,,   Gentleman

London—
  See Corner
  ,,   Public . . .

Longman (M. & T.) *Publishers. See* Sh— Much ado . . . 1757

Longman (T.) *Publisher*—
  See Sh— Macbeth, 1785
  ,,   Sh— Othello, 1753, 1784
  ,,   Sh— Works, 1750-51, 1760

Look into Sh—'s Sonnets. *See* Birmingham

Lord (John) *Stratford-on-Avon Mayor. See* Brassington

Lord chamberlain—
  See Sh— Thomas . . . (*heading*)
  ,,   Sh— Troilus . . . (*heading*)

Loutherbourg *Artist* (*p. 199, add*) (Philip James)

Lowndes (T. & W.) *Publishers. See* Sh— Othello, 1784

Lowndes (W.) *Publisher*—
  See Sh— Macbeth, 1785
  ,,   Sh— Works, 1793

Lubbock *Lord Avebury* (*Sir* John) *Editor. See* Sh— Works, 1890, 1892, 1898

Lucy. Sh— and the supernatural, 1908 (*p. 200, read*) 1906

Lusty Juventus. *See* Wever

Lyly (John). *See* Gentleman

M—— (I.) A health to the gentlemanly profession of seruingmen . . . Imprinted at Ln. by W. W——, 1598. Fcp. 4°
With the anecdote of the 'guerdon' and the 'remuneration,' illustrating a passage in 'Love's labours lost.' Douce says the book supplied several hints to Sh— for this play.
Reprinted in 'Inedited tracts' (*q.v.*)

M—— (J.) *Printer. See* Cowley, 1668, 1681

MacCracken (H. W.) Introduction to Sh—. Ln: Macmillan . . . 1910. Cr. 8°

Mackay (Charles) *Editor. See* Percy Society

Macklin (T.) *Publisher. See* Sh— Works: Ext. 1792-96 (*p. 204, read*) Sh— Works, 1792-96

Maclean (*Sir* John) History of the manor and advowson of Clifford Chambers [near Stratford-on-Avon] and some account of its possessors [In ' Bristol and Gloucestershire Archæological Society's Transactions,' pp. 49-116. 1889-90]. 8°. With seven plates and other illustrations, including one of Clifford Manor   BM
Michael Drayton, Sh—'s friend, is said to have lived at Clifford Manor. His early home was Polesworth Hall, near Nuneaton, where he resided with Sir Henry Goodere and his two daughters, Anne and Frances. Anne Goodere married Sir Henry Raynesford, of Clifford Manor.
'John Sh—, husbandman, of Clifford Chamberer,' lies buried in the churchyard. His will, made 24 Dec., 1608, was proved 7th Feb., 1611. In it he mentions his 'cosen (nephew) John Sh— and his brothers Thomas and Anthonie Sh—.' He bequeathed an ancient wooden bier to Clifford Church, which is still preserved and bears a brass plate indicating the donor and date.

Macpherson (David) *Editor. See* Wyntown

Macready (W.) *Portrait. See* Sh— Titus . . . 1903

Madden (*Rt. Hon.* D. H.) Representation of Sh—. *See* Dowden

Madox-Brown (F.) *Artist. See Sh—*] Sh—'s portrait

Magnes (M.) *Publisher. See* Sh— King Henry VI., i., 1681

Malone (E.) Catalogue of early English poetry (*p. 205, add*) and other miscellaneous pieces illustrating the British drama . . . presented to the Bodleian Library, 1836
The entries under Sh— number 124, including first editions of 'Venus,' 'Lucrece,' several of the early quartos, and copies of the two first folios.

Malone Society publications (*p. 207, add*)—
See Brandon
„ Fidele . . .
„ Sh— Second . . .

Man *or* Mann (Samuel) *Stationers' Warden.* *See* Sh— King Henry IV., i. (*heading*)

Mangin (Edward) Stories for short students. *See Sh—*] Mangin

Manuscripts. *See* Public . . .

Marlowe (C.)—
See Crawford
„ Gentleman
„ Steevens

Marriott (E.) Bacon or Sh— . . . Second edition, with an appendix. Ln: Stock . . . 1898. 8°, pp. 46-24 (including printed wrappers) SML

Marston (John)—
See Camden
„ Crawford
„ Gentleman

Martin (P. J.) Parallel . . . (*p. 210, add*) CPL

Marvin (Frederic Rowland) Excursions of a book-lover, being papers on literary themes. Boston [U.S.]: Sherman, French & Co., 1910. Cr. 8°, pp. xii.-332 SML
Contains a chapter headed 'Sh—'s bones,' at pp. 215-234, written from the Baconian standpoint.

Massinger (Philip) The bondman. An ancient storie, as it hath been often acted with good allowance at the Cockpit in Drury Lane by the most excellent Princesse the Lady Elizabeth her servants. Ln: . . . 1638. Fcp. 4°
Contain imitations of 'Coriolanus' and 'Othello.'
See Gentleman

Matthews (Brander) Molière. *See* Molière

Mazell (P.) *Engraver*—
See Sh— All's well . . . 1773
„ Sh— King John, 1773

Meadows *Engraver. See* Sh— Works: Ext. 1792-96 (*p. 213, read*) *See* Sh— Works, 1792-96

Mendenhall (*Dr.* T. C.) Mechanical solution of a literary problem. [Privately] Reprinted from the 'Popular Science Monthly.' Roy. 8°, pp. xiv., including printed wrappers SML
By a microscopic examination of the style of composition it seeks to prove that Bacon was incapable of writing Sh—'s works, and discovers by the same process a marked resemblance between Marlowe and Sh—, which other writers had already observed superficially.

Merridew (J.) Catalogue of engraved portraits . . . (*p. 215, read*) Coventry : John Merridew, 1848. 4°, pp. viii.-84 and portrait of Sir Wm. Dugdale
Pp. 53-58 are occupied by 'Sh—, the pride and glory of Warwickshire.'

Meyer (H.) *Engraver. See* Hardinge

Middleton (Thomas). *See* Gentleman

Miller (Wm.) *Publisher. See* Sh— Works, 1793, 1797, 1807

Millington (Thomas). *See* Sh— Titus . . . (*heading*)

Milton (John). *See* Seward

Mitan (J.) *Engraver. See* Sh— Works, 1807

Molière.] Matthews (Brander) Molière : his life and his works. Ln : Longmans . . . 1910. 8° BM | BLO | CTC
With many allusions to Sh— and a chapter devoted to a parallel between Molière and Sh—.

Montaigne (Michael). *See* Crawford

Moore (T. S.) *Editor*—
See Sh— Twelfth night, 1901
„ Sh— Two gentlemen . . . 1901
„ Sh— Venus . . . 1903

Morgan (James Appleton) *Editor*—
See Sh— Comedy . . . 1894
„ Sh— King Henry VI., iii., 1892
„ Sh— King John, 1892
„ Sh— Merry wives . . . 1888
„ Sh— Pericles, 1891
„ Sh— Titus . . . 1890
„ Sh— Troilus . . . 1889
„ Sh— Works, 1888-1908, 1898-1908

Morgan (John) *Publisher. See* Taylor (John)

Mullins (John D.) (*p. 225, read*) Mullins (John David)

Murray (John) *Publisher*—
See Sh— Macbeth, 1785
„ Sh— Othello, 1784
„ Sh— Works, 1793, 1797

Murray (John Tucker) English dramatic companies, 1558-1642 : I. London companies, II. Provincial companies . . . Appendices. Ln : Constable . . . 1910. 2 vols. 8°, pp. xvi.-370 and xii.-434 BM | BLO | CTC | SML
It is no reflection upon, but rather a compliment to this work to say it is a disgrace to England that such an undertaking was left to America to perform. It is the kind of work which the trustees of Sh—'s birthplace might have subsidised with propriety.

N—— (G. S.) Sh— diary and almanack (*p. 226, read*) A daily chronicle of events, with appropriate quotations from the poet's works. Ln : 1869. 8°, pp. 28, including printed wrappers BPL | SML

Nash *or* Nashe (Thomas). *See* Gentleman

Neagle (James) *Engraver. See* Sh— Works, 1807

Neidig (Wm. J.) False dates on Sh— quartos;
a new method of proof applied to a controversy of scholars [In the 'Century
Magazine,' pp. 912-919, Oct., 1910]. Roy.
8°   BUS | NY
By applying a millimetre rule to the disputed title-
pages, and then photographing them, Mr. Neidig
and Dr. Manly of Chicago demonstrated beyond
cavil that Dr. Greg is correct in his assumption that
the suspected quartos are falsely dated.
Sh— quartos of 1619 [In 'Modern Philo-
logy,' pp. 1-19. Chicago, Oct., 1910]
                                      BUS | NY
New England Historic Society: Tercentenary
... (p. 227, add)   BM
New Place, Stratford-on-Avon—
See Gentleman
,, Public ...
Newberie (Ralph) Printer. See Hakluyt
Newbery (E.) Publisher—
See Sh— Macbeth, 1785
,, Sh— Works, 1793, 1797
Newbery (W. F. & E.) Publishers. See Sh—
Othello, 1784
Nicholls (J.) Publisher—
See Sh— Macbeth, 1785
,, Sh— Othello, 1784
,, Sh— Works, 1793
Nichols (J.) Memoirs of George Hardinge.
See Hardinge
Nichols (J.) Publisher. See Sh— Works, 1797
Norton (Thomas). See Buckhurst & Norton
Nunn (J.) Publisher. See Sh— Works, 1797

Of education ... p. 237, read [by Obadiah
Walker]. Oxon: At the Theater, anno
1673. Cr. 8°, pp. vi.-292
Offor (G.) Publisher. See Sh— Works, 1820
Ogilvy Publisher. See Sh— Works, 1793
Ogilvy & Son (D.) Publishers. See Sh—
Works, 1797
Okes (N.) Printer. See Camden
Osteler v. Hemyngs. See Public ...
Owen (John). See Camden
Owen & Son (W.) Publishers—
See Sh— Macbeth, 1785
,, Sh— Othello, 1784

P—— (H. T.) Sh— (a poem). See Birmingham
Painter (W.) Palace ... (p. 241, read) 1567-69
(and add)—
Largely consisting of tales from Bandello, Boccaccio,
and Margaret Queen of Navarre.
Parfre (John) Candlemas day, 1512. See
Hawkins
Pavier (Thomas) Publisher. See Sh— Titus
... (heading)
Payne jun. (T.) Publisher. See Sh— Works,
1793, 1797
Payne & Son (T.) Publishers—
See Sh— Macbeth, 1785
,, Sh— Othello, 1784

Pearson (Howard S.) Secret of Sh—.   See
Birmingham
Peele (George) King David and fair Bethsabe.
See Hawkins
See also Gentleman
Pembroke (Mary Herbert Countess of).   See
Gentleman
Percy Bp. (Thomas) Editor. See Sh— Works,
1770-71
Phillip (John) Commemoration of the right
noble and vertuous Ladye, Margrit
Duglasis good grace Countis of Lennox
... Imprinted at Ln. by Iohn Charlewood
dwelling in Barbycan at the signe of the
halfe Eagle and Key, 1578. Fcp. 4° BM
Curious for its acrostic use of the prototype of Sh—'s
'Hamlet' in the following verse:—
'Hautinesse came on to martch with his traine,
And treason the ensine and standert did beare,
Myschiefe made speede the innocent to paine,
Bouldnesse stept vp his rancor to reare,
Lust longed to haue the blood of my deare,
Enuy prest on at vnitie to grudge,
Treason in this case presumed to be iudge.'
Phillips (Augustine) Editor (p. 247, read) See
Sh— Works, 1898-1908
Phonographic type (p. 247, add) Sh— Works,
1875
Platt (Isaac Hull) Editor. See Sh— Love's
labours lost, 1906
Playbills. See Taylor
Poel (Wm.) Should Sh—'s plays be produced
with scenery.   Ln: Sh— league [c.
1907 ?] 8°
A discussion at a meeting of the London Sh— league,
in which G. Bernard Shaw, Mrs. Stopes, and others
took part.
Pollard (A. W.) False dates in Sh— quartos
[In 'The Library,' pp. 101-107, Jan.,
1911]. Roy. 8°   BM | BLO | CTC
Ponsonby (Wm.) Publisher. See Brandon
Preston (Thomas) Lamentable tragedie ...
(p. 253, read) Percia (and add)—
Of peculiar interest as illustrating the transition in
English stage presentations from the early morality
play to historical drama.
See Gentleman
See also Hawkins
Price (Thomas R.) Editor. See Sh— Works,
1888-94
Proescholdt (Ludwig) Editor. See Sh— Merry
devil ... 1884
Prowett (Septimus) Publisher.   See Sh—
Merry devil ... 1825
Public Record Office: Exhibition of a col-
lection of original documents of Shake-
spearean interest ... Sh— day, 23 April,
1910. 8°, pp. 4
The manuscripts described are of surpassing interest.
They include:—
I. 'Payment to Sh—, Kempe and Burbage for
performing in Dec., 1594, before Q. Eliza-
beth at Greenwich (Pipe Office; Declared
Accounts).

II. Wm. Sh—, a defaulter, in St. Helen's parish, Bishopsgate, in the sum of 13/4, in respect of the first of three subsidies granted to Q. Elizabeth, Nov., 1596—Nov., 1597 (Lay Subsidies).

III. Exemplification of the fine levied when Sh—purchased New Place from Underhill in 1597 (Feet of Fines, Warwick, East).

IV.-V. Proceedings in the Star Chamber concerning the removal of the theatre from Shoreditch to Bankside, 1598-99 (Star Chamber Proceedings & Coram Rege Roll).

VI. Signet Bill, 17 May, 1603, which authorised the Lord Chancellor to grant letters patent 19 May, 1603 to Sh— and his associates.

VII. Enrolment of letters patent, 19 May, 1603, to Sh— and his associates, giving permission to perform plays (Patent Rolls).

VIII. King's Company of players summoned 2nd Dec., 1603, to perform in the royal presence at Wilton, owing to London plague (Audit Office ; Declared Accounts).

IX. Expenses incurred for dresses by participants in the procession of James I., 15 March, 1604. Sh—, whose name heads the list, received 'four and a half yards of skarlet red cloth.'

X. Memorandum of plays performed at Whitehall in 1604-05 (Audit office accounts).

XI. Account book of the Master of the revels, 1611-12, mentioning performances of some of Sh—'s plays. [Probably contains entries forged by P. Cunningham.] Audit office accounts.

XII. Osteler v. Hemyngs, Feb., 1615-16. Claim for damages. Mentions the shares held by Sh— in the Globe playhouse, together with matter concerning the site of that theatre (Coram Rege).

XIII. Sale by Wm. & John Combe to Sh—, 107 acres of land and 20 acres of pasture in Old Stratford for £100 (Feet of Fines, Warwick).

XIV. Enrolment 11th Mar., 1612-13, of the conveyance of a house in Blackfriars from Hy. Walker to Sh—, 10 Mar., 1612-13 (Close Rolls).

XV. Documents in an action, 1615, where Sh— was one of the plaintiffs and Mathew Bacon the defendant for delivery of title deeds of the Blackfriars property.

XVI. Bellot v. Mountjoy: Documents in the suit, with signed deposition by Sh— (Court of Requests).

XVII. Enrolment 11th April, 1628, of the conveyance of property on Bankside, 11 Dec., 1626, from Sir Mathew Brend to Hillarie Memprise. The property included 'premises . . . bounded with the alley or way leading to the Gloabe playhouse, commonly called Gloabe Alley.' This document helps to identify the site of the Globe theatre (Close Rolls).

XVIII. Papers in a Chancery suit, 1597, concerning a messuage and yardland in Wylmcote, near Stratford-on-Avon. Sh—'s father and mother were the plaintiffs, and John Lambert the defendant (Chancery Bills and Answers).

XIX. Holograph letter from Lord Burghley to Sir Thomas Walsingham concerning the 'Watch' at Theobald's, 1586 (S.P. Dom. Eliz.)

Purcell (Hy.) Two-part song. See Sh— Timon . . . 1680

Quarles (Francis). See Gentleman

Radclyffe (C. W.) See Jaffray

Raimback Engraver. See Sh— Works, 1807

Rainoldes DD (John) Overthrow . . . (p. 256, add)—
The idea of the 'Authorised version' of the Bible, 1611, was due to Rainoldes, who was president of Corpus Christi College, Oxford, and puritan leader at the Hampton Court conference, 1604.

Raleigh (Prof. Walter) Six essays on Johnson. Ln : Frowde, 1910. 8° BM | BLO | CTC
Includes a chapter on Johnson's Essay on Sh—.

Ramsay (Sir James H.) Roll of Coventry [In ' The Athenæum,' No. 4,331, p. 521, 29 Oct.] 1910 BM | BPL

Ravenscroft Editor (p. 257, read)—
See Sh— Works, 1898-1908

Raynesford (Sir Henry). See Maclean

Red Bull playhouse. See Gentleman

Reed Actor. See Stage player's . . .

Rehan (Ada) Actress. See Sh— Two gentlemen . . . 1895

Remaines concerning Britaine. See Camden

Repton (Humphry)] The bee (p. 260, add) SML

Return from Parnassus, 1606. See Hawkins

Reynolds (William) Editor—
See Sh— Merchant . . . 1888
   ,, Sh— Midsummer . . . 1890
   ,, Sh— Works, 1888-94

Rhodes Engraver. See Sh— Works, 1820

Richardson & Co. (J.) Publishers. See Sh— Works, 1821

Richardson (W.) Publisher. See Sh— Works, 1797

Ricketts (Charles) Artist—
See Sh— Twelfth night, 1901
   ,, Sh— Two gentlemen . . . 1901

Ridley Artist. See Sh— Works, 1798-1800, 1800

Rivington (F. & C.) Publishers. See Sh— Works, 1793, 1797

Rivington (J.) Publisher—
See Sh— Much ado . . . 1757
   ,, Sh— Works, 1760

Rivington (J. F. & C.) Publishers—
See Sh— Macbeth, 1785
   ,, Sh— Othello, 1784

Roberts (James) Printer & Publisher—
See Sh— Troilus . . . (heading)
   ,, Southwell

Robinson (G.) Publisher. See Sh— Othello, 1784

Robinson (G. G. J.) Publisher. See Sh— Works, 1793

Robinson (G. G. J. & J.) Publishers. See Sh— Macbeth, 1785

Robinson (H.) Engraver. See Sh— Poems, 1895

Robinson (J.) Publisher. See Sh— Works, 1793

Robinson (M.) Poems . . . portrait by T. Smirke (p. 266, read) R. Smirke

Robson (J.) *Publisher—*
See Sh— Macbeth, 1785
,, Sh— Othello, 1784
,, Sh— Works, 1793, 1797
Rodd & Maddox. Catalogue... (*p. 266, add*)—
BM
Rossetti (Dante Gabriel) Collected works, edited by W. M. Rossetti. Ln : Ellis ... 1886. 2 vols. Cr. 8° BM
On p. 285, Vol. i., occurs the scathing sonnet on the miserable Gastrell, headed '*On the site of a mulberry tree, planted by Wm. Sh—; felled by the Rev. F. Gastrell*':—
'This tree, here fall'n, no common birth or death
Shared with its kind. The world's enfranchised son
Who found the trees of life and knowledge one,
Here set it, frailer than his laurel wreath,
Shall not the wretch whose hand it fell beneath
Rank also singly—the supreme unhung?
Lo! Sheppard, Turpin, pleading with black tongue
This viler thief's unsuffocated breath;
We'll search thy glossary, Sh—! whence almost
And whence alone, some name shall be reveal'd,
For this deaf drudge, to whom no length of years
Sufficed to catch the music of the spheres,
Whose soul is carrion now—too mean to yield
Some *Starveling's* ninth allotment of a ghost.'
Rowley (Wm.) *See* Gentleman
Rudland (E. Marston) Sh— (a poem). *See* Birmingham
Ruskin (John) Mystery of life and its arts. 1869
'It does not matter how little, or how much, any of us have read either of Homer or Sh—: everything round us, in substance or in thought, has been moulded by them. All Greek gentlemen were educated under Homer; all Roman gentlemen by Greek literature; all Italian, and French, and English gentlemen by Roman literature and by its principles. Of the scope of Sh—, I will say only that the intellectual measure of every man since born, in the domain of creative thought, may be assigned to him, according to the degree in which he has been taught by Sh—.'
Russell (*Sir* Edward Richard) Introduction. *See* Sh— Midsummer ... 1880

S——. Sh— (a sonnet). *See* Birmingham
S—— (W.) Sh— (a poem). *See* Birmingham
Sackville *Baron Buckhurst* (Thomas). *See* Gentleman
Saint John *Editor* (*Sir* Spenser) Essays (*p. 273, add*)— SML
Saintsbury (George) Sh— and the grand style [In ' Essays and studies by members of the English Association']. Ln : Frowde, 1910. 8°— BM | BLO | CTC
Savage (Frederick George) Notes on plants mentioned in Sh—'s plays [In ' Stratford-on-Avon Herald,' 2nd April, 1909-18th Nov., 1910]. F°. [*In progress*]
BPL | SML | SPL
On the migration of midland birds. Avon Club lecture [In ' Stratford Herald,' 17th Feb., 1911] BPL | SML
Illustrates Sh—'s ornithology.
Scatcherd (J.) *Publisher. See* Sh— Works, 1793, 1797

Schelling (*Prof.* Felix E.) English literature during the lifetime of Sh—. Ln : Bell ... 1910. 8° BM | BLO | CTC
Schiavonetti (Luigi) *Engraver. See* Sh— Works, 1807
Schmidt (Heinrich) *Engraver. See* Sh— Works, 1804-13
Scudery (G. de) Amaryllis ... (*p. 278, add*)—
Says:—' I can't, without infinite ingratitude ... omit the first famous masters in it, of our nation, venerable Sh— and the great Ben Jonson.'
Secret history of Mack-beth (*p. 278, read*) Ln : J. Woodward
Sedley (Charles) *Editor. See* Sh— King Richard III., 1873
Selby (Charles) *Actor-Editor. See* Sh— Antony ... 1842
Selimus. *See* Crawford
Sewell (J.) *Publisher. See* Sh— Works, 1793-1797
Seymar (Wm.) Conjugium conjurgium, or some serious considerations on marriage, wherein by way of caution and advice to a friend its nature, ends, events, concomitant accidents, etc. are examined. Ln : Roger Clavell ... 1694. 12°
At p. 74 Sh— is included among the 'priests of Cupid.
Shadwell (T.) *Editor* (*p. 280, read*)—
See Sh— Works, 1898-1908
Shakespeare *of Clifford Chambers* (Anthony). *See* Maclean
Sh— *of Clifford Chambers* (John) *Husbandman. See* Maclean
Sh— *Poet's mother* (Mary). *See* Stopes
Sh— *of Hinckley* (Richard). *See* Harris
Sh— *of Clifford Chambers* (Thomas). *See* Maclean
Sh— (Wm.) All's well ... 1714 (*p. 281, read*) [Ln : Jacob Tonson] Printed in the year MDCCXIV. Cr. 8°, pp. 363-444 (excerpt) and copperplate frontispiece
All's well ... (*p. 281, read*) Ln : Printed for J. Tonson, and the rest of the proprietors ; and sold by the booksellers of Ln. and Westminster, 1734. Cr. 8°, pp. 84 and frontispiece by P. Fourdrinier SML
[*Add to footnote*]—
On the last page of Tonson's issue occurs this passage :—
' N.B. Whereas one R. Walker has proposed to pirate all Sh—'s plays; but, through ignorance of what plays are Sh—'s, did in several advertisements propose to print "Œdipus King of Thebes" as one of Sh—'s plays, and has since printed Tate's "King Lear" instead of Sh—'s, and in that and "Hamlet" has omitted almost one-half of the genuine editions printed by Tonson and proprietors. The world will therefore judge how likely they are to have a compleat collection of Sh—'s plays from the said R. Walker.'
All's well ... 1773 (*p. 281, add*) pp. 72 and frontispiece engraved by P. Mazell after E. Edwards

Sh— All's well . . . A comedy . . . 'Sherwood's dramatic library.' Ln : W. Strange . . . 1846. 16°, pp. 76, including printed wrappers

Antony and Cleopatra. A tragedy. [Ln : Jacob Tonson] Printed in the year MDCCXIV. Cr. 8°, pp. 189-284 (excerpt) and copperplate frontispiece

Antony . . . 1734 (*p. 283, add*)—   SML

Antony and Cleopatra, 1842 ? (*p. 284, read*) A burletta in one act by Charles Selby, comedian. The only edition correctly marked, by permission, from the prompter's book. To which is added . . . the costume . . . cast . . . stage business . . . situations . . . properties, and directions, as performed at the London theatres. Embellished with a fine engraving by Mr. Findlay from a drawing taken expressly in the theatre. Ln : Printed and published by J. Duncombe, &c. [c. 1837]. 12°, pp. 22 (including printed pink wrappers) and etched frontispiece

[Antony . . .] Anthony and Cleopatra. The text of the folio of 1623, with that of ' All for love or the world well lost.' As done by John Dryden in 1678, with an introduction touching the environment of the Restoration drama, whereby Sh— was perpetuated through the Restoration period, by Francis A. Smith. New York : Sh— Society of New York, 1908. Roy. 8°, pp. xvi.-386. With facsimiles
               BPL | BUS | NY
Issue limited to 500 numbered copies.

'Arden of Feversham' references. *See* Hopkinson

As you like it. A comedy. [Ln : Jacob Tonson] Printed in the year MDCCXIV. Cr. 8°, pp. 215-290 (excerpt) and copperplate frontispiece

As you like it. A comedy. By Mr. Wm. Sh—. [*Ornament.*] Ln : Printed for J. Tonson, and the rest of the proprietors, and sold by the booksellers of Ln. and Westminster, 1734. 12°, pp. 72, and frontispiece by P. Fourdrinier   SML
An issue hitherto unrecorded.

As you like it . . . 1773 (*p. 287, add*) pp. 80, and frontispiece engraved by M. Liart after E. Edwards

As you like it, 1829 (*p. 288, add*)   SML
As you like it. Dowden, 1887 (*p. 290, add*) pp. xxiv.-44   SML

As you like it . . . with glossary. Edited by Lord Howard de Walden and Acton Bond. ' British Empire Sh— Society edition.' Ln : Farmer . . . 1910. 16°, pp. 118   BM | BLO | CTC

Sh— As you like it . . . Arranged for class reading, with introduction and notes by A. P. Graves. Ln : Dent . . . 1911. 16°, pp. 154   BM | BLO | CTC

Autograph.] Holy Bible . . . Ln : Imprinted by the deputies of Christopher Barker, 1584. F°   SML
Bequeathed to the Sh— Memorial, 23rd April, 1881, by Shirley Forster Woolmer, a barrister, and descendant of an old Stratford family, who stated the volume once belonged to Sh— and had borne his signature. It is bound in wooden boards, covered with stamped leather and brass bosses of the period.
The three titles (to the old and new testaments and the apocrypha) are missing.

Birth of Merlin . . . ' Sh—'s doubtful plays.' Edited with an introduction by A. F. Hopkinson. Ln. [Privately printed by] M. E. Sims & Co. . . . 1892. Cr. 8°, pp. xvi.-84   SML

' Birth of Merlin ' references—
  See Hopkinson
  ,, Sh— [Works] Sh— apocrypha, 1908

Comedy of errors, 1734 (*p. 294, add*) SML
Comedy of errors, 1829 (*p. 295, add*) SML
Haywell's corrected prompt copy is at Stratford.

Comedy of errors . . . with notes by Charles Knight. [*Chandos portrait.*] ' Cabinet Sh—.' Ln : W. S. Orr & Co., 1854. 16°, pp. 81-148 (excerpt)   SML
Haywell's prompt copy is at Stratford.

Comedy of errors . . . 1873 (*p. 295, read*) With notes critical and explanatory. Adapted for scholastic or private study and for those qualifying for university or government examinations, by John Hunter . . . Ln : Longman . . . 1873. Cr. 8°, pp. viii.-78   BPL

Coriolanus. A tragedy. [Ln : Jacob Tonson] Printed in the year MDCCXIV. Cr. 8°, pp. 295-396 (excerpt) and copperplate frontispiece by Lud. du Guernier

Coriolanus, 1734 (*p. 297, read*) Ln : Printed for J. Tonson, and the rest of the proprietors and sold by the booksellers of Ln. and Westminster, 1734. 12°, pp. 86. With copperplate frontispiece by Lud. du Guernier   BPL | SML

Coriolanus . . . 1773 (*p. 297, add*) pp. 86, and frontispiece engraved by M. Liart after E. Edwards

'Coriolanus' references (*p. 300, add*)—
  See Massinger

Cupid's cabinet . . . *See* Sh— Poems, 1669

Cymbeline. A tragedy. [Ln : Jacob Tonson] Printed in the year MDCCXIV. Cr. 8°, pp. 285-384 (excerpt) and copperplate frontispiece by Lud. du Guernier

Cymbeline, 1734 (*p. 301, add*)—   SML

Sh— Cymbeline . . . 1773 (*p. 301, add*) pp. 84, and frontispiece engraved by M. Liart after E. Edwards

Cymbeline . . . ' Penny Sh—.' Ln : G. Vickers, Holywell Street, Strand [c. 1830]. 12°, pp. 74   SML
Haywell's corrected prompt copy is at Stratford.

Cymbeline . . . with notes and appendices by H. W. Lindsey. ' Normal tutorial series.' Ln : Normal Press, 1910. Cr. 8°
BM | BLO | CTC

Fair Em, the miller's daughter of Manchester, with the love of William the conqueror. Edited with an introduction by A. F. Hopkinson. Ln : [Privately printed by] M. E. Sims & Co. . . . 1895. Cr. 8°, pp. xviii.-58   SML

[Hamlet] Songs in the opera of ' Hamlet ' as they are perform'd at ye Queen's theatre . . . [Ln : . . . c. 1712]. F° BPL

Hamlet, prince of Denmark. A tragedy. [Ln : Jacob Tonson] Printed in the year MDCCXIV. Cr. 8°, pp. 301-406 (excerpt)

Hamlet, 1734 (*p. 308, add*)—   SML

[Hamlet] Slender's ghost . . . 1748 (*p. 308, add*) [by W. Shenstone]

Hamlet, prince of Denmark . . . as performed at the Theatre Royal, Covent Garden. Regulated from the prompt book, with permission of the managers, by Mr. Younger, prompter. An introduction, and notes critical and illustrative, are added by the authors of the ' Dramatic censor ' [F. Gentleman]. Ln : Printed for John Bell . . . and C. Etherington at York, 1773. 8°, pp. 84, and frontispiece engraved by J. Hall after E. Edwards
An issue unnoticed elsewhere.

Hamlet . . . 1829 (*p. 311, add*) embellished with a fine engaving (*sic*) by Mr. White, from a drawing taken in the theatre by R. Cruikshank   SML
Haywell's corrected prompt copy is at Stratford.

[Hamlet] The barrow diggers . . . 1839 (*p. 311, read*) Written by the Rev. C. Woolls (*and add*)—   BPL

[Hamlet] Bubble ghost . . . 1869 (*p. 313, add*)—   BM

[Hamlet] A throw . . . 1870 (*p. 314, add*) [By J. E. Wilson]

Hamlet . . . notes . . . by Oliver Smeaton, 1903 (*p. 317, read*) Oliphant Smeaton

[Hamlet] Polonius's advice to his son. Liverpool . . . 1910. Cr. 8°

Hamlet . . . Illustrated with plates in colour by W. G. Simmonds. Ln : Hodder . . . 1910

Sh— ' Hamlet ' references—
    See Birmingham
    ,, Phillip

Julius Cæsar. A tragedy. [Ln : Jacob Tonson] Printed in the year MDCCXIV. Cr 8°, pp. 161-232 (excerpt)

Julius Cæsar, 1734 (*p. 320, add*)—   SML

Julius Cæsar . . . 1773 (*p. 320, read*) 8°, pp. 84, and frontispiece engraved by James Basire after E. Edwards
The last eight pages bear a list of Bell's publications.

Julius Cæsar . . . c. 1830 (*p. 321, add*) SML
Haywell's prompt copy is at Stratford.

King Edward III. An historical drama. Edited with an introduction by A. F. Hopkinson. Ln : [Privately printed by] M. E. Sims & Co. . . . 1891. Cr. 8°, pp. xvi.-92   SML

'King Edward III.' references—
    See Hopkinson

King Henry IV., i. (*add to heading, p. 327*)
It was registered at Stationers' Hall :—
' *25th Feb., 1597-98. Andrew Wyse. Entred for his copie vnder thandes of Master Dix and Master warden Man a book intituled the Historye of Henry the IIIIth, with his battaile of Shrewsburye against Henry Hotspurre of the northe, with the conceipted mirthe of Sir John Falstoff . . . VId.*'

[King Henry IV., i.] The first part of Henry IV. With the life and death of Henry sirnam'd Hot-Spur. [Ln : Jacob Tonson] Printed in the year MDCCXIV. Cr. 8°, pp. 313-396 (excerpt) and copperplate frontispiece

King Henry IV., i., 1734 (*p. 329, add*) SML

King Henry IV., i. . . . as performed at the Theatre Royal, Drury Lane. Regulated from the prompt-book, with permission of the managers, by Mr. Hopkins, prompter. An introduction, and notes critical and illustrative, are added by the authors of the 'Dramatic censor' [F. Gentleman]. Ln : Printed for John Bell . . . and C. Etherington at York, 1773. 8°, pp. 74, and frontispiece engraved by J. Hall after E. Edwards
An issue unnoticed elsewhere.

King Henry IV., i., c. 1831 (*p. 330, add*) SML
Haywell's prompt copy is at Stratford.

King Henry IV., i., edited by J. H. Lobban. 'Granta Sh—.' Cambridge : University Press, 1910. 16°

King Henry IV., ii. (*add to heading, p. 332*)
It was registered at Stationers' Hall :—
' *23 Aug., 1600. Andrew Wyse. William Aspley. Entred for their copies vnder the handes of the wardens two bookes . . . Thother the second parte of the history of*

Kinge Henry the IIIIth, with the humours of Sir John Fallstoff : Wrytten by Master Shakespere . . . XIId.'

Sh— King Henry IV., ii., 1734 (*p. 332, add*)
SML

[King Henry IV., ii.] Falstaff's wedding . . . by Mr. Kenrick . . . Second edition. Ln : Printed for J. Wilkie in St. Paul's Churchyard ; F. Blyth at St. John's Coffee house near the Royal Exchange ; T. Lowndes and W. Owen in Fleet Street ; Becket and De Hondt in the Strand ; T. Lewis in Russel Street, Covent Garden ; J. Walter at Charing Cross ; and J. Almon in Piccadilly opposite Burlington House, 1766. Cr. 8°, pp. viii.-80   SML
Differs in imprint and pagination from the other 1766 edition.

King Henry IV., ii. . . . as performed at the Theatre Royal, Drury Lane. Regulated from the prompt book, with permission of the managers, by Mr. Hopkins, prompter. An introduction, and notes critical and illustrative, are added by the authors of the 'Dramatic censor' [F. Gentleman]. Ln : Printed for John Bell . . . and C. Etherington at York, 1773. 8°, pp. 78, and frontispiece engraved by J. Hall after E. Edwards
An edition unchronicled elsewhere.

[King Henry IV., ii.] Falstaff's wedding . . . by W. Kenrick. Adapted for theatrical representation, as performed at the Theatre Royal, Covent Garden. Regulated from the prompt book, by permission of the managers. Ln : Printed by George Cawthorn, British library, Strand, 1795. 16°, pp. 96 (including printed wrappers), and frontispiece engraved by Heath after Stodhart [Stothard ?]
SML

King Henry IV., i. and ii., 1887 (*p. 335, add*) pp. xxiv.-88
SML

' King Henry IV.' references—
See Harris
   ,, Stopes, Roll . . .
   ,, Stronach

King Henry V., 1734 (*p. 337, add*)   SML
King Henry V. . . . 1773 (*p. 337, add*) With frontispiece engraved by J. Hall after E. Edwards

King Henry V. . . . 1849 (*p. 338, read*) Ln : Sherwood & Co., 23, Paternoster Row, 1849. 32°, pp. 64   SML
Haywell's corrected prompt copy is at Stratford.

' King Henry V.' references—
See Harris
   ,, Stopes, Roll . . .

King Henry VI., i., 1735 (*p. 343, add*) SML

Sh— King Henry VI., ii., 1734 (*p. 343, add*)
SML

King Henry VI., iii., 1734 (*p. 344, add*) SML
[King Henry VIII.] The famous history of the life of King Henry VIII. [Ln : Jacob Tonson] Printed in the year MDCCXIV. Cr. 8°, pp. 107-198 (excerpt) and copperplate frontispiece

King Henry VIII., 1734 (*p. 347, read*) Ln : Printed for J. Tonson, and the rest of the proprietors, and sold by the booksellers of Ln. and Westminster, 1734. 12°, pp. 96 and frontispiece   BM | SML

King Henry VIII. . . . as performed at the Theatre Royal, Covent Garden. Regulated by Mr. Younger, prompter of that theatre. An introduction, and notes critical and illustrative, are added by the authors of the ' Dramatic censor ' [F. Gentleman]. Ln : Printed for John Bell . . . and C. Etherington at York, 1773. 8°, pp. 72, and frontispiece engraved by J. Hall after E. Edward
An edition unchronicled elsewhere.

King Henry VIII. . . . Dolby, 1824 (*p. 347, read*) An historical play in five acts. Printed under the authority of the managers from the prompt book, with notes critical and explanatory, also an authentic description of the costume and the general stage business, as performed at the Theatres Royal, London. Embellished with a wood engraving . . . by I. R. Cruickshank, executed by Mr. White. Ln : Printed and published by T. Dolby . . . and sold by all booksellers, 1824. 12°, pp. 60   BPL | SML
Haywell's corrected prompt copy is at Stratford.

King Henry VIII. . . . 1872 (*p. 348, read*) With introductory remarks and critical and explanatory notes. Adapted for scholastic or private study, and for those qualifying for university and government examinations, by John Hunter. New edition. Ln : Longmans . . . 1872. Cr. 8°, pp. xii.-134   CPL

King Henry VIII., Dowden, 1892 (*p. 349, add*) pp. xxiv.-54   SML
' King Henry VIII.' references. See Stopes

King John (*add to heading, p. 350*) *Apparently this play was not registered at Stationers' Hall.*

[King John] The life and death of King John. [Ln : Jacob Tonson] Printed in the year MDCCXIV. Cr. 8°, pp. 165-236 (excerpt) and copperplate frontispiece

King John, 1734 (*p. 351, add*)   SML
With piracy warning by Jacob Tonson at end against R. Walker.

Sh— King John . . . 1773 (*p. 351, add*) With frontispiece engraved by P. Mazell after E. Edwards

King John, 1829 (*p. 352, add*) Embellished with a portrait of ' Macready as King John' SML
Haywell's prompt copy is at Stratford.

King John . . . with explanatory and illustrative notes and numerous extracts from the history on which the play is founded. Adapted for scholastic or private study, by John Hunter. New edition. Ln : Longmans . . . 1877. Cr. 8°, pp. xvi.-112

King Lear . . . Printed for Simon Stafford . . . 1605 (*p. 355, read*) by Simon Stafford

King Lear. A tragedy. [Ln : Jacob Tonson] Printed in the year MDCCXIV. Cr. 8°, pp. 92, and copperplate frontispiece by Lud. du Guernier
Until now an unrecorded issue, off-printed from Tonson's anonymous edition of Sh—'s works for playgoers.

King Lear . . . 1734 (*p. 356, add*)— SML

King Lear . . . as performed at the Theatre Royal, Drury Lane. Regulated from the prompt book, with permission of the managers, by Mr. Hopkins, prompter. An introduction, and notes critical and illustrative, are added by the authors of the ' Dramatic censor ' [F. Gentleman]. Ln : Printed for John Bell . . . and C. Etherington at York, 1773. 8°, pp. 84, and copperplate frontispiece engraved by J. Hall after E. Edwards
Hitherto an unrecorded issue.

King Lear . . . edited by K. Harvey. ' Sh— for home reading.' Ln : . . . 1910. Cr. 8°

[King Richard II.] The life and death of King Richard II. [Ln : Jacob Tonson] Printed in the year MDCCXIV. Cr. 8°, pp. 237-312 (excerpt), and copperplate frontispiece by Lud. du Guernier

King Richard II., 1734 (*p. 363, add*) SML

[King Richard III.] The life and death of Richard III. ; with the Landing of the Earl of Richmond and the battel at Bosworth Field. [Ln : Jacob Tonson] Printed in the year MDCCXIV. Cr. 8°, pp. 106 and copperplate frontispiece
Until now an unrecorded issue, and off-printed from Tonson's anonymous edition of Sh—'s works for playgoers.

King Richard III., 1734 (*p. 370, add*) SML

King Richard III. . . . as performed at the Theatre Royal, Drury Lane. Regulated from the prompt book, with permission of the managers, by Mr. Hopkins, prompter. An introduction, and notes critical and illustrative, are added by the authors of the ' Dramatic censor ' [F. Gentleman].

Ln : Printed for John Bell . . . and C. Etherington at York, 1773. 8°, pp. 70 and frontispiece
An edition hitherto unchronicled.

Sh— King Richard III. . . . 1829 (*p. 373, add*) SML
Haywell's corrected prompt copy is at Stratford.

King Richard III. Lacy, c. 1857 (*p. 374, add*) pp. 68 SML
Haywell's prompt copy is at Stratford.

King Richard III. . . . with explanatory and illustrative notes and numerous extracts from the history on which the play is founded. Adapted for scholastic or private study, by John Hunter. Ln : Longmans . . . 1872. Cr. 8°, pp. xxviii.-144

King Richard III. . . . with explanatory and illustrative notes and numerous extracts from the history on which the play is founded. Adapted for scholastic or private study, by John Hunter . . . New edition. Ln : Longmans . . . 1878. Cr. 8°, pp. xxviii.-144

Locrine . . . (*add to heading, p. 377*)—
'*20th-22nd July, 1594. Thomas Creede. Entred for his copie vnder thandes of the wardens the " Lamentable tragedie of Locrine, the eldest sonne of Kinge Brutus, discoursinge the Warres of the Brittans, &c." . . . VId.*'

Locrine . . . ' Sh—'s doubtful plays.' Edited with an introduction by A. F. Hopkinson. Ln : [Privately printed by] M. E. Sims & Co. . . . 1892. Cr. 8°, pp. xvi.-80 SML

' Locrine ' references. *See* Hopkinson

London prodigal . . . (*add to heading, p. 378*)
Apparently this work was not registered at Stationers' Hall originally. The following entry may relate to the play :—
'*27th Nov., 1598. Nicholas Linge. Entred for his copie vnder the handes of Master Swinhowe and the wardens a booke called the " Portraiture of the prodigall sonne " . . . VId.*'

London prodigal . . . ' Sh—'s doubtful plays.' Edited with an introduction by A. F. Hopkinson. Ln : [Privately printed by] M. E. Sims & Co. . . . 1893. Cr. 8°, pp. xxviii.-76 SML

'London prodigal' references. *See* Hopkinson

Love's labours lost. A comedy. [Ln : Jacob Tonson] Printed in the year MDCCXIV. Cr. 8°, pp. 80. With copperplate frontispiece by Lud. du Guernier
Hitherto an unrecorded issue.
Off-printed from Tonson's anonymous edition of Sh—'s works for playgoers.

Sh— Love's labours lost . . . J. Tonson, 1735 (*p. 379, read*) Ln : Printed for J. Tonson and the rest of the proprietors and sold by the booksellers of Ln. and Westminster, 1735. Cr. 8°, pp. 84. With frontispiece by L. Du Guernier   SML

[Love's labours lost] 'Bankside Sh— XXI.' Loues labours lost. (The players' text of 1598, with the Heminges and Condell text of 1623.) With an introduction touching the question whether this play was originally written or 'only newly corrected and augmented' by Wm. Sh—, by Isaac Hull Platt. New York : Sh— Society of New York, 1906. Roy. 8°, pp. viii.-xl.-158 and facsimile
Restricted to 500 numbered copies. BPL | BUS | NY

[Macbeth] The tragedy of Macbeth. [Ln : Jacob Tonson] Printed in the year MDCCXIV. Cr. 8°, pp. 233-300 (excerpt)

Macbeth, 1734 (*pp. 381-382, read*) pp. 68-iv.   SML

[Macbeth] Three conjurers . . . 1763 (*p. 382, add*) BPL | W

[Macbeth] Three conjurers . . . Second edition . . . [c. 1763.] Fcp. 4°

Macbeth . . . C. Bathurst, 1785 (*p. 383, read*) Ln : Printed for C. Bathurst, W. & A. Strahan, J. F. & C. Rivington, L. Davis, W. Lowndes, W. Owen & Son, B. White & Son, T. Longman, B. Law, C. Dilly, T. Cadell, T. Payne & Son, J. Robson, G. G. J. & J. Robinson, T. Davies, T. Bowles, R. Baldwin, H. L. Gardner, J. Nicholls, J. Bew, W. Cater, J. Murray, W. Stuart, S. Hayes, W. Bent, S. Bladon, W. Fox, and E. Newbery, 1785. 12°, pp. 72 and frontispiece
The last five pages contain a list of plays issued by W. Lowndes.

Macbeth . . . 1829 (*p. 384, add*) Embellished with a fine engraving by Mr. White from a drawing taken in the theatre by R. Cruikshank   SML
Haywell's corrected prompt copy is at Stratford.

Macbeth. 'School Sh—,' 1902 (*p. 389, add*) Edited by L. W. Lyde

Macbeth, ed. by L. W. Lyde, 1902 (*p. 390, delete*)

Macbeth, edited by J. H. Lobban. 'Granta Sh—.' Cambridge : University Press, 1910. 16°

'Macbeth' references—
See Birmingham
  ,, Character . . .

Merchant of Venice. A comedy. [Ln : Jacob Tonson] Printed in the year MDCCXIV. Cr. 8°, pp. 141-214 (excerpt) and copperplate frontispiece

Merchant . . . 1734 (*p. 374, add*)— SML

Sh— Merchant . . . c. 1830 (*p. 396, add*) With portrait of 'Mrs. West as Portia,' engraved on steel by Mr. Woolnoth from an original painting by Mr. Wageman
Haywell's corrected prompt copy is at Stratford. SML

Merchant . . . Arranged for reading aloud. With introduction and notes by A. P. Graves. Ln : Dent . . . 1911. 16°, pp. 144   BM | BLO | CTC

'Merchant . . .' references. See Sherley

Merry wives . . . 1734 (*p. 405, add*)— SML

Merry wives . . . printed from the quarto of 1602. With introduction by W. W. Greg. Ln : H. Frowde . . . 1910. Cr. 8°
  BM | BLO | CTC

Merry wives . . . Illustrated by Hugh Thomson. Ln : Heinemann . . . 1910. Fcp. 4°, pp. 180   BM | BLO | CTC

Midsummer night's dream. A comedy. [Ln : Jacob Tonson] Printed in the year MDCCXIV. Cr. 8°, pp. 81-140 (excerpt) and copperplate frontispiece

Midsummer . . . 1830 (*p. 411, add*) Embellished with a fine wood engraving by Mr. Bonner from a drawing taken in the theatre by R. Cruikshank   SML
Haywell's corrected prompt copy is at Stratford.

Midsummer . . . Orr. 1854 (*p. 411, read*) With notes by Charles Knight. [*Chandos portrait.*] 'Cabinet Sh—.' 16°, pp. 84 (including printed wrappers)   SML
Haywell's prompt copy is at Stratford.

[Midsummer . . .] Midsummer night . . . by L. Tieck, 1854 (*p. 411, add*)— BUS

Midsummer night's dream . . . edited by W. H. Hudson. 'Elizabethan Sh—.' Ln : Harrap . . . 1910. Cr. 8°
  BM | BLO | CTC

Othello, the Moor of Venice. A tragedy. [Ln : Jacob Tonson] Printed in the year MDCCXIV. Cr. 8°, pp. 93-188 (excerpt), and copperplate frontispiece by Lud. du Guernier

Othello . . . 1829 (*p. 425, add*) With portrait of 'Mr. Young in Iago' by Woolnoth after Wageman   SML
Haywell's corrected prompt copy is at Stratford.

'Othello' references. See Massinger

Passionate pilgrim (*add to heading, p. 429*)—
The publication was not recorded at Stationers' Hall.

Pericles, prince of Tyre [vignette. Ln :] From the Chiswick Press, 1813. 32°, pp. 72   SML
Haywell's prompt copy is at Stratford.

Phaethon to his friend Florio (*p. 433, add*)—
This sonnet Florio stated was 'written by a gentleman, a friend that loved better to be a poet than to be counted so.' It runs :—
'Sweete friend, whose name agrees with thy increase, How fit a rivall art thou of the spring ;

For when each branche hath left his flourishing,
And green-lockt sommers shadie pleasures cease,
She makes the winter's stormes repose in peace,
And spends her franchise on each living thing ;
The dazies sprout, the little birds do sing,
Hearbes, gummes, and plants doo vaunt of their release.
So when that all our English witts lay dead
(Except the laurell that is evergreene),
Thou with thy "frutes" our barrenness o'respread,
And set thy flowrie pleasance to be seene :
Sutch frutes, sutch flowrets of moralitie
Were nere before brought out of Italie.'
—*Phaethon.*

Sh— Poems and sonnets . . . 'Chiswick series.'
Ln : G. Bell & Sons . . . 1895. Cr. 8°, pp.
iv.-214. With Droeshout portrait engraved by H. Robinson

Romeo and Juliet. A tragedy. [Ln :
Jacob Tonson] Printed in the year
MDCCXIV. Cr. 8°, pp. 90
Until now an unrecorded edition, off-printed from
Tonson's anonymous issue of Sh—'s works for the
use of playgoers.

Romeo and Juliet . . . 1813 (*p. 445, read*)
[vignette. Ln :] From the Chiswick
Press, 1813. 32°, pp. 88   SML
Haywell's prompt copy is at Stratford.

Romeo . . . Cumberland, 1831 (*p. 446, read*)
12°, pp. 70 and portrait of 'Miss F. H.
Kelly as Juliet'
Haywell's corrected prompt copy is at Stratford.

Sonnets [In 'American Review.' New York
. . . 1847]. 8°   BUS

' Sonnets ' references—
See Fitton
,, Look . . .

Taming . . . 1734 (*p. 444, add*)—   SML
[Taming . . .] Sh—'s part . . . 1890 (*p. 461,
add*)—   BM
[The tempest] The virgin queen, 1797 (*p.
464, add*)—   BPL

'The tempest' references. *See* Country club
Troilus and Cressida [Critique in 'Oxford
& Cambridge Magazine,' 1856]. 8° BUS
Twelfth night, edited by J. H. Lobban.
'Granta Sh—.' Cambridge : University
Press, 1910. 16°
Twelfth night . . . adapted by E. Fogerty.
Ln : Sonnenschein . . . 1911. Fcp. 4°
                              BM | BLO | CTC
'Two gentlemen . . .' references. *See* Benson
'Will and testament' references—
See Jeaffreson
,, Yeatman
Winter's tale . . . 1866 (*p. 492, add*)— BPL
Winter's tale, edited by J. H. Lobban.
'Granta Sh—.' Cambridge : University
Press, 1910. 16°
Works . . . 1623 (*p. 495, add footnote*)—
'There are indeed many misprints, omissions, and
strange press-room matters in the first folio . . . but
they are trifles compared with the wonderful accuracy
which prevails.'—*Allan Park Paton.*
For its first appearance at auction *see* Worsley.

Sh— Works . . . 1632 (*p. 496, add*)—
A variant copy belonging to the late Wm. Hughes
Hilton, of Sale, Cheshire, was sold 16th Dec., 1610,
for £105. On the title the word 'copies' was spelt
'coppies.' It bore the Cotes-Allot imprint.
Works, 1768. 9 vols. (*p. 502, add*)— SML
[Works] Bunbury (Hy. Wm.) A series of
prints, illustrative of various interesting
scenes in the plays of Sh—, engraved by
F. Bartolozzi, P. Tomkins, T. Cheesman,
and — Meadows. Ln : T. Macklin [1792-
96]. Oblong f°. Twenty-two plates
                                 BM | BPL | MPL
Executed for Boydell's Sh— gallery (*q.v. under*) Sh—
Works, 1802.
[Works] Sh— illustrated by an assemblage
of portraits and views appropriated to
the whole suite of our author's historical
dramas, to which are added portraits of
actors, editors, etc. Ln : S. & E. Harding,
1793. F°. 148 plates   BM | W
[Works] Plays . . . 1807. 12 vols. 8° (*p.
511, read*) Ln : Printed [by James Bal-
lantyne & Co., Edinburgh] for Longman,
Hurst, Rees & Orme, Paternoster Row ;
William Miller, Albemarle Street. Edin-
burgh : A. Constable & Co., 1807. 12
vols. 8°   BPL | MPL | NY
Some sets were produced on large paper, roy. 8°.
Each play is preceded by a pretty copperplate vignette.
The artists were H. Howard, Singleton, Smirke,
T. Stothard, H. Thompson, and S. Woodforde. The
engravers were C. Armstrong, W. Bromley, Cromek,
T. S. Engleheart, Fittler, J. Heath, J. Mitan, James
Neagle, Raimback, L. Schiavonetti, E. Smith, and
C. Warren.
[Works] 'Granta Sh—,' edited by J. H.
Lobban. Cambridge : University Press,
1910. 4 vols. 16°. [*In progress*]
Contents :—Winter's tale
          King Henry IV., I.
          Macbeth
          Twelfth night.
' Works ' references. *See* MacCracken
[Works : Ext.] Flowers of Sh—, by 'Viola'
(*p. 577, add*)—   BPL | SML
[Works : Ext.] Webb, Beauties . . . 1762
(*p. 561, add*)—   BPL
[Works : Ext.] Clarke (*Mrs.* C. C.) Complete
concordance to Sh—, being a verbal index
to all the passages in the dramatic works
of the poet. Ln : Bickers . . . 1910.
Roy. 8°, pp. 872

Shakespeare.] A—— (I.) Sh—'s birthday,
1899 [by Ion Atkins ?]. *See* Birmingham
] 'Achespè.' Sh— (a sonnet). *See* Birming-
ham
] Atkins (Ion) The immortal memory. *See*
Birmingham
] Bradley (Isaac) The immortal memory . . .
See Birmingham
] Brierley (Leonard) The immortal memory.
See Birmingham

Soliman and Perseda. *See* Hawkins
<small>An early English tragedy, from which Sh— borrowed
many passages and ideas.</small>
Southampton (Henry Wriothesley *third Earl
of*). *See* Willobie
Spence (E. F.) Our stage and its critics. Ln :
Methuen . . . 1910   BM | BLO | CTC
<small>Reviewed in 'The Athenæum,' No. 4338, 17 Dec., 1910.</small>
Spenser (Edmund)—
  See Bodenham   *See* Crawford
   ,, Camden   ,, Gentleman
Springthorpe (J. T.) Sh—'s day, 1901. *See*
  Birmingham
Stage—
  See Albright   *See* Spence
   ,, Drinkwater   ,, Taylor
   ,, Public . . .
Star chamber. *See* Public . . .
Steevens (George) *Forger. See* Jaggard
Still *Bp.* (John) Gammer Gurton's needle.
  See Hawkins
<small>This is the first known English comedy.</small>
Stoker (G. J.) Sh—'s day. *See* Birmingham
Stokes (Henry Paine) *Editor*—
  See Sh— King Henry V., 1892
   ,, Sh— Works, 1888-94
Stothard (T.) *Artist. See* Sh— Works, 1807
Strahan (W. & A.) *Publishers. See* Sh— Mac-
  beth, 1785
Stratford-on-Avon—
  See Avon club   *See* Catalogue, 1871
   ,, Barnard   ,, Clements
   ,, Brassington
Stuart (W.) *Publisher. See* Sh— Macbeth, 1785
Supposes. *See* Hawkins
Sutherland (J.) *Edinburgh Publisher. See*
  Sh— Works, 1820
Symons (Arthur) *Editor. See* Blind

Taverns. *See* Inns
Taylor *Waterman* (John). *See* Gentleman
Taylor (W. H.) A bundle of old playbills.
  See Birmingham
Theatre (The) *afterwards* 'The Globe' play-
  house. *See* Public . . .
Theobald (Lewis) *Forger. See* Jaggard
Thomas (Charles W.) *Editor*—
  See Sh— King Henry VI., ii., 1892
   ,, Sh— Works, 1888-94
Thompson (H.) *Artist. See* Sh— Works, 1807
Thomson *Engraver. See* Sh— Works, 1825
Thomson (Hugh) *Artist. See* Sh— Merry
  wives, 1910
Thurston *Artist. See* Sh— Works, 1820
Todd (Edgar) The immortal memory. *See*
  Birmingham
Tonks (J. W.) Sh—(a poem). *See* Birmingham
Sh—'s day, 1906. *See* Birmingham
Tonson (Jacob) *Publisher. See* Sh— As you
  like it, 1734
True and exact catalogue . . . 1732 (*p. 671,
add*) by Francis Kirkman ? *q.v.*

Underhill family of Stratford-on-Avon. *See*
  Public . . .

Van der Gucht (G.) *Engraver. See* Sh— Troilus
  . . . 1735
Vince (C. A.) John Smith, dramatist [Bacon-
  Sh— controversy]. *See* Birmingham
One more Bakespearean. *See* Birmingham
The immortal memory. *See* Birmingham
Vining (Edward P.) *Editor*—
  See Sh— Hamlet, 1890
   ,, Sh— Works, 1888-94

W—— (W.) *Printer. See* M—— (I.)
Waites (Alfred) *Editor*—
  See Sh— King Richard II. 1892
   ,, Sh— Works, 1888-94
Walker (J. A.) *Artist. See* Sh— Works : Ext.
  1910
Walker (Obadiah). *See* Of education
Walsingham (*Sir* Thomas). *See* Public . . .
Ward (*Dr.* A. W.) Representation of Sh—.
  See Dowden
Warner (Wm.) *See* Gentleman
Warren (C.) *Engraver. See* Sh— Works, 1807
Warwickshire—
  See Baker   *See* Brassington
   ,, Birmingham   ,, Jerrold
   ,, Bradley
Waterson (Simon) *Publisher. See* Camden
Watkins (*Dr.* John). *See* William IV.
Watts (John) *Printer. See* Cibber
Watts-Dunton (Theodore) Representation of
  Sh—. *See* Dowden
Webster (John)—
  See Crawford
   ,, Gentleman
Wever (R.) Lusty Juventus. *See* Hawkins
Whetstone (George). *See* Gentleman
White & Son. (B.) *Publishers. See* Sh— Mac-
  beth, 1785
Whitehall. *See* Public . . .
William IV.] Watkins (*Dr.* John) Life and
  times of William the fourth. Ln : . . .
  1831. 8°
<small>Contains an account of the performance of ' Vortigern,'
Ireland's forged play.</small>
Wilmcote, near Stratford-on-Avon. *See* Public
Wilson (G. B.) On the tragedy of ' Macbeth.'
  See Birmingham
Wilton. *See* Public . . .
Wily beguiled. *See* Hawkins
Winter (Wm.) Portrait. *See* Sh— Twelfth
  night, 1893
Wit's theater . . . *See* Allot
Wolfe (John) *Printer. See* Stowe
Woodforde (S.) *Artist. See* Sh— Works, 1807
Woolmer (Shirley Forster). *See* Sh— Auto-
  graph, 1584

Zincke (W. F.) *Forger. See* Jaggard